THE DICTIONARY OF DATES

THE MACMILLAN COMPANY
NEW YORK · CHICAGO
DALLAS · ATLANTA · SAN FRANCISCO
LONDON · MANILA

THE MACMILLAN COMPANY
OF CANADA, LIMITED
TORONTO

THE DICTIONARY
OF DATES

By HELEN REX KELLER

IN TWO VOLUMES

VOLUME II
THE NEW WORLD

3378

THE   MACMILLAN   COMPANY

NEW YORK   MCMLV

902

PRINTED IN THE UNITED STATES OF AMERICA

CONTENTS

AMERICA

v

THE NEW WORLD

AMERICA

America, the land of the western Hemisphere comprising the connected continents of North and South America, extends from Point Barrow, Alaska, in the north at 71° 24' N. Lat. to Cape Horn, Tierra del Fuego, in the south at 55° 58' S. Lat., about 8,700 miles. The length of the mainland is extended to about 9,600 miles by the archipelago of islands north of Canada, the most northern point of Grant Land, Cape Columbia, at 83° 7' N. within 450 miles of the North Pole. Cape Prince of Wales, Alaska, at 167° 30' W. Long. is the most western point, and Cape St. Roque, Brazil, the most eastern point at 35° 20' W. Long. Cape Horn is about 2,350 miles from the South Pole. The total area is about 16,000,000 square miles. The name America is derived from Amerigo Vespucci, a Florentine merchant (1451–1512) who accompanied Ojeda (Hojeda) on a voyage to South America in 1499 (*see infra*) and described the country in letters sent to his friends in Italy. He is charged with inserting "Tierra de Amerigo" in his maps. Washington Irving discussed the question in the appendix to his life of Columbus but comes to no conclusion. Humboldt asserted that the name was given to the continent in the popular works of Waldseemüller, a German geographer, without the knowledge of Vespucci, where it appears (1507) for land corresponding to continent of South America.

In 986 Bjorni Herjulfson sailing from Iceland sighted land to the southwest. Lief Ericsson reached the mainland of North America at Nova Scotia or New England in 1000, and named the land Vinland. Thorwald, brother of Lief, came to Vinland (1002–1003) and explored the coast. Thorfinn Karlsefne (1007–1009) made unsuccessful attempt to establish a colony in Vinland, as did Helgi and Finnborge with Thorwald and Freydis, his wife (1011–1012). After the Northmen John and Sebastian Cabot in service of England were the first to reach the continent of North America in 1497 (*see infra*), except for alleged voyage of John Scolp, a Dane, to Labrador in 1472. Columbus is hailed as the discoverer of America in his voyage in 1492, sighting Guanahani Island now identified as Watling Island in the Bahamas Oct. 11/20, and making first landfall Oct. 12/21. The native inhabitants of the Americas at the time of the discovery were the Indians. America is the native place of maize, the turkey, the potato, tobacco, Peruvian bark, and the tomato.

1492

Martin Behaim's terrestrial globe represents the known geography of the time; globe preserved in his native city of Nuremberg, Germany, Ptolemy's estimate of the length from Spain to eastern Asia at 183° accepted

April 17, Agreement signed between Columbus (Christoforo Colombo), a native of Genoa, Italy, and the Spanish monarchs, Ferdinand and Isabella, for voyage to find a new route to the East Indies by sailing west, Columbus to be admiral and to have a tenth of spices, precious stones, and gold in newly discovered lands

Aug. 3. Columbus, with 3 ships supplied by Ferdinand and Isabella, sailed from Palos in search of westward route to Indies, the "Santa Maria," the "Pinta," under Martin Alonso Pinzon, and the "Niña" under Vicente Yañez Pinzon

Oct. 12, Columbus reached one of the Bahama Islands called by the Indians Guanahani, named by Columbus, San Salvador, generally identified as Watling Island

Oct. 15, Columbus discovered and named Santa Maria de la Concepcion

Oct. 28, Columbus discovered Cuba which he named Juanna. He believed he had reached the coast of Asia

Nov. 20, Entry in Journal of Columbus notes the smoking of tobacco by the Indians

1

Dec. 6, Haiti discovered, named Hispaniola (Española), and fort, La Navidad, built by Columbus, and a garrison of 37 men left

1493

Jan. 4, Columbus set sail for Spain, reaching Lisbon March 4, and Palos, March 15, and was received with distinguished honors by the Spanish court at Barcelona

Feb. 15, Letter of Columbus to Luis de Sant Angel announced his discovery and gave extracts from his Journal

May 3–4, Bull of demarcation of Pope Alexander VI established a meridian line 100 leagues west of the Azores and Cape Verde Islands divided all newly-discovered lands between Spain and Portugal, all west of the line to fall to Spain, all east to Portugal

Sept. 25, Columbus (second voyage) sailed from Cadiz in fleet of 17 ships with 1,500 men, and animals for colonization, and reached an island of the Carribbean or Lesser Antilles group which he named Dominica, Nov. 3; Guadaloupe discovered and named Nov. 4; Antigua, San Martin, Santa Crux, and Puerto Rico, which he named St. John

Nov. 27, Columbus arrived at La Navidad, Haiti, to find his fort destroyed and the Spaniards he had left there had been killed by Indians

Dec., Columbus founded a new settlement about 30 miles east of Monte Cristi, Haiti, which he named Isabella

1494

April 24, Columbus sailed along south shore of Cuba leaving a Council of Regency headed by his brother, Diego, at La Navidad

May 4, Columbus discovered Jamaica

June 7, Treaty of Tordesillas between Spain and Portugal established new line of demarcation in the New World making it 370 leagues west of the Cape Verde Islands

June 13, Columbus discovered the Isle of Pines which he named Evangelista

Sept. 24, Columbus touched at and named the Island of La Mona in the channel between Hispaniola and Puerto Rico; returned to Isabella Sept. 29, and illness of 5 months duration kept him from further exploration

1495

March 27, Columbus started on march from Isabella to subdue Indians in rebellion against the Spaniards

June 24, Five ship-loads of Indians sent to Seville by Columbus to be sold as slaves

Oct., Juan Aguado arrived at Isabella with royal commission to report on the state of the discontented colonists and the government of Columbus

1496

March 10, Columbus sailed for Spain with Aguado to answer charges against him, his brother, Bartholomew, remaining at Isabella as *adelanto* at head of the administration, reaching Cadiz June 11. During the summer Bartholomew founded Santo Domingo, the oldest European settlement in the New World which still exists

1497

May 2–Aug. 6, Voyage of John and Sebastian Cabot (Venetians) from Bristol in the ship "Matthew" under letters patent of March 5, 1496 from Henry VII

of England, the first to reach the continent of North America after the Northmen

May 10, Alleged first voyage of Amerigo Vespucci from Cadiz. Claim that he discovered the continent of America June 16 in 16° N., 70' W. doubtful. *See infra* 1499

June 2, Former privileges of Columbus reaffirmed in patent

June 24, The Cabot expedition sighted the "Island of St. John," first identified as Newfoundland, now generally believed to be Labrador (Biddle, Harrisse. Biggar makes first land sighted the western extremity of Cape Breton Island). Cabot named Cape North, Cape Discovery, Cape Ray, St. Georges Cape, and England's Cape (Cape Race), the mainland of North America sighted on this date

Aug. 10, King Henry VII granted £10 from the Privy Purse "to him that founde the new isle," either to John Cabot or the sailor who first saw land

Dec. 13, Pension of £20 a year granted to John Cabot by Henry VII with authority to take at his pleasure 6 ships to the "lond and isles of late founde by the said John"

1498

April 1, Grants of £30 to Thomas Bradley and Launcelot Thirkill going to the "new isle," and of £2 to James Carter. From this date contemporary records show voyages of the English to North America. De Witt says, "The navy of England became formidable by the discovery of the inexpressible rich fishing bank of Newfoundland"

April, Under a new patent of Feb. 3, 1498 John and Sebastian Cabot sailed on second voyage which explored the coast of North America from the north coast of Labrador to as far south as 38 degrees at Cape Henlopen, Delaware. The map of Juan de la Cosa (1500) probably shows the result of this expedition, Cape Race or Cape English being the Cavo de Ynglaterra. John Cabot not heard of after this time

May 30, Columbus (third voyage) sailed from San Lucar with 6 ships; discovered and named Trinidad off the coast of Venezuela July 31

May 30–Nov. 25, 1500, Bartholomé de Las Casas at Indies in service of Columbus

Aug. 1, Columbus landed on the continent of South America near the Orinoco River, Venezuela. Believing the land an island he named it Isla Santa. Aug. 2 he sailed into the Gulf of Paria, coasted along the continent, and after sighting Tobago, Grenada, and naming Margarita sailed for San Domingo where he arrived Aug. 31

1499

March 25, John Cabot's pension paid on this date, last authentic knowledge

May 20–June, 1500, Voyage of Alonzo de Ojeda (Hojeda) and Amerigo Vespucci with Juan de la Cosa reached the continent of South America near Paramaribo in Surinam, and coasted Guiana (British), and Venezuela to the Gulf of Maracaibo, southeast and west of coast seen by Columbus. This is considered to be the first voyage of Amerigo Vespucci by most authorities

May 21, Francisco Bobadilla appointed Governor and judge of Hispaniola with authority to examine into the complaints of the colonists

June–April, 1500, Pedro Alonso Niño made voyage

from Palos to the Gulf of Paria, the pearl coast, Venezuela. This profitable expedition promoted further exploration of northern South America

Aug. 24, Ojeda expedition discovered Lake Maracaibo, Venezuela, naming the land "Little Venice" because of the Indian villages built on piles in the water

Sept. 5, Ojeda expedition arrived at Hispaniola

Nov. 18–Sept. 30, 1500, Voyage of Vicente Yañez Pinzon, a captain of Columbus, from Palos, the first to explore South American coast below the equator

Dec., Diego de Lepe sailed from Spain for South America

1500

Jan. 20, Pinzon sighted the coast of Brazil at Cape St. Augustine, doubled Cape San Roque and reached 10° south below the Cape, "farthest south"

Feb. 28, Pinzon discovered the estuary of the Amazon and sailed past the mouth of the Orinoco River and as far as the Gulf of Paria, Venezuela, arrived at Hispaniola June 25

March 9, Pedro Alvarez Cabral sailed on voyage to reach the East Indies

April 22, Cabral driven by storm onto the coast of Brazil took possession of the country for Portugal in about Lat. 10° South

May 1, Cabral again took possession of country for Portugal at Porto Seguro and named it Vera Cruz

May 12, Charter issued to Gaspar de Cortereal (Portuguese). He sailed from Lisbon and believed to have landed at Newfoundland, Conception Bay; rediscovered Greenland which he named "Terra Verde"

Aug. 23, Bobadilla arrived at Hispaniola with full powers of administration and commissioned to investigate charges against Columbus whom he arrested

Oct., Columbus sent to Spain in chains by Bobadilla

Oct.–Sept., 1502, Voyage of Roderigo de Bastidas, accompanied by Balboa with La Cosa for pilot, traced the northern coast of South America west of Cape de la Vela where expedition of Ojeda had turned back, to the later Nombre de Dios on the Isthmus (the coasts of Venezuela, Colombia, and Panama)

Dec. 17, Columbus received at court with honors and Bobadilla's proceedings repudiated by the Spanish monarchs

Map of the New World by Juan de la Cosa who sailed with Columbus as pilot on his second voyage; preserved in Royal Library at Madrid

1501

March 19, Charter from Henry VII of England to Richard Warde, John Thomas, and John Fernandez for 10 years, probably replacing the charter of John Cabot

May 14–Sept. 7, 1502, Voyage of Amerigo Vespucci, in service of Don Nuño Manuel of Portugal, from Lisbon, coasted Brazil and discovered island identified as South Georgia

May 15, Gaspar de Cortereal sailed from Lisbon (second voyage) with 2 ships to Newfoundland. One ship returned Oct. 8, the other with Cortereal not heard from again after Aug. 20

Dec., Patent for 40 years granted by Henry VII to Hugh Eliot, Thomas Ashenhurst, John Gonzalo, and Francis Fernando gave a monopoly of trade in the new lands

Annual trips made from this time to the Gulf of St. Lawrence and the Banks by Portuguese, Norman, and Breton fishermen

Cape Race on Newfoundland coast shown as Cape Raso on Portuguese map

1502

Jan. 7, £5 paid to the "men of Bristol that founde the Isle," possible record of expedition of Richard Warde and his associates

Jan. 15, King Manoel ratified the claim of Miguel Cortereal to Newfoundland explored by his brother, Gaspar

Jan.–Sept., Second voyage of Alonzo de Ojeda from Cadiz to the Gulf of Paria to establish a colony which was not successful

Feb. 13, Nicolas de Ovando sailed from San Lucar to succeed Bobadilla as Governor arriving at Santo Domingo April 15 accompanied by Bartolomé de Las Casas

May 9, Columbus (fourth voyage) sailed from Cadiz to find a route to the Spice Islands with 4 caravels and 150 men

May 10, Miguel de Cortereal under royal grant of Jan. 15 sailed in search of his brother, Gaspar, and was never heard from again

June 15, Columbus discovered the Island of Martinino, probably St. Lucia

June 29, Columbus arrived off Santo Domingo and was refused shelter for his ships from impending storm by Ovando

July 14, Columbus sailed westward from small port near Santo Domingo

July 30, Columbus discovered the Island of Guanaja off the coast of Honduras

Aug. 14, Columbus landed at Cape Honduras

Aug. 17, Columbus landed at mouth of the Tinto River and took possession of the country which is now Honduras for Spain

Sept. 12, Columbus rounded and named Cape Gracias á Dios

Sept. 25, Columbus off the San Juan River dividing Costa Rica from Nicaragua took shelter for his ships for a few days behind the Island of Quiribiri and landed at Indian village of Cariay in Costa Rica

——, Francis Fernandez and John Gonzalez probably in consideration of voyages made in 1501 and 1502 for merchants of Bristol made "captains of the New Found Land" and granted pension of £10 yearly

Sept. 30, Grant of Henry VII to the merchants of Bristol that have "bene in the Newfounde Launde," £20. Newfoundland in the 16th century the name applied to Nova Scotia, New Brunswick, Cape Breton, Prince Edward's Island, and islands and coast of the St. Lawrence River, and even Maine

Oct. 5, Columbus sailed from Cariay, Costa Rica, and on second day reached Laguna de Chiriqui

Nov. 2, Columbus arrived at and named the harbor of Portobello (Puertobello) Panama

Dec. 5, Columbus turned back from El Retrete where he had found a harbor about Nov. 23, place not identified but according to Bancroft at or near Nombre de Dios

Dec. 9, Letters patent granted to Fernandez Gonzalez, Hugh Eliot, and others of Bristol to make further explorations

Map of Alberto Cantino based on the Cortereal and other Portuguese voyages of North America with 22 names on mainland distinct from Asia, and including Cuba, Jamaica, Haiti, and Puerto Rico

1503

Jan. 6, Columbus reached mouth of river he named Santa Maria de Belen near Veragua River, Panama, where he made an attempt to leave colonists, but the hostility of the Indians forced the Spaniards to return to the ships

Jan. 20 and June 5, Decrees established the Casa de Contratacion or House of Trade at Seville to have charge of all matters relating to the Indies

April 6–Sept. 16, 1504, Voyage of Alfonso de Albur- querque from Lisbon to India in which he touched at Brazil and later published "Chronicle" of his voyage with a chapter on the islands of Columbus

May 10–June 18, 1504, Vespucci made voyage from Lisbon with Gonzalo Coelho to coasts of Brazil and Patagonia (May 10, Vespucci's own account, June 10, Bancroft)

June 23, Columbus landed at St. Christopher's Cove at Jamaica and remained there until the following June waiting for the return of his lieutenant, Diego Mendez, sent to Ovando for assistance, sailing for Hispaniola June 28, 1504

1504

Sept. 12, Columbus sailed for Spain arriving at San Lucar Nov. 7, ending his fourth and last voyage

Island of Cape Breton discovered and named by fisher- men from Brittany

1505

Third voyage of Alonzo de Ojeda to Gulf of Uraba, Colombia

1506

May 20, Death of Columbus at Valladolid, Spain, at about 70 years of age

Voyage of Jean Denys of Honfleur and Camaert of Rouen to Newfoundland recorded (Justin Winsor considers evidence insufficient of map by Denys of this date as cited by Charlevoix)

1507

The name "America" first used in a French geography by the German, Waldseemüller. Ignorant of the achievements of Columbus he had read the letters of Amerigo Vespucci about his voyages and believed him the discoverer of the New World

1508

June 29–1509, Voyage of Vicente Pinzon and Diaz de Solis to discover route to the Spice Islands. Sailing along the southern shore they discovered Cuba to be an island. They sailed to Honduras and coasted South America as far as the mouth of the Colorado River of Argentina

Thomas Aubert made unsuccessful attempt to found colony in Newfoundland. See Canada

1509

"Tierra Firme" (New Spain) divided for colonization by the King between Alonzo de Ojeda and Diego de Nicuesa, Ojeda appointed Governor of the eastern part called Nueva Andalucia from Cape de la Vela to the Atranto River, and Nicuesa of region from the

Gulf of Uraba or Darien to Cape Gracias á Dios named Castilla del Oro

July, Diego Colon, son of Columbus, commissioned Governor to succeed Ovando, arrived at Santo Domingo

Nov. 10, Alonzo de Ojeda sailed from Hispaniola to Cartagena, Colombia, to found colony, accompanied by Francisco Pizarro and Juan de la Cosa. Nicuesa arrived later in the month in time to help Ojeda fight the Indians. Ojeda founded his settlement on the Gulf of Uraba and named it San Sebastian, the first settlement on the mainland of South America

Nov. 20, Nicuesa sailed from Cartagena making his capital city on the Belen River, Veragua. See Panama

1510

Ojeda sailed for Hispaniola for relief for his colonists leaving Pizarro in charge, and was never able to return, dying there in poverty. Balboa who came to San Sebastian with relief ship of Encisco long expected took the lead and moved the settlement to Darien named by Encisco, Santa Maria de la Antigua del Darien

1511

March 1, Nicuesa, claiming jurisdiction over the settle- ment of Darien, driven from there by Balboa and not heard from again; probably lost in shipwreck of his vessel

Aug. 11, Bishoprics created in Cuba, Puerto Rico, and Santo Domingo

Council of the Indies first established. (See Aug. 1, 1524)

1512

March 3–Sept. 23, Voyage of Juan Ponce de Leon, Governor of Puerto Rico sighted land March 27 and anchored April 2 at site probably near the present St. Augustine, and named the country Florida taking possession for the King of Spain; sailed as far south as the Florida Keys

April, Death of Amerigo Vespucci at Seville, Spain (61)

Sept. 13, Sebastian Cabot entered the service of Spain, engaged on account of his knowledge of Newfound- land

Dec. 12, Laws of Burgos proclaimed established regula- tions for government of Indians of New Spain

1513

July 27, By royal order the mainland of New Spain hitherto called Tierra Firme to be called Castilla del Oro except Veragua, Paria, and land discovered by Pinzon and Solis; Darien province renamed Andalucia la Nueva. Pedro Arias de Avilla known as Pedrarias Davilla appointed Governor. See also Panama

Sept. 6, Vasco Nuñez de Balboa set out from Antigua de Darien to find "the other sea" described by the Indians, marching across the Isthmus discovered the Pacific Ocean Sept. 25, and took possession of the "Southern Sea" in the name of the sovereigns of Spain, and again on the 29th when the expedition reached the shore

1514

Jan. 19, Balboa arrived at Antigua de Darien with treasure of gold and pearls

April 11, Pedrarias Davilla sailed from San Lucar to supersede Balboa as Governor of Castilla del Oro, arriving June 30 at Darien. Balboa brought to trial was acquitted of charges against him

Nov. 12, Juan Diaz de Solis commissioned by King Ferdinand to find western route to the Spice Islands

1515

March, Gonzalos de Badajos sailed from Antigua to Nombre de Dios, crossed the Isthmus taking gold from the Indians who finally defeated the Spaniards in battle and drove them from the region

Oct. 8-1516, Juan Diaz de Solis sailed from San Lucar and coasted South America from Cape San Roque to Argentina

First printed account of voyage of Cabot in Peter Martyr's "Decades"

1516

Jan. 1, Solis reached the Bay of Rio de Janeiro and proceeded south to the estuary of the La Plata which he named Mare Dulce; killed by Guarani Indians near mouth of the Parana River

July 29, Expedition of Espinosa of exploration and gold hunting from Panama to the Pacific

Sept. 17, Decree declared Bartolomé de Las Casas official protector of the Indians

1517

Feb. 8, Francisco Hernandez de Cordova sailed from Cuba and on March 3 sighted land which he named Punta de Catoche (Point Catoche), Yucatan

Balboa, accused of treason by the jealous Governor Pedrarias Davilla, executed in the public square at Acla

Disputed voyage of Sebastian Cabot in service of Henry VIII in company of Sir Thomas Pert to North American coast at 67° 30′ N. Lat.

1518

Feb. 5, Sebastian Cabot again in service of Spain made pilot major

April 8-Nov. 1, Juan de Grijalva in voyage from Cuba followed the coast of Yucatan and Mexico beyond Vera Cruz. *See* Mexico

Nov. 13, Diego Velasquez, Governor of Cuba, appointed adelanto over all lands discovered by him or at his cost

Baron de Léry sailed from France and landed colonists on Sable Island, first attempt at settlement of North America (Lescarbot)

1519

Feb. 18, Hernando Cortes sailed from Cuba landing at St. Juan de Uloa April 21. For conquest of Mexico for Spain *see* Mexico

July 10, First letter of Cortes to Charles V of Spain on conquest of Mexico

Sept. 20-Sept. 6, 1522, First circumnavigation of the globe by the expedition of Magellan (Fernão de Magalhaes) which sailed from San Lucar

Nov. 29, Magellan sighted South America at Cape St. Augustine near Pernambuco, Brazil

Alonzo Alvarez de Pineda explored the coast of the Gulf of Mexico from Florida to province of Panuco, Mexico; river he mentions believed to be either the Mississippi or the Mobile

The Maggiolo map published, anonymous Portuguese map now preserved in museum at Munich, detailed representation of eastern coast of North America, first known map to note Balboa's discovery of the Pacific Ocean

1520

Jan. 11, Magellan at mouth of the La Plata River examined the estuary in hope of finding a passage at this point

March 31-Aug. 24, 1521, Magellan in winter quarters at Port Saint Julian, Argentina

Oct. 21-Nov. 28, Magellan made the passage to the Pacific through the straits named after him and named the Pacific Ocean, *Mare Pacificum*

Oct. 30, Second letter of Cortes to Spain enclosed map showing Gulf coast and west Cuba

Nov., Las Casas left Spain to make attempt to colonize the pearl coast (South America)

Dec., Lucas Vasquez de Ayllon sent Francisco Gordillo from Hispaniola to explore the mainland

1521

Feb. 20, Ponce de Leon sailed to found settlement in Florida, an unsuccessful expedition which occupied about 5 months

March 6, Magellan arrived at the Ladrones Islands which he named

March 13, Grant of King of Portugal to Joãm Alvarez Fagundez of coast and islands in Gulf of St. Lawrence discovered on voyage of summer and autumn of 1520

March 15, Magellan sighted Philippine Islands according to Pigafetta, chronicler of voyage

March 16, Magellan discovered the Island of Samar in the Philippines. *See also* Philippine Islands

April 25, Magellan mortally wounded in battle with the natives in Philippine Island of Mactan and died on the 27th

June 30, Gordillo with Quexos sent out by Juan Ortiz de Matienzo landed in the vicinity of Cape Fear, North Carolina, and took possession of the country for Spain

1522

Jan. 21-June 25, 1523, Expedition of Andrés Nino and Gil Gonzalez Davila from Panama; Nino sailed the length of the coast of Nicaragua and Davila explored the interior discovering Lake Nicaragua

April 28, See of Santiago de Cuba created, Fra Juan Umite, first bishop

May, All the religious orders authorized to undertake religious work in New Spain

Oct. 15, Emperor Charles V made Cortes Governor and Captain General of New Spain

Nov. 6, Thirty-one survivors of the Magellan expedition reached the Moluccas and by way of the Cape of Good Hope reached San Lucar Sept. 6, 1522 accomplishing the first circumnavigation of the globe

Voyage of Pascual de Andagoya southward from Panama first heard of the Inca Empire, this expedition giving the information and motive for the voyage of conquest of Pizarro

1523

Turin map of the world preserved in Royal Library at Turin gave entire coast line of the Gulf of Mexico westward from the mouth of the Mississippi, Florida is represented as an island and the coast north of Florida omitted

1524

Jan. 17-July 8, Giovanni Verrazano, a Florentine in the service of France, sailed from the Desertas Islands near Madeira west for 25 days and then north for 24 days until he sighted land near Cape Fear in North Carolina. His course is traced to Raleigh, New York, Block Island, Newport, and Portsmouth, New Hampshire, and along the coast of Maine, Nova Scotia, to Cape Breton, and the south and east coast of Newfoundland; arrived at Dieppe, July 8

March 6, Verrazano sighted Cape May, New Jersey according to Ramusio

April 11–May 31, The Badajoz Congress held to decide claim of Spain to the Spice Islands

Aug. 4, Council of the Indies formally reorganized and established for government of New Spain

Nov. 14, Francisco Pizarro sailed from Panama and entered Biru River passing Pueryo de Pinas where voyages of Vasco Nuñez Balboa and Andagoya had ended. Almaça following Pizarro 3 months later coasted as far as river he named the San Juan a few miles north of the port of Buenaventura in New Granada in search of Pizarro

1525

Feb. 10, Stephen Gomez, Portuguese, appointed a pilot in service of Spain, sailed from Corunna either in Nov. 1524 or Feb. 1525, instructed to search for passage to India and examine "all the coast from Florida to Bacallos"; sailed from Cape Race, Newfoundland to Florida, explored harbors of the present Halifax and the Bay of Fundy, and brought back charts of Nova Scotia, Newfoundland, and Maine coasts

March 4, Sebastian Cabot appointed commander of expedition to discover route to the Moluccas and Cathay

July 24, Garcia de Loaisa sailed from Corunna to repeat voyage of Magellan; landed at Tehuantepec, Mexico, July 25. Visited the Philippines

1526

Feb. 23, Death of Diego Columbus in village of Montal-van near Toledo, Spain

March 10, Pizarro expedition back in Panama; contract signed between Pizarro, Almagro, and Father Luque divided Empire of Peru between them. *See* Peru

April–Aug. 1530, Sebastian Cabot, in service of Spain, sailed for South America en route for the Moluccas, entered the La Plata River Feb. 1527, and spent 4 years exploring the La Plata, Uruguay, Parana, and Paraguay rivers

June, Ayllon with 500 persons sailed from Hispaniola to establish a colony, San Miguel, which failed because of the hostility of the Indians; site probably near Jamestown, Virginia (Harrisse favors the Cape Fear River, North Carolina)

Sept. 14, First Audiencia of the New World established at Santo Domingo by decree

Oct. 18, Death of Ayllon, and Virginia colony soon abandoned

1527

May 8, Sebastian Cabot discovered the Parana River, South America

June 10, English expedition of John Rut in "Mary of Guildford" sailed from Plymouth following Cabot's course in search of North-West Passage, and followed coast from Lat. 53° along New England returning by way of the West Indies in Nov. Verrazano may have been the pilot killed by Indians

June 17, Pamphillo de Narvaez with grant of Gulf coast from Mexico to Cape of Florida sailed from San Lucar and arrived at Trinidad Nov. 5

1528

Feb. 20, Narvaez sailed from Havana and landed at Tampa Bay, Florida, April 14, for overland journey to reach Mexico. The ships eventually sailed away without meeting the party as planned

May 1, Narvaez with 300 men began march across Florida reaching Indian town near the present Tallahassee June 25, from there proceeding to Appalachee Bay (Charlevoix and Prince) where boats were built

Sept. 22, Narvaez with 242 survivors embarked in boats from Appalachee Bay, and following the coast past the Mississippi River Narvaez was swept out to sea and lost

Nov. 6, Cabeça de Vaca of the Narvaez expedition was cast ashore on an island probably near Matagorda Bay and was kept in slavery by the Indians until 1534

1529

July 26, Pizarro received commission signed at Toledo, Spain, making him governor, captain-general, and mayor of any lands he might discover 200 leagues south from Santiago

Verrazano map, drawn by Hieronymo Verrazano, brother of the navigator, preserved in museum at Rome, first Italian map in which the name America appears, Atlantic coast line as far as Labrador, Pacific coast line following the Maggiolo map, delineation of Isthmus of Panama an important feature

1530

Dec. 28, Pizarro (third expedition) sailed from Panama for Peru, arriving at Bay of San Mateo in 13 days and from there marching overland to Tumbez. *See* Peru for conquest 1531–1532

1533

Discovery of the peninsula of Lower California by Jiminez. *See* Mexico Oct. 29

Expedition of Sebastian de Benalcazar explored Ecuador and Colombia. *See* Colombia and Ecuador

1534

April 20–Sept. 5, First voyage of Jacques Cartier. *See* Canada

Sept., Simon de Alcazaba sailed from San Lucar to explore and settle South America south of Peru and made extensive explorations in Patagonia

1535

April 17, Antonio de Mendoza commissioned first Viceroy of New Spain

May 3, Expedition of Cortes from Mexico to Lower California reached Bay of Santa Cruz. *See* Mexico

May 12–July 6, 1536, Second voyage of Jacques Cartier. *See* Canada

1536

April 1, Cabeça de Vaca escaping from the Indians reached San Miguel in New Galicia with 3 companions, and July 24 arrived at City of Mexico having crossed the continent in their journey. Sailed from Vera Cruz and reached Lisbon Aug. 9, 1537

The Harleian map supposed to be the work of Pierre Desceliers gives the discoveries of Cartier in the St. Lawrence region and uses the names "Canada" and "Sagne" (Saguenay)

1539

March 7–Aug., Spanish expedition under Fra Marcos from Culiacan last outpost of Spanish civilization in search of the "seven cities" of legend discovered the Zuni villages of western New Mexico, and turned back after seeing Cibola with exaggerated reports of cities beyond

May 18, Ferdinand de Soto, Governor of Cuba, sailed from Havana to complete the discovery and conquest of Florida, arriving at bay on Sunday the 25th which he named Espiritu Santo Bay (Tampa Bay), and took possession of the country for Spain June 3

July 8, Francisco de Ulloa sent by Cortes sailed from Acapulco and Oct. 18 anchored in Santa Cruz Bay; reported Santa Cruz (Lower California) a peninsula not an island as asserted by Jiminez. He reached the Cedros Islands and probably as far as the 28th degree North Lat. on this voyage

Aug. 1, De Soto started march from Tampa into the interior of Florida, spending the winter at Apalachen, discovered Pensacola Bay

Aug., Alonso de Camargo sailed from Seville to the Straits to reach India by westward route. Arrived at Cabo de las Virgenes Jan. 20, 1540, one vessel reaching Arequipa in Peru

Dec. 25, Expedition of Gonzalo Pizarro and Francisco de Orellana started across the Andes from Quito (Ecuador) and reached the Napo River

1540

Feb. 23, Francisco Vasquez Coronado with large force of Spaniards and Indians mobilized at Compostella started march up the west coast. Expedition left Culiacan April 22 marching up the Sonora Valley and down the San Pedro to Gila and Zuni rivers, entered Cibola July 7, and wintered in province of Tiguex on Davis River

March 3, De Soto marching from Florida entered the territory of the present State of Georgia, and July 26 reached Ceca in present Talladega county, Alabama

May 9, Alarcon sailed from Acapulco to coöperate with the land expedition of Coronado

July, Tobar from the Coronado expedition explored the Moqui pueblos north of the Zuni

Aug., Alvarado from the Coronado expedition discov- ered "Acuco" identified as the pueblo of Acoma, and reached province of Tiguex, and "Cicuye," Old Pesos, and Don Gracia Lopez de Cardenas reached the Colorado River and discovered the Grand Canyon

Aug. 26, Hernando de Alarcon discovered the mouth of the Colorado River and proceeded up the river for some distance

Sept., Melchior Diaz and Juan Gallegos joined Coro- nado from Cibola, and Diaz, proceeding by land from San Geronimo to the Colorado to communicate with Alarcon, failed and perished

Oct. 18, De Soto in battle with the Mobilian Indians at Mavilla between the Tombigbee and Alabama rivers; remained here until Nov. 17

Dec. 17, De Soto reached Chicaça in province of that name in present State of Mississippi where he re- mained until April 25

1541

April 23, Coronado left Tiguex and journeyed from the Upper Brazos across the Texas Panhandle and

Oklahoma to Quivira in eastern Kansas, back at Tiguex Oct. 20

May 8, The De Soto expedition, the first Europeans to reach the Mississippi River at place identified as probably the lower Chickasaw Bluffs

Aug. 26, Orellana deserting the Pizarro expedition reached the sea, sailing down the Napo to the Amazon and down the Amazon, voyage of 7 months

1542

April, Coronado started on return journey

May 21, Death of de Soto after voyage from Oklahoma down the Arkansas River to its mouth

June 5, Luis Moscoso appointed by de Soto to succeed him as leader led expedition across Arkansas and Texas and is believed to have gone as far west as the Trinity River and possibly the Brazos River; win- tered on the Mississippi River at Minoya and built boats

June 27, Juan Cabrillo (Rodriguez) sailed from La Navidad and explored the outer coast of the Cali- fornia Peninsula, Aug. 21 at Port of San Quintin, Sept. 28 discovered San Diego Bay, Oct. 7 Catalina Island, Nov. 16 Drake's Bay, taking possession of the country for Spain Nov. 17, named the Sierra Nevadas; wintered on San Miguel Island

Nov. 1, Lopez de Villabos sailed for the Philippines to take possession for Spain

1543

Jan. 19, Ferrelo, after death of Juan Cabrillo Jan. 3, continued northward to the mouth of the Rogue River, Oregon, at Cape Mendocino March 1, and claimed he reached the 43d parallel

Feb. 2, Expedition of Ruy Lopez de Villabos from Mexico reached Mindanao. See Philippine Islands

July 2, Luis Moscoso de Alvarado led survivors of de Soto expedition down the Mississippi from point close to its junction with the Arkansas, reaching Tampa Bay in the Gulf of Mexico July 18, and coasted the Gulf to Panuco which he reached Sept. 10

1544

De Soto map of the explorations of de Soto and Mos- cosco preserved in Seville, the first representation of any part of the interior of the southern States between Georgia and Texas

1546

Map by Giacomo Gastaldi published in Venice united North America with Asia, shows the "seven cities" of the early Spanish explorers

1551

Dec. 18, Company of Merchant Adventurers incor- porated with Sebastian Cabot as Governor for dis- covery and exploration of America

1555

May 14, Nicolas Durand de Villegagnon sailed from Havre with Huguenot colonists reaching Rio de Janeiro Nov. 10. See Brazil

1557

Sept. 6–Sept. 26, 1580, Voyage of Sir Francis Drake from Plymouth, England, to South America and through the Straits of Magellan raiding Spanish ports on the Pacific coast

Nov. 15, Sir Francis Drake made the passage through the Straits of Magellan

1559

June 11, Tristan de Luna y Arellano sailed from Vera Cruz with colonists and landed at port he named Ichuse on Aug. 14 which Shea locates on Santa Rosa Bay and Bolton and Fairbanks on Pensacola Bay

1560

April, Colonists from Ichuse reached the Alabama River and in June reached Coçca on the Coosa River. De Luna replaced by Villafañe and after unsuccessful attempt to settle Santa Elena the enterprise was abandoned

1561

May 27–July 9, Angel de Villafañe sent to supersede de Luna brought colonists from Pensacola Bay to Santa Elena (Port Royal Sound), ascended the Pedee River June 8, June 14 at Cape Hatteras

1562

Feb. 18, Jean de Ribaut sailed from Dieppe with Huguenot colonists reaching the coast of Florida April 30, and entered the St. John's River May 1, built Fort Charles on the present Parris Island in stream emptying into the Beaufort River

Oct.–Sept. 1563, Voyage of Captain John Hawkins from England to Sierra Leone where he took 300 negroes which he sold in Hispaniola, the first slave-trading voyage

1564

April 22, René de Laudonnière sailed from Havre de Grace with Huguenot colonists arriving off St. Augustine, Florida June 22, and at the mouth of the St. John's River June 24, and built Fort Caroline June 29

May, Hernando Manrique de Rojas sent from Cuba destroyed pillars and Fort Charles erected by Ribaut

Oct. 18–Sept. 20, 1565, Captain John Hawkins (second voyage) sailed from Plymouth and arrived off the St. John's River at end of July, proceeded to coast of Central America trading slaves and goods, and coasted north as far as the Newfoundland Banks (Aug. 23) on return voyage

Nov. 21, Miguel Lopez de Legazpi sailing from Navidad reached the Philippine Islands Feb. 13, 1565, and occupied Cebu; left Cebu June 1, and arrived at Acapulco Oct. 8

1565

March 20, Pedro Menéndes de Avilés made adelanto of Florida

May 10, Jean Ribaut sailed from Havre reaching Fort Caroline Aug. 28

June 29, Pedro Menéndes de Avilés sailed from Cadiz commanded by Philip of Spain to destroy French colony in Florida

Aug. 3, Captain John Hawkins on second voyage plundering Spanish ships and settlements saved Laudonnière's Huguenot colony from starvation and sold them a ship to return to France

Aug. 28, Menéndes reached the coast of Florida and sailing north attacked the French fleet at the San Juan River

Sept. 8, Menéndes founded St. Augustine, Florida, the oldest European settlement in existence in America

Sept. 10, Ribaut sailed from the St. John's River in search of Spanish fleet which he had encountered and fled from Sept. 4, failed to find Spaniards and some of his ships were wrecked in tempest

Sept. 16, Menéndes began march overland from St. Augustine to attack Fort Caroline which he reached Sept. 20, massacred the French settlers "not as Frenchmen but as Lutherans," and Sept. 29 massacred those who had escaped from the ships

Oct. 11, The younger Ribaut and Laudonnière sailed for France with survivors of the Florida colony

Oct. 12, The elder Ribaut and other French colonists who had escaped surrendered to Menéndes and were massacred

1566

April, Menéndes established post on St. Catherine's Island, Georgia, which he named Guale, name afterwards extended to coast of northern Georgia where Spanish settlements and missions founded

Nov., Menéndes sent Juan Pardo from Santa Elena "to discover and conquer the interior country from there to Mexico." He reached the Alleghany Mts. in North Carolina

Jesuit missions established in Florida

1567

Aug. 2–June 6, 1568, Voyage of Dominique de Gourges from Bordeaux to avenge the destruction of the French colony in Florida by the Spaniards

Oct. 2–Jan. 25, 1568, Third slave-trading voyage of Captain John Hawkins from Plymouth to Sierra Leone and then with cargo of slaves to the West Indies

1568

March 27, Captain Hawkins reached Dominica Island

May, De Gourges burned the forts and killed the Spaniards in the Florida settlement

Sept. 24, Captain Hawkins in battle with the Spanish fleet in harbor of Vera Cruz, the port of Mexico, escaped with only 2 ships, his own and that of his cousin, Francis Drake

Oct., Journey of 3 Englishmen, David Ingram, Richard Browne, and Richard Twide from near the Rio Panuco in Mexico to Canada after shipwreck in the Gulf

1569

Map by Gerard Mercator published at Duisberg, Germany, using the increased-cylindrical, or Mercator, projection, original at Breslau, Germany, shows results of French exploration in the northeast and Spanish in the southwest

1570

The Jesuit, Father Segura, founded Spanish mission in Virginia; destroyed by Indians and all killed

1572

May 24–Aug. 9, 1573, Voyage of Sir Francis Drake from Plymouth to the West Indies and July 6 sighted the high land of Santa Marta and a few days later reached the Gulf of Darien and attacked and plundered the Spanish town of Nombre de Dios July 29

1573

Feb. 3, Drake crossed the Isthmus of Panama and saw the Pacific

Pedro Menéndes Marques, nephew of earlier Spaniard

of same name, coasted northward from the Florida Keys to Chesapeake Bay

Dec. 1, Cedula of Philip II, of Spain, on colonization promulgated

1574

Sept. 17, Death of Pedro Menéndes de Avilés in Spain

Nov. 22, Juan Fernandez discovered Juan Fernandez Islands opposite Chile, named after him

1576

June 7–Oct. 2, Martin Frobisher (first voyage) in search of passage to China, sailed from Blackwall, England, sighted Cape Farewell, Greenland, July 11, high land which he named Queen Elizabeth's Foreland (Resolution Island) July 20, and inlet north of Hudson Straits named after him Frobisher's Bay, July 21. He explored Baffin Land which was named by Queen Elizabeth, "Meta Incognita"

1577

May 26–Sept. 23, M. Frobisher (second voyage) sighted Friesland (Greenland) July 4, arrived at Hall's Island at north entrance of Frobisher's Bay July 4, and July 17 landed and explored "Meta Incognita" (Baffin Land) hunting for gold

Nov. 15–Sept. 26, 1580, Voyage of Sir Francis Drake around the world, sailing from Plymouth arrived off coast of Brazil April 6, and entered the Rio de la Plata

1578

May 31–Oct. 1, M. Frobisher (third voyage) sailed from Harwich, landed at Friesland (Greenland) June 20 and named it West England. July 2 stormy weather drove him into new strait (Hudson's)

June 11, Sir Humphrey Gilbert obtained a patent from Queen Elizabeth for discovery and colonization in northwest America

June 19–Aug. 17, Drake at port of St. Julian

Aug. 20, Drake entered the Straits of Magellan, made the passage to the Pacific in 16 days, arrived at Mocha Island off the coast of Chile Nov. 25, and continued north along coasts of Chile and Peru plundering Spanish ships and settlements

Sept. 23–May 15, 1579, Voyage of Sir Humphrey Gilbert to found a colony in North America unsuccessful

1579

April 16, Drake left Guatulco, Oaxaca in Mexico and sailed north along Pacific coast

June 17, Drake sailed into harbor believed to be Drake's Bay north of San Francisco Bay, and took possession of the country for England, calling it New Albion

July 26, Drake set sail for the Moluccas returning by way of the Cape of Good Hope (June 15, 1580) arriving in England Sept. 26, 1580

1581

Father Augustin Rodriguez led expedition northeast from Mexico to Puara near the present Albuquerque, all killed by Indians

1582

Nov. 10–Sept. 20, 1583, Anthony de Espejo left San Bartolome and journeyed to the Rio Grande in search of Fra Rodriguez, following the river to the "Tiguex" of Coronado and to pueblo of Puara, and explored the Pecos River

1583

June 11, Sir Humphrey Gilbert sailed from Plymouth with 5 ships, reached north coast of Newfoundland July 30 and St. Johns Aug. 3, took formal possession of the country for England and his colony Aug. 5, continued on his voyage to *Terra Florida* Aug. 20, and on Sept. 9 his ship lost in storm and all on board drowned

1584

March 25, Sir Walter Raleigh secured the patent of his half-brother Sir Humphrey Gilbert for discovery and colonization of America

April 27–Sept. 1584, Voyage of Arthur Barlow and Philip Amidas sent by Sir Walter Raleigh. Arrived at coast of North Carolina July 4, landed at Wokokon Island and at Roanoke Island and named the region Virginia in honor of Queen Elizabeth

1585

April 9–Oct. 18, Expedition of Sir Richard Grenville (second expedition sent by Sir Walter Raleigh) left colonists at Roanoke Island, North Carolina

June 7–Sept. 30, John Davis (first voyage) sighted Greenland July 20, explored the strait named after him and entered Baffin Bay in search of a passage to India, proceeded to Cape Dyer and sailed nearly to the head of Cumberland Sound

Sept. 14, Sir Francis Drake sailed from Plymouth to destroy New Spain. Among the commanders of his fleet were Martin Frobisher, Francis Knollys, and Christopher Carlisle

1586

Jan. 1, The Drake expedition took Santo Domingo

May 7–Oct. 6, John Davis (second voyage) arrived at Gilbert's Sound June 15, named Cape Walsingham, explored Baffin Land, upper Frobisher Bay, and coasted Labrador

May 27, Sir Francis Drake attacked St. Augustine, Florida, and destroyed the Spanish fort

July 21–Sept. 9, 1588, Circumnavigation of the globe by Thomas Cavendish, sailing from Plymouth and by way of Sierra Leone, Cape Verde Islands, Cape Frio, Brazil, to Patagonia, discovered "Port Desire," passed through the Straits of Magellan and plundered Spanish settlements on west coast of Central and South America

July 27, The colonists on Roanoke Island rescued from starvation by Sir Francis Drake (June 10) arrived in England in one of Drake's ships

1587

April 26–Nov. 5, Voyage of John White sent as governor to Raleigh's colony at Roanoke Island, arrived at the Island July 22, and left colonists

May 19–Sept. 15, John Davis (third voyage) sighted Greenland June 14, reached farthest north June 30 at 72° 12′ N. Lat. 56° W. Long. off west Greenland, at Cumberland Sound July 20, passed Frobisher Strait which he named Lumley Inlet on his way south, and Hudson Straits

Aug. 18, Birth of Virginia Dare, first child of English parents born in the present United States at Roanoke Island

Hakluyt map entitled "Novus Orbis" published in Hakluyt edition of Peter Martyr's *De Orbe Novo* in Paris

1589

Ortelius map first published in 1590 in Antwerp the first map to designate the two Americas by the names "North" and "South"

1590

March 20–Oct. 24, Voyage of Sir John White to Roanoke Island which he reached Aug. 17, found no trace of the colonists and returned to England

1591

Lemoyne map by Jacques le Moyne de Morgues who was with the Laudonnière expedition to Florida, map of coast and interior of Florida

1592

Juan de Fuca's discovery of straits named after him on expedition from Mexico at this date now discredited

1595

Feb. 9–Aug., Voyage of Sir Walter Raleigh from Plymouth, arrived at Trinidad off the coast of Venezuela March 22, and entered the Orinoco River in search of gold mines

July 5, Sebastian Roderiguez Cermenho sailed from port of Cavite in the Philippines and on Nov. 4 sighted New Spain, entered Drake's Bay and took possession of the country in the name of the King of Spain, noted and described the entrance to Monterey Bay, arrived at Navidad Jan. 7, 1596

Sept. 21, Juan de Onate appointed Spanish Governor of New Mexico and commissioned to explore and settle the country

1596

Jan. 28, Death of Sir Francis Drake, and burial at sea off east coast of Porto Bello, Panama

March, Sebastian Vizcaino sailed from Acapulco to found colony in Santa Cruz (Lower California); at La Paz abandoned in Oct.

Sept. 9, Onate expedition to New Mexico crossed the Rio de la Nazas and Nov. 1 reached the Minas de Caxco where he remained 19 months

1597

Aug. 1, Onate expedition started north from the Rio de la Nazas

1598

Jan. 30, Onate expedition reached the Rio de Conchas and Feb. 7 left there for New Mexico with 400 men, reached the Rio Grande April 26, and April 30 opposite El Paso took formal possession of the country for Spain, crossed the Rio Grande to site of El Paso May 4, and July 7 received submission of chiefs, and Aug. 11 began work for "city of San Francisco"

July 11, Indian pueblo in the Chama River valley rechristened San Juan de los Caballeros became first capital of New Mexico

July 12, Onate founded settlement which he named San Gabriel (the present Chamita), New Mexico

Sept. 9, Celebration of completion of first church in New Mexico at San Juan de los Caballeros

1599

Jan. 21, General Vicente Zaldivar with 70 men reached Indian stockade at Acoma, New Mexico, in battle with attacking Indians Jan. 22, took possession of Acoma, Jan. 24

1600

Tattonus map engraved by Benjamin Wright, "delineation of the lands and kingdoms of California, New Spain, Mexico and Peru," and "shores of the Gulf of Mexico," etc.

Molineaux-Wright map, attributed to Emerie Molineaux, and to Edward Wright, the first world map on the Wright-Mercator projection engraved in England, and also known as the "New map of Shakespeare" as mentioned by the dramatist in "Twelfth Night," Act III, Scene II

1601

June, Onate with 70 men descended the Canadian River and crossed the Arkansas to Indian settlement called Quivira on site of the present Wichita, Kansas

1602

March 26, Bartholomew Gosnold under Raleigh's patent and sent by the Earl of Southampton sailed from Falmouth to explore "the north part of Virginia." He landed at and named Cape Cod May 14, and made unsuccessful attempt to establish a settlement on Cuttyhunk Island; sailed for England June 18

May 2–Aug. 5, Voyage of Captain George Weymouth explored coast of Maine

May 5, Sebastian Vizcaino sailed from Acapulco, coasted California renaming points visited by Cabrillo, viz., Santa Catalina, San Diego, Santa Barbara, Point Conception, Monterey, Carmel, taking possession of the country at Monterey Dec. 16, sailed as far north as Cape Mendocino

1603

Jan. 12, Vizcaino reached the 41st parallel. On this expedition Martin d'Aguilar sighted entrance to river which may have been the Columbia; Cape Blanco named

March 15–Sept. 20, First voyage of Samuel de Champlain. See Canada

April 10–Oct. 2, Voyage of Martin Pring sent by Richard Hakluyt from Milford Haven to New England coast arrived at Casco Bay in June and sailed as far south as Cape Cod

1604

March 7, Second voyage of Champlain from France to Canada. See Canada

Sept. 2–Oct. 2, Champlain on voyage of exploration from Acadia visited coast of Maine. See Canada

Oct. 7–April 25, 1605, Onate made journey to California from New Mexico, descended Bill Williams Fork and the Colorado to Gulf of California

1605

Jan. 25, Onate took possession for Spain at port at head of Gulf of California

March 5, George Weymouth sailed from Ratcliffe, England, sighted Nantucket Island May 14, at Monhegan Island May 18 off coast of Maine, and explored either the Penobscot or the Kennebec River, returning arrived at Dartmouth July 18

June 18–Aug. 8, Voyage of Champlain along the New England coast. See Canada

1606

April 10 (O.S.), Charter from King James I of England for the incorporation of 2 companies for the purpose of establishing trading colonies in America, the London Company, granted all land between the 34th and 41st degrees of latitude, and the Plymouth Company, the land between the 41st and 45th degrees

Sept. 5–Nov. 14, Voyage of Champlain exploring the New England coast. *See* Canada

Dec. 20, Colonists of the London Company in 3 ships commanded by Captain Christopher Newport, Captain Bartholomew Gosnold, and Captain John Ratcliffe sailed for Virginia

1607

April 26, Colonists of the London Company entered Chesapeake Bay and on the 29th erected a cross and named the place Cape Henry

May 13, The colonists entered the James River and May 14 landed and made first permanent settlement at Jamestown, Virginia

May 31, Colonists from Plymouth sailed in 2 ships commanded by George Popham and Raleigh Gilbert and arrived at the Sagadahoc River Aug. 12 and 16 (Gorges Society)

June 22, Captain Christopher Newport sailed from Jamestown, Virginia, returning to England

Aug. 19, The colonists from Plymouth (Popham's colony) began establishing settlement on Kennebec River, Maine

Sept. 10, Edward M. Wingfield, president of Virginia colony deposed, and John Ratcliffe made president

Dec. 10, John Smith left Jamestown and ascended the Chickahominy River to get provisions. Smith was captured by the Indians and held for several weeks, and his 2 companions killed, the legend being that Smith was saved by the entreaties of Pocahontas, the daughter of Powhatan, the chief. In letter to Queen Anne in 1616 asking her favor for Pocahontas he said, "she hazarded the beating out of her own brains to save mine"

1608

Jan. 8, Arrival of the "first supply" of men and provisions brought by Captain Newport returning to the Jamestown colony, 120 men joining the 38 who had survived the winter. He sailed for England April 10 arriving May 20

July 24–Sept. 7, Captain John Smith made voyage of exploration of Chesapeake Bay and made a map of the region which was published in England in 1612 in the "Oxford Tract"

Sept. 10, Captain John Smith made president of the Jamestown colony

Oct. 17, The Popham colonists abandoned their settlement on the Kennebec River and sailed for England discouraged at news of the death of their leader

1609

April 6–Nov. 4, Voyage of Henry Hudson in service of the Dutch in the "Half Moon" from the Texel in search of northwestern passage, explored the coast from Newfoundland as far south as Chesapeake Bay, then turning north anchored in Delaware Bay Aug. 28, rounded Sandy Hook Sept. 3, and Sept. 11 entered the Hudson River, anchored at site of Albany Sept. 19 and sent a boat 8 or 9 leagues up the river before he turned back. Oct. 2 the "Half

Moon" anchored in the bay where "one side of the river was called Manna-hatta," sailed out of the river named after him Oct. 4 reaching Dartmouth, England, Nov. 4 where his ship was seized by the English Government

May 23, New charter granted to the Virginia settlement making the Jamestown colony independent of the "North Virginia" or Plymouth Company, and grant extended north and south from Point Comfort 200 miles in each direction, and "from sea to sea"

June 1, First expedition for Virginia under the new charter sailed from Plymouth in 9 ships, Captain Newport in command, Sir Thomas Gates, Lieutenant-General, and Sir George Somers, Admiral of Virginia

June 22–Sept. 24, Expedition of Francisco F. de Ecija from St. Augustine, Florida, to the "Rio Jordan"

July 4, Champlain discovered Lake Champlain named after him

July 23, Fleet sailing for Virginia wrecked in hurricane and Newport, Gates, and Somers with 150 settlers cast ashore on the Bermudas, 3 vessels without the commanding officers arrived at the James River in August

Oct. 5, Captain John Smith left the Virginia colony returning to England

The Jesuit fathers, Biard and Massé with settlers from Port Royal established a French colony on Mount Desert Island, Maine

Santa Fé, New Mexico, founded

1610

Feb. 28, Patent to Lord De La Warre (Delaware) as Lord Governor and Captain General of Virginia

April 17, Henry Hudson sailed from Gravesend in the "Discovery" and on June 24 entered the Straits and Bay named after him. *See* Canada

May 10, The Virginia colonists embarked from the Bermudas in newly completed vessels, the "Patience" and the "Delivery" reaching Jamestown May 23

June 10, Arrival of Lord Delaware (De La Warre) with 3 ships and provisions saved the Virginia colony about to abandon Jamestown and sail for the Newfoundland Banks and England

1611

March 28, Dutch expedition of Ernest van de Wall and Pieter Aertzdale de Jonge sailed from the Texel, passed North Cape April 14 in search of North-West Passage, decided to examine the coast of North America, giving up the attempt. Sighted Newfoundland Oct. 29, and sailed south past the Hudson River. The result of this expedition was the founding of the "Compagnie van Nieuw Nederland," forerunner of the Dutch West India Company

Adriaen Block and Hendrick Christiaensen sailed to Manhattan Island, trading with the Indians

1612

March 12, Third charter to Virginia granted by James I transferred control to the stockholders of the London Company

April 15, Sir Thomas Button sailed from the Thames to Port Nelson reached Aug. 15, which he named after the commander of his vessel, Aug. 27, wintered on creek on north side of estuary of the Nelson River, erected a cross July 7, 1613, and July 29 he discovered the inlet known as Sir Thomas Roe's Welcome, the expedition the first to explore the entire western coast of Hudson Bay from Wager Bay to Port Nelson

April 22, Captain Robert Bylot and William Baffin, pilot, sailed from the Humber and explored the coast of Greenland north of Gilbert Sound

July 26, Grant of royal charter to the Merchant Discoverer's of the North-West Passage

Louis XIII of France granted region between Florida and the St. Lawrence claimed by France by virtue of the discoveries of Verrazzano to Mme. de Guercheville

Cultivation of tobacco begun in Virginia by John Rolfe

Champlain map published gave the New England coast for the first time and the St. Lawrence region given with fair accuracy

1613

May and Nov., French settlements on Mount Desert Island and Port Royal and on the St. Croix River destroyed by 2 expeditions of Samuel Argall from Virginia

Captain Samuel Argall on expedition to obtain food from the Indians captured Pocahontas and brought her to Jamestown

1614

March 3, Captain John Smith sailed from London to the Kennebec River, was at Monhegan Island off Maine April 30, and explored the coast as far as Cape Cod. He made a map which was published in London in 1616 of Norumbega or North Virginia to which Prince Charles gave new name of New England

April 5, Pocahontas married to John Rolfe which brought about peace for the Virginia colony with Powhatan and the Chickahominy Indians

Oct. 11, The United Netherland Company formed by Amsterdam merchants granted a charter by the States General of Holland with territory of "New Netherland" between 40° and 45° N. Lat.

Hendrick Christiaensen associated with Adriaen Block constructed a trading house on Castle Island within the present limits of Albany, New York, which he named Fort Nassau

Voyage of Adriaen Block from Amsterdam to the Hudson River where he built boat to replace his own which had been burned and explored the coast to the east, ascending the Connecticut River to an Indian village at 41° 48', named Block Island, explored Narragansett Bay, and went as far as Cape Cod

1615

Jan. 31, Dutch navigators Jacob Lemaire and Willem Schouten discovered a route to the Pacific by passage around Cape Horn, the southernmost promontory of Tierra del Fuego which they named

March 18–Sept. 8, Voyage of Captain Robert Bylot and William Baffin to Hudson Straits and up Fox Channel

Oct. 15, Sir Richard Hawkins, president of the Plymouth Company sailed for New England, and coasted New England and south to Virginia, and thence to Spain, which Sir Ferdinando Gorges says "was all that was done by any of us that year"

1616

Jan. 30, Sir Walter Raleigh released from the Tower to prepare for voyage to Guiana

March 8, Edward Brawnde sailed from Dartmouth and reached Monhegan Island April 20 and proceeded to Cape Cod in search of pearls

March 26, Captain Bylot and William Baffin sailed from Gravesend, discovered Baffin Bay, and Smith's Sound, Jones Sound, and Lancaster Sound, reached 77° 45' N. Lat.

April, Sir Thomas Dale, Governor, with John Rolfe and Pocahontas, and several other Indians sailed for England, arriving June 12. Pocahontas was presented at court by Lady Delaware

1617

March 21, Death of Pocahontas in England aged 22. She left a son from whom descendants can be traced in England and America

June, Raleigh sailed with 11 ships from Plymouth and arrived at Trinidad in December, searched in vain for gold and returned to England, reaching Plymouth in July 1618

Dec. 23, Royal proclamation banished notorious offenders in England to the Virginia colony

1618

Jan. 1, Charter of the United New Netherland Company expired by its own limitation and renewal refused by the States General

1619

Feb. 2, Patent granted to Puritans at Leyden in name of John Wincob for settlement within the limits of South Virginia Company "at some place about the Hudson River"; voided later by fact of their settlement within territory of the Council for New England

July 30–Aug. 6, First colonial legislature in America called the House of Burgesses met at Jamestown, Virginia, no legislation to be valid without approval of the English Company

Aug., A Dutch man-of-war brought 20 negroes for sale to Jamestown and negro slavery introduced in Virginia

First tobacco cargo of 20,000 pounds shipped to England from Virginia

1620

July 22, The religious sect of the Puritans called the "Separatists," congregation of Scrooby, England, who had taken refuge in Holland with their minister, John Robinson, left Leyden for England to emigrate to America; became the "Pilgrim Fathers" of New England

Sept. 6 (O.S.), The Puritans led by Elder Brewster sailed from Plymouth in the "Mayflower," and sighted Cape Cod Nov. 9

Nov. 3 (O.S.), Incorporation of the Council for New England, "The Council established at Plymouth in the county of Devon, for the planting, ruling, ordering and governing New England in America," conferring on 40 of the English nobility with unlimited powers of legislation and government the territory from 40° to 48° N. Lat. and from the Atlantic to the Pacific oceans

Nov. 11 (O.S.), The first exploring party of the colonists landed on Cape Cod, and before landing the colonists signed an agreement to form themselves into a body politic and be governed by just and equitable laws for the general welfare of the Colony, the "Mayflower Compact," John Carver elected Governor. The date of landing is disputed. *See Atlantic Monthly*, Nov. 1881, p. 612

Dec. 11/21, The colonists landed at Plymouth and called their first settlement New Plymouth

1621

Jan. 29, Death of Rose Standish, wife of Miles Standish

Feb. 17, Miles Standish made captain with military authority over settlement

March 9, Grant to John Mason of "Mariana," Cape Ann region south of the Merrimac River, Massachusetts

March 16, Samoset, Indian chief from Island of Monhegan, the first to visit the Plymouth Colony, followed March 21 by visit of Massasoit with about 60 Indians

March 23, John Carver reëlected Governor

April 5, The "Mayflower" sailed for England

——, Death of Governor John Carver, William Carver elected Governor with Isaac Allerton as assistant

June 1, The Council for New England granted the Plymouth Colony a patent in the name of John Pierce and other London merchants who had given them financial assistance

June 3, The Dutch West India Company chartered by the Netherlands States General to protect trade and establish colonies in America and Africa

Sept. 10, Grant of Nova Scotia (Acadia), French by occupation, to Sir William Alexander. *See* Canada

Sept., First Thanksgiving celebrated at Plymouth

Nov. 11, Arrival of the "Fortune" bringing 36 colonists to Plymouth

Dec. 3, The "Fortune" sailed for England carrying beaver and other furs and lumber, cargo valued at $2,400

Alleged discovery of Lake Superior by Brulé and Grenolle. *See* Canada

1622

March 22, Massacre of colonists in Virginia by Indians, 347 persons killed

April 20, New patent from the Council for New England obtained by John Pierce more to his private advantage than to the "Adventurers"; canceled on complaint of Plymouth colonists May 28, 1623

July, Sixty-seven "rude fellows" sent over by Thomas Weston to Plymouth arrived and settled Wessagusset (Weymouth)

Aug. 10, Grant of land between Merrimac and Kennebec rivers to F. Gorges and John Mason, called province of Maine

Oct. 6, Piscataqua (N.H.) at mouth of the Piscataqua River settled by 3 Plymouth merchants

Nov. 3, Patent for that part of New England called Massachusetts granted to Robert Gorges empowered to act as Governor

Dec., The yacht "Mackerel" sent by Dutch West India Company went up the Hudson River trading with the Indians

——, Grant of ten miles "upon the northeast side of Boston Bay" to Robert Gorges

Abraham Jennings became owner of Monhegan Island, Maine

1623

Jan. 1 (O.S.) or Jan. 12 (N.S.), 1624, Patent granted to Roger Conant and associates for Cape Ann, Massachusetts

March, The Dutch West India Company sent settlers to New Netherland, chiefly Walloons, French Protestant refugees, in ship commanded by Cornelis Jacobsen May, who arrived at the mouth of the Hudson River after voyage of 2 months. Eight men left in Manhattan, several families sent to the Delaware River, 6 men to the Connecticut River, and others to Long Island, 18 families under direction of Adriaen Joris proceeding up the Hudson to site of present Albany began construction of Fort Orange

March 23, General Court of Plymouth sent Captain Miles Standish to Wessagussett to settle quarrel with the Indians provoked by the settlers sent by Thomas Weston, the Indians subdued and the settlement abandoned

April 7, Avalon (Newfoundland) granted by charter to George Calvert, Lord Baltimore

June 29, The Council for New England divided the North Atlantic coast from the Bay of Fundy to Narragansett Bay among 20 patentees including Lord Sheffield and Lord Edward Gorges

June, New Netherland made a province and management given to the Amsterdam Chamber

——, Francis West sent to New England commissioned as Admiral of New England to exclude fishermen who came without license from the Council

July, Rain ended drought since planting-time at Plymouth bringing encouragement to colonists on the verge of starvation

Aug., The "Anne" and the "Little James" arrived at Plymouth with 60 colonists and provisions and supplies

Sept., Arrival of Robert Gorges and settlement made at Wessagusset (Weymouth) but the settlement abandoned a second time except by a few persons when Captain Gorges returned to England

Dec. 17, The Colony of Plymouth established trial by jury

First settlement made in New Hampshire by David Thomson, a Scotchman, in the Spring, at Little Harbor on south side of the mouth of the Piscataqua River

English merchants under the proprietors settled Portsmouth and Dover, Casco and Saco bays and Monhegan Island

1624

March, Cornelis Jacobson May (Mey), first Governor of New Netherland, sailed with 30 families, mostly Walloons, and arrived at Manhattan in May

June 16, Charter of the Virginia Company annulled by James I and Virginia became a crown colony. The Company had spent £150,000 and sent out 9,000 settlers

Dec. 21, Charter of a Swedish West India Company granted to William Usselinx under which colony established on the Delaware River

1625

July, Peter Eversen Hulft of Amsterdam with 3 vessels, horses, cattle, pigs, and farming implements established settlement at Governor's Island

July 15, Deed of land from the Indians to John Brown "of New Harbor" of land in Maine which included most of the present towns of Bristol, Nobleborough, Jefferson, and part of town of Newcastle; earliest settlement called Pemaquid

Captain Wollaston with about 30 persons settled at Mount Wollaston (Quincy, Mass.) but soon took his colonists to Virginia, and Thomas Morton with settlers occupied the place, Mount Wollaston becoming Merry Mount

1626

Jan. 9, Peter Minuit, Governor of New Netherland, sailed from Amsterdam arriving

May 24, He bought Manhattan Island from the Indians for goods to value of $24, founded settlement of New Amsterdam

Sept.–Oct., Roger Conant, John Lyford, and about 25 others from the Cape Ann settlement removed to Naumkeag (Salem)

Abraham Shurt purchased the Island of Monhegan from Abraham Jennings for Robert Aldworth and Giles Eldridge of Bristol, England, for £50

1627

Nov., Members of the Plymouth Colony bought the stock and interest from the London merchants who had financed the Colony for $9,000

1628

Feb. 2, Grant to Sir William Alexander by Charles I of islands and trade of the St. Lawrence River and Gulf

March 19, Patent for land between the Merrimac and Charles rivers by the Council for New England to 6 grantees including John Endicott and John White, the Massachusetts Bay Company

June, Settlement at Merry Mount broken up and settlement dispersed by Captain Standish for the Plymouth Colony

Sept. 6, A company of colonists under John Endicott as Governor arrived at Salem, beginning the permanent settlement of Massachusetts Bay Colony, the name Salem chosen in allusion to Psalm lxxvi-2

1629

Jan. 13, Charter of Colony of New Plymouth granted to William Bradford and his associates

Feb. 4, Monopoly of trade in the St. Lawrence River and Gulf granted to Sir William Alexander and his partners

March 4, The Massachusetts Bay Company obtained charter from Charles I confirming land grant of 1628

March 12, Grant to Edward Hitton within Mason's grant of land which included Dover and Exeter, the "Swampscott patent"

April 24, Treaty of peace between France and England

June 7, Charter of 31 articles for the colonization of New Netherland by the Dutch West India Company established the patroon system

June 24, Settlement of Charlestown, Mass. by Ralph, Richard, and William Sprague and others

July 20, Samuel Skelton appointed pastor and Mr. Higginson teacher of first church in Massachusetts at Salem, and the church constituted Aug. 6 by association of 30 persons

Aug. 26, The Cambridge Agreement by which John Winthrop and 11 other Puritans assembled members of the Massachusetts Bay Company agreed to emigrate to New England provided that the charter and administration of the Company be transferred from England to America, this transfer made Aug. 29, and John Winthrop chosen Governor of the Massachusetts Bay Colony

Oct. 30, Grant of Carolina or Carolana, the territory between 31° and 36° N. Lat. to Sir Robert Heath by Charles I

Nov. 7, Grant of all that part of the Province of Maine between the Merrimac and Piscataqua rivers to John Mason by the Council for New England. He named it New Hampshire

Nov. 17, Sir F. Gorges and John Mason received a grant of land in the region of Lake Champlain to be called Laconia

Edward Ashley acting for the Plymouth colonists opened a trading house on the Penobscot River at place which later became Castine

First tannery erected at Lynn, Mass. by Francis Ingalls

1630

Jan. 13, New patent for the Plymouth Colony obtained by Mr. Allerton conveying to William Bradford and his associates tract of land including Plymouth which fixed the boundaries and another on the Connecticut River according to Palfrey, and in Maine according to J. K. Wright, location disputed. See infra Oct. 28, 1783

Feb. 12, Grants made on south bank of Saco River, Maine, to John Oldham and Richard Vines and on north bank to Thomas Lewis and Richard Bonighton

March 13, Grant of the Muscongus or Waldo patent (Maine) made to John Beauchamp of London and Thomas Leverett of Boston, England

April 7, Governor John Winthrop sailed from England in fleet of 14 sail with about 840 persons including Isaac Johnson and his wife Lady Arbella in the "Arbella"

May, The first colonists sent by Killian van Rensselaer to the Upper Hudson arrived at Rensselaerwyck which he had purchased April 18, the first patroon

June 26, The "Plough" or "Lygonia" patent granted 40 miles in length and breadth on Sagadhoc River by Council for New England

July 12, Michael Paauw bought lands on west side of Hudson under patroon system and named his territory Pavonia, the present Hoboken, Aug. 10 Staten Island, Nov. 22 what is now Jersey City

July 15, Samuel Godyn and Samuel Blommaert of Amsterdam obtained ratification from Governor Peter Minuit of New Netherland of deed of land of June 1, 1629 purchased from the Indians extending from Cape Henlopen to the mouth of the Delaware River

July 30, First church in Boston constituted established at Charlestown and transferred to Boston in 1632, Mr. John Wilson elected teacher

Aug. 10, Kiliaen (Killian) van Rensselaer purchased lands about Fort Orange from the Council of New Netherland which he had purchased from the Indians July 27 or July 28. He eventually became owner of over 700,000 acres of land which now is the counties of Albany, Rensselaer, and part of Columbia county, New York

Sept. 17, The peninsula called Shawmut by the Indians named Boston by order of the Court of Charlestown

Oct. 19, A General Court, the first in New England, met in Boston

Dec. 12, David Petersen de Vries, member of a company formed by Godyn, with Pieter Heyes and Gillis Hosset sailed from the Texel and arrived March, 1631 founding first settlement in Delaware on Lewes Creek within Cape Helopen, which they called Swaanendael

Grant of land 120 miles southeast from the Narragansett River extending from the Atlantic to the Pacific by the Council of Plymouth to the Earl of Warwick

Map of Joannes de Laet published in Leyden gives view of the geographical knowledge of this period, and that of Henricus Hondius published in Amsterdam

1631

Feb. 5, Arrival of ship "Lyon" from Bristol with 26 passengers including Roger Williams brought provisions ending long famine of the Massachusetts Bay Colony

Feb. 29, Grant of 12,000 acres near the Pemaquid River to Robert Aldworth and Giles Elbridge

March 19, Grant of Robert, Earl of Warwick, to Lord Say and Seal and associates including Lord Brooke, John Hampden, and John Pym of land west from the Narragansett River extending from the Atlantic to the Pacific

April 30–Oct. 31, 1632, Voyage of Luke Foxe in search of North-West Passage. *See* Canada

May 3–Oct. 22, Voyage of Captain Thomas James. *See* Canada

May 16, Royal grant of license to trade for furs in or near the coasts of America for which patents not granted to others to William Clayborne. He established a trading post on Kent Island in Chesapeake Bay

May 18, Second meeting of General Court of Massachusetts Bay Colony decreed "No man shall be admitted to the body politic but such as are members of some of the churches within the limits" of the Colony

July, Ten settlers under the "Plough" patent arrived in ship, the "Plough" and remained in Massachusetts instead of going to their land in Maine

Nov. 3, Arrival of Rev. John Eliot, "Apostle to the Indians" at Massachusetts Bay Colony

——, Grant of land along the Piscataqua River, the "Piscataqua patent," to 6 London merchants under the Gorges and Mason patent

Dec. 2, Grant of 24,000 acres on both sides of the Agamenticus (York) River to Ferdinando Gorges, Walter Norton, and others by Council for New England, and settlements established

The Earl of Warwick granted land 120 miles southeast from the Narragansett River

1632

April 15, Lord Baltimore received grant of Maryland, a part of the Virginia territory, the charter of Maryland

May 23, De Vries sailed for Swaanendael, arriving in December, and found that colonists had been attacked and killed by the Indians

May, Cornhill, Boston, fortified

June 20, Charter of Lord Baltimore of Maryland grant transferred to his son, Cecilius Calvert, second Lord Baltimore, after death of his father

June, Patent to George Way and Thomas Purchas for tract of land along the Androscoggin River

Settlement of Duxbury, Massachusetts

Map of New France by Samuel de Champlain published, enlarged his map of 1612, important for delineation of Great Lakes region

1633

April 24, Jacob Eelkens in English employ sailed up Hudson River, the first English ship, and established trading post a mile above Fort Orange

June 8, The Dutch bought land from the Indians and erected a fort where Hartford, Connecticut, now stands

July 3, The Privy Council gave decision confirming the grant of Maryland to Lord Baltimore in answer to protests of the Virginia Colony against cession

Sept. 3, Arrival at Boston of Thomas Hooker, John Cotton, John Haynes, and Samuel Stone from England

Oct. 10, Thomas Wiggin brought settlers to Cocheco (Dover) on the Piscataqua River, New Hampshire

Oct., William Holmes and other settlers from Plymouth established a trading post at Winsor on the Connecticut River

1634

Jan., John Endicott cut red cross from the flag as a "relic of antichrist and a popish symbol"

Feb. 27, Leon Calvert reached Point Comfort with settlers for Maryland, landed on St. Clement's Island March 25 and made first settlement at St. Mary's March 27

1635

March 3, Provisional Government instituted under commission General Court of Massachusetts to 8 persons resolved to settle on the Connecticut River

April 22, Grant of Long Island to Sir William Alexander and New Hampshire to John Mason

June 7, Council at Plymouth renounced their charter to Crown of England

Philip Kertland began the manufacture of boots and shoes at Lynn, Massachusetts

1636

Jan., Roger Williams with his family left Salem to escape from Captain Underhill sent from Boston to arrest him and put him on board a ship for England because of his religious opinions; spent the winter with the Indians and started a settlement at Seekonk in the Spring

March 25, First meeting of "councillors" of "New Somersetshire" at Saco, Maine, with Captain William Gorges, sent as deputy-governor by Sir Ferdinando Gorges appointed Governor Oct. 1, 1635

April 26, First court held at Newtown (Hartford) Connecticut

May 14, William Pynchot and others from Roxbury near Boston settled Agawam (Springfield), Massachusetts, Agreement signed May 16

June 16, Jacob van Curler bought land on Long Island from the Indians, first recorded grant in King's county

June, Roger Williams founded Providence, Rhode Island, with a government based on complete religious toleration

——, Thomas Hooker emigrated with his congregation to Newtown (Hartford)

July, John Oldham killed by the Indians near Block Island, one of the chief causes of the war of the colonists with the Pequot Indians of Long Island and Connecticut

Aug. 24, John Endicott sent with 100 men by Governor Vane from Boston to destroy the Pequot settlements on Block Island as punishment for murder of Oldham

Oct. 28, Harvard College founded, to be built at Newtown (Cambridge) by Act of the General Court of Massachusetts granting £400 towards a school or college

1637

Feb. 21, Newtown, Connecticut, named Hartford, and in Massachusetts, Watertown and Dorchester named

——, The Court at Newtown (Hartford) applied to Massachusetts for aid to fight the Pequot Indians

April, Wethersfield (Connecticut) attacked by the Pequot Indians

May 1, The towns of Hartford, Wethersfield, and Winsor united in a self-governing confederation under the name of Connecticut

May 26, Captains John Mason and John Underhill with men from the Massachusetts and Connecticut colonies destroyed the Pequot Indian fort at Mystic, Conn. and more than 600 Indians killed

June 16, Wouter Van Twiller for his private estate bought the present Governor's Island to add to settlement on Long Island which is now Flatlands which he had purchased from the Indians July 16, 1636

June 26, Arrival at Boston of Theophilus Eaton, Edward Hopkins, and John Davenport

July 13, Captains Mason and Stoughton from Massachusetts pursued the Pequots and practically annihilated the tribe in battle near Fairfield, Conn.

July 23, Sir Ferdinando Gorges commissioned Governor-General of New England

Nov. 7, Anne Hutchinson sentenced by the General Court of Massachusetts to banishment for her religious opinions, allowed to remain in the Colony until March

Dec. 30, George Evelyn commissioned commander of Kent Island by the Governor of Maryland

1638

Jan. 14, "Fundamental Orders," a constitution framed for the government of Connecticut at Hartford by delegates from Hartford, Winsor, and Wethersfield adopted, the provision made that the entire body of freemen should hold 2 meetings a year to elect a governor and assistants and deputies from each town, Springfield later in Massachusetts included

Jan. 25, Second Assembly of Maryland met to consider body of laws proposed by Lord Baltimore which were rejected

Feb. 14, Springfield made decision that settlement should be part of Massachusetts instead of Connecticut

Feb., The "Ancient and Honorable Artillery Company" organized in Boston

March 7, Mrs. Anne Hutchinson settled in exile on the island of Aquedneck (Rhode Island), group of 19 settlers formed themselves into a body politic and elected William Coddington Chief-Magistrate, and called the settlement by the Indian name of Pocasset, later named Portsmouth

March, First settlement in Delaware by Swedes under Peter Minuit, formerly of the Dutch West India Company, at Christiana, New Sweden, the present Wilmington

March 24, Deed of sale by Canonicus and Miantinomo, the 2 chief sachems of Narraganset, of lands between the Pawtucket and Pawtuxet rivers to Roger Williams who conveyed lands to 12 associates reserving only an equal share for himself

March 29, Peter Minuit concluded purchase of land from the Iroquois Minquas on west shore of the Delaware River from near Bombay Hook to the Schuylkill River for colony of New Sweden

March 30, Rev. John Davenport, Mr. Eaton, and other settlers sailed from Boston arriving at Quinipiack (New Haven) April 15, Mr. Davenport preached first sermon April 18

April 4, Claim of Lord Baltimore to Kent Island declared valid

April, John Wheelwright and others of the religious sect of Antinomians bought land from the Indians and settled Exeter, New Hampshire

May 6, Governor Kieft of New Netherland protested against Swedish settlement on the Delaware claiming prior possession by the Dutch

June 1, Great earthquake in Plymouth and surrounding country

Sept. 14, John Harvard at his death bequeathed in Charlestown, Mass. his library and half of his estate for a college

Nov. 24 and Dec. 11, The Quinipiack (New Haven) settlement purchased land from the Indians

1639

Jan. 14, Fundamental Orders for government of Connecticut ratified at Hartford for Hartford, Winsor, and Wethersfield

Jan. 15, Purchase of part of Long Island from the Indians by Governor Kieft for New Netherland

March 13, Newtown (Cambridge) selected as site of college to be called Harvard after John Harvard

March, First printing press set up by Stephen Daye at Harvard College in house of the president, Henry Dunster, the "Freeman's Oath" and "An Almanac Calculated for New England" by William Pierce, Mariner, printed

——, First Baptish Church, with Roger Williams, pastor, established at Providence, R.I.

April 3, Royal grant of the Province of Maine to Sir Ferdinando Gorges by Charles I, between the Piscataqua River on the west and the Sagadahocke (Kennebec) on the east, and extending 120 miles northward

April 11, General election at Hartford, Conn. John Haynes chosen Governor

April 29, William Coddington and John Clarke founded settlement at Newport, Rhode Island

May 22, Hampton township laid out by Massachusetts within the territory of New Hampshire

June 4, Free planters met at Quinipiack (New Haven) and framed a constitution

July, Saybrook, Connecticut, founded by George Fenwick, one of the patentees. In 1644 Fenwick sold the fort and the town to Connecticut

Aug. 22, Governor Winthrop of Massachusetts bought tract of land on the Androscoggin River from a settler at Pejepscot (Brunswick) securing first hold on Maine

——, Settlers led by Rev. Mr. Prudden to harbor on Long Island Sound near mouth of the Housatonic bought land of Indians and after a year of residence called their town Milford

Sept. 29, Settlers led by Mr. Whitefield founded Guilford, Connecticut

Oct. 4, John Wheelright and other Antinomians at Exeter, N.H. constituted a body politic and a church. Agreement for government signed Dec. 4

Oct. 25, Samuel Eaton elected magistrate at Quinipiack

(New Haven) and Theophilus Eaton, Governor (Palfrey. Winsor, Oct. 29)

Nov. 5, The General Court of Massachusetts appointed Richard Fairfield of Boston to take care of letters "brought from beyond the seas or to be sent thither," and to receive a penny for each

Nov., Milford, Connecticut settled

1640

Jan. 24, Charter granted by Queen Christina to Dutch settlers of land in New Sweden to be held hereditarily under the Crown of Sweden

Feb. 7, Second company of colonists for New Sweden left for America, arriving at Christiana April 17

March 2, William Bradford and associates surrendered their patent of Plymouth Colony to the freemen

March 10, Gardiner's Island, N.Y. purchased by Lyon Gardiner from the Indians

——, Thomas Gorges appointed deputy-governor of Maine

March 12, Newport, and Portsmouth, Rhode Island, united

April 16, Agawam took name of Springfield from this date

June 12 (O.S.), A Scotchman named Farrett in the name of the Earl of Stirling made grant of Southampton, Long Island, to a company of settlers from New England

June 25, First General Court under the Gorges Charter of the "Province and County of Maine" held at Saco

Aug. 27–Sept. 6, Meeting of inhabitants of Providence Plantations at Providence, R.I. adopted 12 articles of government

Sept. 1, Quinipiack took the name of New Haven

Oct. 22, Provisional government established at Portsmouth, N.H.

Nov. 2, Dutch settlers under grant of land in New Sweden arrived at Delaware River

The "Bay Psalm Book," a metrical version of the Psalms by Richard Mather, Thomas Wilde and John Eliot, the first book printed in British America at the press of Stephen Daye in Cambridge

1641

March 16–19, A General Court declared Rhode Island a democracy and adopted new constitution granting freedom of religion to all citizens

April 10, Sir Ferdinando Gorges made Agamenticus (York) a borough by charter

June 2, Springfield recognized by General Court at Boston as within the jurisdiction of Massachusetts instead of Connecticut

June 14, Dover and the settlement at Piscataqua or Strawberry Bank (Portsmouth) New Hampshire annexed by Massachusetts

Aug. 30, Town meeting at New Haven, Conn. voted authority over region on Delaware Bay bought from the Indians the previous year for the Delaware Company by Captain Turner

Oct. 22, Agreement of the settlers on the Piscataqua River, New Hampshire, for government signed

Dec., Ninety-eight laws adopted in Massachusetts, the "Fundamentals" or "Body of Liberties"

1642

March 1, Agamenticus (York) made a city by Sir Ferdinando Gorges and named Gorgeana

April 19, Settlers from New Haven on the Delaware River expelled by the Dutch

Nov. 1, Fourth Swedish expedition sailed for New Sweden, arriving at Fort Christiana, Feb. 15, 1643

1643

Jan. 12, Samuel Gorton founded settlement at Shawomet (Warwick) Rhode Island

Feb. 15, Johan Printz, appointed Governor of New Sweden arrived at Fort Christiana (fifth Swedish expedition)

Feb. 25, Governor Kieft of New Netherland began Indian war by attack on Indians at Pavonia and Corlaer's Hook because of refusal of the Indians to give up the murderer of a colonist

March 14, Patent for the Providence Plantations (Providence, Newport, and Portsmouth) obtained from Robert, Earl of Warwick, by Roger Williams

April 7, Alexander Rigby purchased the "Plough" or "Lygonia" patent and appointed George Cleaves deputy president

April 15, Death of Elder William Brewster of Plymouth

May 10, Massachusetts divided into 4 counties, Essex, Norfolk, Suffolk, and Middlesex. The 4 New Hampshire towns, Dover, Portsmouth, Exeter, and Hampton, with Salisbury in the county of Norfolk

May 19, The United Colonies of New England was formed for protection against the French, the Dutch, and the Indians, Massachusetts Bay, Plymouth, and the New Haven and the other Connecticut colonies included in the confederation

Sept., Mrs Anne Hutchinson and her family except one daughter carried into captivity massacred by the Indians at their home near Pelham Bay, New York

Oct. 27, Fundamental Orders for the government of the New Haven Colony agreed on by General Court at New Haven

Nov. 3, Samuel Gorton and 6 others brought from Shawomet (Warwick, R.I.) and sentenced by General Court at Boston to confinement at hard labor for blasphemy

1644

March 11, Sixth Swedish expedition arrived at Christiana

March 13, Portsmouth-Newport General Court changed name of Aquedneck Island to Isle of Rhodes or Rhode Island

March 14, Union of Providence, Portsmouth, and Newport under a charter obtained from the Parliamentary commissioners by Roger Williams

April 18, Second massacre of the settlers in Virginia by the Indians, 300 persons killed in outlying districts

May 29, Sentence of banishment against John Wheelwright removed

Oct. 8, Peace Treaty with d'Aulnay. (*See* Canada)

Nov. 16, New England settlers at Hempstead, Long Island, obtained a patent of incorporation from the Director-General and Council of New Netherland

Dec. 5, George Fenwick sold the fort at Saybrook to Connecticut (union of 8 towns called Connecticut)

1645

Feb., Great seal of the Province of Maryland at St. Mary's destroyed by rebels led by Ingle and Claiborne in possession of the Province and Kent Island in the name of the Parliamentary Party

April 22, Treaty of peace with the Indians signed ended war in New Netherland (New York), and Treaty of peace signed at New Amsterdam Aug. 30

1646

Oct. 28, John Eliot preached his first sermon to the Indians at Nonantum in Massachusetts

In last part of the year Governor Calvert with troops organized in Virginia regained St. Mary's and part of Province of Maryland

1647

April, Leonard Calvert established his authority at Kent Island, and appointed Robert Vaughan, Governor

May 19–21, The Rhode Island communities united into one Colony with John Coggeshall, President under the Charter of 1644, and 4 assistants, one from each town, Newport, Providence, Warwick, and Portsmouth, the confederation had been delayed by the hostility of Massachusetts and Plymouth

May 27, Peter Stuyvesant, Governor to New Netherland, arrived at New Amsterdam

Sept. 25, Seventh expedition of colonists from Sweden sailed for America, arriving Oct. 1

Nov. 11, Massachusetts law required every township in the jurisdiction of the General Court which contained 50 householders to maintain a school, and every town with 100 families to maintain a grammar school

1648

Jan., Eighth Swedish expedition sailed for America

May, Samuel Gorton arrived in Boston from England where he had sought redress with a letter from the Earl of Warwick asking only that he might have liberty to return to Shawomet, which was granted after much opposition by majority of a single vote by the General Court

1649

Jan. 30, Virginia announced its allegiance to the House of Stuart after the execution of Charles I, and during the year 330 adherents including Colonel Henry Norwood, Francis Morrison, and Richard Fox took refuge in Virginia

March 26, Death of Governor John Winthrop of Massachusetts

April 21, Toleration Act passed by Legislature of Maryland provided that "no person professing to believe in Jesus Christ shall from henceforth be any waies troubled, molested, or discountenanced for, or in respect of, his or her religion, nor in the free exercise thereof within this province . . . nor any way compelled to the beleefe or exercise of any other religion against his or her consent"

June 15, First trial for witchcraft and execution of Margaret Jones at Charlestown in Massachusetts

July 3, Ninth expedition of colonists from Sweden, boat wrecked off Puerto Rico Aug. 26

Charles II granted to Lord Hopton the tract bounded by and within the heads of the Rappahannock and Potomac rivers, etc., the tract confirmed to Lord Culpepper in 1689 on whose death it descended to Lord Fairfax, rights of soil only, jurisdiction left to Virginia; generally known as the Fairfax grant

1650

May 31, Charter granted to Harvard College

June, Norwalk, Connecticut settled by 20 families from Hartford

Sept. 19, Treaty of Hartford settled the boundaries between New Netherland (New York) and Connecticut

1651

April 3, William Coddington obtained a patent from the Council of State in England making him governor of Rhode Island and Connecticut for life with a council of 6 to assist him, this order later revoked by efforts of Roger Williams

July 18, John Clarke and John Crandall of Newport and Obadiah Holmes of Seekonk, Baptists, arrested at Lynn and sent to Boston for trial, and received sentence of fines, Clarke, £20, Holmes, £30, and Crandall, £5

July 19, The Dutch of New Netherland bought from the Indians the lands already sold by the Indians to the Swedes, and built Fort Casimir at site of the present Newcastle, Delaware

Sept. 26, Council of State in England appointed commission of five including Richard Bennett and William Claiborne "to use their best endeavors to reduce all the plantations upon the bay of Chesapeake to their due obedience to the Parliament and Commonwealth of England"

Oct. 9, Navigation Act limited carrying trade to English vessels. *See* England, 1660, 1662, 1663

1652

March 12, Virginia surrendered to Captain Robert Dennis sent from England by Parliament to reduce the Colony to the authority of the Commonwealth

March 29, The Commissioners forced submission of Maryland to the Commonwealth of England, taking control of the government from Lord Baltimore in spite of Governor Stone's refusal of allegiance, and established a provisional government

April 30, Provisional Government established in Virginia, Richard Bennet, Governor

May 19, The Rhode Island towns of Providence and Shawomet (Warwick) in General Assembly enacted that no man, white or negro, should be held in slavery longer than 10 years on penalty of £40

May 31, Massachusetts General Court claimed boundary under charter 3 miles north of the head-waters of the Merrimac River and assumed jurisdiction

June 10, General Court established a mint at Boston, John Hull the first mint-master, and the coiner of the "pine tree" shillings

June 28, Governor Stone reinstated in Maryland by the Commissioners

Oct. 2, Roger Williams in England acting for the mainland and John Clarke for the island towns of Rhode Island secured repeal of Coddington's patent

Oct. 23, The Massachusetts General Court appointed 6 commissioners to settle civil government in Kittery, Maine and in the Isle of Shoals, and settle boundary

Nov. 20, Forty-one inhabitants of Kittery signed declaration acknowledging the jurisdiction of Massachusetts, and Nov. 22 the same procedure followed at Agamenticus (York)

1653

Feb. 2, Governor Stuyvesant by proclamation brought into effect the burgher government granted to New Amsterdam

June 27, Connecticut colonists seized Dutch post at Hartford

July, Colonists from Virginia started a settlement at Albemarle on the Chowan River in North Carolina

Aug., The Jesuit, Father Antoine Poncet, the first to view the Thousand Islands of the St. Lawrence River. *See* Canada

Nov., Middletown, Connecticut, settled by families from Hartford, Wethersfield, and some settlers just arrived from England

——, Convention met at New Amsterdam to consult on measures for protection against the Indians; adjourned until the following month

Dec. 10, Convention met at New Amsterdam with delegates from Breuckelen (Brooklyn), Flushing, Middleburg, Heemstede (Hempstead), Amersfoort, Flatbush, and Gravesend to consult as to the welfare of the country, and adopted address to the Governor protesting against laws made, appointments, and grants of land without the consent of the people

1654

March 1, Death of John Haynes

March 7, Plymouth obtained from Parliament confirmation of tract of land on the Kennebec River, Maine, and sent Thomas Prince to organize a local government

May 6, Governor Stone by proclamation declared the government of Maryland to be under Oliver Cromwell, Lord Protector of the Commonwealth of England

May 23, The Swedes at the Delaware River took possession of the Dutch Fort Casimir (Newcastle, Delaware) and Governor John Claude Rysingh named it Fort Trinity

July 2, Father Simon Le Moyne began journey from Quebec which took him as far as the Oswego River. *See* Canada

July 8, Jacob Barsimon, a Jew, arrived in New Amsterdam, followed during the year by 23 other Jewish emigrants

July, Bennett and Claiborne again displaced Governor Stone in Maryland and placed the administration in charge of a council headed by William Fuller

Aug. 6–Aug., 1656, Expedition of P. E. Radisson and M. Chouart which may have reached the upper Mississippi. *See* Canada

Aug. 16, Port Royal surrendered by Le Borgne (French) to Major Robert Sedgwick sent by Cromwell to take Manhattan from the Dutch

1655

March 25, Governor Stone of Maryland defeated in attack on Puritans in possession of Providence

April 26, The Dutch West India Company instructed Governor Peter Stuyvesant that Jews should have permission to sail to, trade and live in New Amsterdam

May 8, Death of Edward Winslow

Sept. 1, Governor Stuyvesant captured Fort Trinity and Sept. 15 Fort Christiana and subdued Swedish colony to Dutch rule, sending back to Sweden those who refused to take oath of allegiance to New Netherland

Sept. 15, Indians attacked New Amsterdam, Pavonia, and Staten Island, killing 100 Dutch settlers in 3 days and taking 150 prisoners

Oct. 1, Governor Rysingh of New Sweden and a number of other Swedes left Delaware for Sweden

1656

March 14 (O.S.), Swedish colonists arrived at Colony on ship "Mercurius" and were turned back by the Dutch in possession in Delaware

July 17, Jesuits from Canada began building house on site of present city of Syracuse, New York. *See* Canada May 7

July, Two Quakers, Mary Fisher and Ann Austin, arrived at Boston from England

Aug. 5, Eight Quakers arrived at Boston from England, all imprisoned and masters of vessels which brought them placed under bonds to take them away

Aug. 16, Fort Casimir, and New Amstel (Delaware) transferred to city of New Amsterdam by the Dutch West India Company, and Articles of government (25) for the "Colony of the City" approved by the States General

Sept. 16, Report of Commissioners of Trade to Cromwell's Council of State favorable to Lord Baltimore's proprietary rights in Maryland

Sept. 17, Federal Commissioners recommended severe laws against Quakers at meeting which were enacted by Massachusetts, Quakers to be committed to the house of correction and kept at hard labor until transported

Oct. 3, Death of Captain Miles Standish

Oct. 14, Massachusetts made fine for harboring Quakers 40 shillings an hour, and every Quaker coming into the jurisdiction after punishment to suffer loss of one ear, for second offense the loss of the other, and for third offense have tongue "bored through with a hot iron" (Palfrey)

Map published in Paris by Nicolas Sanson which remained an authority until superseded by that of Delisle

1657

June 1, Five Quakers landed in New Amsterdam and were arrested and imprisoned but after 8 days permitted to sail for Rhode Island

1658

Jan. 7, Death of Theophilus Eaton of New Haven

March 24, Puritans in Maryland surrendered to Josias Fendall, appointed Governor by Lord Baltimore

June 1–Aug. 19, 1660, Expedition of Radisson and Groseilliers which claimed to have reached the Mississippi River. *See* Canada

July 13, Settlements of Casco Bay, Blue Point, Black Point, and Spurwinke acknowledged the jurisdiction of Massachusetts

Aug. 12, A "rattle-watch" of 8 men established in New Amsterdam (New York City), the first police force

Oct., The Massachusetts General Court made it a capital offense for a Quaker to return to the Colony after banishment

1659

Oct. 27, William Robinson and Marmaduke Stevenson, Quakers, hung on Boston Common on return after banishment

1660

March 23, Sir William Berkeley elected Governor by the Virginia Assembly, and commissioned by the King July 31

May, General Court of Massachusetts forbade celebration of Christmas under penalty of 5 shillings fine

June 1, Mary Dyer, Quaker, returning to Boston was hung

July 27, Two judges who condemned Charles I, Edward Whalley and William Goffe, reached Boston and were concealed from the royal officers. From 1664 they were hidden in the house of the Rev. John Russell at Hadley

1661

March 14, William Leddra, Quaker, returning to Boston was executed

May 15–Aug. 19, The regicide judges, Whalley and Goffe, hidden in cave on east side of West Rock, New Haven, while search for them by royalists sent from England in progress

Sept., Governor Endicott of Massachusetts released Quakers from prison and stopped proceedings against them as ordered by Charles II

Dec. 20, Roger Williams executed formal deed of conveyance to his associates of lands sold to him personally by the Indians in March, 1638

1662

April 23, Grant of liberal Charter to Connecticut by Charles II which added Hartford to the New Haven colony and all the lands west of it to the extent of its breadth from sea to sea, boundaries defined as Naragansett Bay on the east, the Atlantic Ocean on the south, Massachusetts on the north, the Pacific on west

June 28, Letter of Charles II confirmed Charter of Massachusetts

1663

March 24, Grant by Charles II of the Carolinas to 8 proprietors, Anthony Ashley Cooper, later Lord Ashley, Lord Clarendon, the Duke of Albermarle, Lord Craven, Sir George Carteret, Lord John Berkeley, Sir William Berkeley, and Sir John Colleton, the territory between 36° and 31° N. Lat. from sea to sea

July 8, Charter of Rhode Island and the Providence Plantations granted by Charles II to Roger Williams and John Clarke, agent for the island towns of Rhode Island

Aug. 25, Declarations and proposals of the proprietors of North Carolina issued

Oct., Sir John Yeamans ascended the Cape Fear River for more than 150 miles

1664

Jan. 11, F. Gorges, grandson of the original proprietor, obtained order from the King that Massachusetts should restore to him the province of Maine

Feb. 10, Philip Carteret, a brother of the proprietor, received a commission as Governor of New Jersey

March 12, Charles II granted to James, Duke of York, land from the St. Croix River west to the Pemaquid, and from the coast to the St. Lawrence, all the islands between Cape Cod and the Narrows, the Hudson River and all the lands from the west side of the Connecticut River to the east side of Delaware Bay; confirmed June 29, 1667

May 15, English fleet commanded by Colonel Nicolls, Carr, and Cartwright sailed from Portsmouth to take possession of New Netherland included in the grant to the Duke of York, reached Boston, July 23, and made arrangements for coöperation of the militia of the colonies

June 24, The region between the Hudson and Delaware rivers (New Jersey) granted by the Duke of York to Lord Berkeley and Sir George Carteret

Aug. 29, New Amsterdam summoned to surrender to English fleet commanded by Colonel Nicolls

Sept. 3, Surrender of New Amsterdam by Governor Stuyvesant to the English, formally completed Sept. 8, and the city named New York, and Fort named Fort James

Sept. 10, Cartwright commissioned to sail up the Hudson and receive the surrender of Fort Orange, which surrendered Sept. 24 and was renamed Fort Albany

Sept. 30, New Amstel and Fort Casimir (Newcastle, Delaware) surrendered to Sir Robert Carr

Oct., Governor Berkeley organized government for northern part of North Carolina calling it Albemarle and naming William Drummond, Governor

Oct. 13, Judges Whalley and Goffe took refuge in Hadley where they lived in the house of the minister, John Russell, in hiding

Nov. 6, Dutch Government demanded return of New Netherland

Nov. 30, Boundary of Connecticut adjusted by commissioners from Connecticut, and the Governor, commissioners from New York and Governor Richard Nicolls, and the King's commissioners; this agreement not accepted by New York or confirmed by the King

1665

Feb. 10, Berkeley and Carteret signed the "Concessions and Agreements of the Lord Proprietors of New Jersey," first Constitution of the Colony, and Philip Carteret commissioned Governor

March 1, At meeting at Hempstead, Long Island, Governor Nicolls published laws for the government of the new province known as the "Duke's Laws"

April 20, Connecticut, the union of Hartford and New Haven, accepted the Charter of 1662, John Winthrop, Governor

May 3, Death of Governor John Endicott of Massachusetts

May 26, The Commissioners from England refused jurisdiction by the General Court of Massachusetts

May 29, Sir John Yeamans brought a group of settlers to the mouth of the Cape Fear River, the present Clarendon, North Carolina

June 23, The King's Commissioners established a provisional government for 8 towns in Maine

June 30, A second patent to the proprietors of the Carolinas extended the boundaries to 36° 30′ on the north and to 29° on the south

Sept. 5, The King's Commissioners organized territory on the west side of the Sagadhock (Kennebec) River which they named Cornwall

1666

May 17, Newark settled by company from New Haven led by Robert Treat and Mathew Gilbert, name given in June, 1667 in honor of minister, Mr. Pierson, who brought his congregation from Branford in the New Haven Colony to Newark, Newark being the name of his former home in England

July, Fort de Chazy built by the French from Canada at Isle La Motte near the north end of Lake Champlain

1667

July, Treaty of Breda confirmed conquest of New York (New Netherland) and New Jersey (the Jerseys) from the Dutch and restored Acadia to France

1668

April 14–15, Baptists had debate with 6 Massachusetts ministers in the First Church of Boston

May 12, Grant of 276 acres at site of present Hoboken to Nicholas Verlett

May 26, First Assembly in East Jersey called by Governor Carteret met at Elizabethtown

May 27, Sentence of banishment of Thomas Gold, William Turner, and John Farnum, Baptists, by the General Court of Massachusetts

July 6, Commissioners from Massachusetts held convention at York calling on citizens of Maine to again recognize the jurisdiction of Massachusetts

July 25, Boundary line between Maryland and Virginia from Chesapeake Bay to the Atlantic Ocean established by a commission

1669

April 20, Queen Regent of Spain commanded war against the English in the Indies

July 21, John Locke's constitution for Carolina, the "Fundamental Constitutions" drafted, went into effect only partially; revised March 1, 1670 by interpolation of a clause against the wishes of Locke which established the Church of England in the Colony

1670

March 17, Captain William Sayle with colonists from England for Carolina made first landing in Sewee Bay at back of Bull's Island and established settlement in South Carolina at Albermarle Point on the west bank of the Ashley River in April

May 2, Hudson Bay Company chartered. *See* Canada

July 18, Treaty between Spain and Great Britain, recognition by Spain of right of England to her colonies in the Caribbean and on the American mainland

Sept. 30, Expedition of La Salle which may have reached Louisville on the Ohio River. *See* Canada

John Lederer, and Captain Collett with party of explorers sent by Governor Berkeley of Virginia left York River, passed the source of the Rappahanock and reached site of Harper's Ferry in the Blue Ridge Mountains

1671

Aug., Sir John Yeamans directed to move his colony from "Old Clarendon" to territory southwest of Cape Carteret established "Old Charlestown" on the Ashley River, North Carolina

Sept. 16, Captain Thomas Batts from site of the present Petersburg, Virginia, traveled west over the Blue Ridge, descended into West Virginia and discovered the falls of the Great Kanawha, and the next day took possession of the region for Charles II

Dec., Dutch settlers from New York arrived in South Carolina

1672

March, "Description geographique et historique des costes de l'Amerique septemtrionale" by Nicholas Denys published in Paris

May 14, Settlers from Jersey towns sent delegates to Elizabethtown who elected James Carteret, Governor

Dec. 12, Death of Governor Richard Bellingham of Massachusetts

Jesuit map probably by Fathers Marquette and Allouez published in the "Relations" in Paris, 1672, first to give a complete map of Lake Superior, and delineation of the lake region and to the westward in advance of earlier maps

1673

Feb. 25, Virginia granted to Lord Arlington and Lord Culpepper for 31 years for rental of 40 shillings a year

April 10, James Needham from South Carolina started from Fort Henry on the Appomattox River, journeyed south and west to the Tennessee River and opened trade relations with the Cherokees

June 17, Louis Joliet and Father Marquette from Canada reached the Mississippi from the Wisconsin River and sailed nearly 1,000 miles down the river. *See* Canada, May 17

Aug. 7, Dutch fleet of 23 vessels carrying 1,600 men anchored off Sandy Hook and the following day demanded the surrender of New York. Delaware also retaken

1674

Feb. 9, New Netherland (New York) including New Jersey surrendered to the English by Holland in the Treaty of Westminster

Feb. 10, Edward Byllinge assigned his interest in Jersey to William Penn and his associates

May 27, Massachusetts made new survey of boundary with Maine and incorporated Cornwall

June 29, The Duke of York received a new patent from the King and appointed Sir Edmund Andros, Governor of Sagadhock and New York

Oct. 15, Governor Colve received orders to surrender New Netherland to the British

Nov. 6, Philip Carteret returning to East Jersey reassumed the government, and met General Assembly at Bergen

Nov. 9, Sir Edmund Andros in anticipation of the surrender of New Netherland proclaimed the "Duke's laws" again in force

Nov. 10, New Netherland formally surrendered to the English

Dec. 4, Father Marquette reached the site of Chicago where he established a mission. *See* Canada, Oct. 25

1675

June 8, Three Indians executed in Boston for murder of Sausaman who had warned the Governor of Plymouth that Philip was preparing for war on the colonists

June 24, King Philip's War begun by Indian massacre of colonists at Swanzey in Plymouth Colony. *See* map "Pageant of America," vol. 6

June, John Fenwick brought settlers to Salem, West Jersey from England

July 13, Sir Edmund Andros appeared before fort at Saybrooke claiming jurisdiction over Connecticut for the Duke of York, surrender refused by Captain Bull

Aug. 2–4, Indian attack on Brookfield, Mass. repulsed by Major Willard

Aug. 25, Indian attack on Deerfield, Mass.

Sept. 1, Indians attacked Hadley, defense led it is said by the regicide judge, William Goffe, who came out of hiding to help the colonists (*see* Scott's "Peveril of the Peak" for this story); Deerfield burned by Indians

Sept. 4, Captain Beers bringing 36 men to relieve the blockhouse at Northfield, ambushed and killed by Indians with 20 of his men

Sept. 9, Meeting of Colonies of Massachusetts, Plymouth, and Connecticut agreed to raise troops for war against the Indians

Sept. 18, Battle with the Indians at Bloody Brook, Mass. in which a large number of the colonists killed, and Indian attack on Saco, Maine, Sept. 18, and on Scarborough, Sept. 20, and during the month other towns in Maine and New Hampshire attacked; 80 Englishmen killed between the Piscataqua and Kennebec rivers

Oct. 5, Indian attack on Springfield, Mass. repulsed

Oct. 19, Indian attack on Hatfield, Mass.

Dec. 19, The fort of the Narragansetts taken by troops of the united Colonies under Governor Josiah Winslow of Plymouth, and over 1,000 Indians killed and captured in fight in the swamp

1676

Jan., Thirty-six Virginians killed by Indians in a single day in this month, the Governor declaring that nothing could be done until the regular meeting of the Assembly in March

Feb. 10, Indians attacked Lancaster, Mass., killed the men and took women and children captives. Mrs. Joseph Rowlandson, wife of the minister, ransomed May 2 for £20, and joined her husband in Boston

Feb. 21, Medfield, Mass. burned by the Indians

Feb. 24, Indians attacked Weymouth, 18 miles from Boston

March 3, "Concessions and Agreements of the Proprietors," a plan of government devised by William Penn published for the Province of West Jersey

March 3, 9, 13, Indian attacks on Groton, Mass.; Northampton, March 14; Marlborough, March 28; Rehoboth and Warwick, Rhode Island, burned by Indians March 17; and Providence attacked March 29 and 30

March, Virginia Assembly declared war on the Indians and a force of 500 men gathered for campaign when Governor Berkeley by proclamation disbanded the force

April 5, Death of John Winthrop of Connecticut

April 20, Death of John Clarke, "Father of Rhode Island"

April 21, Captain Wadsworth and his men surprised and defeated in fight with the Indians at Sudbury, Mass.

May 11, Indians attacked Plymouth; Turner's Falls, May 18; Scituate, May 20; May 30 and June 12, Hatfield; and Hadley, June 12

May, The planters of Virginia with Nathaniel Bacon chosen by them as leader without commission from Governor Berkeley marched against the Indians and defeated them

May 29, Proclamation of Governor Berkeley commanded Bacon's army to disperse declaring Bacon a traitor, and himself took the field against Bacon until recalled by revolt at Jamestown

June 5, Nathaniel Bacon publicly acknowledged his offense in marching against the Indians without a commission and was pardoned by the Governor

June 10, Edward Randolph arrived in Boston as agent

from the Royal Government to inquire into the condition of the country, brought request that the Colony should send agents to England to answer charges of Gorges and Mason as to the provinces of Maine and New Hampshire

July 1, Deed of revision fixed boundaries between East and West Jerseys

July 29, Governor Berkeley again proclaimed Bacon a rebel

Aug. 3, Meeting at Middle Plantation, Virginia took oath to support Bacon

Aug. 11, Falmouth, Maine, attacked by Indians, English fort on Arrowsick Island captured Aug. 18, no English settlement remaining between Casco Bay and the Penobscot River

Aug. 12, King Philip surprised and shot by an Indian in the troops of Captain Church in swamp near New Hope, and Indian war ended with his death

Aug. 18, Richard Hartshorn and Richard Guy, residents of East Jersey, with James Wasse sent from England, commissioned by the proprietors to establish a government for West Jersey

Sept. 16, Major Waldron at Dover by strategy captured 400 Indians and sent them to Boston

Sept. 19, Bacon successful in armed conflict with Governor Berkeley burned Jamestown, the stronghold of the Governor's party

Oct. 1, Rebellion in Virginia ended by the death of Bacon of fever at house of a friend

1677

Jan., An English fleet arrived with troops to suppress rebellion and commission to investigate affairs in Virginia

——, William Stoughton and Peter Bulkeley sent to England as agents for Massachusetts presented memorial to Privy Council in London asking that Gorges and Mason should present them with copies of papers recording their claims

Feb. 26, Indian war continued in Maine, Pemaquid attacked, and Black Point April 13 and May 23

March 3, Code of laws adopted for West Jersey

March 13, Province of Maine purchased by John Usher who paid Gorges £1,250, indenture dated May 6

March 15, Province of Maine deeded to the Governor and Colony of Massachusetts Bay by John Usher

July, Miller, secretary of Governor Eastchurch, arrived in North Carolina, and assumed the government as deputy

July-Aug., Force sent by Sir Edmund Andros to build fort at Pemaquid, Maine

Aug., Large number of Quakers from England arrived in West Jersey

Dec., The colonists of Albemarle, North Carolina, led by John Culpepper, rebelled against Miller, deputy-Governor, because he tried to collect the customs and shut off the New England trade

1678

April 12, A peace with the Indians of Maine made at Casco by commission from Massachusetts

1679

Jan., La Salle and Henry de Tonty, and Louis Hennepin at Niagara Falls, and launched the "Griffin" on Lake Erie

March 16, Death of Governor John Leverett of Massachusetts, Simon Bradford made Governor in May

July 10, New Hampshire made a royal province, the royal commission brought to Portsmouth by Edward Randolph, Jan. 1

Sept. 18, John Cutts of Portsmouth made president of New Hampshire

Dec., Stoughton and Bulkeley returned from England, not successful in their mission

1680

April 30, Philip Carteret seized by soldiers of Sir E. Andros and brought from Jersey to New York where he was kept in prison until May 27

May 10, Lord Culpepper arrived as Governor of Virginia succeeding Sir Henry Chicheley

May 18, Codification of laws for government of the Indies completed and promulgated by Charles II of Spain

June 2, Sir Edmund Andros appeared before the General Assembly at Elizabethtown and claimed jurisdiction of Jersey, his authority not recognized

Aug. 6, Second Grant of the Duke of York of West Jersey to William Penn, Edward Byllynge, and other Quaker proprietors

Aug. 9, Revolt of the Indians drove Spanish settlers out of New Mexico for 10 years, 400 colonists killed, Santa Fé sacked Aug. 15

South Carolina settlement moved from "Old Charlestown" to site of present Charleston in the Spring of this year

1681

March 4, Charter granted Pennsylvania and Delaware to William Penn in payment of a claim on the Crown for £16,000 bequeathed to him by his father, proclaimed April 2

March 27, Death of President Cutts of New Hampshire, succeeded by Major Richard Waldron

April 8, William Penn prepared a letter to be read to settlers on his grant by his representative promising them laws of their own making

April 10, William Penn appointed a young relative, William Markham, deputy-Governor and sent him with a party of colonists to settle in Pennsylvania where he arrived in June

July 11, Agreement between William Penn and purchasers of his land in paper known as "Certain Conditions or Concessions"

Sept. 13, William Markham held a court at Upland, Pennsylvania

Nov. 25, Fundamental Orders issued for the government of West Jersey, Samuel Jennings, chosen deputy-Governor by first Assembly at Burlington

1682

Jan. 25, Mason secured the appointment of Edward Cranfield as Governor of New Hampshire, commissioned May 9

Feb. 1–2, The heirs of Carteret sold East Jersey to William Penn and associated proprietors

March 14, William Penn and other Quaker proprietors now increased to company of 24 obtained charter from the Duke of York confirming their purchase of East Jersey

April 9, La Salle descending the Mississippi arrived at the Gulf of Mexico, named the country Louisiana and took possession in the name of the King of France

April 25, Frame of government signed by William Penn, the government of Pennsylvania vested in Governor and freemen with a provincial Council and an Assembly

May 11, General Court of Massachusetts repealed laws against keeping Christmas and capital punishment for returning Quakers

July 15, Deed given to Governor Markham by the Indians of Pennsylvania, cession of land

Aug. 13, First Welsh emigrants, Quakers, arrived in Pennsylvania, and settled on west side of the Schuylkill, north of Philadelphia

Aug. 21, William Penn obtained from the Duke of York a deed for any right he might have to Pennsylvania as a part of New Netherland in order to perfect his title

Aug. 24, Penn acquired from the Duke of York the town of Newcastle and 12 miles around it, and land south extending to Cape Henlopen in present State of Delaware

Aug. 31, William Penn sailed from England with 3 ships and Quaker settlers, arriving at Newcastle Oct. 27 (O.S.), landing the following day

Aug. or Sept., Philadelphia laid out in streets (Winsor)

Oct. 4, Edward Cranfield assumed office as Lieutenant Governor of New Hampshire

Oct. 10, Governor Cranfield dismissed Waldron and Richard Martyn from the Council of New Hampshire; recalled in Dec. and displaced a second time

Oct. 29, Penn changed name of Upland to Chester

Dec. 4, First Pennsylvania Assembly met at Chester

Dec. 13, Penn met Lord Baltimore to confer as to boundary between Maryland and Pennsylvania, and again in May, 1683, but no agreement reached

1683

Jan. 20, Meeting of Assembly of New Hampshire, dissolved by Governor Cranfield

Feb. 1, Edward Gove sentenced to imprisonment in the Tower of London for leading rebellion against Governor Cranfield of New Hampshire

June 23, Penn made treaty with the Indians at Schackamaxon near Philadelphia by which he purchased their land; no copy extant

Aug. 28, Governor Thomas Dongan arrived in New York

Oct. 6, German emigrants from Crefeld arrived at Philadelphia, 13 Mennonite linen-weavers with their families

Oct. 17, First Assembly under the English government met in New York at Fort James, in 3 weeks session

Oct. 20, Commissioners appointed by the King decided boundary dispute between Rhode Island and Connecticut in favor of Connecticut as to jurisdiction over the Narragansett country in dispute

Oct. 24, Francis Daniel Pastorius, representing the Frankfort Land Company of Germany which had purchased 25,000 acres from William Penn, began settlement of Germantown

Oct. 30, The New York Assembly adopted the "Charter of Liberties" in which declaration was made that under the King and proprietor "the supreme legislative authority shall forever be and reside in a governor, council, and the people met in a general assembly"

Nov. 7, Edward Randolph presented the writ of *quo warranto* against Massachusetts in the General Court

Nov. 28, Agreement made between New York and Connecticut as to boundary line
Scotch settlers brought to South Carolina by Henry Erskine, Lord Cardross, settled on Port Royal Island

1684

Jan. 14, Assembly of New Hampshire convoked by Governor Cranfield refused to appropriate money for expenses of government and for money appropriated without their consent for repair of fort at Portsmouth
Feb. 14, Governor Cranfield levied taxes without consent of the Assembly of New Hampshire
June 18, The Charter of Massachusetts declared forfeited by Court of Chancery in England
July 24, La Salle expedition to the Mississippi sailed from France. See Canada, July 24, Sept. 27, Nov. 25
July 30, Governor Dongan, and Stephen van Cortland from Massachusetts in conference with the Four Nations at Albany received the submission of the chiefs to the King of England
Oct. 23, Court of Chancery by suit of scire facias obtained judgment against Massachusetts
Dec. 28, La Salle expedition from France to the Mississippi River sighted the continent of America at Florida

1685

Jan. 6, The La Salle expedition passed the mouths of the Mississippi without recognizing the river. See Canada, Jan. 19, Feb. 4, March 12, March 24, July, Oct. 31
——, Governor Cranfield left New Hampshire on leave of absence to England, Walter Barefoot succeeding him as his deputy at head of government
Feb. 18, First settlement made in Texas by La Salle
March 2, Colonial post-office established in New York
June 2, Plymouth Colony divided into 3 counties, Plymouth, Bristol, and Barnstable
Nov. 7, Dispute between Pennsylvania and Maryland as to boundary decided by the King and Council in favor of Penn
Nov. 23, Edward Randolph appointed postmaster for the colonies by James II
William Bradford established a printing press in Philadelphia, the first in the middle colonies, first publication an almanac, the "Kalendarium Pennsilvaniense"

1686

April 27, Charter (Dongan's) granted to New York City
April, La Salle left Fort St. Louis near Lavaca Bay for the Illinois country
May 12, Last election in Massachusetts under the Charter
May 14, Edward Randolph arrived from England with commission of provisional government which he presented to the General Court of Massachusetts
May 17, Joseph Dudley, president and William Stoughton, deputy, for the Council for Massachusetts Bay, Maine, and Narragansett
May 25, Charter government formally displaced and possession taken of the government of Massachusetts by proclamation of Joseph Dudley
May 28, Provisional royal government constituted at Narragansett
June 3, Sir Edmund Andros commissioned as Captain General and Governor of New England including the colonies of Massachusetts Bay, Plymouth, New Hampshire, Maine, and Narragansett

Sept. 12, Death of John Alden at Roxbury, Massachusetts
Oct. 15, Spanish expedition from St. Augustine destroyed the Scotch settlement at Port Royal, Carolina; plans for invasion of Spanish territory abandoned by order of new governor, James Colleton
Dec. 20, Sir Edmund Andros arrived in Boston and assumed office as Governor of New England

1687

March 19, La Salle shot and killed by members of his party. See Canada
March 25, Episcopal church established in Old South Meeting House (Congregational) Boston by order of Governor Andros
Oct. 31, Sir Edmund Andros demanded the surrender of the Connecticut Charter. The lights in the Assembly room at Hartford were extinguished and the Charter taken from the table by Captain William Wadsworth and hidden in a hollow oak tree, the "charter oak" on estate of Samuel Wyllys

1688

Jan.–April, Oppressive legislation enacted in Massachusetts destructive of the liberties of the Colony; additional duties imposed Feb. 15, town meetings forbidden except once a year for the election of officers March 17, and the militia subordinated to a commander-in-chief brought from England March 24
April 7, Commission of Sir Edmund Andros extended to include jurisdiction over Rhode Island, Connecticut, New York, and East and West Jersey
May 30, Increase Mather sent by the people of Massachusetts to present their grievances had audience with the King, and again June 1, Sept. 26, and Oct. 16
June 23, New Rochelle, New York, founded
Aug. 13, Indians attacked North Yarmouth on Royals River, Maine, in King William's War
Francis D. Pastorius, Gerhard Hendricks, and other Germantown Quakers sent a written protest to the Friends' Meeting against the buying and selling of slaves (Subject of Whittier's poem, "The Pennsylvania Pilgrim")
Raffeix map published in Paris shows results of French exploration

1689

Feb. 19, Proclamation of William and Mary confirmed appointments of all existing officials in the colonies
March 23, Alonso de Leon, Governor of Coahuila, Mexico, sent by Mexican Government to destroy La Salle's fort and establish Spanish settlement in Texas, left Monclova with 110 soldiers and 3 missionary priests
April 18, The Andros government overthrown by the colonists, Andros and his associates imprisoned in fort in Boston, and the New England colonies reestablished their former governments; New Hampshire without a colonial government until Feb. 20, 1690
April 20, Simon Bradstreet chosen head of a provisional government in Massachusetts
April 22, Spanish force from Mexico reached La Salle's empty fort
April, "An Association in Arms for the Defense of the Protestant Religion, and for asserting the right of King William and Queen Mary to the Province of Maryland" formed with John Coode, president

May 9, The Connecticut Charter restored and the General Court reëstablished free government

May 31, Militia in New York in revolt demanded keys of Fort James from Governor Nicholson, Jacob Leisler promised to hold the fort until orders arrived from the Prince of Orange

June 1, The Spaniards formally established the mission of San Francisco de los Tejos (Texas)

June 6, Governor Nicholson sailed for England

June 8, Jacob Leisler's Committee of Safety made him captain of Fort James, and Aug. 16, commander-in-chief

June 11, Richard Wilkins appointed postmaster by the General Court of Massachusetts

June 27, Cocheco (Dover, New Hampshire), attacked by Indians, the inhabitants massacred including Major Richard Waldron

——, Governor Andros impeached by the General Court of Massachusetts and sent to England

July 25, John Coode at head of the "Associators" took possession of St. Mary's, Maryland, the Council taking flight to fort on the Patuxent River, but surrendered in a few days

Aug. 15, Pemaquid surrendered to the Abenakis, allies of the French, by Lieut. Weems

Sept. 2, Colonel Henry Sloughter commissioned Governor of New York by King William and Queen Mary

Public grammar school set up in Philadelphia which was chartered in 1697 as the William Penn Charter School

1690

Jan. 22, The Indians of the Five Nations in council at Onondaga made renewed declaration of adherence to the English

Jan. 24, The people of Exeter, Hampton, Dover, and Portsmouth sent representatives to Portsmouth who framed a constitution for New Hampshire; failure of Hampton to fulfil conditions caused failure of plan

Feb. 9, Schenectady, New York, burned by French and Indians from Canada

Feb., Rhode Island resumed government under Charter which had been hidden in 1687 from Governor Andros

March 12, New Hampshire effected governmental union with Massachusetts

March 27, Salmon Falls (Berwick) New Hampshire burned by French and Indians

April 28–May 30, Successful expedition of Sir William Phipps from Boston with Massachusetts troops to Acadia, Port Royal taken May 11

May 1, First colonial congress, attended by representatives of New York, Massachusetts, Connecticut, and Plymouth met, called by Jacob Leisler April 2

May 20, Surrender of Fort Loyal attacked by French and Indians at Falmouth (Portland) Maine

July 31, Jacob Leisler commissioned Fitz John Winthrop to make land attack on Quebec to coöperate with expedition of Church attacking by sea

Aug. 13, Capt. John Schuyler led raiding party from Albany into Canada. *See* Canada

Sept. 10, Major Richard Ingoldsby arrived at New York, claimed to represent Governor Sloughter, and prepared to seize the fort on refusal of Jacob Leisler to recognize his authority

Sept. 25, First American newspaper *Publick Occurrences Forreign and Domestick* published in Boston

by Benjamin Harris, to be published once a month or oftener "if any glut of occurrences happen"

Oct. 16–21, Sir William Phipps with fleet from Boston of 35 ships carrying 2,000 militia in unsuccessful siege of Quebec

Nov. 19, Truce concluded by Captain John Alden with the Indians at Sagadhac in King William's War

1691

Feb. 17, Thomas Neal given patent under the Great Seal to establish postoffices in the chief ports of the British colonies

March 1, Samuel Allen appointed Governor of New Hampshire which he purchased (April 27) for £750 from the sons of Robert Mason after his death; John Usher, son-in-law of Allen appointed lieutenant-governor

March 17, Leisler from Fort James exchanged shots with British troops commanded by Major Ingoldsby in parade, 8 men killed and several wounded

March 19, Governor Sloughter reached New York from England

March 20, Jacob Leisler and his supporters imprisoned

——, Charter of incorporation of Philadelphia by William Penn

April, Delaware placed under separate government headed by William Markham, dissolving union with Pennsylvania

May 16, Spanish expedition established a mission in California. *See* Mexico

——, Jacob Leisler and Milbourne hanged

July 23, Death of Governor Sloughter of New York, the administration conducted by Major Ingoldsby until the arrival of Governor Fletcher, Aug. 29, 1692

Aug., Sir Lionel Copley sent to Maryland as royal Governor, the palatinate overthrown

Aug. 11, Peter Schuyler with English and Dutch from Albany in battle with the French at La Prairie, Canada

Oct. 7, William and Mary granted charter to the Province of Massachusetts including Nova Scotia as well as the colony of Massachusetts Bay, New Plymouth, Maine, and the tract of land between Maine and Nova Scotia

The Jesuit Father Eusebio Kino entered the present Arizona and founded mission of Xavier del Bac, 9 miles from the present Tucson

1692

Feb. 5, Attack of French and Indians on York, Maine, half of the inhabitants killed or captured, and the town burned

Feb. 29, Indian servant, Tituba, in family of the Rev. Samuel Parris of Salem, along with Sarah Good accused of witchcraft, tried before magistrates March 1, and sent to jail in Boston March 3

May 14, Sir William Phipps appointed Governor of Massachusetts arrived in Boston

June 10, Bridget Bishop accused by the Rev. Samuel Parris hanged as a witch in Salem

June 21, Wells, north of York, Maine, successfully defended against attack by French and Indians

July 19, Five women hanged as witches in Salem, Sarah Good, Sarah Wildes, Elizabeth Howe, Rebecca Nourse, and Sussanah Martin

Aug. 19, George Burroughs, graduate of Harvard College and former minister of Salem, John Proctor,

John Willard, George Jacobs, and Martha Carrier hanged in Salem charged with witchcraft

Aug. 22, Eight more persons accused of witchcraft hanged in Salem

Sept. 13, New Mexico reconquered by Spanish force from Mexico commanded by Diego de Vargas Zapata Lujan, Santa Fé occupied

Sept. 16, Giles Corey, a man of 80 years, accused of witchcraft and refusing to plead, pressed to death

Sept. 22, Eight more persons executed for witchcraft in Salem including Martha Corey, wife of Giles

Sept., Fort at Pemaquid recaptured by Sir William Phipps and rebuilt as Fort William Henry; withstood attack by d'Iberville

Oct. 21, Governor Fletcher of New York commissioned by William III to take over the government of Pennsylvania and Delaware from Penn

Oct., Cotton Mather published his "Wonders of the Invisible World," a defense of witchcraft

——, Mrs. Hale, wife of the minister of the church at Beverley, Rev. Jeremiah Shepherd, the wife of Governor Phipps, and others of the "better class of church members" accused of witchcraft, and the witchcraft delusion began to be discredited

1693

Feb. 19, College of William and Mary at Williamsburg, Virginia, received royal charter. Founded Feb. 1692 through efforts of Rev. James Blair, its first president

Feb., Mrs. Dayton of Charlestown, Mass., accused of witchcraft, acquitted by jury

April 26, Governor Fletcher assumed the government of Pennsylvania

April, The proprietors of the Carolinas abandoned the "Fundamental Constitutions"

May, Sir William Phipps by proclamation released about 150 persons accused of witchcraft from prison. He put an end to prosecution for witchcraft in Boston by organization of a special court of oyer and terminer or commission of 7 magistrates for consideration of cases

June 9, Massachusetts established a "general letter office" in Boston

Aug. 11, Submission of the eastern Indians at Fort William Henry at Pemaquid

Oct. 26, Governor Benjamin Fletcher of New York demanded command of the militia of Connecticut under commission of the King, which was refused by the Assembly at Hartford, Captain Wadsworth preventing him from reading his commission by beating of drums and threats of death

Oct., The Spanish mission of San Francisco de los Tejas (Texas settlement) abandoned

Nov. 30, William Penn in England acquitted of charges against him

1694

March, Vargas leading Spanish colonists to New Mexico repulsed by the Indians at San Ildefonso, but in the summer made successful attack on the mesa

April, Connecticut Charter confirmed by William III

June 23, Durham, New Hampshire, attacked and the inhabitants massacred by Indians led by French from Canada

Aug. 20, Penn's chartered rights in Pennsylvania and Delaware restored

1695

Feb. 18, Death of Sir William Phipps in England where he had been summoned to vindicate his government of Massachusetts

1696

Aug. 15, Fort William Henry at Pemaquid surrendered by Captain Pascho Chubb to Canadians under d'Iberville

New revolt of New Mexico Indians against the Spaniards, 26 Spaniards killed including 5 missionaries

1697

March 15, Indian attack on Haverhill, Massachusetts, Mrs. Hannah Dustin taken captive with her baby succeeded in killing her captors and making her escape

March 27, Death of Governor Bradstreet at Salem

Sept. 11, The French claimed eastern Sagadhock as part of Nova Scotia

Sept. 20, Treaty of Ryswick ended war between England and France and territory mutually restored

William Penn Charter School established in Philadelphia

1698

April 2, Richard Coote, Earl of Bellomont, appointed in 1695 Governor of New York, Massachusetts, and New Hampshire, arrived in New York

July 23, D'Iberville instructed to proceed to the mouth of the Mississippi to take possession of the region for France. See Canada, 1699, Jan. 23, Feb. 11, March 2, April 8, May 3, Sept. 15, Dec. 7

Aug. 22, Lord Bellomont sent warning to Frontenac that if the French invaded the Iroquois country again he would resist with arms

Oct. 24, Pierre Le Moyne d'Iberville with 4 ships sailed from Brest (Charlevoix, Winsor. Sept. 24, Journal historique, from Rochefort) with 200 emigrants to establish a colony at the mouth of the Mississippi

Nov., Andrés de Arriola sent by Spain fortified Pensacola, Florida

1699

Jan. 7 and Sept. 8, Submission of Indians at Brunswick, Maine

March 2, D'Iberville entered the Mississippi River from the sea

May 26, The Earl of Bellomont, Governor of Massachusetts, New Hampshire, and New York arrived in Boston from New York

June 8, Captain William Kidd imprisoned in Boston and sent to England for trial for piracy and murder, hanged May 23, 1701, in London

Aug. 29, British ship sent by Daniel Cox entered the Mississippi River, turned back Sept. 15 by the French claiming jurisdiction and possession, at the "English Turn"

Oct. 7, Fathers de Montigny and de St. Cosmet from Canada on journey to the Mississippi to establish mission (Cahokia) visited the site of the present Milwaukee

1700

Jan. 6, D'Iberville established a fort on the Mississippi about 38 miles below the present New Orleans. See also Canada, Feb. 16, March 22, May, July 12

March–May, Bienville made expedition from Indian village near the Mississippi River to the Red River and up the Red River into northwest Louisiana

Oct. 1, Le Sueur reached the mouth of Blue Earth

River by the Minnesota River from the Mississippi River

The Sulpician mission to the Indians at Cahokia moved to Kaskaskia (Illinois)

Map published in Paris by Guillaume Delisle a better presentation of coasts and interior than any previous map. He published maps in 1718, 1722, and 1750 probably revisions, the map of Abbé Gentil also published in 1700 shows La Salle's route

1701

March 5, Death of the Earl of Bellomont in New York

July 24, Detroit founded by La Mothe Cadillac, first settlement in Michigan. *See also* Canada

Oct. 9, Yale College, founded in 1700, chartered by the General Court at New Haven, Connecticut, and established at Saybrook

Oct. 25, Government of Pennsylvania reorganized under new constitution, the "Charter of Privileges" by Penn, the Delaware counties given permission to separate from Pennsylvania

——, Philadelphia incorporated as a city, Edward Shippen appointed mayor

Dec. 15, D'Iberville reached Louisiana returning from France and directed Dec. 18 that the colony be moved from Biloxi to the Mobile River

1702

Jan. 6, Bienville established capital of Louisiana on west side of Mobile Bay, first settlement of Alabama

March 10, Joseph Dudley commissioned Governor to succeed Lord Bellomont arrived in Boston June 11

March 20–23, D'Iberville laid out streets of Mobile, the new capital of the Louisiana Colony

April 17, The proprietors of East and West Jersey surrendered their rights to the Crown and the 2 colonies were united

May 15, War declared against France by England (Queen Anne's War)

Sept. 16, Yale College opened for term, one student registering in March

Sept., Governor Moore and Colonel Daniel led the colonists against the Spaniards as allies of France, plundered the town of St. Augustine, Florida, but were not able to take the fort

1703

May 12, Boundary of Connecticut with Massachusetts established

June 20, Governor Dudley of Massachusetts in council with the Abenaki Indians at Falmouth made effort to prevent Indian war

Aug. 10, On the same day Wells, Cape Porpoise, Saco, Scarborough, Casco, Spurwink, and Purpooduck in Maine attacked by French and Indians

Oct. 6, Black Point, Maine attacked by French and Indians

Oct., First separate Assembly for Pennsylvania met at Philadelphia

1704

Feb. 8, Indians took garrison house at Haverhill, Mass. by surprise attack

Feb. 28–29, Destruction of Deerfield, Mass. by French and Indians, about 40 persons killed and 100 taken captive

April 24, The Boston *News-Letter*, first newspaper in the British colonies, a weekly, published; editor, John Campbell

May 21, Colonel Benjamin Church with nearly 600 men sailed from Boston for Nova Scotia, destroyed French settlements near Port Royal. *See also* Canada

1706

Aug. 27–Sept. 2, Unsuccessful attempt of French and Spanish fleet commanded by Le Feboure to take Charleston, South Carolina

Nov. 30, The Church of England made the established religion in the Carolinas

1707

June 6–17, Siege of Port Royal by expedition of Col. March, Wainwright, and Hilton with 1,000 men from New England a failure. *See* Canada

Sept. 21, Winter Harbor, Maine attacked by 150 Indians, the settlers making their escape in ships

1708

Aug. 29, French and Indians attacked Haverhill on the Merrimac River

1709

Sept. 3, Land grant made by the proprietors of the Carolinas to Baron Christopher de Graffenried of 10,000 acres and to Lewis Michel of 3,500 acres for establishment of emigrants from the Swiss canton of Berne

1710

March, Governor Robert Hunter sailed for New York in fleet of 10 ships bringing 3,000 to 4,000 German refugees from the Palatinate on the Rhine who settled at Germantown in Columbia county

April, Large numbers of Quakers arrived to settle on the Neuse and Cape Fear rivers in North Carolina, and about 15,000 Swiss and Palatinates brought by Baron de Graffenried established town of New Berne at junction of the Neuse and Trent rivers

June, Governor Alexander Spotswood arrived in Virginia bringing the writ of *habeas corpus* conceded by the King

Sept. 18, Col. Francis Nicholson, Sir Charles Hobby with British troops sailed from Boston arriving before Port Royal Sept. 24, and received the surrender of the French garrison Oct. 2. The fort renamed Annapolis and Samuel Vetch left as Governor

1711

Aug. 23, Sir Hovenden Walker's fleet from England proceeding to attack of Quebec with troops and colonists from Boston wrecked on reefs off Egg Islands and 10 ships and 742 men lost, and expedition abandoned

Sept. 22, The Tuscaroras began war against the white settlers on the frontier of North Carolina along the Roanoke and at Newbern (New Berne) and Bath

1712

Jan. 28, Colonel John Barnwell defeated the Tuscaroras in fight on the Neuse River, 400 Indian warriors killed and treaty made which was not kept by the Indians

May, Detroit besieged by the Outagamies and Mascoutins. The return of the friendly Ottawas and Hurons enabled du Buisson to defeat the besiegers who lost 1,000 in flight

Sept. 14, Antoine Crozat received a private grant of Louisiana and the French possessions on the Mississippi from the King of France

1713

March 20, Colonel James Moore from South Carolina attacked the Tuscarora Fort Nohucke in North Carolina defeating the Indians who migrated to central New York and joined the Iroquois, the Five Nations thus becoming the Six Nations

April 11, Treaty of Utrecht ended the war. *See* Canada *and* South America

June 5, La Mothe Cadillac arrived at Dauphin Island from France as Governor of Louisiana

Aug. 18, Governor Hunter proclaimed the peace at New York

1714

Feb. 12, Date of deed of purchase for land in Pennsylvania of Thomas Ruuter for iron forge works. His obituary notice March 5, 1729 says of him "the first that erected an iron work in Pennsylvania." Jenkins

April 5–Dec., Expedition of Bienville up Mobile River established Fort Toulouse at junction of the Coosa and the Tallapoosa, Fort Assumption on Chickasaw bluff on the Mississippi, and Fort Paducah at mouth of the Cumberland

Aug.–Aug. 1716, Expedition of Louis Juchereau de Saint Denis sent by Cadillac, Governor of Louisiana, into Texas to open trade with the Indians, was arrested and sent to City of Mexico by Mexicans; from Dauphin Island up the Mississippi to Red River and overland from Natchitoches to Rio Grande

1715

Feb. 20, Death of Lord Baltimore, his son the 4th Lord Baltimore, Benedict Leonard Calvert, a Protestant and the proprietary government of Maryland restored

April 5, Death of the 4th Lord Baltimore, succeeded by his son, Charles Calvert, fifth Lord Baltimore, John Hart, proprietary governor

Expedition of St. Denis up the Red River trading and exploring and west to the Neches River and southwest to the Rio Grande

1716

April 24–25, Lands in Vermont sold to a company of 21 persons at Hartford, Conn.

April 27, Captain Domingo Ramon with 22 soldiers, 12 friars and 31 colonists left the Rio Grande and made journey to the present Texas reëstablishing the Spanish mission of San Francisco

June 3, The Assembly of South Carolina repealed law of 1707 under which land had been set aside for the Yamassees, and under permission of letter of March 3 from the proprietor opened these lands to settlers from abroad

June 6, Two vessels sent by the Company of the West arrived at Louisiana from the coast of Guinea with "five hundred head of negroes"

Aug. 3, Fort Rosalie at Natchez (Miss.) completed by Bienville

Aug.–Sept., Governor Spotswood of Virginia led expedition across the Blue Ridge Mountains and to the Shenandoah Valley, taking possession for England

Sept. 17, Superior Council for Louisiana made perpetual

Oct. 4, Governor Samuel Shute arrived in Boston

1717

March 9, D'Epinay, new Governor of Louisiana arrived in colony, replacing La Mothe Cadillac recalled

June, Grant of land between the Savannah and Altamaha rivers to Sir Robert Montgomery under condition of settlement. He issued pamphlet for colonists calling his land the "Margravate of Aziliz," but failed to establish colonists and forfeited land in 1720

Aug. 23, Crozat remitted the remainder of the term of his exclusive privilege in Louisiana

Sept. 6, Charter of the Company of the West controlled by John Law registered in France based on attempt to fund that part of the debt of France outstanding as *billet d'états* in a form of annuity bonds. *See also* Canada

Sept. 20, Bienville appointed commander general of Louisiana

Sept. 27, French Ordinance incorporated the Illinois country as part of Louisiana

1718

Feb. 9, Arrival of ships from France with emigrants and commission of Bienville as Governor of Louisiana. In this month he began settlement at present New Orleans

June 13, Indian war begun in Maine by seizure by Indians of 9 families at Merrymeeting Bay

July 30, Death of William Penn in England

Sept. 27, William Rhett commanding fleet of South Carolina defeated the notorious pirate, Stede Bonnet, and arrived with his captives at Charleston Oct. 3, the crew executed Nov. 8 and Bonnet, Dec. 10

Oct., Samuel Nutt bought land in Pennsylvania for iron forge works

Nov. 4, Governor Johnson of South Carolina defeated pirate fleet and killed Richard Worley, leader

Nov. 18, Name of Saco changed to Biddeford (Maine)

Nov. 21, Lieutenant Maynard sent by Governor of Virginia captured and killed the pirate, Edward Teach known as "Blackbeard," in engagement in Pamlico Bay. Thirteen of the pirates hanged at Williamsburg. Benjamin Franklin, then an apprentice in Boston, wrote a ballad on Blackbeard's fate which was sold and sung in the streets

Martin de Alarcon, Governor of Coahuila, established the Presidio de Antonio de Bejar, on the San Antonio River at site of present San Antonio, Texas

1719

Jan. 9, France declared war against Spain

Jan. 10, Company of the West absorbed the Senegal Slavery Company to provide slaves for Louisiana

April 25, Ordinance of the Company of the West required that the Louisiana colonists buy and sell only to the Company and at fixed prices

May 3, Company of the West changed name to Company of the Indies

May 14, De Bienville made successful attack on the Spaniards by sea and land at Pensacola, Governor Matamora surrendered and was taken prisoner

June, French and Indians seized Spanish mission of San Miguel de los Adaes (Texas)

Aug. 6, Chateaugne left in command by Bienville at Pensacola forced to capitulate to Spanish force, but de Bienville recaptured Pensacola Sept. 17

Dec. 21, The *Boston Gazette*, second newspaper, published by William Brooker
——, Convention of the people of South Carolina published declaration of their grievances against the proprietors and assumed the government, appointing James Moore, Governor
Dec. 22, Andrew S. Bradford established the *American Weekly Mercury* at Philadelphia
The French established a post on the Wabash which they named Ouiatenon near site of present Lafayette, Indiana, Sieur Dubuisson in command
Bernard de la Harpe established fortified trading post at Arkansas bend of the Red River and explored the country to northwest as far as the villages of the Toucaras
Du Tisné went up the Missouri River to near junction with Grand (Kansas) River and returning made journey into present northeast Oklahoma

1720

Aug. 11, Spanish expedition under Lieut. Gen. Don Pedro de Villasur which left Santa Fé June 16 massacred by the Indians at the Platte River
Sept. 20, Sir Francis Nicholson appointed provisional Governor of South Carolina, the English government recognizing the rebellion of the colonists against the proprietors

1721

Jan. 8, Arrival of 25 girls from house of correction in Paris at Louisiana
March, A company of 200 Germans settled near New Orleans
April, Small-pox in Massachusetts, 844 deaths of the 5,889 persons stricken with the disease in Boston
Aug. 5, The Marques San Miguel de Aguayo reëstablished missions in eastern Texas
Sept. 5, Louisiana divided into 9 military districts united under 4 general commanderies, New Orleans, Biloxi, Arkansas, and Illinois

1722

May 16, Louisiana divided into 3 spiritual jurisdictions
June 4, 250 German settlers arrived at Mobile
June 18, Indians seized 5 English settlers on the Kennebec River as hostages for 4 Indians held in Boston
July 25, The Governor and Council in Boston declared war on the eastern Indians, confirmed by the Assembly, Aug. 8 (Lovewell's War)
Expedition of B. La Harpe up the Arkansas River and into central Arkansas

1723

Aug., New Orleans made capital of Louisiana
Oct., Benjamin Franklin arrived in Philadelphia
——, Bienville led 700 of the Louisiana colonists against the Natchez destroying 2 of their villages
Nov. 15, Etienne Veniard, Sieur de Bourmond, began building Fort Orleans on north bank of the Missouri, about 300 miles from its mouth

1724

Feb., Fort Dummer built by Massachusetts on the Connecticut River at Brattleboro, the first permanent English settlement in Vermont
April 1, Bienville recalled to France to answer charges made against him and arrived in France Aug. 20, 1725
Aug. 23, English attack on Abenaki village of Norridg-

wock, Father Sebastian Rale, French-Canadian leader of the Indians, killed
Sept. 10, "Black Code" of March published by Bienville in New Orleans, 55 articles regulating the government of slaves; declared all Jews should leave the Louisiana colony
Sept. 20, Bourgmont, trader and explorer, starting from Fort Orleans on the Missouri River reached Indian village in western Kansas Oct. 18

1725

Feb. 5, Vitus Bering with Martin Spanberg, and Alexei Chirikov left St. Petersburg (Leningrad) and proceeded across Siberia to Okhotsk, reached Kamchatka by boat in July, crossing the peninsula in sledges during the winter to the Bering Sea
July 11, Jacques de la Chaise appointed first Intendant of the Louisiana colony
Sept. 15, Submission of Indians of Nova Scotia and New England to George II at Boston
Nov. 8, The *New York Gazette*, first newspaper in Province of New York issued by William Bradford
Dec. 15, Dummer's Treaty with the Indians signed in Boston

1726

Feb. 8, Order in Council as to boundary of Connecticut with Rhode Island
Aug. 9, Bienville dismissed and Périer appointed Governor of Louisiana

1727

May 9, Letter of Governor William Burnet, of New York, to Board of Trade that he had built fort at Oswego and established trading post as rival to French post at Niagara with consent of the Six Nations
Morgan Morgan built home at site of the present village of Bunker Hill in Berkeley county, West Virginia
July, The Ursuline nuns arrived in Louisiana to undertake hospital service and maintain a school

1728

Feb. 13, Death of Cotton Mather
July 20, Bering expedition sailed from Kamchatka following and charting the coast to the northeast, sighted and named the Island of St. Lawrence, and reached 67° 18′ N. Lat. Aug. 15 proving that America and Asia were separated by strait which bears his name; returning arrived at the Kamchatka River Sept. 20 (O.S.), at Okhotsk, July 23, and St. Petersburg, March 1, 1730
Sept. 27, Boundary line between Rhode Island and Connecticut agreed upon by joint commission
Arrival of the "casket girls" at Louisiana, each given a present of a dress in a casket. As they were not from houses of correction in France like their predecessors in later times it became a matter of pride to be a descendant of a "casket girl"

1729

June, The proprietors of Carolinas surrendered seven-eighths of their grant to Parliament for £17,500, the same then to be vested in the Crown, Lord Carteret reserving his eighth
Sept. 7, Death of Governor William Burnet of Massachusetts

Oct. 29, David Dunbar appointed Lieutenant-Governor of New Hampshire on the death of Wentworth in spite of the protests of Governor Belcher, Governor of Massachusetts and New Hampshire

Nov. 29, Massacre of the French settlers at Fort Rosalie (Natchez) by the Natchez and Chickasaw Indians

Dec. 11, The British Government repealed prohibition on trade in Indian goods between Albany and Canada

1730

Jan. 27, Le Seuer with Choctaws attacked and defeated Natchez in retaliation for massacre at Fort Rosalie

Jan., The Carolinas divided into North and South Carolina and George Burrington appointed Governor of North Carolina

Feb. 8, Force led by de Loubois attacked Natchez fort. The Indians pretended to surrender on the 25th to Périer and during night of the 28th evacuated the fort and escaped across the Mississippi

Nov. 15–Feb. 5, 1731, Expedition of Governor Périer of Louisiana colony with 650 soldiers and 350 Indians to the Black River against the Natchez

1731

Jan. 23, The Company of the West surrendered charter to the King, and Louisiana became a royal province to take effect Jan. 1, 1732

Jan. 31, Périer reached Natchez fort, captured 450 women and children and 45 men

Aug. 11, Massachusetts and New Hampshire boundary fixed by commission

Nov. 8, Library Company of Philadelphia founded by Benjamin Franklin, a subscription library

1732

Feb. 26, A Catholic church built and mass celebrated in Philadelphia. According to Hildreth this was the only Catholic church allowed in any Anglo-American colony previous to the Revolution

Feb. 28, Lord Carteret sold his land under charter of March 24, 1663 to trustees for establishment of Colony of Georgia

May 7, Superior Council of Louisiana reorganized, Governor Périer continued in office

May 12, Commissioners appointed by Pennsylvania and Maryland to settle boundary line; not settled until 1762 by the Mason and Dixon line

June 9, James Oglethorpe secured charter conveying to himself and associate proprietors land between the Savannah and Altamaha rivers extending to the sea for 21 years to be erected into Province of Georgia

July 25, Bienville appointed Governor of Louisiana

Sept. 27, First issue of the *Rhode Island Gazette* published by James Franklin, brother of Benjamin, at Newport

Oct. 1, Library Company of Philadelphia opened with arrival of books from England

Nov. 17, Oglethorpe with about 120 colonists sailed for Georgia, arriving in Rebellion Roads, South Carolina, Jan. 12

Dec., First number of "Poor Richard's Almanac" issued by Benjamin Franklin in Philadelphia

1733

Feb. 12, Oglethorpe and colonists settled at site of the present Savannah, Georgia, after making treaty with the Indians by which they purchased the land

March 3, Governor Bienville arrived in Louisiana from France and assumed office

April 4, David Dunbar, Governor of Sagadhoc since 1729, removed because of arbitrary acts

July, Forty Jews arrived at Savannah under arrangement with the proprietors

Aug. 25, Massachusetts resumed jurisdiction of Sagadhoc

Map of Henry Popple published in 20 sheets in London

1734

March 17, Forty-two families numbering 78 persons, Protestant refugees from Salzburg sent by the Society for the Propagation of Christian Knowledge, arrived in Georgia and settled 30 miles from Savannah naming their town Ebeneezer

Nov. 17, John Peter Zenger, editor of the *New York Weekly Journal* arrested for libel for criticism of the administration in his paper

1735

July, Zenger acquitted and released, defended by Andrew Hamilton of Philadelphia, Hamilton given franchises of the City of New York by the Council for "his learned and generous defence of the rights of mankind and the liberty of the press"

Eight French families, the first white settlers in Indiana, came to military post at Vincennes established about 1727 by François Margane, sieur de Vincennes on site of trading post founded in 1702

1736

Jan., Scotch settlement established near the mouth of the Altamaha River in Georgia which they named New Inverness

Feb. 5, John and Charles Wesley, Methodist preachers, arrived in Georgia with Oglethorpe and Moravian and Salzburg colonists, returning to England in July

Feb., Fort Frederica established on St. Simon's Island, Georgia

March 26, Campaign of forces of French Louisiana colonists against the Chickasaw Indians who had harbored the Natchez Indians begun by Bienville and d'Artaguette, who was defeated and taken prisoner May 20, and Bienville's attack on Indian fort (the battle of Akia) unsuccessful May 26 and the French forced to retreat May 27

Aug. 6, The *Virginia Gazette* published by William Parks at Williamsburg, the first newspaper in Virginia

1738

May 3–Aug. 28, George Whitefield, Methodist preacher, in Georgia

1739

March 5, The King in Council fixed the boundary between Maine and New Hampshire "to pass through the entrance of Piscataqua harbor and the middle of the river to the farthermost head of Salmon Falls River, thence north 2; west, true course, 120 miles"

May 29, Illinois traders, Pierre and Paul Millet (Mallet) left central Nebraska and following south fork of the Platte River and then the Colorado River arrived at Santa Fé, New Mexico July 22, and from there made journey to New Orleans May 1, 1740

June, A force of French and Indians sent by Bienville from Louisiana established a garrison at Fort Assumption on the Mississippi at Chickasaw bluff

July 20, Captain Edward Vernon sailed from England to raid Spanish American ports in Central and South America. *See* Panama Nov. 21–22, Colombia April 9, 1740

Aug. 14, George Whitefield sailed for America from England

Aug. 21, Treaty of peace with the Creek Indians made by Oglethorpe

Sept. 12–April 1740, Bienville on expedition from Louisiana against the Chickasaws

1740

Jan. 1, Governor Oglethorpe captured Fort Picolata on the St. John's River, Florida, from the Spaniards

Feb. 13, The *American Magazine* published by John Webbe, first American magazine

Feb. 21, Successful attack of French force of de Celeron on Chickasaw Indians, a peace arranged

May 10, Spanish Fort St. Diego near St. Augustine taken by Oglethorpe

——, Marquis de Vaudreuil, new Governor of Louisiana, arrived at French colony

June 15, General Oglethorpe gave up siege of St. Augustine after 3 weeks

Aug. 5, Boundary between Massachusetts and New Hampshire settled by Decree of the King in Council which gave New Hampshire a better line than she had asked for and deprived Massachusetts of 30 or more towns, surveyed later by G. Mitchell and R. Hazen, the Mitchell-Hazen line

Sept. 4, Expedition of the Russians, Bering and Chirikov, left Okhotsk and wintered in Avacha Bay

Sept. 14, Arrival of the Methodist George Whitefield at Newport, R.I. from Charleston, S.C., reached Boston Sept. 18 and preached in New England towns for about a month

1741

March 18–April 6, Nine fires in New York City charged to plot of negroes incited by Spaniards, 20 white men and 160 negroes imprisoned, 4 white men and 18 negroes hanged, and 13 negroes burned at the stake

June 4, Expedition of Bering sailed from Petropavlovsk since named for his 2 ships, "St. Peter" and "St. Paul," sighted Mt. St. Elias July 16, accepted as first discovery of Alaska (Bering's Journal. Heaton gives July 29 N.S.) Chirikov reached the coast of America in about 56° N. Lat. a few days earlier than Bering, and was at Avacha Bay Oct. 11

Nov. 15, Bering passed the Shumagin and the Aleutian Islands and reached island called by his name where he died Dec. 19

First strike in America of New York City journeymen bakers

Cultivation of indigo begun on the Ashley River, South Carolina

1742

June 21, Spanish fleet appeared off the coast of Georgia and made unsuccessful attack in attempt to take possession of Amelia Island

July 5, Spanish vessels entered St. Simon's harbor and forced the English to abandon the fort

July 7, Spaniards defeated in march against Frederica in fight called the "Battle of the Bloody Marsh"

July 14, Spanish fleet sailed away led to believe by decoy letter sent by General Oglethorpe that they were in danger

Aug. 21, The remaining members of the Bering expedition under leadership of the scientist, Steller, sailed from Bering Island reaching Petropavlovsk Sept. 5

1743

Map of Bellin, French cartographer, published the following year in Charlevoix's History of New France

Aug. 17, Bienville left Louisiana, and died in France March 7, 1768

1744

June, Treaty with the Indians signed at Lancaster, Pennsylvania, by the Six Nations and Maryland, Virginia, and Pennsylvania by which they ceded the Ohio Valley

Sept. 17, Lord John Carteret surrendered political power in Carolina and land in South Carolina

Oct. 19, George Whitefield, Methodist, arrived at York, Maine, on second visit to New England, in Boston, Nov. 26

1745

March 25, Expedition against Louisburg organized by Governor Shirley and commanded by William Pepperell sailed from Massachusetts for Canceau (Canso) where they arrived April 1, and there waited a month for ice to break, and landed at Gabarus Bay April 30–May 1 beginning siege

April 23, Commodore Warren arrived at Canceau to join in attack on Louisburg, commanding 5 vessels of 60 guns and 6 frigates to add to the provincial vessels

June 16, Surrender of French fortress at Louisburg, Cape Breton Island to New England force, Pepperell made the first and only baronet of Massachusetts by the King in reward for this victory, and Warren made a vice-admiral

July 19, Fifth Indian war begun in Maine with attacks on St. George and Damariscotta

Aug. 23, Massachusetts declared war on the Indians of eastern Maine

Nov. 28–29, Saratoga, New York, destroyed by attack of French and Indians

1746

Aug. 28, William Johnson appointed commissioner to the Six Nations

Oct. 22, Charter granted to the College of New Jersey afterwards Princeton College, opened in May 1747 in Newark

——, A Bill ordered to raise £250 by lottery toward establishing a college in New York, the beginning of King's College afterwards Columbia University

Large numbers of Scotch Highlanders, supporters of Prince Charles, arrived in North Carolina and settled on the upper Cape Fear River

1747

Oct., The Spanish in New Mexico defeated the Comanches and Utes in battle at Abiquiu, and made treaty with the Comanches

Nov. 17, Riots in Boston because of impressment of seamen by Commodore Charles Knowles of the British navy, and officers seized as hostages, later released by order of the General Court, and Knowles gave up most of the men impressed. Governor Shirley took refuge in Castle

1748

Oct. 18, Treaty of Aix-la-Chapelle ended King George's War and restored Louisburg to France

Nov. 9, First commencement of College of New Jersey at Newark

Dr. Thomas Walker discovered the Cumberland Gap

1749

Jan., Governor Wentworth of New Hampshire made grant of township west of the Connecticut River in Vermont which was named Bennington, territory claimed by New York under Charter from Charles II to Duke of York, beginning boundary dispute

May 8, Peace proclaimed in Boston in accordance with the terms of the Treaty of Aix-la-Chapelle

May 19, Grant to John Hanbury of London, Thomas Lee, and other Virginians organized as the Ohio Company of 200,000 acres of land on the south side of the Ohio River on condition of settlement and erection and maintenance of a fort

June 15–Nov. 9, Journey of Bienville de Celoron taking formal possession of the Ohio Valley for France. *See* Canada

Aug. 6, De Celoron captured a party of English traders with license from the Governor of Pennsylvania, and discharged them with warning and notice to the Governor that traders were not allowed in the Ohio Valley, territory belonging to France

Oct. 12–Dec. 12, Journey of Moravian missionaries, Brothers Leonhard Schnell and John Brandmuller to scattered settlements of Virginia in Bath and Alleghany counties

Oct. 16, Treaty of peace with the Indians made at Falmouth (Portland), Maine, by Thomas Hutchinson and James Otis commissioned by the government of Massachusetts, which was not observed, French and Indian attacks continued

Oct. 26, Importation and use of negro slaves permitted in Georgia

Nov. 7, English post at Minas near Nova Scotia boundary attacked by Indians

1750

March 16, Dr. Thomas Walker sent by Virginia Council to survey public lands began journey to the Cumberland Mountains and entered Kentucky by the Cumberland Gap, first authentic report of journey beyond the Alleghanies, proceeded as far west as the Rockcastle River (May 11) and as far north as site of present Paintsville, Kentucky

April 25, Dr. Thomas Walker completed the first house built in Kentucky at a point near the present town of Barbourville

Sept. 11–25, Indians from Canada attacked settlements in Maine on the Kennebec River

Sept. 16, Christopher Gist instructed by the Ohio Company to explore the western country as far as the falls of the Ohio and look for level tracts suitable for settlement

Sept. 26, The General Court of Massachusetts again declared war on the Indians and ordered levy of 150 men to defend the Maine settlements

Nov. 1, Captain Christopher Gist began journey descending the Alleghany and Ohio rivers to the Big Beaver and across country arriving Dec. 5 at point near line between present counties of Stark and Tuscarawas, and at Wyandot town met George

Croghan (Dec. 14) on an official expedition to protect traders against French and Indians; returned to Virginia through Kentucky

1751

Jan. 7, William Penn Academy opened in Philadelphia

March 13–May 18, Expedition of Capt. Gist into Kentucky territory, up the Licking River and crossing the divide to the Kentucky River he ascended that river and east to the head of the Clinch River, thence to New River, and over the mountains to the head springs of the Roanoke River, traversing Ohio, Kentucky, West Virginia, Maryland, and Pennsylvania

July 16–March, 1752, Journey of Gist to find a passage from Wills Creek to the Monongahela which he accomplished Nov. 4, and a trading house was built at this point (Cumberland, Maryland) because of his favorable report

Sugar cane from San Domingo introduced into Louisiana by the Jesuits

1752

Feb. 18, The *Pennsylvania Gazette* published advertisement proposing to insure houses against fire in and near Philadelphia

April 13, First fire insurance company organized in Philadelphia

June 5, Benjamin Franklin identified electricity and lightning

June 9–13, Indians at Logtown signed deed confirming cession of land at Lancaster, Pa. in 1744, and permission given to build a fort at the forks of the Ohio

June 21, French and Indians from Detroit attacked and destroyed English trading post at Tawightis and fort of Picqualinny ending plans for the Ohio for a time

Expedition of the Marquis de Vaudreuil, French Governor of Louisiana, against the Chickasaw not successful, unable to take their towns he destroyed their cornfields

June 22, Trustees under Charter held last meeting, Georgia becoming a Crown Colony

Dec., Bishop Spangenberg led party of Moravians with surveyors to locate 100,000 acres in North Carolina granted them the previous year by Lord Granville

John Finley, pedler, former fur trader, descended the Ohio with the Indians to site of Louisville and traveled widely through Kentucky. His descriptions of the country inspired Daniel Boone to go to Kentucky

Small-pox again in Boston, and more than a quarter of the population, 5,550 persons had the disease, 514 died

1753

July 13, William Penn Academy in Philadelphia chartered, later became the University of Pennsylvania

Oct. 8, Bernhard Grube, minister, led company of 12 men from Bethlehem, Pennsylvania, to North Carolina, in the present Anson county to establish settlement on land granted

Oct. 30, Instructed by Governor Dinwiddie of Virginia George Washington proceeded to the Ohio Valley to order French settlers to remove from territory claimed by the English on the basis of charters which made the Pacific Ocean the western boundary of the colonies

Nov. 24, Fort Prince George built on the Savannah River near its source by Governor Glenn of South Carolina in 1754 by treaty with the Indians concluded at Saluda promising protection to the Cherokees and their allies

Dec. 11, George Washington reached Fort Le Boeuf (Waterford, Pa.) and presented letter of Governor Dinwiddie to St. Pierre, French commander

1754

Feb., Captain William Trent began to build fort at the junction of the Monongahela and Alleghany rivers at site of the present Pittsburgh

April 17, Ensign Ward forced to surrender fort at the forks of the Ohio (Pittsburgh) to the French led by Contrecoeur, who continued building of the fort which they named Duquesne

April 25, First theatrical performance given in Philadelphia by Hallam's company, the play, the "Fair Penitent"

May 28, George Washington in skirmish at Great Meadows defeated the French from Canada led by de Jumonville, and built a stockade which he named Fort Necessity

June 19, A colonial Congress with representatives from New Hampshire, Massachusetts, Rhode Island, Connecticut, New York, Pennsylvania, and Maryland met at Albany, New York to organize a union of the colonies for defense against the French and Indians. Benjamin Franklin presented a plan which was rejected, and another plan as agreed upon July 4 was rejected by the colonies and the King

July 3, Washington compelled to surrender Fort Necessity to a French force sent from Fort Duquesne and the French were left in complete possession of the Ohio Valley, Washington allowed to retire to Wills Creek (Fort Cumberland)

July 11, Connecticut citizens of the Susquehanna Company purchased land on the Susquehanna River including the Wyoming Valley in Pennsylvania from the Six Nations and established a settlement

Oct. 31, Charter of King's College, later Columbia University, signed by Governor De Lancy of New York

Map by Gerhard Friedrich Müller, member of Bering's second expedition, gave the Alaskan region

1755

Jan., General Braddock with 2 regiments of 500 men each sailed from England

April 12, The *Connecticut Gazette* published at New Haven, first newspaper in Connecticut

April 14, General Braddock at Alexandria, Virginia, in conference with the governors of Pennsylvania, New York, Maryland, and Virginia planned 4 expeditions to repel the encroachment of the French from Canada on the American frontier

May 10, Braddock's army reached Fort Cumberland

May 14, New charter granted to the William Penn Academy which became the College of Philadelphia, and celebrated its first commencement May 17, 1757

June 8, French ships in engagement with the British off Newfoundland, and Treaty of Aix-la-Chapelle broken. *See* Canada

June 16, Expedition of Colonel Monckton and Colonel John Winslow from Boston with 3,000 troops took French forts of Nova Scotia

June, Governor Shirley left Massachusetts on expedition to capture Niagara from the French with 1,500 regular troops, and arrived at shore of Lake Ontario Aug. 31 where he waited for supplies and end of rains before proceeding to Niagara

July 9, Battle of Monongahela, General Braddock defeated by the French and Indians and mortally wounded, remnant of army led in retreat by George Washington

Sept. 8, Battle of Lake George, General Johnson defeated the French led by Baron Dieskau who was wounded and taken prisoner

Sept. 11, Sir William Johnson held conference with the Indians

Sept. 27, In council of war at Oswego Shirley decided to abandon the attack on Niagara as planned at Alexandria until the following year, and retired to Albany leaving a garrison at Oswego

Nov. 27, Joseph Salvador purchased 100,000 acres of land near Fort Ninety-Six for a Jewish settlement in South Carolina

Nov. 30, Nearly 900 Acadian French exiled and transported from Nova Scotia by the English had arrived in Maryland. *See* Canada

Map of Lewis Evans based on actual surveys gave delineation of the Ohio River system according to the explorations of Gist, Walker, and others, and map of John Mitchell which was used by the commissioners who negotiated the Treaty of Peace in 1783 also delineated the Ohio River Valley, the best map until superseded by Arrowsmith's map in 1814

1756

March 27, Fort Bull (Rome, New York) captured and destroyed by de Léry from Montreal

April 14, Pennsylvania proclaimed a war against the Delaware Indians

May 18, Declaration of war by Great Britain against France

June 15, Forty German officers landed at New York to take commissions in Lord Loudon's regiment of Royal Americans

June 25, French and Indians captured and burned Vaux's Fort at headwaters of the Roanoke, Virginia, Captain John Smith captured

Aug. 14, Fort Oswego, New York, taken by French commanded by General Montcalm and destroyed

Sept. 8, Delaware Indian village of Kittaning on the Alleghany River north of Pittsburgh surprised and destroyed by Pennsylvania troops commanded by Colonel John Armstrong

Oct. 7, The *New Hampshire Gazette* published at Portsmouth, the first newspaper in the State

Fort Loudon built on the Tennessee River about 30 miles from the present town of Knoxville by Andrew Lewis sent by Governor Loudon of Virginia

1757

Jan. 21, Captain Robert Rogers' scouts defeated by French near Ticonderoga

July 26, Colonel Parker defeated by French at Sabbath Day Point, Lake George

Aug. 9, Fort William Henry at head of Lake George, besieged by French commanded by General Montcalm since Aug. 2, surrendered by Colonel Monroe. Massacre of British garrison Aug. 10 as they marched out by Indian allies of the French

1758

March 16, Massacre of Spaniards by the Comanches at San Saba mission on the San Saba River near the present town of Menard, Texas, the Comanches antagonistic because of Spanish friendship with the Apaches

June 4, Siege of Louisburg begun and troops landed June 8 at Gabarus Bay. *See* Canada

June 20, Thomas Carr granted 300 acres in Georgia, founded Sunbury

July 5, The largest army yet seen in America assembled at Lake George commanded by General Abercromby, 7,000 British regulars and 10,000 provincial troops, and marched to attack Ticonderoga

July 8, British attack on Ticonderoga repulsed by General Montcalm with loss of 1,967 in killed and wounded, forced to retreat

July 26, Surrender of Louisburg to Admiral Boscawen and Gen. Amherst. *See* Canada

Aug. 27, Fort Frontenac surrendered to English force led by Colonel John Bradstreet

Sept. 14, Major Grant sent by Bouquet to reconnoitre defeated by the French on heights above Fort Duquesne now called Grant's Hill. Lost 273 killed and wounded

Nov. 25, John Forbes occupied Fort Duquesne at forks of the Ohio (Pittsburgh) which the French had blown up and abandoned

1759

June 26, British fleet ascended the St. Lawrence and anchored below Quebec

July 5, Fort Oswego, New York, repulsed an attack of French and Indians led by Saint Luc de la Corne

July 25, Fort Niagara surrendered by the French

July 26, French evacuated fort at Ticonderoga

Aug. 4, French evacuated fort at Crown Point

Sept. 13, Battle of Quebec, General Wolfe killed. *See* Canada

Sept. 18, Surrender of Quebec to the British by de Ramezay, and occupation by the British on the 19th

Oct. 7, Colonel Diego Ortiz with army of over 600 Indians from Mexico, Apaches and Spaniards, defeated by Comanches and northern Indians in battle near Ringgold on the Red River, the Spaniards retreating to San Antonio, and San Saba remained unpunished

Oct. 12, Daniel Boone bought tract on Sugar Creek, tributary of Dutchman's Creek where he lived 5 years

1760

Feb. 16, Fort Prince George attacked by Indians but Captain Hugh Waddell repulsed attack

May 28, Colonel Archibald Montgomerie with 295 South Carolina rangers left Fort Ninety-Six to relieve Fort Loudon invested by Cherokees, crossed Twelve-Mile River June 1, burned Indian villages and captured 100 Cherokees

June 27, Colonel Montgomerie drawn into ambush 8 miles south of the present Franklin, North Carolina and forced to retreat with heavy loss in killed and wounded

Aug. 8, Captain Demere besieged by Indians at Fort Loudon (Tenn.) compelled to surrender to Cherokees, condition of capitulation made that the garrison should not be molested in retreat

Aug. 9, Garrison from Fort Loudon marching in retreat

to Fort Prince George massacred by Indians about 15 miles from Fort Loudon

Sept. 8, Capitulation of Montreal. *See* Canada

Nov. 29, Major Robert Rogers took possession of Detroit

1761

Feb., James Otis before the Supreme Court of Massachusetts denied the right of the British Government to issue "writs of assistance" applied for by customs officials in revival of navigation laws of 1651 and 1660

July 7, Colonel James Grant marched from Fort Prince George with 2,600 men, defeated the Indians June 10 about 2 miles south of where Colonel Montgomerie was ambushed the previous year and laid waste 15 Indian towns during the summer

Oct. 30, Proclamation of Colonel Henry Bouquet at Fort Pitt forbid settlement or hunting in land reserved to the Indians

Dec., Instructions to governors of Nova Scotia, New Hampshire, Virginia, North Carolina, South Carolina, and Georgia forbidding grants of land or settlement which might interfere with Indians on frontiers of the colonies

1762

Jan. 2, England declared war on Spain

Feb., The English fleet in the West Indies captured Martinique, and presently occupied Granada, the Grenadines, and St. Lucia; Havana, Cuba, surrendered Aug. 13

Oct. 5, Manila in the Philippines surrendered to the English fleet

Oct. 12, Association of Philadelphia Baptists voted to establish a college in Rhode Island

Nov. 3, Secret Treaty of Ildefonso between France and Spain by which Louisiana west of the Mississippi and the island of Orleans on the east bank to be transferred to Spain; approved by the Spanish Escurial in secret session Nov. 13 and by the King of France Nov. 23

———, Preliminaries of peace signed at Fontainbleau ended war of France with Great Britain and Spain

James Otis published a pamphlet "A Vindication of the Conduct of the House of Representatives of the Province of Massachusetts Bay"

1763

Jan. 21, General Amherst in New York announced to Colonel Bouquet at Fort Pitt the cessation of hostilities

Feb. 10, Treaty of Paris between England, France, and Spain signed, ended the French and Indian War, France ceding to England Canada, Nova Scotia (Acadia), Prince Edward Island, Cape Breton Island, Louisiana east of the Mississippi except New Orleans, France receiving the islands of St. Pierre and Miquelon in the Gulf of St. Lawrence for fishing stations, and in the West Indies, Martinique, Guadeloupe, Marie Galante, and St. Lucia, Spain ceding Florida to England in exchange for Cuba and the Philippines which the English had taken by conquest

April 17, The *Georgia Gazette*, first newspaper in the State published in Savannah by James Johnson

April 27, Pontiac, chief of the Ottawa tribes, held a council of war on the River Ecorce a few miles south of Detroit, and organized a general revolt of the western Indians against the English which was not suppressed until 1765

May 9–Nov. 1, Major Gladwin withstood attack of Indians led by Pontiac on garrison at Detroit

May 13, Lieutenant Cuyler left Fort Schlosser on southeastern end of Lake Michigan with 10 boats and provisions for the western posts

May 16, Fort Sandusky under command of Ensign Paulli taken by the Indians in surprise attack

May 25, Fort St. Joseph held by Ensign Schlosser taken by the Indians

May 27, Fort Miami on the Maumee River commanded by Holmes taken by the Indians

May 28, The Wyandots attacked Lieutenant Cuyler coming from Lake Michigan at Point Peléeon, Lake Erie, sinking 2 boats

June 1, Indians appeared before Fort Pitt and began attacks in that region

——, Lieutenant Edward Jenkins forced to surrender post at Ouatenon (Indiana) on the Wabash to Indians led by Godefroy, a Canadian

June 4, Fort Michillimackinac, second in importance to post of Detroit, taken by the Ojibwas and English garrison massacred, Captain Etherington, in command was unaware that Indian war had begun, but he and 11 others were saved by a friendly Ottawa

June 17, Fort Presque Isle surrendered by Ensign Christie to the Indians

June 18, Fort Le Boeuf surrendered by Ensign Price to the Indians, Price with 7 men escaping to Fort Pitt

June 20, Fort Venango surrendered to the Indians and communication between Fort Pitt and the lakes cut

June 21, Blaine in command at Fort Ligonier succeeded in repelling Indian attack on way from Bedford to the Ohio

——, Fort at Green Bay abandoned by the English

July 9, Expulsion of the Jesuits from Louisiana, from Illinois Sept. 24, embarked at New Orleans Nov. 24

July 21, Colonel Henry Bouquet started from Carlisle, Pennsylvania to relieve Fort Pitt

July 27–Aug. 1, Captain Ecuyer successfully defended Fort Pitt besieged by the Indians

July 31, Sortie from Fort Detroit led by Captain Dalyell attacked Indians at Parents Creek, the commander killed, and a fourth of the force of 250 wounded or killed

Aug. 3–Sept. 3, Journey of Pierre Lacléde Ligueste from New Orleans to Fort Chartres

Aug. 5–6, Colonel Bouquet marching to Fort Pitt attacked by Indians defeated them at Bushy Run (Edge Hill)

Aug. 10, Colonel Bouquet reached Fort Pitt and relieved the garrison

Sept. 14, British near fort at Niagara at landing above Falls attacked by Senecas and with relief parties sent a total of over 80 men killed

Sept. 30, Major Robert Farman arrived at Mobile to take over Louisiana territory ceded by the Treaty, formal transfer made Oct. 20

Oct. 7, Proclamation of George III provided for the government and defined the boundaries of the new provinces, Quebec, East and West Florida, Grenada, including the Island of Grenada, the Grenadines, St. Vincent's and Tobago, made Crown Colonies, all land between the Alleghanies and the Mississippi reserved for the Indians thus excluding settlers and limiting colonial expansion westward

Oct. 30, Letter of Pontiac made submission to General Gladwin

Nov. 6, Jesuit property in Illinois sold at auction by French commander

Nov. 16, General Gage arrived in New York from England

Dec. 1, Patrick Henry's speech in Virginia in the "parson's cause," a suit brought by the clergy against the laws of 1755 and 1758 fixing the price of tobacco in which their salaries were paid, Henry opposing the right of the Crown to interfere in the internal affairs of the Colony, the clergy supported by the King

Dec. 27, The "Paxton boys" broke into workhouse in Lancaster, Pennsylvania, where the magistrate had placed the peaceful Conestoga Indians for protection, and killed them in attempt to exterminate Indians

1764

Jan. 20, James Wright commissioned as Governor of Georgia

Feb. 6, General James Grant assumed office as first English Governor of East Florida

Feb. 15, St. Louis, Missouri, founded by the French as a fur-trading station by Pierre Lacléde Liguest and Auguste Chouteau

March 20, Major Loftus, from New Orleans, commissioned to take over the French Fort de Chartres on the Illinois under the Treaty, attacked by Indians at Davions Bluff (Fort Adams) on the Mississippi and driven back

April 3, Sir William Johnson arranged a peace with the Senecas by which the Crown secured a large tract of land on the Niagara River

April 5, The Sugar Act passed in England confirmed and modified the Molasses Act of 1733, raising duty on sugar and lowering that on molasses

June 6, Massachusetts Assembly sent a memorial to England to urge repeal of Sugar Act, and a committee of correspondence appointed to inform the other Colonies of this action and ask their coöperation

——, George Johnstone appointed Governor of West Florida

July 20, Royal Order declared the region west of the Connecticut called the "New Hampshire Grants," so-called because of the grant of 131 townships by the Governor of New Hampshire, to belong to New York

July, Colonel Bradstreet from Niagara passed up Lake Erie where at Presque Isle he met Delawares and Shawnees who pretended to sue for peace

Aug. 6, Sir William Johnson made treaty with the Senecas, and the Chenussios

Aug. 12, Colonel Bradstreet made treaty with the Shawnees and Delawares, engaging not to attack tribes within 25 days, which General Gage later refused to ratify

Aug. 26, Colonel Bradstreet arrived at Fort Detroit

Oct. 3, Colonel Bouquet left Fort Pitt for march into the Indian country, the first expedition since that of the French led by de Celoron in 1749 from Canada

Oct., The New York Assembly appointed a committee of correspondence and sent statement of grievances to King and Parliament

Nov. 4, General Bradstreet's "inglorious march" reached the Niagara portage

Nov. 17, Colonel Henry Bouquet at place appointed at junction of the 2 main branches of the Muskingum received the submission of the Indians who delivered up their captives

Nov. 26, First issue of the Connecticut *Courant* published by Thomas Green at Hartford, announced by prospectus of Oct. 26

Nov. 28, Colonel Bouquet with Pennsylvania and Virginia troops returned to Fort Pitt unopposed by the Indians

Nov., Rhode Island Assembly sent a petition to the King in which the principle stated that an essential privilege of Englishmen was that they should be governed by laws made by their own consent

——, Connecticut sent address to Parliament protesting against proposed Stamp Act and any other Bill for internal taxes

Dec. 25, Virginia passed vote of thanks to Colonel Bouquet, Pennsylvania, Jan. 15, 1765, Pennsylvania instructed the colonial agent, Mr. Jackson, to remonstrate against the proposed Stamp Act and to ask for repeal of the Sugar Act, and Benjamin Franklin sent to England to act with him

Virginia sent addresses to the King and Parliament in which the principle of no taxation without representation was laid down

Currency Act forbade the Colonies to issue paper money

1765

March 22, The Stamp Act required revenue stamps to be placed on commercial and legal documents, pamphlets, newspapers, almanacs, playing cards, and dice

May 15, Colonel George Croghan left Fort Pitt on expedition to receive the oath of allegiance from French citizens, descended the Ohio River, at Great Bone Licks, Kentucky, May 30–31, was taken prisoner by the Indians at Vincennes, June 8, but released, started for the Illinois country

May 29, Patrick Henry in the House of Burgesses introduced resolutions stating that the Virginia Assembly had the sole right and power to lay taxes upon the inhabitants of Virginia

Aug. 14, Andrew Oliver, Secretary of Massachusetts, who had accepted the office of stamp collector, hanged in effigy and his house damaged by a mob

Aug. 17–25, George Croghan at Detroit received the submission of the Indians

Aug. 26, Lieutenant-Governor Hutchinson's house destroyed by a Massachusetts mob

Sept. 19, Jared Ingersoll, stamp-collector for Connecticut, forced by the citizens to resign the office

Sept. 28, The "Diligence" arrived in Cape Fear River with stamped paper for use in North Carolina, but was prevented by an armed forced led by Colonel Ashe and Colonel Hugh Waddell from landing the paper, and James Houston, stamp distributor, forced to take oath that he would not distribute stamped paper

——, Maryland adopted a Bill of Rights and protested against the Stamp Act

Oct. 7, Stamp Act Congress with delegates from 9 colonies met in New York in response to a circular letter from Massachusetts; Virginia, North Carolina, Georgia, and New Hampshire not represented

Oct. 10, Fort Chartres and the left bank of the Mississippi surrendered by St. Ange to Captain Thomas Sterling who assumed the government

Oct. 19, The Congress at New York adopted a "declaration of rights and grievances" drafted by John Dickinson of Pennsylvania protesting against taxes imposed except by consent of the Colonies or their representatives, and address to the King, and memorial to the House of Lords, and petition to the House of Commons adopted

Oct. 25, Merchants and traders of Philadelphia subscribed to a non-importation agreement until the Stamp Act should be repealed

Nov. 1, The Stamp Act came into effect

Dec. 3, Major Farman relieved Captain Sterling in command at Fort Chartres

The Quartering Act required the colonists to house British troops in public hostels and vacant buildings if barracks insufficient, persons giving houses for troops and furnishing supplies were to be reimbursed by the Province

1766

Jan. 6, *Pennsylvania Chronicle and Universal Advertiser* issued by William Goddard

Feb. 3–13, Benjamin Franklin in London questioned before the House of Commons on the effect of the Stamp Act in America, and made it clear that the Act could not be enforced

March 5, First Spanish Governor of Spanish Louisiana, Don Antonio de Ulloa, arrived at New Orleans

March 7, The British Parliament passed the Declaratory Act asserting right to make laws to bind the colonies in all cases

March 18, The Stamp Act was repealed by vote of 275 to 167 in the House of Commons

June–Oct., 1768, Journey of Jonathan Carver from Boston to the far West, arrived at Mackinac in August, at Green Bay, Sept. 18–20, ascended the Fox River and arrived at island at east end of Lake Winnebago Oct. 10, reached Lake Pepin Nov. 1, the Falls of St. Anthony Nov. 17, ascended the Minnesota River to stream which bears his name Nov. 25–Dec. 7, and wintered at Prairie du Chien at Indian village

July 24, Treaty of peace with Pontiac at Oswego signed, negotiated by Sir William Johnson

Sept. 6, Illegal commercial decree of Governor de Ulloa of Spanish Louisiana published that all captains of vessels from France or San Domingo must report on arrival with bills of lading and passports, and agents for sale of cargoes must submit the prices of their goods to examiners to be subject to reduction if judged too high

Nov. 10, Queen's College at New Brunswick chartered, later Rutger's University

1767

May, The Townshend Acts passed by Parliament imposed taxes on tea, glass, wine, lead, oil, paper, and painter's colors, the revenue collected to be used to pay the salaries of governors and judges thus making them independent of the colonial Assemblies. A central board of commissioners of customs was established with headquarters in Boston

June 15, The New York Assembly was suspended for non-compliance with the Quartering Act

——, "Farmer's Letters" by John Dickinson expressed the colonial viewpoint on the Townshend Acts

Oct. 28, Boston town-meeting adopted a non-importation agreement

——, Mason and Dixon, surveyors, completed boundary line between Pennsylvania and Maryland

Oct. 28, Spain sent Franciscans to displace the Jesuits in America

North Carolina frontiersmen organized as the "Regulators" to defend themselves against "excessive taxes, dishonest sheriffs, and extortionate fees"

1768

Feb. 11, The General Court of Massachusetts sent petition to the King against the taxes, and circular letter to the other Colonies asking them to join in petition for redress. The British Ministry demanded that the Court rescind the letter and on their refusal to comply the Court was dissolved

March, The people of Orange county, North Carolina, formed association headed by Herman Husbands and William Hunter for regulation of public grievances

May 21, Meeting of the "Regulators" of North Carolina sent James Hunter and Rednap Howell to the Governor with a statement of grievances

June 10, John Hancock's sloop "Liberty" seized for defiance of customs collector. Rioters drove the customs officers to the British warship "Romney"

Aug. 11, Spanish troops under Captain Rios took possession of St. Louis in the name of the King of Spain

Aug. 12, Order in Council confirmed boundary between New York and Canada

Sept. 5, Colonel John Wilkins succeeded Colonel John Reed as military commander of Illinois

Sept. 23–28, Convention of delegates from 96 Massachusetts towns formulated statement of grievances

Sept. 28, Two British regiments arrived in Boston from Halifax commanded by General Thomas Gage

Oct. 28–29, Meeting of Superior Council of Louisiana demanded freedom of commerce and expulsion of Governor de Ulloa

Nov. 1, Governor de Ulloa placed on ship in harbor, and escaped to Havana

Nov. 5, Treaty of Fort Stanwix signed with the Six Nations by representatives of New Jersey, Pennsylvania, and Virginia defined boundaries between the English colonies and the Indian lands

Travels of Father Francisco Tomas Hermengildo Garces in Arizona and New Mexico begun in which he reached Casa Grande on the Gila River

1769

Jan. 9 and Feb. 15, Colonizing expedition sent by José de Galvez from Baja California to California sailed in 2 small vessels commanded by Captain Vicente Vila and Captain Juan Pérez, and arrived at present San Diego April 11 and 29

March 22, Captain Rivera y Moncada at head of land expedition to California sent by Galvez accompanied by Father Juan Crespi began march from Santa Maria and arrived at San Diego May 14

March 24, Second land expedition sent by Galvez to California commanded by Governor Gaspar de Portolá accompanied by Father Junipero Serra began march from Santa Maria de los Angeles mission and reached San Diego June 29

April 5, Pontiac on visit to St. Ange in Upper Louisiana killed by a Peoria Indian at Cahokia. He was buried with military honors at St. Louis

May 1, Daniel Boone, John Finley, John Stuart, and 3 men in their employ left North Carolina and crossed the mountains by the Cumberland Gap into Kentucky, reaching Red River, June 7; captured by Indians Dec. 22 and plundered of furs and stores but made their escape, and Boone spent 2 more winters hunting and trapping and exploring the country

May, House of Burgesses of Virginia adopted resolutions asserting right of taxation to be vested in itself and right of persons accused of treason or any crime or felony committed in the Colony to trial in the courts of the Colony

July 14, Governor Portolá left San Diego on expedition to find Monterey and reached the mouth of the Salinas River on Bay of Monterey Sept. 30 but missed Monterey, at Point Pinos Oct. 5, and compelled by lack of provisions to return to San Diego Dec. 9. He named on this expedition Santa Margarita, Santa Ana, Carpinteria, Gaviota, Canada de los Osos, Pajaro, San Lorenzo, and other places, and on Nov. 2 discovered San Francisco Bay

July 16, Serra at San Diego founded the first of the California missions which he named San Diego de Alcalá

——, The "Watauga Association" pioneers from Virginia and North Carolina began settlement of Tennessee

Aug. 18, Spanish Governor O'Reilly reached New Orleans and took possession of the government, the leaders of the party who expelled Governor Ulloa arrested Aug. 21, and imprisoned, and 5 shot Oct. 25

Sept. 5, James Otis brutally assaulted in the Coffee House on King St., Boston, by Robinson, a commissioner of customs, and some British officers

Sept., First commencement at Rhode Island College, later Brown University

Oct. 7, Report of commissioners on boundary between New York and New Jersey, approved by New York in 1771, and by New Jersey in 1772, and confirmed by the King in Council in 1773

Dec. 30, Dartmouth College at Hanover, New Hampshire, chartered

1770

Jan. 13, Liberty pole in New York cut down by British soldiers

Jan. 24, Portolá reached the Colony at San Diego, California from Monterey

Feb. 22, A boy shot and mortally wounded from house of Richardson in Boston, supposed to be an informer, the "first victim"

March 5, The Boston "Massacre," street encounter of British soldiers and townspeople in which 3 citizens killed and 8 wounded by the guard at the custom house

March 23, Captain Juan Perez entered San Diego Bay, bringing relief to the Spanish colonists

April, Repeal of the Townshend duties except the tax on tea retained in order to maintain the principle that Parliament had the right to tax the colonies

Sept. 10, Castle William in Boston Harbor occupied by British soldiers

Sept. 30, Death of George Whitefield, revivalist, at Newburyport, Massachusetts

Sept., The "long hunters" a company of 40 under Joseph Drake and Henry Skaggs journeyed to Kentucky spending 11 months hunting and trapping

1771

May 16, The North Carolina "Regulators" defeated in battle at Alamance Creek by Governor Tryon's troops, those taken prisoners executed June 19

Aug., A summer of fighting between Penn's guards and the Connecticut Susquehanna colonists in Wyoming Valley ended in eviction of Penn's men

——, Expedition of Father Francisco Garces to mouth of the Gila River, to Yuma country, followed the lower Colorado River to its mouth in Gulf of California, and crossed Imperial Valley to San Felipe Pass in San Jacinto Mountains

1772

June 9, The revenue boat "Gaspee" enforcing the Navigation Acts ran aground near Providence and was burned by Rhode Islanders, the commission appointed to investigate the affair could get no evidence against the offenders though the leaders were known and a large reward offered

Sept. 10, Order of the King based on report of the Marques de Rubi who traversed the Spanish frontier from Louisiana to California in 1766, the "New Regulation of Presidios," to abandon the missions in eastern Texas and withdraw frontier line southward

Nov. 2, First Committee of Correspondence instituted in Boston

1773

March 12, The Virginia House of Burgesses appointed a committee for intercolonial correspondence to keep informed of matters of interest particularly on proposal to transport Americans to England for trial, and a circular letter to the other colonies urged appointment of committees. By July 8 Rhode Island, Connecticut, New Hampshire, Massachusetts, and South Carolina had appointed committees

June 1, Surrender of large tract of land in Georgia by Indians

June 2, Letters of Governor Hutchinson of Massachusetts obtained by Franklin and sent to America by him under seal of confidence read in the Massachusetts Assembly

June 22, Spanish settlement of California. *See* Mexico

Aug., Rev. Samuel Hopkins and Rev. Ezra Stiles of Newport, Rhode Island, issued circular asking for subscriptions for colonization of free negroes on west shore of Africa, beginning of American Colonization Society

Sept. 25, Daniel Boone with his family and 5 other families and 40 men of the "Bryan party" started for the West. Shawnee Indians killed some of the party Oct. 10 and the others except the Boones returned to Virginia and Carolina. Boone built cabin on bank of the Clinch River

Sept., Expedition of Peter Pond, native of Connecticut, to Green Bay, ascended the Fox River, portaged to the Wisconsin, and wintered on plains between the Missouri and Mississippi

Oct. 28, Grant of land including West Virginia to company including Thomas Walpole, Benjamin Franklin, and Samuel Wharton for colony of "Vandalia"

Nov. 28, First ships carrying tea arrived in Boston Harbor

Dec. 16, "Boston Tea Party." On Dec. 17 the cargo of tea sent by George III to Boston would have been seized by the collector for non-payment of duty, but the night of the 16th fifty or sixty men disguised as Indians boarded the ships and threw the tea overboard

——, Tea landed at Charleston, South Carolina, and Dec. 20 stored in damp cellars where it soon spoiled.

New York and Philadelphia sent the tea back to London

1774

Jan., Dr. John Connolly, Dunmore's agent, fired without provocation upon a delegation of Shawanoe chiefs assembled at Fort Pitt

Jan. 8, Captain Juan Bautista de Anza with Father Garces started on overland route from Sonora to San Francisco Bay crossing the Imperial Valley and the San Jacinto Mts. reached mission of San Gabriel March 22 and Monterey April 18

March 9, Governor Tryon of New York by proclamation commanded Ethan Allen, Seth Warner, and other Vermonters to surrender and offered reward for their capture

March 21, Governor Dunmore of Virginia issued proclamation demanding surrender of territory by "one Richard Henderson and other disorderly persons, his associates"

March 31, The Boston Port Bill, the first of 5 measures passed by the British Parliament relating to Massachusetts called the "Intolerable Acts" closed port of Boston to all shipping from June 1, and moved the seat of government from Boston to Salem

April 23, The "Nancy" bringing tea not allowed to land in New York

April 30, Murder of the family of Logan, chief of the Mingoes by a frontier man, Greathouse, and his drunken companions, began war of Logan on settlers on borders of Virginia and Tennessee

May 13, General Gage arrived in Boston as Governor of Massachusetts and Commander-in-Chief of army

May 20, Regulating Act deprived Massachusetts of its chartered rights, and after July 1 the Council to be appointed by the King instead of by the colonial Assembly, the appointment and removal of judicial officers to be by the Governor, and town meetings not permitted without the written consent of the Governor

——, Administration of Justice Act provided that magistrates charged with capital offenses should be sent for trial to some other colony or to England

June 1, Day that the Boston Port Bill to take effect celebrated as a day of fasting

June 2, Quartering Act provided for billeting of soldiers if suitable quarters were not voluntarily provided

June 8, Public Meeting in Boston adopted non-importation agreement

June 11, Juan Perez sailed from Monterey in the "Santiago" and reached 55° N. Lat. July 21. On return voyage he named Nootka Sound, San Lorenzo, Aug. 7, and sighted a mountain which he named Santa Rosalia, later called Mount Olympus Aug. 10 or 11, reached Queen Charlotte Islands July 18, and Monterey Aug. 27. No landing made on entire trip but Spain claimed right to occupy Nootka on basis of this exploration mainly

June 16, Harrod from Virginia founded settlement in Kentucky of Harrodsburg, which was destroyed by the Indians but refounded the following year

June 22, Quebec Act extended the boundaries of Quebec to the Ohio River thus depriving the colonies of western lands claimed under their charters. *See also* Canada

——, Convention at Annapolis, Maryland, proposed an absolute cessation of intercourse with England and nominated delegates to Continental Congress,

Samuel Chase, Robert Goldsborough, William Paca, Matthew Tilghman, and Thomas Johnson

July 11, Death of Sir William Johnson at Albany, New York

July 14, Arrival of British troops in Boston to enforce "Intolerable Acts"

Aug. 25, Convention to form provincial congress met at New Berne, North Carolina, decided that after Sept. 1 all use of East India tea should be prohibited, and after Nov. 1 all importation of African slaves should cease

Aug. 27, Judge Richard Henderson, Colonel John Luttrell, William Johnston, and others met at Hillsborough, North Carolina, and organized company, the "Louisa Company" to purchase land from the Indians for settlement

Sept. 1, Governor Gage issued writ convening the General Court of Massachusetts at Salem but dissolved it by proclamation of Sept. 28

Sept. 5–Oct. 26, First Continental Congress on invitation from Massachusetts met in Philadelphia with 55 delegates from 12 colonies, Georgia only not represented, Peyton Randolph, of Virginia, elected president

Sept. 6, Convention at Suffolk, Massachusetts, resolved "that no obedience is due" to the recent Acts of British Parliament; these "Suffolk Resolutions" approved by the Continental Congress Sept. 17

Sept. 27, The Continental Congress resolved that after Dec. 1 there should be no importation or consumption of British goods in the colonies

Sept. 28, The Continental Congress rejected plan for perpetual colonial dependence on Great Britain proposed by Joseph Galloway of Pennsylvania

Sept. 30, The Continental Congress voted that all exportation to Great Britain, Ireland, and the West Indies should cease after Sept. 10, 1775

Oct. 5, Assembly of Massachusetts met in Salem in defiance of prohibition of Governor Gage, declared themselves a provincial congress, and appointed a committee of safety empowered to call out the militia, and committees to promote military organization

Oct. 10, Battle of the Great Kanawha, Colonel Andrew Lewis defeated the Indians led by Cornstalk ending Lord Dunmore's war caused by hostility of the Indians to the settlement of Kentucky and Tennessee

Oct. 14, Declaration of Rights and Grievances adopted by Congress included list of the Acts of Parliament held to be infringements

Oct. 18, Agreement known as the "Association" pledged the colonies to non-importation of British commodities enumerated after Dec. 1, non-exportation suspended until Sept. 10, 1775, and then not to include rice, committees to be chosen in every county and town for enforcement

Oct. 21, "Address to the people of Great Britain" drafted by John Jay reviewing the history of the relations of the colonies with the mother country adopted by Congress, and also "Memorial to the people of the Colonies" drafted by Richard Henry Lee on the policy of commercial retaliation of the "Association," and a review of grievances

Oct. 22, Henry Middleton, of South Carolina, elected president of Congress on resignation of Randolph

Oct. 26, A letter to the inhabitants of Quebec drafted by John Dickinson urging union in the cause of civil and religious liberty adopted by Congress, and a petition to the King drafted by John Dickinson

Oct. 26, Congress adjourned, another meeting for May 10, 1775 provided for

Peter Pond trading with the Indians on the Minnesota River according to his map preserved in the British Museum

1775

Jan. 6, The "Louisa Company" formed by Judge Richard Henderson and associates in 1774 to settle between the Cumberland and Kentucky rivers enlarged and given name of Transylvania Company, land secured by treaty with the Cherokee Indians

Jan. 18, Provincial Congress met in Savannah, Georgia, to organize the government, a council of safety created June 22

Feb. 1, Second Provincial Congress of Massachusetts met at Cambridge

Feb. 27, Lord North's plan for conciliation adopted by Parliament provided for exemption of any colony from taxation which would agree to contribute a fixed amount for the support of civil officials and army

March 10, Daniel Boone with 30 men started to clear the "Wilderness Road" from the Holston River to Kentucky for Henderson's Transylvania settlement, and April 6 built log fort on the Kentucky River, the beginning of the settlement of Boonesborough

March 16–Oct. 7, Spanish expedition of Bruno Heceta and Juan Francisco de la Bodega y Quadra sailed from San Blas on voyage of exploration to northwest, landed and named Trinidad June 11, July 14, took possession of land at Cape Grenville at Lat. 47° 20'. On July 30 the leaders separated Heceta reaching 49° discovered Trinidad Bay and the mouth of the Columbia River Aug. 17 which he believed a bay and named Assumption Inlet, and Bodega reached 58° and discovered Bodega Bay Oct. 3

March 17, Judge Richard Henderson bought from the Indians the territory between the Ohio, Kentucky, and Cumberland rivers including all of Kentucky and part of Tennessee, and May 23 formed provisional government for Transylvania

March 19, Watauga Association purchased land from the Indians for settlement of Tennessee, deed of conveyance made to Charles Robertson

March 20, Patrick Henry in speech before Virginia Convention at Richmond urged resistance to England

March 30, Restraining Act confined trade of New England to Great Britain and Ireland and British West Indies

April 6, Boonesborough, Kentucky, founded by Richard Henderson

April 8, Governor Martin dissolved the Assembly of North Carolina ending royal rule in State

April 11, Convention at Westminster voted that the New Hampshire Grants must "wholly renounce and resist the administration of the government of New York"

April 18, The countryside warned by Paul Revere and William Dawes of expedition sent by General Gage to seize military stores of Massachusetts and arrest John Hancock and Samuel Adams

April 19, Battle of Lexington began the Revolution. British troops commanded by Major Pitcairn fired on the assembled "minute men" at Lexington killing 8, and marching to Concord were opposed by patriots and several on both sides killed in encounter at the Old North Bridge. The British destroyed military stores and began march back to Boston under continuous fire from the provincial patriots and must have surrendered but for strong relief force sent to Lexington by Lord Percy

April 20, Richard Henderson with settlers arrived at Boone's stockade at mouth of Otter Creek and Kentucky River

May 2, Letter to oppressed inhabitants of Canada drafted by John Jay adopted by Congress

May 5, Benjamin Franklin returned to Philadelphia after 10 years absence in England and was elected May 6 to Congress

May 10–Dec. 12, 1776, Second Continental Congress met in Philadelphia with delegates from the thirteen colonies, Rhode Island delegates arriving May 18, and Georgia acceding July 20

May 10, Fort Ticonderoga on the west side of Lake Champlain taken in surprise attack by Ethan Allen accompanied by Benedict Arnold

May 12, Crown Point on Lake Champlain captured by Colonel Seth Warner

May 16, Fort St. John on the Sorel captured by Benedict Arnold

May 17, Congress voted that exports to Quebec, Nova Scotia, Cape Breton Island, and East and West Florida cease, and adopted "Address to the Inhabitants of Canada" urging them to unite with the colonies in defense of the common liberty

May 23, Transylvanian colonists in convention at Boonesborough, Kentucky, adopted "the earliest form of government in the region west of the Alleghanies"

May 24, John Hancock of Massachusetts chosen president of Congress

May 25, Generals Howe, Clinton, and Burgoyne arrived from England with troops to reënforce General Gage in Boston

May 31, The Mecklenburg Resolves dated May 20 adopted at meeting of frontiersmen at Charlotte, Mecklenburg county, North Carolina, declared that crown commissions in the colonies were null and void, and colonial constitutions suspended (May 20 not accepted as authentic)

June 3, Congress appointed a committee to borrow £6,000 to purchase gunpowder

June 8, Governor Dunmore of Virginia fled to British ship at Yorktown

June 14, Congress voted to raise 20,000 troops and a committee appointed to draft rules for the army which was organized June 16

June 15, George Washington appointed Commander-in-Chief, received his formal commission June 19

June 16, During the night the Americans led by Colonel William Prescott, Thomas Knowlton, and Captain Samuel Gridley constructed fortifications on Breed's Hill, Charlestown, which commanded Boston

June 17, Battle of Breed's and Bunker Hill. At Bunker Hill to which the Americans retreated the British were repulsed twice, but captured Bunker Hill on the third attack with loss of 1,000 men. Charlestown burned by the British

June 22, Continental Congress resolved to issue $2,000,000 in bills of credit, the "Confederated Colonies" pledged for their redemption

——, William Ewen appointed president of Georgia Council of Safety, Seth John Cuthbert, secretary

July 3, General George Washington took command of the army at Cambridge

July 3–March 17, 1776, Siege of Boston by the continental army

July 4, Congress adopted resolution against the Restraining Acts as unconstitutional and cruel

July 5, Petition to the King drawn up by John Dickinson, according to resolutions adopted May 29, signed by Congress July 8

July 6, Declaration of the Cause and Necessity of Taking up Arms, a statement to the army, adopted by Congress

July 12, Continental Congress organized 3 depts. of Indian Affairs, northern, middle, and southern

July 14, Heceta (Spanish expedition) first Europeans to land on northwest coast near Cape Grenville

July 21, Plan of a confederacy submitted to Congress by Franklin but not acted upon

July 26, Post Office established and Benjamin Franklin elected Postmaster General

——, Constitution for Maryland adopted by convention, the "Association of the Freemen of Maryland"

July 27, Army hospital established by Congress

July 31, Lord North's conciliatory proposal of Feb. 27 rejected in formal report

Aug. 1, Statement issued by Congress of the prohibition of the "Association" of Oct. 1774 of export and import from the dominions of Great Britain in retaliation for the Restraining Act of March which in April had been extended to include New Jersey, Pennsylvania, Delaware, Maryland, Virginia, and South Carolina

Aug. 5, Captain Don Juan Manuel Ayala sailed through the Golden Gate, first recorded entrance by a white man, and remained in San Francisco Bay 44 days exploring shores and islands

Aug. 13, General Gage in letter to General Washington refused to accord to Americans the rights of prisoners of war

Aug. 16, Spanish Royal Decree established capital of California at Monterey with Felipe de Neve, Governor

Aug. 17, Spanish expedition of Heceta and Bodega y Quadra at mouth of Columbia River. *See supra* March 16–Oct. 7

Aug. 23, George III proclaimed the American Colonies to be in "open and avowed rebellion"

Sept. 8, Bonvouloir, a French gentleman commissioned by Vergennes to report on American affairs, sailed from London for Philadelphia where he arrived after voyage of 100 days, and sent in report dated Dec. 28 favorable to the colonists

Sept. 13, Benedict Arnold left Cambridge with 1,000 volunteers and sailed from Newburyport at mouth of the Merrimac River to Augusta, Maine, and Sept. 25 began overland march of 300 miles to attack Quebec

Sept. 25, Proprietors of Transylvania met at Oxford, North Carolina, and chose James Hogg as delegate to the Continental Congress. On arrival in Philadelphia he was prevented from taking seat as representative of 14th State by protest of Virginia

——, Ethan Allen and 38 men captured in attack on Montreal and sent prisoners to England where he remained until released by exchange of prisoners May 6, 1778

Oct. 10, Sir William Howe succeeded General Gage as Commander-in-Chief of British army in America

Oct. 13, A "Marine Committee" appointed to control naval affairs, and 2 cruisers ordered

Oct. 18, British vessels sailed into the harbor and burned town of Falmouth (Portland) Maine

——, Fort Chambly on the Sorel River taken by a detachment of Montgomery's troops

Oct. 23, Anza with colonists marched from Tubac over overland route he had discovered, reaching San Gabriel Jan. 4, 1776

Nov. 2, Fort Saint Johns at head of first rapids of the Richelieu besieged since Sept. 18 surrendered to Montgomery, the garrison marching out Nov. 3

Nov. 8, Arnold reached St. Lawrence River at Point Levis

Nov. 10, A marine corps of 2 battalions authorized

Nov. 13, Montgomery occupied Montreal

Nov. 14, Arnold arrived before Quebec, summoned city to surrender and retired to Pointe aux Trembles

Nov. 19, General Prescott surrendered vessels at Lavaltrie in St. Lawrence River

Nov. 23, Rules and regulations for the navy drawn up and adopted by Congress Nov. 28

Nov. 25, Regulations regarding prizes adopted

Nov. 29, Committee on Secret Correspondence of 5 members appointed "for the sole purpose of corresponding with our friends in Great Britain and Ireland and other parts of the world"

Dec. 5, Montgomery and Arnold united before Quebec began siege

Dec. 6, Formal reply by Congress to the King's Proclamation of rebellion repudiating charge of treason

Dec. 9, The Virginia militia under Colonel William Woodford defeated Lord Dunmore's troops in battle at Great Bridge near Norfolk

Dec. 13, Provision made for building 13 war vessels

Dec. 14, Marine Committee reorganized and membership increased to include one member from each colony

Dec. 21–Jan. 5, Convention at Exeter, New Hampshire adopted constitution, the first framed by an American State

Dec. 22, Esek Hopkins made Commander-in-Chief of the fleet, and captains appointed, Paul Jones, a first-lieutenant

Dec. 31, Montgomery and Benedict Arnold defeated by Carleton in attack on Quebec, Montgomery killed

NORTH AMERICA

North America is the third largest of the continents with an approximate area of 8,500,000 square miles and including 16% of the land surface of the globe. Like South America the shape is triangular with maximum width in the north. Included in North America are Canada and Newfoundland (British), Greenland (Danish), the United States with outlying possessions, Central America, Mexico, Panama, and the West Indies. *See also* America and names of countries for detailed account of exploration and history.

UNITED STATES

United States, Federal Republic, situated in the central part of North America bounded on the north by Canada, the outlying Territory of Alaska with the Arctic Ocean as northern boundary, and on the east by the Atlantic Ocean, on the west by the Pacific Ocean, and on the south by Mexico and the Gulf of Mexico. The United States consists of 48 States joined together by a Federal Government to which the original 13 States delegated powers in the Constitution adopted in 1787. The official title is the United States of America. The outlying possessions of the United States are Alaska, Hawaiian Islands, Philippine Islands, Puerto Rico, Guam, Virgin Islands, Samoan Islands (American), and Panama Canal Zone. *See infra.* The most northern point of the United States excluding Alaska is in Minnesota at 49° 23′ N. Lat. and 95° 9′ W. Long., the most southern, Cape Sable, Florida, 25° 7′ N. Lat. and 81° 5′ W. Long., most eastern West Quoddy Head, Maine, at 66° 57′ W. Long. and 44° 49′ N. Lat., and most western Cape Alva, Washington, 124° 45′ W. Long. and 48° 10′ N. Lat. The longest distance north and south from the Canadian boundary to southern Texas is 1,598 miles in a straight line, the 49th parallel, and the longest distance from east to west in a straight line from the Atlantic to the Pacific from West Quoddy Head to Yaquina Head, Oregon, is

2,807 miles, the shortest distance from Charleston, South Carolina, to near San Diego, California, 2,152 miles. The length of boundary as given by the Coast and Geodetic Survey is 10,758 miles as follows: Atlantic Ocean, 1,883; Gulf of Mexico, 1,639; Pacific Ocean, 1,316; Mexico, 1,975; Canada, 3,898. The geographical center of population is near Lebanon in Smith County, Kansas, 39° 50′ N. Lat., and 98° 35′ W. Long., and the center of population according to the 1930 census is near Hymera, Indiana.

The 13 original States as constituted in 1790 after the separation from England were New Hampshire, Massachusetts, Rhode Island, Connecticut, New York, New Jersey, Pennsylvania, Delaware, Maryland, Virginia, North Carolina, South Carolina, and Georgia, with a gross area of 892,135 square miles, of which 24,155 was water, as including claims to western lands later ceded to the Federal Government, present area 326,378 square miles. For settlement and history of the American Colonies *see* America.

Population of the United States at each census from 1790. Residents of Hawaii, Alaska, Puerto Rico, the Philippine Islands, Guam, Samoa, Virgin Islands, and Panama Canal Zone, and persons in the military and naval service stationed abroad are not included in the figures of this table. The residents of Indian reservations are not included prior to 1890.

YEAR	WHITE	NEGROES	OTHER COLORED [1]	TOTAL	DECENNIAL INCREASE, PER CENT.
1790	3,172,006	757,208	—	3,929,214	—
1800	4,306,446	1,002,037	—	5,308,483	35.1
1810	5,862,073	1,377,808	—	7,239,881	36.4
1820	7,866,797	1,771,656	—	9,638,453	33.1
1830	10,537,378	2,328,642	—	12,866,020	33.5
1840	14,195,805	2,873,648	—	17,069,453	32.7
1850	19,553,068	3,638,808	—	23,191,876	35.9
1860	26,922,537	4,441,830	78,954	31,443,321	35.6

[1] The other colored, in 1860, comprise 34,933 Chinese and 44,021 Indians; for 1870, 63,199 Chinese, 55 Japanese, and 25,731 Indians; for 1880, 105,465 Chinese, 148 Japanese, and 66,407 Indians; for 1890, 107,488 Chinese, 2,039 Japanese, and 248,253 Indians; for 1900, 89,863 Chinese, 24,326 Japanese, and 237,196 Indians; for 1910, 71,531 Chinese, 72,157 Japanese, 265,683 Indians and 3,175 other races; for 1920, 61,639 Chinese, 111,010 Japanese, 244,437 Indians, and 9,488 all others.

Year	White	Negroes	Other Colored	Total	Decennial Increase, per Cent.
1870 [1]	33,589,377	4,880,009	88,985	38,558,371	22.6
1870 [1]	*34,337,292*	*5,392,172*	*88,985*	*39,818,449*	*26.6*
1880	43,402,970	6,580,793	172,020	50,155,783	26.0
1890	55,101,258	7,488,676	357,780	62,947,714	25.5
1900	66,809,196	8,833,994	351,385	75,994,575	20.7
1910	81,731,957	9,827,763	412,546	91,972,266	21.0
1920	94,820,915	10,463,131	426,574	105,710,620	14.9
1930	—	—	—	122,775,046	16.1

[1] Enumeration in 1870 incomplete. Figures in italics represent estimated corrected population.

Total population in 1920 comprised 53,900,431 males, and 51,810,189 females; 54,304,603, or 51.4%, were urban, and 51,406,017, or 48.6%, rural. In 1930, 68,955,521, or 56.2%, were urban. In the following table of population statistics for 1930 and 1920, the dates indicate the year in which the constitution was ratified by each of the original thirteen States, the year of the admission of each of the other States into the Union, and the years of organization of Territories:—

Geographic Divisions and States	Land Area: English Sq. Miles, 1930	Population in 1920	Population in 1930	Population per Sq. Mile, 1930
Continental United States	2,973,776	103,710,620	122,775,046	11.3
New England	61,976	7,400,909	8,166,341	131.8
Maine (1820)	29,895	768,014	797,423	26.7
New Hampshire (1788)	9,031	443,083	465,293	51.5
Vermont (1791)	9,124	352,428	359,611	39.4
Massachusetts (1788)	8,039	3,852,356	4,249,614	528.6
Rhode Island (1790)	1,067	604,397	687,497	644.3
Connecticut (1788)	4,820	1,380,631	1,606,903	333.4
Middle Atlantic	100,000	22,261,144	26,260,750	262.6
New York (1788)	47,654	10,385,227	12,588,066	264.2
New Jersey (1787)	7,514	3,155,900	4,041,334	537.8
Pennsylvania (1787)	44,832	8,720,017	9,631,350	214.8
East North Central	245,564	21,475,543	25,297,185	103.0
Ohio (1803)	40,740	5,759,394	6,646,697	163.1
Indiana (1816)	36,045	2,930,390	3,238,503	89.8
Illinois (1818)	56,043	6,485,280	7,630,654	136.2
Michigan (1837)	57,480	3,668,412	4,842,325	84.2
Wisconsin (1848)	55,256	2,632,067	2,939,006	53.2
West North Central	510,804	12,544,249	13,206,915	26.0
Minnesota (1858)	80,858	2,387,125	2,563,953	31.7
Iowa (1846)	55,586	2,404,021	2,470,939	44.5
Missouri (1821)	68,727	3,404,055	3,629,367	52.8
North Dakota (1889)	70,183	646,872	680,845	9.7
South Dakota (1889)	76,868	636,547	692,849	9.0
Nebraska (1867)	76,808	1,296,372	1,377,963	17.9
Kansas (1861)	81,774	1,769,257	1,880,999	23.0
South Atlantic	269,073	13,990,272	15,793,589	58.7
Delaware (1787)	1,965	223,003	238,380	121.3
Maryland (1788)	9,941	1,449,661	1,631,526	164.1
District of Columbia (1791) . . .	62	437,571	486,869	7,852.7
Virginia (1788)	40,262	2,309,187	2,421,851	60.2
West Virginia (1863)	24,022	1,463,701	1,729,205	72.0
North Carolina (1789)	48,740	2,559,123	3,170,276	65.0
South Carolina (1788)	30,495	1,683,724	1,738,765	57.0
Georgia (1788)	58,725	2,895,832	2,908,506	49.5
Florida (1845)	54,861	968,470	1,468,211	26.8
East South Central	179,509	8,893,307	9,887,214	55.1
Kentucky (1792)	40,181	2,416,630	2,614,589	65.0
Tennessee (1796)	41,687	2,337,885	2,616,556	62.8
Alabama (1819)	51,279	2,348,174	2,646,248	51.6
Mississippi (1817)	46,362	1,790,618	2,009,821	43.4
West South Central	429,746	10,242,224	12,176,830	28.3
Arkansas (1836)	52,525	1,752,204	1,854,482	35.3
Louisiana (1812)	45,409	1,798,509	2,101,593	46.3
Oklahoma (1907)	69,414	2,028,283	2,396,040	34.5
Texas (1845)	262,398	4,663,228	5,824,715	22.2

Geographic Divisions and States	Land Area: English Sq. Miles, 1930	Population in 1920	Population in 1930	Population per Sq. Mile, 1930
Mountain	859,009	3,336,101	3,701,789	4.3
Montana (1889)	146,131	548,889	537,606	3.7
Idaho (1890)	83,354	431,866	445,032	5.3
Wyoming (1890)	97,548	194,402	225,565	2.3
Colorado (1876)	103,658	939,629	1,035,791	10.0
New Mexico (1912)	122,503	360,350	423,317	3.5
Arizona (1912)	113,810	334,162	435,573	3.8
Utah (1896)	82,184	449,396	507,847	6.2
Nevada (1864)	109,821	77,407	91,058	0.8
Pacific	318,095	5,566,871	8,194,433	25.8
Washington (1889)	66,836	1,356,621	1,563,396	23.4
Oregon (1859)	95,607	783,389	953,786	10.0
California (1850)	155,652	3,426,861	5,677,251	36.5
Non-contiguous Territory	711,606 [1]	12,112,545	14,233,389	20.0
Alaska (1867)	586,400 [1]	55,036	59,278	0.1
Hawaii (Ter.) (1898) [5]	6,407 [1]	255,912	368,336	57.5
Puerto Rico (1899)	3,435 [1]	1,299,809	1,543,913	449.5
Philippine Islands (1899) . . .	114,400 [1]	10,314,310 [2]	12,082,366 [7]	105.6
Virgin Islands (1917)	133 [1]	26,051 [3]	22,012	165.5
American Samoa (1900) [6] . . .	76 [1]	8,056	10,055	132.3
Guam (1899)	206 [1]	13,275	18,509	89.8
Panama Canal Zone (1904) . . .	549 [1]	22,858	39,467	71.9
Soldiers. etc., abroad	—	117,238	89,453	—
Grand Total	3,685,382 [4]	117,823,165	137,008,435	37.2

[1] Including both the land and water area.
[2] Population in 1918.
[3] Population in 1917.
[4] Gross Area (Land and Water)—Continental United States, 3,026,789; Non-contiguous Territory, 711,606. Total, 3,738,395 square miles.
[5] Includes Midway Islands.   [6] Includes Swain Island.   [7] Estimated July 1, 1929.

The total area of Indian reservations in the United States, exclusive of Alaska, was on June 30, 1929, 50,023 square miles (in 1900, 121,665 square miles), with an Indian population of 345,575 (in 1900, 270,544).

Cities	Land Area in Acres July 1, 1929	Population, April 1, 1930	Cities	Land Area in Acres July 1, 1929	Population, April 1, 1930
New York	191,360.0	6,930,446	Philadelphia, Pa. . .	81,920.0	1,950,961
Borough:			Detroit, Mich. . . .	88,975.4	1,568,662
Manhattan . .	14,080.0	1,867,312	Los Angeles, Calif. . .	281,509.6	1,238,048
Bronx	26,240.0	1,265,258	Cleveland, Ohio . . .	45,289.0	900,429
Brooklyn . . .	45,440.0	2,560,310	St. Louis, Mo. . . .	39,040.0	821,960
Queens	69,120.0	1,079,220	Baltimore, Md. . . .	50,560.0	804,874
Richmond . . .	36,480.0	158,346	Boston, Mass. . . .	27,634.8	781,188
Chicago, Ill. . . .	129,155.0	3,376,438	Pittsburgh, Pa. . . .	32,833.7	669,817

Herbert Clark Hoover, President (1930)

1776

Jan. 1, Flag of the "United Colonies" first raised by General Washington at Cambridge, 13 stripes, alternate red and white, with the crosses of St. George and St. Andrew

——, Norfolk, Virginia, burned by Governor Dunmore after the defeat of some of his loyalist supporters at Great Bridge

Jan. 6, Constitution for New Hampshire adopted by convention

Jan. 9, Agreement to provide German troops for war in America signed with Brunswick, with Hesse Cassel Jan. 15, with Hesse Hanau, Feb. 5. In all 29,166 men sent to America

——, "Common Sense," a pamphlet by Thomas Paine published, urged independence for the colonies, "a firebrand which set aflame the ready political material in America." Van Tyne

Jan. 24, Proclamation of General Wooster in command of Montreal of Address to the inhabitants of Canada

Feb. 11, The Governor of Georgia who had been placed under arrest in Jan. escaped to the British

Feb. 17–April 7, Cruise of Esek Hopkins to the West Indies, captured New Providence, and off Long Island captured 2 small English vessels, one, the "Glasgow" escaped

Feb. 21, Anza with colonists left San Gabriel, arriving at Monterey, California March 10

Feb. 27, Donald McDonald's army of loyalists defeated in Battle of Moore's Creek in North Carolina

March 4, Washington occupied and fortified Dorchester

Heights commanding Boston, "redoubts were raised as if by the genii belonging to Aladdin's wonderful lamp" wrote a British officer

March 17, Boston rendered untenable evacuated by the British, Lord Howe with troops and loyalists sailing for Halifax, Nova Scotia

March 25, Canadians defeated in attempt to relieve Quebec by attack on American battery at Point Levis

March 26, Constitution adopted in South Carolina

April 6, Ports opened to world commerce except trade with Great Britain and her possessions

April 7, John Barry in the "Lexington" in engagement with the British ship "Edward"

April 9–July 25, Journey of Father Garces from California to the Colorado River. *See* Mexico

April 10, Provincial Congress of Georgia elected Archibald Bulloch, president and commander of army

April 12, North Carolina the first State to instruct its delegates to Congress to declare for independence

April 13, Washington arrived in New York to make preparations for defense of the city

——, Committee appointed by Congress of North Carolina to prepare a constitution

April 27, American commissioners arrived in Montreal

May 1, General Thomas reached Arnold's camp with 8 regiments and took command of the army before Quebec

May 3, Attempt to send fire ship past ships at Quebec unsuccessful

——, Lord Cornwallis with the British fleet appeared off Cape Fear

May 6, British reinforcements forced Americans to abandon the siege of Quebec and fall back to Sorel, beginning retreat from Canada

May 15, Virginia Convention adopted resolutions written by Edmund Pendleton directing the delegates in Congress to propose to "declare the United Colonies free and independent States"

May 27, Cartel for exchange of prisoners signed by General Arnold with General Forster

June 4, Clinton and Cornwallis appeared before Charleston, South Carolina

June 5, General John Sullivan, succeeding General Thomas who died of smallpox June 2, arrived at Sorel to take command

June 7, American troops defeated in attack on town of Three Rivers on the St. Lawrence halfway between Quebec and Montreal

June 10, France loaned Americans a million livres through the company of "Hortalez et Cie" organized for the purpose by Beaumarchais, adventurer and playwright, by which large quantities of clothing, military stores, and sums of money were turned over to the Americans

June 12, Virginia Convention adopted Declaration of Rights prepared by George Mason

June 14, General Sullivan retreated from Canada as English fleet carrying Carleton's army came up the St. Lawrence, reaching Crown Point July 1. During July General Gates withdrew the depleted force to Ticonderoga

June 15, Both houses of the New Hampshire Assembly adopted declaration of independence of the United Colonies of Great Britain for instruction of delegates in Congress

June 22, New Jersey authorized its delegates to Congress to agree to independence

June 28, Moultrie repulsed British bombardment from rude fortifications thrown up on Sullivan's Island saving the city of Charleston

June 28, Convention in Maryland ordered delegates to Congress to unite in declaring the colonies free and independent, reserving to State complete internal sovereignty

June 29, Virginia adopted State Constitution

June, Silas Deane arrived in France instructed to appear as a merchant but secretly to negotiate with the government for field artillery, ammunition, and equipment for troops

July 2, Constitution for New Jersey adopted framed by committee which met June 24 and reported June 26

July 3, General Howe with 9,000 troops arrived at Staten Island from Halifax

July 4, Declaration of Independence. *See infra* Congress

July 5, Patrick Henry, elected in June, took oath as Governor of Virginia

July 9, Provincial Congress met and assumed name of Convention of Representatives of the State of New York, and appointed a committee with John Jay as chairman to prepare a form of government

July 10, Declaration of Independence read to the army in New York by order of General Washington

——, Statue of George III in Bowling Green, New York City, thrown down

July 14, Lord Howe sent letter addressed to George Washington, Esq., which Washington refused to receive, with the King's promise of pardon to all who would desist from rebellion

July 15–28, State Convention at Philadelphia assumed government of Pennsylvania

July 17, Silas Deane presented Vergennes with a memorial setting forth the condition of the colonies

July 18, Beaumarchais in letter to Deane of this date agreed to furnish supplies to the American Congress, Deane (July 20) promising payment in tobacco

July 21, British fleet sailed from South Carolina for New York

July 29–Jan. 2, 1777, Expedition of Fathers Dominguez and Escalante with Captain Bernardo de Miera y Pacheco and 9 soldiers left Santa Fé, New Mexico, to find a northern route to Monterey, reached the Navajo River Aug. 12, at the Rio Dolores, at Green River Sept. 13, and Utah Lake Sept. 23

Aug. 1, General Howe in accordance with instructions of Lord George Germain of Dec. 19, 1775, in note to General Washington agreed to exchange of prisoners

Aug. 27, Battle of Long Island, Americans defeated by Howe and Clinton

——, Convention at Newcastle assumed name Delaware State, appointed Dover the capital, and adopted Constitution proclaimed Sept. 21

Aug. 29, During the night Washington withdrew army from Long Island to Manhattan Island

Aug., Newport, Rhode Island occupied by the British

Sept. 15, Howe occupied New York City

Sept. 16, British attack repulsed at Harlem Heights by American army

Sept. 17, Presidio at San Francisco formally dedicated

Sept. 22, Nathan Hale executed by the British in New York as a spy

Oct. 11 and 13, Benedict Arnold harassed the advance of the British fleet on Lake Champlain in 2 attacks at Valcour Island and off Crown Point, and then withdrew to Ticonderoga, 12 out of 15 American vessels lost. Carleton occupied Crown Point but the strength of the American position and lateness of the season determined his evacuation Nov. 3, and withdrawal to Canada

Oct. 12, General Howe moved his main army from New York to Westchester and sent warships up the Hudson to cut off retreat to New Jersey

Oct. 18, Thaddeus Kosciuszko, Pole, commissioned as Colonel of Engineers and sent to the northern army

Oct. 21, Washington withdrew the army to White Plains

Oct. 25, General Howe took position a few miles south of White Plains

Oct. 26, Benjamin Franklin sailed for France on the "Reprisal," arriving in Paris Dec. 18, two prizes taken by the ship in Nov.

Oct. 28, Battle of White Plains, Howe failed to win a decisive victory

Oct. 31, Washington retired to heights in back of White Plains

Nov. 5, General Howe moved army to Dobbs Ferry on the Hudson

Nov. 10–30, John Paul Jones with the "Providence" and the "Alfred" captured many prizes, including (Nov. 13) the "Mellish" transporting stores for Carleton's army and 2 other ships valued at £6,000, off Nova Scotia

Nov. 11, State Constitution adopted by convention in Maryland

Nov. 16, Fort Washington, New York City (between 181st and 186th streets) commanded by Colonel Robert Magaw captured by Lord Howe

Nov. 20, Cornwallis captured Fort Lee, New Jersey, opposite Fort Washington across the Hudson, General Greene making a successful evacuation of the fort before the attack, but lost his stores and cannon

Nov. 20–Dec. 8, Washington led the army in retreat across the Hudson to New Jersey to the west bank of the Delaware, leaving Newark as advance guard of British entered the town Nov. 28

Nov. 30, The Howe brothers, Lord Howe and Admiral Howe, issued a proclamation offering pardon to all who would renounce the cause of independence

Nov., Watauga settlement (Tennessee) annexed to North Carolina as District of Washington

Dec. 1, Cornwallis reached Raritan River and waited for reinforcements

Dec. 6, Kentucky established as a county of Virginia

Dec. 9, British force under General Clinton captured Newport, Rhode Island

Dec. 13, Major-General Charles Lee captured by the British at a tavern in Baskingridge, New Jersey. His troops joined Washington who was thus able to take the offensive

Dec. 18, Constitution adopted by North Carolina in convention which met Nov. 12, Richard Caswell elected Governor

Dec. 26, Battle of Trenton. Washington recrossed the Delaware and defeated the Hessians, outpost of Howe's army, capturing 900 prisoners and a large quantity of ammunition and stores

Dec. 28, Commission received in France by Vergennes, Foreign Minister

Dec. 30–31, Washington again crossed the Delaware making camp near Trenton

CONTINENTAL CONGRESS

Jan. 1, Benjamin Franklin appointed commissioner to Spain, did not go and Arthur Lee appointed in his stead May 1

Jan. 2, Proposed that strong measures be taken against Tories

Feb. 15, Franklin, Carroll, and Chase appointed a commission to go to Canada to try to effect union

March 3, Silas Deane appointed political agent to the Court of France

March 19, Privateering authorized, and general letters of marque and reprisal issued March 23

April 6, Ports ordered open to all nations except Great Britain. Importation of slaves forbidden

May 7, Ralph Izzard appointed commissioner to Court of the Duke of Tuscany

May 10, Rules adopted for better government of troops

——, Congress recommended the establishment of State governments. A preamble to this resolution adopted May 15 stated that the exercise of every kind of authority under the British Crown should be suppressed and all the powers of government exerted under the authority of all the people of the Colonies

May 21, Congress published copies of the treaties which Great Britain had made with the German States to furnish troops to be used against the Americans

June 3 and July 8, Washington authorized to employ Indians to number of 2,000 for the war

June 7, Resolution introduced by Richard Henry Lee of Virginia that "these United Colonies are and of right ought to be free and independent States." Delegates from Massachusetts, Connecticut, and New Hampshire instructed to support Lee's Resolution to substitute "God save the United Colonies" for "God save the King"

June 11, Committee appointed, Thomas Jefferson, John Adams, Benjamin Franklin, Roger Sherman, and Robert R. Livingston, to prepare a declaration of independence and draft treaties to propose to European Powers

June 12, Board of War and Ordinance appointed

——, Committee appointed to prepare Articles of Confederation and Perpetual Union; report with plan of 20 articles reported July 12

July 4, Declaration of Independence prepared by Committee, draft by Thomas Jefferson, adopted by vote of 12 colonies, and on July 9 by New York making it unanimous

Aug. 2, Declaration of Independence signed by 54 delegates

Sept. 9, Resolved that all continental commissions in which heretofore the words "United Colonies" have been used, bear hereafter the words "United States"

Sept. 27, Benjamin Franklin, Silas Deane, and Arthur Lee appointed a commission to the Court of France to seek recognition and negotiate a treaty

Oct. 26, Address to the Inhabitants of Quebec inviting the Canadians to make common cause with the Colonies adopted

Nov. 1, Raising of $5,000 for military purposes by lottery authorized

Dec. 12, Congress adjourned

Dec. 20, Third Continental Congress opened at Baltimore, Maryland

Dec. 30, Resolution adopted agreement to assist Spain to possession of the town and harbor of Pensacola, Florida, held by the English if Spain would join the war against Great Britain

1777

Jan. 3, Battle of Princeton, New Jersey. Washington led his army from Trenton during the night of Jan. 2

and defeated 3 regiments of Cornwallis at Princeton obliging Cornwallis to retire from Trenton to New Brunswick to preserve his communications with New York

Jan. 5, Benjamin Franklin and the other commissioners arrived in Paris and made formal appeal for French naval aid

Jan. 6–May 28, Washington occupied the strong position of Morristown, New Jersey

Jan. 15, Convention in Vermont proclaimed New Connecticut (Vermont) an independent State and appointed delegates to petition for admission to the Union

Feb. 3, Felipe de Neve, Spanish Governor, arrived at Monterey, which he made the capital of the Californias

Feb. 5, Constitution of Georgia framed in convention of Oct. 1775 adopted by ratification

March 3, Lord Germain directed Clinton to negotiate with Vermonters for union with Canada

April 15, Indians made unsuccessful attack on fort at Boonesborough, Kentucky

April 20, Constitution for New York State adopted by Convention

April 25–28, British troops commanded by Tryon raided Connecticut towns, destroyed patriot stores at Danbury and burned the town April 27, the British checked at Ridgefield by Benedict Arnold with 600 troops and local militia

May 4 and 7, G. Conyngham in the "Surprise" captured British ships off the coast of Holland

May 29, Washington took strongly entrenched position at Middlebrook a few miles from the British camp at Brunswick

June 19, Howe began withdrawal of his army to Staten Island

June 27, Burgoyne advancing from Canada reached Crown Point

June, John Paul Jones in command of the "Ranger" raised first "stars and stripes" on an American vessel

——, Captain Lambert Wickes in the "Reprisal" with the "Lexington" and the "Dolphin" made 2 circuits of Ireland capturing or destroying 17 British vessels

July 2, Burgoyne began siege of Fort Ticonderoga, and July 5 fortified Sugar Loaf Mountain making the fort untenable

July 2–8, Convention at Windsor named the State Vermont and adopted a Constitution which contained a clause prohibiting slavery

July 4, Attack of Indians on fort at Boonesborough, Kentucky, repulsed

July 6, St. Clair abandoned Fort Ticonderoga and made a disastrous retreat to Fort Edward on the Hudson, joining Schuyler

July 7, British under Generals Fraser and Riedesel dispersed rear guard of St. Clair's army under Colonels Francis and Warner at Hubbardton, Vermont

July 8, Fight at Fort Anne. Americans fired fort and fell back to Fort Edward, British occupying Fort Anne on the 25th

July 23, Howe left Staten Island sailing for the Delaware River with 18,000 men

July 27, Lafayette, De Kalb, and other foreign officers reached Philadelphia

July 30, Burgoyne occupied Fort Edward which Schuyler had evacuated, after despoiling the country,

Americans taking a position at Stillwater on the west bank of the Hudson

Aug. 3, St. Leger with army of British, Hessians, Tories, and Indians invested Fort Stanwix in the Mohawk Valley

Aug. 6, Battle of Oriskany. General Herkimer leading the militia of Tryon county to relieve the fort was surprised and ambushed by Sir John Johnson's Tories and Indians, and killed in most bloody battle of the war. Both sides claimed the victory

Aug. 16, Battle of Bennington. Colonel Baum sent by Burgoyne with 500 men to capture supplies at Bennington defeated by the local militia led by John Stark, and reinforced by Seth Warner, entire British force wounded or captured and reinforcements sent under Breymann driven from field with loss of a third

Aug. 19, General Gates arrived in Albany with a commission to take the command, superseding General Schuyler

Aug. 22, St. Leger hearing that Benedict Arnold was leading a relief force to Fort Stanwix up the Mohawk Valley retreated leaving stores, tents, and artillery behind, and reached Montreal with a mere remnant of his army

Aug. 24–25, Washington marched through Philadelphia to Wilmington

Sept. 4, Captain T. Thompson in the "Raleigh" in engagement with the British "Druid" was obliged to abandon prize

Sept. 10, First Assembly under the Constitution met in New York at Kingston

Sept. 11, Battle of the Brandywine at Chadd's Ford. Washington attempted to stop Howe's advance to Philadelphia. British troops commanded by Cornwallis and Knyphausen defeated the Americans under Wayne, Greene, and Sullivan

Sept. 13, Burgoyne's army crossed the Hudson and encamped at Saratoga

Sept. 15, Count Casimir Pulaski (Pole) made a major-general

Sept. 19, First Battle of Bemis Heights at Freeman's farm (Stillwater) a drawn battle between General Gates and General Burgoyne, but disastrous to Burgoyne who fell back to his camp to wait for reinforcements which did not arrive

Sept. 21, General Grey surprised a detachment of American troops under General Wayne near Paoli in Pennsylvania, killing and wounding over 300 men who failed to escape

Sept. 23, John Paul Jones in the "Providence" captured or burned 10 prize vessels

Sept. 26, Philadelphia occupied by Cornwallis and Germantown by Howe, plan to effect junction with Buygoyne at Albany not carried out

Oct. 4, Battle of Germantown. Washington with Sullivan and Wayne made attack and was defeated by Howe, obliged to retreat after 3 hours with loss of about 600

——, British fleet arrived in Delaware Bay

Oct. 6, Sir Henry Clinton captured Fort Clinton and Fort Montgomery on the Hudson near Peekskill as he advanced to relief of Burgoyne

Oct. 7, Second Battle of Bemis Heights. Burgoyne attacked Gates and was defeated by Americans commanded by Benedict Arnold

Oct. 8, Burgoyne retreated towards Saratoga

Oct. 13, Kingston on the Hudson burned by the British

Oct. 14, Burgoyne at Schuylerville asked Gates for terms of surrender

Oct. 17, Surrender of Burgoyne marked turning point of the war. Over 5,000 troops surrendered of whom 2,412 were Hessians commanded by Baron Riedesel

Oct. 22, Colonel Christopher Greene at Red Bank on the Delaware repulsed attack of Hessians commanded by Von Donop on Fort Mercer, Von Donop mortally wounded and captured

Nov. 1, John Paul Jones in the "Ranger" sailed for France

Nov. 10–15, Fort Mifflin on the Delaware reduced by Howe's fleet, evacuated by Lieutenant-Colonel Smith on the 16th

Nov. 20, Americans evacuated Fort Mercer on approach of Cornwallis with 5,500 troops

Nov. 28, British troops occupied Rhode Island

Nov. 29, Governor Neve founded pueblo of San José, California

Dec. 1, Baron Steuben, a Prussian, reached Portsmouth in New Hampshire, and offered his services to the American army

Dec. 4–8, Howe with 14,000 men marched from Philadelphia to attack Washington but returned without making the attack

Dec. 6, France recognized the independence of the United States

Dec. 17, Washington led his army into winter quarters on the bleak hills of Valley Forge

During the year the national navy of 25 vessels, state cruisers, and privateers captured 467 vessels

CONTINENTAL CONGRESS

March 4, Third Continental Congress (Baltimore) adjourned

——, Fourth Continental Congress met at Philadelphia

April 17, Resolved that Committee on Secret Correspondence be named Committee on Foreign Affairs, and Thomas Paine elected Secretary of Foreign Affairs

May 9, William Lee appointed commissioner to the courts of Vienna and Berlin

June 14, Flag of 13 stars and stripes adopted on resolution introduced by John Adams

July 2, Application of Vermont organized as an independent State for admission to the Union

Sept. 18, Fourth Congress (Philadelphia) adjourned

Sept. 27, Fifth Congress met at Lancaster, Pennsylvania in session of one day

Sept. 30, Sixth Congress met at York, Pennsylvania

Oct. 14, Resolved that all charges of war and expenses for the general welfare be defrayed from common treasury to be supplied by the several States in proportion to value of land to be estimated by Congress

Oct. 15, Maryland made the proposal that Congress should exercise sovereign jurisdiction over the western country

Nov. 1, Henry Laurens elected president to succeed John Hancock, resigned on account of ill health

Nov. 15, "Articles of Confederation and Perpetual Union," thirteen in number, adopted and sent to the States for ratification

Nov. 21, and Dec. 8, Resolved to recall Deane as a result of Arthur Lee's misrepresentations and criticisms

Nov. 28, John Adams appointed commissioner to France in place of Silas Deane

Nov., "Conway Cabel." Congress vested the management of military affairs in a Board of War of which General Gates was president, and Thomas Conway (Thomas, Count de Conway) made Inspector-General of the army, an intrigue to make Gates commander-in-chief in place of Washington, but the prestige of Washington was so great that the plot failed

1778

Jan. 2, Governor Patrick Henry of Virginia appointed George Rogers Clark to lead expedition into the Illinois country

Jan. 22, Board of War induced Congress to arrange for invasion of Canada by Lafayette with Conway second in command, the expedition impracticable and Lafayette recalled from Albany (Secret Jour. March 2)

Jan. 27, Captain J. P. Rathburne in the "Providence" captured Fort Nassau at New Providence Island and 6 prize vessels

Feb. 6, Treaty of Commerce and Alliance with France signed, provided for recognition of American independence, and offensive and defensive alliance against England, and guarantee of possessions of both in America. A separate and secret agreement reserved for the King of Spain the right to become a party to the Treaty

Feb. 7, Daniel Boone with about 30 men engaged in making salt at Blue Licks, Kentucky, captured by the Indians, all except Boone delivered to the English commander at Detroit. Boone taken to Chilicothe made his escape and reached Boonesborough June 20 after journey of 160 miles through the forest

Feb. 23, Baron Steuben arrived at Valley Forge and began work of organizing and disciplining Washington's crude troops

March 7, Captain James Cook reached the Pacific coast from the Sandwich (Hawaiian Islands) at 44° 55′ N. Lat. and made almost continuous survey to 65° 48′, named Cape Flattery March 22, named King George's Sound (Nootka Sound) discovered March 29, sighted Mt. Edgecombe May 1, and named most northwest point Cape Prince of Wales Aug. 9

——, Captain N. Biddle and his ship, the "Randolph" blown up in engagement with the British ship "Yarmouth"

March 19, Constitution of South Carolina adopted by General Assembly

March 28, Conrad Alexander Gérard appointed by France Minister to the United States

March 31, John Adams replacing Silas Deane on the commission arrived in France

March, Count Pulaski, Polish patriot, recruited legion of cavalry and infantry in Baltimore

——, Crown Commission sent from England to arrange details of pacification of the alienated Colonies

April 10, John Paul Jones sailed from Brest to raid British coast and ships

April 22, General Charles Lee exchanged for General Prescott. Lee joined the army at Valley Forge May 20

April 23, J. P. Jones burned ships in the harbor at Whitehaven, England

April 24, J. P. Jones captured the sloop-of-war, "Drake," 2 other prizes and many prisoners

May 8, Sir Henry Clinton arrived to succeed General Howe in command of the British army, Howe recalled at his own request. The "wearing down policy" threatened by the Crown commissioners begun

May 18, The Mischianza, festival in honor of Sir William Howe, given in Philadelphia, a regatta, tournament, ball, and fireworks

May 19–20, Expedition of General Grant sent by Howe to capture Lafayette stationed at Barren Hill 12 miles from Philadelphia failed

May 29, Washington at Middlebrook

June 1, Joseph Brant, Mohawk chief, plundered and burned Cobleskill, New York

June 9, Admiral Byrom arrived off Sandy Hook to reinforce Admiral Howe

June 10, Convention at Concord, New Hampshire, adopted constitution; rejected by people

June 18, Evacuation of Philadelphia by the British in view of probable blockade by French fleet, 3,000 Tories accompanying the British to New York

——, Springfield, New York, attacked by Indians led by Brant

June 20, Death of Pierre de Laclede, founder of St. Louis

June 28, Battle of Monmouth Court House (Freehold). Washington in pursuit of Clinton's army marching across New Jersey gained a qualified success in spite of the disorganization of the troops due to the disgraceful retreat of General Charles Lee at the beginning of the engagement

July 3–4, Massacre by Indians and Tories led by John Butler of Connecticut settlers at Wyoming Valley, Pennsylvania, Colonel Zebulon Butler leading the defense

July 4, Battle of Kaskaskia in which George Rogers Clark captured British post in the Northwest territory. Within a month Cahokia, Vincennes, and other posts in the Illinois country surrendered, and the region organized by the Legislature of Virginia in October as Illinois county

, Trial by court martial of General Charles Lee for disobedience of orders and disrespect to General Washington

July 8, French fleet commanded by Count d'Estaing arrived off New York blockading Howe at Sandy Hook July 11–22, then sailed for Rhode Island

July 20, Vincennes declared allegiance to Virginia by oath of its citizens

July 29, French fleet arrived off Newport and plan of attack agreed on by d'Estaing in conference with General Sullivan

Aug. 12, Storm prevented engagement of British and French fleets off Newport

Aug. 22, French fleet and 4,000 French soldiers sailed for Boston for repairs in spite of remonstrances of Generals Sullivan, Greene, and Lafayette

Aug. 29, Battle of Rhode Island (Quaker Hill). Attack by Pigot repulsed by Americans entrenched on Butts Hill

Aug. 30, The American forces evacuated Rhode Island, campaign a failure due to lack of support of French fleet

Aug. 31, The British fleet bringing Clinton's army arrived off Newport

Sept. 4, British under General Grey made a raid on American shipping in Buzzard's Bay and at Martha's Vineyard, the towns of New Bedford and Fairhaven burned as "nests of American privateers"

——, Tentative plan for commercial treaty with the Netherlands agreed on by William Lee and Van Bercke, grand pensionary of Amsterdam

Sept. 7–16, Daniel Boone successful in defense of Fort Boonesborough in Kentucky attacked by Indians and Tories led by Quindre

Sept. 17, German Flats, New York, attacked by Brant

——, Treaty of peace negotiated with the Delawares at Fort Pitt

Sept., Grey captured Baylor's troop of Virginia cavalry at Old Tappan on the Hudson

Oct. 3, The Crown commissioners in farewell manifesto threatened the recalcitrant colonies with the "extremes of war" and the desolation of the country

Oct. 15, British under Captain Fergusson raided Egg Harbor, New Jersey, destroying American vessels

Nov. 4, The French fleet sailed from Boston for the West Indies, arriving at Martinique Dec. 9

Nov. 11, Massacre of the inhabitants of Cherry Valley, New York, by Indians and Tories led by Joseph Brant and Walter Butler, defended by Ichabod Alden

Nov. 27, British ships under Hyde Parker sailed from New York for Georgia

Nov., Washington stationed the army at points on the Hudson, and at Elizabethtown, and Middletown, New Jersey, for winter quarters

Dec. 4, General Benjamin Lincoln appointed to command the southern army arrived at Charleston, South Carolina

Dec. 9, Act of Virginia legislature made territory conquered by G. R. Clark the county of Illinois

——, Convention of towns of the Connecticut River including 8 from Vermont and 16 from New Hampshire met at Cornish, N.H. and proposed to form a separate State

Dec. 13, Byrom sailed from Rhode Island, following the French fleet to the West Indies

Dec. 15, Maryland refused to sign the Articles of Confederation until the question of rights in the territory northwest of the Ohio should be settled

Dec. 17, Henry Hamilton, the British Governor of Detroit, recaptured Vincennes

Dec. 19, First of military land reserves for officers and soldiers created by Virginia

Dec. 29, Savannah captured by the British under Campbell reducing Georgia to submission, General Robert Howe retreated up the Savannah River and reached South Carolina

The national navy numbered only 14 at the close of the year

Dec., C. W. F. Dumas became agent of the United States in Holland

CONTINENTAL CONGRESS

Jan. 8, Voted that the embarkation of Burgoyne and the troops under his command, surrendered, be suspended, violating the engagement made in the Convention of Saratoga that they should go to England on parole not to serve again in the war

April 22, Resolved to hold no "conference or treaty with any commissioners on the part of Great Britain until they shall, as a preliminary thereto, either withdraw their fleets and armies, or else . . . acknowledge the independence of the said States"

May 4, Ratification of the Treaty with France

June 27, Sixth Congress (York) adjourned. Lord North's conciliatory proposals presented by the Crown commissioners in letter to the president of the Congress of June 10 formally rejected

July 2, Congress met at Philadelphia, seventh

July 9, Articles of Confederation signed by delegates of 8 States

Aug. 6, M. Gérard, Minister from France, introduced to Congress

Sept. 14, Benjamin Franklin appointed Minister to France to conduct negotiations instead of the commission

Sept. 26, Benjamin Lincoln appointed commander of the southern army

Sept., Resolved that the free navigation of the Mississippi River is a clear and essential right of the United States

Oct. 22, Instructions to Franklin as Minister to France adopted

Dec. 5, Resolved that the sentence of the court-martial of General Charles Lee be executed

1779

Jan. 1, Burgoyne's army, prisoners of war, sent to Virginia

——, First Universalist Society organized at Gloucester, Massachusetts

Jan. 6, Fort Sunbury below Savannah captured by General Prevost with British troops from Florida

Jan. 11, Lafayette sailed from Boston in the "Alliance" to ask for aid of French troops, reaching Paris Feb. 11

Jan. 29, British commanded by Campbell captured Augusta, Georgia

Jan., A list of charges and grievances against Benedict Arnold in command of Philadelphia sent to Congress by the Executive Council of Pennsylvania, only 2 of the charges reported on by congressional committee as worthy of attention, acting without authority in permitting a vessel to come into port, and using some wagons of the State for transportation of private property

Feb. 3, General Moultrie defeated the British under Major Gardiner at Port Royal, South Carolina

Feb. 6, James Robertson with 8 men left Holston settlement for West Tennessee to plant corn for coming settlers

Feb. 11–Nov. 21, Voyage of Captain Ignacio Arteaga accompanied by Quadra from San Blas north along Pacific coast sighted Mount Saint Elias

Feb. 12, Vermont Assembly declared union with Connecticut towns null and void

Feb. 14, A company of 800 loyalists marching across South Carolina defeated by Colonel Andrew Pickens

Feb. 23, Vincennes recaptured by George Rogers Clark, the fort surrendered by Governor Hamilton Feb. 25

March 3, Battle of Brier Creek. General Ashe defeated by Lieutenant-Colonel Prevost in attempt to take Augusta, Georgia, from the British

March 26, General Tryon destroyed salt works at Horseneck, Connecticut

April 10, Colonel Evan Shelby with Colonel John Montgomery and troops from North Carolina and Virginia descended the Holston River from Rogersville, Tenn., surprised and defeated the Chickamaugas, destroying 11 Indian towns

April, Robert Patterson built block house where Lexington, Kentucky, now stands

April 12, Spain by secret Treaty of Aranjuez joined France in war against Great Britain but did not recognize the independence of the Americans, and in June Spain entered the war

——, Tarleton surprised and routed 3 regiments of American cavalry at Biggin's Bridge

April 19, Generals Van Schaick and Willet destroyed the settlement of the Onondagas in retaliation for the massacres at Wyoming and Cherry valleys

April, Benedict Arnold began treasonable correspondence with Sir Henry Clinton

May 8–June 16, Spain declared war against Great Britain

May 9, British force of 2,500 from New York commanded by General Matthew anchored in ships in Hampton Roads

May 10, Matthews occupied Portsmouth and Norfolk and plundered and burned all perishable property

May 11, General Prevost summoned Charleston to surrender. Governor Rutledge reinforced by Count Pulaski refused and the British returned to Savannah as General Lincoln approached

May 12, Colonel Todd, commissioned governor Dec. 12, 1778, arrived at Kaskaskia

May 31–June 1, Sir Henry Clinton seized Verplanc and Stony Point on the Hudson

May, First settlement of West Tennessee by James Robertson

June 16, Note of this date from the Spanish ambassador to British Secretary amounted to declaration of war

——, General McLean from Halifax established fort at Castine, Maine

June 18, Du Romain sent by d'Estaing captured St. Vincent in the West Indies

June 22, Washington moved his headquarters from Middlebrook to New Windsor

July 4, Grenada occupied in the West Indies and 30 merchant ships captured by d'Estaing

July 5, New Haven taken by Tryon ravaging the Connecticut coast, Fairfield, July 8, Norwalk and Green Farms July 11

July 6, Byrom in command of English fleet attacked d'Estaing off Grenada, d'Estaing, a soldier rather than a sailor, failed to follow up his advantage

July 8, Spain authorized her American subjects in Louisiana to capture English posts on the Mississippi

July 15, Stony Point on the Hudson recovered from the British in midnight attack by General Wayne who destroyed the works and abandoned the fort July 18

——, Captain A. Whipple captured 10 British merchantmen and brought 7 valued at $1,000,000 into Boston

July 22, Indians led by Joseph Brant surprised and burned the village of Minisink, New Jersey, only 30 out of 150 of the Orange County militia in pursuit escaped

Aug. 13, Massachusetts fleet failed to capture fort at Castine established in June by loyalists on Penobscot Bay besieged since July 25, dispersed by British fleet

Aug. 15, Juan Bautista Anza left Santa Fé on journey north and northwest of New Mexico, getting as far as the head waters of the Arkansas River

Aug. 19, The fort on Paulus Hook at site of Jersey City taken from British by Harry Lee of Virginia in surprise attack

Aug. 25, Arbuthnot with 3,000 troops arrived at New York from England

Aug. 27, Commissioners from Pennsylvania and Virginia met at Baltimore in conference on boundary and reached agreement on line Aug. 31

Aug. 29, Battle of Newton (Elmira). General Sullivan and James Clinton defeated the Indians and Tories and laid the country waste, and another expedition under General Brodhead from Pittsburgh destroyed the Seneca town on the upper branch of the Alleghany

Sept. 1, The French fleet arrived off Georgia and anchored at the mouth of the Savannah River Sept. 3 with 35 ships and several thousand troops

Sept. 1–March 2, 1780, Convention met in Boston and continued with adjournments to frame a constitution for Massachusetts

Sept. 7, Galvez, the Spanish Governor of Louisiana, took Fort Bute at Manchak

——, Dominica captured by French force under the Marquis de Bouillé from Martinique

Sept. 21, Galvez took Baton Rouge and later other British posts on the Mississippi

Sept. 23, John Paul Jones in the "Bon Homme Richard" captured the British "Serapis" off Flamborough Head, England, in the most famous naval battle of the war. The "Pallas" captured the "Countess of Scarborough." Both prizes taken into the Dutch port of Texel

Sept. 23–Oct. 9, General Lincoln with aid of French made unsuccessful siege of Savannah in possession of British commanded by General Prevost, the French fleet sailed for Europe and Lincoln retreated to South Carolina

Sept. 24, New York, New Hampshire, and Massachusetts requested to send representatives to Philadelphia on Feb. 1, 1780 to meet with representative from Vermont to settle status of Vermont

Oct. 11, Death of Brigadier-General Casimir Pulaski from wounds received Oct. 9 in attack on Savannah

Oct. 25, Clinton withdrew British forces from Rhode Island in expectation of arrival of French fleet

Nov. 29, Pueblo of San José founded in California by Lieutenant José Joaquin Moraga

Dec. 6, General Lincoln with southern army reached Charleston, South Carolina

Dec. 14, Washington went into winter quarters in Morristown, New Jersey

——, St. Lucia in the West Indies captured by the British

Dec. 19, Trial by court martial of Benedict Arnold on trivial charges preferred by the Council of Pennsylvania, and a sentence of reprimand to be given by the commander-in-chief given Jan. 26, 1780 as a concession to Pennsylvania instead of full acquittal

Dec. 22, Settlers led by John Donelson left Fort Patrick Henry on the Holston River, descended the Tennessee River, ascended the Cumberland to French Lick, April 24, and founded Nashborough, Tennessee. James Robertson had crossed the country overland with settlers in May and reached the "Big Salt Lick"

Dec. 26, Clinton, Cornwallis, and Arbuthnot with 8,000 men sailed from New York for Charleston

CONTINENTAL CONGRESS

Jan. 14, Resolved that neither France nor the United States would "conclude either truce or peace with the common enemy, without the formal consent of their ally first obtained"

Feb. 17, The French Minister, Gérard, stated that the price which Spain put on her friendship was Pensacola and the exclusive navigation of the Mississippi

——, Peace terms referred to a special committee of five, Gouverneur Morris, chairman

Feb. 23, Report of committee on peace terms on boundaries and fishing rights, adopted March 19

March 19–July 12, Debate on the peace terms, resolutions offered, amendments passed and reconsidered

Aug. 14, Terms of peace agreed upon, and instructions for a peace commissioner included statement of boundaries (Secret Jour.), that of boundaries as adopted March 19

Sept. 17, The Floridas guaranteed to Spain if Spain took them from Great Britain

Sept. 27, John Adams appointed peace commissioner with title of minister plenipotentiary, to negotiate a treaty of peace and eventually a treaty of commerce with Great Britain, John Jay chosen commissioner to Spain

Oct. 21, Henry Laurens elected to negotiate a loan in Holland

Oct. 28, Board of Admiralty provided for of 3 commissioners and 2 members of Congress to have charge of naval affairs

Nov. 31, Chevalier de Luzern succeeding Gérard as Minister from France presented credentials

1780

Jan. 1, James Robertson with settlers reached the site of Nashville, Tennessee

Jan. 8, Washington wrote from winter quarters at Morristown, "For a fortnight past the troops, both officers and men, have been almost perishing with want." He was obliged to requisition grain and cattle from the counties of New Jersey to save the army from starving

Jan. 26, Court martial sentenced Benedict Arnold to public reprimand. See 1779, Jan. and Dec. 19

Feb. 11, British force landed at St. Johns Island, south of Charleston, S.C.

Feb. 19, New York, the first of the States to authorize cession of western lands claimed, by legislative Act, but with certain conditions

March 1, Act of Pennsylvania legislature provided for gradual emancipation of slaves

March 2, Constitution adopted by Massachusetts in convention which began meetings Sept. 1, 1779 continued with adjournments to March 2, 1780; ratified by the people. A clause prohibited slavery

March 8, Armed neutrality in the war proclaimed by Russia, and a league for the mutual protection of their commerce formed by Russia, Sweden, and Denmark later joined by other Powers

March 14, Mobile, Alabama, captured by Don Bernardo de Galvez, Spanish Governor of Louisiana

March 27, Spanish fleet appeared before Pensacola but did not attack

April 11, Clinton began siege of Charleston, South Carolina

April 19, New York legislature authorized Congress to restrict their western boundaries

April 28, Lafayette landed in Boston and proceeded to Morristown, bringing commission from the Government of France to General Washington appointing him lieutenant-general and vice-admiral of France in order that he might command the united forces of France and the United States

April, British fleet commanded by Rodney in indecisive engagement off West Indies with French under de Guiche

May 6, Fort Moultrie (then Fort Sullivan) on Sullivan's Island surrendered to Captain Hudson (British navy)

May 12, Charleston surrendered to the British, General

Lincoln and 5,000 American troops became prisoners of war, and 4 ships captured, leaving only 6 vessels in the national navy

May 13, The "Cumberland Compact" drawn up for the Cumberland settlements in Tennessee and signed at Nashborough

May 15, The people of Kentucky and Illinois counties petitioned Congress to form them into separate State

May 21, Johnstown, New York, burned by Tories and Indians led by Sir John Johnson and Joseph Brant

May 26, Raid on St. Louis by 1,500 Indians and 140 English and Canadians under Sinclair, commander of Mackinac, repulsed by Spanish commander, de Leyba with aid of G. R. Clark

May 29, Massacre of American force of Colonel Buford at Wauxhaw Creek, North Carolina, by British under Tarleton

June 2, Captain J. Nicholson in the "Trumbull" in drawn battle with the British ship "Watt"

June 7, Knyphausen invading New Jersey checked by the militia at Springfield

June 20, Francis Locke with North Carolina Whigs defeated the Tories led by Lieutenant-Colonel John Moore at Ramsour's Mill near Lincolnton

June 23, Battle of Springfield, New Jersey. General Greene checked advance of Clinton's army toward Morristown. At midnight the British army crossed to Staten Island, "and thus relieved New Jersey of her five years' warfare"

June 28, Death of Governor de Leyba of Upper Louisiana; succeeded Sept. 24 by Cruzat

June, John Long, a trader, reached Green Bay and Prairie du Chien

July 10, The French fleet arrived at Newport, bringing Count de Rochambeau and 6,000 French soldiers

July 12, Colonel Sumter routed the British under Captain Huck at the village of Cross Roads, South Carolina

July 13, Admiral Groves with 6 ships arrived at New York from England

July 30, Colonel Sumter failed in attempt to surprise the British post at Rocky Mountain

July–Aug., Sir John Johnson and Joseph Brant with Tories and Indians ravaged settlements of New York, destroying Canajoharie and Normanskil

Aug. 3, Benedict Arnold at his own request took command of the fortress at West Point on the Hudson

Aug. 6, Unsuccessful attack of Colonel Sumter on British and Tories at Hanging Rock, South Carolina

Aug. 16, Battle of Camden, South Carolina. Gates defeated by Cornwallis with loss of 700. Baron de Kalb held the field and was mortally wounded and taken prisoner

Aug. 18, Colonel Sumter's force routed and captured at north bank of Fishing Creek by Tarleton, and wagons and British prisoners captured by Sumter on the 15th recovered by British

——, Battle of Musgrove Mills, South Carolina. The British attacked and routed by Americans commanded by Colonel Isaac Shelby, Lieutenant-Colonel Clark, and James Williams

Aug., Convention of eastern States in Boston resolved that "the union of these States be fixed in a more solid and permanent manner"

Sept. 3, Laurens captured off Newfoundland on his way to Holland, and imprisoned in the Tower of London, the draft commercial treaty in his possession made a pretext for British war with Holland

Sept. 14, British ships under Admiral Rodney arrive off Sandy Hook instead of the expected French fleet

Sept. 14–18, Americans under Clarke repulsed by British in attack on Augusta, Georgia

Sept. 21, Arnold met Major John André acting for Sir Henry Clinton to arrange details for the surrender of West Point

Sept. 22, Major André captured by Americans near Tarrytown

Sept. 25, Arnold at breakfast learned of the capture of André and made his escape to the British ship "Vulture"

Sept. 26, Battle of Charlotte, North Carolina

Sept. 29, Major André found guilty and condemned to death as a spy by court martial of which General Greene was president and Lafayette and von Steuben, members

Oct. 2, Major André hanged at Tappan, New York

Oct. 7, Battle of King's Mountain, South Carolina. Ferguson killed and his troops asked for quarter from the American frontiersmen under William Campbell, Sevier, and Shelby

Oct. 10, Conditional Act of cession of western lands by Connecticut

Oct. 16, Leslie sailing from New York for Portsmouth, Virginia, proceeded to Charleston, S.C.

Oct. 25, First legislature of Massachusetts under the Constitution met in Boston

Oct., Schoharie Valley, New York, ravaged by about 1,000 Tories and Indians led by Sir John Johnson and Joseph Brant

——, Corn sold in Boston at $180 a bushel, tea at $90 a pound, butter at $12 a pound, and flour at $1,575 a barrel, in depreciated paper money

Nov. 1, Kentucky divided into 3 counties by the Virginia legislature, Jefferson with seat at Louisville, Lincoln with seat at Harrodsburg, and Fayette with seat at Lexington

Nov. 20, Tarleton attacked Sumter at Blackstock's plantation, South Carolina, the British retired

Dec. 2, General Greene superseding Gates took command of the southern army at Charlotte, North Carolina

Dec. 11, British regiment commanded by Benedict Arnold embarked for Virginia

Dec., John Paul Jones in the "Ariel" in engagement with the British "Triumph"

CONTINENTAL CONGRESS

Jan. 10, Charles Lee dismissed from the army by Congress for insolence

Feb. 9, The States asked to furnish 35,211 men by drafts or otherwise before April 1, and to bring to the continental Treasury, $1,250,000 every month to April, 1781, bills to be issued in the names of the several States

March 18, Congress acknowledged the depreciation in money and fixed ratio between paper and specie at 40 to 1

May, Bills issued by Congress had practically ceased to circulate, the phrase "not worth a continental" dates from the financial stress of this period

June 2, The request of Vermont to be ranked among the independent States denied

June 13, General Gates placed in command of the southern army and made independent of the Commander-in-Chief

Sept. 6, The States advised to surrender their claims to

western lands following the example of New York. *See supra* Feb. 19

Oct. 6, General Washington asked to name a successor to Gates as commander of the southern army, and his choice of Nathaniel Greene approved Oct. 30

Oct. 10, Resolved to form new republican states out of western lands ceded

Oct. 13, Daniel Morgan finally given the rank of brigadier-general

Oct. 21, Army officers promised half-pay for life

Dec. 19, Francis Dana constituted Minister to Russia

Dec. 23, John Laurens chosen to present the needs of the army to the French Government and secure a loan

1781

Jan. 1, Mutiny of Pennsylvania troops at Morristown due to lack of food and clothes, demanded back pay. Marching to Philadelphia to ask redress of Congress they were met by the president of the Pennsylvania Council and a congressional committee at Trenton (Jan. 10) and their demands granted

Jan. 2, Virginia legislature passed Act ceding western lands, modified in Oct.

——, Benedict Arnold with 2,000 men and 27 ships appeared in the James River, Virginia

Jan. 4, Leslie with British troops arrived at Charleston

Jan. 5–6, Benedict Arnold with British troops plundered and burned Richmond, Virginia

Jan. 15, Settlers at Freeland's Station on the Cumberland in middle Tennessee repulsed Indian attack

Jan. 17, Battle of Cowpens, South Carolina. Tarleton's force almost annihilated by the American force under Daniel Morgan

Jan. 30–Feb. 14, Retreat of General Greene drawing Cornwallis 200 miles away from his base into difficult and hostile country, uniting with Huger at Guilford Feb. 8, and continuing the retreat across the Dan River into Virginia, Feb. 20

Jan. 31, Washington wrote to Robert R. Livingston, "There can be no radical cure till Congress is vested by the several States with full and ample powers to enact laws for general purposes, till the executive business is placed in the hands of able and responsible men. Requisitions will then be supported by law"

Feb. 1, At Cowan's Ford, North Carolina, General Davidson opposed the crossing of Cornwallis in pursuit of General Greene's army, Davidson killed and his 300 militia dispersed

Feb. 3, Admiral Rodney captured the Dutch Island of St. Eustatius in the West Indies with 200 merchant ships, 6 men of war, and stores to value of £3,000,000. Rodney wrote "this rock only 6 miles in length and 3 in breadth has . . . alone supported the infamous American rebellion"

Feb. 12, Spanish invasion of Michigan led by Captain Eugenio Pourré captured the British fort, St. Joseph, near present site of Niles, in retaliation for attack on St. Louis

——, *Vermont Gazette* published at Westminster, first newspaper in State

March 1, New York ceded her claims to western territory provided that Congress would confirm her western boundary

——, Ratification of the Articles of Confederation completed by the assent of Maryland

March 9, Spanish fleet of 38 ships commanded by Admiral Solana and Galvez began siege of Pensacola

March 15, Battle of Guilford Court House, North

Carolina. Cornwallis proclaimed his victory over Greene, the Americans repulsed, but Fox in the House of Commons said, "another such victory would ruin the British army"

March 16, Detouches with French ships from Newport in engagement with the British under Arbuthnot off the Virginia Capes, compelled to return to Newport for repairs

March 18, Cornwallis began retreat to the coast, arriving at Wilmington April 9

March, Massachusetts assented to independence of Vermont

April 2, Captain J. Barry in the "Alliance" captured the British ships "Mars" and "Minerva"

——, The Cherokees defeated at the Battle of the Bluffs (Nashborough) and the existence of middle Tennessee assured

April 9, Washington wrote to Laurens "I give it decisively as my opinion that without a foreign loan, our present force (which is but the remnant of an army) cannot be kept together this campaign. . . . It may be declared in a word that we are at the end of our tether . . ."

April 23, Lee and Marion captured Fort Watson on the Santee from the British, breaking Lord Rawdon's communications with the coast

April 25, Battle of Hobkirk's Hill, South Carolina. Lord Rawdon attacked and defeated American army of General Greene 2 miles north of Camden but found his position untenable and marched to the sea near Charleston

——, Steuben obliged to retire from Petersburg, Virginia, as the British under Phillips and Arnold approached to take the town, 4,000 hogsheads of tobacco and a number of vessels destroyed

April 27, Phillips marched to Chesterfield Court House and burned the barracks, and Arnold to Osborne where some vessels were burned

April 29, De Grasse fought indecisive engagement with British fleet commanded by General Hood in the West Indies

——, Lafayette, assigned the command in Virginia by Washington, arrived at Richmond

April 30, Phillips and Arnold marched to Manchester and destroyed 1,200 hogsheads of tobacco

May 8–25, Ira Allen and Captain Sherwood, British commissioner, in negotiations respecting union of Vermont with Canada

May 9, Pensacola and entire province of West Florida surrendered by General Campbell to the Spanish under Governor Galvez

May 10, The British evacuated Camden position, South Carolina

May 11, Sumter occupied post of Orangeburg, South Carolina

May 12, Marion and Lee captured Fort Motte, South Carolina, from the British

May 13, By the death of General Phillips, Benedict Arnold became the commander-in-chief of the British army in Virginia until the arrival of Cornwallis at Petersburg May 20

May 15, Fort Granby, South Carolina, surrendered to Lee

May 21, Conference of Washington and Rochambeau at Wethersfield, Connecticut

May 22, Greene and Kosciuszko began siege of Fort Ninety-Six the only post held by the British in northern South Carolina

May 25, Lafayette abandoned Richmond to unite with Wayne

May 29, Captain Barry in the "Alliance" in engagement with the British ships "Atlanta" and "Trepassy"

June 1–9, Raids of Simcoe and Tarleton in Virginia

June 2, De Grasse captured the British Island of Tobago after an unsuccessful attack on St. Lucia

June 5, Augusta, Georgia, besieged by the Americans since April 16, capitulated to Generals Lee and Pickens

June 12, Second Constitutional Convention met at Exeter, New Hampshire, and the constitution again rejected by the towns

——, Lafayette reinforced by Wayne took strong position near Charlottesville, Virginia, preventing Tarleton from seizing military stores at Albemarle

June 19, Greene obliged to raise the siege of Fort Ninety-Six on approach of Lord Rawdon with reinforcements

June 20, Cornwallis evacuated Richmond

June 22, The legislature of Vermont appointed 3 delegates to proceed to Philadelphia and negotiate for the admission of the State into the Union

June 29, The British evacuated Fort Ninety-Six, unable to hold it because of fall of other inland posts

July 6, Battle of Greene Springs Farm, Virginia. An American force led by Wayne routed by Cornwallis

Aug. 2, Cornwallis established his army at Yorktown at the mouth of the York River flowing into Chesapeake Bay

Aug. 14, A letter from de Grasse announcing that he would sail for the Chesapeake on Aug. 13 determined Washington to abandon plan to attack Clinton in New York

Aug. 20, American and French army started from the Hudson River to capture Cornwallis

Aug. 25, John Laurens arrived at Boston from France with clothing, ammunition, and half a million dollars, and with promise of more money

Aug. 30, The French fleet commanded by Admiral de Grasse entered Chesapeake Bay

Sept. 3, The Moravian settlers driven from Salem, Ohio, by British and Indians

Sept. 4, Los Angeles, California, founded under instructions of Aug. 26 of Spanish Governor Neve by 12 families

Sept. 5, British fleet of 19 ships commanded by Admiral Graves reached Chesapeake Bay, and in engagement with the French fleet were disabled and forced to return to New York

Sept. 6, New London, Connecticut, plundered and burned by Benedict Arnold; and 157 militia at Fort Griswold, attacked by 600 troops, forced to surrender

Sept. 8, Battle of Eutaw Springs, South Carolina. The British commanded by Colonel Stewart drove the Americans commanded by General Greene from the field

Sept. 9, Colonel Stewart withdrew to Monck's Corners near Charleston during the night and General Greene took possession of the battle-field and sent detachments in pursuit

Sept. 13, Colonel Hector McNeill leading the Tories, captured and plundered Hillsborough, North Carolina, taking Governor Burke and his staff

Sept. 14, General Washington reached Lafayette's headquarters at Williamsburg

Sept. 28, Siege of Cornwallis in Yorktown begun

Oct. 19, Surrender of Cornwallis with army of 7,000 men at Yorktown

——, Clinton with British fleet sailed from New York for Yorktown but learning of the surrender returned to New York 9 days later

Oct. 20, Robert Livingston took office as Secretary of Foreign Affairs

——, Robert Morris took office as Secretary of Finance

Nov. 4, The French fleet sailed for the West Indies

Nov. 18, The British evacuated Wilmington, North Carolina

Dec. 1, General Greene in engagement with Colonel Stewart at Dorchester forced retreat within British lines at Charleston

Dec. 22, Lafayette sailed from Boston for France

CONTINENTAL CONGRESS

Jan. 10, Office of Secretary of Foreign Affairs established

Jan. 15, Circular letter to the States called attention to the failure of previous requisitions, "aids of men, provisions and money," "the States alone have power to execute"

Feb. 1, Plan for executive departments agreed to, a superintendent of finance, a secretary of war, and a secretary of marines

Feb. 3, The States asked to vest power in Congress to levy an impost duty of 5% on importation of articles of foreign growth and manufacture; the refusal of Rhode Island to agree prevented ratification of this plan

Feb. 19, Full statement made of debts of the United States and estimate of funds necessary to carry on the government for a year

Feb. 20, The Treasury Commission abolished and Robert Morris elected Superintendent of Finance

March 1, Ratification of the Articles of Confederation completed by the assent of Maryland

March 2, "Journals" of Congress read "The United States in Congress assembled"

April 5, Ordinance established federal courts for trial of piracies

May 26, Memorial of the French Minister presented to Congress offered the mediation of the Emperor of Russia and the Emperor of Germany

——, Resolved to establish a Bank of North America, plan submitted by Robert Morris May 17 approved

June 11, Decided to place the peace negotiations in the hands of a commission

June 13, John Jay appointed member of Peace Commission

June 14, Benjamin Franklin, Henry Laurens, and Thomas Jefferson appointed to serve with John Adams as members of Peace Commission, the appointment declined by Jefferson

June 15, Instructions as to terms of peace to the commissioners adopted, and included reference to boundaries of previous instructions of Aug. 14, 1779; amended at instance of Luzern to undertake that nothing should be done without the knowledge and concurrence of the Ministers of France

Aug. 15, Robert R. Livingston elected Secretary of Foreign Affairs

Aug. 18, Delegates from Vermont presented boundary statement to a committee

Aug. 20, Resolution adopted that the condition of admission of Vermont to the Union would be its relinquishment of claims to territory on east side of the west bank of the Connecticut River, in New Hampshire, and west of the present New York line, west of the Massachusetts line as extended northward in New York

Aug. 29, An Agent of Marine appointed

Oct. 24, Washington's despatch announcing the victory at Yorktown read, and the members of Congress went in procession to the Dutch Lutheran Church to return thanks

Oct. 30, Benjamin Lincoln chosen Secretary of War

——, Resolution adopted to requisition $8,000,000 from the States for federal expenses

Nov. 2, Recommended that each State lay a tax entirely separate from levies of its own expenses for raising its share of the $8,000,000 requisitioned for federal expenses

Dec. 31, Ordinance incorporated the Bank of North America in Philadelphia

1782

Jan., Wilmington, North Carolina, evacuated by the British

Jan. 20, British Island of Nevis in the West Indies surrendered to the French

Jan. 22, Circular letter to the Governors of the States from General Washington urged that measures be taken to pay sums requisitioned by Congress

Feb. 23, Vermont accepted conditions of admission to the Union specified by Congress; was not admitted until 1791

Feb. 27, The British House of Commons resolved against "the further prosecution of offensive war on the continent of North America"

March 5, Bill passed in Parliament enabling the King to make a peace or truce with America

March 8, Massacre of Christian Indians at Gnadenhutten on the Tuscaroras River, Ohio, by a company of men from western Pennsylvania

March 20, Resignation of Lord North as Prime Minister of England, "the decisive battle of freedom in England as well as in America" won against the personal and arbitrary government of George III

March 22, The Marquis of Rockingham, Whig leader, took office as head of new Cabinet upon condition that the independence of the United States should be acknowledged

April 4, Sir Guy Carleton made General-in-Chief of the British forces in America and commissioner to negotiate and carry out the conditions of peace

April 12, Richard Oswald introduced to Franklin in Paris by letter of April 6 from Shelburne, Secretary of the Colonies, asked informally on what terms the Americans would make peace

——, Rodney defeated the French fleet in the West Indies taking Admiral de Grasse prisoner

April 19, Holland recognized the independence of the United States and received John Adams as Minister

April 21, Presidio and military town of Santa Barbara, California, founded

April 23, The British Cabinet agreed to send Richard Oswald to Paris with promise of American independence in return for a peace on the basis of the treaties of 1763, Grenville, representing Fox, Secretary of Foreign Affairs, to make a similar proposal to Vergennes; instructions as to boundary issued to Oswald, April 28

May 9, Sir Guy Carleton, succeeding Sir Henry Clinton in command, arrived in New York

May 23, The British Cabinet agreed to propose American independence

May 25–June 6, Colonel William Crawford's campaign to exterminate the Wyandots and Moravian Delawares routed by the Indians

June 23, John Jay joined Franklin in Paris

July 1, Death of Lord Rockingham, succeeded by Lord Shelburne as Prime Minister

July 11, Savannah, Georgia, evacuated by the British

July 16, Treaty with France stated exact amounts of financial advances of France and periods at which Congress engaged to repay in 12 annual instalments of 1,500,000 livres to commence in 3 years. Other loans negotiated in France brought the total to $7,037,037. Entire foreign debt $7,885,085

July 19, New York proposed a convention of the States to revise and amend the Articles of Confederation; Congress did not act on the recommendation

Aug. 10, Franklin and Jay conferred with Vergennes as to Oswald's commission to treat with the American "colonies or plantation" instead of with the United States, and Jay refused to negotiate on this basis

Aug. 15, Bryan's Station, 40 cabins enclosed in palisades in Fayette county, Kentucky, repulsed attack of Captain Caldwell and Captain McKee of the British army with Samuel Girty and nearly 1,000 Indians

Aug. 18, Oswald wrote to Lord Shelburne that nothing could be done "until independence is acknowledged"

Aug. 19, Battle of Blue Licks, Kentucky. Indians led by Samuel Girty defeated the settlers at Hinkston's fork of the Licking River

Aug. 27, Battle with British foraging party at the Combahee ferry near Charleston, South Carolina, in which the younger Laurens was killed

Sept. 2, The "America," a seventy-four gun battleship, presented by the United States to Louis XVI to replace the "Magnifique" lost in Boston Harbor

Sept. 27, Oswald, in Paris, received new commission dated Sept. 21 replacing that of Aug. 7, empowering him to treat with "the United States of America," and negotiations continued without consulting France

Sept., Pedro Gages succeeded Neve as Governor of the Californias

——, Benjamin Vaughan, Englishman, personal friend of Shelburne, sent to England by Jay to present the American position

Oct. 1, Franklin, Jay, and Oswald began formal negotiations

Oct. 8, Treaty of peace and commerce with the Netherlands signed

——, Agreement of peace commissioners, proposals of Americans provided for boundaries to the Mississippi, free navigation of that river, and the right to participate in the Canadian fisheries, the boundary with Nova Scotia to be settled by a commission which was not accepted by the British Government

Oct. 17, Expedition of Pickens begun against the Cherokees resulted in a treaty confirmed the next year which gave Georgia the land south of the Savannah and east of the Chattahoochee

Oct. 20, Virginia legislature authorized delegates to cede territory northwest of the Ohio to the United States

——, Henry Strachey commissioned by the British Government to go to Paris to assist R. Oswald in the negotiations to "obtain a favorable boundary of Nova Scotia," instructed to include Maine in Canada, and proposals for the line of the Royal Proclamation of 1763, or the line of the Quebec Act of 1774

Oct. 26, John Adams joined Franklin and Jay in Paris

Oct. 29, New York's deed of cession of western lands accepted by Congress

Nov. 5, Boundary line passing through the Great Lakes accepted by the peace commissioners

Nov. 12, Board of commissioners opened court at Trenton, New Jersey, and held session of 41 judicial days on disputed boundary, giving decision Dec. 30 in favor of Pennsylvania and against the Connecticut settlers of the Wyoming Valley

Nov. 25, Oswald, Strachey, and Fitzherbert presented British proposals containing provision for collection by English merchants of debts in America, and compensation and protection for loyalists

Nov. 30, Provisional Treaty signed at Paris between Great Britain and the United States, by John Adams, Benjamin Franklin, John Jay, and Henry Laurens, and by Richard Oswald representing Great Britain. The Americans agreed that Congress should recommend to the States that there should be no more confiscations of property or prosecutions of loyalists

Nov., Statement of Vergennes to Lafayette that France had expended 250,000,000 livres in the war. Arthur Young placed cost at £50,000,000. By Report of the Treasury of the United States the amount of expenditure was estimated as follows: 1775–1776, $20,064,666; 1777, $24,986,646; 1778, $24,289,438; 1779, $10,794,620; 1780, $3,000,000; 1781, $1,942,465; 1782, $3,632,745; 1783, $3,632,745; 1784, $548,525. Total cost of the war as reckoned by Jefferson, $140,000,000, by John Fiske as $170,000,000

Dec. 14, Charleston, South Carolina, evacuated by the British, and General Greene marched into the city with his army

Dec. 19, Protest by Vergennes against the negotiation of the Peace Treaty with Great Britain without consultation with France

Dec. 24, The French troops left Boston for the West Indies

CONTINENTAL CONGRESS

May 31, Resolution reaffirmed to make no peace with Great Britain except in conjunction with France and at Paris

June 20, Great seal of the United States adopted

Sept. 13, Agreement to accept cession by Virginia of western lands. See also March 1, 1784

Oct. 29, Agreement to accept cession by New York of western lands, deed of March 1, 1781

1783

Jan. 1, Public debt of the United States estimated at $42,000,000

Jan. 20, Declaration of suspension of hostilities between Great Britain and the United States signed at Versailles, and Provisional Treaty of Nov. 30 held to take effect, and Preliminary Treaties signed between France and England and Spain and cessation of hostilities

Feb. 16, "A Dissertation on the Political Union and Constitution of the thirteen United States of North America," by Pelatiah Webster published, first proposed a new federal system of government

Feb. 25, Contract made with France for new loan of 6,000,000 livres

March 7, Captain J. Barry in the "Alliance" in engagement with the British ship "Sybille" compelled to abandon prize to escape squadron

March 10, An anonymous address, the work of John Armstrong, aide-de-camp of General Gates, called officers at Newburgh to a meeting to consider grievances and urged the soldiers not to disband until the question of their compensation had been adjusted

March 15, General Washington addressed meeting of officers and rebuked the conspirators who were plotting to disgrace the army and involve the country in civil war, and offered to intercede with Congress in behalf of the army

April 3, Treaty of amity and commerce with Sweden signed

April 8, Captain Joshua Barry in the "Hyder Ali" captured the British ship "General Monk"

April 19, Washington published to the army the proclamation by Congress of cessation of hostilities

April 26, 7,000 loyalists sailed from New York for Nova Scotia

April, Plan for organization and settlement of the Northwest drawn up by Timothy Pickering and other army officers at Newburgh

May 6, General Carleton met General Washington and Governor Clinton at Tappan, New York, to arrange for liberation and exchange of prisoners

May 13, Society of the Cincinnati of officers of the army founded, Washington president until his death

June 8, Washington sent letter to Governors of States urging stronger union of the confederated republics, "his legacy" on retirement to private life

June 16, Officers at Newburgh petitioned Congress to assign bounty lands to them in the district between Lake Erie and the Ohio River; no action taken

June 21, Mob of soldiers in Philadelphia demanding back pay threatened Congress

July 2, British Order in Council placed vessels of the United States on an equal footing with those of Great Britain as to direct trade between the 2 countries but restricted trade between the United States and the British West Indies to British ships and restricted products from the United States even in British vessels

——, General Haldiman, British commander, refused to surrender Oswego, Niagara, Detroit, and other western posts

July 28, Morris sent letter of appeal to governors of States asking them to fulfil their financial engagements as his payments had exceeded his receipts

Aug. 13, By act of incorporation Charlestown, South Carolina, changed to Charleston

Sept. 3, Definitive Treaty of Peace with Great Britain signed in Paris, independence recognized and boundaries established, rights of fishing on the Grand Banks retained, payment of outstanding debts pledged, navigation of the Mississippi free to both countries, and Congress to recommend that confiscated estates be restored

——, Florida ceded to Spain by Great Britain by the Treaty of Paris. Spain disputed the boundary with the United States and refused to allow free navigation of the Mississippi

Oct. 20, Virginia legislature authorized cession of territory northwest of the Ohio River

Oct. 31, Fourth constitutional convention in New Hampshire framed constitution acceptable to the people, was ratified and became effective June 2, 1784. A clause prohibited slavery

Nov. 3, Army disbanded by Proclamation of Congress of Oct. 18

Nov. 25, The British evacuated New York City

Dec. 4, Long Island and Staten Island evacuated by the British

——, General Washington took leave of his officers at headquarters in Fraunce's Tavern

Dec. 23, Washington resigned his commission at the state house at Annapolis and retired to his home at Mount Vernon

CONGRESS OF THE CONFEDERATION

Jan. 6, Petition from the officers at Newburgh of Dec., 1782 presented asking for back pay

Jan. 10, Resolved to continue to draw bills of exchange on credit of foreign account already overdrawn in order "to prevent a stop to the public service"

March 22, Half pay for life voted to officers of the army commuted into a sum equal to five years full pay for which certificates bearing interest at 6% to be issued

April 11, Cessation of hostilities on land and sea proclaimed

April 18, Congress asked the States for power to levy certain impost duties on goods imported for a period of 25 years, the revenue to be applied to war debts. The refusal of New York prevented passage of this measure

——, Resolution adopted substituted population in place of land as a basis for proportion of requisition on the States

April 26, Address to the States urged cession of their claims to western territory and assent to resolutions of April 18

April 28, Committee on the New York resolutions of the preceding July in favor of a general convention appointed

June 12, Resolutions adopted on subject of armed neutrality, that the States must not be "entangled in the politics and controversies of European nations." Ministers to negotiate peace instructed to avoid "engagements which shall oblige the contracting parties to support these stipulations by arms"

June 21, Congress adjourned threatened in Philadelphia by soldiers demanding back pay

June 30, Congress met at Princeton, New Jersey

Aug. 26, Committee appointed charged to receive advice from General Washington in preparing plans for peace

Sept. 13, Voted to accept the cession of land offered by Virginia

Oct. 15, Committee in secret session established region north of the Ohio for colonization in which no Indian to be allowed

Oct. 18, Resolution adopted to disband the army by proclamation on Nov. 3

Oct. 20, Resolved that Congress meet alternately in Annapolis and Trenton until site selected for permanent residence be made by committee appointed

Oct. 31, National welcome to Van Berckel, the first Minister from Holland accredited to the United States

Nov. 4, Third Congress of the Confederation adjourned

Nov. 26, Congress met at Annapolis, Maryland

1784

Feb. 23, General Assembly of Rhode Island authorized freeing of slaves and declared free all negroes and mulattoes born in State after March 1

May 1, The University of New York established by legislative act

June 2, Act of cession of western lands by North Carolina but repealed Nov. 20

June 6, The boat of Thomas Amis and his cargo coming down the Mississippi seized at Natchez by the Spanish Governor

June 25, Letter of the Spanish Government of this date declared seizure of vessels navigating the Mississippi through Spanish territory. *See infra* Congress Nov. 19

June, Zespedez, Spanish Governor, assumed the government of Florida at St. Augustine

Aug. 4–Dec. 25, Visit of General Lafayette to the United States, received with enthusiastic welcome in tour

Aug. 23, Convention of the Watauga settlers met at Jonesboro, Tennessee, and adopted resolution to form a state independent of North Carolina to be named "Frankland" or "Franklin," John Sevier elected president, Landon Carter, secretary

Aug. 30, The American ship "Empress of China" commanded by Captain John Green the first to enter the port of Canton

Sept. 1–Oct. 4, Washington on a tour of the Ohio Valley to ascertain by what means it could be most effectually bound to the Union, which eventually led to the formation of the Potomac Land Company

Sept. 7, Affidavit of George Washington of this date that he had seen in operation on the Potomac River model of steamboat of James Rumsey

Sept. 21, The first daily newspaper began publication in Philadelphia, the *Pennsylvania Packet and Daily Advertiser*, later merged into the *North American*

Oct. 22, Second Treaty of Fort Stanwix negotiated with the Six Nations in which they formally relinquished claims to land of Pennsylvania or country north of the Ohio River

Nov. 1, Resignation of Robert Morris as Superintendent of Finance (*see* Congress) because he felt it wrong to "increase our debts while the prospects of paying them diminished"

Nov. 13, Massachusetts General Court authorized cession of claims of western lands

Nov. 14, Samuel Seabury consecrated by the nonjuring Jacobite bishops of the Episcopal Church in Scotland, after refusal of his application in England, as the first bishop of the Protestant Episcopal Church in America

Nov., The Potomac Land Company chartered

Dec. 14, The State of Frankland adopted a temporary convention and chose John Sevier, Governor, before news of repeal of cession of lands west of the Alleghanies by North Carolina received

Dec. 21, John Jay took office as Secretary of Foreign Affairs

Dec. 27, Convention at Danville, Kentucky, proposed separation of Kentucky from Virginia

CONGRESS OF THE CONFEDERATION

Jan. 1, Congress assembled, 6 States only represented, Jeremiah T. Chase elected president

Jan. 14, Treaty of Peace with Great Britain ratified by 23 delegates from 9 States

March 1, Bill, later known as the Ordinance of 1784, providing for the government of the western territory presented by Thomas Jefferson

——, Cession of lands to northwest of the Ohio by Virginia accepted as modified by the omission of the guarantee of her remaining territory previously demanded

March 26, Resolved that in treaties and in all cases arising under them the United States form "one nation"

April 23, Ordinance for division of the Northwest Territory into from 14 to 16 States as reported by Jefferson passed, names suggested, Sylvania, Michigania, Assenisippia, Illinoia, Polypotamia, Cheeronesus, Metropotamia, Saratago, Pelisipis, and Washington; never went into operation

April 29, Compliance of States with recommendations of Sept. 6 and Oct. 10, 1780, urged as to the western territory

April 30, Resolutions passed declared it advisable to meet the restrictions of England with a navigation act, and proposal to the States that Congress be given the power to pass commercial law discriminating against foreign powers refusing to make commercial treaties with the United States, prohibiting for 15 years the importation, or the exportation, of goods in ships belonging to, or navigated by, subjects of these powers

May 7, John Jay elected Secretary of Foreign Affairs, and Thomas Jefferson, Adams, and Franklin elected commissioners to negotiate commercial treaties

May 27, Ordinance passed putting the Treasury in the charge of 3 commissioners

June 2, The army reduced to 80 men ordered to guard the storehouses at Fort Pitt and West Point

June 3, Resolution postponed consideration of the application of Vermont to be constituted an independent State

——, Instructions to Minister of Foreign Affairs not to cede the rights of citizens of the United States to free navigation of the Mississippi

——, Congress adjourned, a Committee of one delegate from each State to act during recess, but unable to act for lack of attendance of quorum of 4 States, adjourned Aug. 19 leaving the Government without any representation

Nov. 1, Congress met at Trenton, New Jersey

——, Congressional Committee of Finance acted in place of Robert Morris, resigned as Superintendent of Finance, and disorder proceeded to a crisis under their management

Nov. 19, Letter of Spanish Government of June 25 received informed Congress that American vessels attempting to navigate the Mississippi River through Spanish territory would be seized

Dec. 24, Congress adjourned

1785

Jan. 1, The *Falmouth Gazette and Weekly Advertiser* published, first newspaper in Maine

Jan. 21, Treaty concluded at Fort McIntosh with the Wyandots, Delawares, Chippewas, and Ottawas by which the Indians relinquished claims to land south of the Ohio, agreeing to be limited to a tract of land on Lake Erie

Jan. 27, The University of Georgia chartered and received 40,000 acres of land; opened in Athens in 1801

March 8, Free School chartered, later Williams College, Williamstown, Massachusetts

March 26, The Duke of Dorset replied to the American commissioners asking for a treaty, "The apparent determination of the respective States to regulate their own separate interests renders it absolutely necessary, towards forming a permanent system of commerce, that my court should be informed how

far the commissioners can be duly authorized to enter into any engagement with Great Britain which it may not be in the power of any one of the States to render totally useless and inefficient"

March 28, Commissioners from Maryland and Virginia met at Mt. Vernon to prepare an agreement for the jurisdiction over Chesapeake Bay and the rivers common to both States

May 15, Don Diego de Gardoqui, Minister from Spain, arrived

May 23, Second convention at Danville, Kentucky, addressed Virginia and the people of Kentucky in favor of separation from Virginia

May 25, Letter from the King of Spain prohibited navigation of the Mississippi in Spanish territory

Aug. 3, First Episcopal ordination held in the United States that of the Rev. Ashbel Baldwin at Middletown, Conn.

Aug. 24, Pitt, Prime Minister of England, received John Adams but declined to make any commercial treaty except on the condition of a preference

Aug., John Fitch launched a boat on a stream in Bucks county, Pennsylvania, propelled by an engine which moved a chain to which paddles were attached, "the first in the world's history to invent and apply steam propulsion of vessels through water"

Sept. 10, Treaty of amity and commerce with Prussia concluded, ratified by Congress May 17, 1786, and ratifications exchanged in Oct.

Sept. 27, Model and drawing of steamboat by John Fitch shown at meeting of the American Philosophical Society in Philadelphia

Oct. 5, Convention met at Falmouth to consider the separation of the District of Maine from Massachusetts

Oct. 22, Building of Fort Finney begun on Big Miami River a mile above its junction with the Ohio

Nov. 14, Convention of State of Frankland met at Greenville and adopted constitution, John Sevier, governor

Nov. 28, Treaty concluded with the Cherokees

Nov. 30, Adams presented a formal demand to the British Secretary of State that the western posts be surrendered

CONGRESS

Jan. 11, Congress met in New York

Jan. 13, Petition received from settlers of Washington county, Virginia, formed in 1777, for proposal of separate state, nothing done and April 7 the settlers drew up proposal for formation of 2 states, the first including the Kentucky settlements, and the second settlements in western Tennessee and southwest Virginia

Feb. 24, John Adams appointed Minister to England, received by George III June 1

March 8, Ordinance regulated office of the Secretary of War, and General Henry Knox appointed

March 10, Thomas Jefferson appointed Minister to France to succeed Benjamin Franklin retiring

April 1, 7, and 12, Organization of the army, 700 men enlisted for 3 years for the defense of the western settlements

April 19, Deed of cession of western lands by Massachusetts accepted, all except 2 tracts now part of New York State

May 20, Ordinance enacted for the survey and sale of the land northwest of the Ohio, townships to be 6 miles square

May 20, Ordinance reserved "one-third part of all gold, silver, lead, and copper mines" established practice of reserving mineral lands

July 2, Don Diego de Gardoqui, Minister from Spain, recognized

July 6, Resolution based on a report of Robert Morris assisted by Gouverneur Morris of Jan. 1782 on the currency adopted as modified by Jefferson, the dollar adopted as its unit and a decimal ratio

July 20, Jay, Secretary of Foreign Affairs, authorized to negotiate a boundary treaty with Spain, and on Aug. 25 instructed to insist on recognition of the 31st parallel as boundary and free navigation of the Mississippi to its mouth

Aug. 29, Letter of John Fitch to Congress about his invention of the steamboat referred to a committee and nothing done

Nov. 4, Congress adjourned

Nov. 7, Congress met in New York

1786

Jan., First Act of Virginia consenting to the separation of Kentucky under certain conditions

Jan. 3, Treaty with the Choctaws

Jan. 4 and Sept. 6, People in Maine in convention resolved in favor of separation from Massachusetts

Jan. 10, Treaty with the Chickasaws

Jan. 21, Resolution of Virginia legislature to invite delegates from the States to meet at Annapolis the first Monday in September " to consider how far a uniform system in their commercial regulations may be necessary to their common interest and their permanent harmony "

Jan. 31, Treaty with the Shawnees

Feb. 22, The Ambassador from Tripoli demanded 30,000 guineas as price of a treaty in interview with John Adams

Feb. 28, The British Secretary of State announced that the western posts would be retained until British creditors were paid

March 3, New Ohio Company formed in Boston to purchase land in the west by fund of continental certificates of $1,000,000, organizers General Rufus Putnam, General Benjamin Tupper, General Samuel H. Parsons, Winthrop Sargent, and Rev. Manasseh Cutter

March 18, New Jersey granted John Fitch exclusive right to make and employ boats by steam in the State for 14 years

March, 1,107,396 acres between the Penobscot and St. Croix rivers belonging to Massachusetts disposed of by lottery

April 14, Proclamation of Governor Caswell of North Carolina warned citizens living in Frankland to return to allegiance of North Carolina

May 11, Connecticut Act of session of western lands and deed of Sept. 13

June 19, Death of General Nathaniel Greene

June 23, La Pérouse expedition sighted land on Alaska coast at 58° 37'

June 28, Treaty of peace and friendship with Morocco signed and additional Article July 15

July 4, Falmouth divided and the peninsula and opposite islands incorporated and named Portland (Maine)

July 27, John Fitch successful with his small model of steamboat on the Delaware River at Philadelphia

Sept. 11, Delegates from Virginia, Pennsylvania, New Jersey, and New York met at Annapolis to consider condition of the nation, and adopted address to the States requesting them to send delegates to a meeting in the following May "for the sole and express purpose of revising the Articles of Confederation"

Sept. 14, Connecticut made a qualified cession of western lands, reserving 3,250,000 acres on the southern shore of Lake Erie

Sept. 15, Jean François Galaup de La Pérouse, French admiral, on geographical and scientific expedition, arrived at Monterey, sailing along the coast from Alaska, and made best map produced to date which was forwarded to France before the ships were wrecked and all lost

Sept. 19–21, Armed mob in New Hampshire threatened the legislature, demanded paper money and distribution of property

Oct., Second Act of Virginia consenting to separation of Kentucky

Dec. 4, Mission founded at Santa Barbara, California

Dec. 5–Feb. 1787, Shay's rebellion led by ex-officer, Daniel Shay, in Massachusetts

Dec. 16, Boundary dispute between Massachusetts and New York due to overlapping grants of charters settled by commission at Hartford, Connecticut, disputed territory except 2 tracts ceded to New York

Dec. 25, Armed rioters prevented session of the Supreme Court at Worcester to stop its issue of writs for the collection of debts (Shay's rebellion)

CONGRESS OF THE CONFEDERATION

July 27, Sale of 5,000,000 acres in region north of the Ohio and east of the Scioto

Aug. 3, Jay laid before Congress his proposal to Gardoqui of suspension of use of the Mississippi for 25 years without relinquishment of rights of free navigation (Secret Jour.), written statement submitted Aug. 13

Aug. 7, Indian Bureau reorganized and made subordinate to the Dept. of War, districts in charge of superintendents organized, a northern and a southern divided by Ohio River

Aug. 8, Coinage established

Aug. 29, Voted to insist on rights of navigation of the Mississippi and Jay so instructed and no treaty with Spain negotiated

Sept. 11, Land cession of Connecticut accepted notwithstanding the reservation claimed

Nov. 3, Congress adjourned

Nov. 6, Congress opened in New York

1787

Jan. 3, The people of Maine in convention resolved in favor of separation from Massachusetts as in earlier conventions in 1786

Jan. 25, Shay's rebels routed by the militia at Springfield in attempt to capture the arsenal in which were stored 7,000 new muskets and 13,000 barrels of gunpowder belonging to the federal government

Feb. 4, Shay's forces completely defeated in engagement at Petersham by State troops commanded by General Benjamin Lincoln

Feb. 28, Pittsburgh Academy founded, becoming University of Pittsburgh in 1908

March 8, South Carolina legislature authorized cession of tract of land extending to the Mississippi River

March 19, New York State granted to John Fitch the sole right to make steamboats

April 3, Mutual Insurance Company, first in New York, organized, became Knickerbocker Company May 12, 1846

April 11, The *Kentuckey Gazette* published at Lexington, first newspaper west of the Alleghanies, by John and Fielding Bradford

May 14, Constitutional Convention met in Philadelphia, first regular session May 25, George Washington elected president, to consider the Articles of Confederation

May 29, Edmund Randolph proposed the "Virginia plan" for a new constitution as a basis for the work of the Convention in a series of 15 resolutions drawn up by Madison

June 15, William Paterson representing the party of the small States introduced the "New Jersey plan," revision and amendment of the Articles of Confederation

June, Captain Barclay discovered Juan de la Fuca Straits. *See* Canada

July 16, The "Connecticut compromise" adopted, in favor of proportional representation in one branch of the legislature and equal representation in the other

July 26, Committee appointed to embody the proposals approved consisting of Nathaniel Gorham, Oliver Ellsworth, James Wilson, Edmund Randolph, and John Rutledge

Aug. 6, Report of the Committee presented rough draft of the Constitution as it now stands

Aug. 9, South Carolina ceded western lands to the United States

Aug. 10–Sept. 30, Voyage of Captain Gray from Boston in the ship "Columbia," first American voyage around the world

Aug. 22, John Fitch tried new model of steamboat on the Delaware River

Sept. 17, Delegates to the Convention signed the Constitution as amended and adjourned

——, Convention at Danville passed resolutions in favor of separation of Kentucky from Virginia

Oct. 1, Captain Gray in the "Lady Washington" and Captain John Kendrick in the "Columbia" sailed from Boston to explore the northwest coast. Gray arrived at "New Albion" at 41° 28′ Aug. 2. At Nootka Sound Sept. 16 and 23, 1788

Oct. 5, Major General Arthur St. Clair appointed Governor of the Northwest Territory

Oct. 27, First issue of the "Federalist," a series of papers written by Alexander Hamilton, Jay, and Madison in defense of the Constitution, printed in the *Independent Journal or Weekly Advertiser*, New York City. The last number appeared April 2, 1788, and it was published in a collection as "The Federalist"

——, Contract of the Ohio Company formally signed by the Treasury Board and by Dr. Cutler and Winthrop Sargent

Oct., John Adams at his own request was permitted to return home since the British Government declined to send a Minister to the United States

Dec. 3, Steamboat invented by James Rumsey went against the current of the Potomac River at rate of 3 miles an hour and on Dec. 11 increased speed to 4 miles

Dec. 7, Delaware the first State to ratify the Constitution

Dec. 12, Ratification of the Constitution by Pennsylvania

Dec. 18, Ratification of the Constitution by New Jersey

Feb. 21, Congress called a convention to meet May 14 at Philadelphia to "devise such further provisions as shall appear to them necessary to render the constitution of the Federal Government adequate to the exigencies of the Union"

April 13, Resolved that State laws in conflict with the Peace Treaty should be repealed

July 13, Ordinance for the government of the Northwest Territory passed constituting one district for temporary government ultimately to be divided into not fewer than 3 or more than 5 states, freedom of religion declared and slavery prohibited

July 27, Sale of 5,000,000 acres in region north of the Ohio and east of the Scioto authorized at two-thirds of a dollar per acre, 1,500,000 for the Ohio Company and the remainder for the Scioto Company, the first great "land job"

Aug. 19, Delegates from South Carolina executed deed of cession of western land

Sept. 20, Draft of the Constitution as prepared by the Convention laid before Congress accompanied by a letter from Washington

Oct. 3, Resolved that corps of 700 troops should be stationed on frontiers to protect settlers from the Indians for a term of 3 years

Oct. 30, Congress adjourned

Nov. 5, Last Congress of the Confederation met in New York

1788

Jan. 2, Ratification of the Constitution by Georgia

Jan. 9, Ratification of the Constitution by Connecticut

Jan. 11, Colonists of the Ohio Company met at Hartford, Conn. to begin their journey

Jan. 23 and Feb. 14, Advance guard of the Ohio Company settlers reached the Youghiogheny and built boats to descend the Ohio in the spring

Feb. 1, Arthur St. Clair appointed Governor of the Northwest Territory

Feb. 6, Ratification of the Constitution by Massachusetts, by Maryland April 28, by South Carolina May 23, by New Hampshire June 21, the ninth State, making the Constitution valid, by Virginia June 26, by New York July 26

Feb. 27–29, John Sevier with 150 men besieged Colonel John Tipton in his home because of his action in harboring some slaves seized under execution of North Carolina court

Feb., Rhode Island General Assembly voted to submit the question of adoption of the Constitution of the United States to popular election in March

March 1, The State of Frankland or Franklin ended with the term of its governor, and John Sevier routed in May by Colonel Tipton acting under authority of North Carolina

March 26, Slave trade prohibited in Massachusetts

April 7, Settlers of the Ohio Company descending the Ohio landed at mouth of the Muskingum and founded a town which they named Marietta July 2 after Marie Antoinette of France

April, Massachusetts sold to Nathaniel Gorham and Oliver Phelps 6,000,000 acres in western New York acquired under boundary arrangement of 1786, and Indian title extinguished by purchase in July of eastern section which is known as the Phelps and Gorham purchase

May 5, Captain Estevan José Martinez sent by the Spanish Viceroy from Mexico to investigate settlements of English, French, and Russians on the coast claimed by Spain arrived at Nootka Harbor and took formal possession, building a fort, 3 English vessels seized but later released. *See also* Canada

June 29, Captain John Meares named Juan de la Fuca Strait and passed mouth of Columbia River. *See* Canada

July 2, Captain John Meares sighted and named Cape Flattery, Washington

July 15, Governor St. Clair made formal entry into Marietta, inaugurating civil government in Northwest Territory

Sept. 1, Trial of Fitch's third steamboat

Sept. 22, Colonists from New Jersey led by Judge J. C. Symmes, Colonel Patterson, and others reached their grant of Ohio land and founded Losantiville which was later named Cincinnati by Governor St. Clair in honor of the Society of the Cincinnati

Oct. 10, John Sevier, former governor of the State of Frankland, arrested by Colonel Tipton in Washington county charged with high treason, released on parole and rescued by his friends soon after

Oct. 12, John Fitch's steamboat made the trip from Philadelphia to Burlington in 3 hours and 10 minutes

Nov. 4-24, Constitutional convention met in Georgia and again Jan. 4, 1789

Nov. 14, Consular Treaty with France signed gave French officials in the United States powers not dissimilar to those given our consuls in more recent times in China

Nov. 21, Massachusetts conveyed and forever quitclaimed the land of the Phelps and Gorham purchase in New York

Dec. 23, Maryland legislature ceded to Congress 10 miles square of land for seat of government

During this year the Spanish intrigue to separate Kentucky from the Union fostered by James Wilkinson

CONGRESS

May 15, Offer of J. C. Symmes of Aug. 29, 1787 to purchase 2,000,000 acres between the Big and Little Miami rivers in the Ohio country accepted

July 2, Announcement of the president that 9 States had ratified the Constitution, and suggested that steps be taken to put the new government in operation

Sept. 13, Report of committee adopted fixing the first Wednesday of January 1789 for the choice of presidential electors, the first Wednesday of February for the electoral choice of a president and vice-president, and the first Wednesday (or 4th day) of March for inauguration of the new government

Oct. 10, Last meeting of the Congress of the Confederation with a quorum of 9 States, only 4 reporting Oct. 15 and thereafter individual delegates attended "occasionally." Last record of a meeting is Nov. 1 and after that no national government for 5 months. Last entry of individual attendance is that of Philip Pell of New York on March 2, 1789

1789

Jan. 7, First national election, the electors chosen in some States by the legislatures and in others by direct vote of the people

Jan. 9, Treaties with the Wyandots and Six Nations at Fort Harmar confirmed earlier treaties and fixed a boundary line

Feb. 4, Electors in the several States voted for president and vice-president, Washington receiving 69 votes (4 not voting, 2 Maryland and 2 Virginia electors) and was therefore the only candidate for president and unanimously elected, John Adams receiving 34 votes elected vice-president

Feb., *The Times and Powtowmack Packet* published at Georgetown, D.C.

April 11, Fenno's *Gazette of the United States* (Federalist) began publication

April 16, George Washington started from Mt. Vernon for New York, arriving April 23, his journey a series of receptions by States and cities

May 6, New Constitution for Georgia adopted by a convention which met May 4, to take effect in October

May 12, The Tammany Society formed as a patriotic association became almost at once a political organization allied with the Anti-Federalists

May 29, Ratification of the Constitution by Rhode Island

June 13, Levi Allen, commissioned by Vermont, presented memorial asking for a commercial treaty with Canada

July, The New York Assembly appointed a commission with full powers to acknowledge the independence of Vermont

July 30, Captain Gray in the "Columbia" sailed from Nootka for Canton, arriving in December

Aug. 10, General Knox reported troops in service as 672

Sept. 11, Alexander Hamilton took oath of office as Secretary of the Treasury

Sept. 29, Army of 700 men organized as of resolution of Oct. 3, 1787

Oct. 3, Proclamation of President Washington appointed Thursday, Nov. 26, as a day of national thanksgiving

Oct. 13, Gouveneur Morris on a visit to London commissioned by Washington as an informal agent to adjust disputes as to execution of the Treaty and to urge a treaty of commerce

Oct. 15-Nov. 13, Visit of Washington to the eastern States except Rhode Island

Nov. 3, General Assembly of Georgia met under new Constitution

Nov. 20, New Jersey ratified the Amendments to the Constitution

Nov. 21, North Carolina ratified the Constitution

Dec. 3, Virginia legislature ceded 10 miles square on the Potomac for seat of government of the United States

Dec. 18, Third Act of Virginia legislature as to cession of Kentucky provided for delegates to a convention to fix date on certain conditions for the erection of the district into an independent state

Dec. 19, Maryland ratified the Amendments to the Constitution

Dec. 21, South Carolina Yazoo Company granted land by Georgia, one of 3 companies receiving millions of acres in Mississippi and Alabama, but never effective as conditions not fulfilled

Dec. 22, North Carolina ratified the Amendments to the Constitution

Dec. 29, Fort Washington at Cincinnati completed and occupied as headquarters by Colonel Harmar

CONGRESS

March 4, First Congress under the Constitution met in New York with delegates from all the States except North Carolina and Rhode Island, the House not having a quorum until April 2, the Senate until April 5

April 6, Congress organized, the electoral vote counted and George Washington declared President with 69 votes and John Adams, Vice-President with 34 votes

April 8, Madison introduced a tariff Bill

April 21, John Adams seated as Vice-President

April 30, President Washington inaugurated in the Federal Hall on Wall St., New York

May 19, The House decided there should be created departments of Foreign Affairs, Treasury, and War

June 1, First Act enacted regulated a form of oath

June 8, Madison asked the House to consider the many amendments to the Constitution presented to the States

July 4, First tariff law enacted laying duty on imports "for the encouragement and protection of manufactures" provided for either specific or ad valorem duties on over 30 classes of commodities, the ad valorem rate varying from 7.5, to 15%, and on articles not enumerated a duty of 5% was fixed, a reduction of 10% when taxed goods were imported by American ships

July 27, Dept. of Foreign Affairs established, name altered Sept. 15 to Dept. of State

July 31, Act for the regulation of collection of duties passed

Aug. 7, Act gave the President power to remove any officer of the United States except judges

——, War Dept. established, the Secretary of War to have supervision of navy

——, Northwest Ordinance reënacted for government of territory northwest of the Ohio

Aug. 22, The House decided to recommend 17 amendments to the Constitution for adoption by the States, the number reduced to 12 by the Senate Sept. 9, and 10 ratified by the States formed a supplementary Bill of Rights guaranteeing freedom of speech, of the press, of petition, of assembly, of religion, to bear arms, etc., against the interference of the federal government

Sept. 1, Act providing for registering and clearing vessels and regulating the coasting trade; explained and amended Sept. 29

Sept. 2, Act forbade any person interested in importing from holding a government office. A. T. Stewart resigned in 1869 under this law

——, Treasury Dept. established

Sept. 11, Act to establish salaries gave the Secretaries of the Treasury and State Depts. $3,500, War $3,000

——, Alexander Hamilton of New York, appointed Secretary of the Treasury

Sept. 12, Henry Knox, of Massachusetts, appointed Secretary of War

Sept. 22, Act provided for compensation to members of Congress, $6 for every day of the session and mileage

——, Act for temporary establishment of the Post Office

Sept. 23, Compensation of Chief Justice fixed at $4,000 supreme court judges, $3,500, judges of courts and Attorney General $1,500

Sept. 24, Salary of the President fixed at $25,000, of the Vice-President, $5,000

——, Federal judiciary system organized substantially as it is at present, and provided for a Supreme Court consisting of a chief Justice and 5 associates, and for inferior courts, and the office of Attorney General created

Sept. 25, The Amendments (10) to the Constitution submitted to the States for ratification

Sept. 26, Thomas Jefferson, Minister to France, appointed Secretary of State, but did not take office until 1790, John Jay continuing to act, and Samuel Osgood, of Massachusetts, Postmaster General, and Edmund Randolph, of Virginia, Attorney General. The appointment of John Jay as Chief Justice of Sept. 24 confirmed by the Senate

Sept. 29, Act provided for recognition and adaptation to the Constitution of the establishment of troops as of Resolution of Oct. 3, 1787

——, First session adjourned

1790

Feb. 1, First meeting of the Supreme Court in Royal Exchange Building, Broad St., New York City

Feb. 25, North Carolina ceded territory southwest of the Ohio, now Tennessee

March 5, Major General Arthur St. Clair, elected by Congress Governor of the Northwest Territory, arrived at Kaskaskia

March 22, Thomas Jefferson took office as Secretary of State

March, French colonists, induced to emigrate by prospectus of the Scioto Company, landed at Alexandria, Va. and proceeded to Ohio where they founded Gallipolis

April 17, Death of Benjamin Franklin (84) in Philadelphia

May 29, Ratification of the Constitution by Rhode Island

June 3, Convention at Columbia, South Carolina, completed State Constitution

June 11, Decree of the French National Assembly that members should wear mourning for Franklin for 3 days

June 27, Lord Dorchester gave secret instructions to George Beckwith who arrived in Philadelphia from Canada in July

July 16, Governor St. Clair sent letter asking troops from Pennsylvania, Kentucky, and Virginia for campaign against the Miami Indians

July 26, Convention of Kentuckians accepted terms of Virginia and appointed June 1, 1792 as date to separate from Virginia

July 13 or 31, First patent granted to Samuel Hopkins for improvement in making potash and pearlash

July, George Beckwith arrived in Philadelphia, sent from Canada

Aug. 7, Peace and Boundary Treaty concluded with the Creek Indians invited to council in New York City. Alexander McGillivray, half-breed, agent for Spain, did not keep the treaty, and kept the position of pretended friend and secret enemy until his death in Feb. 1793

Aug. 10, Captain Gray in the "Columbia" reached Boston, first American vessel to make the voyage around the world, completing voyage begun Oct. 1, 1787

Sept. 2, New Constitution for Pennsylvania proclaimed in effect

Sept. 28, Captain Robert Gray left Boston on second voyage to Pacific Northwest

Sept. 30–Nov. 4, Expedition of General Harmar and Colonel Hardin against the Miami Indians from Fort Washington, defeated by the Indians Oct. 19 and 22 in Ohio

Oct. 7, New York renounced all claims to Vermont territory in consideration of $30,000 paid to New York grantees

Oct. 28, Spain signed agreement to restore land and buildings at Nootka Sound claimed by the British. *See* Canada

Census gave population as 3,929,214 including 697,681 slaves distributed as follows: Virginia, 747,610; Pennsylvania, 434,373; North Carolina, 393,751; Rhode Island, 68,825; Vermont, 85,425; Kentucky, 73,677. The center of population was 23 miles east of Baltimore. Philadelphia had a population of 43,000, New York, 33,000, Baltimore, 13,000

CONGRESS

Jan. 4, First Congress, 2d sess. met in New York, both Houses met in the Senate to hear President Washington deliver his first annual address

Jan. 14, Hamilton's first report on public credit on the settlement of the foreign and domestic debt proposed that the Federal Government assume the State debts incurred in support of the war, and that the whole should be funded and paid at par, foreign debt chiefly French estimated at $11,710,000, domestic at $27,383,000 principal and accrued interest $13,030,000

Jan. 18, General Knox's plan for organization of the army submitted

March 1, Act provided for the first federal census

March 26, Act established a uniform rule for naturalization on basis of 2 years residence

April 2, North Carolina's deed of cession of land of Feb. 25 accepted

April 10, First patent law vested the granting of letters patent jointly in the Secretaries of State and War, and the Attorney General

April 30, Military establishment of 1,216 non-commissioned officers and privates authorized, and permission given to the President to call on the militia of the States

——, Act defined and provided for punishment of certain crimes against the United States

May 26, The "Territory Southwest of the Ohio River" organized, to be governed as the Northwest Territory, slavery not to be permitted

May 31, First copyright law passed

July 6, Provided that a federal city should be established in a district 10 miles square on the Potomac River, but that until 1800 the capital should be Philadelphia

July 22, Hamilton, as requested by Congress Jan. 20, submitted a report on the public domain, recommending that it should be used to put money into the Federal Treasury, the providing homes for settlers a second consideration

——, Act provided that there should be no trading with the Indians except under license

July 26, Vote providing for assumption of State debts to the amount of $21,500,000, passed by 34 against 28, 3 not voting

Aug. 4, Act made provision for debt of the United States, the State debts assumed and proceeds of sales of public lands pledged to the redemption of the debt

Aug. 4, Act organized revenue cutter service, coast guard created

Aug. 5, A commission appointed to arrange for the settlement of accounts between the United States and the States

Aug. 10, New tariff raised the duties to the equal of an 11% ad valorem rate to make further provision for payment of the debts of the United States

Aug. 12, Act made provision for reduction of public debt

——, Congress adjourned

Dec. 6, First Congress, 3d sess. met in Philadelphia

Dec. 13, Report of Hamilton (second) on the public credit recommended an increase of duties and an excise on foreign and domestic and distilled spirits

Dec. 14, Report of Hamilton of plan for establishment of a national bank. The Anti-Federalists now called Democratic-Republicans led by Jefferson opposed this as unconstitutional

Dec. 27, Act supplementary to the Tariff Act provided for the collection of duties

Dec. 30, Message of the President transmitted report of the Secretary of State of Dec. 28 respecting citizens of the United States held captive in Algiers

1791

Jan. 10, Ratification of the Constitution by Vermont

Jan. 22, A commission consisting of Thomas Johnson, and Daniel Carroll of Maryland, and David Stuart of Virginia, appointed by the President to survey the federal district

March 4, Arthur St. Clair appointed Commander-in-Chief

March 30, Proclamation of the President defined boundaries of the federal territory

April–July, Washington made a tour of the southern States

July 1, Alexander McKee, British Indian Agent at Detroit, advised the Indians to make peace with the United States only on terms consistent with their "honor and interest"

July 2, Treaty with the Cherokees concluded

July 27, Mass meeting in Brownsville, Pennsylvania, in protest against the tax on domestic spirits

Aug. 7, George Hammond, first regularly accredited Minister from Great Britain appointed, arrived in Philadelphia, presented his credentials in Oct.

Aug. 12, Timothy Pickering appointed Postmaster General, took office on the 19th

Sept. 7–Sept. 5, 1792, Convention at Concord to revise the Constitution of New Hampshire

Sept. 9, The Commission informed Major L'Enfant, chosen to plan the federal city, that they had agreed to call the district the Territory of Columbia, and the capital the city of Washington

Sept. 29, Act of Pennsylvania legislature authorized incorporation of company to build canal between the Schuylkill and Susquehanna rivers

Oct. 31, The first appearance of the anti-Federalist paper, *The National Gazette* by Philip Freneau

Nov. 2, University of Vermont at Burlington chartered, opened in 1800

Nov. 4, General St. Clair surprised and defeated by the Indians at camp on the Wabash River near the present Ohio-Indiana State line, 894 men killed

Nov. 5, First issue of the *Knoxville Gazette* published at Rogersville, Tenn. by George Roulstone

Dec. 15, Ratification of the Amendments to the Constitution by Virginia, the first 10 Amendments declared in force. No evidence that Massachusetts, Georgia, and Connecticut ever ratified them

Dec. 20, Samuel Slater started 3 cards with 72 spindles working on Arkwright plan, the first successful cotton mill, in Pawtucket, Rhode Island (McMaster. Avery and E. F. Humphrey, 1790)

CONGRESS

Jan. 28, Hamilton as requested by Congress April 15, 1790, reported on the establishment of a mint

Feb. 4, Kentucky authorized to frame a constitution after 7 years of petitions, 4 acts of cession by Virginia, and 9 conventions of the people of Kentucky

Feb. 18, Act provided for the admission of Vermont to the Union, to take effect March 4

Feb. 25, Act incorporated the Bank of the United States, a national bank, chartered for 20 years with a capital of $10,000,000

March 3, Act established the District of Columbia

——, Act increased duties by excise tax on distilled liquors not only imported but distilled in the United States which produced general dissatisfaction, and the legislatures of North Carolina, Virginia, Maryland, and Pennsylvania passed resolutions of disapproval

——, Organization of army Act authorized an additional regiment to make further provision for protection of frontier settlements

——, Lands granted to settlers of Vincennes and Illinois country

——, Congress adjourned

Oct. 24, Second Congress, 1st sess. opened in Philadelphia

Dec. 5, Hamilton sent report on American manufactures, a strong presentation of the case for protection

Dec. 22, Washington sent to the Senate nominations for the diplomatic positions, Gouverneur Morris for France, Thomas Pinckney for England, William Short for Holland

1792

Jan. 12–July 28, 1796, Thomas Pinckney, first Minister to Great Britain

March 5, Anthony Wayne appointed Commander-in-Chief in place of St. Clair

April 3, State convention at Danville, Kentucky, framed a constitution, and General Isaac Shelby elected first Governor in May, holding office until 1796

April 9, Philadelphia and Lancaster Turnpike Road Company chartered, the road completed in 2 years

April 10, Act of Pennsylvania legislature authorized canal between the Delaware and Schuylkill rivers

April 17, Vancouver sailing from Hawaiian Islands reached Drake's "New Albion"

April 27, Vancouver passed Columbia River mouth as "small river" noted, and identified it as Meare's Deception Bay

April 28, Vancouver named Cape Grenville, Washington

May 7, Captain Robert Gray in the ship "Columbia" discovered a bay which he named Bulfinch Harbor, the name afterwards changed to Gray's Harbor

May 8, Vancouver discovered and named Mt. Rainier for Rear Admiral Peter Rainier

May 11, Captain Robert Gray entered the mouth of the Columbia River which he named, this discovery the basis for claim of the United States to the Oregon region

May 11, Connecticut General Assembly gave to citizens who had suffered loss of property during the war half a million acres at west end of Western Reserve in Ohio, known in Connecticut as "The Sufferer's Lands," in Ohio as "The Fire Lands"

June 1, Kentucky admitted to Union as 15th State

June 4–29, First legislature of Kentucky met at Lexington, Frankfort named as capital

June 12, Constitution adopted by convention at Newcastle, Delaware, and name established, the "State of Delaware"

Aug. 21, Convention at Pittsburgh, Pennsylvania, passed resolutions against the excise law, and sent petition to Congress stating the grievances of the western distillers

Sept. 7, Proclamation of the President warned the people not to resist the law against the excise riots in Pennsylvania and the South

Sept. 27, Treaty of peace with the Wabash and the Illinois Indians

Oct. 13, Corner-stone of the White House in Washington laid

Nov. 1–Dec. 4, General election for president and vice-president

Nov. 14–Nov. 26, Vancouver entered San Francisco Bay, the first vessel other than Spanish, at Monterey Nov. 27

Dec. 5, The electors voted, for Washington, 132, not voting, 3, one elector in Vermont and two in Maryland, the only candidate, but for vice-president there were contests between Federalists and anti-Federalists, John Adams receiving 77 votes, and George Clinton, opposition, 50

Dec. 17, South Carolina law prohibited importation of slaves; amended Dec. 18, 1817 and repealed Dec. 16, 1818

CONGRESS

Jan. 12, Gouverneur Morris confirmed as Minister to France

Feb. 8, Report of the Secretary of State (Jefferson) on the impressment of American seamen

March 5, Whiskey Act amended and modified

——, Organization of the army provided for 3 additional regiments for protection of frontiers

April 2, Act provided that mint should be established at Philadelphia. Any person could have gold or silver coined at the mint. Coinage of copper cents, and half-cents provided for

April 5, First presidential veto of Apportionment Bill of members of House

April 14, First Apportionment Act increased the number of members of House to 105, one to 33,000 inhabitants

May 2, Tariff Act amended and rate raised to 13.5% for protection of home industries

May 5, Act granted public lands to J. C. Symmes and his associates under contract of Oct. 15, 1788

May 8, Universal militia law enrolled white citizens between the ages of 18 and 45

——, Sinking fund established

——, Congress adjourned

Nov. 5, Second Congress, 2d sess. met in Philadelphia

1793

Jan. 9, J. P. F. Blanchard made first balloon ascent in America in Philadelphia rising 5,812 feet in 46 minutes and landing in Depford Township, New Jersey Feb. 1

Feb. 18, Decision of the Supreme Court in case of Chisholm vs. Georgia that a State might be sued by the citizens of another State, which later led to adoption of 11th Amendment to the Constitution

Feb. 22, Williams College, Williamstown, Mass. received charter

March 4, Inauguration of President Washington and Vice-President Adams, second term

April 8, Edmond Genêt appointed French Minister to the United States, arrived in Charleston, S.C. and began to enlist an army and commission privateers to attack the enemies of France

April 22, Proclamation of neutrality of the President as to France warned citizens to abstain from acts of hostility towards any of the warring powers, in effect annulling the Treaty with France of 1778

May 9, The French Government ordered the capture of vessels carrying supplies to an enemy's port

May 18, President Washington received "Citizen" Genêt, Minister from France

May 27, Eli Whitney made contract partnership with Phineas Miller, Connecticut teacher in Georgia, to get funds for perfecting his invention of cotton gin

June 5, The Secretary of State (Jefferson) communicated to M. Genêt the formal opinion of the President that "granting military commissions within the United States" was an "infringement of our national sovereignty"

June 8, British Order in Council directed seizure of vessels carrying corn, flour, or meal to France

June 17, Genêt notified that equipping and arming vessels brought into American ports to attack British commerce not allowed by Treaty

June 22, The Middlesex Canal, the first extensive canal in America, begun, completed in 1808 from the Merrimac River to Woburn

July 2–Aug. 13, Commission to negotiate with hostile Indians of northwest insisted on Ohio River as boundary

July 4–9, Constitutional Convention at Windsor, Vermont framed constitution which was adopted by the legislature Nov. 2, 1796

July–Oct., Epidemic of yellow fever in Philadelphia

Aug. 2, The Cabinet decided to demand the recall of Genêt since in the face of expressed prohibition he persisted in arming and sending out the "Little Democrat," a captured British ship, and encouraged by popular sympathy for the French Revolution threatened to appeal from the President to the people

Aug. 13, Commissioners to negotiate with the hostile tribes of the northwest received written statement from the Indians assembled in council denying the validity of former treaties and insisting on the Ohio River as a boundary

Sept. 26, Corner-stone of the Capitol laid by Washington with masonic ceremonies

Oct. 7, General Wayne moved into the Indian country with 2,600 troops

Oct. 15, Spanish "Commercial Company for the Discovery of the Nations of the Upper Missouri" founded at St. Louis to develop the fur trade, which sent several unsuccessful expeditions to find a way to the Pacific

Oct. 16, The French government of the "Reign of Terror" issued orders for the arrest of Genêt, but the President refused to allow his extradition "upon reasons of law and magnanimity," and he became a

citizen of the United States, marrying the daughter of Governor Clinton of New York

Oct. 19, Vancouver again at San Francisco, at Monterey, Nov. 1, at Santa Barbara Nov. 10, San Diego Nov. 27, and sailed Dec. 9 for Hawaiian Islands

Oct. 28, Invention of the cotton-gin by Eli Whitney reduced the cost of removing the seed from cotton to a neglible figure, made the growing of cotton the leading industry of the South, and thus increased the demand for slave labor. Date is that of original specifications before a notary public in New Haven, the patent date is March 14, 1794

Nov. 6, British Order in Council to seize all ships carrying property of French subjects or supplies to France or French colonies under which hundreds of American vessels were condemned

Nov. 9, First appearance of the newspaper *The Centinel of the North-Western Territory* in Cincinnati

Nov., Genêt sent 4 French agents to Kentucky to raise force to attack Spanish Louisiana, G. R. Clark given a commission as general

Dec. 31, Jefferson retired from the Cabinet because of his opposition to the administration. Followers of Jefferson assumed the name Republicans (anti-Federalists)

Canal built around the rapids of the Connecticut River at South Hadley in Massachusetts, the first in America

Jan. 23, Resolutions attacking policy of Hamilton submitted, answered by him in reports of Feb. 4, 13, and 14, a vindication of his administration of financial affairs

Feb. 3, Act providing for salaries of president and vice-president duplicated that of Sept. 24, 1789

Feb. 12, Fugitive Slave Act passed which empowered pretended owner or his agent to bring fugitive before a magistrate in order to obtain decision ordering the return of fugitive

Feb. 13, Electoral count announced and election of George Washington for second term as President, and John Adams, Vice-President

Feb. 21, Patent law repealed and new law passed

March 2, Congress adjourned

Dec. 3, Third Congress, 1st sess. met in Philadelphia

Dec. 16, Report of Secretary of State Jefferson on the commercial restrictions of France, Spain, and Great Britain in trade relations with the United States

1794

Jan. 2, Edmund Randolph, of Virginia, appointed Secretary of State

Jan. 8, The British Government modified the Order of Nov. 6, 1793, to make it apply only to ships carrying the produce from the French West Indies to Europe thus releasing the trade between the islands and the United States

Jan. 11, Nootka Sound Convention signed by Great Britain and Spain

Jan. 27, William Bradford, of Pennsylvania, appointed Attorney General, entering on duties Jan. 29

Feb. 10, Lord Dorchester, Governor of Canada, in speech to a deputation of Indians said that the British and Americans would probably be at war within the year over the Treaty, and the Indians might recover the Northwest territory

Feb. 21, M. Fauchet replaced Genêt as Minister from France

March 14, Eli Whitney received patent for his cotton gin

March 26, The President proclaimed an embargo for 30 days which was subsequently extended for another month on all foreign bound vessels in American ports in retaliation against England

April 14, Insurance Company of North America incorporated (Pennsylvania)

——, Lieutenant-Governor Simcoe of Canada built and garrisoned a fort within the limits of the village of Maumee in northwestern Ohio from which the Indians were given aid and almost open support

June 7–Nov. 4, Journey of Truteau, trader, from St. Louis to Indian villages near the mouth of the Cheyenne River reached Oct. 9, and then descended the Missouri River to the present South Dakota

June 24, Bowdoin College, Brunswick, Maine, received charter

July–Nov., The "Whiskey Rebellion" in western Pennsylvania where whiskey was the money "the, circulating medium of the country" (McMaster)

July 15–17, Armed mob fired on the revenue collector and fought with soldiers from Fort Pitt

July 28, General Wayne reinforced by Major General Charles Scott with 1,600 volunteer cavalry from Kentucky began advance from Fort Greenville, reaching site of present Defiance, Ohio, Aug. 8 and spent a week building Fort Defiance where a garrison of 100 men was left

Aug. 1–2, Meeting at Braddock's Field of the whiskey rioters with avowed purpose to capture the military stores at Pittsburgh, but design abandoned, and the insurrectionists merely marched through the town

Aug. 7, The President issued a proclamation against the whiskey rioters commanding them to disperse

Aug. 14, The Parkinson Ferry Convention adopted resolutions of protest against the excise laws

Aug. 15, James Monroe succeeding G. Morris as Minister to France received by the National Convention

Aug. 20–Sept. 11, A committee appointed by the Convention conferred with commissioners sent by the President who returned to Philadelphia with an unfavorable report

Aug. 20, Defeat of the Indians by General Wayne in the Battle of Fallen Timber at the Maumee Rapids ending 40 years' warfare with the Indians of the northwest

Sept. 10, Blount College chartered which later became the University of Tennessee

Sept. 24, The President issued second proclamation of warning and ordered the militia to suppress the rebellion in Pennsylvania. The approach of the troops ended the first rebellion and it was proved that the government could exercise force and restore order

Sept., James Robertson led 500 men from Tennessee and Kentucky in attack on the Chicamauga towns, driving Indians from that region

Sept.–Oct., General Wayne built Fort Wayne at head of Maumee River where General Harmar had suffered defeat 4 years before

Nov. 13, 200 of the insurgents were arrested, and some taken to Philadelphia for trial, but all pardoned

Nov. 17, John Jay in England secured promise that the western posts still held by the British should be evacuated by June 1, 1796

Nov. 19, Treaty of amity, commerce, and navigation with Great Britain signed (the Jay Treaty) provided for the settlement of debts, and the surrender of the western posts, but the British did not renounce claim to right of search or the impressment of American seamen; Great Britain given the freedom of the Mississippi

Nov. 28, Death of Baron Steuben, major-general in the revolutionary army

CONGRESS

Jan. 13, Two stars and two stripes for Kentucky and Vermont added to the flag making 15 stars and stripes

Feb. 20, Senate debates opened to the public

March 4, Amendment (XIth) to the Constitution approved securing States against suits in United States courts

March 20, Act to provide for the fortification of ports and harbors, with supplementary Act, May 9

March 22, Act prohibited carrying on the slave trade by American citizens from one foreign country to another, under penalty of forfeiture of vessel and fine of $2,000

March 27, The construction of 4 frigates of 44 guns and 2 of 36 guns authorized, the "Constitution," the "United States," and the "Constellation," launched in 1797

April 17, A proposal to suspend all commercial relations with Great Britain passed the House by a large majority and was defeated in the Senate only by the casting vote of Vice-President Adams

April 19, The Senate confirmed the President's nomination of April 16 of John Jay as envoy to Great Britain to try to adjust disputes and negotiate a commercial treaty

May 8, Post Office permanently established

May 9, Act allowing the President to raise the militia of the States

——, A corps of artillerymen and engineers added to the army bringing nominal force to 6,000

May 27, James Monroe confirmed as Minister to France

May 30, John Quincy Adams appointed Minister to the Netherlands

June 5, John Barry, Samuel Nicholson, Silas Talbot, Joshua Barney, Richard Dale, and Thomas Truxton chosen as captains to serve in the new navy, all had served in the revolutionary war

——, Neutrality Act forbade citizens to accept commission to serve a foreign state or give aid to any hostile force that might be directed against any nation with which the United States at peace

June 7, Additional duties imposed on tobacco, snuff, refined sugar, and some other imports classed as luxuries

June 9, Congress adjourned

Sept. 5, The eleventh Amendment to the Constitution approved securing States against suits in the United States courts by a citizen of another State or a foreign State

Nov. 3, Third Congress, 2d sess. opened in Philadelphia

Nov. 19, Message of the President to Congress denounced the clubs formed by the Democratic-Republicans in imitation of and in association with the Jacobin clubs of France as "self-created societies" which had encouraged the insolence of Genêt and the "Whiskey Rebellion"

Nov. 29, Act authorized the President to call out the militia in the 4 western counties of Pennsylvania for a limited time

1795

Jan. 2, Timothy Pickering, of Pennsylvania, appointed Secretary of War

Jan. 7, The Georgia Company and 2 others (Yazoo land companies) secured 25 million acres of land along the Mississippi in Mississippi and Alabama to which Georgia had not a clear title by bribing the legislature. The Act was repealed Feb. 13, 1796 and the sale declared unconstitutional and null and void

Jan. 31, Alexander Hamilton retired from the Cabinet

Feb. 2, Oliver Wolcott, Jr. of Connecticut, succeeded Alexander Hamilton as Secretary of the Treasury, Hamilton resigning from the Cabinet to practice law in New York

Feb. 19, Day of public thanksgiving appointed by statute of Jan. 1

Feb. 25, Joseph Habersham, of Georgia, appointed Postmaster General

July 1, John Rutledge, of South Carolina, appointed Chief Justice of the Supreme Court by President Washington, and took the oath Aug. 1 and served one term; not confirmed by the Senate

Aug. 3, General Wayne signed treaty with 12 Indian tribes at Greenville by which the Indians ceded 25,000 square miles of territory now southeast Indiana and southern Ohio, and established a boundary line

Aug. 19, Edmund Randolph resigned as Secretary of State in consequence of the capture by the British of a dispatch from Fauchet to French Government which represented Randolph in intrigue to defeat the Jay Treaty

Aug. 20, Timothy Pickering became Secretary of State ad interim, and was regularly appointed Dec. 10 to the office

Sept. 5, Treaty of peace with Algiers signed, purchased at total cost of $992,463.25 with agreement that the United States should pay an annual tribute of about $27,500

——, Connecticut Land Company organized which purchased for $1,200,000 the remainder of the "Western Reserve" in Ohio

Oct. 27, Treaty of San Lorenzo with Spain signed of friendship, boundaries, commerce, and navigation, fixed the southern boundary at the 31st parallel and opened the Mississippi to navigation, and gave Americans the right to deposit their produce in New Orleans for 3 years

Dec. 10, Charles Lee, of Virginia, appointed Attorney General

CONGRESS

Jan. 29, New Naturalization Act made the time of residence for citizenship 5 years, and required that allegiance to a former sovereign must be renounced and any title of nobility

Feb. 28, Provision made for calling out the militia to execute the laws of the Union, suppress insurrection, and repel invasion

March 3, Gallipolis land in the Northwest granted to its French inhabitants who had been induced by the Scioto Company of Boston to emigrate, representing the country as settled and cultivated

——, Congress adjourned

June 8, The Senate convened in special session to consider the Jay Treaty which was ratified June 24

Dec. 7, Fourth Congress, 1st sess. met in Philadelphia

Dec. 15, The Senate rejected appointment of John

Rutledge as Chief Justice of the Supreme Court because of his attitude expressed in a speech against the Jay Treaty previous to his appointment by the President

1796

Jan. 27, James McHenry, of Maryland, appointed Secretary of War, entered on duties Feb. 6

Feb. 6, State Constitution adopted for Tennessee by convention which met Jan. 11

Feb. 15, Monroe informed of the resolution of the French Directory that the Treaty with the United States was annulled

Feb. 29, Proclamation of the Jay Treaty of Nov. 19, 1795 as the law of the land

March 11, The French Government presented Monroe with a summary exposition of complaints against the United States, offended by the Treaty with Great Britain

May 4, Treaty with Great Britain signed explanatory of Jay Treaty, Article 3

May 31, Treaty with the Six Nations concluded

May, General Moses Cleaveland led company of settlers from Connecticut to the Western Reserve in Ohio, arriving July 4 and naming their settlement Port Independence, Cleveland settled in Sept.

——, Successful strike of journeymen shoemakers for increase

June 1, According to terms of Treaty Great Britain was to surrender the western posts held since the revolutionary war on this date. The American flag was raised over Fort Lernault at Detroit July 7, at Fort Ontario (Oswego), and Fort Miami July 11, and at Niagara Aug. 11. A British garrison was maintained at Mackinac until Oct.

——, Tennessee with a population of 76,000 was admitted to the Union (16th State)

June 29, Treaty with the Creek Indians signed

July 2, A French Decree announced that France would treat neutrals as they suffered England to treat them as to search and capture, and all goods destined for England declared contraband

Aug. 22, Monroe recalled because of his failure to press American interests in France, and C. C. Pinckney appointed Minister to France Sept. 9

Sept. 19, Washington published his farewell address to the American people (dated Sept. 17) in the Daily Advertiser, in which he refused to accept office again, and warned against "permanent alliances" with "any portion of the foreign world"

Oct. 29, First vessel from the United States in a California port that of Captain Ebenezer Dorr of Boston at Monterey

Oct., P. A. Adet, French Minister to the United States, recalled in protest against the Treaty with Great Britain. He remained in America until March, 1797 and attempted to influence the vote for Jefferson for President

Nov. 3–Dec. 6, Election for President and Vice-President, and the electors voted Dec. 7, the electoral vote for President gave John Adams 71 against 68 cast for Thomas Jefferson, his Democratic-Republican opponent. Thomas Pinckney (Federalist) received 59 votes, and Aaron Burr (Democratic-Republican) 30

Nov. 4 and Jan. 3, 1797, Treaty of peace and friendship with Tripoli signed

Dec. 11, The French Minister of Foreign Affairs in

note to Monroe refused to receive Charles C. Pinckney or any other Minister from the United States until France received redress of grievances, and Dec. 30 Monroe took formal leave

March 24, The House demanded the papers relating to the Jay Treaty with England which request was refused by the President

April 18, The President authorized to establish trading houses at western and southern frontiers or in the Indian country

April 28, Speech of Fisher Ames before the House on the Jay Treaty ("the most eloquent speech ever heard in Congress by his generation." Schouler)

April 30, The House agreed to pass the laws necessary to carry the hated Jay Treaty into effect after a period of debate as to whether the House had a share in the treaty-making power and threats of civil war if the Treaty was violated by the votes of the members from the South

May 17, Grant of land made to Ebenezer Zane to aid in construction of road from Wheeling, Virginia, to Limestons

May 18, Act provided for the survey of the public lands and authorized the President to grant patents for lands, provided for sale at auction at $2 an acre

June 1, Act directed that the United States military district in Ohio be laid off into townships

June 6, Congress adjourned

Dec. 5, Fourth Congress, 2d sess. met in Philadelphia

Dec. 16, The first Committee on Ways and Means appointed on motion of Mr. Gallatin

1797

Jan. 3, Treaty of peace and friendship with Tripoli signed

Feb. 3, C. C. Pinckney sent as Minister to France ordered out of that country

March 2, The French Directory decreed that the Treaty with the United States of 1778 was modified by the engagements of the Treaty of Nov. 19, 1794 between the United States and Great Britain

March 4, John Adams and Thomas Jefferson inaugurated as President and Vice-President

May 2, A letter from Jefferson written to Philip Mazzei April 24, 1796 published in the New York *Minerva*, an exaggerated denunciation of the Federalists as an Anglican party drawing the United States to the "form" of the British government

May 10, The first vessel of the new navy, the "United States" launched at Philadelphia

July 17, Philip Nolan obtained passport from the Governor of Louisiana to buy horses in Texas

Aug. 28 and March 26, 1799, Treaty of peace and friendship with Tunis signed

Oct. 4, Commission to France appointed by the President May 31, C. C. Pinckney, and John Marshall (Federalists) and Elbridge Gerry (Republican) reached Paris, and were received by Tallyrand Oct. 8. Agents of Tallyrand on Oct. 18 designated in report to Congress of April 3, 1798 as X, Y, and Z, demanded that the United States should assist France with a loan and pay the Directory approximately $240,000 as a present. Marshall and Pinckney retired from the negotiations after failure of mission, but Gerry stayed in France as a private citizen for which he was severely criticized

Feb. 8, The electoral votes counted and John Adams (Federalist) declared President, and Thomas Jefferson (Democratic-Republican) receiving the next highest number of votes Vice-President

Feb. 27, Report of Secretary of State presented on French injury to American commerce

Feb. 28, Washington vetoed a Bill to reduce the army

March 3, Congress adjourned

March 4, Fifth Congress, 1st sess. met in Philadelphia, Administration of John Adams

May 15–July 10, Congress met in special session called March 25 to consider relations with France

May 19, President Adams announced that the Directory in expelling Pinckney from French territory (*see supra* Feb. 3) had treated the United States "neither as allies, nor as friends, nor as a sovereign state," and recommended measures of defense be taken

May 31, The President sent to the Senate nominations for a commission to France to consult, negotiate, and treat on all claims and causes of difference with the United States. *See supra* Oct. 4

June 14, Privateering against nations at peace with the United States prohibited, and the exportation of arms forbidden

June 22, Report of Secretary of State Pickering of June 21 presented regarding depredations committed on American commerce since Oct. 1, 1796 by the armed vessels of France, Great Britain, and Spain

June 24, The President authorized to raise 80,000 militia for 3 months

July 1, The President empowered to use the frigates, "United States," "Constitution," and "Constellation"

July 3, First federal impeachment against William Blount, senator from Tennessee, shown to have led an expedition for the conquest of Florida and Louisiana in the interests of England then at war with Spain. The Senate expelled him but the Republicans interposed obstacles to the trial and the case was ultimately dropped

July 6, Act laid duties on stamped vellum, parchment, and paper to increase the revenues, a temporary measure

July 8, Duty on imported salt increased

July 10, Congress adjourned

Nov. 13, Fifth Congress, 2d sess. met in Philadelphia

1798

Jan. 31, Memorial drafted by Marshall delivered to Talleyrand became the basis of the successful negotiation of a later mission to France. Talleyrand's reply of March 18 offered to treat with the Republican member only of the commission

March 15, Explanatory Article to Article 5 of the Jay Treaty with Great Britain signed

April 25, The national song "Hail Columbia" composed and first sung in theater

April, Fitch's third steamboat and the first to carry passengers completed

May 21, Benjamin Stoddert, of Georgetown, D.C., appointed Secretary of the Navy

May 30, Revised Constitution of Georgia proclaimed

June 16, John Marshall arrived in New York and was accorded reception never before received by any American other than Washington. The crowds in the streets acclaimed him as "an honest gentleman who would not sell his countrymen to the sans-culottes." The war party adopted the slogan "not one cent for tribute; millions for defense"

June, George Logan, a Philadelphia Quaker, went to France on a self-constituted mission of peace, and returned in Nov. with verbal assurance that France would negotiate for peace

July, Yellow fever epidemic in Philadelphia caused the Government to move to Trenton for a few weeks

July 7, Captain Stephen Decatur, in the ship "Delaware" captured a French privateer, "Croyable"

July 13, George Washington accepted office of Commander-in-Chief of army

July 18, The President nominated Alexander Hamilton, C. C. Pinckney, and Henry Knox as major-generals. Knox declined appointment ranking him below Hamilton and Pinckney

Sept. 28, An official dispatch from Talleyrand transmitted through W. V. Murray, American Minister in Holland, gave assurance that a Minister would be received in France with "the respect due the representative of a free, independent and powerful nation"

Oct. 2, Treaty with the Cherokees by which they ceded land in Tennessee, and allowed passage through their lands by the Cumberland Gap to Kentucky

Oct. 4, Matthew Lyon, Republican congressman from Vermont, the first to be tried under the Sedition Act, sentenced to imprisonment for 4 months and a fine of $1,000 for criticism of the President in a campaign speech

Oct. 25, The St. Croix River identified as the northeast boundary of the United States by a commission acting under the Jay Treaty

Nov. 14, The Kentucky legislature passed resolutions written by Jefferson denouncing the alien and sedition laws as unconstitutional and claiming the right of the States as a party to the compact of the Constitution to take steps to declare them null and void; approved by the Governor Nov. 16

Nov. 16, The American ship "Baltimore" off Cuba stopped by a British squadron and 5 seamen impressed into British service

Dec. 21, Virginia resolutions written by Madison passed, which like the Kentucky resolutions laid down the principle that the Constitution was a compact and the States have the right to interpose to maintain the rights and liberties appertaining to them, and also denounced the alien and sedition Acts as unconstitutional

CONGRESS

Jan. 8, Eleventh Amendment to the Constitution declared in force. *See* Sept. 5, 1794

Jan. 30, First personal encounter on floor of House between Matthew Lyon of Vermont and Roger Griswold of Connecticut

March 27, Act provided for the equipment of the 3 frigates, "United States," "Constitution," and "Constellation"

April 3, The President submitted report of the commission in France which roused Congress and the country to indignation at treatment accorded to representatives of the nation

April 7, Mississippi Territory created with boundaries including the present State of Alabama

April 27, May 4, June 22, 30, July 9 and 16, Acts to provide additional naval armament for the protec-

tion of American commerce, and additional regiment of artillery and engineers (April 27)

May 3, Act to establish an executive department to be called Department of the Navy

May 21, Benjamin Stoddert appointed Secretary of the Navy, entered on duties June 18

May 28, The President authorized to raise a "provisional army" of 10,000 men for 3 years

——, Act allowing capture of armed vessels of France

June 13, Commercial intercourse with France and dependencies of France suspended

June 18, Naturalization Act amended to require 14 years residence and declaration of intention 5 years before application for citizenship

June 25, Merchant vessels authorized to "repel by force any assault" committed upon them by French vessels and to capture the aggressor

——, Alien Act allowed the President for 2 years to deport any alien dangerous to the "peace and safety" of the country

——, Act to authorize grants of land in the Northwest Territory to the inhabitants of Gallipolis

July 1, Resolved to raise $2,000,000 by direct tax on lands, houses, and negro slaves

July 2, George Washington nominated Commander-in-Chief of the army

July 6, Second Alien Act gave the President power in state of war to arrest, imprison, and banish from the country resident aliens, natives, or citizens of the hostile nation; expired by limitation

July 7, All treaties with France declared void on ground that they had already been violated by France

July 9, Machinery set up for valuation of lands and dwellings

July 11, Marine corps established

July 14, Sedition Act made it a crime to write, utter, or publish "any false, scandalous, and malicious" statements about the Government, Congress, or the President. 10 Republican editors and printers were convicted under this law

——, Act to lay direct tax of $2,000,000 to be apportioned among the States

July 16, Congress adjourned

Dec. 3, Fifth Congress, 3d sess. met in Philadelphia

Dec. 17–Jan. 14, 1799, The Senate sat as court of impeachment in case of William Blount

1799

Feb. 9, Captain Thomas Truxton in the "Constellation" attacked and captured the French frigate "L'Insurgente" off the Island of Nevis

Feb. 18, W. V. Murray nominated envoy to France and Feb. 25 Oliver Ellsworth, and Patrick Henry who declined to serve, and W. R. Davis appointed

March 7–12, Rebellion in Pennsylvania led by John Fries against the collection of the direct tax of July 1, 1798

March 26, Treaty of peace and friendship with Tunis signed again with some alterations

March 29, New York legislature provided for gradual emancipation of slaves

May 18, Beaumarchais died a refugee from France in Hamburg. The debt due him from the United States for aid in revolutionary war not recognized until 1835

May 28, The *Western Spy and Hamilton Gazette*, edited by Joseph Carpenter. first weekly newspaper in the Northwest, published in Cincinnatti

July 8, Edict of Paul I of Russia granted concession to Russian-American Company on the Russian coasts in America on the Pacific

July 11, Treaty of amity and commerce with Prussia signed in substitution for that of 1785 expired; proclamed in force Nov. 4, 1800

Aug. 17, Constitutional Convention at Frankfort, Kentucky, adopted a State Constitution

Sept. 24, Assembly of Northwest Territory organized at Cincinnati

Nov. 5, The second commission sent by the President to France, in opposition to the pro-British Federalists led by Hamilton who wanted war not negotiations for peace

Dec. 14, Death of George Washington at Mt. Vernon

Dec. 24, Proclamation of President Adams of Resolution of Congress recommending that the people of the United States wear crêpe on the left arm as mourning for 30 days in honor of the memory of George Washington

The Spanish Intendant at New Orleans, Juan Ventura Morales, refused to continue the right of deposit in New Orleans or to designate any other place

CONGRESS

Jan. 14, Charges against William Blount dismissed by the Senate on ground of lack of jurisdiction

Jan. 30, The "Logan Act" made it a high misdemeanor subject to fine and imprisonment for any citizen to carry on unauthorized correspondence with a foreign government in any controversy in which the United States was engaged

March 2, Act provided for the collection of duties and tonnage, and established ports of entry

——, A general postoffice established at the seat of government under direction of the Postmaster General

——, First rules and regulations for the navy; revised and reënacted April 23, 1800

May 14, Congress adjourned

Dec. 2, Sixth Congress, 1st sess. met in Philadelphia

1800

Feb. 2-3, Captain Thomas Truxton in the "Constellation" in 5 hour battle defeated the French frigate "La Vengeance"

March 2, The second commission to France reached Paris, were presented to Napoleon March 8, and begun negotiations April 7 which were concluded Sept. 30 with agreement on a convention

April 23, Regulations for navy revised

May 10, President Adams asked for the resignation of Timothy Pickering and James McHenry from the Cabinet, charging them with conspiracy with Hamilton to defeat his reëlection

May 12, Pickering, who refused to resign, dismissed, and Charles Lee, Attorney General, appointed Secretary of State ad interim May 13, and John Marshall appointed entered on duties June 6

May 13, Samuel Dexter, of Massachusetts, appointed Secretary of War

May 30, Connecticut ceded title to narrow tract of land known as "The Gore," 220 miles long between the Delaware River and western boundary of New York and northern boundary of Pennsylvania

July, The Santee and Cooper Canal from the Cooper River above Charleston, South Carolina, 22 miles, completed

Sept. 30, Treaty of Morfontaine with France for period of 8 years signed, abrogated the Treaty of 1778 which bound the United States to France as an ally, but released France from payment of spoliation claims arising out of attacks on American vessels

Oct., Hamilton issued a pamphlet criticizing the President for initiation of the commission to France and denouncing him as egotistical, jealous, and of ungovernable temper

Oct. 1, Secret Treaty signed at San Ildefonso by which Spain ceded Louisiana back to France

Oct. 12, Captain Little in the "Boston" captured the French ship "Le Berceau"

Oct. 19, Captain William Bainbridge forced by the Dey of Algiers to carry his ambassador to Constantinople in the "George Washington"

Nov. 8, A fire destroyed books and papers in the Dept. of War

Nov. 11, Election for President and Vice-President, candidates, John Adams and Charles C. Pinckney (Federalists), Thomas Jefferson and Aaron Burr (Democratic-Republicans). *See infra* Congress, Feb. 11, 1801

Census gave total population as 5,308,483 including 896,849 slaves. The center of population had shifted to 18 miles southwest of Baltimore. Virginia population 880,200, Pennsylvania 602,365, New York 589,051

CONGRESS

Jan. 6, Imprisonment for debt abolished on debtor taking oath of poverty

Feb. 25, Committee of the House reported on the petitions sent in from every State asking for repeal of the alien and sedition laws, and resolution taken against any action

April 4, A general Bankruptcy Act on the model of the English law enacted, extended only to merchants and traders

April 23, Act created a general stamp office in charge of a Superintendent

April 24, Act provided for removal of the government to Washington

——, The Library of Congress founded by the purchase of $5,000 worth of books

May 2, The jurisdiction of the Connecticut "Western Reserve" accepted, and executed May 30

May 7, The Northwest Territory divided into 2 separate governments, Indiana Territory, and the Territory northwest of the River Ohio

May 10, Act established government in the Mississippi Territory

——, Four land offices established for sale of public lands in the northwest at Steubenville, Marietta, Cincinnati, and Chillicothe, size of minimum tract which might be sold reduced from 640 acres to 320 acres, and the credit system extended, minimum price $2 an acre, land to be sold at auction

——, United States war vessels authorized to seize ships engaged in trade of carrying slaves from one foreign country to another contrary to law

May 14, Army reduced to 4 regiments of infantry, 2 of artillery, and 2 of light dragoons, to take effect June 15

——, Congress adjourned

Nov. 17, Sixth Congress, 2d sess. the first to meet in the new federal city of Washington

1801

Jan. 1, Samuel Dexter, of Massachusetts, appointed Secretary of the Treasury

Jan. 10, Governor William Henry Harrison arrived at Vincennes, John Gibson, Secretary, having had charge of the government since its organization July 4, 1800

Jan. 20, A fire in the Treasury Dept. destroyed records

——, John Marshall appointed Chief Justice of the Supreme Court, an office he held for 34 years during which time 1,106 opinions of the court were filed, and in 519 of these Marshall delivered the opinion of the court

March 4, John Marshall appointed Secretary of State for one day

——, Inauguration of President Jefferson. *See infra* Congress

March 5, James Madison appointed Secretary of State, Levi Lincoln, Attorney General, and Henry Dearborn, Secretary of War

——, Trading expedition of Philip Nolan which had penetrated Spanish territory as far as the Brazos River attacked by Spanish force sent to arrest him, and in battle near the Tehuacana Hills Nolan was killed and his surviving followers taken prisoners

——, Columbian Insurance Company of New York organized

March 21, The Treaty of Madrid confirmed the Treaty of San Ildefonso of 1800 by which Spain ceded Louisiana to France

May 6, Albert Gallatin appointed Secretary of the Treasury

May 14, The Pacha of Tripoli cut down the flag staff at the American consulate as a declaration of war

May 20, Naval demonstration in the Mediterranean ordered under command of Richard Dale

June 10, Formal declaration of war by Tripoli

July 15, Robert Smith of Maryland appointed Secretary of the Navy

Aug. 1, Lieutenant Sterrett in the "Enterprise" captured a Tripolitan cruiser of 14 guns

Oct. 19, Philadelphia first supplied with aqueduct water

Nov. 28, Gideon Granger, of Connecticut, appointed Postmaster General

CONGRESS

Jan. 26, John Beckley, of Virginia, appointed Librarian, and room at Capitol provided for the Library

Feb. 11, Electoral votes counted resulted in a tie, Thomas Jefferson and Aaron Burr (Democratic-Republicans) each receiving 73 votes, Adams and Pinckney (Federalists) received 65 (Adams) and 64 (Pinckney), and Jay 1. The election had to be made by the House of Representatives, each State having 1 vote

Feb. 13, Judiciary Act created a distinct class of circuit courts, and increased the number of judges, marshals, attorneys, and clerks

Feb. 17, On the 36th ballot Jefferson was chosen President by the votes of 10 States, and Burr became Vice-President. The defeat of the Federalists was due to dissention within the party

Feb. 27, Congress assumed jurisdiction over the District of Columbia

March 3, The Navy placed on a "peace establishment" and all but 13 vessels sold

——, Congress adjourned

March 4, Thomas Jefferson inaugurated President and Aaron Burr Vice-President in a special session of the Senate. In speech President Jefferson announced his foreign policy as "peace, commerce, and honest friendship with all nations, entangling alliances with none"

Dec. 7, Seventh Congress, 1st sess. convened with Republican majority

Dec. 8, Jefferson established a precedent by sending a written message to Congress. He emphasized economy and retrenchment in federal expenditure, revision of the new federal judiciary system, and enactment of more favorable naturalization law

1802

Jan. 8, Agreement with Great Britain signed regarding Articles 6 and 7 of the Jay Treaty and Article 4 of the Definitive Peace, payment of indemnities, settlement of debts, etc.

Feb. 6, Declaration of war against Tripoli

April 24, Commissioners of the United States and Georgia agreed to articles of cession of western lands claimed by Georgia, Georgia receiving $1,250,000, and the United States to acquire territory of Creeks and Cherokees within the State, into effect June 16 with ratification by Georgia

July 4, Military Academy at West Point, N.Y. formally opened

Aug. 11, Claims Convention with Spain signed set up commissions to settle claims for damages filed by citizens of both countries; ratified by the Senate and the President Jan. 9, 1804, and proclaimed Dec. 22, 1818

Oct. 16, The Spanish Intendant at New Orleans proclaimed that New Orleans could no longer be used as a place of deposit by Americans, again withdrawing right restored in 1801

Nov. 18, Sheet copper first manufactured in Boston

Nov. 29, Convention which met at Chillicothe, Ohio, Nov. 3 ratified for the people the first Constitution. A clause prohibited slavery. This is one of the 3 dates assigned as date of admission of Ohio as a State

CONGRESS

Jan. 26, Library of Congress placed under a joint committee of the Senate and House and a librarian to be appointed by the President

March 8, The Federalist Judiciary Act repealed

March 16, Army reduced to 1 regiment of artillery and 2 of infantry, to take effect June 1, and military academy at West Point established

April 6, Internal revenue taxes removed on domestic spirits, stamped paper, refined sugar, pleasure carriages, etc.

April 14, The naturalization law of 1798 repealed and that of 1795 requiring 5 years' residence for citizenship reënacted

April 29, Judiciary Act reduced terms of Supreme Court to one annually, and 6 circuits constituted with semi-annual courts

——, Act made provision for redemption of the public debt

April 30, Act enabled the eastern district shortly named Ohio to become a State and prescribed boundaries

May 3, Washington, D.C. incorporated as a city with a mayor to be appointed by the President

——, Congress adjourned

Dec. 6, Seventh Congress, 2d sess. convened

1803

March 1, First legislature of Ohio met at Chillicothe, the capital; this the date accepted by the Ohio Archæological and Historical Society as proper one for origin of State

March 24, Chief-Justice Marshall gave decision in favor of William Marbury appointed justice in the District of Columbia on March 3, 1801. President Jefferson had ordered that the "midnight appointments" made after the Republicans had carried the election be null and void

April 11–13, Livingston and Monroe in Paris in negotiation with Marbois for purchase of New Orleans and the Floridas offered all of Louisiana, and May 2 agreement reached for cession for 60 million francs, while American claims against France estimated at 20 million francs to be assumed by the United States, making the purchase price about $15,000,000

April 19, The King of Spain ordered the restoration of the right of deposit at New Orleans

April 30, Treaty transferring Louisiana to the United States signed with France, signed May 2 and antedated April 30, and agreement for payment of 60 million francs by the United States to France, and payment by the United States of sums due by France to citizens of the United States

May 12, King-Hawkesbury boundary agreement as to line south and west of the Lake of the Woods

June 7, Governor Harrison negotiated treaty with Indians at Fort Wayne by which land around Vincennes ceded Aug. 3, 1795 defined, further confirmed by other tribes Aug. 7 to include most of Illinois

June 20, Date of instructions of the President to M. Lewis and Capt. W. Clark for expedition to the West

Aug. 13, Treaty with the Kaskaskias by which territory south and east of Illinois River ceded

Aug. 23, Pinckney, American Minister at Madrid, instructed that the Spanish Government would not include in the Convention of 1802 indemnity for condemnation of American shipping by French consuls on Spanish soil

Aug. 31, Lewis and Clark expedition began descent of Ohio from Pittsburgh

Sept. 29, First Roman Catholic Church erected in Boston dedicated

Oct. 31, Captain Bainbridge in the "Philadelphia" in pursuit of a Tripolitan cruiser ran on a reef and was captured by Tripolitan gun-boats

Nov. 30, Napoleon's agent, Laussat, received possession of the Spanish province of Lower Louisiana from Count of Casa Calvo, the Governor

Nov., Sailor's strike in New York City for increase in wages unsuccessful

Dec. 12, The Lewis and Clark expedition settled in winter quarters at Wood River opposite the mouth of the Missouri

Dec. 20, W. C. C. Claiborne, Governor of Mississippi Territory, took formal possession of Louisiana for the United States. The original area of the United States of 827,844 square miles more than doubled by this acquisition of about 875,025 square miles

CONGRESS

Jan. 12, Nomination of James Monroe by the President a special envoy to assist Livingston in Paris confirmed. Instructed by the President to negotiate for the purchase of New Orleans to safeguard the navigation of the Mississippi and the Floridas

Jan. 18, President Jefferson in secret message to Congress proposed an exploring expedition to the western ocean to extend the commerce of the United States

Feb. 19, Act accepted conditions agreed upon by Ohio Convention of Nov. 29, 1802 admitting Ohio as a State, equivalent to customary act of admission of a State, "whereby the said State has become one of the United States of America"

Feb. 26, $2,000,000 appropriated under head of "foreign intercourse" as fund towards proposed purchase of New Orleans

Feb. 28, Introduction of slaves into States which had forbidden slave trade prohibited

March 3, The President authorized to call out 80,000 militia and build arsenals in the West

——, Conditions agreed upon by Ohio in ordinance in convention Nov. 29, 1802, accepted

March 3–March 12, 1804, Senate sat as court of impeachment in case of Judge John Pickering of United States district court for New Hampshire; removed from bench for drunkenness and profanity

March 7, Congress adjourned

Oct. 17, Eighth Congress, 1st sess. convened by proclamation

Oct. 31, The President authorized to take possession of the territory of the Louisiana purchase, and a provisional government for the new territory established

Nov. 10, Act provided for execution of the Treaty with France for the cession of Louisiana

Nov. 16, Act by which the claims of American citizens on the government of France taken over by virtue of Convention of April 30

Dec. 12, The 12th Amendment to the Constitution approved, providing for the election of president and vice-president on separate ballots

Dec. 19, Unpopular Bankruptcy Act of 1800 repealed

Dec. 21, President Jefferson presented to Senate adverse opinion from 5 prominent American lawyers respecting Franco-American spoliations

1804

Feb. 15, New Jersey law provided for gradual abolition of slavery by granting freedom to all persons born in the State after July 4

Feb. 16, Lieutenant Stephen Decatur in the "Intrepid" burned the "Philadelphia" captured and held in the harbor at Tripoli

March 4, Royal Decree divided the 2 Californias, Upper California having capital at Monterey, and José Joaquin de Arrillaga appointed Governor

March 7, Protest of Yrujo, the Spanish Minister in the United States, against the Mobile Act which established a customs district in the Spanish territory of West Florida

March 10, Upper Louisiana formally transferred by France to the United States, Major Amos Stoddard assuming the government at St. Louis, receiving possession from Delassus representing the French

March 12, Judge John Pickering, of New Hampshire, removed from office by Senate acting as court of impeachment

March 27, Navy-yard established at Washington, D.C.

May 14, Meriwether Lewis and Captain William Clark left winter camp at the Dubois (Wood) River and proceeded up the Missouri, passing La Charette, the home of Daniel Boone, and the last settlement on the river May 25

May 20, Proclamation of the President limited the customs district in the disputed territory east of the Mississippi to waters and shores within the boundaries of the United States

July 2, After negotiations of several months Cevallos informed Pinckney that the Spanish Government would not ratify the Convention of 1802 without further concessions from the United States

July 11, Aaron Burr provoked a duel with Alexander Hamilton and mortally wounded him in revenge for Hamilton's opposition in Burr's unsuccessful campaign for the governorship of New York

July 13, The *Indiana Gazette*, later the *Western Sun* first published at Vincennes, Indiana, by Elihu Stout

Aug. 3, Commodore Preble bombarded Tripoli and sunk 2 gunboats in the harbor, further attacks Aug. 28 and Sept. 5

Aug. 13, Governor Harrison purchased the claims of the Delawares to land between the Wabash and Ohio rivers

Aug. 18 and 27, Treaties with the Indians signed at Vincennes ceded land north of the Ohio River and south of the Vincennes tract

Sept. 4, Captain Richard Somers and Lieutenant Henry Wadsworth undertook to carry the "Intrepid" transformed into a fireship into Tripoli harbor. The vessel exploded before reaching the objective point and all on board were lost

Sept. 25, 12th Amendment to the Constitution declared in force, ratified by 13 States

Oct. 1, William C. C. Claiborne, Governor, inaugurated the territorial government of Louisiana at New Orleans

Oct. 16–Jan. 31, 1805, William Dunbar with Dr. George Hunter sent by the President on official tour of exploration of the Louisiana purchase from village 15 miles below Natchez to the Red River and up the Red River and its tributaries the Black and Washita (Ouachita), arriving at Hot Springs Dec. 9

Oct. 27, Lewis and Clark established winter quarters at the Mandan Indian villages near present site of Bismarck, North Dakota

Nov. 3, The Sauk and Fox tribes at St. Louis ceded to the United States 50 million acres of land for an annuity of $1,000, comprising the eastern third of Missouri, territory between the Wisconsin River on the north, Fox River on the east, Illinois River on the southeast, and Mississippi on the west. Article 7 allowed the Indians to continue to live, hunt, and fish as long as the tract remained public lands

Nov. 13, Presidential and other elections, candidates for president, Thomas Jefferson (Democratic-Republican) for reëlection, Charles Cotesworth Pinckney, of South Carolina (Federalist)

Middlesex Canal completed from Merrimac River to banks of the Charles River opposite Boston

CONGRESS

Jan. 5, Proceedings begun against Judge Chase by the House and on March 26 a committee reported articles of impeachment, and writ of summons delivered to Chase Dec. 12 because of his attack on the President and his principles in charging a jury on May 2

Feb. 24, The Mobile Act established a customs district in West Florida claimed by the United States as part of the Louisiana purchase

March 26, The Territory of Orleans established south of the 33d parallel, and north of the line made the District of Louisiana subject to government of Indiana Territory

——, Act provided for a Mediterranean fund for protection against the Barbary pirates by an ad valorem duty of 2.5% on imports

——, Land law reduced area that might be sold to 160 acres, retaining the credit features of Act of 1800

March 27, Congress adjourned

Nov. 5, Eighth Congress, 2d sess. convened

1805

Jan. 9, "Black laws" of Ohio passed, negroes not to give evidence in any court, etc.

Jan. 10, University of South Carolina chartered in 1801 opened at Columbia

Jan. 28, Monroe and Pinckney presented note and project of a convention by which Spain was to acknowledge the Perdido as the eastern boundary of Louisiana, and commissions appointed to settle disputed boundaries and claims. Monroe left Madrid May 26 after Cevallos had refused to pay claims or to cede the Floridas in lieu of other claims

March 4, Inauguration of President Jefferson and George Clinton, Vice-President

March 8, William Eaton with Hamet, elder brother of Yusuf, the Pacha of Tripoli, started across the desert from Alexandria to make a land attack

April 7, The Lewis and Clark expedition, 132 persons, left the Mandan villages and ascended the Missouri to source of the Jefferson branch in Montana, and reached the mouth of the Yellowstone River April 25

April 27, Eaton's force captured Derna, second city of importance in Tripoli

May–Sept., Aaron Burr traveled through the Mississippi Valley with General Wilkinson, with project of eventually founding a new empire and perhaps driving the Spaniards from Mexico

May 26, Lewis and Clark had first sight of the Rocky Mts. from near Cow Creek, Montana

June 4, Treaty of peace and amity with Tripoli signed which relieved the United States from payment of tribute. The prisoners were ransomed for $60,000

June 11, Detroit destroyed by fire

June 13, Advance party of Lewis and Clark expedition reached the falls of the Missouri

July 4, Aug. 21, and Nov. 14, Treaties signed with the Indians which ceded land, including claim to tract known as the Connecticut Reserve

July 23, Admiralty decision in the case of the "Essex" that the cargo was a prize because though the cargo from Spain had been reshipped for Havana in the United States the intention had been to carry on forbidden trade

July 25, Lewis and Clark at the forks of the Missouri named the rivers Jefferson, Madison and Gallatin

July 29, First Assembly of Indiana Territory met at Vincennes

July 30, The Lewis and Clark expedition began the ascent of the Jefferson River

Aug. 7, John Breckenridge, of Kentucky, appointed Attorney General

Aug. 9–April, 1806, Zebulon M. Pike left St. Louis with 20 men to explore the sources of the Mississippi, directed to report on the country by General James Wilkinson

Aug. 12, Lewis and Clark reached the source of the Jefferson River and marching overland for three-quarters of a mile reached the Lehmi River one of the upper branches of the Columbia running westward

Aug. 21, Treaty with the Indians signed at Grouseland by Delawares ceded land along the Ohio River in eastern Indiana between the tracts ceded in 1795 and 1804

Aug. 25, Proclamation forbade traders, canoe men, and others not citizens of the United States from traffic on the Missouri River; aimed at the Canadian fur companies

Sept., Pike reached Prairie du Chien and proceeded to Lake Pepin

Oct. 7, Lewis and Clark reached the Clearwater River overland and in canoes started down the river, and on Oct. 17 floated in canoes from the Snake River into the Columbia River and Nov. 7 sighted the Pacific

Nov. 1, Strike for increase of wages of journeymen shoemakers of Philadelphia unsuccessful

Nov. 12, The Cabinet adopted Jefferson's plan of reopening negotiations for purchase of Florida

Nov. 15, Lewis and Clark reached the mouth of the Columbia River. Part of the claim of the United States to Oregon based on this successful accomplishment

CONGRESS

Jan. 2, Trial of Judge Samuel Chase by the Senate begun on 8 articles framed by the House. The final vote March 1 acquitted him of charges except on 2 articles, namely of partisanship and rudeness at the trial of Callender under the Sedition Act, and of making a political harangue before the Baltimore grand jury, and no article received the two-thirds vote essential to sustain a vote of impeachment

Jan. 11, Michigan Territory formed out of a part of the Indian Territory

Feb. 13, The electoral vote counted gave Jefferson 162 votes for President, Pinckney (Federalist) receiving 14 carrying all the votes of Connecticut and Delaware and 2 from Maryland. George Clinton received 162 for Vice-President, and Rufus King (Federalist) 14

March 2, Twenty-five gunboats ordered for the protection of ports and harbors

March 3, District of Louisiana made a Territory and James Wilkinson appointed Governor

——, Act changed designation of Doorkeeper of the Senate to Sergeant-at-Arms

——, Congress adjourned

Dec. 2, Ninth Congress, 1st sess. convened

1806

Jan. 20, The Governor of Upper California, de Arrillaga, arrived at Monterey

Feb. 1, Francesco de Miranda sailed from New York with troops in unsuccessful attempt to free his native Caraccas from Spanish rule

——, Lieutenant Pike reached Leech Lake, at Red Cedar Lake, Feb. 25, at mouth of Minnesota River April 11, and at Prairie du Chien April 18, turning back April 22

March 8, Nikolai Petrovitch Rezanov, Chamberlain of the Czar of Russia, sailed from Sitka for California to obtain supplies of food for starving Russian

settlers, and arrived at San Francisco Bay April 5, sailing back May 21

March 23, Lewis and Clark expedition started on return journey from the Pacific coast

March 29, Commissioners appointed to lay out the Cumberland Road, Wheeling selected as crossing place on the Ohio

April 2, Lewis and Clark discovered the Multnomah (Willamette) River

April 4, The Eagle Fire Insurance Company of New York incorporated

April 19, Thomas Freeman instructed to explore the Red River to source left Fort Adams, Mississippi and proceeded up the river until July 29 when at point near present western boundary of Arkansas he was turned back by Spanish troops sent to stop him

April 25, The British vessel "Leander" off Sandy Hook shot across the bow of a passing ship and killed John Pierce, the helmsman

May 14, Lewis and Clark made camp on the Clearwater in Idaho

May 16, British Order in Council declared the coast of Europe from the Elbe River to Brest under blockade

May 17, Monroe and William Pinckney made commissioners extraordinary to settle matters in dispute with Great Britain

June 15, Lewis and Clark expedition started to cross the Rocky Mts. and on July 1 at mouth of the Traveller's Rest Creek the party divided in effort to discover the best route to the Missouri

July 7, Captain Lewis recrossed the great divide that is now known as Lewis and Clark's Pass, reached the Falls of the Missouri July 16

July 15, Captain Clark reached the Yellowstone River and descended it to junction with the Missouri Aug. 3

——, Lieutenant Z. B. Pike with Lieutenant James B. Wilkinson, and Dr. John H. Robinson left mouth of the Missouri, ascended the Missouri to the Osage villages and across Kansas in September to Republican River on border of the present Nebraska, and southwest to the Arkansas River which they ascended to site of present Leadville, arriving near mouth of river Jan. 9, 1807

Aug. 7, Captain Lewis at mouth of the Yellowstone after exploration of the Maria and Yellowstone rivers, and Aug. 12 united with Captain Clark, the expedition reaching the Mandan villages Aug. 14

Aug. 28, Coal first mined in the United States (Ann. Cyc.)

Aug., Aaron Burr started on second journey to the west and began to collect men, boats, and munitions of war for his enterprise

Sept. 23, Lieutenant Pike at site of Fort Snelling made treaty with the Dakotas and obtained grant of land

——, Lewis and Clark expedition reached end of their journey at St. Louis

Nov. 15, Lieutenant Pike sighted peak of Colorado Mts. named after him Pike's Peak

Nov. 21, Napoleon by the Berlin Decree declared a blockade of Great Britain injuring American trade although for 9 months the decree was not enforced against the United States

Nov. 27, Proclamation of the President warned citizens against persons conspiring against Spain, and ordered the arrest of persons concerned in military expeditions

Dec. 2, Aaron Burr acquitted in court at Frankfort, Kentucky, of charge of Daveiss that Burr was raising forces to invade Mexico and to break up the Union

Dec. 10, H. Blennerhassett and 30 conspirators fled down the Ohio River

Dec. 14, Death of Attorney General John Breckenridge

Dec. 22, Burr joined Harman Blennerhassett and with 9 boats and 60 men reached the mouth of the Bayou Pierre 30 miles above Natchez

Dec. 31, William Pinckney and James Monroe negotiated treaty with Great Britain in place of unexpired articles of the Jay Treaty of 1794, the trade with the West Indies was to be permitted under certain regulations, but as there was no provision as to impressment of seamen or seizure of vessels President Jefferson refused to submit it to the Senate

CONGRESS

Feb. 13, Appropriation of $2,000,000 for "extraordinary expenses of foreign intercourse" for purchase of the Floridas and Texas to the Colorado River

Feb. 28, Commercial intercourse with Santo Domingo in revolt against France suspended

March 9, National road from Cumberland, Maryland, to the Ohio authorized

March 26, Senate rules revised

April 18, The Nicholson Non-Intercourse Act provided that after Nov. 15 certain articles of British growth or manufacture should not be imported from Great Britain or British colonies

April 21, Superintendent of Indian trade established whose duty was to take charge and to purchase all goods intended for trade with the Indians

——, Congress adjourned

Dec. 1, Ninth Congress, 2d sess. convened

1807

Jan. 7, British Order in Council decreed that no neutral vessels should be permitted to trade from port to port with France or her Allies

Jan. 17, Burr surrendered to the Governor of Mississippi Territory and was released on bail

Jan. 20, Cæsar A. Rodney, of Delaware, appointed Attorney General

Jan. 30, The Pike expedition reached the upper waters of the Rio Grande del Norte by way of Sand Hill Pass into San Luis Valley, and Feb. 7 was in Spanish territory west of the Rio Grande

Feb. 19, Aaron Burr in flight arrested by Lieutenant Gaines near Fort Stoddert, Alabama

Feb. 27, One hundred Spaniards arrived at Pike's camp and took him prisoner to Sante Fé

March 30, Burr brought before Chief Justice Marshall in Richmond and bound to appear for trial May 22 on charges of misdemeanor

May 22–Oct. 20, Trial of Aaron Burr at Richmond

June 22, British war vessel "Leopard" fired on American frigate "Chesapeake" commanded by Captain Barron to compel surrender to allow search for deserting British seamen

July 1, Members of the Pike expedition arrived at Natchitoches, Louisiana, sent under Spanish escort. This expedition gave first accurate information of New Mexico and Texas

July 2, Proclamation of the President required all British warships to leave American waters

Aug. 17, Robert Fulton made first trip from New York to Albany on the Hudson River in his steamboat "Clermont" in 32 hours

Aug. 22, Burr trial opened on 2 indictments of grand jury of having levied war against the United States on Blennerhassett's Island Dec. 10, 1806, and that further purposes of preparations for war was an invasion of Mexico

Sept. 1, Burr acquitted by the jury on Marshall's decision of Aug. 31 that no overt act sustained by the testimony of 2 witnesses could prove the charge of treason

Nov. 11, British Order in Council prohibited neutral trade with France or her Allies between Copenhagen and Trieste unless the vessel had first entered a British port, paid customs there, and received new clearance papers

Nov. 17, Treaty with the Chippewa, Ottawa, Pottawotami, and Wyandot tribes by which all lands north of the middle of the Maumee River and extending north to Lake Huron and Canadian boundary ceded to the United States

Dec. 17, Napoleon issued the Milan Decree which declared that any vessel touching at a British port or submitting to search by British naval authorities would be considered thereby "denationalized" and lawful prize subject to capture

Dec. 26–March 21, 1808, George Rose, envoy from Great Britain, conducted unsuccessful negotiations for adjustment of "Chesapeake" affair. He refused to offer reparation until the Proclamation of July 2 was withdrawn

Stephen Whitney built a railway on Beacon Hill, Boston

CONGRESS

March 2, Importation of slaves forbidden from Jan. 1, 1808

March 3, Duty on salt repealed

——, Congress adjourned

Oct. 26, Tenth Congress, 1st sess. convened

Dec. 18, Building of 188 gunboats authorized making total 257

Dec. 22, Embargo Act prohibited all foreign commerce

1808

April 6, American Fur Company incorporated by John Jacob Astor

April 17, By the Bayonne Decree Napoleon ordered seizure of all American vessels in French ports as they could not by the embargo laws of their own country be lawfully on the sea

May 6, The steamboat "Phœnix" of John Stevens made first ocean trip from Hoboken to Philadelphia

July 12, Publication of the *Missouri Gazette* begun by Joseph Charles at St. Louis, later the *St. Louis Republican*, first newspaper west of the Mississippi

Oct. 22, The Cabinet agreed to instruct American agents to Cuba and Mexico to say that the United States was satisfied to see them under Spanish rule, but that if they should declare independence in case of danger from England or France it would act according to circumstances but with a "firm belief that our interests are intimately connected"

Nov. 8, Presidential election

Nov. 10, Osage Treaty signed, ratified April 28, 1810, by which Indians ceded nearly all of present Missouri, and Arkansas north of the Arkansas River

Nov. 25, Treaty with the Indians at Brownstone, Michigan, by which land for road from the lowest rapid on the Maumee River to the Connecticut Reserve granted to the United States

CONGRESS

Jan. 9, Coasting and fishing vessels required to give bond to land cargo in the United States

Feb. 27, Articles allowed to be imported under the embargo defined

March 12, The President authorized to permit vessels to transport American property home from foreign ports

——, The embargo extended to all vessels owned by American citizens on lakes and rivers

April 4, Gallatin presented report urging the opening of roads and making of canals in plan of internal improvement, some of the canals to be deep enough to accommodate ocean going vessels

April 12, Army raised to 5 regiments of infantry, 1 of riflemen, 1 of light artillery, and 1 of light dragoons to be enlisted for 5 years

April 23, Act made provision for the army and for equipment of the whole body of militia

April 25, Additional regulations supplemented the embargo laws, and foreign vessels forbidden to engage in the coasting trade

——, Congress adjourned

Nov. 7, Tenth Congress, 2d sess. convened

1809

Feb. 17, Miami University, Oxford, Ohio chartered

March 4, Inauguration of President Madison and Vice-President Clinton

——, First inaugural ball

March 6, Robert Smith, of Maryland, appointed Secretary of State

March 7, William Eustis, of Massachusetts, appointed Secretary of War, entered on duties April 8, and Paul Hamilton, of South Carolina, Secretary of the Navy, entered on duties May 15

——, St. Louis Missouri Fur Company formally organized

April 18 and 19, Notes from Erskine, British Minister in Washington, promised that the Orders in Council of Jan. and Nov. 1807 would be withdrawn as to the United States on June 10 if the President would issue proclamation renewing trade with Great Britain

April 19, Proclamation of the President renewed intercourse with Great Britain

April 26, British Order in Council revoked Order of Nov. 11, 1807 but declared the ports of Holland, France, and Italy to be blockaded

June 15, Expedition of the St. Louis Missouri Fur Company started to return Mandan chief to his people which was accomplished Sept. 24, and then built post Fort Mandan and sent out trapping parties

June 28, Trade with Great Britain legalized under Proclamation of the President

July 31, French Convention expired

Aug. 4, In secret Decree of Vienna never published Napoleon ordered the capture of every American vessel in retaliation for the Non-Intercourse Act (Channing)

Aug. 9, Proclamation of the President renewed the Non-Intercourse Act of March 1 against Great Britain

Sept. 30, General Harrison negotiated a treaty with the Indians at Fort Wayne by which he obtained a cession of nearly 3,000,000 acres on the Wabash River above Terre Haute

Thomas Leiper built tramway to quarries on Crum Creek, Delaware county, Penn.

CONGRESS

Jan. 9, Enforcing Act to supplement the embargo increased the powers of collectors in making seizure of vessels and authorized the President to use the militia and navy

Jan. 31, Employment of the 4 frigates "United States," "Essex," "John Adams," and "President," and additional naval force authorized

Feb. 3, Illinois Territory established by the division of Indiana Territory into two separate governments

Feb. 8, Electoral vote counted gave James Madison, of Virginia, 122 votes of the total 176, for President, Charles C. Pinckney, of South Carolina (Federalist) 47, George Clinton, of New York (Democratic-Republican) 6, not voting 1. George Clinton was elected Vice-President

March 1, Embargo Act passed as to England and France

March 3, Congress adjourned

May 22, Eleventh Congress, 1st sess. convened

June 28, Recruiting service authorizing enlistment for 5 years suspended

——, Congress adjourned

Nov. 27, Eleventh Congress, 2d sess. convened

1810

March 16, Chief Justice Marshall gave decision that the Yazoo land titles under Act of Georgia legislature in 1795 were good in law

March 23, Napoleon's Rambouillet Decree closed the ports of France and countries subject to France to ships of the United States to take effect May 20, 1809. American vessels in port in violation of this act to be condemned and sold. The decree was not published until May 14, by which date cargoes to the value of ten millions of dollars had been seized

March 24, Death of Julien Dubuque, French-Canadian trader, and end of his colony at site of the present Dubuque, Iowa, as the settlers were driven from the lead mines by Sauks and Fox Indians

April 12, Instructions from Castlereagh to the British Minister in Washington stated that the Orders in Council would not be revoked until France absolutely and unconditionally withdrew her decrees as to neutral nations

April 30, General Post Office established in Washington under direction of the Postmaster General

June 16, William Shaler appointed by the Secretary of State as "Agent for seamen and commerce in the port of Vera Cruz and all other ports in the said province" (Mexico), and June 28 policy begun of sending informal agents to Mexico

June 23, Pacific Fur Company formed by John Jacob Astor and 4 others, 3 of whom had served in the Northwest Company

June 28, J. Poinsett instructed to go to Buenos Aires as an observer

July 22, Decree of Napoleon forbade any ship to leave a French port without a license, the license giving the character of a French ship. American ships sailed under these conditions

Aug. 5, Napoleon signed Decree condemning American ships which had arrived in French ports between May 20, 1809 and May 1, 1810

——, Letter of Duke of Cadore to Government of the

United States announced French decrees were withdrawn on the understanding that the United States should by Nov. 1 enforce their rights against England

Aug. 12, Tecumseh in conference with General Harrison at Vincennes pledged himself as ally of the United States if the President would give up lands recently purchased and agree not to make another treaty without the consent of all the Indian tribes

Sept. 8, John Jacob Astor sailed from New York in the ship "Tonquin" to establish a trading station for the Pacific Fur Company on the Columbia River

Sept. 23, Inhabitants of West Florida in revolt captured fort at Baton Rouge

Sept. 26, Convention of delegates from several of its districts proclaimed independence of Spain and applied for admission to the American Union

Oct. 21, William Hunt left Lachine for St. Louis to lead party overland to the Columbia River

Oct. 27, Proclamation of President Madison took possession of West Florida to the Perdido as part of the Louisiana purchase

Nov. 2, Proclamation of the President, deceived by Napoleon, announced that Berlin and Milan decrees had been revoked

Dec. 7, William Claiborne, Governor of Orleans, occupied the 4 districts of West Florida west of the Pearl River and put down the insurrection

Dec. 19, The Czar of Russia issued an ukase admitting American goods thus breaking down Napoleon's "continental system"

Census gave total population as 7,239,903, the white race, 5,862,093, the colored, 1,378,110 of whom 1,191,364 slaves. The center of population 40 miles northwest of Washington. New York and Philadelphia each had 96,000 inhabitants, Baltimore. 46,000, Boston, 32,000

Map published by Major Z. M. Pike contributed to the cartography of the region between the Mississippi River and the Rocky Mts., and map of Alexander von Humboldt of New Spain the best that had yet appeared included country later southwestern United States

Dec. 10, Jonathan Russell, in charge of the American legation in Paris, protested the seizure of 2 American vessels after Nov. 1 at Bordeaux (see supra Aug. 5, and Nov. 2)

CONGRESS

May 1, Act known as "Macon Bill No. 2" modified the Non-Intercourse Act, and provided that if either France or Great Britain should before March 3, 1811, revoke edicts against neutrals the President authorized to prohibit commerce with the other nation, and if the other nation should not take similar action within 3 months, the Non-Intercourse Act would be revived against the nation refusing to revoke its edicts. Armed ships of foreign nations excluded from ports of the United States

——, Congress adjourned

Dec. 3, Eleventh Congress, 3d sess. convened

Dec. 18, Committee of House appointed to inquire if General James Wilkinson had taken bribes from Spain or had in any way been an accomplice of Aaron Burr

1811

Jan. 28, South West Company organized, later the American Fur Company, J. J. Astor having a two-thirds interest

March 4, Russian fur trapping expedition of Kuskov reached Bodega Bay

March 12, William P. Hunt, partner of Astor, left St. Louis with party for overland journey to the Columbia River

March 22, The "Tonquin" reached the entrance of the Columbia River, anchored on March 25, and April 12 began building of Fort Astoria

March 31, "Boston Resolutions" adopted by meeting of citizens at Fanueil Hall, attacked the President and Congress for subserviency to the French Emperor

April 2, James Monroe, of Virginia, appointed Secretary of State, entered on duties April 6

May 1, British frigate "Guerrière" off Sandy Hook impressed John Steggins, a native-born American, from the American brig "Spitfire," and 3 days later another American from the sloop "George"

May 6, Commodore John Rodgers in frigate "President" directed to proceed to Sandy Hook to protect American commerce from British and French cruisers

May 10, Bassano, French Minister, sent Russell, in charge of legation in Paris, copy of an alleged decree dated April 28, 1811 which formally declared in view of Act of March 2 the Berlin and Milan decrees not to be considered in force against American vessels since Nov. 1, 1810

May 16, The "President" riddled the British sloop-of-war "Little Belt" in engagement about 40 miles off Cape Cod. "Evidence conclusive that the 'Little Belt' fired first" (Channing)

July 31, Meeting of citizens of Vincennes adopted resolutions demanding that the settlement at Tippecanoe River of Tecumseh and his brother, the "Prophet" should be broken up

Sept. 2, Court martial of General James Wilkinson opened, charged with receiving money from Spain, of complicity in the conspiracy of Burr, and for disobedience to instructions of the War Dept.; acquitted Dec. 25

Sept. 6, The Hunt party traveling overland to Astoria reached stockade near present Elgin, Idaho

Sept. 11, The "New Orleans" built by Nicholas Roosevelt, the first steamboat to be launched on the Ohio and Mississippi rivers, left Pittsburgh for New Orleans

Oct. 28, Fort Harrison on the Wabash near the present Terre Haute, Indiana, completed

Nov. 1, A. J. Foster, British Minister to the United States, disavowed the act of search of the "Chesapeake" and offered reparation

Nov. 7, General W. H. Harrison defeated Indians who attacked his camp in the absence of Tecumseh, Indians led by brother of Tecumseh, the "Prophet," at Tippecanoe River within present Indiana and in territory belonging to the Indians

Nov. 8, Joel R. Poinsett appointed Consul-General for Buenos Aires, Chile, and Peru

Dec. 5, Resignation of Cæsar Rodney, Attorney General

Dec. 11, William Pinckney, of Maryland, appointed Attorney General

CONGRESS

Jan. 15 and March 3, By secret Acts the President authorized to take possession of East as well as of West Florida in case the local authorities should consent or a foreign power should attempt to occupy it

Feb. 20, Preliminary Act by which the people of Orleans Territory authorized to form a State government, and boundaries fixed by the Iberville and the Sabine for east and west

——, Recharter of the United States Bank defeated in the Senate by the casting vote of Vice-President Clinton

March 2, Non-Intercourse Act revived against Great Britain unless Orders in Council revoked, confirming the President's Proclamation

——, Trading posts first established among the Indians

March 3, Congress adjourned

Nov. 4, Twelfth Congress, 1st sess. convened

Nov. 29, Committee on Foreign Affairs presented report offering 6 resolutions in favor of preparations for war

Dec. 24, Bounty of $16 offered to recruits to the army with 3 months extra pay at time of discharge and 160 acres of land

1812

Jan. 10, Arrival of the "New Orleans," first steamboat on the Mississippi at New Orleans from Pittsburgh

Jan. 18, Donald McKenzie of the Hunt party arrived at Astoria

Jan. 22, Constitutional Convention at New Orleans adopted Constitution

Jan. 30, Louisiana authorized the enrollment of regiments of free persons of color

Feb. 10, The President paid John Henry, political adventurer, $50,000 for papers purporting to give important facts on the disaffection of the New England States and implicating the British Government in attempt to alienate these States

Feb. 15, William P. Hunt party reached Astoria

March 4, Charter of United States Bank expired

March 16, General Matthews, appointed as commissioner under Act of Jan. 15, 1811, took possession of Spanish fort at Fernandina on Amelia Island, East Florida, supporting insurrection of the inhabitants begun on the 14th

April 12, Spanish Governor Don Jose Lopez surrendered port of Fernandina and Island of Amelia to patriots of South America led by Americans, Commodore Campbell and Colonel Ashley

April 20, Death of George Clinton, Vice-President, at Washington

April 30, Louisiana admitted as a State (18th)

May 6, The "Beaver" sent by Astor from New York Oct. 10, 1811 arrived at Astoria

June 19, Proclamation of the President declared war on Great Britain

June 21, Commodore Rodgers with squadron of 5 ships, "President," "United States," "Congress," "Hornet," and "Argus" instructed to clear the American coast by forcing the British to protect their merchantmen on the ocean highways

June 22, Mob destroyed the office of the *Federal Republican* at Baltimore for denunciation of the war

June 23, Announcement of repeal of the British Orders in Council

June 29, Stuart left Astoria, wintered on the Platte River, and at St. Louis April, 1813

July 2, Capture of American schooner "Cayahoga" on the Detroit River by Lieutenant Rolette

——, The Governor of Connecticut refused to supply militia for garrison duty as called for by the Federal Government

July 5, Battle of Chippewa Creek near Niagara Falls, Canadian commander, Riall, forced to withdraw by Winfield Scott's brigade

July 12, General Hull, instructed to invade Canada, made his headquarters at Sandwich, a village on the Canadian side of the Detroit River 3 miles below Detroit (the British retreating to Amherstburg), and issued a bombastic and threatening proclamation to the inhabitants of Canada

July 15, 19, and 24, Americans repulsed at bridge on the Canard River

July 17, The garrison at Mackinac at junction of Lakes Huron and Michigan taken by a combined force of British and Indians led by Captain Roberts. This victory for the British allied the Indians definitely with the British

——, The "Constitution" encountered fleet of 5 British frigates but Captain Hull eluded capture

July 22, General Brook issued counter proclamation to that of General Hull

July 26, Russell, in London, authorized by Monroe to propose a suspension of hostilities if Great Britain would make an informal agreement against impressments and blockades

July 27, The *Federal Republican* circulated in Baltimore from a private house, which was attacked by a mob, the defenders finally taken to jail for protection but jail stormed the following day in attempt to capture the Federalists, General Lingan was killed, General Harry Lee crippled, and others seriously injured

Aug. 5, Captain Talon and Indians under Tecumseh ambushed company of Americans at Brownstown about 20 miles from Detroit and established post

——, The Governor of Massachusetts refused to send militia on call of the Federal Government, denying that the danger of invasion justified the President in making the request under the law

Aug. 7, Lieutenant Rolette captured a convoy of 11 American boats

Aug. 8, General Hull retreated to Detroit, having delayed assault on the British Fort Malden until reinforcements had made it imprudent to attack

——, General Brook embarked on Lake Erie at Long Point reaching Amherstburg Aug. 13

Aug. 9, General Dearborn at Albany agreed to proposal of British Colonel Baynes of Aug. 2 for an armistice instead of supporting General Hull as ordered by a vigorous offensive at Niagara

——, Colonel James Miller defeated the Canadians and Indians led by Major Muir and Tecumseh in battle at Maguaga 14 miles south of Detroit

Aug. 13, Captain Porter in the "Essex" off Newfoundland disarmed the British "Alert" and sent her as cartel into St. Johns

Aug. 15, Madison disavowed Dearborn's arrangement to confine his operations to defensive operations

——, Garrison in retreat from Fort Dearborn, Chicago, massacred by Indians

Aug. 16, General Hull surrendered Detroit to General Brock (British) without firing a gun. In 1814 he was court-martialed for thus giving up the fort and 2,500 men to an enemy numbering only 330 regulars, 400 militia, and about 600 Indians

Aug. 19, Captain Isaac Hull in the "Constitution" off Nova Scotia in engagement lasting 30 minutes defeated the British "Guerrière" and burned the vessel which was too badly damaged to take into port as a prize

——, Meeting in New York in opposition to war attended by John Jay, Rufus King, and Gouverneur Morris

Aug. 25, General Assembly of Connecticut in special session condemned the war

Aug., Filibustering expedition into Texas of Augustus W. Magee with Mexican refugee, Bernardo Gutierrez, captured Nacogdoches, and fort at Spanish Bluffs on the Trinity River

Sept. 4–5, Captain Zachary Taylor successfully defended Fort Harrison against night attack by Indians

Sept. 5, Lieutenants Hamilton and Vasques repulsed attack on Fort Madison on the Mississippi River of 200 Indians after 3 days fight

Sept. 10, Russians completed Fort Ross at site selected by Baranov for settlement 18 miles north of Bodega in violation of the treaty between Russia and Spain

Sept. 12, Siege of Fort Wayne by Indians relieved by General Harrison with Kentucky and Ohio troops

Sept. 17–18, Convention attended by delegates from 34 cities and counties of New York met to protest against the war

Sept. 21, Gananoque raided by Americans

Oct. 4, Colonel Lethbridge failed in attempt to take Ogdensburg from Americans

Oct. 9, British vessels "Detroit" and "Caledonia" attacked off Black Rock, and the "Detroit" captured and burned by Lieutenant Elliot

Oct. 13, General Van Rensselaer in premature advance from Lewiston to attack Queenstown Heights across the Niagara River defeated by British and Indians with loss of 1,000 men killed, wounded, and missing. 23 Irishmen of the prisoners sent to England to be tried for treason

Oct. 18, Captain Jacob Jones in the "Wasp" defeated the British "Frolic" in engagement off North Carolina

Oct. 18–Nov. 20, Armistice between General Smythe at Niagara and General Sheaffe; rejected by Monroe

Oct. 23, Raid of Indian village of St. Regis by Major Young, Union Jack seized

Oct. 25, Captain Decatur in the "United States" defeated the British "Macedonian" off the Madeira Islands, and took the prize to Newport

Nov. 10, Election for president and vice-president

Nov. 19, General Dearborn marched about 20 miles from Plattsburg to the Canadian border where the militia refused to leave the United States, and he returned to Plattsburg and winter quarters

Nov. 20, Attack of Dearborn on Odelltown repulsed by British

Nov. 21, Bombardment of Fort Niagara by British artillery at Forts George and Newark

Nov. 23, American post on Salmon River near St. Regis surrendered to Colonel McMillan

Nov. 28–30, General Smythe with 3,000 troops from Buffalo on the Niagara River at Black Rock demanded surrender of British Fort Erie but decided in council of war that the attack was too hazardous, and the army "dissolved" in confusion

Dec. 7, First General Assembly of Territory of Missouri met at St. Louis

Dec. 29, Captain Bainbridge in the "Constitution" defeated the British "Java" off the Brazilian coast and destroyed the vessel

CONGRESS

Jan. 11, Act provided for 25,000 additional men for the army for 5 years, and granted bounties of public lands

Jan. 14, $1,500,000 appropriated for the purchase of arms, ordnance, camp equipment, and quartermaster's stores, and $400,000 for powder, ordnance, and small arms for the navy

March 9, The President laid before Congress documents purchased for $50,000 from John Henry, political adventurer, sent by the Governor General of Canada to visit New England and find out sentiments of Federalists towards separation from the Union at time of opposition to the Embargo Act in 1809

March 14, A loan of $11,000,000 at 6% authorized to meet military expenses

April 3, Veto of the President of Bill regulating trials in district courts

April 4, Embargo laid upon American shipping for 90 days

April 8, Louisiana (Orleans Territory) admitted to the Union as 18th State to date from April 30, one condition that the Mississippi River be forever free to citizens of the United States

April 10, The President authorized to call on States and Territories for their respective quotas of 100,000 militia

April 14, Louisiana enlarged by the annexation of that part of West Florida between the Mississippi and Pearl rivers

May 6, Six million acres of public lands reserved to satisfy bounties to soldiers

May 14, West Florida between the Pearl and Perdido rivers annexed to Mississippi Territory

June 1, Message of the President suggested provisions for "opposing force to force in defense of their national rights" and recited grievances of the United States—violation of the American flag on the sea, the blockade, impressment of American seamen, refusal of Great Britain to repeal the Orders in Council, and supply of arms by British traders to Indians in the Northwest

June 4, Act providing for the Territory of Missouri comprising all of the Louisiana purchase north of the present boundary of the State of Louisiana

June 18, Declaration of war against Great Britain

June 26, Under Act consolidating the army the regular force numbered 36,700 officers and men, but the actual force was only 10,000 of whom about half were raw recruits

June 30, An issue of $5,000,000 of treasury notes authorized

July 1, Duties on imports doubled

July 6, Congress adjourned

Nov. 2, Twelfth Congress, 2d sess. convened

1813

Jan. 1, James Monroe, Secretary of State, served as Secretary of War until Feb.

Jan. 9, Manifesto of the British Government stated that the war was continued by the Americans on the questions of impressment and search, rights which could not be relinquished except by provision of the United States to prevent deserting British seamen taking refuge in American ships

Jan. 12, William Jones, of Pennsylvania, appointed Secretary of the Navy, entering upon duties on the 19th

Jan. 13, Attempted blockade of coast begun by British

fleet under Vice-Admiral Cockburn in Chesapeake and Delaware bays

——, John Armstrong, of New York, appointed Secretary of War, entering on duties Feb. 5

Jan. 18, Americans occupied Frenchtown (Monroe, Michigan) on the Raisin River

Jan. 22, General Proctor (British) surprised General Winchester at Frenchtown, and nearly 400 Americans killed in battle or in flight, Proctor's Indians massacred the wounded after the surrender

Feb. 6, Americans commanded by Major Forsyth raided Elizabethtown (Brockville) Canada and rescued a number of prisoners held there

Feb. 23, British force under Lieutenant Colonel McDonnell raided and looted Ogdensburg, New York, driving Americans commanded by Major Benjamin Forsyth from the town

Feb. 24, Captain Lawrence in the "Hornet" defeated and sank the British ship "Peacock" near mouth of the Demerara River, South America

Feb. 27, Maine Literary and Theological Institute chartered, name changed Feb. 5, 1821 to Waterville College, and in 1867 to Colby University

March 4, Inauguration of President Madison and Vice-President Elbridge Gerry

March 8, Russian Minister at Washington offered mediation of Russia

March 29, Magee-Gutierrez expedition captured San Antonio, Texas, where Governor Salcedo had retreated after defeat in October at La Bahia (Goliad), and treacherously put to death Governor Salcedo and Governor Simon de Herrera and many Spanish officers

April 15, General Wilkinson summoned Fort Charlotte at Mobile to surrender and took possession of country as far as the Perdido

April 27, York (Toronto) Canada captured by Americans under General Pike; abandoned May 2

May 1-9, Siege of Fort Meigs on the Maumee River in Wood county, Ohio, by British and Indians led by General Proctor and Tecumseh, successfully defended by General Harrison

May 5, General Green Clay coming to relief of General Harrison took possession of British batteries but was routed by Canadian militia and Indians, and 500 Kentuckians captured, only 170 escaping, and 40 prisoners tomahawked

May 9, Albert Gallatin and James A. Bayard appointed by the President to join John Quincy Adams to negotiate peace sailed, arriving in St. Petersburg July 21 where they learned that Great Britain in May had declined Russian mediation

May 12, Cartel for exchange of prisoners of war signed with Great Britain

May 16, Amelia Island evacuated by American troops

May 27, Fort George on west side of the Niagara River occupied by 3 American brigadiers, Boyd, Winder, and Chandler after evacuation of the British under General Vincent retreating to Queenstown and westward along the shore of Lake Ontario

May 28-29, British attack on Sackett Harbor a failure, General Prevost on Sir James Yeo's ships from Kingston, repulsed by General Jacob Brown Adams

June 1, The "Chesapeake" off Boston defeated and captured by the British frigate, "Shannon." Dying appeal of Captain Lawrence to his untrained crew, "Don't give up the ship" became the battle cry of the American navy for the rest of the war

June 3, American gunboats the "Growler" and "Eagle" captured on Lake Champlain

June 6, Generals Chandler and Winder sent in pursuit of British by General Dearborn surprised and captured in Battle of Stony Creek by General Vincent

June 12, Sebastian Kinderlan with royal troops expelled the patriots and occupied Amelia Island

June 22, Virginians at Craney Island repulsed British assault

June 24, General Boyd, who had succeeded in command after resignation of General Dearborn, sent Colonel Boerstler to bombard and take a stone house 17 miles from Fort George, Americans defeated at Beaver Dams (Homer) Ontario, force of 540 Americans surrendering to Lieutenant Fitzgibbon with 47 regular troops and 260 Indians

July 4, Canadians under Lieutenant Colonel Thomas Clark surprised American militia at Fort Schlosser and took prisoners, arms, and provisions

July 11, British under Lieutenant Colonel Bishop defeated by General Peter B. Porter in attack at Black Rock

July 13, Force from St. Louis commanded by Lieutenant John Campbell coming to relief of Fort Shelby at Prairie du Chien defeated at Rock Island and the same day Fort Shelby forced to surrender to Lieutenant Colonel William McKay with British and Indians from Mackinac

July 15, British fleet appeared in Potomac River to the alarm of Washington

July 17, Fifteen *bateaux* and small gunboats seized by Americans in Sackett's Harbor

July 20, British defeated at Goose Creek in attempt to retake boats

July 21, Fort Meigs again besieged by General Proctor

July 27, Battle of Burnt Corn Creek, Alabama, Colonel James Caller defeated by superior number of Indians led by the half-breed, Peter McQueen

July 31, Plattsburg taken by the British and Lake Champlain swept clear of American shipping

——, York, Canada, captured a second time and again abandoned

Aug. 1 and 2, Major George Croghan at Fort Stephenson (Fremont, Ohio) attacked by General Proctor while Tecumseh held the roads to the fort to cut off reinforcements

Aug. 3, General Proctor repulsed in attack on fort at Sandusky

Aug. 14, The American sloop "Argus" with Captain Allen defeated and captured off English coast by the "Pelican." The "Argus" had captured 27 British merchant ships

Aug. 30, Creek war begun by massacre of garrison and refugees at Fort Mimms on the Alabama River

Sept. 3, Fort Madison, Iowa, evacuated by commander in face of large company of Indians

Sept. 4, Captain William Burrows in the "Enterprise" defeated and captured the British "Boxer" off the coast of Maine

Sept. 6, San Antonio, Texas, captured by Colonel Samuel Kemper

Sept. 10, Victory of Lieutenant O. H. Perry over British fleet under Barclay on Lake Erie in which 2 ships, 2 brigs, 1 schooner, and 1 sloop captured, which forced the abandonment of Malden (Amherstburg) and Detroit by the British

Sept. 11, Partial and indecisive naval action off the Genesee River between Chauncey and Yeo

Sept. 22, Failure of Hampton's attempt to enter Lower Canada by Odelltown

Sept. 24, The British abandoned Amherstburg and marched toward Moraviantown

Sept. 26, Wade Hampton leading force from Plattsburg on Lake Champlain reached Chaguenay Four Corners where his position threatened Montreal and the St. Lawrence

Sept. 27, Perry's flotilla landed General Harrison's troops below Amherstburg already evacuated by General Proctor along with Detroit

Sept. 28, Naval action on Lake Ontario between Chauncey and Yeo

Oct. 5, Battle of the Thames. General Harrison in pursuit of Proctor overtook and defeated him at the Thames River. Tecumseh killed in this battle. The territory lost by General Hull regained

Oct. 17, Expedition directed against Montreal led by General Wilkinson embarked on Lake Ontario and coasted to the entrance of the St. Lawrence

Oct. 21, Wade Hampton reached Spear's within 10 miles of the St. Lawrence and 15 miles from the mouth of the Chateaugay

Oct. 23, Duncan McDougal sold Astoria posts to the Northwest Company (British) for $42,000 in absence of Hunt and in view of possible seizure

——, Post at Indian village of St. Regis attacked by Americans

Oct. 25, Hampton led force to dislodge Lieutenant Salaberry and 800 Canadians obstructing the road, but flanking party failed to find the way, and Hampton retired deceived by bugles of the enemy, believing himself opposed by large force

Oct. 27, Forty-six American officers placed in close confinement as hostage for 23 British soldiers confined by the United States as hostages for 23 British born subjects taken to England for legal trial for treason

Nov. 3, General Coffee defeated the Indians in Battle of Tallushatches in present Calhoun county, Alabama

Nov. 4, British Note offered to negotiate directly with the United States for peace; received at Washington Jan. 3, 1814

Nov. 5, Americans led by General Wilkinson began descent of the St. Lawrence with Montreal as their goal

Nov. 8, Battle of Talladega. General Jackson defeated hostile Creeks

Nov. 10, British gunboats effected landing of troops at Hamilton, New York

——, Governor Chittenden ordered recall of Vermont brigade summoned for service outside the State

Nov. 11, General Boyd ordered by General Wilkinson to attack British disgracefully beaten at Chrysler's Farm about 90 miles above Montreal, 2,000 regular troops routed by 800 Canadians commanded by Colonel Morrison

Nov. 12, General Wilkinson moved his troops to winter quarters at French Mills, and campaign against Montreal abandoned

Nov. 29, Brigadier General John Floyd with militia and Indians destroyed 2 Autlose Indian villages in Georgia in retaliation for Fort Mimms

Dec. 10, General McClure evacuated Fort George and burned the Canadian village of Newark as the British marched to retake fort which they occupied Dec. 12

Dec. 12, British sloop of war "Racoon," Captain Black, arrived at Astoria and Dec. 13 took formal possession, renaming post Fort George

Dec. 18, Fort Niagara on the American side taken by Colonel Murray, 67 Americans killed by the bayonet in this surprise attack

Dec. 29–31, The British and their Indian allies crossed the river and burned Black Rock and Buffalo and ravaged 30 miles of frontier in retaliation for Newark (Dec. 10)

CONGRESS

Jan. 2, Four new 74 gunboats and 6 first class frigates authorized

Jan. 20, Bounty for recruits increased

Jan. 29, The President authorized to raise 20 regiments of regular troops for one year

Feb. 2, The Senate refused to authorize the occupation of East Florida

Feb. 8, Loan of $16,000,000 ordered. Not a success and bought by capitalists at high rate of interest, Astor of New York and Parish and Girard of Philadelphia taking $9,000,000

Feb. 10, The electoral vote counted gave Madison 128 out of 218 for president, De Witt Clinton (Federalist) 89, 1 not voting, and Elbridge Gerry 131 votes for vice-president

Feb. 12, The President authorized to occupy Florida west of the Perdido, i.e., Mobile

Feb. 25, Treasury notes for $5,000,000 issued

March 3, Six sloops of war authorized besides provision made for suitable light fleet on the lakes

——, The President authorized to retaliate upon the British for injuries done by Indians and to adopted citizens

——, Act provided that from termination of the war it should be unlawful to employ any person not a citizen of the United States on public or private vessels

——, Congress adjourned

May 24, Thirteenth Congress, 1st sess. convened

July 22, The States divided into collection districts for direct taxes and internal duties

July 24, Duties levied on carriages, refined sugars, licenses to distillers, auction sales

July 29, Duty levied on imported salt

Aug. 2, Notes and bills of exchange were made subject to a stamp duty

——, Duties on licenses to retailers of wines, spirituous liquors, and foreign merchandise levied

——, Loan of $7,500,000 authorized

——, Congress adjourned

Dec. 6, Thirteenth Congress, 2d sess. convened

Dec. 17, Stringent embargo enacted; repealed April, 1814

1814

Jan. 6, English vessel, the "Bramwell" arrived at Annapolis under flag of truce with offer of peace

Jan. 21 and Feb. 21, The President appointed Jacob Brown and George Izard major-generals, and 6 new brigadier-generals, Alexander Macomb, T. A. Smith, Daniel Bissell, E. P. Gaines, Winfield Scott, and E. W. Ripley

Jan. 22, General Jackson defeated the Creek Indians at Emucfau on the Tallapoosa River, Alabama

Jan. 24, General Jackson defeated the Creeks at Enotachopco Creek

Jan. 27, General Floyd repulsed Indian attack on his camp at Calebee Creek, Alabama

Feb. 9, George W. Campbell, of Tennessee, appointed Secretary of the Treasury

Feb. 10, Richard Rush of Pennsylvania, appointed Attorney General

Feb. 26, Death of Judge John C. Symmes at Cincinnatti

March 17, Return J. Meigs, of Ohio, appointed Postmaster General, entered on duties April 11

March 22, The Secretary of State refused to release 23 British soldiers held as hostages for the 23 Irish-Americans sent to England for trial for treason

March 27, Generals Jackson and Coffee defeated the Creeks at Great Horsehoe Bend on the Tallapoosa River, not more than 100 out of 1,000 Indians escaping alive

March 28, Captain Porter in the "Essex" surrendered to the British ships "Phoebe" and "Cherub" in the harbor of Valparaiso, Chile

March 30, General Wilkinson in new advance on Montreal repulsed in attack on stone mill at Lacolle Mills, Lower Canada, by Major Hancock and retired to Plattsburg. Relieved of command by orders dated March 24

April 15, Convention entered into at Montreal between Colonel Baynes and American General Winder for mutual exchange of prisoners-of-war except hostages

April 20, Joseph Bainbridge in the "Frolic" captured by the British "Orpheus"

April 23, British Proclamation added New England to the coast blockade and raids on the Connecticut and Massachusetts coasts followed

April 29, Captain Warrington in the "Peacock" captured the British "Epervier" off the Florida coast with $118,000

May 1–5, Bombardment of Fort Meigs, Ohio, commanded by General Harrison, by British and Canadians under Colonel Proctor with batteries erected at Maumee City

May 6, Sir James Yeo from Kingston attacked and destroyed the fort at Oswego on Lake Ontario

May 9, Pring's attack at Otter Creek, Lake Champlain

May 15, Unauthorized attack on Long Point, Lake Erie, by American troops in which Canadian mills and dwellings burned

May 28, Andrew Jackson commissioned major-general in place of General Harrison resigned

May 29, A fleet of American transports took refuge in Big Sandy Creek and captured their British pursuers from Lake Ontario

June 2, General William Clark, Governor of Missouri, began building Fort Shelby at Prairie du Chien

June 22, Lieutenant Renshaw in the "Rattlesnake" captured by the British "Leander"

June 28, Captain Blakely in the "Wasp" captured the British brig-sloop "Reindeer"

July 3, American troops under General Brown captured Fort Erie, and pushed ahead 15 miles to the British defensive line on the Chippewa River where it flows into the Niagara

July 5, Battle of Chippewa Plains. Generals Brown and Scott forced the British General Riall to retreat to Queenstown, but the failure of Commodore Chauncey at Sackett's Harbor to coöperate with the army made it expedient for the Americans to retire westward

July 11, Fort Sullivan, Eastport, Maine, surrendered by Major Perley Putnam to British force from Halifax and fleet commanded by Sir Thomas Hardy

July 18, Twenty-three British officers held as hostages and the 46 Americans held by the British released

July 19, British and Indian force from Mackinac under Major William McKay took Fort Shelby at Prairie du Chien commanded by Lieutenant Joseph Perkins after siege of 2 days

July 22, Treaty of Greenville, Ohio, with the Indians

July 23, Major Nicholls with British troops landed at Pensacola, Florida, and garrisoned the forts with the consent of the Spanish governor

July 25, Battle of Lundy's Lane or Bridgewater, near Niagara Falls, Upper Canada. General Brown (American) and Generals Riall and Drummond (British) both claimed the victory. The British resumed position July 26 and held it unattacked

July–Aug., 16,000 British veteran troops sent from Europe after the downfall of Napoleon reached Canada

Aug. 3, British advance across the Niagara River toward Buffalo checked at Black Rock by Morgan's rifles

Aug. 4, Expedition from Detroit of Colonel Croghan and Commodore Sinclair against Mackinac repulsed by British

Aug. 8, John Quincy Adams, James A. Bayard, Albert Gallatin, Jonathan Russell, and Henry Clay, American Peace Commission, met the British Commission, Lord Gambier, Henry Goulburn, and William Adams. The British claimed for their Indian allies the establishment of an Indian state between Canada and the United States with the boundary line of the Greenville Treaty of 1795, the country which is now Michigan, Wisconsin, and Illinois, four-fifths of Indiana, and one-third of Ohio, and a revision of the Canadian boundary to include the conquered part of Maine, and the United States was to renounce the right to keep armed vessels or establish military posts on the Great Lakes

Aug. 9, Nantucket Island in negotiation with the British fleet promised to remain neutral in return for permission to bring provisions from the mainland

——, Treaty with the Creeks concluded in which General Jackson forced the Indians to cede two-thirds of their vast territory to the United States

Aug. 9–12, Stonington, Connecticut, bombarded by British fleet under Colonel Hardy

Aug. 12, Capture of the "Ohio" and "Somers" at Fort Erie by Captian Dobbs

Aug. 15, General Drummond repulsed in attack on Fort Erie defended by General Gaines

Aug. 19, General Ross landed British troops at Benedict, Maryland about 50 miles southeast of Washington

Aug. 22, Joshua Barney's flotilla of boats on the Pautuxent destroyed on approach of British fleet led by Admiral Cockburn

Aug. 24, Battle of Bladensburg. General Winder with militia mobilized for the defense of Washington retreated before the British advance which was held back for a time by Joshua Barney and his 400 sailors with 5 guns across the main highway

——, Note of American Peace Commission declined British conditions as having no relation to the causes of the war, and inconsistent with principles of public law

Aug. 25, All the government buildings except the Patent Office, the President's house, and numerous private houses burned in retaliation for the burning of the capital of Upper Canada, York, in 1813

Aug. 26, Expedition of Sir John Sherbrooke against the coast between the New Brunswick frontier and the Penobscot River sailed from Halifax

Aug. 29, Alexandria, Virginia, saved from destruction

by British fleet by payment of over $100,000 in flour, tobacco, naval stores, and shipping

Aug. 30, James Monroe, Secretary of State, appointed *ad interim* Secretary of War and regularly appointed Sept. 27, entering on duties Oct. 1

Sept. 1, Fort at Castine, Maine, and Belfast taken by British fleet from Halifax

Sept. 3, Hampden, Maine, captured by the British and the frigate "Adams" in the Penobscot River for repairs burned by Americans to prevent capture

——, Capture of American vessels "Tigress" and "Scorpion" on upper Lake Huron

Sept. 6, Major Zachary Taylor at Credit Island (Davenport, Iowa) attacked and driven down the river by British and Indians, and the region of the Upper Mississippi abandoned to British control

——, Sir George Prevost encamped before Plattsburg

Sept. 11, The American fleet under Commodore Thomas Macdonough won decisive victory on Lake Champlain in the Bay of Plattsburg over British squadron commanded by Captain Downie. Prevost began retreat to Canada, leaving wounded and stores

Sept. 12–13, The British commanded by General Ross and Admiral Cockburn joined in unsuccessful attack on Baltimore, Maryland. Detained by the British fleet while effecting an exchange of prisoners Francis Scott Key watched Fort McHenry in the light of the artillery fires and composed "The Star Spangled Banner"

Sept. 15, Major Nicholls with marines and Indians repulsed in attack on the garrison at Fort Boyer on east side of entrance to Mobile Bay established by General Wilkinson, and under command of Major William Lawrence

Sept. 16, Colonel Patterson broke up resort of pirates at Barataria Harbor on Grande Isle and Grande Terre ruled by Jean and Pierre Lafitte

Sept. 17, General Brown organized a sortie from Fort Erie which overhwlemed the British batteries and forced General Drummond to give up the siege

Sept. 21, General Drummond began retreat to Canada

——, Territory between Penobscot River and New Brunswick annexed to Great Britain by proclamation

——, Captain Blakely in the "Wasp" captured the British brig "Atlanta"

Sept. 24, General Proctor abandoned Amherstburg

Sept. 26, Captain Reid in the privateer "General Armstrong" in engagement off Fayal in Azores with the British 74 gunboat "Plantagenet," the 38 gun "Rota" and the 18 gun "Carnation," burned his ship Sept. 27 to avoid capture

Oct. 6, Alexander J. Dallas of Pennsylvania appointed Secretary of the Treasury

Oct. 15, British fleet commanded by Sir James Yeo shut Chauncey and his fleet in Sackett's Harbor, keeping them there until the end of the war

Oct. 19, General Drummond (British) and General Izard in skirmish at Cook's Mills 12 miles inland from Chippewa

Oct. 29, The "Fulton," the first steam war vessel launched

Nov. 5, Fort Erie abandoned and blown up by Americans and war ended on the Niagara frontier

Nov. 7, General Jackson occupied Pensacola, clearing West Florida of the British

Nov. 23, Death of Vice-President Elbridge Gerry, Senator John Gaillard, of South Carolina, president of Senate, succeeding

Nov. 26, The British sailed from Jamaica with intention of capturing New Orleans and gaining control of the Mississippi

Dec. 2, General Jackson took command at New Orleans

Dec. 14, Captain Lockyer (British) captured American fleet on Lake Borgne, Louisiana

Dec. 15, The Hartford Convention attended by disaffected New Englanders from Massachusetts, Connecticut, Rhode Island, New Hampshire, and Vermont

Dec. 19, Benjamin W. Crowninshield, of Massachusetts, appointed Secretary of the Navy, entering on duties Jan. 16, 1815

Dec. 23, Advance guard of British under General Keene disembarked from the Villeré Canal on the banks of the Mississippi 7 miles below New Orleans and were checked by attack of General Jackson

Dec. 24, Treaty of Peace with Great Britain signed by the commissioners at Ghent, the provisions including a return of captured territory, the appointment of commissions to settle disputed northeastern boundary and possession of certain islands in Passamaquody Bay, and for steps toward abolition of the slave trade, but nothing about impressment, right of search, blockade, neutral rights or indemnities, fisheries, or navigation of the Mississippi

Dec. 28, Battle of Chalmette's Plantation, near New Orleans. General Pakenham's advance against General Jackson's fortified position halted and army ordered to retire beyond cannon-shot of the "Louisiana"

CONGRESS

Jan. 25, Act relieved the people of Nantucket from rigid enforcement of the embargo prohibiting intercourse with the mainland

Jan. 27, Act to fill the ranks of the army increased the bounty to $124 together with 320 acres of land as already established. As reorganized the army consisted of 62,773 men enlisted for term of 5 years

Feb. 2, The President communicated report from the Secretary of War dated Jan. 25 regarding failure of the war on northern frontier

March 4, $320,000 appropriated for a steam frigate or floating battery for which Robert Fulton offered a plan

——, The issue of $10,000,000 treasury notes authorized

March 25, Loan of $25,000,000 authorized

March 31, Payment of $8,000,000 to the claimants under the Georgia land laws selling Mississippi lands (Yazoo Act)

April 14, Repeal of Embargo Act

April 18, Congress adjourned

Sept. 19, Thirteenth Congress, 3d sess. convened, meeting in Patent Office

Oct. 27, Bill introduced in House proposing conscription defeated

1815

Jan. 1, Battle of Rodriguez Canal. British guns silenced by Americans trained by General Jackson in artillery duel

Jan. 8, Battle of New Orleans in which General Jackson with 4,500 men defeated General Pakenham with 8,000 British troops, General Pakenham killed and the British advancing across the plain towards American fortified entrenchments lost 2,600 of whom 700 were killed, 1,400 wounded, and 500 taken prisoners, the American loss only 8 killed and 13 wounded

Jan. 14, Hartford (Conn.) Convention adjourned, report and resolutions adopted declared that the Constitution had been violated, and that the "States which have no common umpire must be their own judges and execute their own decisions." Amendments to Constitution proposed were intended to restrict the power of Congress over commerce and war, and to prevent naturalized citizens from holding office, the States to retain the proceeds of the national customs duties collected within their borders. Implied in the document was the right to secede if demands not complied with

Jan. 15, Captain Decatur in the "President" captured by the British frigates "Endymion," "Pomone," "Tenedos," and "Majestic"

Feb. 6, John Stevens obtained from New Jersey the first railroad charter granted in the United States to build railroad from New Brunswick to Trenton

Feb. 11, Surrender of Fort Bowyer, Mobile, to the British fleet and troops commanded by General Lambert

——, Treaty of Peace reached New York in British war vessel "Favorite"

Feb. 20, Captain Stewart in the "Constitution" off Lisbon captured 2 British sloops-of-war, the "Cyane," and the "Levant"

Feb. 28, James Monroe, of Virginia, appointed Secretary of State, and March 1, *ad interim* Secretary of War

March 5, General Jackson arrested Louallier as a spy, Judge Hall for granting Louallier a habeas corpus, and Hollander; all later released and March 30, Jackson tried and fined by Judge Hall $1,000

March 14–Aug. 8, A. J. Dall, Secretary of the Treasury, *ad interim* Secretary of War

March 15, Schuylkill Navigation Company incorporated in Pennsylvania, which completed canal between Philadelphia and Reading in 1824 and between Reading and Port Carbon in 1825

March 23, Captain Biddle in the "Hornet" captured the British "Penguin" in the south Atlantic

April 6, American sailors in conflict with guards in attempt to escape from prison in Dartmoor, England, 7 killed and 33 wounded

May 1, Georgetown College at Washington, D.C. chartered as a university

May 20, Captain Stephen Decatur with 10 vessels sailed from New York for Algiers

May 22, Captain A. H. Bulger (British) received word of the peace and evacuated fort at Prairie du Chien

June 17, Decatur's squadron defeated and captured the Algerian 46 gun frigate "Mashouda"

June 19, Decatur's squadron captured the Algerian 22 gun frigate "Estido"

June 30 and July 3, Treaty with the United States signed by the Dey of Algiers by which Algiers renounced all claims to tribute and promised to reduce no more prisoners of war to slavery

——, Captain Warrington in the "Peacock" captured the British "Nautilus" in the Indian Ocean

July 3, Treaty of commerce with Great Britain abolished discriminating duties and admitted American commerce to the East Indies but gave no specific concessions as to the West Indies

July 18, Mackinac formally transferred to the Americans

July 18 and 19, Governor Clark of Missouri and Governor Edwards of Illinois opened negotiations with the Indians of the Northwest who had been allies of the British in the late war, making a series of peace treaties

July 26, Captain Decatur demanded and received $46,000 from Tunis for American prizes allowed to be retaken by the British from neutral port

Aug. 1, William H. Crawford, of Georgia, appointed Secretary of War, entering on duties Aug. 8

Aug. 5, Captain Decatur demanded and received from the Bashaw of Tripoli $25,000 for American prizes allowed to be retaken by British from neutral port

Sept. 1, Peace made with the Indians of the Northwest at council held at Detroit

Sept. 10, Auguste P. Chouteau and Jules de Mun with party of trappers left St. Louis and arrived at Huerfano Dec. 8

Sept. 24, Death of John Sevier

CONGRESS

Jan. 9, Direct tax raised to $6,000,000

Jan. 18, Tariff Act increased customs duties as a revenue measure, added duties on household furniture, watches, etc.

Jan. 27, Act authorized the President to accept the services of State troops

Jan. 30, The library of Thomas Jefferson purchased for the national library

——, Bill to establish a national bank vetoed by the President

Feb. 7, A Board of Navy Commissioners established

——, Flotilla Act repealed and remaining gunboats ordered to be sold

March 3, Repeal of Acts prohibiting entrance of foreign vessels into waters of the United States

——, Loan for $18,000,000 authorized

——, Hostilities authorized against the Dey of Algiers for the protection of American commerce

——, Military peace establishment fixed at 10,000 men

——, Congress adjourned

Dec. 4, Fourteenth Congress, 1st sess. convened

Cost of war estimated at about $200,000,000. The issue of bonds and treasury notes added over $80,-000,000 to the national debt which reached $127,-335,000, about $15 a head for the population as compared with $20 a head in 1791. The number killed in battle was estimated at 1,500, the total of killed and wounded in land battles about 5,000, and total of losses including prisoners 9,700

1816

March, Columbus made the capital of Ohio

May 10, Fort Armstrong at Green Bay begun, one of chain of frontier forts built at this time

May 13, Treaty with the Sauk and Fox of Nov. 3, 1804, formally recognized and confirmed, ending their forays along the Upper Mississippi

June 10–29, Constitutional Convention at Corydon accepted enabling act and adopted Constitution for Indiana, slavery prohibited

June 27, New Hampshire legislature amended charter of Dartmouth College, increasing the number of trustees and changing the name to Dartmouth University, creating a new corporation

July 9, Agreement with Indians made by W. L. Lovely, American agent, by which large tract of land in northeast Oklahoma ceded by the Cherokees, the "Lovely purchase"

July 27, Fort Appalachicola built by Major Nicholls and left by him in possession of his negro allies, fugitive slaves from Georgia, destroyed by General Loomis by artillery fire from gunboats, 270 killed of the 300 negroes and 20 Indians in the fort

Sept. 4, Treaty of friendship and commerce with Sweden and Norway signed

Oct. 22, William H. Crawford, of Georgia, appointed Secretary of the Treasury

Oct., Champlain Canal begun in New York, opened in 1823

Nov. 4, First session of territorial legislature of Indiana met at Corydon

Nov. 12, Presidential election held. *See* 1817, Congress, Feb. 12

Nov. 16, Baltimore, Maryland, the first American city to be lighted by gas

Dec. 13, The Boston Provident Savings Institute incorporated, the first savings bank in the United States

Dec. 22 and 23, Treaty of peace and amity with Algiers signed

Dec. 25, American Colonization Society formed to settle free colored people in Africa

CONGRESS

Feb. 22, Act of Jan. 11, 1815, duty on gold, silver, and plated ware, etc., manufactured in the United States repealed

March 5, The direct tax reduced to $3,000,000

March 19, Compensation of members of Congress changed to $1,500 per annum with mileage, president of Senate and speaker of House each $3,000. This change from the "daily wage" voted in 1789 strongly disapproved as a change "from the simple habits of republicanism into the emoluments of power," and constituents, legislatures, grand juries, and public meetings joined in election of members of Congress who would repeal the law

April 9, Repeal of Act of Jan. 18, 1815 taxing household furniture, watches, etc.

April 10, Second National Bank established for 20 years with capital of $35,000,000 of which the Government to hold $7,000,000

April 19, Indiana authorized to form a State government

April 27, Tariff Act, the first avowedly protection measure, provided for duties of from 7.5 to 30% ad valorem on a large number of manufactured articles, textile industries granted a rate of 25% to 1819 and then 20%, coarse cotton cloths given a minimum valuation of 25 cents a yard, 45 cents a hundredweight placed on hammered iron, $1.50 on rolled iron, 3 cents a pound on sugar

April 29, Act excluded aliens from engaging in fur trade other than as employees by prohibiting trade with the Indians, licenses not granted

——, $1,000,000 a year for 8 years appropriated to build warships

April 30, Joint Resolution fixed Feb. 20, 1817 as date for resumption of specie payments by the Government, all taxes to be paid in legal currency of the United States

——, Congress adjourned

Dec. 2, Fourteenth Congress, 2d sess. convened

Dec. 11, Resolution admitted Indiana as a State

1817

Jan. 1, American Colonization Society organized at Washington to encourage the emancipation of slaves by providing a place outside the United States to which they might emigrate

——, Second Bank of the United States opened for business

March 4, Inauguration of President James Monroe and Vice-President Daniel D. Tompkins

March 5, John Quincy Adams, of Massachusetts, appointed Secretary of State, entered on duties Sept. 22, John Graham, chief clerk *ad interim* March 4, and Richard Rush, Attorney General, *ad interim* March 10 to Sept.

——, William H. Crawford, of Georgia, recommissioned Secretary of the Treasury

March 31, New York law prohibited slavery, to take effect in 1827

April, Jean Lafitte, pirate, occupied Galveston Island after departure of Louis de Aury to join expedition against Mexico, invading Texans led by General Javier Mina and Captain Perry

April 15, New York legislature authorized construction of the Erie Canal and created a Canal Board

April 28, Convention with Great Britain signed by which each agreed to limit war vessels on the Great Lakes to 1 vessel on Lake Ontario and Lake Champlain and 2 on the upper lakes

May 24, A. P. Chouteau and Jules de Mun and party taken prisoners by Spanish New Mexican authorities and their goods to about $30,000 confiscated. Claim settled by Mexico with the United States Government many years later

June 29, Gregor MacGregor, a British subject, demanded and received the surrender of the fort at Amelia Island from the Spanish Governor in the name of the independent South American Republics

July 4, Ground broken at Rome, New York, for the Erie Canal to unite the Atlantic with the Great Lakes; completed in 1825

July 8, Treaty with the Cherokees granted tract of land in Arkansas to United States, the United States agreed to give reservation of 640 acres to every head of Indian family resident on east side of Mississippi River who might wish to become citizen of the United States

Aug. 2, First steamboat to touch at St. Louis, the "Zebulon M. Pike"

Aug. 15, Constitution adopted by Mississippi by convention which met July 7; ratified at special session

Aug. 26, University of Michigan established in Detroit by Act of legislature

Sept. 24, Colgate University organized at meeting at Hamilton, New York, receiving charter 1819 and opened 1820

Oct. 4, In absence of MacGregor another South American adventurer, Louis Aubry, took possession of Amelia Island and declared it part of the Mexican Republic

Oct. 8, John C. Calhoun, of South Carolina, appointed Secretary of War, entering on duties Dec. 10

Nov. 13, William Wirt, of Virginia, appointed Attorney General

Nov. 14, Commission to decide ownership of islands in Passamaquoddy Bay reported a settlement

Nov. 20, Skirmish between Seminoles and soldiers sent by General Gaines from Fort Scott under authority of the War Dept. to expel hostile Indians from their village of Fowltown in ceded Creek district north of the Florida line

Nov. 24, Commission appointed under the 4th Article of the Treaty of Ghent awarded Moose Island, Dudley Island, and Frederick Island in Passamaquoddy Bay to the United States and all other islands in the Bay, and Grand Menan in Bay of Fundy to Great Britain

Nov. 30, Indians attacked boat on Appalachicola River, Florida, and killed all of 40 women and children except 6 men and one woman

Dec. 14, Founding of mission of San Rafael, in northern California

Dec. 23, Major Bankhead raised the American flag over Fort Fernandino and took possession of Amelia Island

Dec. 25, Expedition of Major Stephen H. Long and Major W. Bradford up the Arkansas River built Post Belle Point afterwards Fort Smith

——, Indians attacked Lieutenant Scott's boat ascending the Appalachicola with supplies for fort and massacred crew

Dec. 26, The President assigned General Jackson to command of troops to take action against the Seminole Indians

CONGRESS

Feb. 6, Compensation Act repealed

Feb. 12, Electoral vote counted gave James Monroe, of Virginia (Democratic-Republican), 183 votes out of 221 for president, Rufus King, of New York (Federalist), receiving 34 votes, and 4 not voting, and Daniel D. Tompkins (Democratic-Republican), 183 votes for vice-president

March 1, The western part of Mississippi Territory authorized to form a State government

March 3, The eastern part of Mississippi Territory made the Territory of Alabama

——, The Neutrality Act authorized collectors to seize and detain "any vessel manifestly built for warlike purposes" presumption of intent to violate the neutrality of the United States by cruising against the commerce of a friendly state

——, Importation of plaster of Paris prohibited from any country from which it could not be brought in vessels of the United States in retaliation for the plaster laws of Nova Scotia and New Brunswick

——, Bill to devote bonus and future dividends accruing to government from the National Bank to fund for internal improvements especially roads and canals vetoed by President Madison

——, Act granted 4 towns of Marengo county, Alabama, to French emigrants

——, Congress adjourned

Dec. 1, Fifteenth Congress, 1st sess. convened

Dec. 10, Resolution admitted Mississippi as a State

Dec. 23, The internal taxes repealed

1818

Jan. 6, General Jackson's "Rhea letter" to Monroe on which he based his authority for conquest of Florida

Jan. 19, First territorial legislature of Alabama met at St. Stephens

Feb. 13, Death of George Rogers Clark

March 9, General Jackson reached Fort Scott on the Appalachicola River

April 6, Generals Jackson and Gaines reached Fort Marks and demanded admittance from the Spanish Governor in order to garrison the fort with American troops until the end of the Indian war to prevent further breaches of neutrality

April 7, General Jackson seized Fort Marks and arrested Alexander Arbuthnot, Scotch trader, who had aided and incited the Indians against the United States

April 18, General Jackson marched troops 113 miles across flat and swampy wilderness to Suwanee, village of Chief Bolegs, which was deserted, warned by Arbuthnot of approach of Americans, Robert C. Ambrister from Arbuthnot's schooner captured with Indians and negroes

April 28, Proclamation of the President of arrangements of April 1817 as to naval force on Great Lakes

April 29, General Jackson ordered the execution of Arbuthnot and Ambrister, tried by court martial for inciting Indians against the United States

May 24, General Jackson in pursuit of Indians taking refuge in Spanish territory captured Pensacola and deposed the Spanish Governor who fled to Fort Barrancas and attempted to make resistance

May 28, "Walk in the Water," first steamer on Lake Erie launched at Black Rock, Capt. Job Fish made trip between Buffalo and Detroit

June 17, Protest of Spanish Minister, Don Onis, against seizure of Spanish territory by General Jackson

July 9, Spain ratified Convention of Aug. 1802

Aug. 9, Captain James Biddle, sent by President Monroe, formally proclaimed Astoria American territory

Aug. 26, Illinois in convention at Kaskaskia adopted Constitution, clause prohibiting slavery included

Aug. 26–Sept. 16, Constitutional Convention at Hartford adopted Constitution for Connecticut. *See infra* Oct. 5

Sept. 17, The Wyandots and other Ohio Indians ceded all their lands in Ohio, about 4,000,000 acres embracing the valley of the Maumee in accordance with treaty negotiated Sept. 27, 1817

Sept. 20, Patent leather first manufactured by Seth Boyden (Ann. Cyc.)

Oct. 2, Expedition of Thomas Nuttall from Philadelphia to Pittsburgh, and then down the Ohio and Mississippi rivers to White River and to the Arkansas River

Oct. 5, Connecticut adopted Constitution in place of royal charter; ratified by popular vote

Oct. 6, Astoria restored to the United States

Oct. 19, Treaty with the Chickasaw Indians by which they ceded land between the Mississippi and the northern course of the Tennessee River

Oct. 20, Treaty with Great Britain signed recognized the right of American citizens to fish along the coasts of Newfoundland and Labrador, and dry and cure fish in any unsettled bays and creeks, and the boundary between the United States and Canada established from the Lake of the Woods to the 49th parallel and westward to the Rocky Mts., the land west of the mountains to be held in joint occupation for 10 years. The Treaty of commerce of July 3, 1815 renewed for 10 years

Nov. 6–Feb. 4, 1819, Journey of Henry R. Schoolcraft with 2 companions in country of the Ozarks, Arkansas

Nov. 9, Smith Thompson, of New York, appointed

Secretary of the Navy, entering on duties Jan. 1, 1819

Nov. 20, Two pirate vessels commanded by Hippolyte de Bouchard, who had served in the Buenos Aires navy, entered harbor of Monterey and demanded surrender of city, sailed away Nov. 27 after sacking and burning Monterey

Nov. 28, Secretary Adams in Note to Spain reviewed conduct in violation of Treaty of 1795 by which both Spain and the United States were bound to keep peace along the frontier, and stated that the President would deliver Pensacola and St. Marks when Spain could guarantee an adequate force to hold the garrisons against the attacks of hostile Indians

——, Academy of Natural Sciences founded in Philadelphia

CONGRESS

Jan. 8, Feb. 2, March 16, and Dec. 18. Petitions from Missouri presented asking for admission as a State

Jan. 27, Compensation for members of Congress fixed at $8 per day with added sum for mileage, the president of the Senate and speaker of the House to receive an additional $8

March 18, Life pension of $20 per month for officers and $8 for privates granted to soldiers of the Revolution

March 25, Clay's motion to recognize South American republics defeated in House by vote of 115 to 45

April 4, The flag of the United States established as 13 horizontal stripes representing the original States in alternate red and white, and a white star in a blue field for each State in the Union

April 14, Office of Surgeon General created as head of Army Medical Dept.

April 18, Illinois authorized to adopt a State Constitution

——, Ports of the United States closed against British vessels from any British colonial port into which American vessels not admitted (West Indies)

April 20, Supplementary Tariff Act continued tariff on cotton (25%) and woolen goods for 8 years until 1826, and duty on bar iron and other articles specified raised for protection of manufactures

——, Penalties of the prohibition of 1807 extended to the fitting out of vessels for the slave trade or transportation of slaves

——, Congress adjourned

Nov. 16, Fifteenth Congress, 2d sess. convened

Dec. 3, Illinois admitted as a State (21st)

Dec. 18, Committee of 5 appointed by Senate to inquire into General Jackson's conduct in the summary execution of Arbuthnot and Ambrister and seizure of Spanish posts in Florida

1819

Jan. 22, Thomas Nuttall reached Arkansas Post, and Fort Smith April 24

Feb. 1, Decision of Supreme Court in case of Dartmouth College vs. Woodward that the charter of the college was a contract and the action of the State legislature in altering the charter without the consent of the trustees was an impairment of that contract

Feb. 22, Treaty with Spain signed, West Florida ceded to the United States and East Florida purchased for about $6,500,000, and the western boundary settled by an irregular line from the Gulf of Mexico to the

42d parallel, the Sabine River made the boundary between Louisiana and Texas; rejected by Spain

Feb. 27, Treaty by which the Cherokees ceded all territory north of Tennessee and of the lower course of the Hiwassee concluded

March 6, Decision of Supreme Court in case of McCulloch vs. Maryland declared that Congress had power under the Constitution to charter the Bank of the United States and that the bank had power to establish branches in the States without their consent, and the State might not tax the branches so established

April 23, The *Missouri Intelligencer and Boon's Lick Advertiser* began publication

May 13, Treaty with the Indians signed at St. Louis reaffirmed Treaty of 1804

May 26, The "Savannah," the first steamboat to cross the Atlantic left Savannah, Georgia, for Liverpool, making the trip in 25 days and using steam 18 days

May 30, Major Stephen H. Long left Pittsburgh for St. Louis sent to explore the country between the Mississippi and the Rocky Mts. and left St. Louis June 21 and established winter camp near present site of Omaha

June, James Long with armed force captured Nacodochez, organized a government and declared Texas a republic, B. Gutierrez of the Magee-Gutierrez filibustering expedition of 1812–13 a member of this expedition. Spanish troops captured the post during the absence of Long

June 19 and Feb. 25, 1820, Acts of Massachusetts legislature consented to erection of the District of Maine as a State

July 4, Territorial Government for Arkansas established at Arkansas Post

Aug. 2, Constitutional Convention at Huntsville adopted Constitution for Alabama

Aug. 14, Lieutenant Colonel Henry Leavenworth established post near mouth of the Minnesota River

Sept. 24, Treaty with Chippewas signed

Oct. 19, First General Assembly of State met at Huntsville, Alabama

Oct. 29, Convention at Portland adopted a Constitution for Maine, ratified by the people in town meetings Dec. 6, 1819.

Nov. 9, William Bill inaugurated as first Governor of Alabama

Dec. 26, The Governor, James Miller, arrived at Arkansas Post, Arkansas

CONGRESS

Jan. 12, Report presented in House condemned General Jackson for execution of Arbuthnot and Ambrister and seizure of Spanish posts in Florida

Jan. 18–Feb. 8, Henry Clay led the debate in House against General Jackson, 33 speeches made of which 20 were against proposed resolution of censure

Feb. 12, Benjamin Dearborn, of Boston, applied to Congress for aid to test utility of his invention of engine for railroad

Feb. 13, Bill to enable the people of Missouri to frame a State Constitution amended by James Tallmadge to provide that the further introduction of slaves into Missouri be forbidden, and that all children born after the admission of Missouri should be free, adopted by the House Feb. 16, adopted by Senate Feb. 27 with the anti-slavery clause struck out, adherence of House 78 to 76 and Bill lost March 2

Feb. 24, Adverse report of Senate Committee on conduct of General Jackson, no action taken

March 2, First statute relating to immigrants made regulations for passenger ships requiring a statement of their number brought on each ship

——, Alabama authorized to form a State government

——, Arkansas organized as a Territory. An amendment moved by J. W. Taylor prohibiting the further introduction of slavery Feb. 17 defeated

March 3, The President authorized to restore to their own country any Africans illegally imported and seized within the United States, and a premium of $50 granted to informers

——, Act to protect the commerce of the United States and punish the crime of piracy

——, Joint Resolution for naming public vessels, ships-of-the-line, after States, frigates after rivers, and sloops-of-war after cities

——, The President authorized to take possession of East and West Florida and establish a temporary government

——, Congress adjourned

Dec. 6, Sixteenth Congress, 1st sess. convened, meeting in new Capitol building

Dec. 8, Memorial presented from the people of Maine asking admission as a State

Dec. 14, Joint Resolution admitted Alabama (22d State)

1820

Feb. 6, The "Mayflower of Liberia" sailed from New York with 86 negroes arriving at Sierra Leone March 9, to settle colonists in Africa

Feb. 25, Cession of Maine by General Court of Massachusetts, separate and independent State provided for with consent of Congress

May 15, New charter granted to Washington, D.C. provided that mayor should be elected by the people

June 6, Major S. H. Long started up the Platte River by way of South Fork and July 5 camped at site of present Denver, Colorado, reached base of Rocky Mts. and rediscovered Pike's Peak, Dr. E. James making first ascent

June 10, First steamboat line between New York and New Orleans established

July 2–25, Expedition of Captain Matthew J. Magee and Captain Stephen W. Kearney explored unknown country between Camp Missouri and Cold Water in northwest Iowa and southeast Minnesota

July 5, Expedition of Governor Cass from Detroit entered the St. Louis River from the lakes, and July 15 reached Sandy Lake and July 21 reached true source of the Mississippi and named Lake Cass

July 14, First steamboat on Lake Michigan at Green Bay

July 19, One party of the S. H. Long expedition led by Captain John Bell descended the Arkansas River to the Mississippi, arriving at Fort Smith, Sept. 9, Major Long descended the Canadian River, arriving at Fort Smith, Sept. 13. Major Long represented the country on map as desert between the 39th and 49th parallels

——, Constitution for Missouri adopted by convention which met June 12 at St. Louis, and ratified by the people at ensuing election. Article 3, section 26 required the legislature "to pass such laws as may be necessary" to prevent free negroes and mulattoes from settlement in the State

Aug. 28, Missouri State legislature, State officials and representative in Congress elected, and Alexander McNair for Governor and William H. Ashley, Lieutenant Governor

Sept. 10, Corner-stone of Fort Snelling in Minnesota laid

Sept. 19, General Assembly of Missouri met in St. Louis and organized a State Government

Sept. 26, Death of Daniel Boone (85) at home of his son in St. Charles county, Missouri

Oct. 2, Missouri elected Thomas H. Benton and David Barton to United States Senate

Oct. 18, Treaty with the Choctaws made first assignment of land in Oklahoma

Nov. 14, Presidential election held. *See infra* Congress, 1821, Feb. 14

Nov. 15, First nine articles of Constitution of Massachusetts submitted to convention as revised; ratified and adopted April 9, 1821

Dec. 18, State University at Tuscaloosa, Alabama, chartered by legislature

Dec. 23, Moses Austin arrived at San Antonio and proposed to Spanish Governor project for settlement of American colony in Texas

Fourth census gave a population of 9,638,191; the white race, 7,861,931; free negroes, 233,504; slaves, 1,538,125

CONGRESS

Jan. 3, Bill for admission of Maine passed the House. In the Senate an amendment proposed that the Maine and Missouri Bills be combined in order to keep the balance of free and slave States. Reported from committee in this form Jan. 6

Jan. 17, Senator Roberts proposed to add to Missouri Bill a prohibition of slavery; voted down Feb. 1

Jan. 18 and Feb. 3, Senator Thomas proposed that no restriction be imposed on Missouri as to slavery but as a compromise an east and west line be drawn across the Louisiana cession at 36° 30', north of which slavery should be prohibited, adopted in final form Feb. 17

Feb. 18, The Senate voted to admit Maine as a State provided that Missouri was admitted at the same time as a slave State, and slavery prohibited in certain territories

Feb. 23 and 28, The House rejected Senate Bill for admission of Maine with Missouri

Feb. 26, Amendment in House to same effect as Thomas amendment in Senate defeated

Feb. 29, Missouri Bill with clause prohibiting the further introduction of slaves adopted in House

March 2, The Senate returned the Missouri Bill to the House with the prohibition of slavery clause struck out, and Thomas's territorial proviso inserted, and this compromise Bill passed by House. The introduction of slaves into the Louisiana cession prohibited north of the Arkansas boundary, 36° 30' except in Missouri

March 3, Missouri Compromise Bill became law, Missouri admitted conditionally, the State never to pass any law preventing admission of any citizens of any of States of the Union

——, Maine admitted (23d State) to take effect March 15

March 6, Act authorized the people of Missouri to form a State Constitution

April 24, Public land Act permitted sales as small as

80 acres, and fixed a minimum price of $1.25 an acre, prohibiting sale of land on credit

May 3, First standing committee on agriculture appointed

May 5, Foreign slave trade declared to be piracy

May 10, Henry Clay in House advocated recognition of independence of Spanish-American Republics

May 12, Uniform mode of discipline and field exercise for the militia established

May 15, A loan of $3,000,000 authorized to meet deficiency of revenue reported by Treasury

——, Four year tenure Act limited term of certain officers unless previously removed

——, Ports within which foreign armed vessels allowed designated, and new tonnage duty imposed on French vessels

——, Congress adjourned

Nov. 13, Sixteenth Congress, 2d sess. convened

Nov. 14, Constitution drawn up by Missouri Convention presented to Senate, and to House Nov. 16

Dec. 12, Resolution to admit Missouri as a State passed the Senate with proviso moved by Mr. Eaton disclaiming assent to any clause which contravened the constitutional rights of citizens of each State

Dec. 13, Senate Resolution as to admission of Missouri tabled by the House, and Lowndes measure for the admission of Missouri rejected on the ground that the measures against free negroes was a violation of that clause of the Constitution which provided that "the citizens of each State shall be entitled to all the privileges and immunities of citizens of the several States"

Dec. 20, Floyd, of Virginia, in House moved to appoint a committee "to inquire into the situation of the settlements on the Pacific Ocean and the expediency of occupying the Columbia River"

1821

Jan. 6, Constitution for Missouri ratified by the people

Jan. 17, Grant of land to Moses Austin for American settlement in Texas, and certified by letter of Spanish Governor Martinez Feb. 8

Feb. 9, Columbia College, Washington, D.C. chartered, made a university March 3, 1873, and name changed to Columbian University, and became George Washington University Jan. 23, 1904

March 3, General Jackson appointed Governor of East and West Florida and commissioned to receive the territory from the Spanish

March 5, Inauguration of President Monroe and Vice-President Tompkins

April 30, College of Detroit became the University of Michigan

May 10, Thomas James and John McKnight, traders from St. Louis, started down the Mississippi on expedition to Santa Fé, New Mexico, prohibited Spanish territory

June 10, Death of Moses Austin in Missouri. His colonization plan for Texas carried on by his son, Stephen

June 26, Legislature of Missouri accepted conditions imposed by Congress by the "Missouri Congress" for admission as a State

July 10, American troops received possession of the Spanish fort at St. Augustine

Aug. 4, General Jackson received cession of East Florida

Aug. 10, Proclamation of the President declared Missouri admitted as a State (the 24th)

Aug. 12, Stephen Austin arrived at Bexar, Texas, to take possession of land granted to his father

Aug. 28–Nov. 10, Constitutional Convention at Albany, New York, framed Constitution

Sept. 1–Nov., First expedition of Captain William Beckneil opening Santa Fé trail from Boone's Lick, Missouri to the Rio Grande

Sept. 4, Russia issued decree claiming for the Russian American Fur Company the entire Pacific coast of America north of the 51st parallel of latitude, and forbade vessels of all other nations to approach within 100 Italian miles of the coast

Sept. 18, Exercises of inauguration of Amherst College, Amherst, Massachusetts, and opened to students Sept. 19

Oct. 4, James Long captured La Bahia, Texas, on filibustering expedition

Nov. 10, Constitution adopted in New York State

Dec. 15, Permanent location purchased at Cape Mesurado, Liberia, for colonization by free negroes

Dec. 17, First party of settlers with Stephen Austin left Nacogdoches for lower Brazos in Texas

CONGRESS

Jan. 4, Mr. Archer, of Virginia, offered resolution in House asking that the Committee on the Judiciary be instructed to inquire into the legal relations of Missouri to the United States; tabled

Jan. 24, Resolution of Mr. Eustis, of Massachusetts, that Missouri be declared admitted on condition that the objectional clause in her Constitution as to the immigration and settlement of free negroes and mulattoes be expunged defeated in House

Jan. 25, Report of Committee to House set forth basis of American rights of sovereignty on northwest coast

Feb. 2, The Senate Resolution as to admission of Missouri referred on motion of Mr. Clay to a committee of 13 in the House

Feb. 12 and 13, The House voted to reject the report of the Committee of Thirteen presented Feb. 10 which recommended amendments similar to those afterwards agreed upon

Feb. 14, Electoral vote counted, and including the disputed vote of Missouri Monroe received 231 votes for president, unanimous except for 1 vote for John Quincy Adams, and Tompkins was reëlected vice-president with 218 votes, no opposition ticket

Feb. 21, The House voted down a resolution to repeal Act authorizing Missouri to form a State government

Feb. 22, Henry Clay proposed a joint conference committee to consider and report on the advisability of admitting Missouri

Feb. 23, Joint Committee of 23 representatives and 7 senators appointed to consider admission of Missouri

Feb. 25, John Quincy Adams in note to Russian Government protested claims of territory on Pacific coast of Sept. 4, 1821

Feb. 26, Recommendations of the Committee in form of a resolution agreed to by the House, and Feb. 28 by the Senate

March 2, Resolution approved to admit Missouri as the 24th State on condition that nothing in the State Constitution should ever be construed as denying to a citizen of any State any of the privileges and immunities to which he might be entitled under the Constitution of the United States, and that Missouri must give assent to this

——, Military establishment reduced

March 3, The President authorized to borrow $5,000,000

——, Congress adjourned

Dec. 3, Seventeenth Congress, 1st sess. convened

1822

April 11, Spanish rule in Alta, California ended as citizens at Monterey took oath to support the new Mexican Government

April 13, Commissioners on Northeast boundary in final session filed dissenting opinions, and made separate reports to their respective governments

April 15, Expedition of William Henry Ashley and Major Andrew Henry left St. Louis to trade in the Indian country, wintered at mouth of the Yellowstone

April 29, Stephen Austin arrived at Mexico to obtain confirmation of his land grant in Texas from the Congress and remained there a year during period of rise and downfall of Iturbide

June 1, James and McKnight, traders, left New Mexico, reaching St. Louis in July after this unsuccessful financial venture

June 18, Report of American Commission filed on northeast boundary east of the passage from Lake Huron into Lake Superior to northwest corner of Lake of the Woods

June 19, Formal recognition of Republic of Colombia, South America

June 24, Convention of navigation and commerce with France signed

July 5, Jacob Fowler, trader, arrived at Missouri River near present Sibley, ascended the Arkansas and explored head waters of Rio Grande

July 12, Treaty of indemnification signed with Great Britain under award of the Emperor of Russia

July 20, Resolution of legislature of Tennessee proposed Andrew Jackson for President

Sept. 3, Treaty with Sac and Fox tribes signed at St. Louis confirmed that of 1804 in which the Indians received right to hunt and live on land ceded while it remained in possession of the Federal Government

Sept. 26, Agustin Fernandez de San Vicente, representing the Mexican Emperor Iturbide arrived at Monterey and California proclaimed province of independent Mexico, and new local government established

Nov. 10, New Mexico declared one of the 5 internal provinces of Mexico subject to military commander at Chihuahua

Nov. 18, Henry Clay nominated for President by the Kentucky legislature

Nov. 20, Strike of journeymen hatters, New York City

Dec. 1, James and McKnight, first traders over the Santa Fé trail reached Santa Fé

Dec. 12, Recognition of Mexico by the United States by presentation by Secretary Adams to the President of José Manuel Zozaya, Minister from Mexico

CONGRESS

Jan. 18, Name Oregon first used in Bill introduced in Congress by John Floyd

March 8, President Monroe in message to Congress proposed recognition of the "independent nations on the American continent,' the Spanish-American republics

March 28, Resolution to recognize the independence of the South American republics passed the House with one dissenting vote

March 30, Territorial government provided for Florida

——, Illinois authorized to construct canal and given right of way through public lands

May 4, Act made provision for diplomatic missions to the "independent nations of the American continent" thus giving recognition, and appropriated $100,000 for expenses

——, Bill appropriating $9,000 to preserve and repair the Cumberland Road vetoed by President Monroe who submitted a paper stating his objections to national appropriations for internal improvements

May 6, Trading houses for Indians abolished and the President authorized to appoint a Superintendent of Indian Affairs to be resident at St. Louis

May 8, Congress adjourned

Dec. 2, Seventeenth Congress, 2d sess. convened

Dec. 17, Speech of John Floyd in the House an argument for occupation of the Columbia River region in the northwest

1823

Jan. 27, Heman Allen, of Vermont, appointed first American Minister to Chile, and Cæsar A. Rodney to United Provinces of La Plata (Argentina)

Jan. 28, James Smith Wilcocks appointed first American consul at Mexico City

Feb. 18, Decree of Emperor Iturbide confirmed by Congress April 10 confirmed grant of land on the Rio Brazos in Texas to Stephen F. Austin, who left Mexico City April 28

March 10, Expedition of W. H. Ashley started up Missouri River, reaching Arika Indian villages May 31, forced by Indians to retire down the river

March 31, Charter granted to John Stevens for railroad between Philadelphia and Columbia, Pennsylvania

April 23, The Delaware and Hudson Canal Company incorporated in Pennsylvania and New York

April, Major Stephen H. Long and William H. Keating left Philadelphia on government expedition to northern boundary, traveling overland to the Mississippi and then up the Minnesota River

May 22, Trinity College, Hartford, Connecticut, founded as Washington College, name changed to Trinity in 1845

June 2, Party of W. H. Ashley of 35 men, fur traders, attacked by Arickara Indians and 13 killed and 10 wounded

June 26, John McLean, of Ohio, commissioned Postmaster General to take effect July 1

July 2, Long expedition reached Mendota and on the 9th began exploration of the Minnesota River valley, July 22 at Big Stone Lake, Aug. 5 at Pembina and there Aug. 8 raised American flag on territory within boundary of the United States occupied by the British

July 17, John Quincy Adams, Secretary of State, declared to the Russian Minister at Washington, that "we should contest the right of Russia to any territorial establishment on this continent, and that we should assume distinctly the principle that the American continents are no longer subjects for any new European colonial establishments"

Aug. 9, W. H. Ashley returned with force to attack villages of Arickara (Arika) Indians and found villages evacuated, and no result gained except enmity of Indians which closed the fur route for many years

Aug. 10–12, Colonel Leavenworth with force from post at Council Bluffs defeated the Arickara Indians

Aug. 18, Colonization law of Mexican Republic regulated immigration to Texas (*see* map of grants in Texas in McMaster, vol. 5, p. 12)

Aug. 20, British Minister of Foreign Affairs, George Canning, proposed to Benjamin Rush, American Minister, that the United States and Great Britain make joint declaration that they would not remain indifferent to an intervention by the Powers of the Holy Alliance to restore Spanish authority over her American colonies in revolt. Reply of Mr. Rush Aug. 27 stated that it would facilitate a joint statement if Great Britain would recognize the independence of the South American States

Sept. 16, Samuel L. Southard, of New Jersey, appointed Secretary of the Navy

Sept. 18, Territory assigned for reservation for Florida Indians who agreed to remove within certain limits

Sept. 21, Joseph Smith, founder of Mormon Church, claimed to have had vision which disclosed to him hiding place of plates of gold on which the Book of Mormon written

CONGRESS

Jan. 27, Senate confirmed appointments of Ministers to Colombia, La Plata, and Chile

Feb. 28, First grant of public land to aid public improvement made for construction of a wagon road in Ohio

March 1, "Auction system" by which foreign goods shipped to the United States undervalued in invoice and sold remedied by deterrent legislation

March 3, Act establishing territorial government of Florida amended

——, Congress adjourned

Dec. 1, Eighteenth Congress, 1st sess. convened

Dec. 2, President Monroe in his message made formal and official statement of the policy since known as the "Monroe Doctrine" that "the American continents, by the free and independent condition which they have assumed and maintained, are henceforth not to be considered as subjects for future colonization by any European Powers." Against intervention he said, "With the governments who have declared their independence and maintained it . . . we could not view any interposition for the purpose of oppressing them, or controlling in any other manner their destiny, by any European Power, in any other light than as a manifestation of an unfriendly disposition toward the United States"

1824

Jan. 24, Chesapeake and Ohio Canal Company incorporated in Virginia

Feb. 14, Congressional caucus nominated William H. Crawford for President

Feb. 15, Meeting at Faneuil Hall, Boston, nominated John Quincy Adams for President

Feb. 24, Treaty of amity, commerce, and navigation with Tunis amended Treaty of 1797–1799

Feb., Indian revolt in California

March 4, Senator Ninian Edwards, of Illinois, commissioned as Minister to Mexico, the first, but he resigned under pressure from the President June 22 before leaving, and Joel R. Poinsett, of South Carolina, appointed in July, and whose credentials were finally issued in March, 1825

——, Convention at Harrisburg, Pennsylvania, nominated Andrew Jackson for President

March 11, Secretary of War, Calhoun, created a Bureau of Indian Affairs

March 13, Convention with Great Britain signed denouncing the slave trade as piracy, not ratified

March 19–20, General William H. Ashley, Jedediah Smith, and Fitzpatrick of the Rocky Mountain Fur Company ascended the Platte to the Sweetwater and discovered the South Pass to Oregon. Some of Robert Stuart's party going east from Astoria said to have used this pass in Nov., 1812

March 20, Franklin Institute, Philadelphia, incorporated

April 17, Treaty with Russia signed fixed southern boundary of Russian possessions in America at 54° 40′ N. Lat., and agreement made that citizens of the United States should not make settlements north of this line

April 20, Colonel Arbuckle began building Fort Gibson on east bank of the Neosho, 3 miles from its mouth

May 4, Death of General Rufus Putnam at Marietta, Ohio

May 7, Mexican law made Texas and Coahuila a State

May 26, José S. Rebello received by the President, constituting recognition of Brazil

May 31, George Canning, British Foreign Secretary, wrote famous dispatch to the British commissioners declaring British policy respecting Oregon

May, State Seminary, chartered in 1820 opened, which later became Indiana University

July 6, New Mexico made a Territory of Mexican Republic

Aug. 15, Lafayette and his son arrived in New York from France

Oct. 3, Treaty of peace, amity, and commerce with Colombia signed

Nov. 3–Sept. 19, 1825, William H. Ashley left Fort Atkinson near present Omaha on a fur trading expedition, crossed the Rocky Mts. and explored part of Great Basin

Nov. 9, Presidential election

Dec. 29, Gambier College, Gambier, Ohio, chartered

Dec. 31, Morris and Essex Canal from Delaware River opposite Eaton incorporated

CONGRESS

Jan. 9, Mr. Todd, of Pennsylvania, chairman of the Committee on Manufactures, presented Bill which provided for an increase in duties on woolens, irons, glass, lead, and coal for protection, and on silks, linens, and cutlery for revenue

Jan. 26, Resolution introduced in House by Daniel Webster proposing appointment of an agent or commissioner to Greece defeated in spite of the support of Henry Clay and others

Jan. 29, Ship voted to bring the Marquis de Lafayette to the United States by House and Senate Feb. 4; declined by Lafayette

April 17, Ninian Edwards preferred charges in House against W. H. Crawford who had been nominated for President by a group of Democratic-Republicans (The "A.B." plot) after appearance in early part of year of letters signed A.B. in Washington newspaper written by Edwards charging Crawford with malfeasance in office as Secretary of the Treasury; charges not sustained

April 30, The President authorized to cause surveys, plans, and estimates to be made for roads, and canals of national importance in a commercial or military way or necessary for the transportation of mail, and $30,000 appropriated; repealed in 1838

May 22, Tariff Act preserved the high tariff of 1816 on cotton goods, and increased the duties on iron and lead and on agricultural raw products like wool and hemp, 37% the average rate

May 25, Report of House Committee exonerated W. H. Crawford of all charges

May 27, Congress adjourned

Dec. 6, Eighteenth Congress, 2d sess. convened

Dec. 10, The Marquis de Lafayette welcomed in the House by address of the speaker, Henry Clay

Dec. 22–23, Congress in both House and Senate voted Lafayette $200,000 and a township to be located in any of the unappropriated public lands, in consideration of his services in the war of the Revolution

Dec. 23, Floyd's Bill for occupation of the Columbia River valley passed in House but failed in Senate

1825

Jan. 8, Henry Clay advised his friends to vote for Adams for President

Jan. 31, Chesapeake and Ohio Canal Company incorporated in Maryland

Feb. 8, Geneva Academy, Geneva, New York chartered, later Hobart College

Feb. 12, Treaty with the Creek Indians signed at "Indian Springs," signed by President Adams March 7, which provided for the cession of all Creek territory in Georgia and Alabama, in exchange for tract between Arkansas and Canadian rivers. The Indians rejected this treaty, killed McIntosh, the chief who signed it, and sent delegates to Washington to protest the treaty

Feb. 21, Charter granted to Amherst College

Feb. 28, Treaty between Russia and Great Britain as to Alaska defined boundaries

March 4, Inauguration of President John Quincy Adams and Vice-President John C. Calhoun

March 7, Henry Clay, of Kentucky, appointed Secretary of State, Richard Rush, of Pennsylvania, Secretary of the Treasury, and James Barbour, of Virginia, Secretary of War

March 8, Appointment of Joel R. Poinsett, Minister to Mexico, presented credentials June 1

March 24, Colonization law of Coahuila and Texas invited immigration and required immigrants to present certificate of character

March 25, University of Virginia opened

March 26, Republic of Mexico proclaimed at Monterey and federal document creating Upper (Alta) and Lower (Baja) California Territories read

March 27, Citizens and troops took oath of allegiance at Monterey to the Constitution of the Republic of Mexico

March 29, Death of Return Jonathan Meigs at Marietta, Ohio

April 11, Commission appointed for a canal between Pittsburgh and Philadelphia by the legislature of Pennsylvania

April 15, Grant of land in Texas from Government of Coahuila and Texas, including Nacogdoches, to Hayden Edwards for colony

May 16, The Potomac Company incorporated in the Chesapeake and Ohio Canal Company

June 17–Sept. 11, Major George C. Sibley, appointed by Congress, made survey from Fort Osage on the Missouri to the Arkansas for wagon road

June 17, Lafayette laid corner-stone of Bunker Hill

monument in Charlestown, the oration delivered by Daniel Webster at the ceremony

July 4, Work begun on the Ohio canal, opened between Portsmouth and Cleveland in 1832

July 21, Miami canal begun between Cincinnati and Dayton, Ohio. Fleet of boats reached Cincinnati March 16, 1828

Aug. 19, Treaty between the Dakotas and Ojibways arranged by the United States established boundaries of the 2 nations

Aug. 27, Ashley and Smith began return journey from the Yellowstone, arriving in St. Louis Oct. 8 with $75,000 worth of furs

Sept. 7, Lafayette left Washington after tour in which he visited every State in the Union, the frigate "Brandywine" waiting at the mouth of the Potomac to give him convoy to France

Oct. 26, Erie canal opened. A flotilla of canal boats headed by the "Seneca Chief" in which Governor Clinton and other dignitaries were passengers moved along the canal, reaching Albany Nov. 2 and New York City Nov. 4 by steam tow. The canal was 40 feet wide, 4 feet deep, 363 miles long. A ton of flour which it had cost $100 to send from Buffalo to Albany overland might now be sent for $10

Oct., José Maria de Echeandia, first civil governor and military commander appointed by Republic of Mexico arrived in California. He made San Diego his capital instead of Monterey

Nov. 7, Treaty with the Shawnees gave them a tract of land 50 miles square west of Missouri line and within purchase made from the Osage Indians June 2, 1825

Dec. 5, Treaty of peace, amity, commerce, and navigation with Central America

Dec. 28, Death of General James Wilkinson

CONGRESS

Feb. 9, The electoral count for president gave Andrew Jackson 99 votes; John Quincy Adams, 84; William H. Crawford, 41; and Henry Clay, 37; and as no one person had received a majority it remained for the House of Representatives to elect one from the three who received the largest number of votes which resulted in the election of J. Q. Adams by 87 votes, Jackson receiving 71, and Crawford 54. John C. Calhoun, of South Carolina, received 182 electoral votes for vice-president

March 3, $150,000 appropriated for extension of the Cumberland road from Canton, Ohio, to Zanesville

——, Act provided for survey of a road from the Missouri River to the Mexican boundary on the Arkansas River

——, Act by which $300,000 subscribed to the stock of the Chesapeake and Ohio canal

——, Congress adjourned

Dec. 5, Nineteenth Congress, 1st sess. convened. The followers of Adams constituted the National-Republicans and those of Jackson, the Democratic-Republicans

Dec. 6, President Adams in message announced receipt and acceptance of invitation to send delegates to a Pan-American Congress at Panama, and Dec. 26, 2 envoys and a secretary nominated by the President to attend, Richard C. Anderson, John Sergeant, and W. B. Rochester, secretary

Dec. 15, Resolution in House instructed its committee on roads and canals to inquire into the utility of railroads

1826

Jan. 3, Society of the War of 1812 founded in New York City

Jan. 24, New Treaty with the Creeks replaced Indian Springs Treaty of Feb. 12 and March 7, 1825, ceding an immense area to the United States but far less than the earlier treaty

Feb. 1, First charter granted to Western Reserve College in Hudson, Ohio

Feb. 25, Act of Pennsylvania legislature committed the State to building of a canal from Hollidaysburg to Pittsburgh on the Ohio, and from the Ohio to Johnstown

March 4, Charter granted for railroad from Quincy to the Neponset River in Massachusetts

March 9, Lafayette College, Easton, Pennsylvania, chartered

March 20, Little Schuylkill Navigation Railroad Company chartered to build a railroad from the river to Reading, Pennsylvania. Transferred to the Reading Railroad March 31, 1837

April 7, Columbia, Lancaster, and Philadelphia Railroad chartered

April 17, New York granted charter to the Mohawk and Hudson Railroad Company, later the New York Central

April 26, Treaty of friendship, commerce, and navigation with Denmark signed

July 4, Death of John Adams and of Thomas Jefferson

——, Pennsylvania canal begun at Columbia on the Susquehanna River

July 10, Treaty of commerce with Mexico signed but never ratified by Mexico

July 27, British Order in Council closed West Indian ports to American vessels after Dec. 1

Aug. 22, Jedediah Smith, of the Rocky Mountain Fur Company, left Ogden, Utah, with party on first overland expedition to California, reaching the Pacific at San Diego where he was arrested by Spaniards

Sept. 11, Arrest and imprisonment of William Morgan in Batavia, New York, on petty charge

Sept. 12, Abduction and alleged murder of William Morgan because he had written a book purporting to reveal the secrets of free-masonry. This led to formation of an Anti-Mason party in New York pledged to oppose the election of any Free Masons to public office

Oct. 7, Tramway railroad, first with metal tracks, opened from the granite quarries at Quincy to the Neponset River to carry stone for Bunker Hill monument, cars drawn by horses

Nov. 13, Convention with Great Britain signed regarding indemnity for slaves under Treaty of July 12, 1822, award of Emperor of Russia provided for payment of $1,204,960

Nov. 27, Jedediah Smith with party of 15 arrived at San Gabriel mission, California, from near Great Salt Lake overland across the Sierre Madre range at Cajon Pass "to open the unknown country of the farthest southwest," the first white men to cross the desert

Dec. 16, Benjamin Edwards proclaimed Nacogdoches an independent republic, Fredonia, after grant of Texas land to H. Edwards had been annulled by Mexico

CONGRESS

Jan. 16, Senate Committee reported adversely on nomination of delegates to the Congress at Panama, but nominees confirmed March 14

March 3, Act provided for survey of route for canal between the Atlantic and the Gulf of Mexico, the "Florida Canal"

——, In Senate during debate on Panama Congress John Randolph referred to the coalition of Adams and Clay as "Puritan and black-leg" in reference to the alleged "corrupt bargain" by which Adams was supposed to have promised Clay the post of Secretary of State in return for his election in the House, and also to the fact that Clay played for high stakes, which caused Clay and Randolph to fight a duel April 8

March 25, Appropriation for expenses of delegates to Panama Congress voted by House, but the delay caused the delegates to arrive after the Congress had adjourned, a failure because of non-participation of the United States

May 18, Subscription for 600 shares of stock in Dismal Swamp canal authorized

Dec. 4, Nineteenth Congress, 2d sess. convened

Dec. 20, Van Buren introduced a Resolution in House denying the right of Congress to construct roads and canals within the States

1827

Jan. 11, Alabama and Tennessee Canal Company incorporated

Jan. 13, Muscle Shoals Canal Company incorporated by Alabama legislature

——, Resolution against the tariff and for abrogation of Indian Springs Treaty with the Indians passed by Alabama legislature

Jan. 18, Jedediah Smith, ordered by Spanish Governor to leave California, set out by San Joaquin valley

Jan., Lehigh Coal and Navigation Company in Pennsylvania began the Mauch Chunk and Summit Hill Railroad from the Lehigh Canal to their coal mines, 9 miles, opened in May, cars descending by force of gravity

Feb. 11, Death of Governor De Witt Clinton, of New York, at Albany

Feb. 17, Governor Troup called out the militia of Georgia to resist United States troops sent to prevent the survey of Indian lands surrendered by the Treaty of 1826, before the transfer completed

Feb. 19, Note of Secretary Clay to Mexico disavowed any sympathy with the Fredonia colonists in Texas

Feb. 28, Baltimore and Ohio Railroad chartered in Maryland, and in Virginia, March 8

——, Chesapeake and Ohio Canal again chartered by legislature of Maryland, confirmed by Virginia March 8, and by Pennsylvania Feb. 22, 1828

March 11, Coahuila and Texas united as one state by Mexico, and constitution proclaimed

March 15, President Adams instructed Poinsett to offer $1,000,000 for boundary line with Mexico to run from mouth of the Rio Grande and by the 42d parallel to the Pacific, substituting the Rio Grande and its tributary, the Rio Puerco, for the Sabine, and $500,000 for line from mouth of Colorado River, substituting that river for the Sabine

May 20, Jedediah S. Smith left his men in camp on Merced River while he with 2 companions began ascent of the Sierra Nevadas (May 27) which took 8 days, the first white men to cross the mountains, and through Nevada to Salt Lake rendezvous with his fur partners which he reached about June 17

June 19, Vera Cruz legislature attacked Poinsett as a

"hypocritical foreign minister" unfriendly to Mexico because of his political activities in establishing York lodges of Masons

July 2, Meeting at Columbia, South Carolina, at which Dr. Thomas Cooper presented resolutions which denied the right of Congress to levy taxes for the purpose of protection

July 4, Slavery abolished in New York from this date under law of March 1817

——, Treaty of navigation, commerce, and regulation of consular powers with Sweden and Norway signed

July 13, Jedediah Smith with party started again for California, attacked by Indians, and the survivors who reached California imprisoned by Spanish authorities. Smith released on promise to leave the country

July 30, National Convention met at Harrisburg called by the Pennsylvania Society for the promotion of manufactures, and adopted memorial to Congress urging further duties on wool and woolens, hammered bar iron and steel, flax, hemp, and their products, and on plain and printed cotton goods

Aug. 6, Great Britain and the United States agreed to continue the joint occupation of Oregon

Aug. 14, Strike of journeymen tailors in Philadelphia

Sept. 16, Manufacture of fire brick begun at Baltimore, Maryland

Sept. 22, J. O. Pattie and father, fur traders, left Santa Fé and proceeded down the Gila and Colorado rivers into Lower and Upper California and were imprisoned by Spanish at San Diego, the father died and the son succeeded in reaching the Russian settlement near Bodega Bay

Sept. 29, Convention with Great Britain referred settlement of northeast boundary to arbitration, the King of the Netherlands chosen as arbiter

Oct. 10, Joseph Henry read a paper before the Albany Institute "On some modifications of the electro-magnetic apparatus"

Nov. 15, The Creeks by treaty ceded all lands in Georgia not included in the Treaty of 1826

——, First lithographic establishment completed in Boston

Dec. 19, South Carolina legislature denounced tariff as encroaching on rights of States

Dec. 20, Treaty of friendship, commerce, and navigation signed with the Hanseatic cities, Bremen, Hamburg, and Lübeck

Dec. 24, Commission under Article 6 of the Treaty of Ghent agreed on boundary through the St. Lawrence River and Lakes Ontario, Erie, and Huron

——, Senate of Georgia passed resolution against the tariff

Fort Leavenworth, Kansas, established as a cantonment, became a fort in 1832, named for colonel of regiment

First general strike begun by carpenters in Philadelphia for the 10-hour day, joined by brick layers, painters, glaziers, and other trades, unsuccessful

First successful silk mill established at Gurleyville, Connecticut, by the Mansfield Silk Company

CONGRESS

Jan. 10, Mr. Mallary, of Vermont, introduced tariff Bill which placed the valuation of coarse woolens at the custom house so high that importation practically prohibited; defeated in Senate

March 2, Land granted in Indiana and Illinois for canals

March 2–3, Senate and House voted resolutions sustaining Georgia's claim to all lands within the limits of the State, declaring the Indians of Georgia tenants at will

March 3, Congress adjourned

Dec. 3, Twentieth Congress, 1st sess. convened

Dec. 24, Memorial of Harrisburg Convention and petitions from State legislatures, chambers of commerce, and from citizens presented, of which 25 asked an increase of duties and 32 opposed an increase

1828

Jan. 12, Treaty with Mexico fixed boundary line as designated in Treaty of 1819

Jan. 28, The New York legislature chartered a line to be called the Ithaca and Oswego Railroad to connect these 2 towns

Jan. 30, The South Carolina Canal and Railroad Company incorporated, the railroad known as the Charleston and Hamburg Railroad opened Jan. 15, 1830

March 24, The Mine Hill and Schuylkill Haven Railroad incorporated in Pennsylvania

——, The Pennsylvania legislature agreed to aid by money grant the construction of the Pennsylvania Railroad (Philadelphia-Columbia), "first railroad undertaken in any part of the world by a government"

April 12, Canal between Delaware and Schuylkill authorized

April 21, Webster's Dictionary published

May 1, Treaty of commerce and navigation with Prussia signed

May 5, Texas law provided that contracts made in foreign countries between emigrants or inhabitants and servants were valid, which included contracts with slaves to work for stipulated wages

May 6, Treaty with the Cherokees by which they ceded lands and removed to new tract beyond the western line of Arkansas

May 26, Peter B. Porter, of New York, appointed Secretary of War, entering on duties June 21

June, Joseph Henry exhibited his electro-magnetic apparatus (W. T. Taylor)

July 4, Charles Carroll, sole surviving signer of the Declaration of Independence, laid first stone for line of the Baltimore and Ohio Railroad

——, President John Quincy Adams threw out first spade of earth breaking ground for the Chesapeake and Ohio Canal

Aug. 19, First American power loom for weaving check and plaid goods patented by E. Burt in Connecticut

Aug., Jedediah Smith arrived at Fort Vancouver from California, the first white man to make overland journey along the coast

Oct. 8, Railroad from Carbondale to Honesdale, Pennsylvania, constructed by the Delaware and Hudson Canal Company to bring coal from their mines reported in use (Niles Register)

Oct. 16, The Delaware and Hudson Canal opened from Honesdale to Rondout

Nov. 11, Presidential election

Dec. 12, Treaty of peace, friendship, commerce, and navigation with Brazil signed

Dec. 19, South Carolina legislature adopted 8 resolutions drafted by Calhoun protesting against the tariff as unconstitutional, a first formal statement of the doctrine of nullification

Dec. 20, Georgia legislature annexed the Cherokee lands to 5 adjacent counties

Jan. 31, Tariff Bill presented in House, discussion begun March 4, and passed May 15, and in Senate May 13

May 19, "Tariff of Abominations" signed by the President, provided for a rate of 41%, and included the duties recommended by the Harrisburg Convention, greatly increased rates on wool and woolen goods, hemp, flax, and iron

May 26, Congress adjourned

Dec. 1, Twentieth Congress, 2d sess. convened

1829

Feb. 5, General Assembly of Mississippi declared tariff "contrary to the spirit of the Constitution"

Feb. 21, Virginia Assembly declared tariff unconstitutional

March 4, Inauguration of President Andrew Jackson, of Tennessee, and Vice-President John C. Calhoun, of South Carolina. With inauguration of Jackson came the introduction of the "spoils system" into national politics, the spoils of office to go to the victor by exercise of the hitherto almost unused privilege of removal from office to create vacancies for the appointment of partisans of the Administration. For advisers the President gathered about him a group which was called the "Kitchen Cabinet," Isaac Hill, Amos Kendall, W. B. Lewis, and Duff Green

March 6, Martin Van Buren of New York, appointed Secretary of State, entering on duties March 28, and Samuel D. Ingraham, of Pennsylvania, Secretary of the Treasury

March 9, William T. Barry, of Kentucky, appointed Postmaster General; John H. Eaton, of Tennessee, Secretary of War; John M. Berrien, of Georgia, Attorney General, and John Branch, of North Carolina, Secretary of the Navy

March 23, Message of the President to the Creek Indians said, "My white children in Alabama have extended their law over your country. If you remain in it you must be subject to that law. If you remove across the Mississippi you will be subject to your own laws and the care of your father, the President"

April 18, Secretary of War Eaton, told the Cherokees to be subject to the laws of Georgia or remove beyond the Mississippi

May 17, Death of John Jay, at Bedford, N. Y.

May 29, Corner-stone of the first lock of the Chesapeake and Ohio Canal laid near Georgetown

July 29, The Chippewa, Ottowa, and Powatomi Indians ceded land in Michigan Territory

Aug. 8, The imported English locomotive named "Stourbridge Lion," first locomotive run on rails in the United States, tested on the railroad between Carbondale and Honesdale, Pennsylvania, built by the Delaware and Hudson Canal Company (Poor. Hadley, 1828)

Aug. 13, 14, and 15, President Jackson instructed Secretary of State to renew proposals for change of boundary with Mexico as fixed by Treaty of 1819 and offer $5,000,000 for line of the Rio Grande, and to include Texas

Aug. 25, Van Buren instructed Poinsett, American Minister to Mexico, to open negotiations for cession of Texas

Aug. 27, Treaty of commerce and navigation with Austria-Hungary signed

Oct. 16, Poinsett recalled from Mexico as requested by the Mexican Government, and Oct. 17, Colonel Anthony Butler instructed to continue negotiations and act as chargé d'affaires

Nov. 7–Jan. 31, 1830, Journey of Antonio Armijo, trader, from Abiqui, New Mexico to California by route north of Grand Cañon of Colorado

Nov. 12–13, Joaquin Solis led soldiers in revolt against Mexican authority in California, hardly more than a strike of the soldiers for their pay

Dec. 2, President Guerrero formally excepted Texas from operation of Decree of Sept. 15, 1829, freeing slaves in Mexico

Dec. 23, Colonel Anthony Butler arrived in Mexico, succeeding Poinsett

Jan. 9, Bill for establishment of a territorial government for Oregon and the erection of a fort defeated in House

Jan. 12, Memorial to Congress from Georgia dated Dec. 30, 1828 against the tariff presented in Senate

Jan. 21, Act allowed drawback on sugar refined in the United States and exported therefrom

Feb. 10, South Carolina "Exposition and Protest" against the tariff presented, declared tariffs unconstitutional except when necessary to raise revenue and regulate commerce

Feb. 11, Electoral vote counted gave Andrew Jackson (Democrat) 178 votes for president as against 83 votes for John Quincy Adams (National Republican). John C. Calhoun elected vice-president with 171 votes. The followers of Jackson assumed the name Democrat in this election, used by the party since

March 3, Petition of Feb. 27 of John Ross and other representatives of the Cherokees presented in House protesting action of Georgia in annexing their lands and declaring their laws null and void after June 1

—, Congress adjourned

Dec. 7, Twenty-first Congress, 1st sess. convened

Dec. 8, President Jackson in message advised an inquiry into constitutionality of the charter of the United States Bank, and proposed the distribution of surplus revenue among the States

Dec. 29, Senator Foote offered a Resolution proposing a temporary restriction of the sale of public lands to those already placed on the market, which was resented by western members as a proposed check to immigration

1830

Jan. 10, The Petersburg (Virginia) Railroad incorporated

Jan. 19, Mississippi law passed extended jurisdiction of State over Indians within the State

Jan. 20, The Pontchartrain Railroad first railroad in Louisiana incorporated to run from New Orleans to the Lake, formally opened April 23, 1831

Jan. 27, Lexington (Kentucky) and Ohio Railroad chartered, opened to Frankfort, Jan. 31, 1833

Feb. 3, Randolph-Macon College chartered

Feb. 4, Camden and Amboy Railroad chartered, the first railroad in New Jersey, completed in the spring of 1834

Feb., Delaware and Raritan Railroad chartered

March 28, Treaty with Denmark for adjustment of indemnity claims signed

April 6, The Mormon Church organized at Fayette, Seneca county, New York

April 8, The Mexican Congress passed law forbidding citizens of the United States to settle in Texas, and slavery prohibited. *See also* Mexico

April 10, Wagon train left St. Louis for Oregon

April 13, At banquet to celebrate Jefferson's birthday President Jackson gave "Our Union, it must be preserved" as toast in reply to toasts designed to emphasize the ultra states rights theory, Vice-President Calhoun replied with "Liberty dearer than Union"

May 7, Treaty of commerce and navigation with Turkey signed, opened Black Sea to American ships

May 24, First train on the Baltimore and Ohio Railroad, line opened about 13 miles to Ellicott's Mills (McMaster, and Humphrey. Meyer, May 22)

June 1, First conference of Mormon Church at Fayette, New York

June 5, Boston and Lowell Railroad chartered, completed and formally opened June 24, 1835

July 10 and 15, Treaties of peace and cession of land signed by Indians of the Upper Mississippi at Prairie du Chien confirming previous treaties and Indians promised to remove from Illinois to lands west of the Mississippi

Aug. 28, The locomotive "Tom Thumb" built by Peter Cooper to demonstrate certain principles regarding curves tested on the Baltimore and Ohio Railroad. A trial of speed with a horse resulted in favor of the horse

Sept. 27, Treaty with the Choctaws by which they ceded to the United States all their lands east of the Mississippi

Oct. 5, Proclamation of the President announced that trade with the West Indies was again opened to American vessels

Nov. 2, The "Best Friend," the first locomotive built for actual service in America made trip on railroad from Charleston to Hamburg, South Carolina

Dec., The Georgia legislature passed law requiring all white persons living in the Cherokee country after March 11, 1831 to obtain licenses and take oath of allegiance to the State

——, The "Comet" wrecked on Bahama Islands and English authorities declared slaves on board free

Fifth census gave total population as 12,866,020, 10,575,378 white persons, 2,328,642 colored, including 2,009,043 slaves. New York with 1,918,608 leading of the 24 States, Pennsylvania second with 1,348,233 and Virginia with 1,211,405 third. New York, the largest city, had population of 202,589, Baltimore next with 80,620, Philadelphia with 80,462, Boston with 61,392, New Orleans with 46,082. Immigrant arrivals as officially recorded since 1821 numbered 143,439 with 75,803 from the British Isles. The area of 1,793,400 square miles included only 628,017 square miles of settled country. Center of population 19 miles west southwest of Moorefield, West Virginia

CONGRESS

Jan. 19, Senator Robert Y. Hayne attacked the Foote Resolution limiting sale of public lands and declared opposition "in any shape to all unnecessary extension of the Legislature or Executive of the Union over the States, or the people of the States"

Jan. 20, Daniel Webster replied to Hayne urging that there be no more utterances tending "to bring the Union into discussion, as a mere question of present and temporary expediency"

Jan. 21, Hayne delivered his first reply to Webster in constitutional debate, and continued on Jan. 25, a statement of the doctrine of strict construction, state rights, and nullification

Jan. 26 and 27, Webster's second reply to Hayne argued that the exercise of sovereignty residing in the people of the United States is entrusted partly to the national government and partly to the state governments and if differences arise the decision rests with the federal courts, his speech "regarded as the greatest piece of forensic eloquence which this country has produced" (MacDonald)

Jan. 27, Hayne in second reply to Webster stated that the Union was a compact between sovereign states and each party to the compact is the rightful judge of violations of the agreement

April 26–Jan. 31, 1831, Senate sat as a court of impeachment in case of James H. Peck, judge of United States district court for district of Missouri, for punishing as contempt of court a criticism of his opinions; acquitted

April 29, McDuffiem of South Carolina, in argument for reduction of the tariff pronounced the tariff unconstitutional and threatened resistance to the execution of the tariff laws

May 20, Act reduced the duties on tea, coffee, and cocoa

May 27, The President vetoed a Bill authorizing the subscription of stock by the Government in a Kentucky turnpike running from Maysville on the Ohio River to Lexington 60 miles inland. The House failed to pass the Bill over the veto May 28

May 28, Act made provision for exchange of lands with the Indians resident in any State or Territory for lands west of the Mississippi, and $500,000 appropriated for their removal

May 29, The President authorized to open ports of the United States whenever British colonial ports opened to American vessels without discrimination

——, Duty on molasses and salt reduced, and a drawback allowed on spirits distilled from foreign materials

May 31, The President vetoed a Bill authorizing a subscription to the stock of the Washington Turnpike Road Company as a work of local not national character

——, The President approved a Bill appropriating $30,000 for extension of the Cumberland Road, and additional sums for other roads

——, Tonnage dues on American vessels and on certain foreign vessels repealed

——, Congress adjourned

Dec. 6, Twenty-first Congress, 2d sess. convened

——, Bill for internal improvements, light houses and beacons, and canal stock vetoed by the President

1831

Jan. 1, William Lloyd Garrison began publication of the *Liberator* in Boston

Jan. 6, Proclamation of the Governor of California for secularization of the missions

Jan. 10, Arbitration award of King of the Netherlands recommended a compromise line for northeast boundary; accepted by Great Britain but declined by the United States

Jan., Sidney Rigdon, converted to Mormonism, brought Joseph Smith to Kirtland, Ohio, where first "stake of Zion" was established

Feb. 9, By a "revelation" of this date the elders of the Mormon Church directed to go out and preach the gospel "two by two"

Feb. 16, The Saratoga and Schenectady Railroad chartered in New York, completed in 1833

March 5, The "West Point," a second locomotive built in America, made first trial trip on South Carolina Railroad

March 18, Decision of Chief Justice Marshall in case of Cherokees vs. Georgia, that Cherokees not a foreign nation and court no jurisdiction

April 5, Treaty of limits, amity, commerce, and navigation with Mexico signed

April 12, University of Alabama founded at Tuscaloosa

April 18, New York University chartered

April 26, New York State abolished imprisonment for debt to take effect March 1, 1832

April, First coal train passed over line of the Mine Hill and Schuylkill Haven Railroad

May 23, Levi Woodbury, of New Hampshire, appointed Secretary of the Navy

May 24, Edward Livingston, of Louisiana, appointed Secretary of State

May 28, Governor Reynolds, of Illinois, called for regular troops from General Gaines and for volunteers against Indians under Black Hawk invading the State

June 6, Date of revelation that Missouri the place for the Mormon City of Zion, and June 19 Joseph Smith left Kirtland, Ohio for Independence, Missouri, to select "land of promise and place for the City of Zion"

June 22, The Boston and Providence Railroad chartered, completed June 1835, progenitor of the New York, New Haven, and Hartford

——, American Society for Encouraging the Settlement of the Oregon Territory incorporated in Massachusetts

June 23, Boston and Worcester Railroad chartered, formally opened April 16, 1834 as far as Newton, and completed July 3, 1835, the first steam railroad in Massachusetts

June 25, General Edmund P. Gaines led 1,600 volunteers in demonstration before Black Hawk's village

June 30, Black Hawk signed agreement to withdraw to west of the Mississippi and not to return across the river without the permission of the Governor of Illinois or the President of the United States

July 4, Treaty signed with France by which France agreed to pay 25,000,000 francs and the United States 1,500,000 francs in final settlement of claims of citizens for spoliation in Napoleonic wars

July 20, Roger B. Taney, of Maryland, appointed Attorney General

July 26, Calhoun's "Address to the People of South Carolina" published

Aug. 1, Lewis Cass, of Ohio, appointed Secretary of War

——, First train run from Albany to Schenectady on the Mohawk and Hudson Railroad

Aug. 2, First log for a house laid by Mormons in what is now Kansas City, Joseph Smith "laying the foundations of Zion"

Aug. 7, Henry R. Schoolcraft, commissioned in April to go to Upper Mississippi and exert influence to make peace between the Dakotas and Ojibways, held conference with the Indians at Rice Lake

Aug. 8, Louis McLane, of Delaware, appointed Secretary of the Treasury

Aug. 9, The "De Witt Clinton," the third locomotive built in America, made trip on the Mohawk and Hudson

Aug. 22, A slave insurrection led by Nat Turner in Southampton county, Virginia, in which more than 60 white persons were massacred

Aug., Morris and Essex Canal completed from the Delaware River to Newark

Sept. 26, The Anti-Masonic Party held a national convention at Baltimore and nominated William Wirt of Maryland for president and Amos Ellmaker of Pennsylvania for vice-president

Sept. 30–Oct. 7, Free Trade Convention met at Philadelphia

Oct. 22, Ground broken for Lexington and Ohio Railroad at Lexington, Kentucky

Nov. 24, Joseph Henry announced discovery of induced currents and invented and demonstrated the first practical electro-magnetic telegraph in Albany, producing sounds at a distance. He reported his achievement in *Silliman's Journal* of this year

Dec. 1, The suspension of Governor Victoria who had succeeded Echeandia demanded by Californians in rising against the government in which Victoria was wounded in skirmish and abdicated, returning to Mexico

Dec. 12, Convention of National Republicans at Baltimore nominated Henry Clay for president

Pennsylvania completed its "portage line" of railroad and canal from Philadelphia to Pittsburgh

CONGRESS

Feb. 3, Copyright law amended making term 28 years instead of 14 with privilege of renewal for 14 more years

March 2, Harbor improvement Bill became law, passed by majorities so large that the President yielded and signed

——, Territory of Florida authorized to open a canal through public lands between Chipola River and St. Andrew's Bay in West Florida

——, Baltimore and Ohio Railroad authorized to build extension into the District of Columbia

——, Contempt of court law passed

March 3, Appropriations made for certain lighthouses, light-boats, beacons, and buoys

——, Congress adjourned

Dec. 5, Twenty-second Congress, 1st sess. convened

Dec. 12, John Quincy Adams presented 15 petitions from Pennsylvania in House asking for abolition of slavery in the District of Columbia

1832

Jan. 6, New England Anti-Slavery Society formed

Jan. 10, Convention of Californians chose Pio Pico as Provisional Governor, but Escheandia, former Governor, assumed office

Jan. 24, Fifty foreign residents of Monterey formed a company under William Hartnell for defense of the town

Jan., Canal connecting Huntsville with the Tennessee River opened

March 3, Second decision of Supreme Court in case of Cherokees vs. Georgia by Marshall declared Georgia statutes unconstitutional and jurisdiction of the Federal Government over the Cherokees exclusive

March 10, Expedition of Nathaniel Jarvis Wyeth left Boston to travel overland to Oregon, arriving at Fort Vancouver Oct. 29, and at Cape Disappointment Nov. 8 and establishing trading post on Watapoo Island

March 24, Treaty with the Creeks signed by which the Indians ceded all lands east of the Mississippi

April 6, The Sacs led by Black Hawk crossed the Mississippi and seized their village taken possession of by white settlers and massacred settlers wherever found (Black Hawk War in Illinois)

April 7, Liggett's Gap Railroad afterwards the Lackawanna and Western incorporated in Pennsylvania

——, Pennsylvania College, Gettysburg, chartered; name changed to Gettysburg College Nov. 14, 1921

April 16, Governor Reynolds of Illinois called for volunteers against Indians to meet at Beardstown

April 24, New York and Erie Railroad from Lake Erie to Hudson River chartered, trial trip of train from Pierpont to Ramapo June 17, 1841, first passenger trip June 30

April 26, Conference at Independence, Missouri, recognized Joseph Smith as president of the high priesthood of Mormons

May 1, Exploring expedition of Captain Benjamin L. E. de Bonneville left Fort Osage on the Missouri and reached Green River in southwest Wyoming July 27, and Fort Walla Walla March 4, 1834. Explored the Snake and Columbia rivers

May 9, Treaty with 15 Seminole chiefs by which they ceded all land in Florida and agreed to remove to country west of the Mississippi in 3 years, and to send commission to view lands allotted to them. $15,400 paid to the Indians

May 16, Treaty of peace, amity, commerce, and navigation with Chile signed and additional Article Sept. 1, 1833

May 21, National Democratic Convention at Baltimore nominated Jackson for president and Martin Van Buren for vice-president

May 22, At Davis farm north of Ottawa, Illinois, 15 persons massacred by Indians

May 24, Indian Creek settlement in La Salle county, Illinois, attacked by Indians, followers of Black Hawk, and 15 persons killed

June 5, The Cincinnati, Sandusky, and Cleveland Railroad incorporated in Ohio

June 14, Five men killed by Indians at Spofford's farm (Wisconsin) and in skirmish Colonel Henry Dodge in pursuit, 11 Indians and 3 white men killed

June 23, Schoolcraft expedition reached Fon du Lac trading house on the St. Louis River 20 miles from mouth, at first portage of river June 25, at Sandy Lake July 3, at Lake Winnibogshish July 9, at Cass Lake July 10, at Elk Lake July 13 which he named Itasca and recognized as the true source of the Mississippi; turned back July 14

June 24, Black Hawk with 150 warriors made unsuccessful attack on Apple River Fort near Galena

June 25, Black Hawk defeated in battle at Kellogg's Grove by General Alexander Posey

June 27, Fort Velasco at mouth of the Brazos surrendered by Colonel Ugartechea to Texan colonists led by Frank W. Johnson

June 27–Oct., Cholera in New York City, 4,000 deaths

July 9, Constitution adopted by the "United Inhabitants of the Indian Stream," territory claimed by both Canada and New Hampshire

July 13, Discovery of source of the Mississippi River by Schoolcraft

July 21, Battle at Wisconsin Heights where Black Hawk was overtaken and defeated by Illinois troops under

General James D. Henry and Wisconsin rangers under Colonel Henry Dodge

Aug. 2, Black Hawk's warriors massacred by Illinois militia and regular troops under General Atkinson as they attempted to cross the Mississippi at mouth of Bad Axe River

Aug. 27, Black Hawk surrendered by the Winnebago with whom he had taken refuge to the Indian agency at Prairie du Chien

Aug. 28, Calhoun's "Fort Hill" letter addressed to Governor Hamilton, a statement of the doctrine of nullification

Sept. 21, Treaty with the Sauk and Fox of submission and cession in which they agreed to remain west of the Mississippi and surrendered a strip 50 miles wide along the right bank of the river

Oct. 1, Convention of Texans met at San Felipe and adopted memorials and petitions to Mexican Government

——, Samuel B. Morse sailed from Havre on S.S. "Sully" for America and on this voyage conceived idea of electric telegraph

Oct. 14, Treaty with the Two Sicilies provided for payment of claims for depredations on American commerce by Murat 1809–1812

——, Treaty with the Chickasaws by which they ceded to the United States all their land east of the Mississippi

Oct. 26, Constitution adopted for Mississippi by convention which met Sept. 10; ratified at the general election following

——, High tariff convention in New York City

Nov. 3, First trip of the locomotive "Old Ironsides," built by Baldwin of Philadelphia, on Germantown and Norristown Railroad

Nov. 8–Dec. 2, Convention met at Dover and revised Constitution of Delaware

Nov. 13, Presidential election

Nov. 19, Convention at Columbia, South Carolina, met to protest against the tariff, and Nov. 24 passed ordinance declaring the Tariff Acts of 1828 and 1832 null and void in the State to take effect Feb. 1, 1833, duties not to be paid

Nov. 24, Joseph Smith and Sydney Rigdon tarred and feathered by mob of Gentiles at Hiram, Ohio where Smith had moved from Kirtland, Sept. 18, 1831

Dec. 10, Proclamation of the President to the people of South Carolina against nullification as "incompatible with the existence of the Union, and destructive of the great object for which it was formed"

Dec. 12, Convention of National Republicans met at Baltimore and nominated Henry Clay for president and John Sergeant for vice-president

Dec. 18, Treaty of commerce and navigation with Russia signed

Dec. 20, Proclamation of the Governor of South Carolina in answer to the President warned the people not to be seduced from their primary allegiance to the State

Dec. 28, Resignation of Vice-President Calhoun

The Bent brothers erected Fort William on the north branch of the Arkansas River 80 miles northeast from Taos in present Colorado

CONGRESS

Jan. 9, Formal application for renewal of charter of the United States Bank presented to Senate

——, Henry Clay proposed changes in tariff in favor

of a protective policy, the "American system" so-called, in Senate, supported by representatives of Delaware, Maine, Massachusetts, New Jersey, Ohio, Pennsylvania, and Rhode Island

Feb. 8, McDuffie for the cotton planters introduced in the House an ultra free-trade Bill

Feb. 15, Message of the President recommended speedy migration of the Indians beyond the Mississippi

April 27, Secretary McLane of the Treasury submitted Bill for sweeping reduction of the tariff

May 23, Adams reported a new tariff which made reductions but maintained the protective principle

June 11, Bill rechartering the National Bank passed the Senate 28 to 20, and the House July 3 by vote of 107 to 85

June 23, Senate voted not to accept award of the King of the Netherlands as to northeast boundary

July 9, The President authorized the appointment of a Commission of Indian Affairs

July 10, The President vetoed the Bill to renew the charter of the National Bank, failed to pass over veto in Senate July 13

July 13, Duty on wines reduced as provided for in French Treaty

July 14, Tariff Act modified duties of 1828 restoring many articles to lower duties of 1824, tax on iron reduced, that on molasses increased, but cotton unchanged, and tax placed on woolen yarn

——, "Railway Iron Act" allowed complete drawback on iron imported to be used for railroads

——, Act provided for settlement of northern boundary of Ohio

July 16, Congress adjourned

Dec. 3, Twenty-second Congress, 2d sess. convened

Dec. 12, Clay introduced a Bill providing for distribution of the net revenue from public lands among the States which received a pocket veto

1833

Jan. 31, Lexington and Ohio Railroad formally opened to Frankfort, Kentucky

Feb. 8, Bangor and Piscataqua Railroad chartered, first railroad in Maine

Feb. 23, Decision of Mormon Church to purchase land and establish a permanent Mormon city at Kirtland, Ohio

March 4, Inauguration of President Andrew Jackson and Vice-President Martin Van Buren

March 11–18, Convention of South Carolina in session rescinded Nullification Ordinance on the 15th, adopted an Ordinance against the "force Bill" the 18th and adjourned

March 15, Western Railroad incorporated in Massachusetts and construction begun at Worcester in 1838, and Andover and Haverhill Railroad chartered, later the Boston and Maine

March 20, Treaty of amity and commerce with Siam signed

March 31, Treasury Building and large number of records destroyed by fire in Washington

April 1–13, Convention at San Felipe de Austin framed a Constitution for Texas; not recognized by Mexico or ever put into operation

April 4, Philadelphia and Reading Railroad chartered

April 29, Utica and Schenectady Railroad chartered

May 3, Mormons adopted the name Latter Day Saints

May 9, Compromise effected in the dispute of the rivals,

Baltimore and Ohio Railroad and Chesapeake and Ohio Canal Company, through disputed territory

May 29, Louis McLane, of Louisiana, appointed Secretary of State

May, Hartford and New Haven Railroad incorporated

June 1, The "Black Hawk Purchase" land opened to settlers

June–July, President Jackson on tour of the eastern States

July 20, Meeting of citizens of Jackson county, Missouri, at Independence adopted formal resolve that Mormons should be required to leave the country, and July 23 large numbers of armed men appeared at Independence and warned the Mormons to leave

July 23, Cornerstone of Mormon temple laid at Kirtland, Ohio

——, Mormon Church leaders forced to sign agreement to leave Jackson county, Missouri, one-half by Jan. 1, 1834 and all by April 1, 1834

July 24, Expedition of fur traders of 40 men headed by Joseph R. Walker left Green River from southwest Wyoming and reached Monterey in Nov.

Aug. 1, Strike of journeymen shoemakers in Geneva, N.Y. successful

Aug. 17, Decree for secularization of missions of California, the first to be put into effect

Sept. 3, First issue of the *New York Sun*, first penny paper in New York

——, Diplomatic relations with Argentina severed because of capture of vessels

Sept. 18, The President read to the Cabinet a paper prepared by Taney, an exposition of his reasons for belief that the public funds deposited in the National Bank should be removed

Sept. 21, Treaty of amity and commerce with the Sultan of Muscat signed

Sept. 23, W. J. Duane, Secretary of the Treasury, removed from office by the President for refusing to withdraw deposits from the National Bank, and Roger B. Taney, of Maryland, appointed in his place

Sept. 26, Instructions given by Secretary of the Treasury Taney to the collector at Philadelphia to remove deposits from National Bank to Girard Bank, and contract with Girard Bank signed Sept. 28

Oct. 1, Federal deposits, about $10,000,000, removed from the National Bank, and distributed among selected State banks

Oct. 19, Mormons in Jackson county, Missouri, asked for protection of Governor of State

Oct. 20, Mormons made public announcement that they intended to defend their lands and homes in Jackson county

Oct. 31 and Nov. 1, Destruction of houses of Mormons and whipping of men, "reign of terror" begun in Jackson county

Nov. 2, Mormons attacked town of Independence and were defeated and made to promise to leave the State before Jan. 1, 1834

Nov. 15, Benjamin F. Butler, of New York, appointed Attorney General

Nov. 20, First cars drawn by horses passed over Pennsylvania's portage railroad from Hollidaysburg to Johnstown, 36.44 miles

Dec. 4, American Anti-Slavery Society constituted

CONGRESS

Jan. 16, Message of the President asked for power to enforce the collection of customs in South Carolina

Jan. 21, Bill to ensure the collection of customs in South Carolina introduced, named by the States-rights men the "force Bill"

Jan. 22, Calhoun, now senator from South Carolina, introduced a series of resolutions concerning the powers of the Federal Government, declaring that the theory that the people of the United States are now or ever have been united in one nation is erroneous, false in history and in reason

Feb. 12, Henry Clay proposed a "compromise tariff" in Senate, and Feb. 21, an amendment providing for home valuation

Feb. 13, Electoral votes counted gave Andrew Jackson 219 votes for president, Henry Clay 49, William Wirt 7, John Floyd 11, and Martin Van Buren, of New York 189 for vice-president

Feb. 18, Senate passed Force Bill by vote of 32 to 1, and House March 1

Feb. 26, Tariff Bill passed the House, and the Senate March 1, opposed by New England and the Middle West but carried by support of South and West

March 2, "Compromise Tariff" Bill signed by the President, provided for gradual reduction of duties above 20% until 1842 when all duties would be 20%

——, "Force Bill" signed by the President gave the President power to suppress opposition to Federal laws in any State

——, House resolved that the deposits "may . . . be safely continued in the Bank of the United States"

——, Use of endowment of public land for railways and canals authorized

——, Creation of office of Commissioner of Pensions

——, First extention of Habeas Corpus Act from original Judiciary Act of 1789 extended the right to, and person restrained "from any act done or omitted to be done in pursuance of a law of the United States or on any order of any judge or court thereof"

——, Congress adjourned

Dec. 2, Twenty-third Congress, 2d sess. convened

Dec. 4, President Jackson vetoed Clay's Bill as to proceeds of land sales of Dec. 12, 1832, and in message to Senate gave his reasons

Dec. 26, Clay introduced a resolution of censure of the President's removal of deposits from the National Bank (Bank of the United States)

1834

Jan. 1, Strike of women shoebinders at Lynn, Massachusetts, unsuccessful

Jan. 3, Wilmington and Raleigh (North Carolina) Railroad incorporated, opened from Wilmington to Weldon, 161 miles, March 9, 1840

——, Stephen Austin arrested at Saltillo and taken to Mexico City where he was imprisoned until 1835, regaining his freedom under general amnesty of May 3

Feb. 7, N. J. Wyeth's second expedition to Oregon left Boston for St. Louis and overland journey

Feb. 17, Indemnity Treaty with Spain signed settled claims

Feb. 18, Death of William Wirt (62) in Washington

Feb. 28, Oberlin College, which had opened in 1833, chartered as Oberlin Collegiate Institute

March 28, Additional Treaty with the Seminoles at Fort Gibson signed by which they promised to begin emigration to west of the Mississippi within 3 years, and lands in the west designated in the Indian Territory

April 10, The Mormons petitioned the President for protection and reinstatement in Jackson county, Missouri

April 16, The Pennsylvania Railroad between Philadelphia and Columbia opened to Newton. The canal extended from Columbia to Hollidaysburg where portage railroad by inclined planes crossed the mountains to the western canal at Johnstown where packet boat started for Pittsburgh

April 28, Expedition of N. J. Wyeth left Independence, Missouri, overland for Oregon. Jason and Daniel Lee, first Methodist missionaries to the Northwest, in the party

May 2, The President through the War Dept. replied to Mormons that laws of the United States must not be violated

May 24, Treaty with the Choctaws signed

May, Delaware College, Newark, founded, later University of Delaware

June 16, Committee of citizens of Jackson county, Missouri, offered to buy Mormon lands at double value or allow the Mormons to buy their lands on same terms

June 21, Cyrus Hall McCormick received a patent for his reaper for harvesting grain, first successful automatic cutting machine

June 27, John Forsythe, of Georgia, appointed Secretary of State, and Levi Woodbury, of New Hampshire, Secretary of the Treasury

June 30, Mahlon Dickerson, of New Jersey, appointed Secretary of the Navy

July 15, Wyeth at the Snake River began building Fort Hall, completed Aug. 4, first settlement in Idaho

Aug. 17, Wyeth expedition left Fort Hall, and reached Oak Point 75 miles from the mouth of the Columbia Sept. 15 where he met his boat

Aug. 30, Constitution for Tennessee adopted by convention which met at Nashville May 19; ratified by popular vote March 5–6, 1835

Oct. 6, Jason Lee established mission to the Indians on the Willamette 10 miles north of the present Salem, Oregon

——, Railroad from Philadelphia to Columbia opened

Oct. 28, General Thompson sent to insist on fulfilment of Treaty by Seminole Indians who refused to move from their lands rejecting treaties signed by chiefs

Nov. 1, Philadelphia and Trenton Railroad completed

Nov. 15, Boston and Worcester Railroad opened

The opponents of Jackson adopted the name Whig in place of National Republicans

CONGRESS

March 28, Senate adopted resolution of censure of the President's removal of deposits from the National Bank, that he had assumed authority not conferred by the Constitution or the laws

April 15, President Jackson entered a formal protest against the resolution of March 28 which was finally expunged from the records on Jan. 16, 1837

June 25, The value of certain foreign silver coins circulating in the United States regulated, and of foreign gold coins June 28

June 28, Coinage of the United States regulated and standardized, the ratio of silver and gold changed from 15 to 1 to 16 to 1

——, Territory west of the Mississippi and north of Missouri added to Michigan Territory

June 30, Act enabled the Secretary of State to purchase papers and books of George Washington

June 30, Dept. of Indian Affairs organized, applied only to the field

———, Indian Territory set apart exclusively for Indians

———, Congress adjourned

Dec. 1, Twenty-third Congress, 2d sess. convened

Dec. 2, The President's message announced the national debt paid off to take effect Jan. 1, and recommended reprisals on French property in case payments under the Treaty of 1831 long overdue remained unpaid

1835

Jan. 29, President Jackson shot at by Richard Lawrence afterwards judged insane

March 14, Rev. Samuel Parker, Presbyterian missionary, started overland for Oregon, arriving at Fort Vancouver on the Columbia River Oct. 16

March 16, Cleveland, Columbus, and Cincinnati Railroad incorporated

March, *Shawanoe Sun* published in Indian language in Kansas by Baptist mission

April 6, Treasury order to receivers and disbursers of public money and to deposit banks prohibited receipt after Sept. 30, 1835 of bank-notes of a denomination less than $5, and after July 4 of bank-notes less than $1

April 24, Time for removal of Seminole Indians to the Indian Territory extended to Jan. 1, 1836 to which 5 chiefs refused to agree

May 1, Amos Kendal, of Kentucky, appointed Postmaster General

May 6, The *New York Herald* first published by James Gordon Bennett

May 7, Mob burned 203 houses of Mormons in Jackson county, Missouri

May 11–June 29, Constitutional Convention held at Detroit adopted Constitution for Michigan which was ratified by the people Nov. 2, included clause prohibiting slavery

May 20, National Democratic Convention at Baltimore nominated Martin Van Buren, of New York, for president, and Richard M. Johnson, of Kentucky, for vice-president; two-thirds rule adopted

May 23, Los Angeles made a city and the capital of California

May 29, Colonel Henry Dodge left Fort Leavenworth on expedition to the Rocky Mts., following the west bank of the Missouri nearly to the mouth of the Platte, traced the Platte to its source, and south to head-waters of the Arkansas

June 2, Boston and Providence Railroad opened

June 23, First railroad chartered in New Hampshire, the Nashua and Lowell

June 30, Texas colonists led by William B. Travis captured Mexican garrison at Anahuac

June, Successful strike gained 10 hour day for all municipal employees of Philadelphia

July 29, Anti-slavery propaganda pamphlets taken from the mail at Charleston, South Carolina and publicly burned

Aug. 6, Proposal to Mexico of boundary of Rio Grande to the 37th parallel and thence to the Pacific and the cession of Texas

Aug. 25, The Baltimore and Washington Railroad opened

Sept. 1, Stephen Austin arrived at Velasco at mouth of the Brazos from Mexico

Sept. 12, Public meeting of Texans chose a committee of safety, Stephen Austin a member

Sept. 29, Death of Governor Figueroa of California

Sept., Mad River and Lake Erie Railroad, Dayton to Sandusky begun, first railroad in Ohio

Oct. 2, Texans and Mexicans in battle at Gonzales in which Texans under Colonel Moore successful in gaining possession of cannon lent for defense against Indians in 1831

Oct. 11, Stephen Austin, elected commander of Texan army, marched to meet Mexican General Cos who had occupied San Antonio

Oct. 17–Nov. 1, Convention in Texas which declared for independence

Oct. 21, Mob prevented George Thompson, Englishman, from speaking at anti-slavery meeting in Boston organized by W. L. Garrison

Oct. 28, Colonel James Bowie and Captain J. W. Fannin defeated Mexicans in battle near Conception Mission

Oct. 29, The name "loco-focos" first applied to the radical section of the Democratic Party at meeting at Tammany Hall, New York, where they produced candles and loco-foco matches when lights were put out to end meeting

Nov. 1–Aug. 14, 1842, Second Seminole War with the Indians of Florida, Osceola taking leadership of the Seminoles

Nov. 2, Joseph Henry announced the discovery of secondary currents in electricity

Nov. 5, Convention of Texans met at San Felipe and Nov. 7 made provisional declaration of independence of Mexico, declaring in favor of the Mexican Constitution of 1824 and local self-government for Texas, but denied right of Mexican federal authorities to govern Texas and asserted right of Texas to withdraw from the Mexican union if necessary to secure its rights

Nov. 7, Ground broken for Erie Railroad

Nov. 13, Texas Convention organized a provisional government with Henry Smith, of Kentucky, governor, James W. Robinson, lieutenant-governor, Sam Houston, major-general, and signed a constitution, and appointed William H. Wharton, T. Archer, and Stephen F. Austin a commission to the United States

Dec. 11, Capitulation signed for surrender of fort at Bexar (Bejar) on western bank of the San Antonio River by General Cos (Mexican) to Texans led by Benjamin R. Milam

Dec. 13, Florida troops advancing from Fort Duane to Withlacoochee River barely escaped defeat in engagement with the Seminole Indians

Dec. 15–16, Fire in New York City destroyed $20,000,-000 worth of property

Dec. 16, Anti-Masonic Convention at Harrisburg nominated William H. Harrison for president and Francis Granger for vice-president

Dec. 26, United States troops under Major Dade massacred in surprise attack by the Seminoles near Withlacoochee River

———, Osceola with about 20 Indians surprised and killed General Thompson and others near Fort King

Dec. 29, Treaty with the Cherokees by which the Indians ceded all lands east of the Mississippi for $5,000,000, and an adequate home in new Indian Territory

Dec. 31, Battle of General Clinch with Indians under Osceola at ford of the Withlacoochee River

Samuel Colt took out first patent in London for revolving pistol

CONGRESS

March 3, Branch mints established at New Orleans, Charlotte, North Carolina, and Dahlonega, Georgia

——, Public lands granted to Tallahassee Railroad of Florida

——, Congress adjourned

Dec. 2, Twenty-fourth Congress, 1st sess. convened

——, President Jackson in message suggested that laws be enacted to prohibit the circulation of anti-slavery documents through the mails

1836

Jan. 4, Constitutional Convention met at Little Rock and adopted Constitution for Arkansas

Jan. 5, Powhatan Ellis commissioned chargé d'affaires to Mexico, and presented credentials May 11

Jan. 20, Treaty of peace, amity, commerce, and navigation with Venezuela signed

Jan., Testimony of Professor L. D. Gale that he had examined the apparatus of Morse's electro-magnetic telegraph

Feb. 18, National Bank rechartered by Pennsylvania

Feb. 27, Texans commanded by Frank Johnson defeated at San Patricio

Feb. 27–March 5, General Gaines besieged by the Seminoles at ford of the Withlacoochee River in Florida

March 1, Convention of Texans met at Washington, Texas, and March 2 adopted a declaration of independence severing all political connection with Mexico, and established new provisional government, and March 4 appointed Sam Houston commander of army

March 6, Mexicans commanded by Santa Anna captured Fort Alamo at Bexar, Texas, besieged since Feb. 23, and massacred the garrison headed by W. B. Travis. David Crockett killed here

March 7, Texans commanded by James Grant defeated at Agua Dulce

March 11, Houston advancing against Mexicans reached Gonzales and hearing of the massacre at Alamo began March 14 precipitous retreat eastward to the Colorado

March 14, Richmond and Petersburg (Virginia) Railroad chartered

March 19, The King of France ordered indemnities under the Treaty paid

——, Captain Fannin advancing from fort at Goliad attacked by Mexicans and forced to surrender the following day

March 27, Captain Fannin and 371 prisoners shot by Mexicans, 27 managed to escape

——, Mormon temple at Kirtland, Ohio, dedicated

March 28, Houston continuing retreat eastward to the Brazos reached San Felipe, and Groce's Ferry 15 miles beyond, March 29

April 11, As Santa Anna arrived at Thompson's Ferry Houston began crossing the Brazos in advance southeast towards New Washington, Galveston Bay

April 21, Battle of San Jacinto. Houston defeated Mexicans in attack and captured Santa Anna

April 25, General Gaines ordered to advance to Nacogdoches if necessary to prevent or meet attacks of Indians on people of Texas

May 11, The *Dubuque Visitor* first issued, Iowa then part of Wisconsin

May 14, Santa Anna signed 2 treaties at Velasco with President Burnet of Texas for cessation of hostilities,

Mexican evacuation, exchange of prisoners, and return of Santa Anna to Vera Cruz, and secret agreement by which he promised to arrange with Mexican Cabinet for recognition of independence of Texas and for establishment of boundaries "to go beyond the Rio Bravo del Norte," these stipulations as obtained under duress repudiated by Mexican Congress May 20 and July 29

June 9, Seminole Indians attacked the stockade at Micanopy

July 4, Government of Wisconsin Territory organized at Mineral Point

July 11, President Jackson issued specie circular directing that only gold and silver should be accepted at the land offices in payment for public lands and as only the "pet banks" which held government deposits could furnish specie the others when called upon for gold and silver in exchange for their notes were compelled to suspend

July 14, First issue of *Milwaukee Advertiser* published

July 20, The Secretary of State sent to Mexico a list of 15 grievances of citizens of the United States against Mexico

Aug. 1, Excursion train left Albany over the Mohawk and Hudson and transferred passengers at Schenectady to new road to Utica

Aug. 21, Seminoles forced General Clinch to abandon Fort Drane, but were soon driven out by Major Pearce

Sept. 1, Marcus Whitman and H. H. Spaulding, missionaries, with their wives, the first white women to cross the plains and mountains, reached Fort Walla Walla on the Columbia River, and established first settlement in northern Oregon

Sept. 5, General election held in Texas at which Sam Houston received nearly 80% of the votes cast for president

Sept. 8, First number of anti-slavery newspaper, the *Alton Observer*, published at Alton, Illinois

Sept. 14, Death of Aaron Burr (80) in New York City

Sept. 16, Treaty of peace with Morocco signed

Sept. 26, Mr. Ellis at Mexico City presented demand of claims of the United States

——, Michigan Convention at Ann Arbor rejected Enabling Act of Congress as giving Ohio 470 square miles belonging to Michigan since 1787

Sept. 27, Treaty with Sacs and Fox Indians confirmed earlier treaties

Oct. 22, S. Houston took oath of office as president of Texas at Columbia

Oct. 25, First session of Wisconsin Assembly held at Belmont

Oct. 26, Benjamin F. Butler, of New York, commissioned *ad interim* Attorney General

Oct. Strike of women operatives of mills in Lowell against reduction of wages

Nov. 3, Revolutionists in California led by Juan Bautista Alvarado seized Monterey

Nov. 7, Alvarado at Monterey proclaimed Alta California a "free and sovereign state" until such time as Mexico should restore the Federalist Constitution of 1824

Nov. 8, Presidential election

Nov. 21, Battle of Wahoo swamp, the Seminoles defeated

Nov. 30, Treaty of peace, friendship, commerce, and navigation with Peru-Bolivian Federation

Dec. 7 and 22, Powhatan Ellis, American envoy to Mexico, demanded his passports

Dec. 14, New convention at Ann Arbor accepted Enabling Act for Michigan to form government

Dec. 15, Fire in Washington destroyed post-office and patent buildings

Dec. 19, Texan Congress declared the Rio Grande the boundary with Mexico

Dec. 27, Death of Stephen Austin, Secretary of State in Texan Republic, and with his father founder of American colony

CONGRESS

Jan. 11, Memorial presented in Senate asked for abolition of slavery in the District of Columbia, one of many anti-slavery petitions

Jan. 18, The President's message reviewed relations with France

Feb. 1, Memorial signed by 56 British authors received asking for copyright protection in the United States

March 1, The Senate voted in favor of recognition of Texas, tabled in House

March 5, Roger Taney, appointed Chief Justice of the Supreme Court Dec. 28, 1835, confirmed by Senate after strong opposition

April 20, Wisconsin Territory established and boundaries defined

May 18, American exploring expedition to the south polar regions authorized

May 26, "Gag Resolution" adopted by House ruled that all petitions which had any relation to slavery should be laid on the table without being debated, printed, or referred

June 7, Missouri boundary extended west to the Missouri River adding the "Platte Purchase," slave territory

June 15, Enabling Act provided for admission of Michigan and established northern boundary of Ohio

——, Arkansas admitted as a State with constitution which made slavery perpetual

June 23, Deposit Act required the Secretary of the Treasury to designate at least one bank in each State and Territory if possible as place of deposit for public funds

——, Surplus Revenue Act distributed all surplus funds over $5,000,000 among the several States subject to recall by the Treasurer of the United States

June 25, Proposal to change the Cumberland Road to a railroad defeated in House

July 1, Senate adopted Resolution that the independence of Texas should be recognized, and the House July 4

July 2, Post Office reorganized

July 4, Act reorganized the General Land Office to attend to all affairs of the public lands under superintendence of the Secretary

——, Act granted to Mississippi and Alabama 5% of the net proceeds of the sales of certain lands within those States ceded by the Indians in 1832 to be applied to internal improvements

——, Congress adjourned

Dec. 5, Twenty-fourth Congress, 2d sess. convened

1837

Jan. 17, Convention with the Choctaws and Chickasaws by which the Chickasaws were settled in the country of the Choctaws west of the Mississippi

Jan. 23, Colonel Canfield with Alabama and other troops in battle with the Seminoles near Ahapopira Lake

Feb. 8, Seminoles made unsuccessful attack on Fort Mellon on Lake Monroe

Feb. 12, Flour and bread riot in New York City, mob broke into stores

March 3, The President named Alcée La Branche as chargé d'affaires to Texas thus recognizing the independence of the Republic; confirmed March 6

March 4, Inauguration of President Martin Van Buren and Vice-President Richard M. Johnson

——, Chicago chartered as a city

March 6, General Jessup concluded an agreement with a delegation of Seminole chiefs which he expected would end the war

——, Powhatan Ellis again appointed Minister to Mexico

March 7, Joel R. Poinsett, of South Carolina, appointed Secretary of War

March 18, University of Michigan organized at Ann Arbor and opened to students Sept. 20

March 25, *Public Ledger* first published in Philadelphia

April 3, Philadelphia and Erie Railroad incorporated as Sunbury and Erie Railroad

April 5, Colonel Jessup issued an army order that no white person not engaged in service of the United States should enter territory between the St. John and Gulf of Mexico south of Fort Drane

April 8, Colonel Jessup demanded that Indian chiefs should surrender all negroes belonging to white persons

April, Failure of the largest cotton house in the Southwest for $15,000,000 followed in 2 days by 8 more companies making an aggregate of $27,000,000

——, New Mexican Constitution changing territory into a department went into effect

May 1, Colonel Jessup notified Osceola, Seminole chief, that he would have the negro slaves tracked by bloodhounds

May 9, First rail on Northern Cross Railroad laid at Meredosia, Illinois, and the first locomotive in the Mississippi Valley placed on the track in May

May 10, New York banks suspended specie payment on demand of British for settlements in specie starting panic caused by Jackson's financial measures, "wildcat" banking and overspeculation in western lands

May 29 and June 6, E. S. Greely, commissioned by authorities of Penobscot county Maine, to take census of town of Madawaska, arrested by order of government of New Brunswick

June, Unsuccessful strike of sailors of Boston for increase in wages lasted a week

July 6, Official reception of Mr. Hunt, Minister from Texas

July 12, Public exhibition of Obed Hussey's reaping machine

July 29, Treaty with the Chippewas signed at Fort Snelling with Governor Dodge of Wisconsin by which they ceded valley of the St. Croix and its tributaries to the United States

Aug. 1, Revolt in northern districts of New Mexico against the new Constitution, Governor Perez and other officials killed

Aug. 3, Colonel Jessup offered soldiers and Indian allies $20 a head for negroes captured and property of Seminoles

Aug. 4, Texas petitioned for annexation to the United States; refused Aug. 25

Aug. 10, Santa Fé, New Mexico, occupied by rebels and José Gonzales elected Governor

Sept. 2, S. F. B. Morse exhibited the apparatus of his telegraph in successful operation, and Sept. 28 filed his application for caveat which was witnessed and signed Oct. 3

Sept., Dakotas signed Treaty at Washington ceding all lands east of the Mississippi

Oct. 21, Osceola, Seminole chief, treacherously seized by Colonel Jessup while under protection of flag of truce

Nov. 6, Second session of first Territorial Council at Burlington, Iowa

Nov. 7, E. P. Lovejoy, publisher of *Alton Observer*, anti-slavery paper, shot dead by mob while defending his press

Nov. 8, Mary Lyon founded Holyoke Seminary later Holyoke College

Nov., Failure of Mormon bank at Kirtland, Ohio

Dec. 7, Secretary of State sent letters to the governors of Vermont, New York, and Michigan asking for arrest of American citizens giving aid to Canada rebellion

Dec. 8, Wendell Phillips made his first abolition speech at Faneuil Hall, Boston, to protest against the murder of Elijah P. Lovejoy

Dec. 12, William Lyon Mackenzie, leader in Canadian revolt, made incendiary speech at Buffalo, and Dec. 13 seized Navy Island just above Niagara Falls, where he set up a government with flag, seal, and paper currency, and was joined by an army of several hundred including many Americans

Dec. 22, Treaty of commerce and navigation with Greece signed

Dec. 25, General Zachary Taylor defeated the Seminoles at Okeechobee Swamp

Dec. 29, Canadian militia captured and burned American steamer "Caroline" in service of the rebels at Navy Island at Schlosser's Landing on the American shore, killing several of the crew

CONGRESS

Jan. 18, "Gag" resolution as to petitions regarding slavery similar to that of Pinckney's of May 26, 1836 passed

——, Coinage regulated as to gold and silver alloys and weight of silver dollar

Jan. 26, Michigan admitted as a State (26th)

Feb. 6, John Quincy Adams presented petition from 22 slaves for abolition of slavery in the District of Columbia, the petition tabled Feb. 9 and Adams censured for disrespect to the House

——, President Jackson submitted a list of 46 claims against Mexico dating from 1816, and recommended reprisals

Feb. 8, Electoral vote counted, Martin Van Buren elected president with 170 votes and Richard M. Johnson received 147 for vice-president, not a majority, and was then elected by the Senate. For president William Henry Harrison received 73 votes, Hugh L. White 26, Daniel Webster 14, and W. P. Mangum 11

March 1, Senate adopted formal resolution to recognize the independence of Texas by vote of 23 to 19

March 3, Act provided for salary of a diplomatic agent to Texas whenever the President should decide that the evidence would justify recognition of independ-ence, and the President that day recommended appointment of La Branche

March 3, Congress adjourned

May 15, Extra session of Congress called for Sept. 4

Sept. 4, Twenty-fifth Congress, 1st sess. convened in extra session

Sept. 5, President Van Buren's message detailed the general suspension of the deposit banks and embarassment of public operations in consequence of deficit in the Treasury, and recommended that the Government should be its own depository, the "independent treasury" or "sub-treasury" plan

Sept. 14, "Sub-Treasury" Bill introduced in Senate, passed Oct. 4, and tabled in House Oct. 14

Oct. 2, Transfer of fourth installment of surplus to States suspended, postponed to Jan. 1839

Oct. 12, Treasury notes to $10,000,000 authorized to relieve financial distress

Oct. 16, Time of payment upon duty bonds extended

——, Congress adjourned

Dec. 4, Twenty-fifth Congress, 2 sess. convened

Dec. 19, Resolutions against slavery from the legislature of Vermont presented and pronouncement against the annexation of Texas or admission to Union of any State whose constitution included slavery, and the abolition of slavery in the District of Columbia and national territories urged

Dec. 27, Calhoun presented 6 resolutions in reply to the memorial from Vermont

1838

Jan. 4, American sympathizers with the Canadian revolt seized arms at Detroit belonging to the State which they took to encampment on Sugar Island

Jan. 5, President Van Buren made proclamation of neutrality warning American citizens not to aid the Canadian revolt by hostile acts against Great Britain

——, General Scott instructed by Secretary of War Poinsett to proceed to the Canadian frontier

——, Wisconsin legislature passed act to establish the University of the Territory of Wisconsin, but nothing done about it for 10 years

Jan. 6, S. F. B. Morse gave demonstration of his completed telegraph in room of factory of Speedwell Iron Works, and private exhibition in New York City Jan. 24

Jan. 12, Joseph Smith and Sydney Rigdon fled from Kirtland, Ohio, to escape arrest on charges in connection with the unchartered Mormon bank which had suspended payments

Jan. 13, Navy Island abandoned by "patriots" who surrendered their arms to force of American militia stationed on Grand Island

Jan. 26, Osceola, Seminole chief, died a prisoner at Fort Moultrie

Jan. 28, General Manuel Armijo proclaimed himself Governor of New Mexico in counter-revolution and practically held office except for short intervals until American possession in 1846

Feb. 16, Kentucky granted limited school suffrage to women

Feb. 22, Constitution of Pennsylvania amended by convention which first met May 2, 1837

April 6, General Winfield Scott sent to forcibly remove the Cherokees to west of the Mississippi in accordance with Treaty of 1835

April 7, S. F. B. Morse filed application for patent for his telegraph

April 8-23, First trip of the passenger steamer "Great Western" from Bristol to New York, the first steamboat built for trans-Atlantic service, and the same day the "Sirius" arrived from London after 17 days trip

April 11, Claims Convention with Texas signed

April 17, Bill prohibiting the sale of spirituous liquors at retail became law in Massachusetts

April 25, Boundary Treaty with Texas signed

April 27, Great fire at Charleston, South Carolina, destroyed property worth $3,000,000

April, Convention of bankers from a majority of States met in New York City and decided not to join New York banks in resuming specie payments

May 8, Northern Cross Railroad begun (Wabash), first trip made by the "Rogers" engine Nov. 8

May 10, New York banks resumed specie payments

——, Proclamation of General Scott to the Cherokees followed by their removal in June from their lands by 9,000 regular troops and militia, their property seized by white settlers while the Indians confined in stockades

May 18, Pennsylvania Hall in Philadelphia destroyed by a pro-slavery mob

May 29, The steamer "Sir Robert Peel" on the St. Lawrence River burned by Americans in revenge for the destruction of the "Caroline" by British

June 25, James K. Paulding, of New York, appointed Secretary of the Navy, entering upon duties July 1

July 1, Boston banks resumed specie payments

July 4, "Danites" or "Sons of Dan," secret organization of Mormons founded, "assassins in the name of the Lord," for defense against Gentiles, owing its origin to revelation of Joseph Smith of Aug. 6, 1833

——, Territorial government inaugurated at Burlington, Iowa, Robert Lucas, Governor

July 5, Felix Grundy, of Tennessee, appointed Attorney General to take effect Sept. 1

July 16, Railroad from Reading to Norristown, Pennsylvania, opened

July 23, Bank Convention at Philadelphia attended by representatives of local banks of Massachusetts, Connecticut, Rhode Island, Pennsylvania, Delaware, Maryland, Virginia, Kentucky, and Missouri resolved to resume specie payments Aug. 13

Aug. 11, Lieutenant Charles Wilkes, of the Navy, commissioned March 20 to command of 6 vessels to explore the Pacific Ocean and southern seas, instructed to proceed to Rio de Janeiro and thence to Patagonia, Tierra del Fuego, in interests of the whaling fisheries. Expedition sailed Aug. 18 from Hampton Roads, Virginia and arrived at Rio de Janeiro Nov. 23

Aug., Alvarado received news of his confirmation as Governor of California from the Mexican Government

Sept. 1, $500,000 paid into Treasury under will of John Smith to found the Smithsonian Institution

Oct. 3, Death of Chief Black Hawk in Iowa

Oct. 12, Texas withdrew offer of annexation to the United States

Oct. 27, "Extermination Order" of Governor Boggs which finally drove the Mormons from Missouri

Oct. 30, Mormons gathered in blacksmith's shop at Hawn's Mill, Caldwell, Missouri, massacred by Missourians in retaliation for rout of militia under Captain Bogart by armed force of Mormons

Nov. 14, Arrival of Catholic Fathers F. N. Blanchet and Modeste Demers at Fort Vancouver overland from Canada

Nov. 21, Second Proclamation of the President issued enjoining strict neutrality as to Canada

Nov. 26, Treaty of commerce and navigation with Sardinia

Dec. 3, Constitutional Convention at St. Joseph framed Constitution for Florida

Dec. 4, "Buckshot War" in Pennsylvania legislature, Whigs and Democrats in conflict charging fraudulent election on which depended the election of a United States Senator. The Whig Senate met and adjourned because of mob invading session, and the Whig Governor tried in vain to get federal aid

Dec. 23, Nashua and Lowell Railroad in New Hampshire completed

Dec. 25, Democratic House of Pennsylvania recognized, ending "Buckshot War"

CONGRESS

Jan. 4, Resolution introduced in Senate and House asking the President to take the necessary steps for annexation of Texas. Tabled in Senate June 14, and vote prevented in House by opposition of John Quincy Adams

Feb. 7, Senator Linn presented Bill asking for military occupation of the Columbia River

Feb. 14, John Quincy Adams presented 350 petitions against slavery and the annexation of Texas

March 26, Sub-treasury Bill with specie clause providing for the exclusive use of gold and silver in public revenues passed in Senate; rejected by House June 25

April 24, W. C. Preston asked the Senate to denounce the Treaty of 1819 under which the region between the Sabine and Rio Grande rivers recognized as Mexican territory, and "reannex" it to the United States with the consent of Texas

May 17 and 22, Cushing, of Massachusetts, in House, urged establishment of post on the Columbia River and territorial government for region west of the Rocky Mts.

May 21, New issue of Treasury notes authorized

May 25, Last appropriation made for the national road

May 31, Joint Resolution directed Secretary of the Treasury to receive notes of specie paying banks in payment for public lands thus annulling the specie circular

June 12, Iowa received a territorial government

June 16, J. Q. Adams began speech on right of petition and freedom of speech which he ended on July 7

July 7, Every railroad in the United States constituted a post route

July 9, Congress adjourned

Dec. 3, Twenty-fifth Congress, 2d sess. convened

Dec. 7, The President transmitted report of Secretary of Treasury on defalcations of Samuel Swartwout, ex-collector of custom house of New York

Dec. 11, The "Atherton Resolutions," a second "gag" law to suppress debates on slavery passed the House

1839

Jan. 6, Father Blanchet established mission at site of present St. Paul, Oregon

Jan. 12, Iron successfully made with anthracite coal at Mauch Chunk, Pennsylvania

Jan. 19, Treaty of commerce and navigation with the Netherlands

Jan. 25, Five vessels of the Wilkes expedition to the south seas reached the Rio Negro from Rio de Janeiro

Jan., Governor Fairfield of Maine asked the legislature to send land agent and men to break up lumber camps established by Canadians

Feb. 8, Aroostook war between the Maine frontiersmen and British tresspassers in disputed region of Aroostook county begun. Captain Stover Rines with armed force drove Canadians cutting timber from the region

Feb. 11, University of Missouri at Columbia chartered, opened 1841

Feb. 12, Rufus McIntire, land agent for Maine, and 2 others arrested at lumber camp south of the Little Madawaska River by Canadians from New Brunswick, and sent to prison at Frederickton

Feb. 13, Proclamation of Sir John Harvey, lieutenant-governor of New Brunswick, claimed exclusive jurisdiction over disputed Aroostook region

Feb. 15, Powhatan Ellis, whose commission as Minister to Mexico of March 1837 had been held up by the President, finally appointed

Feb. 27, Agreement of Secretary of State and British Minister in Washington that territory in dispute should remain under British jurisdiction until boundary line settled; this decision greatly resented by Maine

March 3, Agricultural Section established in the Patent Office

March 4, First express in the United States begun by W. F. Harnden between New York and Boston

March 5, General Scott reached Augusta, Maine to take charge on frontier

March 23, Sir John Harvey agreed to proposal of General Scott of March 21 not to take military possession of the disputed territory

March 25, The Governor of Maine agreed not to disturb New Brunswick in the possession of the Madawaska settlements, and war averted

April 6, Joseph Smith and a number of other Mormons arrested and charged with murder, treason, and other crimes. They escaped from their guards on journey to Columbia, Missouri

April 11, Arbitration Convention with Mexico signed for submission of claims of American citizens to a mixed commission, 2 Mexicans, 2 Americans, and a Prussian umpire

April 20, Last of the Mormons left Missouri, ending civil war

May 1, Mormon agents began buying land in Commerce, Illinois, on east bank of the Mississippi, and renamed town City of Nauvoo

May 15, Wilkes expedition at Valparaiso, Chile

May 16, First printing press in Northwest received at Lapwai mission in present Idaho

May 21–Oct., Journey of Thomas J. Farnham from Independence, Missouri through western Colorado to Fort Vancouver

June 13, Treaty of peace, navigation, friendship, and commerce with Ecuador signed

July 2, Joseph N. Nicollet left Fort Pierre (Pierre, S.D.) and journeyed through eastern Dakotas and western Minnesota and descended the Minnesota River to Fort Snelling

July 3, John Augustus Sutter, Swiss-German-American, reached Monterey from the Sandwich Islands and obtained permission of Governor of California to found colony and erect fort on tract along the Sacramento

——, Syracuse and Utica Railroad opened

July 23, Battle of Carloosahatchee River in the Seminole war

Aug. 12, John Augustus Sutter took Mexican citizenship, and settled on south bank of the American River, a branch of the Sacramento

Aug. 26, Lieutenant Gedney, in command of brig "Washington," captured the "Amistad" off Long Island, a Spanish slave ship from Havana in possession of slaves who had killed the captain and seized the ship, which Gedney brought into New London Aug. 29 to jurisdiction of Connecticut courts

Sept. 4, "Harmony" Convention, anti-Van Buren, met at Harrisburg and declared for William Henry Harrison for president

Sept. 6, Demand of the Spanish Minister that the "Amistad" be delivered to her Spanish owners

Sept. 23, Judge Thompson in Hartford gave first decision in the "Amistad" case that ship, cargo, and negroes should be surrendered to the judicial decision of the United States

Sept. 25, Treaty of navigation and commerce between France and Texas signed

Oct. 5, Nauvoo, Illinois, formally adopted as "stake" of Mormon Church

Oct. 9, Jason Lee with settlers sailed from New York, arriving on the Columbia River May 21, 1840

Oct., S. F. B. Morse made his first successful daguerreotype portraits

Nov. 13, Convention of abolitionists afterwards called the Liberty Party met at Warsaw, New York, and nominated James G. Birney for president and Thomas Earle for vice-president

Dec. 4, National Convention of Whigs met at Harrisburg and nominated William Henry Harrison for president (Dec. 6) and John Tyler for vice-president (Dec. 7), though Henry Clay led on first ballot with 103 votes, Harrison, 94, and Scott, 57. *See infra* Feb. 7

Dec. 26, The Wilkes expedition sailed for the south seas from Sydney, Australia

Chapin map published included Texas and part of Mexico as western possessions of the United States

CONGRESS

Jan. 28, Petition from settlers on the Willamette River asking the United States to take formal possession of Oregon laid before the Senate

Feb. 7, Speech of Henry Clay against the abolitionists exerted marked influence on the presidential election

Feb. 16, Report on Oregon region presented by Caleb Cushing

Feb. 20, Anti-dueling law passed

Feb. 28, Act abolished imprisonment for debt in certain cases

March 3, The President given authority to send troops to Maine for protection of the frontier

——, Congress adjourned

Dec. 2, Twenty-sixth Congress, 1st sess. convened

——, Contest over seats of 5 New Jersey members in House delayed organization for several days

Dec. 24, President Van Buren's message again urged adoption of the sub-treasury plan

Dec. 27, Mr. Benton introduced resolution in Senate against the assumption of State debts

1840

Jan. 11, Henry D. Gilpin, of Pennsylvania, appointed Attorney General

Jan. 19, The Wilkes expedition sighted Antarctic Continent, earliest recorded discovery of the continent

Jan. 23, District court awarded the vessel "Amistad" captured Aug. 1839 to lawful owners, slaves to be transported to Africa

March 27–Dec. 3, Expedition of Father Peter John de Smet from St. Louis to visit the Flathead Indians in the Gallatin Valley

March 31, Executive Order of President Van Buren established ten-hour day on government work with no reduction of wages

April 1, Liberty Party of abolitionists in national convention at Albany confirmed the nominations of J. G. Birney for president and Thomas Earle for vice-president

April 28, Battle of Fort King in the Seminole war

May 5, National Democratic Convention met at Baltimore and nominated Van Buren for president, the nomination of vice-president left to the States

May 19, John M. Niles, of Connecticut, appointed Postmaster General

May 20, Treaty of commerce and navigation with Hanover signed

May–Nov., The "log cabin and hard cider campaign" for Harrison and Tyler, with stump speaking, monster processions, and other methods of influencing voters which were later adopted by all parties

June 20, S. F. B. Morse received patent for his telegraph

July 19, First Cunard line steamer, the "Brittania" arrived in Boston from Liverpool, trip of 14 days and 8 hours

Aug. 26, Treaty of commerce and navigation with Portugal signed

Sept. 6, Battle with Indians at Wacahoota, Florida

Sept. 15, Governor Boggs, of Missouri, issued request for surrender of Joseph Smith and Sydney Rigdon, extradition not granted by Illinois

Nov. 10, Presidential election

Nov. 13, Treaty of commerce and navigation between Great Britain and the Texan Republic signed; not ratified by Great Britain

Nov., Alexander McLeod, a deputy sheriff in Canada, who had boasted that he had killed Amos Durfee in the affair of the "Caroline" arrested in New York, and confined in Lockport prison to await trial for murder

Dec. 3–24, Battle of the Everglades with the Florida Indians

Dec. 13, British Minister in Washington asked for release of McLeod

Dec. 26, Secretary of State replied to British Minister that offense with which McLeod was charged was committed in New York and came under the jurisdiction of the courts of the State

First successful daguerreotype portraits made in New York by S. F. B. Morse, introducing photography invented in France by L. J. M. Daguerre

The sixth census gave the total population 17,069,453 (14,195,805 whites, 386,293 free negroes, and 2,487,355 slaves). The number of immigrants arriving between 1830 and 1840 was 599,125 according to the official reports, of whom 283,191 were from the British Isles and 212,497 from European countries. New York led in population with 2,378,890 white inhabitants, 50,027 free negroes, and 4 slaves. Pennsylvania came second with 1,676,115 whites, 47,854 free negroes, and 64 slaves, and Ohio, third, with 1,502,122 whites, 17,342 free negroes, and 3 slaves. The center of population had moved west to a point south of Clarksburg in what is now West

Virginia. Only eight and a half per cent of the total population lived in cities of 8,000 or more inhabitants. The cities having over 100,000 inhabitants were New York, 312,000, Philadelphia, 220,000, Baltimore, 102,000, and New Orleans, 102,000

CONGRESS

Jan. 8, The House reënacted the "gag law" against discussion of slavery as a standing rule

Jan. 25, Message from the President declared England ready to pay £23,500 for claims for damages by slave holders, some of them pending since 1830

March 10, New Jersey election contest settled

July 4, Sub-Treasury Act passed by Senate Jan. 23 and House June 30 became law, providing for the care of the public revenue in sub-treasuries established by the Government

——, Secretary of the Treasury instructed to pay to the heirs of Matthew Lyon $1,062.50 with interest for fine imposed on Lyon under the Sedition Act of 1798

July 20, $25,000 appropriated for exploration and survey of boundary line between Maine and New Hampshire and the British provinces

July 21, Congress adjourned

Dec. 7, Twenty-sixth Congress, 2d sess. convened

1841

Jan. 15, Bank of the United States in Philadelphia resumed specie payments, but suspended Feb. 4

Feb. 17–18, Meeting of settlers of Oregon elected judges, Ira L. Babcock, "supreme judge" and other officers and appointed a committee to draft a code of laws

March 2, Battle at Orange Creek Bridge in Seminole war

March 4, Inauguration of President William Henry Harrison, of Ohio, and Vice-President John Tyler, of Virginia

March 5, Daniel Webster, of Massachusetts, appointed Secretary of State; Thomas Ewing, of Ohio, Secretary of the Treasury; John Bell, of Tennessee, Secretary of War; John J. Crittenden, of Kentucky, Attorney General; George E. Badger, of North Carolina, Secretary of the Navy

March 6, Francis Granger, of New York, appointed Postmaster General

March 9, Decision of the Supreme Court in the "Amistad" case sustained the lower courts and freed the negroes, who were defended by John Quincy Adams

March 12, Formal demand of the British Minister for the release of McLeod

March 17, Claims Convention with Peru signed

April 4, Death of President Harrison of pneumonia

April 6, Vice-President Tyler inaugurated as President

——, The cornerstone of Mormon temple laid at Nauvoo, Illinois

April 10, The New York Tribune first published by Horace Greeley

April 24, Note of Secretary of State Webster to British Minister, Fox, reviewed the destruction of the "Caroline" and stated the responsibility of the British government as acknowledged in British correspondence regarding McLeod

April 27, The Wilkes expedition returning reached Oregon at the Columbia River and carried out survey of the river as far as Walla Walla

May 1, Company of 47 emigrants led by Paul Geddes, John Bartleson, and John Bidwell left Independence,

Missouri, in caravan which became known as "the first emigrant train to California," reaching camp of the American Dr. John Marsh on the Stanislaus River Nov. 4

May 19, The vessel "Star of Oregon" built on Swan Island in the Willamette River launched

June 21, Expedition of President Lamar of Texas commanded by General Hugh McLeod began march against Spanish in New Mexico towards Santa Fé, reaching San Miguel Sept. 4 after journey across unknown desert country

June 30, First passenger train made trip on the Erie Railroad

Aug. 2, The "Star of Oregon" descended the Willamette River, left Cape Disappointment Sept. 12 and arrived at San Francisco Sept. 17

Aug. 21, Letter of John M. Botts of the House to Virginia constituents spoke with contempt of President who would be "headed" yet, which influenced President Tyler to veto the Bank Bill

Sept., James Grogan seized by armed band of Canadians at village of Alburg, Vermont, and held as hostage of McLeod

Sept. 11, Resignation of Cabinet except Secretary of State because of veto of fiscal corporation Bill

Sept. 13, Walter Forward, of Pennsylvania, appointed Secretary of the Treasury; Abel P. Upshur, of Virginia, Secretary of the Navy; Charles A. Wickliffe, of Kentucky, Postmaster General; Hugh L. Legare, of South Carolina, Attorney General

Sept. 25, Proclamation of the President against secret lodges on the border preparing for armed invasion of Canada

Oct. 4, First convention met in Rhode Island to consider charter revision

Oct. 5, Texan invaders of New Mexico under General McLeod captured by Mexicans and jailed and taken prisoners to Mexico City

Oct. 12, McLeod acquitted by New York court, his alibi establishing that he had no part in the "Caroline" affair

——, John C. Spencer, of New York, appointed Secretary of War

Oct. 19, John C. Fremont reached Sutter's fort in California

Oct. 27, The "Creole" with slaves sailed from Hampton, Virginia, for New Orleans, and on Nov. 7 the slaves gained possession of the ship and sailed to the British West Indies where the British gave them their freedom

Nov. 1, Father Lucian Galtier dedicated log cabin to St. Paul on site of present St. Paul, Minnesota, from which name of city taken

Nov. 15, Convention in Rhode Island met in opposition to the legislature, which refused to consider revision of the charter, and framed the "People's Constitution"

Dec. 21, First passenger train on Western Railroad reached Albany from Worcester

Dec. 27–29, "People's Constitution" adopted in Rhode Island by majority of vote cast by opponents of old charter

CONGRESS

Feb. 10, Electoral votes counted, W. H. Harrison, Whig, receiving 234 votes for president; Van Buren, Democrat, 60; and John Tyler, 234 for vice-president; Richard M. Johnson, Liberty Party, 48

March 3, Congress adjourned

May 31, Twenty-seventh Congress, 1st sess. convened in extra session

June 7, Henry Clay introduced Whig program in Senate in a series of resolves, the repeal of the Sub-Treasury Act, incorporation of a bank, provision for raising revenue by new duties and a loan, a prospective distribution among the States of the proceeds of public lands etc.

July 21, Treasury loan of $12,000,000 authorized in 6% notes

July 27, Bill for establishment of a fiscal bank with $30,000,000 capital to be located in Washington with power to establish branches independent of the assent of the States passed Senate, and House Aug. 6

Aug. 13, Sub-Treasury Act repealed

Aug. 16, The President vetoed the Fiscal Bank Bill

Aug. 19, The Senate failed to pass the Fiscal Bank Bill over the veto by vote of 25 to 24

——, Bankruptcy Act established a uniform system of bankruptcy throughout the United States

Aug. 23, New Bank Bill for establishment of a "fiscal corporation" cut down capital to $21,000,000, provided for local agencies instead of offices for discount and deposit, and limited the branch dealings to foreign and interstate bills of exchange passed the House, and the Senate Sept. 6

Sept. 4, Public Land Act, the "general pre-emption law" provided for the distribution of the proceeds of the public lands, but on condition that it should be suspended if the duties were raised above the maximum of the "compromise" Act of 1833

Sept. 9, Second Bank Bill, "fiscal corporation" vetoed by the President, objecting to the bank as unconstitutional, and that the new plan covertly authorized local discounts under the form of exchange

Sept. 10, Bank Bill failed to obtain the two-thirds vote necessary to pass over veto in Senate

Sept. 11, Tariff Act provided for average rate of 33%, "home valuation" dropped

——, Repeal of Act of July 14, 1832 which had released from duty iron used for railroad construction

Sept. 13, Congress adjourned

Dec. 6, Twenty-seventh Congress, 2d sess. convened

Dec. 16, Senator Lewis F. Linn introduced a Bill providing for a line of forts from Missouri to Oregon and at the mouth of the Columbia River

1842

Jan. 1, Bank of the United States in Philadelphia closed its doors

Jan. 18, Riots in Cincinnati after bank failures

Jan. 21, Charles Dickens arrived in Boston from England on visit to America

Jan., Decision given by Supreme Court in case of Prigg vs. Pennsylvania nullified state laws granting trial by jury in case of arrest of fugitive slaves which had rendered nugatory the provisions of the federal fugitive slave law

Feb. 21, Patent granted to John Greenough for a sewing machine

March 3, Massachusetts passed law limiting hours of work for children under 12 in factories to 10 hours a day

March 5, Resolution of legislature of Florida that delegate in Congress be requested to obtain from Congress law authorizing rewards for Indian scalps and for every Indian taken alive

March 5, General Vasquez with 500 Mexicans captured San Antonio, Texas, which he held 2 days

April 16, Waddy Thompson succeeding Poinsett as Minister to Mexico arrived in Mexico City, his first official act to visit the Texan prisoners whose release he was able to obtain on June 16

April 18, Thomas W. Dorr chosen Governor of Rhode Island under the new Constitution, and inaugurated at Providence by supporters of the Constitution

April 19, Battle of Big Hammock in the Seminole war

April 21, P. Ellis left Mexico

May 16, Second emigrant wagon train left Independence, Missouri, for the Pacific, arriving at Whitman's Oregon mission about Sept. 11

May 18, Dorr party, declared by General Assembly at Newport to be in insurrection, failed to gain possession of Rhode Island State Arsenal, and Dorr fled to Connecticut the following day

June 10, Return of the Wilkes exploring expedition after 4 years

June 15, First exploring expedition of John C. Fremont with Kit Carson as guide left the ford of the Kansas near present site of Kansas City, sighted summit of Long's Peak in Rocky Mts. July 9, and Aug. 8 reached South Pass which was crossed

June 27, Texan Congress declared war of invasion on Mexico, but measure vetoed by President Houston

Aug. 9, Treaty with Great Britain (Webster-Ashburton) signed settled boundaries between Maine and the British provinces on the northeast, line extending westward beyond the Great Lakes practically that suggested by the King of the Netherlands earlier and rejected by the United States, the United States receiving seven-twelfths of the 12,000 square miles in dispute. A cruising Convention for the mutual suppression of the slave trade was concluded, and an extradition agreement reached

Aug. 14, Colonel Worth made formal proclamation that the Seminole war had ended

Sept. 11, Mexicans under General Adrian Woll captured San Antonio but evacuated the city Sept. 20 because of advancing Texan troops

Sept., Father de Smet established a mission on the St. Mary's River in the Bitter Root Valley for the Flathead Indians

Oct. 1, Fremont expedition returned to St. Louis

Oct. 3, Whitman left his Oregon mission on the Walla Walla for mid-winter journey to Washington and Boston in interest of mission

Oct. 14, Celebration in New York City of opening of Croton aqueduct

Oct. 19, Morse's submarine telegraph laid between Goose Island and New York City destroyed in test by sailors who cut the cable

Oct. 20, Commodore Thomas A. C. Jones led by reports to believe that Mexico and the United States were at war took possession of Monterey and Mexican fort, territory restored on the 21st and act disavowed by President Tyler and reparation made

Nov. 5, Convention which first met Sept. 12 framed a Constitution for Rhode Island to supersede the charter of 1663, ratified by vote of people Nov. 21–23, a clause abolished slavery

Nov. 22, Abel Stearns sent to Alfred Robinson 20 ounces weight of California placer gold to be forwarded to the mint in Philadelphia for assay

Dec. 7, First concert given by the New York Philharmonic Orchestra

Dec. 19, Official letter of Daniel Webster, Secretary of State, of superior interest of United States in Hawaiian Islands

Dec. 26, Disastrous engagement of Texans under Colonel William S. Fisher at Mier on right bank of Rio Grande with Mexicans ended in surrender

Dec. 31, Message of the President recognized independence of Hawaiian Islands

CONGRESS

Jan. 21, John Quincy Adams presented a petition from citizens of Haverhill, Massachusetts, asking for a peaceful dissolution of the Union

Jan. 25, Resolution of censure of Adams presented and discussed in House until Feb. 7. Adams asked the clerk to read the first paragraph of the Declaration of Independence which recognizes the right of every people to alter or abolish their form of government when it ceases to accomplish its end. The resolution tabled and the House voted Feb. 7 to refuse to receive the petition from the citizens of Haverhill

Jan. 31, Act authorized further issue of Treasury notes to $5,000,000 for temporary relief

Feb. 17, The President's exchequer Bill reported in House

March 21, Joshua Giddings presented a series of resolutions against slavery in House on the "Creole" case, and resolution of censure against him adopted March 23, whereat he resigned, but was reëlected from Ohio with large majority

March 31, Henry Clay resigned from Congress after 40 years of service

April 15, The $12,000,000 loan increased by $5,000,000 and term extended to relieve the Treasury

June 29, President Tyler vetoed the "Little Tariff Bill" because it suspended for 1 month the provisions of the Compromise Act of 1833 which forbade a distribution of the sale of public lands when the duties were raised above 20% ad valorem

Aug. 9, The President vetoed the second tariff Bill presented which included provision that the proceeds of land sales should be distributed notwithstanding the increase of tariff rates above 20% ad valorem

Aug. 26, Fiscal year changed from Jan. 1 to July 1

Aug. 29, Judiciary Act amended so that offenses committed under color of foreign authority and affecting foreign relations might be controlled by the federal courts to avoid such a situation as the McLeod case presented, foreigners restrained by State or court in violation of international rights given right to habeas corpus with appeal to Supreme Court

Aug. 30, Tariff Bill approved without the land distribution clause, duties raised from 20% to 30% ad valorem except on railroad iron; tea and coffee grown east of the Cape of Good Hope and imported in American vessels admitted free of duty

Aug. 31, Congress adjourned

Dec. 5, Twenty-seventh Congress, 3d sess. convened

Dec. 14, President Tyler vetoed Bill as to designation of proceeds of public land sales, and Bill for testimony in contested elections

Dec. 18, President Tyler vetoed Bill regarding payment of Cherokee certificates

1843

Jan. 11, Death of Francis Scott Key, author of the "Star Spangled Banner" in Baltimore

Jan. 30, Claims Treaty with Mexico signed by which Mexico agreed to pay principal and interest on sum awarded under Treaty of 1839

Feb. 2, First of "Wolf meetings" in Oregon, and committee appointed to devise means "for the protection of our herds," and collection of dues from settlers provided for

March 2, Marcus Whitman reached Washington from Oregon

March 3, Death of Commodore David Porter at Pera

——, John C. Spencer, of New York, appointed Secretary of the Treasury

March 8, James M. Porter, of Pennsylvania, appointed Secretary of War

May 2, Second meeting of settlers of Oregon at Champoeg appointed committee to draw up plan for provisional government

May 8, Daniel Webster, Secretary of State, retired from the Cabinet

May 14, The vessel "Star of Oregon" sold in California for 350 cows and the party of 42 started overland to return to Oregon with cattle, horses, and sheep

May 22, About 1,000 emigrants under leadership of Marcus Whitman began journey from near Independence, Missouri, to Oregon

May 29, Fremont's second expedition to discover a new pass through the Rocky Mts. started from near present Kansas City along Kansas River

June 17, Bunker Hill Monument completed, dedicated, address delivered by Daniel Webster, President Tyler at ceremony

June 20, Death of Hugh S. Legare, Attorney General

June 24, Abel P. Upshur, Secretary of the Navy, appointed *ad interim* Secretary of State

July 1, John Nelson, of Maryland, appointed Attorney General

July 5, "Fundamental laws" of Oregon provisional government ratified by meeting of settlers at Champoeg, to serve until the United States extended jurisdiction over the region. The Constitution prohibited slavery in the "Territory" and laws of Iowa adopted as far as they were applicable

July 9, Fremont expedition sighted Pike's Peak

July 12, "Revelation" of this date sanctioned plural marriage among the Mormons

July 24, Abel P. Upshur, of Virginia, appointed Secretary of State, David Henshaw of Massachusetts, Secretary of the Navy

July, Party of emigrants led by Lansford W. Hastings reached Sutter's fort from Oregon; other emigrants of this year to California the Chiles-Walker party

Aug. 7, Fremont gave up attempt to cut through the mountains to South Pass by way of the valley of the Cache de la Poudre River to find more southern route to Oregon and northern California because of roughness of the country, and reached Salt Lake Sept. 6, made scientific examination of northern part, and Fort Hall on the Snake River Sept. 18

Aug. 15, Fremont climbed peak in Rocky Mts. since named for him

Aug. 23, President Santa Anna notified the United States that the Mexican Government would "consider equivalent to a declaration of war against the Mexican Republic the passage of an act of the incorporation of Texas in the territory of the United States"

Aug. 27, Emigrants journeying from Missouri to Ore-

gon reached Fort Hall at junction of Snake and Portneuf rivers

Aug. 30, National Liberty Party in convention at Buffalo, N.Y. nominated J. G. Birney for president and Thomas Morris for vice-president

Oct. 16, Secretary of State Upshur in note to Isaac Van Zandt, Texan Minister in Washington, offered to reopen negotiations as to annexation of Texas

Oct. 20, Instructions of Upshur to Thompson, Minister to Mexico, to demand apology from Mexico for offensive statement of Aug. 23, that if war ensued Mexico would be the aggressor, and Texas to be considered an independent sovereign power competent to treat for herself

Oct. 31, T. W. Dorr returned to Providence and was arrested shortly

——, Vermont Central Railroad chartered

Nov. 5, Fremont expedition reached the Pacific coast at the Dalles of the Columbia River where camp made and proceeded to Vancouver, thus connecting the expedition with that of Captain Wilkes

Nov. 9, Treaty of extradition with France signed providing for surrender of criminals, and additional Article April 15, 1844

Nov. 25, Fremont expedition started south on journey through Oregon, Utah, and across the Sierra Nevadas into California, reaching Klamath Lake Dec. 10, and Lake Albert which Fremont named Dec. 20

CONGRESS

Jan. 10, Resolution offered by J. M. Botts in the House for impeachment of President Tyler rejected

Feb. 3, Linn's Oregon Bill of Dec. 16, 1841, passed in Senate but was defeated in House

Feb. 18, Act provided for relief of owners of fund received from British Government as indemnity for loss of slaves on board the "Comet" and "Encomium"

March 3, Bankruptcy Act of Aug. 19, 1841 repealed

——, Appropriation of $30,000,000 to aid S. F. B. Morse to establish the first telegraph line between Washington and Baltimore

——, Congress adjourned

Dec. 4, Twenty-eighth Congress, 1st sess. convened

Dec. 21, Proposal from legislature of Massachusetts presented by John Quincy Adams to amend the Constitution by repealing the three-fifths clause respecting apportionment of representatives

1844

Jan. 10, Fremont expedition reached Pyramid Lake which Fremont named, crossed the Sierras Feb. 2–29, and reached Sutter's fort March 6, and made camp at junction of American and Sacramento rivers to reëquip for return journey

Feb. 13, *Louisville Courier* established

Feb. 15, William S. Murphy took responsibility of giving in writing the assurance requested by Texas that the United States would aid in protection of Texas against Mexico pending proposed negotiations regarding annexation

——, William Wilkins, of Pennsylvania, appointed Secretary of War, and Thomas W. Gilmer, of Virginia, appointed Secretary of the Navy

Feb. 28, Explosion of gun on warship "Princeton" during pleasure excursion killed Upshur, Secretary of State, and Gilmer, Secretary of the Navy, David Gardiner, and others, and wounded 12 of crew

March 6, Mexican Government severed diplomatic relations in view of joint Resolution for the annexation of Texas

——, John C. Calhoun, of South Carolina, appointed Secretary of State

March 14, John Y. Mason, of Virginia, appointed Secretary of the Navy

April 11, Calhoun in letter to Texas agents, Van Zandt and Henderson, promised that the President would use his constitutional power to defend Texas from attack by any foreign power

April 12, Secret Treaty of annexation with Texas concluded; rejected by Senate June 8

April 20, Van Buren stated in letter that he regarded the annexation of Texas without the consent of Mexico dishonorable, the letter published and cost him nomination for the presidency

April 27, Letter of Henry Clay dated April 17 from Raleigh and letter of Van Buren of April 20 published, both opposing the immediate annexation of Texas

April 30, Mexico failed to pay the 4th quarterly installment due under Treaty of Jan. 30, 1843; protested by the United States July 24

May 1, Whig National Convention in Baltimore nominated Henry Clay for president and Theodore Frelinghuysen for vice-president

May 12, The Fremont expedition reached Las Vegas de Santa Clara, later named Mountain Meadows (Utah) and then the terminus of the desert journey from the West, and Utah Lake May 24

May 24, First message sent by Morse's telegraph between Washington and Baltimore: "What God hath wrought"

May 27, Democratic National Convention at Baltimore nominated James K. Polk for president and George M. Dallas for vice-president on third day (May 29). News of the convention sent from Baltimore to Washington by the new telegraph

——, The Tyler Democrats met in Baltimore to nominate Tyler for president, no vice-president named

May, The Stevens-Murphy party of emigrants left Missouri, reaching the Humboldt Sink Nov. 1, and taking a western course by the Walker River broke a new path to California which they reached in March 1845

June 7, The first and only issue of the Nauvoo *Expositor* appeared attacking Joseph Smith and polygamy

June 10, Office of the Nauvoo *Expositor* wrecked and burned by order of Joseph Smith

June 15, George M. Bibb, of Kentucky, appointed Secretary of the Treasury

June 24, Oregon enacted a prohibition law

——, Joseph and Hiram Smith, Mormons, surrendered to arrest at Carthage, Illinois, charged with resistance of Illinois law in connection with riots after suppression of the *Expositor*

——, Lord Aberdeen proposed to Ashbel Smith, Minister from Texas to Great Britain, "a diplomatic act" by which England and France acting with Mexico and Texas should settle boundaries of Texas and guarantee its independence, Texas to be pledged not to be annexed to the United States

June 25, T. W. Dorr sentenced in Rhode Island to life imprisonment for treason

June 26, Public meeting at Warsaw declared the destruction of the Nauvoo *Expositor* revolutionary and tyrannical and that the time had come to drive the Mormons from Illinois

June 26, Vermont Central Railroad opened 25 miles from White River Village to Bethel

June 27, Joseph Smith, Mormon leader, and his brother, Hiram Smith, in jail in Carthage, Illinois, murdered by a mob which broke into the jail

June 28, The Fremont expedition reached Pueblo, Colorado

July 1, Clay's first "Alabama letter" to Stephen F. Miller, of Tuscaloosa, stated that he had no objection to the annexation of Texas, but in view of abolitionist objection he was unwilling to see the Union dissolved for the sake of acquiring Texas

July 3, First Treaty with China signed of peace, amity, and commerce, permitting Americans to trade and reside at the open ports, and to be tried for crimes only by consul of the United States

July 27, Second "Alabama letter" to Thomas M. Peters and John M. Jackson in which Clay said he had no objection to the annexation of Texas "without dishonor, without war"

July 31, Fremont expedition reached town of Kansas on the Missouri and Aug. 1 took steamboat reaching St. Louis Aug. 6

Aug. 13, Constitution framed by convention which met at Trenton, New Jersey, May 14–June 29, ratified by people, restricted ballot to "white male citizens"

Aug. 22, Tyler withdrew as candidate for presidency

Sept. 1, Wilson Shannon, succeeding W. Thompson as Minister, received in Mexico City

Oct. 23, Day set by William Miller, founder of the Millerite sect, for the end of the world and the second Advent

Nov. 1, Constitution for Iowa adopted by convention which first met Oct. 7 at Iowa City

Nov. 12, Presidential election, Texas the chief issue

Nov. 22, Governor Micheltorena met California rebels led by Alvarado and José Castro near San José, and agreed to settle trouble by sending his convict army out of the country

Dec. 12, Jones succeeded Houston as president of Texas

Dec. 24, Brigham Young elected president of the Mormon Church; confirmed Oct. 7, 1845

CONGRESS

April 22, President Tyler submitted the Texas Annexation Treaty with message urging ratification

May 31, Judiciary Act of Sept. 24, 1789 amended, appeal from circuit courts to Supreme Court in any suit arising under revenue laws

June 8, Texas Annexation Treaty rejected by Senate 35 to 16

June 17, Congress adjourned

Dec. 2, Twenty-eighth Congress, 2d sess. convened

Dec. 3, John Quincy Adams carried the repeal of the "gag" rule against discussions of slavery

1845

Jan. 20, Los Angeles captured by Castro and Alvarado and about 50 of the foreign residents joined him

Feb. 1, Baylor University at Waco, Texas, chartered

Feb. 20–21, Armies of Micheltorena and Castro met in long range artillery duel at Cahuenga Pass. Micheltorena agreed to leave California with his convict army which he did in March

March 3, President Tyler sent official dispatches which tendered proposals of the United States to Texas for immediate annexation

March 4, Inauguration of President James K. Polk, and Vice-President George M. Dallas

March 6, General Almonte, Mexican Minister, protested to State Dept. against the annexation of Texas and demanded his passports

——, James Buchanan, of Pennsylvania, appointed Secretary of State; Robert J. Walker, of Mississippi, Secretary of the Treasury; William L. Marcy, of New York, Secretary of War; Cave Johnson, of Tennessee, Postmaster General; and John Y. Mason, of Virginia, Attorney General

March 10, George Bancroft, of Massachusetts, appointed Secretary of the Navy

March 19, Michigan passed local option laws

March 28, Shannon, American Minister in Mexico, notified by Mexican Government that diplomatic relations with the United States were ended

——, Buchanan, Secretary of State, instructed William S. Parrott, as secret agent, to reopen diplomatic relations with Mexico

March 29, Texan Secretary of State, Ashbel Smith, signed a preliminary treaty with Mexico by which Mexico would recognize the independence of Texas if that Republic would pledge itself against annexation to the United States

April 1, A. J. Donelson, American Minister, presented offer of the United States of annexation to President Jones at Texas capital

April 8, Convention at Champoeg, Oregon, for choice of candidates for governor, supreme court judges, and other officers

April 10, Pittsburgh, Pennsylvania, almost completely destroyed by fire

April, Mormon colony founded by James Jesse Strang on White River near Burlington, Wisconsin, which he named Voree

May 13, W. S. Parrott, American agent in Mexico, wrote that Great Britain had increased her naval forces in the Pacific with object of taking possession of Upper California in case of war between the United States and Mexico

May 14, New York adopted local option laws, and Rhode Island during the month

——, Louisiana in convention adopted a new Constitution

May 18, Colonel S. W. Kearney with 5 companions from Fort Leavenworth journeyed to South Pass, holding councils with the Indians

May 19, Mexican Government agreed to terms of proposed treaty with Texas

June 4, President Jones, of Texas, issued proclamation of cessation of hostilities with Mexico

June 8, Death of General Andrew Jackson (78), former president, near Nashville, Tenn.

June 13, Anti-Mormons to number of 400 appeared before Nauvoo, Illinois, but new citizens forced them to retreat

June 15, Buchanan, in letter to Donelson, agreed to repel invasion of Texas by Mexico if the Texas Congress accepted annexation terms

——, General Taylor ordered to occupy a point "on or near the Rio Grande" but to limit his action to defense of Texas unless war declared by Mexico

June 21, The Texan Senate rejected proposed Treaty with Mexico

June 23, Texan Congress voted for annexation to the United States

June 27, T. W. Dorr, under life sentence for treason, released under Act of amnesty of the Rhode Island legislature

——, Oregon organic law amended, the executive committee replaced by a governor, to be elected by the people, and a House of Representatives to replace the legislative committee

July 4, Texas people in convention accepted terms of annexation offered by the United States

July 5, Oregon legislative committee made final report amending organic laws

July 5–7, First Native American Party Convention held in Philadelphia

July 12, Buchanan, Secretary of State, offered Great Britain the boundary line of the 49th parallel for Oregon without free navigation of the Columbia

July 19, Great fire in New York City, property loss $6,000,000

July 26, Revised organic law for Oregon ratified by vote of people at special election

July 29, Pakenham refused Buchanan's offer of boundary line for Oregon, and asked for another proposal "more consistent with fairness and equity, and with the reasonable expectations of the British Government"

Aug. 16, Fremont started from Bent's Fort on the Arkansas on third exploring expedition through Colorado, Utah, and Nevada to California

Aug. 27, Constitution for Texas framed in convention which met at Austin July 4–Aug. 27, and ratified Oct. 13 by vote of the people

Aug. 30, President Polk instructed Buchanan to withdraw Oregon offer and negotiations with Great Britain ended

Sept. 9, Armed conflict began between Mormons and anti-Mormons in Hancock county, Illinois, houses of Mormons in the country burned forcing their withdrawal to towns

Sept. 16, The President appointed John Slidell, of New Orleans, secret agent to Mexico to negotiate to secure a permanent boundary by the purchase of Upper California and New Mexico

Sept. 24, Father de Smet reached the Flathead Lake Valley and established the St. Ignatius mission

Oct. 1, Meeting of anti-Mormons at Carthage, Illinois, representing several counties resolved that the Mormon settlement at Hancock should be broken up

Oct. 10, Naval Academy formally opened at Annapolis, Maryland, the consolidation of several small schools in New York, Boston, Norfolk, and Philadelphia

Oct. 15, The Foreign Minister of Mexico, Pena y Pena, in letter to Mr. Black, American consul, agreed to receive an envoy from the United States with power to adjust questions in dispute provided the American fleet be withdrawn from Mexican waters

Oct. 17, T. O. Larkin, American consul at Monterey, appointed confidential agent in California to defeat "any attempt which may be made by foreign governments to acquire a control over that country," and instructed as to American policy to acquire California without war but with the spontaneous wish of the Californians

Nov. 3, Lieutenant A. H. Gillespie sent to California to watch over interests of the United States and with messages to Larkin, Commodore Sloat with fleet at Mazatlan, and Captain John C. Fremont

Nov. 10, Instructions to John Slidell of this date to settle American claims, to adjust boundary with Texas, and negotiate for purchase of California and New Mexico, $25,000,000 offered for one line and $20,000,000 for another

——, Treaty of commerce and navigation with Belgium signed

Nov. 24, Fremont expedition reached Walker's Lake making a new trail across Nevada, and Dec. 9 reached Sutter's fort in California

Dec. 6, Slidell arrived at City of Mexico, and Dec. 21 was officially informed that he would not be received by the Herrera Government as envoy extraordinary and minister plenipotentiary, but must get new credentials as a mere "commissioner"

Dec. 27, Pakenham, British Minister, asked that offer of 49th parallel as boundary of Oregon be renewed and that the matter be submitted to arbitration

CONGRESS

Jan. 23, Uniform election day established as the Tuesday following the first Monday in November for all future presidential elections throughout the Union

Jan. 25, Joint Resolution for annexation of Texas passed the House, amended by Senate and passed Feb. 27, and passed Feb. 28

Feb. 12, Electoral vote counted elected James K. Polk, of Tennessee (Democrat) president with 170 votes, and George M. Dallas, of Pennsylvania, vice-president, with 105 votes. Henry Clay (Whig) received 105 votes for president, defeated by the abolitionist vote of the Liberty Party which lost him the votes of New York and Michigan, and Theodore Frelinghuysen (Whig) 105 votes for vice-president. Horace Greeley said: "the triumph of annexation [of Texas] was secured by the indirect aid of the more intense partisans of abolition"

Feb. 20, The President vetoed Bill forbidding the payment for some armed vessels which he had ordered built without lawful authority; passed over veto by Congress, the first veto overruled

March 1, Joint Resolution for the annexation of Texas signed by President Tyler

March 3, Florida admitted as the 27th State

——, Post routes established, and the transportation of mail with foreign countries provided for. Postage on letters reduced to 5 cents within 300 miles and 10 cents for greater distances

——, Enabling Act for Iowa passed, the boundaries therein defined rejected by Iowans. Iowa assigned 5% of the net proceeds of land sales for internal improvements

——, First measure to pass over any president's veto. See supra Feb. 20

——, Congress adjourned

Dec. 1, Twenty-ninth Congress, 1st sess. convened

Dec. 2, President Polk devoted one-fifth of his message to the Oregon question

Dec. 9, The President sent special message to Congress to announce that Texas had accepted proposed terms of admission to the Union

Dec. 29, Texas admitted to the Union as the 28th State on an equal footing with the original States by Joint Resolution

1846

Jan. 13, Secretary Marcy instructed General Taylor to advance and "occupy positions on or near the left

bank of the Rio del Norte (Rio Grande)" which meant invasion of Mexican territory

Jan. 15, Fremont with small party of men and without passports went by water by way of San Francisco Bay to Monterey to obtain consent of Mexico to visit settlements to refit his surveying expedition, and Jan. 27 visited Larkin, American consul, and visited General Castro (Mexican) explaining his purpose to determine the nearest practical route to the Pacific

Feb. 2, Charter for Beloit College approved by Governor of Wisconsin, opened 1847

Feb. 10, Exodus of Mormons from Nauvoo across the Mississippi for the West begun

Feb. 16, First legislature of Texas met at Austin, inaugurating the state government

March 3, Fremont encamped at the Hartwell ranch about 25 miles from Monterey, and on March 5 he was ordered by General Castro and the Mexican prefect to retire northward to the uninhabited region of the San Joaquin, which he refused to do, and March 6 began building a log fort on summit of Hawk's Peak in the Gavilan Mts.

March 8, General Castro issued proclamation against Fremont as leader of a "band of robbers"

——, General Taylor began march from Corpus Christi

March 9, Fremont threatened by large force retired toward the San Joaquin reaching Sutter's fort March 21, and leaving there March 24 reached Klamath Lake May 8

March 15, Slidell received the refusal of the Paredes Government of Mexico to give him an audience

March 28, General Taylor reached Point Isabel which threatened the Mexican town of Matamoras on the opposite bank of the Rio Grande

April 12, General Taylor warned by General Ampudia in command at Matamoras to retire beyond the Nueces River

April 13, Pennsylvania Railroad incorporated

April 21, President Polk informed the Cabinet that he should recommend to Congress the adoption of energetic measures for the redress of grievances against Mexico

April 24, Arista sent a military force across the Rio Grande to force Taylor's troops into an engagement

April 25, Hostilities with Mexico begun by capture of Captain Thornton with 60 dragoons by Mexicans

April 28, Oregon Treaty of 1827 abrogated

May 1, General Taylor left Fort Texas which he had built at the Rio Grande under charge of Major Brown and marched back to relief of Point Isabel

May 1–2, Dedication of completed Mormon temple at Nauvoo

May 3–8, Fort Texas (renamed Fort Brown after death of its defender) bombarded by Mexicans

May 8, Battle of Palo Alto. General Taylor marching from Point Isabel to relieve Fort Texas with artillery forced General Arista to retreat toward Matamoras

May 9, Battle of Resaca de la Palma. General Taylor routed army of Arista posted in new position, and General La Vega taken prisoner. From one-fifth to one-third of Arista's army of 6,000 lost in these 2 battles

——, Lieutenant Gillespie overtook Fremont going toward Oregon at Lake Klamath with secret instructions which made him return to the American settlements on the upper Sacramento which he reached May 24

May 18, General Taylor took possession of Matamoras

June 3, General Kearney ordered to occupy New Mexico and California, and began march from Fort Leavenworth on the Missouri June 5

June 10, Treaty of commerce and navigation with Hanover signed

June 11, American settlers led by Ezekiel Merritt and starting from Fremont's camp captured village of Sonoma 15 miles north of San Francisco Bay in surprise attack

June 14, Americans at Sonoma raised flag of California Republic with one star and a black bear which gave the revolt the name of the Black Bear War

June 15, Treaty with Great Britain signed which secured for the United States the territory of Oregon lying south of the 49th parallel of latitude in settlement of northwest boundary

June 23, Fremont joined the insurgents at Sonoma taking command of the Bear forces July 5

July 7, Monterey surrendered to Commodore J. S. Sloat who raised the American flag and proclaimed annexation of California to the United States

July 9, San Francisco occupied by Americans under Captain Montgomery

July 14, Camargo on the San Juan occupied by Americans under Captain Miles

——, British war vessel "Collingwood" commanded by Sir George Seymour arrived at Monterey, California "intending to take possession of that portion of the country" in case of disturbance to prevent American occupation

July 23, Commodore Robert F. Stockton succeeded Sloat in command of Pacific fleet, and took Fremont and his men into service ordering them to Los Angeles

July 24, General Worth occupied Camargo

July 31, General Kearny issued proclamation that he was going to New Mexico "for the purpose of seeking union with and ameliorating the condition of its inhabitants"

Aug. 3, Constitution for Iowa, adopted by a convention held May 4–19, ratified; a clause prohibited slavery

Aug. 7, First attack on Mexican fort at Alvarado by American frigates, "Mississippi" and "Princeton" under command of Captain David Conner

Aug. 8, General Taylor made Camargo his headquarters

Aug. 10, Smithsonian Institution at Washington incorporated

Aug. 13, Los Angeles occupied by Commodore Stockton and Fremont

Aug. 15, *The Californian* issued at Monterey, first newspaper in California, by Robert Semple and Walton Colton

Aug. 18, Santa Fé, New Mexico, occupied by General Kearny, and New Mexico declared annexed to the United States

Sept. 9, John V. Mason, of Virginia, appointed Secretary of the Navy

Sept. 10, Elias Howe patented his first sewing machine, with eye-pointed needle

——, Siege of Nauvoo begun, which ended in surrender of city and arms and signing of a peace Sept. 16 which forced the last Mormons to leave Illinois

Sept. 21–23, Siege of Monterey, Nuevo Leon, Mexico by General Taylor, who had advanced from Camargo, forced General Ampudia to ask for terms

Sept. 22, General Kearny promulgated code of laws for New Mexico and appointed Charles Bent, Governor

Sept. 23, General Wool began march from San Antonio toward Saltillo

Sept. 24, General Taylor occupied Monterey

Sept. 25, General Kearny left New Mexico for California ordered to proceed to Pacific coast by way of the Gila River and take possession of California

Sept. 29–30, Mexicans led by Captain José Maria Flores in successful revolt against American rule drove Gillespie, who had been appointed in command at Los Angeles by Stockton Aug. 17, from the city, and Talbot from Santa Barbara

Sept. 30, Dr. William Morton, a dentist, made first successful use of ether as an anæsthetic

Oct. 5–Dec. 16, Constitutional Convention at Madison, Wisconsin, framed constitution which was rejected by the people April 1847

Oct. 8, General Wool arrived at the Rio Grande

Oct. 15, Second attack on Alvarado a failure

Oct. 17, Nathan Clifford, of Maine, appointed Attorney General

Oct. 24, San Juan Bautista captured by Captain Perry

Oct. 29, General Wool occupied Monclova

Nov. 5, Orders of the Secretary of the Navy to Commodore Stockton ordered him to recognize General Kearny as Governor and Commander-in-Chief in California

Nov. 15, Tampico captured by Captain Conner

Nov. 16, General Taylor occupied Saltillo without opposition (Smith, McMaster, Nov. 13)

Nov. 19, General Scott accepted command of expedition to Vera Cruz under blockade by Captain Conner

Dec. 5, General Wool occupied Parras about 90 miles from Saltillo and joined General Worth at Saltillo about Dec. 20

Dec. 6, General Kearny worsted in engagement with Spanish Californians at San Pasqual a few miles below Escondido, and retreated to San Diego

Dec. 12, Treaty with New Granada (Colombia) signed of peace, amity, navigation, and commerce, right of free transit across the Isthmus granted and the United States agreed to protect the neutrality of the Isthmus and Colombian sovereignty over it

Dec. 25, Battle of El Brazito. Colonel Doniphan defeated the Mexicans at Temascalitos on east bank of the Rio Grande

Dec. 29, General John A. Quitman entered Victoria without opposition

CONGRESS

April 27, The President authorized to give notice to Great Britain of termination of joint convention for the occupation of Oregon

May 11, The President in message declared that "war exists by the act of Mexico," the boundary of the United States had been passed and American blood shed

May 13, Congress declared war begun by Mexico, appropriated $10,000,000, and empowered the President to use the army and navy

May 19, Establishment of military stations on the route to Oregon authorized and appropriation made

June 10, Proposal of Great Britain for settlement of Oregon boundary at the 49th parallel laid before the Senate by the President, and accepted by Senate June 12

July 30, The "Walker Tariff" Act named from Robert J. Walker, Secretary of the Treasury, reduced the duties on imports to about the rate of the "Compromise" Act of 1833, with high duty on luxuries only, duty on woolen goods lowered from 40 to 30%, and reduced scale for cotton fabrics, and iron

Aug. 3, Veto of River and Harbor Bill on constitutional grounds

Aug. 4, Boundaries of Iowa fixed and Mississippi boundary referred to Supreme Court

Aug. 6, Wisconsin authorized to form a state government

——, Independent Treasury reëstablished

——, "Warehouse system" established by which goods on which duties had not been paid were to be kept in public storehouses

——, First Bill for organization of Oregon as a Territory introduced in House with amendment and adopted that slavery should never exist in Territory; Bill not reported from committee in Senate

Aug. 8, Bill introduced in House embodying the President's request for an appropriation of $2,000,000 to negotiate a peace with Mexico and arrange a boundary, and an amendment added, known as the Wilmot proviso, originated by Jacob Brinkerhoff but presented by David Wilmot prohibiting slavery in any territory acquired from Mexico

Aug. 10, Appropriation Bill with Wilmot proviso failed in Senate where Davis of Massachusetts prevented it from coming to a vote

——, Congress adjourned

Dec. 7, Twenty-ninth Congress, 2d sess. convened

Dec. 28, Iowa admitted as the 29th State

1847

Jan. 3, General Scott arrived at Camargo Dec. 30, and ordered General Butler to move 9,000 of Taylor's best troops and 2 batteries of artillery without consulting General Taylor

Jan. 8, Americans under Stockton and Kearny defeated Californians across the San Gabriel River

Jan. 9, The Californians again defeated near Los Angeles, and the following day the Americans again in possession of Los Angeles

Jan. 13, Treaty of Cahuenga (Couenga). The Californian army under command of Don Andreas Pico surrendered to Fremont who arranged generous terms of capitulation

Jan. 15, Governor Bent, Sheriff Elliott, and 20 others murdered by insurgent Mexicans at San Fernando de Taos, New Mexico

Jan. 17, John Fremont assumed office of Governor of California, commissioned by Commodore Stockton. General Kearny warned Fremont that in accepting appointment from Stockton and thus recognizing Stockton as his chief instead of himself he was guilty of disobedience to his superior officer. The orders of Nov. 5 which settled the conflict of authority between General Kearny and Commodore Stockton were not communicated to Fremont

Jan. 23, Revolt against American government in New Mexico suppressed by Colonel Sterling Price in battle at village of Cordova

Jan. 28, Santa Anna began march from San Luis Potosi with 20,000 men to attack Taylor's depleted army

Feb. 22, Santa Anna sent General Taylor a peremptory summons to surrender

Feb. 23, Battle of Buena Vista. General Taylor with about 7,500 men at narrow mountain pass of Buena Vista near the valley of Saltillo repulsed attack of army of Santa Anna and forced them to retreat during the night to Agua Nueva

Feb. 25, First general Assembly for Territory of Iowa met at Iowa City

——, Pennsylvania Railroad received charter

——, Rockford College, Rockford, Illinois established

Feb. 28, Battle of Sacramento. Colonel A. W. Doniphan on march from New Mexico to join General Wool defeated Mexicans at the pass of Sacramento

March 1, Doniphan occupied Chihuahua which brought the entire southern valley of the upper Rio Grande under military control of the United States

March 9, Major General Winfield Scott's campaign in Mexico begun with landing of troops from Lobos Island 3 miles below Vera Cruz

March 10, Treaty of commerce and navigation with Oldenburg

March 22, Bombardment of Vera Cruz and the castle of San Juan d'Ulloa begun on refusal of General Morales to surrender

March 29, Vera Cruz surrendered to General Scott

April 8, General Scott began march from Verz Cruz toward the City of Mexico

April 14, Brigham Young with large party of Mormons left Council Bluffs for the far West

April 15, N. P. Trist, appointed commissioner to Mexico, received instructions to negotiate for the cession of the two Californias, New Mexico, and privilege of right of way across the Isthmus of Tehuantepec, for $30,000,000, or $20,000,000 for New Mexico and Upper California without the Tehuantepec transit and Lower California, and started on his mission the following day

April 16, Advance party of Mormons led by Young, "the Pioneers," started from camp at Elkhorn River along north bank of the Platte for Fort Laramie, route known thereafter as the Mormon Trail

April 18, Battle of Cerro Gordo. General Scott defeated the Mexicans, driving Santa Anna from a strong position on high hill from which the battle named

April 19, Scott occupied Jalapa

——, Battle of Atlixo. General Lane defeated the Mexicans commanded by Rea

April 27, The Collins Line began service with trip of the "Atlantic" sailing from New York to Liverpool

May 1, Cornerstone of the Smithsonian Institution in Washington laid

May 15, Part of Scott's army under General Worth occupied Puebla

May 31, General Kearny left California, succeeded in military and civil command by Colonel Richard B. Mason

May, Strang established a Mormon settlement on Big Beaver Island near outlet of Lake Michigan

June 6, Trist opened negotiations with Mexican Government through the British legation, as a result of which General Scott paid Santa Anna a bribe of $10,000

June, Grinnell College, at Grinnell, Iowa, chartered

July 7, Brigham Young's party of Mormons reached Fort Bridger

July 22, Advance company of Mormons led by Anson Pratt camped on site of Salt Lake City, and the following day Brigham Young with other settlers arrived at the camp, which day was afterwards celebrated by the Mormons as the anniversary of their deliverance

Aug. 20, General Scott defeated the Mexicans in engagements at Contreras and Cherubusco and called on the City of Mexico to surrender

Aug. 22, City of the Great Salt Lake given as name for Mormon settlement

Aug. 24, Armistice proposed by Scott became effective which lasted until Sept. 7 while Mexican commissioners conferred with Trist

Aug. 31, Convention which met at Springfield June 7 adopted Constitution for Illinois, ratified by popular vote March 6, 1848

Aug., George M. Evans found gold in the mountains between San Diego and the Gila River

Sept. 4, *Santa Fé Republican* issued, first newspaper in English in New Mexico

Sept. 8, Battle of El Molino del Rey (The King's Mill). Hostilities resumed against Santa Anna resulted in American victory. Ulysses S. Grant appointed brevet first lieutenant for gallant conduct in this engagement

Sept. 13, General Scott successfully stormed the fortress of Chapultepec and Mexican army left the capital Sept. 13–14, taking northern road to Guadalupe Hidalgo

Sept. 14, General Scott occupied the City of Mexico and raised the American flag at the palace. Among the members of his staff were Captain Robert E. Lee, Lieutenant P. G. T. Beauregard, and Lieutenant George B. McClellan

——, Siege of American garrison at Puebla under Colonel Childs begun by Rea, reinforced by Santa Anna Sept. 22, but ended with arrival of American force under General Joseph Lane from Vera Cruz

Sept. 25, Mexican General Ampudia surrendered Monterey to forces of General Taylor

Oct. 4, Letter of Buchanan to Trist which he received Nov. 16 ordered his return

Oct. 9, Battle of Huamantla. Captain Walker, part of army of General Lane advancing to reinforce garrisons between Vera Cruz and Mexico City, killed in engagement with forces of Santa Anna, but reinforcements gave Americans the victory

Oct. 13, Aztec Club, veterans of Mexican War, founded in City of Mexico

Oct. 24, The first locomotive west of Chicago, the "Pioneer" made trip on Galena and Chicago Union Railroad

Nov. 18, Revised Constitution for New York State adopted and ratified

Nov. 22, The new Mexican Government after resignation of Santa Anna (Sept. 16) notified Trist that it had appointed commissioners to negotiate a peace

Nov. 29, Massacre of Dr. Whitman and his wife and 7 other persons by the Indians in Oregon, and captives taken later ransomed by efforts of the British

Dec. 24, Lewis Cass in letter to A. O. P. Nicholson of Nashville, Tennessee, first promulgated the doctrine of "squatter sovereignty"

CONGRESS

Jan. 15, Mr. Rhett in House made noted speech in discussion on the Oregon Bill expressing view of the South that the "States" were joint owners of the Territories and "co-sovereigns" in them, and that the Government was only the agent of the States

Jan. 16, Bill for territorial organization of Oregon which excluded slavery by repeating the restrictions of the Northwest Ordinance passed the House; tabled by Senate

Jan. 28, Treasury notes at 6% to $23,000,000 authorized

Feb. 5–March 1, Discussion of a $3,000,000 appropriation Bill in Senate which passed without the "Wilmot proviso"

Feb. 11, Ten additional regiments for regular army authorized

Feb. 15, Appropriation Bill for $2,000,000 with "Wilmot proviso" excluding slavery from all subsequent territorial acquisitions passed in House

Feb. 19, Calhoun introduced his new slavery resolutions in Senate, affirming that the Territories belonged to the several States composing the Union and are held by them as joint and common property, and that Congress as the agent or representative of the States has no right to make any law which shall make any discrimination between the States, *i.e.*, prohibit slavery in Territories under the Constitution

March 3, Postage stamps adopted, the Postmaster General to issue 5 and 10 cent stamps as evidence of prepayment of postage

——, Appropriation of $3,000,000 authorized to bring war with Mexico to a close

——, Resolved to light the Capitol and grounds with gas

——, Wisconsin admitted as a State conditionally provided that the people assembled assented to the Constitution

——, Congress adjourned

Dec. 7, Thirtieth Congress, 1st sess. convened

1848

Jan. 2, First official conference of Trist with Mexican commissioners acting under instructions of Pena y Pena of Dec. 30 to negotiate a peace

Jan. 3, Girard College, Philadelphia, opened

Jan. 24, James W. Marshall struck gold in Eldorado County, San Joaquin Valley, California, while building a mill-race for John A. Sutter

Jan. 31, A court-martial found John Fremont guilty on charges preferred by General Kearny of mutiny from Jan. 17–May 9, 1847, disobedience of the lawful command of a superior officer, and conduct prejudicial to good order and discipline, and sentenced him to dismissal from the service. President Polk immediately canceled the punishment though he approved the sentence. Fremont resigned from the army March 15 protesting his innocence

Feb. 2, Treaty of Guadalupe Hidalgo signed with Mexico ending the war, New Mexico and California including the present California, New Mexico, Nevada, Utah, most of Arizona, and a part of Colorado were ceded by Mexico to the United States on payment of $15,000,000 by the United States and the assumption of $3,250,000 representing claims of American citizens against Mexico, and the Rio Grande and thence to the Pacific south of San Diego accepted as the boundary line

Feb. 18, General William O. Butler, next in rank, succeeded General Scott in command of the army in Mexico

Feb. 19, The Treaty with Mexico negotiated by Trist received by President Polk

Feb. 23, Death of John Quincy Adams (81) former president, in Washington

March 6, Constitution for Illinois ratified by vote of the people, to come into effect April 1

March 13, Constitution for Wisconsin framed by con

vention which met Dec. 15, 1847–Feb. 1 ratified by popular vote, a clause prohibited slavery

March 16–April 28, Court of inquiry to consider charges against General Scott as to bribing Mexicans and distribution of military merit in war sat in Mexico City, and later in the United States

March 29, Death of John Jacob Astor (85) in New York City

April, Pacific Mail Steamship Company organized to bring gold seekers to California

May 1, Main body of Mormons left Missouri for Salt Lake City led by Brigham Young

May 3, Pennsylvania prohibited holding of fugitive slaves in jails of the State

May 22, The National Convention of the Democratic Party met in Baltimore and nominated Lewis Cass of Michigan for president, thus condemning the "Wilmot proviso," and William O. Butler of Kentucky for vice-president

May 29, The *Californian* suspended publication, announcing that the majority of the subscribers had left for the gold fields

——, Wisconsin admitted. *See infra* Congress

June 2, The Liberty League, abolition group, held convention in Rochester, New York, and nominated Gerrit Smith for president and Charles E. Foot for vice-president

June 5, Meeting of first legislature of Wisconsin

June 7, Whig National Convention met in Philadelphia and nominated Zachary Taylor of Louisiana for president and Millard Fillmore of New York for vice-president

June 13, An industrial congress of representatives of labor organizations met in Philadelphia and nominated Gerrit Smith and William S. Waitt for president and vice-president

June 21, Isaac Toucey, of Connecticut, appointed Attorney General

July 4, Mexican Treaty proclaimed by President Polk

——, Cornerstone of the Washington monument laid

July 19–20, First Women's Rights Convention held at Seneca Falls, New York, Lucretia Mott, speaker

Aug. 9, National Convention of an anti-slavery party which called the "Free Soil Party" met in Buffalo and nominated Van Buren for president on a platform which affirmed the power of Congress to exclude slavery from the Territories and its duty to exercise that power, Charles Francis Adams, of Massachusetts, nominated for vice-president

Aug. 19, Letter published in the *New York Herald* announced discovery of gold in California

Sept. 28, Tigre Island ceded to the United States by Honduras on conditions

Nov. 7, Presidential election held, the popular vote 1,360,099 for General Zachary Taylor, Lewis Cass receiving 1,220,544, and Van Buren 291,263

Dec. 5, The publication of President Polk's annual message made authentic the reported discovery of gold in California and the "gold rush" began to California

Dec. 11, William Tweed joined in organization of a volunteer fire company and painted on engine the tiger which he later adopted as emblem of Tammany Society, New York City

CONGRESS

Jan. 10, Mr. Douglas presented in Senate a Bill for the organization of a territorial government in Oregon

which provided that the laws of Oregon should remain in force as far as compatible with the Constitution and laws of the United States until the Territorial legislature should change them

Jan. 31, Resolution authorized the erection of a monument to George Washington on the public grounds in Washington

Feb. 9, The House reintroduced their Bill for organization of Oregon

March 10, Treaty with Mexico ratified by the Senate

March 31, Loan of $16,000,000 authorized

April 13, Resolution congratulated the people of France on the establishment of a Republic

May 29, Message of the President urged immediate action on Oregon, transmitting a petition from the provisional government of Oregon asking the aid and protection of the United States

——, Wisconsin finally admitted to the Union as the 30th State under different State Constitution

May 31, $25,000 appropriated to buy the unpublished papers of James Madison

July 27, Senate committee reported a Bill for the organization of Oregon, New Mexico, and California, the "Clayton Compromise" which provided for the organization of Oregon with its existing anti-slavery laws and referred questions of slavery in New Mexico and California to the territorial courts with right of appeal to the Supreme Court; tabled in House

Aug. 2, Bill passed in House for the organization of Oregon with application of conditions and prohibitions of the Northwest Ordinance, and passed Senate in the early morning of Sunday, Aug. 13

Aug. 14, Oregon Bill signed by the President, slavery prohibited

——, Congress adjourned

Dec. 4, Thirtieth Congress, 2d sess. convened

Dec. 5, President Polk in his message announced the discovery of gold in California

1849

Jan. 15, The "Jackson Resolutions" introduced in Missouri Senate by Carty Wells from committee of which Claiborne F. Jackson, chairman, questioned the right of Congress to legislate for the territories on slavery and declared that "the right to prohibit slavery in any Territory belongs exclusively to the people thereof," passed in both Houses

Jan. 18, The Astor Library, New York City, incorporated

Jan. 30, The *New York Herald* listed 99 vessels sailing for California and carrying 5,700 passengers to the gold fields during the month

Feb. 8, The *New York Tribune* listed 131 vessels sailing for California with over 8,000 passengers for the gold fields

Feb. 12, Mass meeting at San Francisco established a temporary government for that district and the legislature of 15 constituted

Feb. 28, The "California," the first vessel to arrive at San Francisco with crowd of gold seekers

Feb., University of Wisconsin opened at Madison

March 3, General Joseph Lane, first Governor, proclaimed the territorial government in Washington

March 4, Convention held in Salt Lake City to frame a system of government for a state to be called the State of Deseret

March 5, Inauguration of President Zachary Taylor (Whig) and Vice-President Millard Fillmore

March 7, John M. Clayton, of Delaware, appointed Secretary of State

March 8, Jacob Collamer, of Vermont, appointed Postmaster General; William B. Preston, of Virginia, Secretary of the Navy; Thomas Ewing, of Ohio, Secretary of the Interior; Reverdy Johnson, of Maryland, Attorney General; William M. Meredith, of Pennsylvania, Secretary of the Treasury; George W. Crawford, of Georgia, Secretary of War

March 18, Charter granted to the Pacific Railroad (Missouri Pacific Railroad) to build a road from St. Louis to Jefferson City

April 7, Panama Railroad Company incorporated by American company

April 12, General Bennet Riley arrived as acting Governor of California and assumed office the following day

April 28, First number of *Minnesota Pioneer* issued at St. Paul by James M. Goodhue

April 28–Sept. 13, Pitt River Indian expedition

April, Merger of railroads in New Jersey, the Somerville and Easton and the Elizabethtown and Somerville forming the Central Railroad of New Jersey

May 26, Thomas H. Benton, United States senator, opposed "Jackson Resolutions" as representing a spirit of nullification and disunion, and appealed from the legislature to the people of Missouri; defeated Jan. 22, 1851

June 1, Proclamation of Governor Alexander Ramsey organized the territorial government of Minnesota

——, Journey of Captain H. Stansbury, begun from Fort Leavenworth to Fort Bridger on Black Forks River, explored deserts west of Great Salt Lake and on return journey followed new route through the Rocky Mts.

June 15, Death of James K. Polk, former President (54)

July 2, General Assembly chosen for the State of Deseret adopted memorial to Congress asking admission to the Union

Aug. 11, Proclamation of President Taylor declared his belief that an armed expedition was being fitted out against Cuba and called on all good citizens to prevent the enterprise

Aug. 12, Death of Albert Gallatin at Astoria, Long Island

Aug. 25, Public meeting at St. Augustine adopted petition to Congress asking removal of Indians from Florida

Sept. 1, Pennsylvania Railroad opened from Harrisburg to Lewiston

Sept. 1–Oct. 13, Convention at Monterey drafted a Constitution for California, and applied for admission to the Union as a free State, ratified by vote of the people Nov. 13, slavery prohibited

Sept. 3, First legislature of Minnesota met at St. Paul

——, Statement of Buchanan that English or French control of Hawaii would be "highly injurious"

Oct. 1, Constitution for Kentucky adopted in convention at Frankfort

Dec. 20, Treaty of friendship, commerce, and navigation with Hawaiian Islands signed

——, State Government of California established, Peter H. Burnett, Governor, San José, the temporary capital

Dec. 24–25, Great fire in San Francisco

Dec. 31, Vermont Central Railroad completed to Burlington

——, Hudson River Railroad opened as far as Poughkeepsie, New York

CONGRESS

Feb. 14, Electoral votes counted elected General Zachary Taylor (Whig) president with 163 votes, and Millard Fillmore received 163 votes for vice-president. Lewis Cass (Democrat) received 127 votes for president, and W. O. Butler 127 for vice-president

March 2, Swamp lands granted to Louisiana to aid in drainage projects

March 3, Territorial government of Minnesota established, slavery automatically prohibited by the Northwest Ordinance

——, Dept. of the Interior created, and the work of the census office, patents, pensions, Indian and public land affairs assigned to it

——, Coinage of the gold dollar and double eagle authorized

——, Survey to mark the boundary of Iowa authorized

——, Congress adjourned

Dec. 3, Thirty-first Congress, 1st sess. convened

Dec. 4, President Taylor informed Congress of the proceedings in California and of his wish to admit California immediately to the Union as a State. The South in general protested against admission which would endanger southern majority in the Senate

1850

Jan. 2, Treaty of amity, navigation, and commerce with Salvador signed

Jan. 21, Florida Indians in conference with General Twiggs agree to move west

April 15, San Francisco incorporated by first legislature

April 19, Clayton-Bulwer Treaty with Great Britain signed provided for a joint protectorate of the United States and Great Britain over proposed canal across Central America, neither government to obtain exclusive control of the canal, or "occupy, or fortify, or colonize, or assume, or exercise any dominion" over any part of Central America, and the neutrality of the canal guaranteed

May 8, University of Rochester (N.Y.) chartered

May 19, Narcisso Lopez with volunteers from the southern States landed at Cuba on unsuccessful filibustering expedition to free Cuba from Spanish rule

May 22, The Henry Grinnell expedition sailed for the Arctic in search of Sir John Franklin in the "Advance" and the "Rescue" lent by Mr. Grinnell to the United States Government, Lieutenant E. J. DeHaven in charge, Elisha K. Kane, surgeon and historian

May 25, New Mexico in convention adopted a Constitution, settling boundaries and excluding slavery

June 3, Convention of 9 of the slave-holding States met at Nashville in favor of dis-union

June 10, Clerk at Fort Laramie reported the total number of emigrants who passed the post en route for California as 16,915 men, 235 women, and 242 children

June 11, Constitution of 1849 ratified by the people of Kentucky

June 23, Treaty of amity and commerce with Borneo signed

July 1, First overland mail route west of Missouri River established with monthly trip from Independence, Mo., to Salt Lake City

July 8, At this date 42,000 emigrants and 9,720 wagons had passed Fort Laramie bound for the California gold fields since Jan. 1

July 8, Strang's Mormon Colony on Big Beaver Island in Lake Michigan organized as Kingdom of St. James, and Strang crowned King

July 9, Death of President Taylor

July 10, Millard Fillmore, Vice-President, took the oath as President

July 22, John J. Crittenden, of Kentucky, appointed Attorney General; William A. Graham, of North Carolina, Secretary of the Navy; Daniel Webster, of Massachusetts, Secretary of State

July 23, Thomas Corwin, of Ohio, appointed Secretary of the Treasury, and Nathan K. Hall, of New York, appointed Postmaster General

Aug. 14–18, Riots in San Francisco and fighting between armed squatters and police and militia

Aug. 15, Charles M. Conrad, of Louisiana, appointed Secretary of War

Sept. 1, Jenny Lind arrived in New York and was greeted at the pier by more than 20,000 persons

Sept. 12, Alexander H. H. Stuart, of Virginia, appointed Secretary of the Interior

Sept. 25, James Hamlet who had lived for 3 years in New York City seized and taken to Baltimore under the fugitive slave law

Sept. 28, Brigham Young appointed Governor of Utah by the President

Oct. 23, First National Woman's Rights Convention held at Worcester, Massachusetts

Oct. 25, Southern Rights Association formed at St. Helena Parish, South Carolina, for concerted action to resist the anti-slavery States

Nov. 5, Constitution for Michigan, adopted by convention which met June 3–Aug. 15, ratified, and negro suffrage defeated

Nov. 25, Treaty of friendship, commerce, and extradition with Switzerland signed

Nov., University of Utah opened at Salt Lake City

Dec. 9, Agreement with Great Britain as to cession of Horseshoe Reef

Dec. 21, Webster, Secretary of State, wrote the famous letter to Mr. Hulsemann, Austrian Minister at Washington, declaring the principles upon which the United States chose to act in recognizing new governments born of successful revolution

Northern legislatures passed "personal liberty laws" to protect free negroes liable to false accusation under the fugitive slave law

The seventh census gave the total population as 23,191,876, nearly 36% greater than in 1840, 19,553,-114 whites, 434,449 free blacks, and 3,204,051 slaves in the southern States and 262 only in the north; 1,713,251 immigrants had arrived from Europe during the decade, 1,047,763 from Great Britain chiefly from Ireland. The center of population 23 miles southeast of Parkersburg, West Virginia

New York Typographical Union No. 6 founded, Horace Greely, first president

CONGRESS

Jan. 29, Clay in Senate introduced a series of 8 resolutions providing for the admission of California as a State with free-State Constitution, New Mexico and Utah to be organized as Territories without provisions for or against slavery, the establishment of boundary of Texas and debt to be assumed by the United States on condition that Texas relinquish claims on New Mexico, for abolition of the slave trade in the District of Columbia, a more effective

law for the rendition of fugitive slaves without jury trial, denial to Congress of all power to interfere with the slave trade as between slave-holding States

Feb. 5, Clay's speech in support of his resolutions

Feb. 12, Resolution adopted for the purchase of the manuscript of Washington's "Farewell Address"

March 4, Calhoun's speech on the Clay Compromise, a plea for the South and slave institutions

March 7, Webster's speech on the Clay Compromise supported Clay giving his influence to pacification

March 11, W. H. Seward's speech on the Clay Compromise urging the admission of California under her free-state Constitution, supporting the President and opposing Clay

March 26 and 27, S. P. Chase's speech on the Clay Compromise

April 18, The Compromise Resolutions referred to a committee of 13 with Clay as chairman to be framed into bills; reported May 8 in series of measures passed Sept. 9–20 known as the "Compromise" or "Omnibus" Bill

June 17, Increase of rank and file of the army provided for and enlistment encouraged

Sept. 9, New Mexico and Utah Territories established

——, Northern and western boundary of Texas established and $10,000,000 paid to Texas to relinquish her claims to New Mexico

——, California admitted as the 31st State with constitution prohibiting slavery

Sept. 18, Fugitive Slave Act of Feb., 1793 amended, imposed fine and imprisonment on any person harboring a fugitive slave or aiding him to escape, marshals and deputy-marshals to obey and execute warrants, trial by jury of a fugitive on the question of his freedom in a competent court done away with, fee of the commissioner made $10 in case he issued a certificate of arrest to the claimant of the fugitive, and only $5 in cases discharged

Sept. 20, Slave trade in the District of Columbia abolished from Jan. 1, 1851

——, First great public land grant to aid construction of a railroad gave right of way and land to Illinois, Mississippi, and Alabama for railroad from Chicago to Mobile

Sept. 27, Oregon Donation Act provided for survey of public lands in Oregon Territory and granted each missionary station 640 acres of land, and to settlers of terms of residence specified 640 acres to each man and wife, and 320 acres to single men

Sept. 28, Flogging abolished in the navy and on vessels of commerce

——, Swamp lands granted to Arkansas and other States to enable them to reclaim swamp lands within their limits

Sept. 30, Congress adjourned

Dec. 2, Thirty-first Congress, 2d sess. convened

1851

Jan. 27, Death of John James Audubon (71) ornithologist

Feb. 10, Illinois Central Railroad incorporated

——, Constitution for Indiana adopted to take effect Nov. 1, framed by convention which met first Oct. 7, 1850

Feb. 15, University of Rochester, New York, which opened in 1850, chartered

——, Shadrach, arrested in Boston as a fugitive slave,

rescued from jail during the night by a mob of colored men and sent to safety in Canada

Feb. 18, Proclamation of the President called on officers and citizens to aid in the recapture of Shadrach

Feb. 26, Convention signed by which Portugal agreed to pay claims amounting to $91,727

March 4, University of Minnesota founded

March 10, Second Constitution for Ohio adopted by convention

April 3, Thomas Sims, a slave who had escaped from Georgia, arrested in Boston

April 20, First electric railroad inaugurated from Washington to Bladensburg, Md.

April 25, President Fillmore issued second Proclamation warning against participation in expeditions aganist Cuba as violation of international law

May 3, Fifth great fire in San Francisco with property loss of $12,000,000, burned 16 blocks and more than 1,500 houses

May 12, Southern Rights Association convened at Charleston

May 13, Constitution for Maryland adopted by convention which met first at Annapolis Nov. 4, 1850; ratified by the people June 4

May 15, The Erie Railroad, chartered in April 1833, opened from Piermont on the Hudson to Dunkirk on Lake Erie, 400 miles, the longest single railroad in the world at this time

May 21, Lieutenant William L. Herndon and Lardner Gibbon started from Lima, Peru on exploring expedition of Amazon River Valley

May 30, Grinnell expedition to the Arctic returned to New York

June 2, Original Maine Act which prohibited the sale of intoxicating liquors in the State

June 9, Committee of Vigilance of San Francisco organized with membership of about 200 leading citizens to deal with prevalent lawless crime, and that night the members called to headquarters by fire bell tried and convicted John Jenkins, ex-convict, who had burglarized a store, and in 2 hours he was hanged. Record of sentences imposed by the committee as follows: 4 hanged, 1 whipped, 14 deported, 1 ordered to leave the State, 15 handed over to authorities, and 41 discharged

June 22, Another great fire in San Francisco with loss of $2,000,000, burned 8 blocks

July 4, Ground broken for Pacific Railroad on shore of Choteau Lake by mayor of St. Louis

——, Cornerstone for extension of the Capitol laid by the President, oration by Daniel Webster

July 10, Treaty of friendship, commerce, and navigation with Costa Rica signed

July 26, Treaty of friendship, commerce, and navigation with Peru signed

Aug. 2, General Lopez left New Orleans on second filibustering expedition to free Cuba from Spanish rule, landing about 60 miles from Havana Aug. 11, Colonel William L. Crittenden, of Kentucky, member of expedition

Aug. 4, Herndon expedition embarked on Hullaga River in 2 canoes and on Sept. 3 reached junction between Hullaga and Maranon rivers, trip of 700 miles

Aug. 13, Colonel Crittenden with 50 other members of the Lopez expedition captured, and shot Aug. 16 at Havana by Cuban authorities

Aug. 21, Spanish consular office at New Orleans sacked and 10 stores kept by Spaniards looted when news received of execution of Americans of the Lopez expedition in Cuba

Aug. 22, The schooner yacht "America" won cup offered by the Royal Yacht Society of England in race around the Isle of Wight; the cup presented to the New York Yacht Club

Aug. 24, Lopez force defeated by Cubans, and Lopez captured Aug. 28

Sept. 1, Lopez executed at Havana and his followers sent prisoners to Spain

Sept. 7, Lieutenant Gibbon of Herndon expedition in South America reached Fort Principe da Beira on boundary of Bolivia and Brazil by way of Mamore and Itenez rivers

Sept. 10, Louis Kossuth, late Governor of the "Hungarian Republic" with refugees, received on board U.S.S. "Mississippi" at the Dardanelles, arriving at Marseilles Sept. 26, where reception accorded to Kossuth, but French Government refused him passage through France to England

Sept. 14, Death of James Fenimore Cooper (62) at Cooperstown, New York

Sept. 17–19, Boston celebrated jubilee at which President Fillmore was the guest of honor on completion of a series of railroads which connected Boston with Montreal, the Great Lakes and 13 States

Oct. 1, The "Jerry rescue," of fugitive slave at Syracuse, New York, from jail

Oct. 11, Hudson River Railroad completed and opened from Poughkeepsie to Albany making through connection with New York City

Oct. 16, Delaware, Lackawanna, and Western Railroad (Liggett's Gap) opened, and first coal train moved out of Scranton for Ithaca where connection was made with the canal

Oct. 21, Lieutenant Gibbon completed voyage from Sao Antonio Falls to mouth of Madeira River

Oct. 22, Proclamation of the President forbidding expeditions into Mexico

Oct. 23, Kossuth left the U.S.S. "Mississippi" at Gibraltar and proceeded to England for visit

Nov. 12, Public meeting at Genoa, Nevada, to organize a squatter government

Dec. 4, Herndon expedition arrived at Tabatinga, Brazilian frontier

Dec. 5, Kossuth reached New York from England, met by mayor, common council, and company of prominent citizens

Dec. 7, Henry Clay resigned his seat in Senate to take effect Sept. 6, 1852

CONGRESS

Feb. 21, Message of the President reviewed the Shadrach case and asked in view of resistance of Massachusetts to the fugitive slave law that the President be confirmed in the use of the army and navy to suppress violence and execute the laws

March 3, Joint Resolution adopted that a war vessel be sent to the Mediterranean to bring Louis Kossuth, escaped from Hungary to Turkey, to America

——, Letter postage reduced to 3 cents for 3,000 miles or less if prepaid and 5 cents if not, and double rate for over 3,000 miles

——, Land Act provided for commission to settle claims of "squatters" in California

——, Congress adjourned. Decided that Congress should end at noon on March 4

Dec. 1, Thirty-second Congress, 1st sess. convened

Dec. 15, Joint Resolution to welcome Louis Kossuth to the capital and the country

1852

Jan. 2–March 3, California Land Commission held sessions in San Francisco

Jan. 7, Louis Kossuth visited both Houses of Congress and attended a banquet given in his honor in the evening

March 4, Louisiana passed local option law

March 20, "Uncle Tom's Cabin," by Mrs. Harriet Beecher Stowe, depicting the "possibilities of horror and tragedy rooted in the institution" of slavery published in book form after it had appeared as a serial in an anti-slavery paper

April 11, Herndon expedition to Amazon River landed at Para

April 21, Tufts College in Massachusetts chartered

April 30, Consular Convention with the Hanseatic cities of Hamburg, Bremen, and Lübeck signed

May 22, Massachusetts enacted prohibition law; repealed 1868

May–July, Captain Randolph B. Marcy explored upper course and sources of the Red River

June 1, Democratic National Convention met in Baltimore. The two-thirds rule adopted. On the 49th ballot on the 5th day General Franklin Pierce, of New Hampshire, nominated for president and William R. King, of Alabama, for vice-president. The compromise measures of 1850 accepted and any further agitation of the question of slavery opposed, and the Virginia and Kentucky resolutions endorsed

June 16 and Nov. 16, Convention of extradition and additional Article with Prussia signed

——, Whig National Convention met at Baltimore, General Winfield Scott nominated for president on the 53d ballot, and William A. Graham for vice-president. The compromise measures of 1850 approved as final settlement of these questions

June 24, Meeting of first National Agricultural Convention in Washington

June 29, Death of Henry Clay (75) in Washington

June 30, San Francisco Vigilance Committee dissolved though members stood ready to be called for civic purposes

July 5, National Convention at Trenton, New Jersey, of the "Know-Nothing Party," later called the American Party, at which 31 delegates represented 9 States, Pennsylvania, New Jersey, New York, Massachusetts, Illinois, Ohio, Maryland, Virginia, and Georgia, nominated Daniel Webster for president, and George C. Washington as vice-president, the name given them because of their declaration that they knew nothing about their secret oath-bound organization

July 22, John P. Kennedy, of Maryland, appointed Secretary of the Navy

Aug. 11, Free-Soil Convention met at Pittsburgh, and nominated John P. Hale for president and George W. Julian for vice-president, declaration adopted that slavery a sin against God and a crime against man, and the compromise measures denounced

Aug. 12, Isaac M. Singer patented a sewing machine stronger than any heretofore and with new valuable features

Aug. 26, Treaty of commerce and navigation with the

Netherlands signed supplementing Treaty of Jan. 19, 1839

Aug. 31, Samuel D. Hubbard, of Connecticut, appointed Postmaster General

Oct. 10, The first passenger train left Chicago for Joliet on the Rock Island Railroad, the first railroad to cross the Mississippi

Oct. 24, Death of Daniel Webster (70) at Marshfield, Massachusetts

Nov. 1, Constitution for Louisiana, adopted by convention which met at Baton Rouge July 5–31, ratified by the people

Nov. 2, Presidential election

Nov. 6, Edward Everett, of Massachusetts, appointed Secretary of State

Nov. 23, Vermont enacted a prohibition law

Nov. 24, Commodore Matthew Calbraith Perry brother of Oliver Hazard Perry, sailed from Norfolk for Japan on special mission to negotiate a treaty

CONGRESS

Feb. 10, $6,000 appropriated to bring home Americans of the Lopez expedition taken prisoners from Cuba to Spain and freed by Queen Isabella

June 10, Right of way and tract of public lands given to Missouri to aid in building railroads

July 3, Branch of the mint established at San Francisco

Aug. 4, General right of way through the public lands given to all railroads, macadamized roads, and turnpikes chartered within 10 years

Aug. 26, Charles Sumner attacked the fugitive slave law in 4 hour speech in the Senate

Aug. 30, Inspection of steamboat boilers and better security of passengers provided for

Aug. 31, Permanent lighthouse board authorized

——, Congress adjourned

Dec. 6, Thirty-second Congress, 2d sess. convened

——, Joseph Lane introduced resolutions requesting the committee on Territories to examine into the expediency of dividing Oregon Territory

1853

Jan. 12, The Baltimore and Ohio Railroad formally opened to Wheeling

Jan., Rhode Island enacted prohibition law; repealed 1863

Feb. 8, Claims Convention with Great Britain signed

——, The "Water Witch" commanded by Lieutenant Thomas J. Page left Norfolk on exploring expedition to La Plata River

Feb. 12, Illinois law enacted that any negro or mulatto who came into the State and remained 10 days should be fined $50 or sold into slavery until the fine was worked out

Feb. 23, Consular Convention with France signed

Feb. and again Jan. 1856, Citizens of Carson Valley, Nevada, petitioned California for annexation

March 4, Inauguration of President Franklin Pierce (Democrat). Vice-President William R. King took the oath in Cuba March 24

March 7, William L. Marcy, of New York, appointed Secretary of State; Caleb Cushing, of Massachusetts, Attorney General; Jefferson Davis, of Mississippi, Secretary of War; James Campbell, of Pennsylvania, Postmaster General; James C. Dobbin, of North Carolina, Secretary of the Navy; Robert McClelland, of Michigan, Secretary of the Interior; James Guthrie, of Kentucky, Secretary of the Treasury

March 30, California law imposed tax of $4 a month on "foreign miners," aimed at the Chinese

April 18, Death of Vice-President William R. King

May 17, Nine small railroads between Albany and Buffalo merged and incorporated as the New York Central

May 19, James Gadsden appointed to negotiate new boundary treaty with Mexico

June 21, Martin Koszta, Hungarian refugee who had declared intention of becoming an American citizen, seized by Austrian cruiser at Smyrna, Turkey, and rescued from Austrians by Captain Ingraham of the U.S.S. "St. Louis"

July 10, Treaty with Argentina signed for free navigation of the Parana and Uruguay rivers

July 14, Commodore Perry arrived in Japan and presented his credentials and President Fillmore's letter to the Emperor of Japan

——, Crystal Palace in New York City opened by President Pierce

July 27, Treaty of friendship, commerce, and navigation with Argentina signed

Aug. 1, New Constitution for Massachusetts framed by convention which met in Boston May 7; not accepted by people

Aug. 29, Kane expedition to the Arctic in search of Sir John Franklin reached 78° 43' N. Lat. which remained for a long time "farthest north"

Sept. 1, Page expedition which reached Buenos Aires from Rio de Janeiro May 25 left there proceeding up the Parana River to junction with the Paraguay about 800 miles and then 900 miles to Brazilian post of Corumba

Sept. 8 and 10, Treaties signed ended war with Indians of Rogue River, Oregon, entire valley sold by Indians for $60,000

Sept. 12, Extradition Convention with Bavaria signed

Sept. 22, First telegraph in California opened connecting the lighthouse at Point Lobos with San Francisco, 8 miles

Oct. 22, Supplementary instructions to Gadsen as to boundary line between the Rio Grande and the Gila rivers, release from Article 11 of the treaty of 1848, and settlement of claims with Mexico

Nov. 4, William Walker's filibustering expedition landed at La Paz, Lower California, proclaimed the Republic of Sonora and himself president

Nov. 25, I. I. Stevens, appointed Governor of Washington, arrived at Olympia

——, Discovery of Heard Island, Antarctic, by Captain John J. Heard

Dec. 7, The New York Central began work of altering the gauges of the Erie Railroad purchased in the consolidation which resulted in the "Erie war," the citizens of Erie destroying tracks and bridges, suspending all traffic in order to preserve their freight business

Dec. 30, Treaty with Mexico negotiated by James Gadsen signed by which the sum of $10,000,000 paid to Mexico for a strip of territory to the south of the Gila River, the Mesilla Valley, making new boundary with Mexico, the southern part of the present New Mexico and Arizona included in this "Gadsden purchase."

CONGRESS

Jan. 20, The part of the Cumberland Road between Springfield, Ohio and the western boundary of the State transferred to Ohio

Feb. 9, Land grants to be transferred to railroads received by Arkansas and Missouri, and Illinois, Mississippi and Alabama also received land grants

Feb. 21, Coinage of $3 gold pieces authorized, the weight of the half dollar fixed at 192 gr. and the quarter, dime, and nickel at proportionate amounts

March 2, Territory of Washington formed out of the part of Oregon north of the Columbia River

——, Provision made for the administration of the oath to W. R. King, Vice-President elect, in Cuba

March 3, Exploration authorized to make a survey for a railroad from the Mississippi River to the Pacific coast

——, Congress adjourned

Dec. 5, Thirty-third Congress, 1st sess. convened

1854

Jan. 9, General Society of the War of 1812 organized as the Pennsylvania Association of the Defenders of the Country

——, Astor Library, New York City, opened

Jan. 15, First protestant church in New Mexico (Baptist) dedicated at Santa Fé, Louis Smith, minister

Jan. 18, Proclamation of President Pierce against invasion of Mexico called forth by Walker's expedition

Feb. 15, The Pennsylvania opened to Pittsburgh

Feb. 17, Mississippi enacted local option law

Feb. 28, American merchant steamer "Black Warrior" seized at Havana by Cuban officials and cargo confiscated on a technical charge of failure to manifest the cargo in transit

March 8, Commodore Perry in conference with the Japanese at Yokohama presented American gifts including a fully equipped miniature railroad, a telegraph line, and a steamboat, representing the arts of western civilization

March 31, Treaty with Japan signed of peace, amity, and commerce, breaking down Japan's policy of isolation, two ports of entry, Hakodadi and Simoda, opened to the United States

April 5, Lieutenant E. G. Beckwith left Salt Lake City to explore route for Pacific railroad between 41st and 43d parallels

April 8, Soulé, American Minister at Madrid, demanded satisfaction for the "Black Warrior" affair in peremptory manner which gave offense to the Spanish Government, exceeding his instructions, the affair later settled with the owners

April 26, Massachusetts Aid Society organized and incorporated by Eli Thayer to promote emigration to Kansas of settlers opposed to slavery

May 6, Cyrus W. Field organized an American company to raise funds to build a submarine cable across the Atlantic Ocean

May 15, San Francisco Vigilance Committee of 1856 organized, William Tell Coleman, president, after shooting of James King, newspaper editor, by James P. Casey May 14. King died May 20

May 24, The arrest in Boston of a runaway slave, Anthony Burns, was the occasion of riots and an attack on the courthouse led by Thomas Wentworth Higginson in attempt at rescue on May 26

May 31, Proclamation of the President against filibustering invasions of Cuba

June 2, Decision of Commissioner E. G. Loring that Burns was a fugitive and must be sent back to slavery

June 5, Treaty with Great Britain signed arranged for commercial reciprocity and opening the sea fisheries of the British provinces to American citizens, enlarging rights granted under the Convention of 1818, and the markets of each country to most of the natural products of the other free of duty; abrogated by the United States in 1866

June 7, First American Young Men's Christian Association met in Buffalo, N.Y.

June 10, Salt Creek Convention of pro-slavery settlers of Kansas called on friends of slavery to aid in its firmer establishment and wider extension

June 13, Association of 32 persons in Weston, Missouri, organized to found Leavenworth, Kansas

June 22, Connecticut prohibited the sale and manufacture of intoxicating liquors with exceptions such as that 5 gallons or more of domestic cider or wine might be sold by the maker; repealed 1872

July 6, Convention of Whigs and Free Soil party in Detroit, Michigan adopted name Republican

July 13, Commander G. N. Hollins of the United States ship "Cyane" bombarded and destroyed Greytown on the Mosquito coast of Central America in demand for satisfaction for insult to American Minister, Borland, in street fight, in spite of protest of Lieutenant Jolley in command of British ship "Bermuda"

July 17, First party of 29 settlers sent from Boston by the Massachusetts Emigrant Society, 600 settlers sent by winter by the Society

——, Claims Convention with Great Britain signed

July 22, Convention with Russia signed as to rights of neutrals at sea

July 30, Emigrants led by Charles H. Branscomb, sent by Massachusetts Emigrant Aid Society, arrived at Kansas frontier, reached the Wakarusa Aug. 1, and founded Lawrence, named in honor of Amos A. Lawrence

Aug. 21, Convention as to disposition of property signed with Brunswick and Luneburg

Sept. 1, Cornerstone of first railroad bridge across the Mississippi between Rock Island and Davenport, Iowa, laid

——, Second party of settlers from New England arrived in Kansas with Dr. Charles Robinson and Samuel C. Pomeroy

Sept. 15, Leavenworth Herald published, first newspaper in Kansas

Oct. 6, Missourians led by John Baldwin claiming site of Lawrence, Kansas, defeated in conflict with settlers

Oct. 7, Andrew H. Reeder, of Pennsylvania, first territorial Governor of Kansas, arrived at Fort Leavenworth

Oct. 18, American Ministers to Great Britain, Spain, and France in conference at Ostend at request of President Pierce, issued declaration that it was desirable that an effort should be made to purchase Cuba from Spain, and if Spain refused to sell the United States would be justified in wresting it from her because of Spanish oppression in Cuba

Nov. 29, Congressional election in Kansas carried for Whitfield by 1,600 armed men of the Blue Lodges, secret societies, formed in Missouri to extend slavery in Kansas

Dec. 5, Topeka, Kansas, founded by C. K. Holliday, M. C. Dickey, F. W. Giles, and others

Dec. 23, Free-state meeting held at Lawrence, Kansas

Dec. 26, First Treaty with the Oregon Indians, land ceded

Dec. 28, Illinois Central Railroad reached Chicago

Expedition of British sportsman, Sir George Gore, from St. Louis to the headwaters of the Powder River. He built fort on the Tongue River 8 miles from junction with the Yellowstone and remained in present Montana 3 years exploring and hunting

CONGRESS

Jan. 4, Report of Stephen A. Douglas introduced Bill in Senate for the organization of Nebraska with a proviso permitting admission to the Union "with or without slavery," the doctrine of popular or "squatter sovereignty" that the settlers should decide whether to be a free or slave State

Jan. 16, Amendment offered to Bill by A. Dixon exempting the territory from the Missouri Compromise prohibiting slavery

Jan. 17, Charles Sumner offered an amendment to the Nebraska Bill expressly reaffirming the Missouri Compromise

Jan. 23, Senator Douglas reported a new Bill creating 2 territories, Kansas and Nebraska, out of the same territory of the former Nebraska Bill, with a section which virtually repealed the Missouri Compromise

Jan. 24, Protest written by S. P. Chase and signed by a group of third party men entitled the "Appeal of the Independent Democrats in Congress to the People of the United States" called on the people of the North to oppose the Kansas-Nebraska Bill

March 3, The Kansas-Nebraska Bill passed the Senate

May 3, President Pierce vetoed Bill granting public lands to the States for benefit of indigent insane persons

May 22, The Kansas-Nebraska Bill passed the House after days of bitter altercation, and as amended, passed the Senate May 25

May 30, Kansas-Nebraska Bill signed by the President organized the Territories of Kansas and Nebraska, leaving decision as to slavery to the Territories, repealing Missouri Compromise of 1820

Aug. 4, Land Act reduced the price of public lands on the market to actual settlers by graduated system until in 30 years it sold for 12 and a half cents an acre; repealed June 21, 1862

——, Joint Resolution presented a medal to Captain Ingraham for conduct in rescue of Martin Koszta from illegal arrest by Austrian brig of war in 1853

——, Veto of Bill for completion of certain public works

Aug. 7, Congress adjourned

Dec. 4, Thirty-third Congress, 2d sess. convened

1855

Jan. 13, Convention with the Two Sicilies signed as to rights of neutrals at sea

Jan. 16, First legislature of Nebraska Territory met at Omaha

Jan. 18, Convention of extradition with Hanover signed

Jan. 22, Consular Convention with the Netherlands signed

——, Iowa law provided for state wide prohibition; nullified by law of 1858

Jan. 22, 26, 31, June 9, 11, 25, Oct. 17, and Dec. 21, Treaties signed with the Indians of Oregon by which they ceded land to the United States

Jan. 31, Treaty with the Wyandots signed by which certain tribes became citizens

Feb. 1, "Water Witch," American vessel, fired on in Parana River, Paraguay

Feb. 3, Michigan enacted prohibition law; repealed 1875

Feb. 16, Indiana passed prohibition law which was declared void by court in Nov.

Feb. 21, Massachusetts Emigrant Aid Society reincorporated as New England Emigrant Aid Society, John Carter Brown, president

Feb. 22, Indians massacred 13 of the garrison at Whaleshead, Oregon, and besieged the settlers in fort for 31 days until relief arrived

——, Pennsylvania State College chartered as Farmer's High School

Feb. 27, Delaware enacted prohibition law; repealed 1857

March 16, Nebraska law provided for state wide prohibition; repealed 1858

March, University of Iowa at Iowa City opened

March 30, First territorial legislature elected in Kansas by bands of Missourians who crossed border to ensure election of pro-slavery men

April 9, New York law provided for state wide prohibition; declared unconstitutional in 1856

April 28, California law enacted imposed "passenger tax" on every Chinese person entering the State of $50 a head to be collected before landing

April 30, California Mining Act amended to impose license tax of $4 a month on aliens and $12 a month on persons ineligible to become citizens

May 4, William Walker sailed from San Francisco for Nicaragua invited by one of the "Liberal" factions and promised tract of land

May 17, Kane Arctic expedition abandoned vessel in ice

May 24–Sept. 8, Winnas expedition against the Snake Indians, Oregon

July 2, Pro-slavery legislature of Kansas met at Pawnee, and later adjourned to Shawnee, adopted a Constitution

July 4, Dr. Charles Robinson in speech at Lawrence, Kansas, urged repudiation of legislature

July 9, Death of James Jesse Strang, his Mormon settlement of St. James destroyed by fishermen and inhabitants driven away

July 14, New Hampshire law provided for state wide prohibition

July 31, Andrew Reeder removed as Governor of Kansas nominally because of his land speculation, and Daniel Woodson, pro-slavery man, made acting Governor

Aug. 14, Convention of settlers at Lawrence repudiated Kansas legislature elected by fraudulent vote and called for constitutional convention to meet Sept. 3

Sept. 3, William Walker landed at Nicaragua with 160 men

——, New Governor, Wilson Shannon, arrived in Kansas

Sept. 5, Convention of free-state settlers met at Big Springs, Kansas, and repudiated territorial legislature and resolved to hold a separate election for a delegate to Congress

Sept. 13, Dr. Kane found on Disco Island, Greenland, which he had reached Aug. 8

Sept. 17, Cornerstone of Boston Public Library laid

Oct. 1, Treaty of peace, commerce, and friendship with the Two Sicilies signed

——, Election for delegate to Congress from Kansas carried for General Whifield by Missourians from across border

Oct. 3, Major G. O. Haller with troops left the Dalles

for the Yakima country, war begun by surprise attack of Indians

Oct. 3, Page expedition in South America reached Tucuman, the first to penetrate the Argentine deserts by steamboat

Oct. 9, Anthony Reeder elected delegate to Congress by free-state men

Oct. 11, The Kane expedition reached New York

Oct. 17, Bessemer received his first patent for process of producing steel

Oct. 28, Massacre of settlers in the White River Valley in present State of Washington by the Indians

Oct. 31, Convention of Free Soilers met at Albany, Oregon, and drafted platform for anti-slavery party

Nov. 1, William Makepeace Thackeray on visit to the United States delivered first lecture in New York City

Nov. 8, State Dept. refused to recognize Rivas Government of Nicaragua

Nov. 26, Rescue by party of free-state men of Jacob Branson, arrested by Sheriff Jones for threat against Franklin N. Coleman, pro-slavery man and murderer of his friend, Charles Dow, on the 21st

Dec. 5, In answer to appeal from Sheriff Jones more than 1,000 men from Missouri camped on the Wakarusa and threatened the town of Lawrence, Kansas

Dec. 7, Governor Shannon put an end to the "Wakarusa War" by written agreement with citizens of Lawrence that they would aid in execution of the laws, and peaceful dispersal of the Missourians

Dec. 8, Proclamation of the President against invasion of Nicaragua

Dec. 15, Constitution for Kansas prohibiting slavery adopted by convention which met at Topeka Oct. 23–Nov. 2, ratified by vote of settlers

CONGRESS

Feb. 3, Resolution authorized expedition for the rescue of Dr. Kane in the Arctic, which sailed from New York about June 1 under command of Lieutenant H. J. Hartstein

Feb. 10, Right of citizenship secured to children of citizens born out of the limits of the United States

Feb. 15, Resolution created temporarily the grade of lieutenant-general and the rank conferred on Major-General Winfield Scott

Feb. 17, Right of way granted to H. O. Alden and James Eddy for line of telegraph from the Mississippi to the Pacific

Feb. 24, Court of Claims established to hear and determine claims against the United States

March 1, Consular and diplomatic service reorganized, and salaries fixed according to grade

March 3, The President vetoed a Bill for subsidy for transportation of mails by ocean steamer and otherwise

——, Appropriation of $30,000 placed at disposal of the Secretary of War for importation of camels and dromedaries from the Orient to be tested in Texas for military purposes

——, Congress adjourned

Dec. 2, Thirty-fourth Congress, 1st sess. convened

1856

Jan. 15, Election for governor and legislature of Kansas under the Topeka Constitution, Dr. Charles Robinson chosen Governor

Jan. 26, U.S.S. "Decatur" repulsed Indians attacking Seattle

Jan. 24, President Pierce recognized the pro-slavery legislature of Kansas Territory and called attempt to establish a free-state government an act of rebellion

Feb. 11, Proclamation of the President warned against unlawful combinations in Kansas against the constituted authority

Feb. 22, National Convention of the American Party ("Know-Nothing") in Philadelphia nominated Millard Fillmore for president and Andrew J. Donelson for vice-president

March 1, Company of emigrants left New Haven for Kansas with Sharpe's rifles called "Beecher's Bibles" because supplied by members of the congregational church of Henry Ward Beecher

March 4, Free-state legislature met at Topeka, Kansas, adopted a memorial to Congress asking for admission to the Union, and elected A. H. Reeder and J. H. Lane United States senators

March 26, First street railroad in New England opened between Boston and Cambridge

———, Massacre of settlers at the Cascades on the Columbia River. Relief brought by Colonel Wright and Lieutenant P. H. Sheridan

April 19, Sheriff Jones, at Lawrence to arrest members of party which rescued Branson, wounded by unknown assassin

April 21, First train crossed the Mississippi on bridge from Rock Island to Davenport, Iowa

May 5, Grand jury in Douglas county, Kansas, indicted Governor Reeder, and Dr. Charles Robinson for high treason in organizing a free-state government

May 9, Governor Reeder in disguise escaped from Kansas City and proceeded to Illinois

May 14, President Pierce received Father Vijil sent by Walker from Nicaragua thus recognizing Walker's government of Nicaragua

May 21, Lawrence, Kansas, captured and sacked by a pro-slavery armed force under Deputy Marshal Fain and Sheriff Jones

May 22, James P. Casey and Charles Cora, another murderer, tried and executed by Vigilance Committee of San Francisco, taken from the jail by guard of 26 companies

May 24, John Brown led party which killed 25 pro-slavery settlers at Dutch Henry's crossing on the Pottawatomie River

May 29, Treaty of amity and commerce with Siam signed

June 2, Convention of the Democratic Party at Cincinnati nominated James Buchanan, of Pennsylvania, for president and John C. Breckinridge, of Kentucky, for vice-president. Franklin Pierce and Stephen A. Douglas withdrew as candidates for presidency on the 15th and 16th ballots, June 5

———, Missouri troops under Captain Pate sent to arrest John Brown captured by Brown's abolitionist band, but later rescued by federal troops under Sumner

June 4, Governor Shannon, of Kansas, issued proclamation commanding all unauthorized military companies to disperse

June 6, Ossawatomie, Kansas, sacked by Captain Pate, with Missouri troops

June 17, Convention of the Republican Party met at Philadelphia and nominated John C. Fremont of California, for president and William L. Dayton of New Jersey, for vice-president

June 29, Chief John surrendered and Indian war and massacre of settlers in Oregon ended

July 3, Convention of extradition with Austria-Hungary signed

July 4, Dispersal of free-state legislature at Topeka, Kansas, by Colonel Sumner with United States troops from Fort Leavenworth

July 22, Convention as to rights of neutrals at sea signed with Peru

Aug. 13, Free-state men captured the town of Franklin, Kansas, stronghold of pro-slavery troops from the South under Colonel Titus, and Aug. 16 took the fortified house of Colonel Titus and brought the men prisoners to Lawrence

Aug. 17, Governor Shannon made treaty with the "Free State Directory" at Lawrence by which they should keep arms captured but release prisoners

Aug. 18, Vigilance Committee of San Francisco disbanded with military review. There had been 4 executions and about 30 undesirable persons had been deported from the State during what H. H. Bancroft called "one of the grandest moral revolutions the world has ever witnessed"

Aug. 21, Governor Shannon received notice of his removal as Governor of Kansas and the appointment of Daniel Woodson as acting Governor

———, Townsend Harris arrived in Japan, first recognized agent of a foreign Power

Aug. 25, Acting Governor Woodson proclaimed the Territory of Kansas "in a state of open insurrection and rebellion"

Sept. 9, John W. Geary, appointed Governor of Kansas, arrived at Fort Leavenworth

Sept. 13, Destruction of free-state town of Ossawattomie, Kansas, by armed Missourians

Sept. 15, Governor Geary with federal troops met army of Missourians marching to Lawrence and forced them to leave Kansas bringing peace to the Territory

Sept. 17, Whig National Convention at Baltimore adopted nominees of American Party, Millard Fillmore for president and Andrew J. Donelson for vice-president

Nov. 4, Presidential election resulted in election of Buchanan and Breckinridge, popular vote 1,838,169 for Buchanan, for Fremont 1,341,264, and for Fillmore 874,534

Nov. 10, New York and Newfoundland telegraph line opened

Dec. 4, Canada permitted free transit of goods through Canada from points in the United States to other points in the United States by bonding system

Dec. 13, Treaty of friendship and commerce with Persia signed

CONGRESS

Feb. 14, Memorial of A. H. Reeder presented in House contesting the election of J. W. Whitfield as representative from Kansas Territory

March 12, Stephen A. Douglas presented a report which placed the blame for the disorder in Kansas on the New England Emigration Aid Society

March 17, Committee of 3 appointed by the House to investigate the state of civil war in Kansas, began sessions at Kansas City April 14

March 24, Topeka Constitution of Kansas presented in Senate by Lewis Cass

May 15, Public land grant to Iowa for aid to railroad

May 17, Public land granted to Alabama and Florida for railroads

May 19, President Pierce vetoed a Bill to remove obstructions to navigation in mouth of Mississippi River at Southwest Pass and Pass a l'Aoutre, which was passed over the veto by the Senate July 7 and by the House July 8

——, President Pierce vetoed Bill for deepening the channel over the Saint Clair Flats in Michigan, which was passed over the veto by the Senate July 7 and the House July 8

May 19–20, "Crime against Kansas" speech of Charles Sumner in Senate in debate on the admission of free-state Kansas, from the abolitionist point of view and a personal arraignment of Douglas of Illinois and Butler of South Carolina

May 22, The President vetoed Bill for deepening the channel of St. Mary's River, Michigan; passed over veto by Senate July 7 and House July 8

——, Criminal assault on Charles Sumner alone in Senate by Preston S. Brooks, nephew of Senator Butler

June 2, Committee report demanded expulsion of Preston S. Brooks from the House; failed for lack of two-thirds majority. He resigned July 14

June 3, Public lands granted to Louisiana and to Michigan for railroads

July 1, House Committee appointed to report on Kansas declared the territorial elections carried by fraud and the territorial legislature illegal

July 2, The Toombs Bill introduced by Douglas provided for a census of Kansas, a constitutional convention, and a vote under supervision of 5 competent persons appointed by the President, passed in Senate, but was not considered in House

July 3, Bill to admit Kansas under free-state constitution passed in House, failed in Senate

July 11, Oliver made minority report of congressional committee on Kansas, telling the story of the Pottawatomie massacre

Aug. 1, Whitfield unseated and Reeder rejected by vote of House

Aug. 11, Public land granted to Mississippi for railroads

——, The President vetoed a Bill for the improvement of the Des Moines rapids in the Mississippi; passed over veto by House Aug. 11 and by Senate Aug. 16

Aug. 14, The President vetoed a Bill for the improvement of the Patapsco River to make port of Baltimore accessible to war vessels; passed over veto Aug. 16

Aug. 18, Army appropriation Bill failed to pass because of provision attached that army should not be used to aid pro-slavery legislature in Kansas

——, Congress adjourned

Aug. 21, Thirty-fourth Congress Extra (second) sess.

Aug. 30, Army appropriation Bill passed without Kansas proviso

——, Congress adjourned

Dec. 1, Thirty-fourth Congress, 3d sess. convened

1857

Jan. 1, National Kansas Committee reported that it had received $90,000 and spent $81,000, Massachusetts giving $27,000, New York $33,000, Illinois $10,000. The Committee forwarded 2,000 emigrants by way of Iowa and Nebraska

Jan. 6, Free-state legislature attempted to meet at Topeka but was dispersed by federal interference

Jan. 12, Territorial legislature (pro-slavery) met at Lecompton, Kansas, and called a constitutional convention to meet at Lecompton in the following Sept.

March 4, Inauguration of President James Buchanan, and Vice-President J. C. Breckinridge (Democratic)

March 6, Chief Justice Taney gave decision in case of Dred Scott, a negro who claimed that having lived with his owner in Illinois, free State, and in Minnesota, free under the Missouri Compromise, he had been made by common law a free man, that the Declaration of Independence and the Constitution of the United States do not include or refer to negroes other than as property, and that no person who had been a slave or was the descendant of a slave could claim rights of citizenship, or become citizens of the United States or sue in the federal courts. The Missouri Compromise Act and similar prohibitory laws declared unconstitutional

——, Aaron V. Brown, of Tennessee, appointed Postmaster General, Jeremiah Black, of Pennsylvania, Attorney General

——, Lewis Cass, of Michigan, appointed Secretary of State; Howell Cobb, of Georgia, Secretary of the Treasury; John B. Floyd, Secretary of War; Isaac Toucey, of Connecticut, Secretary of the Navy; Jacob Thompson, of Mississippi, Secretary of the Interior

March 27, Memphis and Charleston Railroad completed joining Mississippi River with Atlantic Ocean, and opened May 10

May 1, William Walker surrendered to Commodore C. H. Davis in U.S.S. "Mary" and was taken to Panama

June 2, Marietta and Cincinnati Railroad opened and Northwest Virginia branch of the Baltimore and Ohio from Grafton to Parkersburg on the Ohio

June 4, Ohio and Mississippi Railroad uniting Cincinnati and St. Louis opened

June 17, Treaty of commerce and consuls with Japan signed

June 27, Meeting Joint Commission North West boundary

July 13, City organization and charter voted by meeting at Lawrence, Kansas

July 13–Aug. 28, Constitutional Convention met at St. Paul, Minnesota, Republicans and Democrats meeting separately, but uniting in presentation of State Constitution Aug. 29, a clause prohibiting slavery

July 15, Free-State Convention met at Topeka

July 17, New instructions of Secretary of State Cass to John Forsyth, Minister to Mexico, authorized him to conclude a treaty with Mexico for acquisition of Lower California, nearly all of Sonora, and part of Chihuahua north of 30° and the Rio Chico, and compensation up to $17,000,000 authorized including $2,000,000 for claims of American citizens

Aug. 3, Constitution for Iowa, adopted by convention which met Jan. 19–March 6, ratified by vote of the people

Aug. 7, First attempt to lay Atlantic cable from Trinity Bay, Newfoundland to Valencia Bay, Ireland, begun with U.S.S. "Niagara" and the British steamer "Agamemnon," but failed as cable broke off the coast of Ireland Aug. 11

Aug. 17–Sept. 18, Constitutional Convention met at Salem, Oregon

Aug. 24, Failure of Ohio Life and Trust Company began financial panic from overcapitalization and building of railroads and speculation following the discovery of gold in California, and resulted in over 5,000 failures of banks and railroads within the year

Sept. 5, Constitutional Convention called by pro-slavery legislature met at Lecompton, but adjourned to meet after the election

Sept. 7, Emigrants on their way from Arkansas to California attacked by Indians and Mormons at Mountain Meadows led by John D. Lee, and after siege of 4 days surrendered under promise of protection and all (120 persons) were massacred Sept. 11, except 17 children under 7 years of age

Sept. 15, Brigham Young by proclamation ordered troops to repel "invasion" of United States troops sent by the President to establish new Governor and officials in Utah

Sept., Maine State Seminary opened, later Bates College

Oct. 5, Elections held in Kansas under supervision of Governor Walker, his secretary, F. P. Stanton, and federal troops, resulted in election of a free-state legislature

——, Major Lott Young under orders from Brigham Young burned 2 trains carrying supplies for federal troops advancing into Utah

Oct. 13, Constitution for Minnesota adopted by convention which met July 13–Aug. 28, ratified by the people; slavery prohibited

Oct. 14, General suspension of specie payment by banks

Oct. 19, Constitutional Convention at Lecompton, Kansas, framed Constitution guaranteeing property in slaves already in the Territory, slavery as a permanent institution to be submitted to popular vote

Nov. 2, 4, 5, 7, Following meetings of Germans in Philadelphia in October "hunger meetings" of the unemployed were held almost daily in Tompkins Square, New York City, and attended by thousands of workmen

Nov. 7, William B. Reed sent by the President to attempt mediation between China and Great Britain arrived at Hong Kong

Nov. 9, Oregon Constitution ratified by vote of the people

Nov. 11, Meeting of unemployed in Philadelphia attended by 10,000 men

Nov. 25, William Walker landed at Greytown, Nicaragua, from New Orleans, again invading the country

Nov. 27, Governor Alfred Cumming, appointed Governor of Utah by the President, at Camp Scott 115 miles from Salt Lake City proclaimed Utah Territory in rebellion

Dec. 6, Commodore Paulding in command of U.S.S. "Wabash" dispersed Walkers camp of filibusters and sent men home disarmed, and sent Walker a prisoner to New York

Dec. 7, Territorial legislature in Kansas ordered that the Lecompton Constitution should be submitted to the vote of the people in January

Dec. 17, Robert J. Walker in letter to Secretary Cass resigned as Governor of Kansas and John W. Denver appointed by the President

Dec. 21, Lecompton Constitution with slavery provision adopted, vote for the Constitution with slavery 6,226, for the Constitution without slavery 569. Later investigation showed that 2,720 of these votes were fraudulent

CONGRESS

Feb. 11, Electoral vote counted gave James Buchanan (Democrat) 173 votes for president, and John C. Breckinridge 174 for vice-president; John C. Fre-

mont, Republican, 114 for president, and Millard Fillmore, American, 8

Feb. 21, Coinage reformed, retirement of Spanish and Mexican coins as legal tender and receipt by Treasury at fixed valuation provided for, weight of cent standardized and coinage of half-cent ceased

Feb. 26, People of Minnesota authorized to form State government and frame a constitution

March 3, Tariff of 1846 modified, duties on iron, cotton and woolen reduced, wool of the cheapest sort admitted duty free, and the former free list extended in favor of raw materials, general level of duties at lowest point since 1815

——, Public lands granted to Alabama and Minnesota for railroads

——, Payment of $70,000 a year to the New York, Newfoundland, and London Telegraph Company organized by Field, authorized for transmission of government messages

——, Congress adjourned

Dec. 7, Thirty-fifth Congress, 1st sess. convened

Dec. 9, Stephen A. Douglas in Senate opposed forcing the Lecompton Constitution on Kansas

1858

Jan. 4, Vote for Lecompton Constitution in its entirety taken resulted as follows: for the Constitution with slavery 138; for the Constitution without slavery 24; against the Constitution 10,226

Jan. 6, University of the South at Sewanee, Tennessee, chartered

Feb. 11, Act of Kansas legislature legalized the city charter of Lawrence of July 13, 1857

Feb. 12, Baker University, Baldwin, Kansas, chartered, and opened in Nov.

March 17, Free zone between the United States and Mexico decreed. See Mexico

April 6, Proclamation of the President declared the Mormon government of Utah in rebellion against the Constitution and laws of the United States, pardon offered to all except those who persisted in disloyal resistance

April 12, Colonel Thomas L. Kane, friend of the Mormons sent by the President as mediator, entered Salt Lake City with Governor Cumming to address the people

April 17, "Sons of Vulcan" union organized which became later the Amalgamated Association of Iron and Steel Workers

April 26, Act of California legislature prohibited all Chinese and other Mongolians from landing at any port in the State unless the vessel on which they were passengers was driven ashore by storm or unavoidable accident

May 12, John W. Denver took the oath as Governor of Kansas

——, W. Green Russell with other miners joined Cherokee expedition leaving the Missouri frontier to hunt for gold in Colorado

May 17, Battle of Steptoe Butte near the present Rosalia, Washington, Colonel Steptoe defeated by the Indians

May 19, Charles A. Hamilton, the leader of a pro-slavery band from Georgia, shot 11 prisoners taken in a raid in Kansas at Marais du Cygnes

June 2, Two peace commissioners sent by the President entered Salt Lake City, and held conference with Brigham Young June 10

June 16, Abraham Lincoln accepted the nomination of the Republicans for senator from Illinois, and in speech said, "A house divided against itself cannot stand. I believe this government cannot endure permanently half-slave and half-free"

June 17, Treaty of commerce and navigation with Belgium signed

June 18, Treaty with China signed of peace, amity, and commerce

June 26, Federal troops passed through Salt Lake City to establish a post in Cedar Valley on Utah Lake by arrangement with Brigham Young and the Mormon rebellion ended

June 30, Governor Alfred Cumming assumed office in Salt Lake City

July 17–Oct. 17, Expedition against the Indians in Washington Territory

July 17, The Atlantic Telegraph fleet sailed from Queenstown to lay Atlantic cable, and July 29 the "Agamemnon" and the "Niagara" proceeded from mid-ocean in opposite directions to pay out the cable

July 29, Treaty of friendship, commerce, and navigation with Japan signed

Aug. 2, The Lecompton Constitution as proposed by the English Act of May 4 with offer of millions of acres of public land rejected by vote of people of Kansas

Aug. 5, The first Atlantic cable successfully laid

Aug. 10–Sept. 3, Puget Sound expedition, Washington Territory, against Indians

Aug. 12, Minnesota passed local option law

Aug. 16, Queen Victoria and Secretary Buchanan exchanged congratulations over the Atlantic cable

Aug. 21, The slaver "Echo" bound for Cuba with more than 300 negroes from Africa aboard captured by U.S.S. "Dolphin" and taken to Charleston, South Carolina

——, Abraham Lincoln and Stephen A. Douglas began joint debates at Ottawa, Illinois in campaign for senator. Lincoln made statement that this government cannot endure permanently half-slave and half-free

Aug. 27, In second debate at Freeport Lincoln forced Douglas to declaration that the people of a Territory had the right to make it free or slave by "unfriendly legislation" and police regulations

Sept. 1, Battle of Four Lakes with the Indians near the present Spokane

——, Atlantic cable ceased to transmit messages

Sept. 9–Dec. 25, Navajo expedition, New Mexico, against the Indians

Sept. 11–Dec. 1859, Wichita expedition, Indian Territory, against the Indians

Sept. 13, Arrest of "Little John," a negro, at Oberlin, Ohio, under the Fugitive Slave Act, and Professor Henry E. Peck, of Oberlin College, arrested for his rescue at Wellington

Sept. 15, The Overland Mail Company began transportation of mail by coach from Memphis and San Francisco to the train at St. Louis, the first east bound stage from St. Louis covering the 2,795 miles in 24 days, 18 hours, and 26 minutes, the time from San Franciso 23 days and 4 hours

Sept. 17, Treaty with the Coeur d'Alene Indians made by Colonel George Wright in Washington Territory

Oct. 5, Crystal Palace, New York City, destroyed by fire

Oct. 19, Resignation of Governor Denver of Kansas

Oct. 25, Seward in speech at Rochester, New York, declared that the United States was engaged in an "irrepressible conflict," that it must become either an entirely slaveholding nation or entirely a free labor nation

Nov. 8, Treaty of tariff and trade regulations, consuls, and emigration with China signed

Nov. 30, Grand jury at Charleston, South Carolina, refused to indict crew of slaver "Echo"

Dec. 1, Samuel Medary took the oath as Governor of Kansas

Dec. 18, *Territorial Enterprise* first published at Genoa, Nevada, by William L. Jernegan

Dec. 30, Brigham Young and other leading Mormons indicted for treason

CONGRESS

Feb. 2, The President sent the Lecompton Constitution to Congress recommending the admission of Kansas under its organic law

March 4, Speech of Senator James H. Hammond on the Lecompton Constitution

March 23, Bill for admission of Kansas under the Lecompton Constitution passed the Senate

April 1, Bill passed in the House provided that the Lecompton Constitution should be resubmitted to vote of the people of Kansas

April 5, Asa Biggs in the Senate denounced the "Impending Crisis" by Hinton R. Helps as unfair representation of southern conditions

May 4, Compromise measure proposed by English, representative from Indiana, became a law, offered Kansas a large grant of land and provided that the Lecompton Constitution should be voted on by the people, if rejected the Territory should not be admitted as a State until population reached the number required for a representative

May 11, Minnesota admitted as 32d State with a Constitution prohibiting slavery

June 14, Loan of $20,000,000 authorized

——, Congress adjourned

Dec. 6, Thirty-fifth Congress, 2d sess. convened

1859

Jan. 14, Claims Convention with Venezuela signed

Jan. 15, Gold discovered in small branch of Boulder Creek, Colorado

Jan. 28, Death of William H. Prescott (63) author, in Boston

Jan. 29, Comstock, Fennimore, and Bishop staked off gold claim in Nevada which they called Gold Hill

Jan. 31, First railroad in Washington incorporated, the Cascades, to transport goods and passengers around the cascades of the Columbia River

Feb. 4, Claims Convention with Paraguay signed respecting attack on the United States vessel "Water Witch"; no settlement ever made

——, Treaty of friendship, commerce, and navigation with Paraguay signed

Feb. 11, Charter granted to the Atchison and Topeka Railroad

Feb. 11–April 28, Colorado River expedition, California, against the Indians

March 7, Secretary Cass instructed R. M. McLane, American Minister to Mexico appointed to succeed Forsyth, to recognize Juarez government, negotiate a treaty of commerce and limits, and offer $10,000.000

for cession of Lower California and the grant of transit across Isthmus of Tehuantepec

March 8, Death of Aaron V. Brown, Postmaster General. Joseph Holt, of Kentucky, appointed March 14

April 16–Aug. 17, Pecos expedition against the Indians

April 23, *Rocky Mountain News*, first Colorado newspaper, published at Auraria now Denver

May 6, George Jackson located gold claim on Clear Creek, Colorado, and May 10 John H. Gregory discovered rich gold diggings on the north fork of Clear Creek

May 9–19, Commercial Convention at Vicksburg, Mississippi, recommended that all laws prohibiting the African slave trade be repealed

June 10–Sept. 23, Antelope Hills expedition, Texas, against the Indians

June 11, Penrod Comstock and Company discovered the famous Comstock lode of silver in Six Mile Cañon, Nevada

June 12–Oct. 18, Bear River expedition, Utah, against the Indians

June 23, John Wise started from St. Louis in balloon and landed at Henderson, New York, 802 miles in 20 hours

June 27, Captain George Pickett acting under command of General Harney took possession of San Juan Island claimed by the British as belonging to Vancouver Island

June 30, M. Blondin (Emile Gravelet) crossed the Niagara River below the Falls on a tight rope

July 5, Constitutional Convention met at Wyandotte, Kansas, and adopted a Constitution July 29 which prohibited slavery but restricted the suffrage to white male persons; ratified by voters Oct. 4

——, Iron Moulders Union of North America founded by William H. Sylvis

July 18, Constitutional Convention met and framed Constitution for Nevada in 10 days session which was adopted by vote of the people Sept. 7

Aug. 27, First oil well drilled at depth of 69½ feet near Titusville, Pennsylvania, by E. L. Drake

Sept. 1, First trip of the first Pullman sleeping car from Bloomington, Illinois to Chicago

Sept. 20, U.S.S. "Niagara" sailed from Charleston, South Carolina, with negroes taken from the slave ship "Echo" for Liberia

Oct. 4, Wyandotte Constitution prohibiting slavery ratified in Kansas by popular vote

Oct. 16, Anti-slavery band led by John Brown on raid into Virginia with aim to free the slaves seized the arsenal at Harper's Ferry, and took citizens as hostages

Oct. 17, Captain Robert E. Lee with company of federal marines arrived at Harper's Ferry to aid militia in attack on captured arsenal which was taken the following day and John Brown made a prisoner

Oct. 25–Oct. 31, Trial of John Brown at Charlestown, West Virginia

Nov. 1, Louisville and Nashville Railroad reached Nashville

Nov. 28, Death of Washington Irving (76) at Tarrytown, New York

Dec. 2, John Brown hanged at Charlestown, West Virginia, and Dec. 16, 4 of his followers, 2 white men and 2 negroes, and 2 others hung March 16, 1860, 6 making their escape and 10 killed in action

Dec. 14, Treaty of transit and commerce with Mexico signed (McLane-Ocampo) for which the United States to pay $4,000,000 for privileges conceded and right of transit across Tehuantepec; failed of ratification by Senate

Dec. 15, First legislative assembly met at Genoa, Nevada

Midway Island in the central north Pacific Ocean discovered and annexed by Captain N. C. Brooks, and again in 1867 claimed by the United States by Captain Reynolds (not included in Hawaiian Islands)

CONGRESS

Jan. 10, Senator Slidell introduced Bill to appropriate $30,000,000 "to facilitate the acquisition of Cuba," discussed until Feb. 26 and then withdrawn

Feb. 14, Oregon admitted as the 33d State

Feb. 24, The President vetoed land grant college Bill

March 3, Treasury notes for $20,000,000 authorized

——, Congress adjourned

Dec. 5, Thirty-sixth Congress, 1st sess. convened

——, J. B. Clark introduced Resolution that no member of the House who had endorsed the book "The Impending Crisis" by H. R. Helper on conditions in the South was fit to be speaker of the House and that the proposal to circulate the book as campaign material was an incipient movement of treason

Dec. 19, President Buchanan in message declared that all lawful means should continue to be employed to execute laws against African slave trade

1860

Jan. 2, Louisiana State University opened

Feb. 18, Mrs. Elizabeth Cady Stanton addressed New York Legislature on woman suffrage

Feb. 27, Abraham Lincoln made first speech before an eastern audience at Cooper Institute, New York City

March 27, Japanese embassy bringing Perry Treaty to be ratified reached San Francisco and proceeded to Washington

——, Geneva College became Hobart College, Geneva, New York

March 30, Joint American and British occupation of San Juan Island

April 3, First "pony express" to carry mail by relays of ponies left St. Joseph, Missouri and arrived at Sacramento, California April 13 bringing 8 letters

April 12–July 9, Pah-Ute expedition, California, against the Indians

April 14, Mormons founded Franklin, first permanent settlement in Idaho

April 23, Democratic Convention met at Charleston, South Carolina, and disagreement on platform followed by withdrawal of the delegates from Alabama, Mississippi, Louisiana, South Carolina, Florida, Texas, Arkansas, Georgia, and 2 delegates from Delaware to meet in separate convention. The convention adjourned May 3 without nomination after 57 ballots to meet again June 18

April 28, First railroad in Kansas completed from Elwood to Wathena (5 miles)

May 9, Constitutional Union Party constituted from the old Whig and the American parties met in Baltimore and nominated John Bell, of Tennessee, for president, and Edward Everett, of Massachusetts, for vice-president; Samuel Houston defeated for nomination for president

May 14–July 15, Carson Valley expedition, Utah, against the Indians

May 16, Republican National Convention met at Chicago, and Abraham Lincoln, of Illinois, received nomination for president and Hannibal Hamlin, of Maine, nominated for vice-president. On the first ballot William H. Seward, of New York, received 173½ votes for president, Abraham Lincoln, 102; Simon Cameron, of Pennsylvania 50½; Salmon P. Chase, of Ohio, 49; and Edward Bates, of Missouri, 48

June 11, The Charleston seceders from the Democratic Convention met at Richmond and adjourned to meet in Baltimore on the 28th

June 18, Democratic Convention reassembled at Baltimore and nominated Stephen A. Douglas, of Illinois, for president, and Herschel V. Johnson, of Georgia, for vice-president

June 28, Charleston seceders met at Baltimore and nominated John C. Breckinridge, of Kentucky, for president, and Joseph Lane, of Oregon, for vice-president

June 30, On this date the army consisted of 16,006 men of which 14,926 were enlisted men

Aug. 27, Treaty of amity, commerce, navigation, and extradition with Venezuela signed

Sept. 12, William Walker captured by Honduras troops and shot at Truxillo

Sept. 12–Feb. 24, Navajo Indian expedition, New Mexico

Sept. 13, Attack and murder of emigrants by Bannock Indians at Salmon Fork, Snake River, Idaho

Sept. 19, The Prince of Wales (later Edward VII) arrived at Detroit from Canada on visit to the United States, and arrived in Washington Oct. 3 after visiting Chicago, St. Louis, Cincinnati, and Pittsburgh; at Philadelphia Oct. 7, New York City, Oct. 11. Oct. 20, The Prince of Wales sailed for England from Portland, Maine

Oct. 5, Governor Gist of South Carolina sent a circular letter on subject of secession in case Lincoln was elected to Governors of other southern cotton States

Oct. 25, Meeting of prominent politicians at home of Senator Hammond to discuss secession

Nov. 5, Governor Gist opening legislature of South Carolina directly advocated armed secession

Nov. 6, Presidential election gave Abraham Lincoln (Republican) 1,866,452 votes for president, and Hannibal Hamlin, the same, for vice-president, Stephen A. Douglas (Democrat) and Herschel V. Johnson (Democrat) for president and vice-president 1,375,157, John C. Breckinridge and Joseph Lane (Seceding Democrats) for president and vice-president 847,953; and John Bell and Edward Everett (Constitutional Union) 590,631

Nov. 10, Legislature of South Carolina passed law calling a convention to meet at Columbia Dec. 17 to consider the question of secession from the Union

Nov. 14, Anti-secession speech of Alexander H. Stephens before legislature of Georgia appealed to the people to maintain the Constitution

Nov. 20, Opinion of Attorney General Black given that the President could use force in a State only to protect public property and aid civil courts in execution of the laws. Congress would declare war on a State and make it a foreign enemy if it authorized the President to send troops into State to uphold United States laws

Dec. 10, Resignation of Howell Cobb, of Georgia, Secretary of the Treasury, and appointment Dec. 12, of Philip F. Thomas, of Maryland

Dec. 11, Verbal instructions of Adjutant-General D. P. Butler at Fort Moultrie to avoid aggression but if attacked to defend the fort

Dec. 12, Resignation of Lewis Cass, of Michigan, as Secretary of State because the President declined to reinforce the forts in Charleston Harbor, and appointment of Jeremiah S. Black, of Pennsylvania, as Secretary of State Dec. 17

Dec. 14, Georgia legislature issued address to South Carolina, Alabama, Florida, and Mississippi asking that delegates be appointed to convention

Dec. 17, Letter of Governor Pickens of South Carolina to the President requested permission to send small State force to take possession of Fort Sumter

Dec. 18, South Carolina Convention met at Charleston and passed Ordinance of secession from the Union Dec. 20, declaring South Carolina an independent commonwealth

Dec. 20, Edwin M. Stanton, of Pennsylvania, appointed Attorney General

Dec. 21, Letter from Abraham Lincoln to Washburne asked him to tell General Scott to be "as well prepared as he can to either hold or retake the forts . . . at and after the inauguration"

Dec. 22, South Carolina appointed 3 commissioners to go to Washington to treat for possession of United States property within the limits of the State, held by the Government as "agent of the Confederated States," Robert W. Barnwell, James H. Adams, and James L. Orr

Dec. 24, South Carolina issued an "Address to the Slave-Holding States"

Dec. 26, Major Robert Anderson in command at Fort Moultrie in Charleston Harbor abandoned that fort as untenable and occupied Fort Sumter during night

Dec. 27, Castle Pinckney and Fort Moultrie occupied by South Carolina troops

——, Surrender of U.S. revenue cutter "William Aiken" to South Carolina

Dec. 28, Letter to President Buchanan from the South Carolina commissioners in Washington requested that Anderson be withdrawn from the port of Charleston

——, Interview of the President with the South Carolina commissioners as "private gentlemen"

——, General Scott asked that troops, ammunition, and provisions be sent to Fort Sumter

Dec. 29, Resignation of John B. Floyd, of Virginia, as Secretary of War, accused of embezzlement and treason to the Union

Dec. 30, Letter of the President to the South Carolina commissioners stated that Fort Sumter would be defended to the last extremity

——, Memorial of Secretary of State Black to the President commended action of Major Anderson and declared against any negotiation with the South Carolina commissioners regarding property of the United States

——, State troops seized arsenal at Charleston

The eighth census gave total population as 31,443,322, including 26,973,843 white persons, 487,970 free negroes, and 3,953,780 negro slaves. 2,598,214 immigrants arrived in the decade, 1,338,093 from the British Isles, and 1,114,564 from Europe. Foreign born population 4,136,000: German 1,301,000, Irish 1,611,000, Swedish and Norwegian 63,000. Center of population 20 miles south of Chillicothe, Ohio

CONGRESS

Feb. 2, Jefferson Davis introduced in Senate 7 resolutions affirming state sovereignty, that any attack on the domestic institution of negro slavery was a violation of the Constitution, that neither Congress or a territorial legislature had power directly or indirectly to impair the right to hold slaves in the Territories, and that the Territories should have the right to be received into the Union with or without slavery according to their constitutions; passed May 24

March 5, Resolution offered by John Covode for appointment of a committee to investigate the conduct of the President adopted in House, because of charges made by 2 anti-Lecompton Democrats that the President had used corrupt influences to induce them to vote for the Lecompton Bill. The 3 Republican members voted to sustain the charges and the 2 Democrats for exoneration of the President, but no action was taken

April 11, Bill to admit Kansas under the Wyandotte Constitution passed the House, but was laid aside by Senate June 5

May 10, Morrill tariff Bill raising the tariff of 1857 by one-third passed the House

June 16, Act to encourage the construction of a telegraph line to the Pacific passed

June 22, Homestead Act for actual settlers vetoed by the President

——, Loan of $21,000,000 authorized

June 25, Congress adjourned

Nov. 9, South Carolina senators resigned from Congress

Dec. 3, Thirty-sixth Congress, 2d sess. convened

Dec. 4, President Buchanan's message declared the threatened danger to the Union due to "long-continued and intemperate interference of the northern people with the questions of slavery in the southern States" and recommended a constitutional amendment which should specifically recognize property in slaves and the duty to protect this property

——, Special committee of 33, one member from each State, appointed by the House, on the condition of the country

Dec. 13, House Committee of 33 adopted a general pacific resolution

——, Manifesto of southern congressmen signed by 23 representatives and 7 senators advised state secession and organization of a southern confederacy

Dec. 17, Loan of $10,000,000 in Treasury notes authorized, to be redeemed in 1 year

Dec. 18, John J. Crittenden, of Kentucky, proposed a constitutional amendment that slavery should be prohibited in all the territory of the United States north of latitude 36° 30', States to be admitted with or without slavery as their constitutions might provide, and protective regulations included as to slave property and the domestic slave trade

——, Senate Committee of 13 appointed including Jefferson Davis, Seward, Crittenden, Wade, Toombs, and Douglas to consider the grievances between the slave-holding and non-slave-holding States, which adopted resolution Dec. 28 that they had been unable to agree on any general plan of adjustment, the Crittenden compromise defeated Dec. 22, and proposal of Seward (Republican) of Dec. 24 that the Constitution should never be altered to interfere with slavery in the States, amendment of Fugitive

Slave Act to grant trial by jury, and that the States be asked to repeal acts which contravened the Constitution and constitutional laws

Dec. 21, South Carolina congressmen formally withdrew from the House

Dec. 24, Seward in Senate Committee of 13 offered Lincoln's proposal of an amendment to the Constitution that Constitution should never be altered to interfere with slavery, amendment of fugitive slave law to grant trial by jury, and that legislatures of States be requested to repeal laws which contravened constitutional laws

1861

Jan. 1, The President declined to receive and returned insolent letter from the South Carolina commissioners

——, Army numbered 16,367 (Phisterer)

Jan. 2, Fort Johnson, Charleston Harbor, seized by South Carolina State troops

Jan. 3, Legislature of Delaware at Dover heard and rejected proposals of Henry Dickinson of Mississippi that the State should join the Confederacy

——, South Carolina commissioners left Washington

——, Fort Pulaski at mouth of the Savannah River on Cockspur Island seized by Georgia State troops

Jan. 4, United States arsenal at Mount Vernon, Alabama, seized by State troops from Mobile

——, Fast day proclaimed by President Buchanan on Dec. 14 celebrated

Jan. 5, Forts Morgan and Gaines on Mobile Bay seized by Alabama State troops

——, A merchant side-wheel steamer without guns, the "Star of the West" sent from New York for relief of Fort Sumter, Lieutenant C. R. Woods in command with 250 men

Jan. 6, United States arsenal at Apalachicola, Florida, seized by State troops

——, Message of Fernando Wood, Mayor of New York City, to Common Council proposed that in the event of disunion New York should constitute itself a free city and retain commerce with both sections

Jan. 7, Forts Marion and St. Augustus, Florida, seized by State troops

Jan. 8, Resignation of Jacob Thompson, of Mississippi, Secretary of the Interior

Jan. 9, Mississippi the second State to secede by ordinance passed by convention 84 to 15

——, "Star of the West" fired on by State battery on Morris Island, South Carolina, and prevented from entering Charleston Harbor

——, Fort Johnson seized by citizens of Smithville, North Carolina

Jan. 10, Ordinance of secession adopted by Florida in convention which first met Jan. 3 at Talahassee by vote of 62 to 7, the Constitution amended by substituting "Confederate States" for "United States"

——, Fort Caswell seized by citizens of Smithville and Wilmington, North Carolina

——, Forts Jackson and St. Philip on the Mississippi below New Orleans seized by Louisiana State troops

——, United States troops transferred from Barrancas Barracks to Fort Pickens, Pensacola, Florida, by Lieutenant A. G. Slemmer in command

Jan. 10 and Feb. 23, Major Robert Anderson in command at Fort Sumter again instructed to act strictly on the defensive

Jan. 11, Ordinance of secession adopted by Alabama in convention which met Jan. 7 by vote of 61 to 39

Jan. 11, Resolution of legislature of New York offered the President men to enforce the laws and uphold the authority of the Federal Government

——, John A. Dix, of New York, appointed Secretary of the Treasury

Jan. 12, Barrancas barracks and Forts Barrancas and McRee, and navy yard at Pensacola, Florida, seized by State troops, who Jan. 12, 15, and 18 demanded surrender of Fort Pickens at entrance of Pensacola Bay which was refused by Lieutenant Slemmer

Jan. 13, Ship Island occupied by Confederates as base against Mississippi, and garrisoned Jan. 20

Jan. 14, Fort Taylor, Key West, garrisoned by United States troops

——, Fort Pike, Louisiana, seized by State troops

Jan. 18, Fort Jefferson, Tortugas, Florida, garrisoned by United States troops

——, Fort Gaines, Alabama, seized by State troops

——, Joseph Holt, of Kentucky, appointed Secretary of War

——, Vassar College chartered, opened in Sept. 1865

Jan. 19, Resolution of legislature of Mississippi called for a convention of representatives of the seceding States

——, General Assembly of Virginia adopted resolution inviting States to send representatives to a peace convention to meet in Washington Feb. 4

——, Ordinance of secession passed by Georgia convention which met Jan. 17 by vote of 208 to 89, Alexander H. Stephens and Herchel V. Johnson voting in the negative

Jan. 24, United States arsenal at Augusta, Georgia, seized by State troops

Jan. 26, Oglethorpe barracks at Savannah, Georgia, and Fort Jackson seized by State troops

——, Ordinance of secession adopted by Louisiana convention by vote of 113 to 17

Jan. 28, University of Washington founded at Seattle

——, Fort Macomb, Louisiana, seized by State authorities

Jan. 30, Surrender of United States revenue schooner "Lewis Cass" to State authorities at Mobile, Alabama

Jan. 31, United States revenue schooner "Washington" undergoing repairs at New Orleans seized by State authorities

Feb. 1, Mint and custom house at New Orleans seized by Confederates and money taken

——, Ordinance of secession adopted by Texas in convention which met Jan. 28 by vote of 166 to 7; ratified by vote of the people Feb. 23

Feb. 4–March 16 (Confederate Provisional Congress) Convention representing 6 of the Confederate States met at Montgomery, Alabama, with delegates from South Carolina, Mississippi, Florida, Georgia, and Louisiana, Howell Cobb, of Georgia elected president, and Johnson Cooper, of Alabama, secretary, adopted a provisional constitution Feb. 8 and elected Jefferson Davis, President, and Alexander H. Stephens, Vice-President of Confederate States Feb. 9

Feb. 4–27, Peace Convention met at Washington, D.C. with delegates from 14 States

Feb. 7, Choctaw nation declared adherence to the Confederate States

Feb. 8, People of Tennessee voted against holding a convention

——, United States arsenal at Little Rock, Arkansas, seized by State troops

Feb. 9, Confederate Provisional Congress declared all laws of the United States not inconsistent with the Constitution of the Confederate States continued in force

Feb. 9, Charles Robinson took the oath as Governor of Kansas

Feb. 12, Confederate Provisional Congress authorized a commission of peace to the United States, and passed resolutions assuming authority in all questions as to forts acquired between States of the Confederacy and the United States

——, Horatio King, of Maine, appointed Postmaster General

Feb. 13, Convention met at Richmond, Virginia to consider secession

Feb. 16, United States arsenal and barracks at San Antonio seized by Texas troops

Feb. 18, Jefferson Davis inaugurated at Montgomery, Alabama, as President of the Confederate States

——, United States posts and military property in Texas surrendered by General Twiggs to Texas troops

Feb. 19, General Twiggs superseded in command by Colonel Waite

Feb. 20, Confederate Provisional Congress authorized the President to make contracts for purchase and manufacture of munitions of war

Feb. 21, Confederate Act created departments of State, War, Treasury, Justice, Navy, and Post Office, and C. G. Memminger appointed Secretary of the Treasury; Leroy P. Walker, Secretary of War; and Robert Toombs, Secretary of State

——, Camp Cooper, Texas, abandoned by federal troops

Feb. 22, National Convention of workingmen in Philadelphia adopted resolutions regarding the war

——, Mass meeting in San Francisco declared for support of the Federal Government

Feb. 23, Abraham Lincoln arrived in Washington after secret night journey, warned of plot of assassination at Baltimore

Feb. 25, Henry T. Ellet appointed Confederate Postmaster General declined appointment, Judah P. Benjamin appointed Confederate Attorney General

Feb. 26, Confederate Act established and organized General Staff for army, and declared for free navigation of the Mississippi

Feb. 27, President Davis as authorized by Resolution of Confederate Provisional Congress of Feb. 15 appointed Martin J. Crawford, John Forsyth, and A. B. Roman, commissioners to the United States to negotiate treaty of amity

——, Washington Peace Convention proposed amendments to the Constitution which were rejected by Congress March 2

Feb. 28, Convention met in Jefferson City, Missouri, Sterling Price, president, loyal members were able to prevent adoption of secession ordinance; adjourned to meet at St. Louis March 4

——, Confederate Provisional Congress authorized President Davis to borrow on bonds of Confederate States the sum of $15,000,000 at 8%, and imposed export duty of $1/8$ of 1% per pound on raw cotton for payment of interest and principle

——, Report from Major Anderson at Fort Sumter reached Washington that he had provisions for only about a month

March 1, P. T. Beauregard appointed Brigadier General in Confederate army, took command at Charleston March 3

March 1, General Twiggs dismissed from service for treachery by President Buchanan

March 2, Act of Confederate Congress provided for admission of Texas to the Confederacy

March 3, General Scott in letter to Seward gave opinion that it was impracticable to relieve Fort Sumter

March 4, Inauguration of President Abraham Lincoln and Vice-President Hannibal Hamlin. Lincoln in inaugural speech declared intention to preserve the Union and execute laws and non-interference with institution of slavery in States where it existed

——, Missouri Convention reassembled at St. Louis addressed by Luther Glenn from Georgia who urged secession

——, Flag of 7 stars and 3 stripes raised over Confederate capitol at Montgomery, Alabama

——, Stephen R. Mallory appointed Confederate Secretary of the Navy

March 5, William H. Seward, of New York, appointed Secretary of State; Simon Cameron, of Pennsylvania, Secretary of War; Edward Bates, of Missouri, Attorney General; Montgomery Blair, of the District of Columbia, Postmaster General; Gideon Welles, of Connecticut, Secretary of the Navy; Caleb B. Smith, of Indiana, Secretary of the Interior

March 6, President Jefferson Davis authorized by Provisional Confederate Congress to employ military and naval forces to number of 100,000 men to serve 12 months

——, John H. Reagan appointed Confederate Postmaster General and Post Office organized March 9

——, At meeting at War Dept. General Scott declared that the Navy must decide as to relief of Fort Sumter

March 7, Missouri legislature by resolution of Judge Breckinridge condemned secession

March 8, Confederate commissioners presented statement of terms on which they would consent to delay hostilities to Secretary Seward

March 9, Confederate Act authorized issue of Treasury notes not to exceed $1,000,000 and of denominations not less than $50

——, Committee of Missouri Convention appointed to consider relations between the United States Government and the State adopted resolution declaring for the Union

——, President Lincoln convened first Cabinet meeting to consider the state of the country

March 11, Permanent Constitution of Confederate States adopted by unanimous vote of the 7 States represented in the Congress at Montgomery, the passage of any "law denying or impairing the right of property in negro slaves" prohibited, and the preamble contained declaration of the "sovereign and independent character of each State"

——, Confederate law fixed pay of members of Congress at $8 per day during sessions and 10 cents mileage for travel to and from the seat of government

——, Brigadier General Braxton Bragg assumed command of Confederate forces in Florida

——, Order for reinforcement of federal Fort Pickens given which was not carried out

March 12, General Scott gave formal opinion that Fort Sumter should be evacuated

——, The Confederate commissioners requested Secretary Seward to name day when they might present their credentials to the President

March 13, Confederate Constitution ratified by Alabama

March 14, Confederate Provincial Congress voted thanks to Louisiana for transfer to Confederacy of $536,000 in coin seized from United States mint and custom house in New Orleans

March 15, Confederate Act imposed ad valorem duty on certain imported articles including coal, iron, railroad rails, paper, and wood

——, Purchase or construction of 10 gunboats authorized by Confederate law and Bureau of Indian Affairs established

——, Secretaries Seward, Cameron, Welles, Smith, and Bates filed written opinions advising the President against provisioning Fort Sumter, Blair and Chase only in favor

——, Secretary Seward declined "official intercourse" with the Confederate commissioners in note of this date which was given to the commissioners April 8

March 16, Settlers of New Mexico in Arizona county declared Arizona out of the Union

——, Provisional Confederate Congress adjourned after making provision for organization of navy, and establishing courts

——, President Jefferson Davis appointed William L. Yancey, Pierre A. Rost, and A. Dudley Mann commissioners to Great Britain to negotiate treaty

——, Confederate Constitution ratified by Georgia

——, Governor Houston in Texas refused to take oath to Confederacy and was deposed

March 18, Arkansas Convention which first met on the 4th rejected secession

——, Order of General Bragg (Confederate) forbade passage of supplies to Fort Pickens and United States squadron at Pensacola, and sloop "Isabella" with supplies seized by Confederates March 21 at Mobile, Alabama

March 21, Confederate Constitution ratified by Louisiana

March 23, Brigadier General Edwin V. Sumner assigned to command of the Dept. of the Pacific

——, Confederate Constitution ratified by Texas

March 28, General Scott advised the evacuation of Fort Pickens as well as Fort Sumter

March 29, Confederate Constitution ratified by Mississippi

——, At Cabinet meeting Secretaries Seward and Smith only opposed holding and provisioning Fort Sumter

March 30, President Lincoln ordered Secretaries of War and Navy to prepare expedition to leave Washington by sea April 6, later orders miscarried

March 31, Decision of the President to reinforce Fort Pickens

April 1, Secretary Seward handed the President "Some thoughts for the President's consideration" proposing scheme of foreign war to unite the country to end secession, and charging Lincoln with lack of policy practically demanding that the President should perform the duties of his office or assign them to Seward

April 3, Confederate battery at Morris Island, South Carolina, fired on schooner "Rhoda H. Shannon" of Dorchester, New Jersey

——, Confederate Constitution ratified by South Carolina

April 5, The yacht "Wanderer" arrived at Key West from Havana and was detained by Lieutenant Craven

April 6, The U.S.S. "Powhatan" commanded by

Lieutenant D. D. Porter left New York for Charleston to relieve Fort Sumter

April 7, Lieutenant J. L. Warden left Washington with orders to Captain H. A. Adams to reinforce Fort Pickens

April 8, General Beauregard (Confederate) instructed not to allow any provisions to go to Fort Sumter

——, The "Harriet Lane" sent to Charleston to participate in relief of Fort Sumter, and the "Baltic" the next day

——, Constitution for South Carolina framed by convention which first met in Dec. 1860 came into effect without ratification by the people

April 9, Confederate orders stopped mails and officially isolated Fort Sumter

April 10, The U.S.S. "Pocahontas" left Norfolk, Virginia, for Charleston to participate in relief of Fort Sumter

——, Captain Talbot and Robert A. Chew sent by the President to Charleston informed Governor Pickens of South Carolina that Fort Sumter would be provisioned

——, Massachusetts Institute of Technology incorporated in Boston

April 11, General P. G. T. Beauregard made formal demand of Major Anderson for the surrender of Fort Sumter which was refused

——, Colonel Earl Van Dorn ordered to take command in Texas and drive out federal troops and take possession of federal supplies for the Confederacy

April 12, Civil War begun with attack on Fort Sumter, bombardment from Fort Moultrie, Fort Johnson, and others at 4.30 A.M. by forces of General Beauregard after demand for surrender refused. At 3 A.M. the "Baltic" arrived off Charleston and at 6 A.M. the "Pawnee" joining the "Harriet Lane" and moving toward Charleston heard the guns of the attack

——, Reinforcements from Fort Monroe landed at Fort Pickens, Florida, and troops from New York arrived on the 17th

April 13, The U.S.S. "Pocahontas" arrived off Charleston

——, Major Anderson surrendered Fort Sumter about 7 in the evening after day of heavy bombardment

April 14, Major Anderson with troops marched from Fort Sumter after salute of 50 guns to the flag, raised and then lowered

April 15, Proclamation of the President called on the States for 75,000 militia to put down the armed assault upon the Union and summoned Congress to meet July 4

——, $3,000,000 appropriated by legislature of New York for public defense and provision for enlistment of 30,000 militia for 2 years

——, Fort Macon, North Carolina, seized by State troops

——, Connecticut, Indiana, Maine, Massachusetts, Vermont, Ohio, and New York responded to call for troops, Kentucky, and North Carolina refused to furnish quotas asked for

April 16, New Jersey, New Hampshire, and Iowa responded to call for troops, and Virginia refused to furnish quota

——, Forts Caswell and Johnson, North Carolina, seized by Confederates

——, Conscription Act passed by Confederate Congress including all white men from 18 to 35 for 3 years service unless exempted

April 17, President Davis invited applications for letters of marque and reprisal

——, Illinois and Rhode Island responded to call for troops, Missouri and Tennessee refused to furnish troops

——, Virginia Convention in secret session voted for secession to be submitted to popular vote May 23

April 18, Five companies from Pennsylvania the first troops to reach Washington

——, Arsenal at Harper's Ferry fired by Union force of 45 men under command of Lieutenant Jones on approach of Confederate troops from Virginia who reached the arsenal after evacuation in time to save the rifles

April 19, New York Seventh Regiment left for Washington, the second contingent of loyal troops to arrive at the capital

——, Troops of the Sixth Massachusetts Regiment marching to Washington in battle with rebel mob while passing through Baltimore

——, President Lincoln proclaimed a blockade of southern ports in the seven seceding States

——, Major General Robert Patterson assigned to command over the States of Delaware, Pennsylvania, and Maryland and the District of Columbia

——, Michigan responded to call for troops

April 20, "Star of the West" captured by Confederates off Galveston, and coast survey schooner "Twilight" at Arkansas, Texas

——, Robert E. Lee resigned his command in the United States army

——, Gosport navy-yard near Norfolk partly destroyed by Union troops under Flag Officer C. S. McCauley and left to possession of Virginians, the "Merrimac" among vessels scuttled and burned later salvaged by Confederates

——, United States arsenals at Liberty, Missouri, and Charlotte, North Carolina, seized

April 20–26, Railroad bridges burned by order of the Mayor of Baltimore to prevent passage of Union troops to Washington

April 21, Meeting of loyal citizens of Monongalia County in western Virginia adopted resolutions against secession

——, Capture of the slave ship "Nightingale" of Boston with cargo of 961 slaves by the U.S.S. "Saratoga"

——, California citizens in New York formed regiment under command of E. D. Baker which was accepted by the Government

——, Exemption Act of Confederate Congress specified offices, trades, businesses, occupations, and duties which exempted men from conscription

April 22, Confederate Constitution ratified by Florida

——, Confederate Commander Raphael Semmes assumed command at Fort Sumter

——, Governor of Arkansas refused to furnish quota of troops asked for by the President

——, United States arsenal at Fayetteville abandoned by Union troops

April 23, Robert E. Lee accepted chief command of the Virginia forces, made a brigadier general May 14, and full general June 14

——, United States troops under command of Colonel Carlos A. Waite, Dept. of Texas, surrendered with his officers to Confederates at San Antonio

April 24, Secretary Seward sent circular letter to American Ministers abroad instructing them to negotiate for accession of the United States to the Declaration of Paris

April 25, United States troops at Saluria captured by Colonel Earl Van Dorn and surrender of Major Caleb C. Sibley near Indianola

——, Address of Stephen A. Douglas for the Union before the legislature at Springfield, Illinois

April 26, General Joseph E. Johnston assigned to command Confederate forces in and about Richmond, Virginia

——, Governor Brown, of Georgia, issued order for repudiation by citizens of all debts due to Northerners

——, Proclamation called for volunteers to provide Delaware quota of troops

April 27, Dept. of Annapolis established with General Butler in charge

——, Proclamation of the President extended blockade to ports of Virginia and North Carolina

——, Order of the President to General Scott authorized suspension of writ of habeas corpus when necessary in military lines

——, Colonel J. K. F. Mansfield assigned to the Dept. of Washington, Colonel T. J. Jackson to command at Harper's Ferry

April 29, Major General Robert Patterson assigned to command the Dept. of Pennsylvania

——, House of Delegates of Maryland voted against secession 53 to 13

April 29–May 21, Confederate Provisional Congress met in second session at Montgomery, Alabama

May 1, Joint Resolution of legislature of Tennessee authorized the Governor to appoint commissioners to enter into a military league with the Confederate States

May 3, Proclamation of the President called for 40 additional regiments of volunteers, the increase of the army by 10 regiments and the enlistment of 18,000 seamen

——, General McClellan appointed in command of Dept. of the Ohio comprising Ohio, Indiana, and Illinois

May 3 and 9, Lord Russell received the Confederate commissioners to Great Britain, William L. Yancey and Pierre A. Rost

May 4, Union meeting held at Kingwood, Preston County, western Virginia, declared against secession

May 5, General Butler sent 2 regiments from Annapolis to occupy the Relay House 9 miles from Baltimore on the Baltimore and Ohio Railroad

——, Naval Academy transferred from Annapolis to Newport, Rhode Island

——, Union mass meeting at Wheeling in western Virginia

May 6, Lord John Russell announced officially in Parliament that the British Government had decided to recognize the Confederate States as belligerents

——, Arkansas legislature declared for secession by vote of 69 to 1, dissenting vote that of Dr. Isaac Murphy

——, Confederate Act recognized state of war between the United States and the Confederate States, and Act authorized letters of marque and reprisal

May 7, Virginia admitted as member of the Confederacy

——, Military league between Tennessee and the Confederate States signed at Nashville

May 8, Steamboat with cannon, muskets, and military stores sent by President Davis in response to call

from secessionist Governor Jackson landed at Camp Jackson, near St. Louis occupied by first brigade of Missouri troops in annual encampment of militia

May 8, Captain Lyon placed in command of United States troops in St. Louis

May 9, United States troops at San Lucas Springs, Texas, under Lieutenant Colonel I. V. D. Reeve surrendered to Confederates

May 10, Camp Jackson, being used as a Confederate recruiting station, seized by Captain Nathaniel Lyon

——, Proclamation of the President declared martial law and suspension of writ of habeas corpus on islands of Key West, Tortugas, and Santa Rosa

——, First Confederate commission of privateer of the "Triton," schooner of Brunswick, Georgia

——, Blockade of Charleston, South Carolina, begun by U.S.S. "Niagara"

——, Meeting of citizens in San Francisco declared for the Union

May 13, General Butler with about 1,000 men entered Baltimore and took possession of Federal Hill

——, Great Britain proclaimed neutrality but recognized the Confederate States as belligerents

——, Charles Francis Adams, Minister to England, reached London

——, Convention of loyal citizens met at Wheeling, Virginia (later West Virginia) and opened communications with General McClellan and President Lincoln

May 14, George B. McClellan appointed major general and assigned to command of the Dept. of Ohio including western Virginia

——, U.S.S. "Crusader" captured the yacht "Wanderer" bound for Key West from Havana

——, Governor Hicks of Maryland issued call for troops in response to the President's proclamation

May 15, Order of General Scott relieved General Butler from command at Annapolis, Butler commissioned major-general of volunteers May 16

May 16, Kentucky legislative committee on federal relations proposed that the State remain neutral

——, Confederate Act authorized loan of $50,000,000 to be raised by bonds or treasury notes, and provision for bounties to enlisted men made

May 17, California legislature pledged support to federal government

——, John T. Pickett appointed special agent of the Confederate States to Mexico

——, Confederate Act admitted North Carolina to Confederacy on condition of ratification of the Constitution

May 18, Admission of Tennessee to Confederacy by Confederate Congress

——, General Butler ordered to command of Fortress Monroe

May 18–19, Engagement at Sewell's Point, Virginia, naval attack on Confederate batteries

May 20, Governor Magoffin of Kentucky proclaimed armed neutrality

May 21, Resolution of Provisional Confederate Congress to remove the seat of government to Richmond, Virginia

——, North Carolina Convention passed secession ordinance refusing by a two-thirds vote to submit question to the people

——, Confederate Act forbade all persons to pay debts to individuals or corporations in the Northern States, and declaration made that during the blockade it should not be lawful to export raw cotton or cotton yarn except though ports of the Confederate States

May 21, Confederate permanent Constitution put into operation, Arkansas admitted into Confederacy, and Congress adjourned

——, Agreement between General Harney, U.S. army, and General Sterling Price, State guard, as to defense and preservation of order in Missouri

——, Confederate General Magruder took command at Yorktown, Virginia

May 23, Virginia adopted secession ordinance by popular vote, and the same day troops at Grafton began hostilities by burning 2 bridges on railroad

May 24, Ulysses S. Grant offered his services to the national government but received no answer

——, United States troops under General Irvin Mc-Dowell crossed the Potomac River and with cooperation of the navy occupied Arlington Heights and Alexandria for the protection of Washington. Colonel Ellsworth killed by a hotel-keeper of the Marshall House after taking down Confederate flag from the roof, first officer of rank killed

——, General Butler refused to give up 3 escaped negroes as "contraband of war"

May 26, Blockade established by U.S.S. "Powhatan," Commander D. D. Porter, at Mobile, Alabama

May 27, General Butler reported to the War Dept. that he had within his lines negroes worth $60,000 and would keep them as laborers

——, General Irvin McDowell assumed command of Dept. of Northeast Virginia

May 27–29, Newport News, Virginia, occupied by Union forces

May 28, Blockade established at Savannah, Georgia, by the U.S.S. "Union"

May 29–June 1, Vessels of the Potomac flotilla under Commander Ward in engagement with Confederate batteries at Aquia Creek, Virginia, not effective

May 30, Secretary of War Cameron directed General Butler not to surrender fugitive slaves to disloyal owners

——, Union Convention held at Knoxville, eastern Tennessee

——, Advance guard of Union troops sent by General McClellan reached Grafton in western Virginia where quarters established, Confederates falling back to Philippi

May 31, Brigadier General Nathaniel Lyon succeeded General W. S. Harney in command of Dept. of the West

June 1, British order forbade naval vessels or privateers of American belligerents to carry prizes into any British ports or territorial waters. Similar orders issued by France, Spain, Belgium, Prussia, Holland, Portugal, Hamburg, Bremen, and Hawaiian Islands

June 2, Confederates led by General Beauregard reached Manassas

June 3, Engagement at Philippi, western Virginia, Union troops of General Morris surprised and routed Virginians commanded by Colonel Porterfield, forcing retreat to Beverly

June 5, Confederate General Beauregard issued proclamation to the people of Loudoun, Fairfax, and Prince William counties, Virginia, declaring that a "reckless and unprincipled tyrant has invaded your soil" with war cry of "Beauty and Booty," and called for help against the "invaders"

June 6, Confederate General Henry A. Wise appointed

to command in the Kanawha Valley in western Virginia

June 7, Blockade of Apalachicola, Florida, announced

June 8, Virginia State troops transferred to the Confederate Government

——, Tennessee voted by majority of nearly 58,000 in favor of separation from the Union and of joining the Confederacy

——, Confederate General R. S. Garnett assigned to command in northwestern Virginia

June 9, Formal organization of Sanitary Commission by order of Secretary of War

June 10, France recognized the Confederates as belligerents

——, Small Union force under General E. W. Peirce sent by General Butler from Fortress Monroe to capture hostile battery defeated by Confederates commanded by General J. B. Magruder, Major Theodore Winthrop among the killed in first real battle of the war

June 11, Second loyal convention at Wheeling, (West) Virginia, adopted declaration of rights June 13, and June 19 elected Francis H. Pierpont, Governor

——, Meeting in St. Louis of Unionists and Secessionists. General Lyon declared for war and notified Governor Jackson that he would have him arrested

——, Colonel E. R. S. Canby placed in charge of the Dept. of New Mexico, and General Banks superseded General Cadwalader in command of the Dept. of Annapolis

June 15, General Lyon occupied Jefferson City, capital of Missouri, driving secessionist Governor Jackson and General Price to retreat to Booneville

——, Confederate General J. E. Johnston retreated from Harper's Ferry to Winchester, Virginia, and General Patterson took possession with Union troops

June 17, Spain proclaimed neutrality in American Civil War, and recognized the Confederates as belligerents

——, General Lyon took Booneville, dispersing troops of Governor Jackson and General Price

——, Action at Vienna station, Virginia, Union troops worsted in engagement and Confederate General Gregg captured train

——, Union Convention at Greenville, eastern Tennessee, petitioned Congress for recognition as a separate State

June 27, Federal vessels landed troops at Mathias Point, Virginia, and Commander Ward killed in attack on Confederates who repulsed landing party

——, Peace Convention at Dover, Delaware, proposed peaceful recognition of the Confederacy

——, Major General Banks arrested George P. Kane, secessionist chief of police in Baltimore, and had a provost-marshal appointed to cause police laws to be executed

June 28, Central Pacific Railroad Company of California incorporated at Sacramento, Leland Stanford, president, and Collis P. Huntington, vice-president

June 29, Council of war held by the President and decision made for advance of army from Washington upon Manassas, Confederate base of operations 30 miles distant. General McDowell's plan of attack provided that the Confederate army under Johnston should be held in the Shenandoah Valley

July 1, The Union army numbered 186,751

——, Four members of the Police Board of Baltimore, avowed secessionists, arrested by federal troops and taken to Fort McHenry

July 2, General Patterson advanced to Martinsburg, crossing the Potomac and was dissuaded by his officers from demonstration against Confederates under Johnston at Bunker Hill

——, Blockade established at Galveston, Texas, by U.S.S. "South Carolina"

July 3, Western Dept. constituted with headquarters at St. Louis and under command of General John Fremont, including Illinois and States and Territories west of the Mississippi and on eastern side of the Rocky Mts. and including New Mexico

——, Fort McLane, New Mexico, abandoned by United States troops

July 5, Engagement at Carthage, Missouri, Colonel Franz Sigel forced to retreat by force of secessionist Governor Jackson and General Sterling Price aided by Confederate Generals Ben McCulloch and Pearce with Texas and Arkansas troops

July 8, Confederate Brigadier General Henry H. Sibley ordered to Texas to organize troops to expel Union forces from New Mexico

July 10, Treaty with the Creek Indians concluded by Confederate States

——, Instructions of Russian Government to Minister in Washington as to neutrality friendly to the Union

——, Fort Breckinridge, New Mexico, abandoned

July 11, Engagement at pass over Rich Mountain between Beverly and Buckhannon, (West) Virginia. Generals McClellan and W. S. Rosecrans defeated Confederates under General John Pegram

July 12, Treaty with the Choctaw and Chickasaw Indians concluded by Confederate States

July 13, Confederate General Leonidas Polk assumed command of Dept. No. 2 (Western Dept.) comprising Kentucky, Illinois, Missouri, and Kansas

July 14, Blockade at Wilmington, North Carolina, established by the U.S.S. "Daylight"

——, General McClellan defeated the Confederates under General R. S. Garnett at Carrick's Ford over the Cheat River as they retreated from Laurel Hill to Beverly, Virginia, General Garnett killed

July 15, Skirmish at Bowman's Place, Cheat River, one of a series of engagements by which General McClellan cleared the western part of Virginia of Confederates making formation of State of West Virginia possible

July 16, Federal army commanded by General Irvin McDowell marched from Washington into Virginia reaching Fairfax Court House, evacuated by the Confederates, the following day

July 17, General Patterson fell back to Charleston instead of advancing to Winchester as ordered and thus allowed the Confederate army of General Johnston to reinforce Manassas

——, Colonel Lowe defeated Confederates commanded by Captain Patton at Scarytown, (West) Virginia

July 18, General Johnston began movement of 9,000 Confederate troops from Winchester through Ashby's Gap in Blue Ridge Mts. to railroad at Piedmont and by train to Manassas Junction the following day

——, Advance of Union troops commanded by General Daniel Tyler encountered Confederates at Blackburn's Ford, and engaged in 3 hour battle with loss of about 80 men, retiring to Centreville in the evening

July 20–Aug. 31, Confederate Provisional Congress met at Richmond, Virginia, in 3d session

July 21, First Battle of Bull Run (Manassas). Union attack begun by advance in early morning by General McDowell on Confederate position at Manassas Junction, Virginia. General P. G. T. Beauregard, Confederate commander, defeated Union army by aid of reinforcements from General Johnston arriving in the afternoon under Colonel T. J. Jackson (Stonewall) and Kirby Smith, and final attack of Early's brigade, the Union forces retreating in confusion to Centreville and Washington reached July 22–23. Federal troops engaged 28,455, total loss in killed, wounded, and missing, 2,708, Confederate troops engaged, 32,072, total loss 1,967

July 22, General W. J. Hardee assumed command of Confederate army in upper Arkansas

——, Convention at Jefferson City, Missouri, passed ordinances affirming loyalty, elected Robert Wilson president in place of Sterling Price now a major-general in the Confederate army, and declared State offices vacant, establishing a new government July 31 with Hamilton R. Gamble, Governor, and transferred capital to St. Louis

July 25, General Fremont assumed command in St. Louis of the Dept. of the West, and General Rosecrans appointed to command Dept. of the Ohio

——, Major Isaac Lynde in command at Fort Fillmore attacked Confederates in possession of La Mesilla, New Mexico, without result, and evacuated fort beginning retreat to Fort Stanton the following day

——, Robert M. T. Hunter appointed Confederate Secretary of State

July 26, Brigadier General F. K. Zollicoffer assigned to command Confederate army in eastern Tennessee

July 27, Surrender of Major Isaac Lynde without resistance to Confederate Lieutenant Colonel John R. Baylor at San Augustine Springs, New Mexico

——, General George B. McClellan, appointed July 22, assumed command of the Dept. of Washington and Northeast Virginia and began organization of troops

July 29, Portuguese proclamation against privateering prohibited entrance to ports or fitting out of vessels

Aug. 1, Brazil recognized the Confederates as belligerents

——, Colonel John R. Baylor by proclamation in name of the Confederacy took possession of Arizona and all of New Mexico south of the 34th parallel

Aug. 2, Fort Stanton, New Mexico, abandoned by United States troops

——, Federal troops under General Lyon defeated Confederates commanded by General James Rains at Dug Springs, Missouri

——, Confederate Act extended provisions of Act of May 21 to apply to export of tobacco, sugar, rice, molasses, syrup, and naval stores, to be exported only through Confederate ports

Aug. 3, Orders of the Secretary of the Navy to Commander H. S. Stellwagen to obstruct certain southern ports by sinking vessels loaded with stone across entrance

——, General Robert E. Lee given command of Confederate operations of the Trans-Alleghany region of Virginia

Aug. 7, Hampton, Virginia, burned by Confederates

——, Contract of the Government with J. B. Eads of St. Louis for construction of 7 ironclad gunboats

Aug. 8, Confederate Act authorized the President to grant commissions to raise volunteer regiments composed of persons who are or have been residents of Kentucky, Missouri, Maryland, and Delaware, and Act made provision for deportation of alien enemies

Aug. 8, General U. S. Grant assumed command of the district of Ironton, Missouri

Aug. 8-9, Attack on emigrant train neat Great Salt Lake, Utah, by Indians

Aug. 10, Battle of Wilson's Creek, near Springfield, Missouri, General Nathaniel Lyon with about 6,000 men attacked Confederate army of 20,000 under General Price advancing on Springfield. Union forces obliged to retreat after battle and death of General Lyon who had saved Missouri to the Union in a series of engagements

Aug. 11, Brigadier General John B. Floyd assumed command of Confederate forces in the Kanawha district of western Virginia

Aug. 12, Home Guard organized in California to act with United States troops

Aug. 14, President Jefferson Davis proclaimed banishment of alien enemies adhering to the Government of the United States

——, Brigadier General Paul O. Hébert relieved General Van Dorn in command of the Confederate forces in Texas

——, Martial law declared in Missouri by General Fremont

Aug. 15, States of Kentucky and Tennessee constituted the Dept. of the Cumberland under command of Brigadier General Robert Anderson

Aug. 16, Proclamation of the President declared the inhabitants of 11 southern States in insurrection and forbade all commercial intercourse with them, and confiscation of goods

——, The *New York Journal of Commerce, Daily News, Freeman's Journal*, and the *Brooklyn Eagle* suppressed as aiding treason

Aug. 17, The Dept. of the Potomac created by union of the Depts. of Northeastern Virginia, of Washington, and of the Shenandoah

Aug. 19, Confederate Act authorized the Secretary of the Treasury to issue notes of any denomination not less than $5, payable 6 months after the peace treaty

Aug. 20, Convention at Wheeling in (West) Virginia provided for organization of new State to be called Kanawha; ratified by popular vote of 18,862 to 514 Oct. 24

——, Brigadier General Richard C. Gatlin assumed command of the Confederate defenses of North Carolina

Aug. 21, Brigadier General Roswell S. Ripley assigned to command of Confederate forces of the Dept. of South Carolina, and Brigadier General John B. Grayson to command of Dept. of Middle and East Florida

——, Confederate Act authorized volunteers for local defense and special service

——, Colonel Benjamin L. Beall assigned to command of the District of Oregon

Aug. 22, Confederate Act established a uniform rule of naturalization for persons enlisted in armies of the Confederacy

——, Order to Post-Office that copies of New York papers suppressed for aid to rebellion should not be received in the mails, and the papers seized on arrival by train in Philadelphia

Aug. 24, President Jefferson Davis appointed Pierre A. Rost Confederate envoy to Spain, James M. Mason, special commissioner to Great Britain, and John Slidell, special agent to France

Aug. 25-Sept. 8, Operations against Indians about Fort Stanton, New Mexico

Aug. 26, Proclamation of neutrality in the war by Kamehameha IV, King of the Hawaiian Islands

Aug. 28-29, Joint army and naval expedition commanded by General Butler and Commodore S. H. Stringham from Fortress Monroe attacked Forts Hatteras and Clark on North Carolina coast and batteries at Hatteras Inlet to end privateering from this base, Fort Clark evacuated by Confederates and occupied by Union troops on the 28th, and Fort Hatteras captured Aug. 29

Aug. 30, General Fremont proclaimed free the slaves of all persons in Missouri who had taken up arms against the United States or given its enemies aid or comfort

——, Confederate Act provided for confiscation of estates and property of alien enemies, and Congress adjourned

Aug. 31, Five full generals gazetted by Confederacy, with seniority as follows: Samuel Cooper May 16, Sidney Johnston May 28, Robert E. Lee June 14, Joseph Johnston July 4, P. G. T. Beauregard July 21

Sept. 1, General U. S. Grant sent from Jefferson City, Missouri, to Cape Girardeau by Fremont to take command of all troops in vicinity of mouth of the Ohio, assumed command in southeastern Missouri

Sept. 2, New legislature of Kentucky ordered stars and stripes of the Union displayed above the State House

——, Letter from President Lincoln to General Fremont asked that he modify his proclamation of Aug. 30 to conform to Act of Aug. 6 respecting confiscation of property used for insurrectionary purposes

Sept. 3, General Polk, Confederate, crossed line from western Tennessee into Kentucky and occupied Hickman and Columbus

——, Confederate Congress met in 4th session and adjourned the same day

Sept. 4, General Grant established headquarters at Cairo, Illinois

Sept. 6, Brigadier General Charles F. Smith assigned to command in western Kentucky

——, Gulf squadron placed under command of Captain W. W. McKean

——, Union troops sent by General Grant occupied Paducah, Kentucky, offsetting Confederate advance gained at Columbus and Hickman

Sept. 8-9, Operations by General John Pope against Martin E. Green's forces, "Green's guerillas" in Missouri

Sept. 9, Proclamation of Governor Henry Connolly of New Mexico organizing the militia to resist invasion of armed force from Texas

Sept. 10, Brigadier General George H. Thomas assigned to command at Camp Dick Robinson in eastern Kentucky to organize loyal troops

——, Confederate General Albert Sidney Johnston appointed in command of Tennessee, Missouri, and Arkansas

——, Engagement at Carnifex Ferry, in (West) Virginia. General Rosecrans attacked Confederate entrenchments on the Gauley River 8 miles south of Nicholas and forced General Floyd to withdraw

Sept. 11, President Lincoln in answer to letter of General Fremont of Sept. 8 asking him to give open order for modification of his proclamation of Aug. 30 disavowed the modification ordering modification to conform to Act of Aug. 6

Sept. 11–17, Operations on Cheat Mountain (West) Virginia, General Reynolds repulsing attacks of General Robert E. Lee at Cheat Mountain Pass, Cheat Summit, Point Mountain Turnpike, and Elk Water

Sept. 12, General McClellan ordered arrest of disloyal members of Maryland legislature to convene in Frederick Sept. 17, and arrests made Sept. 12–17 of members suspected of disloyalty

Sept. 15, Confederate General A. S. Johnston superseded General Polk in command of Dept. No. 2 (Western)

Sept. 16, Ship Island, Mississippi Sound, evacuated by Confederate Colonel H. W. Allen and occupied by Union troops the following day

Sept. 18, Kentucky legislature resolved to expel invaders from the State

——, Bowling Green, Kentucky, seized by Confederate General Simon B. Buckner, who assumed command in central Kentucky

——, South Atlantic Squadron placed under command of Captain S. F. Dupont

Sept. 19, North Atlantic Squadron authorized to operate to the southern line of North Carolina and placed under command of Captain L. M. Goldsborough succeeding Captain Stringham Sept. 23

——, Dept. of Western Virginia constituted, and Dept. of the Ohio reorganized

——, Confederate force commanded by General Zollicoffer advanced from Tennessee and at Barboursville, Kentucky, dispersed a regiment of Kentucky Union forces

Sept. 20, Robert Anderson made brigadier general in command at Cincinnati authorized to organize Union forces in Kentucky, his native State. He established headquarters at Louisville

——, Colonel James A. Mulligan besieged at Lexington, Missouri, by Confederate force of General Sterling Price since Sept. 9, compelled to surrender

——, Maryland political prisoners sent to Fort Lafayette

Sept. 20–Oct. 7, Operations against Indians from Camp Robledo, New Mexico

Sept. 21, Brigadier General O. M. Mitchell assumed command of the Dept. of the Ohio

Oct. 1, Dept. of New England constituted, Major General Benjamin F. Butler, in command

——, Confederate Council of war at Centreville, Virginia. Generals Johnston, Beauregard, and G. W. Smith urged President Davis to reinforce army at Manassas and carry the war into the North. He refused to grant the additional 20,000 men to make army of 50,000 required

Oct. 2, Confederate States made treaty with Great Osage Indians

Oct. 3, Engagement at Greenbrier River on Buffalo Hill in western Virginia, Confederate General H. R. Jackson repulsed attack of General Reynolds

Oct. 4, Contract with John Ericsson of New York by Government for construction of ironclad vessel to meet the "Merrimac" salvaged at Gosport Navy Yard by Confederates and renamed "Virginia"

——, Treaty of Confederate States with Senecas and Shawnees, Oct. 7 with Cherokees

Oct. 5, Brigadier General Joseph K. F. Mansfield assigned to command at Hatteras Inlet

Oct. 7, The "Pony Express" officially discontinued

Oct. 8, Brigadier General William T. Sherman superseded Brigadier General Anderson in command of the Dept. of the Cumberland

Oct. 9, Battle of Santa Rosa Island, Florida. Confederates made surprise attack on camp of Wilson's Zouaves about a mile from the fort, camp set on fire, and Major Vogdes with 2 companies sent from fort to relief of camp captured, Confederates retired to their boats after attack

Oct. 10, Brigadier General C. Kirby Smith, Confederate, assigned to command of Dept. of Middle and East Florida

Oct. 11, Brigadier General William S. Rosecrans assumed command of the Dept. of Western Virginia, and Lieutenant Colonel Albemarle Cady assigned to command District of Oregon assumed command Oct. 23

——, James M. Mason of Virginia and John Slidell of Louisiana, commissioners to Great Britain, ran the blockade from Charleston, South Carolina, in the Confederate vessel "Theodora" and proceeded to Nassau

Oct. 11–16, Operations against the Indians from Fort Inge, Texas

Oct. 12, Launching of first ironclad steamer of the United States navy, the "St. Louis" at Carondelet, Missouri

——, At Head of the Passes, Mississippi River, the blockading vessels attacked by Confederate squadron including the ironclad ram "Manassas" and driven to mouth of the Southwest Pass

Oct. 14, Secretary of War Cameron authorized General T. W. Sherman commanding at Port Royal, South Carolina, to organize and if necessary arm squads of fugitive and captured negroes

——, Colonel James H. Carleton took command of District of Southern California

——, Confederate Dept. of Alabama and West Florida constituted, General Bragg in command

Oct. 16, Union troops reoccupied Lexington, Missouri

Oct. 19, Engagement between U.S.S. "Massachusetts" and C.S.S. "Florida" near Ship Island in Mississippi Sound

Oct. 20, Colonel George Wright succeeded General E. V. Sumner in command of the Dept. of the Pacific

Oct. 21, Battle of Ball's Bluff (Leesburg, Virginia). General Charles P. Stone ordered Colonel Devens to cross the Potomac to destroy Confederate camps, and retreating was attacked by Confederates and defeated with loss of 894 men to Confederate 302. Colonel Baker who came with reinforcements bringing Union force to number of 1,900 killed in action

——, General Zollicoffer checked at Wild Cat Mountain near London, Kentucky, by Union force under Colonel Garrard

——, Confederate Dept. of Northern Virginia organized under command of General Joseph E. Johnston

Oct. 22, Rev. William Blount Carter entered eastern Tennessee to organize bands to destroy railroad bridges

——, Brigadier General Benjamin F. Keeley assigned to command of the Dept. of Harper's Ferry and Cumberland

Oct. 24, Major General David Hunter ordered to supersede General Fremont at St. Louis and took command Nov. 2

——, Action of Wheeling Convention to form new State in western Virginia ratified by popular vote

Oct. 24, First ocean to ocean telegraph completed with line from Denver to Sacramento

Oct. 25, Keel of John Ericsson's ironclad vessel "Monitor" laid in Greenpoint, Long Island

Oct. 26, Action at Romney, (West) Virginia. General Kelley drove Confederate troops from the town

Oct. 27, General Fremont in pursuit of Confederate General Price in retreat established headquarters at Springfield, Missouri

Oct. 31, General Scott, aged 75, retired at his own request

Nov. 1, General McClellan appointed Commander-in-Chief of United States army

——, General Grant ordered to make a demonstration on both sides of the Mississippi

Nov. 1-9, Confederate expedition from Rolla, Missouri, against Fremont's forces

Nov. 2-12, Operations from Bud's Point, Cape Giradeau, against Confederates under General Thompson

Nov. 6, Treaty with Hanover signed abolishing the Stadt or Brunshausen dues

——, Jefferson Davis elected Confederate President under new Constitution

Nov. 7, Capture of Forts Beauregard and Walker on Port Royal Sound defended by Confederate Commodore Tatnall and General T. F. Dayton by expedition from Annapolis (Oct. 21) commanded by General Thomas W. Sherman and Commodore Dupont

——, Battle of Belmont, Missouri, in which General Grant with force from Cairo attacked and captured Confederate camp opposite Columbus successful against Generals Pillow and Cheatham, but compelled to withdraw as Confederate reinforcements arrived from Columbus

Nov. 8, The "Trent Affair." Captain Charles Wilkes in the U.S.S. "San Jacinto" stopped the British mail steamer "Trent" in the Old Bahama Channel and arrested Confederate commissioners, James M. Mason and John Slidell, on their way to England, and took them to Boston where they were confined in Fort Warren

——, Uprising of loyal mountaineers in East Tennessee, the burning of railroad bridges begun by organized bands

——, Confederate General R. E. Lee appointed in command Dept. of South Carolina, Georgia, and East Florida

Nov. 9, Dept. of the Ohio reorganized to include Kentucky and Tennessee, General Buell in command, Dept. of the Missouri constituted, General Halleck in command, Dept. of Kansas, General Hunter in command, and Dept. of New Mexico reëstablished under Colonel Canby

Nov. 14, Ex-Senator Gwin and Attorney General Benham arrested by General Sumner who traveled with them from California as they journeyed to join Mason and Slidell

Nov. 15, General Robert E. Lee appointed in charge of Confederate defenses, coasts of South Carolina, Georgia, and Florida

Nov. 18-Feb. 17, 1862, Provisional Confederate Congress met in 4th session

Nov. 18, Commander D. D. Porter ordered to purchase vessels for and organize mortar flotilla

——, Colonel James H. Carleton relieved from command of District of Southern California

Nov. 19, Lucius C. Lamar appointed special agent to Russia for the Confederate States

Nov. 19, Brigadier General George Wright formally assigned to command of the Dept. of the Pacific, and Major General H. W. Halleck assumed command of the Dept. of the Missouri

Nov. 20, Major General David Hunter assumed command of the Dept. of Kansas

Nov. 21, J. P. Benjamin appointed Confederate Secretary of War, Thomas Bragg, Attorney General

Nov. 26, Union Constitutional Convention at Wheeling adopted Constitution for a new state to be called West Virginia

Nov. 28, Confederate Act admitted Missouri to the Confederacy (of no effect)

Nov. 29-Dec. 9, South Carolina planters near the coast burned the year's crop of cotton to prevent capture

Nov. 29, Brigadier General John M. Schofield assumed command of the Missouri militia

Dec. 2, Order to General Halleck authorized suspension of writ of habeas corpus within the limits of his command

Dec. 4, The *Richmond Enquirer* announced burning of cotton at Edisto and all islands between Charleston and Port Royal to prevent capture by Union forces

Dec. 5, Confederate General William J. Hardee assumed command of Kentucky army

Dec. 7, Commander Daniel B. Ridgely in U.S.S. "Santiago de Cuba" off the coast of Mexico overhauled British schooner "Eugenia Smith" and seized J. W. Zacharie, Confederate agent

Dec. 9, 100 bales of cotton on 1 plantation and 4,000 on some others on Paris Island burned to prevent capture by Union troops

Dec. 10, Confederate Act admitted Kentucky to the Confederacy (of no effect)

Dec. 11, Extradition Treaty with Mexico signed

Dec. 14, Confederate General H. H. Sibley assumed command in New Mexico and Arizona

Dec. 17-21, Confederates effected a breach in Chesapeake and Ohio Canal at Dam. No 5

Dec. 18, Lord Lyons, British Minister in Washington, received instructions to demand release of Mason and Slidell, declared their seizure an "affront to the British flag and a violation of international law"

Dec. 19, Confederate supplementary tax law authorized issue of treasury notes and made provision for war tax for their redemption

Dec. 20, Captain C. H. Davis sunk 17 vessels loaded with stone across the entrance to harbor of Charleston, South Carolina

Dec. 21, Confederate General Henry A. Wise assigned to duty in North Carolina

Dec. 23, Lord Lyons, British Minister, presented officially the British Note demanding surrender of Mason and Slidell

Dec. 26, Note of the Government in reply to British Note announcing that Mason and Slidell would be released delivered to Lord Lyons

——, Martial law proclaimed in St. Louis and in and about all railroads in Missouri

Dec. 28, Beckley (Raleigh Court House) in western Virginia captured by Union forces preventing communication between Confederates in central and western parts of State

——, Meeting of New York City banks agreed to immediate suspension of specie payment

Dec. 30, Banks of Boston, Albany, Philadelphia, Cleveland, Pittsburgh, and the Government suspended specie payment

CONGRESS

Jan. 3, Members from the 14 border States met and appointed a committee to consider compromise proposals

——, Senator Crittenden proposed that his compromise plan be submitted to vote of people

Jan. 5, Senators from Georgia, Alabama, Mississippi, Florida, Louisiana, Texas, and Arkansas held caucus and advised people of these States to secede from the Union

Jan. 12, Representatives from Mississippi withdrew

Jan. 14, House Committee of 33 proposed amendment to the Constitution which should make provision against initiation of any amendment as to slavery except at instance of the slave-holding States, and ratification of any amendment except by vote of every State in the Union, jurisdiction under fugitive slave law to be transferred to State from which fugitive escaped

Jan. 16, Crittenden compromise killed in Senate by the adoption of Senator Clark's resolution that the provisions of the Constitution are ample for the preservation of the Union

Jan. 21, Senators and representatives from Georgia, Florida, and Alabama withdrew from Congress, Clement C. Clay, Stephen R. Mallory, and David L. Yulee

Jan. 29, Kansas admitted under the Wyandotte Constitution prohibiting slavery, 34th State

Feb. 4, Judah P. Benjamin and John Slidell withdrew from Senate, Slidell reading Ordinance of secession of Louisiana, and Benjamin making a defiant speech

——, Electoral vote gave Lincoln 180, Breckinridge 72, Bell 39, Douglas 12

Feb. 8, Loan of $25,000,000 at 6% for 10 to 20 years authorized for current expenses and redemption of outstanding treasury notes

Feb. 28, Territory of Colorado created

March 2, Territories of Nevada and Dakota created

——, Senate rejected proposal of Crittenden to substitute amendment proposed and presented by the Peace Convention Feb. 27 in place of compromise resolution originally presented and then declared against Peace Convention resolutions

——, Joint Resolution adopted to amend the Constitution to provide that "no amendment shall be made to the Constitution which will authorize or give Congress the power to abolish or interfere within any State with the domestic institutions thereof, including that of persons held to labor or service by said State"; never ratified by States

——, A $10,000,000 loan authorized to be redeemed after 10 years from July 1, 1861 on stock at 6%

——, Morrill Tariff Act substituted specific for ad valorem duties and increased duties from 5 to 10%, increases specially on iron and wool

March 4, Congress adjourned

July 4, Thirty-seventh Congress, 1st (extra) sess. convened

July 10, Act provided for refund and remission of duties on arms imported by States for use of troops in putting down insurrection against the United States

July 11, The Senate expelled Mason and Hunter of Virginia, Clingman and Bragg of North Carolina,

Chestnut of South Carolina, Nicholson of Tennessee, Sebastian and Mitchell of Arkansas, and Hemphill and Wigfall of Texas, all of whom had vacated their seats at the previous session

July 13, The President empowered to collect customs at ports of delivery and declare existence of insurrection where law could not be executed

July 17, Loan of $250,000,000 authorized, the Treasury to issue bonds at 7% and notes at 7.30%

July 22, Resolution of Crittenden that the war was waged simply "to defend and maintain the supremacy of the Constitution and to preserve the Union" and not for "the purpose of overthrowing established institutions" passed in House and in Senate July 25

——, Levy of 500,000 men for army authorized

July 25, Employment of volunteers to aid in enforcing the law and protecting public property authorized

——, Act provided for more efficient organization of Marine Corps

July 27, Act provided for indemnification of the States for expenses incurred by them in defense of the United States

July 29, The President authorized to call out the militia for suppression of rebellion and resistance to the laws, amending Act of Feb. 28, 1795

——, Nine regiments of infantry, one of cavalry, and one of artillery added to the regular army

July 31, Act to define and punish conspiracy against the United States enacted

——, Office of Assistant Secretary of the Navy created

Aug. 3, Act provided for construction of 1 or more armored ships and floating batteries, and of Aug. 5 for 12 small side-wheel steamers for use of the navy

——, Act to provide for better organization of the army enacted

Aug. 5, The President authorized to enlist seamen for period of the war

——, Direct tax of $20,000,000 on real estate apportioned among the States, customs duties on certain classes of imports, and the first income tax imposed of 3% on all incomes of more than $800 a year

——, Tariff increased rates on sugar, hemp, hides, rubber, silk, lead, salt, brandy, spices, and other articles

——, Issue of bonds authorized bearing 6% interest payable in 20 years exchangeable for 7.30 treasury notes, the entire amount not to exceed entire amount of 7.30 treasury notes issued

Aug. 6, Confiscation Act declared forfeit all claim by the owner to service of slaves employed in arms or labor against the Government of the United States

——, Act provided for increase of pay of soldiers in regular army and of volunteers in service of the United States

——, All acts, proclamations, and orders of the President as to army and navy issued after March 4 preceding approved and legalized

——, Congress adjourned

Dec. 2, Thirty-seventh Congress, 2d sess. convened

Dec. 4, John C. Breckinridge of Kentucky expelled from the Senate

Dec. 14, Joint Committee on the conduct of the war appointed

Dec. 24, Tea and coffee removed from free list and duty on sugar raised as a war measure, and specific duty placed on wool in place of ad valorem rates of 1846 and 1857

1862

Jan. 1, United States army numbered 575,917

——, Mason and Slidell and their secretaries placed on board the British sloop of war "Rinaldo" at Provincetown, Cape Cod, sailing for Halifax

Jan. 7, Dept. of North Carolina constituted with General A. E. Burnside in command

Jan. 10, Engagement at Middle Creek and Prestonburg, Kentucky, General Garfield defeating Confederates under Humphrey Marshall

——, Union troops evacuated Romney in western Virginia which was occupied by Confederates

Jan. 11, Dept. of North Carolina constituted, Brigadier General John M. Brannan in command

Jan. 13, Expedition from Fortress Monroe under General Ambrose E. Burnside and Commodore L. M. Goldsborough reached Hatteras Inlet

Jan. 15, Edwin M. Stanton, of Pennsylvania, appointed Secretary of War

Jan. 18, Confederate Territory of Arizona formed, General Baylor appointed in command

Jan. 19, Battle of Mill Springs, Kentucky. Brigadier General George H. Thomas defeated Confederates under General Felix K. Zollicoffer who was killed

Jan. 20, Second stone fleet sunk at entrance to Charleston Harbor

Jan. 27, President Lincoln issued General War Order No. 1 directing that an advance of all the Union forces should take place on Feb. 22

Jan. 30, Ironclad steamer "Monitor" launched at shipyard of Thomas Rowland, at Greenpoint, Long Island

Feb., The "Battle Hymn of the Republic" by Julia Ward Howe published anonymously in the *Atlantic Monthly*, written during a visit to the camps in Washington in 1861

Feb. 3, The C.S.S. "Nashville" left Southampton, England, under convoy of a British frigate

Feb. 6, Fort Henry on the Tennessee River commanded by Confederate General Tilghman stormed and captured by joint attack of army under General Grant and naval force under Commodore A. H. Foote, General Tilghman making unconditional surrender, the greater part of his garrison escaped to Fort Donelson

Feb. 8, Expedition of General Burnside and Commodore Goldsborough took Roanoke Island, North Carolina, key to rear defenses of Norfolk, garrison under General Wise of 2,675 officers and men captured, and the Confederate fleet driven up Croatan Channel pursued to Elizabeth City and destroyed Feb. 10, and Elizabeth City captured

——, Martial law declared throughout Kansas

Feb. 12, Siege of Fort Donelson, Tennessee, commanded by Confederate General Floyd, begun by General Grant and Commodore Foote, and attack repulsed Feb. 14

Feb. 14, Executive order released political prisoners who would give parole not to give aid or comfort to the enemy

——, Brigadier General Grant assigned to command of District of West Tennessee, and General W. T. Sherman to command of District of Cairo

Feb. 15, Brigadier General John M. Schofield assumed command of District of St. Louis, Missouri

——, Confederate attack from Fort Donelson at first successful but routed by Union attack. During the night after the battle General Floyd surrendered the command to General Pillow, and he to Buckner, and the 2 former with Nathan B. Forrest escaped by way of the river

Feb. 16, Unconditional surrender of Fort Donelson to General Grant by Confederate General Buckner. General Grant made Major General of Volunteers

Feb. 17, Provisional Confederate Congress adjourned

Feb. 18–April 21, First Confederate Congress met in 1st session at Richmond

Feb. 21, Seizure of Lieutenant John Smith alias Henry Myers and T. T. Turnstall of C.S.S. "Sumter" by James De Long, United States consul at Tangier, Morocco

——, Engagement at Valverde near Fort Craig, New Mexico. Confederate Major Henry H. Sibley defeated Union force from Fort Craig under Colonel Edward R. S. Canby in severe all day fight

Feb. 22, President Davis took oath as President under permanent Confederate Constitution

Feb. 23, Dept. of the Gulf constituted under command of General Benjamin F. Butler, and Brigadier General John Pope assumed command of the Army of the Mississippi assembling at Commerce, Missouri

Feb. 25, Nashville, Tennessee, evacuated by Confederates after the surrender of Fort Donelson, occupied by Union forces

——, Treaty of commerce and navigation with Turkey signed

Feb. 27, Confederate Act gave the President authority to suspend writ of habeas corpus

March 1, President Davis proclaimed martial law in Richmond

March 1, *circa*, General McClellan occupied Harper's Ferry, (West) Virginia, and the line of the Baltimore and Ohio Railroad

March 1–3, Evacuation of Columbus, Kentucky, by Confederates, and occupation by Union troops, General Beauregard planning to make next stand at New Madrid and Island No. 10

March 2, Albuquerque, New Mexico, abandoned by Union forces and occupied by Confederate Major Sibley

March 3, Cubero, military post, New Mexico, captured by Confederates

——, General Robert E. Lee assigned to duty at Richmond

March 3–4, Amelia Island, Florida, evacuated by Confederates and occupied by Union force

March 4, General Grant's command transferred to General C. F. Smith by General Halleck because of supposed disregard of orders which Grant had not received

——, Andrew Johnson confirmed by Senate as military governor of Tennessee with rank of brigadier general

——, Santa Fé, New Mexico, abandoned by Union forces and occupied by Confederate force of Major Sibley

March 6, The "Monitor" left New York for Fortress Monroe

March 6–8, Battle of Pea Ridge or Elkhorn Tavern, Arkansas. General Samuel R. Curtis defeated Confederate attack of Generals Earl Van Dorn, Sterling Price, Ben McCulloch, breaking Confederate power in Arkansas and Missouri, General McCulloch and General McIntosh killed, and Price and Slack wounded. Confederate loss about 1,300, Union 1,351 in killed, wounded, and missing

144 UNITED STATES 1862

March 6, Engagement at Bentonville (Battle of Pea Ridge)

March 7, Engagement at Leetown (Battle of Pea Ridge)

March 7–9, Withdrawal of Confederate forces under General Joseph E. Johnston from Manassas to the south bank of the Rappahannock for defense of Richmond

March 7–11, Advance of the Union forces to Centreville and Manassas, Virginia

March 8, Naval engagement at Hampton Roads, Virginia. The C.S.S. "Virginia" (former "Merrimac") attacked and destroyed federal vessels "Cumberland" and "Congress"

——, Confederate General Kirby Smith reached Knoxville and assumed command of troops in East Tennessee, Chattanooga occupied

——, General Sherman's division embarked at Paducah, Kentucky, for the Tennessee River

——, Leesburg, Virginia, occupied by Union force

March 9, Battle between the U.S.S. "Monitor" commanded by Lieutenant John L. Worden and the C.S.S. "Virginia" ("Merrimac"), commanded by Commodore Franklin Buchanan the "Virginia" badly disabled forced to withdraw from the conflict

March 11, General McClellan relieved by the President of command of all military departments except the Potomac, the Dept. of the Mississippi enlarged to include departments of Kansas, Missouri, and in part Ohio, to give General Halleck sole command of forces in the West, and the Dept. of Western Virginia merged into the Mountain Dept. General Rosecrans assuming command March 14, and General J. C. Fremont succeeding him March 29

March 11–12, Winchester, Virginia, evacuated by Confederates and occupied by Union forces

——, Jacksonville, Florida, occupied by Union forces

March 13, Army corps organized in the Army of the Potomac and Generals McDowell, Sumner, Heintzelman, Keyes, and Banks assigned as commanders

——, An additional Article of war forbade officers and soldiers of the United States army from aiding in the capture and return of fugitive slaves to disloyal owners

March 14, Capture of New Madrid, Missouri, by General Pope, after bombardment, Confederate General McCown removing the garrison during the night to Island No. 10

——, President Davis proclaimed martial law in counties of Elizabeth City, Warwick, Gloucester, and Mathews, Virginia

——, Capture of New Berne, North Carolina, in joint attack of army and navy by the Burnside expedition, gave Union forces a base from which to threaten advance on Richmond and caused retention of large Confederate force in the State

March 15, South Carolina, Georgia, and Florida constituted the Dept. of the South, General David Hunter in command

March 16, Action at Pound Gap, Kentucky, General Garfield driving Marshall from the town, freeing eastern Kentucky from Confederates

March 17, Army of the Potomac (Heintzelman's corps) began embarkation from Alexandria, Virginia, for Peninsula campaign, McClellan's plan of advance on Richmond by Yorktown and West Point, name from peninsula between James and York rivers emptying into Chesapeake Bay

March 17, General Grant restored to command in Tennessee

March 18, Judah P. Benjamin appointed Confederate Secretary of State; George W. Randolph, Secretary of War; Thomas H. Watts, Attorney General

——, The Confederate army of General Johnston retreating after surrender of Fort Donelson reached Corinth in Mississippi where he was joined by forces of Generals Bragg and Beauregard

March 20, Major General B. F. Butler assumed command of the Dept. of the Gulf and March 25 arrived at Ship Island to coöperate with Farragut in campaign to capture New Orleans

March 22, The "Oreto" (later C.S.S. "Florida") built in England for the Confederacy sailed for Nassau registered as an English ship

——, Middle Military Dept. constituted under command of General John A. Dix

March 23, General James Shields and General Kimball defeated the Confederates under General T. J. Jackson (Stonewall) at Kernstown near Winchester in the Shenandoah Valley, Virginia

March 28, Engagement at La Glorieta Pass (Apache Cañon) Colonel Slough and Major Chivington with troops from Colorado with Confederates commanded by Major Pyron and Colonel W. R. Scurry. Before battle began Major Chivington marched to the Confederate camp at Johnson's ranch and destroyed their supplies and ammunition, 60 train wagons

March 29, Confederate General A. S. Johnston assumed command of Army of the Mississippi

March 31, United States army numbered 637,126

——, Capture of Union City, Tennessee, with Confederate stores

April 1, Headquarters of Army of the Potomac transferred to near Fortress Monroe

April 3, West Virginia adopted a state constitution by ratification by popular vote

April 4, Army of the Potomac under General McClellan began march from Fortress Monroe and advance up the peninsula, attack on Yorktown repulsed by Confederate General Magruder

——, Dept. of the Rappahannock constituted under General Irvin McDowell and first army corps detached from Army of the Potomac, and Dept. of the Shenandoah under General N. P. Banks and fifth army corps detached

——, Canal cut 12 miles through swamps at New Madrid, Missouri, for passage of Union troops completed after 19 days labor, and vessels able to pass to New Madrid without passing Island Number 10 forcing its capture April 7

April 6–7, Battle of Shiloh or Pittsburg Landing, Tennessee. General A. S. Johnston, Confederate, attacked General Grant and the first day succeeded in driving Union army from vicinity of Shiloh nearly to the river about 3 miles, General Johnston killed, General Beauregard taking command the second day, and ordering retreat in the afternoon after severe battle, General Grant reinforced by General Buell, Confederate total loss 10,699, Union 13,573

April 7, Treaty with Great Britain signed for suppression of the African slave trade

——, Surrender of Island Number 10, important Confederate fort on the Mississippi, to General John Pope and Flag-Officer A. H. Foote, included 3 generals, 273 field and company officers, 6,700 privates, 123 heavy guns, 35 field pieces, 7,000 small arms, tents for 12,000 men, and immense quantities of provisions, ammunition, supplies

April 8, Martial law proclaimed in East Tennessee by President Jefferson Davis and suspension of writ of habeas corpus

April 10, Brigadier General John M. Schofield placed in immediate command in Missouri, Brigadier General Samuel D. Sturgis assumed command of the District of Kansas, and Colonel Ferris Forman of District of Southern California

April 11, Huntsville, Alabama, occupied by General O. M. Mitchell in surprise attack, taking possession of 100 miles of the Memphis and Charleston Railroad

——, Fort Pulaski, Cockspur Island, Georgia, at entrance of the Savannah River compelled to surrender by General Quincy A. Gillmore by bombardment from batteries placed on Tybee Island

——, General Halleck arrived at Pittsburg Landing, Tennessee, headquarters of Grant's army (5 divisions under Generals W. T. Sherman, Hurlbut, W. H. L. Wallace, McClernand, and Prentiss, and including division of General Lew Wallace 7 miles distant, about 40,000 men) to assume command

——, Confederate ironclad "Virginia" ("Merrimac") appeared in Hampton Roads and directed the capture of 3 merchant vessels

April 12, Confederate General Sibley began evacuation of Albuquerque and the Territory forced by Canby to make disastrous retreat to Texas

April 13, Major General David Hunter ordered emancipation of slaves at Fort Pulaski and on Cockspur Island, Georgia

April 16, First Confederate Conscription Act included white men between ages of 18 and 35

April 18–28, Bombardment of Forts Jackson and St. Philip, 25 miles from the mouth of the Mississippi guarding the approach to New Orleans, by Flag Officer D. G. Farragut, Commodore D. D. Porter, and Lieutenant J. M. Wainwright

April 20, Breaking of the obstructions below Forts Jackson and St. Philip on the Mississippi by the U.S.S. "Itasca" and "Pinola" commanded by Captain Bell

April 21, General Grant formally given command of the Army of the Tennessee

——, Confederate Act declared certain persons exempt from military service

——, Confederate Congress, first session, adjourned

April 22, Franklin's division of McDowell's corps joined General McClellan's army before Yorktown, Virginia

April 23, Union naval expedition successfully blocked the Chesapeake and Albermarle Canal, North Carolina

April 24, Farragut's fleet ran past Forts St. Philip and Jackson below New Orleans with 13 of his 17 vessels in successful battle with barreries, fireships, gunboats, and 2 ironclad rams

April 25, Socorro, New Mexico, surrendered to Texan Confederates

——, Farragut silenced the Chalmette batteries 3 miles below New Orleans and dropped anchor off the city

April 25–26, Union army and naval forces commanded by Brigadier General J. G. Parker and Admiral Dupont combined in 10 hour bombardment which forced surrender of Fort Macon, North Carolina, commanding the entrance to the Newport River on April 26

April 26, California Act to protect white labor against Chinese coolie competition provided that every Chinaman over 18 years of age should pay a monthly tax of $2.50 except those engaged in the production of sugar, rice, coffee, and tea. Declared unconstitutional by State Supreme Court in July

April 27, Forts Livingston, Pike, and Wood, Louisiana, recaptured by Union forces

April 28, Surrender of Forts St. Philip and Jackson to General B. F. Butler and Commodore D. D. Porter

——, The "Oreto" (C.S.S. "Florida") reached Nassau in the Bahamas from England

April 29, New Orleans surrendered to naval force of Flag-Officer Farragut. The Confederate army of General Mansfield Lovell had evacuated the city when Forts St. Philip and Jackson were taken

April 30, Reorganization of the Army of the Mississippi, Major Generals Thomas, Pope, and McClernand assigned to command of right wing, left wing, and reserve, Major General Buell remained in command of the Army of the Ohio, and General Grant made second in command to General Halleck but deprived of any actual command of troops

——, Resolution of Confederate Congress ordered that negro slaves captured in arms and their white officers should be delivered to Confederate States to be dealt with according to their respective laws

May 1, General Benjamin F. Butler received possession of New Orleans from Farragut

——, Dept. of Kansas reëstablished, Brigadier General James G. Blunt assuming command May 5

May 3, Proclamation of President Jefferson Davis extended martial law over counties of Lee, Wise, Buchanan, McDowell, and Wyoming in Virginia and suspended writ of habeas corpus

May 4, Army of the Potomac occupied Yorktown, Virginia, evacuated by the Confederates

May 5, Battle of Williamsburg, Virginia. General Hooker engaged Confederates retreating from Yorktown suffering heavy loss, the arrival of reinforcements under Kearny about 4 P.M. caused Confederates to retire toward Richmond

——, Action at Lebanon, Tennessee. General Dumont drove Confederate force of General Morgan from the town

May 6, Williamsburg, Virginia, occupied by Union forces

May 7, Confederate General Braxton Bragg assumed command of the Army of the Mississippi

——, Engagement at Eltham's Landing, West Point, where General Franklin was landing Union force and defeat of Confederates under General Whiting (Peninsula campaign)

May 8, Confederate Major General W. Loring assigned to command of the Army of Southwest Virginia

——, Engagement near McDowell (Bull Mountain Pasture). Confederate General Edward Johnson defeated Milroy

May 9, Major General David Hunter proclaimed martial law in Georgia, Florida, and South Carolina, and declared all slaves free in his military dept. and authorized arming of negroes; disavowed by President Lincoln

May 10, General Wool occupied Norfolk, Virginia, evacuated by Confederates

——, Commodore Porter took possession of Pensacola, Florida, dislodging Confederate force which had threatened Fort Pickens and made it headquarters for the Gulf Squadron

May 10, General Butler seized $800,000 in gold from Netherlands Consulate, New Orleans

May 11, The C.S.S. "Virginia" ("Merrimac") blown up by her commander, Commodore Tattnall, off Craney Island, Virginia, to prevent capture by Union forces

May 12, Proclamation of the President opened ports of Beaufort, Port Royal, and New Orleans to commerce

May 15, United States gunboats commanded by Commodore John Rodgers repulsed in engagement with Confederate batteries at Drewry's Point below Richmond

——, General Butler at New Orleans issued Order No. 28 that "any female" who by "word, gesture or movement" should "insult or show contempt for any officer or soldier of the United States" was thereupon to be "regarded and held liable to be treated as a woman of the town plying her vocation"

——, The C.S.S. "Alabama" launched at Liverpool, England, as the "290"

——, Confederate General Johnston crossed the Chickahominy and encamped 3 miles from Richmond, Virginia

May 16, General McClellan established headquarters at White House on the Pamunkey River

May 17, Major General Irvin McDowell ordered to join the Army of the Potomac

May 18, Surrender of Vicksburg, Mississippi, demanded by General Butler and Flag-Officer Farragut; Confederates refused

May 19, President Lincoln disavowed General Hunter's Proclamation freeing the slaves in his military district

May 20–23, Operations about Bottom's Bridge, Chickahominy River, Virginia, corps of Keyes and Heintzelman crossed the river dividing federal army

May 23, General "Stonewall" Jackson captured Union outpost at Front Royal, Virginia, forcing General Banks to retreat from Strasburg to Winchester, Virginia

May 24, General McDowell's order to join in movement on Richmond suspended in view of General Jackson's advance, recalled for defense of Washington

May 25, Battle of Winchester (Va.) General Jackson routed General Banks forcing Federals to retreat across the Potomac

——, Secretary of War Stanton telegraphed to governors of the northern States to organize and forward all militia and volunteers to defend Washington

May 26, Confederate General Hindman assigned to command of the Trans-Mississippi District charged with defense of Arkansas with authority to organize a force under new conscription law

May 27, General FitzJohn Porter took Hanover Court House 16 miles north of Richmond in battle with Confederates

——, General Stoneham ascended in a captive balloon for reconnoissance

May 30, Confederates evacuated Corinth, Mississippi, invested by Union army, General Beauregard withdrawing 52,000 men and stores without knowledge of Union forces, retiring to Tupelo, 50 miles south. Corinth occupied by General Halleck

May 31–June 1, Battle of Fair Oaks or Seven Pines, near Richmond, Virginia. Confederate General Johnston attacked left wing of the Army of the Potomac which had crossed the Chickahominy

River (*see supra* May 20) which was saved from crushing defeat only by reinforcements under General Sumner so that the second day the Union troops were able to repulse attack, General Johnston severely wounded

June 1, General Robert E. Lee assumed command of the Confederate Army of Northern Virginia

——, The Dept. of Virginia extended under command of General McClellan, General John C. Wool assigned to the Middle Dept., and General John A. Dix to command at Fortress Monroe

June 3, Gold, now become "a measure of the Union fortune" sold at 3.5% premium

——, Colonel George F. Shepley appointed military governor of Louisiana

June 3–4, Evacuation of Fort Pillow on the Mississippi above Memphis by the Confederates after fall of Corinth and occupied by Union force June 5

June 4, The *New York Tribune* reported 20,000 bales of cotton burned to prevent capture by Union troops between Vicksburg and Greenville, and 9,000 between Greenville and Grand Gulf on the Mississippi River

June 6, Memphis, Tennessee, surrendered by Confederates to Commodore C. H. Davis after battle and defeat and destruction of Confederate fleet under Commodore Montgomery

June 7, William B. Mumford hanged at New Orleans for taking down and destroying the United States flag over the Mint, by order of General Butler

June 8, General McDowell ordered under certain stated conditions to operate in the direction of Richmond

——, Martial law proclaimed in Arizona

June 8–9, Battle of Cross Keys in the Shenandoah Valley. Confederate General Jackson's rear guard under Ewell in engagement with Fremont, Ewell retiring during the night

——, At Port Republic, Virginia, Confederate General Jackson in engagement with advance guard of Shields from Fremont's army scattered and dispersed the Union troops

June 13–15, Confederate cavalry commanded by General J. E. B. Stuart in raid including skirmishes at Hawe's Shop, Old Church, and Garlick's Landing passed entirely around the Army of the Potomac from Richmond to Pamunkey River and back

June 16–Oct. 30, Armed escort led "Emigrant road expedition" from Omaha, Nebraska to Portland, Oregon

June 17, General Fremont resigned declining to serve under General Pope as a junior and was replaced by Franz Sigel

——, Confederate General Beauregard turned over command to General Bragg because of ill health

June 18, Skirmish at Wilson's Gap and occupation of Cumberland Gap by Union force under General G. W. Morgan

——, Federal squadron under Farragut assembled below Vicksburg, and 17 schooners of the mortar flotilla under Porter

June 20, Confederate General Bragg assigned to permanent command of the Western Dept.

June 23, C. F. Adams, American Minister in London, forwarded letter to Earl Russell giving information of the building of vessel No. "290" at Liverpool, for the Confederacy, later the C.S.S. "Alabama"

June 24, Confederate General Lee sent two-thirds of his

army to north side of the Chickahominy to strike McClellan's right wing

June 25–July 1, The "Seven Days' Battles" in the Peninsula campaign between Army of the Potomac under McClellan and Confederate army under R. E. Lee, in vicinity of Richmond, which ended with retreat of McClellan to Harrison's Landing

June 25, General Lee attacked at Oak Grove, Confederates repulsed by Hooker's division (Peninsula campaign)

June 26, Major General Pope given command of new Army of Virginia composed of the Mountain Dept. and the Depts. of the Rappahannock and the Shenandoah, Generals Banks and Irvin McDowell commanding the second and third corps respectively

——, Battle of Mechanicsville. General FitzJohn Porter repulsed Confederate attack of Generals A. P. Hill, D. H. Hill, and James Longstreet, General Jackson did not arrive as expected (Peninsula campaign)

June 27, Battle of Gaines Mill. FitzJohn Porter attacked at Gaines Mill Heights about 5 miles east of his former position shortly after noon by Confederate Generals A. P. Hill, Longstreet, and Jackson, reinforced by Slocum's division increasing Union force to 35,000 against Confederate 60,000. Porter was able to hold approaches to the bridges across the Chickahominy over which he retreated during the night destroying the bridges (Peninsula campaign)

——, General Thomas Williams began construction of a canal to change the course of the Mississippi to isolate Vicksburg

——, General McClellan began retreat to the James River from the Pamunkey, abandoning first siege of Richmond

June 28, Naval bombardment of Vicksburg and passage by Farragut's fleet of the Confederate batteries at 3 A.M.

——, Letter of General McClellan to Secretary Stanton from Savage's Station, Virginia, in which he complained that the Government had not sustained the army, accusing the Secretary of doing his "best to sacrifice this army"

June 29, Battle of Savage's Station on Richmond and York River Railroad. General Sumner repulsed attack of Confederate General Magruder and secured passage of the White Oak Swamp for the rear guard of the Federal army (Peninsula campaign)

June 30, Battle of Frayser's Farm, or Glendale. Attack of Confederate Generals Longstreet and Hill in pursuit of McClellan's retreating army attacked McCall's division of which nearly one-fourth were killed (Peninsula campaign)

——, Battle of White Oak Swamp. General Franklin stopped Confederate General Jackson at White Oak Swamp (Peninsula campaign)

July 1, Battle of Malvern Hill. Attack of Confederate Generals D. H. Hill, Magruder, and Armistead repulsed by Generals Porter, Morell, and Couch (Peninsula campaign) General McClellan continued retreat to Harrison's Landing during the night

July 2, President Lincoln by proclamation called for 300,000 volunteers for 3 years service

——, General John H. Forney assigned to command of the Confederate District of the Gulf

July 6, Order from the Secretary of the Navy made the James River flotilla an independent division of the North Atlantic blockading squadron under command of Commodore Charles Wilkes

July 7, Letter of General McClellan to the President an uncalled for summary of his ideas and advice as to the general conduct of affairs

July 9, Confederate General Morgan attacked and dispersed Union cavalry at Tompkinsville, Kentucky, and destroyed equipment carrying away train of 20 wagons, 40 horses, and 50 mules, and July 12 took Lebanon, destroying property

July 10, Gold sold at 117 in New York

July 11, Major General Halleck assigned to command as General-in-Chief of all the land forces of the United States with headquarters in Washington

July 13, Confederates under General Jackson advanced from Hanover Court House upon Gordonsville, Virginia which was occupied on the 16th

——, Confederate cavalry captured Federal cavalry in action at Murfreesborough, Tennessee, the town surrendering to Forrest

July 14, General Pope made address to the Army of Virginia which was regarded as a slur and made almost every officer of the Army of the Potomac an enemy

July 15, The Confederate ram "Arkansas" on the Mississippi above Vicksburg in successful action with Union fleet at mouth of the Yazoo River and ran through Farragut's fleet safely to protection under the guns of Vicksburg

July 16, Slidell, Confederate commissioner, received by Napoleon, asked for recognition of the Confederate States and for war ships to break the blockade for which he offered cotton worth $12,500,000

July 17, Major General Grant assumed command of all troops in the Armies of the Tennessee and the Mississippi, and in the districts of Cairo and the Mississippi

July 22, Confederates repelled attack of D. D. Porter and Ellet on the ram "Arkansas" near Vicksburg

——, Cartel for exchange of prisoners arranged between General Dix and Confederate General D. H. Hill which continued until Dec. 28

——, War Dept. issued order authorizing military and naval commanders within States in rebellion to seize and use for military purposes any real or personal property, and to employ as laborers persons of African descent

——, President Lincoln submitted to the Cabinet the draft of an Emancipation Proclamation

July 23, Major General H. W. Halleck arrived in Washington and took command

July 24, Death of Martin Van Buren at Lindenwold, New York (80)

——, Farragut started for New Orleans, leaving 3 gunboats and the "Essex" and the "Sumter" to guard river between Vicksburg and Baton Rouge

July 26, Confederate Major General Samuel Jones assigned to command District of the Gulf, relieving General John H. Forney

July 28, Confederate General Morgan reached Livingston, Tennessee, reported that he had captured 17 towns in raid into Kentucky

July 29, The "Enrica" (290) sailed from Liverpool and Aug. 24 off the Azores the Confederate flag raised and the vessel became the "Alabama," Semmes taking command

——, Naval attack on Confederate Fort McAllister on Ogeechee River, Georgia

July 31, President Davis ordered that any commissioned officers captured from Pope's army would be treated as felons not as prisoners of war

July 31–Aug. 1, Attack on Union camps and shipping between Shirley and Harrison's Landing, Virginia

Aug. 2, Instructions of Secretary Seward to C. F. Adams forbade him to receive or debate any offer of mediation in war from Great Britain, and if Great Britain acknowledged the insurgent government to suspend his functions as Minister

Aug. 3, General Halleck ordered the withdrawal of McClellan's army from the Peninsula to Aquia Creek on the basis of McClellan's statement that Lee's army numbered 200,000, to unite with Pope's Army of Virginia for overland advance on Richmond

Aug. 4, The President called for 300,000 militia for 9 months, draft subsequently fixed for Sept. 3

——, General Burnside with his entire command arrived from Fort Monroe at Aquia Creek and on the 5th his troops were at Falmouth

Aug. 5, Confederates led by Major John C. Breckinridge made unsuccessful attack on General Williams at Baton Rouge, Louisiana, General Williams killed

Aug. 6, Confederate ram "Arkansas" blown up by her officers near Baton Rouge, Louisiana

Aug. 7, Colonel F. M. McCullough shot at Kirksville by order of General John McNeil in command of District of Northeast Missouri

——, General Canby defeated Confederates at Fort Fillmore, New Mexico

Aug. 9, Battle of Cedar Mountain, Virginia. Confederates led by General Jackson and General A. P. Hill defeated General Banks (Pope's Army of Virginia) Federal losses 314 killed, 1,445 wounded, and 620 missing, Confederates lost 229 killed, and 1,047 wounded

Aug. 11, Property in Louisiana of John Slidell, Confederate commissioner in France, confiscated by order of General Butler

Aug. 12, Capture of Gallatin, Tennessee, and destruction of bridges in that vicinity by Confederates under Colonel J. H. Morgan

Aug. 14, The President received a deputation of colored men and discussed emigration and colonial proposals for Liberia and Central America

Aug. 14–19, Cavalry operations covered rear of the Army of the Potomac from Harrison's Landing to Williamsburg

Aug. 17–23, Massacres by Indians at New Ulm and vicinity in Minnesota

Aug. 18–Oct. 13, Second session of First Confederate Congress

Aug. 18, General instructions issued by the Secretary of the Navy regarding the right of search

Aug. 19, Letter of Horace Greeley addressed to President Lincoln published in the *New York Tribune*, the "Prayer of Twenty Millions," in which he said that "all attempts to put down the rebellion and at the same time uphold its inciting cause are preposterous and futile"

Aug. 19–21, Confederates led by Colonel Morgan in raid on Louisville and Nashville Railroad, General Johnson defeated in action at Gallatin, Tennessee, on the 21st

Aug. 19–Oct. 11, Expedition against the Snake Indians in Idaho

Aug. 20–Sept. 10, Army of the Potomac embarked for Aquia Creek and Alexandria, Virginia

Aug. 21, Issue of postal currency begun

Aug. 22, President Lincoln answered letter of Horace Greeley stating his policy

——, Catlett's Station, Virginia, captured by Confederate cavalry led by Stuart

——, Action with Sioux Indians at Fort Ridgely, Minnesota

Aug. 27, At Kettle Run, Virginia, General Hooker defeated Confederates under General Ewell

——, Confederate General Jackson arrived at Manassas Junction, Virginia, and burned General Pope's main depot of supplies, General Pope arriving at noon after Confederates had left

Aug. 27–28, Confederate General Bragg crossed the Tennessee River at Chattanooga marching north to invade Kentucky

Aug. 28, Battle of Gainsville. King's division of McDowell's corps in conflict with Jackson's troops

Aug. 29, Battle of Groveton. General Jackson reinforced by General Longstreet who marched unopposed through Thoroughfare Gap to join him repulsed Union troops of Pope's army though Pope claimed the victory. FitzJohn Porter did not join action

——, Confederate General G. T. Beauregard assigned to command of the Dept. of South Carolina and Georgia relieving General J. C. Pemberton

Aug. 30, Confederate General Kirby Smith with Bragg's right defeated Union forces under General Manson at Richmond, Kentucky

——, Second Battle of Bull Run called by Confederates Second Battle of Manassas. General Pope renewing Battle of Groveton defeated by Confederates and forced to retreat taking position on heights of Centreville

——, Major General Gustavus W. Smith (Confederate) assumed command of the defenses of Richmond

Aug. 31, The James River flotilla commanded by Captain Charles Wilkes disbanded with withdrawal of McClellan from the Peninsula

Sept. 1, Battle of Chantilly (Pope's Army of Virginia) Confederate General Jackson attacked right flank of Union army under Generals McDowell, Hooker, and Kearny. Neither side gained any ground, Generals Philip Kearny and Isaac I. Stevens killed. Federal loss 1,300, Confederate 800. Pope fell back towards Fairfax Court House

——, Major General Ormsby M. Mitchell assigned to command of the Dept. of the South

——, Confederate Major General J. P. McCown assumed command of the Dept. of East Tennessee

Sept. 2, Surrender of Spencer Court House to Confederate General A. G. Jenkins

——, Confederate General Kirby Smith occupied Lexington, Kentucky and Lew Wallace in charge of defenses of Cincinnati, Covington, and Newport proclaimed martial law and began drilling men

——, Action with Indians at Acton (Birch Coolie) Minnesota

——, Army of Virginia ordered by General Halleck to retire to intrenchments in front of Washington

——, Flag-Officer Goldsborough relieved of command of North Atlantic Blockading Squadron

——, General McClellan again placed in command of the Army of the Potomac and defenses of Washington

Sept. 3, General Pope relieved of command of the Army of Virginia and transferred to command of Dept. of the Northwest to act against Indians in insurrection

Sept. 3, Joseph Holt of Kentucky appointed Judge Advocate General of the United States

——, Army of Northern Virginia (Confederate) marched towards Leesburg, Virginia, occupying Winchester

Sept. 4, Confederate General Morgan joined General Kirby Smith at Lexington, Kentucky

Sept. 4–5, Confederate army under General D. H. Hill began crossing the Potomac River at Leesburg for Maryland campaign

Sept. 5, Armies of the Potomac and Virginia consolidated

——, Confederate General Bragg established headquarters at Sparta, Tennessee

Sept. 6, Dept. of the Northwest created to include Wisconsin, Iowa, Minnesota, Nebraska, and Dakota, General Pope in command

——, Advance guard of Confederate army led by General Jackson reached Frederick City, Maryland

——, Evacuation of Aquia Creek, Virginia, by Union forces and destruction of property there

Sept. 8, General Robert E. Lee issued address to the people of Maryland declaring the aim of the South to aid in "throwing off this foreign yoke," and give them "an opportunity of liberating themselves"

——, Formation of West India Squadron under Commodore Charles Wilkes for protection of Union commerce

——, Major General N. P. Banks assumed command of defenses of Washington, and Major General Samuel P. Heintzelman in command of defenses south of the Potomac on Sept. 9

Sept. 12, Confederate General Bragg occupied Glasgow, Kentucky, and issued proclamation calling on citizens to take oath of allegiance, followed by Union General Buell, both in race to reach Louisville

——, Siege and bombardment of Harper's Ferry, West Virginia, begun by Confederates

Sept. 13, General Butler issued order in New Orleans requiring registration of "foreigners"

——, General McClellan reached Frederick City, Maryland, and by chance acquired a dispatch from General Lee which detailed his plan of campaign and division of his army

Sept. 14, Battles on South Mountain, Maryland. General D. H. Hill reinforced by General Longstreet held Turner's Gap against repeated assaults of Union army of McClellan, corps of Hooker and Burnside, Confederates retiring during the night, and General Franklin took possession of Crampton's Gap 6 miles below held by Confederates under Howell Cobb. Federal loss at Turner's Gap 328 killed and 1,463 wounded and missing, and at Crampton's Gap 115 killed and 418 wounded and missing, Confederate loss at both 934

——, Confederates under General Duncan made unsuccessful attack on Munfordville, Kentucky, defended by Colonel Wilder

——, Confederate General Price occupied Iuka, northeast Mississippi

——, General Buell with bulk of his army reached Bowling Green, Kentucky, to find Bragg in position across railroad between him and Louisville

Sept. 15, Harper's Ferry, West Virginia, surrendered by Colonel Dixon S. Miles to Confederates under General Jackson after bombardment, Colonel Miles mortally wounded

——, Advance guard of Confederates under General Kirby Smith appeared before Covington, Kentucky, threatening Louisville and Cincinnati, but retired

Sept. 15, McClellan's army left South Mountain and took position on east bank of Antietam Creek opposite General Lee

Sept. 16, Hooker's division crossed Antietam Creek and met Confederates in attack

Sept. 17, Battle of Antietam, Maryland (Sharpsburg) General McClellan attacked General Lee, Confederate invasion of the north checked, but Lee's center unbroken, both sides claiming the victory

——, Munfordville, Kentucky, captured by Confederates under General Bragg defeating Colonel J. T. Wilder

Sept. 18–19, General Lee during the night withdrew his army across the Potomac into Virginia and proceeded towards Martinsburg

Sept. 19, Battle of Iuka, Mississippi. Confederates under General Price in engagement with General Rosecrans forced General Price to retreat, and occupied Iuka the following day

——, Dept. of the Missouri established including Dept. of Kansas discontinued, Missouri and Arkansas, General S. R. Curtis appointed Sept. 24 in command, West Virginia transferred to the Dept. of the Ohio

——, Confederate Dept. of Virginia and North Carolina constituted under Major General Gustavus Smith

Sept. 20, Union forces occupied Maryland Heights

Sept. 21, Confederates commanded by General Bragg marched to Bardstown to make connection with Kirby Smith, leaving road to Louisville open

Sept. 22, Preliminary Emancipation Proclamation of President Lincoln freed the slaves in the Confederate States to take effect on Jan. 1, 1863

——, Union troops reoccupied Harper's Ferry evacuated by Confederates

Sept. 23, President Lincoln asked each member of his Cabinet to consider the subject of acquisition of territory to which the negroes might be deported

——, Action with Indians at Wood Lake, Minnesota, in which the Indians were defeated and a large number of prisoners taken

Sept. 24, President Lincoln issued proclamation suspending writ of habeas corpus for persons in rebellion and insurgents arrested, declaring them subject to trial by court-martial or military commission

——, District of West Tennessee reorganized, Major Generals Sherman, Ord, Rosecrans, and Brigadier General Quinby assigned to divisions

——, Confederate General Beauregard succeeded General J. C. Pemberton in command of Dept. of South Carolina and Georgia

——, Convention of governors of 16 States at Altoona, Pennsylvania, approved Lincoln's Emancipation Proclamation

——, Office of Provost-Marshall-General created by Secretary of War and Simeon Draper of New York appointed to office Oct. 1

Sept. 25, General Buell arrived at Louisville, Kentucky, a day in advance of Confederates under General Bragg thus insuring the safety of the city

——, Randolph, Tennessee, burned by order of General W. T. Sherman because citizens fired on packet Steamer "Eugene" from St. Louis

Sept. 27, Confederate General J. P. McCown assigned to command of the Dept. of East Tennessee and General Samuel Jones the District of Middle Tennessee

Oct. 1, Confederate Dept. of Mississippi and East Louisiana constituted, Major General John C. Pemberton taking command Oct. 14, Generals Van Dorn and Price acting under him

Oct. 3–4, Battle of Corinth, Mississippi. General Rosecrans repulsed Confederate attack of Generals Van Dorn, Price, and Lovell

Oct. 4, Confederate Government inaugurated at Frankfort, Kentucky, Richard Hawes, Governor, Generals Bragg and Kirby Smith attending the ceremony

Oct. 7, General Halleck wrote General McClellan, "The country is impatient at the want of activity of your army and you must push it on"

——, W. E. Gladstone in speech at Newcastle, England, stated that the South had "made a nation"

Oct. 8, Battle of Perryville or Chaplin Hill, Kentucky. Drawn battle between General Buell and Confederates under General Bragg begun by attack of Confederate Generals Hardee and Polk and A. M. McCook commanding the Union left. The Confederates retired through Cumberland Gap during the night and from there to Chattanooga

Oct. 9, Confederate Act organized military courts for armies in the field and defined their powers

Oct. 10, Confederate General Stuart crossed the Potomac at McCoy's Ferry, rode to Mercersburg, and demanded and received the surrender of Chambersburg, Pennsylvania, destroying machine shop station and rolling stock of railroad, and seizing 500 horses, government uniforms, and all clothing and food in shops, in skirmish near Gettysburg on the 11th, and at White's Ford, Maryland on the 12th, and recrossed to Potomac, having a second time passed entirely around the Union army

Oct. 11, Confederate Act amended exemption law to greatly increase number of exempted classes

Oct. 13, Confederate Act renewed law authorizing suspension of writ of habeas corpus but provided for investigation of cases of persons arrested; authority to suspend writ expired Feb. 12, 1863

——, Second Session of First Confederate Congress adjourned

Oct. 16, Dept. of the Tennessee constituted including northern Mississippi and Kentucky and Tennessee west of the river, Major General Ulysses S. Grant in command on Oct. 25, and began advance from Holly Springs, Mississippi, Oct. 29

——, Confederate General John Echols succeeded General William H. Loring in command of the Dept. of Western Virginia

Oct. 17–25, Resistance to draft in Carbon, Luzerne, and Schuylkill counties, Pennsylvania

Oct. 18, Ten Confederate prisoners shot at Palmyra, Missouri, by order of General McNeil because of Confederate capture and non-return of Andrew Allsman

Oct. 23, General Lee sent two-thirds of his army to the north side of the Chickahominy to strike McClellan's right wing, driving army towards Yorktown

Oct. 24, Dept. of the Cumberland reëstablished and General W. S. Rosecrans placed in command, succeeding General Buell in command of the Army of the Ohio Oct. 30

Oct. 26, General McClellan led Army of the Potomac across the river from Maryland into Virginia

——, Major General Samuel P. Heintzelman succeeded General Banks in command of the defenses of Washington

Oct. 30, Napoleon proposed to Russia and Great Britain that they should unite in formal proposal of mediation in American civil war

Nov. 4, Elections in northern States declared for Lincoln as president, but the Democrats made important gains except in the New England and border slave States

Nov. 5, General FitzJohn Porter relieved from command of his corps because of charges of General Pope

Nov. 7, Major General A. E. Burnside received appointment of Nov. 5 as Commander of the Army of the Potomac to succeed General McClellan

Nov. 14, Army of the Potomac organized in 3 divisions under command of Major Generals E. V. Sumner, Joseph Hooker, and W. B. Franklin

——, Brigadier General Andrew J. Hamilton appointed military Governor of Texas

Nov. 17, G. W. Smith appointed Confederate Secretary of War (temporary assignment)

Nov. 20, Brigadier General John H. Martindale assumed command as military Governor of the District of Columbia

Nov. 21, Confederate General Bragg in command of Army of Tennessee sent General Forrest to cut General Grant's communications in western part of the State

——, James A. Seddon appointed Confederate Secretary of War

——, General Burnside summoned Fredericksburg, Virginia, to surrender

Nov. 22, Order of Secretary of War effected discharge of practically all of the political prisoners

Nov. 24, Confederate General Joseph E. Johnston appointed to command of army in the west including the depts. of Generals Bragg, Kirby Smith, and Pemberton

Nov. 27, Court martial proceedings begun in Washington in case of General FitzJohn Porter on charge of General Pope of disobedience to orders to attack in Battle of Groveton Aug. 29

Nov. 28, Consul Dudley reported to Secretary Seward that 21 steamers had recently been built or purchased in England for running the American blockade as a part of "the business of the country"

——, Confederates under General Marmaduke defeated at Cane Hill (Boston Mts.) Arkansas by General Blunt

Dec. 7, Battle of Prairie Grove, Arkansas. Generals Francis J. Herron and James G. Blunt defeated Confederates under Generals Hindman, Marmaduke, Parsons, and Frost who retired during the night, Federal loss 1,148, Confederates 1,317

Dec. 12, Confederate Major General Arnold Elzey assigned to command of the defenses of Richmond

Dec. 13, Battle of Fredericksburg, Virginia. General Burnside defeated by General Lee in unsuccessful attack on the Confederate works, Federal loss 12,653, Confederate 5,377

Dec. 14, General Simon B. Buckner assigned to command of the Confederate District of the Gulf, took command Dec. 23

Dec. 15, General Burnside withdrew his demoralized army to the north side of the Rappahannock during the night

Dec. 15–Jan. 3, 1863, Raid of Confederate General Forrest into Tennessee

Dec. 17, General N. P. Banks assumed command of the

Dept. of the Gulf with headquarters at New Orleans, succeeding General Butler

Dec. 17, Resignation of Secretary of State Seward on learning of opposition of the Senate; not accepted by the President

Dec. 18, South Carolina law enacted providing for organization and supply of negro labor for coast defense

——, Confederate General Forrest defeated Union cavalry at Lexington, Tennessee, taking the town and Colonel R. G. Ingersoll

——, Committee of 9 senators presented address to the President asking that Seward be removed from the State Dept.

Dec. 20, Secretary of the Treasury Chase presented his resignation to the President which was not accepted by the President

——, Capture of Union garrison at Holly Springs, Mississippi, by Confederate General Van Dorn and destruction of supplies of General Grant worth $500,000

——, General Sherman embarked from Memphis and moved down the Mississippi under escort of Porter's gunboats

——, Humboldt and Trenton, Tennessee, taken by Confederates led by Forrest

Dec. 21, Union City, Tennessee, taken by Confederate General Forrest

Dec. 23, President Jefferson Davis issued proclamation declaring General B. F. Butler an outlaw and common enemy of mankind and threatened that if caught he should be hanged

Dec. 24–30, Confederate General Morgan in second raid into Kentucky occupied Glasgow the 24th, destroyed Louisville and Nashville Railroad from Munfordville to Shepherdsville the 28th, took Upton and Nollin the 26th, Elizabethtown the 27th

Dec. 25, General Sherman and Commodore Porter (Vicksburg campaign) reached Milliken's Bend above Vicksburg. General Sherman sent troops which destroyed roadway and bridges of the Vicksburg and Shreveport Railroad cutting off supplies from Vicksburg

Dec. 28, Secretary Stanton ordered the discontinuance of exchange of commissioned officers

Dec. 29, Battle of Chickasaw Bayou (Vicksburg campaign) General Sherman attacked the Confederates under General Pemberton and was repulsed with great loss

Dec. 31, The U.S.S. "Monitor" foundered off Cape Hatteras in storm

——, Confederate General Forrest defeated in engagement with Colonel Rinaker at Parker's Cross Roads, Tennessee

——, President Lincoln made contract with Bernard Kock to carry 5,000 negroes to Isle à Vache, Haiti, at $50 each

Dec. 31–Jan. 3, Battle of Stone River or Murfreesboro, Tennessee. Confederate General Bragg attacked General Rosecrans and won the first day's battle, and on Jan. 2 compelled the Union forces to retreat across the Stone River, but was unable to hold the ground gained, and retreated southward Jan. 3 occupying Murfreesboro which he evacuated on the 5th, and General Rosecrans occupied Murfreesboro and claimed the victory. Federal loss about 12,000, Confederates about 11,000. Formby considers this battle the military turning-point of the war

Dec. 31–Jan. 25, 1863, Confederate General Marmaduke on raid into Missouri

CONGRESS

Jan. 20, Jesse Bright of Indiana expelled from the Senate charged with disloyalty

Jan. 31, Act authorized the President to take possession of the railroads and telegraph lines of the United States when the public safety might require it

Feb. 12, Demand notes to the amount of $10,000,000 authorized

Feb. 19, Act prohibited trade in citizens of China, the "coolie trade" by American citizens in American vessels

Feb. 25, Legal Tender Act adopted paper currency known as "greenbacks" declared legal tender, and $150,000,000 authorized

——, Issue of United States notes provided for bonds to an amount not exceeding $500,000,000 payable 20 years from date and bearing interest at 6% (the 5.20s), sinking fund established

March 1, Issue of certificates of indebtedness to public creditors authorized payable 1 year from date in settlement of audited claims against the Government

March 6, Special message of the President recommended compensated emancipation of slaves by coöperation of the United States with any State which might adopt gradual abolition

March 15, Act established a joint commission with Great Britain and France for preservation of the Atlantic fisheries

March 17, Act authorized the Secretary of the Treasury to purchase coin with bonds or notes of the United States

April 7, House Committee on emancipation and colonization of negroes appointed

April 10, Joint Resolution adopted the President's plan for pecuniary assistance to States adopting gradual abolition of slavery

April 16, Act abolished slavery in the District of Columbia

——, Medical Dept. of the Army reorganized for increased efficiency

May 7–June 26, Senate sat as court of impeachment in case of West H. Humphreys, judge of U.S. district court in Tennessee charged with aiding the rebellion, found guilty, and removed from office

May 15, Act established the Dept. of Agriculture

May 20, Homestead Act granted public land not exceeding 160 acres to actual settlers at $1.25 an acre, to receive a patent of ownership after 5 years residence, into effect Jan. 1, 1863

May 21, Act provided for education of colored children in Washington and Georgetown in the District of Columbia

June 5, The President authorized to appoint diplomatic representatives to the negro republics of Haiti and Liberia

June 7, Act provided for the collection of direct taxes in insurrectionary States and the sale of land for taxes

June 19, Slavery abolished in the Territories of the United States

July 1, Act to aid in the construction of a railroad and telegraph line from the Missouri River to the Pacific Ocean chartered the Union Pacific Central Railroad and made grant of public land estimated as 35,000,000 acres according to McPherson

——, Anti-Polygamy Act passed to punish and prevent polygamy

——, Internal Revenue Act revived excise duties repealed in 1802 and created Division of Internal Revenue, George S. Boutwell appointed first Commissioner. Special tax imposed on luxuries, spirits, ales, beer, tobacco, whiskey 20 cents a gallon, tax on products of iron and steel, glass manufactured articles, coal oil, paper, leather, silks, cotton, woolens. General ad valorem tax on other manufactured articles. Licenses on trades established and a general income tax established, railroads, steamboats, and express companies taxed on gross receipts

July 2, National legacy tax enacted; repealed in 1870

——, Act required "iron-clad" oath of every person elected or appointed to office that he had "never voluntarily borne arms against the United States" or "given aid or encouragement" to persons hostile, or yielded voluntary support to any pretended government within the United States

——, Land grant made to agricultural and mechanical colleges

July 4, Boundary of Nevada adjusted

July 5, Bureaus of Navigation, Equipment, and Steam Engineering created in Act reorganizing the Navy Dept.

July 11, Act authorized $150,000,000 in treasury notes, $35,000,000 of which might be of denominations of less than $5

——, Act provided for carrying into effect the Treaty with Great Britain for suppression of the African slave trade

July 12, Resolution passed provided for presentation of "medals of honor" to non-commissioned officers and privates

July 16, Increased temporary protective tariff passed to compensate for internal duties, adding duty on sugar, tobacco, and spirits

——, All pecuniary interest in public contracts forbidden to members of Congress, and officers and agents of the Government

——, Act "to establish and equalize the grade of line officers of the United States Navy"

——, Grade of rear-admiral created, the rank to be conferred on all flag-officers

July 17, The President authorized to call out the militia between 18 and 45 and to receive colored persons for military service

——, Confiscation Act authorized seizure of property of rebels for payment of expenses of the army, and declared free the slaves of all persons engaged in rebellion

——, Currency Act authorized use of postage stamps as currency for amounts less than $5 and prohibited the issue and circulation of notes by private corporations or persons of sum less than $1

——, Congress adjourned

Dec. 1, Thirty-seventh Congress, 3d sess. convened. President Lincoln in message recommended amendments to Constitution to make valid the emancipation of slaves, for bonds to provide compensation for States which would abolish slavery before 1900, and for provision for colonization of free negroes

Dec. 31, Act for admission of West Virginia to date from June 20, 1863, as the 35th State on condition of amending the Constitution

1863

Jan. 1, President proclaimed slaves free within the borders of the seceding States

Jan. 1, Union army numbered 918,191, absent from duty 8,987 officers and 280,073 enlisted men

——, Confederate General Forrest recrossed the Tennessee at Clifton, ending raid

——, Galveston, Texas, recaptured by Confederate General Magruder, proclamation Jan. 5 declared blockade raised

Jan. 7, Springfield, Missouri, successfully defended from attack by Confederate General Marmaduke

Jan. 8, John P. Usher, of Indiana, appointed Secretary of the Interior

Jan. 9, Garrison at Hartville, Missouri, surrendered to Confederate General Marmaduke

Jan. 10, General FitzJohn Porter sentenced by court-martial at Washington to be cashiered and forever disqualified from holding government office

Jan. 11, General McClernand and Commodore Porter took Confederate Fort Hindman at Arkansas Post on Arkansas River 40 miles from its mouth, 5,000 prisoners surrendered, Federal loss 977

Jan. 12, Colonel Merrill defeated Confederates under General Marmaduke at Hartville, Missouri

——, Thomas Carney took office as second Governor of Kansas

Jan. 12–May 1, First Confederate Congress, 3d session

Jan. 13, Letter of Adjutant General authorized raising of South Carolina volunteer infantry of colored troops, Colonel Thomas Wentworth Higginson, the commander

Jan. 15, Letter of Adjutant General to Governor of Rhode Island stated that the President would accept infantry regiments of volunteers of African descent

Jan. 20, General Burnside began advance against Fredericksburg, but storm prevented action, the "mud march"

——, Confederate General Marmaduke took Patterson, Missouri

Jan. 22, General Grant, Sherman's corps, recommenced work on canal to isolate Vicksburg begun by General Thomas in June 1862, but it proved a failure

Jan. 23, General Burnside in interview with the President asked approval of an order dismissing Generals Hooker, Franklin, W. F. Smith, and a number of others from military service for "unjust and unnecessary criticism of his superior officers"

Jan. 25, Major General Joseph Hooker appointed to command the Army of the Potomac in place of General Burnside relieved by the President, Major General Darius N. Couch superseded General E. V. Sumner in command of right grand division, Major General George G. Meade placed in command of center grand division

Jan. 26, Governor Andrews of Massachusetts authorized by Secretary of War Stanton to enlist "persons of African descent organized in separate corps"

Jan. 27 and Feb. 1, 28, and March 3, Union naval attacks on Fort McAllister, Genesis Point, on the Ogeechee River, Georgia, repulsed

Jan. 29, Battle of Bear River or Battle Creek against the Banmack tribe of Indians in Utah

——, Confederacy authorized loan of $15,000,000 to be placed abroad with Emilie Erlanger & Cie

Jan. 30, General Grant assumed immediate command of expedition against Vicksburg, relieving General McClernand

Feb. 2, Passage of the Vicksburg and Warrenton batteries by the U.S.S. "Queen of the West," Colonel C. R. Ellet in command

Feb. 3, M. Mercier, French Minister at Washington, called on Secretary of State to offer mediation of France; declined in letter of Feb. 6

——, Confederate General Wheeler repulsed in attack on Fort Donelson, Tennessee, attempt to stop Union navigation of Cumberland River

Feb. 7, Major General Samuel P. Heintzelman assumed command of the Dept. of Washington, recreated Feb. 2

Feb. 13, U.S.S. "Indianola," ironclad, ran past Vicksburg batteries at night in effort to break Confederate control of the Mississippi from Vicksburg to Port Hudson; the "Indianola" captured by Confederates Feb. 24 and blown up

Feb. 14, Confederates captured U.S.S. "Queen of the West" on Black River below Vicksburg

Feb. 20, Confederate Act provided for issue of bonds for funding treasury notes

Feb. 22, Ground broken for Central Pacific Railroad at Sacramento, California, by Governor Stanford

Feb. 26, Confederate General James Longstreet assumed command of the Dept. of Virginia and North Carolina

March 3, National Academy of Sciences incorporated

March 5, General Van Dorn defeated Federals in engagement at Thompson's Station, Tennessee, Colonel Coburn surrendered with 1,221 prisoners

March 7, Confederate General Kirby Smith assumed command of forces west of the Mississippi

March 10, Major General Edwin V. Sumner assigned to command the Dept. of the Missouri

——, Union forces under Colonel T. W. Higginson reoccupied Jacksonville, Florida

March 11, 13, and 16, Engagements at Fort Pemberton near Greenwood, Mississippi, in Yazoo Pass expedition (Feb. 24–April 8, Admiral Porter), effort to clear the pass to gain the Yazoo River and rear of Vicksburg

March 14, Admiral Farragut sent 7 vessels past the Confederate batteries at Port Hudson, Louisiana, the "Hartford," flagship, making the trip successfully, the "Mississippi" destroyed

March 14–27, The Steele's Bayou expedition in Mississippi commanded by General Sherman and Admiral Porter, an attempt to get in rear of Vicksburg. Channel found impracticable

March 18, Emilie Erlanger & Cie, in Paris opened loan of £3,000,000 to Confederacy on 20 year 7% bonds

March 19, Passage of the Grand Gulf Mississippi batteries by U.S.S. "Hartford" and "Monongahela"

March 23, Confederate Act provided for funding of treasury notes issued previous to Dec. 1, 1862 and for further issue of denominations not less than $5 or more than $50 in treasury notes

March 25, General A. E. Burnside superseded Major General Horatio G. Wright in command of the Dept. of the Ohio

——, Passage of the Vicksburg batteries by U.S.S. "Switzerland," the "Lancaster" exploded and sank

March 26, Confederate agent John Slidell went to Spain

——, Confederate Act authorized impressment of forage or other property including slaves necessary for the army in the field when absolutely necessary

——, Amended Constitution of West Virginia providing for gradual emancipation of slaves ratified by popular vote

March 29, General Grant ordered McClernand to march to New Carthage from Milliken's Bend, Sher-

man and McPherson to follow in due time; arrived April 4

March 30–April 20, Siege of Washington, North Carolina, commanded by General Foster, by Confederates

March 31, Proclamation of the President concerning internal and coast commerce and order of the Secretary of the Navy prohibiting intercourse with the Confederate States

April 2, Bread riot in Richmond, Virginia, mob headed by huckster in the market, Mary Jackson, broke into shops. Dispersed by threats of the militia, of the Governor and President Davis

April 2 and 4, Engagements at Fort Pemberton, Mississippi

April 6, Confederate vessel "Alexandra" fitting out at Liverpool seized by British Government

——, Contract made with Forbes and Tuckerman, New York capitalists, by the Government for colonization of Isle à Vache, Haiti by 500 negroes; enterprise a failure

April 7, Fort Sumter, Charleston, South Carolina, bombarded by federal monitors commanded by Admiral Dupont

April 7–8, Passage of Port Hudson, Louisiana, by Edward C. Gabaudau, Admiral Farragut's secretary at night in a skiff

April 10, Proclamation of President Davis urged the Confederacy to plant crops of corn, beans, peas, and other foods instead of cotton and tobacco

——, Action at Franklin, Tennessee. General Granger defeated the Confederates under General Van Dorn

April 11–May 3, Siege of Suffolk, Virginia, by Confederate General Longstreet by order of War Dept. thus absent from Lee's army at Chancellorsville

April 12–13, Engagement at La Bayou Teche, Louisiana, and Union attack on and occupation of Fort Bisland

April 13, General Burnside issued his General Order No. 38 in which he gave warning that "the habit of declaring sympathy for the enemy" would not be allowed in the Dept. of the Ohio

April 16, Confederate Act to allow minors to hold commissions in the army, and Act passed to prevent absence of officers and soldiers without leave

——, Admiral Porter with 7 ironclads, 3 steamers and 10 barges in tow loaded with supplies passed the batteries at Vicksburg during the night arriving at New Carthage at 2.30 A.M. Every vessel was hit by Confederate fire but all passed except the steamer "Henry Clay"

April 17–May 2, Confederate General John S. Marmaduke in raid into Missouri

April 18–May 2, Raid of Union Colonel Benjamin Grierson from La Grange, Tennessee, to Baton Rouge, Louisiana, in which he destroyed between 50 and 60 miles of railroad and telegraph, army stores, and Confederate government property, captured 1,000 horses and mules, which "attracted the attention of the enemy from the main movement against Vicksburg" (Grant. "Personal Memoirs")

April 18, Confederate Act to establish a volunteer navy

April 20, Proclamation of the President announced the admission of West Virginia as the 35th State to date from June 20

April 22, National Academy of Sciences held first meeting, Alexander D. Bache elected president

April 24, Confederate Internal Revenue Act made

provision for taxes and imposed tax of one-tenth in kind of agricultural products

April 27, Confederate Act provided for issue of 8% bonds or stock to discharge certain agreements prior to Dec. 1, 1862

April 28, General Hooker's army began crossing the Rappahannock marching towards Lee's army at Fredericksburg by the right bank (Chancellorsville campaign)

April 29, Admiral Porter with 7 ironclads bombarded Grand Gulf, Mississippi, but failed to silence the Confederate batteries

April 29–May 1, Demonstration against Haynes and Drumgould's Bluffs by General Sherman at Snyder's Mill, Mississippi

April 29–May 7, Raid of Union General George G. Stoneman with 10,000 cavalry in Virginia

April 30, General Grant began transfer of troops across the Mississippi to Bruinsburg on east bank (Vicksburg campaign)

——, General Hooker arrived at Chancellorsville establishing headquarters of the Army of the Potomac

——, Confederate Acts provided for 10 year bonds and 2 year treasury notes issued under Act of May 16, 1861, and for impressment for supplies for the navy, and Joint Resolution established a seal

May 1, General Hooker ordered advance from Chancellorsville and then withdrew troops after engagement of advance guard with enemy on the Fredericksburg Road leaving Confederates the better position

——, Battle of Port Gibson or Thompson's Hill, Mississippi. General Grant defeated the Confederates under General J. S. Bowen, Federal loss 875, 1,000 prisoners and 5 cannon taken

——, Confederate Acts created a provisional navy in addition to the regular navy, President Davis authorized to contract for construction and equipment of vessels in Europe, abolished all ports of delivery in the Confederate States, provided for elections for delegates to Congress from certain Indian nations entitled by treaty to representation, provided for creation of office of Commissioner of Taxes, repealed clause of Act of Oct. 11, 1862 as to exemption of one person on each plantation of 20 negroes altered to provide for protection of property of women and minors and persons absent from home on military service, and for each person exempted $500 to be paid into Treasury, and adopted national flag. Joint Resolution declared that white officers commanding negro troops should if captured be put to death or otherwise punished at discretion of court martial as inciting insurrection

——, First Confederate Congress, 3d sess. adjourned

May 2–4, Battle of Chancellorsville, Virginia. Confederate General "Stonewall" Jackson by forced march led army of 32,000 to attack federal right under command of General O. O. Howard, General Lee remaining to face Hooker's 72,000 army with about 14,000. Confederate attack at 6 P.M. surprised Federals who fled in panic, General Jackson mortally wounded by fire of his own men mistaken in the dark for an enemy. Attack resumed the following day under command of Confederate General Stuart reinforced by Anderson a victory in general for Confederates, Union General Sedgwick forced General Early out of the Fredericksburg Heights, but was pushed back over the Rappahannock May 4 to

unite with Hooker's beaten army. Federal loss 17,197 of whom 5,000 were prisoners, Confederate about 13,000

May 2, Confederates evacuated Grand Gulf, Mississippi, after Union victory at Port Gibson

May 3, Union Colonel Streight in raid from Tuscumbia, Alabama (April 26) towards Rome, Georgia to cut Georgia railroad south of Dalton surrendered to Confederate General Forrest after action at Cedar Bluff, Alabama

——, Confederate General Longstreet abandoned siege of Suffolk, Virginia

May 4, Clement L. Vallandigham arrested at Dayton, Ohio, for public expression of sympathy with those in arms against the Government, and taken before military tribunal May 6

——, At midnight General Hooker called meeting of his corps commanders to consider withdrawal of army and supported by Couch and Sickles recrossed the Rappahannock in retreat from Chancellorsville against the advice of Generals Meade, Reynolds, and Howard who favored an advance to bring on another battle

May 6, Confederate Major General Ambrose P. Hill assigned to command of second corps Army of Northern Virginia

May 8, Proclamation of President Lincoln that no plea of alienage be received to exempt person of foreign birth who had declared intention of citizenship from military service

May 9, Confederate General Joseph E. Johnston ordered to Mississippi to assume command

May 14, Jackson, Mississippi, captured in battle by Grant's advance commanded by Generals Sherman and McPherson defeating General Johnston

May 16, Battle of Champion Hills, or Baker's Creek, Mississippi. General Grant with Generals McClernand and McPherson defeated Confederate army under Colonel Pemberton who had left Vicksburg to attempt to join Johnston's forces. Federal losses 2,441, Confederate about 4,000

——, Clement L. Vallandigham convicted by court-martial at Cincinnati, Ohio, of violation of General Order No. 38 and sentenced to confinement in fortress during the continuation of the war

——, Resolution of meeting of Democrats at Albany, New York, condemned arrest of Vallandigham

May 17, Confederate General Pemberton made stand at Big Black River Bridge, and was again defeated by Grant, and retired to Vicksburg

May 18, Capture of Haynes' Bluff, Mississippi, Confederates evacuating on approach of fleet

May 19, President Lincoln commuted sentence of imprisonment of C. L. Vallandigham for treasonable utterance in speech of May 1 at Mount Vernon, Ohio, to banishment "beyond our military lines," and he was sent by General Rosecrans to Confederate headquarters of General Bragg at Shelbyville May 25

——, General Grant made unsuccessful assault on Vicksburg and began siege

May 21, Siege of Port Hudson, Louisiana, begun by Union force commanded by General N. P. Banks

May 22, General Grant again repulsed in attack on Vicksburg

——, War Dept. established bureau in Adjutant General's Office for all matters regarding organization of colored troops

May 24, Major General John W. Schofield superseded

General S. R. Curtis in command of the Dept. of the Missouri assuming command May 29

May 26, Gold discovered in Alder Gulch near present Virginia City, Montana, by William Fairweather and other prospectors

May 27, General Banks repulsed in assault on Port Hudson, Louisiana

June 1, United States Consul at Nassau reported that 28 steamers had sailed from there since March 10 for Confederate ports, 13 of these captured or destroyed

June 3, General Lee began to move his army from Fredericksburg for invasion of the North

——, General Burnside stopped publication of the *Chicago Tribune* by order of June 2; order rescinded by President Lincoln June 4

——, Colored troops (54th Massachusetts) Colonel Robert Gould Shaw in command arrived at Port Royal, South Carolina

June 6, First issue of labor paper *Fincher's Trade Review* published in Philadelphia

June 9, Cavalry engagement at Brandy Station or Beverly Ford, Virginia between Confederate General Stuart and General Pleasanton

June 11, Democratic Convention in Ohio nominated Clement L. Vallandigham for governor

June 13, General Hooker's army left position before Fredericksburg, Virginia, marching north in pursuit of Lee's army

June 14, General Banks made unsuccessful assault on Port Hudson, Louisiana, defended by Confederate Major General Frank Gardner

June 15, Battle of Winchester, Virginia. Confederate General Ewell defeated General Milroy in attack, General Milroy escaped capture by retreat to the Potomac River during the night but lost over 3,000 men taken as prisoners

——, Proclamation of President Lincoln called for 100,000 militia from the States for 6 months service to resist Confederate invasion of the North

——, Confederate cavalry raided Chambersburg, Pennsylvania

June 17, American Emigrant Company chartered in Connecticut to assist emigration from foreign countries to the United States

June 18, Napoleon in interview with Confederate agent, Slidell, sanctioned building ironclads for the Confederacy at Bordeaux and Nantes if destination concealed

June 19, West Virginia admitted to the Union as a separate State as from June 20 (35th) with a Constitution providing for gradual abolition of slavery

June 24, General Rosecrans began advance towards the south from Murfreesborough against General Bragg at Tullahoma manœuvring Bragg out of middle Tennessee into Georgia

June 26, Confederates under General Early entered Gettysburg, Pennsylvania

June 27, Confederate General Early received the surrender of York, Pennsylvania, and demanded $100,000 and supplies of foodstuffs and clothing

——, General Lee's main army encamped at Carlisle, Pennsylvania

June 28, Citizens of Columbia, Pennsylvania, in skirmish with Confederate General Early burned bridge across the Susquehanna to prevent its seizure, defeating Confederate plan to cut Pennsylvania Railroad in advance on Harrisburg

——, Major General George Gordon Meade assumed command of the Army of the Potomac superseding General Hooker

June 30, Gladstone in House of Commons stated that the reunion of the North and South was "unattainable"

——, General Kilpatrick in engagement with Confederate General Stuart at Hanover, Pennsylvania

July 1–3, Battle of Gettysburg, Pennsylvania, Union victory of General Meade over General Lee

July 1, Claims Convention with Great Britain. *See* Canada

——, First day of Battle of Gettysburg begun on Seminary Ridge where Buford's cavalry was driven by encounter with Confederate advance under Hill, Pickett, and Heth. General Reynolds in command killed, replaced by Howard and by General W. S. Hancock later in the day. The Confederates reinforced by Ewell forced retirement of Reynold's and Howard's corps to Cemetery Hill south of Gettysburg with loss of nearly 10,000 men

——, Cavalry engagement at Carlisle, Pennsylvania, between General Kilpatrick and the Confederates under General Stuart returning from raid to join Lee's army before Gettysburg

——, Missouri Convention adopted ordinance declaring that slavery should cease in the State July 4, 1870

——, Tullahoma, Tennessee, occupied by Union forces

——, Claims Convention with Great Britain signed

July 2, Second day of Battle of Gettysburg, entire Union army in position on Cemetery Ridge from Culp's Hill to Round Top attacked in afternoon by Confederates, no decisive success gained by Lee in heavy battle with great loss on both sides, Ewell (Confederate) holding Culp's Hill

July 2–26, Confederate General John H. Morgan on raid in Kentucky, Indiana, and Ohio

July 3, Third day of Battle of Gettysburg opened with Union counter-attack which regained possession of Culp's Hill, and in afternoon Confederate assault led by General Pickett on federal center commanded by Hancock which broke Meade's first line but lack of support forced his retreat ending the battle. Federal loss in entire action 3,155 killed, 14,529 wounded, and 5,365 missing, total 23,049; Confederate, 2,592 killed, 12,709 wounded, and 5,150 taken prisoners, total 20,451, official account not including the artillery losses, total about 30,000. Of Pickett's division 3,393 officers and men out of 4,500 left on the field

July 4, General Lee began retreat from Gettysburg during the night unpursued by the Army of the Potomac reaching the Potomac River July 7

——, Vicksburg, Mississippi, surrendered by Confederate General Pemberton to General Grant and Admiral Porter, the garrison of 27,000 paroled by Grant as prisoners of war, entire Mississippi Valley in Union control

——, Confederate attack of General Holmes on Helena, Arkansas, repulsed by General B. M. Prentiss

July 5, Confederate General Morgan captured Lebanon and Bardstown, Kentucky

July 7, Union army reoccupied Maryland Heights

——, Draft under the Conscription Act begun in Rhode Island

July 8, Draft under the Conscription Act begun in Massachusetts

July 8–9, Confederate Colonel Morgan crossed the Ohio River at Cummings Ferry into Indiana on raid

July 9, Port Hudson, Mississippi, untenable after the fall of Vicksburg, surrendered by Confederate General Gardner to General Banks after 6 weeks of siege

July 11, Ambassador Adams told Lord Russell that building warships for the Confederacy must be regarded by the Government of the United States as "virtually tantamount to a participation in the war by the people of Great Britain . . ."

——, Assault on Confederate Fort Wagner, South Carolina, by General Gillmore and Admiral Dahlgren repulsed

July 13, Confederate General Morgan entered Ohio at Harrison.   Martial law declared in Cincinnati, Covington, and Newport, Morgan within 13 miles of Cincinnati marched around the city

——, General Lee's army crossed the Potomac at Williamsport

——, Yazoo City, Mississippi, taken by Major General F. J. Herron and Admiral Porter

July 13–16, Draft riots in New York City, Troy, and Boston, hundreds of persons killed and wounded

July 16, The U.S.S. "Wyoming" fired on by Japanese at Shimonoseki, Japan, returned fire

——, Jackson, Mississippi, evacuated by Confederate General Johnston after siege of 7 days by General Sherman, occupied by Union forces the next day

July 18, Proclamation of President Davis called for enrollment in Confederate army of persons coming under the Conscription Acts

——, Second Union assault on Fort Wagner, Morris Island, South Carolina, repulsed by Confederates commanded by General L. M. Keitt, Colonel Robert Shaw in command of storming party of colored troops killed in action

July 19, Confederate General Daniel H. Hill assigned to command of second army corps relieving General William J. Hardee

——, Confederate Colonel Morgan in engagement with Union forces attempting to cross the Ohio River above Buffington Island forced to abandon guns to escape capture, lost about 600 men and as many more surrendered

July 25–Aug. 6, Raid of Confederate General J. Scott into eastern Kentucky

July 25, Confederate General Bragg appointed in command in Tennessee

July 26, Surrender of Confederate Col. John H. Morgan with remnant of his force at Salineville, Ohio, to cavalry of General Schackelford

——, Death of General Sam Houston at Huntsville, Texas, and John J. Crittenden at Frankfort, Kentucky

July 30, Proclamation of President Lincoln announced protection of colored soldiers and retaliation upon enemy prisoners for acts of Confederates against them

Aug. 5–31, Raid of Union General Averell in West Virginia

Aug. 11, Major General Frederick Steele assumed command of all troops in Arkansas north of the Arkansas River

Aug. 12, Confederate General Holmes placed in command of the Mississippi region

Aug. 16, General Burnside left Camp Nelson near Lexington, Kentucky, to go to relief of loyal East Tennessee reaching the Tennessee River Aug. 20

Aug. 17, Brotherhood of Locomotive Engineers organized

Aug. 17–23, Bombardment of Fort Sumter in Charleston Harbor and Fort Wagner on Morris Island in joint Union attack until forts practically demolished

Aug. 19, Draft resumed in New York City under protection of troops proceeded without disorder

Aug. 20–28, Confederate guerilla leader Quantrell made raid into Kansas, attacking Lawrence in surprise attack on the 21st killing citizens and burning and looting property

Aug. 26, Death of Confederate General John B. Floyd at Abingdon, Virginia

Sept. 2, Election in Nevada for constitutional convention, Constitution rejected

Sept. 4, General Burnside's army led by Colonel John W. Foster occupied Knoxville, Tennessee, evacuated by Confederates

Sept. 5, Letter of Ambassador Adams to Earl Russell regarding ironclads under construction in England for the Confederacy said "It would be superfluous for me to point out to your Lordship that this is war"

——, Earl Russell directed that rams at Birkenhead should not leave Liverpool pending investigation

Sept. 6–7, Evacuation of Fort Wagner, Morris Island, South Carolina by Confederates, damaged by joint army and navy bombardment of Sept. 5

Sept. 8–9, Union naval attack on Fort Sumter unsuccessful, 130 soldiers landed and were captured

Sept. 9, Surrender of Cumberland Gap, Tennessee, by Confederate General Frazer to General Burnside

——, Advance of General Rosecrans' army entered Chattanooga, Tennessee, evacuated by Confederate General Bragg retiring to Lafayette where he was joined Sept. 18 by General Hood

Sept. 10, Union General Steele captured Little Rock, capital of Arkansas

Sept. 12, Letter of Arman, builder at Bordeaux, France, acknowledged check of 720,000 francs first payment of Captain Bullock on 2 ships for the Confederacy

Sept. 13, General Meade occupied Culpeper Court House, Virginia, evacuated by Confederates, as his headquarters, beginning advance of Union forces from the Rappahannock to the Rapidan

Sept. 15, Proclamation of President Lincoln declared general suspension of writ of habeas corpus when necessary, cases specified

Sept. 16, Message of President Lincoln to Andrew Johnson, military Governor of Tennessee, authorized him to take measures to enable the loyal people to establish a state government

Sept. 19–20, Battle of Chickamauga, Georgia, between General Rosecrans with Army of the Cumberland and Confederate General Bragg, a Confederate victory

Sept. 19, First day of battle General Bragg with General Polk began by attack on federal left, no decisive results

Sept. 20, Second day of battle Longstreet broke federal line in gap caused by withdrawal of Wood's division due to a misunderstanding, and federal right wing including Rosecrans, McCook, and Crittenden swept off the field leaving General George H. Thomas on the left to face entire Confederate army and prevent the battle from becoming a complete rout.   He retreated at night from the field taking a position covering Rossville and on the 21st the Union army withdrew to Chattanooga followed by Confederates who took position along Missionary Ridge and

Lookout Mt. investing Chattanooga. Federal loss 16,336, Confederate 18,000

Sept. 22–Oct. 26, Confederate Joseph Shelby made raid into Arkansas and Missouri

Sept. 24, Major General Hooker appointed to command of 11th and 12th army corps of the Army of the Potomac and ordered to reinforce General Rosecrans at Chattanooga

——, Confederate Government appointed Dudley Mann special agent to the Holy See

Sept. 28, Generals Alexander McDowell, McCook, and T. L. Crittenden relieved of commands and ordered to Indianapolis to court of inquiry as to their conduct at Chickamauga

Sept. 29, The *Boise News* published at Boise, Idaho

Oct. 3, War Dept. Order issued regulations for enlistment of colored troops in Maryland, Missouri, and Tennessee

Oct. 11–12, Capture of Boonville, Missouri, by Confederate General Shelby

Oct. 13, General E. B. Brown defeated Confederate Generals Shelby and Coffee 8 miles southwest of Arrow Rock, Missouri

——, Vallandigham defeated in election for governor in Ohio by large majority

Oct. 14, Engagement at Bristow Station, Virginia, General Warren in skirmish with Confederate General A. P. Hill

Oct. 16, Military Dept. of the Mississippi consisting of the Depts. of the Cumberland, Ohio, and Tennessee created and Major General Grant assigned to the command, taking office Oct. 18, and arriving at Chattanooga Oct. 23, General George H. Thomas appointed to command of the Dept. of the Cumberland relieving General Rosecrans, General W. T. Sherman of the Dept. of the Tennessee Oct. 24

Oct. 17, Proclamation of President Lincoln called for 300,000 volunteers for military service for 3 years or the duration of the war

Oct. 18, Confederate Army of Northern Virginia established on line of Rappahannock River

Oct. 19, Custer and Kilpatrick in cavalry engagement with Confederate FitzHugh Lee at Gainesville or Buckland Mills, Virginia, Confederate victory

Oct. 23, Confederate General Leonidas Polk transferred to the Army of the Mississippi, and General W. J. Hardee to Army of Tennessee

Oct. 26–Nov. 4, Joint Union attack on Fort Sumter, South Carolina

Oct. 28, Attack on Union garrison at Pine Bluff south of Little Rock, Arkansas, repulsed. Federal cavalry occupied Arkadelphia and Confederates retreated towards Red River

——, Battle at Wauhatchie, Tennessee. Confederate attack by General Longstreet repulsed by General Hooker

Nov. 3, First National Congress of Fenians met in Chicago

Nov. 6, Brownsville, Texas, and Point Isabel occupied by Union General Dana of General Banks' expedition

Nov. 7, Union forces advanced to the line of the Rappahannock. At Kelly's Ford General Birney of Sedgwick's corps defeated Confederates and at Rappahannock Station General Sedgwick carried enemy works and took 1,500 prisoners

Nov. 8, Confederate General John C. Breckinridge superseded General Daniel A. Hill in command of

the Second Corps, Army of Tennessee, General N. B. Forrest assigned to command of West Tennessee on the 14th

Nov. 12, Meeting at Little Rock, Arkansas, to consult on measures for restoration of State to the Union

Nov. 15, General Sherman arrived at Chattanooga, Tennessee with 4 divisions

Nov. 17–Dec. 4, Siege of Knoxville, Tennessee, by Confederate General Longstreet detached from Bragg's army

Nov. 19, Ceremony of dedication of the national cemetery at Gettysburg, Pennsylvania, Edward Everett, the orator of the day, President Lincoln made memorable address

Nov. 22–30, General Banks' Rio Grande expedition (Oct. 27–Dec. 2) captured Fort Esperanza and made important lodgement at Matagorda Bay, Texas

Nov. 23–25, Battle of Chattanooga, Tennessee. General Grant with Generals Thomas, Sherman, and Hooker defeated Confederates under General Bragg

Nov. 23, First day of battle advance movement of General Thomas developed into a successful action which gained possession of Orchard Knob, a rocky hill in front of Confederate line between the defenses of Chattanooga and the foot of Missionary Ridge

Nov. 24, Second day of battle, General Hooker in the "Battle above the Clouds" drove Confederates from Lookout Mountain into the Chattanooga valley, and General Sherman gained part of Missionary Ridge

Nov. 25, Third and decisive day of battle. General Sherman repulsed in attack on Confederate position on Missionary Ridge, but in afternoon General Thomas ordered by Grant to relieve pressure on General Sherman attacked and carried first trenches and then without orders the entire line of the Army of the Cumberland made the assault and carried the ridge breaking the Confederate center. Confederate loss 8,684, Union about 6,000

——, The C.S.S. "Rappahannock" sailed in unfinished condition from London to Calais to avoid possible detention by the British Government

Nov. 26, Battle of Ringgold, Georgia. General Hooker in pursuit of Confederates in action with General Cleburne

——, Army of the Potomac crossed the Rapidan but retired Dec. 1–2 going into winter quarters

Nov. 27, Confederate General J. H. Morgan escaped from prison at Columbus, Ohio

Nov. 29, Battle of Knoxville, Tennessee. Confederates under General Longstreet attacked Fort Sanders and were repulsed with loss of 1,000 men

Dec. 2, Confederate General William J. Hardee superseded General Bragg in command of the Army of Tennessee

Dec. 3, Confederate General Longstreet began retreat raising the siege at Knoxville, Tennessee, as Sherman approached from Chattanooga to relieve Burnside; General Sherman entered Knoxville, Dec. 6.

Dec. 7–Feb. 17, 1864, First Confederate Congress, 4th session

Dec. 7, First territorial legislature of Idaho met

Dec. 8, President Lincoln proclaimed amnesty to all Confederates who would return to their allegiance and take oath to support the Union, excepting civil and diplomatic officers of "so-called Confederate Government" and military officers of a certain rank and certain others

Dec. 8, Message of the President stated that there were 100,000 colored men in service of whom 50,000 had borne arms

Dec. 8–25, Union raid of W. W. Averell on Virginia and Tennessee Railroad and demonstrations up the Shenandoah Valley and from the Kanawha Valley cut the railroad on the 16th at Salem, destroyed 5 railroad bridges and Confederate supplies, and took about 200 prisoners

Dec. 9, Major General Ambrose E. Burnside superseded in command of the Dept. of the Ohio by Major General John G. Foster

Dec. 11, Nevada Constitutional Convention adjourned; the Constitution not ratified

Dec. 16, Confederate General Joseph E. Johnston assigned to command of the Dept. of Tennessee leaving General Leonidas Polk in command of Army of Mississippi to which he was assigned Dec. 22

Dec. 21, *Savannah Republican* (Georgia) announced cost of grits as $16 a bushel and flour $120 a barrel

Dec. 24, Agreement with Austria-Hungary as to exportation of tobacco from the United States signed

Dec. 28, Confederate Acts ended exemption from military service of those who had heretofore furnished substitutes, authorized tax in kind on bacon to be commuted by collection of salt pork or an equivalent, and amended law which required one-tenth of sweet potatoes produced paid to Government. Bill introduced to receive into military service that part of population known as Creoles in Alabama, Louisiana, and Florida referred to committee on military affairs

CONGRESS

Jan. 17, Joint Resolution authorized Secretary of the Treasury to issue $100,000,000 United States legal tender notes for payment of army and navy

Feb. 24, Arizona organized as Territory, slavery prohibited

Feb. 25, Act provided for a national currency, national banks required to base their note issues on government bonds deposited in Washington

——, Currency Bureau of the Treasury established with a Comptroller of the Currency appointed by the President

——, Act passed to prevent correspondence with "present pretended rebel government"

March 2, Act increased number of major-generals and brigadier-generals in the regular army and in volunteer service

March 3, Resolution adopted against foreign mediation as an encouragement to rebellion and therefore an unfriendly act

——, Act to prevent and punish frauds on revenue provided penalties for presenting fraudulent claims or giving false military vouchers

——, Act turned over to Treasury in trust all captured and abandoned cotton, sugar, rice, and tobacco in States in insurrection

——, Loan Act authorized loans of $300,000,000 for 1863 and $600,000,000 for 1864

——, Act fixed number of supreme court judges at 10, new circuit (tenth) established composed of California and Oregon and a 10th associate judge

——, The President authorized during the War to suspend privilege of writ of habeas corpus in any case necessary

March 3, Issue not to exceed $50,000,000 in fractional currency authorized to replace postage currency or other stamps

——, First Conscription Act by which all male citizens of the United States and persons of foreign birth who had declared intention to become citizens between the ages of 20 and 45 to be enrolled in national army, exemption allowed at cost of $300

——, Idaho made a Territory

March 4, Congress adjourned

Dec. 7, Thirty-eighth Congress, 1st sess. convened

1864

Jan. 1, Union army numbered 860,737

Jan. 2, George Davis appointed Confederate Attorney General

——, Gold sold in New York at 152 and reached 175 in April

Jan. 7, William Preston appointed Confederate envoy to Mexico

Jan. 8, Convention held at New Orleans to advance the work of reconstruction

Jan. 9, Confederate Act authorized cancellation of certain 8% bonds dated Oct. 18 and 27, 1862 for $1,000,000 each, an equal number of like character to be substituted

Jan. 12, Decree of the President fixed western base of the Sierra Nevada Mts. at Arcade Creek in the Sacramento Valley where Central Pacific Railroad should cross

Jan. 16, Major General Samuel R. Curtis assumed command of Dept. of Kansas reëstablished Jan. 1

Jan. 18, James M. Mason appointed a commissioner of Confederate States in different foreign countries as directed

Jan. 21, Meeting of loyal citizens of Tennessee at Nashville declared in favor of a constitutional convention and abolition of slavery

Jan. 22, Isaac Murphy inaugurated Provisional Governor of Arkansas

Jan. 28, Major General John M. Schofield assigned to command of the Dept. of the Ohio, General W. S. Rosecrans to the Dept. of the Missouri, and General Polk to Dept. of Alabama, Mississippi, and East Louisiana

——, Treaty with Japan provided for reduction of import duties

Feb. 1, President Lincoln called for 500,000 men for 3 years military service or during the war, draft to be made March 10

Feb. 3, Confederate Act to organize Treasury Note Bureau

Feb. 3–March 6, General Sherman marched from Vicksburg with 20,000 men for Meridan, Mississippi (coöperating expeditions from Memphis, Tennessee, and up the Yazoo River) and occupied Yazoo City Feb. 9 and Meridan Feb. 14

Feb. 6, Confederate Acts prohibited circulation of United States paper money, prohibited importation of luxuries after March 1, and under regulations for foreign commerce no cotton, tobacco, naval stores, sugar, molasses, and rice could leave ports except under regulations giving the Government half the tonnage

Feb. 7, Jacksonville, Florida, occupied by Union force of General T. Seymour to restore Florida to her allegiance, and proclamation of Feb. 13 called on citizens to take oath

Feb. 9, Ohio State University at Columbus received grant of public land

——, Escape of Union prisoners including Colonel Streight and Colonel Thomas E. Rose from Libby Prison by tunnel under the walls

Feb. 11, Confederate Act authorized issue of certificates for interest on the "fifteen million loan"

Feb. 15, Confederate Act suspended writ of habeas corpus until Aug. 2 in order to enable Government to meet resistance to law making liable for service all who had sent substitutes to the army, suspension restricted to arrests made under authority of the President and Secretary of War

Feb. 17, Confederate Act provided for an Invalid Corps for such duty as they shall be qualified to perform, all white men between 17 and 50 requisitioned for military service, number of exempted classes reduced by more than one-half, free negroes and slaves liable to service in hospitals, on fortifications, and in production of materials of war, additional taxes laid on profits and incomes, and Funding Act reduced the currency and authorized a new issue of notes and bonds, earlier issues of paper money practically repudiated under plan of compulsory funding

Feb. 18, Confederate Congress adjourned

Feb. 20, Battle of Olustee, Florida, General Seymour defeated marching inland about 50 miles west of Jacksonville by Confederates commanded by General Joseph Finnegan, Seymour losing about 2,000 men

Feb. 22, Resignation of Secretary Chase because of publication of Pomeroy Congressional Committee circular urging his election as President

——, In Louisiana election for State offices ordered by General Banks took place, Michael Hahn elected Governor, inaugurated March 4

Feb. 28–March 1, Raid of Union General G. A. Custer into Albemarle County, Virginia

Feb. 28–March 4, Failure of Union expedition of General Kilpatrick and Ulrich Dahlgren against Richmond and attempt to free prisoners, Colonel Dahlgren killed March 2

March 4, Andrew Johnson confirmed as military Governor of Tennessee

March 5, By Confederate regulation the Government exacted from every vessel the use of one-half of her freight capacity, and one-half of net proceeds of owner's part of cargo to be invested in goods to be shipped to the Confederate States

——, Colorado Seminary chartered, reorganized 1880 as University of Denver

——, Confederate General John C. Breckinridge assigned to command of the Trans-Alleghany or Dept. of Western Virginia relieving General Samuel Jones

March 9, General Ulysses S. Grant commissioned Lieutenant-General at the White House, the highest rank in the army, the same that was conferred on Washington in 1798, and the following day assumed the chief command, and March 11 left Washington for the West

March 10, Major General Franz Sigel superseded General Benjamin F. Kelley in command of the Dept. of West Virginia

March 12, General Halleck appointed Chief of Staff, General J. B. McPherson in command of the Army of the Tennessee, and General W. T. Sherman of Division of the Mississippi

March 12, Rear Admiral D. D. Porter coöperating with General N. P. Banks and A. J. Smith in Red River campaign for recovery of Louisiana entered the river

March 14, Order of the President called for additional draft of 200,000 men for service for 3 years

——, Fort De Russy, Louisiana, carried by assault of General A. J. Smith

March 15, Michael Hahn, elected Governor of Louisiana, given military authority

March 16, Confederate Major General Sterling Price superseded General T. H. Holmes in command of the District of Arkansas

March 16–April 14, Confederate General Forrest on expedition into Kentucky and West Tennessee

March 17, Notice of abrogation of Reciprocity Treaty with Great Britain given by the United States

March 18, Constitution for Arkansas which abolished slavery ratified by vote

March 20, Survivors from the negro colony at Isle à Vache landed at Alexandria

March 24, Capture of Union City, Tennessee, by Confederate General Forrest

March 26, General Grant established his headquarters at Culpeper Court House, Virginia

——, President Lincoln made second amnesty Proclamation

March 28, The U.S.S. "Niagara" fired on by Portuguese fort at Lisbon

April 4, Major General Philip H. Sheridan assigned to command of cavalry corps, Army of the Potomac

April 6–July 23, Constitutional Convention at New Orleans adopted Constitution for Louisiana which abolished slavery

April 8, Battle of Sabine Cross Roads, Louisiana. General Banks advancing up the Red River from Alexandria, Louisiana (March 25) encountered force of Confederate Gen. Richard Taylor of Kirby Smith's army and was badly defeated losing 3,000 in killed, wounded, and missing, Confederate loss 2,000. Banks retired to Pleasant Grove where Confederate pursuit was checked and during the night the retreat continued to strong position at Pleasant Hill

April 9, General Banks attacked at Pleasant Hill by Confederate General Taylor but attack was repulsed with aid of reinforcements under General A. J. Smith, and Generals Emory and Mower, Union retreat continued the following day unpursued to Grand Encore

——, General Grant instructed General Meade to follow Lee's army as his objective

April 11, New State Government with Dr. Isaac Murphy, Governor, inaugurated in Arkansas

——, Constitution adopted by loyal Virginians abolished slavery

April 12, Fort Pillow, on the Mississippi River, Tennessee, attacked and captured by Confederate General Forrest who on the following day massacred the negro soldiers in the garrison

April 17, General Grant refused to exchange prisoners of war giving explanation later that it prolonged the war to release prisoners and would ensure defeat

April 17–20, Attack and capture of Plymouth, North Carolina, by Confederate General Hoke

April 18, Confederate General G. T. Beauregard assigned to command the Dept. of North Carolina and Southern Virginia

April 20, The War Dept. reduced rations of Confederate prisoners hitherto the same as the army's ration

20% in retaliation for alleged inhuman treatment of Union prisoners

April 27, Confederates Jacob Thompson and C. C. Clay appointed commissioners to Canada

April 27–Sept. 6, Constitutional Convention met at Annapolis, Maryland

May 2–June 14, First session of Second Confederate Congress

May 3–4, Army of the Potomac began during the night crossing of the Rapidan advancing into the "Wilderness"

May 4, General Sherman with Generals McPherson and Schofield began march from Chattanooga towards Dalton, Georgia, headquarters of Confederate General Johnston and made demonstration on Rocky Face Mountain northeast of Dalton

May 5, General Butler landed troops from Fortress Monroe at City Point and Bermuda Hundred, James River, Virginia, to coöperate with Army of the Potomac in attack on Lee

May 5–6, Battle of the Wilderness, near Chancellorsville, Virginia. General Lee attacked Army of the Potomac commanded by Generals Grant and Meade, fighting severe but indecisive, Confederate General Longstreet wounded, Union General Wadsworth killed. Union losses 17,666, Confederates about 11,500

May 7, General Grant started for Spotsylvania Court House in night march of army with plan to turn Lee's right flank and place army between the latter and Richmond but found on arrival that Lee had sent advance guard which blocked his approach

May 9, Sherman made demonstration against Dalton, Georgia

May 9–13, A series of dams built by Lieutenant Colonel Joseph Bailey at junction of Cane and Red rivers made it possible for the Union fleet commanded by Admiral D. D. Porter to descend river relieving a critical situation with the constant falling of the river

May 9–24, Cavalry raid of General P. H. Sheridan towards Richmond to harass Confederate rear and cut Lee's communications

May 10, Battle of Spotsylvania Court House, Virginia, second Battle of the Wilderness. General Grant attacked, Colonel Emory Upton gained position in Confederate works but failed to hold it for want of support

May 11, Major General Canby assumed command of Division of West Mississippi

——, Ordinance of emancipation of slaves without compensation to owners adopted by Constitutional Convention in Louisiana, added to Constitution by popular ratification July 22

——, Sheridan's cavalry defeated Confederates in action at Yellow Tavern, Virginia, General James E. B. Stuart mortally wounded in action

May 12, Battle of Spotsylvania Court House, third Battle of the Wilderness. General Grant attacked. An advance of Hancock's corps under Francis C. Barlow captured "the salient" and an entire Confederate division, that of General Edward Johnson. Position held in face of 5 Confederate assaults, but Federal assault on Confederate line checked

May 13, Confederate General Johnston forced to retreat from Dalton to Resaca

May 14–15, Battle at Resaca, Georgia. General Sherman defeated Confederates, General Johnston re-

treating during the night towards Dalton, General Sherman captured Rome, Confederate center for supplies and manufacture

May 15, General Sigel defeated by Confederate General Breckinridge at New Market, Virginia

May 16, Confederate General Beauregard attacked and defeated General Butler at Drewry's Bluff, Virginia, and Butler's army "bottled up" at Bermuda Hundred

May 18, Forged Proclamation of the President bearing date of May 17 published by speculators in gold in *New York World, New York Journal of Commerce* and other Democratic papers, calling for 400,000 more troops, editors arrested but released on explanation

May 19, Edward Stanley confirmed as military Governor of North Carolina

——, Death of Nathaniel Hawthorne at Plymouth, New Hampshire

May 21, Major General David Hunter superseded General Franz Sigel in command of the Dept. of West Virginia

May 25, Sherman's Atlanta, Georgia, campaign began with repulse of Hooker's attack on Confederates at New Hope Church

May 26, General Grant withdrew during the night to north bank of the North Anna River, moving towards Hanovertown, Virginia

May 28, General McPherson repulsed attack of Confederates under General Hardee at Dallas, Georgia

May 30–June 20, Raid of Confederate General Morgan into Kentucky

May 31, Convention of radical members of Republican Party met in Cleveland, Ohio, and nominated General John C. Fremont for president and General John Cochrane for vice-president. Platform contained statement that the reconstruction of the rebel States belonged to the people through their representatives in Congress and not to the Executive

June 1, Allatoona, Georgia, captured by cavalry under Major General George Stoneman and made a depot of supplies by Sherman

June 3, Battle of Cold Harbor, Virginia. General Grant attacked General Lee's strong position and was repulsed with loss of probably 7,000

June 4, Confederate General Johnston compelled to retreat from New Hope Church (Georgia) to new position between Lost and Brush Mts. north of Kenesaw

June 5, Battle at Piedmont, Virginia, General Hunter won victory which placed him in command of the Shenandoah Valley, General W. E. Jones, Confederate, killed

June 7, Union National Convention met in Baltimore, Maryland, Lincoln nominated, received all votes except those of Missouri cast for General Grant, later altered to make it unanimous for Lincoln, Andrew Johnson, of Tennessee, nominated for vice-president

——, National Republican Convention at Chicago nominated Lincoln

June 10, Confederate Act provided for organization for military service of men between ages of 17 and 18, and 45 and 50

June 11, Battle of Trevilian Station, Virginia. Sheridan defeated attack of FitzHugh Lee and Hampton

June 12, Grant's loss in men from May 4 to this date in Richmond campaign 54,926 (Rhodes)

——, Confederate General Morgan defeated General Burbridge at Cynthiana, Kentucky

June 12–15, Grant moved the Army of the Potomac across the Chickahominy and James rivers

June 13, Confederate General Richard S. Ewell assigned to command cf the Dept. of Richmond

June 14, Confederate Acts placed additional taxes on property and incomes, and provided that States holding old issues of treasury notes might exchange one-half for new issues and fund the other half

——, Confederate Congress adjourned

——, Army of the Potomac began crossing the James River at City Point

——, Confederate General Leonidas Polk killed on Pine Mountain by cannon ball from Union battery

June 15–18, General Grant made unsuccessful assaults on Petersburg, Virginia, with loss of 7,881 men

June 16, Lieutenant Bennett H. Young authorized by Confederate Secretary of War to organize companies to raid New England towns from Canada

——, General Hunter reached and invested Lynchburg, Virginia, but failed to take it withdrawing during the night of the 18th as reinforcements came to aid of Confederate Generals Early and Breckinridge

——, Confederate General Johnston retired to new line behind Mud Creek, Georgia

June 17, Gold sold at 197 in New York City

June 19, Captain Winslow in the U.S.S. "Kearsarge" off Cherbourg, France, attacked and compelled the surrender of the C.S.S. "Alabama" which sank about 20 minutes later

June 22, Grant made unsuccessful attempt to seize Weldon and South Side Railroad, Lee's lines of communication

June 24, Constitutional Constitution in Maryland voted to abolish slavery

June 27, Battle of Kenesaw Mt., Georgia. General Sherman attacked strong position of Confederate General Johnston and was repulsed with loss of 3,000 men including Generals Harker and McCook, Confederate loss 600

June 30, Gold sold at 250 and continued at this price as average during July and August which made paper money in circulation less than 40 cents on the dollar, and made the Government pay 15% on loans represented by government bonds

——, Secretary Chase resigned from the Cabinet

July 1, William P. Fessenden, of Maine, appointed Secretary of the Treasury succeeding Chase

July 1–Sept. 26, 1869, Second Arctic expedition made by Captain Charles F. Hall, sailed for Arctic, wintered at Repulse Bay (1864–68)

July 2, Confederate General Johnston evacuated position at Kenesaw Mt. during the night

——, Confederate General Early reached Winchester, Virginia, marching towards Washington, and occupied Martinsburg and crossed the Potomac unresisted

July 5, Horace Greeley received letter which he sent to the President announcing that "two ambassadors of Davis and Co.," were in Canada "with full and complete powers for a peace"

——, Proclamation of the President suspended writ of habeas corpus and declared martial law in Kentucky

July 6, Admiral Dupont superseded in command by J. A. Dahlgren

July 8, Proclamation of President Lincoln gave his reasons for not signing the Wade-Davis Reconstruction Bill

July 9, Battle of the Monocacy River, Maryland. General Lew Wallace was defeated by Confederate General Early but checked his advance on Washington by 8 hours

July 11, Confederate General Early appeared on Seventh Street Road north of Washington at noon but attack on outworks repulsed by General Wright

——, Gold in New York City reached 285 highest price during War

July 12, Confederate General Early in engagement with General Bidwell at Fort Stevens 6 miles from Washington, but retreated from region of Washington during the night

July 14, General A. J. Smith defeated Confederate General Forrest near Tupelo, Mississippi

July 17, Confederate General Johnston superseded in command by General J. B. Hood by order of this date, and Johnston censured for failure to arrest the advance of Sherman on Atlanta, President Davis not understanding his Fabian policy

——, Colonel James F. Jacques and J. R. Gilmore had interview with Jefferson Davis without the knowledge of President Lincoln in the interests of peace. Davis would consider no terms but recognition of right of the South to self-government, and no negotiations except on the basis of independence

July 18, Horace Greeley sent to Niagara Falls by President Lincoln to meet Confederates in Canada and ask for their credentials and peace terms, instructed to receive any proposal which embraced the integrity of the Union and the abandonment of slavery from an "authority that can control the armies now at war against the United States." The Confederates refused to negotiate on these terms

——, George A. Trenholm appointed Confederate Secretary of the Treasury

——, President Lincoln called for 500,000 volunteers for service in the army

July 20, Battle of Peach Tree Creek, Georgia. Confederate General Hardee (Hood's army) attacked Sherman's army, mainly divisions of Newton and Johnson, approaching Atlanta and was defeated

July 22, Battle of Atlanta, Georgia. Confederate General Hardee attacked and was defeated by left wing of Sherman's army under McPherson, General J. B. McPherson killed and General John A. Logan assumed command of the Army of the Tennessee, Major General Oliver O. Howard appointed to succeed McPherson July 27

July 27–Aug. 6, General Stoneman started on raid to Macon, Georgia, captured

July 28, Battle of Ezra's Church, third battle before Atlanta, Georgia. Confederate General Hood attacked Logan's corps of General Howard's Army of the Tennessee and was successfully repulsed

July 30, Part of Confederate works at Petersburg, Virginia, blown up by mine, "the crater," but failure of division commander to follow up with attack as planned gave enemy chance to recover and attack storming party with sacrifice of about 4,000 Union soldiers and no advantage gained

——, Chambersburg, Pennsylvania, burned by Confederate General McCausland of General Early's command because of failure to receive requisition of $100,000 in gold demanded

Aug. 1, General Sheridan appointed to take command of the Army of the Shenandoah and began campaign Aug. 10

Aug. 5, Battle of Mobile Bay, Alabama. Union fleet

commanded by Admiral Farragut passed Confederate Forts Morgan, Gaines, and Powell and captured C.S.S. "Tennessee" in battle in the Bay, the U.S.S. "Tecumseh" sunk by torpedo. Fort Powell was destroyed and abandoned by Confederates during the night

Aug. 6, Fort Gaines, Mobile Bay, bombarded by the U.S.S. "Chickasaw" and invested by General G. Granger surrendered to Admiral Farragut Aug. 7

Aug. 7, Middle Military Division constituted, General Sheridan in command

Aug. 17, Railroad union formed a year earlier became the Grand International Brotherhood of Locomotive Engineers

Aug. 18–21, Battle of the Weldon Railroad, Virginia, General Warren permanently gained the railroad for the Union forces, General Lee repulsed on the 24th (Ream's Station) in attempt at recapture

Aug. 18–22, General Kilpatrick in cavalry raid to destroy the Macon Railroad made circuit of Atlanta

Aug. 23, Fort Morgan, Alabama, surrendered to Admiral Farragut and General Granger and Mobile Harbor in Federal possession

Aug. 25, General Sherman gave up the direct siege of Atlanta, Georgia, moving to gain possession of the Macon Railroad to the south, destroyed on the 29th

Aug. 29, Democratic National Convention met in Chicago. General George B. McClellan nominated for president on first ballot, George H. Pendleton for vice-president on second ballot. Convention controlled by the "Copperheads" committed to declaration that the war was a failure

Aug. 29–Dec. 2, Confederate General Price in expedition in Missouri

Aug. 31–Sept. 1, Battle of Jonesborough, Georgia. General Howard repulsed attack of Confederate General Hardee from Jonesborough. Confederates retreated from the town during the night to Lovejoy's Station

Sept. 1, General Hood evacuated Atlanta seeing his position as indefensible and retired to Lovejoy's Station 30 miles southeast on the Savannah Railroad, to place army between Sherman and Andersonville where 34,000 Union prisoners were confined

Sept. 2, Union forces occupied Atlanta, and Sept. 4, General Sherman ordered civilian evacuation

Sept. 4, At Greeneville, Tennessee, Confederate General J. H. Morgan shot by Union soldier at his headquarters

Sept. 5, Election in Louisiana ratified adoption of Constitution

Sept. 6, Convention at Annapolis, Maryland, adopted Constitution, and adjourned, clause abolished slavery, and all who had aided or encouraged rebellion against the United States disenfranchised

Sept. 17, John Fremont withdrew as a candidate for the presidency, letter published in newspapers on the 22d

Sept. 19, Battle of Winchester or Opequan Creek, Virginia. General Sheridan attacked and defeated Confederate General Early inflicting loss of 5,500 men to his own 4,873

Sept. 22, Battle of Fisher's Hill, Virginia. General Sheridan attacked and defeated Confederate General Early 12 miles south of Winchester and drove him from the Shenandoah Valley

Sept. 23, President Lincoln requested the resignation of Montgomery Blair opposed by extreme Republicans from the Cabinet

Sept. 24, William Dennison, of Ohio, appointed Postmaster General succeeding Blair

Oct. 5, Battle of Allatoona, Georgia. Confederate General Hood attacked Generals Tourtelotte and Corse but was repulsed and withdrew

Oct. 7, At Bahia, Brazil, Commander N. Collins in the U.S.S. "Wachusett" attacked the C.S.S. "Florida" in harbor and forced her surrender regardless of neutral rights

Oct. 8, The C.S.S. "Shenandoah" cleared from London for Bombay, India, and at Madeira was taken over for Confederacy by Captain I. T. Waddell

——, Report on secret treasonable associations gave number of the Knights of the Golden Circle also known as Order of American Knights as stated by Vallandigham to be 500,000

Oct. 12, Death of Chief Justice Roger B. Taney in Washington

——, Admiral D. D. Porter assumed command of the North Atlantic Blockading Squadron

Oct. 12–13, Maryland ratified Constitution by popular vote, declared adopted Oct. 29 by Governor Bradford to come into effect Nov. 1

Oct. 13, Surrender of Dalton, Georgia, by Tilton to General Hood

Oct. 19, Raid on St. Albans, Vermont, from Canada by Confederate Lieutenant Bennett H. Young, money in banks seized and town burned

——, Battle of Cedar Creek, Virginia. Confederate General Early made surprise attack on General Wright's division and captured 24 guns and 1,500 prisoners, but arrival of General Sheridan and renewal of battle changed victory to defeat, Federal loss 5,590, Confederate 4,200; last effort of the Confederates to occupy the Shenandoah Valley

Oct. 22, Treaty with Japan signed provided for indemnity for Shimonoseki affair

Oct. 27, Battle of Hatcher's Run or Boydton Plank Road, Virginia. Generals Hancock, Warren, and Gregg repulsed in attempt to turn the Confederate lines and get possession of the South Side Railroad

Oct. 27–28, Destruction of the Confederate ram "Albermarle" at Plymouth, North Carolina, by torpedo exploded under the ram under heavy fire, Lieutenant W. B. Cushing and 4 of 15 men engaged escaped

Oct. 28, Confederate General Price made a stand at Newtonia, Missouri, and was driven from the field, ending raid into Missouri (Sept. 24–Oct. 28)

Oct. 30, Confederate General Hood crossed the Tennessee at Florence beginning invasion of Tennessee

Oct. 31, Nevada admitted as 36th State by proclamation of the President

Nov. 7–March 18, 1865, Second Confederate Congress, second session

Nov. 8, Presidential election gave Lincoln a majority popular vote of 494,567, 2,213,665 votes cast for Lincoln, 1,802,237 for McClellan, including vote of soldiers in the field, 116,887 for Lincoln and 33,748 for McClellan

——, General G. B. McClellan resigned his commission in the army, succeeded by Philip H. Sheridan commissioned major-general

Nov. 12, General Sherman sent last message to General Thomas, left to oppose Confederate General Hood, cutting wires, and was out of communication for 32 days during his "March to the Sea"

Nov. 13, Confederate General Hood made Florence, Alabama, his headquarters

Nov. 15, Sherman began systematic destruction of Atlanta

Nov. 16, General Sherman with army of about 60,000 left Atlanta, Georgia, for Savannah, the army to live on the country, field orders prohibited destruction of property in districts where the army was unmolested, but relentless devastation ordered in case of local hostility, shooting soldiers, burning bridges, &c.

Nov. 19, Proclamation of the President declared the ports of Norfolk, Fernandina, and Pensacola open to commerce

——, Proclamation of Governor Brown of Georgia called all men from 16 to 55 to come to Macon to serve for 40 days to defend State from Sherman

Nov. 21, Confederate General Hood began advance from Florence, Alabama, towards Nashville, Tennessee

Nov. 23, Georgia legislature at Milledgeville passed law to levy the population en masse and fled as Sherman's army arrived driving out the Confederate troops

Nov. 24, Death of Benjamin Silliman, chemist, at New Haven, Connecticut

Nov. 25, The Astor House, Barnum's Museum, and 10 other hotels in New York City set on fire in Confederate conspiracy to burn the city

Nov. 28, Confederate General Rosser surprised and captured Fort Kelley at New Creek, West Virginia, and also Piedmont destroying government buildings, railroad, and stores

——, Dept. of Mississippi created, General Napoleon J. T. Dana assigned to command

Nov. 30, Battle of Franklin, Tennessee. Confederate General Hood repulsed in attack on Generals Schofield and J. D. Cox making stand on the Harpeth River, Union loss 2,326, Confederate 6,252. General Schofield crossed the river during the night marching to Nashville which he reached Dec. 1

Dec. 2, James Speed, of Kentucky, appointed Attorney General

Dec. 6, Salmon P. Chase, of Ohio, appointed Chief Justice

Dec. 10, General Sherman arrived before Savannah, Georgia, and began investment (Dec. 11–21) Confederate General Hardee retiring to inner line of defense

Dec. 12–29, Stoneman's raid from Bean's Station, Tennessee to Saltville, Virginia

Dec. 13, Fort McAllister on the Ogeechee River, defense of Savannah, taken by assault by General Hazen, and communication established between Sherman's army and the South Atlantic Blockading Squadron under Rear Admiral Dahlgren

Dec. 15–16, Battle of Nashville, Tennessee. General Thomas attacked Confederate army of General Hood formed before Nashville driving him back with capture of 16 guns and 1,200 prisoners the first day, and defeating him in complete rout on the second day, 4,875 Confederate prisoners in all taken with 53 guns, Confederates retreated towards Franklin

Dec. 19, President Lincoln called for 300,000 men to make up numbers of call of July 18

Dec. 20, Confederate General Hardee evacuated Savannah, Georgia, during the night retreating to Charleston

Dec. 21, General Sherman took possession of Savannah, Georgia

Dec. 24–25, Joint attack by Generals Butler and Weitzel and Admiral Porter on Fort Fisher, North Carolina, unsuccessful, declared by Butler impregnable

Dec. 26–27, Confederate army of General Hood retreating from Nashville crossed the Tennessee River and Union pursuit stopped

CONGRESS

Jan. 11, Proposal for constitutional amendment abolishing slavery presented in Senate by John B. Henderson of Missouri, and referred to Judiciary Committee which reported Feb. 10 recommending resolution

Feb. 24, Debate begun on recognition of the new federal government of Louisiana, resolution defeated by opposition of Sumner

——, The President authorized to call for such numbers of men for military service as needed and provision made for draft in any division where quota assigned not filled by volunteers, every Union master to receive compensation not exceeding $300 for slaves enlisting in the Union army, the volunteer to be free

Feb. 29, Grade of lieutenant-general revived in the army

March 3, Secretary of the Treasury authorized to borrow $200,000,000 on bonds due in 40 years paying 6% (the 5.40s)

March 21, Enabling Acts for Colorado and Nevada passed

April 4, Joint Resolution passed the House that the United States would not allow the establishment of a monarchical government in Mexico

April 8, Joint Resolution abolishing slavery (XIIIth Amendment) passed in Senate

April 19, Enabling Act for Nebraska passed

April 29, Joint Resolution raised all duties 50% for 60 days and later extensions continued rate until July 1

May 17, Money Orders Division of Post Office established

May 26, Montana Territory created out of part of Idaho and provisional government established

May 31, Joint Resolution abolishing slavery rejected in House by vote of 76 to 55

June 3, Act provided for a national currency secured by pledges of government bonds, and for circulation and redemption thereof, Bureau of Currency constituted and Comptroller of the Treasury to be appointed by the President

June 4, Joint Resolution provided for State of West Virginia

June 15, Joint Resolution abolishing slavery (XIIIth Amendment) failed in House by vote of 95 to 66 lacking the required two-thirds

June 17, Gold Act declared unlawful any contract to purchase or sell gold to be delivered on any day subsequent to day of making contract in order to prevent gambling on the price; repealed July 2

June 28, Fugitive slave law of 1850 repealed

June 30, Secretary of the Treasury authorized to borrow $400,000,000 and to issue therefore bonds or treasury notes not to exceed $200,000,000

——, Tariff Act increased duties increasing average rate from 37.2 to 47.06%, many articles hitherto free made dutiable, glass manufactures raised from 35 to 40%, silks increased 10%, specific duty on woolens to 24 cents a pound and ad valorem to 40%, and duties on raw wool doubled

——, Internal Revenue Act taxed business by means

of licenses especially high on liquor dealers, theaters, and amusements generally, tax on spirits made $1.50 a gallon from July 1, and $2 after Feb. 1, 1865. Income tax of 5% placed on incomes over $600 and less than $5,000, increasing to 10% on excess over $10,000

July 2, Act granted public lands to aid in construction of a railroad and telegraph line from Lake Superior to Puget Sound on the Pacific coast by northern route chartering the Northern Pacific Railroad

——, Act regulated commercial intercourse with the insurrectionary States and provided for collection of captured and abandoned property

July 4, Office of Commissioner of Immigration established, immigrants allowed to come under labor contracts

——, Act supplementary to Enrollment Act repealed exemption clauses which were responsible for the New York draft riots

——, Wade-Davis Reconstruction Bill passed by Congress, was not signed by the President

——, Congress adjourned

Dec. 5, Thirty-eighth Congress, 2d session convened

Dec. 15, Ashley introduced Bill in House assuming for Congress power to regulate reconstruction, laid on table Feb. 21, 1865

Dec. 21, Grade of vice-admiral established in navy; conferred on Admiral Farragut

1865

Jan. 1, Union army numbered 959,460

Jan. 7, General Butler removed from command of the Army of the James as requested by General Grant Jan. 4 and Major General Edward O. C. Ord assumed command on the 8th

Jan. 9, Samuel J. Crawford inaugurated as Governor of Kansas succeeding Carney

Jan. 11, Constitutional Convention at St. Louis (Jan. 6–April 10) adopted ordinance which abolished slavery for Missouri

——, General Robert E. Lee made statement in favor of employing slaves as soldiers and proposed immediate freedom to all who should enlist and a plan for gradual emancipation

——, Confederate General Rosser captured garrison at Beverly, West Virginia, commanded by Colonel Robert Youart in surprise attack taking 580 prisoners

Jan. 12, Francis P. Blair, senior, received by President Davis in confidential interview proposed negotiations for peace and a war of the united North and South against Maximilian in Mexico

Jan. 13, Confederate General Hood in retreat reached Tupelo, Mississippi, and sent his resignation from command to Richmond, Beauregard taking command Jan. 14

Jan. 13–15, Troops landed by General Terry before Fort Fisher under protection of bombardment of fleet commanded by Rear Admiral D. D. Porter, a small advance work taken the second day, surrendered by Confederate General Whiting after battle in evening of the third day, General Whiting mortally wounded, and Colonel Lamb taken prisoner, Federal loss 100 killed and 530 wounded, Confederate loss about 500, 2,083 prisoners taken. Entrance to Cape Fear River now in Union control and Wilmington, North Carolina, the last Confederate port closed

Jan. 15, Legislature of Virginia passed Vagrant Act

authorizing hiring out of persons without employment, and permission given to employer in case of flight to use ball and chain to prevent repetition

Jan. 15, Death of Edward Everett (71) in Boston

Jan. 18, Letter from President Lincoln to Montgomery Blair stated that he was willing to receive informally agents from Mr. Davis with a view of securing peace

——, Confederate Congress adopted resolution asking President Davis to restore General Joseph Johnston to command of the Army of the Tennessee

Jan. 19, Confederate Congress made General Robert E. Lee Commander-in-Chief of army superseding President Davis

——, Advance of Sherman's army began march from Savannah for Goldsborough, North Carolina, to establish base and to open communications with the sea by New Berne Railroad, forts and city transferred to command of General Foster in charge of Dept. of the South

Jan. 23, Confederate General Richard Taylor assumed command of the Army of Tennessee

Jan. 23–24, Confederate Commodore John K. Mitchell sent fleet down James River to try to pass obstructions in river. The C.S.S. "Virginia" and the "Richmond" ran aground and were in engagement with federal batteries next day at Trent's Reach

Jan. 24, Confederate General Nathan B. Forrest assumed command of the District of Mississippi, East Louisiana, and West Tennessee

——, Confederate Government repeated offer of exchange of prisoners, man for man, which Grant accepted

Jan. 25, The C.S.S. "Shenandoah" reached Melbourne, Australia, and from there Captain Waddell sailed for the northern Pacific to destroy the Union whaling industry

Jan. 28, President Davis appointed 3 commissioners, A. H. Stephens, R. M. T. Hunter, and J. A. Campbell, for informal conference as to peace with President Lincoln

Jan. 30, Major General John Pope assigned to command of the Division of the Missouri, Major General Samuel R. Curtis transferred to Dept. of the Northwest

——, The Danish ironclad ram "Sphinx" commissioned off France as C.S.S. "Stonewall"

Jan. 31, Major General John M. Schofield assigned to Dept. of North Carolina

Feb. 1, Confederate Major General J. B. Magruder assumed command of the District of Arkansas

——, Sherman left Savannah marching north to Carolinas

——, Illinois ratified the XIIIth Amendment to the Constitution

Feb. 2, Rhode Island and Michigan ratified the XIIIth Amendment

Feb. 3, Maryland, New York, and West Virginia ratified the XIIIth Amendment

——, Hampton Roads Conference on board vessel near Fort Monroe of President Lincoln and Secretary Seward with Confederate commissioners failed because the Confederates instructed to insist on recognition of independence of the Southern States as basis of negotiations

Feb. 5, Battle of Hatcher's Run, Virginia. Grant unsuccessful in attempt to turn Confederate lines

——, President Lincoln submitted draft Resolution to

Cabinet which proposed provision for compensation to States for slaves freed, $400,000,000 in 6% bonds

Feb. 6, General Robert E. Lee finally appointed Commander-in-Chief of Confederate armies

——, John C. Breckinridge appointed Confederate Secretary of War

——, Major General Edward O. C. Ord assigned to command Dept. of Virginia

Feb. 7, Maine and Kansas ratified the XIIIth Amendment, Delaware voted against, and Texas Constitutional Convention met at Austin (Feb. 7–April 2), voted against ordinance abolishing slavery on the 26th, declared secession ordinance null and void March 15 and Confederate debt void

Feb. 8, Massachusetts and Pennsylvania ratified the XIIIth Amendment

Feb. 9, General Robert E. Lee assumed command of the Confederate armies

——, Virginia ratified the XIIIth Amendment

——, Defenses of New Orleans assigned to Brigadier General Thomas W. Sherman

Feb. 10, Ohio and Missouri ratified the XIIIth Amendment

——, Major General George H. Thomas assigned to the Dept. of the Cumberland, and Major General John M. Palmer to the Dept. of Kentucky

Feb. 13, Earl Russell made formal protest to Mason, Slidell, and Mann, Confederate agents, against attack on St. Albans from Canada and on the "Philo Parsons" as violation of neutrality

Feb. 16, Indiana, Nevada, and Louisiana ratified the XIIIth Amendment

Feb. 17, Columbia, capital of South Carolina, evacuated by Confederates, and partially burned, cause of fire disputed, stated by General Sherman to have started from cotton set on fire by Confederate General Wade Hampton before leaving. General Beauregard retreated to Charlotte

——, Confederate General Hardee evacuated Charleston, South Carolina, setting fires in city, which was occupied by union army

Feb. 18, Columbia occupied by General Sherman, and Charleston by General Gillmore

——, General Robert E. Lee declared it "not only expedient but necessary" that the Confederate army use the slaves as soldiers

——, Fort Anderson, North Carolina, bombarded by Admiral Porter, evacuated by Confederate General Hoke in the evening before arrival of Union troops of Generals Schofield and Terry marching to cut off retreat. Occupied by Union troops on the 19th

Feb. 20–21, Joint expedition of Admiral Porter and General Terry captured Fort Lee and Fort Strong in Cape Fear River, North Carolina

Feb. 21, Bill authorizing use of slaves as soldiers passed by House Feb. 20 indefinitely postponed by action of Confederate Senate, later forced to reconsider

Feb. 22, Kentucky rejected the XIIIth Amendment, Tennessee by popular vote ratified Constitution abolishing slavery, all ordinances and laws of secession and Confederate debts contracted

——, Confederate General Johnston appointed by General Lee to command the Army of Tennessee and all troops in the Depts. of South Carolina, Georgia, and Florida

——, Wilmington, North Carolina, evacuated by Confederates, occupied by General Schofield

Feb. 23, Minnesota ratified the XIIIth Amendment, Maryland rejected

——, General Sherman arrived at Goldsborough, North Carolina

Feb. 25, Governor Johnson of Tennessee proclaimed adoption of the new Constitution

Feb. 27, General Sheridan with General Wesley Merritt, General G. A. Custer, and Colonel Capehart left Winchester on raid to destroy enemy supply depots and communications in central Virginia

March 1, Wisconsin ratified the XIIIth Amendment, New Jersey rejected

March 2, General Robert E. Lee wrote to General Grant asking for conference to consider settlement of difficulties, proposal declined as directed by President Lincoln unless in military matter as to surrender of army

——, At Waynesboro, Virginia, General Custer of Sheridan's cavalry surprised and defeated General Early who escaped but most of his command captured

March 3, General Howard of Sherman's army defeated Generals Hardee and Hampton near Cheraw and occupied Cheraw, South Carolina, capturing large quantities of Confederate guns and ammunition

March 4, President Lincoln inaugurated for second term, Chief Justice Chase administering the oath, Andrew Johnson, Vice-President

——, William G. Brownlow elected Governor of Tennessee

——, New Confederate flag established by Act of Congress

March 5, General Sheridan defeated Confederate General Early in battle between Staunton and Charlottesville, Virginia

March 7, Hugh McCulloch, of Indiana, appointed Secretary of the Treasury

March 8–10, Battle of Kinston, North Carolina. Attack of Confederate General Bragg repulsed by General Cox. Bragg retreated to join General Johnston at Goldsborough, Kinston occupied by General Schofield on the 14th

March 9, Vermont ratified the XIIIth Amendment

March 10, General Sherman occupied Fayetteville, North Carolina, and destroyed the arsenal and ironworks

March 11, Executive Proclamation required all absentees from army and navy to return to duty within 60 days or forfeit their rights and privileges as citizens

March 13, President Davis signed Bill authorizing use of slaves as soldiers in the Confederate armies

March 14, Death of Jared Sparks, historian and biographer, and former president of Harvard College

March 15, Sherman's army started march north from Fayetteville, North Carolina

March 16, Battle of Averysborough, North Carolina. General Slocum attacked and defeated Confederate army commanded by General Hardee who retired during the night pursued by Union forces

——, Confederate General G. T. Beauregard announced as second in command of Johnston's army

March 18, Second Confederate Congress, second session adjourned

March 19, Sheridan arrived at White House, Pamunkey River, Virginia. He had destroyed the Virginia Railroad for miles and the James River Canal besides driving General Early from the Shenandoah Valley

March 19-21, Battle of Bentonville, North Carolina. Confederate attack under General Johnston on General Slocum of Sherman's army repulsed by arrival of reinforcements under General Howard. General Johnston retired during night of the 21st towards Raleigh

March 21-April 25, General Stoneman made raid in eastern Tennessee, southwestern Virginia, and western North Carolina

March 21, General Schofield occupied Goldsborough, North Carolina

March 22-April 24, General Wilson in cavalry raid from Chickasaw to Selma, Alabama and Macon, Georgia

March 23, General Sherman reached Goldsborough, North Carolina

March 25, Fort Stedman in front of Petersburg, Virginia, attacked and taken by Confederate General J. B. Gordon after a number of pretended deserters had got into fort, but was unable to hold it for lack of support, retaken March 27

March 27, General Sheridan with 10,000 cavalry joined the Army of the Potomac before Petersburg, Virginia, returning from raid through the Shenandoah Valley

——, General Canby began siege of Mobile, Alabama, with investment of Spanish Fort

March 29, General Grant began Appomattox campaign with movement to southwest of Petersburg, line from the Appomatox River to Dinwiddie Court House

March 31, Confederate General Pickett's attack defeated Warren and forced Sheridan to retire from Five Forks to Dinwiddie Court House, Virginia

——, General Wilson destroyed furnaces and collieries at Montevallo, Alabama

, Union army numbered 980,086

April 1, Battle of Five Forks near Richmond, Virginia. General Sheridan with Generals Warren, Ayres, and Merritt turned the front of the Confederates and defeated Pickett. General Sheridan relieved General Warren of command of the fifth corps substituting Griffin in the afternoon. More than 5,000 prisoners taken, Sheridan's loss about 1,000 of whom 634 were of Warren's corps

——, Scientific expedition of Louis Agassiz sailed from New York reaching Rio de Janeiro, Brazil, April 23, where party divided into groups to explore rivers

——, At Ebeneezer Church, Alabama, General Wilson defeated Confederate General Forrest forcing his retreat towards Selma

April 2, General Grant in assault carried fortified lines in front of Petersburg, Virginia, General Wright capturing main works in their front and General Parke the outer lines. Confederate General A. P. Hill killed in this battle

——, President Davis in church received telegram from General Lee advising the evacuation of Richmond and of his intention to evacuate Petersburg that night. President Davis and his Cabinet except the Secretary of War left the city that night, arriving in Danville the next afternoon, and the army began evacuation

——, General Wilson again defeated Confederate General Forrest and took Selma, Alabama, Colonel Roddy and 3,000 prisoners taken, arsenal and armory destroyed

April 2-3, Evacuation of Richmond and Petersburg

completed by the Confederate Army of Northern Virginia in the early morning hours of the 3d

April 3, General Weitzel entered Richmond, Virginia, and received surrender of the city, and put out fire started by burning of cotton and tobacco by retreating Confederates, and Union troops occupied Petersburg

April 4, President Lincoln arrived at Richmond from City Point, spending the night

——, General Lee's army reached Amelia Court House, Virginia, on the Richmond and Danville Railroad, where he found supplies ordered for his starving soldiers had been sent on by error to Richmond

——, General Wilson captured and destroyed Tuscaloosa, Alabama

April 5, Sheridan at Jetersville, Virginia, held the Richmond and Danville Railroad, keeping supplies from Danville from reaching Lee's army, and cutting off Confederate retreat in that direction

April 6, Battle of Sailor's Creek, Virginia. General Custer with Crook and Devin in engagement with Confederate General Ewell, and with Wright with the sixth corps forced surrender of Ewell, 5 generals and more than 7,000 men with several hundred wagons and many guns taken

——, General Ord's troops in engagement with advance of Lee's army advancing to Farmville at High Bridge, Confederates checked

April 7, General Grant sent note to General Lee calling upon him to surrender to prevent further bloodshed, and Lee replied asking what terms would be offered

——, Federal advance under Humphreys attacked Confederates north of Farmville and was repulsed

——, W. G. Brownlow inaugurated as civil Governor of Tennessee, XIIIth Amendment ratified

April 8, General Grant and General Lee exchanged notes, General Grant gave terms as disqualification of officers and men from taking up arms against the United States until properly exchanged, Lee proposed to treat for peace, to which Grant replied that he had no authority to treat for peace (April 9)

——, Confederate Spanish Fort, defense of Mobile, Alabama, evacuated as result of joint Union attack of army and navy

——, General Custer seized Confederate supply train at Appomattox station and barred road before Lee's retreating army

——, Missouri Convention adopted Constitution; ratified by popular vote June 6

April 9, General Lee in early morning attacked Sheridan's cavalry, General Gordon leading charge which failed as Generals Ord and Griffin arrived to support

——, General Lee sent flag of truce to General Grant asking to have interview to arrange terms of surrender. The two generals met at Appomattox Court House at 11 o'clock, and General Grant received surrender of 27,805 men, officers gave paroles not to take up arms against the United States until exchanged

——, Confederate Government moved to Greensborough, North Carolina

——, Fort Blakely, Alabama, defense of Mobile, carried by Union assault, and garrison of 4,000 captured

April 10, General Sherman's army left Goldsborough arriving at Raleigh, North Carolina, April 13

April 11, Forts Huger and Tracy on Mobile Bay, Alabama, evacuated by Confederates after bombardment, occupied by Union naval force commanded by Commander W. W. Low

April 12, Mobile, Alabama, surrendered to General Granger. Confederate force of General Maury had evacuated the city the night before retiring towards Meridian

——, Montgomery, Alabama, surrendered to General Wilson

April 14, The Union flag raised over Fort Sumter, Charleston, South Carolina

——, General Sherman received letter from General Johnston asking for terms of surrender

——, President Lincoln shot and mortally wounded in box at Ford's Theatre, Washington, by John Wilkes Booth, who made his escape. Secretary Seward stabbed while ill in bed at same hour in the evening by Lewis Powell, alias Payne, a fellow conspirator of Booth, both members of group of fanatical secessionists

April 15, Death of President Lincoln at 7.22 A.M.

——, Andrew Johnson, Vice-President, took the oath of office as President

——, Military Order of the Loyal Legion organized

April 16, West Point, Georgia taken by Colonel O. H. La Grange of Wilson's command, and General Upton at Columbus took 1,500 prisoners and destroyed navy yard and arsenal

April 17, Surrender of Confederate General Mosby to General Hancock at Berryville, Virginia

April 18, General Sherman and Confederate General Johnston signed a memorandum of agreement of terms of peace providing for disbandment of Confederate armies, political recognition of existing State governments of Confederacy on the taking of oath of allegiance by executives and legislators, all persons to be guaranteed in their political rights. Sent to Grant for approval it was not accepted by President Johnson, disavowal communicated by General Grant in person to General Sherman April 24

——, Confederate Government moved to Charlotte, North Carolina

April 19, Funeral services of Abraham Lincoln held in Washington, and at Springfield, Illinois, where he was buried May 4

April 20, Arkansas ratified the XIIIth Amendment

——, General Wilson occupied Macon, Georgia, surrendered by Confederate Generals Howell Cobb, G. W. Smith, and W. W. Mackall held as prisoners of war

April 26, J. W. Booth and his accomplice, Herold, captured at Garrett farm beyond the Rappahannock, Herold surrendered, and Booth refusing was shot

——, Surrender of Confederate General Johnston to General Sherman with 31,243 men near Durham Station, North Carolina, on same terms as those given to General Lee

April 27, Cornell University chartered

April 29, Executive Order discontinued restrictions on domestic trade in all parts of territory east of the Mississippi River as far as that territory within the Union military lines

May 1, Union army numbered 1,100,516

——, Executive Order for trial of alleged assassins of Abraham Lincoln by a military commission, and commission appointed May 6, meeting May 8

May 2, Executive Order for arrest of Jefferson Davis, Clement C. Clay, Jacob Thompson, George N. Sanders, Beverly Tucker, William C. Cleary charged with complicity in assassination of Lincoln. $100,000 offered for capture of Davis

May 4, Surrender of Confederate General Richard Taylor to General Canby of all troops east of the Mississippi River at Citronelle near Mobile, Alabama, negotiations including fleet by Commodore Farrand to Admiral Thatcher

May 5, Connecticut ratified the XIIIth Amendment

May 9, Executive Order of the President put laws of the United States in operation in Virginia and supported Governor Francis H. Pierpont in his office

May 10, Jefferson Davis and Secretary Reagan captured at a camp in southern Georgia near Irwinville by a detachment of General Wilson's cavalry commanded by Lieutenant Colonel Benjamin D. Pritchard, and taken to Macon, Davis taken from Savannah to Fortress Monroe

——, Surrender of Confederate General Sam Jones at Tallahassee, Florida, to General McCook

——, Proclamation of President Johnson announced that "armed resistance to the authority of the Government in the insurrectionary States may be regarded at an end"

May 11, Formal surrender of Confederate fleet on Tombigee as agreed on May 4 to Captain Edward Simpson at Nanna Hubba Bluff, 4 vessels, 112 officers, 285 enlisted men, and 24 marines

——, Surrender of Confederate General Jeff Thompson to General Dodge's troops at Chalk Bluff, Arkansas

May 12, Major General Oliver O. Howard assigned to duty as Commissioner of the Bureau of Refugees, Freedmen, and Abandoned Lands

May 13, Colonel Barrett defeated in skirmish at Palmetto Ranch, Texas, by Confederate General Slaughter

May 15, James Harlan, of Iowa, appointed Secretary of the Interior

May 17, Dept. of the Gulf constituted of the States of Louisiana, Mississippi, Alabama, Florida, and District of Key West and the Tortugas, General E. R. S. Canby assigned to command, and Major General Philip H. Sheridan assigned to general command west of the Mississippi River and south of the Arkansas River

May 17–20, Surrender of Confederate troops in Florida to General Israel Vogdes

May 19, Surrender of the C.S.S. "Stonewall" by Confederate Commander Page to the Captain General of Cuba at Havana

——, Major General John A. Logan assigned to command Army of the Tennessee

May 22, Commercial restrictions on southern ports removed to take effect July 1 by Executive Order with certain exceptions

——, Insurrection declared ended in Tennessee and disabilities and disqualifications removed by Executive Order

——, Jefferson Davis imprisoned in Fortress Monroe

May 23, Review of the Army of the Potomac in Washington, and then disbanded

——, Loyal Government of Virginia which had existed during entire period of the war established itself at Richmond after recognition by the President of May 9

May 24, Sherman's army reviewed in Washington and disbanded

May 25, Sabine Pass, Texas, evacuated by Confederates

May 26, Confederate General E. Kirby Smith surrendered troops in Trans-Mississippi region to Major General E. R. S. Canby

May 26–June 9, Operations against Indians in Dakota and Colorado Territories

May 29, President Johnson's first proclamation of amnesty on condition of taking oath of obedience to the Constitution excluded those who had held civil, diplomatic, or military office under the Confederacy

——, Proclamation of President Johnson appointed William W. Holden Provisional Governor of North Carolina

June 2, L. P. Milligan, and W. A. Bowles condemned to be executed on this date as Sons of Liberty conspiring against the Government to aid Confederates; reprieved and sentence changed to imprisonment for life

——, Surrender of Galveston, Texas, last seaport held by Confederates

June 3, Lieutenant-Commander W. E. Fitzhugh received surrender of Lieutenant J. H. Carter and Confederate naval force under his command in Red River

June 8–14, Operations against Indians in Kansas and Colorado

June 13, Proclamation of the President appointed William L. Sharkey Provisional Governor of Mississippi

——, Proclamation of the President removed restrictions on commerce east of the Mississippi except as to contraband which remained under prohibition until Aug. 1, and Trans-Mississippi region included June 24

June 17, Proclamation of the President appointed James Johnson Provisional Governor of Georgia, and Andrew J. Hamilton Provisional Governor of Texas

June 21, Proclamation of the President appointed Lewis E. Parsons Provisional Governor of Alabama

June 23, Proclamation of the President rescinded the blockade as to foreign commerce

June 30, Proclamation of the President appointed Benjamin F. Perry Provisional Governor of South Carolina

July 1, New Hampshire ratified the XIIIth Amendment

July 7, According to decision of military tribunal appointed for trial of alleged assassins of Lincoln, David E. Herold, George A. Atzerodt, Lewis Payne (Powell), and Mrs. Mary E. Surrat were hanged, Michael O'Laughlin, Samuel Arnold, and Samuel A. Mudd received sentence June 30 of imprisonment for life and Edward Spangler to 6 years in military prison

July 11, International Commercial Convention at Detroit favored reciprocity with Canada

July 13, Proclamation of the President appointed William Marvin Provisional Governor of Florida

July 25, Agassiz scientific expedition left Rio de Janeiro and Aug. 20 Para, proceeding up the Amazon, and from Manaos Sept. 12 into Amazon valley

July 29, President Johnson provided for release of prisoners of war who would take the oath of allegiance

Aug. 14–26, Convention met at Jackson, Mississippi, adopted ordinance prohibiting slavery in the State Aug. 21, and declared secession ordinance null and void Aug. 22; provision made for election of officers and members of Congress

Aug. 29, Proclamation of the President removed all restrictions on trade with southern ports after Sept. 1

Sept. 1, National debt amounted to $2,846,000,000

Sept. 12–30, Constitutional Convention in Alabama adopted Constitution which was not submitted to popular vote, slavery abolished Sept. 22, secession ordinance declared null and void Sept. 20, and Confederate debt repudiated Sept. 28

Sept. 13, Convention met at Charleston, South Carolina, repealed ordinance of secession Sept. 15, declared slavery abolished Sept. 19, adopted Constitution Sept. 27

Oct. 2, Connecticut voted against negro suffrage

——, Instruction begun in the Massachusetts Institute of Technology in Boston

Oct. 2–19, Constitutional Convention met in Raleigh, North Carolina, passed ordinance prohibiting slavery forever Oct. 9, declared secession ordinance null and void Oct. 7, and Oct. 19 repudiated Confederate debt

Oct. 5, Benjamin G. Humphreys elected Governor of Mississippi, inaugurated Oct. 16

Oct. 11, Executive Order of the President paroled Alexander H. Stephens, John H. Reagan, George A. Trenholm, Charles Clark, and John A. Campbell

Oct. 12, Proclamation ended martial law in Kentucky

Oct. 17, Bricklayers and masons union founded

Oct. 21, Convention met at Milledgeville, Georgia, repealed ordinance of secession Oct. 30, declared slavery abolished Nov. 4, repudiated Confederate debt Nov. 8, sent memorial asking executive clemency for Jefferson Davis Oct. 31

Oct. 25, Convention at Tallahassee, Florida, declared secession ordinance annulled Oct. 28, and abolished slavery and repudiated the Confederate debt Nov. 6

Nov. 2, Commander Alexander Murray in the "Rhode Island" received Confederate ram "Stonewall" from Spanish authorities at Havana, Cuba

Nov. 6, The C.S.S. "Shenandoah" surrendered by Lieutenant James Waddell to British authorities at Liverpool, who delivered it to American Consul Dudley

Nov. 7, Minnesota and Wisconsin voted against negro suffrage. Only 6 northern States allowed colored men to vote, Maine, New Hampshire, Massachusetts, Vermont, and Rhode Island, New York requiring property qualification

Nov. 9, North Carolina elected officers and members of Congress. Ordinances repealing secession ordinance and the anti-slavery ordinance ratified by popular vote

Nov. 10, Captain Henry Wirz in charge of Union prisoners at Andersonville, Georgia, hanged by order of military commission before whom he was tried for cruelties to prisoners

Nov. 13, South Carolina ratified the XIIIth Amendment to the Constitution

Nov. 20, Legislature of Alabama met and ratified the anti-slavery Amendment Dec. 2

Nov. 22, Mississippi Act provided for regulation of master and apprentice for freedmen, free negroes, and mulattoes

Nov. 24, Mississippi Vagrant Act passed, Nov. 25, Act to confer civil rights on freedmen with supplementary laws Nov. 29 and Dec. 2 which practically enacted a slave code as to crimes and misdemeanors

Dec. 1, The President revoked the suspension of the writ of habeas corpus for all the United States except States of the former Confederacy, Kentucky, the District of Columbia, and Arizona and New Mexico Territories

Dec. 4, North Carolina legislature ratified the XIIIth Amendment

———, Mississippi legislature rejected the XIIIth Amendment (anti-slavery)

Dec. 5, Georgia legislature ratified the XIIIth Amendment

Dec. 9, Jonathan Worth declared elected Governor of North Carolina and took oath of office on the 15th

Dec. 11, Oregon ratified the XIIIth Amendment

Dec. 13, Robert M. Patton inaugurated Governor of Alabama

Dec. 16, Napoleon's Government informed that the United States would not tolerate the presence of French troops or a foreign monarchy in Mexico

Dec. 18, Secretary Seward declared the XIIIth Amendment to the Constitution abolishing slavery ratified by 27 States and in effect

Dec. 20, California ratified the XIIIth Amendment

Dec. 28, Florida ratified the XIIIth Amendment

CONGRESS

Jan. 30, Joint Resolution reserved mineral lands from operation of laws granting public lands

Jan. 31, Joint Resolution of the XIIIth Amendment to the Constitution reconsidered in House and passed by vote of 121 to 24, 37 not voting

Feb. 1, Resolution authorizing submission of the XIIIth Amendment to the Constitution abolishing slavery to the States for ratification signed by the President

Feb. 8, Joint Resolution declared that States which had rebelled against the Government not entitled to representation in the Electoral College for choice of president and vice-president

Feb. 12, Electoral votes counted gave Lincoln and Johnson 212 out of 314 for reëlection, McClellan and Pendleton 21

Feb. 17, Confederate debt repudiated by the Senate

———, Act authorized establishment of ocean mail service with China

Feb. 18, Senator Trumbull moved for recognition of Louisiana, decision postponed by opposition of Charles Sumner

March 3, Freedmen's Bureau in the War Dept. for the care of refugees and freedmen established with a chief commissioner and assistant commissioners for each State in insurrection, May 12 Major General Oliver O. Howard appointed Commissioner

———, Freedmen's Bank incorporated in Washington

———, Permission to recruit in Confederate States repealed and stringent provisions against "bounty jumping" and fraudulent enlistment of convicts and insane enacted

———, Resolution adopted for appointment of joint commission to inquire into condition of Indian tribes and their treatment by civil and military authorities

———, Secretary of the Treasury authorized to borrow $600,000,000 and to issue bonds or treasury notes, bonds due in 40 years, rate of interest 6%

———, Joint Resolution made the wives and children of colored soldiers free

———Tax, of 10% imposed on notes issued by State banks after July 1, 1866

———, National Bank Act amended

———, Confederate debt repudiated by the House

———, Congress adjourned

March 4–11, Senate met in special session

Dec. 4, Thirty-ninth Congress, 1st session. Members elected from the reorganized former Confederate States refused recognition and admission

Dec. 14, Joint Committee on Reconstruction constituted by appointment by House of Thaddeus Stevens, Elihu B. Washburn, Justin S. Morrill, Henry Grider, John A. Bingham, Roscoe Conklin, George S. Boutwell, Henry T. Blow, and Andrew J. Rogers

Dec. 18, Mr. Stevens in House spoke on reconstruction advocating doctrine that the territory which had seceded was a conquered district and if States should ever be erected again it must be by the provision of the Constitution that declared that "new States may be admitted by Congress into this Union"

Dec. 21, The Senate appointed as members of Joint Committee on Reconstruction William Pitt Fessenden, James W. Grimes, Ira Harris, Jacob M. Howard, Reverdy Johnson, and George H. Williams

1866

Jan. 17, Strike of engineers and firemen on Michigan Southern and Northern Indiana railroads against new system of work and pay

Jan. 23, New Jersey ratifies the XIIIth Amendment to the Constitution

Jan. 24, Iowa ratified the XIIIth Amendment

Feb. 3–18 and March 2–Sept. 1, Strike of street car employees in New York City

Feb. 22, President Johnson made speech from steps of the White House denouncing attitude of Congress towards reconstruction, calling the Joint Committee on Reconstruction "an irresponsible central Directory" that had assumed "all the powers of Congress"

———, Mass meetings held in northern cities to sustain President Johnson. In New York City meeting at Cooper Union at which Francis B. Cutting presided and Seward was the chief speaker

March 6, Club formed in Washington of leading senators and other supporters of the President, which in June issued call for a "National Union Convention" to meet in Philadelphia in August

March 17, Termination of Reciprocity Treaty of June, 1854 with Canada

April 2, Proclamation of the President declared the Civil War at an end except in Texas

April 5, Official announcement made that French troops would be removed from Mexico. See Mexico

April 6, First post of the Grand Army of the Republic organized at Decatur, Illinois, by Dr. Benjamin F. Stephenson, General Isaac C. Pugh, post commander

April 10, Henry Bergh organized the Society for the Prevention of Cruelty to Animals

May 25, L. D. Campbell appointed Minister to Mexico, accredited to President Juarez

May 29, Death of General Winfield Scott at West Point, New York (80)

May 31, Fenians from Buffalo, New York, made raid across the Niagara River into Canada

June 1, Fenians led by John O'Neill seized Fort Erie across from Buffalo, but were defeated by Canadian troops the next day at Ridgeway and retreated across the border June 3

June 6, President Johnson issued a Proclamation against the Fenians invading Canada, ordering strict enforcement of the neutrality laws

June 7, Fenians occupied St. Armand just over the Vermont border in Quebec

June 14, Muscogee or Creek Indians released lands in Indian Territory to the United States by treaty

June 17, Death of General Lewis Cass, statesman, at Detroit, Michigan

June 25, Tariff Treaty with Japan signed

June 30, Connecticut ratified the XIVth Amendment

July 4, Great fire in Portland, Maine, in which 1,500 buildings burned

July 7, Proclamation revoked Louisiana Constitution of 1864 and appointed July 4 as date of reconvoking the Constitutional Convention of 1864

——, New Hampshire ratified the XIVth Amendment

July 13, War Dept. Order released all persons undergoing sentences by military courts with certain exceptions

July 19, Tennessee ratified the XIVth Amendment

——, First faculty elected for University of Kansas at Lawrence

July 23, Henry Stanberry, of Ohio, appointed Attorney General

July 25, Alexander W. Randall, of Wisconsin, appointed Postmaster General

July 26, American Association for the Relief of Misery on Battlefields organized in New York, Dr. W. H. Bellows, president

July 27, The "Great Eastern" steamship brought Cyrus W. Field's Atlantic cable into fishing village of Heart's Content, on Trinity Bay, Newfoundland, establishing connection with Ireland and successfully completing the work; 2 earlier attempts had failed

——, Orville H. Browning, of Illinois, appointed Secretary of the Interior

July 30, Race riot in New Orleans on occasion of the assembling of the Constitutional Convention. Police fired on citizens, and more than 200 persons killed or wounded, mostly negroes

Aug. 2–4, Constitution adopted for North Carolina May 24 and rejected by the people in election

Aug. 14, National Union Convention of supporters of President Johnson met in Philadelphia

Aug. 20, Proclamation of the President declared the insurrection and Civil War at an end in every part of the country (including Texas)

——, Second Labor Conference held in Baltimore, Maryland, 72 delegates from 13 States and the District of Columbia

Aug. 28, President Johnson accompanied by Seward, Welles, Randall, General Grant, and Admiral Farragut left Washington for Chicago to take part in ceremony of laying corner stone of monument to Stephen A. Douglas (Johnson's electioneering tour, popularly called "swinging around the circle")

Aug., The American vessel "General Sherman" believed by the Koreans to be on expedition to plunder tombs of the Korean kings burned and crew killed

Sept. 3, Convention of Southern Republicans met in Philadelphia to confer with Republican members of the Congressional Party of the North opposed to policy of the President

——, President Johnson defended his policy in speech in Cleveland

Sept. 6, President Johnson laid the cornerstone of the monument to Stephen A. Douglas in Chicago

Sept. 7, The cable broken in 1865 raised and landed in Newfoundland

Sept. 8, President Johnson in speech at St. Louis accused the "radical Congress" of planning the New Orleans riot

Sept. 11, New Jersey ratified the XIVth Amendment

Sept. 17, Convention of war veterans supporting the President met in Cleveland, Ohio, the "Soldiers' and Sailors' Convention"

Sept. 19, Oregon ratified the XIVth Amendment

Sept. 25–26, Convention of Republican war veterans met in Pittsburgh, General J. D. Cox, presiding, and upheld Congress in its opposition to the Administration over the question of reconstruction

Oct. 12, Attorney General Stanberry advised transfer of case of Jefferson Davis to the civil authorities

Oct. 13, Texas voted against ratification of the XIVth Amendment

Oct. 24, Peabody Institute formally inaugurated in Baltimore, Maryland, George Peabody present

Nov., The Government of Brazil contracted with Lansford Warren Hastings, Confederate, for land for colony at the mouth of the Tapajos River. The first 115 colonists arrived in Sept. 1867

Nov. 9, Georgia voted against ratification, and Vermont ratified the XIVth Amendment

Nov. 20, First National Convention of the Grand Army of the Republic met at Indianapolis

Dec. 3, Florida voted against ratification of the XIVth Amendment

Dec. 7, Alabama voted against ratification of the XIVth Amendment

Dec. 8, Act of Georgia recognized the Freedmen's Bureau by making all contracts of apprenticeship made through its agents valid

Dec. 13, North Carolina voted against ratification of the XIVth Amendment

Dec. 17, Arkansas voted against ratification of the XIVth Amendment

Dec. 20, South Carolina rejected the XIVth Amendment

Dec. 21, Sioux Indians massacred troops commanded by Lieutenant-Colonel Fetterman at Fort Philip Kearney near Big Horn, Wyoming

——, John H. Surratt arrested in Alexandria, Egypt, and taken on board American vessel "Swatara"

CONGRESS

Feb. 19, Bill to enlarge powers of the Freedmen's Bureau passed by the Senate Jan. 25 and by the House Feb. 6, vetoed by President Johnson

Feb. 20, The House adopted a Resolution which was later concurred in by Senate that no senator or representative should be admitted from any of the 11 Southern States until Congress had declared such State entitled to representation

Feb. 26, Resolution to authorize and detail a steam vessel from the Pacific squadron to assist in laying cable at Bering Strait

March 2, Enacted that neither House should admit a member from any State which had seceded until a vote of Congress had declared the State entitled to representation

March 27, Civil Rights Bill passed by Congress March 16 vetoed by President Johnson because it conferred citizenship on the negroes when 11 out of 36 States were unrepresented, and attempted to fix by Federal law "a perfect equality of the white and black races in every State of the Union"

April 9, Civil Rights Bill became law passed over the

veto of the President, gave same civil rights to all persons born in the United States (except Indians) and provided for protection of persons in their civil rights and furnished the means of their vindication

April 12, Act authorized the gradual retirement of greenbacks from the currency

May 5, The boundary of Nevada extended one degree east to include territory formerly in Utah

——, International Ocean Telegraph Company granted right to lay cable from Florida to the Bahamas, Cuba, and other West Indian islands

May 15, Bill to admit Colorado as a State returned to Senate with the President's objections

June 16, The XIVth Amendment to the Constitution giving the negro rights of citizenship which was passed by the Senate June 8 and the House June 13 sent to the States for ratification

June 18, Committee on Reconstruction presented report declaring that the Confederate States were not entitled to representation, but must be reconstructed with special legislation and special guarantees

June 21, Hydrographic Office established in the Navy Dept.

July 2, Bill introduced in the House for the admission of Canada to the Union

July 13, First reduction of war time internal revenue to take effect Aug. 1, tax on coal and pig iron, and on slaughtered cattle removed. The taxes on manufactures lowered but tax on cotton raised from 2 to 3 cents per pound, working great hardship for the South

July 16, Act to continue the Freedmen's Bureau for 2 years passed over the veto of the President

July 24, Tennessee readmitted by Joint Resolution

July 25, Act regulated time and manner of holding elections by legislatures of States for senators of the United States

——, Grades of admiral (for D. G. Farragut), vice-admiral (for D. D. Porter), and general in the army (for U. S. Grant) revived

——, Public lands granted to California, Kansas, Arkansas, Oregon, and Missouri for railroad and telegraph

July 27, The Southwest Pacific reorganized as the Atlantic and Pacific Railroad, to run from Springfield, Missouri to the Pacific on or near the 35th parallel, 2,000 miles; subsidized by grant of 42,000,-000 acres of land

July 28, Members of Congress from Tennessee readmitted

——, Act authorized the use of the metric system of weights and measures

——, Internal Revenue Act made tax on cigars $3 per pound with 50% ad valorem in addition, and three cents a pound on cotton

——, Act increased and fixed military peace establishment at 5 regiments of artillery, 10 of cavalry, and 45 of infantry

——, Congress adjourned

Dec. 3, Thirty-ninth Congress, 2d sess. convened

Dec. 14, Bill passed by Congress established universal male suffrage in the District of Columbia, including negroes. Exception made of persons who had given "aid and comfort to the rebels"; vetoed by the President Jan. 5

Dec. 17, Decision of Supreme Court in Milligan case that no branch of the Government had the power to suspend the writ of habeas corpus where the

courts were open, and against the action of the military commission, and the Secretary of War directed the release of Milligan, Bowles, and Horsey from the Ohio State Penitentiary. "This decision of the court overthrew the whole doctrine of military arrest and trial of private citizens in peaceful states" (Lalor. Cyclopedia of Political Science)

1867

Jan. 8, Maryland voted against ratification of the XIVth Amendment; Virginia, Jan. 9; Mississippi Jan. 30

Jan. 10, New York ratified the XIVth Amendment; Ohio, Jan. 11; Illinois, Jan. 15; West Virginia, Jan. 16; Kansas, Jan. 18; Maine, Jan. 19; Nevada, Jan. 22; Missouri, Jan. 26; Indiana, Jan. 29

Jan. 14, In case of Cummings vs. Missouri the Supreme Court decided that a State test oath excluding Confederate sympathizers from professions was a violation of the prohibition of *ex post facto* laws. The Court applied the same rule to the Federal test oath

Jan. 20, Death of Nathaniel P. Willis (born 1807) at Idlewild on the Hudson

Jan. 23, Mrs. Elizabeth Cady Stanton addressed New York State Assembly in behalf of woman suffrage

Jan. 30, Mississippi voted against the XIVth Amendment

Feb. 1, Minnesota ratified the XIVth Amendment, Rhode Island, Feb. 7; Wisconsin and Pennsylvania, Feb. 13; Michigan, Feb. 15

Feb. 6, Louisiana and Delaware voted against ratification of the XIVth Amendment

Feb. 8, Treaty of amity, commerce, and navigation with the Dominican Republic signed

Feb. 13, Acts of Mississippi repealed severe provisions of 1865 against the negro and gave him nearly full civil rights

Feb. 17, Death of Alexander Dallas Bache at Newport, Rhode Island

Feb. 19, Treaty with certain bands of the Dakotas by which the Indians ceded Lake Travere reservation

Feb. 23, Treaty with the Kansas Indians provided for their removal to Indian Territory

March 1, Proclamation of the President declared Nebraska admitted to the Union (37th State)

March 2, The University of Illinois, at Urbana, incorporated Feb. 28, opened

March 6, Death of Charles F. Browne (Artemus Ward) at Southampton, England

March 11, General Order issued by the President through the Adjutant-General's Office assigned commanders to military districts created by the Reconstruction Act, General J. M. Schofield to first district; General D. E. Sickles, second district; General G. H. Thomas, third district; General E. O. C. Ord, fourth district; General P. H. Sheridan, fifth district

March 16, Henry Barnard appointed Commissioner of Education

March 20, Massachusetts ratified the XIVth Amendment

March 23, Maryland voted against ratification of the XIIIth and XIVth Amendments

March 26, Michigan granted limited school suffrage to women

March 30, Treaty signed for the purchase of Alaska from Russia for $7,200,000; proclaimed June 20

April 15, Decision of Supreme Court in the case of the appeal of Mississippi to have Andrew Johnson enjoined from executing the Reconstruction Acts that the Court lacked jurisdiction

——, Stevens Institute of Technology at Hoboken, New Jersey, founded by will of Edward A. Stevens

April 30, Expedition against the Indians in western Kansas begun by Generals Hancock and Custer. General Hancock in this campaign burned village of 300 Cheyenne and Sioux lodges considering the Indians hostile. The Commissioner of Indian Affairs asked $100,000 to reimburse Indians for the destruction of property

May 1, Howard University, Washington, D.C. opened, organized Nov. 17, 1866, at missionary meeting of First Congregational Church

May 8, New Constitution framed by constitutional convention at Annapolis, Maryland; ratified by vote of the people Sept. 18

May 13, Decision of the Supreme Court that it had no jurisdiction in the case of Georgia against Stanton, Grant, and Pope, asking the Court to enjoin them against enforcing the Reconstruction Acts

——, Jefferson Davis brought before Judge Underwood of the United States Circuit Court for district of Virginia at Richmond, and admitted to bail. Horace Greeley volunteered to be one of the bondsmen

June 10, Trial of John H. Surratt in criminal court of the District of Columbia begun, concluded July 26, and discharged Aug. 10, the jury failing to agree; Surratt released from prison June 22

June 15, Nebraska ratified the XIVth Amendment

June 20, Instructions of the President to the commanders of the southern military districts issued

July 31, Death of Catherine Maria Sedgwick near Roxbury, Massachusetts

Aug. 5, Secretary Stanton asked to resign by the President for "public considerations," refused

Aug. 12, Executive Order of the President suspended Secretary Stanton and appointed General Grant to act as Secretary of War *ad interim*

——, Wrangel Island named by American Captain Thomas Long on offshore survey landing from U.S.S. "Corwin" and possession taken for the United States

Aug. 16, Contract between the Union Pacific Railroad Company and Oakes Ames by which he was to build 677 miles of railroad, profits to be divided among stockholders of the Crédit Mobilier

Aug. 17, Order of the President relieved General Sheridan as commander in the fifth military district embracing Louisiana and Texas because of unconciliatory measures in dealing with the conquered South, and General Hancock appointed in his stead

Aug. 23, Secretary Seward tendered his resignation to the President who refused to accept it

Aug. 26, General Sickles replaced by General Canby as commander in second military district of the Carolinas

Sept. 7, General amnesty proclaimed by the President

Sept. 17, National cemetery dedicated at Antietam

Sept. 18, Maryland Constitution ratified by popular vote

Sept. 19, First newspaper in Wyoming, the *Cheyenne Evening Leader* by N. A. Baker, began publication, followed Oct. 25 by the *Daily Argus* established by L. L. Bedell

Oct. 3, Death of Elias Howe, inventor, at Brooklyn, New York

Oct. 18, Formal transfer of Alaska to the United States, General Rousseau taking possession

Oct. 24, Treaty for the purchase of the Danish West Indies concluded; rejected by Senate March, 1870

Nov. 5, Amendment to Kansas Constitution to strike out the word "white" is defeated by vote of 19,421 against to 10,483 in favor. For striking out the word "male" the vote 19,875 against and 9,070 in favor

Nov. 5–Dec. 6, Constitutional Convention in Alabama framed Constitution

Nov. 13, Coast Artillery School at Fort Monroe, Virginia, established

Nov. 19, Charles Dickens arrived in Boston on second visit to the United States

Nov. 22, Constitutional Convention at New Orleans adopted new Constitution for Louisiana which prohibited slavery, declared secession ordinance null and void, and disenfranchised Confederate soldiers

Nov. 29, General Hancock assumed command in New Orleans (fifth district)

Nov., Votes to amend Constitution to extend suffrage without regard to color were taken in Kansas and Minnesota and decided in the negative

Dec. 3–20, Constitutional Convention met at Richmond, Virginia

Dec. 4, The Grangers organized in Washington as Patrons of Husbandry by employees of the Dept. of Agriculture, beginning of large political associations throughout the United States

Dec. 9–March 11, Constitutional Convention met at Atlanta and framed Constitution for Georgia

Dec. 28, General I. McDowell appointed to command the fourth military district, and Major General George C. Meade to the third district succeeding General Pope removed

The Wool Growers Association and the Wool Manufacturers Association met at Syracuse and formed an alliance to recommend to Congress increase of tariff on wool

Midway Island 1,200 miles northwest of Honolulu taken possession of by the United States

CONGRESS

Jan. 7, James M. Ashley in House charged President Johnson "with a usurpation of power and violation of law" in corruptly using the powers of appointment, pardon, and veto, corruptly disposing of public property, and interference in elections; charges referred to Committee on the Judiciary for investigation by vote of 108 to 39

Jan. 8, Act passed over the veto of the President ordered negro suffrage in the District of Columbia

Jan. 21, Act passed which repealed the clause in Act of July 17, 1862 giving the President authority to proclaim general amnesty

Jan. 22, Act provided that the next Congress and all succeeding ones should first assemble March 4 instead of in December

Jan. 24, Universal suffrage for all the Territories established by Act which the President allowed to become a law without his signature

Jan. 29, Bill to admit Colorado as a State vetoed by the President

Jan. 30, Bill to admit Nebraska as a State vetoed by the President

Jan. 31, Elective Franchise Act for the Territories provided that there should be no denial of elective franchise to any citizen on account of race, color, or previous condition of servitude

Feb. 5, Appeals from the federal circuit courts to the Supreme Court in habeas corpus cases extended to "all cases where any person may be restrained of his or her liberty, in violation of the Constitution or of any treaty or law of the United States"

Feb. 9, Nebraska admitted as a State (37th) over the President's veto, condition made that negroes should have the vote

Feb. 13, Reconstruction Bill passed House by vote of 109 to 55, not voting 26, providing for establishment of military government in 10 States not restored to the Union, restoration to be effected only after constitutional reorganization on basis of enfranchisement of the negroes and limited disenfranchisement of Confederates, and passage by legislature of the XIVth Amendment to the Constitution

March 2, Reconstruction Act passed over veto of the President, the States not restored to the Union declared to have no legal government, and divided into 5 military districts to be placed under military governors

——, Cyrus W. Field presented with gold medal and vote of thanks for his successful achievement of the Atlantic cable

——, Tenure of Office Act prohibited the President from removing civil officers except with consent of the Senate, became law over the President's veto

——, Third federal Bankruptcy Act established uniform system of bankruptcy throughout the United States

——, Act established Dept. of Education and Commissioner of Education

——, Joint Resolution prohibited payment by any officer of the Government to any person not known to have been opposed to the Rebellion and in favor of its suppression

——, Act declared valid certain proclamations and acts of the President in suppression of rebellion from March 4, 1861 to July 1, 1866 as to martial law and military trials

——, Duty increased on imported wools and woolens

——, Peonage abolished in New Mexico and other parts of the United States

——, Internal revenue Act reduced rate on cotton to 2.5 cents, removed tax on steel, certain articles of clothing and manufactured products, and exempted incomes under $1,000, incomes in excess of $1,000, 5%

——, "Rider" to Army Appropriation Act provided that the headquarters of the Army of the United States should be in Washington and all orders and instructions from the President or Secretary of War should be issued through it. Section 5 prohibited whipping or maiming negroes in view of certain State laws

——, Act provided that the Federal Government should assume the government of Virginia

March 3, Coal land Act regulated and limited sale of public lands bearing coal

March 4, Congress adjourned (39th) and Fortieth Congress, 2d sess. convened

March 23, Supplementary Reconstruction Act passed over veto of the President provided in detail for administration of districts by military commanders. Registration by vote based on oath which disenfranchised the majority of the white people

March 29, Congress adjourned to July 3

April 1–19, The Senate met in special session

April 9, Treaty for purchase of Alaska ratified by the Senate

July 3, Congress reassembled

July 19, Second supplementary Reconstruction Act passed over veto of the President substituted instructions for those issued by the President to commanders of southern military districts extending military government

July 20, Peace Commission constituted to treat with the Indians

——, Congress adjourned to Nov. 21

Nov. 21, Congress reassembled

Nov. 25, Report of the Committee of the Judiciary on charges against the President resolved that President Johnson "be impeached for high crimes and misdemeanors"

Dec. 2, Congress adjourned

1868

Jan. 7, Constitutional Convention in Arkansas adopted new Constitution Feb. 11, ratified March 13

Jan. 7–May 15, Constitutional Convention in Mississippi at Jackson under the Reconstruction Act framed Constitution; rejected by popular vote June 28

Jan. 9, General Gillem took command of the fourth district

Jan. 13, Edwin M. Stanton reinstated as Secretary of War

Jan. 14–March 16, Constitutional Convention under the Reconstruction Act met at Raleigh, and framed Constitution for North Carolina; ratified by popular vote April 23

Jan. 15, Ohio withdrew ratification of the XIVth Amendment

Jan. 30, Governor Charles J. Jenkins of Georgia removed by General Meade

Feb. 3, Will of Matthew Vassar left money to found Vassar College

Feb. 4, Alabama rejected new Constitution by popular vote

Feb. 8, Consular Treaty with Italy signed

Feb. 21, President Johnson dismissed Secretary Stanton from office of Secretary of War and appointed General Lorenzo Thomas Secretary *ad interim*

Feb. 22, Naturalization Treaty with Prussia (North German Union) signed, the first of a series by which European nations recognized the right of expatriation, the naturalization of Germans in the United States after 5 years' residence recognized

——, Secretary Stanton refused to give up his office to General Thomas and had the latter arrested

March 2, University of Illinois opened at Urbana

——, Constitutional Convention in Louisiana completed Constitution

March 11, New Constitution for Georgia adopted by Convention; ratified by vote of the people April 20

March 23, Extradition Treaty with Italy signed

——, University of California chartered (College of California of 1855)

March 27, Resolution of New Jersey legislature to withdraw previous ratification of the XIVth Amendment to the Constitution passed over veto of the Governor

March 28, General Hancock succeeded by General Buchanan as commander of the fifth military district, superseded because of interference with politics in the interests of honest government

March 31, Chinese embassy accompanying Anson Burlingame, retiring American Minister, to America, reached San Francisco
April 3, Iowa ratified the XIVth Amendment; Arkansas, April 6
April 6, Michigan voted against granting the vote to negroes
April 7, Constitution for Virginia adopted by Convention which had reassembled Jan. 2
April 14–16, New Constitution for South Carolina ratified by popular vote
April 18, New Constitution for Virginia ratified by popular vote and Henry C. Warmouth elected Governor
May 5, Commander-in-Chief John A. Logan of the Grand Army of the Republic issued a general order designating May 30 as Memorial Day for decoration of graves of soldiers who died for their country in the late Rebellion
May 12, Worcester Polytechnic Institute chartered
May 20, Republican National Convention met in Chicago, and nominated U. S. Grant for president on the first ballot, Schuyler Colfax, of Indiana, for vice-president on the fifth ballot
May 26, Resignation of Secretary of War Stanton in letter to the President
May 27, Treaty concluded with the Great and Little Osages
May 28, John M. Schofield, of Illinois, appointed Secretary of War, as of June 1
June 1, Death of James Buchanan, former President, at Wheatland, Pennsylvania
——, Chinese embassy received by Secretary Seward, and reception given for them at the White House June 5
——, General George Stoneman assigned to command in first military district relieving General Schofield
June 4, General I. McDowell assumed command in fourth military district
June 9, Florida ratified the XIVth Amendment
June 22–28, Mississippi in election rejected Constitution proposed
June 25, General Reynolds appointed to command the fifth military district
July 2, North Carolina legislature adopted the XIVth Amendment
July 4, Governor Holden inaugurated in North Carolina
——, General amnesty Proclamation of the President, with a few exceptions
——, Democratic Convention met in New York City, nominated Horatio Seymour for president July 9 on 22d ballot, Frank P. Blair for vice-president on first ballot
——, Legislature of Georgia met, Governor Bullock inaugurated and Sept. 3 expelled negro members; adjourned Oct. 6
July 8, *Daily New Mexico*, first newspaper in New Mexico published
July 9, Louisiana and South Carolina ratified the XIVth Amendment
July 11, Alabama legislature ratified the XIVth Amendment; approved by the Governor July 13
July 15, William M. Ewarts, of New York, appointed Attorney General
July 20, Secretary Seward announced the XIVth Amendment to the Constitution ratified in 29 States
July 21, Georgia ratified the XIVth Amendment to the Constitution

July 22, Governor Warmoth inaugurated Governor (civil) of Louisiana
July 28, Burlingame Treaty with China as to trade, consuls, and emigration concluded in Washington
——, Proclamation of ratification of the XIVth Amendment, and validity as part of Constitution
Aug. 11, Louisiana State Lottery established in New Orleans received charter
——, Death of Thaddeus Stevens at Washington
Aug. 17–18, Popular vote in Louisiana ratified Constitution
Sept. 22, Riot in New Orleans because of attempt to place white people under control of the colored people
Sept. 28, Race riot at Opelousas, Louisiana
Sept., The Louisiana legislature expelled the negro members
Oct. 11, Edison's first invention, the electrical vote recorder, patented
Oct. 15, Oregon withdrew consent to ratification of the XIVth Amendment
Oct. 26, Race riot at Parish of St. Bernard, Louisiana
Nov. 3, Election for president. Ulysses S. Grant, Republican, received 214 electoral votes and Schuyler Colfax, the same for vice-president. The popular vote was 3,015,071 against 2,709,613 cast for the Democratic candidates Horatio Seymour and F. P. Blair
Nov. 5–Feb. 13, 1869, Canadian River expedition against the Indians of New Mexico
Nov. 10, Claims Convention with Great Britain signed
Nov. 16, Naturalization Treaty with Belgium signed
Nov. 30–Dec. 1, Constitution of May 15 for Mississippi submitted to popular vote a second time was adopted, the vote against disenfranchisement of Confederate soldiers almost unanimous
Dec. 3, Trial of Jefferson Davis begun
Dec. 11, "Oyster" boundary line established temporary boundary between Maryland and Virginia
Dec. 25, Proclamation of the President gave final amnesty pardoning all concerned in the Rebellion including Jefferson Davis

CONGRESS

Jan. 13, Senate passed resolution refusing to concur in the suspension of Secretary of War Stanton from office. This decision immediately accepted by Stanton and Grant as lawful under the Tenure of Office Act
Feb. 3, Internal Revenue Act removed tax from cotton
Feb. 4, Contraction of greenbacks prohibited in Act to suspend further reduction of the currency
Feb. 21, Senate resolution declared the removal of the Secretary of War by the President on Feb. 21 illegal
——, Motion presented in House by Mr. Covode to impeach the President referred to Committee on Reconstruction
Feb. 22, Committee on Reconstruction (House) reported recommending resolution for impeachment of the President
Feb. 24, Resolution to impeach the President before the Senate carried in House by vote of 126 to 47
Feb. 25–May 26, The Senate sat as Court of Impeachment in case of President Andrew Johnson
March 2, Nine articles of impeachment against the President agreed upon in House and 2 more added the following day, Thaddeus Stevens, B. F. Butler, John A. Bingham, George S. Boutwell, James F. Wilson, Thomas Williams, and John A. Logan elected managers

March 5, The Senate convened as Court of Impeachment under presidency of the Chief Justice, summoned the President to appear and answer charges, and adjourned until March 13

March 11, Fourth Reconstruction Act provided that a majority of votes cast should decide adoption or rejection of proposed State Constitutions

March 13, Senate Court of Impeachment formally reopened and adjourned until March 23 giving the President 10 days instead of the 40 he asked for preparation of his answer to the 11 charges of violation of the Tenure of Office Act, and of high misdemeanors in his speeches

March 23, Answer of President Johnson to charges read in Senate Court, denial that Stanton's case was affected by the Tenure of Office Act, and defense of his right to make appointment *ad interim* in order to make up an issue before the Supreme Court whereby the constitutionality of the Act might be tested

March 27, Habeas Corpus Act of Feb. 5, 1867 repealed, passed over the veto of the President

——, Act to amend Judiciary Act repealed authorization of certain appeals from judges of circuit courts to Supreme Court thus preventing appeal to Supreme Court of cases under Reconstruction Acts

March 30, Trial of the President begun, the prosecution opened by B. F. Butler

March 31, Internal Revenue Act removed all taxes upon goods, wares, and manufactures except those on gas, illuminating oils, tobacco, liquors, and articles on which tax collected by stamps. Tax on all products of petroleum reduced one-half

April 9, Benjamin R. Curtis, counsel for the President, made opening speech in the defense before Senate Court

May 16, Senate voted on 11th article of impeachment as to whether or not the President of the United States was guilty of high misdemeanor as charged, resulting in 35 votes cast in the affirmative (not the two-thirds necessary) and 19 in the negative, making the vote an acquittal

May 26, Senate voted on 2d and 3d articles of impeachment with same result as upon the 11th, and adjourned *sine die* by vote of 34 to 16

May 28, General Schofield appointed Secretary of War to succeeded General Stanton resigned

June 22, Arkansas readmitted to Congress over the President's veto

June 25, Act established eight hour day for laborers employed by the Government

——, North Carolina, South Carolina, Alabama, Florida, Georgia, and Louisiana admitted to representation in Congress over the President's veto on condition of ratification of the XIVth Amendment

July 6, Act provided for discontinuance of the Freedmen's Bureau after Jan. 1 in States restored to former political relations with the United States

July 11, Act prescribed oath of office to be taken by persons from whom legal disabilities shall have been removed

July 20, Internal Revenue Act reduced taxation on spirits and tobacco and removed tax on petroleum

——, Education Dept. made an office of the Interior Dept. to take effect July 1, 1869

——, Joint Resolution excluded electoral votes of the former Rebel States

July 21, Concurrent Resolution declared the XIVth Amendment adopted by three-fourths of the States

of the Union naming States and including the "newly-constituted" legislatures of former Confederate States as qualified to vote

July 23, Act to authorize temporary supplying of vacancies in the executive departments

July 25, Wyoming Territory organized out of parts of Dakota, Utah, and Idaho

——, Act for payment of the public debt and reduction of rate of interest

——, Act removed legal and political disabilities of several hundred persons in Southern States

——, Act provided for discontinuance of Freedmen's Bureau after Jan. 1, 1869

July 27, Act provided for American line of mail and emigrant passenger steamers between New York and various ports of Europe

——, Act defined the rights of American citizens in foreign States

——, Alaska organized as a Territory

——, Congress adjourned

Dec. 7, Fortieth Congress, 2d sess. convened

1869

Jan. 13, National Convention of Colored Men met in Washington, Frederick Douglass, president

Jan. 14, Johnson-Clarendon Treaty with Great Britain signed in London provided for a commission for settlement of all claims against Great Britain since 1853 including the Alabama claims; rejected by Senate in April

Jan. 19–20, National Woman Suffrage Convention held in Washington

Jan. 21, Additional Consular and Extradition Agreement with Italy signed

Jan. 23, Massachusetts established the first Bureau of Labor in the United States

Feb. 11, A *nolle prosequi* entered in the case of Jefferson Davis

——, Treaty with the Sacs and Foxes of the Missouri and Iowa tribes, and Feb. 13 with the Otoe and Missouria Indians

Feb. 15, University of Nebraska chartered

Feb. 19, The case of Jefferson Davis dismissed from the docket

March 1, Nebraska ratified the XVth Amendment to the Constitution; West Virginia, March 3; North Carolina, Louisiana, and Illinois, March 5; Wisconsin, March 9; Michigan, March 8; Massachusetts and Maine, March 12; South Carolina, March 16; Pennsylvania, March 26; Arkansas, March 30

March 4, Inauguration of President Ulysses S. Grant, and Vice-President Schuyler Colfax

March 5, Executive Order of the President assigned General A. H. Terry to command of the Dept. of the South, General Meade to the Military Division of the Atlantic, General Sheridan to the Dept. of Louisiana, General W. S. Hancock to the Dept. of Dakota, General Canby to the first military district, General Reynolds to the fifth military district, General W. H. Emory to the Dept. of Washington, General Ames to the fourth military district superseding General Gillem

——, Elihu S. Washburn, of Illinois, appointed Secretary of State; Jacob D. Cox, of Ohio, Secretary of the Interior; Adolph E. Borie, of Pennsylvania, Secretary of the Navy; Ebenezer R. Hoar, of Massachusetts, Attorney General; John A. J. Creswell, of Maryland, Postmaster General

March 8, University of Deseret at Salt Lake City, Utah, organized

March 9, Convention of Republicans met at Petersburg, Virginia, and nominated H. H. Wells for Governor

——, A. T. Stewart nominated as Secretary of the Treasury withdrew because of Act of 1789 prohibiting an importer from holding office

March 11, George S. Boutwell, of Massachusetts, appointed Secretary of the Treasury; Hamilton Fish, of New York, Secretary of State; John A. Rawlins, of Illinois, Secretary of War

March 13, Treaty with the Kansas or Kaw Indians signed

——, Law against the Ku Klux passed in Arkansas

March 16, Lieutenant General P. H. Sheridan assigned to command of the Military Division of the Missouri, General Halleck to the Military Division of the South, General G. H. Thomas to the Military Division of the Pacific, and General Schofield to the Dept. of the Missouri to which Illinois added

March 27, General Stoneman removed Acting-Governor Wells of Virginia

April 2, Governor Wells, of Virginia, reinstated by General Webb who relieved General Stoneman, March 30

April 3, Chief of Staff to the General commanding the army abolished

April 12, Decision of the Supreme Court in the McCardle case that the Court lacked jurisdiction under Act of March 27, 1868, and in case of Texas vs. White that Texas had always legally remained a State of the Union in an "indissoluble relation" under the Constitution

——, Anti Ku Klux law passed in North Carolina

April 14, New York ratified the XVth Amendment

April 20, General E. R. S. Canby assumed command of the first military district (Virginia)

April 21, Governor Wells of Virginia resigned and G. C. Walker appointed Governor, by Canby

April 28, Convention of Conservatives at Richmond, Virginia, nominated G. C. Walker for Governor

May 4, Ohio rejected the XVth Amendment to the Constitution

May 10, The Union Pacific and the Central Pacific Railroad joined at Promontory Point near Ogden, Utah, and the Atlantic and Pacific coasts united. This event, the first trans-continental line, celebrated in many cities, in Chicago with a procession 7 miles long, in New York with a salute of 100 guns, and a thanksgiving service at Trinity Church

May 14, Proclamation of the President commanded that the new Constitution framed by Virginia Convention (Dec. 3, 1867) be submitted to the voters for ratification July 6

——, Indiana ratified the XVth Amendment, and Connecticut May 19

May 15, National Woman Suffrage Association formed by Lucy Stone Blackwell

May 18, Southern Commercial Convention met at Memphis, Tennessee, with 1,100 delegates from 22 States

May 19, Proclamation of the President directed heads of departments to see that no cut in wages accompanied the reduction of hours of labor to eight under law enacted

May 25, National Commercial Convention met at New Orleans, Louisiana

May 28, Colored Convention at Richmond, Virginia, adopted the Petersburg platform of March 9

June 1, Thomas A. Edison received first patent for electric apparatus for recording votes

June 12, Proclamation of the President removed discriminating dues levied on merchandise in French vessels

June 15, Florida ratified the XVth Amendment

——, Massachusetts appointed Board of Railroad Commissioners to supervise railroads, the first state railroad law

June 15–20, National Peace Jubilee held in Boston, Massachusetts, with chorus of 10,000 singers and orchestra of over 1,000 pieces conducted by P. S. Gilmore

June 23, Bureau of Labor Statistics established in Massachusetts

June 25, George M. Robeson, of New Jersey, appointed Secretary of the Navy, succeeding A. E. Borie, resigned

July 2, James G. Blaine "hesitated" over "liberal proposition" from Fisher, and subsequently accepted railroad bonds and received a commission on sales to friends in Maine

July 4–5, Irish National Republican Convention met in Chicago

July 6, Virginia adopted State Constitution at election, which recognized equal civil rights irrespective of race, color, or former condition. The disenfranchising clauses separately voted at polls and rejected. Gilbert C. Walker elected Governor

July 7, New Hampshire ratified the XVth Amendment

July 13, Chinese Immigration Convention met at Memphis, Tennessee, and adopted resolution that "the best interests of the South" required that "all legitimate inducements" should be offered "to encourage the immigration of Chinese laborers in large numbers . . ."

——, White laborers in San Francisco stoned Chinese in street riot

——, Proclamation of the President commanded resubmission of Constitution adopted by Mississippi Convention of May 15, 1868 to voters

July 23, French cable landed at Duxbury, Massachusetts, from St. Pierre Island off Newfoundland and connected with Brest, France

July 27, *New York Tribune* declared the plan to revive coolie trade in the South under plea of want of labor was "monstrous"

Aug. 16, National Labor Convention met in Philadelphia

Aug. 19, Proclamation of President Grant recognized the Cuban insurgents as belligerents. This paper "pigeon-holed" by Secretary Fish and never published

Sept. 1–2, National Temperance Convention met in Chicago, Illinois

Sept. 7, Commercial Convention met at Keokuk, Iowa

Sept. 8, Death of William Pitt Fessenden at Portland, Maine

Sept. 9, William T. Sherman, of Ohio, appointed Secretary of War

Sept. 12, National Prohibition Party organized by convention in Chicago

Sept. 24, "Black Friday" on Wall St., a panic due to attempt headed by Gould and Fisk to corner gold. Sale of gold by the Government prevented corner, bringing price down from 162 to 135

22</2>9424121410

Sept. 28, Horace Mann School for the Deaf opened in Boston

Oct. 4, Blaine in letter to Fisher asked him to inform Caldwell, director of Arkansas and Little Rock Railroad of Blaine's advice which saved Bill. *See infra* Congress, April 10

Oct. 5, Legislature of Virginia assembled at Richmond, the first regular session in ten years; ratified the XIVth and XVth Amendments Oct. 8

Oct. 8, Death of Franklin Pierce, former President, at Concord, New Hampshire

Oct. 9, Jefferson Davis arrived at Baltimore from England

Oct. 13, Commercial Convention held at Louisville, Kentucky

Oct. 19, Charles William Eliot inaugurated president of Harvard College

——, Adolph Sutro began work on tunnel to the Comstock lode from the foothills near the Carson River which was reached Sept. 1, 1878

Oct. 21, Vermont ratified the XVth Amendment

Oct. 25, William W. Belknap, of Iowa, appointed Secretary of War

Nov. 1, Columbus Delano, of Ohio, appointed Secretary of the Interior

——, United States Mint (branch) opened at Carson City, Nevada

Nov. 2, Election in New York ratified the new Constitution, but a majority of 40,000 voted against abolishing the property qualification for colored men

——, The people of Florida west of the Choctawhatchee River voted for annexation to Alabama with "the consent of Congress and consideration of $1,000,000 paid to Florida by Alabama"

Nov. 4, Death of George H. Peabody in London, England

Nov. 6, Death of Admiral Charles Stewart at Bordentown, New Jersey

Nov. 24, Alabama ratified the XVth Amendment

——, National Woman's Suffrage Convention met at Cleveland, Ohio, Reverend Henry Ward Beecher, president, and organized the Woman's Suffrage Association

Nov. 29, Annexation Treaty with Santo Domingo concluded; rejected by Senate in 1870

Nov. 30, Mississippi ratified new State Constitution rejected June 28, 1868, and rejected the disenfranchising and disqualifying clauses in separate vote

——, Texas by popular vote ratified adoption of State Constitution. E. J. Davis, aided by federal patronage and federal troops, elected Governor

Dec. 6, Colored National Labor Convention met in Washington

Dec. 9, A secret society organized by Stephens as Garment Cutter's Assembly of the Knights of Labor, in Philadelphia

Dec. 10, Territorial law enacted in Wyoming gave women the right to vote and hold office, first to grant full suffrage to women

Dec. 15, Resignation of Judge Grier of the Supreme Court to take effect Feb. 1, Edwin McMasters Stanton appointed Dec. 20 to succeed him

Dec. 24, General A. H. Terry assigned to the Georgia military district

——, Death of Edwin M. Stanton, former Secretary of War, in Washington, 4 days after his appointment to the Supreme Court

Dec. 30, The "Noble Order of Knights of Labor" organized by garment cutters in Philadelphia, first founded as a secret society by Smith Stephens, a tailor

CONGRESS

Jan. 11, The House voted to repeal the Tenure of Office Act in accordance with the known wishes of President-Elect Grant

Jan. 23, Miss Susan B. Anthony and Elizabeth Cady Stanton presented cause of woman suffrage before Committee of Senate, first congressional hearing granted to women

Feb. 18, Joint Resolution provided for removal of civil officers in Virginia, Texas, and Mississippi who would not take oath prescribed by Act of July 2, 1862

——, Senate Committee recommended rejection of Treaty Claims with Great Britain

Feb. 19, National banks prohibited from making loans on United States notes

Feb. 24, Duty on imported copper and copper ores passed over President's veto

Feb. 26, Fifteenth Amendment to the Constitution passed and by Resolution of Feb. 27 sent to the States for ratification, provided that the right of citizens to vote shall not be abridged or denied by the United States or by any State on account of race, color, or previous condition of servitude

March 3, Act provided for giving effect to treaty stipulations with foreign governments for extradition of criminals

——, Grant to Oregon for Coos Bay wagon road the last grant to State in aid of internal improvements

——, Congress adjourned

March 4, Forty-first Congress, 1st sess. convened

March 15, Joint Resolution introduced proposing Amendment to Constitution granting woman suffrage

March 18, Act gave equal political rights regardless of color to persons in the District of Columbia, striking out the word "white" in all laws and ordinances

——, Public Credit Act pledged the payment of all outstanding bonds and notes in coin or its equivalent and early redemption of greenbacks

April 5, Tenure of Office Act modified by substitution of certain clauses. "Congress let Lincoln remove any one he pleased from office; it refused Johnson the same privilege; and now it gives Grant a tether." *Nation*

April 10, Act imposing tax on spirits and tobacco amended

——, Act extended time for Little Rock and Fort Smith Railroad Company to complete first 20 miles extended, due to Blaine's ruling and recommendation

——, Act authorizing submission of the constitutions of Virginia, Mississippi, and Texas to popular vote required that the XVth Amendment to the Constitution must be ratified before admission to representation in Congress

——, Act amended the Judiciary Act to authorize the appointment of circuit judges, the first since 1802; the Supreme Court to consist of a Chief Justice and 8 associates, and for purposes of Act an additional judge to be appointed

April 12–23, Senate met in special session

April 13, The Senate rejected the Johnson-Clarendon Treaty with Great Britain of Jan. 14 by vote of 54 to 1

Dec. 6, Forty-first Congress, 2d sess. convened

Dec. 14, Act removed legal and political disabilities under the XIVth Amendment from a large number of persons in the South mentioned by names

Dec. 22, Act provided that Georgia should be restored to statehood, membership of the legislature to be determined by Governor Bullock, tests applied to exclude persons by the XIVth Amendment, legislature to ratify the XVth Amendment to the Constitution, and the negro members of the legislature who had been expelled to be restored

1870

Jan. 4, General Terry authorized by the President to resume in Georgia the powers of commander of a military district

Jan. 5, New York withdrew ratification of the XVth Amendment to the Constitution

Jan 8, Canadian Order ended system of licenses to American fishing vessels in force since termination of Reciprocity Treaty

Jan. 10, First act of incorporation of the Standard Oil Company at Cleveland, Ohio

——, Missouri ratified the XVth Amendment to the Constitution; Mississippi, the XIVth and XVth, Jan. 17; Rhode Island, Jan. 18; Kansas, Jan. 19; Ohio, Jan. 27

Jan. 20, The Lenox Library, New York City, incorporated

Jan. 22, California Southern Railroad Company chartered

Jan. 24, Prince Arthur (Duke of Connaught), third son of Queen Victoria, presented to President Grant

Jan. 26, Canal Treaty with Colombia signed; not ratified

Jan. 27, Government of Virginia, readmitted by Act of Congress of Jan. 26, turned over to civil authorities by General Canby

Feb. 2, Georgia ratified the XVth Amendment; Iowa, Feb. 3; Nebraska, Feb. 17; Texas, Feb. 18, the XIIIth, XIVth, and XVth Amendments; Minnesota, the XVth, Feb. 19

Feb. 4, Museum of Fine Arts, Boston, incorporated

Feb. 7, Supreme Court decision declared the legal tender feature of the Act of 1862 as to greenbacks unconstitutional as far as concerned debts contracted prior to the passage of the law (Hepburn vs. Griswold)

Feb. 12, Utah law gave full suffrage to women

Feb. 23, Death of Anson Burlingame in St. Petersburg, Russia

Feb. 24, Treaty with Great Britain signed as to the Northwest boundary

March 7, A grand jury of both men and women impanelled at Fort Laramie, Wyoming

——, Governor Holden of North Carolina issued proclamation declaring Alamance county in state of insurrection on account of activities of the Ku Klux

March 21, Justice Bradley appointed judge of Supreme Court

March 30, Secretary Fish proclaimed the ratification of the XVth Amendment by 29 States and in force consequently

April 5, Tweed charter for New York City adopted for which Tweed said to have spent a million in bribes to members of the legislature (Rhodes)

April, Party of American engineers reported that Hudson Bay Company post north of Pembina was on American territory

April 8, Iowa passed local option law

April 9, American Anti-Slavery Society dissolved

April 13, Metropolitan Museum of Art, New York City, incorporated

April 14, Expiration of time for ratification of Treaty of Oct. 1867 for purchase of Danish West Indies

May 13, Naturalization Treaty with Great Britain signed

May 24, Corcoran Gallery of Art, Washington, D.C. incorporated

——, Proclamation of President Grant against Fenian invasion of Canada

May 25–27, Invasion of Canada by Fenians from Fairfield, Vermont. See Canada

June 1, The ninth census gave the total population as 38,558,371, an increase in the decade of 22.6. Immigrants arrived 2,466,752, of whom 1,106,970 were from Great Britain, and 1,073,429 from other parts of Europe. The colored population numbered 4,880,009; Chinese, 63,199; Japanese, 55; civilized Indians, 25,731. The center of population reckoned as 48 miles east by north of Cincinnati. New York City led with a population of 942,292, Philadelphia second with 674,022; Brooklyn, 396,099; St. Louis, 310,864; and Chicago, 298,977

June 3, Treaty for the suppression of the African slave trade signed with Great Britain

June 23, Amos T. Akerman, of Georgia, appointed Attorney General to succeed E. R. Hoar, resigned

July 1, St. Paul and St. George Islands, Alaska, declared a special reservation for protection of fur seals

July 8, Governor Holden declared Caswell County, North Carolina, in state of insurrection, and a week later sent Colonel Kirk into the county with militia

July 11, Consular Treaty with Austria-Hungary signed

July 12, Death of Admiral John A. Dahlgren

July 24, First through car from the Pacific coast arrived in New York City

Aug. 4, Democrats in North Carolina election carried the State by 1,000 majority gaining control of the legislature and ending domination of "carpet-bag" Republicans

Aug. 14, Death of Admiral David C. Farragut at Portsmouth, New Hampshire

Aug. 15, National Labor Congress met at Cincinnati, Ohio

Aug. 22, Proclamation of President Grant of neutrality in the Franco-Prussian war

Aug. 23, More than 100 citizens of North Carolina arrested by Colonel Kirk and held prisoners discharged by United States judge from "unlawful custody"

——, Irish National Congress met at Cincinnati

Sept. 20, First editorial attacking Tweed rule appeared in the New York Times

——, Naturalization Treaty with Austria-Hungary signed

Oct. 4, National Commercial Convention met at Cincinnati, Ohio (southern convention)

Oct. 12, Death of General Robert E. Lee at Lexington, Virginia

Oct. 13, Proclamation of the President prohibited illegal military expeditions against nations with whom the United States at peace

Oct. 17, Vice-Admiral D. D. Porter made admiral succeeding Admiral Farragut

Nov. 10, Governor Holden of North Carolina revoked his proclamations of insurrection in Alamance and Caswell counties

Dec. 6, Treaty of peace, friendship, commerce, and consular privileges with Salvador signed

Dec. 16, Colored Methodist Episcopal Church of America organized by Bishop Paine at Jackson, Tennessee

Dec. 28, William M. Tweed resigned as Commissioner of Public Works in New York

Dec. 31, State debt of Louisiana which had been $11,182,377 on Dec. 1, 1865, increased to $22,589,628

CONGRESS

Jan. 26, Virginia readmitted to representation in Congress, members to take "iron-clad" oath

Feb. 23, Mississippi readmitted to representation in Congress

Feb. 25, Hiram R. Revels, first colored Senator, from Mississippi, qualified

March 24, Treaty for the purchase of the Danish West Indies of Oct., 1867, rejected by Senate

March 30, Texas readmitted to representation in Congress

May 31, Act to enforce the right of citizens of the United States to vote in the several States of the Union provided heavy penalties for infringement upon the right to vote under the XIVth and XVth Amendments to the Constitution

June 13, Message of the President announced that the attitude of strict neutrality would be maintained in the war between Spain and Cuba

June 22, Act created the Dept. of Justice with Attorney General at head

June 30, The Senate refused to ratify the Treaty for annexation of Santo Domingo by the United States of 1869

——, Bankruptcy law amended, and also July 14

July 8, Act to revise, consolidate, and amend laws of patents and copyrights, copyright extended to 28 years with right of renewal for 14 years and rights to widow or children

July 9, Placer mining law enacted

——, Act authorized the Secretary of War to establish a Weather Bureau

July 13, Act provided for an increase of 54 millions of national banknotes above the 300 millions already authorized, and for redemption of the 3% temporary loan certificates

July 14, Grant of pension of $3,000 a year to Mary Lincoln, widow of Abraham Lincoln

——, Internal Revenue Act and Tariff Act reduced internal duties leaving liquor and tobacco excise, bank tax, and stamp duties, 130 articles mostly of the nature of raw materials placed on the free list. Income tax reduced to 2.5% with an exemption of $2,000. Pig iron reduced from $9 to $7 per ton, and reduction of duties on tea, coffee, wines, sugar, molasses, and spices

——, Act for refunding the debt of the United States in coin bonds at reduced rate of interest, lowered from 5 to 4%

——, Naturalization Act amended to punish crimes against the same and extending laws to apply to aliens of African nativity or descent

——, Bankruptcy law amended

July 15, Georgia readmitted to representation in Congress ending Reconstruction legislation era

——, Act provided for removal of Osage Indians to Indian Territory and for sale of their lands to settlers

——, Congress adjourned

Dec. 5, Forty-first Congress, third sess. convened

Dec. 7, "Anthony rule" for expedition of business in the Senate adopted

Dec. 12, J. H. Rainey, of South Carolina, first colored member of the House of Representatives, took the oath

1871

Jan. 12, Commission appointed to report on annexation of the Dominican Republic including B. F. Wade, A. D. White, and Dr. S. G. Howe

Jan. 16, Supreme Court decision declared the Legal Tender Act of 1862 unconstitutional

Jan. 26, Death of George Ticknor, historian, at Boston, Massachusetts

Feb. 20–22, Grand carnival in Washington

Feb. 21, New Jersey ratified the XVth Amendment to the Constitution

Feb. 23, Naturalization Treaty with Great Britain signed

Feb. 26, Treaty of commerce and navigation with Italy signed

Feb. 27–May 8, Joint High Commission of the United States and Great Britain met in Washington to settle Alabama claims and other differences, the fishery question, San Juan affair, &c.

March 1, The Southern Improvement Company incorporated in Pennsylvania by the oil magnates

——, Arivapa Indians surrendered to Lieutenant Whitman at Fort Grant, Arizona

March 4, George William Curtis, of New York, appointed head of first Civil Service Commission by the President

March, Smith College for women opened at Northampton, Massachusetts

March 15, A paid fire department inaugurated in Philadelphia

March 22, Governor Holden impeached for malfeasance in office and removed from office by the Senate of North Carolina restoring Democratic control

March 24, Proclamation of the President against unlawful combinations of persons (the Ku Klux) in South Carolina

April 6, Public meeting at Cooper Union, New York City, at which W. E. Dodge, Henry Ward Beecher and W. M. Evarts denounced William Tweed, corrupt political boss

April 7, Illinois Railroad Act to prevent extortion and unjust discrimination in rates charged by different railroads in the State, the first "Granger" legislation

April 17, Agricultural and Mechanical College of Texas authorized by the legislature

April 18, First National Bank opened in New Mexico at Santa Fé

April 30, Massacre of Arivapas Indians at Camp Grant, Arizona, in attack of Papago Indians and white persons

May 1, Supreme Court reversed decision of previous year and declared legal tender feature of the greenbacks constitutional and greenbacks legal tender in payment of debts contracted before 1862

May 3, Proclamation of the President warned the people that the Enforcement Act applied to the entire country and urged the newly reconstructed States to suppress unlawful combinations in order that he might not be called upon to use extraordinary powers confirmed by the Act

May 8, Treaty of Washington with Great Britain signed

provided for arbitration of the Alabama claims (Geneva arbitration), submitted the Oregon boundary dispute (San Juan Island) to arbitration of the Emperor of Germany, restored inshore Canadian fisheries to Americans, placed fish products on the free list, and provided for a commission to decide what the United States should pay for fishing privileges (Halifax Commission)

May 16–June 11, Expedition to Korea, Mr. Low, American Minister to China, on mission to Korean Government to investigate affair of the "General Sherman" steamer of Aug., 1866, arrived off Chempilpo May 30

June 1, American vessels fired on by fort in Kang-Yang River, Korea, while taking soundings

June 4, General George Crook took command of the Dept. of Arizona

June 10–11, American force commanded by Commander L. A. Kimberley landed from U.S.S. "Monachy" and "Palos" in Salee River and shelled and captured 5 Korean forts

June 29, Captain Hall's Arctic expedition sailed from New York in the "Polaris" and proceeded to Smith Sound through Kane Basin to Robeson Channel where he wintered in Thank God Harbor 81° 38' N. Turned back at 82° 11' N. Lat. 61° W. "farthest north" at that time

July 4, Treaty of Washington of May 8 proclaimed

July 8, In the fight against the corrupt Tweed ring the *New York Times* began publication of transcripts of the accounts of the Controller supplemented by cartoons by Nast

July 12, Riot between Irish Catholics and Irish Protestants in New York City during parade of Orangemen, many persons wounded and some killed

Aug. 10, National Labor Conference met at St. Louis

Aug. 26, Death of Ezra Stiles Gannett, clergyman and author

Aug. 28–Oct. 25, Yellowstone expedition against the Indians

Sept. 4, Mass meeting at Cooper Institute appointed a Committee of Seventy to work for reform and against the Tweed ring in New York City

Sept. 7, University of Nebraska opened at Lincoln

Sept. 16, Meeting of Boundary Commission at Pembina under the Treaty with Great Britain of May 8

Sept. 19, The body of President Abraham Lincoln removed to Springfield, Illinois

Sept., Stevens Institute of Technology at Hoboken, New Jersey, incorporated Feb. 15, 1870, opened

Oct. 4, University of Alabama at Tuscaloosa reorganized and opened

Oct. 8, Fire in a stable on the west side of the river started the great Chicago fire which lasted 24 hours and destroyed an area of 2,100 acres, 17,500 buildings and property worth $200,000,000

Oct. 9, Brigham Young appeared in court to answer charges of polygamy, and of murder of a man named Buck

Oct. 12, Proclamation of the President to the people of South Carolina declared that hostile combinations of persons were making armed resistance to the civil authorities in the counties of York, Marion, Chester, Laurens, Newberry, Fairfield, Lancaster, and Chesterfield, commanding them to disperse and surrender their arms

Oct. 17, Proclamation of the President suspended writ of habeas corpus in counties in South Carolina named in Proclamation of Oct. 12

Oct. 17, Special State Attorney O'Conor named to bring civil suit against Tweed and his associates to recover money taken fraudulently from the New York City Treasury

Oct. 24, Riot against the Chinese in Los Angeles, California, resulted in hanging of 15 and shooting of 6 by a mob

Oct. 27, Governor Bullock, of Georgia, resigned fearing impeachment and fled from the State

——, Tweed arrested and held on bail of $1,000,000, Jay Gould, chief bondsman

Nov. 3, Proclamation of the President took Marion County, South Carolina, from the list in which privilege of writ suspended, and in Union County, Nov. 10

Nov. 8, Death of Captain Charles F. Hall, Arctic explorer, on his ship, the "Polaris" frozen in the Arctic ice since September

Nov. 19, Arrival of Grand Duke Alexis, third son of the Czar of Russia, with a fleet of war vessels, on visit

Nov. 25, The Russian envoy to the United States, Katakazy, recalled because of differences with Secretary Fish (undue interference)

Dec. 11, Consular treaty with Germany signed

Dec. 14, George H. Williams, of Oregon, appointed Attorney General

Dec. 15, Tribunal of Arbitration under Washington Treaty met at Geneva, Switzerland, and adjourned the following day for 6 months after formal presentation of the case

Dec. 16, The Union Pacific Railroad bought $75,000 worth of Little Rock and Fort Smith Railroad land grant bonds paying an amount in excess of their market value supposedly to J. G. Blaine expecting to recoup themselves through legislative favors (Rhodes)

——, Tweed again arrested and committed to prison but released on writ of habeas corpus on bond of $5,000

Dec. 19, James M. Smith elected Governor of Georgia

Dec. 22, Treaty of friendship, commerce, and extradition with the Orange Free State signed

Dec. 28, William Tweed resigned his office as president of the Board of Supervisors, and as state senator

CONGRESS

Jan. 19, Senate Committee of Five appointed to inquire into conditions in the South and in particular the activities of the Ku Klux in North Carolina

Jan. 20, Refunding Act authorized increase of amount of bonds in the 5% class authorized July 14, 1870 from $200,000,000 to $500,000,000

Feb. 9, Joint Resolution established Fish Commission

Feb. 15, Act prescribed oath of office to be taken by persons who participated in the Rebellion but who were not disqualified from holding office by the XIVth Amendment

Feb. 21, District of Columbia made a territorial government

Feb. 28, Federal election law placed control of congressional elections and registration under United States officers, to protect negro voters in the South

March 3, Texas-Pacific Railroad incorporated and land grant made to aid in construction of road through El Paso to San Diego, the last grant to railroad of public land

March 3, Act provided that hereafter no Indian nation or tribe within the territory of the United States should be acknowledged or recognized as an independent nation, tribe, or power with whom the United States might contract by treaty, government of the Indians to be by legislation and executive orders

——, First Civil Service Commission authorized, but not effective because Congress made no appropriations for expenses

——, Act provided for an exhibition of American and foreign arts, products, and manufactures to be held in 1876 in Philadelphia, the first capital

March 10, Charles Sumner deposed from chairmanship of Senate Committee on Foreign Relations because of opposition to Grant's plan for annexation of Santo Domingo

March 27, Speech of Senator Charles Sumner against the annexation of Santo Domingo

April 5, Report of Santo Domingo Commission sent to Congress by President Grant with message recommending annexation

April 7, Joint congressional investigation of "condition of affairs in the late insurrectionary States" (Ku Klux Committee) authorized. This committee held meetings throughout the South and took a large amount of testimony

April 20, Second Enforcement Act (Ku Klux Act) gave the President the right to suspend the writ of habeas corpus when combinations of private persons had successfully defied the laws of the State as embodied in the XIVth Amendment in any instance, making it the duty of the United States Government to secure enforcement

——, Congress adjourned

Dec. 4, Forty-second Congress, second sess. convened

Dec. 19, Special message of the President announced that he had adopted civil service to go into effect Jan. 1. Congress refused to make adequate appropriation

1872

Jan. 1, Civil service regulations came into effect

——, Total actual and contingent debt of Louisiana $41,194,474

Jan. 7, Tweed trial begun in New York; defended by David Dudley Field, and John Graham, leading members of the Bar, the young lawyer, Elihu Root, on this case

Jan. 8, Trial of Brigham Young begun

Jan. 12, James M. Smith inaugurated Governor of Georgia restoring home rule

Jan. 15–22, Actual bill for furnishing the State House at Columbia, South Carolina, for $40,189.87, increased by Legislature to $90,000 and passed, which included clocks at $480 each, mirrors at $750, and chandeliers at $650, selected by colored legislators. Actual value of furniture reckoned in 1877 to be $17,465

Jan. 18, The Southern Improvement Company (oil) completed contracts with the Pennsylvania, New York Central and Erie railroads which gave the company rebates

Jan., University of Arkansas opened

Jan. 24, Missouri Convention at Jefferson City issued call to all Republicans opposed to the administration and in favor of reform to meet in Cincinnati in May

Jan. 31, The jury disagreed in Tweed trial and case dismissed

Feb. 7, Death of Martin J. Spalding Roman Catholic archbishop of Baltimore

Feb. 22, National Labor Convention held at Columbus, Ohio, Justice David Davis nominated for President, Joel Parker, Governor of New Jersey for Vice-President

——, National Prohibition Convention met at Columbus, Ohio, and nominated James Black, of Pennsylvania, for President, and Joel Parker, of New Jersey, for Vice-President

Feb. 27, Mass meeting of the citizens of Titusville, Pennsylvania, against the Southern Improvement Company

March 4, The Japanese visiting embassy formally received at the White House by President Grant, and reception given by the House of Representatives March 6

March 25, The railroads abrogated contract with the Southern Improvement Company as to rebates

March, Total expense of legislative session, South Carolina, $1,174,177.78 included payment of members $102,900, messengers $58,737.50, sundries including wine, cigars, &c., $282,514.50

April 2, Death of Professor Samuel F. B. Morse, inventor, in New York

April 6, The Southern Improvement Company deprived of charter by the Pennsylvania legislature

April 10–14, National Convention of colored men met at New Orleans, Frederick Douglas, president

April 22, Supreme Court decision in case of Osborn vs. Nicholson confirmed the validity of slave contracts entered into before the Emancipation Proclamation

April 25, Brigham Young dismissed by the court on the writ of habeas corpus

May 1, National Convention of Liberal Republicans met in Cincinnati, Carl Schurz, president, nominated Horace Greeley, of New York, for President and Gratz Brown, of Missouri, for Vice-President

May 15, The President recognized Elisha Baxter, Republican, as lawful Governor of Arkansas in disputed election claimed by Joseph Brooks, Liberal Republican

May 17, The "Pittsburgh Plan" presented at meeting of standard oil magnates

May 23, Workingmen's National Convention at New York nominated General U. S. Grant, of Illinois, for President, and Henry Wilson, of Massachusetts, for Vice-President

June 1, Death of James Gordon Bennett, founder of the *New York Herald*

——, Government mail contract concluded with the Pacific Mail Company calling for 2 departures from and arrivals of steamers in San Francisco

June 5, National Republican Convention met in Philadelphia and renominated U. S. Grant for President on first ballot, and Henry Wilson for Vice-President

June 15, Meeting of Arbitration Tribunal at Geneva under the Washington Treaty reassembled; announced June 19 that they would not consider claims for indirect damages

June 17–July 4, World's Peace Jubilee and International Music Festival held in Boston, conducted by P. S. Gilmore, with a chorus of 20,000, orchestra of 2,000 pieces, and band of the U. S. Marine Corps, and military bands from England, France, and Germany

June 21, Convention of Liberal Republican Revenue Reformers met in New York and nominated William

S. Groesbeck, of Ohio, for President, and Frederick Law Olmsted, of New York, for Vice-President

July 9, National Democratic Convention met at Baltimore, the Cincinnati platform accepted, and Horace Greeley nominated for President and Gratz Brown for Vice-President

July 20, Naturalization Treaty with Denmark signed

July 26–Oct. 15, Yellowstone Indian expedition, Dakota

Aug. 1, Connecticut passed local option law

Aug. 22, National Labor Reform Convention at Philadelphia nominated Charles O'Conor for President and Eli Saulsbury for Vice-President; O'Conor declined the nomination

Sept. 3, The "Straight-Out" Democrats met at Louisville, Kentucky, and nominated Charles O'Conor, of New York, for President and John Quincy Adams, of Massachusetts, for Vice-President; both declined nomination

Sept. 4, Since Sept. 1, 1871 to this date the Indians had made 54 attacks on the white people of Arizona (Dunn)

——, The "Crédit Mobilier" exposed in the *New York Sun*

Sept. 14, Final award of the Geneva Arbitration Tribunal rejected claims for all indirect damages and awarded $15,500,000 as indemnity due the United States from Great Britain; found that the British Government had "failed to use due diligence in the performance of its neutral obligations" as to the Confederate cruisers "Alabama" and "Florida," and of the "Shenandoah" after that vessel left Melbourne Feb. 18, 1865

Sept. 25, Colored Liberal Republican National Convention at Louisville, Kentucky, nominated Horace Greeley for President and B. Gratz Brown for Vice-President

Oct. 10, Death of William Henry Seward, former Secretary of State, at Auburn, New York

Oct. 21, Award of Emperor William, of Germany, as to boundary line with Canada, that the line should be through the Haro Strait according to the Treaty of June 15, 1846, the San Juan Island commanding the strait between British Columbia and the United States awarded to the United States; the Island was evacuated by the British Nov. 22

Nov. 4, Election held in Louisiana, William Pitt Kellogg, Republican, chosen Governor, John McEnery nominee of Democrats claimed the election

Nov. 5, Presidential election. U. S. Grant reëlected President by 286 electoral votes out of 352, with a popular majority of 750,000, and Henry Wilson for Vice-President, popular vote for Grant and Wilson, 3,597,070, for Greeley and Brown, 2,834,079, for Black and Russell, 5,608

——, Second trial of Tweed begun in New York. Convicted of forgery and grand larceny and sentenced to 12 years imprisonment and fine of $12,750

Nov. 9, Fire in Boston started which destroyed about 65 acres and property worth about $73,000,000 in 3 days

Nov. 29, Death of Horace Greeley at Pleasantville, New York

——, Modocs surrounded in camp in Oregon to be returned to reservation refused to surrender to troops and fought their way to liberty

Dec. 11, Governor Warmoth of Louisiana impeached and suspended by legislature

Dec. 12, Death of Edwin Forrest, tragic actor, at Philadelphia

——, Attorney General Williams telegraphed to "Acting Governor Pinchbeck" that he was recognized by the President as the lawful executive of Louisiana and that all necessary assistance would be given to him and the Republican Legislature to protect the State from disorder and violence

Dec. 13, Attorney General Williams telegraphed refusal of President Grant to receive committee of 100 representative citizens of Louisiana

CONGRESS

Feb. 2, Apportionment or representatives among the several States according to the ninth census authorized, representatives numbered 283. Election day fixed as the first Tuesday after the first Monday in Nov. to begin in 1876

Feb. 19, Report of Joint Committee to investigate conditions in Southern States presented, an extreme indictment of the Ku Klux

March 1, Act established Yellowstone National Park

March 5, Act provided that foreign works of art be admitted free of duty for public exhibition

April 4, Homestead Act amended to enable honorably discharged soldiers and sailors to acquire land, and amended June 8

April 23, Ransom, senator of North Carolina, took the oath, and for the first time since 1861 every State represented

May 1, Duty on tea and coffee removed

May 2, Supplementary Act regulated construction of the Texas Pacific Railroad

May 7, Joint Resolution adopted to appoint commission to investigate frontier depredations on Mexican border, and commission reported in Dec. recommending larger cavalry force to prevent raids from Mexico into Texas

May 8, Act provided for removal of the Kansas Indians to Indian Territory and sale of their lands to actual settlers

May 10, Act provided that all valuable mineral deposit lands should be free and open to exploration and purchase by citizens of the United States

May 22, Amnesty Act removed political disabilities under Article 3 of the XIVth Amendment, removed except from senators and representatives in the 36th and 37th Congresses, officers of the judicial, military, and naval services of the United States, and foreign Ministers, exceptions from the Act numbered about 500 persons

May 23, Sion H. Roberts took the oath in the House under Amnesty Act of May 22 as representative from North Carolina making full representation in the House from all States

May 31, Speech of Charles Sumner in the Senate against the President, seeking to prevent his renomination

June 6, Tariff and Internal Revenue Act made 10% horizontal reduction on all manufactured products imported, duties on salt and coal reduced and some raw materials placed on the free list. The reduction affected cotton goods, wool, iron, steel, metals, paper, glass, and leather, and caused a reduction of $53,000,-000 in government revenues

June 8, Post Office established as an executive department

June 10, Act provided for discontinuance of Freedmen's Bureau on June 30

June 10, As part of the Civil Appropriation Act the Federal Election Act of Feb. 28, 1871 modified

——, Congress adjourned

Dec. 2, Forty-second Congress, third sess. convened

——, The Speaker called attention to the charges made during election campaign by Democrats that Republican members of Congress had been bribed in 1867 and 1868 by presents of stock in the "Crédit Mobilier" to vote and act for the benefit of the Union Pacific Railroad. A committee appointed to investigate charges

——, The President recommended Congress to appoint joint commission to determine boundary of Alaska

1873

Jan. 14, William Pitt Kellogg inaugurated Governor of Louisiana, and John McEnery claiming election inaugurated also by Conservatives

Jan. 17, Colonel Wheaton and 400 soldiers forced to retire before Captain Jack and "Curly-Headed Doctor" commanding the Indians in the Lava Beds of northern California (Modoc Indian War)

Jan. 18, Additional Articles to Treaty of May 8, 1871 signed as to fisheries, amendment Article 12

Jan. 31, Jury disagreed in the Tweed trial

Feb. 20, Report of Committee of Congress declared McEnery *de jure* Governor of Louisiana, and Kellogg, supported by troops, the *de facto* Governor (*See infra* Congress), but President Grant declared Feb. 25 for support of the Kellogg Government

March 1, Contract signed by Philo Remington with Carlos Gladden, C. L. Sholes, and S. W. Soule, for manufacture of their typewriter, and manufacture begun Sept. 12 of first commercial typewriter

——, Mass meeting in New Orleans protested against President Grant's support and protection of the Kellogg Government

March 4, Inauguration of President Grant and Vice-President Wilson for second term

March 6, McEnery legislature which had assembled Dec. 11, 1872 dispersed, and 5 members refusing to leave arrested by police under orders from General Longstreet commanding the militia

March 10, Protocol signed with Great Britain regarding the Northwest Water Boundary, Haro Strait

March 17, William A. Richardson, of Massachusetts, appointed Secretary of the Treasury

April 11, Indians led by Captain Jack killed General E. R. S. Canby and Dr. Thomas, near Fort Klamath, California, commissioners sent to negotiate a peaceful settlement

April 14, Supreme Court decision in Slaughter-House cases declared that the XIIIth, XIVth, and XVth Amendments to the Constitution "must be construed in general not as setting up a new and comprehensive system of natural rights and jurisdiction, but as having for their primary if not exclusive purpose to secure and protect the freedom of the negro." The Court said that the United States by the XIVth Amendment did not assert jurisdiction over "the entire domain of civil rights heretofore belonging exclusively to the States," thus recognizing the police power of the State of Louisiana

April 22, Captain Randall captured Del-Shay's band of Tontos in the Sierra Anchas

April 23, In Grant Parish on the Red River in Louisiana a fight between whites and negroes in contest of McEnery supporters for possession of the court houses ended in shooting of 60 or more negroes

April 30, Nineteen survivors of the "Polaris" expedition rescued from floating ice in Baffin Bay by steamer "Tigress" of Newfoundland, and reached Newfoundland May 9

May 1, One-cent postal cards first issued by the Government

May 2, Illinois enacted law for control of transportation within the State

May 7, Death of Chief Justice Salmon P. Chase in New York City

——, American marines landed in Panama to protect lives and property during the revolution

May 22, President Grant ordered forces of McEnery in Louisiana to disperse

——, The main body of the Modocs surrendered ending Indian war in Oregon and California

May 23, United States troops arrived in Louisiana

June 1, Captain Jack and 20 other Indians captured after defeat in Oregon, and Captain Jack and 2 other Modoc Indians executed at Fort Klamath Oct. 3

June 4–Oct. 4, Yellowstone Indian expedition, Dakota

June 7, Protocol signed with reference to Treaty of May 8, 1871 as to fisheries

June 12, Surrender to Captain McGregor of the Jamaspies band of Hualapaes in the Santa Maria Mts.

June 18, Susan B. Anthony fined $100 for illegally voting on election day at Rochester, New York

June 30, Second Report of congressional committee blamed laxity of Mexican Government for Mexican raids into Texas and recommended border cavalry force be increased

Aug. 13, Anti-Monopoly Convention at Des Moines, Iowa

Aug. 18, First recorded ascent of Mt. Whitney, in the Sierra Nevadas, highest peak in the United States excluding Alaska, by John Incas, C. D. Begole, and A. H. Johnson

Sept. 8, Failure of the New York Warehouse and Security Company due to advances on railroad bonds, beginning the panic of 1873

Sept. 13, Failure of Kenyon Cox and Company caused by loans to Canada Southern Railroad

Sept. 18, Failure of Jay Cooke and Company, bankers of Philadelphia, marketing the Northern Pacific Railroad bonds, Jay Cooke, "the financier of the Civil War," and the Morgan of his day

Sept. 19, Nineteen members of the New York Stock Exchange went into bankruptcy including banking house of Fisk and Hatch

Sept. 20, Union Trust Company closed its doors

Sept. 20–30, The New York Stock Exchange closed

Oct. 31, The "Virginius," steamer flying the American flag, carrying supplies to Cuban insurgents captured by Spanish gunboat "Tornado," taken to Cuba where the captain and several of the crew, 8 American citizens, executed Nov. 4–7

——, Failure of Hoyt, Sprague, and Company, mill owners of Providence and New York

——, International bridge across the Niagara River completed

Nov. 24, Election held by Conservatives in New Orleans, Kellogg Government denounced and committee appointed to present appeal to Congress

Nov. 27, The Hoosac Tunnel near North Adams, Massachusetts, completed

Nov. 29, The "Virginius" affair settled by agreement

for restoration of the steamer and surviving passengers to the United States and punishment of Spanish officials responsible for illegal acts

Dec. 2, Election in Texas a Democratic victory, Richard Coke, for Governor

Dec. 12, Procession of unemployed in Chicago

——, Death of Professor Louis Agassiz at Cambridge, Massachusetts

Dec. 14, One hundred women of Fredonia, New York, invaded the saloons in a movement for temperance, singing and praying

Dec. 15, New Constitution for Pennsylvania ratified by popular vote

Dec. 16, The steamer "Virginius" delivered by Spanish Admiral Pole to American navy at Cuba, and the surviving prisoners the following day. The "Virginius" foundered at sea Dec. 19 on way to New York off Cape Fear

——, During the year more than 5,000 business failures occurred with loss estimated at $228,500,000

CONGRESS

Jan. 24, Grades of admiral and vice-admiral in the Navy abolished, offices when vacant not to be filled

Jan. 31, Postal franking privilege abolished

Feb. 12, Coinage Act revised the laws relating to mints, assay offices, and coinage, the silver dollar abolished and a "trade" dollar of 420 grains authorized for use in trade with China and Japan, gold to be the sole monetary standard

Feb. 18, Official report of the Committee of the House investigating the Crédit Mobilier affair (Poland Committee) found Oakes Ames and James Brooks guilty of selling stock of the Crédit Mobilier (or carrying it on their books without any payment) to members of Congress at price below true value in order to influence votes, and recommended their expulsion from the House

Feb. 20, House Committee on privileges and elections reported after investigation that McEnery was de jure Governor of Louisiana in the contested election on the face of the returns although the election was not fairly conducted, but that Kellogg, supported by troops, was the de facto Governor, and recommended passage of an act "to secure an honest reelection"

Feb. 27, Vote of censure of Oakes Ames and James Brooks passed, Ames for selling shares in the Crédit Mobilier at low prices to influence votes, and Brooks as guilty of corruption as member of the House and a government director of the Union Pacific Railroad

March 3, Act provided for sale of coal lands belonging to the United States under specified conditions of sale and fixing of minimum price

——, Timber act to encourage growth of timber on western prairies granted patents on condition of cultivation of part of the land, trees to be planted, title received at end of 8 years

——, "Salary Grab" Act raised the President's salary from $25,000 to $50,000 a year, and made increases for salaries of the Vice-President, members of the Cabinet, Speaker of the House, justices of the Supreme Court, and raised salaries of senators and representatives from $5,000 to $7,500. The fact that the Act was retroactive giving senators and representatives about to retire a bonus of $5,000 gave the law its name

March 3, Act provided for establishment of 10 life-saving stations on the Atlantic coast

March 4, Congress adjourned

Dec. 1, Forty-third Congress, first sess. convened

1874

Jan. 5, Decision of Supreme Court of Texas that law authorizing election of Dec. 1873 void and unconstitutional

Jan. 12, Request of Republican Governor Davis of Texas for federal troops refused

Jan. 13, Procession of the unemployed in New York City in battle with the police at Tompkins Square, hundreds of workmen injured

Jan. 15, Governor Coke inaugurated in Texas

Jan. 26, Kentucky adopted local option

Feb. 4, National Congress of the Grange reported membership of 12,000 subordinate granges with about 1,000,000 members

Feb. 12, Charles Kingsley arrived from England on visit to America

Feb. 13, United States troops landed at Honolulu during riots attending the election of the King

Feb. 13–Aug. 19, Sioux Indian expedition in Wyoming and Nebraska

Feb. 16, North Carolina adopted local option

March 8, Death of Millard Fillmore, former President, at Buffalo, New York

March 11, Death of Charles Sumner at Washington

——, Wisconsin railroad law passed fixed rates of transportation in the State for railroads, express, and telegraph companies

March 22, First Young Men's Hebrew Association met in New York

March 23, Iowa enacted railroad law to establish reasonable maximum rates on the railroads in the State

March 28, Joint Commission began negotiations as to questions in dispute with Canada

April 15, Joseph Brooks, defeated candidate for Governor in Arkansas, obtained a judgment of "ouster" from the circuit court and took forcible possession of the State House claiming election frauds

April 16, Governor Baxter with 200 men surrounded the State House at Little Rock, Arkansas, held by Brooks

April 19, Call for troops made by Elija Baxter, Republican, and the following day by Joseph Brooks, Liberal Republican, each claiming to be the elected Governor of Arkansas

April 27, The White League organized at Opelousas, Louisiana

April 30, Twenty-five men killed or wounded in battle of Brooks and Baxter supporters at Little Rock, Arkansas

May 7, Supreme Court affirmed decision of circuit court in favor of Brooks as Governor of Arkansas

May 10, A large number of distilleries seized in connection with evasion of tax on whiskey

May 11, Legislature of Arkansas convened by Governor Baxter telegraphed for federal assistance

May 15, The President in proclamation against turbulent gatherings in Arkansas upheld the Joseph Brooks claims as against Elisha Baxter for Governor in disputed election of 1872

May 30, Arkansas passed a local option law

June 2, Benjamin H. Bristow, of Kentucky, appointed Secretary of the Treasury

June 20–Aug. 30, Black Hills Indian expedition, Dakota

July 4, Steel bridge across the Mississippi at St. Louis opened

——, First Chautauqua Assembly met at Chautauqua, New York

July 7, Henry Ward Beecher demanded investigation by his church of charges of scandal preferred against him by Theodore Tilton

——, James W. Marshall, of Virginia, appointed July 3, took office as Postmaster General

Aug. 1, Campaign against Kiowa, Cheyenne and Comanche Indians in Indian Territory begun which ended Feb. 16

Aug. 11, Treaty of extradition with Turkey signed and agreement giving right to hold real estate in Turkey

Aug. 13–Oct. 10, Big Horn Indian expedition, Wyoming

Aug. 21, Theodore Tilton brought suit for damages against Henry Ward Beecher for alleged improper relations with Tilton's wife

Aug. 24, Convention of "white people of Louisiana" met at Baton Rouge, and denounced Governor Kellogg as a usurper maintained by federal troops

——, Marshall Jewell, of Connecticut, appointed Postmaster General

Aug. 26, Sixteen negroes taken from jail in Tennessee by men in disguise and shot, because of shooting of 2 white men by negroes on the 22nd

Sept. 14, Citizens of New Orleans reinstated the McEnery Government forcing Governor Kellogg to take refuge in the custom house on his refusal to resign

Sept. 15, Proclamation of the President against disorderly and turbulent gatherings in Louisiana

Sept. 18, McEnery surrendered the State House of Louisiana to United States troops commanded by General Brooke appointed military Governor sent by the President to restore the Kellogg Government

Nov. 4, Congressional elections resulted in a Democratic House, and Democratic victories in state elections in such Republican strongholds as Pennsylvania, Ohio, and Massachusetts, the Republicans retaining control in Senate because only one-third of the members were up for reëlection

Nov. 18–19, National Womens Temperance Union organized at a meeting in Cleveland, Ohio, Mrs. Anna Wittenmeyer, of Philadelphia, the first president, and Miss Frances E. Willard, of Chicago, corresponding secretary

Dec. 1, D. H. Chamberlain, of Massachusetts, inaugurated Republican Governor of South Carolina

Dec. 7, Race riot in Vicksburg, Mississippi, in attempt to reinstate a carpetbag sheriff who had been forced to resign, 75 negroes killed

Dec. 9, Death of Ezra Cornell at Ithaca, New York

Dec. 18, The legislature of Mississippi asked the President for troops to suppress rioting in Warren County

Dec. 21, Proclamation of the President against domestic violence in Mississippi

Dec. 28, Death of Gerrit Smith, abolitionist, at New York City

CONGRESS

Jan. 20, Act repealed "Salary Grab" Act of 1873, all increases repealed except those of the President and justices of the Supreme Court

Jan. 21, Appointment of Morrison R. Waite to succeed Chase as Chief Justice confirmed by the Senate

Jan. 29, Coinage of coins for foreign nations at the mint authorized

April 22, Bill to inflate the currency fixing a maximum of greenback inflation at $400,000,000 vetoed by President Grant

May 24, Joint Commission appointed to report on permanent reclamation and redemption of Mississippi Valley from inundation

June 20, Life Saving Service made a separate service to operate under the Treasury Dept.

——, Currency Act fixed amount of United States notes at maximum of $382,000,000 and limited the paper circulation of national banks

——, Territorial Government of the District of Columbia replaced by government by a commission of three appointed by the President

June 22, Bankruptcy Act of 1867 amended

June 23, Act reorganized the territorial courts of Utah. Writs of error allowed to bring a person convicted of bigamy before the United States Supreme Court

——, Hazing forbidden at Naval Academy at Annapolis, under penalty of investigation by court-martial and dismissal

——, Congress adjourned

Dec. 1, Forty-third Congress, 1st sess. convened

1875

Jan. 4, Legislature of Louisiana met, organized, and appointed Wiltz, Conservative, temporary chairman and speaker of the House. Republicans unable to control proceedings left the hall, and Governor Kellogg sent troops to clear out contested members, not permitting a legislature with a legal quorum to judge the qualifications of its own members as prescribed by law, and then the Republicans organized as suited them under military protection

——, Trial of Henry Ward Beecher begun in suit instituted by Theodore Tilton

Jan. 5, General Sheridan telegraphed to the Secretary of War urging that Congress pass law to enable him to bring the "White Leagues" of Louisiana before military tribunals, describing them as "banditti"

Jan. 15, William Tweed, who had been released from the penitentiary on a technicality, rearrested, bail placed at $3,000,000

Jan. 22, Congressional Committee of investigation reached New Orleans, William Wheeler, George F. Hoar, and 2 others

Jan. 30, Commercial Reciprocity Treaty with Hawaii signed which admitted sugar duty free into the United States

Feb. 9, First train passed through the Hoosac tunnel

Feb. 27, Claims Convention with Spain signed by which the Spanish Government engaged to pay $80,000 for relief of families of American citizens shot in the "Virginius" affair

March 3, Anti-Monopoly Convention at Harrisburg, Pennsylvania

March 8, Treaty of commerce and navigation with Belgium signed

March 11, Independent (Greenback) Convention at Cleveland, Ohio

March 14, Gold discovered in Deadwood and Whitewood gulches, South Dakota

March 15, Archbishop John McCloskey, of New York, made the first American cardinal with title of Sancta Maria supra Minervam, and invested in St. Patrick's Cathedral, New York City, April 27

March 22, Decision of Supreme Court that certain

corporations created by the Georgia legislature while in rebellion were legal

March 26, Raid from Mexico robbing and looting to within a few miles of Corpus Christi, Texas

April 5, Massachusetts legislature repealed the prohibitory liquor law

April 14, "Wheeler Adjustment" agreed to in Louisiana, Congressional Committee passed on candidates for legislature and 12 Conservatives fraudulently excluded by the returning board seated in House. Joint Resolution adopted by legislature, agreement not to disturb the Kellogg Government for the remainder of executive term ending Jan., 1877

April 26, Edwards Pierrepont, of New York, appointed Attorney General

May 1, Exposure of whiskey frauds in the western States by which the Government defrauded of internal revenue taxes on distilled liquors estimated as $1,650,000 during 10 months; the headquarters of the "Whiskey Ring" was in St. Louis, and John McDonald, appointed by Grant to revenue position over protest of both Missouri senators, its chief accomplice

May 10, Seizure of 16 distilleries in St. Louis, Milwaukee, and Chicago, and indictment of 238 persons in whiskey frauds

May 17, Death of John C. Breckinridge at Lexington, Kentucky

June 2, The principle of the telephone discovered by Alexander Graham Bell at Boston, transmitting by wire the sound of a twanging clock spring

June 25, Rhode Island adopted local option

July 2, Jury disagreed in case of Tilton vs. Beecher and were dismissed

July 31, Death of Andrew Johnson, former President, near Jonesborough, Tennessee

Aug. 1, Strike of cotton mill workers at Fall River, Massachusetts, against a reduction of wages begun

Sept. 1, Riots at Yazoo City, Mississippi, and Sept. 4 at Clinton, race and political

——, Murder of Thomas Sanger, young English mine official, by the Molly Maguires. The murderers were convicted by detective work of James McParlan who joined their order employed by the president of the Pennsylvania and Reading Coal and Iron Company

Sept. 6, Constitutional Convention met at Montgomery, Alabama

Sept. 7–27, Expedition against Indians in eastern Nevada

Sept. 8, Governor A. Ames (son-in-law of Benjamin F. Butler) of Mississippi asked the President for troops, which were refused

Oct. 1, Fall River strike ended as workers accepted reduction in wages

Oct. 16, University of Provo founded by Brigham Young in Utah

Oct. 19, Zachariah Chandler, of Michigan, appointed Secretary of the Interior

Oct. 22, Sons of the American Revolution organized at San Francisco

Oct. 30, Constitution for Missouri, adopted by convention which met at Jefferson City May 5–Aug. 19, ratified by vote of the people. Went into effect Nov. 30

Nov. 2, Election in Mississippi restored Democratic control by drastic suppression of the negro vote

Nov. 16, Constitution for Alabama ratified by popular vote

Nov. 22, Death of Vice-President Henry Wilson; Thomas W. Ferry, of Michigan, president *pro tem* of the Senate becoming acting Vice-President

Nov. 24, Death of William B. Astor in New York City

——, Texas Convention called attention of the Congress of the United States to the Mexican depredations in Texas border raids

Dec. 4, Tweed escaped from prison and made his way to Cuba and from there on a sailing vessel in disguise to Spain

Dec. 9, Grand Jury at St. Louis indicted O. E. Babcock, secretary and friend of President Grant, in prosecution of the Whiskey Ring

CONGRESS

Jan. 14, Specie Resumption Act authorized the sale of bonds "to prepare and provide for" redemption of notes in coin on and after Jan. 1, 1879. Provision made for accumulation of gold reserve, free banking, substitution of silver coin for paper fractional currency

March 1, Civil Rights Act (Sumner's Bill) decreed privilege of equal rights and enjoyment in inns, public conveyances, theaters, and other public places of amusement without distinction of color. Forbade exclusion of negroes from jury duty

March 3, Act granted railroad companies right of way to extent of 100 feet on each side of railroads through public lands under prescribed conditions

——, Enabling Act for Colorado to form a State Government passed

——, Part of Island of Mackinac, Michigan, made a national park

——, Act enlarged powers of the circuit courts by granting them for the first time jurisdiction in all suits under the Constitution and laws of the United States

——, Tariff and Internal Revenue Act restored the 10% reduction in duties given in 1872 increasing rates on sugars, and increased the internal revenue tax on tobacco, snuff, and cigars, and raised rate on distilled spirits from 70 to 90 cents

——, Act forbade entrance into the United States of persons convicted of crime other than political in their own country, and provided for inspection of passenger ships

March 4, Congress adjourned

April 15, Joint Resolution created a monetary commission to study the currency situation and make a report

Dec. 6, Forty-fourth Congress, 1st sess. convened

1876

Jan. 9, Death of Samuel Gridley Howe, surgeon for the blind and philanthropist, in Boston

Feb. 10, Death of Reverdy Johnson at Annapolis, Maryland

Feb. 14, Alexander Bell applied for patent for his telephone as an "improvement in telegraphy" which was granted March 17

Feb. 17–June 13, 1877, Big Horn and Yellowstone expeditions against Indians in Wyoming and Montana

Feb. 22, Sons of the Revolution organized

March 8, Alphonso Taft, of Ohio, appointed Secretary of War

March 10, First complete intelligible sentence transmitted by Bell on telephone

March 27, Supreme Court decision in case of U.S. vs.

Reese declared 2 sections of the Act of May 31, 1870 unconstitutional which penalized inspectors in elections for refusing to receive the count of votes and for obstruction of any citizen from voting

April 5, Anti-Chinese mass meeting at San Francisco at which the Governor made an address; an address to Congress adopted

April 10, Death of Alexander T. Stewart in New York City

April 15, Arrival in New York of Don Pedro II, Emperor of Brazil, and the Empress Theresa

May 10, The Centennial Exposition opened with ceremony by President Grant at Fairmount Park, Philadelphia

——, Bell demonstrated his telephone before the American Academy of Arts and Sciences

May 11, Prohibition Convention met at Cleveland, Ohio, and nominated General Green Clay Smith, of Kentucky, for President, and G. T. Stewart, of Ohio, for Vice-President

May 15, Meeting of Liberal Republicans from 17 States met in New York, and pronounced against Blaine, Conkling, and Morton; no candidates named

May 17, National Greenback Convention met in Indianapolis and nominated Peter Cooper, of New York, for President, and Newton Booth, for Vice-President, and on refusal of Booth to accept the nomination, Samuel F. Cary, of Ohio, substituted, attended by 240 delegates from 18 States. Platform advocated issue of legal tender notes, suppression of national bank notes, and repeal of Specie Resumption Act

May 17–Sept. 26, Expedition against the Sioux Indians in Dakota

May 22, James D. Cameron, of Pennsylvania, appointed Secretary of War, and Alphonso Taft, of Ohio, appointed Attorney General

May 29, Final demarcation of boundary with Canada certified and attested in London

June 14, National Republican Convention met in Cincinnati. On the 7th ballot, June 16, Rutherford B. Hayes, of Ohio, nominated for President, and on the first ballot, William A. Wheeler, of New York, for Vice-President. James G. Blaine had received 285 votes on the first ballot, Hayes, 61, Oliver P. Morton, 125, Roscoe Conkling, 99, and B. H. Bristow, the prosecutor of the whiskey ring, 113

June 21, Lot M. Morrill, of Maine, appointed Secretary of the Treasury

June 24, Texas adopted local option

June 25, General G. A. Custer and his entire force outnumbered and massacred by Indians commanded by Sitting Bull in a ravine of the Little Big Horn River in Montana

June 27, National Democratic Convention met at St. Louis. Nomination of Samuel J. Tilden, of New York, for President, made unanimous on the second ballot June 28. Thomas A. Hendricks nominated for Vice-President by acclamation

July 8, Armed conflict between negroes and whites at Hamburg, Aiken County, South Carolina, 5 negroes killed

July 12, James N. Tyner, of Indiana, appointed Postmaster General

Aug. 1, Colorado admitted (38th State) by proclamation of the President

Sept. 27, Death of Braxton Bragg (Confederate General) at Galveston, Texas

Oct. 4, Agricultural and Mechanical College of Texas opened for instruction

Oct. 6, American Library Association organized at meeting in Philadelphia

Oct. 12, New Constitution for North Carolina ratified by popular vote

Oct. 17, Proclamation of the President commanded the "rifle clubs" in South Carolina to disperse

Oct. 18, Death of Francis Preston Blair in Missouri

——, University of Oregon opened at Eugene

Oct. 26, President Grant sent federal troops to South Carolina to disperse turbulent gatherings

Nov. 1–Dec. 31, Powder River Indian expedition, Wyoming

Nov. 7, Presidential election. Popular vote according to Republican count, gave Hayes, 4,033,768, and Tilden, 4,285,992, and according to the Democratic count, Hayes, 4,036,298, Tilden, 4,300,509, Cooper (Greenback) 81,737, and Smith (Prohibition) 9,522. Double returns were sent in from South Carolina, Florida, Louisiana, and Oregon. Republican headquarters at Washington declared Rutherford B. Hayes elected by electoral majority of one

Nov. 9, Federal troops sent to Tallahassee, Florida

Nov. 10, President Grant requested prominent northern Republicans to go to New Orleans "to witness the count" of votes. Democrats sent also by the Democratic chairman

——, Centennial Exposition at Philadelphia closed

Nov. 23, William Tweed brought back to New York from Europe to serve his prison sentence

Nov. 24, Sioux Indians defeated by Colonel McKenzie in pass in the Big Horn Mountains

Dec. 6, Electors in the States met and voted, two sets of returns coming from South Carolina, Florida, Louisiana, and Oregon. In Oregon Republican electors were ousted and the vacancies filled by Democrats. In Florida the majority for the Tilden electors was made a majority for Hayes by 2 of the 3 members of the Board of State Canvassers because of alleged frauds and irregularities. South Carolina votes were for Hayes. In Louisiana the Board controlled by Republicans, the former Governor, Wells, chairman, declared for Hayes which gave him the presidency. In Louisiana "on the face of the returns the Tilden electors had majorities varying from 6,300 to 8,957," which result was changed by the Board by throwing out "13,250 Democratic votes, and 2,042 Republican" (Rhodes). The returning boards gave Hayes 185 electoral votes and Tilden 184

Dec. 24, Death of Charles Tufts, manufacturer, founder of Tufts College, Massachusetts

CONGRESS

Jan. 10, Blaine introduced motion to refuse amnesty to Jefferson Davis

March 2, A committee of the House reported Secretary of War, William W. Belknap, guilty of malfeasance in office, and impeachment voted. Belknap resigned the same day to avoid the proceedings

April 4, The Senate organized as Court of Impeachment in case of W. W. Belknap, charged with selling of privileges at trading posts in the Indian Territory and receiving several thousand dollars each year since 1870 for concessions. He was acquitted Aug. 1, but 23 of the 25 senators who voted not guilty declared they did so because they believed they had no jurisdiction over an officer who had resigned

April 18, General Grant vetoed Bill to reduce salary of President from $50,000 to $25,000 after March 4, 1877

April 24, James G. Blaine denied in the House that he had received $64,000 from Union Pacific Railroad for bonds of the Little Rock and Fort Smith Railroad as charged in the newspapers

May 2, Committee of House ordered to investigate charges against Blaine relating to Union Pacific transaction

May 4, Message of President Grant justified absence of the executive from the seat of government by precedents cited

May 31, James Mulligan before the House Committee testified that he had kept accounts for Fisher for Little Rock and Fort Smith bonds, and that Blaine had indirectly sold the bonds to the Union Pacific as charged, and mentioned letters of Blaine in his possession which Blaine had borrowed from him and refused to return, the "Mulligan letters"

June 5, Blaine made speech of defense in the House reading selected parts of the Mulligan letters. The investigating committee made no report

July 22, Joint Resolution provided for the issue of silver coin to amount not to exceed $10,000,000. The trade dollar declared no longer legal tender

Aug. 1, W. W. Belknap acquitted by Senate Court of Impeachment. *See supra* April 5

Aug. 15, "Silver Commission" appointed of 3 senators and 3 representatives to study the silver question with a view to a "restoration of the double standard"

——, Congress adjourned

Dec. 4, Forty-third Congress, 2d sess. convened

Dec. 27, Proposal to prohibit the sale of intoxicating liquors by amendment of the Constitution first introduced by Henry W. Blair of New Hampshire in the House

1877

Jan. 1, Governor Kellogg barricaded the State House in Louisiana admitting only members of the legislature certified by Election Board of Returns

Jan. 2, Republican legislature of Louisiana declared Packard and Antoine elected and the Democrats declared Nicholls and Wiltz elected

——, Governor Drew inaugurated as Governor in Florida after Supreme Court of the State had by mandamus ousted Stearns ending Republican domination

Jan. 4, Death of Cornelius Vanderbilt, in New York

Jan. 8, S. B. Packard inaugurated as Republican Governor at the State House in Louisiana, and Francis T. Nicholls inaugurated by the Democrats at St. Patrick's Hall, and 2 legislatures met

Jan. 11, Incorporation of Jesuit Fathers of New Mexico by Act of the legislature passed over veto of Governor. Annulled by Congress of the United States Feb. 4, 1879

Jan. 16, Commission declared boundary line between Maryland and Virginia; approved by Maryland and Virginia in 1878, and ratified by Congress in 1879

Jan. 29, Electoral Count Act provided for a commission of 5 senators, 5 representatives, and 5 justices of the Supreme Court to count votes for the President; count begun Feb. 1, the decision in favor of receiving the votes regularly attested by the Republican election board in each State, therefore there was no attempt to "go behind the returns" and investigate

the justice or injustice of the count. The members stood 8 Republicans and 7 Democrats

Feb. 9, Commission awarded the vote to the Republicans of disputed election in Florida by 8 to 7

Feb. 12, Professor Alexander Graham Bell exhibited his telephone at the Essex Institute, Salem, Massachusetts

Feb. 16, Commission awarded the electoral vote of Louisiana to the Republicans by vote of 8 to 7

Feb. 23, Commission awarded the electoral vote of Oregon to the Republicans by vote of 8 to 7

Feb. 28, Commission awarded the electoral vote of South Carolina to the Republicans by vote of 8 to 7

March 2, Report of Monetary Commission presented

——, Electoral Commission declared Hayes and Wheeler elected by majority of one vote

March 3, Rutherford B. Hayes took the oath as President privately Saturday evening

March 5, President Hayes inaugurated and took public oath of office. Vice-President Wheeler took the oath at special session of Senate

March 8, John Sherman, of Ohio, appointed Secretary of the Treasury

March 12, William M. Evarts, of New York, appointed Secretary of State, George W. McCrary, of Iowa, Secretary of War, Charles Schurz, of Massachusetts, Secretary of the Interior, Richard W. Thompson, of Indiana, Secretary of the Navy, Charles Devens, of Massachusetts, Attorney General, and David M. Key, of Tennessee, Postmaster General

March 15, Professor Bell gave a demonstration of his newly invented telephone to a group of scientists who heard conversation between Salem and Boston

March 20, Tennessee law prohibited sale of liquor within 4 miles of a school

March 23, President Hayes notified Wade Hampton and D. H. Chamberlain, rival claimants for governorship of South Carolina, that federal troops would be withdrawn which decided the controversy in favor of Democratic candidate, Hampton

——, John D. Lee executed for complicity in the Mountain Meadows massacre of 1857

April 2, President Hayes sent a commission to Louisiana to report on conditions: Wayne MacVeagh, former Minister to Turkey, Charles B. Lawrence, ex-chief justice of Illinois, General John M. Harlan, of Kentucky, former attorney general, General Hawley, and John C. Brown, former Governor of Tennessee. They recommended recognition of the Nicholls Government

April 10, United States troops withdrawn from Columbia, South Carolina, and Chamberlain withdrew from office of Governor

April 14, Strike on the Philadelphia and Reading Railroad for recognition of the Union

April 20, United States troops withdrawn from the public buildings of New Orleans and the Packard Government obliged to abdicate. The Nicholls Government took possession of the State House of Louisiana

April 21, The Packard legislature dispersed and Packard left Louisiana returning eventually to Maine

May 17, General Grant with his family left Philadelphia for visit to Europe to "encircle the globe"

May 29, Death of Fletcher Harper, publisher, New York City

——, Death of John Lothrop Motley, historian and diplomat, at Dorchester, England

June 1, General Ord ordered to cross the border into Mexico in pursuit of bandits raiding Texas; Mexico protested

June 14–Oct. 5, Nez Perce Indian campaign

June 14, Massacre began Battle of White Bird Canyon with Wallowa Indians in Idaho

June 15, First meeting of Fisheries Commission at Halifax

June 17, Idaho Indians killed Captain Perry and 18 of his volunteer company

——, General Shafter crossed the border into Mexico

June 21, Leaders of the "Molly Maguires," secret organization which had attacked and murdered owners and officials of mines in Pennsylvania, hanged at Pottsville and Mauch Chunk, Pennsylvania

June 22, Civil service order of President Hayes that "no officer should be required to take part in the management of political organizations or election campaigns"

July 11–12, General Howard defeated the Idaho Indians in battle

July 14, Strike of employees of the Baltimore and Ohio Railroad begun in Baltimore because of 10% reduction in wages, the fourth since 1870, to take effect July 16

——, Strike of firemen on freight trains at Martinsburg, West Virginia, men prevented by force from taking their places

July 18, Proclamation of President Hayes warned mobs to cease obstruction and troops sent to Martinsburg

July 19, Conductors and brakemen of the Pennsylvania Railroad went on strike at Pittsburgh

July 20, Riots in Baltimore and fighting between strikers and militia, in which 9 strikers killed

——, Firemen and brakemen of the New York and Erie Railroad joined the strike

July 21, Troops from Philadelphia in battle with strikers in Pittsburgh as they tried to clear the tracks, 10 strikers killed and many wounded, the troops lost 4 killed and 13 wounded

——, Proclamation of the President against turbulent gatherings in Maryland along the line of the Baltimore and Ohio Railroad

July 23, Proclamation of the President against domestic violence in Pennsylvania

——, Mass meeting in San Francisco in sympathy with the railroad strike in the East

July 26, Battle of police and communists as police broke up meeting at Turner Hall, Chicago

July 31, Thomas A. Edison took out first patent in which he indicated the principle of the phonograph

Aug. 11, Asaph Hall in charge of 26" telescope at the Naval Observatory in Washington discovered first satellite of Mars

Aug. 29, Death of Brigham Young at Salt Lake City, Utah. Survived by 17 wives and 47 children

Sept. 12, Unemployed in San Francisco assembled in vacant lot and led by Dennis Kearney organized the Workingman's Trade and Labor Union of San Francisco

Oct. 4, Surrender of Chief Joseph ended war with the Idaho Indians

Oct. 5, Dennis Kearney chosen president of the Workingman's Party of California, called the "Sand-lot" party because of Sunday meetings on vacant lots

Oct. 17, Pennsylvania Railroad contract with the Standard Oil Company gave that company practically a monopoly of production and transportation of oil in the United States

Oct. 24, The President nominated Theodore Roosevelt for Collector of the Port of New York, Edward A. Merritt for Surveyor General, and L. B. Prince for Naval Officer. All rejected by the Senate 5 days later

Oct. 29, Mass meeting of San Francisco workmen at Nob Hill where railroad magnates lived, speeches made by Dennis Kearney and other leaders

Nov. 3, Dennis Kearney arrested on charge of using incendiary language

Nov. 23, Decision of Fisheries Commission condemned the United States to pay Great Britain $5,500,000

CONGRESS

March 2, Electoral Commission declared Hayes and Wheeler elected President and Vice-President by Republican majority of one electoral vote

March 3, Act provided for the sale of desert land in certain States and Territories on satisfactory proof of arrangements for irrigation, entry of 640 acres permitted

March 4, Congress adjourned

Oct. 15, Forty-fifth Congress, 1st sess. (extra) convened

Oct. 29, Nominations of the President of Oct. 24 rejected by Senate

Nov. 5, Bill introduced by Richard P. Bland, of Missouri, provided for free and unlimited coinage of silver, passed in House, amended in Senate to limit amount

Nov. 23, Bill to repeal that part of Specie Resumption Act which authorized the Secretary of the Treasury to dispose of United States bonds and redeem and cancel greenback currency passed by House

Dec. 3, Congress adjourned

——, Forty-fifth Congress, 2d sess. convened

Dec. 6, Nominations of the President again sent to Senate and rejected, only that of L. B. Prince for Naval Officer accepted on the 16th

1878

Jan. 3, Dennis Kearney led procession to City Hall in San Francisco to demand work or bread for the unemployed

Jan. 5, Dennis Kearney indicted, tried and released Jan. 22

Jan. 6, Attack of Newfoundland fishermen on American fishermen violating the Newfoundland Sunday prohibition of fishing in Fortune Bay

Jan. 16, Death of Samuel Bowles, journalist

Jan. 19, California "gag law" imposed severe penalties on those inciting to riot

Jan. 21, First State Convention of the Workingmen's Party of California

Jan. 28, First telephone switchboard installed for service in New Haven

Feb. 11, Death of Gideon Wells, former Secretary of the Navy

Feb. 19, Edison's phonograph patented

Feb. 22, "National Party" organized at a convention in Toledo, Ohio, with over 800 delegates from 28 States, successor of the Greenback Party of 1874 joined by the Laborites and referred to as the Greenback-Labor Party

March 2, Death of Benjamin F. Wade at Jefferson, Ohio

April 3–Sept. 9, Ute expedition, Colorado, against the Indians

April 12, Board of army officers convened to reëxamine

and report on the case of General FitzJohn Porter cashiered in Jan., 1863

April 12, Death of William Tweed in prison in New York City

April 29, First train run on the Sixth Avenue Elevated Railroad in New York City

May 1, From this date the Standard Oil Company received the rebates of 10 cents on all freight on the Pennsylvania Railroad

May 8, Consular Treaty with Italy signed

May 13, Death of Professor Joseph Henry of the Smithsonian Institution

May 30–Sept. 4, Campaign against the Bannock and Piute Indians

June 12, Death of William Cullen Bryant in New York

July 10–15, Beginnings of yellow fever epidemic in New Orleans

July 11, President Hayes removed General Arthur, Collector of the Port of New York, and Alonzo B. Cornell, the Naval Officer, whose resignations he had requested, in order to separate the offices from politics. With Senators Conkling and Platt these two men constituted the "Big Four" who ran New York State politics. He appointed in their places *ad interim* General E. A. Merritt and Silas Burt

July 25, Treaty of commerce with Japan signed

Sept. 28, First Chinese resident Embassy to the United States presented credentials, Chen Lan Pin, Yung Wing, and 36 others

Oct. 7, Proclamation of President Hayes warned free-booters led by "Billy the Kid" to stop robbing ranches in New Mexico

Oct. 8, Thomas A. Edison announced his successful subdivision of the electric current

Oct. 16, Publication of telegrams in the *New York Tribune* written either to Tilden's nephew, Pelton, or by him, during the presidential election campaign, showed that Pelton had tried to bribe elector of Oregon, and had offered money to secure the returning boards of South Carolina and Louisiana, stopped Democratic attacks on title of Hayes to the presidency

Dec. 17, Gold reached par in New York City for the first time since Jan. 13, 1862

Dec. 18, "Big Jack" Kehoe, Molly Maguire leader, hanged at Pottsville, Pennsylvania

Dec. 19, Death of Bayard Taylor in Berlin, Germany, author and diplomat

CONGRESS

Jan. 10, Resolution introduced in Senate by Senator Sargent that women be given a hearing on suffrage

Feb. 28, Bland-Allison Act provided for coinage of a limited amount of silver at 16 to 1, and resumed coinage of silver dollars as legal tender. The Secretary of the Treasury directed to buy each month 2 to 4 million dollars worth of silver and coin it into standard dollars. Passed over veto of the President

May 17, Select Committee appointed by the House to investigate alleged election frauds of Nov., 1876, in Louisiana and Florida

May 31, Act forbade the further retirement of United States legal tender notes providing that when redeemed they should be reissued and paid out again and kept in circulation in number as of that day

June 7, Bankruptcy Act to take effect Sept. 1, repealed that of March, 1867 and June, 1874

June 11, Act provided for permanent Commission of three for government of the District of Columbia

June 14, Timber and Stone Lands Act for limited sale of western lands valuable only for these purposes amended that of March 13, 1874

June 18, Act restricted the use of the army as a *posse comitatus* in the execution of laws except in such cases as are expressly provided for in the Constitution (rider to the Army Appropriation Act)

——, Provision made for additional life saving services

June 19, Act to relieve political disabilities of General E. Kirby Smith

June 20, Congress adjourned

Dec. 2, Forty-fifth Congress, 3d sess. convened

1879

Jan. 1, Specie payments resumed

Jan. 2, The New York Sub-Treasury began to exchange gold for greenbacks on demand with a reserve of $133,508,000 in coin to control the $346,681 outstanding greenbacks

——, Death of Caleb Cushing at Newburyport, Massachusetts

Feb. 4, Open letter of President Hayes, the equivalent of an executive order, to E. A. Merritt, successor of Arthur at the New York Custom House, desired the office to be conducted on "strict business principles" and "according to the rules of the Civil Service Commission"

Feb. 27, Secretary of the Navy authorized to accept the ship "Jeanette," gift of James Gordon Bennett for Polar exploration

March 19, Board of army officers reported that the sentence of court-martial of FitzJohn Porter should be set aside

March 31, The Pennsylvania Railroad ceased payment of rebates

April 21, New Constitution for Louisiana adopted by convention, capital changed from New Orleans to Baton Rouge

April 26, Proclamation of the President ordered removal of squatter settlers not of the Indian race from Oklahoma in the Indian Territory

May 24, Clarence King, first Director of the United States Geological Survey, entered on duties

——, Death of William Lloyd Garrison, abolitionist, in New York City

July 8, The yacht "Jeanette," James Gordon Bennett expedition, sailed for the Arctic under command of Captain G. W. De Long

Aug. 30, Death of Confederate General John B. Hood at New Orleans

Sept. 3, Apache Indians led by Vitorio began war in New Mexico by raid at Ojo Caliente

Sept. 11, Apaches attacked ranch near Hillsboro, New Mexico

Sept. 20, General Grant arrived at New Orleans from his trip around the world and received a great popular ovation

Sept. 21–Nov. 8, 1880, Campaign against the Ute Indians in Colorado and Utah

Oct. 13, Death of Henry C. Carey, economist, at Philadelphia

Oct. 20, Albuquerque Academy, New Mexico, formally opened under charter of Oct. 6

Oct. 21, Edison's invention of the first incandescent lamp put in circuit, maintained incandescence for more than 40 hours

Nov. 4, Thomas A. Edison filed patent for his incandescent electric lamp

Dec. 8, Constitution for Louisiana adopted in April ratified by popular vote, and Louis A. Wiltz, Democrat, elected Governor. State lottery renewed in Constitution

Dec. 10, Alexander Ramsey, of Minnesota, appointed Secretary of War, succeeding McCrary, resigned

Dec. 13, Wyoming gave women the vote

CONGRESS

Jan. 25, Act to facilitate the refunding of the national debt

——, Arrears of pension Act provided that Civil War pensions should begin with date of death or service disability, date of injury in the case of all claims filed before July 1, 1880. Under this law the applications rose from 36,832 to 110,673 in a single year

Feb. 15, Act permitted women to practice before the Supreme Court

March 1, Internal Revenue Act provided for tax on snuff and tobacco

——, President Hayes vetoed Willis Bill to restrict Chinese immigration as a violation of treaty with China

March 3, National Board of Health of 7 members authorized, to be appointed by the President, by Act to prevent introduction of infectious and contagious diseases

——, Amendments to Homestead Act provided additional regulations, and additional rights to homesteaders on public lands within railroad limits granted

March 4, Congress adjourned

March 18, Forty-sixth Congress, 1st sess. (extra) convened, the Democrats in control in both Houses for the first time

April 29, Army Appropriation Bill carrying amendment forbidding the use of troops at the polls, and prohibiting civil officers of the United States from employing any adequate civil force at places where congressional election held, vetoed by the President

May 12, Bill "to prohibit military interference at elections" vetoed by the President

May 29, The Appropriation Bill for the legislative, executive, and judicial expenses vetoed by President Hayes because of riders attached amending the election laws of 1870 and 1871

June 28, Act authorized commission of seven to be appointed by the President to consider improvements in the Mississippi River

July 1, Salts and sulphate of quinine placed on free list

——, Amendment to Homestead Act to grant additional rights to settlers within the railroad limits in Missouri and Arkansas

——, Congress adjourned

Dec. 1, Forty-sixth Congress, 2d sess. convened

Dec. 19, House Committee of 11 appointed to report on an interoceanic canal

1880

Jan. 2, Arrival of Charles S. Parnell, president of the Irish Land League and John Dillon, in New York, to raise money for Ireland; addressed large meeting in New York Jan. 4, in Toledo, Jan. 17, in Boston, Jan. 22

Jan. 15, Claims Convention with France signed

Jan. 23, Alleged letter of Garfield of this date, pronounced by him a forgery, circulated, in which he advocated buying labor where it was cheapest, and standing by the Treaty with China

Jan. 24, General Grant arrived in Florida beginning trip through the South and West

Feb. 12, Second Proclamation of the President against settlers in Oklahoma (Indian Territory)

March 8, Statement of President Hayes on proposed Isthmian Canal, that it must be "under American control" as it would be "virtually a part of the coast line of the United States"

March 9, Consular Treaty with Belgium signed

March 10, Order of June 1, 1877 as to crossing of Mexican border in pursuit of bandits protested by Mexico, withdrawn

March 11, Dennis Kearney, and other leaders arrested in San Francisco on charge of using incendiary language, and sentenced to 6 months in prison. Released by Supreme Court order

March 18, The Southern Pacific Railroad of Arizona and New Mexico completed to Tucson, Arizona

March 30, The Metropolitan Museum of Art in New York City opened

May 1, Strike of longshoremen in New York City

May 6, Republican Anti-Third Term Convention met at St. Louis, General J. B. Henderson, presiding, with delegates from 13 States, and 4 other States represented unofficially

May 14, First street railway in New Mexico chartered at Albuquerque

May 26, Strike of miners at Leadville, Colorado, for increase of wages from $3 to $4 a day, and a reduction of working hours to eight for a shift

June 1, The tenth census gave total population as 50,155,783, increase of 11,597,412 since 1870. Immigrants arrived from Europe during the decade 2,944,695, of whom 989,163 were from the British Isles. The colored population numbered 6,580,793; Chinese, 105,465; Japanese, 148; civilized Indians, 66,407. The center of population was 8 miles south of Cincinnati

June 2, Republican Convention in Chicago nominated James A. Garfield, of Ohio, for President on the 36th ballot June 8 receiving 399 votes. Chester A. Arthur, of New York, was nominated for Vice-President on the 1st ballot. On the first ballot, June 7, Grant led with 304 votes, James G. Blaine, 284, and John Sherman, 93. Garfield received 1 vote on the second ballot, 17 on the 34th, and 250 on the 35th. On the last ballot (36th) Grant had 306 votes, Blaine, 42, and Sherman, 3

June 9, National (Greenback) Party met in Chicago, and nominated James B. Weaver, of Iowa, for President, and B. J. Chambers, of Texas, for Vice-President

June 17, Prohibition Party met in Cleveland, and nominated Neal Dow, of Maine, for President, and A. M. Thompson, of Ohio, for Vice-President

June 22, Democratic National Convention met at Cincinnati and nominated General Winfield S. Hancock, of Pennsylvania, for President, and William H. English, of Indiana, for Vice-President

July 3, Treaty with Morocco as to protection signed

July 4, Death of Reverend George Ripley in New York City

July 20, Arrival in New York of the Egyptian obelisk, "Cleopatra's Needle," which was placed in Central Park

Aug. 25–28, Survey of Wrangel Island made by officers of the U.S.S. "Rodgers," Lieutenant Berry in command

Aug. 28, Public return of Benjamin F. Butler to the Democratic Party celebrated at Faneuil Hall, Boston

Oct. 20, Death of Mrs. Lydia Maria Child at Wayland, Massachusetts

——, The "Morey" letters forged in Garfield's name and addressed to a fictitious Mr. Morey, favored cheap labor and by implication Chinese labor. Used as a campaign document

Nov. 2, The popular vote cast for Garfield for President was 4,454,416. Hancock, the Democratic candidate received 4,444,952; Weaver, National Greenback, 308,578; and Dow, Prohibition, 10,305. Garfield received 214 electoral votes, and Hancock 155. All the former slave States carried by the Democrats, and also New Jersey, California, and Nevada

Nov. 11, Death of Lucretia Mott, suffrage leader, near Philadelphia

Nov. 17, Treaty with China signed which permitted the United States to "regulate, limit or suspend" but not absolutely to prohibit entrance of Chinese laborers. Commercial intercourse and judicial procedure Agreements also signed

Nov. 18, Sarah Bernhardt, actress, made first appearance in the United States at Booth's Theatre, New York City

Nov. 27, Death of General George B. Crittenden, at Danville, Kentucky

Dec. 6, States, except Georgia, cast electoral votes

Dec. 10, Texas, Santa Fé, and Northern Railroad Company incorporated

Dec. 20, Broadway, New York City, lighted by electric arc lights invented by Charles F. Brush

Dec., Settlers led by Payne from Kansas into Oklahoma in defiance of laws and proclamations of the President dispersed by federal troops

CONGRESS

March 3, Act to facilitate refunding of the national debt

March 18, De Lesseps had hearing before the House Committee, and testified that the French Government had no official connection with his canal company

May 4, Appropriation Bill vetoed by President because of rider attached providing that army should not be used at elections

June 8, The President authorized to appoint a judge advocate general of the Navy

June 16, Deficiencies Appropriation Act provided that deputies should not be paid for services rendered at elections

——, Act for relief of certain settlers on public lands, to provide for repayment of certain fees, commissions, &c., on void entries

——, Congress adjourned

Dec. 6, Forty-sixth Congress, 3d sess. convened

1881

Jan. 5, International Sanitary Conference met in Washington

Jan. 6, Nathan Goff, Jr., of West Virginia, appointed Secretary of the Navy

Jan. 22, "Cleopatra's Needle," Egyptian obelisk, set up in Central Park, New York City

Jan. 31, First meeting of new Interoceanic Canal Company, de Lesseps presiding, in Paris

Feb. 2, Young People's Society of Christian Endeavor organized in the Williston Congregational Church of Portland, Maine, by the Rev. Francis E. Clark, an organization which became national and international

Feb. 19, Kansas adopted state wide prohibition

Feb. 22, Executive Order of President Hayes that the Secretary of War take steps to prevent sale of intoxicating liquor at army camps, posts, and forts

Feb. 24, Arrival of Count de Lesseps in New York City

——, Supplementary Consular Treaty with Italy signed

Feb. 28, Limited measure of local option adopted in Nebraska

March 1, Santa Fé Railroad completed to join the Southern Pacific Railroad at Deming

March 3, Massachusetts adopted local option

March 4, President James A. Garfield inaugurated President and Chester A. Arthur, Vice-President

March 5, James G. Blaine, of Maine, appointed Secretary of State, William Windom, of Massachusetts, Secretary of the Treasury; Robert T. Lincoln, of Illinois, Secretary of War; Wayne MacVeagh, of Pennsylvania, Attorney General; Thomas L. James, of New York, Postmaster General; William H. Hunt, of Louisiana, Secretary of the Navy; Samuel J. Kirkwood, of Iowa, Secretary of the Interior

March 12, Dennis Kearney, San Francisco agitator, speaking against Chinese and for the Sand Lot squatters, arrested

March 15, Strike of puddlers in Pennsylvania

March 23, Judge William H. Robertson nominated by the President as Collector of Customs at the port of New York, political and personal enemy of Senator Conkling of New York, leader of the "Stalwarts" so-called, who had acquired control of distribution of offices under the Federal Government

March 28, Protest against the appointment of Mr. Robertson and the removal of General Merritt from the position of Collector of the Port of New York presented to the President by Senators Conkling and Platt of New York, which was signed by Thomas L. James, Chester A. Arthur, Roscoe Conkling, and Thomas C. Platt

March 30, Boston Symphony Orchestra founded and endowed by Henry Lee Higginson, George Henschel, the first conductor

April 9, Report of discovery of "star route" fraud cases by the Postmaster General and Special Agent Woodward to the President, of millions of dollars paid in contracts annually for mail never delivered on routes not opened, so-called because marked by stars in postmaster's list

April 18, Rio Grande, Mexico, and Pacific Railroad chartered

April 20, Resignation of Assistant Postmaster General Thomas A. Brady on account of exposure of "star route" frauds

May 16, Resignation of Senators Conkling and Platt of New York in protest against the appointment of Robertson on the ground that they had not been consulted by the President. *See infra* Congress

May 19, The New Mexico and Southern Pacific Railroad chartered

May 21, The American Red Cross Society organized, Miss Clara Barton, president

May 29–June 1, Strike of miners at Leadville, Colorado

June 1, Strike of iron workers at Covington and New-
port, Kentucky, which lasted 21 weeks, for new scale
of prices
June 13, The "Jeannette" crushed in the polar ice.
Two boats with crew reached mouth of the Lena,
Siberia. De Long and 14 other members of the ex-
pedition died of cold and starvation near the mouth
of the Lena
June 15, The whaler "Rodgers" sent by the Navy
Dept. in search of the "Jeannette" left San Francisco
June 17, Consular Treaty with Rumania signed
June 24, Letter of Secretary Blaine to American Min-
isters in Europe stated that any attempt of European
Powers to jointly guarantee the neutrality of canal
at Panama would be regarded by the United States
as uncalled-for interference
June 26, Resignation of Mr. McGrew, auditor in
Treasury Dept. in charge of post office accounts on
account of exposure of "star route" frauds
July 2, President Garfield shot in railroad station at
Washington by Charles Jules Guiteau, a disappointed
office seeker
July 7, Adolphus W. Greely sailed from St. Johns,
Newfoundland, in the "Proteus" to establish an
Arctic observing station in accordance with the plan
of the Hamburg International Geographical Con-
gress of 1879 to erect a chain of stations
July 16, Warner Miller appointed to succeed Thomas
Platt as senator from New York
July 22, Elbridge G. Lapham appointed to succeed
Roscoe Conkling as senator from New York
July 25, Death of Judge Nathan Clifford at Cornish,
Maine
Aug. 2, Conference of disaffected Knights of Labor
and Amalgamated Labor Union called convention to
establish a new organization, and in preliminary
national convention at Terre Haute called for dele-
gates to an international trades union congress to be
held in Pittsburgh in November
Aug. 12, Wrangel Island off the coast of Siberia taken
possession of by Captain Hooper in revenue cutter
"Corwin" in name of the United States
——, Greely expedition reached Discovery Harbor
where he established station, N. Lat. 81° 44', W.
Long. 64° 45'
Aug. 18, Anti-Monopoly League met at Utica, New
York
Aug. 26, Professor Amos E. Dolbear announced new
system of telephone with improved receiver
Sept. 2, Strike of 10,000 cotton handlers in New Orleans
for increase in wages
Sept. 12, Captain De Long in one boat reached the
western mouth of the Lena River, Siberia, and Mel-
ville, chief engineer, in second boat reached eastern
mouth of the Lena delta
Sept. 13, Death of General Ambrose E. Burnside at
Bristol, Rhode Island
Sept. 19, Death of President Garfield at Elberon, New
Jersey, where he had been moved on the 6th, from
the effects of the bullet wound of July 2
Sept. 20, Vice-President Arthur took the oath as Presi-
dent at his home in New York
Sept. 26, Funeral services for President Garfield held
at Cleveland, Ohio
Oct. 5, International Cotton Exposition opened at
Atlanta, Georgia
Oct. 9, Two of De Long's party started to find help
and on the 19th reached the Tunguses, native Asi-

atics, who kept them during the winter but would not
go to the rescue of De Long's party
Oct. 12, Death of Josiah Gilbert Holland, author
editor, in New York City
Oct. 14, Treaties of commerce and navigation and
consular service with Serbia signed
Oct. 27, Charles J. Folger, of New York, appointed
Secretary of the Treasury
Nov. 4, Denver made the permanent capital of Colorado
Nov. 10, Star route case dismissed on ground that
proceeding by information could not be sustained
Nov. 14, Trial of Charles J. Guiteau for assassination
of President Garfield begun in Washington
Nov. 15, Labor Convention at Pittsburgh organized the
Federation of trade and labor unions of the United
States and Canada
Nov 19, Secretary Blaine addressed Note to Great
Britain proposing modification of the Clayton-Bulwer
Treaty of 1850
Nov. 29, Secretary Blaine invited the Latin American
States to send representatives to a convention in
Washington to discuss methods of prevention of war
between the nations of America. The invitations
were withdrawn by his successor in office, F. L. Fre-
linghuysen Nov. 24, 1882
Dec. 1, Last spike driven near El Paso connecting New
Orleans with the Pacific on railroad later the "South-
ern Pacific"
Dec. 3, Electric lighting introduced on the streets of
Philadelphia
Dec. 12, Frederick T. Frelinghuysen appointed Secre-
tary of State succeeding Blaine, entering on duties
Dec. 19
Dec. 19, Benjamin H. Brewster, of Pennsylvania, ap-
pointed Attorney General
Dec. 20, Timothy O. Howe, of Wisconsin, appointed
Postmaster General
Dec. 24–31, Exodus of 5,000 colored people from Edge-
field County, South Carolina to settle in Arkansas

CONGRESS

Jan. 31, Foreign Decorations Act allowed decorations
to be tendered through the State Dept.
March 3, Act authorized registration of trade marks
and provided for their protection
——, Refunding Bill vetoed by the President because
of clause which affected the national banks
——, Congress adjourned
May 4–May 20, Special session of the Senate
May 16, Resignation of Senators Conkling and Platt
of New York in protest against appointment of
W. H. Robertson as Collector of Port of New York
by the President on the ground that they had not
been consulted about the appointment
May 18, The appointment of W. H. Robertson ratified
by the Senate
Dec. 5, Forty-seventh Congress, 1st sess. convened

1882

Jan. 2, Standard Oil Company organized into a trust
Jan. 16, Meeting of society organized by Father Joseph
M. Givney at New Haven, Connecticut, which be-
came the Knights of Columbus later
Jan. 25, Charles Guiteau convicted of murder and
sentenced March 4 to be hanged
Feb. 2, Catholic Society, the Knights of Columbus,
founded at New Haven, Connecticut
Feb. 9, South Carolina adopted local option

March 1, Adhesion of the United States to Geneva Convention for amelioration of wounded in time of war; proclaimed July 26

March 4, John W. Dorsey, John M. Peck, John R. Miner, Stephen W. Dorsey, M. C. Rerdell, Thomas J. Brady, William H. Turner, and J. L. Sanderson indicted in the star route frauds in court of the District of Columbia

March 14, Strike of 5,000 weavers and spinners at Lawrence, Massachusetts, against reduction of wages which lasted 23 weeks

March 23, Chief Engineer George W. Melville, of the expedition, found bodies of De Long and his 14 companions near the mouth of the Lena River, Siberia

March 24, Death of Henry Wadsworth Longfellow at Cambridge, Massachusetts

April 1, Unsuccessful strike of coal miners of western Pennsylvania against reduction of wages begun which lasted 20 weeks

April 2, Successful strike of 3,000 bricklayers of Chicago for increase in wages which lasted 68 days

April 3, Jesse James, notorious bandit, shot and killed by 2 members of his own band at St. Joseph, Missouri

April 6, Henry M. Teller, of Colorado, appointed Secretary of the Interior

April 12, William E. Chandler, of New Hampshire, appointed Secretary of the Navy

April 17, Strike of 5,000 cotton mill employees at Cohoes, New York, against reduction of wages begun which lasted 19 weeks

April 27, Death of Ralph Waldo Emerson at Concord, Massachusetts

May 3, Proclamation of the President called on outlaw "cowboys" in Arizona to disperse

May 4, President Arthur remitted the unexecuted part of sentence disqualifying General FitzJohn Porter

May 6, Claims Convention with Spain signed

May 9, Strike of Amalgamated Association of Steel and Iron Workers declared at Cleveland, Ohio, for advance in wages which lasted 95 days until the workers were starved into returning to the mills

May 15, Lieutenant James B. Lockwood and Sergeant Brainard of the Greely expedition to the Arctic reached "farthest north" at Lat. 83° 24½' N. and Long. 40° 46½' W.

May 20, New indictment in star route cases

May 22, Treaty of peace, amity, commerce, and navigation with Korea signed

May 28, Four survivors of the De Long Arctic expedition reached New York

June 1, Thirty thousand iron workers in Pennsylvania struck for new scale of prices

——, New trial begun in star route cases, ended in acquittal June 14

June 13, Extradition Treaty with Belgium signed

June 30, Charles J. Guiteau, murderer of President Garfield, executed in Washington

July 6, Tariff Commission met in Washington, John L. Hayes, president

July 14, One hundred marines landed at Alexandria, Egypt, by Admiral Nicholson, extinguished fire caused by English bombardment, and guarded American consulate

July 16, Death of Mrs. Lincoln, widow of Abraham Lincoln

July 19, Claims Convention with France signed

July 29, Treaty with Mexico signed by which troops of either country authorized to pursue fleeing marauding Indians across the border under certain conditions, and Boundary Treaty signed

Aug. 16, The Harvard Annex later Radcliffe College chartered in Cambridge for college for women

Sept. 4, Thomas A. Edison inaugurated first commercial electric lighting in the New York Central Station

Sept. 11, Verdict of jury in trial in star route postal fraud cases of S. W. Dorsey, Brady, and others accused found only 2 minor employees guilty

Sept. 13, G. W. Melville, with William Noros and William Ninderman, survivors of the "Jeannette" arrived in New York from the Arctic

Sept. 20, Strike of iron workers in Pennsylvania ended

Nov. 21, Second International Federation of Trades Unions met at Cleveland, Ohio, only 19 delegates

Nov. 22, Death of Thurlow Weed, journalist and politician, in New York City

Nov. 25, President Arthur at suggestion of the Attorney General removed from office the postmaster and assistant postmaster of the District of Columbia, and the foreman of the Government Printing Office involved in star route frauds

Dec. 4, New trial begun in star route postal fraud cases

——, Tariff Commission submitted a voluminous report recommending amendments to the customs laws

CONGRESS

Feb. 25, Apportionment Act on basis of the tenth census increased number of congressional representatives to 325

——, $100,000 appropriated for Mississippi River flood sufferers, and March 21 another $50,000 for relief

March 22, Anti-Polygamy Act imposed penalties on the practice and disqualified all those who practiced or approved polygamy from voting, holding public office, serving on juries dealing with prosecutions for polygamy. Elections in Utah placed under supervision of a board of 5 persons appointed by the President

March 28, Northern boundary of Nebraska extended to the 43d parallel

March 31, Annual pensions of $5,000 each granted to widows of ex-Presidents Garfield, Polk, and Tyler

April 4, President Arthur vetoed Bill prohibiting Chinese immigration for 20 years

April 26, Special message of the President to Congress on conditions in Arizona where a band of armed "cowboys" were engaged in robbery and resistance to laws and murder and asked for authority to act

May 6, Exclusion Act restricted the immigration of Chinese laborers for the ensuing 10 years to go into effect Aug. 5

May 15, A Tariff Commission constituted of prominent manufacturers, J. L. Hayes, H. W. Oliver, A. M. Garland, J. A. Ambler, Robert P. Porter, J. W. H. Underwood, A. R. Boteler, and Duncan F. Kennon, to examine the industrial situation and make recommendations as to rates of duty

July 1, President Arthur vetoed Bill providing for better protection of ocean travel because of defects due to bad wording which would have caused confusion in clearing vessels

July 12, Act passed to enable national-banking associations to extend their corporate existence

July 31, Indian Act penalized persons who attempted to reside in Indian Territory as traders or traded without authorization of federal agents

Aug. 1, President Arthur vetoed River and Harbor Appropriation Bill for $18,748,875 as extravagant expenditure of public money. Passed over his veto the following day

——, Copyright law passed

Aug. 2, Act to regulate carriage of passengers by sea provided for safety and sanitation

——, River and Harbor Appropriation Act passed over veto

Aug. 3, The President authorized to call an international conference to establish a common prime meridian for the world

——, Act barred paupers, criminals, convicts, and the insane from the United States requiring that they be returned at expense of owners of vessels in which they were brought. Head tax of fifty cents imposed on each alien passenger

Aug. 5, Construction of 2 steam cruising vessels of war authorized, to be steel and of domestic manufacture

——, Act to establish diplomatic relations with Persia passed

Aug. 7, General U. S. Grant and William H. Trescot commissioned by Senate to negotiate a commercial treaty with Mexico

Aug. 8, Export tax on tobacco repealed

——, Congress adjourned

Dec. 4, Forty-seventh Congress, 2d sess. convened

1883

Jan. 10, Death of Lot M. Morrill at Augusta, Maine

Jan. 20, Treaty of commerce with Mexico signed

Feb. 8, Claims Convention with France

Feb. 9, Death of W. E. Dodge at New York City

Feb. 15, The Ohio River flooded, reached highest point at Cincinnati of 66 feet, 4 inches

Feb. 23, University of North Dakota at Grand Forks founded

March 4, Death of Alexander H. Stephens at Atlanta, Georgia

March 5, Decision of Chief Justice Waite in the case of New York and New Hampshire vs. Louisiana that "one State cannot create a controversy with another State . . . by assuming the prosecution of debts owing by other States to its citizens"

March 9, Civil Service Commission organized, Dorman B. Eaton appointed chairman

March 24, Telephone communication opened between New York and Chicago

March 25, Death of Timothy C. Howe, Postmaster General

April 3, Walter Q. Gresham, of Indiana, appointed Postmaster General

April 4, Death of Peter Cooper in New York City

May 8, New civil service rules published by the President

May 22, Treaty of peace, amity, commerce, and navigation with Korea signed

May 24, Bridge over the East River connecting New York and Brooklyn opened for traffic

June 7, Extradition Treaty with Norway signed

June 19, Strike of telegraphers begun demanding one day's rest in seven, an eight hour day shift and a seven hour night shift, general increase of 15% in wages. At end of July the men went back to work on the same terms

June 21, Star route case trial of postal frauds ended with acquittal of Dorsey

June 28, Treaty with Mexico signed as to pursuit of Indians across border

June 29, The steamers "Yantic" and "Proteus" left St. Johns, Newfoundland, to go to relief of Greely Arctic expedition

July 1, The President gave notice of intention to terminate fishery articles of Treaty of Washington

July 15, Death of Charles Sherwood Stratton, dwarf (General Tom Thumb)

July 22, Death of General Edward O. C. Ord at Havana, Cuba

July 23, The "Proteus" was crushed in ice at entrance to Smith's Sound, and the "Yantic" returned to St. Johns arriving Sept. 13

July 27, Death of Montgomery Blair at Silver Spring, Maryland

July 29, International Boundary Treaty with Mexico signed

Aug. 1, Southern Exposition opened at Louisville, Kentucky

Aug. 19, Death of Jeremiah S. Black at Brockie, York, Pennsylvania

Sept. 1, Strike of glass blowers of western Pennsylvania against reduction of wages begun which lasted 23 weeks

Sept. 8, Completion of the Northern Pacific Railroad, the last spike driven at mouth of Gold Creek, Montana, by Henry Villard

Sept. 15, University of Texas at Austin opened

Sept. 18, Korean embassy received by President Arthur at the Fifth Avenue Hotel, New York City

Sept. 21, Direct telegraph communication established between the United States and Brazil via Central America

Oct. 15, Supreme Court decision declared the Supplementary Civil Rights Act of March 1, 1875 giving colored persons equal privileges in hotels, inns, theaters, and public conveyances unconstitutional except in the District of Columbia and the Territories

Oct. 22, Death of Thomas Mayne Reid, novelist, in London, England

Nov. 1, General Philip H. Sheridan succeeded General W. T. Sherman, retired, in command of the army of the United States

Nov. 3, Decision of Supreme Court that an Indian was by birth an alien and dependent

Dec. 4, Sons of the Revolution reorganized in New York City

Dec. 20, The cantilever railroad bridge across the Niagara River at the Falls opened

CONGRESS

Jan. 16, Civil Service Act to reform and improve the civil service of the United States passed. It passed in the Senate by vote of 25 Republicans and 13 Democrats, 33 senators not voting, and the House by vote of 102 Republicans and 49 Democrats, and 4 Nationalists (155 to 47) 87 members not voting

March 3, Tariff Act made first general revision since the Civil War, the protective principle maintained, iron ore, pig iron, and sugar included in the protected articles. Ad valorem rate on wool removed, and duties on woolen goods lowered, and those on pig iron and steel rails

——, Pensions increased for soldiers and sailors who have lost arm or leg in the service

——, Four war vessels authorized, 3 steel cruisers, the

"Chicago," "Boston," and "Atlanta," and one dispatch boat, the "Dolphin"

March 3, Joint Resolution gave notice of termination of certain articles of the Canadian Reciprocity Treaty to take effect in 1885

——, Letter postage reduced to 2 cents the half ounce

March 4, Congress adjourned

Dec. 3, Forty-eighth Congress, 1st sess. convened

1884

Jan. 1, New York and West Shore Railroad opened

Jan. 2, Suit vs. the Louisiana lottery decided against the United States

——, Treaty of commercial relations with Spain signed

Jan. 5, Death of Eduard Lasker, German Liberal, in New York City

Jan. 23, Conference of Independent Republicans met in New York City

Feb. 2, Strike of the Fall River spinners begun for increase of wages. Defeated in May by introduction of Swedish strike breakers

——, Death of Wendell Phillips in Boston

Feb. 8, Death of Arnold H. Guyot, geographer, at Princeton, New Jersey

Feb. 10, Devastating floods in the West, Ohio River reached height of 71 feet and ¾ inches Feb. 14 at Cincinnati, Ohio

Feb. 13, Treaty of commerce with Spain signed as to relations with Cuba and Puerto Rico, abolition of discriminating duties

Feb. 26, Strike of 3,000 miners at Brazil, Indiana, begun which lasted 14 weeks against reduction of wages

March 3, Supreme Court decision declared in favor of the Legal Tender Act of May 31, 1878, for reissue of Treasury notes in time of peace, such notes lawful tender for all debts

March 4, Iowa adopted state wide prohibition

March 14, The United States signed international Convention for protection of submarine cables

March 17, Successful three weeks strike of New York City painters for increase in wages

March 28, Riot in Cincinnati, Ohio, because of failure to punish a confessed murderer, William Berner, the court house burned, militia in conflict with mob, 42 persons killed, and 120 injured

March–April, 1885, Lockout of the Cigar Makers' International Union at Cincinnati

April 21, Discovery of natural gas in Pittsburgh, Pennsylvania

May 3, Sons of the Revolution, patriotic society, chartered

May 4, Strike of shopmen in Denver on reduction of wages by the Union Pacific Railroad. Managed by Knights of Labor and successful on third day

May 6–7, Failure of Marine Bank, New York City, and of firm of Grant and Ward in which General Grant as silent partner lost his fortune and suffered in reputation

May 8, Death of Judah Philip Benjamin in Paris, France

May 12, Death of Charles O'Conor, prosecuting lawyer of the Tweed Ring in New York City

May 12–13, Panic in stock market, New York City

May 13, Death of Cyrus Hall McCormick, inventor of reaping machine, at Chicago

May 14, National Anti-Monopoly Convention in Chicago nominated Benjamin F. Butler for President,

name of Vice-President left to nomination of the national committee

May 19, Race riot, whites and blacks, in conflict in Danville, Virginia

May 26, End of strike of spinners at Fall River, Massachusetts

May 28–29, National Greenback Party met in Indianapolis and nominated General B. F. Butler for President and A. M. West of Mississippi for Vice-President

May–Sept., Strike of the Troy, New York, stove mounters against reduction of wages and disbanding of union unsuccessful

June 2, Woman suffrage Amendment defeated by popular vote in Oregon

June 3, Republican National Convention met at Chicago and nominated James G. Blaine for President on first ballot, June 6, receiving 334½ votes and on the fourth, 541. General John A. Logan nominated for Vice-President. On the first ballot Chester A. Arthur received 278 votes for renomination, and on the fourth, 207

June 16, Strike of miners in western Pennsylvania for increase of wages begun, which lasted 22 weeks and was unsuccessful

——, Conference of Independent Democrats (Mugwumps) in New York, George W. Curtis, presiding, declared against the nomination of Blaine and Logan

June 18, Death of Bishop Matthew Simpson at Philadelphia

June 20, American Prohibition Party Convention at Chicago nominated Samuel C. Pomeroy, of Kansas, for President, and John A. Conant, of Connecticut, for Vice-President. These candidates withdrawn in favor of John P. St. John, of Kansas, for President, and William Daniel, of Maryland, for Vice-President

June 22, Strike of the Hocking Valley (Ohio) coal miners begun against reduction of wages which failed after 6 months

——, Lieutenant A. W. Greely and 6 other survivors of the Arctic expedition rescued at Cape Sabine, Smith's Sound, by relief expedition of Captain Winfield Schley

July 1, Proclamation of the President warned persons not to settle on Oklahoma territory

July 7, Massachusetts Reform Club declared against the Republican nominations

July 8–11, Democratic National Convention met at Chicago, and nominated Grover Cleveland, Governor of New York, for President, receiving 392 votes on first ballot, 475 on second, amended, 683. Thomas A. Hendricks, of Indiana, nominated for Vice-President unanimously

July 17, Lieutenant A. W. Greely arrived at St. Johns, Newfoundland, and at Portsmouth, New Hampshire, Aug. 1

July 23–24, National Prohibition Convention at Pittsburgh nominated John P. St. John of Kansas, for President, and William Daniel, of Maryland, for Vice-President

July 30, National Labor Party at Chicago declared for Cleveland and Hendricks for President and Vice-President

Aug. 16, General A. M. West nominated for Vice-President by National Committee of the Anti-Monopoly Party

Sept. 2, International Electrical Exhibition opened at Philadelphia

Sept. 4, Death of Charles J. Folger, at Geneva, New York

Sept. 9, American Historical Association formed at Saratoga, New York

Sept. 16, James Mulligan and Warren Fisher republished the letters of J. G. Blaine to Fisher upon which he was charged with corruption in favoring legislation while in office to help the Little Rock and Fort Smith Railroad, with a new lot of letters, letters in which Blaine expressed gratitude for being "admitted to participation" in certain enterprises, in his "present state of crippled and deranged finances," and promised he would not be a "deadhead" in the business

Oct. 1–Nov. 1, Meridian Conference opened at Washington, 25 nations represented, the meridian of Greenwich recommended

Oct. 6, Naval War College established by the Navy Dept.

Oct. 14, Frank Hatton, of Iowa, appointed Postmaster General

——, Appeal of FitzJohn Porter to the President for relief

Oct. 20, Meridian Conference at Washington agreed on normal day

Oct. 28, Hugh McCulloch, of Indiana, appointed Secretary of the Treasury

Oct. 29, Speech of Rev. Samuel D. Burchard at the Fifth Avenue Hotel in New York City at meeting of clergymen to pledge support to Blaine in which he described the Democratic Party as "the party of rum, Romanism and rebellion." Blaine in reply did not rebuke Burchard and disavow the insult which was resented by Catholics and featured by the anti-Blaine press. Blaine later attributed his defeat in the election to this unfortunate incident

Nov. 4, New Constitution for Montana ratified by popular vote

——, Presidential election. Grover Cleveland and T. A. Hendricks, Democrats, received popular vote of 4,911,017; Blaine and Logan, Republicans, 4,848,334; St. John and Daniel, Prohibition, 151,809; B. F. Butler and A. M. West, Greenbacks, 133,825. The electoral vote stood 219 for Cleveland and 182 for Blaine. The Republicans gained 18 seats in the House reducing Democratic majority to 45

Nov. 16, Treaty of commerce and customs regulations with Egypt signed

Nov. 20, Strike of carpet weavers of Philadelphia against reduction of wages which lasted 22 weeks

Dec. 1, Draft Canal Treaty with Nicaragua signed, the Zavala-Frelinghuysen Treaty by which title to canal conveyed to the United States. This Treaty later withdrawn by President Cleveland

Dec. 6, Completion of the Washington monument, Washington, D.C.

——, Treaty of commercial reciprocity with Hawaii extended

Dec. 16, World's Industrial Cotton Exposition opened at New Orleans

CONGRESS

Feb. 4, Morrison introduced Tariff Bill in House which proposed a reduction of 20% with exceptions which made it an average of about 17%

Feb. 12, Appropriation of $300,000 made for relief of flood sufferers in the Ohio Valley, and $200,000 more on Feb. 15

Feb. 13, Joint Resolution for expedition to Greenland to relief of the Greely Arctic expedition adopted

April 7, The Blair School Bill carried in the Senate for national aid to common schools; no action taken in House

May 6, Morrison Tariff Bill defeated in House by motion to strike out the enacting clause

May 13, Official "test" oath of 1862 repealed

May 17, Act passed for the civil government of Alaska

May 29, Bureau of Animal Industry created to inaugurate federal meat inspection

June 9, Act fixed second class postage at one cent for each 4 ounces

June 26, Act provided that graduates of the Naval Academy should be commissioned as ensigns

June 27, Bureau of Labor organized as part of Interior Dept.

July 2, Bill to place FitzJohn Porter on retired list as a colonel vetoed by the President. Passed over veto in House, but defeated in Senate July 3

July 5, Second Chinese Exclusion Act amended the first, limiting the meaning of the word "merchant," made additional requirements of identification for "visitors," and placed stringent requirements on masters of vessels bringing Chinese who had been in the country Nov. 17, 1880, and admitted on certificate from Chinese Government endorsed by American diplomatic representative abroad

——, Bureau of Navigation established in the Treasury Dept.

July 7, Organization of the Office of Naval Records of the Rebellion authorized

——, Congress adjourned

Dec. 1, Forty-eighth Congress, 1st sess. convened

1885

Jan. 13, Death of Schuyler Colfax at Mankato, Minnesota

Feb. 21, Dedication of the Washington monument at Washington

Feb. 27, Strike on the Missouri, Kansas, and Texas Railroad

March 1, New Southern Pacific Railroad Company formed by consolidation of the Central Pacific and the Southern Pacific

March 4, Inauguration of President Grover Cleveland, first Democratic President since the Civil War, and Thomas A. Hendricks, Vice-President

March 5, Unsuccessful strike of miners of western Pennsylvania begun which lasted 54 days against reduction of wages

March 6, Thomas F. Bayard, of Delaware, appointed Secretary of State; Daniel Manning, of New York, Secretary of the Treasury; Augustus H. Garland, of Arkansas, Attorney General; William C. Whitney, of New York, Secretary of the Navy; Lucius Q. C. Lamar, Secretary of the Interior; William F. Vilas, Postmaster General; William C. Endicott, of Massachusetts, Secretary of War

March 9, Strike on the Wabash Railroad which was joined by the Missouri Pacific and the Gould system, 4,500 men on strike

March 11, Woman suffrage Bill vetoed by the Governor of Dakota

March 12, University of Arizona chartered

March 13, Proclamation of the President warned against attempt of persons to settle on Oklahoma territory

——, President Cleveland withdrew the Frelinghuysen-

Zavala Canal Treaty negotiated with Nicaragua in Dec. 1884

March 18, Death of Susan Warner, author of the "Wide Wide World" and other novels, in New York City

March 31, Rebels in Panama seized an American ship. *See* Panama

April 2, American marines sent to Panama to protect freedom of communications between Panama and Colon, landed at Panama April 8, and occupied Colon, April 24

April 8, Death of Richard Grant White, Shakespearean scholar, in New York City

April 13, The McCormick Observatory in Virginia dedicated

April 17, Second Proclamation of the President declared Arthur's order opening Winnebago and Crow Creek reservations on east bank of Missouri River in Dakota inoperative and void and gave persons who had entered 60 days to vacate

May 16, Strike of Pittsburgh iron workers begun which ended in compromise

May 17, Apache Indians under Chief Geronimo took the warpath in Arizona and New Mexico

May 20, Death of Frederick T. Frelinghuysen at Millstone, Somerset County, New Jersey

May 25, United States troops in fight with Geronimo and Indians on the Blue River, Arizona

May 26, Surrender of Indian Chief Poundmaker to United States troops

May 28–June 5, Labor lockout in iron mills in Pennsylvania and Ohio, ended in Pennsylvania district

June 14, Death of Benjamin Silliman at New Haven, Connecticut, second of the name, son of the first

June 19, Bartholdi's Statue of Liberty Enlightening the World presented by the French people arrived at New York and was received with ceremonies

July 1–Sept. 27, Strike of rolling mill workers in Cleveland against reduction of wages

July 1, Provisions of Washington Treaty of 1871 with Great Britain extended for 6 months after expiration, as to privileges of American fishermen in Canadian waters and ports, and entry of Canadian fresh fish into the United States free of duty

July 1–7, Strike of street car drivers in Chicago

July 6–Sept. 1, Strike of workmen in the lumber and shingle mills in the Saginaw Valley, Michigan

July 23, Death of General Ulysses S. Grant at Mount McGregor, near Saratoga, New York

——, Proclamation of the President required cattle men to vacate the Indian lands of the Cheyenne and Arapahoe reservations within 40 days

July 28, Twelve months strike of coal miners at Mount Carmel, Pennsylvania, ended

Aug. 7, Proclamation of President Cleveland against illegal enclosures of public lands, and agents of the Land Offices sent to destroy fences. "One rancher took down 34 miles of fence after Cleveland's order." (Nevins)

Aug. 12, Death of Mrs. Helen Hunt Jackson in San Francisco, California

Aug. 18, Second strike on the Wabash Railroad system because of what was practically a lockout of members of the Knights of Labor in violation of agreement made

Aug. 29, White miners attacked and massacred Chinese laborers at Rock Spring, Wyoming. Federal troops sent

Aug. 29, First cable railroad opened in New York City

Sept. 2, Chinese laborers imported to work in the Union Pacific coal mines again attacked at Rock Spring, Wyoming, and a large number killed

Sept. 3, Naval War College, Newport, Rhode Island, opened

Sept. 8, Anti-Chinese outbreaks in Wyoming and Washington Territory

Sept. 18, Georgia adopted local option

Oct. 5–8, Unsuccessful strike of street car employees in St. Louis, Missouri

Oct. 10, Death of Cardinal John McCloskey

Oct. 14, Death of Henry W. Shaw (Josh Billings) at Monterey, California

Oct. 29, Death of General George B. McClellan at Orange, New Jersey

Nov. 5, End of long strike of miners in the Hocking Valley, Ohio

Nov. 7, Proclamation of the President against unlawful gatherings in Washington Territory, the anti-Chinese excesses

Nov. 10, Kansas prohibition law declared constitutional

Nov. 11, Stanford University, California, founded; opened in 1891

Nov. 12, Grand Jury at Seattle indicted 13 persons for anti-Chinese disturbances. No one convicted

Nov. 25, Death of Vice-President Thomas A. Hendricks at Indianapolis, Indiana

Dec. 8, Death of William H. Vanderbilt (born 1821) in New York City

Dec. 15, Death of Robert Toombs, Confederate General, at Washington, Georgia

CONGRESS

Jan. 8, Reagan Interstate Commerce Bill introduced which passed House Feb. 3. Failed Feb. 27, after Senate had passed substitute Bill Feb. 4

Jan. 20, French Spoliation Claims Act submitted claims of American citizens to a court

Feb. 14, Act authorized retired list at three-quarters pay for private and non-commissioned officers in army or marine corps who had served 30 years

Feb. 25, Act to prevent and provide penalties for illegal enclosures of public lands

Feb. 26, Contract Labor Act prohibited the entrance of contract laborers into the United States except domestic servants or skilled labor not otherwise obtainable for new industries

Feb. 28, Act of March 3, 1871, granting land to the Texas Pacific Railroad declared forfeit, and all amendments to Act, and lands returned to the public domain

March 3, Amendment to Postal Act raised the maximum weight on letter postage to one ounce for 2 cents and rates on second class matter lowered to one cent a pound

——, Revised international regulations for preventing collision at sea adopted

——, Act restored the right of appeal to the Supreme Court in cases of habeas corpus arising out of the restraint of any person in violation of the Constitution or laws of the United States. Right had been in abeyance for 17 years since Act of Feb. 5, 1867 granting such appeal had been repealed in 1868

——, Act authorized creation of one general from among those who had been generals of the army in addition to the number allowed by law. President Arthur appointed General Grant which gave him a pension of $13,500 on retired list

March 3, Construction of 2 cruisers and 2 gunboats authorized at aggregate cost of $3,000,000

——, Congress adjourned

Dec. 7, Forty-ninth Congress, 1st sess. convened

1886

Jan. 1, Council of the Cherokee Nation passed resolutions denying jurisdiction of the United States over Cherokee lands

——, Strike of glove makers of Gloversville, New York, begun for increase in wages

Jan. 4, Strike for 12 hour day on principal railroads of New York City. Ultimately granted

Jan. 11, Captain Emmet Crawford shot and mortally wounded by Mexicans while he was pursuing Apaches 50 miles southwest of Nacori, Mexico

Jan. 18, King's Daughters, religious society, organized in New York City

Jan. 19, Lockout of 8,000 cigar makers who refused to accept reduction of wages

Feb. 7, Anti-Chinese riot in Seattle after 400 Chinese have been driven out and sent to San Francisco

Feb. 9, Death of General Winfield Scott Hancock at Governor's Island, New York

Feb. 12, Death of Horatio Seymour at Utica, New York

Feb. 18, Death of John B. Gough at Frankford, Pennsylvania

Feb. 21, Chinese merchant, member of firm in San Francisco with certificate from consul at Hong Kong, refused permission to land on his return to San Francisco

Feb. 26, Virginia adopted local option

Feb. 27, Strike of stove molders of Troy, New York, begun which lasted 17 weeks and gained increase in wages

March 1, Strike on the Texas and Pacific Railroad on issue of discrimination against the Knights of Labor which spread to the Missouri Pacific, affected more than 5,000 lines of railroad and lasted 2 months

March 2–April 20, Strike of street car employees in New York City begun against hours and discharge of men which lasted 60 days

March 4, University of Wyoming at Laramie chartered, and opened in 1887

March 17, Race conflict at Carrollton, Mississippi, 20 colored men killed

March 21, Chief Geronimo surrendered to Lieutenant M. P. Maus, but escaped from guard March 31

March 26, Government troops sent to St. Louis to protect mail in transit against the railroad strikers

March 28, Railroad strikers ordered back to work by the Knights of Labor

April 5, Railroad strike on Gould system resumed because of refusal to take back all the strikers

April 7, Bloody riots of railroad strikers and special deputies guarding the bridge on the Louisville and Nashville Railroad crossing

April 9, Deputy sheriffs fired on strikers in railroad yard at East St. Louis killing six

April 16–20, Strike of employees of the street railroads in New York City begun on the Third Avenue line

April 20, General Miles began war on the Apache Indians

April 27, Apache raid in the Santa Cruz Valley, New Mexico

May 1, Strikes all over the country in demand for the eight hour day particularly in the building trades

May 3, Conflict of strikers and police at the McCormick Reaper Works in which one man killed and 6 injured

May 4, Knights of Labor declared the railroad strike on the Gould system ended, not more than one-fifth of men taken back on the Missouri-Pacific

——, State militia sent by Governor Rusk dispersed 7,000 strikers at Bay View, Wisconsin

——, Meeting of anarchists in Haymarket Place, Chicago, to denounce police shooting of workmen May 3. Police ordered crowd to disperse and a bomb was hurled killing seven of police and wounding 60

May 5, Anarchist riot at Milwaukee, Wisconsin, 10 persons killed and 15 wounded, the leader, John Mott, escaping arrest

May 7, American schooner "David J. Adams" seized at port of Digby, Nova Scotia, by Captain Scott of the steamer "Lansdowne," alleged violation of fishing laws

May 10, Appeal of Malietoa, King of Samoa, for American protection under the Treaty of Jan. 17, 1878. The American flag raised by Greenebaum, American consul, at Samoa proclaiming protectorate May 14, but this act disavowed. *See* Samoa

May 15, Strike of 180 women laundry workers, the "Joan of Arc" assembly of the Knights of Labor, in Troy, New York, for higher wages

May 17, General Trade Union Convention met in Philadelphia in opposition to the Knights of Labor

——, The American schooner "Ella M. Doughty" seized by Canadians at Englishtown, Nova Scotia

May 18, Lockout declared by employers of striking laundry workers at Troy, New York, and 15,000 laundry workers joined the strike which lasted 5 weeks, ending with acceptance of terms of employers

May 27, Twenty-two anarchists indicted by Grand Jury at Chicago for murder of policemen, trial begun June 1

May 28, In New York City John Most, A. Schenk, and R. Braunschweig, anarchists, convicted and imprisoned for inciting riots, sentenced June 2, Most for 1 year and the others for 9 months

June 1, Strike of Philadelphia carpenters

June 2, President Cleveland married Miss Frances Folsom of Buffalo, New York, the ceremony taking place in the White House

June 5, Street railroad strike in New York City stopped by order of the Knights of Columbus

June 7, Death of Richard M. Hoe, inventor of the revolving press, at Florence, Italy

June 30, James Gibbons, created cardinal priest with the title of Santa Maria in trastevere by Pope Leo XIII on June 17, invested

July 6, Death of Paul Hamilton Hayne near Augusta, Georgia

July 21, A. K. Cutting, American editor of Texas paper, arrested in Mexico, because of libel in his paper of Spanish-Mexican, Emilio Medina, as a "fraud and dead-beat," release demanded by Secretary Bayard Aug. 2, refused by Mexican Government

July 23, Camp of Geronimo surprised by General Miles

July 28, Lockout of cigar makers in New York to number of 3,500

Aug. 1, FitzJohn Porter reinstated in the army as a colonel and placed on retired list

Aug. 1, Seizure of British ships "Carolina" and "Thornton" in Bering Sea by the "Corwin"

Aug. 4, Death of Samuel Tilden at Greystone, New York

Aug. 5, A. K. Cutting sentenced by Mexican court to imprisonment for one year and payment of $600 fine

Aug. 12, Strike in Chicago stock yards

Aug. 20, Seven Chicago anarchists convicted of murder, August Spies, Michael Schwab, Samuel Fielden, Albert A. Parsons, Adolph Fischer, George Engel, and Louis Lingg sentenced to death, Oscar W. Neebe to 15 years imprisonment

Aug. 23, A. K. Cutting released from prison by the Mexican Government

Aug. 25–27, Convention of Populist Party at St. Paul, Minnesota, 27 States represented

Aug. 31, Earthquake shock which particularly affected Charleston, South Carolina, 57 persons killed, and property worth $5,000,000 destroyed

Sept. 4, Geronimo, Natchez and band surrendered to Captain Lawton

Sept. 16, First national convention of Anti-Saloon Republicans met at Chicago

Oct. 7, Federation of Organized Trades and Labor Unions met at Chicago, delegates from 8 unions

Oct. 8–10, Lockout of Chicago meat packers when men suspended work on notification of return to 10 hour day

Oct. 12–13, Storms on Gulf of Mexico and floods in Texas; Sabine Pass destroyed and 247 lives lost

Oct. 16, Lockout of Knights of Labor at Amsterdam and Cohoes, New York, because of strike in knit goods industry which lasted 5 months

Oct. 21, Protest of British Minister at seizure of Canadian fishing vessels in Bering Sea

Oct. 25, Chief Geronimo and 14 other Apaches remanded to Fort Marion, St. Augustine, Florida

Oct. 28, Bartholdi's statue of Liberty Enlightening the World, gift of the French people, set up on Bedloe's Island; dedicated by President Cleveland

Nov. 2, Strike of packers of Swift and Company, Chicago, became general throughout the stockyards, for the eight hour day

——, Florida ratified new Constitution by popular vote; local option established

——, Working men first nominated candidate for office in mayoralty election New York City, Henry George. Election won by Hewit defeating George and Theodore Roosevelt

Nov. 15, Chicago packers ordered back to work by union officials

Nov. 18, Death of Chester A. Arthur, in New York City

Nov. 21, Death of Charles Francis Adams at Boston, Massachusetts

Nov. 27, Reception given to Henry M. Stanley, African explorer, in New York City

Dec. 2, Panic on the San Francisco stock exchange

Dec. 15, Panic on the New York City stock exchange

Dec. 21, President Cleveland nominated J. C. Matthews, of New York, a colored man, to succeed Frederick Douglass as recorder of deeds in the District of Columbia. Controversy over the appointment, but eventually confirmed by the Senate

Dec. 26, Death of General John Alexander Logan at Washington

Dec. 28, Hearings begun in the Andover heresy trials

Dec., The sixth annual Convention of the Federation of Trades and Labor Unions became the first annual Convention of the American Federation of Labor

CONGRESS

Jan. 19, Presidential Succession Act provided for performance of duties of office of President and Vice-President in case of removal, death, resignation, or inability by members of Cabinet in the order of the creation of offices

Feb. 15, Morrison Tariff Bill introduced in House by which lumber, wood, fish, salt, flax, hemp, jute, and wool placed on free list, specific duties on woolen textiles replaced by lower ad valorem duties, rates reduced on cotton, pig iron, steel rails, and window glass

March 1, Special message of President Cleveland as to right of President of dismissal of federal officers

March 10, President Cleveland sent first pension veto to Congress. In all he vetoed over 200 pensions

April 8, Bill for free coinage of silver defeated in House by vote of 163 to 126

April 15, Act provided for new building for the Library of Congress

April 22, First message of a President on labor proposed board for settlement of disputes

May 17, Act provided that graduates of the United States Military Academy should be commissioned as second lieutenants

May 20, Act to provide for study of the nature of alcoholic drinks and their effect on the human system

June 17, Defeat of the Morrison Tariff Bill, vote against consideration in the House 157 to 140

June 19, Act to abolish certain fees for official services to American vessels amended Shipping Act, and authorized the President to exclude vessels of any country from privileges which were denied to American vessels by that country

June 29, Act legalized the incorporation of national trades unions

July 1, Act for relief of FitzJohn Porter authorized the President to appoint him a colonel in the army of the United States on the retired list

July 9, President Cleveland vetoed Bill for public building in Dayton, Ohio

July 10, President Cleveland vetoed Bill for public building in Asheville, North Carolina

July 30, President Cleveland vetoed Bill for public building in Springfield, Ohio

——, Act prohibited the passage of local or special laws in the Territories to limit territorial indebtedness and other specified subjects

Aug. 2, Act imposed tax on oleomargarine of 2 cents a pound and imposed regulations for manufacture, marking, sale, export, and import. Imported oleomargarine to pay internal revenue tax of 15 cents a pound

Aug. 3, Construction of 2 armor-clad vessels, 1 cruiser, and 1 torpedo boat, all steel, and of domestic manufacture, authorized

Aug. 4, One, two, and five dollar silver certificates authorized

Aug. 5, Congress adjourned

Dec. 6, Forty-ninth Congress, 2d sess. convened

1887

Jan. 1, Strikes begun by New Jersey coal handlers of the Philadelphia and Reading Railroad and by New

York longshoremen which spread to other roads; assisted by the Knights of Labor

Jan. 3, Free delivery system extended by the Post Office to include all towns having a population of 10,000 or any post-office with gross revenue of $10,000

Jan. 10, Death of John Roach, ship builder, at New York City

Jan. 18, Death of Edward L. Youmans, scientist, at New York City

Feb. 11, The Philadelphia and Reading Railroad Company settled strike by giving the 85 coal handlers who started strike their former rate of wages, and the approximately 28,000 in sympathy returned to work

Feb. 15, Act of Kansas legislature gave women the right to vote in cities of the first, second, and third classes in city elections and for school officers

Feb. 21, Oregon passed the first law recognizing Labor Day as a holiday, the first Monday in September; the celebration of Labor Day begun by Knights of Labor who paraded in New York City in 1882

Feb. 22, Union Labor Party organized in meeting at Cincinnati

March 1, Hospital Corps of the Army organized

March 3, Colonel Gilder's overland Polar expedition returned to Winnipeg

March 8, Strike of workers of the Bridge and Beach Manufacturing Company in St. Louis for increase in wages, and conflict between the Union and the National Defense Association of the employers continued until June when both sides claimed victory

——, Death of Henry Ward Beecher at Brooklyn, New York

——, Death of James B. Eads, engineer, at Nassau, New Providence, Bahama Islands

March 13, American Protective Association (A.P.A.) secret society, organized at Clinton, Iowa, objects to secure restrictions on immigration and naturalization, prevent State aid to parochial schools, and the exclusion of Catholics from political affairs

March 15, Strike of engineers on the Atchison, Topeka, and Santa Fé Railroad

March 22, First Interstate Commerce Commission appointed by the President

March 28, Extradition Treaty with Russia signed

March 31, Death of John Godfrey Saxe, poet, at Albany, New York

April 1, Charles S. Fairchild, of New York, appointed Secretary of the Treasury succeeding Daniel Manning, resigned

April 2, 9, 12, and 17, British sealing vessels in North Pacific seized

April 19, Catholic University of America incorporated

May 12, Strike of the building trades in Chicago

May 30, Death of Benjamin Perley Poore at Washington

June 4, Death of William A. Wheeler, former Vice-President, at Malone, New York

June 7, War Dept. Order to return flags captured in the Civil War to the States, both Union and Confederate; order revoked by President Cleveland June 16 as to Confederate flags because of protests

July 2–4, Reunion of both Union and Confederate soldiers held at Gettysburg, Pennsylvania

July 17, Death of Dorothea Lynde Dix, philanthropist, at Trenton, New Jersey

Aug. 9, State troops of Colorado in battle with the Ute Indians

Aug. 11, Failure of H. S. Ives and Company, stock-brokers, New York City, liabilities $20,000,000

Aug. 19, Death of Spencer F. Baird, naturalist, at Wood's Hole, Massachusetts

Aug. 24, The Utes led by Chief Colorow who had left their reservations in Utah to roam in their former home lands in Colorado fired on by Colorado militia in camp on their return, and a number of Indians killed and wounded and their possessions stolen. They had been promised immunity

Sept. 10, Strike declared against Lehigh Company by anthracite coal miners

Sept., American Tariff Reform League incorporated with headquarters in Chicago, John A. King, president, Franklin MacVeagh, vice-president

Sept. 21, Proclamation of the President revoked discriminating duties on Spanish imports

Oct. 1, Sugar Refineries Company trust organized in August became effective

Oct. 14, Pomona College, Claremont, California, founded

Oct. 22, Death of Elihu Benjamin Washburne, former Secretary of State, at Chicago

Oct. 25, Decision of Supreme Court in Wabash Railroad case denied the States power to regulate interstate traffic

Nov. 11, The Chicago anarchists, Spies, Fischer, Engel, and Albert R. Parsons convicted in May riot case, hanged. Fielden and Schwab sentenced to imprisonment for life, and Oscar Neebe for 15 years. Lingg escaped sentence by suicide in prison

Nov. 15, Meeting of Fisheries Commission in Washington

Nov. 17, John Most, anarchist, arrested in New York City for incendiary language, and sentenced Dec. 8 to imprisonment for one year

Nov. 28, Phonograph invented by Thomas Edison as announced Nov. 21 exhibited

Dec. 22, Death of Ferdinand V. Hayden, geologist, at Philadelphia

Dec. 24, Strike of employees of Reading Railroad for increase in wages

Dec. 30, Proclamation of the President asserted title of the United States to land in dispute with Texas between forks of river made Greer County by Texas Feb. 8, 1860

CONGRESS

Jan. 29, Mexican War Pension Act provided for pension of $6 and $8 per month to veterans who had actually served 60 days, a pension to be paid other officers and soldiers physically disabled or over 62 years of age. Not to include persons under disability of the XIVth Amendment to the Constitution

Feb. 3, Electoral Count Act fixed day for meeting of electors and made regulations for counting of votes and decision of questions arising throwing upon each State as far as possible the responsibility of determining its own vote, Congress to accept electoral vote certified by the executive of the State in case of disputed returns. Aim to prevent recurrence of disputed election as had happened in 1876

Feb. 4, Interstate Commerce Commission created by Act to regulate commerce making regulations for railroads passing through more than one State. Special rates to special shippers, rebates, drawbacks, discriminations between persons, places, and commodities prohibited, and greater compensation for a shorter than for a longer haul over same line in same direction with conditions the same, pooling operations made illegal, the Commission to have the right to require carriers to file annual reports and to install uniform system of accounts

Feb. 8, Act provided for allotment of lands in severalty to Indians on various reservations, citizenship to be accorded to allotees and Indians adopting a civilized life, 160 acres allotted to each head of family and 80 acres to each adult single person in division of tribal lands, surplus to be sold and held in trust by the Government for the entire community

Feb. 11, President Cleveland vetoed Pension Bill "for the relief of dependent parents and honorably discharged soldiers and sailors who are now disabled and dependent upon their own labor for support"; failed to pass in House Feb. 24 over veto

Feb. 23, Amendment to Act of Feb. 26, 1885 prohibited convict labor from landing in the United States with penalties and regulations for masters of vessels. Domestic convict labor prohibited

——, Canadian Retaliation Bill passed House authorizing suspension of goods to and from Canada by President

——, Importation of opium from China by Chinese or American citizens prohibited

Feb. 24, $147,748 voted for indemnity to Chinese for the Rock Springs, Wyoming, massacre of Sept., 1885

Feb. 25, President Cleveland vetoed appropriation for public building in Lynn, Massachusetts, of the same in Portsmouth, Ohio, Feb. 26, and in Lafayette, Indiana, Feb. 28

March 2, Hatch Act gave each State $15,000 a year to establish agricultural experiment station in connection with agricultural college

——, The President authorized to protect and defend rights of American fishermen and fishing vessels in fishery dispute with Canada, in retaliatory measures, to exclude Canadian vessels from American waters and stop importation of Canadian goods

March 3, Act to limit ownership of land and mines in Territories to American citizens

——, Act directed Secretary of the Interior to adjust railroad land grants and make investigation as to fulfillment of contracts

——, Trade dollar retired and provision made for recoinage

——, Tenure of Office Act of 1867 repealed

——, Anti-Polygamy Act with special reference to the Territory of Utah authorized the United States Government to seize and administer the property of the corporation of the Church of Jesus Christ of the Latter Day Saints

——, Congress adjourned

Dec. 5, Fiftieth Congress, 1st sess. convened

Dec. 6, President Cleveland's message devoted to subjects of taxation and revenue and urged revision of tariff

1888

Jan. 7–14, Strike of 20,000 miners in Schuylkill region against reduction of wages

Jan. 16, Don M. Dickinson, of Michigan, appointed Postmaster General, and William F. Vilas, of Wisconsin, appointed Secretary of the Interior

Jan. 30, Death of Asa Gray, botanist, at Cambridge, Massachusetts

Feb. 15, Death of David Ross Locke (Petroleum Vesuvius Nasby) at Toledo, Ohio

——, Treaty and *modus vivendi* with Great Britain as to Canadian fisheries signed; rejected by Senate Aug. 21 partly because it contained reciprocal tariff privileges by Republican straight party vote

Feb. 27, Strike of locomotive engineers and locomotive firemen on the Chicago, Burlington, and Quincy Railroad for new wage scale unsuccessful. Officially called off Jan. 3, 1889

March 3, Ohio adopted local option

March 4, Death of Amos Bronson Alcott at Boston

March 6, Death of Louisa May Alcott at Boston

March 14, Reading Railroad strike declared ended

March 15, Engineers and firemen of the Atchison, Topeka, and Santa Fé Railroad declared a sympathetic strike

March 22, Award of President Cleveland in boundary dispute between Nicaragua and Costa Rica

March 23, Death of Chief Justice Morrison R. Waite at Washington

April 18, Death of Roscoe Conkling at New York City from effects of exposure in the blizzard of March 12–13

April 25, Convention of representatives from nearly all the Southern States east of the Mississippi met at Hot Springs, North Carolina, to discuss ways of directing immigrant labor to the South

April 30, Melville W. Fuller appointed Chief Justice, confirmed July 20

May 15, Two Conventions of the Labor Party met at Cincinnati, Ohio, the "Union Labor" nominated Alson J. Streeter, of Illinois, for President and C. E. Cunningham, of Arkansas, for Vice-President, and the "United Labor" nominated Robert H. Cowdrey, of Illinois, for President and W. H. T. Wakefield, of Kansas, for Vice-President

——, Equal Rights Convention at Des Moines nominated Belva A. Lockwood, of Washington, for President, and A. H. Love, of Philadelphia, for Vice-President

May 26, Treaty of commerce with Spain signed (tonnage dues)

May 30, The Prohibition Party in convention at Indianapolis nominated General Clinton B. Fisk, of New Jersey, for President, and John A. Brooks, of Missouri, for Vice-President

June 1, Lick Observatory transferred by the trustees to the University of California

——, Philip H. Sheridan appointed by the President General of the Army. *See infra* Congress

June 5, Democratic National Convention met at St. Louis, Missouri, and nominated President Cleveland for reëlection and Allen G. Thurman, of Ohio, for Vice-President

June 16, Thomas A. Edison perfected the cylinder type of phonograph

June 19, Republican National Convention met at Chicago and nominated Benjamin Harrison, of Indiana, for President, and Levi P. Morton, of New York, for Vice-President. The first ballot June 22 gave Harrison 80 votes, John Sherman, 229; Russell A. Alger, 84; and Walter Q. Gresham, 111. Harrison nominated on the eighth ballot, June 25, with 544 votes

——, Lieutenant C. D. Halloway with 25 armed men landed from the U.S.S. "Essex" at Chemulpo, Korea, for the protection of American residents at Seoul

July 13, Secretary Bayard issued invitations to the independent Latin American States to a conference to be held in Washington, Oct., 1889

July 19, Death of Edward P. Roe, novelist, at New York City

Aug. 5, Death of General Philip H. Sheridan at Nonquitt, Massachusetts

Aug. 14, "American" Party met at Washington and nominated James L. Curtis, of New York, for President, and James R. Greer, of Tennessee, for Vice-President. Mr. Greer declined the nomination and P. D. Wigginton nominated Oct. 2

——, General J. M. Schofield appointed General of the Army succeeding General Sheridan

Sept. 4, Letter purporting to come from naturalized American, former British subject, addressed to the British Minister, Lord Sackville-West, asked for advice about his vote in the coming election. Reply of the British Minister Sept. 13 to the fictitious "Murchison letter" indirectly suggested that his correspondent should vote for the Democratic Party

Oct. 4, Alleged contract signed by John E. Campbell, Democrat, published in the Cincinnati *Commercial Gazette* in which he used political office for personal gain. Denied directly but used in Republican campaign

Oct. 6, Strike of street car employees in Chicago

Oct. 24, The "Murchison letter" and reply of Lord Sackville-West published in the newspapers

Oct. 30, Passports of the British Minister handed to him when his recall refused by the British Government

Nov. 6, Presidential election. Cleveland received popular vote of 5,540,329, to 5,439,853 for Harrison, Republican. Benjamin Harrison was elected President by 233 electoral votes to 168 for Cleveland. Fisk, Prohibition, received 249,506 votes; Streeter, Union Labor, 146,935; Cowdrey, United Labor, 2,818; Curtis, American, 1,591

Dec. 6, Claims Convention with Denmark signed

Dec. 24, Strike on Reading Railroad begun when men refused to handle a car of flour consigned to firm which employed non-union labor

——, Appeal of King Malietoa for protection against the Germans. *See* Samoa

CONGRESS

April 2, $1,000,000 voted to Esquimaux of the Atlantic coast of the Arctic for acts of humanity to shipwrecked seamen of the American whaler "Napoleon"

May 9, President Cleveland vetoed Bill under which $100,000 was to be appropriated to build a postoffice at Allentown, Pennsylvania, where adequate housing for the postoffice was rented for $1,300 a year

May 24, The President authorized to invite Latin American States to a conference in Washington in 1889 to consider certain specified measures which would promote peace and prosperity

June 1, Grade of lieutenant-general merged into general and the President authorized to appoint a General of the Army

June 13, Bureau of Labor made Dept. of Labor to take effect June 30

July 21, Mills Tariff Bill passed the House, providing for removal of duty on wool and reduction of customs duties by about $50,000,000, reducing duties on pig iron and cotton and woolen goods, and placed

salt, tin plate, hemp, flax, lumber, and wool on free list

Aug. 21, Bayard-Chamberlain Treaty with Great Britain providing for mixed commission to delimit territorial rights of American fishermen in Canadian waters rejected by Senate, the *modus vivendi* which accompanied the Treaty accepted

Aug. 23, President Cleveland sent message to Congress asking for power to suspend by proclamation the operation of laws and regulations as to transit of goods, wares, and merchandise in bond across or over the territory of the United States to and from Canada

Sept. 8, Canadian Retaliation Bill as proposed by the President passed in House; shelved in Senate

Sept. 13, Chinese Exclusion Act prohibited the coming of Chinese laborers to the United States, Chinese officials, students, traveling merchants, and visitors to be admitted on certificate. This Act to repeal the Act of May 6, 1882, and to take effect after exchange of ratifications of Treaty with China

Oct. 1, First law enacted dealing with adjustment of labor disputes on railroads created boards of arbitration and conciliation for voluntary arbitration of disputes between railroad corporations and other common carriers (Interstate) and their employees

Oct. 20, Congress adjourned

Dec. 3, Fiftieth Congress, 2d sess. convened

Dec. 5, The Senate substituted tariff Bill of its own for the Mills Bill

1889

Jan. 4, American Historical Association incorporated

Feb. 11, Death of John C. Dalton, physiologist, New York City

Feb. 13, Norman J. Coleman, of Missouri, appointed first Secretary of Agriculture

Feb. 20, The Maritime Canal Company of Nicaragua chartered for construction of a canal with express condition that the United States should not be financially liable but should control the canal as provided for in Treaty of 1867 with Nicaragua

March 4, Inauguration of President Benjamin Harrison. Levi P. Morton took the oath as Vice-President in the Senate

March 5, James G. Blaine, of Maine, appointed Secretary of State; William Windom, of Minnesota, Secretary of the Treasury; Redfield Proctor, of Vermont, Secretary of War; William H. H. Miller, of Indiana, Attorney General; John Wanamaker, of Pennsylvania, Postmaster General; Benjamin F. Tracy, of New York, Secretary of the Navy; John W. Noble, of Missouri, Secretary of the Interior; Jeremiah M. Rusk, of Wisconsin, Secretary of Agriculture

March 5–7, First conference of railroad commissioners at Washington

March 7, Catholic University of America given a charter by Pope Leo XIII

March 8, Death of John Ericsson, scientist and inventor, designer of the "Monitor" at New York City

March 9, Kansas passed first anti-trust law, and Maine, North Carolina, Tennessee, and Michigan during the year passed similar laws

March 15, Railroad mail service brought under the classified civil service

March 15–16, Hurricane at Apia, Samoa, and wreck of the U.S.S. "Trenton," "Vandalia," and "Nipsic" and 3 German war vessels. *See also* Samoa

March 16, The Seminole formally conveyed their lands to Congress

March 21, Proclamation of the President warned persons not to enter the Bering Sea for the purpose of unlawful killing of fur bearing animals

March 22, Death of Associate Justices Stanley Matthews and John A. Campbell of the Supreme Court

March 23, Proclamation of the President opened Oklahoma to settlers on April 22 at noon

April 16, President Harrison appointed Charles Foster, William Warner, and General George Crook a Commission to the Indians

April 16, The Standard Oil Company absorbed the Ohio Oil Company

April 22, Opening of Oklahoma for settlement, and official race of more than 50,000 settlers, Guthrie and Oklahoma City established as tent colonies before night

April 24, Wisconsin adopted local option

April 27, Death of Frederick A. P. Barnard, educator, at Sheffield, Massachusetts

April 29, Conference in Berlin of Great Britain, Germany, and the United States on Samoa

April 30, Sons of the American Revolution organized in 1875 became a national society

May 13, Supreme Court affirmed the constitutionality of the Chinese Exclusion Act of Oct. 1, 1888

May 14, Sioux Falls Constitution of 1885 for South Dakota adopted by popular vote, and as amended by convention of July 4-Aug. 5

May 31, The Johnstown flood caused by breaking of a dam in western Pennsylvania which wiped 7 towns out of existence in 15 minutes, and carried away the greater part of Johnstown. At least 5,000 persons lost their lives and property worth $10,000,000 destroyed

June 14, Treaty on Samoa signed by the United States with England and Germany at Berlin by which a tripartite protectorate over Samoa was established. *See* Samoa

June 20, The name Madison University changed to Colgate University, New York

June 26, Death of Simon Cameron, first Secretary of War in Lincoln's Cabinet, in Donegal, Lancaster, Pennsylvania

——, Death of Maria Mitchell, astronomer, at Lynn, Massachusetts

June 28, The District of Columbia criminal court ordered a *nolle prosequi* in the star route trial cases

June 29, Granting of liquor licenses placed with local authorities by Michigan

July 1, Death of Theodore Dwight Woolsey, former president of Yale University at New Haven, Connecticut

July 4, Constitutional Convention for North Dakota met at Bismarck, for South Dakota at Sioux Falls, for Montana at Helena, and for Washington at Olympia

July 4-6, Constitution for Idaho framed by Convention; ratified Nov. 5

July 12, New Extradition Treaty with Great Britain signed

Aug. 6, Sioux reservation (11,000,000 acres) ceded to the United States

Sept. 11, Enforced resignation of James Tanner, Commissioner of Pensions, owing to disagreement with the Secretary of the Treasury

Sept. 14, Jane Addams and Ellen Gates Starr took up residence in Hull House at 800 South Halsted St., Chicago

Oct. 1, Constitution for North Dakota including prohibition adopted by vote

Oct. 2, Clark University, Worcester, Massachusetts, formally opened

Oct. 2-April 19, 1890, International American Conference (first Pan-American) met in Washington to "consider measures for preserving the peace." Bureau of American Republics established to bring about a closer union of the Americas for purposes of trade and mutual advantage

Oct. 16-Dec. 31, International Marine Conference in Washington

Nov. 2, Proclamation of the President declared North Dakota (39th State) and South Dakota (40th State) added to the Union

Nov. 8, Proclamation of the President declared Montana (41st State) added to the Union

Nov. 11, Proclamation of the President declared Washington (42d State) added to the Union

Nov. 13, School of Theology opened in Catholic University of America

Nov. 13-15, Convention of the Populist Party at Montgomery, Alabama, described as "the largest gathering of representative agriculturists of the United States ever assembled"

Nov. 26, National Silver Convention met at St. Louis, Missouri

Dec. 6, Death of Jefferson Davis, Confederate President, at New Orleans, Louisiana

Dec. 14, American Academy of Political and Social Science organized at Philadelphia

Dec. 23, Death of Henry W. Grady, journalist, at Atlanta, Georgia

Dec. 25, Oklahoma enacted licensing act for liquor

CONGRESS

Jan. 22, Mills Tariff Bill passed by Senate and returned to House so amended as to be a new Bill

Feb. 9, The Dept. of Agriculture made a Cabinet Office

Feb. 13, Joint Committee for counting electoral votes, first under Act of Feb. 3, 1887, declared Republicans elected, Benjamin Harrison and Levi P. Morton receiving 233 votes and Grover Cleveland and A. G. Thurman, Democrats, 168 votes

Feb. 22, Enabling Act for North and South Dakota, Montana, and Washington passed to form constitutions and state governments

Feb. 25, $250,000 appropriated to enable the President to protect interests of the United States in Panama

Feb. 27, Special Act reappointed William S. Rosecrans brigadier general, and placed him on the retired list

March 2, $100,000 appropriated for a permanent coaling station at Pago Pago, Tutuila, Samoa

——, Act for protection of salmon fisheries of Alaska declared "all the dominion of the United States in the waters of the Bering Sea"

——, Bill to refund to the States and Territories the direct tax levied by Act of Aug. 5, 1861, vetoed by President Cleveland; repassed by Senate over veto but defeated in the House

——, Powers of Interstate Commerce Commission increased

March 4, Congress adjourned

1890

Jan. 2, Death of George Henry Boker, poet and dramatist, at Philadelphia

Jan. 22, Death of Adam Forepaugh, circus manager, at Philadelphia

Jan. 25, Miss Nellie Bly (Pink E. Corkran) of the New York *World* completed trip around the world eastward in 72 days, 6 hours, and 11 minutes

Feb. 2, Supreme Court decision sustained Anti-Lottery Act

Feb. 10, Protocol of explanation of Treaty of commerce and navigation with Greece of 1837 signed

——, Proclamation of the President declared part of the Great Sioux reservation in Dakota opened for settlement

——, Gentiles in Salt Lake City obtained control in a local election for the first time electing George A. Scott, mayor

Feb. 17, Proclamation of the President against use of the Cherokee strip by cattlemen under private contracts with the Cherokees

Feb. 22, Death of John Jacob Astor in New York City

March 15, Proclamation of the President again warned persons against entering the Bering Sea for purpose of unlawful killing of fur bearing animals, directed against British sea poaching

March 23, Invasion of the Cherokee strip by "boomers"

——, Death of General Robert C. Schenck at Washington

March 28, State College of Washington founded at Pullman

March 29, Massachusetts the first State to establish a naval militia

——, International Union of American Republics established Bureau in Washington

March 31, Bill to introduce the Australian ballot system in New York vetoed by the Governor

April 19, International American Congress (Pan-American) adjourned. Declarations in favor of compulsory arbitration. International Bureau of American Republics established (March 29). *See also* South America

——, Sons of the Revolution organized in New York

April 28, Supreme Court decision denied the validity of State prohibition laws affecting intoxicating liquors during the period of interstate transportation

May 1, Failure of Bank of America at Philadelphia followed by failure of other banks and of the American Life Insurance Company of Philadelphia

——, Strike of carpenters for the eight hour day claimed success in 137 cities and a nine hour day in many other cities

May 2, Proclamation of the President assigned Greer County in dispute with Texas to Oklahoma

May 3, Death of James B. Beck at Washington

——, The Merchants Bridge across the Mississippi River at St. Louis completed

May 19, Decision of the Supreme Court sustained the constitutionality of Act dissolving the Mormon Church Corporation

May 20, Indian lands in Iowa ceded to the United States

May 23, National Society of the Colonial Dames of America organized in New York City

May 24, George Francis Train completed trip around the world at Tacoma in 67 days, 13 hours, 3 minutes, and 3 seconds, beating Nellie Bly's record by about 5 days

May 29, University of Florida founded at Tarpon Springs

June, The eleventh census gave total population 62,622,250, an increase of 12,466,467 since 1880. 5,246,613 immigrants arrived from Europe during the decade, 1,462,839 from the British Isles, and 3,258,743 from other European countries. Center of population 20 miles east of Columbus, Indiana. Population of New York City 2,492,591; Chicago, 1,099,850; Philadelphia, 1,046,196; St. Louis, 451,770; Boston, 448,471

June 12, Convention at Topeka, Kansas, formed People's or Populist Party

June 25, Pottawatomie Indians ceded their lands to the United States, and the Shawnees the following day

June 27, National Commission of the World's Columbian Exposition appointed by the President, Thomas W. Palmer, former senator, of Detroit, permanent chairman, and John T. Dickinson, of Texas, permanent secretary

July 2, International Treaty for suppression of African slave trade signed

July 3, Idaho admitted as 43d State

July 7, Bill for renewal of Louisiana State Lottery which was due to expire in 1894 vetoed by the Governor

July 10, Wyoming admitted as 44th State

July 13, Death of Major General John C. Fremont at New York City

July 14, Bureau of American Republics organized

July 15, New Croton Aqueduct opened for use in New York

July 18, Death of Christian H. F. Peters, astronomer, at Clinton, New York

Aug. 2, Statement of Lord Salisbury of British claim for free navigation of Bering Sea

Aug. 9–Sept. 17, Strike of switchmen and yardmen of the New York Central Railroad because of dismissal of Knights of Labor begun

Aug. 10, Death of John Boyle O'Reilly, Irish-American journalist and poet, at Hull, Massachusetts

Aug. 12–Nov. 1, Constitutional Convention met at Jackson, Mississippi, and adopted Constitution which limited suffrage

Aug. 13, First annual convention of letter carriers of the United States held in Boston

Aug. 22, Arbitrator rendered award under Claims Treaty with Denmark of Dec. 6, 1888, that no compensation due from Danish Government to the United States on the Carlos-Butterfield claim

Aug. 25, Tunnel under St. Clair River at Port Huron, Michigan, completed

Sept. 1, Strike of carpenters in Cincinnati, Ohio

Sept. 2, Award under Claims Conventions with Venezuela of Dec. 5, 1885, and March 15 and Oct. 5, 1888, gave the United States $912,036.88 for claims approved

Sept. 2–3, Single Tax Convention met in New York City and adopted a platform

Sept. 4, United States Geographic Board created by Executive Order

Sept. 18, Death of Dion Boucicault, dramatist, at New York City

Sept. 19, George R. Davis, of Illinois, appointed Director General of the World's Columbian Exposition, at Chicago

Oct. 1, Official notice of the New York Central that no Knights of Labor would be employed on the railroad

Oct. 6, President of the Mormon Church issued manifesto proclaiming that the Church no longer sanctioned plural marriage

Oct. 11, Daughters of the American Revolution organized at Washington

Oct. 13, Death of Justice Samuel Miller of the Supreme Court at Washington

——, Death of William W. Belknap, former Secretary of War, at Washington

Oct. 15, David C. Hennessy, Chief of Police of New Orleans, killed at door of his home by members of Italian "Maffia" society, to which he had traced many crimes

Nov. 1, Mississippi Constitution adopted by Convention which met Aug. 12–Nov. 1, first of southern constitutions to limit suffrage, to take effect Jan. 1, 1891

Nov. 2, Irish leaders, Dillon and O'Brien, escaped from Ireland, arrived in New York

Nov. 4, Elections for Congress in 39 States in general defeat for Republicans

Nov. 24, Death of August Belmont at New York City

Nov. 25, Death of Benjamin P. Shillaber (Mrs. Partington) at Chelsea, Massachusetts

Dec. 2, National Convention of the Farmer's Alliance and Industrial Union at Ocala, Florida

Dec. 4, David Kalakaua, King of the Hawaiian Islands, landed at San Francisco, en route for Washington to negotiate as to tariff

Dec. 6, Cotton firm of V. and A. Meyer and Company in New Orleans failed with liabilities of about $2,000,000

Dec. 13, Sioux Indians in battle with troops near the Bad Lands in South Dakota

Dec. 15, Chief Sitting Bull killed while resisting arrest near Fort Yates, North Dakota

Dec. 16, Death of General Alfred H. Terry at New Haven, Connecticut

Dec. 19, State University of Oklahoma founded at Norman, opened in 1892

Dec. 29, Battle of Wounded Knee Creek, South Dakota, of Sioux Indians and troops commanded by General Miles in which 500 Indians were killed and 30 soldiers

CONGRESS

Jan. 29, Conflict in the House as to power of the Speaker to count a quorum when those actually present refused to respond to roll call

Feb. 14, New rules in the House enabled the Speaker to include in the quorum those present even if not responding to roll call, and that no dilatory motions should be entertained by the Speaker

Feb. 19, Joint Resolution adopted congratulations to Brazil on adoption of Republic

Feb. 24, Vote in the House for site for the World's Columbian Exposition gave Chicago 157 votes, New York 107, St. Louis 26 and Washington 18

March 5, Act authorized an assistant Secretary of War at salary of $4,500

March 20, Blair Education Bill for national support of common schools defeated in the Senate 37 to 31

March 27, Public Health Act to prevent introduction of contagious diseases from one State to another

March 31, $25,000 appropriated for tents for relief of flood sufferers in Arkansas, Mississippi, and Louisiana

April 16, Tariff Bill reported by William McKinley laid high duties on foreign goods coming into competition with home manufactures and admitted free those which did not

April 19, The President authorized to place John C. Fremont on the retired list with rank of major-general

April 25, Joint Resolution appropriated $150,000 for relief of flood sufferers on the banks of the Mississippi River

——, Act provided for the celebration of the 400th anniversary of the discovery of America by Columbus by an International Exhibition of Arts, Industries, and Manufactures to be held at Chicago

May 2, Act provided for a temporary government for the Territory of Oklahoma

May 21, McKinley Tariff Bill passed by the House by vote of 164 to 142 after debate May 7–10, the yeas all Republicans, the nays all Democrats except two

June 17, Free coinage Bill passed in Senate by vote of 28 Democrats and 15 Republicans against 3 Democrats and 15 Republicans; defeated in House by vote of 152 to 135

June 18, McKinley Tariff Bill reported in the Senate

June 19, Bill reported in House provided for federal control of federal elections to protect negro voters, called by its opponents, the Force Bill. Passed the House July 2 but killed in Senate

June 27, Dependent Parents and Disabilities Act granted pensions to soldiers and sailors who had served 90 days in the Civil War now or hereafter disabled and to widows and minor children and dependent parents. Number of pensioners increased under it from 537,944 to 976,014 in 1897, and annual expenditure during this period from $72,052,143 to $141,263,880

June 30, Three sea-going coast line battleships authorized

July 2, The United States signed the General Act for repression of the African slave trade

——, Sherman Anti-Trust Act to protect trade and commerce against unlawful restraints and monopolies. "Every contract, combination in the form of trust or otherwise, or conspiracy, in restraint of trade or commerce among the several States or with foreign nations" prohibited

July 11, Act incorporated the North River Bridge Company and authorized the construction of a bridge over the Hudson River between New York and New Jersey

July 12, American Merchant Marine Bill passed Senate to place trade on equality with that of other nations

July 14, Sherman Silver Purchase Act passed by which the Treasury Dept. was required to purchase each month 4,500,000 ounces of silver, and issue legal tender Treasury notes redeemable in gold or silver at the option of the Government in payment. Repealed the Silver Act of 1878

Aug. 8, "Original Package" Act made imported liquors subject to provisions of the laws of the State or Territory into which transported

Aug. 19, Act to adopt regulations for prevention of collisions at sea. Adoption postponed later to date to be designated

Aug. 30, Act provided for inspection by the Dept. of Agriculture of salted pork and bacon for export, and of foods and drink and cattle imported, and the

President empowered to use retaliatory measures against foreign nations discriminating against the United States

Aug 30, Act provided for annual appropriation from sale of public lands to the Colleges of Agriculture and Mechanics Arts established by Congress July 1862, each State and Territory to receive $15,000 the first year increased by $1,000 annually until $25,000 reached as a permanent annual grant

Sept. 4, Act extended criminal jurisdiction of United States Circuit Courts and District Courts to the Great Lakes and connecting waters

Sept. 10, McKinley Tariff Bill passed Senate 40 to 29

Sept. 19, Anti-Lottery Act amended statutes relating to transmission of lottery matter by mail

——, River and Harbor Act appropriated $24,981,295

Sept. 25, Act provided for forfeiture of certain public lands granted for construction of railroads when conditions not fulfilled

——, Act reserved for public park the big tree groves of townships 17 and 18 in California

Sept. 26, Act discontinued the coinage of three dollar and one dollar gold coins and three cent nickel pieces

Sept. 27, Rock Creek Park established in the District of Columbia

Oct. 1, McKinley Tariff Act signed by the President, raised average duty 48.2%. The duty on sugar abolished and a bounty given to domestic production of sugar in Louisiana. Duty raised on all foreign articles which under previous tariff laws could compete with similar articles of domestic production. Provision made for limited reciprocity treaties to encourage reciprocity between the United States and countries that produce sugar, molasses, coffee, tea, and hides

——, Weather Bureau transferred to the Dept. of Agriculture

——, Act set apart tracts of land in California as forest reservations

1891

Jan. 1, Engagement with Indians of troops commanded by Captain Kerr and Major Tupper on White River

Jan. 5, Fight with Indians near Pine Ridge Agency, South Dakota

Jan. 7, Forces of General Miles surrounded hostile Indians in Dakota

——, Meeting of International Monetary Conference in Washington

Jan. 12, Canada brought suit in Supreme Court of the United States in regard to seizure of Canadian sealer "W. P. Sayward" in Bering Sea

Jan. 15, Indians held council with General Miles at Pine Ridge Agency, South Dakota, ending Indian war

Jan. 17, Death of George Bancroft, historian, at Washington

Jan. 20, Professor Charles A. Briggs at Union Theological Seminary, New York City, delivered address on "The Authority of Scriptures" which was the cause of his trial for heresy later

Jan. 22, Conference of labor organizations in Washington created permanent organization and agreed upon platform

Jan. 24, Treaty of amity, commerce, navigation, and extradition with the Congo signed

Jan. 29, Death of William Windom, Secretary of the Treasury, in New York City

Feb. 5, Proclamation of the President announced commercial reciprocity with Brazil

Feb. 9–March 6, Strike of 10,000 miners in coke district of Pennsylvania begun at Connellsville, for advance in wages and against reduction of wages, successful

Feb. 10, Strike on the Pittsburgh and Western Railroad

Feb. 13, Death of Admiral David Dixon Porter at Washington

Feb. 14, Death of General William T. Sherman at New York City

Feb. 19, Death of Alexander Winchell, geologist, at Ann Arbor, Michigan

Feb. 24, Charles Foster, of Ohio, appointed Secretary of the Treasury

March 7, Lockout in clothing industry in Rochester, New York

March 12, Strike of weavers at Providence, Rhode Island

March 13, Italians charged with murder of Police Chief Hennessy in New Orleans acquitted in trial

March 14, Eleven Italians acquitted of murder of Police Chief Hennessy taken from prison by body of citizens of New Orleans and massacred, three of them citizens of Italy

March 15, Baron Fava, Italian Minister, protested the lynching of Italians in New Orleans

March 18, Death of William H. Herndon, law partner and biographer of Lincoln

March 21, Death of Lawrence Barrett, tragic actor, at Paterson, New Jersey

——, Death of Joseph E. Johnston, Confederate General, at Washington

March 25, Committees of the Union and the Defense Association met and worked out a plan of organization for stove molding industry, first written trade agreement with a local union

March 30, Proclamation of the President set apart a forest reserve in Wyoming

March 31, Italy recalled Minister, Baron Fava, because of massacre of Italians in New Orleans

April 1, Reciprocity Treaty with Brazil came into effect

April 2, Death of General Albert Pike at Washington

——, Fight of coke workers at the Moreland works in the Connellsville region in Pennsylvania with deputy sheriffs, 11 killed and 40 wounded

April 4, American Academy of Political and Social Science, organized in 1889, incorporated

April 5, San Francisco Chinese merchants send protest to Government against appointment of Henry W. Blair as Minister to China because of speech in Congress against the Chinese

April 6, Strike of journeymen printers for eight hour day and higher wages

April 7, Death of Phineas T. Barnum, showman, at Bridgeport, Connecticut

April 13, National Society of the Colonial Dames of America incorporated

April 14, President Harrison left Washington for trip through the Southern and Western States, returning from the Pacific coast to Washington May 15

April 22, Strike of building trades workers in New Orleans ordered by unions

April 28, China made formal objection to appointment of H. W. Blair as Minister to China

April 29, Death of John Le Conte, physicist, former president of the University of California

May 1, Strike of miners in Indiana for new wage scale which lasted 2 months

May 5, New Orleans Grand Jury refused to indict lynchers of the Italians

May 6, United States Marshal at request of Chilean Minister took possession of the Chilean transport "Itata" charged with carrying arms to Chilean rebels

May 7, The "Itata" sailed from San Diego, California, carrying the United States Marshal a prisoner. The Marshal landed south of San Diego and the cargo of arms taken on board

May 9, The U.S.S. "Charleston" sailed in pursuit of the "Itata"

May 19, Political Convention at Cincinnati called by the Citizen's Alliance and the Knights of Labor, organized new political party, the People's Party of the United States of America

——, Rice Institute, Houston, Texas, chartered

May 20, Proclamation of the President declared lands ceded by Indians on Fort Berthold Indian Reservation, about 1,600,000 acres, in North Dakota, open to settlement

May 25, Supreme Court upheld constitutionality of the "Original Package" Act

May 27, Registration of labels practically done away with by decision of Supreme Court in case of Higgins vs. Keuffel

June 3, Death of Benson John Lossing, historian, near Dover Plains, New York

June 4, Surrender of the "Itata" to the U.S.S. "Charleston" with cargo of rifles

June 6, Lieutenant Robert E. Peary and Mrs. Peary sailed from New York on expedition to Greenland

June 8, Daughters of the American Revolution incorporated

June 12, The Sac and Fox Indians ceded their lands in Oklahoma to the United States

June 15, Great Britain agreed to a *modus vivendi* in regard to Bering Sea seal fishing, a closed season and limited privileges until May 1, 1892

June 19, Treaty with Spain signed regarding commerce with Cuba and Puerto Rico

June 23, Rain making experiments in Texas under direction of the Dept. of Agriculture

June 29, Lake suddenly appeared in lowlands of the Colorado desert

July 1, Proclamation of the President extended privileges of the Copyright Act to Great Britain, Switzerland, France, and Belgium

——, Strike of 2,000 coal miners in Ohio for the nine hour day and "Columbus scale"

——, Pike's Peak Railroad opened in Colorado

——, Coinage of silver dollars suspended by the Treasury Dept.

July 4, Death of Hannibal Hamlin, former Vice-President, at Bangor, Maine

July 8, The Secretary of the Treasury accepted $5,000 from the "Itata" for violation of the navigation laws, cargo libelled at San Diego July 14

July 12, Immigration Bureau established

July 20, One thousand miners at Briceville, Tennessee, forced militia to withdraw from the mines with the convicts leased to work in the mines in competition with free labor

July 22, Steel workers on strike in Allegheny, Pennsylvania, returned to work on the company's terms

July 22-24, Compromise agreement that convicts should return to work in the Tennessee mines without mil-

itary protection but the Legislature must change the law and abolish convict labor within 60 days

July 31, Proclamation of the President announced commercial reciprocity with Spain

Aug. 1, Proclamation of the President announced commercial reciprocity with Santo Domingo

——, Eight hour day law went into effect in Nebraska

Aug. 5, Death of Thomas W. Bocock, in Virginia, Speaker of the Confederate Congress

Aug. 12, Death of James Russell Lowell at Cambridge, Massachusetts

Aug. 13, Miners took possession of the iron mines at Tracy City, Tennessee, and set the convicts who were working under the leasing system free

Aug. 15, Miners took possession of iron mines at Inman, Tennessee, and freed the convict laborers, and at Coal Creek, Aug. 18 after battle

Aug. 20, Daughters of the Revolution organized at New York City

Aug. 24, Patent for motion picture camera applied for by Thomas A. Edison, issued 1897

Sept. 1, Daughters of the Revolution incorporated as a national society

Sept. 5, Germany removed prohibition on American hogs and hog products officially certified by American Government

Sept. 6, Colored cotton pickers in Texas organized for better wages

Sept. 7, Chilean Government of President Jorge Montt officially recognized

Sept. 8, Denmark removed prohibition on American hogs and hog products

Sept. 9, Agreement with the Kickapoo Indians in Oklahoma by which they ceded lands to the United States

Sept. 10, Second Proclamation of the President set aside forest reservation in Wyoming adjoining Yellowstone Park

Sept. 18, Proclamation of the President declared the ceded Indian lands (June 12) in Oklahoma opened to settlement Sept. 22

Sept. 19, Tunnel under the St. Clair River between the United States and Canada opened

Oct. 1, Stanford University, California, founded

——, General strike in railroad coal mines

——, Miners in Briceville, Tennessee, set convict laborers in mines free

Oct. 4, New York Presbytery acquitted Dr. Charles Briggs of charge of heresy

Oct. 16, Proclamation of the President set apart the White River Forest Reserve in Colorado

——, Assault of mob in streets of Valparaiso, Chile, killed one sailor and wounded several from the U.S.S. "Baltimore"

Oct. 17, Death of James Parton, author, at Newburyport, Massachusetts

Oct. 19, Italy removed prohibition on American hogs and hog products

Oct. 23, Indictment of officers of the Louisiana Lottery at Sioux Falls, North Dakota

Oct. 26, First Empire State Express on the New York Central Railroad made the run from New York to Buffalo in 8 hours and 42 minutes, distance 436½ miles

Nov. 1, Failure of the Maverick National Bank in Boston, liabilities about $8,000,000

Nov. 4, New York Presbytery dismissed charge of heresy against Professor Charles Augustus Briggs;

case referred Nov. 16 to General Assembly of the Presbyterian Church

Nov. 6, Strike of iron workers against increase of hours without increase of pay

Nov. 16, France removed prohibition on American hogs and hog products

Nov. 17, Letters patent issued for Berliner microphone

Nov. 18, Mining Conference opened at Denver, Colorado

——, Farmer's Alliance Convention met at Indianapolis

Nov. 27, Attack of armed mob drove negroes from mines, Oliver Springs, Tennessee, employed after miners had forced convict laborers out Nov. 1

——, Post Office Dept. announced award of contracts for subsidized mail service

Nov. 29, The Cherokees agreed to sell the "Cherokee Strip" for $8,700,000

Dec. 4, The *Northwestern Miller*, Minneapolis newspaper, published an appeal for flour to send to starving Russians

Dec. 17, Drexel Institute of Art, Science, and Industry, dedicated at Philadelphia

Dec. 18, Colorado troops ordered to the Crested Butte to prevent conflicts between the miners and strikers

——, Agreement with Great Britain signed as to Articles for insertion in the Bering Sea Arbitration Agreement

Dec. 19, Petition of Mormon Church pledged obedience to laws and asked for amnesty for past offenses against the laws

Dec. 22, Stephen B. Elkins, of West Virginia, appointed Secretary of War

Dec. 31, Proclamation of the President announced commercial reciprocity with Salvador

CONGRESS

Feb. 7, Apportionment Act provided that after March 3 the House should have 356 members

Feb. 10, Penalties imposed for counterfeiting money or securities

Feb. 13, Act ratified and confirmed agreement with Sac and Fox Indians of Iowa and Indiana as to surrender of lands to the United States

March 2, Refunding Act required the Secretary of the Treasury to credit each State and Territory with sum collected under the Direct Tax Act of 1861 amounting in all to $15,227,632

March 3, Timber Culture Act of June 14, 1878, repealed and supplements. The President authorized to set apart reserve land in any part of the public lands

——, French Spoliations Claims Act appropriated $1,304,095.37 to pay indemnity according to findings of Court of Claims

——, Franking privileges for letters addressed to any official of the Government given to members of Congress

——, Act made provision for creation of a Court of Appeals and an additional circuit judge in each of the 9 districts, the Court of Appeals to have final jurisdiction in certain cases relieving the Supreme Court. Court of Private Land Claims provided for

——, The Postmaster General authorized to enter into contracts with American citizens for carrying mails on American steamships. Subsidy of $4 a mile run for first class vessels carrying foreign mails

——, Act amended that of 1877 providing for the sale of desert land in certain States and Territories

——, Act provided regulations to ensure safe transport

and humane treatment of exported cattle and for government inspection, which resulted in removal of foreign restrictions which excluded American meats

March 3, Amendment to Immigration Acts excluded alien idiots, insane persons, paupers liable to become a public charge, persons suffering from contagious diseases, polygamists, and felons. Established Office of Superintendent of Immigration

——, International Copyright Act gave rights to foreign authors of such countries as granted the same privileges to American authors

——, Homestead Act amended as to residence requirement by "commutation clause" providing that title may be obtained for fixed price per acre

March 4, Congress adjourned

Dec. 2, Fifty-second Congress, 1st sess. convened

1892

Jan. 2, Reciprocity Agreement with Salvador proclaimed

——, Tennessee convict miners returned to Coal Creek with military guard

Jan. 4, Chile reported the affair of Oct. 16 as begun by a quarrel of drunken sailors and not attack on the dignity of the United States

Jan. 10–March 18, Strike of employees of street car lines in Indianapolis

Jan. 11, Proclamation of the President set aside reservation of public land in New Mexico

Jan. 15, Death of Randolph Rogers, sculptor, at Rome, Italy

——, Copyright Agreement with Germany signed

Jan. 19, Claims Convention with Venezuela provided for submission to arbitration seizure of 3 American steamers during revolution

Jan. 20, Chilean Government asked that American Minister Egan be recalled

Jan. 21, Ultimatum presented to Chile demanded suitable apology, and reparation for assault on sailors of the U.S.S. "Baltimore" and that the Matta circular be withdrawn. (*See* Chile, Dec. 11, 1891)

Jan. 25, Reply of Chile dated Jan. 23 received proposed to submit Baltimore case to arbitration of a neutral nation or to decision of Supreme Court of the United States, and withdrew Matta note of Dec. 11 and request for recall of Minister Egan

Jan. 27, Chile accepted all demands of the United States; announced by the President Jan. 28 as satisfactory

Feb. 1, Proclamation of commercial reciprocity with Germany, British West Indies, and British Guiana

——, Supreme Court decision upheld Act of Congress excluding lotteries from use of the mails

Feb. 2, Commercial Reciprocity Agreement with Germany

Feb. 6, Letter of James G. Blaine to chairman of the Republican National Committee stated that he was not a candidate for the presidency

Feb. 8–March 4, Bering Sea Commission in session agreed to make separate reports

Feb. 11, Proclamation of the President set apart forest reservation, Pike's Peak, Colorado, and in New Mexico

Feb. 22, National Industrial Conference called by the Farmer's Alliance and the Knights of Labor met at St. Louis, Missouri, announced decision to act with the People's Party in nomination for President

Feb. 29, Supreme Court decision upheld constitutionality of the Tariff Act
——, Treaty of Arbitration signed with Great Britain
referring Bering Sea dispute to a judicial international
tribunal of 7 members, arbiters to be appointed by
Italy, France, and Sweden
March 1, Decision of Supreme Court of Ohio against
the Standard Oil Company dissolved the trust
——, Classified service extended to include physicians,
superintendents, assistant superintendents, school
teachers, and matrons in the Indian service
March 2, Indictment of the officers of the Whiskey trust
(Distilling and Cattle Feeding Company) in district
court in Boston
——, Death of Henry B. Hyde, founder of the Equitable
Life Insurance Company, New York
March 4, Death of Noah Porter, educator and philol-
ogist, and former president of Yale University, at
New Haven
March 12, Proclamation of the President announced
commercial reciprocity with Nicaragua
March 15, Proclamation of the President announced
retaliatory duties on certain articles imported from
Colombia, Haiti, and Venezuela
——, Commercial Agreement with France signed
March 16, The "Missouri" of the American Transport
Line sailed from New York carrying American gift
of 5½ million pounds of flour and meal to starving
Russians. Arrived at Libau April 3
March 21, Standard Oil Company dissolved at meeting
of trust certificate holders in formal action
March 23, Court of Arbitration for Bering Sea fisheries
dispute with Great Britain began formal sessions at
Paris: Justice John Harlan, of the Supreme Court,
Senator John T. Morgan of Alabama, Lord Hannan,
and Sir John Thompson, Canadian Prime Minister,
Senator Baron Alphonse de Courcelles, former
French Minister to Berlin, Senator Marquis E.
Visconti Venosta, of Italy, and Judge Mons Gregers
Gram, of Sweden
April 1, Lockout involving 3,000 miners begun in the
Cœur d'Alene mining district in Shoshone County,
Idaho
April 11, Proclamation of the President declared the
lands of the Lake Traverse Indian Reservation in
North and South Dakota opened to settlement on
April 15
April 12, Proclamation of the President opened to
settlement the Cheyenne and Arapahoe Indian
reservations in Oklahoma, about 3,000,000 acres, to
take effect April 19
——, Termination of difficulties with Italy by payment
of $25,000 to relatives of the victims of the New
Orleans riot and lynching
April 13, United States troops ordered out to enforce
peace between the cowboys and "rustlers" in
Wyoming
April 18, Renewal of the *modus vivendi* with Great
Britain as to the Bering Sea
April 19, Gasoline automobile operated by its inventor,
C. A. Duryea. Machine is on exhibition at the
Smithsonian Institution in Washington
April 21, Fight between cowboys and "rustlers" at
Powder River, Montana
April 27, Cornerstone of the Grant monument on River-
side Drive, New York, laid
——, Cornerstone of the Catholic University at Wash-
ington laid

April 30, Proclamation of the President announced
commercial reciprocity with Honduras
May 2–Sept., Strike of granite cutters and quarrymen
in New England unsuccessful
May 18, Proclamation of the President announced
commercial reciprocity with Guatemala
May 19, Society of the Colonial Dames of America
organized at Wilmington, Delaware
May 22, Spain removed prohibition on American hogs
and hog products
May 25, Meeting of the General Assembly of the
Presbyterian Church and consideration of the
charge of heresy against Dr. Charles A. Briggs.
Remanded to New York Presbytery May 30
May 26, Proclamation of the President announced
commercial reciprocity with Austria-Hungary
May 27, First elevated railroad in Chicago opened
June 4, Resignation of James G. Blaine as Secretary of
State 3 days before the Republican National Conven-
tion
June 5, Flood and fire caused by bursting of dam at
Spartansburg, Pennsylvania, and breaking of tanks
containing 5,000 gallons of gasoline which ignited on
oil creek between Titusville and Oil City, 100 persons
perished
June 7, Republican National Convention met at
Minneapolis, Minnesota, and nominated Benjamin
Harrison for second term, and Whitelaw Reid, of
New York, for Vice-President, June 10. On first
ballot Blaine received 182 votes to 155 cast for
Harrison
June 21, Democratic National Convention met in
Chicago and nominated Grover Cleveland for
President (June 23) and Adlai E. Stevenson, of
Illinois, for Vice-President. On the first ballot
Cleveland received 617 votes, David B. Hill 115,
and Boies 103, Gorham 36, and Carlisle 14
June 25, Strike begun of the Amalgamated Association
of Steel and Iron Workers against the Carnegie Com-
pany over new wage scale introduced in the mills at
Homestead, Pennsylvania
June 29, William F. Wharton, of Massachusetts, ap-
pointed Secretary of State
——, National Prohibition Convention met at Cin-
cinnati, Ohio, and nominated General John Bidwell,
of California, for President and James B. Cranfill, of
Texas, for Vice-President June 30
June 30, The mills at Homestead closed on account of
the strike
July 2, First National Convention of the People's
Party met at Omaha, Nebraska, and nominated
General James B. Weaver, of Iowa, for President,
and General James G. Field, of Virginia, for Vice-
President and adopted platform July 4
July 4, Peary Arctic expedition reached Independence
Bay
July 6, Pinkerton detectives hired by Carnegie Mills
at Homestead attacked by strikers as they came up
the river in barges and driven away in battle in
which 10 men killed and 60 wounded before the
Pinkerton men who had surrendered reached the
train for Pittsburgh
July 11, Strikers in the Cœur d'Alene silver mining
district in Idaho attacked and drove away non-
union men imported, many lives lost and property
destroyed
July 12, National Guard of Pennsylvania entered
Homestead by order of the Governor to protect the

Carnegie properties. Harrison attributed his defeat in the election to this strike

July 12, Death of Cyrus W. Field, founder of the Atlantic Cable Company, in New York

July 14, Three thousand workers in Pittsburgh, Pennsylvania, struck in sympathy with the Homestead strikers

——, Martial law declared in the Cœur d'Alene district in Idaho, and troops occupied Wardner and other towns

July 16, Proclamation of the President ordered persons in insurrection in Idaho to disperse

July 17, Indemnity of $75,000 received from Chile for relief of families of sailors in affair of Oct. 16, 1881

July 22, Treaty with Great Britain signed delimiting northeastern and northwestern boundaries

July 23, H. C. Frick, chairman of the Carnegie Company, shot and wounded by Russian Jewish anarchist, Alexander Berkman

Aug. 7, Claims Convention with Chile settled claims

Aug. 13, Strike of switchmen in Buffalo railroad yards begun for 10 hour day on Erie Railroad. Freight cars and other railroad property burned

——, Miners took possession of Tracy City in Tennessee and took convicts leased to the coal mines working in competition with free labor from the mines placing them on the train for Nashville

Aug. 17, Tennessee miners captured stockade at Oliver Springs and sent convict laborers and guards from the mines to Knoxville

——, Strike at Buffalo extended to the West Shore and New York Central Railroad

Aug. 18, State troops arrived at Buffalo to stop rioting of strikers

——, Society of Colonial Wars organized in New York City and chartered Oct. 18

——, Troops and miners in conflict near Coal Creek, Tennessee

Aug. 20, Proclamation of the President imposed tolls on freight through St. Mary's Canal bound for Canada as long as rebate on Montreal freight allowed in Welland Canal, retaliatory measure which went into effect Sept. 1

Aug. 22, Switchmen of the Western New York and Pennsylvania joined the strike, and also car handlers of the Lehigh. Conflict with National Guard at Buffalo

Aug. 24, Railroad strike in Buffalo declared off

Aug. 28, Socialist Labor Party met in New York and nominated Simon Wing, of Massachusetts, for President, and Charles R. Matchett, of New York, for Vice-President

Aug. 30, The "Moravia" of the Hamburg-American Line arrived in New York with 385 steerage passengers and cases of cholera reported

Aug. 31, Death of George William Curtis at Staten Island, New York

Sept. 1, Treasury Circular required 20 days quarantine for every vessel carrying immigrants

Sept. 7, Death of John Greenleaf Whittier at Hampton Falls, New Hampshire

Sept. 11, The Peary Arctic expedition brought to St. Johns, Newfoundland, by relief steamer "Kite"

Sept. 12, Citizens of Long Island towns of Islip, Bay Shore, and Babylon, prevented landing of passengers of cholera stricken steamer "Normannia" on Fire Island where the State had established a quarantine station

Sept. 13, National Guard and Naval Reserves enforced landing of passengers of the "Normannia" at quarantine station on Fire Island, New York

Sept. 19, Alexander Berkman, anarchist assailant of H. C. Frick sentenced to imprisonment for 22 years

Sept. 22, Grand Jury returned true bills in case of 169 strikers arrested at Homestead

Sept. 23, Death of General John Pope at Sandusky, Ohio

Sept. 30, Arrest of Chairman Crawford, Hugh O'Donnell, John McLuckie, and 30 other men of the Amalgamated Association of Iron and Steel Workers on charge of treason against the Commonwealth of Pennsylvania

Oct. 1, The University of Chicago opened

Oct. 3, University of Idaho chartered Jan., 1889 opened

Oct. 5, Four of the Dalton gang killed, 1 wounded, and 1 escaped in fight with citizens at Coffeeville, Kansas, in attempt to rob the bank, and 4 citizens killed

Oct. 13, Pennsylvania troops withdrawn from Homestead after 95 days service in protection of the Carnegie mills from strikers

Oct. 15, Proclamation of the President opened 1,800,000 acres in the Crow Reservation, Montana, to settlers

Oct. 20, Violence renewed by strikers at Homestead

Oct. 21, The World's Columbian Exposition at Chicago formally dedicated on Oct. 21 corresponding to Oct. 12, Old Style Calendar, the date of discovery of America by Columbus in 1492, and opened to the public the May 1 following

Oct. 31, Proclamation of the President extended privileges of the copyright to Italy

Nov. 5–11, General strike at New Orleans, Louisiana

Nov. 8, Presidential election. Grover Cleveland, Democrat, received 5,556,553 votes of total popular vote cast of 12,154,542; Harrison, Republican, receiving 5,175,577; Weaver, People's Party, 1,122,045; Bidwell, Prohibition, 279,191; Wing, Socialist Labor, 21,191

Nov. 19, General Society of the War of 1812 incorporated under present name. See 1854, Jan. 9

——, Letter of John Stevens, American Minister in Hawaii, to State Dept. argued the case of American annexation of Hawaii on moral, economic, and political grounds

Nov. 20, The Homestead strike declared off and most of the workers returned as non-union

Nov. 27, The Pittsburgh strikers refused to return to work unless the union recognized by the Carnegie mills

Dec. 2, Death of Jay Gould, capitalist, New York City, leaving property valued at $72,000,000

Dec. 5, Formal decree published in France removed prohibition on American pork

Dec. 8, Crow Indians ceded land in Montana to the United States

Dec. 9, Proclamations of the President reserved forest reservations, the South Platte, in Colorado, San Gabriel, in California, Dec. 20, Afognak Island, Alaska, Dec. 24

Dec. 27, Cornerstone laid of Protestant Episcopal Cathedral of St. John the Divine in New York City

——, Proclamation of the President announced commercial reciprocity with Salvador

Dec. 31, The Yankton Indian Reservation ceded and sold to the United States by Sioux Indians

CONGRESS

Jan. 11, Ratification of the General Act of the Brussels Anti-Slavery Convention of July 2, 1890, by the Senate

Jan. 21, Bland Free Coinage Bill introduced in House

Feb. 4, New House rules adopted did not include innovations of Speaker Reed as to counting of quorum, but did adopt restrictions as to filibuster

Feb. 9, Financial Committee of Senate reported against Free Coinage bills

Feb. 13, Resolution calling for an investigation of the "sweating system" adopted in House

March 24, Motion to lay Free Coinage Bill on table defeated in House

May 5, Chinese Exclusion Act (Geary) renewed prohibition of coming into the United States of Chinese persons for another 10 years, and made regulations for deportation of Chinese not lawfully entitled to remain in the United States. All Chinese laborers entitled to remain in the United States must obtain certificates of residence from district collectors of internal revenue

May 10, Act to encourage American shipping granted registration as vessels of the United States to foreign built vessels engaged in freight or passenger service from United States ports

July 1, Stewart Bill for free coinage of silver passed in Senate 29 to 25

July 13, Stewart Bill for free coinage of silver defeated in House by vote of 154 to 136

July 14, Act provided that pensions for soldiers and sailors totally incapacitated for manual labor by injury or disease contracted in service should be $50 a month

July 23, Act prohibited introduction of liquor of any kind into the Indian country, and penalties imposed

July 26, Act to enforce reciprocal relations with China

——, Act authorized the President to suspend free passage through St. Mary's Canal by foreign vessels

July 27, Act granted pensions of $8 a month to survivors of Indian Wars of 1832 to 1842

Aug. 4, Placer law extended to apply to lands chiefly valuable for building stone

Aug. 5, Act provided for coinage of the Columbian silver half-dollars for benefit of the World's Columbian Exposition

——, Pensions of $12 per month granted to all women nurses of the Civil War now dependent

——, Congress adjourned

Dec. 5, Fifty-second Congress, 2d sess. convened

1893

Jan. 4, President Harrison proclaimed amnesty for past offenses against Anti-Polygamy Act on condition of obedience to the law

Jan. 6, The Great Northern Railroad extension from Pacific Junction, Montana, to Lowell on Puget Sound completed

Jan. 9, Presidential electors met at State capitals to vote

Jan. 11, Death of General Benjamin F. Butler at Washington

Jan. 14, Extradition Treaty with Sweden replaced that of March 31, 1860

Jan. 16, American marines landed at request of J. L. Stevens, American Minister in Hawaii as urged by Committee of Citizens at outbreak of revolution. *See* Hawaii

Jan. 17, Provisional Government of Hawaii proclaimed and recognized by American Minister Stevens

——, Death of Rutherford B. Hayes, former President, at Fremont, Ohio

Jan. 23, Death of Lucius Q. C. Lamar, associate justice of the Supreme Court, and former Secretary of the Interior, at Macon, Georgia

——, Death of Philips Brooks, Bishop of Massachusetts, at Boston

Jan. 27, Death of James G. Blaine, in Washington

Feb. 1, American Minister Stevens assumed protectorate of Hawaii

Feb. 4, Commissioners of the Provisional Government of Hawaii received by the State Dept., and Feb. 11 by the President

——, Indians and cowboys in fight near Pine Ridge Agency

Feb. 14, Treaty of annexation signed with Hawaii

——, Proclamation of the President set apart the Sierra Forest Reserve, and the 25th the Trabuco Cañon Forest Reserve in California, and Feb. 20, the Pacific Coast Reserve, Washington, and Grand Cañon Reserve, Arizona

Feb. 15, Death of Samuel Colgate, merchant of New York

Feb. 17, Envoys of Liliuokalani, deposed Queen of Hawaii, reached Washington

——, State University of Montana established

Feb. 18, Sales on Stock Exchange, Wall St., New York reached unprecedented amount of 888,000 shares

Feb. 20, Death of Pierre G. T. Beauregard, Confederate General, at New Orleans

Feb. 21, Proclamation of the President suspended retaliatory tolls against Canada through St. Mary's Canal since discrimination against the United States terminated by Canadian Order of Feb. 13

Feb. 22, Steamers "City of New York" and "City of Paris" transferred from British to American registry

Feb. 23, Bering Sea Tribunal met in Paris and adjourned to meet March 23

Feb. 26, Bankruptcy of the Philadelphia and Reading Railroad with debts of more than $125,000,000

March 4, Inauguration of President Cleveland (second administration) and Vice-President Adlai E. Stevenson

March 6, Idaho law made it unlawful for any employer to enter into agreement requiring promise of employee not to become a member of a union

——, Walter Q. Gresham, of Illinois, appointed Secretary of State; John G. Carlisle, of Kentucky, Secretary of the Treasury; Daniel S. Lamont, of New York, Secretary of War; Richard Olney, of Massachusetts, Attorney General; Wilson S. Bissell, of New York, Postmaster General; Hilary A. Herbert, of Alabama, Secretary of the Navy; Hoke Smith, of Georgia, Secretary of the Interior; Julius Sterling Morton, of Nebraska, Secretary of Agriculture

March 10, Death of Andrew Preston Peabody, author

March 15, J. H. Blount sent a special commissioner to Hawaii to investigate the revolution which deposed Queen Liliuokalani, and American support of it

March 23, Bering Sea Tribunal met in Paris

March 25, Treasury reserve reached $107,000,000

——, Strike of clothing cutters in New York City because of discharge of union men

March 26, Sixty-seven Chinese illegally landed at Portland, Oregon, from Vancouver

March 27, End of unsuccessful strike of coal miners in Monongahela Valley which had lasted 7 months and thrown 70,000 men out of work

March 28, Death of Edmund Kirby Smith, Confederate General, at Sewanee, Tennessee

——, Rival factions of Choctaws in battle on the Reservation, Indian Territory

April 1, Commissioner Blount in Hawaii declared the American Protectorate established by Minister Stevens ended

April 3, Thomas F. Bayard took oath of office as ambassador to Great Britain, the first to hold that diplomatic rank

——, Decision of Supreme Court in case of Sidney Lascelles arrested in New York on a warrant of extradition in Georgia that a person extradited from one state to another is not exempted from trial for any other offense different from the one on which his exemption was secured

April 4, Arguments of English and American representatives begun before Court of Arbitration on Bering Sea question in Paris

April 5, American consulate at Mollendo, Peru, invaded by mob attacking a masonic lodge, and consul shot in foot; reparation demanded by Secretary Gresham April 6

April 6, Mormon Temple at Salt Lake City, 40 years in building, dedicated

April 7, Law of Colorado granted full suffrage to women; proclaimed by the Governor Dec. 2

April 12, American Railway Union organized at Chicago including all railroad employees

April 15, Arrival of the Duke of Veragua, successor to the honors of Columbus, invited by Congress to attend the Columbian Exposition; received by the President April 24

April 16, Secretary Carlisle suspended issue of gold certificates as by law required when greenback redemption fund fell below $100,000,000

April 17, Death of Lucy Larcom, poet

April 19, Miners in Tennessee attacked prison in Tracy City in demonstration against convict labor

April 21, Gold reserve fell below the $100,000,000 mark precipitating panic

April 24, The Spanish caravel "Santa Maria," reproduction of the flag-ship of Columbus given to the United States by Spain, arrived in New York

April 27, Columbian naval review in New York harbor, 10 nations represented by 35 warships led by the 3 caravels "Pinta," "Santa Maria," and "Nina," reviewed by President Cleveland on board the "Dolphin"

——, Death of General John Murray Corse at Winchester, Massachusetts

April 29, The Liberty Bell arrived at Chicago to be placed on exhibition at the Exposition

May 1, World's Columbian Exposition at Chicago formally opened by President Cleveland

——, Strike of 20,000 coal miners in Ohio

May 4, Secretary Carlisle issued order delaying arrests of Chinese who had not registered as required under the Chinese Exclusion Act to come into effect May 5

——, National Cordage Company went into bankruptcy resulting in panic in the West and South

May 8, Benefits of Copyright Act of 1891 extended to Denmark

May 9, Resignation of John L. Stevens as Minister to Hawaii and James H. Blount appointed

May 10, Death of Joseph Francis, inventor of the life-saving car, at Cooperstown, New York

——, New York Central Railroad engine No. 999, Charles Hogan, engineer ran a mile in 32 seconds between Batavia and Buffalo establishing a world record for speed

May 12, Bridge across the Mississippi at Memphis, Tennessee, opened

May 15, The Supreme Court declared the Geary Chinese Exclusion Act constitutional

——, Forty-seven delegates from miners locals met in Butte, Montana, the beginning of the Western Federation of Miners

May 17, The Cherokee Strip between Kansas and Oklahoma containing 6,072,754 acres purchased by the United States from the Indians for $8,595,736.12

May 18–21, General Assembly of the Presbyterian Church began session in Washington, and in case of Professor Charles A. Briggs on trial for heresy, May 31 reversed judgment of acquittal of New York Presbytery, and Dr. Briggs formally suspended June 1 from the ministry

May 19, Princess Eulalie, Infanta of Spain, special representative of the Queen Regent of Spain to the Columbian Exposition, arrived in New York

May 22, Trial cruise of the U.S.S. "New York" developed speed of 21.09 knots establishing world record for speed

May 31, Body of Jefferson Davis, brought from New Orleans, buried in Hollywood Cemetery, Richmond, Virginia

June 5, Proclamation of the President announced ratification of the Treaty of extradition with Russia of March 28, 1887 and March 3, 1893, to go into effect June 24

June 6, Convention of citizens of Canada and the United States met at St. Paul, Minnesota, to discuss question of reciprocity

June 7, Death of Edwin T. Booth, actor, in New York City

June 8, Gold reserve in Treasury fell below $89,600,000

——, Battle at Romeo, Illinois, between strikers and negro employees on Chicago drainage canal, 8 killed and many wounded, troops sent

June 9, Collapse of Ford's Theatre building used as office by the Pension Bureau in Washington caused death of 21 persons and injury to 68

June 20, Death of Leland Stanford at Palo Alto, California

June 26, India closed its mints to free coinage of silver, but was prepared to issue silver rupees at value of 1s. 4d., leaving the United States and Mexico the only important countries attempting by legislation to uphold silver either in price or as legal tender money *per se*

——, Governor Altgeld, of Illinois, pardoned Chicago anarchists convicted in connection with the Haymarket riot in 1886, Fielden, Schwab, and Neebe

June 27, Panic caused by fear of silver standard

June 29, First International Conference of the Epworth League held at Cleveland, Ohio

——, Seizure of steamer "Haitian Republic" with 500 contraband Chinese

July 1, Evans Dispensary law went into effect in South Carolina under which the State assumed control of sale of liquor in drug stores and State Dispensaries to be established, a total abstainer to be at head of each Dispensary and to receive definite salary regardless of sales made, no drinking to be allowed on the premises, and no quantity less than one-half pint to be sold

July 2, Peary Arctic expedition sailed from New York

July 7, Death of Samuel Blatchford, Justice of the Supreme Court, at Newport, Rhode Island

July 11, Convention in Denver, Colorado, in the interests of silver, made appeal for free and unlimited silver coinage

July 13, Convention at Salt Lake City in interest of silver standard

July 14, Suspension of 2,500 pensions by order of Secretary Smith

July 17, Stage employees and moving picture operators organized a union in affiliation with the American Federation of Labor

——, Report of Mr. Blount to Secretary Gresham represented the revolution in Hawaii as a conspiracy managed by aliens and chiefly Americans supported by Mr. Stevens, the American Minister. Report published Nov. 20

July 20, Benefits of Copyright Act of 1891 extended to Portugal

July 22, Since May 1 301 banks suspended, 93% in the South and West

July 26, The steel cruiser "Columbia" launched

July 27, Ten banks in the Northwest suspended

Aug. 1, First Convention of the National Bimetallic League in Chicago

Aug. 3, Peary Arctic expedition arrived at Greenland

Aug. 9, Suspension of Madison Square Bank, New York City

Aug. 10, First deportation under Chinese Exclusion Act from San Francisco of Chinaman who had not registered

——, Two deaths from yellow fever at Pensacola, Florida, the first on shore since 1888

Aug. 12, The steel cruiser "Minneapolis" launched at Cramp's ship-yards, Philadelphia

Aug. 15, Decision of Bering Sea Arbitration Court denied exclusive jurisdiction of Russia after 1825, and the right of the United States to a closed sea, but regulations prohibited the killing, capture, or pursuit of seals within a zone of 60 miles around the Pribilov Islands or outside that limit from May 1–July 31

Aug. 19, Proclamation of the President opened the Cherokee Strip to settlement on Sept. 16

Sept. 7, Agreement with Canada provided for stationing American agents at designated Canadian ports of entry to inspect immigrants landing destined for the United States

——, Death of Hamilton Fish at Garrison, New York

Sept. 16, Cherokee Strip opened to settlers, 90,000 persons in rush to take up land, 8 persons killed and many injured

Sept. 17, Yellow fever became epidemic in Brunswick, Georgia

Sept. 28, Proclamation of the President set apart the Cascade Range Forest Reserve, and the Ashland Forest Reserve, Oregon

Oct. 13, Union Pacific Railroad placed in hands of a receiver

Oct. 18, Death of Lucy Stone Blackwell, suffragist, at Dorchester, Massachusetts

——, Albert S. Willis, nominated Minister to Hawaii Sept. 8, instructed to support reinstatement of Queen Liliuokalani on condition that she grant full amnesty to those who participated in movement

against her, and assumes obligations of the Provisional Government; finally agreed to by the Queen Dec. 18

Oct. 19, American Federation of Musicians founded in affiliation with the American Federation of Labor

Oct. 20, Death of Philip Schaff, church historian, at New York City

Oct. 25, Rear Admiral Stanton removed from command of the South Atlantic Squadron on charge of saluting the flag-ship of Admiral Mello, Brazilian insurgent leader

Oct. 26, The U.S.S. "Oregon" launched at San Francisco

Oct. 28, Assassination of Carter Harrison, Mayor of Chicago, by P. E. Prendergast, disappointed office seeker

Oct. 30, World's Columbian Exposition closed, total attendance 27,539,041

Nov. 3, Ruling of Acting Secretary of the Treasury defined immigrants as "persons not naturalized" citizens arriving for purpose of establishing "permanent residence" without reference to part of vessel in which they traveled

Nov. 7, Mr. Willis presented his credentials to the Provisional Government of Hawaii headed by S. F. Dole

——, Elections in 12 States gave Republican gains

Nov. 8, Death of Francis Parkman, historian, at Jamaica Plain, Boston

Nov. 8–Dec. 5, Strike begun on the Lehigh Valley Railroad because of grievances which threw 27,000 miners out of work in coal mines controlled or dependent on the company. Both sides claimed victory

Nov. 23, President Dole representing the Provisional Government of Hawaii refused the request of the American Minister, Mr. Willis, that he turn over the government of Hawaii to Queen Liliuokalani

Nov. 26, Resignation of Terence V. Powderly as head of the Knights of Columbus. Succeeded by James R. Sovereign of Iowa

Dec. 23, Atchison, Topeka, and Santa Fé Railroad went into hands of a receiver, largest railroad system in the world

Dec. 30, Gold reserve at $80,000,000

CONGRESS

Jan. 5, Pension Act increased pensions for Mexican war veterans from $8 to $12 a month when absolutely needed for necessities of life

Feb. 6, Motion to take up consideration of repeal of the Sherman Silver Act of 1890 rejected by Senate

Feb. 7, Extradition Treaty with Russia ratified by the Senate

Feb. 8, Electoral votes counted, Grover Cleveland receiving 277 for President declared elected. Benjamin Harrison received 145 votes and General Weaver 22

Feb. 11, Compulsory Testimony Act provided that no person should be excused from testifying and documents, contracts, &c., required by Interstate Commerce Commission must be produced

Feb. 15, Quarantine Act added powers to and imposed added duties on the Marine Hospital service

——, Act established the Sierra Forest Reserve

March 1, Diplomatic Appropriation Act authorized the President to make rank of Minister correspond to that of the representative to the United States of country to which he was accredited. Ministers to

Great Britain, France, Germany, and Russia became ambassadors under this Act

March 2, Safety Appliance Act required automatic couplers and continuous brakes for cars and driving brakes on locomotives of interstate trains after Jan. 1, 1898

March 3, Commission created to negotiate with the Five Civilized Tribes of Indians as to their relations with the Government, extinguishing national or tribal titles, and allotment of their lands in severalty

——, Amendment to Immigration Acts established regulations for inspection and information as to conforming with laws

——, Free postal delivery extended to rural communities

——, Congress adjourned. This Congress called the "Billion Dollar" Congress because of appropriation of $1,026,822,049.72

March 9, President Cleveland withdrew Hawaiian Annexation Treaty submitted Feb. 15

Aug. 7, Fifty-third Congress, 1st sess. (extra) convened

Aug. 8, President Cleveland's message to Congress recommended repeal of the purchase clause of the Sherman Silver Act

Aug. 11, Wilson Bill introduced in House for repeal of purchase clause of the Sherman Silver Act

Aug. 18, Senator Voorhees introduced amended Wilson Bill in Senate

Aug. 28, Bill to repeal Sherman Silver Act passed in House by vote of 239 to 108

Oct. 30, Bill to repeal Sherman Silver Act passed in Senate by vote of 48 to 37

Nov. 1, Silver Purchase Clause of the Sherman Silver Act of July 14, 1890 repealed, passed the House and signed by the President the same day

Nov. 3, Time of registration for Chinese extended 6 months from date by the McCreary Act

——, Congress adjourned

Dec. 4, Fifty-third Congress, 2d sess. convened. Cleveland's message recommended reform of tariff

Dec. 18, President Cleveland in message defined his position on Hawaii, denouncing action of American Minister Stevens in supporting revolution, and his view that the status quo before the revolution should be restored

Dec. 19, Wilson Tariff Bill reported to the House provided for adoption wherever practicable of ad valorem duties instead of specific, and extension of free list to include raw materials of every description including such commodities as iron ore, coal, lumber, and wool, reduction of duties on manufactured articles as on steel rails for example from 75% to 25%, and woolen schedule 50%

1894

Jan. 1, Charter of the Louisiana State Lottery Company expired

Jan. 3, Death of Elizabeth Palmer Peabody, educator, at Jamaica Plain, Boston who opened first kindergarten in America in Boston

Jan. 17, Secretary of the Treasury Carlisle offered the ten year 5% bonds to amount of $50,000,000, which sold at a premium of $8,660,917 and brought gold reserve in Treasury up to $107,440,802 in February

Jan. 18, Gold reserve at $69,000,000

Jan. 24, Death of Constance Fenimore Cooper, novelist, at Venice, Italy

Jan. 25, A large number of strikers in Danbury hat mills returned to work after being out 9 weeks

Jan. 30, United States vessel fired on by revolutionists in harbor at Rio de Janeiro, Brazil

Jan. 31, New York Senate adopted resolutions for investigation of the New York City Police Dept. and Committee (Lexow) appointed because of public charges of the Rev. Dr. Charles Parkhurst, president of Society for the Prevention of Crime

Feb. 2 and 28, Miners in the Kanawha coal mining region in West Virginia on strike in riots in attempt to compel cessation of work in neighboring mines. Troops sent and martial law declared March 2

Feb. 3, Term of Alaskan Boundary Commission extended

——, Death of George William Childs, publisher, at Philadelphia

Feb. 16, Strike of silk weavers in New York City for advance in wages

Feb. 18, Strike of miners in Massillon district which ended in agreement March 7

Feb. 25, Death of Steele MacKaye, actor, in California

March 1, Death of William F. Poole, librarian, at Evanston, Illinois

March 2, General strike of silk weavers of Paterson, New Jersey

——, Death of Jubal A. Early, Confederate General, at Lynchburg, Virginia

March 9, First meeting of the Lexow Committee to hear testimony on blackmail levied by members of the New York police

March 13, Riots of strikers at Paterson, New Jersey

March 17, Governor Waite of Colorado ordered troops to Cripple Creek, where miners, on strike for $3 for an eight hour day or $3.25 for nine hours, in riots

——, Chinese Exclusion Treaty signed absolutely prohibiting immigration of Chinese laborers except in certain specified cases for period of 10 years

March 19, Miners at Cripple Creek, Colorado, agreed to arbitrate dispute, and troops withdrawn

March 25, Jacob S. Coxey, of Massillon, Ohio, led march of the unemployed for Washington to proclaim the wants of the people on the steps of the Capitol on May 1, the "Commonweal Army" numbering 75 planning to gather recruits at each town they passed through

March 29, Iowa mulct law established system of local option and license instead of prohibition

March 30, "Whiskey War" in 3 counties of South Carolina against the dispensary liquor law. Armed conflict in Darlington

April 1, State militia in South Carolina ordered out to stop rioting

April 2, Strike of miners in the coke region of Pennsylvania in Fayette and Westmoreland counties begun which resulted in murder of Joseph H. Paddock, Chief Engineer of the H. C. Frick Company at Connellsville by mob of Hungarians and arrest of district president and secretary of the United Mine Workers charged with murder by body of armed citizens

——, The Coxey Army reached Pittsburgh, Pennsylvania

——, Strike of 5,000 painters and plumbers at Chicago

April 3, Martial law declared in South Carolina cities by the Governor

April 4, Kelly's "industrial army" started from San Francisco to march to Washington

April 9, The coke miners of Pennsylvania agreed to return to work on the H. C. Frick scale

April 13, Strike of employees of the Great Northern Railroad for higher wages begun which by the 28th included all divisions of the road and 3,700 miles of railroad, which was settled May 1 by efforts of committee of leading business men of Minneapolis and St. Paul in most points in favor of the strikers

April 16, Railroad strike spread to the Northern Pacific Railroad

April 18, Judge Sanborne issued injunction against strikers interfering with trains on the Northern Pacific

April 19, State Supreme Court declared South Carolina dispensary liquor law of Dec. 24, 1892 unconstitutional and the Governor ordered dispensaries closed

April 21, General coal strike ordered April 11 by the United Mine Workers in convention in Cleveland, Ohio, begun because of low wages, lack of steady employment and lack in uniformity in rates, which affected 125,000 bituminous miners

April 29, Coxey's Army arrived at Brightwood Park, near Washington

April 30, Strike of 2,000 painters in Chicago

May 1, Arctic expedition of Walter Wellman sailed from Tromso, Norway and reached Table Isle May 12 off Spitzbergen but unable to proceed north because of broken ice, his ship crushed May 28, and the explorers conveyed back to Tromso by fishing yacht "Berntine" arriving Aug. 15

——, Coxey and his Army arrived in Washington and Coxey was arrested on the grounds of the Capitol on the technical charge of trespassing

May 4, Fur Seal Fisheries Treaty signed with Russia

May 9, President of the Pullman Company refused demand of committee for increase in wages

May 11 Strike begun of employees in shops of Pullman Company at Pullman, Illinois for increase in wages

May 12, Coxey's Army, forced to leave the District of Columbia, camped in Maryland while their leader toured the country trying to obtain supplies

May 16, United States Bering Sea patrol fleet sailed for sealing grounds

May 24–26, Trial of Professor Henry Preserved Smith of the Lane Theological Seminary, Cincinnati, Ohio, by the General Assembly of the Presbyterian Church on charge of heresy resulted in conviction by vote of 306 to 101

June 1, Strike of St. Louis street car employees for union scale of 40 cents an hour

June 2, Dedication of the Field Columbian Museum at Chicago

June 5–6, Strike at the National Tube works at McKeesport, Pennsylvania, and riots with violence

June 7, Death of William Dwight Whitney, philologist, at New Haven, Connecticut

June 9, Strike of coal miners in Iowa begun

June 11, Agreement on wage scale in coal strike concluded at Columbus, Ohio, and signed June 15 by operators and miners of region from Pennsylvania to Illinois, fixing wage basis at 60 cents a ton in Ohio and 69 cents in Pennsylvania

June 17, Miners in Pennsylvania, Ohio, and West Virginia agree to return to work. Indiana miners continued strike

June 20, 2,000 miners in Michigan on Gogebic range on strike

June 21, Officers of the American Railway Union ordered its members not to haul trains containing Pullman cars unless the demands of the strikers were granted

June 25, General Managers' Association of the railroads met in Chicago to discuss strike methods

June 26, American Railway Union ordered sympathetic railroad strike as the Pullman Company refused to arbitrate

——, Indiana coal miners returned to work

June 28, Mob of strikers at Hammond, Indiana, took Pullman coaches from the trains

——, The Attorney General instructed the District Attorney in Chicago to protect mail trains with United States marshals

July 2, Federal injunction issued by United States Judges Grosscup and Woods of northern district of Illinois enjoining President Eugene Debs of the American Railway Union and others from interference with trains carrying mails or engaged in commerce between the States

July 3, President Cleveland ordered federal troops to Chicago to protect the mails

July 4, Elwood Haynes at Kokomo, Indiana, drove gasoline engine automobile which he had invented. The machine is now on exhibition at the Smithsonian Institution

——, Federal troops from Fort Sheridan arrived in Chicago and were stationed by Colonel Crofton in stock yards, at Grand Crossing and Blue Island

——, Hawaiian Republic proclaimed. See Hawaii

July 5, Governor Altgeld, of Illinois, telegraphed protest to the President against invasion of federal troops

July 6, Mob of railroad strikers burned 225 cars along line of the Panhandle road

——, Governor Altgeld ordered out the militia to stop riots of strikers in Chicago

July 7, Troops dispersed mob of strikers at Hammond, Indiana

July 8, Proclamation of President Cleveland to the people of Illinois and of Chicago in particular warning them that those "taking part with a riotous mob in forcibly resisting and obstructing the execution of the laws . . . cannot be regarded otherwise than as public enemies"

July 9, Proclamation of the President against "unlawful obstructions, combinations and assemblages of persons" in North Dakota, Montana, Idaho, Washington, Wyoming, Colorado, California, Utah, and New Mexico

July 10, Knights of Labor called for general sympathetic strike which received no general response

——, E. V. Debs, president of the American Railway Union, Vice-President Howard, and other officials of the union, arrested on charge of interfering with the execution of the laws of the United States by complicity in the obstruction of the mails and conspiracy in restraint of trade under the Sherman Anti-Trust Act. Released on $10,000 bail

July 11, Strike in the potteries of Trenton, New Jersey, which began Jan. 1 against reduction of wages settled by agreement of workers to accept reduction of 12.5% instead of the 25 to 40% first proposed

July 12, Delegates from 25 unions connected with the American Federation of Labor met in Chicago and decided against calling a general strike in sympathy with the railroad strike

July 13, Railroad strikers in large numbers returned to work

July 17, E. V. Debs and other leaders of the American Railway Union arrested a second time on charge of contempt of court for disregarding the injunction of July 2, and sent to prison on refusal to give bail

July 19, Federal troops withdrawn from Chicago

——, Trial of police officials begun before Police Board, New York City

July 21, The cruiser "Columbia" started for Bluefields, Nicaragua, to protect American interests

——, Strike on Southern Pacific Railroad declared off

July 23, Proclamation of the Governor of South Carolina that the State Dispensaries for selling liquor would reopen Aug. 1 since the State Supreme Court had not declared the Act of Dec. 23, 1893 unconstitutional which was practically the same as that of Dec. 24, 1892. *See* April 19 *supra*

July 26, President Cleveland appointed Carroll D. Wright, of Massachusetts, John D. Kernan, of New York, and Nicholas E. Worthington, of Illinois, a commission to investigate the railroad strike

——, Coxey after a short term in District of Columbia jail disbanded his army

July 27, Completion of new Atlantic cable from Ireland to Newfoundland

Aug. 2, The Pullman shops in Chicago reopened

Aug. 3, Railroad strike officially called off by American Railway Union

——, Arrest of 12 persons, prominent citizens, of Darlington County, South Carolina, for participation in whiskey riots

Aug. 7, President Cleveland in formal letter to President Dole recognized the Hawaiian Republic

——, Gold reserve in Treasury fell to lowest point of $52,189,500

Aug. 11, Militia drove last of "industrial armies" of "Generals" Kelly and Fry across the Potomac

Aug. 14, Death of John Quincy Adams at Quincy, Massachusetts

Aug. 20, Strike of textile workers begun at New Bedford, Massachusetts, and becoming a lockout in Fall River, Aug. 22 on account of 10% reduction in wages. Ended by agreement Aug. 23

Aug. 21, Secretary of State Gresham offered $425,000 in settlement of claims for seizure of British vessels in Bering Sea. Not granted by Congress until Dec. 1897

Aug. 26, Death of Mrs. Celia Thaxter, poet, on Appledore Island of Isles of Shoals

Sept. 1, Death of General Nathaniel P. Banks at Waltham, Massachusetts, and of Samuel J. Kirkwood at Des Moines, Iowa

Sept 3, Royal Spanish Decree published canceled Reciprocity Treaty and ordered customs officials in Cuba and Puerto Rico to impose duties in force prior to Sept. 1, 1891, on all American imports

Sept. 4–13, Strike of United Brotherhood of Tailors and United Garment Workers of America in New York City and Brooklyn affecting 20,000 workers against the "task system" and the "sweating system" and for increase to a living wage

Sept. 9, Troops withdrawn from Cœur d'Alene mine district, Idaho

Sept. 11, Cases of 16 strikers of Great Northern Railroad charged with obstruction of mails dismissed by district court of Minnesota

Sept. 14, The "Lucania" of the Cunard Steamship Line made record eastern trip from New York to Queenstown in 5 days, 8 hours, and 38 minutes which at the time equaled the best westward record made by the same ship. Record western trip made on this date from Southampton to New York by the "New York," 6 days, 7 hours, and 14 minutes

Sept. 15, Peary Arctic expedition arrived at St. Johns, Newfoundland

Sept. 17, Sugar Planters' Convention in New Orleans declared against Democratic party

Sept. 20, Strike of 5,000 garment workers in Boston for shorter hours and increase of wages

Sept. 25, Trial of Eugene Debs begun

Sept. 27, President Cleveland proclaimed a general amnesty to Mormons convicted of polygamy under the Edmunds Act

Sept. 29, New York Constitutional Convention dissolved, had adopted 33 amendments to Constitution to be submitted to popular vote Nov. 6

Oct. 1, Indictment by Grand Jury of Washington of H. O. Havemeyer and John E. Searles of the Sugar Trust for refusing to testify before Senate Investigating Committee

Oct. 7, Death of Oliver Wendell Holmes, in Boston, Massachusetts, and of Andrew G. Curtin, at Bellefonte, Pennsylvania

Oct. 8, South Carolina Supreme Court declared liquor dispensary law constitutional

Oct. 8 and 29, Textile strike in New Bedford and Fall River ended in defeat

Oct. 17, Wheat reached lowest price ever recorded at 54.5 cents a bushel

Oct. 22, Pennsylvania Supreme Court permanently enjoined Standard Oil Company from absorbing several minor companies

Oct. 28, Prohibitions against American cattle at Bremen and Hamburg

Nov. 3, President Cleveland extended the classified civil service

Nov. 12, Cotton quoted at 5.56 cents, lowest price on record

Nov. 13, Secretary Carlisle issued call for loan of $50,000,000 on United States 5% ten year bonds; awarded Nov. 26 to syndicate of 39 firms

Nov. 14, Gold reserve down to $61,000,000

——, Report of Pullman Strike Commission published adverse to Pullman Company

Nov. 16, Death of Dr. James McCosh in Princeton, New Jersey

Nov. 21, Indian Commission Report declared the Indians have perverted the trust confided to them by the Federal Government and shown inability to protect their own interests and demonstrated their political incapacity

Nov. 22, Treaty of commerce and navigation with Japan signed

Dec. 1, John Burns, English Labor member of House of Commons arrived in New York

Dec. 14, Eugene V. Debs sentenced to 6 months imprisonment for contempt of court and the other leaders of the American Railway Union to 3 months each

Dec. 18, Decision of Judge Carpenter of the United States circuit court declared the Berliner microphone letters-patent void (application of June 4, 1877)

Dec. 22, Mayflower Society organized of descendants of those who came over in the "Mayflower"

Dec. 27, First meeting of the Venezuela Claims Commission

Dec. 27, Military and Naval Order of the United States organized. Incorporated Jan. 1, 1895
Dec. 28, Daughters of the Cincinnati formed in New York
Dec. 29, Last meeting of the Lexow Committee investigating charges against the New York Police Dept., charges confirmed by the evidence received

CONGRESS

Jan. 8, Debate begun in House on the Wilson Tariff Bill
Jan. 15, Senate led by David B. Hill of New York rejected nomination of the President of William B. Hornblower, of New York, as justice of the Supreme Court, by vote of 30 to 24, because President Cleveland had not submitted to Senate rule that nomination to offices should be subject to approval of the senators from the State to which the nominees belonged
Feb. 1, Wilson Tariff Bill passed the House with income tax and internal revenue added by vote of 204 to 140, average rate of duty 35.52%
Feb. 7, The House passed resolutions condemning American Minister Stevens for illegally aiding in overthrow of the constitutional government of Hawaii
Feb. 8, Federal Election Laws Repeal Act repealed clauses as to federal supervision of elections of the "Force Bills" of May 31, 1870 and April 20, 1871, the conduct of elections becoming entirely the affair of the States
Feb. 16, The Senate rejected the nomination by the President of Wheeler H. Peckham, of New York, as justice of the Supreme Court by vote of 41 to 32
Feb. 19, Senator E. D. White, of Louisiana, nominated by the President, confirmed as justice of the Supreme Court according to Senate practice when one of its own members was nominated to office
March 29, President Cleveland vetoed the Bland Seigniorage Bill to coin purchased silver bullion held in Treasury which had passed the House March 1 by vote of 168 to 129, and the Senate March 15 by vote of 44 to 31
April 2, Debate of Tariff Bill begun in Senate
April 6, Act gave effect to award of Bering Sea Tribunal
April 17, House Rules amended to count as quorum members present but not voting on roll-call
May 28, Act of Aug. 19, 1890 to adopt regulations to prevent collisions at sea amended
May 31, The Senate agreed on declaration that the Hawaiian Islands should maintain their own government, that the United States would not interfere but that interference by any other government would be regarded as unfriendly to the United States
June 28, The President signed Bill making Labor Day, the first Monday in September, a legal holiday
June 29, Compromise Tariff Bill reported from Committee to Senate radically changed from the House Bill, the sugar trust protected and other "interests"
July 3, The Gorham Compromise Tariff Bill passed the Senate with 634 amendments to original Wilson Bill of the House by vote of 39 to 34
July 17, Utah enabling Act passed with condition that polygamy be forever prohibited in the State
July 19, Letter of President Cleveland of July 2 to W. L. Wilson read in House condemned the Tariff Bill as amended by Senate
July 20, Joint Resolution passed in House provided that Constitution should be amended to provide

for the election of senators by the people of the states; no action taken in Senate
Aug. 13, Tariff Bill passed in House after unsuccessful attempt to break the combination against free sugar, free coal, and free iron ore; average rates of duty 37% as against 49.58 in the McKinley Tariff Act
Aug. 18, Carey Act provided that the United States should donate to the States desert lands not to exceed 1,000,000 acres to each as the State may cause to be irrigated, reclaimed, and settled
——, Head money for alien passengers on and after Oct. 1 to be increased, to one dollar
Aug. 28, Tariff Bill became law without the President's signature. Income tax last imposed in 1861 renewed for incomes over $4,000. Ad valorem tax on sugar 40%, wool and lumber placed on the free list. Reciprocity repealed
——, Congress adjourned
Dec. 3, Fifty-third Congress, 3d sess. convened
Dec. 10, House Committee on banking and currency began hearings on 4 plans, the Bill prepared by Secretary Carlisle, the Baltimore Plan submitted by the Baltimore Clearing House Association, and Plan of Mr. Eckels, all favoring repeal of laws requiring deposit of United States bonds as security for circulation

1895

Jan. 10–Feb. 24, Unsuccessful strike in Brooklyn, New York, of street car employees for 10 hour day and increase from $2 to $2.25
Jan. 16, Coal strike at Massilon, Ohio, ended on condition of reinstatement of strikers
Jan. 17, Lexow Committee submitted report to New York legislature
Jan. 18, The Mayor of Brooklyn called for troops to suppress rioting of strikers
Jan. 19, Brooklyn strikers in conflict with militia
Jan. 20, The U.S.S. "Philadelphia" sailed from San Francisco for Hawaiian Islands in view of uprising there
Jan. 21, Supreme Court decision that the sugar trust neither a conspiracy nor a combination in restraint of trade in case of E. C. Knight Company
Jan. 24, Eugene V. Debs and associates placed on trial in Chicago
Jan. 28, The Government undertook to arbitrate dispute between Mexico and Guatemala
Jan. 31, Gold reserve in Treasury reached new low of $45,000,000
Feb. 4, Assembly of 2,000 strikers at City Hall, Brooklyn
Feb. 5, The President declared in favor of Brazil in missiones boundary dispute between that country and the Argentine Republic
Feb. 7, The President in conference with J. Pierpont Morgan, Secretary Carlisle, and Attorney-General entered into contract with the Morgan-Belmont-Rothschild syndicate by which the bankers furnished 3,500,000 ounces of gold coin to the Treasury to be paid for by 4% bonds to run 30 years
Feb. 8, Gold reserve in Treasury at $41,340,181
Feb. 11, New York law gave power to Reform Mayor Strong of New York City to remove administrative and other officials
Feb. 12, New trial in Debs case ordered
Feb. 18–March 20, Strike in New York building trades begun by electricians demanding that eight hour

rule be brought into immediate effect; settled by agreement

Feb. 20, Death of Frederick Douglass, colored leader, near Washington

Feb. 21, Secretary Gresham asked for recall of Mr. Thurston, Minister to Hawaii, on ground that he had given the press material reflecting on the Administration

Feb. 25, France published decree prohibiting entry of live American cattle

Feb. 27, Resignation of W. S. Bissell, Postmaster General

March 1, Mexican Free Zone Joint Resolution suspended privilege of free transportation across United States territory to Mexico

——, William L. Wilson, of West Virginia appointed Postmaster General

March 6, New American Bimetallic Party issued platform

——, Strike of coal miners in Pittsburgh region

March 8, American steamer "Allianca" bound from Colon for New York fired on by Spanish gunboat 6 miles off Cuba; disavowal and apology asked March 14, settled May 6 by apology

March 11-12, Organized attack of New Orleans white laborers on negroes working at lower rates, 6 negroes killed, troops called out

March 12-13, Mob of miners at Walsenburg, Colorado, killed 6 Italians accused in killing of an American

March 15, Illinois Supreme Court declared eight hour law unconstitutional

March 18, Two hundred negro emigrants sailed for Liberia from Savannah, Georgia

——, Indictment of Police Inspector McLaughlin and 7 police captains in New York City

March 23, Indictment of C. P. Huntington, president of the Southern Pacific Railroad by Federal Grand Jury for violation of the interstate commerce law

March 26, Venezuela Claims Commission rendered judgment in favor of the United States for $143,500

April 2, Iowa liquor law, the "mulct law" declared constitutional by State Supreme Court

April 8, Income tax clauses of the Tariff Act of 1894 on real estate pronounced unconstitutional and void by the Supreme Court of the United States in case of Pollock vs. Farmer's Loan and Trust Company; rehearing May 20 on other income tax as the Court evenly divided

April 9, Strike of coat makers in Cincinnati and vicinity which was settled by agreement of April 17 with 25% advance

April 14, Death of Professor James Dana Dwight, geologist, at New Haven

April 19, Garment workers strike at St. Louis for clean shop and sanitary conditions

April 29, Secretary of the Navy ordered war ships to Nicaragua to protect American interests

April 30, Strike of garment workers of Baltimore against the sweating system

May 3, Order of Attorney General stopped proceedings against E. V. Debs in California riots

May 7, United States District Court declared South Carolina dispensary law unconstitutional in part as interference with interstate commerce

May 8, Judge Goff of the United States District Court at Columbus declared the law requiring registration unconstitutional but in June was over-ruled by the Court of Appeals

May 8, Coat makers at Philadelphia win strike

——, New York Bi-partisan Police Act passed

May 12, Death of Julius H. Seelye, former president of Amherst College

May 13, Admiral Meader declined to answer inquiry of the Navy Dept. as to his criticism of the Administration; resignation accepted May 17

May 15, Silver Convention at Salt Lake City attended by representatives from 17 States and Territories

May 16, Proclamation of the President declared the Yankton Indian Reservation in South Dakota opened to settlers to take effect May 21 at noon, and May 18 the Kickapoo Indian Reservation in Oklahoma to take effect May 23

May 18, Decree of Judge Carpenter of Dec., 1894, reversed as to Berliner microphone patent which was declared valid, victory for the American Bell Telephone Company

May 20, Decision of the Supreme Court pronounced the income tax clauses of the Tariff Act of 1894 unconstitutional because not apportioned as a direct tax

May 22, General strike in the brickyards of Chicago

May 23, New York Public Library, Astor, Lenox, and Tilden foundations, formed by consolidation of the Astor and Lenox libraries and the Tilden trust under law of March 20, originally incorporated March 26, 1887

——, Sound Money Convention of the Southern States met at Memphis, Tennessee

May 24, The President placed all positions in the Dept. of Agriculture above the grade of laborer and excepting half a dozen of the highest offices in the classified service

——, Ballington Booth and his wife of the Salvation Army became naturalized citizens of the United States

May 25, The Supreme Court in the Debs case upheld injunction issued by the lower court restraining the defendant from obstructing trains engaged in interstate commerce or obstructing mails

May 27, Supreme Court denied application for habeas corpus in case of Debs and his associates

May 28, Death of Secretary Walter Q. Gresham at Washington

June 1, Coal miners on strike reached agreement at Columbus

June 4, Free Silver Convention at Springfield, Illinois

June 6, Free Silver Convention at Des Moines, Iowa

June 8, Richard Olney, of Massachusetts, appointed Secretary of State, and Judson Harmon, of Ohio, appointed Attorney General to succeed Olney

June 12, Proclamation of the President warned American citizens against violation of the neutrality laws by giving aid to Cuban insurgents

June 12-13, Bi-Metallic Convention at Memphis, Tennessee

June 13, 2,700 employees of the Government Printing Office put under classified service

——, Supreme Court of Illinois declared the Distilling and Cattle Feeding Company (Whiskey Trust) illegal

June 18, Missouri Supreme Court declared unconstitutional law forbidding discharge of employees for connection with a labor organization

June 19, Committee of Seventy of New York organized Sept., 1894, to lead campaign against Tammany misrule in New York City disbanded

June 23, Death of James Renwick, architect of St. Patrick's Cathedral, New York

June 25, Gold reserve at $100,000,000 for first time since Dec., 1894

July 3, National Reform Conference met at Staten Island, New York City

July 4, In Boston a parade of the American Protective Association (A.P.A.), the "Little Red School House" and kindred associations attacked by Roman Catholics, one man killed and 40 injured

July 15, Pension Office clerks placed under the classified service

July 16, General strike of iron miners demanding $2 a day, ended Sept. 1

July 19, Boycott of national bank notes in attack on gold system ordered by J. R. Sovereign, head of the Knights of Labor, to begin Sept. 1

July 20, Note of Secretary of State Olney protested to Great Britain against the enlargement of British Guiana in arbitrary rectification of the boundary with Venezuela in derogation of the rights of Venezuela as an extension of European dominion in the Western Hemisphere, and that the settlement of the dispute should be by "peaceful arbitration"

July 23, Employees of the Geological Survey placed under the classified service

July 24, United States troops ordered to Wyoming on account of Indian outbreaks

July 26, Secretary Morton ordered abolition of Seed Division of the Dept. of Agriculture to take effect Oct. 1 stopping free distribution of seeds

July 28, General strike of tailors in New York City and Brooklyn which extended to Newark affecting 150,000 men against the "task system" which was settled Aug. 10

Aug. 4–7, Race war of Italians and negro miners in coal region, Spring Valley, Illinois, negro settlement broken up

Aug. 14–15, Silver Democrats in conference in Washington organized a National Bimetallic Committee, Senator I. G. Harris, chairman

Sept. 5, Decision of Comptroller of Treasury that sugar bounty granted by Sundry Civil Bill of the 53d Congress unconstitutional

Sept. 11, The Empire State Express on the New York Central Railroad made long distance record for speed from New York to Buffalo in 6 hours, 54 minutes, and 27 seconds, 436½ miles, average 64.34 miles an hour as compared with English record of Aug. 20 on London and Northwestern of 63.27 miles an hour

——, State University of Montana opened

Sept. 14, Mora claim paid by Spain of $1,449,000 for estate seized in Cuba in 1869, sugar plantation of Antonio M. Mora

Sept. 18–Dec. 31, Cotton States and International Exposition at Atlanta, Georgia, with exhibits from 37 States and 13 foreign countries

Sept. 19, Dedication of National Park on site of the Chickamauga battle field in Tennessee

Sept. 20, Executive Order of President Cleveland for improvement of the consular service providing for promotion and transfer in certain class of positions carrying salary or fee of not more than $2,500 or less than $1,000. Positions to be filled by persons either in the State Dept. in the past or present or qualifications tested by competitive examination

Sept. 29, General John M. Schofield retired from active military service and General Nelson A. Miles succeeded him as Commander-in-Chief of the United States Army

Oct. 7, Death of William Wetmore Story, sculptor, in Italy

Oct. 24, World long distance speed record made on Lake Shore and Michigan Southern Railroad from Chicago to Buffalo, 510 miles in 8 hours, 1 minute, and 7 seconds, average 64.98 miles an hour exclusive of stops

Nov. 4, Death of Eugene Field, poet, at Chicago

Nov. 5, Elections in 11 States a victory for Republicans

Nov. 8, Proclamation of the President declared the unallotted and unreserved lands acquired from the Nez Percé Indians in Idaho under Agreements with the Indians of May 1 and June 9, 1893 to be opened to settlers Nov. 18

——, Fourth class post-masters placed under classified civil service

Nov. 16, Death of Dr. Samuel F. Smith, author of the anthem "America"

Nov. 18, Sentences of Eugene V. Debs and other American Railway Union officials in case of strike of 1894 of lower courts confirmed by the Supreme Court

Nov. 18–Dec., Strike of house smiths and bridgemakers union in New York

Nov. 26, Notes of Lord Salisbury in answer to Note of Secretary Olney of July 26 declined to submit boundary dispute between British Guiana and Venezuela to arbitration and denied that the Monroe Doctrine was applicable to the case

Dec. 4, New Constitution adopted by South Carolina Convention which first met Sept. 10 to go into effect Jan. 1, 1896. Mississippi plan adopted for 2 years excluding illiterates from the suffrage but admitting persons who could not read but could explain section of Constitution to satisfaction of registry officer, with effect of disfranchising from two-thirds to three-fourths of the negro voters

Dec. 8, Lord Salisbury declined to arbitrate Venezuela boundary

Dec. 17–23, Strike of street car employees in Philadelphia for 10 hour day at $2 a day unsuccessful

Dec. 17, Strike of tailors in New York and Brooklyn because of repudiation of July agreement by employers

Dec. 18, Anti-Saloon League founded in Washington

Dec. 19, Death of Charles B. Atwood, architect, at Chicago

CONGRESS

Jan. 25, The Nicaragua Canal Bill passed by the Senate; no action taken by the House

Jan. 28, Springer Bill to authorize the Secretary of the Treasury to issue bonds to maintain a sufficient gold reserve and to redeem greenbacks introduced in the House; rejected by House Feb. 7 and Senate Feb. 14

Feb. 8, Message of the President to Congress notified of loan of $62,317,500 on 4% bonds for 30 years under Act of Jan. 14, 1875. See supra, Feb. 7

Feb. 20, Joint Resolution of Congress approved suggestion of the President that Great Britain and Venezuela submit boundary dispute to arbitration

Feb. 25, Congress rejected arrangement for payment of British claims

March 2, Commission authorized to examine cost and practicability of a Nicaragua canal

March 2, Penalties imposed for using the mails for lotteries

——, Two members added to Indian Commission appointed in 1893

——, Congress adjourned

Dec. 2, Fifty-fourth Congress, 1st sess. convened

Dec. 17, President Cleveland's Venezuela message affirmed the Monroe Doctrine as applicable to boundary dispute of Venezuela and British Guiana, and recommended appointment of commission to determine the true boundary. Should Great Britain not accept the decision of commission the United States must "resist by every means in its power"

Dec. 21, Act authorized appointment of a commission to determine the boundary line of Venezuela and appropriated $100,000 for the expenses of its work

Dec. 26, Dingley Bill to temporarily increase revenues and a Bond Bill to maintain and protect the redemption fund introduced in House; passed Dec. 27 and 28

1896

Jan. 1, Venezuela Boundary Commission to determine the true boundary between British Guiana and Venezuela appointed by the President: Justice D. J. Brewer, of the Supreme Court; Judge R. H. Alvey, of the Court of Appeals, District of Columbia; Andrew D. White, Frederick R. Coudert, and Daniel G. Gilman

Jan. 4, Proclamation of the President admitted Utah as the 45th State; clause in Constitution prohibited polygamy

——, Venezuelan Boundary Commission held first meeting, Justice Brewer elected president

Jan. 6, The Treasury Dept. offered $100,000,000 in 4% bonds for thirty years; sale oversubscribed

——, Strike of stone cutters at Chicago

——, Recall of Ballington Booth and his wife to England, commanders of the Salvation Army in America for 9 years

Jan. 15, Arthur J. Balfour in speech at Manchester, England, asserted cordial assent of the British Government to the Monroe Doctrine, and Mr. Chamberlain also in speech at Birmingham Jan. 25

Jan. 16, Strike of employees of the Westinghouse Electric Company of Pittsburgh against a 25% reduction in wages

Jan. 22–23, Conference of free silver advocates at Washington which formally adopted name of the American Bimetallic Union, General A. J. Warner, of Ohio, chosen president

Jan. 25, Settlement of strike of tailors of New York City and Brooklyn, agreement signed provided for continuance of arrangement of Aug. 10, 1895

Feb. 3, Meeting in Carnegie Hall, New York City, presided over by Chauncey Depew and at which Mayor Strong spoke, protested against recall of Salvation Army leaders Mr. and Mrs. Ballington Booth and sent telegram to English headquarters

Feb. 8, Bering Sea Treaty with Great Britain signed, commission provided for; ratified by Senate April 15

——, Richard Croker withdrew from leadership of Tammany Hall and was succeeded by John C. Sheehan

Feb. 18, The Cave of the Winds at Niagara Falls was practically dry for the first time in about 50 years

Feb. 20, National Society of Daughters of the American Revolution incorporated

Feb. 22, Death of Edgar Wilson Nye ("Bill"), writer and humorist near Asheville, North Carolina

Feb. 24, Capture of the "Bermuda," British steamer, leaving New York harbor with cargo of ammunition for Cuban rebels

Feb. 27, Strike of garment workers at Baltimore

——, Privileges of Copyright Act of March, 1891, extended to Mexico

——, Lord Dunraven expelled as honorary member of the New Yacht Club after committee had declared unfounded his charge of unfairness against owners of the yacht "Defender" in race for the "America's" cup

Feb. 29, The Baltimore and Ohio Railroad passed into receivership

March 1, United States Supreme Court decision sustained lower court against the United States and in favor of the estate of Leland Stanford of California in suit to recover $15,000,000 liability for bonds of the Central Pacific Railroad

——, 311 negro colonists sailed for Liberia from Savannah, Georgia

——, Mob in Madrid made demonstration against Americans, in Barcelona March 2, and in Valencia March 8 because of friendly attitude of the United States toward Cuban insurgents. Troops protected American consulates

March 6, New liquor dispensary law passed by the South Carolina legislature

March 11 and 25, Greater New York Consolidation Bill passed the New York State Senate and Assembly respectively

March 12, Commander Frederick S. Tucker, son-in-law of General Booth, appointed head of the Salvation Army in America, and arrived in the country April 2

——, Strike of 13,000 tailors and cutters in Chicago

March 19, Secret conference of Republican senators in Washington favoring free coinage of silver

March 20, American marines from the "Alert" landed at port of Corinto, Nicaragua, for protection of life and property in revolution

——, Classified service extended to offices at Indian agencies and schools except to Indians who are subject to tests of Secretary of the Interior

March 21, Ballington Booth appointed officers of new organization "Volunteers of America" formed by him after resignation from the Salvation Army

March 23, Raines Liquor Bill signed by the Governor of New York

April 1, Decision of Supreme Court that the Interstate Commerce Commission could compel railroad officials summoned as witnesses to give evidence tending to incriminate themselves

April 4 and 18, Secretary of State Olney offered mediation of the United States in Cuba to Spain on basis of reforms in the Cuban Government and a more complete autonomy; refused June 4

April 22, International Arbitration Congress met at Washington

April 23, Death of George Munro, publisher, in New York City

April 27, John Hayes Hammond, civil engineer, and other Americans pleaded guilty of treason in Transvaal court and were given sentence of death the following day which was changed to exile April 29

——, First showing of a moving picture in the United States by Thomas A. Edison's vitascope at Koster and Bial's Music Hall, New York City

May 2, American and British marines landed at Corinto, Nicaragua, to protect property

May 4–June 19, Unsuccessful strike of street car employees of Milwaukee, Wisconsin, for increase of wages of one cent an hour and reduction of working day from 12 to 10 hours

May 6, Professor Samuel P. Langley launched his "aërodrome" with wings and miniature steam engine over the Potomac River, which twice sustained itself in the air for 1½ minutes, the time for which it was supplied with fuel and water, and traversing a distance each time of over half a mile

——, Order of President Cleveland extended classified service to bring 30,000 more government employees under the civil service increasing the number to 85,135

May 11, Governor Morton of New York signed Greater New York Bill for consolidation of counties of Kings and Richmond, and of Long Island City and New-town with the City of New York

May 18, Supreme Court decision sustained constitu-tionality of Louisiana law requiring railroads to provide separate cars for colored passengers

May 19, Death of Kate Field, journalist, in Hawaii

May 22, Spain declined offer of the United States of April 4 of mediation on the ground that Cuba had "one of the most liberal political systems in the world"

May 25, Supreme Court decision sustained validity of appropriation bill providing for payment of sugar bounties reversing decision of the Comptroller of the Treasury

——, Privileges of the Copyright Act of 1891 extended to Chile

May 27–28, National Convention of the Prohibition Party met at Pittsburgh and nominated Joshua Levering, of Maryland, for President, and Hale John-son, of Illinois, for Vice-President. Minority nom-inated Charles E. Bentley, of Nebraska, for Presi-dent, and J. H. Southgate, of North Carolina, for Vice-President organizing in another hall as the "National Party"

June 1, National University incorporated in the District of Columbia

June 4, Agreement with Mexico signed as to pursuit by troops of criminals across the border to suppress raids of Indians, criminals, and outlaws

June 9, Commission to draft charter for Greater New York City named by the Governor: Seth Low, General Benjamin F. Tracy, John F. Dillon, Ashbel P. Fitch, General Stewart L. Woodford, Silas B. Dutcher, William C. Dewitt, George M. Pinney, Jr., Garret J. Garretson

June 13, Indemnity paid by the Government to families killed in Colorado raid, and to Great Britain for outrages on British subjects in New Orleans and Nebraska

June 16–18, National Republican Convention met at St. Louis, and nominated William McKinley, of Ohio, for President on first ballot by 661½ votes against a combined total of his opponents of 240½ including Senator W. B. Allison, of Iowa, Thomas B. Reed, Speaker of the House, Governor Levi P. Morton, of New York, and Matthew Quay, of Pennsylvania. Garret A. Hobart, of New York, nominated for Vice-President. Platform adopted stood for protective tariff and gold standard, and the Monroe Doctrine affirmed. The "silver" Republicans led by Senator Teller withdrew from the Party

June 19, Mark A. Hanna, of Cleveland, Ohio, made chairman of Republican National Committee

June 24, Adelphi College, Brooklyn, incorporated

June 25, Death of Lyman Trumbull, jurist, in Chi-cago

June 26, Florida East Coast Railroad reached Miami

June 29, "City of Richmond" which left Key West June 24 with men and munitions for Cuba, and the "Three Friends" captured and captains brought before United States Court charged with organizing military expeditions against Spain, but released as nothing proved

July 1, Death of Mrs. Harriet Beecher Stowe, author of "Uncle Tom's Cabin" at Hartford, Connecticut

——, Grant of 2.5 cents per ton to coal miners at Birmingham, Alabama

July 4–10, Socialist Labor Party met in New York City and nominated Charles H. Matchett, of Brooklyn, for President, and Mathew Maguire, of Paterson, New Jersey, for Vice-President

July 7–11, Democratic National Convention met at Chicago, and nominated William J. Bryan for Presi-dent on the 5th ballot, and Arthur Sewall for Vice-President on platform favoring adoption of free and unlimited coinage of silver at 16 to 1. On July 9 Bryan made his "crown of thorns" and "cross of gold" speech. The first ballot July 10 gave Richard P. Bland, of Missouri, the lead with 235 votes to Bryan's 119

July 13, Note of Secretary Olney asked Great Britain to submit the Venezuelan boundary dispute to unre-stricted arbitration "with the period for the acquisi-tion of title by prescription fixed by agreement of the parties in advance at 60 years"

July 15, Lieutenant Robert E. Peary started on 6th Arctic expedition sailing from Sidney, Cape Breton, and returning Sept. 26 with scientific collections for the American Museum of Natural History

July 15–Sept. 26, Strike of miners at Leadville, Colo-rado, for increase in wages to $3 a day and recognition of the union unsuccessful

July 22, Strike of tailors in New York City and Brook-lyn to prevent restoration of the "task" system be-cause of repudiation of previous agreements by em-ployers, for a 10 hour day, and payment of wages by the week at rate of $8 to 18

July 22–24, National Silver Republicans who favored free coinage of silver met at St. Louis and accepted Democratic nominations of Bryan and Sewall

July 22–25, Populist or People's Party held national convention at St. Louis, and nominated William J. Bryan for President and Thomas E. Watson for Vice-President

July 27, Strike of boiler makers and machinists and lockout begun in Cleveland, Ohio, in May, ended by agreement

——, Proclamation of the President warned citizens to observe the laws of neutrality and not take part in Cuban insurrection

Aug. 4, Failure at Chicago of Moore Brothers organizers of the Diamond Match Company and New York Biscuit Company with liabilities of $8,000,000

Aug. 8, Lynching of 3 Italians at Hahnville, Louisiana

Aug. 11, Decision of Judge Welborn in United States Circuit Court at Los Angeles denied right of land-grant railroads to fix rates of compensation which they may demand from federal government for trans-portation of mail, troops, etc.

Aug. 12, Gold found in Klondike region, Alaska, by George Cormack

Aug. 17, Death of Mary Abigail Dodge (Gail Hamilton) writer, at Hamilton, Massachusetts

Aug. 18, Strike of painter's unions, New York City, for $3.50 a day

Aug. 19, Death of Professor James Dwight Whitney, geologist, at New Haven, Connecticut

Aug. 22, Resignation of Hoke Smith, Secretary of the Interior

Aug. 24, Letter of Bismarck to Governor Culbertson of Texas favoring bimetallism which was used as a campaign document to influence German vote

Aug. 28, Arrival of the Chinese statesman, Li Hung-Chang in New York. Received by President Cleveland the following day

Sept. 1, David R. Francis, of Missouri, appointed Secretary of the Interior

——, Indian Territory passed from alien juridical jurisdiction

Sept. 2–3, "Sound-Money" Democrats organized as the "National Democratic Party" met in Indianapolis and nominated John M. Palmer, of Illinois, for President, and Simon B. Buckner, of Kentucky, for Vice-President, repudiating the Chicago platform and declaring for a single gold standard

Sept. 11, Death of Professor Francis James Child at Cambridge, Massachusetts

Sept. 17, Death of Enoch Pratt, of Baltimore

Sept. 21–23, Strikers at Leadville, Colorado, in riots, leaders arrested on the 23d and district placed under martial law

Sept. 26, Treaty of extradition with Argentina signed

Sept. 27, Death of Professor Benjamin A. Gould, astronomer, at Cambridge, Massachusetts

Oct. 2, Strike of 1,500 garment workers in Boston

Oct. 17, Death of Henry E. Abbey, theatrical manager, New York City

Oct. 21, Judge R. M. Cole of Circuit Court, Florida, declared unconstitutional the Sheats law making it a punishable offense to allow white and colored children to be educated in the same school

Oct. 28, Treaty of extradition with the Orange Free State signed

Nov. 3, Presidential election a Republican victory, McKinley and Hobart receiving 7,104,779 votes; Bryan and Sewall (Democrats) 6,502,925; Joshua Levering (Prohibition) 132,007; J. M. Palmer (National Democratic) 133,148; C. H. Matchett (Socialist) 36,274; C. E. Bentley (National Party) 13,969. The Republicans received 271 electoral votes to 176 for Democrats

——, Idaho granted full suffrage to women in amendment to Constitution ratified by popular vote

Nov. 7, Strike of 3,500 miners at Jackson, Ohio, against reduction of wages

Nov. 9, Supreme Court of Illinois declared Torrens Land Title Act unconstitutional

Nov. 12, Agreement signed with Great Britain as to arbitration of Venezuela boundary

Nov. 24–Feb. 3, 1897, Meeting of Bering Sea Claims Commission at Victoria

Nov. 28, Professor S. P. Langley launched his steam-driven miniature "aërodrome" a second time over the Potomac River in flight of about ¾ of a mile at a speed of about 30 miles an hour

Nov. 30, Death of William Steinway, piano manufacturer

Dec. 3, Proclamation of the President revoked that of Jan. 26, 1888, suspending tonnage duties imposed on German vessels because of taxes on American vessels by Germany

Dec. 10, Arrival of Liliuokalani, former Queen of Hawaii, at San Francisco

Dec. 11, Woman suffrage became effective in Idaho

Dec. 18, Agreement with the Choctaw tribe signed providing for allotment of lands, town sites, school sites, and relinquishment of tribal government within 8 years

Dec. 19, Statement of Richard Olney, Secretary of State, in the newspaper press that the power and right to recognize foreign governments was vested exclusively in the President

Dec. 24, Recognition of the Union of the Greater Republic of Central America

Dec. 24–25, Strike of street car employees in Boston over grievances

Dec. 26, The "Three Friends" in custody of customs officials at Jacksonville, Florida, after a successful landing of men and ammunition in Cuba

Dec. 29, Wheat at 90 cents a bushel

CONGRESS

Jan. 20, Resolution adopted in Senate reaffirming the Monroe Doctrine

Jan. 27, Resolution protesting against the Armenian outrages adopted and the President requested to communicate it to the Powers, signatories of the Berlin Treaty of July 13, 1878, and ask for protection of Christians in the Turkish Empire in their rights

Feb. 1, Dingley Bond Bill in Senate changed by adoption of provision for free coinage of silver passed by vote of 42 to 35

Feb. 7, Report of Nicaraguan Canal Commission submitted to Congress adverse as to cost of construction

——, Prize fights prohibited in the District of Columbia and the Territories

Feb. 14, The House voted against accepting Senate amendments to Dingley Bond Bill by vote of 215 to 90 and the Bill dropped

Feb. 28, Senate Resolution adopted by vote of 64 to 6 that the United States should accord belligerent rights to Cuba and offer friendly offices to Spain for recognition of independence of Cuba

March 31, "Act of Oblivion" repealed the law that persons who had held commissions or served in any official capacity in the Confederate States were not eligible to any position in the army or navy of the United States

April 3, Provision made for distribution of 15,000 packages of seed to each senator and representatives for public distribution as done in previous years reversing decision of Secretary of Agriculture

April 6, Resolution adopted by House by vote of 245 to 27 as to Cuba practically the same as that of the Senate of Feb. 28

June 2, Butler Anti-Bond Bill passed in Senate; no action taken by House after adverse report from committee June 7

June 6, Pure Food Act defined cheese and imposed tax and regulations on manufacture; tax on filled cheese designed to be prohibitory

June 8, Regulations for fourth class mail matter enacted

June 10, Regulations to prevent collisions at sea enacted

——, Act provided that there should be no further appropriation for Indian sectarian schools

June 11, Congress adjourned

Dec. 7, Fifty-fourth Congress, 2d sess. convened

1897

Jan. 5, Death of Francis A. Walker, economist, in Boston

Jan. 6, Bimetallic Conference at Lincoln, Nebraska

Jan. 8, Striking miners in riots at Rutland, Vermont

Jan. 11, Arbitration Treaty with Great Britain signed; rejected by Senate May 5

——, Meeting of electors in the several States cast formal ballots for President and Vice-President

Jan. 12–13, Non-Partisan Monetary Convention of business men met at Indianapolis, representing 64 cities in 26 States, and adopted resolutions in favor of present gold standard and for monetary reforms and appointing a commission of 11 members to investigate conditions

Jan. 13, Agreement with Japan signed to put into immediate effect the arrangements of the Treaty of Nov. 22, 1894 for protection of patents and trade marks

Jan. 18, Decision of Supreme Court that the South Carolina dispensary liquor law in part unconstitutional

Jan. 22, Foreclosure proceedings against the Pacific Railroads on part of the United States Government announced

Jan. 30, Treaty with Great Britain signed appointed joint commission to ascertain the Alaska boundary

Feb. 2, Anglo-Venezuelan Convention signed in Washington, agreement to arbitrate the boundary dispute as to Venezuela and British Guiana

Feb. 6, The President reduced the number of pension agencies by one-half effecting annual saving of $160,000

Feb. 12, Death of Homer Dodge Martin, artist, at St. Paul, Minnesota

Feb. 13, Death of J. O. Shelby, Confederate General, at Adrian, Missouri

Feb. 17, Death of General Alfred Pleasonton at Washington

Feb. 22, Proclamations of the President set aside 13 new forest reserves in the West including 20,000,000 acres in California, Wyoming, Montana, Utah, Washington, and Idaho, the name of the Pacific Forest Reserve in Washington changed to Mount Rainier Forest Reserve

——, Manifesto of Silver Republicans of Congress called for coöperation in political action

Feb. 27, Commission to ascertain boundary between Venezuela and British Guiana presented report to the President

March 1, The Supreme Court sustained seizure and forfeiture of the notorious filibustering steamer, the "Three Friends"

March 4, Inauguration of President William McKinley and Vice-President Garret A. Hobart

March 5, John Sherman, of Ohio, appointed Secretary of State; Lyman J. Gage, of Illinois, Secretary of the Treasury; Russell A. Alger, of Michigan, Secretary of War; Joseph McKenna, of California, Attorney General; James A. Gary, of Maryland, Postmaster General; John D. Long, of Massachusetts, Secretary of the Navy; Cornelius N. Bliss, of New York, Secretary of the Interior; James Wilson, of Iowa, Secretary of Agriculture

March 6, Miners of Leadville, Colorado, voted to end strike which had begun in June 1896

March 22, Supreme Court decision that pooling contracts between railroads unlawful under anti-trust law in case of the United States vs. Trans-Missouri Freight Association, fixing and maintaining uniform freight rates defined by joint agreement and regulations reversing decision of lower court

——, Death of William T. Adams (Oliver Optic) writer, in Boston

March 30, Strike of 1,500 tanners to enforce demand for eight hour day

April 3, Commission made agreement with the Choctaws and Chickasaws

——, Filibustering tug and lighter prevented from sailing from Fernandia, Florida, by torpedo boat U.S.S. "Vesuvius," but not the "Bermuda" which escaped to waters outside the jurisdiction of the United States and raised the British flag

April 7, Mayor Strong, of New York City, vetoed the Greater New York Charter. Approved by mayors of Brooklyn and Long Island City

April 8, John W. Foster and Charles S. Hamlin appointed a commission to investigate the protection and preservation of seals destroyed in the Bering Sea in spite of the regulations

April 11, Organization of beet sugar company at Minneapolis with $20,000 capital to fight the sugar trust

April 12, Commission appointed to sound sentiment of Europe on international bimetallism and to promote the calling of an international monetary conference, Senator E. O. Wolcott, General Charles J. Paine, and Adlai E. Stevenson

April 26, Death of Theodore A. Havemeyer, capitalist, in New York City (58)

April 27, Dedication of the Grant Mausoleum on Riverside Drive, New York City. Addresses by President McKinley and General Horace Porter

April 29, The "Mayflower Log" formally presented to T. F. Bayard by the Bishop of London, and on May 26 formally transferred by him to the Commonwealth of Massachusetts

May 1, Receivers appointed for 3 New Bedford cotton mills

May 3, Strike of New York carpenters and woodworkers

May 4, Death of Rear Admiral Richard W. Meade

May 5, Greater New York Charter signed by Governor Black after repassage by New York legislature

——, International Postal Union Congress met at Washington

May 9, A cruiser ordered to Honduras to protect American interests

May 10, Supreme Court decision in favor of the validity of the Berliner microphone patent of the Bell Telephone Company

May 14, Strike of union plasterers in New York City

——, Treaty of extradition with Brazil signed

May 15, Decision of Judge Gibbons declared American Tobacco Company an illegal corporation in Illinois

May 16, Strike of garment workers in New York, Brooklyn, and Newark to sustain previous agreements and for better conditions and increase of wages

——, Tribal war among the Piute Indians of California

May 17, Dissolution of the American Railway Union, Chicago, and substitution of organization of the Social Democracy of America

May 24, Claims Treaties with Chile provided for revival of Claims Commission of 1892

May 24, Supreme Court decision that the Interstate Commerce Commission had no power to prescribe the tariff of rates which shall control in the future, and therefore cannot invoke a judgment in *mandamus* from the courts to enforce any such tariff by it prescribed

May 25–27, Trial of Henry O. Havemeyer in Washington District of Columbia Court for contempt of court for refusal to answer questions of congressional investigating committee; acquitted

June 8, Trial of officials of the American Tobacco Company under Anti-Trust Act begun in New York

June 9, Death of Alvin Graham Clark, astronomer, at Cambridge, Massachusetts

June 10, New State Constitution went into effect in Delaware. Provided that after Jan. 1, 1900 no citizen may vote who cannot read and write, and a registration fee of $1

June 15, Universal Postal Union signed

June 16, Second Treaty of annexation signed with Hawaii

June 19, Japan made formal protest against annexation of Hawaii by the United States

June 25, Proclamation of the President set apart the public reservation of Nogales, Arizona

June 27, Note of Secretary Sherman to the Spanish Minister protested against Spanish methods of war in Cuba complaining against "the inclusion of a thousand or more of our own citizens among the victims of this policy"

June 29, Indian tribes in Idaho began ghost dance and the Governor requested protection of federal troops

July 1, Indian sectarian schools abolished after this date

——, Union mills of the Amalgamated Association of Iron and Steel Workers closed pending wage agreement, about 75,000 men idle

July 5, Strike of bituminous coal miners ordered July 2 by the United Mine Workers begun for increase of wages, chief grievance the 54 cent rate paid by W. P. De Armitt of the New York and Cleveland Gas Coal Company which was 10 cents a ton below payment by other operators in return for which he abolished company stores and gave other concessions. The De Armitt miners refused to go on strike but were later forced to join

July 10, Cheyenne and Arapahoe Indians held council and war dance at Darlington, Oklahoma, threatened migration to Mexico

July 13, Death of Alfred M. Mayer, physicist, at Maplewood, New Jersey

July 14, President McKinley revoked Order of President Cleveland reducing the number of pension agencies

July 17, Arrival of steamship "Portland" at Port Townsend, Washington, with first large shipment of gold from the Klondike, Alaska, starting the gold rush

July 19–Sept. 20, Lieutenant R. E. Peary sailed from Boston for the Arctic in the "Hope" carrying several scientific expeditions and returned with the famous Cape York meteorite estimated to weigh about 100 tons

July 24, Nicaragua Canal Commission under chairmanship of Rear Admiral John G. Walker appointed

Aug. 10, Decision of South Carolina Court defined "original package," and an order filed recognizing as "original packages" bottles of liquor loosely packed in cars, the importation and sale of which was permitted

Aug. 11, Decision of Attorney General that goods imported into Canada and then exported into the United States must pay discriminating duty of 10%

Aug. 12, Judge Collier of the United States Court at Pittsburgh granted injunction restraining striking miners from assembling, marching, and encamping with intention to intimidate

Aug. 13, Strike of workmen on public school buildings in Chicago because of refusal of Board of Education to employ only union men

Aug. 15, Nearly 1,000 gold-seekers sailed from Victoria, British Columbia, for the Klondike, and 3,000 said to be waiting at the entrance to White Pass in Alaska to cross the mountains to the Yukon River

Aug. 17, Death of Judge David G. Swaim, in Washington

Aug. 20, Bar silver worth 52¾ cents per ounce. The United States had purchased 291,272,018.56 ounces of silver costing $308,279,260.71 under the Bland-Allison Act of 1878, and 168,674,682.53 ounces costing $155,931,602.25, average price paid $1.0093 an ounce

——, September wheat sold in New York at $1 per bushel for the first time in 5 years and 5 months

Aug. 25, Meeting at St. Louis of new political party calling itself the "American Party" with 50 delegates from 9 States

——, Strike of cloakmakers in New York City for increase of wages

Aug. 31, Death of Louisa Lane Drew (Mrs. John Drew) actress at Larchmont, New York

——, Patent for motion picture camera issued to Thomas A. Edison

Sept. 3, Strike of 5,000 postmasters for increase in salary

Sept. 6, Official statement issued of the existence of yellow fever in Mississippi, the last epidemic occurred in 1888

Sept. 10, Conflict of striking miners at Latimer, Pennsylvania, with sheriffs in which 22 men killed and 44 wounded

Sept. 12, Coal strike ended in agreement signed at Columbus, Ohio, which first met Sept. 8, for uniform rate of 65 cents per ton

Sept. 17, Death of Henry W. Sage at Ithaca, New York

Sept. 22, National Monetary Commission met at Washington

Sept. 27, Agreement with the Creek Indians made by Commission

Oct. 2, Death of General Neal Dow at Portland, Maine

Oct. 17, Death of Charles A. Dana, editor of the New York *Sun*

Oct. 18, Death of Rear Admiral John L. Warden in Washington

Oct. 19, Death of George M. Pullman, at Chicago, Illinois

Oct. 20, Military Reservation ordered on St. Michael's Island, Alaska, to preserve order in the gold fields

Oct. 21, The Yerkes Observatory, built and equipped for the University of Chicago by Charles T. Yerkes at Williams Bay near Lake Geneva in Wisconsin, opened and dedicated

Oct. 21–25, Strike of workmen on the Cornell dam near Croton, New York, on grievances

Oct. 22, Death of Justin Winsor, historian, and librarian of Harvard University, at Cambridge

Oct. 23, Meeting of representatives of the United States, Russia, and Japan at Washington to act on sealing questions

——, Dr. Fridtjof Nansen, Arctic explorer arrived in New York, received by the President Oct. 26

Oct. 28, Thomas A. Edison announced the success of his new process for recovering the iron in low grade ores

Oct. 29, Death of Henry George, economist and author, in New York City

Nov. 1, The new Library of Congress in Washington opened

Nov. 6, Treaty between Russia, Japan, and the United States provided for suspension of pelagic sealing during a period of time to be decided by experts

Nov. 12, Proclamation of the President suspended collection of discriminating tonnage duties on Mexican vessels

Nov. 29, The North German Lloyd steamer "Kaiser Wilhelm der Grosse" in trip from New York to Southampton, England, in 5 days, 17 hours, and 8 minutes made new record beating that of the American "St. Louis," and made hourly record of 22.35 knots for the 3,065 knots of the trip bettering the previous hourly average made by the "Lucania" of the Cunard Line by 34 knots

——, The revenue cutter "Bear" commanded by Captain Francis Tuttle sailed from Seattle in search of whaling fleet

Dec. 9, Wheat in Chicago sold at $1.09 a bushel, highest price since 1891

——, Strike of cotton operatives at Atlanta, Georgia

Dec. 22, Award of arbitrators in Bering Sea case granted Great Britain $463,454 in claims for British vessels seized by United States

Dec. 25, 15,000 window glass makers on strike in Indiana returned to work

CONGRESS

Jan. 6, Senator Eugene Hale introduced a Resolution asking Secretary Olney for a report covering precedents in matter of recognition of foreign governments

Jan. 7, Resolution of Senator Mills stated that the expediency of recognition of foreign governments belonged to Congress, and that when Congress should so determine the executive should act in harmony with Congress, and that the independence of Cuba ought to be and hereby is recognized; not acted on

Jan. 15, Cases for the death penalty reduced, the jury given discretion to substitute imprisonment for life in cases of murder and rape

Jan. 30, Sale of intoxicating liquors to Indians prohibited under penalties of imprisonment and fine

Feb. 8, Act to prevent carrying of obscene literature from one State or Territory into another

Feb. 11, Act to authorize entry and patenting of lands containing petroleum and other mineral oils under placer mining laws

Feb. 27, Postal Act provided for indemnity for loss of registered mail up to $10 for one registered piece

March 2, Act of 1887 as to alien ownership of real estate in the Territories amended making certain exceptions

——, President Cleveland vetoed Immigration Bill containing literacy test, and prohibiting the employment of aliens on any public works of the United States, and 45 Bills received pocket veto

March 3, Act provided for the representation of the

United States by commissioners at any international monetary conference hereafter to be called and to enable the President to otherwise promote an international agreement

March 4, Congress adjourned

March 15, Fifty-fifth Congress, 1st sess. (extra) convened. Message of the President devoted to the tariff urged revision for protection and revenue

March 30, The Pooling Bill introduced by Senator Foraker to overcome the effect of decision of Supreme Court of March that pooling contracts illegal under the anti-trust law

March 31, Dingley Tariff Bill passed the House by vote of 205 to 121

April 7, Joint Resolution appropriated $200,000 for relief of flood sufferers in the Mississippi River Valley

May 5, The Senate voted against ratification of the Arbitration Treaty with Great Britain negotiated by Richard Olney and Lord Salisbury by vote of 43 to 26, two-thirds majority lacking

May 24, Joint Resolution appropriated $50,000 for relief of American citizens in Cuba

June 4, Act created a commission to examine all routes possible for canal through Nicaragua and report on cost

——, Suspension of Proclamation of Feb. 22, of President Cleveland setting aside forest reserves

June 7, Act abolished tribal courts of Indians and provided for establishment of United States courts

June 9, Appropriation of $10,000 for relief of flood sufferers in Rio Grand River district

June 30, From this date no money to be appropriated for sectarian education

July 7, The Dingley Tariff Bill with amendments passed the Senate by vote of 38 to 28

July 19, Amended Dingley Tariff Bill passed the House by vote of 189 to 115, and the Senate July 24 by vote of 40 to 30

July 24, Dingley Tariff Act signed by the President reimposed duties on wool and lumber and hides, and high compensating duties placed on woolens averaging 55%, the duty on raw sugar made specific and practically doubled, and the differential of protection for the refiner was maintained. The lower rates on iron and steel products of 1894 were retained, and copper, tea, coffee, tonka beans, and vanilla beans placed on the free list. The average rates were 49.5%, the highest in the history of the country. The policy of reciprocity was revived

——, The President authorized to suspend discriminating duties in case of countries not imposing like duties against the United States

——, Congress adjourned

Dec. 6, Fifty-fifth Congress, 2d sess. convened

Dec. 18, Joint Resolution appropriated $200,000 for relief of the Klondike miners and authorized the Secretary of War to purchase subsistence stores, supplies, &c., and provide for their transportation and distribution

Dec. 29, Act prohibited killing of seals in the Pacific Ocean north of 35 degrees N. Lat. Importation of sealskins taken elsewhere than in the Pribilov Islands forbidden

1898

Jan. 1, City of Greater New York inaugurated with ceremonies, ranking in population below London only making it second city in the world in population estimated as 3,438,899 boroughs as follows: Manhattan, 1,911,755; Brooklyn, 1,197,100; The Bronx, 137,075; Queens, 128,042; Richmond, 64,927

Jan. 8, Public announcement of the organization of a Cuban Relief Committee with headquarters in New York City, and first distribution of supplies for starving natives delivered at Havana Jan. 9

Jan. 12, Demonstration against the American Consulate in Havana because of relief project of the United States

Jan. 18–April 21, Strikes of cotton mill workers in New England because of reduction of wages in 150 mills

Jan. 20–26, Monetary Conference (second) at Indianapolis accepted and discussed report of Commission published Jan. 3

Jan. 24, The U.S.S. "Maine" ordered to proceed from Key West, Florida, to Havana, Cuba on friendly visit, and arrived Jan. 25, Captain C. D. Sigsbee entertained by the Governor General as guest of honor

Jan. 25, John W. Griggs, of New Jersey, appointed Attorney General

Jan. 26, President S. F. Dole of the Hawaiian Republic arrived in Washington

Jan. 28, Interstate Agreement signed by bituminous miners and operators in Chicago of Illinois, Indiana, Ohio, and West Pennsylvania and plan to unionize West Virginia mines

Feb. 6, Government relief expedition sailed from Oregon for the Klondike

Feb. 9, Facsimile of private letter of Dupuy de Lôme, Spanish Minister to the United States, printed in newspapers in which he described President McKinley as "weak and catering to the rabble" and a timeserving politician. Spain accepted his cabled resignation

Feb. 15, The U.S.S. "Maine" destroyed in the harbor of Havana by an explosion in which 2 officers and 264 of the crew were killed

Feb. 17, Two courts of inquiry on the "Maine" disaster appointed, one by the Navy Dept. of the United States and one by the Spanish Government

Feb. 18, Death of Frances E. Willard, temperance leader, in New York City

Feb. 27, Death of William M. Singerly, newspaper editor and publisher, in Philadelphia

March 2, Proclamation of the President set apart the Pine Mountain and Zaca Lake Forest Reservation, California

March 11, Death of General William S. Rosecrans near Redondo, California

March 12, A Board appointed to make examination of vessels desirable for purchase by the Navy Dept.

March 21, United States Naval Court of Inquiry on the "Maine" reported that the ship was destroyed by explosion of a submarine mine, the upheaval of the bottom of the ship the chief reason for this decision that the explosion was external

March 23, S. L. Woodford, Minister to Spain, presented formal statement to Spanish Minister of Foreign Affairs that unless agreement ensuring an honorable peace with Cuba were reached the United States must submit to Congress the entire question of relations between the United States and Spain including the destruction of the U.S.S. "Maine"

March 27, Proposals of President McKinley to Spanish Government submitted for armistice until Oct. 1

for negotiation of peace with Cuba, negotiations with the insurgents by Spain to be conducted through the President, and the reconcentration policy to cease immediately

March 28, Report of Spanish Court of Inquiry published reported the explosion in the forward magazine of the "Maine" caused its destruction

——, Commodore Schley took command of "flying squadron" at Hampton Roads

March 29, The relief expedition from the "Bear" reached Point Barrow with herd of reindeer and relieved starving whalers

March 31, Spanish Note in answer to Note of March 27 offered to arbitrate the questions arising out of the sinking of the "Maine" and to abolish the reconcentration system, but an armistice would be granted only if the insurgents asked for it

April 1, Regular army of the United States numbered 28,183 officers and men

April 3, Cable from American Minister Woodford in Madrid to State Dept. suggested that the President ask the Pope to intervene and that the United States abstain from all show of force. He said, "If you can still give me time and reasonable liberty of action I will get you the peace you desire so much . . . "

April 5, Consul General Fitzhugh Lee recalled from Cuba by the President and instructed to bring to the United States all American citizens who desired to return

April 7, Joint Note presented to the President by Sir Julian Pauncefote, British Minister, from representatives of Great Britain, Germany, France, Austria-Hungary, Russia, and Italy making a "pressing appeal to the feelings of humanity and moderation of the President and of the American people, in their existing differences with Spain," and expressing hope that "further negotiations will lead to an agreement which, while securing the maintenance of peace, will afford all necessary guarantees for the reëstablishment of order in Cuba"

April 9, Foreign Ministers in Madrid called on the Minister of Foreign Affairs and asked that Spain grant armistice in Cuba

——, Armistice granted to Cuba by Spain, and this information cabled to the Secretary of State by General Woodford

April 10, New proposals of Spain announced armistice granted and asked for arbitration of the "Maine" affair

April 18, Resignation of Postmaster General James A. Gary

April 21, State of war with Spain begun. *See infra* Congress April 20 and 25

——, Spain declared diplomatic relations with the United States severed

——, Charles Emory Smith, of Pennsylvania, appointed Postmaster General

——, Captain William T. Sampson appointed to command Atlantic fleet with rank of rear admiral and ordered to blockade coast of Cuba from Cardenas to Bahia Honda

April 22, Blockade of certain ports on the north coast of Cuba and of Cienfuegos proclaimed by the President

——, Capture of the first Spanish prize vessel "Buena Ventura" bound from Sierra Morena to Cardenas with cargo valued at $150,000 by the U.S.S. "Nashville"

April 23, The President called for 125,000 volunteers for war with Spain

April 24, Spain issued declaration of state of war with the United States

——, Great Britain proclaimed neutrality in the war

——, General Emilio Aguinaldo, exiled Philippine leader, had secret interview with Mr. Pratt, American Consul General at Singapore, and promised cooperation with the United States fleet

——, Orders to Commodore George Dewey in command of the Asiatic squadron then at Hong Kong to proceed to the Philippine Islands and capture or destroy the Spanish fleet

April 25, Resignation of General Sherman as Secretary of State

——, Supreme Court decision affirmed validity of inheritance tax law of Illinois

——, Commodore Dewey received orders to proceed to the Philippines at Mirs Bay where he had proceeded from Hong Kong after notice from the British authorities that he must leave that neutral port after the declaration of war

April 26, Proclamation of the President as to treatment to be accorded to vessels and their cargoes as to blockade, contraband, right of search, &c.

——, William R. Day, of Ohio, appointed Secretary of State

——, Aguinaldo, invited by Commodore Dewey, to go to the Philippines, with other leaders sailed from Singapore for Hong Kong in disguise on British steamer "Malacca"

April 27, First engagement of the war between American fleet and batteries at Matanzas, Cuba

——, Commodore Dewey's fleet left Mirs Bay, China, for the Philippines, 628 mile voyage

——, President Dole of Hawaii offered to transfer Islands to the United States and to furnish the United States war vessels with coal, ammunition, and supplies

April 28, France declared neutrality

April 29, Portugal issued proclamation of neutrality, and Admiral Pascual Cervera left the Cape Verde Islands and Portuguese waters for San Juan, Puerto Rico, and the relief of blockaded Havana

April 30, American squadron commanded by Commodore Dewey entered Manila Bay at midnight

May 1, Battle of Manila Bay. Commodore Dewey arrived off Manila at daybreak and was fired on by Spanish batteries and fleet at 5.15 A.M. beginning attack. The Spanish fleet was destroyed with only seven men in the American squadron slightly wounded, and none killed, Spanish loss very heavy

May 2, American squadron took position at Cavite, and landing party sent to destroy guns and magazines. The arsenal at Cavite occupied by marines the following day after evacuation by Spanish forces

May 9, Supreme Court decision declared that part of South Carolina dispensary liquor law which provided for inspections equivalent to denial of right of interstate commerce and illegal, but affirmed validity of the part of law regulating sale of original packages

May 10, Wheat was quoted for cash at $1.91, the highest point touched in 21 years

——, Proclamation of the President set apart Prescott Forest Reservation in Arizona

May 11, Cruiser "Wilmington" and torpedo boat "Winslow" unsuccessful in attack on batteries at Cardenas. Ensign Bagley and 4 of crew of the "Winslow" killed

May 11, Major General Wesley Merritt ordered to the Philippines to support Dewey and occupy Manila

May 12, Admiral Sampson attacked forts at San Juan, Puerto Rico, and ascertained that the Spanish fleet was not in the bay

——, Third German warship arrived in Manila harbor

——, Louisiana Constitution adopted to take effect Sept. 1, containing restriction of suffrage operating against the negro called the "grandfather clause," providing that no man entitled to vote at the beginning of 1867 and no son or grandson of such person be denied the right to vote by reason of his failure to possess the educational or property qualification ($300) demanded by the Constitution for voting

May 16, Aguinaldo sailed from Hong Kong for Cavite, Philippines, on the U.S.S. "McCulloch," where he arrived May 19 and proceeded to organize a native army under the protection of the American fleet

May 19, Admiral Cervera commanding Spanish fleet arrived at Santiago de Cuba

——, "Flying squadron" of Commodore Schley left Key West, Florida, to patrol the southern coast of Cuba, and engaged in blockade of Cienfuegos May 21–24

May 21, The cruiser "Charleston" sailed from San Francisco to join Dewey's fleet

——, Admiral Sampson ordered Comm. Schley to proceed to Santiago if satisfied Spanish fleet not at Cienfuegos

May 22, Death of Edward Bellamy, author of "Looking Backward" at Chicopee Falls, Massachusetts

May 23, Decision of Supreme Court in oleomargarine cases that Pennsylvania by prohibiting the importation and New Hampshire by restricting the importation were interfering with interstate commerce

——, Second order of Admiral Sampson to Schley to to proceed to Santiago disregarded by Schley

May 24, Capt. McCalla communicated with Cubans and found out that Spanish fleet had never been at Cienfuegos and on this information Schley left Cienfuegos but proceeded toward Key West to coal

May 25, The President issued call for 75,000 additional volunteers for war with Spain

——, Third order of Admiral Sampson to Schley to proceed to Santiago

——, 2,491 troops under command of Brigadier General T. M. Anderson sailed from San Francisco for Manila

May 27, Proclamation of the President set apart the Pecos River Forest River Reserve, New Mexico

——, Reply of Schley to Sampson regretted cannot obey order as necessary to go to Key West to coal

May 28, Commodore Schley on discovery of the presence of Cervera's fleet at Santiago de Cuba began blockade after coaling at sea

——, Commercial Treaty with France signed, the first under the new tariff law

May 30, First troops from Honolulu reached Manila conveyed by the cruiser "Charleston"

——, Bombardment of forts north of Santiago harbor by Schley's squadron

——, Agreement concluded for Joint High Commission to negotiate a treaty to settle disputed questions between the United States and Canada

June 1, Admiral Sampson arrived at Santiago harbor and took command of the blockading squadron

June 1, Death of Thomas W. Keene, actor, on Staten Island

June 1–Oct. 31, Trans-Mississippi International Exposition at Omaha, Nebraska

June 3, Lieutenant Richmond P. Hobson with crew of 6 men sunk the collier "Merrimac" in mouth of harbor at Santiago de Cuba to bottle up the Spanish fleet. A shell disabled the steering gear and the vessel sunk too far in to block the entrance completely. Hobson and his men picked up from raft by Spaniards

June 4, Lieutenant Hobson and crew sent prisoners to Morro Castle

June 6, Bombardment of fortifications at entrance of harbor of Santiago. A battleship played searchlight every night making it impossible for the Spanish fleet to escape unobserved at night

June 7, Cuban cable cut and Island isolated

——, General Miles authorized to assemble 30,000 troops for invasion of Puerto Rico

——, Two vessels from American squadron entered harbor of Guantanamo, Cuba, in anticipation of its use as an invading point, and 600 marines landed June 10

June 11, At conference of the "Social Democracy" at Chicago, Eugene V. Debs with 30 others representing membership of about 2,000, withdrew and founded new "Social Democratic Party of America" June 13, and adopted platform favoring public ownership of all utilities, mines, gas, &c.

June 12, The German Vice-Admiral von Diedrichs arrived in the harbor of Manila on his flag-ship, the "Kaiserin Augusta," third German warship in harbor

——, Filipino proclamation of independence of Spain

June 14, General Shafter's army of 16,887 sailed from Tampa, Florida, arriving off Santiago in 6 days

——, United States marines routed Spaniards in attack at Guantanamo, Cuba

June 16, Bombardment of forts at Santiago by American squadron

June 17, Dewey reported that there were assembled in Manila Bay a French and a Japanese warship, 2 British and 3 German, and that another German warship was expected

June 20, Guam Island seized by Captain Glass commanding the U.S.S. "Charleston." Captain Henry Glass entered harbor of Guam and opened fire on fort whereat the Spanish commander sent apology not returning "the salute" on account of lack of ammunition, having heard nothing of the war

——, General William R. Shafter in command of army of 17,000 on 32 transports arrived off Santiago from Tampa, Florida

June 21, Formal surrender of Island of Guam by Spanish Governor to Captain Glass of the U.S.S. "Charleston"

June 22, American troops began to disembark at Daiquiri, 15 miles east of Santiago, and on the next day at Siboney, Cuba

June 23, Conflict of strikers, woodworkers, at Oshkosh, Wisconsin; the strike called off June 29

——, Aguinaldo proclaimed himself President and Dictator in the Philippines

June 24, General Young's brigade of General Wheeler's Division moving against Santiago in engagement with Spaniards commanded by General Linares at Las Guasimas and drove enemy from superior position on high ground

June 26, Spanish fleet of Admiral Camara reached Port Said where Egyptian Government refused to permit the ships to take coal

June 27, Captain Joshua Slocum arrived at Newport, Rhode Island, in his sloop yacht "Spray" the end of a voyage alone around the world begun from Boston April 24, 1895

June 28, Proclamation of the President extended blockade to entire south coast of Cuba and to San Juan, Puerto Rico

June 30, First American troops from San Francisco, commanded by General T. M. Anderson, arrived in Manila Bay, 2,500 officers and men

July 1, Battle of El Caney. General Lawton in command of about 7,000 troops captured Spanish blockhouse after 8 hour fight losing 440 killed and wounded, Chaffee, Miles, and Ludlow commanding brigades

——, Battle of San Juan. General Hawkins took the Spanish blockhouse, and Generals S. S. Sumner and Kent and Colonel Wikoff (killed), and Colonel Theodore Roosevelt commanding the "Rough Riders," first volunteer cavalry regiment took Kettle Hill and then San Juan Hill. The Spanish General Linares wounded

——, General Anderson and Admiral Dewey in interview with Emilio Aguinaldo, Filipino leader, said they had no authority to recognize his Government proclaimed June 28

July 1–6, Strike of stereotypers of Chicago newspapers for 7 hour day and increase from $3.25 to $4 a day unsuccessful

July 2, 4,000 Spanish troops led by Colonel Escario entering Santiago by the Cobre Road intercepted by General Garcia with Cubans stationed on extreme right to prevent reinforcements

July 3, Spanish fleet of Cervera made attempt to escape from Santiago harbor between 9.31 and 10 A.M. trying to run the American blockade and making for Cienfuegos, and were totally destroyed in engagement with the American fleet commanded by Admiral Sampson. Admiral Cervera taken prisoner

July 3–Aug. 17, 1899, Arctic expedition of Walter Wellman from Tromsoe, Norway

July 3, General Shafter sent letter to General Toral, Spanish commander, asking for surrender of Santiago before noon on July 5 under threat of bombardment

July 4, Information as to naval victory of July 3 conveyed under flag of truce to Spanish General Toral with suggestion that he surrender to save further bloodshed

——, United States flag raised over Wake Island in the Pacific Ocean

July 6, Lieutenant Hobson and his crew released in exchange for Spanish prisoners of war

——, General Shafter gave General Toral time and facilities to consult the Government in Spain as to his action

July 8, General Toral offered to march out of Santiago and surrender territory occupied by him provided he was allowed to take arms and baggage and would not be molested before reaching Holguin 60 miles west; unconditional surrender insisted on by the United States

July 9, The President appointed a Commission as provided for in Joint Resolution annexing Hawaii, Senators S. M. Cullom, and J. T. Morgan, Representative Robert R. Hitt, and Sanford B. Dole and Justice W. F. Frear of Hawaii, to recommend legislation to Congress

July 10, General Shafter began bombardment of Santiago

July 11, General Miles arrived at Santiago with reinforcements for General Shafter's army, and the bombardment renewed. General Shafter again asked General Toral for the surrender of Santiago

——, Death of Rear Admiral Daniel Ammen in Washington

July 13, Conference of General Miles, and General Shafter with General Toral asking for surrender of Santiago

——, Anglo-American League organized in London

July 14, General Toral agreed to surrender of Santiago, the capitulation including eastern Cuba east of a line passing from Acerraderos on the south to Sagua de Tanamo on the north via Palma Soriano, and the return of his army to Spain

July 17, Formal surrender of Santiago and 24,000 troops by Spanish General Toral to General Shafter; casualties in American operations against Santiago in 5 battles 1,344

——, Second contingent of American troops commanded by General F. V. Greene arrived at Manila Bay, 3,515 men

July 19, Proclamation of the President announced suspension of tonnage duties on vessels from Denmark

July 25, General Wesley Merritt arrived with third contingent of American troops bringing number at Manila Bay to about 10,000

——, General Miles landed troops on the south coast of Puerto Rico 15 miles west of Ponce at harbor of Guanica and after skirmish with Spaniards the American flag raised

July 26, The Government of Spain through the French Minister, M. Cambon, asked the United States to state terms upon which it would be willing to make peace

July 28, The steamer "Bear" arrived at Point Barrow, distributed supplies, and brought 146 persons back to Seattle, arriving Sept. 13

——, Formal surrender of Ponce, second largest city of Puerto Rico to Gen. Miles

July 30, Terms of peace presented to the Duke of Almodovar, Spanish Minister, the independence of Cuba, cession of Puerto Rico, and one of the Ladrones Islands to the United States, and the Philippines to be retained pending final disposition

July 31, Night attack of Spanish troops repulsed by Colonel Greene's brigade on the "Calle Real" between Cavite and Manila at Malate

——, Troops commanded by Major General John R. Brooks disembarked at Arroyo, Puerto Rico

Aug. 1, General Shafter reported 4,255 sick in American army in Cuba, 3,164 cases of yellow fever

——, Juana Diaz, Puerto Rico, taken by American troops

Aug. 3, Generals Kent, Bates, Chaffee, Sumner, Ludlow, Ames, Wood, and Colonel Theodore Roosevelt signed "round robin" addressed to General Shafter on the condition of the army asking that the men be moved at once to save thousands of lives

Aug. 4, Instructions from the War Dept. authorized removal of troops from Cuba to Montauk Point, Long Island, New York

——, The monitor "Monterey" arrived in Manila Bay

Aug. 7, Joint letter of General Wesley Merritt and Admiral Dewey to Spanish Captain General notifying him to remove non-combatants within 48 hours as bombardment of Manila would be begun

Aug. 7, Death of Dr. James Hall, geologist, at Bethlehem, New Hampshire

Aug. 8, Transportation of Spanish troops to Spain from Santiago district begun in Spanish ships paid by the United States

Aug. 9, Formal demand for surrender of Manila made by General Merritt and Admiral Dewey

Aug. 10, Spanish Note dated Aug. 7 accepted terms imposed by the United States except as to Philippine Islands

Aug. 12, Protocol signed ended war with Spain, Spain to relinquish all title to Cuba, to cede Puerto Rico and other islands in the West Indies under Spanish sovereignty, and also an island in the Ladrones group to be selected by the United States, the United States to hold Manila, city, harbor, and bay, pending arrangements of Treaty of Peace

——, Proclamation by the President of suspension of hostilities

——, Engagement with Spaniards at Coamo, Puerto Rico, General Wilson's force retired because of lack of ammunition

——, Formal transfer of Hawaiian Islands to the United States

——, Aguinaldo notified to prohibit Filipino insurgents under his command from entering Manila thus refusing their coöperation in attack planned

Aug. 13, Manila bombarded, assaulted, and occupied by American forces except the walled town which presently surrendered

Aug. 14, General Merritt proclaimed military occupation of the Philippine Islands. Formal articles of the capitulation signed at Manila

——, Blockade of Cuba ended

Aug. 15, Enlisted forces in the Navy on this date 24,123

Aug. 16, American Commission appointed to arrange for and execute the details of Spanish evacuation of Cuba, Rear Admiral Sampson, Major Generals James F. Wade and Matthew C. Butler

Aug. 17, San Francisco Mountains Forest Reserves in Arizona set apart by proclamation of the President

Aug. 18, Muster-out of 100,000 volunteers ordered

Aug. 21, Death of Dr. William Pepper, former provost of the University of Pennsylvania

Aug. 23–Oct. 10, Joint Tribunal of the United States and Canada met in Quebec, adjourned to meet in Washington Nov. 10

Aug. 23, General Merritt assumed duties as Military Governor of the Philippine Islands

Aug. 24, Votes for "Atoka Agreement" taken by Indians, counted and proclaimed in force in the Chickasaw and Choctaw nations Aug. 30; adhered to by Creeks Nov. 1

Aug. 25, General Shafter turned over command to General Lawton and sailed from Cuba arriving at Montauk Point, Long Island, Sept. 1

Aug. 26, The President appointed a Commission of five to conclude a Peace Treaty with Spain: William R. Day, Cushman K. Davis, William P. Frye, Whitelaw Reid, Edward D. White who declined to serve and George Gray appointed in his stead. An equal number of commissioners represented Spain

Aug. 29, General Otis became Military Governor of the Philippines, General Merritt sailing on the steamer "China" from Manila to attend the Peace Conference in Paris, transferring his command to Major General Otis

Aug. 31, Army of the United States numbered 272,618 including 56,362 regular army and 216,256 volunteers

Sept. 6, National Populist Convention at Cincinnati nominated Wharton Barker, of Pennsylvania, for President, and Ignatius Donnelly, of Minnesota, for Vice-President

Sept. 8, Commission appointed by the President to investigate conduct of the war by the War Dept., Major General Grenville M. Dodge, chairman, began work Sept. 24

Sept. 12, Death of Judge Thomas McIntyre Cooley at Ann Arbor, Michigan

Sept. 17, Peace Commission headed by Judge W. R. Day sailed for Paris

Sept. 19, Proclamation of the President set apart the Black Hills Forest Reserve, South Dakota and Wyoming

Sept. 26, Death of Fanny Davenport (Mrs. Melbourne McDowell) actress, at Duxbury, Mass.

Sept. 28, Death of Thomas Francis Bayard, diplomatist, at Dedham, Mass.

Sept. 29, Illinois State troops called out to maintain order among striking miners at Pana

——, John Hay, of the District of Columbia, appointed Secretary of State to succeed Judge Day resigned

Sept. 30, From May 1 to this date 80 officers and 2,520 enlisted men died in camps from disease

Oct. 1, Meeting of Peace Commission in Paris

Oct. 5, Chippewa Indians in outbreak at Leech Lake Reservation because of tyrannical oppression of white settlers. Suppressed by troops commanded by Major Wilkinson who was killed with 5 others, 16 wounded

Oct. 12, Striking coal miners in strike begun in May in Illinois about wage agreement in riot at Virden where mine owners attempted to bring in 200 negroes to work the mines, 14 persons killed and 25 wounded; strike ended Nov. 16, the company conceding the 40 cent rate

Oct. 18, The United States took formal possession of Puerto Rico, General John R. Brooke, Military Governor

Oct. 24, Supreme Court decision in case of the Joint Traffic Association declared railway pooling illegal

Oct. 26, The Paris Peace Commission instructed to ask for cession of entire archipelago of the Philippine Islands; formal demand made Nov. 1

Oct. 29, Death of Colonel George E. Waring, sanitary engineer, in New York City

Nov. 1, Speech of Senator Hoar at Worcester, Mass., against imperial expansion

Nov. 4, Spanish Government refused to cede Philippines

Nov. 6, Elections gave Republicans a majority in the House

Nov. 10, Joint High Commission of Canada and the United States met in Washington

——, Race riot at Wilmington, North Carolina, 8 negroes killed

Nov. 14, Strike of 2,500 shoemakers at Marlborough, Mass., against free shops

Nov. 16, Death of Dr. Samuel Colcord Bartlett at Hanover, New Hampshire

Nov. 19, Death of General Don Carlos Buell at Rockport, Kentucky

Nov. 21, Ultimatum of the United States offered $20,000,000 for the Philippine Islands which was accepted by Spain Nov. 28

Nov. 21, Strike of cotton operatives in Augusta, Georgia, against a reduction of wages

——, Bills of indictment against Senator Quay and his son, former State Treasurer, charged with misuse of Pennsylvania State funds

Dec. 2, Boundary Treaty with Mexico signed

Dec. 10, Treaty of Paris signed between the United States and Spain by which Spain relinquished all claim and title to Cuba, and ceded to the United States Puerto Rico and other islands in the West Indies, Guam, and the Philippine Islands for which the United States to pay Spain $20,000,000

Dec. 15, Death of Calvin Stewart Brice, former senator from Ohio, in New York City

Dec. 21, Ethan A. Hitchcock, of Missouri, appointed Secretary of the Interior

——, Instructions of the President to Secretary of War as to temporary government of Philippines

Dec. 26, Rear Admiral Walker submitted preliminary report on Nicaragua Canal as feasible from engineering and financial standpoints

Dec. 27, Death of Mrs. Isabel A. Mallon who wrote under pseudonym of Ruth Ashmore

CONGRESS

Jan. 17, Lodge Immigration Bill subjecting all aliens seeking admission to the United States to a literacy test passed the Senate by vote of 45 to 28

Jan. 28, Teller Resolution that the bonds of the United States be paid in silver dollars passed Senate by vote of 47 to 32

March 4, Amendment to Act prohibiting the passage of local or special laws in the Territories and limiting indebtedness permitted issue of bonds by chartered municipal corporations for certain purposes specified

March 8, Act authorized additional regiments of artillery

March 9, Appropriation of $50,000,000 for emergency fund for the national defense

March 11, Act dispensed with proof of loyalty during the War of the Rebellion as prerequisite in any application for bounty lands

March 28, Message of the President communicated the findings of the Court regarding the destruction of the U.S.S. "Maine"

April 1, Joint Resolution provided for duty free admission until Jan. 1, 1899 of naval and military supplies procured abroad

April 11, Message of the President asked for authority to intervene by force and end war in Cuba

April 20, Joint Resolution recognized the independence of Cuba and demanded that Spain relinquish authority and withdraw land and naval forces from Cuba. The President directed to use forces of the United States to carry Resolution into effect. Any intention to exercise sovereignty over Cuba disclaimed by the United States

April 22, Volunteer army authorized by Act providing for temporary increase of the military establishment of the United States

April 25, Act declared existence of war between the United States and Spain to be considered to have begun April 21

April 26, Act authorized increase of the regular army

May 4, Act making appropriation for the naval service authorized building of 3 coast-line battleships, 4 harbor defense vessels of the monitor type, 16 torpedo boat destroyers, and 12 torpedo boats at cost of $20,900,000.   Aggregate amount carried by Act $56,098,783

May 10, Joint Resolution tendered thanks of Congress to Commodore George Dewey and through him to the officers and men under his command at Manila

May 11, Act provided for organization of a volunteer naval battalion in the District of Columbia

——, Act provided for volunteer brigade of engineers, and additional force of 10,000 men, both in addition to volunteer forces already authorized

May 12, Additional assistant surgeons in army authorized

May 14, Act extended the homestead laws to Alaska and provided for right of way for railroads, wagon roads, &c.

May 18, Volunteer signal corps authorized

——, Act to furnish assistance of arms, equipment, military stores, and supplies, &c., to people of Cuba as required by them in war with Spain

May 26, Joint Resolution authorized organization of an auxiliary naval force not to exceed 3,000 men

June 1, Act provided for the arbitration of disputes between employers and employees engaged in interstate commerce

June 3, Joint Resolution appropriated $10,000 for presentation of a sword to Commodore George Dewey and for bronze medals to officers and men of the Asiatic Squadron in commemoration of the Battle of Manila Bay

June 6, Disabilities imposed by Section 3 of the XIVth Amendment to the Constitution amended

June 13, Coinage of silver bullion purchased under Sherman Act authorized

——, War Revenue Act imposed taxes on fermented liquors, tobacco, seats in parlor cars and for berths, mixed flour, legacies and distributive shares of personal property. A duty of 10 cents a pound placed on imported tea. The Secretary of the Treasury authorized to borrow sums necessary to meet public expenditures on certificates not to exceed $100,000,000

June 14, House Joint Resolution appropriating $473,151.26 to pay Bering Sea claims to Great Britain adopted in Senate

June 18, Act created United States Industrial Commission, a "non-partisan commission to collate information and to consider and recommend legislation to meet the problems presented by labor, agriculture, and capital"

June 28, Curtis Act ratified Agreement of Commission with Choctaws and Chickasaws in April and Creeks in Sept., to become effective by ratification of tribal votes

July 1, National Bankruptcy Act passed

July 7, Joint Resolution provided for annexation of the Hawaiian Islands

July 8, Act provided for reimbursement to the States for expenses incurred on account of war with Spain

——, Congress adjourned

Dec. 5, Fifty-fifth Congress, 3d sess. convened

1899

Jan. 1, Cuba formally transferred to American control. *See* Cuba

Jan. 12, Commissary General Eagan in testimony before Commission investigating the War supplies charged General Miles with falsehood

Jan. 13, Death of Nelson Dingley, Jr., congressman from Maine, in Washington

Jan. 14, Treaty with the Cherokees provided for dissolution of tribal relations; not ratified by Congress because of conditions attached

Jan. 17, Commodore Taussig of the U.S.S. "Bennington" raised the American flag over Wake Island discovered by Charles Wilkes in 1841, taking formal possession for the United States

——, Death of John Russell Young, Librarian of Congress

Jan. 18, Court martial ordered for General Charles P. Eagan because of criticism of the Administration

Jan. 19, U.S.S. "Philadelphia" under command of Rear Admiral Kautz ordered to Samoa to protect American interests, where German and British warships already stationed

Jan. 20, First Philippine Commission appointed by the President: Jacob G. Schurman, Admiral George Dewey, General Elwell S. Otis, Charles Denby, and Dean C. Worcester

Jan. 28, Court martial in the case of General Eagan recommended dismissal from the service on charge of unbecoming conduct "to the prejudice of good order and military discipline." Sentence altered by the President to suspension from duty for 6 years

——, Death of General George S. Greene

Feb. 1, American flag raised on Island of Guam by Commodore Taussig of the U.S.S. "Bennington" who assumed temporary government

Feb. 4, Armed conflict between American forces and Filipinos begun as Filipinos deliberately invaded American lines though warned and were fired on beginning battle. *See* Philippine Islands

Feb. 8, Announcement of the Government disclaimed responsibility in case of shooting of Austro-Hungarian striking miners at Lattimer, Pennsylvania, in Sept., 1897

Feb. 9, Military Court of Inquiry appointed to investigate charges of General Miles against the Commissary Dept. as to beef furnished to the army

Feb. 10, Proclamation of the President set apart forest reservations in Montana and Utah, and March 2 in New Mexico

Feb. 17, Anti-Imperialist League founded in favor of early recognition of independence of the Philippines

Feb. 20, Last meeting of Canadian-American Boundary Commission met in Washington, and adjourned to meet in Quebec in August; no treaty concluded as to boundary

Feb. 22, New Treaty of Extradition with Mexico signed

March 2, Mount Rainier National Park proclaimed as name of former Pacific Coast Reservation

March 3, Rear Admiral Dewey made Admiral of the United States Navy

——, Commodore Sampson commissioned Rear Admiral

March 13, Herbert Putnam appointed Librarian of Congress

March 16, Death of Joseph Medill, newspaper proprietor, in Chicago

March 17, Orders issued for a military exploration of Alaska

March 18, Death of Professor Othniel Charles Marsh, geologist, at New Haven

March 31, Committee to investigate Tammany administration of New York City under Richard Croker charged with extravagance and corruption, and as to blackmail levied by policemen, and alleged exactions from policemen for funds for corruptly influencing legislation at Albany, Robert Mazet, chairman

April 1, Attack on British and American sailors at Samoa. *See* Samoa

April 9, Death of Stephen Johnson Field, associate justice Supreme Court, in Washington

April 11, Formal ratifications exchanged of the Treaty with Spain of Dec. 10, 1898 and the Treaty proclaimed

——, Conflict between white and negro non-union miners at Pana, Illinois, 6 persons killed and 8 wounded

April 14, Commodore Schley commissioned Rear Admiral

April 21, Ex-Senator Quay, of Pennsylvania, acquitted of charge of misuse of State funds

April 24, Miners at Wardner, Idaho, asked for $3.50 a day for men underground and that only union men be employed, the latter demand refused

April 26, Joint Commission of British, Germans, and Americans sailed from San Francisco for Samoa to investigate conditions

April 29, Miners at Wardner, Idaho, blew up mills with dynamite, destruction of property valued at $250,000

——, Military Court dismissed charges of General Miles as to quality of beef furnished to the army as not sustained

May 1–2, Federal troops sent to Wardner, Idaho, to prevent riots of striking miners

May 2, Death of Henry Hyde, founder of the Equitable Life Assurance Society

May 4, Ute Indian Reservation, Colorado, opened to settlers

May 5–24, Strike of grain shovelers at Buffalo against new schedule of wages

May 8, All mines closed at Wardner, Idaho, and district placed under martial law

May 10, Striking miners at Pana, Illinois, in riots

May 12, Death of Roswell Flower, former Governor of New York

May 14, Dr. Charles A. Briggs, suspended from the Presbyterian Church in 1893 on charge of heresy, ordained priest in the Protestant Episcopal Church

May 22, Commercial Treaty with Portugal signed

May 29, Order of President McKinley modified civil service rules releasing about 4,000 offices from their operation

May 31, Nicaragua Canal Commission dissolved. Report recommended the Childs route from Brito on the Pacific to Lake Nicaragua (survey of 1852) and the Lull route (survey of 1873) from Lake Nicaragua to Greytown on the Atlantic

June 5, Death of Frank Thomson, president of the Pennsylvania Railroad

June 7, Death of Augustin Daly, playwright, in Paris, France

June 10, New Isthmian Canal Commission appointed, Rear Admiral Walker again president

June 10–24, Strike of street car employees of Cleveland, Ohio, with riots and violence, mobs attacking the cars, settled by agreement to arbitrate

June 13–24, Strike of street car employees of Rochester, New York, for $1.50 for an eight hour day successful

June 15, First meeting of the Venezuela Arbitration Commission in Paris

——, Death of Richard Parks Bland, Democratic congressman from Missouri, and advocate of free silver

June 16–Aug., Strike of miners in Colorado against new

law reducing working day from 12 to 8 hours as to adjustment of wages ended by decision of the court that the law unconstitutional

July 5, Death of Bishop John Philip Newman, at Saratoga, New York

July 6, Death of Robert Bonner, editor, New York City

——, General Order 122 called for 10 regiments of volunteers to suppress revolt in the Philippines

July 16, Strike of street car employees in Brooklyn begun, and joined by New York employees on the 19th, failed for lack of support

July 17, Strike of street car employees in Cleveland renewed, the men claiming the company had not fulfilled agreement, which lasted 2 months and was characterized by violence and riots. Troops sent July 22 to preserve order

July 18, Death of Horatio Alger, writer, at Natick, Massachusetts

July 19, Resignation of Secretary of War Alger

July 21, Death of Robert Green Ingersoll, lawyer and agnostic, at Dobbs Ferry, New York

——, Five Italians, 2 of them subjects of Italy, accused in murder of an American, lynched in Tallulah, Louisiana

July 22, Commercial Reciprocity with Portugal proclaimed

July 24, Reciprocity Treaty with France signed

July 29, The United States signed the Hague Peace Conventions for the pacific settlement of disputes, launching of projectiles and explosives from balloons, adaptation to maritime warfare of the principles of the Geneva Convention, and laws and customs of war on land

July 31, Death of Daniel Garrison Briton, geologist

Aug. 1, Elihu Root, of New York, appointed Secretary of War

Aug. 20, Treaty with the Sultan of Sulu negotiated by General John C. Bates signed established sovereignty of the United States over the Sulu Archipelago

Aug. 24, Death of Judge Henry Hilton, merchant

Sept. 6, Note of Secretary Hay to Great Britain, Germany, and Russia and subsequently to Japan, France, and Italy asked for maintenance of the "open door" in China, that the powers claiming spheres of influence in China should keep the treaty ports open, allow the application of the Chinese treaty tariff to ports under their control, and that they would not discriminate against other nationals in the matter of railroad rates or harbor dues; accession of Great Britain first on Nov. 30, France Dec. 16, Russia Dec. 30, Japan Dec. 26, Italy Jan. 7, 1900, Germany Feb. 19, 1900

Sept. 12, Death of Cornelius Vanderbilt, railroad magnate, New York City

Sept. 29–30, Naval and land parades in New York City in honor of Admiral George Dewey, who arrived in New York harbor on the 26th

Oct. 3, Court of Arbitration gave award in case of boundary line between Venezuela and British Guiana

Oct. 16, Dismal Swamp Canal opened in Virginia, original survey made by George Washington

Oct. 19, Death of William Henry Appleton, publisher, at New York City

Oct. 20, Agreement with Great Britain fixed provisional boundary line between Alaska and Canada about the head of the Lynn Canal

Oct. 28, Death of Ottmar Mergenthaler, inventor, in Baltimore

Oct. 30, Death of William Henry Webb, shipbuilder, New York City

Nov. 2, Preliminary Report of the Philippine Commission

Nov. 7, The United States, Great Britain, and Germany agreed to submit claims for bombardment of Samoan villages by British and American warships to arbitration of the King of Sweden

Nov. 21, Death of Vice-President Hobart. The Secretary of State became successor of the President as provided by law

Nov. 28, Extradition Treaty with Peru signed

Dec. 2, Treaty signed with Germany and Great Britain by which the Samoan Islands partitioned between Germany and the United States, the United States receiving Pago Pago, Tutuila, and some small islands lying east of the 171st meridian

Dec. 4, Supreme Court decision in Addyston Pipe and Steel Company case that an agreement between corporations which prevented competition in public bidding for contracts violated the Anti-Trust Act

Dec. 12, W. S. Taylor, Republican, inaugurated Governor of Kentucky, election disputed

Dec. 22, Boundary Agreement with Mexico extended Convention of March 1, 1889

——, Death of Dwight L. Moody, evangelist, at Northfield, Mass.

Dec. 25, Death of Elliott Coues, naturalist, at Baltimore

CONGRESS

Jan. 9, Speech of Senator Hoar against interference of the United States with the Philippine Islands

Jan. 14, Resolution of Senator Hoar submitted "that the people of the Philippine Islands of right ought to be free and independent . . ."

Feb. 6, Treaty with Spain of Dec. 10, 1898 ratified by the Senate by vote of 57 to 27

Feb. 11, Secretary Long submitted report to Senate which charged Commodore Schley with "reprehensible conduct" in delay off Cienfuegos from May 24–26, and retrograde movement to Key West to coal May 26–27 thus raising the blockade of the harbor of Santiago temporarily

Feb. 14, Resolution introduced by Senator McEnery, of Louisiana, adopted by vote of 26 to 22 declared it "is not intended to incorporate the inhabitants of the Philippine Islands into citizenship of the United States nor is it intended to permanently annex said Islands as an integral part of the United States . . ."

March 2, Regular army increased to 65,000 enlisted men and a force of 35,000 volunteers authorized for service in the Philippine Islands to suppress the rebellion

——, Office of Admiral of the Navy created, provided that office should cease to exist when vacated by death or otherwise. Rear Admiral George Dewey appointed Admiral under this law

——, General law enacted for acquiring of rights by railroad companies through Indian reservations

March 3, Act provided for reimbursement of States and Territories for expenses incurred in raising volunteers for war with Spain

——, Navy Personnel Act reorganized the navy and marine corps

March 3, Naval appropriation provided for construction of 3 battleships, 3 armed cruisers, and 6 protective cruisers

——, Act provided for codes of criminal law and procedure for Alaska

——, Commission created to examine and report on all routes possible for a canal through Panama or Nicaragua and cost, "placing it under the control, management and ownership of the United States"

——, Act authorized development of Muscle Shoals for navigation and power; nothing done

March 4, Congress adjourned

Dec. 4, Fifty-sixth Congress, 1st sess. convened

Dec. 18, Gold Standard Bill passed House by vote of 190 to 150

1900

Jan. 2, Secretary Hay announced to the Cabinet that he had completed negotiations for "open door" policy in China. *See infra* March 20

——, The Chicago drainage canal opened, 40 miles long, 22 feet deep, constructed at cost of $45,289,000

——, First electric automobile omnibus on the Fifth Avenue Line, New York City

Jan. 11, Treaty of commerce with Portugal signed

Jan. 15, Report of Mazet Committee presented 8 bills for reform of government of the City of New York

Jan. 30, William Goebel, Democratic candidate for Governor of Kentucky shot by an assassin. He had been defeated in Nov. election but refused to accept the returns

Jan. 31, Kentucky legislature declared recognition of William Goebel as Governor, and J. C. W. Beckham as Lieutenant Governor, and oaths administered

——, Final Report of the Philippine Commission presented favored government analogous to a territory, with home rule in local affairs

Feb. 1, Republican Governor Taylor, of Kentucky, asked President McKinley for recognition as elected Governor

Feb. 2, Cabinet declared against interference in disputed Kentucky election

Feb. 3, Death of William Goebel. J. C. W. Beckham sworn in as Governor

Feb. 5, First Hay-Pauncefote Treaty as to Panama Canal signed modifying the Clayton-Bulwer Treaty. Great Britain renounced all right to joint construction, ownership, and maintenance. Neutrality of the Canal agreed upon, and no fortifications to be erected commanding the Canal or adjacent waters

Feb. 6, Judge William H. Taft appointed chairman of the new Philippine Commission to establish civil government in the Philippines

Feb. 6–8, Farmer's Alliance and Industrial Union met in Washington and pledged support to candidates for President and Vice-President of the Democratic Party

Feb. 8, Commercial Reciprocity Treaty with Italy signed

Feb. 10, Commodore Seaton Schroeder appointed Naval Governor of Samoa

——, Lockout and strike in the building trades in Chicago begun of 7,000 men which lasted a year and affected 50,000 men

Feb. 11, Commercial Reciprocity Treaty with Argentina proposed by wool interests lapsed because of failure of ratification by the Senate

Feb. 13, Commercial Reciprocity Treaty concluded with British Island of Trinidad

Feb. 18, Death of Miss Sarah Porter, educator, at Farmington, Connecticut

Feb. 22–23, Anti-Imperialist League held in Philadelphia

Feb. 23, Anti-Imperialist mass meeting held in Faneuil Hall, Boston, George S. Boutwell presiding

Feb. 24, Death of Richard Hovey, poet

March 1, Strike of 6,000 granite cutters in New England for $3 for an eight hour day

March 5, Council of New York University accepted gift of $100,000 later increased from unnamed donor for erection of a "Hall of Fame"

March 9, Social Democratic Party held national convention at Indianapolis, and nominated Eugene V. Debs for President and Job Harriman, of California, for Vice-President

——, Death of Edward J. Phelps, lawyer and diplomat, at New Haven

March 10, Decision of Judge of circuit court in favor of J. C. W. Beckham as Governor of Kentucky. Caleb Powers, Secretary of State, and Captain Davis, arrested charged with complicity in murder of William Goebel

March 20, Public announcement of Secretary Hay of correspondence concluded by which pledges from Great Britain, France, Germany, Russia, Italy, and Japan that existing commercial privileges in China secured by Treaty should not be prejudiced, and Chinese sovereignty in spheres of influence respected

March 24, New Carnegie Steel Company incorporated in Trenton, New Jersey, with capital of $160,000,000

March 29, Order of Secretary of War announced discontinuance of the Dept. of the Pacific, and creation of the Military Division of the Philippines, General Otis in command, comprising 4 departments, with Generals MacArthur, Bates, Hughes, and Kobbe in command

April 1, End of strike in Chicago following agreement March 24

April 4, Admiral Dewey announced his intention to be a candidate for the presidency by authorized statement in newspaper

April 7, Second Philippine Commission headed by Judge W. H. Taft appointed

April 10, Proclamation of the President opened part of the Colville Indian Reservation in Washington to settlers on Oct. 10

April 12, Treaty with the Cherokees negotiated by the Dawes Commission provided for allotment of their lands

April 13, Death of Henry Scripps, newspaper publisher, in California

April 15, Strike of the laborers on the Croton Dam, New York, for advance from $1.25 to $1.50 a day. Troops sent to preserve order

May 1, Convention of United Christian Party at Rock Island, Illinois, nominated the Rev. S. C. Swallow, of Pennsylvania, for President, and John G. Wooley, of Illinois, for Vice-President. Both declined the nomination, and subsequently Jonathan F. R. Leonard, of Iowa, and David H. Martin, of Pennsylvania, nominated

——, Charles H. Allen inaugurated first Civil Governor of Puerto Rico

May 3, Strike of 8,000 men in building trades at Philadelphia for increase in wages and eight hour day

May 4, Sanford B. Dole, former President, nominated first Governor of Hawaii by President McKinley, and Henry E. Cooper, former Minister of Foreign Affairs, Secretary

May 7, Mass meeting in San Francisco passed resolution urging extension of Chinese Exclusion Act to include the Japanese

May 8–July 2, Strike of street car employees in St. Louis. Cars run June 15 with aid of 2,000 deputies

May 9–10, Two conventions of the Populist (People's) Party met at Cincinnati, Ohio and Sioux Falls, South Dakota. At Cincinnati, Wharton Barker, of Pennsylvania, named for President and Ignatius Donnelly, of Minnesota, for Vice-President. At Sioux Falls, William J. Bryan nominated for President and Charles A. Towne for Vice-President

May 12, Proclamation of the President revived Claims Convention with Chile of 1892 and 1897

May 14, Supreme Court decision sustained constitutionality of inheritance tax provisions of the War Revenue Act of 1898, and held that government bonds are not exempt from taxation either under federal or state laws

——, Agreement concluded in New York City with machinists representing 100,000 workmen throughout the United States

——, Extradition Treaty with Switzerland signed

May 21, Supreme Court decision that the court had no jurisdiction in the matter of the disputed election for governor in Kentucky

——, Secretary Hay assured Boer delegation that the United States would maintain strict neutrality in South African War

June 1, American marines sent to Peking to guard Legation arrived with guards of other nations

June 2–8, Socialist Labor Party met in New York City and nominated Joseph P. Maloney, of Massachusetts, for President, and Valentine Remmel, of Pennsylvania, for Vice-President

June 5, Death of Stephen Crane, novelist, at Badenweiler, Germany, and of the Rev. Dr. Richard Salter Storrs in Brooklyn

June 10, Chippewa Indians of the Leech Lake Reservation, Minnesota, again on the war path

June 19, American Legation in China joined the other foreign legations in Peking at British Embassy and prepared for siege. See China

June 19–21, Republican National Convention met in Philadelphia and nominated President McKinley for a second term and Theodore Roosevelt, of New York, for Vice-President. Platform declared for gold standard, approved the foreign policy of the Administration, advocated federal aid for shipping industry, and for an isthmian canal to be constructed, owned, and controlled by the United States

June 24, General A. R. Chaffee assigned to command of United States troops for the relief of the Legation in Peking besieged by Chinese. See China

June 25, Death of Mellen Chamberlain, jurist and librarian, in Boston

June 26, United States Army Commission headed by Dr. Walter Reed appointed to investigate yellow fever in Havana. Experiments resulted in discovery that the disease was spread solely by the female stegomyia mosquito

June 27–28, National Prohibition Party met in Chicago and nominated John G. Wooley, of Chicago, for

President, and Henry B. Metcalf, of Rhode Island, for Vice-President

June 30, Death of Rear Admiral John Woodward Philip in Brooklyn

July 3, Circular Note issued by Secretary Hay to the Powers declared purposes of the United States Government as to China

July 4–6, Democratic National Convention met at Kansas City and nominated William J. Bryan for President by acclamation. The Vice-Presidency was offered to David B. Hill who had been a candidate for the Presidency and when he refused Adlai E. Stevenson, of Illinois, received the nomination. Platform denounced imperialism, the Currency Act of the last Congress, and advocated free silver

——, Silver Republican Party Convention met at Kansas City and endorsed W. J. Bryan for President and eventually A. E. Stevenson for Vice-President by action of the national committee

July 5, Death of Henry Barnard, educator, at Hartford

July 9, Death of Rear Admiral George Cochran in Philadelphia

July 10, Treaty of commerce with Germany signed

July 14, Death of Senator John Henry Gear, of Iowa, in Washington

July 16, Strike of iron miners in New Jersey against reduction of wages

July 18, Anti-Imperialists and Gold Democrats met in New York City and denounced Mr. McKinley, Mr. Roosevelt, and Mr. Bryan

July 20, Message dated July 16 from Mr. Conger received of siege in British legation at Peking and saying that only quick relief would prevent massacre by Chinese

July 22, Death of Lucius E. Chittenden, lawyer, at Burlington, Vermont

July 24–27, Race riots in New Orleans after 2 police officers killed by a negro resisting arrest. A negro schoolhouse and 30 negro tenements burned and a large number of persons injured

July 31, Death of John Clark Ridpath, historian, in New York City

Aug. 4, Death of Jacob D. Cox, former Governor of Ohio

Aug. 13, Death of William Steinitz, chess player, in New York City

——, Death of Collis P. Huntington, railroad magnate, in the Adirondacks, New York

Aug. 15–16, Liberty Congress of the American League of Anti-Imperialists met at Indianapolis and endorsed the nomination of William J. Bryan

Aug. 16, Death of John James Ingalls, lawyer, in New Mexico

Aug. 18, Caleb Powers, former Secretary of State of Kentucky, convicted of complicity in the murder of William Goebel in Jan. and sentenced to imprisonment for life

Aug. 31, Relief authorized for destitute miners at Cape Nome, Alaska

Sept. 5, Anti-Imperialists met in New York City as the "National Party" and nominated Senator Donelson Caffery, of Louisiana, for President and Archibald M. Howe, of Massachusetts, for Vice-President

Sept. 8, Hurricane and flood devastated Galveston, Texas, loss of life estimated as 6,000 and property loss $15,000,000

Sept. 11, Death of William Saunders, horticulturist, in Washington

Sept. 14, Death of Rear Admiral Montgomery Sicard, at Westerville, New York

Sept. 17–Oct. 25, Strike of anthracite coal miners in Pennsylvania

Sept. 23, Renewal of wage scale of amalgamated iron and steel workers

Oct. 12, American representatives to the Permanent Court of Arbitration at the Hague appointed: Benjamin Harrison, Melville W. Fuller, John W. Griggs, and George Gray

Oct. 17, Death of William Lyne Wilson, lawyer and educator, at Lexington, Virginia

Oct. 20, Death of Charles Dudley Warner, author, at Hartford, Connecticut

Oct. 22, Death of John Sherman, former Secretary of State, in Washington

Oct. 25, Strike of anthracite miners declared off, certain companies agreeing to abolish sliding scale and granting advance in wages

Nov. 1, Census at this date gave total population as 76,304,799, a gain of 13,235,043 since 1890 representing an increase of nearly 21%. The center of population was in southern Indiana about 7 miles north of Columbus. New York City led with population of 3,437,202, Chicago 1,698,575, Philadelphia 1,293,697, St. Louis 575,238, Boston 560,892. Jewish people numbered 1,058,000 as compared with 130,000 in 1890

Nov. 2, Death of William L. Strong, former Mayor of New York City

Nov. 6, Presidential election a Republican victory, McKinley and Roosevelt receiving popular vote of 7,217,677, and 292 electoral votes to 155 cast for Bryan and Stevenson, Democrats. The popular vote for Bryan was 6,967,853; for J. G. Wooley, Prohibition, 207,368; for Wharton Barker, People's Party, 50,192; for E. V. Debs, Social Democrat, 94,552; for James F. Maloney, Socialist Labor, 33,450

Nov. 7, Treaty with Spain signed, cession of islands in Philippine Archipelago outside lines of Treaty of 1898, particularly the islands of Cagayan Sulu and Sibutu for sum of $100,000

Nov. 12, Death of Marcus Daly, copper magnate, New York City, and of Henry Villard, financier

Nov. 15, Carnegie Institute of Technology founded by Andrew Carnegie, accepted by City of Pittsburgh Jan. 28, 1901 and opened Oct. 1905

Nov. 21, Water Boundary Treaty with Mexico signed

Nov. 29, Death of Burke Aaron Hinsdale, educator, at Atlanta, Georgia

Nov. 30, Report of Walker Commission presented favored Nicaraguan route for trans-isthmian canal rather than through Panama

Dec. 1, Protocols signed with Costa Rica and Nicaragua as to right to construct canal

Dec. 6, Strike of telegraphers on Santa Fé railroads

Dec. 7, Report of new gold field, the richest since the Klondike, on the Yellow River, branch of the Kuskokwim

Dec. 13, Supplementary Extradition Treaty with Great Britain signed

Dec. 21, Death of Roger Wolcott, former Governor of Massachusetts

Dec. 23–30, Strike of street car employees at Scranton, Penn. gained 10 hour day and increased pay to 20 cents an hour

Dec. 28, Death of Moses Coit Tyler, historian, in Ithaca, New York

CONGRESS

Jan. 16, Samoan Treaty ratified by the Senate

Jan. 25, The House refused to allow elected Congressman Brigham H. Roberts from Utah to take his seat because of his plural marriages by vote of 268 to 50

Feb. 10, Provided that vessels owned by citizens of Cuba should thereafter be entitled in ports of the United States to the rights and privileges of vessels of the most favored nations

Feb. 16, Gold Standard Bill passed the Senate by vote of 46 to 29

March 14, Currency Act signed by the President declared the gold dollar the standard unit of value and decreed the parity of all kinds of money with gold, provided for gold reserve of $150,000,000 for redemption of legal tender notes, the redemption not to be allowed to fall below $100,000,000 in which case sales of bonds to replenish the gold reserve

March 24, Act appropriated all duties collected on produce of Puerto Rico in ports of the United States to the expenses of Puerto Rico

April 10, The Senate voted not to seat W. A. Clark from Montana because of extraordinary expenditure of money preventing a free election

April 12, Organic Act for Civil Government and Tariff to temporarily provide revenues for Puerto Rico enacted. The duties on merchandise entering the United States from Puerto Rico and entering Puerto Rico from the United States shall be 15% of the duties levied on like merchandise from foreign countries. Residents become citizens of Puerto Rico except those Spaniards who elect to remain Spaniards. The navigation laws of the United States are extended to the Island and the statute laws of the United States with some exceptions to be in force. Charles H. Allen appointed first Civil Governor under this Act to take effect May 1

April 17, Speech of Senator Hoar denied the right of the United States under the Constitution to hold the Philippine Islands as subject state, and presented program of the Anti-Imperialists

April 24, The Senate refused to seat Matthew S. Quay appointed by the Governor of Pennsylvania, the vacancy to which he was named having been in existence while the legislature was in session

April 30, Act provided territorial form of government for the Hawaiian Islands to take effect June 14

May 26, Appropriation of $20,000 for establishment of an Army War College. This lapsed and new appropriation made March 2, 1901

June 6, Civil Government Act for Alaska constituted a civil and judicial district with a governor and a district court. Civil Code provided and land laws

——, Act provided for extradition for countries occupied by or under control of the United States

——, Act to incorporate the National Red Cross Society

——, Secretary of the Treasury authorized to designate bank or banks in the Philippines, Puerto Rico, and Cuba in which public moneys may be deposited, said depositories to give satisfactory security by deposits in the United States Treasury

——, Act created the senior major general of the Army, Lieutenant General, and the present Adjutant General to have the rank, pay, and allowances of a major general

June 7, Congress adjourned

Dec. 3, Fifty-sixth Congress, 2d sess. convened

Dec. 20, Hay-Pauncefote Treaty as to Panama Canal signed in Feb. ratified by Senate with amendments which were not accepted by Great Britain

1901

Jan. 6, Death of Philip D. Armour at Chicago

Jan. 9, The War Dept. closed the canteens, army post exchanges, selling liquor

Jan. 10, Texas oil boom began with spouting of a well at Beaumont which began with a delivery of 25,000 barrels a day with a column of oil 200 feet high

Jan. 14, Supreme Court decision in case of Neely vs. Henkel directed extradition of Neely to Cuba on charge of embezzlement of public funds, under Extradition Act of 1900. Cuba declared foreign territory

Jan. 21, Death of Elisha Gray, inventor, at Newtonville, Mass.

Feb. 4, Major William C. Gorgas began campaign against yellow fever mosquitos in Havana

——, Arrest of Mrs. Carrie Nation leading a band of women against illicit liquor selling in Kansas, wrecking restaurants and saloons

Feb. 15, Death of Maurice Thompson, author, at Crawfordsville, Indiana

Feb. 16, Russian Decree to take effect March 1 withdrew from specified imports from the United States the privileges of the most favored nation clause of Treaty of 1832 in retaliation for American duty on sugar

Feb. 25, United States Steel Company filed articles of incorporation in New Jersey, capitalization $1,319,-000,000; advertised by J. P. Morgan Company March 3

Feb. 27, New decision in Berliner microphone patent case of Boston circuit court declared patent void

Feb. 28, Death of William M. Evarts, lawyer, in New York City

March 4, President McKinley inaugurated for second term, Theodore Roosevelt, of New York, Vice-President

March 5, All members of the Cabinet continued from preceding administration and recommissioned

March 11, Great Britain refused to accept the Senate amendments to the Hay-Pauncefote Treaty abrogating the Clayton-Bulwer Treaty of 1850

March 12, Letter of Andrew Carnegie offered $5,200,000 for 65 branch libraries for the public system in New York City, the city to provide the sites

March 13, Andrew Carnegie gave $4,000,000 for fund for disabled and superannuated workmen of the Carnegie Company, and $1,000,000 for maintenance of the Carnegie libraries at Braddock, Homestead, and Duquesne

——, Death of Benjamin Harrison, former President, at Indianapolis

March 23, Capture of Aguinaldo, Filipino leader. *See* Philippine Islands

April 5, Philander C. Knox, of Pennsylvania, appointed Attorney General

——, Death of General Alexander Caldwell McClurg, publisher, Chicago

April 10, Death of William Jay Youmans, editor, Mount Vernon, New York

April 11, Proclamation of the President established San Isabel Forest Reserve, Colorado

April 15, Supreme Court decision in the Atherton vs.

Atherton case as to extraterritorial validity of decree of divorce affirmed validity of Kentucky court on the ground that Kentucky was the state of marital residence, and reversed that of New York that the divorce was invalid, and reversed judgments of courts of Pennsylvania and North Dakota in cases where the state of the marital residence was New York

April 16, Death of Professor Henry Augustus Rowland, physicist, in Baltimore

April 18, Threatened strike of iron, steel, and tin workers at McKeesport, Pennsylvania, averted by compromise

April 30, Lincoln College and Decatur College in Illinois united as the James Milliken University

May 1–Nov. 2, Pan-American Exposition at Buffalo, New York

May 5, Americans the first of the international troops to leave Peking, sailing from Tientsin for Manila May 22, a single company remaining as a legation guard

May 6–18, Strike of street car employees in Albany, Troy, Cohoes, and Rensselaer on refusal of company to recognize union and discharge non-union men, troops sent because of violence fired on crowd May 16 and 2 persons killed and 20 injured. Settlement provided for increase and redress of grievances

May 9, Panic on stock exchange, New York City, caused by struggle for control of the stock of the Northern Pacific Railroad Company

May 20, Strike of machinists for 9 hour day begun

May 21, Death of Charles Addison Boutelle, congressman and journalist, and of General Fitzjohn Porter

May 27, Supreme Court decisions in the insular cases as to status of the new territorial possessions that the "Constitution does not follow the flag," and that "Islands appertain to but are not a part of the United States," and consequently duties could be collected on Puerto Rican exports under the Foraker law

June 2, Death of James A. Hearne, actor, New York City

June 7, Andrew Carnegie gave $10,000,000 to provide for free education of young persons born in Scotland at the Scotch universities

June 12, The Platt Amendment adopted as part of Constitution of Cuba

June 18, Death of Hazen S. Pingree, former Governor of Michigan

June 21, Order of War Dept. ended military government in the Philippines, authority transferred to Civil Governor appointed, W. H. Taft, except in districts still in insurrection; to take effect July 4

June 22, General Chaffee appointed Military Governor in the Philippines

June 24, Final court decision that Berliner telephone patent invalid

——, Death of Rev. Joseph Cook, lecturer and writer, at Ticonderoga, New York

June 29, Iron, steel, and tin-plate workers refused to sign wage scale agreement unless scale signed for non-union as well as union mills

July, Strike of teamster's union, San Francisco, begun

July 1, Strike of molders in Cleveland, Ohio, for increase in wages

July 4, Proclamation of the President set apart the Wichita Forest Reserve in Oklahoma

——, Death of John Fiske, historian, at Gloucester, Mass.

July 6, Death of Joseph Le Conte, scientist, in California

July 11, Italians killed by armed mob at Erwin, near Vicksburg, Mississippi; representations to State Dept. made by Italian Minister

July 13, Proclamation of commercial agreement with Italy

July 15, Strike of Amalgamated Association of Iron, Steel, and Tin Workers begun

July 21, Charles Fitzmorris, sent by Chicago newspaper, completed record breaking trip around the world in 60 days, 13 hours, 29 minutes and 42¾ seconds; previous record, G. F. Train in 1890

——, Further extension of the classified civil service, 1,600 places in War Dept. taken out by General Alger returned, and the rural postal carriers placed under civil service

July 25, Court of Inquiry on conduct of Rear Admiral Schley at Santiago named by Secretary of the Navy, Admiral Dewey, president, to meet Sept. 12

——, Proclamation of the President established free trade between Puerto Rico and the United States

July 30, Death of Herbert B. Adams, historian, at Amherst, Mass.

Aug. 3, Proclamation of the President established Payson Forest Reserve, Utah

Aug. 11, General strike of the iron, steel, and tin workers under second order of Aug. 6

Sept. 3, Ellen N. Stone, missionary, captured by Turkish brigands in the Salonica district of Bulgaria, and held for ransom of £25,000

Sept. 6, President McKinley fatally shot by Leon Czolgosz, anarchist, at a reception at Buffalo, New York, while visiting the Exposition

Sept. 7, Protocol with China signed as to Boxer indemnity gave the United States $24,440,000 covering losses of American citizens and expenses of military expedition to Peking, discovered later to be in excess of amount required and readjustment of payments made July, 1908, to return $10,000,000 to China

Sept. 14, Death of President McKinley at Buffalo, New York. Theodore Roosevelt, Vice-President, took the oath as President

——, End of strike of the Amalgamated Association of Iron, Steel, and Tin Workers without gaining its object

Sept. 16, Death of Bishop Henry B. Whipple in Minneapolis

Sept. 17, Funeral services of President McKinley at Washington, and on the 19th at Canton, Ohio

Sept. 23–26, Trial and sentence of Czolgosz, assassin of President McKinley, at Buffalo, and execution Oct. 29

Sept. 26, Death of John G. Nicolay, biographer of Lincoln, at Washington

Oct. 2, Strike of teamsters, stevedores, and longshoremen at San Francisco begun July 30 ended

Oct. 17, President Roosevelt entertained Booker Washington, colored leader, at dinner at the White House, causing great indignation in the South

Oct. 19, Death of Rear Admiral Francis M. Bunce at Hartford, Conn.

Oct. 20, Death of General James A. Walker in Virginia

Oct. 26 and June, 6, 1902, Extradition Treaty with Belgium signed

Nov. 11, New Constitution for Alabama adopted by popular vote contained the "grandfather clause" by which soldiers in wars, Mexican, Indian, Civil, and their descendants can vote without being able to read and write. Suffrage granted also to those paying taxes on $300 worth of land

Nov. 11, Death of Richmond Mayo-Smith, economist, in New York City

Nov. 12, The Northern Securities Company organized under the laws of New Jersey

Nov. 18, Hay-Pauncefote Treaty with Great Britain signed with respect to the Panama Canal provided for complete abrogation of the Clayton-Bulwer Treaty of 1850, neutrality of canal maintained under supervision of the United States, the United States to have sole right of construction, maintenance, and control, fortification permitted

Nov. 19, Order of the President revoked the civil service modification effected by President McKinley in May, 1899

Nov. 27, President Roosevelt authorized application of civil service rules to Indian agencies

——, Army War College formally established at the Washington Barracks, District of Columbia, as a post-graduate school for officers, Tasker H. Bliss, president

Dec. 2, Supreme Court decision in the "fourteen diamond rings case," Pepke vs. United States, declared the status of the Philippines to be domestic territory for tariff purposes, and collection of import duty on the rings brought from Manila illegal. All goods from the Philippines will be admitted to American ports without duty until law enacted similar to the Foraker law for Puerto Rico

Dec. 13, Decision of Court of Inquiry pronounced Rear Admiral Schley guilty of charges of delay in locating the Spanish squadron, and his conduct prior to June 1, 1898 as "characterized by vacillation, dilatoriness and lack of enterprise." Recommended that no action be taken. Bill of exceptions filed by Schley Dec. 19 to findings

Dec. 16–17, Conference on the peaceful settlement of labor disputes held under auspices of the National Civic Federation in New York City, Oscar S. Straus, presiding, representatives of labor and capital present. A Board of Industrial Arbitration appointed

Dec. 17, Death of Dr. Rush S. Huidekoper, physician and editor, in Philadelphia

Dec. 19, Claims Convention with Salvador signed

Dec. 23, Death of William Ellery Channing, poet, at Concord, Mass.

Dec. 24, Death of Clarence King, geologist and mining engineer, in Arizona

CONGRESS

Jan. 10, Petition of Filipinos asking for independence for their country presented in Senate by Senator Teller

Jan. 26, Act to allow the commutation of homestead entries in certain cases

Feb. 2, Army reorganized fixed at 58,000 as a minimum, the President empowered to raise it to 100,000 if needed. The "army canteen" abolished by section 38. Provision made for "Philippine Scouts," a force not to exceed 12,000 to be composed of Filipinos and Americans. Artillery to be organized as a separate corps

March 2, Regulations for the government of Cuba passed included the Platt Amendment by which Cuba to agree to make no agreements with foreign governments which would impair independence of Cuba, granted naval stations to the United States, and granted the United States the right to intervene for maintenance of government, the protection of life, property, or for preservation of Cuban independence. Accepted by Cuba June 12

March 2, Spooner Amendment to Army Appropriation Act authorized the President to establish civil government in the Philippine Islands. He had hitherto acted under his war powers

——, Act directed suppression of hazing at Military Academy at West Point

——, Act providing for reduction of war taxes affected beer, cigars, documentary and check stamps, proprietary articles, legacies, &c., to extent of $40,000,000

March 3, Common carriers required to report to the Interstate Commerce Commission on railroad accidents

——, National Bureau of Standards established

——, Act made provision for the Louisiana Purchase Exposition in St. Louis in 1903

——, Congress adjourned

Dec. 2, Fifty-seventh Congress, 1st sess. convened

Dec. 3, Message of President Roosevelt on public affairs of over 30,000 words called for regulation of corporations and trusts, conservation of natural resources, reciprocity treaties, better army and larger navy, extension of civil service, extended powers for Interstate Commerce Commission, encouragement of merchant marine

Dec. 16, The Senate ratified the Hay-Pauncefote Canal Treaty by vote of 72 to 6

1902

Jan. 4, The Panama Canal Company made formal offer of property and franchises to the United States for $40,000,000

Jan. 6, Treaty of extradition with Denmark signed

——, Dr. Nicholas Murray Butler elected president of Columbia University to succeed Seth Low, installed April 19; Rev. Henry Hopkins elected president of Williams College Jan. 17; Rev. Dan F. Brady elected president of Iowa College Jan. 28; Dr. Edmund J. James elected president of Northwestern University, Jan. 21

Jan. 7, Death of Elbridge S. Brooks, historian, at Somerville, Mass.

Jan. 9, Leslie M. Shaw, of Iowa, appointed Secretary of the Treasury

——, Henry C. Payne, of Wisconsin, appointed Postmaster General

Jan. 11, Lewis Nixon succeeded Richard Croker as chairman of finances of Tammany Hall, New York City

——, Death of Horace Elisha Scudder, editor and author, at Cambridge, Mass.

Jan. 15, Death of Alpheus Hyatt, naturalist, at Cambridge, Mass.

Jan. 24, Treaty with Denmark signed by which Denmark ceded the Islands of St. John, St. Croix, and St. Thomas in the West Indies to the United States for sum of $5,000,000; not ratified by Danish Parliament

Jan. 27, International Convention on literary and artistic copyrights and on exchange of publications signed by the United States

Jan. 28, Carnegie Institution of Washington founded by Andrew Carnegie for promotion of original research, gift of $10,000,000

Jan. 28, Death of Eugene Dupont (61)

Jan. 30, Convention for arbitration of Pan-American Claims signed by the United States

Feb. 1, Secretary Hay addressed Note to 11 Governments as to policy of "open door" in Manchuria

Feb. 14, John Mitchell asked for a conference with the coal operators to present case of miners which was refused on ground that there could not be two masters in management of the coal business

——, Death of Professor James B. Thayer at Cambridge, Mass.

Feb. 18, Death of Albert Bierstadt, painter (71) and of Charles L. Tiffany (90) in New York City

Feb. 19, President Roosevelt refused to reopen the Sampson-Schley case sustaining the judgment of the Court of Inquiry

Feb. 20, Announcement of Attorney General Knox that the Government would bring suit against the Northern Securities Company organized Nov. 12, 1901, by James J. Hill

Feb. 22–March 11, Visit of Prince Henry of Prussia, brother of the Emperor of Germany, entertained in Washington, Annapolis, West Point, Philadelphia, Boston, and New York, and made a six days trip to the West

Feb. 23, Miss Ellen Stone, American missionary, captured by Turkish brigands in Sept., 1901, with Mme Tsilka, released on payment of ransom of $72,500 raised by subscription and paid Jan. 21

Feb. 24, General Order increased pay of rural free delivery carriers $100 a year

Feb. 26, Death of Henry Gordon Marquand, railroad magnate, in New York City

Feb. 27, Constitution of the General Education Board. Offices opened in New York City April 1

——, Colombia forbade French Panama Canal Company to transfer concessions to the United States until it had fulfilled certain obligations to Colombia

March 2, Death of Francis Wayland Parker, educator, at Chicago

March 6, Death of John Daniell, merchant, New York City

March 9, Death of Bishop John F. Spaulding, in Colorado

March 10, Supreme Court decision declared Illinois anti-trust law unconstitutional because of exceptions made in cases of combinations of farmers and live-stock raisers. This decision annulled anti-trust laws enacted by Illinois, Georgia, Indiana, Louisiana, Michigan, Mississippi, Montana, Nebraska, North Carolina, South Dakota, Tennessee, Texas, and Wisconsin

——, Suit brought by the United States vs. the Northern Securities, Great Northern, and Northern Pacific companies under Sherman Anti-Trust Act in the circuit court at St. Paul, the combination of corporations through a holding company

——, Resignation of John D. Long, Secretary of the Navy

March 12, Death of John Peter Altgeld, former Governor of Illinois, at Joliet

March 13, Strike of 6 days of 20,000 teamsters, dock laborers, and freight handlers in Boston settled by conciliation

March 22, Attorney General Knox sustained right of possession of the United States to public lands of Puerto Rico claimed by Puerto Rico

March 25, Executive Order provided for evacuation of

Cuba and transfer from American to Cuban control on May 20

April 1, Death of Dr. Thomas Dunn English, lawyer, and author of "Ben Bolt"

April 3, New political party, the "Allied People's Party" created by congress of reformers at St. Louis

April 4, Will of Cecil Rhodes published gave $10,000,000 to provide for scholarships at Oxford University in England, 2 scholarships assigned to "each of the present States and Territories of the United States"

April 11, Proclamation of the President set apart the Santa Rita Forest Reserve, Arizona

——, Death of Wade Hampton, Confederate General, at Columbia, South Carolina

April 12, Death of the Rev. Thomas De Witt Talmage, at Washington

April 16, Proclamation of the President established Niobrara Forest Reserve, Nebraska, and the Dismal River Forest Reservation

April 20, Death of Frank R. Stockton (68), novelist, at Washington

April 20–26, Strike of street car employees in San Francisco gained increase in wages and shorter hours

April 24, Attorney General Knox announced intention to proceed against the beef trust as a combination in restraint of trade

April 28, Death of Sol Smith Russell, actor, in Washington

——, Claims Convention with Dominican Republic signed

April 29, William H. Moody, of Massachusetts, appointed Secretary of the Navy

May 4, Death of Potter Palmer (74) in Chicago

May 5, Death of Francis Bret Harte (66), author, at Camberley, Surrey, England, and of Archbishop Michael A. Corrigan (63) in New York City

May 6, Death of Rear Admiral William T. Sampson in Washington

May 7, Proclamation of the President set apart Fort Hall Reservation, Idaho

May 8, Death of Paul Leicester Ford, novelist, in New York City

——, Anthracite coal miners offered to submit their grievances and demand for a 20% increase in wages and eight hour day to arbitration which was refused by the operators

May 9, W. H. Taft instructed to go to Rome to negotiate with the Pope for sale of friars' lands in Philippines and withdrawal of friars

May 12, Anthracite coal strike ordered May 9 begun in Pennsylvania

May 15, Death of Dr. William Todd Helmuth, physician and editor, in Philadelphia

May 20, Government of Cuba formally transferred to the President of Cuba. See also Cuba

——, Death of Edwin L. Godkin, journalist, at Brixham, England

May 22, Treaty with Mexico as to the "Pious Fund" case signed

——, Proclamation of the President set apart Medicine Bow Forest Reserve, and Yellowstone and Teton Forest Reserve, Wyoming

May 24, Dedication of the Rochambeau monument in Washington, representatives of the families of Marshal de Rochambeau and the Marquis de Lafayette the guests of the United States

May 28–June 5, Strike of teamsters in Chicago

May 29, Civil service employees and officers of the

classified list arranged into 6 classes according to salary received

June 3, Death of Dr. John Henry Barrows, president of Oberlin College, Ohio

June 6, Constitutional Convention in Virginia which first met Jan. 2 adopted new Constitution which was rejected by the electorate June 16

June 7, President Roosevelt directed Commissioner Wright to investigate the causes of the anthracite coal strike and make recommendations. He held conference on June 9

——, Death of Dean Eugene Augustus Hoffman, of the General Theological Seminary, New York

June 13, International Waterways Commission authorized

June 15, Death of Anson Judd Upson, educator, Glenn Falls, New York

June 25, Extradition Treaty with Mexico signed

July 1, Society of the Army of Santiago de Cuba incorporated

——, Permanent Census Office established

July 3, Governor Taft proposed purchase of the lands of the friars in the Philippines, price to be fixed by 5 arbiters, and the friars to withdraw from the Islands within a specified time

——, Treaty of friendship and general relations with Spain signed

——, Suspension of tonnage dues on Cuban vessels entering ports of the United States declared

——, Strike of smelters in Denver for eight hour day; militia sent Sept. 4

July 8, Death of Dr. John D. Runkle, educator

July 9, Proposals of the Vatican as to lands of friars in the Philippines declared it impossible for the friars to be withdrawn

July 16, Note of the United States Secretary of War presented to the Pope asked for withdrawal of the 4 religious orders in the Philippines

July 17–19, Conference of bituminous coal miners at Indianapolis decided not to join strike

July 20, Death of John W. Mackay, "bonanza king," in England

July 22, Proclamation of the President set apart Mount Graham Forest Reserve, Arizona, the Lincoln Forest Reserve, New Mexico, July 26, and the Chiricahua Forest Reserve, July 30

July 25, Strike and boycott of Loewe hat manufacturers in Danbury, Conn., begun

July 26, Death of Charles K. Adams, educator and historian, in California

Aug. 1, Largest known tree in the world discovered in the Sierras, California, of the species sequoia gigantea sempervirens, circumference 1 foot from the ground 108 feet, and 6 foot from the ground 93 feet as measured by John Muir

Aug. 11, Note of the United States to signatory Powers of the Berlin Treaty of 1878 published Sept. 17 protested against the oppression of Jews in Rumania

Aug. 16, Proclamation of the President set apart the Little Belt Mountains Reserve and the Madison Forest Reserve, Montana, and the Alexander Archipelago Forest Reserve, Alaska, Aug. 20

Aug. 20, Treaty of commerce with France signed

Aug. 21, Death of General Franz Sigel in New York City

Aug. 31, Suit brought against trade union in Danbury hat boycott on ground of violation of the Sherman Anti-Trust Act

Sept. 3, Death of Edward Eggleston, author, at Lake George, New York

——, Report of Commissioner Wright to the President published, the demands of the coal miners on strike modified to demand for 10% wage increase and 8 to 10 hour day, refused by operators

Sept. 18, Lieutenant Robert E. Peary reached Sydney, N.S., from the Arctic

Sept. 23, Death of Major John Wesley Powell, geologist, in Maine

Sept. 28–Nov. 28, Strike of street car employees in New Orleans for eight hour day at 25 cents an hour

Oct. 1, Incorporation of the International Mercantile Marine Company including the American, Red Star, White Star, Atlantic Transport, Leyland, and Dominion lines

——, Secretary of the Treasury authorized banks holding government deposits secured by United States bonds to substitute specified state and municipal bonds for the latter

——, Death of Rear Admiral James Edward Jouett in Maryland

Oct. 2, Death of Mrs. Elizabeth Cady Stanton, suffragist

Oct. 3, President Roosevelt invited the mine owners and presidents and John Mitchell, president of the United Mine Workers, to conference at the White House, and asked for agreement by which mining of coal should be resumed pending examination of the case by a commission. The mine operators refused, and President Roosevelt made arrangements with the Governor of Pennsylvania, known only to 3 or 4 other persons, to send Major General Schofield to the mines with United States troops to take charge of the mines and operate them for the public good as receivers from the government

Oct. 6, Entire National Guard of Pennsylvania ordered to anthracite region because of riots, and demand of mine operators of President Roosevelt that federal troops be sent to protect the mines

Oct. 9, Simmons College for women opened in Boston

Oct. 11, Raids in Boston and New York by federal immigration officers and local police on Chinese quarters requiring Chinese to show certificates of residence, and many Chinese arrested and imprisoned when certificates not forthcoming

Oct. 12, Secretary Root in conference with J. P. Morgan as to coal strike

Oct. 13, Draft proposal for settlement of strike published to which operators agreed

Oct. 14, Permanent Court of Arbitration at The Hague in "Pious Fund" case decided in favor of the United States, Mexico to pay $1,420,682 and successive annual installments of $43,050

——, Decision of King of Norway and Sweden under Convention of Nov. 7, 1899 in favor of Germany and against the United States and Great Britain in the Samoa case

Oct. 15, Army reduced to minimum of 59,600 by War Dept.

——, Death of Rear Admiral Thomas O. Selfridge at Waverley, Mass.

Oct. 16, Coal Strike Commission appointed: Judge George Gray, Edgar E. Clark, Chief of the Order of Railway Conductors, Thomas H. Watkins, Bishop John L. Spalding, and Carroll D. Wright, and organized at White House Oct. 24, Judge Gray, president

Oct. 21, Strike of anthracite coal miners declared at end by President John Mitchell accepting plan of arbitration of commission appointed by President Roosevelt

Oct. 22, Danish legislature failed to ratify Treaty of Jan. 24 ceding West Indian islands to the United States

Oct. 23, Coal miners resumed work

Oct. 25, Death of Frank Norris, novelist

Oct. 28, The steamship "Korea" reached San Francisco from Yokohama in 10 days, 15 hours, and 15 minutes, fastest trip on record

Nov. 4, Election for members of Congress gave Republican majority for 58th Congress

Nov. 8, Reciprocity Treaty with Newfoundland signed

Nov. 19, Amendment to Treaty of commerce with Portugal of May 22, 1899, signed

Nov. 29, Arbitration decision of King of Sweden and Norway condemned Russia to pay damages for seizure of American sealing vessels

Dec. 4, Dr. Charles W. Stiles published his discovery of hookworm as cause of disease in the South

Dec. 6, Death of Alice Freeman Palmer (Mrs. Herbert Palmer) former president of Wellesley College, in France

Dec. 7, Death of Thomas B. Reed, former Speaker of the House, in Washington, and of Thomas Nast, cartoonist, in Ecuador where he was United States Consul General

Dec. 11, Vermont legislature passed high license local option law with a referendum

——, Commercial Reciprocity Convention with Cuba signed

Dec. 12, Proposal for arbitration of President Castro of Venezuela submitted to Great Britain and Germany by the United States. *See also* Venezuela

Dec. 16, New Pacific cable laid at San Francisco with ceremonies, to stretch to Shanghai by way of Honolulu and Manila

Dec. 18, Teamster's strike in New Orleans declared off

——, New Hampshire Constitutional Convention adopted woman suffrage amendment to be submitted to popular vote

Dec. 26, Death of Mary Hartwell Catherwood, novelist, in Chicago

Dec. 29, Standard Oil Company announced establishment of pension system for employees

CONGRESS

Jan. 20, Report of Canal Commission recommending purchase of property and rights of Panama Canal as offered by the French company for $40,000,000 sent to Congress by the President

Feb. 17, The Senate ratified Treaty of Jan. 24 for purchase of Danish West Indies; rejected by Danish legislature Oct. 22

Feb. 22, Personal encounter of Senators Tillman and McLaurin, Tillman charging McLaurin with having been bribed to vote for the Treaty of Paris

March 6, Permanent Census Bureau created to date from July 1

March 8, Act established tariff for the Philippines and allowed Philippine exports to enter the United States at a 25% reduction from the rates of the Dingley tariff, not the 50% asked by the Commission or the 75% asked for by Governor Taft

April 12, Comptroller of the Currency authorized to extend the charters of the national banks for a further 20 years

April 12, War revenue taxes left unrepealed by law of 1901 repealed except tax on mixed flour

April 15, Act for relief of bona fide settlers on forest reserves

April 29, Chinese Exclusion Act extended to the Territories and all territories under jurisdiction of the United States

May 9, Act regulated manufacture and sale of butter and substitutes. Oleomargarine and other substitutes made subject to laws of State or Territory into which they are transported

June 2, Pension Act amended as to Indian wars, extending provisions and benefits

June 7, Act provided for protection of game in Alaska

June 17, Newlands Reclamation Act devoted almost entire amount of proceeds of sales of public lands in 16 western and southwestern States to fund for the construction and maintenance of irrigation works

June 28, Act provided for construction of a canal across the Isthmus of Panama and establishment of an Isthmian Canal Commission. $40,000,000 appropriated for purchase of the property and rights from the French Canal Company. In case of failure of negotiations recourse to be had to the building of canal through Nicaragua

July 1, Organic Act constituted the Philippine Islands as "unorganized" territory, recognized inhabitants as citizens of the Philippine Islands and entitled to protection of the United States, and confirmed act of the President in appointment of the Philippine Commission for government of the Islands

——, Act to prevent false branding and marking of foods and dairy products as to State or Territory in which produced

——, The United States Marine Hospital Service made the Public Health and Marine Hospital Service

——, Congress adjourned

Dec. 1, Fifty-seventh Congress, 2d sess. convened

1903

Jan. 1, United States Steel Company announced plan for sharing profits with employees and for purchase of stock by employees

Jan. 6, New York Court of Appeals decided against William S. Devery in his suit for reinstatement as Chief of Police, New York City

Jan. 12, General Education Board incorporated to promote education in the United States regardless of race, creed, or sex, funds from John D. Rockefeller

Jan. 18, President Roosevelt greeted King Edward by wireless telegraph from Marconi station at Wellfleet, Mass., to England

——, Death of Abram Stevens Hewitt, manufacturer and former Mayor of New York City

Jan. 22, The Hay-Herran Treaty with Colombia signed providing for Panama Canal; not ratified by Colombia

Jan. 24, Treaty with Great Britain as to Alaska boundary agreed to formation of a joint commission to interpret boundary

Jan. 26, Supplementary Commercial Treaty with Cuba signed

Jan. 27, Gift of John D. Rockefeller of $7,000,000 announced in Chicago for research for tuberculosis serum

Jan. 31, Claims Convention with Santo Domingo (Dominican Republic) signed

Feb. 1, Henry Phipps Institute founded for study of causes, treatment, and prevention of tuberculosis; incorporated Sept. 1

Feb. 7, Bituminous coal miners voted to accept offer of operators of increase in wages averaging 14%

Feb. 16, George B. Cortelyou, of New York, appointed first Secretary of new Dept. of Commerce and Labor, and James R. Garfield Commissioner of Corporations

Feb. 16 and 23, Agreement with Cuba signed provided for lease of lands for coaling and naval stations. *See also* Cuba

Feb. 17, Protocol with Venezuela signed agreement to refer claims to mixed commission

Feb. 21, Cornerstone of Army War College laid

Feb. 23, Supreme Court decision that Congress under interstate commerce law may prohibit sale of lottery tickets between States

Feb. 27, Strike of structural iron workers at Pittsburgh

March 10, Nevada established local prohibition through local petitions

March 11, Woman suffrage defeated by vote in New Hampshire

March 18, Anthracite Coal Commission Report presented

March 20, The Mississippi River at New Orleans the highest ever known at 19 feet and 8 inches above normal

——, Death of Charles Godfrey Leland (Hans Breitman) humorist and writer (78) in Florence, Italy

March 21, Award of Anthracite Coal Commission increased wages on the basis of a minimum wage, sliding scale from April 1, 1903 to April 1, 1906, contract miners receiving 10% increase, and hours shortened, and the union recognized

March 27, New Hampshire substituted local option for state wide prohibition by system of licenses to take effect May 1

March 28–June 21, Strike of mill operatives at Lowell, Mass.

March 31, Death of Ebenezer Butterick (73) originator of the tissue paper dress pattern

April 1, Award of Anthracite Coal Commission went into effect

——, Indiana Supreme Court declared unconstitutional the law providing for minimum wage in public works and on April 8 the weekly payment law

April 7, Death of Rear Admiral George Belknap at Key West, Florida

April 8, Andrew Carnegie gave $250,000 for branch public libraries in Cleveland, Ohio

April 9, United States Court of Appeals decided case against the Northern Securities Company as an illegal combination in restraint of trade in violation of the Anti-Trust Act

April 11, Death of Brigham Young in Salt Lake City, Utah

April 15, Civil service rules amended and classified list amended

April 18, Decision of Circuit Court in Illinois declared the "beef trust," Swift and Co. *et al.* guilty of combination in restraint of trade in their agreement to refrain from bidding against each other

April 20, Reading Coal and Iron Company ordered lockout because men refused to work 9 hours a day on Saturday but returned to work April 21 on order

of United Mine Workers pending adjustment of grievance by conciliation board

April 27, United States Supreme Court sustained clauses in Alabama Constitution which disenfranchised the negroes

April 28, New York Court of Appeals declared eight hour day law unconstitutional

April 29, Death of Paul B. DuChaillu (68) explorer, and Robson Stuart (Stuart Robson) actor

May 1, South Carolina law providing that no children under 10 should work in the cotton mills went into effect

May 1–June 5, Strike of Chicago laundry workers settled by agreement to submit dispute to board of arbitration

May 7, Claims Convention with Venezuela signed

May 12, Death of Richard Henry Stoddard (78) poet and essayist

May 14, President Roosevelt named umpire of claims in case of Great Britain, Germany, and Italy against Venezuela

May 22, Treaty of relations with Cuba signed which embodied the Platt Amendment

May 27, Mass meeting in New York City denounced the Kishinev massacres in Russia

——, Strike in Union Pacific Railroad shops ended

May 31, Floods of the Kansas, Missouri, and Des Moines rivers destroyed property estimated at $17,-000,000 in Topeka and Kansas City, and 200 persons drowned

June 10, State troops sent to Morenci, Arizona, and federal troops asked for and sent on account of riots of miners on strike against reduction of wages

June 12, Death of General Alexander McDowell Cook (73)

June 21, Death of Major James B. Pond (65) lecture manager

June 23–26, The United States fleet entertained by the Emperor of Germany at Kiel

June 23, New Springfield rifle formally adopted for use of the army

June 30, Immigration records broken with admittance during fiscal year ending this date of 812,870 persons, increase of 32% over previous year

July 2, Treaties with Cuba signed by which Isle of Pines transferred to the sovereignty of Cuba and Cuba ceded coaling and naval stations to the United States; not ratified within time prescribed

July 4, Pacific cable from San Francisco by way of Hawaii and Guam to the Philippines. President Roosevelt sent first message to the Philippines and second around the world in 12 minutes time

July 6–17, Visit of United States fleet to England

July 17, Death of James McNeill Whistler, artist, in London, England

July 22, Death of General Cassius Marcellus Clay, diplomat, in Kentucky

July 24, Serious decline in Wall St. stocks in New York City

Aug. 1, American Minister Bowen ordered to protest against seizure of asphalt properties of American company in Venezuela

Aug. 8, Major General Nelson A. Miles Commander of the Army retired and was succeeded by the General Staff of which General S. B. M. Young became the first head Aug. 15

Aug. 9, Death of William E. Dodge, merchant, New York City

Aug. 12, Announcement of rejection of Panama Canal Treaty by Colombian Senate

Aug. 16, Death of Noah Brooks (73) author and journalist

Aug. 17, Joseph Pulitzer gave $1,000,000 for establishment of School of Journalism, Columbia University

Aug. 22, Award of arbitration commission in the Alabama coal strike

Aug. 24, The horse "Lou Dillon" trotted a mile in 2 minutes breaking the world record, and Oct. 24 reached 1.585

Aug. 27, The United States squadron ordered to Beirut to support any demand that might be made by the United States on Turkey

Aug. 28, Death of Frederick Law Olmstead (81) landscape architect

Aug. 31, A Packard automobile completed 52 day journey from San Francisco to New York City, first time an automobile had crossed the continent under its own power

Sept. 26, Alabama passed law against boycotting, picketing, &c., first United States law of the kind

Sept. 28, Death of Henry Demarest Lloyd, sociologist and writer

Oct. 7, Professor S. P. Langley launched his "aërodrome" over Widewater, Virginia, where it immediately sank in the Potomac River

——, Document signed by which Andrew Carnegie gave $1,500,000 for building a "temple of peace" at The Hague to house the Permanent Court of Arbitration

Oct. 8, Treaty of commerce with China signed

Oct. 16, John A. Dowie with 3,500 of his followers from Zion City opened an evangelical campaign in New York City

Oct. 20, Decision of Alaskan Boundary Commission sustained the claims of the United States as to boundary line barring Canada from the ocean inlets

Oct. 26, Supreme Court decision that canals are under the federal courts

Nov. 2, Commanders of the U.S.S. "Nashville" and "Marblehead" stationed at Colon and Acapulco directed to prevent landing of troops of either Colombia or Panama within 50 miles of Panama under Article 35 of Treaty of 1840 with Colombia

Nov. 6, Independence of Panama from Colombia recognized by the United States

——, The University of Chattanooga, Tennessee, chartered under present name

Nov. 7, Request of Colombia for permission to land troops at Panama for the purpose of maintaining integrity of her territory refused by commanders of the American warships

——, Death of William L. Elkins (71) street railroad magnate

Nov. 12–25, Strike of 3,000 street car employees in Chicago

Nov. 13, Señor Bunau-Varilla formally received as Minister from Panama

Nov. 14, Rhode Island cotton mills reduced wages 10%

Nov. 16, Death of James Roberts Gilmore (Edmund Kirke) author (80)

Nov. 18, Hay-Varilla Treaty signed with Panama for construction of a ship canal across the Isthmus by the United States, the United States to guarantee the independence of Panama, and for cash payment of $10,000,000 and annual payments of $250,000 the United States to have full sovereignty over strip of land 10 miles wide across the Isthmus

Nov. 19, Mrs. Carrie Nation, refused admission to the White House, proceeded to the Senate and began harangue on temperance for which she was arrested and later fined $25

Nov. 23, Troops sent to Cripple Creek mining district, Colorado, on account of riots of strikers

Nov. 29, Bristow Report of postoffice published, showed existence of conspiracy to defraud the government and estimated losses in postal contracts, &c., at $1,000,000

Dec. 3, International Sanitary Convention signed by the United States

Dec. 4, Martial law declared at Cripple Creek, Colorado, where coal miners on strike since Nov. for eight hour day and employment of union labor only

Dec. 8, Second failure of Professor S. P. Langley to launch his "aërodrome" capable of carrying a man, with result that government support of his experiments withdrawn

Dec. 10, Death of Rear Admiral Bancroft Gherardi (71)

Dec. 11, United States marines formally occupied naval station ceded to the United States by Cuba at Guantanamo

Dec. 17, First successful airplane flight made by the brothers, Orville and Wilbur Wright, at Kitty Hawk, North Carolina, with power machine, which lasted 12 seconds, Orville Wright, pilot. The same day Wilbur Wright made flight which lasted 59 seconds

Dec. 19, Williamsburg Bridge over the East River from New York City to Brooklyn opened

Dec. 20, Death of Frederic R. Coudert (72) lawyer, New York City

Dec. 22, Negotiations for purchase of the friar's lands, for $7,250,000, about 400,000 acres, concluded. All agricultural lands except 10,000 acres transferred to the Philippine Government. Followed by voluntary withdrawal of the friars

Dec. 23, Death of Rear Admiral Edwin White (60)

Dec. 27, Treaty of commerce with Abyssinia (Ethiopia) signed

Dec. 30, Iroquois Theatre in Chicago burned with loss of life of 588 persons chiefly women and children because of defective provisions for safety and exit

Dec. 31, Immigration records broken this year with admittance of 857,046 persons

CONGRESS

Jan. 9, The House rejected amendment in favor of Panama and passed Nicaragua Bill for canal, but Senate subsequently substituted Panama and the House concurred

Jan. 15, Free Coal Act suspended duties on coal imported for one year, and placed anthracite coal permanently on the free list

Jan. 21, Dick Act reorganized and nationalized the militia making it a reserve of the regular army. Every able bodied male citizen between ages of 18 and 45 included with certain exceptions

Feb. 2, Supplementary Animal Contagious Diseases Act to prevent spread of disease passed

Feb. 5, Bankruptcy Act amended

Feb. 9, System of extradition with the Philippines established

Feb. 11, Expedition Act for control of trusts made it possible to prosecute with quick results by giving precedence on court dockets to federal suits dealing with trusts

Feb. 12, Salaries of federal judges increased, Chief Justice to receive $13,000, and associates $12,500

Feb. 14, Department of Commerce and Labor created and Bureau of Corporations

——, General Staff Act organized corps to increase efficiency of army

Feb. 19, Elkins Act defined what constituted unfair discrimination between shippers in interstate commerce dealing chiefly with procedure and penalties imposed on the receiver as well as the giver of rebates

March 2, Civil Government Act of Alaska amended

——, Act established standard of value and coinage for the Philippines

March 3, Act regulating immigration provided for levy of $2 for every passenger not a citizen of the United States or of Canada, Cuba, or Mexico

——, Navy increased by 3,000 men and 5 battleships and 2 training ships authorized

——, Appropriation Act for the Dept. of Agriculture provided regulations for inspection of imported foods to prevent adulteration

——, Five Acts revised laws as to steamboat inspection and safety of steamship travel

——, $20,000,000 appropriated for public buildings

——, Congress adjourned

Nov. 9, Fifty-Eighth Congress, 1st sess. convened

Dec. 7, Fifty-Eighth Congress, 2d sess. convened

Dec. 17, Act passed to carry into effect Commercial Convention with Cuba

1904

Jan. 2, Death of General James Longstreet (83) Confederate

Jan. 4, Supreme Court decision held that citizens of Puerto Rico are not aliens to the United States and therefore cannot be excluded as such from admission to mainland of the United States, but they are not necessarily citizens of the United States

——, Death of Mrs. Mary Elizabeth Wormely Latimer, writer and translator of Balzac

Jan. 9, General S. B. M. Young retired as Chief of Staff of the Army and succeeded by General Adna R. Chaffee

——, Death of Francis L. Wayland, jurist and educator (78)

Jan. 11, Judge William H. Taft, of Ohio, appointed Secretary of War to take effect Feb. 1

Jan. 18, Death of George Francis Train (74) author

——, Supreme Court decision that negroes cannot be debarred from serving on juries in cases of crimes committed by members of their race

Jan. 20, Convention extended time of ratification of Treaty with Cuba of May, 1903

Feb. 2, Death of William C. Whitney (62) former Secretary of the Navy

Feb. 7, Death of James B. Colgate (86) financier

Feb. 7–8, Fire in Baltimore, Maryland, the largest fire since that of Chicago in 1871, destroyed entire business section, burning 30 hours, loss of 2,600 buildings estimated at $125,000,000

Feb. 15, Death of Marcus A. (Mark) Hanna (66) senator from Ohio

Feb. 19, Cash price of wheat in Chicago market $1.08

Feb. 22, Decision of Hague Tribunal announced in favor of preferential treatment of Great Britain, Germany, and Italy in collection of claims growing out of the revolution in Venezuela (30%) and against the United States

Feb. 22, President Roosevelt sent Admiral Dewey and Asst. Sec. Loomis to investigate conditions in Santo Domingo

Feb. 26, A. W. Machen, former superintendent of rural free delivery service, the Groff brothers, and George E. Lorenz convicted of complicity in the postal frauds and sentenced the following day to 2 years imprisonment and $10,000 fine each

——, American marines landed at Santo Domingo and fought against insurgents

Feb. 28, Special Commission appointed by the President to investigate immigration service exonerated officials of charge of maladministration

Feb. 29, Isthmian Canal Commission appointed by the President, Rear Admiral John Walker, chairman

March 1, Conference of bituminous coal miners and operators in Indianapolis failed to reach agreement on wage scale. the miners refusing to accept 10% reduction

March 2, New Treaty with Cuba signed by which the United States relinquished sovereignty over the Isle of Pines, identical with treaty of July 2, 1903, which had expired by time limitation

——, Abrogation of Bates Treaty of Aug. 1899 with the Sultan of Sulu in view of his participation in the Moro revolt in the Philippines

March 8, Death of Robert Taber (38) actor

March 14, Supreme Court decision upheld decision of lower court that the Northern Securities Company an illegal corporation and ordered its dissolution

March 15, Convention with France signed as to relations in Tunis

——, Wage agreement of bituminous coal miners accepted wage reduction of 5½% for 2 years

——, Executive Order of the President established a service pension for all veterans of the Civil War over 62 years of age, to take effect April 13, minimum $6 a month, maximum at 70, $12

March 22, General Davis appointed Governor of the Panama Canal Zone

March 28, Senator Joseph E. Burton, of Kansas, found guilty of using his influence with the Post Office Dept. to prevent fraud order being issued, and accepting bribes

March 29, Death of General Henry Payne (74) Confederate

April 1, Coal miners in Central Pennsylvania accepted 6% reduction in wages

April 4, Supreme Court decision that coal railroads must answer questions asked by the Interstate Commerce Commission and produce contracts required

April 5, Chicago voted in favor of municipal ownership of street railroads

April 6, Extradition Treaty with Cuba signed, and amended Dec. 6

April 11, Supreme Court decision held that books issued periodically cannot be sent through the mails as second class matter

April 15, National Farmer's Exchange organized for coöperation, headquarters at Pierre, South Dakota

——, Andrew Carnegie established "hero fund" with fund of $5,000,000 for those who risk their lives for others

April 20, Death of Mrs. Sara Jane Lippincott (Grace Greenwood) author (80)

April 22, Contract for transference of Panama Canal property to the United States signed in Paris

April 28, Carnegie Institution of Washington founded in 1902 incorporated

April 30–Dec. 1, Louisiana Purchase Exposition at St. Louis

April 30, Claims Convention with Santo Domingo signed

May 1–6, Socialist Party Convention met in Chicago and nominated Eugene V. Debs, of Indiana, for President, and Benjamin Hanford, of New York, for Vice-President (May 5)

May 2, Convention of United Christian Party at St. Louis adopted platform of resolutions but made no nominations

May 4, Formal transfer of property of French Panama Canal Company to the United States

May 7, Death of Andrew McNally (66) publisher, in Chicago

May 9, The President promulgated rules for government of the Panama Canal Zone, instructions to the Commission

May 10, John F. Wallace appointed Chief Engineer of the Panama Canal

May 13, Proclamation of the President opened 382,000 acres of land in the Rosebud Reservation in South Dakota to settlers to take effect in July, the last large government land grant to settlers

May 14, Miss Clara Barton resigned as president of the American Red Cross and was succeeded by Mrs. John A. Logan

May 18, International Convention for suppression of white slave traffic signed by the United States

May 20, United States warships ordered to Tangier because of kidnaping of American naturalized citizen, Ion Pericardis, by Moroccan bandit chief, El Raisuli, demanding ransom of $70,000

May 23, The German, French, Belgian, and Dutch steamship lines announced cut in steerage rates to $10 to compete with English ships carrying immigrants to the United States

——, Death of Colonel Augustus C. Buell (57) author and engineer

May 25, Extradition Treaty with Panama signed

May 28, Death of Matthew S. Quay, senator from Pennsylvania (71) in Washington

May 31, Supreme Court decision upheld tax on oleomargarine

June 3, Walter J. Travis won the British amateur championship at golf at Sandwich, England

June 8, Strikers at Dunnville, Colorado, in battle with militia, 6 strikers killed and 15 made prisoners by General Bell. Riots at Cripple Creek

June 12, Strike of meat packers begun in Chicago because of reduction in wages

June 15, The steamer "General Slocum" with excursion party from St. Mark's German Lutheran Church, New York City, burned and sank in the East River, and more than 900 persons chiefly women and children lost their lives

June 17, Death of Rear Admiral James A. Grier in Washington

June 21–23, Republican National Convention met at Chicago and nominated Theodore Roosevelt for President by acclamation, no other candidates named. Charles W. Fairbanks, of Indiana, nominated for Vice-President

June 22, Secretary Hay cabled "We want Pericardis alive or Raizuli dead"

June 24, Ion Pericardis released on payment of ransom of $70,000

——, Executive Order extended Dingley Tariff Act to the Panama Canal Zone

June 29–30, Prohibition Party Convention at Indianapolis named Silas C. Swallow, of Pennsylvania, for President, and George W. Carroll, of Texas, for Vice-President

July 1, Victor H. Metcalf, of California, appointed Secretary of Commerce and Labor, Paul Morton, of Illinois, Secretary of the Navy, and William H. Moody, of Massachusetts, Attorney General

——, Charles H. Moyer, and William Haywood, president and secretary of the Western Federation of Miners and 46 others indicted as inciting riot and murder

July 2–8, Socialist Labor Party met in New York and nominated Charles Hunter Corregan, of New York, for President, and William Wesley Cox, of Illinois, for Vice-President

July 4–5, Populist or People's Party met in convention at Springfield, Illinois, and nominated Thomas E. Watson, of Georgia, for President, and Thomas H. Tibbles, of Nebraska, for Vice-President

July 6–9, Democratic National Convention met at St. Louis and nominated Alton B. Parker, of New York, for President, and Henry G. Davis, of West Virginia, for Vice-President. Judge Parker notified the party that he would accept the nomination only if it were understood that the gold standard was "irrevocably fixed"

July 7, National Liberty Party met at St. Louis and adopted platform of principles

——, Death of General Thomas B. Howard (84)

July 11, Death of Bishop Frederick Dan Huntington (85) New York

July 12 20, General strike of employees of meat packing companies because of reduction of wages of unskilled labor settled by reference to arbitration

July 22, Strike of meat packers renewed in Chicago because of discrimination against union men, but gave up fight Sept. 8

——, Death of Wilson Barrett (58) actor

July 25, Strike of 25,000 workers in cotton mills in Fall River, Mass. begun because of reduction of wages

July 26, Death of John Rogers, sculptor of the "Rogers' groups," and of Rear Admiral Henry Clay Taylor (59), and Colonel Paul F. de Gournay, Confederate veteran

July 27, Death of William Davenport Adams (53) author and critic

July 28, Decision of Treasury Dept. that Panama Canal Zone not United States territory, and under sole control of the President until Congress should provide a form of government

July 29, Seizure of land and asphalt lakes of New York and Bermudez Company by Government of Venezuela; protested by the United States July 30 and Aug. 1

Aug. 31, New "Continental Party" met in Chicago. The candidates named for offices declined the nomination and were replaced later by Austin Holcomb, of Georgia, for President, and A. King, of Missouri, for Vice-President

Sept. 9, New York City mounted police first went on duty

Sept. 18, Death of Daniel Willard Fiske

Sept. 25, Death of Frederick W. Rhinelander, president of the Metropolitan Museum of New York City, and of Louis Fleischmann, baker-philanthropist (68)

Sept. 30, Death of George F. Hoar (78) senator from Massachusetts

Oct. 4, Death of Henry C. Payne, Postmaster General

Oct. 10, Robert J. Wynne, of Pennsylvania, appointed Postmaster General

Oct. 21, Circular Letter sent by State Dept. to signatories of Act of Hague Convention of 1899 proposing a second Peace Conference at The Hague. *See also* Hague Conferences

Oct. 27, New York City subway opened from the City Hall to 145th St. on the west side

Nov. 1, Arbitration Treaty with France signed, not ratified by Senate

Nov. 8, Presidential election elected Republican nominees, Theodore Roosevelt, and Charles Warren Fairbanks, receiving 7,623,486 votes to 5,077,971 cast for the Democrats; 402,283 Socialist; 258,356 Prohibition; 117,183 Populist; 31,249 Socialist

——, President Roosevelt made public statement accepting custom which limited the presidency to 2 terms, that under no circumstances would he be a candidate for reëlection

Nov. 12, Atlantic steamship rate war ended

Nov. 15, Civil service extended to the Panama Canal Zone

Nov. 18, Case against 37 members of Western Federation of Miners abandoned and men released

Nov. 22, Arbitration Treaty with Germany signed; not ratified by Senate

——, Death of Rear Admiral John Russell Bartlett at St. Louis

Nov. 23, Arbitration Treaty with Portugal signed

Nov. 27, Secretary Taft as representative of the President arrived at Colon, Panama, to hold conference on matters in dispute with the United States

Nov. 28, Dept. of Commerce began investigation of the petroleum industry

——, Death of Rev. William M. Paxon (80) former president of Princeton Theological Seminary, and of Rev. Jeremiah E. Rankin, former president of Howard University

Nov. 30, Strike of Colorado miners declared off

Dec. 2, Death of Mrs. George H. Gilbert (83) actress

Dec. 4, Executive Order of Secretary Taft settled points in dispute between Panama and the United States as to Canal Zone

Dec. 10, Extradition Treaty with Norway signed

Dec. 16, Decision of Supreme Court of New York, Appellate Division, that labor unions may lawfully strike, boycott and picket within reasonable limits

Dec. 19, Supreme Court decision that railroads are compelled to provide safety appliances

Dec. 25, First car run on first municipally owned line in United States at Seattle, fare 2.5 cents

Dec. 27, Decision of Attorney General's Office that laws of the United States do not apply to the Canal Zone

Dec. 28, Cotton went above 14 cents a pound on New York and New Orleans exchanges

Dec. 30, Negotiations begun which resulted in request of Santo Domingo that the United States take control of its finances

Dec. 31, Senator John H. Mitchell, of Oregon, and Congressman Binger Hermann, former Commissioner of the Land Office, indicted for complicity in public land frauds in Oregon

CONGRESS

Jan. 9, House voted appropriation of $250,000 to be used for emergency caused by destruction of cotton by the boll weevil

Feb. 23, Panama Canal Treaty ratified by Senate by vote of 66 to 14

March 7, Report read in the House named 140 representatives and senators as guilty of impropriety in using influence with officials in the Post Office Dept. to increase salaries of postmasters or secure lease of buildings

——, Resolution adopted in House asks the Secretary of Commerce and Labor to investigate the causes of the low prices of beef cattle, and the large margins between the prices of beef cattle and the selling of fresh beef

March 12, McCall Committee appointed in House to investigate postal charges of March 7; report made April 12 exonerated senators and representatives from charge of using undue influence

March 22, Treaty with Cuba embodying the Platt Amendment of May 22, 1903, ratified by Senate

April 15, Act to regulate shipping in the Philippines provided for transportation in American vessels

April 27, Provided that existing laws as to exclusion of Chinese should remain in force

——, First class battleships authorized, 2 first class armed cruisers, 3 scout cruisers, and 2 colliers

April 28, Merchant Marine Commission created, 5 members from the Senate, and 5 members from the House

——, Act provided for temporary government of the Panama Canal Zone

——, Congress adjourned

June 8, Isle of Pines Treaty with Cuba ratified by Senate

Dec. 5, Fifty-Eighth Congress, 3d sess. convened

Dec. 6, Message of President Roosevelt announced doctrine of "international police power" as a corollary of Monroe Doctrine to be applied in cases of flagrant "chronic wrong doing"

Dec. 14–Feb. 27, 1905, The Senate sat as a Court of Impeachment in case of Charles Swayne, judge of United States District Court, northern district, Florida, charged with incompetence and corruption

1905

Jan. 4, Death of Theodore Thomas, orchestra director (69) in Chicago, and of Henry V. Poor, authority on railroads (92) in Washington

Jan. 13, Note of Secretary Hay to European Powers as to open door and integrity of China at close of war

Jan. 15, Death of Robert Swain Gifford (64) painter

Jan. 18, Settlement of strike of cotton mill operators in Fall River, Massachusetts, after six months, by mediation of the Governor and promise of future increase

Jan. 21, Protocol with Santo Domingo signed by which the United States guaranteed the integrity of the Dominican Republic and agreed to undertake adjustment of obligations domestic and foreign, taking charge of the customs, to go into effect Feb. 1

Jan. 30, Supreme Court decision declared the "Beef Trust," Swift and Company *et al.* illegal affirming decree of lower court, and the packers were enjoined from making agreements among themselves not to bid against each other, fixing of prices, maintenance of blacklist, obtaining rebates from railroads and other methods to strangle competition, but the National Packing Company was not dissolved

Jan. 31, Federal Grand Jury indicted Binger Hermann and John H. Mitchell for conspiracy to defraud the government in public land deals

Feb. 1, Care of the forests transferred to Forest Service Division, later Forestry Bureau of the Dept. of Agriculture, and Gifford Pinchot appointed Chief

——, Attorney General Miller ruled that rebates of 99% of duty on Canadian wheat should be made on flour made from Canadian wheat exported

Feb. 3, The Interstate Commerce Commission declared the Atchison, Topeka, and Santa Fé Railroad guilty of making rebates in violation of the law to the Colorado Fuel and Iron Company

Feb. 7, Convention with Santo Domingo provided that the United States should take over the customs April 1

Feb. 8, Reorganization of Red Cross Society, W. H. Taft elected president

Feb. 13, Second indictment of Senator J. H. Mitchell and Congressman Binger Hermann, and also Congressman John N. Williamson in public land frauds by Federal Grand Jury at Portland, Oregon

Feb. 15, Death of General Lew Wallace, author of "Ben Hur" (78) in Indiana

Feb. 16, Death of Jay Cooke (83) financier of the Civil War

Feb. 17, Parcels Post Treaty with Great Britain signed

Feb. 23, The *San Francisco Chronicle* began publication of articles on the menace of the Japanese invasion, labor willing to work for low wages

Feb. 26, The Panama Canal Engineering Commission recommended a sea-level canal to be constructed in 12 years at cost of $230,500,000

Feb. 27, Death of George S. Boutwell, former Secretary of the Treasury and Senator from Massachusetts (87)

Feb. 28, The State Dept. notified that Colombia would resume diplomatic relations

March 1, Extradition Treaty with Nicaragua signed

——, Confederate battle flags returned

March 2, Resolution of legislature of California asked that action be taken against the immigration of Japanese laborers

March 4, President Roosevelt inaugurated for second term, and Charles Warren Fairbanks, of Indiana, as Vice-President

March 6, George B. Cortelyou, of New York, appointed Postmaster General

——, Death of John H. Reagan, of Texas, last surviving member of the Confederate Cabinet

March 6–11, Strike of employees of subways and elevated railroads in New York City

March 11, Extradition Treaty with Uruguay signed

March 20, Convention with Mexico signed as to elimination of bancos in the Rio Grande River, and Nov. 14

——, The United States and Great Britain refused to pay $160,000 for German claims as to Samoa; referred to arbitration

March 22, Death of Elmer H. Capen (67), president of Tufts College

March 23, Newfoundland took steps to prevent American fishermen from obtaining bait there

March 24, President Castro of Venezuela refused request of the United States for arbitration of the asphalt controversy

March 25, Arrangement made for collection of revenue in Santo Domingo by United States Commissioner

March 25, Report of Alaskan Boundary Commission accepted by United States and Great Britain

——, Death of Maurice Barrymore (55) actor

March 28, Death of Adrian Iselin (87) banker, New York City

March 29, Resignation of the Panama Canal Commission as requested

March 31, *Modus vivendi* with Santo Domingo signed provided that until the Treaty of Feb. 7 be ratified the President of the Dominican Republic should appoint a person nominated by the President of the United States to receive revenue of customs, 55% to be applied to liquidation of the Dominican debt and deposited in New York banks, and 45% be used for Dominican current expenses

April 1, Bituminous coal operators of Pennsylvania renewed wage scale agreement averting strike

——, New Panama Canal Commission appointed, Theodore P. Shonts, chairman, B. M. Harrod, Rear Admiral M. T. Endicott, General P. C. Haines, and Colonel O. H. Ernst

April 5, The Government invited Germany, France, and Great Britain each to nominate engineer to serve on advisory board of Panama Canal Commission

April 7, Strike of the teamsters employed by Montgomery Ward and Co., Chicago, to support strike of the garment worker's union

April 9, Death of Sarah Chauncey Wordsworth (Susan Coolidge) writer (60)

April 12, Extradition Treaty with Great Britain signed

April 14, The six years search for the body of Admiral John Paul Jones buried in Paris July 20, 1792 ended in discovery, and arrangements immediately made for bringing the coffin to the United States

April 17, Supreme Court decision that a state law limiting number of hours of the day and week a man might work was unconstitutional

April 18, Newfoundland legislature passed measure to exclude American fishermen

April 23, Death of Joseph Jefferson (76) actor, at Palm Beach, Florida

April 27, Andrew Carnegie gave $10,000,000 for pension fund for college professors

April 28, Injunctions served on striking teamsters in Chicago

——, Employers ended lockout of Brotherhood of Carpenters and Amalgamated Carpenter's Society which had lasted 9 months

April 29, American Minister Bowen recalled from Venezuela to explain certain charges he had made against Assistant Secretary of State Loomis, his predecessor in office

May 1, Riots of striking teamsters in Chicago, 1 man killed and 150 injured

May 4–13, International Railway Congress met in Washington

May 5, Decision of United States Attorney General that Congress has power to fix railroad rates and can delegate its power

——, President Roosevelt ordered investigation of the tobacco trust

May 6, San Francisco Board of Education adopted resolution to provide for separate schools for Chinese and Japanese children beginning Oct. 15; not carried out

May 7, San Francisco Convention of Labor organized, speeches made against Japanese labor

May 7, Arrival of 12,039 immigrants, chiefly Italians, in New York, broke immigration records

May 10, Investigation of affairs of the Equitable Insurance Company begun by New York State Insurance Company

May 11, Strike of rockmen and excavators against Contractors' Protective Association for new wage scale and recognition of union, New York City, followed by lockout May 23

May 12, Proclamation of the President set apart the Chesnimnus Forest Reserve, Oregon

May 13, Edwin Anderson Alderman inaugurated as president of University of Virginia

May 16, Death of Thomas Brigham Bishop, author of "John Brown's Body" (70)

May 23, Death of Mrs. Mary A. Livermore (83) suffragist, at Melrose, Mass.

May 24, Mayor Dunne, of Chicago, called for 1,000 volunteer police in the strike of teamsters

May 25, First meeting International Joint Commission on use of waters adjacent to boundary between Canada and United States

May 31, Resignation of Paul Morton, Secretary of the Navy

June 1, Lewis and Clarke Exposition at Portland, Oregon, opened

June 3, New York Act abolished the Raines law hotels

June 6, Teamsters in Chicago agreed to appoint a peace committee

June 7, International Convention as to International Institute of Agriculture signed by the United States

——, Death of George W. Elkins (77) street railroad magnate, Philadelphia

June 8, Decision of Attorney General that the eight hour law applied to mechanics and laborers on the Panama Canal but not to railroad or office force

——, President Roosevelt addressed identical Notes to Russia and Japan urging an end to the conflict. Both accepted his overtures

June 19, Boycott of American goods in China because of exclusion of Chinese

June 20, Herbert W. Bowen, Minister to Venezuela, dismissed by President Roosevelt because of unfounded charges against his predecessor F. B. Loomis, and Mr. Loomis reproved for indiscretion

June 23, Order of the President made Chinese merchants, students, officials, and travelers exceptions and exempt from provisions of the Chinese exclusion law

June 26, Resignation of John F. Wallace, Chief Engineer, Panama Canal

June 28, John D. Rockefeller gave $1,000,000 to the endowment fund of Yale University and other gifts aggregating an additional $1,000,000

June 30, John F. Stevens appointed Chief Engineer, Panama Canal

——, Secretary Taft with party including members of both Houses of Congress started for the Philippines

——, John D. Rockefeller gave $10,000,000 to General Education Board for the endowment of small colleges

July 1, Charles J. Bonaparte, of Maryland, appointed Secretary of the Navy

——, Seventeen indictments against the beef trust, Armour and Company *et al.* for violation of anti-trust law presented by Federal Grand Jury at Chicago against individuals and five against corporations

——, Grand Jury indicted C. P. Shea and John Sheridan, president and secretary of the International

Brotherhood of Teamsters charged with conspiracy to injure the business of Montgomery Ward and Co.

July 1, Death of John Hay (66) Secretary of State

July 3, Senator John H. Mitchell convicted in Oregon land fraud cases and sentenced to 6 months imprisonment and fine of $1,000

July 7, Elihu Root, of New York, appointed Secretary of State

——, Industrial Workers of the World organized in Chicago in opposition to the American Federation of Labor

July 8, Edwin S. Holmes of the Dept. of Agriculture dismissed for giving advance information to cotton brokers

July 16, Robert E. Peary started from New York on seventh trip to the Arctic, and from Sydney July 26

July 20, Yellow fever reported in New Orleans

——, Armstrong Committee appointed by the New York legislature to investigate conditions and methods of life insurance companies in the State and to recommend legislation

——, Teamster's strike in Chicago of 105 days ended in defeat

July 23, Death of Colonel Daniel S. Lamont, former Secretary of War (54)

July 24, Investigation of the "cotton scandal," sale of cotton crop reports by officials of the Dept. of Agriculture, begun by Grand Jury at Washington

——, The body of Admiral John Paul Jones placed in tomb in Annapolis, Maryland

July 29, Agreement with Japan by which Japan recognized American sovereignty over the Philippines, and the United States recognized Japanese sovereignty over Korea, and the United States became a party to the Anglo-Japanese Alliance of 1902 and 1905 for maintenance of peace in the Far East "as if the United States were under treaty obligations"

July 31, The Attorney General asked the Supreme Court of New York to order accounting and restitution by officials of the Equitable Life Assurance Society of $10,000,000 withheld from policy holders

Aug. 1–19, Strike of telegraphers of the Great Northern and Northern Pacific railroads

Aug. 5, The Russian and Japanese peace commissioners met with President Roosevelt at Oyster Bay, New York, and Peace Conference opened at Portsmouth, New Hampshire Aug. 9

Aug. 7, The United States Marine Hospital Service as ordered by the President took charge of the yellow fever district in Louisiana

——, General strike ordered against the American Bridge Company

——, Death of Alexander Melville Bell (86) inventor of visible speech for deaf mutes

Aug. 9, Death of Archbishop P. L. Chapelle at New Orleans of yellow fever

Aug. 21, Death of Mrs. Mary Mapes Dodge (67) editor of *St. Nicholas*

Aug. 26, Strike of job printers in Chicago for eight hour day

Sept. 1, Chinese boycott of American goods ended

——, Strike called by amalgamated sheet metal workers in New York City for increase of wages

Sept. 5, Death of Hezekiah Butterworth (66) author, and of General Thomas T. Crittenden (77)

Sept. 6–30, Strike of United States mail wagon drivers in New York City for shorter hours and increase of wages

Sept. 8, Public Printer Frank W. Palmer dismissed by President Roosevelt when he refused to resign because of troubles in office

Sept. 12, Senator Burton, of Kansas, again indicted for acceptance of money for practice before the executive departments, and Nov. 10 for complicity in postal frauds, and convicted Nov. 27

Sept. 18, Death of General Isaac J. Wistar (78) in Philadelphia

Sept. 22, Death of Francis H. Peabody (74) banker, in Boston

Sept. 27, Agreement with China as to Whanh Pu (Hwangpu) signed

Sept. 28, Death of Frank Beard (63) illustrator and cartoonist

——, Congressman Williamson, Dr. Van Gessner, and Marion R. Biggs convicted in Oregon land fraud cases

Oct. 5, The Wright brothers flew 24.2 miles in 38 minutes over Dayton, Ohio

Oct. 12, Formal complaint made because Americans forbidden to fish on the "treaty coast," Newfoundland

Oct. 14, International Sanitary Convention (Central and South America) signed by the United States

Nov. 1, British squadron commanded by Rear Admiral Prince Louis of Battenburg arrived at Annapolis, and Prince Louis received by the President Nov. 3

Nov. 6, Housesmiths on 50 buildings in New York City went on strike

——, Supplementary Extradition Treaty with Denmark signed

Nov. 14, Death of Robert Whitehead, inventor

Nov. 17, At Ziegler, Illinois, strikers fired on train bringing in Italian strike breakers

——, Board of Consulting Engineers in Washington reported by majority of 3 out of 13 for sea-level canal

Nov. 28, Directors of the Chicago, Milwaukee, and St. Paul Railroad authorized extension of road from the Missouri River to the Pacific

Nov. 30, Strike of Colorado miners called off, agreement by which miners received minimum wage of original demand and eight hour day

Dec. 3, Death of John Bartlett (85) author of "Familiar Quotations"

Dec. 9, Death of Edward Atkinson (78) economist, in Boston

Dec. 14, Death of Henry Harlan (45) novelist

Dec. 20, Secretary Bonaparte ordered trial by court martial of midshipmen at the Naval Academy at Annapolis for hazing

Dec. 25, Building trades in New York City except housesmiths and bridgemen signed agreement

Dec. 30, Frank Steunenberg, former Governor of Idaho, murdered by bomb placed at his gate by Harry Orchard, who claimed to be employed by officials of the Western Federation of Miners

——, End of public hearings of New York Armstrong Legislative Committee investigating insurance companies conducted by Charles E. Hughes which led to discovery of abuses and under which "great reputations became great notorieties"

CONGRESS

Jan. 5, National Red Cross Society reincorporated, the new organization to be operated under government supervision

Feb. 1, Act granted rights of way within or across na-

tional forests for dams, tunnels, canals, or for the purposes of milling and reduction of ores

Feb. 6, Philippine Acts amended for administration of civil government, to provide revenue, and construct railroads

Feb. 8, Electoral vote counted gave Roosevelt and Fairbanks, Republicans, 336, and Parker and Davis, Democrats, 140

Feb. 9, The House passed Hepburn Bill giving the Interstate Commerce Commission power to fix railroad rates definitively; no action by Senate

Feb. 12, The Senate amended the Roosevelt Arbitration Agreements with Great Britain, France, Germany, Switzerland, Italy, Spain, Portugal, Austria-Hungary, Sweden and Norway, and Mexico to require a special treaty for each case of arbitration, refusing to ratify them in the form submitted, substituting the word "treaties" for "agreements" in text, taking power from the executive and making any arrangement with foreign powers again referable for final action to the Senate

Feb. 20, Trade Mark Act repealed that of 1881

Feb. 21, Metal and Hall Mark Act (gold and silver articles) passed

Feb. 23, Medals of Honor Act passed

Feb. 27, Senate Court of Impeachment acquitted Judge Charles Swayne

Feb. 28, Joint Resolution authorized the Secretary of War to deliver Union and Confederate flags to respective States

March 3, Copyright Act amended, Enlarged Animal Quarantine Act passed, and Philippine Tariff Act revised and amended. Two first class battleships authorized

——, Congress adjourned

Dec. 4, Fifty-Ninth Congress, 1st sess. convened

1906

Jan. 1, New England woolen manufacturers raised wages of 30,000 employees

Jan. 2, Strike of chorus of the Metropolitan Opera, New York City, and strike of typographical union for eight hour day and closing of shops to non-union labor

Jan. 10, Extradition Treaty with San Marino signed

——, Death of William Rainey Harper, president of the University of Chicago; succeeded by Harry Pratt Judson

Jan. 16, The United States represented at the Algeciras Conference, Morocco, by Henry White, Minister to Italy

——, Death of Marshall Field (70) Chicago merchant

Jan. 17, Midshipmen at Annapolis dismissed for hazing

Jan. 23, Case of the Government against the beef packers opened in Chicago

Jan. 25, Death of General Joseph Wheeler (69) Confederate cavalry leader

Feb. 1, General Chaffee retired as Chief of Staff and was succeeded by Major General John C. Bates

Feb. 9, Death of Paul Lawrence Dunbar (34) negro poet

Feb. 17, Charles H. Moyer, W. D. Haywood, and George A. Pettibone arrested in Colorado on extradition proceedings implicated by confession of Harry Orchard in murder of Frank Steunenberg, and taken to Idaho for trial

Feb. 18, Death of John B. Stetson (76) hat manufacturer, in Philadelphia, and of John A. McCall, insurance president

Feb. 19, Supreme Court decision on subject of common carriers dealing with commodities

——, Western Federation of Miners officially charged with responsibility for the death of former Governor Steunenberg, of Idaho

——, Decision of President Roosevelt for lock canal for the Panama Canal

Feb. 22, Report of the Armstrong Insurance Investigating Committee presented to the New York legislature

Feb. 27, Commercial Agreement with Germany signed

——, Decision of United States Circuit Court that Interstate Commerce Commission had power to compel witnesses to answer questions

——, Death of Samuel P. Langley (72) scientist and inventor

March 4, Death of Lieutenant General John M. Schofield (74)

March 10, Carnegie Foundation for the Advancement of Teaching incorporated

March 12, Supreme Court decision against the tobacco trust in case of Hale vs. Henkel, that in proceedings under the anti-trust law witnesses may be compelled to testify and must produce books and papers asked for

March 13, Death of Susan B. Anthony (86) suffragist

March 21, In case of the U.S. vs. Armour and Company et al. Judge Humphrey sustained the claim of the defendants as individuals for immunity under clause of Fifth Amendment to the Constitution, but denied immunity to the packing corporations

March 24, Order of the Postmaster General excluded from the mails advertising matter of 52 fraudulent medical concerns in New York City

March 31, End of three year agreement between operators and miners in anthracite coal, and of two year agreement in bituminous coal, and failure of operators and miners to reach agreement

April 1, Suspension of work in coal mines

——, John A. Dowie deposed from leadership of Zion City

April 5, Death of Eastman Johnson (82) portrait painter

April 7, The United States signed the General Act of the International Conference at Algeciras

April 11, Death of James A. Bailey (59) circus owner

April 12, Benjamin J. Greene and John F. Gaynor convicted of embezzlement and conspiracy to defraud the government, and sentenced April 13 to four years imprisonment and heavy fines. Extradited from Canada under decision of the English Privy Council of Feb. 8, which reversed decision of Justice Caron of Quebec of Aug. 13, 1902

April 14, President Roosevelt in laying the cornerstone of the House of Representatives Office made his famous "muckrake" speech

April 16, Strike of 4,000 linemen and other electrical employees of the Southern Bell Telephone Company

April 17–28, Trial for heresy of the Rev. Algernon Sidney Crapsey, at Batavia, New York

April 18–20, Earthquake followed by fire destroyed great part of the City of San Francisco, California. Hundreds of persons killed and thousands injured, and property loss estimated at $300,000,000

April 21, Convention as to the boundary of Alaska with Great Britain signed

April 25, Death of John Knowles Paine (67) composer and musician

April 27, Ground broken for City of Gary east of Chicago by the United States Steel Corporation

May 4, Federal Grand Jury indicted New York Central and Hudson River Railroad for giving rebates and the American Sugar Refining Company for receiving them

May 7, Union executives signed agreement with operators to continue the award of the Anthracite Coal Commission for 3 years to March 31, 1909

May 9, Rev. Algernon S. Crapsey found guilty of heresy and suspended from office May 15

May 11, Suit against the paper trust in United States Circuit Court in St. Paul decided in favor of the Government

May 14, Death of General Carl Schurz (77) in New York City

——, All Bills proposed by Armstrong Committee for regulation of insurance companies passed by the legislature of New York

May 17, Extradition Treaty with Japan signed

May 18, Forest fires devastated 200 square miles in northern Michigan destroying 8 towns and villages, and May 20 another 200 square miles devastated

May 21, Agreement with Mexico signed as to equitable distribution of the waters of the Rio Grande River

June 1, Convention of coal miners and operators of Illinois adopted wage agreement to hold until March 31, 1908

June 4, Armed conflict between striking miners and guards at Steubenville, Ohio

June 10, The Christian Science Cathedral in Boston dedicated

June 12, Armour, Swift, Cudahy, and Nelson Morris packing companies found guilty of violation of the Elkins Act and fined $15,000 each for accepting rebates

June 13, Chicago, Burlington, and Quincy Railroad found guilty of receiving rebates from Chicago packers

June 22, Announcement of Attorney General Moody that suits would be brought against the Standard Oil Company for accepting rebates, and against the railroads for violation of safety appliances law

June 25, Death of Stanford White (53) architect

June 27, Executive Order of the President provided a system of examination and promotion in the consular service

July 6, International Red Cross Convention for the amelioration of the condition of wounded of armies in the field signed by the United States

July 10, In strike of housesmiths and bridgemen in New York City a murderous attack made on special police guarding non-union men

July 13, Agreement signed which ended coal strike in bituminous fields, increase in wages given and right of check off

July 16, Japanese killing seals illegally near St. Paul's Island fired on by guard, 5 killed and 12 captured

July 19, Death of Michael H. Cardoza (55) lawyer, and Walter S. Logan (59), lawyer, in New York City

July 20, Pure Food Commission named

July 22, Death of Russell Sage (90) financier, New York City

July 23, Death of Major John Eagan (69)

July 28, Death of George T. Bispham (68) lawyer and author, in Philadelphia

July 31, Announcement of payment by the United

States of $20,000 to Germany in settlement of Samoan claims

Aug. 1, Commercial Reciprocity Tariff Treaty with Germany signed

Aug. 2, Anthony Comstock raided the Art Student's League, New York City

Aug. 3, Death of Rear Admiral Charles J. Train commanding Asiatic Squadron in China (51)

Aug. 8, Standard Oil Company indicted at Chicago for receiving rebates

Aug. 9–11, Strike of railroad switchmen in New York

Aug. 13, Death of Mrs. Pearl Mary Teresa Richards Craigie (Mrs. John Oliver Hobbes) novelist, in London, England

——, Brownsville, Texas, affair. Soldiers of a colored regiment fired at midnight into houses of the town killing one man and wounding another, and seriously injuring the Chief of Police, for revenge because of alleged insults. President Roosevelt ordered discharge of the entire battalion Nov. 6

——, International Conventions as to status of naturalized citizens and as to pecuniary claims signed by the United States

Aug. 16, Death of Rebecca S. Clark (Sophie May) writer (74)

Aug. 22, Death of Albert G. Lane (65) educator, Chicago

Aug. 26, Strike of street car employees in San Francisco for increase in wages

Aug. 27, Federal Grand Jury at Chicago returned 10 indictments against the Standard Oil Company

——, President Roosevelt ordered the Public Printer to use simplified spelling, order subsequently withdrawn

Aug. 28, Failure of the Real Estate Trust Company, Philadelphia, liabilities $10,000,000

Aug. 29, Two days before Railroad Rates Act went into effect over 5,000 notices of voluntary reduction of rates were filed with the Interstate Commerce Commission

Sept. 12, President Roosevelt ordered war ships to Cuba, and marines landed the following day in view of revolution

Sept. 16, National Conservation Association formed in Chicago, Dr. Charles W. Eliot, president

Sept. 19, Proclamation extended eight hour day to all government work

——, Proclamation opened 500,000 acres in Oklahoma to settlers

Sept. 20, Captain John J. Pershing made a brigadier general in recognition of service in the Philippines

Sept. 21, Death of General James C. Hill (76) Confederate officer

Sept. 22–23, Anti-negro riots in Atlanta, Georgia, 12 negroes killed and many injured, the city put under martial law

Sept. 25, Strikers at Standard Oil Company works at Whiting, Indiana, in riots

Sept. 28, Death of George E. Poor (61) inventor of air brake

Sept. 29, Secretary Taft proclaimed the intervention of the United States in Cuba. *See also* Cuba

Sept. 30, Electric locomotives installed on the New York Central Railroad

Oct. 6 and 8, *Modus vivendi* as to Newfoundland fisheries extended

Oct. 11, Resolution of the Board of Education of San Francisco that on and after Oct. 15, Chinese, Japanese,

and Korean children should attend the Oriental Public School separating oriental from white children

Oct. 12, Death of Richard B. Borden (72) New England cotton manufacturer

Oct. 19, Standard Oil Company of Ohio at Findlay convicted of violations of Ohio Anti-Trust law

——, Death of Henry Altemus, publisher, Philadelphia

Oct. 22, Riot of 3,000 negroes in Philadelphia in connection with presentation of Thomas Dixon's "The Clansman" at theater

Nov. 3, International Convention as to importation of spirituous liquors into Africa and Convention as to wireless telegraphy signed by the United States

Nov. 6, Project for union of New Mexico and Arizona defeated by rejection in Arizona

——, Delegates elected for Constitutional Convention to frame Constitution for Oklahoma

Nov. 9–26, President Roosevelt left for Panama, the first instance of a President in office leaving the United States; inspected the Canal Nov. 16, at Puerto Rico Nov. 21

Nov. 12, Death of Major General William Rufus Shafter (71)

Nov. 15, Suit brought by the United States in St. Louis against the Standard Oil Company of New Jersey and 70 other corporations and partnerships and 7 persons including John D. Rockefeller, H. H. Rogers, and others under the Sherman Anti-Trust Act

——, New York Central Railroad found guilty of giving rebates to the American Sugar Refining Company, and fined $18,000 Nov. 22

——, Mayor Eugene Schmitz, of San Francisco, and Abe Ruef, political boss, indicted on 5 bills charging extortion

Nov. 21, Negro regiments implicated in the Brownsville riot in Texas dismissed from the service, the War Dept. upholding executive order of the President, and by Senate Committee March 11, 1907

Nov. 23, Joseph Smith, president of Mormon Church of Utah convicted of polygamy

Dec. 5, Formal ceremony of deposal of Dr. Algernon S. Crapsey from ministry of the Protestant Episcopal Church

Dec. 10, President Roosevelt officially notified that the Nobel Peace Prize had been awarded to him for his services in bringing peace to Russia and Japan

Dec. 12, Charles J. Bonaparte, of Maryland, appointed Attorney General, Victor H. Metcalf, of California, Secretary of the Navy, and Oscar L. Straus, of New York, Secretary of Commerce and Labor

Dec. 28, Death of Alexander J. Cassatt (67) president of the Pennsylvania Railroad

CONGRESS

Feb. 8, The House again passed Hepburn Bill giving the Interstate Commerce Commission power to fix railroad rates definitively by vote of 346 to 7

April 5, Act reformed the consular service and provided for classification, and grading and fixing salaries

June 4, Report of the President's Commission to investigate the meat packing establishments in Chicago sent to Congress, resulting in sensation in the United States and other countries equal to that of Sinclair's book, "The Jungle" published during the year

June 11, Employer's Liability Act extended to common carriers, the first attempt to make corporations engaged in interstate commerce responsible for injuries received by their employees

June 13, Metal and Hall Mark Act amended

June 15, Bankruptcy Act amended

June 16, Enabling Act for Indian Territory and Oklahoma to unite to form the State of Oklahoma, the people authorized to adopt a constitution, and provision made for vote for union in each Territory. The same offer was made to Arizona and New Mexico to form the State of Arizona

June 19, Enlarged National Quarantine Act passed

June 29, The Hepburn Act amended the Interstate Commerce Act giving the Commission the power to fix railroad rates and to establish uniform systems of accounting. Express companies, sleeping car companies, and oil pipe lines brought under jurisdiction of the Commission. The issuance of private passes prohibited. The Commission authorized to call a hearing and fix maximum rate in case of dispute. Membership of Commission raised from 5 to 7. Carriers forbidden to engage in transport of commodities they themselves produced with certain exceptions

——, Plan for a lock canal at Panama authorized

——, Bureau of Immigration and Naturalization established and uniform and stricter rules for naturalization prescribed. Aliens to be registered at port of entry. No alien unable to read and write allowed to become a citizen

——, Cruelty to Animals Act passed

June 30, Act established United States Court in China to have jurisdiction in cases formerly decided by United States consuls

——, Pure Food and Drugs Act prohibited misbranding and adulteration of foods

——, Meat Inspection Act made slaughtering or preparing meats to be shipped over state lines subject to inspection of the Dept. of Agriculture

——, Immunity of Witnesses' Act provided that officers of corporations must testify to misdeeds of company without recourse to plea of immunity

——, Congress adjourned

1907

Jan. 12, Three-cent carfare went into effect in Cleveland, Ohio, Mayor Johnson acting as motorman of the first car

Jan. 14, The Standard Oil Company of New Jersey indicted at Findlay, Ohio, on 939 counts for illegal acceptance of rebates

Jan. 15, James R. Garfield, of Ohio, appointed Secretary of the Interior, George B. Cortelyou, of New York, Secretary of the Treasury, George von L. Meyer, of Massachusetts, Postmaster General

Jan. 20, Death of Josiah Flynt Willard (Josiah Flint), sociological writer (38)

Jan. 22, Two hundred Japanese laborers from Honolulu refused permission to land in San Francisco under instructions from Washington

Jan. 23, Resignation of Theodore P. Shonts as head of Panama Canal Commission and Chief Engineer

Feb. 8, Treaty with Santo Domingo (Dominican Republic) signed by which the debt of the Republic converted and collection of customs assumed by the United States, receipts to be used for purchase and redemption of bonds issued and creation of sinking fund for liquidation of indebtedness

Feb. 19, Death of John Carter Brown (67) banker, Providence, Rhode Island

Feb. 21, C. P. Shea and 10 others of teamster's union at

Chicago acquitted of charge of conspiracy after trial of 138 days

Feb. 23, Death of Archibald Clavering Gunter (59) playwright and publisher

Feb. 25, Supreme Court decision that under rate law all complaints must be made through the Interstate Commerce Commission

Feb. 26, Announcement that bids for construction of Panama Canal would not be accepted as the Government had decided to continue the work of construction. The lowest bid had been 6.75% of money to be expended

Feb. 27, Death of Wendell Phillips Garrison (67) editor of the *Nation*

Feb. 28, Death of Orson D. Munn (83) publisher

Feb., Strike on railroads west and southwest of Chicago

March, The American Federation of Labor proclaimed a boycott against the Bucks Stove and Range Company

March 4, John F. Stevens succeeded T. P. Shonts as Chief Engineer and head of Panama Canal Commission

March 8, Supreme Court decision that Isle of Pines under the jurisdiction of Cuba

March 9, Death of John Alexander Dowie, founder of Zion City and the Christian Catholic Apostolic Church at Zion

March 11, Strike of 2,000 ship-builders begun in Cleveland, Chicago, and other ports on the Great Lakes and the American Shipbuilding Company

March 12, The Russell Sage Foundation founded by Mrs. Russell Sage with endowment fund of $10,000,-000 " for the improvement of social and living conditions in the United States"

March 13, San Francisco Board of Education rescinded resolution segregating Japanese in schools

March 14, Inland Waterways Commission appointed, Theodore E. Burton, chairman, to study problems of waterways and forest preservation

——, Executive Order of the President excluded from the mainland of the United States all Japanese laborers from Mexico, Canada, or Hawaii

——, Sharp decline of stocks on the stock exchange, New York City

March 15, Constitutional Convention of Oklahoma adopted Constitution

March 18, Death of Brigadier General John Moore (81) former Surgeon General

March 19, Death of Thomas Bailey Aldrich (70) author and journalist, Boston

March 21, American marines landed in Honduras for protection of life and property during revolution

——, Delaware adopted local option

March 25, Colorado adopted local option

April 1, Resignation of John F. Stevens. Major George W. Goethals succeeded him as Chief Engineer of the Panama Canal

April 3, Strike of brewery employees in St. Louis begun in March ended with signing of 3 year contract providing for 15% increase in wages and arbitration of disputes

April 6, First case under new law decided by Secretary of Commerce and Labor against 5 Japanese who had been refused admission to the country without passports

April 8, Supreme Court decision that in the matter of customs the Isle of Pines must be treated as part of the Republic of Cuba

April 13, The Standard Oil Company of Indiana found guilty on 1,463 counts by United States District Court of receiving rebates from the Chicago and Alton Railroad

April 14, First National Peace Congress initiated by Andrew Carnegie met in New York City

April 22 and May 2, Commercial Agreement with Germany signed by which American goods imported continued to enjoy privileges of minimum tariff rates

April 24, Death of Dennis Kearney (60) San Francisco labor leader

April 26, Tercentenary Exposition at Jamestown, Virginia, opened by President Roosevelt

May 2–June 14, Strike of longshoremen in New York for increase in wages

May 3, Textile operators and manufacturers in Fall River agreed on wage scale with 10% increase

May 6, Labor crisis in San Francisco on account of strike, no street cars running

——, Death of Rev. John Watson (Ian Maclaren) author, at Mount Pleasant, Iowa

May 9, Trial begun of W. D. Haywood of the Western Federation of Miners charged with complicity in murder of former Governor Steunenberg, of Idaho, Dec., 1905

May 12, Death of Charles H. Haswell (98) engineer

May 16, Treaty of commerce with the Netherlands signed

——, The Chicago, Milwaukee, and St. Paul Railroad pleaded guilty to giving rebates and paid fine of $20,000

May 18, Death of Edwin Hurd Conger (64) former Minister to China

May 20, The Chicago, Rock Island, and Pacific Railroad pleaded guilty to granting rebates and was fined $20,000

——, Strike of trackmen of the New York, New Haven, and Hartford

May 25, Death of Edward Payson Terhune (76) of New York

May 26, Death of Professor Albert Harkness (84) classical scholar

June 1, General strike at Birmingham, Alabama

——, Waters Pierce Company, affiliate of the Standard Oil Company, fined $1,623,900 by Texas court at Austin for illegal practices

June 4, Fines aggregating $284,000 imposed on 31 promoters of the Honduras Lottery in United States Court at Mobile, Alabama

June 6, Act of New York State established 2 public service commissions for the State, the one with authority in the first district which included New York, Kings, Queens, and Richmond counties, and the other in the second district which included all other counties

June 9, Death of Julia Magruder (53) novelist

June 11, Death of Senator John T. Morgan, from Alabama

June 13, Mayor Eugene Schmitz, of San Francisco, found guilty of extorting money from keepers of illegal resorts and giving them protection, removed from office, and sentenced July 8 to 5 years imprisonment

June 28, Strike of ice-wagon drivers in New York City

June 30, Immigration for the year 1,285,349 surpassing previous records

July 10, Suit brought against 65 corporations and 27 persons of the American Tobacco Company in the Circuit Court for the Southern District of New York as a combination in restraint of trade

July 10, Atchison, Topeka, and Santa Fé Railroad indicted in Chicago on 65 counts on charge of giving rebates

July 17, Death of Angelo Heilprin (54) scientist and explorer

July 23, Death of Will S. Hay (70) poet, in Kentucky, and of William Hamilton Russell (51) architect

July 28, W. D. Haywood acquitted at trial for murder of Governor Steunenberg in 1905 for lack of corroborative evidence

Aug. 3, The Standard Oil Company of Indiana fined $29,240,000 by Judge K. M. Landis in United States District Court for accepting freight rebates in violation of the law. Decision reversed July 22, 1908

——, Death of Augustus Saint Gaudens (60) sculptor, at Cornish, New Hampshire

Aug. 6, Prohibition Act for Georgia approved to go into effect Jan. 1, 1908

——, Strike of trainmen of the Colorado and Southern Railroad

Aug. 8, Strike of men in the building trades in Washington, D.C.

Aug. 10, Strike of telegraphers begun in Chicago which spread to about 15 other cities and lasted until Nov. 6

Aug. 17, Secretary Taft concluded agreement with representatives of Colombia and Panama, settlement of issues arising from creation of Canal Zone

Aug. 19, John A. Bensar and Edward Perrin convicted in federal court at San Francisco of conspiracy to obtain 12,000 acres of public lands in California by fraud

Aug. 23, Strike of packing-house teamsters in New York City

Aug. 27, Death of Nelson Morris (68) packer, Chicago

Aug. 30, Death of Richard Mansfield (50) actor

Sept. 4, *Modus vivendi* continued as to Newfoundland fisheries

Sept. 5, International Harvester Company in suits brought in Texas under anti-trust laws pleaded guilty and paid fine of $35,000

——, Race riot in Bellingham, Washington, Hindus employed in the mills attacked, 750 fled to Canada

Sept. 11, Strike of dockmen at Galveston, Texas

Sept. 12, Arrival of the "Lusitania" in New York from Queenstown on first voyage, the largest ship in the world, breaking all previous speed records by trip in 5 days and 54 minutes

Sept. 13, Airship "America," Wellman expedition, made trial trip in Arctic and descended on glacier

Sept. 17, Constitution including prohibition adopted by the people of Oklahoma

——, Suit to dissolve the Standard Oil Company begun in New York

Sept. 22, Death of Wilbur O. Atwater, physiological chemist, at Middletown, Conn.

Sept. 30, Strike of longshoremen and teamsters at New Orleans

Oct. 2, Strike of bookbinders throughout the country

Oct. 7, Death of Mrs. Mary Jane Hawes Holmes, novelist, at Brockport, New York

Oct. 11, The Atchison, Topeka, and Santa Fe Railroad found guilty of rebating by federal court at Los Angeles, and fined $330,000 Nov. 7

Oct. 18, Wireless telegraph established by Guglielmo

Marconi from Glace Bay, Nova Scotia, to Clifden, Ireland

Oct. 18, Conventions of the Second Hague Conference signed regulating land, sea and aërial warfare, rights of neutrals, &c., with limited sanction of the Drago doctrine prohibiting the use of force by a State for collection of financial claims of its citizens or subjects against another State. *See also* Hague Conferences

Oct. 22, Suspension of the Knickerbocker Trust Company in New York inaugurated panic, and advertised failure of the Currency Act of 1900 to stabilize the currency

Nov.-Jan., 1910, Scientific expedition of John D. Haseman in Brazil, Uruguay, Argentina, Paraguay, and Bolivia

Nov. 15, Death of Moncure D. Conway (75) author, in Paris

Nov. 16, Oklahoma admitted to the Union, 46th State, proclaimed by the President, Charles N. Haskell made 1st Governor

Nov. 19, Treaty of commerce with Great Britain signed provided that all samples of goods taken to Great Britain by American commercial travelers should be passed through the custom house without delay and without examination merely on the authority of their seals, marks, or officially attested lists

Nov. 20, United States Treasury agent discovered fraudulent weighing machines on Jersey City docks of the American Sugar Refining Company by which the Government was defrauded of duty

Nov. 22, Death of Professor Asaph Hall (78) astronomer

Nov. 26, World air record made by Glenn H. Curtiss at Hammondsport, New York, in the "All America" balloon, remaining in the air 4 hours with 7 persons

Nov. 27, Edward Payson Weston, pedestrian, completed walk from Portland, Maine, to Chicago, 1,375 miles in 24 days, 19 hours, and 15 minutes

Dec. 1, Executive order extended merit system to nearly one-third of the fourth class postmasters

Dec. 3, 1,500 men locked out by building contractors in open shop contest in Duluth, Minnesota

Dec. 5, National Council of Commerce organized in Washington by Secretary Strauss of the Dept. of Commerce and Labor

——, Governor Sparks of Nevada asked for and received federal troops to stop riots of striking miners in Goldfield

——, The Cunard liner "Mauretania" made new east bound transatlantic record from Sandy Hook to Daunt's Rock, Queenstown, of 4 days, 22 hours, and 29 minutes

Dec. 9, International Convention as to Office of Public Health signed

Dec. 11, President Roosevelt appointed a commission to go to Nevada to investigate the strike, Assistant Secretary of Commerce and Labor Murray, Commissioner of Labor Neill, and Commissioner of Corporations Smith

Dec. 16, World round cruise of American fleet sailed from Hampton Roads under command of Rear Admiral Robley D. Evans, 16 battleships with officers and crew numbering about 12,000 men. At San Francisco Rear Admiral Charles S. Sperry took command

Dec. 20, Conventions concluded at Central American Peace Conference signed by the United States. *See* Central America

CONGRESS

Jan. 25, Act authorized the enlargement and reorganized the artillery

Jan. 26, Act prohibited corporations from making money contributions in connection with political elections

Feb. 6, Graduated age pensions authorized for Mexican and Civil war veterans of 62 and over following executive order

Feb. 20, The Senate voted 42 to 28 confirming Reed Smoot, of Utah, in his seat, defeating proposal to unseat him because of his membership in Mormon Church

——, Act to regulate immigration excluded undesirable classes of aliens, the insane, feeble minded, &c., contract labor, raised tax on aliens to $4 each, and created a Joint Commission. The President authorized to refuse entrance to immigrants who, to obtain entrance to the mainland, were using passports originally issued to "any country other than the United States"

——, White Slave Act passed

Feb. 25, The Senate ratified the Treaty with Santo Domingo

March 1, Act to amend Act providing for the public printing, &c., stopped use of simplified spelling

March 2, Foundation for the Promotion of Industrial Peace established, endowed by President Roosevelt with money he received with award of the Nobel peace prize

——, Trade Mark Act amended

March 4, Railroads engaged in interstate commerce prohibited from requiring employees to be continuously on duty over 16 hours

——, Act provided for establishment of an agricultural bank in the Philippines

——, National Banking Act amended authorized deposits of customs receipts in national banks, supply of small bills increased

——, Meat inspection Act passed

——, Congress adjourned

Dec. 2, Sixtieth Congress, 1st sess. convened

1908

Jan. 1, State wide prohibition went into effect in Georgia

Jan. 4, George A. Pettibone indicted with W. D. Haywood for complicity in murder of former Governor Steunenberg, of Idaho, acquitted (Western Federation of Miners case)

Jan. 6, Supreme Court decision that Employer's Liability Act of June, 1906, transgressed constitutional limits imposed on interstate commerce

Jan. 9, East River Tunnel from the Battery, New York City, to Brooklyn opened

——, District Court of Appeals set aside judgment against Mayor Schmitz of San Francisco on a technicality

Jan. 10, Decision of United States District Court at Denver dismissed cases of prominent business men indicted in Colorado land frauds; reversed by Supreme Court Dec. 14

Jan. 12, Report of the President's Commission to investigate strike in Nevada declared that there had been no warrant for calling for federal troops to do police duty

——, American battleship fleet arrived at Rio de Janeiro, Brazil

Jan. 13, Theater fire in Boyerstown, Pennsylvania, in which 200 persons perished

Jan. 14, Petition of legislature of Nevada asked the President to allow federal troops to remain until police force could be organized, which was done in spite of criticism

Jan. 18, Death of Edmund Clarence Stedman, poet and critic (74) in New York City

Jan. 21, The Sullivan Ordinance, New York City, made smoking by women in public places illegal

Jan. 22, Death of Morris K. Jessup, New York City. His will left $1,000,000 to the American Museum of Natural History of which he was president

Jan. 24, Death of Edward Alexander MacDowell (46) musical composer, in New York City

Jan. 28, Treaty of commerce with France signed

Jan. 31, State wide prohibition enacted in North Carolina

Feb. 3, Supreme Court decision in Danbury hatters case (D. E. Loewe and Co.) that the anti-trust law covered labor combinations and prohibited boycott by union

Feb. 4, Strike of 3,000 miners near Pittsburgh, Pennsylvania, because of enforcement of rule requiring use of smokeless powder

——, Kentucky masked night riders at Dycusburg, Kentucky, burned tobacco warehouse destroying $40,000 worth of property, terrorized Eddyville Feb. 16, and burned 15,000 pounds of tobacco at Brookside March 10, in tobacco war

Feb. 10, Arbitration Treaty with France signed

Feb. 12, New York to Paris automobile race started with 6 cars, by way of Alaska, Siberia, and Russia

Feb. 18, The "Gentlemen's Agreement," Japanese Note to American Ambassador outlined plan by which emigration might be restricted

Feb. 19, State wide prohibition enacted in Mississippi

Feb. 21, Death of Harriet Hosmer (78) sculptor

Feb. 22, Conference of Mr. Hearst's Independence League in Chicago, and decision that nominations for President and Vice-President should be made after conventions of the Republican and Democratic parties

Feb. 24, Death of Edward Gaylord Bourne, historian, at Strykersville, New York

Feb. 25, The first of the tunnels under the Hudson River between New York and New Jersey opened

Feb. 29, Arbitration Treaty with Switzerland signed

March 4, Death of Redfield Proctor (76) senator from Vermont since 1891

March 10, The St. Louis and San Francisco Railroad found guilty of rebating and fined $13,000

March 12, Successful trial trip of the Curtiss airplane "Red Wing" over Lake Keuka, New York

——, The American battleship fleet arrived at Magdalena Bay, Mexico

——, A 10% reduction in wages in cotton mills of Lowell, Massachusetts, affected 20,000 workers to begin March 30, and in mills in Manchester and Nashua, New Hampshire, March 13

March 13, Decision that Andover Theological Seminary be removed from Andover to Cambridge and affiliated with Harvard University

March 14, Naturalization Treaty with Salvador signed

March 16, Machinists and other workers in the shops of the Denver and Rio Grande Railroad at Denver on strike

——, Supreme Court sustained conviction of Armour,

Swift, Morris, and Cudahy packing houses for rebating

March 18, Henry Orchard sentenced to death for murder of former Governor Steunenberg of Idaho; sentence commuted to life imprisonment July 1

March 23, Supreme Court decision that the railroad rate laws in Minnesota and North Carolina unconstitutional

——, Permanent injunction of Supreme Court of District of Columbia in the Bucks Stove and Range Company case

March 24, Arbitration Treaty with Mexico signed

March 25, Death of Rev. Cuthbert Hall (55) president of Union Theological Seminary

March 28, Arbitration Treaty with Italy signed

April 1, Bituminous coal miners began strike

——, Trial of land fraud cases begun in Washington

——, Agreement of 7 southern railroads to continue existing wage scale averted strike

April 2–3, Populist Party Convention in St. Louis nominated Thomas E. Watson, of Georgia, for President and Samuel W. Williams, of Indiana, for Vice-President

April 4, Treaties of arbitration with Great Britain and with Norway signed

April 6, Arbitration Treaty with Portugal signed

April 7 and 16, Memorandum to Belgium on administrative reforms in Congo Free State

April 11, Convention with Great Britain signed as to protection, preservation, and propagation of food fishes in waters contiguous to the United States and Canada, and Convention providing for delimitation of boundary line through all border waters from Passamaquoddy Bay to Puget Sound

April 12, Troops ordered to Pensacola, Florida, to suppress rioting of striking street car employees

——, Chelsea, Mass., destroyed by fire, 10,000 people homeless and property loss $10,000,000

April 14–17, Joint conference of operators and miners of Ohio, Indiana, and Pennsylvania

April 20, Agreement reached between bituminous coal miners and operators and work resumed

——, Arbitration Treaty with Spain signed

April 21, Dr. Frederick Cook claimed to have reached the North Pole on this date; claim not proved

April 27, Naturalization Treaty with Brazil signed

May 1, United Christian Party met at Rock Island, Illinois, and nominated Daniel B. Turney, of Illinois, for President, and L. S. Coffin, of Iowa, for Vice-President

——, The "commodities clause" of the Hepburn Act became operative

May 2, Arbitration Treaty with the Netherlands and with Sweden signed

May 5, Arbitration Treaty with Japan signed

May 7, Naturalization and extradition treaties with Portugal signed

May 10–18, National Convention of the Socialist Party in Chicago nominated Eugene V. Debs for President and Benjamin Hanford for Vice-President

May 13–15, Conference of Governors of the States and Territories at the White House on invitation of the President to discuss the question of means to conserve the natural resources of the country, and of invited prominent citizens including Grover Cleveland, William J. Bryan, Andrew Carnegie, James J. Hill, John Mitchell, and Judge George Gray

May 18, Arbitration Treaty with Denmark signed

May 18, Motto "In God We Trust" restored to coins of the United States

May 21, New York law prohibited operation of "bucket shops" in the State

May 23, Death of Peter Dailey (50) actor

May 25, Death of Homer H. Merriam (95) publisher, Springfield, Mass.

May 26, Deputation from Liberia received by the Secretary of State asked for aid of the United States to establish peace and order in Liberia

June 1, Supreme Court decision that a retail dealer of copyright book can sell book below price fixed by publisher

June 5, The Government began action against 7 coal carrying railroad companies for violation of the commodities clause of the Act to regulate commerce, namely the Pennsylvania, Reading, New Jersey Central, Delaware, Lackawana and Hudson, Delaware and Hudson, and Erie and Lehigh Valley railroads

June 6, President Roosevelt appointed a Conservation Commission of 57 members, Gifford Pinchot, chairman

June 10, Death of Oliver H. P. Belmont (50) financier, New York City

June 11, Anti-Race Track Gambling Act signed by the Governor of New York

June 12, The Cunard steamer "Lusitania" made record trip from Queenstown to New York, 2,890 miles in 4 days, 20 hours, and 7 minutes

June 13, Governor Willson, of Kentucky, announced pardon of Caleb Powers and James Howard, sentenced in 1900 in case of murder of Governor Goebel after jury disagreed on 4th trial June 4

June 16–19, Republican National Convention met in Chicago, and nominated William H. Taft, of Ohio, for President on the first ballot, and James S. Sherman, of New York, for Vice-President

June 19, William H. Taft resigned as Secretary of War to take effect June 30

June 23, Conviction of F. A. Hyde and J. H. Schneider in land fraud cases, Hyde sentenced to 2 years in prison and $10,000 fine. 100,000 acres restored to the Government as a result of proceedings in this case

——, Secretary of the American Legation left Caracas, Venezuela, severing diplomatic relations on account of controversy as to claims

——, Naturalization Treaty with Honduras signed

——, Louisiana passed anti-racing gambling law

June 24, Death of Grover Cleveland (71) former President, at Princeton, New Jersey

June 29, Luke E. Wright, of Tennessee, appointed Secretary of War

July 1, Direct primary law went into effect in Illinois

July 2, Socialist Labor Convention met in New York City, platform as of 1904 adopted, and Martin B. Preston, of Nevada, in prison for killing a man when on picket duty, nominated for President. August Gilhaus, of New York, later placed at head of ticket in view of ineligibility of Preston. Donald L. Munro nominated for Vice-President

July 3, Death of Joel Chandler Harris (60) author, at Atlanta, Georgia

July 4, Glenn H. Curtiss at Hammondsport, New York, in flight in his "June Bug" of 5,090 feet in 1 hour and 42 minutes won Scientific American Cup

July 6, Commander Robert E. Peary sailed from New York on polar expedition

July 7–10, National Democratic Convention met in Denver, and nominated William J. Bryan for President and John W. Kern, of Indiana, for Vice-President

July 14, Death of William Mason, musician

July 15, Modus vivendi as to fisheries off Newfoundland signed with Great Britain pending final settlement

July 15–16, Prohibition Party Convention at Columbus, Ohio, nominated Eugene W. Chafin, of Illinois, for President, and Aaron S. Watkins, of Ohio, for Vice-President

July 16, American battleship fleet arrived at Honolulu

July 17, Commander R. E. Peary left Sydney, Nova Scotia, proceeding to Etah on western coast of Greenland and through Smith Sound to northern coast of Grant Land, and arriving at Cape York, Greenland Aug. 1

July 21, Death of Bishop Henry Codman Potter (74) at Cooperstown, New York

July 22, Fine of $29,240,000 imposed on Standard Oil Company Aug., 1907, set aside by United States Circuit Court of Appeals of the Chicago district. The following day the President directed the Attorney General to take steps for immediate retrial

July 23, Dismissal of 8 West Point cadets recommended for hazing

July 24, Socialist Labor Party met in New York City and nominated August Gilhaus, of New York, for President, and Donald L. Munro, of Virginia, for Vice-President

July 27, Independence Party Convention (Hearst's Party) in Chicago and nominated Thomas L. Hisgen, of Massachusetts, for President, and John Temple Graves, of Georgia, for Vice-President

July 28, American car "Thomas" pronounced victor in New York to Paris automobile race begun Feb. 12

Aug. 4, Death of Bronson Howard, dramatist (66) at Avon, New Jersey, and of Senator William B. Allison (79) at Dubuque, Iowa, and of Katherine Prescott Wormeley, author

Aug. 8, American battleship fleet at Auckland, New Zealand

——, Wilbur Wright made first European flight at Le Mans, France, 3 kilometers in 1 minute and 46 seconds

Aug. 9, Riots of striking miners in Birmingham district, Alabama, resulted in killing of 3 men and wounding 11. State militia sent

Aug. 10, President Roosevelt appointed Country Life Commission, Professor L. H. Bailey, chairman, Henry Wallace, Kenyon L. Butterfield, Gifford Pinchot, and Walter H. Page

——, Death of Louise Chandler Moulton (73) author

——, Naturalization Treaty with Uruguay signed

Aug. 11, Death of Ainsworth R. Spofford (84) former librarian of Congress

Aug. 13, Death of Ira D. Sankey (67) evangelist and composer

Aug. 14–19, Race riot at Springfield, Illinois, troops sent

Aug. 18, Death of Dr. Henry Hopkins (71) former president of Williams College

——, Peary Arctic expedition left Etah, Greenland, and arrived at Cape Sheridan, Grant Land, where the winter was spent

Aug. 20, The "Lusitania" made new record from Queenstown to New York in 4 days and 15 hours

Aug. 21, Claims Convention with Venezuela signed

Sept. 3, Strike of Alabama coal miners declared off, men returning to work on non-union basis

Sept. 4, American battleship fleet left Melbourne, Australia

Sept. 10, United States Circuit Court of Appeals in Philadelphia decided that the "commodities clause" of the Hepburn Act was unconstitutional

Sept. 12, Orville Wright made flight of 45 miles in 1 hour and $14^1/_3$ minutes, established new record by remaining in the air 1 hour and $14^1/_3$ minutes at Fort Myer near Washington

Sept. 17, W. R. Hearst published correspondence destined to show that Senator Joseph B. Foraker, of Ohio, had acted as counsel for the Standard Oil Company, which he denied as to date on the 25th

——, Orville Wright making record flight over Fort Myer had accident resulting from breaking of a propeller-blade, the machine falling 75 feet injuring Wright seriously and killing Lieutenant Selfridge, his companion

Sept. 19, Convict lease system ended in Georgia by statute

Sept. 21, Wilbur Wright at Le Mans, France, made flight of 56 miles in 1 hour, 31 minutes, and $25^4/_5$ seconds

Oct. 1, Postal Convention which lowered rate on letters between the United States and Great Britain to 2 cents came into effect

Oct. 2, American fleet arrived at Manila, Philippines

Oct. 8, Arbitration Treaty with China signed

Oct. 13, Death of Daniel Coit Gilman (78) former president of Johns Hopkins University

Oct. 20–25, American battleship fleet at Japan

Oct. 21, Death of Charles Eliot Norton (81) writer, at Cambridge, Mass.

Oct. 29, American fleet arrived at Amoy, China

Nov. 3, Presidential election. W. H. Taft and J. S. Sherman, Republicans, received popular vote of 7,637,676; W. J. Bryan, Democrat, 6,393,182; Socialist, 420,464; Prohibition, 231,252; Independence Party, 83,183; Populist, 33,871; Socialist Labor, 15,421; electoral votes were 326 for Taft and Sherman, and 157 for Bryan and Kern

Nov. 4, Resignation of President Eliot of Harvard University after 39 years of service

Nov. 5, Charles W. Morse and Alfred H. Curtis found guilty of misapplication and false entry of funds of National Bank of North America in New York City and sentenced Nov. 6 to 15 years imprisonment; sentence of Morse commuted Jan. 18, 1912 after 2 years in prison

——, Resignation of E. B. Andrews, chancellor of the University of Nebraska

Nov. 7, Decision of Circuit Court of New York against the American Tobacco Company as a trust and combination in restraint of trade

Nov. 11, San Francisco voted for "Hetch Hetchy" project for water supply

Nov. 13, Francis J. Heney in charge of the prosecution of bribery cases in San Francisco shot and seriously wounded in court by an ex-convict during the trial of Ruef on bribery charges

Nov. 15, Strike of street car employees in Louisville, Kentucky, for increase of wages

Nov. 16, Supreme Court decision in boundary dispute between Washington and Oregon in favor of Oregon

Nov. 23, National Monetary Commission held first session

——, Riots of striking pottery workers at Perth Amboy, New Jersey

Nov. 30, Identical Notes exchanged between Japan and the United States, declaration of common policy in the East, to maintain status quo in the Pacific, the open door and independence and integrity of China

——, Supreme Court decision in case of Virginia Railroads against the State Corporation Commission of Virginia

——, Executive Order of the President brought all the 15,000 fourth class postmasters north of the Ohio River east of the Mississippi into classified civil service

Dec. 1, Truman H. Newberry, of Michigan, appointed Secretary of the Navy

Dec. 5, Arbitration Treaty with Peru signed

Dec. 7, Naturalization Treaty with Nicaragua signed

Dec. 8, Second Conference of Governors in Washington, President-Elect Taft presiding

Dec. 10, Abraham Ruef convicted in San Francisco bribery cases and sentenced Dec. 29 to 14 years imprisonment

Dec. 15, Death of Donald Grant Mitchell (Ik Marvel) author (86) at Edgewood, Conn.

——, Circuit Court of the United States issued final decree against the tobacco trust, the American Tobacco Company et al., restrained the combined companies from interstate and foreign trade

Dec. 17, Glen Curtiss in airplane "Silver Dart" flew over a mile at rate of 40 miles an hour

Dec. 18, Wilbur Wright made continuous flight of 95 miles in 1 hour and 54 minutes at Le Mans, France, and in second flight rose to height of 360 feet, breaking all previous records

Dec. 21, Arbitration Treaty with Salvador signed

Dec. 23, Justice Wright at Washington sentenced Samuel Gompers, John Mitchell, and Frank Morrison, officers of American Federation of Labor, to imprisonment of 1 year for Gompers and 6 months each for the others, for contempt, violation of injunction in the Bucks Stove and Range case

——, Supreme Court of Missouri decision ousted Standard Oil of Indiana, Republic Oil Company of Ohio, and Waters Pierce Company from the State, each fined $50,000

——, Arbitration Treaty with Argentina; not ratified

Dec. 31, State wide prohibition went into effect in Mississippi and Alabama

——, Wilbur Wright at Le Mans, France, made world endurance record in flight of 2 hours, 20 minutes, and $23\frac{1}{2}$ seconds, and flight of 77 miles and 2,280 feet, winning Michelin prize for longest distance flight of the year, a second world record

CONGRESS

April 22, New Employer's Liability Act replaced that of 1906 declared unconstitutional. Gave right to claim damages to "any person suffering injury while he is employed by such carrier in such (interstate) commerce. Provisions of this law confined to interstate railroads and to common carriers in Territories, the District of Columbia, and other parts of the United States subject immediately to the control of Congress

May 11, Consular Service Act amended

May 23, Mail subsidy provision for ocean steamers rejected by House

——, Senate killed resolution to choose members by popular vote

May 25, Joint Resolution passed remitted to China half of the $24,440,778 imposed on China on account of Boxer affair

May 27, Militia Act of 1903 amended

May 28, Act regulated employment of child labor in the District of Columbia; intended for a model law

May 30, Aldrich-Vreeland Currency Act provided that national banks in the same locality might form "national currency associations." Provision made to authorize national banks in time of emergency to obtain circulating notes by deposit of securities. All banks in association jointly and individually liable for redemption of notes. Individual banks by deposit of bonds with the Treasurer of the United States might obtain additional circulating notes. Appointment of National Monetary Commission authorized

——, Act to promote safety of employees on railroads enacted, known as the Locomotive Ash Pan Act

——, Congress adjourned

Dec. 2, Sixtieth Congress, 2d sess. convened

1909

Jan. 1, Supreme Court decision that Chicago and Alton Railroad should pay $60,000 fine for giving rebates

——, Death of George Washington Hough (72) astronomer

Jan. 3, American fleet at Suez Canal

Jan. 4, Supreme Court refused rehearing to the Government in the case of fine of $29,240,000 against Standard Oil Company imposed in 1907

Jan. 6, Extradition Treaty with France signed

Jan. 7, Arbitration Treaty with Haiti signed and with Ecuador

——, In "night rider" trials at Union City, Tennessee, 8 of the Reelfoot Lake band convicted of murder and death penalty imposed on 6 and 2 given 20 years in prison Jan. 9

Jan. 9, Arbitration Treaty with Uruguay signed

Jan. 11, Convention as to boundary waters between the United States and Canada signed with Great Britain

——, Secretary Root demanded from the Government of Belgium assurance of certain reforms in the Belgian Congo as to natives, and guarantee of free trade between Belgian Congo and the United States

Jan. 12, State wide prohibition passed by the Senate of Tennessee, and the Assembly on the 13th

Jan. 13, Arbitration Treaty with Costa Rica signed

——, Abbott Lawrence Lowell chosen president of Harvard University

Jan. 15, Arbitration Treaty with Austria-Hungary signed and Extradition Treaty with Honduras

Jan. 18, Secretary Garfield announced discovery of western land frauds involving $110,000,000

——, Supreme Court sustained decision of Supreme Court of Texas against the Waters Pierce Oil Company ousted from the State and fined $1,623,500 for violation of anti-trust laws; paid April 24

Jan. 21, Legislature of Tennessee passed state wide prohibition over the veto of the Governor of Jan. 19

Jan. 23, Arbitration Treaty with Brazil signed

——, In collision of steamers "Florida" and "Republic" in fog off Nantucket the passengers were rescued by the "Baltic" of the White Star Line guided by wireless telegraph from the "Republic," 1,500 persons saved

Jan. 25, President Elect Taft sailed from Charleston, South Carolina, to Panama Canal Zone, and Feb. 1 with engineers who accompanied him examined the Culebra Cut

Jan. 27, Newfoundland Fisheries Treaty signed submitted to arbitration the interpretation of Fisheries Treaty of 1818

——, Robert Bacon, of New York, appointed Secretary of State

Jan. 30, Death of Martha Finley (81) author of the "Elsie Books"

Feb. 1, United States troops withdrawn from Cuba

Feb. 3 and May 27, Governor C. N. Haskell, of Oklahoma, indicted by United States Grand Jury for fraud in connection with scheduling town lots at Muskogee

Feb. 4, California House passed Drew Bill prohibiting aliens from owning land

Feb. 6, American fleet left Gibraltar for Hampton Roads, Virginia, ending world cruise

Feb. 9, Wyoming prohibited sale of liquor outside incorporated cities and towns

Feb. 10, Bill barring Japanese from schools reconsidered and rejected by legislature in California

Feb. 11, Death of Russell Sturgis (73) architect and writer, New York

Feb. 13, Aug. 21, and Sept. 9, Claims Conventions with Venezuela signed as to Orinoco Steamship Company and Corporation

Feb. 15, Peary expedition for the North Pole (7 persons and 50 Esquimaux) left the "Roosevelt" and proceeding on sledges arriving at Cape Colombia

Feb. 17, Dr. James B. Angell resigned as president of the University of Michigan

——, Federal Grand Jury indicted Joseph Pulitzer, and editors of the New York *World* for criminal libel of President Roosevelt and W. H. Taft in connection with purchase of Panama Canal

Feb. 20, Supplemental Treaty of commerce with Spain signed

——, Death of Carroll D. Wright, economist and educator (69) at Worcester, Mass.

——, Idaho passed local option liquor law

Feb. 21, The fleet reached Hampton Roads, Virginia, after world cruise, and was reviewed by President Roosevelt the following day

Feb. 23, Patent Agreement with Germany signed

——, Supreme Court decision sustained verdict of Circuit Court of New York imposing fine of $134,000 on New York Central Railroad for granting rebates to the American Sugar Refining Company, which was paid May 12

March 1, Robert E. Peary with Henson and 4 Esquimaux began dash for North Pole from Cape Columbia

March 2, Peary expedition passed the British record

——, The S.S. "Mauretania" established new eastbound record making trip in 4 days, 20 hours, and 2 minutes

——, Treaty of commerce with Italy signed

March 4, Inauguration of President William Howard Taft and Vice-President James S. Sherman

——, Verdict of guilty brought in Circuit Court of southern district of New York against Sugar Refining Company for defrauding the Government by false weighing machines

March 5, James Wilson, of Iowa, recommissioned Secretary of Agriculture; Philander C. Knox, of Pennsylvania, appointed Secretary of State; Franklin MacVeagh, of Illinois, Secretary of the Treasury; Jacob M. Dickinson, of Tennessee, Secretary of War; George W. Wickersham, of New York, Attorney General; Frank H. Hitchcock, of Massachusetts, Postmaster General; George von L. Meyer, of Massachusetts, Secretary of the Navy; Richard A. Ballinger, of Washington, Secretary of the Interior; Charles Nagel, of Missouri, Secretary of Commerce and Labor

March 7-9, Strike of street railroad employees in Trenton, New Jersey

March 9, Supreme Court of Missouri confirmed decree ousting Standard Oil Company from the State

March 11, Court of Appeals in District of Columbia modified decree in Bucks Stove and Range Company case in which Samuel Gompers and other leaders of American Federation of Labor convicted, providing that the decree should restrain the defendants from only such publications referring to Bucks Company as were made in furtherance of an illegal boycott

——, Conference of anthracite operators in Philadelphia proposed renewal of agreement for 3 years and refused demands of coal miners

March 12, Washington adopted local option

——, Diplomatic relations with Nicaragua severed because of treatment of Americans

March 13, Arbitration Treaty with Paraguay signed

——, Death of Lieutenant Petrosini of the detective force of New York City, assassinated at Palermo, Sicily, by agents of the Black Hand Society

March 16, Death of George T. Angell (68) "friend of dumb animals"

March 18, The President named Commission to investigate conditions in Liberia, Robert C. Ogden, W. Morgan Schuster, and Emmet J. Scott, which sailed for Liberia in April

March 22, The S.S. "Mauretania" established new eastbound transatlantic record of 4 days, 18 hours, and 25 minutes

March 23, Theodore Roosevelt sailed from New York on a scientific expedition to Africa under auspices of the Smithsonian Institution, Washington

——, The Peary expedition to the North Pole passed the Norwegian record, the Italian record on the 24th, and the American record on the 28th

March 23-24, Anthracite coal miners in convention at Scranton, Penn. refused offer of operators for renewal of agreement for 3 years unless union recognized

March 25-29, Rising of Creek Indians suppressed by Oklahoma militia

March 29, Death of Dr. James H. Canfield (62) educator and librarian, New York

March 30, Queensborough Bridge over East River, New York, opened

——, American miners drove 150 Hungarians from Boyle mines near Jasonville, Indiana

March 31, Convict lease system in Georgia ended under law of Sept. 1908

April 1, Chicago, Milwaukee, and St. Paul Railroad completed to Seattle and Tacoma making the seventh transcontinental line

April 2, Peary expedition to the North Pole passed the 88th parallel, and the 89th the day following

April 5, Supreme Court decision in favor of dispensary liquor system, South Carolina

April 6, Discovery of the North Pole by Robert E. Peary, the first to reach the Pole

April 8, Death of F. Marion Crawford, novelist, at Sorrento, Italy, and of Mme Helena Modjeska, actress, in California

April 9, Death of Ethan Allen Hitchcock (74) former Secretary of the Interior

April 16, Cudahy Packing Company indicted in Kansas City on 695 counts for alleged oleomargarine frauds

April 21, Death of Dr. Samuel June Barrows, author and criminologist

April 23, Governor Willson, of Kentucky, pardoned former Governor Taylor and 5 others charged with complicity in murder of Governor Goebel in 1900

——, R. E. Peary arrived at Cape Columbia from the North Pole and at the ship "Roosevelt" April 27

April 29, Agreement of anthracite coal miners and operators renewed that of 1902 for another 3 years as to wage schedule

——, Announcement of Attorney General Wickersham that the American Sugar Refining Company paid penalty awarded in March of $134,411.03 and in addition $1,239,088.97 of $2,000,000 to be paid representing duties unpaid during previous 12 years due to fraudulent practices

April 30, Strike of laborers on the Great Lakes, and of bakers in New York City

May 3, Supreme Court decision reversed decision of lower court and upheld the constitutionality of the "commodities clause" of the Hepburn Act of June 1906 amending the interstate commerce law

May 7, Indictments presented by Grand Jury of the Circuit Court, New York, against Oliver Spitzer, and 6 other employees of the American Sugar Refining Company

May 8-Aug. 13, Strike of Chicago street railroad employees

May 10, The S.S. "Mauretania" made new eastbound transatlantic record of run in 4 days, 18 hours, and 11 minutes

May 13, Executive Order of the President established a central committee to purchase all supplies for government use doing away with payment of several prices instead of one for the same supplies

May 14, Colonel S. F. Cody at Laffan's Plain, England, made flight of 3,600 feet

May 17, Strike of white firemen on Georgia Railroad against employment of negroes as firemen, joined by white engineers May 23

May 18, Interstate Commerce Commission ruled that negro passengers paying fares cannot legally be discriminated against in accommodations

May 19, Death of Henry H. Rogers (69) financier, New York City

May 21, Death of Charles G. Bush (67) cartoonist, New York City

May 22, The President opened 700,000 acres of public land to settlers in the States of Washington, Montana, and Idaho

May 25, Claims Convention with Nicaragua signed

May 29, Strike of white miners of Georgia ended, both sides making concessions

May 29-June 4, Successful strike of street railroad employees in Philadelphia

May 30, Indictment of 5 prominent citizens at Denver, charged with defrauding the government of coal lands in Colorado valued at $1,000,000

May 30–June 4, Strike of street car employees in Philadelphia successful

June 1–Oct. 16, Alaska-Yukon Pacific Exposition at Seattle, Washington

June 8, Pennsylvania Sugar Refining Company suit for damages against the American Sugar Refining Company settled out of court for $10,250,000, the Pennsylvania company ruined by means in contravention of anti-trust law

——, Hat makers strike over use of union labels settled in favor of employers

June 10, Death of Rev. Edward Everett Hale (87) writer and chaplain of the Senate

June 11, Memorandum of Secretary Root of American view of obligations of Belgium in the Congo under international conventions to which the United States a party

June 15, Death of Louis Prang (85) lithographer

June 16, Death of Dana Estes (69) publisher, Boston

June 19, Extradition Treaty with Santo Domingo signed

June 22, Construction of Cape Cod Canal begun

June 24, Death of Sarah Orne Jewett (60) author

June 27, Board of Arbitration in Georgia strike decided that negroes when employed to be paid same wages as white men in similar positions thus removing incentive to their employment as cheap labor

——, Strike of street car employees at Pittsburgh, Penn.

June 28, Treaty of commerce with Portugal signed

——, 6,000 coal miners on strike in Pittsburg, Kansas

June 30, State wide prohibition went into effect in Tennessee

——, Strike of 10,000 men in tin-plate industry begun because of open shop order

July 1, American Sugar Refining Company indicted in New York on charge of violation of criminal clause of Sherman anti-trust law

July 5–9, Champlain Tercentenary Celebration at Lake Champlain in New York and Vermont

July 9, Gift of John D. Rockefeller of $10,000,000 to General Education Board bringing gifts to total of $53,000,000

July 11, Death of Simon Newcomb (74) astronomer, in Washington

July 14, July wheat at $1.27 a bushel in Chicago

July 22 and Sept. 8, Convention with Great Britain signed as to Newfoundland fisheries

July 26, Death of Rev. William R. Huntington, of New York City

July 27, Orville Wright demonstrated his airplane at Fort Myer near Washington, carrying 2 persons in sustained flight of 1 hour, 12 minutes, and 40 seconds, covering 50 miles at average rate of 40 miles an hour

July 29, National Conservation Association organized, Dr. Charles W. Eliot first president, first convention held at Seattle Aug. 26–28

July 30, Orville Wright broke all speed records in flight over measured course of 10 miles in 14 minutes and 42 seconds, the demonstrations of July 27 and 30 securing acceptance of his machine by the Government

July, Serious riots of strikers of the Pressed Steel Car Company at McKees Rocks, Pennsylvania

Aug. 13, 87,360 acres withdrawn by the Interior Dept. along the Colorado River in Utah to prevent "monopolies" of water power sites

Aug. 17, Alabama the first State to ratify the Income Tax Amendment to the Constitution (XVIth)

Aug. 21, Walter Wellman returned to Spitzbergen with balloon which burst shortly after his attempt to start for the North Pole

——, President Taft ordered army reduced to 80,000

Aug. 26, Peary Arctic expedition reached Indian Harbor, Labrador

Aug. 28, Glenn H. Curtiss won Gordon Bennett Cup at Reims, France, in first international air meet, in flight of 12.42 miles in 15 minutes and $50^3/_5$ seconds

Sept. 1, Message received from Dr. Frederick Cook in which he claimed to have reached the North Pole on April 21, 1908

Sept. 4, Death of (William) Clyde Fitch (44) playwright

Sept. 6, Message from Robert E. Peary from Indian Harbor, Labrador, announcing his discovery of the North Pole April 6, 1909

Sept. 7, Strike of pressed steel workers ended at McKees Rocks, Pennsylvania, after 53 days, all demands granted, and compromise on wage scale

——, Death of General James Schackelford

Sept. 9, Death of Edward H. Harriman (62) railroad magnate

——, Claims Convention with Nicaragua signed

Sept. 11, President Taft appointed Tariff Commission, Professor H. C. Emery, James B. Reynolds, and Alvin H. Sanders

Sept. 12, Death of William Lloyd Garrison (71) reformer

Sept. 13, Statement of Commander R. E. Peary denied claim of Dr. Frederick Cook that he had reached the North Pole

Sept. 14, Death of Charles F. McKim (62) architect, New York City, and of James David Smillie, artist and engraver (79)

Sept. 15, President Taft upheld Secretary Ballinger and ordered dismissal of L. R. Glavis, Land Office agent, who had made charges against him

Sept. 18, Orville Wright set new carrying endurance passenger record, staying in air 1 hour, 35 minutes, and 47 seconds in Berlin, Germany

Sept. 21, Dr. Frederick Cook reached New York from Europe and was acclaimed as discoverer of the North Pole

Sept. 22, Death of Robert Hoe (70) printer

Sept. 23, President Taft opened the Gunnisson Irrigation Tunnel in Colorado

Sept. 25–Oct. 2, Hudson-Fulton Celebration in New York of the 300th anniversary of the arrival of Henry Hudson, and the 100th anniversary of the work of Robert Fulton

Sept. 27, President Taft withdrew 3,000,000 acres of public lands in California and Wyoming from "location" to meet future needs of the government

Sept. 29, University of Redlands, California, opened

Oct. 2, Orville Wright, in Berlin, Germany, reached height of 1,637 feet making unofficial world record

Oct. 4, Wilbur Wright made flight from Governor's Island up the Hudson River to Grant's Tomb and back, 19½ miles in 33½ minutes

Oct. 6, Death of Dudley Buck (70) organist and composer

Oct. 13, In Danbury hatters case verdict assessed damages for labor boycott at $232,240

Oct. 15, Walter Wellman with 3 companions started from Spitzbergen in flight for the North Pole, but forced to turn back after only 12 miles by the breaking of the equilibrator

Oct. 16, President Taft met President Diaz, of Mexico, at El Paso, Texas

Oct. 24, Death of Judge Rufus Wheeler Peckham at Altamont, New York

Oct. 26, Death of Major General Oliver O. Howard (79) author

Oct. 27, Secretary Ballinger made statement defining policy of protection of western public lands

Oct. 28, Announcement that John D. Rockefeller had given $1,000,000 for fight against the hook-worm disease in the South

Nov. 1, Secretary of the Navy reported warship tonnage as 682,785 as compared with 758,350 of Great Britain, and 609,700 of Germany

Nov. 2, District of Columbia Court of Appeals affirmed decree of Supreme Court of District as to sentences of imprisonment of Samuel Gompers, John Mitchell, and Frank Morrison, officers of the American Federation of Labor, for contempt of injunction in Bucks Stove and Range Company case

——, General strike of shirt-waist makers of New York, chiefly women, begun for recognition of the union, sanitary conditions in shops, and humane treatment by foremen and forewomen

Nov. 3, Commander Robert E. Peary's records of his journey to the North Pole approved by the National Geographic Society

Nov. 4, Death of Major General John J. Coppinger (75)

Nov. 5, Death of William Torrey Harris (74) educator

Nov. 9, Secretary Knox suggested plan for neutralization of Manchurian railroads

——, Death of Joseph M. Asher, Talmudic scholar

Nov. 10, President Taft returned to Washington from tour of the South and West of 13,000 miles of travel, having made 266 speeches

——, Adoption of employees pension system by New York Central Railroad

——, Warships sent to Nicaragua and explanation demanded as to execution of 2 Americans in service of insurgent army

Nov. 11, Pearl Harbor, Hawaiian Islands, selected for naval base in Pacific

Nov. 12, Indictment of former employees of New York Custom House and of James Bendernagel and 6 other employees of American Sugar Refining Company

Nov. 16, American Telephone and Telegraph Company announced control secured of the Western Union Telegraph Company

——, Death of Charles N. Crittenden (76) reformer

Nov. 17, Strike of 5,000 granite workers at Barre, Vermont

Nov. 18, Death of Richard Watson Gilder (65) poet and editor, New York City

——, Strike of railroad employees in the Northwest

Nov. 19, Death of William Laffan (61) newspaper proprietor, New York City, and John R. Tabb (64) poet

Nov. 20, Decision of United States Circuit Court of Appeals at St. Louis held the Standard Oil Company of New Jersey to be an illegal corporation and decreed its dissolution

Nov. 26, President Taft approved regulations for collection of corporation tax submitted to him by the Secretary of the Treasury

——, Executive Order provided that promotion in consular service should be based on efficiency records

Nov. 29, Formal notice to President Zelaya that Nicaragua Government held responsible in execution of 2 Americans

Nov. 30, Two weeks strike of 2,000 switchmen in railroad yards between St. Paul and the Pacific for increase in wages ended in defeat

Dec. 1, Claims Convention with Chile signed referred Alsop claim to arbitration

——, Diplomatic relations with Mexico severed

Dec. 10, Ice trust convicted of violation of New York State anti-monopoly law and $5,000 fine imposed

Dec. 14, Union presented list of grievances against the United States Steel Corporation, to President Taft and Congress

Dec. 15, Major General Leonard Wood appointed Chief of Staff of Army

——, International School of Peace founded in Boston on initiative of Edward Ginn, publisher

——, Arbuckle Company paid the government $695,573 of sugar duties in fraud case

Dec. 20–Feb. 6, 1910, Strike of shirt-waist makers in Philadelphia in sympathy with the New York strike

Dec. 21, Committee of the University of Copenhagen examining records of Dr. Frederick Cook declared that no proof existed that he had reached the North Pole

Dec. 22, Death of Timothy P. Sullivan (40) Tammany politician, New York City

Dec. 26, Death of Frederick Remington (48) artist and sculptor, and of Claus Spreckels (80) California financier

Dec. 31, Manhattan Bridge over the East River between New York and Brooklyn opened for traffic

——, Death of Spencer Trask (65) New York banker

CONGRESS

Jan. 19, House passed Pension Appropriation Bill abolishing all but 1 of 18 pension agencies

Jan. 22, Joint Resolution provided for special Lincoln postage stamp

Feb. 9, Act prohibited the importation and smoking of opium

Feb. 18, Trade Mark Act amended as to registration

Feb. 19, Act provided for enlarged homesteads in certain States on lands designated as not susceptible of successful irrigation

March 4, Act provided that no senator or representative should solicit or receive contributions for a political purpose

——, Criminal Code Act passed

——, Amendment to Sundry Civil Bill cut off appropriation of Conservation Commission

——, Congress adjourned

March 15, Sixty-First Congress, 1st (special) sess. convened

April 9, Payne Tariff Bill placing coal, iron ore, hide, flax, and wood pulp on the free list, and reducing duties on iron, steel, lumber, chemicals, and refined sugar passed House by vote of 217 to 161. Inheritance tax included

May 29, Resolution of Senate created a Committee on Public Expenditures

July 8, Aldrich Tariff Bill restored iron ore and flax to dutiable list, placed increased tax on iron and steel goods, reporting some 600 increases over the House schedules, passed by Senate by vote of 45 to 34

July 13, The XVIth Amendment to the Constitution permitting an unapportioned income tax, adopted by House July 12 and Senate July 5, submitted to the States for ratification

July 15, Olmstead Act again vested jurisdiction over Puerto Rico in War Dept.

Aug. 5, Payne-Aldrich Tariff Act increased the Dingley tariff duties in 300 instances and reduced them in 584, 65% of total imports remained subject to old rates. Raw hides, wood pulp, and oil were placed on the free list, duties lowered on lumber, window glass, harnesses, and agricultural implements, and bituminous coal. Tax of 1% placed on corporations with net earnings in excess of $5,000. A Tariff Board was created and a Customs Court of Appeals. The maximum and minimum clause provided for tariff discrimination against nations maintaining a tariff discrimination against the United States. The importation of Hawaiian and Puerto Rican sugar free of duty continued, and the 20% reduction on Cuban sugar, and importation free of 300,000 tons of sugar from the Philippines. Average rate of duties 36.86%

——, Congress adjourned

Dec. 6, Sixty-first Congress, 2d sess. convened

1910

Jan. 1, Law prohibiting manufacture of liquor in Tennessee came into effect

Jan. 3, Death of Darius Ogden Mills (84) banker

Jan. 7, President Taft directed removal of Gifford Pinchot, Chief of Forest Service from office because of letter to Senator Dolliver (*see infra* Congress Jan. 6) in violation of a rule forbidding subordinates to carry on direct correspondence with Congress in such cases

——, Paper Board Association of 140 paper manufacturers indicted on charge of illegal combination in restraint of trade; pleaded guilty Feb. 7 and paid fine of $52,000

Jan. 10, Four employees of the sugar trust sentenced to imprisonment of 1 year

——, Supreme Court decision in Illinois Central Railroad case upheld Interstate Commerce Commission

Jan. 11, Death of Theodore T. Munger (79) author and clergyman

——, Glenn Curtiss made new record at Los Angeles carrying passengers at speed of 55 miles an hour

Jan. 12, Louis Paulhan, French aviator, at Los Angeles reached altitude of 1,383 yards in biplane making world record

——, Henry S. Groves appointed Chief Forester

Jan. 14, Charles R. Heike, Secretary of the American Sugar Refining Company, E. W. Gerbracht, J. V. Bendernagel, and 3 others indicted by Grand Jury, New York, charged with making false entries in conspiracy to defraud the government; sentenced in September to fines and imprisonment. Jury disagreed as to Bendernagel

Jan. 17, Shoshone dam, Wyoming, completed

Jan. 18, Proclamation of the President of minimum rates under tariff law to Great Britain, Italy, Russia, Switzerland, Spain, Turkey, and on the 29th to 8 other countries

Jan. 21, Japan and Russia declined to agree to Secretary Knox's proposal for neutralization of the railroads of Manchuria

Jan. 22, Settlement of shirt waist strike in New York City by agreement of certain companies

——, Death of Henry T. Coates (67) publisher

Jan. 23, Gifford Pinchot elected president of the National Conservation Association

Jan. 24, Renewed proceedings against the beef trust begun by Grand Jury and Judge Landis at Chicago, Swift and Co., Armour and Co., and Morris and Co. with reference to the National Packing Company and the increased prices of meats

Jan. 24, Death of Benjamin Hanford (49) socialist leader

Jan. 26, Case of libel suit of the United States vs. the New York *World* as to statements about Panama Canal purchase quashed by Judge Hough of the United States Circuit Court at New York

Jan. 28, Death of Brigadier General William J. Draper (68)

Jan. 29, Death of Bishop Cyrus D. Foss (76) Methodist

Feb. 3, Proclamation of the President announced tariff agreement with Germany, and Feb. 21 with 18 other countries

——, Court at Hartford, Conn., awarded damages of $74,000 against hatter's union and American Federation of Labor in Danbury case of D. E. Loewe and Co.

Feb. 7, Proclamation of the President announced minimum tariff agreement with Germany

Feb. 8, National Sugar Refining Company paid the Government $604,304.37 in back duties withheld

——, Boy Scouts of America organized and incorporated in District of Columbia

Feb. 9, Secretary of Agriculture Wilson opened 4,000,-000 acres of forest reserves to settlement

——, Death of John S. Ogilvie (67) publisher

Feb. 11, Death of Brigadier General Robert L. Meade (69)

Feb. 17, Secretary Ballinger withdrew more than 2,000,000 acres of coal lands for conservation purposes in Wyoming and Montana

Feb. 18, 23, and 25, National Packing Company indicted in New Jersey on charges of conspiracy to raise prices by keeping food stuffs in cold storage

Feb. 19, Strike of street car employees in Philadelphia for increase in wages and recognition of the union. 300 cars wrecked Feb. 20

——, Fatal race riots at Cairo, Illinois

Feb. 23, Death of Amos E. Dolbear (72) educator and inventor

Feb. 24, Two hundred State Police arrived in Philadelphia to keep order in strike

Feb. 25, Bethlehem Steel Company closed because of rioting strikers

Feb. 27, Central Labor Union of Philadelphia declared general sympathetic strike to begin March 5 when 40,000 men stopped work

March 1, Rockefeller Foundation established by John D. Rockefeller for benefit of humanity

March 6, Death of Thomas Collier Platt (76) former senator, New York City

March 16, Barney Oldfield at Daytona, Florida, broke world automobile speed record at 27²/₃ seconds a mile

March 20, Conference of President Taft with the Premier of Canada on tariff relations

March 21, Federal Grand Jury at Chicago indicted National Packing Company and 10 subsidiary companies for violation of anti-trust laws

March 22, General strike in Philadelphia declared after peace negotiations rejected by street car employees

March 23, Agreement of firemen on western railroads to arbitrate dispute averted strike

March 27, Death of Alexander Agassiz (75) scientist and engineer, and of David D. Wood (72), blind musician and composer

March 28, Death of Justice Josiah Brewer (73) of Supreme Court

March 30, Proclamation of the President granted minimum tariff rates under tariff law to Canada and Australia thereby completing extension of minimum rates to all the countries of the world

——, Death of Charles Sprague Smith (56) educator, and of Myra Kelly (Mrs. Allan MacNaughton) writer

March 31, 300,000 bituminous coal miners suspended work pending wage settlement

——, Woman's College of Baltimore founded in 1885 became Goucher College

April 1, Executive Order of the President placed assistant postmasters of first and second class post offices in classified service list

——, Death of Robert W. Patterson (59) educator, Chicago

April 2, Maryland legislature passed Bill to disenfranchise the negro in municipal and State elections on ground that the State had never adopted the XVth Amendment to the Constitution; not adopted, the Governor announced April 8 that he would veto it

April 6, Military Court of Inquiry found negro soldiers of the twenty-fifth infantry guilty in Brownsville shooting affair of 1906

April 10, Interstate Commerce Commission ordered reduction in Pullman car rates

April 12, Dispute of New York Central Railroad with trainmen and conductors submitted to arbitration

——, Death of William Graham Sumner (69), sociological writer

April 15, Census as of this date gave total population as 91,972,226 and including Alaska, Hawaii, and Puerto Rico 93,402,151, including 81,732,687 white persons, 9,828,294 negroes, and 411,285 all other including Indians, Chinese, and Japanese. The center of population was in the city of Bloomington, Indiana.

Origin of the foreign-born white population, 1910 census:—

England	876,455
Wales	82,479
Scotland	261,034
Ireland	1,352,155
Total United Kingdom	2,572,123
Germany	2,501,181
Canada	1,196,070
Sweden	665,183
Norway	403,858
Russia and Finland	1,732,421
Italy	1,343,070
Denmark	181,621
Austria	1,174,924
France	117,236
Switzerland	124,834
Holland	120,053
Mexico	219,802
Cuba and West Indies [1]	23,169
Hungary	495,600
Belgium	49,397
Portugal	57,623
Spain	21,977
China	333
Japan	198
Greece	101,264
Turkey	91,923
Other foreign countries	151,685
Total	13,345,545

[1] Except Puerto Rico.

April 17, Settlement of strike of street car employees in Philadelphia

April 21, Secretary Ballinger withdrew from entry 13,500,000 acres of coal lands in Montana

——, Death of Samuel Langhorne Clemens (Mark Twain) at Redding, Connecticut (74)

April 26, Dedication of International Bureau of American Republics Building, gift of Andrew Carnegie, in Washington

April 29, 40,000 bituminous coal miners returned to work in Pennsylvania with 5.55% wage increase

April 30, 6,000 bakers in New York City struck on question of open shop

May 1, Death of John Q. A. Ward (80) sculptor, and of Admiral Philip Hichborn (71)

May 2, Local option won over state wide prohibition in Alabama

——, International Convention for Repression of the Circulation of Obscene Documents signed

May 11, Glacier National Park in northern Montana created

May 21, World record broken by 2 special trains on Michigan Central Railroad between Detroit and Niagara Falls, 224 miles in 224 and 217 minutes respectively

——, Boundary Treaty with Great Britain settled boundary in Passamaquoddy Bay

May 29, Glenn H. Curtiss made flight from Albany to New York City, 137 miles in 2 hours and 32 minutes surpassing any previous record

May 31, Twenty-five western railroads restrained from making general advance in freight rates to go into effect June 1 charged with fixing agreement in violation of Sherman anti-trust law

——, Death of Charles H. Treat, former Secretary of the Treasury, and of Dr. Elizabeth Blackwell (89) at Hastings, New York

June 5, Death of William Sydney Porter (O. Henry) writer (42)

June 10, The Western Union Telegraph Company indicted by Federal Grand Jury in Washington charged with 42 violations of bucket shop law

June 11, Charles R. Heike and Ernest Gebrach found guilty of fraud against the government in sugar refining cases

June 13, Flight of Charles K. Hamilton from New York to Philadelphia, 172 miles in 3 hours and 29 minutes

June 13 and 17, Walter Brookins at Indianapolis reached altitude of 4,384 and over 4,500 respectively breaking record

June 15, Philadelphia and Reading Railroad and Lehigh Valley and Bethlehem Steel Company found guilty of rebating

June 18, Theodore Roosevelt landed in New York from hunting and exploring trip in eastern Africa and tour of Europe

June 24 and Dec. 5, Treaty with Mexico submitted Chamizal boundary dispute to arbitration. See also Mexico

June 28, Henry B. Hutchins chosen president of the University of Michigan

June 29, Interstate Commerce Commission ordered reduction in freight rates on large number of railroads

July 1, Strike of cigar workers, Tampa, Florida begun

July 3 and 7, President Taft withdrew 8,495,731 acres of water power sites and petroleum lands in Alabama and 35,073,164 coal lands in West

July 4, Death of Chief Justice Melville W. Fuller (77) at Sorrento, Maine

July 7, Death of William J. Rolfe (83), Shakespearean scholar

July 8, Strike of cloak and suit makers union in New York City begun which lasted 10 weeks

July 9, Walter Brookins in biplane reached altitude estimated at 6,175 feet in flight at Atlantic City

July 17, Report of congressional committee investigating the Dept. of the Interior and Bureau of Forestry vindicated Secretary Ballinger

July 18–Aug. 2, Strike of conductors and trainmen on Grand Trunk and Central Vermont Railroads because of failure to agree on wages and rules

July 19, Agreement of Bucks Stove and Range Company with labor unions to employ only union labor ending long controversy

July 24–Sept. 3, Secretary of War and the Chief of the Bureau of Insular Affairs on tour of inspection of the Philippines

July 24–Oct., Riots and violence in street car strike, Columbus, Ohio

July 31, Death of John G. Carlisle (74), former Secretary of the Treasury

Aug. 2, Oklahoma voted for amendment to Constitution which adopted "grandfather clause" of North Carolina to disenfranchise the negro; later declared illegal by Supreme Court

Aug. 11, International Copyright Convention signed by the United States, and Pan-American Claims Treaty

——, Death of Robert Treat Paine (75), philanthropist, in Boston

Aug. 12, Uhlan, trotting horse, established new record at 1.58 minutes per mile

Aug. 13, War Dept. sent troops to fight forest fires ranging over 100,000 acres in Montana and Idaho

Aug. 18, Pecuniary Claims Convention signed with Great Britain for arbitration of claims of private citizens of each country

——, Death of David Ranken (74) St. Louis

Aug. 20, International Patent Convention signed by the United States

Aug. 26, Death of William James (68) psychologist and philosopher, in Chocorua, New Hampshire

Aug. 31, At Osawatomie, Kansas, Theodore Roosevelt made speech defining the "New Nationalism" in favor of control of trusts by publicity of accounts and proceedings, tariff revision, graduated income tax, adequate army and navy, conservation, protection of labor, and the direct primary with the recall of elective officers

——, Turkey granted to American religious and educational institutions exemption from Ottoman law and permission to own land

——, Glenn Curtiss made new world record in flight near Cleveland, Ohio, of 60 miles in 1 hour and 18 minutes

Sept. 2, New York City cloakmaker's strike begun in July and involving 70,000 workers settled on basis of the "preferential shop" a compromise in favor of the employees

Sept. 7, Permanent Court of Arbitration at The Hague handed down award as to Newfoundland fisheries, affirmed right of Americans ·to fish on "treaty" coasts of Newfoundland and Magdalen Island, Canada and Newfoundland to make reasonable regulations

Sept. 8, Strike of Illinois coal miners ended after 5 months, wage increase of 8% and other demands granted

Sept. 9, Minority Report of Congressional Committee upholding charges of Pinchot and Glavis against Secretary Ballinger published

Sept. 12, Ten chief officials of the beef trust, the Armour, Swift, and Morris companies, indicted by Federal Grand Jury at Chicago in second suit for conspiracy in restraint of interstate trade

Sept. 23, International Convention on assistance and salvage at sea signed

Sept. 29, Death of Winslow Homer (74) artist, and of Mrs. Rebecca Harding Davis (79), author

Sept. 30, The President placed all assistant postmasters under the classified civil service

Oct. 1, The Los Angeles *Times* Building destroyed by bomb explosion in which 21 persons killed

Oct. 3–Nov. 21, Constitutional Convention at Santa Fé, New Mexico

Oct. 5, St. Patrick's Cathedral in New York City dedicated by Archbishop Farley

Oct. 9–10, Forest fires in northern Minnesota destroyed 6 towns with loss of life of 400 persons, property loss estimated $100,000,000

Oct. 10, Death of William B. Dana (81) editor, New York City

Oct. 11, Constitutional Convention met at Phœnix, Arizona

Oct. 15, Walter Wellman's transatlantic expedition launched his dirigible airship at Atlantic City for flight to Europe. The trip lasted 71 hours and covered 1,008 miles, the crew picked up by steamer "Trent" on the 18th

Oct. 16, Death of Willard Stephen Whitmore (68)

Oct. 17, A. R. Hawley and Augustus Post made trip from St. Louis to North Lake, Chilogoma, Canada by balloon

——, Death of Mrs. Julia Ward Howe (91) author of the "Battle Hymn of the Republic" at Newport, Rhode Island, and of William Vaughan Moody (41) poet and playwright

Oct. 20, Death of David B. Hill (67) former Senator and Governor, at Albany, New York

Oct. 24, The Secretary of the Interior ordered sale at auction of 1,650,000 acres of Indian lands in Oklahoma

Oct. 25, Permanent Court of Arbitration at The Hague awarded the United States $48,867 in Orinoco Steamship Company case in controversy with Venezuela

Nov. 1–12, Strike of expressmen, New York City, company granted demands as to wages and hours but not recognition of union

Nov. 5, Death of Lyman C. Smith, type manufacturer, New York City

Nov. 8, Constitutional Amendment adopted by popular vote in Washington granted suffrage to women; woman suffrage rejected in Oregon, Oklahoma, and South Dakota. 225 Democrats were elected to Congress, 165 Republicans, and 1 Socialist, the first to be elected to any Congress, Victor L. Berger, of Milwaukee, Wisconsin

Nov. 14, Eugene Ely in Curtiss plane with undergear of wheels took off the deck of the armored cruiser "Birmingham" at Hampton Roads, Virginia

——, Death of John La Farge (75) artist, at Providence, Rhode Island

Nov. 27, Pennsylvania Railroad began train service through tunnels completed under the Hudson River into New York City

Nov. 28, United States Attorney Wise entered suit in New York City for dissolution of the sugar trust

Nov. 30, Dr. Frederick Cook in his "own story" admitted that he was not absolutely sure that he had reached the North Pole

Dec. 3 and 8, Convention with Great Britain signed as to exemption of commercial traveler's samples from inspection of customs

Dec. 3, Death of Mrs. Mary Baker Eddy (89) founder of the Christian Science Church, at Newton, Mass.

Dec. 5, Strike of taxi drivers in New York City ended

——, Immigration Commission submitted Report, result of labor of 3 years. Recommended restriction of immigration of unskilled labor

Dec. 7, Death of George N. Johnstone (78), Confederate brigadier general

Dec. 8, Death of James Huff Stout (62), educator and philanthropist in Wisconsin

Dec. 10, Death of Henry Guy Carleton (64), playwright

Dec. 12, Edward Douglas White appointed and confirmed Chief Justice of the Supreme Court

Dec. 14, Andrew Carnegie established the Carnegie Peace Fund endowed with $10,000,000 to "hasten the abolition of international war"

Dec. 21, Trainmen and conductors on 50 railroads operating west of Chicago received a flat increase wage of 10% after negotiations which averted strike

Dec. 24, American Sugar Refining Company agreed to refund drawbacks to Government amounting to $700,000

Dec. 26, Arch Hoxsey, of Illinois, made world record altitude flight, his barograph registering 11,474

Dec. 27, Civil suit at Chicago against beef trust dismissed at request of Government

Dec. 28, Death of Ben Pitman (68) lecturer and writer on phonography

Dec. 31, Arch Hoxsey killed by fall from his airship in flight at Los Angeles, and John B. Moisant, aviator, in flight at New Orleans

CONGRESS

Jan. 6, Letter of Gifford Pinchot, Chief of the Forestry Service, read by Senator Dolliver, a criticism of Secretary of the Interior Ballinger because of his policy as to water power sites and coal lands; Pinchot dismissed by order of the President. See supra Jan. 7

Jan. 19, Joint Resolution to hold congressional investigation of the Dept. of the Interior signed by the President (Ballinger-Pinchot controversy)

Jan. 26, Joint Committee appointed to investigate Dept. of the Interior

Feb. 19, Enlarged Homestead Act provided for entry of 320 acres of non-mineral land designated by the Secretary of the Interior as not susceptible of successful irrigation in certain specified western States

March 19, Amendment to House rules took appointment of the Committee on Rules away from the Speaker making it elective by the House itself, and enlarging it to 10 members

March 25, Report of Liberian Commission submitted to Congress recommended aid to Liberia in reform of its finances, refunding debt, and settling boundary disputes, and suggested the United States establish naval coaling station in Liberia

March 26, Immigration Act of 1907 amended to extend

and define limitation of aliens admitted, and White Slave Act of 1907 amended

April 5, Employer's Liability Act amended as to time limits of actions

April 26, Insecticide Act passed

May 6, Act required common carriers engaged in interstate and foreign commerce to make full reports of all accidents to Interstate Commerce Commission and authorized investigation by the Commission

May 16, Mines Bureau established by Act, to take effect July 1

May 17, Commission of Fine Arts established

June 18, Mann-Elkins Act increased the jurisdiction of Interstate Commerce Commission to include terminals, telegraph, telephone, and cable service, and to suspend changes in rates. A new Federal Court of Commerce established to determine appeals arising from the orders of the Commission

June 20, Enabling Act for people of New Mexico and Arizona to form governments and frame constitutions

June 22, Act provided for agricultural entries on coal lands

June 24, Act required apparatus and operators for radio communication on certain steamers on the Great Lakes and on ocean steamers

June 25, Act established Postal Savings Bank system

——, Contract system of surveying public lands abolished and the Secretary of the Interior authorized to select competent surveyors

——, The President authorized to withdraw from entry public lands to reserve them for power sites, irrigation works, &c.

——, Publicity of Campaign Contributions Act made for purpose of influencing elections for representatives of Congress

——, Repeal of Act of June 17, 1901, and appropriation of $20,000,000 to complete works of irrigation begun

——, Employer's Liability and Workmen's Compensation Commission appointed by Joint Resolution

——, Bankruptcy and White Slave Acts amended

——, Congress adjourned

Dec. 5, Sixty-first Congress, 3d sess. convened

Dec. 7, Joint Committee of Investigation exonerated Secretary Ballinger but indirectly condemned his policy as to coal lands by recommendation that such lands should be held by the Government and leased for limited periods. The minority reported against Secretary Ballinger. See supra Sept. 9

Dec. 21, Senate Committee reported that charges of bribery against Senator Lorimer had not been sustained

1911

Jan. 3, First postal savings banks established in 48 selected post offices in every State and Territory

——, Supreme Court decision that it lacked jurisdiction in Panama libel suit

Jan. 4, Death of Stephen B. Elkins (70)

——, Government brought suit under Sherman Act to dissolve Atlantic steamship combination

——, Bethlehem Steel Company and the Lehigh and Reading railroads fined $40,000 each in United States District Court for rebating

Jan. 5, The Grand Jury returned 22 indictments for murder in connection with the bombing of the Los Angeles Times building

Jan. 7, New York State Banking Dept. closed the Carnegie Trust Company, New York City

Jan. 9, Reargument of suit against tobacco trust begun in Supreme Court

Jan. 9–12 and 13–14, Agreement with Great Britain as to North Atlantic Coast Fisheries

Jan. 10, Agreement with Honduras for loan

Jan. 11–18, Meeting of International Joint Commission of Canada and the United States provided for in Convention of Jan. 1909 met in Washington to discuss regulation of the draught of water from Lake Champlain to supply a Canadian canal connecting the Lake with the St. Lawrence River and the construction of a dam across the Long Sault of the St. Lawrence

Jan. 14, 12,000 striking garment workers in Chicago returned to work pending arbitration

Jan. 15, Death of former Congressman C. J. Erdman

Jan. 19, Death of Paul Morton, former Secretary of the Navy

Jan. 20, Andrew Carnegie gave $10,000,000 to Carnegie Institution in Washington increasing endowment to $25,000,000

Jan. 21, Commercial Reciprocity Agreement with Canada by exchange of Notes on basis of exchange of Canadian food stuffs for American manufactured goods, free trade as to grain, vegetables, eggs, cattle, fish, &c., and reduction of duties on flour, meats, and manufactured goods; failed of ratification in Canada

——, National Progressive Republican League organized by insurgent Republicans with Jonathan Bourne, of Oregon, as president, with program of reform which included direct election of United States Senators, direct primaries, initiative, referendum, and recall to be incorporated in the constitutions of the States, direct election of delegates to national conventions, and the passage of corrupt practices laws

——, Constitution of New Mexico ratified by popular vote

Jan. 24, Death of David Graham Philips (43) novelist

Jan. 25, Cavalry sent to frontier to preserve neutrality in Mexican revolt

Jan. 28, Death of Mrs. Elizabeth Stuart Phelps Ward (66) author

Jan. 31, California Anti-Racing Gambling Track Bill signed by the Governor

Feb. 1, Death of Rear Admiral Charles S. Sperry (63)

Feb. 3, President Taft offered services to assist in restoration of peace in Honduras

——, Garment worker's strike in Chicago ended in submission of workers

Feb. 4, Death of Owen Kildare (46) author

Feb. 6, Death of James B. Weaver at Des Moines, Iowa

Feb. 7, Fur Seals Convention with Great Britain signed for protection of seals in the North Pacific

Feb. 9, Constitution ratified by vote of people of Arizona

——, Oklahoma City declared the permanent capital of Oklahoma

——, Arrival of Count Apponyi of Hungary on official visit

Feb. 10, Death of Dr. Edward G. Janeway (70) New York City

Feb. 11, Death of Archbishop Patrick J. Ryan (79) at Philadelphia

Feb. 12, Death of General Alexander S. Webb, former president of College of the City of New York

Feb. 13, W. Morgan Shuster appointed Treasurer General of Persia to reorganize the finances

Feb. 15, First public session of the new Commerce Court at Washington

Feb. 16, Death of Mrs. Alice Morse Earle (57) author

Feb. 18, Death of the Rev. Amory Howe Bradford (64) writer and clergyman, New Jersey

Feb. 21, Treaty of commerce and navigation with Japan signed replacing that of 1854. Appended to Treaty a declaration that the Government of Japan was "fully prepared to maintain with equal effectiveness the limitation and control which they have for the past three years exercised in regulation of the emigration of laborers to the United States"

Feb. 23, Secretary of State Knox left Key West on visit to Latin American Republics on the Caribbean Sea

Feb. 26, Death of Sam Walter Foss (53) poet, Somerville, Mass.

March 1, Western Union Telegraph Company began night letter system

——, Death of John M. Carrère (52) architect, New York City

March 7, Twenty thousand troops and 15 warships ordered to points near Mexican frontiers

——, Resignation of Secretary of the Interior Ballinger accepted by the President, Walter Lowrie Fish, of Illinois, appointed

——, Death of Rear Admiral John C. French (61)

March 9, Strike of white firemen of the Cincinnati, New Orleans, and Texas Pacific Railroad against employment of negroes

March 13, Supreme Court decision affirmed constitutionality of the corporation tax

March 17, Death of Rear Admiral George Wallace Melville (72) at Batavia, New York

March 18, Roosevelt Dam at Phœnix, Arizona, opened by Theodore Roosevelt

——, About 5,000 miners in eastern Ohio went on strike in sympathy with strikers in Tuscarawas district begun in April 1910

March 21 and 24, Claims Convention with Nicaragua signed

March 25, 145 lives lost in fire in Triangle Shirt-Waist Company in New York City due to inadequate means of escape, chiefly girls; the proprietors indicted for manslaughter April 11, but acquitted Dec. 7

March 27, Death of George Hall Baker, former librarian of Columbia University

March 29, Death of Sir Caspar Purdon Clarke, former head of Metropolitan Museum of Art, New York City

March 31, Death of Otto Ringling, circus owner

April 1, Death of Dr. Seaman A. Knapp (78) of the Dept. of Agriculture

April 3, Supreme Court decision that under the "commodities clause" of the Hepburn Act the railroads must be actually independent of the coal companies

April 4, California adopted local option

April 6, Death of Craig Lippincott (64) publisher, Philadelphia

April 10, United States Court of Appeals reversed decision of lower court in Danbury hatter's case against union for boycott assessing $232,000 damages

——, Death of Tom L. Johnson (57) Mayor of Cleveland, Ohio

April 13, 17, and May 8, American citizens at Douglas, Arizona and El Paso, Texas, killed by wild bullets fired in battles of Mexican revolution near the border

April 13, Death of William Keith (72) artist, California

April 14, Death of Denman Thompson (77) actor, and

of George Cary Eggleston (72) author, in New York

April 14–May 2, Strike of pearl button makers at Muscatine, Iowa

April 15, The United States participated in Chinese loan concluded at Peking by international banking group

April 18, Extradition Treaty with Salvador signed

April 19, The completed part of Cathedral of St. John the Divine in New York City consecrated

——, Strike of 6,000 furniture workers at Grand Rapids, Michigan

April 22, James B. and John McNamara and Ortie M. McManigal arrested in Indianapolis charged with dynamiting the Los Angeles *Times* building in Oct. 1910; 21 indictments made against them May 4

April 24, Dr. Elmer E. Brown chosen Chancellor of New York University

April 30, Conference of Progressive Republicans decided that Senator Robert La Follette should be nominated for President by the Party

May 1, Supreme Court decision that the Federal Government controlled the forest reserves not the States

——, Strike of shopmen of the Pennsylvania Railroad between Pittsburgh and Altoona for recognition of union, of 9,000 machinists of New York and New Jersey railroads for eight hour day, of carpenters in Los Angeles for daily wage of $4, and of building and metal trades and brick making industries in Chicago

May 6, Agreement with Nicaragua as to customs control and loans

May 8, First direct telephone conversation held between New York City and Denver, 2,000 miles

May 9, New York Clearing House admitted trust companies to membership to take effect June 12

——, Death of Thomas Wentworth Higginson (87) author and soldier, at Cambridge, Mass.

May 15, Supreme Court decision confirmed decree of Circuit Court against the Standard Oil Company of New Jersey as a monopoly and combination in restraint of trade and ordered its dissolution, suit begun Nov. 1906

——, Supreme Court decision set aside sentence of imprisonment imposed on Samuel Gompers, John Mitchell, and Frank Morrison, of American Federation of Labor, imposed by District of Columbia Court

——, International Seal Conference at Washington opened

May 16, Henry L. Stimson, of New York, appointed Secretary of War

May 17, German-American conference on potash questions reached agreement

May 19, The Government brought suit against the lumber trust in the eastern States as a combination in restraint of trade

May 20, Thirty million dollar loan to China for construction of railroads signed by American, British, French, and German bankers

May 23, New York Public Library Building dedicated by President Taft, Governor Dix, Mayor Gaynor, and others

May 26, Announcement that Russia had promised better treatment for Jewish travelers from the United States

——, Proclamation extended copyright benefits to Sweden

May 29, Supreme Court decision dissolved the American Tobacco Company as an illegal combination in restraint of trade

June 2, International Convention as to industrial property signed by the United States

June 6, Commercial Protectorate over Nicaragua established by Treaty, and loan to Nicaragua to be secured by customs; not ratified by United States Senate

June 10, Naturalization Treaty with Costa Rica signed

June 12, The Baldwin Locomotive Works employing 12,000 men shut down because of strike

June 17, Naturalization Treaty with Nicaragua signed

June 19, Recognition of Portuguese Government

June 21, Supreme Court decision ordered dissolution of the Du Pont de Nemours Company as a combination in restraint of trade

June 24, Decision of Circuit Court at St. Louis that Union Pacific-Southern Pacific merger not a combination in restraint of trade

June 26, United States Commissioner of the Land Office declared Cunningham claims involving 5,250 acres of coal lands in Alaska invalid

June 29, Proclamations of the President set apart Selway National Forest, St. Joe National Forest, Idaho and Durango National Forest, Colorado, and opened Pine Ridge and Rosebud reservations in South Dakota to settlers

June 30, Flight of Harry N. Atwood from Boston to Washington

July 1, Interstate Commerce Commission ordered investigation of express companies engaged in interstate business

July 4, Death of Kester Vaughan (41) novelist

——, First Workmen's Compensation Act became effective in State of New Jersey

July 5, Award of George V as arbitrator in dispute between the United States and Chile in Alsop claim in favor of the United States

——, Note of the United States, Great Britain, France, Germany, and Italy to Haiti insisted claims of citizens of respective countries must be settled within 3 months

——, Strike of coal miners in Westmoreland County, Pennsylvania, ended with submission of strikers and no gains after 16 months

July 7, Fur Seals Convention signed with Great Britain, Russia, and Japan prohibited pelagic sealing on the high seas and arranged for apportionment of the legitimate catch

July 12, The Attorney General recommended dismissal of Dr. H. H. Wiley head of the Bureau of Chemistry in the Dept. of Agriculture for alleged violation of law

July 17, Government suit begun against Philadelphia and Reading to dissociate it from coal companies it controlled

July 18, United States gunboat sent to Haiti to protect American interests

July 22, Prohibition defeated in Texas by majority of 6,000 out of 462,000 votes

July 29, Austrian Premier announced opposition to importation of American meats

Aug. 1, Death of Edwin Austin Abbey (59) painter, in London, England

Aug. 4, Government suit to dissolve soft coal companies begun in Circuit Court at Columbus, Ohio

Aug. 14–25, Flight of Harry N. Atwood from St. Louis to New York City established new world record for distance flight

Aug. 17, Death of Mrs. Myrtle Read McCullough (37) author, at Chicago

Aug. 20, Death of Gamaliel Bradford (80) author

Sept. 1, Announcement of Standard Oil Company of New Jersey that shares of 33 subsidiary corporations would be distributed to them pro rata by Dec. 1

Sept. 11, The "Hai Chi" first Chinese cruiser to enter New York harbor

Sept. 14, Refined sugar quoted at 7¼ cents per pound wholesale in New York City as compared with 4³/₅ cents in Feb.

Sept. 15, President Taft exonerated Chief Chemist Wiley of charges against him. *See infra* Congress July 14

Sept. 16, Strike of 1,200 firemen and laborers on Lackawana Railroad for increase in wages and better conditions

Sept. 17–Nov. 5, First transcontinental flight of Calbraith B. Rodgers from New York to Pasadena, California, in 49 days in 68 hops, total flying time 82 hours, distance 3,390 miles

Sept. 21, Death of Dr. James C. Hepburn (96) first medical missionary to Japan

Sept. 23, Death of Charles Battell Loomis (50) author, at Hartford, Conn.

——, Strike of 1,500 shopmen of Missouri, Kansas, and Texas railroads for increase in wages and recognition of the union

Sept. 30, Strike of 18,000 railroad shopmen of the Illinois Central Railroad and Harriman lines

Oct. 2, Death of Rear Admiral W. S. Schley (72)

Oct. 7, Firemen of Georgia and Florida railroads returned to work after 10 weeks strike for 50% of pay of engineers which was granted

Oct. 9, Death of Cornelius N. Bliss (78) former Secretary of the Interior

Oct. 10, California adopted woman suffrage

Oct. 14, Death of John M. Harlan, associate justice of the Supreme Court

Oct. 16, Conference of Progressive Republicans met in Chicago and adopted declaration of principles. Senator Robert M. La Follette declared to be the "logical Republican candidate for President of the United States"

Oct. 17, Strike of shoe cutters at Lynn, Mass. for eight hour day

Oct. 19, Strike of carmen of the Schenectady Railway Company

Oct. 26, Suit of the United States to dissolve the United States Steel Corporation brought in Circuit Court at Trenton, New Jersey

Oct. 29, Death of Joseph Pulitzer (64) journalist and proprietor of the New York *World*

Nov. 1, Mobilization of the Atlantic fleet at New York City and the Pacific fleet at San Diego, California, 98 war vessels assembled in the Hudson River including 4 dreadnoughts and 20 battleships, and 26 vessels on the Pacific

——, American Steel and Wire Company indicted July 1 under Sherman Act paid fine of $128,720

Nov. 2, Death of Kyrle Bellew, actor

Nov. 5–20, Strike of drivers of the New York City Cleaning Dept. against night work

Nov. 8, Constitutional Amendment for prohibition defeated in Missouri leaving the State under local option

——, Strike of telegraphers on the Southern Railroad and the Baltimore and Ohio settled

Nov. 10, Andrew Carnegie gave $25,000,000 to the Carnegie Corporation to take over and carry on his own philanthropic work

Nov. 14, Missouri Supreme Court fined the International Harvester Company $50,000 and forbade it to do business in the State

Nov. 24, Death of John F. Dryden, founder and president of the Prudential Insurance Company of America

Nov. 30, The Standard Oil Company of New Jersey passed out of existence as decreed by Supreme Court, each subsidiary company assuming control of its own affairs

Dec. 1, The MacNamara brothers pleaded guilty to attempt to wreck the Los Angeles *Times* building by a bomb, and Dec. 5, James B. MacNamara received life sentence, and John J. MacNamara a sentence of 15 years for complicity in that and other dynamiting outrages

Dec. 8, National Drainage Association organized at Chicago to promote drainage and reclamation of lands

Dec. 11, Death of Thomas Ball (92) sculptor

Dec. 19, Death of John Bigelow (94) author, diplomat, and lawyer

Dec. 28, Death of Ben Pitmann, Anglo-American stenographer, at Cincinnati, Ohio

CONGRESS

Jan. 12, Message of the President asked for appropriation of $5,000,000 to begin work for fortification of the Panama Canal

——, Constitutional Amendment for popular election of United States Senators passed by Senate

Feb. 15, Act provided for quadrennial elections for members of the Philippine Assembly and for resident commissioners to the United States

Feb. 17, Provision made for purchase or erection of embassy, legation, and consular buildings abroad, and Railroad Locomotive Inspection and Boiler Inspection laws enacted

Feb. 18, Lands in 11 townships of Red Lake Indian Reservation in Minnesota opened for homesteads

Feb. 24, The Senate ratified the new Treaty with Japan of Feb. 21 with the understanding that it "shall not be deemed to repeal or affect any of the provisions of the Act of Congress entitled 'An Act to Regulate the Immigration of Aliens into the United States'" of Feb. 20, 1907

March 1, Act provided for purchase of land for forest reserves in the eastern States in order to protect watersheds of navigable rivers

——, The Senate by vote of 46 to 40 decided against unseating of Senator Lorimer on charge of bribery

March 2, Act prohibited the use of future issues of bonds of Panama Canal as security for national bank notes

March 3, Federal Judicial Code amended and revised to take effect Jan. 1, 1912

——, Act to prevent disclosure of national defense secrets passed

March 4, Thanks of Congress extended to Robert E. Peary retired with rank of rear admiral

——, Clause in Appropriation Act provided for fortifications in Panama Canal Zone

——, Act provided for entry under bond of exhibits of arts, science, and industries

——, Marine Schools established

March 4, Congress adjourned

April 4, Sixty-Second Congress, 1st (extra) sess. convened

June 1, New Senate Committee appointed to investigate charges against Senator Lorimer

July 14, Congressional investigation of charges against Dr. H. W. Wiley, Chief Chemist, ordered, that an expert in his department had received recompense exceeding the legal rate

July 26, Canadian Reciprocity Act provided for free trade between United States and Canada in grain, vegetables, domestic animals, fish, and other food products, and lowered duties on certain manufactured articles and meat, flour, &c. Rejected by Canada

Aug. 8, Apportionment of representatives according to 13th Census fixed members of House at 433

Aug. 15, President Taft vetoed Resolution admitting Arizona and New Mexico because of certain provisions of their constitutions

Aug. 17, President Taft vetoed Revision of Schedule K (wool) of the Payne-Aldrich Tariff passed by combination of Democrats and Republican insurgents

Aug. 19, President Taft vetoed Farmer's Free List Bill

——, Publicity of Contributions Act as to elections of members of Congress amended, its application extended, and expenditure limited

Aug. 21, Joint Resolution for admission under certain conditions of Arizona and New Mexico signed by the President

Aug. 22, President Taft vetoed the Cotton Bill

——, Congress adjourned

Dec. 4, Sixty-Second Congress, 2d sess. convened

Dec. 21, Russian Treaty of Commerce of 1832 abrogated as protest against treatment of American Jews in Russia to take effect Jan. 1, 1913, Joint Resolution, ratifying abrogation by President Taft on the 17th

1912

Jan. 2, Request of 5 European countries for free entry of wood pulp, print paper, and paper board refused

Jan. 3, Death of Rear Admiral Robley D. Evans (64)

Jan. 6, New Mexico (47th State) admitted by proclamation of the President, W. C. McDonald inaugurated as first Governor on the 15th

——, 25,000 operatives of cotton mills in Lawrence, Massachusetts, went on strike because of reduction of wages

Jan. 15, Supreme Court decision upheld the constitutionality of the Employer's Liability Act of 1908

——, Militia ordered to Lawrence to suppress rioting of strikers

——, U.S.S. "Maryland" ordered to Ecuador to protect American interests

Jan. 16, Cuba warned by President Taft that continuance of political strife will lead to intervention by the United States

Jan. 17, International Sanitary Convention signed by the United States

——, Death of Brigadier William Smith (80), late Paymaster General

Jan. 19, American troops landed in China to protect railroad connecting Tientsin and Peking

——, Government brought suit against Erie Railroad for keeping firemen on duty more than 16 hours

Jan. 23, The Standard Oil Company of New York fined $55,000 by Federal Court for accepting rebates

Jan. 23, International Opium and Drugs Convention signed by the United States

Jan. 30, Copyright Treaty with Austria-Hungary signed

Feb. 5, Four battalions of troops sent to Mexican border by order of President Taft

Feb. 9, United States marines landed at Honduras to protect American property

Feb. 10, Meeting in Chicago of 7 Republican Governors and 70 other Republican leaders representing 24 States to forward nomination of Theodore Roosevelt for the presidency

Feb. 14, Arizona (48th State) admitted by proclamation of the President

Feb. 15, Major General F. C. Ainsworth acting in opposition to the policy of the War Dept. removed from office of adjutant-general by order of the President for insubordination

Feb. 23–April 23, Secretary of State Knox made official visit to Latin American Republics bordering on the Caribbean Sea

Feb. 24, Letter of Roosevelt announced candidacy for a third term as President leading the insurgent Republicans against Taft

——, Additional troops sent to El Paso, Texas for protection of American border

Feb. 29, The Dept. of State notified President Madero, of Mexico, that export of military supplies to the insurgents could not be prohibited under existing laws. *See infra* Congress March 14

March 2, Proclamation of the President warned Americans to observe neutrality laws and abstain from taking any part in Mexican disturbances

March 12, Suit begun by Federal Government in New York City against the sugar trust

March 14, The Dept. of Justice began suit for dissolution of the Southern Pacific and Union Pacific merger

——, Proclamation of the President prohibited exportation of war material to Mexico

——, A band of Virginia mountaineers "shot up" the court at Hillsville, Va. killing the judge and other officials in attempt to rescue prisoner

——, Textile workers at Lowell, Massachusetts, accepted terms offered by operators ending strike, wages increased

March 16, The hulk of the battleship "Maine" towed from Havana Harbor and sunk 3 miles out at sea with ceremonies

March 17, Death of Rear Admiral George W. Melville (72) arctic explorer and former Engineer-in-Chief of the Navy

March 18, General wage advance in cotton mills of Rhode Island, Maine, and Massachusetts

March 21, Death of Professor Ralph S. Tarr (48) geographer and explorer

March 23, Funeral services at National Cemetery, Arlington, and interment of 59 bodies removed from the battleship "Maine"

——, Legislature of Maine rejected local option Amendment to Constitution

——, Floods in the Mississippi Valley began which devastated 200 square miles with property damages of $50,000,000 between Cairo and the Gulf

March 24, Interstate Commerce Commission established principle that freight rates between equidistant points must be the same regardless of State lines

March 26, Ten officials of Swift and Company, Armour and Company, and Morris and Company, packers, acquitted by court in beef trust investigation

March 28, New Bedford cotton manufacturers agreed on 10% wage increase

March 29, Demands of bituminous coal miners settled by compromise agreement, slight advance in wages for day labor, and general advance of 5 cents a ton on screened lump coal

March 31, Jury disagreed and were discharged in case of the United States against the American Sugar Refining Company

——, Strike of anthracite coal miners begun

April 4, Death of Dr. Isaac K. Funk (72) editor and publisher

April 7, Socialist Labor Party Convention in New York City nominated Arthur E. Reimer for President and August Gillhaus for Vice-President

April 10, Ira Remsen resigned as president of Johns Hopkins University

April 12, Death of Clara Barton (90) organizer of the American Red Cross Society, and of Major General Frederick Dent Grant (62)

April 14, The White Star liner "Titanic" struck an iceburg at 11.40 Sunday night on first trip from Liverpool bound for New York and sunk less than 3 hours later with loss of 1,635 persons out of 2,340 including John Jacob Astor, Major Archibald Butt, Jacques Futrelle, Francis D. Millet, Benjamin Guggenheim, Henry B. Harris, Charles M. Hays, John B. Thayer, George D. Widener, and Isidor Straus and his wife

——, Mexican Government and insurgent forces warned to respect the lives and property of American citizens

April 15, At 4 A.M. the Cunard liner "Carpathia" reached the scene of the disaster and picked up 20 boatloads of survivors of the "Titanic"

April 17, Miss Julia Lathrop appointed head of the new Children's Bureau by President Taft

April 18, The "Carpathia" commanded by Captain Rostrom arrived in New York with 705 survivors of the "Titanic"

April 19, Strike of coal miners begun in the Kanawha district, West Virginia, after failure of negotiations

April 22, Locomotive engineers of eastern railroads accepted offer of mediation of Commissioner of Labor Neill, and the railroads the day following

April 29, Government suit against the International Harvester Company begun under the Sherman Act in District Court of Minnesota

May 1, Compromise settlement made by union operators in West Virginia with coal miners except those on Paint Creek, and work resumed

May 2, Strike of pressmen of Chicago newspapers

May 11, Dr. John Grier Hibben installed as president of Princeton University

May 12–18, Socialist Party Convention at Indianapolis, Indiana, nominated Eugene V. Debs for President and Emil Seidel, former Mayor of Milwaukee, as Vice-President on the 17th

May 17, Dr. Alexander Meiklejohn elected president of Amherst College

May 18, Government suit begun in New York to break up alleged coffee trust

May 20, Anthracite Coal Agreement signed continued award with modifications for 4 years, 10% increase in wages allowed

May 23, Two battalions of marines sent to Cuba to protect American interests

May 24, Government suit against alleged wall paper trust in Chicago resulted in acquittal of defendants

May 29, Mine guards attacked by miners at Mucklow, West Virginia, in Paint Creek district, beginning of many conflicts

May 30, Death of Wilbur Wright (45) pioneer aviator and aëroplane builder

May 31–June 25, Strike of 5,000 waiters in New York City

June 1, Ohio Constitutional Convention which began sessions Jan. 9 adjourned after adoption of 41 Amendments

——, Death of Daniel Hudson Burnham (66) architect in Germany

June 3, Death of Mrs. Mary Elizabeth Sangster (74) author and editor

——, Visiting German warships welcomed by the President at Hampton Roads, Virginia

June 9–July 29, Strike of employees of Boston elevated railroads on question of organization of unions successful

June 13, United States Circuit Court at Wilmington, Delaware, ordered dissolution of powder trust

June 18, Republican National Convention met in Chicago and on the 22d nominated President Taft and Vice-President Sherman for a second term, Taft receiving 561 votes, Roosevelt 107, Senator La Follette 41, Senator Cummins 17, Charles E. Hughes 2, with 344 delegates not voting

June 22, Roosevelt followers met and invited Roosevelt to head a third party, and adopted resolutions declaring that the nomination of Taft had been accomplished by a fraud. The next day a committee to lead in future action was appointed

June 24, Supreme Court of the District of Columbia reaffirmed sentences of Samuel Gompers, John Mitchell, and Frank Morrison to various terms of imprisonment for contempt of court in the Bucks Stove and Range case

June 25–July 3, Democratic National Convention met in Baltimore. On the first ballot on the 28th Speaker Champ Clark received 440½ votes, Woodrow Wilson 324, Judson Harmon 148, Congressman Underwood, of Alabama, 117½, and scattering vote of 56 for Baldwin, Sulzer, and Bryan. On the 14th ballot W. J. Bryan announced that he would transfer his vote from Clark who had the majority to Wilson. On the 46th ballot July 2 Woodrow Wilson was nominated for President receiving 990 votes to Clark's 84 and Harmon's 12, afterward vote made unanimous. Thomas R. Marshall, of Indiana, nominated for Vice-President by acclamation July 3

July 2, The dirigible "Akron" destroyed by explosion at height of 2,000 feet over Atlantic City, New Jersey, killing Melvil Vaniman, its builder, and crew of 4

July 5, International Radiotelegraph Convention signed by the United States

July 7, Death of Mrs. Sarah Platt Decker, suffragist leader, in California

July 10–15, National Prohibition Party met at Atlantic City and nominated Eugene W. Chafin, of Arizona, for President, and Aaron S. Watkins, of Ohio, for Vice-President

July 16, Murder of Herman Rosenthal, gambler, New York City, as he was about to reveal relations of gamblers with police to the District Attorney

July 20, Convention with Great Britain signed as to North Atlantic Coast Fisheries

July 21, Death of Dr. Gerrit Smith (52) organist and composer

July 23, State militia brought to Paint Creek district in West Virginia to stop violence in coal mine strike

July 29, Lieutenant Charles Becker of the New York City police force indicted for instigation of the murder of Herman Rosenthal

July 31, Death of Dr. Maurice Howe Richardson (60) surgeon, in Boston

Aug. 3, Arrival of Admiral Togo, of Japan, on official visit

Aug. 5–7, Progressive Party Convention at Chicago of 2,000 men and women from 40 States nominated Theodore Roosevelt for President and Hiram W. Johnson, of California, for Vice-President, and adopted a platform called "A Contract with the People"

Aug. 13, Death of Dr. Horace Howard Furness (79) Shakespearean scholar, Philadelphia

Aug. 15, Death of Brigadier General Edward M. Hayes (69)

Aug. 16, Government suit begun in Federal Court in Philadelphia to dissolve alleged motion picture combination

Aug. 28, Great Britain presented Note protesting against grant of free passage through the Panama Canal of American coastwise shipping by Act of Aug. 24 as in contravention of terms of the Hay-Pauncefote Treaty

Aug. 31, The Interstate Commerce Commission suspended until Dec. 31 proposed increase of freight rates from eastern points to the Pacific coast

Sept. 2, President Taft created Naval Oil Reserve Number 1 at Elk Hills, California, to contain 38,969 acres

Sept. 3, New Constitution of Ohio ratified by popular vote, Amendment proposing woman suffrage defeated

Sept. 8, Strike of 10,000 furriers in New York City settled after 12 weeks, concessions made by employers, and joint board of sanitary control established

Sept. 9, Professor V. Stefansson arrived at Seattle after 4 years of exploration in Arctic

Sept. 13, "Cunningham claims" to Alaskan coal lands canceled by Secretary of the Interior

Sept. 18, Price of steers in Chicago stock yards reached $11 a hundred pounds

Sept. 23, Rice Institute, Houston, Texas, opened

Sept. 24, The United States intervened in Santo Domingo to restore order and protect the custom house

Sept. 27, Augusta, Georgia, placed under martial law because of serious riots of striking street car employees

Sept. 30, Strikers at Lawrence, Massachusetts, in riots during 24 hour strike

Oct. 3, California Supreme Court ruled that names of Taft electors could not be printed on the ballot as Republicans on which ballot the Progressive candidates had been given official place as winners in the Republican primary election

Oct. 8, New world record made by Uhlan, trotting horse, at Lexington, Kentucky, of a mile in 1.58

——, Death of Dr. Morris Loeb (49) chemist, New York City, and of Frank C. Bostock (50) animal trainer

Oct. 10, Nobel prize for medicine awarded to Dr. Alexis Carrel, New York

Oct. 11, United States District Court at Hartford gave verdict of $252,130 to plaintiff D. E. Loewe and Company (Danbury hatters case) in damages

Oct. 14, Theodore Roosevelt shot and seriously wounded by John Schrank, a maniac, at Milwaukee

Oct. 15, President Taft placed all remaining fourth class postmasters in the classified civil service

Oct. 16, Lieut. John H. Towers established duration record of 6 hours, 35 minutes, and 10 seconds in air in Curtiss hydro-aëroplane at Annapolis

Oct. 18, Death of Alfred Tyler Perry (54) president of Marietta College, Ohio

Oct. 24, Lieut. Charles Becker of the New York police force convicted of the murder of Herman Rosenthal July 16, and his 4 hired assassins on Nov. 19

Oct. 30, Death of Vice-President James S. Sherman (57) at Utica, New York

Nov. 4, New federal equity rules promulgated by the Supreme Court to take effect Feb. 1, 1913

——, Death of Dr. Arthur T. Cabot (60) surgeon, in Boston

Nov. 5, Presidential election. Woodrow Wilson elected President and Thomas R. Marshall, Vice-President, Democrats. The popular vote was 6,293,120 for Wilson, 4,119,582 for Roosevelt, 3,485,082 for Taft, 901,839 for Debs, 206,427 for Chafin, and 28,750 for Reimer. The electoral vote for Wilson was 435, Roosevelt receiving 88 votes and Taft 8. Woman suffrage adopted in Arizona, Kansas, and Oregon and rejected in Michigan and Wisconsin

——, American altitude record made by Harry B. Brown in flight at Staten Island carrying one passenger, 5,300 feet

Nov. 13, Proclamation of the President fixed rate of tolls for vessels using the Panama Canal

Nov. 18, Supreme Court upheld decision of Maryland Federal Court, and decreed dissolution of the Standard Sanitary Manufacturing Company et al., the bathtub trust

Nov. 24, Award of Board of Arbitration in case of locomotive engineers on eastern railroads adopted standard minimum wage and general wage increase

Nov. 30, Death of Rev. Robert Collyer (83) Unitarian clergyman, New York City

Dec. 2, Supreme Court decision that the Harriman merger of Union Pacific and Southern Pacific railroads constituted a combination in restraint of trade and dissolution ordered, reversing decision of lower court of June, 1911

——, Death of Albert K. Smiley (84) founder of the Lake Mohonk conferences, in Redlands, California

Dec. 3, President Taft created Naval Oil Reserve No. 2 near Buena Vista Hills, California, containing 29,341 acres

Dec. 5, Executive Order of the President declared land and water within the limits of the Panama Canal Zone a military reservation

Dec. 7, All skilled labor, about 20,000 persons including artisans and supervisory artisans under jurisdiction of the Navy Dept. placed in classified civil service

Dec. 9, Formal protest of Great Britain dated Nov. 14 as to discrimination against foreign vessels traveling through the Panama Canal demanded that the United States either repeal clause in Act of Aug. 24 giving free passage to American coastwise vessels or submit the matter to arbitration

Dec. 11, Warship ordered to Santo Domingo

Dec. 14, Government suit to dissolve alleged butter trust begun in District Court, Chicago

Dec. 15, Death of Whitelaw Reid (75) American Ambassador to Great Britain, in London

Dec. 16, Supreme Court decision that the Government had failed to prove existence of combination in restraint of trade of coal carrying railroads in Eastern States, but ordered dissolution of interests in control of the Temple Coal Company

Dec. 18, Death of Will Carleton (77) poet, in Brooklyn

Dec. 19, President Taft left Washington for Canal Zone arriving at Colon Dec. 24

———, Death of Brigadier General Theophilus F. Roden (74) in New York

Dec. 20, Government suit begun in District Court, Los Angeles, to compel the Southern Pacific Railroad to release oil lands in California valued at $250,000,-000 patent for which alleged to be obtained by fraud

Dec. 23, Federal Grand Jury in New York indicted President Charles S. Mellen, E. J. Chamberlain, and Alfred W. Smithers on charge of conspiracy to form combination in restraint of trade in handling of freight traffic by the New Haven and Hartford and Grand Trunk railroads

Dec. 30, Prison sentences varying from 1 year to 7 given to 33 convicted labor union officials in dynamite conspiracy trial of iron workers at Indianapolis

———, Strike of 75,000 men's garment workers begun in New York City

Dec. 31, Death of Henry Carey Baird (87) publisher, in Philadelphia

CONGRESS

Jan. 22, Congressional Committee reported exonerating Dr. Harvey W. Wiley, Chief Chemist, of charges against him

Jan. 29, Iron and steel schedule revision of tariff with estimated reduction of duties from average of 34.51% to 22.42% ad valorem passed the House

Feb. 15, Criminal Code Act amended

March 7, Act authorized that commission of ensign be given midshipmen upon graduation from Naval Academy

March 14, Joint Resolution provided that whenever in any American country conditions of domestic violence existed which were promoted by the use of arms or ammunition procured from the United States the President might by proclamation make it unlawful to export such supplies to that country except under conditions prescribed by him

March 23, Philippine Legislature authorized to provide for acquisition of citizenship. All resident Spanish subjects in 1899 and their children deemed citizens

April 1, Revised wool schedule passed House by vote of 189 to 92

April 3, $350,000 appropriated for purpose of maintaining and protecting the levees on the Mississippi River from impending floods, and an additional $300,000 appropriated April 16

April 9, Act taxed white phosphorus matches 2 cents per hundred and forbade export and import after Jan. 1, passed in interests of industrial hygiene

———, Children's Bureau created in Dept. of Commerce and Labor

April 17, Concurrent Resolution congratulated the people of China on assumption of republican form of government

April 24, Act provided for the use of the American National Red Cross in time of actual or threatened war

April 27, Congressional inquiry into "money trust" begun by Committee of House, the "Pujo Committee"

May 6, Joint Resolution made appropriation for relief of sufferers from floods in the Mississippi and Ohio River valleys

May 11, Act granted pensions to veterans of Mexican and Civil Wars of a dollar a day involving additional expenditure of $25,000,000 a year for pensions

May 15, Joint Concurrent Resolution submitted Amendment to Constitution providing for direct election of Senators by popular vote to the States for ratification

May 28, Senate Committee reported on "Titanic" disaster and offered thanks to officers and crew of the "Carpathia"

May 30, House Steel Bill passed Senate with 4 amendments, 1 repealing Canadian reciprocity

June 6, Land Act reduced the period of residence required of the homesteader from 5 to 3 years by "commutation clause" for fixed price per acre

June 17, President Taft vetoed Army Appropriation Bill which would have retired General Wood

June 19, Eight hour day extended to all labor in federal service

June 27, Report of President's Commission on Economy and Efficiency presented recommended a national budget

July 13, The Senate voted by 55 to 28 to unseat Senator William Lorimer, of Illinois, for buying votes for his election; he had occupied seat for 2 years

July 13–Jan. 13, 1913, Senate sat as Court of Impeachment in case of Judge Robert W. Archibald charged with using his position to enhance his personal fortunes

July 23, Act required radio equipment for every steamer licensed to carry 50 or more passengers

July 25, La Follette Bill revising the wool schedule passed by Senate

July 27, Bill revising sugar schedule passed Senate

July 31, Senate passed Resolution to the effect that "when any harbor or other place on the American continents was so situated that the occupation thereof for naval or military purposes might threaten the communications or safety of the United States" our government could not "without grave concern" see any non-American power take possession

Aug. 2, Bill revising cotton schedule passed House

———, Congressional Committee investigating the steel corporation presented report with recommendations of legislation for control of corporations

Aug. 3, Act established standard barrel and standard grade for apples packed in barrels

Aug. 9, President Taft vetoed compromise wool tariff schedule which had passed the House Aug. 3 and the Senate Aug. 5; passed over veto by House Aug. 13, but no action taken by Senate

Aug. 13, Act to regulate wireless telegraphy authorized the President to take over all radio stations as might be needed in case of war

Aug. 14, President Taft vetoed the steel and iron schedule which was passed over veto by House by vote of 173 to 83

Aug. 15, President Taft vetoed the Legislative, Executive, and Judicial Appropriation Bill because of provision to abolish Court of Commerce

Aug. 17, Pension Act amended, 18 independent agencies to be abolished Jan. 31, 1913, and distribution made from Pension Bureau, carried appropriation of $153,682,000

Aug. 20, Plant Quarantine Act regulated the importation of nursery and plant stocks

Aug. 23, Commission on Industrial Relations established to be appointed by the President, 3 members to be employers of labor, and 3 representatives of organized labor

——, Publicity of Campaign Contributions Act amended

Aug. 24, Act provided for opening, maintenance, protection, and operation of the Panama Canal. American coastwise shipping exempted from tolls

——, Copyright Act amended to protect motion pictures and plays

——, Act gave effect to Convention of July 7, 1911 prohibition of killing of fur seals for 5 year period at Pribilov Island

——, Post Office Appropriation Act contained clause requiring regular statement from newspapers of ownership, &c. (the newspaper publicity law) $500,-000 voted for construction of experimental parcels post and rural delivery routes

——, Act provided for creation of a legislative assembly in Alaska, territorial form of government provided for

——, Civil Service Act made many executive rules bearing on removals statutory

——, Entry into the United States of certain adulterated grains and seeds unfit for seeding purposes prohibited

——, Act provided for agricultural entries on oil and gas lands

Aug. 26, Congress adjourned

Dec. 2, Sixty-Second Congress, 3d sess. convened

Dec. 3, Impeachment proceedings against Judge Robert W. Archibald begun in Senate on 13 articles charging him with corrupt collusion with coal mine owners and railroad officials while in office as Associate Judge of Commerce Court

Dec. 12, Seat of Charles C. Bowman, of Pennsylvania, in House declared vacant because of methods of his election

1913

Jan. 1, Parcels post system went into effect throughout the country. Official estimate that 6,000,000 parcels were transmitted during the first week

——, Sumter, South Carolina, the first city in the United States to adopt the city manager plan

Jan. 1–17, Strike of street car employees in Yonkers, New York

Jan. 2, Strike of textile workers of Little Falls, New York, which began in Oct. 1912 settled with increase in wages

Jan. 3, Thomas A. Edison gave demonstration in his laboratory in Orange, New Jersey, of talking moving pictures

Jan. 14, Death of Samuel D. Coykendall (75) railroad president, in New York

Jan. 14–18, Strike of dress and waist makers in New York City settled by adoption of grievance committee and board of arbitration composed of representatives of employers and employees

Jan. 15, General Cipriano Castro, deposed President of Venezuela, refused admittance to the United States

under the immigration law, and Jan. 30 by the Dept. of Commerce and Labor to which he appealed

Jan. 17, Secretary Knox in reply to British Note of Nov. 14, 1912, stated that "no specific acts had occurred" of discrimination against foreign vessels at the Panama Canal

Jan. 27, Death of James B. Hammond (73) inventor and manufacturer of typewriters

Jan. 29–Feb. 6, Strike of employees of the American Steel and Wire Company

Jan. 30, American Hospital in Paris, France, incorporated

Jan. 31, Offer for settlement of points in dispute with Colombia refused by Colombia

Feb. 3, Delaware and Wyoming ratified the XIth Amendment to the Constitution completing ratification by the necessary 36 States

Feb. 4, National Institute of Arts and Letters incorporated

Feb. 6, United Shoe Machinery Company dissolved at Detroit in accordance with demand of the Government

Feb. 8, Convention with Nicaragua respecting construction of an interoceanic canal signed; not ratified by Senate

Feb. 9, Death of Dr. Homer Eaton (78) clergyman and publisher

Feb. 10, Sixteen persons killed in conflict of striking coal miners with sheriffs and police near Mucklow, West Virginia

Feb. 12, Suit begun by Government for dissolution of the shoe last trust

Feb. 13, Arbitration Treaty with France extended Convention of May 2, 1908

——, Twenty-nine officials of the National Cash Register Company including President J. H. Patterson found guilty of violation of the Sherman Act by Federal Court at Cincinnati, and on the 17th received prison sentences of from 3 months to a year, President Patterson sentenced to imprisonment for one year and to pay $5,000 fine

Feb. 14, Individuals and corporations of bath tub trust found guilty under Sherman law in Detroit court and fined $51,000

Feb. 15, Ex-President Castro, of Venezuela, finally permitted to enter the United States under ruling of United States District Court

——, Formal submission of proposals for settlement of points in dispute over Panama Canal by American Minister J. T. DuBoise to Colombian Minister of Foreign Affairs at Bogota; rejected by Colombia who asked for arbitration before the Hague Tribunal

Feb. 17, Death of Joaquin Miller (72) poet at Oaklands, California (originally Cincinnatus Heine Miller)

Feb. 18, Death of General George Washington Custis Lee (80) Confederate general and educator, at Ravensworth, Virginia

Feb. 19, The "Seven Sisters" anti-trust laws signed by Governor Woodrow Wilson in New Jersey

Feb. 22 and 24, Additional troops sent by the President to Galveston, Texas, for possible service in Mexico where revolution in progress

Feb. 24, Supreme Court decision upheld constitutionality of Mann White Slave Act

Feb. 25, President Elect Woodrow Wilson resigned as Governor of New Jersey to take effect March 1

Feb. 25, Treaty of commerce and navigation with Italy signed

——, Proclamation of Secretary Knox declared the Income Tax Amendment (XVIth) to the Constitution adopted and in effect which empowered Congress to "lay and collect taxes on incomes from whatever source derived"

——, Strike of silk weavers in Paterson, New Jersey, begun for increase in wages, eight hour day, better sanitary conditions, and non-introduction of the three- and four-loom system in place of the one- and two-loom. The Industrial Workers of the World assumed leadership after the strike began

Feb. 27, Great Britain replied to Note of Secretary Knox of Jan. 17 in "observations" presented by Ambassador James Bryce and asked for reference of case of tolls of Panama Canal to arbitration of Hague Tribunal

——, Death of Dr. Philip Hanson Hiss (45) bacteriologist, New York City

Feb. 28, Strike of garment workers in New York City ended, settlement reached March 1, and final agreement April 21, wages increased and hours submitted to arbitration

March 3, Order of President Taft for reorganization of customs service to go into effect July 1 under Sundry Civil Appropriation Act of Aug. 24, 1912, the number of collectors reduced from 152 to 49, salaries placed on fixed basis and many ports of entry abolished

March 4, Inauguration of President Woodrow Wilson and Vice-President Thomas R. Marshall, the first Democratic Administration since Cleveland (1893–1897)

March 5, William Jennings Bryan, of Nebraska, appointed Secretary of State; William Gibbs McAdoo, of New York, Secretary of the Treasury; Lindley M. Garrison, of New Jersey, Secretary of War; James Clark McReynolds, of Tennessee, Attorney General; Albert Sidney Burleson, of Texas, Postmaster General; Josephus Daniels, of North Carolina, Secretary of the Navy; Franklin Knight Lane, of California, Secretary of the Interior; David Franklin Houston, of Missouri, Secretary of Agriculture; William C. Redfield, of New York, Secretary of Commerce; William Bauchop Wilson, of Pennsylvania, Secretary of Labor

March 10, Hearings on arbitration of railroad firemen's dispute begun in New York

March 11, President Wilson in statement on Latin-American policy refused recognition of the Huerta Government of Mexico as based on military seizure

——, Death of Dr. John Shaw Billings (65) surgeon and librarian; succeeded as Director of the New York Public Library May 14 by Edwin H. Anderson

March 15, Trial under martial law of 48 men and one woman on charges growing out of the coal strike begun at Paint Creek Junction, West Virginia

March 18, President Wilson announced disapproval of the conditions of the proposed Six Power Loan to China and withdrawal of American bankers from participation

March 19, The first territorial legislature of Alaska inaugurated March 3 extended the suffrage to women

March 22, Death of Francis S. Black (60) former Governor of New York

March 23, Death of Samuel Judson Roberts (55) editor, Lexington, Kentucky

March 25–26, Great floods in Ohio, Indiana, and Pennsylvania cause great loss of life and property damage estimated at $50,000,000. Officers of the Public Health Service and the Army sent to district and the National Red Cross

March 26, Extradition Treaty with Paraguay signed

March 28, Death of James McCrea (65) former president of the Pennsylvania Railroad

March 29, Arbitration Treaty with Spain signed

March 31, Death of John Pierpont Morgan (75) financier, at Rome, Italy

April 2, The United States invited other Powers to join in recognition of the Chinese Republic

April 4, Baron Chinda, the Japanese Ambassador, protested against proposed California land law as an infringement of the treaty rights of Japan

April 6–11, Strike of street railway employees in Buffalo for increase in wages and recognition of union accompanied by riots and violence

April 7, Woman suffrage defeated in Michigan a second time by vote of 168,738 yeas to 264,882 nays

April 9, Death of Judge Addison Brown (83) of New York

April 15, California Assembly passed Bill to prohibit aliens from ownership of land in the State, directed against the Japanese

April 18 and 22, President Wilson protested to Governor Johnson, of California, against passage of land legislation excluding aliens from ownership

April 18, Death of Lester F. Ward (71) sociologist

April 24, Award published in arbitration of dispute of firemen representing 52 eastern railroads granted most of demands as to conditions of work, and compromise as to wages, provision made for arbitration of certain cases

April 25, Strike of coal miners in West Virginia begun April 1912 ended with ultimatum from Governor Hatfield that the "strife and dissension must end within 36 hours," terms proposed by the Governor accepted, into effect May 1

April 27, Death of Dr. Andrew Sloan Draper (64) educator, in Albany, New York

May 2, President Wilson formally recognized the Republic of China

May 3, Legislature of California passed revised measure as to ownership of land which was objected to by the Japanese and by President Wilson

May 5, The Lower House in Arizona passed Bill prohibiting aliens from owning land, and the Senate May 12

——, Court of Appeals of the District of Columbia upheld conviction of Samuel Gompers and other officials of the American Federation of Labor for contempt in the Bucks Stove and Range case but modified sentence

May 7, Order of President Wilson amended previous orders to require that no fourth class postmaster having a salary of as much as $180 a year should be given a classified status in the civil service unless he had been, or should be appointed as a result of a competitive examination

May 9, Secretary of State announced ratification of the XVIIth Amendment to the Constitution by Connecticut, the 36th

——, Ten day strike of 1,800 employees of street railways of Cincinnati begun for higher wages and recognition of union settled by submission of wages to arbitration and recognition of union

May 9, Japan made formal protest against passage of California Land Bill

May 11, Death of Francis Fisher Browne (69) editor, Chicago

May 13–17, Meeting of Claims Commission of the United States and Great Britain in Washington; adjourned to meet in Ottawa June 9–18

May 14, Rockefeller Foundation chartered in New York, work chiefly along lines of public health and medical education

May 16, Arizona Act prohibiting alien ownership of land signed by Governor Hunt

——, Death of Bishop William C. Doane (81) in Albany, New York

May 18, Death of Stephen Dudley Field (67) inventor, Stockbridge, Mass.

May 19, California Land Act signed by Governor Johnson provided that aliens not eligible to citizenship are limited to rights specifically secured by treaty thus prohibiting Japanese from ownership of agricultural land

——, Dr. David Starr Jordan resigned as president of Leland Stanford Junior University. Succeeded by Dr. John Casper Branner

May 20, Government suit to dissolve the United Shoe Machinery Company under Sherman Act begun in Boston

——, Death of Henry M. Flagler (83) financier, at West Palm Beach, Florida

May 26, President Wilson issued statement denouncing the "extraordinary exertions" of insidious lobby to procure changes in the Underwood Tariff Bill in the interests of a group of manufacturers

——, Supreme Court decision that a retailer may sell a patented article at less than price fixed by patentee

——, Death of James Heaton Baker (84) editor and historian, Minneapolis

May 28, Treaty of arbitration with Italy signed

May 29, Treaty of arbitration with Spain signed extending that of April 20, 1908

May 31, Proclamation of adoption of XVIIth Amendment to the Constitution providing for direct election of Senators by popular vote instead of by State Legislatures

——, Treaty of arbitration with Great Britain signed

June 4, Japan in second Note protested against California Land Act

June 7, The summit of Mt. McKinley, in Alaska range, first reached by Hudson Stuck, Harry P. Karstens, and Robert Tatum

——, John P. White, president of the United Mine Workers and 18 other officials indicted in Federal Court at Charleston, West Virginia, for violation of anti-trust law by controlling coal prices

June 8, Death of Dr. Charles Augustus Briggs (72) theologian, New York City

June 9, Supreme Court decision in Minnesota rate cases upheld right of States to regulate interstate traffic by fixing reasonable rates of railroad transportation within their borders. Congress might regulate such rates as against state control for the reason that intrastate rates are indirectly determined by interstate rates

June 9–18, Meeting of Claims Commission in Ottawa of Great Britain and the United States

June 10, Supreme Court decision affirmed constitutionality of law of Aug. 1912 requiring newspapers to publish statements of circulation and ownership

June 16, Supreme Court decision in railroad rate cases upheld laws of Missouri, Oregon, Arkansas, and West Virginia as to right of states to fix intrastate rates on interstate railroads

——, Arbitration Treaty with Norway signed extending Convention of April 4, 1908

——, Death of Della Fox (40) actress

June 17, Operation of the Food and Drugs Act extended to cover meat and meat products

June 18, Death of Thomas A. Janvier (64) author, New York City

June 23, Death of Rev. Edgar Gardner Murphy (44) Southern educator

June 26, Equal Suffrage Act for Illinois signed by Governor Dunne

——, Federal Commission on Industrial Relations named by the President, Frank P. Walsh, chairman; nominations confirmed by Senate Sept. 10

June 28, Arbitration Treaties with Japan, Sweden, and Portugal signed extending Conventions of 1908

June 29, Miners on Paint Creek and Cabin Creek, West Virginia, declared another strike which was settled July 15 on terms of agreement of May 1 with grant of check-off in addition

June 30, Plan for dissolution of Union Pacific-Southern Pacific merger approved by the United States District Court at Utah

July 1–5, Reunion of Union and Confederate veterans of the Civil War at Gettysburg, Pennsylvania, on 50th anniversary of the Battle of Gettysburg

July 2, Conference of leaders of the Progressive Party held at Newport, Rhode Island

——, Crocker Land expedition of Dr. Donald B. MacMillan under auspices of the American Museum of Natural History of New York, and the American Geographical Society left New York for 3 years exploration in the Arctic

——, Mayor Hunt of Cincinnati seized ice plants and operated them until the ice companies agreed to arbitrate dispute with their striking employees

July 8, Trainmen and conductors of 45 eastern railroads voted for strike for higher wages

July 9, Second International Opium Convention signed by the United States

July 14, The President held conference at the White House with representatives of the railroads and the railroad brotherhoods and Congressmen Clayton and Mann and agreement reached on amendments to the Erdman Act to avert strike of conductors and trainmen

July 15, Augustus O. Bacon, of Georgia, the first Senator to be elected by popular vote

July 23, Strike of silk workers of Paterson, New Jersey, which had lasted 5 months and affected 25,000 persons, abandoned

July 24, Strike of copper miners in Calumet district begun in which the right to organize was one of the main points of dispute. The entire Michigan Guard called out to keep order

——, Government suit against the American Telephone and Telegraph Company begun in Portland, Oregon, under the Sherman Act

July 26, Formal agreement concluded by representatives of 52 eastern railroads for arbitration of wage dispute under the Newlands Act of July 15

Aug. 1, The Pennsylvania Railroad fined $4,900 for infraction of Federal Hours of Service Act

Aug. 3, Death of Timothy D. Sullivan (60) former

Congressman, New York, and of William P. P. Long-fellow (76) architect and author, at Gloucester, Mass.

Aug. 4, Resignation of Henry Lane Wilson, Ambassador to Mexico, accepted, and John Lind, former Governor of Minnesota, appointed special envoy to Mexico by the President. He arrived in Mexico Aug. 10. *See also* Mexico

Aug. 6, John H. Mears arrived in New York City after trip around the world for the New York *Evening Sun*, breaking previous records, time 35 days, 21 hours, and 35 minutes

——, Death of Robert C. Ogden (77) merchant and philanthropist

Aug. 7, Advancement of Peace Treaty with Salvador signed

——, Colonel S. F. Cody killed in aviation accident in England

Aug. 11–26, Lind negotiations in Mexico a failure

Aug. 13, New York Assembly adopted resolution to impeach Governor William Sulzer by vote of 79 to 45 on charges of false statement of campaign receipts and expenditures in his election

Aug. 16, Death of Joseph Nelson Larned (77) librarian, Buffalo, New York

Aug. 26, Japan presented fourth Note protesting California land legislation

Sept. 1 and 23, Extradition Convention with Great Britain signed

Sept. 2, Government suit begun in Philadelphia under Sherman Act to dissolve Reading Company in control of coal mine and coal carrying railroad

Sept. 10, Death of William J. Gaynor, Mayor of New York City (62) at sea on way to Ireland

Sept. 11, Arbitration of wages of conductors and trainmen of eastern railroads begun by board under Newlands Act

Sept. 15, Convention of United Mine Workers of America held in Trinidad, Colorado, operators invited did not attend. Voted to strike Sept. 23 if demands not granted

Sept. 17, First Southern Labor Congress met at Nashville, Tennessee, affiliated with the American Federation of Labor

Sept. 18, Trial of Governor William Sulzer, of New York, on impeachment charges begun

Sept. 20, Advancement of Peace Treaty with Guatemala signed

Sept. 23, Strike of Colorado miners begun in southern part of State

Sept. 26, A tug boat successfully passed through the Gatun locks of the Panama Canal. *See also* Panama Canal, Oct.

Oct. 4, Theodore Roosevelt left New York for Brazil and Argentina on lecturing and hunting trip, and to hold conferences under auspices of Pan-American Union

Oct. 7, Death of Benjamin Altman (73) merchant, New York City, and of Francis H. Lee (77) banker, Boston

Oct. 12, Death of Timothy L. Woodruff (55) former lieutenant-governor of New York

Oct. 16, William Sulzer, Governor of New York, found guilty on 3 of the 8 articles of impeachment charged against him

Oct. 17, Governor Sulzer removed from office as Governor of New York

Oct. 18, Mrs. Emmeline Pankhurst, English suffragist, arrived in New York, and was ordered deported as an undesirable alien; order reversed by direction of President Wilson on the 20th

Oct. 22, Death of Reuben Gold Thwaites (60) historian, at Madison, Wisconsin

Oct. 27, Speech of President Wilson at Mobile, Alabama, declared that the United States would never again seek an additional foot of territory by conquest, this called the Wilsonian interpretation of the Monroe Doctrine

——, State troops sent to strike district by Governor of Colorado

Nov. 1–7, Strike of street railway employees in Indianapolis with riots and violence

Nov. 2, Resignation of President Huerta, of Mexico, formally demanded by the United States

Nov. 3, Arbitration Treaty with Switzerland signed extending Convention of Feb. 29, 1908, and Advancement of Peace Treaty with Honduras

——, Government suit to dissolve the International Harvester Company begun in St. Paul

Nov. 11, Award of Board of Arbitration of Nov. 10 published gave trainmen and conductors on eastern railroads an increase in wages averaging 7% but rejected other demands of the railroad brotherhoods

Nov. 13, 25,000 employees of the Southern Pacific Railroad between El Paso and New Orleans went on strike

Nov. 26–27, Secretary of Labor Wilson attempted mediation in strike of coal miners in Colorado

Nov. 27–29, 15,000 employees of the General Electric Company at Schenectady, New York, on strike, settled by compromise

Nov. 29, Suit of Government against American Can Company begun (tin trust)

Nov. 30, Strike of teamsters in Indianapolis begun

Dec. 1, Supreme Court decision in Kansas City Southern Railway case affirmed the power of the Interstate Commerce Commission to regulate not only rates but the internal administration of railroad companies

Dec. 3, Supreme Court decision reversed decision of lower courts and declared that agreements of publishers to fix prices on both copyrighted and uncopyrighted books illegal, a violation of the Sherman Act

Dec. 7, Death of A. Montgomery Ward (70) mail order merchant, Chicago

Dec. 10, The New York, New Haven, and Hartford Railroad suspended payment to its stockholders (21,716) after unbroken record of more than 40 years

——, Nobel peace prize awarded to Elihu Root

Dec. 17, Advancement of Peace Treaty with Nicaragua signed

Dec. 18, Advancement of Peace Treaty with the Netherlands signed, referred all disputes to a permanent international commission; proclaimed March 12, 1928

Dec. 19, Agreement of American Telephone and Telegraph Company to dispose of its holdings of stock in the Western Union Telegraph Company and reorganize in full conformity with the terms of the Sherman Act

Dec. 31, Commerce Court created by Tariff Act of 1909 abolished

CONGRESS

Jan. 7, Investigation of shipping trust begun by House Committee

Jan. 8, Trade mark Act amended

Jan. 13, Decision of Senate Court of Impeachment in case of Judge R. W. Archibald a verdict of guilty on 5 out of 13 of the articles of impeachment, and sentence of removal from office and disqualification from holding any office under the United States

Jan. 14, Bill proposing to grant independence to the Philippine Islands within 8 years introduced in House by Mr. Jones

Jan. 16, Legislative, Executive, and Judicial Appropriation Bill passed by Senate

Jan. 27, Act opened Fort Niobrara Military Reservation, Nebraska, to homestead settlement

Feb. 1, The Senate passed proposed Amendment to Constitution to limit tenure of office of the President and Vice-President to one term of 6 years by vote of 47 to 23; action postponed indefinitely by House Feb. 11

Feb. 14, Immigration Bill containing literacy test for immigrants vetoed by President Taft; passed over veto by Senate Feb. 18 by vote of 72 to 18, but failed in House on the 19th by vote of 213 to 114

Feb. 19, Pensions for veterans of the Indian Wars increased

Feb. 28, President Taft vetoed the Webb-Kenyon Bill prohibiting the illicit interstate shipment of intoxicating liquors into dry States as in violation of the Constitution, a delegation by Congress of powers of regulation of interstate commerce; passed over veto by Senate the same day

——, Pujo Committee on investigation of money trust presented report statement that concentration of credit and money existed in the control of a few leaders of finance brought about by mergers of competing banks and trust companies, stock ownership, interlocking directorates, extension of banking influence into insurance companies, railroad companies, and public utilities, syndicate financing of security issues, &c., but existence of any so-called money trust denied. Two draft bills submitted of proposed reforms

March 1, Webb-Kenyon Act divesting intoxicating liquors of interstate character in certain cases passed by House over veto and became law

——, Valuation Act made it the duty of the Interstate Commerce Commission to "investigate, ascertain and report in detail" on all property owned or used by common carriers as to cost and physical valuation, to be the basis of rate-making and reasonable profit for the railroads

March 3, Federal Eight Hour Day Act extended in application

March 4, Copyright law amended to provide for additional facts in certificates of registration

——, Dept. of Labor as an executive dept. created with membership in the Cabinet "to foster, promote, and develop the welfare of the wage earners of the United States, to improve their working conditions, and to advance their opportunities for profitable employment." The jurisdiction transferred of Children's Bureau, Bureau of Labor, to be called Bureau of Labor Statistics, and the Bureau of Immigration and Naturalization to be divided into the 2 bureaus, the Bureau of Immigration and the Bureau of Naturalization. The Dept. of Commerce and Labor to be continued as the Dept. of Commerce

——, Serums and toxins regulated by clauses of Agriculture Appropriation Act

March 4, Sundry Civil Appropriation Bill passed over veto of President by House exempted by rider attached labor unions and farmer's organizations from prosecution under the Sherman Act

——, Seamen's Bill for improvement of conditions of labor in mercantile marine received pocket veto

——, Act for protection of migrating birds passed

——, Congress adjourned

April 7, Sixty-Third Congress, 1st (special) sess. convened, to consider tariff

April 8, President Wilson appeared in person before the two Houses to deliver his message, reverting to custom abandoned since administration of John Adams

May 8, Underwood Tariff Bill passed the House by vote of 281 to 139, average rate reduced from 42% to below 30%

May 27, The Senate adopted resolution providing for investigation of the industrial situation in bituminous coal district of West Virginia

May 29, The Senate authorized inquiry on activity of tariff lobby as charged by President Wilson May 26. *See supra*

June 23, Sundry Civil Appropriation Bill vetoed by Taft signed by President

July 9, The House ordered an independent investigation of the lobby against the Tariff Bill

July 15, Newlands Arbitration Act replaced the Erdman Act of 1898. Provided for a permanent Board of Mediation and Conciliation appointed by the President to act at request of either in a railroad labor dispute as to wages, conditions of labor, &c.

Sept. 9, Underwood Tariff Bill passed the Senate by vote of 44 to 37

Sept. 18, Glass Banking and Currency Bill passed the House by vote of 285 to 85 after adoption of amendment affirming the gold standard by providing that nothing in the Act should be construed to repeal the parity provisions of Act of March 14, 1900

Sept. 30, Conference Report on Tariff Bill passed House with amendment to Senate clause imposing tax on cotton futures

——, Act authorized the President to provide method for opening lands restored from reservation or withdrawal

Oct. 2, Senate passed Conference Report on tariff receding as to tax on cotton futures

Oct. 3, Underwood Tariff Act reduced average rates from about 37% to 27%. The free list included wool, cotton, hemp, flax, agricultural implements, hides, leather, boots and shoes, wheat, flour, cattle, meats, eggs, milk and cream, coal, lumber, iron ore, and steel rails. Duty on sugar to be gradually reduced until in 1916 all sugar admitted free. Duties on woolen manufactures reduced from average of 50% to 35%. Duties were reduced on 958 articles, increased on 86 chiefly chemicals, and 307 items were left unchanged. Income tax included based on a one per cent rate on incomes over $4,000 and surtax on incomes over $20,000. Corporation tax of 1% on net incomes in excess of $5,000 retained. Tariff Board not retained

Dec. 1, Sixty-Third Congress, 2d sess. convened, the extra session merging into the regular session without recess

Dec. 9, House Report on tariff lobby presented

Dec. 10, Amendment to Constitution providing for national prohibition introduced in House by Mr.

Hobson and in Senate by Mr. Sheppard, sponsored by the Anti-Saloon League, Women's Christian Temperance Union, and other allied societies, whose representatives to number of about 3,000 representing every State in the Union marched to the Capitol steps and held public exercises before the presentation of the amendment

Dec. 19, Act granted the City of San Francisco right to draw water supply from the Hetch-Hetchy Valley, a part of the Yosemite National Park

———, Currency Bill passed by Senate

Dec. 23, Federal Reserve (Owen-Glass Currency) Act established the Federal Reserve Board and district federal reserve banks in which all national banks required to take membership

1914

Jan. 4, Death of Dr. Silas Weir Mitchell (84), Philadelphia

Jan. 5, Ford Motor Company announced profit sharing plan for employees

Jan. 6, United States Circuit Court of Appeals at Chicago confirmed sentences of 24 members of Ironworker's Union convicted of conspiracy to transport dynamite for illegal purposes, and granted new trial to 6

Jan. 8, Death of Simon B. Buckner (91) Confederate General, at Munford, Kentucky

Jan. 10, Agreement signed for dissolution of New Haven Railroad avoiding suit, announced March 21

Jan. 13, The United States Circuit Court of Appeals in New York City upheld Wright aëroplane patents as against Curtiss machine

Jan. 15, Western Federation of Miner's officials indicted for conspiracy in connection with Michigan copper strike

Jan. 16, Death of Benjamin H. Ticknor (71) publisher, Boston

Jan. 18–19, Strike on Delaware and Hudson Railroad settled by reinstatement of 2 men discharged at suggestion of Federal Board of Mediation and Conciliation

Jan. 21, Death of Edwin Ginn (76) Boston publisher and peace advocate

Jan. 22, Advancement of Peace Treaty with Bolivia signed

Jan. 27, Executive Order of the President established permanent civil government for Panama Canal Zone to take effect April 1. George W. Goethals confirmed as first Governor by Senate Feb. 4

Jan. 28, Direct wireless communication with Germany established from Sayville, Long Island

Jan. 29, Death of Samuel Billings Capen (71) merchant, in Shanghai, China

Feb. 1, Death of James Grant Wilson (81) Civil War General and author

Feb. 3, Proclamation of the President lifted embargo on export of arms to Mexico

Feb. 4, Advancement of Peace Treaty with Portugal signed

Feb. 9, Harry Post killed in collision of his aëroplane after establishing an American record for altitude flight of 12,120 feet at San Diego Bay, California

Feb. 11, Government suit to dissolve the control of the Southern Pacific Railroad over the Central Pacific

Feb. 13, Advancement of Peace Treaty with Costa Rica signed

Feb. 16, Death of Theodore Low De Vinne (85) printer and author, New York City

Feb. 22, Death of Joseph Fels (61) manufacturer, Philadelphia

Feb. 23, Supreme Court decision that Food and Drug's Act does not prohibit use of injurious substances except in quantities sufficient to affect health

Feb. 27, Expedition of Theodore Roosevelt in Brazil embarked on the Rio da Dúvida (River of Doubt) which was traced and surveyed in its entirety, most of it unexplored hitherto

March 1, Prohibition became effective in Tennessee under new law

March 3, "General" Kelly with 2,000 unemployed began march from San Francisco for Washington

March 4, Frank Tannenbaum, International Workers of the World leader, arrested with 189 of his followers for invading the churches in New York City, and March 27 Tannenbaum sentenced to imprisonment for one year

March 9, Supreme Court refused to review conviction of 24 of the Iron Workers for dynamite outrages

March 11, Additional troops sent to Mexican frontier

March 12, Death of George Westinghouse (67) engineer and inventor

March 14, Death of Bishop John Scarborough (82) at Trenton, New Jersey

———, Claims Commission, Great Britain and the United States, met in Washington

March 16, Arbitration Treaty with Costa Rica extended Convention of Jan. 13, 1909

March 18, Government suit filed against Lehigh Valley Railroad Company under Sherman Act alleging monopoly of anthracite coal industry through subsidiary companies

March 20, Death of Marie Jansen (Hattie Johnson) actress

March 21, Advancement of Peace Treaty with Venezuela signed

March 23, Death of Professor Harry Thurston Peck (57) author

April 1, Strike of coal miners begun in eastern Ohio over terms of an agreement embodying provisions of new Ohio law which required that the miners be paid on the run-of-the-mine rather than on the screen-coal basis

———, Civil government inaugurated in the Panama Canal Zone

April 4, Order of Secretary Daniels to take effect July 1 prohibited use of alcoholic liquors on naval vessels or in naval stations

April 6, Treaty with Colombia signed providing for settlement of differences and for payment of $25,000,-000 by the United States as compensation for loss of canal zone; not ratified by Senate because of expressions of regret in Treaty which was interpreted as slur on Ex-President Roosevelt

———, Strike begun in Arkansas coal mines

April 8, Suit of the Government against the Delaware, Lackawanna, and Western Railroad and Coal Company as an illegal monopoly dismissed by United States District Court at Trenton

April 9, American marines landing at wharf at Tampico, Mexico, for supplies, arrested, but released with apology after short detention. Rear Admiral Mayo demanded reparation from Mexico in form of salute to American flag

April 11, Apology of Huerta for Tampico affair ignored request for salute of American flag

April 12, Secretary Bryan insisted that Huerta comply with demand for salute of flag

April 13, President Huerta agreed to salute American flag on condition of return salute

——, Announcement of Secretary of the Western Federation of Miners of return to work of the copper miners on strike since July 1913 at Calumet, Michigan; recognition of union waived

April 14, Fourteen battleships ordered to Mexican waters

April 16, President Huerta agreed to salute of American flag, the United States to return the salute as a matter of international courtesy

——, "General" Coxey with army of unemployed began his second march to Washington from Massillon, Ohio

April 17, Advancement of Peace Treaty with Denmark signed

April 18, Ultimatum of President Wilson to President Huerta demanded unconditional salute to American flag before 6 P.M. the next day

April 19, President Huerta refused to comply with demand of President Wilson

April 20, Conflict of armed miners with militia at Ludlow, Colorado, resulted in death of 25 persons including 11 children and 2 women when soldiers set fire to striking miners' tent colony

April 21, Vera Cruz, Mexico, occupied by American marines, and custom house seized

April 22, Major General Leonard Wood succeeded as Chief of Staff of the Army by Major General William W. Wotherspoon

——, President Huerta handed Nelson O'Shaughnessy, American chargé d'affaires at Mexico City, his passports

April 23, President restored embargo on arms to Mexico

April 25, The United States accepted offer of mediation of the "A.B.C." Powers, Argentina, Brazil, and Chile, and Huerta the following day "in principle"

April 26, Admiral Fletcher placed Vera Cruz under martial law after 19 Americans killed and 70 wounded

——, Death of George F. Baer (71) president Philadelphia and Reading Railroad

April 28, President Wilson ordered federal troops to the mining district of Colorado to take the place of the militia

April 30, General Funston landed at Vera Cruz and took command establishing military government May 3

May 3, Death of Major General Daniel E. Sickles (88) in New York

May 5, Advancement of Peace Treaty with Italy signed

——, Death of John Forrest Dillon (82) lawyer, New York, and of Hiram Duryea (80) merchant

May 6, Arbitration Treaty with Austria-Hungary signed extending Convention of Jan. 15, 1909

May 9, Arbitration Treaty with the Netherlands extended Convention of May 2, 1908

May 10, Death of Mme Lillian Norton Nordica (57) singer, at Batavia, Java

May 11, Supreme Court set aside sentence imposed by Supreme Court of the District of Columbia on Samuel Gompers, John Mitchell, and Frank Morrison, officials of the American Federation of Labor, for contempt of court in alleged violation of injunctions against boycott in Bucks Stove and Range cases under statute of limitations

May 11, Death of Daniel De Leon (51) Socialist leader and editor, New York City

May 13, Arbitration Treaty with Salvador signed extending Convention of Dec. 21, 1908

May 18, Panama Canal opened for barge service

May 19, Theodore Roosevelt landed in New York City after 8 months of travel and exploration in South America

May 20–June 30, Conference opened at Niagara Falls with representatives of the United States and the Huerta Government of Mexico, and of the "A.B.C." Powers. Constitutionalists of Mexico joined the Conference in June

May 22, Charles Becker convicted a second time for instigation of the murder of Herman Rosenthal

May 25, Supreme Court decision sustained reversal of decision of Interstate Commerce Commission in tap line cases declaring the lines connecting lumber industries with railroads common carriers and entitled to freight charges

May 26, Death of Jacob A. Riis (65) author and social worker

June 3, American College in Turkey opened

June 5, Strike of 10,000 workers begun which lasted a month at Westinghouse Electric and Manufacturing Company, Pittsburgh district, under leadership of Industrial Workers of the World caused by introduction of premium and bonus system of payment, failed to accomplish its object

June 8, Supreme Court decision in Shreveport rate case ruled that federal control and orders of Interstate Commerce Commission take precedence of State control

——, American Thread Company agreed to dissolve to avoid suit under Sherman Act

June 12, Strike of West Virginia coal miners begun in Sept. 1913 ended, recognition of union waived, some other demands gained

June 13, Riots in Butte, Montana, in conflict between members of the Industrial Workers of the World and the Western Federation of Miners

——, Death of Adlai E. Stevenson (78) former Vice-President, in Chicago

June 15, Federal Reserve Board members nominated by the President

June 22, Supreme Court decision in Intermountain long and short haul rate case affirmed power of Interstate Commerce Commission to fix rates

June 24, Advancement of Peace Treaty with Norway signed

June 25, Third International Opium Convention signed by the United States

——, Silas Christofferson made flight over Mt. Whitney in the Sierras, highest summit in the United States excluding Alaska, attaining aëroplane altitude record of 15,728 feet

June 27, Treaty of commerce with Abyssinia (Ethiopia) signed

July 1, End of mediation conference at Niagara Falls, New York, without positive results

——, Order of Secretary Daniels prohibiting use of alcoholic liquors in the Navy went into effect

——, Prohibition went into effect in West Virginia

July 12, Death of Horace H. Lurton (70) associate justice of the Supreme Court

July 14, Advancement of Peace Treaty with Peru signed

July 20, Advancement of Peace Treaty with Uruguay signed

July 20, Death of James McCutcheon (72) merchant, New York City

July 23, Government suit to dissolve the New York, New Haven, and Hartford Railroad Company begun in District Court, New York

July 24, Advancement of Peace Treaties signed with Argentina, Brazil, and Chile

July 29, The Cape Cod Canal between Barnstable and Buzzards Bay formally opened reducing distance between New York and Boston by 70 miles on safer route

——, Interstate Commerce Commission granted 5% rate increase in Central Freight Association territory

July 31, New York Stock Exchange closed in financial crisis due to war in Europe, procedure unknown since 1873, and the New York and New Orleans cotton exchanges

——, Railroad Brotherhoods made announcement that strike order would go into effect Aug. 7 if railroad managers did not accept plan of settlement proposed by Board of Mediation

Aug. 3, Representatives of the Railroad Brotherhoods and of the managers of the companies signed agreement to arbitrate dispute with their firemen and engineers

Aug. 4, Proclamation of neutrality of the President based on Washington's Proclamation of April 22, 1793 and the Neutrality Act of 1794, in war between Austria-Hungary and Serbia, Germany and Russia, and Germany and France

Aug. 5, Proclamation of neutrality of the President in war of Great Britain and Germany

——, Treaty with Nicaragua signed gave the United States naval bases near the terminals of the Panama Canal on Fonseca Bay on the Pacific and on Corn Island on the Caribbean, and the perpetual right to build an interoceanic canal, $3,000,000 paid for these concessions

——, President Wilson offered mediation by the United States as a signatory of the Hague Convention to reëstablish peace in Europe

——, Censors placed in all wireless stations to enforce neutrality

Aug. 6, The U.S.S. "Tennessee" left for Europe with $6,000,000 in gold for the assistance of Americans stranded in Europe

——, Death of Mrs. Woodrow Wilson (Ellen Louise Axen Wilson) at the White House, Washington

Aug. 7, Proclamation of neutrality in war between Austria-Hungary and Russia

Aug. 10, *The Fatherland*, issued as a weekly by German-Americans in New York began publication

——, Members of Federal Reserve Board took oath of office, Charles S. Hamlin, of Boston, chairman

——, Personal message of German Emperor to President Wilson explained German entrance into war and justified Belgian invasion

——, Commission sent to Santo Domingo with plan for restoration of peace

Aug. 12, The International Harvester Company declared to be a monopoly and dissolution ordered by United States District Court at St. Paul

Aug. 13, Proclamation of neutrality in war between Great Britain and Austria-Hungary

Aug. 14, Proclamation of neutrality in war between France and Austria-Hungary

——, American marines landed at Bluefields to preserve order with consent of Nicaraguan Government

Aug. 14, Executive Order of the President established Food Administration Grain Corporation incorporated in Delaware to buy, sell, and store grain, Herbert Hoover, chairman

Aug. 15, The Panama Canal opened to traffic, the Panama Railroad steamer "Ancon" making the passage in 9 hours

——, Statement of Secretary Bryan that "loans by American bankers to any foreign nation which is at war is inconsistent with the true spirit of neutrality"

Aug. 18, Proclamation of neutrality in war between Belgium and Germany

Aug. 24, Proclamation of neutrality in war between Japan and Germany

Aug. 25, Strike of 1,500 glove cutters at Gloversville, New York

Aug. 27, Proclamation of neutrality in war between Japan and Austria-Hungary

Aug. 29, Advancement of Peace Treaty with Paraguay signed

Sept. 1, Proclamation of neutrality in war between Belgium and Austria-Hungary

——, State militia sent to Butte, Montana, and martial law declared, because of riots between rival unions of miners

Sept. 2, Convention with Panama signed defined boundaries of Panama Canal Zone and gave the United States control over the harbor waters of Colon and Ancon and certain other rights

Sept. 5, Executive Order of the President provided for government operation of all wireless stations

——, President Wilson submitted plan for settlement of Colorado strike to miners and operators; accepted by miners Sept. 15, but declined by operators Sept. 23

Sept. 15, Advancement of Peace Treaties signed with France, Great Britain, Spain, and China

——, Panama Canal closed for 4 days because of earth slide in the Culebra Cut

Sept. 19, Interstate Commerce Commission granted request of railroads for rehearing of case for increase of freight rates

Sept. 20, Advancement of Peace Treaty with Portugal signed

Sept. 22, Prohibition law enacted in Virginia to take effect Nov. 1, 1916

Sept. 24, Wireless telegraph communication with Japan became effective

Sept. 26, Federal Trade Commission established. *See infra* Congress

Sept. 28, Death of Richard Sears (50) mail order merchant, Chicago

Oct. 1, Advancement of Peace Treaty with Russia signed

——, Announcement of agreement between Great Britain and Holland by which American food stuffs may be shipped to Holland but not reshipped to Germany

——, Phenomenal cotton crop estimated on this date as 16,135,000 bales

Oct. 3, Rustem Bey, Turkish Ambassador, left the United States because of official dissatisfaction with his public criticism of American affairs, notably the treatment of Filipinos and lynching of negroes in the South

Oct. 8, Dr. Simon Flexner, of New York, announced that he had succeeded in isolating and transmitting the germ of infant paralysis

Oct. 10, Protocol with Panama signed as to neutrality of Canal Zone

Oct. 13, Advancement of Peace Treaties with Sweden and Ecuador signed

——, United States District Court at New York dismissed all but one of contentions of Government suit to dissolve Atlantic steamship combination

Oct. 15–20, Panama Canal closed by slide of earth in Culebra Cut

Oct. 17, Dissolution decree signed by the New York, New Haven, and Hartford Railroad Company, agreement of company to dispose of holdings in trolley and steamship lines, and in Boston and Maine Railroad

Oct. 18, Letter of President Wilson to Representative Underwood urged reëlection of every member of Congress "who had sustained and advanced the plans of the party," offered as substitute for speech in campaign

Oct. 19, American marines landed at Cap Haitien to preserve order during revolution

Oct. 22, Note to belligerent powers insisted on observance of existing rules of international law

——, Commission for Relief in Belgium organized in London, England, by resident Americans and English citizens

Oct. 23, Protest to Great Britain against seizure of Standard Oil Company tank steamer "Platuria" bound for neutral port

Oct. 27, American ship "Kroonland" detained at Gibraltar pending inquiry into ultimate destination of its cargo of copper, the unusually heavy shipments of copper to Italian ports believed by Great Britain to be destined for transshipment; ship ultimately released but cargo seized

Oct. 30, First shipment of food (2,500 tons) for relief of Belgium

Oct. 31, Panama Canal again closed because of earth slide in Culebra Cut

——, December wheat quoted in Chicago at $1.12¼ as compared with $.83 of previous year

Nov. 1, Death of Lieutenant General Adna R. Chaffee (72) at Los Angeles

Nov. 2, Federal Grand Jury at New York indicted 21 directors of the New York, New Haven, and Hartford Railroad for conspiracy to drive other carriers from the field

Nov. 3, Congressional election resulted in gain for Republicans reducing Democratic majority in the House from 147 to 29. Constitutional Amendments granting suffrage to women adopted in Nevada, and Montana, and prohibition in Arizona, Washington, Colorado, and Oregon

——, Federal troops sent to Fort Smith, Arkansas in coal strike to enforce order of United States District Court, ending strike

Nov. 5, Death of Henry Gannett (68) geographer, in Washington

Nov. 6, Neutrality proclaimed in war between Great Britain and Turkey

Nov. 13, Proclamation of the President of neutrality of Panama Canal Zone, and further orders as to regulations Nov. 20

Nov. 16, Cotton exchanges of New York and New Orleans reopened

——, Brigadier General Hugh L. Scott appointed Chief of Staff of Army

——, Federal Reserve System inaugurated by opening of 12 federal reserve banks

Nov. 23, American troops withdrawn from Vera Cruz, Mexico

——, Chicago stock exchange opened

Nov. 29, President Wilson named Seth Low, Charles W. Mills, and Patrick Gilday a commission to go to Colorado to adjust differences between coal miners and operators

Nov. 30, Arbitration begun of wage dispute of locomotive engineers and firemen of 98 western railroads in Chicago

Dec. 1, National Security League organized at meeting in New York City

——, Death of Rear Admiral Alfred Thayer Mahan (74) author, in Washington

Dec. 2, National Committee of the Progressive Party met in Chicago

Dec. 7, Death of Madison Julius Cawein (49) poet, at Louisville, Kentucky

Dec. 8, Troops sent to Naco, Arizona, after 52 Americans had been killed or wounded by intermittent firing across the border by Mexican revolutionists, and additional troops on the 15th

——, Colorado coal strike declared at end by United Mine Workers

Dec. 12, The New York Stock Exchange reopened for limited trading

Dec. 17, American Marines landed at Port au Prince and at request of Bank removed $500,000 to prevent seizure by the President

Dec. 18, The Interstate Commerce Commission granted the application of 125 eastern railroads for 5% increase in all freight rates except on coal and coke, and iron ore

Dec. 21, Government suit against Lehigh Valley Railroad Company under the Sherman Act dismissed by United States District Court at New York

Dec. 24, Death of John Muir (76) naturalist, in Los Angeles, and of Thomas Whitaker (73) publisher, New York City

Dec. 26, Note delivered Dec. 28 protested to Great Britain against interference with neutral shipping and trade, and policy of search

CONGRESS

Jan. 17, Acts regulated the manufacture and importation of opium, taxes increased and bond required of manufacturers

Jan. 20, Message of President Wilson recommended legislation to strengthen and supplement the Sherman Anti-Trust Act of 1890

Jan. 27, Resolution adopted by House to investigate the strikes of miners in Colorado and Michigan

Feb. 16, Act to promote efficiency of naval militia prescribed organization and authorized the President in the event of war, threat of war, or rebellion to call upon the militia, orders to be issued through governors of States

March 4, Congress adjourned

March 5, Formal request of President Wilson for repeal of the tolls exemption clause of the Canal Act of 1912

March 12, Act authorized the President to construct, maintain, and operate 1,000 miles of railroads in Alaska

March 19, The Susan B. Anthony Amendment to the Constitution providing for women suffrage failed of passage in Senate by vote of 35 to 34, with 26 members not voting, the constitutional two-thirds lacking

March 28, Copyright Act amended

April 20, Message of the President on the Tampico incident. Resolution passed by House that the President justified in use of armed force in Mexico to enforce demands made on Huerta

April 22, Bill passed in Senate providing for use of armed force in Mexico and any hostility to Mexican people or purpose to make war disclaimed

April 25, Act provided for raising volunteer forces in case of war

May 8, Smith-Lever Act provided for agricultural extension work to be carried on by coöperation between the Dept. of Agriculture and the land grant colleges

June 15, Panama Tolls Act repealed clauses exempting American vessels from payment of tolls of Act of Aug. 24, 1912

July 18, Act to increase the efficiency of the aviation service in the Army provided for an Aviation Section as a part of the Signal Corps, and additional officers and men

Aug. 3, Joint Resolution for relief, protection, and transportation of American citizens in Europe appropriated $250,000

Aug. 4, Act provided for issue of emergency currency extending time of national currency associations and National Monetary Commission of the Aldrich-Vreeland Act of 1908 due to expire

Aug. 5, Second Joint Resolution for relief of American citizens in Europe appropriated $2,500,000

Aug. 13, Reclamation Extension Act extended period of payment under reclamation projects

Aug. 15, Federal Reserve Act amended to enable state banks to continue holding reserves during months federal reserve system put into operation

Aug. 18, Ship Registry Act amended to permit foreign-built ships of American ownership to American registry for purposes of the over-seas trade

——, United States Cotton Futures Act placed tax on privilege of dealing on exchanges, boards of trade, or elsewhere in sales of cotton for future delivery in order to minimize market manipulation

Aug. 24, Bill providing for Federal licensing of warehouses for cotton, grain, and other nonperishable agricultural products passed Senate

Sept. 2, Act provided for War Risk Bureau in Treasury Dept. to underwrite insurance at a reasonable rate for American ships, crews, &c.

Sept. 26, Federal Trade Commission created to represent the Government in supervision of trusts taking over work done formerly by the Bureau of Corporations

Oct. 14, The House passed Jones Bill declaring the intention of the United States to withdraw from the Philippine Islands as soon as a stable government should be established, replacing the Commission by an elective Filipino Senate; not acted on by Senate until 1916

Oct. 15, Clayton Anti-Trust Act prohibited interlocking directorates in business, the acquisition by any corporation of the stock in another corporation where the effect may be to "substantially lessen competition" and discrimination in prices, and government by injunction. Human labor declared not to be a commodity and therefore labor and agricultural organizations not to be considered combinations in restraint of trade

Oct. 20, Act provided for leasing coal lands in Alaska under direction of the Secretary of the Interior, leases not to run for more than 50 years

Oct. 22, War Revenue Act passed to produce extra revenue of about $100,000,000 chiefly by internal taxation. Excise duties on liquors increased, license taxes imposed on bankers, brokers, theaters and other amusement enterprises, tobacco dealers and manufacturers. Stamp taxes laid on promissory notes, insurance policies, bills of lading, steamer tickets, parlor car seats, sleeping car berths, telegraph and telephone messages for 1 year

Oct. 24, Congress adjourned

Dec. 7, Sixty-Third Congress, 3d sess. convened

Dec. 17, Act imposed tax on importation, manufacture, and sale of opium in any form

Dec. 22, Resolution proposing national prohibition by constitutional amendment passed the House by 197 to 189 votes failing to secure the two-thirds vote needed for adoption

1915

Jan. 1, Prohibition went into effect in Arizona, and Idaho

Jan. 2, German reservists traveling under false passports taken from the "Bergenfjord" of the Norwegian-American line in New York Harbor

——, Strike of 900 fertilizer employees near Elizabeth, New York

Jan. 4–30, Strike of employees of chemical companies at Roosevelt, New Jersey, settled with grant of increase of wages

Jan. 5, United States Supreme Court in the Danbury hatters boycott case sustained verdict of lower court in final decision that union had been guilty of restraint of trade and must pay damages imposed of $252,130 against the 186 members of the hatter's union

Jan. 7, British preliminary reply to American Note of Dec. 26, 1914, conceded principles underlying American contentions but referred to fraudulent measures of shippers and increase in certain branches of neutral commerce supporting belief that contraband was passing into enemy countries

Jan. 10, Neutralization Pact for protection of American-Mexican border signed at Naco by Mexican General Maytorena and Colonel Calles with General Hugh L. Scott

Jan. 15, Price of wheat $1.45 a bushel, highest since 1898

Jan. 18, Incendiary fire at works of John A. Roebling's Sons Company with loss of $1,500,000, the first of many fires in plants supplying Allies

Jan. 19, Twenty rioting strikers shot by factory guards at Roosevelt, New Jersey, one killed

——, Strike of coal miners of Bache-Denman Company in Hartford Valley, Arkansas, ended with purchase of property by the United Mine Workers

——, Germany protested to the United States against sale of hydro-aëroplanes to the Allies; reply of Secretary Bryan Jan. 29 that hydro-aëroplanes not war vessels

Jan. 25, Supreme Court declared Kansas law unconstitutional which prohibited an employer from requiring that an employee should not be a member of a labor union

——, Telephone communication established between New York and San Francisco, Alexander Graham Bell talked with his assistant, Thomas W. Watson, in San Francisco in first conversation across the continent

Jan. 26, Rocky Mountain Park in Colorado established

Jan. 28, The German cruiser "Prinz Eitel Friedrich" sunk the American sailing vessel "William P. Frye" carrying a cargo of wheat to England in the South Atlantic

Feb. 2, Unsuccessful attempt of Werner Horn, a German, to blow up Canadian Pacific railroad bridge across the St. Croix River at Vanceboro, Maine

Feb. 6, State wide prohibition law for Arkansas to take effect Jan. 1, 1916, signed by the Governor

——, The "Lusitania," British Cunard steamer, arrived at Liverpool, under American flag, flown during passage through Irish Sea

Feb. 7, British Foreign Office issued memorandum justification of use of neutral flag by belligerents

——, The Lackawanna Railroad made successful test of wireless telegraph communication from moving train to station

——, British Note replied to protest regarding seizure and detention of American vessels that British policy and practice was consistent with the rules of international law

——, Note of the United States to Germany regarding attacks on American shipping warned that Germany would be held to "strict accountability" and protested war zone proclamation of Germany of Feb. 4

Feb. 10, Note of the United States to Great Britain protested against use of American flags on British vessels as "an indefensible violation of rights"

Feb. 11, The American steamer "Wilhelmina" with cargo of wheat, which had put into port of Falmouth, England, on the 9th, seized and held for British prize court, and settlement made with owners April 12

——, The Interstate Commerce Commission reversed earlier ruling in part in intermountain freight rate cases allowing higher rate for through traffic on account of opening of Panama Canal and consequent competition for railroads

Feb. 12, Death of James Creelman (55) journalist

Feb. 15, Death of Simon Brentano (56) publisher, New York City

——, German Note to the United States agreed to modify submarine policy only if England would allow shipments of food stuffs to Germany for use of civilians

Feb. 16, South Carolina passed law establishing state wide prohibition

Feb. 18, Iowa House agreed with action of Senate of Feb. 12 to repeal Mulct Act and reëstablish prohibition to take effect Jan. 1, 1916

——, Oregon enacted state wide prohibition to take effect Jan. 1, 1916

Feb. 19, British reply referred case of ships to prize courts

——, American steamer "Evelyn" with cotton consigned for Bremen sunk by German mine off Borkum Island

Feb. 20, Identical Notes sent to Germany and Great Britain proposed compromise settlement for termination of submarine warfare and blockade

Feb. 20–Dec. 4, Panama-Pacific International Exposition at San Francisco

Feb. 22, Federal Trade Commission nominated by the President, Joseph E. Davies, W. J. Harris, W. H. Parry, E. N. Hurley, and George Rublee

Feb. 23, American steamer "Carib" sunk by mine off German coast in North Sea

Feb. 23, The "easy divorce" law enacted in Nevada reducing required residence period to 6 months

Feb. 24, Rising of Piute Indians near Bluff, Utah, escaped into desert

Feb. 27, American vessel "Dacia" recently transferred from German to American ownership with cotton consigned for Bremen seized by French warship, and seizure declared valid by French prize court March 22

March 1, Federal Grand Jury in New York indicted 5 officers of the Hamburg-American line charged with swearing to false manifests to secure clearance papers for vessels sent to supply German warships on the high seas

——, State wide prohibition law enacted in Idaho to take effect Jan. 1, 1916

March 3, Colorado enacted prohibition law

March 5, Note to France and Great Britain asked for details as to scope of the blockade of Germany

March 6, Constitutional Amendments for prohibition and woman suffrage signed by Governor of Iowa to be submitted to vote of people

March 8, Supreme Court decision overruled West Virginia 2 cent a mile railroad passenger fare, and North Dakota statute fixing rate for transportation of coal

——, Price of loaf of bread which had risen to 6 cents a loaf on Feb. 10 reduced to 5 cents after public investigation

March 10, The German cruiser "Prinz Eitel Friedrich" arrived at Newport News, Virginia, and reported the sinking of the "William P. Frye" on Jan. 28, the first deliberate attack on American vessel

March 11, Central Railroad of New Jersey found guilty of rebating on 185 counts in favor of the Lehigh Coal and Navigation Company

March 13, United States Circuit Court of Appeals reversed judgment of lower court of conviction of 28 officials of the National Cash Register Company under the Sherman anti-trust law

——, Notes to China and Japan stated that the United States could not recognize any agreements impairing treaty rights, the "open door," or the integrity of China

March 14, Death of Samuel Bowles (63) editor, Springfield, Mass.

March 15, British Note transmitted copy of Order in Council of March 11 giving list of contraband and prescribing measures as to neutral merchant vessels

March 20, Outlaw Piute Indians surrendered after conference with General Scott

——, Death of Charles Francis Adams (79) publicist and historian, in Washington

March 28, British steamer "Falaba" sunk by German submarine, L. C. Thrasher, American citizen, lost his life

March 29, Agreement of American rubber interests to export only to Great Britain

March 30, New Note to Great Britain as to blockade policy refused to recognize British right to interfere with legitimate commerce of neutrals or of non-contraband goods even if their ultimate destination Germany

April 4, German Note criticized the failure of the United States to safeguard legitimate commerce with Germany and condemned as unneutral the sale and export of arms and munitions of war to the Allies, the "enormous new industry of war materials of every kind" in the United States, supplying "only Germany's enemies, a fact which is no way modified by the purely theoretical willingness to furnish Germany as well if it were possible" . . .

April 5, Demand for reparation from Germany made for sinking of the "William P. Frye," accepted by Germany subject to proof that the vessel and cargo were proved to be of American ownership

April 7, Death of F. Hopkinson Smith (76) artist, author, engineer, New York

April 9, Death of Professor Thomas R. Lounsbury (77), New Haven, Conn.

April 10, The "Prinz Eitel Friedrich" interned at Norfolk, Virginia

April 11, The German cruiser "Kronprinz Wilhelm" entered harbor of Hampton Roads, Virginia

April 13, Death of William Rockhill Nelson (74) editor, Kansas City

April 16, Strike of carpenters begun in Chicago for increase of wages

——, Death of Nelson W. Aldrich (73) former senator from Rhode Island

April 20, The Chicago, Rock Island, and Pacific Railroad went into hands of a receiver

April 21, Reply to German Note of April 4 denied that the United States had yielded any of its rights as a neutral and declared that any embargo on export of war supplies during the war would constitute an unjustifiable departure from the principles of strict neutrality

April 26, Death of John Bunny (52) motion picture actor

——, The German raider "Kronprinz Wilhelm" interned at Newport News, Virginia

April 28, German aëroplanes dropped 3 bombs on American Standard Oil tank steamer "Cushing" in the North Sea flying American flag, with name painted in large letters on the side

April 29, German Foreign Office wireless message to German Ambassador in Washington read "Warn 'Lusitania' passengers through press not voyage across the Atlantic"

April 30, Award of Board of Arbitrators in railroad dispute conceded a substantial part of the demands of the Brotherhoods but was not satisfactory to them, and signature refused

——, President Wilson created Naval Oil Reserve Number 3 near Casper, Wyoming, containing 9,481 acres, popular name the "Teapot Dome"

May 1, The American oil steamer "Gulflight" torpedoed by German submarine without warning off the Scilly Islands, 3 deaths resulting

——, Notice published in American newspapers by the German Embassy warned travelers that vessels flying the British flag were liable to destruction in the war zone

May 3, Strike of 1,700 weavers at the Borden Mill, Fall River, Mass.

May 4, Death of Gerrit Smith (76) inventor, at Amityville, New York

May 7, 114 Americans lost on the Cunard steamer "Lusitania" sunk by German submarine, including Charles Frohman, Alfred G. Vanderbilt, Charles Klein, Elbert Hubbard, Herbert S. Stone. See World War

May 8, Strike of coal miners in eastern Ohio which had lasted more than a year settled by efforts of the Governor, the operators conceding rate of payment per ton asked, and the miners agreed to certain changes in working conditions

May 13, President Wilson sent Note to Germany demanding disavowal of the sinking of the "Lusitania" and indemnity, and again warned Germany of "strict accountability" for any infringement of American rights

May 15, Decision of Interstate Commerce Commission under Panama Canal Act of Aug. 24, 1912, that railroads cannot own steamship lines on the Great Lakes

May 20, Employers in cloak and suit industry in New York City abrogated the "peace protocol" after 5 years

May 21, Dr. Frank J. Goodnow inaugurated president of Johns Hopkins University

May 25, American steamer "Nebraskan" torpedoed by German submarine off Fastnet, but succeeded in returning to Liverpool

May 26, Decision of Court of Customs Appeals granted 5% discount on imports in American bottoms and in ships of countries entitled to most-favored-nation treatment

May 28, German reply to first American Note on the "Lusitania" declared that the "Lusitania" was armed with concealed cannon and was carrying British troops and munitions of war, and gave justification of self-defense

May 30, 9 of the 10 deputies accused found guilty of manslaughter in the Roosevelt, New Jersey, strike case (See Jan. 19 supra) and sentenced June 7 to terms of imprisonment varying from 2 to 10 years

May 31, Note of British Ambassador to Secretary of State Bryan declared that the "Lusitania" was not carrying any guns and never had at any time during the war

June 1, German Note apologized for attack on American steamer "Gulflight" and offered reparation

June 2, Warning Note of the United States to leaders of warring factions in Mexico to come to an agreement or the United States would take steps to bring about order

June 3, District Court of New Jersey decision dismissed suit of Government under anti-trust law and refused to order dissolution of the United States Steel Corporation

June 7, German Note referred case of the "William P. Frye" to a prize court

June 8, Resignation of W. J. Bryan as Secretary of State tendered and accepted by the President, in disagreement with policy of the President on the "Lusitania" affair

June 9, Second Note to Germany on the "Lusitania" repeated former representations and asked for definite pledges that attacks on unresisting non-combatants should cease

June 17, League to Enforce Peace formed at meeting at Independence Hall, Philadelphia, its aim to provide a substitute for war as a means of settlement for international disputes, W. H. Taft, president, Herbert S. Houston, treasurer, A. Lawrence Lowell, chairman of the executive committee

June 20–22, Strike of street railroad employees in Chicago settled by reference to board of arbitration which granted wage increases

June 21, Supreme Court declared the "grandfather clause" in the Oklahoma and Maryland Constitutions imposing a general literacy test but exempting those persons entitled to vote prior to 1866, and their lineal descendants and those who were in 1866 foreigners, a violation of the XVth Amendment and unconstitutional

June 23, Robert Lansing, of New York, appointed Secretary of State

June 24, Note to Germany made renewed demand for reparation for sinking of the "William P. Frye" without reference to a prize court

June 27, General Victoriano Huerta and General Pascual Orozco arrested at Newman, New Mexico, accused of plotting against Mexico, released on bail

June 29, Austrian Note protested against export of munitions to Great Britain and her Allies and asked the United States to place an embargo thereon, and to threaten the Allies with an embargo on export of foodstuffs if legitimate commerce with the Central Powers was not allowed

June 30, Exports for the fiscal year ending on this date amounted to $2,768,643,532 as compared with the previous year $2,364,579,148. United States exports to Germany were only $28,863,354 as compared with $344,792,276 in the previous year, and to Austria-Hungary, $1,240,167 against $22,718,258, and exports to Great Britain rose to 911 millions as compared to 594 millions in the preceding year, to France 369 millions as compared to 159 millions, 143 millions to the Netherlands as compared to 112 millions, to Norway from 9 to 39 millions, to Sweden from 14½ to 78 millions, and to Italy from 74 millions to 184 millions

——, Average price of wheat for fiscal year ending on this date $1.28 as compared with .95²/₁₀ cents the preceding year

July 1, Dept. of Agriculture reorganized, and States Relations Service established

——, State wide prohibition became effective in Alabama, law passed over veto Jan. 22

July 2, Bomb placed by Erich Muenter alias Frank Holt, instructor in German in Cornell University, exploded in the Senate reception room

July 3, J. P. Morgan, acting as agent of the British Government in the matter of war contracts, attacked and slightly wounded by shot of Erich Muenter, at Glen Cove, Long Island. Muenter committed suicide in jail 3 days later

July 4, Death of Charles A. Conant (54) financial expert

July 8, German reply to American Note of June 9 made proposals to safeguard Americans from German submarine warfare, the installation of a reasonable number of neutral steamers under American flag, &c.

July 9, The Government took over the operation of the German wireless station at Sayville, Long Island

July 10, Strike of carpenters in Chicago settled by reference to arbitration, and increase of wages granted and continuance of closed shop, the unions conceding open market for materials and agreeing to arbitrate any differences

July 12, German Note acknowledged responsibility for submarine attack on the "Nebraskan" and offered reparation

July 16, The Panama Canal used for the first time by American battleships, the "Missouri," "Ohio," and "Wisconsin," passing through to California to the San Diego Exposition

——, Death of St. Clair McKelway (70) editor, Brooklyn, New York

July 18–27, Strike of the employees of the Standard Oil Company at Bayonne, New Jersey, for higher wages and shorter hours, successful as to increase

July 19, Strike of machinists at Remington Arms Company at Bridgeport, Conn. averted by increase of wages and grant of eight hour day. Other companies at Bridgeport forced by strikes during the next 6 weeks to give wage increase or shorter hours

July 20, Strike of 60,000 clothing workers in New York averted by reference to arbitration and award which increased wages from 12 to 15%

July 21, Third Note regarding the "Lusitania" warned Germany that further infringements of American rights on the high seas would be considered as "deliberately unfriendly"

July 22, Death of Martha Baker Dunn (67) author

——, The Interstate Commerce Commission allowed advance of express rates except in zone north of the Ohio and east of the Mississippi

July 23, British reply to American Note of March 30 defended blockade as adaptation of the old principles to the peculiar circumstances confronting Great Britain with reference to American declaration of blockade of some 3,000 miles of coast line in Civil War and application of doctrine of continuous voyage

July 24, The excursion steamer "Eastland" capsized at pier at Chicago with loss of 852 persons

July 25, The American steamer "Leelanaw" carrying cargo of flax declared contraband by Germany sunk by German submarine off the coast of Scotland after removal of crew

July 27, First direct wireless communication established between Japan and the United States

July 29, American marines landed at Haiti and stopped riots

——, Death of Thomas Y. Crowell (80) publisher

July 30, Charles Becker finally executed for murder of Herman Rosenthal in 1912 after refusal of the Governor of New York to commute the sentence

July 31, British reply to American caveat on British prize procedure of July 14 against the substitution of British municipal enactments for international law

Aug. 4, Case of the "Dacia" decided, the cargo of cotton which was not contraband at time of voyage purchased by the French Government, the vessel condemned by prize court

——, Strike of 60,000 garment workers in New York City prevented by arbitration and wage increase

Aug. 5, Representatives of Latin American Republics met with the Secretary of State in Washington to discuss means of ending anarchy in Mexico, and issued appeal to Mexico Aug. 11 to establish a provisional government and hold election for president

Aug. 6, American marines took possession of Port au Prince, Haiti, to establish order. See also Haiti

Aug. 9, Death of George Fitch (38) author

Aug. 10, Training camps for citizens established at Plattsburg, New York, by military authorities

Aug. 11, Interstate Commerce Commission permitted increase per car load on 41 railroads in the Middle West on coal, grain, fruits, and vegetables

Aug. 12, Interstate Commerce Commission ruling reduced freight rates on anthracite coal between the producing district and tidewater from 10 to 80 cents a ton

——, Note to Austria-Hungary in reply to protest of June 29 stated that the Central Powers had always furnished belligerents with war supplies and that peaceful nations would be at the mercy of aggressive and prepared enemies if they could not procure arms and ammunition from neutral nations in case of foreign attack

Aug. 14, Death of John W. Harper (84) publisher

Aug. 15, The New York *World* published papers lost by Dr. Albert, financial adviser of the German Embassy, on July 31, signed by Albert, Ambassador von Bernsdorff, and Captain Franz von Papen, which revealed plans for fomenting disorder among the American people in the interests of Germany

Aug. 19, The White Star liner "Arabic" sunk without warning off Fastnet by a German submarine, 2 Americans lost their lives; the committing of "deliberately unfriendly" act disavowed by Germany, and apology offered

Aug. 23, Federal Commission on Industrial Relations expired by limitation, majority and minority reports presented

Aug. 24, The United States District Court at Buffalo declared the Eastman Kodak Company an illegal corporation in restraint of trade and ordered it dissolved

Aug. 30, Dr. Dumba, Austro-Hungarian Ambassador, admitted authorship of letter seized in England in which he asked authority from his government to pursue certain methods which would "disorganize and hold up for months, if not entirely prevent, the manufacture of munitions in Bethlehem (Pennsylvania), and in the Middle West"

Sept. 1, German Government gave assurance that "liners will not be sunk by our submarines without warning and without safety of the lives of non-combatants, provided that the liners do not try to escape or offer resistance"

Sept. 2, Railroad strike ordered to take effect Sept. 4 rescinded after passage of the Adamson Act

Sept. 7, German Note refused indemnity in case of the sinking of the "Arabic" and deaths of American citizens, claiming self-defense

Sept. 8, The State Dept. asked for formal recall of Dr. Dumba as no longer acceptable as Ambassador from Austria-Hungary for the reason of "admitted purpose and intent" to conspire to "cripple legitimate industries of the people of the United States" . . . which was granted Sept. 28

——, Gustav Stahl, German reservist arrested June 10 who swore to having seen guns mounted on the "Lusitania" pleaded guilty to perjury and was sentenced to 18 months imprisonment

Sept. 14, State wide prohibition adopted in South Carolina by majority vote, system of dispensaries to end Jan. 1

Sept. 16, Treaty with Haiti signed established a virtual protectorate of the United States for 10 years. Provided for the appointment of an American receiver of customs, an American financial adviser, and American officers to organize an armed police force, the United States to "lend an efficient aid for the preservation of Haitian independence and the maintenance of a government adequate for the protection of life, property, and individual liberty"

——, British Prize Court condemned cargoes of American meat and meat products seized in Nov. 1914 (the packer's cases). Memorandum to the State Dept. of Oct. 12 explained that the ships were carrying to Denmark more than 13 times the amount of goods consigned in non-war time and the inference was that their ultimate destination was Germany

Sept. 19, German Note on the "William P. Frye" case promised not to sink American ships carrying conditional contraband

Sept. 21, Death of Anthony Comstock (71) Secretary of the New York Society for the Suppression of Vice

Sept. 23, Convention with Russia signed for exportation of embargoed goods from Russia

——, Advancement of Peace Treaty with China signed

Sept. 24, Second Austro-Hungarian Note of protest against supplying of munitions of war to the Allies questioned validity of American position; not answered as American Note of Aug. 12 closed discussion

Sept. 27, Strike of garment workers in Chicago to obtain agreement similar to the protocols in the women's garment trade

Sept. 29, Anglo-French loan of $500,000,000 at 5% arranged, money to remain in the United States to be used only in payment for goods; contract signed Oct. 15

Sept. 30, Death of Richard R. Williams (72) editor of the *Iron Age*

Oct. 1, Cotton crop estimated on this date to be 10,950,000 bales

——, Value of export of explosives since Aug. 1914 $121,842,937

Oct. 4, Strikes at General Electric Company, Schenectady, and at the International Silver Company at Meriden, Conn. for the eight hour day

Oct. 5, Case of the "Arabic" disavowed by Germany and agreement made to pay reparation

——, Dr. Dumba, Austro-Hungarian Ambassador recalled, sailed from New York

Oct. 6, First meeting of Naval Advisory Board of Inventions, Thomas Edison, chairman

Oct. 12, Further Note to Germany respecting the "William P. Frye" case and as to provision for safety of crews of ships sunk as carrying contraband

Oct. 19, Recognition of *de facto* Government of Mexico of General Venustiano Carranza

——, Embargo declared on export of arms to Mexico except to territory controlled by Carranza

——, Woman suffrage defeated in New Jersey by vote of 133,282 to 184,390

Oct. 21, Note of Secretary Lansing to Great Britain declared the blockade "ineffective, illegal, and indefensible" especial protest being made against the ruling by which American shipowners were compelled to seek redress in British prize courts rather than through diplomatic channels, and asked that the blockade should be conducted according to rules of international law and not according to mere expediency

Oct. 24, Arrest of Robert Fay and Walter Scholz of the German secret service charged with conspiracy to destroy at sea by time bombs merchant ships leaving New York for England and France with munitions

Oct. 27, Oscar A. Brindley flew 544 miles along the California coast in 10 hours making new American seaplane record

Oct. 28, Final decision of District Court ordered dissolution of Reading Company, hard coal combination

Nov. 1, Supreme Court declared the anti-alien labor law of Arizona requiring 80% of employees of any company to be of American nationality unconstitutional

——, Death of Herman Ridder (64) editor of *New Yorker Staats-Zeitung*

Nov. 2, Constitution for New York State framed by convention which met April 6–Sept. 10 rejected by voters, and prohibition in Ohio, and woman suffrage in Massachusetts, New York, and Pennsylvania

Nov. 6, Death of Peter A. B. Widener (80) financier and art collector, Philadelphia

Nov. 10, Ordinance shop at Bethlehem Steel Company destroyed with heavy loss by fire believed to be incendiary

Nov. 11, Wire rope shop of John A. Roebling Sons Company at Trenton, New Jersey, destroyed by fire believed to be incendiary

——, Proclamation of neutrality in war between the Allies and Bulgaria

Nov. 12, Nobel prize for physics awarded to Thomas A. Edison and Nicola Tesla, and the 1914 prize for chemistry to Professor Theodore W. Richards

Nov. 14, Death of Booker T. Washington (56) negro educator

Nov. 19, Death of Dr. Solomon Schechter (67) rabbi and author, New York City

Nov. 21, Dept. of Justice issued appeal to state authorities to aid in bringing conspiracies against American industries in the interests of Austria-Hungary and Germany to justice

Nov. 26, Announcement of loan of $50,000,000 credit to 8 London banks

Nov. 27, Claims Convention with Panama signed as to damages caused by a riot at Panama City

Nov. 30, Death of Paul Fuller (67) lawyer, New York City

——, Explosion at a Du Pont Powder Company plant near Wilmington, Delaware, caused death of 31 persons and injury of others, believed to be part of the organized war on munition factories

Nov., Ku Klux Klan reorganized by William Joseph Simmons at meeting on Stone Mountain, Georgia

Dec. 1 and 4, Recall of Captain Franz von Papen and Captain Karl Boy-Ed, German military naval attachés, asked for by State Dept. because of alleged improper activities in military and naval matters; granted Dec. 10

Dec. 2, Conviction of Karl Buenz, director of the Hamburg-American line with 3 other officials charged with conspiracy to dispatch supply ships to German cruisers on the high seas, and sentenced Dec. 4 to terms of imprisonment

Dec. 4, Henry Ford with delegation of advocates of peace sailed from New York on the "Oscar II" chartered by him "to try to get the boys out of the trenches and back to their homes by Christmas day" and stop the war in Europe

——, The Ku Klux Klan reorganized under charter granted in Georgia

Dec. 5, The "Petrolite," Standard Oil steamer, fired on by German submarine

Dec. 6, Note to Austria-Hungary demanded disavowal and indemnity for the sinking of the Italian steamer "Ancona" Nov. 7 in which 9 Americans lost their lives

Dec. 9, Fire believed to be incendiary destroyed Du Pont Powder Company factory town and factory at Hopewell, Virginia

Dec. 11, Interstate Commerce Commission authorized increase in passenger fares in western territory on nearly 50 railroads

Dec. 15, Austria made evasive reply as to sinking of the "Ancona" raising technical objections, and in-

viting the United States to an exchange of views on principles of record

Dec. 19, Second Note to Austria-Hungary renewed demands for disavowal and reparation

Dec. 22, Henry Ford left his peace party at Christiania and returned to the United States

Dec. 23, Federal Grand Jury indicted Paul Koenig of the Hamburg-American line, R. E. Leydendecker, and Fred Metzler in New York City on charge of conspiracy to destroy the Welland Canal

——, Price of copper in New York market reached 21 cents a pound

Dec. 27, Strike of iron and steel workers at Youngstown, Ohio, begun for increase in wages

Dec. 28, Federal Grant Jury at New York indicted Captain Franz Rintelen of the German army, Representative Frank Buchanan, of Illinois, H. R. Fowler, general counsel, and 5 other officers of Labor's National Peace Council on charge of conspiracy to restrain the foreign commerce of the United States by fomenting strikes and by propaganda in munitions plants

——, Colonel Edward House sailed for Europe as representative of President Wilson on mission to suggest a peace conference which had no result

Dec. 29, Austria-Hungary accepted American demands as to the "Ancona" and gave assurance that its submarines would not imperil the safety of passengers who did not offer resistance or attempt to escape

Dec. 30, American consul at Aden, R. N. McNeely, drowned when British steamer "Persia" torpedoed without warning in the Mediterranean

Dec. 31, Laws prohibiting sale of liquor became effective in Arkansas, Iowa, South Carolina, Washington, Oregon, Indiana, and Colorado

CONGRESS

Jan. 12, Proposed Amendment to Constitution to establish woman suffrage defeated in House by vote of 174 to 204

Jan. 28, President Wilson vetoed the Immigration Bill disapproving the literacy test and the restrictions which would tend to deny asylum to political refugees

——, Coast Guard established combining life saving and revenue cutter services

Feb. 4, The House failed to pass the Immigration Bill over veto by vote of 261 to 136, lacking the necessary two-thirds majority

Feb. 5, Act for improvement of the consular service graded and classified the foreign service

Feb. 10, Senate adjourned after a continuous session of 52 hours and 10 minutes of filibuster to defeat Ship Purchase Bill favored by the President

March 2, Committee investigating Colorado strike reported criticizing John D. Rockefeller and the state militia and recommending legislation to promote arbitration in industrial disputes

March 3, Federal Reserve Bank Act amended

——, Resolution adopted in both Houses to strengthen the power of the President to enforce neutrality

——, National Advisory Committee for Aëronautics authorized

——, Double pensions granted for disability for aviators in Navy and Marine Corps

March 4, Interstate Commerce Act amended

——, Act to promote the welfare of American seamen in the merchant marine, to abolish arrest and imprisonment for desertion, and to promote safety at sea. Language test required that 75% of crew should be able to understand orders given by the officers

March 4, Railroad Locomotive Inspection Act amended

——, Congress adjourned

Dec. 6, Sixty-Fourth Congress, 1st sess. convened

Dec. 17, Emergency Internal Revenue Act imposed taxes

——, Joint Resolution extended operation of War Revenue Act of Oct. 1914 for another year

1916

Jan. 1, Prohibition into effect in Colorado, South Carolina, Oregon, Washington, Arkansas, and Idaho

Jan. 2, Death of Justice Joseph Rucker Lamar, of the Supreme Court

Jan. 4, Secretary Lansing protested against the seizure of American mails to and from the Scandinavian countries by Great Britain

Jan. 6, President Wilson in address to the second Pan-American Scientific Congress in Washington declared that the States of America should unite in guaranteeing to each other political independence and territorial integrity

Jan. 7, Striking steel workers in riot in Youngstown, Ohio, burn and loot in business section destroying property valued at $800,000

Jan. 8, German undated Note received declared that American vessels would be sunk only when carrying absolute contraband and when passengers and crews could reach port in safety

——, Death of Ada Rehan (55) actress, in New York

Jan. 10, Eighteen Americans taken from a train by followers of Villa at Santa Ysabel, Mexico, mining officials and employees, and shot

——, Government suit begun Oct. 13, 1915, against 11 former directors of the New York, New Haven, and Hartford Railroad for conspiracy to monopolize New England transportation facilities ended, 6 acquitted and jury disagreed in case of 5 to be placed on trial again

Jan. 11, National Conference of the Progressive Party held in Chicago with delegates from every State but one

Jan. 12, Government demanded punishment and capture of Mexicans responsible for murder of American citizens at Santa Ysabel; accepted by Carranza on the 16th

Jan. 13, Increase of 10% in wages granted in mills in Youngstown, Ohio, ending strike

Jan. 17, German Note denied responsibility for sinking of the "Persia" Dec. 30, 1915

Jan. 18, Note to belligerents proposed regulations for submarine warfare and disarming of merchant ships

Jan. 22, Austria-Hungary disclaimed responsibility for sinking of the "Persia"

Jan. 24, Supreme Court decision upheld constitutionality of federal income tax law

——, Death of John A. Hill (57) publisher, East Orange, New Jersey

Jan. 25, Note to Great Britain protested against restraints on neutral commerce

Jan. 28, Note of Secretary Lansing asked Allies to discontinue the practice of arming liners

Jan. 31, Strike of copper miners in southern Arizona begun in Sept. 1915 ended with increase of 20%

Feb. 1, United States Steel Corporation granted a 10% increase in wages averting strike

——, The British steamer "Appam," captured in Jan. by German cruiser "Moewe" off the Canary Islands, brought into Newport News, Virginia, by German Lieutenant Berg

Feb. 3, Strike of nearly 60,000 clothing workers in New York ended by agreement and formation of Board of Protocol Standards March 10

Feb. 4, Death of Alexander Wilson Drake (73) editor and artist, New York

Feb. 8, Federal Grand Jury at San Francisco indicted 32 persons including Francis Bopp, German Consul, charged with conspiracy to wreck ammunition factories and to furnish supplies to German vessels

——, Death of Charles Willard Hayes (56) geologist, Washington

Feb. 9, 350,000 railroad trainmen in the freight service demanded an eight hour day and higher pay for overtime

Feb. 9–May 1, Strike of jewelry workers of New York City for increase in wages successful

Feb. 10, German Note announced that from March 1 armed enemy merchant ships would be treated as war vessels

——, Resignation of L. M. Garrison as Secretary of War because of refusal of the President to accept his plan for army of volunteer force of over 400,000 men under national control, instead of reliance on the militia for national defense. Henry Breckinridge, Assistant Secretary of War, also resigned

Feb. 12, Death of John T. Trowbridge (88) author, Arlington, Mass.

Feb. 15, Announcement of Administration given to the press that "merchant vessels have an international legal right to arm for the sole purpose of defense"

Feb. 16, Germany recognized liability and offered indemnity in the "Lusitania" case

Feb. 18, British cruiser at entrance to the Yangtze River, China, removed from the American steamer "China" 28 German citizens, 8 Austrians, and 2 Turks, passengers

Feb. 21, Reply of Great Britain and France to Note of Jan. 25 offered to submit case to international tribunal after the War

Feb. 23, American Can Company declared by United States District Court at Baltimore to be a legal combination denying suit of Government

Feb. 25, Henry P. Fletcher appointed Minister to Mexico

Feb. 28, Death of Henry James (72) novelist, in London. He had become an English citizen

Feb. 29, South Carolina law raised minimum age from 12 to 14 for children employed in factories, mines, and textile establishments

March 2, Note of Secretary Lansing to Germany denied right of asylum to the "Appam"

March 7, Note of Turkish Government denied destruction of the "Persia"

——, Newton D. Baker, of Ohio, appointed Secretary of War

March 9, Agreement reached of bituminous coal operators and miners to begin April 1 and last 4 years, wages increased 5%, payment on the mine run system, recognition of union, but not demand for 8 hour day to begin when entering mine and end when leaving, that is for travel underground to place of work

——, Villistas crossed the frontier into New Mexico

and raided town of Columbus killing 17 Americans

March 12, State Dept. ruling as to arming of merchant vessels issued

March 13, Agreement made with General Carranza by which he allowed American troops to enter Mexico in pursuit of Villa on condition that his own forces should have same right to pursue bandits across the American frontier

——, Death of Seymour Eaton (57) author

March 15, Punitive expedition organized by General Frederick Funston and commanded by Brigadier General John J. Pershing with 6,000 troops crossed the border into Mexico in pursuit of Villa, Colonel Dodd in command of cavalry

March 29, Colonel Dodd in engagement with Villa at San Geronimo, Mexico, dispersing Mexicans

April 1, Engagement with Mexicans at Aguascalientes

——, Death of James B. Angell (87) president emeritus of University of Michigan

April 2, Lockout in the clothing industry in New York City

April 3, Reply of Great Britain and France as to interference with transoceanic mails to Scandinavian countries

——, Strike of unskilled laborers working on construction of subway New York City for wage of $2 a day instead of $1.50 to $1.75 which was granted

April 10, German Note denied sinking the "Sussex" and suggested it was destroyed by a floating mine

April 11, Death of Richard Harding Davis (52) journalist and author

April 12, American troops entering Mexican town of Parral more than 400 miles south of the border attacked by Carranza force. Note of Carranza proposed withdrawal of American troops from Mexico

April 14, Agreement reached in London with Chicago meat packers whose cargoes had been seized in 1914, and payment by British Government

April 15, Panama Canal which had been closed for 7 months on account of earth slides reopened

April 16, Note of Carranza demanded withdrawal of American troops from Mexico

April 17, Federal Grand Jury in New York indicted Captain Franz von Papen and Captain Hans Taucher on charge of conspiracy to destroy the Welland Canal

——, American Academy of Arts and Letters incorporated

April 18, Office of von Papen raided by officers of the Dept. of Justice and papers seized which provided data for prosecutions and exposed secret activities of the German Embassy. Wolf von Igel arrested in office on charge of complicity in attempt to destroy the Welland Canal

——, Note of President Wilson to Germany in regard to sinking of the "Sussex" with loss of Americans warned that unless Germany made immediate declaration of abandonment of submarine warfare against passenger and freight carrying vessels diplomatic relations must be severed

April 22–29, Strike of laborers working on construction of government railroad in Alaska for increase in wages settled by compromise

April 22–May 9, Unsuccessful strike of employees of the Westinghouse plant at East Pittsburgh for eight hour day and wage increase, the militia called out to suppress rioting

April 22, Strike of bituminous coal miners at Pittsburgh because promised increase not received

April 23, Socialist Labor Party met in New York City and nominated its candidates of 1912, Arthur Reimer, of Massachusetts, for President. The Socialist Party held no convention but nominated Allen L. Benson, of New York, for President and George R. Kirkpatrick, of New Jersey, for Vice-President, by mail referendum

April 24, British Note in answer to American Note of Oct. 21, 1915, which had filed an elaborate documented list of complaints as to blockade defended detention and seizure of neutral cargoes and yielded nothing

April 26, Offer of the National Academy of Sciences to organize educational and research institutions in the interests of national preparedness accepted by the President

April 28, Federal Grand Jury in New York indicted Walter T. Scheele and other Germans on charge of conspiracy to destroy ships carrying munitions

——, Death of Rev. Josiah Strong (69) author, New York

——, Strike of cloak, suit, and skirt industries begun in New York City when the manufacturers locked out 30,000 workers

April 29, Conference of Generals Scott and Funston with Mexican Generals Obregon and Treviso begun, and agreement drafted as to conditions of withdrawal of American troops May 3, which was approved by President Wilson and by President Carranza except on minor points

May 1, Second increase of 10% given in wages by United States Steel Company

——, Prohibition laws of Georgia went into effect

May 4, German reply to Note of April 18 as to "Sussex" pledged enforcement of orders given to submarine commanders not to sink merchant vessels without warning unless ships offered resistance or attempted to escape

May 5, Agreement in anthracite coal industry renewed to run until March 31, 1920, hours reduced from 9 to 8, 3 to 7% increase in wages

——, Villistas raided and looted towns of Glen Springs and Boquillas in Texas. Rescue party in pursuit recovered American prisoners

May 8, Germany acknowledged responsibility for sinking of the "Sussex" by a submarine in error and offered indemnity

——, Robert Fay, Walter Scholz, and Paul Doecke convicted of conspiracy to destroy ocean vessels engaged in transportation of munitions by jury in New York, and sentenced to terms of imprisonment

——, Carl A. Lüderitz, German consul, indicted in Baltimore on charge of procuring a fraudulent passport for Major von der Goltz

——, The Secretary of State accepted assurances of German Note of May 4, but refused to consider conditions making it contingent upon the course of negotiations with Great Britain as to modification of blockade as suggested

May 9, President Wilson ordered the mobilization of the militia of Texas, Arizona, and New Mexico for service on the Mexican border, and sent 4,000 additional troops of the regular army

May 10, Secretary Lansing offered to extend the organization of the Belgian Relief Commission to Poland; accepted by Russia May 20, conditions proposed by Great Britain rejected by Germany May 30

May 12, Federal District Court affirmed decision of Interstate Commerce Commission, the "Lake lines divorce decision" refusing to authorize railroads to continue ownership of steamship properties on the Great Lakes

May 13, Death of Clara Louise Kellogg (Mrs. Carl Strakosch) singer

——, Agreement of Great Britain to release enemy citizens taken from American steamer "China"

May 22, Second Note of President Carranza demanding withdrawal of American troops from Mexico, and asking intent and purposes of the United States be declared

May 24, Note to French Government protested against seizure and detention of neutral mails by France and Great Britain on the high seas

May 26, Death of Timothy Dwight (87) former president of Yale University

May 26–27, League to Enforce Peace held first annual meeting in Washington. President Wilson in address on the 27th declared that every people should have sovereignty under which it shall live, that small States have same rights as large ones, and that the United States would be willing to become part of any feasible association of nations to maintain freedom of the seas, and stop wars begun in violation of international treaties

May 29, Note to Great Britain as to importation of German machine knitting needles needed for American manufacturers

——, Death of Thomas R. Slicer (69) Unitarian clergyman, New York City, and James J. Hill (77) financier, St. Paul

June 1, Conference of railroad managers and representatives of the four Railroad Brotherhoods begun in New York which ended in 2 weeks without agreement

——, National Committee on Red Cross Medical Service organized, composed of 47 distinguished physicians and surgeons

——, Strike of longshoremen on the Pacific coast for increase in wages settled in San Francisco by agreement July 20, and in other sections in Oct.

June 2–Sept. 17, Strike of 15,000 miners in the Mesaba Iron Range, Minnesota, for eight hour day, minimum wage of $3, and abolition of contract labor system, partially successful

June 5, Iowa in special election rejected woman suffrage

June 7–10, Republican National Convention met at Chicago and on June 10 on third ballot nominated Charles E. Hughes for President with 949½ votes, and Charles W. Fairbanks nominated for Vice-President

——, Progressive Party Convention met in Chicago and nominated Theodore Roosevelt for President, and John M. Parker, of Louisiana, for Vice-President. Roosevelt declined the nomination

June 9, Oregon-California Railroad Land Grant Act restored to the United States the lands granted for railroads April 10, 1869 and May 4, 1870, except rights of way

——, Death of John R. McLean (67) newspaper publisher, Washington

June 11, Death of Jean Webster (Mrs. Glenn F. McKinney) novelist, New York

June 14–16, Democratic National Convention met at St. Louis. President Wilson was renominated by acclamation in spite of the one-term declaration of the platform of 1912 introduced by Bryan, and Vice-President Marshall also

June 15, Mexicans attacked American border patrol at San Ugnacio, Texas, several killed and wounded on both sides

June 16, General Treviso, instructed by General Carranza, informed General Pershing that any further invasion of American troops into Mexico would be resisted

June 18, The President ordered mobilization of militia of all the States for service on the Mexican border

——, A boat from the American gunboat "Annapolis" landing at Mazatlan, Mexico, fired on by Mexicans

June 20, Secretary Lansing notified Mexican Government that American troops would not be withdrawn until order was restored on the border

June 21, American force commanded by Captain Charles T. Boyd attacked by Mexicans at Carrizal and greatly outnumbered, Captain Boyd and Lieutenant H. R. Adair and 7 soldiers killed, 9 wounded and 22 taken prisoners, and the Mexican commander, General Gomez, and 38 Mexicans killed

June 22, Notes sent to diplomatic representatives of South and Central American Republics as to position of the United States regarding Mexico

June 24, Federal District Court of New York ordered dissolution of the Corn Products Refining Company as an illegal combination in restraint of trade

June 25, Note to Mexican Government demanded release of Americans taken prisoners at Carrizal; released on the 28th

June 26, National Committee of the Progressive Party endorsed Charles E. Hughes for President

June 30, Captain Hans Tauscher, representative of the Krupp Works, acquitted of charge of conspiracy to violate the neutrality laws of the United States

July 3, Death of Hetty Green (Mrs. Edward H.) capitalist (80), New York City

July 4, President Carranza returned conciliatory answer to American notes of June 20 and 25 and proposed negotiations, which was accepted by Secretary Lansing

July 9, The German submarine "Deutschland" arrived at Norfolk with a cargo of dyestuffs, and proceeded to Baltimore

July 12, Proposal of Mexican Government for a joint commission to draw up a protocol covering the retirement of American troops and rights of each nation to send troops across the border

July 17, Note to Ambassador Gerard from the Dept. of State declared that the "Deutschland" was an unarmed merchant vessel

July 18, Blacklist of 82 American firms, chiefly German, published by Great Britain, and dealings with them forbidden to British subjects under the Trading with the Enemy Act; protested by the United States July 26

——, Death of Anna Fuller, author (62), Boston

July 19–21, National Convention of the Prohibition Party met at St. Paul and nominated J. Frank Hanly, of Indiana, for President, and Dr. Ira D. Landrith, of Tennessee, for Vice-President

July 20, British memorandum defended censorship of mails

July 22, During a preparedness parade in San Francisco a bomb exploded in the crowd caused the death of 6 persons and injury to 25. Of labor leaders accused in connection with the affair Warren K. Billings was subsequently convicted and sentenced to life imprisonment, and Thomas Mooney received death sentence

July 22, Death of James Whitcomb Riley (63) poet, at Indianapolis

July 23, Employees of street railroads north of New York City in Yonkers, New Rochelle, and Mount Vernon struck for minimum wage of 30 cents an hour, and strike spread to New York City July 27

July 24, National Research Council reorganized by the National Academy of Sciences received formal approval of the President

July 26, Note of protest sent to British Government regarding blacklist of American firms

July 28, Death of Rev. Daniel Bliss, missionary and educator, at Beirut, Syria

July 29, United States District Court at Norfolk, Virginia, decided that the steamer "Appam" and cargo should be restored to British owners, declaring that "the manner of bringing the 'Appam' into the United States, as well as her presence in these waters, constitutes a violation of the neutrality of the United States"

——, Employees on the Third Avenue Elevated in New York City joined the strike, and of the Interborough system Aug. 4

July 30, Explosion and fire at munitions plant on Black Tom Island, New Jersey, destroyed property worth $20,000,000. Believed to be work of German incendiaries but Mixed Claims Commission in Oct. 1930 disallowed claim for damages finding no evidence

Aug. 1, The German submarine "Deutschland" sailed from Baltimore on return trip arriving at Bremerhaven, Germany, Aug. 16

——, Prohibition law for Utah signed by the Governor

——, Death of Eben Jordan (58) merchant, Boston

Aug. 3, Conference of the Progressive Party at Indianapolis nominated John M. Parker for Vice-President and condemned action of National Committee in endorsing Charles E. Hughes for President

Aug. 4, Treaty with Denmark signed provided for purchase of the Danish West Indies (Virgin Islands) for $25,000,000; ratified by Senate Sept. 7

——, Agreement signed ended strike of cloak, suit, and skirt industries in New York City

Aug. 7, Street car strike in New York City ended with compromise settlement

Aug. 8, At joint meeting of the managers of the railroads and representatives of the Brotherhoods the former were notified that the men had voted for a strike if no satisfactory agreement was reached as to eight hour day, which was refused by the managers Aug. 9

Aug. 14–15, The President met the managers of the railroads and the representatives of the Brotherhoods in separate conferences to discuss settlement of dispute to avoid strike

Aug. 17, Proposal of the President of compromise agreement to avoid railroad strike rejected by managers. President Wilson summoned the railroad presidents to conference

Aug. 18, The President met presidents of 31 railroads in conference. The officials of the Brotherhoods voted to accept President Wilson's plan

Aug. 19, President Wilson issued public statement of his endorsement of the eight hour day for railroad workers which the railroad presidents had rejected

Aug. 20, Death of James Seligman (92) banker, New York

Aug. 24, Protocol to Treaty with Haiti signed arranged for establishment of native constabulary under American control

Aug. 25, Death of Archbishop John Lancaster Spalding at Peoria, Illinois

Aug. 26, Death of James Harper (61) publisher

Aug. 28, 637 delegates of the Brotherhoods received sealed orders for nation wide strike to begin Sept. 4

——, Death of William H. Ward (81) late editor of the *Independent*

Aug. 31, Memo to France, Great Britain, Japan, and Russia and subsequently to Italy and Portugal in answer to protests as to the "Deutschland" reserved liberty of action in regard to the treatment of submarines, and declared the existing rules of international law as applicable had been complied with

Sept. 2, Railroad strike order rescinded after passage of Eight Hour Bill by House and Senate

——, Death of Samuel W. Pennypacker (73) former Governor of Pennsylvania

Sept. 4–Jan. 15, 1917, Joint American-Mexican Commission held meetings to settle dispute first in New York City, then in New London, Conn. and finally at Atlantic City Oct. 1

Sept. 6, New strike of surface and elevated railway lines begun in New York City

Sept. 8, Frank W. Taussig appointed chairman of the new permanent Tariff Commission

Sept. 16, Death of Horace White (82) editor and author, New York

Sept. 17, Death of Seth Low (66) former president of Columbia University and Mayor of New York

Sept. 19, Naval Consulting Board organized by Secretary Daniels to give scientific advice on the manufacture of naval munitions

Sept. 25, New York Stock Exchange transacted record sales shares representing $2,192,300

Oct. 1, Death of Brigadier General Galusha Pennypacker (72)

Oct. 5, President Wilson appointed General George W. Goethals, Edgar E. Clark, and George Rublee a board to investigate the effect of the railroad eight hour day

Oct. 6–19, Strike of employees of the Standard Oil Company at Bayonne, New Jersey, begun for increase in wages of 30%, an eight hour day, and better conditions of labor

Oct. 7, The German submarine "U-53" entered harbor at Newport, Rhode Island, and proceeded Oct. 8 to sink 6 merchant vessels off Nantucket Island and 3 more on the 9th

Oct. 11, British Note replied to protest as to blacklist of July 26 defending action

——, Council of National Defense organized with Secretary of War Baker as chairman and W. S. Gifford, director. The Advisory Commission included Daniel Willard, Hollis Godfrey, Howard E. Coffin, Bernard M. Baruch, Julius Rosenwald, Samuel Gompers, and Dr. Franklin H. Martin

Oct. 15, Death of Rev. Francis Brown (66) president of Union Theological Seminary, New York

Oct. 24, Chicago Dec. wheat quoted at $1.68³/₄ a bushel as compared with $1.03¹/₈ of the previous year, Dec. corn at $.82¼ as compared with $.58, cotton in New York at $.17 a pound (Oct. 12), and established

average price levels of food in New York City estimated to have increased 40% within the year

Oct. 25, Death of William M. Chase (66) portrait
painter, New York

Nov. 1, The German submarine "Deutschland" on
second voyage to the United States arrived at New
London, Connecticut, with $10,000,000 cargo of
chemicals, gems, and securities

——, State wide prohibition went into effect in Virginia

Nov. 2–3, Flight of Victor Carlstrom from Chicago to
New York, 900 miles in 8 hours and 28½ minutes
actual flying time, establishing new American non-
stop record in first hop from Chicago to Erie, Pennsylvania, made in 4 hours, 17½ minutes, 452 miles

Nov. 7, Presidential election a victory for the Democrats, President Wilson reëlected by popular vote
of 9,128,837 and electoral vote of 277, Hughes,
Republican receiving popular vote of 8,536,380 and
electoral vote of 254. Benson (Socialist) received
590,415 votes; Hanly (Prohibition), 221,196; Reimer
(Socialist-Labor), 13,922; John Parker on a headless
Progressive ticket received 42,836 votes for the vice-
presidency. The Democratic majority in Congress
slightly reduced. Prohibition adopted in Michigan,
Montana, South Dakota

Nov. 10, Death of Charles N. Flagg (67) painter,
Hartford, Conn.

Nov. 12, Death of Percival Lowell (61) astronomer,
Flagstaff, Arizona

Nov. 15, Marconi wireless telegraph service established
with Japan with relay at Hawaii

——, National Conference Board established by 12
large employers' associations

——, Death of Mollie Elliot Seawell (56) novelist,
Washington

Nov. 20, Ruth Law in a Curtiss biplane made trip
from Chicago to Hornell, New York, flying time
8 hours, 55½ minutes, non-stop flight of 590 miles
establishing new American record

Nov. 22, United States Circuit Court at Kansas City
pronounced the Adamson Eight Hour Day Act unconstitutional in suit brought by the Missouri,
Oklahoma, and Gulf Railroad

——, Death of Jack London (40) novelist, at Glen
Ellen, California

Nov. 24, Protocol with Mexico signed at Atlantic City
providing for withdrawal of American troops on
certain terms which were not accepted by President
Carranza

Nov. 25, Death of Mrs. Inez Mulholland Boissevain (30)
suffragist

Nov. 27, Federal Reserve Board issued statement opposing purchases of short term British treasury
notes by banks, the liquid funds of which should
be available for short-term credits for domestic needs:
withdrawal announced by J. P. Morgan and Co.
Dec. 1

Nov. 29, Military occupation of Santo Domingo by
the United States

——, The Government protested to Germany against
the deportation of Belgian civilians

Dec. 5, Death of John D. Archbold (68) president of
the Standard Oil Co. of New Jersey

Dec. 12, Agreement signed in New York City for 49
hour week with the clothing workers of the United
Garment Workers union

Dec. 13, Strike of 60,000 clothing workers of Amalgamated Clothing Workers union in New York City
for increase in wages and the 48 hour week

Dec. 18, Note of President to the warring nations suggested that they communicate their terms of peace

Dec. 22, The President nominated 5 members of the
new Shipping Board, John B. White, William Denman, Bernard N. Baker, John A. Donald, and Theodore Brent

Dec. 26, Central Powers and Turkey replied to Note
of Dec. 18 proposing a conference of belligerents but
giving no statement of peace terms

Dec. 31, Death of Hamilton Wright Mabie (70) editor
and author, New York

CONGRESS

Feb. 15, Number of cadets at Naval Academy increased,
2 assigned to each congressional district, 2 to each
Territory, 4 to the District of Columbia, 2 to Puerto
Rico, 4 to each State at large, 80 to the United
States at large, and 180 to the enlisted men of the
National Guard

Feb. 28, Bureau of Efficiency of Civil Service Commission made an independent bureau

March 3, Gore Resolution in the Senate declaring that
if an armed liner were attacked without warning
and if an American lost his life, the incident would
be "a just and sufficient cause of war," tabled by
vote of 68 to 14

March 16, Clause of Underwood Tariff Act making
sugar duty-free after May 1, 1916 repealed by House
by vote of 346 to 14; accepted by Senate April 22

March 17, Joint Resolution provided for increasing
the number of enlisted men in the army in an emergency

March 30, The House passed the Burnett Immigration
Bill by vote of 308 to 87 with clause prescribing a
literacy test for immigrants, and the Senate Dec. 14

April 19, President Wilson informed Congress that he
had demanded abandonment of submarine warfare
by Germany if diplomatic relations with the United
States to be maintained

April 27, Free sugar clause of the Underwood Tariff
Act repealed because of need of revenue

May 1, The House rejected Senate Bill as to Philippines
and substituted Jones Bill of 1914

May 4, Number of cadets at Military Academy doubled

May 15, Anti-Trust Interlocking Directorates Act
passed

June 3, National Defense Act authorized increased
regular army to 186,000, a total of 223,000 to be
reached in 5 years, and a federalized national guard
of 424,800, civilian training camps provided for and
a reserve officers training corps at colleges and universities, and construction of a plant for the production of nitrates and munitions, a signal corps constituted, and $640,000,000 appropriated for purchase
and maintenance of airships. The President given
power to fix prices under this Act

June 12, Act authorized the President to detail officers
and enlisted men of Navy and Marine Corps to serve
in Haiti

June 15, Boy Scouts of America incorporated

July 3, Act provided for incorporation of organized
militia into the regular army

July 11, Federal Aid Road Act authorized Federal aid
to extent of $5,000,000 for 1917, with increase of
$5,000,000 a year for 4 years to States for construc-
tion of rural post roads

July 17, Federal Farm Loan Act divided the country into 12 districts in each of which there was to be a Federal Land Bank, and a Loan Association made up of farmers who desired to borrow money, and Federal Farm Loan Board created to administer the system, the Secretary of the Treasury, chairman

Aug. 3, $540,000 appropriated for flood sufferers in Southern States and West Virginia

Aug. 9, Lassen Volcanic National Park, California, established, 80,000 acres

Aug. 11, Agricultural Appropriation Act contained the Grain Standards Act, the Warehouse Act, and the Cotton Futures Act of 1914 repealed and new one substituted

Aug. 18, President Wilson vetoed the Army Appropriation Bill because of clause providing for exemption of retired army officers from trial by court martial

Aug. 21, Act authorized the President to make rules and regulations for the Panama Canal Zone as to health, sanitation, quarantine, taxes, police powers

Aug. 25, Act established National Park Service in Dept. of Interior

Aug. 29, President Wilson addressed both Houses on the railroad strike threatened and recommended legislation to establish the eight hour day as basis of work and wages

——, Bill of Lading Act established carriers' liability

——, Army Appropriation Act provided for creation of Council of National Defense, and authorized the President to take possession of and assume control of the transportation systems.   Amount carried $267,596,530

——, Naval Appropriation Act carried appropriation of $313,300,555 and authorized three year building program for addition of 156 vessels

——, Number of midshipmen in the Naval Academy increased

——, Jones Act "to declare the purpose of the people of the United States as to the future political status of the people of the Philippine Islands, and to provide a more autonomous government for those Islands," granted larger measure of self government and promised independence "as soon as a stable government can be established"

Sept. 1, Child Labor Act passed to take effect in 1 year, prohibited the interstate shipment of the products of child labor, minimum age and hours fixed in different industries, 14 years for factories, 16 years for mines and quarries

Sept. 3, Adamson Act made the principle of the eight hour day mandatory on interstate railroads, overtime to be paid on pro rata basis, to become effective Jan. 1, 1917. Signed by the President Sept. 3 and 5

Sept. 7, Workmen's Compensation Act provided for compensation for injuries for federal employees

——, Shipping Act established a Shipping Board of 5 members, authorized to obtain by purchase or construction an American merchant marine to value of $50,000,000

Sept. 8, New Revenue Act doubled normal rate of the income tax for both individuals and corporations, surtaxes on incomes exceeding $40,000 increased on a graduated scale rising to 13% on incomes of $2,000,000 or more. An estate tax was laid on inherited estates, an excise tax on the net profits of manufacturers of explosives, firearms, and other munitions.   A Tariff Commission of 6 members appointed. Anti-dumping clause included to protect

American industries from unfair competition. Duties imposed on dye stuffs, beer, and fermented liquors

Sept. 8, Congress adjourned

Dec. 4, Sixty-Fourth Congress, 2d sess. convened

1917

Jan. 1, The eight hour day of the Adamson Act did not come into effect because of suits of railroads to declare law unconstitutional

——, Prohibition in force in 19 States: Alabama, Arkansas, Arizona, Colorado, Georgia, Idaho, Iowa, Kansas, Maine, Mississippi, North Carolina, North Dakota, Oklahoma, Oregon, South Carolina, Tennessee, Virginia, Washington, and West Virginia

Jan. 3, Colonel Chester Harding nominated by the President to succeed Goethals as Governor of the Panama Canal Zone

Jan. 4, Death of Brigadier General Peter J. Osterhaus (94)

Jan. 5, Employees Compensation Commission established for administration of system

Jan. 8, Supreme Court decision upheld the constitutionality of the Webb-Kenyon Act prohibiting the transportation of intoxicating liquors in interstate commerce from wet to dry States

Jan. 10, Congressional Union for Woman Suffrage posted 6 pickets at the gates of the White House because of President Wilson's failure to declare for the proposed suffrage amendment

——, End of clothing strike in New York City, demands conceded including 48 hour week

——, The German Consul-General in San Francisco and 4 of his employees found guilty of violation of neutrality laws in conspiracy to blow up shipments of munitions to Entente Allies

——, Note of Entente Powers in reply to Note of Dec. 18, 1916 stated war aims. See World War

——, Death of William F. Cody, "Buffalo Bill," scout and showman (71)

Jan. 11, Ammunition plant of the Canadian Car and Foundry Company near Kingsland, New Jersey, destroyed by fire believed to be incendiary

——, Death of Wayne McVeagh (84) lawyer and diplomat

Jan. 15, American-Mexican Joint Commission formally dissolved, failed to settle the border patrol disputes

——, Supreme Court upheld the constitutionality of the so-called White Slave Act

Jan. 16, Death of Admiral George Dewey (79)

Jan. 17, The Virgin Islands passed from the sovereignty of Denmark to that of the United States

Jan. 19, The German Government instructed Minister in Mexico to negotiate with Mexico and propose alliance between Mexico and Japan against the United States in the event of war, Mexico to receive the lost territory of New Mexico, Texas, and Arizona

Jan. 22, The Supreme Court upheld the constitutionality of the "blue sky" laws of Ohio, Michigan, and South Dakota which regulated the sale of securities

Jan. 23, North Dakota granted suffrage to women in vote for presidential electors and certain state officers and local officers

——, Message of Ambassador von Bernsdorff to German Foreign Office asked for $50,000 to influence Congress to prevent war

Jan. 24, Prohibition law enacted in Arkansas

Jan. 28, Announcement of Secretary Baker that American troops under General Pershing had been ordered to withdraw from Mexico followed by withdrawal on Feb. 5

Jan. 30, Decision to recognize Carranza Government in Mexico

Jan. 31, German Note to State Dept. announced unrestricted submarine warfare

Feb. 3, American steamer "Housatonic" sunk by German submarine after warning; all on board saved

——, Diplomatic relations with Germany severed. See *infra* Congress

Feb. 4, The Government invited neutral nations to break off relations with Germany

Feb. 5, The pacifist organizations including the American Union against Militarism, the Women's Peace Party, American Neutrality League, and the Anti-Conscription League opened headquarters in New York City under the name of the Emergency Peace Federation

Feb. 7, Foreign workmen employed by 3 sugar refining companies in Philadelphia went on strike for increase in wages

——, President Wilson directed the Federal Trade Commission to investigate and report on packers and stockyards

Feb. 9, Thomas Mooney convicted on charge of murder and sentenced to be hanged

——, Prohibition Bill signed by the Governor of Indiana to take effect April 2, 1918, and women granted right to vote for presidential electors

Feb. 10, Mr. Gerard, American Minister in Germany, finally permitted to leave the country, and American affairs placed in charge of the Spanish Minister

Feb. 12, Statement of Secretary Lansing in answer to German proposal through the Swiss Minister for negotiations as to blockade that there could be no discussion unless the proclamation of Jan. 31 by which Germany cancelled assurances of May 4 as to submarine warfare was withdrawn

Feb. 13, Committee on Labor of the Council of National Defense formally constituted, Samuel Gompers, chairman

Feb. 14–April 21, Unsuccessful strike of white goods workers in Chicago

Feb. 15, Wyoming enacted prohibition law

——, Great Britain agreed to issue permits for importation of German needles after State Dept. pointed out that the importation refused was freely granted in England at expense of American commerce

Feb. 19, Death of Major General Frederick Funston (51) at San Antonio, Texas

Feb. 21, Woman suffrage became effective in Ohio

Feb. 23, Federal Board for Vocational Education created

Feb. 27, Statement of President Wilson that sinking of the "Laconia" constituted "overt act"

Feb. 28, Preliminary Conference of American Federation of Labor called by the president, Samuel Gompers, and meeting March 9

——, Munitions Standard Board created by the Council of National Defense

——, Woman suffrage became effective in Indiana

——, Publication of German (Zimmermann) Note of Jan. 19 to Mexico by Associated Press in Washington

March 3, Diplomatic relations with Mexico renewed, Henry P. Fletcher presenting credentials as Minister

——, Daniel Willard appointed chairman of Advisory Committee of Council of National Defense

March 5, (Monday) Inauguration of President Wilson and Vice-President Marshall for second term

March 6, Arkansas gave women the right to vote at primary elections

——, Supreme Court upheld decision of lower court to restore the "Appam" to British owners

——, Supreme Court decision that clause of Underwood tariff law granting 5% rebate on goods imported in American vessels unconstitutional

March 7, Major General Scott reappointed Chief of Staff

March 8, The prisoners taken from British steamer "Yarrowdale" raided in South Atlantic released by Germany in accordance with request of the United States of Feb. 3, and sent to Switzerland

March 9, Resolution adopted by American Federation of Labor that workers should be given representation on national boards "coequal with that given to any other part of the community"

March 12, Announcement of the President that merchant ships entering the submarine zone would be armed and supplied with naval gunners

——, Conference of union leaders in Washington declared support of government in event of war

——, The four railroad brotherhoods called a strike for March 17 as part of fight for 8 hour day; postponed March 17 for 48 hours

March 16, Note to Mexico gave reasons and expressed regret at inability to accept proposals for peace

March 19, Decision of United States Supreme Court upheld the constitutionality of the Eight Hour Day Act, and the same day the railroad companies yielded obedience to law

March 21, American oil steamer "Healdton" torpedoed without warning off the coast of Holland

March 22, Recognition of the new Government of Russia

March 24, Proclamation of the President suspended the operation of the eight hour day for government work and provided for pay for overtime

——, Commercial Economy Board created by the Council of National Defense, A. W. Shaw, chairman, "to investigate and advise in regard to the economic distribution of commodities so as to conserve both capital and personnel for the national defense"

March 25, War Dept. Order called out units of National Guard in nine eastern States and the District of Columbia "for police purposes"

——, Order directed increase of navy personnel to 87,000

March 26, Texas gave women the right to vote at primary elections

——, Order directed increase of Marine Corps to 17,400

March 28, Rear Admiral James H. Oliver named as Governor of the Virgin Islands

March 31, The United States took formal possession of the Virgin Islands, St. Thomas, St. Croix, and St. John, former Danish West Indies

——, Executive Order of the President placed more than 10,000 postmasters of the first, second, and third classes under the merit system, future appointments to be under competitive examination

——, General Munitions Board created by the Council of National Defense

April 1, The regular army numbered 5,791 officers and 121,797 enlisted men, the national guard about 3,733 officers and 76,713 enlisted men and the reserve

4,000 enlisted men according to statement of Secretary Baker

April 1, American steamer "Aztec" torpedoed and sunk

April 4, Price of wheat on the Chicago Board of Trade passed $2

April 6, Proclamation of the President declared the United States at war with Germany

——, Eighty-seven German ships in American harbors taken over by the Government

April 7, Convention of the Socialist Party in Chicago passed resolutions against the War. The minority left the Party

——, Statement of Samuel Gompers at Washington Conference pledged support of the Government by the American Federation of Labor during the War

——, The Navy Dept. assumed control of all the wireless stations

April 8, Death of Richard Olney (81) former Secretary of State

——, Austria-Hungary severed diplomatic relations with the United States

April 9, Fourteen Austrian vessels in American ports seized by the Government

——, The price of cotton reached 21¼ cents a pound on the New York Stock Exchange, the highest price since the Civil War

——, General Munitions Board created with Frank A. Scott, chairman

——, Admiral Sims arrived in England

——, The Eddystone Ammunition Corporation plant at Chester, Pennsylvania, destroyed by internal explosion, 122 persons killed

April 10, Bulgaria severed diplomatic relations

——, Death of Dr. John K. Mitchell, neurologist (57) in Philadelphia

April 11, As requested by the Council of National Defense the American Railway Association named a board of 5 members to direct the operation of the railroads during the War, Fairfax Harrison, president

April 13, Convention of the Progressive Party at St. Louis with radicals of other parties to form new organization of Liberals

April 14, Executive Order of the President established a Committee on Public Information consisting of the Secretaries of State, War, and Navy with George Creel as chairman

April 16, United States Shipping Board Emergency Fleet Corporation organized as a corporation under laws of the District of Columbia, Charles M. Schwab, at head

April 18, Rhode Island granted women right to vote for presidential electors

——, Woman suffrage became effective in Michigan

——, Lockout begun in shoe factories in Lynn, Massachusetts

——, Death of Herbert W. Conn, bacteriologist

April 19, First shot of American gun in the War, the steamer "Mongolia" repulsed submarine attack

April 20, Turkey severed diplomatic relations with the United States

April 21, Woman suffrage and state wide prohibition laws enacted in Nebraska

April 22, British War Commission headed by Arthur J. Balfour arrived in Washington

April 24, French War Commission headed by Marshal Joffre and including M. Viviani arrived at Hampton Roads, Virginia

April 25, First loan made to the Allies under the Liberty Loan Act, $200,000,000 to Great Britain

——, Anthracite coal miners in the eastern States received wage increases averaging 20%

April 27, Names of American persons and firms removed from the British "black list"

April 29, Executive Order of President Wilson provided for censorship of cables and telegraphs into Mexico

——, Death of Rear Admiral Samuel L. Ayres (81) in Philadelphia

April 30, All Reserve Corps officers ordered into active service

——, Bituminous coal miners in Central Pennsylvania received an increase of 20 to 30% in wages

May 1, New immigration law became effective

——, Prohibition went into effect in Nebraska

——, The "Rockingham," American armed vessel, sunk by German submarine off coast of England

May 3-4, First American destroyer flotilla arrived off Queenstown, Ireland

May 3, Loan to Italy of $100,000,000

May 6, Death of Mrs. Ruth McEnery Stuart (Mrs. Alfred O.), author

May 8, Loan to France of $100,000,000 under Liberty Loan Act

May 9, American Commission headed by John F. Stevens left New York for Russia to aid in rehabilitation of railroads

May 9-10, Italian High Commission headed by Enrico Erlotta and Prince Udine arrived in New York

May 10, Major General John J. Pershing appointed to command American Expeditionary Forces in France; formal appointment May 26

——, Death of former Senator Joseph Benson Foraker, Cincinnati, Ohio

——, Red Cross War Council established, Henry P. Davison, chairman

May 11, Secretary Baker sent final refusal to Theodore Roosevelt of his request to be allowed to organize a Division of Infantry for service in France

——, Commission to Russia announced, Elihu Root, Charles Crane, John R. Mott, Cyrus McCormick, Rear Admiral James H. Glennon, Major General H. L. Scott

May 12, Chicago Board of Trade ordered discontinuance of trading in May wheat the price of which had reached unprecedented high of $3.25 a bushel, similar action taken by exchanges at St. Louis, Duluth, Kansas City, Minneapolis, and Toledo

May 14, Circular issued by the Secretary of the Treasury announced first Liberty Loan of $2,000,000,000 in 3½% convertible gold bonds dated June 15

——, President Wilson ordered immediate increase of army to full war strength provided for under Act of June 3, 1916, of 223,000

——, Death of Joseph H. Choate (85), lawyer and diplomat, New York

May 15, New series of training camps opened modeled on citizen training camps of Plattsburg to prepare more reserve officers

May 16, Aircraft Production Board established

——, Loan to Russia of $100,000,000 and to Belgium $45,000,000

——, Strike of carpenters, joiners, and calkers in 3 shipyards at Camden, New Jersey

May 18, President Wilson ordered an expeditionary force of one division under command of General Pershing to proceed to France

May 19, Herbert Hoover appointed Food Controller by the President to organize a Food Administration

——, Death of Mrs. Belva A. B. Lockwood (86) lawyer and suffragist, Washington

May 21, Franz von Rintelen, David Lamar, and H. B. Martin sentenced to fine and imprisonment for conspiracy to restrain the manufacture, transportation, and export of munitions of war

May 23, Proclamation of the President as to regulations for maintenance of neutrality of Panama Canal

May 24, President Wilson received Italian War Commission headed by Ferdinand of Savoy, Prince of Udine

——, 88 individuals and corporations indicted in Boston on charge of conspiracy to monopolize interstate commerce in onions

——, Samuel Gompers declined participation of American Federation of Labor in proposed Labor Conference to be held at Stockholm

May 26, General Pershing appointed Commander in Chief of forces in France, and instructed to proceed to Paris with staff

May 27–30, Race riots in East St. Louis, Illinois

May 28, General Pershing sailed from New York, and arrived in London June 9, and in Paris June 13

May 29, Rear Admiral Albert Gleaves appointed in command of operations for convoy of the army to France

May 30, The People's Council for Democracy and Terms of Peace organized at Madison Square Garden, New York City, by Socialists and Pacificists

——, Gun crew on merchant ship "Silvershell" sunk submarine attacking in the Mediterranean

June 2, Federal Grand Jury in Chicago indicted Baron Kurt von Reiswitz and 13 others including 9 Hindus charged with conspiracy to instigate revolution in India

——, 25 individuals and firms indicted in Chicago charged with conspiracy to monopolize interstate trade in butter and eggs

June 5, 10,679,814 men registered for the draft for selective conscription

June 7, Official announcement that fleet of 25,000 airplanes would be created

June 8, Judge Thomas signed decree ordering sale of homes of members of hatter's union to pay fine in Danbury hatter's case in the courts since 1903

June 9, Loan of $3,000,000 to Serbia under Liberty Loan Act

June 11–Sept. 17, Strike of copper miners in Butte, Montana, for increase in wages and grievances finally settled by increase in wages

June 13, First American combatant troops sailed from New York

——, General John J. Pershing arrived in France

——, American Mission headed by Elihu Root arrived in Russia, and Railroad Commission headed by John F. Stevens

June 14, United States Public Service Reserve created by Secretary of Labor for registration for government service with or without compensation

June 15, Emma Goldman and Alexander Berkman, anarchists, arrested for interference with registration under the Conscription Act

June 18, Belgian Mission headed by Baron Ludovic Moncheur received by the President

June 19, Trading in cotton for future delivery reached 27 cents a pound on the New York Cotton Exchange, highest prince since 1871

June 20, Proclamation of the President called for enlistment of 70,000 men in the regular army

——, Russian Mission headed by Boris A. Bakhmetieff arrived

——, Death of Digby Bell (67) actor, New York

June 22, Exports Council (later Exports Administrative Board) appointed by the President composed of the Secretaries of State, Agriculture, and Commerce and the Food Administrator to formulate policies and make recommendations, and the United States Millers' Committee by Mr. Hoover

——, American medical units took over control of 6 British field hospitals in France

——, Convoy of troops ships repulsed submarine attacks June 22, 25, and 26 on voyage to France

June 24–25, Katharine Stinson made flight from Buffalo to Washington with stops at Albany, New York, and Philadelphia, and during the month Ruth Law made 2,500 mile trip in the interests of the Liberty Loan in the Middle West

June 25, First American troops arrived in France of the Expeditionary Force

June 26, Anthracite and bituminous coal operators met in Washington and agreed to establish a fixed lower price for coal

——, Strike of copper miners called at Bisbee, Arizona, to begin the following day, demanding a minimum wage of $6 a day for underground and $5.50 for work above ground, and changes in working conditions which were refused by the operators

June 28, Price of bituminous coal fixed at $3 a ton by conference of boards and operators, not accepted by Secretary of War and of Navy

June 29, Interstate Commerce Commission refused request of railroads for 15% increase in freight rates because of higher operating costs due to advances in prices of labor and of steel and coal

June 30, Imports for the fiscal year totaled $2,659,355,-185 and exports $6,293,806,090 an increase of 35% over 1916

——, Death of William Winter (80) dramatic critic and author, New York

July 1, Prohibition went into effect in South Dakota

——, Referendum vote of Socialist Party condemned entrance of the United States into the war by 21,639 to 2,752, whereupon a number of prominent members left the Party, John Spargo, William English Walling, J. G. Phelps Stokes and Mrs. Stokes, Upton Sinclair, Allan Benson, Dr. J. Bohn, and Charles Edward Russell

——, Plant Disease Survey established by the Dept. of Agriculture

July 2, The Rumanian Mission received by the Secretary of State

——, Strike of copper miners in the Globe-Miami district of Arizona

——, First convoy escorting merchant ships sailed from Hampton Roads

——, Strike of machinists and boilermakers in shipyards of Hoboken and New York for a minimum wage of $4.50 a day and improved working conditions which was settled Aug. 26 by reference to Adjustment Board

——, Death of William H. Moody (66) former Secretary of the Navy and Supreme Court judge

July 2–3, More than 100 negroes killed or wounded in

race riot in East St. Louis, Illinois, caused by importation of negro labor during strike. Martial law proclaimed

July 3, Proclamation of the President called out the national guard and reserve for military service

——, The "Liberty" engine, designed by a group of prominent aëronautical and automobile engineers for airplanes, sent to Washington for test as standard motor

July 4, Attack of German submarines on United States transports defeated

——, General Pershing with American troops marched through the streets of Paris

July 7, Emma Goldman and Alexander Berkman, anarchists, sentenced to 2 year imprisonment and $10,000 fine for interference with registration of soldiers, decision sustained by Supreme Court Jan. 14, 1918

July 9, Proclamation of the President placed export of food stuffs, flour, meats, fats, &c., coal, fuel oils, iron and steel and war materials under government control to begin July 15

July 11, President Wilson made statement to mine operators, manufacturers, and shipping interests that the prices for the public must be the same as for the Government

July 12, 1,186 I.W.W. members deported from the Warren district of Arizona to Columbus, New Mexico, by the sheriff of the county, because of the belief that the Industrial Workers of the World were inciting the miners to strike and working in the interests of Germany

——, Strike of employers of revolver factory in Springfield Mass. for higher wages

July 13, Order of the President drafted into military service 678,000 men from those who had registered June 5

July 15, 50,000 lumber men went on strike in Washington, Oregon, Idaho, and Montana for eight hour day and increase in wages. The eight hour day granted in Dec.

July 17, Sixteen suffragettes arrested for picketing the White House and sentenced to 60 days in the workhouse, but were pardoned by the President July 19

July 18, Censorship ordered for all transatlantic cable messages by the Navy Dept. and across land frontiers by the War Dept.

July 20, Drawing for first draft for military service held in the Senate Office building. Every registrant given a number which established his order of liability to be called for service

July 24, General Goethals resigned from Shipping Board because of disagreement with William Denman, chairman, as to building of ships. The President requested resignation of Mr. Denman, and Edward N. Hurley appointed chairman, and Rear Admiral W. L. Capps succeeded General Goethals as manager of the Emergency Fleet Corporation, and Bainbridge Colby succeeded J. B. White resigned

July 26, The Federal Trade Commission recommended that Congress enact legislation to protect the public against the "indefensible" and "extortionate" prices being charged for commodities in special demand since the United States entered the War

July 27, Governor James E. Ferguson, of Texas, and other officials arrested charged with misapplication of public funds

July 28, War Industries Board created by the Council

of National Defense succeeding the General Munitions Board, Frank A. Scott, of Cleveland, chairman, designed to concentrate and standardize buying

July 28, Switchmen of 19 railroads in Chicago region went on strike for changes in the rules regarding employment, promotion and dismissal, and the closed shop, settled 2 days later the men waiving the matter of the closed shop

July 29, First keel of a contract ship laid down and delivery made by Emergency Fleet Corporation Jan. 5, 1918

July 30, Death of Brigadier General Harrison Gray Otis (80) publisher of the *Los Angeles Times*

July 31, American oil steamer "Montano" torpedoed by German submarine without warning off the coast of Ireland, and 16 of the crew and 8 naval gunners lost

Aug. 1, Prohibition (statutory) went into effect in Utah

Aug. 3, The Emergency Fleet Corporation requisitioned all steel ships over 2,500 deadweight tonnage under construction in American shipyards

Aug. 8, National Adjustment Commission constituted to fix wages and conditions of labor employed in loading and unloading ships

Aug. 10, Food Commission legally established, and Herbert Hoover appointed Food Administrator

Aug. 11, Announcement of Secretary Lansing that passports would not be granted for attendance at the Labor Conference at Stockholm

Aug. 12, Commission headed by H. A. Garfield appointed to fix the price of wheat

Aug. 12–Oct., Strike of employees of the street railroads of San Francisco for increase in wages to $3.50 a day and time and one-half for overtime, and eight hour day

Aug. 13, Japanese Mission arrived on the Pacific coast headed by Viscount Ishii

Aug. 14, 105 persons indicted in connection with the race riots in East St. Louis, Illinois, in July

——, Food Administration Grain Corporation organized to engage in buying, storing, transporting, and selling grain

——, Proclamation of the President required licensing by Sept. 1 of all persons or corporations engaged in business of storing or distributing wheat or rye or their products

Aug. 15, Arsenals and Navy Yards Wage Commission created, F. D. Roosevelt, Stanley King, and R. B. Mahaney

Aug. 16, Announcement of Food Administration that the production of distilled spirits for beverage purposes must cease Sept. 8 under Food Control Act

——, Nine day strike of street car employees of Kansas City settled by compromise agreement

Aug. 19, 26 I.W.W. leaders arrested at Spokane, Washington, on charge of inciting strikes in the lumber and fruit industries

Aug. 20, Agreement of the Emergency Fleet Corporation and the American Federation of Labor created the Shipbuilding Labor Adjustment Board to have jurisdiction over disputes concerning wages and working conditions in shipbuilding plants

——, United States District Court at Atlanta upheld constitutionality of the Selective Draft Act in decision as to "slackers" in Georgia

Aug. 21, Exports Administrative Board established

——, Price of bituminous coal fixed by the President

Aug. 23, Harry A. Garfield appointed Fuel Administrator. Price of anthracite coal fixed by the President

——, Race riot at Houston, Texas, negro soldiers at Camp Logan in conflict with the citizens, 17 persons killed, and martial law declared

Aug. 24, Board of Control for Labor Standards in Army Clothing created in the War Dept.

——, Announcement of loan of $100,000,000 to Russia making a total of $275,000,000

——, Agreement of 100,000 workers in the shipbuilding trades of the Pacific coast signed to submit differences to arbitration avoiding strike

Aug. 25, The Shipbuilding Labor Adjustment Board created to provide for adjustment of disputes for all union laborers doing work of shipbuilding except carpenters

Aug. 27, President Wilson replied to Pope Benedict's peace note of Aug. 1 that the guarantee of the present rulers of Germany could not be accepted for an enduring peace, and declared that a preliminary condition for peace negotiations would be the establishment of a government representing the German people

——, Proclamation of the President prohibited exportation of a list of specified articles except by license

Aug. 30, Basic price of wheat at Chicago fixed at $2.20 a bushel by the President, and of print paper for official bulletins at 2½ cents a pound

Aug. 31, Federal Child Labor law declared unconstitutional by Federal Circuit Court of North Carolina

Sept. 1, Federal Child Labor law of 1916 came into effect

——, Grain Corporation under the Food Administration began operations buying and distributing wheat and urging cultivation of every patch of land that could be utilized

Sept. 5, Federal agents raided I.W.W. headquarters in 23 cities. In Chicago William D. Haywood, president, arrested with 167 others

Sept. 7, Proclamation of the President prohibited the export of coin, bullion, and currency

——, Proclamation of the President licensed the importation of sugar, sirups, and molasses

——, American Atlantic transport "Minnehaha" sunk by submarine off the coast of Ireland, 48 persons lost

Sept. 8, Secretary Lansing published message of German Ambassador in Argentina recommending that Argentine vessels either be spared or sunk without a trace. See also Argentina

Sept. 10, Woman suffrage defeated in election in Maine

Sept. 15, Strike of shipyard workers on the northwest coast

Sept. 16–20, Strike of longshoremen in New York City ended with acceptance of arbitration

Sept. 17–29, Strike of 25,000 employees in iron trades and shipbuilding trades in San Francisco for wage increase

Sept. 19, Mediation Council of 5 members headed by the Secretary of Labor appointed by the President to investigate and settle various strikes on the Pacific coast

——, Caleb Bragg established a new American aëroplane altitude record at 22,000 feet

Sept. 19–22, Non-Partisan League held convention at St. Paul, Minnesota, Governor Frazier, of North Dakota, presiding, A. C. Townley president, asked

that the Government fix not only the price of wheat but of other materials that enter into the products that the farmers must buy, coal, iron, steel, and oil, &c.

Sept. 20, Lockout in shoe factories in Lynn, Massachusetts

——, Price of copper fixed by the President at 23½ cents a pound

Sept. 21, State Dept. published message of Ambassador von Bernstorff to the German Government of Jan. 22 asking for $50,000 to expend to influence Congressmen in favor of peace

Sept. 22, Senate of Texas sustained charges against Governor James Ferguson on charges of misappropriation of funds

——, General Tasker H. Bliss became Chief of Staff of the Army succeeding General Hugh L. Scott

Sept. 24, The President approved maximum prices fixed for iron ore, iron, and steel involving reductions of from 43 to 70%

——, Socialist Party National Council went out of existence, and affairs placed in charge of a National Executive Committee of 4 members, Morris Hillquit, Victor Berger, John M. Work, and Anna A. Maley

Sept. 27, Shipping Board announced that on Oct. 15 all American ocean vessels over 2,500 tons would be requisitioned for government service

Sept. 30, Death of Isaac N. Seligman (62) banker, philanthropist, New York

Oct. 1, Second Liberty Loan offered of $3,000,000,000 at 4% to run for 25 years

——, Award to 45,000 longshoremen in Atlantic ports gave eight hour day and increase in overtime rates, and new wage scale signed May 4, 1918

Oct. 3, Members of the National Progressive Party supporters of the single tax met with some members of the Socialist Party in Chicago to discuss organization of a new radical party

Oct. 6, Bituminous coal miners and operators reached agreement (the Washington Agreement) providing for an increase in wages and for an automatic penalty clause to be introduced into wage contracts to prevent strikes and lockouts

——, War Risk Insurance Bureau of the Treasury Dept. authorized to make provision for support of dependent families of the men under arms, and evolve compensation grants program for soldiers and sailors killed or injured in the service, and offer insurance policies against death or total disability

——, Major General Pershing and Tasker Bliss commissioned generals

Oct. 7, Strike of street car employees at Chattanooga, Tenn. which had prevented operation of cars for a month settled

Oct. 8, Proclamation of the President required licensing of 64 staple commodities by importers, manufacturers, and distributors under Food Administration

——, Strike of longshoremen on piers of the North River, New York City, threatening interference with the shipment of war supplies begun, which was settled by reference to arbitration

Oct. 12, New Catskill Aqueduct (Ashokan) for water supply of New York City completed

——, War Trade Council and War Trade Board and Censorship Board created by orders of the President

Oct. 15, Constitutional amendment for state wide prohibition defeated at election in Iowa, prohibition already in existence by legislative enactment

Oct. 15, Strike of window cleaners begun which lasted 32 days and gained increase in wages and recognition of union

Oct. 17, Transport "Antilles" torpedoed and sunk on return voyage from France in spite of convoy of armed vessels with loss of 70 persons

Oct. 18, 58 enemy aliens arrested at dry docks, Hoboken, New Jersey

——, Strike of employees of shipyards on the Pacific coast settled

Oct. 18–19, 2,000 milk drivers in New York struck for increase in wages, settled by arbitration

Oct. 20, Gupta, Jacobsen Wehde, Boehm, and others in California convicted of conspiracy to violate neutrality of the United States, and wreck vessels at sea and sentenced to imprisonment and fines

——, New York Harbor Wage Adjustment Board organized

Oct. 21, Americans entered the line in Toul sector, France, and in first action Oct. 23. For war *see* World War

Oct. 22, A. Mitchell Palmer assumed office as Custodian of Enemy Property, appointed by the President

Oct. 24, Death of James Carroll Beckwith (65) painter, New York

Oct. 25, President Wilson in address endorsed woman suffrage as a state issue

Oct. 29, Order of President Wilson increased price of bituminous coal by 45 cents a ton in order that wage increases promised should be effected

Oct. 30, Death of Elisha Benjamin Andrews, educator (73), at Interlaken, Florida

Nov. 1, Prohibition went into effect in the District of Columbia

——, Prices as published by the Dept. of Agriculture for this date showed general rise, the average rise in 9 products, wheat, corn, oats, barley, rye, buckwheat, white potatoes, sweet potatoes, and flaxseed showed increase of 31% as compared with 1916 and slightly over 100% in comparison with a 5 year average (1911–1915)

——, Tax of 1% collected for each 10-cent admission to places of amusement and on club dues 10%

Nov. 2, Lansing-Ishii Agreement signed by which the United States recognized Japan's special interests in China, the "open door" policy as to China and maintenance of integrity of China reaffirmed; protested by China

——, New loan to Russia of $31,700,000

——, On and after this date tax imposed on cigars, cigarettes, and tobacco in addition to existing taxes

——, Rate on first class mail increased from 2 to 3 cents an ounce and post cards from 1 to 2 cents

Nov. 4, Award of Shipbuilding Labor Adjustment Board fixed basic wage rates for the entire Pacific coast from 10 to 30% higher than the old scale

Nov. 6, In elections New York adopted woman suffrage by constitutional amendment by majority of 102,353, but was defeated in Ohio as was also prohibition. Prohibition was adopted by New Mexico

Nov. 7, Proclamation of the President required all manufacturers of bakery products to be licensed by Dec. 10

Nov. 9, Maximum basic prices for coke fixed

Nov. 15, "Lightless" nights inaugurated by the Fuel Administration to conserve supply, lights of electric signs in cities restricted as to hours (Nov. 9)

Nov. 16, Proclamation of the President prescribed registration of enemy aliens, surveillance and exclusion from the District of Columbia, the Canal Zone, and waterfronts throughout the country

——, The Post Office took over control of the cables

Nov. 19, Daniel Willard appointed chairman of the War Industries Board

Nov. 20, Arsenic industry brought under government control

Nov. 22, Conference of the President with representatives of the railroad brotherhoods as to increase of wages demanded, the contention being that the eight hour day granted not equivalent to wage increase

——, Decision of court against unions awarded $200,000 damages in Bache-Denman Co. case against United Mine workers

Nov. 24, All railroads east of Chicago pooled to facilitate movement of freight

——, Admiral F. R. Harris appointed manager of the Emergency Fleet Corporation succeeding Admiral Capps resigned

Nov. 26, Cotton for Dec. delivery in New York City priced at 30.5 cents a pound

Nov. 27, Executive order vested power to fix prices in Food Administration

——, New War Council including 6 Cabinet members appointed

——, Bishop Hayes (later Cardinal) appointed chaplain of all the United States forces in the war

——, Conviction by court martial of David A. Henkes charged with disloyalty, and sentence of imprisonment for 25 years

Nov. 28, First Army General Staff College opened at Langres, France, under supervision of General James W. McAndrew, a 3 months' course

——, Proclamation of the President provided for system of licenses for imports

Nov. 29, The United States represented at Inter-Allied Conference in Paris by General Tasker H. Bliss, Colonel E. M. House, Admiral Benson, and Messrs. Crosby, McCormick, Taylor, and Perkins

Nov. 30, The "Rainbow Division" representing every State in the Union reached France

Dec. 1, Price of anthracite coal at mines increased 35 cents a ton by order of the President

——, The United States represented at Supreme War Council at Versailles by Colonel E. M. House, and Admiral Bliss

——, War stamp taxes imposed after this date on bonds, stock certificates, drafts and checks, steamer tickets, playing cards, &c.

——, Railroad conductors and trainmen demanded wage increase of 40%

——, Death of Henry Marcus Leipziger (62) educator, New York City

Dec. 3, War savings and thrift stamps placed on sale

Dec. 4, War Trade Board published black list of more than 1,600 German controlled firms in Latin America

Dec. 6, A division of United States battleships joined the Allied fleet at Scapa Flow

Dec. 7, War declared on Austria-Hungary. *See infra* Congress

Dec. 8, Rules and regulations for control of slaughtering and meat packing industries published, and production of malt liquor and its alcoholic content limited by proclamation of the President

Dec. 10, Supreme Court decision sustained injunctions

restraining activities of unions from attempt to organize where workmen are under contract with employers not to join unions

Dec. 11, 13 colored soldiers hanged for participation in riot at Houston, Texas, in Aug.

——, Proclamation of the President declared existence of state of war with Austria-Hungary

——, Non-stop flight of Katharine Stinson from San Diego to San Francisco, 610 miles, in 9 hours and 10 minutes

Dec. 15, New War Council created of Secretary of War and officers of Army to consider problems of supply

Dec. 17, Charles A. Piez appointed manager of the Emergency Fleet Corporation succeeding Admiral Harris

——, Death of Zenas Crane (77) paper manufacturer, Dalton, Mass.

Dec. 20, Diplomatic Mission from Serbia arrived

Dec. 24, Price of wood alcohol fixed by War Industries Board at 50 cents a gallon

——, Death of Francis Griffith Newlands (69) Senator from Nevada, in Washington

Dec. 26, Proclamation of the President placed the railroads under government control and operation, William G. McAdoo appointed Director General of Railroads, to take effect Dec. 28. Actual transfer made at midnight Dec. 31

Dec. 27, Death of Dr. Theodore C. Janeway (45) diagnostician and professor, Baltimore

Dec. 29, First order of Director General of Railroads ordered pooling of all traffic, common utilization of all facilities, haulage of freight by the shortest routes, and called on all employees to continue in the performance of their duties

Dec. 31, Railroad War Board resigned

——, The Regular Army on this date numbered 10,250 officers and 475,000 enlisted men; National Guard 16,031 officers and 400,000 enlisted men; National Army 480,000 men; Reserve 84,575 officers and 72,750 enlisted men (Baker); increase in 9 months from 9,524 officers to 110,856, and from 202,510 enlisted men to 1,428,650

CONGRESS

Jan. 18, House Committee ordered to investigate charges that the contents of the Peace Note of the President of Dec. 18 was made known to financiers in Wall St. in advance by high officials in Washington for pecuniary benefit in speculation resulted in exoneration of officials

Jan. 22, President Wilson in address to the Senate declared that a just peace must be "a peace without victory," must recognize equality of right among great and small nations, security for "subject people," freedom of the seas, limitation of armaments, and replacement of the old system of alliances by a general concert of powers

Jan. 29, President Wilson vetoed the Immigration Bill because of inclusion of the literacy test and a provision which permitted immigration officials to exempt from test foreigners who were fleeing from religious persecution

Feb. 1, Immigration Bill passed in House over veto by vote of 211 to 196

Feb. 3, The President addressed Congress in joint session announcing that he had directed the Secretary of State to sever diplomatic relations with Germany, recalling Ambassador Gerard from Berlin, and that

passports would be handed to Count von Bernsdorff that day

Feb. 5, The Senate passed the Immigration Bill over the President's veto by vote of 62 to 19 making it the law

Feb. 14, Act prohibited the manufacture and sale of intoxicating liquors in Alaska Territory

——, Appropriations for fortifications, &c., provided for $3,600,000 for airships

——, Act to punish threats against the President passed

Feb. 23, Federal Board for Vocational Education created, and provision for financial aid to States for promotion of vocational education

Feb. 26, President Wilson's "armed neutrality" message asked for authority to arm merchant ships for defense in case of submarine attack

——, Mt. McKinley National Park created in Alaska

Feb. 28, Filibuster against the Armed Merchant Ship Bill begun in Senate which prevented passage before expiration of Congress March 4, by 7 Republicans and 5 Democrats, the "little group of wilful men"

March 1, The House passed the Armed Ship Bill by vote of 403 to 13 in modified form

——, First Mississippi Flood Control Act appropriated $45,000,000

March 2, New Organic Act for Puerto Rico made it a Territory and extended American citizenship to all inhabitants, the suffrage to all males of 21 and over, and replaced the Executive Council as the upper legislative chamber by a Senate of 19 members elected by the people

——, Bankruptcy Act amended

——, National Military Park established at battlefield of Guilford Court House

March 3, Organic Act for the Virgin Islands vested all military, civil, and judicial powers in a Governor to be appointed by the President, Danish code of law continued in force

——, War Revenue Act of $350,000,000, the Legislative, Executive, and Judicial Appropriation, Pension Appropriation, and increased appropriations for War Risk Insurance Bureau and army and navy. An excess profits tax established under the War Revenue Act and increased inheritance tax

——, Prohibition established in the District of Columbia after Nov. 1

——, Joint Resolution made appropriation for construction and operation of railroads in Alaska

——, Congress adjourned

March 8, At special session of the Senate a new closure rule adopted by vote of 76 to 3, the Senate remaining in session for the purpose, providing procedure by which a majority might force the termination of a debate

March 21, The President called Congress to meet in special session on April 2 to "receive a communication concerning grave matters of national policy"

April 2, Sixty-Fifth Congress, 1st (extra) sess. convened. President Wilson recited grievances of the United States against the German Government and asked for a declaration of war against "this natural foe to liberty," and that Americans should fight "for the ultimate peace of the world and for the liberation of its peoples, the German people included; for the rights of nations, great and small, and the privilege of men everywhere to choose their way of life and of obedience." In this address he said "The world must be made safe for democracy." Resolutions for war introduced in both House and Senate

April 4, War Resolution passed Senate by vote of 82 to 6, Stone, Vardaman, and Lane (Democrats), and La Follette, Norris, and Gronna (Republicans) voting against. Passed in the House April 6 by vote of 373 to 50

April 6, Joint Resolution declaring a state of war with the Imperial German Government signed by the President

April 17, First Deficiency Appropriation Act for expenses of year ending June 30, 1917 and prior to fiscal year

April 24, Liberty Bonds Act authorized the issue of bonds to meet expenditures for the national defense, $5,000,000,000 at 3½%, and an issue of short term notes of $2,000,000,000, of which $3,000,000 to be invested in bonds for the Allies

April 25, Number of midshipmen in the Naval Academy again increased

May 12, Army Appropriation Act provided for $10,800,000 for construction and purchase of airplanes

——, Joint Resolution authorized the President to take possession of vessels of nations at war with the United States

May 18, Selective Conscription Act provided that all men between ages of 21 and 31 should be enrolled for military service, and from this number should be drafted the men for the army by the President, the Regular Army to be increased 287,000, and an additional 500,000 to be chosen by selective draft, and 500,000 more later, and the President authorized to call the entire National Guard into service

May 22, Act increased Navy and Marine Corps

May 29, Act amending Interstate Commerce Act organized Bureau of Car Service with power to regulate use of rolling stock without reference to ownership

June 12, War Risk Insurance Act amended, and $45,150,000 appropriated to insure American vessels and their cargoes

June 15, $43,450,000 additional appropriation made for purchase and construction of airships

——, Espionage Act imposed penalties on persons who interfered with foreign relations, neutrality, or the mobilization of the military or naval forces, or gave information concerning national defenses. Provision for the control of exports made and an Exports Administrative Board created

——, Urgent Deficiency Act gave the President power to take over the shipyards and their output

——, War Appropriation Act carried $3,281,904,541.60 for expenses of Army and Navy arising out of the War

June 21, Federal Reserve Act amended, establishment of branches authorized, regulations as to admissions of State banks and trust companies, accounts, &c.

July 2, Act authorized condemnation of lands for military purposes

July 24, Aviation Act provided for additional officers and men and appropriated $640,000,000 for purchase and construction of airplanes

July 28, Act provided relief for homestead entrymen and settlers who had entered army or navy

Aug. 10, Food Production and Food Control and Fuel Acts signed authorized the President to buy, transport and sell wheat and to fix a price which was not to go below $2 a bushel, and extensive powers given the government over fuel and food stuffs, and the im-

portation and manufacture of distilled spirits forbidden during the period of the War

Aug. 10, Preferential Shipments Act gave right of way on railroads to national defense commodities

Sept. 24, Second Liberty Loan Act authorized the Secretary of the Treasury to borrow by certificates of indebtedness from $2,000,000,000 to $4,000,000,000, and War Saving Certificates authorized

Oct. 1, Act created an Aircraft Board of 9 members and appropriated $100,000 for its maintenance

Oct. 3, New War Revenue Act provided for an increased income tax beginning with 4% on individual incomes over $1,000, graduated excess profit taxes, and increased taxes on tobacco, alcoholic liquors, on transportation, amusements and luxuries, automobiles, stamp taxes on bonds, deeds, &c., and parcel post packages, on transfer of estates, postal rates on letters and second class matter. Munitions tax of Sept. 8, 1916 reduced from 12½% to 10% for 1917, and made inoperative after Jan. 1, 1918

Oct. 6, Military and Naval Insurance Act appropriated $176,250,000 providing for family allowances, and compulsory allotment of pay for the support of dependents, compensation for death or disability due to injury or disease resulting from the service, and additional insurance at low cost

——, Second Deficiency War Appropriation Act carried $5,356,666,016.93

——, Trading with the Enemy Act prohibited commercial intercourse with an enemy or ally of an enemy, authorized the President to establish censorship of messages between the United States and any foreign country, to place an embargo on imports, and provided for the establishment of a custodian of alien property

——, Prohibition extended to all places under jurisdiction of Navy Dept.

——, Congress adjourned

Dec. 3, Sixty-Fifth Congress, 2d sess. convened

Dec. 4, President Wilson in address to Congress stated that "the wrongs . . . committed in this War will have to be righted . . . But they cannot and must not be righted by the commission of similar wrongs against Germany and her Allies." President Wilson recommended declaration of war on Austria-Hungary

Dec. 7, Resolution declaring a state of war with Austria-Hungary adopted

Dec. 12, Committee on Military Affairs headed by Senator Chamberlain began investigation of the War Dept.

Dec. 14, House Committee on Naval Affairs ordered investigation into conduct of war by the Navy Dept.

Dec. 17, Resolution proposing Prohibition Amendment to the Constitution passed the House by vote of 282 to 128, and the Senate the following day by vote of 47 to 8

Dec. 18, Resolution adopted submitting to the States an Amendment to the Constitution to prohibit "the manufacture, sale or transportation of intoxicating liquors within, the importation thereof into, or the exportation thereof from the United States and all territory subject to the jurisdiction thereof for beverage purposes"

1918

Jan. 3, and March 9, United States Employment Service established as distinct unit of the Dept. of Labor

——, Proclamation of the President licensed ammonia industry

Jan. 4, President Wilson requested Secretary of Labor Wilson to organize a program of war labor administration

Jan. 6, Railroad Administration ordered demurrage rates doubled, sliding scale of charges ranging from $3 to $10 per car per day into effect Feb. 10

Jan. 7, Supreme Court decision sustained the constitutionality of the Selective Draft Act

Jan. 8, Mississippi ratified the XVIIIth (Prohibition) Amendment to the Constitution

——, Death of Ellis H. Roberts (90) former Secretary of the Treasury, at Utica, New York

Jan. 9, Naval Overseas Transportation Service created by Navy Dept.

Jan. 10, Proclamation of the President further extended the licensing system

Jan. 11, Virginia ratified the Prohibition Amendment to the Constitution; by Kentucky Jan. 14, by South Carolina Jan. 23, and by North Dakota Jan. 25

Jan. 16, Fuel Administration Order provided that on Jan. 18–22 inclusive and on every Monday from Jan. 28 to March 25 inclusive no manufacturing plant should burn fuel or use power derived from fuel except such industries as needed to operate 7 days a week to avoid injury to plant or product, stores selling food or drugs, printing and publishing establishments to extent necessary to issue periodical publications, with some other exceptions, in order to restrict use of coal in that part of the United States east of the Mississippi because of wartime demand, and no manufacturing industries allowed to operate on days specified even if supply of coal on hand in order to place all industry on equal footing

Jan. 17, American gunboat "Monacacy" fired on by Chinese above Yoochow, apology made Jan. 24

Jan. 18, Railroad Administration appointed Railroad Wage Commission and divided country into 3 operating districts, eastern, southern, and western with regional directors

Jan. 19, Food Administration announced agreement with trade and fixed prices for butter

Jan. 23, Railroad Administration placed embargo on all freight other than food, fuel, and munitions on 3 eastern railroads to relieve the coal shortage

Jan. 25, Provisional Agreement with the Netherlands for use of Dutch ships in American ports for Belgian relief cargoes

Jan. 26, Proclamation of the President asked for voluntary observance of 2 days a week without wheat and pork and 1 day a week without any meat

Jan. 28, War Labor Conference Board organized by the Secretary of Labor

Jan. 30, Proclamation of the President announced licensing of bakery products

Jan. 31, Proclamation of the President established licensing system for producers and dealers in fuel oil

Feb. 2, Executive Order of the President provided for taking over of enemy property

——, Death of John L. Sullivan (59) pugilist, in Massachusetts

Feb. 3, Compulsory baking regulations for making bread required that 5% of other cereals be mixed with white flour, and this proportion raised to 20% later in the month and to 25% in April

——, Death of Judge William M. Chase (80), Concord, New Hampshire

Feb. 5, General Peyton C. Marsh appointed Acting

Chief of Staff, recalled from France; assumed office March 4

Feb. 5, Franz von Rintelen and 10 other Germans convicted of conspiracy to destroy the British vessel "Kirk Oswald" with bombs and sentenced to fines and imprisonment

Feb. 8, Monday closing rescinded by Fuel Administration for 8 Southern States

——, 55 members of the I.W.W. indicted at Sacramento, California, for conspiracy against war measures

Feb. 11, Carpenters in New York shipyards went on strike for same wage as given on the Pacific coast

Feb. 13, Maryland ratified the Prohibition Amendment, Montana Feb. 19

——, Monday closing order rescinded but the State authorities given power to keep it in effect where needed

Feb. 14, The President ordered an investigation of charges of waste and irregularities in shipyard contracts at Hog Island

——, Award of Shipbuilding Labor Adjustment Board in Delaware River and Baltimore district increased wages and established basic 44 hour week

——, Proclamation of the President prohibited export of all articles without license, and of all imports, formally taking control of all foreign trade by the Government

Feb. 16, New Jersey "anti-loafing" law required all able-bodied males to be regularly employed in some useful occupation

——, Inland Waterways Commission appointed headed by General W. M. Black

Feb. 18, Striking carpenters in shipyards of New York and Baltimore returned to work after letter from President Wilson of Feb. 17 to the officers of the union in which he condemned their strike at critical time for the nation until every method of adjustment had been tried

Feb. 21, Proclamation of the President fixed $2.20 per bushel as minimum price for 1918 wheat at Chicago

Feb. 22, Canteen work in France taken over by the Y.M.C.A. at request of General Pershing

Feb. 25, Conference of representatives of capital and labor in Washington to consider basis for adjustment of disputes during period of the War

——, Samuel Gompers, head of the American Federation of Labor, announced that he had refused invitation from the head of the German Federation of Trades Unions to confer as to peace terms

——, Proclamation of the President ordered licensing of the fertilizer industry

——, Construction of Dam No. 2 at Muscle Shoals authorized by the President. During this year 2 nitrate plants completed

Feb. 27, Arbitration Convention with France extended that of Feb. 10, 1908

March 2, Supreme Court of California denied new trial to Thomas J. Mooney and affirmed conviction and death sentence

——, Death of Hubert Howe Bancroft (85) historian, in California

——, General strike in Kansas City declared in sympathy with laundry workers who had been out several weeks, settled by arbitrators from the Dept. of Labor

March 3, Food Administration reduced number of

"meatless" days and meals, beef and pork only forbidden on Tuesdays

March 4, War Industries Board reorganized, Bernard M. Baruch, chairman, succeeding Daniel Willard

——, Prohibition Amendment ratified by Texas, South Dakota March 10, Delaware March 18. Rejected by Rhode Island March 12 and by New York March 20

——, Strike at the Pullman Palace Car works at Wilmington, Delaware

——, Award Shipbuilding Labor Adjustment Board in South Atlantic and Gulf States increased wages

March 5, Maximum price of aluminum fixed by agreement

——, Agreement with Spain by which United States received mules and blankets for cotton and petroleum

March 6, Sale of liquor within 5 miles of any naval training station prohibited by the Navy Dept.

——, Strike of employees in 7 department stores in St. Louis, and in 3 chemical factories, became general

March 8, New National Party formed by John Spargo, William English Walling, and other Socialists who had seceded from the Socialist Party, and some Progressives meeting in Chicago, adopted platform endorsing prohibition, woman suffrage, government ownership of public utilities and industries dependent on public franchises or requiring large scale noncompetitive operation

March 9, Order of Fuel Administration to take effect April 1 established rationing system of coal for domestic consumers

March 10, Secretary of War Baker arrived in France

March 11, President Wilson sent message to Russian National Congress of Soviets of sympathy as to German Treaty of March 3

March 14, Price Fixing Committee of War Industries Board created, Robert Brookings, chairman

March 15, Proclamation of the President established licensing system for coal and coke industry

——, Interstate Commerce Commission allowed 15% increase in commodity rates on eastern railroads

——, Death of James Stillman (67) banker, New York

March 20, Proclamation of the President ordered taking over of 40 Dutch vessels in American ports for government service in view of military needs, full compensation to be given

——, The "War Cabinet" meetings begun by conference of the President with the Secretary of the Navy and Acting Secretary of War, and 6 heads of War boards, weekly meetings held thereafter

——, Prohibition Amendment ratified by South Dakota

March 21, Scott Nearing indicted in New York for articles in which he denounced the Liberty Loan and Selective Service Act

March 22, Prohibition law enacted by Texas to take effect June 26

——, Railroad Board of Adjustment No. 1 constituted

March 23, Voluntary rationing measures issued by Food Administration for saving wheat

——, Death of Homer B. Sprague (88) former president of University of North Dakota

March 24, Mrs. Rose Pastor Stokes arrested in Kansas City after speech denouncing the War on March 17

——, Award in packing industry gave basic eight hour day and increase in wages

March 25, Railroad Wage Commission in General Order 27 provided for annual increase in wages aggregating about $300,000,000 a year with eight hour day and special rates for overtime

March 25, Secretary of the Treasury announced the third Liberty Loan as $3,000,000,000 at 4½%, offered April 6

——, Karl Muck, conductor of the Boston Symphony Orchestra, arrested as an enemy alien

March 27, Railroad Board of Adjustment No. 1 to settle disputes as to wages created by Director General, C. P. Neill, chairman

——, Death of Henry Adams (80) historian, in Washington

March 29, President Wilson appealed to the Governor of California for executive clemency for Thomas J. Mooney

March 30, Arbitration Treaty with Norway extended that of 1908

April 2, Prohibition Amendment ratified by Massachusetts, and prohibition went into effect in Indiana

——, Note to Mexico protested against Mexican decree of Feb. 19 imposing new tax on oil lands and contracts made previous to May 1, 1917 when new Constitution came into effect

April 6, Shipbuilding Labor Adjustment Board granted increase in wages to carpenters in North Atlantic District, common labor 49 cents an hour, provided for shop committees to take up matters in dispute

April 8, Proclamation of the President created War Labor Board to be a supreme court for labor disputes, Frank P. Walsh and former President Taft co-chairmen

April 9, General Munitions Board created with Frank A. Scott as chairman

April 11, Proclamation of the President declared taking over of the 4 principal coast line steamship companies of the Atlantic coast, placed under control of the Railroad Administration

April 12, Death of Rudolf Blankenburg (75) former mayor of Philadelphia

April 14, Death of William J. Stone (69) Senator from Missouri

April 15–17, First trial of editors of the *Masses*, Max Eastman, Floyd Dell, and Arthur Young, under Espionage Act for publication of cartoons, poems, and editorials, failed to secure conviction

April 16, Charles M. Schwab appointed Director General of the Emergency Fleet Corporation

April 17, Railroad Administration took over the new enlarged New York Barge Canal system nearing completion

April 19, Rhode Island Act required men between 18 and 50 to be employed at least 36 hours a week in useful labor

April 21, Towns of San Jacinto and Hemet in California destroyed by an earthquake

April 23, Death of Edwin O. Wood (56) editor and author, Pasadena, California

April 24, John D. Ryan appointed head of new Bureau of Aircraft Production and William L. Kenly Chief of new Division of Military Aëronautics

April 27, Interstate Commerce Commission granted increase in class freight rates and passenger fares on New England railroads

April 28, Strike of telegraph operators scheduled to begin on the 9th postponed pending arbitration proceedings by the War Labor Board

April 29, W. P. G. Harding nominated manager of War Finance Corporation

April 30, Franz Bopp, German consul, and E. H. von Schack, vice-consul, San Francisco, sentenced to imprisonment for 2 years and fines of $10,000 each for conspiracy against the British Government in India

——, Agreement with Norway for supplies not needed by Allies

May, Strike of 15,000 textile workers in the mills of Massachusetts and Rhode Island terminated by agreement

May 1, Fixed prices of rubber became effective

——, Prohibition became effective in Michigan and New Hampshire

May 3, Major General James W. McAndrew appointed Chief of Staff of American Expeditionary Force

——, Police raided I.W.W. headquarters in Seattle and arrested 213 persons

——, Strike of machinists of 22 shops of ammunitions plants in Bridgeport, Connecticut for increase in wages and the eight hour day

——, Death of Robert M. Oliphant (93) former railroad president

May 4, Death of James Ripley Wellman Hitchcock (60) author and publisher, New York

——, New wage agreement signed with longshoremen of Atlantic ports

May 7, Death of Judge Marcus P. Knowlton (79) Springfield, Mass.

May 8, Strike of employees of the Remington Arms Company

May 13, New York law required all able bodied male citizens between ages of 18 and 50 to be engaged in useful occupations until termination of War

May 14, War Trade Board announced licensing of all commodities imported

——, Death of James Gordon Bennett (77) owner of the *New York Herald*

May 15, Airplane mail service between Washington and New York begun

——, New York State Barge Canal opened for through traffic from ports on Lake Ontario to the Hudson River

May 17, Announcement of creaton of War Labor Policies Board to represent all depts. to standardize labor conditions, constituted June 8, Felix Frankfurter, chairman

May 20, Executive Order of the President reorganized Signal Corps, functions pertaining to aircraft production transferred to Air Service

——, General Peyton C. Marsh appointed Chief of General Staff of Army, confirmed on the 24th

——, Supreme Court decision refused to dissolve the United Shoe Machinery Company as an illegal combination in restraint of trade

——, The Director General of Railroads authorized 182 railroads to expend $938,000,000 during the year next for repairs, equipment, and improvements

May 21, The Director General of Railroads announced removal of all railroad presidents and reorganization under federal managers

May 22, Death of Rev. Minot J. Savage (77) Boston, Mass.

May 23, War Dept. ordered that after July 1 all draft registrants should be engaged in useful work

——, Rose Pastor Stokes convicted under the Espionage Act by court at Kansas City and June 1 sentenced to 10 years imprisonment

——, Death of John B. Castelman (76) Louisville, Kentucky

May 25, Railroad Administration General Order No. 28 ordered average increase of 25% in freight rates to meet increased expenses, and passenger fares increased to 3 cents a mile

——, Board of Railroad Wages and Working Conditions established to investigate matters presented to it

——, Director General of Railroads granted railroad employees earning $249 or less a month increase beginning at 43% for lowest employees and minimum advance of 2½ cents an hour to common labor, and eight hours made the basic day, wage raise totaling $300,000,000 came into effect May 26

May 26, Food Administration proposed limit of 2 pounds of meat per person per week

May 27, Prohibition Amendment ratified by Arizona

May 28, The Director General of Railroads authorized the merger of 4 express companies into a Federal Express Company to handle all business on the railroads

——, Executive Order of the President reorganized and reëstablished the War Industries Board as a separate administrative agency

——, American First Division commanded by Gen. R. L. Bullard in engagement at Cantigny, France. *See* World War

May 29, Announcement of Secretary Lansing of sympathy of the United States with the nationalist aspirations of the Czechs and Yugoslavs

May 31, Railroad Board of Adjustment No. 2 established, E. F. Potter, chairman, to settle disputes of railroad shopmen

June 1, Order of the President permitted furloughing of conscientious objectors for agricultural service or work in connection with the Friends Reconstruction Service

June 1–12, Strike of employees of street railroads of Schenectady for increase in wages

June 3, Supreme Court by vote of 5 to 4 declared the Federal Child Labor Act of Sept. 1, 1916 unconstitutional

——, Air mail service established between New York, Boston, and Montreal

——, Reciprocal Military Service Convention with Great Britain and Canada signed provided for military service of nationals in the country in which they were under the draft

——, Arbitration Treaty with Great Britain signed renewed that of 1908

June 4, Death of Charles Warren Fairbanks (66) former Vice-President, at Indianapolis

——, Second American Division entered the line on the Marne. *See* World War

June 5, Registration of 745,000 men who had come of draft age within the year

June 6, Agreement for control of distribution of manufactured steel and iron products published by War Industries Board

June 7, Jeremiah O'Leary, John T. Ryan, and 5 others of the pro-German Irish-American group indicted at New York for conspiracy under the Espionage law, and O'Leary arrested at Sara, Washington, on the 13th

June 11–16, Strike of subway workers, New York City

June 15, Maximum prices for lumber fixed by the Government

June 18, Proclamation of the President required licensing of stock yards for live cattle, sheep, swine, and goats and traffic at the yards

June 19, Federal Trade Commission fixed maximum price for newsprint paper

June 26–28, Munition workers at Bridgeport, Connecticut, struck because the manufacturers refused to accept the award

June 26, Sugar rationing system came into effect, limiting consumption to 3 pounds per month per person

——, Prohibition Amendment ratified by Georgia legislature

June 27, Second drawing for the draft held in Washington, 745,000 men

June 28, Chemical Warfare Service created in the Army

June 29, State Dept. reaffirmed Note of April 2 to Mexico protesting against confiscatory tax on oil lands

——, Railroad Administration returned over 1,700 short line railroads to private management

——, Award of 20% increase in wages and basic eight hour day to employees of paper mills in Maine and northern New York

——, Piers of German steamship lines at Hoboken taken over

——, Death of John A. Mitchell (73) editor of *Life*

June 30, Imports for the fiscal year totaled $2,946,-059,403, and exports $5,928,285,641

——, Eugene V. Debs arrested in Cleveland, Ohio, charged with violation of the Espionage Act, on basis of speech made at Canton June 16 against war interpreted as an interference with recruiting

July 2, Death of Rev. Washington Gladden (82) author, Columbus, Ohio

July 3, Death of Benjamin R. Tillman (70) Senator from South Carolina

July 4, President Wilson in address at Mount Vernon laid down the "Four Ends," as Allied War aims as the destruction or reduction to impotence of every arbitrary power that can disturb the peace of the world, a settlement on the basis of the free acceptance of the conditions of the settlement by the peoples immediately concerned, the consent of all the nations to be governed by the same principles of honor and of respect for the common law of civilized society that govern individual citizens of modern states, and the establishment of an organization of peace

——, 95 merchant ships and 14 destroyers launched

July 5, Excursion steamer "Columbia" sunk near shore in Illinois River near Peoria with loss of 200 persons

——, Award of National Labor Board accepted by employers of 53 companies at Bridgeport, Connecticut, representing 50,000 machinists and tool makers, and wage increase announced Sept. 4 established a minimum wage of 42 cents an hour for all men employees and 38 cents for women, and recognition of union

——, Food Administration announced establishment of Cereal Division and extension of operations to purchase, store, and sale of all cereals

——, Operatives in cotton mills at Lowell, Mass. returned to work after 5 days strike, granted an increase in wages of 5%

July 6, John Purroy Mitchell (38) former Mayor of New York, killed by fall from airplane at Lake Charles, Louisiana

July 6, Decision to unite with Japanese in intervention in Siberia to protect supplies and help Czechs to get out of Russia

July 8, Strike of telegraph operators ordered June 30 for this date postponed at request of the Secretary of Labor pending action by the Government. The Western Union Company refused to accept award and union membership of its employees

——, Edward A. Rumely arrested in New York City for perjury in concealing German ownership of the New York *Evening Mail,* and indictment Aug. 2

July 9, Price of charcoal fixed

July 12, Strike of employees of the Smith and Wesson Company at Springfield, Mass. for increase in wages and better working conditions

July 13, Sugar Equalization Board created to control the prices and distribution of sugar

July 15, Strike of 10,000 employees of the General Electric Company at Lynn, Mass. for wage increase and better working conditions

July 17–20, Strike of metal workers at Newark, New Jersey, for wage increase and eight hour day ended by reference to arbitration and increase granted

July 22, Prohibition Amendment ratified by Georgia

——, Proclamation of the President announced taking over of the telephone and telegraph systems placed under the Postmaster General from Aug. 1

——, Proclamation of the President placed the Cape Cod Canal under the Railroad Administration

July 25, Wage order of Railroad Administration gave shop mechanics basic minimum wage of 58–68 cents an hour in place of 55, clerks, maintenance of way, common labor in shops, station employees an increase of 12 cents an hour

——, Death of Professor Walter Rauschenbusch (56) theologian, Rochester, New York, and James C. Nicoll (70) painter

July 26, Food Board reduced allowance per person of sugar from 3 to 2 pounds per month

July 27, Thomas J. Mooney reprieved by Governor of California to Dec. 13

——, Death of Gustav Kobbe (60) musical critic and author, New York

July 31, Fourth Liberty Loan campaign announced for Sept. 28 to Oct. 19

——, During this month 306,000 soldiers transported to Europe, the highest record during the War (Ayres)

——, Death of Henry S. Williams (71) geologist, Ithaca, New York

Aug. 1, Wage increases on electric railway systems approved by War Labor Board, and Aug. 8 settlement included Cleveland, Columbus, Detroit, Albany, Rochester, and Buffalo, 35 to 40% increase in large cities and as high as 65% in some small towns, and right to organize sustained

——, Joyce Kilmer (31) journalist and poet, killed in action in France

Aug. 2, American Vice-Consul at Petrograd notified that state of war existed between Russia and the United States

——, Indiana state wide prohibition law came into effect

Aug. 3, Announcement of State Dept. of participation of the United States in Allied intervention in Russia

——, Prohibition Amendment ratified by Louisiana

Aug. 4, Government suit against the International Harvester Company begun in 1912 ended by agreement as to adoption of certain measures of dissolution

Aug. 5, American affairs in Russia turned over to Swedish Consul General

Aug. 7, Major General William S. Grove appointed to command American forces in Vladivostok

——, Fuel Administration assumed preparation and adoption of standardized specifications for supply of petroleum and products

Aug. 9, Restrictions as to use of meat abolished by the Food Administration

Aug. 11, American troops landed at Vladivostok

Aug. 16, Secretary Daniels prohibited use of alcohol at naval camps except for medicine

Aug. 17, 112 I.W.W. leaders indicted at Chicago charged with conspiracy to interfere with the prosecution of the War

Aug. 21, Award of the War Labor Board in the Smith and Wesson Company strike granted a number of the demands of the employees; not accepted by company

Aug. 23, Arbitration Treaty with Japan extended that of May 5, 1908

Aug. 24, Reciprocal Military Service Convention with Italy signed providing for drafting Americans in Italy and Italians in the United States

——, Death of William H. Brett, librarian, Cleveland, Ohio

——, Registration of 158,000 men who had reached draft age since previous registration

——, United States District Court of New York declared the sinking of the *Lusitania* an act of piracy

Aug. 25, Death of Professor Arlo Bates (67) author, Boston

Aug. 27, Fuel Administration asked discontinuance of automobile riding on Sundays in region east of the Mississippi, except in cases of necessity, in order to save gasoline

——, Resignation of Walter Hines Page, Ambassador to Great Britain, on account of ill health; succeeded in Sept. by John William Davis, of West Virginia

Aug. 28, Death of Ollie James (47) Senator from Kentucky

Aug. 30, Reciprocal Military Service Convention with Greece signed

——, William D. Haywood and 14 other I.W.W. leaders sentenced to 20 years in prison and $20,000 fine each for violation of the Espionage Act, and 80 others to lesser terms of imprisonment

——, Death of James D. Cameron (85) former Secretary of War and Senator from Pennsylvania

Aug. 31, Death of Luther Halsey Gulick (52) educator and author

Sept. 2, Proclamation of the President continued the basic price of wheat at $2.20 per bushel for 1919 crop

——, The United States recognized the Czecho-Slovaks as belligerents

Sept. 3, Reciprocal Military Service Convention with France signed

Sept. 4, American troops arrived at Archangel, Russia

——, Alien Property Custodian took over vessels of American Transatlantic Company and other lines

Sept. 6, Machinists of the Smith and Wesson Co. at Bridgeport, Conn. voted for strike against award. (*See supra* July 5)

——, Food Administration ordered closing of all breweries after Nov. 30

Sept. 8, Secretary of War Baker arrived at Brest

Sept. 10, Postal aviator, E. V. Gardner completed trip from Chicago to New York in a single day for the first time, actual flying time 10 hours and 5 minutes

Sept. 12, Registration of about 13,228,000 men between ages of 18 and 45 under Man Power Act of Aug. 31

——, Eugene V. Debs convicted in Cleveland of violation of the Espionage Act and Sept. 14 sentenced to 10 years imprisonment

Sept. 13, The President warned machinists on strike at Bridgeport, Conn. that they must accept award of the War Labor Board, and the men returned to work Sept. 17

——, War Dept. announced taking over of the plant and business of the Smith and Wesson Company at Springfield, Mass. for refusal to accept award of War Labor Board

——, Death of Frederic Crowninshield (72) artist, in Italy

Sept. 15, Austro-Hungarian Note to the United States and all belligerents suggested "confidential and non-binding" discussion of peace terms; rejected by President Wilson on the 16th

Sept. 16, Proclamation of the President prohibited the use of food stuffs in production of malt liquors, closing the breweries

Sept. 17, Death of Cardinal John Murphy Farley (76) Cardinal Archbishop of New York

Sept. 18, Captain R. W. Schroeder at Wright Field, Dayton, Ohio, made world aëroplane altitude record at 28,900 feet

Sept. 25, Death of John Ireland (80) Roman Catholic Archbishop of Minnesota

Sept. 27, President Wilson in speech in New York City, the "Five Particulars," promised justice even "to those to whom we do not wish to be just," and declared that "the constitution of a League of Nations must be a part, and in a sense the most essential part, of the peace settlement itself"

Sept. 28, Fifth Liberty Loan subscription opened, closing Oct. 19 with total subscriptions of $6,989,-047,000

Sept. 29, Death of Frederic Robert Halsey (71) print collector, New York

Sept. 30, Draft drawing for new classes of registrants held in Washington

Sept. 30–Oct. 4, Second trial of the editors of the *Masses* failed to secure convictions

Oct. 1, State wide prohibition became effective in New Mexico

——, Students' Army Training Corps organized in 500 colleges for training

Oct. 2, War Industries Board fixed prices for shoes

Oct. 2–3, Influenza epidemic at height, over 12,000 cases reported among soldiers

Oct. 4, Note from Germany to President Wilson asked that steps be taken for restoration of peace, received Oct. 6 and Note from Austria-Hungary Oct. 7

Oct. 4–5, Destruction of shell-loading plant at Morgan, New Jersey, by explosion which wrecked neighboring villages, 90 persons killed

Oct. 5, Death of Charles G. Roebling (69) engineer, at Trenton, New Jersey

Oct. 6–9, Strike of street car employees at Minneapolis and St. Paul

Oct. 8, President Wilson replied to Central Powers. *See* World War

——, Henry Bruere appointed Director United States Employment Service

Oct. 9, First American Army organized under command of Major General G. H. Liggett, and Second, Oct. 12 under command of Major General R. L. Bullard. *See also* World War Oct. 12

Oct. 12, Forest fires in Minnesota and Wisconsin destroyed homes and killed hundreds of persons

——, Death of Rev. Madison Clinton Peters (58) New York City

——, Twelve rules for public eating places proposed by Food Administration

Oct. 14, The Spanish Ambassador at Washington presented Note from Turkey dated Oct. 12 asking President Wilson to take steps toward ending hostilities

——, Note of President Wilson to Germany imposed further conditions as essential to armistice in reply to German Note of Oct. 12

Oct. 18, Note of President Wilson to Austria-Hungary proposed recognition of independence of Czechs and Yugoslavs

Oct. 20, German Note to President Wilson accepted proposal of evacuation of occupied territories and declared that the present government was supported by the approval of the overwhelming majority of the German people

Oct. 21, Death of Dr. Edwin B. Cragin (59) physician, New York

Oct. 22, Death of Francis Key Brooke (65) Bishop of Oklahoma

Oct. 23, Note of President Wilson agreed to submit German proposals for an armistice to the Allied and Associated Powers

Oct. 24, Increase of wages to bituminous miners refused by Fuel Administrator

Oct. 25, Open letter of President Wilson to the American people asked for the election of a Democratic Congress to give him effective support at home and abroad in negotiations for peace

Oct. 26, Reply of Republicans to President Wilson's letter of Oct. 25 signed by H. C. Lodge and others accused the President of using the War as a "party asset"

——, Death of Ella Flagg Young (73) educator, Chicago

——, Representatives of 11 subject nationalities of Central Europe met at Independence Hall, Philadelphia, and adopted declaration of independence

Oct. 27, Shipbuilding Labor Adjustment Board made new wage award granting basic minimum rate of 80 cents an hour in skilled trades, and increases averaging 15% on eastern coast and Great Lakes, and 20% on western coast

——, Note from Germany declared peace negotiations conducted by a government of the people and that the military powers of Germany were under control of the civil government

——, Note from Austria-Hungary to President Wilson accepted all conditions and asked for armistice

Oct. 28, Strike of Amalgamated Clothing Trade Workers begun in New York City for 44 hour week

Oct. 31, Former Republican Presidents Roosevelt and Taft made joint appeal to the country for election of a Republican Congress

——, Fuel Administration ordered wage increase of $1 per day to anthracite coal miners

Nov. 1, Since Sept. 12 the number of influenza cases reported among troops in America 306,719, approximately one in every five, 48,079 cases of pneumonia and 19,429 deaths

Nov. 2, Proclamation of the President placed all marine cables under control of the Postmaster General to take effect Nov. 16

Nov. 4, Death of Andrew Dickson White (86) educator and diplomat, at Ithaca, New York

Nov. 5, Election gave Republicans a majority in both Houses of Congress, woman suffrage adopted in Michigan, Oklahoma, Nebraska, and South Dakota, and prohibition in Washington, Ohio, Wyoming, Florida, Nevada

——, Last Note of President Wilson to Germany announced that Marshal Foch was authorized to represent the Allied Powers to communicate terms for armistice

Nov. 7, Celebrations of signing of armistice throughout the country on publication by press of false report

Nov. 8, Death of Robert J. Collier (42) editor and publisher, New York City

Nov. 9, President Wilson directed Herbert Hoover to go to Europe to represent the United States in organization of food relief

——, Lockout of 30,000 cutters of men's clothing

Nov. 11, Armistice signed ending the War. Army on this date 3,665,000 of whom 2,000,000 were in France

——, New regulations issued for "lightless nights"

Nov. 13, International Labor Conference at Laredo, Texas, attended by representatives from the United States, Central American States, and Colombia

Nov. 14, Regulations requiring wheat substitutes in making bread suspended by the Food Administration

——, United Lutheran Church formed by union of 3 branches of the denomination

Nov. 15, Secretary of War Baker issued first demobilization order

——, Death of Robert A. Van Wyck (71) former Mayor of New York

——, Board of Censorship abolished

Nov. 16, Proclamation of the President took over the American Railway Express Company to take effect Nov. 18

——, Cable lines taken over by the Post Office Dept. on this date

——, Wages of railroad telegraphers increased 13 cents an hour

Nov. 17, Independent Labor Party formed at meeting in Chicago, adopted platform of "Fourteen Points of Labor"

Nov. 18, President Wilson announced that he would attend the Peace Conference in Paris and named as delegates Robert Lansing, Henry White, Colonel E. M. House, and General Tasker H. Bliss

——, Supreme Court refused to consider the case of Thomas J. Mooney

Nov. 19, Death of Joseph F. Smith (80) president of the Mormon Church, at Salt Lake City

Nov. 20, Regulations as to "lightless nights" abolished by Fuel Administration

Nov. 21, Resignation of William G. McAdoo as Secretary of the Treasury and Director General of Railroads

Nov. 22, Death of William D. Hoard (82) publisher, former Governor of Wisconsin

Nov. 27, NC-1, largest seaplane in the world, established record for flight with 50 passengers, the largest number carried in any type of airplane, at Naval Air Station, Rockaway

Nov. 28, Sentence of Thomas J. Mooney commuted to life imprisonment by the Governor of California

Nov. 30, Announcement of casualties in War (as revised) killed in action in Army 37,568, died of wounds received in action 12,942, wounded 182,674, total 233,184; killed in action in Navy 356, died of wounds 58, lost at sea 457, total 871; Marine Corps, killed in action 1,450, died of wounds 1,007, other causes 46, wounded 7,714, total casualties 10,521. Of total mobilized forces of 4,057,101, killed and died 119,956; wounded 193,663 (not including 12,942 who died of wounds), prisoners 4,423, total casualties of the A.E.F. 318,042

A total of 44 vessels manned by the Navy were lost during the War, and 151 merchant vessels of 315,588 tons with loss of 409 persons, and of these 21 vessels representing 67,815 tons and 67 persons lost before the United States entered the War

——, Loans to the Allies to this date, total $8,184,-576,666 as follows: Great Britain $3,945,000,000; France $2,445,000,000; Italy $1,210,000,000; Russia $325,000,000; Belgium $198,120,000; Greece $15,000,-000; Cuba $15,000,000; Serbia $12,000,000; Rumania $6,000,000; Liberia $5,000,000; Czecho-Slovak National Council $7,000,000

Dec. 1, First American troops returned from Europe to New York on the "Mauretania"

Dec. 3, Harry A. Garfield resigned as Fuel Administrator

Dec. 4, President Wilson and delegates to the Peace Conference sailed on the "George Washington" arriving at Brest Dec. 13

Dec. 5, Steamship lines not owned by railroads released from control by Railroad Administration

Dec. 6, Carter Glass, of Virginia, appointed Secretary of the Treasury

Dec. 14, Prohibition Amendment ratified by Florida

Dec. 16, State wide prohibition law for Colorado signed by the Governor, and prohibition became effective in Nevada

——, Citizenship of Paris conferred on President Wilson

Dec. 18, Five editors and officials of the Philadelphia *Tageblatt* sentenced to prison term for violation of the Espionage Act

Dec. 21, Death of Walter Hines Page (63) diplomat and publisher, at Pinehurst, North Carolina

Dec. 22, All food regulations suspended by Food Administration

Dec. 23, Supreme Court decision sustained property rights in news in favor of Associated Press vs. International News Service

——, Return of 3,798 soldiers from Europe at New York

Dec. 24, Death of Henry M. MacCracken (78) chancellor emeritus of New York University

Dec. 25, Death of J. Wilbur Chapman (59) presbyterian evangelist, and of "Olive Thorne" Miller, author, Los Angeles, California

Dec. 26, Review of overseas battleship fleet in New York harbor by Secretary Daniels

Dec. 26–31, President Wilson on visit to England

Dec. 27–28, Executive Council of the American Federation of Labor decided not to support the new Independent Labor Party

Dec. 31, War Industries Board dissolved, and Railroad War Board

——, State wide prohibition became effective in Montana

Jan. 8, President Wilson in address to Congress on war aims and peace terms laid down his "Fourteen Points," project for a League of Nations the 14th point

Jan. 10, Resolution providing for woman suffrage, the Susan B. Anthony Amendment to the Constitution passed the House by vote of 274 to 136

Jan. 28, Secretary Baker defended conduct of the War Dept. before Senate Committee on Military Affairs to answer charges of Senator Chamberlain and others that "the military establishment of America (had) fallen down because of inefficiency in every bureau and department of the United States Government"

Feb. 11, Address of President Wilson to Congress in which he laid down the "four principles," additional terms

March 1, Emergency Fleet Corporation Housing Act appropriated $50,000,000 to provide for housing for shipyard employees and their families

March 3, Double pension provided for in case of disability on account of aviation duty for Navy and Marine Corps

——, Office of Chief of Naval Operations created and National Advisory Committee for Aëronautics

March 8, Soldiers and Sailors Civil Relief Act provided for matters of rents, taxes, mortgages, insurance, &c., giving temporary suspension of legal proceedings

March 19, Daylight Saving Act advanced the time one hour from May 31 to Oct. 27

March 21, Railroad Control Act placed the management of all railroads under the Government with a Director General and regional directors

April 4, Third Liberty Loan Act authorized added credit of $1,500,000,000

April 5, War Finance Corporation created with capital stock of $500,000,000 and power to issue $3,000,-000,000 in bonds, authorized to lend to banks to cover loans made to assist war industries, and to persons and corporations engaged in business necessary to prosecution of war

April 10, Webb-Pomerene Export Trade Act provided that exporters might organize associations for export trade without becoming liable for violation of the anti-trust laws, unfair methods of competition prohibited

April 19, Espionage Act extended to include female enemy aliens

April 20, Sabotage Act provided for punishment of injury and destruction of war material and war transportation facilities

April 23, Pittman Act authorized replacement of silver dollars and certificates by Federal Reserve bank notes, and the sale of silver bullion to be used in the Far East to aid the exchange rate

May 7, Act provided for enlistment of foreign nationals by their governments in the United States

May 9, Naturalization laws amended to provide for naturalization of aliens serving with the A.E.F. and those aliens who had taken out first papers

May 10, Act authorized the Secretary of War to sell surplus war material remaining in Europe after the War to foreign governments and accept their obligations in payment thereof

May 16, Espionage Act amended to provide penalties for false reports and statements made to interfere with military or naval forces or hinder prosecution of war. Act made persons liable to a fine of $10,000 or 20 years imprisonment or both found guilty of abusive language regarding the American form of government, the Constitution, the Army, the Navy, or the flag

May 20, Selective Draft Act amended to provide for registration of men who had reached age of 21 since June 5, 1917

——, Overman Act "to coördinate or consolidate executive bureaus, agencies, and offices" gave the President powers for the period of the War to create new agencies, alter existing ones, and transfer their powers

May 22, Passport Control Act to prevent departure from or entry into the United States in time of war contrary to public safety

May 23, Act prohibited sale, manufacture, or importation of liquor in Hawaii until after peace concluded and then a referendum to be held

June 10, Pension Act provided for minimum pension of $30 a month for anyone who had served 90 days in the Civil War, maximum $40 granted according to length of service

——, Resolution of Senator King proposed intervention in Russia, and appointment of a civil commission to be sent there

June 27, Smith-Sears Vocational Rehabilitation Act provided for vocational reëducation for disabled soldiers and sailors

July 1, Naval Appropriation Act granted credit of $1,573,468,415, and authorized increase of personnel from 87,000 to 131,485

July 8, Army Appropriation Act granted $12,085,-000,000 and granted the President authority to increase Army by calls under the draft law

July 9, Fourth Liberty Loan Act added credit of $1,500,000,000

July 16, Resolution adopted provided for government control of the telephone, telegraph, cables, and radio

July 18, Act authorized the President to take over shipping and shipping agencies for period of the War

Aug. 22, Senate Committee published report of investigation of aircraft situation and declared that airship production had been subordinated and delayed by creation of special "Liberty" motor, and charged incompetency, waste, and profiteering

Aug. 31, Man Power Act required registration with a view to military service if needed of men between ages of 18 and 45

Sept. 12, Joint Resolution authorized the President to establish zones around coal mines, munition plants, shipbuilding plants where war materials made in which intoxicating liquors might not be manufactured, sold, or distributed

Sept. 26, Federal Reserve Act amended gives Board discretion in grouping of member banks and changed manner of election of directors, and authorized issue of Federal reserve notes in denominations of $500, $1,000, $5,000, and $10,000, the largest note heretofore authorized being $100

Sept. 30, President Wilson in address before the Senate declared that the Woman Suffrage Amendment should be adopted as "a vitally necessary war measure"

Oct. 1, The Senate rejected the Woman Suffrage Amendment by vote of 53 to 31, less than the required two-thirds in favor

Oct. 16, Immigration Act amended to exclude alien anarchists and the Secretary of Labor authorized to deport aliens who advocated overthrowing the government or unlawful destruction of property

——, Act provided for fine and imprisonment of persons who should promise or offer anything of value or contract for purchase of vote for senator or representative of the United States

Nov. 4, Amendment to Trading with the Enemy Act authorized the seizure of certain enemy owned patents

Nov. 7, National Bank Consolidation Act

Nov. 21, Food Production Act prohibited the manufacture (after May 1, 1919) and sale of intoxicating liquors from June 30, 1919, until the completion of demobilization, the date of demobilization to be determined and announced by the President

——, Congress adjourned

Dec. 2, Sixty-Fifth Congress, 3d sess. convened

Dec. 5, Secretary McAdoo asked Congress to continue power to establish credits for Allied Governments for 1 year

1919

Jan. 1, Business of War Industries Board transferred to War Trade Board and Dept. of Commerce

——, Henry Ford raised minimum wage of his employees from $5 to $6 a day

——, Prohibition became effective in Florida and Utah by constitutional amendment

Jan. 2, Prohibition Amendment ratified by Michigan, by Ohio and Oklahoma Jan. 7, Idaho, Maine, and Tennessee Jan. 8, West Virginia Jan. 9, California and Washington Jan. 13, Alabama, Arkansas, Illinois, Indiana, Iowa, Kansas, and North Carolina Jan. 14, New Hampshire, Colorado, Oregon, and Utah Jan. 15, and by ratification of Nebraska Jan. 16 the necessary two-thirds secured. Missouri and Wyoming also ratified on the 16th, and Wisconsin and Minnesota on the 17th

Jan. 3, Herbert Hoover appointed head of international relief organization to minister to liberated and enemy countries

Jan. 3-6, President Wilson on visit to Italy

Jan. 6, Death of Theodore Roosevelt (60) at Oyster Bay, Long Island, New York

Jan. 8, Federal Jury at Chicago found Victor Berger and 4 other Socialists guilty of conspiracy to interfere with prosecution of the War ending trial which had begun Dec. 9

Jan. 9, Strike of 16,000 harbor workers in New York employed on North River piers demanding an increase in wages and eight hour day, and 30,000 longshoremen also kept from work

Jan. 10, Walker D. Hines appointed Director General of Railroads succeeding W. G. McAdoo

Jan. 11, Harbor workers in New York returned to work pending decision of War Labor Board

Jan. 12, President Wilson and Secretary Lansing represented the United States at Supreme War Council in Paris

Jan. 13, Supreme Court decision upheld prohibition of interstate transportation of liquor from wet into dry territory

——, Death of Horace Fletcher (69) author and dietitian, in Denmark

Jan. 15, Death of Henry J. Duveen (64) art dealer, New York City

Jan. 16, Release of 131 conscientious objectors imprisoned at Fort Leavenworth ordered by Secretary of War

Jan. 17, Prohibition Amendment ratified by Minnesota

——, Regulations fixing price of bituminous coal abolished to take effect Feb. 1

Jan. 18, The United States represented at Peace Conference in Paris by President Wilson, Secretary Robert Lansing, Henry White, Edward M. House, and General Tasker H. Bliss

Jan. 20, Interstate Commerce Commission in Pacific Lumber Company case declared itself in authority to overrule rates established by Railroad Administration

Jan. 21, Railroad Wage Commission organized

——, Strike of 25,000 shipyard workers ordered Jan. 16 begun in Seattle and Tacoma for increase in wages

Jan. 23, Forty-six members of the I.W.W. found guilty of conspiracy by Federal District Court at Sacramento, California, in connection with dynamiting home of the Governor Dec. 17, 1917, and sentenced to terms of from 1 to 10 years in prison

Jan. 25 and Feb. 11, Proclamations announced licenses for exports and imports no longer necessary for many articles

Jan. 26, Strike of dress and waist makers of New York City for increase in wages and shorter hours and over the "right to discharge" which lasted 11 weeks for 35,000 employed by the manufacturer's association, ended by agreement retaining board of discharge and grant of 44 hour week

Jan. 27, Agreement in clothing trade ended strike, the 44 hour week granted in Rochester, New York, and to the 20,000 employees of the Hart, Schaffner and Marx Company in Chicago

Jan. 28, Death of Brown Ayres (62) president of University of Tennessee

Jan. 29, Proclamation of the Secretary of State of the ratification by the States of the Prohibition Amendment (XVIIIth) to the Constitution to take effect Jan. 16, 1920

——, Strike of employees of the American Woolen Company in Lawrence, Mass. for increase in wages ended May 22 with 15% increase

Jan. 31, Death of Nathaniel (Nat) Goodwin (61) actor, New York City

——, All restrictions on margins of profit of foodstuffs canceled except eggs and cottonseed products

Feb. 1, Institute of International Education under the Carnegie Endowment for International Peace established

Feb. 2, Shipping Board announced that Dutch ships would be returned to the Netherlands

Feb. 3, General strike of textile workers of New England, New Jersey, and New York for 48 hour week without reduction in wages successful in general

Feb. 4, Prohibition Amendment rejected by Connecticut Senate

Feb. 6, Legislature of Ohio asked U.S. Senators to support Federal Woman Suffrage Amendment

——, General strike begun in Seattle in support of striking shipyard workers which spread to Tacoma and to San Francisco

——, Indiana granted women the right to vote for presidential electors

Feb. 8, Martial law declared in Seattle and Citizen's Committee appointed to confer with strikers

Feb. 11, General strike in Seattle ended but strike in shipyards continued

Feb. 14, President Wilson left Paris and sailed on the "George Washington" from Brest on the 15th arriving in Boston Feb. 24

Feb. 16, Paterson silk-mill workers locked out since Feb. 3 returned to work pending decision of War Labor Board

Feb. 20, Victor Berger and 4 other Socialists convicted Jan. 8 under the Espionage Act received sentence, Berger to 20 years imprisonment. Released on bail pending appeal

Feb. 21, Death of Dr. Mary Walker (87) commissioned assistant-surgeon Civil War

Feb. 24, General strike of carpenters and builders settled by reference to arbitration

Feb. 25, Announcement of Secretary of Commerce of creation of Industrial Board in the Dept. of Commerce to effect stabilization of prices of basic commodities, George N. Peek, chairman

——, Rear Admiral Thomas Snowden assumed charge of military government of Santo Domingo and military representation of the United States in Haiti

——, Award of Shipbuilding Labor Adjustment Board in case of harbor workers, New York piers granted eight hour day but no increase in wages

——, Prohibition Amendment ratified by Pennsylvania

Feb. 28, Executive Order of the President provided for continuation of the Fuel Administration pending legislation by Congress

——, Wisconsin granted women the right to vote for presidential electors

March 1, American Red Cross War Council dissolved

March 3, Bishop Patrick J. Hayes made Roman Catholic Archbishop of New York, and Rev. Albert Anthony Daeger Archbishop of Santa Fé, New Mexico

——, Francis P. Garvin succeeded A. Mitchell Palmer as Alien Property Custodian

March 4, Longshoremen and harbor workers of New York went on strike a second time against award of Feb. 25 (Macy award)

March 5, A. Mitchell Palmer, of Pennsylvania, appointed Attorney General

——, Sentence of 52 persons convicted under the Espionage Act commuted by the President

——, President Wilson sailed for France

March 7, Concessions granted by Railroad Administration and subsequently by War and Navy Depts. ended strike of longshoremen and harbor workers on railroad boats, and on April 19 by grant of private owners of 10 hour day and reference of wage dispute to arbitration

March 8, Arbitration Conventions with Spain and the Netherlands signed extending those of 1908

March 9, Shipyard workers on strike in Seattle and Tacoma voted to return to work under same conditions

March 10, Supreme Court upheld conviction of E. V. Debs under the Espionage Act

——, Death of Amelia Barr (Mrs. Robert) novelist, New York City

March 11–18, Strike of employees of street railroads in northern New Jersey

March 14, President Wilson arrived in Paris

——, Death of Judge Roger A. Pryor (90) Confederate General and lawyer

March 15, American Legion informally organized at meeting in Paris

March 17, Death of Kenyon Cox (62) artist, New York City

March 18, Prohibition Amendment rejected by New Jersey

March 20, Arbitration Treaty with Italy signed extended that of March 28, 1908

March 23, American border troops in pursuit of bandits who had stolen cattle and horses from American ranch at Nuez, Texas, in skirmish with Mexicans after crossing the Mexican frontier, 5 Mexicans killed

——, Jury disagreed in trial of Jeremiah O'Leary for violation of the Espionage Act

March 24, William H. Taft proposed an amendment to the Covenant of the League of Nations to provide for recognition of the Monroe Doctrine

March 26, Charles E. Hughes in speech in New York proposed 7 amendments to the Covenant of the League of Nations

March 27, Woman suffrage law enacted in Minnesota

March 28, Maine granted women the right to vote for presidential electors

——, Death of Samuel Train Dutton (69) educator and author

March 30, Elihu Root proposed 6 amendments to the Covenant of the League of Nations

March 31, State Dept. ordered investigation of report that Mexico had granted concessions of land in Lower California to Japanese corporations; denied by Baron Otori, Japanese Minister to Mexico April 1

April 1, Meat packing industry released from government control by license

April 2, War Trade Board announced partial resumption of trade with German Austria

——, Director General of Railroads refused to accept steel prices suggested by Industrial Board of the Dept. of Commerce

April 4, Filipino delegation headed by Manuel Quezon presented memorial to Secretary of War asking for complete independence of the Philippines

April 6, Death of John Rogers Hegeman (74) president of Metropolitan Life Insurance Company

April 8, Death of Frank W. Woolworth (66) founder of the 5 and 10 cent stores

April 9, Death of Sidney Drew (54) actor, New York City

April 10, Railroad Administration granted wage increase to trainmen estimated at $65,000,000 annually

——, Alien Property Custodian sold 45,000 patents to Chemical Foundation for $250,000

April 13, Secretary of the Treasury announced Fifth (Victory) Loan

——, Eugene V. Debs began 10 year term in the penitentiary at Moundsville, Virginia

April 14, Railroad Administration granted increase in wages to 69,000 employees of the American Railway Express Company average $15 a month

April 15, Hugh Gibson appointed first Minister from the United States to Poland

April 15–20, Successful strike of telephone operators of New England for increase in wages

April 16, Death of Henry Morse Stephens (61) author, San Francisco

April 17, Richard Crane appointed first Minister to Czechoslovakia

April 19, Strike of marine harbor workers in New York ended with return of non-government employees to work

April 21, Victory Loan campaign opened, 2 series of

bonds offered, one at 3¾% fully exempt from all taxation except estate and inheritance taxes, and one at 4¾% subject to all Federal taxes except normal income tax

April 22, Recognition of British Protectorate over Egypt by the United States

April 23, President Wilson appealed to the Italian people as to Fiume. *See* Peace Conference

——, Rhode Island law declared non-intoxicating beverages containing "not more than 4 per centum by weight of alcohol"

April 25, Tax on profits of industries employing child labor (Act of Feb. 24) went into effect

——, Iowa enacted law granting women the right to vote at presidential elections, to be submitted to legislature of 1921

April 28, United States District Court in United Mine Workers *v.* Coronado Coal Company assessed damages of $600,000 as liability of the union for destructive acts committed by members in 1914 in the Prairie Creek district of Arkansas

April 29, All enemy trading lists withdrawn on this date and restrictions of trade except as to Germany, Austria, and Hungary

April 30, Cost of War from April 1, 1917 to this date announced as $21,354,867,000: War Dept. $13,987,-202,000; Navy Dept. $3,056,400,000; Civil and miscellaneous $4,311,265,000

May 2, Child Labor Section of War Revenue Act as to tax on products of child labor declared unconstitutional by United States District Court at Greensboro, North Carolina

——, Cables returned to private ownership

May 3, The Government purchased German owned piers at Hoboken, New Jersey, from the Alien Property Custodian

May 8, Transatlantic flight of Navy seaplanes begun from Rockaway Beach, Long Island, to Halifax, Nova Scotia, Lieut.-Com. P. N. L. Bellinger in the NC-1, Com. J. H. Towers in the NC-3, and Com. A. C. Read in the NC-4 which was forced to make a landing at Chatham, Mass. for repairs

May 8–10, American Legion formally organized and draft constitution drawn up

May 9, Industrial Board of Dept. of Commerce abolished

May 10, Seaplanes NC-1, and NC-3 make flight from Halifax to Trepassy, Newfoundland where they were joined by NC-4 on the 14th

May 14, Strike of 45,000 garment workers begun in New York City (ladies' cloak and suit makers) for 44 hour week, guarantee of work for 48 weeks a year, and increase of wages on time basis instead of piecework basis

May 15, Cleveland to Chicago air mail route established

May 16–17, Navy seaplanes NC-1, NC-3, and NC-4 left Trepassy, Newfoundland for the Azores. NC-4 reached Horta in 15 hours and 13 minutes, NC-1 forced to descend in fog and sank, the crew reaching Horta on passing steamship, NC-3 reached Ponta Delgada on the 19th but so damaged as not to be able to proceed. Navy dirigible C-5 which had left Montauk Point, Long Island on the 14th under command of Lieut. Com. Coil, carried out to sea and destroyed from St. Johns, Newfoundland on the 16th

May 19, R. G. Cholmeley-Jones appointed head of War Risk Bureau by Secretary Glass, replacing Henry D. Lindsley

May 19, Death of Bishop David H. Greer (75) of New York

May 20 NC-4 made flight from Horta to Ponta Delgada, 160 miles in 1 hour and 44 minutes

May 22, Strike of textile workers in Lawrence, Massachusetts, ended with grant of increase in wages

May 23, United States District Court at New York granted preliminary injunction enjoining Federal interference with the manufacture of 2.75% beer

May 24, Texas voted for adoption of constitutional amendment prohibiting manufacture and sale of intoxicants by vote of 158,982 to 138,907, but voted against woman suffrage amendment proposed

May 27, Prohibition became effective in Ohio

——, NC-4 left Ponta Delgada, Azores and arrived at Lisbon, Portugal, 810 miles in 9 hours and 43 minutes, completing first successful flight across the Atlantic, actual flying time from Newfoundland to Portugal 26 hours and 51 minutes, 2,472 miles

——, Death of George Hodges (62) author and dean of Theological School at Cambridge, Mass.

May 29, Death of Robert B. Fulton (70) former chancellor of the University of Mississippi

May 31, Proclamation of the President ended licensing of designated cottonseed projects

——, The NC-4 arrived at Plymouth, England, from Ferrol, Spain, completing transatlantic flight from New York as scheduled

June 2, Supreme Court decision in a number of cases upheld power of Federal Government to fix rates on railroads, telephones, and telegraphs under war laws and within States as well as between States

June 3, First contingent of American troops from northern Russia sailed from Archangel

——, Bombs sent by mail to Attorney General Palmer, Postmaster General Burleson, Justice O. W. Holmes, Judge Landis of Chicago, and Mayor Ole Hanson of Seattle, and anarchist attacks on officials in 8 cities

June 8, Nicaragua asked the United States for aid to protect frontier from invasion from Costa Rica

June 9, Treaty of Versailles (draft) published by *New York Times* and *Chicago Tribune*

June 10, Woman Suffrage Amendment (XIXth) to the Constitution ratified by Michigan and Wisconsin, by Kansas, New York, and Ohio on the 16th, by Illinois on the 17th, by Pennsylvania on the 24th, Massachusetts on the 25th, and Texas on the 27th

June 11–July 2, Strike of members of Commercial Telegraphers' Union for recognition of union and increase in wages unsuccessful

June 14, Demonstration of 10,000 members of trade unions in Washington against prohibition of beer and light wines

June 14–15, First non-stop flight across the Atlantic by Captain Alcock and A. W. Brown, British aviators. *See* Canada

June 15, American troops crossed into Mexico to protect El Paso, Texas, in battle between Carranza and Villista forces, assisting the Carranza troops

June 17, Marine workers working for private employers received wage increase averaging $15 a month

——, Strike of telephone operators of California begun for increase in wages, which spread to Nevada the following day

June 20, Announcement of War Dept. that 26,450 men would be enlisted to patrol the Mexican border

June 21, Postal censorship ended

——, Police in New York City raided headquarters of Socialists and I.W.W.s and the Rand School of Social Science

June 23, President de Valera, of Ireland, arrived in New York

——, Proclamation of the President announced licensing of wheat and wheat flour

June 24, Proclamation of the President prohibited import and export of wheat and wheat flour

June 28, President Wilson left Paris, sailing from Brest on the 29th, and arriving in New York July 8

——, 900 interned Germans sailed from Charleston, South Carolina

——, Peace Treaty with Germany signed in Paris, and Treaty between France and the United States, agreement of the United States to undertake defense of France in case of unprovoked aggression of Germany; never in force for the United States as not ratified by the Senate

June 29, Prohibition under War Time Prohibition Act of Nov. 21, 1918 came into effect at midnight

June 30, Exports totaled $7,225,084,257 and imports $3,095,876,582 for fiscal year

——, Rear Admiral Henry B. Wilson assumed command of the Atlantic fleet succeeding Admiral H. T. Mayo

——, Statutory state wide prohibition into effect in Wyoming

July 1, War Trade Board dissolved, personnel, powers, and duties transferred to the Dept. of State

——, Air mail route from New York to Cleveland established and from there to Chicago

——, Public debt $25,482,034,418

——, Herbert Hoover resigned as head of the Food Administration Grain Corporation and was succeeded by Julius Barnes

——, Admiral Hugh Rodman took command of the Pacific fleet

July 2, Woman Suffrage Amendment ratified by Iowa and Missouri, by Arkansas on the 28th, and Montana on the 30th; rejected by Alabama on the 17th, and Georgia on the 24th

——, Death of Anna Howard Shaw (72) suffragist leader, at Moylan, Pennsylvania

July 4, Heavy weight championship of the world won by Jack Dempsey in a fight with Jess Willard at Toledo, Ohio

July 5, Death of Nathaniel B. Potter (49) physician, at Santa Barbara, Cal.

July 6, British dirigible R–34 arrived at Mineola, Long Island, and left on return trip July 9, making first transatlantic round trip

July 8, Major General H. T. Allen took command of American Army of Occupation in Germany

——, Death of John W. Fox (56) author, at Big Stone Gap, Virginia

July 10, H. P. Dodge appointed first Minister to Yugoslavia

——, Death of Abraham Jacobi (89) physician, New York City

July 11, Army reduced to 325,000 men

——, Edward N. Hurley resigned as chairman of the Shipping Board, succeeded by John Barton Payne

——, Federal Trade Commission reported to the President as to the control of the market by the 5 packing companies charging them with fixing prices and acting in combination in restraint of trade

——, Death of William M. Payne (61) educator and author, Chicago

July 12, Proclamation of the President against illegal exportation of arms to Mexico

July 13, Race riots in Longview and Gregg County, Texas, martial law declared

July 14, Trade relations with Germany authorized with certain limitations

July 16, Proclamation of the President of control of wheat by Wheat Director J. H. Barnes

July 17–20, Strike of street railway and elevated employees in Boston gained increase from 48 cents an hour to 62, and an eight hour day

July 19–21, Race riots in Washington begun by attacks on colored quarters by white soldiers

July 23, W. H. Taft proposed 6 reservations to the Covenant of the League of Nations

July 25, Proclamation of the President placed embargo on passage of arms and ammunition to Mexico

———, Strike of Amalgamated Clothing union workers against the Michaels, Stern Company, Rochester, New York

July 26, Strike of seamen firemen and shipyard workers settled by increase in wages

July 27–31, Race riots in Chicago, order restored by troops, many persons killed and injured

July 29–Aug. 1, Strike of street railway employees in Chicago settled by compromise agreement of wage increase from 48 cents an hour to 67 cents, and 50% increase in pay for overtime over 8 hours

July 30, American airplane altitude record made by Roland Rohlfs of 30,700 feet at Mineola, Long Island

July 31, Telephones and telegraphs returned to private ownership at midnight as to control of operations

———, Statement published by "Bradstreet's" reported wholesale prices of food for 31 articles higher by 3.7% than on Dec. 19, 1918

———, Committee to investigate high cost of living appointed by the Cabinet

Aug. 1, Outlaw strike of railroad shopmen begun in Chicago which spread to other parts of the country because of delay in wage increase promised

———, Death of Oscar Hammerstein (72) theater and opera manager, in New York

———, Resignation of F. W. Taussig as head of Tariff Commission

Aug. 2, The president of the 4 Railroad Brotherhoods asked for adoption of the "Plumb plan" providing for government ownership of railroads

———, Woman Suffrage Amendment ratified by Nebraska

Aug. 5, Strike of textile workers at Paterson, New Jersey, for the 44 hour week begun, granted after 3 weeks

Aug. 6, Attorney General Palmer announced intention to bring suit against the 5 meat packers companies as a combination in restraint of trade

Aug. 6–9, Strike of employees of street railways, Brooklyn for recognition of union settled by reference to arbitration

Aug. 7, Report of Federal Trade Commission stated that there was plenty of food but that tens of millions of eggs, millions of pounds of butter, and large quantities of meat and vegetables were hoarded by wholesale dealers and packers to be sold at exorbitant prices

———, Death of Will N. Harben (60) author, New York

Aug. 7–Sept. 6, Actors in New York City went on strike for recognition of the Actors' Equity Association, which closed theaters and also theaters in Boston, Philadelphia, and Chicago

Aug. 11, Death of Andrew Carnegie (83) capitalist and philanthropist, at Lenox, Mass.

Aug. 12, War Labor Board dissolved for lack of funds

Aug. 14, First air delivery of late mail to ocean outgoing steamer by aëroplane flying boat to the "Adriatic" of the White Star line

———, Seizure of hoarded food stuffs begun by Federal officers in Chicago, St. Louis, and Birmingham

Aug. 16, Bureau of Labor Statistics announced that the cost of living had increased 79% in New York City since 1914

Aug. 17–18, Strike of employees of the Interborough Rapid Transit Company, New York City, gained increase of 25% in wages

Aug. 17–Sept. 6, Sympathetic strike of stage workers and musicians

Aug. 18, Railroad shopmen returned to work, and later voted to defer strike for 3 months pending government action

———, Rescue of Lieutenants Davis and Peterson, aviators, captured by Mexican bandits demanded

Aug. 19, Death of Rudolph E. Schirmer (60) music publisher, New York

———, Davis and Peterson ransomed by United States War Dept. for $15,000 and American cavalry and airplanes entered Mexico in pursuit of bandits

Aug. 21, Pearl Harbor Dry Dock, Hawaii, formally opened by Secretary Daniels

Aug. 21–30, Strike of railroad employees in southern California

Aug. 23, Death of Floyd W. Triggs (47) cartoonist, Darien, Conn.

Aug. 24, Death of Theodore Cooper (80) engineer, New York

Aug. 25, President Wilson offered the railroad shopmen increase of 4 cents an hour which was accepted Sept. 21

Aug. 30, Race riots in Knoxville, Tennessee

Aug. 31, Public debt reached peak at over 26 billions

Sept. 2, Mexicans fired on American airplane near Laredo, Texas

———, Communist Labor Party organized at Chicago, adopted emblems of scythe and hammer of the Russian Soviet and motto "Workers of the World Unite"

Sept. 4, President Wilson started for the West on speaking tour to make direct appeal to the people for the German Peace Treaty and the League of Nations

Sept. 6, Actors' strike ended in New York with compromise agreement to run 5 years

———, Death of Horace Traubel (60) author, in Canada

Sept. 8, General J. J. Pershing arrived in New York from Europe

———, Woman Suffrage Amendment ratified by Minnesota, by New Hampshire Sept. 10, and by Utah, Sept. 30; rejected by Virginia, Sept. 3

Sept. 9, 1,500 policemen in Boston went on strike to enforce recognition of right to form a union which resulted in riot and disorder in the city

———, Cardinal Mercier, of Belgium, arrived in New York, to express the thanks of his country for American relief

Sept. 10, International Convention as to Liquor Traffic in Africa signed by the United States

———, Martial law declared in Boston and streets

patrolled by cavalry and the State Guard, and new police force formed at increased wage

Sept. 10, Senators Johnson and Borah began tour in Chicago in opposition to President Wilson, speaking against the German Peace Treaty

——, Treaty of Peace with Austria signed at St. Germain; not ratified by Senate

Sept. 16, American Legion incorporated

Sept. 17, Alabama rejected Woman Suffrage Amendment

Sept. 18, Roland Rohlfs established new world altitude record at 34,500 feet at Mineola, Long Island

Sept. 21, Death of Theodore P. Shonts (63), New York City

Sept. 22, Strike of employees of the United States Steel Corporation begun at Gary, Indiana, for recognition of union, affecting 268,710 employees, which lasted until Jan., 1920

——, Death of David N. Fell (78) chief justice supreme court of Pennsylvania

Sept. 24–27, First meeting of Roman Catholic hierarchy of the United States in Washington, and National Catholic Welfare Council organized

Sept. 25, Death of Charles Lang Freer (63) capitalist and art collector, New York

Sept. 26, President Wilson at Pueblo, Colorado, on return from Pacific coast, forced by illness to give up his speaking tour and return to Washington

Oct. 1, 10,000 printers locked out in New York by 250 firms because of refusal to abide by contract causing suspension of more than 200 periodicals, the men demanding higher wages and a 44 hour week

——, Race riots at Elaine, Arkansas, 9 persons killed

Oct. 2–31, Visit of King Albert and Queen Elizabeth, of Belgium, and the Crown Prince Leopold, landed in New York, and made a tour of the Pacific coast, sailing from New York on the "George Washington"

Oct. 3, Claims Convention with Haiti signed

Oct. 6, National Industrial Conference called by President Wilson met in Washington, ended without results Oct. 23 in disagreement as to collective bargaining

——, General Leonard Wood with federal troops occupied Gary, Indiana, to suppress riots and disorder due to steel strike. Martial law declared at Gary, Indiana Harbor, and East Chicago, Indiana

Oct. 7, Unauthorized strike of longshoremen and harbor workers in New York City demanding increase in wages tying up shipping and causing tons of food on the piers to spoil

——, Death of Henry Mills Alden (82) editor, New York City

Oct. 8–18, Race of 63 army airplanes from Mineola, Long Island, to San Francisco and return won by Lieutenant B. W. Maynard, time 9 days, 4 hours, 26 minutes and 5 seconds, 10 airplanes completing the round trip

Oct. 10, Longshoremen's strike spread to Baltimore, Norfolk, and Boston

——, Strike of railroad shopmen of the Pennsylvania Railroad at Altoona and Hollidaysburg, Pa.

——, United States Employment Service abandoned because of failure of Congress to provide funds for support

Oct. 11, Chesapeake and Delaware Canal taken over by purchase by the Government

Oct. 13–23, Strike of drivers of American Railway Express Company begun in New York City

Oct. 19, W. O. Jenkins, American consular agent in Mexico, kidnapped by bandits for ransom

Oct. 21, 500 regular troops began loading and unloading ships in New York City

——, Death of Alfred T. Ringling (56) circus proprietor

Oct. 23, Death of George W. Elkins (61) capitalist, Philadelphia

Oct. 24, Appeal of President Wilson to coal miners and operators who had suspended negotiations in Washington against proposed bituminous strike as "unjustifiable" and "unlawful"

Oct. 26, William O. Jenkins released by Mexican bandits on payment of ransom

Oct. 29–Nov. 29, First International Labor Conference met in Washington as authorized by the German Peace Treaty

Oct. 30, Executive Order of President Wilson restored war powers to the Fuel Administration over prices and distribution of coal

——, Death of Ella Wheeler Wilcox (Mrs. Robert J.) author (64) at Branford, Conn., and Charles H. Steinway (62) piano manufacturer, New York

Oct. 31, Judge Anderson of Indiana District Court issued injunction to restrain officers of unions from sending out strike orders in coal strike under War Time Food and Fuel Control Act

Nov. 1, 425,000 bituminous coal miners went on strike for increase in wages and shorter hours

——, Woman Suffrage Amendment ratified by California, by Maine Nov. 5

Nov. 4, Elections gave Republicans a majority; Ohio rejected Prohibition Amendment

Nov. 5, Strike of longshoremen in New York ended with compromise agreement and wage increase granted Nov. 21 of 22½%

Nov. 7, Arrest of 250 members of radical organizations in 12 cities including a large number of Russians

Nov. 8–14, First annual convention of the American Legion held at Minneapolis, Franklin D'Olier elected national commander, and permanent constitution adopted

Nov. 10–22, Visit of the Prince of Wales who entered the country at Rouse's Point, New York, and sailed from New York City

Nov. 11, Strike orders to bituminous coal miners formally recalled but few of the miners returned to work and great shortage of coal resulted

——, Armistice Day parade at Centralia, Washington, fired on and 6 wounded and 3 killed; the I.W.W. accused

Nov. 12, John F. Kramer appointed National Prohibition Commissioner

——, Death of Thomas S. Martin (72) Senator from Virginia

Nov. 13, Further I.W.W. raids in western cities including Seattle, Portland, and Spokane

Nov. 14, Conference of representatives of operators and bituminous coal miners opened in Washington which ended Nov. 27 without agreement

——, Death of Major Henry L. Higginson (85) founder of the Boston Symphony Orchestra and of the Harvard Union

Nov. 15, W. O. Jenkins arrested in Mexico charged with connivance with the bandits who kidnapped him

Nov. 17, Supreme Court ordered cancellation of patents of 6,000 acres of oil lands in California granted to the Southern Pacific Railroad

Nov. 20, Note of the State Dept. demanded immediate release of W. O. Jenkins

Nov. 21, Proclamation of the President reëstablished functions of the Food Administration, authority transferred to Attorney General

——, Grain Corporation announced removal of embargoes on wheat and flour to take effect Dec. 15

Nov. 22, New National Labor Party organized at Chicago with platform of "Labor's Fourteen Points"

——, Railroad wage agreement for maintenance of way and track men and establishment of basic eight hour day affected 400,000 workers

Nov. 25, Printers strike in New York City ended with increase of $6 a week

Nov. 26, Mexico refused to release Jenkins as he was under custody of State of Puebla and not under national jurisdiction

Nov. 29, New Note to Mexico demanded release of W. O. Jenkins and stated that consular cases came under Mexican federal courts

——, Senator T. H. Newberry and 133 other persons indicted at Grand Rapids, Michigan, for corrupt practices in election campaign

Dec. 1, Second Industrial Conference called by the President met in Washington, and made recommendations for creation of machinery for settlement of industrial disputes, and suggested extension of employee representation in industry

——, Woman Suffrage Amendment ratified by North Dakota, by South Dakota Dec. 4, and Colorado Dec. 12

——, Thirty-three I.W.W. members brought to trial in Kansas Federal Court charged with attempt to overthrow the government, and 25 sentenced Dec. 18 to terms of imprisonment varying from 3 to 9 years and fines ranging from $3,000 to $10,000

——, Ultimatum to Mexico demanded release of W. O. Jenkins

Dec. 2, Death of Henry Clay Frick (69) financier, New York

Dec. 3, United States District Court at Indianapolis summoned 84 officers of the United Mine Workers of America to answer charges of contempt

Dec. 4, W. O. Jenkins released on bail by Mexican authorities

——, Federal Trade Commission charged the 5 packing companies with control of 31 corporations handling food and other products in violation of the anti-trust laws

Dec. 5, Martial law declared in Oklahoma coal regions and mines reopened with volunteers

Dec. 6, President Wilson submitted written proposal for ending bituminous coal strike, the miners to return to work with a 14% wage increase and a commission to be appointed to work out a new wage agreement

Dec. 8, Peace Treaty with Austria signed at Saint Germain-en-Laye; not perfected

——, Death of Julian A. Weir (67) painter, New York City

Dec. 10, United Mine Workers accepted President Wilson's offer of Dec. 6, and strike ended

Dec. 11, Joshua W. Alexander, of Missouri, appointed Secretary of Commerce

Dec. 15, Supreme Court decision upheld constitutionality of the War Time Prohibition Act of Nov. 1918

Dec. 17, Rhode Island brought suit in Supreme Court to declare the Prohibition Amendment void and enjoin enforcement of the Prohibition Enforcement Act

Dec. 19, Bituminous Coal Commission appointed, Henry M. Robinson, John P. White, and Rembrandt Peale

——, Announcement of the Dept. of Justice of agreement with the meat packing companies, the "Big Five" by which they agreed to dissociate themselves from all lines of industry unrelated to meat packing

——, Victor L. Berger, Socialist, reëlected to Congress from Wisconsin

Dec. 22, The United States transport "Buford" sailed from New York for Russia with 249 deported aliens, chiefly Russians, including Emma Goldman and Alexander Berkman

Dec. 24, Proclamation of the President returned railroads and express companies to private control to take effect March 1

Dec. 28, National Industrial Conference Board published figures showed that cost of living in the United States had advanced more than 80% since July, 1914 and 5.8% since July 1919

CONGRESS

Jan. 9, Association of Railway Executives representing 92% of railway mileage presented to Senate Committee proposals for management of railroads under private ownership under Federal supervision with a Federal Transportation Board appointed by the President, and regulation of rates by the Interstate Commerce Commission

Jan. 16, Charges of disloyalty dismissed against Senator La Follette by Senate

Jan. 29, Resolution of Senator Johnson demanded withdrawal of troops from Russia

Jan. 31, National Association of Owners of Railroad Securities presented plan to Senate Committee calling for private ownership of railroads under Federal regulation and guarantee of 6% return to investors by fixing of rates by Interstate Commerce Commission to enable payment

Feb. 7, Glenn E. Plumb plan approved by railroad unions for government ownership of railroads and operation of roads by railroad employees presented to Senate Committee

Feb. 10, Woman Suffrage Amendment again defeated in Senate by one vote less than the necessary two-thirds

Feb. 19, Senator Poindexter attacked Covenant of the League of Nations as surrendering high functions of sovereignty

Feb. 21, Senator Borah made speech against the Covenant of the League of Nations

Feb. 22, Senator Reed denounced League of Nations as abrogation of the Monroe Doctrine

Feb. 24, War Revenue Act levied income, profits, and estate taxes, excise, privilege, or occupation taxes and tax on the employment of child labor. Excess profits tax on individuals repealed, tax to apply only to corporations. A section made available to public inspection the names and addresses of persons making income tax returns

Feb. 25, $100,000,000 appropriated for relief fund for newly-liberated people of Austria, Poland, Turkey, and Western Russia to be used "as a revolving fund until June 30, 1919." Herbert Hoover as Director General of the American Relief Administration administered this fund

Feb. 26, President Wilson met members of Senate and House Committees on Foreign Relations at the White House in conference on the League of Nations
——, Grand Canyon National Park in Arizona and the Lafayette National Park in Maine established
Feb. 28, Army Voluntary Enlistment Act
——, Senator Lodge made speech against the Covenant of the League of Nations
March 1, Senator Knox attacked the Covenant of the League of Nations as productive of future wars
March 2, War Contracts Relief Act passed
March 3, Federal Reserve Act amended as to surplus fund, and prohibition of Secretaries of the Treasury and Comptroller of the Currency from holding any office in member banks during term of office or 2 years thereafter
——, Victory Loan Act (5th) authorized issue of $7,000,000,000 of notes and created cumulative sinking fund, and War Finance Corporation authorized to promote commerce with foreign nations by making advances to persons and firms to assist in exportation of domestic products
March 4, Resolution presented recommending rejection of proposed League of Nations presented in Senate and "Round Robin" signed March 2 by H. C. Lodge and 38 other Senators read stating that the Covenant of the League "in the form now proposed to the Peace Conference should not be accepted by the United States"
——, Wheat Guarantee Act placed wheat and flour trades under license, powers of President under Food Control Act continued, and $1,000,000,000 appropriated
——, Congress adjourned. Seven appropriation Bills failed to pass because of filibuster to force calling special session
May 19, Sixty-Sixth Congress, 1st (extra) sess. convened, Republicans in a majority in both Houses
May 21, Woman Suffrage Amendment passed in House by vote of 304 to 89
June 2, Speech of Senator Johnson against the League of Nations
June 4, Woman Suffrage Amendment passed the Senate by vote of 56 to 25
June 5, Woman Suffrage Amendment (XIXth) adopted by Joint Resolution and referred to the States for ratification
——, Speech of Senator Borah against the League of Nations
June 9, Treaty of Peace with Germany, unofficial text brought from Paris by a newspaper correspondent, ordered printed in the "Congressional Record"
June 10, Senator Knox introduced Resolution advocating separation of the Covenant of the League of Nations from the German Peace Treaty
July 10, President Wilson formally presented the Peace Treaty with Germany to the Senate urging ratification
July 11, Joint Resolution authorizing the President to take over telephone, telegraph, and cables repealed
——, Army reduced to 325,000 men
July 12, President Wilson vetoed Agricultural Appropriation Bill because of repeal of daylight saving clause, and Sundry Civil Appropriation Bill because of lack of adequate provision for disabled soldiers
July 14, Debate begun in Senate on the German Peace Treaty, Mr. Swanson making speech in support of Treaty and League of Nations

July 15, Senators Lodge and Norris speak against the Shantung clause of the Treaty as an outrage perpetrated on China
July 22, Approval of nominations of the President for members of Reparation Commission provided for in German Treaty rejected by Senate Committee on ground that the Treaty not yet ratified
July 26, Treaty with France of June 28 submitted to Senate
July 31–Sept. 12, Public hearings on the German Peace Treaty by Foreign Relations Committee of the Senate
Aug. 6, War Risk Insurance Act amended to provide total disability compensation
Aug. 8, President Wilson addressed joint session on high prices and high cost of living recommending legislation to check hoarding, regulation of cold storage, and extension of Food Control Act
——, Resolution adopted by Senate for investigation of the Mexican situation
Aug. 12, Senator Lodge made speech against the proposed League of Nations as a "deformed experiment"
Aug. 15, President Wilson vetoed Bill to repeal daylight saving a second time; passed over veto in House Aug. 19, and in Senate Aug. 20 becoming law
Aug. 19, Senate Committee on Foreign Relations in conference with President Wilson at the White House on the German Peace Treaty
Aug. 23, Senate Committee on Foreign Relations voted for adoption of amendment to German Peace Treaty providing for reversion of German rights in Shantung to China instead of Japan
Aug. 26, Senate Committee on Foreign Relations voted for adoption of amendment to German Peace Treaty to eliminate the United States from membership on all commissions except that on reparations
Sept. 3, Act conferred permanent rank of general on General Pershing
Sept. 10, Senator Lodge, chairman of Foreign Relations Committee, presented majority report of Committee on the German Peace Treaty presenting 38 amendments and 4 reservations
Sept. 11, Senator Hitchcock submitted minority report of the Senate Committee on Foreign Relations
Sept. 15–Oct. 20, Formal debate in the Senate on the German Peace Treaty and the amendments and reservations
Sept. 17, Officers in army increased to 18,000
——, Federal Reserve Act amended to allow banks to invest in stock of corporations engaged in financing exports
Sept. 25, Senate investigation of conditions causing steel strike begun
Sept. 29, Absence of soldiers from homesteads authorized when in training under Vocational Rehabilitation Act
Oct. 2, Senate rejected amendments to German Peace Treaty offered by Senator Fall which would eliminate the United States from serving on any international commissions to be created by Treaty
——, Federal Reserve Act amended provided that national banks might lend to extent of 25% of their capital and surplus instead of 10% on shipping documents, warehouse receipts, &c., based on cotton and livestock under certain specified conditions
Oct. 16, Lodge amendments to German Peace Treaty as to restoration of Shantung to China rather than Japan, and as to Reparation Commissions defeated in Senate

Oct. 18, $17,000,000 appropriated for completion of Alaskan railroads

Oct. 22, Food Control Act amended to include clothing and food containers, and hoarding and profiteering made punishable by fine and imprisonment, administration assigned to Attorney General and food administrators in States revived and local "fair price committees" to formulate lists

Oct. 24, House Committee recommended exclusion of Victor Berger of Wisconsin on ground of disloyalty during the War

Oct. 27, President Wilson vetoed the Prohibition Enforcement Bill (Volstead) passed over veto by House the same day and by the Senate Oct. 28

——, Senator Johnson's amendment to German Peace Treaty proposing to equalize votes of the United States and the British Empire in the League defeated

Oct. 28, National Prohibition Enforcement Act became law, ½ of 1% fixed as maximum of alcohol in non-intoxicating beverages, and responsibility of enforcement placed with the Commissioner of Internal Revenue and his assistants

Oct. 29, Three amendments to German Peace Treaty calculated to equalize votes of United States and British Empire in League of Nations rejected by Senate

Nov. 4, Senator Lodge's motion to strike from the German Peace Treaty the articles dealing with the Shantung award defeated

Nov. 5, Amendments to German Peace Treaty eliminating labor sections defeated in Senate

Nov. 6, Act conferred citizenship on Indians in military service

Nov. 7, Pay of postal employees increased

——, Senate adopted reservation on the Preamble to League of Nations Covenant as to ratification

Nov. 10, Act further restricted entry of aliens by extension of provisions of passport control, and provision made for punishment for violation of immigration law

Nov. 12, The House voted to permanently unseat Victor Berger, of Wisconsin, because of his conviction under the Espionage Act, vote 309 to 1

Nov. 13, Senate adopted reservation to Article X of Covenant of League of Nations, declaring that military or naval forces of the United States can not be used under the Article without consent of Congress

Nov. 15, Ten more drastic amendments to German Peace Treaty adopted by Senate

Nov. 19, Motions for ratification of German Peace Treaty with and without reservations defeated in Senate

——, Senator Hitchcock read letter from President Wilson in which he said that the majority reservations amounted to nullification

——, Act extended war time restrictions on importation of dyes and coal tar products

——, Congress adjourned

Dec. 1, Sixty-Sixth Congress, 2d sess. convened

Dec. 18, Copyright Act of 1809 amended modifying regulations for filing of copies of works by foreign authors

Dec. 24, War Risk Insurance Act amended to increase compensation

——, Federal Reserve Act amended to allow organization of corporations to extend credit in Europe to stimulate export trade

Dec. 31, Sugar Control Act continued the Sugar Equalization Board for one year

1920

Jan. 1, Census of this date gave total population as 105,710,620 exclusive of outlying possessions and dependencies, and including outlying possessions 117,823,165, outlying possessions including Alaska, Hawaii, Philippines, Puerto Rico, Guam, American Samoa, Virgin Islands, and Panama Canal Zone 12,115,545. Total white population 94,820,915; colored 10,463,131; Indian 244,437; Chinese 61,639; Japanese 111,010; all other 9,488. The center of population was 8.3 miles southeast of Spencer, Washington township, Owen County, Indiana. New York City led in population with 5,620,048, Chicago second with 2,701,705, Philadelphia 1,823,779, Detroit 993,678, Cleveland 796,841

——, Prohibition by constitutional amendment became effective in Wyoming

Jan. 2, Raids by agents of the Dept. of Justice in 30 cities resulted in arrest of 2,700 persons, about three-fourths of them Russians

Jan. 5, Supreme Court decision sustained the Prohibition Enforcement Act popularly known as the Volstead Act

Jan. 6, Woman Suffrage Amendment ratified by Rhode Island and Kentucky, by Oregon Jan. 12, Indiana Jan. 16, Wyoming Jan. 27; rejected by Mississippi Jan. 21, and South Carolina Jan. 28

Jan. 8, Steel strike officially ended with no gain to workers

——, Death of Maud Powell (Mrs. H. G. Turner) violinist

Jan. 12, President Wilson announced recall of American troops from Russia, withdrawal completed Jan. 17–April 3

Jan. 13, President Wilson called meeting of the Council of the League of Nations

Jan. 14, Death of Charles E. Magoon (59) former Governor of Canal Zone, and John F. Dodge, automobile manufacturer

Jan. 15, Death of Richard C. Maclaurin (50) president of the Massachusetts Institute of Technology

Jan. 16, Prohibition Amendment (XVIIIth) came into effect

——, Death of Reginald De Koven (59) musical composer, New York City, and Isaac Sharpless (72) college president

Jan. 21, The President reappointed members of Permanent Court of Arbitration at The Hague, J. B. Moore, Elihu Root, George Gray, O. S. Straus

Jan. 24, Return of the American Expeditionary Forces completed

——, Death of Cyrus Townsend Brady, clergyman and novelist (59) at Yonkers, New York

Jan. 26, 50,000 garment workers in New York City given 15% increase ending strike

Jan. 30, Bureau of Internal Revenue issued regulations as to medical use of wine and liquor, limiting prescriptions to 1 pint in 10 days

Jan. 31, Edwin T. Meredith, of Iowa, appointed Secretary of Agriculture succeeding D. F. Houston resigned

——, President Wilson removed Frank S. Myers, postmaster at Portland, Oregon, appointed for 4 year term beginning July 21, 1917

Feb. 2, Kansas Court of Industrial Relations organized

under law of Jan. 23, taking over functions of Public Utilities Commission

Feb. 4, Death of E. P. Ripley (75) railroad president, Santa Barbara, California

Feb. 7, Woman Suffrage Amendment ratified by Nevada, by New Jersey Feb. 10, Idaho Feb. 11, Arizona Feb. 12, New Mexico Feb. 19, Oklahoma Feb. 28; rejected by Maryland Feb. 17, and by Mississippi Feb. 18

Feb. 9, Strike of 30,000 ladies' garment workers in New York City against the open shop which lasted a week

Feb. 11, Benjamin Gitlow in New York received the maximum sentence of imprisonment for publication in his paper of the manifesto of the Communist Party

Feb. 13, Resignation of Secretary of State Lansing accepted by the President, offered the 12th after letters from the President Feb. 7 and 11 which accused him of usurpation of presidential powers in summoning meetings of the Cabinet during the illness of the President

——, Executive Order returned commercial radio stations to private ownership to take effect Feb. 29

Feb. 19, Bureau of Labor Statistics reported wages in past year had risen from 25% to 125% in 11 leading industries

Feb. 20, Death of Admiral Robert E. Peary (63) discoverer of the North Pole

Feb. 21, Strike of waist and dressmakers in New York City

Feb. 24, Death of John Charles Olmstead (68) landscape architect

Feb. 25, Death of James Gayley (65) metallurgist

Feb. 27, Packer's consent decree entered in Supreme Court of District of Columbia enjoined the "Big Five," Swift, Armour, Morris, Wilson, and Cudahy companies, from engaging in business of handling any food products except meat and meat products, from establishing retail markets, from owning stockyards, stock in stockyards, stockyard terminal railways, market newspapers, from dealing in milk and cream, from employing any illegal trade practices

Feb. 28, John Barton Payne, of Illinois, appointed Secretary of the Interior

——, Altitude record made by Rudolf C. Schroeder to height of 33,114 feet in a La Pere biplane

——, Executive Order of the President provided for division of powers of the Fuel Administration between the Director General of Railroads and a commission of four

March 1, Railroads returned to private ownership

——, The Shipping Board turned over ships to private operators as agents

——, Supreme Court decision that United States Steel Corporation not an illegal monopoly under Sherman Act

——, Supreme Court decision sustained right of States to impose income tax on non-residents

March 2, Governor of New Jersey signed Bill permitting manufacture and sale of 3.50 beer, and other States enacted similar measures

March 4, New Jersey filled suit to declare the Prohibition Amendment and the Prohibition Enforcement (Volstead) Act null and void

——, Death of George D. Smith (50) rare book collector, and Louis J. Duveen, art collector

March 6, Strike of express clerks, Chicago

March 8, Supreme Court decision that stock dividends not taxable

March 10, Woman Suffrage ratified by West Virginia, and by Washington March 22

March 11, Coal Strike Commission majority report in favor of increase of 27% in wages without change in working conditions

——, Federal Grand Jury at Indianapolis indicted 125 coal operators and miners on charge of conspiracy to raise the price of fuel, agreement in violation of the Lever Act

March 13, 7 I.W.W.s convicted of murder of war veterans in parade at Centralia

——, Death of William Henry Lippincott (71) artist

March 15, Death of George Louis Beer (48) historian

March 20, Senator Newberry and 16 codefendants found guilty of corrupt practices in election and sentenced to various terms of imprisonment, Newberry to 2 years and $10,000 fine

March 22, Bainbridge Colby, of New York, appointed Secretary of State

March 23, President Wilson abolished government price fixing for coal to take effect April 1

March 29, Joint conference of operators and coal miners accepted award of Coal Commission of increase of 27% in wages to take effect April 1, the agreement signed March 31

——, Strike of live stock handlers in Chicago

March 30, G. C. Bergdoll, millionaire draft dodger of Philadelphia, sentenced to imprisonment for 5 years. He was captured Jan. 7

——, Death of Charles Francis Browne (61) artist, Chicago

April 1, Last American troops sailed from Siberia for the Philippines

April 2, Unauthorized strike of railroad switchmen and yardmen begun on Chicago and Milwaukee Railroad which spread over the country from Los Angeles to New York because of delay in wage award

April 5, Bituminous coal miners of Kansas struck against the award

April 9, Alexander Howat, district president of United Mine Workers and other union leaders sentenced to prison because of refusal to answer summons of April 6 to appear before the Kansas Court of Industrial Relations

April 10, Arthur T. Hadley resigned as president of Yale University

April 12, United States marines occupied Guatemala City to protect life and property during revolt

April 13, Railroad Labor Board named by the President, nine members, 3 representing the employees, 3 representing the management, and 3 representing the public, R. M. Barton, chairman

——, Mrs. Helen H. Gardener, first woman civil service commissioner, assumed duties

April 14, President Wilson met with the Cabinet the first time since Sept. 2, 1919

April 15, Strike of elevated railroad employees in New York City for increase in wages

——, Murder of F. A. Parmenter, paymaster of a shoe factory, and Alessandro Berardelli, his guard, at South Braintree, Massachusetts, for which Sacco and Vanzetti, Italians, subsequently arrested

April 16, Death of Theodore N. Vail (75) organizer of telephone industry

April 20, Formal dedication of the Grand Canyon of Colorado as a national park

April 24, Resignation of Director General of Railroads, W. D. Hines, to take effect May 15

April 25, Supreme Council requested the United States to assume mandate for Armenia

April 26, Supreme Court decision ordered dissolution of railroad and mining companies in Reading anthracite coal case

April 30, Kansas Court of Industrial Relations adjudged constitutional

May 1, Wage increase to all classes of railroad employees came into effect

May 3, Strike of textile workers in Massachusetts for wage increase

May 5, Nicola Sacco and Bartolomeo Vanzetti, Italians, arrested for murder of paymaster and guard on April 15

——, Secretary of Labor Wilson announced decision that membership in the Communist Labor Party was not a deportable offense ending raids

May 5–10, Socialist Labor Convention in New York City nominated W. W. Cox of St. Louis for President and August Gilhaus of Brooklyn for Vice-President

May 8–14, Socialist National Convention met in New York and nominated E. V. Debs serving 10 year sentence for violation of the Espionage Act for President, and Seymour Stedman for Vice-President

May 11, Death of William Dean Howells (84) novelist

May 12, Note to Great Britain insisted on equal treatment for all nationals in mandated territories

May 14, John B. Payne appointed Director General of Railroads

May 15, Airmail between Chicago and Omaha inaugurated

——, First labor bank opened in Washington

May 16, Death of Levi P. Morton (96) former Vice-President, Senator and Governor of New York

May 20, Interstate Commerce Commission ordered rerouting of freights to shorten hauls and other measures to relieve congestion on railroads

——, Escape of Grover C. Bergdoll, draft evader, from his guards after automobile broke down in Philadelphia, and from Canada to Germany

May 22, President Wilson accepted invitation of Allied Powers to fix the boundaries of Armenia

May 24, New York State enacted law for manufacture and sale of 2.75% beer

May 25, Strike of truckmen, New York City

——, Proclamation of the President terminated licensing of designated cereals

May 26, Federal Grand Jury indicted American Woolen Company of Massachusetts and New York on charge of profiteering

May 27, National Popular Government League published protest signed by 12 prominent lawyers denouncing as illegal the raids of the Dept. of Justice

May 27–Dec. 21, Strike of fur workers, New York City

May 28, New England shoe, woolen, and cotton mills shut down or went on part time for lack of demand, throwing out 20,000 workers

June 1, Supreme Court decision reversed decision of Ohio Supreme Court that referendum was necessary on prohibition, and affirmed that ratification of Prohibition Amendment by legislatures was sufficient

——, Sugar Equalization Board and Grain Corporation dissolved

June 2, Fine of $50,000 imposed on John A. Roberts Company of Utica, New York for profiteering

June 3, Anthracite Coal Commission named by the President, Dr. W. O. Thompson, W. L. Connell, and N. J. Ferry

June 4, Treaty of peace with Hungary signed at Trianon; never perfected

June 7, Final Supreme Court decision sustained validity of the Prohibition Amendment and the Prohibition Enforcement Act and declared State laws authorizing light wines and beer invalid, that Congress had authority to define "intoxicating liquors"

June 8, Woman Suffrage Amendment rejected by Louisiana

June 8–12, National Republican Convention met in Chicago. Candidates on the first ballot were Leonard Wood, F. O. Lowden, Hiram Johnson, W. E. Borah, W. G. Harding, N. M. Butler, W. C. Sproul, Herbert Hoover, Calvin Coolidge. General Wood received 287½ votes on the first ballot and 314½ at the fourth, and Governor Lowden came second with 211½ votes on the first and 289 on the fourth, Harding receiving 65½ on the first and 61½ on the fourth. Warren G. Harding was nominated for President on the tenth ballot receiving 692½ votes, Wood 156, Lowden 11, and Johnson 80⁴/₅. Governor Coolidge of Massachusetts received nomination for Vice-President on first ballot with 674½ votes

June 11, Indictment of American Woolen Companies for profiteering quashed by Federal District Court on ground that woolen cloth was not wearing apparel and therefore did not come under law

June 16–19, American Federation of Labor in annual convention pledged fight against Kansas Industrial Court, and supported the League of Nations

June 17, Death of Dr. James H. Hyslop (86) founder of the American Institute for Psychical Research

June 18, Death of George W. Perkins (58) financier and leader of Progressive Party

June 19, Supreme Court decision made injunction against Amalgamated Clothing Workers in case of Michaels, Stern Company of Rochester, New York, and awarded the company $100,000 damages caused by activities of union

——, Order reduced 23 emergency officers from rank of major general to brigadier general, and 16 brigadier generals to ranks lower from major to colonel

June 20, Strike of railroad employees at Baltimore against delay in wage award

June 25, Silk mills of Paterson, New Jersey, shut down or went on part time because of lack of demand and labor troubles

June 28, National Democratic Convention met in San Francisco, and James M. Cox, Governor of Ohio, received the nomination for President July 5 on the 44th ballot, and Franklin D. Roosevelt, Assistant Secretary of the Navy, was chosen for Vice-President by acclamation. On the first ballot W. G. McAdoo led with 266, and A. Mitchell Palmer received 256, and Cox 134, Alfred E. Smith 109, E. I. Edwards 42, R. L. Owen 33, J. W. Davis 32, E. T. Meredith 27, Carter Glass 26½. The platform endorsed the League of Nations

July 1, Strike of miners of Ming County, West Virginia

——, Constitutional prohibition became effective in Kentucky

July 1–25, Strike of employees of street railways in New Orleans settled by reference to conciliation

July 4, Death of Major General William C. Gorgas (66) sanitary engineer and former Surgeon General of the Army

July 7, Admiral Sims in speech in London criticized activities of Sinn Fein in the United States

July 8, State Dept. announced raising of embargo on trade with Russia but declared that political recognition was not thereby granted or implied

July 10, Committee of 48 met in Chicago with Progressives and dissenters from the other parties

July 11–16, Farmer Labor Convention met in Chicago and nominated P. P. Christensen, of Salt Lake City, for President, and Max S. Hayes, of Cleveland, for Vice-President

July 12, Formal declaration of opening of the Panama Canal

——, Single Tax Convention met in Chicago and nominated Robert C. Macauley, of Philadelphia, for President, and Richard C. Barnum, of Cleveland, for Vice-President

July 15–Oct. 20, Flight of 4 Army Air Service planes from Mineola, New York, to Nome, Alaska, with object to establish a route to Asia and photograph area of Alaska north of the 66th parallel, actual flying time 55 hours

July 20, Railroad Labor Board handed down award granting wage increases retroactive to May 1 averaging 21% and adding $586,340,000 to railroad pay rolls; accepted July 22

July 21, National Convention of the Prohibition Party at Lincoln, Nebraska, nominated W. J. Bryan for President, and when he declined the nomination, A. S. Watkins July 22

July 22, Outlaw strike of coal miners of Illinois which spread to Indiana, closing all mines

——, Death of William K. Vanderbilt (71) railroad president, New York

July 23, Board appointed headed by Assistant Secretary of the Navy Roosevelt to readjust wages in navy yards

July 28, Death of William M. Reedy (58) editor, St. Louis

July 29–Aug. 8, First transcontinental air mail from New York to San Francisco

July 30, Letter of President Wilson to John Lewis, president of the United Mine Workers, asked the striking coal miners to return to work pending negotiations

July 31, Interstate Commerce Commission announced increase in railroad freight and passenger rates to take effect Aug. 26, passenger rates 20% increase, freight rates on eastern roads 40%, Mountain Pacific 25%, in the West 35%, and in the South 25%

Aug. 1–7, Strike of employees of street railways in Denver for wage increase ended when Federal troops sent to restore order

Aug. 1, 15 coal profiteers arrested in Tennessee

——, Agreement in hosiery industry created unemployment fund

——, Death of Frank Hanley (57) former Governor of Indiana

Aug. 2, Coal miners of Indiana and Illinois returned to work

Aug. 6, War Dept. announced that 6 army depts. would be abolished and 9 army corps organized

Aug. 7, The Dept. of Justice reported 151 convictions for profiteering, 1499 indictments and 1854 arrests

Aug. 10, Note of Secretary Colby to Italian Minister stated that the Russian Soviet Government would not be recognized by the United States, but insisted on territorial integrity of Russia and Poland

Aug. 10, Railroad Labor Board granted wage increase to 75,000 express workers retroactive to May 1

Aug. 13, Woman Suffrage Amendment ratified by Tennessee

——, Interstate Commerce Commission raised express rates by 12½%

Aug. 16, Bartolomeo Vanzetti convicted and given prison sentence by Judge Thayer for participation in attempted robbery of a pay truck at Bridgewater, Mass.

——, Air mail route established between Chicago and St. Louis

Aug. 17, Striking longshoremen, New York City, returned to work after 5 months

Aug. 18, Death of Charles E. Hasbrook (73) editor, Virginia

Aug. 19, Death of Alpheus H. Snow (61) international lawyer and author, and Samuel M. Roosevelt (66) portrait painter

Aug. 25, Death of John H. Hanan (71) shoe manufacturer

Aug. 26, Secretary Colby proclaimed adoption of the XIXth Amendment (Woman Suffrage) to the Constitution by ratification of two-thirds of the States

——, Death of James Wilson (85) former Secretary of Agriculture

Aug. 28, Contract signed providing for air mail service to Cuba

Aug. 29, Strike on surface and elevated railways, Brooklyn, and of baggage men in New York which gained 25% wage increase

Aug. 30, President Wilson approved report of Anthracite Coal Commission of wage increase from 17 to 20%

——, Death of George E. Bissell (81) sculptor, and Benjamin S. Lyman (85) geologist

Sept. 1, Government 6 months guarantee of railroad earnings expired

——, Dr. L. S. Rowe succeeded John Barrett as Director of the Pan-American Union

Sept. 3, Agreement of anthracite coal miners and operators signed accepting award, but miners dissatisfied decided "to take a vacation" and practically all miners were out until the 19th

Sept. 8–11, Transcontinental air mail established between Mineola, New York, and Marina Field, San Francisco, 16,000 letters carried

Sept. 10, California Anti-Alien Land Leasing Act passed to prevent Japanese from owning agricultural land

Sept. 14, Arbitration Convention with Portugal signed renewing that of April 1908

——, Death of Alexander Dunnett (67) lawyer, Vermont

Sept. 16, Bomb exploded at noon hour opposite the J. P. Morgan offices, Wall St. New York, killing 35 persons and injuring 130

Sept. 18, State troops sent to keep order in coal mine district near Birmingham, Alabama, during strike

Sept. 21, Nebraska adopted 41 amendments to Constitution

——, The 5 Socialists expelled from New York Assembly in March and reëlected Sept. 16 again unseated

Sept. 25, Death of Jacob H. Schiff (73) banker, New York

Sept. 28, Attorney General Palmer rejected plan of meat packers for disposal of properties

Sept. 29, Professor Walter Dill Scott made president of Northwestern University

Oct. 1, Charles Ponzi, speculator, Boston, indicted on 86 counts for use of the mails to defraud

Oct. 2, Revived Ku Klux Klan made demonstration on streets at Jacksonville, Florida

——, Death of Winthrop Murray Crane (67), Senator from Massachusetts

Oct. 3, President Wilson in letter addressed to voters asked for endorsement of the League of Nations at the election in Nov.

Oct. 5, United States Circuit Court of Appeals affirmed verdict against 94 members of the I.W.W., including William D. Haywood, of conspiracy to overthrow the government, sustaining sentence of Judge K. M. Landis of Aug. 1918

Oct. 8, Silk, cotton, and shoe factories of Massachusetts shut down in part for lack of demand

Oct. 9, Proclamation of the President set apart the Custer State Park Game Sanctuary in South Dakota

Oct. 11, Night riders in Georgia terrorized cotton ginners who asked for federal aid

Oct. 12, President Wilson reopened anthracite wage award and called for new conference

Oct. 17, Death of John Reed (33) Socialist leader and author

Oct. 18, Death of Charles Ernest Acker (52) inventor and electrochemist

Oct. 20, Housing and building investigation begun in New York which resulted in advanced legislation

——, Tariff Treaty with China provided for application of ad valorem 5% duty on imports of American goods into China by citizens of the United States

——, Cotton mills of Fall River, Massachusetts, cut wages from 15 to 20%

Oct. 25, Governor Parker of Louisiana required cotton ginners to close down for a month until cotton prices higher

Oct. 28, Death of Milton See (67) architect, and James A. Gary (87) former Postmaster General

Oct. 30, Sugar licensing ended

Nov. 2, In election Warren G. Harding and Calvin Coolidge, Republicans, received 16,181,289 votes for President and Vice-President. The Democratic candidates James M. Cox and Franklin Roosevelt received 9,141,753 votes. The electoral vote for President Harding was 404, Cox receiving 127. The Socialists polled 941,827 votes, Prohibition Party 195,923, Farmer Labor 350,267, Socialist 941,827 exclusive of 8 States

Alice Robertson elected to Congress from Oklahoma, the one woman member. The California Alien-Land Act approved by voters by majority of 220,000

——, Westinghouse Electrical and Manufacturing Company inaugurated the first general broadcast for this election

——, Death of Louise Imogen Guiney (59) poet, in London

Nov. 4, Proclamation of the President revoked Federal licensing to take effect Nov. 15

Nov. 8, Supreme Court ruled that private stocks of liquor might be moved and stored by owners

Nov. 9, Note to Japan protested Japanese mandate for Island of Yap in the Pacific

Nov. 11, Price of raw sugar dropped to 6 cents a pound wholesale and refined sugar to 10 cents a pound from prices as high as 30 cents a pound in Aug.

Nov. 13, The President of Haiti asked for investigation

by Congress of American civil administration in Haiti

Nov. 20, Secretary Colby made formal protest against San Remo Agreement as to oil interests and insisted that drafts of mandates must be communicated to the United States for criticism

Nov. 22, Boundary of Armenia transmitted by President Wilson to Supreme Council

Nov. 24, 600 conscientious objectors ordered released from prison

Nov. 31, First regular evening radio program broadcasted by the Westinghouse Electrical Company

Dec. 6, Supreme Court decision against Lehigh Valley Railroad Company under trust laws

Dec. 8, Strike in clothing industry in New York begun which extended to Boston and Baltimore against individual bargaining, piece work, and wage reductions

Dec. 10, California Alien Land Act declared in force

——, National Health Council organized

Dec. 16, Treaty of amity, commerce, and navigation with Siam signed

Dec. 17, 16 individuals and 14 corporations of New York Cut Stone Contract Association fined $80,000 for stifling competition

Dec. 23, Wage cut of 22½% affected 35,000 cotton mill workers

Dec. 31, Association against the Prohibition Amendment incorporated, C. W. H. Stayton, chairman, membership 530,000

CONGRESS

Jan. 10, House voted a second time by 328 to 6 against seating of Victor Berger reëlected from Wisconsin

Feb. 9, The Senate suspended rules and permitted reconsideration of the German Peace Treaty referred to Foreign Relations Committee which reported it Feb. 16 when debate in Senate begun

Feb. 21, Senate voted 45 to 20 to adopt Lodge reservation to German Peace Treaty making the United States the sole judge of right to quit League of Nations

Feb. 25, Oil and Coal Land Leasing Act authorized the Secretary of the Interior to lease to persons and corporations deposits of coal, phosphate, sodium, oil, shale, and gas in lands belonging to the United States

——, Motion to repeal the Volstead Act defeated by vote of 80 to 39, and again March 4

Feb. 26, Senate adopted Lodge mandate reservation to German Peace Treaty

Feb. 28, Transportation Act provided for return of railroads to private ownership and created Railroad Labor Board for settlement of disputes, guarantee of net revenue equal to government rental for 6 months (to Aug. 31) offered to companies on condition that any net earnings in excess of amount be turned over to government

March 3, The Senate voted to accept the Lodge reservations to German Peace Treaty as to domestic questions and Monroe Doctrine

March 4, Lodge amendment on Shantung and Walsh reservation on American representation adopted by Senate

March 9, Lenroot reservation as to equality of voting power in the League of Nations adopted by Senate

March 15, New Lodge reservation as to Article X of the Covenant adopted by Senate

March 18, Reservation (15th) to German Peace Treaty adopted declared adherence to Resolution of sympathy with national aspirations of Ireland as adopted by Senate June 6, 1919, and admission to League of Nations when national government attained

March 19, German Peace Treaty again failed to obtain necessary two-thirds vote in Senate for ratification, vote 49 to 35

March 30, United States Grain Corporation authorized to sell 5,000,000 barrels of flour to buy food for relief of populations of Europe

April 9, Joint Resolution to end war with Germany passed House by vote of 242 to 150

April 13, Federal Reserve Act amended as to discount rates

April 20, Farm Loan Act amended

April 30, Foreign Relations Committee reported in Senate in favor of Knox Resolution proposing repeal of Joint Resolution of April 6, 1917 declaring state of war with Germany, and new treaty

May 1, Civil War Pension Act increased pensions of veterans to $50 a month, $72 for total disability. Widows granted $30 a month and $6 for each child

May 10, Act provided for deportation of undesirable aliens

May 13, Senate Resolution expressed congratulations to Armenian people on recognition of independence

——, Knox Resolution amended by elimination of request that the President should negotiate a separate treaty with Germany

May 15, Knox Resolution as amended adopted by Senate by vote of 43 to 38

May 21, Knox Resolution adopted by House by vote of 228 to 139

——, Joint Resolution proposing adoption of Woman Suffrage to the Constitution passed in House by vote of 304 to 89

May 22, Civil Service Retirement Act provided for pensions for persons within the classified civil service compulsory retirement at age of 70 and annuity if 15 years of service had been rendered

May 26, Federal Farm Loan Act amended as to bonds

May 27, Knox Resolution providing for peace with Germany vetoed by President Wilson

May 28, Motion to pass Knox Resolution over veto defeated in House by vote of 219 to 52

June 1, Senate by vote of 62 to 12 refused to accept mandate for Armenia as requested by the President on May 24

June 2, Vocational Rehabilitation Act amended to include persons disabled in industry

June 4, Army Reorganization Act revised the National Defense Act, providing for a peace army of 297,000 officers and men, continuation of the National Guard, and organization of an enlisted Reserve Corps

——, Budget Bill vetoed by the President as unconstitutional in that it gave Congress authority to remove Comptroller General and his assistant, appointees of the President

——, Diplomatic and Consular Appropriation Act provided that validity of passports be limited to 2 years and visa fee to be $9 with $1 for execution

——, Joint Resolution for Woman Suffrage Amendment passed Senate by vote of 56 to 25

——, Naval Appropriation Act provided that naval oil reserves be transferred to control of the Navy Dept.

June 5, Women's Bureau established in the Dept. of Labor

June 5, First Act for release of sequestrated property in certain cases by Alien Property Custodian

——, Amendment to Immigration Act provided for exclusion and deportation of anarchists and all aliens belonging to organizations that advocate sabotage, destruction of property, &c.

——, Act reclassified postal service and readjusted and increased salaries to take effect July 1

——, Pensions granted for disability for service in the war with Spain, and in China and the Philippines

——, Jones Mercantile Marine Act provided for continuance of the United States Shipping Board, ships to be sold and the proceeds and funds derived from government operation of ships up to $25,000,000 a year for 5 years to be loaned to ship owners to build new ships. Coastwise commerce to be carried in United States vessels

June 10, Water Power Act provided for development of water power reserves under public control, and created Water Power Commission consisting of the Secretaries of War, Agriculture, and the Interior to have jurisdiction over Federal water power

——, Congress adjourned

Dec. 6, Sixty-Sixth Congress, 3d sess. convened

——, Message of President Wilson recommended granting immediate independence to the Philippine Islands on the ground that the "stable government," condition set by the preamble of the Jones Act had been fulfilled

1921

Jan. 1, Pennsylvania Railroad set up joint reviewing committee "for amicable settlement by joint conference of all controversial questions affecting the engine and train service men"

Jan. 3, Supreme Court decision in Duplex Printer's case held that labor unions were liable to prosecution in case of interference with interstate trade

Jan. 10, Wage cut of 22½% in 50 mills of the American Woolen Company

Jan. 16, Bethlehem Steel Company made reductions in wages ranging from 8 to 20%

Jan. 18, Financial Consortium in China signed with China and other Powers; not perfected

Jan. 26, Death of Professor William T. Sedgwick (56) biologist

Jan. 30, Death of John Francis Murphy (68) artist

Jan. 31, President Wilson refused to commute sentence of Eugene V. Debs as recommended by Attorney General Palmer

——, Supreme Court reversed conviction of Victor Berger

Feb. 2, Standard Oil Company announced 10% wage cut

——, Decision of Attorney General, permits for sale of intoxicating liquors in wholesale quantities limited to manufacturers and wholesale druggists

Feb. 7, Arrest of Alexander Howat by Kansas Industrial Relations Court for calling a strike in violation of injunction; sentenced to 1 year in prison on the 16th

Feb. 8, Death of Professor Barrett Wendell (66) author

——, Robert Brindell sentenced to term of 5 years for extortion in building trades in New York

——, Riots in street car employees strike in Albany and Troy, and State Police called to restore order

Feb. 9, Strike of 30,000 needleworkers to enforce standardized conditions

Feb. 9, Death of James G. Huneker (68) musical critic and author

Feb. 19, Dr. James Rowland Angell elected president of Yale University

Feb. 21, Note of Secretary Colby asked that affair of mandate of Island of Yap be reopened, and proposed internationalization for cable purposes

Feb. 22, Strike of coal miners of Alabama begun in previous Sept. ended in defeat

Feb. 23, Strike of Kansas coal miners ended with settlement by Kansas Industrial Relations Court as to matters in controversy

Feb. 24, John T. Hettrick, lawyer, convicted of coercion in maintenance of building ring and given prison sentence, New York

Feb. 28, Supreme Court decision declared invalid penalty clauses of Lever Act as to penalties for profiteering

March 1, 74 cement companies and 40 officers indicted by Federal Grand Jury in New York for $600,000,000 combination in restraint of trade

March 3, Decision of Attorney General, limit of permits for liquors for medicinal purposes not authorized

——, Death of Champ Clark (71) Speaker of the House, representative from Missouri

March 4, Inauguration of President Warren G. Harding, and Vice-President Calvin Coolidge

——, Charles Evans Hughes, of New York, appointed Secretary of State; Andrew W. Mellon, of Pennsylvania, Secretary of the Treasury

——, Resignation of J. B. Payne, Director General of Railroads, succeeded by James C. Davis March 26

March 5, John W. Weeks, of Massachusetts, appointed Secretary of War; Harry M. Daugherty, of Ohio, Attorney General; Will N. Hays, of Indiana, Postmaster General; Edwin Denby, of Michigan, Secretary of the Navy; Albert B. Fall, of New Mexico, Secretary of the Interior; Henry C. Wallace, Secretary of Agriculture; Herbert Hoover, of California, Secretary of Commerce, and James J. Davis, of Pennsylvania, Secretary of Labor

——, Secretary of State Hughes made offer of mediation of boundary dispute between Costa Rica and Panama, which was accepted

March 7, Dennis J. Dougherty, Archbishop of Philadelphia, created a Cardinal

March 8, Packers of Chicago announced wage reduction of 15%

March 17, Death of Frank W. Gunsaulus (65) clergyman and author

March 22, German Court convicted 2 Americans who attempted in Jan. to kidnap G. C. Bergdoll, draft evader, from German territory

March 23, Meat packers of Chicago made agreement for eight hour day and a wage cut of from 12½ to 15%, overtime rates restored

——, President Harding appointed General Leonard Wood and William C. Forbes a commission to investigate conditions in the Philippines

March 24, Death of Cardinal James Gibbons, Archbishop of Baltimore (87)

March 25, Secretary of State Hughes declined request of Russian Soviet Government of March 20 for resumption of trade relations

March 26, Death of Charles McCarthy (48) legislative reference librarian, Wisconsin

March 28, René Viviani, former Premier of France, arrived in New York

March 29, Death of John Burroughs (84) naturalist and essayist

April 4, Death of Charles W. Ames (66) publisher, St. Paul, Minnesota

April 5, Death of George H. Mifflin (75) publisher, Boston

April 6, Notes to Great Britain, France, Italy, and Japan insisted on participation of the United States in disposal of German colonies and equal rights in mandated territories

April 11, President Harding opened telephone line between the United States and Cuba

April 14, Railroad Labor Board ordered abrogation of the "national agreements" defining working conditions on railroads referring disputes over rules to conference between each road and its employees

April 18, Supreme Court upheld legislation of New York and the District of Columbia limiting rent increases

April 20, Death of George F. Wright (83) geologist and author

April 23, Death of John P. Young (71) editor, San Francisco

April 25, Nebraska law prohibited aliens from ownership of land

April 27, Resignation of Melville E. Stone as general manager of the Associated Press since 1893, succeeded by F. R. Martin

April 28, Philadelphia builders reduced wages from over $1.16 an hour to 88 cents

April 29, Federal Trade Commission entered complaint against United States Steel Corporation for unfair competition through Pittsburgh basic price and plus price

May 1, Strike of 10,000 printers to enforce 44 hour week begun

May 1–June 13, Strike of 140,000 marine workers begun in New York ended with wage reduction of 15%, strike spread from Maine to California

May 1–13, Strike in building trades in Cleveland ended with award which gave wage reduction of 17%

May 2, Note to Panama insisted on acceptance of boundary award of March 16. *See also* Panama

——, Supreme Court reversed conviction of T. H. Newberry for violation of Federal Corrupt Practices Act, declared Acts of 1910, 1911, and 1912 as to campaign expenses unconstitutional and void

May 3, United States Steel Corporation reduced wages of common labor 20% affecting 150,000 men

——, Three day battle of miners with guards along Kentucky border

May 10, Executive Order of the President transferred from the Navy Dept. to that of the Interior the management of naval oil land reserves at Elk Hills, and Buena Vista Hills, California, and Teapot Dome, Wyoming

May 11–June 25, Visit of Mme M. S. Curie, discoverer of radium

May 14, Preliminary Agreement of Sinclair Company with Government of Far Eastern Republic for oil concessions in North Sakhalin

May 15, Death of Major General Francis V. Greene (70) author

May 18, Death of Franklin K. Lane (56) former Secretary of the Interior

May 19, Death of Edward D. White, Chief Justice of the Supreme Court (76)

May 20, Mingo County, West Virginia, placed under martial law because of riots of striking miners

——, State troops quelled riots of striking street car employees in Albany, New York

May 21, Claims Convention with Peru provided for arbitration of Landreau claim

May 29, Death of Abbot H. Thayer (72) painter

May 31, Trial of Sacco and Vanzetti begun. 11 witnesses supported the alibi of Vanzetti and 10 of Sacco

——, Note to Japan protested invasion of Russia by Japan. *See also* Japan

June 1, Decision of Railroad Labor Board to order reduction in wages averaging 12% to go into effect July 1

——, Supreme Court decision that former internal revenue laws superseded by Volstead Act

——, Strike of clothing workers in New York City ended with settlement on basis of agreement drawn up by Sidney Hillman, president of the Amalgamated Clothing Workers and wage reduction of 15%

——, Strike in building trades in Pittsburgh begun

——, Race riots in Tulsa, Oklahoma, 25 white persons and 60 negroes killed

June 3, Death of Simon Baruch (71) physician and Confederate veteran

June 4–6, Floods of the Arkansas and South Platte River in central and southern Colorado caused property loss of $25,000,000, of which $15,000,000 represented damage in city of Pueblo where 350 city blocks were under water

June 7, Secretary Hughes proposed treaty of amity and commerce with Mexico to include provision by which Mexico guaranteed to safeguard property rights existing prior to promulgation of the Mexican Constitution of 1917; declined by Mexico. *See* Mexico Sept. 1

June 8, Secretary Denby asked explanation from Admiral Sims of his speech in London of June 7 criticizing activities of Sinn Feiners in the United States, recalled and publicly rebuked June 24

——, New Shipping Board organized with A. D. Lasker, chairman

June 10, Roy A. Haynes, of Ohio, appointed National Prohibition Commissioner

June 12, Death of George P. Morris (57) journalist and author

June 13, Marine workers strike ended with 15% wage reduction

——, Death of Henry Clay Ide (76) former chief justice in Samoa, and governor in the Philippines

June 15, Death of Judge William A. Blount (70) president of the American Bar Association

June 18, Vice-Admiral H. P. Jones appointed to command of Atlantic fleet, and Rear Admiral E. W. Eberle the Pacific fleet

June 21, Charles G. Dawes appointed Director of the Budget

June 22, Death of Professor Morris Jastrow (60) Orientalist and author

June 27, Livingston Farrand elected president of Cornell University

June 28, Railroad Labor Board issued order continuing all national agreements as negotiations between individual railroads and their employees had proved a failure

June 30, Claims Agreement with Norway signed as to requisitioned ships

June 30, William H. Taft appointed and confirmed Chief Justice of the Supreme Court

——, Prosecution of the cement trust begun by Federal Court, New York

July 1, General J. J. Pershing appointed Chief of Staff succeeding General March

——, Wages of railroad employees reduced on this date

July 1–25, Strike of street railway employees in New Orleans

July 3, Death of John F. Wallace (69) former chief engineer of the Panama Canal

July 11, Ships forbidden to bring liquor within 3 miles of shores of the United States

July 14, Sacco and Vanzetti convicted of murder of paymaster at South Braintree, Massachusetts, in April, 1920

July 22, Interborough Rapid Transit Company, New York, and Brooklyn Rapid Transit Company announced wage reduction of 10%

July 23, Herbert Hoover, chairman of American Relief Administration, replied to appeal of Russia of July 16 for aid to famine sufferers and promised assistance on condition of release of American prisoners; terms accepted July 30

July 25, Secretary Weeks rejected offer of Henry Ford to purchase the Muscle Shoals plant for nitrate and water-power development

July 28, The Interstate Commerce Commission refused request of New England railroads for readjustment of freight rates as between New England roads and connecting United States roads

Aug. 1, Sidney Hatfield leader of striking miners shot by private detectives employed by mine owners in West Virginia

Aug. 2, British schooner "Henry L. Marshall" seized outside the 3 mile limit with invoice for 15,000 cases of liquor and 12,000 cases on board

——, Death of Enrico Caruso (48) singer, in Naples, Italy

Aug. 8, Death of Professor George T. Ladd (79) author, and Charles E. McDonnell (67), Roman Catholic bishop

Aug. 9, Bureau of War Risk Insurance abolished, duties transferred to new Veteran's Bureau established

Aug. 11, Formal invitations issued by President Harding to Great Britain, France, Italy, and Japan to conference at Washington to discuss limitation and reduction of armaments, and interchange of views on Pacific and Far Eastern problems, and China invited to discuss the latter, and date fixed for Nov. 11

Aug. 16, Arbitration award in paper industry reduced wages of unskilled labor an average of 25% and skilled labor 10%

Aug. 17, Death of John S. Crowell (71) publisher

Aug. 18, William J. Burns appointed head of the United States Secret Service, succeeding William J. Flynn

Aug. 19, United States Steel Corporation reduced wages a third time in the year to take effect Aug. 29, unskilled labor receiving $3 for a 10 hour day, 40% below wage paid Feb. 1, 1920, but 50% above wage of 1915

Aug. 20, Relief Agreement signed with Russia at Riga, Colonel William N. Haskell appointed Director of American Relief Administration with headquarters in Moscow, and by the end of the year 1,000,000 children were being fed, and by Aug. 1922, 11,000,000 children and adults daily

Aug. 23, March of union miners begun from Marmet, West Virginia, on Mingo County to force unionizing of mines; turned back Aug. 26

——, Death of General James F. Wade (78)

Aug. 24, Peace Treaty with Austria signed at Vienna declaring war ended July 2, date of resolution of Congress

Aug. 25, Peace Treaty with Germany signed in Berlin terminating state of war as of July 2

——, Death of Peter Cooper Hewitt (60) scientist and inventor

Aug. 28, Death of Frederick U. Adams (62) inventor and author

Aug. 29, Peace Treaty with Hungary signed at Budapest terminating state of war as of July 2

Aug. 30, Proclamation of the President ordered marching miners of West Virginia to return to their homes

Aug. 31, Federal Trade Commission issued complaint against the Famous Players Lasky Corporation as a film trust

——, New York Court of Appeals ruled that the New York State Bonus Act providing for bond issue of $45,000,000 for payment of bonus to soldiers unconstitutional

Sept. 2, Federal troops sent to West Virginia ending strike in mining districts

Sept. 3, Agreement of executives of American oil companies in Mexico with the Government. *See also* Mexico

Sept. 6, Indiana by ratification of voters adopted constitutional amendment giving full suffrage to women and prohibiting aliens from voting until fully naturalized

Sept. 7, Award of Judge Landis in the building trades dispute in Chicago provided for reduction in wages varying from 10 to 33%. Recognition of the union included in declaration of principles as to working agreements. Ruled that owner be allowed a representative upon his own work, that an employer might use non-union labor when supply of union labor inadequate, and that labor rulings designed to prolong work be abolished along with other abuses named

Sept. 8, Death of Thomas O'Gorman (78) Roman Catholic bishop and author

Sept. 9–10, Floods at San Antonio, Texas, put center of city including the business district under from 3 to 10 feet of water, region inundated 6 miles long and from $^1/_3$ of a mile to a mile wide, 250 deaths, and $3,000,000 property loss

Sept. 10, Supreme Court of California declared alien poll tax law unconstitutional in violation of the Constitution and of treaties of the United States with Japan

Sept. 11, Death of George P. Wetmore (75) former Governor and Senator, Rhode Island

Sept. 13, Thomas W. Lamont arrived in Mexico on mission as to Mexican foreign debt

Sept. 21, Bureau of Aëronautics established in Navy Dept.

Sept. 26–Oct. 13, Unemployment Conference met in Washington at invitation of the President, Secretary Hoover, chairman, and adopted program

Sept. 28, Lieutenant John A. Macready set altitude record at 37,800 (figures officially corrected) feet at Dayton, Ohio

Oct. 2, Death of David Bispham (65) singer

Oct. 8, Report of Philippine Commission submitted

did not favor granting independence at present time

Oct. 12, Death of Philander C. Knox (68) Senator from Pennsylvania

Oct. 19, Agreement with Russia signed by which persons were enabled to purchase food remittances of $10 and more from the American Relief Administration for their friends and relatives in Russia, food packages to amount of remittances delivered to consignees from American Food Relief

Oct. 22, Interstate Commerce Commission ordered 20% rate reduction for freight of certain commodities including hay and grain between points Western and Mountain and Pacific divisions

Oct. 27, Railroad strike which had been ordered for Oct. 30 against wage reduction of July 1 called off by labor leaders

Oct. 28, Agreement for $5,000,000 loan to Liberia signed

——, Marshal Ferdinand Foch arrived in New York from France on visit

Oct. 31, Judge Anderson, Indianapolis Federal District Court, granted injunction forbidding further efforts to unionize miners of West Virginia, and enjoined further collection of check-off

Nov. 1, Record for parachute leap made by Serg. E. Chambers from army plane of 26,000 feet—slightly less than 5 miles—at Kansas City

Nov. 2, Federal Court in New York City declared 8% a fair rental profit, as against ruling of State Supreme Court Aug. 31 ruling that 10% on present market value a reasonable return

Nov. 4, United States Circuit Court of Appeals suspended injunction of Oct. 31 as to check-off

Nov. 5, Death of Antoinette Louisa Brown Blackwell (96) pioneer suffragist

Nov. 11, Burial of unknown soldier at Arlington National Cemetery, Virginia

Nov. 11–18, First American Birth Control Conference held in New York City under auspices of American Birth Control League organized Nov. 2, Mrs. Margaret Sanger, president

Nov. 12–Feb. 6, International Disarmament Conference in Washington, Secretary Charles Evans Hughes, chairman, presented proposal for "naval holiday," cessation of naval construction for 10 years, and scrapping of 66 capital ships by the United States, Great Britain, and Japan. Nov. 16 China presented 10 principles as to policy in Far East

Nov. 14, Proclamation of the President of termination of war with Germany as of July 2

——, Strike of women's garment workers union in New York City begun against resumption of piece work system, in which the union secured an injunction against the employers prohibiting violation of contract which ran until June, 1922

Nov. 17, Proclamation of the President of termination of war with Austria as of July 2

Nov. 22, American speed record for airplanes broken by Bert Acosta in Curtiss navy racer at Mineola, Long Island, officially timed average speed of 184.8 miles an hour, the maximum 197.8 miles an hour

Nov. 27, Death of Willie Olcott Burr (78) journalist, at Hartford, Connecticut

Nov. 29, Death of Augustus H. Strong (85) theologian and college president

Dec. 1, Railroad Labor Board promulgated 148 new working rules for shopcrafts

Dec. 4, Full diplomatic relations resumed with Bulgaria

Dec. 5, Strike of packing house workers begun

Dec. 12, Agreement in the Cincinnati building trades

Dec. 13, Four Power Pacific Treaty signed with Great Britain, France, and Japan at the Washington Conference, purpose "to respect their rights in relation to their insular possessions and insular dominions in the region of the Pacific Ocean," and committed signatories to settlement of disputes arising out of Pacific questions to conciliation. American reservation made as to mandated islands in north Pacific

——, Navy reduced by 5,000 men

Dec. 19, Supreme Court decision declared Arizona law prohibiting the issuance of injunctions in labor disputes unconstitutional

Dec. 20, Proclamation of the President of termination of war with Hungary

Dec. 22, Death of Henry Watterson (81) journalist of Louisville, Kentucky

Dec. 23, President Harding pardoned Eugene V. Debs and 23 other persons convicted under the Espionage and other war time laws, on Christmas Day

Dec. 24, Judge Thayer denied new trial in the Sacco-Vanzetti case

Dec. 25, Workers Party of America organized

Dec. 30–31, Duration altitude airplane record established by Edward Stinson and Lloyd Bertrand in continuous flight near Mineola, Long Island, 26 hours, 19 minutes, and 35 seconds

Dec. 31, Death of Boies Penrose (61) Senator from Pennsylvania

CONGRESS

Jan. 3, President Wilson vetoed Resolution to revive War Finance Corporation

Jan. 4, Joint Resolution revived War Finance Corporation for relief of depression in agricultural sections, passed over veto

Jan. 19, House voted against increase of membership under census, retaining membership of 435

Feb. 26, Amendment to Transportation Act provided for payment to railroads in advance of final accounting of about $370,000,000

Feb. 27, Act provided for return by Alien Property Custodian of property of women citizens of the United States and Allied countries who had married enemy subjects before declaration of war by the United States

March 3, President Wilson vetoed the Fordney Emergency Tariff Bill levying high duties on imported agricultural products

——, Joint Resolution declared that certain laws, resolutions, and proclamations should be construed as if war with Germany and Austria-Hungary officially ended

March 4, President Wilson vetoed Immigration Bill and Army Appropriation and measure reorganizing war risk insurance

——, Congress adjourned

April 11, Sixty-Seventh Congress, 1st sess. convened

April 20, Treaty with Colombia of April 1914 ratified by Senate as modified with the "sincere regrets" clause removed

May 9, Farm Bloc organized in Senate and May 16 in House to support agricultural measures

May 19, First Immigration Quota Act provided that the number of aliens of any nationality to be admitted under immigration laws should be limited to 3% of the number of foreign born persons of such nationality resident in the country as stated in the census of 1910 with certain exceptions, and provided that not more than 20% of any nationality admissible during any year should be admitted during any single month

May 21, Act provided regulations for landing and operation of submarine cables

May 27, Emergency Tariff Act imposed temporary duties on certain agricultural products for protection from foreign competition. Provisions included against dumping these products on the market at prices lower than those prevailing abroad. Among rates prescribed were wheat at 35 cents a bushel, corn 15 cents a bushel, beans 2 cents a pound, cotton 7 cents a pound, cattle 30% ad valorem, fresh meats 2 cents a pound, butter 6 cents a pound, wool 15 to 45 cents a pound

June 8, Appropriation made for relief of flood sufferers in Colorado

June 10, Budget Act provided for a national budget system and an independent audit of government accounts. Budget Bureau established in the Treasury Dept. with director and assistant director to be appointed by the President

June 30, Army Appropriation Act carried appropriation of $31,000,000 and reduced army to 150,000

July 2, Joint Resolution terminated war with Germany and Austria-Hungary, the United States reserving rights and advantages accorded under armistice, Treaty of Versailles or as a result of the War

July 12, Navy Appropriation Act carried appropriation of $417,000,000 and established a Bureau of Aëronautics

July 27, Senate adopted Resolution providing for investigation of American occupation and administration of Haiti and Santo Domingo, hearings held Oct. 4–Nov. 16

July, Majority report as to administration of the War by the Navy Dept. in answer to charges of Admiral Sims chiefly of administrative delays declared criticisms justified

Aug. 9, United States Veterans' Bureau established as independent bureau directly responsible to the President taking over all forms of veterans' relief, Colonel Charles R. Forbes appointed head

Aug. 15, Packers and Stockyards Act prohibited unfair and discriminatory practices, manipulating and controlling prices, or otherwise creating a monopoly or acting in restraint of commerce, regulating interstate and foreign commerce in livestock, livestock products, dairy products, poultry, and eggs. Enforcement of the law entrusted to Dept. of Agriculture

Aug. 22, Joint Resolution permitted admission of certain aliens who sailed from foreign ports on or before June 8

Aug. 24, Future Grain Trading Act imposed a prohibitive tax on speculative transactions of 20 cents a bushel, and a similar tax on grain sold for future delivery except by owners or certain authorized contract markets

——, War Finance Corporation Act amended to provide special credit facilities in foreign markets, the corporation reorganized to include the Secretary of Agriculture as one of its members, and empowered to issue securities to July 1, 1922

——, Dye and Chemical Control Act

Oct. 18, Peace Treaties with Germany, Austria, and Hungary ratified by the Senate

Nov. 16, Emergency Tariff Act of May extended until other provisions made by law

Nov. 23, Supplementary Prohibition Act prohibited the use of beer or malt liquors except for medicinal purposes, extended prohibition to the Hawaiian and Virgin Islands, and made regulations as to search and seizure, requiring a warrant for search of a private residence

——, Revenue Act abolished the war taxes on war profits, excess profits, transportation, soft drinks, sales at soda fountains, furs, toilet articles, and so-called luxuries, on theater tickets, cigars, tobacco products, the publicity clause as to income tax returns reënacted

——, Sheppard-Towner Maternity and Infancy Act for protection of maternity and infancy passed to continue in effect for 5 years, $1,500,000 appropriated to aid the States, Board of Maternity and Infant Hygiene created

——, Congress adjourned

Dec. 5, Sixty-Seventh Congress, 2d sess. convened

Dec. 22, $20,000,000 appropriated for relief of starving Russians for purchase of seed grain

1922

Jan. 3–11, General lockout of engravers in the printing trades in New York, Chicago, St. Louis, Cleveland, and Philadelphia, award Jan. 21

Jan. 11, New York cloak makers secured permanent injunction requiring employers to keep to terms of contract, and strike ended on the 16th

——, Interstate Commerce Commission ordered 49 railroads to equip main lines with automatic train control devices by March 15

Jan. 15, Meat packers strike in New York City ended

Jan. 17, Notes sent to Chile and Peru inviting representatives to Washington to discuss Tacna-Arica dispute; both accepted

Jan. 19 and 21, Extradition Agreement with Venezuela signed

Jan. 21, Death of John Kendrick Bangs (60) author

Jan. 22, South Carolina rejected the Woman Suffrage Amendment to the Constitution

Jan. 23, Agricultural Conference began 5 days session in Washington

Jan. 25, Death of Alonzo Barton Hepburn (75) financier and author

——, Request of Cuba for withdrawal of American troops from Camaguey granted, withdrawn Feb. 7

Jan. 31, Meat packers strike in Chicago ended

Feb. 6, Nine Power Treaty on the Chinese Customs Tariff signed at the Washington Conference by the United States. Provided for revision of the tariff to make it equivalent to 5% ad valorem instead of 3½%, eventual abolition of likin

——, International Treaty on Chinese integrity and the "open door" signed by the United States

——, International Treaty embodying Resolutions adopted by Washington Conference regulating submarines in time of war, prohibiting use of poison and asphyxiating gases, &c., signed by the United States

——, Five Power Treaty for limitation of naval armaments signed by the United States with Great Britain, France, Italy, and Japan, is concerned mainly with capital ships, defining for each Power what her replacement tonnage shall be, and fixing the maximum displacement of such ships at 35,000 tons, and their heaviest armaments at the 16 in. gun. There is no

restriction as to the number of cruisers, but they are not to exceed 10,000 tons, nor to have a heavier gun than the 8 in. Destroyers and submarines are not affected by the Treaty, but there are special restrictions as to aircraft-carriers

Feb. 7–15, Successful strike of 15,000 New York dressmakers to organize shops

Feb. 11, Treaty with Japan signed as to equal rights in former German Islands in the Pacific Ocean as to cable, radio-telegraph, &c., the "Yap Treaty"

Feb. 13, Textile strike begun in New Hampshire and Rhode Island against 20% cut in wages in cotton mills

Feb. 17, Woman Suffrage Amendment rejected by Maryland

Feb. 21, Foreign Debt Funding Commission nominated by the President, Secretaries Mellon, Hughes, and Hoover, Senator Smoot, and Congressman Burton

——, United States Army airship "Roma" crashed near Hampton Roads killing 25 of crew of 34

——, Strike of cotton operatives in North Carolina

Feb. 27, First National Radio Conference met in Washington

——, Supreme Court sustained constitutionality of Woman Suffrage (XIXth) Amendment to the Constitution, and authorized Interstate Commerce Commission to fix railroad passenger rates in New York and Wisconsin

——, Miss Marion Edwards Park elected president of Bryn Mawr College

March 1, Strike of dress and waist makers in Philadelphia called off after 26 weeks

March 4, Hubert Work, of Colorado, appointed Postmaster General to succeed Will H. Hayes resigned

——, Proclamation of the President prohibited export of arms or munitions to China

March 8, Note of Secretary Hughes declined invitation to participate in Genoa Conference giving reason that the proposed conference was political rather than economic, and could not be entered into with any advantage by the United States

——, Strike of silk workers at Paterson, New Jersey

March 9, Prohibition Amendment (XVIIIth) ratified by New Jersey, completing ratification by all the States except Rhode Island and Connecticut

March 20, Supreme Court decision upheld rent laws of New York State

——, President Harding ordered withdrawal of all American troops from Germany to be completed by July 1

March 22, Note to Allied Governments as to costs of American Army of Occupation in Germany asked priority of payment on a parity with them

March 27, First settlement in New England textile strike at Lawrence, Mass.

March 28, New York law prohibited aliens from teaching in the public schools unless immediate steps towards naturalization taken

March 31, Executive Order of President Harding reorganized Bureau of Engraving and Printing, dismissing the director, James L. Wilmeth and 25 others "for the good of the service"

April 1, Strike of both anthracite and bituminous coal miners begun after reduction of wages proposed by operators when wage scale agreement of 1920 expired March 31

——, Woman Suffrage Amendment rejected by Delaware

April 7, Secretary Fall leased Naval Reserve No. 3 (Teapot Dome) to Harry F. Sinclair without competitive bids who turned it over to the Mammoth Oil Company for $160,000,000 of stock

April 11, World War Foreign Debt Commission appointed, Secretary Mellon, chairman

April 25 and Dec. 11, Secretary Fall leased Elk Hills Reserve to Edward L. Doheny without competitive bids

April 29, Death of Richard Croker (81) Tammany politician, near Dublin, Ireland

May 1, Agreement of Amalgamated Clothing Workers of Association with Chicago employers for reduction in wages of about 10% affecting 50,000 workers

May 6, Death of Henry P. Davison (55) banker, chairman Red Cross War Council

May 7, Death of John H. Patterson (78) founder of National Cash Register Company

May 9, Government suit against American Sugar Refining Company and other sugar corporations ended when Circuit Court filed dissolution and injunction decree

May 15, Supplementary Extradition Convention with Great Britain signed

——, Supreme Court decision that the transportation of liquors from foreign countries through an American port to another foreign port prohibited by Volstead Act

——, Supreme Court decision that Child Labor Clauses of Revenue Act of Feb. 24, 1919 unconstitutional

——, Supreme Court decision that Future Trading Act of Aug. 1921 unconstitutional, and constitutionality of the Packers and Stockyards Act of 1921 sustained

——, Representatives of Chile and Peru began session in Washington on the Tacna-Arica dispute

May 17, Mississippi River floods covered 55,000 square miles in Louisiana and Mississippi, below Cairo the highest levels ever recorded were reached

May 18, Conference of members of the American Iron and Steel Institute at the White House favored abolition of the 12 hour day in the industry

May 24, Interstate Commerce Commission declared reduction of 10% freight rates below those effective Aug. 26, 1920, to take effect July 1

May 28, Railroad Labor Board issued order for wage reductions of about 13% affecting 400,000 employees, effective July 1

May 29, Supreme Court decision ordered Southern Pacific Railroad to sever its control of the Central Pacific Railroad Company under anti-trust laws

——, Last advance of money under the Liberty Loan Acts to Czechoslovakia of $717,834.36

June 1, Agreement of International Ladies Garment Workers in New York with the Merchants Ladies Garment Association, and July 17 with the Cloak, Suit, and Skirt Manufacturers' Association

June 3, Death of Mrs. Mary Virginia Terhune (Marion Harland) author of cookbooks

June 5, Supreme Court decision that labor unions can be sued under anti-trust laws and damages collected from strike funds of union, in Coronado coal case

June 6, Railroad Labor Board authorized wage reduction of shopworkers from 5 to 10 cents an hour

——, Death of Lillian Russell (Mrs. Alexander P. Moore) actress and singer, and Richard A. Ballinger (64) former Secretary of the Interior

June 15, Woman Suffrage Amendment rejected by Louisiana

June 17, Railroad Labor Board authorized wage reduction for employees other than shopmen, clerks, station employees, and freight handlers to take effect July 1

——, President Harding received Filipino delegation headed by M. Quezon and refused June 22 request for independence

June 19, Death of Frederic C. Penfield (67) writer and diplomat

June 21–22, In retaliation for killing by mine guards of 2 union miners attempting to induce strike breakers to leave coal mine an armed mob of miners attacked the mine at Herrin, Illinois, killing 19 non-union miners and wounding 30

June 21–July 3, Strike of men's clothing workers, New York City

June 22, Exchange of Notes established commercial relations with Yugoslavia

June 24, Death of William G. Rockefeller (52) one of founders of Standard Oil Company

July 1, Strike of railroad shopmen begun against reduction of wages effective on this date

——, President Harding ordered Alien Property Custodian to secure return to the Government of the German dye and drug patents and other enemy alien patents from the Chemical Foundation of New York City on ground that the prices paid were insufficient to protect interests of former German owners for whom Alien Property Custodian acted as trustee, refused by Foundation

July 10, President Harding made proposal to coal miners and operators in conference in Washington that the miners return to work on terms and conditions in force March 31 including the check off, and that a coal commission be appointed to consider all phases of the industry

July 11, Proclamation of the President against interference with the mails in the shopmen's strike

July 13, The Secretary of War promised federal police protection in event of need to preserve order

——, Joint Conference begun regarding armaments on Great Lakes with Canadians

July 15, Death of Edward J. Wheeler (63) editor

July 18, Death of Charles R. Miller (73) editor, New York City

July 20, Protocol signed by Chile and Peru submitted Tacna-Arica dispute to the President of the United States

July 25, Interstate Commerce Commission declared public emergency existed and formulated regulations for distribution of coal

——, Death of Simon N. Patten (70) economist

July 28, Note of Secretary Hughes to Mexico suggested that "effective action" on the land question might be substituted for treaty of amity and commerce hitherto asked for

July 31, Death of Mary N. Murfree (Charles Egbert Craddock) author

Aug. 1, Miners and operators met in conference in Cleveland

Aug. 1–4, Strike of street car employees in Chicago settled with grant of eight hour day and 70 cents an hour wage

Aug. 2, Railroad shopmen accepted President Harding's proposal of July 31 to end strike by reference to Railroad Labor Board, but operators refused to agree to proposal to allow employees to return to work with their seniority rights unimpaired

Aug. 2, Death of Alexander Graham Bell, telephone inventor

Aug. 7, Second proposal of President Harding for settlement of railroad strike to leave question of seniority to Railroad Labor Board accepted by operators but rejected by strikers

Aug. 10, Mixed Claims Commission established under agreement with Germany

Aug. 11, Death of Merrill E. Gates (74) educator, and William Sloan (50) merchant

Aug. 14, Contract signed in Washington which provided that Dr. A. C. Millspaugh, economic adviser of the Dept. of State should become Administrator General of the finances of Persia

Aug. 15, Agreement at Cleveland Conference by bituminous coal miners and operators for maintenance of previous wage scale to March 31, 1923, and for joint conference to make new agreement before that date, ending strike

Aug. 22, United States Steel Company gave increase in wages of 20% to day labor affecting about 156,000 men, to receive $3.60 for 10 hour day

Aug. 24, Statement of Secretary Mellon answer to Note of Balfour of Aug. 1. (*See* Great Britain)

Aug. 30, Bituminous coal miners returned to work

Sept. 1, Injunction issued by Judge Wilkerson at request of Attorney General Daugherty forbade issue of instructions to unions by labor leaders to induce any railroad employee to leave his work or cause any person to abstain from entering employment of a railway, and public statements, telephone messages, picketing, or any form of interference with operation of railroads prohibited

Sept. 2, Agreement of anthracite coal miners and operators of Pennsylvania extended the contracts and working conditions in force March 31, 1922 to Aug. 31, 1923, ending strike; agreement ratified by miners Sept. 9

Sept. 4, Resignation of Associate Justice John H. Clarke who had succeeded C. E. Hughes on the Supreme Court; Senator George Sutherland succeeded

Sept. 5, Death of Bishop Samuel Fallows (87) at Chicago

Sept. 8, Government suit filed against Chemical Foundation charging a monopoly in dyestuffs, and asking return of German patents

Sept. 11, Sixteen railroads made agreement with shopmen, the Baltimore Agreement, acceptance of decisions of Railroad Labor Board, and seniority rights of strikers restored; strike cost railroads about 20% of 1923 income, and the government nearly $2,000,000 for deputies to preserve order

——, Anthracite coal miners returned to work

Sept. 12, Wooden ships built during the war sold by Emergency Fleet Corporation to George D. Perry, of San Francisco, for $750,000, cost of each had been $700,000, but value had depreciated

Sept. 13, Railroad Shop Crafts Conference announced that the shopmen would return to work on railroads which accepted the Baltimore Agreement

Sept. 26, Death of Thomas P. Watson (66) Senator from Georgia

Sept. 28, Death of Rush Taggart (73) lawyer and vice-president, Western Union Telegraph Company

Oct. 1, World duration record made by Lieutenants J. A. Macready and O. G. Kelly at San Diego remaining in air 35 hours, 18 minutes, and 35 seconds

Oct. 2, United Mine Workers and operators met in conference

——, Death of Lucius F. Clarke, former Governor of Rhode Island

Oct. 6, Decision of Attorney General that American ships on the high seas are under prohibition laws, and foreign ships within the 3 mile limit and may not bring liquors even under seal into American ports

Oct. 9, Death of Frank S. Washburn (62) engineer, New York City

Oct. 10, Coal Commission appointed by the President, John Hays Hammond, chairman

Oct. 12, National Aëronautic Association organized at Detroit, Michigan

Oct. 13, Award of Permanent Court of Arbitration at The Hague ordered the United States to pay Norway $12,239,652.47 in compensation for Norwegian ships requisitioned during the War; protested by the United States but paid Feb. 26, 1923

Oct. 14, World speed aëroplane record made at Detroit by Lieut. R. L. Maughan on 160 miles course at average speed of 205.8 miles an hour. Second place won by Lieut. Maitland at 198.8 miles an hour, and third by Lieut. H. J. Brow at 193.8, all exceeding previous world records

Oct. 16, World speed aëroplane record (unofficial) made by Lieut. R. L. Maughan at St. Clemens, Michigan, at rate of 248.5 miles an hour, but electrically timed and met usual requirements for a record

——, British Government protested against seizure by United States of vessels engaged in illegal liquor traffic outside the 3 mile limit, and declined to adopt proposed extension to 12 mile limit

Oct. 17, World speed aëroplane record (official) made by Brig. Gen. William Mitchell at rate of 224.05 miles an hour

Oct. 20, Note of this date ended American occupation of Santo Domingo

Oct. 22, Death of Lyman Abbot (87) author and editor, New York City

Oct. 25, Death of Lloyd Warren (52) architect

Oct. 26, President Harding ordered prohibition officers not to act outside the three mile limit

Oct. 27, End of strike of coal miners in Mingo County, West Virginia

Nov. 1, Death of Thomas Nelson Page (69) author and diplomat, in Virginia

Nov. 2, Loan to Cuba approved, request of Cuba of Oct. 18 to State Dept.

Nov. 3–4, World aëroplane record for distance flight made by non-stop flight of Lieuts. J. A. Macready and O. G. Kelly from San Diego, California to Indianapolis, Indiana, 2,060 miles

Nov. 6, Minimum wage law of District of Columbia declared unconstitutional by Court of Appeals, D. C.

Nov. 7, Election increased number of Democrats in both Houses of Congress

——, Death of Jacob Gimbel (72) New York merchant

Nov. 13, Supreme Court decision that Japanese not eligible to American citizenship

——, Trial for murders at Herrin, Illinois, during coal strike ended in acquital as did later trials

Nov. 15, Death of Edward L. Burlingame (74) editor, New York City

Nov. 17, Death of Luke E. Wright (76) former Secretary of War, at Memphis, Tenn.

Nov. 19, Death of Frank Bacon (58) actor

Nov. 20, The United States represented at the Lausanne Conference by "observers" Admiral Bristol, Ambassador R. W. Child from Rome, and Joseph C. Grew, Minister in Switzerland

Nov. 20, Conference of Governor of Louisiana with the President as to lawlessness of Ku Klux Klan in State

——, Death of George Bronson Howard (38) novelist and playwright

Nov. 23, Pierce Butler appointed Associate Justice, Supreme Court, to succeed W. R. Day

——, Death of Henry N. Cary (64) general manager of Chicago Newspaper Publishers' Association since 1911

Nov. 24, Colorado River Compact signed by representatives of 7 States for control and utilization of waters of river; Arizona subsequently refused ratification

——, Federal Government began suit to recover $20,-000,000 for fraud in connection with army cantonment contracts

Nov. 26, Textile strike in New Hampshire ended in defeat, workers returning to 54 hour week

Dec. 4–Feb. 7, 1923, Conference at Washington of representatives of the five Central American Republics with the United States

Dec. 4, Death of Josephine Preston Peabody (Mrs. L. S. Marks) author, Cambridge, Mass.

Dec. 5, Death of Andrew McLean (74) author and editor, Brooklyn, N. Y.

Dec. 7, Atlantic and Pacific fleets consolidated under single command of Admiral Hilary P. Jones

——, Georges Clemenceau, War Premier of France, received by the President

Dec. 11–Feb. 19, 1923, The United States represented at meeting of Commission of Jurists at the Hague, meeting for the purpose of formulating a code of rules for the regulation of the use of aircraft and of radio in time of war

Dec. 11, Second agreement by which Secretary Fall leased Elk Hills Naval Oil Reserve in California to E. M. Doheny

Dec. 12, Death of John Wanamaker (84) merchant and former Postmaster General, at Philadelphia

Dec. 29, Secretary Hughes in speech at New Haven proposed plan of international non-partisan commission of financial experts to name figures for German reparations payments

Dec. 30, Extradition Treaty with Siam signed

Dec. 31, Public debt reduced to $22,986,318,018.09 on this date

CONGRESS

Jan. 12, Senate by vote of 46 to 41 declared Truman H. Newberry entitled to his seat as Senator from Michigan, but criticized his expenditure of $195,000 for campaign expenses

Jan. 19, Resolution of Senator Borah as to outlawry of war, plan of S. O. Levinson

Jan. 26, Dyer Anti-Lynching Bill passed in House by vote of 230 to 119 making lynching a federal crime

Jan. 31, Joint Resolution prohibited export of arms or munitions to certain American countries in which domestic violence existed

Feb. 7, Ford proposal for purchase of Muscle Shoals referred to Senate Committee of Agriculture

Feb. 9, Foreign Debt Funding Act provided for a debt commission of 5 members, the Secretary of the Treasury, chairman

Feb. 18, Coöperative Marketing Act authorized asso-

ciations of producers of agricultural products exempt under anti-trust laws to allow coöperative buying and selling by farmers

Feb. 19, Resignation of Congressman Joseph Cannon announced, member of Congress 1873–91, 1893–1913, 1915–1922, and speaker of the House 1903–1911

Feb. 21, Offer of Alabama Power Company for Muscle Shoals referred to Congress by Secretary of War

Feb. 24, Offer of F. E. Engstrom for Muscle Shoals referred to Congress by Secretary of War

March 2, Report of Committee headed by Walsh investigating Shipping Board revealed cases of graft and embezzlement and waste in purchase of supplies

March 20, Additional appropriation of $107,764 made for European food relief

March 23, Soldiers' Bonus Bill passed by House by vote of 333 to 70

March 30, Seed Grain Act appropriated $1,500,000 for purchase of seed by farmers in the crop failure regions

April 4, Offer of Charles L. Parsons for Muscle Shoals referred to Congress

May 4, Senate declared in favor of restoration of Palestine as national home for Jewish people

May 11, Joint Resolution extended operation of the Immigration Restriction Act to June 30, 1924. Amendment required foreigners to have had residence of 5 years in Mexico, Cuba, or Canada and Central and South America before admission to the United States from those countries

May 15, Privileges of Federal Farm Loan Act made specifically available to farmers on reclamation projects regardless of liens already given

May 26, Federal Narcotics Control Board established, and the importation of narcotics except as necessary for medicinal purposes prohibited with heavy penalties for violation

June 3, Amendment to Federal Reserve Act provided for agricultural representation on the Federal Reserve Board

June 10, Powers of War Finance Corporation to make loans for agricultural purposes extended to June 30, 1923

June 26, Report of Senate Committee investigating American occupation of Santo Domingo and Haiti recommended indefinite military occupation of Haiti

Aug. 31, Soldiers' Bonus Bill passed Senate by vote of 47 to 22

Sept. 19, China Trade Act provided law and administrative machinery for organization of American corporations in China

——, President Harding vetoed the Soldiers' Bonus Bill

Sept. 20, Soldiers' Bonus Bill passed over veto in House by vote of 258 to 54, but defeated in Senate by vote of 44 to 28, lacking 4 votes to make the necessary two-thirds

Sept. 21, New Grain Futures Act for prevention and removal of obstacles in interstate commerce in grain

——, Fordney-McCumber Tariff Act raised duties established in 1913 to high rates of the Payne-Aldrich Act, levying higher duties on agricultural products than in any previous tariff, and almost prohibitive duties on certain manufactured articles as cutlery, yarns, laces, and embroideries. Pig iron, manufactures of iron and steel, salt, wool, hemp, and many food products taken from the free list. Duties increased on woolens, cottons, silks, pottery, hardware, and on dyestuffs and chemicals. The President empowered to increase or decrease the rates within a limit of 50% in order to equalize costs of production at home and abroad. The ad valorem duties were to be assessed on the foreign value of the goods or their export value at port of shipment

Sept. 22, Act required women to become citizens independently of their husband's naturalization, an American woman not to lose citizenship on marriage to alien or gain citizenship by marriage to an American citizen

——, Government Coal Distribution and Price Control Act declared a national emergency in the production and transportation of coal, and increased the powers of the Interstate Commerce Commission to act as to car service, and purchases and sale of coal during the emergency

——, United States Coal Commission created, John H. Hammond, chairman

——, Congress adjourned

Nov. 20, Sixty-Seventh Congress, 3d sess. convened

——, Resignation of Senator Newberry because of continued public criticism of excessive campaign expenses

Nov. 21, Mrs. Rebecca Latimer Felton (87) the first woman Senator seated, appointed Oct. 3 by Governor of Georgia to fill out unexpired term of Senator Watson

——, President Harding appealed for financial aid to American merchant marine

Nov. 23, Proposed loan to Liberia of $5,000,000 defeated in Senate

Nov. 29, Ship Subsidy Bill passed House by vote of 208 to 184

Dec. 1, Representative Keller submitted Resolution for impeachment of Attorney General Daugherty on account of injunction of Sept. 1 during strike

——, New *bloc* formed of 32 Progressives and Radicals under leadership of La Follette, including Senators McNary, Capper, Brookhart, Norris, Fraser, and Ladd; France, Sheppard, Owen, and Wheeler, and Borah joined later, as an organized protest against the Harding administration policy

Dec. 4, Congress adjourned

——, Sixty-Seventh Congress, 4th sess. convened

——, Dyer Anti-Lynching Bill withdrawn from Senate

Dec. 22, Appropriation of $20,000,000 for relief of starvation in Russia

1923

Jan. 4, British Debt Commission headed by Stanley Baldwin arrived in New York, and negotiations for funding war debt begun on the 8th

Jan. 7, Death of Rabbi Emil Gustav Hirsch (72) editor and author

Jan. 10, New York State Court of Appeals in case of Wolfsohn vs. Soviet Government of Russia gave decision that Soviet Government could not be sued as a foreign corporation

——, President Harding ordered return of American Army of Occupation on the Rhine

Jan. 14, Wireless telephone message heard between New York and London, first transatlantic radio

Jan. 15, Ernest DeWitt Burton elected president of the University of Chicago

Jan. 18, Death of Wallace Reid (31) motion picture actor

Jan. 19, Death of Lady Cook, the former Tennessee

Claflin of New York, suffragist leader of the 1870's, in London

Jan. 23, New wage scale signed by bituminous coal miners and operators in New York covering Illinois, Indiana, and Ohio, $7.50 a day wage, and $1.08 on tonnage basis

Jan. 29, President Harding selected as arbiter in Tacna-Arica dispute between Peru and Chile

——, Death of Elihu Vedder (87) mural painter, at Rome

Feb. 3, Strike of textile workers in Rhode Island because of wage reduction extended to Massachusetts and New Hampshire

——, Strike of clothing workers in New York City begun for a 40-hour week

Feb. 7, Treaty of peace and amity, 11 Conventions and 3 Protocols signed by the Central American Republics and the United States. *See also* Central America

——, Death of Edward Emerson Barnard (66) astronomer, at Williams Bay, Wisconsin

Feb. 10, Soldier's Compensation law of North Dakota declared unconstitutional by State Supreme Court

Feb. 13, Treaty with France signed by which the United States consented to administration by France of mandates over former German Cameroon and Togo

Feb. 15, Resignation of Charles R. Forbes, Director of the Veterans' Bureau, under charges of mismanagement

——, President Harding ordered troops on Mexican border to be ready to protect American lives and property

Feb. 16, A news dispatch broadcasted by radio from Newark, New Jersey, for publication in newspapers in England

Feb. 19, Supreme Court decision that Hindus not eligible to American citizenship

Feb. 20, New York Assembly adopted petition to Congress asking for amendment of Volstead Act to permit manufacture and traffic in light wines and beer

Feb. 24, Death of Charlemagne Tower (74) diplomat and author

Feb. 26, Award paid to Norway under Hague Court decision of Oct. 13, 1922

Feb. 27, Meeting of manufacturers of automobiles and accessories protested against British rubber monopoly

——, Executive Order of President Harding ordered 35,000 square miles in Alaska set aside as naval oil reserve

March 1, Strike of workers in textile knit goods in New York City for increase in wages, 44-hour week and recognition of union

——, Death of W. Bourke Cockran (69) lawyer and former member of Congress from New York

March 2, Treaty with Canada signed for preservation of the halibut fisheries in the North Pacific, the first direct treaty between the United States and Canada

March 5, Trial begun of Klan murders at Mer Rouge, Louisiana, no convictions

——, Death of Francis W. Ayer (75) pioneer advertiser, Philadelphia

March 13, Death of James Roscoe Day (77) educator and author

March 14, Miss Ada Louise Comstock elected president of Radcliffe College

March 15, Great Britain made first payment of $4,128,-685.74 in gold under Debt Refunding Act of Feb. 28

March 20, Supreme Court decision declared New York

UNITED STATES 1923 333

State law exempting new buildings from taxation unconstitutional

March 20, Death of Henry Edward Krehbiel (69) musical critic and author, New York

March 26, Cotton mills of New England raised wages 12½%

March 27, President Harding ordered Tariff Commission to investigate high prices of sugar; report April 19 that price not due to tariff

March 29, World aëroplane speed record established by Lieut. Russell L. Maughan at 236.5 miles an hour at Mineola, Long Island

April 1, Bituminous coal miners and operators signed agreement renewing wage scale for one year

April 5, Trial of radicals including William Z. Foster charged with criminal syndicalism begun March 15 ended in hung jury and dismissal of case

April 6, Trial in case of murders of miners at Herrin, Illinois, June 1922, ended with acquittal of 6, and the rest were nolle prossed the following day

April 9, Supreme Court decision that minimum wage law of the District of Columbia unconstitutional interfering with liberty of contract guaranteed the individual

——, United States Steel Corporation granted 11% wage increase to day labor affecting 214,000 men

April 10, Nationalist Assembly of Turkey ratified grant of concession of oil fields and for building railroad in Anatolia to American Company headed by Rear Admiral Colby M. Chester, and Agreement signed April 30; protested by France April 11

——, Death of Stuyvesant Fish (71) banker, New York City

April 13, Packing industry raised wages 11%

April 14, Ishii-Lansing Agreement of Nov. 2, 1917, recognizing special interests of Japan in China canceled by exchange of notes

April 16–17, World aëroplane duration record established by Lieuts. Macready and Kelly at 36 hours and 5 minutes at Dayton, Ohio, and world maximum distance record of 2,541 miles

April 17, 20 individuals and 23 corporations in pottery industry found guilty of violation of anti-trust laws

——, Death of George Clarke Houghton (72) clergyman, New York City

April 18, Treaty with Belgium signed and amendment of Jan. 21, 1924 by which the United States consented to Belgian mandate over Ruanda-Urundi, East Africa

April 20, Florida Senate ended loan of convicts to private corporations

April 22, Dept. of Agriculture announced large exodus of southern negroes to northern cities, 32,000 from Georgia during the year representing 13% of farm labor, 3% from South Carolina, 3½% from Arkansas, 2% from Florida

April 24, 275,000 acres in western States set aside for homesteads for ex-service men

April 26, Florida Senate in executive session ordered removal of Sheriff J. R. Jones charged with beating prisoners at convict camp

April 28, Convention for protection of trade marks and commercial names signed with Latin American Republics

——, Death of Knute Nelson (80) Senator from Minnesota

April 30, Supreme Court decision that Volstead Act did not apply to American ships on the high seas, but that neither American nor foreign ships could bring intoxicating beverages within the three mile limit as ship's stores, in bond or sealed

April 30, Death of Emerson Hough (66) author, at Evanston, Illinois

May 1, Debt Funding Agreement with Finland signed

——, Successful strike of 4,000 bricklayers in New York City for basic wage of $12 per day begun

——, Strike of 5,000 bakers of the Ward Company against open shop

May 2–3, First transcontinental non-stop aëroplane flight of Lieuts. Kelly and Macready from New York to San Diego, 2,516 miles in 26 hours and 50 minutes

May 3, Treaties as to avoidance and prevention of conflicts between the American States and as to publicity of customs documents signed by the United States

——, 220,569 additional acres in western States set aside for homesteads for ex-service men

May 10, Edward P. Farley appointed to succeed Lloyd D. Lasker resigned as chairman of the Shipping Board

May 14–Aug. 15, Conference at Mexico City for settlement of questions in dispute, the United States represented by Charles B. Warren and John Barton Payne

May 14, Florida legislature abolished flogging at convict labor camps, this legislation following publicity given by newspapers of the country to death of prisoner in 1921 following punishment for trivial offense

May 16, Strike of shoe factory workers at Brockton, Mass. for wage increase begun which lasted 11 weeks with no gain

——, Death of George Jay Gould (59) capitalist, at Mentone, France

May 20, Bills for $1,479,064,313.92 presented against Germany to Mixed Claims Commission

May 25, Agreement with France, Great Britain, Italy, and Japan signed in Paris by which the Allies guaranteed to collect from Germany 1,000,000,000 gold marks due the United States as cost of the American Army of Occupation to be paid in 12 annual installments; approximately $15,000,000 received under this Convention

——, Lusk anti-sedition laws in New York State repealed

May 26, Protest to State Dept. of Supreme Court ruling of April 30 as to liquor on foreign ships by Great Britain, France, Italy, Spain, and the Netherlands

May 28, Death of Joseph W. Folk (53) former Governor of Missouri

June 1, Mullan-Gage State Prohibition Enforcement Act repealed in New York

June 3, Treasury Dept. ruling ordered all American and foreign ships in territorial waters to be "dry" to take effect after June 10

June 4, Supreme Court decision declared invalid State laws prohibiting the teaching of foreign languages in the schools

——, Suit of the Government against the Chemical Foundation begun in Federal Court, Washington, as to German dyes and chemical patents

June 11, Supreme Court decision that wage fixing by Kansas Court of Industrial Relations unconstitutional

June 14, Rise of the North Canadian River begun May 22 resulted in floods which reached new high water mark sweeping away all bridges at Oklahoma City

June 15, Alaska Railroad completed with completion of railroad bridge across the Tanana River giving train service from Seward to Fairbanks

June 19, Enforced resignation of President Alexander Meiklejohn, of Amherst College, following disagreement with trustees, and Professor George D. Olds succeeded as president

——, Debt Funding Agreement with Great Britain signed, $4,128,085.74 paid at time of settlement leaving total of $4,600,000,000, the interest is computed at 3% for the first 10 years and at 3½% for the remaining 52 of payments in annual installments ranging from $23,000,000 in 1923 and 1924 to $175,000,000 for last 2 installments in 1983 and 1984

June 20, President Harding left Washington on trip to the Pacific coast

——, Building strike in New York City begun in April 1922 ended with settlement of payment of bricklayers basic wage of $1.50 an hour, $12 a day

June 23, Arbitration Treaty with Great Britain extended that of April 4, 1908

——, Treasury Dept. ruling directed that liquor for medicinal purposes and a given amount per capita carried for crew allowed on foreign ships where laws of the country so required, and all liquors not coming within this purview found within territorial waters subject to seizure

June 26, Strike of 3,950 telephone operators in New England begun for increase in wages which lasted a month

June 27, Illinois anti-Ku Klux law prohibited assemblies of white persons masked or robed to conceal identity

July 6, Strike of 3,725 coal miners near Scranton, Pennsylvania, over grievance which lasted a week

July 8, Report and recommendations of United States Coal Commission presented recommended regulation through the Interstate Commerce Commission, and a number of proposals made to the Government and to the industry

July 9, Death of William R. Day (74) former justice of the Supreme Court

July 19, Arbitration Treaty with France renewed that of Feb. 10, 1908

——, Death of William Holabird (69) architect, at Evanston, Illinois

July 24, Treaty of Peace with Turkey signed at Lausanne; not ratified by Senate

July 27, Conference of anthracite coal miners and operators ended in disagreement, the operators granting increase asked for of 20% for contract miners and $2 a day for day workers but refused the check-off, collection of union dues by the operators and the closed shop

July 28, Strike of cigar makers in northern New England for increase in wages

Aug. 1, Strike of 3,734 employees of street railroads in New Jersey for 30% wage increase ended Aug. 23 with compromise of 20% increase, men returned to work Sept. 21

——, Procter and Gamble (soap manufacturers) guaranteed employees 48 weeks a year employment

Aug. 2, Death of President Harding in San Francisco after illness of 7 days

Aug. 3, Calvin Coolidge, Vice-President, took oath of office as President, at Plymouth, Vermont

Aug. 6, Treaties of amity and commerce and of ex-

tradition with Turkey signed granting the United States the same rights and privileges as were granted to signatories of the Turko-Allied Treaty; not ratified by Senate

Aug. 10, Death of Raphael Pumpelly (85) geologist and author

Aug. 14, Martial law declared by Governor of Oklahoma in attempt to end alleged rule of Ku Klux Klan

Aug. 15, Agreement with Mexico signed as to foreign debts, oil disputes, &c., by delegates at conference in Mexico City. See also Mexico

Aug. 16, Eight hour day established by Carnegie Steel Company, and by the end of the year all employees of United States Steel Corporation were working on shorter day, and a large number of the independent plants

Aug. 23, Arbitration Treaty with Japan signed extending that of May 5, 1908

——, Death of Kate Douglas Wiggin (Mrs. George C. Riggs) author, in London

Aug. 24, Governor Pinchot appointed commissioner to deal with the anthracite coal strike by President Coolidge after failure of renewed conference of miners and operators

Aug. 27–28, World aëroplane duration record established by Lieuts. Lowell H. Smith and J. P. Richter of 37 hours, 15 minutes, and 43.8 seconds at San Diego, California

Aug. 27, Death of Alonzo Kimball (49) artist, at Evanston, Illinois

Aug. 31, Official recognition of Obregon Government of Mexico

Sept. 1, Strike of anthracite coal miners in Pennsylvania begun

Sept. 3, Diplomatic relations with Mexico resumed

Sept. 5, Arbitration Convention signed with Portugal extending that of April 6, 1908

Sept. 6, Death of Edward P. Dutton (92) publisher, New York

Sept. 7, Death of William Roscoe Thayer (64) historian, Cambridge, Mass.

Sept. 8, Settlement of anthracite coal strike on terms proposed by Governor Pinchot, 10% increase in wages, but the check-off not granted or closed shop. Miners resumed work Sept. 18

Sept. 8 and 10, General Claims Convention with Mexico signed

Sept. 12, International Convention for suppression of obscene literature signed by the United States

Sept. 15, Governor Walton declared Oklahoma in "state of rebellion and insurrection" and placed entire State under martial law because of alleged Ku Klux Klan activities

Sept. 16, Death of Charles F. Millspaugh (69) botanist and explorer

Sept. 18–26, Strike of pressmen in New York City for increase of wages and improvement of working conditions. Award Sept. 21 gave $3 increase in weekly wage and reduced hours

Sept. 18, Death of Paul J. Rainey (46) explorer and lecturer

Sept. 22, Final report of Coal Commission which expired by limitation on this date

Sept. 28, World speed record for seaplanes established by Lieut. David Rittenhouse of 177.38 miles per hour at Cowes, England

Oct. 5–Nov. 4, Visit of David Lloyd George, War Prime Minister of England

Oct. 6 and 22, Treaty of commerce with Spain signed

Oct. 9, Death of Ralph Peters (69) railroad president, Long Island

Oct. 10, ZR1 named the "Shenandoah," largest rigid airship of Zeppelin type commissioned

Oct. 14, Death of George Whiting (81) organ composer

Oct. 15, Floods in Oklahoma due to rise of North Canadian River exceeded damage of June, bridges destroyed and 15,000 people rendered homeless

Oct. 16, Extradition Treaty with Latvia signed

Oct. 18, Most Favored National Treaty as to customs signed with Brazil

Oct. 24, Death of Dr. Boris Sidis (56) psychologist and psychopathologist

——, Federal Court ordered dissolution of Cement Manufacturers Protective Association consisting of 9 large manufacturers

——, Dept. of Labor estimated that nearly 500,000 negroes had left the South during the previous 12 months

Oct. 26, Death of Charles P. Steinmetz (58) electrical expert, Schenectady, New York

Oct. 29, Most Favored Nation Treaty as to customs signed with Czechoslovakia

Nov. 4, Final world airplane speed record made by Lieut. Alford J. Williams at Mineola, Long Island, with average speed of 266.6 miles an hour. Of aviation records during this year the United States held 35 out of 42 world records, the Army 12 and the Navy 23

Nov. 5, Decision of Mixed Claims Commission that Germany liable for actual "Lusitania" losses, $23,790,-000

Nov. 8, Extradition Treaty with Estonia signed

——, Death of George Wharton James (65) explorer and ethnologist, at St. Helena, California

Nov. 11, National Vigilance Association incorporated in Washington to wage fight on the Ku Klux Klan and similar organizations

——, Death of John B. Robinson (70) architect and educator

Nov. 12 and 19, Supreme Court decision upheld laws of California and Washington prohibiting alien ownership of land

Nov. 13, Conference on Tacna-Arica dispute begun in Washington, Chile and Peru presenting arguments to President Coolidge, arbitrator

——, Nobel prize for physics awarded to Professor Robert A. Millikan, who first isolated and measured the electron

Nov. 15, Petition of American Chamber of Commerce at Manila asked for repeal of Jones Act and establishment of territorial government for the Philippines

Nov. 17, Death of Anthony Caminetti (69) former Commissioner of Immigration

Nov. 19, Supreme Court decision that interstate exchange of motion picture films was subject to antitrust laws

——, Governor Walton, of Oklahoma, impeached and dismissed from office by the legislature

Nov. 23, Naturalization Treaty with Bulgaria signed

Nov. 25, Railroad Labor Board authorized wage increase for railroad telegraphers and station agents on 26 railroads

Nov. 26, Arbitration Treaty with Norway extended convention of April 4, 1908

Dec. 8, Treaty of friendship, commerce, and consular rights with Germany signed

Dec. 11, Death of William A. Pinkerton (78) detective, in California

——, President Coolidge accepted invitation to participate in Reparations Conference, and announcement Dec. 15 that Charles G. Dawes, H. M. Robinson, and Owen D. Young would serve as experts on committees to investigate finances of Germany

Dec. 18, Secretary Hughes in answer to Russian Note of Dec. 16 refused to negotiate regarding reëstablishment of diplomatic relations

Dec. 19, Notice given by Turkey that Chester concession canceled because of failure to begin railroad construction within time specified

——, Norman H. Davis appointed head of League of Nations Commission to investigate Memel situation

Dec. 21, Death of Frank Irving Cobb (54) editor, New York City

Dec. 24, Claims Agreement with Turkey

Dec. 27, Notes exchanged with Canada constituted agreement as to reciprocal application of copyright regulations

Dec. 29, Agreement to sell munitions to Obregon Government of Mexico

Dec. 31, Station at East Pittsburgh transmitted radio program to Great Britain on short wave

CONGRESS

Jan. 3, President Harding vetoed the Bursum Pension Bill providing for increase of pensions to veterans of Civil War from $50 to $72 a month, and to widows from $24 to $50

Jan. 6, Senate voted for immediate withdrawal of American Army of Occupation from the Rhine

Jan. 25, House vote of 204 to 77 dismissed Congressman Keller's impeachment charges against Attorney General Daugherty

Feb. 12, Senate directed investigation of charges of mismanagement of the United States Veterans' Bureau

Feb. 13, Second Resolution of Senator Borah as to outlawry of war

Feb. 23, Warehouse Act amended to extend its provisions to additional agricultural commodities

Feb. 24, Message of the President urged consent of Senate to adherence of the United States to Protocol of Dec. 16, 1920, establishing the Permanent Court of International Justice subject to 4 reservations as to League of Nations as set forth by Secretary Hughes in letter of Feb. 17 transmitted

Feb. 28, British Debt Refunding Act provided for payment of $4,600,000,000 in annual installments on a fixed schedule. *See also supra* June 19

——, Ship Subsidy Bill defeated by filibuster in Senate

March 3, Naval Stores Act established standard grades of naval stores

March 4, Butter Standards Act defined butter and provided standard thereof

——, Cotton Standards Act established official cotton standards

——, Agricultural Credits Act authorized creation of 12 Intermediate Credit Banks, each with a capital of $5,000,000 subscribed by the Government, and authorized to make loans not only on land but on farmers' crops, live stock, personal notes, and equipment

——, Filled Milk Act prohibited milk in which the butterfat had been replaced by vegetable oils

March 4, Classification Act established a Personnel Classification Board to make rules and regulations for civil employees, to establish grades and define duties of position and qualifications required thereof

——, Further release of enemy property in certain specified cases

——, Second Flood Control Act provided for continued improvements on the Mississippi, $10,000,000 annual appropriation for 6 years to begin July 1, 1924

——, Congress adjourned

Oct. 23, Mr. Fall denied to Senate Investigating Committee that he had ever been in the pay of Sinclair or Doheny oil interests

Dec. 3, Sixty-Eighth Congress, 1st sess. convened

Dec. 6, First annual message of President Coolidge declared in favor of adherence to Permanent Court, the tax reduction plan of Secretary Mellon, coal control, and prohibition enforcement, and opposed soldier bonus, and cancellation of Allied debts

1924

Jan. 1, General S. D. Butler assumed office as Director of Public Safety in Philadelphia

——, Death of James B. Reynolds (63) lawyer and settlement worker of New York

Jan. 3, United States Court at Wilmington sustained sale of 5,700 German dye and chemical patents to the Chemical Foundation of New York by the Alien Property Custodian

Jan. 7, Proclamation of the President prohibited sale of arms and munitions to Mexican rebels

Jan. 8, Death of George Chase (75) lawyer and educator, New York

Jan. 14, Death of Dr. Emmett Holt (55) physician and specialist in pediatrics, in China

Jan. 15, Death of Maurice Francis Egan (71) diplomatist and author, and Peter Newell (61) author and illustrator

Jan. 19, Death of Charles H. Grasty (60) newspaper proprietor, in England

Jan. 23, Liquor Smuggling Treaty with Great Britain signed which permitted search of British vessels within one hour's sailing distance from the coast if suspected of smuggling liquor, and right granted to British vessels to bring intoxicating liquors under seal into American ports

Jan. 27, Announcement of President Coolidge that anyone who seemed guilty of fraud would be prosecuted in answer to accusation of Chairman of Democratic National Committee of Jan. 26 that Republicans guilty of fraud and corruption in office were being protected

——, Death of William Appleton (78) publisher, New York

Jan. 28, Strike of clothing workers in New York City who remained out 12 days

Jan, 29, Diplomatic relations with Greece resumed

——, Conviction of W. H. Anderson, superintendent of Anti-Saloon League on charge of forgery, and sentenced Feb. 8 to prison term of 1 or 2 years; sentence sustained by Supreme Court July 1

Feb. 3, Death of (Thomas) Woodrow Wilson (68) former president, in Washington

Feb. 4, Rev. H. E. Fosdick by vote of 111 to 28 cleared of charge of heresy by New York Presbytery of Baptist Church

Feb. 8–9, Commonwealth Land Party (former Single

Tax) nominated W. J. Wallace for President and J. C. Lincoln for Vice-President

Feb. 11, Death of Jacques Loeb (64) biologist and research worker

Feb. 13, Arbitration Convention with the Netherlands signed extending that of May 2, 1908

——, Diplomatic relations with Honduras severed pending result of revolution

Feb. 16, J. P. Morgan presented the $8,500,000 Library of his father including the building on East 36th St. to New York City

——, Death of Henry Bacon (58) architect, New York City

Feb. 18, Resignation of Edwin Denby, Secretary of the Navy, as of March 10

——, Bituminous coal agreement as to wage scale for 3 years signed

——, Death of Frederick S. Church (82) artist and illustrator

Feb. 21, Letter of President Coolidge to Manuel Rozas, chairman of Philippine Independence Commission in Washington, in reply to request of Jan. 31 for removal of Governor General Wood gave emphatic support to General Wood and stated that the Philippines were not yet ready for independence. Letter published March 5

Feb. 26, Death of George R. Chester (54) author and dramatist

Feb. 29, Charles R. Forbes, former chief of Veterans' Bureau, and John Thompson, contractor, indicted by Federal Grand Jury, Chicago, for conspiracy to defraud the government in hospital contracts, &c.

March 7, Proclamation of the President raised tariff rates on wheat and wheat products to equalize differences in costs of production, 12 cents a bushel on wheat, and 26 cents a hundredweight on flour

March 8, Death of Alfred H. Smith (61) railroad president, New York

March 10, Death of Orison S. Marden (74) editor and author

March 12, Death of Judge Edward E. McCall (61) New York City

March 13, Federal Judge at Cheyenne, Wyoming, granted temporary injunction against further exploitation of Teapot Dome by Sinclair oil interests

March 14, St. Lawrence-Great Lakes Waterways Commission of 9 members appointed, Secretary Hoover at head

March 17, United States Army Air Service of 4 airplanes started flight around the world from Santa Monica, California, proceeding to Seattle, official starting point. Commanded by Major F. L. Marvin, Lieut. Lowell H. Smith, Lieut. Leigh Wade, Lieut. Eric Nelson

——, Federal Court at Los Angeles granted injunction against further operation of Naval Reserve No. 1 by Doheny oil interests

March 18, Curtis D. Wilbur, of California, appointed Secretary of the Navy

——, Three weeks' strike of Boston dressmakers won 42 hour week

March 19, Treaty of extradition with Bulgaria signed

March 21, Kentucky enacted law requiring daily reading of the Bible in the public schools

March 24, Archbishop Patrick J. Hayes, of New York, and Archbishop George W. Mundelein, of Chicago, appointed Cardinals

March 26, Death of Bishop Charles T. Olmsted (82) at Utica, New York

March 27, Death of John G. Leishman (67) diplomat, at Monte Carlo

March 28, President Coolidge asked for resignation of Attorney General Daugherty

March 31, Federal District Court at Portland declared Oregon law requiring attendance of children from 8 to 16 at public schools unconstitutional

April 1, Jacksonville (Florida) wage agreement for bituminous coal industry extended existing scale for 3 years

April 2–May 3, Strike of 40,000 coal miners in Missouri, Kansas, Arkansas, and Oklahoma as to wage agreement successful

April 3, Death of Charles A. Munn (43) editor and publisher, New York City

April 4, Treaty with France assured equal rights in mandated territory of Syria and Lebanon

April 6, Army Air Service planes left Seattle on round the world flight proceeding to Prince Rupert, British Columbia, and to Alaska at Sitka, April 10

——, Jeremiah Smith, Jr. appointed Commissioner General under League of Nations plan for financial reconstruction of Hungary, arriving at Budapest May 1

April 7, Harlan F. Stone, of New York, appointed Attorney General

April 8, Senator B. K. Wheeler indicted in Montana charged with unlawful receiving of retaining fee to influence oil and gas permits

April 9, Extradition Treaty with Lithuania signed

April 10, Note of Ambassador Hanihara to Secretary Hughes protested against immigration provision excluding the Japanese, declaring the effect would involve serious consequences in relations with Japan if "Gentleman's Agreement" abandoned

April 16, Coal miners of Kentucky and Tennessee went on strike after failure to negotiate new agreement

April 22, Death of Lindon W. Bates (66) engineer, in France

April 23, Death of Bertram G. Goodhue (55) architect, New York

April 24, Death of Granville Stanley Hall (78) educator and author, at Worcester, Mass.

April 25, Death of Charles F. Murphy (66) Tammany Hall political leader, New York City

——, Debt Funding Agreement with Hungary signed for debt for purchase of food stuffs

April 30, Plane of Major Martin and Sergeant Harvey forced down in fog and pilots made their way to Point Moller, Alaska, abandoning world trip

——, Governor McCray, of Indiana, sentenced to 10 years in jail and $10,000 fine for fraud and fraudulent use of the mails

April 30–May 3, Strike of 15,000 miners of the Glen Alden Coal Company, Pennsylvania

May 1–27, Strike of ironworkers in New York City and northern New Jersey gained wage increase

May 2, Proclamation of the President prohibited export of arms and munitions to Cuban rebels

May 6–16, Strike of taxi drivers in New York demanding 40% of receipts

——, Death of Victor Herbert (65) musical composer and conductor

May 9, Three remaining planes of Army Air Service continued world flight, Lieut. Lowell H. Smith taking

command, flight from Nazan to Chicagooff on Island of Attu

May 9, Resignation of W. J. Burns as head of Secret Service because of charges of espionage of members of Congress

May 10–12, Successful strike of street car employees of Pittsburgh against reduction of wages

May 11–13, Socialist Labor Party Convention met in New York and nominated F. T. Johns for President and V. L. Reynolds for Vice-President

May 12, Death of George Kennan (79) author and lecturer

May 17, Army Air Service planes landed in Kashiwabara Bay, Kurile Islands, Japan, from Paramoshiri

May 19, Liquor Smuggling Treaty with Germany signed

May 22, Liquor Smuggling Treaty with Sweden signed

May 24, Liquor Smuggling Treaty with Norway signed

May 29, Liquor Smuggling Treaty with Denmark signed

June 3, American Party met at Columbus, Ohio, and nominated Judge Gilbert O. Nations for President and C. H. Randall for Vice-President

——, Liquor Smuggling Treaty with Italy signed

——, Army Air Service planes reached Shanghai, China

June 5, National Convention of the Prohibition Party met at Columbus, Ohio, and nominated H. P. Faris for President and Miss M. C. Brehm for Vice-President

June 6, Liquor Smuggling Treaty with Panama signed and with Great Britain in respect of Canada

June 7, Executive Order provided regulations for execution of the Rogers Act setting up a Foreign Service Personnel Board, an Executive Committee, a Board of Examiners, a Foreign Service School, and a Foreign Service School Board

June 9, Supreme Court decision ruling declared that "only spirituous and vinous liquors may be prescribed for medicinal purposes" thus ruling out beer as a medicine

June 10–12, Republican National Convention met at Cleveland, Ohio, and nominated President Coolidge for reëlection on first ballot, with vote of 1,605 as against 34 for La Follette and 10 for Hiram Johnson, and vote made unanimous, and General Charles G. Dawes, of Illinois, on third ballot for Vice-President by vote of 682½ as against 334½ for Herbert Hoover, and 75 for Judge Kenyon. Governor Frank A. Lowden, of Illinois, was nominated on second ballot but declined the nomination

June 11, Army Air Service planes reached Haip-Hong, French Indo-China

June 11 and July 11, Most Favored Nation Treaty with Nicaragua signed as to customs

June 12, Convention with Santo Domingo as to evacuation of the United States validated all orders and resolutions made during the American occupation

June 16, Note of Secretary Hughes to Japan asserted right of United States to exclude citizens of any other country

June 17–19, National Convention of the Farmer Labor Party nominated Duncan MacDonald for President and William Bouck for Vice-President, the Executive Committee given authority to make substitutions later

June 18, Army Air Service planes reached Bangkok, Siam

June 19, Gas bomb exploded in Rhode Island Senate

Chamber ended filibuster, with result that 20 Republican members went across the State line into Massachusetts where they remained until close of the year, preventing a quorum

June 20, Army Air Service planes flew across the Malay Peninsula to Tavoy in Lower Burma and from there to Rangoon

June 23, Transcontinental flight from New York to San Francisco made by Lieut. R. L. Maughan, 2,700 miles in 21 hours and 44 minutes with 3 stops, total flying time 17 hours and 52 minutes, the "dawn to dusk" flight

June 24, Treaties of Arbitration signed with Denmark and Sweden

——, Death of Terence Powderly (75) labor leader, in Washington

June 24–July 10, National Convention of the Democratic Party met in New York City and nominated John W. Davis, of West Virginia, for President on the 103d ballot on July 9, and Charles W. Bryan, Governor of Nebraska, for Vice-President July 10. On the first ballot William G. McAdoo led with 431½ votes, with Alfred Smith second with 241 votes. On the 69th ballot McAdoo received 530 votes

June 25, Ambassador Kellogg instructed to attend the London Conference for consideration of German Reparations

——, American marines ordered to withdraw from Santo Domingo

June 25–July 12, Strike of 40,000 men's clothing workers in New York City against reduction in wages and use of non-union shops gained wage increase

June 26, Army Air Service planes reached Calcutta

June 28, Death of Adolph B. Spreckels (67) sugar manufacturer, in San Francisco

June 30, Liquor Smuggling Treaty with France signed

——, Federal Grand Jury of the District of Columbia found indictment against Albert B. Fall, Harry F. Sinclair, Edward L. Doheny, and Edward L. Doheny, Jr. for bribery and conspiracy to defraud the government

July 1, New transcontinental air mail service between New York and San Francisco established delivery of mail within 24 hours

——, New immigration law came into effect

——, Army Air Service planes left Calcutta, flying across India to Karachi on July 4 and at Constantinople July 10

July 2–3, Child Labor Amendment rejected by Georgia

July 4–6, Conference for Progressive Political Action met at Cleveland, Ohio, and nominated Robert La Follette for President and Burton K. Wheeler for Vice-President

July 8, Supreme Court of Pennsylvania declared State bonus law unconstitutional

July 8–21, Successful strike of 50,000 clothing workers, New York City for wage increase and 40 hour week; agreement signed July 16

July 9, National Independence Party held convention in Cleveland and nominated John Zahnd for President

July 10, Nominees of Farmer Labor Party withdrew in favor of Senator La Follette. Executive Committee substituted Foster and Gitlow

July 11, Workers' Party nominated W. Z. Foster for President and Benjamin Gitlow for Vice-President

July 13, Army Air Service planes flew from Bucharest to Vienna, and the following day from Vienna to Paris, and reached London July 16

July 16, George W. Olvany named to succeed C. F. Murphy as leader of Tammany Hall

July 17, Death of Mrs. Isabella Stewart Gardner (Mrs. John L.) art patron, Boston

July 18, American Vice-Consul at Teheran, Persia, killed by mob of fanatics. See Persia

July 22, Federal Trade Commission declared Pittsburgh plus plan a violation of Clayton Act

July 23, Extradition Treaty with Rumania signed

——, Baltimore clothing workers went on strike for New York agreement terms

July 24, Death of Palmer Cox (84) artist and writer, at Granby, Quebec

July 28–Aug. 15, Visit of Secretary Hughes to London, Paris, and Berlin

July 31, Persia pledged indemnity and satisfaction as to murder of Vice-Consul Imbrie

Aug. 1, Extradition Treaty with Finland signed

Aug. 2 and 5, Army Air Service planes reached Iceland, Lieut. Wade's plane wrecked, and Lieut. Lowell H. Smith and Lieut. Nelson proceeded on trip reaching Greenland Aug. 21 and landing on American continent at Labrador Aug. 31

Aug. 5, Resignation of Charles B. Warren as Ambassador to Mexico

Aug. 6–14, Successful strike of 3,500 clothing workers to organize the shops in Philadelphia

Aug. 10, Death of Mary S. Cutting (73) author

Aug. 11–Jan. 6, 1925, Strike of the Waltham Watch Company against wage reduction

Aug. 11–18, Successful strike of 4,000 clothing workers in Boston to eliminate the sweat shop

Aug. 12–Dec. 14, Strike of silk weavers in Paterson, New Jersey, gained wage increase but not demand for 44 hour week and restriction of looms to 2 per operator

Aug. 14, Most Favored Nation Treaty as to customs signed with Guatemala

Aug. 21, Liquor Smuggling Treaty with the Netherlands signed

Aug. 21–29, Clothing workers in Boston went on strike for terms of the New York agreement

Aug. 28, Universal Postal Union Convention signed by the United States

Aug. 28–Sept. 21, Visit of the Prince of Wales

Aug. 30, First meeting of American-Mexican Claims Commission in Mexico City

——, Plan of Dawes Committee accepted by Allies and Germany

Sept. 3, Seymour Parker Gilbert appointed Agent General for German Reparations Payments

——, Death of Adam W. Wagnalls (80) publisher

Sept. 5, Army Air Service planes landed in Casco Bay, Maine, and Sept. 8 proceeded to Mitchell Field, Long Island, escorted by General Patrick, Chief of Air Service

Sept. 10, In Chicago N. F. Leopold, Jr. and R. A. Loeb, murderers of Robert Franks, sentenced to life imprisonment

Sept. 12, Retirement of General John J. Pershing from active service at statutory age of 64

Sept. 14, Death of Charles Zueblin (58) author, in Switzerland

Sept. 18, Last American marines left Santo Domingo

Sept. 20, Return of D. M. MacMillan scientific Arctic expedition of 1923–1924

Sept. 22, Debt Funding Agreement with Lithuania signed

Sept. 25, Most Favored Nation Treaty as to customs signed with Santo Domingo

——, Death of Charlotte Crabtree (Lotta) actress, in Boston

Sept. 25–Oct. 18, Strike of 12,500 cigar workers at Tampa, Florida, gained wage increase of 25%

Sept. 28, Army Air Service planes reached Seattle officially completing the first round the world airship flight by 2 of the 4 planes, the "Chicago" commanded by Lieut. L. H. Smith, and the "New Orleans" commanded by Lieut. Erik H. Nelson, time 175 days, flying time approximately 351 hours, average length of flights 480 miles, 57 stops had been made

Oct. 1, Payment of $60,000 indemnity by Persia to widow of Vice-Consul Imbrie

Oct. 2, Death of William B. Ross, Governor of Wyoming (51), his wife elected to fill out his unexpired term in special election becoming first woman governor in the United States

Oct. 5, Federal Trade Commission declared Aluminum Company of America a monopoly

Oct. 6, Death of William A. Shanklin (62) educator, New York City

Oct. 7–26, Airship "Shenandoah" made transcontinental flight from Lakehurst, New Jersey, to San Diego, California, returning Oct. 25–26

Oct. 9, Strike of 22,000 miners of the Hudson Coal Company, settled by arbitration

Oct. 10, James R. Sheffield succeeded C. B. Warren as Ambassador to Mexico

Oct. 12, Death of Laurenus Clark Seelye (87) president emeritus of Smith College, at Northampton, Mass.

Oct. 13, Supreme Court decision in case of Ziang Sung Wan ruled out confessions obtained by "third degree" methods

——, Henry Ford withdrew offer to take over Muscle Shoals on 100 years lease

Oct. 15, The ZR-3 airship built for the United States in Germany as reparation for certain airships destroyed by Germans after the Armistice arrived in New York under command of Dr. Hugo Eckener (Oct. 12–15), and was rechristened the "Los Angeles" by Mrs. Calvin Coolidge Nov. 25

Oct. 17, Death of Herman Henry Kohlsaat (71) Chicago editor

Oct. 20, Supreme Court decision sustained the Clayton Act of 1914 by which workers empowered to demand trial by jury for charges of criminal contempt arising out of the issuance of an injunction

Oct. 25, Death of Henry C. Wallace (58) Secretary of Agriculture, and Laura Jean Libbey (62) novelist

Oct. 26, Death of Lew Dockstader (G. A. Clapp) vaudeville actor (70)

Oct. 29, Death of Frances Hodgson Burnett (Mrs. Stephen Townsend) novelist

Nov. 4, Election gave President Coolidge, reëlected President, 15,718,789 votes, John W. Davis (Democrat) receiving 8,378,962, and 4,822,319 votes cast for La Follette. Charles G. Dawes, of Illinois, elected Vice-President. The Worker's Party received 33,605 votes; Socialist-Labor 33,901; Prohibition 48,671; American Party 22,873; Commonwealth Land Party less than 3,000. The electoral vote for Coolidge was 382 representing 35 States, and for Davis 136 from 12 States. Two women were elected governors,

Mrs. Nellie G. Ross in Wyoming, and Mrs. Miriam Ferguson in Texas

Nov. 7, Transactions on New York stock exchange in 2,336,160 shares exceeded records for 5 years

——, Commission to study agricultural conditions appointed by the President, former Governor Cary, of Wyoming, chairman

Nov. 9, British Note protested American claim to German reparations payments under Dawes Plan; had been agreed to by France Oct. 15

——, Death of Henry Cabot Lodge (74) Senator from Massachusetts

Nov. 14, Pan-American Sanitary Convention signed by the United States

Nov. 15, Debt Funding Agreement with Poland signed, total $178,560,000

Nov. 17, The United States represented at International Opium Conference, Geneva

Nov. 21, Howard M. Gore, of West Virginia, appointed Secretary of Agriculture

Nov. 26, Agreement with Austria and Hungary signed for appointment of a Claims Commission

Nov. 28, Conference of 34 Republican Senators read insurgents, La Follette, Brookhart, Ladd, and Frazer out of the Party, and agreed they were not to be invited to act on committees

Nov. 30, Radio Corporation of America demonstrated transmission of pictures by wireless telegraph from London to New York

Dec. 3, Convention with Great Britain gave American nationals rights in Palestine

Dec. 5, Most Favored Nation Treaty as to customs with Czechoslovakia extended that of Oct. 29, 1923

Dec. 9, Most Favored Nation Treaty as to customs signed with Greece

Dec. 12, Note to Great Britain maintained claim to Reparations payments

Dec. 13, Death of Samuel Gompers (74) president of the American Federation of Labor since 1882 except for the year 1894 when he was defeated by Socialists, at San Antonio, Texas

Dec. 14, Death of Martin H. Glynn (53) former Governor of New York and member of Congress

Dec. 19, Federal Oil Conservation Board appointed by the President, of the Secretaries of War, Navy, Commerce, and Interior

Dec. 20, Death of Arthur I. Keller (57) artist and illustrator

Dec. 27, Treaty with Santo Domingo replaced and modified Convention of Feb. 8, 1907 and provided for loan of $25,000,000 to the Dominican Republic

CONGRESS

Jan. 16, McNary-Haughen Farm Bill introduced in both Houses

Jan. 24, Testimony of E. L. Doheny before Senate Committee that he had "lent" A. B. Fall $100,000 without interest or security on Nov. 30, 1921

Jan. 31, Senate adopted Resolution charging fraud and corruption in execution of oil leases and contracts in April 1922 by A. B. Fall, then Secretary of the Interior, and Edwin Denby, Secretary of the Navy, and instructed the President to institute court action to cancel Doheny and Sinclair land leases in California and Wyoming. Joint Resolution to this effect signed by the President Feb. 8

Feb. 11, Senate Resolution asked the President to call

for resignation of Secretary of the Navy Denby on account of the oil leases

Feb. 20, Act extended life and power of the War Finance Corporation for 9 months

Feb. 24, Message of the President urged adherence of the United States to the Permanent Court of International Justice

Feb. 27, Joint Resolution granted $100,000 to the President to employ special counsel in civil and criminal cases in connection with the naval oil reserves

March 1, Senate Resolution called for investigation of the administration of the Attorney General's Office under Harry M. Daugherty

March 10, The House voted by 227 to 142 to accept offer of Henry Ford to lease Muscle Shoals power plant and nitrate works for 100 years

March 18, Soldiers' Bonus Bill providing for a 20 year endowment insurance and ultimate expenditure of $2,000,000,000 passed in House by vote of 355 to 54

——, Joint Resolution passed in Senate proposing constitutional amendment providing that the President should take office in January following the presidential election, and that Congress should meet on the third Monday in January, elimination of the short "lame duck" session

March 22, H. F. Sinclair refused to answer questions of the Senate Committee as to oil leases on ground that the validity of the leases was still in litigation

April 10, Senate Committee headed by Borah appointed to investigate the indictment of Senator Wheeler

April 12, House passed Immigration Bill with clause prohibiting Japanese immigration, and Senate April 17

April 21, Coast Guard increased for enforcement of prohibition

April 23, Soldiers' Bonus Bill passed by Senate

April 26, Seed Grain Act authorized appropriation of $1,000,000 for relief of drought-stricken farm areas of New Mexico

——, Child Labor Amendment to the Constitution adopted by House by vote of 297 to 69

May 3, Bursum Pension Increase Bill for Civil and Spanish War pensions vetoed by the President

May 15, Soldiers' Bonus Bill vetoed by the President; passed over veto on the 17th by the House and on the 19th by the Senate

May 19, World War Adjusted Compensation (Soldiers' Bonus) Act authorized payment of adjusted compensation to all veterans of the World War, not including any officer above grade of captain, the adjusted service certificates in form of 20 year endowment policies against which veterans might borrow money from the government, $1.25 being credit per day for overseas service and $1.00 per day for home service, certificates to bear compound interest at 4%

May 21, Joint Resolution remitted unpaid balance of Boxer indemnity of $6,137,552.90 to China for educational and cultural purposes

May 24, Diplomatic and Consular Services merged into one to be called the "Foreign Service of the United States" to take effect July 1

May 26, Immigration Quota Act amended to base quota on 2% of foreign-born individuals of any nationality resident in the United States as determined by census of 1890, reducing number of aliens to be admitted from July 1, 1924 to July 1, 1927, and provided that only 150,000 immigrants should be admitted in any year, and divided among the various countries in the proportion that the number of their nationals bore to total population in 1920, preference within quota given to members of families already resident and of persons skilled in agriculture, and American consular officers abroad to decide on eligibility of candidates thus avoiding as far as possible deportation after arrival. Aliens ineligible to citizenship barred thus ending "Gentleman's Agreement" with Japan which had excluded only laborers. The quota system was not to apply to Canada, Mexico, and the independent nations of Central and South America

May 29, Dairy Bureau in the Dept. of Agriculture established

June 2, Act authorized the Secretary of the Interior to issue certificates of citizenship to Indians

——, Child Labor Amendment to the Constitution passed in Senate and was sent to States for ratification

——, Revenue Act reduced tax on incomes earned in 1923 by 25%, and new rates established 2% tax on incomes less than $4,000, and 4% on incomes from $4,000 to $8,000, and 6% above $8,000. Range of surtaxes from 1% on incomes between $10,000 and $14,000, to 40% on incomes over $500,000. Tax placed on gifts. Excise taxes on candy, yachts, motor boats, telephone and telegraph messages, drafts, and promissory notes among those repealed. Taxes on automobiles selling for less than $1,000 exempted from the 3% tax. Rates of estate taxes increased to highest ever imposed

June 3, Inland Waterways Corporation constituted controlled by the Government through the Secretary of War

——, McNary-Haugen Farm Relief Bill defeated in House by vote of 224 to 154

June 7, Act provided for decentralization of activities of the Veterans' Bureau by establishment of regional offices, laws affecting the Bureau, and administration of War Risk Insurance and Vocational Rehabilitation revised and consolidated

——, Clarke-McNary Reforestation Act passed

——, Bill raising postal salaries $68,000,000 a year vetoed by the President

——, Congress adjourned

Dec. 1, Sixty-Eighth Congress, 2d sess. convened

1925

Jan. 2, Republican Senators returned to legislature in Rhode Island

Jan. 5, Harlan F. Stone resigned as Attorney General to accept appointment as associate justice of Supreme Court succeeding Joseph McKenna resigned

——, Supreme Court decision sustained lower courts in suit of Sanitary District of Chicago vs. the United States prohibiting diversion of water from Lake Michigan in excess of that allowed by the Secretary of War

——, Mrs. Nellie T. Ross, first woman Governor, inaugurated in Wyoming

Jan. 5–6, Strike of 3,000 coal teamsters in Chicago for wage increase ended with agreement to arbitrate dispute

Jan. 6, Commission appointed to study equitable use of waters of the Rio Grande

Jan. 8, Child Labor Amendment to Constitution ratified by California, and by Lower House, New Mexico,

Jan. 28; rejected by South Carolina Jan. 14, by legislatures of Oklahoma, Ohio, Kansas, Texas Jan. 26,
and by North Dakota Senate, and by Delaware and
Washington on the 28th

Jan. 8, Extradition Treaty with Great Britain signed
in respect of breaches of narcotic laws as to Canada

——, Death of George Wesley Bellows (42) artist,
New York City

Jan. 10, Resignation of Charles Evans Hughes as
Secretary of State as of March 4

——, Adjustment of claims of the United States to
payments from Germany under the Dawes Plan at
Interallied Financial Congress in Paris (Jan. 7–14),
$255,000,000 for cost of American Army of Occupa-
tion, and $350,000,000 for war damage; signed by
the United States Jan. 14

Jan. 19, New cable opened between the United States
and Spain, President Coolidge and King Alfonso
exchange greetings

Jan. 20, Mrs. Miriam A. Ferguson, second woman
governor in the United States, inaugurated in Texas

Jan. 23, Agreement with the Netherlands for settlement
by arbitration of the question of sovereignty of
Island of Palmas

Jan. 27, Announcement made that 13 States had rejected the Child Labor Amendment

Jan. 30, Gaston B. Means and Thomas B. Felder convicted by Federal Jury in New York of conspiracy to
bribe United States Government officials and fined
$10,000 each, and Means sentenced to 2 years in
prison

——, Colonel Charles R. Forbes, former head of
Veterans' Bureau, and John Thompson, contractor,
convicted by Federal Court in Chicago of conspiracy
to defraud the Government in hospital contracts,
and given sentences Feb. 4 of 2 years in prison and
$10,000 fine each

Jan. 31, Death of George Washington Cable (80) author
and reformer

Feb. 2, Nome, Alaska, diphtheria epidemic broken by
arrival of anti-toxin brought 650 miles from Nenana
by dog sleds

Feb. 3, Child Labor Amendment rejected by Connecticut Senate and Nevada Assembly, by Vermont
House Feb. 12, and Pennsylvania Senate Feb. 17

Feb. 3 and 4, Agreements signed in ladies garment
workers industry in New York City for 2 years, and
unemployment insurance fund provided for

Feb. 5, Harlan F. Stone appointed associate justice,
Supreme Court, taking the oath March 2

Feb. 6, American delegates to Opium Conference at
Geneva, Switzerland, withdrew from Conference,
Mr. Stephen G. Porter reporting that American plan
of restriction of production to medical and scientific
needs, and progressive reduction of use of raw opium
not accepted. *See* League of Nations

Feb. 7, Death of Thomas W. Lawson (68) broker and
author, in Boston

Feb. 8, Death of Edward Penfield (59) artist, illustrator,
and editor

Feb. 10, Most Favored Nation Treaty as to customs
signed with Poland

——, Renewal of strike of Structural Iron Worker's
League against the open shop

——, Three Conventions with Great Britain signed by
which rights of the United States in mandated territories of the Cameroons, Togoland, and East Africa
recognized

Feb. 11–28, Successful strike of 2,500 municipal employees in Chicago, teamsters and street cleaners,
begun for increase in wages, gained increases of 15
and 25 cents a day

Feb. 12, Death of Carlton T. Chapman (64) marine
and landscape artist

Feb. 14, Death of Arnold W. Brunner (67) architect,
New York

Feb. 16, Frank B. Kellogg, of Minnesota, appointed
Secretary of State

Feb. 17, Secretary of the Navy Wilbur certified that
under the Washington Conference Treaty of Feb.
1922 the Dept. had scrapped $197,418,620 of capital
ships

——, Strike of garment workers (underwear and children's dresses) New York City for wage increase, 40
hour week, and closed shop ended with compromise
agreement after 20 days

Feb. 18, William M. Jardine, of Kansas, appointed
Secretary of Agriculture

——, Death of James Lane Allen (75) novelist, Marion
Leroy Burton (50) president of University of
Michigan, and Robert A. Woods (60) Boston settle-
ment worker

Feb. 22, Announcement of endowment of $3,000,000
for fellowships for international study by Simon
Guggenheim

——, Death of Job E. Hedges (63) lawyer and Republican party leader, and Major General James H.
Wilson (87) Civil War veteran

Feb. 24, Treaty with Great Britain signed supplementary to Canada Boundary Treaty of April 11,
1908

Feb. 27, Death of Joseph Medill McCormick, Senator
from Illinois (48) in Washington

March 1, Dr. Harry Emerson Fosdick left the First
Presbyterian Church, New York City, refusing to
accept the requirements of the General Assembly

March 2, Most Favored Nation Customs Treaty with
Estonia signed

——, Supreme Court decision denied right of States
to regulate motor bus companies engaged in interstate commerce

——, Supreme Court decision that railroads not required to arbitrate disputes with their employers
before the Railroad Labor Board

——, Supreme Court decision in Grossman case held
that the President has power of pardon as to persons
held guilty by judge for contempt of court

March 3, Death of Frank Moore Colby (60) encyclo-
pedia editor, New York

March 4, Inauguration of President Coolidge and Vice-
President Charles G. Dawes. Photographs of the
ceremonies transmitted by American Telephone
and Telegraph Company to New York, Chicago, and
in Washington published in evening newspapers

——, Child Labor Amendment rejected by Missouri,
by Indiana March 5, by New Hampshire March 18

March 6, Lieut. Col. James E. Fechet replaced Brig.
General Mitchell as Assistant Chief of Air Service

March 9, President Coolidge as arbitrator in Tacna-
Arica case declared that plebiscite should be held

——, Strike of 2,360 employees of the American Thread
Company at Willimantic, Conn. against a 10% reduction which lasted into 1926

——, Death of William A. Quayle (65) Bishop of
Kansas

March 9–26, Teapot Dome naval oil reserve trial at Cheyenne, Wyoming

March 10, Successful strike of 30,000 clothing workers in New York City against violation of agreement by employers lasted 6 days

March 14, Death of Walter Camp (65) athletic authority, at New Haven, Conn.

March 16, First direct cable between Italy and the United States opened, between Rome and New York City

March 17, John G. Sargent, of Vermont, appointed Attorney General succeeding Harlan F. Stone resigned

March 18, Tornado in Illinois, Indiana, Missouri, and Kentucky killed more than 830 persons and destroyed property valued at $10,000,000

——, Receivership appointed for Chicago, Milwaukee, and St. Paul Railroad

March 19, Patent Office transferred from the Interior Dept. to the Dept. of Commerce

March 19–April 3, Bricklayers, masons, and plasterers in jurisdictional strike against each other in New York, Philadelphia, and Chicago

March 23, General John J. Pershing appointed chairman of Plebiscite Commission for Tacna and Arica vote in dispute between Chile and Peru

——, Tennessee enacted law forbidding the teaching of evolution in any school or college supported by public funds

March 24, Soviet Court at Moscow canceled Sinclair concession in Northern Sakhalin

March 26, President Coolidge appointed a commission to report on practical methods of utilizing the facilities of Muscles Shoals

March 27, Senator Burton K. Wheeler indicted by a Grand Jury in District of Columbia on charge of conspiracy to secure more than legal number of permits to prospect on public lands for oil and gas

April 1, Strike begun in coal mines of northern West Virginia to unionize the coal fields of the district, and enforce the Jacksonville wage agreement, and a series of strikes in the building trades in Boston

——, Colonel Lincoln C. Andrews placed in charge of prohibition enforcement in drastic reorganization and decentralization of administration

April 3, Indictments in oil lease cases against E. L. Doheny, H. F. Sinclair, and A. B. Fall quashed on ground of technicality. The Government appealed

April 3 and 7, Child Labor Amendment rejected by West Virginia House and Senate, by Minnesota Senate, April 14, and by Florida legislature April 29

April 8, Lieut. Commander Robert E. Byrd appointed to command flying unit of MacMillan Polar Expedition

April 9, Frederick C. Hicks, of New York, appointed Alien Property Custodian

April 13, Supreme Court decision declared the clause which authorized the fixing of hours of labor by compulsory arbitration of industrial disputes by Kansas Court of Industrial Relations invalid

——, Henry Ford started first commercial aviation on regular schedule by airplane freight line between Detroit and Chicago

April 15, Lucille Atcherson, first woman to be appointed in the Diplomatic Service, made third secretary of the American Legation at Berne, Switzerland

——, Death of John Singer Sargent (69) artist, in London

April 20, Foreign Service School opened by the Government in Washington with 25 students

April 24, Senator B. K. Wheeler acquitted by Montana jury of receiving fees for cases before the Interior Dept.

April 29, Florence Rena Sabin elected first woman member of the National Academy of Sciences

May 1–2, New record for sustained flight made by Lieuts. C. H. Schildhauer and J. R. Kyle in the air 28 hours, 35 minutes, and 27 seconds

May 2, Most Favored Nation Customs Treaty with Finland signed, and Treaty of commerce with Spain

——, Nicholas Murray Butler succeeded Elihu Root as head of the Carnegie Endowment for International Peace

May 4, The United States represented at Conference on Traffic in Arms, Geneva

May 5, John Scopes arrested in Dayton, Tennessee, for violation of State law forbidding teaching of evolution in a high school class

May 10, Death of Herbert Quick (64) novelist, at Columbia, Missouri

May 12, Death of Amy Lowell (51) poet, at Brookline, Mass.

May 13, American sovereignty proclaimed over Swain's Island, Samoa

May 15, Death of General Nelson A. Miles (85) Civil War veteran

May 16, Foreign representatives instructed to notify the 9 nations of the 14 which had borrowed from the United States during the World War and had not made debt adjustments that negotiations were invited by the United States

May 20, Glenn Frank accepted presidency of the University of Wisconsin

May 21–June 15, Amundsen-Ellsworth airplane expedition unsuccessful in attempt to reach North Pole. *See* Arctic Regions

May 25, Supreme Court decision declared publication of income tax payment records valid

——, John Scopes indicted by Grand Jury at Nashville, Tennessee, in evolution case

May 27, A. B. Fall, E. L. Doheny, and H. F. Sinclair reindicted in Washington in naval oil cases, the bribery charge dropped, the charge being criminal conspiracy to defraud the Government of property through the negotiation of the oil land leases

May 28, Federal Judge McCormick at Los Angeles declared lease of Elk Hills oil reserve lands to private companies void as contracts secured by fraud

May 29, Death of Donn Barber (53) architect, New York

June 1, Supreme Court decision declared Oregon law requiring children between ages of 8 and 16 to attend the public schools unconstitutional. Law directed against the parochial schools. The Court recognized that the State may regulate private schools

——, Death of Thomas R. Marshall (71) former Vice-President

June 1–Aug., Strike of clothing workers in St. Louis for 25% wage increase, 44-hour week, and recognition of union unsuccessful

June 4, Executive Order of the President transferred the Bureau of Mines from the Interior Dept. to the Dept. of Commerce

June 5, William MacFarlane beat Robert T. Jones for

"open" golf championship of America at Worcester, Mass.

June 8, Supreme Court decision in case of Gitlow convicted in New York State of publication of Communist manifesto upheld State law as valid exercise of police power, but held that the guarantee of due process includes the guaranty of freedom of speech and the press

June 12, Note of Secretary of State Kellogg to the press stated that Mexico could command the support of the United States "only so long as it protects American lives and rights," and that Mexico was "on trial before the world." Reply of President Calles of June 14 declared he saw "threat to sovereignty of Mexico" in this statement

——, "The Cloisters" and collection of Gothic art purchased by the Metropolitan Museum of New York from George G. Barnard, sculptor, with gift of $600,000 of John D. Rockefeller, Jr.

June 14, School of Aëronautics for Yale University endowed with $500,000 by Daniel Guggenheim

June 15, Gertrude Ederle swam 21 miles from the Battery to Sandy Hook in 7 hours, 11 minutes, and 30 seconds establishing a record beyond that of George R. Meehan of July 20, 1914

——, Death of Julius Kruttschnitt (71) railroad executive

June 17, Protocol for prohibition of use in war of asphyxiating gases and bacteriological methods of warfare signed in Geneva (in force April 3, 1928), and Convention for the Supervision of the International Trade in Arms, and Ammunition and in Implements of War signed

——, Admiral Samuel S. Robison appointed Commander-in-Chief of fleet

June 18, Death of Robert M. La Follette (70) Senator from Wisconsin, at Washington

June 19, Judge T. B. Kennedy at Cheyenne gave decision against the Government and in favor of Harry F. Sinclair in case of Teapot Dome Naval Oil Reserve lease, appeal taken

——, Death of Edmund J. James (70) former president of the University of Illinois

June 20, Scientific expedition headed by D. B. MacMillan left for base at Etah, Greenland, reached Aug. 1, and returned in October, the first airplane flights in Arctic made by naval flyers commanded by Lieut. Commander R. E. Byrd

June 22, Death of Edwin F. Ladd (65) Senator from North Dakota

June 24, Treaty of commerce, friendship, and consular rights with Hungary signed

June 25–30, Italian Debt Commission in negotiations in Washington

June 29, Earthquake destroyed business section of Santa Barbara, California, property loss $20,000,000

July 1, Strike of Amalgamated Clothing Workers in New York and Illinois against employer refusing to renew agreement and against the open shop lasted 19 weeks and ended with victory of union

——, Overnight air mail service established between New York and Chicago

——, Death of Dwight W. Tryon (75) artist and educator

July 2, Extradition Treaty with Czechoslovakia signed

July 6, Judge T. B. Kennedy at Cheyenne, Wyoming, denied motion for rehearing of government suit to cancel Teapot Dome oil lease, and appeal taken to Circuit Court of Appeals

July 6, Building trade laborers on strike in Boston since April 1 returned to work

July 10, Trial of John Scopes begun in Dayton, Tennessee, in anti-evolution case, the prosecution in charge of Attorney General A. T. Stewart, the defense undertaken by the American Civil Liberties Union who employed as counsel Clarence Darrow, Dudley Field Malone, and Dr. John R. Neal. William Jennings Bryan aided the prosecution

July 11, Final decree confirmed revocation of Elk Hills Naval Reserve oil leases to E. L. Doheny

July 13, Standard Oil Company of New Jersey established the eight hour day

July 19, Last of the Boxer indemnity of $6,137,552 remitted to China for educational purposes by executive order of the President of July 16

July 21, John Scopes found guilty of having taught the doctrines of evolution in violation of law of Tennessee and fined $100 and costs of suit

July 26, Death of William Jennings Bryan (65) former Secretary of State, and Democratic leader, at Dayton, Tennessee, and of Mrs. Helen H. Gardener (71) author and educator, in Washington

July 27, George Seldes, correspondent of Chicago Tribune ordered out of Italy because of his reports of conditions of minorities

July 29, Georgia House voted against prohibition of teaching of evolution

Aug. 3, American marines withdrawn from Nicaragua, force placed there as legation guards in 1912

Aug. 4, Shipping Board accepted offer of Henry Ford of $1,706,000 for 200 ships to be scrapped

Aug. 5, First meeting of Plebiscite Commission in Tacna-Arica case, General John J. Pershing presiding

Aug. 7, Death of Judge George Gray (85) of Permanent Court of Arbitration, The Hague, and former senator from Delaware

Aug. 15, Strike of textile workers at Pittsfield, Mass. begun which was settled at end of month by reference to arbitration

Aug. 18, Agreement as to Belgian debt, pre-armistice debt of $171,780,000, and post-armistice of $556,050,500, total debt including arrears of interest $727,830,500 to be paid in annual installments spread over 62 years with interest rate of 3½% on post-armistice debt

Aug. 19, Death of Francis Lee Higginson (83) Boston banker and philanthropist

Aug. 24, Strike of baggage handlers in New York City for increase in wages and eight hour day settled Sept. 16 with increase of $1 per day

Aug. 31, Navy seaplanes began flight to Hawaii from San Francisco, 2,100 miles. No. 1 commanded by Comm. John Rodgers made distance record of 1,730 miles and was lost at sea for 9 days reaching within 15 miles of Kauai Island by sailing the plane as a boat before picked up

Sept. 1, Strike of anthracite coal miners in Pennsylvania for wage increase, 5 day week, and check-off begun, affecting 158,000 workers

——, Federal income tax records opened to public inspection, largest personal amount paid by John D. Rockefeller, Jr. of $6,278,000, and largest corporation tax paid by Henry Ford Company of $16,493,000

Sept. 3, Navy dirigible "Shenandoah" wrecked in

storm over Ava, Ohio, and 14 of crew including Lieut. Comm. Zachary Lansdowne killed

Sept. 5, Colonel William Mitchell of the Air Service criticized Government air administration as incompetent and criminally negligent resulting in his summons to Washington Sept. 21

Sept. 8–Oct. 1, Radio Broadcasting Convention with Great Britain, Canada, and Newfoundland signed

Sept. 9–24, Strike of large numbers of seamen in New York and other ports in sympathy with British strike

Sept. 10, Death of James H. Baker (76) president emeritus of University of Colorado

Sept. 12, National Aircraft Board appointed by the President to investigate question of relation of government to aëronautics, Dwight W. Morrow, chairman

Sept. 16, Shapurji Saklatvala, Communist member of the British Parliament, and delegate to Inter-Parliamentary Union at Washington, refused admission to the United States by Secretary Kellogg

——, Death of Herbert Parsons (56) lawyer and former member of Congress from New York

Sept. 17, 500 Chinese arrested in New York City under the Exclusion Act

Sept. 24–Oct. 3, French Debt Commission headed by Joseph Caillaux in negotiations with American Debt Commission in Washington; no agreement reached

Sept. 24, Agreement as to Latvian war debt reached, total funded at $5,775,000

Sept. 25, Submarine S-51 sunk in collision with steamer "City of Rome" off Block Island, the commanding officer Lieut. Rodney H. Dobson, 5 other officers, and 31 enlisted men drowned

Sept. 28, Government filed appeal in Teapot Dome oil lease case alleging errors in trial

Sept. 29, Col. William Mitchell before the National Air Board advocated an independent department for aviation

Oct. 5, Dispute as to sovereignty of the Island of Palmas referred by the Netherlands and the United States to Judge Max Huber, of Switzerland, as arbitrator

Oct. 7, Death of Christy Mathewson (45) base ball player and manager

Oct. 10, Death of James B. Duke (68) tobacco industrialist and founder of Duke University, North Carolina

Oct. 12, Bishop William M. Brown, of Arkansas, convicted of heresy by the Protestant Episcopal Church Convention, and unfrocked

Oct. 12–23, 600 American troops policed Panama City at request of Government during riots

Oct. 13, Debt Funding Agreement with Czechoslovakia, total $115,000,000

——, Dwight F. Davis, of Missouri, appointed Secretary of War, succeeding John W. Weeks resigned

Oct. 15, Strike of enginemen on Western Maryland Railroad for increase in wages

Oct. 16, Texas State Book Board barred evolution from school textbooks

Oct. 19, Supreme Court dismissed case of Charlotte Anita Whitney vs. California under California Criminal Syndicalism Act for lack of jurisdiction

Oct. 22, Announced that Countess Karolyi, wife of President of the Hungarian Republic of 1919, refused a passport to come to the United States because of her political views

Oct. 26, Death of Henry J. Waters (59) editor, Kansas City

Oct. 28, Trial by court-martial of Colonel William Mitchell of the Air Service for criticism of the Administration begun; he pleaded not guilty on the 30th

——, Debt Funding Agreement with Estonia, total fixed at $13,830,000

Nov. 2, Clarence Cook Little inaugurated president of University of Michigan

——, New Italian Commission headed by Count Volpi began sessions with World War Debts Commission in Washington

Nov. 6, International Convention for Protection of Industrial Property signed by the United States which revised that of March 20, 1883

Nov. 10, Testimony at court-martial of Colonel Mitchell that of 505 aviators killed in line of duty all but 12 were using planes inherited from the World War

Nov. 14, Debt Funding Agreement with Italy, total $2,042,199,466.34 reduced from $2,148,000,000, payment as with other agreements to be spread over 62 years which with reduction of interest made actual value $360,000,000

Nov. 17 and 27, Secretary Kellogg protested against proposed Mexican land laws

Nov. 18, Confession of Celestino Madeiros of participation in South Braintree murders and statement that neither Sacco nor Vanzetti had committed the crime

Nov. 27, Proposal of Governor Pinchot, of Pennsylvania, for settlement of anthracite coal strike of 5 year agreement without price increase, and a commission to decide on wages, accepted by miners and rejected by operators

Dec. 1, Debt Funding Agreement with Rumania, total $44,591,000

Dec. 2, Report of Aircraft Board to the President recommended creation of assistant secretaryships of War, Navy, and Commerce to handle aviation affairs, and reported against unified air service

Dec. 6, German-American Claims Commission settled "Lusitania" claims at $2,409,443, total of all claims awarded $167,663,102

Dec. 9, Liquor Smuggling Treaty with Belgium signed

Dec. 11, Benjamin Gitlow pardoned by Governor Smith of New York

Dec. 17, Col. William Mitchell found guilty by court martial of conduct "to the prejudice of good order and military discipline" in violation of the 96th Article of War, by his criticisms of preparations for the "Shenandoah" trip, and the flight to the Hawaiian Islands. Sentenced to suspension from rank, command, and duty with forfeiture of all pay and allowances for 5 years

Dec. 21, Treaty as to tonnage dues with Finland signed

Dec. 22, Brigadier General Butler dismissed as Director of Public Safety of Philadelphia, returning to Marine Corps Service on refusal of the President to further extend his leave of absence

——, Death of Frank A. Munsey (71) publisher, New York City

Dec. 23, Treaties with Mexico as to smuggling and extradition signed, and of friendship, commerce, and consular rights with Estonia, and Most Favored Nation as to customs with Lithuania

Dec. 29, Indictment of Senator Wheeler of Montana quashed at Washington

Dec. 30, Presentment of Grand Jury against Harry F. Sinclair, W. S. Burns, Sheldon Clark, Henry M. Day, Charles G. Ruddy, and Frank J. O'Reilly charged with conspiracy to obstruct justice in Fall-Sinclair case

CONGRESS

Jan. 14, Underwood Bill adopted by Senate giving the President authority to lease government properties at Muscles Shoals for the manufacture of nitrate and production of electric power by vote of 52 to 30

Jan. 18, Feb. 6, 12, and 20, General William Mitchell testified before House Committee urging separate dept. for aviation and criticized Army and Navy aviation service, and held that "capital ships are absolutely at the mercy of aircraft"

Jan. 20, Resolution condemning lease of naval oil reserves to private companies adopted by Senate

Jan. 27, Resolution instructing the Interstate Commerce Commission to regard farm products as basic industry in adjusting freight rates adopted in Senate

Feb. 2, Air Mail Act to promote commercial aviation authorized the Postmaster General to ask bids from civilian air transport companies for services in connection with existing government routes

Feb. 12, Arbitration Act to take effect Jan. 1, 1926 made valid in the Federal Courts agreements for arbitration of disputes arising from contracts, maritime transactions, or commerce

Feb. 13, Amendments to Judicial Code provided for direct review by Supreme Court of judgments of United States District Courts limited to certain cases specified, and direct review by Supreme Court of cases decided in the territorial courts and courts of insular possessions abolished. Appeals from the United States Court for China may be taken to United States Circuit Courts

Feb. 24, Purnell Act authorized increased appropriation for the more complete endowment of agricultural experiment stations, and included subjects of agricultural economics, home economics, and rural sociology in scope of investigation

——, American War Mothers incorporated

Feb. 25, Act authorized the President to reduce or abolish visa fees for aliens (not immigrants) visiting the United States

Feb. 26, Rear Admiral H. P. Jones testified before House Committee that the "battleship is dominant" in naval warfare though airships indispensable

Feb. 27, Admiral Sims testified before House Committee declaring that all ships are at mercy of aircraft but was not in favor of an air dept.

Feb. 28, Postal Pay and Rate Increase Act increased rates for second class matter raising revenue $60,000,-000 and increased salaries to extent of $68,000,000

——, Resolution declared Swain's Island north east of Samoa under sovereignty of the United States

——, Federal Corrupt Practices Act as to lawful campaign expenses amended

March 3, Act provided for disposal of automobiles and vessels forfeited for violation of the prohibition laws

——, 11 projects for inland waterways improvements and 6 for Great Lakes' harbors adopted

——, House expressed approval of Permanent Court of International Justice and recommended early adherence of the United States with reservations by vote of 302 to 28

March 4, Congress adjourned. Muscle Shoals Lease Bill failed of passage

——, Sixty-Ninth Congress convened. Vice-President Dawes made speech in Senate as presiding officer

criticism of rules and procedure which allowed filibuster, and advocated limitation of debate. House adjourned *sine die*

March 4, Salary Act raised salaries of the Vice-President, Speaker of the House, and Cabinet members from $12,000 to $15,000, and members of Congress from $7,500 to $10,000

——, Act allowed Secretary of the Navy authority to accept men for the Navy on terms of 2, 3, 4, and 6 years together with minority enlistments

——, World War Veterans Act amended

March 4–18, Special Session of Senate. On March 10 the nomination of Charles B. Warren as Attorney General rejected because of his connection with the sugar trust, the first time the Senate had refused to confirm a Cabinet officer since 1868. The vote was 40 to 40, a tie in the absence of Vice-President Dawes who would have cast deciding vote in favor of the President's nomination, vote a second time changed to 41 to 39

March 12, Senate abolished caucus rules for members, the insurgent members La Follette, Brookhart, Ladd, and Frazier allowed patronage

March 13, Isle of Pines Treaty with Cuba of March 3, 1904, ratified by Senate after 20 years discussion, claim of Cuba to Island recognized

——, Agreed by Senate vote of 72 to 2 to consider proposal that the United States join Permanent Court on Dec. 17

March 16, Senate again rejected renomination of the President of March 12 of Charles B. Warren for Attorney General by vote of 46 to 40

March 17, The President nominated John G. Sargent, of Vermont, for Attorney General, which was confirmed by Senate

Dec. 7, Sixty-Ninth Congress, 1st sess. convened

Dec. 17, Debate opened in Senate as to adherence of the United States to Permanent Court

Dec. 21, Message of President Coolidge recommended adherence to Permanent Court

1926

Jan. 4, United States Circuit Court of Appeals sustained decision of lower court of cancellation of Elk Hills Naval Reserve oil lease

Jan. 7, Plan for compulsory arbitration agreed upon by Labor Board and representatives of railroad workers

Jan. 8, Note of Secretary Kellogg protested against petroleum and alien land laws of Mexico as affecting American citizens

Jan. 11, General William Lassiter appointed to succeed General Pershing as head of Tacna-Arica Plebiscite Commission, the latter retiring because of ill health

Jan. 14, Child Labor Amendment rejected by Virginia General Assembly

——, Additional Extradition Treaty with Cuba signed

Jan. 15, Announcement that all treaties signed by the United States would be transmitted to Geneva for insertion in League of Nations series

Jan. 17, Fund of $2,500,000 established for promotion of aëronautics by Daniel Guggenheim

Jan. 21, Agreement with Austria signed as to passport visas

Jan. 22, The United States refused to recognize the Chamorro Government of Nicaragua

Jan. 25, Strike of 11,700 textile workers in Passaic, New Jersey organized by Communists against 10%

wage cut of summer of 1925 and for 50% for over-time

Jan. 25, Rescue of entire crew of steamer "Antinoe" in mid-Atlantic by Captain George Fried of the "President Roosevelt" after standing by for 4 days in storm

Jan. 28, Note to Mexico again protested against petroleum and alien land laws of Dec., 1925, and feature of requiring aliens to wave protection of their government, and the retroactive and confiscatory features in answer to Mexican Note of Jan. 20

Jan. 29, Resignation of Colonel William Mitchell of the Army Air Service accepted

——, John A. Macready established American altitude aëroplane record at 35,900 feet

Feb. 1, Most Favored Nation Treaty as to customs signed with Latvia

Feb. 3, Death of Laura Drake Gill (65) educator

Feb. 9, Board of Education of Atlanta, Georgia, prohibited teaching of evolution in the public schools

Feb. 10, Arbitration Convention with Liberia signed, and Liquor Smuggling Treaty with Spain

Feb. 11, Anthracite coal strike begun Sept. 1925 ended with signing of agreement for 4½ years at wage scale in effect before the strike began. Miners returned to work on the 18th

——, Death of William C. Bobbs (65) publisher, Indianapolis

Feb. 13, Death of Henry Holt (86) publisher and author, New York City

Feb. 15, Awards totaling $5,397,368.26 granted by German-American Mixed Claims Commission to American citizens for claims arising out of War

——, Original Gutenburg Bible sold in New York for $106,000 and was presented to Yale University

Feb. 16–June 16, Strike of fur workers in New York for increase of 10% and 40 hour week

Feb. 17, Secretary of Labor affirmed act of immigration authorities refusing admission of Countess Cathcart on ground of moral turpitude; opinion of Federal Judge that delinquency not recognized by any federal statute March 5

Feb. 22, Treaty of commerce and consular rights with Salvador signed

Feb. 25, President Coolidge confirmed rulings of Tacna-Arica Plebiscite Commission as to rulings, registration, and voting regulations. *See also* Chile

Feb. 26, Most Favored Nation Treaty as to customs signed with Rumania

March 1, Note to Mexico of Secretary Kellogg asked for information as to retroactive character of petroleum and alien land laws; answer of Mexican Government stated that the laws would not be retroactive

March 2, Interstate Commerce Commission denied proposed Van Sweringen Nickel Plate railroad merger of the Chesapeake and Ohio, Hocking Valley, Erie and Père Marquette and New York, Chicago, and St. Louis

March 4, Liquor Smuggling Treaty with Cuba signed

March 6, Death of Rear Admiral Richard Wainwright (77) in Washington

March 7, First successful radio telephone conversation held between New York and London

March 11, Mississippi law prohibited teaching that man "ascended or descended from a lower order of animals" in state supported schools

——, Liquor Smuggling Treaty with Cuba signed

March 12, Death of Edward W. Scripps (71) newspaper proprietor

March 13, Interstate Commerce Commission denied request of western railroads for reduction in long haul freight rates to meet competition of the Panama Canal

——, John A. Macready established airplane altitude record at 37,579 feet over Dayton, Ohio

March 21, Death of Alfred D. F. Hamlin (70) architect, New York City

March 24, Death of Dr. Albion Small (71) sociologist and educator

March 26, Death of Franz Kneisel (61) violinist and conductor

March 27, Bahama Agreement with Great Britain permitted "specified United States revenue cutters to enter British territorial waters" under certain conditions to enforce prohibition

April 1–Jan. 14, 1927, Strike of carpenters of San Francisco against the open shop unsuccessful

April 2, Colonel Carmi A. Thompson appointed by the President to investigate and report on economic and political conditions in the Philippines

April 3, Ward Food Products Corporation (baking trust) dissolved by consent decree in government suit under anti-trust laws begun Feb. 8 in Baltimore

April 5, Arctic expedition, Byrd-MacMillan, sailed from New York on the S.S. "Chantier" arriving at Kings Bay, Spitzbergen April 29

April 6, Conference of Chile and Peru begun in Washington as to Tacna-Arica

April 9, Death of Henry Miller (66) actor, New York City

April 10, Flight of Capt. George H. Wilkins with Lieut. Carl Ben Eielson (Detroit-Arctic expedition) from base at Point Barrow. *See* Arctic Regions

April 11, Death of Luther Burbank (77) horticulturist, at Santa Rosa, California

April 13, Death of Edmund Munroe Smith (71) legal historian, New York City

——, Ku Klux Klan feud revived at Herrin, Illinois, Deputy Sheriff Charles Briggs and 5 others killed at polls

April 15, Proposal of Secretary Kellogg for establishment of Tacna-Arica as a separate neutral State, or sold to third power (Bolivia), or be divided between Peru and Chile

April 19, Note of Secretary Kellogg refused invitation of League of Nations that the United States participate in conference on Permanent Court reservations of American Senate

April 20, Death of Ogden T. McClurg (46) publisher, Chicago

April 22, Consular Convention with Cuba signed

April 23, French Debt Commission headed by Senator Henri Bérenger began new negotiations in Washington

——, Death of Joseph Pennell (66) artist, author, and illustrator

April 24, American Cyanamid Company made proposal for operation of Muscle Shoals

April 25, Dr. Henry S. Coffin elected president of Union Theological Seminary, New York City

April 29, Debt Funding Agreement with France signed, total $6,847,674,104.17 to be paid during period of 62 years, no interest to be paid for first 5 years, then 1% for 10 years gradually increased until 3½% reached for last 22 years

April 30, Photographs sent by radio from London published in New York newspapers

May 3, Debt Funding Agreement with Yugoslavia signed

——, Death of Oscar S. Straus (75) diplomat, New York City

May 4–June 5, American marines at Bluefields, Nicaragua, during war

May 4–23, The United States represented at International Economic Conference at Geneva

May 7, Federal indictment against Harry M. Daugherty, Thomas M. Miller, and John T. King, charged with conspiracy to defraud the Government in case of return of $7,000,000 worth of stock of the American Metal Company in 1921 to a Swiss corporation which paid a fee of $441,000, the charge of bribery being impossible because of the statute of limitations

——, Death of Howard Van Doren Shaw (57) architect, Chicago

May 8, Executive Order of President Coolidge authorized employment of state or local officers as federal prohibition enforcement agents, amending and adding to an executive order of Jan. 17, 1873

May 9, Flight of Commander Richard Byrd with Floyd Bennett, pilot, in the "Josephine Ford" from King's Bay, Spitzbergen, to the North Pole and return in 15½ hours. *See also* Arctic Regions

May 10, Death of Alton B. Parker (73) judge and Democratic leader, New York City

May 10–14, Conference on International Relations held at Briarcliff, New York, under auspices of the Carnegie Endowment for International Peace and the Academy of Political Science

May 11–14, Amundsen-Ellsworth-Nobile expedition in the airship "Norge" made flight from King's Bay, Spitzbergen crossing the North Pole May 12. *See also* Arctic Regions

May 12, Massachusetts Superior Court denied new trial to Sacco and Vanzetti

——, New $1,000,000 American hospital dedicated at Paris, France

May 18–26 and Sept. 22–27, &c., The United States represented at Preparatory Commission for Disarmament Conference at Geneva

May 26, United States Shipping Board authorized sale of 5 American Oriental Mail Liners to R. Stanley Dollar of San Francisco

May 27, Charles Edward Russell, Socialist, barred by immigration authorities from landing at Plymouth, England, on complaint of the Irish Free State

——, Gustavus Adolphus, Crown Prince of Sweden, and the Crown Princess Louise arrived in New York on their way to San Francisco to sail for the Far East

June 6, Death of Meyer London (54) Socialist, member of Congress from New York

June 8, Admiral C. F. Hughes appointed in command of fleet, succeeding Admiral S. S. Robison

——, American Minister withdrawn from Nicaragua, and refusal to recognize the Chamorro Government

June 9, Death of Louis Sherry (71) restaurateur and caterer, New York City

June 10, End of 17 weeks' strike of fur workers, New York City, granted 40 hour week

June 14, President Coolidge appointed Board of Mediation which succeeded the Railroad Labor Board

——, Death of Mary Cassatt (81) artist, in France

——, General Lassiter presented report declaring that conditions were not favorable for Tacna-Arica plebiscite and recommended termination of the proceedings placing the blame for the situation on Chile

June 16, Edward S. Evans and Linton O. Wells began from New York City trip which established new record for encircling the globe arriving in New York July 14 after journey of 20,100 miles by train, airplane, and motors of 28 days, 14 hours, 36 minutes, and 5 seconds

June 21, International Sanitary Convention revising that of Jan. 17, 1912, signed by the United States

June 24, Death of Cleveland H. Dodge (66) financier and philanthropist, New York City

June 25, Robert Jones, of Atlanta, won British open golf championship

June 27, University of Michigan expedition headed by Professor William H. Hobbs left Sydney, Nova Scotia, with the Putnam Greenland expedition of the American Museum of Natural History in the "Morrissey" for study of weather over Greenland, returning Oct. 1

June 30, Strike of professional engineering employees, Chicago

July 1, Baumes laws went into effect in New York State including law providing for life sentence in case of fourth offenders

——, Air mail established between Boston and New York City

——, Strike of cloakmakers in New York City begun for maintenance of decent working conditions which lasted 19 weeks, and strike of oil workers in California

July 5–30, Strike of employees of New York City subway for increase in wages unsuccessful

July 6–29, Strike of 6,000 cloth cap millinery workers in New York City settled by arbitration, wage increases granted and 40 hour week to take effect July 1, 1927

July 8, United States Circuit Court of Appeals ruled out the 12 mile limit as applied to American ships, suspected cargo liable to search anywhere on the high seas

——, Most Favored Nation Treaty as to customs with Haiti signed

July 13, War Time Sugar Equalization Board dissolved

July 14, Statement of Secretary Mellon that large proportion of funds advanced to Great Britain was advanced after the War to save Government from borrowing at home; debated in British House of Commons July 19 and denied

July 21, Death of Washington A. Roebling (89) engineer, builder of Brooklyn bridge

July 24–April 20, 1927, Expedition of Comm. George M. Dyott to South America explored Roosevelt's "River of Doubt"

July 28, Treaty with Panama signed of alliance and amity. Rejected Jan. 1927 by Panama because of Article XI providing that Panama should consider itself in a state of war in case of any war in which the United States should be a belligerent

July 30, Death of Albert B. Cummins (76) Senator from Iowa

July 31, Note to Mexico protested oil and land laws as retroactive and confiscatory

Aug. 5, Warner Brothers' Theater, New York, showed vitaphone in connection with the moving picture "Don Juan"

Aug. 6, Gertrude Ederle, of New York, the first woman

to swim across the English Channel, crossing from Gris Nez to Dover in 14 hours and 31 minutes

Aug. 10–Sept. 3, Strike of textile workers of Manville and Woonsocket, Rhode Island

Aug. 16, Death of Judge Henry W. Rogers (72) international jurist, Pennington, New Jersey

Aug. 22, Death of Dr. Charles W. Eliot (92) president emeritus of Harvard University

Aug. 23, Death of Rudolph Valentino (31) motion picture actor, New York City

Aug. 28, American marines landed at Bluefields, Nicaragua, at request of Diaz

——, Mrs. Clemington Carson, of New York, swam across the English Channel in 15 hours and 32 minutes

Aug. 29, Statement of Newton D. Baker, Secretary of War in the Wilson Cabinet, that he was in favor of mutual cancellation of war debts

Sept. 1, Conference of signatories of the statute of the Permanent Court of International Justice met at Geneva to consider reservations of the Senate of the United States. *See also* League of Nations

Sept. 1–6, Strike of musicians of motion picture theaters of San Francisco, and Sept. 6–10, of Chicago

Sept. 2, Government announced receipt of $5,900,000 first annual payment of German reparations under the Dawes Plan

Sept 5, Death of Charles Hopkins Clarke (78) editor, Hartford, Conn.

Sept. 7, Death of Professor Henry A. Beers (79) writer, at New Haven, Conn.

Sept. 8, Strike of building trades begun in Boston

Sept. 12, Motion for new trial of Sacco and Vanzetti argued at Dedham, Mass.

Sept. 13, Ku Klux Klan parade of from 15,000 to 20,000 in Washington

Sept. 15, Proclamation of the President prohibited illegal shipment of arms and ammunition to Nicaragua

——, Murder of Jacob Rosenthal, New York merchant, by Mexican brigands

Sept. 17–18, Florida hurricane in the Miami region caused death of 370 persons, injury to thousands, and rendered 50,000 persons homeless, property loss estimated at $100,000,000

Sept. 20–30, Strike of shirt workers in New York City against proposed reduction of wages

Sept. 21, Major General Charles P. Summeral appointed Chief of Staff of Army succeeding Major General John L. Hines

Sept. 22, Gene Tunney became world heavyweight champion defeating Jack Dempsey in bout at Philadelphia

Sept. 25, International Convention as to slavery signed by the United States

——, Henry Ford adopted the 5 day week, eight hour day

Sept. 28, Circuit Court of Appeals at St. Louis reversed decision of Judge Kennedy in Wyoming and canceled as fraudulent the lease of the Teapot Dome district to the Sinclair interests

Sept. 28–Oct. 2, Strike of the employees of the worsted mills in Bristol, Rhode Island, gained 5% increase

Sept. 29, Death of William J. Tucker (87) president emeritus of Dartmouth College

Sept. 30, Charles E. Hughes designated by President Coolidge to succeed Judge Gray as member of the Permanent Court of Arbitration at the Hague

Oct. 1, Return of Putnam Greenland expedition with specimens for the American Museum of Natural History, George Palmer Putnam, director, and the Michigan University scientific expedition

——, Death of Henry T. Finck (72) musical critic of New York

Oct. 5–12, Successful strike of tailors in New York City for wage increase and 40 hour week

Oct. 5–Feb. 11, 1927, Unsuccessful strike of paper box manufacturers in New York City for increase in wages and 40 hour week

Oct. 11, Supreme Court sustained sale of seized German dye and chemical patents, trade marks, and copyrights to the Chemical Foundation in 1919 by the Alien Property Custodian

——, The jury reported disagreement in conspiracy case of the Government against former Attorney General H. M. Daugherty and former Alien Property Custodian T. W. Miller after trial of 23 days; case appealed

Oct. 12–16, Strike of coal miners in the Hocking Valley, Ohio

Oct. 13–Nov. 23, Successful strike of textile workers at New Bedford, Mass. against working conditions

Oct. 18–Nov. 24, Visit of Queen Marie of Rumania with Prince Nicholas and the Princess Ileana

Oct. 20, Death of Eugene V. Debs (70) Socialist candidate for President, at Elmhurst, Illinois, and Thomas Mott Osborne (67) penologist, at Auburn, N.Y.

Oct. 23, Judge Webster Thayer, of Massachusetts, denied new trial to Nicola Sacco and Bartolomeo Vanzetti

Oct. 25, Supreme Court decision sustained constitutionality of Act of Kansas Court of Industrial Relations in provision of punishment for anyone inducing or ordering others to take part in an unjustifiable strike, declaring strikes for certain purposes illegal

——, Supreme Court decision in appeal of F. S. Myers, postmaster removed from office in 1920, held valid the removal by the President of executive officers from their positions, declaring laws of 1867 and 1876 restricting power of removal of the President invalid

Oct. 28, Death of Professor William J. Hussey (64) astronomer, in London

Oct. 30, Final Note of Secretary Kellogg to Mexico stated position of the United States as to petroleum and alien land laws; reply Nov. 17 maintained that protest as to laws should be made only after specific examples of confiscation of American property had occurred under them

Oct. 31, Death of Harry Houdini (Eric Weiss), magician (52) at Detroit, Michigan

Nov. 1, Supreme Court decision that an offender against the prohibition laws may be prosecuted in both State and Federal courts for the same offense

Nov. 2, Election ended Republican majority in Senate almost evenly divided, and reduced majority in House with 237 Republicans and 195 Democrats; prohibition referendum in 8 States gave wets victory in 5 including New York and Illinois. The Ku Klux Klan elected a number of candidates in this election

Nov. 4, Resignation of Judge George W. English of the United States District Court for eastern Illinois facing impeachment trial

Nov. 8, Death of James K. Hackett (57) actor, in France

Nov. 11, Partial settlement of strike at Passaic, New Jersey, with some gain for workers in certain mills, recognition of the union and a preference for union workers

Nov. 11, President Coolidge in Armistice Day address at Kansas City mentioned the question of adherence of the United States to the Permanent Court of International Justice as "a closed incident"

Nov. 12, Death of Joseph G. Cannon (90) former member of Congress and Speaker of the House for 4 terms, at Danville, Illinois

Nov. 13, Strike of clothing workers of New York City, begun in July, ended with agreement for wage increase and fewer working hours, the 40 hour week to succeed a 42 hour week after 18 months

Nov. 15, Death of Lafayette Young (78) newspaper editor and former Senator

Nov. 17, Death of James F. Kemp (67) geologist, of New York City

——, Diaz Government of Nicaragua recognized by the United States

Nov. 21, Death of Joseph McKenna (83) former Supreme Court justice

Nov. 22, Trial of Fall-Doheny conspiracy to defraud the Government case on appeal in respect of the lease of the Elk Hills Naval Oil Reserve begun

——, Agreement of Chicago building trades by which employers agreed to employ only union labor and men agreed to place no limits on day's work, and both agreed to arbitrate disputes

Nov. 26, Death of John M. Browning (72) gun inventor of Utah, at Brussels

Nov. 29, Supreme Court decision sustained that part of prohibition law which limited prescriptions of alcoholic liquors by physicians to 1 pint per patient every 10 days

Nov. 30, Proposal of Secretary Kellogg for settlement of Tacna-Arica dispute by sale of the 2 provinces to Bolivia; accepted by Bolivia Dec. 2, and by Chile "in principle" Dec. 5, and rejected by Peru Jan. 12, 1927

——, Death of Carl E. Akeley (62) explorer, at Kabale, Uganda, Africa

Dec. 2, First decision of United States Board of Mediation granted increase of 7½% to 89,000 conductors and trainmen employed on eastern railroads

Dec. 3, Death of Charles Ringling (62) circus owner, at Sarasota, Florida

Dec. 4, Report on the Philippines of Colonel Carmi A. Thompson, filed and published Dec. 22, recommended that the granting of absolute independence be postponed for some time to come. He recommended creation of a new colonial dept. to supervise administration, that coöperation between the legislative and executive branches be reëstablished, that the Governor General's military advisers be replaced by civilians, and that the policy of home rule be enlarged

Dec. 5, Debt Funding Agreement with Greece signed

Dec. 7, American warships ordered to Nicaraguan ports to prevent importation of arms by Sacasa

Dec. 9, Firestone Rubber Company lease for 1,000,-000 acres for 99 years in Liberia ratified by the Liberian Government

Dec. 10, Nobel peace prize for 1925 awarded to General Charles G. Dawes

Dec. 13, More of strikers in Passaic, New Jersey, those employed in the Botany Mills reached agreement winning right to organize, and strikers returned to work after 10 months

Dec. 15, William B. Shearer engaged by Bethlehem Shipbuilding Company, Newport News Shipbuilding Company, and Dry Dock Company to "stimulate interest in the merchant marine"

Dec. 15, Death of Paul Haupt (71) semitic scholar, at Baltimore, Maryland

Dec. 16, Albert B. Fall, E. L. Doheny, and E. L. Doheny, Jr., acquitted in conspiracy case of charge of defrauding the Government in lease of Naval Oil Reserve at Elk Hills, California

Dec. 19, Statement issued by Political Science Faculty of Columbia University urged reconsideration and reduction of foreign debt settlements

Dec. 21, Good Will flight of 5 Army planes to Central and South America begun from San Antonio, Texas

Dec. 31, Death of Colonel Henry A. du Pont (88) former Senator from Delaware

CONGRESS

Jan. 5, Resolution for investigation of the Aluminum Company of America said to be under control of Secretary Mellon and his brother ordered by both Houses

Jan. 6, Senate Judiciary Committee ordered to investigate failure of the Dept. of Justice to bring action against the Aluminum Company of America

Jan. 19, Senate refused to ratify Treaty of Peace with Turkey signed at Lausanne July 24, 1923

Jan. 22, Senate invoked closure rule on debate on adherence to World Court

Jan. 27, Resolution of Senate gave consent to adherence to the World Court (Permanent Court of International Justice of the League of Nations) subject to 5 reservations and 2 explanatory paragraphs by vote of 76 to 17, 3 Senators absent

Feb. 19, Dept. of Justice made statement of reasons why charges against the Aluminum Company of America under anti-trust laws could not be sustained

Feb. 26, Revenue Act reduced income taxes by about $387,811,000, personal exemption of single persons raised from $1,000 to $1,500, and of married persons from $2,500 to $3,500, and normal rates from 2% to 1½% on first $4,000 of taxable income, and from 4% to 3% on the next $4,000, and 5% on the remainder. The surtax rates begin at 1% to apply to amounts of net income over $10,000, the maximum surtax rate reduced from 40% to 20%. Tax on corporations increased from 12½% to 13% for 1925 and 13½% for 1926 and subsequent years. Gift tax abolished. Tax on passenger automobiles reduced from 5% to 3%. A large number of excise and occupation taxes dropped. Schedule of inheritance taxes modified. Publicity clause as to income tax returns repealed. Tax on auto trucks removed. Tax on theater admittances retained

Feb. 27, Better Government Association of Chicago and Cook County asked the Senate for investigation of crime and lawlessness in Chicago

March 24, Long and short haul freight Bill defeated in the Senate by vote of 46 to 33

April 1, The House voted to impeach Federal Judge George W. English of Illinois charged with depositing funds and assets under court jurisdiction in institutions in which he had an interest as stockholder, and with alleged tyrannical and oppressive actions, vote 306 to 62

April 5–24, Public hearings held by the Judiciary Committee of the Senate on prohibition, as to its success or failure, ended with conviction that enforcement with modifications is possible

April 7, District Attorney Buckner in prohibition hearing estimated violators of the Volstead Act in New York City as 180,000, and the country's bootlegging at $3,600,000,000

April 8, The House by vote of 265 to 87 declined to take action to set aside the rules and reapportion congressional districts on basis of the 1920 census

April 12, S. W. Brookhart, of Iowa, deprived of seat in Senate by vote of 45 to 41, in favor of Capt. Daniel F. Steck, Democrat

May 20, Air Commerce Act placed civil aviation under control of the Secretary of Commerce and assistant secretary in charge to be appointed

——, Railroad Labor Act abolished the Railroad Labor Board and substituted the United States Board of Mediation, and the principle of mediation for compulsory arbitration of disputes between railroad employers and employees. Provision made for appointment of an emergency board by the President to investigate and report in cases of unadjusted disputes

May 21, Haugen Bill for farm relief to maintain price of farm products by sale of surpluses by a Federal Farm Board defeated in House because based on principle of price-fixing by the Government by vote of 212 to 167

May 25, Public Buildings Act authorized expenditure of $165,000,000 in 5 years in construction of federal buildings, $50,000,000 to be expended in the District of Columbia

——, 70,000 acres in Kentucky including the Mammoth Cave made a national park

May 26, Immigration Act amended to admit to the United States and to extend naturalization privileges to alien veterans of the World War, and to exempt certain Spanish subjects resident in Puerto Rico on April 11, 1899 from the provisions of the Immigration Act of 1924

June 22, Federal Aid in road building continued for 2 years with annual appropriation of $82,500,000 for 1928 and 1929 to be used largely in the West and Southwest

June 24, McNary-Haugen Farm Relief Bill defeated in Senate by vote of 45 to 39

July 2, Act created a Division of Coöperative Marketing in the Dept. of Agriculture to provide for the acquisition and dissemination of information pertaining to coöperation

——, Act expanded Army Air Corps to 1,800 planes, 1,650 officers, and 15,000 enlisted men, increase to be reached at end of 5 years

July 3, Immigration Act of May 26 amended to permit entry of wife or unmarried child under 18 of alien who was resident prior to July 1, 1924, minister of religious denomination or professor of college, university, seminary, or academy under certain conditions

——, Copyright Act amended to secure protection for books not printed from type set

——, Civil Service Retirement Act replaced that of May 1920, increased maximum annuity from $720 to $1,000 and provided for contribution from employees of 3½% of salary

——, Pension Act granted $65 per month to Mexican and Civil War veterans in receipt of less than $72 per month and $90 per month for total disability, and $50 per month to widows

July 3, Congress adjourned

Nov. 10, Senate convened as Court of Impeachment for trial of Judge George W. English adjourned the same day because of resignation of the defendant

Dec. 6, Sixty-Ninth Congress, 2d sess. convened

Dec. 11, Impeachment charges against Judge English dismissed by vote of House as primary purpose, the removal from office accomplished

Dec. 13, Salaries of Supreme Court judges increased

1927

Jan. 3, Supreme Court decision fixed boundary between Texas and Oklahoma

Jan. 4 and Feb. 23, Agreements with Great Britain as to release of property seized under American and British Trading with the Enemy Acts

Jan. 5, Death of George S. Huntington (66) anatomist, New York City

Jan. 7, Transatlantic commercial telephone service opened between New York and London

Jan. 13, Death of Arnold Daly (51) actor, in New York City

Jan. 15, Tennessee Supreme Court upheld law against teaching of evolution but dismissed case on appeal against John T. Scopes and voided fine of $100

Jan. 17, Supreme Court decision declared that Congress had the right to compel attendance of witnesses at hearings where inquiry is solely for the purpose of gathering information that might lead to legislative enactments

Jan. 22, Death of James Ford Rhodes (78) historian, at Brookline, Mass.

Jan. 24, German-American Mixed Claims Commission announced awards in 428 cases of claims against Germany amounting to $3,707,000 and dismissal of claims in 399 cases

Jan. 26, Secretary Kellogg stated that the United States was willing to negotiate with China on subject of tariff and extraterritoriality with a central government which could speak for the whole of China

——, Death of Lyman J. Gage (90) former Secretary of the Treasury

Jan. 30, Death of Simeon E. Baldwin (87) jurist, at New Haven, Conn.

Feb. 2, Death of Clarence L. Brownell (63) author and educator

Feb. 3, William Phillips appointed first Minister from the United States to Canada

Feb. 5, State Dept. announced that German firms doing business in the United States would deposit amounts to be credited to reparations payments in the Federal Reserve Bank, and would be reimbursed by Germany

——, Federal Board of Mediation granted increase of wages of 7½% to enginemen and firemen employed on 27 railroads east of Chicago and north of the Ohio River

Feb. 6, Federal Reserve Board established a rediscount rate of 3½% for Federal Reserve Bank of Chicago, the first time this power had been used by the Board of direct determination of rate of discount for member bank

Feb. 8, Federal Board of Mediation granted 7½% wage increase to trainmen of southern railroads

——, Retrial of case of H. M. Daugherty and T. W. Miller on charge of defrauding the Government as to alien property seized during the War

Feb. 9, World War Foreign Debt Commission dissolved,

after having negotiated settlements with 13 countries for eventual payment of $11,522,354,000 of principal and interest

Feb. 9, Death of Charles D. Walcott (77) geologist, at Washington

Feb. 10, President Coolidge invited Great Britain, France, Italy, and Japan to Naval Conference for further limitation of armaments to be held at Geneva in June; accepted by Japan Feb. 19 and Great Britain Feb. 28; declined by France Feb. 15 and by Italy Feb. 21

Feb. 13, Death of Rev. Percy Stickney Grant (67) Protestant Episcopal clergyman, New York City

Feb. 14, 16, 28, Strike at Passaic, New Jersey, begun in Jan. 1926 of textile workers finally settled in all mills

——, Death of Lucy Maynard Salmon, educator, at Poughkeepsie, New York

Feb. 17, Agreement provided for resumption of diplomatic relations with Turkey severed by Turkey April 20, 1917, and most favored nation treatment as to customs

Feb. 18, The $12,000,000 Moffat Tunnel under James Peak, Colorado, nearly 7 miles long, formally opened

——, Hon. Charles V. Massey, first Minister from Canada, received by the President

——, Death of Elbridge T. Gerry (89) lawyer and philanthropist

Feb. 21, Supplementary Extradition Treaty signed with Honduras

——, Supreme Court sustained conviction of 20 individuals and 23 corporations in pottery industry for conspiracy to fix prices

Feb. 21 and March 7, American marines landed at Corinto, Nicaragua. *See also* Nicaragua

Feb. 21–April 11, Strike and lockout of textile workers in Rhode Island

Feb. 22, Death of Dr. Judson Harmon (81) former Attorney General, and Sydney G. Fisher (71) lawyer and historian

Feb. 24, Supreme Court declared constitutional decision of Kansas Court barring Ku Klux Klan from the State as an unauthorized foreign corporation

Feb. 25, Death of Rev. Henry Preserved Smith (80) theologian and Orientalist

Feb. 26, Radio telephone conversation held between San Francisco and London established new long distance record, 7,287 miles

Feb. 28, Supreme Court decision declared oil contracts and leases granted E. Doheny by former Secretary Fall of Elk Hills Naval Oil Reserve, California, canceled as illegal, fraudulent, and corrupt, and also the lease for construction of naval oil station at Pearl Harbor, Hawaii

——, Supreme Court decision that New York law forbidding resale of theater tickets above a fixed price unconstitutional

——, General Enrique Estrada and 12 of his staff convicted of conspiracy to violate neutrality laws and sentenced to prison terms by court at Los Angeles. *See also* Mexico

March 1, Federal Board of Radio Control appointed by the President, Rear Admiral Bullard, of Pennsylvania, chairman, held first meeting on the 15th

——, Letter of President Poincaré made new arrangement for immediate payment of $10,000,000 a year under unratified Bérenger-Mellon Debt Agreement in addition to $20,000,000 annual payment

charges on debt for surplus war material, which was accepted, and first payment made June 1

March 2, Death of Walter Lippincott (77) publisher, Philadelphia

March 4, New York Federal District Court found Thomas W. Miller, former Alien Property Custodian, guilty of conspiracy to defraud the Government *in re* the American Metal Company, and sentenced him to 18 months imprisonment and fine of $5,000, but jury disagreed as to former Attorney General Harry M. Daugherty, and he was freed

——, Direct cable service with Germany formally reestablished

——, Death of Harry Pratt Judson (77) president emeritus of the University of Chicago

March 5, Death of Dr. Ira Remsen (81) president emeritus of Johns Hopkins University, and Abbie Farwell Brown, author

March 7, Supreme Court decision declared Texas law prohibiting negroes from voting in Democratic primary election unconstitutional

March 10, Note to League of Nations opposed international supervision of armaments

——, Public statement of Faculty of Princeton University endorsed that of Faculty of Columbia University urging reduction of foreign debt settlements

March 15, Death of Edwin S. Balch (74) author and explorer, at Philadelphia

March 16, Harry F. Sinclair judged guilty of contempt by Supreme Court of the District of Columbia for refusal to answer questions before Walsh Committee of the Senate

——, Secretary Mellon in reply to criticisms of Faculties of Columbia and Princeton universities upheld capacity-to-pay principle, and declared that the principal debtor companies were already receiving from Germany more than enough to pay their debts to the United States, and that cancellation would leave out of account goods bought for cash in France and England during the War; letter published March 17

March 17, William B. Shearer commissioned by shipbuilding companies to attend Geneva Disarmament Conference and "report his observations"

March 19, Bureau of Prohibition and office of Commissioner of Prohibition created by Secretary of the Treasury under Act of March 3

March 21–22, Successful strike of cleaners, dyers, and pressers in Missouri

March 22, Death of Archbishop Robert Seton (87) titular archbishop of Heliopolis, Egypt, and dean of all the monsignori of Catholic Church in the United States

March 23–28, Strike of clothing workers in Baltimore

March 24, Roy A. Haynes appointed Acting Commissioner of Prohibition

——, American consulate at Nanking attacked and looted by Chinese troops

March 26, Arbitration decision granted wage increase to railroad station employees

March 29, Major H. O. D. Segrave drove his racing automobile on the beach at Daytona, Florida, at average rate of 203.79 miles an hour

——, Italian aviator, Colonel F. de Pinedo, reached New Orleans in flight from Havana, Cuba on trip from Italy begun Feb. 13 in airplane "Santa Maria"

April 1, Bituminous coal miners began strike in Illinois, Indiana, Ohio, and Pennsylvania after failure of conference to reach agreement to follow contract which expired March 31, involving 200,000 men

April 1, Dept. of Labor placed non-native inhabitants of Canada under the immigration quota laws, affecting those who crossed the border for employment in the United States especially at Detroit and Buffalo

April 1–May 19, Strike and lockout of plumbers in New York City gained wage increase, and strike of plumbers in Brooklyn April 1–June 14 for a 5 day week

April 2, Order of the President revoked order of May 10, 1921, placing naval oil reserves under control of the Secretary of the Interior, returning them to control of the Navy Dept.

April 4, Death of Charles J. Bartlett (83) Arctic explorer

April 5, Election of William Hale Thompson as Mayor of Chicago on campaign appeal to racial groups hostile to England, declaration of friendship for negro and anti-prohibition, pledged to "have recognition given to the heroes of Irish, Polish, German, Dutch, Italian and other extractions who had been dropped from the histories"

April 6, Supreme Court of Massachusetts overruled exceptions of the defense in case of Sacco and Vanzetti and declared "new trial is not necessary to prevent a failure of justice"

——, President Coolidge vetoed Act of Legislature of the Philippines passed over veto of Governor General Wood to hold a plebiscite on independence for Islands

——, Proposal of Aristide Briand, Foreign Minister of France, in statement to Associated Press that France and the United States should make mutual engagement for the outlawry of war to replace Treaty of Arbitration of 1908

April 7, First successful demonstration of television made, Secretary Hoover in his office in Washington shown in New York while talking over the telephone to President Gifford of the Bell Telephone Company

April 8, Death of William P. W. Dana (94) artist, in London, England

April 9, Henry L. Stimson, appointed as personal representative of the President April 7 to go to Nicaragua to negotiate for end of hostilities, sailed from New York

——, Judge Webster Thayer, of Massachusetts Superior Court, sentenced Sacco and Vanzetti to death

April 11, Reparation demand made of China for Nanking outrage of March 24, the United States joining with Great Britain, France, Italy, and Japan in Joint Note to Hankow Government

April 12–14, World air endurance record established by Bert Acosta and Clarence D. Chamberlin remaining in air 51 hours, 11 minutes, and 25 seconds at Roosevelt Field, Long Island

April 15, J. Ramsay MacDonald, former British Prime Minister, and daughter, arrived in New York for American visit

April 16, Disastrous floods in the Mississippi Valley affecting especially Arkansas and Missouri, breaking all previous records, the flood of 1922 taking second place and that of 1822 third

April 20, Coal miners of Indiana signed 2 year agreement on basis of the Jacksonville wage scale

April 21, Suit for libel brought against Henry Ford for alleged anti-Jewish activities by Aaron Sapiro ended in mistrial

April 22, President Coolidge appointed Committee of

5 cabinet members with Secretary Hoover, chairman, to coöperate with the Red Cross in relief in the Mississippi flood district where it was estimated 700,000 persons needed assistance and 28,573 square miles inundated

April 25, Secretary Hoover arrived at Memphis, Tennessee, to take charge of flood relief

——, Public letter of Nicholas Murray Butler called attention to proposal of Briand of April 6

April 27, Death of Albert J. Beveridge (64) historian and former Senator from Indiana

April 29, Army engineers dynamited section of levee 15 miles below New Orleans to make outlet for flood waters to save the city

May 2, Army airplanes reached Washington ending good will flight to Mexico, Central and South America which started Dec. 21, 1926 from San Antonio, Texas, and covered 22,065 miles in 263¼ hours of actual flying time

——, Note of British Government answered and challenged statements of Secretary Mellon of March 16 on interallied debts; answered by Secretary Kellogg May 4

——, Death of Benjamin Ide Wheeler (73) educator, in Vienna, Austria

May 4–23, The United States represented at the International Economic Conference at Geneva

May 6, Death of Hudson Maxim (74) engineer, inventor, and author

May 7, Death of Bruce McRae (60) actor, in New York

May 13, Break of the Bayou des Glaises levee at Moreauville, Louisiana, flooded the sugar cane region

May 19, Death of Joseph Swain (70) educator, at Swarthmore, Pennsylvania

——, Exchange of Notes with Great Britain settled unadjusted pecuniary claims arising out of the World War

——, Interstate Commerce Commission rejected plan of L. F. Loree for merger of St. Louis-Southwestern Railroad and Missouri-Kansas-Texas Railroad companies

May 20, James M. Doran appointed Prohibition Commissioner, and Seymour Lowman, Assistant Secretary of the Treasury in charge of enforcement of prohibition, succeeding L. C. Andrews, resigned, and took office Aug. 1

May 20–21, Airplane flight of Charles A. Lindbergh alone in the monoplane "Spirit of St. Louis" in first non-stop flight from New York to Paris, 3,610 miles in 33 hours and 39 minutes, leaving Roosevelt Field at 7.52 A.M. and arriving at Le Bourget Field at 5.21 P.M., average speed about 108 miles an hour. Greeted by over 100,000 persons on the field at Paris

May 23, Death of Henry E. Huntington (77) railroad executive and art and book collector of California

May 24, Break of the levee at McCrea on east bank of the Atchafalaya River inundated 4 parishes of Louisiana

May 26, Secretary Mellon authorized reduction in size of paper money by about one-third, new bills to be $6\frac{1}{8}$ by $2\frac{5}{8}$ inches

——, Death of Rev. Francis Edward Clark (75) founder of the Christian Endeavor Society, at Newton, Mass.

May 31, Draft Plan to Outlaw War prepared by Professor James T. Shotwell and Professor Chamberlain of Columbia University published

June 1, Governor Fuller, of Massachusetts, appointed President Lowell, of Harvard University, President

Stratton, of the Massachusetts Institute of Technology, and Judge Robert Grant, a committee to study and make report on the Sacco-Vanzetti case. Independently of the committee Felix Frankfurter published review of case and opinion that the identity of the defendants and the evidence as to their subsequent consciousness of guilt were faulty

June 1–11, Strike of bricklayers of Pittsburgh, Pennsylvania gained increase of 60 cents a day, of carpenters at Providence, R.I. June 1–July 25 which was settled at $1.175 an hour

June 3, Flood Credits Corporation created to assist flood sufferers in Mississippi and Louisiana to purchase material to resume farming

June 4, Illinois $1,025,000 suit against Governor Len Small for taxes alleged withheld when he was State Treasurer settled by agreement and Governor Small exonerated

——, Charles Chamberlin with Charles Levine as first transatlantic passenger left New York in the "Colombia" a Bellanca monoplane, and made forced landing at Hefta near Eisleben, Saxony, Germany, after flight of 43 hours of 3,905 miles establishing new world non-stop record

June 5, Judge Ben B. Lindsey, founder of Juvenile Court, Denver, ousted from office after 25 years by decision of State Supreme Court declaring his election illegal

June 6, Supreme Court exonerated International Harvester Company of charge of violation of anti-trust laws

June 7, Death of Thomas Willing Balch (58) international lawyer and author, in Philadelphia

June 9, Death of Virginia Claflin Woodhull (Mrs. J. B. Martin) pioneer suffragist (89) in England

June 11, Charles A. Lindbergh arrived at Washington from Europe on the U.S.S. "Memphis," and received the Distinguished Flying Cross from President Coolidge, and then flew to New York where great public demonstration held in his honor

June 12, Putnam expedition to Arctic regions left New York. *See* Canada

June 15–July 27, Successful strike of 1,300 barbers in New York City for wage of $35 per week and half of receipts over $50 a week, and of barbers in Newark June 20–July 1

June 18, Arthur S. Pease elected president of Amherst College succeeding Professor George D. Olds resigned Nov. 12, 1926

June 20, Draft and Pact of Perpetual Friendship between France and the United States, the Briand proposal for outlawry of war transmitted to the Government of the United States

——, Charlotte A. Whitney pardoned after 7 years fight against conviction under the criminal syndicalism law of California

June 20–Aug. 4, Naval Conference of the United States, Great Britain, and Japan at Geneva, Switzerland, called by President Coolidge, failed to agree as to disarmament, the American proposal that the 5–5–3 ratio of the Washington Conference established for capital ships be extended to cruisers, destroyers, and submarines with other plans not accepted

June 21, Death of Mrs. Clara Louise Burnham (71) novelist

June 25, Rawson-MacMillan scientific expedition left for 15 months exploration of Labrador and Baffin Land

June 28–29, Lieuts. Albert F. Hegenberger and Lester J. Maitland made first successful flight from California to Hawaii, from Oakland to Honolulu, 2,400 miles in 25 hours and 15 minutes

June 29–July 1, Comm. Richard E. Byrd in the "America," tri-motor Fokker airplane, with Bert Acosta, Bernt Balchen, and Lieut. George O. Noville made transatlantic flight from New York and after flight of 43 hours and 21 minutes made forced landing due to exhaustion of fuel supply at Ver-sur-Mer on coast of France in fog and rain

June 30, Retraction by Henry Ford of charges against Jews published during several years in his weekly newspaper, the *Dearborn Independent*

July 2, President Coolidge announced appointment of General F. R. McCoy to supervise election in 1928 in Nicaragua as arranged by H. L. Stimson

July 4, World altitude record for seaplanes made by Lieut. C. C. Champion at Washington at height of 37,995 feet

July 8–9, Strike of tank-wagon drivers and filling station attendants in Chicago of the Sinclair Refining Company for wage increase, and lockout of employees of the Standard Oil Company, Texas Company, and others settled by compromise agreement of $7.50 per month for drivers and $5 per month increase for filling station attendants

July 9, Death of John Drew (73) actor, on tour in San Francisco

July 12–22, Strike of building trades workers in Baltimore in jurisdictional dispute

July 14, Flight of Ernest L. Smith and E. B. Bronte from San Francisco to Molokai, Hawaii, 2,348 miles in 25½ hours, plane wrecked in forced landing due to lack of gasoline

July 15, Death of Henry White (67) diplomat

July 15–21, Successful strike of 8,000 cleaners and dyers in New Jersey for the union shop

July 16, The $1,000,000 libel suit of Aaron Sapiro against Henry Ford settled out of court after withdrawal by Mr. Ford on June 30 of anti-Semitic charges

July 20–Oct. 23, Colonel Charles A. Lindbergh made tour of the United States in his airplane the "Spirit of St. Louis," visited every State, traveled 20,350 miles, total flying time 260 hours

July 23, Last meeting of American-Mexican Claims Commission, awards of $2,221,659.46, made in 36 out of 51 claims of the United States, and in 5 out of 9 claims of Mexico of $39,000

July 25, World altitude airplane record made by Lieut. C. C. Champion at 38,474 feet at Anacostia, D.C.

Aug. 2, President Coolidge at summer camp at Rapid City, South Dakota, gave newspaper statement "I do not choose to run for President in 1928"

Aug. 3, Governor Fuller, of Massachusetts, refused clemency in Sacco-Vanzetti case, and published statement declaring his own opinion and that of his advisory committee that they had had a fair trial

——, Death of Edward Bradford Titchener (60) educator, psychologist, and author, at Ithaca, New York

Aug. 4–Sept. 19, Strike of unorganized textile workers at Henderson, North Carolina, for 12½% increase in wages

Aug. 7, International Peace Bridge at Buffalo, New York, dedicated by Vice-President Dawes and the Prince of Wales

Aug. 7, Death of General Leonard Wood (65) Governor General of the Philippines, at Boston, Mass.

Aug. 13, Death of Thomas W. Salmon (51) psychiatrist, New York

Aug. 14, Death of Alexander C. Humphreys (77) educator and engineer, at Morristown, New Jersey

Aug. 15, Death of Elbert H. Gary (80) lawyer and steel manufacturer, in New York City

Aug. 16, Agreement to continue American-Mexican Claims Commission of Sept. 8, 1923

———, Death of Jonathan Ogden Armour (63) meat packer of Chicago, in London

Aug. 16–17, Arthur C. Goebel and Lieut. William V. Davis won first prize in Dole air race from Oakland, California, to Honolulu, in the "Woolaroc," 2,407 miles in 26 hours, 17 minutes, and 33 seconds. The second prize went to Martin Jensen and Paul Schulter in the "Aloha," making flight in 28 hours and 16 minutes

Aug. 19, Massachusetts Supreme Court rejected final appeal for Sacco and Vanzetti

Aug. 21, The Attorney General of the United States refused to intervene in the Sacco-Vanzetti case

———, Death of Fannie B. Zeisler (64) pianist, at Chicago

Aug. 23, Sacco and Vanzetti executed in Charlestown prison in Massachusetts and also Celestino Madeiros who had confessed to participation in the crime at South Braintree in April 1920 and had exonerated Sacco and Vanzetti in his statement

Aug. 25, Paul Redfern left Brunswick, Georgia, in the "Port of Brunswick," monoplane, for non-stop flight to Rio de Janeiro, Brazil, and was never heard from again

Aug. 27, Edward F. Schlee and William S. Brock left Harbor Grace, Newfoundland in the monoplane "Pride of Detroit," in transatlantic flight, landing at Croydon, England, and ending flight at Tokio, Japan, after visiting 15 cities, making flight of 12,295 miles in 145½ hours of flying

Aug. 28, Dept. of Agriculture estimated flood areas as 4,417,500 acres in Kentucky, Tennessee, Missouri, Arkansas, Mississippi, and Louisiana

Aug. 29, Treaty with France provided for acquisition of sites for battle monuments

———, Strike in Chicago of motion picture machine operators closed 350 or more theaters, and lockout which followed affected about 15,000 employees, settled Sept. 3

Sept. 1, Death of Amelia Bingham (58) actress, New York City

Sept. 4, Death of Isadora Duncan (47) dancer, at Nice, France

Sept. 5, Death of Wayne B. Wheeler (58) lawyer and counsel of the Anti-Saloon League, and Marcus Loew (66) motion picture producer, New York

Sept. 6, Lloyd W. Bertaud and James De Witt with Philip A. Payne as passenger left Old Orchard Beach, Maine, in the "Old Glory," a single-motor Fokker monoplane, for Rome, Italy, and were lost at sea

Sept. 7–15, Strike of 6,000 teamsters and truckmen in New York City for wage increase and increase of overtime pay settled by compromise agreement gave wage of $45 a week instead of $40, but no advance for overtime paid for at $1 an hour, and retained the 9 hour day

Sept. 9, Protest made to France against new French tariff of Sept. 6, which placed maximum rates on certain American goods, in cases of electrical equip-

ment as high as 800%, settled Nov. 21 with return to rates as before Sept. 6

Sept. 16–23, American Legion Convention held in Paris, France

Sept. 20, Dwight Morrow appointed Ambassador to Mexico to succeed J. R. Sheffield, to take effect Oct. 6

Sept. 29, Tornado swept St. Louis killing 90 persons and injuring 1,500, and destroying 5,000 buildings, property loss estimated at $50,000,000

Sept. 30, First injunction of Judge F. P. Schoonmaker at Pittsburgh, in coal strike against the United Mine Workers prohibited any act which might interfere with the production, mining, transportation, or shipment of coal, and forbade union pickets to enter company grounds and from using "abusive language"

Oct. 1, Agreement of Illinois coal miners and operators renewed Jacksonville wage scale until April 1, 1928, and settlements in Missouri and Kansas followed

Oct. 1–6, Strike of glass blowers in a number of States for wage increase settled by renewal of old wage scale

Oct. 2, Death of John Dalzell (82) former member of Congress from Pennsylvania

Oct. 4–Nov. 25, International Radio Conference met in Washington, Secretary Herbert Hoover, chairman

Oct. 5, Death of Sam L. Warner (40) motion picture producer, in Los Angeles

Oct. 6, Agreement of miners and operators in coal strike in Oklahoma on basis of Jacksonville wage agreement, and Oct. 7 in Indiana

Oct. 10, Supreme Court decision sustained lower courts holding that lease and agreement of Teapot Dome Naval Oil Reserve with the Mammoth Oil Company was obtained by fraud, and cancellation of lease and all agreements with Sinclair interests ordered

Oct. 11, Ruth Elder (Mrs. Lyle Womack) with George W. Haldeman as pilot left New York in the monoplane "American Girl," and was forced down northeast of the Azores and rescued by Captain Goss in the Dutch ship "Barendrecht" on Oct. 13

———, Second injunction of Judge Schoonmaker at Pittsburgh in the coal strike

Oct. 17, Trial of Harry F. Sinclair and Albert B. Fall on charges of criminal conspiracy to defraud the Government in lease of Teapot Dome Naval Oil Reserve begun in Supreme Court of the District of Columbia

Oct. 18, Strike of coal miners in Colorado for a "flat scale of $8.50 a day for all classes of mine workers, a six hour day and a five day week," and restoration of the Jacksonville agreement

Oct. 19, Additional Protocol amending the Pan-American Sanitary Convention of Nov. 14, 1924 signed by the United States

Oct. 20, Mayor Thompson, of Chicago, in effort to "drive King George out of Chicago" sent emissaries to the Public Library to find and burn all pro-English books

Oct. 24, Death of Solomon D. Warfield (64) banker and railroad organizer, at Baltimore

Oct. 26 and Nov. 7, Treaty of commerce with Spain signed

Oct. 31, Death of John Luther Long (66) novelist and playwright

Nov. 1, Mistrial declared in Fall-Sinclair case in Teapot Dome Naval Oil Reserve case because of attempts of agents of the defense, William J. Burns and others, to tamper with the jury

Nov. 2, Floods begun in New England caused by heavy rainfall and unprecedented rise of White River which swept away roads and houses in Vermont

Nov. 4, National Guard of New York ordered out to aid in rescue and preserve order because of floods of upper Hudson River

Nov. 7, A large number of I.W.W. leaders in southern Colorado arrested in connection with the coal strike

——, United States army took charge of flood relief in Burlington, Vermont, district

Nov. 8, International Convention and Protocol for abolition of import and export prohibitions and restrictions signed by the United States

Nov. 9, Death of Samuel M. Crothers (70) clergyman and author, at Cambridge, Mass.

Nov. 12, Holland Tunnel under the Hudson River between New York City and Jersey City, the largest vehicular tunnel in the world, formally opened for traffic. Named for Clifford M. Holland, first chief engineer

Nov. 14–Dec. 10, Publication in the Hearst newspapers of text of alleged documents as to payment of $1,215,-000 to Senators Borah, La Follette, Heflin, and Norris for pro-Mexican propaganda, names of Senators not given in the newspapers but supplied by W. R. Hearst. *See infra* Congress Dec. 15

Nov. 15, Supreme Court of District of Columbia ordered seizure of $100,000 of property of Harry M. Blackmer, fugitive witness for the prosecution of Harry F. Sinclair

Nov. 16, Mexican Foreign Office declared the documents published in the Hearst newspapers as to payment of propaganda fund to United States Senators and financing of Sacasa revolt in Nicaragua forgeries

Nov. 17, Death of Charles S. Mellen (76), railroad president, at Concord, N.H.

Nov. 21, Striking coal miners fired on by mine guards and State police at Columbine mine near Denver, Colorado, 6 killed and 27 wounded. National Guard sent to the district by the Governor

Nov. 22, Extradition Treaty with Poland signed

Nov. 24, Death of Israel C. White (79) geologist, at Baltimore, and of Rear Admiral William H. G. Bullard (61) at Washington

Nov. 25, International Radio Convention and General Regulations signed by the United States at the Washington Conference. An International Technical Consulting Committee created

Nov. 26, Death of Charles B. Manville (93), manufacturer and inventor, New York

Nov. 29, Announcement of State Dept. that native Canadians only would receive permits to cross the border, and non-native commuters would receive priority treatment in application for immigration passport visas

——, Death of Henry W. Savage (68) theatrical manager, Boston

Dec. 1, Six Colorado coal mines opened under guard of State troops

Dec. 5, Debt Funding Agreement with Greece negotiated providing for payment of $19,659,836 at 3% over period of 62 years, and additional loan granted of $12,167,000 at 4% over period of 20 years

——, Supreme Court decision in boundary dispute between New Mexico and Texas awarded 25,000 acres of land on Rio Grande to Texas

Dec. 5, Hearings begun before Supreme Court, District of Columbia, H. F. Sinclair, and W. J. Burns and others of the Sinclair Oil interests and the Burns Detective Agency charged with contempt of court in connection with Fall-Sinclair trial

Dec. 7, Treaty of friendship, commerce, and consular rights with Honduras signed

Dec. 10, Nobel prize for physics awarded to Professor Arthur Compton, of the University of Chicago, and Professor C. T. R. Wilson of England

Dec. 11, Supreme Court decision ruled that liquors seized by New York State troopers without search warrant were illegally obtained and not admissible as evidence

Dec. 12, W. S. Hill, member of the Shipping Board, removed by the President because of acceptance of large loan of money from a Pacific shipping company

Dec. 13, Henry L. Stimson appointed Governor General of the Philippine Islands

Dec. 13–14, Colonel Charles A. Lindbergh made good will flight from Washington to Mexico City, in the "Spirit of St. Louis" non-stop flight of 2,031 miles in 27 hours and 10 minutes

Dec. 16, Troops called out by Governor H. S. Johnston, of Oklahoma, to bar out legislature convened to hear impeachment charges against him; impeachment proceedings dropped on the 29th

Dec. 17, Submarine S–4 sunk in collision with coast guard destroyer "Paulding" off Provincetown, Mass. and all 40 men aboard lost

——, Arbitration Board awarded increase to western locomotive firemen; rejected by carriers

Dec. 23, Mrs. Francis W. Grayson and Bruce Goldsborough left Roosevelt Field, Long Island, for flight to Europe, and were lost off Cape God

——, Buffalo Federal Court sustained immigration regulations of April 1

Dec. 28, Draft Treaty submitted to France by the State Dept. providing for a multilateral treaty to outlaw war

Dec. 28–Feb. 13, 1929, Colonel Lindbergh left Mexico for Guatemala and visited the Central American Republics, British Honduras, Panama, Colombia, and Venezuela, and on return flight the Virgin Islands, Puerto Rico, Santo Domingo, Haiti, and Cuba

Dec. 29, Decree signed by Judge Blake Kennedy at Cheyenne, Wyoming, returned Teapot Dome Reserve to the Navy Dept.

Dec. 30, Grand Jury presentment against Harry F. Sinclair, William J. Burns, and 5 others charged conspiracy to obstruct justice

Dec. 31, Death of Rev. Algernon S. Crapsey (80) who was deposed from the Protestant Episcopal Church in Dec., 1906 after trial for heresy

CONGRESS

Jan. 10, Message of the President defended his policy of intervention in Nicaragua, and declared that Mexico was attempting to establish a Government there hostile to the United States and sending arms and munitions to the revolutionists

Jan. 12, Note of Secretary Kellogg to Senate Committee on Foreign Relations gave particulars of Communist activities in Mexico and Latin America hostile to the United States

Jan. 18, Treaty of amity and commerce with Turkey signed Aug. 6, 1923, rejected by the Senate

Jan. 20, The Senate refused to seat Senator Elect Frank L. Smith appointed to fill vacancy caused by death of W. B. McKinley, of Illinois, because of large amount spent on campaign for election

Jan. 21, Nine projects for Great Lakes harbors and 24 for inland waterways adopted

Jan. 22, Maternity and Infancy Act extended for 2 years

Jan. 25, Resolution adopted by Senate in favor of arbitration of questions as to American property rights in Mexico

Feb. 9, Resolution to rescind the action of the previous session as to adherence to World Court defeated in Senate by vote of 59 to 30

——, Act provided that women might serve on juries in the District of Columbia, but jury service not compulsory

——, $10,000,000 appropriated for eradication or control of the European cornborer

Feb. 11, McNary-Haugen Farm Relief Bill passed in Senate by vote of 47 to 39

Feb. 15, Milk Importation Act provided for regulation of importation of milk and cream

Feb. 17, McNary-Haugen Farm Relief Bill of Senate passed House by vote of 214 to 178

Feb. 21, Act changed name of Emergency Fleet Corporation to Merchant Fleet Corporation

Feb. 23, Radio Control Act created a Federal Radio Commission of 5 members appointed by the President with power to make regulations and to issue and revoke licenses

Feb. 25, National Bank Consolidation Act provided for indefinite extension of the charters of the Federal Reserve Banks, and allowed national banks to establish branches

——, McNary-Haugen Farm Relief Bill vetoed by the President as fixing prices by government. He condemned the "equalization fee" as "a tax for the special benefit of particular groups." Opinion of Attorney General Sargent accompanied the message stating that the measure was unconstitutional

——, Act granted American citizenship to certain inhabitants of the Virgin Islands, and the District Court of the Islands authorized to grant citizenship by naturalization of aliens on application

March 2, Naval Appropriation Act provided for appropriation of $316,215,107, fixed navy personnel at 83,200 men and provided for construction to be begun on 3 cruisers authorized in 1924 and for additional naval airplanes

March 3, Director of Veteran's Bureau authorized to make loans to veterans on the security of their adjusted compensation certificates

——, Produce Agency Act to prevent destruction or dumping of farm produce by commission merchants

——, Prohibition Reorganization Act to become effective April 1 created a Prohibition Bureau in the Treasury Dept., and placed enforcement agents under the civil service

March 4, Longshoremen's Compensation Act to go into effect July 1 covers longshoremen and other workers upon navigable waters not entitled to compensation under State laws

——, Operation of national origins clause of Immigration Act of 1924 postponed until 1928

——, Act to prevent discrimination by boards of trade

and similar organizations against Farmers' Coöperative Associations

March 4, Organic Act of Puerto Rico amended

——, Congress adjourned

Dec. 5, Seventieth Congress, 1st sess. convened

Dec. 7, The Senate by vote of 53 to 28 refused to seat Senator Elect Frank L. Smith from Illinois because of campaign fund amounting to $458,782

Dec. 9, The Senate by vote of 56 to 30 refused to seat Senator Elect William S. Vare from Pennsylvania because of amount spent on campaign

——, Senate appointed a committee to investigate statement of Hearst newspapers of that day that 4 unnamed Senators had been paid over a million by Mexico according to alleged text of documents published

Dec. 15, Hearings begun by Senate Committee investigating documents submitted by W. R. Hearst

Dec. 19, Statement of Senate Committee on examination of Hearst documents that there was no evidence that any "slush fund" had been paid to Senators Borah, Heflin, Norris, and La Follette

1928

Jan. 2, Death of Emily Stevens (45) actress, New York City

Jan. 5, French Note in answer to American proposal of Dec. 28, 1927, limited renunciation of war to wars of aggression

Jan. 7, Death of Mrs. Sara Agnes Conboy (58) labor leader, at Brooklyn, New York

Jan. 10, Death of Louis F. Post (78) lawyer, economist, and author, at Washington

Jan. 11, Note of Secretary Kellogg in reply to Briand Note of Jan. 5 insisted on renunciation "of all war as an instrument of national policy"

Jan. 14, Death of Archibald Cary Coolidge (61) historian, Boston, Mass.

Jan. 16–Feb. 20, Pan-American Conference at Havana, Cuba. President Coolidge delivered the opening address, Charles Evans Hughes, chairman of the delegation from the United States

Jan. 19–29, Successful 10 day strike of 6,500 shoe workers at Haverhill, Mass. against reduction of wages

Jan. 20, William Cosgrove, President of the Executive Council of the Irish Free State, arrived in New York on visit to the United States

Jan. 21, Dispute of 21,000 employees of street railroads of Chicago settled by award of arbitrators of increase in wages and provisions as to health and accident insurance

——, Note of Briand called attention to obligations of France as member of the League of Nations and signatory of the Locarno treaties under which certain wars were legitimate and even obligatory, and also right of self-defense

——, Death of Major General George Washington Goethals (69) engineer of the Panama Canal

Jan. 24, Death of Talcott Williams (78) journalist, author, and educator, New York City

Jan. 26–31, Strike of clothing workers, New York City

Jan. 27, Death of Clarence W. Alvord (59) historian, in Italy, and John Spencer Bassett (61) historian, in Washington

Feb. 1, Dept. of State issued statement objecting to flotation of Russian loan by United States banks

Feb. 4, Death of Aram J. Pothier (74) banker and

Governor of Rhode Island, 1909–1915 and 1925–1928

Feb. 5, Death of Rev. William Elliot Griffis (85) author and educator

Feb. 6, New Arbitration Treaty with France signed

Feb. 8, Costes and Lebrix, French aviators, reached Washington from New Orleans where they had entered the country from Mexico, Feb. 4, and were received by the President, and on March 2 began flight from New York across the continent to San Francisco, reached March 7

Feb. 13, Adolfo de la Huerta and 4 other Mexicans charged in July, 1927 with violation of the neutrality laws acquitted by Federal Court at Los Angeles

Feb. 16, Three remaining government owned cargo lines in the Pacific were sold by the Shipping Board

——, Death of Edward Fitzgerald (Eddie Foy) actor (73)

Feb. 19, End of Colorado coal strike which began in October

Feb. 20, International Conventions as to rights and duties of states in the event of civil strife and as to status of aliens signed by the United States at Havana with other American Republics

Feb. 20–March 10, Successful strike of 25,000 employees of dyeing and cleaning establishments in New York City to stabilize industry and end competition

Feb. 21, District of Columbia Court found Harry F. Sinclair, H. M. Day, W. J. Burns, and Sherman Burns guilty of contempt in view of attempts of the detectives in following and spying on members of jury in trial of the oil lease case. Sinclair sentenced to 6 months in prison, and the others received shorter terms

Feb. 22, Announcement that the Ku Klux Klan had on this date discarded masks and changed name to Knights of the Green Forest

Feb. 27, Note of Secretary Kellogg to Briand expressed belief that the unequivocal renunciation of war would not violate the obligations imposed by the Covenant of the League of Nations, but declared that the right of self-defense "is inherent in every sovereign state and is implicit in every treaty"

Feb. 29, Unsuccessful strike of paper box makers in New York City for recognition of union and standard wage

March 5, New York Circuit Court of Appeals decided that Canadians having business in the United States and daily crossing the frontier were not immigrants and not subject to the Immigration Act of 1924

March 5–6, First non-stop flight from New York to Havana, Cuba, made by Charles A. Levine in the "Columbia"

March 6, Circuit Court of Appeals declared Jay Treaty of 1794 applied to Canadians crossing the border for employment

March 7, Death of William Henry Crane (82) actor, at Hollywood, California

March 9, Bank of France filed suit in New York court to recover $5,210,000 in Russian gold held in banks in New York

——, Death of Rodman Wanamaker (65) merchant, of Philadelphia and New York

March 13, St. Francis Dam on Santa Clara River 40 miles north of Los Angeles gave way flooding the country and sweeping away buildings and bridges in the river valley, 350 persons killed

March 15–24, The United States officially represented at the meeting of the Preparatory Commission for the Disarmament Conference of the League of Nations at Geneva

March 16, Convention as to safety of livestock interests through prevention of contagious diseases signed with Mexico

March 20, Death of James Ward Packard (64) automobile manufacturer, at Cleveland, Ohio

March 23–26, Floods in Sacramento River Valley, California, the river reaching highest level at Sacramento since the flood of 1862

March 30, Settlement by exchange of notes with China as to compensation for Nanking affair of March, 1927. A joint commission to negotiate, and regret expressed

——, World airplane duration record without refueling made by Edward Stinson and Capt. George Halderman at Jacksonville, Florida, remaining in air 53 hours, 36 minutes, and 30 seconds

——, Note of Briand in reply to Kellogg Note of Feb. 27 agreed to submission of correspondence as to pact to outlaw war to the powers

——, Death of Frank B. Willis (57) Senator from Ohio, and educator

April 2, Strike of 1,500 granite quarrymen in Maine for wage increase and 44 hour week, gained 2 cents an hour increase instead of the 5 cents asked for and 44 hour week with half day on Saturday

April 3–May 25, Successful strike of 2,500 union barbers in New York City

April 4, Award of Professor Max Huber, of Switzerland, arbitrator, gave the Island of Las Palmas (Miangas) between the Dutch East Indies and the Philippines to the Netherlands

——, The American Telegraph and Telephone Company transmitted a moving picture by wireless for the first time

——, Death of Delos F. Wilcox (55) author and public utility expert, New York

April 5, Death of Chauncey M. Depew (93) lawyer and railroad president, New York

April 10, Treaty with Colombia signed as to status of Serrana and Quito Sueño Banks and Roncador Cay in the Caribbean

April 11, Resignation of Judge John Bassett Moore from Permanent Court of International Justice

April 12–13, First non-stop western transatlantic flight made by the "Bremen" from Dublin and landing forced down at Greenly Island, Strait of Belle Isle, Labrador. *See also* Germany

April 12–27, The United States represented at meeting Advisory Opium Committee (11th session) Geneva

April 13, Proposed Treaty for renunciation of war (American draft) sent to Great Britain, France, Germany, Italy, and Japan

April 13–18, National Socialist Party Convention held in New York City nominated Norman Thomas for President and James H. Maurer for Vice-President

April 16–Oct. 6, Strike of cotton textile operatives in New Bedford, Massachusetts, after announcement of manufacturers on April 9 that general wage reduction of 10% would become effective on the 16th. Settled by 5% wage cut and promise of 30 days notice for any future wage change

April 18, Death of Samuel B. McCormick (69) former chancellor of the University of Pittsburgh

April 19, Treaty of arbitration with Italy signed

April 20, Treaty of friendship, commerce, and consular rights with Latvia signed

——, Relief plane started from Detroit piloted by Floyd Bennett and Bernt Balchen with parts to repair the "Bremen"

April 21, H. F. Sinclair in second trial acquitted by District of Columbia jury of conspiracy with A. B. Fall to defraud the Government in the naval oil leases

April 22, Ray Keech made world speed automobile record at Daytona Beach, Florida, at average speed of 207.5526 miles an hour

April 25, Liquor Smuggling Treaty with Greece signed

——, Death of Floyd Bennett (37) aviator, of pneumonia in Quebec. Serum carried by Col. Charles A. Lindbergh in flight to Quebec failed to save him

April 28, First emergency board appointed by the President to investigate railroad dispute

April 30–May 5, The United States represented at meeting of Health Committee of the League of Nations (12th sess.) Geneva

May 5, Treaties of arbitration and of conciliation with Germany signed

May 14, Provisional Agreement with Persia by exchange of notes as to commerce

May 16, Unsuccessful strike of 1,000 dental workers in New York City for minimum wage scale of $25 per week and 44 hour week

May 16–27, Successful strike of 2,500 employees of the Standard Oil plant at Bayonne, New Jersey for improvement of working conditions

May 18, Death of William D. Haywood (58) I.W.W. leader, at Moscow, Russia

May 19, Exchange of Notes with Turkey extended Customs Agreement

May 21, Death of Hideyo Noguchi (51), bacteriologist, at Accra, in West Africa

May 24, Circuit Court of Appeals affirmed award of wage increase of Dec. 17, 1927, to western locomotive firemen

May 26, Mrs. Florence E. Knapp, former Secretary of State of New York, found guilty of larceny of census funds, and sentenced Sept. 4 to 30 days in prison

——, Death of Thomas S. Butler (73) member of Congress from Pennsylvania

May 27, First National Convention of Workers Party (Communist) met in New York City and nominated William Z. Foster for President and Benjamin Gitlow for Vice-President

May 30, Roosevelt Memorial Park of 38 acres of water front dedicated at Oyster Bay, Long Island, New York

May 31, Liquor Smuggling Treaty with Japan signed

May 31–June 1, Flight of Capt. Charles Kingsford Smith with C. T. P. Ulm, Lieut. Harry Lyon, and James Warner from Oakland, California, to Honolulu, in 27 hours and 28 minutes, 2,400 miles; second hop to Suva, Fiji Islands, 3,138 miles in 34 hours and 33 minutes, June 3–5; third to Brisbane, Australia, 1,762 miles in 19 hours and 18 minutes, June 9

June 1–3, The United States represented by official observer at International Copyright Union at Rome, Italy

June 1–7, Successful strike of 2,100 carpenters at Buffalo, New York, for wage increase, and June 1–July 5, of carpenters at Bridgeport, Conn. for increase of $1 per day and 5 day week settled by compromise

June 2, Newton D. Baker appointed fourth member for the United States of the Permanent Court of Arbitration at The Hague

June 4, Supreme Court decision that wire tapping of private telephone conversation to secure evidence permissible in a prohibition case (Olmstead vs. U.S.) and evidence usable at trials

June 5, Treaty of friendship, commerce and consular rights with Norway replaced that of July 4, 1827

——, Cases of 5 women employed by the United States Radium Corporation at Orange, New Jersey, bringing action for poisoning, settled for $10,000 each and yearly pension of $600

June 7, Treaties of arbitration and conciliation with Finland signed

June 10–12, Strike of artist's models and manikins in Chicago for increase in wages and better working conditions

June 12, Emilio Carranza on good will flight from Mexico City arrived in Washington

June 12–15, Republican National Convention met in Kansas City, and nominated Herbert Hoover for President on first ballot June 14, Hoover receiving 837 out of 1,089 votes, Frank O. Lowden 74, and Charles Curtis 64. Curtis was nominated for Vice-President on first ballot June 15

June 14, Robert W. Stewart acquitted by Supreme Court of the District of Columbia of contempt charges for refusal to answer questions of Senate Committee in investigation of the naval oil leases

——, Treaty of arbitration with Denmark signed

June 15, Henry M. Blackmer, oil operator, who had fled to France to avoid questioning as a witness in Teapot Dome oil case, indicted by Federal Grand Jury at Denver on charge of perjury and evasion of income tax law, and on Aug. 4 President Kellogg and Secretary Coolidge signed a warrant for his arrest

June 17, Break in St. Francis River levee inundated northeastern Arkansas and Missouri

——, Death of Edwin T. Meredith (52) former Secretary of Agriculture at Des Moines, Iowa

June 17–18, Miss Amelia Earhart with Wilmer Stultz as pilot and Louis Gordon as mechanic, the first woman to make transatlantic flight, from Trepassey, Newfoundland to Burry Estuary, Wales, in trimotor Fokker monoplane "Friendship" in 20 hours and 49 minutes

June 18, Death of Donn Byrne (39) Irish-American novelist, in Ireland

June 19, Virginia adopted revised Constitution involving 47 major changes

——, Treaty of friendship and commerce with Austria signed

June 20, Arthur Kill cantilever bridges joining Staten Island and New Jersey dedicated and opened to traffic on the 29th

——, Death of William R. Mead (81) architect, of New York, in France

June 22, Mrs. Helen Tufts Bailie, of Cambridge, Mass. expelled from the National Society of the Daughters of the Revolution on charges arising from publication of the so-called black list of the Society

——, Death of Basil King (69) novelist, at Cambridge, Mass.

June 23, Note of Secretary Kellogg presented new draft treaty to outlaw war to all signatories of the Locarno treaties

June 24, Death of Holbrook Blinn (56) actor and producer

June 26–28, Strike of clothing workers, New York City against violation of contract

June 26–29, Democratic National Convention met at Houston, Texas, and nominated Alfred E. Smith, Governor of New York, June 28 on first ballot for President with 849²/₃ votes of the 1,100 cast, and Senator Joseph T. Robinson, of Arkansas, June 29 on first ballot for Vice-President

June 27, Death of Robert B. Mantell (74) actor, at Atlantic Highlands, New Jersey

June 29–July 22, Capt. C. B. D. Collier and John H. Mears made record trip around the world from New York City by steamer, train, airplane, and automobile, in 23 days, 15 hours, 21 minutes, and 3 seconds

June 30, Abolition of Alabama State convict leasing system completed with withdrawal of 800 prisoners from the coal mines and 200 from the lumber camps

June 30–July 1, The United States represented at meeting of Permanent Committee of International Association of Road Congresses at Chantilly, France

July 3, Order of the Interstate Commerce Commission allowed increased pay to railroads for transportation of mail

July 6, First all-talking motion picture, "The Lights of New York" produced in New York City by the Warner Brothers

July 11, Farm Labor Party nominated George W. Norris for President and W. J. Vereen for Vice-President

July 12, National Prohibition Convention met in Chicago and nominated William F. Varney for President and James A. Edgerton for Vice-President

July 16, Naturalization Treaty with Czechoslovakia signed

July 18, United Mine Workers in convention at Indianapolis gave up demand for the Jacksonville wage agreement in bituminous coal fields allowing each district to settle with operators on "basis mutually satisfactory"

July 18–19, Southern Dry Democrats representing 14 States in conference at Asheville, North Carolina, voted to support Herbert Hoover for President

July 20, Roy O. West nominated by President Coolidge as Secretary of the Interior to succeed Dr. Hubert Work

July 22, Death of William C. Brownell (76) author and literary critic, of New York

July 25, New Tariff Treaty signed with China gave de jure recognition of the Nationalist Government of China and recognition of tariff autonomy effective Jan. 1, 1929

July 27, Secretary Kellogg refused request of Conservative Party of Panama to supervise Panama election

July 28, Death of Mrs. Crystal Eastman Fuller (47) feminist leader

July 30, First public demonstration of colored motion pictures by George Eastman at Rochester, New York

Aug. 14, Diplomatic relations with Ecuador severed since 1925 resumed by recognition of the Ayora Government

Aug. 16, Arbitration and Conciliation Treaties with Austria, Czechoslovakia, and Poland signed

Aug. 17, The Savannah River at Augusta, Georgia, in flood reached high record

Aug. 20, Death of George Harvey (64) journalist and diplomat, of New York

Aug. 20–21, Record non-stop flight of Arthur Goebel and Harry Tucker from Los Angeles, California to New York in 18 hours and 51 minutes surpassing previous record of May 1923 by 8 hours

Aug. 21, William F. Whiting, of Massachusetts, appointed Secretary of Commerce by the President succeeding Herbert Hoover resigned

Aug. 23, Agreement of bituminous coal miners with Central Ohio Coal Operators' Association to take effect Sept. 1 and terminate March 31, 1930, on basis of $5 per day and 70 cents per ton for cutting and loading

Aug. 24, Wage agreement concluded at Kansas City by bituminous coal miners with Southwestern Coal Operators' Association to take effect Sept. 1 and terminate March 31, 1931, based on 1917 wage scale

Aug. 25, Byrd Antarctic expedition left New York in the "City of New York," ice breaker boat, Commander Byrd following later on the "Larsen" which left San Diego Oct. 12

Aug. 27, International Treaty for the renunciation of war (Briand-Kellogg Peace Pact) as an instrument of national policy signed at Paris by the United States

——, The United States sent invitations to other nations than the 15 who signed the Paris Peace Pact to adhere to Pact

Aug. 29, Death of Mary Garrett Hay (71) suffragist leader, at New Rochelle, New York

Sept. 1, Illinois bituminous coal miners signed wage agreement effective Sept. 16 and terminating March 31, 1932, miners accepting wage reduction of from 16 to 19%, basic scale of 91 cents a ton, and $6.10 per day

Sept. 5, Death of Robert H. Ingersoll (69) watch manufacturer

Sept. 8, Charles Evans Hughes elected to succeed John Bassett Moore resigned as member of Permanent Court of International Justice of the League of Nations

Sept. 12, Death of Professor William M. Sloane (77) historian

Sept. 16–17, Hurricane in southern Florida and flood of Lake Okeechobee caused great damage and loss of life estimated by the Red Cross at 2,300, property loss $25,000,000

Sept. 25, The "American Palmetto," Atlantic coast line of steamers, sold by the Shipping Board

——, Death of Richard F. Outcault (65) newspaper artist and humorist, originator of colored comic sheets, the "Buster Brown" series and others

Sept. 28, Wage agreement of bituminous coal miners of Iowa concluded a reduction of 14% from the Jacksonville wage scale agreement

——, The United States notified France and Great Britain that the Anglo-French naval accord was not acceptable as a basis for naval disarmament

Sept. 29, Emergency Board appointed by the President to investigate wage dispute between 47 western railroads and conductors and trainmen which recommended (Oct. 30) increase of 6½% without change in rules which was accepted by trainmen

Oct. 1, Government suit filed in District Court at Albany against International Brotherhood of Paper Makers and Alden Paper Company charging conspiracy under Sherman anti-trust law to monopolize trade in union-made watermarked paper by agreement

Oct. 2, Death of Oscar George Theodore Sonneck (55)

musician and author, and of Clarence Walker Barron (73) financial editor

Oct. 3, Chicago officially opened new 32 mile northside sewage disposal plant

Oct. 6, Textile strike in New Bedford ended after 25 weeks with acceptance by workers of a 5% wage reduction

Oct. 9–11, Unauthorized strike of 7,000 employees of American Railway Express in New York City for recognition of union

Oct. 10–Jan. 2, Strike of 3,000 silk workers at Paterson, New Jersey, for union recognition and increase in wages and better hours

Oct. 12, Death of Mrs. Augusta E. Stetson (87) Christian Science leader, at Rochester, N.Y.

Oct. 15, The "Graf Zeppelin" commanded by Dr. Hugo Eckener with crew and 23 passengers arrived at Lakehurst, New Jersey, from Friedrichschafen, Germany, trip made in 111 hours and 35 minutes; return trip Oct. 29–Nov. 1 in 69 hours, pioneer round trip commercial flight

Oct. 17, Lieut. H. C. MacDonald left Harbor Grace, Newfoundland, in plane the "Gypsy Moth" for flight to England and was lost at sea

Oct. 22, Treaties of arbitration and conciliation with Albania signed

Oct. 23, Death of George Barr McCutcheon (62) novelist, in New York City

Oct. 25, Flight of Capts. Collyer and Tucker from New York to Los Angeles in 18 hours and 25 minutes; on the return trip both aviators killed when plane crashed Nov. 3 in Crook Canyon south of Prescott, Arizona

——, Death of Reuben A. Torrey (72) evangelist, at Asheville, North Carolina

Oct. 27, Treaty of arbitration with Sweden signed

Oct. 30, Death of Robert Lansing (64) former Secretary of State, in Washington

Nov. 5, Death of Frank Crane (67) journalist, at Nice, France

Nov. 6, Election gave Republicans, Hoover and Curtis, majority vote of 21,429,109, though Governor Alfred E. Smith, Democratic candidate for President received more votes than any previous Democratic candidate, 15,005,497; Thomas, Socialist, received 267,835 votes; Foster, Worker's Party, 48,228; Reynolds, Socialist Labor, 21,181; Webb, Farmer Labor, 6,391. The electoral vote for Hoover and Curtis was 444, and for Smith and Robinson 87. The Republicans gained in both Houses

Nov. 14, Treaties of arbitration and conciliation with Lithuania signed

Nov. 15, Death of Thomas C. Chamberlin (85) geologist, author, and educator, in Chicago

Nov. 17, James River Bridge at Newport News, Virginia, opened, the longest highway bridge in the world

——, Note of Great Britain as to sovereignty in Antarctic *in re* Byrd expedition

Nov. 19, Supreme Court decision upheld New York law aimed at the Ku Klux Klan requiring all organizations except trade unions and fraternal orders to give publicity to their regulations, oaths, and memberships

——, President-Elect Hoover left San Pedro, California, on U.S.S. "Maryland" for visit to Latin American countries for the purpose "of laying a basis for personal relations between himself as the

next President . . . and the leaders and governments of these countries and for mutual assistance in dealing with problems that confront them"

Nov. 19, Supreme Court decision reversed decision of Oct. 8 and sustained regulations of Labor Dept. of April, 1927 as to Canadians crossing the border and also April 9, 1929

Nov. 23, Death of Thomas Fortune Ryan (77) financier, New York City

——, New debt agreement with Austria

Nov. 24, President Coolidge announced intention to renew negotiations for American membership in the Permanent Court of International Justice

Nov. 25, Death of Charles F. Lummis (69) author, at Los Angeles

Nov. 26, The United States represented at Conference on Economic Statistics at Geneva

Dec. 2, Commander Byrd sailed from Dunedin, New Zealand, in the "City of New York" for the Ross Sea and Ice Shelf, preparatory for flight to South Pole. *See also* Antarctic

Dec. 3, Striking textile workers in Rhode Island accepted 5% wage cut

Dec. 4, French Government refused extradition of Harry M. Blackmer, fugitive witness wanted in Teapot Dome oil lease case

Dec. 5, Death of Paxton Hibben (48) author and diplomat, New York City

Dec. 10–Jan. 5, 1929, International American Conference on conciliation and arbitration held in Washington, all independent Latin American States except Argentina sending representatives

Dec. 11, International Civil Aëronautic Conference held in Washington

Dec. 16, Death of Elinor Hoyt Wylie (Mrs. William Rose Benet) poet (42), in New York City

Dec. 19, Death of John Hartley Manners (58) playwright, in New York City

Dec. 23, Death of John M. Coulter (77) botanist, author, and educator

Dec. 24, Invitation accepted to send representatives to serve on experts committees on German reparations

Dec. 29, Dept. of Justice filed suit against Sinclair Crude Oil Purchasing Company and the Mammoth Oil Company on charge of depriving the Government of at least 20,000,000 barrels of crude oil by fraud

Dec. 31, Agreement with Germany extended jurisdiction of Mixed Claims Commission

CONGRESS

Jan. 11, Senate Committee reported the Hearst documents as to bribery by Mexican officials of United States Senators as fraudulent and spurious

Jan. 17, Senate Committee declared Frank L. Smith elected from Illinois ineligible because of $452,782 contribution in the primary campaign, and Jan. 19 declared his seat vacant

Jan. 26, Appropriation of $500,000 granted for aid in rehabilitation of farm lands in flooded areas

Feb. 10, La Follette Resolution against third presidential terms adopted by Senate by vote of 56 to 26

Feb. 25, Jurisdiction over oil and gas leases issued on land in naval oil reserves transferred from Secretary of the Interior to the Secretary of the Navy

March 9, Clayton Anti-Trust Act amended to permit limited interlocking of bank directorates

March 9, Senator Norris raised question of authority of President to supervise election in Nicaragua

March 10, Settlement of War Claims Act provided for ultimate return of property held by Alien Property Custodian seized during War of Austrian, German, and Hungarian citizens, and for payment of claims

March 16, Senate refused to confirm J. J. Esch as member Interstate Commerce Commission

March 28, Radio Commission continued for another year

March 31, Adoption of national origin quota plan of Immigration Act of 1924 postponed until July 1, 1929

April 2, Immigration Act of 1924 amended to provide for rights of American Indians born in Canada to cross the border

April 12, Fifth McNary-Haugen Farm Relief Bill passed the Senate by vote of 53 to 23, and House May 3 by vote of 204 to 121

May 7, Act provided that State banks might be designated by the Federal Reserve Board as general depositories of public money by the Treasury

May 15, Flood Control Act adopted plan of army engineers for control of floods in the Mississippi Valley, $325,000,000 appropriated and 10 year program endorsed, and board created to report plans to the President

May 16, Bill to empower the Government to operate plants at Muscle Shoals passed the House by vote of 251 to 165, and the conference report both Houses on the 25th

May 17, Minimum air mail rate established made 5 cents per ounce instead of 10 cents per half ounce the rate

May 21, Standard Hamper Act fixed standards for hampers and baskets for fruits and vegetables

——, $5,000,000 appropriated for eradication of pink bollworm in cotton

May 22, Capper-Ketcham Extension Act provided for further development of agricultural extension work in the States and Territories receiving benefits of the Smith-Lever Act of May 8, 1914, authorized annual appropriation of $980,000 in 1929 and $500,-000 thereafter

——, Two postal pay measures increasing pay of certain employees and the maintenance allowance of fourth class postmasters passed in House over veto

——, Merchant Marine (Jones-White) Act increased construction loan fund from which builders of merchant ships could borrow up to 75% of the cost of the vessel, and gave long term contracts for carrying mail, and authorized sale of government-owned vessels at low prices

May 23, President Coolidge vetoed the McNary-Haugen Bill on ground that it involved a price-fixing policy, that the equalization fee involved a relinquishment of the taxing power of Congress, that it would encourage profiteering and stimulate overproduction, and aid foreign agricultural competitors

——, Act authorized appropriation of $15,000,000 to provide additional hospital, domiciliary, and outpatient dispensary facilities for persons entitled to hospitalization under World War Veterans' Act

——, Copyright Act amended, fee for registration of published works increased to $2

May 25, Muscle Shoals Bill conference report passed Senate by vote of 43 to 34, and the House by 211 to 146

May 25, McNary-Haugen Bill failed to pass in Senate over veto

May 26, Army, Navy, Marine Corps, and Coast Guard enlisted officers who had served in the World War placed on equal retirement status with officers of regular establishment, and public Health Service included

May 28, Joint Resolution requested the President to negotiate with nations to protect American citizens from forced military and naval service when sojourning in countries of their own or parent's origin

May 29, Quota Act amended to preserve entity of families. Non-quota status class increased in certain specified cases, classes of aliens entitled to preference in issue of immigration visas increased and to include wives and children under 21 of aliens previously admitted

——, Revenue Act reduced corporation income tax from 13½% to 12%, repealed the 3% tax on automobile manufacturers, exempted theater ticket admissions up to $3 from tax, club dues from $10 increased to $25 for 10% tax, taxes on wine reduced, and 25% of normal tax allowed on all net income under $5,000, and on all "earned" net income under $30,000. Estimated net reduction in revenue $222,-495,000

——, Postal rates revised and reduced on second, third, and fourth class matter

——, Senate Committee investigating Tariff Commission presented Report which recommended repeal of flexible provisions of the 1922 law, and that the Commission be made an agency of Congress and propose tariff revisions directly to Congress

——, Congress adjourned, Muscle Shoals Bill killed by pocket veto, and action on Boulder Dam prevented by Senate filibuster

Dec. 3, Seventieth Congress, 2d sess. convened

Dec. 21, Boulder Dam Act provided for construction of a dam at Boulder Canyon authorizing Arizona, California, and Nevada to enter into agreement as to division of the 7½ million acre-feet to be apportioned annually as specified, the Colorado River Interstate Compact to be ratified by 6 States, and an all-American canal into the Imperial Valley to be constructed from point lower on the Colorado River. Appropriations totaling $165,000,000 authorized

——, Joint Resolution created Puerto Rico Relief Commission

1929

Jan. 2, Convention for preservation of Niagara Falls signed with Canada

——, Strike of Paterson, New Jersey silk workers begun in Oct. ended

Jan. 5, Inter-American Arbitration and Conciliation Convention signed by the United States on last day of Pan-American Conference

Jan. 6, President Elect Hoover arrived at Hampton Roads from visit to 11 Latin-American countries, and proceeded to Washington

Jan. 7, Record flight of army airplane "Question Mark" commanded by Major Carl Spatz in southern California remained in air 150 hours, 40 minutes, and 15 seconds refueling from another plane

Jan. 8, Death of Benjamin N. Duke (73) capitalist, in New York City, and of Wallace Eddinger (47) actor

Jan. 9, Airmail lines between the United States and

Cuba, Puerto Rico, Haiti, Santo Domingo, Nassau, and the Bahamas inaugurated

Jan. 15, Treaty of extradition supplementary to that of Jan. 6, 1909, with France signed

Jan. 18, Board of Mediation awarded increase of 40 cents per day to shop workers of New York Central Railroad

Jan. 19, Owen D. Young and J. P. Morgan named as American experts on Committee on German Reparations, with Thomas N. Perkins and T. W. Lamont as alternatives

——, Death of Caspar Whitney (65) editor and author, New York City

Jan. 21, Treaties of conciliation and arbitration signed with Yugoslavia and Bulgaria

Jan. 23, Capt. George Fried in the "America," the "Antinoe" rescuer of 1926, saved 32 men from the sinking Italian freighter "Florida" 700 miles off Virginia

Jan. 25, Death of Oscar W. Underwood (67) former member of Congress from Alabama

Jan. 26, Treaties of arbitration and conciliation with Hungary and Ethiopia signed

Jan. 28, Death of Ogden Mills (72) financier, New York City

Feb. 4, Col. Charles A. Lindbergh opened air mail service to Central America, carrying mail from Miami, Florida, to Havana, Cuba, and from there to Belize, British Honduras

Feb. 4–5, Record non-stop flight made by Capt. Frank M. Hawks and Oscar E. Grubb from Los Angeles to Roosevelt Field, Long Island, 2,700 miles in 18 hours, 21 minutes, and 59 seconds

Feb. 6, First air mail from the United States to Panama Canal Zone with arrival of Col. Lindbergh at Colon

Feb. 8, Death of Edwin Denby (58) former Secretary of the Navy, in Detroit, Michigan

Feb. 9, The Shipping Board accepted bid of the P. W. Chapman Company of Jan. 16 of $16,082,000 for the "Leviathan," the "George Washington," the "America," the "Republic," the "President Harding," and the "President Roosevelt" and 5 ships of the American Merchant Line, thus virtually retiring from the shipping business

Feb. 11, Owen D. Young, of New York, appointed chairman of the Experts Committee on Reparations meeting in Paris to revise the Dawes Plan of 1924

Feb. 12, Rio Grande Compact between Colorado, New Mexico, and Texas signed

Feb. 15, Death of Melville E. Stone (80) former general manager of the Associated Press

Feb. 19, Notes sent by State Dept. to the Secretary General of the League of Nations and to the 40 States which had ratified the Protocol of Signature of the Permanent Court setting forth reasons why the recommendations of Geneva Conference not accepted and defining attitude of the United States, especially emphasizing the fifth American reservation, and willingness to adhere if Senate reservations could be met

Feb. 20, Trade Marks and Commercial Convention signed by the United States with other American Republics, and Arbitration Convention with Norway

Feb. 21, Col. C. A. Lindbergh appointed Technical Adviser to the Aëronautics Branch of the Dept. of Commerce

Feb. 25, Death of Rev. Newell Dwight Hillis (70) at Brooklyn, New York

Feb. 27, Convention of Arbitration with the Netherlands of May 2, 1908 extended

Feb. 28, Death of Harvey O'Higgins (52) novelist and playwright, in New York City

Feb. 28–March 4, Strike of shoe workers at Lynn, Massachusetts, and complete settlement March 14 with agreement of unions to draw up new price list to be submitted

March 1, Arbitration Treaty with Portugal signed

March 3, Death of Haley Fiske (77) lawyer and capitalist, New York City

March 4, President Herbert Hoover and Vice-President Charles Curtis inaugurated in Washington

March 5, Cabinet appointed: Henry L. Stimson, of New York, Secretary of State; Andrew W. Mellon, of Pennsylvania, Secretary of the Treasury; James W. Good, of Iowa, Secretary of War; William D. Mitchell, of Minnesota, Attorney General; Walter F. Brown, of Ohio, Postmaster General; Charles Francis Adams, of Massachusetts, Secretary of the Navy; Ray Lyman Wilbur, of California, Secretary of the Interior; Arthur M. Hyde, of Missouri, Secretary of Agriculture; Robert P. Lamont, of Illinois, Secretary of Commerce; James John Davis, of Illinois, Secretary of Labor

——, President Hoover announced that the embargo on arms to Mexico would be maintained

March 6, Death of Thomas Taggart (72) Democratic leader, in Indianapolis, and of David Buick (74) manufacturer, at Detroit

March 9, Col. Charles A. Lindbergh opened 500 miles air mail line between Brownsville, Texas and Mexico City

March 11, Major H. O. D. Segrave, English racing driver, established automobile world speed record at Daytona Beach, Florida, with average speed of 231.36246 an hour

——, The "Root Formula" proposal as to fifth American reservation to Permanent Court discussed by Committee of Jurists at Geneva

March 12, President Hoover announced policy of neither selling nor leasing oil lands except by mandatory provision of Congress, and directed that all outstanding leases be examined as to compliance of holders with the law

March 12–May 25, Strike of textile workers in the rayon mills at Elizabethton, Tennessee, for wage increase, settled through efforts of representative of the Dept. of Labor, who obtained a conciliatory offer from the employers

March 14, Heavy rains and swollen streams inundate towns in southern Alabama, Georgia, and western Florida. In Alabama the town of Elba wiped out and highways totaling 1,350 miles damaged in worst floods on record

——, Executive Order of the President declared that all future decisions of the Commissioner of Internal Revenue dealing with tax refunds in excess of $20,000 shall be open for public inspection, following criticism of rebates to corporations

March 15, Strike of cotton workers at Ware Shoals, South Carolina, began a series of strikes in South and North Carolina against new efficiency system

——, George W. Olvany who succeeded Murphy in 1924 as head of Tammany Society, New York, resigned, and was succeeded by John F. Curry

——, Death of Daniel Appleton (77) publisher, at White Plains, New York

March 17, The American Red Cross undertook full charge of flood-relief in Alabama, Florida, Georgia, and Mississippi

March 20, Arbitration and Conciliation Treaties with Belgium signed

——, Governor Henry S. Johnston, of Oklahoma, found guilty by State Senate on one of impeachment charges brought by House, general incompetence, and removed from office

March 21, Arbitration and Conciliation Treaties with Rumania signed

March 22, Canadian steamer "I'm Alone" with cargo of liquor fired on and sunk by U.S. Coast Guard vessel "Dexter" within 10.8 miles off the coast of Louisiana. Capt. J. T. Randall and crew taken prisoners to New Orleans

——, Proclamation of the President declared nationals origin clause of the Immigration Act of 1924 effective from July 1

March 24, Death of Samuel Rea (73) engineer and railroad official, in Philadelphia

March 26, Trading on the New York Stock Exchange totaled 8,246,740 shares, highest record, marked by severe declines with call money 20%. Over 300 low records of year made

March 27, Death of Bishop Charles H. Brent (66) at Lausanne, Switzerland

March 28, Death of Katharine Lee Bates (69) educator, at Wellesley, Mass.

March 29, Third emergency board appointed by the President to report on dispute on Texas and Pacific Railroad

March 30, Governors of Wyoming, Utah, and Colorado in conference at Denver agree on protest against President Hoover's order of March 12 canceling oil exploration permits

March 31, Death of Myron T. Herrick (74) Ambassador to France, in Paris, and of Professor Brander Matthews (77) author, in New York City

April 1, Privilege of suing the United States denied to citizens of the Russian Soviet Republics by decision of United States Court of Claims

April 2, Referendum in Wisconsin declared for repeal of State Prohibition Enforcement Act; accepted by Assembly April 17

——, Strike of textile workers at Gastonia, North Carolina, for minimum wage of $20 for a 40 hour 5 day week, and improved conditions

April 2–23, Dawes Committee to reorganize finances at Haiti

April 3, Attorney General Mitchell ruled that oil limitation plan impossible under anti-trust laws

——, National Guard sent to Gastonia, North Carolina, strike district

April 6, Treaties of Arbitration and Conciliation with Luxemburg signed

——, Discovery of the Mediterranean fruit medfly for first time on North American continent at Orlando, Florida, and quarantine established

April 8, Interborough Rapid Transit Company of New York City lost seven cent fare case, the Supreme Court reversing the decision in their favor by lower court of May 10, 1928

——, Supreme Court sustained sentence of Harry F. Sinclair of lower court for contempt in refusal to answer Senate Committee investigating oil cases, began to serve his sentence May 6

April 9, Canada entered formal protest with State Dept.

against seizure of rum runner "I'm Alone" outside legal limit of one hour's sailing distance from coast; referred to international arbitration April 25

April 16–May 13, United States represented at International Conference on Safety of Life at Sea in London

April 22, Presentation of policy of the United States as to disarmament at session of Preparatory Commission for Disarmament Conference of League of Nations

April 24, New solo endurance flying record for women established by Elinor Smith at Roosevelt Field, Long Island, of 26 hours, 21 minutes and 32 seconds

——, Death of Professor Theodore S. Woolsey (77) author, New Haven, Conn.

April 29, Note from Norway claimed rights in Antarctic regions being explored by Admiral R. E. Byrd

May 1, Night transcontinental air service established between New York and San Francisco on 31 hour schedule

May 1–June 12, Strike of building trades in Missouri begun in St. Louis for increase in wages ended in compromise agreement and wage increase

May 2, Several important railroads announced reductions from 2 to 5 cents a bushel on freight charges for export shipments of wheat, because a farm "emergency of national proportions exists," reductions to hold until Sept. 30

May 4, A five day week and 10% wage increase granted to 150,000 workers in the building trades in New York City

May 4–6, Records for free balloon distance and duration broken by Lieut. Thomas W. G. Settle and Ensign Wilfred Bushnell who left Pittsburgh May 4 and landed on Prince Edward Island May 6, distance 952 miles, time 43 hours, and 20 minutes

May 8, New world altitude air record made by Lieut. Apollo Soucek, U.S. Navy, in flight over Washington at 39,190 feet

May 10, Final settlement for Greek War Debt signed at $18,000,000 to be paid during 62 years, and new loan of $12,000,000 provided for

May 11, Death of Birge Harrison (73) artist

May 15, Fire destroyed clinic at Cleveland, Ohio, X-ray films in storage cellar created a poisonous gas which circulated rapidly through the building with explosions causing death of 124 persons immediately or in the 2 days following, doctors, nurses, patients, and visitors

May 17, Formal announcement by President Hoover of settlement of Tacna-Arica boundary dispute between Chile and Peru. See s.v.

——, Dwight L. Davis appointed Governor General of the Philippines

——, Governor Huey P. Long, of Louisiana, relieved of impeachment charges brought by the House with announcement of majority in Senate that they will acquit

——, Death of Mary Shaw (69) actress, in New York City

May 19–26, New endurance record of 172 hours and 32 minutes, refueling in air 17 times made by Reginald Robbins and James Kelly in airplane "Fort Worth" above Fort Worth, Texas

May 20, Supreme Court decision in the O'Fallon case overruled the Interstate Commerce Commission as to method for fixing railroad valuations, declaring the Commission had failed to consider present reproduction costs in valuation of railroad property as directed by Congress; decision gives estimated increase of $1,200,000,000 in income for the railroads

May 20, National Commission on Law Enforcement named by the President of 10 prominent lawyers, and one woman, Ada L. Comstock, president of Radcliffe College, George W. Wickersham appointed chairman, which made first report Jan. 19, 1931, dealing with enforcement of prohibition, all but one member signing report which opposed repeal of the XVIIIth Amendment or modification of Volstead Enforcement Act, but in appended statements only Judge Grubb expressed confidence in efficacy of law as it stood, and 3 members expressed themselves in favor of further trial of the Amendment, 4 were for immediate modification, and 2 for outright repeal, making it a self-contradictory document

——, Record flood in lower Mississippi Valley reached crest with about $10,000,000 damage to property, though all levees held

May 22, Stocks break in New York Stock Exchange from 2 to 18 points with 200 stocks at new low for year due to news that Federal Reserve Advisory Council recommended 6% New York Reserve bank rate, but rallied the following day on failure of bank to advance rate

May 23, Theodore Roosevelt appointed Governor of Puerto Rico

May 24, Death of Garrett P. Serviss (78) writer and astronomer

May 26, Mrs. Mabel W. Willebrandt resigned as Assistant Attorney General in charge of prohibition prosecutions

May 27, Supreme Court refused citizenship to Rosika Schwimmer, Hungarian pacifist, because of declaration that in case of war she would not bear arms in defense of the United States

——, Supreme Court decision upheld the right of the President to block legislation by means of the "pocket veto," failure of the President either to sign or return to Congress within 10 days a measure passed by Congress and sent to him

——, Wheat at Chicago fell below $1 for the first time since 1915 but recovered June 3

May 29, State Prohibition Enforcement Act repealed, by signature of the Governor of Wisconsin

June 1–Aug. 19, Strike of shoe workers at Haverhill, Mass. for wage increase of 10% and a 5 day week of 44 hours, settled by agreement to continue wages and hours in effect for 3 years

June 3, Supreme Court decision upheld contempt conviction of 6 months imprisonment of Harry F. Sinclair for having jury shadowed by detectives, and also sentences of H. M. Day and W. S. Burns

June 7, Chief of Police Aderholt killed in raid on tent colony of strikers at Gastonia, North Carolina, 15 men and women arrested for the murder

——, Young Plan to supersede Dawes Plan presented for reparations

June 8, Death of William Bliss Carman (68) Canadian-American poet, in New Canaan, Conn.

June 10, Conference of Governors met at Colorado Springs to consider working out plan for curtailment of production of oil

June 11, At Chicago the Standard Oil Company of Indiana and 51 associated companies found guilty and enjoined by District Court from further violation of the Sherman anti-trust law by pooling 77 patents relating to oil cracking processes

June 12, Resolution of Council of the League of Nations accepted draft protocol (plan of Elihu Root as amended in meeting of Committee of Jurists) for adherence of United States to Protocol and Statute of Permanent Court of International Justice

June 13, The "Yellow Bird," French monoplane with Armond Lotti, in command, and Jean Assolant and René Le Fèvre, pilots, left Old Orchard, Maine, reaching Santander, Spain, in 29 hours and 52 minutes, in non-stop flight, and continued to Paris June 16

June 15, Federal Farm Board constituted, Alexander Legge, chairman

——, Death of Charles Francis Brush (80) inventor of the arc light, in Cleveland, Ohio

June 18, President Hoover announced that the United States would not sign the Young Agreement as to reparations but that Congress would be asked for authority to sign a separate commitment with Germany as to those parts of the settlement affecting the United States

——, Interoceanic Canal Board appointed to investigate proposed canal route across Nicaragua as authorized by Congress

June 24, U.S. Court at New Haven, Conn. refused application for citizenship of Professor D. C. MacIntosh, of Yale University, because he had said he would not feel obliged to fight in the event of war. He had served 4 years in France in the World War

June 25, Proclamation of the President that the Boulder Dam project in effect as agreed upon by California, Colorado, Nevada, New Mexico, Utah, and Wyoming

——, Death of Dion Boucicault (70) actor and producer, in England

June 27, Demonstration of color television at Bell Telephone laboratories New York City

June 27–29, Capt. Frank M. Hawks made transcontinental flight from Roosevelt Field, Long Island, to Los Angeles, California, and return in 44 hours, 3 minutes, and 2 seconds, actual flying time 36 hours, 48 minutes, and 48 seconds, west to east trip a record in 17 hours, 38 minutes, and 16 seconds

June 30, The Sheppard-Towner Maternity and Infant Welfare Act lapsed

July 1, The "national origins" clause of the Immigration Act of 1924 came into effect

July 1–Sept. 5, Unsuccessful strike of street car workers in New Orleans for wage increase and recognition of union, accompanied by riots and violence

July 2–9, Refueling endurance airplane record made by L. W. Mendell and R. S. Reinhart at Culver City, California, of 246 hours and 44 minutes

July 2–11, Strike of union of International Ladies' Garment Workers in New York City affecting 30,000 workers for new agreement, 40 hour week and end of sweating system. A favorable settlement with new 3 year agreement signed in Mayor's Office, July 16, but no wage increase

July 3, Death of Dustin Farnum (55) actor, New York City

July 8–9, Non-stop flight of Roger Q. Williams and Lewis A. Yancey in the "Pathfinder" from Old Orchard, Maine, bound for Rome, landed at Santander, Spain, because fuel tanks exhausted, 3,410 miles in 31 hours and 42 minutes. Continued to Rome reached July 10

July 9, Announcement of State Dept. that protests

against the new high tariff rates had been received from 38 nations

July 10, The new smaller sized national currency went into circulation

July 11, Textile workers at Marion, North Carolina, went on strike

——, Death of Mrs. Katherine Tingley (79), theosophist, in Visingso, Sweden

July 12, Death of Robert Henri (64) artist, in New York City

July 13–30, New refueling endurance airplane record made by the "St. Louis Robin," Dale Jackson and Forrest O'Brine, pilots, at St. Louis, remaining in air 420 hours and 21 minutes

July 15, First meeting of newly-created Federal Farm Board, Alexander Legge, chairman

——, Four week tour of first American trade delegation to visit Soviet Russia begun, 99 business men

July 17, Two large banks at Tampa, Florida, and 12 smaller banks with about $22,000,000 deposits suspended payments because of depression caused by damage done by the Mediterranean fruit fly

July 18, Proclamation of the President revoked embargo on export of arms and munitions to Mexico as of Jan. 7, 1924

——, Conference of anthracite coal miners and operators in New York City reached agreement as to wages, and recognition of check-off

July 19, Note of Secretary Stimson to China and Russia reminded them of their peace obligations under the Pact of Paris, as pledged to settle dispute by peaceful means; both formally assured Secretary Stimson on the 22d that they have no intention of war

July 22, New transatlantic record of 4 days, 17 hours, and 42 minutes from Cherbourg to New York established by German liner "Bremen" on first voyage

July 24, Formal ceremony in Washington inaugurated the coming into force of the Briand-Kellogg Treaty for Renunciation of War (Pact of Paris), proclaimed by President Hoover in the presence of representatives of 43 nations

Aug. 3, Death of Emile Berliner (78) inventor of disk phonograph record and the gramophone, in Washington

Aug. 4, The airship "Graf Zeppelin" landed at Lakehurst, New Jersey, from Friedrichshafen, Germany, on second visit to the United States, Hugo Eckener in command, leaving on return trip Aug. 8

Aug. 6, Forest fires in Washington, Idaho, and Montana destroyed 30,000 acres of timber land

Aug. 7, Death of Victor L. Berger (69) Socialist leader and former member of Congress, in Milwaukee

Aug. 8, Federal Farm Board made first loan, an advance of $300,000 to Florida Citrus Exchange to relieve growers affected by quarantine imposed in April because of Mediterranean fruit fly

Aug. 10, Note to Nanking Government declined to accept immediate abolition of extra-territoriality on ground that China was not yet in position to guarantee justice to Americans in Chinese courts

Aug. 13, Rioting strikers in New Orleans invaded City Hall under pretext of presenting a petition and beat the Mayor and councilmen

Aug. 16–20, Round trip non-stop transcontinental flight of N. B. Mamer and Arthur Walker from Spokane to New York and return, 7,200 miles in 115 hours, 45 minutes, 10 seconds

Aug. 17, Special Claims Convention with Mexico prolonged that of Sept. 10, 1923

Aug. 19, Southern Cotton Coöperatives obtained loans from the Federal Farm Board

Aug. 21, W. B. Shearer filed suit against 3 shipbuilding firms for payment for services as propagandist, lobbyist, and naval expert at Geneva Naval Conference in 1927, for $257,655

Aug. 24, Death of Jeremiah W. Jenks (72) economist, author, educator, New York City

Aug. 26, The airship "Graf Zeppelin" landed at Los Angeles from Tokio, Japan, and proceeded to Lakehurst, New Jersey, Aug. 29, completing trip around the world begun from there Aug. 8

Aug. 27, Treaties of arbitration and conciliation with Egypt and with Estonia signed

Aug. 31, Death of Dr. Morton Prince (75) neurologist, at Brookline, Mass.

Sept. 1, The United States had received on costs of army of occupation from Germany $39,000,000, under Paris Agreement of $194,000,000 due, and of awards of Mixed Claims Commission $32,000,000 approximately out of $256,000,000

Sept. 2, General Claims Convention with Mexico prolonged that of Sept. 8, 1923

Sept. 4–12, Conference of members of Permanent Court of International Justice accepted draft protocol (Root formula) for American adherence to Court

Sept. 5, Interoceanic Canal Board headed by Lieut. Gen. Edgar Jadwin, appointed to investigate and survey route for canal across Nicaragua

Sept. 6, Plan for arbitration of New Orleans street car strike signed

——, President Hoover instructed Attorney General Mitchell to study the possibility of government action against William B. Shearer who states that he was paid by shipbuilding companies to spread propaganda against naval armament reduction at the Geneva Conference

Sept. 8, League for Independent Political Action with Professor John Dewey as chairman formed to organize a new political party

Sept. 9, Claudius H. Huston succeeded Hubert Work as chairman Republican National Committee

Sept. 11, Death of Louis Marshall (73) lawyer, in Zurich, Switzerland

Sept. 14, Protocol for adherence of the United States to the Permanent Court adopted by Assembly of the League of Nations and opened for signature

——, Death of Jesse Lynch Williams (58) novelist and playwright, New York City

——, Ella May Wiggins, striking mill worker and mother of 5 children, killed when group of Anti-Communists fired at truck in which strikers were riding near Gastonia, North Carolina

Sept. 15, Morris Hillquit, of New York, elected national chairman of the Socialist Party succeeding Victor L. Berger deceased

Sept. 17, Supreme Court of District of Columbia fined Harry M. Blackmer, fugitive oil case witness, $60,000 on 2 charges of contempt arising from his failure to obey subpœnas to appear in trial of H. F. Sinclair and A. B. Fall

Sept. 22–26, Flood caused by rise of the Rio Grande in New Mexico covered 52 miles of valley at average width of a mile, the greatest inundation in 300 years

Oct. 1, Treaty of commerce and navigation with Turkey signed

——, President Hoover appointed John McNab to make special study of law enforcement of prohibition and formulate plan for its improvement

Oct. 2, Six strikers killed and 20 wounded by Sheriff O. F. Adkins and deputy sheriffs at Marion, North Carolina in clash at picket line

Oct. 3, Death of Jeanne Eagels (35) actress, New York City

Oct. 4, British Prime Minister J. Ramsay MacDonald accompanied by his daughter, Miss Ishbel MacDonald arrived in New York and proceeded to Washington to confer with President Hoover on naval reduction

Oct. 6–8, Strike of 2,000 market teamsters and truck drivers in New York City for wage increase successful

Oct. 7, Trial of former Secretary of the Interior A. B. Fall begun on an indictment charging acceptance of a $100,000 bribe from Edward L. Doheny in leasing Elk Hills Naval Oil Reserve; found guilty Oct. 25 and sentenced Nov. 1

Oct. 9, Joint statement of Premier MacDonald and President Hoover issued, repeating pledge to support Briand-Kellogg Pact (Paris Peace Pact) and expressing confidence in the Five Power Naval Agreement

Oct. 10, Invitation of Great Britain to participate in Naval Disarmament Conference to be held in London in Jan. 1930 accepted by State Dept.

Oct. 13, Russian aviators in "Land of the Soviets" arrived in Seattle in flight from Moscow to New York, proceeding by way of Vancouver, Oakland, Salt Lake City, Chicago, Detroit, arriving at Curtiss Air Port, Long Island, Nov. 1

Oct. 15, Death of Dr. Edwin E. Slosson (64) chemist, author, and editor, in Washington

Oct. 16, Committee of Investment Bankers Association reports that speculation in public service stocks has reached a danger point, and many stocks are selling for prices far above their intrinsic value

Oct. 17, Celebration at Pittsburgh begun of completion of thousand mile deep waterway from Pittsburgh to the Mississippi River

——, James R. Garfield appointed chairman of President's Commission on Conservation and Management of the Public Domain

Oct. 21, Second trial of textile strikers for murder of Police Chief Aderholt at Gastonia, North Carolina ended, the first a mistrial, found 7 men guilty, and sentences given of from 17 to 20 years in prison

Oct. 22, Rio Grande Tia Juana International Water Commission met at Washington

——, Death of Thomas Hastings (69) architect, of New York City

Oct. 24, New York Stock Exchange in most severe break in its history, trading of 12,894,650 shares set record, and on Curb of 6,337,415 shares, industrial average down 12$^1/_8$ points

——, Grand Jury in case of murder of Ella May Wiggins, striking textile worker of Gastonia, on Sept. 14, failed to bring indictment because of "insufficient evidence," and in Nov. another attempt made to obtain indictment unsuccessful

——, Death of Moorfield Storey (85) lawyer and author, Lincoln, Mass.

Oct. 25, Albert B. Fall found guilty of accepting a bribe in the naval oil lease case when Secretary of the Interior and sentenced to 1 year in prison and $100,000 fine Nov. 1

Oct. 28, Secretary Stimson permitted Count and Countess Karolyi, former Hungarian president and his wife, to visit the United States for 6 months

——, Death of Theodore E. Burton (77) former member of Congress and senator from Ohio

Oct. 29, Farmers' National Grain Corporation incorporated to be central marketing agency for grain coöperatives with program of handling of 500,000,000 bushels of grain annually

——, Death of John Roach Straton (54) Baptist fundamentalist clergyman of New York City

Oct. 30, President Hoover presented Mme Marie Curie, co-discoverer of radium, with $50,000 to purchase a gram of the mineral, a gift from American admirers

——, Death of Edwin B. Parker, international financier

Nov. 1, G. Aaron Youngquist succeeded Mrs. Mabel Walker Willebrandt as Assistant Attorney General in charge of enforcement of prohibition

——, Arrival in New York from Moscow of monoplane "Land of the Soviets"

——, Note to China declared willingness to enter into negotiations as to abolition of extraterritoriality in answer to Note from China of Sept. 5

Nov. 2, Death of William G. Lee (69) railroad labor leader, at Cleveland, Ohio

Nov. 3, Statement issued by Italian Embassy that American born sons of Italian parents, American citizens of Italian birth, and even citizens of Italy resident in the United States might return to Italy without fear of conscription in time of peace

Nov. 6, Death of Dr. Edward Norton Libby (61) dean of Tufts College Medical School

Nov. 10, New record set for group parachute jumping as 16 persons leap from a single plane at 2,000 feet at Roosevelt Field, Long Island

Nov. 11, The Ambassador Bridge over the Detroit River between the United States and Canada, largest suspension span in the world, dedicated at Detroit 1,850 feet long

Nov. 12, Stock market collapse in New York City, transactions of sales 6,452,770 on the Stock Exchange in 3 hour market (10 A.M. to 1 P.M.), and 2,204,700 on the Curb Exchange, average of industrials down 16 points

Nov. 13, Bishop Charles P. Anderson, of Chicago, elected Presiding Bishop of the Episcopal Church in the United States, succeeding the late John Gardner Murray, deceased Oct. 3

——, Stocks reach lowest prices of 1929 on New York Stock Exchange in 7,761,000 share market

Nov. 14, Federal Reserve Bank of New York lowered rediscount rate from 5 to 4½%, second cut in 2 weeks

Nov. 15, President Hoover announced a series of conferences of agriculture, labor, and industrial leaders to meet at the White House to discuss "continued business progress"

——, Note to Great Britain in reply to Note of Nov. 27, 1928 reserved opinion on British claims in the Antarctic

Nov. 17, Death of James Melvin Lee (51) director of Dept. of Journalism, New York University

Nov 18, Death of James W. Good (63) of Iowa, Secretary of War

Nov. 22, Chicago Federal Reserve Bank lowered discount rates from 5 to 4½%

Nov. 28, Commander Richard E. Byrd with Bernt Balchen as pilot, Harold I. June as radio operator, and Capt. Ashley C. McKinley, photographer, left base

"Little America" in Bay of Whales in the Antarctic for flight to South Pole

Nov. 29, Byrd expedition reached the South Pole at about 8.55 A.M. New York time, flying up the Liv Glacier to Polar Plateau (1.25 P.M. Greenwich mean time) dropping American flag at Pole, and returned to "Little America" at 5.10 P.M. New York time with one stop of an hour at refueling base, the entire trip made in 19 hours Nov. 28–Nov. 29

Dec. 2, Note of Secretary Stimson appealed to Russia and China to adjust dispute by pacific means as to Manchuria and Chinese Eastern Railroad

Dec. 3, Memorandum of Litvinov, Acting Commissary of Foreign Affairs of Russia, declared Secretary Stimson's peace move as outside interference and non-friendly act, as Russia and China negotiating for an armistice

Dec. 4, Note from China attributed military action to self-protection and stated that China was ready to make peaceful settlement

Dec. 5, Alabama Supreme Court declared the purchasers of liquor guilty under the state law

——, Air Corps increased by 536 men

Dec. 6, San Francisco Federal Reserve Bank lowered discount rates from 5 to $4\frac{1}{2}\%$

——, Patrick J. Hurley of Oklahoma appointed Secretary of War

Dec. 8, Telephone service established from shore to ship at sea as New York talks with the "Leviathan" 200 miles distant

Dec. 9, Protocol of Signature of the Statute of the Permanent Court of International Justice of the League of Nations, and the Protocol of Accession of the United States, and Protocol of Revision of the Statute of the Court signed by American chargé d'affaires in Switzerland on authorization of President Hoover for the United States

Dec. 12, Stocks decline in New York Stock Exchange in worst break since Nov. 13 from 2 to 22 points

Dec. 19, Social Research Council headed by Wesley C. Mitchell appointed by the President

Dec. 20, James A. DeLacy, Boston bookseller, sentenced to a month in jail and $500 fine for selling the book "Lady Chatterly's Loves" by D. H. Lawrence, though both prosecuting attorney and judge condemn methods of the "Watch and Ward Society" by which evidence was secured

Dec. 21, Commander Richard E. Byrd made a rear admiral by the President

——, Interstate Commerce Commission announced plan for consolidation of railroads into a series of 19 systems: two New England systems, to be built around Boston & Maine and New Haven; five trunk lines between New York, Philadelphia, Baltimore, Chicago, and Kansas City, to be built around New York Central, the Pennsylvania, the Baltimore & Ohio, the Chesapeake & Ohio-Nickel Plate, and the Wabash-Seaboard; nine systems in the west to be grouped around Great Northern-Northern Pacific; Chicago, Milwaukee, St. Paul & Pacific; the Chicago, Burlington & Quincy; the Union Pacific; the Southern Pacific; the Atchison, Topeka & Santa Fé; the Missouri Pacific; and the combined Chicago, Rock Island & Pacific-St. Louis & San Francisco; three systems in the south to be built about the Atlantic Coast Line, the Southern, and the Illinois Central; and two systems composed of Canadian-controlled lines in the United States

Dec. 22, Fascist League of North America with headquarters in New York City formally disbanded

Dec. 27, Federal Farm Board drafted charter for American Cotton Growers' Exchange to be capitalized at $30,000,000 to market the cotton crop, expected to be the largest coöperative group in the world

Dec. 31, Death of Charles P. Taft (86) editor and former member of Congress, in Cincinnati, Ohio

CONGRESS

Jan. 8, James M. Beck, former Solicitor General, sustained as member of House from Pennsylvania in seat contest

Jan. 11, House agreement upon method of apportionment of its seats to take effect after 1930 census

Jan. 15, Senate ratified the Briand-Kellogg Treaty for Renunciation of War with an explanatory resolution by vote of 85 to 1

Jan. 19, Cooper-Hawes Act provided that after 5 years any goods produced by convict labor transported into any State shall be subject to its laws as if made there, the interstate commerce subjected to federal regulation

——, Establishment of 2 narcotic farms primarily for prisoners authorized to be under the Public Health Service

Feb. 4, Joint Resolution authorized uniting with creditor nations to float loan to Austria

Feb. 5, Appropriation of $500,000 authorized for aid to States in vocational education

Feb. 13, Fifteen new cruisers authorized of 10,000 tons and 1 air craft carrier, all to cost $274,000,000

Feb. 18, Migratory Bird Conservation Act authorized purchase and rent of land for preservation of game birds

Feb. 20, Resolution provided for confirmation of cession of certain Samoan Islands to the United States

——, Potash Investigation Act authorized appropriations for joint investigation by Depts. of Agriculture and Commerce

Feb. 23, Act provided that Chief of Staff of Army should have rank of General

Feb. 25, Seed, Feed, and Fertilizer Resolution authorized appropriation of $6,000,000 for loans to farmers in storm and flood stricken areas of the southeastern States

Feb. 28, $3,654,000 appropriated for restoration of roads and bridges in flooded areas

March 1, Compacts between the States, New Mexico and Oklahoma, Oklahoma and Texas and New Mexico, New Mexico and Arizona, Colorado and New Mexico, Colorado, Oklahoma, and Kansas ratified as to protection of titles of land transferred

——, Philippine Legislative Act of Dec. 3, 1928 approved

——, Act of 1915 amended to give double pensions to aviators in Army as well as to aviators in Naval and Marine Corps

March 2, "Jones Act" increased penalties for violation of prohibition law to "a fine not to exceed $10,000 or imprisonment not to exceed 5 years, or both," the court to discriminate "between casual or slight violations and habitual sales of intoxicating liquor, or attempts to commercialize violations of the law"

——, Act to enable mothers and widows of soldiers, sailors, and marines of World War now interred in cemeteries in Europe to make pilgrimage to cemeteries

March 2, Act provided that aliens who had entered the United States before June 3, 1921, who had no legal record of admission should be permitted to register entry by application for certificate which would enable them to establish residence by giving proof of meeting requirements of laws

March 4, Act provided for imprisonment and fine for aliens returning to the United States after having been arrested and deported

——, Radio Commission continued until Dec. 31, 1929

——, Congress adjourned

April 15, Seventy-First Congress, 1st (extra) sess. convened to consider farm relief and limited tariff revision

April 25, Administration Farm Relief Bill providing for Federal Farm Board, &c., but not the debenture plan of Senate Bill disapproved by the President passed in House by vote of 366 to 35

May 1, Appropriation of $4,250,000 made available for fighting the Mediterranean fruit fly, and Dec. 21 an additional $1,290,000

May 7, Hawley Tariff Bill proposing an increase in duties introduced in House

May 8, Senate voted 47 to 44 to retain export debenture scheme in Farm Relief Bill in spite of President Hoover's opposition

May 14, Senate adopted Farm Relief Bill with debenture plan by vote of 54 to 33

May 17, The House refused to accept Senate Farm Relief Bill as substitute for Bill of House of April 25 by vote of 249 to 119

May 27, Prohibition Reorganization Act transferred to Attorney General certain functions of the prohibition law and created a Bureau of Prohibition in the Dept. of Justice

May 28, Hawley Tariff Bill passed in House by vote of 264 to 147

June 7, The Senate adopted Norris Resolution to move forward presidential inaugurations to Jan. 15 and terms of Senators and Representatives to Jan. 2 for fifth time

June 11, Senate refused to eliminate debenture clause of Farm Relief Bill by vote of 46 to 43, and House again rejected it June 13 by vote of 250 to 113

June 14, Both Houses accept conference report of Farm Relief Bill without debenture clause

June 15, Agricultural Marketing Act created Federal Farm Board of 8 members with the Secretary of Agriculture making 9 to promote effective merchandizing of agricultural products in interstate commerce, and authorized a revolving fund of $500,000,-000 for loans to coöperative associations at rate of interest not to exceed 4%. $151,500,000 of this fund appropriated for the ensuing year on June 18

June 17, Borah Motion to limit tariff revision to duties on farm produce defeated in Senate by vote of 39 to 38

June 18, Census and Congressional Reapportionment Act for 1930 provided that in case no measure passed by Congress the number of the House remain fixed at existing 435 members under an executive reapportionment

June 24, Immigration Act amended to provide penalties for deported aliens returning to the United States

Sept. 11, Resolution adopted by Senate to investigate alleged activities of William B. Shearer as agent of the ship building interests at the Naval Disarmament Conference at Geneva in 1927

Sept. 20, Hearings begun by Senate Committee on Shearer case

Sept. 25, Senator Black, of Alabama, moved for general investigation of lobbying which was adopted Oct. 1

Oct. 2, Power of the President to change tariff duties under tariff law of 1922 withdrawn by Senate by vote of 47 to 42

Oct. 7, Senator Sheppard, of Texas, introduced Bill to extend scope of the Prohibition Amendment by making the purchase of intoxicating liquor a crime

Oct. 9, King Amendment to grant independence to the Philippines defeated in Senate

Oct. 19, Norris farm export debenture plan added to Tariff Bill adopted by Senate

Nov. 4, Senate adopted Resolution declaring that Senator Bingham in placing Charles L. Eyanson, a worker for tariff-seeking manufacturers, upon the official rolls of the Senate as his aid was "contrary to good morals and senatorial ethics"

Nov. 22, Congress adjourned

Dec. 2, Seventy-First Congress, 2d sess. (1st regular) convened

Dec. 6, The Senate denied seat to Senator Elect William S. Vare, of Pennsylvania, on the grounds of fraud, and also declared the election of his opponent William B. Wilson void, and Dec. 11, Joseph R. Grundy, appointed by the Governor, seated, ending the controversy

Dec. 16, Federal Income Tax Reduction Act cut normal tax for 1929 on incomes under $4,000 from 1½% to ½%, those of $4,000 to $8,000 from 3 to 2%, and over $8,000 from 5 to 4%, and tax on corporations from 12 to 11%

Dec. 18, Radio Commission continued until otherwise provided by law by amendment to Radio Act of 1927

1930

Jan. 1, A Curtiss "Tanager" biplane won the $100,000 Guggenheim prize for "fool-proof" airplanes, after many tests

Jan. 2, Convention with Great Britain signed as to boundary between the Philippines and North Borneo, by which the sovereignty of the United States was recognized as extending over the Turtle Islands, a group of 8 small islands off the eastern coast of British North Borneo

——, Note to China as to procedure for extra-territoriality negotiations

——, Death of George Edward Woodberry (74) author and educator, at Beverley, Mass.

Jan. 3, Death of Claire Briggs (54) newspaper cartoonist, New York City

Jan. 8–13, Successful strike of garment workers, Cleveland, Ohio, won five day and forty-two hour week, elimination of sweat shop and preference of work before sent outside the city

Jan. 9, Treaty with Great Britain signed as to rights of nationals in Iraq

——, Death of Edward W. Bok (66) editor and author, at Mountain Lake, Florida

Jan. 13, Arbitration Treaty with the Netherlands replaced that of May 2, 1908

——, American Cotton Coöperative Association incorporated by Federal Farm Board

Jan. 14, Treaties of arbitration and conciliation with Latvia signed

Jan. 15, Floods in the Wabash-White system of Indiana which caused nearly $7,000,000 loss. National Guard ordered out to protect weakened dam at Hazelton

Jan. 18, Five hundred families evacuated their homes when the St. Francis River levee broke flooding 50,000 acres in southeastern Missouri and northeastern Arkansas

Jan. 20, Secretary of War Hurley extended prohibition to United States military forces throughout the world as a military law

Jan. 21, Unknown planet recorded at Flagstaff, Arizona, Lowell Observatory given the name "Pluto"

Jan. 21–April 22, Naval Conference in London, the United States represented by Henry L. Stimson, Secretary of State, Charles F. Adams, Secretary of the Navy, Charles G. Dawes, Ambassador to Great Britain, Ambassador Dwight Morrow, Admiral William V. Pratt, Rear Admiral Hilary P. Jones, Senator Joseph T. Robinson, Senator David A. Reed, and Ambassador Hugh Gibson

Jan. 25, Riots against Filipino laborers at Watsonville, California

——, The airplane of Carl Ben Eielson and his mechanic, Frank Dorbandt, missing since Nov. 9, found wrecked on the ice near the coast of Siberia at mouth of the Anguema River by Pilots Joseph Crosson and Harold Gillam, and the bodies of the aviators buried in the snow

——, Death of Dr. Harry B. Hutchins (82) former president of University of Michigan

Jan. 30, Death of Bishop Charles P. Anderson (65) head of Protestant Episcopal Church

Jan. 31, Death of William H. P. Faunce (70) president emeritus of Brown University

——, Treaty of extradition with Austria signed

Feb. 3, Federal Farm Board and Cotton Coöperative Association took over handling of cotton

——, Resignation of Chief Justice W. H. Taft of the Supreme Court because of ill health, Charles Evans Hughes nominated by the President to succeed, and appointment confirmed by the Senate Feb. 13

Feb. 4, Strike of 30,000 dress and suit workers in New York City to eliminate piece work (the sweat shop) and regularize employment. Settlements Feb. 10 and 12 included the five day forty hour week

Feb. 7, President Hoover appointed 2 commissions to study conditions in Haiti, W. Cameron Forbes, chairman of the first, and Dr. R. E. Moton of the second to investigate education

——, Federal Reserve Bank of New York reduced rates from 4½ to 4%

Feb. 9, Speech of Philip Snowden, British Cabinet, pointed out that the United States spends more for armaments than any other great power

Feb. 15, Suit filed by the Government against 19 California oil companies to enjoin them from conspiracy to maintain a uniform price for gasoline

——, Charles Evans Hughes resigned as member of Permanent Court of International Justice

Feb. 16, Bishop Manning, of New York, endorsed action of Vatican and Archbishop of Canterbury in denunciation of anti-religious policy of Soviet Russia and invited all faiths to join in special services at the Cathedral of St. John

Feb. 17–March 24, The United States represented at Preliminary Conference for Concerted Economic Action by E. C. Wilson as an observer, at Geneva

Feb. 18, The "City of New York" reached Little

America, and the following day the Byrd Antarctic expedition embarked for New Zealand

Feb. 24, First 5,000,000 share day on New York Stock Exchange since Oct. 10

——, National Bean Marketing Association incorporated by Federal Farm Board

Feb. 27, Death of George Haven Putnam (85) publisher, New York

March 1, Forbes Commission began sessions in Haiti. *See* Haiti

March 3, United States Circuit Court of Appeals reversed conviction of Mrs. Mary Ware Dennett of sending obscene matter through the mails in tract "The Sex Side of Life"

March 4, State memorandum of Dec. 1928 published, held that the Monroe Doctrine covers protection against European aggression and not interference in internal affairs of Latin American countries

——, Coolidge Dam near Globe, Arizona, dedicated by former President for whom it is named

March 6, Death of Arthur Twining Hadley (73) former president of Yale University, at Kobe, Japan

——, Jury acquitted 5 men accused of murder of Ella May Wiggins during strike in Gastonia, North Carolina in Sept. 1929

——, Cotton at 14.5 cents, lowest price since 1927

March 8, Death of William Howard Taft (72) former President and Chief Justice of the Supreme Court, in Washington, and of Edward T. Sanford (64) Justice of the Supreme Court

March 10, Byrd Antarctic Expedition reached Dunedin, New Zealand

——, Miss Elinor Smith established world altitude aëroplane record for women at height unofficially estimated at between 30,000 and 32,000 feet

March 11, Death of Samuel M. Felton (77) engineer and railroad president, Chicago

March 13, Harvard University announced discovery of a hitherto unknown ninth planet, photographed by astronomers of the Lowell Observatory, Flagstaff, Arizona

——, Trial of Edward L. Doheny, oil operator, begun, charged with giving bribe to A. B. Fall, when Secretary of the Interior, for award of Elk Hill oil leases, in District of Columbia Supreme Court

——, New York Reserve Bank rate reduced to 3½%

——, Death of Arthur Sherburne Hardy (82) diplomat and author, at Woodstock, Conn., and Mrs. Mary Eleanor Wilkins Freeman (68) author

March 13–24, Strike of 2,000 garment workers in Boston for 5 day week and 8 hour day and wage increase settled by agreement which granted all demands except wage increase and creation of unemployment fund

March 14, Death of Martin G. Brumbaugh (67) educator and former Governor of Pennsylvania

March 15, The U.S.S. frigate "Constitution" ("Old Ironsides" first launched in 1797) reconditioned by popular subscription, relaunched in Boston

March 17, Death of Frederick Trevor Hill (63) lawyer and author, at Yonkers, New York

March 18, Merger of the Chase National Bank of New York, the Equitable Trust Company, and the Interstate Trust Company, aggregate resources total $3,000,000,000, the combination becoming the world's greatest bank

March 19, Death of Edward Nelson Dingley (68) tariff expert, in Washington

March 20, Death of Rear Admiral Walter R. McLean (74) at Annapolis, Md.

March 21, President Hoover nominated Judge John J. Parker, of North Carolina, as Associate Justice of the Supreme Court; not confirmed by Senate

——, Death of V. Everit Macy (58) banker and philanthropist of New York City

March 22, Edward L. Doheny, oil operator, acquitted of charge of giving a bribe to former Secretary of the Interior Albert B. Fall in connection with the Elk Hills naval oil leases

March 25, New North German Lloyd liner "Europa" on first voyage makes transatlantic record from Cherbourg to New York in 4 days, 17 hours, and 6 minutes

March 26, Forbes Commission Report on Haiti presented, recommended that the United States limit intervention to affairs specifically provided for by treaty or agreement, and existing treaty be further modified, and criticized measures for preparation of Haitians for political and administrative responsibilities as hitherto inadequate

April 1, Census of this date gave total population as 122,775,046 of Continental United States, land area 2,973,776 square miles, representing an increase of 17,064,426 (16.1%) since Jan. 1, 1920. The area of the non-contiguous territory including Alaska, Guam, Hawaii, Philippine Islands, Puerto Rico, American Samoa, the Virgin Islands, Panama Canal Zone, and certain Pacific Islands is 711,606 square miles with a population of 14,233,389, making grand total for territory including both land and water area 3,738,395 square miles, with population of 137,008,435. Total white population 108,864,207, colored 11,891,143, Indians 332,397, Mexicans 1,422,533, Chinese 74,954, Japanese 138,834. The center of population is announced as near Hymera, Indiana, 20 miles from western boundary of State, and nearly 30 miles west of center of 1920. Population of New York City 6,930,446, of Chicago 3,376,438, of Philadelphia 1,950,961, of Detroit 1,568,662

——, Number of unemployed officially announced as 2,508,151 about 2% of population

April 1–2, Flight from New York to Bermuda of Capt. Lewis A. Yancey accompanied by W. H. Alexander and Z. Bouck, actual flying time approximately 8 hours and 30 minutes, in hydroplane "Pilot Radio," spending the night on the ocean when overtaken by darkness 70 miles from Bermuda

April 3, President Hoover opened direct radio telephone communication with South America through station near Buenos Aires, Argentina, talking with Presidents of Chile and Uruguay

April 4, Federal Trade Commission dismissed all monopoly charges instituted against the Aluminum Company of America

April 9, Two-way telephone television demonstrated by officers and engineers of American Telephone and Telegraph Company in New York City

April 10, Stocks on New York Exchange touch year's highest average, 5,600,000 shares sold

April 13, President Hoover issued a Dept. of Justice memorandum defending decision of Judge John J. Parker upholding a "yellow dog" contract injunction, which is one of reasons of opposition to his appointment to the Supreme Court

April 15, Roland W. Boyden, of Boston, appointed by the President to succeed Charles Evans Hughes,

resigned, as member of the Permanent Court of Arbitration at the Hague

April 19, Death of Charles Scribner (76) publisher, New York

April 20, Col. and Mrs. Charles A. Lindbergh make transcontinental flight from Glendale, California, to Roosevelt Field, Long Island, with one stop for fuel at Wichita, Kansas, breaking previous records in 14 hours, 45 minutes, 32 seconds, actual flying time 14 hours, 23 minutes, and 27 seconds

April 22, Gates W. McGarrah made president of Bank for International Settlements at Basle, Switzerland

——, International Treaty for Limitation and Reduction of Naval Armament signed at London by the United States

April 23, First Anti-Prohibition Conference called by women met in Cleveland, Ohio, attended by 400 women who pledged themselves to work for repeal of the Eighteenth Amendment

April 26, Col. C. A. Lindbergh inaugurating air mail service between Miami, Florida and Havana, Cuba, made flight in 2 hours and 3 minutes, and from there on April 27 to Panama Canal Zone, May 1 to Puerto Cabezas, Nicaragua, May 2 at Havana, and Miami, and ended trip at Roosevelt Field, Long Island, May 3, actual flying time less than 9 hours for 12,000 miles

April 27, Telephone communication established between Montreal-Chicago train of the Canadian National Railways, and Washington, Ottawa, and Fort Worth, Texas

April 30, Jack Barstow, in a glider, set an unofficial world record for motorless sustained flight by remaining aloft over San Diego, California, 15 hours and 12 minutes

May 1, Federal Reserve Bank of New York reduced rate of discount from 3½ to 3%

May 1–9, Successful strike of teamsters handling building materials, New York City, for increase of $1 per day and an extra helper

May 3–4, Forest fires destroyed several villages, many farm dwellings, and homes in New Jersey, New Hampshire, Rhode Island, Long Island, and Staten Island

May 5, Supreme Court decision held that sale of liquor-making paraphernalia is illegal when "offered for sale in such a way as purposely to attract purchasers who want them for the unlawful manufacture" of illicit intoxicants, sellers of barrels, bottles, labels, cartons, &c., liable to penalties under the Volstead Act

May 5–31, Successful strike of chauffeurs in the building trades, New York City, for 55 hour week and wage increase gained increase of $2.50 a week

May 6, Interstate Commerce Commission decision that general level of rates relatively low in western trunk line territory and increase justified

May 8, Agreement with Austria signed for settlement of relief indebtedness to the United States

May 9, Treaty with Canada signed for preservation of halibut fishery of northern Pacific and the Bering Sea

——, President Hoover nominated Owen J. Roberts as Associate Justice of Supreme Court which was confirmed by the Senate

May 10, National Livestock Marketing Association incorporated

——, Interstate Commerce Commission decision in eastern rate case gave increase based on principle of mileage basis and increased number of classifications

May 15, Arbitration Treaty with Iceland signed

May 19, Bishop James Cannon, Jr. is exonerated by Committee of the Methodist Episcopal Church, South, of stock market speculation charges brought against him

——, Supreme Court decision that holders of liens on automobiles seized by prohibition officers in connection with alleged violation of the prohibition laws shall be protected

——, Opinion of Chief Justice Hughes in railroad rate case that interstate rates lawful until Interstate Commerce Commission decided they were discriminatory

May 22, For the first time in any theater a television feature act shown in a theater in Schenectady, New York, by Dr. E. F. W. Alexanderson of the General Electric Company

May 23, Nation wide poll on prohibition of the *Literary Digest* announced total votes cast 4,806,464 of which 1,943,052 were for repeal of the Eighteenth Amendment, 1,464,098 for enforcement, and 1,399,-314 for modification to permit sale of light wines and beer

May 24, Most Favored Nation Treaty as to customs signed with Egypt

May 26, Supreme Court decision that the purchaser of intoxicating liquor was not guilty of criminal action under the Eighteenth Amendment and the Volstead Act

——, Provisional Commercial Agreement with Lithuania signed

May 27, Liquor Smuggling Treaty with Chile signed

——, East to west transcontinental flight record made by Lieut. Col. Roscoe Turner in 18 hours and 42 minutes with stop to refuel at Wichita

May 30, Petition signed by over 1,000 leading economists asked the President to refuse to sign the Hawley-Smoot tariff

May 31, The "Graf Zeppelin," Dr. Hugo Eckener in command, arrived at Lakehurst, New Jersey, from Pernambuco, Brazil, with 20 passengers and crew of 42 on board, and left June 2 on return trip to Germany

June 2, Death of Brig. Gen. Herbert M. Lord (70) former Director of the Budget, Washington

June 4, World airplane altitude record made by Lieut. Apollo Soucek, U.S.N. at Anacostia, D.C. at height of 43,166 feet

June 8–9, Stocks break heavily on New York Exchange taking sharpest fall since Dec. 1929

June 10, Decision of Judge James W. Remick, War Claims Arbiter that the United States pay Germany $74,243,000 for 94 ships seized in American ports during the War, payment to be made to the Hamburg-American and North German Lloyd lines during 27 years, chief claimants

June 11–July 4, Kenneth and John Hunter in refueling airplane endurance flight that lasted 553 hours, 41 minutes, and 30 seconds, near Chicago

June 12, German Republic's 5½% "mobilization loan" offered, American part, $98,250,000, offered at 90, and immediately subscribed

June 14, Wheat falls below $1

June 16, Death of Elmer Ambrose Sperry (69) inventor of the gyroscope, in Brooklyn, N.Y.

June 18, Transcontinental airplane record flight made

by Edward F. Schlee and William A. Brock between Jacksonville, Florida, and San Diego, California in 13 hours and 55 minutes

June 18, Sales on New York Stock Exchange totaled 6,425,630, and on Curb Exchange 2,019,000, prices setting new lows for the year

June 19, Official welcome of New York City to Rear Admiral Richard E. Byrd and members of Antarctic polar expedition arrived in New York harbor in the "City of New York," and the "Eleanor Bolling" on the 18th

——, Liquor Smuggling Treaty with Poland signed, and treaties of arbitration and conciliation with Greece

——, Federal Reserve Bank of New York reduced rate to 2½%, lowest in history

June 20, Price of wheat falls to 93¾ cents, and June 25 to 87¾ cents, lowest since 1914

——, President Hoover proposes year's suspension of payment on intergovernmental war debts and German reparations

——, Rear Admiral Byrd and members of Antarctic polar expedition received by the President and Congress, and medal of the National Geographic Society presented to Byrd by President Hoover

——, Roger Q. Williams and 2 companions make non-stop flight of 1,560 miles from New York to Bermuda and back in the "Columbia," in 17 hours and 1 minute

June 23, Reparation Debt Agreement with Germany signed for payment of war claims of the United States and cost of American Army of Occupation

——, Price of cotton fell to 13½ cents, to 13¼ June 24, and 13 cents on June 25

June 25, Stocks break to lowest of year and then recover

——, Death of James K. Vardaman (68) former Senator from Mississippi, of William Barnes (64) Republican leader, New York, and Kuno Francke (74) German-American author, and professor at Harvard University

June 26, Maj. Charles Kingsford Smith in the "Southern Cross" landed at Roosevelt Field, Long Island from Harbor Grace after flight from Ireland to Newfoundland June 23–25, the first airplane to make east-west flight across the North Atlantic to the United States

June 27, Arbitration Treaty with China signed

June 30, Number of aliens admitted during fiscal year 446,214 of whom 241,700 were classed as immigrants, and 272,425 left the United States of whom 50,661 were classed as emigrants, 8,233 aliens denied admission

——, Exports $3,843,181, imports $3,060,908

——, Public debt $16,185,308,299

——, Record of prohibition *see* July 10 and Oct. 4 *infra*

——, United States Circuit Court of Appeals admitted Rev. Douglas C. MacIntosh, of the Yale Divinity School, to citizenship, reversing decision of court of June 24, 1929

——, Death of Dr. Harvey W. Wiley (85) former Chief of Division of Chemistry, in Washington

June–Aug., Drought in mid-western and southern States, rainfall lowest ever recorded

July 1, Enforcement of prohibition transferred from Treasury Dept. to Dept. of Justice on this date, Major Amos W. W. Woodcock in charge as Director of Bureau of Prohibition, Dr. James H. Doran becoming Commissioner of Industrial Alcohol, and head of new Bureau of Industrial Alcohol in the Treasury Dept.

July 1, Decision of Interstate Commerce Commission reduced grain rates in western territory with result of estimated loss to railroads of $20,000,000

——, Italy increased duties on American automobiles by average of 100% as reprisal against new tariff

——, Republican State Convention in New Jersey which nominated Dwight Morrow for United States Senator adopted his demand for repeal of Prohibition Amendment as a plank in its platform, and the Democrats also adopted a repeal plank

July 2–4, Flight of Maj. Charles Kingsford Smith from New York to Oakland, California, completed airplane trip around the world begun May 31, 1928

July 4, John and Kenneth Hunter in the "City of Chicago" landed near Chicago after setting a new world endurance airplane record of 553 hours, and 41½ minutes in air

——, California Supreme Court refused to recommend to the Governor pardon of Thomas J. Mooney and Warren K. Billings

July 6, Miss Amelia Earhart made average speed record of 181.18 miles an hour over a measured 64 mile course, establishing first women's international flight record

July 7, Work begun on Boulder Dam project

July 10, Last report of Prohibition Bureau under the Treasury Dept. stated that during fiscal year ending June 30, 68,186 persons were arrested by federal agents, 1,308 more than the previous year, and 24,373 stills captured as against 17,146 in previous year

July 11, Strike of textile workers at Marion, North Carolina, begun

——, Wheat fell to 86.5 cents, lowest price of year to date

July 12, Treaty of Extradition with Germany signed

July 15, Death of Leopold Auer (85) naturalized Hungarian-American, musician, in Germany, and of Rudolph Schildkraut (65) actor at Hollywood, California

July 18, Agreement of anthracite coal operators and miners on wages for 5½ years, recognition of check-off system, and a modified form of arbitration of disputes

July 22, Spain and New Zealand increased tariff against American goods in reprisal for American tariff

——, Interstate Commerce Commission denied petitions of carriers for modification of railroad consolidation plan of Dec. 21, 1929

July 23, Death of Glenn H. Curtiss (52) pioneer aviator and aviation inventor, at Buffalo, New York

July 23–Aug. 4, Strike of garment workers at Baltimore gained 3 year contract with recognition of the union, a 44 hour week for the first year, and a 40 hour week for the third year, and a definite procedure as to discharge

July 24, Cotton sold at 12.65 cents, lowest of year to date

July 25, Agreement signed with Mexico by Thomas Lamont and De Oca, Mexican Finance Minister, as to foreign debt and debt of national railways of Mexico, to supersede Agreements of 1923 and 1925, providing for total payment of approximately $500,000,000 at 5% over period of 45 years beginning in 1931, and provision made for reorganization of railroads

July 25, Embargo placed on importation of pulpwood from Russia by the Treasury Dept. because of alleged handling by convict labor

July 26, Republicans agreed upon Simeon D. Fess, of Ohio, to succeed Claudius H. Huston as chairman of the Republican National Committee on resignation of Mr. Huston, and Robert H. Lucas, of Kentucky, as chairman of the Executive Committee

July 28, Two cargoes of pulpwood from Archangel, Russia, barred from entry at New York in accordance with embargo of the Treasury Dept., as product of convict labor and therefore barred by tariff law

July 29, Announcement that no discriminatory action against Russian imports into the United States would be taken except as to convict-made goods or those created by forced labor

July 30, Wheat at new low price of 83³/₈ cents selling below corn for first time in 35 years, cotton at 12.45 cents lowest since 1921 except for one day in 1927

July 31, President Hoover announced appointment of a commission headed by Robert T. Lamont, Secretary of Commerce, to investigate problems of home-building and ownership

Aug. 1, Embargo on Russian pulpwood revoked by Treasury Dept. since evidence does not conclusively prove that convict labor is employed in its production, decision affecting 80 cargoes en route to American ports

Aug. 2, National program for coöperation adopted by meeting of representatives of 17 sugar beet producing States at Greeley, Colorado

Aug. 6, Capt. Frank Hawks made flight from New York to Los Angeles establishing new transcontinental record in 14 hours, 50 minutes, and 43 seconds, averaging 179 miles an hour, made 5 stops for fuel

Aug. 7, Corn sold at $1.02¾, highest price of year

Aug. 8, Agreement signed by anthracite coal miners and operators renewed for 5½ years wage agreement and check off in modified form, to take effect Sept. 1

Aug. 13, Capt. Frank Hawks made flight from Los Angeles to New York establishing new record in 12 hours, 25 minutes, and 3 seconds at average rate of 215 miles per hour, making 3 stops for refueling, previous record made by Col. and Mrs. C. A. Lindbergh of 14¾ hours in April

——, National Beet Grower's Association incorporated

Aug. 14, Conference of Governors of States affected by drought called by the President met at the White House, agreed that a federal committee should be appointed and state drought committees composed of state officials, and farmers and bankers, and representatives of the Red Cross to recommend relief measures. National Drought Committee, Secretary Hyde, chairman, appointed by the President on the 19th

——, Death of Bishop James H. Darlington (74) of Harrisburg, Pennsylvania

Aug. 15, Col. Lindbergh received from President Hoover special medal awarded by Congress

Aug. 17, World airplane duration record refueling during flight made by Dale Jackson and Forrest O'Brien near St. Louis, remaining in air 647 hours, 28 minutes and 30 seconds, making 223 contacts with refueling planes

Aug. 18, Cotton sold at 11 cents lowest price since 1921

Aug. 18–25, Strike of cotton employees at Bessemer City, North Carolina, against proposed wage reduction of 20% successful

Aug. 19, Federal Farm Board agreed to make loans on cotton

Aug. 20, State Convention of Illinois Democrats demanded repeal of Volstead Act and laws legalizing light wines and beers

——, Most Favored Nation Treaty as to customs signed with Rumania

Aug. 21, Rio Grande Boundary Commission Report as between Mexico and the United States recommending straightening of river between El Paso and Fort Quitman signed by President Hoover

Aug. 22, Henry P. Fletcher, of Pennsylvania, appointed chairman of the new Tariff Commission to take office Sept. 16

Aug. 23, Death of Henry Rogers Seager (60) economist, author, educator, in Russia

Aug. 25, Mid-Hudson Suspension Bridge connecting Poughkeepsie and Highland, New York opened to traffic

Aug. 26, Baron von Gronau and 3 companions arrived in New York in flight from Germany begun Aug. 18 from Isle of Sylt, after stops at Faroe Islands, Iceland, Greenland, Labrador, and Nova Scotia

Aug. 30, Death of Major General Henry T. Allen (71) who commanded American Army of Occupation in Germany, in Washington

Sept. 1, William Randolph Hearst, newspaper proprietor, expelled from France by the authorities because of his alleged anti-French journalist activities in publishing secret document relative to the Franco-British naval negotiations

Sept. 2, Capt. Dieudonné Coste and Maurice Bellonte landed at Curtiss Airport, Long Island, in first nonstop airplane flight from Paris to New York, in the "Question Mark," time 37 hours and 18 minutes, and 30 seconds, distance 4,100 miles, the 5th westward transatlantic flight, and first non-stop from Europe to the United States

Sept. 3, First electric passenger train on the Lackawanna Railroad from Hoboken to Montclair, New Jersey, operated by Thomas A. Edison

Sept. 7, Death of Simon W. Straus (64) banker and philanthropist, New York City

Sept. 9, State Dept. ordered labor immigration restricted because of unemployment

Sept. 13–18, In races for the cup "America" the American yacht "Enterprise" of Harold S. Vanderbilt, beat Sir Thomas Lipton's yacht "Shamrock V" in 4 races out of 7

Sept. 16, Eugene Meyer, Jr., of New York took oath of office as Governor of the Federal Reserve Board, succeeding Roy A. Young resigned

——, Canada raised tariff rates on 130 articles in retaliation for American tariff

Sept. 17, Judge Frank B. Kellogg elected by Assembly and Council of the League of Nations at Geneva to fill the unexpired term of Charles Evans Hughes resigned

——, Work begun on $165,000,000 Boulder Dam at Las Vegas, Nevada, in official ceremony, Secretary of the Interior Wilbur announcing that the name Hoover Dam will be given in honor of the President

——, Admiral William V. Pratt succeeded Admiral Hughes as Chief of Naval Operations, and Admiral J. V. Chase made Commander-in-Chief of the Navy

Sept. 18, The United States formally recognized new provisional governments of Argentina, Bolivia, and Peru

Sept. 18, Death of Ruth Alexander (Mrs. R. A. Elliott) aviator (24) in crash of her monoplane near San Diego, California

——, Copper reached new low price at 10.5 cents

Sept. 19, Secretary of Agriculture Arthur M. Hyde accused the Russian Government of contributing to the fall in the price of wheat by selling short 7,500,000 bushels in Chicago market

——, Louisiana Senate concurred in action of House of Sept. 17 voting a nolle prosse of impeachment proceedings of 1929 against Governor Huey P. Long, and adjourned Sept. 22 after ratification of practically the entire Long program of expenditure, bond issue, and taxation

Sept. 22, Cotton sold at 10.75 cents, lowest since 1912 except during brief period at beginning of World War in 1914

——, Death of Henry Phipps (90) steel manufacturer and philanthropist, at Great Neck, Long Island

Sept. 25, Judge Frank B. Kellogg, filling unexpired term of C. E. Hughes as member of Permanent Court of International Justice, elected for 9 year term beginning Jan. 1, 1931

——, Strike of 2,550 women's tailors and dressmakers in New York City for increase in wages and improved working conditions begun which lasted 2 months

Sept. 26, Republican State Convention of New York State declared for repeal of prohibition law by vote of 733 to 258

Sept. 27, Prohibition Commissioner Woodcock announced that "search warrants issued against private homes can be obtained only on the presentation of evidence of sales," and the difficulty of getting evidence places manufacture of wine and beer in the home virtually beyond the reach of federal interference

Sept. 28, Representative John M. Garner, member of congressional committee, made public list of 17 men contributing $10,000 each to the congressional campaign expenses of Republican Party, who, he says, received heavy personal tax refunds or were connected with corporations that have received such refunds

——, Death of Daniel Guggenheim (74) capitalist and philanthropist notably in the development of aviation, at Port Washington, Long Island

Sept. 29, Wheat sold at 72.75 cents, the lowest since Jan. 1907

——, Unsuccessful strike of 4,000 cotton mill workers at Danville, Virginia, for recognition begun which lasted until Jan. 29, 1931

Oct. 1, Capt. Frank Hawks made flight from Detroit to New York in 2 hours and 41 minutes, new record

Oct. 3, Joshua R. Clark, Jr., of Salt Lake City, appointed to succeed Dwight Morrow, resigned, as Ambassador to Mexico

——, Secretary Wilbur suspended Ralph S. Kelley from Land Office, Denver, and asked him to name companies he has accused of obtaining land grants by fraud and political pressure

Oct. 4, Bureau of Prohibition estimated the possible production of illicit liquor for fiscal year ending June 30 as 876,320,718 gallons

Oct. 7, Cotton sold at 10.15 cents, new low

Oct. 8, Secretary of the Navy Adams issued orders converting or decommissioning 46 ships and reducing enlisted men by 4,800 to conform with London Naval Treaty, the reduction of tonnage amounting to about

120,000 tons including 14 submarines, 16 destroyers, and the battleship "Utah"

Oct. 8, Capt. Frank M. Hawks made flight from Philadelphia to New York in 20 minutes averaging 270 miles an hour, the fastest time ever made off a standard race course

Oct. 9, Trading on the New York Stock Exchange totaled 5,050,600 shares with severe break in stocks led by U.S. Steel and establishment of new lows. Failure of Prince & Whitely announced and receivership

Oct. 9–10, Capt. J. Errol Boyd (Canadian) and Lieut. Harry P. Connor (U.S. Naval Reserve Officer) made flight from Harbor Grace, Newfoundland, to Tresco, Scilly Islands, off coast of England, on attempted non-stop flight to London, time 24 hours and 5 minutes

Oct. 17, President Hoover announced creation of Committee for Employment of Secretaries of the Cabinet and Governor of Federal Reserve Bank to formulate and submit plans for relief, Col. Arthur Woods chosen to manage program

——, On New York Stock Exchange average of stocks go for first time below low of Nov. 1929

Oct. 21, Resignation of Felix Warburg, chairman of the administrative committee of the Jewish Agency for Palestine as protest against British policy as published Oct. 20

Oct. 22, President Hoover declared arms embargo against the revolutionists of Brazil

Oct. 23, Copper reached price of 9.275 lowest since 1895 followed by agreement to reduce output

Oct. 26, Federal Farm Board offered to loan to cooperative associations on wheat up to stated values

——, Dept. of Commerce decision that no merit or substance in charges of Ralph S. Kelley that valuable oil shale lands are in danger of being lost to the Government

Oct. 29, Nobel prize for medicine awarded to Dr. Karl Landsteiner, member of Rockefeller Institute of Medical Research

——, Statement of Secretary Mellon that "the underlying causes of the present world-wide depression could be traced primarily to overproduction"

Nov. 1, Tunnel under Detroit River between Detroit and Windsor, Canada, formally opened

——, Treaty with Norway signed regulating liability for military service for persons of so-called dual nationality

Nov. 4, Congressional elections resulted in Democratic gains, and reduction of Republican majorities in House from 103 to 2, and in Senate from 16 to 0. Massachusetts voted for repeal of state prohibition enforcement law, Illinois voted repeal of Prohibition Amendment and state prohibition enforcement law, and modification of Volstead Act, and Rhode Island for repeal

Nov. 5, Break in stock market carried prices to new low for the year

——, Sinclair Lewis awarded Nobel prize for literature for his novel "Babbitt"

Nov. 6, Capt. Frank Hawks made flight from New York to Havana, Cuba, in 8 hours, 38 minutes

Nov. 7, Seven national leaders of the Democratic party—James M. Cox, John W. Davis, Alfred E. Smith, Joseph T. Robinson, John M. Garner, John J. Raskob, and Jouett Shouse—unite in a statement offering the minority party's coöperation in every measure conducing to the public welfare

Nov. 8, New Government of Brazil recognized by the United States

Nov. 9, Capt. Frank Hawks makes flight from Havana, Cuba, to New York, return trip, actual flying time 8 hours and 44 minutes

——, Death of General Tasker Howard Bliss (77) Chief of Staff of Army in World War, in Washington

Nov. 9–10, First solo non-stop flight from New York to Panama Canal Zone made by Capt. Roy W. Ammel in 24 hours and 35 minutes

Nov. 11, Death of Gen. Coleman du Pont (67) former Senator from Delaware in Wilmington, Delaware

Nov. 13, State Dept. issued statement on extraterritoriality

——, Receivership entered into by Caldwell and Co., investment brokers, Nashville, Tennessee, caused failure of several banks including the State Bank of Tennessee

Nov. 14, Mixed Claims Commission at Hamburg decided against $40,000,000 claim of Americans in connection with Black Tom explosion in July, 1916, and destruction of munitions plant at Kingsland, N.J. 6 months later allegedly by German agents. On Sept. 24 the German chief counsel before Commission admitted that German agents had infected horses and mules in American cities during 1915 and 1916, but denied responsibility for the Black Tom and Kingsland explosions, the Black Tom believed to be caused by sparks from watchman's fire

Nov. 17–28, United States represented by Prentiss Gilbert as official "observer" at Preliminary Conference for Economic Action of the League of Nations, 2d session, at Geneva

Nov. 18, American Bar Association announced that a vote of its members taken by mail resulted in 13,779 for repeal of Prohibition Amendment and 6,340 against

Nov. 20, Maj. Gen. Douglas MacArthur succeeded Gen. Charles P. Summerall as Chief of Staff of Army

Nov. 24, Treasury Dept. placed on importers the burden of proof that goods alleged to have been produced by convict labor not so produced

——, Supreme Court decisions found motion picture producers, one group headed by the Paramount-Famous-Lasky Corporation, and the other by First National Pictures guilty of violation of the Sherman Anti-Trust Act

Nov. 27, Nobel Peace Prize awarded to Judge Frank B. Kellogg, former Secretary of State

Nov. 28, President Hoover appointed William N. Doak, of Virginia, legislative agent of the Brotherhood of Railway Trainmen, Secretary of Labor, to succeed James J. Davis resigned; confirmed by Senate Dec. 8

Nov. 30, Death of Mary Jones (Mother Jones) labor leader (100) at Silver Spring, Maryland

Dec. 1, California Supreme Court refused to recommend a pardon for Warren K. Billings convicted of charges of complicity in bomb case of July, 1916 at San Francisco on basis of testimony of J. MacDonald who declared his testimony of 1916 false. Decision also affects Thomas J. Mooney also serving life sentence for complicity in same crime

——, Farm price of wheat of 61 cents a bushel lowest price reported on this date since 1899, 41.5% lower than average price of Dec. 1, 1929, and the farm price of corn for grain 66 cents a bushel compared with 78 cents of 1929

Dec. 1, Court of Appeals District of Columbia upheld federal authority to refuse permits to prospect for oil and gas on public lands

Dec. 6, Interstate Commerce Commission ordered the Pennsylvania Company, subsidiary of the Pennsylvania Railroad, to divest itself within 6 months of its 48% stock ownership of the Wabash Railroad and 30% stock ownership of the Lehigh Valley, aggregate investment of $106,592,757, as violation of Clayton Anti-Trust Act; announced that Pennsylvania Railroad will take divestment order to the courts

Dec. 7, Judge Ben B. Lindsey, of Denver, ejected from Cathedral of St. John the Divine, New York City, on charge of disturbing public worship, after challenging Bishop Manning's denunciation of his book on companionate marriage. Set free by court Dec. 17

Dec. 10, Miss Ruth Nichols established new transcontinental airplane record for women in flight from Los Angeles to Roosevelt Field, Long Island, with stop at Wichita, Kansas, actual flying time 13 hours and 22 minutes, more than an hour less than the time of Col. and Mrs. Lindbergh, and within 2 hours of time of Capt. F. M. Hawks

——, Announcement of new denaturing element discovered making possible elimination of poisons from industrial alcohol

Dec. 11, Bank of United States in New York City with 60 branches and 400,000 depositors suspended payments, closed by the State Superintendent of Banks, largest banking suspension in history of the State, and first failure of New York City Bank since the depression

Dec. 12, Sale of American-Diamond and American-France Lines by Shipping Board

——, Death of Lee Slater Overman (76) Senator from North Carolina, in Washington

Dec. 14, National Economic League announced result of a vote of members that 55% favored repeal of Prohibition Amendment

Dec. 15, Heavy break in bonds on New York Stock Exchange. Cotton falls below 9.50 cents, decline of 15% during the month

——, Foreign Governments paid the United States $122,989,449 on war debts, Great Britain paying $86,000,000

Dec. 16, Judge William Clark in Federal District Court of Northern New Jersey ruled that the Prohibition Amendment (XVIIIth) to the Constitution was invalid because not adopted by constitutional conventions as prescribed by Article 10 of the Constitution

Dec. 17, Agreement with Sweden signed as to war claims

Dec. 21, New Federal Water Power Commission appointed Claude L. Draper, R. B. Williamson, Marcel Garsaud, G. O. Smith, and Frank R. McNinch

Dec. 23, First act of Federal Water Power Commission to dismiss 2 employees of the former Commission, Charles A. Russell, solicitor, William V. King, chief accountant, much criticized and Senate in Jan. requested the President to return the nominations of the members for reconsideration

——, Chelsea Bank, New York City, closed as result of run on bank

——, Federal Reserve Bank of New York reduced discount rate to 2%, lowest in history

Dec. 23, Death of Christina Merriman, first Secretary of Foreign Policy Association, New York

Dec. 26, Price of wheat at 62.75 cents. Reserve System's gold holdings at lowest of year

——, Ruling of Secretary Hyde that the presence of corn sugar (dextrose) in prepared foods need no longer be declared on the label, removing restrictions of Food and Drug Act in effect since 1906

Dec. 30, President Hoover announced agreement of Eastern Railroads on plan for creation of 4 systems to be submitted to Interstate Commerce Commission calling for creation of a greater Baltimore and Ohio Railroad with mileage of 11,156, a combined Chesapeake and Ohio and Nickel Plate system with 12,554 mileage, a greater New York Central with mileage of 12,920, and a greater Pennsylvania Railroad with mileage of 16,548

Dec. 31, International Convention on military obligations in cases of double nationality signed by the United States

——, Commercial failures as reported by R. G. Dun and Co. 26,355 with liabilities of $668,283,842 as compared with 22,109 in 1929, and bank failures reported as 1,326 representing 903,954,000 depositors

Dec., National Wool Marketing Corporation incorporated with assistance of Federal Farm Board

CONGRESS

Jan. 13, President Hoover submitted preliminary Report of the Wickersham Law Enforcement Committee which reported the criminal law enforcement of the country entirely inadequate with covering message urging strengthened prohibition enforcement with 6 specific recommendations

Jan. 16, Senate voted to leave sugar duties unchanged by 48 to 38

Jan. 22, An additional $3,000,000 appropriated for Puerto Rican Hurricane Relief Commission

Jan. 31, Cement restored to free list by vote of 40 to 35 in Senate

Feb. 7, $5,386,367 appropriated to enable mothers and widows of members of the military and naval forces of the United States whose graves were in Europe to make pilgrimages to cemeteries. During the calendar year 3,634 of the 14,134 listed as eligible made the trip to Europe

Feb. 17, Senate voted 41 to 39 to reduce the duty on aluminum

March 3, Appropriation of $7,000,000 authorized for loans to farmers by Secretary of Agriculture in drought and flood stricken States

March 5, Increased sugar duties adopted by Senate by vote of 47 to 39, duty on Cuban sugar raised from 1.76 to 2 cents a pound, and on foreign sugar from 2.20 of House Bill to 2.50 cents a pound

March 7, Senate adopted a duty on cement by vote of 45 to 37 of 6 cents a hundredweight

March 20, Duty on lumber (soft woods) of $1.50 per thousand feet favorable to views of Grundy high tariff group adopted in Senate by vote of 39 to 38, reversing vote of Feb. 27

March 24, Tariff Bill passed in Senate by vote of 53 to 31, with a total of 1,253 amendments to original House Bill

March 31, Act authorized appropriation of $230,000,000 for erection of public buildings in all sections of the country, half of the total to be expended in the District of Columbia, expenditure to cover a term of years

April 4, Federal Aid Road Act amended, appropriated $300,000,000 for highway construction assistance to States, $50,000,000 for 1931, and the regular subsidy for 1932 and 1933 increased to $125,000,000

——, Norris Resolution for government operation of Muscle Shoals properties adopted in Senate by vote of 45 to 23

April 10, Wagner Relief Bill creating a Federal Employment Service passed the Senate

April 12, Federal Reserve Act amended as to limitations upon the rediscount by member banks

April 15, Testimony of Representative Tinkham before Committee that the Anti-Saloon League had not made full report of its expenditures as required by law and that Bishop James J. Cannon had not reported $48,000 of $65,300 contributed by E. C. Jameson during campaign in 1928. Cannon denied authority of Committee to require testimony from him

April 17, Federal Reserve Act amended to permit member banks to withdraw without waiting 6 months after filing intention

April 21, Senate Judiciary Committee voted 10 to 6 to report adversely upon the nomination of Judge John J. Parker, of North Carolina, to the Supreme Court because of opposition of negroes because of derogatory remarks about them made by the Judge in political campaign in 1920, and of labor because of a decision upholding individual contracts between employers and workers in which workers agreed to refrain from joining a union during the period of their employment in 1922

April 23, Federal Reserve Act amended as to bank liquidation

April 29, Air Mail Act amended, award of contracts to lowest responsible bidder provided for

May 1, London Naval Treaty sent to Senate by the President and referred to Committee on Foreign Relations

——, Testimony to Senate Committee gave expenditures of Representative Ruth Hanna McCormick in campaign in senatorial primary election in Illinois as $244,857.49 in which she won Republican nomination over Senator Charles S. Deneen whose expenditure was $24,493.21

May 3, House rejected Senate amendments to Tariff Bill, the debenture plan of an export bounty on certain farm products by vote of 231 to 161, and the repeal of the flexible provision of tariff law giving President power to raise or lower rates by vote of 236 to 154

May 6, Testimony of Edward C. Jameson before Senate Lobby Investigation Committee that at direction of Bishop Cannon he had divided amount paid to Bishop Cannon for campaign expenditures so that it would appear as $17,300 paid to the headquarters committee of the anti-Smith Democrats, and $48,000 to Virginia Committee of the anti-Smith Democrats

May 7, The Senate by vote of 41 to 39 refused to confirm appointment of Judge John J. Parker by the President to be an Associate Justice of the Supreme Court, first Supreme Court rejection in 36 years

May 13, Act approved settlement of suit against Sinclair Crude Oil Purchasing Company in naval oil lease case for $2,906,484

May 14, Act to Reorganize the Administration of Federal Prisons created Bureau of Prisons

May 19, Deadlock over Tariff Bill ended by Senate surrender to House and the Administration on export debenture clause of Senate Bill by vote of 43 to 41, and on flexible provision as to power of President to reduce rates by 43 to 42

May 20, Senate confirmed nomination by the President of May 9 of Owen J. Roberts to Supreme Court to succeed the late Edwin T. Sanford

May 26, Act established National Institute of Health

May 27, Prohibition Reorganization Act transferred enforcement from the Treasury Dept. to the Dept. of Justice, Bureau of Prohibition created, and Director of Bureau to be appointed by the President

May 28, Bill proposing an $11,712,000 pension increase for Spanish War veterans vetoed by the President, as omitting exception as to cases of disability resulting from vicious habits, and pension granted when disability not incurred in service

——, House Committee substituted measure for leasing Muscle Shoals plant to private interests for operation rejecting Norris plan adopted by Senate April 4 for government operation

June 2, Spanish War Pension Increase of $11,712,000 passed over the veto, in the Senate by vote of 61 to 18 and in the House by 298 to 14. Minimum length of service required reduced from 90 to 70 days

——, Report to Senate Committee disclosed that $362,547 was spent in campaign in Pennsylvania for Davis-Brown ticket, $338,000 for Senator Grundy, and $200,000 for Francis H. Bohlen

June 3 and 11, Bishop Cannon refused to answer questions of Senate Lobby Investigating Committee as to his anti-Smith activities in campaign in 1928, challenging authority of Committee and declaring he believed the inquiry an attack to impair his influence and persecution by "the wet and Roman Catholic press" and June 5 walked out of hearing room, challenging Committee to subpœna him

June 5, Act provided for expansion of foreign service of the Dept. of Agriculture

——, Act to authorize settlement of indebtedness of Germany to the United States as to reparations according to plan as negotiated

June 9, Pensions of Civil War veterans and their widows increased at cost estimated to be upwards of $13,000,000, minimum rate $75 a month

——, Vocational Rehabilitation Act amended

June 11, Act provided for Division of Identification and Information in the Dept. of Justice as clearing house for criminal identification records

June 13, Conference Report on Tariff adopted in both Houses, in House by vote of 222 to 153, and in Senate by 44 to 42

——, Act provided for admission of Chinese wives of certain American citizens in cases where marriage prior to May 26, 1924, as nonquota alien

June 14, Bureau of Narcotics created in Treasury Dept. replacing Federal Narcotics Board

June 17, Tariff Act raised duties on 890 articles, chiefly on agricultural products including cattle, meats, dairy products, fruits and vegetables, placed duty of 7 cents a pound on cotton of $1\frac{1}{8}$ inch staple or over, raised general duty on sugar to 2.5 from 2.2, on Cuban sugar from 1.76 to 2 raw, duties on wool increased, and on building materials. Cement, bricks, hides, and boots and shoes removed from free list. Average *ad valorem* rate estimated as 41.57% as compared with 38.24 of the Fordney-McCumber Act of 1922 for dutiable articles. Automobiles taxed 10%. Average *ad valorem* increase on earthenware and glass ware from 29.22 to 31.40%, metals and metal manufactures from 33.71 to 35.01%, wood and wood manufactures from 7.97 to 10.49%, sugar, molasses, and manufactures from 67.85 to 77.21%, tobacco and manufactures from 63.09 to 64.78%, agricultural products from 19.86 to 33.62%, wool and woolen manufactures from 49.54 to 59.83%, cotton 40.27 to 46.42%, &c.

June 17, Censorship of books imported as to judgment for obscenity or treason vested in the district courts by the Tariff Act

June 18, Senate Resolution directed Tariff Commission to investigate differences in cost of production in this country and abroad of shoes, cement, furniture, farm implements, bells, wire fencing and netting

June 21, Act authorized repatriation of war veterans who had lost citizenship by taking oath of allegiance to enter military service of countries later allies of the United States

June 23, Federal Water Power Act amended provided for appointment of a Commission of 5 members to replace Cabinet Secretaries

June 26, World War Veteran's Bill carrying an appropriation of $102,000,000 vetoed by the President as giving war disability benefits to from 75,000 to 100,000 men not disabled as a result of the war, and increase of the $102,000,000 to $225,000,000 as ultimate maximum

——, Federal Reserve Act amended as to election of directors of banks, trust powers rights, and assessments of costs of examinations

July 1, Passport fees reduced from $9 to $5

July 3, Act of Sept. 22, 1922 amended to permit American women who lost citizenship by marriage to aliens to become citizens if eligible by simplified procedure

——, Act authorized international tribunals to administer oaths

——, Veterans' Administration Act consolidated all agencies for relief of veterans, Veterans' Bureau, National Home for Disabled Soldiers, former Bureau of Pensions, &c., disability allowances authorized in case "of 25% of more permanent disability" though "not acquired in the service during the World War, or, for which compensation is not payable," but not to be paid for illness incurred through wilful misconduct

——, Rivers and Harbors Act authorized 15 year program of waterway development at estimated cost of $144,881,902 and federalization of Erie Canal and Illinois Waterway

July 3, Congress adjourned

July 7, One of Wagner's relief measures as to statistics on unemployment passed

July 7-21, Special Session of Senate to consider the London Treaty for Limitation of Naval Armaments of April 22

July 8, Amendment to Pure Food Act of 1906 granted authority to the Secretary of Agriculture to make legal standards for food products and enforce them

July 10, Resolution adopted requesting the President to transmit to the Senate all documents and other data bearing on the Treaty, which was refused by the President July 11 as a breach of trust which would betray foreign confidence necessary to the "protection of future negotiations" and as against the public interest

July 15, Congressional Committee headed by Hamilton Fish, Jr., began investigation of communist propaganda in schools

July 21, Naval Armaments Treaty ratified by the Senate conditional to there being no "secret files, documents, letters, understandings or agreements" modification of the Treaty, and the President signed it the following day

Nov. 18, Reapportionment of seats in the House announced by the President, on basis of new census 21 States losing 27 seats which 11 States with increased population gain. House membership of 435 not changed. California gained 9 additional seats, Michigan 4, Texas 3, New York, New Jersey, and Ohio 2, Connecticut, Florida, North Carolina, Oklahoma, and Washington each 1

Dec. 1, Seventy-First Congress, 3d sess. convened

Dec. 2, President Hoover asked Congress for $150,000,-000 to aid unemployed

Dec. 10, President Hoover submitted to Senate for ratification the 3 Protocols signed Dec. 9, 1929 for adherence of the United States to the Permanent Court of International Justice

Dec. 20, Joint Resolution appropriated $45,000,000 for agricultural relief in drought and storm stricken areas for loans for purchase of seed, fertilizer, feed, and gasoline, &c.

——, Act provided for emergency construction to provide employment and appropriated $16,000,000 for building of roads, harbors, &c.

Dec. 22, $150,000,000 appropriated for addition to Federal Farm Board revolving fund

Since the adoption of the Constitution the offices of President and Vice-President have been occupied as follows:—

PRESIDENTS OF THE UNITED STATES

NAME	FROM STATE	TERM OF SERVICE	BORN	DIED
George Washington	Virginia	1789-1797	1732	1799
John Adams	Massachusetts	1797-1801	1735	1826
Thomas Jefferson	Virginia	1801-1809	1743	1826
James Madison	Virginia	1809-1817	1751	1836
James Monroe	Virginia	1817-1825	1759	1831
John Quincy Adams	Massachusetts	1825-1829	1767	1848
Andrew Jackson	Tennessee	1829-1837	1767	1845
Martin Van Buren	New York	1837-1841	1782	1862
William H. Harrison	Ohio	March-Apr. 1841	1773	1841
John Tyler	Virginia	1841-1845	1790	1862
James K. Polk	Tennessee	1845-1849	1795	1849

PRESIDENTS OF THE UNITED STATES (Continued)

NAME	FROM STATE	TERM OF SERVICE	BORN	DIED
Zachary Taylor	Louisiana	1849–1850	1784	1850
Millard Fillmore	New York	1850–1853	1800	1874
Franklin Pierce	New Hampshire	1853–1857	1804	1869
James Buchanan	Pennsylvania	1857–1861	1791	1868
Abraham Lincoln	Illinois	1861–1865	1809	1865
Andrew Johnson	Tennessee	1865–1869	1808	1875
Ulysses S. Grant	Illinois	1869–1877	1822	1885
Rutherford B. Hayes	Ohio	1877–1881	1822	1893
James A. Garfield	Ohio	March–Sept. 1881	1831	1881
Chester A. Arthur	New York	1881–1885	1830	1886
Grover Cleveland	New York	1885–1889	1837	1908
Benjamin Harrison	Indiana	1889–1893	1833	1901
Grover Cleveland	New York	1893–1897	1837	1908
William McKinley	Ohio	1897–1901	1843	1901
Theodore Roosevelt	New York	1901–1909	1858	1919
William H. Taft	Ohio	1909–1913	1857	1930
Woodrow Wilson	New Jersey	1913–1921	1856	1924
Warren Gamaliel Harding	Ohio	1921–1923	1865	1923
Calvin Coolidge	Massachusetts	1923–1929	1872	1933
Herbert Clark Hoover	California	1929–1933	1874	—

VICE-PRESIDENTS OF THE UNITED STATES

NAME	FROM STATE	TERM OF SERVICE	BORN	DIED
John Adams	Massachusetts	1789–1797	1735	1826
Thomas Jefferson	Virginia	1797–1801	1743	1826
Aaron Burr	New York	1801–1805	1756	1836
George Clinton	New York	1805–1812	1739	1812
Elbridge Gerry	Massachusetts	1813–1814	1744	1814
Daniel D. Tompkins	New York	1817–1825	1774	1825
John C. Calhoun	South Carolina	1825–1832	1782	1850
Martin Van Buren	New York	1833–1837	1782	1862
Richard M. Johnson	Kentucky	1837–1841	1780	1850
John Tyler	Virginia	March–Apr. 1841	1790	1862
George M. Dallas	Pennsylvania	1845–1849	1792	1864
Millard Fillmore	New York	1849–1850	1800	1874
William R. King	Alabama	1853	1786	1853
John C. Breckinridge	Kentucky	1857–1861	1821	1875
Hannibal Hamlin	Maine	1861–1865	1809	1891
Andrew Johnson	Tennessee	March–Apr. 1865	1808	1875
Schuyler Colfax	Indiana	1869–1873	1823	1885
Henry Wilson	Massachusetts	1873–1875	1812	1875
William A. Wheeler	New York	1877–1881	1819	1887
Chester A. Arthur	New York	March–Sept. 1881	1830	1886
Thomas A. Hendricks	Indiana	Mar.–Nov. 25, 1885	1819	1885
Levi P. Morton	New York	1889–1893	1824	1920
Adlai E. Stevenson	Illinois	1893–1897	1835	1914
Garret A. Hobart	New Jersey	1897–1899	1844	1899
Theodore Roosevelt	New York	March–Sept., 1901	1858	1919
Charles W. Fairbanks	Indiana	1905–1909	1855	1920
James S. Sherman	New York	1909–1912	1855	1912
Thomas R. Marshall	Indiana	1913–1921	1854	1925
Calvin Coolidge	Massachusetts	1921–1923	1872	1933
Charles G. Dawes	Illinois	1925–1929	1865	—
Charles Curtis	Kansas	1929–1933	1860	—

UNITED STATES DEPENDENCIES

ALASKA

Alaska, Territory of the United States, is situated in northwest North America bounded on the north by the Arctic Ocean, on the east by Canada, on the south by the Pacific Ocean, and on the west by the Bering Sea and Strait and Arctic Ocean, total area 590,884 square miles, nearly equal to one-fifth of continental United States and twice the size of Texas the largest State. The total coast line is 15,132 miles, the mainland 6,542 miles, the adjacent islands 8,590 miles. The Aleutian Islands extend 1,200 miles west from the southwestern end of the Alaskan peninsula toward the Kamchatka Peninsula with an area of 6,391 square miles. Other Alaskan islands include the Pribilof Islands, the Hall and St. Matthew Islands, St. Lawrence Island, and Nunivak, and Kodiak. Alaska was purchased by the United States from Russia under Treaty of March 30, 1867 for $7,200,000; General Rousseau took formal possession Oct. 18. Organized as a Territory Aug. 24, 1912. For discovery and exploration see America. Gold was discovered in the Klondike region in 1896. The total population in 1930 was 58,758 as compared with 55,036 in 1920 not including about 20,000 persons employed in mines, canneries, and railway construction who spend a few months in the year in the Territory. The largest town, Juneau, the capital has a population of 4,037; the second largest, Ketchikan with 3,786; Fairbanks, 2,099; Anchorage, 2,276; Petersburg, 1,249; Nome, 1,213; Sitka, 1,053.

George A. Parks, Governor.

GUAM

The Island of Guam, situated at the southern extremity of the Mariana Archipelago, in latitude 13° 26′ N., longitude 144° 43′ E., is the largest island of that group. It was ceded by Spain to the United States by the Treaty of Paris (December 10, 1898). It is a Naval Station and saluting port under the jurisdiction of the Navy Department of the United States. A garrison of marines and a shore naval force are maintained.

Guam lies 3,300 miles west by south from Honolulu and is 1,500 miles east of Luzon, Philippines.

The length of the island is 32 miles, the breadth from 4 to 10 miles, and the area 210 square miles. Agaña, the seat of Government, is about eight miles from the anchorage in Apra Harbor. The port of entry is Piti. The number of inhabitants (including the military establishment and non-native residents) on June 30, 1930, was 19,139, of whom 17,437 were classed as natives.

Willis W. Bradley, Jr., Commander United States Navy, Governor.

1521

March 6, Island of Guam discovered by Magellan on his voyage around the world. He first named the group of islands "Islas de Velas Latinas" because of the prowess of the natives in canoes with huge triangular sails but changed the name before he left to "Ladrone" (Robber Islands). In the seventeenth century they were renamed "Marianas" in honor of Maria Anna de Austria

1565

Jan. 22, Expedition from Spain commanded by Miguel Lopez de Legaspi rediscovered the "Marianas" and landed and took possession for the Crown of Spain
Jan. 25, Augustinian fathers celebrated first mass on Islands

1588

Jan. 3, Guam visited by the English buccaneer Thomas Cavendish

1638

The ship "Concepcion" wrecked on shores of "Tinian," and a few survivors made their way to Guam. One man Pedro found there in 1668

1668

June 15, Padre Diego Luis de Sanvitores, Jesuit, from Mexico founded first mission
June 16, Captain Juan de Santa Cruz, military commander of Island

1669

Feb. 2, First church named *Dulce Nombre de Maria* built of stone and lime formally opened

1672

April 2, Murder of Padre Sanvitos by natives who were in continuous war with the Spaniards
May 2, Captain Damian de Esplana appointed military commander

1674

June 16, Don Damian de Esplana arrived and began campaign for conquest of the natives

1676

June 10, Captain Francisco de Irisarri, Governor, arrived and continued war to subdue the natives

1678

June 21, Arrival of new Governor Captain Juan Antonio de Salas

1680

June 5, Major Jose Quiroga, Governor. He captured Matapang and Hirao, murderers of Sanvitores and Aguarin, leader of insurrection, and executed them

1681

Captain Antonio Saravia, Governor

1683

Nov. 3, Death of Governor Saravia. Succeeded by Major Damian de Esplana

1688

Major Jose Quiroga again Governor

1690

June, General Damian de Esplana, Governor

1694

Aug. 16, Death of Governor de Esplana. Succeeded by Major Jose Quiroga

1695

July, Battle in Aguigan in which Quiroga decisively defeated the natives and received their submission ending warfare of over a century

1696

Aug. 1, General Jose Madraso, Governor

1700

Sept. 15, Major Francisco Medraso y Asiam, Governor

1704

Sept. 1, Major Antonio Villamor y Vadillo, Governor

1709

Sept. 1, Lieutenant General Juan Antonio Pimentel, Governor

1720

Nov. 21, Captain Luis Antonio Sanchez di Tagle, Governor

1725

April 4, Captain Juan de Ojeda, Governor
Sept. 28, General Manuel Arguelles Valda, Governor

1730

Feb. 12, Major Pedro Laso de la Vega, Governor

1734

Aug. 21, General Francisco Cardenas Pacheco, Governor and commander of the fleet

1740

April 2, Major Miguel Fernando de Cardenas, Governor

1746

Sept. 21, Captain Domingo Gomez de la Sierra, Governor

1749

Sept. 8, Lieutenant Enrique de Olavide y Michelena, Governor

1756

Nov. 6, General Andres del Darrio y Rabago, Governor

1759

Nov. 20, Lieutenant Jose de Soroa, Governor

1768

June 9, Lieutenant Enrique de Olavide y Michelena, Governor

1771

Sept. 15, Major Mariano Tobias, Governor

1774

June 15, Major Antonio Apodaca, Governor

1776

June 6, Captain Felipe de Cerain, Governor

1786

Aug. 21, Lieutenant Colonel Jose Arlegue y Leon, Governor

1794

Sept. 2, Lieutenant Colonel Manuel Muro, Governor

1802

Jan. 12, Captain Vicente Blanco, Governor

1806

Oct. 18, Captain Alexandro Parreño, Governor

1812

July 26, Lieutenant Jose de Medinilla y Pineda, Governor

1822

Aug. 15, Captain Jose Montilla, Governor

1823

May 15, Captain Jose Ganga Herrero, Governor

1826

Aug. 1, Lieutenant Colonel Jose de Medinilla y Pineda, Governor

1831

Sept. 26, Captain Francisco Ramon de Villalobos, Governor. "He systematized the affairs of the treasury, especially the schedule of port fees; he personally superintended the building of roads and bridges . . . built a pottery; opened the Atattano Valley for the culture of rice . . ." L. M. Cox

1837

Oct. 1, Lieutenant Colonel Jose Casillas Salazar, Governor

1843

Oct. 1, Major Gergorio Sta. Maria, Governor

1848

April 4, Death of Governor Maria. Succeeded by Treasurer, Acting-Governor Felix Calvo
Sept. 8, Lieutenant Colonel Pablo Perez, Governor

1855

May 16, Lieutenant Colonel Felipe Maria de la Corte, Governor

1866

Jan. 28, Lieutenant Colonel Francisco Moscoso y Lara, Governor

1871

Aug. 17, Colonel Luis de Ybanez y Garcia, Governor

1873

March 24, Lieutenant Colonel Eduarto Beaumont y Galafat, Governor

1875

Jan. 15, Lieutenant Colonel Manuel Brabo y Barrera, Governor

1880

Aug. 15, Lieutenant Colonel Francisco Brochero y Parreno, Governor

1884

March 14, Colonel Angel de Pazos Vela-Hidalgo, Governor
July 17, Lieutenant Colonel Enrique Solano, Governor
Aug. 4, Colonel Antonio Borreda, Governor
Nov., Lieutenant Colonel Francisco Olive y Garcia, Governor

1890

April 20, Lieutenant Colonel Joaquin Vara de Rey, Governor

1891

Aug. 14, Lieutenant Colonel Luis Santos, Governor

1892

Aug. 23, Lieutenant Colonel Vicente Gomez Hernandez, Governor

1893

Sept. 1, Lieutenant Juan Godoy, Acting Governor on death of Governor Gomez Hernandez

1895

Dec. 24, Lieutenant Colonel Jacobo Marina, Governor

1897

Feb. 15, Lieutenant Angel Nieto, Acting Governor
April 17, Juan Marina, Lieutenant Colonel, Governor

1898

June 20, Captain Henry Glass proceeding to join Admiral Dewey at Manila requested the surrender of the Island and troops to the United States
June 21, Capitulation by Governor Juan Marina at Piti. Taken on board transport as prisoner of war

with troops. The Treasurer Don Jose Sisto took charge of the administration

Dec. 28, Executive order of the President placed Guam under control of Department of the Navy

1899

Feb. 1, Commander Edward D. Taussig, U.S.N. arrived and took formal possession. He appointed Joaquin Perez "commissioner" in charge of the administration

March 1, Arrival of Ensign L. A. Kaiser, U.S.N. to take charge

April 20, Ensign Kaiser appointed William Coe, Acting Governor

Aug. 7, Captain Richard P. Leary, first American Governor arrived and assumed office

Aug. 21, Order prohibited sale of land without consent of the Government

1900

Jan. 5, Spanish system of taxation of real estate abolished and new system established

Jan. 22, System of public education provided for

Feb. 22, Slavery abolished and system of peonage from this date

1901

July 19, Commander Seaton Schroeder succeeded Captain Leary as Governor

Aug. 11–Nov. 2, Commander William Swift, Acting Governor during absence of Governor Schroeder in the United States

1903

Feb. 6, Commander W. E. Sewell, Governor

1904

Jan. 28, Lieutenant R. Stone, Acting Governor

May 16, Commander G. L. Dyer, Governor after death of Governor Sewell in the United States

1905

Nov. 2, Lieutenant L. McNamee, Acting Governor

1906

March 3, Commander T. M. Potts, Governor

1907

Oct. 3, Lieutenant L. McNamee, Acting Governor

Dec. 28, Captain E. J. Dorn, Governor

1909

July 1, Currency changed to American from Mexican

1910

Nov. 5, Lieutenant F. B. Freyer, Acting Governor

1911

Jan. 12, Captain G. R. Salisbury, Governor

1912

April 30, Captain R. E. Coontz, Governor

1913

Sept. 23, Commander A. W. Hinds, Acting Governor

1914

March 28, Captain W. J. Maxwell, Governor

1916

Jan. 1, Bank of Guam opened

April 29, Lieutenant Commander W. P. Cronan, Acting Governor

May 8, Captain E. Simpson, Acting Governor

May 30, Captain R. C. Smith, Governor

1918

July 6, Typhoon devastated the island destroying cocoanut trees

Nov. 15, Captain William W. Gilmer, Governor

1919

Nov. 22, Lieutenant Commander W. A. Hodgman, Governor

Dec. 21, Captain W. W. Gilmer, Governor

1920

July 7, Captain Ivan C. Wettengel, Governor

1921

Feb. 27, Lieutenant Commander James S. Spore, Acting Governor

1922

Feb. 7, Captain A. Althouse, Governor

Nov. 8, Commander John P. Miller, Acting Governor

Dec. 14, Captain A. Althouse, Governor

1923

Aug. 4, Captain H. B. Price, Governor

1924

Aug. 26, Commander A. W. Brown, Acting Governor

1926

April 7, Captain L. S. Shapley, Governor

1929

June 11, Commander Willis W. Bradley, Governor

HAWAIIAN ISLANDS

Hawaiian Islands (former Sandwich Islands) Territory of the United States, lie in the North Pacific Ocean, between 18° 54' and 20° 14' north latitude, and 154° 48' and 160° 13' west longitude. They are about 2,020 miles southwest of San Francisco, and are in the line of steamer travel between Victoria, B.C., and Australia and New Zealand. The total area of the islands is 6,449 square miles. The principal islands of the group are Hawaii, 4,015; Maui, 728; Oahu, 598; Kauai, 547; Molokai, 261; Lanai, 139; Niihau, 97; Kahoolawe, 69. According to the census taken in 1920, the total population of the islands numbered 255,912, an increase of 64,003, or 33.4 per cent since 1910, in 1930, 368,336. The capital, Honolulu, in the Island of Oahu, had 116,260 inhabitants on July 1, 1929.

The Islands were discovered in 1555 by the Spaniard Juan Gaetano according to some accounts now disputed. Capt. James Cook is celebrated as the real discoverer, landing at Waimea,

Kauai in 1778. The annexation to the United States was July 7, and Aug. 12, 1898. June 14, 1900 the Territory of Hawaii was constituted. Lawrence M. Judd, Governor.

1778

Jan. 18, Capt. James Cook on voyage from England to settle the question of a North West passage discovered or rediscovered the Sandwich Islands which he named after Lord Sandwich, then head of the British admiralty. Feb. 14, 1779 he was killed in a fight with the natives who had stolen a boat he was trying to recover

1795–1819

Period of Kamehameha I who conquered all the Islands except Kauai and Nihau which were ceded to him in 1810 and consolidated his kingdom. Died May 8, 1819

1819

May 20–July 14, 1824, Reign of Kamehameha II

1820

March 31, American missionaries from New England reached Hawaii, Hiram Bingham, Asa Thurston, Dr. Thomas Holman, Samuel Whitney, Samuel Ruggles, Elisha Loomis, D. Chamberlain

1824

July 14, Death of King Kamehameha II and his Queen on a visit to England. Lord Byron of the British Navy brought back their bodies in May 1825

1825

June 6–Dec. 15, 1854, Reign of Kamehameha III

1826

Dec. 23, Treaty of friendship, commerce, and navigation with the United States

1829

Oct. 7, Proclamation of Kamehameha III named King and Regent and 10 Chiefs entitled to sit in Council

1836

Nov. 16, Treaty with England as to rights of English subjects

1839

June 7, Declaration of Rights (Hawaiian Magna Charta) promulgated by Kamehameha III
July 12 and 17, Treaties with France as to rights of French citizens

1840

Oct. 8, First Constitution promulgated
Nov. 2–14, House of Nobles met at Lahaina, Maui, and first election law passed providing for choosing annually "certain persons to sit in Council with the Nobles and establish laws," 2 each from Hawaii, Maui, and Oahu, and 1 from Kauai

1841

April 1–May 31, Meeting of Nobles at Luaehu, Lahaina, "and 3 persons came forward appointed by the people, and joined the Council of Nobles." Of the 14 Nobles 3 were women chiefs

1842

Dec. 31, Message of the President of the United States recognized independence

1843

Feb. 25, Lord George Paulet raised British flag claiming Islands, but action disavowed and restored July 31
Nov. 28, Joint Convention of France and England recognized independence and promised non-annexation

1845

April 2–April 27, 1846, First meeting of Council now generally known as Legislature at Honolulu, with 2 Houses, House of Nobles and House of Representatives

1846

March 26, Treaties with Great Britain and France signed the same day, of friendship and recognition
July 31, Speech of King to the Legislature announced appointment of William Richards as head of a Dept. of Public Instruction
W. L. Lee appointed Chief Justice

1848

Jan. 8, Treaty with Free Hanseatic City of Hamburg signed
June, Kamehameha III abolished feudal land tenure and surrendered the greater part of the Royal Domain

1849

Aug. 25, French Admiral de Tromelin after making impossible demands seized forts and held government buildings until Sept. 5. *See also* United States
Dec. 20, Treaty of friendship, commerce, and navigation with the United States signed
Dec. 21, Resolutions passed with view of giving "industrious cultivators of the soil an allodial title to the portions they occupied, and to facilitate the acquisition of land in fee simple, by others inclined to be industrious," confirmed by laws of July 10, and Aug. 6, 1850

1850

July 30, Act increased the number of House of Representatives to 24

1851

Jan. 6, First election by ballot held for members of House
March 10, Deed of cession of the King placed Islands under provisional protection of the United States to be annexed in case the French seized the Islands; confirmed by Joint Resolution of Legislature June 21
April 30, Legislative Council with enlarged House met
June 18, Secretary of State Daniel Webster instructed American Minister in France to inform the French Government that enforcement of French demands on Hawaii amounting to subjugation would disturb friendly relations with the United States
July 10, New Treaty with Great Britain signed
July 14, Secretary Webster in message to American Minister at Honolulu stated that the United States could not consent to possession of Islands by any European Power
Aug. 7, Treaty with the Republic of Bremen signed

1852

June 14, New Constitution granted by the King
July 1, Treaty with Norway and Sweden signed

1854

Dec. 15, Death of King Kamehameha III

1855

Jan. 11–Nov. 30, 1863, Reign of Kamehameha IV (Liholiho)
June 16, Proclamation of the King dissolved the Legislature because of disagreement of the two Houses on the Bill of Supplies, and election called for July 10
July 20, Treaty of commercial reciprocity with the United States signed; not ratified

1856

April 18, Law provided that the Legislature should meet biennially instead of annually

1857

Oct. 29, Treaty with France signed

1863

Nov. 30, Death of Kamehameha IV. Succeeded by his brother Kamehameha V (1863–Dec. 11, 1872)

1864

June 13, Constitutional Convention called by the King which he dissolved Aug. 13
Aug. 20, New Constitution promulgated by the King

1867

May 21, Commercial Reciprocity Treaty with the United States; failed of ratification

1868

Aug. 14, Contract by which Japanese labor imported

1872

Dec. 11, Death of Kamehameha V and end of the dynasty

1873

Jan. 8, William C. Lunalilo elected King by the Legislature

1874

Feb. 3, Death of King Lunalilo
Feb. 12, David Kalakaua elected King by the Legislature and proclaimed on the 18th

1875

Jan. 30, Commercial Reciprocity Treaty with the United States signed under which Hawaiian sugar admitted to the United States free of duty in return for general remission of duties and use by the United States of Pearl Harbor for coaling and naval station, and Protocol Sept. 9, 1876

1879

Jan. 24, Treaty with Germany signed by which Germans acquired Saluafala Harbor

1881

Dec. 1, Secretary of State James G. Blaine in dispatch to American Minister Comly at Honolulu said: "This Government firmly believes that the position of

the Hawaiian Islands as the key to the dominion of the American Pacific demands their benevolent neutrality . . ." and in later dispatch that "under no circumstances will it permit the transfer of the territory or sovereignty to any of the great European Powers"

1884

Aug. 28, Treaty with England by which England acquired harbor to be designated
Dec. 6, New Commercial Reciprocity Treaty with the United States signed

1887

June 30, Bloodless revolution against a corrupt ministry deposed. Committee of Public Safety at mass meeting adopt resolution for better government and sent ultimatum to King to give pledges of good government and revised Constitution
July 6, New Constitution granted by the King and promulgated July 7
Nov. 9, Reciprocity Treaty with the United States extended and exclusive rights as to Pearl Harbor

1889

July 31, Insurrection against the Government led by Robert Wilcox defeated, and Wilcox surrendered

1891

Jan. 20, Death of King Kalakaua in San Francisco soon after landing on visit to the United States. Succeeded by his sister Lydia Liliuokalani, proclaimed Queen Jan. 29
Feb. 26, New Ministry formed after political differences, the old Ministry at first refusing to resign
March 3, Act of United States Congress provided that tariff should not affect arrangements of Treaty of Jan. 30, 1875
March 9, Princess Victoria Kawekui Kaiulani declared heir apparent
Aug. 27, Privy Council of 40 members including John Owen Dominis, her husband, nominated by the Queen

1892

May 20, Conspiracy of Robert Wilcox and others to form a Republic suppressed
Oct. 16, New Ministry appointed by the Queen forced to resign and Ministry elected by the Legislature appointed
Nov. 19, Letter of John Stevens, American Minister, to United States State Dept. argued in favor of annexation on moral, economic, and political grounds

1893

Jan. 13, The Queen appointed a Ministry arbitrarily chosen by herself in defiance of constitutional principles and popular representation
Jan. 14, The Queen prorogued the Legislature and promulgated new Constitution which proposed to disenfranchise more than one-fourth of the voters and the owners of nine-tenths of the private property to abolish upper elected House of Nobles and substitute one appointed by the Sovereign
Jan. 16, American residents organized a Committee of Safety
——, United States marines landed at request of American Minister Stevens from the U.S.S. "Boston" as urged by members of Committee of Safety for protection of life and property

Jan. 17, Proclamation of the Committee of Safety of organization of Provisional Government, Executive and Advisory Councils named as Legislative Power. Executive Council included Sanford B. Dole, James A. King, Peter C. Jones, and William O. Smith. The monarchy declared abolished and the Queen deposed. Provisional Government recognized by the American Minister and other foreign diplomats

Jan. 18, Appeal of the Queen to President Harrison and on the 31st to President-Elect Cleveland

Feb. 1, Mr. Stevens, American Minister, declared an American Protectorate

Feb. 4, Commissioners of the Provisional Government received by the State Dept. in Washington, and Feb. 11 by President Harrison

Feb. 14, Treaty of annexation with the United States signed

Feb. 17, Envoys of Liliuokalani, deposed Queen, arrived in Washington

March 9, President Cleveland withdrew the Hawaiian Annexation Treaty which had been submitted to the Senate by President Harrison, his predecessor in office

March 15, James H. Blount appointed by President Cleveland special commissioner to investigate conditions in Hawaii and American support of revolution, arrived in Hawaii March 29

March 31, Commissioner Blount withdrew American Protectorate and American flag ordered to be taken down on the day following

May 9, John L. Stevens resigned as American Minister and James H. Blount appointed to succeed him as Envoy Extraordinary and Minister Plenipotentiary

June 5, Provisional Government formally took possession of the Palace

July 17, Report of Mr. Blount represented the revolution in Hawaii as a conspiracy managed by aliens and chiefly by Americans supported by Mr. Stevens, the American Minister. Report published Nov. 20

Sept. 8, Albert S. Willis appointed American Minister and instructed to support and reinstate Queen Liliuokalani on condition she grant full amnesty to those who participated in revolt and assumed obligations of the Provisional Government

Nov. 7, Mr. Willis presented his credentials to Provisional Government headed by President Sanford F. Dole

Nov. 13, Liliuokalani refused to submit to American conditions but finally agreed and signed pledge on Dec. 18

Nov. 23, President Dole refused request of Mr. Willis that he turn over the Government to Queen Liliuokalani

Dec. 18, Message of President Cleveland to United States Congress on Hawaii denounced support of American Minister Stevens of the revolution and declared the Queen should be restored

Dec. 19, Mr. Willis presented copy of amnesty pledge of Liliuokalani to President Dole asking that he resign the government

1894

Jan. 11, President Dole submitted grievances against the United States to Mr. Willis

May 31, United States Senate agreed on declaration that the Hawaiian Islands should maintain their own government without interference by the United States, and that interference by any foreign government would be regarded by the United States as an unfriendly act

July 3, Constitution of the Republic of Hawaii adopted and proclaimed July 4 and permanent Government formally installed

Aug. 7, President Cleveland in formal letter which was presented to President Dole on the 27th recognized the Republic

Nov. 8, Republic recognized by Germany

Dec. 8, Royalist revolt begun

1895

Jan. 6, Martial law declared after seizure of arms landed by revolutionists at Waikiki Beach near Honolulu

Jan. 19, Liliuokalani arrested charged with complicity in revolt

Feb. 5, Trial of royalist leaders of revolt begun and sentence of court martial of death pronounced commuted March 1 to imprisonment for 35 years and fine of $10,000 each

March 13, Liliuokalani sentenced to imprisonment for 5 years and fine of $5,000

May 22, Last meeting of the Executive and Advisory Councils named by the Committee of Safety

June 12–Aug. 15, Special Session of elected Legislature. Address of President Dole declared that the Republic had been recognized by the United States, France, Switzerland, Mexico, Russia, Italy, Belgium, Guatemala, Great Britain, Germany, Japan, the Netherlands, Chile, Peru, Brazil, China, Sweden and Norway, Austria-Hungary, Spain, Portugal, and Denmark

——, Land law enacted to replace Homestead Act of 1884 and Land Commission appointed

June 30, Liliuokalani renounced rights to the throne

1896

Jan. 1, Eight persons in prison for complicity in revolt released on taking oath to support the Government

Feb. 7, Liliuokalani pardoned

Census gave total population as 109,020 including 31,019 native Hawaiians, and 8,485 Americans

1897

March-April, Japanese immigrants refused permission to land as not conforming to requirements of laws appertaining to landing of aliens; protested by Japan

June 16, Treaty of annexation with the United States signed; ratified by Hawaiian Senate Sept. 9, and by the United States July 7, 1898 in Joint Resolution of Congress

1898

Jan. 26, President Dole arrived in Washington as guest of the United States

July 7, Joint Resolution of the United States for annexation of Hawaiian Islands

Aug. 12, Formal transfer of sovereignty to the United States by President Dole to the American Minister Harold M. Sewall, the Hawaiian flag lowered and the American flag raised

——, Proclamation of American Minister that civil, judicial, and military officers be continued as prior to transfer of sovereignty on taking oath of allegiance to the United States

Dec. 15, Supreme Court decision that Chinese contract laborers should not be permitted to land; reversed Jan. 7, 1899

1899

Jan. 17, Wake Island, 2,000 miles from Hawaii, taken over by United States

March 6, Death of Princess Kaiulani, former heiress to throne, at Honolulu

July 4, Violent eruption of Kilauea and Mauna Loa volcanoes after 12 years quiet

1900

April 30, United States Act provided territorial form of government for Hawaii to take effect June 14. Contract Labor Act of the United States of Feb. 26, 1885 to apply to Islands

June 14, Sanford B. Dole, appointed first Governor May 4, inaugurated, and territorial government in effect

Sept. 24, Conventions of political parties nominated candidates for Congress and the territorial legislature

Nov., Election in which Home Rule Party (Hawaii for the Hawaiians) as against Republican and Democratic parties elected 9 of 15 senators, and 22 of 30 representatives to legislature, and R. W. Wilcox to Congress

Census gave total population as 154,001 increase of 41.2% since 1896

1901

Feb. 20–May 1, First Legislature of the Territory in session

Aug. 31, Between June 14, 1900 and this date 4,079 Japanese left Hawaii, only 589 arriving, creating shortage of labor

1903

Jan. 14, Act provided for substitution of silver coins of the United States for Hawaiian, Hawaiian to be recognized as legal tender until Jan. 1, 1904

Nov. 23, George R. Carter inaugurated Governor

1905

May 21–22, Strike of Japanese laborers

1906

Government assistance given to immigration from Spain, Portugal, and Russia. From 1906–1912, 13,000 laborers entered the Islands

1907

Feb. 20, Protest of Japanese in Hawaii against exclusion law of the United States

Aug. 15, Walter F. Frear inaugurated Governor

1909

Feb. 3, Executive Order created Hawaiian Island Reservation on small islands and reefs northwest of Hawaii as preserve and breeding ground for birds

1910

April 15, Census gave total population as 191,909, increase of 24.61% since 1900, Honolulu, the capital, having 52,183 inhabitants

The number of Hawaiians in the islands in 1910 was 26,041; the part-Hawaiians 12,506. The decrease in the number of Hawaiians in the ten years 1900–1910 was 3,746, and increase in part-Hawaiians 4,658. Of the part-Hawaiians, 8,772 are Caucasian-Hawaiian and 3,734 Asiatic-Hawaiian. There are 21,674 Chi-

nese and 79,674 Japanese. The Portuguese number 22,303; the Spanish, 1,990; other Caucasians, chiefly Americans, British, and Germans, 14,867; and Puerto Ricans, 4,890. Chinese, Japanese, and Korean immigration is prohibited

May 27, Organic Act of 1900 amended, changed land laws

June 26, Special election resulted in 2,262 votes in favor of prohibition and 7,511 against

1911

Feb. 2, Revolt in northern Hawaii

Oct. 1, District of Hawaii constituted as a geographical department

1913

Nov. 29, Lucius E. Pinkham inaugurated Governor

1915

June 30, During fiscal year 1,307 Filipino immigrants introduced

1916

Aug. 1, National Park created including the volcanoes Kilauea and Manua Loa on Hawaii and Haleakala on Maui by Act of Congress of the United States

1918

May 23, United States Act prohibited sale, manufacture, or importation of liquors in the Territory. After conclusion of peace a referendum to be held as to prohibition; prohibition effective Aug. 21

May 28, Proclamation called National Guard into service of the United States

June 13, United States Act empowered Hawaii to give women the vote

June 22, Charles J. McCarthy appointed May 4 inaugurated Governor

Oct. 11, Engineering and Signal Corps and Hawaiian cavalry disbanded with approval of the Secretary of War

Nov. 11, Death of ex-Queen Liliuokalani

1919

Aug. 21, Pearl Harbor Dry Dock at Hawaii completed and officially opened by the Secretary of the Navy of the United States

1920

Jan. 1, Census gave total population as 255,912

Feb. 1–June 30, Unsuccessful strike of several thousand plantation workers on Oahu Island for increase in wages

Nov., Foreign language schools rendered subject to supervision by Dept. of Public Instruction, permits required for teachers; to take effect July 1, 1921

1921

June 28, Acquisition by the United States of private rights as to fishing in and about Pearl Harbor, Hawaii

July 5, Wallace R. Farrington appointed Governor to succeed C. J. McCarthy retired

July 9, Formal dedication of Hawaiian National Park

1924

April 1, Strike of sugar plantation workers begun for increase in wages and reduction of hours which was defeated by importation of Japanese labor

Sept. 9, Riots among strikers on Kauai Island, 19 killed and many injured

1925

Feb. 18–April 29, Session of Legislature enacted pension retirement system covering all public employees and teachers, and provided for defining and declaring citizenship status, and commission authorized to go to Washington to present matter of recognition of American citizens of Hawaii in other parts of the United States

July 25, Governor Wallace R. Farrington reappointed

1926

April 18, Village of Hoopulos destroyed by eruption of Mauna Loa volcano

June 9, Death of Sanford B. Dole, President of the Republic, and first Governor, in Honolulu

1927

Feb. 21, United States Supreme Court declared invalid law of 1920 regulating foreign language schools

April 11–16, Pan-Pacific Conference on education, reclamation, rehabilitation, and recreation met in Honolulu

April 21, Order of the President set aside 2 tracts of land for military purposes

July 16, Institute of Pacific Relations met at Honolulu

1928

Aug. 15–20, Celebration commemorated the 150th anniversary of the discovery of the Hawaiian Islands by Capt. James Cook

All previous records for tourist travel to Hawaii were exceeded in this year with arrival of 19,980 non-resident persons, a gain of 15% over 1927 and estimated as worth $10,000,000

1929

Feb.–May, Legislature passed law creating a tax board, and providing for an appraisal of all taxable property and an economic study of the taxation laws

July 5, Lawrence M. Judd assumed office as Governor

1930

Sept. 30, For year ending on this date sugar plantations produced 924,463 tons of sugar and 12,672,000 cases of pineapples packed

PANAMA CANAL ZONE

On November 18, 1903, a treaty between the United States and Panama was signed, providing facilities for the construction and maintenance of the inter-oceanic Canal. In this treaty, Panama granted in perpetuity the use of a zone (Canal Zone) five miles wide on each side of the Canal route, and within this zone the exclusive control for police, judicial, sanitary, and other purposes. For subsidiary canals other territory was ceded and, for the defense of the Canal, the coastline of the zone and the islands in Panama Bay were also ceded. The cities of Panama and Colon remain under the authority of Panama, but complete jurisdiction was granted to the United States in both the cities and in their harbors in all that relates to sanitation and quarantine. In return for these grants the United States paid 10,000,000 dollars on the ratification of the treaty, and is paying 250,000 dollars yearly, beginning after nine years. The treaty was ratified on February 26, 1904, and in July, 1904, the agreement for the provisional delimitation of the boundaries of the United States territory on the Isthmus was signed.

The area of the Canal Zone, including land and water, but not including the water area within the 3-mile limit from the Atlantic and Pacific ends, is 553.8 square miles. The area of Gatun Lake, when its surface is at its normal elevation of 85 feet above sea level, is 163.4 square miles.

The Canal has a summit elevation of 85 feet above the sea. It is 50.72 statute miles in length from deep water in the Caribbean Sea to deep water in the Pacific Ocean. The distance from deep water to the shore line in Limon Bay is about 5 miles, and from the Pacific shore line to deep water is about 5½ miles; hence the length of the Canal from shore to shore is approximately 40¹/₅ miles. The channel ranges in width from 300 to 1,000 feet. The average bottom width of the channel in this project is 649 feet, and the minimum width is 300 feet. The Canal has a minimum depth of 41 feet. The average time of passage through the Canal is from 7 to 8 hours. The record passage is 4 hours 10 minutes. The maximum traffic capacity of the Canal is estimated at 48 ships of usual size in a day or about 17,000 in a year.

The Gatun dam along the crest is 8,400 feet long, including the spillway, or over 1½ miles, and ½ mile wide at its greatest width. The crest of the dam is at an elevation of 105 feet above sea level, or 20 feet above the normal level of Gatun Lake, and 100 feet wide. The width of the dam at the normal water level of the lake, i.e., 85 feet above sea level, is about 388 feet. The length of the cut through the Continental divide (Culebra, now Gaillard Cut), is 8 statute miles. The minimum bottom width of the cut is 300 feet. The bottom is 40 feet above sea level, giving a normal depth of 45 feet.

The civil population of the Canal Zone in April, 1930, was 28,500, of whom 8,000 were Americans. Of this population, 3,344 Americans and 11,780 of other nationalities (chiefly British West Indian negroes) were employed by The Panama Canal and Railroad. No land in the Zone is privately owned and the Zone is, in effect, a Government owned reservation dedicated to the operation, maintenance, and protection of the Canal and its appurtenances. However, building sites and agricultural lands are licensed to responsible companies and individuals.

The appropriations for the construction, operation, and maintenance of the Canal to June 30, 1930, totaled 522,100,028 dollars, and the net revenues from tolls and other sources since it was opened to navigation have totaled 136,226,489 dollars. The current expenses of operation and maintenance, exclusive of depreciation and amortisations during the fiscal year 1929–30 were 8,351,583 dollars, and the gross revenue was 27,426,373 dollars.

The Canal was informally opened to commerce by the passage of the 9,000 ton steamer *Ancon* on August 15, 1914, with specially invited guests. The journey was made without mishap in ten hours. It was formally opened to commerce July 12, 1920 by Proclamation of the President of the United States.

Governor of Canal Zone.—Colonel H. Burgess. Appointed October 16, 1928.

1550

Antonio Galvao, Portuguese navigator, published a book to prove that a canal could be cut at Tehuantepec, Nicaragua, Panama, or Darien

1551

F. L. de Gomara, Spanish historian, presented memorial to Philip II urging that a canal be undertaken

1620

Diego de Mercado submitted report to Philip III of Spain proposing canal by San Juan River and Lake and then through Costa Rican territory along the Quebrada or Barranca Honda to Salinas Bay (Puerto del Papagayo)

1825

June 16, Congress of Central America enacted decree providing for construction of a canal but dissolution of the Congress prevented action

1850

April 19, Clayton-Bulwer Treaty by which the United States and Great Britain agreed not to "obtain or maintain" any exclusive control of a proposed canal across the Isthmus, or unequal advantage in its use, and guaranteed its neutrality

1855

Jan. 28, Railroad across the Isthmus from Aspinwall to Panama City completed

1858

May 1, Costa Rica and Nicaragua granted concession for canal to Felix Belly, French writer, supported in undertaking by the Emperor Napoleon

1868

Oct. 6 and June 18, 1869, Nicaragua and Costa Rica respectively signed the Ayon-Chevalier contract for canal; title conveyed to United States in 1884 (Zavala-Frelinghuysen Treaty)

1878

May 18, Colombia granted French company headed by Count Ferdinand de Lesseps exclusive privileges for construction of interoceanic canal, concession obtained by Lieutenant L. A. B. Wyse March 20

1879

May 1, Congress respecting a canal with 135 delegates including representatives from Great Britain and the United States and Germany met in Paris, F. de Lesseps, president

Aug. 17, French Panama Canal Company organized and selected route for sea-level canal following the railroad; suspended for lack of funds

1880

Jan. 1, Ceremony of beginning construction of canal, Mlle de Lesseps struck first blow with pickaxe

Dec., French Company reorganized

1881

Feb. 24, French engineers began work on canal

1882

Jan. 20, First excavation of canal made

1888

Dec. 14, Canal Company stopped payments, and M. de Lesseps resigned the following day and proposed liquidation

1889

Feb. 4, French Court, acting as receiver for Panama Canal Company, dissolved, found that of $265,000,000 collected only $156,000,000 had been spent on the project

May 15, Work on canal stopped

1891

Jan. 10, Contract of Colombia with the Company extended time for completion of canal

1892

Nov. 25, Trial of F. and Charles de Lesseps and directors for fraud. *See* France

1894

Oct. 20, Second French Canal Company organized with capital of 65,000,000 francs

Nov. 1–June 3, 1899, Work on canal

1897

June 4, Act of Congress of the United States created Canal Commission. *See* United States

1898

Nov. 16, Report of international engineers in favor of a lock type of canal

1899

May 31, Nicaragua Canal Commission, organized in 1889 for construction of interoceanic canal, dissolved

June 10, Isthmian Canal Commission appointed under Act of Congress of the United States of March 3 to examine and report on all routes possible for a canal through Panama to be placed under control, management, and ownership of the United States, Rear Admiral Walker, president

Dec. 27, Panama Canal Company formed in New Jersey to purchase the canal from the French Company

1900

Feb. 5, First Hay-Pauncefote Treaty between the United States and Great Britain to modify Clayton-Bulwer Treaty by which Great Britain renounced right to joint construction and ownership in canal; not accepted by Great Britain as amended by the United States Senate

Nov. 30, Report of Isthmian Commission to the President of the United States favored the Nicaraguan route rather than through Panama for canal

Dec. 1, Treaties made by the United States with Costa Rica and Nicaragua providing for control of territory for negotiations for interoceanic canal; not acted on by Senate of the United States

1901

Nov. 18, Second Hay-Pauncefote Treaty between the United States and Great Britain signed provided for abrogation of the Clayton-Bulwer Treaty of 1850, the United States to have sole right of construction, maintenance, and control of interoceanic canal; "general principle" of neutrality maintained

1902

Jan. 4, French Canal Company offered to sell rights to the United States for $40,000,000

Jan. 18, Isthmian Commission issued a supplementary report recommending the Panama route for canal

June 28, Spooner Bill became law authorizing the President of the United States to purchase rights and property of the French Panama Canal Company and enter into treaty with Colombia for building interoceanic canal

1903

Jan. 22, Hay-Herran Treaty between the United States and Colombia signed by which the United States to acquire Canal Zone on payment of $10,000,000 and annual payment of $250,000 to begin 10 years later; ratified by Senate of the United States March 17

Aug. 12, The Colombian Senate refused to ratify the Treaty with the United States (*see also* Colombia) and adjourned Oct. 31 without action

Nov. 3, Revolution in Panama and declaration of independence of Colombia. *See* Panama

Nov. 18, Treaty between Panama and the United States signed by which the United States was granted the use, occupation, and control of a strip of land ten miles wide for Canal

1904

Feb. 29, President Roosevelt appointed first Canal Commission, Admiral John G. Walker, chairman, and John F. Wallace, Chief Engineer, appointed in May

April 23, Properties of the French Canal Company transferred to the United States on payment of $40,000,000

May 4, Americans began work on canal as transfer of property of French Canal Company became effective

May 9, Rules for government of Zone issued by the President

May 10, John F. Wallace appointed Chief Engineer

June 24, Dingley Tariff extended to Zone

July 28, Decision of United States Treasury Dept. as to sole control of the President until Congress provided form of government

Dec. 19, Report of Chief Engineer of the Isthmian Canal Commission presented before Committee of the House of Representatives recommended return to original plan of M. de Lesseps for a sea-level canal, period of construction 20 years

1905

Feb. 26, Report of Engineering Committee recommended a sea-level canal, period of construction 12 years, submitted by Secretary of War Taft to President Roosevelt

April 1, Commission reorganized, Theodore P. Shonts, chairman, and advisory board to be appointed

May 25, Charles E. Magoon inaugurated as Governor

May 30, Eight hour day established

June 30, John F. Stevens appointed Chief Engineer

June, Advisory Board of consulting engineers, 5 nominated by European governments, appointed to consider whether the canal should be made at sea-level without locks, or above sea-level with locks; majority report in favor of sea-level canal Nov. 18

1906

Feb. 5, Isthmian Canal Commission presented report in favor of the lock canal representing opinion of minority of the Advisory Board of consulting engineers

June 29, Act provided for building a lock canal

Nov. 14, President Roosevelt landed at Colon on visit to inspect the Canal

1907

March 4, John F. Stevens appointed chairman of the Canal Commission to succeed T. P. Shonts resigned

March 30, Secretary Taft arrived at Colon to inspect the Canal

April 1, Lieutenant-Colonel George W. Goethals, army engineer, appointed to succeed John F. Stevens, resigned, and Major Gaillard and Major Siebert as assistant engineers

April 2, Colonel Goethals appointed chairman of the Canal Commission

1911

July 13, Secretary of War Stimson arrived to inspect the Canal

1912

Aug. 24, Act for administration of the Panama Canal contained the provision that "no toll shall be levied upon vessels engaged in the coastwise trade of the United States"; this exception in favor of the United States protested by Great Britain as a violation of the Hay-Pauncefote Treaty

Dec. 24, President Taft arrived at Colon to inspect Canal

1913

June 14, Gatun locks on the Canal completed

Sept. 26, First passage of Gatun locks made by tug boat

Oct. 1, Water turned into Culebra Cut

Oct. 10, The Gamboa Dyke blown up and waters of the Atlantic and Pacific joined across the Isthmus, small boats able to pass from Gatun Lake into Culebra Cut

Oct. 14, First lockage on Pacific made by tug "Miraflores"

Nov. 13, Proclamation of President Wilson fixed canal

tolls at $1.20 per net ton on laden ships and $.72 on vessels in ballast on basis of tonnage as determined

1914

Jan. 7, The craneboat "Lavallex" made first complete passage of the Canal

Jan. 27, President Wilson signed Order establishing new government of Panama Canal Zone to take effect April 1

Jan. 29, President Wilson nominated Colonel George W. Goethals as first Governor, confirmed by Senate Feb. 4

Feb. 2, Executive Order provided for conditions of employment for permanent force for Canal

March 2, Washington Office of the Panama Canal established

April 1, Colonel Goethals took office as Governor

——, Isthmian Canal Commission ceased to exist

May 15, Barge service through the Canal opened

June 8, First passage of Gatun locks by ocean steamer, made by the "Allianca" of the Panama Railroad fleet

June 15, Act repealed exemption clause of Act of 1912 as to American vessels

Aug. 3, Passage of ocean steamer "Cristobal" from ocean to ocean in test trip

Aug. 15, The steamer "Ancon" made trip officially opening the Panama Canal in 9 hours

Sept. 15-20, Oct. 15, Oct. 31, Slide closed the Canal to all shipping

Oct. 10, Protocol signed with Panama as to use of Canal by ships of belligerents

Nov. 13, Proclamation of the President of the neutrality of the Canal

1915

Feb. 15, Supplementary instructions as to canal tolls issued by President Wilson

1916

April 15, Canal opened but suspended 6 days in latter part of Aug. due to activity of Curacha slide

Aug. 21, The President of the United States authorized by Congress to make rules and regulations for Zone

1917

Jan. 10-11, Suspension due to Culebra slide

Jan. 11, Colonel Chester Harding succeeded Colonel Goethals as Governor

April 9, Order of the President to commanding officer of troops to take jurisdiction over Canal making it in effect a military reservation

May 23, Proclamation of the President for maintenance of neutrality

1918

June 28, United States troops assumed police powers in terminal cities of Colon and Panama to prevent disorder

1919

Oct. 28, Act to prohibit manufacture and sale of alcohol extended to Canal Zone

1920

July 12, The President of the United States proclaimed the official and formal opening of the Canal

1921

March 27, Colonel Chester Harding resigned and was succeeded as Governor by Colonel Jay J. Morrow

June 6, Special Commission to investigate and report on the Canal appointed by the President, arrived at Zone June 18 and submitted report Sept. 15

1924

Oct. 15, Resignation of Governor Morrow, succeeded by Colonel Meriwether L. Walker

1928

Oct. 16, Colonel H. Burgess appointed Governor

1929

Feb. 18, Order of President Coolidge opened the Canal to aircraft of all nations

PHILIPPINE ISLANDS

Philippine Islands, archipelago named after Philip II of Spain, the largest group of the Malay Archipelago, ceded to the United States by the Treaty with Spain Dec. 10, 1898, extend almost due north and south from Formosa to Borneo and the Moluccas, embracing an extent of 16° of latitude and 9° of longtitude.

The group is composed of 7,083 islands and islets, of which only 466 have areas of one square mile or over. The eleven most important islands are Luzon, with an area of 40,814 square miles; Mindanao, 36,906 square miles; Samar, 5,124 square miles; Negros, 4,903 square miles; Palawan, 4,500 square miles; Panay, 4,448 square miles; Mindoro, 3,794 square miles; Leyte, 2,799 square miles; Cebu, 1,695 square miles; Bohol, 1,534 square miles; and Masbate, 1,255 square miles.

The total population was estimated in 1930 at 12,204,100. Philippine Census of 1918 gave 10,314,310, chiefly of Malay race, 91% of whom are Christians, and only 932,953, or 9%, are Moros and Pagans, though these are fast taking advantage of the all-pervading system of public schools. The population of Manila, the capital and the leading commercial and industrial center, was 285,306, of whom 259,437 were Filipinos, 17,760 Chinese, 1,612 Japanese, 2,916 Americans, 2,050 Spaniards, 664 English, 201 Germans, 121 French, 71 Swiss, and the rest of other nationalities. About 1,500,000 have some knowledge of English and about 660,000 some knowledge of Spanish; for Government and commercial purposes these two languages are used.

Other towns with their estimated present population, including suburbs, are: Iloilo on Panay, 67,143; Cebu on Cebu, 86,152; Legaspi (formerly Albay), 33,048; Laoag, 40,879; Vigan, 19,939; Naga, 9,468 (all on Luzon); and Zamboanga on Mindanao, 47,302. Baguio, in the Mountain

Province, is the summer capital, corresponding to Simla in India, and has a population of 8,449.

Dwight F. Davis, Governor General.

1521

March 15, Discovery of the Philippine Islands by Magellan, sighted this day according to Pigafetta, chronicler of the voyage

March 16, Magellan expedition landed at island south of Samar which Pigafetta called "Humunu," still known as Homonhon and Malhon

April 7, Magellan reached the harbor of Cebu where 2,200 "Indians" were baptized by the Spaniards and proffered submission. The expedition then proceeded to northwestern coast of Mindanao at site of Quipit

April 25, Magellan mortally wounded in battle with the natives and died April 27

1525

July 24, Expedition of Loaisa and Don Juan Sebastian del Cano of the Magellan company sailed from Corunna, Spain, and visited Mindanao

1528

Expedition of the Spaniard, Alvaro de Saavedra, visited the Islands

1542

Nov. 1, Expedition of Ruy Lopez de Villalobos sailed from Navidad, Mexico, and took formal possession Feb. 2 at Mindanao. He named the Islands Filipinas in honor of Crown Prince Don Felipe of Spain, afterwards Philip II

1564

Nov. 21, Expedition of M. L. de Legazpi sailed from Navidad, Mexico, arrived at Abuyog, Island of Leyte Feb. 13, touched at Mindanao and Bohol and proceeded to Cebu and founded first Spanish settlement which he called San Miguel

1569

Aug. 14, Legazpi's title as Governor and Captain General of the Philippine Islands confirmed by royal decree

1571

Jan. 1, Legazpi organized the government of Cebu dividing the natives among the Spaniards into royal grants

May 19, Manila, the fortified town of the Mohammedan chief, Rajah Soliman, taken after battle with the natives, and June 24 made the Spanish capital

1574

Nov., Attack of Chinese pirate Limahong, but Manila saved by arrival of Juan de Salcedo with troops

1581

March, Arrival of Domingo de Salazar, first Bishop of Manila, and Jesuits

1583

May 5, The Audiencia, high court of justice, created by royal decree

1584

May 29, Dr. Santiago de Vera, first president of the Audiencia, arrived at Manila

1589

Aug. 9, The Audiencia abolished by royal decree after petition of citizens and Gomez Perez Dasmarinas appointed Governor, arriving in May 1590

1596

May 25, Audiencia reëstablished and Antonio de Marga appointed Auditor

1600

Oct., Spaniards defeated Dutch under Van Noordt in naval battle

1603

Chinese insurrection resulted in massacre of Chinese on evening of the Feast of St. Francis

1604

Earliest account of the Islands, the "Relacion de las Islas Filipinas," by Padre Pedro Chirino, published in Rome

1639

Nov., Revolt of Chinese suppressed but disturbances lasted until the following March

1645

Pampangan revolt against the Spaniards suppressed, and again in 1660

1719

Oct. 11, Fernando de Bustamante, Governor since 1717, murdered by mob led by friars because of his efforts to reform management of public money

1755

June 30, Governor Arandia (1754–1759) ordered all Chinese who had not become Christians to leave the Islands

1759

Miguel Ezpelela succeeded as Governor

1762

Sept. 22, English fleet entered harbor and bombarded Manila on refusal of city to surrender. City taken by the English Oct. 5

1764

March 31, The British withdrew from Manila under Peace of Paris of Feb. 10, 1763, on notification of termination of the war with Spain, leaving Don Simon de Anda, Spaniard, in possession

1770

Jesuits expelled by Governor Raon in accordance with decree of April 2, 1767

1785

May 10, Royal decree announced organization of the Royal Company of the Philippines for trade between Manila and Cadiz, dissolved 1830

1810

Feb. 14, Royal decree provided that the Islands should send representative to the Cortes in Spain, Don Ventura de los Reyes elected as delegate

1816

June 4, Royal decree established Council of Administration, advisory body, Governor General, president

1823

Native rebellion against Spaniards led by Captain Novales captured the palace and barracks in Manila but ended in defeat and leaders shot

1830

Dec. 11, Provincial governments organized

1832

July 26, Commercial Court established

1836

Sept. 23, Treaty of commerce with the Sultan of Sulu (Jolo) concluded by Spain

1841

Oct., Revolt in Apolinario Province of Tayabas, and Jan. 21, 1843

1849

Jan. 15, Order forbade religious orders to alienate their property

1851

Spaniards attacked and took town of Jolo on Jolo Island, Sulu archipelago

Aug. 1, Banco-Espanol-Filipino established

1852

Oct. 19, Reinstatement of Jesuits, first band arrived in 1859

1861

July 4, The Governor General ceased to be president of the Audiencia

1872

Native revolt against Spaniards suppressed and leaders imprisoned, and executed

1878

July 20, The Sultan of Sulu acknowledged Spanish sovereignty and again May 7, 1885 by Treaty

1884

Sept. 4, Code of criminal procedure established to go into effect Jan. 1, 1888

1886

Feb. 26, Civil governorships established in 18 provinces, and territorial audiencia of Cebu

1888

Feb. 3, Royal decree extended law of civil procedure to the Philippines

Aug. 6, Spanish commercial code established

1889

July 31, Spanish civil code established

1892

July 3, Dr. Jose Rizal, patriot, organized secret society, the "Liga Filipina" at Manila, and the "Katipunan," another secret society, organized by Andres Bonifacio July 6

1895

March 10, Severe fighting in Mindanao; the Malay Mohammedans defeated and their Sultan killed

1896

Aug. 17, The "Katipunan" decided on revolt against Spain and 3 days later declared for a republic

Aug. 26, "Cry of Balintawak" began insurrection at Cavite, led by General Emilio Aguinaldo

Aug. 30, Insurgents made unsuccessful attack on the outposts of Manila

Nov. 11, Spaniards repulsed in engagement at Novaleta

Dec. 13, Gen. Camillo de Polavieja succeeded Gen. Blanco as Governor General

Dec. 30, Dr. Jose Rizal executed after farcical trial, charged with inciting revolution

1897

Jan. 1, Battle at Cacaron near Santa Maria, the insurgents under Eusabio (also known as General Dimaluga) routed by General Rios

Jan. 11, Señor Rojas and 11 insurgents shot as instigators of revolt

Jan. 16, Insurgent General Eusebio Roque captured and shot

Feb. 25, Rising in Manila suppressed

April 20, Gen. Primo de Rivera succeeded Polavieja as Governor General

May 10, Andres Bonifacio and his brother Procopio killed by followers of Aguinaldo, charged with promoting counter revolution

Dec. 14, Pact of Biac-na-bato concluded with General Aguinaldo by Governor General Primo de Rivera ended rebellion, armistice for 3 years for the application of reforms promised, Aguinaldo and other leaders to leave the Islands, and the sum of $1,000,000 to be paid by the Spanish Government to the rebels and $700,000 to families who had sustained loss by reason of the war

1898

April 9, Gen. Basilio Augustin arrived at Manila to succeed Rivera as Governor General

April 21, War between the United States and Spain. *See* United States

May 8, Rebel town Panay Island captured by Spaniards, reported 672 rebels killed

May 11, Telegram of Prince Henry of Prussia in command of Asiatic squadron from Hongkong to the Kaiser that the Philippines had decided on revolt against Spain and "would gladly place themselves under protection of a European Power, especially Germany"

May 13, Assembly of 15 members of natives and others constituted by Governor General, Señor Paterno, president

May 19, Aguinaldo arrived from Hongkong on the U.S.S. "McCulloch" and under protection of United States troops at Cavite organized native army

June 12, General Aguinaldo proclaimed independence of Spain and provisional government organized, Aguinaldo, President and Daniel Perindo, Vice-President

June 23, Proclamation of General Aguinaldo declared establishment of revolutionary government

July 18, General Aguinaldo named Cabinet

Aug. 6, General Aguinaldo made appeal to foreign governments to recognize the independence of the Islands

Aug. 12, Protocol of Agreement between Spain and the United States signed

Aug. 14, General Merritt assumed duties as Military

Governor and proclaimed military occupation of the Islands by the United States. Formal articles of capitulation signed

Aug. 30, General Elwell S. Otis became Military Governor

Sept. 9, The Filipinos established their capital at Malolos, 25 miles north of Manila

Sept. 15, Congress of the Filipinos opened session, and General Aguinaldo, President, named his Cabinet: Apolinario Mabini, Dr. Trinidad H. Pardo de Tavera, Don Cayetano Arellano, Don Gregorio Araneta, Don Benito Legarda, and General Antonio Luna

Sept. 28, General MacArthur captured Porac but evacuated it the following day and it was reoccupied by insurgents Oct. 4

Oct. 1, Envoys from Aguinaldo received by General Otis

Oct. 7, General Order permitted civil courts to resume jurisdiction under supervision of the military government

Nov. 7, Insurgent Assembly met at Iloilo, organized Provisional Government of the Visayas, Roque Lopez President

Nov. 29, Constitution adopted by Filipino Congress, and approved by President Aguinaldo Dec. 23

Dec. 10, Treaty of Paris signed by which Spain ceded the Philippine Islands to the United States for $20,000,000

Dec. 21, Proclamation of this date of President McKinley of administration of the Islands published by General Otis Jan. 4

Dec. 24, The Spaniards evacuated Iloilo which was occupied by forces of Aguinaldo

1899

Jan. 4, Proclamation of General Otis announced terms of Treaty of Peace with Spain giving control, disposition, and government of the Philippine Islands to the United States

Jan. 5, Counter-Proclamation of General Aguinaldo protested American sovereignty and administration and called on Filipinos to declare their independence

Jan. 20, Constitution formally adopted by Filipino Congress and promulgated the following day

——, First Philippine Commission appointed by President McKinley. See United States

Feb. 4, Revolution against American rule begun by Filipinos invading American lines at Manila resisted by United States troops

Feb. 5–6, Continued attacks of Filipinos in effort to push back American outposts and advance their line at Manila repulsed

Feb. 10, Battle of Caloocan. Filipinos gathering for attack dispersed and Caloocan captured

Feb. 11, City of Iloilo on Island of Panay occupied by Americans after bombardment by General Miller

Feb. 22, Rising in Manila as ordered by Malolos Government on the 15th for massacre of Americans and Europeans suppressed by American troops

——, Cebu surrendered to Capt. Cornwall in the "Petrel"

Feb. 28, American garrison established at City of Cebu on Cebu Island

March 1, Visayan Military District constituted of Islands of Cebu, Panay, and Negritos, placed under command of General Marcus Miller

March 4, City of Bacolod, capital of Negros, occupied by American troops

March 4, The Schurman Commission arrived at Manila from the United States

March 10, United States troops commanded by Major General Henry W. Lawton arrived at Manila from New York

March 13, General Wheaton occupied Pasig and seized line of the Pasig River March 13–15 placing gunboats on the Laguna de Bay, dividing the Tagal forces

March 31, General MacArthur occupied Malolos, insurgent capital, General Aguinaldo retiring to Tarlac

April 4, Proclamation of the Schurman Commission promised "the amplest liberty of self-government reconcilable with just, stable, effective, and economical administration, and compatible with the sovereign rights and obligations of the United States"

April 5–22, Gunboat "Wilmington" proceeded up Amazon River 100 miles from Manaos to Iquitos

April 10, General Lawton began assault on Santa Cruz

April 11, Treaty between Spain and the United States of Dec. 10, 1898, proclaimed

April 23, Engagement at Quingan near Malolos, insurgent attack repulsed by Major Bell

April 28, Filipino commission, Colonel Manuel Arguleses and Lieutenant Jose' Bernal proposed armistice and terms of peace. General Otis refused to accept anything but unconditional surrender

——, Americans occupied the town of Calumpit

May 4–5, Gen. Lawton occupied San Tomas and San Fernando, Luzon Island

May 5, Colonel James F. Smith assumed temporary command of the Visayan Military District, General R. P. Hughes assigned to command on the 29th

May 6, Municipal government established by General Lawton at Baliuag, Bulacan

May 8, Office of Auditor of the Philippine Islands created by President McKinley

May 17, Chief Scout William H. Young of General Lawton's command occupied San Isidro

May 19, Spanish troops in garrison at Jolo relieved by American troops

May 20–22, Commission from insurgents received by Schurman Commission but negotiations for peace failed

May 29, Audiencia of Manila reconstituted as Supreme Court of the Islands, Cayetano S. Arellano appointed Chief Justice

——, Gen. R. P. Hughes assigned to command Visayan Military District

June 5, Lower courts of Manila Province reëstablished

——, Gen. Antonio Luna killed by body guard of Aguinaldo at Cabanatuan

June 13, General Lawton defeated the insurgents entrenched on bridge across the Zapote River in decisive battle south of Manila

June 21, Tarlac made capital of Filipino Republic

June 30, Siege of Spanish garrison at Baler on coast of Luzon raised by General Aguinaldo and Spaniards allowed to leave

——, Filipino attack on American defenses at San Fernandez

July 3, Public schools at Manila opened

July 11, Engagement at Muntinlupa

July 22, Gen. Otis organized local government at Negros which became basis of similar governments in other islands

July 27, General R. H. Hall captured Calamba

——, Aguinaldo issued appeal to the Powers

Aug. 8, General Order issued for organization of municipal government in occupied towns

Aug. 9, Capture of Angeles by General MacArthur and enemy driven north from San Fernando

Aug. 20, Bates Treaty with Sultan of Sulu established American sovereignty

Sept. 16, Lieutenant Babson authorized to organize 100 Macabebe scouts to act as police

Sept. 28, Advance of General MacArthur from Bacolor to Porac, clearing country of rebels

Oct. 1, Members of insurgent commission headed by Gen. Alejandrino had interview with General Otis

Oct. 2, Insurgents reoccupied Porac but were driven out on the 17th

——, Attack of insurgents on Imus, Island of Luzon, repulsed

Oct. 6, General F. D. Grant advanced from Imus, driving insurgents from entire west bank of the Imus River

Oct. 8-13, In Province of Cavite General Schwan began advance from Bacoor driving insurgents from Old Cavite, Noveleta, Santa Cruz, San Francisco de Malabon, Saban, and Perez das Marinas

Oct. 12, Generals Lawton and Young began advance northward up the Rio Grande from Arayat against insurgents, reaching Cabiao on the 18th

Oct. 19, San Isidro captured and garrison established

Oct. 27, Cabanatuan occupied and garrison established

Nov. 1, Aliaga and Talavera occupied by Americans

Nov. 2, Preliminary Report of the Philippine Commission advised keeping of Islands by United States

Nov. 4, Insurgent attack on Vigan repulsed

Nov. 5, General MacArthur advancing from Angeles captured Magalang

Nov. 7, General Wheaton with force from Manila disembarked at San Fabian on the Gulf of Lingayen in face of strong opposition from Filipinos

Nov. 8, General MacArthur occupied Mabacalat

Nov. 11, Aguinaldo and his chiefs in conference at Bayombong agreed to scatter and maintain guerilla warfare as more effective than resistance in battles

——, General MacArthur took Banban, Capas, and Concepcion

Nov. 12, Colonel Bell occupied Tarlac, General Aguinaldo and his government escaping capture, General Aguinaldo with a few followers going to the mountains of Benguet

——, Colonel Hare attacked and routed insurgents near San Jacinto

Nov. 15, Lieutenant Johnston captured San Nicolas

Nov. 17-18, General MacArthur occupied Gerona and Panique, north of Tarlac

Nov. 19-20, General Wheaton occupied Dagupan

Nov. 21, Engagement with insurgents on Island of Panay

Nov. 23, General Young's troops reached Namacpacan, 30 miles north of San Fernando in Union province

Nov. 24, Port of Vigan occupied by marines from U.S.S. "Oregon"

Dec. 2, Lieutenant Munro captured Bayambang on Manila-Dagupan Railroad

——, Insurgent General Pilar defending the escape of General Aguinaldo killed in engagement with Major March in Lepanto Province, Tila Pass

Dec. 11, Insurgent General Tirona surrendered province of Cagayan to Captain McCalla

Dec. 12, Colonel Hayes captured the rebel stronghold of Biacnabato

Dec. 19, General Henry W. Lawton killed supervising movement of troops over the Mariquina River in attack near San Mateo in the Island of Luzon

Dec. 21, Colonel Charles C. Hood appointed Military Governor of northeastern provinces of Luzon

Dec. 25, General Young appointed Military Governor of northwestern Luzon with headquarters at Vigan

Dec. 26, Bubonic plague discovered at Manila

Dec. 27-29, Colonel Lockett attacked insurgents at and about Montalban, driving them back into the mountains

1900

Jan. 1-17, Generals Schwan and Lloyd Wheaton advanced against insurgent positions on shores of Laguna Bay, General Wheaton cleared rebels from Cavite Province, and General Schwan from Batangas Province

Jan. 2, Brigadier General Bates appointed major general succeeding General Lawton in command

Jan. 20, General William A. Kobbé with force from Manila entered Sorsogon Bay, garrisoned Sorsogon and subsequently took Bulan and Donsal

Jan. 21, Gen. Schwan captured San Diego

Jan. 29, Board constituted by Military Governor to prepare plans for municipal government, headed by C. Arellano

Jan. 31, Final Report Philippine Commission presented in favor territorial form of government with home rule in local affairs

Feb. 6, Second Philippine Commission headed by Judge William H. Taft appointed

March 20, Brigadier General William A. Kobbé appointed Military Governor of Mindanao and Jolo and adjacent islands, and Gen. James M. Bell placed in command of District of Southeastern Luzon

March 29, Law provided for election and institution of municipal governments

March 30, Captain Albert Todd assigned to head Dept. of Public Instruction

April 1, Walter G. Coleman, Auditor, arrived at Manila

April 7, Military Division of the Philippines created which General Otis divided into 4 departments commanded by Generals MacArthur, Bates, Hughes, and Kobbé

——, Insurgent attack at Cagayan, Island of Mindanao, repulsed

April 15, American reverse at Catubig, Samar

May 1, Insurgent attack at Catarman, Island of Samar, repulsed

May 5, General Otis relieved at his own request and Major General Arthur MacArthur assigned to succeed him as Military Governor

——, General Pantelon Garcia, highest Filipino officer next to Aguinaldo, captured near San Isidro at Jaen

May 7, Insurgent attack near San Jacinto repulsed

May 15, New code of criminal procedure went into effect, American judicial system as far as applicable

May 16, Engagement near Malibicong, Ilocos Province

June 3, Second Philippine Commission headed by Judge W. H. Taft reached Manila

June 6, Act of United States Congress authorized designation of banks in which public moneys might be deposited

June 8, Insurgent General Pio del Pilar captured at Guadalupe

June 15, Insurgent General Macabulos with 8 officers

and 124 men surrendered to Colonel Liscum at Tarlac, Luzon

June 21, General MacArthur, Military Governor, issued amnesty proclamation to those who within 90 days would renounce connection with insurgent government and accept sovereignty of the United States

June 27, Order of General Aguinaldo urged attacks on outposts of Americans and continued resistance in period before the election in the United States

June 29, College of primary and secondary education opened in Manila

——, Surrender of Insurgent General Aquina

July 1, Capture of Insurgent General Ricarti

July 15, Appeal of citizens of Manila to Congress of the United States signed by 2,006 persons; presented in United States Senate Jan. 10, 1901

July 25, General Young installed municipal government at Vigan, northern Luzon

Aug. 1, Insurgent Colonel Grassa surrendered at Tayug, Luzon, with 182 armed men

Sept. 1, Philippine Commission began exercise of legislative powers, Judge W. H. Taft superseding the Military Governor

——, Dr. David P. Barrows appointed superintendent of schools in Manila

Sept. 12, First session and first legislative act of Philippine Commission the appropriation of $2,000,000 (Mexican) for construction and repair of roads and bridges

Sept. 17, Engagement at Siniloan, Laguna Bay, Captain D. D. Mitchell and Lieutenant G. A. Cooper killed

Sept. 19, Act of Commission adopted civil service rules

Nov. 7, Treaty for cession of outlying islands concluded between Spain and the United States

Dec. 12, Municipal police force created by the Commission

Dec. 20, Proclamation of General MacArthur established laws of war in occupied towns

Dec. 23, Federal Party formed by Filipinos, platform adopted recognized the sovereignty of the United States

1901

Jan. 7, Order of General MacArthur for deportation to Island of Guam of Generals Ricarte, del Pilar, Hizon, Llanera, and Santos, and 9 lower officers and 8 civilians including Trias, Tecson, and Mabini

Jan. 9, Lieutenant Steele in engagement with insurgents at Tenaguna, Island of Leyte

Jan. 21, Commission established a Dept. of Public Instruction, and provided that as soon as practicable the English language should be the basis of all instruction. Normal schools and a trade school in Manila authorized, and schools organized by the Military Government taken over as public school system

Jan. 25, General Funston in engagement near San Isidro, Tagunton, insurgent leader, killed

Jan. 29, Lieutenant Hicken repulsed surprise attack of insurgents near Fiesta San Lucia, Island of Cebu

Jan. 31, Municipal Code Act passed by the Commission creating form of government for municipalities other than Manila or tribal settlements, and tax on real estate imposed

Feb. 6, Provincial Government Act passed by the Commission provided for provincial governors in each province, and provincial board of 3 members with legislative functions

Feb. 13, Civil government established at province of Pampanga, Luzon, Secrina Joven, Governor

——, Insurgent Major Maximo Angeles surrendered 112 rifles

March 2, "Spooner Amendment" to Army Appropriation Act authorized the President of the United States to establish civil government in the Islands

March 3, President Taft of Philippine Commission reported provincial governments established in Pampanga, Pangasinan, Tarlac, Bulacan, and Bataan

March 12, Provincial Government of Tayabas organized, Colonel Gardener made Governor

March 15, Surrender of Insurgent General Mariano Trias at San Francisco de Malabon, equal in prestige in southern Luzon to Aguinaldo

March 18, Insurgent General Diocino captured, and surrender of last insurgent band in Island of Panay commanded by Fullon followed on the 22d

March 23, Capture of Aguinaldo, insurgent president, by General Frederick Funston, and a group of officers, at Palanan, province of Isabela, pretending to be prisoners of Filipino Macabebe scouts and brought into Aguinaldo's camp

April 2, Aguinaldo took oath of allegiance and accepted authority of the United States

April 19, Aguinaldo issued manifesto advising submission. 1,000 prisoners released on taking oath of allegiance

April 30, Insurgent General Tinio surrendered at Sinait, northern Luzon

June 15, Supreme Court constituted by decree of Commission, Cayetano Arellano, Chief Justice, associate justices, Florentino Torres, Victorino Mapa, and J. F. Cooper, of Texas, Charles A. Willard, of Minnesota, Fletcher Ladd, of New Hampshire, and L. R. Wilfley, of Missouri, appointed Attorney General with native Filipinos as assistant and solicitor

June 21, Order of President McKinley through the War Dept. established civil government to take effect July 4 except in districts where insurrection continued to exist, W. H. Taft, President of the Philippine Commission, appointed Civil Governor

June 23, Surrender of Insurgent General Cailles in Laguna

July 4, Judge William Howard Taft installed as Civil Governor, and Major General Adna R. Chaffee relieved General MacArthur as Military Governor of districts not yet under civil jurisdiction, and as Commander of American army in the Philippines. Insurrection continued in provinces of Batangas, Samar, Cebu, and Bohol, and Island of Mindoro

——, Surrender of Insurgent General Belarmino in Albay

July 16, Proclamation of Miquel Malvar, successor of Aguinaldo as rebel leader, announced continuance of warfare

July 17, Batangas, Cebu, and Bohol provinces returned to military from civil control

July 18, "Philippines Constabulary," insular police force appointed, not to exceed 150 men for each province

July 24, Surrender of Insurgent General Zunbano at Zabayas

July 31, General Henry T. Allen appointed Chief of Constabulary

Aug. 31, Brigadier General George W. Davis relieved

General Kobbé as Military Governor of Mindanao and Jolo

Sept. 1, Three Filipinos added to the Commission, Trinidad H. Pardo de Tavera, Benito Legarda, and Jose de Luzuriaga

Sept. 17, Tariff law enacted by Commission to take effect Nov. 15

Sept. 22, Major Alhambra with 3 officers and 28 followers of Aguinaldo captured at Casiguran

Sept. 28, Garrison of the town of Balangiga, Samar, massacred by Filipinos in surprise attack

Oct. 2, Bureau of Non-Christian Tribes created

Nov. 24, Capture of fort in Bohol by Captain Edward P. Lawton

Dec. 20, Civil authority in Cebu reëstablished to take effect Jan. 1, 1902

1902

Jan. 1, Cebu returned to civil government

Jan. 14, Surrender of Col. Marsignan of Batangas to Gen. Bell with 240 armed insurgents

Jan. 21, Bureau of Education established by the Commission, Dr. Fred W. Atkinson, head

Feb. 22, Rebel leader Gen. Lukban captured in Samar and in April insurgents under Gen. Guevara surrendered

Feb., First elections for provincial governors held during the month

March 3, Civil government restored to Bohol to take effect April 1

March 7, Law authorized provincial schools of secondary instruction

March 8, United States Tariff Act provided that products of the Islands coming into the United States should pay only 75% of charges of imports imposed for foreign countries

April 12, $50,000 appropriated for a leper colony

April 16, Gen. Miguel Malvar leading insurrection in Island of Mindoro surrendered

April 25–May 3, Court martial to try Brig. Gen. Jacob H. Smith held in Samar charged with ordering troops to kill natives over 10 capable of bearing arms and ordering ravaging of the Island; reprimanded and retired from service July 16

April 29, Chinese Exclusion Act extended to the Islands by United States

May 1, Ports of Batangas and Laguna opened for trade and later of Samar

May 2, Fort at Bayan in Mindanao taken by Americans

May 12, Trial by court martial of Maj. Edwin F. Glenn charged with administering "water cure" to Filipinos

June 17, Island of Samar placed under civil government

June 23, Act of Commission restored civil government in Batangas to take effect July 4

June 30, From May 1, 1898, to this date cost of pacification $177,000,000

July 1, Organic Act for government of the Philippine Islands as "unorganized" territory, recognized inhabitants as citizens of the Philippine Islands and entitled to protection of the United States, and Act of President in appointment of Commission to govern Islands confirmed

——, $7,000,000 granted to Philippine Government for purchase of friar's lands. *See also* United States, July 3, 9, and 16 as to negotiations, and *infra* Dec. 22, 1903

——, Civil Government organized in Province of Laguna

July 4, War Dept. Order declared office of military governor of the Philippine Islands terminated

——, Peace and amnesty proclaimed by President Roosevelt to Filipinos on subscription to oath of allegiance in case of crimes committed before May 1, 1902

July 6, Aguinaldo and other political prisoners released under amnesty proclamation

July 10, Brig. Gen. Samuel S. Sumner relieved Gen. Davis as Military Governor of Mindanao and Jolo

July 14, Maj. Gen. G. W. Davis appointed to chief command Army of the Philippines succeeding Gen. Chaffee to take effect Sept. 30

Aug. 16, Battle with band of *Ladrones* near Caloocan

Aug. 18, Moros began hostilities, skirmishes near Manila and Cavite

Aug. 22, Governor Taft returned from conferences at Rome on friar's lands

Aug. 30, Cholera epidemic, 19,640 deaths reported

Sept. 2, *Official Gazette* of the Philippine Islands established

Sept. 3, Rios, a fanatical leader, routed in Tayabas

Sept. 17, Capt. J. J. Pershing started expedition against the Sultan of Bulig which was successful during the month, but a serious skirmish with the Moros at Mindanao Sept. 29–30

Oct. 1, Capt. Pershing began bombardment of chief Moro fort which was abandoned the following day

Oct. 6, Act provided for taking a census

Oct. 27, Bishop Aglipay forms independent Catholic Church which adheres to modern science, proclaims that science is superior to Biblical tradition, denies the possibility of miracles, and conceives God as an invisible Father with one essence and a single gender. The ritual resembles somewhat that of the Roman Church. Latin was originally prescribed, but the Spanish language is now the official tongue, and encouragement is given to the vernacular dialects. Marriage is allowed to its apostles. According to the Government Census of 1918, the Independent Filipino Church had 1,417,448 followers, but in the last Church Census its followers numbered 4,000,000

Dec. 7, Governor Taft established zones of concentration for aggressive campaign against the *Ladrones*

1903

Jan. 30, Act to promote efficiency of the constabulary

Feb. 8, Insurgents defeated near Mariquira

Feb. 9, United States Act provided system of extradition with the Philippines

Feb. 11, Land reserved in hills of northern Luzon for summer capital, the City of Baguio

March 2, United States Act established standard of value and new coinage system, the silver peso ($.50) made unit and legal tender to be guaranteed by gold

——, First census gave total population as 7,635,426 including 647,740 classed as wild tribes; only 20% of population over 10 years of age able to read and write in any language, and of these less than 10% could read and write Spanish

March 22, *Ladrones* captured town of Surigao, Mindanao

March 27, Insurgents routed with loss near Mariquira

April 10, Capt. Pershing captured Moro stronghold at Bacolod

April 27, Report of Gen. Miles published confirmed some American cruelties during the war

May 31, Rios, insurgent leader captured Sept. 1902, condemned to death

June 1, Most of the Mindanao and Sulu Archipelago established as Moro Province by Commission, Gen. Leonard Wood becoming first civil governor in July

July 16, United States warships took formal possession of 7 small islands adjacent belonging to the Philippines under Treaty

July 25, Maj. Gen. James F. Wade succeeded Gen. Davis in command of Army

Aug. 25, Luke E. Wright appointed Governor to succeed Judge Taft

Nov. 17, Gen. Leonard Wood defeated Moros at Siet Lake, Jolo Islands, after 5 day battle

Dec. 22, Agreement for purchase of lands of friars about 400,000 acres concluded, for $7,250,000

——, Commission appropriated $75,000 to enable Filipino Commission to visit the United States and attend Louisiana Purchase Exposition

1904

Jan. 14, Importation of Mexican silver prohibited

Jan. 26, Gen. V. Lukban arrested charged with seditious activities

Feb. 1, Governor Luke E. Wright inaugurated

Feb. 5, Sixto Lopez sentenced to deportation for refusal to take oath of allegiance

Feb. 29, Moros defeated in engagement Island of Jolo, Lieut. West and 6 privates killed

March 2, The Sultan of Sulu formally notified by the United States of abrogation of Bates Treaty of Aug. 1899 in view of his connection with Moro revolt

March 14, Gen. Wood defeated Moros in battle at Catobolo, Mindanao Island

May 8, Detachment of United States infantry attacked by Moros near Lake Liguasan, Mindanao and 2 lieutenants and 15 men killed

May 23, 53 Filipinos killed by Moros near Malabang

May 30, A Ricarte, insurgent leader, captured in Luzon and deported to Guam

July 2, Internal Revenue Act of Commission repealed many taxes of the Spanish régime on industries, imposing tax on articles of luxury, tobacco and tobacco products, and alcoholic liquors, and provided for certain license taxes

Aug. 22, Bond issue of $5,000,000 authorized for municipal improvement oversubscribed

Aug. 25, Detachment of constabulary ambushed on Island of Seyte by bandits

Oct. 18, Constabulary force defeated Pulayanes in mountains of eastern Samar, Oyomo, notorious outlaw and 50 of his followers killed

Dec. 23, Lieut. S. K. Hoyt and 37 men ambushed and killed in Samar

1905

Jan. 3, Writ of habeas corpus suspended in Cavite and Batangas and campaign begun

Jan. 24, Attack on town of San Francisco de Malobon in Cavite, family of Gov. Trias captured for ransom

Feb. 6, United States Act amended Organic Act to provide revenue and for construction of railroads. Title of chief executive changed from Civil Governor to Governor General

March 3, United States Tariff Act for the Philippines reduced rates on manufactured tobacco and on gasoline about one-half, and duty on agricultural, electrical, and other machinery made nominal rate of 5% ad valorem

March 4, Report of Committee appointed by Philippine

Commission including Major Carter, Dr. Albert, and Bishop Brent to investigate methods of dealing with sale and use of opium recommended that opium and the traffic be made a strict Government monopoly, and use prohibited except for medicinal purposes after 3 years, and licensed for use until then

May 17, Engagement with the Pulajanes on coast of Samar, Col. Wallace Taylor and 10 privates wounded

June 10, Gen. Carter reported capture of main stronghold of the Pulajanes and killing of Chief Daguhob

June 11, War Dept. made public plan for construction of railroads and invited proposals

Oct. 22, Ali, chief Moro insurgent on Mindanao Island killed in engagement, also a large number of his followers

Oct. 26, Reorganization Act reduced number of bureaus and reassigned duties improving efficiency and reducing expenses

1906

Jan. 31, Maj. Gen. Leonard Wood appointed commander of Military Division of the Philippines

March 6–9, Gen. Wood in battle with Moros at Mt. Dajo crater, Sulu Islands, near Jolo, 600 Moros killed and 50 Americans

March 24, On Island of Samar Pulajanes who had agreed to surrender opened fire

April 2, Governor General Henry C. Ide inaugurated succeeding L. E. Wright resigned to become Ambassador to Japan

April 16, *Ladrones* raided town of Malolos near Manila

——, Gen. Tasker H. Bliss succeeded Gen. Wood as Governor of Moro Province

May 24, Postal savings banks created by Commission

June 19, Pulajanes attacked town of Burauen, Leyte

July 22–24, Aug. 6 and 9, Engagements with the Pulajanes

Aug. 3, Act of the Commission made metric system legal for all weights and measures

Sept. 20, James F. Smith inaugurated as Governor General succeeding H. C. Ide resigned

Sept. 28, W. Morgan Shuster appointed Secretary of Public Instruction to succeed James F. Smith

Oct. 1, Conference of provincial governors, Governor Osmeña of Cebu presiding, held at Manila

Nov. 15, Majority of members of provincial boards and provincial governors made elective

Dec. 5, Capt. Ham and troops ambushed, Island of Leyte

1907

Jan. 9, Election law passed by the Commission, the provinces inhabited by Moros or other non-Christian tribes divided into 78 assembly districts, each province to constitute at least one district. 80 delegates to Assembly provided for, 2 representing the City of Manila

Feb. 13, Pulajanes attacked and burned 2 towns in Occidental Negros Province

March 12, "Partido Independista Immediata" formed, official party for independence

March 28, Resolution of the Commission certified that for 2 years "a condition of general and complete peace" had existed in the Islands not inhabited by the Moros or other non-Christian tribes

——, Proclamation of the President of the United States called for general election to be called by the Commission

April 1, Proclamation of the Commission called for

election for delegates to a popular assembly be held July 30

May 18, Pure Food and Drugs Act enacted by Commission

July 30, Election for first Assembly held of 80 members representing 34 provinces. Total number of votes registered 104,966 and result the election of 32 Nationalists, 20 Independents, 1 Central Catholic, 4 Independistas, 16 Progresistas, and 7 Immediastistas

Aug. 23, Display of Filipino flag for purposes of rebellion prohibited

Oct. 16, First Assembly met opened by William H. Taft, Secretary of War, and former Governor General of the Philippines, becoming the lower House of the Legislature of which the Commission the upper House

Nov. 7, Benito Legarda and Pablo Ocampo appointed Resident Commissioners to represent the Philippine Islands in Washington

1908

Feb. 1, First (inaugural) Assembly closed, 125 measures introduced and 5 passed. Voted to continue use of Spanish jointly with English as official language until 1913 when English to become sole official language

Feb. 4, First regular Assembly opened

Feb. 20, Maj. Gen. John F. Weston succeeded Gen. Wood in command of Army

April 29, United States Act repealed application of coastwise laws of April 30, 1906 to Philippines

May 11, Philippine Commission increased by one member

June 18, Agricultural Bank of the Philippine Islands created with capital of $500,000, and University of the Philippines opened in 1909

——, Bureau of Labor created by Legislature

June 30, Rafael Palma appointed member of Commission without portfolio

July 1, Gregorio Araneta succeeded H. C. Ide as Secretary of Finance and Justice, and Newton W. Gilbert succeeded Commissioner Legarda elected Resident Commissioner in Washington, W. Cameron Forbes appointed Vice-Governor

Aug. 18, Mountain Province established for government of tribal peoples, William Pack, first Governor

Dec. 14, Gen. Tasker H. Bliss succeeded as commander of Army

1909

Feb. 1–May 20, Second session of first legislature

March 1, Newton W. Gilbert made Secretary of Public Instruction succeeding W. Morgan Shuster, resigned

March 27, Joint Resolution of Assembly against extension of free trade to the Islands

April 6–22, Gen. W. H. Carter in command of Army, and April 23, Gen. W. P. Duvall

May 20, All libraries consolidated into the Philippines Library

Aug. 5, Payne-Tariff Act provided for limited free trade with the United States, a restriction placed on the amount of sugar and tobacco admitted free of duty

Nov. 11, W. Cameron Forbes appointed Governor General on resignation of James F. Smith, inaugurated Nov. 23

Nov. 28, Gen. John J. Pershing succeeded Gen. Tasker H. Bliss as Governor of the Moro Province

1910

Feb. 14, Charles B. Elliot became Secretary of Commerce and Police

Feb., Commissioner Gilbert became Vice-Governor

April 19, Deportation of 12 Chinese, leaders in a tong, as undesirable citizens

Sept. 1, Formal opening of the General Hospital at Manila

Dec. 5, Joint Resolution of Legislature asked Congress of the United States to recognize right to prepare and adopt own Constitution

Dec. 28, Brig. Gen. John J. Pershing in command of Army

1911

Jan. 13, Maj. Gen. J. Franklin Bell in command of Army

Jan. 30, Eruption of Mt. Taal, 39 miles south of Manila, accompanied by earthquake and tidal wave. 1,335 persons killed in 3 days

Feb. 15, United States Act provided for quadrennial election of members of Philippine Assembly and Resident Commissioners to the United States

Oct. 1, Noted outlaw, Otloy, in Samar killed, captured by Filipino, member of Constabulary

1912

March 15–Jan. 17, 1913, Vice-Governor Gilbert acted as Governor General

March 23, Philippine Legislature authorized to provide for acquisition of citizenship. All Spanish subjects resident in 1899 and their children deemed citizens

June 10, School of Household Industries in Manila formally opened by Bureau of Education

1913

Feb. 11, Act recognized English as "the" language of the courts, and Spanish as "a" language of the courts

May 5, Decision of Supreme Court of the United States upheld right of the Governor General to deport aliens in case of Chinese deported in 1910

June 1, English became the official language but use of Spanish extended to Jan. 1, 1920

June 12, Gen. Pershing in surprise attack routed rebel Moros who had established a stronghold on Mt. Bagsak

Aug. 21, Francis Burton Harrison appointed Governor General by President Wilson

Sept. 2–Oct. 6, Vice-Governor Gilbert acted as Governor General until arrival of Governor Harrison

Sept. 15, Dean C. Worcester resigned from the Commission

Oct. 3, Underwood Tariff Act of the United States removed limitations on amount of sugar and tobacco that might be admitted free of duty into the United States, and repealed duty on rice

Oct. 6, Inauguration of Governor General Francis B. Harrison. In address the Governor General declared immediate majority representation would be given to Filipinos on the Commission (Upper House)

Nov. 24, President Wilson nominated 3 American members of the Commission, Clinton L. Riggs, Secretary of Commerce and Police; Winfred T. Denison, Secretary Interior, Henderson S. Martin appointed Vice-Governor with portfolio of Public Instruction

Dec. 13, Act transferred management of rinderpest quarantine from Dept. of Agriculture composed of Americans to provincial boards with the result that deaths of cattle increased from 2,787 in 1913 to 35,740

Dec. 20, Act changed name of Moro Province to Dept.

of Mindanao and Sulu, and the Province of Agusun placed under its jurisdiction

In 1913 there were 6,363 Americans connected with the Government and 2,623 Filipinos. Resignations asked for by Governor General Harrison included Vice-Governor Gilbert, Commissioner F. A. Branagan and the 4 Filipino commissioners. Enforced resignations asked for by Governor General Harrison included First Assistant Executive Secretary T. C. Welch; Director of Lands, C. H. Sleeper; and Assistant Director, J. R. Wilson; Assistant Director, Bureau of Civil Service, J. E. Enright; Director of Posts, C. M. Cotterman; Collector of Customs, H. B. McCoy; Deputy Collector, H. B. Steere; Director of Printing, J. S. Leech; and Assistant Director, J. A. Hoggsette; Prosecuting Attorney, City of Manila, W. H. Bishop; and Chief of Police, City of Manila, J. E. Harding. A large number of voluntary resignations on account of reductions of salary

1914

Feb. 28, Abolition of Land Court, duties transferred to other courts

April 16, Maj. Gen. Thomas H. Barry in command of Army

July 23, Commission enacted new Organic Act for government of Dept. of Mindanao and Sulu

Dec. 24, Small organized insurrection of followers of Artemio Ricarte, fugitive revolutionist in Hong Kong, in Navotas, suburb of Manila, soon suppressed

1915

March 22, Agreement with the Sultan of Sulu signed by the Sultan and the Governor General by which the Sultan recognized the sovereignty of the United States

April 3, Ricarte arrested at Shanghai charged with inciting revolt at Manila

Dec. 31, In Constabulary there were 341 officers of whom 223 were Americans and 118 Filipinos, and 4,981 enlisted men, all Filipinos

1916

Feb. 4, Retirement Act provided allowances for those who had served for 6 years but proviso that official who desired to avail himself thereof must resign in writing before July 1 of ensuing year

——, National Bank of the Philippine Islands chartered and made depository of public funds

March 31, Resignation of W. T. Denison, Secretary of the Interior

April 16, Maj. Gen. Hunter Liggett in command of Army

Aug. 29, Jones Act of Congress of the United States, the Constitution of the Philippines, abolished the Commission and gave Filipinos the right to elect members to an Upper House of the Legislature to have power to confirm or decline appointments made by Governor General except members of Legislature to represent Moros and other tribes. Ultimate independence promised as soon as "a stable government" established

Oct. 16, Commission ceased to exist

——, First session of Philippine Legislature under new Organic Act. Elected Senate inaugurated. Non-Christian tribes represented for the first time

Nov. 7, Sulu Public Hospital at Jolo opened, and Rizal

Memorial Hospital at Zamboanga, Mindanao, Dec. 30

1917

Jan. 1, At this date there were 31 Americans acting as chiefs and assistant chiefs in the Government and 22 Filipinos

March 10, National Coal Company created as a private company but most of the stock owned by the Government

April 16, Brig. Gen. Charles J. Bailey in command of Army

April 25, Filipino National Guard constituted and services offered to United States in World War

May 29, Act provided for construction of a destroyer and a submarine for the United States

June 28, Resignation of Vice-Governor Martin

Aug. 15, Brig. Gen. Robert K. Evans in command of Army

1918

Aug. 6, Brig. Gen. Henry A. Greene in command of Army, and succeeded Dec. 6 by Col. Edwin A. Root

Oct., Executive Order of the Governor General created a Council of State composed of presiding officers of both Houses of the Legislature and the Secretaries of the executive depts. (Executive Order No. 25)

Nov. 7, Commission of Independence constituted composed of members of the Legislature to consolidate all efforts for independence

Nov. 20, Filipino Division mustered into the federal service

Dec. 31, Total population given by second census as 10,314,310 of whom 9,332,960 reported as Christians and 443,037 as Mohammedans or Moros, and 508,-596 as pagan tribes, 24,263 as Buddhists and 5,454 as "all others." Resident foreigners estimated as 64,-037

1919

Jan. 20, Col. Samuel E. Allen in command of Army, succeeded Feb. 16 by Gen. F. H. French

March 6, Act extended time of use of Spanish language as well as English in the courts until Jan. 1, 1930

March 19, Income tax law adopted including tax on undivided profits

April 4, Filipino Delegation headed by Manuel Quezon presented memorial to Secretary of War Baker in Washington asking for fulfilment of promises for complete independence of the Islands

Oct. 22, Act repealed that of 1907 forbidding display of Filipino flag

Nov. 21, Maj. Gen. Francis J. Kernan in command of Army

1920

Feb. 5, Resignation of Governor General F. B. Harrison to take effect March 4 on which date he left the Islands

March 24, Act granted life pension of $6,000 a year to General Aguinaldo

March 26, Act provided for use of Filipino flag with American

July 1, Victorino Mapa appointed Chief Justice of the Supreme Court to succeed Justice Arellano retired April 1

——, 20 Americans head of Government offices and 30 Filipinos on this date, and 760 Americans connected with the Government as compared with 12,047 Filipinos

Dec. 15, Act provided for annual appropriation of a

million pesos for use of Independence Commission

1921

March 23, President Harding appointed General Leonard Wood and W. Cameron Forbes a commission to investigate conditions in the Philippines

May 4–Sept. 12, Wood-Forbes Commission in the Philippines

June 9, Petition of Sulu Chiefs to President of the United States of grievances

Oct. 5, Gen. Leonard Wood appointed Governor General

Oct. 8, Report of Wood-Forbes Commission submitted did not favor granting independence to the Filipinos at present time

Oct. 15, Inauguration of Governor General Leonard Wood

Nov. 1, Manuel Araullo appointed Chief Justice of the Supreme Court succeeding Justice Mapa retired Oct. 31

1922

June 13, Gold Standard Funding Act passed

June 29, President Harding made reply to Filipino delegation that time for independence had not arrived but that "no backward step" contemplated

Sept. 11, Maj. Gen. Omar Bundy in command of Army succeeded Oct. 3 by Gen. George W. Read

Oct., Collectivist (National) Party adopted platform demanding complete independence for Islands and immediate curtailment of powers of Governor General

Nov. 22, House adopted Resolution asking the United States to recognize right of Islands to independence

1923

Feb. 16, Resolution introduced in United States Senate proposed independence for the Philippines

——, Message of Gov. Gen. Wood to Legislature as to closing of Philippine National Bank because of incompetent management which permitted loan of large amounts without adequate security and use of funds for speculation

March 19, Act of Legislature provided for medical inspection of school children annually

May 19, Engagement with Moros on Island of Pala, 30 reported killed

June 1, Clash of Constabulary force with Moros on Island of Pala led by Akbara who was killed with 52 of his followers

July 2, Manuel Quezon, president of Senate, charged Gov. Gen. Wood with undue interference in domestic affairs

July 13, Resignation of Secretary of the Interior because of reinstatement of Ray Conley, American Chief of the Secret Service, after he had been acquitted of charges made against him for the third time. Conley's suppression of gambling had brought him into conflict with local interests

July 17, Resignation of Filipino members of the Cabinet demanding resignation of Gov. Gen. Wood

July 23 and Oct. 17, Resolution adopted in both Houses requested recall of Gov. Gen. Wood

July 24, Filipino Independence Commission requested the United States to appoint a Filipino Governor, and about this time a boycott of American goods begun in San Miguel

Aug. 6, Conflict of Moros with Constabulary near Lake Laona on Mindanao Island

Nov. 15, American Chamber of Commerce in Manila petitioned Congress to repeal the Jones Act and establish a territorial government in Islands

Nov. 24, Gov. Gen. Wood vetoed remission of penalty of land tax for 1923 voted by Legislature Oct. 24

Dec. 28, Gov. Gen. Wood vetoed measure appropriating $50,000 for relief of destitute persons as contrary to Jones law since it vested discretionary control in Secretary of the Interior

1924

Jan. 8, Filipino Independence Commission addressed petition to Congress asking for immediate action on independence of the Islands

Jan. 31, Filipino Independence Commission filed charges against Gov. Gen. Wood and asked for his removal

Feb. 15, Auditor refused to honor vouchers on million pesos fund for Independence Commission

Feb. 21, Letter of President Coolidge in reply to demand for independence declared that "the Philippine people are by no means equipped either in wealth or experience to undertake the heavy burden which would be imposed upon them with political independence." Published March 5

March 18, Petition of Legislature to the President against use of veto power by Gov. Gen. Wood

May 6, Special Independence Commission headed by Manuel Quezon arrived in Washington

July 26, Death of Chief Justice Araullo of the Supreme Court. Succeeded by E. Finley Johnson, Acting

Nov. 18, Maj. Gen. James H. McRae in command of Army

Nov. 19, Resolution adopted by Legislature demanding complete independence

Nov. 24, Act to rehabilitate Philippine National Bank

1925

Feb. 28, Ramon Avanceña appointed Chief Justice

March 10, Rafael Palma elected president of the University of the Philippine Islands

June 2, General election reduced majority of Nationalist Consolidated Party

Nov. 9, House passed Senate Bill providing for plebiscite on Philippine independence

Dec. 7, Petition for independence from the Philippine Legislature presented to Congress of the United States

——, Tax levied on gasoline by Legislature to provide for maintenance of roads

1926

Feb. 25, Maj. Gen. William Weigel in command of Army succeeded May 4 by Maj. Gen. Fred W. Sladen

June 7, Act of Legislature making it unlawful for any business firm to keep accounts in any language other than English or Spanish or a local dialect declared invalid by Supreme Court of the United States

July 9–Oct. 4, Col. Carmi Thompson appointed by the President to investigate political and economic situation at Manila

July 16, Legislature adopted Resolution for plebiscite vote on independence

July 26, Gov. Gen. Wood issued appeal to American people for subscription fund of $2,000,000 to eradicate leprosy in the Islands

Aug. 17, Gov. Gen. Wood for second time vetoed Resolution for plebiscite vote on independence; passed over veto Aug. 30

Nov. 9, Executive Order of Gov. Gen. Wood abolished Board of Control and provides that duties and powers shall be exercised solely by Governor General

Dec. 4, Report of Col. Carmi Thompson recommended reforms but suggested granting of absolute independence to the Islands be postponed

Dec. 7, House of Representatives increased its members to 94

1927

April 6, President Coolidge vetoed Act of Philippine Legislature for plebiscite on independence which had been twice passed over veto of Governor General

June 26, Direct radio communication with the United States opened

July 16–Nov. 9, Legislature passed Workmen's Compensation Act which became law without signature of Governor

Aug. 7, Death of Gov. Gen. Leonard Wood on leave of absence in the United States

Dec. 13, Henry L. Stimson appointed Governor General

Dec. 31, On this date 470 Americans and 18,246 Filipinos in the Government service

1928

March 1, Inauguration of Governor General Henry L. Stimson

March 5, Resignation of Isauro Gabaldon, Resident Commissioner at Washington, as protest against failure of the United States to grant independence

May 14, United States Supreme Court sustained decision of Supreme Court of the Philippines declaring Board of Control Act invalid

June 5, General election an overwhelming defeat of Democratic Party demanding immediate independence

June 20, Workmen's Compensation Act adopted 1927 came into effect

Aug. 9, Act provided for technical advisers and civilian assistants to the Governor General and carried annual appropriation of $125,000

Aug. 30, Executive Order of Governor General created an advisory Council of State

Nov. 23–25, Typhoon in central and southern Islands the most destructive ever in history, 500 persons killed, 25,000 rendered homeless, and damage estimated at $25,000,000

Dec. 3, Corporation law amended provided for authorization of no par stock and stock dividends and repealed provisions which prohibited an investor from being interested in more than one agricultural corporation

1929

Feb. 7, Special Session of Legislature called to provide funds for relief of typhoon sufferers passed measures for reorganization of system of bank inspection, amended insular irrigation law and gasoline tax law

Feb. 23, Governor General Stimson left Manila to become Secretary of State of the United States

May 17, Dwight F. Davis appointed Governor General and arrived in Manila July 8

Oct. 9, King Amendment to Tariff Act for independence of the Philippines defeated in United States Senate

1930

Jan. 2, Convention between Great Britain and the United States signed by which sovereignty of the United States recognized as extending over the Turtle Islands

Feb. 22–26, Independence Congress held in Manila on initiative of private citizens

May 7, Moros in clash with Constabulary in Lanao Province, Mindanao Island

July 16–Nov. 8, Legislature increased number of judges of the Supreme Court from 9 to 15, approved revision of Penal Code, provided for employment of experts for general revision of tax and tariff laws, and for a permanent legislative service office to furnish technical assistance needed

July 29, Nicholas Roosevelt, of New York, appointed Vice-Governor, but appointment withdrawn because of opposition. He had expressed himself as against independence

Nov. 15, New National Party, the *Bagong Katipunan* launched by Manuel Roxas, Speaker of the House

PUERTO RICO

Puerto Rico, the most easterly of the Greater Antilles group of the West Indies Islands lying about 70 miles east of Haiti, about 40 miles west of St. Thomas, and about 1,400 miles southeast of New York City, total area 3,434 square miles, with average length from east to west of about 100 miles, and a width of from 35 to 40 miles, and a population, according to the census of April 1, 1930, of 1,543,913, or 449.5 per sq. mile.

The population in 1920 was 1,299,809 or 378.4 per sq. mile, distributed according to color, as follows:—White, 948,709; black, 49,246; mulatto, 301,816; Chinese, 32; Japanese, 4; all other (Filipino and Hindu), 2. During the decade ending 1920 the white population increased by 29.5%, while the black population decreased by 2%, and the mulatto by 10%. Of the working population, 63% were engaged in agriculture, fisheries, and mining; 21% in domestic and personal service; 8% in manufacturing industries; 8% in trade and transportation.

Chief towns, San Juan, the capital, 114,715 inhabitants (1930); Ponce, 53,430; Mayaguez, 37,060. Puerto Rico was ceded to the United States by Spain by Treaty of Dec. 10, 1898. It is governed by the "Organic Act" of the Congress of the United States of March 2, 1917.

Theodore Roosevelt, Governor.

1493

Nov. 17, Columbus on second voyage anchored his caravels off the shore of Puerto Rico near Aguada

Nov. 19, Columbus anchored in Bay naming Island San Juan Bautista to which later was added "de Puerto Rico" and took possession for Ferdinand and Isabella

1506

Rights of colonization granted to Captain Yanez Pinzon, pilot of Columbus

1508

Juan Ponce de Leon discovered harbor of San Juan and established settlement he named Villa de Caparra

1509

May 2, Ponce de Leon authorized to colonize Island of San Juan

Oct. 28, Ponce de Leon relinquished government to Juan Ceron

1510

March 20, Order of King made Ponce de Leon again Governor

1511

June, Rising of Indians against Spaniards

Nov. 8, King Ferdinand granted coat of arms to Island still in use as the official seal

Nov. 28, Juan Ceron again Governor

1512

March 3, Ponce de Leon sailed to find the fountain of youth and discovered Florida, April 11

June 2, Rodrigo de Moscoso, Governor

1513

Cristobal de Mendoza, Governor

1515

July 15, Ponce de Leon returned as Governor

1519

Sept.19, Antonio de la Gama, Governor

1520

Nov. 16, Report to the Emperor that City of San Juan Bautista de Puerto Rico transferred as commanded to more healthful present site

1533

Fortress begun at Santa Catalina, completed in 1538

1595

Nov. 22–25, Francis Drake expedition failed in attack on San Juan. Sir John Hawkins killed by shot

1598

June 6, Expedition of Lord George Clifford, Earl of Cumberland arrived off San Juan and landed soldiers

June 21, Spanish Governor Mosquera forced to surrender

July 7, Governor Mosquera and Spaniards deported by the English sent to Cartagena

Aug. 14, Cumberland left his colony

Nov. 23, The surviving English with Sir John Berkeley left Puerto Rico

1625

Sept. 25–Oct., Dutch expedition commanded by Captain Enrico besieged fort successfully defended by Governor

1791

March 29, Royal order authorized founding of Seminario Conciliar. Collection of funds begun

1797

April 17–May 2, Attack and invasion of English expedition of General Abercromby successfully repulsed by Captain General Ramon de Castro

1808

July 6, Spanish Cortes authorized the Government to send representatives

1813

Feb. 12, First Intendant Alejandro Ramirez assumed office

1832

April 10, Private primary schools opened

July 23, Supreme Court inaugurated

Oct. 12, Seminario Conciliar opened

1844

Aug. 1, First public English class established at the Seminario Conciliar

1848

First sugar mill built by Santaolaya near the capital

1868

Sept. 23, Rebellion at Lares led by Matthew Bruckman, American, and Manuel Rojas, a Venezuelan, declaring for a republic unsuccessful

1869

Jan. 20, Amnesty granted to all connected with Lares revolt

1870

Dec. 19, Cable laid between San Juan and St. Thomas by West India and Panama Telegraph Company

1871

April 1, "Diputacion Provincial" local elected governing body began sessions

1873

March 22, Abolition of slavery

1879

May 23, Criminal Code promulgated

1885

Sept. 25, Civil procedure promulgated

1886

Jan. 28, Commercial Code adopted

1889

July 31, Civil Code promulgated

Oct. 1, Liberal Party organized

Oct. 19, Code of criminal procedure adopted

1897

Feb. 11, Autonomous government inaugurated. Proclaimed by royal decree Nov. 25

1898

Feb. 10, Cabinet consisting of 5 heads of departments and a President appointed

March 25, First Socialist Party meeting

March 27, Election for legislature

April 21, Spanish-American War. See United States

May 12, American fleet commanded by Admiral Sampson searching for the Spanish fleet appeared off San Juan

July 25, First landing of American troops. General Nelson A. Miles took possession of Guanica

July 27, Ponce occupied by Americans, formal surrender on the 28th

July 31, American force commanded by General John R. Brooks landed at Arroyo

Aug. 9, Skirmish of Spaniards and Americans at Coamo

Aug. 10, Skirmish near Hormigueros

Aug. 13, Fighting ended with news that Protocol had been signed in Washington Aug. 12

Oct. 16, Spanish Governor General Macias vacated the palace and sailed for Spain the following day

Oct. 18, American military government established. General John R. Brooke took formal possession and raised the American flag

Nov. 29, General Brooke ordered discontinuance of legislature, the "Provincial Deputation"

Dec. 6, Major General Guy V. Henry succeeded General Brooke as Military Governor

Dec. 10, Treaty of peace between the United States and Spain by which Spain relinquished sovereignty over Puerto Rico

1899

Jan., "State constabulary" organized to succeed Spanish guard

Feb. 5, The Cabinet resigned because of appointment of 2 Americans at head of Bureaus instead of Puerto Ricans

Feb. 6, Cabinet discontinued by General Henry and Secretaries of State, Treasury, Justice, and Interior substituted

March 6, The American "Insular Commission" arrived, General Robert P. Kennedy, C. W. Watkins, and H. G. Curtis appointed to investigate and report on matters of administration

March 23, Republican Party organized

March 24, Puerto Rican regiment organized

April 29, Resignation of Governor Henry because of ill health

May 8, Auditing system for accounts established, J. R. Garrison appointed Auditor

May 9, Brigadier General George W. Davis became Military Governor

July 8, Board of Education appointed

July 15 and Aug. 12, Military orders created Judicial Board of 3 Puerto Ricans and 2 American lawyers. Work of State, Treasury, and Interior Departments transferred to a civil Secretary, a Board of Public Works, a Board of Charities, and a number of advisory Boards

July 25, Election for municipal officers held

Aug. 8, Terrific hurricane first, since 1867, and most destructive in history of the Island, killed 2,600 persons and destroyed the coffee plantations

Aug. 15, General Davis reorganized the civil government

Aug. 30, Insular Commission filed report with the War Department

Oct. 16, Census taken gave population as 953,243 including 941,751 natives, 11,492 foreigners, whites 589,426, colored 363,817

1900

March 24, Act of United States Congress appropriated all duties collected on produce of Puerto Rico in ports of the United States to expenses of Puerto Rico

April 1, First Normal and Industrial School opened

April 12, Organic Act for government of Puerto Rico (Foraker Act) established free trade with the United States, passed by United States Congress, slightly amended May 1, and March 2, 1901

May 1, Charles H. Allen, first civil Governor inaugurated

June 6, Joint Resolution of Congress of the United States empowered the Spanish Bank of Puerto Rico to amend its by-laws

June 9, William H. Hunt appointed Secretary of the Island

June 28, Executive Council (Upper House) organized

June 29, Supreme Court organized

Aug. 17, Political riot at Mayaguez

Sept. 14, Mob broke into office of "El Diario" in clash between Federals and Republicans

Nov. 6, First general election for members of House of Delegates

Dec. 3–Jan. 31, 1901, First session of the Legislature. 36 laws passed establishing civil government and system of taxation and internal revenue

1901

Jan. 12, Act established trial by jury

Jan. 31, General Jury Procedure Act passed

——, School law placed public education under control of an elected School Board and provided for "school funds"

——, Revenue Act revised taxation, provided for general property tax, system of excises, and an inheritance tax

Feb. 23, Puerto Rican army replaced American troops

April 15, Petition of workingmen presented to President of the United States describing destitute condition and lack of work

May 27 and Dec. 2, United States Supreme Court decisions as to status of insular possessions. *See* United States

May 30, Puerto Rican provisional regiment organized

July 25, Proclamation of President McKinley announced free trade with Puerto Rico

Sept. 15, William H. Hunt became Governor

Dec. 6, Gold standard adopted

1902

March 1, New municipal law reduced number of municipalities from 66 to 46

1903

Jan. 17, Proclamation of the President of the United States set apart the Luquillo Forest Reserve

March 12, Law provided that the Supreme Court should be a court of appeals rather than a court of cassation

Sept. 29, University of Puerto Rico opened at San Juan

1904

Jan. 4, Decision of United States Supreme Court that Puerto Ricans not aliens and therefore cannot be excluded. *See also* United States

Feb. 20, Assembly voted for statehood in the United States or independence by 60 to 15

March 10, Revenue and Judiciary Acts amended adopting American system of civil procedure. Universal suffrage adopted

July 4, Beekman Winthrop inaugurated Governor

1906

Nov. 21–22, President Roosevelt on visit to Island

1907

April 18, Regis H. Post, appointed Governor March 5, inaugurated

1909

July 15, Olmstead Act placed Puerto Rico under Executive Department of the United States (War Department)
Nov. 6, George H. Colton became Governor

1910

Census gave total population as 1,118,012

1912

Jan. 11, House of Delegates passed resolution declaring against American citizenship unless accompanied by full self-government

1913

Nov. 6, Arthur Yager became Governor

1915

June 6, Committee representing Free Federation of Workingmen petitioned President Wilson for American investigation of labor conditions

1916

June 3, National Defense Act. National Guard authorized

1917

March 2, New Organic Act (Jones Act) made Puerto Rico a Territory of the United States. Six executive departments created. Conferred American citizenship on Puerto Ricans collectively. Provision of Foraker Act prohibition of holding by corporations of more than 500 acres repealed

1918

March 2, Prohibition of all alcoholic beverages went into effect
June 2, The S.S. "Carolina" sunk by German submarine on voyage from San Juan to New York
Oct. 11 and 24, Destructive earthquake caused loss of life and property on western part of Island

1919

March 1, Legislature adopted resolution in favor of statehood or independence
June 30, Act passed to prevent and help in settlement of strikes

1920

Census gave population total as 1,299,809

1921

May 15, E. Mont Reily succeeded as Governor
Strike of agricultural workers on sugar plantations

1923

April 6, Horace M. Towner inaugurated as Governor
Dec. 10, New Banking law came into effect

1924

Nov. 4, Elections a victory for the Unionist Party

1926

Aug.–Jan. 1927, Strike of cigar makers

Sept. 22, School of Tropical Medicine opened, run in coöperation with Columbia University, New York

1927

March 4, Organic Act of March 2 and June 7, 1924 amended

1928

Jan. 21, Treaty of arbitration with Spain signed
Feb. 2, Colonel Charles A. Lindbergh arrived at Puerto Rico in the "Spirit of St. Louis"
March 15, President Coolidge replied to resolution of legislature of Feb. 28 asking for independence, pointing out benefits of American rule
Sept. 13–14, Hurricane in which 200 lives lost, and crops ruined, damage estimated at $85,000,000; 400,000 homeless. The American Red Cross helped rebuild 50,000 homes, expending $3,150,288 for relief work
Dec. 21, Act of United States Congress appointed Relief Commission and appropriated $8,150,000 for relief

1929

Sept. 9, Theodore Roosevelt appointed Governor

1930

April 28, Joint Resolution created Bureau of Commerce and Industry with a branch office in New York City which included an employment exchange

SAMOAN ISLANDS

Samoan Islands (American) group of 4 inhabited and several uninhabited islands of the Samoan Islands in south Pacific Ocean confirmed to possession of the United States by Treaty with Great Britain and Germany of Dec. 2, 1899. They include Tutuila and Aunu'u, the Manu'a group including Ta'u with Ofu and Olosega, the coral atoll of Rose Island, and all of the islands east of 171° W. Long. Pago Pago, Tutuila, is the capital.

The total area of American Samoa is 60 square miles and according to the 1930 census, contained 10,055 inhabitants. The Island of Tutuila 70 miles from Apia, has an area of about 40.2 square miles with a population of 9,768 (including the Island of Aunu'u) according to the 1930 census. Ta'u has an area of 14 square miles, and the other islets (Ofu and Olosega) of the Manu'a group have an area of about 4 square miles with a population of 2,069. Swain's Island, annexed in 1925, is from a mile and a half to two miles in diameter. Population (1930) is 99. The harbor at Pago Pago, which penetrates the south coast like a fiord, is the only good harbor in Samoa. It is a United States naval station.

The Commandant is also the Governor of American Samoa by commission from the President of the United States. He appoints officers and frames laws or ordinances, but native customs (not inconsistent with United States laws) are not changed without the consent of the people.

The Samoan Islands were discovered by Jacob Roggewein, navigator of the Dutch East India Company, May 19 and June 14, 1722. Louis Antoine de Bougainville, French circumnavigator of the globe, sighted the Islands May 3, 1768, and the J. F. de G. La Pérouse expedition were the first to make a landing, a party from the ships being killed by natives Dec. 11, 1787. Capt. Edward Edwards was the first English navigator at the Islands, June 18, 1791 at Savaii, and at Tutuila and Upolu July 14. Lieut. Charles Wilkes visited Samoa in Oct. 1791 and American consular representatives date from this time.

Captain Gatewood S. Lincoln, Governor.

1872

March 2, Admiral Meade on his own authority made compact with Chief for exclusive privileges for the United States of the harbor of Pago Pago on Tutuila Island in return for the friendship and protection of the United States; not ratified by Senate

April 9, Petition of Chiefs of Samoa for annexation to the United States

1873

Aug. 7–Oct. 13, Visit of Col. A. B. Steinberger, sent as special agent by President Grant

Oct. 2, Code of laws adopted Aug. 21 proclaimed by Samoan Chiefs and declaration of union at Mulinuu, and the flag saluted by foreign consuls, Mauga recognized as Chief

1875

Jan. 2, Malietoa Laupepa and Pulepule vested jointly as Kings

April 1, Col. Steinberger as special agent arrived at Apia on second visit

May 18, New Constitution adopted and Malietoa made sole King, and Colonel Steinberger accepted office as Premier July 4; not recognized as special agent of the United States after taking office as Premier

1876

Jan. 13, Memorandum signed by 3 consuls, Williams, Poppe, and Foster, British, German, and American, refused to recognize laws of the Steinberger government

Feb. 8, Col. Steinberger arrested by group headed by the American and English consuls and taken to British ship and presently deported, and Malietoa forced to resign

1877

March 13, Meeting of Samoans representing the old Party of Taimua and Faipule of the Steinberger régime and the Puletua, the opposition party, asked advice of the foreign consuls who advised an election

April 3, Petition of the Taimua and Faipule to Great Britain for protectorate

April 13, Petition of Le Mamea, Secretary of State, and other chiefs for protection of the United States

1878

Jan. 16, Treaty with the United States signed of friendship and commerce by which privileges at Pago Pago as coaling and naval station granted, and free trade and extraterritorial jurisdiction

1879

Jan. 24, Treaty of commerce with Germany signed and privileges of Apia Harbor obtained

May 15, Instructions of State Dept. to American Minister in London to present claim of A. B. Steinberger against Great Britain for outrage at Samoa at hands of Capt. Stevens of the H. M. S., "Barracouta" including his deportation, but responsibility denied by Great Britain as acting at request of United States Consul

Dec. 15, Treaty of peace signed by warring factions of Samoans on board German warship

Dec. 23, Agreement signed on German warship by Samoans recognizing Malietoa Talavou as King during his lifetime, and his nephew Malietoa Laupepa appointed Regent

1880

March 24, Agreement drawn up by consuls of Great Britain, Germany, and the United States signed by the King and Regent recognized Malietoa Talavou as King and Malietoa Laupepa as Regent, and provided for an executive council of 3 members to assist the King, to consist of an American, a German, and a British subject

May 3, Malietoa Talavou crowned at Mulinuu

Aug. 28, Treaty of commerce with Great Britain and provision for naval and coaling station

Nov. 8, Death of King Malietoa Talavou followed by civil war

1881

March 19, Malietoa Laupepa crowned, supported by the foreign consuls, and a few days later Chief Tamasese of the House of Tupua crowned by the old party chiefs as King of Atua and Aana at Leulumoega

June 26, Meeting of representatives of all parties and the consuls with Capt. Gillis of the U.S.S. "Lackawanna" who presented "four articles" to be considered to bring about a peace, and an armistice arranged

July 12, Agreement signed on board U.S.S. "Lackawanna." Peace recognized Malietoa Laupepa and Tupua Tamasese as Vice-King

1884

Jan. 23, Dr. Stubel, German Consul, seized Apia, charging that Malietoa had failed to carry out treaty engagements, declaring it a neutral zone, and raising the German flag. Act disavowed by German Government and flag taken down May 29, 1886

Nov. 10, Malietoa under duress signed Treaty which provided for appointment of German-Samoan Commission which should approve all laws, the German consul to be secretary and adviser to the King. Malietoa disowned treaty and appealed to the Emperor of Germany

1886

May 10, Malietoa asked for protection of the United States under Treaty of Jan. 1878

May 14, American Consul, Greenebaum, proclaimed an American Protectorate which was disavowed by the United States

May 27, Proclamation of the 3 consuls declared against recognition of Tamasese as King

Aug., Commission sent to Samoa to investigate conditions, Travers (German), Bates (American), and Thurston (British)

1887

Feb. 17, Political Confederation with King of Hawaii signed

June 25–July 26, Conference at Washington of Germany, Great Britain, and the United States on Samoa

July 24, German troops landed and recognized Tamasese as King

Aug. 19, German squadron entered Apia Harbor

Aug. 23, Ultimatum to King Malietoa demanded reparation for alleged grievances amounting to $13,000

Aug. 24, War declared by Germans on Malietoa and Tamasese proclaimed King

Sept. 9, Mataafa crowned King at Faleula and declared war on Tamasese

Sept. 17, Malietoa surrendered and was sent into exile by the Germans

1888

Sept. 4, The natives led by Mataafa rose against the Germans and Tamasese

Sept. 11–12, Battle which ended in complete rout of Tamasese forces

Dec. 18, Mataafa ambushed a German landing party and killed 20 and wounded 30

1889

March 15–16, Hurricane in Apia Harbor and 3 American warships and 3 German driven ashore and destroyed, only the British "Calliope" saved by steaming out of the harbor, 50 Americans lost and 96 Germans

April 29–June 14, Conference on Samoan affairs at Berlin of England, Germany, and the United States

June 14, Treaty signed by the United States, Germany, and Great Britain, agreement to establish and maintain Malietoa Laupepa as King of Samoa, provided for a municipal council for the District of Apia with a foreign president who should act as adviser to the King, a foreign court, a court for settlement of land titles, and a revenue system

1893

June, Mataafa surrendered and was exiled to Marshall Island

1894

Dec. 3, Death of Robert Louis Stevenson (44) writer, at his home at Vailima, buried the day following at summit of precipitous peak of Mt. Vaea, carried there by 60 Samoans who acknowledged him as chief

1898

Aug. 22, Death of King Malietoa Laupepa

Sept. 19, Mataafa and other exiled chiefs, allowed to return, landed in Apia from German warship

Nov. 12, Mataafa elected King, considered ineligible because of Berlin Treaty of June 1889 by foreign consuls in favor of Tanu, son of Malietoa

Dec. 31, Decision of Mr. Chambers, Chief Justice of the Supreme Court, that Malietoa Tanu the rightful king, and civil war begun

1899

Jan. 1, Mataafa attacked and defeated the Malietoans, Tanu taking refuge on British warship

Jan. 4, Foreign consuls recognized de facto government

of the victorious Mataafa party, and Provisional Government headed by Dr. Raffel, president of the municipal court. Dr. Raffel proclaimed himself acting Chief Justice; protested by British and American consuls, and Chief Justice Chambers (American) resumed his office

March 6, Admiral Kantz arrived on U.S.S. "Philadelphia" at Apia, instructed to carry out Berlin Treaty

March 11, Consuls of Great Britain and United States and naval commanders declare Provisional Government illegal under Berlin Treaty, refuse to continue to recognize Mataafa as King

March 13, Rose, German Consul, made counter proclamation. Dr. Wilhelm Solf appointed president of the municipal council, succeeding Dr. Raffel, recalled to Germany

March 15, Rear Admiral Kantz (American) and British warships began bombardment of Apia in demonstration against Mataafa and his German supporters

March 23, Malietoa Tanu crowned King by British and American officials at Mulimni

March 30, Villages held by Mataafa shelled by British and American warships

March 31, Proclamation of British and American consuls warned Mataafa that he would be treated as a rebel unless he laid down arms

April 1, Samoans made surprise attack at Vailele, killing 2 American officers and 2 marines, and 3 British marines

May 13, Joint Commission, American-British-German, arrived at Apia to investigate conditions, Bartlett Trip, American, president

June 10, Office of King of Samoa declared abolished by Commission

——, Decision of Chief Justice Chambers as to king confirmed. Tanu voluntarily abdicated kingship

July 4, Fighting between followers of Mataafa and Malietoa Tanu

July 14, Chief Justice Chambers resigned and left the Islands

Nov. 7, Claims Convention signed by the United States, Great Britain and Germany agreed to submit claims for bombardment of Samoan villages by British and American warships to arbitration of the King of Sweden

Nov. 14, Anglo-German Treaty signed by which Great Britain renounced all rights over the Islands as regarded Savaii and Upolu in favor of Germany, and in favor of the United States as regarded Tutuila and other islands east of 171° W. Long.

Nov. 27, Agreement of the United States to arrangements for partition of Samoa by Treaty of Nov. 14

Dec. 2, Treaty signed by the United States, Great Britain, and Germany confirmed Anglo-German Treaty of Nov. 14 for partition of Samoa, and ratifications exchanged Feb. 16, 1900

1900

Feb. 10, Commander Seaton Schroeder appointed Governor of Tutuila Island under the Navy Dept.

Feb. 19, Islands placed under control of the Navy Dept. by the President

April 17, "Instrument of Cession" signed by the Chiefs of Tutuila conveying sovereign rights of islands west of 171° W. Long. to the United States and American flag raised at naval station at Pago Pago

1902

Oct. 14, King Oscar of Sweden decided in favor of Germany and against the United States and Great Britain in Samoan case

1904

July 14, "Instrument of Cession" signed by Chiefs of Manu'a group of islands conveying sovereign rights to the United States

1929

Feb. 20, President Coolidge signed Resolution of Congress accepting cession of Chiefs of Samoan Islands
Aug. 2, Capt. Gatewood S. Lincoln took office as Governor

VIRGIN ISLANDS

Virgin Islands, group of small islands numbering about 100 lying about 60 miles due east of Puerto Rico between the Atlantic Ocean and the Caribbean Sea, comprises in the main the Islands of St. Thomas (28 square miles), St. Croix (84 square miles), and St. John (20 square miles), total area 132 square miles. The population according to the census of April 1, 1930, was 9,834, 11,413, and 765 respectively, total 22,051 as compared with 26,051 in 1917, decrease said to be due to unemployment and emigration to the United States and other islands of the West Indies. The islands contain 3 towns, St. Thomas (formerly Charlotte Amalie) on St. Thomas Island with a population of 7,036, and Christiansted and Frederiksted on the Island of St. Croix with populations of 3,767 and 2,698 respectively. St. Thomas is the capital. By Treaty with Denmark of Aug. 4, 1916, the Islands, formerly the Danish West Indies, were purchased by the United States for $25,000,000, ratified Jan. 17, 1917. An Organic Act of March 3, 1917 vested all military, civil, and judicial powers in a Governor appointed by the President, the Danish code of laws dated April 6, 1906 with tax and customs laws continued in force except where incompatible with the new sovereignty. Danish citizens were held to have accepted citizenship in the United States unless they declared their Danish citizenship before a court of record. On March 31, 1917 Rear Admiral James H. Oliver took formal possession, named as first Governor. Capt. Waldo Evans, Governor.

CANADA

Canada, Dominion of the British Empire, in North America, bounded on the north by the Arctic Ocean, on the east by Labrador and the Atlantic Ocean, on the south by the United States, and on the west by Alaska and the Pacific Ocean. Ottawa is the capital. The total area is 3,684,723 square miles, larger than the United States excluding Alaska. The territories which constitute the Dominion came under British power at various times by settlement, conquest, and cession. Nova Scotia was ceded by France by the Treaty of Utrecht in 1713, and Canada including New Brunswick and Prince Edward Island was ceded by France in 1763. Vancouver Island was acknowledged to be British by the Oregon Boundary Treaty of 1846. British Columbia was established as a separate colony in 1858.

As originally constituted, the Dominion was composed of the provinces of Canada—Upper and Lower Canada, now Ontario and Quebec—Nova Scotia, and New Brunswick. They were united under the provisions of an Act of the Imperial Parliament known as "The British North America Act, 1867," which came into operation on July 1, 1867, by royal proclamation. The Act provides that the Constitution of the Dominion shall be "similar in principle to that of the United Kingdom"; that the executive authority shall be vested in the Sovereign of Great Britain and Ireland, and carried on in his name by a Governor-General and Privy Council; and that the legislative power shall be exercised by a Parliament of two Houses, called the "Senate" and the "House of Commons." The present position of Canada in the British Commonwealth of Nations was defined at the Imperial Conference of 1926: "The self-governing Dominions are autonomous Communities within the British Empire, equal in status, though united by a common allegiance to the Crown. The Dominion has its own representatives in foreign countries, and was elected a member of the Council of the League of Nations in 1927. Provision was made in the Act for the admission of British Columbia, Prince Edward Island, the North West Territories, and Newfoundland into the Dominion; Newfoundland alone has not availed itself of such provision. In 1869 Rupert's Land, or the North West Territories, were purchased from the Hudson's Bay Company; the province of Manitoba was erected from this territory, and admitted into the confederation on July 15, 1870. On July 20, 1871 the province of British Columbia was admitted, and Prince Edward Island July 1, 1873. The provinces of Alberta and Saskatchewan were formed from the provisional districts of Alberta, Athabaska, Assiniboia, and Saskatchewan and admitted on Sept. 1, 1905.

The estimated population in 1930 was 9,934,500.

The census population of the Prairie Provinces as at June 1, 1926, was as follows: Manitoba, 639,056; Saskatchewan, 820,738; Alberta, 607,584; Total, 2,067,378. Total rural, 1,313,681; Total urban, 753,697.

The following are the areas of the provinces, &c., with the population at recent censuses:—

PROVINCE	LAND AREA SQ. MILES	WATER AREA [1] SQ. MILES	TOTAL AREA SQ. MILES	POPULA- TION, 1901	POPULA- TION, 1911	POPULA- TION, 1921
Prince Edward Island [1]	2,184	——	2,184	103,259	93,728	88,615
Nova Scotia [1]	20,743	685	21,428	459,574	492,338	523,837
New Brunswick [1]	27,710	275	27,985	331,120	351,889	387,876
Quebec [1][2][3]	571,004	23,430	594,434	1,648,898	2,005,776	2,361,199
Ontario [2]	363,282	49,300	412,582	2,182,947	2,527,292	2,933,662
Manitoba [1]	224,777	27,055	251,832	255,211	461,394	610,118
British Columbia [1]	349,970	5,885	355,855	178,657	392,480	524,582
Alberta	248,800	6,485	255,285	73,022	374,295	588,454
Saskatchewan	237,975	13,725	251,700	91,279	492,432	757,510
Yukon	205,346	1,730	207,076	27,219	8,512	4,157
North West Territories	1,258,217	51,465	1,309,682	20,129	6,507	7,988
Royal Canadian Navy						485
Totals	3,510,008	180,035	3,690,043	5,371,315	7,206,643	8,788,483

[1] The water areas here assigned to Prince Edward Island, Nova Scotia, New Brunswick, and British Columbia are exclusive of the territorial seas, that to Quebec is exclusive of the Gulf of St. Lawrence. Ontario is inclusive of the Canadian portions of the great lakes of the St. Lawrence system.

[2] By Federal Act passed during the session of 1912, the boundaries of the provinces of Ontario, Quebec, and Manitoba were extended at the expense of the North West Territories. Ontario was enlarged by 146,400 square miles, Quebec by 351,780, and Manitoba by 178,100.

[3] As amended by the Labrador Boundary Award.

YEAR	POPULATION	YEAR	POPULATION
1806–07 (est.)	433,000	1881	4,324,810
1825	860,000	1891	4,833,239
1851–52	2,383,500	1901	5,371,315
1860–61	3,183,000	1911	7,206,643
1871	3,689,257	1921	8,788,483

CITIES	POPULATION	CITIES	POPULATION
Montreal (1929)	1,098,409	Calgary (1929)	102,470
Toronto (1929)	690,645	London (1929)	68,400
Winnipeg (1929)	336,202	Edmonton (1928)	69,744
Vancouver (1929)	277,631	Halifax (1929)	64,000
Hamilton (1929)	134,566	Saint John, N. B. (1929)	60,500
Ottawa (1929)	165,987	Victoria (1929)	39,394
Quebec (1929)	135,000	Windsor (1929)	66,893

Viscount Willingdon, Governor General, appointed 1926.

1497

June 24, John and Sebastian Cabot, first after the Northmen, Bjorni Herjulfson, Lief Ericsson, Thorwald, and others, to discover Canada, sighted the "Island of St. John" and the coast of the mainland. The "Island of St. John" is identified as Newfoundland by Judge Prouse, as Labrador by Harrisse, R. Biddle, and Biggar, as Cape Breton by Sir Clements Markham, R. G. Thwaites, S. E. Dawson, and J. G. Bourinot. For voyage of the Cabots See also America. Spain claimed prior discovery of Newfoundland, and Pitt in a despatch speaks of the "stale and inadmissible pretensions of the Biscayans and Guipuscoans to fish at Newfoundland." There is record of an alleged voyage to Labrador of John Scolp, a Dane, in 1472

1500

May 12, Gaspar de Cortereal, Portuguese, sailed from Lisbon, and is believed to have landed at Conception Bay, Newfoundland, rediscovered Greenland. He sailed on second voyage May 15, 1501, to Newfoundland with 2 ships, and was not heard from after Aug. 20, one ship making the return voyage
From 1501 it is known that Portuguese, and Norman

and Breton fishermen made yearly trips to the Newfoundland Banks and Gulf of St. Lawrence. Cape Breton Island was discovered and named by fishermen from Brittany in 1504. Jean Denys of Honfleur and Camaert of Rouen made voyage to Newfoundland. See also America

1508

Thomas Aubert in the ship "La Pensée" owned by Ango of Dieppe made unsuccessful attempt to found a colony in Newfoundland. Brought back American Indians to France

1518

Baron de Léry sailed from France, landed colonists on Sable Island

1521

March 13, Grant of King of Portugal to Joam Alvarez Fagundez of large territory of coast and islands of the Gulf of St. Lawrence which included Nova Scotia, discovered by him it is claimed on voyage in the summer and autumn of 1520

1524

Jan. 17, Jean Verrazano in service of France sailed from the Desertas Islands near Madeira and northward along coast of North America from Cape Fear to Nova Scotia and Newfoundland. Claim of France to Canada based on this voyage

1527

Aug. 3, John Rut in the "Mary of Guildford" from Plymouth, England, reached harbor of St. Johns, Newfoundland, "where they found eleven sails from Normandy, one from Brittany, and two Portuguese barks, all a fishing." He sailed south visiting and landing on shores of Cape Breton, Nova Scotia, and New England, reaching Puerto Rico in Nov. before he returned to England

1534

April 20–Sept. 5, First voyage of Jacques Cartier from St. Malo, France, reached Cape Bonavista on Newfoundland coast May 10, at entrance of the Straits of Belle Isle May 24, and June 9 weather permitted sailing through and landing made at Brest on Esquimaux Bay June 10. On July 1 he landed probably at North Cape, Prince Edward Island, which he believed the mainland, was at Port Daniel July 4–12 and named Chaleur Bay, and at Gaspé Bay July 16–25 where on the 24th he landed and erected a cross taking possession of the country for France, coasted Anticosti Island July 27–Aug. 5, and sighted north shore of Gulf of St. Lawrence Aug. 1; arrived at Blanc Sablon Aug. 9, and sailed on return voyage Aug. 15

1535

May 19–July 6, 1536, Second voyage of Jacques Cartier from St. Malo and entered the Straits of Belle Isle July 8, anchored in small bay on north shore, the present Pillage Bay, Aug. 10, which he named St. Lawrence in honor of the day. He named Anticosti Island Assomption Aug. 15, and Aug. 24 started up the St. Lawrence River exploring the mouth of the Saguenay Sept. 1, landed at the Island of Orleans which he named Bacchus Sept. 7, reached Indian village of Stadacona on site of the present Quebec Sept. 14, and Hochelaga, the present Montreal, Oct. 2, and named the mountain Mont Royal. Wintered at mouth of the Lairet River near Stadacona until May 6 when he descended the river and passed through Cabot Strait, sailing for France. On May 3 Cartier erected a cross on bank of the St. Charles River taking possession of the land for France

1540

Jan. 15, Royal grant to Jean François de la Roque, sieur de Roberval, as Lieutenant General, to take possession of the countries of Canada, Hochelaga, and the land of Saguenay for France. Roberval took oath of office as Lieut. Gen. Feb. 6. Francis I appointed Jacques Cartier pilot of the Roberval expedition Oct. 17

March 9, The Parliament of Rouen authorized Roberval to take certain classes of criminals to New France

1541

May 23, Jacques Cartier on third voyage to Canada sailed from St. Malo and reached Stadacona Aug. 23, and the Lachine Rapids Sept. 11. Wintered at Cap Rouge above Stadacona and returned to France in the spring, meeting the delayed expedition of Roberval at Newfoundland in June, 1542 but refusing to return with him to Canada. Death of Cartier at St. Malo Sept. 1, 1557

Act provided penalty for buying fish in Flanders or at sea, "half the sea over," to be sold in England (Henry VIII, cap. 2) the origin of the phrase "half-seas over" from the carousal when the English ships met the Picardese

1542

April 16, Roberval sailed from La Rochelle for New France, reached St. Johns, Newfoundland, June 7, and Stadacona in July and his colonists wintered at Ste. Croix, 4 leagues west of Orleans

1543

June 6, Roberval left Stadacona where he had built a "fair fort" to explore the Saguenay before returning to France; no further account of voyage except that the colonists all returned with him to France

1544

The Basques established fisheries at Tadousac on the St. Lawrence River at mouth of the Saguenay

1558

Map of Diego Homen showed Bay of Fundy for first time on map

1560

April 15, At St. Malo, France, 25 fishing vessels waited for a fair wind to start for the Newfoundland Banks, and 5 more at Carcolle

1576

June 7–Oct. 2, First voyage of Martin Frobisher to Frobisher's Bay named after him and to Baffin Land. *See* America

1577

March, First commission to Troilus du Mesgonez, Marquis de la Roche, from Henry III to trade in New France and settle colonists

May 26–Sept. 23, Second voyage of Martin Frobisher reached Hall's Island at north entrance of Frobisher's Bay and July 17 landed and explored Baffin Land

1578

Jan. 3, Letters patent of Henry III appointed the Marquis de la Roche Viceroy of Newfoundland, and Jan. 12 Lieutenant General of Canada

May 31–Oct. 31, Third voyage of Martin Frobisher to Greenland reached June 20, and discovery of Hudson's Strait July 2

1581

Merchants of St. Malo, France, began the trade for furs up the St. Lawrence River

1583

Aug. 3, Sir Humphrey Gilbert reached St. John's Harbor, Newfoundland, from Plymouth, England, and Aug. 5 took possession of the land for England and his colony. He found 36 sail of Portuguese and French fishing vessels in the harbor

1585

June 7–Sept. 30, First voyage of John Davis on which he explored the strait named after him, entered Aug. 11, and discovered land in 66° 40′ N. Lat.

1586

May 7–Oct. 6, Second voyage of John Davis to Baffin Land arrived at Gilbert's Sound June 15, discovered land in N. Lat. 66° 33′ and 70° W. Long., continued exploration of Baffin Land, and named Cape Walsingham

1587

May 19–Sept. 15, Third voyage of John Davis to Arctic Canada reached Gilbert's Sound June 16, Cumberland Straits July 20, and discovered Hudson Straits July 31 and reached farthest north June 30 at 72° 12′ N. Lat. and 56° W. Long.

1588

Jan. 14, La Jaunaye and Jacques Nouel received a grant of the monopoly of the fur trade in the St. Lawrence for 12 years from Henry III and permission to take out 60 criminals as colonists; revoked July 9

1598

Jan. 12, Letters patent of Henry IV, registered March 2, appointed La Roche Lieutenant General in Canada, Hochelaga, Newfoundland, Labrador, Saguenay, Sable Island, and Nova Scotia called Norumbega, the same monopoly as granted to Roberval. La Roche landed 40 convicts at Sable Islands on voyage of this year in attempt to found a settlement

1599

May, Pierre Chauvin, sieur de Tonnetuit, and Pontgravé granted a monopoly of the fur trade in Canada on condition of taking out settlers. Made voyage to Tadousac, built stone house according to account of Champlain, and left 16 men for the winter. No letters patent issued

The St. Malo Company for trading in Canada established by de Chastes

1600

June, Second voyage of Chauvin and Pontgravé to Tadousac with colonists

1601

Voyage of Chauvin to St. Lawrence Valley

1602

Dec. 28, Order issued to summon merchants of Rouen and St. Malo with Capt. Chauvin to draw up agreement for regulation of fur trade and for colonization of New France, Chauvin's patent of 1599 which apparently was not registered reaffirmed

1603

Jan. 12, Vizcaino coasting western North America from Mexico reached 41st parallel, and Martin d'Aguilar sighted entrance to a river which may have been the Columbia. Cape Blanco named

Jan. 20–May 15, Death of Chauvin sometime between these dates (Dionne) and his patent granted to Aymar de Chastes, Governor of Dieppe, for trading privileges in New France

March 15, Samuel de Champlain (first voyage) under commission of Aymar de Chastes, with Sieur de Monts, Pontgravé (Pont-Gravé) and Baron de Poutrincourt sailed from Honfleur, and arrived at Tadousac by mouth of the Saguenay River May 24 where post established. June 11 they ascended the

Saguenay about 40 miles, started up the St. Lawrence June 18 reaching Island of Orleans June 22, and entered Lake St. Peter June 29, proceeded as far as the Lachine Rapids and up the Richelieu to the St. Ours Rapids. Sailed on return voyage from Gaspé Aug. 24 and arrived at Havre-de-Grâce, France, Sept. 20

May 13, Death of Aymar de Chastes voided his patent, and his commission given to Sieur de Monts

Sept. 17, English royal proclamation made provision for banishing and conveying to "New-found Land, the East and West Indies," &c., of vagabonds and rogues

Sept. 20, Chedotel, Norman pilot, reached Sable Island and brought 11 survivors of the La Roche colonists back to France

Nov. 8, Pierre du Guast, Sieur de Monts, received royal commission to undertake the colonization of New France (La Cadia) from the 40th to the 46th degrees

Dec. 18, Sieur de Monts received letters patent granting monopoly in furs in New France for 10 years

1604

Feb. 10, Agreement signed of articles of association of the de Monts company and the merchants of St. Malo and Rouen in regard to fishing, timber, mineral, and fur trade and colonization of New France

March 7, Champlain (second voyage) with de Monts, Poutrincourt, and colonists left Havre-de-Grâce, and arrived at Cape de la Have near the present Lunenburg in Nova Scotia May 8, reached Port Royal May 16, and settled on an island in the St. Croix River believed to be the present Dochet Island June 25. Date of embarkation March 7 according to Champlain, Lescarbot gives April 7

June 1, French East India Company founded

June 24, De Monts named the St. John River

Aug. 31, Poutrincourt sailed for France

Sept. 2–Oct. 2, Champlain on voyage of discovery coasted Maine, ascended the Penobscot almost to the site of Bangor and turned back before reaching the Kennebec River Sept. 23. Mt. Desert Island named Sept. 5

1605

June 15, Pontgravé arrived from France with supplies

June 18–Aug. 8, Champlain and de Monts on voyage of exploration from the St. Croix reached the Kennebec River July 5, entered Massachusetts Bay July 16, left Boston Harbor July 17, and reached Plymouth Harbor July 18 and Nauset Harbor, Cape Cod, July 20 (Prince Soc.)

Aug., The St. Croix colony moved to Port Royal, Acadia, the present Annapolis Royal, Nova Scotia, granted by de Monts in fief to Poutrincourt

1606

At Port Royal de Monts built 2 small vessels in which they intended to sail to Ile Royale

March 16, Champlain set out on another voyage of exploration and reached Port aux Coquilles, island at mouth of St. Croix River, driven back by storms

May 13, Poutrincourt accompanied by Marc Lescarbot sailed from France with colonists and provisions reaching Port Royal July 27

Sept. 5–Nov. 14, Champlain and Poutrincourt sailed on voyage of exploration reaching Martha's Vineyard Oct. 20

1607

May 24, Chevalier arrived at Port Royal bringing word from de Monts that his grant had been revoked because of protests of French merchants and fishermen and the colonists must return to France

July 30, The colonists left Port Royal followed by Champlain and de Poutrincourt Aug. 11, and sailed from Canso (spelled variously Canseau, Canceau) for France Sept. 3

1608

Jan. 7, Commission of de Monts renewed for one year

April 5, Pontgravé sailed from Honfleur and Champlain (third voyage) April 13 arriving at Tadousac June 3

July 3, The ground cleared and Quebec founded by Champlain. The Indian name Quebeio in the Algonquin language meant a narrowing in, the river at that part narrows until it is only a mile wide (Charlevoix)

Sept. 18, Pontgravé sailed for France taking 3 of the party who had conspired to murder Champlain prisoners. It had been arranged by Champlain that Stephen Brulé should winter with the Hurons and that a Huron he named Savignon should go to France

1609

April 6–Nov. 4, Voyage of Henry Hudson, an Englishman in service of the Dutch in the "Half Moon" coasted Newfoundland. *See* America

June 28, Champlain ascended the St. Lawrence River with a party of Hurons and Algonquins on the war path against the Iroquois, and discovered Lake Champlain July 4, proceeding by the Richelieu River, and then Lake George

July 30, Champlain helped the Hurons to defeat the Iroquois in battle near Crown Point

Sept. 1, Champlain and Pontgravé left Pierre Chauvin with 15 men at Quebec and proceeded to Tadousac where they sailed Sept. 10 for France, arriving at Honfleur Oct. 13

Marc Lescarbot published his "History of New France" this year

1610

Feb. 26, Poutrincourt sailed from Dieppe for Port Royal with his son, Charles de Biencourt, the Abbé Fléche, Claude de la Tour and his son Charles, and a number of colonists and reëstablished his settlement

March 7–Sept. 27, Champlain (fourth voyage) left Honfleur and arrived at Tadousac April 26. He returned to France, leaving Quebec Aug. 8, Tadousac Aug. 13

April 17, Henry Hudson sailed from Gravesend, England, in the "Discovery," and June 24 entered Strait which bears his name and Hudson Bay on Aug. 3 and wintered in James Bay where his ship was run aground Nov. 1. He explored the eastern coast from Cape Wolstenholme to foot of James Bay and west coast to Cape Henrietta Maria

May 2, Grant of James I of land in Newfoundland between Cape Bonavista and Cape St. Mary to John Guy, of Bristol, who with William Colston took out a party of colonists to Cupid's Cove in Conception Bay, arriving May 10, 1611

June 14, Champlain left Quebec with the Indians and Three Rivers June 18 and led attack on the Iroquois near mouth of the Richelieu June 19

1611

Jan. 20, Antoinette de Pons, Marchioness de Guercheville, who had bought the rights of de Monts, entered into partnership with M. de Biencourt, son of Poutrincourt, to settle colonists in New France

Jan. 26, Biencourt sailed from France for Port Royal accompanied by the Jesuit Fathers Pierre Biard and Ennemond Massé, and arrived May 11 according to Shortt and Doughty, May 22 according to Shea, and June 12 according to Winsor and Charlevoix

March 1, Champlain (fifth voyage) left Honfleur and arrived at Tadousac May 13 and at Quebec May 21

May 26, Champlain ascending the St. Lawrence arrived at the Grand Sault where he began clearing the ground for settlement (Montreal) while he waited for the Indians to arrive. Named the mountain near Mt. Royal. Reached Lake of the Two Mountains on this expedition

June 13, The Hurons with Brulé met Champlain and Savignon at Lachine Rapids as arranged the year before for the fur trade and exchange of the 2 young men. Claimed that during the year Brulé was the first European to ascend the Ottawa to Lake Nipissing and Lake Huron and Lake Ontario

June 22, Henry Hudson turned adrift by mutinous crew with 8 others and never heard from again. Robert Bylot elected master brought the ship back to England where the crew were thrown into prison but 7 years later acquitted because they alone knew the lands Hudson had discovered

July 20, Champlain left Quebec and arrived in La Rochelle Sept. 16, remaining in France during 1612

1612

April 15, Sir Thomas Button sailed from the Thames in the "Discovery" and the "Resolution" to discover the North West Passage. He anchored at Digges Island and reached Port Nelson Aug. 15, which he later named after the commander of his ship and made his winter quarters on small creek on northern side of the estuary of the Nelson River. Erected a cross July 7, 1613 and named the country New Wales. He explored the entire western coast of Hudson Bay from Wager Bay to Port Nelson

April 22, Voyage of Capt. Robert Bylow with William Baffin, pilot, to coast of Greenland explored north of Gilbert Sound

Oct. 8, Charles de Bourbon, Count de Soissons, Governor of Dauphiny and Normandy, appointed Viceroy of New France. He commissioned Champlain as his deputy Oct. 15

Nov. 13, Letters patent to Henry de Bourbon, Prince de Condé, after death of Soissons as Viceroy of New France and new commission to Champlain Nov. 22

Louis XIII granted region between Florida and the St. Lawrence to the Marchioness de Guercheville for a Jesuit mission

1613

March 6, Champlain (sixth voyage) left Honfleur arriving at Tadousac April 29 and at Quebec May 7, and at the Sault St. Louis May 21. Deceived by story of Nicholas Vignau of "the northern sea" he left Sault St. Louis (Montreal) May 27, ascending the Ottawa River as far as Allumette Island in search of the North West Passage reached June 7 where Vignau's lying story was disproved. Described Lake of Two Mountains, mouth of the Rideau River, the Chaudière Falls (site of Ottawa) and Chats Falls

March 12, Colonists sent by the Marchioness de Guercheville under Capt. de la Saussaye sailed from Honfleur with the Jesuit Fathers Quentin and du Thet. Reaching Port Royal they were joined by Fathers Biard and Massé, and sailed across the Bay of Fundy to Saint Desert Island where they began clearing ground for settlement to be called Saint Sauveur. The colony was destroyed and the colonists taken prisoners to Virginia by Capt. Samuel Argall in May

June 7, Champlain on portage road from the Ottawa River to Mud Lake lost his astrolabe, instrument for taking observations; found Aug. 1867

July 8, Champlain left Tadousac for France, arriving at St. Malo Aug. 26. Company of Rouen and St. Malo (Champlain's company) established for trade in New France

Nov. 9, Second expedition of Capt. Argall from Virginia left Port Royal after destroying the French settlements in Acadia at Port Royal and on St. Croix River

Fort Pentagoet built by Claude de la Tour at Penobscot

1614

Oct. 4, Capt. Benjamin Joseph and Robert Fotherby with William Baffin as pilot made voyage to Greenland

1615

March 18–Sept. 8, Capt. Robert Bylot and William Baffin, pilot, sailed from Gravesend to Hudson Straits and up Fox Channel beyond Cape Comfort

April 24, Champlain (seventh voyage) with Pontgravé and the Recollet friars Fathers Denis Jamet, Jean d'Olbeau, Joseph Le Caron, and a brother named Pacifique du Plessis, sailed from Honfleur and arrived at Tadousac May 25

May 11, Capt. Richard Whitbourne sailed from England commissioned to establish order in Newfoundland and correct abuses of fishermen, held first court June 4

June 24, First mass celebrated in Canada by the Recollet Fathers on day of feast of St. John the Baptist near eastern extremity of Island of Montreal at Rivière des Prairie

June 25, First mass celebrated at Quebec by the Recollet Fathers

July 1, Father Le Caron left Island of Montreal with the Hurons to establish mission south of Georgian Bay

July 9, Champlain with Etienne Brulé and 10 Indians began ascent of the Ottawa following the Hurons and Father Le Caron, crossed the divide by the Mattawa to Lake Nipissing July 26, and from there to Georgian Bay and along Lake Huron, Hurontown village reached Aug. 1, and joined Father Le Caron Aug. 4

Aug. 12, First mass celebrated in the Province of Ontario by Father Le Caron at Carhagonha, Huron village, south of Thunder Bay

Sept. 8, Etienne Brulé left Lake Simcoe with party of Indians to urge the Andastes (Carantounnais) to send war party against the Iroquois, traveling along east shore of Lake Simcoe to Talbot Creek, to Sturgeon Lake and Trent River to Bay of Quinte, and across Lake Ontario to northern New York. He re-

mained with the Indians the first white man to visit western New York and central Pennsylvania and is believed to have reached Chesapeake Bay by the Susquehanna River. Returned Oct. 1615 to Huron Indian village Carhagonha and returned to Three Rivers July 7, 1618 to meet Champlain

Oct. 10, Champlain led the Hurons in unsuccessful attack on their enemies, the Iroquois, their fort located on Nichols pond southeast of Oneida Lake in Madison county, New York, by Parkman, E. F. Slafter, J. S. Clark, Winsor, and Dawson, and on Lake Canandaigua by O'Callaghan, on Lake Onondaga by O. H. Marshall, Brodhead, and J. V. H. Clark

Dec. 2, Father Jean d'Olbeau set out to winter among the Montaganis at Tadousac

1616

March 26, Capt. Robert Bylow and William Baffin sailed from Gravesend in Hudson's ship, the "Discovery" and sailed up Davis Strait and reached farthest north at 77° 45′ N. Lat., discovered Baffin Bay, Smith's Sound, Jones Sound, July 11, and Lancaster Sound July 12

May 20, Champlain left the Huron country and reached Sault St. Louis July 1, and Quebec July 11, and sailed from Tadousac for France Aug. 3

June 15, Father Le Caron reached Three Rivers from the Huron country

First schools for Indians opened by Brother Pacifique Duplessis at Three Rivers and by Father d'Olbeau at Tadousac

Sale to Sir William Vaughan by Guy's Company of part of Avalon Peninsula, Newfoundland, and a Welsh colony founded in Trepassey Harbor

1617

April 11, Champlain (eighth voyage) left Honfleur and arrived at Tadousac June 14. Left no record of this period. Louis Hébert, the first settler to take land in Quebec, arrived with Champlain

First marriage in Canada that of Anne Hébert and Etienne Jonquest in the autumn. Father Joseph Le Caron officiated

Welsh settlement established at Cambriol, now Little Britain, by Capt. Whitbourne

1618

May 24, Champlain (ninth voyage) sailed from France arriving at Tadousac June 24. Helped Hurons in battle with the Iroquois along the Richelieu River. Left Quebec July 26 and arrived at Honfleur, France, Aug. 28

Jean Nicolet arrived and went with the Hurons to the Ottawa River and to Lake Nipissing. It is stated in "Jesuit Relations" that he remained with the Indians until 1632, Kellogg until June 1633

Nov. 27, Marc Lescarbot received permission to print his "History of New France" published in this year in Paris

1619

May 16–Sept. 1920, Jens Munck, a Dane, sailed for Hudson Bay in search of the Northwest Passage, reached Digges Island Aug. 20 and sailed across the Bay to Port Churchill reached Sept. 5 where he wintered. Probably he was the discoverer of the mouth of the Churchill River Sept. 7. July 18 Munck sailed on return voyage with only 2 of crew of 65, the others had died of scurvy, reached Europe in Sept.

1620

Feb. 25, First commission of Henry, Duke of Montmorency as Viceroy

May 8, Champlain (tenth voyage) sailed from France with his young wife arriving at Tadousac

June 3, The Recollect Fathers laid cornerstone of their church, Notre Dame des Anges, at Quebec, and May 25, 1621 the church was opened as a parish church

July 7, He began building Fort St. Louis on site of the present Chateau Frontenac

Nov. 26, Articles of new company, the Montmorency, to trade in France signed by the de Caen brothers, rival of the Rouen company

1621

Aug. 18, Louis XIII appointed Henry, Duke of Montmorency, Viceroy of New France, and Champlain, Lieutenant-General. Montmorency bought commission and formed a company headed by William and Emery de Caen with which the St. Malo and Rouen Company united

Sept. 10, Sir William Alexander granted all the territory between the St. Lawrence River and the sea lying east of the St. Croix River, named in the patent Nova Scotia, by James I, of England, and comprising the present Nova Scotia and New Brunswick and the Gaspé peninsula

Etienne Brulé and Grenolle explored Georgian Bay and are believed to be the discoverers of Lake Superior in 1623 according to account of Sagard. Claim rests largely on the fact that they located copper mines. Reached Quebec July 2, 1623

Code of laws issued and a register of births, marriages, and deaths first kept in Quebec

1622

April 1, Commission to the Duke of Montmorency, Viceroy of New France

June, Sir William Alexander sent colonists from Kirkcudbright on the Dee for New Scotland, Acadia, who wintered at St. Johns, Newfoundland

1623

Feb. 4, Seignorial grant made by the Duc de Montmorency to Louis Hébert, described as "head of the first family settled in the country" at Quebec

April 7, Grant of the Province of Avalon in Newfoundland to George Calvert, 1st Lord Baltimore

June 5, Second company of settlers sent from London in March by Sir William Alexander arrived at Newfoundland, and June 23 the colonists sailed for Nova Scotia

Aug. 15, Fathers Le Caron, Nicolas Viel, and Gabriel Sagard, historian, arrived at Huron village to revive mission

Death of Biencourt, son of Baron de Poutrincourt, his property in Acadia bequeathed to Charles de la Tour

Nov. 17, Roadway to the upper town completed in Quebec

1624

Aug. 15, Champlain left Quebec for France arriving at Dieppe Oct. 1, after making a peace at Three Rivers between the Hurons and Algonquins and the Iroquois

Nov. 30, Proclamation of King James created baronets

of New Scotland (Acadia) each of the 10 baronetcies carrying hereditary title and grant of land in Nova Scotia for which Alexander to be paid 3,000 marks

1625

Feb. 15, Champlain created representative of the Duke of Ventadour, new Viceroy of New France, appointed in Jan. His commission mentions the finding of a passage to China and the Indies

April 1, New Scotland (Acadia) divided into 2 provinces with counties, bishoprics, and baronetcies

April 26, The Jesuit Fathers sailed from Dieppe arriving June 15 at Quebec, Jean de Brébeuf, Enemond Massé, François Charton, Gilbert Bural, and Charles Lalemant. Brébeuf went immediately to the Huron country

July 12, Charles I confirmed grant of Sir William Alexander to Nova Scotia, and of Lord Baltimore to Avalon, Newfoundland

Sept. 23, The Jesuits at Quebec selected land beyond the St. Charles at the confluence of the Lairet where Champlain believed Cartier had wintered, and began to clear the ground to build habitation

Dec. 2, Father John d'Olbeau left to winter with the Montagnais at Tadousac

1626

March 10, The seigneury of Notre Dame des Anges along the Charles River near Quebec the first of a series of grants to the Jesuits. Convent dedicated April 6

April 24, Champlain (eleventh voyage) sailed from Dieppe accompanied by Fathers Noyrot, de la Noue, Le Caron, and Brother Gaufestre, arriving at Percé June 20 and Quebec July 5. Established a farm near Cape Tourmente

July, The Jesuit Fathers Brébeuf, Noue, and Daillion left Quebec with the Hurons and reëstablished mission on Georgian Bay at present site of town of Penetanguishene. Father Viel had been drowned in 1625

Oct. 18-March 8, 1627, Father Daillion (La Roche d'Aillan) on mission to the Neutral Indians in region east of the Niagara River

1627

Jan. 25, Death of Louis Hébert at Quebec

March-April 24, 1629, War between England and France

April 25, Company of New France or the Hundred Associates organized by Cardinal Richelieu, charter signed by the King April 29, and by the Council of State May 6, 1628. Thenceforth no Calvinist to be allowed to enter New France. The de Caen Company charter canceled because they had failed to take out colonists

July 23, Calvert, Lord Baltimore, brought colonists to Ferryland, Newfoundland

Charles de la Tour built Fort St. Louis near Cape Sable, Acadia

War resumed with the Iroquois

1628

Feb. 2, King Charles granted patent to Sir William Alexander of the Islands in the Gulf and River of the St. Lawrence and trade

April 27, Couillard at Quebec used first plough in Canada drawn by oxen

May, Son of Sir William Alexander sailed from Scotland bringing 70 colonists to Port Royal. Built new fort

July 10, David Kirke, commissioned by Sir William Alexander, arrived in the St. Lawrence River and sent his brother Lewis Kirke with summons to Champlain to surrender the fort at Quebec which Champlain refused though the garrison was without provisions

July 18, David Kirke in battle in Gulf of St. Lawrence with the French squadron sent out with provisions and settlers by the Hundred Associates under command of Claude de Roquemont captured such ships as he did not sink and sailed for England with his prizes

Fort Pentagoet built by Claude de la Tour at Penobscot in 1613 captured by Kirke after destruction of Port Royal

1629

Feb. 4, Royal patent to Sir William Alexander as "sole trader" of the St. Lawrence valley

March 21, Commission appointed Champlain lieutenant for Richelieu in New France

March 25, David Kirke with 6 ships left Gravesend accompanied by son of Sir William Alexander with colonists for Port Royal and Lord Ochiltree with 60 settlers, arriving at Gaspé June 15

April 4, Scottish and English Company for trade in Gulf and River of St. Lawrence formed by union of Alexander and Kirke interests with monopoly of fur trade

April 24, Treaty of Susa established peace between France and England, and agreed that all land conquered should be restored; ratified by England Sept. 6 and by France Sept. 16

July 1, James Stuart, Lord Ochiltree, to whom Sir William Alexander had granted a barony, landed colonists at Baleine, Cape Breton Island

July 19, Sir David Kirke appeared before Quebec forcing Champlain to surrender, the English flag raised over fort July 22

July 23, Sir William Alexander granted part of Acadia to the two La Tours

July 25, French ship under Emeric de Caen surrendered to Kirke after battle on the St. Lawrence

Sept. 8, Capt. Daniel of the French Company who had arrived at Cape Breton Island from Dieppe Aug. 28 attacked Lord Ochiltree's settlement and captured fort and made the colonists prisoners

Sept. 14, The English fleet sailed taking Champlain and nearly all the colonists from Quebec, as prisoners reaching Plymouth Oct. 20

Nov. 30, Claude de St. Etienne de la Tour carried to England as a prisoner by Kirke enrolled as a baronet of Nova Scotia, transferring his allegiance to the English

1630

April 30, Grant of Sir William Alexander of part of territory of Acadia to Claude de St. Etienne, sieur de la Tour, and his son Charles, confirmed

May 12, Charles de la Tour enrolled as an English baronet by Claude, his father, who now sailed from England for Cape Sable where he made unsuccessful attempt to secure allegiance of his son for the British and to capture the fort

1631

Feb. 11, Charles de la Tour commissioned Lieutenant General of Acadia by Louis XIII of France. He built Fort St. Jean at mouth of St. John River, Bay of Fundy in this year

April 30–Oct. 31, 1632, Voyage of Luke Foxe in search of North West Passage from London made landing June 20 on north side of Frobisher Bay, explored Hudson Strait, July 27 at Sir Thomas Roe's Welcome Island, and Aug. 27 entered mouth of the Nelson River where he wintered. He explored hitherto unknown coast of Hudson's Bay from Port Nelson to Cape Henrietta Maria. Sept. 15–20 he made a series of observations on Foxe Channel named for him on west shore of Baffin Land and convinced himself that there was no passage, his farthest north 66° 47′ N. Lat.

May 3–Oct. 22, 1632, Voyage of Capt. Thomas James from Bristol reached Port Churchill Aug. 11, Hudson's Bay, sailing over practically same waters as Foxe whom he met in the Bay. He named Cape Henrietta Maria after his ship, and wintered at Charlton Island Oct. 3, leaving there July 3, 1632, reached Cape Esquimo Aug. 19, and ended his voyage at point on southeast coast of the Melville Peninsula near Winter Island

June 12, King Charles informed his ambassador that he would surrender Quebec and Port Royal to France according to treaty terms when the balance of dower of Queen Henrietta Maria, about $240,000 paid

July 10, Sir William Alexander instructed by King Charles to give up Port Royal and destroy fort built by his son

Nov. 8, Cape Breton Island allotted to Sir Robert Gordon of Lochinvar and his second son, Robert, by King of England, to form province of New Galloway

1632

March 1, Champlain appointed Governor of New France

March 27, Isaac de Razilly commissioned by Louis XIII to receive Port Royal from the English for the Company of New France

March 29, Treaty of St. Germain-en-Laye between England and France restored Quebec and Acadia to France

April 18, Two Jesuit Fathers Le Jeune and de Noüe sailed for Quebec from Havre

May 19, Razilly commissioned Governor May 10, granted concession on the St. Croix River, lands, and adjacent islands, by the Company of New France. He designated as his lieutenants Charles de la Tour for part east of the St. Croix and Charles de Menou, sieur d'Aulnay-Charnisay for part west of the St. Croix, and from Canso to Gaspé, Nicolas Denys

June 12, Sir William Alexander, Robert Charlton, and William Berkeley commissioned by the King to receive forts from Capt. Lewis Kirke, Governor, and deliver them to the French

July 5, Emery de Caen, commissioned to take over posts, landed at Quebec with religious fathers

July 13, Fort at Quebec surrendered to the French, Emery de Caen and Duplessis Bochart in charge until the return of Champlain

1633

March 23, Champlain (twelfth voyage) sailed from Dieppe and arrived at Quebec May 22

May 11, Sir William Alexander received royal patent for sole right to trade in St. Lawrence River and

Gulf; made 1st Earl of Stirling, and Viscount of Canada June 14

1634

Jan. 15, Seigniory of Beauport granted to Robert Giffard by Company of Hundred Associates of 1 league of land along the St. Lawrence River, and he arrived at Quebec June 4 with settlers brought from his home in France at Mortagne

July 1, Jean Nicolet left Three Rivers proceeding up the Ottawa River and by Lake Nipissing and the French River to the Huron villages at Georgian Bay, was the first European to reach Sault Ste. Marie. From there he journeyed to the Straits of Mackinaw, to Green Bay, discovering Lake Michigan, and up the Fox River in 1635 and through the upper river as far as portage to the Wisconsin, returning with the Indian trading fleet of 1635. J. G. Shea and Henri Jouan believed that he reached the Mississippi

July 4, Settlement of Three Rivers, founded by M. de la Violette

July 7, Fathers Jean de Brébeuf, Davost, and Daniel left Three Rivers and reëstablished the Jesuit mission among the Hurons Aug. 5

Sept. 8, Fathers Le Jeune and Buteux established a mission at Three Rivers

1635

Jan. 15, Charles de St. Etienne, sieur de la Tour, granted land and fort at the mouth of the St. John River, Acadia, by the Company of New France

April 22, Sir William Alexander, now Earl of Stirling, granted Canada and Long Island by Council for the Affairs of New England

July 20, Father Le Mercier arrived in Canada and went to Huron mission at Ihonatira where he arrived Aug. 13 and remained 15 years

July 22, Champlain met the Indians in council at Quebec

Nov., With death of Isaac de Razilly civil war began in Acadia with strife between La Tour, Charnisay, and Denys. Razilly said to have appointed d'Aulnay Charnisay his successor

Dec. 25, Death of Governor Samuel de Champlain (68) at Quebec. Marc Antoine Bras de fer de Châteaufort succeeded as Administrator

Jesuit College at Quebec opened, money given for foundation by the Marquis of Gamache in 1626

1636

June 15, Charles Hualt de Montmagny, the new Governor appointed March 10, arrived at Quebec from France

July 29, Concession of the Island of Montreal to M. de Lauzon

1637

Jan. 16, Grant of Company of New France for establishment of a nunnery at Quebec. Act recorded of possession taken by the Ursulines Sept. 12, 1646

March 18, Grant of Company of New France of land for Jesuit church and seminary in Quebec

July, The Village of Sillery founded for the Algonquin and Montagnais, money and skilled workmen sent from France by the Chevalier de Sillery, gift to Father Lalemant

Aug. 16, Donation of 22,440 livres by the Duchesse d'Aiguillon for Hôtel Dieu, hospital, at Quebec

Nov. 13, Grant of Newfoundland to Sir David Kirke, the Duke of Hamilton, and others on ground that Lord Baltimore had forfeited his grant because no settlement made. Sir David settled at Ferryland where he remained until his death 20 years later

Dec. 1, Establishment of the Customs of Paris in Canada. Mentioned in grant of fief of Dautre to Jean Bourdon

1638

Feb. 10, Letter of King Louis to Charles de Menou, sieur d'Aulnay Charnisay, in possession of lands of Razilly, deceased, defined limits of territory in dispute between Charles de la Tour and d'Aulnay Charnisay, which gave d'Aulnay the north shore of the Bay of Fundy but not St. John, and La Tour the peninsula but not Port Royal

June 11, Earthquake in Canada, first recorded

1639

April 15, Deed for foundation of Hôtel Dieu at Quebec by the Duchesse d'Aiguillon

May 4, Mme. de la Peltrie, the founder, accompanied by 3 Ursuline nuns, Mère Marie de l'Incarnation, Marie de St. Joseph, and Cécile de la Croix sailed from Dieppe to establish convent at Quebec where they arrived Aug. 1, date generally given as that of the foundation

1640

Jan. 31, The Duchesse d'Aiguillon gave 18,000 francs for foundation of hospital at Quebec, this date generally accepted as foundation

June 15, Fire destroyed the Chapel of Notre Dame de la Recouvrance and the parish registers of Quebec

Aug. 7, M. Lauzon gave over Montreal Island to the Sulpicians

Nov. 2–Feb. 1641, Visit of Fathers Jean de Brébeuf and Joseph Marie Chaumont starting from the Huron mission on Georgian Bay to the Neutral Indians on the Niagara River and Lake Erie, giving first information of the Lake which Champlain had mapped as a river connecting Lakes Huron and Ontario

Dec. 17, Grant by Company of New France of the Island of Montreal to representatives of the Seminary of St. Sulpice; ratified by the King Feb. 13, 1644

First census of New France gave population as 375 persons

1641

Feb. 13, Intrigue of d'Aulnay obtained order from the King for arrest of Charles de la Tour summoned to France for alleged misconduct because of negotiations with the merchants of Boston

June 2, Fathers Raymbault and Jogues started for Sault Ste. Marie to establish a mission. Father Raymbault drowned at rapids between Lakes Huron and Superior in Sept.

Oct. 14, Ceremony of taking possession of the site of Ville Marie or Montreal by Paul de Chomedy, Sieur de Maisonneuve, Mlle Jeanne Mance, and other representatives of the Company of Notre Dame de Montreal

Oct. 15, De Maisonneuve declared the Governor of the Island of Montreal

1642

Jan. 16, Deeds of transfer of lands in Acadia granted to Razilly to d'Aulnay

May 18, Formal founding of Ville Marie (Montreal) in

service of consecration by Father Vimont. Montmagny handed over the fief to Governor Maisonneuve

Aug. 3, Huron canoes attacked on the Richelieu by the Iroquois and Father Jogues carried captive to New York, the first European on Lake George. Rescued by the Dutch in the following year

Aug. 13, Fort Richelieu established by Governor Montmagny at mouth of the Richelieu, now named Sorel

1643

June 21, De la Tour and his wife escaped from Fort St. John besieged by d'Aulnay and sought help in New England

July 14, De la Tour with squadron sailed from Boston and was successful against d'Aulnay

D'Aulnay erected a new fort, at Port Royal, site of present town of Annapolis Royal, Nova Scotia

Aug., Gift of Mme de Bullion founded Hôtel Dieu, Montreal

Nov. 5, Father Jogues sailed for France from New Amsterdam arriving at Rennes, Jan. 5, 1644

1644

Feb. 13, Cession of Montreal Island to the Sulpicians by Lauzon and the Company of New France ratified by the King

March 30, Maisonneuve defeated the Iroquois at Montreal

April 27, Father Joseph Bressani captured and tortured by the Iroquois. Ransomed by the Dutch in Sept. and sent to France

Sept. 23, Father Lalemant and Governor Montmagny laid cornerstone of church of Notre Dame de la Paix. First mass celebrated Dec. 25, 1650

Oct. 8, Hôtel Dieu, Montreal, opened by Mlle Mance

——, Peace Treaty with d'Aulnay signed by Governor of Massachusetts; ratified March 6, 1645

Nov., François, Duc de Levis, appointed Viceroy

1645

Jan. 14, The Company of New France transferred its trading rights to the *Compagnie des Habitans* made up of the chief colonists in Canada; ratified by the King's Council March 6, the Company reserving the seigneurial ownership of the colony and feudal dues and appointment of colonial officers

April 17, Fort La Tour at mouth of St. John River taken by d'Aulnay Charnisay after siege of 3 days of the fort defended by Lady de la Tour in the absence of her husband, and gained control over Acadia

July 14, Peace between the French and Iroquois made by Montmagny, the Treaty of Three Rivers

D'Aulnay took possession of forts of Denys on Cape Breton at Chedabucto (Guysboro) and St. Peters

1646

Aug. 26, Father Druillettes sent on mission to the Abenakis on the Kennebec River, and Father Jogues to the Mohawks, the first white man to reach Lake George according to Parkman, on Corpus Christi Day

Sept. 12, Act recording taking possession of nunnery at Quebec by *Les Dames Ursuline*

Oct. 18, Fathers Jogues and Lalande killed by the Iroquois breaking the peace

Dec. 31, Corneille's "Le Cid" performed by the Jesuit pupils

1647

Feb., Acadia granted to d'Aulnay Charnisay as a hereditary fief

March 27, Royal regulations for the fur monopoly, the first political constitution for Canada, provided for a Council composed of the Governor, the Superior of the Jesuits or the bishop, and the Governor of Montreal, the "Council of Quebec," and Quebec, Montreal, and Three Rivers to elect municipal officers called syndics to look after interests of the people and attend Council

June 12, First stone of Jesuit College at Quebec laid

June 25, First horse in Canada arrived in Quebec, a present of the inhabitants to the Governor

July 16, Lake St. John discovered by Father de Quen on expedition to the Porcupine Indians, ascending the Saguenay and the Chicoutimi rivers

Governor Winthrop of Massachusetts opened negotiations for a treaty of commerce and free trade between New England and New France which came to no result

Fort Richelieu burned by the Iroquois

1648

March 5, Royal warrant modified regulations of March 27 for government of the colony until 1663, the Governor to be appointed for 3 years only and the retiring governor to be included in the Council, and 2 or more inhabitants of the country to be elected by the appointed members of the Council. The King named the additional members for the first Council, François de Chavigny, Paul Godefroy, and Robert Giffard

July 4, The Huron village of St. Joseph destroyed by the Iroquois and Father Daniel killed

Aug. 20, D'Ailleboust de Coulonge succeeded Montmagny as Governor

Jacques Boisdon granted privilege of keeping the first inn on condition that he "settled in the square in front of the Church" and "keeps nobody in his house during high mass, sermons, the catechism, or vespers"

1649

March 16–17, The Huron villages of St. Ignace and St. Louis destroyed by the Iroquois, and the Jesuit Fathers Brébeuf and Lalemant captured and subsequently burned at the stake

June 14, Father Rageneau abandoned Huron mission at St. Marie removing to St. Joseph

Dec. 7, Huron town of St. Jean destroyed by the Iroquois and Fathers Garner and Cabanel killed

1650

March, The Iroquois attacked outlying houses of the European settlements

May 15, The Iroquois defeated the powerful Neutral Indians

May 24, D'Aulnay Charnisay drowned

June 10, The Jesuits abandoned mission on the Isle of St. Joseph, the last in the Huron country, and the Hurons dispersed by the Iroquois, abandoned their country

Sept. 1–June 4, 1651, Father Druillettes on unsuccessful mission to Boston to negotiate a treaty of commerce and alliance with New England

Dec. 30, Ursuline Convent at Quebec burned

Martin Boulet opened a school at Quebec
Population of New France 705 persons

1651

Jan. 17, Jean de Lauzon appointed Governor and Lieutenant General of Canada
Feb. 25, Charles de la Tour commissioned by the King as Governor and Lieutenant General in Acadia, and reinstated in possession of his lands Sept. 23

1652

May, New Ursuline Convent building opened in Quebec
Aug. 18, A surgeon named Plassy and 4 inhabitants of Three Rivers in canoe killed by Iroquois, and the following day Governor Duplessis Bochart killed in attack on same Indians near Three Rivers with 15 men
Pierre Esprit Radisson, captured by the Iroquois, escaped to Dutch fort at Albany, New York, according to his journal Oct. 29, 1653 and sailed to Europe from New Amsterdam
Iroquois repulsed in attack on Montreal

1653

Feb. 24, Marriage contract of Charles de la Tour with the widow of d'Aulnay Charnisay for "the peace and tranquility of the country, and concord and union between the two families"
June 26, Peace arranged at Montreal with the Onondagas (central Iroquois)
Aug.–Oct., The Jesuit Father Antoine Poncet, seized by the Mohawks at Cap Rouge near Quebec, kept a captive. Winsor says he was the first white man to view the Thousand Islands of the St. Lawrence. T. J. Campbell gives his route as up the Richelieu and Lake Champlain, and return journey up Mohawk River and West Canada Creek to the St. Lawrence near Ogdensburg
Sept. 22, De Maisonneuve reached Quebec from France bringing new settlers including Margaret Bourgeois who established the Sisters of the Congregation
Nov. 5, Peace arranged between the French and the Iroquois at Quebec
Dec. 3, Nicolas Denys received grant of all lands from Cape Canso to Cape Rosiers in Acadia from the Company of New France. He was subsequently attacked and made a prisoner by Emmanuel Le Borgne, creditor of d'Aulnay claiming all his property, and taken to Port Royal also seized

1654

Jan. 30, Royal letters patent to Nicolas Denys as Governor and Lieutenant General over "la Baye St. Laurent" and adjacent islands confirmed rights in lands from Cape Canso to Cape Rosiers of which he had been unjustly deprived by d'Aulnay Charnisay. He settled at St. Peters in Cape Breton
May 17, Radisson landed in Canada
July 2, Father Simon Le Moyne left Quebec and Montreal on the 17th to visit the Iroquois. Reached Lake Ontario by the St. Lawrence River July 29, and from Aug. 2–15 at village of the Onondagas south of Oneida Lake on Indian Hill about 2 miles from the present town of Manlius. Return journey by Lake Onondaga and Seneca and Oneida rivers and Lake Ontario and the first white man to voyage on the Oswego River. Reached Montreal Sept. 7
Aug. 6–Aug. 1656, First voyage westward of Pierre

Esprit Radisson with his brother-in-law, Médart Chouart, sieur de Groseilliers, believed to be the 2 unnamed *voyageurs* of "Jesuit Relations." Wintered at Green Bay, Lake Michigan, and explored the Fox River country (H. C. Campbell). Warren Upham states that they were at Prairie Island, Lake Pepin, an expansion of the upper Mississippi from April or May 1655 to June 1656 (Minn. Hist. Soc. X)
Aug. 16, Port Royal surrendered by Emanuel Le Borgne, creditor of d'Aulnay, who had seized the fort, to Major Robert Sedgwick commanding expedition from New England after capture of Pentagoet and La Tour's Fort St. John

1655

Oct. 7, Fathers Chaumont and Dablon left Montreal for the Onondaga country, arriving at Indian village Nov. 5 by the St. Lawrence and Salmon rivers and Lake Ontario and the Oneida River, and began return journey from Oneida Lake March 2, 1656
Oct. 15, Decree of the King's Council gave judgment against Le Borgne in suit of Denys for recovery of his lands and property
Nov. 3, Treaty of Westminster between France and England signed restored Acadia to the French, the status of the forts at Pentagoet, St. John, and Port Royal referred by Article 25 to a commission. Restitution did not take place until the Treaty of Breda

1656

May 7, Four Jesuit Fathers François Le Mercier, Fremin, Dablon, and Menard with soldiers commanded by Major Zachary Dupuys left Quebec to establish a post in the Onondaga country, reaching the mouth of the Oswego River July 7 and Lake Onondaga July 11, and July 17 began building house at site of the present city of Syracuse, New York (Prince Soc. May 7, Parkman May 17)
May 19–20, The Iroquois killed and captured Huron refugees on Island of Orleans
Aug., Return of the 2 Frenchmen believed to be Radisson and Groseilliers escorting 50 canoes laden with furs
Aug. 9, Grant by Cromwell of Acadia to Sir Charles La Tour, son of Charles de La Tour and a Nova Scotian baronet, Sir Thomas Temple and William Crowne. On Sept. 20 La Tour made over his interest to his associates for the twentieth part of the products of the country

1657

Jan. 26, Letters patent made Viscount d'Argenson Governor of New France
March 7, Decree of the King prohibited sale of liquor to the Indians
July 29, The Sulpician priests, Fathers de Queylus, Souart Gallinée, and d'Allet arrived at Quebec, sent to found seminary and take charge of Montreal Island
July, Fathers Paul Raguenay, Joseph Imbert Duperon, with P. E. Radisson started for the Onondaga mission
Sept. 2, Ship brought word of appointment of Father de Queylus as Vicar General of Quebec by the Archbishop of Rouen who claimed jurisdiction in Canada
Nov. 20, Le Borgne received grant of land in Acadia from the Company of New France from entrance of the river of the Isle of Verte to New England except the lands granted to La Tour

Nov. 25, Marguerite Bourgeois opened a school for Indian and French children at Ville Marie (Montreal)

Dec. 10, Commission Royal appointed Le Borgne Governor and Lieutenant General in Acadia from Canso to New England

1658

March 12, Order forbade inhabitants of New France to leave the colony without permission of the Governor

March 19–20, Major Dupuys, Father Le Mercier, Radisson, and the rest of the company, 40 Frenchmen, 10 soldiers, and 6 Jesuits escaped during the night from the hostile Onondagas and reached Montreal April 3 and Quebec April 23

March 30, New commission to Father de Queylus as Vicar General to Montreal only

June 1–Aug. 19, 1660, Radisson and Groseilliers on second expedition to the west, traveled to Lake Superior, Chequamegon Bay by the Ottawa River and by Lake Nipissing route to Sault Ste. Marie, and to Lake Courte Oreille. In the spring of 1659 they visited the Sioux country between the St. Croix and upper Mississippi. H. C. Campbell, Thwaites, Parkman, Burpee, Sulte, and Scull claim that they reached the Mississippi at this time, and Campbell that they also traveled overland to Hudson Bay

July 11, Father Claude Allouez reached Quebec, crossing from France with the new Governor d'Argenson

Aug. 10, Hôtel Dieu, Quebec, completed and consecrated

Sept. 1, First patent of nobility granted to resident of Canada to Robert Giffard

Dec. 8, François de Laval ordained Bishop of Petrea, and Vicar Apostolic of Canada; arrived in Canada June 16, 1659

1659

Sept. 7, Marguerite Bourgeois and Jean Mance who had returned to France for assistance for their work arrived at Montreal bringing 62 men and 47 women, and established the Congregation of Notre Dame

Sept. 12, The Abbé de Queylus arrived at Quebec from Montreal, opposed by Jesuits, and in conflict of authority with Bishop Laval who had arrived June 16, arrested Oct. 22 and sent to France

Sept. 26, A "Brandy Parliament" called by Bishop Laval to consider the traffic in liquor with the Indians. He threatened those who disobeyed his mandate of prohibition with excommunication

Dec. 25, Bishop Laval insisted that priests of the choir should receive incense at midnight mass before Governor d'Argenson, one of many slights in his quarrel with the Governor for precedence

1660

Feb. 27, The Abbé de Queylus in France refused permission to return to Canada

May 5, Bishop Laval excommunicated those who persisted in the sale of liquor to the Indians; excommunication suspended in Jan., 1662 and renewed in Feb.

May 21, Adam Dollard des Ormeaux and 15 companions killed in stockade at rapids at the Long Sault on the Ottawa River by band of Iroquois after siege of 10 days, saving the colony at Montreal by their sacrifice

Aug. 28, Father Menard left Three Rivers and reached Keweenaw Bay, Lake Superior Oct. 15 and estab-

lished St. Teresa mission about 7 miles north of the present village of L'Anse, Michigan

Aug. 30, Isaac de Pas, Marquis de Feuquères, appointed Viceroy

1661

June 1, Fathers Dablon and Dreuilletes from Tadousac ascended the Saguenay to Lake St. John and established a mission a short distance north of the Lake. They entered the Chamouchouan River and by the Chegobich River and Lake reached the Nikaubau River and Lake on July 2

July 13, Father René Menard left Keweenaw Bay to visit Hurons who had migrated to the mouth of the Blackwater River in Wisconsin to escape from the Iroquois, and was lost on the trail Aug. 7–10, Thwaites places spot at present city of Merrill, Wisconsin. His mission of St. Teresa continued by Father Allouez

Aug. 4, Bishop Laval forbade the Abbé de Queylus who had appeared at Quebec Aug. 3 from proceeding to Montreal

Aug. 28–Aug. 1662, Journey of Radisson and Groseilliers without permission of the Governor who had asked for too large a share in the enterprise from Montreal west by way of the Ottawa River, Lake Nipissing, French River, and Lake Huron to the Sault Ste. Marie and Lake Superior at Chequamegon Bay. On this expedition Thwaites claims that they reached Lake Assiniboine, Sulte, Burpee, Laut and others that they traveled overland to Hudson Bay in the spring of 1662, which is denied by Campbell and Bryce

Sept. 19, Baron d'Avaugour succeeded d'Argenson as Governor

Oct. 23, Queylus sent back to France

Oct., Two men put to death under law prohibiting sale of liquor to the Indians

1662

Feb. 24, Bishop Laval again excommunicated persons selling liquor to the Indians but was obliged to revoke his act the same day because of riots

May 2, Groseilliers left Quebec for Hudson Bay according to statement of Father Lalemant in "Jesuit Relations"

Aug. 12, Bishop Laval sailed for France to secure support against the Governor for his measures against the liquor traffic with the Indians

Nov. 6, Pierre Boucher returned from France with 100 soldiers and 300 colonists

The French settled Placentia, Newfoundland, which was occupied by the Dutch the same year

Godefroy, Comte d'Estrades, Viceroy

1663

Feb. 5, Earthquake in Quebec

Feb. 24, The Company of New France of the One Hundred Associates resolved to restore property in New France to the King; accepted by the King in March

March 21, Louis Robert named first Intendant of New France by the King; he never came to Canada

——, Decree of the Council that all lands in Canada not cleared within 3 months should be resumed by the Crown and granted to actual settlers

March 26, Sovereign Council established by royal charter registered Oct. 10, the Governor, the Bishop or other head of the Church, and 5 other members to be appointed by the Governor and Bishop

March 26, Laval obtained royal grant to establish a theological seminary at Quebec, registered by the Council Oct. 10, the later Laval University

April, Edict of the King declared that the laws and ordinances of France as practiced within the jurisdiction of the Parliament of Paris to govern in Canada

May 1, Augustin de Saffray, Sieur de Mézy appointed Governor

May 5, M. Souart representing the Seminary of St. Sulpice assumed obligations of the Associates of Montreal, the Company of Notre Dame, ceremony of taking possession Aug. 18. Christie gives date of deed as March 9

May 7, Louis Gaudais Dupont appointed special commissioner to go to Canada to take possession for the King and end rule of the Company of New France, and investigate conditions and make report

July 21, Father Claude Allouez created Vicar General of the Church in the West

Sept. 15, Governor de Mézy arrived from France at Quebec with 159 colonists including 35 young girls, and accompanied by Bishop Laval

Sept. 18, First meeting of the Sovereign Council empowered to carry on the government under the Royal Province

Sept. 20, The Council sent soldiers to seize incriminating papers of M. Dumesnil, lawyer, sent by the Company of New France to the Colony to investigate alleged peculations of the Company of the Habitants

Sept. 28, Ordinance of the Council prohibited trade in liquor with the Indians

Oct. 7, Sovereign Council called meeting of citizens to elect a mayor and 2 aldermen for Quebec, Jean Baptiste Legardeur de Repentigny chosen mayor

Nov. 19, Patent appointed Alexander de Prouville, Marquis de Tracy, Lieutenant General

Nov. 26, Order in Council for colonial coinage

Dec. 16, Merchants permitted to charge 65% advance on selling price of goods in France out of which they paid a revenue of 10% import duty

The "Galiote" built by the Sovereign Council, the first vessel launched at Quebec

1664

March 12, Grant of Charles II to James, Duke of York, of the territory between the St. Croix and the Kennebec rivers

April 17, Decree of the Sovereign Council prohibited bartering or giving intoxicating drinks to the Indians

May 28, Edict of the King creating the new West India Company (*Compagnie des Indes Occidentales*) and registered July 11 placed trade under the Company of lands and islands in America including Canada

July 26, Sovereign Council fixed the price of brandy at 190 livres per barrel, lard at 80 livres in wheat, or 75 in silver, and a 55% profit allowed on all other commodities. Officers appointed at Quebec to attach tags to goods showing retail prices

Sept. 19, Governor de Mézy autocratically dismissed 4 members of the Council, and appointed new members in their places Sept. 28

Cost of passage from Quebec to France fixed at 33 livres

1665

Jan. 29, Act for union of Seminary in Quebec with Seminary of Foreign Missions in Paris

March 23, Intendant ranking in importance with the Governor and the Bishop appointed, Jean Talon, commissioned

——, Sieur Daniel Rémy de Courcelles commissioned Governor and Lieutenant General of Canada, Acadia, and Island of Terre Neuve. Governor Mézy recalled

May 5, Death of Governor Augustin de Saffray, Chevalier de Mézy

June 30, Alexander de Prouville, Marquis de Tracy, Lieutenant Governor, arrived at Quebec with 4 companies of the Carignan-Salières regiment from France for campaign against the hostile Iroquois and began building forts on the Richelieu, Fort St. Louis, later known as Fort Chambly from the builder, established by La Vérendrye, and Forts Sorel and Ste. Thérèse

July 16, 12 horses landed at Quebec from France, the first in the colony since the solitary horse presented to Governor Montmagny. The Indians called them the "moose from France"

Aug. 1, Radisson and Groseilliers sailed from Nantucket for England with the English Commission, after failure to interest French authorities in an expedition to Hudson Bay

Aug. 8, Father Allouez left Three Rivers, reached Sault Ste. Marie Sept. 2 and Chequamegon Bay Oct. 1 where he established a mission called La Pointe du Saint Esprit, soon shortened to La Pointe. He named Lake Superior Lake Tracy after the Lieutenant Governor

Sept. 12, Governor de Courcelles and Talon, the Intendant, arrived, and 2 days later 8 companies of soldiers, and 400 settlers, artisans, and laborers in the "Justice"

Sept. 23, Members of the Council illegally dismissed by de Mézy reinstated

Oct. 15, Judgment against Le Borgne in suit of Nicolas Denys before King's Council

Dec. 13, Treaty of peace with the Iroquois concluded at Quebec

The Sanctuary of St. Anne de Beaupré erected by Bishop de Laval

Talon had a vessel of 120 tons built with his own private means to encourage shipbuilding

Successful attack of the Dutch on St. Johns, Newfoundland

1666

Jan. 9–March 17, Governor de Courcelles led armed reconnaissance into the Mohawk country from Quebec, reached Schenectady Feb. 20

May 25, Peace Treaty with the Senecas concluded at Quebec

July 12, Peace Treaty with the Oneidas concluded at Quebec

July, Fort de Chazy built by the French at Isle La Motte near north end of Lake Champlain

Sept. 14–Nov. 5, The Marquis de Tracy commanded second expedition into the Mohawk country which systematically destroyed their 5 main towns, burning palisades and stores and standing crops

Sept. 20, Father Jacques Marquette arrived at Quebec

Oct. 25, Radisson and Groseilliers in England had audience with King Charles who promised them ships for expedition to America

Dec. 6, The Council abolished the death penalty for violation of the ordinance prohibiting sale of liquor to the Indians, and substituted discretionary fines and corporal punishment

La Salle established Lachine on Lake St. Louis, named 1669 in mockery of La Salle's search in the west for route to China

Census of New France gave population as 3,215 persons including 2,034 men and 1,181 women, 528 married couples. Population of Quebec 547, of Montreal 455, Three Rivers 457, Orleans 532, Beaupré 523, Beauport 185. One thousand soldiers and 400 servants not included in this enumeration

1667

Feb. 1, M. de la Barre commissioned Governor General

Feb. 4, First ball in Canada given at Quebec by Chartier de Lotbinière

April, Ordinance of Louis XIV for regulation of the courts, the first civil code

May, Royal letters patent confirmed establishment of Seminary at Montreal, and of the Island of Montreal to the Sulpician Seminary in Paris

May 17–June, Father Allouez crossed Lake Superior by canoe on perilous journey to Lake Nepigon to visit the Nepissiriens

July 7, Treaty of peace with the Iroquois made by the Marquis de Tracy. He left Canada for France Aug. 28, his work accomplished

July 21, Treaty of Breda ended war between England and France and restored Acadia to France

Sept. 4, Ordinances of the Council ruled that tithes should be paid at rate of the 26th bushel

Nov. 9, The Company of the West Indies confirmed grant of Nicolas Denys in Acadia of Dec. 3, 1853

First roads made from Quebec to outlying districts

Census of Canada gave 1,667 families including 4,312 persons. Talon records the arrival of 286 immigrants in this year

1668

March 12, Royal regulation excluded military officers from rank in churches

April 8, M. de Bouteroue commissioned Intendant until 1670 while Talon absent in France

April 21, Father Marquette left Montreal to establish a mission at Sault Ste. Marie

June 3–June, 1669, Voyage of Capt. Zachary Gillam from the Thames in the "Nonsuch" with Groseilliers in service of England to Hudson Bay, the "Eaglet" with Radisson damaged by storm forced to turn back. Reached Rupert Bay Sept. 25 and the mouth of Rupert River Sept. 29, where Fort Charles erected

Oct. 2, The Sulpician Fathers Trouvé and Fénelon left Lachine to establish a mission at the Bay of Quinté reached Oct. 28

Oct. 9, The Petit Séminaire (smaller seminary) founded by Laval at Quebec and opened with 8 French pupils and 6 Hurons

Nov. 10, The Council gave permission to Frenchmen in Canada to give or sell liquor to the Indians, the reason to prevent the fur trade from going to the English

Talon advanced 3,268 livres to François Bissot to establish a tannery at Pointe de Levy, and in this year established a brewery at Quebec which is mentioned in the "Jesuit Relations," and constructed 2 vessels to establish trade with the West Indies

Queylus reconciled with Laval during the latter's sojourn in France returned to Canada as Grand Vicar of Montreal

Census of Canada gave 1,139 families including 5,870 persons

1669

April 5, Ordinance of the King ordered a pension to encourage large families and marriages in Canada, 300 livres a year to families with as many as 10 legitimate children, and 400 for 12 children

April 8, Agreement of King to establishment of a religious hospital in Montreal; registered in Quebec Oct. 20, 1670

May 15, Colbert wrote to Governor de Courcelles that henceforth trade was to be free in New France, the West India Company losing its monopoly

June 26, Ordinance forbade carrying liquor into the Indian country

July 6, Robert René Cavelier, later sieur de La Salle and Fathers Dollier de Casson and Galinée left Montreal reaching Lake Ontario Aug. 2 and Irondequoit Bay Aug. 26, Galinée's journal the first description of the Niagara River which they reached the middle of Sept. On the way to west shore of Lake Erie Sept. 24 they met Louis Joliet who had been sent by Governor de Courcelles to find copper on Lake Superior and returning by Lakes Huron, St. Clair, and the Detroit River was the first white man known to have been on Lake Erie

July 9, Declaration of the King confirmed by Parliament established Company of the North for 20 years

Sept. 13, Father Marquette left Sault Ste. Marie to succeed Father Allouez at La Pointe mission

Sept. 30, Fathers Dollier de Casson, and Galinée left La Salle and wintered on shore of Lake Erie at site of the present Port Dover near Long Point

Nov. 3, Father Allouez left Sault Ste. Marie to establish a mission at Green Bay

1670

March 23, Fathers Dollier de Casson and Galinée erected a cross on the shore of Lake Erie taking possession for France

March 24, Decree of King's Council, and of the King Feb. 19 ordered coinage of silver and copper pieces to 100,000 livres for use in America

April 16, Father Allouez left Green Bay to visit the Outagamis, ascended the Fox River and portaged to Lake Winnebago, April 19, which he named St. Francis and established St. Mark's mission, and by the Wolf River to junction of Little Wolf and Embarass April 24. He entered the Fox River on return journey April 29 to visit the Mascoutens. On April 20 on shore of Lake Winnebago Father Allouez celebrated first mass in Wisconsin

May 2, The Hudson Bay Company incorporated as "The Governor and Company of Adventurers of England trading into Hudson's Bay" under Prince Rupert as the first governor, granted sole trade and commerce in Hudson Bay region

May 25, Fathers Dollier de Casson and Galinée, Sulpicians, arrived at the Jesuit mission at Sault Ste. Marie from site of Detroit known from this time by Galinée's rude map, and returned to Montreal reached June 18

June, Radisson with Capt. Newland in the "Waveno" and Groseilliers with Capt. Gillam in the "Nelson" sailed for Hudson Bay and there erected arms of England at Port Nelson where York factory was later established, named the southern river Hayes after Sir Jasper Hayes and wintered at Fort Charles gathering furs

Aug. 5, Surrender of fort at Pentagoet by Walker to the French by order of Sir Thomas Temple of July 7 for surrender of Acadian forts

Aug. 18, Talon arrived in Quebec accompanied by 3 Recollet priests brought to break up the monopoly of the Jesuits, and a large number of immigrants

Aug. 27, Surrender of Fort Gemisick on the St. John River by the English to de Soulange

Sept. 2, Port Royal surrendered by the English to French possession

Sept. 30, La Salle crossed the isthmus to the south shore of Lake Erie. Claim that he explored the Ohio River as far as Louisville conceded by Parkman, Wrong, and Margry, but Shea and others believe he reached only the Illinois River

Oct. 20, Decree of the Council abolished duty of 10% on dry goods and imposed duties on tobacco and liquors

Oct. 23, Jean Talon reappointed Intendant May 14, 1669, took office

Privilege given to Sieur Colinet to establish a potash and soft soap factory in New France

1671

April 29, Royal letters patent approved establishment of the Sisters of the Congregation of Montreal; registered in Quebec, Oct. 17, 1672

May 5, Nicolas Perrot reached Sault Ste. Marie in advance of Lusson to notify tribes of meeting to be held. Made peace between the Pottawattomies and the Menominees and Miamis

June 3, Governor de Courcelles led expedition from Montreal which entered Lake Ontario June 12 to make demonstration by armed force of the power of the French

June 14, Simon François Daumont, Sieur de St. Lusson, met great assembly of Indians representing 14 tribes at Sault Ste. Marie and with religious and civil ceremonies took possession of the land for France, and of Lakes Huron and Superior, and all countries adjacent and bounded by the Northern and Western Seas and the South Sea

Aug. 6, Father Albanel and Sieur Denys de St. Simon left Quebec and reached Lake St. John up the Saguenay River Sept. 17, where they wintered and making the overland journey arrived at Hudson's Bay at the English Fort Charles on James Bay, June 28, 1672

Nov. 18, Death of Mme. de la Peltrie

The Hurons driven from Chequamegon Bay by the Sioux settled at the Island of Mackinac, and Father Marquette went with them and established mission of St. Ignace which he later moved from the island to the mainland

1672

March 12, Father Dollier de Casson traced the main street of Montreal which he named Notre Dame

April 7, Louis de Buade, Comte de Frontenac, appointed Governor and Lieutenant General, and arrived in Canada Sept. 12

April 30, Death of Mère de l'Incarnation

Oct. 10–Nov. 8, Talon granted about 60 seignorial concessions to officers and others desirous of forming settlements

Oct. 23, The three estates convoked by Governor Frontenac

Nov. 3, St. Helen's Island named by Champlain for his wife granted to M. Lemoine

Nov., Talon and de Courcelles left Canada

1673

March 23, Ordinances established police regulations, rules for cleaning the streets and prevention of fires, and concerning markets

May 17, Louis Joliet, Father Marquette, and 5 others started from Mackinac in canoes on Lake Michigan for Green Bay, and by the Fox and Wisconsin rivers reached the Mississippi on June 17 at Prairie du Chien, the first white men to descend the river. They turned back at the mouth of the Arkansas River, July 17, 1674, and returned to Green Bay by the Illinois River

May 29, Proclamation of Frontenac gave the Recollets title to their land on the St. Charles River of which title deeds lost after the English occupation of Quebec, ratified April 1676

June 5, Royal decree condemned the *coureurs de bois* and forbade the inhabitants to go into the woods for 24 hours without permission in an effort to control the trade in furs, the only effect being to make the *coureurs de bois* outlaws and divert trade to the English

June 13, Cataraqui (Kingston) founded by La Salle on north shore of Lake Ontario

July 12, Frontenac with a large company landed at Cataraqui and Fort Frontenac begun on the 13th, and on the 17th a grand conference held with the Iroquois

Successful attack of the Dutch on Ferryland, Newfoundland

Second census of New France gave 6,705 as population

1674

Jan. 26, Frontenac arrested and imprisoned François Perrot, Governor of Montreal, charged with illegal dealings with the *coureurs de bois* in the fur trade

Feb. 9, Treaty of Westminster signed made peace between England and Holland, ending raids of the Dutch in English settlements at Newfoundland

Aug. 3, Father Albanel arrived at Hudson Bay on second overland journey, his passport dated Oct. 7, 1673, Quebec, among papers of the Hudson Bay Company

Aug. 7, Permission given for revival of trade in liquor with the Indians

Aug. 10, Capture of the French forts of Pentagoet and St. John (Jemseg or Gemisick), Acadia, by the Dutch, but possession only temporary

Aug. 31, The Council ordered beggars to leave Quebec. Begging had been begun in 1673 by 5 women

Oct. 1, Pope Clement X established the bishopric of Quebec, Laval appointed first bishop

Oct. 25, Father Marquette left the St. Francis Xavier mission at mouth of the Fox River on mission to the Illinois Indians, and reached the Chicago River Dec. 4 where he spent the winter

Dec. 16, Grant of French West India Company revoked

1675

April 8, Father Marquette on return journey from the Illinois mission begun March 29 reached Indian village of Kaskaskia and established the first mission in Illinois

May 11, Decree of Council gave Jean Oudiette monopoly of the beaver trade for 7 years beginning June 1

May 13, Patent of nobility and the seignory of Fort Frontenac at Cataraqui (Kingston) granted to La Salle in France

May 18, Death of Father Marquette on east shore of Lake Michigan near the present Ludington on journey returning to St. Ignace mission

May 19, Letter of union of Sulpician Seminary in Quebec with the Seminary in Paris

May 30, Jacques Duschesneau appointed Intendant, the first since Talon left Canada in 1672, took office Sept. 16

June 5, Edict increased ordinary members of the Council from 5 to 7

1676

April 15, Royal ordinance forbade trade in furs in the Indian villages, compelling the Indians to come to the settlements for needed supplies, and royal edict forbade issue of permits to sell liquor to the Indians, registered by the Council Oct. 5

——, Tax on furs in Canada farmed out to Nicolas Oudiette and his associates, Oudiette, *Fermier-Général du Domaine d'Occident*, licenses for private trade with the Indians revoked

May 11, Ordinance prohibited begging in Montreal without certificates of parish priest

May 20, Royal edict empowered the Governor and Intendant acting jointly to make land grants on condition that the land should be cleared within 6 years

——, Under terms of edict of Louis XIV Nashwaak and Jemseg on the St. John River granted to Pierre de Joibert, Sieur de Soulanges, and Marson, tract of more than 100 square miles, held in 1759 by the Marquis de Vaudreuil, grandson, when Quebec surrendered

June 15 and Nov. 15, The chief inhabitants of Quebec summoned to semi-annual meetings to fix the price of bread, and make recommendations for the prosperity of the colony

Sept. 11, The Dutch West India Company issued a commission authorizing John Rhoade to take possession of Acadia and Nova Scotia, and Cornelius Steenwyck named Governor Oct. 27

Oct. 11, Decree of Council established public markets in Quebec, Three Rivers, and Ville Marie (Montreal), and trade forbidden in other places

Baron de St. Castine occupied Pentagoet

Oct., Father Allouez started from De Pere for the Illinois mission, wintered near Green Bay, and reached Kaskaskia April 27, 1677

1677

May 9, Tribunal called the *Prévôté de Quebec* established by Louis XV, to be composed of a lieutenant-general, a King's attorney, and a clerk, for civil and criminal cases; registered Oct. 25

May 16, Decree of Council fixed price of furs

May, Grant of Island of Montreal to St. Sulpice Seminary, Paris, confirmed by letters patent

June 7, La Durantaye at head of strait leading from Lake Huron to Lake St. Clair formally took possession of the country for France

1678

May 12, Royal edict ordered that the matter of liquor traffic with the Indians be discussed in meeting of the inhabitants and magistrates and report sent to France

May 12, Patent signed at St. Germain-en-Laye, La Salle authorized to discover western lands and to build forts to the south and west, and his seigneurial tenure of Fort Frontenac at Cataraqui confirmed

July 14, La Salle and Henri de Tonty sailed from Rochelle, France, for Quebec arriving Sept. 15

Sept. 1–May, 1681, Du Lhut, Daniel Greysolon, and Charles de Greysolon, Sieur de la Tourette, left Montreal and journeyed to the region beyond Lake Superior, in this year built fort at Lake Nepigon which he discovered unless it had been seen earlier by Radisson, and built Fort Kaministikquia on Thunder Bay

Oct. 20, The "Brandy Parliament" summoned, 20 of chief merchants and seigneurs met with Superior Conference and after debate voted for continuance of liquor traffic with the Indians

Oct. 30, Parish of Notre Dame, Montreal united with the Seminary of Montreal

Nov. 7, Civil Code of April, 1667, as amended approved by ordinance of Louis XIV; registered Oct. 23, 1679

Nov. 18, La Salle sent party under Sieur de la Motte-Lussière and including Tonty and Father Hennepin to the Niagara River near Lake Erie to establish post, where La Salle himself arrived Dec. 6

1679

Jan. 26, Keel of the "Griffin," La Salle's vessel, laid, and ground broken Feb. 1 by La Salle for Fort Conty at site of present Fort Niagara (Margry)

April 25, Earlier regulations as to fur trade confirmed but the Governor allowed to grant hunting permits

May 24, Royal decree permitted sale of liquor at the settlements but provided that permits for sale in Indian villages be reduced to smallest possible number

July 2, Du Lhut reached the Sioux village of Izatys on shore of Lake Mille Lacs and planted arms of France and took possession of the country for France, the first white man in Minnesota

Aug. 7, La Salle launched the "Griffin" towed from the Niagara River on Lake Erie, sailed up the Detroit River to Lake Huron Aug. 23, reached St. Ignace mission at Mackinac Aug. 27

Aug. 29, Domain of Seminary of St. Sulpice enlarged by grant of islands near Montreal and later by grant of the seignory of the Two Mountains

Sept. 15, Du Lhut met Indians in grand council at head of Lake Superior and arranged a peace between the Sioux and the Assiniboines, Saulteurs, and Crees

Sept. 18, La Salle sent the "Griffin" from Green Bay with cargo of furs which never reached the post at Niagara, the ship probably sunk in a storm or scuttled by crew. La Salle Sept. 19, continued by canoe along Wisconsin shore of Lake Michigan

Oct. 16, At meeting of the Council voted that liquor should not be carried into Indian villages

Nov. 1, La Salle reached the St. Joseph River near southeast end of Lake Michigan and built Fort Miami

Nov. 10, Duchesneau, the Intendant, formally accused Governor Frontenac of encouragement of the *coureurs de bois* roving the woods in illegal trade in furs

Dec. 3, La Salle and Tonty ascended the St. Joseph River and proceeded by portage to the Kankakee and from there to the Illinois River to Peoria Lake reached Jan. 5, 1680

1680

Jan. 5, La Salle at Peoria Lake on the Illinois River and began building Fort Crèvecœur, the second French fort in the West, on the east bank of the Illinois River about a mile from Lake Peoria

Feb. 29, Father Hennepin, Antoine du Gay Anguel and Michel Accault left Fort Crèvecœur commissioned by La Salle to explore the upper Mississippi and trace its source

March 1, La Salle with 6 Frenchmen and an Indian started from Fort Crèvecœur on long overland journey to Montreal leaving Tonty at the fort, and reached fort on St. Joseph River March 24, and Niagara on April 21, and Fort Frontenac May 6

March 12, Hennepin and his companions entered the Mississippi from the Illinois River and turning north discovered the Falls of St. Anthony which they named

April 11, Hennepin and the other Frenchmen captured by the Sioux Indians and taken to village of Issati near Mille Lac

May 29, Grant of Louis XIV of Le Sault near St. Louis rapids to Jesuits for a settlement for converted Indians

June, Du Lhut ascended the Bois Brulé River from Lake Superior to its source and by portage reached the St. Croix River which he descended to the Mississippi

July 22, La Salle received word that in the absence of Tonty to examine Starved Rock as base for permanent post his men mutinied and destroyed Fort Crèvecœur on the Illinois and the fort on the St. Joseph, and at Niagara

July 23, La Salle left Fort Frontenac and proceeded to Detroit reached Aug. 10, Mackinac in Sept. and the St. Joseph River Nov. 28 and the Illinois village Dec. 1 and down the Illinois to the Mississippi in search of Tonty

July 25, Du Lhut rescued Father Hennepin and the other Frenchmen from the Sioux

Sept. 11, Tonty left Starved Rock in view of probable Iroquois attack and made the journey to Green Bay

1681

May 22, La Salle started for Mackinac and from there proceeded to St. Joseph River

May, Amnesty granted to the *coureurs de bois*, but trade in furs with the Indians in the West without a license forbidden

Sept. 25, Radisson arrived in Quebec

Dec. 21, Tonty, Father Membre, and the Indians and 23 Frenchmen left Fort Miami on the St. Joseph to begin journey to descend the Mississippi, La Salle following later

1682

Feb. 2, Commission of Nicolas Denys to his son Richard now in charge of holdings in Acadia

Feb. 6, La Salle expedition entered the Mississippi River from the Illinois, camped near the third Chickasaw bluffs Feb. 24 and built Fort Prudhomme

March 14, La Salle expedition at the mouth of the Arkansas took possession of the country for France

April 6, La Salle expedition reached point where the Mississippi divided into 3 channels, and La Salle descended one, Tonty, the second, and d'Autray the third

April 9, La Salle expedition reached the mouth of the Mississippi, the first to descend the river to the Gulf,

and took possession of the country for France naming it Louisiana after Louis XIV; began return journey April 10 and reached mouth of the St. Joseph in Sept.

May 1, Le Febre de la Barre commissioned Governor and Lieutenant General to replace Frontenac recalled, and Sieur Jacques de Meulles as Intendant

July 11–July 1683, Voyage of Radisson for La Chesnaye, merchant of Quebec, with his nephew Jean Baptiste Chouart de Groseilliers, to Hudson Bay, reached Hayes River Sept. 2 where fort built. Radisson captured vessel of Capt. Gillam, burned English forts, and carried Bridgar, representing the Hudson Bay Company, and also a son of Capt. Gillam representing a New England trading company, prisoners to Quebec. On this expedition Radisson made journey up the Hayes River in 1682

Oct. 9, Commissions of appointment of Governor de la Barre and Intendant de Meulles read at meeting of Council and letter recalling Frontenac and Duchesne because of their continued conflict in administration

Oct. 19, Licenses for the fur trade reissued

New Company of the North formed at Quebec for the Hudson Bay fur trade by Charles A. de Chesnaye and other merchants

Dec., La Salle established Fort St. Louis on Starved Rock on the Illinois River and Tonty left in command

1683

Jan. 5, Father Hennepin published his book on America, "Nouvelle decouverte d'un tres grand pays situé dans l'Amerique entre le Nouveau Mexique et la Mer Glaciale"

May, Oliver Morrel, Sieur de la Durantaye, sent to post at Mackinac by Governor de la Barre, to guard against threatened Iroquois attack, commanded post until 1690

Aug. 8, Du Lhut left Mackinac and reached the Mississippi by way of Green Bay

Sept., La Salle left Canada in disguise to seek protection of the King against the hostile Governor de la Barre

Nov. 16, Royal ordinance forbade trade in furs except under license

Fort La Tourette on Lake Nipigion at mouth of the Ombabika River built by Claude Greysolon, sieur de la Tourette, to control fur trade of the region

Nov. 26–29, Du Lhut held council with the Ojibwas at Sault Ste. Marie and compelled judgment and execution of 2 Indians who had murdered 3 Frenchmen

Nov., Baron Lahontan arrived in Quebec with company of French marines

Nicolas Perrot again in the West to gather Indian allies of the French to join La Barre at Niagara in expedition against the Iroquois

1684

March 28, Chevalier de Tonty repulsed the attack of the Iroquois on Fort St. Louis on Starved Rock, on the Illinois, after siege of 6 days

April 10, Ordinance forbade emigration to English colonies

April 14, Commission to La Salle from the King as Commander of country he had discovered

May 10, Radisson arrived in London from France and May 12 took service with the Hudson Bay Company and sailed for the Bay, May 17, took over French fort Aug. 15 and store of furs from his nephew, Jean Chouart, and sailed for England Sept. 4, carrying the 5 Frenchmen prisoners

July 9, Governor de la Barre left Quebec on unsuccessful expedition against the Iroquois

July 24, La Salle with Commander Beaujer and colonists sailed from La Rochelle, France, for the Gulf of Mexico and the Mississippi River

Sept. 5, La Barre in conference with the Iroquois makes concessions and accepts their terms of peace

Sept. 27, Commander Beaujer cast anchor at Petit Goave, Santo Domingo, instead of at Port de Paix as La Salle directed, remained at Santo Domingo until the 25th of Nov.

Nov. 6, Ordinance established a cathedral chapter at Quebec with 12 canons and 4 chaplains, inaugurated Nov. 12

Nov. 14, Laval sailed for France to resign the bishopric of Quebec

Dec. 28, The La Salle expedition sighted the continent of America at Florida

1685

Jan. 1, The Marquis de Denonville appointed Governor

Jan. 6, La Salle expedition passed the mouths of the Mississippi without recognizing the river

Jan. 14, Party landed for exploration for a few hours

Jan. 19, La Salle landed at point on the coast believed by most authorities to be Matagorda Bay, Texas

Feb. 4, Party by land led by La Salle started to find the Mississippi, and the boats led by Beaujer Feb. 9 uniting on the 13th

Feb. 18, Colonists made first settlement in Texas

Feb. 20, The "Amiable," La Salle's ship, wrecked on reef, one boat had been lost to the Spaniards on the voyage

March 12, Beaujer sailed for France reaching La Rochelle about July 1

March 24–April 2, La Salle with 47 men on expedition to find the Mississippi reached head of the Bay and built a stockade

June 8, Proclamation of Demeulles (De Meulles) Intendant, issued "card money," certain notes made out of playing cards cut in four to pay the wages of the soldiers; withdrawn Sept. 5

July 30, Jean Baptiste de la Croix, Chèvrière de Saint Vallier, appointed Vicar General of Canada, arrived in Quebec

July, La Salle's colonists occupied stockade believed to have been built on the Garcitas River, 5 miles from its junction with Lavaca Bay, which he named Fort St. Louis

Aug. 6, Three ships of the Hudson Bay Company in battle with French ships commanded by La Martinière in Hudson Bay, and the English "Merchant of Perpetuana" commanded by Edward Hume captured

Aug. 15, Letters patent appointing the Marquis de Denonville Governor enregistered

Oct. 29, Jean Pére La Martinière captured by the English at Hudson Bay and sent a prisoner to England

Oct. 31–March 24, 1686, La Salle with 50 men on exploring expedition from Fort St. Louis to search for the Mississippi

Nicolas Perrot in command at Green Bay traveled to the Mississippi River

Population of New France 12,263 including 1,538 Indians collected in villages

1686

Feb. 9, Second issue of card money; recalled in Oct.

Feb. 13–April 20, Tonty engaged in fruitless expedition to find La Salle's colony, camped at mouth of the Mississippi and left letter dated April 20, 1686, for La Salle with the Indians which was given by them to d'Iberville 12 years later

Feb. 18, Parish of Lachine established a convent, branch of the Congregation of Notre Dame of Montreal

March 20, Pierre le Moyne, Sieur d'Iberville left by the Ottawa River route for Hudson Bay arriving in June

April 22–Oct. 17, La Salle with party of 28 men in search for the Mississippi

April 24, Jean Bochart de Champigny appointed Intendant replacing de Meulles

May 1, Survivors of the wreck of La Salle's last boat, the "Belle" reached Fort St. Louis where Joutel had been left in charge

May, Gabriel Gautier received a grant of Cape Breton Island, the Island of St. John, and the Magdalen Islands

June 6, Daniel Greysolon, Sieur Du Lhut, commissioned commander of fort to be built by him between Lakes Erie and Huron near the present Detroit, Michigan

June 18, Moose factory (Fort St. Louis) on Hudson Bay taken from the English by d'Iberville and de Troyes

July 1, Fort Rupert, English post on Hudson Bay, taken by d'Iberville, and Governor Bridgar made a prisoner a second time

Aug. 8, Fort Albany on Hudson Bay surrendered by Governor Sargeant to de Troyes and d'Iberville after siege

Sept. 15, Abbé Souart and La Faye in name of the Seminary granted half an arpent of land to the citizens of Ville Marie (Montreal) for a school

Oct. 20, The Ursuline convent at Quebec founded 1639 burned

Nov. 16, Treaty of Neutrality concluded by Louis XIV and James II governing their possessions in America in the event of war in Europe

Quebec merchants built ship to carry timber to La Rochelle, France

1687

Jan. 7, La Salle with half of his colonists started on the journey to Canada to get relief

March 19, La Salle (43), shot and killed by two of his company, Duhaut and Liotot

April 17, Grant of Nicolas Denys in Acadia revoked giving him in lieu another seigneury to be assigned later

June, Champigny seized a number of Iroquois chiefs invited to Fort Frontenac and sent them to France to the galleys

June 13, Starting from Montreal Denonville reached Fort Frontenac July 1 and July 12 led nearly 3,000 men from rendezvous at Irondequist Bay into the Seneca country defeating the Indians in battle and burning their villages July 13–14

July 12, Du Lhut, Tonty, and La Durantaye in battle with Iroquois on upper Lakes

July 31, Fort Niagara constructed by Denonville at mouth of Niagara River at site of La Salle's post; abandoned Sept. 15, 1688

Aug. 1, Jean, Comte d'Estrees, Viceroy

Aug. 3, Baron Louis de Lahontan sent by Denonville left Fort Niagara for Fort St. Joseph

Sept. 14, The remainder of La Salle's party led by Joutel reached Tonty's fort at Starved Rock on the Illinois, concealed the death of La Salle and obtained money to return to France

Oct. 27, Tonty returned to Fort St. Louis, Starved Rock, on the Illinois and heard from Joutel false account of La Salle

Dec. 11, Report of French and English Commission under Treaty of Neutrality to decide as to Hudson Bay practically gave the territory to the French

1688

Jacques de Noyon made the journey from the Kaministikwia River to Rainy Lake where he spent the winter and built small fort. In the spring he descended the Rainy River to the Lake of the Woods

Jan. 4, Decree of Council called meeting of inhabitants of Quebec to decide on the price of bread and make recommendations as to the colony

Jan. 25, Abbé de St. Vallier consecrated (second) Bishop of Quebec, succeeding Bishop Laval, resigned

March 21, Remainder of La Salle's party left fort on the Illinois and reached Montreal July 14

May, French prisoners took possession of Hudson Bay ship, the "Churchill," and delivered it to d'Iberville

June 15, Three Iroquois tribes signed a declaration of neutrality

June 24, Radisson again in service of the Hudson Bay Company sailed for Hudson Bay

July 1, Lahontan sent by Denonville from Fort Niagara reached Fort St. Joseph which he burned Aug. 27 and abandoned and proceeded to Mackinac arriving Sept. 10

Aug. 15, Laval arrived from France and took up residence in Seminary he had founded

Sept. 24, Baron Lahontan from Mackinac made journey to Green Bay and by the Fox and Wisconsin rivers arrived at the Mississippi Oct. 23 and descended the river to junction with the Ohio. Returned to Montreal from Mackinac by the Ottawa River route July 9, 1689

Dec., Tonty made second journey to the rescue of La Salle's colonists but the Indians deserted and he was obliged to give up the attempt

Fort Prince of Wales built at the mouth of the Churchill River by the Hudson Bay Company

Population of New France 11,562 persons

1689

Jan. 28, The French left Three Rivers to attack New England frontier

April 22, The Spaniards from Mexico reached La Salle's fort in Texas and found the post deserted and plundered by the Indians

May 8, Nicolas Perrot at Fort St. Antoine which he had built on the Wisconsin side of Lake Pepin took possession of that region for France

May 15, Frontenac appointed Governor

May 17, King William's War begun between the English and the French, the Iroquois allies of the English against the French in Canada

June 27, Cocheco (Dover, New Hampshire) attacked and the inhabitants massacred by French and Indians

July 23, Jesuit Father Sebastian Rale arrived at Quebec from France and was sent on mission to the Abenaki Indians on the Kennebec River

Aug. 5, Iroquois massacred the sleeping inhabitants of the village of Lachine on the St. Lawrence

Aug. 15, Fort Pemaquid on point between the Penobscot and the Kennebec rivers captured by the Abenaki allies of the French

Aug. 27, Death of Father Allouez at Kaskaskia mission

Sept. 20, English fleet withdrew from unsuccessful attack on Placentia, Newfoundland

Oct. 16, Du Lhut defeated a party of Iroquois at the Lake of the Two Mountains

Oct. 18, Governor Frontenac with instructions of June 7 to expel the English from Hudson Bay and to capture New York, arrived at Quebec

Oct., Fort Frontenac at Cataraqui (Kingston) abandoned by the French

——, D'Iberville forced surrender of Fort New Severn on Hudson Bay and defended Fort Albany against English attack

Nov. 13, Iroquois attacked and massacred inhabitants of La Chenaye about 4 miles east of present village of Terrebonne

Dec. 3, Tonty left Fort St. Louis on the Illinois to find La Salle's colonists

Peace with the Iroquois defeated by cunning deception of the Huron chief, Kondiaronk

1690

Jan., Frontenac organized 3 expeditions against the English, one to New York, one to Maine, and one to New England

Feb. 9, French and Indians led by d'Iberville destroyed Schenectady, New York

Feb., Captain H. Wilson plundered Placentia, Newfoundland

March 27, Salmon Falls, the present Berwick, New Hampshire, destroyed by French and Indians led by François de Hertel

April 18, Decree of Intendant Champigny defined boundaries of grant in Acadia of Nicolas Denys under grant of April 17; ratified by the King March 16 1691

April 24, Tonty arrived at Asinai Indian village near the Neches River in attempt to find La Salle's colonists and turned back

May 11, Port Royal, Nova Scotia, commanded by Menneval surrendered to fleet from New England commanded by Sir William Phipps

May 20, Fort Loyal, at the present Portland, Maine, captured by French and Indians led by Portneuf

May 22, M. de Louvigny with Nicolas Perrot and 143 Canadians left Montreal to relieve La Durantaye at Mackinac

June 12, Henry Kelsey left York Factory on Hudson Bay to explore the western country and ascended the Hayes River with the Assiniboines and the Saskatchewan, no record of his route from the Hayes but July 10 was 600 miles southwest from the Factory

July 14, The King gave consent to grant of Fort St. Louis on the Illinois to Tonty and La Forest

Aug. 13, Captain John Schuyler led party from Albany on invasion into Canada, reached Crown Point Aug. 24 and La Prairie Sept. 2, took 19 prisoners in surprise attack, burned houses, and slaughtered cattle

Oct. 16–21, Sir William Phipps with fleet of 35 sail carrying 2,000 militia from Boston in unsuccessful siege of Quebec

Oct. 19–20, Major Whalley landing at Beauport from the Phipps expedition Oct. 18 defeated by the French, retreated to the ships leaving 5 guns and stores, the ships retreating down the river on the 23d

1691

Jan. 7, Ordinance provided for issue of card money, no specific redemption provided for

June 7, At Repentigny the Iroquois killed François Le Moyne de Bienville and 5 others

July 15, Henry Kelsey left Deerings Point where he may have wintered and journeyed up the Saskatchewan with the Indians and the Carrot River and to the prairies where he was the first white man to see a buffalo hunt on Aug. 23, end of his journey probably the Swan River country, no record between Sept. and July, 1692 when he returned to York Factory with a fleet of Indian canoes

Aug. 11, Peter Schuyler leading party of English and Dutch from Albany in battle with the French led by de Valrenne near La Prairie

Oct. 7, Charter of William and Mary to Massachusetts included "Accada or Nova Scotia"

Nov. 26, Villebon took possession of Port Royal abandoned by the English

1692

Feb. 5, Abenakis attacked and burned York, Maine, killing and capturing half the inhabitants

June 21, Attack of French and Indians on Wells, Maine, repulsed

Aug.–Sept., Sir William Phipps again in possession of Pemaquid built a fort

Sept., Unsuccessful attack of the English on Placentia, Newfoundland

Oct. 22, Defense of Fort Verchères against attack of the Iroquois by fourteen year old Madeleine de Verchères with 2 younger brothers, 2 soldiers, and a man of eighty

1693

Pierre Le Sueur commissioned by Frontenac established post at Chequamegon Bay (La Pointe) and traveled to the Mississippi by the Wisconsin River

Feb. 16–17, Canadians in battle with the English and Indians in raid on Mohawk villages within 36 miles of Albany, New York

Aug. 4, A flotilla of nearly 200 canoes with furs arrived at Montreal from the western country, the route again opened for trade

The Hudson Bay Company with help of British ships commanded by Capt. Grimmington recovered all posts on the Bay from the French

1694

Jan. 17, Bishop St. Vallier denounced all comedies and tragedies and prohibited all persons from attending a performance of Molière's "Tartuffe"

March 24, Death of Talon in France

April 15, Royal letters patent permitted establishment of a hospital at Ville Marie (Montreal)

June 23, French and Indians led by de Villieu massacred inhabitants of Durham, New Hampshire

Sept. 25–Oct. 14, Siege of Fort Nelson (York Factory), Hudson Bay, by d'Iberville ended with capitulation of the English Governor Thomas Walsh

Sept., Frontenac sent Antoine de la Motte Cadillac to command post at Mackinac where he remained until 1697

D'Orvilliers and de Beaucourt defeated the Iroquois at Lake St. Francis

1695

July 20, De Chrisay commissioned by Frontenac to rebuild Fort Frontenac at Cataraqui on Lake Ontario left Montreal, Du Lhut placed in command

Le Sueur built posts on islands in the Mississippi between Lake Pepin and the mouth of the St. Croix

First saw mill in New Brunswick at mouth of Nashwaak River built by Sieur de Chauffours and de Freneuse

1696

May 21 and 26, Royal ordinances received by Frontenac Sept. 12 reversed his policy in New France, settlers ordered not to go beyond the prescribed limits of the colonies, no more licenses to be issued for fur trade in the western country, and western posts to be abandoned and destroyed, the Indians to come to the settlement for trade. Peace to be made with the Iroquois

July 4, Frontenac led expedition from Lachine of more than 2,000 men which destroyed the Onondaga villages beyond Lake Onondaga Aug. 4–5, and Vaudreuil with a detachment went to destroy the town of the Oneidas, with the result that the Iroquois sued for peace

July 14, D'Iberville and Bonaventure in battle with the English fleet attacking French forts captured the British ship "Newport" near St. Johns, Newfoundland

Aug. 15, Fort Pemaquid surrendered by Capt. Pascho Chubb to French and Indians led by d'Iberville

Aug. 31, Capitulation of Fort Nelson at Hudson Bay in absence of d'Iberville. Two English warships commanded by Capt. Allen forced de la Forest to surrender

Nov. 10, English settlement at Ferryland, Newfoundland attacked and destroyed by d'Iberville

Nov. 30, St. Johns, Newfoundland, surrendered to d'Iberville and de Brouillon and fort destroyed and inhabitants sent to England

1697

Sept. 3, D'Iberville with warships sent from France under command of Serigny April 7 appeared before Fort Nelson (York Factory) Hudson Bay, sighted the English ships Sept. 5, and sank 3 English ships in battle

Sept. 13, Bayley surrendered Fort Nelson to d'Iberville. He renamed it Fort Bourbon

Sept. 20, Peace of Ryswick brought a 5 years' truce with the English. Places taken during the war mutually restored

1698

May 1 and July 14, Acts of Bishop Laval granted to the Seminary at Quebec the right to establish a mission on the Illinois at Cahokia

July 23, D'Iberville instructed to "reconnoitre the mouth of the Mississippi" and raise fort to prevent other nations from occupation of country claimed by France

Oct. 24, D'Iberville sailed from Brest with 4 ships and 200 emigrants to establish a colony at the mouth of the Mississippi

Nov. 28, Death of Governor Frontenac (78) at Quebec

1699

Jan. 22, De Saint Vallier established an elementary

school for children in the Upper Town of Quebec which was opened in Oct. 1700

Jan. 23, D'Iberville expedition sighted American continent, off Pensacola on the 26th, and anchored at mouth of the Mobile River on the 31st at Massacre (Dauphin) Island

Feb. 11, D'Iberville with 11 men landed on northeast coast of Bay of Biloxi to search for the Mississippi

March 2, D'Iberville entered the Mississippi, the first to enter the river from the sea, and ascended to probably the mouth of the Red River, and returned to ships on the 31st by 2 lakes which he named Maurepas and Pontchartrain

March 28, Fathers Francis Jolliet de Montigny, J. F. Buisson de St. Cosme, and Antoine Davion, guided by Tonty by Mackinac to the Chicago portage and the Illinois River, established mission at Cahokia (Tamaroa) house and chapel completed May 20

April 8, D'Iberville began to build a nine foot palisade fort which he called Maurepas about 15 miles north of Ship Island at Biloxi in present Mississippi which was completed May 1

April 20, Chevalier de Callières appointed Governor of Canada

May 3, D'Iberville sailed for France from Ship Island leaving the colonists under command of Sauvole and Jean Baptist Le Moyne de Bienville

June 2, Sauvole appointed Governor of Louisiana

Sept. 15, Bienville met an English ship which had entered the Mississippi Aug. 29, and turned it back claiming French jurisdiction. This bend of the river still called the English Turn

Dec. 7, Cannon on Ship Island announced return of d'Iberville from France to Biloxi. Le Sueur with 30 miners accompanied him from France to work in the copper mines.

1700

Jan. 17, D'Iberville built fort on the Mississippi about 38 miles below present city of New Orleans and 54 miles above the mouth of the river

Feb. 1, Tonty abandoned Fort St. Louis on the Illinois and joined the Biloxi colony arriving Feb. 16 with 60 *voyageurs* and 5 canoes laden with furs

March 22–May 18, Bienville on exploring expedition up the Red River

May 3, D'Iberville sailed for France leaving Sauvole in command

July 12, Le Sueur ascended the Mississippi, reached Lake Pepin in Aug., passed the Wisconsin River Sept. 1, and entered the Minnesota River which he named St. Peter's River Sept. 19, and arrived at Blue River Oct. 1, and completed Fort l'Huillier at entrance of this river Oct. 14

Sept. 8, Peace Treaty concluded between the French and the Iroquois signed at Montreal

Oct. 13, Bishop St. Vallier sailed for France

Oct. 15, Company of Canada organized and all trade in furs restricted to its members; registered Oct. 30 before a notary

1701

May 31, Royal edict approved regulations for the Company of Canada

June 4, Letters patent of Louis XIV granted Charles Jucherau de Saint Denys to establish tanneries in the Mississippi Valley, one at Mackinac and one near the present Cairo, Illinois

July 19, The Iroquois deeded their hunting grounds north of Lake Ontario and west of Lake Michigan to the King of England

July 24, Fort Pontchartrain built and Detroit founded by La Mothe Cadillac

Aug. 4, General peace with the Iroquois at Montreal

Aug. 22, Death of Sauvole, Governor of Louisiana, succeeded by Bienville

Oct. 31, Company of Canada leased privileges of the Company of the Indies

Dec. 15, D'Iberville reached Louisiana from France and Dec. 18 directed removal of colony to Massacre (Dauphin) Island preparatory to settlement on the Mobile River

1702

Jan. 6, Bienville left Biloxi and ten days later broke ground for Fort St. Louis and new settlement on west side of Mobile Bay, the first settlement in Alabama

Feb. 10, Le Sueur arrived at mouth of Mississippi with blue and green earth from the Sioux country

March 20–23, D'Iberville laid out streets of the Mobile Bay settlement

March 31, Bienville commissioned Governor of Louisiana

April 27, D'Iberville sailed for France

May 4/15, Queen Anne's War begun between England and France (War of the Spanish Succession)

May 15, Ordinance of the Council of State and letters patent in June united parish and Sulpician Seminary, Montreal

May, Royal letters patent permitted establishment of a hospital at Three Rivers to be administered by the Ursuline nuns

Oct. 5, François de Beauharnois, commissioned Intendant April 1, took office

1703

May 26, Death of Governor de Callières at Quebec

June 16, Royal decree registered in Canada Oct. 29 increased number of members of the Council from 7 to 12 and name changed from Sovereign Council to Superior Council

Aug. 1, The Marquis de Vaudreuil appointed Governor and Lieutenant General of Canada, Acadia, and Isle de Terreneuve

Aug. 10, French and Indians attacked Wells and other New England settlements

1704

Feb. 8, Indians took garrison at Haverhill, Massachusetts, in surprise attack

Feb. 28–29, Indians and French led by Hertel de Rouville destroyed the town of Deerfield, Massachusetts, about 40 persons killed and 100 taken prisoners

June 20, Col. Benjamin Church with 600 men from Boston attacked and destroyed the town of Menis near Port Royal, Nova Scotia

July 1, New England fleet arrived before Port Royal and summoned the garrison to surrender, but sailed away without making any attack on the 18th after Church had held council of war July 4/15 which decided against attack

July 28, Church attacked and destroyed the town of Beaubassin (Chigneto) Acadia

Aug. 18–29, French and Indians from Placentia destroyed English settlement of Bonavista, Newfoundland, and burned 4 English vessels

1705

Jan. 1, Jacques Raudot, commissioned Intendant, took office Sept. 17

Jan. 21–Feb. 23, St. Johns, Newfoundland, besieged by French Governor Subercase of Placentia, and attack repulsed

July 26, French ship "La Seine" captured by the English with cargo worth 1,000,000 francs and Bishop de St. Vallier, returning to Canada, taken prisoner

Oct. 20, Vaudreuil at Quebec proposed peace and neutrality between Canada and New England, that "both should hinder all acts of hostility on the part of the Indians"

Oct. 24, Ordinance prescribed uniform circulation as money of all card money outstanding

1706

June 22, Order of Council to inhabitants of Ville Marie (Montreal) to repair roads and build sidewalks at street corners, and forbade inhabitants to keep pigs in their dwellings on penalty of fine of 3 francs for each pig

July 9, Death of d'Iberville at Havana, Cuba

July 24, Decree of Council granted monopoly of the beaver trade to the Company of Canada

Population of New France 16,417

1707

May, V. M. Comte d'Estrees, Viceroy

May 13/24, Colonel March and Colonel Wainwright sailed from Boston with 1,000 men to attack Port Royal, arrived before the fort June 6 and abandoned attack sailing away June 17, Colonel Wainwright superseding Marsh in command returned to Port Royal Aug. 21–30, but no serious attack made

June 30, De Muy, appointed Governor of Louisiana but died on voyage out

——, Royal order forbade sale of liquor to the Indians, corporal punishment the penalty

Population of New France 17,124

1708

Feb. 25, Bienville again Governor of Louisiana

May 6, Death of Bishop Laval at Quebec

Aug. 29, French and Indians commanded by Hertel de Rouville attacked and massacred inhabitants of Haverhill on the Merrimac River, Massachusetts

Dec. 21, St. Johns, Newfoundland, taken again by the French commanded by de St. Ovide, heavy ransom exacted, and English inhabitants of the east shore forced to accept French sovereignty. Fort William destroyed

1710

March 31, Michel Begon appointed Intendant, took office Oct. 14

May 15, Antoine de la Mothe Cadillac appointed Governor of Louisiana

June 12, Widow of Radisson given £6 by Hudson Bay Company "as a charity"

Oct. 2, Port Royal besieged by New England fleet under Francis Nicholson since Sept. 24 forced to surrender, Governor Subercase marching out Oct. 16; name changed to Annapolis, and Samuel Vetch remained in command at the fort

Oct. 10 (O.S.) First Anglican service in Canada held at Halifax, Nova Scotia

1711

March, Fort Condé built on the Mobile River a few miles above the present city of Mobile, Alabama, and the Louisiana colony moved there

July 6, Ordinance of Royal Council of State ordered the inhabitants and the seigneurs to cultivate their lands, seigniories without settlers to be resumed by the Crown one year from date

Aug. 23, Sir Hovenden Walker's fleet from England proceeding from Boston to join force under Nicholson in attack on Quebec wrecked among reefs off the Egg Islands and 8 transports and 2 store ships lost and 742 troops. Council of war on Aug. 25 decided to abandon the attack and the expedition returned to England, and Nicholson's force waiting at Lake Champlain for news of ships made retreat abandoning attack on Montreal

1712

Aug. 19, Treaty of Paris signed, four months' truce between Great Britain and France

Sept. 12, Father Druilletes and Jean Godefroy commissioned ambassadors to New England to negotiate a commercial treaty

Sept. 14, Louisiana granted by charter to Antoine Crozat with exclusive commercial rights for 15 years from the sea to the Illinois and the Wabash rivers

Nov. 7, Report of the French engineer, Gédéon de Catalogne, on the seigniories of France

Dec. 18, Superior Council for Louisiana created for 3 years

Population of Canada 18,440

1713

Jan. 5, Fire in Quebec destroyed the Intendant's palace and Talon's brewery

April 11 (March 31/April 11), Treaty of Utrecht by which France ceded Newfoundland to England, and Acadia (Nova Scotia) and the Hudson Bay Territory. Cape Breton and Prince Edward Islands remained in possession of the French. The Iroquois recognized as subjects of Great Britain

May 17, La Mothe Cadillac, Governor of Louisiana under Crozat, arrived at Dauphin Island

June 23, Warrant of Queen Anne gave the French inhabitants of Nova Scotia a year to remove from the country, those remaining must take oath of allegiance to Great Britain

Aug. 17, Bishop St. Vallier reached Quebec after an absence of 13 years, had been a prisoner of the English since 1704

Sept. 8, Mandate published the constitution "Unigenitus" against the Jansenists

Sept. 13, French expedition took possession of Cape Breton Island, and fort at Louisburg built, the name of the Island changed to Isle Royale

1714

March 19, Ordinance of the King granted amnesty to the inhabitants of New France who had sojourned among the Indians on certain conditions

April 5–Dec., Voyage of Bienville up the Mobile River. See America

June 12, Placentia, Newfoundland, surrendered by M. Costabelle to Col. John Moody, appointed British Lieutenant Governor

July 10, Royal decree allowed the issue of 15 licenses to

trade for furs to be used only at the posts of Detroit, Mackinac, and the Illinois, increased April 28, 1716 to 25

July 25, Jeremie surrendered Port Nelson and other Hudson Bay posts to Governor James Knight and Henry Kelsey of the Hudson Bay Company

Aug. 23, Riot near Quebec mob threatening march on the city unless prices of merchandise reduced

Aug.–Aug. 1716, Expedition of Louis Juchereau de Saint Denis from the Mobile Bay colony up the Mississippi and Red rivers and from Natchitoches across Texas to San Juan Bautista on the Rio Grande where he was arrested by Mexican officials and sent back to Louisiana

Population of Canada 18,964

1716

March 3, De l'Epinay appointed Governor of Louisiana

May 1–Oct. 2, Successful expedition of de Louvigny from Montreal against the Outagamis (Fox) villages

A Jesuit, Father Joseph François Lafitau, discovered the ginseng plant in Canada, which was exported to China

1717

May 11, Royal edict permitted the merchants and traders of Quebec and Montreal to meet daily to confer on matters of business as petitioned by them, establishing a commercial exchange

July 5, Decree accepted redemption of card money at one-half of the face value, and all card money to be withdrawn

Sept. 6, Company of the West chartered in Aug. registered, receiving all the privileges granted to Crozat who had surrendered his monopoly Aug. 23, and the monopoly of Canadian export trade granted to the Company. Controlled by John Law

Sept. 27, Ordinance of the King's Council incorporated the Illinois country into Louisiana, separating it from New France

Dec. 11, Ordinance of the King's Council applied letters patent of April, regulating commerce of French colonies to Canada

Zacharie Robutel, Sieur de la Nouë, sent from Montreal, established posts on Rainy Lake and at Kaministikwia

1718

Jan. 1, Company of the West (Compagnie d'Occident) obtained exclusive privilege of the beaver trade, and order of July 11 required that all beaver skins be delivered to their stores

March 21, Supplementary ordinance made debts contracted since 1714 payable with card money (reduced to one half of its face value) and prohibited its issue after 1720

1719

Jan. 9, Ordinance of the King declared war against Spain

May 3, Ordinance united the East India and China Companies to the Company of the West and the name changed to Company of the Indies

June 3, James Knight commissioned by the Hudson Bay Company to find the North West Passage sailed from England about June 5 with Capt. George Berley or Barlow or Bailey in the "Albany" and Capt. David Vaughan in the "Discovery." Wrecked on Marble Island and fate unknown until 1867 when a whaling expedition found relics of the ships

June 19–Aug. 10, Expedition of Capt. Henry Kelsey from Fort York in the "Prosperous," Hudson Bay Company vessel in search of the North West Passage

July 2–Aug. 10, Expedition of Capt. John Hancock from Fort Prince of Wales in Hudson Bay Company vessel, the "Success" in search of North West Passage

July 5, Richard Phillips appointed Governor of Placentia and Captain General and Commander-in-Chief of Nova Scotia; arrived at Annapolis Royal April 1720

Aug., Concession of St. Jean and Miscou Islands in the Gulf of the St. Lawrence to the Comte de St. Pierre

1720

April 15, Three ships bringing 300 settlers for Island of St. Jean sailed, arriving at Port La Joye Aug. 23; abandoned when letters patent recalled concession to Comte de St. Pierre except settlement at present site of Georgetown, Cape Breton Island

May 6, First meeting of Council appointed by the Governor of Nova Scotia

Sept., Father Charlevoix arrived in Quebec commissioned to survey the French colonies of Canada and Louisiana and route to the "Western Sea," traveled through the country making surveys from 1720–1723, and recommended expedition up the Missouri to find some western waterway to western sea

Dec. 28, Letters of British Lords of Trade proposed removal of French Acadians

Henley House, 150 miles up the Albany River, built by the Hudson Bay Company

Joincaire and de La Corne built a trading post at Niagara

1721

Jan. 27, Mail stages established between Quebec and Montreal

May 31–July 25, 1722, Expedition of Capt. John Scroggs in the "Whalebone" from Gravesend in search of the Knight expedition and the North West Passage; wintered at Fort Prince of Wales, Hudson Bay, and sailed June 21 from the fort

June 19, Fire in Montreal burned large part of the town

June 26, James Napper sailed from Fort York, Hudson Bay, in the "Success" in search of North West Passage; lost June 30

June 26–Sept. 2, Voyage of Capt. Henry Kelsey in the "Prosperous" from Fort York, Hudson Bay, in search of North West Passage

July 21, Father Charlevoix making survey of the French dominion in America left Mackinac, at Kaskaskia Oct.–Nov. and started down the Mississippi Nov. 10

Governor Phillips of Nova Scotia started a settlement at Canso

1722

Jan. 5, Father Charlevoix reached New Orleans where he remained until July and then proceeded to Biloxi

March 3, Colony of New France divided into parishes by an edict of the Council of State confirming adoption of schedule drawn up by Michel Begon, Intendant, and Monseigneur l'Eveque of Quebec in Sept., 1721: Government of Quebec, 41 parishes; Three Rivers, 13; Montreal, 28

June 22, The Seminary of Foreign Missions received cession of land which became the village of Cahokia near the present East St. Louis, Illinois

1723

March 22, Company of the Indies given exclusive monopoly of tobacco trade, and March 24 edict of Council of State reëstablished the Company with commercial but not political privileges

Nov. 15, Etienne Veniard, Sieur de Bourmond, began building Fort Orleans on north bank of the Missouri about 300 miles from the mouth of the river

1724

Feb. 22, Edme Nicolas Robert appointed Intendant

May 13, Royal edict for better defense of the city of Montreal; stone wall built around the city

Aug. 23, The English commanded by Capt. Moulton and Capt. Harmon attacked Abenaki village of Norridgwock on the Kennebec River, and Father Sebastian Rale, Jesuit, who had led the Indians in many attacks on New England settlements

Sept. 10, "Black Code" of March regulating government of negro slaves in Louisiana published in New Orleans. *See also* America

1725

Sept. 15, Indians of Nova Scotia with those of New England made submission at Boston to George II in connection with the Treaty of Utrecht, and Dummer's Treaty of peace signed Dec. 15

Oct. 10, Death of Philippe de Rigaud, Marquis de Vaudreuil at Quebec. He had been Governor since 1703

Nov. 23, Claude Thomas Dupuy appointed Intendant

The French built 2 ships on Lake Ontario

1726

Jan. 11, The Marquis de Beauharnois appointed Governor of New France

April 28, Charles Le Moyne appointed first commander of fort to be built at Niagara, and a stone fort begun by Chaussegross de Léry on site of trading house built by Denonville which was completed in 1727

June 15, Peace made by M. de Lignery with the Foxes, Sakis, Puans, and Winnebagos

Sept. 25, The Acadians signed oath of allegiance to Great Britain with the proviso inserted by Governor Phillips that they might not be obliged to carry arms

Sept., Treaty with Iroquois ceded region west of Lake Erie and north of Erie and Ontario to Great Britain

Pierre Gaultier de Varennes, Sieur de la Vérendrye, last great explorer of New France, in command of trading post at Lake Nipigon

1727

June 6, Company formed at Montreal to trade on the upper Mississippi, and René Boucher, Sieur de La Perrière, sent by them, left June 16 for Lake Pepin where he arrived Sept. 17 by Green Bay and the Fox River and built Fort Beauharnois completed Nov. 14

Sept. 6, Acadian deputies summoned to appear before Council of Nova Scotia to sign oath of allegiance insisted on reservation of freedom of religion, exemption from bearing arms, and liberty to withdraw from the province

Nov. 10, Declaration of the King confirmed letters patent of Oct. excluding all foreign commerce from the French colonies

Dec. 26, Death of Bishop de Saint Vallier. Succeeded by François Duplessis de Mornay, appointed the same day. Quarrel over ceremony of funeral of the Bishop between the Governor and the Intendant began feud which lasted for months until recall of M. Dupuy

1728

June 5, Expedition of Marchard de Lignery left Montreal and Mackinac Aug. 10 arriving at Winnebago villages Aug. 24, burned crops and destroyed the villages of the Fox Indians

Captain Henry Osborne appointed first Governor of Newfoundland by Order in Council

Settlement of Prince Edward Island begun by Acadians

1729

March 2, French Government authorized the issue of 400,000 livres of card money as a temporary measure

Nov. 29, Massacre of French settlers at Fort Rosalie (Natchez). *See* America

Dec. 7, The Mississagas surrendered 3,000,000 acres comprising the present Norfolk, Haldimand, and Wentworth counties, and parts of Wellington, Oxford, Elgin, Welland, Waterloo, and Lincoln

1730

Population of Canada estimated as 33,682

Aug. 17–Sept. 9, Fox fort besieged by St. Ange and Villiers. The Indians escaped from the fort in retreat but were pursued and killed by the troops

Dec., Edict of the King ordered making of pieces of silver money for the American colonies

La Vérendrye given monopoly of trade of Lake Winnipeg region and commissioned to search for the Western Sea

1731

Feb. 21, Gilles Hocquart appointed Intendant, second after Talon in developing Canadian industries especially shipbuilding and iron works

June 8, La Vérendrye left Montreal for Grand Portage at mouth of Pigeon River near west end of Lake Superior reached Aug. 26 with party of 50 including his 3 sons and his nephew Christophe Dufrost, Sieur de la Jemmeraye, who during that year reached Rainy Lake and built Fort St. Pierre

The King offered a bounty of 500 livres on each ship over 200 tons built in the Colony

Fort Frédéric built at Crown Point on Lake Champlain by de la Fresnière

1732

Feb. 19, Ordinance forbade convents to give refuge to deserters and fugitives from justice

May 27, La Vérendrye sent his eldest son, Jean Baptiste, to build fort at mouth of Winnipeg River, named Fort Maurepas. First person known to have reached Lake Winnipeg

June 8, La Vérendrye left winter quarters on the Kaministikwia for Rainy Lake, descended the Rainy River and discovered the Lake of the Woods where he built Fort St. Charles July 14

Oct. 17, The Hurons crossed from Detroit to Fox village on the Wisconsin River and killed most of the warriors in surprise attack

1733

May 12, Ordinance of the King provided for increase of 200,000 livres in card money, making total sum authorized 600,000 livres

May 29, Right to hold Indians in slavery and sell them decided by Judge Hocquart according to ordinance of April 13, 1709

Sept. 12, Bishop de Mornay resigned and Pierre Hermann Dosquet appointed Bishop of Quebec

Sept. 16, Repentigny, de Villiers, Duplessis, and several other Frenchmen killed by the Sauk Indians

1734

April 1, First lighthouse in Canada established at Louisburg, referred to in letter of Governor de St. Ovide of Oct. 21, 1734

Post road opened from Montreal to Quebec, and first vehicle on wheels passed from Quebec to Montreal

1735

June 6, La Vérendrye left Montreal, reaching Fort St. Charles on Lake of the Woods Sept. 6

The Bishop of Quebec tried to exact as tithe the 13th bushel of grain instead of the 26th allowed for the support of the church, and also on vegetables, flax, and tobacco

1736

June 8, Jean Baptiste La Vérendrye and Father Jean Aulneau, Jesuit, left Lake of the Woods to go to Mackinac for supplies and were massacred with party of from 20 to 25 Frenchmen by the Sioux while in camp on island 20 miles from the lake

Ships made in dock yards of Quebec sold in the West Indies

1737

April 22, St. Maurice iron forges company formed in 1736 established by royal decree and iron first smelted in Canada Oct. 15 at the forges near Three Rivers

July 7–Aug. 18, Capt. James Napper in the "Churchill" sailed from Fort Prince of Wales on Hudson Bay to search for North West Passage. The Captain died Aug. 8 and vessel returned

July 7–Aug. 22, Capt. Robert Crow in the "Musquash" in voyage from Fort Prince of Wales in search for North West Passage

Aug. 24, La Vérendrye in Montreal engaged to visit the Mandan Indians

1738

July 20, La Vérendrye left Mackinac and reached Fort St. Charles Aug. 31

Sept. 11, La Vérendrye left Lake of the Woods and Fort Maurepas at mouth of Winnipeg River on the 22d for unknown western country across Lake Winnebago to Red River, and on 24th at junction of Red and Assiniboine rivers where Winnipeg now stands built Fort Rouge, and Oct. 3–15 built Fort La Reine at Portage La Prairie, and on the 18th left with party of 52 including his 2 sons for the Mandan villages on the Missouri River 250 miles distant in North Dakota reached Dec. 3. Started on return journey Dec. 13 for Fort La Reine reached Feb. 19

Oct. 30, Founding of the Grey Nunnery at Montreal by Mme d'Youville

1739

April 16, La Vérendrye sent his son, Louis Joseph, north from Fort La Reine to explore rivers flowing into Lake Winnipeg especially the Saskatchewan, and Fort Dauphin built on west side of Lake Manitoba discovered by them and called Lac des Prairies and Fort Bourbon at Cedar Lake

May 29–July 22, Expedition of Canadians Pierre and Paul Mallet to New Mexico. See America

July 20, François Louis Pourroy de Lauberivière appointed Bishop of Quebec, succeeding Bishop Dosquet who resigned June 25

Population of New France 42,701

1740

Feb. 21, Successful attack of de Celeron on Chickasaw Indians, peace concluded

April, Joseph La France, a half-breed, reached Rainy Lake from Sault Ste. Marie after a winter on the north shore of Lake Superior, and proceeded down the Rainy River to the Lake of the Woods reached the end of May, and at Lake Winnipeg in Sept.

Aug. 20, Death of Bishop de Lauberivière 10 days after his arrival in the country

1741

March 6, Henri Marie Dubreuil de Pontbriand appointed Bishop of Quebec, consecrated April 9

June 26, La Vérendrye left Montreal for the west arriving at Lake of the Woods Sept. 16 and Fort La Reine Oct. 13

Nov. 28, Death of Bishop Mornay of Quebec in Paris

Exports from Canada exceeded imports for only time during the French régime

1742

Feb. 27, French Government conceded an additional 120,000 livres of card money

April 20, Royal edict suspended all licenses for the western trade and ordered all posts auctioned off to highest bidder for monopoly exploitation

April 29, The sons of La Vérendrye left Fort La Reine to explore country to the southwest in search of Western Sea and at the Mandan villages from May 19–July 23 for the "Horse Indians" from the south to be their guides, and then traveled through the region between the Little Missouri and Cheyenne rivers and saw the Black Hills, and returned to the Missouri March 19, 1743, and at Fort La Reine June 2

June 4, The first war vessel built at Quebec, the "Canada" launched and sailed to Rochefort, France

June 29, Joseph La France descending the Nelson River from Lake Winnipeg ended his journey at York Factory on Hudson Bay

July 1–Aug. 18, Capt. Christopher Middleton with 2 ships from Fort Churchill, Hudson Bay, on voyage of search for the North West Passage. Rediscovered Roe's Welcome, Wager Bay, Repulse Bay, and Frozen Strait

1743

Jan. 1, The sons of La Vérendrye may have sighted the Rocky Mts. On Jan. 12 they were at the foot of mountains from the top of which they were told they could view the sea, perhaps the Big Horn, but obliged to retreat with the Mandans who were in fear of their enemies the Serpent tribe probably Cheyennes. For various theories see Champlain Soc. Publications

March 30, Plate buried by La Vérendrye expedition claiming the country for France at the present Pierre, South Dakota, found Feb. 16, 1913

May 2, Regulations made by Governor and Intendant on importation of liquors into the colony

Nov. 25, Royal ordinance by which all religious communities restrained in acquisition of property and law of mortmain defined

1744

March 15, France declared war against England, and April 9, England declared war on France

May 13, Canso, British Nova Scotia settlement, destroyed by the French from Louisburg under Duvivier, the fort surrendered by Capt. Patrick Heron on the 24th

July 12, English fort at Annapolis Royal attacked by Indians incited by French priest, Father Le Loutes

Oct. 6, Duvivier abandoned siege of fort at Annapolis defended successfully by Mascarene against the French attack

Nov. 24, Ordinance suppressed the observance of 19 saint's days thus extending time for labor

History of New France published by Father Charlevoix

1745

April 30, and May 1, New England ships and army commanded by William Pepperell landed at Gabarus Bay and began seige of Louisburg

May 19, Battle between French and the English fleet from the West Indies commanded by Admiral Warren, "Le Vigilante"

May 24, Night attack on Louisburg defeated with loss of 189 men

June 16, Duchambon surrendered the fortress of Louisburg, Cape Breton Island, to Col. William Pepperell after siege of 47 days, the strongest French fortification in America

Nov. 28–29, Marin led attack of French and Indians on Saratoga, New York

1746

March 15, La Jonquière appointed Governor of Canada, Acadia, and Louisiana

May 24–Oct. 14, 1747, Capt. William Moore and Capt. Francis Smith sailed from the Thames to Port Nelson, Hudson Bay reached Aug. 26 where they wintered, and June 14, 1747 coasted Hudson Bay in last attempt to find North West Passage through the Bay (the Dobbs expedition)

June 22, Expedition of the Duc d'Anville sailed from Rochelle, France, for recovery of Louisburg, failed because of storm of Sept. 2 which wrecked the fleet which arrived at Chebucto (Halifax), Sept. 10

Aug. 30, Major R. de Vaudreuil with force from Three Rivers attacked fort at Crown Point which surrendered Aug. 31, and settlement of Fort Masson on site of present town of South Adams attacked and destroyed

1747

Jan. 23, Ordinance of the Royal Council of State increased duties on wine, brandy, and rum imported into colony for 3 years

Feb. 4, Grand Pré (Horton) Nova Scotia taken in surprise attack by the French

March 15, The Marquis de Jonquière appointed Governor

May 3, Capt. Anson Ortegal and Admiral Warren defeated French fleet of La Jonquière off Cape Finistère, with stores for Canada, and Governor Jonquière taken prisoner to England

June 10, Comte de la Galissonnière named Commander General of New France and Governor *ad interim*

Oct. 14, Admiral Hawke defeated French fleet bound for Canada in engagement

1748

Jan. 1, François Bigot appointed Intendant, took office Aug. 20

Feb. 25, Royal edict established duties on exports and imports

Sept., Ordinance of Bigot issued treasury notes

——, La Présentation (now Ogdensburg, N.Y.) founded by Abbé Picquet at head of rapids of the St. Lawrence

Oct. 18, Treaty of Aix-la-Chapelle ended King George's War and restored Cape Breton Island and Louisburg to France

1749

April 18, Royal order increased card money from 720,000 livres to 1,000,000

June 15–Nov. 9, Expedition led by Bienville de Celoron from Montreal instructed to take formal possession of the Ohio country at selected points and drive out the English traders. Metal plates recording the French occupation were buried, generally at mouths of rivers, July 22 expedition at headwaters of the Ohio, at Lake Chatauqua. July 29 the expedition embarked on the Alleghany. Proceeded down the Ohio as far as the mouth of the Great Miami not far from present site of Cincinnati, turned up that stream at end of Aug. Sept. 20 the river left and crossing made to the Maumee Sept. 25. Reached Detroit Oct. 6

June 21, Cornwallis gazetted as Governor of Nova Scotia arrived at Chebucto with 2,500 English colonists, began fort and named his capital Halifax June 30

July 12, Louisburg evacuated by Colonel Hobson and given over to French representative M. Desherbier

Aug. 1, Cornwallis issued proclamation to the Acadians calling upon them to take oath of allegiance before Oct. 15

Aug. 5, Peter Kalm, Swedish scientist and philosopher, landed at Quebec for visit to Canada

Aug. 6, De Celoren captured a party of English traders and warned them not to trespass in Ohio valley

Aug. 15, La Jonquière began term as Governor

Sept. 6, Deputies of the Acadians gave answer to Governor Cornwallis that the French inhabitants of Nova Scotia would not take oath of allegiance and asked permission to leave the country

Dec. 6, Death of Pierre de La Vérendrye (64) at Montreal as he was preparing to make another journey to discover the Western Sea by exploration of the Saskatchewan

Fort Rouillé (Toronto) established

1750

April 19 and May 25, Deputations of Acadians appeared before the Council at Halifax asking permission to leave Nova Scotia; not granted

June, Jacques Repentigny Legardeur de Saint Pierre given charge of western exploration succeeding La Vérendrye, disregarding petitions of his sons for the post

Aug. 16, Major Lawrence began construction of Fort Lawrence on the Chignecto isthmus connecting Nova Scotia with the mainland

Aug., 300 German immigrants from the Palatinate arrived in the "Anne" at Nova Scotia

Sept. 2, St. Paul's Church in Halifax opened by Rev.

William Tutty, oldest Protestant church in Canada

Sept., Canadians established Fort Beauséjour directly opposite Fort Lawrence and Fort Gaspareau on Baie Verte

1751

May 29, Joseph Boucher, Sieur de Niverville, sent by Saint Pierre to The Pas and instructed to go up the Saskatchewan. Fort La Jonquière built near the Rocky Mts. probably near site of the present town of Calgary, as it was evident that to reach the Western Sea the mountains must be crossed

Aug., First printing press set up in Nova Scotia by Bartholomew Green at Halifax

Sept. 26, 1,000 emigrants from Montbeliard, Würtemberg, Germany reached Halifax

1752

March 1, Marquis du Quesne de Menneville appointed Governor of Canada, Louisiana, Isle Royale

March 23, First issue of the *Halifax Gazette*, first newspaper in Canada, published

May 17, Death of Governor La Jonquière

1753

June 3, Royal letters patent granted to Grey Nuns of Montreal founded by Mme d'Youville

Lunenburg, Nova Scotia, settled early in the year by Germans from Halifax

Dec. 11, George Washington presented claim of Virginia to the Ohio Valley on basis of charters to St. Pierre at Fort Le Bœuf (Waterford, Pennsylvania). French claim based on rights of discovery

1754

April 17, French force led by Contrecœur attacked Virginians building fort at forks of the Ohio (Pittsburgh) and forced surrender of Ensign Ward. Fort completed as French post and named Fort Duquesne

May 28, George Washington with force of Virginians and South Carolinians defeated French force at Great Meadows, the French commander Coulon de Jumonville killed

June 26–June 20, 1755, Expedition of Anthony Hendry from York Factory, Hudson Bay, ascending the Hayes and Steel rivers to Oxford Lake reached July 6, and west to Cross Lake on the Nelson River, and up the Pine River to Moose Lake reaching the Saskatchewan July 21, the first Englishman ever on the river. Visited French Fort St. Louis at The Pas July 22. The region between the north and south branches of the Saskatchewan explored and farthest west reached Nov. 21 at 114° W. and south of 52° N. Wintered with the Blackfeet Indians

July 3, Washington attacked at Fort Necessity which he had built at Great Meadows by Coulon de Villiers with force from Montreal and defeated signed capitulation and retreated leaving the French in possession of the Ohio region

Oct. 21, Jonathan Belcher appointed first Chief Justice of Nova Scotia

A seventy-four gun war vessel built at Quebec

Population of New France 55,000

1755

Jan. 1, Pierre de Rigaud, Marquis de Vaudreuil de Cavagnal appointed Governor

June 8, French fleet bringing General Dieskau to Canada in engagement with English fleet under Vice-Admiral Boscawen off coast of Newfoundland. The French lost 2 ships and 8 companies of soldiers June 10

June 16, Col. Monckton with troops from Massachusetts forced surrender of French Fort Beauséjour, Nova Scotia, commanded by du Chambon de Verger, and fort renamed Fort Cumberland

July 9, General Braddock advancing with Virginia troops against Fort Duquesne ambushed by French and Indians led by de Contrecœur and de Beaujeur, defeated and mortally wounded, de Beaujeur killed

July 25, Deputation of Acadians appeared before the Council at Halifax and refused to take oath of allegiance without reservations

July 28, Decision of Council at Halifax to deport the Acadians from Nova Scotia, and July 31 Col. Monckton, Col. Winslow, and Capt. Murray ordered to collect the Acadians

Aug. 11, Acadians summoned to Fort Cumberland and 400 imprisoned

Aug., Baron Dieskau began to fortify Ticonderoga

Sept. 2, Col. Winslow at Grand Pré on Minas Basin summoned Acadian male inhabitants to assemble in the church on Sept. 5 where they were kept prisoners until the transports arrived Oct. 8

Sept. 8, French and English in battle on Lake George. The English under General William Johnson were ambuscaded but later rallied and defeated the French under Baron Dieskau who was wounded and taken prisoner

Oct. 13, Fleet of 10 ships carried 960 Acadians to South Carolina and Georgia, and between Oct. 29 and Dec. 20, 6,000 Acadians deported to the American colonies, by Governor Lawrence without authority from British Government

Dec. 9, 1,600 Acadians sailed from Annapolis Royal

First post office in Canada opened at Halifax

1756

March 27, Indians and French commanded by de Léry captured Fort Bull at site of the present Rome, New York, destroyed fort and carried 30 prisoners to Montreal

May 13, General Montcalm appointed March 11 to command of forces in Canada landed at Quebec accompanied by the Chevalier de Levis, Colonel de Bourlamaque, and Captain de Bougainville, and bringing 1,189 soldiers

May 18, Declaration of war against France by Great Britain, and Ordinance of King of France of June 9 declared war against England, beginning the Seven Years' War

July 3, Colonel Bradstreet defeated French and Indians led by de Villiers near Oswego

Aug. 5, General Montcalm transported his army to Sackett's Harbor on Lake Ontario

Aug. 14, Oswego, New York, surrendered to General Montcalm after siege of 4 days

1757

Jan. 21, Captain Robert Rogers' scouts defeated by French near Ticonderoga

July 26, Montcalm and de Levis defeated British commanded by Colonel Parker at Sabbath Day Point, Lake George

Aug. 9, Fort William Henry on Lake George surrendered to Montcalm. The British garrison massacred by the Indian allies of the French as they marched out Aug. 10 in spite of the terms of the capitulation promising protection

Famine in Quebec 1757–1758

1758

May 9, British fleet commanded by Admiral Edward Boscawen and with troops commanded by General Jeffrey Amherst from England reached Halifax for attack on Louisburg

April 1, Rations of bread to citizens of Quebec and Montreal reduced to 2 ounces, and the population forced to eat horse flesh before arrival of relief from France in May

June 2, Admiral Boscawen and General Amherst arrived at Gabarus Bay before Louisburg, operations begun June 4 and troops landed June 8. James Wolfe and Isaac Barré officers in expedition

July 8, British attack on Ticonderoga defeated by Montcalm. Lord Howe killed in advance engagement July 6, and Abercromby forced to retreat with heavy loss

July 26, Drucour surrendered Louisburg to the British with more than 5,500 men after siege of 48 days, the French marching from the fort on the 27th

Aug. 8, Captain Rogers' scouts defeated the French led by Marin near Fort Anne

Aug. 27, Fort Frontenac on site of modern city of Kingston, Ontario, surrendered to Colonel John Bradstreet, fort and ships in harbor destroyed

Aug. 29, James Wolfe sailed to destroy French settlement in Gaspé, and reported from Louisburg Sept. 30 that this had been accomplished

Sept. 14, Grant defeated by the French on heights above Fort Duquesne

Sept. 20, General Monckton landed troops at mouth of St. John River and English settlement of western New Brunswick begun

Oct. 2, First legislative assembly in British Canada met at Halifax, Nova Scotia, meeting proclaimed by ringing a bell

Nov. 25, Fort Duquesne abandoned by de Ligneris occupied by the English under John Forbes, and French rule on the Ohio ended

1759

May 25, Record of official message sent from New Orleans Feb. 19 reaching Montreal, 95 days

June 26, Admiral Charles Saunders with British fleet anchored below Quebec on the St. Lawrence and occupied Island of Orleans on the 27th

June 28, Fire rafts sent against the British ships at Island of Orleans

June 29, Point Lévis facing Quebec and only 1,200 yards from the walls taken by General Monckton, and occupied by General Wolfe July 2 with 5,000 men and siege guns

June 30, Canadians in engagement with Monckton's brigade at entrenchments of the Beauport lines

July 9, Townshend's brigade occupied the left bank of the Montmorency

July 12, General Wolfe began bombardment of Quebec, and repulsed attack of Dumas July 12–13 on entrenchments at Lévis Heights

July 16, Upper town of Quebec set on fire by shells from British batteries

July 21, Carleton led expedition 20 miles up the St. Lawrence against Pointe aux Trembles above Quebec

July 24, French force under de Ligneris coming to relief of Fort Niagara defeated by Sir William Johnson at La Belle Famille

July 25, Fort Niagara surrendered to the British

——, The French under de Repentigny repulsed British troops making a reconnaissance up the Montmorency

July 26, Bourlamaque blew up fort at Ticonderoga, retreating to Crown Point as General Amherst started siege operations

July 31, Battle of Montmorency. French victory at Beauport Flats. Attack of Wolfe repulsed with over 400 British casualties

Aug. 4, Fort Frédéric at Crown Point evacuated by the French retiring to Ile aux Noix

Aug. 8, At Pointe aux Trembles Murray received severe check from Bougainville

Aug. 9, Lower town of Quebec set on fire by British shells burned all except 4 or 5 houses

Aug. 31–Sept. 3, Camp at Montmorency evacuated by the British and troops transferred to Point Lévis

Sept. 7, Part of the British fleet moved up the St. Lawrence to Cap Rouge

Sept. 12, Saunders began bombardment of the Beauport lines covering advance of Wolfe to 2 miles above Quebec at Anse du Foulon (Wolfe's Cove) landing troops an hour before sunrise on the 13th

Sept. 13, At sunrise General Wolfe had 4,500 men on the Plains of Abraham above Quebec taking the French completely by surprise, and the battle begun General Montcalm advancing to attack about 9 A.M. The victorious General Wolfe killed and Montcalm, mortally wounded, died the following day. Vaudreuil retreated to the St. Charles valley

Sept. 17, Lévis at Pointe aux Trembles took command of the French troops and withdrew to Montreal after capitulation of Quebec

Sept. 18, De Ramezay made the surrender of Quebec to the British, unable to hold out for lack of supplies

Sept. 19, British troops under the Marquis of Townshend entered Quebec

Sept. 29, British army marched into Quebec

Oct. 5, Raid led by Major Rogers destroyed Abenaki Indian village of St. Francis between Montreal and Quebec

Oct. 15, Royal Council of State ordered suspension of payment of bills of exchange

Nov. 12, General Murray appointed Colonel John Young, chief judge, in Quebec

Nov. 22, French fleet descended the St. Lawrence and anchored above Quebec at Sillery; first attempt to run past the city a failure but several of the ships succeeded a few nights later in escaping to France

1760

Jan. 6, Jacques Allier commissioned civil and criminal judge on south bank of the St. Lawrence from Berthier to Kamouraska

Jan. 9, Submission of Nova Scotian Indians begun with peace overtures from the Micmacs

April 28, Francis Gaston de Lévis in command of French army in Montreal began advance against Quebec and defeated General Murray who advanced from Quebec to Ste. Foy to meet the French, and was forced to retreat

——, Last meeting of French Superior Council

May 9, First British ship the "Lowstoff" appeared in the St. Lawrence

May 11, De Lévis began siege of Quebec

May 14, French fleet from France arrived but retreated to Bay of Chaleur on news of capture of Quebec

May 16, De Lévis abandoned siege of Quebec on approach of British fleet under Commodore Swanton who destroyed the French ships in the river

June 8, Death of Bishop de Pontbriand

July 8, Captain John Byron in battle off La Petite Rochelle, Bay of Chaleurs, defeated the French fleet which had taken refuge there

July 14, General Murray left Quebec for Montreal with 2,500 troops arriving before the city Aug. 27

Aug. 10, General Amherst embarked from Oswego with troops to descend the St. Lawrence

Aug. 22, Church fortified by the inhabitants at Sorel attacked by the British and the town destroyed

Aug. 25, Fort Lévis above the St. Lawrence rapids taken by General Amherst

Aug. 27, The Ile aux Noix taken by General William Haviland

Sept. 7, General Murray effected junction under the walls of Montreal with General Haviland who had come by the Richelieu and Amherst descending the St. Lawrence

Sept. 8, Montreal, the last French stronghold in Canada, surrendered by the Marquis de Vaudreuil to General Jeffrey Amherst

——, British military rule set up in Canada divided into the 3 districts of Quebec, Montreal, and Three Rivers

Sept. 9, De Lévis reviewed his army for the last time, present only 1,953 soldiers and 179 officers

Sept. 13, Major Robert Rogers sent by General Amherst from Montreal to receive submission of the French forts on the Lakes

Sept. 16, Colonel Ralph Burton appointed Governor of Three Rivers by General Amherst and Brigadier General Thomas Gage, Governor of Montreal

Oct. 31, Proclamation of General Murray established military courts

Oct., Governor Whitmore completed destruction of fort at Louisburg

Nov. 7–12, Major Rogers encamped on Lake Erie near site of the present Cleveland met Pontiac who agreed to submit to the English

Nov. 29, Detroit surrendered by French Commander Belêtre to Major Rogers

Population of Canada estimated as 70,000

1761

Feb. 14, Mackinac occupied by the British

Aug., Alexander Henry, the first "fur pedlar" left Montreal for Mackinac to trade with the Indians

Sept. 28, The English flag replaced the French at Fort Michillimackinac (Mackinac)

Dec. 17, Royal letters issued by King of France ordered trial for those responsible for abuses in Canada, and as a result Bigot was condemned to banishment for life and his property confiscated

1762

Jan. 2, War declared by England against Spain

April 27, Grant by General Murray of seigneuries to Capt. John Nairne and to Capt. Malcolm Fraser

May 16, New Englanders sailed from Newburyport, Massachusetts, and settled at Maugerville afterwards Sunbury, New Brunswick, first British settlement

June 27, French expedition commanded by the Comte d'Haussonville surprised and captured St. Johns,

Newfoundland, and the sloop of war "Grammont" in harbor

Sept. 18, St. Johns retaken by British Colonel William Amherst and d'Haussonville granted passage to France

Nov. 3, France agreed to preliminaries of peace with Great Britain and Spain

Dec. 24, Decree of Royal Council of State of France that Canadian bills of exchange and money notes must be declared

1763

Feb. 10, Treaty of Paris signed between Great Britain, France, and Spain provided that Canada, Nova Scotia, Cape Breton, Island of St. John (Prince Edward), and all islands in the Gulf and River of St. Lawrence except St. Pierre and Miquelon be ceded by France to Great Britain, and Louisiana east of the Mississippi except New Orleans

Feb. 10–Dec. 25, 1791, Quebec, the capital of the Province of Canada

April 27, Pontiac, Chief of the Ottawas, held council of war against the English. For Pontiac's War *see* America

May 27, Governor Murray published French decree of Dec. 24, 1762 regarding declaration of Canadian paper money

July 4, Grant of seigneury on Bay of Chaleurs by Lord Dorchester to John Shoolbred

July 14, Baron de L'Esperance given possession of Islands of St. Pierre and Miquelon settled by Acadians

Sept. 7, Proclamation of the King invited British subjects to settle in Canada

Oct. 7, Proclamation of George III established civil government in Canada (the Province of Quebec) defined boundaries, name of Canada changed to Quebec, Isle Royale or Cape Breton, and Isle St. Jean (Prince Edward Island) annexed to Nova Scotia, Labrador, Anticosti, and Magdalen Islands to Newfoundland

Oct. 20, Brigadier General Thomas Gage received instructions of Aug. 13 to vacate the government of Montreal succeeding General Amherst as commander-in-chief, and Colonel Ralph Burton made Governor of Montreal, and Colonel Frederick Haldimand, Governor at Three Rivers

Oct., Petition of de Glapion, head of the Jesuits, asked the King that the Jesuits be placed in possession of their property and allowed to continue their schools

Nov. 21, General James Murray commissioned "Governor in Chief" of the Province of Quebec, royal instructions dated Dec. 7

First post offices established at Montreal, Quebec, and Three Rivers by Benjamin Franklin

1764

Feb. 13, John, Earl of Egremont, presented memorial to the King of feudal scheme for settlement of the Island of St. John

Feb. 17, William Gregory appointed first Chief Justice of Supreme Court; new commission Aug. 24

March 5, Proclamation of Governor Murray ordered inhabitants to make declaration of French Canadian paper money before April 1

March 23, Captain Samuel Holland commissioned by the Lord Commissioners for Trade and Plantations to make survey of the Island of St. John arrived at Island in Oct. and presented his report a year later

April 29, Sulpicians in Paris conveyed their title to property in Montreal to the Sulpician Seminary in Montreal

June 21, First issue of *Quebec Gazette*, second oldest newspaper in Canada

June 29, Decree of French Royal Council of State ordered liquidation of Canadian bills of exchange and money notes

Aug. 10, Governor Murray assumed office and civil government formally established. Aug. 13 date of Egremont's letter to Murray sometimes given as date

——, After this date property transmitted through death subject to English law

Sept. 3, Governor and Council decided that the sixpenny white loaf of bread should weigh 4 pounds and the brown loaf 6 pounds as long as flour sold for 14 shillings per cwt. and every loaf to be stamped with the initials of the baker

Sept. 14, Ordinance of Governor Murray established the currency

Sept. 17, Ordinance of the Governor in Council established a Court of King's Bench, and a Court of Common Pleas, and directed that judgment be given in common courts by the laws of England as far as circumstances permitted; in cases arising before Oct. 1 French law might be applied

——, Government of the District of Three Rivers abolished. Colonel Haldimand turned over the civil government to Cramahé on the 28th, keeping command of the troops

Sept., Governor Murray appointed a receiver general, Walter Murray, the first

Oct. 4, Ordinance provided regulations for foreign currency

Oct. 16, Presentments of the Grand Jury at Quebec stated objections of the British inhabitants to the administration; statement of French jurists Oct. 26

Oct. 29, Petition of French Canadians asked for rights as jurors, that laws be published in French, &c.

Nov. 3, Ordinance regulated the markets of Quebec and Montreal

Nov. 6, Ordinance regarding property established age of majority as 21; titles of cession and rights of heritage obtained previous to the Treaty declared legal

——, Ordinance declared that until Aug. 10 following tenure of lands should remain as prior to Treaty

——, Ordinance for the benefit of creditors forbade persons to leave the Province without a pass

Nov. 10, Ordinance prohibited selling of liquor to the Indians

Dec. 6, Assault on Thomas Walker, a magistrate in Montreal who had made himself particularly obnoxious to the soldiers, by a party of soldiers who beat him and carried off part of his ear as a souvenir

Dec. 8, Second registration of paper money

1765

Jan. 7, Address of French citizens to the King protested against the legal system

Feb. 9, Decree of Royal Council of France in accordance with decree of Dec. 15, as to liquidation of Canadian paper money placed credit certificates on same footing as bills of exchange and money notes

May 18, Fire destroyed a quarter of the city of Montreal

June 4, Alexander Henry made captain of the western

posts with headquarters at Mackinac with license for exclusive trade of Lake Superior

Nov. 15, Ordinance admitted French Canadian jurors to courts and permitted lawyers to plead in French

First Presbyterian Church organized in Canada at Quebec by Rev. George Henry

First printed book in Canada "Catechism du diocese de Sens"

Population of Canada 69,810

1766

Jan. 21, Jean Olivier Briand appointed Bishop of Quebec, the first head of the Roman Catholic Church since the death of Bishop de Pontbriand in 1760

March 27, Ordinance provided for repairing highways and bridges in the Province

March 29, Convention between Great Britain and France signed for liquidation of the Canadian paper money, bills of exchange to be paid on basis of 50% of face value and card money of 25%

April 1, Governor Murray ordered to London to give account of his administration, unpopular because he refused to call an Assembly that would place 65,000 Canadians at the mercy of the small Protestant minority and the merchants whom he described in letter to Lord Shelburne (Aug. 20) as "the most immoral collection of men I ever knew . . . little calculated to make the new subjects enamoured with our laws, religion and customs"

April 7, Sir Guy Carleton appointed Lieutenant Governor of the Province, took office Sept. 24

June 28, Governor Murray sailed for England, retaining governorship until April 1768, but did not return to Canada, Paulus Irving, Acting, until Sept. 24

——, Arrival of Bishop Jean Olivier Briand at Quebec

July 17, Ordinance provided regulations for granting licenses for selling of liquor retail, and a proclamation fixed scale of duties on wine and spirits

Aug. 11, William Campbell commissioned Governor of Nova Scotia

Aug. 15, First issue of the *Nova Scotia Gazette*

Sept. 22, Sir Guy Carleton arrived in Quebec and took oath of office the following day

Sept. 25, William Hey commissioned Chief Justice replacing the incompetent William Gregory

Oct. 13, Remonstrance of members of the Council to Carleton in connection with his removal of Irving and Mabane, chief friends of Murray, from the Council

1767

Feb. 3, Petition of seigneurs of Montreal to the King asking that subjects be admitted to any office without any distinction of religion

July 12, Thomas Curry on license of this date to travel to the Kaministiquia with 2 canoes and £1,000 worth of goods reached the Saskatchewan, the pioneer trader on both rivers according to Mackenzie. According to Matthew Cocking's Journal of 1772, and Bain, editor of Henry's travels James Finlay the first

July 23, Lottery held by Lord Commissioners for Trade and Plantations by which the land of Prince Edward Island (former Island of St. John) granted to proprietors

Dec. 24, Ordinance provided for continuation of the laws and customs of the French régime as to tenor of inheritance and alienation of land

Trader on the Saskatchewan wintering at the French Fort Nepawee below the Forks

First book published at Quebec "Catechisme Montag-
naise"
First public library at Montreal College

1768

April 11, Great fire at Montreal
Aug. 12, Order in Council confirmed boundary between
Canada and New York
Oct. 25, Sir Guy Carleton appointed Governor
Port La Joie, Prince Edward Island founded by the
French about 1750 given name of Charlottetown

1769

Aug. 4, Prince Edward Island under Order in Council
of June 28 separated from Nova Scotia and made a
separate colony, Walter Paterson appointed first
Lieutenant Governor July 14, arrived in the country
Aug. 30, 1770 and sworn in Sept. 19
Nov. 6–Dec. 11, Journey of Samuel Hearne from Fort
Prince of Wales, Hudson Bay, in search of the Copper-
mine River; deserted by the Indians he was obliged
to turn back
A rum distillery established in Canada

1770

Feb. 1, Ordinance for regulating the courts by which
Carleton increased courts of common pleas from one
to 2 for each district to sit continuously, costs reduced
and debtors protected by depriving justices of the
peace of jurisdiction in cases affecting private property exercised to injury of French Canadians
Feb. 23–Nov. 25, Second journey of Samuel Hearne in
search of the Coppermine River, traveled up the
Seal River to Lake Shethani, at the Kathawachaga
or Kazan River June 30, at Dubawnt the end of
July, broke his quadrant Aug. 11 and decided to
return, crossed southeast to Angikuni Lake and
reached Fort Prince of Wales on Hudson Bay Nov. 25
July 3, First ordination of a Presbyterian minister in
Halifax, Nova Scotia, of Bruin Romcas Comingoe,
pastor to Dutch Calvinistic Church at Lunenburg
Sir Guy Carleton turned over Government to Hector T.
Cramahé, made Lieutenant Governor in the following
year, and sailed for England remaining until 1774
Dec. 7–June 30, 1772, Samuel Hearne on third journey
in search of the Coppermine River left Hudson Bay
with Indian guide, Matonabbee, and reached Neultin
or Bland Lake Dec. 31, Feb. 6, crossed the Kazan
River and came to Kasba or Partridge Lake, crossed
Snowbird Lake Feb. 21, and camped at Wholdaia
Lake March 2, and camped at Clowey Lake in May
to build canoes, at Peshew Lake May 30, at Rum
Lake June 20 and reached the Coppermine River
about 40 miles from its mouth July 13, 1771. Hearne
erected a cross at the mouth of the river traced to the
Arctic Ocean July 18 and took possession for the
Hudson Bay Company. On return journey discovered
the Great Slave Lake Dec. 24, and proceeding east
from the mouth of Slave River reaching Fort Prince
of Wales June 30, 1772. This journey proved that
there was no North West Passage across the continent
Thomas Curry traveled west of Montreal as far as Fort
Bourbon at west end of Cedar Lake on the Saskatchewan, reported by the Hudson Bay Company the
following year as intercepting a "great part of York
Fort trade"

1771

July 2, Royal instructions authorized reversion to
French system of grants of crown lands in fief or
seigneury
Sept. 26, Hector T. Cramahé appointed Lieutenant
Governor
188,000 bushels of grain shipped from the ports of the
St. Lawrence

1772

Jan. 22, L. P. M. D'Esglis (Desgly) appointed Bishop
and coadjutor of Bishop Briand
June 27, Matthew Cocking left Hudson Bay, ascended
the Hayes River and portaged across to the Nelson
River through Cross Lake, and reached the lower
Saskatchewan July 23 by Moose Lake, and wintered
with the Blackfeet Indians
June 30, Hearne reached Fort Prince of Wales from
journey to the Arctic
Aug. 8–9, Surrender of Fort Prince of Wales at mouth
of the Churchill River to the French commanded by
Admiral La Pérouse, and of York Factory 12 days
later
Thomas and Joseph Frobisher built a trading post at
Sturgeon Lake on the Saskatchewan, sending furs to
Hudson Bay by the Churchill River

1773

July, Meeting of first Assembly Island of St. John
(Prince Edward Island)
Oct. 8, Arrival of Governor Legge commissioned Gov-
ernor of Nova Scotia July 22
Oct. 30, Meeting at Montreal presided over by Thomas
Walker, magistrate, drafted petition to the King
asking for an Assembly
Nov. 29, Petition of British citizens of the Province of
Quebec to the Lieutenant Governor for an Assembly,
to the King Dec. 31
Dec., Petition of Roman Catholics to the King for
equal rights and privileges of citizens of England

1774

May 17, Quebec Bill introduced in the British House of
Lords
May 31, Petition of British merchants trading to
Quebec presented in House of Commons asked revival of the French code of laws
June 22, Quebec Act restored French civil law but retained English criminal law, granted religious freedom, abolished the test oath and substituted an oath
of allegiance for Roman Catholics, liberty given to
French inhabitants to profess "the religion of the
Church of Rome," existing rights of property confirmed except property of religious orders, provided
for a nominated Legislative Council, and postponed
indefinitely calling of an Assembly, gave legal recognition of tithes for support of churches for the Roman
Catholics and Protestants. The Illinois country was
restored by extension of the boundaries on the west
to the Mississippi including all regions north of the
Ohio to the territories of the Hudson Bay Company
to the east. Labrador and Anticosti and a number
of islands in the St. Lawrence added to the Province.
Effective May 1, 1775 (14 Geo. III, cap. 83)
Quebec Revenue Act to provide for support of the
Government imposed customs duties and a fee for
public-house licenses, and continued "the territorial
or casual revenues" as belonging to the Crown before
the conquest (14 Geo. III, cap. 88)

Aug. 10, Expedition of Perez sighted Mt. Olympus, British Columbia, and named San Lorenzo Sound believed to be present Nootka. *See* America

Oct. 26, "Letter to the Inhabitants of the Province of Quebec" from the Continental Congress urged union in the cause of civil and religious liberty and invited delegates to second meeting of Congress in Philadelphia in May

Nov. 12, Petition for repeal of the Quebec Act from British inhabitants deprived of the protection of the writ of habeas corpus and trial by jury under restored French law

Samuel Hearne built Cumberland House, Hudson Bay Company post, on Pine Island Lake north of the lower Saskatchewan River a few miles west of Lake Winnipeg

1775

Jan. 3, Instructions to Sir Guy Carleton provided for governments for communities in the districts of Illinois, Vincennes, Mackinac, and Detroit restored to the Province under the Quebec Act

April 19, American Revolution begun (*see* United States) Canada remained loyal to Great Britain

May 1, The Quebec Act, the "Magna Carta" of the French Canadian citizens came into effect

May 10, Fort Ticonderoga taken by American revolutionists, Crown Point May 12

June 9, Governor Carleton called upon the seigniors to muster their inhabitants for military service under the old French law to repel threatened American invasion, and proclaimed martial law in Montreal

June 10, Alexander Henry left Sault Ste. Marie with goods and provisions valued at £3,000 in 16 canoes, proceeded westward by the Grand Portage and by the Pigeon River reached Rainy Lake, the Lake of the Woods, descended the Winnipeg to its mouth, and to the mouth of the Saskatchewan by Lake Winnipeg, and up the Saskatchewan to The Pas Oct. 1, and Oct. 26 at Cumberland House. Peter Pond joined the expedition at Lake Winnipeg

Aug. 17–Sept. 7, First Legislative Council established by Governor Carleton under the Quebec Act met at Quebec

Sept. 25, Ethan Allen and 38 men from Vermont captured in attack on Montreal and sent prisoners to England

Oct. 18, Fort Chambly on the Sorel surrendered by Major Stopford to the Americans Major Brown and James Livingston

Oct. 30, Governor Carleton made unsuccessful attempt to cross the river from Montreal to relieve Fort St. John, but unable to effect landing at Longueil

Nov. 2, Fort St. John at head of first rapids of the Richelieu besieged by Americans under General Montgomery since Sept. 18 surrendered by Major Preston making defense of Montreal impossible. The garrison marched out Nov. 3

Nov. 13, American army commanded by General Montgomery occupied Montreal

Nov. 14, Benedict Arnold who had marched overland from New England arrived before Quebec and summoned the city to surrender without effect and then withdrew his force to Point aux Trembles to wait for General Montgomery

Nov. 17, American privateers captured and sacked Charlottetown, Island of St. John (Prince Edward

Island) and carried away members of the Government as prisoners

Nov. 19, Carleton in disguise left Montreal on the 11th and succeeded in reaching Quebec on the 19th, but his fleet in the St. Lawrence was forced to surrender to the Americans

Dec. 5, Generals Montgomery and Arnold began the siege of Quebec

Dec. 31, American attack on Quebec defeated by Carleton, General Montgomery killed, and General Arnold wounded, and his men forced to retreat and nearly 450 surrendered and 30 killed, Carleton's loss only 7 killed and 11 wounded

Population of Lower Canada estimated at 90,000

1776

Jan. 1–April 9, Alexander Henry from Beaver Lake explored the country between the branches of the Saskatchewan

March 25, Attempt to relieve Quebec by attack on American battery at Point Lévis unsuccessful

April 12, Thomas Frobisher sent to construct a fort on the Churchill River to intercept the fur trade down this river to the Hudson Bay Company

April 27, Three commissioners from the American Congress arrived at Montreal

May 3, Attempt of Americans to send fire ships against Quebec unsuccessful

May 6, British ships coming to relief of Quebec arrived on the St. Lawrence and Americans led by General Thomas began retreat from Canada

May 19, Major Forster forced surrender of American post at the cedars on north bank of the St. Lawrence between Lake Francis and Lake St. Louis commanded by Major Butterfield with between 400 and 500 prisoners

May 20, Americans defeated at Quinze Chênes 7 miles north of the Cedars on the Ottawa River, and Major Sherburne taken prisoner by de Lorimer

May 25, Lieutenant Richard Pickersgill left Deptford, instructed to make survey of Baffin Bay. Reached 65° 37′ N. Lat. Aug. 4 and turned back without having accomplished anything

May 27, Cartel for exchange of prisoners between Forster and Arnold signed by General Arnold at St. Anne which was later repudiated by the American Congress

June 8, American General Thompson cut off in attempt to regain Three Rivers and taken prisoner with 200 men

June 14, General Sullivan began retreat from Canada to Crown Point and General Arnold embarked his forces from La Prairie June 18 and American invasion of Canada ended

June 16, Joseph Frobisher and Alexander Henry left fort on Churchill River ascending river to meet Chipewyan Indians at Lake Ile à la Crosse. Reached Montreal by way of the Grand Portage Oct. 15

June 25, Warrant of Governor Carleton prohibited sale of liquor without license

June 28, Governor Carleton held meeting with 300 Iroquois at Montreal and received their declaration of allegiance to Great Britain

July 7, Sir John Johnson, loyalist from Albany, New York, in Canada, granted leave to raise an American loyalist battalion, the King's Royal Regiment, the first of a number of such companies

Aug., Peter Livius appointed Chief Justice by Lord

Germain in spite of protest of Carleton, succeeding Hey in office since 1766

Aug. 7, Carleton constituted a Privy Council of 5 members and such other persons as should be called for by the Lieutenant Governor

Aug. 22, Letter of Lord Germain to Carleton which was not received until May, 1777 instructed him to retire to Quebec and attend to civil duties, notifying him of Burgoyne's appointment to command the troops

Oct. 11 and 13, Fleet commanded by Carleton in engagement with Americans on Lake Champlain destroyed 12 out of 15 vessels. General Benedict Arnold escaped through the British blockade; Crown Point occupied but evacuated Nov. 3 and return made to Canada

Nov. 6, Americans from Machias, Maine, attacked Fort Cumberland, Nova Scotia, but were dispersed by marines from Windsor

First book printed at Montreal by Berger and Mesplet who had come with the American commissioners, "Règlement de la confrérie de l'adoration perpétuelle du Saint Sacrement et la bonne mort"

1777

May 6, General Burgoyne arrived in Canada and took command of army

May 9, Plan for establishment of a Board of Trade prepared

May 27, Governor Carleton asked to be recalled on receipt of letter of Lord Germain of Aug. 22, 1776 and second letter dated March 26, 1777 which removed him from military command, and second letter censured him for retiring from Lake Champlain in the fall of 1776

July 8, Engagement at Fort Anne. *See* United States

Aug. 3, St. Leger invested Fort Stanwix called Fort Schuyler by the Americans

Aug. 6, Battle of Oriskany. *See* United States

Sept. 18, Frederick Haldimand nominated Governor to succeed Carleton

Provisions, provender, and livestock brought in by vessels not to be disposed of before hour's notice given by bell man so all inhabitants might have equal chance to buy (17 Geo. III, cap. 4)

1778

March 29, Captain James Cook on third voyage striking the American Pacific coast at 44° 55′ made continuous survey to Bering Strait. March 29 discovered Nootka Sound which he named King George's Sound, sighted Mount Edgecombe May 1

April 2, Petition of merchants of Quebec for repeal of the Quebec Act

May 1, Carleton dismissed Chief Justice Livius from office

June 3, First issue of the Montreal *Gazette* (*Gazette Littéraire*)

June 27, Governor Frederick Haldimand took office, and Sir Guy Carleton sailed for England

Peter Pond commissioned by group of fur traders to find Lake Athabaska left Sturgeon Lake and by the Churchill from Lake Ile à la Crosse continued northwest to Clear, Buffalo, and La Loche lakes and by portage to Clearwater River which he descended and discovered the Athabaska River and Lake and built a fort 40 miles from Lake Athabaska on the Deer River

1779

March 1, Governor Haldimand in letter proposed establishment of public library at Quebec

March 29, Royal instructions to Governor Haldimand reversed Carleton's interpretation of general instructions by which he created a permanent Privy Council

——, Peter Livius cleared and reinstated as Chief Justice of Canada but did not return to Canada

April 24, The first North West Company formed

June 17, Colonel Francis McLean with 650 men from Halifax established fort at Castine at mouth of the Penobscot River at site of La Tour's Fort Pentagoet as a refuge for loyalists; besieged by New England fleet July 23–Aug. 13

Sept. 13, Letter of Governor Haldimand to the dramatist, Richard Cumberland, asked him to select books and buy for a library at Quebec. 50 cases arrived from England in 1780

1780

March 9, Ordinance of Governor Haldimand regulated fees of office for 2 years as too high and exacted in excessive amount from the French Canadians

Oct. 25, Governor Haldimand in accord with his predecessors Governors Murray and Carleton expressed himself in letter to Lord Germain in condemnation of the British merchants declaring that in making laws and regulations regard should be paid to the 60,000 Canadians rather than the 2,000 minority, "three-fourths of whom are traders and cannot with propriety be considered as residents of the Province"

1781

Feb. 15, First canal completed to overcome the Cedar, Cascades, and Coteau rapids on the St. Lawrence (7 miles)

May 12, The Chippewas ceded the Island of Mackinac (Michilimac) to George III for £5,000

July, Indecisive naval encounter between ships from Halifax with 2 French frigates near Sydney

Aug. 28, Annapolis Royal raided and plundered by American privateers

1782

March 14, Sir John Johnson placed in charge of Indians of Canada by royal commission

April 23, Henry Hamilton appointed Lieutenant Governor of Province of Quebec, assumed office June 24

June 11, William Black, first Canadian Methodist minister, preached at Halifax, Nova Scotia

July 1, Lunenburg, Nova Scotia, plundered by American privateers

Aug. 9, Governor Hearne surrendered Fort Prince of Wales on the Churchill River, Hudson Bay, to French Admiral La Pérouse who burned the fort

Aug. 21, Governor Humphrey Martin surrendered York Factory, Hudson Bay, to La Pérouse

Dec. 7, Governor Parr of Nova Scotia announced that 501 loyalists had arrived from Charleston, South Carolina

1783

May 18, 7,000 loyalists, the first refugees, from New York arrived at Parrtown, New Brunswick, the present St. John, this day celebrated as anniversary day

May 26, Surveyor General Major Samuel Holland given instructions to survey the land from the last

French seigneury to Cataraqui (Kingston) and from there to Niagara

July, British Parliament appointed a commission of 5 to report on services and losses of loyalists

July 16, Royal instructions to Governor Haldimand granted land to American loyalists, every head of family to have 100 acres and 50 to each member of family, 50 to single men, and 200 to non-commissioned officers, the seigneury of Sorel divided among them

July 22, Governor Parr named loyalist settlement of Shelburne, Nova Scotia, in ceremony

Aug. 7, Instructions to Governor Haldimand to grant every field officer 1,000 acres, captains 700, staff officers 500

Sept. 3, Treaty of peace between the United States and Great Britain defined boundaries of the United States with Canada, Great Britain surrendering the territory between the Great Lakes and the Ohio River which had been included in the Province of Quebec by the Quebec Act in 1774

Sept. 8, Loyalists headed by Van Alstine sailed from New York reaching Quebec Oct. 8 and settled at Adolphustown

Nov., Packet service between Halifax and New York restored

Dec. 13, Number of loyalists arrived in Nova Scotia from the United States estimated as 30,000

Dec. 17, *Royal St. John Gazette and Nova Scotia Intelligencer* founded

Repeal of the penal laws against Catholics in Nova Scotia (cap. 9)

The North West Company formed of leading merchants of Montreal in opposition to the Hudson Bay Company

1784

April 29, Ordinance provided "for securing liberty of the subject and for the prevention of imprisonments out of this province" in response to demand for habeas corpus

May 13, Orders issued to officers to embark the loyalists and proceed to townships allotted

June 20, First of the Johnston regiment of loyalists arrived to settle townships of Edwardburg, Augusta, and Elizabethtown

Aug. 16, New Brunswick separated from Nova Scotia and made a separate Colony, Thomas Carleton, first Governor appointed Nov. 22

Aug. 26, Cape Breton separated from Nova Scotia and made a separate Colony

Sept., David Thompson arrived at Churchill Factory, Hudson Bay. He was 14 when he entered service of the Company

Oct. 25, Proclamation of Governor Haldimand assigned land to the Six Nations, Indian allies in the war, of 6 miles on the Ouse or Grand River

Nov. 15, Sir Frederick Haldimand left Canada, the Government administered by Henry Hamilton, Lieutenant Governor from Nov. 16 to Nov. 2, 1785

Nov. 22, Parrtown (St. John) made the capital of New Brunswick

Nov. 24, Petition of the British inhabitants for repeal of the Quebec Act and for an Assembly

Nov. 25, George Duncan Ludlow appointed first Chief Justice of New Brunswick

Nov. 29, Louis Philippe Mariauchaud Desgly appointed Roman Catholic Bishop of Quebec, the

first native Canadian bishop, on resignation of Bishop Briand

Population of Lower Canada 113,012, and of Upper Canada estimated as 10,000

Mail route established between Halifax and Quebec

Fredericton, New Brunswick, founded by American loyalists

1785

April 8, Order in Council prohibited importation by sea of any goods from the United States

April 11, Sir John Johnson and other loyalists in the western country petitioned for division of the Province and repeal of the Quebec Act

April 21, Ordinance established trial by jury

April, Captain James Hanna sailed from the Typa, China, reaching Nootka Sound in Aug., and in Sept. sailed with cargo of furs for China, arriving in Dec.

May 18, Parrtown, New Brunswick, incorporated under new name of St. John, the oldest incorporated town in Canada

Sept. 15, First journey of David Thompson from Churchill to York Factory 150 miles along Hudson Bay

Oct. 11, *Royal Gazette and New Brunswick Advertiser* published

Nov. 2, Colonel Henry Hope appointed Lieutenant Governor and administered the Government until arrival of Lord Dorchester as Governor in Oct. 1786

Dec. 25, Christ Church in Sorel, oldest Protestant church in Province of Quebec opened

1786

Jan. 9, First meeting of the Legislature of New Brunswick at St. John

March 12, First Presbyterian church service held in Montreal by Rev. John Bethune

April 22, Guy Carleton, Baron Dorchester, nominated Governor

July 21, David Thompson in party which left York Factory, Hudson Bay, to establish posts on the Saskatchewan to trade with the Blackfeet Indians; Manchester House built on the north Saskatchewan near present station of Birling on the Canadian Northern Railway

Sept. 7, Rev. Alexander Macdonell arrived at Quebec with 526 immigrants from Scotland en route for Upper Canada, their settlement named Glengarry after their home town

Oct. 23, Lord Dorchester arrived in Quebec and assumed office as Governor

——, Government of New Brunswick moved from St. John to Fredericton

First Methodist minister in Upper Canada, George Neal, began to preach on the Niagara frontier

1787

April 30, Ordinance regulated proceedings in civil courts and as to trial by jury in actions of a commercial nature

June, Captain Barclay who had sailed from Ostend the previous autumn reached Nootka Sound, and discovered in July the Strait of Juan de la Fuca

July 1, Captain Dixon discovered Bay named after him and named Dixon Straits and named Queen Charlotte Islands July 25

July, Captains Colnett and Duncan at Nootka Sound

Aug. 12, First Anglican Bishop of Nova Scotia with

jurisdiction over Quebec, Charles Inglis, consecrated at Lambeth by the Archbishop of Canterbury, arrived at Halifax Oct. 16, first colonial bishopric in British Empire

Aug. 12, Arrival of Prince William Henry, third son of George III, afterwards William IV, at Quebec on H.M.S. "Pegasus"

Oct. 19, Grant of land and £2,000 to the Mississaugas in region of Kingston, Indian allies in late war

David Thompson from Manchester House visited and wintered with the Pigeon Indians on the Bow River 1787–1788

1788

May 5, Captain Estevan Jose Martinez from Mexico arrived at Nootka Sound claimed by Spain on voyage of exploration to the south, June 11–July 26

May 13, Captain John Meares and Captain William Douglas reached Nootka and established a settlement for fur trade, and May 13–Aug. on voyage of exploration, the "Felice" returning Aug. 24 and the "Iphegenia" Aug. 27

May 16, Adam Lymburner, of Quebec, representing the British minority of Canada, heard in the House of Commons in support of petitions for repeal of Quebec Act and for an Assembly

June 4, Death of Bishop Desgly, head of Roman Catholic Church in Canada, Jean François Hubert appointed Bishop of Quebec to succeed him

June 29, Captain John Meares sighted inlet discovered in previous year by Barclay which he named Strait of Juan de Fuca after alleged Greek discoverer, sighted and named Mt. Olympus July 4, named Cape Disappointment July 6 and passed the mouth of the Columbia River which he named Deception Bay

June 30, Charles François Bailly de Messein elected coadjutor to Bishop Hubert

July 24, Western part of the Province (the present Ontario) divided into 4 districts, Lunenburg, Mecklenburg, Nassau, and Hesse, English law introduced. Boards established assigned land to loyalists

Sept. 20, First vessel built and launched on the Pacific coast, the "North West America" by John Meares

Sept. 24, Captain John Meares sailed for China with cargo of furs

Nov. 1, Religious and Literary Institution which eventually became King's College formally opened at Windsor, Nova Scotia, by Bishop Inglis; incorporated in 1789 (cap. 4)

John Young erected a distillery at Quebec

"Scarce year" in Upper Canada

Sailing packet service established between Great Britain and Halifax

1789

Jan. 6, First agricultural society of Canada established in Quebec by Lord Dorchester, and first meeting held April 6, Henry Caldwell, president

May 5, Spanish expedition of Estevan Martinez sent from Mexico to take formal possession of lands claimed by Spain in view of discovery by Heceta and Bodega in 1775 arrived at Nootka Sound

May 14, Martinez seized the British ship "Iphigenia" commanded by Captain William Douglas, flying Portuguese flag to avoid paying port charges in China

May 15, Final report of Commission appointed by British Parliament in 1783 to classify services and

losses of loyalists in the American Revolution, 1,401 claims, and $2,745,000 paid in sums ranging from $221,000 to Sir John Johnson to $50

June 3–Sept. 12, Alexander Mackenzie on journey to the Arctic from Fort Chipewyan on southern shore of Lake Athabaska reached Slave River June 4 and Slave Lake June 9, and June 29 embarked on the unknown river later named the Mackenzie for its discoverer, and the Arctic Sea sighted July 12 from island which he named Whale Island and established record post on the island July 14, and then turned back

June 8, Spaniards seized Meares' vessel the "North West America"

June 24, Martinez at Nootka Sound took formal possession of land for Spain and of the 4 ships of Meares seized taken as prizes to Mexico

July 3, Captain Colnett arrived from China July 2 sent by Meares began building Fort Pitt at Nootka defying Spaniards and was made a prisoner by Martinez and taken to Mexico

July 13, The "Princess Royal," British ship commanded by Captain Hudson seized by Spaniards at Nootka Sound

Aug. 5, First conference of the Protestant Episcopal Church held in Quebec summoned by Bishop Inglis

Nov. 9, Lord Dorchester in Council ordered that land boards keep a registry of the "United Empire Loyalists" as a mark of honor to American loyalists

1790

April 13, Charles Justin McCarthy ordered by Court of Quarter Session to leave the district as a "vagabond, impostor, disturberer of the peace" for preaching after the manner of the Methodists

April 17, Ordinance prohibited the export of wheat, pease, oats, flour, and meal in effort to reduce high price of wheat

May 13, Memorial of Captain Meares of April 30 claiming damage for ships seized at Nootka Sound presented in House of Commons

May 16, Formal demand for release of Colnett and British ships seized at Nootka Sound in 1789 secured release by Viceroy of Mexico

May 19, Surrender of 2,000,000 acres of land, parts of Essex, Kent, Middlesex, and Elgin counties by the Ottawas, Chippewas, Pottawatamies, and Hurons

June 4, Letter of Spain to European Governments on Nootka affair

June 8, King's College, Windsor, Nova Scotia, opened

June 9, David Thompson left Cumberland House, surveyed Saskatchewan River reaching its mouth June 15, and by Lakes Winnipeg, Buscucoggan, Oxford, Knee, and Swampy and Hayes River reached York Factory on Hudson Bay

June 16, Spain claimed assistance of France under family compact in case of war

July 24, Spain agreed to make full reparation for seizure of vessels in Nootka Sound

Oct. 8–June 24, 1795, Alured Clarke, Lieutenant Governor of Province of Quebec

Oct. 28, Spain signed Nootka Sound Convention with Great Britain abandoning claims to the region

Belleville, Vancouver, founded by Captain Myers

Population of Lower Canada estimated as 161,311

1791

Jan. 25, Royal message to House of Commons announced intention to divide Province of Quebec into Upper and Lower Canada

Feb. 20, First Methodist class held at Hay Bay near Napanese in Upper Canada

March 4, Canada Bill introduced in British House of Commons by Mr. Pitt

March 23, Adam Lymburner in England as representing Canadian merchants heard in House of Commons in opposition to Canada Bill asked for total repeal of the Quebec Act, opposed division of the Province

May, Major Edward Jessup, United Empire Loyalist, granted land on which he built the town of Prescott in 1797

June 10, Canada Constitutional Act received royal assent, the Province of Quebec divided into Upper and Lower Canada, Upper Canada chiefly settled by the English, Lower Canada by the French, each with its own Government, a Lieutenant Governor, House of Assembly elected by the people for 4 years, and Legislative Council appointed for life by the Lieutenant Governor, went into effect Dec. 26. Under the Act land set aside "for the support and maintenance of a Protestant clergy," the "clergy reserves" of land in each province amounting to about one-seventh of crown lands

Aug. 11, Arrival of Prince Edward, later Duke of Kent, in command of the 7th Royal Fusiliers, remained 3 years

Aug. 18, Lord Dorchester sailed for England leaving the Lieutenant Governor, Sir Alured Clarke in charge of the Government

Aug. 24, Order in Council divided the Province into Upper and Lower Canada

Sept. 12, Lord Dorchester received new commission as Governor in Chief of Upper and Lower Canada, and Alured Clarke as Lieutenant Governor of Lower Canada and John Graves Simcoe as Lieutenant Governor of Upper Canada

Sept. 28, Class meeting of Methodist Church organized at St. John, New Brunswick

Nov. 11, Lieutenant Governor Simcoe arrived at Quebec

Nov. 14, Death of Lieut. Governor John Parr in Nova Scotia

Nov. 18, Proclamation of Lieutenant Governor Clarke acting for Lord Dorchester announced that the division of the Province into Upper and Lower Canada would take effect Dec. 26, and the Constitutional Act become effective

Dec. 26, Constitutional Act came into effect. Quebec became the capital of Lower Canada, Newark of Upper Canada

Dec. 31, William Osgoode appointed first Judge of King's Bench, Upper Canada, new commission July 29, 1792

Imperial Act created Court at Newfoundland, John Reeves, Chief Justice

1792

April 27, Captain George Vancouver (voyage from England of April, 1791–Oct. 20, 1794) sailing along the Pacific coast from California noted entrance of "small river," but passed the mouth of the Columbia, Meares' Deception Bay as not worthy of note, named Point Grenville April 28, at Juan de Fuca Strait April 29 and proceeded as far as 52° 18′ N., reached the ocean Aug. 9, discovered Gulf of Georgia and circumnavigated Vancouver Island

May 7, Lower Canada divided into 27 electoral districts returning 50 members

May 8, Moravian mission established in Upper Canada at Oxford by David Zeisberger

May 14, John Wentworth became Lieutenant Governor of Nova Scotia

June 4, Captain Vancouver landed at site of present city of Everett and took possession of the land for England calling the country New Georgia

June 15, Captain James Knight appointed Governor at Hudson Bay

June 27, Prince Edward speaking at Charlesbourg in Quebec County stopped election riot saying "Let me hear no more of the odious distinctions, English and French: you are all his Brittanic Majesty's Canadian subjects"

July 1, Lieutenant Governor Simcoe arrived at Kingston and organized the Government of Upper Canada

July 8, First Executive Council for Upper Canada appointed by Lieutenant Governor Simcoe

July 16, Proclamation of Lieutenant Governor Simcoe divided Upper Canada into districts and counties

July 17, First meeting of Executive Council of Upper Canada took steps to organize Legislative Council

Aug. 28–Oct. 12, Vancouver at Nootka Sound

Sept. 5, David Thompson from York Factory ascended the Hayes and Nelson rivers arriving at Split Lake Sept. 28, and the Saskatchewan Sept. 30, and at Sipiwesk Lake Oct. 8 where he built Hudson Bay Company trading post

Sept. 7, Supreme Court opened in Newfoundland

Sept. 17–Oct. 15, First session of first Parliament of Upper Canada held at Newark (Niagara) English civil law introduced and trial by jury. Provision made for regulation of tolls to be taken in grist mills, for collection of small debts and for building jails and courthouses in each district

Oct. 10, Alexander Mackenzie of the North West Company returned from visit to England left Fort Chipewyan on Lake Athabasca and spent the winter in fur trading with the Indians above the forks of the Peace River which he reached Nov. 1

Oct. 21, Ordered by the Council that an annual fair should be held at Newark on the second Monday of each October to last 6 days

Dec. 17–May 9, 1793, First session of first Parliament of Lower Canada met in Quebec. Framed rules of procedure, agreement made to use both French and English languages, provided for payment of members of Assembly and Council, adopted resolution to assist Great Britain against France in any war which might occur. Act granted indulgence to Quakers to make affirmation instead of taking oath, and tax imposed on wine and spirits for revenue. Act provided for returning officers for Knights, citizens, and burgesses to serve in Assembly, thereafter voted annually. Bill to abolish slavery discussed but was not passed

1793

Feb. 1, France declared war against Great Britain

Feb. 4–March 10, Lieutenant Governor Simcoe on official tour of inspection of Upper Canada, at Detroit Feb. 18–23, March 2 at present site of London favored site for capital

Feb. 12, Spain agreed to pay John Meares and his associates compensation for vessels seized

April 13, Upper Canada *Gazette* first published newspaper issued at Newark on the first printing press in Upper Canada established by Louis Roy

May 9–July 22, Alexander Mackenzie started journey to the Pacific up the Peace River by canoe with his lieutenant, Alexander Mackay, 6 Frenchmen, and 2 Indians, ascended the Parsnip to its source and portaged to the Fraser River and June 17 down the Fraser River to present Quesnel, July 4 left Fraser River (Tacouche Tesse) and by overland trail, reached the Bella Coola River July 17 about 30 miles from the Pacific Ocean where the Indians of "Friendly Village" provided them with canoes and they reached the Ocean July 22 where Mackenzie set up inscription of his journey. On return journey reached the "Friendly Village" July 26, the Fraser River Aug. 4 and the fort at forks of the Peace River from where he started Aug. 24

May 14, Brigadier General Ogilvie took possession of St. Pierre and Miquelon Islands in war with France, inhabitants deported

May 31–July 9, Second session of first Parliament of Upper Canada. Acts made valid marriages heretofore contracted before any person in the public employment, and made provision for laying and collection of assessments, provided for better regulation of the militia, for keeping roads in repair, established courts of probate and surrogate in every district, for payment of salaries of members of the Assembly and Legislative Council, for appointment of parish and town officers beginning representative local government, further introduction of slaves prohibited, destruction of wolves encouraged

June 28, Letters patent established bishop's see of Provinces of Upper and Lower Canada, and Dr. Jacob Mountain appointed Bishop

July 7, Meeting of Commission with the Indians at Niagara

July 21, Thompson at York Factory from Seepaywisk House from Seepaysisk or Sipiwesk Lake through Landing, Wintering, Red Paint, Wuskwating, and Burntwood lakes to the Churchill River, and then by the Burntwood and Nelson rivers

July 22, Alexander Mackenzie reached the Pacific Ocean overland. *See supra* May 9

Aug. 27, Publicly announced that the name of Toronto had been officially changed to York Aug. 26 "in consideration and compliment of the Duke of York's victories in Flanders"

Sept. 23, Lord Dorchester, Governor, arrived in Canada from England after 2 years absence

Sept. 28, Provision made in Upper Canada for gradual emancipation of negro slaves in the Province

Oct. 5–8, Vancouver again at Nootka Sound, explored as far north as 56° 44′

Oct. 5, David Thompson reached Cumberland House from York Factory by the Hayes River route, began ascent of Saskatchewan Oct. 8, reaching the Forks Oct. 15, at Manchester House Oct. 28, and at Buckingham House on the north Saskatchewan Oct. 31 where he wintered

Nov. 1, Dr. Jacob Mountain, first Anglican bishop of Canada, arrived at Quebec

Nov. 11–May 31, 1794, Second session of first Parliament of Lower Canada, 5 measures passed, commission authorized to treat with commission of Upper Canada to arrange about division of customs duties, Alien Act provided for registration of French immigrants entering the Province, directed against foreigners spreading treasonable doctrines of the French Revolution, law courts reorganized, militia regulated, and the Province divided into the 3 districts of Quebec, Montreal, and Three Rivers

Nov. 23, John Young, member of Assembly, arrested on suit of James Hunt, arrest contested by him as breach of privilege claimed as of members of House of Commons on Nov. 25

Dec. 6, Death of William Smith, Secretary of Lower Canada

1794

Feb. 10, Speech to the Indians of Lord Dorchester in which he stated that the patience of Great Britain with the United States was "almost exhausted" and would not be surprised if war followed "during the course of the present year"

May 10, The Duke of Kent (later Prince Edward) took command of the troops at Halifax

May 16, David Thompson surveyed the north Saskatchewan from Buckingham House to the Forks, arrived at Cumberland House June 2, journeyed to Goose and Athapapuskow, Cranberry, and Reed lakes and arrived at York Factory on Hudson Bay July 5 where he remained 21 days, and then proceeded to Reed Lake reached Sept. 2 where he wintered

May 29, Bishop Mountain given seat in Legislative Council, and assumed title given to him and his successors by royal letters patent of "Lord Bishop of Quebec"

June 2–July 9, Third session of first Parliament of Upper Canada, established a Court of King's Bench and district courts, the Lieutenant Governor or Chief Justice or any 2 members of Executive Council constituted a Court of Appeal, the Governor or Lieutenant Governor authorized to license practitioners in the law, regulations for juries provided, and for licensing of public houses, a duty placed on stills, and Road Act amended, and Act to restrain custom of permitting cattle, sheep, horses, and pigs from running at large

Sept. 14, Chief Justice Osgoode took oath of office at Quebec, and as member of Executive Council of Lower Canada

Oct. 16, Vancouver sailed from Nootka Sound after third voyage of exploration to the North West

Nov. 19, Treaty between the United States and Great Britain (Jay's Treaty) provided for withdrawal from western posts within the territory of the United States by June 1, 1796, provided for a boundary commission to determine boundary of Canada with the United States west of the Lake of the Woods, the identity of the St. Croix River as part of the boundary, and mutual commercial concessions as to the United States

Governor Simcoe by labor of the Queen's Rangers (loyalist regiment) begun in 1793 opened portage road of 33 miles from Toronto (York) to Lake Simcoe, the former Lac aux Claies, and named the road Yonge St. for Sir George Yonge in Government of George III. Dundas St. also laid out

Fort Augustus built on northern Saskatchewan about one and one-half miles above mouth of the Sturgeon River by Angus Shaw and Duncan McGallivray

1795

Jan. 5–May 7, 1796, Third session of first Parliament of Lower Canada. Inspectors of quality of potash and pearl ashes appointed, provisional agreement as to customs with Upper Canada confirmed, form of register for baptism, marriage, and burial established for both Protestant and Catholic churches, licenses imposed for peddlers, public houses, and retail selling of wine, brandy, &c., and new tax placed on wines, sugar, coffee, tobacco, salt, and playing cards. Act obliged vessels to perform quarantine. Regulation of trade with the United States voted and thereafter annually

Feb., Agreement of commissioners from the 2 Provinces for allowance by Lower Canada of return of customs dues to Upper Canada on its own imports passing through Lower Canada

March 28, Spanish at Nootka Sound surrendered post to the British and sailed for Mexico

July 6–Aug. 10, Fourth session of first Parliament of Upper Canada, passed laws to regulate the practice of medicine, to ascertain eligibility of persons for election to Assembly, to establish a superior court, to register deeds and wills, and to ratify provisional agreement with Lower Canada as to customs

July 18, David Thompson and Malcolm Ross who had arrived at York Factory July 5 ascended the Nelson River to west end of Sisipuk Lake, Sept. 6, where trading post built and the winter spent

Nov. 20–May 7, 1796, Fourth session of first Parliament of Lower Canada passed laws for registration of letters patent granting crown lands, regulations for guides and journeys to the Indian country, for weights and measures, for repair of roads and bridges, and for apprehension of felons from other provinces. Deficit in revenue of over £14,000 later met by British Treasury

Some members of the North West Company formed a new and rival trading company calling themselves the "New North West Company" and known as the X Y Company

1796

Jan. 21, General Robert Prescott appointed Lieutenant Governor of Lower Canada

Feb. 1, Offices of Government of Upper Canada transferred to York

April 6, Proclamation of Lieutenant Governor Simcoe directed magistrates to find out under oath the names of persons entitled to land grants because of loyalty in the late war

May 16–June 3, Fifth session of first Parliament of Upper Canada. Regulations as to foreign silver coins passed, commissioners appointed to act with Lower Canada, license law amended

June 10, David Thompson started northward from Fairford House built by Ross a mile below mouth of the Reindeer River, proceeded through Reindeer and Wollaston lakes and down the Black River to east end of Lake Athabaska. He had in the Spring surveyed the Kississing River to its mouth and the Churchill to Fairford House. Wintered on Reindeer Lake

July 9, Lord Dorchester sailed for England leaving General R. Prescott, Lieutenant Governor in charge

July 20, Peter Russell, Administrator of Upper Canada, on Lieutenant Governor Simcoe's departure for England

Aug. 11, Niagara post surrendered to the United States

Sept. 1, French attack on St. Johns, Newfoundland, led by Admiral Richery unsuccessful

Sept. 7, Parts of present Middlesex and Oxford counties, 132,000 acres ceded by the Chippewas, and 88,000 in Lambton county

Nov. 2, The Six Nations authorized Captain Brant by formal power of attorney to sell certain lands which were transferred by deed of Feb. 5, 1798

Dec. 15, Directed that the Lieutenant Governor of Upper Canada manage the Indian affairs of that Province

Thomas Dunn of Quebec obtained grant of township thereafter named Dunham for himself and associates

1797

Jan. 24–May 2, First session of second Parliament of Lower Canada. Agreement with Upper Canada as to proportion of customs duties to be allotted to Upper Canada of goods imported ratified, regulations as to aliens from France suspected of high treason continued, more effective provision for pilotage in the St. Lawrence between Quebec and the Island of Bic arranged for

April 27, Robert Prescott, nominated Dec. 15, 1796, took office as Governor in Chief succeeding Lord Dorchester

May 23, David Thompson left the service of the Hudson Bay Company for the North West Company

June 1–July 3, First session, second Parliament of Upper Canada met at York. Acts passed for better securing the Province against the King's enemies, for regulation of ferries, of the practice of law, for more easy barring of dower, for dealing with felons from other provinces, for the Court of King's Bench, for securing titles of land, and for trade with the United States. Address to King George III asked for appropriation for education

July 3, Law Society of Upper Canada established by statute

July 22, David Thompson reached headquarters of the North West Company and received instructions to locate the 49th parallel of latitude and to go as far as the Missouri River visiting Indian villages and locating the company posts

Aug. 9, David Thompson left Lake Superior and by Rainy Lake and River and Lake of the Woods reached Lake Winnipeg Sept. 1. From Pigeon Bay he descended the Dauphin River and through St. Martin's Lake reached Lake Manitoba and by Meadow Portage Lake Winnipegosis. Sept. 19 he ascended the Shoal River to Swan Lake. Surveyed upper waters of Assiniboine and Red Deer rivers

Aug. 21, Mississagas surrendered part of Halton county, 3,450 acres

Aug. 25, Last slave publicly sold at Montreal, Emanuel Allen aged 33 for £36

Sept. 1, Pierre Denaut appointed Bishop of Quebec succeeding Bishop Hubert, resigned

Oct. 17, Death of Bishop Hubert, Roman Catholic Bishop of Quebec

Prescott founded by Major Edward Jessup

Nov. 4, Robert Shore Milnes commissioned Lieutenant Governor of Lower Canada

Nov. 28, Thompson left post on Assiniboine and Dec. 7 reached Ash House on the Souris River and Dec. 29 the Mandan Indian villages on the Missouri. Started back Jan. 10, 1798 and reached McDonnel's House Feb. 3 at mouth of the Souris River

Sault Ste. Marie Canal begun by the North West Company to overcome the rapids of the St. Mary's

River connecting Lakes Superior and Huron; destroyed by Americans in War of 1812

1798

Feb. 20–May 11, Second session of second Parliament of Lower Canada. Act allowed proportion of revenue duties to Upper Canada for period between March 1 and Dec. 31, 1797, and for making valid certain marriages performed by ministers other than those of the Anglican Church

Feb. 26, Thompson started to explore the head waters of the Mississippi, reaching site of the present Winnipeg at forks of the Assiniboine and Red rivers March 7, ascended Red River and March 14 at site of present town of Pembina, North Dakota, March 24 at Red Lake Falls, proceeded to Red Lake by portages and reached Turtle Lake which he believed the source of the Mississippi April 27. At Red Cedar (Cass) Lake April 29–May 3. Descended the Mississippi to the mouth of the Sand Lake River which he ascended to Sandy Lake, and by portage to the St. Louis River and Lake Superior and May 20 at Sault Ste. Marie

March 15, Treaty between Great Britain and the United States; explanatory of the Jay Treaty, River Ste. Croix boundary

May 22, 28,000 acres ceded by the Chippewas, a part of Simcoe county

June 5–July 5, Second session of second Parliament of Upper Canada. Act for better division of the Province established the county system proclaimed Jan. 1, 1800, and for confirmation of marriages by ministers other than the Church of England, and commission appointed to settle boundary lines of townships

June 14, Thompson started from the Grand Portage, arrived at Winnipeg House at mouth of the Winnipeg July 31, and by east shore of Winnipeg Lake at mouth of the Saskatchewan Aug. 9, and Aug. 18 Cumberland House. Aug. 24 reached Churchill River by Frog portage from the Sturgeonweir River and Lake Amisk, and ascended the Churchill to mouth of the Rapid River and up this stream to Lake La Ronge, and by the Churchill to Isle à la Crosse Lake. Sept. 8 began ascent of Beaver River and Red Deer Brook to Red Deer Lake (Lake La Biche) Oct. 4 where he wintered and built fort

June 30, Island of St. Joseph ceded by the Chippewas

Oct. 7, Company of 44 émigrés from the French Revolution reached Quebec and were allotted lands in Upper Canada of townships of Uxbridge, Gwillimburg, and part of Whitechurch

Oct. 23, Prince Edward sailed for England

Oct. 25, Declaration of boundary commission acting under Jay Treaty identified the Scoodic River with the St. Croix River of Champlain as boundary with the United States

Nov., Provincial Legislature changed name of Island of St. John to Prince Edward Island; confirmed by King

Dec. 29, Royal Proclamation gave assent to laws making valid marriages performed by ministers other than those of the Church of England

First stage in Upper Canada established by Mr. Macklem of Chippewa between Queenstown and Fort Erie, distance 25 miles, fare $1

Coal first discovered in Pictou county, Nova Scotia

1799

Jan. 7, Quebec Library established, incorporated 1840

Feb. 14, French émigrés settled Windham near York where Joseph de Puisaye had erected houses on Yonge St.

March 28–June 3, Third session of second Parliament of Lower Canada, commission appointed to adjust customs duties with Upper Canada reappointed, erection of court houses in Quebec and Montreal districts provided for and houses of correction in all districts, road law amended, and new revenue duties on commodities imposed, tea, sugar, wine, salt, playing cards

March, Thompson traveled to Fort Augustus on the North Saskatchewan a mile and a half above the mouth of the Sturgeon, reaching the Pembina River April 21, at mouth of the Athabaska April 25, surveyed the Athabaska and the Lesser Slave Lake River, May 10 at mouth of the Clearwater, and by Clearwater, Methy portage, and Churchill River to Isle à la Crosse May 20, and thence to Grand Portage. Wintered at Fort George on the Saskatchewan

April, The mouth of the Stikine River on Alaska coast first explored by Capt. Cleveland

May 17, Edward, Duke of Kent, made Commander-in-Chief of army

June 12–June 29, Third session of second Parliament of Upper Canada passed law to provide for education and support of orphan children

June 13, Name Prince Edward Island first used in an official document

July 24, Colonial Secretary authorized building of Anglican Metropolitan Church at Quebec

July 25, Governor Robert Prescott sailed for England, Lieut. Governor Robert Shore Milnes, in charge of the Government

Aug. 17, Peter Hunter took office as Lieutenant Governor of Upper Canada succeeding Simcoe

Nov. 11, Committee appointed to supervise building Cathedral of Quebec

1800

Jan. 1, Act for division of Upper Canada into counties proclaimed

Jan. 3, Duel between John White, Attorney General, and John Small, Clerk of the Executive Council, White died of wounds a few days later

Feb. 12, New Brunswick College, Fredericton, founded by provincial charter

March 5–May 29, Fourth session of second Parliament of Lower Canada. Resolution passed as to expediency of encouragement of cultivation of hemp, salaries of judges increased causing deficit, commissioners appointed to treat with Upper Canada as to duties, penalties imposed for harboring runaway seamen, and provision made for bridge over Jacques Cartier River

March 7, Hull founded by Philemon Wright

March 12, Jesuit estates taken over by the Government on death of last of the order, Father Casot

March 25, Thompson from south shore of the Saskatchewan started overland to Fort Augustus which he reached March 28, and the Rocky Mountain House April 7 and from the Rocky Mountain House May 5 made a survey of the North Saskatchewan River to "The Elbow," May 9 at Fort Augustus, May 12 at Fort George, May 28 camped at the Forks, and June 7 reached mouth of the Saskatchewan

June 2–July 4, Fourth session of second Parliament of Upper Canada. Criminal law of England introduced, regulation of special juries, qualifications of electors defined, and provision made for conviction of persons selling liquor without license. Act passed for the more equal representation of the commons in Parliament and for better definition of the qualifications of electors

June 13, Daniel Williams Harmon in service of the North West Company started from Grand Portage, reached Rainy Lake July 24, at mouth of the Winnipeg River July 31, and Aug. 10 started for the Swan River which he reached Oct. 9 and built post, proceeded to Fort Alexandria on bank of Upper Red River Oct. 23 where he wintered

Aug. 18, Alexander Henry, Jr. reached forks of the Assiniboine and Red River and built post on the Park River in North Dakota

Oct. 5, Thompson left the Rocky Mountain House on visit to the Piegan Indians on the Red Deer River, Nov. 17–Dec. 3, and surveyed the Bow River

Duncan McGillivray, fur trader, ascended the North Saskatchewan River and discovered the Howse Pass, and the first on upper waters of the Columbia

First public library in Upper Canada established at Niagara

Sherbrooke, Province of Quebec, founded as Little Forks by Daniel Moe and associates

1801

Jan. 8–April 8, First session of third Parliament of Lower Canada. Free schools to be supported by grants of land authorized, royal assent given April 7, 1802, and became law by proclamation Aug. 12, 1802. Act provided for demolition of walls around Montreal, proclaimed Aug. 12, 1802, billiard tables licensed, and new duty imposed on manufactured tobacco and snuff, provision made for water supply for Montreal, Agreement with Upper Canada of Feb. 2 ratified as to customs duties. Act passed for relief of persons holding lands of the Crown *en roture* on which mutation fines due

May 28–July 9, First session of third Parliament of Upper Canada, militia regulated, market established at Kingston, provision of funds for government, appointment of inspectors of flour, potash, and pearl ashes. Provided that duties on goods from the United States should be the same as those from Great Britain

June, Thompson made "a journey into the Rocky Mountains by land," left Saskatchewan 28 miles above Rocky Mountain House, and followed Sheep River to its source in one of the eastern ranges

1802

Jan. 11–April 5, Second session of third Parliament of Lower Canada. Appropriation of £1,200 voted for encouragement of growth of hemp, regulations made for police, Act disqualified Charles Baptiste Bouc from acting as member of Assembly on conviction of Bouc of crime against Etienne Drouin

Feb. 10, Alexander Mackenzie knighted

May 12, King's College, Nova Scotia, received a royal charter

May 25–July 7, Second session of third Parliament of Upper Canada. Acts passed to better ascertain and secure title to lands. Governor authorized to name additional ports

May, Thompson descended the Saskatchewan and continued to Lake Superior to Fort William, head-

quarters of the North West Company at mouth of the Kaministiquia

Oct. 21–Nov. 9, Thompson from the mouth of the Lesser Slave River ascended to Lesser Slave Lake, and from there to "Forks of the Peace River" where he made his headquarters during 1803

Nov. 6, Petition from congregation of Church of Scotland in Quebec for grant of land for a church presented by Alexander Spark, minister

1,010,033 bushels of wheat exported from Canada in this year

1803

Jan. 24–March 5, Third session of third Parliament of Upper Canada. Acts provided for allowance of time for sale of land and tenements by the sheriff, to authorize Governor and Lieutenant Governor to license practitioners of law, to declare right of certain grantees of crown waste lands, particularized property subject to assessment, and regulated property of married women, and for encouragement of destruction of bears and wolves

Feb. 8–April 18, Third session of third Parliament of Lower Canada. Six measures passed. Provision made for better regulation of the militia

May 12, Convention between Great Britain and the United States signed provided for a boundary commission to define frontiers from northwest angle of Nova Scotia to the Highlands; not ratified

May 21, Thomas Talbot arrived at Dunship with settlers for 5,000 acres granted to him Feb. 15

Aug. 2–Aug. 11, Special session fourth of third of Parliament of Lower Canada renewed Alien Act regulations and Act for better preservation of His Majesty's Government because of war between Great Britain and France

Aug. 7, 9, and 27, In 3 ships the first Scotch immigrants sent by Lord Selkirk arrived at Island of St. John (Prince Edward Island) to settle on land bought by him

Aug. 11, Imperial Act provided that offenses committed in Indian lands and other parts of British North America should be tried as if committed in provinces of Upper and Lower Canada

Aug. 28, Lord Selkirk with 800 Scotch settlers arrived at Charlottetown, Island of St. John (Prince Edward Island)

Nov. 5, Weekly public market established at York (Toronto)

Chief Justice Osgoode in giving decision declared slavery illegal which practically abolished it in Lower Canada

First paper mill at St. Andrews, Province of Quebec

1804

Feb. 1–March 9, Fourth session of third Parliament of Upper Canada. Act passed for better securing the Province against all sedition and provision made for punishment for harboring deserters. Grant for encouragement of growth and export of hemp, and £1,000 voted for repair of roads and bridges

Feb. 10–May 2, Fifth session of third Parliament of Lower Canada. Commissioners appointed to treat with Upper Canada as to customs duties, marriages as solemnized by ministers of dissenting Protestant sects since Sept. 13, 1759 confirmed and made valid as to the future, provision made for the insane, and Act for encouragement of persons apprehending deserters. 13 laws enacted

Feb. 29–March 13, Thompson on journey to most westerly post of North West Company which he built in 56° 12′ 54″ N. Lat., and 120° 38′ W. Long. 5 miles above Smoky River in present Alberta. March 15 he descended the Peace River to Lake Athabaska, May 12, reached mouth of the Clearwater from the Athabaska River May 19 and then journeyed to Lake Superior and Sept. 8 at Cumberland House where he wintered

May, Scotch colonists sailed on the "Oughton" from Tobermory Island of Mull to settle on Baldoon Farm in Upper Canada near Lake St. Clair where Lord Selkirk had purchased 950 acres

Sept., Metropolitan Church at Quebec completed

Nov. 5, The North West and X Y Companies united

Nov. 19, Mr. Ormsby, Scottish actor, opened a theater in Montreal, first play "The Busy-Body and the Sultan"

1805

Jan. 5, First issue of the *Quebec Mercury*

Jan. 9–March 25, First session of fourth Parliament of Lower Canada. Law passed for taxing trade to pay for erection of common jails in Montreal and Quebec which was very unpopular. Acts established a turnpike from Montreal to Lachine, prohibited sale of goods on Sunday, for erection of hotel, coffee house, and assembly room at Quebec, for better regulation of pilots and shipping in port of Quebec and harbors, and for road from Montreal to Lachine

Jan. 24, Justice Robert Thorpe took seat as judge of King's Bench in Upper Canada

Feb. 1–March 2, First session of fourth Parliament of Upper Canada, laws enacted provided for regulation of controverted elections, and for relief of insolvent debtors, and for relief of persons entitled to claim crown lands where no patents issued

May 27–28, Thompson made journey to post at south end of Indian (South) Lake and Churchill River about 250 miles from Fort Churchill on Hudson Bay, arrived at Forks of the Churchill June 4, at Cumberland House June 17, at Cranberry Lake June 27, at Reindeer Lake Aug. 4, and returned to Cumberland House Aug. 24. Wintered on Reed Lake

June, Simon Fraser from Cumberland House crossed the Rocky Mountains by the Peace River Pass, ascended the Parsnip River to Lake which he named after Norman McLeod of the North West Company

July 22, Harmon left Fort William at the mouth of the Kaministiquia and reached Cumberland House (North West Company post on the Saskatchewan near Hudson Bay post of same name) Sept. 5, and continued up the Saskatchewan reaching South Branch post 120 miles above the Forks Sept. 21. Wintered at the Cumberland House

Aug. 1, 250,850 acres, part of York county, ceded by the Mississagas

Aug. 5, Governor Milnes left for England transferring the administration to Thomas Dunn

Aug. 21, Death of Lieutenant Governor Peter Hunter of Upper Canada. Succeeded Sept. 11–Aug. 25, 1806 by Alexander Grant as Administrator

Paper made at St. Andrews, Lower Canada

1806

Jan. 17, Death of Bishop Pierre Denaud (Roman Catholic) Bishop of Quebec

Jan. 27, Joseph Octave Plessis appointed Bishop of Quebec to succeed Denaud

Feb. 4–March 3, Second session of fourth Parliament of Upper Canada. Act made provision for sheriffs, £400 voted for purchase of scientific instruments and apparatus, appropriation made for building roads and bridges, and provision made for assessment and collection of municipal rates

Feb. 20–April 19, Second session of fourth Parliament of Lower Canada. £1,000 voted for inland navigation between Montreal and Lake St. Francis

May 20, Simon Fraser with James Stuart crossed from headwaters of the Parsnip to the south fork of the Fraser River which he descended to the Nechaco to mouth June 10, July 26 at lake which he named after James Stuart and where he established Fort St. James. Visited Lake Fraser and built Fort Fraser. Wintered at Stuart Lake

June 10, Thompson left Reed Lake, arrived at Cumberland House June 14, and journeyed from there to Fort William on Lake Superior, and thence to Rocky Mountain House Oct. 29, where he wintered trading and exploring between the Peace and Saskatchewan rivers

June, First raft of logs went down the Ottawa River beginning the lumber trade

Aug. 12, Bernard Claudet Panet appointed Bishop of Sardes and coadjutor to the Bishop of Quebec (Roman Catholic)

Aug. 25, Francis Gore, Lieutenant Governor, of Upper Canada

Sept. 6, 85,000 acres ceded by the Mississagas, parts of Halton and Peel counties

Oct. 26, Death of John Graves Simcoe, former Lieutenant Governor of Upper Canada

Nov. 22, First issue of *Le Canadien* by Panet and Pierre Bedard, French newspaper

Dec. 31, Treaty of London signed by Great Britain and the United States; not ratified by United States. *See also* United States

Population of Upper Canada 17,718, of Lower Canada 250,000, of Nova Scotia about 65,000, of New Brunswick 35,000, of Island of St. John (Prince Edward Island) 9,676

1807

Jan. 21–April 16, Third session of fourth Parliament of Lower Canada. Proposal to defray expenses of members living at a distance from Quebec defeated by 2 votes, Mr. Hart, a Jew, elected to the Assembly, not allowed to take his seat. Act passed for regulation of fisheries of Gaspé, and for regulation of provincial post houses

Feb. 2–March 10, Third session of fourth Parliament, of Upper Canada, schools for every district provided for

Feb. 4, Petition of York electorate against election of Judge Thorpe as member of Assembly of Upper Canada as illegal and unconstitutional

April 16, Quebec Benevolent Society incorporated by statute; proclaimed March 30, 1808

May 10, Thompson left Rocky Mountain House on the North Saskatchewan and followed the river to its source, discovered and crossed Howse Pass June 25 (*see also* 1800) and arrived at the Columbia River June 30 which he ascended to Windemere Lake reached July 18 where he built Fort Kootenay at junction of Columbia with Toby Creek July 29, the first trading post on the Columbia

May 28–Aug. 6, Fraser and Stuart left Fort George

which they had built at the confluence of the Nechaco and the Fraser, descended the Fraser River, and proceeding partly by land around the cascades reached the mouth of the Coquihalla at site of present Hope June 30, and July 2 within sight of the Pacific Ocean, but prevented by hostility of Indians from going farther. Aug. 6 at Stuart Lake on return journey

July 8, Judge Thorpe, leader of Opposition in Assembly of Upper Canada, suspended for having exceeded his duties as judge by his political activities

July, Harmon again at New Fort (Fort William) at mouth of Kaministiquia, wintered at Lake Nipigon

Oct. 24, Sir James Henry Craig, nominated Governor in Chief Aug. 29, took office, his rule in Lower Canada called by the French-Canadians the "reign of terror" because of his hostility to French and Catholics

Nov. 27, Death of Joseph Brant, Chief of the Six Nations

1808

Jan. 20–March 16, Fourth session of fourth Parliament of Upper Canada, 16 laws enacted, regulations governing the militia consolidated into one act, increase of electoral districts to 22 by redistribution act provided for better representation of commons

Jan. 29–April 14, Fourth session of fourth Parliament of Lower Canada. Bill to render judges ineligible to membership in Assembly passed but thrown out by Legislative Council. Permanent fund provided for improvement of navigation of the St. Lawrence River. Act providing for jails in Gaspé passed, reserved, and received royal assent Nov. 15, 1809, and was proclaimed April 12, 1810. Act regulated controverted trial of elections. Ezekiel Hart, a Jew, reëlected to Assembly from Three Rivers, expelled, because of his alleged inability to subscribe to oath of office

Feb. 20, Joseph Willcocks arrested on charge of contempt of Assembly of Upper Canada, because of alleged libel in newspaper which he owned

April 13, Sir George Prevost took office as Lieutenant Governor of Nova Scotia

April 20, Thompson descended the Columbia River reaching mouth of St. Mary's April 24 and the Tobacco River in Montana April 27, May 6 Thompson at Kootenay Falls and at Kootenay House June 5, descended the Saskatchewan to Rainy Lake Aug. 2, and back at Kootenay House Nov. 10

May 8, Alexander Henry, Jr. left the Red River district for the Saskatchewan, and wintered at Fort Vermillion on the North Saskatchewan

May 21, Proclamation dissolved Parliament of Upper Canada

Aug. 12, Harmon from Cumberland House started for the Athabaska district up the Churchill River, reaching Isle à la Crosse post Aug. 25 and Lake Athabaska Sept. 6, Fort Chipewyan Sept. 7. On Sept. 22 he entered the Peace River and by canoe proceeded to Fort Vermillion opposite entrance to Vermillion River, reaching Dunvegan Oct. 10 and wintered on left bank of Peace River about Lat. 56°, Long. 118° 40'

Sept. 30, Death of Peter Russell, former Lieutenant Governor of Upper Canada

Oct. 10, Death of Guy Carleton, Lord Dorchester, former Governor

Nov. 29, N. Francis Burton appointed Lieutenant Governor of Lower Canada. He held the office as a sinecure, remaining in England until 1822, held office until Jan. 27, 1832

1809

Feb. 2–March 9, First session of fifth Parliament of Upper Canada. Act provided for billeting of troops and the provincial militia on occasion, grant provided for bridge over Grand River, and grant for encouragement of destruction of wolves

March 30, Labrador Act reannexed Labrador to Newfoundland

April 10–May 15, First and only session of fifth Parliament of Lower Canada, 5 laws enacted. Assembly expelled P. A. de Bonne as a judge of the King's Bench. Dissolved by Governor Craig

April 17, Thompson left Kootenay House, crossed the Rocky Mountains to the Saskatchewan, reached Fort Augustus on site of present city of Edmonton June 24, at the Columbia River Aug. 13 on return journey, and descended the Kootenay Aug. 20, reached Lake Pend d'Oreille and built Fort Kullyspell Sept. 10 on east shore at site of present Hope, Idaho, and explored lake and river making surveys Sept. 27–Oct. 6, the Saleesh River Oct. 11–30, and Nov. 2 built Saleesh House at site of the present Woodlin on the Northern Pacific Railroad in Montana

Oct., Election for Assembly in Lower Canada

Oct. 9–Oct. 13, 1812, Isaac Brock, Administrator of Upper Canada

Nov. 2, Communion plate, gift of the King for the Cathedral (Metropolitan Church) at Quebec received

Nov. 4, John Molson in the steamer "Accomodation," first steamboat on the St. Lawrence, arrived at Quebec from Montreal, time of passage 66 hours, 30 of which the steamer at anchor, speed 5 miles an hour, fare $8

Halifax Fire Insurance Company in Nova Scotia established, the first insurance company recorded

1810

Jan. 29–Feb. 26, First session of sixth Parliament of Lower Canada. Bills for appointing a provincial agent to London to solicit passing of laws, and that judges of his Majesty's Bench should not sit in the Assembly not passed because of dissolution of the Assembly by the Governor

Feb. 1–March 12, Second session of fifth Parliament of Upper Canada. Acts provided for repair of roads, prevention of forgery, and counterfeiting of foreign bills and notes, duty laid on billiard tables for revenue. James Wilson and John Roblin expelled as preachers coming within specific disqualification under Constitutional Act

Feb. 23–March 6, March 8–14, and March 17–25, Thompson from Saleesh House made journeys to camp of the Saleesh Indians on Flat Head River 20 miles from its mouth

March 17, Soldiers headed by magistrate seized type and press of French journal Le Canadien and imprisoned M. Panet because of abuse of the administration; published again in 1830

March 19, M. Bédard, Blanchet, and Taschereau, members of Parliament, imprisoned on charge of sedition

April 19, Thompson left Saleesh House, arrived at Kullyspell House April 21, crossed Lake Pend 'Oreille April 24, and surveyed the Pend 'Oreille River to within 22 miles of its mouth, and returned to Kullyspell House May 1, leaving May 9 for the Kootenay River, at McGillivray Portage on Kootenay River June 6, descended the Columbia to Mountain Portage arriving June 16, crossed to the Saskatchewan and arrived at the Forks in the mountains June 19, July 4 at Cumberland House and July 22 at Rainy Lake House

Oct., Harmon left Dunvegan for Stuart Lake and Fraser's Lake where he remained until the spring of 1811 when he returned to Stuart's Lake making it his headquarters until May 1819

Dec. 12–March 21, 1811, First session of seventh Parliament of Lower Canada. Provision made against forging and counterfeiting foreign bills of exchange, and Act passed disqualifying judges of Court of King's Bench from sitting in the Assembly. Resolution of Dec. 24 protested against imprisonment of Pierre Bédard

1811

Jan. 10–11, Thompson crossed the mountains by the Athabaska Pass which he discovered and descended Wood River to the Columbia which he reached Jan. 18, returned to the Canoe River Jan. 26 to camp for the winter at the Big Bend

Feb. 1–March 13, Third session of fifth Parliament of Upper Canada. 9 laws enacted. Regulations as to arrest adopted, personal arrest extended to sum of 40 shillings

March 18, Governor Craig authorized Morier, the *chargé d'affaires* to inform the United States of hostility of Indians and efforts of the Government to quiet them

April 17, Thompson ascended the Columbia River, reaching McGillivray's Portage May 14 at head of Upper Columbia Lake, and descended the Kootenay, crossed to Saleesh House and to Spokane House 10 miles northwest of present Spokane, and to the Columbia River at Kettle Falls, and July 3 began descent of the Columbia and July 15 arrived at Fort Astoria. Finished survey of river on return trip

May, Petition of the North West Company for a charter

May 30, Meeting of Hudson Bay Company in London accepted proposal of Lord Selkirk, who had purchased a controlling interest, of purchase of land on Rupert River for colonists

June 12, Grant to Lord Selkirk of 116,000 square miles in present Province of Manitoba, and States of Minnesota and North Dakota in the United States, by the Hudson Bay Company

June 19, Sir James Craig sailed for England and died in Jan. 1812, Thomas Dunn, acting as Lieutenant Governor of Lower Canada and Administrator

July 26, Colonists led by Captain Miles Macdonell sailed from Scotland for Lord Selkirk's Red River land arriving at York Factory, Hudson Bay, Sept. 24 too late to travel to the river that season

Sept. 14, Sir George Prevost succeeded Thomas Dunn as Administrator

Oct. 21, Sir George Prevost commissioned Governor-in-Chief

1812

Feb. 3–March 6, Fourth session of fifth Parliament of Upper Canada. Special militia law provided for raising troops of volunteers or by ballot, and £5,000 voted for training militia. Act to prevent desertion of soldiers passed

Feb. 21–May 19, Second session of seventh Parliament of Lower Canada. £2,000 granted for defense of Province and £3,000 more in case of war with the United States. Provision made for enrollment of militia and regulation of militia. Act to secure liberty of subjects extended powers of courts as to writs of habeas corpus

March 13, Thompson left Saleesh House for Fort William, traveling east by Athabaska Pass, leaving Fort William Aug. 12 and arriving at Montreal Aug. 24, his last journey

April 9, General Isaac Brock, commissioned as Administrator, did not act

June 19, The United States proclaimed war against Great Britain, news received in Canada on the 24th through an agent of the North West Company

June 24, Second company of Lord Selkirk's colonists sailed, and arrived at Red River Oct. 27, led by Owen Keveney

June 30, Proclamation of the Lieutenant Governor of Upper Canada gave Americans 14 days to leave the Province. An embargo imposed on shipping in port

July 12, Invasion of Canada by Americans commanded by General Hull at Sandwich, village on the Detroit River. *See* United States

——, Bank of Kingston incorporated

July 16–Aug. 1, Third session of seventh Parliament of Lower Canada. Act to facilitate the circulation of army bills assented to issue payable in government bills of exchange on London to £250,000 to relieve financial situation

July 17, Mackinac taken by force from St. Joseph's Island commanded by Captain Roberts

July 22, General Brock issued counter proclamation to that of General Hull of the 13th addressed to Canadians

July 27–Aug. 5, First session of sixth Parliament of Upper Canada. Act provided for defense of Province. 5 laws enacted. Legislature prorogued

Aug. 7, General Brock held conference with the Indians and received promise of support from 60 Mohawk chiefs

Aug. 16, Surrender of Detroit by General Hull to General Brock. *See also* United States

Aug. 30, The Selkirk colonists reached Forks of the Red River after winter at York Factory; first Governor Captain Miles Macdonell who on Sept. 4 took formal possession of the District of Assiniboia

Oct. 13, General Isaac Brock killed in Battle of Queenston Heights, Sir Roger H. Sheaffe succeeding to command

Oct. 20–June 19, 1813, Roger Hale Sheaffe Administrator of Upper Canada

Oct. 27, Second party of Selkirk colonists led by Owen Keveney arrived at Red River

Dec. 29–Feb. 15, 1813, Fourth session of seventh Parliament of Lower Canada. Additional duties placed on sugar, tobacco, snuff, wines and brandy, and on licenses for billiard tables. Circulation of army bills increased to £500,000 and grant made for annual interest, and grant of £25,000 made for war with the United States. Duties of 2.5% laid on all merchandise imported except provisions, royal assent received June 2 and proclaimed Oct. 1, 1813

1813

Feb. 20–March 16, and May 12–June 14, Francis Baron de Rottenburg, Administrator of Lower Canada

Feb. 25–March 14, Second session of sixth Parliament of Upper Canada. Sale of liquor to the Indians prohibited. Army bills issued in Lower Canada legalized. Temporary prohibition of export of grain to avoid scarcity of food. Pensions granted to persons disabled in His Majesty's service and to widows and children of persons killed

June 14–Sept. 25, George Glasgow, Administrator of Lower Canada

June 19–Dec. 13, Francis, Baron de Rottenburg, Administrator of Upper Canada

June 22, 93 Selkirk colonists led by Archibald MacDonald reached Red River settlement by way of York Factory

Nov. 17, Regiments of sedentary militia temporarily disbanded as campaign against Montreal abandoned by American General Wilkinson on the 12th

Nov. 22, Proclamation declared limited martial law in Upper Canada

Dec. 10, Newark burned by American troops

Dec. 13–April 25, 1815, General Gordon Drummond Administrator of Upper Canada

Dec. 19, Death of James McGill. By his will he bequeathed £10,000 to college to be founded

Dec. 30–31, Raid on Black Rock and Buffalo in retaliation for Newark. *See* United States

Hamilton founded by George Hamilton

1814

Jan. 8, Proclamation of Governor Miles Macdonell of the Red River Colony imposed an embargo on provisions in order to keep a supply of food in the colony and prohibited fur trade without a license as against the hostile fur traders

Jan. 13–March 17, Fifth session of seventh Parliament of Lower Canada. Provisions of Army Bill Act extended to permit issue of £1,500,000 in currency. Impeachment of Chief Justice Jonathan Sewell of Quebec, and of Chief Justice James Monk of Montreal, chief charge being the publication on their own authority of rules and order of practice for their courts. Bill to have judges disqualified from membership in Legislative Council rejected by Council

Feb. 15–March 14, Third session of sixth Parliament of Upper Canada. The seats of Abraham Marcle and John Willcocks who had joined the American army declared vacant as "traitors." Act declared certain persons (from the United States) aliens and vested their estates in the Crown. Issue of government notes for 1 year authorized. Grant made for repair of roads and bridges. Additional duty imposed upon stills. Militia Bill passed. Government empowered for a limited time to secure and detain persons suspected of treason. Bill passed by Assembly to appoint a special agent to represent the Province in London thrown out by Legislative Council by refusal to pass money bill for expenses of agent

March 30, American attack on La Colle (Lacolle's mills) Lower Canada repulsed

May 22, Alexander Henry, Jr. and Donald McTavish of the North West Company drowned in the Columbia River

July 20, Eight Canadian traders hanged at Ancaster

Sept. 18, Gabriel Franchère who had sailed to the Columbia River from New York with the Astor expedition traveled overland from Astoria on the Pacific coast and by the Athabaska Pass reached Montreal

Dec. 21–Jan. 28, Court martial of Major General Procter for retreat and loss of fleet on Lake Erie in fall of 1813. *See* United States

Dec. 24, Treaty of Ghent signed between Great Britain and the United States, the provisions including return of captured territory, and boundary commissions to settle disputed boundaries between United States and Canada and ownership of islands in Passamaquoddy Bay

Dec. 31, Court martial assembled at Montreal to try General Pring for Plattsburg and Lake Champlain failure

Population of Lower Canada estimated as 335,000 and of Upper Canada as 95,000

1815

Jan. 10, Instructions of British Colonial Office prohibited the settlement of Canada from the United States causing great hardship in Upper Canada where land the only wealth

Jan. 21–March 25, First session of eighth Parliament of Lower Canada. £1,000 voted for salary of the Speaker, received royal assent Jan. 22, 1817. New duties placed on tea, strong spirits, and goods sold at auction. £8,600 granted to improve internal communications, £25,000 for the Lachine-Montreal Canal, and grant of £1,000 for encouragement of vaccine inoculation, and grant to Joseph Bouchette to publish geographical and topographical maps of Canada. Militia Act amended to provide for substitutes. £300 voted for a parliamentary library. Louis Joseph Papineau elected speaker

Feb. 1–March 14, Fourth session of sixth Parliament of Upper Canada. Pension Act providing for persons disabled in war, &c., amended, grants made for militia and for repair of roads and jails

March 1, Troops of Lower Canada disbanded

March 9, Treaty of Ghent of Dec. 24, 1814, proclaimed at Quebec

April 7–June 7, Letters (10) signed "Veritas" appeared in the *Montreal Herald* attacking the conduct of the war with the United States by Sir George Prevost

May 29, Order in Council declared the Province open to citizens of the United States for commerce

June 11, Duncan Cameron, trader of the North West Company led attack on the Selkirk Colony on the Red River

June 15, 140 Selkirk colonists left the Red River for Upper Canada, induced by grants of land and free transportation from the North West Company, arriving at Holland Landing Sept. 5

——, Captain Lock of the ship "Jaseur" warned American fishing vessels off Cape Sable not to come within 60 miles of the coast; action disavowed by the British Government

June 25, Alexander Macdonell and Cuthbert Grant of the North West Company attacked the fort at Selkirk settlement on the Red River and took Governor Miles Macdonell prisoner and forced settlers to leave

June 27, Red River colonists started for Hudson Bay post at Lake Winnipeg

July 3, Treaty of London between Great Britain and the United States as to commerce

July 25, Executive Council recommended dismissal of Stephen Sewell, Attorney General, because of connection alleged which he denied with letters published in the *Montreal Herald* signed "an Englishman," criticism of the Government, immediately acted upon by Sir John Sherbrooke

Sept. 21, Lieutenant Governor Gore returned to Upper Canada after absence of 4 years

Sept., Perth settled by 250 Scotch immigrants

Nov. 3, 100 new colonists led by Governor Robert Semple arrived at the Red River to reëstablish the settlement, Fort Douglas built

Nov., Lighting of the streets of Montreal begun with 22 lamps put up by private citizens

Nov. 16, Court of Appeals for Lower Canada constituted

Nov. 17, 250,000 acres, part of Simcoe County, ceded by the Chippewas

1816

Jan. 1, First through stage established between Montreal and Kingston by Barnabas Dickinson, trip made in 3 days

Jan. 8, Death of Sir George Prevost prevented his trial by court martial appointed

Jan. 26–Feb. 26, Second session of eighth Parliament of Lower Canada. In opening speech Governor Drummond announced that Imperial Government declined to interfere in matter of the 2 impeached judges. Only one measure passed to provide regulations for trial of election petitions. The Assembly dissolved because of resolutions respecting the impeached judges

Feb. 6–April 1, Fifth session of sixth Parliament of Upper Canada. Common schools established. Appropriation made for a parliamentary library, for cultivation of hemp, for support of civil service. Agreement with Lower Canada as to duties which was to expire May 1 renewed. Act afforded relief to persons possessing lands in Niagara district due to losses during the war. Counties of Prescott and Russell constituted a separate district under name of Ottawa, and District of Gore established out of Home and Niagara

Feb. 12, St. Johns, Newfoundland, nearly destroyed by fire, loss £100,000

March 17, Hudson Bay Company traders attacked and destroyed Fort Gibraltar, North West Company post at the Forks

March 25, Sir John C. Sherbrooke commissioned Governor in Chief, assumed office July 12

May 1, New Agreement of Upper and Lower Canada for $1/8$ of net produce of customs dues renewing agreements of Feb., 1795, and Jan., 1797

June 4, A company of soldier settlers followed by Lord Selkirk on the 16th left Montreal for the Red River

June 19, Battle of Seven Oaks in which Governor Semple and about 20 colonists killed by the Métis incited by traders of the North West Company led by Cuthbert Grant. Fort Douglas seized and the Red River settlers driven away in second exodus June 22

June 22, 150 French families returned to St. Pierre Island restored to France by treaties

Aug. 13, General order of Secretary of the Colonies placed control of Indian affairs under military commander of the North West Province

——, Lord Selkirk seized North West Company post on the Kaministiquia, Fort William, and arrested partners of the Company sending them prisoners to York, and seized incriminating papers

Sept. 7, The steamer "Frontenac" launched at Ernestown for service on Lake Ontario

Pictou Academy (Presbyterian) in Nova Scotia chartered (56 Geo. III, cap. 29)

1817

Jan. 10, Lord Selkirk's forces recaptured Fort Douglas on the Red River

Jan. 15–March 22, First session of ninth Parliament of Lower Canada. The Governor empowered to pay £20,000 to Upper Canada as share of duties as agreed upon by a commission. £55,000 granted to improve internal communications, £20,000 granted for purchase of seed grain for relief of poor as a loan. Justice Louis Charles Foucher impeached Jan. 25 but no action taken by the Government. Salary of £1,000 voted to each of the Speakers of the 2 Houses. Bill disqualifying judges of King's Bench from sitting in the Legislative Council again passed and again thrown out by Council

Jan., First stage service established by Samuel Purdy between Kingston and York (Toronto), fare $18

Feb. 4–April 7, First session of seventh Parliament of Upper Canada. Market established at Niagara. Eleven resolutions passed as to impolicy of checking immigration from the United States, unsatisfactory land policy, inefficiency of post office and other matters

April 28–29, Exchange of Notes between Great Britain and the United States as to naval forces and war vessels on the Great Lakes. *See also* United States

April, The steamer "Ontario" the first on Lake Ontario, made round trip between Lewiston and Ogdensburg in 10 days

May 19, Articles of association of the Bank of Montreal adopted, published in the *Montreal Herald* 10 days later

May, New Agreement between Upper and Lower Canada by which Upper Canada granted $1/5$ of the net proceeds of the customs dues

——, Commission sent to investigate Red River disturbances made impartial statement of events and recommended withdrawal of charges against Lord Selkirk

June 5, The steamboat "Frontenac" launched Sept. 7, 1815, made trip from Kingston to York on Lake Ontario

June 11–Aug. 13, 1818, Samuel Smith, Administrator of Upper Canada

July 4, Edmund Burke appointed titular Bishop of Sion and first Vicar-Apostolic of Nova Scotia

July 17, Lachine Canal begun, first sod removed

July 18, Lord Selkirk in the name of George III made first treaty with the Indians of the North West

Sept. 9, Lord Selkirk left Red River settlement for Montreal

Oct. 30, Robert Gourlay who had arrived in Upper Canada from England in June published his first address to resident land owners in the *Upper Canada Gazette*

Nov. 3, Bank of Montreal opened; royal sanction to incorporation May 18, 1822

Nov. 24, Award of commissioners under Article 4 of the Treaty of Ghent gave Moose, Dudley, and Frederick Islands to the United States and all others in Passamaquoddy Bay to Great Britain, and also Grand Menan in Bay of Fundy

1818

Jan. 7–April 1, Second session of ninth Parliament of

Lower Canada. Acts established watch and night lights in cities of Quebec and Montreal, and a House of Industry in Montreal. £2,000 granted for promotion of agriculture. House passed resolution that in the next session the estimates should be presented to it under detailed heads, to place the question of supplies on more constitutional basis

Jan. 10, Lord Selkirk reached York and became involved in lawsuits with the North West Company in which he was unable to obtain justice

Jan. 30, Monseigneur Plessis, Roman Catholic Bishop of Quebec, became member of the Legislative Council by mandamus

Feb. 5 and 12, Robert Gourlay dissatisfied at not receiving grant of land published addresses attacking the land system

Feb. 5–April 1, Second session of seventh Parliament of Upper Canada. Duties laid on selling liquor wholesale, on licenses to auctioneers and on goods sold at auction. Eligibility of persons to be returned to the Assembly defined and amendments to law enacted. The Assembly (March 27) insisted on its right to initiate money bills. Act provided for registration of wills, deeds, &c. Report on grievances by committee of Assembly

April 1, Canal between Chambly and St. John incorporated

April 13, Gourlay called convention to meet at Niagara to consider the condition of the country

May 3, Captain John Ross and Lieutenant W. E. Parry sailed from Lerwick in search of North West Passage. Reached farthest north at 76° 54′ northwest of Carey Island. Sailed 50 miles up Lancaster Sound but concluded it was a bay

May 8, Charles, Duke of Richmond, commissioned Governor in Chief to succeed Sir John Sherbrooke, took oath of office July 30

May 19, Father Norbert Provencher and Father Dumoulin left Montreal to establish mission of St. Boniface on the Red River, reached Fort Douglas July 16

May 27, Halifax and St. John declared free ports

June 13, Richard Talbot with company of nearly 200 Irish immigrants sailed for Canada arriving at Quebec July 27, and proceeded to York, leaving there Sept. 11 to settle in London townships

July 9, Articles of association signed founded Bank of Quebec with capital of £75,000

July 20, Sir C. Hamilton, first resident Governor of Newfoundland, arrived and took up residence at Fort Townsend

Aug. 13, Sir Peregrine Maitland commissioned Lieutenant Governor of Upper Canada

Aug. 15 and 30, Robert Gourlay tried at Kingston and at Brockville for sedition was acquitted

Aug. 25, Second bank opened in Montreal, the Bank of Canada, but failed to obtain charter

Sept. 17, Lord Selkirk sold Baldoon tract to John McNab, Hudson Bay trader

Oct. 8, The Royal Institution for the progress of education formally established

Oct. 12–Nov. 27, Third session of seventh Parliament of Upper Canada. Assemblies held for certain "seditious" purposes declared unlawful. Marriage Act amended. £2,000 granted for survey of the St. Lawrence River

Oct. 17, The Chippewas ceded 1,592,000 acres, parts of Dufferin, Grey, and Simcoe counties, and Oct. 28

the Mississagas 648,000 acres, parts of Peel, Halton, Wellington, and Dufferin counties

Oct. 20, Convention between the United States and Great Britain as to the fisheries and boundaries, the country west of the Rocky Mountains to be occupied by the 2 countries jointly for 10 years. *See also* United States

Nov. 5, The Chippewas surrendered 1,951,000 acres, parts of Northumberland, Durham, Ontario, Haliburton, and Hastings counties and the District of Muskoka

Dec. 15, Central Agricultural Society of Nova Scotia organized, John Young, author of "Letters of Agricola," the Secretary

Dec. 21, Robert Gourlay arrested on charge of sedition under Act of Upper Canada of 1804, and ordered to leave the Province by Jan. 1

Welland Canal begun by inhabitants of the Niagara District

1819

Jan. 4–Aug. 20, 1820, Robert Gourlay a prisoner in jail at Niagara, after refusal to leave Jan. 1 as ordered

Jan. 12–April 24, Third session of ninth Parliament of Lower Canada. Supply Bill voted as annual grant by office and salary rejected by Legislative Council as unconstitutional. Provision made for a canal from Montreal to Lachine, weights and rates of gold and silver coins of France regulated, grant made for public library in Montreal

April 21, Proclamation of incorporation of Bank of Upper Canada

May 17, Presbyterians of Niagara presented petition to the Lieutenant Governor of Upper Canada asking for funds from the clergy reserves, their church having been burned by the Americans in the war

June 7–July 12, Fourth session of seventh Parliament of Upper Canada. Act gave effect and validity to deeds executed by married women. Bank of Kingston incorporated. Additional duty laid on stills. All wild lands held in fee were taxed one penny in the pound. Governor Maitland announced that he was authorized to grant land to militia for service in war

July 1, Customs Agreement between Upper and Lower Canada expired

July 12, Bank of Kingston incorporated, but charter forfeited because not used

Aug. 28, Death of Charles Lennox, Duke of Richmond, Governor in Chief

Sept. 9–June, 1822, Voyage of Captain John Franklin (later Sir John), Dr. John Richardson, George Back, and Robert Hood from York Factory to the Coppermine River, reached the Cumberland House on the Saskatchewan from the Red River, Oct. 22, where they wintered

Sept. 19, Charter of the Quebec Friendly Society received royal assent

Oct. 13, The Earl of Dalhousie commissioned Administrator of Lower Canada, delegated authority to Sir Peregrine Maitland

Nov. 15, Opinion of Law Officers of the Crown in England given that the Church of Scotland in Canada entitled to share in the clergy reserves

Halifax Fire Insurance Company founded as the Nova Scotia Fire Association in 1809 incorporated (N.S. cap. 17)

Large immigration of Irish to Canada on account of

crop failure in Ireland and the decline in manufacture of linen due to introduction of machinery in England

1820

Jan. 18, The Franklin expedition left Cumberland House on the Saskatchewan and arrived at Chippewyan March 26 after a journey on foot of 856 miles, and on Aug. 2 from north side of Great Slave Lake ascended the Yellow Knife River and Aug. 20 reached Winter Lake where winter quarters established

Jan. 21, Father Joseph Norbert Provencher appointed Bishop of Juliopolis and assigned to the Red River District as Vicar Apostolic in the North West Territories

Feb. 21–March 7, Fifth session of seventh Parliament of Upper Canada. Members of Assembly increased. Government authorized to appoint inspectors of flour, and pot and pearl ashes. Common School Act of 1816 renewed

Feb. 28, The Mississagas surrendered 2,000 acres, part of present Peel County

March 8–June 30, Lieut. Colonel Samuel Smith, Administrator, of Upper Canada

March 25, Bank of New Brunswick, St. John, incorporated, first in New Brunswick

April 8, Death of Lord Selkirk (49), at Pau in the Pyrenees

April 11–April 24, First session of tenth Parliament of Lower Canada dissolved on official news of the death of George III

April 12, The Earl of Dalhousie commissioned Governor in Chief, assumed office June 19

July 20, The Mohawks of the Bay of Quinte ceded 33,280 acres, the town of Tyendinaga

Aug. 20, Coronation of George IV celebrated in Canada 11 months before the ceremony in London of July 10, 1821

Aug. 21, Robert Gourlay sentenced to banishment from Canada

Oct. 9, Proclamation made necessary regulations for reannexation of Cape Breton Island to Nova Scotia

Nov. 12 and 18, Presbyterians of Quebec and Montreal petitioned for share of the clergy reserves

Dec. 14–March 17, 1821, First session of eleventh Parliament of Lower Canada. Agent for the Province in London again considered but rejected by the Legislative Council. Supply Bill rejected by Council because the supply was not made permanent and did not cover the deficiency. An address presented protesting against position of the Lieutenant Governor drawing salary of £1,500 and resident in England having never visited Canada, and other similar absentee officers drawing salaries. Grant of £2,500 made for encouragement of agriculture and a grant for the Montreal-Lachine Canal

Dec. 14, Bank of Montreal incorporated

Rev. John West, chaplain to Hudson Bay Company, went to the North West as first Church of England missionary

1821

Jan. 31–Feb. 14, First session of eighth Parliament of Upper Canada. Acts provided for better division of the Province into counties and districts, for preservation of deer and of salmon, small notes and inland bills of exchange made legal, currency made uniform, acts for punishment of persons illegally solemnizing

marriage, and respecting conveyance of real estate by married women. Provided that no tithes or ecclesiastical rates should ever be levied in Upper Canada, proclaimed Feb. 20, 1823

March 26, The North West Company merged with the Hudson Bay Company under name of the latter

March 31, The Royal Institution for the Advancement of Learning established in 1818 obtained charter in order to establish McGill University

April 21, Bank of Upper Canada incorporated in York, royal assent proclaimed. Had been established at Kingston in 1818

May 8–Oct. 10, 1823, Voyage of Captain Parry to Hudson Bay, and Aug. 23 through the Fox Channel, wintered on Melville Peninsula, and second winter at Igloo in 69° 20' N. Lat. and discovered Fury and Hecla Strait July, 1822

June 6, Corner stone of Montreal General Hospital laid

June, The Franklin expedition descended the Coppermine River to Coronation Gulf and traced the Arctic coast eastward to point on Kent Peninsula which he named Cape Turnagain in 109° 25' W. Obliged to return to Fort Enterprise at Winter Lake to escape starvation

July 2, Imperial Act regulated fur trade in the West and established civil and criminal jurisdiction, Hudson Bay Territory included

July 7, The Province of Lower Canada took over the Montreal-Lachine Canal from private company, and construction begun at Lachine on the 17th

Sept. 4, Ukase of Alexander I of Russia granted to Russian American Company exclusive rights of commerce and fishing on west coast of America above the 51st degree N. Lat. claiming sole jurisdiction over the Bering Sea to distance of 100 Italian miles from the coast, officially communicated to the British Government Nov. 12

Nov. 21–Jan. 17, 1822, Second session of eighth Parliament of Upper Canada

Nov. 24, Disallowance of the election of Barnabas Bidwell, citizen of the United States, to the Assembly as an alien

Dec. 5, Terms of the Hudson Bay Company renewed for 21 years and grant of exclusive trade to the Company

Dec. 11–Feb. 18, Second session of eleventh Parliament of Lower Canada. Resolutions of Assembly declared that the expenses of the Government should be voted annually instead of permanent provision being made, and refusal to renew laws under which the revenue raised. Refused to grant larger proportion of customs duties to Upper Canada as requested. 13 laws passed. Act provided for better inspection of flour

Dalhousie College, Halifax, Nova Scotia, chartered (1 and 2 Geo. 4, cap. 39) founded in 1820 by Lord Dalhousie

1822

Feb., First Presbyterian Church opened in York (Toronto)

Feb. 25, Papineau and Neilson arrived in London and asked audience of Lord Bathhurst, Colonial Secretary, to submit protest of Canadian people against proposed legislative union of the 2 Canadas without consultation of wishes of either Province, carrying petition against Bill

April 13, Commission on northeast boundary of the United States with Canada as to northwest angle of Nova Scotia held final session in New York and filed dissenting reports and opinions

May 1, Montreal General Hospital opened for patients

June 1, Alexander Stewart and Robert Reid left Quebec and in Nov. began settlement of Douro township

June 18, Award of Boundary Commission under Article 6 of the Treaty of Ghent of boundary line through the St. Lawrence and the Great Lakes

July 5, Lieutenant Governor Nathaniel Francis Burton of Lower Canada arrived from England, assumed office

July 8, 580,000 acres ceded by the Chippewas, parts of Lambton, Middlesex, and Kent counties

July 12, Captain Parry sailed north discovering Fury and Hecla Strait

July 22, Proclamation of royal assent of May 18 to incorporation of the Bank of Montreal

July 29, Pioneer saw mill opened in New Brunswick at St. John by Otty and Crookshank Company

Aug. 5, Imperial Canada Trade Act regulated commercial and financial relations between Upper and Lower Canada. The Parliament of Lower Canada forbidden to impose new duties on imported goods without consent of Upper Canada or the King, and duties of the last Agreement of apportionment of share of duties of one-fifth which Lower Canada had refused to reënact made permanent, and provision made for settlement by arbitration of the proportion to go to respective provinces in case of future dispute. Provision made for commutation of tenor of land held *en seigneurie*

Sept. 3, Failure of Bank of Upper Canada at Kingston

Oct. 7, Public meeting of Anti-Unionists at Quebec, Louis Guy presiding

Oct. 14, Public meeting of Anti-Unionists at Montreal, calling themselves constitutional committees, John Richardson, presiding

Nov. 21–Jan. 17, Second session of eighth Parliament of Upper Canada. Regulations as to practice of King's Bench consolidated into one law, and militia law and laws as to district courts amended. Grant for purchase and erection of machinery to prepare hemp for exportation. Commission to England appointed to present claim of Upper Canada to larger share of customs duties from Lower Canada. Marshall Spring Bidwell, citizen of the United States, expelled as alien from the Assembly

Nov. 28, The Mississagas ceded 2,748,000 acres, parts of Hastings, Addington, Frontenac, Lanark, Carleton, and Renfrew counties

Nov. 30, Proclamation of royal assent of Sept. 16 to incorporation of "Quebec Bank," and Bank of Canada at Montreal

John M. McLeod in service of Hudson Bay Company crossed the Rocky Mountains and descended the Fraser River to Strait of Georgia on the Pacific

1823

Jan. 10–March 22, Third session of eleventh Parliament of Lower Canada. District of St. Francis created and provincial judge appointed. Further regulation of licenses for public houses and sale of liquor and wines. Act established provincial fairs, grant of £2,100 to promote agriculture made and for canal from St. John to Basin of Chambly

Jan. 15–March 19, Third session of eighth Parliament

of Upper Canada. Marshall Spring Bidwell, an American citizen, elected to Assembly; not allowed to take seat. 38 laws enacted. Construction of Burlington Bay Canal authorized

Aug. 5, Expedition of Majors Long and Keating raised American flag at Pembina

Aug. 20, J. C. Beltramé with Major Long at Turtle Lake. *See also* United States, July 2

Nov. 5, Archibald McNab granted township in Renfrew County which he named McNab and settled with immigrants from his home in Scotland

Nov. 11–Jan. 19, 1824, Fourth session of eighth Parliament of Upper Canada. Laws as to election of members of Assembly consolidated into one law, trial of election petitions committed to special committee of eleven, £150 a year granted for common schools and Sunday schools, and Common School Act of 1820 made permanent. Bill passed declared marriages performed by Methodist ministers legal, but thrown out by Legislative Council. Welland Canal Company incorporated. M. S. Bidwell again expelled

Nov. 23, John Caldwell, Receiver General of Lower Canada, suspended from office for misappropriation of funds, defalcation of about £96,000. He held office without bonds and accounts not subject to provincial audit

Nov. 25–March 9, 1824, Fourth session of eleventh Parliament of Lower Canada. An elementary education endowment established, law for encouragement of useful arts enacted first patent law. Repeal of laws as to capital punishment for theft amounting to 5 shillings from warehouse, shop, or stable, and 40 shillings from dwelling house or wharf or river. Supply Bill not passed, Assembly claiming right to approve entire revenue of Province including that raised by imperial statutes for administration

Dec. 26, Chamber of Commerce established at St. Johns, Newfoundland

Library established at St. Johns, Newfoundland

1824

Jan. 6, Literary and Historical Society of Quebec founded

Jan. 19, Welland Canal Company for canal between Lakes Erie and Ontario incorporated; promoted by W. H. Merritt

April 17, Boundary Treaty between the United States and Russia fixed line of 54° 40′ as boundary of settlements on west coast of North America

May 18, William Lyon Mackenzie, leader of Reform Party, began publication of the *Colonial Advocate* which attacked the privileged class, who held office and political control in Upper Canada, called the "family compact," first published at Queenston

May 19–Oct. 12, 1825, Voyage of Captain Parry, entered Lancaster Sound Sept. 10, and wintered at Port Bowen on Prince Regent Inlet, prevented by storm and ice from further progress

June 7, Sir Francis N. Burton, Administrator, to Sept. 16, 1825, during absence of Dalhousie who sailed June 6

June 8, First patent issued to Noah Cushing of Quebec for a washing machine

Aug., John Galt proposed formation of Canada Land Company for colonization of the Huron grant

Aug. 25, First Conference of the Methodist Church in Canada

Sept. 20, School opened in Newfoundland by English Society for Educating the Poor of Newfoundland

Oct. 28, Lectures begun at Montreal Medical Institute

Nov. 30, Ground broken for Welland Canal to connect Lakes Ontario and Erie

Dec. 30, Fire destroyed parliament building of Upper Canada

First tow boat, the "Hercules" brought the ship "Margaret" of Liverpool from Quebec to Montreal. Waiting for favorable tides and winds often had delayed ships for weeks

John McLoughlin, appointed in 1823 to charge of the Columbia District of the Hudson Bay Company arrived at Fort Astoria on the Pacific coast in the spring of 1824

John Finlay of the Hudson Bay Company crossed the Rocky Mountains by the Peace River Pass and explored river which bears his name to its source in Thutage Lake

Captain G. F. Lyon made voyage through Hudson Bay to Roe's Welcome in search of North West Passage

First circulating library in Halifax

1825

Jan. 8–March 22, First session of twelfth Parliament of Lower Canada. Resolutions passed disqualifying judges from sitting in either legislative or executive councils. Supply Bill for civil list limited expenses to 1 year without mention of any class of revenue, reduced all salaries 25% naming each specifically, rejected by Legislative Council. Request of Upper Canada for imposition of additional duties on account of suffering the greatest losses in the war with the United States refused. Act for enumeration of census passed

Jan. 13–April 13, First session of ninth Parliament of Upper Canada. 7 laws enacted. Provision made for fixing price of bread. Reform Party in majority, Dr. John Rolf, M. S. Bidwell, W. W. Baldwin, W. L. Mackenzie, members of Assembly

Feb. 28, Treaty between Russia and Great Britain signed by which Russia renounced extravagant claims to jurisdiction on the North West Pacific coast, and the boundaries of Alaska defined

May, 400 families from Ireland induced to settle in Peterborough County by Peter Robinson sailed from Cork for Canada

May 27, Settlers under McNab grant of Nov. 5, 1823, arrived from Scotland and proceeded to McNab township in Renfrew County

June 18, Death of Bishop Jacob Mountain, Anglican Bishop of Quebec, succeeded by Bishop Charles James Stewart

June 22, Imperial Canada Trade and Tenures Act provided for extinction of feudal and seigniorial rights

June 27, Canada Land Company incorporated in Upper Canada on advice of John Galt under which great tract of land on Lake Huron opened to settlement

July 5, Imperial Acts repealed certain duties of customs, regulated the trade of British North America and the West Indies, and encouraged British shipping and navigation

July 9, Fort Douglas on the Red River sold to Robert Logan for £400

July 12, Captain Parry continued along west coast of Prince Regent Inlet

Aug., First sale in Montreal of tea brought directly to Canada from East Indian ports helped to check smuggling from the United States

Sept. 3, Halifax Banking Company (Collins Bank) founded by Enos Collins, Samuel Cunard, and 5 other shareholders

Oct. 7, The "Miramichi fire" on the banks of that river in New Brunswick in which several hundred persons perished and several hundred square miles burned

Oct. 8, Captain Sir Thomas Cochrane, first civil Governor of Newfoundland

Nov. 7–Jan. 30, 1826, Second session of ninth Parliament of Upper Canada. 31 laws enacted. Desjardin Canal Company incorporated to connect Burlington Bay with Lake Ontario. Act to encourage useful arts regulated patents for inventors. Bounty of £125 authorized to any paper mill established. Tax on dogs imposed in towns regulated by police. Act modified capital punishment by reducing the number of capital offenses. Bill passed for repeal of sedition law, under which Robert Gourlay imprisoned, thrown out by Legislative Council

Nov. 10, McGill University received charter

Dec. 4, Bishop Panet (Roman Catholic) made Archbishop

Population of Lower Canada 479,288, and of Upper Canada 157,923

1826

Jan. 1, Captain Matthews, member of Assembly of Upper Canada, called for hats off for American music "Yankee Doodle" as for the national anthem, and for this sent to England for trial in spite of protest of the Assembly

Jan. 2, Supreme Court of Newfoundland constituted by royal charter opened by the Governor

Jan. 21–March 29, Second session of twelfth Parliament of Lower Canada. Act enabled courts to abstain from pronouncement of death sentence in certain felonies. Supply Bill again voted by items as an annual grant again rejected by Legislative Council. Assembly adopted resolution that to the legislature alone appertained right to distribute money raised by levy in the Colony

Jan. 30, Desjardin Canal Company chartered connecting Burlington Bay with Lake Ontario

Feb. 4, First issue of La Minerva, Montreal

Feb. 14, Alexander Macdonell appointed Bishop of Kingston

March 29, Quebec Fire Assurance Company incorporated

April 14, Proclamation of Governor Dalhousie made regulations for voluntary commutation of lands held under seigneurial tenure

May 26, Imperial Act granted that persons naturalized in Upper Canada might vote for and become members of Assembly

June 1, Shubenacadie Canal chartered by Nova Scotia statute and work begun on canal in July

June 8, Band of younger members of the "family compact" wrecked printing office of Mackenzie's Colonial Advocate at York

June 22–Sept. 21, Journey of Franklin from Great Bear Lake, where he had wintered, to the Arctic by the Bear River and descent of the Mackenzie, traced coast for 374 miles west. Richardson explored the shore between the mouths of the Mackenzie and Coppermine and sighted land to the west named by him Wollaston Land, the dividing channel being called Union and Dolphin Strait. Franklin turned back at Return Reef in 70° 11′ N. Lat. and 145° 50′ W. Long.

June 24, The De Meurons and Swiss settlers left for Canada

July 1, Burlington Bay Canal in Upper Canada opened by the Lieutenant Governor

Sept. 21, Rideau Canal, below the Chaudière Falls to Kingston, on Lake Ontario, begun, expense of construction borne by Imperial Government. Founding of Bytown (Ottawa) by Colonel John By, builder of the canal

Dec. 5–Feb. 17, 1827, Third session of ninth Parliament of Upper Canada. Laws of practice of medicine regulated, law enacted for relief of insolvent debtors, and appointment of guardians

London, Ontario, founded by Peter McGregor

1827

Jan. 23–March 7, Third session of twelfth Parliament of Lower Canada. Act confirmed that of 1795 establishing registration of births, deaths, and marriages, and declared marriages by ministers of the Church of Scotland legal

March 15, King's College, Toronto, chartered, issued March 22 and registered in Upper Canada Nov. 22

April 23, John Galt arrived at York and April 28 founded the town of Guelph named in honor of the reigning dynasty

May 18, Proceedings against William Forsythe, tavern keeper, at Niagara, the fence about his property removed by the sheriff by order of the Lieutenant Governor; his later suit against the Government failed

July 2, Imperial Act amended customs, and Ac authorized sale of part of the clergy reserves in Upper and Lower Canada

July 5, Governor Dalhousie issued general order calling for meetings of the militia in Lower Canada in view of refusal of Assembly to renew militia act

July 10, Chippewas ceded 2,200,000 acres, parts of Lambton, Middlesex, Oxford, Perth, Wellington, Waterloo, and Hudson counties

July 30, Work of clearing the ground for Fort Langley at the mouth of the Fraser River begun

Aug. 6, Convention of Oct. 20, 1818 between Great Britain and the United States as to the Oregon Territory indefinitely renewed, and also Treaty of Commerce of July 3, 1815

Aug. 16, First stone of lock at Ottawa of Rideau Canal laid by Captain, afterwards Sir John, Franklin, Arctic explorer

Sept. 29, Judge John W. Willis arrived from England

——, Treaty of London signed between Great Britain and the United States, for arbitration of the northeast boundary of the United States (northwest angle of Nova Scotia)

Nov. 20–22, First session of thirteenth Parliament of Lower Canada. Lord Dalhousie disapproved the reëlection of Louis Joseph Papineau as Speaker, and asked for election of another Speaker. Resolutions of Assembly declared that Mr. Papineau had been Speaker in 6 Parliaments, had been elected, and "ought to be and was the Speaker." Parliament prorogued and Lord Dalhousie condemned assumption of executive authority by legislative branch as to Supply Bill

Population of Lower Canada 471,875, and of Upper Canada 177,174

1828

Jan. 10, King's College received a land endowment by royal charter

Jan. 15–March 25, Fourth session of ninth Parliament of Upper Canada. Act passed conferred British citizenship rights on certain inhabitants and on those resident since 1820 and after 7 years for others, the assent of the King given May 7. Alien Act amended to close proceedings under Act. Act for relief of religious societies allowed Presbyterians, Lutherans, Calvinists, Congregationalists, and Quakers to hold 5 acres of land for church or burial ground

March 18, Royal charter of King's College (later University of Toronto)

May 2, Committee to inquire into the government of Canada appointed by British House of Commons; report presented July 22

June 9, First public temperance meeting in Canada held at Montreal

June 20, Judge Willis of Upper Canada removed from office by Sir Peregrine Maitland for criticism of the Attorney General

July 12, Report of select committee of the British House of Commons recommended recognition of claim of the Church of Scotland to proceeds of sale of the "clergy reserves"

July 15, Charter of Canada (Land) Company amended by imperial statute

July 22, Report of Committee of Imperial House of Commons declared that legal right of appropriation of revenue arising from Imperial Act of 1774 was vested in the Crown, but recommended placing entire revenue collected in Province under control of Assembly

July 28, Governor Simpson started from York Factory for Fort Vancouver on the Columbia River, and by the Peace River and by portage to the Fraser reaching Fort Langley at its mouth in 3 months

Aug. 23, Sir John Colborne appointed Lieutenant Governor of Upper Canada

Sept. 8, Sir James Kempt, succeeded Lord Dalhousie as Administrator, at Quebec

Oct. 2, The Methodist Church in Upper Canada in conference at Ernestown adopted resolutions separating from the Church in the United States

Oct. 25, Francis Collins on trial for libel of the Attorney General in Upper Canada condemned to imprisonment for 1 year and payment of exorbitant fine

Nov. 4, Sir John Colborne assumed office as Lieutenant Governor of Upper Canada

Nov. 21–March 14, 1829, Second session of thirteenth Parliament of Lower Canada. Papineau elected as Speaker and his election confirmed by Sir James Kempt. Act of representation in the Assembly created 44 counties, increasing members from 50 to 84. Robert Christie expelled from the House on charge that he had obtained the dismissal of some justices of the peace by partisan support of the Governor General. Act extended benefit of trial by jury. Supply bills for 1828 and 1829 passed, the budget voted after the model of 1825, that of 1829 passed in Legislative Council by casting vote of Speaker, afterwards decided as contrary to law. The request of the Governor for a permanent civil list set aside. 16 resolutions as to grievances dated Dec. 6 adopted, asked for control of revenue

1829

Jan. 8–March 20, First session of tenth Parliament of Upper Canada. Act restored to ordinary courts the duty of dealing with sedition and seditious practices repealing statute of 1804 under which Robert Gourlay prosecuted, the admission of evidence of Quakers, Tunkers, and Moravians in criminal cases provided for. Resolution passed claiming control of funds. An address to the King asked for royal clemency for Francis Collins, denied by the Lieutenant Governor, which was granted. 21 Bills rejected by the Legislative Council

Jan. 29, McGill College, Montreal, opened, Archbishop Mountain, president

Feb. 10, King's College (New Brunswick College) at Fredericton, New Brunswick, incorporated by royal charter

March 14, Grant made by Parliament of Lower Canada to Pierre Chasseur for collection of objects illustrating the natural history of Canada to be placed on public exhibition

May 23–Oct., 1833, Voyage of Captain John Ross from England, passed Lancaster Sound Aug. 10 and to south to mouth of and through Prince Regent Inlet, traced north Somerset to southern extremity; wintered at Felix Harbor

June 28, Montreal Medical Institute became the Medical Faculty of McGill University

Oct. 5, Proclamation of royal assent of Aug. 17 to Act redistributing and increasing seats in Assembly of Lower Canada of March 14, 1829

Nov. 21, First number of the *Christian Guardian* published by Egerton Ryerson in interests of Methodists in religion and politics

Nov. 30, The first Welland Canal connecting Lake Erie and Lake Ontario opened. The 2 schooners "Anne and Jane," and "R. H. Boughton" started from Port Dalhousie cutting through ice 3 inches thick in some places and reached Buffalo Dec. 2

Horton Academy, Wolfville, Nova Scotia, chartered, established by Baptists

1830

Jan. 1, Grand Lodge of Orange Order for British North America instituted at Brockville, Upper Canada, beginning Orange movement

Jan. 4, Upper Canada College at York opened

Jan. 8–March 6, Second session of tenth Parliament of Upper Canada. Act provided for remuneration of war losses incurred during war with the United States, better regulation of currency provided for, law for encouragement of agricultural societies, loan for Welland Canal. 27 bills rejected by Legislative Council, including Act to make marriages by Methodists and certain others valid

Jan. 22–March 26, Third session of thirteenth Parliament of Lower Canada. Acts incorporated the Quebec Exchange, provided for erection of Marine Hospital and Custom House at Quebec, for stone wharves at Montreal, and provided for lighthouses and courthouses. Militia Bill passed superseded the ordinances of Lord Dalhousie. Mr. Christie again expelled from the Assembly. Death of George IV dissolved this Parliament

March 6, Grantham Academy chartered

April, Town of Brantford founded in Ontario

June 26, Death of George IV

July 16, Constitutional Amendment to Act for government of Province of Quebec provided that persons naturalized might sit in Assembly and Legislative Council

Sept. 2, Keel of the "Royal William" laid at Cape Cove

Oct. 20, Baron Aylmer succeeded Sir James Kempt as Administrator, and was appointed Governor of the 2 Canadas Nov. 24

Dec. 10, At meeting presided over by Robert Baldwin petition signed by more than 10,000 settlers of Ontario asked that proceeds of sale of the clergy reserves be applied for purposes of general education and internal improvement

1831

Jan. 7–March 16, First session of eleventh Parliament of Upper Canada. 27 laws enacted. Royal assent given to Marriage Act March 2 which made valid marriages performed by dissenting ministers including Methodists and Moravians

Jan. 20, Award of the King of the Netherlands for northeast boundary of the United States with Canada (the northwest angle of Nova Scotia). The United States refused to accept, and Dec. 28, 1835, British withdrew acceptance of award

Jan. 23–March 31, First session of fourteenth Parliament of Lower Canada. Papineau again elected Speaker. Act declared persons of Jewish religion entitled to all rights and privileges of other subjects, royal assent given April 12, 1832 and proclaimed June 5. Acts granted relief to Presbyterians not of the Church of Scotland, grant made for encouragement of education, for encouragement of useful arts and regulation of patents for inventors. Act conferred civil and political rights of natural born British subjects on certain residents, proclaimed June 5, 1832. Mr. Christie again expelled. Attorney General James Stuart impeached for alleged impropriety in administration of office. Resolutions of grievance reported. The Assembly again refused to grant permanent civil list

Feb. 4, Baron Aylmer assumed office as Governor in Chief

March 28, Attorney General James Stuart suspended by the Governor for engaging as private counsel for the Hudson Bay Company in case of William Lamson against the Company for destruction of his property

March 31, Quebec and Montreal incorporated as cities by statutes which received royal assent April 12, 1832 and were proclaimed June 5

——, Quebec and Halifax Steam Navigation Company incorporated

April 29, The "Royal William" launched by the Quebec and Halifax Navigation Company. A public holiday proclaimed in Quebec in honor of the occasion

June 1, Discovery of position of the north magnetic pole southwest of Boothia by J. C. Ross. He discovered and named King William Land

Aug. 24, The steamer "Royal William" left Quebec on first trip to Halifax

Sept. 8, Petition of the Methodist Episcopal Church for share in the proceeds of sale of the "clergy reserves"

Sept. 22, Canada Revenue Control Act (Imperial) transferred to control of the Province of Quebec the proceeds of the customs duties, the entire permanent revenue. Colonial Office made provision that a fixed civil list of £19,500 only should be reserved

Oct. 5, Literary and Historical Society of Quebec incorporated by statute

Nov. 15–Feb. 25, 1832, Second session of fourteenth Parliament of Lower Canada. Act created fund for relief of emigrants, protection of copyrights provided for first copyright law, Boards of Health established, and provision made for effectual system of quarantine. Grant made for elementary schools in country districts, and provision made for instruction of the deaf and dumb. Act authorizing erection of jails and courthouses in counties received royal assent and was proclaimed Jan. 8, 1833. Dispatch of Lord Goderich of July 7, answer to report on grievances, read. The Assembly again refused to grant permanent civil list, and recommended that members of the Legislative Council be elected by the people. Mr. Christie again expelled

Nov. 17–Jan. 28, 1832, Second session of eleventh Parliament of Upper Canada. Additional duty placed on licenses to sell wines and liquor. Act provided for making stock companies liable for debts. W. L. Mackenzie expelled from Assembly for criticism of that body in his paper the *Colonial Advocate* by vote of 24 to 15 on Dec. 12, 1831. W. L. Mackenzie reëlected from York again expelled from Assembly Jan. 6, 1832 by vote of 27 to 19

Population of Lower Canada 553,134, of Upper Canada 236,702

1832

Jan. 2, William Lyon Mackenzie again elected from York to the Assembly of Upper Canada and presented with a gold medal by his constitutents in appreciation of his political career; expelled from the House again Jan. 6

Jan. 28, Commercial Bank of the Midland District incorporated in Upper Canada

Feb. 25, Quebec Fire Society incorporated by statute

——, Champlain and St. Lawrence Railroad Company, now part of Grand Trunk system, incorporated for construction of a railroad from Lake Champlain to the St. Lawrence River, first railroad legislation in Canada

March 23, Political riot in Toronto

March 30, Bank of Nova Scotia incorporated, first chartered bank in Province

April 13, Rev. Mr. Cochrane chose site for Indian village of St. Peters, Manitoba

April 24, Death of Baron Francis de Rottenburg, former Administrator, in England

May 1, W. L. Mackenzie sailed from New York for England to present petition for redress of grievances in Upper Canada

May 21, Election riot in Montreal, troops sent fired on jeering crowd killing 3, and wounding others

May 29, Rideau Canal opened, the "Pumper" making first trip from Bytown (Ottawa) to Kingston

June 5, Proclamation of royal assent of April 12 to incorporation of cities of Montreal and Quebec

June 7, Corner stone of Upper Canada Academy (Methodist) at Cobourg laid

June 8, Ship from Dublin, the "Carrick," arrived at Quebec with 59 deaths from the cholera of 133 passengers on board

July 9, Constitution adopted by the "United Inhabitants of the Indian Stream," territory claimed by both Canada and New Hampshire

Aug. 18, The Methodist Church in conference at Halowell adopted resolutions uniting with the British Wesleyans

Sept. 30, Total of deaths from cholera in Quebec since June 8, 3,292

Oct. 31–Feb. 13, 1833, Third session of eleventh Parliament of Upper Canada. Act reduced number of cases for capital punishment, partition of real estates provided for, for legal remedies against corporations. W. L. Mackenzie again expelled

Grant made for erection of a penitentiary. Boards of Health provided for

Nov. 8, Charter of King's College (later University of Toronto) amended

Nov. 15–April 3, 1833, Third session of fourteenth Parliament of Lower Canada. Act provided for summary trial of small cases, received royal assent April 13, 1834 and was proclaimed Aug. 13. Supply Bill passed with conditions which caused its rejection by the Legislative Council. Petition of Assembly asked for remodeling of Legislative Council on elective basis

1833

Jan. 1, First representative Assembly of Newfoundland met

Jan. 8, Natural History Society at Montreal incorporated by proclamation of royal assent of Oct. 12, 1832

Feb. 13, Hamilton, Ontario, incorporated

——, British American Assurance Company of Toronto incorporated; began business in 1835, fire and life insurance, oldest in Ontario

Feb. 14, Death of Archbishop Panet (Roman Catholic). Succeeded as Bishop of Quebec by Joseph Signay

March 6, Attorney General Boulton and Solicitor General Hagerman removed from office by the British Government because of their part in the expulsion of W. L. Mackenzie from Assembly of Upper Canada

April 16, Public meeting of British residents of Quebec disapproved of proceedings of Assembly and adopted 23 resolutions

May 24, First university degree granted in medicine to W. Logie, of Montreal

Aug. 5, The "Royal William," the first vessel to cross the Atlantic Ocean wholly under its own steam, left Quebec, coaled at Pictou, Nova Scotia, and left there Aug. 18, and arrived at Gravesend, England, Sept. 11

Aug. 28, Imperial Act regulating trade of possessions abroad established free ports to which imports and exports confined

——, Slavery abolished throughout the British Empire to take effect Aug. 1, 1834

Nov. 19–March 6, 1834, Fourth session of eleventh Parliament of Upper Canada. Act rendered judges of King's Bench independent of the Crown to hold office during good behavior. Act respecting appointment and duties of township officers amended. Grant for roads and bridges. W. L. Mackenzie again expelled from Assembly by vote of 22 to 18 on Dec. 17, 1833, and again on Feb. 10, 1834, after being sworn before Clerk of the Privy Council. Law as to real property and law of inheritance conveyance amended. *See also infra* March 6, 1834 incorporations

Father Georges Antoine Belcourt established an Indian mission, St. Paul's, on the Assiniboine River

1834

Jan. 7–March 18, Fourth session of fourteenth Parliament of Lower Canada. Acts passed to relieve distress due to failure of crops, new system introduced to deal with contested elections and new places of election established in certain counties, establishment of mutual fire insurance companies authorized. Act for encouragement of elementary education received royal assent Aug. 15, proclaimed Jan. 7, 1835. The "Ninety-Two Resolutions" introduced in Assembly Feb. 21 by Elzéar Bédard, the grievances of Papineau and his followers as French-Canadian Declaration of Rights adopted. Owing to disputes with the executive no vote on estimates

Jan. 23, Chateau St. Louis, the second one built by Frontenac in Quebec, destroyed by fire

March 6, London and Gore Railroad incorporated (Great Western) the first railroad in Upper Canada

——, York, Upper Canada, incorporated under name of Toronto, W. L. Mackenzie, first mayor

——, Cobourg Railway Company incorporated (London and Gore Railway Company)

——, Port Hope and Rice Canal Company and Richmond Canal Company incorporated

——, Village of Prescott, Upper Canada, incorporated

——, Bath School established at Bath in 1812 by Barnabas Bidwell chartered

March 18, College of Sainte Anne de la Pocatière founded in 1829 in Quebec incorporated, received royal assent Aug. 15, proclaimed Jan. 7, 1835

March 22, Central Bank of New Brunswick chartered

May, Hudson Bay Company boat, "Dryad," sent to establish post on Stikine River, British Columbia, boarded by Russian officer and refused entrance to the River. Claims for damages eventually settled by fur companies

June 6, The sixth Earl of Selkirk consented to convey Assiniboia back to the Hudson Bay Company for £15,000 of stock in the Company

June 7, Sir George Back with Dr. R. King in search of Sir John Ross expedition left Fort Reliance which he had built at east end of Great Slave Lake and where he had wintered, and descended the Great Fish (Backs) River for 530 miles to its mouth in Arctic Ocean reached July 29, and traced coast as far as Point Ogle, back at Fort Reliance, Sept. 27

Aug. 15, Imperial Act amended customs

Sept. 24, Resolutions passed in Montreal meeting amplification of the 92 Resolutions of Quebec

Nov. 20, Address of Constitutional Society of Montreal stated rights and grievances of British residents of Lower Canada in answer to 92 Resolutions

Dec. 9, Canadian Alliance Society formed at Toronto, W. L. Mackenzie, Corresponding Secretary

Dec. 30, Fire destroyed Parliament Building of Upper Canada

Another epidemic of cholera

John M. McLeod explored upper waters of the Liard to Simpson Lake in the Yukon, and the Dease to Dease Lake and from there reached upper waters of the Stikine River which he descended to below Thomas Falls

1835

Jan. 1, Joseph Howe published article in his paper for which he was indicted for libel upon the magistrates of Halifax. He conducted his own trial and was triumphantly acquitted and free press in Nova Scotia victorious

Jan. 7, Mutual Fire Insurance Company established by proclamation of royal assent of Aug. 15, 1834

Jan. 15–April 17, First session of twelfth Parliament of Upper Canada. Act provided for payment of members of Assembly representing towns. Sale of liquor to Indians prohibited after Jan. 5, 1836. Seventh Report of Grievances presented by Mackenzie April 10. Touched on patronage, official salaries, status of the churches, land grants, pensions, public accounts, and system of government

Feb. 21–March 18, First session of fifteenth Parliament of Lower Canada. Act passed to authorize counsel to address jurors in behalf of prisoners in capital cases, received royal assent Feb. 23, and proclaimed May 18, 1836. The Governor announced that to avoid embarrassment due to failure of Supply Bill he had taken £31,000 from military chest. This action disapproved by House. Resolved that petitions be sent to the King and Imperial Parliament which were presented in London in March. Supply Bill granted only for limited period rejected by Council

April 16, Erie and Ontario and Hamilton and Port Dover railroads incorporated

April 30, Sir Francis Bond Head appointed Lieutenant Governor of Upper Canada

July 1, The Earl of Gosford appointed Governor of the two Canadas

Aug. 24, Sir Charles Grey and Sir George Gipps appointed commissioners to Quebec with Lord Gosford, arrived in Canada to investigate conditions

Oct. 5, Meeting of citizens of St. Andrews, New Brunswick, formed an association to build a railroad from St. Andrews to Quebec

Oct. 27–March 21, 1836, Second session of fifteenth Parliament of Lower Canada. Acts provided for building of custom house in Montreal, for lighting Montreal by gas, establishment of normal schools, and to extend certain privileges to Methodists. The Assembly refused to make vote of supply because of warrant for contingencies withheld. Act provided for transportation of certain offenders to New South Wales or Van Diemens Land. Members of Assembly granted 10 shillings per day of attendance in Parliament and 4 shillings for each league of distance from residence

Nov., "Constitutional Associations" formed by British loyalists in Quebec and Montreal, and "Committees of Correspondence" organized by the radicals

Dec. 28, Great Britain withdrew assent to boundary award of the King of the Netherlands of Jan., 1831

1836

Jan. 14–April 20, Second session of twelfth Parliament of Upper Canada. Sir F. B. Head announced that request for elective Legislative Council would not be granted. Assembly refused to vote supplies because of lack of confidence in the administration. April 15, The Assembly passed an Address to the Imperial House of Commons condemning arbitrary conduct of Governor Francis Bond Head

Jan. 18, Upper Canada Academy opened at Cobourg

Jan. 25, Sir Francis Bond Head assumed office as Lieutenant Governor of Upper Canada

Jan. 30, First report of the Gosford Commission sent to investigate conditions in Lower Canada, others March 12, May 3, June 17, and Oct. 15

Jan., Lieutenant Governor Colborne of Upper Canada in Council created 57 rectories of the Church of England and endowed them with valuable lands out of the "clergy reserves," 44 actually endowed

Feb. 1, Death of Colonel By, engineer and founder of Ottawa

Feb. 20, Robert Baldwin, Dr. John Rolph, and John Henry Dunn of the Reform Party appointed members of the Executive Council by Sir F. B. Head in Upper Canada

March 4, The Executive Council of Upper Canada made formal complaint that they had no part in the administration

March 8, New Brunswick and Canada Railroad chartered by New Brunswick to run from St. Andrews to Quebec. The Imperial Government agreed to make the survey but work postponed on account of boundary dispute with Maine

March 10, Sir F. B. Head replied to Council in answer to complaint of March 4 that he recognized responsibility to the Colonial Office only

March 12, Members of the Executive Council of Upper Canada resigned as a protest because not consulted by the Lieutenant Governor

March 16, Railroad from Shediac to St. John chartered in New Brunswick; reincorporated in April, 1848

March 18, The steamer "Beaver" of the Hudson Bay Company arrived at Fort Vancouver, first steamer on the northern Pacific Ocean

March 21, College of Chambly chartered in Lower Canada

April 20, Company for erection of a suspension bridge over the Niagara River incorporated

——, City of Toronto and Lake Huron Railway Company incorporated, and a company to construct a railroad from Burlington Bay to Lake Huron

May 13, Bishop Jean Jacques Lartigue made first Bishop of Montreal erected into a Roman Catholic bishopric

July 4, W. L. Mackenzie began publication of the *Constitution* which advocated a republican form of government

July 16, Constitutional Reform Society, Dr. William Baldwin, president, organized in Upper Canada

July 21, First railroad in Canada opened from Laprairie on the St. Lawrence to St. Johns on the Richelieu, 16 miles (the Champlain and St. Lawrence). Operated by horse power for the first year, the only railroad in operation until 1847

Aug. 9, Chippewas ceded 1,500,000 acres, parts of Bruce, Grey, Wellington, and Huron counties

Aug. 27, Grant of £2,000 first installment of £10,000 by William IV to the St. Andrews and Quebec Railroad

Sept. 22–Oct. 4, Third session of fifteenth Parliament of Lower Canada. Two bills introduced, for appointment of an agent in London, and to amend the Imperial Act of 1791 as to the Legislative Council, but no act passed. Assembly refused to vote Supply Bill. Provision made for lighting the city of Montreal by gas. Railroad from the St. Lawrence River to the Province line authorized

Oct. 12, Upper Canada Academy, the later Victoria College, received charter

Oct. 25, Moravians of the Thames surrendered the township of Zone, 26,000 acres

Oct. 29, Royal assent proclaimed for construction of a railroad from the St. Lawrence River to the Province line

1837

Jan., Joseph Howe, elected to Assembly of Nova Scotia from Halifax County, presented his famous "Twelve Resolutions" asking for a system of responsible government

Feb., Address of Assembly of Nova Scotia to William IV based on Howe's "Twelve Resolutions"

March 4, Charter granted to London and Davenport Railway and Harbor Company, Upper Canada

——, Royal assent given to incorporation of Regiopolis College, Kingston, under direction of the Roman Catholic Church

——, Charter of King's College, Toronto, amended

——, Fort Erie Canal Company incorporated

——, Bank of British North America incorporated in Upper Canada

March 6, Lord John Russell, as Chancellor of the Exchequer, introduced a series of 10 Resolutions in the Imperial Parliament on affairs in Lower Canada, the lack of provision since Oct. 1, 1832 for charges of administration, and recommended that the Governor-General be empowered to take funds for the purpose from the revenues without authorization of the Assembly

May 7, Meeting of French-Canadians at St. Ours on the Richelieu River organized by Dr. Wolfred Nelson on the Lord Russell Resolutions, Papineau elected leader. One of resolutions passed forswore the use of English imported goods

May 18, Lower Canada banks suspended payment until June 23, 1838

June 10, Upper Canada Academy at Cobourg opened

June 15, Lord Gosford issued a proclamation calling on all loyal subjects to discountenance writings of a seditious tendency, and avoid meetings of turbulent or political character

June 19–July 11, Second session of thirteenth Parliament of Upper Canada, 4 laws enacted, 2 dealing with banking, the suspension of specie payment to meet commercial crisis allowed without penalty of suspension of charter

June 20, Death of William IV and accession of Queen Victoria. News received in Canada July 31, and Victoria proclaimed Aug. 1

July 9, Thomas Simpson and Peter Warren Dease, of the Hudson Bay Company, reached the mouth of the Mackenzie from Fort Chipewyan, and Franklin's "Return Reef" 14 days later. Simpson with 5 men marched overland to Point Barrow

July 13, Death of Bishop Stewart, Anglican Bishop of Quebec. Succeeded by George J. Mountain

July 31, Meeting in Quebec formed a "Committee of Vigilance" of Upper Canada with William Lyon Mackenzie as "agent and corresponding secretary" with purpose to form a Provisional Government

——, "Declaration of the Reformers of Toronto" drawn up by Mackenzie and others and published in the "Constitution" Aug. 2

Aug. 18–Aug. 26, Fourth session of fifteenth Parliament of Lower Canada. No business done at this last meeting

Sept. 10, Sir F. B. Head refused to carry out instructions of Lord Glenelg, Colonial Secretary, to reinstate Judge George Ridout whom he had unjustly deprived of office, and to offer next vacant judgeship to Barnabas Bidwell

Oct. 23, Meeting of 1,000 of the British party at Montreal

——, Meeting of representatives of 6 counties bordering on the Richelieu at St. Charles, Wolfred Nelson, chairman, and extravagant resolutions adopted.

Papineau was against revolution but Dr. Nelson asserted: "The time has come to melt our spoons into bullets"

Oct. 27, Resignation of Lord Gosford accepted

Nov. 4 and 12, Proclamation prohibited meetings for military drill at Quebec and Montreal

Nov. 6, Riots in streets of Montreal in conflict of the *Fils de Liberté* and the Doric Club of the British party

Nov. 16, Warrants for arrest of Papineau, Dr. Nelson, Thomas Storrow Brown, Edmund Bailey O'Callaghan and several others issued by the Government

Nov. 18, The political prisoners Davignon and Demaray under escort of Lieut. Ermatinger rescued by armed party led by Bonaventure Viger at Longueuil

Nov. 23, Shops in Montreal first lighted by gas

——, Government troops sent to arrest Dr. Nelson under Colonel Gore repulsed in attack on Dr. Nelson's fortified stone distillery at St. Denis. Lieut. Weir, captured by insurgents, killed trying to make his escape to join Colonel Gore. It was on the eve of this engagement that Papineau fled to St. Hyacinthe and from there to the United States

Nov. 24, Lord Glenelg, Colonial Secretary, accepted resignation of Lieut. Governor Head in letter of Sept. 10

Nov. 25, Insurgents led by Thomas S. Brown defeated at St. Charles by Colonel Wetherall, fort taken and rebellion in the Richelieu country ended

——, Proclamation of W. L. Mackenzie declared the Provisional Government of the State of Upper Canada

Nov. 28, Capture of Chartrand, loyal volunteer, near St. Johns, executed by rebels after a mock trial as a spy

Dec. 1, Proclamation declared Papineau a rebel and reward of £1,000 offered for his capture

——, Colonel Gore entered St. Denis without opposition. Government troops set fire to the village in retaliation for the death of Lieutenant Weir

Dec. 4, Rebels met at Montgomery's Tavern, north of Toronto, under leadership of W. L. Mackenzie and Dr. Rolph, beginning revolt in Upper Canada on this date instead of on the 7th as had been planned

Dec. 5, Fitz Gibbon's rifles, a company of 90 young men, led charge which dispersed insurgent force led by Samuel Lount and W. L. Mackenzie attacking Toronto. At eleven at night Sir Allan McNab arrived with the Gore militia to defend city

——, Proclamation of martial law for Montreal district

——, Sir F. B. Head in interview with Marshall Spring Bidwell forced him to promise to leave Canada, which he did, becoming a citizen of the United States

Dec. 6, Mackenzie seized mail at Peacock Inn on its arrival in order to learn the movements of the Government. Dr. Rolph, hearing of arrest of Dr. Morrison, escaped from Toronto

Dec. 7, Loyalist forces headed by Sir F. B. Head attacked and dispersed the insurgents near Montgomery's Tavern, and Sir F. B. Head ordered the Tavern burned. Mackenzie fled to the United States 4 days later

——, Proclamation of Sir F. B. Head offered £1,000 for capture of W. L. Mackenzie

Dec. 12, Dr. Wolfred Nelson captured and brought to prison in Montreal, and was later exiled

Dec. 13, Mackenzie crossed from Buffalo, New York, to Navy Island, about 2 miles above Niagara on the Canadian side and proclaimed the establishment of

a Provisional Government. He was joined by a number of Americans

Dec. 14, Rebels at St. Eustache, commanded by Dr. J. O. Chénier, retreated before loyalist troops led by Sir John Colborne, Chénier shot and killed in attempt to escape, and Amury Girod shot himself 4 days later to escape capture

Dec. 28–March 6, 1838, Third session of thirteenth Parliament of Upper Canada. Acts authorized apprehension, detention, and trial of persons suspected of high treason, the Government authorized to extend conditional pardon to persons concerned in the late insurrection, and commission appointed to investigate losses caused by the insurrection. Loan of £80,000 authorized to provide funds for completion of improvement of the St. Lawrence River

Dec. 29, Destruction of the American steamer "Caroline," used by Mackenzie, by Captain Drew, burned and sent over Niagara Falls by Canadians at the command of Allan McNab at Schlosser's Landing on the American shore of the Niagara River, an invasion of American territory complained of by the United States

1838

Jan. 13, Navy Island abandoned by Mackenzie "patriots" on the approach of the 24th regiment of Canadians, and the island occupied by the militia on the 15th. Mackenzie arrested for breach of neutrality laws of the United States

Jan. 16, Lord John Russell introduced Bill in Imperial House of Commons making provision for government of Lower Canada by a Governor and Special Commission

Feb. 10, Constitution of Lower Canada suspended and Special Council created for the government, proclaimed March 29

Feb. 27, Sir John Colborne, Administrator, in place of Lord Gosford, who left the Province on the 26th

Feb. 28, Robert Nelson, brother of Wolfred, crossed the border from the United States leading band of insurgents from Alburg, Vermont, but driven back by Missiquoi militia recrossed the border March 1 and were disarmed by General Wool

March 3, 500 American sympathizers with insurgents took possession of Point Pelé Island on Lake Erie, but were driven back to United States by Canadian militia commanded by Colonel Maitland

March 5, Bank of Upper Canada suspended specie payment until Nov. 1, 1839

March 6, Town of Kingston incorporated

——, Kingston Marine Railway Company incorporated

March 23, Sir George Arthur, appointed Lieutenant Governor in Upper Canada Dec. 22, 1837, arrived in York, and assumed office on the 24th

March 27, Act suspending the Constitution of Lower Canada came into effect

March 30, Lord Durham appointed Governor-in-Chief of all British North American Provinces except Newfoundland, High Commissioner in Upper and Lower Canada, and Governor General of British North America

April 2, Special Council of 22 members appointed by Sir John Colborne for the government of Lower Canada to meet April 18, James Cuthbert elected chairman

April 12, Peter Matthews and Samuel Lount, rebel leaders in Upper Canada, hanged

May 29, Lord Durham landed at Quebec with his Staff including Charles Buller, Edward G. Wakefield, and Thomas Turton

——, Americans led by Bill Johnson set fire to Canadian steamer "Sir Robert Peel" on the St. Lawrence in retaliation for the "Caroline"

May 30, New charter for 21 years granted to the Hudson Bay Company

May, Banks of Lower Canada resumed specie payments

June 1, Lord Durham dissolved the Special Council nominated by Sir John Colborne, members notified May 31, and appointed new Council of 5, of his 3 secretaries, the commissary-general, and one Canadian official, Mr. Daly, the provincial secretary included

June 28, Ordinance of Lord Durham passed sentence of banishment without trial of Dr. Nelson and 7 other prisoners including R. S. M. Bouchette, Bonaventure Viger, and Siméon Marchesseault, leaders in the rebellion, to Bermuda, and an amnesty granted to all political prisoners not actively engaged in the rebellion, the 16 who had fled from justice including Papineau were held to be liable to punishment of death if they should return to the Province

July 4, Lord Durham left Quebec for tour of the Province, arriving at Montreal on the 5th and proceeding from there to Kingston and Niagara, Fort Erie, and Toronto

Aug. 10, Ordinance of Lord Durham of June 28 disallowed by the Imperial Government

Aug. 16, Imperial Act provided for indemnification of those who had acted under ordinance of June 28 "which cannot be justified as law" now made void

Sept. 25, Letter of Lord Durham to Lord Glenelg announced his resignation

Oct. 9, Proclamation of Lord Durham announced his resignation because of lack of support of home government, defended his policy, and promised to defend Canadian interests against influence of "persons too apt to legislate in ignorance and indifference"

Oct. 16, Escape of Theller, Dodge, Culver, Hull, and Parker, political prisoners, from the citadel of Quebec, Hull and Culver recaptured

Nov. 1, Lord Durham sailed for England arriving in Plymouth Sound Nov. 26

——, Dalhousie College, Halifax, opened in Nova Scotia

Nov. 1–Jan. 17, 1839, Sir John Colborne, Administrator, succeeding Lord Durham

Nov. 3, New insurrection in counties on the Richelieu, the steamer "Henry Brougham" attacked at Beauharnois

Nov. 4, Robert Nelson declared president of Canadian Republic by insurgents

——, "Patriots" of Chauteauguay attacked Indian village of Caughnawaga to obtain arms, defeated by Indians who took 70 prisoners who were taken to Montreal

Nov. 5, Banks of Lower Canada again suspended until June 1839

——, Toussaint Pothier elected chairman of new Special Council, Lower Canada

Nov. 7, Insurgents led by Dr. Cyrile Coté defeated at Lacolle as they marched toward Rouse's Point

——, Lafontaine, Vigers, and other leading French Canadians arrested and imprisoned

Nov. 9, Insurgents and American sympathizers, led by Robert Nelson, defeated at Odelltown by Colonel Taylor. Sir John Colborne entered Napierville without opposition

Nov. 10, Defeat of insurgents at Beauharnois by Colonels Carmichael and Philpotts

Nov. 11, American border organization, the "Hunters" led invasion of Prescott, and "Battle of the Windmill" resulted in heavy casualties Nov. 13–16

Nov. 14, First Catholic missionaries, Francis Norbet Blanchet, Vicar General and afterwards Archbishop, and Father Modeste Demers arrived at Vancouver from Quebec in answer to petitions from French Catholic settlers

Dec. 4, Defeat of insurgents and Americans led from Detroit by General Bierce and Colonels Putnam and Havell at Sandwich by Colonel Prince

Dec. 6, Defeat of insurgents at Philipsburg

——, Rebels entering Canada from Vermont defeated at Moore's Corners by volunteers under Captain Kemp. Robert Shore Bouchette, in command of advance guard of insurgents, wounded and taken prisoner

Dec. 8, Ordinance suspended Judges Panet and Bédard of Quebec in controversy about *habeas corpus* in case of T. A. Young, whom they had served with writ, police magistrate, who had arrested alleged insurgent Teed

Dec. 21, Joseph Narcisse Cardinal and Joseph Duquette, insurgent leaders, hanged at Quebec after sentence by court martial

Robert Campbell ascended the Liard River to headwaters in Dease Lake, present British Columbia, and built post where he remained a year

1839

Jan. 18, 5 more political prisoners executed, P. T. Decoigne, J. J. Robert, F. X. Hamelin, the Sanguinet brothers

Jan. 21, Acadia College, Wolfville, Nova Scotia, opened

Feb., Agreement between the Hudson Bay Company and the Russian American Fur Company for lease of land to the Canada Company under Treaty of Feb. 28, 1825, between Great Britain and Russia

Feb. 8–March 23, "Aroostock War" on borders of New Brunswick and Maine. *See* United States

Feb. 11, Lord Durham's Report dated Jan. 31 submitted to Parliament, celebrated document of Canadian history. He proposed to unite the Provinces of Upper and Lower Canada in a legislative union and the establishment in them of responsible government, and outlined a program of reforms to be embodied in legislation

Feb. 15, 6 more political prisoners executed, P. R. Narbonne, M. T. Chevalier de Lorimier, Charles Hindenland, François Nicolas, and Amable Daunais

Feb. 27–May 11, Fourth session of thirteenth Parliament of Upper Canada. Militia laws amended. Grant of £5,650 to schools. Act regulated practice of the Court of King's or Queen's Bench. Resolutions in favor of union of Upper and Lower Canada adopted, and that a commission be sent to England to advocate the union

April 11, Death of John Galt

May 11, College of Physicians and Surgeons of Upper Canada incorporated

June 1, Banks of Lower Canada resumed specie payment suspended in fall of 1838

June 3, Resolution of Lord John Russell introduced in British House of Commons proposed formation of a legislative union of Upper and Lower Canada

June 20, Lord John Russell withdrew Resolution of June 3 and introduced another providing for reunion of Upper and Lower Canada and for government of the United Provinces

June, Thomas Simpson and Peter Dease descended the Coppermine River and reached Cape Alexander by boat July 26, Point Ogle Aug. 13, their farthest point Castor and Pollux Bay 68° 28′ N. Lat. and 94° 14′ W. Long., back at mouth of the Coppermine Sept. 16 after an Arctic boat journey of 1,408 miles following south shore of King William Land and Victoria Land

July 27, Meeting at Hamilton passed 8 resolutions expressing attachment to the British Crown and approval of Lord Durham's Report

Aug., Anglican Diocese of Toronto formed and John Strachan appointed first Bishop

Sept. 18, Joseph Howe in Nova Scotia published "Letters to Lord John Russell" on responsible government enshrined with Durham's Report in political literature

Sept. 26, 151 prisoners sent to penal colony in Australia by Special Council of Quebec

Oct. 16, Despatch of Lord John Russell authorized Governors to change Executive Council at will upon "motives of public policy," and declared tenure of colonial offices not during good behavior, officers might be called upon to retire when expedient

Oct. 19, Charles Poulett Thompson now Lord Sydenham appointed Governor-in-Chief Sept. 6, took oath of office

Nov. 1, Bank of Upper Canada resumed specie payment

Dec. 3–Feb. 10, 1840, Fifth session of thirteenth Parliament of Upper Canada. Resolutions in favor of union of Upper and Lower Canada adopted, that the representation of each province be equal and that a sufficient civil list be granted, the public debt to be charged to the united Province. Expenditure of £40,000 authorized to indemnify loyalists for property losses during the rebellion, but no funds provided

The Erie and Ontario Railroad, a horse tramway, opened between Queenston and Chippewa in Upper Canada

Small coal tramway from Albion coal mines to tidewater opened in Nova Scotia

1840

Jan. 17, Resolution adopted at meeting of French Canadians at Quebec declared that inhabitants of Lower Canada had not been consulted on the subject of the union of Upper and Lower Canada

Feb. 10, College at Kingston chartered by provincial legislature

March 27, Queen's College (Baptist) established at Horton, Nova Scotia, the former Horton Academy, and later Acadia College

April 19, Ignace Bourget appointed Roman Catholic Bishop of Montreal

June 8, Ordinance gave Sulpicians legal possession of their estates

June 26, Ordinance divided Lower Canada into 4 districts and reconstituted the courts

July 4, The "Brittania," Cunard Line steamer sailed for Halifax, Nova Scotia, and Boston from Liverpool, making the trip in 14 days and 8 hours, to Halifax in

12 days and 10 hours. Samuel Cunard received with enthusiasm by citizens of Boston. Had "1,800 invitations to dinner during the first 24 hours after his arrival"

July 23, Union Act to reunite the Provinces of Upper and Lower Canada received royal assent, to become effective Feb. 10, 1841

July 28, Death of Lord Durham at Cowes, England

Aug., New charters granted to Quebec and Montreal,

Aug. 7, Imperial Act provided for sale and distribution of the "clergy reserves," funds to be divided, one-third to the Church of England, one-sixth to the Church of Scotland, and the remainder applied to "purposes of public worship and religious instruction in Canada"

Aug. 19, The steamer "Ontario" descended the Lachine Rapids

Nov., McLeod arrested in New York in affair of steamer "Caroline." *See* United States

Robert Campbell of the Hudson Bay Company from Fort Halkett ascended the Liard River to its source and entered lake he named Francis and to Lake Finlayson which he discovered and named, and discovered the Pelly River

1841

Jan. 28–Feb. 10, George Moffatt chairman of Special Council, Lower Canada

Feb. 10, Proclamation of Lord Sydenham of the Union of Upper and Lower Canada

Feb. 10–May 10, 1844, Kingston, the capital of Canada

Feb. 13–Sept. 1842, Draper-Ogden Ministry. Robert Baldwin accepted seat in the Executive Council and appointed Solicitor General

March 3, Sir George Simpson, governor-in-chief of the Hudson Bay Company, sailed from London in trip around the world. Traveled by sleigh from Boston to Montreal which he left May 4. Arrived at Sault Ste. Marie, May 16, at Fort Gary, June 10, at Fort Vancouver, Aug. 24, and sailed for California Dec. 3

March 29, St. Mary's College at Halifax, Nova Scotia, chartered, and Queen's College at Horton became Acadia College by statute

April 10, Halifax, Nova Scotia, incorporated

May 17, Landslide from Citadel Rock, Quebec, 32 persons killed

June 9, Legislative Council of 24 members appointed by Lord Sydenham, which held first meeting at Kingston June 11

June 14, Robert Baldwin resigned as Solicitor General

June 14–Sept. 18, First session of first Parliament of Canada at Kingston. Opened by Governor General Lord Sydenham. Board of Works established, local government organized in Upper Canada by the District Council Act, currency regulated, customs tariff consolidated and revised, the Bible exempted from duty, regulation of the public lands ceded by the Crown under the Union Act, in Lower Canada district and division courts established, criminal law modified, number of capital offenses reduced and pillory abolished, civil and political rights conferred on aliens resident 7 years. Banking Act provided unified system of banking. The Government authorized to purchase the Welland Canal from private company, grants made for construction of canals, and roads, and navigation of the St. Lawrence, and annual grant of $200,000 provided for common schools, three-fifths to Lower Canada, two-fifths to

Upper Canada. Grant made for geological survey of the Province. First Act for disposal of public lands received royal assent April 27, 1842, and was proclaimed May 30. The "September Resolutions" presented by Baldwin in favor of responsible government carried Sept. 3 as amended by Harrison and Sydenham

Aug. 27, Upper Canada Academy incorporated as Victoria College, Mr. Ryerson, first president, opened the college Oct. 21, Mr. Ryerson formally inaugurated June 21, 1842

Sept. 18, Roman Catholic College of L'Assomption chartered in county of Leinster

Sept. 19, Death of Governor General Lord Sydenham from injuries after fall from horseback, Sir Richard Downes Jackson acted as Administrator

Oct. 7, Sir Charles Bagot commissioned Governor

Oct. 12, McLeod acquitted in "Caroline" affair in trial in New York Oct. 4–8

Oct. 14, Royal charter issued for University at Kingston (Presbyterian)

Oct. 16, Royal charter issued to Queen's College (Presbyterian) at Kingston

Dec. 1, First copyright granted to Alexander Davidson for Canadian spelling book published by Henry Roswell, Toronto

Dec. 31, Report of Commission appointed in Oct. 1840 to investigate the post office; report used as basis of reorganization

Population of Lower Canada estimated as 625,000 and of Upper Canada as 455,688

1842

Jan. 12, Sir Charles Bagot assumed office as Governor in Kingston

March 7, First classes held at Queen's College, Kingston

March 29, New charter granted to Acadia College, Horton, Nova Scotia

April 23, Corner stone of King's College building laid, later University of Toronto, by Sir Charles Bagot

May 8, Michael Power consecrated first Roman Catholic Bishop of Toronto

July 16, Imperial Act regulated trade of British possessions abroad, last tariff framed by Great Britain for Canada

Aug. 9, Ashburton Treaty respecting boundaries, slave trade, and extradition signed. On northeast boundary Massachusetts surrendered $5/12$ of territory claimed, and received $300,000 compensation. Great Britain surrendered $7/12$ of territory claimed. The United States received rights on St. John River

Aug. 12, Amalgamated Assembly of Newfoundland constituted by Imperial statute and Constitution suspended until 1847

Sept. 8–Oct. 12, Second session of first Parliament. New election law enacted, the ancient boundaries of Quebec and Montreal restored reversing Sydenham's separation of cities and suburbs. Duty on wheat from the United States imposed. Resolution passed declaring Kingston not suitable for the seat of government

Sept. 13, Lafontaine at first refused a seat in the Cabinet

Sept. 16, First Baldwin-Lafontaine Ministry, the first liberal Executive Council in the Canadas, representing Reform Party and French Canadians

Oct. 5, Election riots drove voters for Mr. Baldwin and Mr. Murney from the polls

Oct. 28, Constitutional Society of Toronto reorganized from that of 1832, opposed to Administration

1843

Jan. 19, Mt. Allison Wesleyan Academy, Sackville, New Brunswick, opened

March 14, James Douglas with 15 men from Fort Vancouver landed at Clover Point to establish a Hudson Bay Company post at Victoria, British Columbia, founded June 4

March 30, Sir Charles T. Metcalfe, commissioned Governor Feb. 24, assumed office

May 29, Death of Sir Charles Bagot

June 8, King's College (Anglican) opened at Toronto, Dr. Strachan, president

June, Cornwall Canal in Upper Canada opened

June 11, William Dollard consecrated Bishop of New Brunswick

June, Captain Henry Lefroy arrived at Red River and passed through Lake Athabaska and from Oct. to Feb. engaged in meteorological and magnetic observations

July 9, The "Prince Albert," first iron steamer in Canada, launched at Montreal

July 12, Imperial Act admitted Canadian corn and flour to British ports with only nominal duty

Aug. 18, The *Banner*, organ of the Presbyterian Free Church, first issued by George Brown

Sept. 28–Dec. 9, Third session of first Parliament. Of 84 members of the Assembly 60 were members of the Reform Party. Resolution advised that the seat of government be removed to Montreal. Provided that permanent officials such as judges and registrars could not hold their positions and be members of Parliament, the judges of King's Bench in Lower Canada made independent of the Crown holding office during good behavior, circuit courts replaced the district and division courts in Lower Canada simplifying the judicial system. Grant made to elementary schools. Bill introduced by Robert Baldwin passed declared all secret societies except Masons illegal, but did not receive royal assent. Duty imposed on imported horses and cattle and on wheat and grain to meet American tariff, and established a differential duty on all goods imported into Canada by inland routes. New school law (Hincks Act) created Superintendent of Schools for Upper Canada. Act to restrain "party processions" enacted

Nov. 24, Baldwin and Lafontaine demanded of Governor Metcalfe that he should make no appointments without consultation with them

Nov. 26, Resignation of the Baldwin-Lafontaine Ministry charging that the Governor did not give them his confidence

Dec. 9, Mercantile Library Association of Montreal incorporated by statute

——, Bishop's College (Church of England) Lennoxville, chartered

Dec. 12–June 1846, Draper-Viger Ministry

1844

March 5, The *Pilot*, journal, established by Frances Hincks at Montreal

——, First issue of the *Toronto Globe* founded by George Brown

March 25, Toronto Reform Association met with Robert Baldwin presiding and William Hume Blake, orator

May 10–Nov. 14, 1849, Montreal, capital of the Province of Canada

June 27, *Banque du Peuple* incorporated by statute of Dec. 9, 1843 which received royal assent May 23 and was proclaimed June 27

July 1, Executive Council met at Montreal

Sept., Egerton Ryerson appointed assistant Superintendent of Schools in Upper Canada, soon became Superintendent and for 30 years controlled the Dept. of Education

Nov. 8, Knox College, Toronto, Presbyterian theological seminary, opened

Nov. 28–March 29, 1845, First session of second Parliament met at Montreal. Acts passed to facilitate the optional commutation of seigneurial dues, provided for high schools in Montreal and Quebec, established municipal government in Lower Canada, clergy given right to vote, and new and elaborate scale of customs duties included almost all articles imported for commercial purposes. Restrictions on official use of French language removed. Ordinance for defense and regulation of the militia revived

1845

March 17, Quebec Library Association incorporated

——, The St. Lawrence and Atlantic Railroad Company chartered to build a railroad from Montreal to the border, and there to meet railroad to be built by the United States from Portland, Maine

——, Geological Survey of Canada established

March 29, The London and Gore Railroad incorporated as the Great Western

——, Town of Niagara in Upper Canada incorporated

——, Mechanics Institute of Montreal for library and lectures incorporated

April 7, Memorial to Queen Victoria from the Board of Trade of Toronto against duties imposed by law of Canadian Legislature of 1843 where "commercial interests of the Colony . . . inadequately represented"

May 19, Sir John Franklin sailed from England in the "Erebus" and the "Terror" and entered Baffin Bay in July, not heard of after July 26 at entrance of Lancaster Sound. In 1859 records found showed that he wintered at Beechey Island in 1845 and was at King William Land in 1846 to 1847, and found channel leading south along west of North Somerset discovered by Parry in 1819 (Peel Sound) and knew that he could reach Bering Strait through it, the long sought North West Passage

May 28–29, Great fire at Quebec destroyed two-thirds of the town, the St. Roch suburbs

June 28, Another great fire at Quebec destroyed the St. John suburbs, 1,300 houses destroyed

June, Robert Campbell descended the Pelly River to mouth of the Lewes where the 2 streams join forming the Yukon discovering that river

Oct., Bishop's College opened to students

Nov. 24, Commission appointed to enquire into losses sustained in rebellion in Lower Canada in 1837

Nov. 26, Earl Cathcart, Administrator, to April 23, 1846

Beauharnois Canal completed

1846

March, Ryerson, Superintendent of Education, submitted report on education for Upper Canada

March 16, Earl Cathcart commissioned Governor, sworn in April 24

March 20–June 9, Second session of second Parliament. Militia Bill passed, civil list salaries now under control of Assembly revised, Ryerson School Act created Board of Education and made provision for common schools in every parish in Lower Canada. Act restored rights to certain persons charged with treason in connection with the rebellion of 1837, received royal assent Oct. 30 and proclaimed Dec. 26. £10,000 voted to Lower Canada for payment of claims for damages during rebellion

April 18, Report of Commission on losses in rebellion

May 12, Address to the Queen from the Assembly against Imperial Corn Act asked the British Government to negotiate with the United States to secure admission of Canadian produce to American ports on same terms as American produce admitted to Canadian and British ports

May 18, Kingston incorporated

May 26, Public meeting in court house at St. Johns, Newfoundland, adopted resolutions in favor of responsible government

June 9, Cobourg Railroad reincorporated as Cobourg and Rice Lake Plank Road and Ferry Company, and Montreal and Lachine Railroad Company chartered

——, Great fire in St. Johns, Newfoundland, destroyed 2 principal streets for a mile

June 15, Oregon Boundary Treaty signed between Great Britain and the United States, the Pacific coast between 49° and 54° 40′ N. Lat. including Vancouver Island declared British

June 18–April 1847, Draper-Papineau Ministry, Papineau had returned to Canada in 1845

June 26, Imperial Act terminating the corn laws destroyed special preference enjoyed by Canada

June, John Rae made first journey from York Factory wintering at Repulse Bay in Lat. 66° 32′ North, and in 1847 surveyed 700 miles of new coast, shores of Committee Bay

July 17, Petition of Free Trade Association of Canada to the Queen asked relief from restrictions in favor of Great Britain and preferences to British goods in view of consequences of the corn law

July 28, Death of Sir George Murray in London

Aug., Provincial Agricultural Association organized at Hamilton

——, Dr. John Rae reached Repulse Bay from Fort Churchill on Hudson Bay and spent the winter

Aug. 28, British Possessions Act (Imperial) gave Province power to enact tariffs and reduce or repeal duties

Oct. 1, The Earl of Elgin commissioned Governor

Oct. 21–22, First exhibition at Toronto of the Provincial Agricultural Association and Board of Agriculture for West Canada

Oct. 22, First telegraph company organized, Toronto, Hamilton, and Niagara

Oct. 30, Great Western Railroad authorized to extend line from Hamilton to Toronto

Dec. 19, Toronto-Hamilton telegraph line opened

Dec. 26, Proclamation of royal assent of Oct. 30 to erection of suspension bridge over Niagara River near the Falls, and of Montreal and Kingston Railroad incorporation by act of Provincial Legislature of June 9, reserved, and of Port Hope, Lindsay and Beaverton Railroad, Peterboro and Port Hope Railroad, and Hamilton and Toronto

1847

Jan. 30, Earl of Elgin assumed office as Governor

April 22, Sir John Harvey succeeded as Governor of Newfoundland by Le Marchant, and old Constitution restored

May 11, Sherwood-Daly Ministry included Papineau, Draper, Morris, Cayley, and Badgley

June 2, John A. Macdonald entered the Cabinet

June 2–July 28, Third session of second Parliament. Lord Elgin announced that England was prepared to give control of the Post Office to the Provincial Legislature. Act extended provincial copyright to persons resident in the United Kingdom, relations between masters and servants regulated, parish and township municipalities abolished and county municipalities substituted in Lower Canada, and limited corporate powers conferred on unincorporated towns and villages in West Canada. Privileges of marriage law of Upper Canada extended to ministers of all denominations. Duties on imports from the United States reduced from 12.5% to 7.5% and duties on British goods raised from 5% to 7.5%. July 1, W. H. Merritt introduced Resolution proposing reciprocity with the United States, and Assembly passed Address to the Imperial Government asking that negotiations with the United States be reopened for free admission of goods. Supplementary School Act regulated city schools. A Board of Registration and Statistics created. First agricultural law enacted authorized agricultural societies and provided for government aid. Bytown incorporated, its limits defined, and town council established, the incorporation disallowed by Imperial Government proclaimed Oct. 12, 1849

June 11, Death of Sir John Franklin on board the "Erebus" in Arctic waters

June 28, Report of Commission appointed to trace boundary between the source of the St. Croix River and the St. Lawrence River

July 9, Joseph Eugene Bruno Guiges appointed first Roman Catholic Bishop of Bytown (Ottawa)

July 22, Imperial Act gave Canada control of taxation confirming civil list granted by Province, and differential duties removed

July 28, Towns of Brantford and London incorporated

——, Agricultural Society of Lower Canada and Agricultural Association of Upper Canada received charters

——, St. Lawrence and Industry Railroad chartered, and Canada, Nova Scotia and New Brunswick Railroad

——, Incorporation of Montreal Mining Company, British North America Company, and British and Canadian Mining Company of Lake Superior

——, Incorporation of companies to operate the "magnetic telegraph"

Aug. 3, First electric telegraph service between Montreal and Toronto

Aug. 16, Royal assent given to Act of June 9, 1846, granting civil list

Aug. 21, Canada Life Insurance Company established

Sept. 11, Great hurricane off Newfoundland, hundreds of fishing boats and 300 lives lost

Oct. 2, Telegraph service opened between Montreal and Quebec

Oct. 23, Ground broken for Great Western Railroad at London but construction not begun until 1851

Oct., Williamsburg Canals on Upper St. Lawrence completed

Nov. 1, Normal School opened at Toronto, T. J. Robertson, head master

Nov. 25, Railroad opened from Montreal to Lachine

Nov. 30, Father Demers consecrated first Roman Catholic Bishop of Vancouver Island

Nov., Ground broken for railroad from St. Andrews, New Brunswick, to Woodstock

A. H. Murray established Fort Yukon for the Hudson Bay Company at mouth of the Porcupine River

John Rae discovered that Boothia Felix was a peninsula, surveyed west coast

Large death rate among the Irish immigrants

1848

Feb. 2, First Liberal Ministry established in Nova Scotia, J. B. Uniacke, Prime Minister

Feb. 25–March 23, First session of third Parliament. Laws enacted for protection of immigrants, inspection of flour, oatmeal, butter, &c., sanitary matters. Motion of lack of confidence in conservative Ministry resulted in formation of the Lafontaine-Baldwin Cabinet known as the "Great Administration" which lasted until the retirement of the 2 leaders in 1851

March 11–Oct., 1851, Second Lafontaine-Baldwin Ministry

March 23, Western Telegraph Company chartered

——, Toronto Athenæum, public library, and museum chartered

——, *Institut Canadien de Quebec* incorporated

March 30, Niagara Falls blocked by jam of ice for several hours, the only time on record

April 14, Railroad from Shediac to St. John chartered by New Brunswick legislature in March 1836 reincorporated

April 15. Charter of Canada, New Brunswick and Nova Scotia Railroad chartered by Provincial Legislature in July 1847 received royal assent, and the Toronto and Goderich Railroad incorporated, proclaimed June 24

April 22, Captain Francis R. M. Crozier in command of Franklin Arctic expedition after death of Franklin left ships frozen in since Sept. 12, 1846, with officers and crew consisting of 105 persons, and all perished, records found in 1859

May 9, John Larkin appointed Roman Catholic Bishop of Toronto, but refused to act

May 30, Fredericton, New Brunswick, incorporated

June 12–Oct. 28, 1849, Voyage of Sir James C. Ross in search of Sir John Franklin. *See* Arctic Regions

June 13, Sir John Richardson and Dr. John Rae in search of Sir John Franklin, sailing from England March 25, reached Cumberland House on the Saskatchewan and Fort Chipewyan July 11, entered the Mackenzie River July 20, and reached its mouth at Arctic Ocean Aug. 3, and proceeded to mouth of Coppermine River. Wintered at Fort Confidence

June 24, The Woodstock and Lake Erie Railroad later the Great Southern incorporated, and the Carillon and Grenville Railroad Company

June, Robert Campbell descended the Pelly River and built Fort Selkirk at forks of Pelly and Lewes rivers

July 24, The "James Ferrier," first locomotive imported from England for use on the Montreal-Lachine Railroad

Aug. 14, Act of Union amended repealing clause which declared English the sole official language in Canada

Oct. 3, Expedition of Lieutenant Pullen ascending the Mackenzie River reached Fort Simpson from the Arctic

Oct. 10, Public Library at Fort Garry, Assiniboia incorporated

Oct. 26, College of Bytown opened

Dec. 14, First session of Newfoundland Legislature after return to the Constitution of 1843

Dec. 26, Railroad opened from Montreal to St. Hyacinthe (toward the Maine border)

1849

Jan. 13, Vancouver Island placed under jurisdiction of the Hudson Bay Company by royal charter

Jan. 18–May 30, Second session of third Parliament. Dual language system, French and English adopted. Commercial reciprocity offered to the United States of certain food stuffs imported. Policy of government aid to railroads inaugurated in connection with grant to Halifax and Quebec Railroad, guarantee of 6% interest on one half of bonds of any company whose lines should extend to 75 miles as less than 50 miles of railroad completed in Canada at this time. New tariff established ad valorem duty of 12.5% on most goods imported. Amnesty granted to rebels of 1837 and 1838. Commission appointed and provision made for indemnification of losses caused by rebellion in Lower Canada. Patent laws consolidated. Court of Error and Appeals established in Lower Canada, and incorporation in Lower Canada of members of law and medical professions. Court of Error and Appeals established in Lower Canada, imprisonment for debt abolished in Lower Canada. Municipal system for Upper Canada established by Baldwin Act, and Court of Chancery Act created office of chancellor and vice-chancellor for Upper Canada and jurisdiction of courts extended. Assent given to Imperial Act authorizing colonial legislatures to establish and regulate posts. New School (Cameron) Act which was never enforced in Upper Canada

Feb., Final Report of survey of Quebec and Halifax Railroad presented to Imperial Parliament

Feb. 1, W. L. Mackenzie returned to Toronto from the United States under pardon from the Government

March 22, Baldwin, Mackenzie, and Blake burned in effigy at Toronto in demonstration against the Rebellion Losses Bill

April 14, Mount Allison Academy at Sackville, New Brunswick (Wesleyan) received a charter

April 25, The Parliament buildings burned in riot in Montreal when Lord Elgin signed Rebellion Losses Bill providing for commission to adjust all "just losses" incurred during the rebellion

——, Canada Life Insurance Company established in 1847 received charter

April 30, Lord Elgin driving to the Government House stoned by a mob

May 29, David Anderson appointed first Anglican Bishop of Rupert's Land

May 30, College of Bytown (Roman Catholic) chartered, later University of Ottawa

——, Hamilton Mercantile Library Association incorporated, and Gore Mechanics Institute

——, Library Association of Teachers of District of Quebec chartered

——, King's College became the University of Toronto by statute to take effect Jan. 1, 1850; secularized

——, Charter of Great Western Railroad altered and amended, and Montreal and Vermont Junction

Railway Company chartered, and Quebec and Halifax Railway

May 30, Construction of a ship canal from Lake Champlain to the St. Lawrence River authorized to enable passage of ships and meet competition of the Erie Canal

June 8, Dr. John Rae left Fort Confidence and descended the Dease River to the Coppermine reaching Cape Krusenstern July 30, obliged to return and give up crossing Wollaston Land June 22 on account of the ice. Sir John Richardson had returned to England in May

June 20, Canadian Institute founded at Toronto by Sandford Fleming, Kivas Tully, and other surveyors, engineers, and architects

June 26, British Navigation Acts abolished restrictions on colonial shipping

July 16, Richard Blanchard appointed Governor of new Vancouver Colony

July 24, Death of John McLeod, explorer

July 26, Convention met at Kingston proposing annexation to the United States because of loss of Canadian economic preference in Great Britain

July 28, Imperial Act enabled colonial legislature to establish inland posts

Aug. 29, Toronto, Sarnia, and Lake Huron Railroad chartered

Oct. 10, Annexation Manifesto published in Montreal favored a North American Confederacy

Nov. 13, Executive Council met at Toronto made the capital because of riots at Montreal in connection with Rebellion Losses Act

Epidemic of cholera

Stewart River discovered by James G. Stewart

1850

Jan. 1, Shipping restrictions on colonial trade with the repeal of British Navigation Acts came into effect on this date, and permitted vessels of all nations to resort to the St. Lawrence

March 10, Richard Blanchard sworn in as Governor of Vancouver

May, The St. Lawrence and Industry Railroad opened from Lanoraie on north bank of the St. Lawrence to village of Industry (later Joliette) third completed railroad in Canada, length 12 miles

May 14–Aug. 10, Third session of third Parliament met at Toronto. Free Banking law passed, only banks incorporated by Parliament or Royal Charter allowed to issue notes, new School Act, the "Great Charter" for Upper Canada passed and Act for protection of the Indians. Duty imposed on foreign reprints of British copyrighted works. Resolutions adopted against seigniorial tenure and in favor of secularization of the clergy reserves. Board of Agriculture established for Upper Canada, and Act to remedy defects in agricultural system of Lower Canada passed

May 26, Armand François Marie de Charbonnel consecrated Roman Catholic Bishop of Toronto

July 12, Joseph Signay, first Metropolitan Archbishop of Quebec (Roman Catholic)

July 17, Lieutenant Pullen descended the Mackenzie River, reaching the Arctic Ocean July 22, and Aug. 9 reached farthest north at Cape Bathurst and Baillie's Islands in 70° 30′ N. Lat., back at mouth of the Mackenzie Aug. 31 and Sept. 4 at Fort Macpherson on the Peel River and at Fort Simpson Oct. 5. Found no trace of Franklin expedition

July 24, The Champlain and St. Lawrence Railroad Company authorized to construct a line to the St. Lawrence River and to Rouse's Point; completed Aug., 1851, now part of Grand Trunk system

Aug. 10, Removal of Victoria College from Cobourg to Toronto authorized

——, Toronto, Sarnia, and Lake Huron became the Ontario, Simcoe, and Lake Huron, part of Northern Railroad in 1858

——, Quebec and Richmond Railroad Company incorporated, and Bytown and Prescott and the Montreal and Lachine Railroad reincorporated

Aug. 20, Caledonia named British Columbia

Sept. 7 and 9, William B. Robinson negotiated 2 treaties with the Indians for land on Lake Huron and Lake Superior, the Indians allowed to hunt and fish on crown domain not conceded

Oct. 3, Death of Archbishop Joseph Signay, succeeded as Bishop of Quebec (Roman Catholic) by Bishop P. Flavien Turgeon Oct. 8

Oct. 11, Railroad opened from Longueil to Richmond (St. Lawrence and Atlantic Company)

Oct. 26, Captain McClure discovered the North West Passage. See Arctic Regions

Nov. 7, Upper Canada School of Medicine became affiliated with the University of Toronto

Dec. 9, Protocol signed between Great Britain and the United States regarding cession of Horseshoe Reef, Lake Erie

Dec. 12, Imperial Order in Council suspended the prohibitions of 1842 against certain foreign reprints of British books entitled to copyright

Robert Campbell descended the Yukon from Fort Selkirk at junction of the Lewes and the Pelly to the mouth of the Porcupine and established identity of the river, first white man on site of Dawson

1851

Feb., Anti-Slavery Society of Canada founded

March 28, New Brunswick passed law to facilitate construction of European and North American Railroad

April 6, Post Office transferred to Canadian control on this date

April 7, Name of Queen's College at Horton, Nova Scotia, changed to Acadia College

April 23, Postage stamps issued

April 24, Lieutenant Governor Sir Alexander Bannerman formed first responsible government in Prince Edward Island, George Coles, first Premier

April 25, Dr. Rae with 2 men left Fort Confidence, on Bear Lake traveled over 942 miles examining shore of Wollaston Land to 110° East and 117° 17' West Long.

May 20–Aug. 30, Fourth session of third Parliament. Acts for trial of controverted elections consolidated, territorial divisions of Upper Canada altered, railroad law clauses as to construction and management consolidated and provision made for a trunk main line through Province, uniform rate of postage adopted, provision made for normal school in Lower Canada and medical schools in Montreal and Toronto. Motion of W. L. Mackenzie to abolish Court of Chancery reorganized by Baldwin 2 years before defeated by support of French

June 30, Resignation of Robert Baldwin and retirement from public life

July 2, Corner stone of Ontario Normal School laid by Lord Elgin

July 17, Death of Sir Roger H. Sheaffe at Edinburgh

Aug. 2, Trinity College (Anglican) at Toronto chartered

Aug. 30, Toronto and Goderich Railroad reincorporated as the Toronto and Guelph

——, First session of first Legislative Council of Vancouver

Aug., The Montreal and Champlain Railroad opened from St. Johns to Rouse's Point

Sept., First sod turned on the Bytown and Prescott Railroad, later the St. Lawrence and Ottawa

Sept. 17–19, Celebration in Boston of establishment of railroad connection with Canada attended by Governor Macdonald, Francis Hincks, and Allan McNab

Sept. 22–Oct. 20, Quebec the capital of Canada

Oct. 22, Executive Council met at Quebec

Oct. 28–Sept. 8, 1854, The Hincks-Morin Ministry, Francis Hincks, Premier, and Inspector General, from Upper Canada, A. N. Morin, Provincial Secretary, from Lower Canada

Oct., Resignation of Lafontaine

Nov. 4, Canadian Institute at Toronto received royal charter

Nov. to March, 1864, James Douglas, Governor of Vancouver Island

Nov. 25, Young Men's Christian Association organized in Montreal

First submarine cable laid between New Brunswick and Prince Edward Island, 10 miles long, by Frederick Newton Gisborne

Epidemic of cholera

Population of Lower Canada 890,261, of Upper Canada 952,004; negroes 2,102

1852

Jan., The Montreal and Champlain Railroad opened from St. Lambert to St. Johns

Jan. 15, Trinity College (Anglican) at Toronto formally opened

March 30, Railroad from Halifax, Nova Scotia, to Quebec authorized

June 8, Thomas Cooke appointed Bishop (Roman Catholic) of Three Rivers

July 8, Fire at Montreal made 10,000 persons homeless

July 15, Victoria College, Toronto, received royal charter

Aug., Montreal and Champlain Railroad opened from Caughnawaga to Moer's Junction

Aug. 7, Montreal and Kingston and Kingston and Toronto Railroad charters proclaimed in force

Aug. 19–Nov. 10, First part of first session of fourth Parliament. Municipal Loan Fund Act for Upper Canada provided for aid in making local improvements, appointment of justices of the peace in remote parts of Lower Canada authorized. Sept. 17 and Oct. 8 Mr. Brown moved in Assembly that measures be taken to recover funds paid for 300,000 acres of land in Upper Canada and 227,000 in Lower Canada obtained by error or fraud of Protestant clergy. Bureau of Agriculture and Minister authorized, and £19,000 annual appropriation for establishment of transatlantic steamship line between Canada and Great Britain, and Act to incorporate the Grand Trunk Railroad

Sept. 6, Robert Campbell began journey from White River in the Yukon district, ascended the Pelly, crossed the mountains to branch of the Liard and arrived at Fort Simpson Oct. 21, and from there on snow shoes by Great Slave Lake, Lake Athabaska,

Ile à la Crosse, to Carleton House, Fort Pelly, Fort Garry, and Pembina to Crow Wing, Minnesota, March 13 and thence to Chicago and at Montreal April 1. Journey of 9,700 miles continuous travel

Sept. 29, New Brunswick made contract for construction of railroad from the boundary of Nova Scotia to the Maine boundary

Nov. 3, Death of Sir Francis Gore

Nov. 10, St. Mary's College, Montreal (Roman Catholic) founded in 1848 received a charter, and royal charter made Bishop's College a University

——, Montreal Ocean Steamship Company established by Hugh and Andrew Allan and other merchants for service between Canada and Great Britain

——, Grand Trunk Railroad chartered and consent to amalgamation with the St. Lawrence and Atlantic, Toronto, and Guelph, Grand Trunk of Canada East and Quebec and Richmond, and the Galt and Guelph Railroad (Great Western) incorporated and Cobourg and Peterboro

——, Charter of McGill University amended

Nov. 24, Normal School of Ontario opened

Dec. 8, Laval University (Roman Catholic) at Quebec received royal charter, the former Seminary of Quebec founded by Bishop Laval

Electric telegraph between St. Johns and Conception Bay of F. N. Gisborne opened

1853

Feb. 1, Robert Campbell left Fort Simpson and arrived at Crow Wing, Minnesota, March 13, and from there proceeded to London, Ontario, journey of 9,700 miles, over 300 on snow shoes

Feb. 9, First sod turned for the Cobourg and Peterboro Railroad

Feb. 14–June 14, Second part of first session of fourth Parliament, called the "railroad session," 28 railroad laws enacted. Franchise extended and provision made for registration of voters, members of Legislative Council increased from 84 to 130. Customs reduced on certain articles including sugar, wines, and molasses, and salt placed on free list. Decimal system of currency adopted. Assembly petitioned Imperial Government for permission to remodel the Legislative Council on elective basis. Grand Trunk Amalgamation Act extended to allow incorporation of intersecting lines

April 4, King's College, Windsor, Nova Scotia, incorporated by provincial statute

April 12, Supplementary Agreement completed amalgamation of Grand Trunk Railroad

April 22, Charter of Toronto University amended to vest teaching in new collegiate institution of "University College," and functions of University limited to examination for and granting degrees

——, The Stanstead, Shefford, and Chambly Railroad chartered, and Montreal and Bytown, and London and Port Sarnia which became Sarnia branch of the Great Western

May 9, British Parliament recognized right of Canada to dispose of the clergy reserves and proceeds thereof on condition that all vested rights respected

May 10, The "Genova," first steamer of transatlantic line to arrive at Quebec from England, beginning fortnightly service between Montreal and Liverpool

May 16, The Northern Railroad opened from Toronto to Aurora, 30 miles, to Bradford June 13, and to Barrie Oct. 1

May 23, Canadian Steam Navigation Company incorporated and ocean mail service to Great Britain established

——, Dalhousie and Thorold Railroad chartered

June 6, Riots in Quebec against converted Italian priest, Gavazzi, lecturing in the Presbyterian Church on the "errors of Rome"

June 7, Death of Mgr. Provencher at St. Boniface

June 9, Gavazzi riot in Montreal, 5 persons killed

June 13, Northern Railroad opened from Toronto to Bradford, first in Upper Canada on which a locomotive used

June 13–June 22, 1854, Second session of fourth Parliament. Municipal Loan Fund Act for Upper Canada amended to make approval of majority of electors necessary for loan, and amount limited to 20% of value of property

June 14, St. Maurice Iron Works incorporated

July 16, Trinity College became Trinity University by royal charter

July, The Grand Trunk Railroad completed from Sherbrooke to the Province Line

Aug. 23–June 10, 1854, William Rowan, Administrator, in absence of Lord Elgin

Sept. 14, First sod of railroad from boundary of Nova Scotia to Maine boundary turned by Lady Head at St. John, New Brunswick (European and North American Railroad)

Oct. 1, The *Toronto Globe* first issued as a daily newspaper

Nov. 10, The Great Western Railroad opened from Suspension Bridge to Hamilton, 43 miles, and from Hamilton to London, 76 miles, Dec. 31

Dec. 2, Governor Douglas established Supreme Court at Vancouver Island, David Cameron appointed Chief Justice, appointment confirmed by Imperial Order in Council April 4, 1856

Meterological Bureau transferred from Imperial to Canadian control

1854

Jan. 27, The Great Western Railroad opened from London to Windsor opposite Detroit connected by Niagara suspension bridge with New York Central and Michigan Central

Feb. 1, Parliament Buildings at Quebec burned

March 31, Nova Scotia Railroad authorized to open road from Truro to Pictou on Gulf of St. Lawrence

——, After winter at Repulse Bay John Rae started to trace west coast of Boothia peninsula and proved King William's Land an island, obtained news of Franklin expedition from the Esquimaux and returned to York Factory Aug. 31

May 3, Bell Ewart branch of the Great Northern Railroad opened

May 6, New York, Newfoundland, and London Telegraph Company founded by Cyrus W. Field

May 30, Death of Sir Peregrine Maitland in London

June 5, Elgin Treaty established commercial reciprocity between Canada and the United States, mutual abandonment of customs duties on most of natural products, came into effect in Canada Oct. 18

June 13, First sod of Nova Scotia Railroad turned at Richmond near Halifax for railroad from Halifax to Truro

July 3, Erie and Ontario Railroad from Lake Ontario to Chippewa, a horse tramway, opened, leased to Great Western

July 20, First stone of the Victoria Railroad Bridge at Montreal laid by Robert Stephenson, celebrated engineer

Aug. 10, Imperial Act consolidated laws respecting merchant shipping

Aug. 11, Union Amendment Act (Imperial) to empower alteration of the constitution of the Legislative Council of Canada to make it elective

Aug. 21, The Harrisburg to Galt branch of the Great Western (Galt and Guelph) opened

Sept. 5–Dec. 18, First part of first session of fifth Parliament. Secularization of clergy reserves and abolition of seigniorial tenure settled at cost of $1,000,000

Sept. 7, Work begun on St. Peter's Canal, Cape Breton

Sept. 8, Resignation of the Hincks-Morin Cabinet

Sept. 11–Jan., 1855, The McNab-Morin Ministry entered office, Sir Allan McNab, President of the Council and Minister of Agriculture (Upper Canada), and A. N. Morin (Upper Canada) Commissioner of Crown Lands. Oct. 13, Committee of Assembly, W. H. Merritt, Francis Hincks, John Young, G. E. Cartier appointed to enquire into commercial intercourse with other countries

Sept. 20, The pioneer steamship "Canadian" of the Allan Line (Montreal Steamship Company) sailed from Liverpool for Quebec and Montreal

Oct., The Carillon and Grenville Railroad built around the Long Sault rapids in the Ottawa opened

Oct. 10, Death of Sir Gordon Drummond in London

Nov. 27, The Grand Trunk Railroad completed from Richmond to Point Levis opposite Quebec

Dec. 18, Quebec and Saguenay Railroad chartered

——, Montreal Ocean Steamship Company incorporated and Canada Ocean Steam Navigation Company

——, Bytown became city of Ottawa

Dec. 19, Sir Edmund W. Head, commissioned Governor Sept. 21, assumed office, succeeding Lord Elgin

Cholera epidemic

1855

Jan., The Northern Railroad opened from Barrie to Collingwood on Georgian Bay 96 miles from Toronto

Jan. 26, Resignation of A. N. Morin for reasons of health caused resignation of entire Cabinet

Jan. 27–May, 1856, The McNab-Taché Ministry, Colonel Taché resuming his portfolio as Receiver General, Mr. Cauchon becoming Commissioner of Crown Lands

Feb. 8, Six new Legislative Councillors appointed

Feb. 23–May 30, Second part of first session of fifth Parliament. Militia laws amended to enable formation of volunteer companies and battalions divided into the 2 classes of sedentary and active, and all lands and works of Imperial Government transferred to Canada by Militia Act. School Act for Upper Canada amended to make further provision for grammar and common schools. Municipal and Road Act for Lower Canada enacted. Postage abolished on newspapers published in the Province. Postal money-order and letter registration systems established. Measure for making the Legislative Council elective passed the Assembly and was rejected by the Council. £900,000 granted to Grand Trunk Railroad Company

Feb., Nova Scotia Railroad opened to Mile House and to Bedford in July

March 9, Niagara Suspension Bridge over the Niagara River completed

April 17, Charlottetown incorporated

May 19, Niagara District Bank chartered, and Molson's Bank in Montreal

——, Amherstburg and St. Thomas Railroad Company chartered

May 30, Hamilton and South Western Railroad chartered

June 18, Sault Ste. Marie Canal built in 1797 by the North West Company rebuilt and reopened

June 25, The Great Western Railroad placed the steamers "Canada" and "America" on Lake Ontario for service between Hamilton and Oswego

Aug. 14, Imperial Merchant Shipping Act of 1854 amended, the erection of colonial lighthouses provided for

Sept. 4, Seigneurial Court met and rendered judgment May 4, 1856

Oct. 1, The London and Port Stanley Railroad completed from Lake Erie to London

Oct. 20–Sept. 24, 1859, Toronto the capital of Canada

Nov. 9, Executive Council met at Toronto

Nov. 29, The Grand Trunk Railroad completed from Montreal to Brockville and from Levis to St. Thomas, Quebec Dec. 23

Dec. 3, The Great Western opened from Hamilton to Toronto

1856

Feb. 15–July 1, Second session of fifth Parliament. Common Law Procedure Act for Upper Canada enacted. Legislative Council (Upper House) formerly appointed by the Crown made elective by Act which received the royal assent June 24, proclaimed July 14

April 16, Governor Douglas made official announcement of discovery of gold in British Columbia and proclamation declared all gold the property of the Crown

May 16, Buffalo and Lake Huron Railroad chartered, and Canadian Western Railway Company

May 18, College and Academy of the Free Church of Nova Scotia chartered

May 24–Nov., 1857, The Taché-Macdonald Ministry, only 2 new members, P. M. M. S. Vankoughnet succeeding Sir Allan McNab as President of the Council and became head of the Dept. of Agriculture, and T. L. Terrill who succeeded Mr. Cartier as Provincial Secretary

July 1, Canadian Marine Insurance Company chartered

Aug. 12, First meeting of Legislature of Vancouver Island

Oct. 1, London and Port Stanley Railroad completed from Lake Erie to London

Oct. 27, First passenger train ran from Montreal to Toronto on the Grand Trunk Railroad, and opened from Quebec to Toronto Nov. 12

Nov. 10, Newfoundland-New York telegraph line opened

Nov. 17, The Grand Trunk completed from Guelph to Stratford, 39 miles, and from St. Mary's to Sarnia Nov. 21

Dec. 4, Canadian Order in Council provided for free transit of goods through Canada from points in the United States to other points in the United States by bonding system

Dec. 22, Buffalo and Lake Huron Railroad opened from Fort Erie to Stratford, later incorporated with the Grand Trunk

1857

Feb. 5, Imperial House of Commons appointed select committee to investigate administration of the Hudson Bay Company over its vast domains

Feb. 10, Death of David Thompson, explorer of western country

Feb. 26–June 10, Third session of fifth Parliament. Election and Franchise Act passed, Act to encourage gradual civilization of the Indians, civil laws, and laws of procedure of Lower Canada codified, and decentralization of justice by division of Lower Canada into 19 judicial districts instead of 7. Resolution asked Her Majesty to select a city for permanent seat of government

March 12, Train on Great Western Railroad broke through bridge over the Desjardin Canal, 70 persons killed

March 17, St. John (New Brunswick) to Shediac Railroad opened for 3 miles out of St. John

March 18, Canadian Literary Institute organized, the later Woodstock Baptist College

May 27, Belleville Seminary (Methodist Episcopal) chartered

——, Richelieu Company incorporated, name changed in 1875 to Richelieu and Ontario Navigation Company

June 10, Toronto and Owen Sound, Eastwood and Berlin, Strathroy and Port Frank, Brantford and Southwestern railroads, chartered. Brantford, a town of less than 5,000 inhabitants, borrowed $500,000 for the railroad from the Municipal Loan Fund

June 20–Nov. 2, Sir William Eyre, Administrator

June 26, Fire on the steamer "Montreal" burned on the St. Lawrence on the way from Montreal to Quebec, 250 persons chiefly Scotch and Norwegian immigrants lost their lives

June 27, Joint Commission on boundary with the United States met, no agreement reached in 6 meetings

Aug. 7–11, Failure of first attempt to lay Atlantic cable from Trinity Bay, Newfoundland to Valencia Bay, Ireland

Sept. 28, Great Western Railroad opened from Galt to Guelph

Oct. 1, St. Andrews (New Brunswick) and Quebec Railroad opened for 34 miles from St. Andrews to Barber Dam

Nov. 25, Resignation of Prime Minister, Colonel Taché

Nov. 26–July 29, 1858, Macdonald-Cartier Ministry, Macdonald continued in office and Mr. Cartier continuing to hold portfolio of Attorney General East represented Lower Canada section of the Cabinet

Dec. 30, Port Hope, Lindsay, and Beaverton Railroad opened from Port Hope to Lindsay, and the Welland Railroad from Port Dalhousie to Port Colborne

Dec. 31, Ottawa chosen by the Queen as the capital of Canada

1858

Feb. 14, Proclamation of Governor Douglas fixed agricultural land in British Columbia at 10 shillings per acre

Feb. 25–Aug. 16, First session of sixth Parliament. Defective Franchise Act of previous session amended. Customs duties raised to 15% as a general rate and protection for home industries discussed. Canadian consolidated stock at 4 and 4.5% authorized. Municipal Act for Upper Canada enacted. Both Houses

petitioned Her Majesty for construction of an intercolonial railroad to connect New Brunswick and Nova Scotia with Canada

Feb., Discovery of gold in the Fraser River valley

April 6, Mount Allison Academy, Sackville, New Brunswick, made Mount Allison Wesleyan College by new charter

April 25, First miners arrived at Victoria, British Columbia

May 30, Revocation of charter of Hudson Bay Company as to the mainland (British Columbia)

June 1, Railroad opened from St. John, New Brunswick, to Rothesay (European and North American)

June 3, Windsor branch of Nova Scotia Railroad opened

June 28, Buffalo and Lake Huron Railroad opened from Stratford to Goderich, leased to Grand Trunk

July 24, Knox College, Toronto, Presbyterian theological seminary, chartered

July 28, The Macdonald-Cartier Ministry defeated on motion that the city of Ottawa ought not to be the permanent seat of government by 14 votes and the Ministry resigned on the 29th

Aug. 2, Imperial Act provided for government of mainland of British North America to be called British Columbia, and Victoria to be the capital

Aug. 2–4, Brown-Dorion Ministry, the so-called "double-shuffle." Governor Head refused his new Premier a dissolution. J. A. Macdonald took advantage of clause in statute providing that when a minister accepted another office within one month he should not thereby vacate his seat, and each minister shifted to a different post and then returned to his normal post

Aug. 5, Completion of the Atlantic cable, laid between July 7 and Aug. 5, but failure of electrical insulation in Oct. made it useless

Aug. 6–May, 1862, The Macdonald-Cartier Ministry

Aug. 16, The Ontario, Simcoe, and Huron Railroad formerly the Toronto, Sarnia and Lake Huron changed its name to Northern Railroad of Canada

——, Bank of Canada chartered

Aug. 18, The Port Hope, Lindsay and Beaverton Railroad opened from Milbrook to Peterborough

Aug. 20, Colony of British Columbia established, and control of Vancouver Island surrendered by the Hudson Bay Company

Sept. 2, Sir James Douglas appointed Governor of British Columbia, and Matthew B. Begbie commissioned Judge

Sept. 27, The Grand Trunk Railroad completed from Stratford to London

Nov. 19, Governor Douglas and Judge Begbie took oath of office for administration of British Columbia

Dec. 1, New Brunswick and Canada Railroad opened to Canterbury

Dec. 9, Death of Robert Baldwin, called the "father of responsible government"

Dec. 15, Nova Scotia Railroad completed from Halifax to Truro (93 miles)

Dec. 27, The Great Western Railroad opened from Komoka to Sarnia

Henry Yule Hind explored the country west of Lake Winnipeg in 1858–1859

1859

Jan., Silver coinage issued

Jan. 1, The Stanstead, Shefford and Chambly Railroad opened from St. John, New Brunswick to West

Farnham, and as far as Granby, Lower Canada Dec. 31

Jan. 29–May 4, Second session of sixth Parliament. Railroad Act passed. Customs duties increased to average of 20% on articles not specifically enumerated. Issue of new municipal loans prohibited except for purposes of renewal and 5% required on obligations instead of 8%. Public Works Act amended and consolidated. Ottawa voted as seat of government. Provision made for facilitating the redemption of Provincial debentures and the consolidation of the public debt, and title of Minister of Finance given to head of Dept. of Finance

April 13, University of New Brunswick at Fredericton chartered by provincial statute, former King's College

April 15, Thomas Louis Connolly appointed Archbishop of Halifax (Roman Catholic)

May 4, Incorporation of the Bank of Western Canada, the Royal Bank of Canada, and *La Banque Nationale*

May 5, New Westminster founded by Colonel R. C. Moody in Feb. made the capital of British Columbia

May 19, First steamboat on the Red River arrived at Fort Gary

May, Allan Steamship Line began weekly service from Quebec to Liverpool

June 8, Proclamation of Governor Douglas constituted the Supreme Court of British Columbia

——, European and North American Railroad opened from Rothesay to Hampton, and from Hampton to Sussex Nov. 10

Sept. 17, Montreal-Victoria railroad bridge over the St. Lawrence completed, and first passenger train crossed the bridge Dec. 17

Sept. 24–Oct. 20, 1865, Quebec, the capital of Canada

Oct. 12–Feb. 22, 1861, Sir William F. Williams, Administrator

Oct. 21, Executive Council met at Quebec

Oct. 27, International Bank suspended

Nov. 20, John Joseph Lynch consecrated Bishop of Toronto (Roman Catholic)

Dec. 16, The Grand Trunk Railroad completed to Victoria Bay, and from St. Thomas to St. Paschal Dec. 31

1860

Feb. 28–May 19, Third session of sixth Parliament. Final abolition of seigniorial rights and duties. Municipal and Roads Acts for Lower Canada consolidated and amended. Mr. Brown introduced 2 measures declaring the Union a failure which were defeated by 66 to 27, and 74 to 32

April 6–Aug. 13, Contract with Allan Steamship Line for weekly postal service to Liverpool

May 2, Prince of Wales College, Prince Edward Island, chartered, the former Central Academy, Charlottetown

July 1, All control of Indian affairs transferred to Province

July 2, The Grand Trunk Railroad completed below Quebec to Rivière du Loup

July 24, The Prince of Wales afterwards Edward VII arrived at Newfoundland, at Halifax July 30, at St. John, New Brunswick Aug. 2, Charlottetown Aug. 9, and Aug. 18 at Quebec

Aug. 1, European and North American Railroad opened from Sussex to Monckton

Aug. 25, The Prince of Wales formally opened Victoria Railroad Bridge across the St. Lawrence at Montreal

Sept. 1, Corner stone of Parliament Buildings at Ottawa laid by the Prince of Wales

Sept. 19, The Prince of Wales left Canada for visit to the United States, and returned to England from Portland, Maine, sailing Oct. 20

Sept. 26, Morrin College (Presbyterian theological) founded by Joseph Morrin at Quebec

Nov. 6, L. B. Vaughan struck oil at depth of 85 feet in first Canadian oil well sunk at Petrolia, Ontario

Nov. 10, Kingston branch of the Grand Trunk Railroad completed

1861

March 16–May 18, Fourth session of sixth Parliament. No important measures passed. Discussion of case of John Anderson, colored slave who had escaped to Canada from Missouri in 1853 and had been discovered and arrested April 30, 1860, in connection with writ of habeas corpus and recommendation made to Imperial Government for legislation to prevent conflict of jurisdiction. Anderson discharged by court

April 15, Resolution introduced by Joseph Howe proposing union of North American Provinces adopted by Parliament of Nova Scotia and sent by despatch of July 6, 1862, to Governors of the various provinces. Resulted in the Charlottetown Conference

May 18, Morrin College, Quebec, chartered, and College of Bytown became College of Ottawa

Aug. 14, Great inundation of Montreal, a quarter of the city under water

Aug. 29, Death of William Lyon Mackenzie

Sept. 10, Meeting of first Anglican provincial synod

Sept. 11, First street railway opened in Toronto, Yonge Street line

Oct. 25–Nov. 27, Viscount Monck, Administrator, commissioned Governor Nov. 2, and assumed office Nov. 28

Dec. 3, 3,000 British troops sent to Canada on account of the "Trent affair" of Nov. 8, seizure of Confederate commissioners from British ship

Population of Lower Canada, 1,111,566, of Upper Canada, 1,396,091, of Nova Scotia, 330,857, of New Brunswick, 252,047, of Prince Edward Island, 80,857, of British Columbia estimated as 3,024, and of Manitoba, 10,000; total, 3,184,442. Included 13,166 negroes

1862

March 20–June 9, First session of seventh Parliament. Criminal law amended. The Legislative Council exercised privilege of electing a Speaker for the first time, Sir Allan McNab chosen. Bureau of Agriculture organized as a separate dept. Announcement that Her Majesty granted free interprovincial commercial intercourse. The Macdonald-Cartier Militia Bill defeated May 20. Grand Trunk Railroad authorized to issue $500,000 of equipment bonds and allowed to postpone payment of government loans. New Militia Bill providing for 10,000 volunteers passed

April 17, Legislative Council of Prince Edward Island made elective

May 21, Resignation of Ministry, defeated May 20 on the Militia Bill

May 24–May 6, 1863, Macdonald-Sicotte Ministry, John Sandfield Macdonald (Upper Canada) Prime Minister and Attorney General West, and L. V.

Sicotte (Lower Canada) Attorney General East, T. D. McGee, President of the Council

May 31, Bank of British Columbia incorporated, opened in Aug. at Victoria

July, New Brunswick and Canada Railroad opened to Richmond

Aug. 2, Victoria, British Columbia, incorporated

Aug. 8, Death of Sir Allan McNab

Sept. 26, Journey of Lord Milton and Dr. W. B. Cheadle of the Royal Geographical Society begun "with a view of exploring a route across the continent to British Columbia through British territory, by one of the northern passes in the Rocky Mountains" reached Carlton House on the Saskatchewan and wintered 70 miles northwest

1863

Jan. 6, Death of Anglican Bishop George J. Mountain, succeeded as Bishop of Quebec by James W. Williams

Feb. 12–May 12, Second session of seventh Parliament. Act restored to Roman Catholics in Upper Canada certain rights respecting separate schools

April 16, Entomological Society of Ontario organized in Ontario

April 29, Dalhousie College and University, Halifax, Nova Scotia, reëstablished

April, Milton and Cheadle left winter quarters and Edmonton, June 3, by Pembina River and following the Athabaska River reached the Fraser July 10, crossing the mountains by the Yellowhead Pass and descended the North Thompson River, British Columbia

May 5, Huron College, London, Ontario, chartered

May 16–March 21, 1864, The Macdonald-Dorion Ministry, John Sandfield Macdonald, Premier and Attorney General West, and A. A. Dorion, Attorney General East (Lower Canada)

June 11, Legislative Council for British Columbia appointed

July 1, Claims Convention between Great Britain and the United States signed at Washington for final settlement of the claims of the Hudson Bay Company and the Puget Sound Agricultural Company, commission appointed, and award Sept. 1869

July 28, Boundaries of British Columbia defined by imperial statute

Aug. 13–Oct. 15, First session of eighth Parliament. New Militia Act included all male inhabitants between ages of 18 and 60

Dec. 8, New mail contract made with the Allan Steamship Line

1864

Jan. 1, Government account transferred to Bank of Montreal

Feb. 19–June 30, Second session of eighth Parliament. Acts passed respecting sale of intoxicating liquor, excise duties, gold mines, insolvency. Committee of Assembly reported in favor of change in federal system

Feb. 26, Death of Sir Louis Hypolite Lafontaine, Chief Justice of Lower Canada, in Montreal

March 21, Resignation of the Ministry

March 30–June 14, Taché-Macdonald Ministry

June 6, First issue of *Cariboo Sentinel*, British Columbia

June 14, Ministry defeated on vote of censure as to financial transactions of Finance Minister Galt with Grand Trunk Railroad

June 30, "Great Coalition" Ministry formed, George Brown joining Macdonald and Taché to form a Cabinet to work for Confederation, new Ministers Oliver Mowat and William McDougall

——, Royal Canadian Bank of Toronto chartered

Aug. 1, The Buffalo and Lake Huron Railroad became part of the Grand Trunk system

Sept. 1, Conference at Charlottetown, Prince Edward Island, of representatives of Nova Scotia, New Brunswick, and Prince Edward Island to discuss union of the maritime provinces, Newfoundland represented, and J. A. Macdonald, George Brown, G. E. Cartier, A. T. Galt, T. D. McGee, H. L. Langevin, W. McDougall, and Alexander Campbell, all members of the Canada Cabinet, attended to present proposal of union of all the Provinces

Oct. 10–28, Quebec Convention to discuss Confederation, 12 representatives from Canada, 5 from Nova Scotia, 7 from New Brunswick, 7 from Prince Edward Island, and 2 from Newfoundland, the "Fathers of the Confederation." Federal Union under the Crown recommended, and 72 resolutions adopted which became the basis of the British North America Act

Oct. 19, Raid on St. Albans, Vermont. Confederates led by Lieut. Bennett H. Young from Canada; discharged by Canadian Judge Coursol Dec. 14 on technical grounds, and $90,000 taken from St. Albans bank returned to them, but eventually paid back by the Government

Dec. 20, Canadian volunteers called for service on the frontier against Fenian attacks from the United States

1865

Jan. 19–March 18, Third session of eighth Parliament. Discussion of Address to Her Majesty praying for submission to Imperial Parliament of measure for union of the provinces of British North America, based on the Quebec Resolutions of Oct. 10, carried in Legislative Council Feb. 20 by vote of 45 to 15, and in Assembly March 10 by vote of 91 to 33. Insolvency Act of 1864 amended

Feb. 24, Cable telegraph line begun at New Westminster, British Columbia, for Russia-American telegraph; never completed

March 7, New Brunswick Assembly rejected Confederation, and again in 1866, 1870, and 1873

March 23, British Parliament granted £50,000 for defense of Canada

March 24, Order in Council appointed committee to England for conference, Macdonald, Cartier, Brown and Galt

May 2, Provision made by Nova Scotia Legislature for construction of St. Peter's Canal

May 19, Robert Machray appointed Anglican Bishop of Rupert's Land, succeeding Bishop Anderson

May, Canadian Land and Emigration Company of London, England, bought 10 townships in Upper Canada and settled present towns of Haliburton and Minden

June 29, Imperial Act to remove doubts as to the validity of colonial laws defined "repugnancy" as to English law

July 1, Quebec made the capital of the Province of Quebec

July 11, Commercial Convention at Detroit, Michigan, adopted resolutions in favor of continued commercial reciprocity, Joseph Howe, of Nova Scotia, one of the speakers

July 30, Death of Sir Etienne Taché, Prime Minister

Aug. 7, Belleau-Macdonald Ministry, Sir Narcisse Belleau succeeding Taché as Premier

Aug. 8–Sept. 18, Fourth session of eighth Parliament received report on the Confederation of the Committee who had returned from England. Civil Code for Lower Canada adopted

Sept. 18, London Collegiate Institute chartered

Sept. 30–Feb. 12, 1866, Sir John Michel, Administrator, during absence in England of Lord Monck

Oct. 20, Proclamation fixed seat of government permanently at Ottawa

Nov. 28, Executive Council met at Ottawa

Dec. 21, George Brown resigned from the Cabinet

American explorer, Charles Francis Hall, made journey to Repulse Bay where he wintered, and in the spring reached Cape Weynton, Simpson Peninsula

1866

March 17, Elgin Reciprocity Treaty of June 5, 1854 terminated by the United States

April 10, Threatened invasion of Fenians gathered at Eastport, Maine, into New Brunswick prevented by arrival of troops

April 17, Nova Scotia Assembly led by Dr. Charles Tupper voted in favor of Union

May 7, St. Francis Xavier College at Antigonish founded in 1854 chartered

May 14, Windsor and Annapolis Railroad chartered

May 31, Fenians from Buffalo, New York, made raid into Canada across the Niagara River near Black Rock

——, Call for 14,000 troops and by June 3 20,000 volunteers were under arms

June 1, Fenians led by John O'Neill seized Fort Erie across from Buffalo

June 2, Fenians defeated at Ridgeway by Canadian force and retreated across the border into the United States June 3

June 4, Fenian invasion of 1,800 Irish-Americans from St. Albans but retired without giving battle after plundering at Pigeon Hill and Frelighsburg

June 7, Fenians occupied St. Armand just over the Vermont border

June 8–Aug. 15, Fifth session of eighth Parliament, at Ottawa. Act passed to protect Lower Canada against lawless aggression from subjects of foreign countries at peace with Canada, and writ of habeas corpus suspended for one year in case of persons suspected on account of Fenian invasions. Common law procedure of Upper Canada amended, and municipal institutions and assessment laws, incomes assessed for first time. Currency Act provided for issue of provincial notes. Duty on manufactured goods raised to 15%, and tax on whiskey increased to 30 cents a gallon

June 30, New Brunswick led by Mr. Tilley voted for Union, and provided for immediate construction of the Intercolonial Railroad

July 27, Atlantic cable completed as the "Great Eastern" with arrival of cable at fishing village of Heart's Content, Trinity Bay, Newfoundland

Aug. 1, Civil Code of Lower Canada came into effect

Aug. 6, Imperial statute established union of Vancouver Island with British Columbia

Aug. 15, Ottawa College charter amended to confer university powers, and College of Regiopolis made a university

Aug. 15, Royal College of Physicians and Surgeons chartered at Kingston, and Belleville Seminary chartered as Albert College

——, Montreal Club, Montreal Literary Club, and *Institut des Artisans des Canadiens de Montreal* chartered

Aug., The Esquimalt and Nanaimo Railroad, first on Vancouver Island, opened by Sir John Macdonald

——, Gold discovered in Madoc township, Ontario, near Eldorado station

Sept., Failure of Bank of Upper Canada

Oct. 14, Fire in the St. Roch and St. Sauveurs suburbs of Quebec, 2,129 houses burned

Nov. 7, Canadian delegates to Conference, Macdonald, Cartier, Howland, McDougall, Langevin, and Galt sailed for England

Nov. 17, Proclamation of union of Vancouver Island to British Columbia

Nov., Discovery of gold in Hastings County, western Canada

Dec. 4–24, Conference in London of representatives of Canada, Nova Scotia, and New Brunswick on the Confederation Bill. Delegates from Nova Scotia included Tupper, Henry, Archibald, McCully, and W. J. Ritchie, and from New Brunswick, Tilley, Fisher, Mitchell, Johnston, and R. D. Wilmot. Mr. Macdonald elected chairman. London Resolutions adopted replaced the Quebec Resolutions, pledge as to building of Intercolonial Railroad made more explicit and imperial aid guaranteed and clause guaranteed to both Protestant and Roman Catholic minorities rights regarding separate schools

Dec. 10, Sir John Michel, Administrator, until June 25, 1867, during absence of Viscount Monck, Governor, in England

Dec. 17, Petrolia branch of the Great Western Railroad opened

Dec. 21, The Bytown (Ottawa) and Prescott Railroad became the St. Lawrence and Ottawa under new charter

1867

Feb. 7, Draft Bill to unite the Provinces into the Dominion of Canada introduced in British House of Lords and sent to Commons Feb. 26, and received royal assent March 29

March 29, British North America Act by which Upper Canada as Ontario and Lower Canada as Quebec, Nova Scotia, and New Brunswick united into the Dominion of Canada

April 12, Imperial Canada Railway Loan Act authorized imperial guarantee of interest on Canadian loan of £3,000,000 for Intercolonial Railroad to be constructed from Quebec to Halifax

May 22, Royal Proclamation declared the Dominion of Canada should come into existence July 1. The term "Dominion" adopted from Psalms 72:8 "dominion from sea to sea and from the river unto the ends of the earth"

——, Senate appointed by the Crown of 72 life members, 24 for Ontario, 24 for Quebec, and 12 each for Nova Scotia and New Brunswick

May 31, Nova Scotia Railroad opened from Truro to Pictou, 52 miles

June 1, Viscount Monck appointed Governor of the Dominion, assumed office July 1

June 27–28, Liberal Party Convention met in Toronto
July 1, British North America Act establishing the
Dominion of Canada came into effect, celebrated
every year as Dominion Day, Quebec established as
the capital of the Province of Quebec and Toronto as
the capital of the Province of Ontario
——, First Dominion Ministry appointed

Office	Name	Date of Appointment
Premier	Sir John A. Macdonald	July 1, 1867
Minister of Justice and Attorney General	Sir John A. Macdonald	July 1, 1867
Minister of Finance	Sir A. T. Galt	July 1, 1867
	Sir John Rose	Nov. 18, 1867
	Sir Francis Hincks	Oct. 9, 1869
	Sir Samuel Leonard Tilley	Feb. 22, 1873
Minister of Public Works	William McDougall	July 1, 1867
	Sir Hector L. Langevin	Dec. 8, 1869
Minister of Militia and Defense	Sir George E. Cartier	July 1, 1867
	Hugh McDonald	July 1, 1873
Minister of Customs	Sir Samuel Leonard Tilley	July 1, 1867
	Sir Charles Tupper	Feb. 22, 1873
Minister of Agriculture	J. C. Chapais	July 1, 1867
	Christopher Dunkin	Nov. 16, 1869
	John Henry Pope	Oct. 25, 1871
Postmaster General	Sir Alexander Campbell	July 1, 1867
	John O'Connor	July 1, 1873
Minister of Marine and Fisheries	Peter Mitchell	July 1, 1867
Minister of Inland Revenue	William Pearce Howland	July 1, 1867
	A. Morris	Nov. 16, 1869
	Sir Charles Tupper	July 2, 1872
	John O'Connor	March 4, 1873
	T. N. Gibbs	July 1, 1873
Minister of the Interior	Sir Alexander Campbell	July 1, 1873
President of Council	A. J. Ferguson Blair	July 1, 1867
	Joseph Howe	Jan. 30, 1869
	Edward Kenny	Nov. 16, 1869
	Sir Charles Tupper	June 21, 1870
	John O'Connor	July 2, 1872
	Hugh McDonald	June 14, 1873
Receiver General	Edward Kenny	July 1, 1867
	J. C. Chapais	Nov. 16, 1869
	Theodore Robitaille	Jan. 30, 1873

Office	Name	Date of Appointment
Secretary of State	Sir Hector L. Langevin	July 1, 1867
	J. C. Aikins	Dec. 8, 1869
Secretary of State for the Provinces	Adams G. Archibald	July 1, 1867
	Joseph Howe	Nov. 16, 1869
	T. N. Gibbs	June 14, 1873
Without portfolio	J. C. Aikins	Nov. 16, 1869

Sept., First general election in general favorable to the
Government, George Brown, opposition leader defeated in Ontario, only in Nova Scotia owing to
opposition of Joseph Howe an opposition majority
returned
Nov. 1, Death of Anglican Bishop John Strachan
Nov. 6–Dec. 21, First part of first session of first
Dominion Parliament. Salary of members fixed at
$6 per day to end of 30 days and mileage granted,
and $600 for the session if longer than 30 days, salary
of Speaker fixed at $3,200. Legislation enacted for
establishment of departments of the Government,
and a Public Works Dept. created. Post Office Act
established uniform rates and regulations and postal
savings banks. Banking Act passed. Stamp duty
placed on bills of exchange and promissory notes.
Resolution adopted for admission of Rupert's Land
and North West Territory into the Dominion, and
Address sent to Her Majesty. Act gave effect to
construction of Intercolonial Railroad provided for
by British North America Act of 1867. The Grand
Trunk Railroad authorized to issue another £500,000
equipment bonds. Act again passed to protect inhabitants against lawless aggression from subjects of
foreign countries at peace with the Government
Dec. 17, Legislature of British Columbia met for first
time at Victoria
Dec. 27, First meetings of Provincial Legislatures of
Quebec and Ontario

1868

Jan. 30, First meeting of Legislature of Nova Scotia
after the Confederation
Feb. 13, First meeting of Legislature of New Brunswick
after the Confederation
Feb. 14, Joseph Howe sailed for England as head of
delegation to ask for repeal of the British North
America Act for Nova Scotia
March 4, Toronto Young Men's Christian Association
incorporated
——, Royal Canadian Yacht Club chartered
——, London Collegiate Institute became Hellmuth
College
March 12–May 22, Second part of first session of first
Dominion Parliament. Legislation enacted for management and collection of revenue, and for establishing and regulating the various Offices of State.
New Customs and Militia Acts passed, and new Act
to secure independence of members of Parliament
made any person holding a position of profit or
emolument under the Government ineligible to seat
in Parliament under penalty of fine. Copyright Act
passed, Act regulating naturalization of aliens, provision made for geological survey, for free entry of
natural products from the United States on condi-

tion of reciprocity. Provided that Government might grant licenses to foreign vessels to fish in Canadian waters. Act passed to enable Parliament to continue in case of decease of sovereign. Railway Act passed, and civil service organized. First Dominion Insurance Act passed

March 23, College of St. Joseph (Roman Catholic) established 1864 at Memramcook, New Brunswick, received charter

April 1, Post Office Savings Bank established

April 7, Thomas Darcy McGee assassinated by Fenians at Ottawa

May 26, Design for Great Seal with arms of the four confederated provinces approved by royal warrant

May, Montreal Mining Company organized an exploring party which discovered Silver Islet silver vein

July 1, Dept. of Marine and Fisheries organized

July 31, Rupert's Land Act authorized acquisition by the Dominion of the North West Territories, and to enable the Crown to accept surrender of lands and privileges of the Hudson Bay Company

Nov. 10, Commercial Bank of New Brunswick suspended payment

Nov. 14, Sir Charles A. Wyndham made Administrator on departure of Viscount Monck for England

Dec. 1, Baron Lisgar (Sir John Young) appointed Governor to succeed Viscount Monck, and acted as Administrator until Feb. 2, 1869

Dec. 11, Order in Council appointed a commission to construct the Intercolonial Railway from Halifax to Quebec

1869

Jan. 30, Joseph Howe appointed President of the Council entering the Dominion Ministry, exacting as price of adherence promise of "better terms" for Nova Scotia

Feb. 2, Lord Lisgar assumed office as Governor

Feb. 11, Patrick J. Whelan hanged at Ottawa for murder of T. D. McGee, last public execution in Canada

Feb., Canadian Society for the Prevention of Cruelty to Animals organized

April 15–June 22, Second session of first Dominion Parliament. Salary of Governor fixed at £10,000 per year. Insolvency laws amended and consolidated, Dept. of Finance formally established and Patent Office constituted. "Better terms" for Nova Scotia adopted provided for increase of amount of provincial debt assumed by the Dominion to $8,968,756 from $8,000,000 and annual grant of $82,968 for 10 years. Temporary Government provided for Rupert's Land and North West Territory. Contract with Hugh Allan for weekly service of ocean steamers ratified. New Immigration law enacted. Loan of $1,460,000 to pay Hudson Bay Company for rights in Rupert's Land, &c., authorized

June 14, London Convention as to water boundary

July 17, First exercise of veto power of Nova Scotia measure respecting Halifax reformatory

Sept. 10, Award of Commission appointed under Claims Treaty of July 1, 1863 of $450,000 to Hudson Bay Company and to Puget Sound $1,168,000

Sept. 28, William McDougall appointed Lieutenant Governor of North West Territories

Oct. 11, French *Métis* (half-breeds) led by Louis Riel stopped survey party of Colonel Dennis alarmed

because of their uncertain land tenure and believing they were to be deprived of their lands

Oct. 30, First issue of *Illustrated Canadian News*, Montreal

Oct. 31, Lieutenant Governor William McDougall warned at Pembina by agent of Louis Riel not to enter North West Territories

Nov. 1, Riel seized Fort Garry (Winnipeg)

Nov. 16, Convention of rebels of the Red River district met and Nov. 24 formed a Provisional Government

Nov. 19, Deed of surrender of the Hudson Bay Company territories to the Crown for £300,000, the Company retaining one-twentieth of the land

——, Death of Joseph Guibord, member of *Institut Canadien de Montreal* condemned by Bishop Bourget (Roman Catholic), beginning of the Guibord case, refusal of Church to allow his burial in consecrated ground

Dec. 1, On day set for official transfer of North West Territories to the Canadian Government Lieutenant Governor McDougall issued proclamation of annexation from Pembina

Dec. 5, List of rights claimed by the Métis published

Dec. 6, Proclamation of Governor Lisgar offered pardon to rebels who would disperse peaceably

Dec. 7, Riel captured Dr. John Christian Schultz and other Canadians and imprisoned them in Fort Garry

Dec. 24, Name of Port Hope, Lindsay, and Beaverton Railroad changed to Midland Railway of Canada

Dec. 27, Riel formally assumed presidency of Rupert's Land and North West

——, Donald Smith appointed commissioner to Red River arrived at Fort Gary and was made a prisoner by Riel

——, First issue of the *Ottawa Free Press*

Dec., Western extension of European and North American Railroad opened from Fairville to St. Croix

1870

Jan. 5, First issue of *Le Courrier d'Ottawa*

Jan. 8, Order in Council ended system of issuing licenses to American fishing vessels as practiced since termination of Reciprocity Treaty in March, 1866

Jan. 18, Railroad completed from Lindsay to Beaverton

Jan. 25–Feb. 10, Convention of rebels at Red River to consider proposals made Jan. 19 by Donald Smith drew up new list of rights

Feb. 15–May 12, Third session of first Dominion Parliament. Customs amended, police laws regulated, civil service superannuation fund established, seizure of foreign fishing vessels in Canadian waters authorized. Act established banking policy regulating issue of notes. Act made provision for government of the Province of Manitoba to take effect when the Queen in Council should admit Rupert's Land and the North West Territory into the Union

Feb. 24, Declaration approved Oregon boundary under Treaty of June 15, 1846

March 4, Riel after mock trial put to death Thomas Scott, one of the Canadian prisoners at Fort Garry, a former resident of Ontario

March 5, Joint Imperial and Canadian military expedition to Red River district agreed upon for the following summer

March 8, Bishop Taché arrived at St. Boniface to negotiate with Riel to end rebellion

March 12, Montreal and Champlain Junction Railroad incorporated

March 15, Council of settlers at Red River addressed by Bishop Taché. New list of rights drawn up by Riel and his associates included claim for separate schools

March 18, Donald Smith allowed to leave Fort Garry by Riel. Submitted report on the situation April 13

——, Bishop John Joseph Lynch appointed first Archbishop of Toronto (Roman Catholic)

March 23, Père Ritchot and Alfred H. Scott left Red River as delegates from Riel and the Provisional Government to negotiate with Canadian Government at Ottawa where they were officially received by the Secretary of State

April 6, Meeting at Toronto expressed sympathy for refugees from the Red River

May 11, On this date $300,000 finally paid to Hudson Bay Company for territorial rights in the North West

May 12, Montreal and Champlain Junction Railroad chartered

——, Manitoba, Rupert's Land and the North West Territory formally established by Dominion statute

——, Society of Canadian Artists incorporated

May 13, Naturalization Convention between the United States and Great Britain signed

May 20, Adams G. Archibald appointed Lieutenant Governor of Manitoba and the North West Territory

May 25, Fenian attack at Eccles Hill led by John O'Neill defeated by Colonel Osborn Smith, and the leaders arrested by the United States Marshal for Vermont

June 7–16, First General Assembly of the Presbyterian Church in Canada

June 23, Imperial Order in Council transferred Rupert's Land and the North West Territory to Canada to take effect July 15, Manitoba constituted a Province

——, Manitoba Act formally accepted by the Provisional Government at Red River

——, Dominion Steamship Line established

July 1, Order in Council respecting entry of British Columbia into the Dominion stated that the Government undertook to construct railroad from the Pacific Ocean to connect with railroad system of Canada

July 15, By royal proclamation all of British North America between Ontario and British Columbia including present Provinces of Manitoba, Saskatchewan, and Alberta became part of the Dominion

Aug. 9, Imperial Loan Act for Canadian Defenses guaranteed payment of loan for construction of fortifications

Aug. 24, Colonel Garnet Wolseley at head of British regular troops and Canadian militia reached Fort Garry by Lake Superior and overland to find that Riel had fled to the United States on news of his approach and the rebellion was ended

Sept. 2, Lieutenant Governor Archibald arrived at Fort Garry (Winnipeg) to assume the government of new Province of Manitoba

Sept. 16, Executive Council of Manitoba organized, and first election for Assembly held Dec. 30

Sept. 23, Death of Louis Joseph Papineau, French-Canadian leader

Dec., Quebec and Gosford Railroad completed

1871

Feb. 14, Constitutional Act passed by Legislative Council of British Columbia constituted Assembly, into effect July 19

Feb. 15–April 14, Fourth session of first Dominion Parliament. First general banking law enacted consolidated all banking laws, currency law, and decimal system applied to entire Dominion. Railroad Act of 1868 amended. Government Savings Bank established

Feb. 23, Supplementary Naturalization Convention signed between the United States and Great Britain

Feb. 27–May 8, Joint Commission met in Washington to settle various claims, Sir John Macdonald attended to guard Canadian interests

March 4, Sandford Fleming appointed first engineer in charge of survey for Canadian Pacific Railroad, beginning survey from Fort William to the coast

March 10, First session of first Legislative Council of Manitoba opened

March 15, First session of first Legislature of Manitoba opened

April 2, First census of the Dominion, total population 3,689,257 including British 2,110,502; French 1,082,940. Quebec 1,191,516; Ontario 1,620,851; Nova Scotia 387,000; New Brunswick 285,594; Prince Edward Island 94,021; British Columbia 36,247; Manitoba 10,000

April 5, Railroad for Prince Edward Island authorized

May 3, St. Boniface College received a charter from the Manitoba Legislature

May 8, Treaty of Washington signed dealing with questions outstanding between Great Britain and the United States: reciprocity, boundaries, &c., which gave Americans right to fish in Canadian waters, and use of Canadian canals in return for navigation of Lake Michigan and the St. Clair Flats Canal for term of Treaty, and of the Alaskan rivers forever, free navigation of the St. Lawrence forever granted by Canada. San Juan Island boundary dispute submitted to arbitration, and a commission to decide what the United States should pay for fishing privileges

May 16, Imperial Order in Council admitted British Columbia as a Province of the Dominion

May 17, Common Schools Act established separate schools in New Brunswick

June 29, British North America Act of 1871 declared Parliament of Canada may establish new provinces by increasing or altering limits

July 1, Currency made uniform from this date, decimal system applied to entire Dominion

July 20, In accordance with Imperial Order in Council of May 16 British Columbia became a Province of the Dominion under agreement of construction by the Government of Canada of a transcontinental railroad, the Canadian Pacific

Aug. 3, Treaty No. 1 concluded with the North West Indians at Lower Fort Garry by Lieutenant Governor Archibald, and Treaty No. 2 with Indians at Lake Manitoba Aug. 21

Oct. 5, Fenians organized in Minnesota crossed the border and captured the Hudson Bay Company fort at Pembina. Followed by United States troops and "General" O'Donoghue and 4 other leaders arrested and marched back

Oct. 19, Last spike driven of European and North American Railroad connecting with railroad system of the United States at Vanceboro

Nov. 11, Last British troops left Quebec

Nov. 28, First issue of post cards by Dominion Post Office

Nov., Telegraph from Winnipeg to Pembina opened

Dec. 23, Legislature of the Province of Quebec revised municipal laws and established code

1872

Jan., Ontario Legislature offered $5,000 for capture of Louis Riel who was living in Manitoba forcing his withdrawal from the Dominion

Feb. 15, First meeting of British Columbia Legislature

March 30, First issue of the *Toronto Mail*

April 11–June 14, Fifth session of first Dominion Parliament. Trades Union Act legalized trade unions. Public Archives Office constituted and Dominion Lands Office. Immigration Aid Societies provided for. Duties on tea and coffee repealed. Acts provided for building of Canadian Pacific Railroad under direction of Sir Hugh Allan, and of the Interoceanic Railroad under direction of Sir David Macpherson. Dual representation abolished. Discussion of motion proposing disallowance of New Brunswick school law declaring that schools receiving legislative aid must be non-sectarian

May 22, The Earl of Dufferin (Frederick T. H. T. Blackwood) appointed Governor to succeed Lord Lisgar

June 22–24, Sir Charles H. Doyle, Administrator, Lord Lisgar leaving for England

June 25, Lord Dufferin arrived in Canada and assumed office as Governor

July 2, Morris Alexander appointed first Chief Justice in Manitoba

July 11, Canada requested the British Foreign Office to take up the question of the boundary of Alaska with the United States

July, Printers of Toronto went on strike for a 9 hour day which lasted 17 weeks

Sept. 25, Interoceanic Railroad Company organized by D. L. Macpherson for construction of the Canadian Pacific Railroad

Oct. 15, Company organized by Sir Hugh Allan for construction of the Canadian Pacific Railroad

Oct. 21, Award of Emperor of Germany as to water boundary between Vancouver Island and the mainland under Treaty of May, 1871 awarded the San Juan Island to the United States and the boundary line through the Haro Strait

Oct. 25, Oliver Mowat who had retired from politics in 1864 retired from the bench and appointed Attorney General and on the 31st assumed office as Prime Minister of the Province of Ontario, assuming leadership of the Liberal Party

Nov. 9, Order in Council constituted the Intercolonial Railroad

Nov. 11, All rail communication established between St. John, New Brunswick and Halifax, Nova Scotia

1873

Jan. 18, Additional Articles to Treaty of May 8, 1871 signed amending Article XII as to fisheries

Feb. 5, Charter of the Canadian Pacific Railroad Company signed by Governor Dufferin, pledge to build transcontinental railway within 10 years from July 20, 1871, Sir Hugh Allan, president of the new company for construction of the railroad

Feb. 12, Order in Council authorized Lieutenant Governor of the North West Territories to make provision for administration of justice

March 5–Aug. 13, First session of second Parliament. Secretary of State for Provinces abolished and Dept.

of Interior which included the Geological Survey constituted. Trial of controverted elections transferred from House Committee to special judges. Labor law, the "Deck Load Act" passed. North West Mounted Police established. Alexander Mackenzie moved resolution Aug. 13 in Assembly asking for investigation of charges against Sir John Macdonald in connection with the Canadian Pacific Railroad which was defeated. Members of provincial Assemblies and Legislative Councils declared ineligible to seats in House of Commons. Act for inspection of staple articles consolidated and amended and extended to entire Dominion. Bill passed by which the Dominion assumed a large proportion of the respective provincial debts. Salary of members increased from $600 a session to $1,000 and those of Ministers and Lieutenant Governors increased. Oaths Bill allowing Committee to examine witnesses on oath passed but disallowed by the Imperial Government

March 10, Protocol defined boundary line through the Haro Strait, northwest boundary

March 29, Charter of University of Toronto amended

——, Ontario relieved municipalities of their indebtedness to the Municipal Loan Fund

——, School of Practical Science for Mining and Mechanical Engineering chartered

May 7, Joseph Howe took the oath as Lieutenant Governor of Nova Scotia

May 20, Death of Sir Georges Etienne Cartier in London

June 1, Death of Lieutenant Governor Joseph Howe, of Nova Scotia. Succeeded July 5 by Adams G. Archibald

June 7, Protocol of a Conference signed as to fisheries in reference to Treaty of May, 1871, Articles 18 to 25, and 30

June 26, Imperial Order in Council admitted Prince Edward Island into the Dominion to take effect July 1

July 1, Disallowance of Oaths Bill by the Queen as *ultra vires* of British North America Act proclaimed

——, From this date Indian affairs administered by the Dept. of the Interior

——, Prince Edward Island entered the Confederation

July 4, *Montreal Herald* published letters of Sir Hugh Allan and George W. McMullen written between Jan. and Oct., 1872, showing that Allan had spent large sums of money in connection with obtaining the grant of the charter of the Canadian Pacific and later letters showed that Macdonald had drawn heavily on Allan for election expenses for himself and his Conservative supporters

July 25, Provincial Government of British Columbia formally protested to Canadian Government of failure to fulfil terms as to connection with railroad system of Canada by northern railroad

Aug. 13, Lord Dufferin refused to interfere in Pacific Railroad affairs against the advice of his Ministers

Aug. 18, Royal Commission on Canadian Pacific Railroad appointed, made report Oct. 17

Aug. 28, News of discovery of gold by Henry Thibert in the Cassiar district of British Columbia

Sept. 23, First Convention of representatives of organized labor met at Toronto with 45 delegates and formed Canadian Labor Union representing 31 unions

——, Ambrose Lepine arrested and sentenced to be hanged Nov. 4, 1874, commuted Jan. 25, 1875 to imprisonment for 2 years

Oct. 3, Treaty No. 3, the North West Angle Treaty with the Indians concluded

Oct. 9, Sir John Macdonald in letter to Governor defended his actions in connection with Canadian Pacific Railroad, insisting there had been no connection between contribution of Sir Hugh Allan to campaign funds and the granting of charter to the railroad

Oct. 23–Nov. 7, Second session of second Parliament. Discussion of Canadian Pacific scandal and defense by Sir John A. Macdonald

Oct. 31, International Bridge over the Niagara River opened

Nov. 5, Resignation of Sir John A. Macdonald as result of exposure of the Pacific scandal

Nov. 7, Second Dominion Ministry appointed

OFFICE	NAME	DATE OF APPOINTMENT
Premier	Alexander Mackenzie	Nov. 7, 1873
Minister of Public Works	Alexander Mackenzie	Nov. 7, 1873
Minister of Justice and Attorney General	A. Aimé Dorion	Nov. 7, 1873
	Telesphore Fournier	July 8, 1874
	Edward Blake	May 1, 1875
	Rodolphe Laflamme	June 8, 1877
Minister of Finance	Sir Richard Cartwright	Nov. 8, 1873
Minister of Militia and Defense	William Ross	May 7, 1873
	William B. Vail	Sept. 30, 1874
	A. G. Jones	Jan. 21, 1878
Minister of Customs	Isaac Burpee	Nov. 7, 1873
Minister of Agriculture	L. Letellier de St. Just	Nov. 7, 1873
	C. A. P. Pelletier	Jan. 26, 1877
Postmaster General	Donald A. Macdonald	Nov. 7, 1873
	Telesphore Fournier	May 19, 1875
	Lucius S. Huntington	Oct. 9, 1875
Minister of Inland Revenue	Telesphore Fournier	Nov. 7, 1873
	Felix Geoffrion	June 8, 1874
	Rodolphe Laflamme	Nov. 9, 1876
	Joseph Cauchon	June 8, 1877
	Wilfrid Laurier	Oct. 8, 1877
Minister of Marine and Fisheries	Albert J. Smith	Nov. 7, 1873
Minister of the Interior	David Laird	Nov. 7, 1873
	David Mills	Oct. 24, 1876
President of Council	L. S. Huntington	Jan. 20, 1874
	Joseph Cauchon	Dec. 7, 1875
	Edward Blake	June 8, 1877
Receiver General	Thomas Coffin	Nov. 7, 1873
Secretary of State	David Christie	Nov. 7, 1873
	Richard W. Scott	Jan. 9, 1874
Without portfolio	Edward Blake	Nov. 7, 1873
	Richard W. Scott	Nov. 7, 1873

Nov. 8, Winnipeg, Manitoba, incorporated

First butter factory established at Athelston (Huntingdon)

1874

Jan. 22, Liberals won in general election for Parliament owing to the Pacific Railroad scandal. Louis Riel elected to Parliament from Manitoba

Feb. 8, Death of Roman Catholic Bishop Guiges of Ottawa

Feb. 23, Annual subsidy of £1,000 voted for 5 years to first sugar beet factory in Quebec Province

Feb. 24, Death of Jean François Jamot, Bishop of Sarepta and Vicar Apostolic of Northern Ontario

March 17, Sir Edward Thornton, British Minister to the United States, and Senator George Brown appointed members of joint commission to negotiate a treaty of fisheries, commerce, and navigation with the United States, conference begun March 28

March 26–May 26, First session of third Parliament. Louis Riel elected from Provencher, Manitoba, did not appear but was expelled from House April 16 by vote of 124 to 68 as a fugitive from justice found guilty by court of murder of Thomas Scott. Customs duties raised from 15% to 17.5%, and large advance in excise duties on spirits and tobacco, and duty averaging 5 cents a pound laid on tea and coffee and 20% on luxuries, silver, silver plated ware, silks, satins. Railroads transferred to jurisdiction of Public Works Dept. General Act as to incorporation of Boards of Trade passed. Act provided for construction of the Canadian Pacific Railroad under the new company. Elections Act included provision for secret voting and all federal elections to be held on the same day, and property qualification abolished for members of Parliament

April 16, Agricultural College and an experimental farm established at Guelph, opened June 1 with 31 students, William Johnston, principal

June 2, Dominion Grange formed at London, Ontario

June 15, Memorial of British Columbia to Imperial Government protested failure of Canadian Government to build Pacific Railroad

July 31, First party of 1,532 Mennonites from Russia arrived at Quebec to settle in Manitoba

Sept. 15, Treaty No. 4, the Qu'Appelle Treaty with the Indians concluded

Oct. 3, Speech of Edward Blake representing the Canada National Association at Aurora on their program of "Canada First" in favor of Federated British Empire, encouragement of free homesteads in the public domain, and of native industry

Nov. 17, Decision of Lord Carnarvon, Colonial Secretary, acting as arbitrator between the Dominion and British Columbia as to the Pacific railway, that Canada begin building railroad from Esquimault to Nanaimo on Vancouver Island, and surveys on mainland, expenditure of at least $2,000,000 a year on construction of British Columbia part of railroad, and completion of line from the Pacific to Lake Superior on or before Dec. 31, 1890

Dec. 18, Lord Dufferin's proposal for settlement of Canadian Pacific accepted by Order in Council

1875

Jan. 1, *Canadian Methodist Magazine* began publication

Jan. 14–28, Caraquet School riot

Feb. 4–April 8, Second session of third Parliament.

Pardon recommended to all participants in North West rebellion except Riel, Lepine, and O'Donoghue. Riel again elected to House from Provencher, Manitoba, again formally expelled from the House. Supreme Court constituted. Seamen's Act as to shipping of inland waters passed, Post Office Act, Copyright Act, Insolvency, and Immigration Acts amended. North West Territories Act consolidated and amended. Land Purchase Act provided for payment of proprietors of Prince Edward Island for land sold under compulsion

Feb. 21, Commercial Travelers Association of Canada organized at Montreal

Feb. 24, Louis Riel declared an outlaw

April 3, Construction of Canadian Pacific Railroad begun at Thunder Bay, Lake Superior

April 8, North West Territories Act established a Lieutenant Governor and Council

May 12, Prince Edward Island Railroad opened

May 13, Death of Lieutenant Governor John Willoughby Crawford of Ontario

June 15, Various Presbyterian churches united as the Presbyterian Church of Canada

June 20, University of Manitoba established

July 19, Imperial Parliament of Canada Act defined powers and privileges of members

July 20, Death of Sir Francis Bond Head

Aug. 2, Imperial Act gave effect to Act of the Dominion respecting copyright

Aug. 4, Bishop Robert Machray made Archbishop

Aug. 23, Indian Treaties No. 1 and 2 revised

Sept. 15–17, National Prohibition Convention met at Montreal

Sept. 20 and 24, Treaty No. 5 concluded with the Indians at Lake Winnipeg

Sept., Riots in Montreal because of attempted burial in consecrated ground of Joseph Guibord who had been censured by clerics of the Roman Catholic Church for having prohibited books in his possession

Oct. 8, Sir William Buell Richards appointed first Chief Justice of the Supreme Court

Dec. 10, Death of General Henry William Stisted

Dec. 28, Union Navigation Company organized

1876

Feb. 1, Branch of Laval University established at Montreal, confirmed by Bull of canonical establishment May 15

Feb. 4, Manitoba abolished Legislative Council

Feb. 10, Crooks Act in Ontario Province established control of sale of intoxicating liquors, and Dept. of Education under Minister of the Crown established

Feb. 10–April 12, Third session of third Parliament. Election laws as to corrupt practices consolidated and amended. Labor legislation amended the criminal code as to conspiracy and intimidation, Indian Acts consolidated and Minister of the Interior made Supt. of Indian Affairs. Better financial terms granted to Manitoba, annual grant of $26,746 for 6 or 7 years

Feb. 22, First general meeting at Ottawa of the Dominion Artillery Association

April 4, University of Halifax chartered

April 12, Beaver Steamship Line established by Montreal merchants, chartered under name of Canada Shipping Company

——, District of Keewatin defined

May 11, Bishop Bourget, Roman Catholic Bishop of

Montreal resigned, and was succeeded by Edouard Charles Fabre

May 30, Fire in suburbs of Montreal, 411 houses burned

June 1, Royal Military College, Kingston, established in 1874, opened

June 5, Manitoba abolished the Legislative Council

——, First session of Supreme Court of the Dominion

July 3, Opening of the Intercolonial Railroad from opposite Quebec to Halifax, completed July 1

July 29, 402 Icelanders arrived at Quebec to settle at Gimli on west shore of Lake Winnipeg, settled by Icelanders in 1874–1875

Aug. 10, First telephone conversation over any distance made by Alexander Graham Bell between Brantford and Paris, 8 miles, Tutela Heights, Brantford, the home of Mr. Bell's father

Aug. 23, 28, and Sept. 9, Treaty No. 6 with the Indians concluded at Forts Carlton and Pitt

Oct., Ontario School of Art opened

Oct. 6, Death of John Young, Baron Lisgar, former Governor

Oct. 7, Organization of the North West Territories with David Laird as Lieutenant Governor and a Council of 3 members, Livingstone, Swan River, temporary capital

Oct. 21, First wheat shipped out of Manitoba

Nov. 16, Joseph Guibord buried under protection of police and militia in Montreal

Dec. 17, Bread riots in Montreal

Dec. 28, Province of Quebec created new Dept. and Supt. of Education. Council of Public Instruction abolished and Catholic and Protestant Committees substituted

1877

Jan. 6, McLean's flour mill, the first in Manitoba, began operations

Feb. 8–April 28, Fourth session of third Parliament. Geological Survey Branch established and provision made for Geological and Natural History Museum. Customs and extradition laws consolidated and amended

Feb. 28, University of Manitoba organized by provincial statute, opened June 20

March 2, Ontario Society of Artists founded in 1872 received a charter

April 17, Order in Council provided for appointment of a Dominion Council of Agriculture, organized April 25 at Ottawa

May, Medical Council of Great Britain decided to recognize Canadian degrees

May 24, George Conroy, Bishop of Armagh, Roman Catholic Apostolic delegate to Canada arrived at Quebec

June, Wilfrid Laurier's speech at Quebec on political liberalism

June 20, First commercial telephone established at Hamilton, Ontario

——, Great fire at St. John, New Brunswick, destroyed entire business section and 1,612 houses, loss $27,000,000

July 12, Orange riots in Montreal

Sept. 22, Treaty No. 7 with the Blackfeet Indians

Sept., First Young Men's Christian Association Convention met in Quebec

Oct., Wycliffe College, Toronto, Protestant Episcopal Divinity School, opened

Oct. 17, First exportation of wheat from Manitoba direct to Great Britain

Oct. 24, Declaration for the protection of trade marks

Nov. 23, Award of Halifax Fisheries Commission of $5,500,000 to be paid by the United States to Great Britain

1878

Jan. 6, Americans fishing in Fortune Bay on Sunday in defiance of Newfoundland regulations forbidding fishing on the Sabbath driven off, and international complications ensued which resulted in eventual award of compensation of £15,000

Jan. 15, Convention of Conservatives met at Toronto and adopted resolutions in favor of "national policy" for tariff and reciprocity

Jan. 22, Canada given right to decide whether to be included in British treaties by dispatch of Lord Carnarvon

Feb. 7–May 10, Fifth session of third Parliament. On April 11, Sir John A Macdonald moved resolution disapproving the dismissal of Cabinet by Lieutenant Governor of Quebec which was defeated after debate at sitting of 24 consecutive hours by vote of 112 to 70. Canada Temperance (Scott) Act introduced by Richard W. Scott passed by which prohibition could be enforced locally by popular vote. Auditor General for Dominion provided for. Sir John A. Macdonald moved resolution advocating national tariff policy. Labor legislation, the "Deck Leads" Act passed. Independence of Parliament further secured

March 7, Western University of London, Ontario, incorporated, and the University of Montreal, by provincial statutes

March 28, Lieutenant Governor Letellier de St. Just of Province of Quebec dismissed de Boucherville from Cabinet on charge of non-submission of important documents for his consideration and signature

July 1, Canada admitted as member of the Universal Postal Union

Aug. 2, J. L. Macdougall appointed first Auditor General of the Dominion

Aug. 3, Award of arbitrators appointed to settle northwest boundary of Ontario, not accepted by Dominion

——, Lease of Pembina branch railroad from Pembina to Winnipeg to the St. Paul and Pacific Railroad, later St. Paul, Minnesota, and Manitoba

Sept. 17, The Mackenzie Liberal Government defeated in general election

Oct. 5, Letters patent constituted the office of Governor General of Canada, and the Marquis of Lorne (John Douglas S. Campbell) appointed

Oct. 10, Resignation of Mackenzie Ministry

Oct. 17, Third Dominion Ministry appointed

Office	Name	Date of Appointment
Premier	Sir John A. Macdonald	Oct. 17, 1878
Minister of Justice and Attorney General	James McDonald	Oct. 17, 1878
	Alexander Campbell	May 20, 1881
	Sir J. S. D. Thompson	Sept. 25, 1885
Minister of Finance	Sir Samuel Leonard Tilley	Oct. 17, 1878

Office	Name	Date of Appointment
	A. W. McLelan	Dec. 10, 1885
	Sir Charles Tupper	Jan. 27, 1887
	George Eulas Foster	May 29, 1888
Minister of Public Works	Sir Charles Tupper	Oct. 17, 1878
	Sir Hector L. Langevin	May 20, 1879
Minister of Railways and Canals	Sir Charles Tupper	May 20, 1879
	John Henry Pope	Sept. 25, 1885
	Sir John A. Macdonald	Nov. 28, 1889
Minister of Militia and Defense	L. F. R. Masson	Oct. 19, 1878
	Sir Alexander Campbell	Jan. 16, 1880
	Sir A. P. Caron	Nov. 8, 1880
Minister of Customs	Mackenzie Bowell	Oct. 19, 1878
Minister of Agriculture	John Henry Pope	Oct. 17, 1878
	John Carling	Sept. 25, 1885
Postmaster General	Sir Hector L. Langevin	Oct. 19, 1878
	Sir Alexander Campbell	May 20, 1879
	John O'Connor	Jan. 16, 1880
	Sir Alexander Campbell	Nov. 8, 1880
	John O'Connor	May 20, 1881
	John Carling	May 23, 1882
	Sir Alexander Campbell	Sept. 25, 1885
	A. W. McLelan	Jan. 27, 1887
	John G. Haggart	Aug. 3, 1888
Minister of Marine and Fisheries	J. C. Pope	Oct. 19, 1878
	A. W. McLelan	July 10, 1882
	George Eulas Foster	Dec. 10, 1885
	Charles Hibbert Tupper	May 31, 1888
Minister of Inland Revenue	L. F. G. Baby	Oct. 26, 1878
	J. C. Aikins	Nov. 8, 1880
	John Costigan	May 23, 1882
Minister of the Interior	Sir John A. Macdonald	Oct. 17, 1878
	Sir D. L. Macpherson	Oct. 17, 1883
	Thomas White	Aug. 5, 1885
	Edgar Dewdney	Aug. 3, 1888
President of Council	John O'Connor	Oct. 17, 1878
	L. F. R. Masson	Jan. 16, 1880
	Joseph A. Mousseau	Nov. 8, 1880
	A. W. McLelan	May 20, 1881
	Sir John A. Macdonald	Oct. 17, 1883
	C. C. Colby	Nov. 28, 1889
Receiver General	Sir Alexander Campbell	Nov. 8, 1878

Office	Name	Date of Appointment
Secretary of State	J. C. Aikins	Oct. 19, 1878
	John O'Connor	Nov. 8, 1880
	Joseph A. Mousseau	May 20, 1881
	J. A. Chapleau	July 29, 1882
Without portfolio	R. D. Wilmot	Nov. 8, 1878
	Sir D. L. Macpherson	Feb. 11, 1880
	Frank Smith	July 29, 1882
	J. J. C. Abbott	May 13, 1887

Oct. 19, Lord Dufferin sailed for England
Nov. 1, Death of Chief Justice Robert Alexander Harrison
Nov. 25, Arrival of the Marquis of Lorne and the Princess Louise at Halifax
Dec. 3, Last spike of Canadian Pacific Railroad, Pembina branch, from Winnipeg to Emerson where it met the St. Paul and Pacific driven, and first train arrived at St. Boniface from Emerson Dec. 9

1879

Jan. 8, First issue of *La Gazette d'Ottawa*
Jan. 11, Sir William Johnstone Ritchie appointed Chief Justice of the Supreme Court
Feb. 13–May 15, First session of fourth Parliament. Resolution condemning the dismissal of the de Boucherville Ministry by Lieutenant Governor Letellier de St. Just carried. Customs Tariff Act inaugurated the "national policy," a protective tariff raised duties, average level on American goods 25%, and on all dutiable commodities 23.35%, average duty on iron articles 16.17%, duty on unenumerated goods raised from 17.5% to 20%, and a specific as well as *ad valorem* duty placed on such staple articles as cottons, woolens, and sugars. Pig iron previously on free list received duty of $2 a ton, coal, 50 cents a ton to enable Nova Scotian coal to compete with American, increased rates on furniture and clocks, carriages, glass-ware, wall-paper, silks, boots and shoes, rubber goods, 25% on agricultural implements. Free entry from United States of certain enumerated articles if reciprocal action. Dept. of Railroads and Canals constituted and Railroad Act of 1868 amended, and Land laws consolidated. Government authorized to make land grants to the *Métis*. Additional money grant made to Manitoba
May 15, Geographical Society of Quebec chartered
May 20, Dept. of Railroads and Canals organized and Sir Charles Tupper became first head
May 23, The St. Paul and Pacific Railroad became the St. Paul, Minnesota, and Manitoba, and sold to J. J. Hill and his associates June 14
July 5, Lieutenant Governor Letellier de St. Just removed from office by the Dominion Parliament
Aug. 15–19, Ship laborers riot at Quebec
Sept. 27, Dominion Industrial Exhibition opened at Ottawa by the Marquis of Lorne
Oct. 31, Seminary of Chicoutimi established in 1875 received a charter, and the Wesleyan Theological College of Montreal chartered

1880

Feb. 12–May 7, Second session of fourth Parliament. Dept. of Indian Affairs constituted and laws respecting Indians amended and consolidated. Acts as to North West Territories consolidated. Office of High Commissioner created to provide representation of the Government in England. Mr. Mackenzie announced his resignation as opposition leader and that his place would be taken by Edward Blake. First revision of Banking Act of 1871
March 6, Royal Canadian Academy of Arts founded by the Marquis of Lorne and the Princess Louise
April 8, First passenger train on the Chicago and Grand Trunk Railroad from Port Huron to Chicago
May 9, Death of George Brown, shot by a discharged printer
May 11, Sir Alexander Galt appointed first High Commissioner for the Dominion in London
May 23, Arrival at Quebec of Prince Leopold, made visits to Montreal, Toronto, and Ottawa
July 31, By Imperial Order in Council all British possessions in North America with the exception of Newfoundland and dependencies annexed to Canada from Sept. 1
Aug. 6, Orange riots in Toronto
Sept. 1, British possessions in North America except Newfoundland annexed to Canada on this date, including Arctic Archipelago
Sept. 14, Agreement for construction of Canadian Pacific Railroad signed in London, England, and executed at Ottawa Oct. 21
Nov. 15, Edward Hanlan, Canadian, rowed on the Thames against E. A. Trickett, Australian, and won world championship
Dec. 9–March 21, 1881, Third session of fourth Parliament. Act by which the contract for construction of the Canadian Pacific Railroad turned over to private company ratified Feb. 15. Boundaries of Manitoba extended eastward. Specific duties in general substituted for *ad valorem* rates as feature of national protective policy. Duty on bituminous coal raised from 50 to 60 cents a ton, and duty placed on livestock. Government Railroad Act, Savings Bank, and Alien and Naturalization laws enacted

1881

Jan. 28, Death of Luc Letellier de St. Just
Feb. 15, Charter for Canadian Pacific Railroad
March 4, Toronto Baptist College incorporated
——, Ontario Judicature Act remodeled the judicial system of the Province
April 4, Population 4,324,810, English 2,548,514, French 1,298,929; Quebec 1,359,027; Ontario 1,926,922; Nova Scotia 440,572; New Brunswick 321,233; Prince Edward Island 108,891; British Columbia 49,459; Manitoba 62,260; North West Territories 56,446
May 2, Work on Canadian Pacific Railroad begun by new company
May 19, Dominion disallowance of Ontario Streams Act for protection of public interest in rivers, streams, and creeks
May 28, Arrangement made as to fisheries under Treaty of 1871, and award of £15,000 in Fortune Bay affair of Jan. 6, 1878 to the United States
June 8, Fire in St. John suburb of Quebec, 642 houses burned
July 12, First sod of Westbourne and North Western Railroad turned at Portage la Prairie
Aug. 9, First sod turned for first Newfoundland railroad from St. John's to Hall Bay

Nov. 11–Jan. 20, 1882, Sir Patrick L. MacDougall, Administrator

Nov. 14, Supreme Court of the Dominion decided the Mercer Escheat Case in favor of claim that Provincial Governments have no right to escheat property to the Crown

Dec. 30, Royal Society of Canada founded

Jules Paul Tardivel founded *La Vérité* at Quebec

1882

Jan. 1, W. C. Van Horne appointed first general manager of the Canadian Pacific Railroad

Feb. 9–May 17, Fourth session of fourth Parliament. Civil Service reorganized and provision made for a Board of Examiners, marriage with deceased wife's sister legalized. Inland Revenue and Extradition Acts amended. Dominion Redistribution (Gerrymander) Act readjusted representation in House on census basis

Feb. 19, Death of Egerton Ryerson

May 7, Manitoba Bank chartered

May 8, Provisional districts of Assiniboia, Saskatchewan, Alberta, and Athabaska formed

May 17, Queen's College, Kingston, given university powers

——, Sisters of Charity of the North West Territories incorporated

May 25, First meeting of Royal Society of Canada founded by the Marquis of Lorne at Ottawa

June 1, Winnipeg, Manitoba, first lighted by gas

June 20, General election declared in favor of the Macdonald Government

June 22, Constitutionality of the Canada Temperance Act confirmed by the Privy Council

Aug. 12, Amalgamation of the Grand Trunk and Great Western railroads

Aug. 16, Peter Redpath Museum (McGill University) opened

Aug. 23, Regina named and made seat of government of the North West Territories

Sept. 20, Second Dominion disallowance of Ontario Streams Bill

Sept. 21, First sod turned on Emerson and North Western Railroad, Emerson, Manitoba

Oct. 3, Hector Fabre commissioned to act as agent of Canada in France

Dec. 9, Death of Sir Hugh Allan

Dec. 12, Michigan Central Railroad agreed to operate the Canada Southern Railroad and leased lines for 21 years beginning Jan. 1, 1883

Dec. 18–Jan. 30, 1883, Sir Patrick L. MacDougall, Administrator

Dec., Labor Congress at Toronto

1883

Jan. 3, Ontario Liberal Convention held at Toronto, 5,000 delegates present

Jan. 23, First Ice Palace Carnival held in Montreal

——, First issue of *L'Estendard*, Montreal

Feb. 1, Woodstock College (Baptist) chartered

Feb. 8–May 25, First session of fifth Parliament. Railroad Act of 1879 amended. Militia and Defense Acts, Customs, Bank, Dominion Lands, and Inland Revenue amended and consolidated. Liquor License Act enacted. Bounty of $1.50 per ton on all pig iron manufactured in Canada authorized

Feb. 9, First Free Library in Ontario opened at Guelph

March 16, Third Dominion disallowance of Ontario Streams Bill

April 19, Parliament Building, Quebec, burned

May 25, Royal Society of Canada received a charter

——, Amalgamation of Grand Trunk and Great Western railroads

——, University of Saskatchewan founded by Dominion statute

July 1, The United States gave required two year's notice of abrogation of fishery clauses of the Washington Treaty

July 18, Mercer Escheat Case on appeal to Judicial Committee of Imperial Privy Council decided in favor of provincial right to escheat real property to the Crown

July 20, First rail laid of Pacific section of Canadian Pacific Railroad at Port Moody

Aug. 18, The Marquis of Lansdowne (Henry C. K. Fitz Maurice) appointed Governor General

Aug. 20, First session of the North West Territories Legislative Council at Regina

Aug. 29, First Salvation Army services held in London, Ontario

Aug. 31, First number of the *Calgarry Herald* issued

Sept. 5, Methodist churches in Canada united in conference

Oct. 21, Henri Smeulders, Apostolic Delegate, arrived at Quebec

Oct. 23, The Marquis of Lansdowne assumed office as Governor General

Nov. 18, Standard time adopted by Canada

Dec. 20, First cantilever bridge over the Niagara River opened

Dec. 26, Orange riot at Conception Bay, Newfoundland

Dec., Canadian Pacific Railroad placed steamers on Lake Superior to connect Owen Sound and Port Arthur

1884

Jan. 17–April 19, Second session of fifth Parliament. Canadian Pacific Act advanced loan of $22,500,000 to the Company from the public funds, Temperance Act of 1878, and Liquor License Act of 1883 amended, and Dominion Land Act, Civil Service, and Act for better independence of Parliament of 1878

March 6, Toronto Free Library established

March 25, Victoria College became Victoria University, and Albert College affiliated

——, First Factory Act in Canada passed by Ontario Province

——, Municipal Amendment Act amended law of 1883 to exempt manufacturers from taxation for 10 years with privilege of renewal for another 10 years

May 24, Sir Charles Tupper appointed High Commissioner for the Dominion in England

June 20, London Convention, postal money orders

July 4, Royal Commission appointed to examine into Chinese immigration, Secretary of State Joseph A. Chapleau, and Judge J. H. Gray of the Supreme Court of British Columbia

July 22, Imperial Order of Privy Council defined boundaries of Ontario; confirmed by her Majesty Aug. 11 and Imperial Act in 1889

Aug. 6, Ordinance established public school system for the North West Territories, included separate schools

Aug. 27, British Association for the Advancement of Sciences met in Montreal

Sept., Meeting of *Métis* at St. Laurent drew up bill of rights as to land grants and grants of money

Sept. 15, Canadian contingent of 400 left Quebec under command of Lieutenant Colonel Frederick C. Denison to take part in the Egypt expedition for relief of Gordon

Oct. 15, First issue of *La Presse*, Montreal

Dec. 17, Meeting of Conservatives of Ontario reaffirmed resolutions of Jan. 15, 1878

1885

Jan. 12, Supreme Court decision that liquor licensing vested in the Dominion Government

Jan. 24, Canadian Pacific telegraph completed from Atlantic to Pacific

Jan. 29–July 20, Third session of fifth Parliament. Dominion Franchise Act provided for Dominion franchise and voter's list distinct from the provincial list hitherto used, and defined qualifications of voters, and provided for Deputy Speaker of House. Chinese Immigration Act imposed head tax of $50 on every Chinese entering the Dominion. Sir John Macdonald made statement as to *Métis* that they could not get both Indian script and white man's homestead. Civil Service laws amended and consolidated

Feb. 23, Death of Joseph E. Cauchon, former Lieutenant Governor, Manitoba

March 17, Meeting of *Métis* at St. Laurent formed a Provisional Government with Louis Riel, President, and Gabriel Dumont, Adjutant General

March 26, Rising of *Métis* and Indians in the North West led by Riel begun at Duck Lake by successful attack on the mounted police under Major Crozier, capturing the post which was burned and then evacuated by rebels April 4

March 30, Ontario School Act established compulsory education, and Torrens system of land registration for certain districts adopted

March 31, Dominion Disallowance of the Chinese Restriction Act passed by British Columbia

April 1, Indians besiege Battleford (Saskatchewan)

April 2, Massacre by Indians of white persons at Frog Lake Indian Station and Mission in Winnepeg

April 24, Defeat of rebels at Fish Creek by Major General Middleton

April 25, Battleford besieged by Indian supporters of Riel relieved by troops commanded by Lieut. Col. Otter

May 1, Ottawa the second city in the Dominion to be lighted by electric lights

May 1–2, Canadian troops under Lieut. Col. W. D. Otter attacked Indians under Poundmaker at Cut Knife Hill but were compelled to retreat by superior numbers of the Indians

May 2, Canadian troops under Maj. Gen. T. Bland Strange reached and relieved Edmonton

——, Torrens system of land transfer or registration of titles adopted in Manitoba

May 9, Canadian branch of Imperial Federation League formed at public meeting in Montreal

May 12, General Middleton defeated rebels and captured Batoche, rebel stronghold on the Saskatchewan River

May 14, Indians led by Poundmaker captured a supply train of 31 wagons

May 15, Riel captured

May 26, Poundmaker with Indian followers and 150 half-breeds surrendered to General Middleton at Battleford

June 2, Skirmish between scouts and Indians at Loon Lake

June 8, Death of Archbishop Ignace Bourget (Roman Catholic)

July 1, Termination of application of fishery clauses of the Treaty of Washington by the United States came into effect, but arrangement made for allowing American fishermen to enjoy privileges of the treaty until end of the season to the dissatisfaction of Canadian fishermen

July 2, Capture of Big Bear and final suppression of rebellion in the North West

July 20, Trial of Louis Riel begun at Regina, found guilty of high treason, and sentenced to death Sept. 18

Aug. 18, Death of Sir Francis Hincks, former Premier, at Montreal

Aug. 18, First census of North West Territories gave population of Assiniboia as 22,083, of Saskatchewan 10,746, Alberta 15,533, grand total 48,362

Sept. 18, Riot in Montreal against compulsory vaccination, City Hall attacked

Sept. 24, Railroad from Dunmore, station on the Canadian Pacific to Galt coal mines at Lethbridge, 109½ miles opened by the Governor General

Oct., During the month there were 1,391 deaths from small-pox in Montreal, 1,286 being French Canadians

Oct. 15, Fraser Institute, free public library, formally opened at Montreal

Nov. 2, First passenger train for Winnipeg over the Canadian Pacific left Montreal

Nov. 5, Death of Bishop David Anderson, former Anglican Bishop of Rupert's Land

Nov. 7, Last spike of the Canadian Pacific Railroad driven by Donald Smith (later Lord Strathcona) at Craigellachie, Eagle Pass, 340 miles from Port Moody

Nov. 16, Louis Riel hanged at Regina

Nov. 25, Order in Council established the Rocky Mountains Park of Canada at Banff, Alberta

Nov. 27, Eight Indians, leaders in the rebellion, hanged at Regina

Dec. 12, First freight train of 16 cars loaded with wheat from Manitoba left Portage La Prairie for Montreal

——, Decision of Judicial Committee of the Privy Council declared the Liquor License Act of 1883 and amending Act of 1884 as not within the legislative authority of the Parliament of Canada, confirming opinion of Supreme Court of Canada of Jan. 12 that both Acts were *ultra vires*

Dec. 28, Death of Adam Crooks, former Cabinet Minister

1886

Feb. 6, Dominion Live Stock Association held first annual meeting at Toronto

Feb. 25–June 2, Fourth session of fourth Parliament. Dept. of Public Printing and Stationery constituted. North West Territories Representation Act provided for representation in the Dominion Parliament. Supreme Court for North West Territories constituted. Post Office Act of 1875 amended. Establishment of experimental farms and school savings banks authorized, Insurance Dept. constituted, Steamboat Inspection Act passed, bounty on pig iron continued, Chinese Immigration Act amended by additional regulations as to women. Debate on execution of Louis Riel. Fisheries Act required licenses from foreign vessels

March 18, First stone of Lachine Bridge of the Canadian Pacific Railroad over the St. Lawrence River laid

March 25, First Workmen's Compensation Act in Canada passed in Ontario Province

April 2, Mount Allison Wesleyan Academy at Sackville, New Brunswick, received college charter

April 6, Vancouver, British Columbia, founded about 1881 by the Canadian Pacific Railroad Company incorporated

April–July, Seizure and counter-seizure of American fishing vessels in Canadian waters

May 23, First train entered Vancouver

May 28, Second branch of the Imperial Federation League established at Ingersoll

June 2, First synod of Reformed Episcopal Church incorporated

June 7, Archbishop Elzéar Alexandre Taschereau made first Canadian cardinal

June 8, Bishop Fabre made Archbishop of Montreal (Roman Catholic)

June 10, Canada Congregational Woman's Board of Missions organized at Ottawa

June 13, Fire destroyed Vancouver, British Columbia, only 4 houses left standing, 50 persons killed

June 25, British North America Act made provision for representation of Territories not included in any Province in the Dominion Parliament

June 28, First through train on the Canadian Pacific Railroad left Montreal for Vancouver, arriving July 4

July 6, First Congress of the Chambers of Commerce of the British Empire met in London

July 9, General amnesty to all persons implicated in the North West rebellion except murderers

July 19, Captain Scott fined for seizure of American fishing vessel "David J. Adams" at Digby, Nova Scotia, May 7

Aug. 14, First Royal Commission on Canadian Railroads appointed, made report in Jan. 1888

Oct. 21, Protest of British Minister in Washington, L. S. Sackville-West at seizure of Canadian sealing vessels in the Bering Sea in Aug. and ships released

Nov. 16 and 20, Final Agreement signed between the Government and the Canadian Pacific Railroad Company

Dec. 6, Branch of Imperial Federation League established at Halifax

1887

Feb. 23, Conservative Government sustained in the Dominion elections

Feb. 24, Canadian Society of Civil Engineers founded, incorporated June 23

March 3, Fisheries Retaliation Act of United States Congress authorized the President to protect and defend rights of Americans in fishery dispute with Canada, to exclude Canadian vessels from United States waters and stop importation of Canadian goods

April 2, University Federation Act passed by Ontario Province

April 2, 9, 12, 17, Sealing vessels in North Pacific seized by Americans

April 4–May 9, Imperial Conference in London, England, Sir Alexander Campbell and Sandford Fleming representing Canada, to consider matters of common concern

April 12, Branch of Imperial Federation League established at Peterborough, Ontario

April 13–June 23, First session of fifth Parliament.

Dept. of Trade and Commerce constituted. Immigration Act and Chinese Immigration Act amended. Employees of incorporated companies empowered to establish pension fund societies. Treasury Board reconstituted. School Savings Bank Act passed. Customs duties raised on printed and dyed cottons, cigars, cigarettes, and on iron and iron products, rate on pig iron to $4 per ton

April 23, McMaster University, Toronto, established by union of the Toronto Baptist College and Woodstock College

April 28, Central Farmers Institute of Ontario organized at Toronto

May 11–28, Visit to Canada of William O'Brien, editor of *United Ireland* on unsuccessful mission

May 12, Society of Jesus reconstituted in Quebec Province, receiving a charter

June 7, Wilfrid Laurier elected Opposition leader succeeding Edward Blake who resigned June 2

——, Resolution adopted in Manitoba against the "monopoly clause" of the Canadian Pacific Railroad, and threat of appeal to the Crown for its abrogation in order to make independent railroad connection with system of the United States

June 14, First Canadian Pacific steamer arrived at Vancouver from Yokohama, Japan

June 22, Jubilee year celebration of reign of 50 years of Queen Victoria

June 23, Halifax and West India Steamship Company chartered, and Canada Atlantic Steamship Company

July 2, Seizure of sealing schooner "Anna Bick" in Bering Sea by Americans

——, First sod turned of Red River Valley Railroad, Manitoba. Charter of May 31 disallowed by Dominion Parliament

July 30, Railroad bridge over the St. Lawrence at Lachine completed

Oct. 12, Sir Richard Cartwright, chief fiscal authority of the Liberal Party, declared for "unrestricted reciprocity" with the United States

Oct. 20, Interprovincial Conference of premiers held at Quebec, Sir Oliver Mowat, president, adopted 21 fundamental resolutions, and endorsed free trade with the United States

Nov. 3, Commercial Union Club organized at Toronto, Goldwin Smith, president

Nov. 15, Meeting of Fisheries Commission in Washington

1888

Jan. 23, Natural gas struck at Kingsville, Ontario

Jan. 24, Union of Grand Trunk Railroad with the Northern and Hamilton and North Western railroads

Feb. 15, Chamberlain-Bayard Treaty with the United States as to fisheries gave certain rights in Canadian inshore waters in return for free fish, but rejected, but *modus vivendi* allowed American fishermen to take out Canadian licenses on payment of a fee

Feb. 23–May 22, Second session of sixth Parliament. Railroad Act established Committee of Privy Council to control railroad affairs. After debate of 3 weeks Sir Richard Cartwright's motion for unrestricted reciprocity with the United States defeated by vote of 124 to 67. Canada Temperance Act amended, and also Civil Service, Customs, Dominion Election, and Indian Acts. Average rate of duties on all imports, dutiable and free, made 22.0% ad valorem

March 1, Parcel post established between Canada and the United States

March 8, Newfoundland Bait Act first put into effect empowered executive to prohibit the capture or sale of bait fishes in Newfoundland waters except under license

March 23, Ontario statute gave a bonus to manufacturers

April 21, Death of Thomas White, Minister of the Interior

May 1, Lord Stanley, of Preston, Earl of Derby (Frederick A. Stanley) appointed Governor General, assumed office June 11

May 12, Death of Archbishop Joseph Lynch (Roman Catholic)

July 12, Jesuits Estate Act passed by the Quebec Legislature authorized payment of $400,000 for confiscated estates which had reverted to the Crown when Jesuit Order suppressed in 1773

Sept. 4, Pioneer Historical Association of the Province of Ontario organized at Toronto

Oct. 31, First Legislative Assembly of the North West Territories met

Nov. 24, William O'Connor of Toronto defeated Teemer at Washington and won rowing championship of America

Dec. 13, Judicial Committee of the Imperial Privy Council decided in favor of Ontario in case of Dominion vs. provincial jurisdiction in the St. Catherine's Milling Company suit

1889

Jan. 26, Death of Sir W. B. Richards

Jan. 29, Canadian Pacific Railroad opened telegraph office at St. John, New Brunswick

Jan. 31–May 2, Third session of sixth Parliament. Act passed to prevent combinations in restraint of trade. Voted to grant licenses to American fishermen. Decision made that Canada should not take part in Paris Exposition. O'Brien's Jesuit disallowance amendment to Quebec provincial law of July 12, 1888, defeated March 29. Sir Richard Cartwright's resolution in favor of assumption of treaty power by Dominion defeated in House. Subsidy granted for steamship and mail service from British Columbia to China and Japan. Copyright Act amended. Average rate of customs duties increased to maximum at 31.9% ad valorem. Disallowance of proposed extension by Manitoba of Red River Railroad across the line of the Canadian Pacific Railroad as interference with monopoly of the Canadian Pacific

Feb. 3, First Convention of the Christian Alliance met at Hamilton

Feb. 5, College of Ottawa made Roman Catholic University by Pope

Feb. 14–March 19, Strike of 200 weavers at Cornwall, Ontario

Feb. 15, Militia of Manitoba suppressed riot of Dakota half-breeds who resisted collection of taxes

Feb. 19, Pardon extended by Dominion to Gabriel Dumont, Riel's first lieutenant in North West Rebellion

March 6, Custom's authorities of Toronto seized and destroyed copies of novels of Zola as obscene literature

March 20, Baptist Convention of Ontario and Quebec established

April 9, Conference of delegates of all dairymen's associations met at Ottawa

April 16, Enlarged Welland Canal opened

May 10, Public Library opened at Victoria, British Columbia

May 15, Epworth League formed

May 18, Death of A. G. B. Bannatyne

June 2, Short line railroad built across Maine to New Brunswick by the Canadian Pacific opened

June 3, First through train for St. Paul, Minnesota, via the Sault Ste. Marie left Montreal (Canadian Pacific)

June 11, Equal Rights Association formed in Toronto to work for disallowance of the Quebec Jesuit Estates Act

July 5, Death of John Norquay

July 12, Supplementary Extradition Treaty between Great Britain and the United States signed

July 15, Contract made by Postmaster of Great Britain for transportation of mails by Canadian Pacific Steamship Company between Halifax or Quebec and Hong Kong, China

July 20, Meeting at Ottawa to protest seizure of Canadian sealing vessels by Americans in Bering Sea

July 25, John Walsh elected Archbishop of Toronto (Roman Catholic)

Aug. 12, Imperial Act defined boundaries of Ontario and Manitoba

Aug. 15, First vessel, the yacht "Surprise" passed through the Murray Canal from the Bay of Quinte to Lake Ontario

Aug. 17, Canadian College of Music opened at Ottawa

Sept. 13, Death of H. J. Clarke

Sept. 19, Land slide, the second, from Citadel Rock, Quebec, killed 45 persons

Nov. 4, Large deposits of coal discovered in Nova Scotia

Nov. 5, The Province of Quebec paid Society of Jesus $400,000 under Jesuit Estates Act, and $60,000 to the Protestant Board of Education

1890

Jan. 1, Ontario and Quebec Railroad opened between London and Windsor

Jan. 11, Telegraph office of the Canadian Pacific Railroad system opened at Halifax, Nova Scotia

Jan. 16–May 16, Fourth session of sixth Parliament. Licenses granted to United States fishing vessels. Bank Act revised regulating issue of bank notes. Bounty on pig iron increased to $2 per ton. Geological Survey made a separate dept. and remained so until 1907

Feb. 1, Professor James W. Robertson appointed first Dominion Dairy Commissioner

March 31, Manitoba School Act abolished separate schools for Protestants and Catholics establishing a non-sectarian system of public education to begin May 1. Dept. of Education created

April 7, Municipalities of Ontario granted local option in regard to prohibition of the liquor traffic

May 16, Grand Orange Lodge of British North America incorporated

May 21–June 12, Visit of the Duke and Duchess of Connaught

June 16, Newfoundland Government made contract for construction of railroad from Placentia Junction on Placentia Railroad north to Hall's Bay, 262 miles

June 24, Resignation of General Middleton under censure, convicted May 12 by Parliament of looting valuable furs while engaged in suppression of the North West Rebellion

July 1, Cable communication with Bermuda established

July 14, National Educational Association met at Toronto

Aug. 15–16, Conference of Church of England at Winnipeg established union between all provincial synods in British North America, and established a General Synod for government of the Church in Canada

Sept. 14, Great strike in lumber mills at Ottawa begun

Sept. 23, Official inauguration of Order of Agricultural Merit and distribution of rewards to meritorious farmers

Nov. 21, Indians of Ontario and Quebec at meeting agreed to petition for release from political franchise and for permission to elect their own chiefs as formerly, still remaining subject to the Queen

Nov. 24, Cape Breton Railroad opened, part of Intercolonial system

1891

March 5, General election gave Government (Conservatives) 124 seats, and 91 to Liberals

March 6, Letters of Edward Blake to the West Durham electors published declaring against "unrestricted reciprocity"

March 14, Order in Council transferred immigration from the Dept. of Agriculture to the Dept. of the Interior

April 5, Population, 4,833,239. Quebec, 1,488,535; Ontario, 2,114,321; Nova Scotia, 450,396; New Brunswick, 321,263; Prince Edward Island, 109,078; British Columbia, 98,173; Manitoba, 152,506; North West Territories, 98,967

April 16, New Brunswick abolished the Legislative Council

April 29–Sept. 30, First session of seventh Parliament, called the "scandal session" because of numerous charges of maladministration of government departments. Accusation of J. Israel Tart against Sir Hector Langevin and Thomas McGreevy, members of his own party. North West Territories Act provided for Legislative Assembly. Bounty granted on beet root sugar produced in Canada of $1 per 100 pounds, removal of taxes on raw sugar, duties on spirits and tobacco increased. Bank Act again revised

April 29, First of new Canadian Pacific steamers arrived at Vancouver from Yokohama, beating record by over 2 days. Mails arrived in New York City in 3 days and 12½ hours from Vancouver

May 4, Bureau of Mines, Ontario, established

May 29, Botanical Club of Canada organized

May 31, Death of Sir Antoine Aimé Dorion

June 6, Death of Sir John A. Macdonald, Prime Minister

June 11, Imperial Act prohibited seal fishing in the Bering Sea

June 16, Fourth Dominion Ministry appointed

Office	Name	Date of Appointment
Premier and President of Council	Sir J. J. C. Abbott	June 16, 1891
Minister of Public Works	Sir Hector L. Langevin	May 20, 1879
	Frank Smith	Aug. 14, 1891
	Joseph A. Ouimet	Jan. 11, 1892
Minister of Customs	Mackenzie Bowell	Oct. 19, 1879
	Joseph A. Chapleau	Jan. 25, 1892

Office	Name	Date of Appointment
Minister of Militia	Sir A. P. Caron	Nov. 8, 1880
	Mackenzie Bowell	Jan. 25, 1892
Minister of Agriculture	John Carling	Sept. 25, 1885
Minister of Inland Revenue	John Costigan	May 23, 1882
Secretary of State	J. A. Chapleau	July 29, 1882
	J. C. Patterson	Jan. 25, 1892
Minister of Justice	Sir J. S. D. Thompson	Sept. 25, 1885
Minister of Finance	George Eulas Foster	May 29, 1888
Minister of Marine and Fisheries	Charles Hibbert Tupper	May 31, 1888
Minister of Interior and Superintendent General of Indian Affairs	Edgar Dewdney	June 3, 1888
	Thomas M. Daly	Oct. 17, 1892
Postmaster General	John C. Haggart	Aug. 3, 1888
	Sir A. P. Caron	Jan. 25, 1892
Minister of Railways and Canals	John G. Haggart	Jan. 11, 1892
Without portfolio	Frank Smith	Jan. 29, 1882

July 27, Last spike driven in Calgary-Edmonton railroad of Canadian Pacific

July 30, Right of appeal from decision of Supreme Court of North West Territories to Her Majesty in Privy Council granted by Order in Council

Aug. 11, Sir Hector L. Langevin resigned his position as Minister of Public Works because of charges made against his Dept., accepted Sept. 7

Aug. 28, All railroads in Quebec, New Brunswick, and Nova Scotia declared to constitute the Intercolonial Railroad

Sept. 14, Sir H. L. Langevin exonerated from all charges except that of negligence. Thomas McGreevy censured with other officials by Parliamentary Committee

Sept. 17, Canadian Electrical Association organized at Toronto

Sept. 19, St. Clair tunnel connecting Canadian railroads with United States railroads to Chicago opened by Sir Henry Tyler, chairman of the Grand Trunk Railroad

Sept. 22, Association of Patrons of Husbandry, organized in Feb., 1890, adopted a political platform

Sept. 29, Thomas McGreevy expelled from the House of Commons in consequence of contracting scandals in Public Works Dept.

Oct. 28, Act of Manitoba abolishing separate schools and making the public school system unsectarian declared unconstitutional by the Dominion Supreme Court

Dec. 8, In consequence of the restriction of Newfoundland in its supply of herring bait to Canadian fishermen the Dominion imposed duty on fish imported from Newfoundland

Dec. 15, Honoré Mercier, Premier of Quebec Province, dismissed from office because of evidence that he had trafficked in public contracts for the benefit of campaign funds for the provincial Liberal Party, the *Baie des Chaleurs* scandal

Dec. 17, Canadian Bankers Association organized at Montreal

Dec. 24, Nicholas Conolly and Thomas McGreevy committed for trial

1892

Jan. 26, Death of Jean P. F. Langevin, Bishop of Rimouski and Archbishop of Leontopolis (Roman Catholic)

Feb. 8–March 4, Bering Sea Commission in session, agreement to present separate reports

Feb. 10–15, Meeting in Washington of representatives of Canada and the United States to consider commercial reciprocity with no result

Feb. 25–July 9, Second session of seventh Parliament. Criminal Code established. Representation in House readjusted. Canada Temperance Act of 1888 amended. Geological Survey made a dept. of Civil Service

Feb. 28, Trinity Bay ice storm in which many fishermen lost their lives

Feb. 29, Treaty of Washington between Great Britain and the United States provided for arbitration of the Bering Sea fishery question

March 14, Royal Commission to investigate the liquor traffic appointed. First public session at Halifax July 25, and final report presented March 29, 1895

April 1, North American Canal Company chartered to build canal from Lake Erie to Lake Ontario, deepen the St. Lawrence channel, and cut canal from Lake Francis to Lake Champlain and thence to the Hudson River

April 4, Order in Council by which Canada discriminated against the United States in use of the Welland Canal

April 17, Death of Alexander Mackenzie, former Premier

April 20, Death of Anglican Bishop James W. Williams

April 30, St. Anne's College, Church Point, Nova Scotia, founded in 1890, chartered with university powers

May 16, Manitoba given right of appeal from Supreme Court decision as to School Act to Her Majesty in Privy Council; revoked March 15, 1893

May 21, Disagreement with Newfoundland as to fishing ended and *status quo* of 1889 resumed

May 24, Death of Sir Alexander Campbell, Lieutenant Governor of Ontario; succeeded May 30 by Sir George A. Kirkpatrick

June 3, Treaty for the surrender of merchant seamen deserters signed between the United States and Great Britain

June 21, A. H. Dunn appointed Anglican Bishop of Quebec

June 27, Imperial British Columbia (Loan) Act authorized an advance to the Province of British Columbia

July 6 and 9, Great fire at St. Johns, Newfoundland, 10,000 persons made homeless

July 12, Privy Council of England gave decision affirming court judgment of Queen's Bench Manitoba in the case of Barret *vs.* Winnipeg, the Manitoba school case, which the Supreme Court of the Dominion had reversed

July 22, Boundary Convention as to Alaska and Passamaquoddy Bay between the United States and Great Britain signed, provided for joint survey

July 23, Manitoba voted in favor of prohibition legislation

July 30, Judicial Committee of the Imperial Privy Council on appeal from decision of Canada Supreme Court upheld right of Manitoba to abolish separate schools

Aug. 30, Death of F. N. Gisborne

Sept. 20, Appeal of Roman Catholic minority of Manitoba to Governor General as to separate schools

Sept. 25, Death of Sir William J. Ritchie, Chief Justice

——, Seizure of sealing vessels at Ounalaska by Americans

Sept. 28, New Brunswick abolished the Legislative Council

Nov. 4, Ex-Premier Mercier acquitted of charge of malfeasance in office

Nov. 26, Right of petition of the Roman Catholics of Manitoba to the Governor General against Manitoba School Act abolishing separate schools denied by Canadian Privy Council

Dec. 3, Dept. of Trade and Commerce brought into effect by proclamation

Dec. 5, Fifth Dominion Ministry appointed

OFFICE	NAME	DATE OF APPOINTMENT
Premier	Sir J. S. D. Thompson	Dec. 5, 1892
Minister of Justice and Attorney General	Sir J. S. D. Thompson	Sept. 25, 1885
Minister of Trade and Commerce	Mackenzie Bowell	Dec. 5, 1892
Postmaster General	Sir A. P. Caron	Jan. 25, 1892
Secretary of State	John Costigan	Dec. 5, 1892
Minister of Finance	George Eulas Foster	May 29, 1888
Minister of Marine and Fisheries	Sir Charles Hibbert Tupper	May 31, 1888
Minister of Railways and Canals	John G. Haggart	Jan. 11, 1892
Minister of Public Works	J. A. Ouimet	Jan. 17, 1892
Minister of Militia	J. C. Patterson	Dec. 5, 1892
Minister of the Interior and Superintendent General of Indian affairs	Thomas M. Daly	Oct. 17, 1892
Minister of Agriculture	A. R. Angers	Dec. 5, 1892
President of Council	William B. Ives	Dec. 5, 1892
Without portfolio	Sir John Carling	Dec. 5, 1892
	Sir Frank Smith	July 29, 1882

NOT IN THE CABINET

Solicitor General	John J. Curran	Dec. 5, 1892
Controller of Inland Revenue	John F. Wood	Dec. 5, 1892
Controller of Customs	N. Clarke Wallace	Dec. 5, 1892

Dec. 13, Sir Samuel Henry Strong appointed Chief Justice

Dec. 17, Thomas McGreevy sentenced to imprisonment for one year in contracts case

J. B. Tyrrell sent by Geological Survey explored unknown country north of Churchill River and southeast of Lake Athabaska proceeding from Prince Albert on the Saskatchewan to Green Lake and descended the Beaver River to Isle à la Crosse Lake on Churchill River which was descended for 90 miles, ascended Mudjatic River and by Cree Lake and Black Lake and Black River to Lake Athabaska, returning by Wollaston Lake and Geikie River to Churchill River and Hudson Bay

1893

Jan., Dominion Coal Company formed in Nova Scotia

Jan. 26–April 1, Third session of seventh Parliament. Act of previous session as to readjustment of representation in the House amended. Railroad Act amended to permit railroad crossing of tracks. Beet sugar bounty continued to 1895. Tariff reduced on binder twine from 25% *ad valorem* to 12.5%. Grand Trunk Railroad Act passed, Dairy Products Act, and subsidy granted to establish steamship and mail service between British Columbia and Australia and New Zealand

Feb. 6, Commercial Treaty with France signed, came into effect Oct. 14, 1895

March 17, Newfoundland Bait Act suspended

March 23, Bering Sea Arbitration Court met in Paris, France, and began hearings April 4

March 25, Magistrate Baxter of Toronto imposed fine of $2 or 10 days in jail on cab driver for driving a lady on Sunday

April 20, Legislative Council in Prince Edward Island merged with Assembly

May 1, Expedition of Joseph B. and James W. Tyrrell left Ottawa to explore the Barren Lands country between Hudson Bay and Lake Athabaska, starting down the Athabaska River May 31 for the Lake

May 22, The Earl of Aberdeen (John C. Gordon) appointed Governor General

May 24, Death of Sir Alexander Campbell

June 6–7, International Reciprocity Convention held at St. Paul, Minnesota

June 8, The "Miowera," first steamer of new line between Canada and Australia arrived at Victoria, British Columbia, had left Sydney May 18

June 20–21, Liberal Party held convention at Ottawa and adopted resolutions on tariff and reciprocity

June 29, Second Imperial Act respecting seal fishing in Bering Sea

Aug. 15, Award of Bering Sea Arbitration Tribunal as to seal fisheries. Regulations prohibited seal fishing within zone defined. (*See* United States.) $425,000 paid by the United States to Great Britain in 1894 as damages for seizure of vessels

Sept. 15, Charles H. Tupper knighted by Queen Victoria in recognition of his services in connection with the Bering Sea arbitration

Sept. 19, Death of Sir Alexander T. Galt

Oct. 26, National Council of Women of Canada founded, the Countess of Aberdeen, president

Oct. 30, Death of Sir John J. C. Abbott, former Premier

Oct. 31, Redpath Library, Montreal (McGill University) opened

Dec. 13, Prince Edward Island voted for prohibition

Dec. 18, Archbishop Machray of Rupert's Land elected first Anglican Primate of all Canada

Dec. 30, Geological expedition of J. Burr Tyrrell and J. W. Tyrrell arrived at Selkirk having surveyed northern shore of Lake Athabaska, and then proceeded to Black Lake and unknown country to the

northeast. On Aug. 25 arrived at 64° 36' N. Lat., at Churchill Oct. 19, York Factory Nov. 24

1894

Jan. 1, Ontario voted in favor of prohibition of the liquor traffic

——, Manchester Canal opened for traffic

Jan. 2, J. B. Tyrrell and J. W. Tyrrell reached Winnipeg from Black Lake and unknown country to the northeast to Dubawnt Lake, Baker Lake, and Chesterfield Inlet, to York Factory on Hudson Bay, and then by Hayes and Hill rivers to Lake Winnipeg. During entire expedition they traveled in addition to railroad journeys, 3,200 miles, in canoes 2,150 miles, on snow shoes 610 miles, 350 miles in conveyances drawn by dogs, and 100 miles in conveyances drawn by horses. Surveys and geological and botanical investigations carried out

Jan. 23, Convention of Protestant Protective Association met at Hamilton

Feb. 3, Convention extended term of the Alaska Boundary Commission

Feb. 20, Supreme Court of the Dominion decided that Roman Catholic minority in Manitoba had no right of appeal to Dominion against the Manitoba Separate School Act of 1890

March 15, Nova Scotia voted in favor of prohibition of the liquor traffic

March 15–July 23, Fourth session of seventh Parliament. Deputy Speaker provided for. Railroad Act amended to empower Railroad Committee to make regulations requiring that proper shelter be provided for workmen operating cars. The arrest, trial, and imprisonment of youthful offenders separated from that of older criminals. Customs readjusted, consolidated and amended in favor of protection, reductions on agricultural products and on agricultural implements, cottons and woolens, and iron and steel and their products and on chemicals and leather. Tea imported from England made duty free. Bounty on iron and steel made in Canada from Canadian ore authorized and $2 per ton on pig iron. Dominion Election Act amended to make all elections come on the same day. Dominion bank notes limited to $25,000,000 outstanding instead of $20,000,000. Land Titles Act consolidated and amended laws respecting land in the Territories. Subsidies granted in aid of 60 railroad enterprises. Ten years' contract and subsidy to weekly steamship service between Canada and the United Kingdom granted. Commercial Treaty with France ratified

April 21, College of St. Joseph (Roman Catholic) at Memramcook received new charter

June 16, Opening of Victoria and Sidney Railroad

June 16, Third journey of J. B. Tyrrell from Selkirk northeast from Reindeer Lake to Yathkyed Lake and to Hudson Bay (Sept. 10) at western end of Chesterfield Inlet by the Ferguson River, and from Churchill overland to the Nelson River and to north end of Lake Winnipeg, covering distance of nearly 3,000 miles in 7 months, reaching Fort Selkirk Jan. 7, 1895

June 22, Death of Archbishop Alexandre Antoine Taché (Roman Catholic)

June 24, Decision Imperial Privy Council granted right of Manitoba Roman Catholic minority in Manitoba to appeal against decision of Feb. 20

June 26, Elections in favor of Liberal Government

June 28–July 11, Second Inter-Colonial Conference held at Ottawa, attended by representatives of the Imperial Government, New South Wales, Cape Colony, New Zealand, Victoria, and Queensland

Sept. 14, Death of Sir Narcisse Fortunate Belleau

Oct. 30, Death of Honoré Mercier, former Lieutenant Governor of Quebec

Nov. 3, First issue of *Le Temps*, Ottawa

Nov. 29, Death of Viscount Monck, former Governor General

Dec. 10, Financial crisis in Newfoundland caused by failure of Prowse, Hall and Morris, London firm, which acted as agent of many Newfoundland companies

Dec. 12, Death of Sir John Thompson, Prime Minister, at Windsor Castle, on visit to England

Dec. 21, Sixth Dominion Ministry appointed

Office	Name	Date of Appointment
Premier and President of Council	Sir Mackenzie Bowell	Dec. 21, 1894
Minister of Justice	Sir Charles Hibbert Tupper	Dec. 21, 1894
	A. R. Dickey	Jan. 15, 1896
Minister of Trade and Commerce	W. B. Ives	Dec. 21, 1894
Postmaster General	Sir A. P. Caron	Jan. 21, 1892
Secretary of State	A. R. Dickey	Dec. 12, 1894
	W. H. Montague	Mar. 26, 1895
	Sir Charles Tupper, Bart.	Jan. 15, 1896
Minister of Finance	George Eulas Foster	May 29, 1888
Minister of Marine and Fisheries	John Costigan	Dec. 21, 1894
Minister of Railways and Canals	John G. Haggart	Jan. 11, 1892
Minister of Public Works	J. A. Ouimet	Jan. 11, 1892
Minister of Militia and Defense	J. C. Patterson	Dec. 5, 1892
	A. R. Dickey	Mar. 26, 1895
	A. Desjardins	Jan. 15, 1896
Minister of Interior	Thomas M. Daly	Oct. 17, 1892
Minister of Agriculture	A. R. Angers	Dec. 5, 1892
	W. H. Montague	Jan. 15, 1896
Controller of Customs	J. F. Wood	Dec. 17, 1895
Controller of Inland Revenue	E. G. Prior	Dec. 17, 1895
Without portfolio	Sir Frank Smith	July 29, 1882
	W. H. Montague	Dec. 21, 1894
	D. Ferguson	Dec. 21, 1894

NOT IN THE CABINET

Solicitor General	John J. Curran	Dec. 5, 1892
Controller of Inland Revenue	John F. Wood	Dec. 5, 1892
Controller of Customs	N. Clarke Wallace	Dec. 5, 1892

1895

Jan. 1, Mackenzie Bowell knighted

Jan. 15, Decision of Supreme Court sustained lower court in prohibition test case

Jan. 29, Decision of Judicial Committee of Imperial Privy Council that Roman Catholic minority of Manitoba have right to appeal to Governor General for redress of grievances as to schools

March 21, Remedial Order relating to Manitoba schools called on Manitoba to take necessary steps to restore rights of Catholics respecting denominational schools

April 4–16, Canada-Newfoundland Confederation Conference met at Ottawa, terms agreed upon not accepted by Newfoundland asking for $650,000 a year instead of $500,000 offered, and assumption of debt of $17,000,000 instead of the $10,000,000 offered

April 18–July 22, Fifth session of seventh Parliament. North West Territories Act amended defined voters. Dominion Election Act amended to establish same day for nomination of candidates. Customs tariff amended to increase duties on certain articles. Bounty on beet sugar extended to July 1, 1897, and bounty granted on silver, lead, and other ores, and silver and gold smelted to July 1, 1900. New Copyright Act passed

April 24, Report of Royal Commission on Liquor Traffic submitted, the majority not in favor of enacting prohibition law for the entire Dominion

June 13, Manitoba Legislature declined to alter status of its schools as suggested by Dominion Order in Council of March 21

July 7–11, Cabinet crisis at Ottawa on Manitoba school question and resignation of A. R. Angers, Lieut. Governor of Ontario

July 15, *Banque du Peuple* suspended payment, resumed operations Nov. 4, depositors getting 25%

Aug. 6, Neil McNeil appointed Bishop of Nilopolis and Vicar Apostolic at St. George, Newfoundland

Sept. 5, Imperial Act for removal of doubts as to validity of Dominion law respecting Deputy Speaker of the Senate

Sept. 9, Sault Ste. Marie again rebuilt, reopened

Oct. 2, Yukon, Mackenzie, Ungava, and Franklin provisional districts of North West Territories defined by Order in Council

Oct. 14, Commercial Treaty with France came into effect

Nov. 1, Independence of Canada Club adopted platform

Nov. 25, Copyright Conference at Ottawa

1896

Jan. 2–April 23, Sixth session of seventh Parliament. Six Ministers resigned during debate on Address Jan. 2. Mining and smelting machinery imported prior to July 1, 1897, placed on free list. Manitoba Remedial School Bill introduced Feb. 11, withdrawn April 16 after debate of 60 hours

Jan. 8, Bowell Ministry resigned but reorganized Cabinet

Feb. 8, Convention for submission to arbitration of British claims in connection with the Bering Sea seal fisheries signed between the United States and Great Britain

Feb. 27, Manitoba Legislature protested interference of Dominion in Manitoba school affairs

March 4, Name of Imperial Federation League changed to British Empire League

March 21, A. R. Dickey, A. Desjardin, and Sir Donald A. Smith appointed a commission to Manitoba to try to arrange compromise on the school question, report of their failure presented to Parliament April 7

March 30, Death of Lieut. Colonel G. Amyot, member of Parliament

April 24, Sir Donald A. Smith appointed High Commissioner in England for Canada

April 27, Bowell Ministry resigned

——, Seventh Dominion Ministry appointed

Office	Name	Date of Appointment
Premier and Secretary of State	Sir Charles Tupper, Bart.	Jan. 15, 1896
Minister of Marine and Fisheries	John Costigan	Dec. 21, 1894
Minister of Finance	George Eulas Foster	Jan. 15, 1896
Minister of Railways and Canals	John G. Haggart	Jan. 15, 1896
Minister of Trade and Commerce	William B. Ives	Jan. 15, 1896
Minister of Justice	A. R. Dickey	Jan. 15, 1896
Minister of Agriculture	W. H. Montague	Jan. 15, 1896
President of Council	A. R. Angers	May 1, 1896
Minister of Public Works	A. Desjardins	May 1, 1896
Minister of Interior	Hugh John Macdonald	May 1, 1896
Postmaster General	L. O. Taillon	May 1, 1899
Minister of Militia and Defense	David Tisdale	May 2, 1896
Controller of Customs	John F. Wood	Jan. 15, 1896
Controller of Inland Revenue	E. G. Prior	Dec. 17, 1895
Without portfolio	Sir Frank Smith	July 29, 1892
	D. Ferguson	Dec. 21, 1894
	J. J. Ross	May 1, 1896

NOT IN THE CABINET

Solicitor General	Sir Charles Hibbert Tupper	May 1, 1896

May 1, Eight-hour day adopted by Public Printing Bureau

May 9, Decision of Judicial Committee of Imperial Privy Council on prohibition test case on appeal gave federal government exclusive right of absolute prohibition as to Dominion or Provinces, but affirmed constitutionality of local option legislation

May 10, Death of Justice Fournier of the Supreme Court

May 17, Roman Catholic bishops issued mandamus respecting Manitoba schools

June 10, Death of Donald Alexander Macdonald

June 23, Sir Charles Tupper's Government defeated in general election, the first Liberal victory since 1874

June 25, Death of Sir Samuel Leonard Tilley

July 6, Order in Council enlarged boundaries of the Province of Quebec to the shores of Hudson Bay, adding 118,450 square miles of territory

July 8, Resignation of Tupper Ministry

July 11, Eighth Dominion Ministry appointed

Office	Name	Date of Appointment
Premier and President of Council	Sir Wilfrid Laurier	July 11, 1896
Minister of Trade and Commerce	Sir Richard J. Cartwright	July 13, 1896
Secretary of State	R. W. Scott	July 13, 1896
	Charles Murphy	Oct. 10, 1908
Minister of Justice	Sir Oliver Mowat	July 13, 1896
	David Mills	Nov. 18, 1897
	Charles Fitzpatrick	Feb. 11, 1902
	Sir Allen B. Aylesworth	June 4, 1905
Minister of Marine and Fisheries	Sir Louis Henry Davies	July 13, 1896
	James Sutherland	Jan. 15, 1902
	J. Raymond F. Prefontaine	Nov. 11, 1902
	Louis P. Brodeur	Feb. 6, 1906
	Rodolphe Lemieux	Aug. 11, 1911
Minister of Militia and Defense	Sir Frederick W. Borden	July 13, 1896
Postmaster General	Sir William Mulock	July 13, 1896
	Allen B. Aylesworth	Oct. 16, 1905
	Rodolphe Lemieux	June 4, 1906
	Henri S. Beland	Aug. 11, 1911
Minister of Agriculture	Sydney A. Fisher	July 13, 1896
Minister of Public Works	J. Israel Tarte	July 13, 1896
	James Sutherland	Nov. 11, 1902
	Charles S. Hyman	May 22, 1905
	William Pugsley	Sept. 13, 1907
Minister of Finance	William S. Fielding	July 13, 1896
Minister of Railways and Canals	Andrew G. Blair	July 13, 1896
	Henry R. Emmerson	Jan. 15, 1904
	George P. Graham	Sept. 13, 1907
Minister of Interior	Clifford Sifton	Nov. 17, 1896
	Frank Oliver	April 8, 1905
Minister of Customs	William Paterson	July 30, 1897
Minister of Inland Revenue	Sir Henri G. Joly de Lothbinière	June 30, 1897
	M. E. Bernier	June 22, 1900
	Louis P. Brodeur	Jan. 19, 1904
	William Templeman	Feb. 6, 1905
Minister of Labor	William Lyon Mackenzie King	June 2, 1909
Without portfolio	Richard R. Dobell	July 13, 1896
	C. A. Geoffrion	July 13, 1896
	James Sutherland	Sept. 30, 1899
	W. Templeman	Feb. 25, 1902
	Charles S. Hyman	Feb. 5, 1904

NOT IN THE CABINET

Solicitor General	Charles Fitzpatrick	July 13, 1896
	Henry Carroll	Feb. 11, 1902

Office	Name	Date of Appointment
	Rodolphe Lemieux	Jan. 29, 1904
	Jacques Bureau	Feb. 14, 1907
Controller of Customs	William Paterson	July 13, 1896
Controller of Inland Revenue	Sir Henri G. Joly de Lothbiniere	July 13, 1896

July 15, The Canadian yacht "Glencairn" won in international race

Aug. 12, George Carmack discovered gold on creek afterwards named Bonanza Creek, Yukon, in the Klondike region

Aug. 19–Oct. 5, First session of eighth Parliament. Fourteen Bills including supply received assent

Aug. 27, Sir Charles Tupper chosen leader of the Opposition by Conservatives at meeting at Ottawa

Sept. 15, First meeting of Bar Association of Canada held in Montreal

Sept. 27–Oct. 7, Strike of telegraph train dispatchers of Canadian Pacific Railroad over grievances and in movement for shorter hours and increase in wages, settled by compromise

Oct. 13, Supreme Court gave judgment on fisheries reference case

Nov. 9, Pacific Cable Conference reassembled in London, England

Nov. 24, Bering Sea Commission met at Victoria, British Columbia

Dec. 5, A "horseless carriage" made in Canada first appeared on streets in Toronto

Dec. 15, Railroad from Gladstone to Dauphin, Manitoba, opened (Canadian Northern)

Dec. 30, Death of Archbishop Fabre, of Montreal (Roman Catholic)

1897

Jan. 30, Convention between Great Britain and the United States provided for demarcation of boundary between Yukon and British Columbia by a boundary commission

March 25, Manitoba Legislature passed a compromise measure on the school question

March 25–June 29, Second session of eighth Parliament. British preferential tariff enacted with duties fixed at $7/8$ of regular duty for first year and $3/4$ after July 1, 1898, and "the reciprocal tariff" $12\frac{1}{2}\%$ reduction on all duties except those on alcoholic liquors and tobacco to all countries giving Canadian products equally favorable rates. Bounty on iron and steel ingots made in Canada authorized. Act restricted the importation and employment of aliens in retaliation for measure adopted in the United States

March 31, Raphael Merry Del Val, Apostolic Delegate to Canada, arrived in Quebec on mission to investigate the Manitoba school situation

June, Gold first discovered at Lake Wawa, and site of Wawa City laid out Sept. 6

June 5, Sir Wilfrid Laurier, Premier, sailed for England to attend the Queen's Diamond Jubilee, celebrated June 22

June 25, Louis Joseph Paul Bruchési appointed Archbishop of Montreal (Roman Catholic)

July 3, G. A. Lancaster located claim on Eldorado Creek later known as Gold Hill

July 28, A royalty of 2% imposed on product of Canadian mines

July 30, Great Britain gave notice of denunciation of Commercial Treaties with Belgium and Germany in accordance with the request of the Dominion, Belgium and Germany claiming benefits of "reciprocal tariff" under treaties of 1861 and 1865 respectively

Aug. 11, Minimum tariff rates extended to France

Aug. 16, Yukon Judicial District formed and proclaimed by the Governor General in Council, and James Morro Walsh appointed first Commissioner on the 17th

Aug. 18, Meeting of British Association in Toronto

Aug. 31, British Medical Association met at Montreal

Sept. 6, The Knapp roller boat launched in Toronto

Sept. 27, Long distance telephone communication established from Quebec and Montreal with Boston, Mass.

Nov. 11, Premier Laurier in conference with Secretary of State Sherman in Washington as to questions in dispute between Canada and the United States

Dec. 8, Judicial Committee of the Imperial Privy Council reported in favor of the Provinces of the Dominion having the right to create Queen's Counsel

——, Encyclical letter of Pope Leo XIV on Manitoba schools urged Catholics to establish separate schools, and accept Manitoba school settlement

Dec. 18, Geographic Board established by Order in Council

——, Order in Council changed boundaries of Yukon, Franklin, and Ungava

Dec. 22, Award of Bering Sea Claims Commission of $463,454 in satisfaction of Canadian claims against the United States

1898

Jan. 14, Colonial premiers of Australasia in conference agreed to contribute one-third of cost of Pacific cable if Great Britain and Canada would contribute the other two-thirds

Feb. 3–June 13, Third session of eighth Parliament. Reciprocal Tariff Act repealed and British preferential tariff enacted to take effect Aug. 1, with duties 25% lower than the general rate. Imperial penny postage established. Prohibition Plebiscite Act passed and Dominion Franchise Act. Provision made for enlargement of boundaries of the Province of Quebec to north, northeast, and northwest. Manitoba Debt Account Act provided for loan for erection of public buildings. Yukon Railway Bill for road to Klondike defeated in Upper House

March 18, St. Joseph's College (Roman Catholic) established in New Brunswick in 1864, given university powers

April 12, Death of Cardinal Taschereau. Louis Nazaire Bégin appointed Archbishop of Quebec

May 3, Pioneer Historical Association became the Ontario Historical Society

May 26, Decision of Judicial Committee of Imperial Privy Council that sole power to make fisheries regulations is vested in the Dominion, the Provinces except Manitoba and the North West Territories may issue licenses and collect revenue

May 30, Agreement for Canadian-American Joint Commission to negotiate treaty to adjust differences as to fisheries and commercial reciprocity, &c·

June 13, Yukon Territory organized, Dawson, the capital, Commissioner, William Ogilvie, appointed July 4

———, Death of Sir Joseph Adolphe Chapleau

July 30, The Earl of Minto (Gilbert J. M. K. Elliot) appointed Governor General

July 31, Death of Archbishop Walsh (Roman Catholic) of Toronto

Aug. 1, Treaty of Great Britain of May 30, 1865 with Germany and containing clauses affecting Canada terminated, German goods entitled henceforth to enter Canada only under general not preferential tariff

———, British preferential tariff came into effect

Aug. 23–Oct. 10, Joint High Commission to consider questions in dispute between Canada and the United States met at Quebec

Sept. 26, Death of Malcolm C. Cameron, Lieutenant Governor of the North West Territories; succeeded Oct. 13 by Amedee E. Forget

Sept. 29, Dominion prohibition plebiscite resulted in vote for prohibition of 278,380 against 264,693

Nov. 10–Feb. 20, Joint High Commission reassembled in Washington. Failed to reach agreement as to Alaska boundary

Nov. 12, Lord Minto took oath of office as Governor General

Dec. 25, Imperial penny postage (2 cent) inaugurated for letters weighing one-half ounce or less, to take effect Jan. 1

1899

Jan. 20, 2,000 Doukhobors arrived in Canada from Russia to settle in the North West Territories; during the year about 7,500 entered the country

Jan. 24, Bishop Denis O'Connor appointed Archbishop of Toronto (Roman Catholic)

Feb. 2, Paris Exposition Commission for Canada appointed, J. I. Tarte, head

March, Dominion Iron and Steel Company incorporated in Nova Scotia

March 10, General education law enacted by Quebec Province

March 16–Aug. 11, Fourth session of eighth Parliament. Pacific Cable Act provided for making arrangements for construction of cable between Canada and Australasia. Bounties on iron and steel continued to June 30, 1907. Report of Yukon Commission presented exonerated officials of charge of selling mining permits

April 1, Ontario Historical Society received a charter

May 23, First celebration of Empire Day

July, Railroad connection between Lake Bennett in the Yukon and Skagaway, Alaska, completed

July 7, Germany deprived Canada of most favored nation treatment in commercial matters

July 8–9, Riots in London, Ontario, on account of a tram strike, troops called out

July 12, Supplementary Treaty as to extradition of criminals between Great Britain and the United States signed

July 21, New suspension bridge over the Niagara River between Queenston and Lewiston formally opened

July 25, Bank Ville Marie suspended payment because of a defaulting teller

Aug. 11, Strikers on the Grand Trunk Railroad accepted compromise agreement

Sept. 4, Royal Victoria College for Women (McGill University) opened; gift of a million dollar endowment by Lord Strathcona announced Dec. 13

Sept. 28, Dawson, Yukon Territory, connected with British Columbia by telegraph

Oct. 1, Diomède Falconio, first permanent Apostolic delegate, arrived at Quebec

Oct. 9, The Soulanges Canal (1,435 miles and 14 feet navigation) from Quebec to Lake Superior opened

Oct. 13, Canada organized a contingent for service in South African War

Oct. 18, Henri Bourassa resigned seat in Parliament in protest against sending Canadian troops to South Africa

Oct. 20, Great Britain and the United States agreed on provisional boundary between Alaska and Canada

Oct. 30, First Canadian troops sailed from Quebec for South Africa, 57 officers, and 1,224 men, and arrived at Capetown Nov. 29

Nov. 18, Death of Sir William Dawson

Dec. 7, General elections in Manitoba resulted in defeat of Thomas Greenaway

1900

Jan. 21 and 27, First and second quota of second contingent of Canadian troops sailed from Halifax for South Africa arriving Feb. 17 and 26 at Capetown

Feb. 1–July 18, Fifth session of eighth Parliament. Dominion Election Act consolidated and amended as to election of members of House of Commons, and Dominion Controverted Election Act, Bank Act, Criminal Code of 1892, and Tariff Act amended. British preferential tariff raised to $^1/_3$ of the general tariff. Conciliation Act provided for aid in settlement of industrial disputes and collection of information and statistics, and established Dept. of Labor. Chinese immigration further restricted and head tax raised to $100

Feb. 21, Third quota of second contingent of Canadian troops sailed from Halifax for South Africa, arriving at Capetown March 22

Feb. 27, Semlin Ministry of British Columbia dismissed by Lieutenant Governor Thomas R. McInnes, which was strongly disapproved, and caused demonstration against the Lieutenant Governor, all but one member of the House leaving the hall when he arrived to prorogue the legislature

———, Battle of Paardeburg, South Africa, where Canadians distinguished themselves

March 7, Canadians in artillery duel of Poplar Grove near Modder River, South Africa

March 16, "Strathcona's Horse," troops equipped at expense of Lord Strathcona, sailed for South Africa arriving April 10

March–Dec., J. W. Tyrrell made 1,729 miles of surveys from east end of Great Slave Lake across the Barren Lands to mouth of the Chesterfield Inlet, Hudson Bay

April 25, Canadians in Battle of Israel's Poort, South Africa

April 26, Great fire at Hull and Ottawa, property loss $10,000,000, 800 acres destroyed

June 9, Prince Edward Island adopted prohibition

June 15, Resolution adopted at mass meeting of Roman Catholics of Manitoba, May 27, presented to the Government of the Dominion asking for relief in matter of the law abolishing separate schools

July, Strike of fishermen on the Fraser River for increase in wages

July 3, Death by drowning of A. R. Dickey

July 23, Proclamation prohibited the landing in Canada of criminals and paupers

July 30, Japan prohibited emigration of Japanese to Canada

Aug. 3, General strike in Canadian Pacific Railroad shops

Sept. 25, Death of F. G. Marchand

Nov. 1, Canadian troops from South Africa arrived on ship "Idaho"

Nov. 7, The Liberal Government sustained in the Dominion elections

Dec. 13, Supplementary Convention for extradition of fugitive criminals signed between the United States and Great Britain

1901

Jan. 15, The Government of Manitoba leased railroad lines in the Province for 999 years to the Northern Pacific Railroad, and on Feb. 11 the lease transferred to the Canadian Northern Railroad Company

Jan. 22, Death of Queen Victoria and accession of King Edward VII

Feb. 6–May 23, First session of ninth Parliament. Canadian branch of Royal Mint established at Ottawa. May 24, Victoria Day, established as a public holiday. Fruit Marking and Inspection Act provided for grading and inspection of fruit. Military Pension Act provided for pensions for the army. Third revision of Bank Act. Alien law amended as to penalties and prohibition of importation of unskilled labor procurable in the country. Resolution adopted in favor of removal from coronation oath of parts offensive to Roman Catholics

Feb. 6, Robert Laird Borden elected leader of the Conservative Opposition to succeed Sir Charles Tupper, resigned

Feb. 15, The "Strathcona Horse" reviewed by King Edward in London; arrived in Halifax March 8

Feb. 23, Manitoba prohibition law of July 3, 1900, declared by court to be null and void

March 11, Reduction of royalties by Yukon gold mines from 10 to 5%

March 22, Newfoundland Government informed of agreement of France and Great Britain as to French shore replacing *modus vivendi* to remain in force until Dec. 31 which had been renewed from year to year by Newfoundland

March 30, Court decision in Delpit marriage case held that marriages of Roman Catholics by Protestant clergymen were valid

April 1, Population 5,371,315, English 3,063,195, French 1,649,371. Quebec 1,648,898, Ontario 2,182,947, Nova Scotia 459,574, New Brunswick 331,120, Prince Edward Island 103,259, British Columbia 178,657, Manitoba 255,211, North West Territories 20,129, Saskatchewan 91,279, Alberta 73,022, Yukon Territory 27,219

April 15, Anglican Archbishop William Bennett Bond elected Metropolitan

June 3, Strike of carpenters in Ottawa for increase in wages and recognition of the union

July 12, Strikers in salmon fisheries on the Pacific marooned and imprisoned 47 non-union Japanese

Aug. 22, First sod turned on Cape Breton Railroad

Aug. 28, Municipal Convention held at Toronto

Sept. 16–Oct. 21, Visit of Duke and Duchess of Cornwall (afterwards King George V and Queen Mary) to Canada

Sept. 24, Telegraph communication established between Dawson City and the rest of Canada

Oct. 2, Marconi wireless telegraph installed in Straits of Belle Isle

Oct. 28, Death of W. E. H. Massey

Dec. 14, Order in Council published Feb. 8, 1902, established Yoho Park Reserve

——, Marconi at wireless station at St. Johns, Newfoundland, received signals from his station at Cornwall, England

1902

Jan. 14, Prince Edward Island Prohibition Act declared valid by Supreme Court

Jan. 14 and 24, Canadian mounted rifles sailed from Halifax for South Africa

Feb. 12, Death of the Earl of Dufferin, former Governor General

Feb. 13–May 15, Second session of ninth Parliament. Acts passed as to administration of justice and representation in House of Commons of Yukon Territory. Immigration Act amended to prohibit landing in Canada of diseased persons. Medical Council established. Marconi granted $80,000 to construct wireless telegraph station on Nova Scotia coast

Feb. 18, Bessemer steel manufactured at Sault Ste. Marie

April 2, Liquor Referendum Act defeated in popular election at Manitoba

May 10, Death of Principal Grant of Queen's University

May 31, Peace signed at Vereeniging ended war in South Africa. Canadian expenditure on the war amounted to $2,000,000 and contributed about 8,000 men

June 4, Conference of Dominion Boards of Trade to discuss relations of Canada with the Empire

June 21–24, Strike of employees of street railroads in Toronto

July 25, Lord Dundonald took over command of the Canadian militia

Aug. 21, Doukhbors in Yorktown district turned their horses, cattle, and sheep free "giving them to the Lord" and began pilgrimage

Sept. 6, Jamaica sugar planters passed resolution in favor of federation with Canada

Sept. 13, Death of Sir John Bourinot

Oct. 31, Sandford Fleming sent first message over completed Pacific cable from Canada to Australia

Nov. 21, Commission appointed to revise, classify, and consolidate public general statutes

——, Sir Henry Elzéar Taschereau appointed Chief Justice

Dec. 2, James H. Ross elected first member from Yukon to the Dominion Parliament

Dec. 4, Liquor Referendum Act voted on in Ontario, 199,749 in favor and 103,542 against

Dec. 8, Vancouver cable between Australia and New Zealand opened

International Nickel Company formed controlling chief deposits

1903

Jan. 3, Donatus Sbarretti, Apostolic delegate, arrived at Ottawa

Jan. 24, Convention between Great Britain and the United States, agreement to refer interpretation of Alaskan boundary to 6 impartial jurists of repute.

Elihu Root, H. C. Lodge, and Senator Turner named by President Roosevelt on Feb. 18, all known opponents of Canadian claims

Jan. 27, Andrew Carnegie offered $350,000 for Central Public Library and 2 branches at Toronto; accepted Feb. 23

March 12–Oct. 24, Third session of ninth Parliament. Bounties on iron and steel continued to 1907. Railroad Act created Railway Commission of the Privy Council to administer railroads and amended and consolidated laws. Grand Trunk Pacific Company authorized to construct another transcontinental railroad. Labor Disputes' Act for settlement of disputes between railroad companies and their employees passed. Act provided for advances to the Government of the North West Territories. Penny Bank Act and Act to readjust representation in the House. Head tax on Chinese entering the country raised to $500 to take effect Jan. 1, 1904

March 31, British colonists sent by I. M. Barr sailed from Liverpool, settled in Saskatchewan valley in vicinity of Lloydminster

April 16, Announcement of Minister of Finance of imposition of surtax of $1/3$ over general tariff on imports from Germany because of German discrimination due to preferential Canadian tariff in favor of Great Britain

April 19, Death of Sir Oliver Mowatt

May 7–10, Strike of dockers at Montreal

June 19, Incorporation of Regina, Saskatchewan

July 7, Cape of Good Hope and other British South African colonies given benefits of preferential tariff by Order in Council

Aug. 17, Congress of Chambers of Commerce of the Empire opened at Montreal

Oct. 5, Alberta College, Edmonton, founded by the Methodist Church

Oct. 10, Canadian Nationalist League under H. Bourassa published platform

Oct. 20, Award of the Alaska Boundary Tribunal adverse to Canada, barring Canada from ocean inlets

Oct. 24, Grand Trunk Pacific Railroad chartered for line from Moncton, New Brunswick, through Quebec to Winnipeg and the Pacific coast at Prince Rupert, the eastern division from Moncton to be built by the Government and the western from Winnipeg to Prince Rupert by the Grand Trunk Pacific Company, to be completed by Dec. 1, 1911

Nov. 17, Canadian Mounted Police occupied Herschel Island and raised the British flag

Discovery of silver at the present Cobalt near town of Haileyburg, Ontario

Nov. 28, German imported goods subjected to surtax of one-third over and above duties of the general tariff

1904

Jan. 20, Act to regulate immigration of British Columbia disallowed by Dominion Government

Feb. 1, Dominion Railway Commission established under statute of 1903 with judicial powers to fix rates, regulate operation and management, and settle disputes

March 10–Aug. 10, Fourth session of ninth Parliament. New militia law enacted. Tariff and Temperance Acts amended, the Tariff Act containing "anti-dumping" clause and levying extra duty on undervalued goods. Provision made for payment of bounties on crude petroleum from Canadian wells

April 8, Lansdowne-Cambon Convention signed in London effected final settlement of "French shore" question in Newfoundland, the French giving up rights of landing under Article XIII of the Treaty of Utrecht, and compensation given to France by territorial concessions elsewhere

April 19, Great fire in Toronto, $12,000,000 property loss

June 7, Speech of Lord Dundonald in criticism of acting Minister of Militia, Sydney Fisher, led to his dismissal from office, and with him the practice of appointment of Imperial officers to command of Canadian militia ended

July 15, Tariff Agreement with South Africa gave preference on a limited list of commodities

Aug. 28, Archbishop of Canterbury arrived at Quebec on visit to Canada

Oct. 8, Edmonton incorporated

Oct. 14, Archbishop Bond (Anglican) made primate of all Canada

Nov. 3, Liberal Government sustained in elections with parliamentary majority of 64

Dec. 10, Earl Grey (Albert H. G. Grey), appointed Sept. 26, assumed office as Governor General succeeding Lord Minto

1905

Jan. 11–July 20, First session of tenth Parliament. Establishment of Alberta and Saskatchewan as provinces provided for. Acts regulated wireless telegraph, provided for inspection and sale of seeds, militia administration reorganized. Census and Statistics Act made provision for permanent census office to take decennial census. Salaries of members of Parliament increased from $1,500 to $2,500, and of Prime Minister from $8,000 to $12,000, and gave salary of $7,000 to leader of the Opposition, and salaries of judges and Cabinet Ministers increased. Pensions provided for certain Kings' Privy Councillors

Jan. 14, François Théophile Zotique Racicot appointed Bishop of Pogla and auxiliary to Archbishop of Montreal

Jan. 25, The Liberal Government of G. W. Ross overthrown in provincial election in Ontario; succeeded Feb. 8 by Sir James Pliny Whitney, first Conservative Ministry since 1872

March 6–7, First meeting of Canadian section of joint international commission to report on boundary waters between Canada and the United States

March 25, Exchange of Notes completed the Alaska boundary award

March 31, During year 146,266 immigrants arrived; from Great Britain 65,359, from the United States 43,543

April 12, New Extradition Convention between the United States and Great Britain signed

May 10, Armorial ensigns granted to Prince Edward Island and Manitoba

May 25, First meeting of joint international commission on use of waters adjacent to boundary between Canada and the United States met in Washington

June 1–Sept. 30, Strike of coal miners at Nanaimo, British Columbia

June 15, Newfoundland prohibited sale of bait to foreign fishing vessels and ended license system

——, The Governor General commissioned Commander-in-Chief

June 18, Canadian Manufacturers' Association reached Liverpool on visit to Great Britain

June 28–July 3, Strike of employees of street railroads at Cornwall, Ontario

July 24, Area of Keewatin not included in North West Territories annexed to take effect Sept. 1

Aug. 11–Oct. 30, Semi-official visit of Prince Louis of Battenberg

Aug. 13, Canadian vessel "Antiope" from Victoria, British Columbia, seized by Japanese as carrier of food, contraband of war

Sept. 1, Provinces of Alberta and Saskatchewan established, George H. V. Bulyea first Lieutenant Governor of Alberta, and A. E. Forget, of Saskatchewan and North West Territories reconstituted

Sept. 11, First sod of Lake Superior branch of Grand Trunk Pacific Railroad turned by Sir Wilfrid Laurier at Fort William

Sept. 29, Carnegie Library at Guelph, Ontario, opened

1906

Jan. 16, Control of military garrison at Halifax, Nova Scotia, transferred to control of Dominion Government, and the British soldiers left Canada

Jan. 31, Convention of Great Britain with Japan respecting commercial relations of Canada and Japan

Feb. 28, Royal Commission appointed to investigate life insurance in Canada; made report Feb. 22, 1907

March 8–July 13, Second session of tenth Parliament. Immigration Act passed repealed those of 1886, 1887, and 1902. Railroad Act of 1903 amended. Lord's Day Observance Act forbade Sunday labor, Sunday transportation with certain exceptions, and Sunday performances for which a fee charged. Forest Reserves' Act set aside certain Dominion lands. Control of Money Lenders' Act limited rate of interest. Gold and Silver Marking Act regulated manufacture, sale, and importation of articles of gold and silver. Yukon Placer Mining Act amended. Immigration Act amended to provide for deportation of criminals and immigrants liable to become a public charge. North West Territories Act amended to appoint a commissioner to administer the government. Bounty on crude petroleum provided for

March 9–Dec. 2, Strike of coal miners at Lethbridge, Alberta

March 27, Prince Arthur of Connaught landed at Victoria, British Columbia, after visit to Japan, and sailed for England May 10

March 29–30, Riots in strike of street railway employees at Winnipeg

March 31, During the year 189,064 immigrants entered the country; 86,796 from the United Kingdom, and 57,796 from the United States

——, Armorial ensigns granted to British Columbia and Saskatchewan

April 21, Convention as to demarcation of Alaskan boundary as constituted by the 141st meridian signed by Great Britain and the United States

May 1, New regulations respecting pay and allowance to Canadian militia came into effect

——, Carnegie Public Library opened in Ottawa

May 7, Strike of cotton workers at Montreal ended with grant of 10% increase in wages

May 9, University of Alberta at Edmonton received a charter from the provincial legislature

May 14, The University of Toronto received a new charter

——, Ontario Hydro Electric Power Commission created

May 19, Death of Gabriel Dumont

May 22, The British garrison left Esquimalt on the Pacific after military occupation which dated from 1858, the last British soldiers in Canada

June 4, Sir Charles Fitzpatrick appointed Chief Justice

Aug. 13, Captain Roald Amundsen reached Nome after navigation of North West Passage for the first time from east to west

Sept. 22–Nov. 13, Strike of 1,600 miners employed at Fernie and Michel, British Columbia

Oct. 6, *Modus vivendi* arranged by which United States' vessels were permitted to use purse-seines for ensuing season, and to engage Newfoundlanders outside the 3-mile limit, but were not to fish on Sunday in Newfoundland waters, to pay dues and conform to customs regulations

Oct. 8–13, Interprovincial Conference at Ottawa

Oct. 9, Death of Archbishop William Bennett (Anglican); succeeded by Bishop James Carmichael, appointed Bishop of Montreal, and Bishop Arthur Sweatman, of Toronto, made primate of Canada

Nov. 22–April 27, 1907, Third session of tenth Parliament. Act provided for inspection of meats and canned goods and of public warehouses for cold storage. Customs tariff included an "intermediate tariff" for use in granting favors on a reciprocal basis to foreign countries, in addition to the general tariff and the British preferential rate. Bounties on iron and steel continued until 1910. Dept. of Mines with the Geological Survey as a branch constituted. Industrial Disputes Investigation (Lemieux) Act to prevent strikes and lockouts passed. Provident fund arranged for pensions for employees of the Intercolonial and Prince Edward Island railroads. Representation of Alberta and Saskatchewan in the House of Commons readjusted. Yukon Act amended to permit appointment of Acting Commissioner. Yukon Placer Mining Act again amended

1907

Jan. 2, Death of Sir W. P. Howland, a "Father of the Confederation"

Jan. 3, Canada adhered to Anglo-Japanese Treaty of commerce of 1894

Jan., Strike of telephone employees at Toronto

Feb. 11, Supreme Court of Alberta Province established

March 8, Supreme Court of Saskatchewan Province established

March 14, Technical schools established at Montreal and Quebec

March 17, Royal Commission appointed to investigate civil service

March 18, Railroad Commission ordered Canadian Pacific and Grand Trunk to reduce passenger fares to 3 cents a mile within 60 days

March 22, North West Territories Act amended to vest executive powers in a commissioner

March 31, For 9 months previous to this date 124,667 immigrants entered the country, 55,791 from the United Kingdom and 34,217 from the United States

April 3, University of Saskatchewan received charter from the provincial legislature

April 15–May 6, Strike of coal miners in Alberta and East British Columbia of 3,450 men

May 1, Convention came into effect by which postage on British newspapers and periodicals from the United Kingdom reduced

May 14–21, Strike of longshoremen of Montreal unsuccessful

May 15–Sept., Strike of plumbers of Toronto

May 30, Royal warrant gave armorial ensigns to Alberta Province

June 7–25, Visit of Prince Fushimi of Japan

Aug. 1–Oct. 31, Strike of coal miners at Springhill, Nova Scotia

Aug. 9, British North America (Provincial Subsidies) Act made further provision with respect to the sums to be paid by the Dominion to the several provinces

Aug. 27, First joint report of the Alaskan Boundary Commission

Sept. 8–9, Riots against the Japanese at Vancouver

Sept. 19, New Commercial Treaty with France gave Canada the minimum rates on live cattle, fresh canned meats, dairy products, fish, lumber, pulp, agricultural implements, various iron and steel manufactures, furniture, boots and shoes, asbestos products and cement; not ratified until 1910

Oct. 12, Agreement to pay damages to Japanese sufferers of Vancouver riots

Oct. 16, Macdonald College opened at Sainte de Bellevue, 20 miles west of Montreal

Oct. 17, First message by Marconi wireless telegraph between Canada and Great Britain

Nov. 28–July 20, 1908, Fourth session of tenth Parliament. $2,850,000 appropriated for purchase and distribution of seed grain to farmers of Alberta and Saskatchewan under easy terms of repayment. Issue of government annuities for old age authorized. Inspection and Sale Act amended to provide penalties for adulteration of cheese, and respecting fruit and fruit markets. The acquisition of historic battlefields for national parks authorized and appointment of a national battlefields' commission. Civil Service Act amended to establish a permanent Civil Service Commission. Other legislation dealt with the treatment of juvenile delinquents, homesteads, immigration, transportation, conduct of elections, tobacco, opium, patent medicines. Dominion Lands' Act, and Dominion Lands' Survey Act amended. North West Territories' Act amended respecting jurisdiction of courts. Yukon Act amended to provide for administration by a commissioner. Chinese Immigration Act amended

Dec. 13, Women's Canadian Club inaugurated at Montreal by Lord Grey

1908

Jan. 1, Doukhobors who started on pilgrimage from Yorktown in July reached Fort William and were returned to their homes by train by the Government of Ontario

Jan. 2, Branch of the Royal Mint opened at Ottawa

March 7, University of British Columbia founded

March 31, During this year 262,469 immigrants arrived, 120,182 from the United Kingdom and 53,312 from the United States, and 83,975 from the continent of Europe

April 11, Conventions signed between the United States and Great Britain regarding protection of food fishes in contiguous boundary waters of Canada and the United States, and as to demarcation of boundary

May 4–June, Strike of cotton mill employees in Quebec

May 18, Treaty between Great Britain and the United States provided for conveyance of persons in custody for trial in one country through territory of the other,

and respecting wreckage and salvage in contiguous boundary waters

May, V. Stefansson and R. M. Anderson left New York on scientific expedition to study the Esquimo and make zoölogical survey east of the Mackenzie River

June 13, Death of the Earl of Derby, former Governor General

June 21–23, Celebration at Quebec of bicentenary of Bishop Laval

July 20–31, Celebration of Quebec tercentenary. Visit of the Prince of Wales July 22–29

Aug. 5–Oct. 5, Strike of machinists and carmen of the Canadian Pacific Railroad

Aug. 6, Fergus Patrick McEvay appointed Archbishop of Toronto (Roman Catholic)

Sept. 1, Dominion Lands' Act came into effect, total area opened 30,000,000 acres

Sept. 12, Civil Service Commission appointed

Sept. 23, University of Alberta, Edmonton, opened with 37 students

Oct. 26, Liberal Government sustained in Dominion elections

Nov. 8, Death of Dr. James Fletcher

Nov. 16, Death of Sir Henri Joly de Lotbinière

Dec. 29, Second joint report of Alaskan Boundary Commission

Dec., First gold coins minted in Canada, sovereigns

1909

Jan. 11, Treaty between Great Britain and the United States relating to boundary waters established an international joint commission of the United States and Canada

Jan. 20–May 19, First session of eleventh Parliament. Dept. of Labor, and Dept. of External Affairs constituted. Yukon Act amended, and Tariff to place duty on sugar imports. Commercial Feeding Stuffs' and Fertilizers' Acts provided for annual licensing of manufacturers, and guaranteed analyses. Secret Commissions' Act for prevention of illicit or secret commissions enacted. Commission of Conservation of Natural Resources authorized. Resolution adopted by House of Commons approved of organization of a Canadian naval service

Jan. 23, Supplementary Convention with France signed by Great Britain at Paris prior to ratification of Treaty of commerce of Sept., 1907

Jan. 27, Special Agreement signed for submission to arbitration of questions relating to fisheries on the North Atlantic coast in dispute between the United States and Canada to the Permanent Court of Arbitration at The Hague

Feb. 27, By royal warrant additional armorial bearings granted to Ontario Province

March 12, Juvenile Delinquent Act of 1908 put in force in Winnipeg by proclamation

March 13, Letter of Lord Strathcona to Minister of Militia and Defense offered to provide an annual fund for physical and military training in the schools; accepted, and "Strathcona Trust" established

March 31, During year ending on this date 146,908 immigrants arrived, 52,901 from the United Kingdom, 59,926 from the United States, and 83,975 from the continent of Europe

April 1–June 30, Strike of coal miners in Alberta involved 2,100 men and 11 mines

April 13, Supreme Court of Ontario established

May 1, Prohibition came into effect in Ontario

May 19, Commission of Conservation appointed

July 6, Strike of coal miners at Glace Bay, Nova Scotia

July 7, Institution of the "king's police medal"

July 17, Juvenile Delinquent Act of 1908 put in force in Ottawa by proclamation

Aug. 10–May 27, 1911, Strike of coal miners at Spring Hill, Nova Scotia

Aug. 12, Fort William placed under martial law because of rioting of strikers

——, Canadian government steamer "Arctic" left Winter Harbor and proceeded to Byam Martin Channel and returned by Austin Channel to Barrow Strait and Lancaster Sound reaching Quebec Oct. 5. On this expedition Banksland and Victoria Islands annexed to Canada

Aug. 25–Sept. 1, British Association for the Advancement of Science met at Winnipeg

Aug. 31, Death of Sir Samuel Henry Strong, former Chief Justice

Sept. 3, Conservation Commission appointed

Oct. 21, Royal Edward Institute for Tuberculosis opened at Montreal

Nov. 11–May 4, 1910, Second session of eleventh Parliament. Dept. of Naval Service constituted under Naval Service Act, a voluntary service established, and regulations for navy adopted. Insurance Act repealed previous legislation. Dept. of Insurance constituted under Minister of Finance, a Supt. of Insurance to be deputy head. Currency Act provided for issue of gold coins and a silver dollar. New Immigration Act still further strengthened laws against admission and for deportation of undesirable persons. Legislation enacted for prevention of importation of destructive insects and pests. Combines' Investigation Act provided for the investigation of combines, monopolies, trusts, and mergers. Intermediate tariff instead of general tariff extended to 13 specified articles imported from the United States

Dec., Third joint report of the Alaskan Boundary Commission

Discovery of silver at Gowganda, and of gold in the Porcupine District, Ontario

1910

Jan. 10, *Le Devoir* first published at Montreal by Henri Bourassa

Jan. 18–20, French Canadian Congress held at Ottawa

Jan. 18–21, First annual meeting of Commission of Conservation

Feb. 1, Ratifications of Treaty of Commerce with France signed Sept. 19, 1907 exchanged in Paris

Feb. 14, Bishop Neil McNeil (Roman Catholic) made Archbishop of Vancouver

Feb. 15, Provisional Agreement by which on and after March 1 Canada removed surtax from German imports and Germany conceded minimum rates of duty on a long list of Canadian exports

March 4, Public Utilities Commission established by Province of Quebec, 4 members appointed

March 31, Number of immigrant arrivals during the year 208,794, including 59,790 from the United Kingdom and 103,798 from the United States

April 25, Quebec prohibited the exportation of pulp wood after May 1; protested by the United States

May 4, Canadian Northern Alberta Railway Company chartered and government aid granted

May 6, Death of King Edward VII and accession of George V

May 20, General Sir John French, Inspector General of the Imperial Army, landed in Quebec to inspect military forces of Canada

May 21, Boundary Treaty as to Passamaquoddy Bay signed between the United States and Great Britain gave Pope's Folly Island to the United States and the fishing grounds south of Lubec to Canada

June 6, Agreement with Italy by which Canadian goods admitted at conventional rates and Canadian intermediate tariff extended to Italy

June 7, Order in Council extended benefit of the intermediate tariff to specified goods, the produce or manufacture of Belgium, Holland, and Italy

——, Death of Goldwin Smith (85) at Toronto

June 18, Blackfoot Indians surrendered 115,000 acres of reserves in Alberta at average of about $14 per acre

June 24, Gold discovered near Stewart, British Columbia

June 30, Royal Ontario Museum opened

July 18–Aug. 2, Strike of employees in train and yard service of the Grand Trunk Railroad settled by compromise agreement, wages increased 15%

July 27–Sept. 25, 1911, Unsuccessful attempt of Captain Joseph Bernier to sail through the North West Passage

Aug. 18, Agreement between Great Britain and the United States for arbitration of certain outstanding pecuniary claims

Aug. 28, The Canadian "Queen's Own Rifles" arrived at Aldershot, England, to take part in the autumn military manœuvers

Sept. 6–10, Eucharistic Congress held in Montreal

Sept. 7, Award of the Hague Tribunal as to North Atlantic coast fisheries settled dispute of near 100 years' standing

Oct. 11, Electrical energy generated by Niagara Falls turned on for the first time at Berlin (now Kitchener), Ontario

Oct. 17, First cruiser of Canada's new navy, the "Niobe" purchased from the British Navy for training officers and men arrived at Halifax

Nov. 7, The cruiser "Rainbow" purchased from the British Navy arrived at Esquimalt, British Columbia

Nov. 17–July 29, 1911, Third session of eleventh Parliament. Grant made for construction of Northern Ontario Railroad to be part of a third transcontinental railroad system. Customs Agreement with Japan continued. Fisheries Act amended provided for licenses in British Columbia to manufacturers of oil from sea fish and animals, and salmon and lobster canneries. Dominion Forest Reserves' Act repealed previous legislation. Opium and Drug Act repealed that of 1908. New Seed Control Act passed. Subsidy granted for steamship service between the Pacific coast and China and Japan. Proposals for commercial reciprocity with the United States debated. Medical Act amended to provide for general and uniform registration of practitioners

Dec. 16, Delegation of 1,000 farmers demanded tariff revision

Dec. 28, Fourth joint report of the Alaskan Boundary Commission

Dec. 31, Agreement with the United States for an international railroad commission to regulate rates

Naval College established at Halifax, Nova Scotia

Agitation over bilingual schools in Ontario and Quebec

1911

Jan. 1, Compulsory military training in force from this date under 1909 statute

Jan. 9–12 and 13–14, Anglo-American Conference at Washington on application of award of Sept., 1910, as to fisheries

Jan. 21, Commercial Reciprocity Agreement with the United States by exchange of letters between Canadian Ministers of Finance, and Trade and Commerce, and American Secretary of State, to establish permanent reciprocal trading relations by concurrent legislation; defeated by Conservative election victory in Canada

Feb. 7, Treaty between Great Britain and the United States provided for preservation and protection of fur seals in the North Pacific

Feb. 19, Japan denounced existing commercial treaty with Canada

March 21, The Duke of Connaught appointed Governor General of Canada

March 24, Bellegrino Francesco Stagni, Apostolic delegate to Canada and Newfoundland, arrived at Ottawa

April 14, Death of Sir Henry E. Taschereau, former Chief Justice

May 1, Philippe Ray appointed Commissioner for Canada to France

May 23–June 30, Sir Wilfrid Laurier, Prime Minister, attended Imperial Conference in London

May 27, End of strike of coal miners at Spring Hill, Nova Scotia, begun in Aug., 1909

June 1, Population 7,206,643, English 3,896,985, French 2,054,890. Quebec 2,005,776, Ontario 2,527,292, Nova Scotia 492,338, New Brunswick 351,889, Prince Edward Island 93,728, British Columbia 392,480, North West Territories 8,512, Saskatchewan 492,432, Alberta 374,295, Yukon Territory 8,512

June 5–July 25, Strike in the building trades at Vancouver

July 4, Gift of 25 acres to McGill University from Sir William Macdonald, "Macdonald Park," on which a stadium erected

July 7, Convention signed by Great Britain, the United States, Japan, and Russia prohibited pelagic sealing on the high seas and arranged for apportionment of the legitimate catch

July 11, Forest fires in Porcupine mining district of Ontario reached height, 70 persons perished

July 21, Olivier Elzéar Mathieu appointed Bishop of Regina, Saskatchewan (Roman Catholic)

July 29, New Customs Tariff Agreement with Japan

——, Railroad branch completed connected Montreal with Port Arthur establishing third transcontinental railroad

Aug. 16–Sept. 6, Visit to England of composite team of Canadian artillery

Sept. 21, General election resulted in defeat of Liberal Government and rejection of proposed commercial reciprocity with the United States

Oct. 6, Resignation of Laurier Ministry

Oct. 10, Ninth Dominion Ministry appointed

Office	Name	Date of Appointment
Premier and President of the Privy Council	Robert Laird Borden	Oct. 10, 1911

Office	Name	Date of Appointment
Minister of Trade and Commerce	George Eulas Foster	Oct. 10, 1911
Minister of Interior	Robert Rogers	Oct. 10, 1911
	William J. Roche	Oct. 29, 1912
Minister of Public Works	Frederick D. Monk	Oct. 10, 1911
	Robert Rogers	Oct. 29, 1912
Minister of Railways and Canals	Francis Cochrane	Oct. 10, 1911
Minister of Finance	William T. White	Oct. 10, 1911
Postmaster General	Louis P. Pelletier	Oct. 10, 1911
Minister of Marine and Fisheries	John D. Hazen	Oct. 10, 1911
Minister of Justice	Charles J. Doherty	Oct. 10, 1911
Minister of Militia and Defense	Samuel Hughes	Oct. 10, 1911
Secretary of State	William J. Roche	Oct. 10, 1911
	Louis Coderre	Oct. 29, 1912
Minister of Labor	Thomas W. Crothers	Oct. 10, 1911
Minister of Inland Revenue	Wilfrid B. Nantel	Oct. 10, 1911
Minister of Customs	John D. Reid	Oct. 10, 1911
Minister of Agriculture	Martin Burrell	Oct. 10, 1911
Ministers without portfolio	George E. Perley	Oct. 10, 1911
	Albert E. Kemp	Oct. 10, 1911
	James A. Lougheed	Oct. 10, 1911

NOT IN THE CABINET

Solicitor General	Arthur Meighen	June 26, 1913

1911

Oct. 11, Inauguration at Kitchener of Ontario Hydro Electrical Power Transmission System

Oct. 13, The Duke of Connaught arrived from England and took oath of office as Governor General

Nov. 2–24, $1,500,000 raised chiefly from the citizens of Montreal as an endowment for McGill University

Nov. 15–April 1, 1912, First session of twelfth Parliament. Extension of boundaries of Province of Quebec by addition of Ungava, the remaining area of the North West Territories south of 60° N. Lat. divided between Ontario and Manitoba, Manitoba gaining littoral on Hudson Bay of 500 miles and 106,304,000 acres added, extensions of boundary to be effective May 15, 1912. Canada Grain Act provided for appointment of a board of 3 commissioners for management and control of grain trade. Provision made for granting subsidies to provincial governments for aid to agriculture. Judges' Act amended to create new judgeships and increase salaries. Dominion Archives placed under jurisdiction of the president of the Privy Council, the Archivist, Arthur G. Doughty, receiving rank of deputy head. Grant of additional subsidy of $100,000 made to Prince Edward Island from July 1. The House of Commons passed bills for creation of a tariff commission and for grant of assistance to provincial highways, but these measures defeated in Upper House. Yukon Act and Yukon Placer Mining Act amended

Dec. 16, Imperial Copyright Act refrained from legislation for Dominion to accept or repeal at will

Dec. 29, Fifth joint report of the Alaskan Boundary Commission

Dec. 31, Immigrants arriving during the calendar year 350,374 including 144,076 from the United Kingdom, and 131,114 from the United States

104 strikes and lockouts during the year involved 28,-918 persons

1912

Jan. 21, Justice Charbonneau of Montreal ruled in favor of legality of marriage contract in Hébert case declared invalid by Archbishop Bruchesi Nov. 12, 1909, under *ne temere* decree

March 1, Death of Edward Blake

March 29–April 9, Conference with representatives of the West Indian Colonies at Ottawa, and April 10 at Toronto, terms of preferential tariff agreement settled for submission to legislatures concerned

March 31, 354,237 immigrants arrived during year ending on this date including 138,121 from the United Kingdom and 133,710 from the United States

April 1, Biological Board of Canada constituted

April 10, Board of Grain Commissioners appointed

April 15, Dominions Royal Commission appointed as proposed by Sir W. Laurier at Imperial Conference in 1911

April 26, Exchange of Notes confirmed first schedule of claims under Agreement of Aug. 18, 1910, with the United States

May, First gold pieces struck in Canadian money, $10 and $5

May 15, Extension of boundaries of Manitoba, Ontario, and Quebec came into effect

June 12, First Congress of French Language at Quebec

June 28, Georges Gauthier appointed Bishop of Philipopolis and auxiliary to Archbishop of Montreal (Roman Catholic)

July 12–15, Strike of transport workers in Montreal

July 20, Convention between Great Britain and the United States respecting the North Atlantic fisheries

July 29, Decision of Imperial Privy Council on marriage question raised by the *ne temere* promulgated by Roman Catholic Church Aug. 2, 1907, declaring marriages between Roman Catholics and persons of other denominations invalid except under certain conditions, held the provincial legislature had power to make marriage laws

——, Strike of 3,000 Winnipeg carpenters

Aug. 20, Strike of dock workers at Fort William, Ontario

Sept. 9, Professor V. Stefansson returned from 4 years' expedition in Arctic

Sept. 21, Death of Sir Richard John Cartwright

Oct. 12, Pupils of the Garneau, Ontario, school walked out in protest when English speaking instructor entered

Nov. 18, The floating steel dry-dock, the "Duke of Connaught," dedicated at Montreal

Nov. 21–June 6, 1913, Second session of twelfth Parliament. Banking Act revised to include better inspection of banks and security for depositors. Agricultural Instruction Act provided for appropriation of $10,000,000 during the ensuing 10 years. R. L. Bor-

den proposed appropriation of $35,000,000 for construction of 3 battleships in the United Kingdom for defense of the Empire which passed in House but was defeated in Upper House, Sir Wilfrid Laurier in opposition advocating a Canadian navy. West India Trade Agreement accepted. Acts passed relating to wireless telegraph. Amendment to Judges' Act settled salaries for certain provincial courts. Parcel post established. New Gold and Silver Marking Act passed

Dec. 12, Sixth joint report of the Alaskan Boundary Commission

Dec. 30, First train from the West with 20 carloads of wheat passed over railroad from North Bay to Cochrane and arrived at Port Colborne

1913

Jan. 5, General Ian Hamilton, Inspector General of Overseas Forces, arrived at Quebec to inspect Canadian troops

March 31, 402,432 immigrants arrived during year including 150,542 from the United Kingdom and 139,009 from the United States

April 23, Death of Sir Richard W. Scott

May 20–Oct. 24, Sir Charles Fitzpatrick Administrator in absence of Governor General

June 2, Trade Agreement with the West Indies came into effect by which about 50 Canadian products received tariff reduction of 20%

July 5, V. Stefansson left Seattle for 3 year expedition in Arctic regions under auspices of the Canadian Government, and sailed from Port Clarence, Alaska, July 29, wintering at Collinson Point

Aug. 17, Ontario Dept. of Instruction issued Circular No. 17 providing that the French language should not be used in the schools beyond the first form

Sept. 1–3, American Bar Association met at Montreal, Viscount Haldane, Lord Chancellor, in attendance

Oct. 4, New customs tariff with the United States went into effect, lower rates

Oct. 8, First issue of the *Daily Mail*, Montreal

Nov. 17, Last rail laid on Grand Trunk Pacific Railroad, eastern division, at point in Quebec near boundary with Ontario

Dec. 8, Order in Council prohibited landing of laborers, skilled or unskilled at ports in British Columbia, because of labor conditions and unemployment

1914

Jan. 11, The "Karluk" of the Arctic expedition under Stefansson crushed by the ice, 8 members of party lost in attempt to reach land. Capt. R. A. Bartlett reached Wrangel Island with others of party and then made journey on foot to Emma Harbor, Siberia, which he reached May 16, 1914 in 59 days

Jan. 12, Death of David Laird

Jan. 15–June 12, Third session of twelfth Parliament. Representation of House of Commons readjusted to consist of 234 members. Naturalization Act gave effect to imperial statute of Aug. 7. Loan and Trust Companies' Act settled conditions under which companies might be formed. Fisheries' Act consolidated all laws respecting fisheries and fishing. Act provided regulations for cold storage warehouses. Customs Tariff Act amended to make alterations in rates of duty on 59 articles. Inspection and Sale Act and Judges' Act amended among others. Naturalization Act gave effect to imperial statute

Jan. 21, Death of Lord Strathcona (Donald Alexander Smith), High Commissioner for Canada in London, aged 94

March 1, Death of Lord Minto, former Governor General

March 7, Death of Sir George Ross

March 14, Claims Commission met in Washington

March 18, Death of William Paterson

March 22, Stefansson with 2 companions left Martin Point, Alaska. Reached 73° N. Lat. on June 25. Landed on Banks Land June 25. Maps of Norway and Berniard islands and Wilkins River made. Sept. 11 went into winter quarters at Cape Kellett. A division of the expedition from Collinson Point base investigated the copper bearing rocks between Cape Parry and Kent Peninsula

March 31, The Canadian Militia numbered 3,000 officers and men in the permanent force, and 5,615 officers and 68,991 non-commissioned officers and men

——, 348,878 immigrants arrived during the year, including 142,622 from the United Kingdom and 107,530 from the United States

April 7, Completion of Grand Trunk Pacific Railroad, western division, at Nechaco River Crossing, British Columbia

April 9, Arrival of first train from Winnipeg at Prince Rupert, British Columbia

April 29, Injunction of Supreme Court of Ontario prohibited employment by Board of Education of teachers not legally qualified

May 2, Death of the Duke of Argyll, who as Marquis of Lorne was Governor General of Canada from 1878 to 1883

May 8, Announcement that Prince Alexander of Teck had been appointed Governor General, but later that the Duke of Connaught would retain position

May 21, Gurdit Singh with 396 Hindus on steamer "Komagata Maru" from India arrived at Vancouver and was not permitted to land under the immigration laws

May 25, Archbishop Bégin, of Quebec, made a cardinal

May 29, Wreck of the "Empress of Ireland" (Canadian Pacific steamer) rammed by Norwegian steamer in the St. Lawrence River with loss of 900 persons

July 1, Canadian flag raised on Wrangel Island and claimed for the British Empire as first sighted by Captain Kellett in 1849

July 28, Montreal and Toronto stock exchanges closed for 3 months

July 28 and Aug. 6, Proclamations prohibited export of cereals, food articles, ammunition, military and naval stores, and coal except to United Kingdom, Japan, France, Russia, and the United States

Aug. 1, The Duke of Connaught cabled offer of Canadian troops to Great Britain which was accepted on the 6th

Aug. 3, Specie payments suspended to conserve supply of gold, and moratorium authorized (never declared), banks authorized to make payments in their own notes in place of gold and Dominion notes, and advances to the banks in the form of Dominion notes to be made against approved securities deposited with the Government

——, Acquisition by Canada of 2 submarines on the Pacific coast

Aug. 4, Mobilization of Canadian Expeditionary force begun as Great Britain declared war on Germany

Aug. 7, Imperial Act provided for issue of a naturalization certificate to an alien by the Secretary of State on proof of 5 years residence and fulfillment of certain conditions. Persons naturalized under legislation by Imperial Parliament or Dominions Parliaments become British subjects throughout the Empire

Aug. 18–22, Fourth session of twelfth Parliament (special war session). War Appropriation Act granted $50,000,000 for military and naval purposes. Financial measures of Aug. 3 adopted as Finance Act. War Measures' Act conferred emergency powers on the Governor General in Council and amended the Immigration Act. Customs Tariff Act and Inland Revenue Act amended raised customs and excise duties chiefly for coffee, sugar, spirituous liquors, and tobacco. Canadian Patriotic Fund for assistance to relatives and dependents of soldiers established. Amendment to Naturalization Act respecting married women and widows. Nationality and Status of Aliens law enacted

Aug. 19, War declared against Germany and Austria-Hungary

Aug. 29, The Princess Patricia Regiment sailed from Montreal for England

Sept. 7, First meeting Shell Committee of 5

——, Rescue expedition from Nome found 8 members of the Stefansson party marooned on Wrangel Island since March 12 and brought them to Nome on the 14th

Sept. 11, Ontario Court ordered Board of Education to reopen schools and employ only qualified teachers

Sept. 24, First Canadian contingent sailed for England, 33,000 men, 7,000 horses, and 144 heavy guns, and arrived at Plymouth Oct. 14 and proceeded to Salisbury Plain

Oct. 28, Order in Council for registration of alien enemies

Nov. 11, First Canadian Stationary Hospital (Unit No. 2) reached France

1915

Feb. 4–April 15, Fifth session of twelfth Parliament. War Appropriation Act provided for further sum of $100,000,000. Customs Tariff War Revenue Act imposed duties or additional duties of 5% under the British preferential tariff and 7½% under intermediate and general tariff on all goods with certain exceptions. The Special War Revenue Act imposed new taxes on railroad and steamship tickets, parlor car seats, sleeping car berths, telegrams, bank checks and notes, and stamp tax on money orders, postal notes, patent medicines, perfumes, spirits and wines, and excess profits trust, insurance and loan companies, &c. War Loan of bonds to value of $50,-000,000 authorized. Controverted Elections Act and Railway Act amended

Feb. 8, Death of Sir François Langelier

Feb. 14, First Canadian troops arrived in France from England and proceeded to Flanders

Feb. 20, Stefansson, Dr. R. M. Anderson, and Mr. Thomson journeyed along coast of Banks Land to Alfred Point. Landed from ice on Prince Patrick Island, west coast, early in May. June 18 sighted land not shown on any chart at N. Lat. 77° 43′, W. Long. 115° 43′ which they took possession of for British Empire. Arrived at Kellett on Aug. 8

Feb. 24, Canadian troops in action in trenches near Armentières

March 10, Canadian troops engaged in battle at Neuve Chapelle

March 16, Second division of Canadian troops began to arrive in England

March 31, 144,789 immigrants arrived during the year, 43,276 from the United Kingdom and 59,779 from the United States

April 8, Ontario Liquor License Act created Board of Commissioners with power to make regulations as to sale of liquor to particular classes of persons and in particular localities

April 22, First Canadian Division in action at Ypres, and gassed on the 24th

April 27, Order in Council prohibited export of certain articles

May 8, War Purchasing Commission appointed

May 9, First Canadian Division in action at Festubert

June 15, Canadian troops in action at Givenchy

June 30, Hospital Commission established to provide for treatment of returning wounded and disabled soldiers. Name changed in Oct. to Military Hospitals Commission

July 12, Supreme Court affirmed decision of lower court of Sept. 11, 1914, as to Ontario schools

July 14, Sir Robert Borden attended meeting of the British Cabinet, the first attendance of a Dominion Prime Minister

July 22, Death of Sir Sandford Fleming, engineer and railroad builder

Aug. 4, Commission of 3 appointed to replace School Board in Ottawa which refused to insist on English language qualifications required for teachers

Sept. 11, Death of Sir William C. Van Horne, financier and railroad builder

Sept. 12, Saint Sulpice Library, Montreal, opened

Sept., First and Second Divisions formed into a Canadian Corps under General E. A. H. Alderson, with A. W. Currie and Richard Turner as divisional commanders

Oct. 30, Death of Sir Charles Tupper, former Prime Minister

Nov. 18, Circular 17, regulations for Ontario schools, declared valid by court

Nov. 20, Corner-stone of Montreal Free Municipal Library laid

——, War declared against Bulgaria and Turkey

Nov. 22, Canadian War Loan of $50,000,000 issued, first Dominion loan, oversubscribed over $100,000, in 5% bonds, and increased Nov. 30 to $100,000,000

Nov. 29, Shell Committee became Imperial Munitions Board, Sir Joseph Flavelle, chairman

Nov. 30, Reported killed and missing 539 officers and 13,017 of other ranks

Dec. 10, Death of Sir C. E. Boucher de Boucherville

1916

Jan. 12, Order in Council authorized increase in troops to 500,000

Jan. 12–May 18, Sixth session of twelfth Parliament. War Appropriation Act authorized expenditure of $250,000,000. Public Service Loan Act authorized loan of $75,000,000. Customs Tariff Amendment Act raised import duty on apples, and reduced duties on fuel oil. Business Profits War Tax enacted imposed tax of 25%. Other measures enacted as to the judiciary (c. 5, 16, 25), prohibition and restriction

of sale or use of liquor in the provinces, and amendments to Shipping, Prison and Reformatories, Railway and Bank laws

Feb. 3, 17 bilingual schools closed in Ottawa with 122 French teachers on strike because they had not been paid on account of their refusal to accept regulations

——, Parliament buildings at Ottawa destroyed by fire

March 2, Ontario Temperance Act passed

March 13, Manitoba Temperance Act adopted by referendum vote of 50,484 to 26,502 banished the saloon but allowed use of liquor in the home

March 31, 48,537 immigrants arrived during the year. *See infra* Dec. 31

——, Total cost of war at this date $150,000,000

April 17, Federal Grand Jury in New York City indicted Captains Franz von Papen and Hans Taucher on charge of conspiracy to destroy the Welland Canal

May 9, Lieutenant General Sir Julian Byng appointed to command of Canadian Expeditionary Force in Europe succeeding General Alderson on May 28

May 25, Prolongation of present Parliament for one year allowed

June 3, Board of Pension Commissioners of 3 members established by Order in Council to deal with grants of military and naval pensions

June 13, First express train of the "Western National," transcontinental railroad, made first run from Quebec to Winnipeg

June 14, Congress of confederated boards of trade held at Sorel

July 1, Newfoundland troops took Beaumont-Hamel in France

Aug. 4, Total cost of war at this date $213,000,000

Aug. 19, The Duke of Devonshire (Victor C. W. Cavendish) appointed Governor General

Sept. 1, Corner-stone of new Houses of Parliament at Ottawa laid by Duke of Connaught

Sept. 12, Sir Thomas Tait appointed Director General of National Service Board created in Aug.

Oct. 1, Second War Loan of $100,000,000 oversubscribed, 5% 15 year bonds

Oct. 28, Sir George Perley, acting High Commissioner in London, appointed Minister of the Overseas Military Forces for Canada in the United Kingdom

Nov. 2, Imperial Privy Council upheld appointment of Commission to control Ottawa schools

Nov. 10, Order in Council for control of prices

Nov. 11, The Duke of Devonshire assumed office as Governor General

——, General Sir Sam Hughes, Minister of Militia and Defense, resigned as requested by the Prime Minister because of disagreement on overseas administration, and was succeeded by Sir Edward Kemp Nov. 23

Dec. 11, Saskatchewan voted to abolish liquor stores

Dec. 31, 65,836 immigrants arrived during the year including 8,596 from the United Kingdom and 51,701 from the United States

1917

Jan. 1, Prohibition became effective in Newfoundland

Jan. 18–Sept. 20, Seventh session of twelfth Parliament. Income War Tax (first Dominion income tax) enacted. Public Service Loan Act authorized loan of $100,000,000. Military Service Act (passed Aug. 29) made every British subject between ages of 25 and 45 with certain exceptions liable for active service. Military Voters' Act gave right to vote to every

British subject in war service, and provided for partial woman suffrage. Provision made for purchase by the Government of the 600,000 shares of the Canadian Northern Railway. Acts created offices during continuance of the War, Minister of the Overseas force, Parliamentary Secretary of the Dept. of Militia and Defense, and Parliamentary Under-Secretary of State for External Affairs. Soldier Settlement Act passed to assist returned soldiers to settle on the land, and Soldier Settlement Board constituted. Business Profits War Tax Act increased and extended

Jan. 26, National Factory for manufacture of steel established at Toronto which became largest electric steel equipment in the world

Feb. 12–May 15, Visit of the Prime Minister to England

Feb. 21, Final report of Dominions Royal Commission

March, Third War Loan of $150,000,000 issued of 20-year bonds at 5%

March 20–May 2, Meetings in London of Imperial War Cabinet

March 21–April 27, Imperial War Conference in London

March 31, 75,374 immigrants arrived during the year, 8,282 from the United Kingdom, and 61,389 from the United States

April 9, Capture of Vimy Ridge (Arras) by 4 Canadian divisions and 1 British brigade

April 16, Wheat, wheat flour, and seminola placed on customs free list by Order in Council

June 8, Dominion Fuel Controller created by Order in Council

June 11, Board of Grain Supervisors for Canada appointed under War Measures Act

June 19, Major General Sir Arthur Currie appointed to command of the Canadian troops at the front succeeding General Byng transferred to command of the Third Army

June 21, W. J. Hanna appointed Food Controller of Canada

July 12, C. A. Magrath appointed Fuel Controller of Canada

Aug. 29, Mass meeting at Montreal of 5,000 persons in demonstration against compulsory military service

——, Death of Earl Grey, former Governor General

Sept. 1, At this date the Canada Expeditionary Force sent overseas numbered 331,578, and training in camps in Canada 831 officers and 20,179 of other ranks

Sept. 20, Parliamentary franchise extended to women, all engaged in war service

——, Completion of Quebec (cantilever) bridge over the St. Lawrence River

Sept. 26, Compulsory military service came into effect, upheld by the Supreme Court

Oct. 13, Proclamation called the first class to service

——, Unionist Government assumed office (Tenth Dominion Ministry)

——, Unionist Government

Prime Minister and Minister of External Affairs	Sir Robert Laird Borden
President of the Privy Council	Newton Wesley Rowell
Minister of Trade and Commerce	Sir George E. Foster
Minister of Public Works	Frank Bradstreet Carvell
Minister of the Interior	Arthur Meighen
Minister of Railways and Canals	John Dowsley Reid
Minister of Finance	Sir William Thomas White
Postmaster-General	Pierre Edouard Blondin
Minister of Marine and Fisheries and Naval Service	Charles Colquhoun Ballantyne
Minister of Justice	Charles Joseph Doherty
Minister of Militia and Defense	Sydney Chilton Mewburn
Secretary of State	Martin Burrell
Minister of Labor	Thomas Wilson Crothers
Minister of Inland Revenue	J. P. Albert Sévigny
Minister of Customs	Arthur Lewis Sifton
Minister of Agriculture	Thomas Alexander Crerar
Minister of Militia—Overseas	Sir Albert Edward Kemp
Minister of Immigration and Colonization	James Alexander Calder
Solicitor-General	Hugh Guthrie
Without portfolio	Gideon Decker Robertson
	Alexander K. Maclean
	Frank Cochrane
	Sir James Alexander Lougheed

Oct. 23, Reconstruction and Development Committee of the Cabinet appointed, the Prime Minister, chairman

Oct. 30, Montreal and Toronto stock exchanges resorted to minimum price system

Nov. 5, Use of grain in manufacture of liquor prohibited for war period

Nov. 12, Fourth War Loan (1st Victory) floated

Dec. 6, Collision of the "Imo" and the "Mont Blanc" laden with explosives at Halifax caused explosion in which 1,500 persons killed, and 25,000 rendered homeless and destitute, money loss about $20,000,000

Dec. 10, Death of Sir Mackenzie Bowell

Dec. 17, General election sustained the Unionist Government

1918

Jan. 24, Resignation of Food Controller

Feb. 1, Soldier Settlement Board appointed

Feb. 7, Order in Council gave War Purchasing Board authority to make all purchases for the Government

Feb. 8, War Trade Board created, Sir George Foster, chairman

Feb. 11, Food Board constituted under control of the Minister of Agriculture in place of Food Controller

Feb. 21, Minister of Soldiers' Reëstablishment appointed

Feb. 22, Canada Registration Board appointed

Feb. 25, Gift of $1,000,000 to McGill University from the Carnegie Corporation of New York in recognition of service of the University in the War

Feb. 28–March 2, Womens' War Conference held at Ottawa

March 18–May 24, First session of thirteenth Parliament. War Appropriation Act authorized expenditure of $500,000,000 and the loans needed to provide for this expenditure. Business Profits War Tax amended to provide that every business with capital from $25,000 to $50,000 should pay tax of 25% on profits exceeding 10% of its capital from Dec. 31, 1917 until Dec. 31, 1918. Income War Tax amended to lower limit of exemption, super-tax increased. Customs Tariff Act amended increased duties on coffee, tea, and tobacco. Special War Revenue increased taxes and created new ones. Dept. of Immigration constituted to administer the Immigration Act, the Chinese Immigration Act and Orders in Council dealing with immigration under the War Measures Act. Soldiers' Civil Reëstablishment created another new dept. Yukon Act amended authorized the Governor in Council to abolish the Council and appoint another, abolish offices, or transfer duties. Amendment to Penitentiary Act created a Supt. of Penitentiaries in the Dept. of Justice. New Civil Service Act passed, Act to confer electoral franchise, Compensation Act for employees of His Majesty injured or killed in performance of duty. Act consolidated all previous statistical legislation and established Dominion Bureau of Statistics. Luxury tax of 10% placed on selling price of passenger automobiles, and on gramophones, records, pianoplayers and records, and jewelry. Employment Offices Coördination Act authorized establishment of public employment offices. Daylight saving prescribed, Dominion Franchise Act included women

March 28, Conscription riots in Quebec

March 31, 79,074 immigrants arrived during the year including 3,178 from the United Kingdom and 71,314 from the United States. 650 Chinese paid head tax as compared with 272 in 1916–1917, 20 in 1915–1916, and 1,555 in 1914–1915

April 1, Royal Air Force formed

April 4, Order in Council provided that every male person between ages of 16 and 60 must be regularly engaged in some useful occupation

April 11, Order in Council created Overseas Military Council, Sir E. Kemp, at head

April 20, Men from 20 to 22 called to military service

May 14, Deputation of farmers refused request for exemption of farmers' sons from conscription by Sir Robert Borden

May 24, Soldiers' Civil Reëstablishment Dept. established

June 11, Board of Grain Supervisors appointed to control grain production and trade

Aug. 4–Nov. 11, "Canada's Hundred Days" in the War, Amiens, Arras, Cambrai, Mons

Sept. 12, Dept. of Public Instruction established to disseminate information relating to the War, using addresses, books, pamphlets, and motion pictures

Sept. 16, Stefannson arrived at Vancouver after 5 years in the Arctic regions

Sept. 19, "Khaki University of Canada" established

Oct. 9, Dominion troops entered Cambrai

Oct. 11, Order in Council enacted regulations for war time labor and prohibited strikes and lockouts

Oct. 16, Order in Council accepted offer of United States of free importation of wheat, wheat flour, and seminola in return for reciprocity

Oct. 21, Commercial Commission for Siberia appointed, and proceeded to Vladivostok

Oct. 28, Fifth War Loan (Victory bonds) issued of $300,000,000

Nov. 7, Canadian Trade Mission established in London, to have branches in France, Italy, and Belgium

Nov. 11, Armistice ended the War. Of 595,441 enlisted Canadian soldiers 422,266 including 4,214 in Siberia served oversea, 218,433 casualties, 35,684 killed in action, and 12,437 died of wounds; wounded 155,839.

Ontario sent 205,808 volunteers, and Quebec 52,993, only eighteen percent of the Expeditionary Force was drafted into service

Nov. 19, Order in Council united all the government railroads

Nov. 29, Canadian Council of Agriculture in meeting at Winnipeg issued a "national farmers' platform" including reduction of tariff, free trade with Great Britain, revival and extension of reciprocity with the United States, Government ownership of public utilities, taxes on incomes, &c.

Dec. 6, Canadian Trade Mission appointed with headquarters at Ottawa to coöperate with the Canadian Mission in London

Dec. 10, Issue of $5 war savings stamps to amount of $50,000,000 authorized

1919

Jan. 4, Sir Robert Borden opened exhibit in London, England, of nearly 400 war memorial paintings by Canadian and British artists

Feb. 16–28, Visit of General Pau from France

Feb. 17, Death of Sir Wilfrid Laurier, former Premier, and Liberal leader

Feb. 26–July 7, Second session of the thirteenth Parliament. Demobilization Appropriation Act appropriated $350,000,000. Business Profits' War Tax renewed for the year 1919. Amendment to the Income War Tax Act increased the general rate of taxation. Extra duty of 5% ad valorem of Customs' War Revenue Act of 1915 repealed and partial repeal of 7½% of intermediate and general tariff rates, and provision made for free importation of wheat, wheat flour, and potatoes from countries not imposing duty on such articles grown in Canada, duties on tea and coffee reduced, and a general reduction on specified articles named. Dept. of Health established and a Board of Commerce. Soldiers' Settlement Act provided for financial assistance to soldiers to enable them to settle on Dominion lands. Immigration Act amended to exclude anarchists and enemy aliens, and persons over 15 years of age unable to read and write with certain exceptions. Various laws relating to railroads consolidated. Annual grants to provinces in aid of technical education and for construction of highways authorized. Air Board appointed for control of aëronautics. Address to His Majesty adopted asking that no more titles of nobility be conferred on residents of Canada

March 7, Government receiver appointed for the Grand Trunk Pacific Railroad

March 10–12, British Columbia Federation of Labor met at Calgary

March 13–15, Western Interprovincial Labor Conference of the 4 western provinces met at Calgary

March 29, Industrial Conditions Act of Manitoba established a joint council for settlement of industrial disputes

March 31, 57,702 immigrants arrived during the year including 9,914 from the United Kingdom and 40,715 from the United States

April 9, Royal Commission of 7 members on industrial relations representing labor and capital appointed to investigate conditions arising from the high cost of living; majority and minority reports presented June 28

May 1–June 26, Great strike at Winnipeg which began in the metal trades and became a sympathetic strike on May 15 in movement toward "One Big Union" which failed, though the strikers had complete control of the city for a time

May 12 and Sept. 9–10, National Conference of Women met at Ottawa to discuss immigration of women

May 17, Citizens' Committee of One Thousand organized to counteract the strike in Winnipeg and supply public and semi-public services

May 18–19, Major Harry Hawker and Commander Mackenzie Grieve made attempt to fly across the Atlantic from St. Johns, Newfoundland, but were forced down after 15 hours and 1,000 miles, and picked up by Danish steamer

May 26, The Prime Minister returned to Canada from the Peace Conference at Paris

June 14, Captain John Alcock and Lieut. Arthur Brown made first non-stop flight across the Atlantic from St. Johns, Newfoundland, to Clifton in Galway, Ireland, 1,960 miles in 16 hours and 12 minutes

June 23, General election in Quebec Province a victory for the Liberal Administration

July 24, General election in Prince Edward Island a defeat for the Conservative Administration

Aug. 5, W. L. Mackenzie King elected leader of the Liberal Party to succeed the late Sir Winfrid Laurier

Aug. 12, Arrival of the Prince of Wales at Newfoundland on official visit to Canada and the United States, and at Quebec Aug. 21

Aug. 18, Convention of journalists at Victoria, British Columbia

Aug. 22, Formal opening of the Quebec Bridge by the Prince of Wales

Sept. 1, Corner-stone of new Parliament Buildings at Ottawa laid by the Prince of Wales

Sept. 1–Nov. 10, Third session of thirteenth Parliament. Resolutions passed to give effect to the Peace Treaties with Germany and Austria. Government authorized to acquire the capital stock of the Grand Trunk Railroad. Civil Service Amendment Act increased salaries of commissioners. Temperance Act amended to give electors of provinces the right to vote to prevent importation of intoxicating liquors. Manufacture of intoxicants for unlawful use forbidden. Amendment to the Criminal Code forbade aliens to have weapons or firearms without permit. Amendment to Patent Act safeguarded interests of those who due to war conditions were unable to fulfil legal requirements. Dominion Lands Act amended to give priority to soldiers to obtain Dominion lands

Sept. 15–21, National Industrial Conference held at Ottawa, Dominion Minister of Labor presiding

Sept. 22–27, Convention of the Trades and Labor Congress held at Hamilton, Ontario

Oct., Issue of sixth War Loan for $300,000,000

Oct. 20, General election in Ontario resulted in defeat of the Conservative Administration, and formation of Ministry by E. C. Drury, United Farmers' Organization

Oct. 20–22, National Education Conference held at Winnipeg

Oct. 30–Nov. 22, Visit of Cardinal Mercier from Belgium

Oct. 31, Werner Horn sentenced at Fredericton, New Brunswick, to 10 years' imprisonment for attempt to destroy the St. Croix bridge Feb. 2, 1915

Nov. 8, Sir Robert Borden, Prime Minister, Sir George Foster, C. J. Doherty, and A. L. Sifton left Ottawa to attend Peace Conference in Paris

Nov. 8–Jan. 1, 1920, Visit of Viscount Jellicoe

Nov. 10, The Prince of Wales left Ottawa for the United States

Nov. 18–19, Waterways Conference held at Windsor, Ontario

Nov. 25, The Prince of Wales sailed from Halifax for England

Dec. 3, $25,000,000 appropriated for housing enterprise to enable purchase of homes by tenants

Dec. 20, Canadian National Railways organized by Order in Council under charter of July 7; stock vested in Minister of Finance on behalf of the Crown

——, Proclamation abrogated War-Time Restrictions' Act raising ban on liquor and horse-racing

Dec. 29, Death of Sir William Osler

298 strikes during the year involved 138,988 persons with loss of 3,942,189 working days

The Canadian Pacific of approximately 13,000 miles the only remaining privately owned line in Canada. Mileage of railroad lines to be operated as a single system as follows:

Intercolonial	1,592.35
Prince Edward Island	278.81
Transcontinental	2,002.92
Canadian Northern	9,479.17
Grand Trunk Pacific	1,794.07
G.T.P. branch lines	1,036.79
Grand Trunk in Canada	3,578.80
Grand Trunk in United States	1,665.00
Lines in maritime provinces	485.00
Total	21,912.91

1920

Jan. 1, Mackenzie, Keewatin, and Franklin admitted by Dominion under Order in Council of March 16, 1918

Jan. 10, Canada became original member of the League of Nations

Feb. 1, Name of Royal North West Mounted Police changed to Royal Canadian Mounted Police

Feb. 14, University of Montreal incorporated under provincial statute

Feb. 19, Shareholders ratify agreement for sale of Grand Trunk Railroad to the Dominion

Feb. 26–July 1, Fourth session of thirteenth Parliament. Canadian National Railways' Act authorized 3 lines, one from Prince Albert, Saskatchewan, north, one from the main line to Meeting Lake, one southwest from point on the Maryfield branch. Opium and Drug Act of 1911 amended to embody conclusions of the International Opium Convention. Dominion Election Act passed. Standard weight of silver and gold coins established. Special War Revenue Act of 1915 amended, stamp duties placed on certain articles. Shipping Act amended and aid to shipbuilding authorized. Indian Act amended to provide for enfranchisement of Indians and attendance of Indian children at schools. Settlement of Returned Soldiers' Act of 1919 amended providing for insurance and increase of pensions. Naturalization Act of 1919 repealed and 1914 revived with certain amendments. Salary of Prime Minister increased to $15,000, and other Ministers to $10,000 a year, Solicitor General to $7,000, Speakers $6,000, Deputy Speaker $4,000. Sessional allowance increased to $4,000. Leader of the Opposition to receive $10,000. Civil Service Acts, Business Profits War Tax, Income War Tax, Customs, Animal Contagious Diseases, Bankruptcy, Criminal Code, Dominion Land, Industrial Disputes Investigation, Irrigation, and Yukon Placer Mining laws amended. Sales tax of 1% imposed

March 31, 117,336 immigrants arrived during the year including 59,603 from the United Kingdom and 49,656 from the United States

May 10, Official announcement that Canada authorized to appoint a Minister Plenipotentiary to the United States

May 31–June 18, Trade Conference of Dominion and West Indian Governments at Ottawa

June 7–19, Convention of the American Federation of Labor held at Montreal

June 29, Provincial election in Manitoba sustained the Liberal Government

July 1, Conservative Party reorganized as the National Liberal and Conservative Party with program of autonomy within the Empire, revision of the tariff, government aid to soldiers and farmers, encouragement of immigration, internal improvements

——, Regulations for trade in food stuffs for animals and poultry except corn, hay, straw, and bran adopted

July 10, Resignation of Prime Minister Sir Robert Borden

——, New Brunswick voted for total prohibition

——, Eleventh Dominion Ministry appointed

OFFICE	NAME	DATE OF APPOINTMENT
Premier, Secretary of State for External Affairs	Arthur Meighen	July 10, 1920
Minister of Finance	Sir Henry L. Drayton	" " "
Minister of Marine and Fisheries, and Naval Service	Charles C. Ballantyne	" " "
Minister of Labor	Gideon D. Robertson	" " "
Minister of Militia and Defense	Hugh Guthrie	" " "
Minister of Agriculture	Simon F. Tolmie	" " "
Minister of the Interior, Supt.-Gen. Indian Affairs Office, and Minister of Mines	Sir Joseph A. Lougheed	" " "
Minister of Public Works	Fleming B. McCurdy	July 13, 1920
Postmaster General	Louis de Gonzagua Billey	Sept. 21, 1920
Minister of Customs and Excise	John B. Macaulay Baxter	" " "
Minister of Railroads and Canals	John A. Stewart	" " "

OFFICE	NAME	DATE OF APPOINTMENT
Minister of Soldiers Reëstablishment	Robert J. Manion	Sept. 21, 1920
Minister of Justice and Attorney General	Richard B. Bennett	" " "
Minister of Immigration and Colonization	John W. Edwards	" " "
President of the Privy Council	Louis P. Normand	" " "
Minister of Trade and Commerce	Henry H. Stevens	" " "
Secretary of State	Rodolphe Monty	" " "
Minister without portfolio	Sir Albert Edward Kemp	" " "
	Edgar Keith Spinney	" " "
	James Robert Wilson	" " "
	Edmund Bristol	" " "

July 27, General election in Nova Scotia sustained Liberal Government

Aug. 5–7, Imperial Press Conference at Ottawa

Sept. 18–23, Congress of Chambers of Commerce of the Empire at Ottawa

Oct. 9, General election in New Brunswick sustained the Liberal Government

Oct. 12, Pupils of Garneau, Ontario, school walked out in protest against English speaking teacher

Oct. 20, British Columbia voted for government control and sale of liquors rejecting previous policy of prohibition

Oct. 25, Plebiscites in Alberta, Manitoba, Saskatchewan, and Nova Scotia resulted in large majorities for prohibition

Oct. 25–28, National Conference held in Ottawa on technical education and statistics of education

Nov. 15–Dec. 18, Canada represented at first meeting of the League of Nations at Geneva, Switzerland, by Sir George E. Foster, C. J. Doherty, and N. W. Rowell

Nov. 15–20, More than $4,000,000 subscribed by citizens of Montreal and alumni to funds of McGill University, and $1,000,000 given by the Province of Quebec, and $1,000,000 by the Rockefeller Foundation

Dec. 1, General election in British Columbia sustained the Liberal Government

——, Order in Council effective Dec. 15 provided that no immigrant should enter the country unless he possessed $250 in his own right, and if accompanied by his family, he must have $125 for each member over 18 and $50 for every child between ages of 5 and 18

1921

Jan. 4, Death of Sir William Peterson, principal of McGill University

Jan. 22, Death of Arthur L. Sifton, Dominion Minister

Jan. 29, Trade Convention with France signed

Feb. 14–June 4, Fifth session of thirteenth Parliament. Income War Tax amended to provide for penalties for failure to return tax, excise duties on liquors increased, copyright law consolidated and amended, sales tax increased, issue of a nickel five-cent coin authorized. Civil Service, Opium and Narcotic Drugs, Pension Acts, and Criminal Code amended.

Dominion Election Act defined as urban districts those which contained 2,500 population instead of 1,000. Immigration Act amended as to amount of money required of immigrants on entrance, and provided that Chinese immigrants claiming exemption must prove their status. Taxes placed on playing cards and wines

March 31, 148,477 immigrants arrived during the year including 74,262 from the United Kingdom, and 48,059 from the United States

April 18, Plebiscite vote in Ontario resulted in vote for prohibition of manufacture, importation, and sale of alcoholic liquors

May 1, Government control of sale of liquor went into effect in the Province of Quebec

May 10, Preferential tariff agreement with the British West Indies came into effect

June 1, Strike of printers begun for a 44 hour week

——, Population 8,788,483, English 4,868,903, French 2,452,751. Quebec 2,361,199, Ontario 2,933,662, Nova Scotia 523,837, New Brunswick 387,876, Prince Edward Island 88,615, British Columbia 524,582, Manitoba 610,118, North West Territories 7,988, Saskatchewan 757,510, Alberta 588,454, Yukon Territory 4,157, Royal Canadian Navy 485

June 9, Election in Saskatchewan sustained the Liberal Government

June 20–Aug. 5, Arthur Meighen, Prime Minister, represented Canada at the Imperial Conference in England

July 15, War legislation which allowed Canadian vessels free access to American ports canceled by the United States

July 18, The United Farmers gained a majority of seats at election in Alberta

July 19, Ontario became legally "bone dry"

Aug. 2, Lord Byng of Vimy (Julian H. G. Byng) appointed Governor General and assumed office Aug. 11

Sept. 5–Oct. 5, C. J. Doherty represented Canada at second meeting of the League of Nations at Geneva

Sept. 16, V. Stefansson sent expedition to Wrangel Island, British possession affirmed. All of the party except the Esquimaux perished as was discovered by relief vessel which arrived Aug. 20, 1923

Oct. 10, New Brunswick voted against importation of liquor for personal use

Nov. 12–Feb. 6, 1922, Sir Robert Borden represented Canada at Washington Conference on Limitation of Armaments

Dec. 6, General Election a victory for the Liberals and defeat of the Meighen Government in every province except British Columbia, the Liberals receiving a plurality of vote and control of 117 seats in the Commons, the Progressives 66 seats, Independents 2, and Conservatives (Government) 50. Miss Agnes McPhail, Ontario, the first woman elected to House of Commons

Dec. 29, Twelfth Dominion Ministry appointed

Office	Name	Date of Appointment
Prime Minister, Secretary of State for External Affairs, President of the Privy Council	William Lyon Mackenzie King	Dec. 29, 1921
Minister of Finance	William S. Fielding	Dec. 29, 1921
	James A. Robb	Sept. 5, 1925
Minister of National Defense	George P. Graham	Dec. 29, 1921
	Edward Macdonald	April 28, 1923
	Edward Macdonald	Aug. 17, 1923
Postmaster General	Charles Murphy	Dec. 29, 1921
Minister without portfolio	Raoul Dandurand	Dec. 29, 1921
Minister of Soldier's Civil Reestablishment and the Minister in charge of and to administer the Department of Health	Henri S. Beland	Dec. 29, 1921
	John C. Elliott	April 15, 1926
Minister of Public Works	Hewitt Bostock	Dec. 29, 1921
	James H. King	Feb. 3, 1922
Minister of Justice and Attorney General	Sir Lomer Gouin	Dec. 29, 1921
	Ernest Lapointe	Jan. 30, 1924
Minister of Customs and Excise	Jacques Bureau	Dec. 29, 1921
	George H. Boivin	Sept. 5, 1925
Minister of Marine and Fisheries	Ernest Lapointe	Dec. 29, 1921
	P. J. A. Cardin	Jan. 30, 1924
Solicitor-General	Daniel D. McKenzie	Dec. 29, 1921
	E. J. McMurray	Sept. 12, 1923
Minister of Immigration and Colonization	James A. Robb	Aug. 17, 1923
	George N. Gordon	Sept. 5, 1925
	Charles Stewart	Nov. 13, 1925
Minister of Trade and Commerce	James A. Robb	Dec. 29, 1921
	Thomas A. Low	Aug. 17, 1923
	James A. Robb	Nov. 13, 1925
Secretary of State	Arthur B. Copp	Dec. 29, 1921
	Walter E. Foster	Sept. 12, 1925
	Ernest Lapointe	Mar. 24, 1926
Minister of Railways and Canals	William C. Kennedy	Dec. 29, 1921
	George P. Graham	April 28, 1923
	Charles A. Dunning	Mar. 1, 1926
Minister of the Interior, Superintendent-General of Indian Affairs and Minister of Mines	Charles Stewart	Dec. 29, 1921
Minister of Agriculture	William R. Motherwell	Dec. 29, 1921
Minister of Labor	James Mudock	Dec. 29, 1921
	James H. King	Nov. 13, 1925
	John C. Elliott	Mar. 8, 1926

OFFICE	NAME	DATE OF APPOINTMENT
Minister without portfolio	John E. Sinclair	Dec. 29, 1921
	H. B. McGiverin	Sept. 30, 1924
	Herbert H. Marler	Sept. 5, 1925
	Charles Vincent Massey	Sept. 12, 1925

1922

Feb. 10, P. C. Larkin appointed High Commissioner for Canada in Great Britain

March 8–June 28, First session of fourteenth Parliament. Provision made for constitution of the Canada Wheat Board. National Defense Act which came into effect Jan. 1, 1923, provided for a Dept. of National Defense presided over by a Minister who is charged with all matters formerly administered by the Depts. of Militia and Defense, Marine and Naval Service, and the Air Board, and a Defense Council constituted to advise the Minister. Customs Tariff provided for moderate tariff reductions on 50 articles. Bankruptcy Act, Insurance, Fisheries, Pensions and Returned Soldiers' Acts amended. Special War Revenue Act amended to increase duties. Canadian Red Cross Society given powers of a corporation. Criminal Code codified

March 19, Stefansson announced taking possession of Wrangel Island for Great Britain in Sept. 1921

March 22–Aug. 24, Strike of coal miners in Alberta and British Columbia

March 31, 89,999 immigrants arrived including 39,020 from the United Kingdom and 29,345 from the United States

April 10–May 19, Canada represented at Economic Conference at Genoa, Italy, by Sir Charles B. Gordon

May 12, Announcement of reduction of navy leaving only 3 small vessels on each coast

May 16, General railroad strike begun in Newfoundland

July 3, Anglo-Russian Trade Agreement of March 16, 1921 extended to Canada

July 13, Conference between Canada and the United States regarding armaments on the Great Lakes

July 18, Canadian Government Arctic expedition left Quebec, sighted Coburg Island Aug. 20, and Aug. 28 established most northern post at Craig Harbor at 76° 10′ N. Lat. and 81° 20′ W. Long.

Aug. 13, V. S. Sriniva arrived from India at Victoria, British Columbia, to discuss franchise and condition of Indians in Canada with the Government

Oct. 4, Separate lines in Canadian National Railway system consolidated and a board of directors appointed

Nov. 5, Treaty of commerce with Italy signed

Dec. 4, International Postal Conference (5th) opened at Ottawa, between representatives of the United States and Canada

Dec. 15, Imperial Importation of Animals Act removed embargo on Canadian cattle

——, Commercial Treaty with France signed

1923

Jan. 1, National Defense Act of 1922 came into effect

Jan. 4, Trade Agreement between Canada and Italy signed

Jan. 24, Resignation of George H. Murray, Prime Minister of Nova Scotia, after 27 years in office; succeeded by E. H. Armstrong

Jan. 31–June 30, Second session of fourteenth Parliament. Immigration Act amended with respect to deportation and prohibition of alien enemies from entering the country removed. Chinese Immigration Act further restricted entry of Chinese. Fifth revision of Bank Act. Duty on sugar reduced by 50 cents per 100 pounds and further reductions in the tariff, but new bounties granted for the copper and hemp industry and on crude petroleum. The sales tax, and taxes on cigarettes, wines, checks reduced. Amendment to Patent Act established a Patent Office in charge of a Commissioner of Patents. Improper use of opium and other drugs prohibited. Marriage declared valid to brother of a deceased husband of the woman, or son of such brother. Amendments made to Bankruptcy, Animal Contagious Diseases, Copyright Acts and Criminal Code

Feb. 5, General election in Quebec a victory for the Liberal Government of Premier Taschereau

March 31, 72,887 immigrants arrived during the year including 34,508 from the United Kingdom and 22,007 from the United States

April 1, Removal of British embargo from Canadian cattle came into effect

May 21, Prohibition established in Prince Edward Island as a result of a plebiscite of Jan. 22

June 22, Manitoba voted for government control of sale of liquor by a majority of over 35,000, repealing Act of March 13, 1916

June 25, General election in Ontario resulted in defeat of the Liberal Drury Government and return to power of the Conservatives with G. Howard Ferguson, Prime Minister

July 5, Strike of miners and steel workers in Sydney, Nova Scotia, for increase in wages and recognition of the union which was lost by the workers in the autumn. An investigating commission appointed by the Dominion Government sustained the strikers in their demands

July 23, Resignation of Sir Richard Squires, Premier of Newfoundland; succeeded by W. R. Warren

July 26, General election in Prince Edward Island defeated the Liberal Government of John H. Bell, and Conservatives returned to power with J. D. Stewart, Prime Minister

Aug. 17, Pension Federal Appeal Board appointed by Order in Council

Aug. 24, Western Canada Coal Operators' Association reached agreement with employees under which 12,000 miners on strike since March 31, 1922 in Alberta and British Columbia resumed work

Nov. 5, Alberta voted for government control of the liquor traffic and sale of liquor after 7 years of prohibition

Nov., Dry dock at St. John, New Brunswick, opened, the largest in the world, extreme length 1,225 feet

Dec. 27, Agreement with the United States as to reciprocal application of copyright regulations

Wheat crop of this year 474,199,000 bushels largest in the history of the country grown on 22,671,864 acres, and representing average of 21 bushels an acre, estimated value $316,934,700

1924

Jan. 2, Death of Louis Philippe Brodeur, statesman

Feb. 28–July 19, Third session of fourteenth Parliament. Bank Act amended providing for appointment of an inspector of banks. Customs duties reduced on agricultural implements, and machinery used in forestry, mining, dairying, fishing, fruit raising, and the lumber industry, and raw materials used for the manufacture of these implements placed on the free list, in effort to reduce cost of "instruments of production" in Canada's basic industries. Representation Act made the decennial census the basis of representation in the House of Commons. Indian Act amended to give the Supt. General of Indian Affairs charge of Eskimos. Research Council Act provided for an "Honorary Advisory Council for Scientific and Industrial Research." Provided that Business Profits War Tax should not extend beyond Dec. 31, 1920. Income War Tax increased exemption allowed for each child from $300 to $500. Immigration Act amended as to details of domicile and deportation. Customs benefits extended to mandated countries

March 27, Death of Sir Byron E. Walker, financier

March 31, 148,560 immigrants arrived during the year including 72,919 from the United Kingdom and 20,521 from the United States

June 6, Treaty signed between the United States and Great Britain in respect of Canada for suppression of smuggling of intoxicating liquors

June 19–29, Strike of postal workers

June 20, General election in British Columbia a victory for the Liberals

July 3, Trade Agreement with Belgium signed

July 11, Trade Agreement with the Netherlands signed

July 16, Saskatchewan voted in favor of government control of the liquor traffic, repealing action of Dec. 11, 1916

Aug. 7–16, British Association for the Advancement of Science met at Toronto

Aug. 11–16, International Mathematical Congress met at Toronto

Sept. 25, Trade agreement with Australia concluded

Oct. 15, The Prince of Wales arrived at Toronto on visit to Canada

Oct. 23, Plebiscite on liquor question in Ontario reduced the majority for continuation of prohibition

Dec. 17, Legislature of British Columbia adopted a resolution opposing further immigration of Orientals to Canada

1925

Feb. 5–June 27, Fourth session of fourteenth Parliament. Commercial reciprocity with Finland and the Netherlands authorized and trade agreement with Australia ratified. Canada Grain Act replaced that of 1912. Post office employees brought under the civil service. Important amendments made to Workmen's Compensation Act. Duty on bituminous coal reduced, and further reductions made for machinery. Amendment to North West Territories Act provided for control and regulation of exploration of northern lands. Discussion of referendum on reform of Senate

Feb. 24, Boundary Treaty with the United States provided for an International Lake of the Woods Control Board and for maintenance of a fixed level in order to secure to both countries the most advantageous use of the waters of the lake

March 6–Aug. 6, Strike of 12,000 coal miners in Nova Scotia, settled by compromise agreement

March 10, Statement of Prime Minister to League of Nations gave reasons for declining to adhere to

Geneva Protocol for Pacific Settlement of International Disputes

March 31, 111,362 immigrants arrived during the year including 53,178 from the United Kingdom and 15,818 from the United States

——, Net public debt on this date $2,417,437,685

April 11, Commercial *modus vivendi* with Spain concluded

June 2, General election in Saskatchewan a victory for the Liberals led by Mr. Dunning

June 10, Union of sections of the Methodists, Congregationalists, and Presbyterians formed the United Church of Canada

June 25, General election in Nova Scotia returned Conservatives under E. N. Rhodes to office

June 28, Official reception at Ottawa to Field Marshal Earl Haig

June 29, New Canadian Building in London opened by the King

July 6, New Canadian-West Indian trade agreement signed at Ottawa

Aug. 10, General election in New Brunswick returned Conservatives under J. B. M. Baxter to power

Sept. 7–26, Senator Raoul Dandurand, president of the Assembly of the League of Nations, at Geneva

Oct. 29, Dominion general election gave Conservatives 116 seats, the Liberals 101, and the Progressives and Independents 28, Labor retaining the 2 they had, the balance of power remaining with the agricultural "bloc," the Liberal (Government) strength reduced in the Commons from 118 to 101

Nov. 10, Total yield of wheat 423,000,000, second largest in history of the country

Dec. 15, Agreement with Imperial Government by which transportation rates for immigrants reduced

1926

Jan. 7–July 2, First session of fifteenth Parliament. Diversion of water of Great Lakes by Chicago discussed. Income War Tax amended to raise exemption limit and reduce rates of taxation. Customs Tariff reduced, and discussion of report of parliamentary committee on smuggling industry in alcoholic liquors and narcotics across the United States border robbing the Dominion Treasury of millions of dollars estimated as at least $35,000,000 annually, and the illegal entry of dutiable articles from the United States such as textiles and cigarettes. Trade Marks Act amended to authorize registration of "union labels." Provision made for additional judge of the Supreme Court and compulsory retirement of all judges of Superior and Exchequer Courts at 75. Increase of pay granted to civil service officials. Resignation of Prime Minister King because of refusal of the Governor General to dissolve Parliament, but defeat of the Meighen Ministry induced him to grant a dissolution. An old age pensions' measure and rural credits passed in the Commons but defeated in the Senate. Opium and Narcotic Act of 1923 amended

Feb., Gold rush to the Red Bank country 1,200 miles northwest of Toronto in Ontario

March 12, Coal miners voted to accept wage contract recommended by Royal Commission, reduction of 10% of wage scale of 1924 and restoration of check off

March 31, 96,064 immigrants arrived during the year including 37,030 from the United Kingdom and 18,778 from the United States

April 7, Advisory Board on tariff and taxation appointed by Order in Council

June 28, Resignation of Mackenzie King Ministry because of customs scandals

June 29, Thirteenth Dominion Ministry appointed

OFFICE	NAME	DATE OF APPOINTMENT
Prime Minister, Secretary of State for External Affairs and President of the Privy Council	Arthur Meighen	June 29, 1926
Secretary of State	Sir George H. Perley	July 13, 1926
Minister of Justice and Attorney-General	E. L. Patenaude	July 13, 1926
Minister of Marine and Fisheries	E. L. Patenaude	July 13, 1926
Minister of National Defense	Hugh Guthrie	July 13, 1926
Minister of Immigration and Colonization	Sir Henry L. Drayton	July 13, 1926
Minister of Agriculture	S. F. Tolmie	July 13, 1926
Minister of Customs and Excise	H. H. Stevens	July 13, 1926
Postmaster General	R. J. Manion	July 13, 1926
Minister of Finance	R. B. Bennett	July 13, 1926
Minister of the Interior, Supt.-General of Indian Affairs and Minister of Mines	R. B. Bennett	July 13, 1926
Minister of Railways and Canals	W. A. Black	July 13, 1926
Minister of Trade and Commerce	J. D. Chaplin	July 13, 1926
Minister of Labor	G. B. Jones	July 13, 1926
Minister of Public Works	E. B. Ryckman	July 13, 1926
Minister without portfolio	D. Sutherland	July 13, 1926
Minister of Soldiers' Civil Reestablishment, Minister in charge of and to administer the Department of Health	R. D. Morand Eugene Paquet	July 13, 1926 Aug. 23, 1926
Minister without portfolio	J. A. Macdonald	July 13, 1926

July 1, Two cent domestic rate of postage restored

——, Gold standard reëstablished

July 2, Meighen Ministry (Conservative) defeated on motion of want of confidence by vote of 96 to 95

Sept. 14, Dominion general election returned the Liberals to power; Liberals received 118 seats, Conservatives 91, Liberal Progressives 11, United Farmers of Alberta 11, Progressives 9, Labor 3, Independent 2

Sept. 24, Meighen Ministry resigned

Sept. 25, Fourteenth Dominion Ministry appointed

OFFICE	NAME	DATE OF APPOINTMENT
Prime Minister, President of the Privy Council and Secretary of State for External Affairs	William Lyon Mackenzie King	Sept. 25, 1926
Member of the Administration as Minister without portfolio	Raoul Dandurand	Sept. 25, 1926
Minister of Justice and Attorney-General	Ernest Lapointe	Sept. 25, 1926
Minister of Finance and Receiver General	James A. Robb	Sept. 25, 1926
Minister of the Interior, Minister of Mines and Superintendent-General of Indian Affairs	Charles Stewart	Sept. 25, 1926
Minister of Agriculture	William R. Motherwell	Sept. 25, 1926
Minister in charge of and to Administer the Department of Health and the Minister of Soldiers' Civil Reestablishment	James H. King	Sept. 25, 1926
Minister of Railways and Canals	Charles A. Dunning	Sept. 25, 1926
Minister of Public Works	John C. Elliott	Sept. 25, 1926
Solicitor General	Lucien Cannon	Sept. 25, 1926
Minister of National Defense	J. L. Ralston	Oct. 7, 1926
Postmaster General	Peter J. Veniot	Sept. 25, 1926
Minister of Customs and Excise	William D. Euler	Sept. 25, 1926
Secretary of State	Fernand Rinfret	Sept. 25, 1926
Minister of Trade and Commerce	James Malcolm	Sept. 25, 1926
Minister of Immigration and Colonization	Robert Forke	Sept. 25, 1926
Minister of Labor	Peter Heeman	Sept. 25, 1926
Minister of Marine and Fisheries	Pierre J. A. Cardin	Sept. 25, 1926

Oct. 2, Lord Willingdon of Ratton (Freeman-Thomas) appointed Aug. 19, assumed office as Governor General

Oct. 28, The Queen of Rumania officially received at Ottawa

Nov. 26, Vincent Massey appointed first Canadian Minister to the United States

Dec. 1, General election in Ontario a victory for the Ferguson Government. Sale of intoxicating liquors by the Government instead of prohibition adopted by voters

Dec. 9–April 14, 1927, First session of sixteenth Parliament. Income and sales taxes reduced and stamp tax on checks, the so-called "nuisance taxes" but made no tariff changes. Farm Loan Act established system of long term mortgage credit for farmers and created Canada Farm Loan Board. Dept. of National Revenue constituted. Arrangement made for coöperation with the provinces in system of old age pensions. Government authorized to form company to be called the Canada National (West Indies) Steamship Company

Dec. 20, Provisional trade agreement with Czechoslovakia signed

1927

March 1, Imperial Privy Council decision in favor of Newfoundland in dispute with Labrador, Newfoundland receiving 12,000 square miles of Labrador territory

March 29, Ten years of prohibition ended in Ontario with passage of law to place liquor under government control, the purpose of the law stated to be "to promote temperance, sobriety, personal liberty and above all to restore respect for law"

March 31, 143,991 immigrants arrived including 49,784 from the United Kingdom and 21,025 from the United States

April 1, Dept. of Labor of the United States placed aliens who crossed the border for purposes of employment under immigration quota

April 19, New Brunswick placed sale of liquor under government control

May 16, General election in Quebec sustained Liberal Government of Taschereau

May 25, Decision of Cabinet that Canada should take the same course as Great Britain and terminate trade relations with Soviet Russia

May 27, Death of Sir John Willison

June 1, William Phillips, first United States Minister to Canada, arrived at Ottawa

——, Sale of liquor at government stores begun in Ontario to persons with permits which were issued to adults not habitual drunkards for $2

June 8, Protest to the United States against order classifying Canadians who crossed the border into the United States as commuters to places of employment as immigrants under the quota law

June 12, Imperial Privy Council dismissed appeal of Roman Catholics for separate schools in Ontario

June 25, General election in Prince Edward Island defeated Conservative Government of J. D. Stewart; succeeded by A. C. Saunders. Vote sustained prohibition as against government control proposed

June 28, General election in Manitoba sustained Government headed by John Bracken

July 1, Direct communication inaugurated between Government of Great Britain and Government of Canada without mediation of Governor General

July 1–3, Diamond jubilee of the Confederation celebrated

July 16, Announced that Canada would not accept invitation of the United States to join in convention for development of St. Lawrence waterway from Great Lakes to the Atlantic Ocean

July 27–Aug. 4, World Poultry Congress held at Ottawa

July 30, The Prince of Wales, Prince George, and Stanley Baldwin arrived at Quebec on visit to Canada

Aug. 5, Putnam expedition from the United States arrived at Cape Dorchester, South Baffin Land, and checked position of the Cape not done since expedition of Luke Foxe in 1631

Aug. 18, Premier Stanley Baldwin sailed from Nova Scotia for England after tour of Canada

Sept. 7, The Prince of Wales and Prince George embarked for England

Sept. 15, Canada elected to one of non-permanent seats of the Council of the League of Nations

Oct. 10, National Conservative Convention met at Winnipeg, and Richard Bedford Bennett elected leader of party in succession to Arthur Meighen, resigned

Nov. 3, Federal and Inter-Provincial Conference at Ottawa on the relations between the Dominion and the Provinces

1928

Jan. 26–June 11, Second session of sixteenth Parliament. Copper bounties extended to 1931. Gold and Silver Marking Act amended to include platinum. Immigration Act amended to provide for deportation of persons seeking to overthrow the Government and deportation for certain causes made dependent upon conviction under the criminal code rather than upon hearings before board. Customs revised. New Electricity Inspection Act passed. Other legislation dealt with the dairy industry, experimental farms, fertilizers, seeds, Dominion lands, soldiers' insurance and pensions, patents, and importation of liquor into the provinces. Income War Tax reduced to 80% of rate paid in 1926. Spanish Treaty Act provided that certain treaties between the United Kingdom and Spain regarding commerce, navigation, and treatment of companies should apply to Canada. Certain other British treaties granting reciprocal most favored nation treatment are to apply to Canada when so ordered by the Governor General in Council, namely with Estonia, Hungary, Latvia, Lithuania, Portugal, Rumania, and Yugoslavia

Jan. 30, Visit of President Cosgrove of the Irish Free State to Ottawa

Feb. 2, Imperial Privy Council upheld decision of Supreme Court of Canada that Jews of Montreal as "protestants" had no right of representation on Protestant School Board, but added that there was nothing to prevent them from serving on the Board if appointed

March 15, Convention with Czechoslovakia provided for most favored nation treatment by each country of goods produced or manufactured in the other

March 31, 151,597 immigrants arrived during the year including 50,872 from the United Kingdom and 25,007 from the United States

April 15, Canadian plane discovered and relieved the German airship "Bremen" stranded on Greenley Island

April 17–18, First National Assembly of Liberal Women met at Ottawa

April 23, Sir William H. Clark appointed first British High Commissioner to Canada, assumed duties Sept. 22

April 24, Supreme Court decision as to right of women to sit in Senate that the term "qualified persons" in the British North America Act did not include women

May 31, Legislative Council of Nova Scotia abolished; Quebec the only province with a bicameral legislature

June 12, Decision of Imperial Privy Council dismissed appeal of Roman Catholic separate schools of Tiny, Ontario, claiming exemption from laws of the Province as to schools

July 18, General election in British Columbia resulted in victory of the Conservatives, and Aug. 21 S. F. Tolmie succeeded J. D. Maclean as Premier

July 20, Japan opened legation at Ottawa

Aug. 11, Bert Hassell and Parker Cramer left Cochrane, Ontario, in attempt to make an America-to-Sweden flight. Rescued after forced landing at Point Sukkertoppen in southern Greenland

Aug. 24–Oct. 5, Empire Parliamentary Association visited Canada

Sept. 1, Manitoba Old Age Pension Act came into effect

Oct. 1, General election in Nova Scotia a victory for the Conservative Government

Oct. 8, United States Supreme Court upheld right of Canadian citizens employed in the United States to cross the border without payment of immigration fee

Oct. 29, Election in Newfoundland a victory for the Liberals led by Sir Richard Squires

Nov. 9, Imperial Privy Council confirmed decision of Supreme Court that gold and silver in lands of the Hudson Bay Company is owned by the Crown in the right of the Dominion Government instead of by the Company

Nov. 16, Georges Jean Knight, first Minister from France to Canada, presented his credentials

Nov. 19, Supreme Court of the United States reversed its decision of Oct. 8 and upheld regulations of Dept. of Labor of April, 1927, as to Canadians crossing the border, and again April 9, 1929

Dec. 25, Penny postage within the Empire discontinued in 1914 restored

1929

Jan. 2, Convention for preservation of Niagara Falls signed with the United States

Feb. 7–June 14, Third session of sixteenth Parliament. Canada Grain Act extensively amended. Other laws amended included the Dominion Election Act, Fisheries Act with regard to licenses and to put into effect the recommendations of the Atlantic Fisheries Commission, the Opium and Narcotic Drug Act to make illicit selling and distribution a criminal offense, and Insurance Act as to casualty and marine insurance. Special War Revenue Act repealed taxes including tax on railroad and steamship tickets, telegrams and cables and sales tax reduced. Juvenile Delinquency Act substituted for that of 1927 based on recommendations of the Council on Child Welfare. Railroad pensions extended. Resolution to repeal previous legislation against Canadian titles defeated

Feb. 23, George Haldeman made flight from Windsor, Ontario, to Havana, Cuba, non-stop flight of 1,404 miles in 12 hours and 56 minutes

March 22, Canadian schooner "I'm Alone" sunk by United States Coast Guard and Captain J. T. Randall and crew taken prisoners to New Orleans. *See also* United States

March 31, 167,722 immigrants arrived during the year including 58,880 from the United Kingdom and 30,560 from the United States

April 9, Canadian Minister in Washington presented protest against sinking of the "I'm Alone"; the case referred to arbitration April 25

May 5, Radio telephone on National Railway train maintained two-way communication with home office in test

June 6, Liberal Government defeated in election in Saskatchewan

July 18, Prohibition law in Prince Edward Island indorsed by plebiscite

Aug. 7, Landing of any immigrant under a labor contract prohibited, not to be applied to farm labor or domestic service

Oct. 15, Prime Minister Ramsay MacDonald and Miss MacDonald entered Canada for visit, reaching Ottawa Oct. 17, Montreal Oct. 21, and sailed for England Oct. 25

Oct. 18, Judicial Committee of the Imperial Privy Council ruled in case appealed from the Supreme Court of Canada that women are eligible to sit in Canadian Senate

Oct. 30, Elections in Ontario sustained the Conservative Government of G. H. Ferguson, and continued system of liquor control by the Government

——, Nova Scotia voted for system of government control of liquor by a large majority, ending prohibition

Nov. 9, Imperial Privy Council confirmed decision of Canada Supreme Court that gold and silver on lands of the Hudson Bay Company are property of the Crown

Nov. 11, Death of James A. Robb, Minister of Finance; succeeded by Charles A. Dunning

Dec. 20, Exchange of Notes with Union of Socialist Soviet Republics resumed diplomatic relations with Russia

1930

Jan. 14, Agreement with Germany as to liquidation of German (alien enemy) property signed at The Hague

Feb. 3, Death of Peter C. Larkin, High Commissioner for Canada in London

Feb. 20–May 30, Fourth session of sixteenth Parliament. Acts amended included the Special War Revenue Act, Income War Tax, Canada Grain, Fish Inspection, Insurance, Pensions and National Health, Soldier Settlement, and Criminal Code. A new Dept. of Marine constituted and a Dept. of Fisheries. Fair Wages and Eight-Hour Day Act enacted to cover all government employees. Iron and steel schedules of the tariff revised, and seasonable rates for fruits and vegetables, duties on tea, porcelain and chinaware, and meats reduced, and increased those on beans and butter, and so-called "countervailing" duties imposed on 16 commodities

March 12, Colonel W. G. Barker, aviator who had brought down 52 German planes in the World War, died in crash of his plane at Ottawa

March 31, 163,288 immigrants arrived in the country during the year including 64,082 from the United Kingdom and 30,727 from the United States

June 19, General election in Alberta resulted in return of Ministry of J. E. Brownlee, United Farmer

June 20, General election in New Brunswick a Conservative victory

June 25, The "Southern Cross" carrying the Australian Major Charles Kingsford Smith and 3 companions landed at Harbor Grace, Newfoundland, after a 31½ hour crossing from Port Marnock, Ireland

July 28, Dominion election a Conservative victory ending nine year rule of the Liberals; returned 138 Conservatives; 87 Liberals; 3 Liberal-Progressives; 10 United Farmers of Alberta; 2 Progressives; 3 Labor; 2 Independent

Aug. 1, The R–100 docked at St. Hubert airport, Montreal, in transatlantic crossing in 78 hours and 51 minutes from Cardington, England

Aug. 6, Resignation of W. L. Mackenzie King, Liberal Ministry

Aug. 7, Fifteenth Dominion Ministry appointed, Richard B. Bennett, Prime Minister

The following is the list of the Cabinet, in order of precedence, which in Canada attaches generally rather to the person than to the office:

Prime Minister, President of the Privy Council, Secretary of State for External Affairs and Minister of Finance (pro tem.), R. B. Bennett; Minister without Portfolio, Sir George H. Perley; Fisheries, E. N. Rhodes (Senator); Labor, Gideon Robertson (Senator); Justice and Attorney-General, Hugh Guthrie; Trade and Commerce, H. H. Stevens; Railways and Canals, R. J. Manion; National Revenue, E. B. Ryckman; Minister without Portfolio, J. A. Macdonald; Postmaster-General, Arthur Sauve; Pensions and National Health, Col. Murray MacLaren; Public Works, H. A. Stewart; Secretary of State, C. H. Cahan; National Defense, Col. D. M. Sutherland; Marine, Alfred Duranleau; Interior and Superintendent-General of Indian Affairs, Thomas G. Murphy; Solicitor General, Maurice Dupré; Immigration and Colonization and Minister of Mines, W. A. Gordon; Agriculture, Robert Weir

Aug. 13, The R–100 left Montreal at 9.32 A.M. and landed at Cardington, England Aug. 16, time 57 hours and 5 minutes for transatlantic crossing

Sept. 8–22, First session of seventeenth Parliament met to enact emergency unemployment and tariff legislation. $20,000,000 granted for construction or improvement of public works, assistance in cost of distribution of products of farms, mines, rivers, &c., and to aid provinces and municipalities in unemployment relief work. The anti-dumping clauses of the tariff rewritten and increased duties placed on 130 articles including most agricultural products, glass, printed matter, manufactures of paper, commodities in the iron and steel group, on boots and shoes, and on a wide range of textile items. Premier Bennett announced in Commons that he would assist the United States in investigating the charge that Soviet interests had been short-selling wheat on the Chicago Board of Trade

Sept. 30, Federal Appeal Board for pensions discontinued

Nov. 12, Announcement that Norway formally recognized sovereignty of Canada over the Sverdrup Islands in the Arctic

67 strikes during the year, the lowest record since 1900 except for 1914 and 1915

GREENLAND

Greenland, largest island in the world except Australia, the only colonial possession of Denmark, situated in north polar regions northeast of North America with area estimated as 827,275 square miles. The most northern point is Cape Morris Jesup in 83° 39′ N. Lat., and Cape Farwell, the most southern point on a small island in 50° 45′ N. The extreme length is about 1,650 miles, and extreme breadth nearly 800 miles. The population by census of 1921 numbered 14,355 including 274 Danes. The largest settlement is Sydproven with population of 901. The capital is Godhaven.

LABRADOR

Labrador, peninsula of northeast North America with area of over 500,000 square miles, the southern part included in Quebec Province of Canada, and the coast a dependency of Newfoundland. By proclamation of Oct. 7, 1763 Labrador from St. Johns River to Hudson Bay placed under jurisdiction of Newfoundland, restored to Canada in 1774, Labrador Act of March 30, 1809, reannexed coast strip to Newfoundland and boundary in dispute with Province of Quebec, Canada, decided in favor of Newfoundland in 1927. See also Newfoundland.

NEWFOUNDLAND

Newfoundland (originally New-found land), British Dominion, tenth largest island in the world forming a separate country and one-fifth smaller than Ireland, with total area of 42,734 square miles, situated on northeast side of the Gulf of St. Lawrence in 46° 37′ and 51° 39′ N. Lat. and 52° 35′ and 59° 25′ West. Long. and including a part of the Labrador peninsula. The greatest length from north to south is 250 miles and average breadth about 130 miles. Newfoundland's Labrador territory comprises about 232,400 square miles. The capital is St. John's. For history see Canada

Population in 1929, 271,553. Dependent on Newfoundland is Labrador, the most easterly part of the American continent. The boundary between the said Dependency and the Province of Quebec, which had, for many years, been in dispute, was defined by the Judicial Committee of the Privy Council in March 1927, as being, in effect, the watershed of the rivers flowing into the Atlantic Ocean, the coastal boundaries being from Blanc Sablon, on the South, to Cape Chidley, on the North. As a result of this decision an estimated area of some 110,000 sq. miles, formerly in dispute, was confirmed as under the jurisdiction of Newfoundland. The population of Labrador in 1929 was 4,163 (2,228 males, 1,935 females). Of the total Newfoundland population in 1921, 65,448 were engaged in the fisheries, 3,227 were farmers, 4,862 mechanics, and 1,117 miners. Capital, St. John's, 41,157 inhabitants (1928); other towns (1921), Harbor Grace, 3,825; Bonavista, 4,052; Carbonear, 3,320; Twllingate, 3,217, and Grand Falls, 3,769.

MEXICO

Mexico, Federal Republic, south of the United States extending southeast to Guatemala and British Honduras, and bounded on the west by the Pacific Ocean and on the east by the Gulf of Mexico, situated between the parallels of 14° 31′ and 32° 43′ North, and 86° 48′ and 117° 8′ West, and comprises, according to Mexican estimates, 757,907 square miles, though English geographers compute it as 767,198 square miles, and German authorities as 767,290 square miles.

The population at the census of May 15, 1930, was 16,404,030, an increase of 2,069,250 or 14.4% since 1921; density was 21.36 persons per square mile; census results are shown in the following table. The capitals of the States and territories are in parentheses.

States and Territories	Area, in Square Miles	Census Population, 1930
Aguascalientes (Aguascalientes)	2,969	132,492
Baja California (La Paz)	58,338	94,469
Campeche (Campeche)	18,089	84,971
Chiapas (Tuxtla Gutiérrez)	27,527	521,318
Chihuahua (Chihuahua)	90,036	491,893
Coahuila (Saltillo)	63,786	434,313
Colima (Colima)	2,272	60,845
Distrito Federal (México City)	578	1,217,663
Durango (Durango)	42,272	395,807
Guanajuato (Guanajuato)	10,950	981,963
Guerrero (Chilpancingo)	25,279	637,530
Hidalgo (Pachuca)	8,637	674,674
Jalisco (Guadalajara)	33,492	1,239,484
México (Toluca)	9,230	978,412
Michoacáan (Morelia)	22,621	1,014,020
Morelos (Guernavaca)	1,895	132,582
Nayarit (Tepic)	10,953	170,054
Nuevo León (Monterrey)	25,032	416,173
Oaxaca (Oaxaca)	35,689	1,070,852
Puebla (Puebla)	12,992	1,148,286
Querétaro (Querétaro)	4,493	234,386
Quintana Roo (Payo Obispo)	19,270	12,150
San Luis Potosi (San Luis Potosi)	24,004	559,106
Sinaloa (Culiacan)	27,557	385,512
Sonora (Hermosillo)	76,633	315,312
Tabasco (Villa Hermosa)	10,374	223,838
Tamaulipas (Ciudad Victoria)	30,831	343,677
Tlaxcala (Tlaxcala)	1,534	204,424
Veracruz (Jalapa)	27,880	1,376,865
Yucatán (Mérida)	15,939	384,790
Zacatecas (Zacatecas)	24,471	465,021
Islands	1,575	1,148
Grand Total	767,198	16,404,030

Of the population in 1930, 4,620,880 were Indian, 9,040,590 of mixed race, 2,444,466 pure white, 140,094 of unknown racial origin, and 158,000 foreigners.

The chief cities, 1921, are:—Mexico City (capital), 968,443 (census of 1930); Puebla, 95,535; Guadalajara, 143,376; San Luis Potosi, 57,353; Leon, 53,639; Monterey, 88,458; Pachuca, 40,802; Zacatecas, 15,462; Guanajuato, 19,408; Mérida, 79,225; Querétaro, 30,073; Morelia, 31,148; Oaxaca, 27,792 Orizaba, 39,563; Aguascalientes, 48,041; Saltillo, 40,451; Durango, 39,091; Chihuahua, 37,078; Vera Cruz, 54,225; Toluca, 34,265; Celaya, 24,035.

Mexico was annexed to the Spanish Crown by conquest in 1521, gained independence in 1821, and became a Republic in 1823. From 1864–1867 Maximilian ruled as Emperor, but Republic re-established

Pascual Ortiz Rubio, President

1517

March 4, Hernandez de Cordova on slave hunting expedition from Cuba landed at Yucatan, Mexico, at Punta de Catoche which he named

1518

April 8, Juan de Grijalva sailed from Cuba and coasted Yucatan and Mexico, reaching Island of Santa Cruz (Cozumel) May 3, June 19 he took possession of country near the present Vera Cruz naming the Island of San Juan de Ulloa which he reached June 18

Nov. 18, Hernando Cortés, commissioned by Governor of Cuba, sailed from Santiago (Cuba) with 6 vessels for Mexico on voyage of discovery

1519

Jan. 24, Papal bull made Julian Garces, a Dominican, bishop of Cozumel Island, Mexico

Feb. 18, Cortés, though recalled by Governor Velasquez, now with his expedition equipped to 12 vessels finally sailed from Cuba for Mexico. Fathers Bartolome de Olmeda and Juan Diaz accompanied the expedition

March 4, Cortés expedition landed at Yucatan. Sailing up coast the Spaniards reached site of San Juan de Ulloa April 2

March 25, Spaniards in battle with Indians at Tabasco and received their submission at end of a series of battles

April 21, Vera Cruz founded by Cortés

Aug. 16, Cortés started march from Vera Cruz with 450 Spaniards for the so-called republic of Tlascala on plateau of Anahuac

Sept. 5, Cortés defeated the Tlascalan Indians in battle and won their allegiance against Montezuma

Sept. 23, Spaniards entered the city of Tlascala

Oct. 13, Cortés started for Cholula where he defeated Indians in battle

Nov. 1, Cortés left Cholula for Aztec capital

Nov. 8, Montezuma, Aztec emperor, received the Spaniards, and lodged them in a palace in his city of Tenochtitlan (Mexico City)

Voyage of Alonzo Alvarez de Pineda commissioned by Governor Garay of Jamaica reached Panuco, Mexico from Florida

1520

April 1, Panfilo de Narvaez, sent by Governor Velasquez to supersede Cortés in command arrived at San Juan de Ulloa with 16 vessels and 1,500 men

May, Cortés marching to the coast defeated Narvaez in night attack and attached his soldiers to his own cause

June 30, Death of Montezuma, captive of the Spaniards
——, The "Noche Triste," sad night. The Spaniards now besieged in Mexico City made night sally to escape and a large number were killed and wounded by superior numbers of Indians

July 7, Cortés defeated the Mexicans in battle on plain of Otumba, and then retreated to his allies the Tlascalans, reaching Tlaxcala on the 12th

Dec. 25, Cortés began reconquest of Mexico

1521

April 28, Cortés began siege of Mexico City

May 20, Alvarado and Olid destroyed part of the aqueduct at Chapultepec, cutting off the water supply from Mexico City

Aug. 13, Cortés recaptured Mexico City

Oct., Sandoval, lieutenant of Cortés, began march to southern Vera Cruz, subdued tribes and founded Medellin and Espiritu Santo
——, Cortés sent Orozco on expedition which subjugated the province of Oajaca and north Colima and Jalisco

Dec., Cristobal de Tapia sent to take charge of government and investigate Cortés arrived at Vera Cruz and was sent out of country

1522

Jan., Pedro de Alvarado started south and added Tututepec on the coast to the Spanish domain

May, All the mendicant orders authorized to undertake religious work in New Spain

June, Olid extended Spanish rule to Michoacan territory of the Tarascos where settlement made at Zacatula

Aug., Three Franciscan fathers from Ghent, Juan de Tecto, Juan de Ayora, and Pedro de Gante reached Mexico and established mission for Indians

Oct. 15, Cortés named governor and captain-general of New Spain by Emperor Charles V, his rebellion against Diego Velasquez, Governor of Cuba, pardoned and his position legalized

Mexico City rebuilt as a Spanish municipality and Pedro de Alvarado made first Mayor

1523

April 24, Royal cedula forbade Garay to interfere in any district conquered or held by Cortés

May 1, Formal founding of San Esteban del Puerto in Panuco by Cortés in expedition which left Mexico in 1522 and conquered that region establishing claim disputed by Garay

June 24, Garay set sail from Jamaica and entered the present Santander River July 25. Sent Gonzalo de Ocampo to explore country, and proceeded eventually to establish settlement in Panuco claiming region between the Tampico River and the Rio Grande on basis of Pineda's expedition

July 26, Royal Order forbade granting of *repartimentos* (allotment of Indians for forced labor) but Cortés succeeded in having it withdrawn

Dec. 24, Death of Garay about 6 weeks after his arrival in Mexico

1523–1524

Pedro de Alvarado sent by Cortés subdued Guatemala and Salvador

1524

Jan. 11, Olid sent by Cortés to Honduras sailed from Vera Cruz. Landed May 3 and took possession for himself not Cortés. *See* Honduras

July 2, The Custodia del Santo Evangelio established by the Franciscans in the City of Mexico. In 1580 it had more than 80 convents

Oct. 12, Cortés with 140 Spaniards and 300 Indians marched over mountains, jungles, and rivers of Southern Mexico and Guatemala to reconquer Honduras from Olid. Returned by sea reaching Mexico in May, 1526

1525

Oct. 13, Bishopric of Mexico created

Nov. 4, Luis Ponce de Leon instructed to proceed to Mexico, assume governorship, and investigate charges against Cortés

Nov. 17, King of Spain issued a cedula for protection of Indian race decreasing under cruel exploitation of Spaniards

Silver deposits first discovered at Tasco in present state of Guerrero

1526

May 24, Cortés returned to Mexico from Honduras, landing at Vera Cruz

June, Ponce de Leon arrived in Mexico to investigate and supersede Cortés. First Dominicans accompanied him

Sept. 19, Royal decree extended see of bishopric of Cozumel over Tabasco and Vera Cruz districts including Tlascala

Nov. 17, Francisco de Montejoy received royal commission to settle Yucatan

1527

Conquest of Yucatan begun by Francisco de Montejoy

June 17, Pamphilio de Narvaez with commission as governor of Las Palmas, north of Panuco, sailed from San Lucar. For expedition *see* America

July, Cortés made first voyage along Pacific coast from Zacatula to Santiago in Colima

Dec. 12, Juan de Zumarraga made bishop of Mexico, later first archbishop

Dec. 13, Charles V created an Audiencia for Mexico, headed by Nuno de Guzman which began to function as council of state and supreme court in Mexico City Jan. 1, 1529

1528

May, Cortés arrived in Spain at port of Palos to defend himself against his enemies in Mexico

1529

July 6, Emperor Charles V made Cortés marques of the Valley Oaxaca and later in the month gave him princely domain of land in Oaxaca and Mexico and appointed him Captain-General of New Spain

Dec.–Oct. 1531, Journey of Nuno de Guzman, Governor of New Spain, from Jalisco, north to find "Island of the Seven Cities." Penetrated and conquered Sinaloa and founded settlements of San Miguel and Culiacan and gave territory name of New Galicia. Reached the present Guadalajara

College of San Juan de Lethran established in City of Mexico

1530

April 12, Second Audiencia with Sebastian Ramirez de Fuenleal president appointed. Arrived from Spain at

Vera Cruz Dec. 23, and assumed office at Mexico City Jan. 12, 1531

July 15, Cortés returned from Spain arrived at Villa Rica

Sept. 9, First cathedral in Mexico City founded by Charles V and a bull of Pope Clement VII of this date

Nov., Guzman expedition first to enter the present Sinaloa at Chametla in region of present Rosario

1531

Jan., Guzman marched north to region of modern Mazatlan and in March proceeded to Culiacan province to Colombo near site of present Culiacan

May–July 25, Guzman on exploring expedition from Colombo crossed the Sierras into Durango

July 25, San Luis de Montanez and Fernando de Tapia, Indian allies, invaded the country of the Chichimec and conquered Queretaro in "bloodless" battle

Oct., Guzman returned to Jalisco. Gave name to all country discovered of Nueva Galicia and established his capital at Compostela

1532

March 20, Royal cedula sanctioned the founding and settlement of town of Puebla de los Angeles. Work begun April 16

May 24 or June 30, Diego Hurtado de Mendoza sent by Cortés sailed from Acapulco, discovered the Tres Marias Islands and reached the Rio Fuerte in Sinaloa. Expedition a failure because of hostility of Guzman who prohibited landing

1533

The Augustinian friars joined the Franciscans and Dominicans in New Spain

April 27, Zumarraga consecrated as first Bishop of Mexico at Valladolid, Spain

July 4–Dec. 30, Expedition of Diego de Guzman left Culiacan Valley, proceeded to the present Sinaloa River and early in August arrived in territory of present state of Sinaloa. Reached Rio del Fuerte River Sept. 8, the 24th at the Rio Mayo and Oct. 4 at Yaqui River and established town of Yaquimi

Oct. 29 or 30, Hernando de Grijalva and Fortún Jiminez sailed from Tehuantepec. Discovered Revilla Gigedo group of islands landing on Socorro Dec. 20. At Acapulco Feb., 1534. On this expedition Jiminez discovered Lower California, the Bay of La Paz

1534

Feb., Royal decree divided New Spain into 4 ecclesiastical provinces and 4 bishoprics, Mexico, Michoacan, Goazacoalco, and Miztecapan

1535

April 15 or 18, Cortés sailed from Chametla northward

April 17, Antonio de Mendoza appointed first viceroy of New Spain and president of the Audiencia. His administration lasted until 1550 notable for encouragement of exploration, effort to suppress *encomienda* system (allotment of Indians for forced labor)

May 3, Cortés entered bay believed to be the present Santa Cruz and May 10 took formal possession of the country and established colonists in Baja California

May 31, Mendoza established a mint in Mexico City

June 27, Bishop Zumarraga appointed inquisitor

Printing press in Mexico City imported by Mendoza and given to Juan Pablos published first book, a translation of the Latin version of the Greek work of St. John Climacus, the Hermit, the "Escala espiritual parallegar al cielo," "Spiritual Ladder"

1536

Franciscans opened College of Santa Cruz de Tlaltelolco for Indian boys

1537

Oct. 27, Permission given by Queen Juana for founding and settlement of Valladolid

1539

March 7, Spanish expedition to New Mexico. *See* America

July 8, Expedition of F. de Ulloa to Lower California. *See* America

Nov. 17, Melchior Diaz left Culiacan and traveled to Cibola

1540

Expedition of Coronado into region of New Mexico. *See* America

Jan., Cortés sailed for Spain to present his claims for exploration at court where he was coldly received. He never returned

1541

The "Mixton War," rebellion of the Indians. Guadalajara founded by Juan de Onate

July 4, Death of Alvarado at Guadalajara in Mixton Indian war

1542

Nov. 20, The "New Laws" achievement of efforts of Bartholomew de Las Casas, signed by the Emperor made Indians vassals of the Crown of Castile and provided for their release from slavery unless their owners could prove a legal title, and decreed that no more should be enslaved

1544

March 24, The "New Laws" published in Mexico City by Don Tello de Sandoval sent from Spain by the Council of the Indies

1545

Oct. 20, The "New Laws" revoked at requests of colonists

1547

July 8, Papal bull made Mexico an archdiocese

Dec. 2, Death of Hernando Cortés near Seville in Spain

1548

June 3, Death of Bishop Zumarraga

June 11, Discovery of San Barnabé lode silver in Zacatecas

1550

Town of Queretaro founded

1551

July, The King ordered all Indian women and males under 14, prisoners of war, to be set free

Sept. 25, Royal cedula authorized founding of University of Mexico

Nov., Luiz D. Velasco, Viceroy arrived (1550–64)

1553

June 3, University of Mexico opened

1554

City of Santa Fé de Guanajuato founded

1562

June, Francisco de Ibarra commissioned as Governor of territory to the north of the Spanish dominions arrived at the San Juan Valley at site of later San Juan del Rio where he made fortified camp and named his province Nueva Vizcaya

1563

April 14, City of Durango founded by Alonzo Pacheco, serving under Ibarra, as capital of Nueva Vizcaya
Oct. 6, Villa of Nombre de Dios formally founded

1564

Ibarra extended his authority to the coast provinces and established the town of San Juan de Sinaloa on the Suaqui River, and crossed the mountains to the west, conquering Topia

1566

Gaston de Peralta, Viceroy (1566–68)
Unsuccessful attempt of *encomenderos* to set up Martin Cortés as king

1567

June, Ibarra ascended the Yaqui Valley, crossed the mountains eastward to river and ruined pueblo of Paquime (Casas Grandes) in northern Chihuahua
Sept. 16, Sir John Hawkins and Francis Drake driven ashore at Vera Cruz

1568

M. Enriquez de Almanza, Viceroy (1568–80)

1569

Jan. 25, Decree of Philip II established the tribunal of the Inquisition
March, Sebastian Vizcaino sailed from Acapulco for La Paz, Lower California, and left colonists. Sailed north on voyage of discovery in August
Oct. 28, Colony at La Paz abandoned. Colonists returned to Mexico with Vizcaino

1571

Nov. 11, Inquisition established in Mexico

1572

Sept. 9, 12 Jesuits under Dr. Pedro Sanchez arrived at Vera Cruz

1573

Great cathedral of Mexico City begun. Finished in 1813

1574

Feb. 28, First great auto da fé took place at Mexico City; 63 persons were punished, 5 publicly burned

1576

June 7, The excise tax, the *Alcabala*, levied 2% on all inheritances or transfers of property, on all sales, barter, or exchange of commodities between any 2 or more persons. Later increased to 6%

1579

May 31, Luis de Carabajal secured contract naming him Governor and Captain-General of kingdom of Nuevo Leon, the region north and west of Panuco, which he settled in 1580

1580

Conde de la Coruna, Viceroy (1580–83)

1581

June 6, Fra Augustin Roderiquez left San Bartolome, descended the Conchos River to the Rio Grande and up the river to New Mexico. Killed by Indians

1583

March 31, A public granary established at Mexico City by order of Philip II

1584

Pedro Moya de Contreras, Viceroy (1584–85)

1585

Oct. 18, Alvara Manrique de Zuniga, Marquis of Villamanrique, seventh Viceroy arrived in Mexico (1585–90)
Humana's expedition into New Mexico

1587

Sept., Thomas Cavendish arrived at Mazatlan and proceeded to capture Spanish galleon the "Santa Ana" commanded by Tomas de Alzola, Nov. 4 near Cape San Lucas, California

1589

The Benedictine friars came to Mexico

1590

Jan. 25, Luis de Velasco, eighth Viceroy reached Mexico City (1590–95)

1595

Conde de Monterey, Viceroy (1595–1603)
Sept. 21, Juan de Onate commissioned Governor of New Mexico

1596

March, Sebastian Vizcaino sailed from Acapulco to establish colony at La Paz, California; colony abandoned in Oct.
Sept. 20, Montemayor established Monterey as capital of Nueva Leon

1598

April 30, Onate made first Spanish settlement in New Mexico. *See* America

1603

Jan. 12, Voyage of Vizcaino along California coast to 41st parallel. *See* America
Marques de Montes Claros, Viceroy (1603–07)

1607

Oct. 23, Decree authorized draining of the valley of Mexico. Work begun Dec. 28
Luis de Velasco, Viceroy, second term (1607–11)

1611

Fray Gracia Guerra, Viceroy (1611–12)

1612

Marques Guadalcazar, Viceroy (1612–21)

1615

March 21, Juan de Iturbe in service of Tomas de Cardona sailed from Acapulco for Gulf of California, making successful search for pearls

1621

Marques de Galvez, Viceroy (1621–24)
Aug. 6, University created at Cordoba by Pope Gregory XV

1624

Marques de Cerralvo, Viceroy (1624–45)

1629

June 20, City of Mexico inundated by floods to depth of more than 3 feet; 30,000 persons said to have perished

1632

March 20, Francisco de Ortega sailed from San Pedro and June 10 entered Bay of Sacramento, California, named port of San Francisco and proceeded up the coast to Lat. 27°

1633

Oct. 7, Ortega on second voyage arrived at La Paz (Lower California) and left 28 men to establish settlement while he sailed north exploring islands

1635

Marques de Cadereyta, Viceroy (1635–40)

1636

Jan. 11–May 15, Third voyage of Ortega on which he sailed from Santa Catalina de Sinaloa to La Paz

1640

Duque de Escalona, Viceroy (1640–42)

1642

Juan de Palafox y Mendoza, Viceroy
Conde de Salvatierra, Viceroy (1642–48)

1648

Marcos Torres y Rueda, Viceroy (1648–49)

1650

Conde de Alva de Liste, Viceroy (1650–53)

1653

Duque de Alburquerque, Viceroy (1653–60)

1656

Feb. 2, First dedication of cathedral in City of Mexico before its completion

1660

Marques de Leiva, Viceroy (1660-64)

1664

D. Osorio de Escobar y Liamas, Viceroy
Marques de Mancera, Viceroy (1664–73)

1667

Dec. 22, Cathedral of Mexico City finally dedicated

1673

Duque de Veraguas, Viceroy
Fr. Payo de Rivera, Viceroy (1673–80)

1679

Gold first coined in Mexico, heretofore sent to Spain as bullion

1680

Aug. 9, Pueblo Indians of New Mexico, led by Chief Pope enslaved by Spaniards rose against them and drove settlers from the country taking possession of Santa Fé Sept. 21
Marques de la Laguna, Viceroy (1680–86)

1683

Jan. 18, Expedition of Isidro Otondo y Antillon sailed from Cacala on Sinaloa coast and landed at La Paz April 1 to found colony which was abandoned July 14. The Jesuit Father Eusebio Francisco Kino on this expedition
May 17, Pirates led by Laurent (Lorencillo) and Van Horn captured and sacked Vera Cruz. Citizens taken as hostages for ransom
Oct. 6, Otondo on second voyage arrived at bay north of La Paz and established settlement of San Bruno in Lower California about 50 miles north of La Paz on Bay of San Juan

1686

Conde de Monclova, Viceroy (1686–88)

1687

March, Father Eusebio Kino entered north Sonora and founded Dolores mission
June 4, Land law provided for survey of Indian towns, to be measured from the last house

1688

Conde de Galve, Viceroy (1688–96)

1691

May 16, Expedition of Domingo Teran de los Rios, Governor of Coahuila left Monclova with soldiers and Franciscan friars. Arrived at Colorado River June 26 and Aug. 4 at mission of San Francisco de los Tejas. Made exploration northward in Nov. and Dec. reaching the Red River

1692

Governor Diego de Vargas reoccupied Spanish missions in New Mexico and northern regions
June 8, Indian and native riot in Mexico City against the Viceroy
July 10–22, Rains brought disastrous floods to Mexico City

1693

Oct. 25, The Texas missions abandoned because of hostile Indians

1696

Juan Ortega y Montanez, Viceroy (1696–1701)

1697

Feb. 5, Spanish Viceroy granted license to Father Juan Maria Salvatierra and Father Kino to undertake conversion of the Indians of Upper and Lower California. The "Pious Fund" collected for this purpose

Oct. 10, Father Salvatierra with 6 soldiers left Yaqui and landed on the 16th at San Bruno and founded first mission in Lower California at Loreto opposite Guaxmas

1701

Juan Ortega y Montanez, Viceroy, second term (1701–02)

1702

Duque de Alburquerque, Viceroy, second term (1702–11)

1703

Oct. 22, Treasureships from Mexico under French and Spanish convoy attacked and captured off Vigo, Spain by allied enemies of Louis XIV

1711

Duque de Linares, Viceroy (1711–16)

1716

Marques de Valero, Viceroy (1716–22)

1722

Marques de Casa Fuerte, Viceroy (1722–34)
First newspaper published in Mexico, the *Gaceta de Mexico*

1724

Nov. 21–June 9, Journey of ex-Governor of Tlascala, Pedro de Rivera, from City of Mexico, of 3,082 leagues inspecting the frontier defenses of New Spain

1734

J. Antonio de Vizarron, Viceroy (1734–40)

1740

Duque de la Conquista, Viceroy (1740–41)

1742

Conde de Fuenclara, Viceroy (1742–46)

1746

Conde Revillagigedo, the Elder, Viceroy (1746–55)

1753

March 31, Royal decree proclaimed Sept. 7 established La Paz College

1755

Marques de les Amarillas, Viceroy (1755–60)

1760

Francisco Cagigal, Viceroy
Marques de Cruillas, Viceroy (1760–66)

1764

Government monopoly on tobacco established

1765

Feb. 20, José de Galvez named Visitador-General of New Spain arrived at Vera Cruz in July instructed to increase the revenues and introduce commercial reforms

1766

Marques de Croix, Viceroy (1766–71)

1767

Feb. 27, Royal decree expelled Jesuits from New Spain

June 25, Jesuits in Mexico arrested and on Oct. 24, sent in ships to Havana to reëmbark for Cadiz, the Franciscans replacing them

1768

Feb. 8, Jesuit fathers in California embarked at Loreto for Vera Cruz and Spain
March 10, Colonel Domingo Elizondo with 1,100 men disembarked at Guaymas to subdue the Indians of Sonora and Sinaloa. Made five unsuccessful attacks on mountain stronghold of Indians at Cerro Prieto during the year
April 8, Galvez left Mexico City to establish the Department of San Blas. Reached San Blas May 13 and left May 24 for Baja California where he spent 10 months reorganizing government and missions
April 13, The Franciscan fathers sent to replace the Jesuits arrived in California

1769

May 14, Mission San Fernando de Velicata founded by the Franciscans in Lat. 30° N., 115° 5′ West Long.

1771

Antonio M. Bucarelli, Viceroy (1771–79)

1773

June 22, The Dominican friars led by Father Palou and escorted by José de Ortega reached San Francisco de Borja and 11 days later arrived at San Diego in Alta California

1774

Jan. 8, Juan Bautista de Anza started on first inland expedition to California from Tubac across the San Jacinto Mountains
Jan. 24, Juan Perez sailed from San Blas for California instructed to carry supplies to Monterey and then to explore coast north and south and take possession of country whenever possible to land
June 11, Voyage of Juan Perez to Nootka Sound. *See* America

1775

March 16–Oct. 7, Voyage of Heceta to North Pacific. *See* America
July 27, Ayala left Monterey and on Aug. 5 sent José Canizares into San Francisco Bay and also made entrance himself, the first white man by way of the Golden Gate, and made thorough exploration of Bay
Oct. 23, Anza led colonists from Tubac to Monterey, reaching San Gabriel Jan. 4, 1776, and Monterey, March 10, San Francisco, March 23, and himself proceeded to San Francisco Bay to select sites for presidio and mission
Nov. 4, The San Diego Mission attacked by Indians and partly destroyed

1776

Feb. 25, Monte de Piedad, first bank begun as a charity pawnshop, opened in Mexico City
March 24, Father Garces reached San Gabriel by Mojava River and through Cajon Pass
April 9, Father Garces left San Gabriel in attempt to reach Monterey by interior route. Through Tejon Pass reached the Moqui July 2 and by San Joaquin Valley to Lake Tulare and recrossed desert to Mojaves on Colorado River reached July 25
July 29, Exploring expedition of Fathers Domininguez

and Escalante, Capt. Bernardo de Miera y Pacheco with 9 soldiers left Santa Fé and marched to Colorado across the San Juan, Dolores, Grand, and Colorado rivers, west to Utah Lake and south past Sevier Lake. In October they returned by Moqui, Zuni, and Santa Fé. *See also* United States

Aug. 22, Decree provided that provinces of New Spain should be under control of a commandant-general independent of the Viceroy

1778

Oct. 12, Ordinance of Charles III extended to 13 ports the right of trade with New Spain

1779

Feb. 11–Nov. 21, Voyage of Captain Ignacio Arteaga and Quadra northward from San Blas along Pacific coast

Martin de Mayorga, Viceroy (1779–83)

1781

July 17, Yuma Indian massacre at Conception and San Pablo California. Lieut.-Governor Rivera killed with all the men including Father Garces. The women and children carried off into slavery by Yuma Indians

Sept. 4, Pueblo of Los Angeles founded by Governor Neve in Upper California

Nov. 5, National School of Fine Arts opened

1783

May 22, Royal decree established school for teaching of metallurgical subjects, the later School of Mines

——, Ordinance of Charles III of Spain established mining code which went into effect 1784 and remained authoritative mining law until 1884

Matfas de Galvez, Viceroy (1783–84)

1785

Bernardo de Galvez, Viceroy (1785–86)

1786

Nov. 30, Death of Viceroy Galvez

1787

May–Aug., Alonzo Nunez de Haro, Viceroy

Manuel Antonio Flores, Viceroy (1787–89)

1789

Feb. 17, Estevan Martinez sailed from San Blas and reached Nootka Sound May 5 claimed by Spain in view of discovery by Heceta in 1775. *See also* Canada

Oct., New Viceroy arrived, Juan Vicente de Guemes Pacheco de Padilla, count de Revillagigedo (1789–94)

1790

March 17, Canal turning surplus drainage of valley of Mexico into the Panuco River completed

Sept. 17, Aztec calendar stone excavated in City of Mexico weighing 24 tons. Placed in wall of Cathedral

1792

Jan. 1, School of Mines opened in Mexico City

Nov. 3, National University of Guadalajara inaugurated

1794

Marques de Branciforte, Viceroy (1794–98)

1798

Miguel de Azanza, Viceroy (1798–1800)

1800

F. Berenguer de Marquina, Viceroy (1800–03)

1803

Jan., Alexander Humboldt and Bonpland landed at Acapulco and remained until 1804 making city of Mexico headquarters and exploring the country as far as Guanajuato in the north, Jorullo in the west, and to Jalapa

J. de Iturigaray, Viceroy (1803–08)

1806

Dec., First opera in Mexico "The Barber of Seville" by Paesiello

1808

Aug. 9, Junta of leading citizens proclaimed that until restoration of Ferdinand VII they would obey no orders of French emperor

Sept. 15, Viceroy Iturigaray seized by Spaniards led by Yermo, leader of natives working for independence. General Pedro de Garibay made Viceroy (1808–09)

1809

July 19, Francisco Javier Lizana, Viceroy (1809–May 8, 1810)

1810

Sept. 16, Don Miguel Hidalgo y Costilla, parish priest of Dolores, began the revolt of Mexicans against Spanish government with Allende as second in command

Sept. 19, Hidalgo and Captain Ignacio Allende summoned town of Celaya to surrender and entered city

Sept. 24, Representatives of New Spain met for first time with the Spanish *Cortes;* presented statement of grievances of the American colonies Dec. 16

Sept. 28, The City of Guanajuato, capital of the Intendancy, taken in battle by Hidalgo and Allende. All the Spaniards killed and city burned and looted

Oct. 17, Valladolid taken by Hidalgo

Oct. 30, Marching toward Mexico City Hidalgo defeated royalist forces under General Torcuato Trujillo in Battle of Monte de las Cruces

Oct., The priest, José Maria Morelos y Pavon, sent by Hidalgo to carry revolution to the south and seize Acapulco as seaport, began operations in Guerrero

Nov. 6, General Felix M. Calleja checked Hidalgo at Acapulco

Francisco J. Venegas, Viceroy (1810–13)

1811

Jan. 17, Calleja defeated Hidalgo's forces on banks of the Lerma at Bridge of Calderon near Guadalajara. Allende now given command above Hidalgo, led retreat

Jan. 21, Calleja entered Guadalajara

Feb. 17, Spanish Colonel Soto repulsed and mortally wounded in attack on Morelos at Izucar

Feb. 21, The rebels under Allende captured by treachery of one of their own number, Ignacio Elizondo at the wells called Acatita de Bajan

March 21, Hidalgo captured

April 15, City of Zacetas recaptured by Ignacio Lopez Rayon in command of remainder of rebels

May 7, Trial of Hidalgo begun

June 26, Allende, Aldama, and Jimenez put to death

July 31, Hidalgo faced the firing squad at Chihuahua. Leadership taken by José Maria Morelos y Pavon, priest of Caracuaro, State of Michoacan

Aug. 19, Revolutionists convened at Zitacuaro by Rayon announced establishment of a supreme national junta of 3 men, the "National Supreme Junta of America for the conservation of the rights of Ferdinand VII . . ."

Aug. 20, Morelos captured Chilapa in Guerrero

Dec. 17, Morelos repulsed royalist attack at Zucar

Dec. 25, Morelos entered Cuautla without resistance

1812

Jan. 1, Zitacuaro fell before attack of General Calleja

Feb. 19–May 2, Morelos besieged by General Calleja at Cuautla. Made successful evacuation of town in brilliant retreat

Feb. 22, Spanish troops commanded by Llano repulsed in attack on Izucar

March 18–19, Rebels took rich town of Huamantla which they sacked and abandoned March 20

May 28, Royalists captured Orizaba

Sept. 28, New Constitution of March 18 published by edict in Mexico

Oct. 5, Liberty of the press proclaimed, a decree of the Spanish *Cortes* of Nov. 10, 1810

Oct. 29, Morelos captured Orizaba

Nov. 25, Morelos captured Oxaca. General Saravia captured and shot by Independents

1813

Feb. 13, Felix M. Calleja del Rey, Viceroy (1813–16)

March 12, Capture of Cerro del Gallo, evacuated by Rayon, by royalists under Castillo

April 12, Morelos captured Acapulco after siege of 6 days

June 10, Ferdinand's restoration celebrated in Spain

Aug. 20, Morelos captured Castle of San Diego, Acapulco

Sept. 14, First Mexican Congress of the insurgents met at Chilpancingo. Morelos elected General-in-Chief with powers of chief executive

Nov. 6, Mexican Congress issued declaration of independence, decreed emancipation of slaves, and adopted a set of laws

Dec. 22, Morelos routed in attempt to recapture Valladolid by Augustin de Iturbide

1814

Jan. 5, The revolutionists routed by Llano and Iturbide

Feb. 3, Matamoros, lieutenant of Morelos, defeated and captured at Puruaran

April 15, Don Miguel Brava captured and shot at Puebla

May 1, Galeana, insurgent leader, defeated and killed at Coyuce

Aug. 16, Decree of Valencia of May 4, by which Ferdinand VII proclaimed his intention of disregarding the Constitution of 1812 and decrees of the liberal *Cortes* published in Mexico

Oct. 22, The first Mexican Constitution, called the "Apatzingan Constitution" from name of place where insurgent Congress met, promulgated. Created a republic and vested executive power in 3 persons

1815

Sept. 16, Royal order reëstablished the Inquisition, set up Jan. 21, 1815

Nov. 5, Morelos escorting Congress toward Tehuacan overtaken, defeated, and captured by royalist troops

Dec. 15, Congress dissolved by Manuel de Mier y Teran as not having been sanctioned by popular election. A provisional executive commission substituted of which he was a member

Dec. 22, Morelos executed by firing squad at San Cristobal Ecatepec, a hamlet near the capital

1816

June 15, Mina defeated the royalists in battle near San Luis Potosi

Sept. 19, Juan Ruiz de Apodaca, Viceroy assumed office (1816–21)

Nov., Insurgent leader Mier y Teran defeated by General Samaniego

1817

April 15, Francisco Javier Mina, Spanish adventurer from England, arrived at port of Sota la Morena with men he had recruited in the United States to aid the Mexican revolution

Oct. 27, Mina after several unimportant victories was captured at ranch called El Venadito in the intendancy of Guanajuato

Nov. 11, Mina executed

Dec. 1, Nicolas Bravo, insurgent, defeated at the hill of Coporo

Dec. 22, Nicolas Bravo, Ignacio Rayon, and Verduzco, members of the first insurgent junta captured

1818

Jan. 1, Fort of Los Remedios the stronghold of the revolution in Guanajuato captured

1819

Feb. 22, Treaty of Spain with the United States. *See* United States. Boundary between Texas and Louisiana established

May 19, The Jesuits reinstated in Mexico under royal decree of Sept. 17, 1815

June, Rebellion in Texas. *See* United States

1820

Feb. 22, Inquisition abolished

May 3, The Viceroy proclaimed the Constitution of 1812 restored by Ferdinand

Nov. 20, Iturbide at head of royalist forces set out from Mexico to meet Vicente Guerrero in command of the insurgents

1821

Jan., Jesuits again expelled under decree of Spanish *Cortes* of Aug. 17, 1820

Jan. 10, Iturbide in conference with the patriot, Guerrero, proposed agreement on plan for independence of Spain

Jan. 17, Government granted land in Texas to Moses Austin for American colony

Feb. 24, The "Plan of Igula" proclaimed. Signed by Iturbide and Guerrero it established an independent limited monarchy in Mexico with equality of all races

March 29, The garrison of Vera Cruz commanded by Captain Antonio Lopez de Santa Anna proclaimed adherence to Iturbide's plan

May 22, Iturbide entered Valladolid which declared for his cause

June 28, Queretaro taken by Iturbide

July 6, Apodaca, the Viceroy, forced by adherents of Iturbide to resign. General Novella made Viceroy

July 30, The last Viceroy, Juan O'Donoju, arrived at Vera Cruz and presently joined the party of Iturbide

Aug. 24, Iturbide and O'Donoju signed the Treaty of Cordoba, which included the Plan de Iguala, and provided that in case no Spanish aspirant to throne the crown should go to "such person as the Imperial *Cortes* may designate"

Sept. 27, Iturbide made triumphal entrance into Mexico City, the capital. ". . . Independence, proclaimed the 16th of Sept. 1810, and completed the 27th of Sept. 1821"

Sept. 28, A Provisional Government signed act of independence and appointed a Regency of 5 with Iturbide President

Oct. 8, Death of former Viceroy, O'Donoju

Nov. 22, Law suppressed all imposts established on mining by the Spanish government

Dec. 7, Circular of the Secretary of the Colonies, Ramon Pelegrin, disavowed the Treaty of Cordoba

Dec. 15, Provisional tariff law prohibited entry of tobacco, raw cotton, manufactured wax, spun cotton of certain definite numbers, some breadstuffs, and other manufactured articles and imposed 25% duty on imports from foreign countries

1822

Jan., The Regency negotiated a loan of 1,500,000 pesos of which about $1/3$ was obtained by levy on the Cathedral chapters, and a certain portion by forced levy on designated persons

Feb. 13, Decree of Spanish *Cortes* declared the Treaty of Cordoba null and void and that recognition of independence of any Spanish colony by a foreign power would be considered an act of hostility to Spain

Feb. 24, Constitution gave foreigners the same civil rights as Mexicans

——, Congress of Mexico including Guatemala, met

April 11–May 18, Second Regency

April 29, Earliest diplomatic Act recognized independence of Colombian Republic

May 18, A popular clamor for Iturbide as Emperor staged by the army

May 19, Mexican Congress summoned and Iturbide elected Emperor by Assembly which did not constitute a legal quorum

May 21, Iturbide took oath of office

June 11, Constituent Congress authorized forced loan of 600,000 pesos upon tribunals of commerce of Mexico City, Puebla, Vera Cruz, and Guadalajara

June 25, Congress authorized foreign loan of 25 to 30 million pesos; not successful in London

July 25, Iturbide crowned Emperor as Augustin I

Sept., Augustin I proclaimed Emperor in Central America

Sept. 25, José M. Zozaya appointed Minister to the United States by the Emperor

Oct. 31, Emperor Augustin I dissolved the Congress which opposed him and established a Junta

Dec. 2, General Santa Anna at Vera Cruz headed a movement against Augustin I for a republic

Dec. 12, The United States recognized the independence of Mexico. Secretary Adams presented Mexican

charge d'affaires, José M. Zozaya, to President Monroe

1823

Jan. 4, National colonization law enacted and regulations as to all land grants; suspended in April

Feb. 1, Proclamation of Plan de Casa Mata signed by Santa Anna, Guadalupe Victoria, and other Republicans pledging the army to support the Assembly, demanding a republic, a constituent congress, and a constitution

March 19, Iturbide abdicated his throne and offered to go into voluntary banishment. The Marques of Vivanco assumed executive office

March 27, The "Army of the Republic" entered the capital

April 7, Congress decreed the coronation of Augustin I illegal and all acts of the imperial government null and void

May 1, Congress authorized new foreign loan of 8,000,-000 pesos

May 11, Iturbide sailed from Vera Cruz banished by Congress to Italy. Arrived at Leghorn Aug. 2

May 31, Congress vested executive power in military triumvirate, Generals Nicolas Bravo, Guadulupe Victoria, and Pedro C. Negret, and decreed that delegates should be chosen to a constitutional congress

Aug. 18, New colonization law enacted regulated immigration to Texas

Sept. 25, Spanish garrison at San Juan de Ulloa, the only post in Mexico in possession of Spain, opened fire on Vera Cruz

Oct. 1, Declaration of war against Spain

Oct. 3, Treaty with Colombia concluded

Oct. 14, First decree as to colonization opened lands of new province to be formed out of Acayucan and Tehuantepec to settlement by natives and foreigners

Oct. 27, Mexican Congress decreed the suspension of the provisions which required foreigners to be naturalized or "tolerated" with express license from the Government to acquire property and work their own mines

Nov. 7, Constituent Congress assembled

Dec. 23, Supreme Court founded

1824

Jan. 8, San Luis Potosi, Vera Cruz, and Guanajuato became States of the Federation

Jan. 31, Fundamental Law of 36 Articles adopted by Congress, the "basis of the future political constitution"

——, Congress approved loan proposed by English consul, Robert Staples, of 1,500,000 pesos in London

——, Oaxaca became a State of the Federation

Feb. 7, Loan of £1,600,000 (8,000,000 pesos) contracted for with London house of Goldschmidt; approved by Congress May 14

April 28, Congress passed decree of outlawry against Iturbide

May 7, Nuevo Leon and Coahuila which included Texas became States of the Federation

May 11, Iturbide sailed from England for America, planning to save his country from foreign enemies planning to reconquer the Spanish colonies

May 22, Durango became a State of the Federation

July 6, Chihuahua became State of the Federation

July 13, Congress forbade African slave trade and further introduction of slaves by immigration

July 15, Iturbide landed at Soto la Marina, was immediately arrested

July 19, Iturbide executed

Aug. 18, First colonization law enacted offered foreigners security in their persons and property provided they subjected themselves to the laws of the country

Aug. 25, Contract signed for loan to Mexico by London firm of Barclay, Herring, Richardson, and Company for £3,200,000 at 6%

Oct. 4, Constitution proclaimed by Congress established a federal republic for Mexico similar to that of the United States and erected provinces into states

——, Mexico, Jalisco, Colima, Michoacan, Puebla, Queretaro, Sinaloa, Sonora Tabasco, Tamaulipas, Zacatecas, and Yucatan became States of the Federation

Oct. 10, First President of the republic, General Guadalupe Victoria took oath of office, General Nicolas Bravo, Vice-President

Nov. 12, Chiapas became State of the Federation

Nov. 18, Federal District formed with Mexico City as capital

——, Pablo Obregon presented his credentials at Washington

Dec. 24, Constituent Congress dissolved

1825

Jan. 1, First constitutional Congress convened in Mexico City

——, Formal recognition of Mexico decided on at British Cabinet meeting of Dec. 14, 1824 communicated to diplomatic corps and to the public 2 days later

June 1, First American minister, J. R. Poinsett received by President Victoria

Sept. 16, President Victoria liberated the slaves with fund collected for that purpose. Not fully carried out

Nov. 18, José Coppinger forced by siege to surrender fort at San Juan de Ulloa (Vera Cruz) to Mexicans. The Spanish garrison allowed to depart with honors of war

1826

May 20, Law abolished the Tribunal of Mining

Aug. 27, Decree permitted establishment of commercial relations with foreign countries on basis of reciprocity

Dec. 26, Treaty between Great Britain and Mexico signed at London of amity, commerce, and navigation

1827

May 9, Convention of commerce with France concluded

June 15, Treaty of commerce and navigation with the Netherlands concluded

July 19, Treaty of friendship, navigation, and commerce with Denmark signed

Nov. 16, New tariff of maritime duties reduced import duties on certain articles and diminished number of prohibited articles to 56. Rates in general high. Importation of raw cotton and yarn prohibited

Nov. 21, Local loan authorized by Congress

Dec. 20, Congress enacted a decree that all Spaniards should be expelled from Mexico

Dec. 23, Plan of Montano proclaimed at Otumba in revolt headed by Nicolas Bravo

1828

Jan. 7, General Bravo, Vice-President and leader of political party of the *Escooés*, the Scotch Free-

Masons, defeated and made prisoner in battle with General Guerrero, leader of the Yorkinos or York Free-Masons

Jan. 12, Treaty with the United States fixed boundary; not ratified by Mexico

Feb. 14, Treaty of amity, commerce, and navigation with the United States; not ratified

March 21, General regulations as to colonization issued

Sept. 1, Gomez Pedraza received votes of 10 out of 19 State Legislatures for president

Sept. 10, Death of Pablo Obregon, Mexican Chargé d'Affaires at Washington, D.C. José Montoya acted *ad interim* until Feb. 16, 1830

Nov. 30, Revolt led by Loballo and Zavalla seized capital

1829

Jan. 12, Congress declared the election of General Manuel Gomez Pedraza as President null and void and elected Guerrero (Yorkino) President and Anastasio Bustamante Vice-President

April 1, General Vicente Guerrero took oath as President

May 22, New customs tariff prohibited entry of cotton goods

July 6, Spanish expedition for reconquest of Mexico sailed from Havana, Cuba. They landed July 27

Aug. 18, Spaniards entered Tampico evacuated by the citizens

Sept. 11, Santa Anna and Teran forced the Spanish troops commanded by Barradas to capitulate on Panuco River after battle in which both sides had heavy losses

Sept. 15, Decree of total abolition of slavery in Mexico signed by President Guerrero, exception the Isthmus of Tehuantepec, and Texas excepted Dec. 2

Dec. 4, At Jalapa Vice-President Bustamante headed a successful revolt under pretence of restoring Constitution and laws

Dec. 15, Pedraza renounced claim to presidency

Dec. 16, José M. Bocanegra chosen acting President

Dec. 22, Quintanar ousted Bocanegra and placed Pedro Velez, Chief Justice, in executive office pending installation of Bustamante

Dec. 25, Guerrero fled to his estate in the south near Tixtla

——, J. Poinsett recalled by letter of Dec. 9 left Mexico. Succeeded as envoy from the United States by Anthony Butler

1830

Jan. 1, Anastasio Bustamante assumed the executive office at Acapulco

Feb. 16, José M. Tornel, Mexican representative at Washington, D.C. presented his credentials

April 6, Law encouraged colonization by Mexicans in Texas and made regulations as to settlement which checked immigration from the United States; negro slavery prohibited

Aug. 24, Tariff law increased duties on "clothes, fruits and goods from abroad" and liquors

Dec. 30, Treaty by which Santa Anna sold the Mesilla Valley to the United States

First stage line established between Vera Cruz and the City of Mexico over the Jalapa route by 3 Americans from New England whose names are not known

1831

Jan. 1–2, Forces of Guerrero and Alvarez routed by General Bravo near Chilpancingo

Feb. 14, Guerrero captured by treachery in January was executed at Cuilapa

Feb. 18, Treaty of commerce and navigation concluded with Prussia

March 7, Treaty of friendship, commerce, and navigation concluded with Chile

April 5, Sept. 17, and Dec. 17, Treaties of limits, and of amity, commerce, and navigation concluded with the United States; proclaimed April 5, 1832

1832

Jan. 2, Revolt of the garrison of Vera Cruz demanded reorganization of Ministry. Santa Anna accepted leadership

March 3, Santa Anna defeated by ministerial forces at Tolome retreated to Vera Cruz

April 12–May 13, Siege of Santa Anna at Vera Cruz by Calderon unsuccessful

May 7, Law on patents enacted

Aug. 3, Rebels under Moctezuma defeated the government force under Colonel Mariano Otero and occupied San Luis Potosi

Aug. 14, General Melchor Musquiz took office with title of president ad interim

Sept. 18, Bustamente defeated forces of Moctezuma at Puerto del Gallinero

Sept. 19, Bustamente resigned as executive in favor of Gomez Pedraza

Sept. 30, Bustamente reoccupied San Luis Potosi

Nov. 16, Treaty of amity, commerce, and navigation with Persia concluded

Dec. 5, Bustamente defeated in battle of Posadas by Santa Anna

Dec. 23, Peace treaty signed which recognized Gomez Pedraza as President until April 1, 1833

Dec. 26, Pedraza took oath of office as President at Puebla serving remaining 3 months of term which he should legally have begun in 1829

1833

April 1, Santa Anna, elected President and Valentin Gomez Farias, Vice-President assumed office

1834

April 24, Santa Anna assumed the presidency. He had allowed Farias to act as President until this date

May 31, Santa Anna dissolved Congress and made himself dictator with a Council composed of Clericals and Centralists

1835

Jan. 4, Congress met

Jan. 28, Santa Anna retired from the presidency leaving General Miguel Barragan in charge of his office

Oct. 3, Congress decreed abolition of the federal system and established centralized government, the States became Departments

Rebellion of Texas. See United States

Dec. 15, Constitutional law promulgated

1836

Feb. 27, José Justo Corro chosen to be Acting-President during illness of President Barragan

March 1, Death of President Barragan from a fever

March 2, A Convention of Texans declared independence of Mexico. See United States

March 6, Siege and capture of the fortress of the Alamo, Texas by Santa Anna and massacre of the garrison

April 21, Texans defeated and captured Santa Anna in battle of San Jacinto

May 14, Agreement made by Santa Anna with the United States. See United States

July 29, Mexican Congress issued a manifesto repudiating the agreement of Velasco made by Santa Anna with the United States May 14

Sept. 19, Law enacted attached endowment for disposal of "Pious Fund"

Sept. 26, Written demands of claims against Mexican government by the United States presented by American envoy. See also United States, Dec. 7

Oct. 15, Gorostiza demanded his passports from the United States because of instructions to Gen. Gaines to advance into Mexico if necessary to protect Texans from Indians

Dec. 7 and 22, Powhatan Ellis, American minister, demanded his passports

Dec. 28, Spain recognized the independence of Mexico. The treaty published in Mexico City March 4, 1838

Dec. 29, Centralist constitution promulgated known as the "Siete Leyes" because of its seven separate but correlated laws

1837

March 11, Tariff law permitted importation of many articles forbidden in 1830

April 5, A second decree declared slavery abolished with compensation to owners

April 12, President Corro decreed issue of warrants at 5 shillings an acre giving title to vacant lands in Texas, Chihuahua, New Mexico, Sonora, and the Californias in order to reduce foreign debt and colonize land

April 19, Bustamente took oath as President

July 10–17, General Nicolas Bravo acted as President

Aug. 22, First charter for Mexico City to Vera Cruz railroad

1838

April 16, French blockade of ports of Mexico begun by French squadron demanding payment of claims of French citizens for property damaged in wars, about $600,000. Called the "Pastry War" because of claim of French baker whose wares had attracted the mob in a revolutionary uprising

Sept. 10, Convention between Mexico and the United States agreed that claims against Mexico should be referred to mixed commission with king of Prussia as umpire. Renewed April 11, 1839. See United States

Oct. 7, Rising of federalists at Tampico headed by General Urrea from Sonora

Nov. 27, French ships bombarded San Juan de Ulloa. Capitulated and occupied by the French Nov. 28

1839

Feb. 4, General Paredes checked federalist uprising at the hacienda de Santa Cruz in Guadalajara

March 9, Treaty and convention with France signed by which Mexico agreed to pay $600,000 and give French citizens privileges of most favored nation

March 18, Santa Anna assumed control as provisional president

April 7, San Juan de Ulloa surrendered by the French and fleet retired

April 11, Claims convention concluded with the United States; proclaimed April 8, 1840

May 3, General Valencia defeated the federalists at Acajete

June 4, General Escalada surrendered Tampico to government forces in absence of General Urrea

June 6, Federalists in Yucatan captured Campeche

July 10, Nicolas Bravo took oath as substitute President

Dec. 19, Angel Calderon de la Barca, first minister to Mexico from Spain, arrived at Vera Cruz

1840

July 15, President Bustamente captured in the palace by federalist General Urrea

July 26, Government accorded a capitulation to federalists, ending civil war

1841

Aug. 8, General Paredes started revolution against the Government

Aug. 25–Feb. 25, 1842, Mixed Claims Commission met in Washington

Aug. 31, Valencia joined the revolution

Sept. 22, Don Javier Escheverria installed as Acting President

Sept. 28, Santa Anna joined successful revolution against President Bustamente and proclaimed the Plan of Tacubaya reorganizing the Government

Oct. 1, Legislature of Yucatan passed resolution declaring Yucatan a free and independent republic

Oct. 10–Dec. 6, 1844, Santa Anna, as President ruled as dictator either directly or by substitutes of his own choosing

1842

March 1, Concession granted for Tehuantepec National Railway

March 11, Decree more extensive than previous ones permitted foreigners to acquire property subject to Mexican laws and with consent of Government as to land on frontiers

April 30, New tariff law increased list of prohibited articles

May 21, Concession of Santa Anna granted for railroad from Vera Cruz to Rio de San Juan (Vera Cruz). Only 3 miles completed in 7 years when taken over by Government (Mexican Railway)

July 30, Treaty of friendship, commerce, and navigation concluded with Austria-Hungary

Aug., First steamers built in London for Mexican Government arrived at Vera Cruz

Oct. 2, Circular declared that foreign partners of companies, discoverers of mines, or restorers of abandoned ones, even though absent from the Republic preserved their property therein

Oct. 15, Convention concluded for benefit of British subjects to whom Mexican government acknowledged liability of 306,931,440 pesos on account of various claims

Oct. 26–March 5, 1843, General Nicolas Bravo, substitute President

Dec. 11, Pronouncement against the Congress started at town of Huejotzingo spread through country which resulted in dissolving of that body on the 19th

1843

Jan. 6, Congress of centralists installed began work on new constitution

Jan. 30, Claims convention with the United States signed

Feb. 28, A bonded warehouse established at Acapulco with reduction of duties on goods imported through it

June 12, New Constitution proclaimed providing for centralized government, the "Bases Organicas" consolidated constitutional laws of 1836 into one instrument

June 21, Decree of Santa Anna gave permission to Jesuit order to return to Mexico

July 14, Decree directed expulsion of Americans from Sonora, California, but withdrawn

Aug. 23, Mexican Government announced that it would consider the annexation of Texas by the United States equal to a declaration of war

Sept. 23, Tariff increased duties. All articles not rated in classifications paid 30%

Oct. 12–June 4, 1844, General Valentin Canalizo, substitute President

Nov. 3, Note of Gen. Almonte stated that annexation of Texas would be considered aggression

Dec. 15, Yucatan reincorporated with Mexico

Nov. 20, Claims Convention with the United States signed; not ratified by American Senate

1844

Jan. 2, Congress declared Santa Anna elected President

Sept. 1, Wilson Shannon, American Minister, succeeding W. Thompson received

Sept. 12–Sept. 21, General José Joaquin de Herrera, Acting President

Sept. 21–Dec. 6, General Valentin Canalizo Acting President

Nov. 2, Paredes at Guadalajara issued manifesto against Government of Santa Anna calling for his suspension from office and examination of his acts by Congress

Nov. 25, Santa Anna reached Queretaro, marching to subdue rebellion

Dec. 5, José Joaquin Herrera made President, deposing Canalizo, Santa Anna's substitute President

1845

Jan. 2, Santa Anna began unsuccessful attack on Puebla which ended in retreat

Jan. 12, Paredes and Alvarez entered Puebla

Jan. 15, Santa Anna captured while trying to escape to the coast

Feb. 24, Grand jury of Congress declared for impeachment of Santa Anna

March 1, Joint resolution of American Congress for annexation of Texas signed by President Tyler

March 6, Gen. Almonte, protested action of United States Congress, and asked for his passports

March 28, American Minister in Mexico notified diplomatic relations severed

March 29, Treaty with Texas signed by which independence to be recognized on condition of pledge against American annexation

May 19, Treaty with Texas of March 29 accepted by Mexican Government

May 24, Decree of amnesty included Santa Anna, and Canalizo on condition they leave the country

June 3, Santa Anna embarked for Havana

June 21, Texan Senate rejected Treaty with Mexico of March 29

July 4, Convention of Texas accepted terms offered by the United States for annexation

Sept. 16, Herrera formally inaugurated as President

Oct. 4, Tariff enacted which forbade the importation of sugar, flour, lard, molasses, rice, coffee, tobacco, raw cotton, &c., 62 articles. Duties increased

Dec. 14, Army of the reserve at San Luis Potosi made ₁ pronunciamento against the Government instead of obeying orders to march to Texas

Dec. 21, John Slidell, commissioner from the United States, officially notified by Herrera Government that he would not be granted an audience

Dec. 30, The revolution proclaimed in the (Citadel) Ciudadela by General Valencia, President Herrera surrendered the Government

1846

Jan. 1, Yucatan again seceded from Mexico

Jan. 4, General Mariano Paredes y Arrillaga installed as President

April 25, Hostilities begun against the United States by General A. Torrejon by attack and capture of American dragoons commanded by Captain Thornton

May 7, Revolution proclaimed in Mazatlan by Colonel Rafael Tellez

May 13, War declared against Mexico by the United States. For Mexican War *see* United States

May 20, Plan de la Guadalajara published by the garrison under leader General José Maria Yanez

Aug. 4, Plan de la Ciudadela announced. Paredes Government overthrown by revolution led by General José Mariano de Salas who deposed Vice-President Bravo, acting as executive Aug. 6. Paredes captured in flight

Aug. 16, Santa Anna landed at Vera Cruz, allowed to pass by the American blockading squadron

Aug. 22, Constitution of 1824 restored

Sept. 14, Santa Anna entered Mexico City

Sept. 17, Santa Anna given command of the army and with 3,000 men left the capital for San Luis Potosi Sept. 28 arriving Oct. 8

Nov. 2, Yucatan reincorporated in Mexico

Dec. 23, Santa Anna chosen President *ad interim*, Gomez Farias, Vice-President assuming executive authority in his absence

1847

Jan. 11, Executive decree provided that the Government should obtain $15,000,000 by mortgaging or selling at auction property held in mortmain except certain educational and charitable institutions

March 9, General Winfield Scott landed American troops 3 miles from Vera Cruz

March 22, President Santa Anna resumed executive office

March 29, Fort San Juan de Ulloa (Vera Cruz) captured by General Winfield Scott, beseiged since March 22

April 2, General Pedro Maria Anaya named substitute President assumed office held until return of Santa Anna May 20

April 15, Nicholas P. Trist appointed commissioner by the United States to conclude treaty of peace with Mexico

May 18, Congress assembled by General Salas passed acts of reform

——, Guerrero became a State of the Federation

May 21, Santa Anna published the *Acta Constitutiva y de Reformas*

Sept. 14, City of Mexico occupied by General Scott

Sept. 16, Santa Anna resigned the presidency

Sept. 26, General Manuel de la Pena assumed office as Provisional President

Oct. 7, Santa Anna deposed as commander oɪ arɪɪy and ordered before court of inquiry

Oct. 20, N. P. Trist, American Commissioner, reopened negotiations

Nov. 11, Pena y Pena appointed Minister of Foreign Affairs by Anaya

Nov. 14, General Anaya made Acting President

1848

Jan. 8–June 2, Manuel de la Pena y Pena, President, and Rosa appointed Minister of Foreign Affairs

Feb. 2, Treaty signed at Guadalupe Hidalgo ended war with the United States. Texas relinquished by Mexico, and American conquest of California and New Mexico acknowledged. Claims against Mexico antedating treaty relinquished. $15,000,000 paid by the United States for territory taken. Territory south of the Rio Grande restored to Mexico

April 5, Santa Anna left Mexico, going to Jamaica

April 23, Peace Treaty signed between Indians and Whites in Yucatan

May 3, Duties reduced to 60% by tariff law

May 4, Treaty of Feb. 2 with the United States accepted by Congress

June 3, General José Joaquin de Herrera elected President assumed office, the second Federalist régime

June 11, Last American troops left Mexico

June 12, Paredes leading new revolution with Governor Cosio and Padre Cenobio Jarauta left Aguascalientes and marched on Guanajuato deposing Governor

July 19, Guanajuato surrendered as Jarauta taken prisoner in assault of July 18 and shot. Paredes and the other leaders escaped and fled the country

1849

Feb., General Leonardo Marquez in command of troops engaged in subduing rebel Indians in the Sierra Gorda announced plan in favor of Santa Anna but revolt reduced by General Bustamente

April 4, Tariff law enacted

May 18, Congress authorized the President to grant concession for railroad from Vera Cruz to Mexico City

Nov. 24, Decree lowered all duties 40%

1850

June 22, Convention signed with the United States to open canal across isthmus of Tehuantepec. Failed because it gave United States permission to send troops to guard construction

July 20, Federal Government made provision for special guard on frontier to prevent smuggling from the United States and to enforce tariff

Sept. 20, Expedition of José M. Carvajal with force of Mexicans and Americans took Camargo

Oct. 20, Carvajal began siege of Matamoros. Retired defeated after 11 days

1851

Jan. 15, General Mariano Arista inaugurated President, the first peaceful transfer of executive authority from a constitutional President to his constitutionally elected successor

Jan. 21, Claims Convention with France concluded

April 5, Tariff Act prohibited importation of sugar

Nov. 14 and Dec. 6, Diplomatic conventions signed with Spain provided for adjustment of claims of Spanish subjects

Dec. 4, "Doyle" Convention signed with England for adjustment of claims for damages

Dec. 5, Padre-Moran claims Convention with Spain signed

1851

Dec. 10 and 17, Convention signed with France as to monetary claims

Dec., The first telegram transmitted between Mexico and Puebla

1852

Feb. 21, José M. Carvajal made unsuccessful attack on Camargo; returned to exile in the United States

July 26, Revolt under the "Plan del Hospicio" begun in Guadalajara which spread over the country. José Maria Blancarte seized palace

Sept. 15, Plan formally issued to recall Santa Anna

Dec. 9, Supplement to Doyle Convention signed

1853

Jan. 5, Arista compelled by revolution resigned as President

Jan. 6, Judge Juan Bautista Ceballos took oath as President *ad interim*

Jan. 24, Ceballos tariff moderated provisions of law

Feb. 4, New plan agreed upon by General Robles in charge of government troops acting in Guadalajara and Governor Ledo, Governor of Guadalajara

Feb. 7, Ceballos resigned the presidency

March 17, Assembly declared Santa Anna *ad interim* President

April 15, Santa Anna inaugurated elected President

April 22, Santa Anna published the *Bases para la Administracion de la Republica*

May 30, Juarez imprisoned in Castle of San Juan de Ulloa at Vera Cruz by Santa Anna

June 1, List of prohibited articles reduced to 53 by new tariff. Merchandise not named in fixed rates paid 20%

June 10, Convention for adjustment of claims with France signed

Nov. 4, William Walker, American filibuster, landed at La Paz, Lower California and proclaimed republic

Nov. 12, Convention for adjustment of claims of Spain signed

Dec. 16, Santa Anna proclaimed himself Perpetual Dictator

Dec. 30, Treaty known in Mexico as sale of the Mesilla Valley for $10,000,000 (Gadsen Treaty) to United States concluded

1854

Jan. 24, Decree defined foreign diplomatic privileges

Jan. 30, Decree on foreign citizenship and nationality declared decree of March 11, 1842 in force on acquisition of real estate by foreigners except in cases in which by treaties any of its dispositions modified

Feb. 16, Law offered land and pecuniary help to European immigrants

Feb. 20, Revolt of Juan Alvarez begun in the south

March 1, The "Plan de Ayutla" by Colonel Villareal announced in Guerrero; modified on the 11th. The removal of Santa Anna demanded and a Congress to frame a federal constitution

March 11, Plan of Ayutla amended in Acapulco

April 20, Santa Anna with 7,000 men made unsuccessful attempt to take Acapulco held by Comonfort

May 16, Commercial Code issued

July 15, Concession granted for railroad from Presidio del Norte to Guaymas

1855

April 28, Tariff law established payment of 15% import duties in bonds of the foreign debt. Repealed Oct. 17

June 25, The "Ley Lerdo" passed by Congress prohibited civil and religious corporations from holding real estate not in actual use

July 10, Treaty with Prussia concluded of commerce and navigation

Aug. 1, Treaty of commerce with Sardinia concluded

Aug. 2, Concession for railroad from San Juan to Acapulco granted to Mosso Brothers and work begun in 1856 (Mexican Railway)

Aug. 9, Santa Anna started for Vera Cruz, embarked on 16th for Havana and went into exile in Cartagena

Aug. 13, Plan of Ayutla proclaimed

Aug. 15, Martin Carrera elected President *ad interim*; resigned Sept. 11

Sept. 8, Contract made for the construction of the Mexican Central Railroad

Sept. 11, General Romulo Diaz de la Vega became President

Oct. 1, American forces under J. H. Callahan arrived at the Rio Grande near Fort Duncan

Oct. 3, Americans in encounter with Indians and Mexicans fell back on Piedras Negras, burning the town Oct. 6

Oct. 4–Dec. 12, General Juan Alvarez, an Indian, was temporary President under Plan of Ayutla

Nov. 23, The "Ley Juarez" promulgated suppressed special courts, military and church, and providing for the first time for legal equality of all citizens, subjecting clergy and army to jurisdiction of civil courts

Dec. 11, Ignacio Comonfort, a creole, acted as President after resignation of Alvarez

Dec. 26, Miramon defeated Constitutionalists at San Joaquin

1856

Jan. 31, New tariff law lowered duties and reduced list of prohibited articles to 18

Feb. 18, Constitutional convention met

May 15, "Provisional Organic Statute" promulgated

June 5, Society of Jesus suppressed by government decree

June 25, The "Ley Lerdo" prohibited religious corporations from ownership of property not used for the specific purpose of the corporation, and decree of President Comonfort ordered sale of all unimproved real estate held by the Church to the lessees at reasonable terms

Dec. 9, The House of Jecker obtained from the Mexican government right to survey the territories of Sonora and southern California, one-third of unclaimed land to become their property. Rescinded by Liberal government in 1859

1857

Jan. 1, College of Juanajuato reorganized

Jan. 11, Mexican Railway line from Mexico City to Guadalupe Hidalgo opened for traffic (3½ miles)

Feb. 2, John Forsythe, American minister in Mexico,

without instructions from Washington signed treaties with Mexico which were not accepted by the United States

Feb. 5, New federal Constitution promulgated to become effective Sept. 16, the anniversary of Hidalgo's *Grito de Dolores*. Superseded the "Organic Statute" of 1856. Placed control of the mining industry in the various States.

March 15, French decimal metric system adopted

Aug. 13, Battle of Ixcapa Oaxaca between the Liberals and Clerical party a victory for the Conservatives

Aug. 31, Mosso concession sold to Antonio Escandon who obtained charter to build railroad from Vera Cruz to a port on the Pacific

Dec. 1, Comonfort took office as reëlected President

Dec. 17, General Felix Zuloaga issued the "Plan of Tacubaya" against the Government, proposing the annulment of the new Constitution. Accepted by President Comonfort

Dec. 23, President Comonfort announced adherence to new Plan

Dec. 26, Siege of Oaxaca begun

1858

Jan. 19, Benito Juarez, legal successor of Comonfort, established a Liberal Government based on Constitution of 1857 at Guanajuato which was recognized by a majority of the States

Jan. 21, President Comonfort fled to the United States

Jan. 23, General Felix Zuloaga representing Clerical party took oath as President and appointed Miramon his Commander-in-Chief

Jan., Porfirio Diaz under General Rosas Lander defended Oaxaca against Spanish General José Maria Cobos who was forced to raise the siege

Feb. 15, Juarez arrived at Guadalajara

Feb. 25, Diaz routed Spaniards at Jalapa, Oaxaca

March 9-10, Battle of Salamanca in Guanajuato a victory for the reactionary Government

March 14, Juarez and his Cabinet arrested at Guadalajara by an inferior officer, Landa, who released his prisoners for a price

March 17, Decree of government of Tamaulipas established a free zone as to tariff 6 miles wide along entire length of Tamaulipas on Rio Grande; formally ratified by Mexican Congress 1861

April 13, Diaz made successful attack on forces of General José Conchado at the hacienda of Jicaras

April 14, Juarez sailed from Manzanillo for Vera Cruz

May 4, Juarez, constitutional President, reached Vera Cruz with his Cabinet

May 5, President Zuloaga opened University closed by President Comonfort in 1857

May 18, Campeche separated from Yucatan became a State

June 1, From this date by the Constitution the *alcabalas* and interior custom houses abolished

July 24, Miramon recaptured Guanajuato from the constitutionalists

Aug. 10, L. C. Otway, British minister, concluded convention increasing interest on bonds issued under Doyle Convention from 3 to 6% and providing for payment of interest

Aug. 12, Battle between constitutionalists under Pueblita and government troops under Leonardo Marquez near Acambaro

Sept. 12, Miramon and Mejia occupied San Luis Potosi

Sept. 21, Defeat of government troops under General Casanova in defile of Las Cuevitas, Jalisco

Sept. 29, Vidaurri defeated by Miramon

Oct. 14, Capital attacked by constitutionalists from Morelia commanded by General Blanco. Forced to retreat

Oct. 27, Guadalajara recaptured by constitutionalists under Santos Degollado. Evacuated later on approach of Marquez

Nov. 16, Reactionary government troops captured Perote

Dec. 23, Zuloaga resigned the presidency and took refuge at British legation

Dec. 25, Miramon recovered Colima

1859

Jan. 26, Juarez Government assumed obligation of French debt

Jan. 31, Zuloaga designated Miguel Miramon as President as his successor

Feb. 5, Aguas Calientes became State of the Federation

Feb. 7, Juarez Government assumed obligation of English debt, the "Dunlop Arrangement"

Feb. 16, Miramon left Mexico City for capture of Vera Cruz

March 22, Tacubaya and Chapultepec taken by Miramon forces under Callejo and Mejia

March 29, In council of war Miramon at Vergara decided assault of Vera Cruz impracticable and siege abandoned without any attempt at attack

April 6, Recognition of the government of Juarez confirmed by the Senate of the United States

April 10, President Miramon arrived at the capital during unsuccessful siege by constitutionalists under Degollada

April 11, Shooting of prisoners of rank under written order of Miramon including physicians and medical students who had come out to attend wounded of both sides

——, Defeat of the constitutionalists at Tacubaya

June 17, Diaz gained victory at La Mixtequilla, Oaxaca over forces of Lieutenant-Colonel Espinosa and was made Lieutenant-Colonel of Infantry

July 7, Juarez issued a proclamation of his political program

July 12, Decree that all property of church be "nationalized," a confiscation, and religious brotherhoods prohibited

July 23, 28, 31, Marriage made a civil contract, civil judges to make regulations as to birth and death, control of cemeteries taken from clergy, and religious tolerance decreed

Aug. 11, The number of church holidays limited

Sept. 26, Miramon's Minister in Paris made treaty with Spain, the Mon-Almonte Treaty, by which the reactionaries were to receive aid from Spain in establishing a foreign protectorate in return for acknowledging Spanish claims for over 10,000,000 pesos

Sept. 28, Mexican bandit, Juan N. Cortina, raided Brownsville, Texas

Oct. 13, Miramon repulsed liberals at Estancia de las Vacas

Oct. 17, Because of inability to get compensation for claims of nationals Great Britain severed diplomatic relations

Oct. 29, Contract made by government with J. B. Jecker and Co. a bank headed by a Swiss national

of bonds for 15,000,000 pesos in return for an actual expenditure of 1,000,000 pesos

Nov. 13, Miramon defeated Degollado's army at La Estancia de las Vacas

Nov. 22, "Law of Juarez" for administration of justice

Nov. 25, Diaz took city of Tehuantepec, Oaxaca defeating conservatives commanded by General Alarcon. Now made a Colonel

Dec. 4, Decree provided for full religious liberty

Dec. 14, The McLane-Ocampo Treaty concluded by Juarez with the United States granted unlimited transit across the Tehuantepec Isthmus for 4 million dollars, half to be used for American private claims. American Senate refused ratification May 31, 1860

Dec. 24, Miramon defeated Ogazon at Tomla south of Jalisco

Dec. 27, Cortina in engagement with United States troops pursued into Mexico

1860

Jan. 21, Diaz defeated by General Cobos at Mitla, Oaxaca

Feb. 2, Diaz defeated forces of Cobos at Fortin de la Soledad

Feb. 8, Miramon left capital on second campaign against Vera Cruz and planned for coöperation of squadron for attack

March 6, Miramon's ships captured off Vera Cruz by American frigates commanded by Capt. Jarvis and 2 Mexican vessels of the Juarez Government

March 9, Diaz in action at Marquesado, Oaxaca

March 15–20, Unsuccessful siege of Vera Cruz by Miramon's troops

May, Failure of House of Jecker, a Swiss firm with whom Miramon had negotiated for loan in 1859 of $15,000,000 of which $1,470,000 had been paid

May 15, Diaz in action at Ixtepeji, Oaxaca

May 25, Liberal General Uraga repulsed in attack on Guadalajara

Aug. 5, Diaz defeated army of Cobos at San Luis and pursued enemy though badly wounded and took city of Oaxaca

Aug. 10, Miramon defeated at Silao by forces of Generals Zaragoza and Gonzalez Ortega

Sept. 9, Juarez Government seized funds at Laguna Seca in transit from port of Tampico owned by foreign nationals, £80,000 to £100,000 of British funds, and also money belonging to French and Spanish

Nov. 6, Juarez issued decree fixing date of election for president and vice-president for the following Jan.

Nov. 10, Liberal army routed army of Marquez at Calderon

Nov. 17, Miramon seized $660,000 left under seal at British legation to pay his troops

Dec. 15, Capt. Dunlop negotiated with Juarez for additional temporary assignment of 10% of customs duties at Vera Cruz and Tampico for British convention and London debt

Dec. 20, Guadalajara taken by Liberals

Dec. 22, Liberal victory in Battle at San Miguel Calpulalpam in which Gonzalez Ortega defeated Miramon and ended Three Years' War

Dec. 25, General Ortega entered Mexico City

1861

Jan. 11, President Juarez entered the capital

Jan. 12, Spanish Minister, Joaquin F. Pacheco the Papal Nuncio, the Minister of Guatemala, and the

Chargé d'Affaires of Equador dismissed because of acting on behalf of the reactionaries at capital

Jan. 23, The University closed by Juarez

Feb. 2, Hospitals and charitable institutions secularized

Feb. 22, British Government recognized Government of Juarez on condition that he assumed responsibility for British funds seized by Mexican leaders

March 2, Degollada defeated the reactionary generals Marquez and Mejia at Las Guayabitas

March 15, Enactment fixed silver dollar as unit of value

May 29, Congress passed act providing that payment on national debt with exception of money due to owners of funds seized at Lagune Seca and those recognized by conventions with Great Britain, France, and Spain to be suspended for 12 months

June, M. de Saligny, French Minister, arrived, instructed to enforce recognition of validity of Jecker bonds to full amount

June 11, Juarez reëlected in March, declared President and formally inaugurated on the 15th

July 17, Congress enacted a law suspending for 2 years payment of interest on external national debt, all obligations including the diplomatic convention debts

July 18, Protest of representatives of Great Britain and France against law of July 17

July 20, Treaty of commerce and navigation concluded with Belgium

July 25, Great Britain and France suspended diplomatic relations

Aug. 13, General Porfirio Diaz after pursuit of 2 months surprised and routed the forces of General Leonardo Marquez, leader of Church party in town of Jalatlaco

Aug. 21 or 23, Decree imposed tax of 10% on all fortunes over $2,000

Sept. 19, General Marquez defeated by General Tapia at Real del Monte

Oct. 4, Count Reichberg sent by Emperor Francis Joseph to Miramare to inform Maximilian of proposal of Napoleon III to reëstablish monarchy in Mexico and offer crown to Maximilian

Oct. 20, Forces of Marquez and Mejia defeated at Pachuca by Generals Tapia and Porfirio Diaz

Oct. 31, By Convention signed in London, France, Spain, and England agreed to send a military force to occupy parts of coast of Mexico to enforce claims of their citizens. The United States invited to join in convention

Nov. 15, Customs tariff modified

Nov. 21, Wyke-Zamaconda Convention provided for payment of British funds seized; rejected by Mexican Congress and British Foreign Office

Nov. 26, Decree revoked law of July 17 and provided for payment of the foreign obligations

Dec. 4, The United States declined to join Convention of Oct. 31 in letter of Seward

Dec. 11, Extradition Treaty concluded with the United States

Dec. 14, Spanish fleet arrived at Vera Cruz and demanded surrender of city within 24 hours

Dec. 17, General Emmanuel Gasset y Mercader in command of Spanish forces entered Vera Cruz without opposition

Dec. 29, Civil marriage law

1862

Jan. 7, French and English soldiers arrived at Vera Cruz

Jan. 14, Joint ultimatum presented to Mexican Government by General Prim for protection of persons and property of nationals and satisfaction of past injuries. Spain and Great Britain refused to support French claim for recognition of Jecker contract

Jan. 27, Miramon who had returned to Mexico under protection of French commissioners arrested by British on their frigate "Avon" and ordered to leave

Feb. 19, Convention at La Soledad of Mexicans and Allies as preliminary to negotiations signed by Generals Doblado and Prim

——, Capeche became State of the Federation

Feb. 27, General Juan Almonte arrived at Vera Cruz from France and Vienna under protection of the French

March 26, Jecker became a naturalized citizen of France and France took over his claim on Mexico of entire amount of bonds not the amount paid. The Duc de Morny reported to have acquired 30% of the bonds

April 6, Thomas Corwin negotiated treaty providing for loan from the United States of $9,000,000; tabled by American Senate

April 7, General Almonte, officially recognized by French, issued proclamation declaring himself supreme chief of Mexican nation

April 8, Final conference of Allies at Orizaba. Spanish and English left for Vera Cruz and Europe

April 16, French issued proclamation at Cordoba declaring war on the Juarez Government

April 19, First skirmish of the war at the village of Fortin

April 20, The French under General Bazaine occupied Orizaba

April 22, English and Spanish soldiers embarked on British ships for Havana, retiring from Mexico

April 28, Diaz in battle with French on heights of Acultzingo (Vera Cruz) forced to retreat to Puebla

——, The Wyke-Doblado Convention as to claims independent of the London loans; not ratified by the British Government

May 5, In Battle of Cinco de Mayo at Puebla the French led by General Laurencez defeated by Mexicans commanded by General Zaragoza and Porfirio Diaz

May 18, Liberals under General Tapia were defeated at Barranca Seca by conservative General Leonardo Marquez assisted by the French

May 31, President Juarez left the capital to establish the government at San Luis Potosi

June 14, Mexicans under Gonzales Ortega defeated in battle with French on the Cerro del Borrego, and Zaragoza failed in attack on Orizaba

Sept. 8, Death of General Zaragoza

Sept. 21, General Forey arrived at Vera Cruz from France to command 30,000 troops

Oct. 23, French made contract for construction of railroad from Tejeria to Chiquihuyte

1863

Jan. 8–10, French squadron bombarded Acapulco for 8 hours doing great damage

Feb. 26, Religious communities for women suppressed

May 17, Puebla besieged by the French since March 23, obliged to surrender. Generals Ortega and Porfirio Diaz, in command of the Army of East among those taken prisoners

June 1, Reactionists at Mexico City directed by General Bruno Aguilar at public meeting adopted resolutions to accept the foreign intervention

June 7, General Bazaine's division of French army entered Mexico City

June 10, Juarez set up his government at San Luis Potosi

——, General Forey entered Mexico City accompanied by Almonte, Saligy, and Marquez

June 16, Decree of General Forey authorized formation of Junta of 35 to elect 3 Mexican citizens for chief authority and 215 Mexican citizens to constitute an assembly of Notables

June 22, Provisional executive of 3 elected, later given title of Regency of the Mexican Empire

June 24, The triumviri, General Juan Nepomuceno Almonte, Mariano Salas, and Pelagio Antonio de Labistida y Davalos, archbishop of Mexico, assumed the executive authority

July 10, Convention of Notables assembled July 8 declared in favor of establishment of a monarchy in Mexico and that the crown should be offered to Maximilian of Austria

July 17, French vessels carried troops to port of Minatitlan on the Rio Goatzacolaco

July 20, Juarez land law first attempt to survey and adjudicate waste lands. Limit of possession established for individual, owners protected in claims and settlement insisted on

July 22, Law favoring colonization defined national lands

July 29, Fall of Cuernavaca

Aug. 11, French ships from Vera Cruz took Tampico

Aug. 18, Deputation headed by Estrada left Vera Cruz for Europe to offer crown to Maximilian

Oct. 1, General Forey recalled to France surrendered his authority to General Bazaine and embarked for France Oct. 21

Oct. 3, A commission from Mexico, headed by José Maria Guttierez de Estrada, at Miramare formally offered crown to Maximilian who agreed to accept on condition that the Mexican people endorsed the monarchy and his name by popular election

Oct. 24, General Bazaine published notice that proceedings pending in courts respecting sales of ecclesiastical property should take their due course thus alienating the clericals

Oct. 28, After severe battle at Taxto Diaz entered Oaxaca

Nov. 8, The Regency at request of General Bazaine issued decree to expedite the ecclesiastical suits in courts

Nov. 14, Comonfort killed in ambush on his way to Guanajuato. General Uraga succeeded him in command of republican forces

Nov. 17, Imperialists under Mejia occupied Queretaro

——, The Archbishop of Mexico expelled from the Regency by his colleagues for protest against decree of Nov. 8

Nov. 30, Morelia evacuated by Beriozabal and imperialists commanded by Marquez and Berthier entered the same day

Dec. 8, National troops commanded by Generals Doblado and Douai occupied Guanajuato

Dec. 18, Liberals led by General Uraga made unsuccessful attack on Morelia

Dec. 22, Juarez with his government left San Luis Potosi for Saltillo, capital of Coahuila

Dec. 25, The imperialists commanded by General Mejia occupied San Luis Potosi

Dec. 26, Protest of Church party signed by the archbishop and bishops of Mexico, Michoacan, Guadalajara, San Luis Potosi, and Oaxaca against the "Sacrilegious laws of spoliation of property of church"

Dec. 27, Liberal General Negrete made unsuccessful attempt to recapture San Luis Potosi

1864

Jan. 1, Districts occupied by French intervention in interior formed triangle with apex at Mexico, sides north to San Luis Potosi and west as far as Guadalajara city

Jan. 2, The Regency dismissed judges who had refused to take cognizance of cases as to church property

Jan. 5, General Bazaine occupied Guadalajara

Jan. 22, Campeche in Yucatan surrendered to the French

Feb. 7, Rich mining town of Zacatecas occupied by imperialists

Feb. 11, Juarez established his government at Monterey but retired on the 14th as Vidaurri refused to surrender the fort

Feb. 16, Castagny took Colotlan and 80 republican prisoners including General Ghilardi who was shot

Feb. 17, Vidaurri declared for the Empire against Juarez and went to Texas

Feb. 18, Ortega routed by Castagny at Colotlan

Feb. 27, San Juan Bautista, capital of Tabasco, defended by garrison and French vessels taken by republicans after siege of 6 weeks

Feb., Santa Anna arrived at Vera Cruz from St. Thomas after nearly 9 years absence

March 7, General Bazaine ordered Santa Anna to leave Mexico. Sailed for Havana on the 12th

March 20, Contract for loan of £8,000,000 to Maximilian concluded in London

March 28, Minatitlan surrendered to the republicans

March 29, Juarez occupied and presently established his government at Monterey

April 4, American House passed resolution in opposition to recognition of a monarchy in Mexico

April 9, Maximilian signed "family compact" demanded by Emperor Francis Joseph, renouncing his right of succession to the Austrian throne

April 10, Maximilian, archduke of Austria, formally accepted the throne of Mexico, offered

———, Treaty of Miramar concluded between France and Mexico settled conditions of sojourn of French troops in Mexico

May 3, Thomas Corwin, American minister, left Mexico

May 13, Colonel Potier took Nochistlan, republican stronghold, by assault

May 17, Doblado defeated by Mejia in attack on Matehuala

May 29, Maximilian and Charlotte landed in Vera Cruz, received by General Juan N. Almonte as president of the Regency

June 3, Acapulco on the coast of Guerrero surrendered to French because of lack of artillery. Abandoned by them in beginning of December

June 12, Maximilian accompanied by his wife, Charlotte, daughter of Leopold I, of Belgium, arrived at Mexico City

June, First modern bank established in Mexico City, the *Banco de Londres y Mexico*

June 30, New law relating to internal taxes changed rates and added taxes

July 1, General J. L. Uraga deserted Juarez for the imperialists

July 3, The French entered Durango

July 4, Claims Convention for submission of all claims arising since Treaty of Guadalupe of United States

Aug. 10, Battle of Nanaguatipam, Oaxaca, Diaz commanding Republicans

Aug. 15, Monterey taken by imperialists and Juarez and his minister narrowly escaped capture by Quiroga, son of Vidaurri

Aug. 20, Imperial Mexican Railway Company incorporated in London, England, later Mexican Railway

Sept. 26, Cortina surrendered Matamoras to the imperialists commanded by General Mejia

Sept. 28, Death of Juan Alvarez

Oct. 15, Juarez established his government at Chihuahua

Oct. 26, General Diaz began siege of town of Tasco which capitulated 3 days later

Oct. 28, Generals Douay and Marquez made attack on Arteaga in ravine of Atenquique, Jalisco and dispersed the republicans

Nov. 12, Juarez Government authorized acceptance of military services of foreigners and a foreign loan for equipment

Dec. 4, Consulting body called Council of State created

Dec. 22, Rosales routed imperialists and French at San Pedro

1865

Jan., The French under Castagny at Mazatlan burned towns and estates and executed prisoners with view of terrifying Republicans into submission

Jan. 1, Corona from Mazatlan successfully defended passage of Espinazo del Diablo by French troops

Jan. 7, Decree of Maximilian declared that papal bulls and briefs were not to be promulgated without imperial sanction

Jan. 28, Defeat and death of General Antonio Rojas at Potrerillos in Jalisco by Douay's forces

Jan. 31, Romero defeated in battle at Apatzingan by Colonel Potier with loss of 200 killed and 160 prisoners, the leader, Romero, executed

Feb. 9, City of Oaxaca surrendered to General Bazaine, besieged since Jan. 8. Diaz sent a prisoner to Puebla

Feb. 26, Decree promulgated provisions for liberty of worship and revision of sales of church property

March 3, New taxes promulgated

March 9, Decree of Maximilian authorized Council of State to revise actions taken as to church property and provided for establishment of office to be called "The Administration of Nationalized Property"

April 1, Cortina joined the imperialists

April 9, Negrete, Juarist leader, occupied Saltillo, driving out imperialists under Olvera and Lopez

April 10, Maximilian created three orders, the Eagle of Mexico, reviving Our Lady of Guadalupe created by Iturbide, and that of St. Charles for women

April 11, Town of Tacambaro taken by republicans, Belgian and Mexican garrison forced to capitulate

April 12, Negrete occupied Monterey

April 23, Ciudad Victoria captured by Col. Mendez, imperialist, after siege of a fortnight

April, Maximilian negotiated a new loan in Paris of bonds for 250,000,000 francs at 6%

May 10, Decree defined extent of freedom to be allowed to the press

June 4, Tula taken by Colonel Mendez

June 6, Negrete evacuated Saltillo; his army dispersed

and he later transferred his allegiance from Juarez to Ortega

July 29, Colonel Garnier with French troops and Indian allies marched into Hermosillo

Aug. 14, Brincourt occupied Chihuahua for the Empire

Aug. 15, Juarez made Pasco del Norte his capital

Aug. 21, Juarist forces under Escobedo captured Catorce

Sept. 11, General José Maria Carbajal acting for Juarez in New York negotiated loan of 30,000,000 pesos with banking house of John W. Corlies and Company

Sept. 20, Diaz made his escape from Puebla and at Guerrero began forming new army

Sept. 22, Diaz captured the garrison at Tehuitzina

Sept. 23, Diaz defeated the French and Imperialists at Piaxtla

Oct. 1, Loan for 30 millions placed in New York by Juarist Government

——, Diaz defeated French and imperialists at Jultzingo

Oct. 3, Maximilian issued "Black Decree" that all Mexicans found bearing arms against the Empire were to be considered beyond the law, and members of "Juarist bands" taken under arms should be executed without trial except court martial

Oct. 7, An Immigration Bureau established and arrangements made for French, German, and American immigration into interior districts under which colonists from the Southern States came to Mexico after the American Civil War

Oct. 13, Generals Arteaga and Salazar defeated by imperialists at Amatlan

Oct. 19, General Escobedo, appointed by Juarez commander-in-chief in the northern states, began siege of Matamoras

Oct. 21, Generals Arteaga and Salazar and 4 colonels, prisoners of war, shot by Mendez under decree of Oct. 3

Oct. 25, Escobedo made unsuccessful attack on Matamoras

Nov. 8, General Escobedo abandoned the siege of Matamoras

Nov. 9, Juarez issued decree extending his presidential term until new election could be held

Nov. 13, Constitutional term of President Juarez expired

Nov. 20, Juarez reëstablished his government at Chihuahua

Nov. 24, Escobedo took possession of Monterey evacuated by the French but was obliged to leave the following day

Nov. 30, Maximilian suppressed the University

——, Ortega claimed presidency as president of the supreme court in 1864 and proceeded to the United States

Dec. 4, Diaz victory at Comitlixa

Dec., Imperial decree granted to J. Stanley Keeling right for 10 years to run line of steamers between Vera Cruz and New York

1866

Jan. 6, Battle of Tlaxiaco, General Diaz commanded patriots

Jan., Negro soldiers from the United States in service of General Cortina sacked Bagdad

Feb. 12, Secretary Seward demanded withdrawal of French troops from Mexico

April 5, Official announcement of Napoleon that the French armies would be withdrawn from Mexico within 19 months

June 5, Santa Anna issued manifesto from Elizabeth Port

July 13, Act reduced a number of the internal revenue taxes. Stamp tax placed on alcoholic liquors

July 15–17, 60 conspirators arrested and sent to Yucatan and Santa Anna's estates confiscated

Aug. 9–29, Charlotte in Paris sent to appeal to Napoleon for aid for Maximilian, received his answer and refusal Aug. 24

Sept. 18, Charlotte left Miramare for Rome in mental condition which became permanent insanity

Sept. 23, Diaz defeated small company of Hungarian cavalry at Nochextlan

Oct. 3, Diaz surprised Oronozo commanding the imperialist forces in Oajaca and killed or captured 1,200 French troops near Miahuatlan

Oct. 18, Diaz won battle at La Carbonera. The town surrendered Oct. 30

Oct. 21, Maximilian with escort of Colonel Kodolitch and his Austro-Hungarian regiment started from Chapultepec for Orizaba where he remained until Dec. 12

Nov. 1, City of Oajaca capitulated to Diaz

Nov. 3, General Ortega and his troops arrested and detained until Dec. 6 by Captain Paulson, American commander at Brazos Santiago in defense of neutrality laws

Nov. 11, Jalapa surrendered to General Alatorre

Nov. 14, Durango occupied by General Azunda

Dec. 1, General Escobedo received possession of Matamoros from American General Sedgwick to whom Canales had surrendered. Action of General Sedgwick in receiving surrender disowned by the United States

Dec. 24, Mazatlan taken by General Corona

Dec. 27, President Juarez entered Durango

1867

Jan. 8, Ortega arrived in Zacatecas, claiming to be president

Jan. 17, Council of 35 men met and voted 27 to 8 against the abdication of Maximilian

Jan. 26, Guanajuato captured by republican generals Antillon and Rincon

Jan. 27, General Miramon in surprise attack took Zacatecas. Juarez narrowly escaped capture

Feb. 5, General Bazaine with French troops left Mexico City

Feb. 6, Miramon defeated at San Jacinto

Feb. 13, Maximilian with 2,000 troops left Mexico to establish base of operations at Queretaro which he reached on the 19th

March 2, Internal taxes reduced

March 5, The Republicans commanded by Gen. Mariano Escobedo appeared before Queretaro and siege begun

March 12, The last French troops sailed from Vera Cruz

March 14, Republicans attack Queretaro

March 22, General Marquez made successful sortie from Queretaro and reached Mexico City the 27th

March 24, Republicans beaten in attack on Queretaro with 2,000 killed and wounded

April 4, Puebla besieged by Diaz since March 9 surrendered

April 10, Marquez defeated by Diaz in battle in hacienda of San Lorenzo, retreated to the capital

April 12, The siege of Mexico City begun by the Republican forces under Diaz

April 27, Imperialists at Queretaro victorious in battle with Republicans

May 14, Maximilian planning to escape from Queretaro sent General Lopez to ask capitulation of Escobedo which was denied, and Republican forces entered city. Bancroft states that Miguel Lopez turned traitor and admitted republican troops

May 15, Maximilian captured at the Cerro de las Campanas, a hill near city

May 27, Imperialist commander, Olvera, surrendered to General Martinez at Huichapan

June 13, Court martial of Maximilian, Mejia, and Miramon opened. Mendez had been shot in retaliation for execution of Arteaga

June 14, Court martial gave verdict of guilty with sentence of death for Maximilian and his generals

June 19, Maximilian shot together with Generals Miramon and Mejia at Cerro de la Campana

June 21, City of Mexico besieged since April 12 surrendered to General Diaz. Marquez escaped from the city and the country

June 27, City of Vera Cruz capitulated to republican Generals Alejandro Garcia and Benavides

July 8, Viadurri arrested in the capital and shot

July 15, President Juarez entered the capital

July 16, Name Mexican Railway adopted by Imperial Mexican Railway Company

July 20, Inayarita, last Clerical stronghold, taken

July 22, Nayarit submitted to Government

Aug. 12, Juarez established an "Administration of Nationalized Property" office

Aug. 14, President Juarez issued regulations providing for the election of state and federal magistrates

Aug. 21, General Tomas O'Horan shot after trial and conviction

Dec. 2, Provision made for 10 model schools in the federal district in new education law which divided education into primary, preparatory, and professional schools

Dec. 8, Congress met, the first since 1863

Dec. 19, Juarez declared President Elect by Congress; assumed office the 25th

1868

Jan. 8, Congress issued manifesto declaring that the Government would reëstablish diplomatic relations with countries which had recognized Maximilian's empire

Jan. 31, Alatorre defeated insurrectionists in Yucatan at Maxcanu

March 27, Decree established a military post of 500 men at Campeche to put down insurrection in Yucatan

April 8, General Corona defeated insurrectionists led by Martinez

May 5, Plan of Aurelio Rivera against Juarez Government published

July 4, Claims Convention with the United States provided for adjustment by arbitration; proclaimed Feb. 1, 1869

July 10, Convention with the United States to determine nationality of citizens of either country migrating to the other

Aug. 19, Jesus G. Ortega, released from prison, renounced his claim to the presidency and also position of Chief Justice to which Lerdo had been appointed June 5

Sept. 16, Mexican Railway, Puebla branch, opened from Apizaco to the city of Puebla; officially opened to the public Jan. 1, 1873

Dec. 1, State of Morelos created by act of Congress. Formally installed April 26, 1869

1869

Jan.–Feb., Insurrection in Yucatan put down by Colonel Ceballos

Jan. 16, The State of Hidalgo created by act of Congress. Antonio Tagle, first Governor, installed May 27

Feb. 3, Pronunciamento at Puebla headed by Miguel Negrete

Feb. 22, Negrete defeated by General Cuellan at Iagunilla near San Martin Atexcal

March, Death of General Almonte at Paris

April 7, Morelos became a State of the Federation

July 31, Mexican and American joint claims and naturalization commission organized at Washington

Aug. 28, Treaty of friendship, commerce, and navigation concluded with the King of Prussia

Dec. 15, Revolution at San Luis Potosi against Juarez Government headed by Generals Francisco Aguirre, Martinez, and Larranga proclaimed

Dec. 30, Proclamation of San Luis Potosi against the Government by Generals Aguirre, Martinez, and Laranga

1870

Jan. 10, Revolutionists joined by Governor Trinidad Garcia de la Cadena at Zacatecas who headed movement

Feb. 18, Rebel General Dominguez defeated by government forces near Olocosco

Feb. 22, Revolution ended with defeat by General Rocha at Lo de Ovejo

April 28, Amendment to Constitution creating a senate passed by Congress; submitted to states for ratification

May 28, Colonel Viscayno, rebel leader, captured the city of Guaymas but evacuated on the 29th on approach of government forces

Oct. 13, General amnesty law enacted and prisoners released

Dec., President promulgated Civil Code to go into effect March 1, 1871

Dec. 14, Treaty of commerce and navigation with Italy concluded

1871

April 19, Claims Convention with United States concluded; proclaimed Feb. 8, 1872

——, Joint commission powers extended by convention

May 2, Revolt of garrison at Tampico against the Juarez Government

June 11, General Rocha commanding federal troops took Tampico

Oct. 1, Insurrection in Mexico City

Oct. 12, Congress chose Juarez as constitutional President, as none of candidates at election had obtained the requisite majority

Nov. 8, Diaz issued *Plan de la Noria* calling for reconstruction of the government beginning revolt against Juarez

Nov. 20, The garrison at Guaymas, Sonora declared for Diaz

Dec. 1, President Juarez began new term of 4 years

Dec. 2, Revolutionists led by General Trevino took Saltillo

Dec. 7, Penal Code promulgated

Dec. 23, Loaeza's brigade of Alatorre's command defeated Diaz forces under General Luis Mier y Teran at San Mateo Xindihui

Dec., Sinaloa legislature declared against Government of Juarez

1872

Jan. 1, Tariff law increased number of articles on free list to 63

Jan. 4, General Alatorre occupied Oajaca ending revolution in that State

Feb. 8, Porfirio Diaz occupied Zacatecas taken by his supporters Jan. 26

Feb. 23, Aguascalientes besieged by Gomez Portugal commanding rebels

March 2, Rocha defeated the army of Trevino supporting Diaz at Cerro de la Bufa in Zacatecas

March 13, Revolution pronounced at Valladolid, Yucatan

March 31, Contract subsidy with Pacific Mail S.S. line established steamers between Panama and San Francisco which should touch Mexican ports

April 1, Penal code of the Federal District went into effect

April 13, The forces of Juarez reoccupied Zacatecas

May 30, General Corella defeated rebels under General Trevino near Monterey

May 31, In surprise attack General Trevino completely routed forces of Corella at Monterey

July 18, Death of President Juarez from heart attack

July 19, Sebastian Lerdo de Tejada, chief justice Supreme Court, and constitutional successor of the president, took office

Aug. 1, Manuel Lozada, bandit of Tepic, declared town of Nayarit independent of the central government

Sept. 14, Mazatlan in Sinaloa taken by revolutionists

Oct. 6, Mazatlan accepted amnesty and was occupied by federal troops Oct. 19 ending revolution in Sinaloa

Oct. 26, Diaz accepted amnesty the day on which elections for Lerdo and himself held for president. Lerdo received 10,000 votes, Diaz 600, and other candidates 136. Lerdo declared President-Elect by Congress Nov. 16

Nov. 27, Claims Convention with the United States concluded, extended powers of joint commission

Dec. 1, Lerdo de Tejada inaugurated as President

1873

Jan. 1, First Mexican Railroad completed to Vera Cruz from Mexico City and formally opened by the President

Jan. 17, The tribes of Nayarit with Lozada as chief declared war against the Government

Jan. 27–28, General Corona in battle with rebels led by Lozada defeated them at Mojonera

Jan. 31, Claims Convention with the United States

Feb. 28, Cavalry of General Ceballos under General Carbo entered Tepic and the rest of the troops on March 2

May 5, Rebels routed at Arroyo de Guadalupe by General Carbo

May 13, Decree that no religious rite may take place outside of a church building

May 29, Congress adopted constitutional amendments which declared for religious tolerance, separation of church and State, marriage a civil contract, and prohibited monastic orders. Incorporated into

Constitution by decree of Sept. 25. Affirmed by State legislatures became part of national Constitution Nov. 12, 1874

July 14, Lozada captured and executed on the 19th ending rebellion in Tepic

Sept. 25, Decree declared adoption of constitutional amendments. *See* May 29

——, Law declared against recognition of monastic orders and their establishment forbidden

1874

Jan., Protestants assaulted in Toluca

April 22, Concession granted for railroad from Merida to Progreso built in 1881 (United Railways of Yucatan)

May 2, John Stephens, American Protestant minister, killed at Ahualuco, Jalisco, by Catholic fanatics

Nov. 20, Claims Convention with the United States

Dec. 1, Decree by which sisters of charity expelled from the country

Dec. 4, Religious exercises and instruction forbidden in all federal, state, and municipal schools

Dec. 14, Legacies in favor of ministers or their relatives to fourth degree declared null and void when they have rendered spiritual aid in last illness of testator

1875

March 26, Raid into vicinity of Corpus Christi, Texas

May 31, Colonization law authorized execution of contracts established on certain conditions

Dec., Diaz established base of operations at Brownsville, Texas

1876

Jan. 15, General Fidencio Hernandez, partisan of Diaz, announced revolutionary Plan de Tuxtepec, Oaxaca

Jan. 28, General F. Hernandez occupied Oajaca and proclaimed himself Governor. Rebellion spread to other States

Jan. 31, Decision of Claims Commission under Convention of July 4, 1864. Balance due from Mexico to the United States $3,975,123

March 31, Diaz proclaimed amended form of *Plan de Tuxtepec* which he called the *Plan de Palo Blanco* declaring against the Lerdo Government

April 2, Diaz occupied Matamoros, key to frontier enabling him to obtain foreign military supplies

April 29 and Dec. 14, Claims Conventions with the United States

May 18, Gen. Cortina released from prison declared for Diaz

May 22, Diaz in disguise landed at Vera Cruz

May 28, General Alatorre defeated revolutionists led by Hernandez, Teran, and Couttolenne at Epatlan

May 31, Decree of President Lerdo granted public lands and subsidy to settlers to encourage immigration

June 21, Death of Santa Anna in Mexico City

July, President Lerdo reëlected

Oct. 31, Iglesias, chief justice, claimed to be constitutional President, published the Plan of Salamanca, and set up his government at Guanajuato

Nov. 16, Diaz with General Gonzalez defeated government forces under General Alatorre in battle at Tecoac

Nov. 20, Lerdo fled from the capital and to New York

Nov. 20 and Dec. 14, Adjustment of claims between the United States and Mexico concluded

Nov. 23, Diaz entered City of Mexico and by decree of

Nov. 28 assumed executive power upholding principle that outgoing president not eligible for reëlection

Dec. 6–Feb. 16, 1877, General Juan N. Mendez, acting President

Dec. 20, Diaz entered Queretaro and on 21st held conference with Iglesias who refused to give up his claim to the executive office

1877

Jan. 2, Iglesias issued final manifesto to the people of Mexico

Jan. 17, José Maria Iglesias embarked at Mazatlan for San Francisco

Feb. 11, Diaz returned to capital from his march through states reorganizing governments which had declared for Iglesias, and assumed provisional presidency on the 15th

May 2, Congress declared Diaz elected President and he was installed May 5

June 1, American General Ord instructed to cross Mexican border in pursuit of bandits which was protested by Mexico

June 18, President Diaz instructed Gen. Trevino to prevent border robberies and pursue robbers within Mexican limits but in case of invasion to repel force by force

Nov. 1, Congress approved law prohibiting the immediate reëlection of the President

Nov., Contract made with James Sullivan and his associates for railroad from American boundary to City of Mexico

Dec. 7, Boundary Treaty with Guatemala concluded

Dec. 25, Railroad law enacted

1878

March 27, Concession granted for railroad from Merida to Peto (United Railways of Yucatan)

April 9, The Diaz Government recognized by the United States

April 16, Concession to State of Morelos for railroad from Mexico to Morelos and Cuernavaca and to Amacusac River which became later the Interoceanic Railroad

May 5, Constitution amended to prohibit immediate reëlection of the President

June 3, Escobedo, partisan of Lerdo, defeated and captured shortly after by Nuncio at Cuatro Cienagas

June 12, Decree reduced import duty on Virginia tobacco from the United States from $1.25 to 16 cents per kilogram net

June 30, Decree reduced duty on imported cotton and linen handkerchiefs

Aug. 24, José Maria Amador, partisan of Lerdo, routed and killed at the Rancho de Guadalupe

1879

June, Mutiny of crew of Mexican warship "Trinidad" at Tlacotalpan on Alvarado River in support of Lerdo under Francisco A. Navarro, sailed for Campeche, Governor Mier y Teran of Vera Cruz seized 9 persons whom he believed conspirators and had them shot. Counter-mutiny brought the "Trinidad" back to Vera Cruz

June 25, 9 young men at Vera Cruz accused of anti-Diaz political activities shot without trial

1880

March 10, Order of June 1, 1877, of the United States

as to crossing border in pursuit of bandits and long protested by Mexico withdrawn

April 3, Concession of 1874 for railroad from Mexico to Leon transferred to Robert R. Symon who organized the "Ferrocarril Central Mexicano" in Boston, Mass. (Mexican Central Railway)

May 25, Work begun on Mexican Central Railroad

July 9, National Government granted concession to State of Guerrero for railroad from Acapulco to Mexico

Aug. 25, First concession for railroad afterwards the Mexico Southern Railroad granted to State of Oaxaca for line from port of Anton Lizardo to Port Angel

Sept. 8, Charter granted to Mexican Central Railway for construction of railroad from Mexico City to Leon, and from Leon to Paso del Norte

Sept. 13, Concession to National Railroad Company approved by Congress Nov. 8 superseded previous concessions beginning Dec. 22, 1877 by which railroad authorized to extend from Mexico City through Toluca, Acambaro, Celaya, San Luis Potosi, Saltillo and Monterey to Laredo, and from Mexico City through Acambaro to port of Manzanillo

Sept. 14, Concession granted for Sonora Railway from Nogales to Guaymas (Southern Pacific Railway of Mexico)

Sept. 25, Manuel Gonzales declared by Congress elected President

Nov. 24, The national Government contracted with State of Morelos for railroad from Los Reyes to Mexican Railroad at Irolo. Completed in 1882 (Interoceanic Railroad)

Dec. 1, President Gonzales inaugurated, the Vice-President according to the Constitution the President of the Supreme Court, Licentiate Ignacio L. Vallarta

Dec. 15, Railroad from Merida to Valladolid authorized, completed in 1906 (United Railways of Yucatan)

Dec. 20 and Feb. 23, 1881, Concessions granted for railroad from Merida to Campeche; completed 1898 (United Railways of Yucatan)

1881

June 7, First concession for Mexican International Railroad granted to John B. Frisbie representative of the Southern Pacific to construct railroad from Piedras Negras to Durango and from Durango through Zacatecas and Guanjuato to Mexico City

Aug. 23, Contract signed for establishment of *Banco-Nacional Mexicano*

Dec. 16, Railroad law enacted

1882

Jan. 21, Concession for railroad from Irolo to Puebla and to Matamoros granted to Francisco Arteaga

March 19, A run on the national bank

March 27, Banco Mercantil, second modern bank, opened in Mexico City

April 26, Charter for Mexican International Railroad from State of Connecticut based on concessions of Nov. 4, 1881 and April 2, 1882

July 29, Convention with the United States signed by which it was agreed that troops of both nations might cross international border in pursuit of hostile bandits on certain conditions; proclaimed March 5, 1883

Sept. 4, Railroad from Mexico City to Toluca opened for passenger traffic (National Railroad)

Sept. 21, Convention with the United States as to pursuit of Indians across frontier

Sept. 27, Treaty signed by which Guatemala resigned pretensions to Chiapas and Soconusco and boundary - line defined

Oct. 19, United Morelos, Iroto, and Acapulco Railway Company organized by Delfin Sanchez

Oct. 25, Sonora Railway opened for traffic

Oct. 26, Railroad from Laredo to Monterey opened (National Railroad)

Nov. 18, Railroad from Manzanillo to Armeria opened for freight (National Railroad)

Dec. 5, Treaty of commerce concluded with Germany

1883

Jan. 20, Commercial reciprocity treaty with the United States concluded; proclaimed June 2, 1884

Feb. 6, Railroad from Toluca to Maravatio opened for passengers and freight (National Railroad)

Feb. 13, Several railroad concessions consolidated to form later Interoceanic Railroad

April 12, Various concessions of Mexican Central Railway consolidated

May 12, Agreement signed in London for settlement of Mexican debt provided for issue of new bonds for £20,000,000 at 3%

June 14, Congress passed law providing for consolidation of public debt of Mexico

June 28, Agreement as to pursuit of Indians across frontier. Renewed Oct. 31, 1884, and Oct. 16, 1885, June 25, 1890, Nov. 25, 1892, June 4, 1896

July 29, Treaty with the United States concluded to create an International Boundary Commission

Dec. 14, Constitutional amendment placed mining under federal jurisdiction

——, Constitutional amendment as to banking passed

Dec. 15, Law enacted provided for survey of national lands by private companies who were to receive as compensation one-third of land surveyed

——, Colonization law promulgated

——, Congress authorized the executive to issue a mining code for the republic

1884

Jan., Mexican International Railroad tracks reached Monclova

March 22, Stamp tax on quoted merchandise law enacted

March 31, New Civil Code adopted superseded that of 1870

April 10, Mexican Central Railroad completed March 8, opened for passenger traffic from Mexico City to El Paso, Texas

April 15, Commercial code promulgated included regulations for establishment of banks

May 14, Commercial Treaty with the United States ratified by the Mexican Senate

May 15, Concession granted for railroad from Merida to Zagmal built in 1890 (United Railways of Yucatan)

May 31, Consolidation of banks became the National Bank of Mexico

Aug. 6, Agreement concluded with Great Britain provided for reëstablishment of diplomatic relations and payment of English bondholders

Nov. 12, Boundary Convention as to Rio Grande and Rio Colorado concluded with the United States

Nov. 22, First Federal Mining code promulgated.

Placed petroleum with those minerals which were the exclusive property of the owner of the soil

Dec. 1, Porfirio Diaz inaugurated President, having received 15,999 out of the 16,462 electoral votes, and began rule that ended with his exile in May, 1911

Dec. 12, Territory of Tepic established by decree of Congress

1885

Jan. 29, New Internal Revenue tax on merchandise

Feb. 25, Reciprocity Convention with the United States concluded; proclaimed May 4, 1886

June 22, Congress enacted law providing for settlement of debt, the "Dublan Conversion"

July, First attempt to assassinate Dr. Ignacio Martinez in Brownsville, Texas, editor of newspaper which criticized Diaz policies

July 29, Treaty of commerce concluded with Sweden and Norway

Dec. 15, Colonization law promulgated

1886

March, Federal Government suppressed Yaqui war led by chief Cajeme in Sonora

May 14, Supplementary Commercial Treaty with the United States signed

May 28, Law governing aliens and their naturalization passed and regulations as to colonization, and foreigners not allowed to acquire land near frontiers

Aug. 5, Cutting affair. *See* United States

Nov. 27, Treaty of commerce and navigation concluded with France

1887

May 3, Earthquake at Sonora and volcanic eruption 14 miles southeast of Bavispe

June 6, Regulations made respecting tax on mining property

——, A tax measure passed and Article 6 defined terms on which executive might grant mining contracts; law exempted quicksilver and coal-mines from taxation and certain other commodities freed from import duties

Aug., Telegraph between Mexico and Guatemala opened

Oct. 21, Law enacted to allow a single reëlection for president

Nov. 10, Concession for building the Monterey and Mexican Gulf Railroad granted to American company

Dec. 13, Congress authorized a loan of not more than £10,500,000

Dec. 14, Lower California divided into 2 political districts, north and south. The Northern District granted to Louis Huller who sold it to International Company of Mexico, a Connecticut corporation

1888

Jan. 12, Main line of the Mexican International Railway an extension of the Southern Pacific completed to Torreon and opened for traffic 2 months later

March 23, Law making education compulsory enacted but not enforced

March 24, Contract for Mexican loan signed at Berlin by international bankers

May 21, The Guadalajara division of the Mexican Central Railroad opened

May 25, Compulsory education act applied to children between 6 and 12

June 5, Law enacted as to public waters and water rights therein

July, Interoceanic Railway Company organized in England

July 10, Treaty of commerce and navigation concluded with Ecuador

July 16, Treaty of friendship, commerce, and navigation with Dominican Republic

Sept. 29, Railroad from Mexico City to Laredo completed

Nov. 1, Mexican National Railroad inaugurated

Nov. 27, Treaty of commerce and navigation with Great Britain concluded

Nov. 30, Treaty of commerce with Japan concluded

Dec. 18, Decree founded National Medical Institute

1889

March 1, Boundary Convention with the United States concluded at Washington

April 29, Railroad law passed

May 9, The Mexico Southern Railway Company organized

Sept. 15, New commercial code omitting regulations on banking, superseded that of 1884

Nov. 28, Patent law enacted

Dec. 1–March 31, 1890, First Congress of Public Education held in Mexico

1890

March 30, Mexican Central Railway completed to Gulf at Tampico

April 16, Treaty of commerce and navigation with Italy signed

May 12, Decree of Diaz that all village communal lands must be expropriated and allotted in severalty, taking land from the people

May 30, Concession to Mexican Cuernavaca and Pacific Railroad

June 7, Patent law enacted

June 25, Agreement with the United States as to pursuit of Indians across frontier

Sept., Railway subvention loan to nominal amount £6,000,000 issued at Berlin, London, and Amsterdam

Dec. 1, Second educational congress met at Mexico City

Dec. 20, Pachuca branch of Mexican Railway from Ometusco to Pachuca opened

——, Amendment to law respecting election of president permitting indefinite reëlection passed

1891

March 21, Law regulating compulsory education to become effective Jan. 17, 1892 as to the Federal District, and Territories of Tepic and Lower California

June 12, Tariff law of protective character enacted to go into effect Nov. 1

Nov. 16, General Reiz Sandival and Catarino Garza in rebellion against the Government attacked Guerrera

1892

June 4, New mining code enacted

June 25, Detailed regulations as to procedure necessary for acquiring mining grants published

Oct. 1, Mexican International Railroad opened to Durango

Nov., Railroad between Puebla and Oaxaca officially

opened by President Diaz (Mexico Southern Railway Company)

Nov. 8, Law of liberation declared nationalized ecclesiastical property free from any further claims by the Treasury

Nov. 12, Law of liberation fixed limit within which Secretariat of Hacienda obliged to issue declaration of renunciation of any eventual rights which might have been considered as acquired by the nation over supposedly private estates

Nov. 25, Agreement with the United States as to right to pursue Indians across the border

Dec. 1, President Diaz began his fourth term of office

1893

April 20, Concession for Coahuila and Zacatecas Railroad (British company)

May 29, Congress authorized an issue of bonds for settlement of debt

July 8, Treaty fixing boundary with British Honduras

1894

March 26, General land law promulgated increased facilities for acquisition of waste lands practically removing all restrictions of land laws of 1863 and 1883, repealed

June 6, First measure which regulated the use of waters under federal jurisdiction by means of concessions

Oct. 1, Regulations published prescribing conditions under permits to fell timber, extract rubber, and as to grazing, fishing, and hunting on national lands

Oct. 15, Tehuantepec National Railway across the Isthmus completed by American company of C. S. Stanhope and associates

1895

March 1, Resolution suspended privilege of Free Zone as to tariff with the United States

April 1, Boundary convention between Mexico and Guatemala concluded; commission appointed

——, Boundary dispute with Guatemala as to territory about the Lacantun River settled by Treaty. Provision made for arbitration as to claims for destruction of property

July 11, Postage reduced from 10 to 5 cents

Aug. 3, Concession granted for railroad from Jalapa to Teocelo

Sept. 16, M. W. Ranson, American Minister as arbitrator in dispute with Guatemala

Oct. 1, Boundary convention with the United States as to Rio Grande and Colorado rivers

1896

Feb. 27, Agreement made with the United States giving citizens reciprocal benefits of copyright

March 24, Concession to New York company to build Rio Grande, Sierra Madre, and Pacific Railroad

May 19, Law respecting public education promulgated

May 27, Patent law amended

June 3, Congress authorized the executive to issue general banking law

June 4, Agreement with United States respecting pursuit of Indians across the border

June 6, Patent law amended

June 6 and 19, Laws passed as to weights and measures and coinage

July 1, Amendment to Constitution prohibiting any interstate tax on commerce came into effect

July 13, President Diaz reëlected
Aug. 12, Yaqui insurrection begun by attack on Nogales to capture arms and money
Aug. 15, Ground broken for Rio Grande, Sierra Madre, and Pacific Railroad
Sept. 16, International decimal metric system of weights and measures the only legal system from this date
Nov. 6, Water Boundary Agreement with the United States signed
Nov. 20, Congress authorized the executive to make free grants of national and waste lands to needy farmers
Dec. 1, President Diaz reëlected in July began his fifth term
Dec. 17, Law designed to revalidate all franchises granted by States as to waters as complement to law of June 4, 1894

1897

March 2, Protocol signed respecting claims of Oberlander and Messenger with the United States
March 13, General banking law passed
March 19, General law relating to institutions of credit passed
April 7, Boundary Convention with British Honduras concluded
June 24, Court of Claims at Washington decided fraud employed in La Alira case and forbade payment of award of Jan. 31, 1876, and in 1902 $412,572 returned to Mexico
June 27, First passenger train passed over the Rio Grande, Sierra Madre, and Pacific Railroad completed to Casas Grandes
Dec. 12, Railroad opened from the capital to Cuernavaca

1898

Feb. 25, First concession for Vera Cruz to Isthmus Railway from Cordoba to Santa Lucrecia. Various concessions acquired by the Government May 13, 1904
March 23, Concession granted for railroad from Mexico City to Chalco (San Rafael and Atlixco Railway)
May 17, New Convention with Guatemala extended term of boundary commission
June 6, Decree granted free entry of certain goods, arms and munition, rolling stock for National Tehuantepec Railroad, and wire for federal telegraph lines for federal and state governments
June, Coahuila and Zacatecas Railroad completed from Saltillo to Concepcion del Oro
Dec. 9, Concession granted for railroad from Cordoba to Coscomatepec; acquired by Mexican Railway Nov. 4, 1909
Dec. 17, Railroad act of Limantour

1899

Feb. 22, Extradition Treaty with the United States concluded; proclaimed April 24
April 29, General railroad law enacted which repealed those previously made except as to acquirement of telephone and telegraph lines by government; franchises granted for term not over 99 years
July 1, New loan contracted for £22,700,000 at 5% signed in Berlin, in Paris, July 2, in London, July 3, and new bonds issued
July, Yaqui Indians in Sonora in revolt against the Government
Sept. 25, Yaquis defeated in battle

Dec. 14, Treaty of friendship, commerce, and navigation with China signed
Dec. 22, Boundary Agreement with the United States

1900

Jan. 1, President Diaz reëlected
Jan. 18, Gen. Torres gained important victory over Yaquis at Macoyate
Feb. 23, Fierce battle with the Yaquis at Macoyate
March 6–9, Engagements with the Yaquis at Cocori
May 17, Canal begun in 1886 to prevent floods in valley of Mexico City completed
July, Work begun on Kansas City, Mexico, and Orient Railway to connect Kansas City, Mo., with Pacific
Oct. 28, Census showed population of Mexico to be 13,570,545 of whom 19% were white, 43% Indian, and 38% of mixed blood. About 80,000 foreigners; 530,723 in Federal District, 357,000 in City of Mexico. The population of the seven states, Jalisco, Guanajuato, Puebla, Vera Cruz, Oaxaca, Michoan, and Mexico is 6,995,880 more than half of the population (Population of Mexico City 368,777, Puebla 88,684, Guadalajara 83,934, San Luis Potosi 69,050)
Nov. 6, Treaty of commerce with Nicaragua concluded
Nov. 21, Water boundary convention with the United States concluded
Dec. 1, President Diaz inaugurated as President for 6th term
Dec., Mexican Petroleum Company organized by E. L. Doheny and C. A. Canfield; drilling begun by this pioneer company May, 1901
Dec. 14, Territory of Quintana Roo created

1901

Feb. 2, Snow fell in Mexico City for first time in 50 years
——, Mexican forces in Sonora ambushed by Yaquis and 100 killed
Feb. 12, Mayas in revolt in Yucatan defeated in battle
April 17, Representatives of Mexico signed convention at Peace Conference at The Hague
April 24, Constitution of 1857 amended
May 14, First oil well brought in at Ebano
Sept. 17, Treaty of commerce and navigation with Austria-Hungary concluded
Oct. 22–Jan. 31, 1902, Second Pan-American Congress held at Mexico City; decision made to adhere to Hague Convention of 1899
Nov. 1, New tariff schedule came into effect

1902

Jan. 18, Arbitration Treaty with Spain signed
Jan. 29, Compulsory Arbitration Treaty signed with Argentina, Bolivia, Dominican Republic, Guatemala, Peru, Salvador, and Uruguay
May 14, Treaty of commerce with Persia concluded
May 16, Contract for railroad signed with S. Pearson and Co.
May 22, Protocol for adjustment of contention under "Pious fund of the Californias" concluded referred to Hague Tribunal for arbitration
May 29, Yaquis defeated at El Tanque and retired to Mazatam Mts.
June 25, Supplementary extradition Convention with the United States concluded
Oct. 14, Award of the Hague Tribunal that Mexico should pay the United States $1,420,682.67 in Pious

funds case and $43,051 annually in satisfaction of California claim

Nov. 25, Decree established basis for calculating and collecting duties on importation of foreign goods

Dec. 3, Decree established surtax of 2% on foreign goods imported through Tampico custom house

Dec. 20, Diaz decree revised legislation as to public lands

1903

Jan. 28, Mexico and China proposed a world agreement on silver

Feb. 20, Meeting of Mexican monetary conference

March 26, Treaty respecting literary, scientific, and artistic copyrights between Mexico and Spain concluded

May 7, Decree as to stamp duty on tobacco

June 10, Mexico joined the International Union for the Protection of Industrial Property

Aug. 25, New patent law enacted

——, New trade mark law enacted repealing law of Nov. 28, 1889 and amendment of Dec. 17, 1897

Sept. 24, Regulations published as to procedure as to patents and trade marks

Oct. 6, Mexico awarded $510,000 in claims against Venezuela

1904

Feb. 25, Quintana Roo made a federal territory

April 3, Rules governing admission of Orientals to the Republic promulgated

May 6, Concession for Inter-California Railway granted. Completed in 1909 from Andrade to Calexico

May 20, Decree as to stamp duty on tobacco

Oct. 31, Contract for new loan of $40,000,000 at 4% signed in New York with international bankers

Dec. 1, President Diaz inaugurated as President, his 7th consecutive term of office. The first Vice-President of Mexico under constitutional amendment, Ramon Corral also inaugurated

1905

March 20, Convention with the United States concluded for elimination of the Bancos in the Rio Grande River; proclaimed June 6, 1907

March 25, Gold standard put into effect in decree for reform of currency

——, Mining tax imposed on precious metals and mines

April 25, Ratification of Geneva Convention of 1864

May 1, New monetary system went into effect, the peso stabilized on gold basis

June 20, New tariff law enacted to take effect Sept. 1, 1905, increased rates on 217 numbers, reduced rates on 175 numbers, and reclassified entire tariff

July 1, The Free Zone ceased to exist

——, Disastrous flood at mining city of Guanajuato

Oct. 27, Concession granted for railroad from Guaymas, Sonora, to Guadalajara, Jalisco (The Southern Pacific Railway of Mexico). Ground broken immediately

1906

Feb. 3, President Diaz and other government officials left Vera Cruz on visit to Yucatan

March 21, Centenary of Benito Juarez celebrated in Mexico by decree of Congress

May 21, Convention with the United States provided for equitable distribution of the waters of the Rio Grande for irrigation purposes

June 1, Riots in connection with strike of Greene Consolidated Copper Company (American) at Cananea, Sonora

——, Federal stamp tax law enacted

July 19, Conference on American battleship in which Mexico agreed to join the United States in mediating with warring states of Salvador, Honduras, and Guatemala

Sept. 29, Ceremony in which President received the insignia of the Order of the Bath from the British minister in Mexico conferred by King Edward

Dec. 26, Mexican Central Railroad and Mexican National Railroad companies combined under government control by resolution of Congress

1907

Jan. 24, Completion of the Tehuantepec Railway connected the Atlantic and Pacific

April 14, Earthquake practically destroyed the towns of Chilapaca, Aytula, and Ometepec

May 12, Southern Pacific completed from Empalme to Navojoa (117 miles)

June 30, Manuel Sarabia, opponent of the government of Diaz resident in Douglas, Arizona, kidnapped by Maza, Mexican consul at Douglas, and taken to Mexico. Brought back because of aroused American public opinion

July 6, Decree authorized combination of Central and National railroads under law of Dec. 26, 1906; combination made April 6, 1908

Aug. 6, Red Cross Society founded

Oct. 16, Arbitration Treaty with Italy signed

Dec. 2–7, Third International Sanitary Convention of American Republics met in Mexico City

1908

March, Personal interview given by President Diaz to James Creelman published in *Pearson's Magazine* in which he said that Mexico was ready for democratic government and that he intended to leave the presidency at the end of his term

March 24, Arbitration convention with the United States concluded; proclaimed June 29, and with Honduras

April 3, San Diego and Arizona Railway obtained concession for road through Mexico to complete road from Tiajuana to Lindero; opened in 1915

April 15, Anti-reëlection party nominated F. Madero and F. V. Gomez for President and Vice-President

May 28, Treaty of amity and commerce with Honduras

June 19, New Banking law

June 20, Constitutional amendment empowered federal government to define and determine waters subject to federal jurisdiction

June 25, Rebels raided and looted Viesca in Coahula

June 26, Engagement with rebels near Las Vacas

July 1, Yaqui Indians in revolt captured by federal troops in mountains of Sonora

Aug., Revision of tariff

Sept. 3, Concession granted for establishment of Loan Bank for Works of Irrigation and Promotion of Agriculture

Dec., Railroad from Guadalajara to Colima opened establishing with connections a second route between the Pacific Ocean and the Gulf

Dec. 29, War with Yaquis ended by peace signed by 3 chiefs with governor of Sonora

1909

Jan. 1, Hidalgo and North East Railroad from Mexico to Tortugas became party of system of National Railroad

Jan. 4, Peace treaty signed by Yaqui Indians

Jan. 7, Contract made for railroad from Durango to Mazatlan

Feb. 1, Merger of Mexican Central Railway and Mexican National Railway became effective

Feb. 15, Theater burned at Acapulco. 300 lives lost

April 11, Treaty of arbitration with Brazil signed

July 30, Earthquake virtually destroyed Acapulco

Sept. 13, Decree proclaimed Mexico a party to International Agreement respecting Trade Marks

Sept. 19 (Oct. 2), Commercial Treaty with Russia

Oct. 16, President Taft at El Paso, Texas, received visit from President Diaz and was entertained at dinner by President Diaz at Ciudad Juarez on the Mexican side of boundary

Nov. 2, Concession granted for construction of Mexico Northwestern Railway from Ciudad Juarez to Tabalaopa

Nov. 9, Regulations for registry of international trade marks published

Nov. 25, New mining code published made absolute restriction against foreign companies; not permitted to hold patent or title to properties within certain area of border, to become effective Jan. 1, 1910

Dec. 1, United States severed diplomatic relations with Mexico

Dec. 15, Regulations as to mining under new law published

Dec. 18, New land law suspended provisions of law of March 26, 1894 relating to filing claims on waste lands

1910

Feb. 2, Failure of Mexican Packing Company with liabilities of $37,000,000

April 18, Concession for railroad from Santa Rosalia to La Boquilla (Camargo and Western Railway)

May 26, Existing schools of law, medicine, engineering, and architecture made parts of University of Mexico

June 7, Arrest and imprisonment for sedition of Francisco I. Madero

——, Troops sent to quell Maya uprising in Yucatan

June 22, Agrarian Bureau created

June 24, Convention with the United States for arbitration of the Chamizal case signed at Washington, as to boundary line at Chamizal tract

July 2, Loan contracted for bond issue of £22,200,000 signed in Paris with international bankers

Sept. 21, Centennial celebration of anniversary of independence

——, Opening of new water supply for Mexico City

Sept. 22, Official inauguration of University of Mexico under new plan

Oct. 4, The reëlection of Diaz and Corral for another 6 years announced

Oct. 5, Madero proclaimed the Plan de San Luis Potosi denouncing the reëlection of Diaz and his lack of opportunity to receive vote for the presidency, promising agrarian, franchise, and administrative reforms

Oct. 7, Madero in disguise escaped across the border into the United States to San Antonio, Texas

Nov., Castulo Herrera and Pascal Orozco started revolt in Chihuahua

Nov. 18, Aquiles Serdan at Puebla in revolt against Diaz shot in his home

Dec. 1, President Diaz took oath of office for his 8th presidential term

Dec. 5, Supplementary protocol to Chamizal convention signed at Washington

Dec. 6, Rebels captured Guerrero; driven out 3 days later

Dec. 13, Battle at Cerro Prieto in state of Chihuahua

Dec. 14, Congress enacted regulations as to enjoyment of waters under federal jurisdiction; restrictions against foreigners embodied forbidding ownership within certain distance of frontiers and coast

Dec. 16, Federal troops defeated at La Junta

1911

Jan. 11, Clash between Mexican regular troops and insurgents opposite Comstock, Texas

Jan. 13, Skirmish on the Rio Grande, 20 killed

Jan. 17, 16 hour battle at Carome, Chihuahua

Jan. 20, International School of American Archaeology inaugurated in Mexico City by Mexican and Prussian governments and Columbia and Harvard universities

Jan. 29, Insurgents take Mexicali

Feb. 5, Federals win at Juarez

Feb. 9, Federals occupied Juarez

Feb. 16, Gen. Navarro placed Juarez under martial law; attack on insurgents at Mexicala unsuccessful

Feb. 20, Navarro takes Guadalupe

March 5, Rebels defeated by Federalist troops at Casas Grandes

March 11, The Government suspended constitutional guarantees

March 12, Rebels defeated by government forces near Agua Prieta

March 13, States of Coahuila and Morelos revolt

March 23, 9 hour battle at Sonora

March 24, Jose Pinto Suarez inaugurated Vice-President. Cabinet resigned and new Cabinet with de la Barra as Premier took office

April 1, Diaz in message to Congress promised abolition of reëlection of president

April 13, The insurgents captured Agua Prieta. American citizens at Douglas, Arizona town, opposite, killed and wounded

April 23, 5 days armistice to discuss peace signed

April 27, Armistice extended until May 6

May 10, Ciudad Juarez taken by rebels. Madero established his government at Ciudad Juarez

May 15–June 15, International Boundary Commission in sessions at El Paso, Texas, and Juarez, Mexico; made decision in Chamizal boundary dispute

May 21, Treaty signed with the successful rebels providing that Diaz and Corral should resign before June 1, and Francisco de la Barra should become ad interim President and call for general election

May 25, Diaz and Corral resigned and De la Barra assumed office the next day

May 26, Escorted by General Victoriano Huerta Diaz left the capital for Vera Cruz and sailed for France

June 7, Madero entered capital

July 13, Federalists and Maderists in 2 day battle at Puebla. 135 killed

Aug. 30, F. I. Madero nominated for president by the Progressive party

Oct. 1 and 15, Elections took place

Oct. 2, The newspapers *La Prensa* and the *Daily Mexican* established

Nov. 6, Madero as President and Pino Suarez, Vice-President, inaugurated

Nov. 18, General Reyes, revolutionist, arrested at San Antonio, Texas, for violation of neutrality

Nov. 24, President Madero signed decree providing for active military service of 2 years of annual quota of 15,000 men

Nov. 25, State of Oaxaca seceded

Nov. 28, Zapata published his Plan of Ayala which called for distribution of one-third of the great estates among the landless

Dec. 25, General Reyes surrendered to Madero Government and was thrown into prison

1912

Jan. 31, Rebels seized the city of Juarez

Feb. 1, Emilio Gomez named provisional President by revolutionists

Feb. 2, Battle at Chihuahua

Feb. 5, Southern Pacific Railroad opened from Nogales, Arizona to Tepic in State of Nayarit

Feb. 18, Gomez resigned as Minister of the Interior and in manifesto accepted presidency

Feb. 23, General Orozco joined the revolution

Feb. 24, Decree provided for new survey of national lands and division into small lots to be sold to needy Mexicans

Feb. 27, Revolutionary General Campa captured Juarez

March 3, Armed revolt against Government led by Pascual Orozco in Chihuahua

March 12, 500 rebels under General Blanco defeated near Agua Prieta

March 14, President Taft placed embargo on arms to Mexico from the United States

March 17, Ex-Provisional President De la Barra left Paris for Mexico

March 22, Federals defeat rebels under Salazar 20 miles south of Jiminez

March 25, Rebels rout federals at Jiminez

March 29, American owned newspaper *El Herlado Mexicano* suppressed by Madero

April 5, Parral taken by rebels

April 6, De la Barra arrived at Vera Cruz

April 9, 500 rebels killed at Jojutla

April 18, Culiacan captured by rebels

April 23, Congress increased army to 60,000

April 24, Yaqui Indians take to the war path

April 25, Federals take Hutzilao

May 4, Emilio Gomez proclaimed President at Vera Cruz

May 9, Federals defeat rebels at Torreon

May 16, Federals defeated at Pedricena

May 21, Escalon sacked. Rebels win Guadaloupe

May 23, Rebels defeated in battle at Rellano retreat to Corralitos

May 26, Rebels establish headquarters at Jiminez but evacuate May 27

May 30, Madero negotiated loan in New York for $10,000,000 at 4.5% with Speyer and Company

June 2, People of western Chihuahua and eastern Sonora rise

June 7, State of Chihuahua authorized a $1,000,000 bond issue to finance the revolution and General Orozco

June 15, Zapata defeated in Morelos

June 25, General Orozco offered to surrender if amnesty granted for himself and his followers

July 3, Orozco defeated in battle at Bachimba by government troops

July 9, Federals took Chihuahua evacuated by rebels

July 11, General Orozco established rebel headquarters at Juarez

July 16, Concession granted to Richard Honey for railroad from Mexico City to Tampico; acquired by Mexican Railway May 21, 1923

July 29, Federals beaten at Cas Grandas and rebels at Ojitos

Aug. 12, Concession granted for a railroad from Monclova to Chihuahua

Aug. 16, Orozco evacuated Juarez

Aug. 20, Federal troops occupied Juarez

Sept. 1, Zapatists beaten near Tenancingo

Sept. 14, Rebels lose at Jajalpa and near Oaxaca

Sept. 15, Federals take Ojinaga

Sept. 19, Federal victory near Agua Prieta

Oct. 4, Rebels take Cholula and Ascension

Oct. 15, Vera Cruz captured by revolutionists led by Felix Diaz

Oct. 22, Felix Diaz arrested and imprisoned after defeat by General Joaquin Beltran sent by Madero to recover Vera Cruz

Oct. 25, Madero saves Felix Diaz from death penalty

Nov. 5, Zapatists take Cuernavaca

Nov. 21, Rebels take Palomas

Dec. 18, Rebels under Orozco captured Casas Grandes

Dec. 30, General Fernandez and 200 rebels surrender

1913

Jan. 9, Ayotzingo burned by rebels

Jan. 20, The volcano Colima in southwest in violent eruption

Feb. 9, General Mondragon and Colonel Aguillon at head of soldiers released General Reyes and Felix Diaz from prison and attacked the Palace. Reyes killed by defenders in attack

Feb. 9–18, The "Tragic Ten Days"; revolution against Government of Madero by Huerta and other leaders

Feb. 10, Bombardment of the National Palace begun

Feb. 11, General Huerta with other rebels defended the arsenal against 4 attacks of loyal federal troops

——, Battle in streets of Mexico City between revolutionists and federal troops

Feb. 15, The Senate convened recommended that President Madero resign

——, E. V. Gomez proclaimed himself President

Feb. 17, General Blanque arrived at capital with 1,200 federal troops and joined Huerta in attack on the Government

Feb. 18, Madero, Suarez, and the cabinet officers arrested by order of General Huerta who acted as chief executive taking title of Provisional President

——, Company formed for construction of Tampico Panuco Valley Railway Company. In 1917 8 miles from Panuco completed

Feb. 19, Madero resigned as demanded by Huerta and asked for escort to Vera Cruz. Huerta took oath of office as President

——, G. Madero, brother of the President, executed

——, Venustiano Carranza, Governor of Coahuila, refused to recognize usurpation of government by Huerta and called on governors of other states to join in revolt, the "Revolution of the Constitutionalist Party"

Feb. 22–23, Madero and Suarez assassinated by Huerta guards while being taken from one prison to another. Crime charged to Major Francisco Cardenas. Huerta denied complicity

March 9, Rebels take Nacozari

March 11, Refusal of President Wilson to recognize the Huerta Government

March 12, Constitutionalists occupy Agua Prieta

——, Pascuale Orozco declared for Huerta

March 13, Constitutionalists occupy Nogales

March 15, General Ojeda defeated rebels at Naco

March 25, Carranza lost Saltillo

March 26, Carranza announced the Plan of Guadalupe against Huerta. Joined by Pascual Orozco, Emilio Vasquez Gomez, and others

April 1, General Obregon took Naco

April 2, Villa recaptured Torreon from the Federalists

April 11, Spain recognized the Huerta Government

April 13, Rebels take Naco, Sonora

May 1, Export tax placed on gold

May 3, Great Britain recognized Huerta Government

May 5, Colombia recognized the Huerta Government

May 7, President Huerta asked recognition of his Government by the United States

May 13, France recognized the Huerta Government

May 22, Rebels win battle near Sacramento, Coahuila gaining possession of all towns between Saltillo and Monclova

May 24, Honduras recognized the Huerta Government

May 29, Italy recognized the Huerta Government

May 31, Federalists routed 200 Carranzists near Laredo, Texas

June 3, Rebels (Constitutionalists) took Matamoras

June 8, Loan of £16,000,000 negotiated by the Huerta Government in Paris with representatives of banking houses of Paris, Berlin, London, and New York at 6% for 10 years

June 9, Norway and Ecuador recognized the Huerta Government

June 12, Japan recognized the Huerta Government

June 13, The Netherlands recognized the Huerta Government

June 15, Uruguay recognized the Huerta Government

June 17, Germany recognized the Huerta Government

June 21, Federals defeated rebels in 2 days battle at Ortiz, Sonora

July 2, Denmark recognized the Huerta Government

July 7, Turkey recognized the Huerta Government

July 14, President Wilson recalled Henry Lane Wilson, American minister in Mexico friendly to Huerta administration, Nelson O'Shaughnessy left in charge

Aug. 10–26, John Lind, sent by President Wilson to Mexico to ask Huerta to agree to an armistice and withdraw as candidate for the presidency, in Mexico City

Aug. 18, President Huerta rejected the Lind proposals

Sept. 9, Obregon and Villa combined to urge Carranza to undertake the solution of the agrarian problem

Sept. 19, Revolutionists dynamited train near Saltillo killing soldiers and passengers

Sept. 30, Huerta obtained loan of 18,000,000 pesos from 9 banks in Mexico City

Oct. 2, Rebels defeated at Santa Rosalia

Oct. 7, General Maas for Huerta took Piedras Negras

Oct. 10, Revolutionists led by Francisco Villa took Torreon after victories at Casas Grandes and San Andres

Oct. 10, *Coup d'état* by which 110 members of Chamber of Deputies ordered under arrest for move to investigate disappearance of Senator Belisario Dominguez on Oct. 7, after his speech against Huerta. Congress dissolved by Huerta

——, Drawn battle at Altes

Oct. 14, Resignation of Henry Lane Wilson, American ambassador to Mexico, took effect

Oct. 20, Huerta ordered 50% increase of import duties

Oct. 23, Rebel attack on Monterey

Oct. 25, Constitutionalist General Jesus Carranza captured Monterey

Oct. 26, Election which occurred fraudulent because of interference of administration was rejected by Congress as to president but accepted as to Congress

——, Huerta decree increased army from 80,000 to 150,000

Nov. 2, Formal request of the United States for resignation of President Huerta

Nov. 4, Zacatecas besieged by rebels

Nov. 5, New banking law made acceptance of silver peso obligatory for any amount, and paper of National Bank of Mexico and Bank of London and Mexico legal tender for all amounts; banks instructed not to redeem their paper

Nov. 6–8, Attack of Pancho Villa on Ciudad Juarez beaten off by federal troops

Nov. 12, William Bayard Hale representing President Wilson made proposals to Carranza Government. John Lind left Mexico City

Nov. 13, General Candido Aguilar captured port of Tuxpan

Nov. 14, Obregon captured Culiacan in Sinaloa

Nov. 15, Rebels captured Tuxpan and Sancho Villa took Juarez

Nov. 18, Lucio Blanco and Pablo Gonzales captured Ciudad Victoria

Nov. 19, Rebels surrendered Tampico

Nov. 20, Huerta nearly doubles the stamp taxes to take effect Dec. 1

——, Tepic captured by rebels

Nov. 24, Federals attacked Juarez but were defeated in battle the following day

Nov. 27, General Obregon captured Mazatlan

Dec. 1, Federals evacuate Chihuahua

Dec. 2, President Wilson announced to Congress his continued policy of non-recognition of Huerta Government

Dec. 5, Revolutionists captured Colima

Dec. 6, A Belgian company authorized to construct more than 3,000 miles of railroad in Mexico

Dec. 7, Zapatists start fighting in state of Morelos

Dec. 8, Villa entered Chihuahua evacuated by the federals

Dec. 9, Congress extended Huerta's term to July 5, 1914, by a resolution which declared the election which had taken place invalid

Dec. 10, Congress authorized an additional loan of 100,000,000 pesos

——, Tampico attacked by rebels but siege raised the following day on protest of American Rear-Admiral Fletcher and his threat to fire on combatants

Dec. 12, Formal declaration of reform program by Constitutionalist group

Dec. 15, Zapatists capture Milpa Alta 20 miles from capital

Dec. 24, Torreon again occupied by rebels

Dec. 29, Federalists defeated in engagement with General Villa at Ojinaga

1914

Jan. 2, 26 deputies imprisoned since October released at Mexico City

Jan. 7, Federals lose 130 in battle at Torreon

Jan. 10, Ojinaga fell on attack led by Villa. Federal force of 4,600 escaped from Villa across the Rio Grande into American territory where they were interned

Jan. 12, Mexico defaulted payment of interest on national debt

Jan. 29, Decree abolished peonage

Feb. 3, Embargo on arms of March 14, 1912, removed by the American Government to assist revolution in Mexico

——, Rebels take Mazatlan

Feb. 14, Federals defeat rebels at Parral

Feb. 16, William G. Benton, an Englishman, killed by Villa when he made complaint of injury to his property by Villista troops

Feb. 21, Mass meeting at El Paso, Texas, adopted formal resolutions declaring Benton's death a case of unprovoked murder

March 3, Declaration of Sir Edward Grey in British House of Commons as to murder of Benton

——, General Carranza appointed a committee to investigate the killing of W. S. Benton

March 4, 200 Zapatists killed by Federals near capital

March 8, Constitutionalists began attack on Tampico

March 17, Villa army checked at Torreon

March 19, All day battle at Escalon

March 21, Villa arrived before Torreon

March 23, Rebels renewed attack on Torreon

March 24, Huerta obtained loan of 45,000,000 pesos from banks of Mexico

April 2, General Villa occupied Torreon driving the federal troops commanded by General Velasco and 6,000 to 7,000 Spaniards from the city

April 3, John Lind left Mexico City

April 4, Villa ordered deportation of 600 Spanish residents of Torreon

April 5, Carranza Committee reported Benton killed by Rodolfo Fierro

April 7, Spaniards driven from their homes in Torreon arrived at El Paso, Texas

——, United States protested against expulsion of Spaniards

April 9, American marines landing at wharf in Tampico for gasoline arrested presently released but demand of Admiral Mayo for apology and salute to flag in satisfaction denied

April 9–10, Villa won battle of San Pedro against General Velasco

April 11, Huerta apology for Tampico affair ignored order to salute American flag

April 12, Secretary Bryan insisted that Huerta comply with Admiral Mayo's demands

April 13, Huerta ordered that no salute should be given American flag except on condition of return salute

April 14, Constitutionalists under Villa captured San Pedro de las Colonias near Torreon

April 16, President Huerta agreed to salute American flag, the United States to return salute as a matter of courtesy

April 18, President Wilson informed Huerta that salute must be fired before 6 P.M. without any written agreement as to returned salute demanded

April 19, President Huerta refused to give unconditional salute to American flag

April 20, Villa troops take suburb of Monterey

April 21, American marines occupied Vera Cruz and seized the custom house in order to prevent landing of guns from German ship

April 22, Carranza protested to President Wilson against American occupation of Vera Cruz as "violation of national sovereignty"

——, Huerta ended diplomatic relations with the United States handing Nelson O'Shaughnessy his passports

April 23, Mexican Chargé d'Affaires in Washington requested his passports

——, President Wilson restored embargo on arms

April 24, Constitutionalists captured Monterey

——, General Funston with the 5th brigade of infantry sailed from Galveston for Vera Cruz

April 25, "A.B.C." powers offered mediation; accepted by the United States

April 26, Huerta accepted offer of "A.B.C." powers for mediation "in principle"

——, Admiral Fletcher placed Vera Cruz under martial law and required the citizens to surrender their arms

April 29, Carranza accepted "A.B.C." mediation "in principle"

April 30, Armistice arranged

May 3, General Funston established military government in Vera Cruz

——, Carranza refused request of "A.B.C." peace commissioners to suspend hostilities with Huerta

May 7, Rebels captured Mazatlan

May 10, American force took Lobos Island between Vera Cruz and Tampico

May 13, Carranza forces led by General Pablo Gonzales captured Tampico

May 16, Dutch marines landed at Tampico to protect oil properties

May 19, Carranza forces captured San Luis Potosi after 3 days battle

May 20, Constitutionalists occupied Saltillo

May 20–June 30, Mediation Conference held at Niagara Falls, Canada of representatives of the United States, Argentine, Brazil, and Chile and Mexico. Constitutionalist delegates were not included at opening because General Carranza would not agree to an armistice

May 21, Saltillo abandoned by Federalists on approach of Villa

May 24, "Uncultivated land tax bill" passed which imposed tax on great landed proprietors; 7,000 families held practically all arable land in Mexico

May 26, German steamer landed arms for revolutionists at Puerto Mexico

May 27, "A.B.C." conference at Niagara Falls agreed on peace plan

May 31, Carranza assumed title of Provisional President and established his government at Saltillo

——, Huerta cabled counter-proposals to the Niagara Conference

June 8, Carranza inaugurated Provisional President

June 10–14, Panfilo Natera, constitutional general, made unsuccessful attack on Zacatecas

June 12, Carranza named three delegates to conference at Niagara Falls

June 13, The Government suspended interest on the national debt for 6 months

June 16, Protests of France, Great Britain, and Germany of suspension of payment

June 23, Villa captured Zacatecas

June 24, Constitutionalists under General Gonzalo took Zacatecas

——, Mediators at Niagara Falls Conference sign Protocol providing that a new government constituted by agreement should be recognized by the United States, no war indemnity be demanded by the United States, and amnesty granted to foreigners for all political offenses

July 1, Conference at Niagara Falls ended

July 5, Huerta elected President

July 6, Villa acknowledged Carranza his chief and resumed his campaign

July 9, General Obregon, Constitutionalist, occupied Guadalajara after battle in which he captured 5,000 prisoners

July, General Pascual Orozco started a revolt against Carranza at Aguascalientes

——, Conference of Constitutionalist generals refused to consider anything but the unconditional surrender of the Huerta Government

July 10, Chief Justice Francisco Carbajal appointed Minister of Foreign Affairs

July 11, Senate approved Niagara Falls Conference Peace Protocol

July 15, Huerta resigned acknowledging that he had been forced out of office by nonrecognition policy of President Wilson and left the country on a German steamer

——, Francisco Carbajal took office as Provisional President

July 17, San Luis Potosi fell to Constitutionalist troops

July 18, Constitutionalist troops took Guaymas

July 19, Fall of Manzanillo

July 22, Constitutionalist troops captured Aguascalientes

July 23, Colima captured by Constitutionalists

July 24, Constitutionalist troops took Manzanillo

July 28, Constitutionalist troops took Guanajuato

July 31, Constitutionalists captured Queretaro

Aug. 5, Government declared neutrality in World War

Aug. 9–10, Pachuca, Toluca, and Morelia taken by Constitutionalists

Aug. 12, Provisional President Francisco S. Carbajal to whom Huerta had turned over the executive office resigned and left the capital, turning over Government to Iturbide, Governor of Federal District

Aug. 13, Protocol signed arranged for peaceful capitulation of Mexico City

Aug. 15, Alvaro Obregon entered the capital at head of soldiers of the Constitutionalist army

Aug. 17, Clash between Villistas and Carranzistas at Durango in new revolt

Aug. 20, Carranza entered the capital and assumed the executive power

Aug. 30, Zapata agreed to support Carranza

Sept. 3, General H. Aguilar proclaimed revolt against Carranza Government at Tehuacan

Sept. 4, Carranza declared himself provisional President and a candidate for permanent President at coming election

Sept. 6, Zapata, bandit, declared war on Carranza Government because of refusal to accept his proposed agrarian reforms

Sept. 7, President Carranza issued decree setting aside restrictions on arbitrary arrest and confiscation of property by which 1,000 persons arrested by the middle of the month

Sept. 25, Francisco Villa announced himself dictator of the north and declared war on the Carranza Government

——, Battle between Villistas and Carranzistas at Torreon

——, Declaration of neutrality in European war repeated

Oct. 1, Meeting of generals at Aguascalientes dominated by Zapata and Villa declared an armistice

Oct. 10, Conference between representatives of Carranza and Villa opened at Aguascalientes

Oct. 12, Carranza Government took possession of street car service of Mexico City following strike of employees

Oct. 17, Lower California seceded

Oct. 26, Decree of Aguascalientes Conference that provisional government be taken over by commission of five whom it nominated

Oct. 30, Conference of generals at Aguascalientes decreed the retirement of both Carranza and Villa

Nov. 4, Constitutionalist government decree promised to enact laws to improve conditions of labor

——, Villa seized Aguascalientes, arresting Carranza delegates to conference and made city temporary capital. Carranza made Puebla his capital

Nov. 5, Clashes between Villistas and Carranza troops south of the city

Nov. 6, Villa routed Carranza troops in an all day battle

Nov. 7, Tehuacan taken from Carranza forces. 200 killed

Nov. 8, Conference of Aguascalientes elected Eulalio Gutierrez provisional President. Villa and Zapata accepted choice. Obregon declared for Carranza

Nov. 10, President Gutierrez took oath of office as provisional President

——, Convention declared Carranza in rebellion

Nov. 11, Aguascalientes Conference made Villa commander-in-chief and ordered war on Carranza. General Obregon pledged loyalty to the Conference

——, Villa in battle at Leon with Carranza troops

Nov. 17, General Obregon seized Mexico City

Nov. 18, Villa occupied Irapuato and Guanajuato

Nov. 19, Villa occupied Quertano evacuated by Carranza

Nov. 21, Emiliano Zapata drove Carranza out of the capital, and a Villa-Zapata group occupied the city calling themselves "Conventionists"

Nov. 23, American marines evacuated Vera Cruz and General Candido Aguilar, Constitutionalist, occupied the city

Nov. 24, 10,000 Villista troops made unsuccessful attempt to wrest Guadalajara from Constitutionalists

——, Carranza forces left Mexico City. Zapata forces took possession

Nov. 26, Carranza, Obregon, and Alvarez entered Vera Cruz which became headquarters of Constitutionalist Government

Nov. 27, Carranza offered to retire if Villa and Zapata would do the same

Nov. 29, Villa troops took city of Pachuca

Dec. 1, Villa arrived at Mexico City

Dec. 3, President Gutierrez installed at capital

——, Carranzists captured Guaymas

Dec. 12, Decree of Carranza at Vera Cruz announced reform program

Dec. 16, Battle near Torreon

Dec. 18, Puebla captured by the Conventionalists Generals Zapata and Angeles but soon evacuated

Dec. 25, Decree abolished the "Jefe Politico"

Dec. 26, Carranza decree established "free municipal elections" for officials by the towns

Dec. 29, Divorce made legal

1915

Jan. 1, The Villa and Zapata delegates of the Aguascalientes Conference met at Mexico City to appoint provisional government

Jan. 3, General Obregon (Carranzista) captured Amazac near Puebla

Jan. 5, General Obregon occupied Puebla captured from the Villistas

Jan. 6, Carranza land decree divided the large estates and annulled all alienation laws, of communal, forests, water rights and lands sequent to Lerdo law of 1856 and restored them to their pueblos; amended Sept. 19, 1916

——, British oil properties at Tampico closed down by order of Carranza. Embargo raised Jan. 16

Jan. 7, Circular of the Government announced oil wells drilled without permits would be taken over on properties whose companies had not complied with decrees

Jan. 10, Neutralization pact made for protection of American border signed at Naco by General Maytorena and Colonel Calles and American General Hugh L. Scott

Jan. 11, General Angeles (Villista) captured Salinas on outskirts of Monterey forcing Carranzistas to evacuate the city

Jan. 12, Convention chose Eulalio Gutierrez as provisional President to serve until April 1, 1916

Jan. 16, Carranza raised embargo on exploitation of oil for the Tampico region

Jan. 17, General Angeles occupied Monterey

——, The Convention chose Roque Gonzales Garza as provisional President to hold office until Dec. 3, ratified Jan. 23, deposing Gutierrez who established headquarters at Pachuca

Jan. 20, General Eulalio Gutierrez surrendered his forces to General Carranza at Vera Cruz

Jan. 20–21, General Caballero in battle with Villistas around Tampico

Jan. 22, Zapata captured city of Puebla

Jan. 24, General Obregon defeated the Zapatistas about 40 miles from Mexico City

Jan. 27, Mexico City evacuated by the Villistas and President Garza

Jan. 28, Obregon occupied the capital for Carranza

Jan. 29, Garza resigned as President

——, Carranza decree assumed federal jurisdiction over labor legislation

Jan. 30, General Pablo de la Garza renounced Villa and surrendered city of San Luis Potosi to Generals Blanco Robler and Aguirre

Feb. 1, General Tomas Urbina captured San Luis Potosi for Villa

Feb. 3, Villa with headquarters at Aguascalientes announced his assumption of the executive power

Feb. 8, Villa won important 5 day battle near Monterey

Feb. 11, Carranza ordered Spanish Minister at Mexico City to leave within 24 hours because of his refusal to surrender Angel Del Caso, Spanish subject, suspected as a Villista who had taken refuge in the legation

Feb. 13, Villista General Medina drove General Miguel Dieguez from Guadalajara, the second most important city in Mexico

Feb. 16, The Spanish Minister left Vera Cruz for Havana

Feb. 17, Agreement between the Constitutionalist Government and organized labor, the *Casa del Obrero Mundial* declared terms of support of workers

Feb. 19, General Dieguez defeated by Villistas at Cuestra de Sayuta near Zapotlan and 400 of his troops captured

Feb. 20, Mexican forces of Cabral and Maytorera in violation of neutrality pact occupied Naco, Sonora

Feb. 23, General Obregon issued decree exacting payment within 72 hours of tax of ¾ of 1% on capital of all business in the Federal District; revoked as to foreigners Feb. 26 on protest of the United States

Feb. 26, General Pablo Gonzales (Carranzista) began attack on Monterey

March 10, General Obregon evacuated Mexico City and the Zapatists entered the following day

March 13, General Carranza abandoned blockade on Mexican port of Progresso under pressure from the United States

March 24, Villa renounced claims to presidency and named Garza as provisional President

March 27, Villa forces defeated in attack on Matamoras

April 1, Decree of Carranza increased wages of employees of textile factories 35%

April 2, 7, 16, and 19, Villa defeated in attacks on Celaya by Obregon

April 9, At Celaya General Obregon fixed 75 centavos daily as a minimum wage

April 15, Carranza declared neutrality in World War in message to Congress

——, Carranza decree modified decree of Jan. 6, 1915, by prohibiting provisional grants of lands

April 15–19, General Obregon repulsed attacks of Villa at Celaya

May 2, Both sides claimed victory in battle south of Aguascalientes occupied by Villa

May 22, General Angeles (Villista) defeated in battle near Trinidad Station, Guanajuato

——, Villa took Silao after all day battle with Obregon

May 31, Conventionalist army under General Urbina attempting to capture Tampico defeated at El Ebano

——, Battle of Leon begun

June 2, President Wilson made statement of policy expressing desire of United States to aid in settlement of country. Copies sent to Carranza, Villa, Zapata, and Garza

June 6, Carranzist forces under General Obregon win victory over Generals Villa and Angeles at Leon after 5 days fighting

June 9, Garza deposed by Convention and Francisco Lagos Chazaro appointed provisional President

June 11, General Carranza issued proclamation inviting warring Mexican factions to join government he proposed to establish at Mexico City and stated his program of reform which included separation of Church and State and freedom of religion

June 27, General Victoriano Huerta and General P. Orozco arrested by federal officers at Newman, New Mexico, accused of plotting revolution in Mexico

June 30, The United States invited the "A.B.C."

powers with Bolivia, Guatemala, and Uruguay to conference on Mexican problems

July 2, Death of Porfirio Diaz at Paris

July 10, Zapatistas evacuated Mexico City and constitutionalist General Gonzales took possession for Carranza

July 15, Carranza returned to capital

July 19, Zapata again occupied Mexico City

July 20, General Calles (Carranzista) captured Naco in violation of neutrality pact

July 31, General Pablo Gonzales again occupied Mexico City

Aug. 11, The "A.B.C." States with Bolivia, Uruguay, and Guatemala in conference at Washington (Aug. 5) issued appeal to Mexicans to establish a provisional government and call for election of president

——, Carranza protested to the United States at foreign intervention in Mexican affairs

Aug. 19, Villa accepted offer of the United States and South American states for peace conference

Aug. 31, General P. Orozco killed by American posse in Texas

Sept. 4, General Obregon captured Saltillo for Carranza

Sept. 10, Carranza rejected offer of United States and South American states for peace conference

Sept. 15, Proclamation of Carranza called for convention to reform the Constitution

Sept. 18, Pan-American Conference adjourned to New York City

Sept. 29, General Obregon captured Torreon

Oct. 12, Carranzistas captured port of Guaymas

Oct. 19, Eight Latin-American republics joined with the United States in recognition of Carranza as *de facto* president. Carranza controlled the larger part of central and southern Mexico at this time, the States of Sonora and Chihuahua and parts of Sinaloa, Durango, and Coahuila in the north controlled by Villa. Lower California remained neutral

——, President Wilson proclaimed embargo on arms to territory not in control of Carranza

Nov. 2, Carranza troops allowed to pass through American territory to Douglas, Arizona, recrossed the frontier and defeated Villa forces at Agua Prieta

Nov. 3, Villa failed in attack on Agua Prieta occupied by General Calles

Nov. 10, Cuba recognized the Carranza Government

Nov. 16, Great Britain recognized the Carranza Government

Nov. 22, Carranza forces captured Cananea in the northern part of Sonora, Villa losing 2,000 men at Hermosillo, 130 miles to the southwest

Nov. 25, Carranza Government recognized by Spain

Dec. 17, Diplomatic relations with Mexico resumed by the United States, Henry P. Fletcher sent as ambassador to Mexico and Eliseo Arredono received in Washington

Dec. 18, In a council of war at Chihuahua Villa announced that he would cease to oppose the Carranza Government and would leave Mexico

Dec. 23, Juarez occupied by General Obregon

1916

Jan. 10, Followers of Villa shot 18 American citizens headed by C. R. Watson at Santa Ysabel on their way to Mexico to open mines

Jan. 12, General José Roderiguez, Almeida, and other Villista leaders captured by General Maximo

Marquez, commander of garrison at Madera. Almeida shot immediately and the others later

Jan. 13, Death of Victoriano Huerta, former President at El Paso, Texas, a prisoner of the United States

Jan. 14, Carranza decree empowered any citizen of Mexico to kill on sight Villa, Rafael Castro, and Pablo Lopez, murderers of Americans at Santa Ysabel

Feb. 13, Capture of Ajusco in Morelos stronghold of Zapata

March 9, Raid of Villa on Columbus, New Mexico in which 17 Americans and a large number of Mexicans killed

March 10, Carranza Note proposed reciprocal rights as to pursuit of border raiders

——, President Wilson ordered General Funston to pursue Villa into Mexico

March 13, American Note accepted Carranza proposal of reciprocal rights in pursuit across frontier

March 15, American troops commanded by General Pershing and Colonel George Dodd crossed Mexican border in pursuit of Villa

——, Protest of Carranza against entry of United States troops into Mexico before terms of reciprocal agreement concluded

March 20, Carranzistas defeat Villa's forces at Namiqulpa, Chihuahua

March 27, Villa attacked town of Guerrero killing 172 men in the garrison

March 29, United States troops commanded by Colonel Dodd in engagement with Villa's troops at San Geronimo dispersed them; Villa escaped

April 1, United States cavalry killed 30 Mexican bandits at Aguascalientes

April 3, Decree provided for commission to reorganize currency system

April 12, Clash between American and Carranza troops at Parral

April 16, Carranza Note to American government demanded withdrawal of American soldiers from Mexico

April 29, Conference of Generals Scott and Funston with Mexican Generals Obregon and Trevino begun which ended without agreement

May 5, Villistas raided and looted Texas villages of Boquillas and Glen Springs

May 10, The State Department of the United States advised American nationals to leave Mexico

May 22, Carranza second Note to American Government demanded withdrawal of United States soldiers from Mexico

May 29, Villa defeated in battle by Colonel Dodd

June 11, American troops at Laredo attacked by Mexicans

June 15, Mexicans attacked American border patrol at San Ignacio; several killed and wounded on both sides

June 16, Carranza notified General Pershing at head of punitive expedition against Villa that further invasion of Mexico would be resisted

June 18, A boat from American gunboat "Annapolis" landing at Mazatlan fired on by Mexicans

June 20, Note of Secretary Lansing refusing to withdraw American troops until order established received by Carranza

June 21–22, Carranza troops and Americans in engagement at Carrizal and 22 American prisoners taken

June 24, Note to United States stated that orders to General Treviso were not to permit American troops to advance either south, east, or west

June 28, American prisoners released by Carranza on demand of American Government

June 30, Order withdrew all notes of over 20 pesos in value

July 4, Carranza returned conciliatory reply to American notes of June 20 and 25 accepting mediation

July 12, The Government proposed to the United States that a joint commission should draw up a protocol covering the retirement of the American troops and the rights of each nation to send soldiers across the border

July 31, New tariff enacted to take effect Nov. 1, certain food stuffs put on free list

Aug. 10, Carranza decree required foreign stockholders of new companies to waive diplomatic protection

Aug. 15, Decree requiring foreigners to renounce their national protection when acquiring rights to certain real property in Mexico

Sept. 6, American-Mexican Joint Commission began sessions at New York which adjourned to New London, Connecticut and subsequently to Atlantic City, ending Oct. 1

Sept. 15, Carranza decree that banks should bring their reserve (metal) up to outstanding notes within 60 days

Sept. 30, Decree provided for abolition of vice-presidency and reduced presidential term to 4 years with no reëlection

Oct. 7, Decree suspended bull fighting until order restored in country

Oct. 20, Villa defeated Carranza forces at Santa Ysabel

——, Concession for Acambaro to Quetaro Railway granted

Oct. 22, General election for constitutional assembly to revise organic law

Oct. 31, Villa captured Parral and occupied Jininez about the same time

Nov. 21–Jan. 31, 1917, Constitutional Convention in session

Nov. 23 and 25, Villistas repulsed in attack on city of Chihuahua by General Trevino who was obliged to evacuate the city on Nov. 27

Nov. 24, Commission signed agreement at Atlantic City that provided for withdrawal of American troops but terms not accepted by Carranza

Nov. 27, General Trevino evacuated city of Chihuahua

Dec. 1, Constitutional assembly met in Mexico City

——, Villa defeated by General Francisco Murguria 36 miles south of Chihuahua

Dec. 3, Carranza troops reëntered Chihuahua City

Dec. 6, Carranza recaptured Parral, Chihuahua

Dec. 15, Decree extended time for compliance with decree of Aug. 15 to April 15, 1917

Dec. 19, German Note proposed alliance in case of war with the United States, Mexico to receive former territory of Arizona, New Mexico, and Texas. Suggestion that Japan be invited to join by Mexico

Dec. 22, Villa captured Torreon

Dec. 25, Villistas captured San Luis Potosi

1917

Jan. 3, Villa at Torreon defeated in battle with General Obregon

Jan. 4, Villa defeated at Jiminez by General Murguria fled to Durango

Jan. 12, Villa forces defeated at Pilar de Concho by General Pablo Gonzales

Jan. 15, American-Mexican Joint Commission adjourned without settlement of disputes as to border patrol

Jan. 19, Zimmerman dispatch of Dec. 19, 1916 in which the alliance of Mexico with Germany proposed in case of war with the United States, published

——, Extension of time granted for compliance with decree of Dec. 15, 1916

Jan. 25, Concession granted to State of Jalisco for railroad from Santa Anna

Jan. 30, Decision of United States to recognize the Carranza Government

Jan. 31, Constitutional Convention at Queretaro adopted a new Constitution which was promulgated Feb. 5 to become effective May 1. Universal suffrage, presidency for only a single term, eight hour day, minimum wage, laws as to church and religious orders included. Article 27 restored communal lands to Indian villages. Each State to fix the maximum amount of land for individual ownership. All minerals and petroleum resources vested in "the nation"

Feb. 5, American troops left Mexico without accomplishing their object through lack of coöperation of Carranza

——, New Constitution promulgated

Feb. 12, Carranza Note to neutral nations proposing embargo on shipments of munitions and foodstuffs to all belligerents in World War

March 3, American ambassador, Henry P. Fletcher, presented his credentials resuming diplomatic relations with Mexico by the United States

March 11, Carranza elected President

——, Herlinda Galindo, first woman elected to Congress, to Chamber of Deputies

March 18, President Carranza issued decree of neutrality in European War

March 27, Villistas defeated at Marpula south of Chihuahua by General Murguria

March 30, Villa failed in attempt to capture Chihuahua

April 15, New Congress assembled, Constitutionalist Liberals in the majority

May 1, Carranza inaugurated as President

——, New Constitution came into effect

June 7, Decree placed tax on petroleum and its by-products

June 24, Department order prohibited issuance of drilling permits for oil wells on lands leased on dates subsequent to Feb. 5

July 9, Evangelical Seminary (Protestant) opened in Mexico City

July 20, Congress authorized loan of 100,000,000 pesos to establish a bank with exclusive right to issue currency

Sept. 1, President Carranza reaffirmed the neutrality of Mexico in the European War

Nov. 28, Concession for La Capilla to Chapala Railway granted to Norwegian company. Work begun July 1918

1918

Jan. 30, Act provided for establishment of Board of Conciliation and Arbitration

Feb. 19, Decree of Carranza under Article 27 of the new Constitution which declared oil an inalienable national resource imposed a tax on petroleum lands and contracts made prior to May 1, 1917. Oil companies required to confirm their titles. In place of titles to oil deposits "concessions" to be given to companies complying with the law

April 2, Foreign oil producers began to protest decrees of Carranza through their state departments. First American Note of protest on this date

May 18, Oil producers required under decree of Feb. 19 to declare and register their holdings given until July 31 to comply with the law

May 24, Diplomatic relations with Cuba severed because of Cuban measures due to state of war

July 31, Decree of Carranza declared that oil producers not declaring their holdings under decree of Feb. 19 were liable to denouncement of holdings; period of registration extended through Aug. 15

Aug. 8, New decree required owner or lessee who had registered to file claim for concession for holdings within 3 months

Aug. 12, Decree provided that no surveyed oil property in which capital invested should be open to claim and that owners might operate until "special contracts" prepared

Aug. 17, Reply of Government to American note of April 2

Oct. 3, Decree provided for mintage of new gold coins of denominations of 20, 10, 5, and 2½ pesos

Nov. 13, Monetary law of March 25, 1905 altered

Nov. 23, Decree carried out principle of government ownership conferring rights to claims to lands filed prior to May 1, 1917

Dec. 13, American Note on petroleum situation affecting American citizens owning property

1919

Feb. 23, International Committee of Bankers organized for protection of holders of securities of Mexican Republic and of various railway systems

March 15, Announced that General Pablo Gonzales, commander of government forces, had recovered control of State of Morelos, for years overrun by bands of Emiliano Zapato

March 20, Circular of Government ordered confiscation of oil wells and destruction of work if drilling permits have not been obtained

March 23, United States troops entered Mexico in pursuit of Mexican bandits stealing cattle and horses. Several Mexicans killed in skirmish

March 29, Government announced concession to Japanese to exploit agricultural lands in Lower California

April 9, Government took possession of Southern Pacific Railroad to end strike

April 17, Gen. Blanquet, rebel leader, killed in engagement near Vera Cruz

April 23, Mexican Minister to France recalled

May 29, Government answered American Note of April 16 protesting confiscation of oil properties of American citizens

June 15, American troops crossed border of Mexico to protect El Paso, Texas, and assisting the Carranza forces in battle with the Villistas

June 27, New schedule of mining taxes put into effect by executive decree

July 15, 13 sailors from United States gunboat "Cheyenne" attacked and robbed near Tampico by bandits

July 25, President of the United States placed embargo on arms and ammunition for Mexico

Aug. 1, Carranza circular announced that oil companies that had not complied with his decrees were prohibited from drilling without a permit

Aug. 16, Carranza ordered British diplomatic agent in charge of archives to leave Mexico

Aug. 30, Decision of Supreme Court of Mexico in case brought by Texas Oil Company upheld contention of American company that Article 27 of Constitution could not affect private titles acquired before May 1, 1917

——, Law provided for claims commission to adjust claims for damages caused by revolutions since 1910

Oct. 19, William Jenkins, American consular agent at Puebla, captured by bandits and held for ransom

Oct. 26, William Jenkins released on payment of ransom. Later arrested on charge of connivance with bandits

Nov. 12, Troops sent by Government stopped drilling in oil fields that had no permit

Nov. 19, General Felipe Angeles captured by government troops at Parral

——, Carranza Order refused permission to take oil from wells already drilled without a permit

Nov. 26, General Angeles, rebel leader, executed at Chihuahua

Dec. 4, William Jenkins set free on bail on request of United States

Dec. 28, An article in the *Excelsior* of Mexico City listed lands in possession of foreigners as 62,600,000 acres

Dec. 29, Decree published Jan. 1 imposed tax of 10% on net value per ton of petroleum exported

1920

Jan. 7, New bronze coin at nominal value of 20 centavos established

Jan. 10, Pan-American Federation of Labor met at Mexico City with delegates from 16 South American republics, and the United States and Mexico, Samuel Gompers presiding

Jan. 17, Carranza agreed to issue permits for drilling additional wells

Jan. 20, Petroleum companies obtained suspension of Carranza decrees pending final decision of courts

——, Agrarian law fixed indemnity for lands confiscated and provided for issuance of 20 year 5% bonds regulated Jan. 26, 1922

March 4, Villa with 150 men held up Mexico City train, robbed passengers, set fire to cars. Joseph Williams, American engineer, captured, released after 4 days

April 3, Strike of employees of Southern Pacific Railroad of Mexico begun

April 6, Ultimatum of Federal Government to Southern Pacific Railroad Company of Mexico and its employees that it would take over the railroad unless they reached agreement in disputes by April 9

April 9, State Government of Sonora seized railroad and began operation with strikers

——, *Plan de Agua Prieta* against Carranza published by Sonora "Triumvirate" composed of Adolfo de la Huerta, Obregon, and General Plutarco Elias Calles and the "Republic of Sonora" declared

April 12, Guaymas taken by anti-Carranza forces

April 17, Revolutionists of Sonora took Culiacan

April 18, The State of Nayarit joined the Sonora revolt

April 21, Colonel Rodolfo Gallegos with garrison of 400 at Linares, Nuevo Leon, joined anti-Carranza forces

April 23, Revolutionists proclaimed provisional government with de la Huerta as President, the Plan of
Agua Prieta

April 25, First clash in war in mountains near Pulpito
pass between the states of Chihuahua and Sonora

——, 18 members of Congress sent by Carranza to
negotiate with the rebels arrived at Hermosillo but
efforts fruitless

April 26, Federal garrison at Chihuahua City joined
the revolt against Carranza

May, La Capilla to Chapala Railway (Jalisco) completed

May 3, General Pablo Gonzales joined the revolt

May 5, President Carranza issued manifesto against
the revolutionists declaring that he would fight to
the end

May 6, Carranza with his troops and officials left Mexico City to establish his government at Vera Cruz

May 8, Obregon entered City of Mexico

May 9, Tampico fell to revolutionists

May 10, Mazatlan captured by General Flores, anti-
Carranzista

May 12, Vera Cruz surrendered to Obregon forces

May 14, Carranza with small force broke through
rebel lines south of Rinconada and started to make
his escape into the mountains between Puebla and
Orizaba

——, Matamoras surrendered to the rebels

May 21, Carranza shot by soldiers of Obregon at
Tlaxcalaltongo, Puebla attacked in his tent in the
night

May 24, A. de la Huerta chosen acting-President by
Congress

May 30, President de la Huerta arrived at the capital,
and June 1–Nov. 30, acted as provisional President

June 8, American war ships arrived at Tampico; withdrawn because of protest

June 14, Concession granted for railroad from Bahia
de la Roca to northern frontier (Arizona and Sonora
Railway)

July 14, General Pablo Gonzales started a revolt but
was captured

July 26, Villa entered Sabinas and wired to President
de la Huerta for permission to surrender

July 27, General Martinez received Villa's surrender
and agreement signed the following day

July 28, Villa's retirement purchased by Huerta with
gift of vast estate

——, General Esteban Cantu, Governor of northern
district of Lower California, declared a revolt

Aug. 3, Cantu forces seized Mexican patrol boat in
harbor of Ensenda and killed the captain, Zapeda

Aug. 6, State of blockade of Lower California proclaimed

Aug. 7, Law established lottery at Mexico City

Aug. 16, Rebellion of Governor Cantu of Lower California ended

Sept. 1, "Informe" of de la Huerta reëstablished the
decree of Jan 15, 1915 which authorized provisional
possession for the villages after their demands had
been passed on by local executives

Sept. 5, Obregon elected President

Sept. 18, "Congress of the Mexican Proletariat" met
in Mexico City

Sept. 24, Decree of President authorized the creation
of 3 free ports, Salina Cruz, Puerto Mexico, and
Guaymas, and an interior free zone "Rincon
Antonio"

Sept. 26, Workmen's parade in Mexico City

Oct. 11, George Creel, confidential agent for President
Wilson, arrived in Mexico to propose conditions of
recognition by the United States. Not accepted

——, General Felix Diaz and some of his followers
deported from Vera Cruz

——, Strike of Coahuila coal miners demanded wage
increase of 100%; Government intervened and 20%
granted

Nov. 13, 22 mines closed because of decline in price
of silver

Nov. 22, Mexican rebels from Texas raided Ramirez
in Tamaulipas

Dec. 1, President Obregon inaugurated

——, Japan recognized the new Mexican administration

Dec. 5, Brazil recognized the Mexican Government

Dec. 11, Diplomatic relations resumed with Holland

Dec. 28, Agrarian law modified

1921

Jan. 8, Preferential rights granted to owners of surface
land to oil in sub-soil

Jan. 27, Colonization decree facilitated settlement,
provided for transportation, and offered subsidies

March 15, Decree reduced army to 50,000 men, to
become effective by March 31, 1922

June 7, Protest of Secretary Hughes against retroactive effect on property of Americans in Mexico
in interpretation of Constitution of 1917 and proposed treaty of amity and commerce to adjust
matters which would guarantee American property
rights in Mexico

——, Decree increased export duties on petroleum by
25%

June 27, Statement of President Obregon to American
people published in the New York World promised
that private rights prior to May 1, 1917, would
be respected, that Mexico would meet every just
obligation without evasion

July, First amendment to Constitution of 1917 enacted
and proclaimed established the Secretariat of Public
Instruction and Belles Arts

July 1, Government decree became effective, increased
export tax on oil by 25% which so injured industry
by reduction of exports that tax had to be reduced
in September

July 10, Riots at Tampico

July 13, President Obregon invited countries interested
to send representatives to constitute a permanent
Mexican claims commission. Invitation accepted
in November by France, Great Britain, Italy, Spain,
and the Netherlands

July 21, Spain and Japan formally recognized the
Obregon Government

Aug. 28–Sept. 3, Conference of American oil producers
in Mexico City, E. L. Doheny, W. C. Teagle, H. F.
Sinclair, A. L. Beatty, and J. W. Van Dyke with
the Government reached agreement as to oil export
tax and subsequently as to production tax

Aug. 30, Decision of Superior Court in Amparo proceedings declared in favor of Texas Oil Company
of Mexico reversing decision of District Court of
Feb. 17 that Article 27 of Constitution of 1917 did
not apply to lands legally acquired before May 1,
1917

Sept. 1, By this date 413,123 acres had been "restored"
to villages and 1,462,293 acres granted

——, President Obregon refused to sign treaty with

the United States, the price of recognition of his government, making pledges to modify constitution as to property and taxation favorable to American citizens

Sept. 13, Arrival of Thomas W. Lamont from the United States for negotiations

Sept. 26, Treaty of friendship, commerce, and navigation with China of 1899 amended

Oct. 7, Chihuahua and Oriente Railroad organized

Nov. 14, The shrine of patron saint of Mexico, the Virgin of Guadalupe, wrecked by bomb

Nov. 26, Decision of Supreme Court in International Petroleum Company case

Dec. 21, Mgr. Philipi received by President Obregon. Since 1910 the Vatican had been unrepresented

Dec. 26, General Francesco Reyna, revolutionary leader, executed at Nogales

Census gave population total as 14,234,799

1922

Jan., Epidemic of yellow fever at Vera Cruz, 116 deaths out of 217 cases reported

Jan. 18, Norway recognized the Obregon Government

Jan. 22–28, Street car strike in Mexico City

Jan. 31, Joint Resolution of United States Congress as to embargo on arms used against rebels

Feb. 1, Revolt of General Miguel Aleman

Feb. 2, Execution of Major José Anaya connected with revolt of General Aleman

March 1, National University of the Southeast founded at Merida, Yucatan

March 10, Concession for railroad begun in 1908 from Acapulco to port of Zihuatanejo (Guerrero)

April 10, Regulations issued as to expropriation and distribution of agricultural lands in accordance with law of Nov. 22, 1921

May 6, Concession granted to Chihuahua and Oriente Railroad

May 12, Decision of Supreme Court in Tamiahua Petroleum Company, 2 cases

May 20, First North American Convention of the Pan-American League of Women in Mexico City

June 2, De la Huerta met International Committee of Bankers in New York in conference

June 16, Lamont-de la Huerta debt refunding agreement concluded in conference of international bankers in New York

July 21, Spain and Japan formally recognized the Government

Aug., Revolt of General Francesco Murguia in Durango

Aug. 22, Chihuahua and Oriente Railroad completed from Lucero to Los Lamentos

Sept. 30, Agreement as to payment of debt to the United States signed by the President

——, League of Nations decision to admit Mexico as a member

——, Revolt of garrison at Juarez in favor of Murguia

Oct. 8, General Eduardo Hernandez, second in command to General Murguia, killed in conflict with home guards

Oct. 11, Mexican ships granted 50% reduction in port dues and charges as compared with vessels of other countries in Mexican ports

Oct. 31, General Murguia captured in Durango, tried by court-martial, and shot

Nov. 11, Elias Zarate lynched by mob at Weslaco, Texas. No one punished for this crime

Nov. 15, Failure of *Banque Française* with headquarters in Mexico City and branches throughout the Republic began suspension of banks

Dec. 1, General strike in Mexico City

Dec. 26, Amnesty bill for all rebel prisoners passed Chamber of Deputies

Dec. 30, Act created National Bureau of Statistics

1923

Jan. 2, National Chamber of Agriculture opened agricultural school at San Rafael

Jan. 5, 256 rebel prisoners released from jail

Jan. 18, Federal tax placed on gross receipts of railroads and express companies, on dining and sleeping cars, and other services

Jan. 19, Papal delegate, Mgr. Filipi expelled from the country for participation in open air religious ceremony forbidden by law

Jan. 20, Decree established Bank of Mexico

Feb. 7, Papal delegate, Filipi, sailed for Rome

Feb. 10, Concession for railroad from Vera Cruz through the Isthmus of Tehuantepec into state of Campeche

Feb. 21, Mexican Government announced that a "dry zone" 50 miles wide in which all alcoholic beverages would be prohibited would be established on the American border

March 5, Work begun on Southern Pacific to connect Tepic and Orendain junction

March 31, Circular from Department of Agriculture ordered all holders of more than 5,000 acres of land to dispose of their surplus to Mexicans. Aimed at large foreign estates

April 26, New petroleum law conferred validity on concessions obtained before May 1, 1917, but required concessionaires to revalidate their claims within 3 years

May 14–Aug. 15, Joint American-Mexican Commission met in Mexico City to discuss proposals leading to recognition of the Mexican Government by the United States, Charles B. Warren and John B. Payne with Ramon Ross and F. Gonzales

May 20, First national convention of women's organizations opened at Mexico City

May 29, Obregon decree exempted from expropriation lands included in contracts of colonization made with the Federal Government

June 16, Strike of 12,000 workers in Orizaba district of Vera Cruz over workmen's compensation law

June 25, Notice served on manager of 100,000 acre ranch of William R. Hearst in Chihuahua that the State Agrarian Commission would take over part of the property

June 27, Decree established free ports at Salina Cruz, Puerto Mexico, and Guayamas

July 14, Inauguration of highway from Dzitas to Chichen Itaza, in Yucatan

July 20, Death of Villa by shots fired at his automobile by assassins

July 23, Decree of the President forbade importation of opium, cocaine, morphine, &c., by any other agency than the national Dept. of Health

July 27, Test of claims conventions of Joint Commission approved

Aug. 4, Presidential decree authorized all Mexicans over 18 who possessed no real estate to seize any national or unappropriated land, planting stakes as sign of possession and notifying the Minister of Agriculture

Aug. 15, Sub-soil rights acquired by Americans in oil and minerals before May 1, 1917 were validated

Aug. 27, General strike begun in August by strike of employees of street railways of Vera Cruz declared off

Aug. 31, The Obregon Government recognized by the United States

Sept. 3, Diplomatic relations with the United States formally resumed

——, France recognized Mexico

Sept. 8, General Claims Convention with the United States concluded provided for adjustment of claims of citizens of either country that had originated since July 4, 1868

Sept. 10, Special Claims Convention with the United States signed for adjustment of claims of American citizens through revolutionary act between Nov. 20, 1910 and May 31, 1920

Sept. 13, Jesus Salas, confessed slayer of Villa, sentenced to 20 years imprisonment

Sept. 14, Mexico declined to enter League of Nations while Mexican Government remained unrecognized by Great Britain

——, Coöperative Party declared in favor of Adolfo de la Huerta and nominated him for President in convention of Nov. 23

Sept. 19, Strike of 4,000 employees of American Smelting and Refining Company at Chihuahua

Sept. 24, Adolfo de la Huerta resigned as Minister of Finance; succeeded by Pani

Sept. 29, Diplomatic relations with Venezuela suspended because of refusal of Venezuela to recognize diplomatic rights of representatives of Mexico in that country

Oct. 18, Huerta announced his candidacy for presidential office

Oct. 19, Finance Minister Alberto Pani in official report charged Huerta with mismanagement of the public funds, and President Obregon in public statement supported the charges

Oct. 21, Clash of supporters of Calles and de la Huerta in Mexico City, 5 persons killed and many wounded

Oct. 25, Pani, Finance Minister, summoned by Chamber to conference on charges made against de la Huerta, his predecessor in office

Oct. 30, Huerta replied to Pani charges and claimed credit for increase of $50,000,000 in national revenues

Nov. 1, Social Reform Party nominated Huerta for President

Nov. 5, National Political League organized at Juarez nominated General Angel Flores for President

Nov. 10, Decree announced that sub-soil rights prior to promulgation of Constitution of 1917 would be respected but in future all titles to land reserved national ownership

Nov. 11, National Agrarian Party nominated Calles for President

Nov. 15, Amendments to the Constitution tending toward autonomy of Congress signed by the President

Nov. 20, Huerta appeared before the Senate to deny Pani charges

Nov. 23, Huerta chosen for President in convention of Coöperative and National Independent parties

Dec. 5, De la Huerta party issued Plan of Vera Cruz against the Government. Accepted in States of Vera Cruz, Chihuahua, Michoacan, Tamaulipas, San Luis Potosi, and soon in additional States

Dec. 6, Revolt against Obregon Government and Calles

candidacy for president of de la Huerta joined by J. P. Laurens, General Guadalupe Sanchez, Fortunato Maycotte, and Enrique Estrada

Dec. 8, Payment of $15,000,000 made on national debt for year 1923

——, Successful assault of rebels on Jalapa capital of State of Vera Cruz. General Berlanga captured

——, Garrison at Frontera, Tabasco declared in favor of de la Huerta

Dec. 13, Federal victory at Ocotlan 250 miles northwest of City of Mexico against General Enrique Estrada

Dec. 15, City of Puebla evacuated by federal troops and occupied by rebels the next day

——, General Obregon established headquarters at Apizaco

——, Rebels captured Yurecuaro

——, Acapulco surrendered to rebels

Dec. 16, Cuautla captured by rebels

Dec. 18, Rebels seized Merida, capital of Yucatan

Dec. 22, General Villareal with 6,000 rebel soldiers evacuated Puebla. Occupied by federals the following day

Dec. 26, Government troops recaptured Tamaculla

Dec. 27, General Lazaro Cardenas defeated and captured with his staff in region south of Lake Chapala by rebels

1924

Jan., Defeat of rebels at Esperanza

Jan. 4, Sale of arms by United States Government to Obregon Government announced

Jan. 7, President Coolidge placed embargo on arms and ammunition to Mexico

Jan. 12, Decree of A. de la Huerta announced blockade of port of Tampico

Jan. 17, Mexican troops permitted to pass through Arizona and New Mexico in pursuit of rebels

Jan. 19, Blockade of Tampico by rebels abandoned because of protest of the United States of the 16th

Feb. 3, Rebels evacuated Vera Cruz and Obregon forces entered Feb. 6

Feb. 9, Defeat of rebel General Salvador at Ocotlan

Feb. 11, Federal troops recapture Vera Cruz

Feb. 12, Defeat of rebel Generals Estrada and Diequez at Penjamo

Feb. 18, Labor Convention in Mexico City voted to seize cotton mills

Feb. 20, Representatives of oil interests expressed alarm at "growing wave of Bolshevism"

Feb. 21, Income tax law signed by the President

Feb. 26, Federal forces reoccupied part of Tuxpan

——, Convention of 27 chambers of commerce met at Monterey

Feb. 28–March 4, Rebels evacuated Puerto Mexico, Alvarado, and Oaxaca City

March 4, Generals Estrada and Dieguez gave up campaign and their troops dispersed

March 31, Charles B. Warren presented credentials as American ambassador

April 27, Secretary Trevino refused to supply troops to break strike of Aguila Oil Company men

May 6, Stadium seating 70,000 persons, erected at cost of 1,000,000 pesos, dedicated at Mexico City

May 14, Joint American-Mexican Conference begun at Mexico City

May 24, Government requested Great Britain to withdraw Minister Cummins because of his letters to the

Government on the subject of attacks by bandits on Mrs. Evans, an English property owner

June 9, Villa Hermosa, capital of Tabasco, occupied by federal troops

June 18, Great Britain recalled Minister H. C. Cummins and broke off diplomatic relations

June 30, Decree of President Obregon suspended debt agreement of 1922 with International Committee

July 3, 300 rebels surrendered at Tabasco

July 6, The election a victory for Calles

July 15, Government granted 10 year concession to Mexican aviators for establishment of air service between Mexico City and Tampico

July 17, Strike of bakers at Vera Cruz for shorter hours

July 21, Strikers at E. Aguila Petroleum Company returned to work on agreement with company of July 17 after four months strike

July 28, Suspension of coinage of silver

Aug. 2, Mrs. Rosalie Evans, American born wife of English citizen, and property owner in Puebla, murdered by Mexicans because of refusal to surrender her land

Aug. 8, Francisco Ruiz and Alejo Garcia confess to murder of Mrs. Evans

Aug. 18, Special American-Mexican Claims Commission met in Mexico City

Aug. 30, General American-Mexican Claims Commission held first meeting in Washington

Sept. 8, Strike ended of employees of the Huastea Petroleum Company. Demands of workers conceded

——, Strike of Mexican Gulf Petroleum Company employees begun. Ended in Oct.

Sept. 15–20, American Industrial Mission in Mexico City

Sept. 25, Claims Convention with France signed

Sept. 27, Decree gave economic autonomy to the National University

Sept. 29, United States of Mexico Oil Production Tax External Loan of 1924 announced, $50,000,000 at 6% in bonds

Oct. 8, Treaty of amity, commerce, and trade concluded with Japan

Oct. 10, James R. Sheffield, American ambassador to Mexico, arrived at the capital

Oct. 11, Surrender of Hippolito Villa, brother of Francisco, with 200 men

Oct. 19, President Obregon ordered expulsion of 100 Chinese members of Tong causing disturbances in northern Mexico

Oct. 23, New Debt Agreement with International Committee of Bankers modified the earlier one

Oct. 24, Department of Foreign Relations ordered closing of Mexican consulates in London and Liverpool and other cities in Great Britain

Oct. 26, General Calles arrived in New York City and proceeded to Washington Oct. 31 where he was received a guest of the nation

Oct. 31, Governor Roderiguez of Lower California announced unalterable opposition to colonization of Japanese or other Orientals

Nov. 7, Vasilio Vadillo Pestkovsky presented credentials as ambassador from Soviet Government of Russia

Nov. 11, President-Elect Calles arrived in Mexico after 4 months tour of Europe and United States

Nov. 12, In Chamber of Deputies shots fired in stormy debate. Deputy Luis Morones, Labor leader, seriously wounded and Deputy Leocadio Guerrero fatally

Nov. 16, Two Mexicans sentenced to death for murder of Mrs. Evans in Aug.

Nov. 30, General P. E. Calles inaugurated President

Dec. 7, Bandits sacked town of Tapala, Jalisco

Dec. 20, Official welcome to Japanese fleet at Acapulco

Dec. 25, One day railroad strike in Vera Cruz suppressed by Government

Dec., Deportation of 200 Chinese from Sonora, Sinaloa, and Lower California because of Tong warfare

1925

Jan. 7, States authorized to issue 25 year 4% bonds to owners of expropriated lands

Feb. 2, Manuel Tellez, ambassador to the United States, presented credentials in Washington

Feb. 10, All railroads of national system placed under control of the Ministry of Communications

Feb. 18, Manifesto of Joaquin Perez priest, announced establishment of independent Mexican Catholic Church

Feb. 21, Armed clash between orthodox Catholics and separatist followers of Perez

March 1, Strike of electric railway employees in Mexico City for recognition of union. President Calles ordered the company to negotiate with the strikers

March 16, Claims Convention with Germany signed

March 18, Income tax law promulgated

March 31, Kansas City, Mexico and Orient Railway Company reorganized

April 1, National highway tax of 3 centavos per liter on all domestic consumers of gasoline went into effect

April 26, Strike of power and rail employees at Puebla

April 29, Decree made monetary unit the gold peso or the silver dollar

May 25, Extradition Treaty with Cuba signed

May, Strike of union of bank clerks

June 10–11, Flight of Carranza to Morresville, North Carolina from Mexico City and June 12 to Washington

June 12, Secretary of State Kellogg in a statement to the press declared conditions in Mexico unsatisfactory, that the United States expected that Americans should be indemnified for property taken under Carranza decrees, that the "government of Mexico is now on trial before the world, and the American government will continue to support the government of Mexico only so long as it protects American lives and rights and complies with its international obligations"

June 14, Reply of President Calles to Secretary Kellogg that his statement embodied "a threat to the sovereignty of Mexico"

June 15, Opening of Puerto Mexico on the Gulf and Salina Cruz on the Pacific as free ports

June 17, Permit issued to a Japanese company to establish an industrial plant near Magdalena Bay

July 1, Mexican National Railways returned to their original owners

July 15, The President signed regulations for National Commission on Banking

Aug. 4, General strike at Orizaba

Aug. 7, Successful one day strike of railroad employees at Chihuahua because of non-payment of wages

Aug. 12, Civil Pension Act signed by the President

Aug. 28, British Government resumed diplomatic relations with Mexico

Sept. 1, Strike of oil workers at Vera Cruz against discharges in British owned Aguila Petroleum Company

Sept. 1, Mexico opened new bank of issue, the *Banco de Mexico*, 51% of the capital of 100,000,000 pesos held by the Government

——, President Calles announced in message to Congress that cordial relations had been restored with the United States

Sept., Strike of employees of Aguila Petroleum Company

Oct. 12, University of Guadalajara, closed since 1860, reopened

Oct. 23, New debt funding agreement made, modifying the Lamont-de la Huerta agreement beginning new schedule of payments on Jan. 1, 1926 and excluding National Railways from Mexico's external debt signed in New York by Alberto J. Pani and Thomas Lamont. Approved by President Calles Nov. 11

Nov. 26, Claims Convention with Spain signed

Dec. 23, Congress enacted law restricting aliens as to acquisition or ownership of land especially within 100 kilometers from the frontiers or 50 kilometers from the coasts

——, Convention with the United States signed for prevention of smuggling and a supplementary Extradition Convention

Dec. 31, Petroleum law promulgated (passed Dec. 18) repeating constitutional provisions of 1917, asserting inalienable ownership of nation of sub-soil deposits, and required foreigners to waive nationality and diplomatic protection as to Mexican owned property, and gave detailed regulations for confirming concessions granted prior to May 1, 1917

1926

Jan. 1, Railroads returned to private ownership under government supervision

Jan. 8, American State Department protested to Mexico against retroactive and confiscatory land and petroleum laws as violation of agreement of Convention of 1923

Jan. 20, Mexican Government replied to American Note of Jan. 9, giving assurance that the "precepts of international law, and of justice and equity" would be recognized

Jan. 21, Alien land law of Dec. 23 promulgated. Repeated constitutional restrictions and included foreigners in Mexican corporations

Jan. 25, Presidential decree withdrew decree of June 30, 1924 suspending service of external debt

Jan. 27, Church announcement of repudiation of Constitution of 1917 signed by all archbishops and bishops

Jan. 28, American Note called attention to distinction between future acquisition of property in Mexico and status of property rights under laws existing at time of acquisition

Feb. 2, Apostolic letter of Pope Pius XI protested against the religions and educational provisions of the Constitution and directed bishops to refrain from political activities

Feb. 5, At Jalapa General José Riveros and 2 other rebel officers executed for treason

Feb. 8, Discovery of sites of 6 ancient Maya cities along east coast of Yucatan

Feb. 10, Arrest of foreign priests for deportation begun

Feb. 11, Mexican Government ordered nationalization of all church property

Feb. 12, Schools and orphan asylums where religious instruction given, closed

Feb. 13, Government ordered deportation of foreign monks and nuns. Closing of convents begun where schools giving religious instruction existed

Feb. 26, Reply of Government to American Note

——, Decree directed registration of all private schools with Ministry of Public Instruction within 60 days

March 6, Sanitary Code enacted

March 8, Decree provided regulations for industrial conciliation and arbitration boards

March 9, Migration law regulated immigration and emigration

March 10, National Agricultural Bank opened in Mexico City

March 27, Note of Mexican Foreign Minister to the United States in answer to Note of March 1 stated that petroleum and land laws would not be given retroactive effect

March 29, Land regulations promulgated with no change in features restricting ownership of property by aliens protested by foreigners. Clause stated that law will not be retroactively applied to prejudice of any interest

March 31, President Calles signed Land and Oil Restriction Act

April 1, New income tax went into effect

April 5, New colonization law as to lands signed by the President, and Forestry Act

April 8, Regulations for Petroleum Act officially promulgated

April 22, Railroad law abrogated that of April 29, 1899

May 1, Agricultural bank founded in Tula Hidalgo and also coöperatives and regional agricultural schools

May 3, New Mining Act signed by the President

May 15, Government decreed deportation of the papal envoy Mgr. George Caruana who had entered the country without disclosing his identity

May 27, Law enacted for regulation of insurance companies

June 8 and 9, New Sanitary Code published in the *Diario Oficial*

June 23, Breaking of Coecillo dam, Guanajuato destroyed the city of Leon. 1,000 lives lost

June 24, Decree of President Calles put into effect religious provisions of Constitution

July 3, Decree defined offenses against Article 130 of the Constitution and prescribed penalties. Ministers required to be of Mexican birth. Churches administered by foreigners to be closed July 31

July 23, Decree of President prohibited the employment of any but lay teachers in the public schools

July 24, New Military School at Mexico City modeled on West Point opened

July 25, Pastoral letter of Mexican Roman Catholic Church announced suspension of all church rites on July 31 as protest against anti-church decrees, the day set for the required registration of priests

July 26, Enactment provided that no Mexican individual or corporation allowed to place insurance in foreign companies which have not complied with regulations including investment of certain percentage of funds in Mexico

July 29, Monsignor Crespi, chief of Roman Catholic Apostolic Delegation, ordered out of the country

Aug. 1, A labor parade of over 50,000 persons in Mexico City in support of President Calles and his decrees as to the Church. Churches taken over by civil committees

——, Pope Pius XI called on Catholics of the world

to pray for deliverance of the Catholics of Mexico from persecution

Aug. 11, Government ordered seizure of property listed as administered by the Catholic clergy

——, Spain signed treaties with Mexico, Guatemala, Italy, and France in a new Pan-American policy

Aug. 15, Gen. Enrique Estrada, former Secretary, arrested with 174 men at San Diego, California, charged with violation of neutrality laws. Munitions seized

Aug. 18, President Calles rejected plea of Mexican Catholics for suspension of religious laws pending further action by Congress

Sept. 15, Jacob Rosenthal, New York merchant, killed by Mexican brigands after his capture for ransom of $10,000 on Sept. 12 as the bandits pursued by government troops

——, General Valente de la Cruz executed for sedition

Sept. 23, Petition of Roman Catholic Church presented to Congress Sept. 7 asking for a modification of the Constitution Articles as to the Church rejected

Sept., Revolt of Yaqui Indians caused by refusal of permission to make pilgrimage to shrine of their patron saint at Magdalena, Sonora

Sept. 27, Ultimatum of Gen. Obregon to Yaquis called for surrender of Luis Matis, leader of revolt

Oct. 6, New Penal Code came into effect

Oct. 7, Note replied to American Note of July 31 stated that the law had not produced confiscatory effects and therefore diplomatic representations were not in order

Nov., President Diaz formally opened the Tehuantepec Railway

Nov. 13, Yaquis defeated in fierce battle

Nov. 15, Insurrection in Chihuahua and Vera Cruz States

Nov. 17, Mexican Note to the United States in reply to that of Secretary Kellogg of Oct. 30 affirmed that protest as to Mexican laws should be made only after actual confiscation of American property thereunder

Nov. 19, Claims Convention with Great Britain signed

Nov. 20, Pope Pius in encyclical addressed to bishops throughout the world condemned alleged persecution of the Catholic Church by Calles Government, and "arbitrary character" of the Constitution

Nov. 25, Chamber of Deputies passed regulations to Article 130 of Constitution granting permission to foreign colonies to have foreign clergymen conduct their services for 6 years

——, Dept. of Industry warned oil companies they must apply for confirmation of titles obtained before 1917 Constitution by Dec. 31 or renounce their holdings

Nov. 29, New banking law came into effect

Dec. 7, Mexico recognized the election of Sacasa as "constitutional President" of Nicaragua

Dec. 10, First children's court opened by the President for the Federal District

Dec. 20, Mexican Minister of Industries submitted draft of proposed new concessions for oil companies

Dec. 27, Chief oil companies decided not to apply for "confirmation" of their rights

1927

Jan. 1, Mexican oil legislation went into effect

——, General regulations for establishment and operation of insurance companies went into effect

Jan. 9, Revolutionists at El Paso, Texas, announced Rene C. Garga provisional President

Jan. 10, Bishop Diaz arrested and deported to Guatemala accused of revolutionary activities

Jan. 13, Claims Convention with Italy signed

Jan. 20, Mexico accepted "in principle" arbitration of all differences with the United States

Jan. 21, Coöperative Societies Act signed by the President

Jan. 22, Decree pronounced the president eligible for reëlection "after a presidential term has intervened"

Feb. 25, A central Board of Commerce and Industry installed in Mexico City to study economic conditions

Feb. 28, General Estrada convicted at Los Angeles, California, of violation of Neutrality Act in effort to raise army to invade Mexico

March 12, Further Claims Convention with France signed

March 15, Executive resolution required that all disputes in textile industry be submitted to the Department of Industry, Commerce, and Labor

March 19, Rebels looted and burned Laredo-Mexico City train

March 27, Edgar M. Wilkins, kidnapped for ransom, killed; murderers shot April 4

March 28, Announcement of possession by President Calles of documents altered to make it appear that the United States was fomenting Mexican revolution

April 19, Rebels stopped train at Limon and massacred 52 soldiers and some 100 passengers

April 21, Abp. Mora y del Rio charged with complicity in Limon massacre made denial before Minister of Interior, but declared Catholics of Mexico had right to fight for their rights

April 22, Archbishop of Mexico and 5 other Roman Catholic dignitaries deported after Limon massacre

April 30, Engagement with Yaquis south of Nogales

June 16, Debt Agreement with the United States signed superseding that of Oct. 23, 1925

June 18, Decree of President forbidding government purchase of American products in the United States published

Aug. 16, General Claims Convention with the United States extended for 2 years

Aug. 17, New compilation of agrarian laws issued

Sept. 28, Hurricane at Vera Cruz caused damage to amount of $5,000,000

Sept. 29, A long distance telephone inaugurated between Mexico City and Washington, D.C.

Oct. 3, Mutiny of 800 soldiers in Mexico City, 2 regiments in Vera Cruz and a battalion at Torreon

Oct. 4, Serrano captured by federals and 13 leaders of revolt shot

——, Torreon captured by federals after battle and its commander Lieutenant-Colonel Manganilla and all his staff shot

Oct. 6, Gen. Alfredo Quijano, Gen. Vincent Gonzales, rebel leaders, and 13 members of Morelos Legislature executed

Oct. 7, 13 Mexican States out of 28 in a state of revolt

Oct. 9, Federals defeated rebels led by General Gomez and Hector Alamada in State of Vera Cruz. Gomez escaped but was pursued and shot Nov. 3

Oct. 16, Treaty of friendship, conciliation, and arbitration with Italy

Oct. 27, Repeal of decree of President Calles prohibiting

purchase by Mexican Departments of goods in the United States

Oct. 29, American ambassador Dwight Morrow presented credentials succeeding J. R. Sheffield

Nov. 1, Telephone connection with Cuba inaugurated

Nov. 13, Attempted assassination of General Alvaro Obregon, former President

Nov. 16, Foreign Office declared false the documents published in American newspapers showing Mexico financed Sacasa revolution in Nicaragua

Nov. 17, Decision of Supreme Court granted appeal of the Mexican Petroleum Company (American) against cancellation of certain drilling permits by the Department of Industry, Commerce, and Labor under the petroleum law requiring companies to exchange their titles for 50 year concessions within one year. Decision that limitation of company's fee right to right not exceeding 50 years a violation of the company's constitutional guarantees

Nov. 18, Announcement of court martial and execution of Gen. Oscar Aguilar, rebel leader

Nov. 20, Bill passed to extend presidential term from 4 to 6 years

Nov. 29, Long distance telephone from Mexico City to Montreal inaugurated

Dec. 3, Rebel General Bertani executed

Dec. 4, Rebel General Hector Lucero executed

Dec. 14, Goodwill "ambassador," Charles Lindbergh, arrived in Mexico City on non-stop flight from Washington

Dec. 27, New petroleum law passed by Congress confirmed all rights in lands where contracts had been made previous to May 1, 1917 by issue of concessions for an indefinite time instead of the 50 year period, to be effective as of Jan. 11 and March 27, 1928

——, Embargo of United States on arms to Mexico removed

Dec. 28, Colonel Lindbergh left Mexico for Guatemala

1928

Jan. 11, Petroleum law of Dec. 27, 1927 became effective

Jan. 12, Treaty with Argentina signed as to literary and artistic rights in Mexico

Jan. 26, Earthquake in State of Oaxaca

Jan. 29, French aviators D. Costes and J. Lebrix visited Mexico City

Feb. 9, Earthquake in Central Mexico especially in State of Puebla

Feb. 13, Gen. Adolfo de la Huerta and 4 associates charged in July, 1927, with violation of neutrality laws of the United States acquitted by Federal Court at Los Angeles

Feb. 14, Decree provided that all lands on islands included in national petroleum reserve

Feb. 26, Bishop Armoro of Tampaulipas in hiding since July, 1926, arrested Feb. 20 and deported to the United States because of acts in opposition to religious decree of Government

Feb. 28, Earthquake in central states particularly severe in State of Puebla

Feb. 29, Decree gave oil companies until Jan. 11, 1929 to comply with laws

March 2, Contract signed to begin air mail service from Mexico City to Tampico and Tuxpan on April 15

March 16, Treaty with the United States signed providing for examination of livestock at frontier for prevention of contagious diseases

March 27, President Calles signed regulations which made amended petroleum laws effective, recognizing as valid titles obtained before May 1, 1917

April 4, Conference of President Calles at Vera Cruz with Father Burke (American)

April 22, Death of Abp. Mora y Del Rio in San Antonio, Texas, in exile

April 26, Customs Act passed to go into effect Sept. 1

May 2, The President laid first stone of the Tepuxtepec dam in Michoacan

May 10, Decree established National Economic Council

May 12, Death of Bishop Ignacio Valdespino in exile at San Antonio, Texas

May 25, 800 rebels attacking seaport of Manzanillo repulsed by federal troops

——, Captain Emilio Carranza flew from San Diego, California, to Mexico City

May 28, Act created Federal Administrative Bureau of the Budget

June 11, Carranza left Mexico arriving at Washington June 12

June 12 and 16, Earthquakes at Mexico City and in State of Oaxaca

July 1, Trans-Atlantic telephone service opened with London

——, General Alvarado Obregon elected President

July 11, Arbitration Treaty with Colombia signed

July 12, Death of Mexican aviator, Emilio Carranza, returning to Mexico from New York in fatal accident of forced landing in New Jersey

July 17, General Obregon, President Elect, assassinated by young student José de Leon Toral, a Roman Catholic fanatic

Aug. 11–Sept. 20, Good will flight of Lieutenant Colonel Roberto Fierro to Havana from Mexico City and to Central American States

Aug. 22, First meeting of British-Mexican Mixed Claims Commission held at Mexico City

Aug. 26, Strike of telegraph operators in Mexico City

Sept. 1, President Calles announced intention to leave office at end of his term

Sept. 7–Oct. 18, American-Mexican General Claims Commission met in Mexico City

Sept. 25, Mexican Congress selected Emilio Portes Gil provisional President for term from Dec. 1, 1928 to Feb. 5, 1930

Oct. 1, Air mail service with the United States inaugurated

Oct. 23, Extradition Treaty with Panama signed

Oct., Revolt in State of Jalisco

Nov. 2, Trial of Toral begun and of the nun, Mother Superior Maria Conception, charged with being the "intellectual leader" of plot to kill Obregon

Nov. 8, Toral pronounced guilty and sentenced to death by firing squad. Maria Conception sentenced to imprisonment for 20 years

Nov. 13, Regulations to govern petroleum industry issued

Nov. 30, President Gil took oath of office

Dec. 25, Summary executions, even in the case of rebels, are abolished in Mexico by order of President Gil

Dec. 28, Maximiliano Vigueras, notorious bandit, executed at Mexico City after court martial

1929

Jan. 1, New patent and trade-mark laws went into effect

Jan. 20, 50 killed and 100 wounded in election riots in State of Hidalgo

Feb. 9, Execution of José de Leon Toral. The Supreme Court refused new trial Feb. 6

Feb. 10, Unsuccessful attempt made to dynamite special train of President Gil near Comonfort

Feb. 11, President Gil issued edict calling on all Catholic priests to register their addresses with Government within 15 days or be declared rebels

Feb. 22, Bandits seized for ransom and later killed 2 Americans, J. M. Underwood and C. G. Aiesthrope, employees of mining company in Guanajuato

March 1, Convention of Revolutionary Party met at Queretaro and nominated P. R. Ortiz for President March 4

March 3, Revolt in Vera Cruz headed by General Jesus Maria Aguirre supported by General Gonzalo Escobar of Coahuila, and Francisco Manzo, Governor, and Governor Fausto Topete of Sonora. Port of Vera Cruz seized

March 4, Revolutionary manifesto published at Vera Cruz declared against attempt of Government to force P. O. Rubio on the people as President

March 5, Rebel General Escobar took possession of Monterey in State of Nuevo Leon

March 6, Government troops commanded by General Calles took Vera Cruz

———, Government troops drove General Escobar from Monterey

March 8, Rebels led by Valles captured Juarez on American border opposite El Paso

March 9, General Calles with 18,000 troops began advance toward the northwest

March 11, Vera Cruz recaptured from rebels

———, Secretary of State Kellogg announced that American Government would not recognize rebels as belligerents, thus depriving them of supplies and loans

March 12, General Escobar, rebel commander, evacuated Saltillo and retired to Torreon. Rebel commander Colonel P. Lopez, and General Simon Aguirre captured

March 14, General Jesus Aguirre, rebel commander, captured

March 15, Durango taken by federal troops

March 18, General Escobar evacuated Torreon on approach of General Calles

March 20, Rebels demanded surrender of city of Mazatlan, Sinaloa

March 21, Law enacted on *dotación* and *restitución* of lands and waters

———, Rebel General Jesus M. Aguirre executed by firing squad

———, Mexican-French-Italian Commission began conference on questions in dispute

March 22, Main rebel attack on Mazatlan repulsed

March 25, Rebels defeated abandoned siege of Mazatlan

March 27, General Calles reached Escalon

March 28, Engagement at Jarai Grande

March 30, Engagement at Corralitos

March 30 and April 2, Naco, Sonora, bombed by rebel troops

———, General Escobar, rebel, in battle with federal troops near Escalon, Chihuahua

April 1, Rebels commanded by General Escobar in 2 days battle with General Calles at Jiminez driven from town in disastrous retreat

April 2, Decisive battle at La Reforma. Rebel General Escobar defeated

April 3, Battle of Naco begun

April 6, Federal troops commanded by Cardenas occupied Culiacan

———, Rebel assault on Naco commanded by Topete failed

April 7, Cities of Parral and Rosario in southern Chihuahua occupied by federal troops commanded by Almazan

April 8, General José G. Escobar proclaimed provisional President by rebels

April 10, Federal troops occupied Chihuahua City and Juarez evacuated by rebels

April 12, Revolutionary General Francisco Manzo from Nogales crossed the international border, was interned and surrendered to President Gil by telegraph

April 28, General Calles announced that the revolt had ended

———, General Simon Aguirre captured and executed

April 30, Surrender of Nogales to federal troops ended the conflict. General Escobar escaped to the United States

May 1, 1,500 rebels at Agua Prieta surrendered to federal troops

———, Government announced that the Catholic clergy might exercise their rites provided they respected the laws of the land as did ministers of other denominations

May 12, General Calles returned to Mexico City

May 21, General Calles, former President of Mexico, retires from his temporary post as Secretary of War, having put down the insurrection. Succeeded by General Joaquin Amaro

May 28–June 5, Strike of students of the University which ended when University declared free of governmental direction but was resumed when President Gil refused to dismiss the rector, A. L. Castro

June 12, 13, and 18, Conferences of Archbishop Ruiz and Pascual Diaz, Bishop of Tabasco, with the President on church in Mexico

June 21, Agreement between President Gil and Archbishop Ruiz settled controversy with Catholic Church. Church services suspended since July 31, 1926 to be resumed

June 22, Bishop Pascual Diaz appointed Archbishop of Mexico City and Primate of all Mexico

July 5, National City Bank of New York opened first branch in Mexico City

July 10, Government decreed national University free from Government control. To be managed by committee of teachers, students, and graduates

July 18, Embargo of arms to Mexico from the United States of Jan. 7, 1924 revoked

July 20, General Calles left Mexico for visit to Europe

July 27, Rebel generals M. Aguirre, Eduardo Garcia, and Jesus Palma exiled

Aug. 11, Advanced labor code promulgated which gave 8 hour day, 6 day week, recognized right to strike, established a minimum wage, made insurance compulsory with other reforms announced adopted by legislatures of 14 States

Aug. 17, Convention with the United States extended duration of special claims commission

Sept. 2, Convention with the United States extended duration of general claims commission

Sept. 17, First Pan-American Institute of Geography and History opened at Mexico City

Sept. 17, Mgr. Pascual Diaz formally installed as Archbishop of Mexico

Oct. 2, Regular air mail service between Mexico and the United States and Canada inaugurated

Nov. 7, Mexican Special Claims Commission established

Nov. 12, Mexico relinquished extraterritorial rights in China

Nov. 17, Pascual Ortiz Rubio elected President representing the National Revolutionary Party defeating José Vasconcelos representing the National Anti-Reëlectionists and P. V. Triana, Communist; announced by Congress Nov. 28

Dec. 3, Vasconcelos, defeated candidate for president, arrived at Nogales, Arizona, and charged a fraudulent election

Dec. 4, President Elect Rubio entered the United States at Brownsville.   Arrived at Washington Dec. 26

Dec. 5, Diplomatic relations resumed with Portugal

Dec. 6–18, Employees of Mexican Railroad between Mexico City and Vera Cruz on strike because of failure of company to sign collective labor contract

Dec. 15, New and radical law code adopted based on reform instead of punishment.   Abolished death sentence, except for crimes of sedition and treason, jury system. To go into effect Jan. 1, 1930

Final conquest of the Yaqui Indians by General Francisco Manzo in campaign begun in 1926—after 400 years resistance

1930

Jan. 3, Announcement of appointment of official observer to follow work of League of Nations

Jan. 20, Law created Labor Bank

Jan. 23, Mexico, because of Communist propaganda, recalls her Minister from Soviet Russia, severing diplomatic relations

Feb. 3, Pascual Ortiz Rubio, President Elect of Mexico, announces the personnel of his Cabinet, in which Provisional President Emil Portes Gil is named Secretary of the Interior.   Genaro Estrada is named Secretary of Foreign Affairs

Feb. 5, Ortiz Rubio, just inaugurated Mexican President, as he returned home was wounded by an assassin, Daniel Flores, a follower of Vasconcelos, who was arrested

Feb. 9, Raid on Soviet Legation at Mexico City

Feb. 20, Calles Immigration Act modified to permit entry of nuns who agree to comply with law forbidding convents

March 10, President Rubio transferred presidential offices from the National Palace, Mexico City, to Chapultepec Castle

April 9, J. E. Barstow, American citizen kidnapped for ransom, released on payment of $1,500, a tenth of amount first asked for

April 22, Portes Gil resigned as Minister of Interior

April 27, Executive decree empowered the President to issue bonds of $25,000,000 on public agrarian debt, 5% redeemable in 20 years

——, Decree authorized every Mexican over 18 years

of age with capital of $2,500 to lease piece of land from national domain under certain conditions

May 11, Death of Colonel Pablo Sidar, aviator, in crash of plane at sea off Costa Rica

May 19, Soviet commercial attaché left Mexico, last representative of Russia in Mexico

June 1, Announcement that Guatemalan invasion at La Fama, Chiapas, in Feb. on chicle plantation had been explained and indemnity arranged for

June 21, Colonel Roberto Fierro, Mexican army aviator, flew with a mechanic 2,200 miles from New York to Mexico City in 16 hours, 35 minutes

June 28, Mexico City Cathedral restored to control of Catholic Church by decree of the President

June 30, Civil Aëronautics Act

——, Communist riots at Matamoros

July 3, Workers University opened in Mexico City

July 6, Election for Senate and Chamber a victory for the Nationalist Revolutionist Party

July 25, Debt Agreement with the United States signed by Thomas Lamont and Senor Montes de Oca as to foreign debt and national railways.   Back interest to be cut, railroads reorganized, and interest payments resumed in 1931

Aug. 2, New mining law promulgated to go into effect Oct. 1 made extraction and commercial preparation of minerals a public utility.   Concessions granted by President

Aug. 12, Decree provided for apportionment of communal grants to small holders of government plantations

Aug. 15, Cathedral of Mexico City formally reopened. Closed since July, 1926

Aug. 16, President Rubio approved Debt Agreement of July 25, $275,302,000 total

Aug. 21, Rio Grande Boundary Commission Report signed by President of the United States. *See also* United States

Sept. 17, Dwight Morrow, American ambassador, left Mexico. Succeeded by J. Reuben Clark, Jr., Nov. 28

Oct. 8, Resignation of Luis Leon as Secretary of Industries, Commerce, and Labor. Succeeded by Aaron Saenz

Nov. 15, Astronomical time restored in Mexico in Mexico City zone

Nov. 23, The Government abolished capital punishment under the new penal code for the Federal District and Territories

Dec. 2, Chamber concurred in action of Senate giving the President extraordinary financial powers to deal with financial and industrial situation effective until Aug., 1931

Dec. 5, Supplementary Claims Commission with Great Britain signed

Dec. 12 and 18, Amendment to agrarian law gave guarantee to foreign capital as to taking over lands for village communities from owners

Dec. 20, Headquarters of Communist publications in Mexico City raided and leaders arrested and documents seized

Dec. 26, Law on granting and restitution of lands and waters made new definitions of lands and new conditions

WEST INDIES

West Indies, archipelago between North and South America in the Atlantic Ocean extending from Florida as far south as Venezuela and enclosing the Caribbean Sea and Gulf of Mexico, total area nearly 100,000 square miles. Cuba, Haiti, Jamaica, and Puerto Rico are called the Greater Antilles, and the rest of the islands except the Bahamas the Lesser Antilles, name taken from "Antilia" which appeared as island on medieval maps. The islands were discovered by Columbus on his first voyage, first land he made in the New World Oct. 11–12, 1492 (*see* America) and named by him in the belief that he had found the western route to India and reached the further coasts of the "Indies" and the fabled land of Antilia. The independent islands are Haiti comprising the Republics of Haiti and Santo Domingo (Dominican Republic), and Cuba, the largest of the islands. The American West Indies are the Virgin Islands (former Danish West Indies), and Puerto Rico. The British West Indies include the Bahamas, Barbados, Jamaica, Turks Island, the Leeward Islands, Trinidad with Tobago, Virgin Islands (Br.), and the Windward Islands. The Dutch West Indies are the Colony of Curaçao.

BAHAMAS

Bahamas, British archipelago, 20 inhabited islands and a large number of uninhabited islands including 661 cays and 2,387 rocks off the southeast coast of Florida, in the Atlantic Ocean, area, 4,404 square miles. Principal islands—New Providence (pop., census 1921, 12,975, containing capital Nassau), Abaco (3,993), Harbour Island (917), Grand Bahama (1,695), Cat Island (4,273), Long Island (4,659), Mayaguana (432), Eleuthera (6,048), Exuma (3,730), San Salvador or Watlings Island (686), Acklin's Island (1,811), Crooked Island (1,481), Great Inagua (937), Andros Island (6,976). Total population in 1921 (census), 53,031. Estimated population January 1, 1930, 60,848.

The islands were discovered by Columbus, but were not settled by the Spaniards, and were included in the English royal grant of the Carolinas to Sir Robert Heath Oct. 30, 1629, and in Aug. 31, 1649 to the Company of Eleutherian Adventurers formed in London by William Sayle and others which resulted in actual settlement of New Providence. Charles II granted the islands to the Duke of Albemarle and other Carolina proprietors, and Dec. 26, 1671, John Wentworth confirmed as Governor. The Government was resumed by the Crown Oct. 28, 1717 and Captain Woodes Rogers appointed first Royal Governor arrived in 1718. Captured by the Spanish in 1781, recaptured 1783 and Treaty of Versailles confirmed British possession the same year. British authority extended to Turks and Caicos islands (discovered by Ponce de Leon 1512) in 1804.

BARBADOS

Barbados, British island, 78 miles east of St. Vincent, the most easterly of the West Indies, 21 miles long, 14½ miles maximum width, total area 166 square miles, population 156,312 census of 1921, estimated population Dec. 31, 1929, 170,391. Capital, Bridgetown, population, 13,486, Speightstown, 1,500

The British ship "Blossom" took possession of the island in 1605 and it was settled by the English in 1625.

BERMUDA

Bermuda, group of islands, British Colony, 580 miles east of North Carolina and 677 miles from New York. Twenty of the 360 islands are inhabited, total area 19.3 square miles (12,360 acres, 2,759 under cultivation), population at census of 1921, 20,127 (7,006 white), estimated civil population, 1928, 30,884 (15,556 white).

The islands were discovered by Juan de Bermudez, a Spaniard, early in the 16th century (the exact date is unknown) for whom they were named. They were uninhabited until Sir George Somers was shipwrecked there in 1609. A company was formed for the "Plantation of the

Somers' Islands," as they were called at first. The Crown took over the Government in 1684.

CUBA

Cuba, Republic, largest island in the West Indies, has a length of about 730 miles, and width averaging about 50 miles ranging from a maximum of about 160 miles to a minimum of about 22 miles, and is about 92 miles south of Key West, Florida. Cuba has an area of 44,164 square miles (41,634 square miles for the island of Cuba, 1,180 square miles for the Isle of Pines, and 1,350 square miles for the other islands), with an estimated population, on June 30, 1929, of 3,607,919, including 82,531 immigrants, and estimated population of 3,638,174 on Dec. 31, 1930. The area, population, and density of population of each of the six provinces, on the former date, were as follows:—

Province	Area	Population (June 30, 1929)	Pop. per Sq. Mile
	Square miles		
Havana . . .	3,170	951,359	300.1
Pinar del Rio .	5,206	304,275	58.4
Matanzas . . .	3,256	349,578	107.3
Santa Clara . .	8,257	764,072	92.5
Camagüey . .	10,064	261,724	26.0
Oriente . . .	14,211	894,380	62.9
Total . . .	44,164	3,607,919 [1]	81.6

[1] Including 82,531 immigrants.

Cuba was discovered by Columbus on his first voyage and except for a brief period of British occupation in 1762–1763 remained a Spanish possession until 1898 when the sovereignty was relinquished under the terms of the Treaty of Paris which ended the armed intervention of the United States in the struggle of the Cubans against Spanish rule, and Cuba became an independent State. The Government of the United States handed over the government to the Cuban people upon the undertaking that they should conclude no treaty with a foreign Power that would endanger the independence of Cuba, that no debts should be contracted for which the current revenue would not suffice, that the United States should have certain rights of intervention, and be granted the use of naval stations. These conditions were accepted and the control of the Island was formally transferred to the national Government May 20, 1902 ending military control of the United States. After political disturbances American control was resumed Sept. 29, 1906 and continued until Jan. 28, 1909.

General Gerardo Machado y Morales, President.

1492

Oct. 28, Columbus discovered Cuba, which he named Juana, and took possession in the name of the King of Spain. It was later called Santiago and Ave Maria and finally regained the original Indian name of Cuba

Nov. 18, Columbus erected a cross on the heights

1494

May 18, On second voyage Columbus named Cape Cruz

June 12, Columbus had a notary draw up document which was signed by all persons on his vessels declaring the land to be a continent

1508

Cuba circumnavigated by Sebastian de Ocampo proving it an island

1511

Diego Columbus appointed Diego de Velasquez commander of force to conquer the natives

1515

April, Santiago de Cuba founded by Velasquez

1516

Nov. 11, A tribunal of Jeronimite monks sailed from San Lucar to establish a court to act on treatment of the Indians

1518

Papal Bull of Leo X established first bishopric at Baracoa

Nov. 13, Velasquez given authority to explore and made Adelanto and Governor of mainland and Island

1521

Jan. 18, Alonso de Zuazo appointed by Diego Columbus to investigate the administration of Velasquez and supersede him in government

Dec. 23, Velasquez restored to office as Lieutenant-Governor

1523

Oct. 22, Bishop Don Juan Ubicte authorized to remove the cathedral from Baracoa to Santiago de Cuba

1524

June 11, Death of Velasquez. Manuel de Rojas succeeded him as Governor

1525

March 14, Juan Altamirano appointed May 20, 1524, assumed office as Governor

April 4, Resignation of Bishop Don Juan de Ubicte

1526

Aug. 1, Gonzalo de Guzman appointed Dec. 1, 1525 assumed office as Governor, succeeding Altamirano deposed because of complaints against him

1527

Jan. 1, Miguel Ramirez appointed Bishop of Cuba and Protector of the Indians

1531

Jan. 25, Royal cedula forbade enslavement of Indians taken in war

Nov. 3, Royal cedula making slavery of the Indians illegal proclaimed at Santiago. Had no effect on the practice

Nov. 6, Juan Vadillo appointed Feb. 27 arrived to investigate the administration and take over the government

1532

March 1, Manuel de Rojas, Governor

1533

Nov., Negro uprising at mines of Jobabo

1535

Oct. 28, Gonzalo de Guzman, Governor

1537

May 4, Hernando de Soto appointed Governor of Cuba, first to hold office by royal appointment, and Adelanto of Florida

1538

June 7 or 9, De Soto arrived at San Juan

1539

May, De Soto sailed for Florida leaving his wife, Lady Isabella, acting Governor, with Juan de Rojas as her lieutenant

1540

March 12, First fort completed at Havana

1544

Feb. 2, Juanes de Avila, appointed Governor by the Crown Aug. 14, 1543, arrived

1546

June 4, Arrival of Antonio Chaves, appointed Governor, Oct. 5, 1545

1549

Nov. 4, Arrival of Dr. Gonzalo Perez de Angulo appointed Governor Sept. 1, 1548

1555

July 10, Havana taken by French expedition of Jacques de Sores. The fort defended by Juan de Lobero also taken
Oct. 9–23, The French again at Havana

1557

Diego de Mazariegas, new Governor, arrived at Havana

1565

Sept. 18, New Governor Garcia Osorio arrived

1567

Aug., Don Diego de Santillan appointed Governor
Oct. 24, Pedro Menendez made Governor in place of Santillan

1573

Dec. 13, Don Gabriel Montalvo appointed Governor

1574

Sept., Death of Pedro Menendez in Santander

1577

Feb. 13, Captain Francisco Carreño appointed Governor

1579

April 27, Death of Governor Carreño
Oct. 3, Provisional Governor Gaspar de Torres arrived

1580

Aug. 17, Captain Gabriel de Luxan appointed Governor Sept. 1, 1579, arrived and assumed office

1585

Dec. 20, Pedro Guera de la Vega arrived to take charge of the government after deposition of Luxan

1721

Sept. 12, University of Havana founded

1762

Aug. 12, Havana surrendered to English commanded by Lord Albemarle and Admiral Sir George Pocock after siege of 12 months

1763

June 6, Cuba restored to Spain when Treaty ended war between Great Britain, France, and Spain and English troops sailed away

1764

Oct. 31, Royal decree created an Intendant of equal rank with the Captain General to manage civil and military revenues

1790

Luis de las Casas, Governor (1790–96)

1799

Marquis de Someruelos, Governor (1799–1813)

1817

Oct. 21, Royal ordinance of colonization promulgated, "domiciled" foreigners required to profess Roman Catholic religion and swear allegiance to Spain and promise to obey laws and ordinances
State tobacco monopoly abolished

1818

Free Commerce with foreigners legalized

1825

May 28, Royal decree defined powers of Captain General, the "constitution of Cuba"

1834

Miguel Tacon, Governor (1834–39)

1837

Nov. 19, First railroad opened from Havana to Bejucal 11 years before any railroads in Spain

1838

Nov. 19, Railroad opened from Bejucal to Guines

1840

June, Railroad opened from Cardenas to Contreras

1841

Railroad from Pijuan to Banaguises opened

1842

Sept., Railroad from Jucaro to Recreo opened

1843

Aug., Railroad opened to Pijuan
Nov. 1, Railroad from Matanzas to Guanabano opened

1844

May, Railroad opened to Sabanilla

1848

June 24, Narciso Lopez set day for beginning of revolt against Spain. The plot discovered. Lopez escaped to the United States

Oct. 1, Railroad opened to Union

1850

May 19, Lopez filibustering expedition from the United States took Cardenas, but retreated to Key West pursued by Spanish vessels

1851

April 14, Railroad opened from Caibarien to Remedios

July 3, Joaquin de Aguero led revolt at Puerto Principe (Camaguey). He was defeated and captured and shot

Aug. 2, Narciso Lopez sailed from New Orleans, landing at Morillo, leading revolt Aug. 12

Aug. 13, Battle at Las Pozas

Aug. 16, William S. Crittenden, American, and 52 members of Lopez expedition captured on the 15th, shot

Aug. 25 and 26, Remainder of Lopez expedition captured and Lopez shot Aug. 31

Oct. 21, Cuban Central Railroad opened from Cienfuegos to Palmira

1852

March 7, Concordat signed by which dispute as to church property settled

1853

Oct. 21, Cedula made the Captain General also Superintendent of Finances

Nov. 15, Cuban Central Railroad opened to Cruces

1854

Feb. 28, The "Black Warrior" affair. American steamer cargo confiscated because not declared as required by law

Aug. 17, Juntas made entirely advisory subordinate to Captain General

Oct. 18, Ostend declaration as to Cuba. *See* United States

1859

April 4, Railroad from Regla to Minas opened

Oct. 4, Railroad opened from Guines to Catalina

Nov. 14, Lieutenant General Francesco Serrano, Duke de la Torre, appointed Governor

1860

Nov. 19, Cuban Central Railroad opened to Santa Clara

1861

June 23, First train run from Cristina (Havana) to Calabazar

Oct. 15, First train run from Guines to Matanzas

1863

July 19, Railroad opened from Concha to Mariano

1866

April 5, Railroad opened to Camajuani

1868

Sept. 17, After this date children of slave mothers decreed free

Oct. 10, "Declaration of the plan of the Yara" revolt led by Carlos Manuel de Cespedes and Manuel de Quesada, General of forces. Provisional government formed. Civil war begun lasted 10 years

1869

Feb. 26, Assembly of the insurrection issued decree proclaiming abolition of slavery

April 10, Constitution adopted by the insurgents and Cespedes made President

1870

May 17, Railroad to Guareiras completed

July, Act gave freedom to slaves who had served under Spanish flag and those who had reached the age of 60

1871

Nov. 27, Execution of 8 young students in Havana charged with revolt

1873

Oct. 31, Capture of vessel of insurrectionists on high seas, the "Virginius" flying the American flag, by Spanish war vessel

Nov. 4, After court-martial General W. A. C. Ryan of the "Virginius" and 4 Cubans shot

Nov. 7, 8, and 12, Captain Frye and entire crew of the "Virginius" and 12 passengers executed

1875

Feb. 27, Spain agreed to pay the United States $80,000 for indemnity, relief for families of "Virginius" victims

1878

Jan. 28, Provincial municipal law promulgated

Feb. 10, Treaty of Zanjon signed by General Martinez Campos and Maximo Gomez, insurgent leader, ended civil war

March 1, Cuba granted representation in the Spanish Cortes

1879

May 23, Spanish penal code extended to Cuba

1880

Feb. 13, Law provided for gradual abolition of slavery

May 1, Spanish mortgage law extended to Cuba

Oct. 1, Railroad opened as far as Placetas

1881

April 7, Decree applied Spanish Constitution of 1876 to Cuba, and nominally rights of Spanish citizenship given to Cubans

1885

Sept. 25, Law of civil procedure applied to Cuba

1886

Jan. 28, Commercial code came into effect

Oct. 17, Decree abolished slavery in the Spanish dominions

1887

Census of population gave total of 1,631,687 inhabitants

Oct. 18, Law of criminal procedure came into effect

1889

July 31, Civil code promulgated

Oct. 19, Code of criminal procedure promulgated

1893

April 24, Proclamation of revolt of Generals Manuel and Ricardo Sartorius near Holgiun, which ended with surrender of the Sartorius brothers on May 2

July 14, Civil code modified

Record crop of sugar cane, million ton mark passed for the first time

1895

Jan. 4, Engagement with rebels near Tapeste, Havana. The Spaniards under Colonel Benedicto saved from defeat by arrival of reinforcements

Jan. 13, Cuban rebels successful in engagement at Gabuquito near Manzanillo when insurgent General Calixto Garcia attacked by General Segura

Feb. 4, The Queen Regent signed decree instituting measures of reform

Feb. 23, General Calleja suspended the constitutional guarantees

Feb. 24, Rebellion in provinces of Santiago, Santa Clara, and Matanzas

Feb. 26, Insurgents entrenched at Vequita attacked by government troops

March 17, Engagement near Ulloa

March 22, Insurgents led by B. Masso ambushed convoy south of Holguin and captured arms, ammunition, and commissary stores

April 1, Antonio and José Maceo with other rebel leaders landed at Duaba

April 11, Maximo Gomez and José Marti, rebel leaders, landed in eastern Cuba

April 13, Insurgents defeated near Palmerito with great loss

April 16, General Arsenio Martinez Campos succeeded General Calleja as Governor and Captain General

April 16 and 18, Insurgents led by Gomez defeated Colonel Bosch at Sabana de Jaibo

April 29, Spaniards defeated in attack on José Maceo at Arroyo Hondo near Guantanamo

May 14, Insurgents defeated at Jobito near Guantanamo but Spanish Colonel Bosch killed

May 18, Bartolome Maso elected President by the Insurgent Assembly and Estrada Palma delegate at large to the United States and other countries

May 19, José Marti, patriot, ambushed in skirmish at Boca dos Rios and killed

June 2, Insurgents commanded by Gomez entered Camaguey

July 13, General Santo Cildes and 70 men killed near Bayamo in surprise ambuscade

July 15, Independence of Spain formally proclaimed by the insurgents

Aug. 31, Battle at Sao del Indio

Sept. 5, Insurgent General Garcia captured important town of Victoriade las Tunas in Santiago

Sept. 9, 150,000 Spanish troops landed

Sept. 13, Insurgent constituent Assembly summoned by Marti at Jimaguayu, and adopted a Constitution on the 16th, and officers of the Government on the 18th

Sept. 22, Government of the Republic of Cuba established at Najasa, Salvador Cisneros Betancourt, President, and Bartolome Maso, Vice-President

Sept. 25, Engagement near the Guayabal River

Oct. 2, Battle at Mount Mogote, insurgents commanded by Maceo attacked and defeated Spaniards under Generals Garcia, Navarro, and Linares

Oct. 6, Cabinet Council decided to give Cuba autonomy under suzerainty of Spain

Nov. 6, Maximo Gomez ordered suspension of work on the plantations to help the revolution and later destruction of buildings and railroads

Nov. 12, Maceo reached La Villas with 800 men

Nov. 18–19, Battle at Taguasco in Santa Clara between insurgents Gomez and Maceo and Spanish Generals Suarez Valdes, Luque, and Aldave, an insurgent victory

Dec. 7, T. Estrada Palma representing the insurgents made statement to the United States State Dept. on causes of the revolt and oppression of Spain

Dec. 10, Spaniards under Commander Garado defeated at La Virginia

Dec. 23, Spaniards defeated at Palmarito

Dec. 26, Insurgents invading loyal province of Havana defeated. More than half the island in possession of the insurgents, including Santiago de Cuba, Puerto Principe, and half of Santa Clara

1896

Jan. 3, Martial law proclaimed in provinces of Havana and Pinar del Rio

Jan. 5, Gomez marched insurgent army into Pinar del Rio

Jan. 11, Insurgents captured San Cristobal and Bahia Honda

Jan. 15, By this date estimated that one-third of the sugar cane crop had been burned

Jan. 17, General Martinez Campos recalled and General Valeriano Weyler appointed Governor and Captain General, arriving Feb. 10

Jan. 29, Gomez defeated with heavy loss at St. Lucia

Feb. 16, Order of Governor Weyler for confinement of the inhabitants of certain districts in rebellion in reconcentration camps

Feb. 28, Senate of the United States adopted resolution that belligerent rights should be accorded to Cuba, and House April 6

March 13, Maceo attacked and took Batabano

March 17, Defeat of the Spaniards near Candelaria, Pinar del Rio, by insurgents led by Maceo and Bandera

March 18, The steamer "Three Friends" from Tampa, Florida, landed General Collazo and Major Hernandez and large cargo of arms and ammunition for insurgents

March 22, General Gomez, insurgent, captured Santa Clara in night attack, and took large quantity of military supplies, evacuated after 5 hours

April 4, Mediation offered by the United States to Spain; refused June 4

April 14, Battle at La Chuza, Pinar del Rio, the Spaniards defeated by General Maceo retreated to the coast, and were rescued by warships

April 25, Spanish gunboat captured by steamer "Competitor" sailing from Key West, Florida, and Captain A. Laborde and 4 others captured and sentenced to death; intervention of United States May 10

May, General Weyler prohibited exportation of tobacco, and of fruit in July

May 1, Conflict at Cacarajicara in Pinar del Rio, General Inclan captured insurgent fort but forced to retreat under fire

May 6, Town of Punta Brava near Havana burned by insurgents forcing the Spaniards to surrender the forts

May 16, British steamer "Laurada" from New York landed General S. Ruiz, insurgent, and large quantity of munitions of war

May 23, The "Three Friends" landed General R. Portuondo and munitions, in spite of pursuit of Spanish war vessels and again on the 29th

July 9–11, Battle at Najasa in Puerto Principe province, insurgents commanded by General Gomez and Spaniards by General Castellanos, no advantage gained by either

July 15, General Maceo, insurgent, defeated Spanish General Inclan, who was taken prisoner, in Pinar del Rio

Aug. 20, Decree of General Weyler ordered compulsory circulation at par of large issue of notes put out by Spanish Bank at Havana; modified Sept. 25 because of complete stoppage of business

Sept. 20, Engagement near Calabazar, Havana, insurgents commanded by Castillo and Delgado routed

Sept. 29, General attack on insurgent position in Pinar del Rio

Oct. 1, General Molina defeated insurgent force under Arango and Sanguilly at Arcos de Diego and Samarones, Havana

Oct. 21, Order of concentration for inhabitants of Pinar del Rio in isolated camps or garrison towns while the country laid waste by Spanish troops

Oct. 23, Cacarajicara occupied by Spaniards

Oct. 27, Guimaro besieged since the 17th surrendered to insurgent General Calixto Garcia

Nov. 8–23, General Weyler took the field in person without any result

Dec. 1, Insurgents raided city of Guanabacoa near Havana

Dec. 7, Antonio Maceo, insurgent commander-in-chief, ambushed by Spaniards and killed; succeeded by General Juan Rius Rivera

1897

Jan. 4, Colonel Benedicto in engagement with insurgents commanded by Aguirre, Aranguren, and Arango near Tapeste, Havana, gained victory

Jan. 13, Insurgent General Garcia attacked at Gabuquito by General Segura forced Spaniards to retreat

Feb. 4, Reform program drawn up by Canovas signed by the Queen Regent to be operative when order restored; put into effect in certain provinces April 29

March 21, Holguin captured by insurgents

March 28, Insurgent General Rivera taken prisoner by Spanish General H. Velasco in surprise attack at Cabezedas in Pinar del Rio

July 6, General Weyler proclaimed amnesty to rebels who would surrender

Sept. 5, Victoria de las Tunas in Santiago captured by insurgent General Garcia with forts

Sept. 12, Domingo Mendez Capote elected President of Cuban Republic, B. Maso, Vice-President, General Garcia, Commander-in-Chief

Oct. 7, General Weyler recalled

——, Spaniards defeated by insurgents at Carmen in Havana

Nov. 1, General Ramon Blanco y Arenas succeeded as Governor and Captain General

Nov. 8, Proclamation of amnesty to rebels by General Blanco

Nov. 10, Edict of General Blanco gave planters permission to grind sugar

Nov. 14, Decree of General Blanco gave permission to reconcentrados to return to their farms and plantations under certain conditions

Nov. 21, Insurgents raided Casa Blanca and took money and silver

Nov. 25, Royal edict published on the 27th granted autonomy to Cuba

Dec. 2, Guisa, in Santiago, captured by insurgents commanded by General Calixto Garcia

Dec. 9, Raid of insurgents on port of Caimanera successful

Dec. 19, Colonel Ruiz sent to Aranguren, insurgent leader, to ask him to surrender and accept autonomy, executed

1898

Jan. 1, Autonomist Government came into effect and Executive Council organized, José M. Galvez, president

Jan. 12–18, Demonstrations against autonomy and riots in Havana

Jan. 21, Surrender of General Juan Masso Parro with 10 officers and 110 men to General Aguirre in Santa Clara

Jan. 25, The United States battleship "Maine" arrived at Havana on friendly visit

Feb. 12, Radical wing of the autonomists adopted program of conciliation

Feb. 15, The U.S.S. "Maine" blown up in harbor of Havana. See also United States

March 30, Decree of Captain General Blanco directed ending of reconcentration camps in the western provinces

April 25, The United States declared war on Spain as from April 21. For events of the war see United States

May 4, First autonomous Congress opened by Captain General Blanco

July 17, Formal surrender of Santiago to Americans by General Toral

Nov. 26, Resignation of General Blanco; succeeded as Governor and Captain General by General Castellanos

Dec. 10, Treaty of Paris signed by the United States and Cuba by which Spain relinquished sovereignty over Cuba. See United States

Dec. 11, Death of General Calixto Garcia in Washington

Dec. 13, Executive Order created Division of Cuba, Major General John R. Brooke in command

1899

Jan. 1, Formal transfer of Cuba to the United States. General Brooke as military Governor issued proclamation declaring protectorate; General Fitzhugh Lee assumed command of province of Havana

——, New customs tariff average 6% reduction put into effect reducing duties and taxes reduced

Jan. 11, Provision made for administration by 4 departments, State; Finance; Justice and Public Instruction; Agriculture, Commerce, Industries, and Public Works

Jan. 12, Domingo Mendez Capote appointed Secretary of State; Pablo Desvernine, Secretary of Finance; José Antonio Gonzales Lanuza, Justice; and Adolfo Saenz Yanez, Agriculture

Feb. 6, Last Spanish soldiers left Cuba

Feb. 10, Decree remitted taxes due under Spanish régime with certain exceptions, abolished the octroi, taxes on food and fuel, and reduced land taxes, but increased taxes on alcoholic liquors

Feb., General Gomez accepted offer of the United States of $3,000,000 for distribution to Cuban soldiers for help to return to civil pursuits

March 11, Cuban Assembly adopted resolution impeaching General Gomez and depriving him of command of army because of his acceptance of financial terms of the United States; later withdrawn

March 18–20, Mobs in conflict with municipal police in Havana

April 4, Assembly voted disbanding of army, surrender of muster roll to General Brooke for distribution of the $3,000,000, and its own dissolution

April 7, Cuban generals voted to reinstate General Gomez as Commander-in-Chief

April 14, Order created the Supreme Court

——, Decree applied immigration law and regulations of the United States to Cuba

April 17, Number of provinces reduced by consolidation of Pinar del Rio with rural Havana, and Mantanazas with Santa Clara

May 6, C. F. W. Neely arrested in New York in connection with postal frauds and held for extradition to Cuba

May 14, Society of Veterans of Independence, the revived Cuban Military Assembly, organized

May 15, General Gomez withdrew from plan agreed to in Jan. for distribution of $3,000,000 because of project of subordinate officers to defeat the apportionment

May 26, Decision allowed Cuban vessels to engage in international trade under Cuban coasting flag

May 27, Payment of the $3,000,000 begun at Havana but only 7 received the money because of opposition of former Assembly, but more applied on following days

——, Disbandment of army begun

May 31, Order made only civil marriage legal

June 1, Decree pardoned all persons convicted of offenses against Spanish military laws

——, Decree made editors and proprietors of newspapers responsible for their contents

June 15, Order provided for establishment of audiencias in each of the six provinces to administer civil and criminal justice

July 28, E. G. Rathbone dismissed as Director of Department of Posts and arrested for embezzlement of funds

Aug. 1, General Ludlow suppressed Cuban newspaper for seditious language

Aug. 2, Appointment of judges for Supreme Court and provincial courts

Sept. 25, General strike at Havana collapsed with arrest of leaders

Oct. 16, Census begun. Total population estimated as 1,572,797

Oct. 28, Courts of First Instance below Audiencias established

Nov. 2, Official order created new office of Superintendent of Schools in the Department of Justice. Alexis E. Frye appointed first Superintendent

Dec. 6, Order issued constituting school law provided for opening of elementary schools by Dec. 11

Dec. 13, Executive Order opened coasting trade to American vessels

Dec. 20, General Leonard Wood appointed military Governor Dec. 13 arrived at Havana succeeding General Brooke

Dec. 30, Governor Wood announced appointment of Cabinet, Diego Tamajo, Secretary of State; Enrique José de Varona, Secretary of Finance; Luis Estevez, Secretary of Justice; Juan Ruis Rivera, Secretary of Agriculture; Juan Bautista Barreiro, Secretary of Public Instruction; José Ramon Villalon, Secretary of Public Works

1900

Jan. 19, Order issued that civil agencies should be employed in preference to methods of military government except when incapable of maintaining public peace

Jan. 24, School Board established, A. E. Frye, E. B. Echeverria, and Lincoln de Zayas

April 11, Expiration of period of time given for Spanish residents to make their election as to citizenship

April 13, Powers of Police Court at Havana increased

April 18, Municipal election law issued

June 15, New tariff took effect

June 16, Election for municipal officers held; 110,816 persons voted

June 26, Dr. Walter Reed appointed to investigate theory of Dr. Charles John Finlay as to transmission of yellow fever by mosquitoes

July, 1,281 Cuban teachers accepted invitation to attend session of Harvard University Summer School, all expenses paid. Visits to New York City and Washington arranged

July 1, Courts established in cities other than Havana

July 25, Order issued providing for elections for delegates to a constitutional convention

Aug. 8, Order declared marriage "may be civil or religious at option of contracting parties"

Sept. 15, Elections held for constituent congress

Oct. 9, Decree provided for introduction of writ of *habeas corpus* in judicial procedure

Nov. 5–Feb. 21, Constitutional Convention met at Havana

Nov. 20, Experimental Sanitary Station opened about 1 mile from Quemados suburb of Havana named for Dr. Lazear

Dec. 31, Order of General Wood for reform of the judiciary, placing judges and court officers on salary and abolishing feeing system

1901

Jan. 14, United States Supreme Court decision extradited American citizen C. F. W. Neely wanted in Cuba on charge of frauds in Post Office under United States law of June 6, 1900

Feb. 4, Major William C. Gorgas began campaign which resulted in eradication of yellow fever in Havana

Feb. 21, Constitution for the Republic adopted by Convention

March 2, Law including Platt Amendment passed in the United States

April 5, Order effected reorganization of the rural guard, the national police

June 12, Platt Amendment adopted and incorporated in Cuban Constitution

July 25, Proclamation of President McKinley putting civil government into effect. Free trade with the United States established

Oct. 1, Convention adopted electoral law providing for general election for government officers, House of Representatives and presidential and senatorial electors

Oct. 3, Constitutional Convention dissolved

Dec. 31, Election held for Congress and President. Tomas Estrada Palma elected first President

1902

Jan. 24, Civil order abolished one-third of the municipalities

Feb. 7, March 3, and April 28, Railroad laws enacted

Feb. 8, Decree created a commission to regulate construction and management of railroads

Feb. 24, President Palma declared elected by presidential electors, Luis Estevez, Vice-President

March 5, Law issued as to land, boundary lines, and individual estates

April 5, Jury system abolished because of difficulty in getting convictions

April 16, Decree safeguarded judicial officers against arbitrary removal or suspension

April 28, Railroad law recommended by Sir W. C. Van Horne came into effect

——, Order provided manual for military law

April 29, Order gave effect to quarantine laws and regulations

May 5, First Congress met

May 11, President Elect Palma arrived in Cuba and was given enthusiastic welcome

May 12, Railroad Commission appointed under law of April 28

May 15, Order applied immigration laws of the United States to Cuba

May 17, Order of General Wood for regulation of sanitary affairs established a "Superior Sanitary Board"

May 20, The Republic inaugurated. General Wood formally transferred the Government to President Palma inaugurated first President

May 26, First message of President Palma to Congress

June 16, Señor Quesada received at Washington as Minister from Cuba

July 3, Suspension of tonnage dues on Cuban vessels entering the ports of the United States

Sept. 22, Assassination of Liberal Representative Enrique Villuendas at Cienfuegos

Nov. 23–24, General strike. Laborers attacked police; 20 killed and over 100 wounded

Dec. 1, Railroad from Santiago to Santa Clara completed

Dec. 11, Commercial and reciprocity Treaty signed with the United States

1903

Jan. 26, Supplementary Commercial Treaty with the United States

Feb. 16 and 23, Agreement for lease of coaling and naval stations in Cuba concluded with the United States, signed by President of Cuba, Feb. 23 by the United States

March 28, Commercial Reciprocity Treaty of 1902 with the United States adopted by the Cuban Senate provided that American goods received should pay from 25–40% less than regular tariff and Cuban goods should received 20% reduction from the regular American tariff

May 22, Treaty with the United States incorporated the Platt Amendment

July 2, Treaty with the United States respecting Isle of Pines signed. Not ratified within the time prescribed

July 14–26, Insurrection at Vicana suppressed

Sept. 13–22, Insurrection at Sevilla near Santiago suppressed

Nov. 9, Commercial Reciprocity Treaty with the United States signed

Nov. 17, Copyright law proclaimed

Dec. 11, United States marines occupied Guantanamo ceded by Cuba for naval station

Dec. 29, Treaty of commerce, navigation and emigration, and arbitration with Italy signed

1904

Jan. 7, President Palma vetoed lottery bill

Jan. 12, Act authorized increased tariff rates, amount not to exceed 30%. Promulgated Feb. 5

Jan. 20, Supplementary Relations with the United States Treaty concluded

Jan. 22, Law authorized recognition of bonds of 1896 and 1897 issued by Cuban Revolutionary Government

Feb. 4, Last American soldiers left Cuba

March 2, Second Treaty as to Isle of Pines with the United States recognized the sovereignty of Cuba; ratified by United States 1925

April 6, Extradition Treaty with the United States signed. Amended Dec. 6

First loan negotiated with Speyer and Company of New York and London for $35,000,000 at 5%

1905

March 3, Cabinet reorganized

May 23, National Liberal Convention nominated José Miguel Gomez for President and Alfredo Zayas for Vice-President

June 17, Death of Maximilian Gomez (82) at Havana

Sept. 23, First election held a Moderate victory

Sept. 27, J. M. Gomez withdrew name from Liberal ticket as candidate for President

Dec. 1, Final election a Conservative victory. President Palma reëlected. Declared elected by Electoral College March 19

1906

Feb. 24–25, Liberal revolt. Barracks at Guanabacoa seized

May 20, President Palma inaugurated for second term

July 1, Decree of the President made effective the budget of 1908–1909 of $24,285,000 because of failure of Senate to pass budget

July 28, Liberals issued manifesto of insurrection

Aug. 16, Insurrection of Liberals led by José Miguel Gomez in Pinar del Rio

Aug. 21, Fighting in Matanzas province, and rebels took Aguines, Havana

Aug. 22, Rebels captured town of San Luis in province of Pinar del Rio

Aug. 23, San Juan y Martinez taken by rebels. Q. Bandera, revolutionary leader, defeated and killed

Aug. 27, Colonel Valle defeated insurgent force commanded by General Guzman at Cienfuegos

Aug. 31, Revolt spread to Santiago and the following day to Puerto Principe

Sept. 8, President Palma appealed to the United States for intervention

Sept. 10 and 13, American marines landed at Havana

Sept. 14, Open letter of the President to Gonzalo de

Quesada, Cuban Minister in Washington announcing that an American Mission would be sent to Cuba and warning of American intervention if hostilities did not cease

Sept. 16, Armistice declared

Sept. 19, Secretary of War Taft and Acting Secretary of State Bacon arrived in Cuba

Sept. 25, President Palma announced his resignation and the 28th presented his resignation to Congress and that of his Cabinet

Sept. 29, American control over Cuba resumed and proclamation of Secretary Taft announced provisional Government

Oct. 10, Provisional Governor Taft issued general amnesty proclamation

Oct. 13, Charles E. Magoon appointed to succeed Taft as provisional Governor of Cuba on Oct. 3 took office

Nov. 3, Meeting of Moderates formally dissolved the party

Nov. 25, Last band of insurgents commanded by former Chief of Police Ruis surrendered near Cienfuegos

Dec. 3, Statement of President Roosevelt that while the United States had no desire to annex Cuba it was impossible for the Island to continue independent if the "insurrectionary habit should become confirmed"

——, Governor Magoon vacated places of Congress

Dec. 24, Governor Magoon appointed Advisory Law Commission of 9 Cubans and 3 Americans headed by Colonel E. H. Crowder

1907

Feb. 5, Order issued directed artillery force increased to 2,000 and rural guard from 6,000 to 1,000 and all able bodied males from 21 to 45 included in the militia

April 8, Visit of Secretary Taft to Havana for 2 days

June 14, Death of General Bartolome Maso (73)

July 7, The Government ratified the Geneva Convention of 1864

Sept. 26, Mazo Parra, revolutionist, arrested day before the time set for beginning revolt

Sept. 30–Nov. 14, Census taken gave total of population as 2,048,980, 1,074,882 males, 974,098 females, 419,342 voters. This included 1,428,176 whites to 620,804 colored, 228,741 foreign-born including 185,393 Spanish, 11,217 Chinese, and 6,713 Americans

1908

April 1, Electoral law promulgated. Revised and promulgated again Sept. 11

May 29, Organic municipal law promulgated replacing Spanish law of 1878. Came into effect Oct. 1 by decree of Sept. 21

Aug. 1, Provincial and municipal election a Conservative victory

Nov. 4, Death of Tomas E. Palma (72), first President

Nov. 14, Election for President and Congress a Liberal victory. José M. Gomez elected President and Alfredo Zayas, Vice-President, defeating General Mario Menocal, Conservative candidate for President

1909

Jan. 13, Congress met

Jan. 26, Act established 8 hour day for government employees

Jan. 27, Judiciary law promulgated

Jan. 28, President José Miguel Gomez inaugurated second President. American administration ended

Feb. 1, United States troops withdrawn

March 10, Red Cross Society founded

March 15–16, Shooting of Manuel Lavastida under arrest charged with revolutionary acts because of alleged attempt to escape

July 3, Act restored cock-fights

July 7, Act established a national lottery

July 18, Congress adjourned

Second Speyer loan negotiated for $16,500,000 at $4\frac{1}{2}\%$

1910

Feb. 5, Two Cuban editors sentenced to imprisonment for libel of President Gomez

April 16, Señor Morua, first negro to hold a Cabinet position, appointed

May 4, Law ordered closing of all places of business, workshops, factories on Sundays

May, Morua law passed prohibited formation of any political party on basis of lines of race or color

June 20, Law authorized establishment of Territorial Bank of Cuba

July 25, Insurrection led by General Vicente Miniet suppressed and Miniet captured 2 days later

Oct. 22, Attempted assassination of General "Pino" Guerra, commander-in-chief

Loan of $10,000,000 concluded with J. P. Morgan and Company of New York

1911

Jan. 25, Proposal of Cuban Ports Company to dredge and improve a specified list of harbors in return for duties to be levied

Feb. 20, Ports Company Concession Bill passed

June 23, Protest of the United States against the Ports Company concession

June 29, Suspension of payment law passed

July 3, General Guillermo Acevedo began unsuccessful revolt

July 23, Law authorized exchange of Arsenal property for Villaneuva

Aug., Revolt headed by General Emilio Nunez supported by the National Council of Veterans

1912

Feb. 1, Territorial Bank of Cuba chartered

March, Veterans' Council reached agreement with the Government

April 26, Treaty of friendship, commerce, and navigation concluded with Peru

May 15, Zayas nominated for President by the Liberals

May 20, Negro insurrection led by General Estenoz at Sagua La Grande in the province of El Oriente

May 28, American marines landed at Guantanamo

May 30, American marines landed at Daiquiri

June 4, Martial law declared by General Monteagudo

June 5, American marines assumed control of Guantanamo City

June 18, Decree of the President granted concessions of forest privileges and public lands to the Campania Agricultora de Zapata on condition swamp land be reclaimed for agriculture within 8 years

June 27, General Evaristo Estenoz killed in engagement near Santiago ending insurrection

July 9, Lottery law amended

July 11, Protest of American Minister in Cuba against the Zapata concession

Aug. 2, Zapata concession repealed

Nov. 1, General Mario Menocal, Conservative, elected President and José Varona, Vice-President

Dec. 27, Treaty with the United States by which the United States relinquished rights at Bahia Honda in consideration for increased advantages at Guantanamo

1913

Feb. 9–10, Visit of William Jennings Bryan to Havana

March 13, President Gomez vetoed Bill granting amnesty to political offenders

April 11, Ciferino Mendez, mayor of Cienfuegos, assassinated

April 21, Congress in joint session proclaimed Menocal President

April 25, Amnesty Bill passed

May 12, Gomez decree provided for method of arbitration to end Ports Company concession

May 20, President Menocal inaugurated

June 18, Decree canceled Ports Company Concession. Work taken over by Department of Public Works Aug. 4

June 30, General retirement law for land and sea forces enacted

July 7, General Armado Riva, Chief of National Police, shot fatally by Eugenio Arias. General Ernesto Asbert, Governor of Havana Province, charged with complicity

Nov., Revolt headed by Crescencio Garcia, mulatto, suppressed

1914

April 6, New Congress met

Aug. 5, Declaration of neutrality in European War

Nov. 7, Law published authorized new coinage issue of gold peso of 1.6718 grammes (1.5046 grammes fine) as monetary unit

Morgan loan of $10,000,000 at 5% negotiated

1915

Feb. 1, Amnesty Bill passed over veto which freed Ernesto Asbert

March 1, New law enacted governing entry of Chinese immigrants went into effect

1916

Jan. 16, Conservative Party Convention in which Menocal won nomination. Fraud claimed

June 12, Workmen's Compensation law enacted

Nov. 1, President Menocal reëlected in disputed election

1917

Feb. 9, Revolt led by ex-President Gomez over disputed presidential election

Feb. 12, Rebels led by Major Regoberto Fernandez took Santiago

Feb. 17, Government forces captured rebel cities of Sancti Spiritus and Ciego de Avila

Feb. 28, American marines landed at Guantanamo

March 7, General José Gomez, rebel leader, captured by government troops after battle near Placetas

March 8, 400 American marines landed at Santiago at request of civil authorities to protect property

April 7, Congress adopted resolution declaring state of war with Germany existed

April 29, Electoral College declared Mario Menocal elected President

May 20, President Menocal inaugurated for second term

July 24, Congress authorized the President to pay indemnity to Ports Company

Aug. 21, Government turned over to the United States 4 German warships in Cuban ports

Sept. 24, Gomez released from prison

Oct. 29, General regulations for importation of contract laborers framed

Dec. 16, War declared on Austria-Hungary

Loans for $7,000,000 and $30,000,000 negotiated

1918

March 18, Amnesty Bill passed

April 3, Decree of the President authorized exchange of $7,000,000 in 5% Cuban Treasury bonds of Cuban Ports Company

April 11, Pension law enacted for Army of Liberation and for civilians who aided independence

April, Cuba received $15,000,000 war loan from the United States

Aug. 3, Military Service Act came into effect providing for compulsory training for citizens between ages of 19 and 25, and draft for those between ages of 21 and 28

Aug. 25, Teacher's Retirement law promulgated

Sept. 11, President Menocal offered the United States Cuban troops for service in the war with the Central Powers. Declined on ground of inadequate shipping facilities

1919

May 30, Senate passed Bill authorizing suspension of Constitutional guarantees because of labor strikes and riots

June 12, Workmen's Accident law passed

Aug. 8, New Electoral law went into effect. Each voter required to have an identification card and provision made for public counting of ballots and the recognition of all political parties

Aug. 15, Law authorized certain gambling games and horse racing

1920

March 8, Cuba became original member of the League of Nations by adherence to Covenant

May 19–26, Height of sugar boom with prices over 20 cents a pound

Sept., Sugar at 8 cents a pound

Oct. 10, Financial moratorium proclaimed in order to avoid panic in the sugar market

Oct. 27, Diplomatic relations with Germany resumed

Nov. 1, First election under new electoral law. Dr. Zayas elected President. Liberals charged fraud

Dec. 13, Sugar sold at 3.75 cents a pound

1921

Jan. 6, General Enoch H. Crowder, appointed by President Wilson "to confer with President Menocal with respect to the political and financial condition of Cuba," arrived

March 15, New elections held in 4 provinces confirmed election of Dr. Zayas, Conservative, as President

April 9, Banco Nacional closed its door with liabilities amounting to $67,660,126.92

April 17, Formal recognition of the election of Zayas by the United States

April 30, Failure of J. I. Lezama, chief sugar speculator, who fled from the country

May 20, President Zayas inaugurated

May–June, Failure of 18 banks representing indebtedness of $130,000,000

June 13, Death of José Miguel Gomez in New York City

Oct. 7, Contract with J. P. Morgan and Company signed formed basis of loan of $5,000,000

Dec. 5, Open shop principle inaugurated by employers in wharfage and lighter operations

Dec. 7, Congress adopted resolution that it would be a friendly act for the United States to withdraw troops in Cuban territory since the War began

Cuba defaulted on bonded debt both domestic and foreign

1922

April 8, General Crowder sent first of a series of memoranda to President Zayas based on investigation of government departments by American experts

April 13, Strike of telegraphers

May 1, Suspension of German Bank of H. Upmann and Co.

May 5, Death of Nunez y Rodriguez at Havana

June 10, Cabinet resigned

June 15, New Cabinet took office headed by Manuel de Cespedes, known as the "Honest Cabinet"

Aug. 30, Financial legislation recommended by General Crowder enacted

Sept. 13, Debt Commission created

Oct. 7, $50,000,000 loan authorized

Oct. 13–Feb. 19, 1925, Meetings of Debt Commission

Nov. 1, Elections a Liberal victory

1923

Jan. 11, American Legation made an embassy

Feb. 9, Major General Enoch H. Crowder appointed first Ambassador from the United States

March 10, Zayas decree for purchase of Santa Clara Convent for a government building for $2,350,000

April 2, Manifesto of Cuban Committee of National and Civic Renovation against corruption of the Government signed by large number of distinguished citizens

April 3, President Zayas dismissed 4 members of the "Honest Cabinet" for "high reasons of State"

April 29, Revolt in Central Cuba chiefly in provinces of Santa Clara and El Oriente

Aug. 4, New Lottery Act enacted

Aug. 12, First meeting of the new association the Veterans and Patriots Association for reform of the Government

Aug. 22, Cuba paid in full World War debt to the United States

Aug. 31, Veteran's Association adopted 12 recommendations practically the Crowder program for presentation to Congress

Sept. 1, Dr. Cosme de la Torriente appointed Ambassador to the United States

Sept. 20, 20 leaders of the Veterans and Patriots Association arrested but later released

Oct. 9, Pension law enacted

——, Tarafa law for consolidation of railroads claiming to cheapen and improve service, closing private ports of sugar planters

Nov. 23, Decree established sales tax on national products to be paid by merchants, manufacturers, and producers

Dec. 19, Strike of railroad employees

1924

March 25, Organ of Veterans and Patriots Association suppressed and its leader General Garcia Velez compelled to leave the country

April 29, Revolt led by Colonel Federico Laredo Bru begun near Cienfuegos, Santa Clara

May 10–14, Strike on United Railways

May 17, General amnesty granted

July 10, Act set up conciliation committees to settle industrial disputes

July 14, General Retirement and Pension Fund Board constituted

July 26, Tariff Commission reported to President Coolidge that $417,568,000 of American capital invested in Cuban sugar mills

Aug. 28, Consolidation of railroads effected

Oct., The "Malecon affair" expropriation by the Government of a piece of land at extraordinary high price to continue ocean front drive

Nov. 1, Election held. Liberal Gerardo Machado elected President, Mendez Capote, Vice-President

Nov.–Dec., Strike of sugar mill employees

Dec. 1, Cardenas Bay Contract Bill signed by the President

1925

March 13, United States Senate ratified the Isle of Pines Treaty

May 20, General Gerardo Machado inaugurated President

1926

Jan. 14, Additional Extradition Treaty with the United States signed

March 4, Liquor Smuggling Treaty with the United States signed and supplement signed March 11

April 10–12, Run on banks especially the Royal Bank of Canada

April 22, Consular Treaty with the United States

May 4, Law promulgated for government control of sugar products. Crop cut down 10%. Penalties provided for violation

Oct. 20, Hurricane killed over 600 persons at Havana and other places and injured thousands

Nov. 15, Agreement signed with sugar producers of Germany, Poland, and Czechoslovakia to seek rational apportionment of exports

Nov. 19, Diplomatic relations severed with Uruguay because of statement of Uruguayan delegate at League of Nations Assembly that sovereignty of Cuba was limited by Treaty with the United States

1927

May 22, Cuban Federation of Labor organized

June 22, Act signed approval of Constitutional Amendments, term of president 6 years, and ineligible to reëlection, number of senators and representatives increased

July 15, Commercial Treaty with Spain signed

Oct. 3, Law created National Commission for protection of the sugar industry

Oct. 19, New customs tariff went into effect

Nov. 21, Commercial Agreement with Canada signed

1928

Jan. 16, President Coolidge delivered opening address at Pan-American Conference at Havana

Feb. 8, Colonel Charles A. Lindbergh in the "Spirit

of St. Louis" arrived at Havana, flight from Port au
Prince, Haiti
May 9, Constitutional Amendments as to suffrage,
presidential term, number of senators, and members
of Chamber approved became part of Constitution
May 11
June 2, Act prohibited night work in bakeries
June 22, Contract signed with New York bankers for
loan of 50,000,000 pesos for construction of public
works
June 29, Radiotelegraph Convention with Mexico
signed
Oct. 5, Extradition Convention with Italy signed
Nov. 1, President Machado reëlected, unopposed

1929

Feb. 27, Arrest of 9 persons charged with plot to over-
turn the Government
May 11, Franchise extended to women over 21 who
can read and write by new Constitution in effect on
this date
May 20, President Machado y Morales inaugurated
for second term. The new term is 6 years instead of 4
July 1, Act amended Civil Code provided that Cuban
woman marrying a foreigner should not lose nationality
Aug. 27, Joseph E. Barlow claiming $9,000,000 for
confiscation of his property arrested
Nov. 6, Most favored nation commercial Treaty with
France signed
Nov. 16, Decree of deportation of 23 Asiatics as undesirable citizens signed by the President

1930

Feb. 6, New divorce law went into effect
Feb. 9, Cuba agreed to arbitrate the claims of Joseph E.
Barlow because of alleged confiscation of property
March 20, Strike in Havana because of unemployment
and the dissolution of 2 unions charged with com-
munism
April 26, Colonel Charles A. Lindbergh landed at
Havana completing first part of inaugural air-mail
flight from Miami across Caribbean Sea to the Canal
Zone
May 17, 4 persons killed and 20 injured when soldiers
break up meeting at Artemisa opposed to President
Machado
Aug. 5, 70 persons arrested in alleged communist plot
against the Government
Sept. 19, Fighting between citizens and troops at Sagua
de Tanamo in province of El Oriente, 37 persons
arrested
Sept. 30, Clash of police with students making a
demonstration against the Government. 12 persons
wounded
Oct. 3 and Dec. 12, Secretary Stimson issued statements that the United States would not intervene
in Cuba
Oct. 4, President Machado signed decree authorizing
suspension of constitutional guarantees which continued in Havana district until Nov. 1
Oct. 14, Presidential decree forbade holding assemblies
of any kind until after the election of Nov.
Nov. 1, Election a victory for Machado
Nov. 13, Havana placed under martial law following
student riots against President Machado
Nov. 15, Act of Congress for stabilization of the sugar
industry

Dec. 3, Student riots in Havana
Dec. 5, Cabinet reorganized by the President
Dec. 11, Constitutional guarantees suspended through-
out Cuba by the President following continued out-
breaks of students. Continued until Feb. 8, 1931
Dec. 16, National University closed

CURAÇAO

Curaçao, Dutch Island, 40 miles from the northern coast of Venezuela, average breadth 10 miles.
The Colony consists of two groups of islands
about 500 miles apart. One group is made up of
the first three islands in the following list; the
other of the last three:—

—	SQUARE MILES	POPULATION DEC. 31, 1929
Curaçao	210	44,344
Bonaire	95	13,450
Aruba	69	5,375
St. Martin [1]	17	2,180
St. Eustatius	7	965
Saba	5	1,408
	403	67,722

[1] Only the southern part belongs to the Netherlands, the
northern to France.

Curaçao was discovered by Hojeda in 1499
and occupied by the Spaniards in 1527, and has
been held by the Dutch since capture from the
Spaniards in 1634 except during English occupation in 1798 and 1806–1814. Willemstad is the
capital.

DOMINICAN REPUBLIC

See Santo Domingo.

GUADELOUPE

Guadeloupe, French Colony, situated in the
Lesser Antilles, consists of two islands separated
by a narrow channel, called " Rivière Salée." That
on the west is called Guadeloupe proper or Basse-
Terre, and that to the east Grande-Terres; they
have a united area of 1,380 square kilometers
(532 square miles), and a circumference of 275
miles. There are five dependencies consisting of
the smaller islands, Marie Galante, Les Saintes,
Désirade, St. Barthélemy, and St. Martin; the
total area with these is 688 square miles. Basse-
Terre is the capital.

HAITI

Haiti, second largest island of the West Indies,
southeast of Cuba, from which it is separated by
the Windward Passage. The Republic of Haiti

occupies the western part of the Island, the larger but less populated eastern division forming the Dominican Republic (Santo Domingo. *See s.v.*) The area of Haiti is estimated at 10,204 English square miles, the entire Island including both Haiti and Santo Domingo 28,242 square miles. On January 1, 1927, the estimated population was 2,300,200, excluding 3,000 white foreign residents and the military forces of the United States. The majority of the population are Negroes; there are also great numbers of Mulatto Haitians, the descendants of the former French settlers. Capital, Port-au-Prince, with about 100,000 inhabitants, situated on a large bay and possessed of an excellent harbor. Cap Haitien has an estimated population of about 22,000; Cayes and Jacmel about 12,000 each; Gonaives, 10,000; Port de Paix, 5,000. The official language of the country is French, though most of the common people speak a dialect known as Creole French.

Haiti was discovered Dec. 6, 1492 by Columbus who named it La Española, which soon became Hispaniola. (*See* America.)

Stenio Vincent, President.

1496

City of Santo Domingo founded by Bartholomew Columbus

1502

April 15, Nicolas de Ovando arrived at Hispanola succeeding Columbus as Governor

1508

Census estimated Indian population as 60,000

1509

May 3, Diego Colon, son of Columbus appointed Governor in 1508 instructed in letter of this date as to his duties as Viceroy of the Indies, "islands and mainland." Arrived in July

1514

Census estimated Indians who had survived slavery as 14,000

1526

Sept. 14, First Audiencia in the New World established at Santo Domingo

1530

French buccaneers settled Isle de la Tortue (Tortuga) on northern coast

1586

Jan. 10, Expedition of Sir Francis Drake from England took Santo Domingo and extracted ransom from the inhabitants of 30,000 ducats

1630

French began to establish settlements on the Island of Santo Domingo

1641

Le Vasseur established French settlement called Port Margot

1652

Chevalier Fontenay sent to supersede La Vasseur in government of French settlements

1655

April 14–28, English expedition defeated in attack on Santo Domingo

1665

Bertrand d'Ogeron sent as Governor of French on Tortuga Island and the settlements on Island of Santo Domingo

1677

April 6, French Governor took formal possession of Island of Santo Domingo

1685

Proclamation of Louis XIV established government by royal council including governor and intendant

1697

Sept. 20, Treaty of Ryswick between France and England, Spain and Holland recognized French settlements in western part of Haiti

1790

April 15, Convocation of new colonial Assembly at Saint Marc discussed plan for constitution, and May 18 proclaimed itself sole legal representative body

May 15, Decree of Assembly in France declared colored persons born of free parents entitled to privileges of French citizens. Delay of the white Governor to make this decree effective

May 28, Assembly issued "Constitutional Bases"

1791

Aug. 14, Boukman Biasson and Jean François in meeting urged negroes to revolt

Aug. 23, Slaves led by Boukman murdered Europeans and burned and looted. Suppressed with troops and help of mulattoes

Sept. 26, Civil Commission arrived from France to restore peace

1792

June 22, Decree of French Commission offered freedom to all slaves who would join their forces

1793

May, M. Galbaud sent from France as Governor driven from Island by insurrection

Aug. 28, Sonthonax, Commissioner, proclaimed freedom of slaves in the northern provinces

1794

May, British troops commanded by General Whitelock captured Port-au-Prince and besieged the French Governor in Port de la Paix

May 6, François Dominique Toussaint L'Overture, negro patriot leader, raised the flag of the Republic and deserting Spanish joined the French with his troops

1795

July 22, Treaty of Basle signed by which Spain ceded entire Island of Santo Domingo to France, but eastern part went back to Spanish Crown after the downfall of Napoleon

1798

May, General Hedoiville landed at city of Santo Domingo from France

1800

Aug. 1, Toussaint occupied Aux Cayes

1801

May 9, Constituent Assembly adopted Constitution. Confirmed title of Toussaint as Governor-General for life

Nov. 22, French and Spanish fleet sailed from Brest to suppress rebellion

1802

Jan. 29, Captain General Charles V. E. Le Clerc, sent by Napoleon, refused entry by Toussaint

Feb., Maurepois surrendered to the French

May 1, Toussaint and Dessalines surrendered

May 7, Peace Treaty signed by Le Clerc and Toussaint

Aug. 23, Toussaint taken to France, imprisoned by Napoleon at Fort de Joux

Nov. 2, Death of Le Clerc. Succeeded as Governor by General Rochambeau

1803

April 7, Death of Toussaint in prison

Oct., Dessalines leading blacks captured Port-au-Prince

Nov. 19, General Rochambeau signed capitulation with Dessalines by which the French surrendered Le Cap and agreed to leave

Nov. 29, Rochambeau sailed from Le Cap. Dessalines made proclamation of independence

1804

Jan. 1, Jean Jacques Dessalines proclaimed Governor for life, and independence of France declared. Name Santo Domingo changed to Haiti

March 29, Dessalines proclaimed massacre of all white persons

Oct. 8, Dessalines crowned Emperor Jacques I

1805

June, First Constitution framed by Dessalines

1806

Oct. 17, Dessalines assassinated because of his tyranny

Dec. 18, First Legislative Assembly met at Port-au-Prince

Dec. 27, Constitution drafted, changed Empire to Republic

Dec. 28, Christophe chosen chief executive, rejected the Constitution and collected army to seize the Government

1807

Jan. 6, Petion defeated Christophe in engagement

Feb. 17, Henri Christophe elected President by group of military leaders, and ruled in the north as President of State of Haiti at Cap Haitien

March 9, Alexandre Sabes Petion elected President at Port-au-Prince

March 10, President Petion took oath to observe the Constitution

1809

July 9, Combined forces of British and Spaniards captured Santo Domingo from the French

1811

June 2, Christophe crowned as King Henri I of Haiti

1814

May 30, Spain's title to eastern half of Island of Santo Domingo reasserted in Treaty of Paris

1816

June, Constitution revised

1818

March 20 or 30, Jean Pierre Boyer inaugurated President after death of Petion

1820

Oct. 8, Revolutionists advanced on palace at Cap Haitien and Christophe shot himself

Nov., Northern State declared for Boyer and the 2 States united

1821

Dec. 1, The Dominicans of eastern Santo Domingo deported the Spanish Governor and proclaimed independence, led by Spaniard, Munez de Caceres

1822

President Boyer invaded eastern part of Island and captured Santo Domingo City and brought entire Island under his rule

1825

April 17, Ordinance of Charles X defined status granting independence on condition of indemnity and free trade

July 11, Senate forced to accept dictation of French squadron. Independence recognized by France on condition that France pay only half duties and an indemnity of 150,000,000 francs be paid for compensation for loss of colony

1838

Feb. 12, Treaty of friendship, commerce, and recognition with France signed

1839

Jan. 31, Treaty of peace, commerce, and friendship with Great Britain signed

Nov. 19, Law suppressed the slave trade

1843

March 13, Resignation of President Boyer forced by revolution led by Charles Herard

March 21, Charles Herard became President

Dec. 30, New Constitution promulgated

1844

Feb. 27, Successful revolution of Dominicans captured gate of City of Santo Domingo and Spanish part of Island resumed autonomy

May 3, Revolution deposed President Herard and proclaimed Philippe Guerrier, President

1845

April 15, Death of President Guerrier

April 16, Jean Louis Pierrot became President

1846

March 1, Jean Baptiste Riche, President (1846–Feb. 27, 1847)
Nov. 14, New Constitution promulgated

1847

March 1, General Faustin Soulouque became President (1847–Jan. 15, 1859)

1848

Dec. 14, Law modified Constitution

1849

Aug. 26, Solouque had himself declared Emperor under title of Faustin I

1856

Feb. 1, Attack of Faustin I on Santo Domingo repulsed

1858

Dec. 22, Fabre Geffrard led insurrection against the Emperor proclaiming a republic

1859

Jan. 15, Faustin took refuge in French Legation
Jan. 20, Fabre Geffrard took oath as President (1858–March 13, 1867)

1861

May 20, Spanish Santo Domingo reunited with Spain. *See* Santo Domingo

1864

Nov. 3, Treaty of amity, commerce, navigation, and extradition with the United States signed and Claims Treaty

1865

May, Insurrection of Sylvain Salnave captured Cap Haitien

1867

March 13, President Geffrard resigned and sailed for Jamaica
May 14, New Constitution adopted which abolished life term for President fixing term of office as 4 years. Sylvain Salnave elected President

1868

May 10–June 3, Unsuccessful insurrection

1869

Dec. 19, President Salnave who had had Council of State make him President for life shot in revolt led by Generals Brice and Boisronde Canal

1870

March 19, Nissage-Saget, President (1870–May 13, 1874)

1874

June 11, Michel Dominique, President (1874–April 15, 1876)
Nov. 9, Treaty of amity, commerce, navigation, and extradition with Dominican Republic signed

1876

March 7, Louis Tanis headed revolt
April 15, Vice-President Rameau assassinated, President Dominique defeated, fled

July 17, General Boisronde Canal, President (1876–July 17, 1879)

1879

May 20, Revolt at Cap Haitien led by Gen. Parisien
July 17, President Boisronde Canal deposed by revolutionists
Oct. 23, Etienne Felicite Salomon inaugurated President (1879–Aug. 10, 1888)

1883

March 25, Revolution breaks out. Suppressed in June

1884

May 28, Arbitration of claims Convention signed with the United States

1888

Aug. 10, President Salomon who had been reëlected in 1886 deposed by revolution and left Haiti
Aug. 24, General Telemaque took over provisional Government
Sept. 19, General Telemaque and 300 others killed in attack on palace at Port-au-Prince
Oct. 22, F. Deus Legitime elected President
Dec. 7, Cap Haitien bombarded
Dec. 16, President Legitime inaugurated (1888–Aug. 22, 1889)
Dec. 21, General Hippolyte and President Legitime in indecisive battle

1889

June 1, President Legitime defeated in battle with General Hippolyte
Aug. 22, Civil war ended when President Legitime left Port-au-Prince on French gunboat
Aug. 23, General Hippolyte entered capital in triumph
Sept. 24, Constitution amended. Hippolyte elected President by Assembly Oct. 9
Oct. 14, President L. M. Florvil Hippolyte inaugurated (1889–March 24, 1896)

1890

May 15, President Florvil Hippolyte reëlected for second term

1891

May 28, Revolt at Port-au-Prince suppressed

1893

April 22, Agreement with President of Santo Domingo concluded

1895

July 3, Boundary Treaty with Santo Domingo

1896

March 24, Death of President Hippolyte
March 31, General P. A. Tiresias Simon Sam succeeded as President (1896–May 12, 1902)

1897

Sept., Arrest of Haitian native, Lueders, who had acquired German citizenship, resisting arrest of his coachman
Dec. 6, 2 German warships forced Government to pay $30,000 for alleged illegal arrest of Lueders

1899

Aug., Revolt planned to overthrow President Sam in favor of M. Fouchard, former Minister of Finance, discovered and leaders arrested

Oct. 18, Claims Convention with the United States signed

1900

June 30, Claims Convention with the United States signed

July 31, Commercial Treaty with France concluded

1902

March 22, Naturalization Treaty with the United States signed

May 12, Resignation of President Sam. Revolution begun by forced adjournment of Chamber to prevent election of General Leconte as President. Government troops defended palace, arsenal, and barracks

May 13, Former President Sam, Mrs. Sam, and General Leconte escorted to steamer to leave Island

May 26, Provisional Government established with General Boisronde Canal as President

July 21, A. Firmin proclaimed President at Artabonite

Sept. 2, During civil war in contest for the presidency Admiral Killick who was supporting Mr. A. Firmin searched German vessel and took goods consigned to Haitian Government

Sept. 7, German gunboat "Panther" sunk Haitian flagship with Admiral Killick who went down with the boat

Oct. 17, Capitulation of St. Marc to General Alexis. General Firmin took refuge on German steamer

Dec. 17, General Nord Alexis proclaimed President by the Army

Dec. 21, General Alexis elected President by the National Assembly took oath on 23d (1902–08)

1904

July 19, Concession for railroad to R. Gardere, later sold to American company

Aug. 9, Extradition Treaty with the United States signed

Nov. 28, Ex-President Sam and 33 prominent citizens placed on trial for issue of fraudulent bonds and sentenced Dec. 27 to various terms

1906

Feb. 6, Chamber of Commerce established

1907

Jan. 30, Commercial Convention with France signed

June 24, Government adhered to Geneva Convention of 1864

1908

Jan. 15, Exiles landed at Gonaives and tried to start insurrection. Not successful

March 15, Reign of terror begun on discovery of alleged revolutionary plot, 11 citizens shot

March 21, General Firmin and other insurgents sailed on French steamer

July 29, Treaty of commerce with Germany signed

Nov. 19, General Antoine Simon led revolt against the Government at Aux Cayes

Nov. 27, General Simon defeated Government troops commanded by General Cyrioque

Dec. 2, President Alexis took refuge on French steamer rescued from mob attack

Dec. 5, General Simon and his victorious army entered the capital

Dec. 17, General Simon elected President by Congress

Dec. 20, President Simon inaugurated (1902–08)

1909

Jan. 7, Arbitration Treaty with the United States signed

1910

April 25, Arbitration Convention with Brazil signed

May 1, Death of General Nord Alexis in Jamaica

Aug. 4, Law opened port of Fort Liberté to foreign commerce

Oct. 21, National Bank established. Loan for $16,-000,000 contracted in Paris

1911

Jan. 17, Peace Convention with the Dominican Republic signed. Provided for withdrawal of troops from the boundary

Feb. 2, Revolution begun in north Haiti

Feb. 7, Leader of revolt General Millionard executed

March 8, National Bank opened at Port-au-Prince

July 5, Notes submitted by the United States, Great Britain, France, Italy, and Germany demanded settlement of claims within 3 months

July 22, American cruiser "Des Moines" sent to Haiti to protect American interests

July 28, Rebels defeated at Aux Cayes

Aug. 1, Revolt successful

Aug. 4, President Simon left the country

Aug. 14, Michel Cincinnatus Leconte elected President. Inaugurated on the 16th (1911–12)

Oct. 6, Earthquake at Port-au-Prince

1912

Aug. 8, Explosion of powder in palace at Port-au-Prince resulted in death of the President. General Tancrede Auguste elected President (1912–13)

1913

May 2, Death of President Auguste, poisoned

May 4, Michel Oreste elected President by Congress

1914

Jan. 1, New currency issued

Jan. 27, Forced abdication of President Oreste in revolt led by Oreste Zamor and Davilmar Theodore. The President took refuge on German warship

Jan. 28, American, British, French, and German marines landed to protect foreign interests

Feb. 8, Oreste Zamor elected President

March 1, Zamor Government recognized by the United States

May, England demanded indemnity of $62,000

June 14, France and Germany demanded control of customs houses to provide for financial claims of their citizens

June, Revolt led by Davilmar Theodore, successful in Oct.

Aug. 7, Neutrality declared in World War

Sept. 20, The National Bank stopped payments of money to the national Government

Oct. 19, Rebels occupied Cap Haitien. American marines landed to preserve order

Oct. 29, President Zamor resigned. American marines ordered to Port-au-Prince

Nov. 7, Joseph Davilmar Theodore elected President

Dec. 17, American marines from the U.S.S. "Machias" landed at Port-au-Prince and removed $500,000 from National Bank at request of Bank in face of threats of seizure by the President

Dec. 24, Law authorized issue of 8,000,000 gourdes in fiat money

1915

Jan. 2, National Bank closed by order of the Government

Jan. 7, Revolt against President Theodore begun. Cap Haitien attacked

Jan. 16, Cap Haitien captured by rebels led by General Vilbrun Guillaume

Feb. 23, President Theodore forced by Zamorists to resign. He took refuge on Dutch steamer at Port-au-Prince

March 4, General Jean V. Guillaume Sam elected President by Congress

March 9, President Guillaume Sam inaugurated

April, New insurrection led by General Bobo. Cap Haitien and Port Liberté occupied

June 19, Insurrection of Bobo suppressed by Government troops

July 3, American marines landed to protect foreign lives and property

July 26, Charles de Delva attacked palace. President Guillaume Sam took refuge in French Legation

July 27, 160 political prisoners including former President Orestes Zamor executed by order of President Guillaume Sam

July 28, Mob took President Guillaume Sam from the French Legation and killed him and General Oscar who had ordered the executions who had taken refuge in consulate of the Dominican Republic. American marines landed to restore order

Aug. 4, American second regiment landed at Port-au-Prince

Aug. 6, American troops took possession of the national Palace, the gunboat "Pacifique," and the office of port of Port-au-Prince

Aug. 10, Proclamation of American Admiral Caperton to people of Haiti that the United States had no object except to insure Haitian independence and establish government

Aug. 12, Election held under American auspices by National Assembly. Philippe Sudre Dartiguenave chosen President

Aug.15, President Dartiguenave inaugurated (1915–22)

Sept. 2, Admiral Caperton took over administration of the customs at Port-au-Prince

Sept. 3, Admiral William B. Caperton proclaimed martial law at Port-au-Prince

Sept. 16, Treaty with the United States signed established American supervision of finances and customs and provided for native constabulary under American officers

Sept. 17, Official recognition of the Dartiguenave Government by the United States

Oct. 6, The Chamber ratified the Treaty with the United States and the Senate on Nov. 11 making the Republic in effect a protectorate of the United States

Nov., Formal apology to France made by the President for invasion of French Legation

Nov. 29, *Modus vivendi* signed with the United States pending ratification of Treaty by United States Senate

1916

Jan. 5, Revolt first week in this month at Puerto Principe suppressed by American troops

Feb. 28, United States Senate gave consent to Treaty

April 5, Decree of the President dissolving Senate approved and upheld by Admiral Caperton

May 3, Ratifications of Treaty with the United States signed

May 4, Cabinet resigned

May 10, Mm. Herrau and Vieux appointed to preside over Departments of Finance and Interior, and Mm. Borno, Audain, and Dorneval retained from former Cabinet

July 9, First American financial adviser assumed duties of office, A. T. Ruan

July 10, Agreement signed by Haitian Commission and National Bank provided for loan of $500,000

Aug. 24, Protocol to Treaty established native constabulary under American control

Aug. 29, Customs taken over by civilian American Receiver General from naval administration

Sept. 22, Decree of the President called for new election to revise Constitution

1917

Jan. 10, The Chamber of Deputies dissolved as terms expired, elections held for both Houses Jan. 15 and 16, and met April 21

March 28, Additional Act extended duration of Treaty with the United States of Sept. 16, 1915 to May 3, 1936

June 17, Haiti severed diplomatic relations with Germany

June 19, Congress dissolved by Admiral Caperton. Replaced by Council of State

Dec. 26, Decree forbade export of foodstuffs to countries at war with the United States

1918

June 12, New Constitution ratified by plebiscite, promulgated June 19

July, Revolt against American control led by Charlemagne Perlate

July 12, War declared on Germany

Aug. 24, Agreement to submit all proposed laws to United States for approval

Oct. 1, Corvée, enforced labor for road work, discontinued

1919

Feb. 25, Rear Admiral Snowden became military representative of the United States in Haiti

Feb. 26, Law established a National Board of Public Hygiene

——, Law passed governing granting of mining rights

May 2, The *gourd*, monetary unit, stabilized at $.20

June 13, Law enacted for protection of trade marks

——, Law provided for retirement and pensions for civil employees

Aug. 4, Electoral law enacted

Oct. 3, Claims Convention with the United States signed provided for commission for settlement of foreign claims

Oct. 31, Rebel leader Charlemagne Perlate captured and killed, ending insurrection begun in 1918

1920

June 30, Haiti became member of the League of Nations

July 21, Law promulgated respecting rights of foreigners to own real property in Haiti

Oct. 20, American marines accused of killing natives placed on trial in naval court

Nov. 13, Appeal of President Dartiguenave to Congress of the United States for investigation of American civil administration in Haiti

Dec. 18, American marines acquitted by naval court

1921

Nov. 29, United States Senate Commission of Inquiry headed by Senator Medill McCormick arrived at Port-au-Prince to investigate American occupation

1922

Feb. 11, President Harding appointed Brigadier General John H. Russell high commissioner to Haiti

May 9, Presidential decree made use of metric system of weights and measures obligatory after July 1

May 15, Joseph Louis Borno elected April 11 inaugurated President

June 3, Notes exchanged with the United States modified Convention of Oct. 3, 1919 respecting finances

June 26, Formal report of United States Senate Commission presented a justification of American occupation

June 26 and Oct. 27, Laws authorized loan of $40,000,-000, floated in New York

Oct. 9, National City Bank of New York offered Haitian loan of $16,000,000 in 30 year bonds at 6%

Oct. 21, Resignation of John A. McIlhenny, financial adviser. John S. Hord appointed

1923

Feb. 5, Civil Pension law enacted for benefit of government employees

Feb. 16, Emigration Law passed

April 17, Protocol to Treaty of 1915 with the United States provided for appointment of American agricultural engineers and the establishment of a Technical Bureau in the Department of Agriculture

Sept. 27, Resignation of Ministry. Donique succeeded

1924

Jan., Dr. Cumberland became Financial Adviser and General Receiver

Feb. 28, New emigration law promulgated

March 18, American marines withdrawn

June 18, Act created new Internal Revenue Bureau under control of American Receiver General of Customs, Dr. W. E. Dunn, first head

1925

Feb. 13, Law as to ownership of real property by foreigners and foreign corporations enacted

1926

April 12, Louis Borno reëlected President

July 8, Exchange of notes with the United States agreed on most favored nation treatment as to customs

July 26, New tariff law passed by the Council of State

July 29, Commercial Agreement with France signed

Sept. 7, Commercial Treaty with the Netherlands signed

Oct. 26, Agreement with France modified Arbitration Protocol of Sept. 10, 1913

1927

Jan. 3, Commercial Convention with Italy signed

March 12, The United States notified that Senator W. H. King would not be allowed in the country

July 6, Law for regulation of lotteries signed

July 26, Land law passed designed to give security to squatters

July 28, Commercial *modus vivendi* with Germany signed

Oct. 3, New School of Medicine and Pharmacy formally opened

Oct. 8, 13 Amendments to the Constitution adopted by the Council of State

Nov. 14, Arthur C. Millspaugh appointed Financial Adviser and Receiver General to succeed W. W. Cumberland

Dec. 21, Law defined authority of Courts of Cassation

1928

Jan. 10, 13 Amendments to Constitution ratified by popular vote increased power of the President

Feb. 6, Colonel Charles Lindbergh at Port-au-Prince on good will flight

Feb. 25, Exchange of notes with Great Britain established commercial *modus vivendi*

March 16 and 23, Laws as to courts and court procedure passed

March 29, Law amended Penal Code

April 5, Treaty of conciliation and arbitration with Denmark signed

July 13, Ministerial Decree prohibited emigration

July 25, Law exempted agricultural machinery, books, printing presses from taxation

Aug. 1, Tariff Act passed

Aug. 10, Hurricane killed 42 persons and destroyed property

Aug. 14, Excise tax law placed moderate imposts on alcoholic beverages and manufactured tobacco

Dec. 24, Passport law passed required every foreigner in the country 30 days to have a passport

1929

Jan. 10, Resignation of Dr. Millspaugh, Financial Adviser

Jan. 21, Boundary Treaty with the Dominican Republic signed

Feb. 20, Treaty of amity, peace, and arbitration with the Dominican Republic signed

June 12, Standardization law enacted, into effect for coffee Oct. 1

Oct. 5, Announcement of the President that no elections would be held in Jan.

Oct. 31, Strike of students against the Government because of reduction of grant to education spread to government employees

Nov. 26, New Cabinet appointed

Dec. 4, Strike in the Customs Office and raid thereon. American marines landed at Port-au-Prince and Cap Haitien

——, Martial law declared by Colonel Richard Cutts, U.S. of A.

Dec. 6, Mob of 1,500 attacked American marines at port of Aux Cayes. 5 Haitians killed and 20 wounded

Dec. 8, U.S.S. "Galveston" arrived and landed marines at Jacmel

1930

Feb. 28, American Commission headed by William Cameron Forbes appointed by President Hoover to investigate conditions in Haiti arrived and held sessions March 1–15

March 10, Most favored nation commercial Treaty concluded with Germany
March 20, Assembly of Peoples Delegates nominated Eugene Roy, banker, to succeed President Borno
March 26, Forbes Commission presented Report to President Hoover which proposed end of American supervision as soon as possible. Approved March 28
April 12, Commercial Convention with France signed
April 21, Eugene Roy elected President by the State Council
May 15, Eugene Roy inaugurated Provisional President
June 15, Commission headed by Dr. R. E. Moton appointed by President Hoover to study educational conditions arrived. Presented final Report Nov. 30
Aug. 14, Resignation of Provisional Cabinet
Aug. 20, New Cabinet appointed
Sept. 20, Military Training School to train native officers to replace Americans opened at Port-au-Prince. O. R. Cauldwell, U.S.N. president
Sept. 30, Public debt reduced from about $24,210,000 in 1924 to $16,541,000
Oct. 14, Election held for constituent Congress a victory for the Anti-American party
Nov. 18, Stenio Vincent elected by Congress convened Nov. 10 as permanent President

JAMAICA

Jamaica, largest island of the British West Indies lying about 80 miles south of Cuba, 144 miles long and 50 wide, total area 4,450 square miles.

Attached to Jamaica are Turks and Caicos Islands, Cayman Islands, Morant Cays, and Pedro Cays. Area of Jamaica, 4,450 square miles; Turks and Caicos Islands, &c., 224 square miles.

Population of Jamaica (census, 1921): total, 858,118 (males, 401,973; females, 456,145); white, 14,476; colored, 157,223; black, 660,420; East Indian, 18,610; Chinese, 3,696; not stated, 3,693. Estimated population, end of 1929, 994,419. Capital, Kingston (census, 1921), 62,707. Other towns (census, 1921)—Spanish Town, 8,694; Port Antonio, 6,272; Montego Bay, 6,580; Savanna-la-Mar, 3,442; Port Maria, 2,481; St. Ann's Bay, 2,090; Falmouth 2,136. Total estimated East Indian population on December 31, 1929, 17,424.

Columbus discovered the island May 3, 1494 and named it St. Jago, and the first settlement made by Juan de Esquivel appointed Governor in 1509 by Diego, the son of Columbus. Admirals Penn and Venables captured Jamaica from the Spaniards May 11, 1655.

Sir R. E. Stubbs, Governor.

LEEWARD ISLANDS

Leeward Islands north of the Windward group and taking their name from situation further down the trade wind than the Windward Islands. They are the most northern of the Lesser Antilles extending from Puerto Rico to Saint Lucia in the southeast, the majority belonging to Great Britain. The Dutch West Indies are Curaçao (see s.v.). The French West Indies are Guadeloupe, and dependencies (see s.v.) and part of St. Martin.

The following table shows the area and population of the British Leeward Islands:—

	AREA: Sq. Miles	POPULATION 1929	POPULATION ACCORDING TO CENSUS TAKEN IN 1921		
			Males	Females	Total
Antigua	108		12,200	16,664	28,864
Barbuda and Redonda	62	30,974	342	561	903
Virgin Islands	58	5,126	2,321	2,723	5,044
Dominica	305	41,482	16,760	20,299	37,059
St. Kitts	65		9,115	13,300	22,415
Nevis	50	35,365	4,678	6,891	11,569
Anguilla	35		1,447	2,783	4,227
Montserrat	32	11,954	5,094	7,026	12,120
Total	715	124,901	51,957	70,247	122,201

PUERTO RICO

Puerto Rico, the most easterly island of the Greater Antilles group, possession of the United States. See p. 400.

SANTO DOMINGO

Santo Domingo (the Dominican Republic), the eastern part of the Island of Haiti (about two-thirds) estimated at 19,332 square miles, with 1,017 miles of coast line and 193 miles of frontier line with Haiti, and a population, according to the census of 1921, of 897,405. The boundary with Haiti, long in dispute, is being resurveyed under a treaty signed in 1929. The population (1921) of the 12 provinces was as follows: Santo Domingo, 146,446; San Pedro de Macoris, 43,612; Seybo, 58,408; Azua, 100,577; Barahona, 48,180; Samaná, 16,915; La Vega, 105,820; Pacificador, 77,620; Espaillat, 50,956; Santiago de los Caballeros 122,773; Puerto Plata, 59,025; and Monte Cristi, 67,073. Total population 1930 estimated as 1,200,000.

The capital, Santo Domingo, on the left bank of the river Ozama, founded 1496 by Bartolomeo

Columbus, brother of Christopher, was destroyed in 1502 by a hurricane, and subsequently rebuilt on the right bank of the same river. According to the census of 1921, the City of Santo Domingo had 30,957 inhabitants and the City of Puerto Plata 7,807; Santiago de los Caballeros 17,052; San Pedro de Macoris, 13,802; La Vega, 6,564; Samaná, 1,656; Sanchez, 3,075; Azua, 4,707; Monte Cristi, 2,580; Pacificador (San Francisco de Macoris), 5,188; and Espaillat (Moca), 3,994.

For earliest history *see* Haiti.

General Rafael Trujillo, President of the Republic (assumed office on August 16, 1930).

Rafael Estrella Urena, Vice-President (also Minister of Foreign Affairs).

1697

Sept. 20, By the Treaty of Ryswick the French settlements ceded to France and the Spanish settlements on eastern part of Island remained under Spanish rule

1795

July 22, By the Treaty of Basle the Spanish settlements ceded to France also, but returned to Spanish Crown after downfall of Napoleon

1809

July 9, English squadron aided by rebels against French captured city of Santo Domingo

1814

May 30, Treaty of Paris reaffirmed Spanish rule in eastern half of the Island

1821

Dec. 1, Santo Domingo proclaimed independence of Spain. Article 4 of Constitution adopted provided for annexation to Colombia

1822

President Boyer of Haiti invaded the Spanish settlements and captured city of Santo Domingo bringing entire Island under his rule

1844

Feb. 27, Successful revolution of Dominicans reëstablished Spanish autonomy

Nov. 6, Constitution promulgated, and Pedro Santana elected President

1849

April 22, Dominicans under Santana defeat Haitians invading under Soulouque

1850

Jan. 24, Appeal to the United States for a protectorate

Feb., Mediation of the Ministers of Foreign Affairs of England, France, and the United States

March 6, Treaty of peace, commerce, and navigation with Great Britain signed

1852

Nov. 26, Treaty of friendship, commerce, and navigation with France signed

1854

Feb. 27, New Constitution promulgated and a second on Dec. 23

1855

Jan. 11, Treaty of recognition, peace, friendship, commerce, and navigation with Spain signed, and of friendship, commerce, and navigation with Sardinia

Jan. 30, Treaty of commerce and navigation with Germany signed

1856

July 24, Treaty of friendship, commerce, and navigation with the Netherlands signed

Santana resigned as President and was succeeded by Buenaventura Baez

1858

Feb. 19, New Constitution promulgated

1859

Jan. 31, Pedro Santana inaugurated President for the third time after revolt

1861

March 18, Proclamation announced voluntary annexation to Spain

May 20, Spanish rule again in Santo Domingo

1863

Aug. 16, Revolution begun at Capotillo headed by Spanish planter, Cabrera, ended Spanish rule

1865

May 1, Law of the Spanish Cortes by which the annexation repealed and Spain renounced all claim to Santo Domingo

Convention proclaimed Constitution of 1858 and elected General Antonio Pimentel President, but revolution deposed him and General Buenaventura Baez became President

1866

Sept. 27, New Constitution promulgated

1867

Feb. 8, Treaty of friendship, commerce, and navigation with the United States

1869

Nov. 29, Baez again President negotiated a Treaty with the United States for annexation which failed of ratification by the Senate of the United States in 1870

1870

Feb., Referendum vote by which Dominicans declared for annexation to the United States

1872

Dec. 28, President Baez rented Samaná Bay to an American corporation for 99 years

1873

Nov. 25, Revolution begun in Puerto Plata which spread to other sections

Dec. 31, President Baez forced to surrender to the revolutionists

1874

Jan. 27, General Gonzales installed as President

April 6, Assumed office as constitutional President

Oct. 14, Treaty of recognition, friendship, commerce, navigation, and extradition with Spain signed

Nov. 9, Treaty of peace, friendship, commerce, navigation, and extradition with Haiti signed

1875

March 8, New Constitution promulgated which led to revolt

1876

Feb. 23, President Gonzales forced to resign

April 29, Ulises F. Espaillat designated President by Council of Ministers

Oct. 5, Revolt against the Government headed by Gonzales started

Nov., Gonzales again President

Dec., Gonzales overthrown by revolt begun in Cibrao and General Baez again President

1877

May 14, New Constitution promulgated

1878

Feb. 24, President Baez overthrown by revolutionists. General Gonzales proclaimed President in Cibao and General Guillermo in Santo Domingo

April 13, General Guillermo appointed Provisional President

July 6, General Gonzales assumed office as constitutional elected President

Sept. 2, Revolutionists led by General Guillermo and General Ulises Heureaux forced Gonzales to resign, and Jacinto de Castro became acting President

Sept. 29, General Guillermo assumed the Government

1879

Feb. 11, Constitution of 1878 promulgated

Feb. 28, General Guillermo assumed office as constitutional elected President

Oct. 6, Revolution begun at Puerto Plata headed by General Gregorio Luperon

Dec. 9, President Guillermo forced to resign

1880

Oct. 12, M. Marino, priest proclaimed President

1882

July 20, General Ulises Heureaux proclaimed President

Sept. 9, Treaty of commerce and navigation with France signed

1883

May 1, Treaty of commerce and navigation with Portugal signed

1884

April 17, Civil Code promulgated and Aug. 20, Penal Code

1886

Oct. 18, Treaty of commerce with Italy signed

1890

March 29, Treaty of commerce with Mexico signed

1891

June 4, Publication of commercial arrangement with the United States

1892

Dec. 16, President Heureaux reëlected

1893

March 8, Revolutionists against President Heureaux entered country from Haiti in successful raid

April 18, Rupture with France in bank dispute

April 22, Agreement with Haiti signed and apology for March raid by Haiti

1894

July 27, Plot against the Government discovered, General Bobadilla ordered shot

1895

July 3, Boundary Treaty with Haiti signed

1896

June 20, New Constitution promulgated

1897

July 1, The United States gold dollar adopted as standard of value

1898

June 2, Revolution led by J. I. Jimenez and General Augustin Morales against the President but soon ended

1899

July 26, President Heureaux assassinated at Moca by Ramon Caceres, succeeded by Vice-President Aug. 1, General Figuereo according to the Constitution

Aug. 24, Revolutionists led by Jiminez occupied San Francisco de Macoris and the towns of Sanchez Blanco and Moca declared in favor of the revolution, and the commander of San José de las Matas the following day

Aug. 26, Puerto Plata surrendered to the revolutionists and the city of Santiago de los Caballeros the following day

Aug. 31, President Figuereo resigned

Sept. 1, Provisional Government headed by Horacio Vasquez as President formed by revolutionists and Sept. 5 Vasquez entered the capital

Sept. 8, Juan Isidro Jiminez arrived at Moca and was made Minister of War

Oct. 20, Jiminez elected President

Nov. 14, President Jiminez inaugurated, General Horacio Vasquez, Vice-President

1900

Jan. 3, French Government demanded payment of $56,000 claims (Boismare-Caccavelli) and sent 3 warships to enforce demands

Nov. 24, Code of commerce and of civil procedure promulgated

1902

Jan. 28, Arbitration Treaty with Spain signed

April 28, Claims Convention with the United States signed to settle claims incurred in successive revolutions

May 2, Revolutionists captured President Jiminez, deposed, succeeded by provisional government under General Horacio Vasquez

1903

Jan. 31, Claims Convention with the United States to settle claims of the American Santo Domingo

Improvement Company against the Republic for damages incurred in revolutions

March 23, Revolt and flight of President Vasquez, and provisional government

April 27, General Wos y Gil became President

Nov. 10, President Wos y Gil took refuge in German consulate from revolutionists

Nov. 25, Articles of capitulation signed surrender to insurgents

Dec. 28, General Jiminez became President

1904

Jan. 17, Government troops captured Puerto Plata

Jan. 23, Battle at Los Llanos

March 24, General N. Arrias, insurgent leader, captured and shot

April 2, Jiminez defeated at Monte Cristi took refuge on German steamer

April 23, Government troops defeated at Guayances, Generals Cabrera, Arroyo, and Luna killed

April 30, Claims Convention with the United States

June 4, Peace established and insurgents recognized General Morales

June 19, Carlos Morales inaugurated elected President and Ramon Caceres Vice-President, former President Jiminez having fled to the United States in April

July 14, Award made that the American Santo Domingo Improvement Company should surrender its properties to the Republic and be paid an indemnity of $4,481,250

Sept. 26, General C. de Las Rosas started revolt in favor of Jiminez

Sept., Public debt estimated at about $32,000,000, the annual revenue $1,850,000

Dec. 16, Jiminez revolutionists repulsed at San Aago

1905

Jan. 18, Comm. A. C. Dillingham, U.S.N., as special commissioner of the United States to restore order, took over customs

Jan. 21, Protocol signed with the United States by which the United States guaranteed integrity and agreed to undertake adjustment of obligations of the Dominican Government and administer the customs for service of the debt

Feb. 7, Convention with the United States signed, the customs to be taken over April 1

March 31, *Modus vivendi* signed created receivership, into effect April 1

Dec. 25, President Morales deposed by revolution led by Vice-President Caceres

Dec. 27, Force led by Rodrigues and Navarro advancing to defense of Morales took Mao

1906

Jan. 4, Rodrigues defeated and killed in battle

Jan. 5, Congress voted impeachment of Morales

Jan. 12, Morales resigned as President

Jan. 17, Peace Treaty signed by contending factions

Aug.–Oct., New revolt settled in Oct. by agreement with Government

1907

Feb. 8, Treaty signed with the United States by which debt of republic converted and collection of customs assumed by the United States

June 25, Santo Domingo adhered to Geneva Convention of 1864

Sept. 9, New Constitution submitted to Congress

1908

Feb. 22, New Constitution adopted to take effect April 1

April 3, Sanitary law passed, proclaimed June 6, to go into effect Jan. 1, 1909, established municipal boards

July 1, General Ramon Caceres inaugurated as elected President

1909

April 26, Patent law enacted

May 28, Law prescribed that obligations incurred before July 1 should be presented to Financial Dept. for examination and settlement before Jan. 1, 1910

Oct. 11, Revolution begun, attack on Dajabon repulsed by government troops

Nov. 15, Banking law promulgated

Nov. 23, Law governing tariffs passed

1910

April 29, Arbitration Convention with Brazil signed

June 27, Law and regulations respecting mines adopted

1911

Jan. 17, Convention of peace with Haiti signed

Nov. 19, Assassination of President Caceres

Dec. 2, Eladio Victoria chosen Provisional President

1912

Feb. 5, Provisional President Victoria elected constitutional President for 6 year term and inaugurated Feb. 28

Sept. 24, The United States intervened in order to restore order and protect custom house

Nov. 28, President Victoria resigned under pressure from the United States and because of revolt of General Horacio Vasquez and others

Dec. 1, Congress elected Archbishop Noel Provisional President, and revolutionary leaders informed that the United States would resist any attempt to depose him

1913

March 9, Provisional President Noel resigned

April 13, General José Bordas Baldez elected Provisional President by Congress

Aug. 1, Metric system adopted

Oct. 21, Peace signed with revolutionists led by General Vasquez, revolt had begun in Sept.

1914

Jan. 12, United States Minister authorized to audit daily expenses of the Government

Feb. 17, Advancement of Peace Treaty with the United States signed

March 20, Agreement of President that financial expert be appointed to supervise finances

April 13, Expiration of term of Provisional President General Bordas Baldez

June 26, United States gunboat entered the inner harbor of Puerto Plata to intervene and compel revolutionists led by Desiderio Arias to stop bombardment of city

Aug. 10, President Wilson sent a commission to plan for restoration of peace

Aug. 21, Peace concluded between contending factions with aid of American commission

Aug. 27, Dr. Ramon Baez elected Provisional President

Nov. 23, Code of education declared in effect

Nov. 25, Dominican Republic declared neutrality in World War

Dec. 5, Juan Isidro Jiminez elected constitutional President in Oct. inaugurated, first regularly elected President since 1911. Cabinet inaugurated with Elias Brache, B. Pichardo, and others

1916

April, Revolution begun led by General Desiderio Arias who proclaimed himself President

May 1, The Chamber of Deputies voted to impeach President Jiminez for violation of the Constitution in connection with the budget

May 4, American marines landed

May 7, President Jiminez resigned and left the country

May 15, American marines landed to guarantee a free election and prevent General Arias from seizing the Government

May 16, Dr. Francisco Henriquez y Carvajal elected Provisional President by Congress

June 1, American marines landed at Monte Cristi and at Puerto Plata to preserve order

July 1, United States troops in decisive engagement with revolutionists at Guayacanes near Esperanza, Maximito Cabral, rebel leader, killed

July 25, Dr. Francisco Henriquez y Carvajal elected Provisional President by Congress and proclaimed the next day

Nov. 29, Captain H. S. Knapp proclaimed the Dominican Republic under military occupation of the United States

Dec. 26, Marriage law amended to allow either civil or religious ceremony

1917

April 12, The German consular service canceled by military government

June 11, Diplomatic relations with Germany severed

June 26 and July 9, Decrees appointed claims commission

Nov. 25, Decree declared maintenance of neutrality

1919

Feb. 25, Rear Admiral Thomas Snowden took charge of the Government as military Governor

Nov. 12, A "Junta Consultiva" appointed

Commission headed by Dr. Henriquez y Carvajal went to Paris to ask for restoration of liberty and then proceeded to Washington

1920

Jan. 1, New tariff reducing duties about 38% came into effect, favored American goods, and provided for an extensive free list including agricultural and industrial machinery, building materials, and petroleum products

Jan. 9, "Junta Consultiva" resigned

April 10, Civil service law promulgated established civil service commission

Dec. 24, Proclamation of Admiral Snowden declared that the United States would inaugurate processes of withdrawal from "responsibilities assumed in connection with Dominican affairs"

1921

March 21, Admiral S. S. Robison appointed Military Governor

June 14, Second Proclamation of Military Governor stated conditions under which United States military forces would be withdrawn and administration transferred to a native government

Aug. 13, Elections set for this date not held, prevented by Junta of Election Abstention, refusing American demand for validation of $2,400,000 loan and other conditions

1922

June 30, Agreement signed with the United States as to evacuation of troops, and establishment of a provisional Government, Acts of the American occupation to be recognized as legal by Dominicans in Washington

July 8, Bankruptcy law published

Oct. 6, Juan Bautista Vicini Burgos named Provisional President by Archbishop Noel and the negotiators of the Agreement of June 30

Oct. 21, Provisional Government inaugurated ending American régime

Oct. 24, Military Governor sailed for the United States

Oct. 27, Decree embodied terms of Treaty with the United States

1923

Sept. 28, Law on registration of trademarks enacted

Nov. 17, Executive Order the "land registration" law published

1924

March 19, General Horacio Vasquez elected President by coalition of Nationalist and Progressive parties

June 12, Convention signed with the United States confirmed that of June 30, 1922 and ratified plan of evacuation of American troops

June 13, New Constitution promulgated provided for direct elections of President and members of Congress, terms of President and Vice-President to be 6 years, capital punishment abolished, issue of paper money prohibited

June 26, Congress ratified Treaty

July 10, Announcement of withdrawal of American forces which was begun July 12 and last marines left Sept. 18

July 12, President Vasquez inaugurated and Vice-President Federico Velasquez

Sept. 25, Most favored nation commercial Agreement with the United States concluded by exchange of Notes

Sept. 29, Santo Domingo became member of the League of Nations

Oct. 31, Naturalization law adopted, promulgated Nov. 18

Nov. 19, Marriage law promulgated

Dec. 27, New Treaty with the United States signed replaced that of Feb. 8, 1907, which contained provisions not in keeping with present needs, modified control over customs to facilitate refunding of debt of the Republic and provide for expenditure on improvements, and provided for loan of $25,000,000

1925

Jan. 14 and 21, Law created domestic postal money order service

Jan. 25, Seventeen of thirty members of Chamber of Deputies signed "Pact of Honor" in opposition to loan from the United States

May 25, Congress approved the Treaty of Dec. 27 and loan Agreement

May 26, Tariff law enacted modified American tariff of 1919

June 1, Sunday closing law came into effect

Nov. 24, Decree amended tariff law to impose additional duties on 102 articles imported from the United States

1927

June 14, Weekly passenger, freight, and mail steamship service inaugurated with the United States

June 16, Revised Constitution promulgated extended terms of President Vasquez and Vice-President Velasquez from 1928 to 1930

July 2, Colonization law published

1928

Feb. 4, Colonel Charles A. Lindbergh reached Santo Domingo in good will flight and Feb. 6 inaugurated air mail service from the Dominican Republic to Cuba

May 23, Act prohibited introduction into country of all plants and seeds not authorized by permit

Nov. 24, Law defined parental obligations

1929

Jan. 9, Revised Constitution promulgated provided for election of president and vice-president and members of Congress for four year term, the outgoing president and vice-president not eligible to election for term succeeding

Jan. 21, Boundary Treaty with Haiti signed

Feb. 20, Treaty of peace and arbitration with Haiti signed

March 1, President Vasquez invited Vice-President Dawes to accept chairmanship of advisory mission and organize economic and financial administration

April 2–23, American commission headed by Charles G. Dawes in Santo Domingo, and presented report on leaving which contained in codified form a budget law and recommendations for establishment of budget system, and an accounting law, modified law of finance and the necessary repealing laws, and statements on government finances and explanations as to how economies might be effected

June 20, Nationality and citizenship law enacted

1930

Feb. 23, Revolt begun in the north against President Vasquez seeking reëlection

Feb. 26, Rebel army of about 2,000 peasants took possession of Santo Domingo forcing the Government to negotiate for settlement of their grievances

Feb. 27, President Vasquez took refuge in American Legation and resigned Feb. 28 naming General Urena Secretary of the Interior and under Constitution therefore Provisional President

Feb. 28, Rafael Estrella Urena, insurgent leader, named Provisional President

March 3, General Estrella Urena, insurgent leader, assumed office as Provisional President

April 9, New election law passed by Congress

April 18, Federico Velasquez, candidate of National and Progressive parties, arrested charged with attempting to start a revolution

May 16, General Rafael L. Trujillo elected President and General Urena, Vice-President

May 20, General Velasquez offered Treasury portfolio by President Elect Trujillo

Aug. 16, President Trujillo and Vice-President Urena inaugurated, Urena also Minister of Foreign Affairs

Sept. 3, Hurricane destroyed City of Santo Domingo killing more than 2,000 persons, 6,000 injured, damage estimated at $40,000,000

TRINIDAD

Trinidad, next to Jamaica the largest of the British West Indies, 16 miles east of Venezuela, lies immediately north of the mouth of the Orinoco, and includes Tobago administratively, was discovered by Columbus in 1498 and colonized by the Spaniards in the 16th century. About the period of the Revolution a large number of French families settled in the island, where the French element is still preponderant. On Feb. 18, 1797, Great Britain being at war with Spain, Trinidad was occupied by the British, and ceded to Great Britain by the Treaty of Amiens in 1802.

Area: Trinidad, 1,862 square miles; Tobago, 114. Population: census 1921, 365,913 (186,802 males and 179,111 females). Estimated population, end of 1929, 403,275. Capital, Trinidad, Port of Spain, 67,877. The white population is chiefly composed of English, French, Spanish, and Portuguese. The large majority of the inhabitants are natives of the West Indies, of African descent, the balance being made up of East Indians, estimated at 130,542, and a small number of Chinese. English is spoken generally throughout the Colony.

Sir Alfred Claud Hollis, Governor.

VIRGIN ISLANDS

Virgin Islands, group of small islands about 100 in number extending east from Puerto Rico, total area about 465 square miles. The British islands number 30, situated between the Greater and Lesser Antilles, total area 58 square miles. The chief islands (British) are Tortola, Virgin Gorda, Anegada, and Jost Van Dykes. Sombrero, a small island in the Leeward group, is attached administratively to the Presidency of the Virgin Islands. The American Virgin Islands, the former Danish West Indies, were purchased by the United States from Denmark in a Treaty ratified by both nations and proclaimed Jan. 25, 1917, and include St. Croix, St. Thomas, and St. John. See also p. 406. The islands were discovered by Columbus on his second voyage in 1493 and named Las Virgenes in honor of St. Ursula and her companions.

WINDWARD ISLANDS

Windward Islands, British Colony, consist of Grenada, St. Vincent, the Grenadines (half under St. Vincent, half under Grenada), and St. Lucia, and form the eastern barrier to the Caribbean Sea between Martinique and Trinidad.

CENTRAL AMERICA

Central America occupies the narrow strip of land between the Atlantic and Pacific oceans from the Isthmus of Tehuantepec in Mexico to the Isthmus of Panama, Panama, lying between 8° and 18° 3′ N. Lat. and between 82° 50′ and 92° 17′ W. Long., total area about 185,000 square miles, greatest length about 600 miles and greatest width 250 miles. Politically Central America includes the five Republics of Costa Rica, Nicaragua, Honduras, Guatemala, and Salvador, the British Crown Colony of British Honduras, and Panama (Republic). Columbus discovered Costa Rica on his last voyage in 1502, and attempted to make the first settlement in the New World there, leaving his brother Bartholomew in charge, but the colonists were driven out by the Indians and rejoined Columbus.

1787

The Captaincy-General of Guatemala at this time included 13 provinces, Soconusco, Chiapas, Suchitepec, San Miguel, Vera Paz, Izaleos, Jerez de la Cholutec, Tegucigalpa, Honduras, San Salvador, Guatemala, Nicaragua, and Costa Rica

1821

Sept. 15, Guatemala declared independence of Spain. *See* Guatemala and names of Central American States

1822

Jan. 5, Decree of Junta at Guatemala that the whole of Central America should be annexed to the Mexican Empire

June 12, Filisola, Mexican, arrived at Guatemala City, to assume government

Nov. 4, Decree of Mexican Government divided Central America into 3 captaincy-generals, Chiapas with capital at Ciudad Real, Sacatepequez with capital at Guatemala City and Nicaragua with capital at Leon

1823

March 29, Decree of Filisola summoned Congress of all provinces of Central America which amounted to recognition of independence of Central America from Mexico after fall of Empire

June 24–Jan. 23, 1825, Meeting of first Central American Congress at Guatemala City under presidency of José Matias Delgado

July 1, New declaration of independence adopted

July 2, Congress assumed title of National Constituent Congress

July 15, Decree divided government into legislature, executive of 3 members, and judiciary. Public debt recognized, freedom of press declared, and Catholic religion declared that of State. M. J. Arce, Dr. Pedro Molina, and Juan Vicente Villacorta presently appointed as executives

Aug. 3, Filisola departed with his troops

Aug. 20, Mexico acknowledged the independence of Central America

Aug. 21, Coat of arms adopted

Oct. 4, Resignation of Villacorta, Molina, and Rivera. José Manuel Arce elected President

Nov. 5, Flag adopted

Dec. 17, Bases of Constitution adopted

Dec. 31, and April 17 and 24, 1824, Law emancipated all slaves, made slaves from other countries coming to Central America free, and prohibited slave trade

1824

April 17, Decree making abolition of slavery absolute. *See* 1823, Dec. 31

May 5, Bases of organization for each State fixed

Aug. 4, Central American Federation recognized by the United States. A. J. Canas, agent from Central America received by President Monroe

Nov. 22, Constitution promulgated for the "Central American Federation"

1825

Jan. 23, National Constituent Assembly ended sessions

Feb. 6, First constitutional Congress met, Mariano Galvez, President, in Guatemala City

March 15, First treaty negotiated, Treaty of union, league, and perpetual confederation with Colombia

April 21, José Manuel Arce elected first President, Mariano Beltranena, Vice-President of the Confederation

April 22, Letters of instruction to William Miller appointed American Minister to Central America. This date also used as date of recognition of United States

April 29, Supreme Court installed

June 16, Decree of Congress authorized construction of an interoceanic canal

Sept. 1, Congress ratified the Constitution of Nov. 22, 1824

Dec. 5, Treaty of peace, amity, commerce, and navigation with the United States signed

Dec. 25, Congress ended session

1826

March 1–June 30, Second Congress met

Oct. 1, Congress met but without quorum owing to absence of opposition members

Oct. 10, President Arce by decree convoked an extraordinary Congress to meet at Cojutepeque in Salvador

1828

Feb. 14, President Arce turned over executive office to Vice-President Beltranena but did not resign

1829

April 13, Beltranena and Arce arrested by General Morazan commander of allied forces of Salvador and Honduras on his occupation of Guatemala City. *See* Guatemala

June 22, Congress called by Morazan met under presidency of Doroteo Vasconcelos

June 25, José Francisco Barrundia assumed office of President of the Confederation

1830

March 27, Congress met

——, Supreme Court installed

Sept. 16, General Morazan inaugurated President succeeding Barrundia, and Mariano Prado, Vice-President

1832

Jan. 7, Secession of State of Salvador from the Confederation, and Act of secession of Feb. 13, 1833

May 2, Act of Congress recognized freedom of conscience and worship allowing other churches than the Roman Catholic

Dec. 3, Nicaragua seceded from the Confederation

1833

Jan. 27, Guatemala seceded from the Confederation, Feb. 13, Salvador, May 19, Honduras, and Costa Rica, Sept. 18, but all returned

July 8, Congress adjourned

1834

Feb. 5, Seat of Federal Government transferred to Sonsonate and later to San Salvador

June 2, Jose Gregorio Salazar, acting Vice-President elected Vice-President

1835

Feb. 2, Morazan declared reëlected President by Congress

Feb. 14, President Morazan inaugurated

Feb. 15, Congress adjourned

1838

April 30, Nicaragua seceded from the Confederation

May 30, Congress passed act declaring the States free to constitute themselves as they might deem best

July 20, The last Federal Congress adjourned

Aug. 4, Costa Rica withdrew from the Confederation, formal statement of secession April 15, 1839

Nov. 5, Honduras withdrew from the Federation

1839

Feb. 1, Term of President Morazan expired

April 17, Guatemala declared the Federal compact dissolved

1842

March 17, Convention met at Chinandega, Nicaragua, with delegates from Honduras, Salvador, and Nicaragua to reorganize Union of Central America and elected Don Antonio Canas president

April 11, Convention made declaration in 7 articles establishing a provisional Government for the Central American Confederation

July 27, Act formed league under name of **Central American Confederation**. Never effective because of opposition of Guatemala

1847

Oct. 7, Assembly met at Nacaome, Honduras, with view of effecting union with Nicaragua and Salvador for maintenance of peace. Planned for committee on national constitutions to meet Aug. 1, 1848

1848

Nov. 8, Representatives from Honduras, Salvador, and Nicaragua met at Leon, Nicaragua, agreed to adopt plan of union and coöperation as to foreign relations

1850

April 19, Clayton-Bulwer Treaty between Great Britain and the United States, agreement that neither country should colonize, exercise dominion, or annex any Central American territory

1851

Jan. 9, Representatives met in Chinandega according to plan of 1849, José F. Barrundia chosen President

1852

Oct. 9, National Constituent Congress which met in January at Tegucigalpa installed Diet for "Republic of Central America"

Oct. 13, Trinidad Cabanas chosen President declined office. Organic law enacted

Oct. 28, Francisco Castellon appointed President. Pedro Molina elected Vice-President

1853

March 21, Salvador seceded declaring the Congress had assumed a dictatorship

April 30, Nicaragua seceded

1872

Feb. 17, Representatives of Honduras, Salvador, Guatemala, and Costa Rica met at La Union, Salvador to establish bases of union and signed pact

1885

Feb. 28, Decree of President Barrios of Guatemala proclaimed the consolidation of the 5 Central American States into one republic

March 7, Honduras adopted resolutions accepting Federation

March 8, Nicaraguan Congress rejected the Union

March 17, Costa Rican manifesto against Union

March 22, Alliance of Costa Rica, Nicaragua, and Salvador against the Union and Guatemala

April 3, Provisional President Alejandro Sinibaldi of Guatemala revoked the decree of Feb. 28 after defeat and death of President Barrios on April 2. *See* Guatemala

1886

Nov. 15, President Barillas of Guatemala invited Costa Rica, Honduras, and Nicaragua to send delegates to a conference to form Union

1887

Jan. 20–Feb. 16, Meeting of representatives of Guatemala, Costa Rica, Honduras, and Nicaragua at

Guatemala City. Treaty of peace and agreement as to customs and extradition signed

1889

Oct. 15, Provisional Pact of Union signed by representatives of Salvador, Honduras, and Guatemala

1895

June 20, Pact of Amapala signed by representatives of Honduras, Nicaragua, and Salvador, agreement to establish common political organization for their external relations

1896

Sept. 15, Diet created by the Pact of Amapala installed at San Salvador

Dec. 24, President Cleveland formally recognized the " Greater Republic of Central America "

1897

June 15, Costa Rica and Guatemala adhered to Pact of Amapala

1898

Aug. 27, Constitution adopted at Managua signed by representatives of Honduras, Nicaragua, and Salvador

Nov. 1, The 3 States took the name of the "United States of Central America" and Council installed at Amapala

Nov. 25, Manifesto of new Government of Salvador declared secession

Nov. 28, Council declared the Union dissolved

1902

Jan. 20, Convention of peace and obligatory arbitration signed at Corinto by representatives of Nicaragua, Salvador, Honduras, and Costa Rica and a Central American court created

March 1, Guatemala signed the Convention

Oct. 4, Central American Court of Arbitration instituted in Costa Rica

1903

Nov. 2, Treaty of peace and arbitration signed by Guatemala, Honduras, Salvador, and Nicaragua

1904

Aug. 21, Meeting of Presidents of Nicaragua, Honduras, and Salvador with a representative from Guatemala held conference at Corinto, Nicaragua, with a view to securing the peace of Central America

1906

July 20, General Peace Treaty signed by Salvador, Guatemala, and Honduras on U.S.S. " Marblehead " in preliminary conference, and agreement to sign Treaty within 2 months

Sept. 15–25, Conference at San José de Costa Rica

Sept. 25, Treaty of peace, amity, and arbitration signed at San José by Costa Rica, Honduras, Salvador, and Guatemala provided that in any future disputes the presidents of the United States and Mexico should act as umpires, Treaty establishing International Bureau and Treaty establishing Pedagogical Institute

1907

Feb. 1–8, Tribunal of Arbitration convened at San Salvador under Treaty of Jan. 20, 1902

Sept. 16–17, Preliminary Conference in Washington

Nov. 13–Dec. 20, First Central American Conference at Washington, D.C.

Dec. 20, General Treaty of peace and amity signed by the 5 Central American republics. Conventions provided for establishment of a Central American Court of Justice, an International American Central Bureau, and a Central American Pedagogical Institute, non-recognition of any government in the 5 republics the result of a coup d'état, and neutrality in war, provided for future conferences

1908

May 25, Central American Court of Justice opened at Cartago, Costa Rica

Sept. 15, Central American International Bureau opened at Guatemala City

Dec. 19, First decision of Central American Court delivered in suit of Honduras against Salvador and Guatemala charged with giving assistance to revolutionists

1909

Jan. 1–21, First Central American Congress at Tegucigalpa, Honduras, discussed program for future action

1910

Feb. 1–7, Second Central American Conference at San Salvador adopted conventions as to unification of the currency, a Central American Pedagogical Institute, a Central American Bureau, unification of weights and measures, consular service, customs duties

1911

Jan. 1, Third Central American Conference at Guatemala City, Convention of 1907 amended to transfer seat of Central American Court of Justice to San José on Jan. 10, Convention signed Jan. 12 to establish a school of agriculture in Salvador, 2 schools of mines at Honduras, and school of arts at Nicaragua, Convention to unify Central American primary and secondary education Jan. 12, Convention to establish liberty of commerce Jan. 14, Convention regarding exchange of parcels post between Central American Republics Jan. 17, and Convention establishing coasting trade Jan. 18

1912

Jan. 1–11, Fourth Central American Conference at Managua, Nicaragua, adopted conventions for unification of the consular service, telegraph service and postal system, maritime communication, and for establishment of railway communication

1913

Jan. 2–16, Fifth Central American Conference at San José de Costa Rica

1914

Jan. 1–10, Sixth Central American Conference at Tegucigalpa

1916

Sept. 30, Decision of Central American Court of Justice in suit brought against Nicaragua by Costa Rica claiming violation by Nicaragua of rights in Treaty with the United States

1917

March 2, Decision of Central American Court of Justice in suit brought by Salvador against Nicaragua that rights of Salvador infringed by Nicaragua in Treaty with the United States of Aug. 5, 1914

March 9, Nicaragua denounced Convention of Dec. 20, 1907 which established Central American Court

1918

March 10, Central American Court of Justice dissolved because of failure of renewal of contract creating the court at expiration after 10 years from last ratification which was that of Guatemala March 11, 1908. Lasting meeting held March 12

1920

June 24, Salvador issued invitations to a general conference to consider free trade, customs duties, law codes, and unification of national constitutions

Nov. 1, Municipal representatives of the 5 Republics in conference at Antigua, Guatemala, adopted resolution in favor of union of the Republics under one government

Dec. 4, Conference to form Confederation met and elected officers

1921

Jan. 19, Pact of Union signed by Costa Rica, Guatemala, Honduras, and Salvador at San José, Costa Rica to become effective Feb. 10, 1922 provided for "a perpetual and indissoluble union" to be designated the "Federation of Central America"; ratified by Honduras April 11, Salvador April 15, Guatemala May 12, May 15 Costa Rica

June 17, Provisional Federal Council met at Tegucigalpa, Honduras, beginning to function, V. Martinez of Guatemala named president

July 20, Constitutent Assembly met at Tegucigalpa to frame a permanent Constitution

Sept. 9, Constitution adopted by signature of Guatemala, Honduras, and Salvador and promulgated Oct. 3

Oct. 10, Federation came into effect

Dec. 8, Revolution in Guatemala caused collapse of the Union, Acts of the former Government declared null and void which included signature by Guatemala of Pact of Union

1922

Jan. 18, Guatemala formally withdrew from the Union

Jan. 29, Federation of Central America dissolved

Feb. 4, Salvador resumed independent status

Feb. 11, Honduras resumed status as independent Republic

Aug. 20, Treaty of peace of Dec. 20, 1907, renewed, signed on board U.S.S. "Tacoma" by Honduras, Nicaragua, and Salvador; Costa Rica invited refused to adhere Sept. 9, and Guatemala Oct. 5

Dec. 4–Feb. 7, 1923, Central American Conference at Washington on invitation of the Government of the United States (second, see 1907 for first) attended by representatives of the 5 Republics

1923

Feb. 7, Treaty of peace and amity signed at Washington Conference, 11 conventions and 3 protocols. The Treaty provided that disputes arising among the Republics should be submitted to commissions of inquiry, and Convention for establishment of permanent Central American Court of Justice, Convention for limitation of armaments, free trade, unification of protective laws for workmen, electoral legislation, reciprocal exchange of Central American students, &c.

1927

May 25, Pact signed by Guatemala, Honduras, and Salvador, agreement to act together in matters affecting the general interest; approved by Governments June 4

1928

Dec. 10–Jan. 5, 1929, International Conference of American States on Conciliation and Arbitration in Washington adopted General Treaty of Inter-American Arbitration, and General Treaty of Inter-American Conciliation

1929

Feb. 4, Air mail service with the United States opened by Colonel Charles A. Lindbergh

BRITISH HONDURAS

British Honduras, Crown Colony of Central America on the Caribbean Sea, south of Yucatan, and 700 miles west from Jamaica, formerly called Belize, is bounded on the north and northwest by Mexico (Yucatan), northeast and east by the Bay of Honduras, and south and west by Guatemala. The total area is 8,598 square miles, population census of 1921, 45,317, estimated population Dec. 31, 1929, 51,228. The capital and chief seaport is Belize, population census of 1921, 12,661. The boundary with Guatemala was settled by Treaty of April 30, 1859 and Treaty of July 9, 1893. The country was discovered by Columbus in 1502, and the earliest settlements were made by woodcutters from Jamaica in 1638 at the mouth of the Belize River. By the Treaty of Paris in 1763 the English "baymen" were recognized, and Spain gave consent in return for the destruction of their fortifications that they should not be "disturbed or molested" in their "places of cutting and loading logwood." The settlement was destroyed by attack of the Spaniards Sept. 15 and the settlers sent to Cuba, but they returned in 1783, and by Treaty of Versailles of Sept. 3, 1783 they were granted right to cut wood in northern part of the present British Honduras. May 27, 1784 the settlements were delivered to Great Britain by Spain. A new Treaty of July 14, 1786, reaffirmed that of 1783, and Great Britain gave up the Mosquito coast to Spain. Another Spanish attack on the settlements was made July 10, 1798, but was not successful, the Spaniards defeated in battles of Sept. 3–5, and Sept. 10 at St. George's Caye. In 1862, May 12, British Honduras declared a Colony and its superintendent, Frederick Seymour, appointed Lieutenant-Governor under Jamaica. In 1884, Oct. 2, British Honduras separated from Jamaica and made an independent Colony, proclaimed Nov. 1.

Major Sir J. A. Burdon, Governor.

COSTA RICA

Costa Rica, most southern of the Central American Republics, bounded on the north by Nicaragua, on the east by the Caribbean Sea (coast line about 181 miles), by Panama on the southeast and east, and by the Pacific Ocean on the west (coast line 360 miles). The area of the Republic is estimated at 23,000 English square miles, divided into seven provinces, San José, Alajuela, Heredia, Cartago, Guanacaste, Puntarenas, and Limón. The last Census, taken in May, 1927, showed a population of 471,525. The population of European descent, many of them pure Spanish blood, dwell mostly around the capital, the city of San José (population, 1928, 51,459, with suburbs, 62,637), and in the towns of Alajuela (8,611), Cartago (16,261), Heredia (10,763), Liberia (7,473), Puntarenas (7,848), and Limón (15,690). There are some 18,000 colored British West Indians, mostly in Limón Province, on the banana farms.

Don Cleto Gonzales Viquez, President.

1502

Sept. 15, Costa Rica discovered by Columbus on his last voyage and probably named by him called Nueva Cartago for a time. The Bay of Almirante (Admiral) named in his honor discovered Oct. 6

1509

Diego de Nicuesa appointed first Governor of the province of Castilla del Oro which included Costa Rica

1513

July 27, Pedrarias de Avila appointed Governor of Castilla del Oro. He sent Captain Gaspar de Espinosa who discovered Burica and the Golfo Dulce on the Pacific

1519

Bartolome de Hurtado in 2 ships constructed by Vasco Nunez de Balboa coasted as far as the Gulf of Nicoya

1522

Gil Gonzales de Avila from Chiriqui marched through the territory of Costa Rica to Nicaragua

1523

Jan., Francisco Hernandez de Cordova sent by Avila founded the city of Bruselas at Urutina near the Gulf of Nicoya

1526

March 16, Pedrarias de Avila took possession of the Island of Chira

1540

April 25, Hernan Sanchez de Badajoz appointed Governor of Costa Rica arrived at the mouth of the Teliri (Sicsola) River and founded the City of Badajoz
Nov., Badajoz forced to surrender to Roderigo de Contreras, Governor of Nicaragua claiming the territory
Nov. 29, Diego Gutierrez named Governor and Captain-

General of Cartago (Costa Rica) and given grant of land

1541

March 5, Badajoz sent by Contreras to the Council of the Indies for trial

1543

Nov., Gutierrez founded the City of Talamanca

1544

Oct. 4, Gutierrez ascended the San Juan River and founded City of San Francisco
Dec., Gutierrez killed in battle with the Indians

1549

Feb. 22, Perez de Cabrera appointed Governor of Cartago

1560

Jan. 30, Licenciado Juan de Cavallon appointed by the audiencia alcalde mayor of Nicaragua and authorized to undertake the exploration of Costa Rica. Confirmed by royal grant Feb. 5, 1561
Oct., Juan de Estrada Ravago with 60 Spaniards founded the Villa del Castillo de Austria

1561

Jan., Cavallon with Ravago left Nicaragua for Costa Rica. He founded the village of Landecho, the present Caldera
March, Cavallon founded the City of the Castillo de Garci-Munoz on left bank of the Ciruelas River

1562

Juan de Estrada Ravago, Governor
April 2, Juan Vasquez de Coronado, the real conqueror of Costa Rica appointed alcalde mayor of the Provinces of Cartago and Costa Rica. His first expedition to Talamanca where he made peace with the Indians
Nov. 20, Coronado became Governor

1564

Miguel Sanchez de Guido, Governor
Coronado took possession of the Bay of Almirante, of the Valley of Guaymi and of the Rio de la Estrella which he named. The City of Cartago founded

1565

April 4, Coronado in Spain appointed Adelanto and Governor of Costa Rica. Lost on return voyage

1566

Pedro Venegas de los Rios, Governor (1566–68)
July 19, Perafau de Rivera appointed Governor (1568–73)

1568

Rivera founded port of his name on the Gulf of Nicoya and the City of Aranjuez

1569

Antonio Pereira, Provisional Governor (1569–72)

1573

Dec. 18, Grant to Captain Diego de Artieda Chirino to explore and settle Costa Rica

1574

Alonso de Anguciana de Gamboa Provisional Governor (1574–76). He removed the City of Aranjuez to the

Coyocho Valley and founded the new Village of Castillo de Austria in the Port of Suerre

1576

July, Diego de Arteida Governor (1576–90)

1578

March 5, Captain Pavon sent by Arteida took possession of the Guaymi Valley

1590

Velasquez Ramirez, Provisional Governor (1590–91)

1591–1595

Captains Antonio Pereira, Bartolome de Lences, and Gonzalo de Palma successively provisional governors

1595

March, The new Governor, Don Fernando de la Cueva, appointed in 1591 arrived in Costa Rica (1595–99)

1600

Gonzalo Vasquez de Coronado son of Juan Vasquez de Coronado, Governor (1600–04)

1605

Don Juan de Ocon y Trillo Governor (1605–10)
Oct. 10, Diego de Sojo y Penaranda sent by the Governor founded the City of Talamanca

1610

July, The Indians rose against the Spaniards and burned Santiago

1612

Gonzalo Vasquez de Coronado again Governor (1612–15)

1615

Juan de Medrano y Mendoza Governor

1622

Alonso de Guzman y Casilla Governor

1628

Fray Juan de Chauz Governor

1637

Don Gregorio Sandoval Governor

1647

Juan de Chaves Governor

1651

Don Juan Fernandez Salinas y Cerda Governor (1651–59)

1659

Andres Arias Maldonado Governor

1660

Rodrigo Arias Maldonado y Velazco Governor

1665

Juan de Obregon and Juan Lopez de la Flor Governors

1666

April 8, The English buccaneers Morgan and Mansfelt arrived at El Portete and began march into the

interior which reached Turrialba. Forced to retreat April 16 by forces of the Governor

1674

April 26, Don Juan Francisco Saenz Vazquez inaugurated Governor (1674–81)

1676

June 30, Pirates landed at El Portete (Moin) and set out for Cartago. Defeated and driven back by forces of the Governor

1679

Francisco Antonio de Rivas Contreras Provisional Governor

1681

July 24, Don Miguel Gomez de Lara inaugurated Governor

1693

April, Manuel de Bustamante y Vivero Governor (1693–98)

1698

May 28, Francisco Bruno Cerrando de Reyna Governor (1698–1704)

1705

May 8, Diego de Herrera Campuzano Governor

1707

Lorenzo Antonio de Granda y Balbin Governor

1713

José Antonio Locayo de Briones Governor and Pedro Ruiz de Bustamante

1718

Nov. 26, General Diego de la Haya y Fernandez Governor

1723

Feb. 16, Eruption of the volcano Irazu began which continued until the 27th

1727

May, Daltazar Francisco de Valderrama Governor

1736

Antonio Vazquez de la Cuadra Governor

1738

Francisco Antonio Carrandi y Menan Governor

1739

Francisco de Olaechea Governor

1740

June 22, Juan Gemmir y Leonard Governor (1740–47)

1747

Dec., Luis Diez Navarro Governor

1750

Jan., Cristobal Ignacio de Soria Governor (1750–March 14, 1754)

1755

Francisco Fernandez de la Pastora Governor (1755–58)

1758

Manuel Soler Governor

1762

Francisco Xavier Oreamuno Governor

1771

José Joaquin de Nava Governor

1773

Juan Fernandez de Bovadilla y Gradi Governor

1778

June, José Perie Governor

1780

Aug., Juan Fernandez de Bovadilla y Gradi Governor (1780–81)

1781

April, Juan Florez Governor

1785

José Perie, Governor (1785–97)

1789

José Antonio Oreamuno Governor

1790

Juan Pinillos Governor
April, José Vazquez y Tellez Governor (1790–97)

1797

April, Tomas de Acosta Governor (1797–1810) the most important of the Spanish governors inaugurated a period of prosperity

1810

Oct., Juan de Dios de Ayala Governor (1810–19)

1813

Aug. 14, Protest to Governor against the prohibition of commerce with Panama by the Captain-General of Guatemala

1819

Ramon Jiminez Provisional Governor with de Canas
Juan Manuel de Canas Governor (1819–21)

1821

Oct. 13, News of the declaration of independence of Guatemala of Sept. 15 received
Oct. 29, Citizens took possession of Cartago and declared Costa Rica independent of all governments
Nov. 12, Provisional government installed the Superior Gubernative Provisional Union. Formal resignation of the Spanish Governor accepted
Dec. 1, "Social, Fundamental, Provisional Compact of Costa Rica" adopted, and a "Provisional Governing Union" elected of 7 members and 3 substitutes headed by Don Pedro Alvarado (ecclesiastic vicar) with Don Joaquin de Iglesias as Secretary

1822

Jan. 10, Union with Mexico formally proclaimed
Jan. 11, The Fundamental Law approved
Jan. 13, Superior Gubernative Union installed, President Licenciado Don Rafael Barroeta, Vice-President Don José Maria Peralta, Secretary Don Juan Mora

1823

Jan. 1, New elected Gubernative Union installed, President, Don José Santos Lombardo, Vice-President Don José Francisco Madriz
March 4, Assembly met. Don Rafael Francisco Osejo, Don Manuel Maria Peralta, and Don Hermenegildo Bonill appointed in charge of the Government
March 29, Imperialist revolution against the Government begun, aided by General Saravia, Governor of Leon
April 5, Republicans commanded by Don Gregorio J. Ramirez defeated the Imperialists in battle on heights of Ochomogo near Cartago
May 10, Superior Gubernative Union under new Political Statute inaugurated
July 1, Costa Rica joined the first Central American Union

1824

Sept. 6, First Constituent Congress met with Licenciado Don Agustin Gutierrez Lizaur Zabal president
Sept. 8, Congress named Don Juan Mora Chief of State and for Vice-President Mariano Montealegre

1825

Jan. 22, Constitution promulgated. The first Juan Mora again elected President under the Constitution and Don Rafael Gallegos, Vice-President
April, First Legislature installed
Dec. 9, The District of Guanacaste or Nicoya of Nicaragua incorporated with Costa Rica

1826

Jan. 29, Unsuccessful attempt of José Zamora at Alajuela to overthrow the government

1829

March 21, Juan Mora reëlected President
April 1, Costa Rica declared independence of the Central American Confederation

1831

Jan., Secession from the Central American Confederation revoked

1833

March 9, José Rafael de Gallegos assumed office as President

1834

Juan José Lara became Provisional President on resignation of Gallegos
June, Augustin G. Lizaur Zabal Provisional President

1835

May 5, Lic. Braulio Carrillo inaugurated as President
Sept. 24, Revolt of San José against Cartago
Oct. 28, Revolutionists at San José defeated by government troops

1836

June, Manuel Quijano led unsuccessful revolt

1837

April 17, Lic. Manuel Aguilar succeeded Carillo as President

1838

May 27, Braulio Carillo overthrew the Jefe Aguilar

and banished him. Vice-Jefe Mora assumed the government
June 25, Assembly declared Carillo President
Aug. 4, Costa Rica withdrew from the Federal Assembly because of unequal representation

1839

April 15, Formal separation from the Central American Confederation declared
July 1, Treaty of friendship and alliance with Honduras signed
Aug. 1, Treaty with Guatemala signed

1841

March 8, Carillo issued decree giving himself life tenure as Jefe

1842

April 7, General Morazan landed at Caldera from Honduras to support revolt against Carillo
April 11, Convention of peace signed at Jacote, Morazan to take charge of the government until constitutional assembly should reorganize the government
July 10, Constituent Assembly met at San José
July 15, Francisco Morazan elected provisional President by Congress
Sept. 11, Revolt against Morazan led by Florentin Alfaro marched on San José
Sept. 14, Morazan escaped from San José to Cartago not knowing that the commander Mayorga had joined the revolution
Sept. 15, Morazan executed
Sept. 27, José Maria Alfaro inaugurated as provisional President and Antonio Pinto proclaimed commander-in-chief of the army

1843

June 1–Sept. 22, Constituent Assembly in session and again on Nov. 13

1844

April 11, New Constitution promulgated
July 3, Chamber of Deputies installed
July 12, Senate and Assembly installed
Nov. 15, Francisco Maria Oreamuno declared elected President by the Chamber of Deputies and the Senate
Dec. 7, Rafael Moya became President on resignation of Oreamuno

1845

May 1, José Rafael Gallegas took office as President

1846

June 7, Revolt of 4 regiments supported by the people to overthrow the Constitution
June 9, José Maria Alfaro assumed office as President
Sept. 15, Constituent Assembly met

1847

Jan. 21, New Constitution promulgated. Formally adopted the title of the Republic of Costa Rica. Declared willingness to negotiate with other Central American States for "a new compact of social union"
May 1, Congress met and on the 5th elected Castro President
May 8, Inauguration of Dr. José Maria Castro, President and Alfaro as Vice-President

1848

March 12, Accession of Costa Rica to Commercial Treaty of Guatemala and France
Aug. 30, Declaration by Congress of sovereignty and independence
Nov. 22, Fundamental law of 1847 revised

1849

Nov. 16, President Castro resigned
Nov. 26, Juan Rafael Mora assumed office as President
Nov. 27, Treaty of friendship, commerce, and navigation with Great Britain signed

1850

May 10, Treaty with Spain concluded by which independence recognized

1851

Feb. 2, Church raised to bishopric independent of Guatemala
July 10, Treaty with the United States signed of friendship, commerce, and navigation
Sept. 7, Padre Anselmo Lorente y Lafuente consecrated first bishop

1852

July 12, Treaty of friendship, commerce, and navigation with Holland

1853

May 3, Juan Rafael Mora reëlected President and Oreamuno Vice-President

1856

March 1, Costa Rica declared war on William Walker, American filibuster in Nicaragua
March 8, President Mora took command of army. For war see Nicaragua
Sept. 17, Vicente Aguilar chosen Vice-President on death of Oreamuno
Oct. 22, Aguilar resigned but remained Minister of Foreign Affairs

1858

Jan. 16, Peace concluded with Nicaragua
April 15, Boundary Treaty with Nicaragua signed. Contained clause providing that Nicaragua should not enter into contracts for canal or transit without consulting Costa Rica
April 23, Colonization law enacted offered inducements to foreign immigrants
May 1, Concession for inter-oceanic canal granted to Felix Belly, French writer
Aug. 31, Commercial Treaty with Belgium signed

1859

May 4, President Mora reëlected, Rafael G. Escalante, Vice-President
Aug. 14, President Mora deposed and exiled and José Maria Montealegre elected President (provisional)
Oct. 16, Constituent Assembly met
Dec. 26, New Constitution adopted. Promulgated Dec. 27

1860

April 22, Congress opened session
May 8, Montealegre inaugurated as constitutional President

July 2, Claims Convention with the United States concluded which provided for appointment of a commission to settle claims due largely to Walker affair in Nicaragua

Sept. 28, Mora who had returned to Costa Rica in attempt to seize the government defeated in battle at La Angostura

Sept. 30, Mora shot

Oct. 1, General J. M. Canas, revolutionist, executed

1861

April 26, Death of Vicente Aguilar

1862

Feb. 8, Claims Convention met in Washington which fixed settlement at $26,704

1863

May 8, Jesus Jiminez, former minister of Mora, inaugurated President

Nov. 24, Decree adopted decimal system for money

1866

May 8, Dr. José Maria Castro inaugurated President

1867

Sept. 20, Port of Limon opened to foreign trade

1868

Nov. 1, Revolutionists led by Generals Lorenzo Salazar and Maximo Blanco proclaimed Licdo. Jesus Jiminez for President at San José

1869

Feb. 18, New Constitution adopted

April 15, Constitution promulgated

May 1, Jiminez assumed office as constitutional President

June 8, Costa Rica with Nicaragua signed contract for inter-oceanic canal

First Central American telegraph completed from Puntarenas to Cartago

1870

April 27, Successful revolt led by Tomas and Victor Guardia, Pedro and Pablo Quiroz and Prospero Fernandez seized the barracks at San José and took the President prisoner declaring Bruno Carranza President

April 28, Bruno Carranza assumed office as provisional President

Aug. 8, Resignation of Carranza. Assembly declared the Constitution of 1869 no longer in force and revived that of Dec. 1859. Tomas Guardia appointed provisional President. Remained in office until 1876

Oct. 10, President Guardia dissolved the Assembly

Oct. 13, President Guardia created a Council of State, appointed Rafael Barroeta his substitute, and took command of the army

1871

July 20, Henry Meiggs granted concession for a railroad. Construction begun in Oct.

Oct. 15, Constitutional Assembly met

Dec. 7, New Constitution promulgated

1872

May 30, Tomas Guardia reëlected President, and J. A. Pinto and Rafael Barroeta first and second Vice-Presidents

June 20, President Guardia granted leave of absence. Vice-President Pinto acted as President

1873

Jan. 26, President Guardia reassumed the executive office

Oct. 24, Note remonstrated against Treaty of Alliance of Guatemala, Salvador, and Nicaragua of Aug. 26

Nov. 21, President Guardia temporarily resigned office to Salvador Gonzales until Dec. 1. Dec. 2 resigned office to Rafael Barroeta

1874

Feb. 28, President Guardia resumed the executive office

1875

May 19, President Guardia granted another leave of absence

1876

May 8, Lic. Aniceto Esquivel inaugurated as President, Tomas Guardia and Vicente appointed Vice-Presidents

July 29–30, Revolt at Cartago deposed Esquivel

July 30, Dr. Vicente Herrera assumed office as President

Aug. 11, President Herrera established censorship of the press

Sept. 11, Revolt overthrew Herrera

Sept. 17, Tomas Guardia inaugurated as President

1878

Jan., Federico Mara led unsuccessful revolt against Guardia

1879

May 12, Constitution of 1871 amended

1880

Feb. 7, The steamer "Earnholm" carried first cargo of bananas from Limon to New York City

Dec. 25, Boundary convention with Colombia signed

1881

Dec. 7, New Constitution adopted

1882

April 26, Modification of Constitution of 1871

July 7, Death of President Guardia. General Prospero Fernandez designated President assumed office July 20

Aug. 10, Fernandez inaugurated constitutional President

1884

July 10, Decree adopted metric system for weights and measures

July 18, Decree expelled the Jesuits and Bishop Thiel

1885

March 12, Death of President Fernandez. First Vice-President Bernardo Soto assumed executive office

March 22, Costa Rica, Nicaragua, and Salvador entered into offensive and defensive alliance against Guatemala

April 19, Peace proclaimed ending war
Aug., Revolt led by General Fadrique Gutierrez unsuccessful

1886

Jan. 20, Boundary Treaty with Colombia signed
Feb. 26, Education law enacted
May 8, Bernardo Soto inaugurated constitutional President
Dec. 20, Law on citizenship and naturalization enacted
Dec. 24, Boundary Treaty with Nicaragua concluded

1888

May 22, Award of President Cleveland in interpretation of Treaty of Limits of April 15, 1858 as to San Juan River with Nicaragua
July 6, Amendment to Constitution promulgated

1890

May 8, Licenciado José Rodriquez inaugurated President
May 13, Citizenship law of 1886 amended

1892

Census gave total population as 255,365

1893

March 27, Revolt led by J. M. Gutierrez against the Government unsuccessful

1894

May 8, Rafael Iglesias inaugurated President

1896

March 27, Boundary Treaty with Nicaragua signed
Oct. 26, Act provided for adoption of gold standard, monetary unit the gold colon
Nov. 4, Boundary Treaty with Colombia signed

1897

June 15, Treaty for Central American Union signed. Not ratified

1898

March 20, Troops in conflict with Nicaraguan force on frontier in boundary dispute
May 8, President Iglesias inaugurated for second term

1899

Feb. 25, Revolt led by "General" Velarde at San José unsuccessful

1900

Sept. 11, Award of President Loubet of France in boundary dispute with Colombia
Dec. 1, Treaty with the United States signed as to an inter-oceanic canal

1901

June 7, Commercial treaty with France signed

1902

May 8, Licenciado Ascension Esquivel assumed office as President

1905

March 6, Agreement with Panama as to boundary under Loubet award of 1900
May 1, Congress met

1906

April 1, Cleto Gonzales Viquez elected President. Inaugurated May 8
Sept. 15–25, General Peace Conference at San José attended by representatives of Costa Rica, Guatemala, and San Salvador, and Treaty signed. *See* Central America

1907

Dec. 20, Treaty of peace signed. *See* Central America

1908

May 25, First Central American Court opened at Cartago

1909

Jan. 13, Arbitration Treaty signed with the United States
Aug. 30, Ricardo Jiminez elected President

1910

March 17, Costa Rica and Panama signed Protocol setting forth basis of fact for boundary arbitration
April, Ricardo Jiminez again elected President, the election of the previous August having been declared annulled
May 4, Earthquake destroyed towns of Cartago and Paraiso
May 8, President Jiminez inaugurated
Dec. 7, Fernandez-Keith agreement provided for refunding foreign debt into bonds

1911

Jan. 14, Railroad between San José and Puntarenas (67 miles) formally opened

1912

Jan. 1, Census gave total population as 388,266
March 3, American Secretary of State Knox arrived at Costa Rica on visit
May 8, President Viquez inaugurated

1913

Aug. 18, Election law adopted universal suffrage for male citizens of age and able to support themselves, except criminals, bankrupts, &c.

1914

Feb. 13, Advance of Peace Treaty signed with the United States
May 8, Alfredo Gonzales Flores inaugurated President
Sept. 12, Award of Chief Justice White of the United States in boundary dispute with Panama favorable to Costa Rica
Oct. 9, Executive decree created International Bank of Costa Rica as a Government Bank of Issue
Dec. 14, Direct taxation law enacted
Dec. 18, Tax placed on incomes and real estate

1915

Jan. 14, Executive decree published rules and regulations for normal school at Heredia
March 4, Law as to insurance companies promulgated
May 8, Workmen's compensation law published in Official Gazette
July 5, College of Dental Surgery opened at San José
Sept. 23, Contract signed with American company for exploitation of oil. Accepted by Congress Nov. 10, published Nov. 12, 1916

1916

March 26, Costa Rica brought suit in Central American Court against Nicaragua alleging infringement of rights in negotiation of canal treaty with the United States

May 1, Destructive earthquake at San José

Sept. 30, Decision of Central American Court in favor of Costa Rica in dispute with Nicaragua as to lease of Fonseca Bay to the United States

1917

Jan. 27, Military coup d'état led by former war minister Federico Tinoco deposed President Gonzales. Tinoco made provisional President

Feb. 21, The United States refused to recognize the Tinoco Government unless legal proof of election

April 11, Tinoco elected President

June 8, New Constitution adopted. Promulgated July 13

Sept. 21, Costa Rica severed diplomatic relations with Germany

Nov. 4, Red Cross Society founded

1918

May 23, War declared on Germany

Oct. 28, New election law passed

1919

May 6, Revolt of Flores party overthrew Tinoco

May 7, Revolutionists proclaimed Julio Acosta President

June 4, American marines landed at Punta Arenas, and Port Limon

June 28, Decree authorized issue of 15,000,000 colones in currency notes

July 8, Decree authorized circulation of notes of 1,000 colones

Aug. 13, Juan B. Quiros assumed office

Dec. 9, Julio Acosta elected President

1920

April 30, Executive decree published new consular rules and regulations to replace those of Oct. 12, 1887. To take effect May 7

May 8, Julio Acosta inaugurated President

June 20, Treaty with Nicaragua signed by which reciprocal use of waters near frontiers arranged for timber commerce

June 30, Decree created a Council of Public Finance to study economic situation

Aug. 2, Acosta Government recognized by the United States

Aug. 16, Eight hour day for workers employed by the Government established

Aug. 21, Decree canceled all acts of the Tinoco régime, and contracts

Aug. 23, Universal suffrage adopted

Dec. 9, Decree published on the 27th established eight hour day in factories

Dec. 16, Costa Rica admitted as member of League of Nations

1921

Jan. 19, Costa Rica signed Provisional Pact of Central American Union

Feb. 21, Troops occupied village in District of Coto (Panama) assigned to Costa Rica by White award of 1914 which was not accepted by Panama

Feb. 27–28, Fighting between forces of Panama and Costa Rica on boundary

March 4, Costa Rican troops occupied Almirante, port of Panama

March 5, Secretary Hughes sent notes to Costa Rica and Panama urging cessation of hostilities and offering the mediation of the United States

March 7, Costa Rica accepted mediation of the United States

March 16, Decision of United States as arbiter that the Loubet and White awards should stand. Panama refused to accept

March 17, Congress voted 24 to 17 to support the President in his refusal to recognize oil concessions granted to British companies by the Tinoco Government. This approved by the United States in note of April 19 to Great Britain

Aug. 23, Panama ceded territory in dispute to Costa Rica after ultimatum from the United States

Sept. 5, Costa Rica assumed possession of Coto District

1922

Jan. 12, Arbitration Agreement with Great Britain signed as to claims against Costa Rica

March 26, Emergency Rent Law Decree

May 19, New law for unification of paper currency promulgated

Sept. 9, Costa Rica declined to adhere to Central American Federation Pact

Oct. 2, Industrial Insurance law enacted

Oct. 17, The President authorized to negotiate loan of 1,200,000 colones to use for construction of houses for workmen

Nov. 10, Extradition Treaty with the United States signed

1923

Feb. 8, Announcement that the United States recognized rights of Costa Rica in San Juan River and Salvinas Bay

Sept. 14, Decree amended education law of 1886 making primary education free and compulsory for children between the ages of 8 and 15

Oct. 18, Award of Chief Justice Taft in favor of Costa Rica as to British claims in Amory oil concession and Royal Bank of Canada case

Dec. 1, Customs Convention with France signed

Dec. 7, Don Ricardo Jimenez elected President

1924

March 14–15, Five towns destroyed by earthquakes

March 22, Presidential Decree prohibited raising rents for dwellings, offices, or shops above rentals charged March 1

May 8, President Jimenez inaugurated

July 7, Banco de Cooperacion National established in San José

Oct. 30, Compulsory insurance law enacted

Dec. 24, Costa Rica gave notice of withdrawal from the League of Nations to take effect from Jan. 1, 1927

1925

Jan. 23, Executive Decree regulated importation of seeds and plants

Jan. 31, Workmen's Compensation law enacted, published Feb. 6

July 26, Law made voting for president, deputies, and municipal councillors secret, direct, and free

Oct. 22, Decree of the President provided that the National Insurance Bank should on Nov. 1 assume the monopoly of all insurance

1926

March 26, Commercial Treaty with France announced in *La Gaceta* of this date

May 14, Constitution amended as to elections, candidates having absolute majority to be elected

Sept. 15, Foundation stone laid for St. Thomas University at San José

1927

Jan. 1, Withdrawal from League of Nations became effective

Jan. 17, New regulations for insurance issued

March 15, Decree prohibited importation, export, and transit of opium for smoking

May, Census gave population as 471,525

Public debt 70,270,740 colones

1928

Jan. 7, Colonel Charles Lindbergh arrived at San José on good will flight

March 15, Council of the League of Nations appealed to Costa Rica to return to membership in the League

May 7, Extradition Treaty with Colombia signed

May 8, Cleto Gonzales Viquez, member of National Union Party, inaugurated as President

July 13 and Aug. 17, Exchange of Notes with Germany as to claims

July 18, Note of Costa Rica to Council of the League of Nations asked for interpretation of Article 21 of the Covenant as to the Monroe Doctrine before accepting invitation to resume membership in the League; reply accepted Sept. 1

Aug. 4, Law nationalized all electrical power available to form a government electric service

Oct. 6, Diplomatic relations with Panama resumed

Oct. 8, Convention with Colombia signed for mutual recognition of professional degrees

Nov. 28, President-Elect Hoover arrived at San José from the United States on good will visit

1929

April 7, Roberto Smith became Minister of Foreign Affairs and Rafael Castro Quesada, Interior

Aug. 12, Law provided for increase in export tax on bananas and for restrictions on their cultivation

GUATEMALA

Guatemala, most northern of the Central American Republics, the second in size and the most populous, bounded on the north and west by Mexico, on the east by British Honduras, the Gulf of Honduras (coast line 70 miles), and Honduras, Salvador on the southeast, and the Pacific Ocean on the south (coast line 200 miles). The name of the country said to mean "land of the eagle" is probably of Aztec origin. The greatest length from north to south is 360 miles and width, Atlantic to Pacific, 390 miles. With the exception of a small strip of land along the coast the altitude is from 4,000 to 11,000 feet. Area estimated at 109,724 sq. kilometers, or 42,353 square miles, but the boundary with Honduras has long been in dispute; in 1930 both countries agreed to submit it to arbitration. The population, according to the 1920 census, was 2,004,900. About 60% are pure Indians, most of the remainder being mixed Indian and Spanish (*ladinos*); the ruling classes are of European descent. A system of peonage prevails on the large plantations. Guatemala is administratively divided into 22 departments.

The capital is Guatemala City, with 120,707 inhabitants, 1928, almost all *ladinos* or descendants of Europeans. Other towns are Quezaltenango, 30,125, Coban, 26,774, and Zacapa, 18,094.

J. M. Andrade, Provisional President (Dec. 31, 1930).

1523

Dec., Pedro de Alvarado, lieutenant of Cortes appointed Governor, started from Mexico for Guatemala to subdue the Indians and explore the country

1524

Feb., Alvarado reached the border of Guatemala from Honduras

July 25, Alvarado founded city of St. Jago (Santiago) as seat of his colony, the later Guatemala City

1525

Indian stronghold of Mixco taken by Alvarado after long siege

1527

March 20, Jorge de Alvarado, brother of the conqueror, substitute Governor arrived

Nov. 22, Jorge de Alvarado founded new capital known as Ciudad Vieja

Dec. 18, Commission to Pedro de Alvarado from Charles V confirmed appointment of governor

1529

April, Gaspar de Arias led expedition against the tribes of Uzpantlan

Aug. 14, Francisco de Orduna arrived from Mexico appointed to investigate commission of Governor

Dec., Stronghold of Uzpantlans taken by Francisco de Castellanos

1530

April 11, Pedro de Alvarado returned from Spain

1534

Jan. 23, Pedro de Alvarado sailed for Peru claiming northern Peru in dispute with Pizarro

March, Alvarado landed in Bay of Caraques and proceeded to march across the Andes to Quito. Conflict avoided by cession of army and ships to Pizarro and Almagro for 100,000 gold ducats for which Alvarado renounced his claim

1536

May 10, Alonso de Maldonado appointed Governor of Guatemala arrived. Pedro de Alvarado sailed for Spain to petition for restoration

1538

April 17, Pedro de Alvarado commissioned as Governor

1539

Sept. 15, Alvarado arrived at capital and resumed office as Governor

1541

June 29, Death of Pedro de Alvarado at Guadalajara, Mexico

Sept. 10, Earthquake destroyed Santiago. Dona Beatrix, wife of Alvarado who had been made Governor *ad interim* Sept. 9, among those killed

Sept. 16–17, The Cabildo elected Francisco de la Cueva and Bishop Marroquin as joint provisional governors

1542

March 2, Alonso de Maldonado appointed Governor by Viceroy Mendoza. He assumed office May 17

Nov. 20, Audiencia created for Guatemala and Nicaragua by royal decree. Opened May 16, 1544

Guatemala City rebuilt

1548

March 1, Formal founding of town of Ciudad Real

May, Alonso Lopez Cerrato appointed substitute Governor for Maldonado

1555

Jan. 14, Dr. Antonio Rodriguez de Quesada succeeded Cerrato as Governor

1558

Nov. 28, Death of Governor Rodriguez de Quesada. Succeeded by Licenciado Ramirez de Quinones

1559

Sept. 2, Juan Nunez de Landecho took office as President of the Audiencia, Governor and Captain General

1563

April 18, Death of Governor Landecho. Succeeded by Francisco Marroquin *ad interim*

1564

Aug. 2, Licentiate Francisco Briseno took office as Governor

1565

July 7, Transfer of Audiencia of Guatemala from Nombre de Dios, Panama to Guatemala City authorized

1570

March, Dr. Antonio Gonzales assumed office as President of the Audiencia and Governor

1572

Jan., Dr. Pedro de Villabos succeeded Gonzales as President and Governor

1578

Nov., New Governor appointed April, 1577, Garcia de Valverde, arrived

1589

July 21, Pedro Mayen de la Rueda took office as Governor and President of the Audiencia

1594

Aug., Dr. Francisco de Sande succeeded de la Rueda as Governor

1598

Sept. 19, Dr. Alfonso Criado de Castilla took office as Governor

1609

Aug., Antonio Peraza Ayala Castilla y Rojas conde de la Gomera appointed Governor. Took office 1611

1626

Juan de Guzman, Governor

1634

Jan., Alvaro de Quinonez y Osorio, marques de Lorenzana took office as President and Governor

1642

March, Diego de Avendano succeeded Osorio as Captain General and President of the Audiencia

1649

Aug. 2, Death of Avendano. Succeeded by Antonio de Lara y Mongrovejo *ad interim*

1654

May, Fernando Altamirano y Velasco took office as Governor

1659

Jan., The new Governor General Martin Carlos de Mencos, Captain General and President of the Audiencia, arrived

1667 or 1668

Jan. 18, The new Governor Sebastian Alvarez Alfonso Rosica de Caldas took office

1669

Oct. 30, Foundation stone of Cathedral laid

1670

May 6, Bishop Juan de Santa Mathia Seanz Manosca appointed *ad interim* Governor

1672

Feb., General Francisco de Escobedo took office as Governor

1676

Jan. 5, Decree of Charles II created the College of St. Thomas Aquinas in which lectures had been first given in 1620, later the University of Guatemala

1678

Lope de Sierra Osorio, *interim* Governor

1681

Juan Miguel Augurto y Alava *interim* Governor

1683

Enrique Enriquez de Guzman, *interim* Governor

1688

Jan. 26, General Jacinto Barrios Leal took office as Governor and President

1695

Nov. 12, Death of President Barrios. Succeeded by Provisional President José de Scals

1696

March, Gabriel Sanchez de Berrospe appointed Governor and President

1699

Berrospe deposed. Amezqueta acted *ad interim*

1702

May, Alonso de Ceballos y Villagutierre succeeded Berrospe as Governor

1703

Oct. 27, José Osorio Espinosa de los Monteros, Governor, assumed office

1706

Sept. 2, Toribio José de Cosio y Campa took office as Governor

1712

Aug. 10–March, 1713, Insurrection of Indians in Chiapas. Nicolas de Segovia in charge of campaign

1716

Oct. 4, Francisco Rodriguez de Rivas took office as Governor and President

1717

Sept. 29, Earthquake and eruption of volcano destroyed city of Guatemala

1724

Dec., Antonio Echevers y Subiza took office as Governor

1729

First issue of the *Gazeta de Guatamala* appeared

1733

March 19, First money coined at mint with dies brought from Mexico received with official ceremonies Feb. 17
July 12, General Pedro Rivera y Villalon succeeded Subiza as Governor

1742

Oct. 16, Tomas Rivera y Santa Cruz took office as Governor and Captain General and President of the Audiencia

1748

Sept., José Araujo y Rio took office as Governor

1752

Jan. 17, José Vasquez Prego took office as Governor

1753

June 24, Death of Governor Vasquez Prego
Oct. 17, Alonso de Arcos y Moreno took office as Governor

1760

Oct. 27, Death of Captain General Arcos y Moreno

1761

June 14, Alonso Fernandez de Heredia took office as Governor

1765

Dec. 3, Pedro de Salazar y Herrera Natera y Mendoza took office as Governor

1767

June 26, Expulsion of Jesuits. Deported July 1

1771

May 20, Death of President Salazar

1773

June, Martin de Mayorga took office as Governor succeeding Salazar
July 29, Severe earthquake destroyed city of Guatemala

1776

Jan. 1, Present city of Guatemala laid out

1779

April 4, General (Coronel) Matias de Galvez proclaimed himself Governor and Captain General. Formally appointed May 5

1781

July 25, Foundation stone of Cathedral laid

1783

April 5, José de Estacheria took office as Governor and Captain General

1789

Dec. 29, Bernardo Troncoso Martinez del Rincon took office as Governor

1794

May 25, José Domas y Valle took office as Governor

1801

July 28, Antonio Mollinedo y Saravia took office as Governor

1802

June 3, First archbishop of Guatemala Luis Penalver y Cardenas reached Guatemala and assumed office on the 26th

1810

March 3, Electors chose deputy for representation in the Spanish Cortes, Manuel José Pavon y Munoz

1811

March 14, Lieutenant José Bustamente y Guerra succeeded Saravia as Governor

1812

Sept. 10, Constitution adopted by Spanish Cortes in March received at Guatemala and sworn to by Audiencia and people Nov. 3

1813

Dec. 21, Conspiracy of Betlen. Plot for independence discovered and leaders arrested except José F. Barrundia who escaped

1817

July 28, Royal order set free prisoners of Betlen conspiracy

1818

March 28, Lieutenant General Carlos de Urrutia y Montoya succeeded Bustamente as Governor

1820

June, Don Pedro Molina began publication of radical paper *El Editor Constitucional*

1821

March 9, Urrutia resigned in favor of General Gainza

Sept. 3, The Province of Chiapas proclaimed separation from Spain and acceptance of Iturbide's Plan of Iguala and was annexed to Mexico

Sept. 15, Junta in Guatemala City proclaimed independence of Guatemala from Spain

1822

Jan. 5, Junta in Guatemala City proclaimed annexation of Guatemala to Mexico

Feb. 21, Provisional Governing Junta in Guatemala City dissolved. Governor Gainza continued in office as Captain General

March 19, Colonel Arzu sent to bring Salvador to subjection

June 12, Mexican commander Filisola arrived at Guatemala to supersede Gainza and 10 days later took possession of the Government

1823

Feb. 21, Filisola returned to Guatemala City from Salvador and convoked a Congress

June 24, Central American Congress met at Guatemala City with delegates from the five States. *See* Central America

July 1, National Constituent Assembly declared the provinces of Guatemala independent States confederated into the United Provinces of Central America

Aug. 3, Filisola with his army left the country for Mexico ending foreign domination

1824

Sept. 13, Captain Ariza y Torres assumed title of commander-in-chief and forced Government to recognize him but unable to retain his position

Sept. 16, Constituent Congress met at La Antigua. A. Diaz Cabeza de Vaca appointed provisional "Jefe"

Oct. 12, Juan Barrundia appointed by Congress Sept. 30 assumed office as Jefe and Cerillo Flores as Vice-Jefe

Oct. 12–Nov. 3, Salvadorian troops called in to aid against revolt of Ariza y Torres in Guatemala City

1825

Jan. 20, Coat of arms adopted

May 2, Installation of executive council and superior court of justice

Oct. 11, Constitution promulgated

1826

Feb. 1, First ordinary legislature met

Sept. 6, Federal President Arce arrested and deposed Barrundia. Vice-Jefe Flores assumed the Government

Oct. 8, Flores arrived at Quezaltenango selected as seat of Government

Oct. 13, Jefe Flores assassinated by a fanatical mob of Indians

Oct. 18, Colonel José Pierzon defeated Quezaltenango rebels near Salcaja and occupied Quezaltenango the following day

Oct. 25, Pierzon left Quezaltenango and was pursued and defeated by Federals commanded by Colonel F. Cascaras at Malacatan

Nov. 15, Colonel Cascaras entered Guatemala City

Dec. 31, New Assembly met, controlled by Servile party

1827

March 1, Mariano Aycinena chosen Jefe

March 23, Salvadorians defeated by Federal President Arce at Arrazola

May 11, Colonel Pierzon, a prisoner, shot by Federal authorities

May 18, Invasion of Salvador. *See* Salvador

Oct. 29, Assembly adjourned

1828

Nov. 5, Revolt at Quezaltenango suppressed

1829

Jan. 22, Revolutionists in Antigua made alliance with General Morazan of Salvador

Feb. 5, Morazan's attack on capital repulsed

Feb. 15, Morazan defeated at Mixco

March 6, Pacheco defeated by Morazan at San Miguelito

March 15, General A. Prado defeated by Morazan at Las Charcas

April 12, General Morazan took Guatemala City

April 13, Morazan occupied Guatemala City and reinstated Juan Barrundia as Jefe

April 21, Deposed Congress of 1826 reassembled

Aug. 22, Pedro Molina, elected Jefe, installed

1830

March 9, Molina deposed and Vice-Jefe Rivera Cabezas superseded him

April 23, Severe earthquake most violent since 1773

1831

Aug. 24, Dr. Mariano Galvez assumed office as elected Jefe succeeding acting Vice-Jefe Gregorio Marquez. Barrundia elected Jefe previously had declined the office

1832

Feb. 24, Invasion of Arce defeated at Escuintla de Soconusco by troops of Morazan

March 1, Decree established Academy of Instruction

1834

Feb. 27, Assembly passed act to enable nuns to leave their convents if they so desired

March 2, Death of José del Valle

1835

Feb. 25, Jefe Galvez inaugurated for second term, Pedro José Valenzuela Vice-Jefe

1837

Jan. 1, Penal Code adopted

March 6, Insurrection of Indians at San Juan Ostuncalco

June 9, Insurrection at Mita in Santa Rosa led by Rafael Carrera

June 15, Insurgents defeated by government troops at Mataquescuintla

1838

Jan. 26, Insurrection of battalion at Guatemala City against the Minister of War

Feb. 1, Rafael Carrera leading revolt against the Government entered Guatemala City

Feb. 2, Vice-President Valenzuela replaced Galvez as provisional President

Feb. 2, The Departments of Los Altos declared independence of Guatemala and organized as a sixth Central American State

March 30, Morazan opened campaign against Carrera

July 22, Valenzuela deposed. Mariano Rivera Paz took office as Governor

Sept. 10, Carrera routed by Federalist troops commanded by General Carlos Salazar at Villaneuva

Nov. 4, Carrera defeated at Chiquimulilla by Colonel Carballo

Dec. 23, Carrera signed capitulation and agreed to recognize the Government

Dec. 28, Marcelo Molina inaugurated as first ruler of new State of Los Altos

1839

March 19, Morazan defeated at Guatemala City by Carrera

April 13, Guatemala declared independence of the Federation of Central America. Carrera reinstated Rivera Paz as Governor, deposed the preceding Jan. by General Carlos Salazar

April 17, Independent government established under title State of Guatemala

May 11, Treaty of amity and alliance with Honduras signed

June 5, Treaty of amity and alliance with Salvador signed

July 24, Treaty of amity and alliance with Nicaragua signed

Aug. 1, Treaty of amity and alliance with Costa Rica signed

Nov. 29, Title President given to chief executive heretofore called Jefe

1840

Jan. 29, State of Los Altos reincorporated in Guatemala

March 18, General Morazan took City of Guatemala

March 19, Morazan defeated by Carrera and forced to retreat from Guatemala City

1841

Dec. 14, Rivera Paz resigned and Venancio Lopez took office as President

1842

May 14, Rivera Paz again President

1844

March 14, Assembly dissolved by order of Carrera

Aug. 5, Convention with Salvador signed ending war

Sept. 20, Revolt of soldiers because of non-payment, shops looted

Dec. 8, Carrera installed a Council of Government to take the place of the Assembly

Dec. 11, Rafael Carrera took office as elected President

1845

April 4, Treaty of peace, amity, and alliance with Salvador

Sept. 16, Constituent Congress adopted Constitution. Rejected by Congress Feb. 1, 1846

1847

March 21, New declaration of independence made and title State of Guatemala changed to Republic of Guatemala

May, Revolt of Indians in Sacatepequez

June 25, Treaty of commerce and navigation with the German Hanseatic States signed

1848

Jan. 25, Vice-President Cruz assumed office as President by decree of Carrera in effort to check revolt

Feb. 4, Carrera resumed office of President

March 8, Treaty with France signed by which independence recognized and with Costa Rica

Aug. 15, Assembly installed with Pedro Molina President. Resignation of Carrera accepted

Sept. 5, Los Altos again reorganized as a State

Sept. 14, Assembly made declaration of the independence of the Guatemalan Republic

Oct. 13, Proscription of Carrera decreed. He went to Mexico. Succeeded by Juan Antonio Martinez as President

Oct. 21, Revolutionists of Los Altos defeated in battle

Nov. 28, José Bernardo Escobar succeeded Martinez resigned as President

Dec. 30, Manuel Tejada chosen President on resignation of Escobar. He declined the office

1849

Jan. 1, Mariano Paredes took office as elected President

Feb. 20, Treaty with Great Britain signed

March 20, Treaty with the United States signed

April 12, Treaty of friendship, commerce, and navigation with Belgium signed

April 13, Carrera with troops announced march on the capital

June 4, Decree ordered hostilities against Carrera to cease after negotiations in which he agreed to submission

Aug. 8, Carrera returned, took command of army

Oct. 13, Attack on capital of President Vasconcelos of Salvador and J. F. Barrundia. General Augustin Guzman defending the capital killed

1850

Dec. 4, War begun by Salvador, Honduras, and Nicaragua against Guatemala

1851

Feb. 2, Battle of Arada. General Cabanas (Salvador) defeated by Carrera in invasion

March 14, Decree changed national flag

June 7, Decree authorized return of Jesuits

Aug. 16, Constituent Assembly installed

Oct. 19, New Constitution adopted, the "Acta Constitutiva de la Republica de Guatemala"

Oct. 21, Rafael Carrera declared President. He took office the following day on the resignation of General Paredes

1853

July 6, Honduran troops commanded by Cerna defeated at Chiquimula

1854

Aug. 18, Claims Convention with France signed

Oct. 21, Carrera proclaimed President for life term

1856

March 22, Treaty of friendship, commerce, and navigation with the Netherlands

July 18, Treaty with Honduras and Salvador ended war

1859

April 30, Treaty with Great Britain as to boundary with Belize (British Honduras)

1862

Sept. 20, Treaty of amity and defensive alliance with Nicaragua concluded

1863

War with Salvador and Honduras. *See s.v.*
May 29, Treaty with Spain signed at Madrid by which Spain recognized the independence of Guatemala

1865

April 14, Death of President Carrera. Pedro de Ayci.nena, Minister of Foreign Affairs, assumed the executive office
May 24, Vicente Cerna elected by Assembly, inaugurated as President

1867

Feb., Revolt of Serapio Cruz in Sanarate, aided by Justo Rufino Barrios, begun which continued to 1870
Aug. 3, Pronunciation against the Government by Barrios and Francisco Cruz

1868

April, Barrios again in unsuccessful revolt
Dec. 31, Treaty of commerce and navigation with Italy signed

1869

May 20, Serapio Cruz defeated and forced to retire to Chiapas
May 24, President Cerna inaugurated for second term. Successful in election against Liberal candidate General V. Zavala

1870

Jan. 15, Serapio Cruz killed in advance on capital to aid Liberal revolt which was defeated

1871

March 5, Vicente Mendez Cruz began invasion from Mexico joining forces with Garcia Granados and J. Rufino Barrios against President Cerna
May 8, Manifesto of Granados against Cerna
May 10, Revolutionists occupied San Marcos
June 1, Granados routed Colonel Calonge and occupied La Antigua the following day
June 3, Miguel Garcia Granados proclaimed provisional President by the liberating army at meeting at Patzicia
June 23, President Cerna in command of troops routed in battle between Tonicapan and Quezaltenango
June 29, Forces of Cerna decisively defeated in battle near San Lucas. Cerna escaped
June 30, Victorious revolutionists entered Guatemala City and Granados proclaimed provisional President
Aug. 17, New flag adopted
Sept., Jesuits deported under decree of the revolutionary government dated May 24, 1870
Sept. 23, Revolt of reactionaries defeated at Cerro Gorda
Sept. 24, Reactionaries defeated at Santa Rosa
Sept. 28, Insurrectionists led by priests and aristocrats defeated at Jalapa
Oct. 17, Archbishop Pinol and Ortiz Urruela, Bishop of Teya, deported for aiding revolt
Nov. 18, New coat of arms adopted
Nov. 26, Garcia Granados made Captain General and Barrios a lieutenant general

1872

Jan. 24, Treaty of amity and alliance with Salvador signed
March 10, Constituent Assembly met
May 8, President Granados declared war on Honduras
June 7, Religious communities of men suppressed
June 10, President Granados returned after successful campaign

1873

March 12, Ecclesiastical court for civil and criminal cases abolished
March 15, Freedom of worship decreed
May 7, General Rufino Barrios declared elected President
June 4, President Barrios inaugurated
July, Unsuccessful revolt led by Palacios who fled to Honduras
Aug. 26, Treaty of alliance with Salvador and Nicaragua concluded, against Costa Rica

1874

Feb. 9, Decree suppressed many religious orders, permitting nuns to leave the cloister
Feb. 13, Treaty of peace, friendship, commerce, and extradition with Nicaragua
March 3, Nuns at Santa Catarina put out of the cloister

1875

April 6, Decree recognized the independence of Cuba. Later necessary to give satisfaction to Spain for this act
July 1, Government decree created University of Guatemala
Sept. 11, Constituent Assembly installed

1876

March 27, Declaration of war with Salvador. *See* Salvador
April 25, Armistice with Salvador signed
Oct. 23, "Pro-Constitution" framed

1877

Jan. 20, Decree made regulations as to immigration
Nov. 1, Revolutionary conspiracy discovered at the capital. 17 leaders executed

1878

March 2, Further regulations as to immigration. Modified Aug. 19
Sept. 8, Death of Garcia Granados
Nov. 9, Constituent Assembly convoked

1879

Dec. 12, Constitution amended
Dec. 13, Decree established system of compulsory free elementary education

1880

March 1, New Constitution went into effect
March 15, President Barrios reëlected, inaugurated
June 18, Central railroad opened from San José to Esquintla with ceremonies attended by Presidents of Guatemala, Honduras, and Salvador
July 17, Treaty of commerce and extradition with Honduras signed

1881

June 15, The Government made appeal to the United States in boundary dispute with Mexico "as the natural protector of the integrity of the Central American territory"

1882

April 26, Constitution amended

Aug. 12, Preliminary Boundary Treaty with Mexico signed. In case of dispute the United States to act as arbitrator

Sept. 27, Boundary Treaty with Mexico signed. In case of dispute the United States to act as arbiter

1883

Jan. 6, President Barrios resumed office after visit to Europe and the United States

Dec. 27, Treaty of friendship, defensive alliance, commerce, navigation, and extradition with Nicaragua signed

1884

Sept. 24, Railroad from San José to Guatemala City completed

1885

Feb. 28, Decree of President Barrios proclaimed the Central American Union consolidation of the 5 States into one republic, and issued manifesto to people of Central America

March 7, Honduras adopted resolutions accepting Federation

March 22, Costa Rica, Nicaragua, and Salvador entered into a defensive alliance against Guatemala

March 28, President Barrios with army crossed the frontier in invasion of Salvador

April 2, President Barrios killed in attempt to storm the fortifications of Chalchuapa. Alejandro Sinibaldi appointed provisional President

April 3, The Legislative Assembly revoked the decree of Feb. 28

April 15, Manuel Lisandro Barillas, Provisional President, after resignation of Sinibaldi, made peace with Salvador and her allies Nicaragua and Costa Rica

Nov. 22, M. L. Barillas elected President

1886

March 15, President Barillas inaugurated, Coronel Vicente Castaneda, Vice-President

1887

June 26, Insurrection at capital suppressed

Sept. 20, Treaty of commerce, navigation, and consular relations with Germany signed

Nov. 5, Constitution amended

1889

Feb. 15, Claims Convention with Mexico concluded

1890

June 22, General Barillas mobilized troops on the frontier against Salvador

July 21, War against Salvador declared and Salvadorians defeated July 23

Aug. 26, War ended by mediation of members of diplomatic corps

1892

March 15, General José Maria Reyna Barrios inaugurated as President

1893

April 19, Decree regulating status of foreign companies

July 9, Boundary Treaty with British Honduras

Nov. 4, New tariff promulgated

1894

Feb. 21, Decree regulated status of foreigners. Amended May 5

1895

March 1, Boundary Treaty with Honduras signed

March 10, Treaty of commerce, navigation, and arbitration with Honduras signed

April 1, Agreement signed ended boundary dispute with Mexico as to territory about the Lacantun River and provided for arbitration of claims

Aug. 17–18, Indians from Salvador invading Guatemala in conflict with Guatemalan troops

1897

June 1, President Barrios dissolved the National Assembly and proclaimed a dictatorship

June 15, Guatemala signed Treaty of Union of the Central American States

Sept. 7, Revolution organized by Prospero Morales, captured Quezaltenango Sept. 13–14

Oct. 3, Government troops defeated revolutionists at Totonicapan

1898

Feb. 8, President Barrios shot and killed by assassin, Zolinger, in revenge for the execution of his employer, Aparicio, in insurrection of 1897

Feb. 9, Insurrection led by General José Najero begun

Feb. 10, Election for President contested. Candidates Morales, Barrios, and Castillo

Feb. 11, Suspension of constitutional guarantees. Manifesto of Najero

July 25, Invasion of Coronel Prospero Morales took possession of the plaza of San Marcos and proclaimed Licenciado Feliciano Aguilar President

Aug. 17, Death of Morales ended insurrection

Aug. 31, Martial law ended. Congress met and elected Licenciado Estrada Cabrera President

Oct. 2, President Cabrera inaugurated

1899

May 8, Boundary Convention with Mexico signed

1900

Feb. 23, Claims Convention with the United States signed, with supplementary article May 10

1901

April 15, Trade Marks Convention with the United States signed

Aug. 27, Treaty with the United States signed as to tenure and disposition of property

1902

Jan. 29, Treaty of Arbitration with Mexico signed

Feb. 28, Treaty of Arbitration with Spain signed

April 8, Eruption of volcano of Santa Maria destroyed country in the west

1903

Feb. 27, Extradition Treaty with the United States signed

March 24, The Government adhered to the Geneva Convention of 1864

Nov. 21, Railroad joining central, southern, and western departments opened

1904

Oct. 30, Revolt led by General S. Toledo with troops from Salvador

1905

March 15, Dr. Estrada Cabrera inaugurated President

1906

May 27, Invasion led by General Manuel Barrilos. Forces of Salvador, Costa Rica, and Honduras joined insurrection against President Cabrera

June 8–10, Engagements of revolutionists and government troops

June 11, Battle at Ayutla

July 9, Second invasion led by General Tomas Regalado who was killed in battle July 13

July 20, Preliminary Peace Treaty signed on board U.S.S. "Marblehead" with Salvador and Honduras

Sept. 25, Treaty of Peace signed. Provided that future disputes should be submitted to arbitration of the United States or Mexico. *See also* Central America

Nov. 21, Workmen's Protection Act established employers' liability for accident and sickness

1907

Dec. 20, Treaty of peace and amity signed. *See* Central America

1908

Jan. 19, Northern Railroad from Puerto Barrios on the Atlantic to San José on the Pacific formally opened

June 30, New Mining Code signed and promulgated

Nov. 21, Foundation stone of railroad laid at Quezaltenango. To run to Zapala

1910

March 1, Boundary Convention of 1895 with Honduras extended

March 5, President Cabrera inaugurated for second term

1911

Jan. 17, Guatemala signed Central American Parcels Post Convention

1912

March 15, Secretary Knox from the United States arrived at Guatemala City

June 30, New National Military Academy opened in Guatemala City

1913

May 15, Agreement made to pay interest on debt to Great Britain suspended since 1894

May 31, Arbitration Treaty with Italy signed

Sept. 30, Advancement of Peace Treaty with the United States signed

1914

Aug. 1, Boundary Treaty with Honduras signed

Aug. 12, Declaration of neutrality in European War

1916

Feb. 28, Treaty of commerce and navigation with Italy signed

1917

March 15, President Cabrera inaugurated for another six year term

April 27, Diplomatic relations with Germany severed

Sept. 15, National University opened

Nov. 17, Earthquake destroyed city of Amatitlan

Dec. 25–29, Earthquake destroyed Guatemala City

1918

Jan. 3–4, Second earthquake completed destruction of Guatemala City

March 1, Executive decree provided for exemption from military service on payment of fixed sum

April 11, Decree established national bank

April 23, Guatemala joined War against Germany

April 28, Tax placed on spirits to be devoted to reconstruction of the capital city

May 2, Decree established the University of Guatemala. Opened Sept. 15

July 3, Amnesty granted for political crimes committed prior to Dec. 25, 1917

1919

Jan. 4, Decree admitted free of duty all building materials for reconstruction of city

March 5, Martial law in force since declaration of war raised

June 28, Guatemala signed Treaty of Versailles

July 19, New road opened from Quezaltenango to Totoni Capan, altitude 13,000 at places

1920

Jan. 10, Guatemala became original member of the League of Nations

April 7, Revolt begun against President Cabrera on issue of Central American Union which he opposed

April 8, Cabrera deposed by the Assembly. Had been in office since 1898. Carlos Herrera named provisional President

April 12, United States marines occupied Guatemala City to preserve order

Aug. 29, Herrera elected President

Sept. 15, President Herrera inaugurated

1921

Jan. 19, Guatemala signed Treaty of Union

Aug. 6, Revolt headed by General Isidor Valdez suppressed

Dec. 5, Military coup d'état led by General Orellana overthrew the Herrera Government. General Orellana organized a provisional Government Dec. 6

Dec. 8, Former Congress recalled declared all acts of the Herrera Government null and void which in effect destroyed the Central American Union

1922

Jan. 18, Guatemala withdrew from the Central American Union

March 4, President José Maria Orellana inaugurated for six year term

May 25, Act regulating hydrocarbons passed

July 28, Treaty of commerce with France signed

1923

Feb. 13, Public Charities Department to include protection and aid of children, women, and aged persons by decree of government

April 22, Red Cross Society formally established

May 8, Commercial Treaty with France came into effect

June 30, Government controlled Banco Central received contract of sole right to issue paper currency for 10 years

July 4, Amnesty proclaimed by President for military offenders

Sept. 20, Decree changed customs tariff regulations

1924

Feb. 12, American army aviators on good will flight arrived at Guatemala City

Feb. 25 and Nov. 21, Decrees of the President changed law of 1922 on hydrocarbons as to taxes, length of contracts, &c.

Aug. 14, Customs Agreement concluded with the United States

Sept. 10, Commercial Convention with Nicaragua concluded

Sept. 14, Decree established the Exchange Bank

Nov. 7, Treaty of commerce and navigation with the Economic Union of Belgium and Luxemburg signed

Nov. 29, Decree adopted gold standard with the quetzal as the monetary unit

1925

Feb. 23 and May 28, Decree and law by which credit institutions to be regulated signed

March 28, Reforestation decree published

April 2, Law passed by which foreign companies in Guatemala must employ 75% native labor exclusive of technical experts

April 17, Act as to rights of women in matters of property and in exercise of a trade or profession approved by Legislature

Sept. 14, New National Observatory near Guatemala City officially inaugurated

Oct. 5, Radiotelegraph service with Mexico opened

Oct. 29, Decree provided for proof of ownership of land for persons without deeds or registration title

1926

April 30, Labor Act passed dealing with wages, hours, rest days, employment of women and minors, of employed mothers, labor disputes, &c.

June 30, Decree created the Central Bank

——, First book of new Civil Code signed by the President

Sept. 27, Death of President Orellana. General Lazaro Chacon, first designate, assumed office *ad interim* and was elected President Dec. 3–5

Oct. 20, Exchange of notes with France constituted commercial *modus vivendi*

Dec. 18, General Chacon inaugurated as elected President

1927

March 15, President Chacon inaugurated as elected President

April 9, Commercial Convention with the Netherlands signed

May 25, Convention with Honduras and Salvador signed, agreement to act together in matters affecting the general interest

July 30, The Chacon suspension bridge over the Motagua River near San Augustin formally opened

Aug. 30, Forestry law passed providing regulation for granting concessions for exploitation of the national forests

Aug. 31, Decree established immigration restrictions for certain European countries

Sept. 15, Treaty of commerce and navigation with Italy signed

Nov. 8, Death of Don Francisco Sanchez Latour, Minister to the United States

Nov. 22, 400th anniversary of founding of Guatemala City by Alvarado on site of the present Antigua celebrated

Dec. 14, New Organic Law of Public Education promulgated

Dec. 21, Amendment to Constitution promulgated

Dec. 28, Colonel Charles A. Lindbergh arrived at Guatemala City from Mexico

1928

Jan. 1, Constitution as amended came into effect

Jan. 19, Decree created Colonization and Immigration Bureau under the Department of Agriculture

Feb. 22, Commercial Treaty with Great Britain signed

March 26, New law regulations for medical profession

April 12, Mixed Boundary Commission constituted to establish boundary with Honduras

June 4, Executive decree granted free building lots under certain restrictions in 3 sections of Guatemala City to workers

July 19, Guatemala accepted proposal of American Secretary of State Kellogg that boundary dispute with Honduras be submitted to Central American Court

Nov. 10, Executive decree created National Property Bureau

1929

Jan. 17, Revolutionists seized towns of Retalhuleu and Mazatanango

Jan. 22, Government announced revolt suppressed

Feb. 3, Cabinet resigned

Feb. 12, New Cabinet organized

March 11, Diplomatic relations with Nicaragua resumed

June 20, Air mail and passenger service opened between Guatemala City and Quezaltenango

Sept. 11, Aëronautical Bureau created in the Ministry of Promotion

Oct. 10, Air service inaugurated between Vera Cruz and Guatemala City

Nov. 3, 300 persons killed by eruption of volcano Santa Maria

Dec. 4, Decree established National Mortgage Bank

Dec. 29, Railroad between Salvador and Guatemala officially opened at Puerto Barrios

1930

Jan. 20, Boundary conference with Honduras opened in Washington

March 30, First national electric railway officially opened between Quezaltenango and San Felipe

July 16, Treaty signed with Honduras. Agreement to submit boundary dispute to arbitration

July 24, Arbitration award in favor of the United States in Shufeldt claim

Aug. 30, Resignation and reorganization of Cabinet

Sept. 11, Constitutional guarantees restored and state of siege proclaimed in Sept. 1929 lifted

Dec. 13, Bautillo Palma chosen provisional President because of illness of President Chacon

Dec. 16, Government of Palma overthrown by General Manuel Orellana who took office as provisional President

Dec. 22, The United States notified General Orellana that his government would not be recognized

Dec. 31, Orellana resigned and J. M. Andrade appointed provisional President

HONDURAS

Honduras, Republic, bounded on the north by the Caribbean Sea with coast line of 400 miles, on the east by Nicaragua, and south by Nicaragua and the Gulf of Fonseca on the Pacific (coast line 40 miles) and Salvador, and on the west by Salvador and Guatemala; area about 44,275 English square miles with population June 29, 1930 (census) of 859,761, or 19.4 inhabitants to the square mile, wild tribes are estimated to number over 35,000. The inhabitants are chiefly Indians with an admixture of Spanish blood. The Republic is divided into 17 departments and 1 territory. La Mosquitia is still practically unexplored and is inhabited by native races.

The capital of Honduras is Tegucigalpa, with (census of June, 1930) 40,049 inhabitants. Other towns are Pespire, 7,132; Nacaome, 8,152; La Esperanza, 11,453; Santa Rosa, 10,574; Choluteca 8,065; San Pedro Sula, 7,820. The main ports are Amapala on the Pacific, and, on the Atlantic, Puerto Cortez (2,500), Omoa (1,000), La Ceiba, Trujillo, Puerto Castilla, and Tela. The port of entry for the Bay Islands is Roatan.

Dr. Vicente Mejia Colindres, President.

1502

July 30, On fourth and last voyage Columbus landed at Island of Guanaja (or Bonacca) which he named the Isle of Pines

Aug. 14, Columbus first landed on continent of America at Cape Honduras which he named Punta de Casinas and is said to have made attempt at settlement at Trujillo which was destroyed by Indians before he sailed away

Aug. 17, He sailed up the Tinto River and took possession of the country for Spain

1524

Gil Gonzales Davila on his way to Nicaragua made attempt to found a settlement in Honduras east of the Golfo Dulce, Caballos

May 3, Christoval de Olid sent by Cortes from Mexico to explore and conquer Honduras took possession of the country for Spain but in his own name not that of Cortes and established town of Triunfo

1525

April 15, Cortes reached Honduras from Mexico to reconquer the country. Founded the town of Natividad de Nuestra Senora on Caballos Bay

May 18, Trujillo founded by Alcalde Medina

Nov. 20, Diego Lopez de Salcedo appointed Governor

1526

April 25, Cortes left Honduras returning to Mexico

1530

Jan. 3, Death of Governor Salcedo. Of 3 claimants for executive office, Andres de Cerceda, Vasco de Herrera, and Diego Mendez, Cerceda, and Herrera chosen for joint rule

1531

Oct. 8, Unsuccessful uprising in favor of Diego Mendez. Mendez captured and beheaded

1532

Oct. 30, New Governor, Diego de Albitez, took office but died within a fortnight

1539

April 2, Francisco de Montejo appointed Governor arrived

Honduras made an Audiencia of the Captain-Generalcy of Guatemala

1540

Alonzo de Caceres founded town of Comayagua which was then called Valladolid

1740

Aug. 30, Royal decree established Fort San Fernando de Omoa on the coast near Puerto de Caballos

1779

Sept. 25, Fort San Fernando de Omoa repulsed English attack

Oct. 20, Second attack of English on Omoa in war between Spain and France successful. Took and looted town

Nov. 26, Spaniards led by Governor of Guatemala recaptured Omoa

1820

April 21-23, Unsuccessful attack of Colombian vessels on Trujillo

April 25-May 6, Unsuccessful attack of Colombians on Omoa

Nov. 25, Armistice signed by Bolivar with General Morillo (royalist)

1821

Oct. 16, Independence of Spain declared

Dec. 1, Patriots supported by Guatemalan force deposed Spanish Governor Tinoco who had declared for annexation to Mexico

1823

May 10, The provincial assembly resolved to enter into the union with the other provinces of Central America

1824

July 1, Independent Constitution adopted

Sept. 16, State Constituent Assembly elected Dionisio Herrera chief of State and Jose Justo Milla vice-chief

Oct. 3, Charter for government adopted

Dec. 11, Constitution promulgated

1827

April 4, Milla supported by Arce in effort to overthrow the Liberal Party began siege of Comayagua

May 9, Surrender of Comayagua, the capital city. President Herrera sent as a prisoner to Guatemala. Francisco Morazan, Liberal, managed to escape

Sept. 13, New legislature appointed Geronimo Zelaya chief but he was not generally recognized

Nov. 11, Morazan victorious in battle at Trinidad

Nov. 16, F. Morazan took temporary control of the Government

1828

June, Geronimo Zelaya, Governor

1829

April, Diego Vijil, Vice-Jefe acted as Governor

Dec., Juan Angel Arias, acted as Governor

1830

Jan. 21, Olancho rebels surrendered to General Morazan at Las Vuellas and bound themselves to obey the Government

Feb. 19, Morazan routed insurgents at Opoteca

July, José Santos del Valle, Governor

1831

March, José Ant. Marquez, Governor

Nov. 21, Ramon Guzman of the Servile party seized fort at Omoa supported by invasion of Arce

1832

Feb. 24, Arce defeated at Escuintla de Soconusco

March 9, Dominguez who had seized Trujillo in Nov. defeated at Tercales

March 26, Dominguez defeated by government troops at Jaitique

March, Francisco Milla, Governor, after death of Marquez

May 5, Dominguez defeated at Opoteca and taken prisoner

Sept. 12, Omoa surrendered by rebels

Sept. 14, Dominguez executed

1833

Jan., Joaquin Rivera, Governor until Dec. 31, 1836. F. Ferrera acting Governor in Sept. and J. M. Bustillo in Sept. 1835

1837

Jan., J. M. Martinez acted as Governor

1838

Oct., Leon Alvarado, Governor

Oct. 7, Constituent Assembly met at Comayagua

Oct. 26, Honduras declared secession and independence of Guatemala

Nov. 5, Act of secession and independence reaffirmed

Nov., Lino Matute, Governor

1839

Jan., Juan F. Molina, Governor

Jan. 11, Constitution amended

Jan. 18, Treaty of alliance with Nicaragua against Salvador signed

April 6, The allied troops of Honduras and Nicaragua defeated by Salvadorians under Morazan at Espiritu Santo

May, José M. Guerrero, Governor

May 11, Treaty of amity and alliance with Guatemala

July 1, Treaty of friendship and alliance with Costa Rica concluded

Aug. 28, Morazan's General Cabanas occupied the capital

Sept. 6, Defeat of Hondurans at Cuesta Grande by Federalists

Sept., Francisco Zelaya, Governor

1840

Jan. 31, Nicaraguans and Hondurans defeated Federalist army of General Cabanas at the hacienda del Potrero and forced them to leave Honduras

Dec. 30, Francisco Ferrera elected President

1841

Jan. 1, Francisco Ferrera inaugurated as first constitutional President

1842

Dec. 31, Francisco Ferrera reëlected President

1843

Jan. 11, State Assembly installed

July 1, Santos Guardiola defeated rebels at Corpus

Dec., Insurrection of troops at Olancho

Dec. 16, Treaty signed with the King of the Mosquito Indians

1844

July 10, Treaty with Salvador signed

Dec. 31, Coronado Chavez elected President

1845

Jan. 4, Rivera, Martinez, Landa, and Julian Diaz in invasion leading revolt against the Government captured and brought to Comayagua in irons and were shot

Nov. 27, Treaty of peace with Salvador signed ending the war

1847

Jan. 14, Juan Lindo chosen President to succeed Chavez. Ferrera continued as commander of the army

1848

Feb. 4, Constitution of the Republic promulgated, allowed freedom of religion

March 10, Treaty of commerce and navigation with the Hanseatic Republics signed

Sept. 28, Tigre Island ceded conditionally to the United States; returned in 1850

1849

Oct. 4, The British landed an armed force at Trujillo to enforce claim of her citizens for $111,061

Nov. 8, Alliance with Salvador and Nicaragua which went into effect Jan. 9, 1851

Nov. 16, British ship seized Island of Tigre and raised British flag at Amapala Nov. 30 in demand of money due; returned Dec. 26

Dec. 29, Preliminary Claims Convention with Great Britain signed by Felipe Jauregui and British chargé Chatfield. Disavowed by Honduran Government in 1850

1850

Feb. 12, Guardiola made pronunciamento against the Government. Lindo fled but invoked aid of Salvador and Nicaragua as allies and Guardiola not supported

March 25, Guardiola submitted to authority of President Lindo

Aug., Lieutenant Jolly took formal possession of the Bay Islands for Great Britain

Sept. 15, Honduras protested act of Great Britain in seizing the Bay Islands

Nov., Alliance with Salvador against Guatemala

1852

Feb. 1, President Lindo reëlected assumed office for a third term but stated his wish to resign

March 1, Trinidad Cabanas inaugurated as elected President

March 20, The Bay Islands, Ruatan, Bonaca and others erected into a British colony by royal warrant and held for several years

March 27, Claims settlement with Great Britain. Honduras agreed to pay $80,000

1853

July 6, Honduran troops under V. Cerna defeated at Chiquimula, Guatemala

Aug. 24, Omoa taken by Guatemalans under Colonel Zavala

1855

July 6, Revolution headed by General S. Guardiola supported by Guatemala overthrew Cabanas government

Oct. 14, Vice-President S. Bueso assumed the executive office. He turned it over to Senator Francisco Aguilar

1856

Feb. 17, General Santos Guardiola, henchman of Carrera, took office as elected President

July 18, Treaty of alliance with Guatemala and Salvador signed

Aug. 27, Treaties with Great Britain signed as to Bay Islands and of friendship, commerce, and navigation

1859

Aug. 9, Convention with Guatemala agreement to recognize the constitutional authority in Salvador

Nov. 28, Treaty with Great Britain signed by which Great Britain ceded the Bay Islands and Mosquito Reserve claims

1860

Aug. 6, Walker on third filibustering expedition to Central America landed at Trujillo and seized the custom-house

Aug. 20, Walker forced by British ships to leave Trujillo

Sept. 3, Honduran troops with aid of British captured William Walker at mouth of the Tinto River

Sept. 12, Walker executed

1862

Jan. 11, President Guardiola assassinated. Succeeded by constitutional successor Victoriano Castellanos

March 25, Treaty of Santa Rosa signed with Salvador

Oct., Death of President Castellanos. Succeeded temporarily by J. F. Montes

1863

April 29, Honduran and Salvadorian troops defeated by Nicaraguan General Martinez

June 16, Honduran and Salvadorian troops defeated by allied Guatemalans and Nicaraguans on plains of Santa Rosa

June 21, The Serviles assisted by Guatemalans and

Nicaraguans overthrew Montes and made Senator José Maria Medina provisional President

July 20, Decree of outlawry against Montes

Dec. 31, Medina surrendered executive office to Francisco Inestroza

1864

Feb. 15, J. F. Medina elected President and F. Xatruch, Vice-President. The election of Xatruch declared unconstitutional Feb. 26, 1865

July 4, Treaty of friendship, commerce, and navigation with the United States signed

1865

Sept. 28, Constitution amended by Constituent Assembly, Roman Catholicism the State religion to exclusion of other faiths

Oct. 29, Constituent Assembly appointed Medina provisional President and fixed date of election for Dec. 1

——, Decree granted amnesty for all political offenses since Feb. 4, 1848

1866

Feb. 1, President Medina reëlected, inaugurated

Feb. 16, Congress decreed change in flag and coat of arms

1868

Feb. 21, Congress established the order of *Santa Rosa y de la Civilizacion de Honduras* promulgated on the 24th

Dec. 31, Treaty of commerce and navigation with Italy signed

1869

June 15, Convention of extradition with Italy signed

1870

Feb. 1, President Medina reëlected, inaugurated

Sept. 1, Boundary Convention with Nicaragua signed

1871

Feb. 7, Decree announced suspension of all treaties with Salvador because of unfriendly acts and treaty violations

March 5, War declared on Salvador

March 17, Hondurans occupied Sensunte and presently Ilobasco

April 10, President Duenas defeated by Hondurans at Santa Anna led by General Santiago Gonzales (Salvadorian) and deposed. *See* Salvador

May 11, Xatruch leading Salvador troops in invasion of Honduras announced intention to leave the country, ending insurrection against Medina

Aug., Revolt of Indians begun

Dec. 13, Agreement with rebel leaders and Indians ended insurrection

Dec. 18, Convention of offensive and defensive alliance with Salvador signed

1872

March 9, General Espinosa, commanding Salvadorian army, occupied Tegucigalpa

March 25, Honduras severed diplomatic relations with Salvador because of refusal of Salvador to pay war indemnity

May 9, Invading Salvador troops defeated Honduran General Velez

May 27, President Medina defeated in attempt to capture Comayagua occupied by Salvadorians
July 20, Omoa surrendered to Salvadorian General Antonio Medina supporting Celeo Arias for President of Honduras
——, President Medina defeated at Potrerillos
July 26, President Medina defeated at Santa Barbara escaped to Omoa where Antonio Medina had proclaimed himself provisional President
Aug. 9, José M. Medina, ex-President, Crescencio Gomez taken prisoners, arrived at Comayagua

1873

June 9, Trujillo surrendered to revolutionary invasion from Colon led by E. Palacios, C. Alvarado, and Miranda Baraona
Aug. 9, Miranda's forces defeated by Guatemalan commander General Solares on north side of the Chamelecon River, Alvarado and Colonel A. Munoz killed
Aug. 19, British warship bombarded Omoa in consequence of looting of revolutionists
Nov. 23, Ponciano Leiva set up a government at Choluteca supported by Guatemala and Salvador as provisional President in place of Arias
Dec. 14, Congress refused to accept resignation of Arias as President

1874

Jan. 6, Allied troops of Guatemala and Salvador began siege of Comayagua
Jan. 13, Arias at Comayagua forced to surrender to besieging forces and the Leiva Government took possession

1875

Feb. 1, President Leiva inaugurated as constitutional President
Dec. 21, Ex-President Medina began revolt at Gracias proclaiming himself provisional President

1876

Feb. 15, The presidents of Salvador and Guatemala met at Chingo and made arrangements to intervene in Honduras
Feb., Battle of Naranjo a decisive victory for President Leiva
June 8, Treaty of peace signed at Los Cedros. Executive office went to Marcelino Mejia who transferred it to Crescencio Gomez
Aug. 12, Gomez transferred executive office to Medina who refused to take the office
Aug. 18, Marco Aurelio Soto made provisional President
Aug. 27, President Soto inaugurated

1877

May 30, President Soto inaugurated constitutional President

1878

Feb. 8, Ex-President Medina, and General Ezequel Marin shot at Santa Rosa after attempt to start a revolt late in 1877
Feb. 25, Debt agreement with Great Britain concluded
March 13, Treaty of commerce and extradition with Nicaragua signed
March 31, Treaty of commerce and extradition with Salvador signed

1880

Feb. 11, Decree created National Library. Officially opened Aug. 27
July 17, Treaty of commerce and extradition with Guatemala signed
Nov. 1, New Constitution promulgated
Nov. 2, National capital removed to Tegucigalpa
Dec. 27, President Soto reëlected

1881

Aug. 23, Boundary Treaty with Salvador signed

1882

Sept. 15, The Government sanctioned plan of Central American Union

1883

Feb. 19, National Assembly met. President Soto again installed as President
March 10, Resignation of President Soto not accepted. Granted leave of absence
May 9, President Soto placed the executive office in charge of the council of ministers, Enrique Gutierrez, Luis Bogran, and Rafael Alvarado and departed for Europe
Sept. 3, President Soto's resignation due to quarrel with President Barrios of Guatemala, sent from San Francisco, accepted
Nov. 30, General Luis Bogran inaugurated as President

1885

March 7, Resolution in favor of Central American Union adopted
April 11, Treaty of alliance with Costa Rica signed

1886

Sept. 28, Boundary Treaty with Salvador

1887

Jan. 21, Treaty of amity, commerce, and navigation with Great Britain signed
Nov. 30, General Luis Bogran inaugurated for second presidential term
Dec. 12, Treaty of commerce, navigation, and consular relations with Germany signed

1888

May 15, Land Law enacted abrogating all previous laws
Sept. 24, Mining Law enacted

1889

Jan. 24, Boundary Treaty with Nicaragua

1890

May 28, Death of Celeo Arias
Nov. 2, Revolution led by General Sanchez begun at first successful but the insurgents defeated Nov. 13–15 and Sanchez captured and shot

1891

Feb. 5, Meeting of Liberals decided to elect Bonilla President
Nov. 10, General Pariano Leiva elected President. Inaugurated Nov. 30
Dec. 12, Insurrection proclaimed Bonilla President

1892

March, Revolution of Liberals led by Leonardo Nuila proclaiming Bonilla President

1893

Jan., Bonilla in second campaign defeated successively at Tatumbla, Tegucigalpa, La Cuestra, Cedros, Guaimaca, and El Salto

April, President Leiva resigned in favor of General Domingo Vasquez

Sept. 15, President Vasquez inaugurated as constitutional President

Dec. 24, Dr. Policarpo Bonilla organized a provisional government

1894

Jan. 23, Rebels attacked Tegucigalpa but were at first repulsed

Feb. 22, Rebels with aid of Nicaraguans took Tegucigalpa and President Vasquez forced to leave. Dr. Bonilla proclaimed President

Oct. 7, Boundary Treaty with Nicaragua

Oct. 14, Constitution amended

Nov. 17, Treaty of peace and amity with Spain signed by which independence of Honduras recognized

1895

Jan. 19, Boundary Treaty with Salvador

Feb. 2, Dr. Bonilla inaugurated as constitutional President

March 1, Boundary Treaty with Guatemala

March 10, Treaty of commerce, navigation, and arbitration with Guatemala signed

June 20, Honduras signed pact of union with Nicaragua and Salvador, agreement to establish a common political organization for their external relations

1897

April 13, Revolutionists seized the towns

1898

May 16, Adherence to Geneva Convention of 1864

Aug. 27, Constitution for the United States of Central America signed with Nicaragua and Salvador

1899

Feb. 1, General Terencio Sierra succeeded Dr. Bonilla as President

1902

Feb. 11, Commercial Convention with France signed

Dec. 25, Presidential decree established stage coach line from Tegucigalpa to Sabanagrande to begin Jan. 1

1903

Jan. 30, President Sierra and a number of members of Congress fled to Salvador and a new Congress proclaimed Dr. Juan Angel Arias President and General M. B. Rosales, Vice-President

Feb. 1, General Manuel Bonilla inaugurated President

Feb. 22, General Bonilla defeated in battle at El Aceituno by ex-President Sierra

Oct. 14, President Bonilla convoked a constitutional congress and proclaimed the political code of 1880

1904

Feb. 8, Coup d'état

Sept. 2, New Constitution promulgated

1905

May 13, Arbitration Treaty with Spain signed

1906

Feb. 8, Immigration law enacted

July 20 and Sept. 25, Through the mediation of the United States and Mexico treaties of peace, amity, and commerce signed which ended war with Guatemala and Salvador. *See also* Central America

Dec. 23, Award in boundary dispute with Nicaragua

1907

Feb. 19, President Bonilla began war with Nicaragua on the frontier, aiding revolt of Davila against his Government. Salvador joined him

Feb. 20, Nicaraguans captured El Triunfo

Feb. 21, Nicaraguans captured San Bernardo

Feb. 25, Nicaraguans captured San Marcos de Colon

March 18, American marines landed at Trujillo and at Ceiba to protect American interests

March 18–24, Battle of Choluteca

March 25, Nicaraguans occupied the capital

April 11, President Bonilla surrendered at Amapala to President Zelaya of Nicaragua and was taken to Mexico on an American gunboat

April 23, Treaty of peace signed

April 24, Provisional Government established by Davila

Aug. 15, General Miguel R. Davila inaugurated President

Dec. 20, Treaty of peace and amity signed. *See* Central America

1908

Feb. 1, President Davila inaugurated as constitutional President

March 2, Dept. of Agriculture organized

March 24, Treaty of friendship, commerce, and navigation with Mexico signed

1909

Jan. 15, Treaty of extradition with the United States signed

Feb. 1, Apology sent to Guatemala by the President for derogatory reference to Guatemala in message to Congress

March 1, Boundary Convention with Guatemala due to expire on this date extended

March 25, Treaty of commerce and navigation with Belgium signed

April 26, Treaty of arbitration with Brazil signed

May 5, Treaty of commerce and navigation with Great Britain signed

July 22, Attack of supporters of Bonilla led by General R. O. Marin on barracks at Puerto Cortés

Dec. 18, Census gave population as 553,446

Dec., Revolt led by General Bonilla begun

1911

Jan. 10, Convention signed in Washington for conversion of foreign debt by which the United States guaranteed a loan without assuming financial protection; not ratified

Feb. 1, M. R. Davila inaugurated as President

Feb. 2, Congress refused to approve negotiations for American loan of $1,000,000

Feb. 8, Armistice arranged between President Davila and General Bonilla, rebel leader. Agreement to abide by election

Feb. 18, Manuel Bonilla, Lee Christmas, and 2 others indicted in New Orleans, U.S. of A. for violation of neutrality laws in connection with filibustering expedition of the gunboat "Hornet"

March 4, President Taft tendered offices of the United States for restoration of peace at request of President Davila

March 19, Government troops defeated in engagement at Puerto Cortés

March 28, President Davila resigned and Congress appointed Francisco Beltran provisional President

April 18, Extradition Convention with the United States signed

Oct. 29, Manuel Bonilla elected President

1912

Jan. 9, American marines landed in Honduras to protect American property

Feb. 2, General Bonilla inaugurated President, Francisco Bertrand Vice-President

Feb. 9, The railroad from Puerto Cortés to Camayagua taken over by the Government on ground that W. S. Valentine had failed to fulfil terms of contract

March 1, Rebel leader Villadares led invasion from Salvador and captured Aramecina

1913

March 1, Bank of Commerce opened

March 21, Death of President Bonilla. Succeeded by Vice-President Bertrand

Nov. 3, Advancement of Peace Treaty with the United States signed

1914

April 1, Law required the establishment of primary schools in factories having more than 100 employees and distant 2 kilometers from public school

1915

July 27, Treaty with Salvador providing for freedom of trade

Aug. 1, Boundary Treaty with Guatemala signed

Aug. 1–Feb. 1, 1916, Alberto Membreño, first designate, in executive office

1916

Jan. 1, Foreign debt owed £25,407,858

March 19, Government troops defeated in battle with revolutionists

March 28, Dr. Francisco Bertrand inaugurated elected President, Alberto Membreño, Vice-President

Dec. 7, Arbitration award of King of Spain in regard to La Masica affray

1917

May 17, Diplomatic relations with Germany severed

1918

Jan. 10, Loan Convention with the United States signed; failed of ratification by United States Senate

Feb. 28, Commercial Treaty with Salvador signed

April 5, Boundary Treaty with Salvador signed, ratified by Congress April 13

April 21, Resolution adopted as to World War to take same attitude as the United States

July 19, Declaration of war on Germany

Legislation enacted during the year included municipal treasury law, pharmacy law, and law establishing bounties for cultivation of fibrous plants

1919

March 22, Law provided regulations for registration of trade-marks

Aug. 3, Revolt led by Lopez Gutierrez against President Bertrand in the Departments of Gracios, Comayagua, and Choluteca

Sept. 8, President Bertrand resigned his office to Council of Ministers and fled from the country

Sept. 11, American marines landed at Puerto Cortés to protect lives and property

Sept. 14, Francisco Bogran appointed Provisional President

Oct. 26, Gutierrez, victorious rebel leader, elected President

1920

Feb. 1, President Gutierrez inaugurated

May 4, Executive Decree provided for establishment of a Superior Board of Health

Nov. 3, Honduras became a member of the League of Nations

Nov. 17, Agreement with Nicaragua signed for surveillance of political refugees

1921

Jan. 19, Honduras signed Pact of Central American Union. *See* Central America

Feb. 2, Death of Dr. Alberto Membreño, statesman

Feb. 5, Honduras the first Central American State to ratify the Federation

1922

Feb. 11, Honduras withdrew from the Central American Federation, Pact rejected by National Assembly

Feb. 15, Martial law declared

April 22, Protest made against occupation of Swan Island by the United Fruit Company (American)

April 27, Revolutionists took Tegucigalpa

April 28, War ended and peace signed May 3

May 30, The Government signed contract for 25 years with the Bank of Honduras whereby the Bank became the Bank of the Republic with a capital of 2,000,000 pesos of which the Government to provide one-fifth. Notes of the Bank to be recognized as currency

Population according to census 673,408, including 332,371 men and 341,037 women

Aug. 20, Conference on board the U.S.S. "Tacoma." Treaty of peace and friendship of Dec. 20, 1907 reaffirmed with Nicaragua and Salvador. *See* Central America

Nov. 15, Honduras gave notification of withdrawal from the League of Nations because of onerous dues but reconsidered

1923

March 29, Decree removed basic customs duties from all automobile vehicles for a period of 5 years

Oct. 28–30, General Tiburcio Carias, Conservative, elected President

Dec. 27, First hydro-airplane to make landing in Honduras arrived at Bay of Puerto Cortés inaugurating mail service with Guatemala and British Honduras

1924

Feb. 1, Dictatorship proclaimed by Lopez Gutierrez

——, General Carias proclaimed himself President and marched on capital

Feb. 13, Diplomatic relations severed by the United

States because of failure of political factions to agree to use constitutional means to restore the government

Feb. 13, General Carias within 25 miles of capital

Feb. 29, American marines landed at La Ceiba to preserve order

March 1, General Gregorio Ferrara (Indian) in rebellion invested capital

March 10, Death of Lopez Gutierrez. General F. Davila proclaimed Provisional President March 27

March 19, Tegucigalpa taken by the rebels

March 31, Rebels occupied the capital

April 24, Conference of revolutionists with representatives of the Government at Amapala and preliminary peace agreement signed May 1

May 3, Pact of Amapala signed by representatives of Costa Rica, Guatemala, Nicaragua, and Salvador and the United States signed on board U.S.S. "Milwaukee" for restoration of peace in Honduras

Aug. 9, Revolt of City of Amapala against Provisional Government headed by General Vicente Tosta led by General Gregorio Ferrera

Sept. 10, New Constitution promulgated to take effect Oct. 3 abrogating that of Oct. 1894

Oct. 9, Press law enacted

Oct. 28, Ferrera revolutionists finally defeated at Chinchayote

Dec. 28–30, Election of Dr. Miguel Paez Barahona for President and P. Quesada, Vice-President

1925

Jan. 1, Homestead Agrarian law governing division of national lands became effective

Feb. 1, President Barahona inaugurated

April 20, American marines landed at La Ceiba to protect lives and property

July 21, Regulations for motion picture censorship issued

Aug. 7, Agreement to submit to arbitration of the United States the boundary dispute with Nicaragua

Oct. 29, Agreement signed for settlement of British debt

1926

March 4, Treaty of commerce with Germany signed

March 26, Code of agrarian procedure governing transference of national lands signed by the President

April 3, Law passed adopted gold standard, the monetary unit to be the lempira equivalent to $.50

April 9, The President authorized to establish a Bank of the Republic

July 29, New lands opened for homestead lots and colonization projects

Sept. 1, Regulations for amortization of internal debt went into effect

1927

May 25, Honduras signed Central American pact. *See* Central America

Oct. 14, Death of M. R. Davila, former President

Dec. 7, Treaty of friendship, commerce, and consular rights with the United States signed replacing that of 1864

1928

Jan. 3, Colonel Charles A. Lindbergh flew from San Salvador to Tegucigalpa

Feb. 22, Act created a Superior Court of Accounts

Feb. 27, Primary Teachers Pension Act passed

April 12, Boundary Commission installed

April 25, Law provided for free nonsectarian public education, compulsory for children between 7 and 15

July 19, Agreement with Guatemala to arbitrate boundary dispute

——, Executive decree condemned as an attempt on the peace of the Republic all propaganda tending to promote revolution or subversive move against a recognized government in any Central American Republic

July 27, Honduras refused to submit boundary dispute with Guatemala to the Central American Court. Suggested the President of the United States as arbiter

Oct. 28, Dr. Vicente Mejia Colindres, Liberal, elected President, and Rafael Diaz Chavez, Vice-President

Nov. 26, President Elect Hoover delivered "good will" speech at Amapala

1929

Feb. 1, Dr. Vicente Mejia Colindres inaugurated President, and Rafael Diaz Chavez, Vice-President

March 11, New immigration law approved by President

Nov. 26, Municipal election resulted in Liberal victory in 175 out of 273 municipalities

Nov. 30, Announcement that Spanish experts were to be employed to cultivate grape vines on large scale and produce native wine

1930

Jan. 30, Commercial Treaty with Nicaragua signed

April 25, President refused to accept resignations of Ministers of Education, Foreign Affairs, War, Interior, and Public Works

May 25, First Congress of journalists met at Tegucigalpa

June 29, Government declared martial law in 4 departments along the Atlantic coast because of communist activities

July 16, Treaty with Guatemala provided for settlement of boundary disputes by arbitration

NICARAGUA

Nicaragua, largest Republic of Central America, bounded on the north by Honduras, on the south by Costa Rica, by the Caribbean Sea on the east, and the Pacific Ocean on the west. The name is probably derived from name of leading chief in 1522, Nicarao. The Republic is divided into 13 departments and 2 "comarcas." The Mosquito Reserve forms a department named Bluefields.

Area estimated at 51,660 English square miles, with a coastline of about 300 miles on the Atlantic and 200 miles on the Pacific. The population, according to the census of 1920, was 638,119. Estimated population in 1930, based on registration of voters, 750,000. This is the most thinly populated of the Central American republics. At least 75% of the inhabitants live in the western half of the country. The two halves of the Republic differ greatly in many respects and there is little communication between them, the journey by trail and river being so slow and difficult that passengers usually go by way of Costa Rica, while the small amounts of merchandise shipped from one side to the other are sent mainly by way of Panama.

The people of the western half of the Republic are principally of mixed Spanish and Indian extraction, though there are a considerable number of pure Spanish descent and many Indians. The population of the eastern half is composed mainly of Mosquito and Zambo Indians and Negroes from Jamaica and other islands of the Caribbean, with some Americans and a comparatively small number of Nicaraguans from the western part of the Republic.

There are within the Republic 105 municipalities of which 28 have from 2,000 to 30,000 inhabitants. The capital and seat of government is Managua, situated on the southern border of the lake of the same name, with (1926) 32,536 inhabitants. León, formerly the capital, had a population of 23,565; Granada, 18,066; Matagalpa, 10,271; Masaya, 13,763; Jinotega, 6,990; Chinandega, 10,307; Rivas, 4,081; Esteli, 4,583; Matapa, 4,561; Somoto, 6,182; Boaco, 4,342; Jinotepe, 6,317; Diriamba, 6,151; Bluefields, 4,706. Other towns are Corinto, 2,307; Cabo-Gracias; and San Juan del Sur on the Pacific.

General Don José Maria Moncada, President.

1502

Sept. 12, Columbus rounded and named Cape Gracias a Dios and coasted Nicaragua
Sept. 25, Columbus landed at mouth of the Rama River and took possession of the country for Spain

1519

Espinosa sent expedition from Panama under Castaneda which reached the Gulf of Nicoya

1522

Jan. 21–June 25, 1523, Joint expedition of Andres Nino and Gil Gonzales Davila explored coast and interior of Nicaragua on voyage from Panama, landing at Chiriqui
April 17, Nino and Gonzales in battle with the Indians

1523

Francisco Hernandez de Cordova with Hernando de Soto sent from Panama by Pedrarias to subdue Nicaragua founded Leon on the edge of Lake Managua

1524

Granada founded by Hernandez de Cordova and at Urutina on Gulf of Nicoya

1526

March, Pedrarias arrived at Leon and beheaded Cordova who had set up government independent of Panama

1527

May 7, Salcedo, Governor of Honduras, inaugurated Governor of Nicaragua at Leon
May 16, Pedrarias Davilla commissioned Governor of Nicaragua

1528

March, Pedrarias arrived at Leon and imprisoned Salcedo
Dec. 25, Salcedo released from prison departed for Honduras

1529

Expedition of Estete sent by Pedrarias to find the outlet to Lake Nicaragua descended the San Juan River to within sight of the sea

1530

July, Death of Pedrarias. Francisco de Castaneda assumed office as Governor

1531

Diego Alvarez Osorio appointed first bishop of Nicaragua

1535

Nov., The new governor Rodrigo de Contreras arrived at Leon

1536

Alonso Carrero and Diego Machuco explored the San Juan and tributary branches

1542

Nov. 20, Royal decree created Audiencia for Nicaragua and Guatemala. Opened May 16, 1544 at Gracias a Dios, Panama

1576

Spanish royal cedula conveyed Mosquito coast to Captain Diego Lopez and Diego Garcia de Palacios to be colonized and governed under explicit regulations

1660

First white settlement made on the Mosquito coast by representatives of an English chartered company of which John Pym was the treasurer and the Earl of Warwick the head

1700

Administration of Pablo de Loyola, first Governor of which any record according to Bancroft during this period. Succeeded by Miguel de Camargo, and José Calvo de Lara

1721

Sebastian de Aransivia y Sasi, Governor

1722

Antonio Poveda, Governor

1728

Tomas Duque de Estrada, Governor

1730

Bartolome Gonzales Fitorio, Governor

1740

April 8, Robert Hodgson from Jamaica arrived on the Mosquito shore, assembled the Indians and took possession of the country for Great Britain

1744

José A. Lacayao de Briones, Governor

1757

Melchior Vidal de Larca y Vellena Vivas, Governor

1759

Colonel Pantaleon Ibanez named as Governor in office in an official report at this time

1760

Alonso Fernandez de Herrera, Governor

1763

Feb. 10, By the Treaty of Paris Great Britain agreed to demolish all fortifications erected on the Mosquito coast as well as in "all other places in the territory of Spain in that part of the world"

1766

Domingo Cabello, Governor

1780

Jan., San Juan surrendered to Captain Horatio Nelson after siege of 10 days

1783

José Estacheria, Governor

1786

July 14, Convention between Great Britain and Spain by which Great Britain gave up Mosquito coast to Spain; evacuated by British July 6, 1787

1810

Jan. 29, Establishment of the Council of the Regency on the Island of Leon

1811

Dec. 11, Insurrection at Leon deposed the intendente
Dec. 22, Granada joined the revolt

1812

Jan. 1, Royal decree established the University at Leon. Opened in 1814
Jan. 8, Insurgents captured Fort San Carlos. Royalists fled to Masaya to wait for aid from Bustamente
April 21, Royal force from Guatemala arrived at Granada
April 28, Spanish royalists entered Granada

1814

Aug. 28, Treaty of Madrid by which provisions of Convention of 1786 confirmed

1821

Sept. 15, Declaration of independence of Spain of Central American colonies
Oct. 11, Leon declared secession from Guatemala
Oct. 21, Leon accepted the Iguala Plan which provided for annexation to Mexico

1823

March 29, Decree of national Government called for a national Congress and declared Nicaragua united with other provinces which had formerly been the reino de Guatemala
April 17, Governing junta at Leon headed by Basilio Carrillo for that province. Cleto Ordonez and Juan Arguello ruled at Leon, Bishop Garcia at Managua

1824

Jan. 13, Insurrection in Leon placed Carmen Salazar at head of junta

July 22, Ordonez had himself proclaimed commandante general by garrison
Aug. 6, Revolt against Ordonez unsuccessful
Aug. 9, Governing Junta established at El Viejo in opposition to that at the capital
Aug. 14, Force from Managua under Colonel Crisanto Sacasa captured part of city of Granada
Aug. 24, Leonese and Granadans attacked Managua

1825

Jan. 4, End of unsuccessful siege of Leon of 114 days by troops from El Viejo and Managua commanded by Sacasa and the Colombian Juan José Salas
Jan. 22, Managua surrendered to Manuel José Arce from Salvador who entered State as a peacemaker
April 10, First constituent assembly met
April 20, Manuel Antonio de la Cerda installed as Governor and Juan Arguello as Vice-Governor
April 23, King of the Mosquito Indians christened Robert Charles Frederick and taken to Belize by British and crowned with ceremonies

1826

April 8, Constitution of the State of Nicaragua promulgated
Aug. 13, National Assembly met at Leon. Cerda presently impeached and Arguello took office pending new elections which Arguello managed to prevent. Cerda did not accept his removal and set up a government at Managua

1827

Feb., Assembly dissolved by Arguello
Sept. 14, Third or fourth unsuccessful attempt of Colonel Cleto Ordonez to overthrow the Arguello Government

1828

Nov. 8, Cerda captured at Rivas
Nov. 29, Cerda executed

1829

Nov. 1, Assembly installed

1830

May 23, Dionisio Herrera, chief of Honduras, who had undertaken pacification of the State under instructions of the Federal Government, in 1829, elected President

1832

Dec. 3, State Assembly declared secession from the Confederation, attaching the federal revenue

1833

March 1, Herrera resigned in face of revolt of Managua, Masaya, and Matagalpa but was reinstated 4 days later
June 29, Taking of Managua by government troops ended revolution

1834

May, Rebellion in Granada and at Metapa under C. Flores
Aug. 13, Rebels defeated and Granada recovered

1835

Jan. 20, Terrific earthquake and eruption of the volcano Cosiguina

Feb. 21, Assembly declared José Zepeda President and José Nunez Vice-President

April 23, President Zepada inaugurated

1837

Jan. 25, Revolt of garrison at Leon led by Braulio Mendiola. President Zepada murdered. Suppressed and Mendiola executed. Nunez assumed the executive office

1838

April 30, Nicaragua seceded from the Federal Confederation

Nov. 12, New Constitution promulgated of the Republic of Nicaragua

1839

Jan. 18, Treaty of alliance with Honduras against Salvador. *See* Honduras

June, Patricio Rivas, *ad interim* President

July, Joaquin Cosio *ad interim* President

July 24, Treaty of alliance with Guatemala

Oct., Senator Hilario Ulloa in charge of the Government

Nov., Senator Tomas Valladares *ad interim* President

1840

Feb., Will of the King of the Mosquito Indians provided that his country be administered by Colonel MacDonald, Superintendent of Belize. Patrick Walker assigned to residence at Bluefields under this document

Sept., Patricio Rivas, *ad interim* President

1841

March 4, Pablo Buitrago inaugurated constitutional President

Aug. 12, Colonel MacDonald brought King of the Mosquito Indians to San Juan del Norte and notified Spaniards of British protectorate

Aug. 15, Spanish Lieutenant-Colonel Quijano imprisoned by MacDonald for refusal to recognize British authority over coast "from Cape Honduras down to the mouth of the River San Juan"

1842

April 11, Declaration of the Convention at Chinandega established a Central American provisional government

July 27, Pact of Chinandega signed by Nicaragua with Salvador and Honduras established the Confederacion Centro Americano

Aug. 19–Jan. 23, 1843, British blockade of San Juan to enforce claims

1843

April 1, Juan de Dios Orozco succeeded Buitrago as provisional President. Later Manuel Perez chosen constitutional President by the Assembly

June 10–Nov. 1, Second British blockade of San Juan to enforce claims

Dec. 16, Honduras in Treaty recognized Mosquito Nation as independent of Nicaragua

1844

Nov. 14, Invasion of Nicaragua by forces of Honduras and Salvador

Nov. 21, Treaty of Zacata made peace with Salvador

and Honduras, but the people of Leon refused to accept the degrading terms

Nov. 26, Bombardment of Leon begun

1845

Jan. 20, Blas Antonio Saez assumed the executive office at San Fernando made the seat of government

Jan. 24, Leon fell in assault of Guardiola and city given over to soldiers for plunder and prominent citizens shot by order of Malespin

April 4, José Leon Sandoval declared elected President

May 6, Treaty of peace with Salvador signed

June 24, Revolt at Leon suppressed by General Munoz

July 26, Munoz repulsed an attack on Leon

July 29, Chinandega captured by insurgents led by José M. Valle

Aug. 16, Munoz reoccupied Chinandega

Nov. 26, Valle recaptured Chinandega but was defeated by government force under Guardiola

1846

Aug., British blockaded port of Realejo in enforcement of claims

1847

April 6, José Guerrero inaugurated as elected President

Oct. 28, Treaty with the Princess Inez recognition of authority of Nicaragua over the Mosquito reserve

1848

Jan., British warships occupied the port of San Juan, ousted the Nicaraguan officials, and placed Robert Hodgson in charge as Governor of the Mosquitos

March 12, Nicaraguans defeated in battle with the English on the Mosquito coast

1849

April 1, Norberto Ramirez took office as Supreme Director

June 14, Bernabe Somoza in revolt defeated by J. T. Munoz and captured at San Jorge

June 17, Somoza executed

Aug. 27, Contract with American Atlantic and Pacific Maritime Canal Company

Sept. 22, Charter granted for a canal to a New York company

Oct. 9, Temporary cession of the Island of Tigre to the United States

1850

April 19, Clayton-Bulwer Treaty between the United States and Great Britain provided that neither should occupy, fortify, or colonize or exercise dominion over any part of Central America or make use of a protectorate

July 25, Treaty of commerce and navigation with Spain signed by which the independence of Nicaragua recognized

Aug. 27, Colonel O. W. Childs arrived and began survey for canal

Dec. 4, War begun by Salvador and Honduras and Nicaragua against Guatemala

1851

May 5, Laureano Pineda inaugurated as Director

Aug. 4, Revolt led by J. T. Munoz at first successful

Nov. 10, Leon held by Munoz taken by government troops and Munoz exiled went to Salvador

1852

Oct. 13, National Constitutent Assembly adopted a provisional constitution

1853

April 1, General Fruto Chamorro elected Director

April 30, Legislative Assembly rejected Constitution of 1852

May 6, The Executive authorized to enter into colonization contracts

Nov., Revolt in Leon led by Liberals Castellon, Jerez, and Mariano Salazar suppressed

1854

Feb. 28, Decree assumed for the State the title of Republic of Nicaragua and gave executive title of President

April 21, Decree established flag and coat of arms

April 30, New Constitution adopted

June 11, Castellon proclaimed himself Director at Leon beginning civil war

July 13, Commander Hollins bombarded San Juan and burned the town because of alleged insults to American minister Solon Borland

1855

March 12, Death of President Chamorro. José Maria Estrada made *ad interim* President

June 13, The American filibuster William Walker invited by the Democrats in revolt at Leon arrived at port of Realejo with force from San Francisco and was made a colonel in the Nicaraguan army

June 27, Walker repulsed in attack on Rivas

Aug. 18, Engagement at El Sauce between Guardiola and Munoz a victory for the Democrats until Munoz killed

Aug. 29, Walker landed at San Juan

Sept. 2, Death of Castellon of cholera. Senator Nazario Escoto succeeded him as head of Democratic Government

Sept. 2-3, Guardiola made unsuccessful attack on Walker at La Virgen

Oct. 11, General Pineda at Pueblo Nuevo attacked by government troops (Legitimists) and driven from the place

Oct. 13, Walker took Granada in surprise attack and made himself master of Nicaragua

Oct. 23, Treaty between Walker and General Corral representing the Government practically a capitulation ended the war. P. Rivas made provisional President, Walker commander of the army. Corral became Minister of War

Oct. 28, Estrada dissolved his government and left the country

Oct. 30, Patricio Rivas inaugurated President; not recognized by United States

Nov. 5, Corral arrested for opposition to Walker and executed on the 8th

Nov. 23, Colonization decree granted each immigrant 250 acres of the public land and 100 additional to each family

1856

March 1, Costa Rica declared war on Walker to free Nicaragua from foreign domination

March 20, Louis Schlesinger sent by Walker against invading Costa Ricans defeated in Battle of Santa Rosa

April 8, Costa Ricans occupied Rivas evacuated by Walker

April 11, Battle of Rivas. Walker attacked Rivas and was defeated. He retreated to the Gil Gonzales River

May 14, The United States received Father Augustin Vigil as minister from Nicaragua which was of advantage to Walker

May, Walker occupied Rivas evacuated by Costa Ricans

June 21, Legitimate President Estrada organized a government at Somotillo

June 25, President Rivas declared Walker a usurper and traitor and ordered officers and men of foreign phalanx to renounce Walker and submit to the government

July 3, Rivas, who had been deposed by Walker who placed Fermin Ferrer in the executive office, issued appeal to the other Central American States for aid against Walker

July 12, Walker inaugurated as President at Granada

July 18, Convention signed by Guatemala, Honduras, and Salvador by which it was agreed to join forces against Walker

Aug. 13, At Ocotal Estrada attacked and defeated by party of Democrats, Estrada killed. Nicasio del Castillo succeeded Estrada as Legitimist President

Sept. 12, Legitimists and Democrats united against Walker recognizing Rivas as President

Sept. 14, Troops commanded by C. J. Dolores Estrada defeated Walker's troops commanded by Byron Cole at San Jacinto

Sept. 22, Walker decree repealed all laws as to abolition of slavery

Oct. 3, Masaya occupied by the Allies

Oct. 12, Attack of Walker on Masaya repulsed

Nov. 2, Costa Ricans commanded by General José M. Canas occupied San Juan and the road to La Virgen cutting Walker's communications

Nov. 13, General Canas occupied Rivas

Nov. 15-18, Walker's army commanded by Bruno von Naztmer and later by Walker himself defeated in second attack on Masaya by Nicaraguans and Guatemalans who forced him to retreat to Granada

Nov. 24, Granada evacuated and the city burned by Walker

———, Allies from Masaya defeated in engagement with Walker's forces

Dec. 1, Indians captured the Island of Ometepec from Walker's guard

Dec. 11, First Honduran troops arrived under command of General Florencio Xatruch

Dec. 21, Costa Ricans commanded by Coronel Barillier and M. M. Blanco took Fort Trinidad in the province of Estero

Dec. 24, General J. J. Mora (Costa Rican) captured 4 of Walker's steamers at San Juan

Dec. 28, General Mora took Castillo Viejo with steamer "Virgen" loaded with rifles and ammunition for Walker

Dec. 30, Costa Ricans captured forts on the San Carlos River

1857

Jan. 3, Costa Ricans captured another of Walker's boats

Jan. 20, Council of 5 ministers installed, organized by the Provisional Government on the 20th

Jan. 23, General F. Xatruch made temporary commander-in-chief of Allied armies

Feb. 6, Commander C. H. Davis of the U.S.S. "Saint Mary's" offered to mediate

Feb. 19 and 20, Orders made General J. J. Mora commander-in-chief of the Allied armies, ending dissensions. Took command at San Jorge March 19

March 23, Allies began siege of Walker in Rivas

March 26, Xatruch took the barrio de la Puebla south of Rivas, the only means of entrance and exit for the filibusters

April 11, Attack on Rivas repulsed by Walker

May 1, Walker surrendered to American Commander Davis, signed capitulation and with 16 officers left under escort of Zavala and were embarked for the United States the following day

May 2, Allies occupied Rivas

June 24, Generals Martinez and Jerez organized joint Government recognized by both Democrats and Legitimists which lasted until Oct. 19

Oct. 19, Costa Rica declared war on Nicaragua, planning to extend her boundaries to the Lake

Nov. 8, Constituent Assembly elected Tomas Martinez President

Nov. 15, President Martinez inaugurated

Nov. 25, William Walker landed at Greytown in second invasion

Dec. 8, Walker with 400 men arrested by American Commander Paulding at Punta da Castilla and sent back to the United States

——, Boundary Treaty with Costa Rica signed

1858

Jan. 16, Peace with Costa Rica concluded and boundary agreement

May 1, Governments of Nicaragua and Costa Rica granted concession to Felix Belly representing a French company for an interoceanic canal

May 3, Decree changed coat of arms

Aug. 19, Constitution adopted

1859

April 11, Treaty of amity, commerce, and navigation with France signed

1860

Jan. 28, Treaty with Great Britain signed by which the Mosquito coast from Gracias a Dios to Greytown surrendered to Nicaragua

Feb. 11, Treaty of amity, commerce, and navigation with Great Britain signed

April 2, Contract with Central American Transportation Company for construction of route between the Atlantic and Pacific Oceans

Aug. 6, Walker landed at Trujillo, Honduras on third invasion. Shot Sept. 12. *See* Honduras

Nov. 23, Decree made San Juan del Norte (Greytown) a free port

1861

Nov. 2, Concordat with Rome concluded

1862

Sept. 20, Treaty of amity and defensive alliance with Guatemala signed

1863

Feb. 28, President Martinez inaugurated for second term

April 29, Martinez gained victory against partisans of Jerez and Salvadorians at San Felipe engaged in war with Salvador as ally of Guatemala

Aug. 31, Martinez returned from the war and resumed the executive office

1864

April 20, Amnesty law passed

1865

March 7, Liberal immigration law enacted under which a number of southern Americans settled in the country after the Civil War

1867

March 1, Fernando Guzman succeeded Martinez as President

June 21, Treaty of friendship, commerce, and navigation with the United States signed

1868

March 6, Treaty of commerce and navigation with Italy signed

March 17, Treaty of friendship and commerce with Salvador signed

Oct. 6, Ayon-Chevalier contract signed by Nicaragua for inter-oceanic canal

1869

June 26, Revolt at Leon of Maximo Jerez, Ex-President Martinez, Hilario Oliva, and Pascasio Bermudez

June 27, Provisional Government organized by insurrectionists with Jerez at head but on the 29th he resigned in favor of Francisco Baca taking command of the army himself

July 28, Government troops commanded by General Urtecho made unsuccessful attack on insurgents in Correvientos and Chocoya or Metapa

Aug. 12, Death of General J. D. Estrada

Sept. 12, President Guzman took command of the army leaving Senator Pedro Joaquin Chamorro as Acting President

Oct. 13, Insurgents defeated in attack on Matagalpa

Oct. 14, Insurgents defeated by Guzman at Niquinohomo

Oct. 24, Convention signed through mediation of the American Minister General C. N. Riotte which ended war. Rebels surrendered

Nov. 25, President Guzman resumed the executive office

Dec. 17, Decree of the President reëstablished the Constitution from Jan. 1. 1870

1870

June 25, Extradition Treaty with the United States signed

1871

March 1, Vicente Quadra inaugurated elected President

1873

Feb. 12, Vote of Chamber of Deputies in favor of permitting Jesuits exiled from Guatemala to remain in the country

March 12, Death of Ex-President Martinez

Aug. 26, Defensive alliance with Guatemala and Salvador concluded

1874

Feb. 13, Treaty of friendship, commerce, peace, and extradition with Guatemala

March 30, Decree as to acquisition of real estate by foreigners

Nov. 3, Revolutionists led by Tinoco left Costa Rica and landed in San Bernardo, Honduras to invade Nicaragua

Dec. 6, Tinoco surrendered to Nicaraguan government force

1875

March 1, Pedro Joaquin Chamorro inaugurated as President

May 8, New law regulating acquisition of unoccupied public lands by foreigners

Nov. 17, Decree of expulsion and partial banishment announced against a number of persons to quiet the country

1878

March 3, Treaty of friendship, commerce, and extradition with Honduras signed

1879

March 1, General Joaquin Zavala inaugurated President

1881

Jan. 1, Railroad from Corinto to Chinandega opened

May 6, Indian insurrection in Matagalpa instigated by Jesuits

June, Jesuits expelled from the country after instigation of revolt at Leon

July 2, Award in favor of Indians in interpretation of Treaty of Jan., 1860

1882

July, Revolt at Gracias a Dios

1883

March 1, Adan Cardenas inaugurated President

1884

Dec. 1, Zavala-Frelinghuysen Treaty signed with the United States as to canal; treaty withdrawn by President Cleveland March, 1885

1885

March 1, The Pacific Railroad reached Granada

March 8, Congress adopted resolution against Central American Union

March 22, Alliance with other States against Barrios

April 5, The Pacific Railroad opened from Managua to Masaya

April 15, Peace with Guatemala

1886

Dec. 24, Arbitration Boundary Treaty with Costa Rica

1887

March 1, Coronel Evaristo Carazo inaugurated President

1888

March 22, Award of President Cleveland declared Ayon-Chevalier contract of 1868 valid

1889

Jan. 24, Boundary Treaty with Honduras

Feb. 20, Maritime Canal Company of Nicaragua incorporated, and organized May 4 (American)

Aug. 30, Death of President Carazo. Roberto Sacasa became ad interim President

1891

March 1, Roberto Sacasa inaugurated President

1893

Jan. 7, Metric system of weights and measures established

April 28, Revolutionists seized the barracks at Masaya

May 20, Government troops decisively defeated at Masaya

June 1, President Sacasa resigned turning over executive office to Salvador Machado

July 11, Liberal insurrection at Leon

July 24, Bombardment of Granada

July 25, Managua taken by insurgents

July 30, Peace signed at Managua

Sept. 15, General Zelaya proclaimed President by Constituent Assembly

Dec. 10, Constitution promulgated

1894

Feb. 1, President Zelaya inaugurated elected President

Feb. 10, Nicaraguan soldiers occupied Bluefields in war with Honduras

Feb. 12, Martial law declared at Bluefields

March 3, Agreement arrived at for temporary provisional government of the Mosquito Reserve of Nicaraguan commissioner, Captain Howe (British) and American consul

Aug. 8, Force sent which ended rebellion on Mosquito coast

Oct. 7, Boundary Treaty with Honduras

Nov. 20, Mosquito Indians voluntarily surrendered autonomy

Dec. 17, Mosquito Reservation formally incorporated with Nicaragua in Department of Zelaya

1895

Feb. 26, British Government demanded £15,500 for damages in connection with Mosquito coast

March 19, Great Britain demanded reparation for expulsion of British representative at Bluefields

April 27, British occupied port of Corinto and seized the custom house

April 28, Nicaragua agreed to accept terms of British ultimatum and pay indemnity. British squadron retired from Corinto

May 16, Indemnity paid to Great Britain

June 20, Pact of Amapala signed. See Central America

1896

Feb. 4, Treaty of commerce and navigation with Germany signed

Feb. 12, Revolt of clerical party proclaiming Vice-President Baca President

March 1, Rebels attacking Nagarote repulsed after 8 hour battle

March 27, Boundary Treaty with Costa Rica signed

April 18, Rebel stronghold of Tablon captured

May 1, Capture of Felix Quinonez, rebel leader, followed by surrender of Leon

May 2, Official announcement of suppression of revolt, British and American marines withdrawn

Oct. 15, Constitution amended

1897

Feb. 1–6, Exchange of notes with Great Britain as to Mosquito claims

Sept. 17–24, Revolt against the Zelaya Government suppressed

Sept. 30, Award of General Alexander in boundary dispute with Costa Rica in favor of Nicaragua

1898

Feb. 1, President José Santos Zelaya inaugurated for a second term

May 16, Adherence to Geneva Convention of 1864

June 24, Constituent Assembly met at Managua

Aug. 27, New Constitution promulgated

1899

Feb. 4–27, Insurrection led by General Juan Pablo Reyes in Bluefields ended with surrender of Reyes to American and British warships

April 19, Nicaragua took possession of Bluefields

May 6, American Minister made temporary arrangement as to funds paid by American merchants to Reyes insurgents pending negotiations with the United States

Oct. 10, Contract of Maritime Canal Company declared forfeit on ground of non-fulfillment within 10 years' period stipulated in the contract

1900

March 22, Claims Treaty with the United States signed

Nov. 6, Treaty of commerce and navigation with Mexico signed

Nov. 30, American Canal Commission presented report to the President of the United States favoring Nicaragua canal route

Dec. 1, Interoceanic Canal Treaty with the United States signed

1902

Jan. 20, American decision in favor of Panama route for interoceanic canal instead of through Nicaragua. *See* United States

Jan. 27, Commercial Convention with France signed

Feb. 1, President Zelaya inaugurated for third term

1904

Aug. 21, Conference at Corinto. *See* Central America

Oct. 4, Arbitration Treaty with Spain signed

1905

March 1, Extradition Treaty with the United States signed

March 30, New Constitution promulgated

April 19, New Treaty of Managua signed with Great Britain

July 28, Treaty of commerce and navigation with Great Britain signed

1906

March 6, Arbitration treaties with Belgium and Guatemala signed

April 17, President Zelaya inaugurated for another term

Dec. 20, Nicaragua refused to sign Treaty of Sept. 25

with other Central American States because of objection to Treaty of Jan. 20, 1902 as to arbitration

Dec. 23, Award of King of Spain in boundary dispute with Honduras

1907

Jan. 9, Refusal of Nicaragua to be bound by Treaty of July 20, 1906. *See* Central America

Feb. 19, War with Honduras. *See* Honduras

April 23, Treaty of peace, amity, commerce, and arbitration with Salvador signed

Dec. 20, General Treaty of peace and amity signed with the other Central American Republics. *See* Central America

1908

Dec. 7, Naturalization Treaty with the United States signed

1909

March 12, The United States severed diplomatic relations because of treatment of Americans by President Zelaya

May 25, Protocol with the United States signed provided for submission of Emery Company claims to arbitration

July 17, Arbitration Treaty with Portugal signed

Oct. 8, Revolution against Zelaya led by General Estrada in coast towns

Oct. 10, Conservatives proclaimed Juan J. Estrada provisional President and organized a de facto Government

Oct. 24, Insurgents successful in battle on San Juan River

Nov. 2, Americans serving in Estrada army, L. R. Cannon and Leonard Grace, captured and executed

Nov. 18, American gunboats ordered to Nicaragua after execution of Americans entitled to receive treatment of prisoners of war

Dec. 1, The United States severed diplomatic relations with the Zelaya Government and recognized the Estrada Government

Dec. 16, President Zelaya resigned and Congress appointed Dr. Madriz President

Dec. 18, The U.S.S. "Des Moines" prevented fighting at Bluefields thus aiding the Conservatives

Dec. 20, American troops landed at Corinto

Dec. 21, President Madriz inaugurated

Dec. 23, Conservative victory at Rama

Dec. 24, Zelaya left the country for Mexico

1910

Jan. 29, Government troops defeated by Conservatives (insurgents)

Feb. 4, President Madriz defeated Conservatives at Santo Tomas

Feb. 18, Conservative victory at San Vicento

Feb. 22, Government troops defeated General Chamorro. Estrada forced to leave Bluefields

May 8, The Bureau of American Republics received appeal claiming to represent 90% of the Nicaraguan people asking intervention of the United States

Aug. 20, President Madriz resigned naming J. D. Estrada brother of the Conservative leader as his successor

Aug. 21, Coronel José Dolores Estrada took office as President at Managua

Aug. 29, President Estrada inaugurated at the capital as provisional President

Sept. 15, Constitution suspended on account of revolution and a law issued for government of the country

Nov. 6, Agreement with United States provided for convention that should elect Provisional President Estrada as President and loan to Nicaragua

Nov. 10, Dawson Pacts signed with the United States

Nov. 27–28, Elections held. General Juan J. Estrada elected President, and Adolfo Diaz Vice-President

Dec. 31, Congress confirmed the election of Estrada as President. Estrada Government recognized by the United States

1911

Jan. 1, President Estrada inaugurated

——, Diplomatic relations with Nicaragua renewed by the United States

Feb. 13, Martial law declared after explosion in government barracks at Managua

March 29, Mixed Claims Commission with the United States signed

April 5, President Estrada dissolved the Assembly because of its control by opposition leader General E. Chamorro

May 9, Resignation of President Estrada because of dispute with Mena, Minister of War

May 10, Vice-President Diaz assumed the presidency

May 31, As a result of a plot of the Liberal Party Fort Loma blown up and 60 persons killed

June 6, Loan Convention with the United States signed, the "Knox-Castrillo" Treaty. Not ratified by American Senate

June 17, Naturalization Treaty with the United States signed

Sept. 1, Loan for $1,500,000 negotiated with Brown Brothers and J. and W. Seligman and Company of New York City at 6%

Oct. 7, Luis Mena elected President by the Assembly in contravention of the Dawson Agreements which provided for free election by the people

Oct. 26, New Ministry appointed

Nov. 7, C. D. Ham, American citizen, designated as Collector General of customs by New York bankers

Dec. 21, New Constitution promulgated to take effect March 1, 1912

1912

Jan. 1, President Mena inaugurated. His election declared invalid

March 5, Secretary Knox from the United States arrived at Corinto

March 12, New Constitution promulgated, came into effect April, 1913

March 20, Monetary Law enacted which provided for gold standard and adopted cordoba as monetary unit

March 26, Claims Convention began sessions

——, New York bankers made another loan of $755,000 for 6 months at 6%

July 29, Mena deposed began revolution. Diaz assumed office as President

July 30, Revolt supporting Mena at Managua

Aug. 4, American gunboat "Annapolis" landed marines near Managua for protection of American citizens and property

Aug. 7, U.S.S. "Tacoma" arrived at Bluefields

Aug. 11, General Zeledon supporting Mena began bombardment of Managua

Aug. 14, American Major Smedley D. Butler arrived at Managua. American marines landed at Corinto

Aug. 19, Rebels took Leon. Massacre of 500 government troops taken prisoners

Aug. 31, Government troops won decisive victory over rebels

Sept. 4, American marines took control of the national railway from Managua to Corinto to keep communications open

Sept. 25, Revolutionary General Mena surrendered to American Admiral Southerland. Allowed to leave Nicaragua on American war vessel at Granada

Oct. 4, American marines captured insurgent position near Masaya, the Barranca forts. Rebel General Zeledon killed in flight after this engagement

Oct. 6, Leon surrendered by the rebels to American force

Oct. 25, United States troops withdrawn except 400 marines left at Managua

Nov. 2, Adolfo Diaz elected President, Fernando Solorzano, Vice-President

1913

Jan. 1, President Adolfo Diaz inaugurated

Jan. 9, American troops withdrawn except Legation guard

Feb. 8, Weitzel-Chamorro Treaty signed respecting Canal. Failed of ratification by American Senate

Feb. 10, New coinage and currency established unit of the cordoba equal to $1

April 5, New Constitution came into effect

April 19, General Luis Mena released from detention at Panama. Proceeded to Costa Rica

Oct. 8, Another $1,000,000 loan from Brown Brothers and the J. W. Seligman Company arranged

Nov. 24, Gold basis for currency adopted

Nov. 26, J. S. Zelaya former President arrested in New York City after conviction for murder in Nicaragua

Dec. 17, Advancement of Peace Treaty signed with the United States

1914

June 24, Protocol signed with Mexico

Aug. 5, Treaty with the United States (Bryan-Chamorro) signed by which the United States paid $3,000,000 for control of the canal route proposed and certain strategic islands

Aug. 14, 500 American marines landed at Bluefields to preserve order during revolt

Oct. 8, Moratorium law passed

Nov. 20, Law placed direct and proportional tax on capital

Dec. 5, Nicaragua proclaimed neutrality in European War

1915

Jan. 1, New direct tax placed on all kinds of property and business

March 18, Act provided for free exportation of sugar from the Atlantic coast

April 2, Revolt suppressed by government troops

1916

April 13, Canal Treaty with the United States of 1914 ratified

Sept. 30, Decision of Central American Court that Canal Treaty with the United States violation of rights of Costa Rica

Oct. 1, Emiliano Chamorro elected President

1917

Jan. 1, President Chamorro, Conservative, inaugurated

March 2, Decision of Central American Court of Justice

in favor of Salvador in case brought by Salvador against Nicaragua on account of lease of Gulf of Fonseca to the United States

March 2, New Agrarian law promulgated

March 9, Nicaragua denounced Treaty of 1907

April 18, Diplomatic relations with Germany severed

July 23, New tax placed on wines and liquor imported

Aug. 31, Financial plan of Government for complete reorganization of finances adopted by Congress

Oct. 20, Agreement signed with foreign bondholders reorganizing and consolidating debt

1918

Jan. 21, Forestry law enacted

March 1, New tariff came into effect

May 8, Nicaragua declared war on Germany and Austria

1919

Feb. 21, Law provided for judges to hear cases relating to labor and agriculture

June 8, Nicaragua asked the United States for troops for protection against invasion of Costa Ricans

1920

June 20, Treaty with Costa Rica provided for reciprocal use of waters near frontier

Oct., Government loan negotiated with J. and W. Seligman and Company and Brown Brothers of New York City for $9,000,000 to be used in construction of a railroad from the Atlantic to the Pacific Ocean

Nov. 3, Nicaragua became original member of the League of Nations

1921

Jan. 1, Diego Chamorro inaugurated President and B. Martinez, Vice-President

Feb. 26, United States marines who wrecked newspaper plant sentenced to 2 years' imprisonment and discharge

Aug. 23, War declared against armed bands invading the country from Honduras

Nov. 11, Rebels repulsed in attack on Santillo

Dec. 10, Clash between American marines and civilians at Managua. 3 Nicaraguan police killed.

Dec. 30, American marines tried by court-martial for part in affair at Managua and sentenced to 10 years' imprisonment at hard labor

1922

Jan. 24, Fighting between American marines and Nicaraguan police at Managua

May 21, Slight uprising against the Government

Aug. 11, Attacks of Liberals and refugees at Chinandego and Leon repulsed

Aug. 15, Government forces defeated rebels 12 miles from Managua

Aug. 20, Conference of presidents of Honduras, Salvador, and Nicaragua on board U.S.S. "Tacoma" at request of Nicaraguan Government. Reaffirmed Treaty of peace and friendship of Dec. 20, 1907. See also Central America Dec. 20

1923

Jan. 31, Labor law enacted

March 20, Electoral law enacted

Oct. 12, Death of President Diego M. Chamorro. Succeeded by Vice-President Martinez Bartolo

1924

March 6, Treaty of commerce with Germany of 1896 extended

March 21, Decree created Upper Board of Education

July 14, Commercial modus vivendi established with the United States

Aug. 1, The Government repurchased 51% of stock of national railways

Oct. 9, Decree published provided regulations for pearl fishing

Dec. 22, British-Nicaraguan Claims Commission met at Bluefields

1925

Jan. 1, Dr. Carlos Solorzano, Conservative-Republican inaugurated President, Juan B. Sacasa, Vice-President, Liberal

Feb. 7, Official statement that the cordoba, unit of currency, would be equal to the American gold dollar

March 20, Patent law promulgated

March 25, Resignation of Cabinet

March 26, Public Health law enacted. Created a National Bureau of Public Health

Aug. 3, American marines stationed in the country since 1912 withdrawn

Aug. 28, New Cabinet appointed

Aug. 29, Armed men opposed to Liberals in new Cabinet seized the Finance Minister and other prominent Liberals. Released the next day through offices of United States Minister

Oct. 25, Coup d'état of General Emiliano Chamorro took Fort Loma, Managua and forced resignation of Vice-President Sacasa and eventually of President Solorzano

Oct. 26, Peace agreement by which Government to be Conservative. All Liberals expelled from the Cabinet, and Chamorro named "designate" for the presidency

Dec. 6, Pharmacy and Pure Food law enacted

Dec. 19, Ex-Vice-President Sacasa arrived in Washington to lay his case before the Secretary of State of the United States

1926

Jan. 12, Congress impeached Vice-President Sacasa who had fled from the country after the coup d'état of Oct. 25, and declared him banished for 2 years

Jan. 14, President Solorzano resigned

Jan. 17, Chamorro declared elected President by Congress

Jan. 22, Secretary of State Kellogg informed Nicaragua that the United States would not recognize the Chamorro Government on ground of usurpation

Feb. 18, Law provided for recognition of religious marriages. By former law only civil marriages recognized

April 30, Highway Labor Construction law published. Provided that all male residents over 18 should contribute to construction and maintenance of roads

May 2, Liberal revolt led by General Sandino in name of Sacasa captured Bluefields and Rama

May 4, Government declared state of war. United States marines landed at Bluefields

June 5, American marines withdrawn

June 8, State Department (United States) served notice that the United States would not recognize Chamorro and withdrew American Minister

Aug. 28, Admiral Latimer landed American marines at Bluefields to protect life and property of foreigners

Sept. 1, Rebels defeated in battle near Coseguima

Sept. 15, United States placed embargo on export of arms to Nicaragua

Sept. 23, Agreement for 17 days' armistice signed

Oct. 16–24, Conference at Corinto on board U.S.S. "Denver"

Oct. 26, Written agreement declared Bluefields a neutral zone

Oct. 30, Hostilities resumed. President Chamorro resigned turning over the executive office to Sebastian Uriza

Nov. 5, Earthquake damaged property to value of $4,000,000

Nov. 11, Congress elected Adolfo Diaz, Conservative, President

Nov. 14, President Diaz inaugurated

Nov. 17, Diaz Government recognized by the United States

Dec. 2, Former Vice-President Sacasa, Liberal leader, inaugurated "constitutional president" by his supporters, landed at Puerto Cabezas

Dec. 7, American warships ordered to Nicaraguan ports to prevent importation of munitions by Sacasa rebels

——, Mexico recognized the Sacasa Government

Dec. 8, Chamorro resigned as commander-in-chief of the army

Dec. 11, Manifesto of the President accused Mexican Government of aiding Liberal revolution

Dec. 18, Salvador recognized the Diaz Government

Dec. 19, President Diaz declined offer of Guatemala of Dec. 8 of mediation with rebels

Dec. 23, American marines landed at Puerto Cabezas, rebel capital, taking possession and at Rio Grande Bar and established neutral zones at request of the President

Dec. 28, Conservative forces defeated by rebels in 3 day battle at Laguna Las Perlas

1927

Jan. 6, American marines sent from Corinto to Managua as "legation guard"

Jan. 11, American marines established neutral zone at mouth of the Wawa River

Feb. 6, Liberal forces captured city of Chinandega. Retaken by government troops Feb. 9

Feb. 19, Forestry law amended

Feb. 21 and March 7, American marines landed on west coast at Corinto to guard railroad

Feb. 25, Contract with United States Government made for sale of arms and munitions

March 14, Liberals defeated government troops at San Geronimo

March 25, Government loan for $1,000,000 negotiated in New York City

April 17, Henry L. Stimson arrived in Nicaragua as personal representative of President Coolidge to discuss situation; began conferences with President on the 18th

April 18, Matagalpa declared a neutral zone

April 22, President Diaz agreed to make peace with rebel leaders and grant general amnesty on certain specified conditions including supervision of an election by Americans

April 30–May 1, Conference of Mr. Stimson and representatives of Señor Sacasa

May 4, Conference of Mr. Stimson with rebel General Moncada in Tipitapa resulted in acceptance of peace terms of President Diaz

May 5, Government decree granted amnesty to all political offenders since Oct. 25, 1925

May 11, Mr. Stimson gave written promise of American supervision of election of 1928 and that certain reforms would be carried out by the President

May 12, General Moncada and other Liberal leaders accepted terms of the President. Not accepted by General Sandino

May 13, Marine patrol fired on at El Paso

May 16, American marines at La Paz attacked by Nicaraguans

June 3, Executive decree prohibited carrying of concealed weapons

June 7, Law provided for government export and slaughter of cattle

June 30, Rebels under Sandino attacked and seized gold mine owned by an American and took dynamite

July 1, Nicaraguan Claims Commission established

July 16, Rebel General Sandino attacked American marines at Ocotal near Honduran border

July 30, Decree provided for organization of a national guard to take over duties of police force

Aug. 24, American General McCoy arrived at Managua to supervise election

Sept. 8, American marines in engagement with rebels

Oct. 9, Engagement of patrol with rebel band of 300

Oct. 12, 7 of men of Santos Lobos captured at Pueblo Nueva and Santos Lobos killed

Oct. 27, Engagement of patrol with rebels at Jicaro

Nov. 23, American marines took part in engagement at Telpaneca

Nov. 29, Dr. William W. Cumberland designated by American State Department to make financial and economic survey of Nicaragua

Dec. 18, Patrol attacked near Macuelizo

Dec. 22, Agreement signed with the United States for creation of a national constabulary with assistance of American Navy and Marine Corps

Dec. 30, Marine patrol proceeding from Matagalpa to Quilai ambushed by rebels

1928

Jan. 5, Charles A. Lindbergh flew to Managua

Jan. 30, 1,000 American marines sent to Nicaragua

Feb. 29, American marines ambushed by rebels. 5 killed and 8 wounded

March 7, Nicaraguan Senate passed amended draft of temporary electoral law to provide for American supervision of election according to Stimson agreement

March 13, Electoral law rejected by Chamber of Deputies by 24 to 18

March 21, President Diaz by decree provided for supervision of presidential election by General McCoy as chairman of National Board of Elections

March 24, Treaty with Colombia and the U.S. awarded Mosquito coast and Great and Little Corn Island to Nicaragua, the latter leased to the United States

April 12, Raid of Sandinistas on American owned mines in Pis-Pis district

May 13, Engagement with rebels at Paso Real

May 31, Colonel C. D. Ham resigned as Collector General of Customs

July 26, American airplane patrol fired on near Honduras border by Sandino rebels

Aug. 11, President Diaz issued decree promising amnesty to all rebels who would surrender by Sept. 15

Aug. 27, American marines in engagement with rebels near Maculezo

Nov. 4, Elections held under supervision resulted in election of General José Maria Moncada, Liberal, for President by a large majority, Adolfo Benaro, Conservative, Vice-President

Nov. 27, Herbert Hoover, President-Elect of the United States, arrived at Corinto on good will visit

1929

Jan. 1, President Moncada inaugurated at Managua, first Liberal in office since 1910

Feb. 3, Government declared rebellion suppressed

March 9, Manuel Maria Jiron, Sandino leader, captured and executed by General Juan Escamillo

March 11, Diplomatic relations with Guatemala resumed

June 29, Rebel General Sandino arrived at Vera Cruz, Mexico in exile

Sept. 5, American Secretary of War Good named Interoceanic Canal Board headed by Lieutenant General Edgar Jadwin with engineering battalion to survey a route for proposed interoceanic canal

Nov. 1, Municipality of Managua created a national district by presidential decree

1930

Feb. 12, Government asked the United States to nominate an American citizen as permanent chairman of National Board of Elections

May 1, Colonel Charles A. Lindbergh flew from Cristobal, Canal Zone, to Porto Cabezas, Nicaragua

May 12, Captain A. W. Johnson nominated by the United States chairman of the National Board of Elections

July 9, Decree raised state of siege in 5 northern departments

July 17, Commercial Treaty with Honduras signed

Aug. 20, Amnesty decree of President

Nov. 2, Congress elected

Nov. 13, Martial law established in certain districts for protection against bandits

Dec. 31, Sandino guerrillas made surprise attack on patrol between Ocotal and Apali. 8 American marines killed

PANAMA

Panama, former Department of Colombia, declared independence Nov. 3, 1903, which was recognized by the United States Nov. 6, and by Colombia in 1914. The Republic is bounded on the north by the Caribbean Sea, on the east by Colombia, south by the Bay of Panama and the Pacific Ocean, and west by Costa Rica. Geographically Panama is part of Central America occupying the narrowest part of the narrow intercontinental strip of land between the Atlantic and Pacific oceans, and is divided into 2 parts by the Panama Canal Zone (see Panama Canal Zone, p. 386).

Extreme length is about 480 miles; breadth between 37 and 110 miles; coast line, 477 miles on the Atlantic and 767 on the Pacific; total area is 32,380 square miles; population according to the census of 1930 (excluding the Canal Zone),

467,459, of whom 52,000 were white, 86,000 Negroes, 33,500 Indians, 3,000 Orientals, and 268,000 mestizos or mixed. There are approximately 40,000 British subjects in the Republic, chiefly colored, from the West Indies. There are 9 provinces with populations (1930) as follows (the capitals in parentheses):—Bocas del Toro (Bocas del Toro), 15,851; Coclé (Penonomé), 48,244; Colón (Colón), 57,161; Chiriquí (David), 76,918; Los Santos (Las Tablas), 41,218; Panama (Panama City), 114,103; and Veraguas (Santiago), 69,543; Herrera (Chitré), 31,030; Darien (La Palma), 13,391. The capital, Panama City, founded in 1518, on the Pacific coast, had (1930) about 60,000 inhabitants, and Colón on the Atlantic coast (1930), 31,940. Smaller ports on the Pacific are Aguadulce, Pedregal, Montijo, Puerto Mutis, and Puerto Armuelles; on the Atlantic, Bocas del Toro, Portobello, and Mandinga.

Florencio Harmodio Arosemena, President.

1501

Rodrigo de Bastidas coasting South America from Venezuela reached Porto Bello

1502

Oct. 6, Columbus entered Bay named in his honor Admiral or Almirante but now known as Bocas del Toro

Nov. 2, Columbus entered the harbor of Porto Bello which he named and tried to leave Colonists but they were attacked by Indians and forced to return to the ships

Nov. 23, Columbus driven into port which he named El Retrete where he remained until Dec. 5

1503

Jan. 7, Columbus reached the mouth of the Belen River which he named Santa Maria de Belen and established settlement he called Nombre de Dios. This was abandoned in April because of the hostility of the Indians

1509

Nov. 20, Diego de Nicuesa appointed Governor of Veragua (Castilla del Oro) sailed from Santo Domingo to Cartagena (Colombia) and established his colony at mouth of the Belen River

1510

Nicuesa left Belen River for better site. Driven from Puerto Bello by Indians, made permanent settlement Nombre de Dios

After the departure of Ojeda from San Sebastian (Colombia) for aid the relief ship of Martin Fernandez de Encisco arrived and Encisco taking charge moved the colonists to Darien called Santa Maria de la Antigua del Darien

Nov., Relief ship of Rodrigo de Colmenares arrived and informed Nicuesa of settlement of Ojeda's colonists at Darien within his grant and their invitation to Nicuesa to assume government. See also America

Dec., Insurrection of colonists at Antigua del Darien against Encisco placed Vasco Nunez de Balboa in charge

1511

March 1, Vasco Nunez refused to surrender government to Nicuesa who had arrived and placed him on ship for Hispanola which was lost at sea

1513

Sept. 6, Vasco Nunez started journey across the Isthmus, the first white man

Sept. 25, Vasco Nunez climbed that "peak of Darien" and viewed the Pacific Ocean

Sept. 29, Vasco Nunez took possession of the Pacific Ocean for Spain. Named Gulf of San Miguel

1514

June 30, Pedrarias Davilla arrived at Darien appointed Governor to supersede Vasco Nunez and instructed to bring him to trial to investigate charges of Encisco. Vasco Nunez acquitted. Pedrarias united the provinces of Nueva Andalusia and Castilla del Oro into one province called Tierra Firma

1515

Acla founded by Gabriel Rojo

March, Expedition of Gonzalo de Badajos found no trace of Nicuesa's colonists at Nombre de Dios

1516

July 29, Expedition of Espinosa to the South Sea. Defeated Indians at Nata in province of Veragua. At Nombre de Dios found no trace of colonists of Nicuesa

1517

Vasco Nunez de Balboa accused of treason executed in the public square at Acla by the jealous Pedrarias

Jan., Fortified post established on the site of Puerto Bello

1519

Aug. 15, Formal founding of old city of Panama by Pedrarias

First road across the Isthmus from Panama to Nombre de Dios completed

1520

Jan., Arrival of Gil Conzales de Avila and Andres Nino at Acla from Spain

May, Lope de Sosa arrived to supersede Pedrarias as Governor. Was taken with sudden illness and died

Nata founded by Espinosa

1521

Sept. 15, Panama made a city by royal decree and granted a coat of arms

1522

Jan. 21–June 25, 1523, Expedition of Nino and Gonzales Davilla to Nicaragua. See America; Nicaragua

Voyage of Pascual de Andagoya southward from Panama. See Peru

1524

Nov. 14, First voyage of Francisco Pizarro and Diego Almagro to find Peru. See America; Peru

1526

Voyage of Pedrarias to Nicaragua to make war on Cordova, his lieutenant sent to establish conquest of Nino and Gonzales who had declared independence of Panama. See Nicaragua

Pedro de los Rios arrived, appointed Governor to supersede Pedrarias

March 10, Contract of Pizarro, Almagro, and Luque for division of Peru and voyage. See Peru

1529

Licentiate Antonio de la Gama sent as acting Governor. Rios ordered to Spain to answer charges

Spanish engineer Alvaro de Saavedra Ceron surveyed Isthmus and made proposal to Charles V for construction of a canal. Este and Rojas, officers of Pedrarias favored plan of canal around falls of the San Juan, Nicaragua and another on the Pacific slope

1530

Dec. 28, Pizarro expedition to Peru. See Peru

1533

Barge canal made by making Chagres River navigable from the Atlantic Ocean to Ventra Cruz and use of the Atrato River in Colombia reducing overland route across the Isthmus by making it a land and water route

1534

Pascual de Andagoya made survey with view to construction of a canal

Captain Francisco de Barrionuevo superseded La Gama as Governor

1535

Feb. 30, Audiencia of City of Panama established

Sept., Felipe Gutierrez with royal grant to settle colony in Veragua sailed from Santo Domingo to Belen River and founded Concepcion

1537

Jan. 19, Don Luis Columbus given title of duke and a domain on Belen River

1538

Pedro Vazquez, Governor of Castilla del Oro, succeeded Barrionuevo

154?

Dr. Robles, Governor, succeeded Vazquez

1545

Oct., Pedro de Hinojosa, lieutenant, set up residence at Panama in interests of Gonzalo Pizarro

1546

Aug. 13, Gasca sent to investigate affairs in Peru entered Panama

1550

March 12, Gasca returned to Panama from Peru to remain in charge until arrival of Viceroy Mendoza

April 20, Hernando and Pedro de Contreras and Bermejo, rebels, took Panama City but were presently defeated by Gasca

1572

July 29, Raid of Sir Francis Drake on Nombre de Dios. Forced to leave without treasure

1577

April 13, Drake plundered port of Guatulco on the Pacific

1595

Nombre de Dios captured and burned by Drake and Hawkins. Defeated by Spaniards, Sir Thomas Baskerville unable to take Panama City

1602

Feb. 7, Capture and looting of Porto Bello by Captain William Parker

1605

Valverde, Governor

1610

Mercedo, Governor

1616

Dec. 31, Diego Fernandez de Velasco, Governor

162?

Rodrigo de Vivero succeeded Velasco as Governor

1621

May 2–Aug. 21, Earthquake shocks almost daily

1668

June 30, Captain Henry Morgan sacked Porto Bello carrying off large amount of treasure

1670

Dec., Morgan captured Castle of San Lorenzo at the mouth of the Chagre River

1671

Jan. 28, Henry Morgan made successful attack on city of Panama
Feb. 24, Morgan burned city of Panama as he left it

1672

Oct. 24, Decree of Governor Don Fernandez de Cordova y Mendoza that all persons should remove to new site chosen for rebuilding city of Panama. Confirmed by royal charter Dec. 31

1673

Jan. 21, Formal act of founding of new city of Panama

1680

April, Bartholomew Sharp and William Dampier made unsuccessful attack on city of Panama

1698

Oct. 30, Scotch colony of William Patterson landed at Acla
Nov. 4, Scotch settlement given name of New Edinburgh and fort St. Andrew built at site still known as Puerto Escoces

1699

June 22, William Patterson and colonists abandoned Darien colony
Nov. 30, Another shipload of colonists from Scotland arrived

1700

April 24, The Scotch colonists made surrender to Spaniards hostile to foreign settlement and abandoned colony

1708

June, Fernando de Haro Monterrosa succeeded the Marquis de Villa Roche, deposed as Governor

1711

June, Hurtado de Amedzaga, Governor, succeeding Villa Roche who had proclaimed himself Governor and was deposed within 24 hours

1713

March 13, Under Treaty of Utrecht the English obtained right to send ship with merchandise to Porto Bello

1716

Bishop José de Llamas y Rivas, Governor after deposition of Villa Roche

1717

May 27, Panama included in new Viceroyalty of New Granada

1725

April 25, Alderete, Governor (1725–30)

1730

Juan José Andia, Marquis de Villa Hermosa, Governor (1730–35)

1737

Feb. 1–2, Fire destroyed city of Panama
Aug. 20, Royal decree embodied captain-generalcy of Panama and Veragua in Viceroyalty of New Granada

1739

Nov. 20–21, Admiral Vernon attacked and captured Porto Bello in war of Spain and England declared Oct. 19

1740

March 24, Castle of San Lorenzo at mouth of the Chagre captured by the English

1745

Dionisio de Alcedo, Governor

1749

Dec. 24, Jaime Munoz de Guzman appointed Governor but same day appointee of Crown arrived, Manuel de Montiano (1749–55)

1751

June 20, Royal decree abolished the Audiencia of Panama

1756

March 30, Fire destroyed half of city of Panama

1758

Antonio Guill, Governor (1758–61)

1762

José Raon, Governor (1762–64)

1764

José Vasco y Orosco, Governor (1764–67)

1769

Jan., Vicente Olaziregui, Governor

1771

April 26, Fire in Panama City burned 55 houses

1774

Andres de Ariza, Governor

1779

Ramon de Carbajal, Governor (1779–86)

1801

Antonio Narvaez y la Torre, Governor

1803

March 15, Colonel Juan de Marcos Urbina, Governor

1805

Feb. 22, Death of Governor Urbina. Succeeded by Juan A. de la Mata

1812

Feb. 19, Viceroy Benito Perez unable to get to Bogota established residence in Panama
Death of Governor Mata. Succeeded by Victor Salcedo and then by Carlos Meyner

1815

Alejandro de Hore appointed Governor (1815–20). Sent with troops from Spain to suppress revolt in Spanish colonies

1819

April 8, Expedition of Englishmen commanded by General M. McGregor attacked and captured Porto Bello in name of the "United Provinces of New Granada" but driven out by royalist Governor Hore
Dec. 17, Congress at Angostura proclaimed Republic of Colombia including Panama

1820

July 8, Death of Governor Hore. Succeeded by Pedro Aguilar
Oct. 22, Viceroy Samano led royalist expedition sailing for reconquest of Ecuador

1821

Aug. 3, Death of Viceroy Samano. Succeeded by Juan de la Cruz Mourgeon
Oct. 22, Royalist expedition of Viceroy Mourgeon sailed for reconquest of Ecuador
Nov. 13, Independence proclaimed at Los Santos
Nov. 28, Panama declared independence of Spain and joined the Republic of Colombia as a State. Former Governor José de Fabrega appointed Supreme Jefe

1822

Feb., José Maria Carreno appointed commander-general of the Isthmus and Fabrega Governor

1826

June 22–July 15, Bolivar's Congress met at Panama City with representatives from Great Colombia, Guatemala, Mexico, and Peru

1831

Sept. 26, Meeting of citizens proclaimed independence of Colombia. José Domingo Espinar assumed control
Dec. 11, Panama reunited with Colombia

1840

Nov. 18, Successful revolt against Colombia. Tomas Herrera made Jefe

1842

Panama submitted to union with Colombia

1849

Feb. 24, First issue of *The Star* in Spanish and English

1850

April 15, Concession for railroad across the Isthmus granted by Colombia to John L. Stephens, City of Colon founded by Americans then called Aspinwall after William H. Aspinwall, one of the builders of the railroad
April 19, Clayton-Bulwer Treaty between Great Britain and the United States proposed ship canal
May 22 and Oct., Revolts against Government

1851

July 22, Revolt of 4 southern provinces
Nov. 14, Revolutionary outbreak at Chagres

1854

Oct. 24, Independence of the Isthmus declared by provincial legislature

1855

Jan. 28, Railroad across the Isthmus from ocean to ocean opened (Colon to Panama)
Feb. 27, Congress of Colombia granted autonomy to Panama made a State
July 15, Constituent Assembly met
July 18, Organization Act. Justo Arosemena appointed chief of State
Sept. 17, Constitution promulgated
Sept. 28, Resignation of Arosemena
Oct. 4, Francisco Fabrega, vice-chief, assumed office

1856

Jan. 26, Protest of consuls of the United States, France, Great Britain, Brazil, Portugal, Denmark, Peru, and Ecuador to Government against neglect of protection afforded in passage across the Isthmus
April 15, "Panama massacre" Riot in which Americans in transit across Isthmus waiting for boat killed and property looted
May 4 and 18, Riots
Sept. 18, Bartolome Calvo declared elected Governor and F. Fabrega, Vice-Governor
Oct. 2, Conflict between two political parties. United States forces landed

1858

Oct. 1, José de Obaldia assumed office as elected Governor
Dec. 18, Attempted secession from Colombia

1859

April 17 and Sept. 27, Race riots

1860

Santiago de la Guardia, Governor
Oct. 4, United States troops landed to preserve order during riot

1861

May 23, Intervention of the United States in insurrection
Oct. 2, Insurrection

1862

June 13, Troops of Mosquera refused admittance to Panama
July, State assumed official name of Estado Soberano de Panama

Aug. 19, Revolt deposed Governor La Guardia who was killed in skirmish. Manuel M. Diaz made provisional Governor. Later Pedro Goitia, Governor

1863

July 4, Constitution adopted, published July 6, to conform with national Constitution

Aug., Spanish squadron commanded by Admiral Pinzon visited Panama

Aug. 13, General Peregrino Santo Colomba took office as President

1865

March and Aug., Riots

May 9, Acting Vice-President J. L. Calancho deposed. Succeeded by Jil Colunje

1866

March, Unsuccessful revolution

Oct. 1, Vicente Olarte Galendo assumed office as elected President

1867

April and August, Insurrectionary riots

1868

March 3, President Olarte poisoned, Juan José Diaz second designado took office

July 5, Revolt of colored citizens led by General Fernando Ponce deposed Diaz and Ponce assumed the executive office

Aug. 29, Second revolution. Ponce resigned

Aug. 30, Buenaventura Correoso assumed office as President

Sept. 30, President Correoso inaugurated as constitutional President

1871

April, Revolution followed by counter revolution

1872

Oct. 1, Resignation of President Correoso. Succeeded by Gabriel Neira

1873

April 5, Revolution deposed President Neira. Succeeded by Damaso Cervera

May 7, American marines landed at Panama by Rear-Admiral Stedman to protect lives and property during revolution

May 9, Peace arranged on condition of restoration of President Neira

Sept. 24, Hostilities renewed and second landing of American marines

Nov. 14, President Neira failed in attempt to dissolve Assembly and was deposed by it

Nov. 16, Gregorio Miro, first designado, assumed executive office

1875

Oct. 1, Pablo Arosemena inaugurated President

Oct. 12, Arosemena deposed and Rafael Aizpuru became provisional President

Dec. 6, President Aizpuru inaugurated constitutional President. Another Constitution adopted

1876

Aug–April, 1877, Civil war

1878

Jan. 1, Buenaventura Correoso elected President inaugurated

May 18, French company granted concession for canal. *See* Colombia

July and Dec., Revolts

Dec. 30, Resignation of President Correoso. Succeeded by J. R. Casorta, designado

1879

June 7, Revolt led by General Aizpuru who proclaimed himself President at Colon. Casorta replaced by J. Ortega

Aug. 17, French Panama Canal Company organized with Count Ferdinand de Lesseps as head to construct sea-level canal

1880

Jan. 1, Mlle de Lesseps struck first blow with pickaxe in ceremony of beginning construction of canal

——, Damaso Cervera inaugurated President

1881

Feb. 24, French engineers began work on canal

June 13, Constitution amended

1882

Jan. 1, Rafael Nunez, President, but D. Cervera, first designado inaugurated *ad interim*. Nunez resigned in November because of ill health

Jan. 20, First excavation made for canal

1883

Jan. 1, D. Cervera inaugurated President

March and May, Riots

1884

Sept. 19, Revolt at David

Nov. 25, Resignation of President Cervera. Succeeded by Vives Leon, second designado

1885

Jan. 6, General Ramon Santo Domingo Vila chosen President

Jan. 18, American marines landed during revolt at request of President

Feb. 17, Pablo Arosemena first designado assumed office. President on leave of absence

March 16, Revolution of General Aizpuru against Government begun

March 24, Resignation of President Arosemena. General Gonima assumed the executive office

March 31, Aizpuru seized Panama and forced surrender of President Gonima. American ship "Colon" seized by revolutionists. Aspinwall set on fire

April 8, American marines landed at Panama to protect railroad

April 24, American marines occupied Colon

April 30, Aizpuru surrendered to government troops and was deported to Colombia May 2

1888

Dec. 14, French Canal Company stopped payment

1889

May 15, Work ceased on canal. Company in hands of receiver Feb. 4

1892

Nov. 25, Prosecution of directors of Canal Company in France

1894

Oct. 20, Second Panama Canal Company organized (French)
Nov. 1, Work begun again on canal

1895

Jan.–April, Revolution
March 8, American marines landed at Bocas del Toro for protection of property

1899

June 3, Work on canal stopped
Oct., Revolution

1900

Feb.–July, Revolutionary uprising. *See also* Colombia
July 16, Rebels entered Colon without fighting
July 26, Surrender of insurgents

1901

Jan. and July, Revolutionary uprisings
Sept. 1, Colon taken by rebels, and again Nov. 20, and surrendered on Nov. 28
Nov. 21, American marines landed at Colon

1902

Jan. 4, French Panama Canal Company offered to sell rights to the United States for $40,000,000
Jan. 20, Steamer "Lautaro" sunk by rebels and Governor Alban drowned
June 28, The President of the United States authorized to purchase rights of French Canal Company and land for canal from Colombia

1903

Jan. 22, Treaty between Colombia and the United States by which the United States to purchase the Canal Zone; not ratified by Colombia Senate. *See also* Colombia
Nov. 2, Arrival of the U.S.S. "Nashville" at Colon
Nov. 3, Revolution in Panama, Colombian officials made prisoners and Colombian warships captured
Nov. 4, Panama declared independence of Colombia
Nov. 5, Arrival of U.S.S. "Dixie" at Colon
Nov. 6 and 13, The independence of Panama recognized by the United States, Señor Bunau-Varilla received by President Roosevelt as Minister from the new State on the 13th
Nov. 10, Independence recognized by France, by Germany Nov. 23
Nov. 18, Treaty with the United States signed by which the United States agreed to guarantee and maintain the independence of Panama and Panama granted to the United States the use, occupation, and control of a strip of land ten miles wide extending from ocean to ocean for ship canal on payment of $10,000,000 on exchange of ratifications and beginning 9 years from that date, an annual payment of $250,000; ratified by Panama Senate Dec. 2, by the United States Senate Feb. 23, ratifications exchanged Feb. 26
Dec. 13, Election ordered for Jan. 15, 1904 for delegates to a constitutional convention
Dec. 19, Recognition of Panama by Peru
Dec. 24, Recognition of Panama by Great Britain

1904

Feb. 13, Constitution framed, adopted by convention, and promulgated Feb. 16

Feb. 20, Manuel Amador Guerrero, elected Feb. 16, inaugurated President, Dr. Pablo Arosemena, first Vice-President, Don Domingo de Obaldia, second Vice-President, Dr. Carlos Mendoza, third Vice-President
March 8, United States Canal Commission appointed. *See* United States, and Panama Canal Zone
May 25, Extradition Treaty with the United States signed
June 28, Gold standard adopted
Dec. 4, The "Taft Settlement" of questions in dispute with United States announced after conference of Judge Taft and President Amador Guerrero Nov. 27–28

1905

March 6, Agreement with Costa Rica as to boundary under Loubet award of 1900

1906

Aug. 25, Extradition Treaty with Great Britain signed

1907

April 24, Boundary Treaty with Brazil signed
July 24, Adherence to Geneva Convention
Aug. 17, Secretary Taft concluded Agreement with representatives of Colombia and Panama, settlement of issues growing out of separation of Panama from Colombia

1908

July 12, José Domingo de Obaldia elected President, and inaugurated Oct. 1

1909

May 2, Death of first President, Dr. Manuel Amador Guerrero

1910

March 1, Death of President Obaldia, succeeded by Dr. Carlos A. Mendoza, Vice-President
March 17, Agreement with Costa Rica to submit boundary dispute to arbitration
Oct. 5, Pablo Arosemena, elected in Sept. to serve for the remainder of term of Obaldia, inaugurated

1911

May 11, Arbitration Treaty with Italy signed
First census gave total population as 336,742 including 36,178 uncivilized Indians

1912

Feb. 28, United States Secretary Knox arrived at Panama on official visit
July 6, Railroad opened from La Union to San Miguel
Aug. 2, Dr. Belisario Porras, Liberal, elected President and inaugurated Oct. 1

1913

Jan. 31, Public land law enacted and regulations by Decree of April 14
Feb. 10, Law enacted to conserve natural resources, regulations April 16
March 24, Immigration law allowed entrance of Chinese, Syrians, Turks under certain conditions, registration required
Sept. 20, Advancement of Peace Treaty with the United States signed

1914

Feb. 13, New Constitution adopted

April 6, Treaty between the United States and Colombia by which Colombia recognized the independence of Panama

June 30, Treaty of arbitration with Portugal signed

Sept. 2, Treaty with the United States giving the United States control of the waters of Colon and Ancon at terminus of canal, transferred to the United States 2 small islands in Ancon harbor, and granted site for battery on waterfront at Ancon; boundary with Canal Zone defined

Sept. 12, Award of Chief Justice White of United States Supreme Court as to boundary with Costa Rica favorable to Costa Rica

Oct. 10, Treaty with the United States signed as to use of Canal by ships of belligerents

Dec. 5, Law created national lottery

Dec. 8, Treaty with the United States of Sept. 2 ratified

Dec. 10, Telephone between Tablas and port of Mensabe opened

1915

Jan. 6, Panama notified Costa Rica that boundary award of Chief Justice White would not be accepted

Jan. 9, Law enacted as to wells or deposits of petroleum enacted; amended Feb. 20

Feb. 25, Law established commercial taxes

Feb. 26, Contract signed for establishment of a branch of the National City Bank of New York

April 30, Large section of Colon destroyed by fire, 11 persons killed, property loss $3,500,000

Nov. 27, Agreement with the United States signed as to damages for riots at Panama City

1916

May 14, The United States Government demanded surrender of rifles of Panama police

July 9, Ramon Valdes elected President, election riots in which 3 persons killed

Sept. 26, The new port of Mandinga, about 80 miles from the city of Colon, opened

Oct. 1, Ramon Valdes inaugurated President

Nov. 16, Industrial Accident law enacted

Dec. 28, Law enacted for encouragement of industrial enterprises

1917

Jan. 13, National Red Cross Society inaugurated

Feb. 1, Immigration law of 1913 amended, regulations for resident Chinese, Syrians, Turks absent from country on passport

Feb. 3, Law authorized the President to grant contracts for public lands

April 7, Panama declared war on Germany

July 1, Seven codes came into effect, civil, penal, commercial, judicial, fiscal, and mining

Dec. 10, Panama declared war on Austria-Hungary

1918

June 3, Death of President Ramon M. Valdes, succeeded by Vice-President Ciro L. Urriola

June 28, American troops assumed police duties in terminal canal cities of Panama and Colon

Oct. 12, Belisario Porras inaugurated President

Nov. 15, Administrative code came into effect

Dec. 26, Amendments to Constitution provided for abolition of death penalty, election of president by direct vote for 4 years, and election of deputies every 4 years beginning in 1924

1919

Jan. 20, Law enacted regarding concessions for search and exploitation of minerals, and law regulating the manufacture and sale of liquor

March 7, Law enacted to promote immigration to develop the land, benefits to any persons under 50 entering the country for agricultural purposes, and preference to immigration from the Canary Islands or Puerto Rico

March 10, Education law made primary education compulsory for children from 7 to 15 years, and penalties provided for parents and guardians responsible for school attendance

June 28, Panama signed the Treaty of Versailles

1920

Jan. 9, Panama adhered to Covenant of the League of Nations

Aug. 1, Belisario Porras elected President under new law by direct vote

Oct. 1, President Porras inaugurated

Census gave population as 401,428 not including about 35,000 uncivilized Indians

1921

Feb. 21, Costa Ricans invaded Panama seizing Coto assigned to Costa Rica by White award of 1914

Feb. 24, Panama asked assistance of United States troops to prevent war

Feb. 28, Fighting on the border and riots at Panama, the palace attacked

March 5, Costa Ricans occupied Almirante, port of Panama

——, Note of Secretary Hughes offered mediation of the United States which was accepted March 7

March 9, Armistice announced

March 16, Decision of the United States as arbiter that the line of the Loubet and White awards should stand

April 7, National Assembly refused to accept award of the United States

May 2, The United States notified Panama that the disputed territory must be ceded to Costa Rica under award

July 25, Panama asked that boundary dispute be referred to the Hague Court

Aug. 18 and 23, Ultimatum of the United States to Panama demanded cession of disputed territory to Costa Rica

Aug. 23, Panama ceded territory to Costa Rica making formal protest the following day

1923

Feb. 14, Loan of $4,500,000 approved by legislature and floated in New York May 25 for building of roads and development of country's resources

Nov. 21, Announcement that the Government had refused proposed vote of women in the 1924 elections

1924

April 9, Immigration Decree

May 8, Protocol with Colombia signed in Washington by which diplomatic relations resumed

June 6, Treaty with the United States signed regarding smuggling of intoxicating liquors

Aug. 3, Dr. Rodolfo Chiari elected President

Aug. 20, Treaty with Colombia signed provided for delimitation of boundary by a mixed commission

Oct. 1, President Rodolfo Chiari inaugurated

Oct. 29, Law enacted that 50% of employees on public works must be nationals

1925

Feb. 21, Uprising of Indians at Tigre Island proclaimed Republic of Tula

Feb. 27, National Assembly declared state of siege in San Blas district because of revolt of Indians. American marines assisted in suppressing uprising

March 5, San Blas Indian revolt ended and peace signed

March 30, Immigration law enacted

June 8, Decree provided regulations for mining code of 1919

Aug. 19 and 20, Decree established passport regulations required of every person entering the country

Oct. 10–11, Riots of workers demanding lower rents

Oct. 12–23, American troops in Panama to maintain order at request of the Government

Oct. 14, Landlords in conference with the President agreed to reduce rents for the cheaper houses 10%

1926

June 18–25, Centenary celebration of first Pan-American Congress of June 22–July 15, 1826 called by Simon Bolivar

June 22, Bolivarian University dedicated in Panama

June 25, Pan-American Congress at Panama attended by delegates from 21 American Republics approved a resolution for creation of an American League of Nations

July 28, Treaty with the United States defined mutual relations provided that in case of war of any power with the United States Panama will consider herself in a state of war and will turn over to the United States if necessary control and operation of wireless and radio communication, aircraft, aviation centers, and other warlike equipment, and in time of peace the armed forces of the United States are granted free transit throughout the Panama Republic for manœuvres or other military purposes, and the United States granted use, occupation, and control of Mazanillo Island and Colon harbor; not ratified by Panama

Oct. 23, New immigration law prohibited entry of Orientals including Chinese, Japanese, Turks, Syrians, East Indians, and Dravidians, and negroes from the West Indies and Guiana whose original language not Spanish

1927

Jan. 26, Treaty of July 28, 1926 rejected by National Assembly

Nov. 21, Treaty of commerce with Germany signed, most favored nation

Dec. 24, Extradition Treaty with Colombia signed

1928

Jan. 9, Colonel Charles A. Lindbergh arrived at Panama City on good will flight

March 29, Immigration law allowed entrance of 10 each of Chinese, Syrians, Turks, and negroes, and allowed Japanese and Hindus to enter the country

June 25, Loan of $12,000,000 5% 35 year bonds floated in New York for construction of public works and redemption of earlier loans

Aug. 5, Florencio Harmodio Arosemena elected President

Oct. 1, President Arosemena inaugurated

——, Diplomatic relations with Costa Rica broken off in 1921 resumed

Oct. 19, Legislative decree amended the Constitution as to citizenship, Article 6

Oct. 23, Extradition Treaty with Mexico signed

Nov. 30, National Board of Health established

1929

April 17, Air mail and passenger service opened to Cristobal, Panama Canal Zone

June 6, Decree of the President reduced salaries of government employees from 10 to 15%

Oct. 16, Treaty of friendship, commerce, and navigation with Italy signed

1930

March 18, Decree reorganized the consular service

March 25, Executive Decree dealing with naturalization of aliens modified that of Oct. 18, 1890

March 30, Immigration Decree required certificates of good character for natives of Syria and Lebanon entering the country with the permission of the Minister of Foreign Affairs, and proof of means of support and deposit required

May 1, Radio-telegraph service with the United States officially inaugurated

Aug. 7, Dr. Enrique Olaya Herrera headed new Cabinet

Sept. 9, Resignation of 5 members of Cabinet in opposition to J. B. Duncan, Secretary of Education, and the following day the entire Cabinet resigned

Sept. 11, Demonstration of 8,000 persons in Panama City in favor of Duncan

SALVADOR

Salvador, smallest Republic of Central America, on the Pacific coast bounded on the north and east by Honduras, west and northwest by Guatemala, the only Central American country with no Atlantic coast line; area 13,176 square miles, greatest length 160 miles, greatest width 60 miles; divided into 14 departments.

Estimated population (Jan. 1, 1929), 1,722,579. Aboriginal and mixed races constitute the bulk of the population, Ladinos or Mestizos being returned as numbering 1,307,200, and Indians 326,800. The language of the country is Spanish. The capital is San Salvador, with (1930) 95,692 inhabitants. Other towns are Santa Ana, population 75,796; San Miguel, 38,620; Zatatecoluca, 34,456; San Vicente, 34,723; Sonsonate, 16,895.

Until 1821 Salvador was a Viceroyalty of Guatemala.

Dr. Pio Romero Bosque, President.

1524

April–July, Pedro de Alvarado marched from Honduras and subdued the natives of Salvador

1525

Alvarado captured the Indian capital of Cuscatlan
City of San Salvador founded

1811

Nov. 5, Two curates N. Aguilar and M. Delgado with
M. Rodriguez, M. J. Arce, and others seized muskets
and $200,000 from the Treasury in San Salvador and
began first Central American revolt against rule of
Spain. Removed intendente
Dec. 3, Colonel José de Aycinena sent by Bustamante
to suppress the revolt reached Salvador and checked
revolution

1814

Jan. 24, Revolt begun by M. J. Arce unsuccessful. Arce
imprisoned

1821

Sept. 21, Independence declared by the ayuntamiento
and proclaimed 8 days after

1822

June 3, Colonel Arzu with 1,000 men from Guatemala
entered San Salvador but was defeated in street fight
and driven from city
Dec. 2, Congress adopted resolution of annexation to
the United States

1823

Feb. 7, Filisola defeated Salvadorians under Arce at
Mejicanos
Feb. 9, Filisola entered San Salvador ending revolt
against annexation to Mexico
Feb. 21, Surrender of remaining Salvadorian troops at
Gualcine

1824

March 5–Nov. 23, Constituent Assembly in session
June 12, Constitution adopted
July 4, First Constitution promulgated
Nov. 22, Salvador entered the Central American Union
as a State
Dec. 13, Juan Vicente Villacorta appointed by Constituent Assembly took office as Jefe, Mariano Prado
as Vice-Jefe, succeeding Juan Manuel Rodriguez who
had held the executive office during period of organization

1826

Dec. 6, Vice-Jefe took over the executive office on resignation of Villacorta

1827

March 22, Salvadorians invading Guatemala defeated
by President Arce at Guadalupe
March 23, Salvadorians routed at Arrazola
May 18, Attack of Arce on San Salvador repulsed
July 14, Arce on second invasion occupied Chalchuapa
July 16, Arce took Santa Ana
Dec. 17, Battle in streets of Santa Ana ended in a
capitulation. The Salvadorians held the city

1828

Feb. 29, Third invasion of Salvador by Federal troops.
Chalchuapa occupied
March 1, Battle at Chalchuapa a victory for the Federal
troops commanded by General Arzu
March 12, General Arzu made unsuccessful assault on
San Salvador
April 13, Action at Quelepa. Federal troops defeated
Salvadorians

April 25, Federal victory at Guascoran
June 12, Peace signed. Not accepted by Salvador
July 6, Federal army defeated at Gualcho by General
Morazan
Sept. 20, Federal force of Colonel Manuel Montufar
compelled to surrender at Mejicanos
Oct. 9, Federal army which had occupied San Miguel
forced to surrender at San Antonio
Oct. 23, General Morazan made triumphal entry into
San Salvador

1829

Jan., José M. Cornejo became Jefe
Feb. 5, General Morazan with Salvadorian army re-
pulsed in attack on Guatemala City, but took city
April 13. *See* Guatemala

1831

Dec. 29, Morazan now President of the Federation left
Guatemala to make his headquarters in Salvador

1832

Jan. 6, President Cornejo ordered President Morazan
at Santa Ana to leave Salvador
Jan. 7, Act declared secession of Salvador from the
Federation
March 14, Morazan defeated Cornejo at Portillo
March 28, Morazan with Nicaraguan and Honduran
troops took San Salvador by assault and assumed
control of the Government until reorganization could
be effected
July 25, Mariano Prado elected Jefe and J. San Martin
y Ulloa, Vice-Jefe, took office
Aug. 21, Moderate direct tax adopted. This brought
about revolt in several places

1833

Feb. 13, Salvador seceded from the Federal Union
July, Indian insurrection led by Aquino against white
rule
July 1, Revolt made J. San Martin y Ulloa, Jefe
July 24, Aquino executed and rebellion ended

1834

Feb., Federal Government took up residence at Sonsonate and in June at San Salvador
June 23, San Martin deposed after street fight with
Federal troops and Carlos Salazar assumed the executive office
July 25, Gregorio Salazar, Vice-President, assumed the
executive office
Oct., Joaquin Escolan assumed executive office. Succeeded same month by Vice-Jefe José M. Silva

1835

April, Nicolas Espinosa became Jefe
Nov. 13, Espinosa deposed. Succeeded by Francisco
Gomez

1836

April, Diego Vijil became Jefe
April 6, Allied Nicaraguans and Hondurans commanded
by Morazan defeated by Salvadorians called Federals
at Espiritu Santo
Sept., Timoteo Menendez, Vice-Jefe, assumed executive
office

1839

May, Antonio J. Canas became Jefe

June 5, Treaty of amity and alliance with Guatemala signed

Aug. 1, Constituent Assembly at Zacatecoluca

1840

April 5, General Morazan unwelcome after his defeat in Guatemala left San Salvador and refused residence in Costa Rica, proceeded to South America where he remained 2 years

May 13, Humiliating Treaty with Guatemala signed

Sept. 20, Insurrection begun by Francisco Malespin, tool of Carrera

Sept. 23, President Antonio Canas forced to resign. Noberto Ramirez became provisional Jefe

1841

Jan. 7, Juan Lindo became provisional Jefe on resignation of Ramirez

Jan. 30, Assembly voted to call the State Republic of Salvador

Feb. 18, Second Constitution adopted. Independence and separation from the Federation declared

Nov. 6, President Lindo dissolved the Assembly by a coup d'état because some of its members friends of Morazan

1842

Jan. 13, Three senators at San Vicente proclaimed restoration of constitutional order and forced resignation of President Lindo

Feb. 1, Antonio Canas chosen President. He resigned and was succeeded successively by Pedro Arce and Senator Escolastico Marin and J. J. Guzman

Sept. 17, Assembly installed at San Vicente

Sept. 20, As no candidate had majority of votes for President Guzman asked by Assembly to continue in office

1844

Feb. 5, Colonel Francisco Malespin assumed office as elected President after forced resignation of J. J. Guzman

May, Invasion of Manuel José Arce supported by troops from Guatemala

June, Invasion of Guatemala by Malespin

July 10, Convention with Honduras signed

Aug. 5, Convention with Guatemala ended war

Sept. 1, Unsuccessful revolt against Malespin at San Miguel led by Trinidad Cabanas and Gerardo Barrios, officers of Morazan

Oct. 25, Malespin turned over the executive office to Vice-President J. E. Guzman and took command of army for war against Salvador because of refusal of that State to give up Cabanas and Barrios

Oct. 31, Malespin and his army entered Honduras

Nov. 7, Malespin made commander in chief of allied armies of Honduras and Salvador against Nicaragua. *See* Nicaragua

Dec. 30–31, Night attack of revolutionists captured the garrison at San Salvador

1845

Jan. 4, Insurrectionists defeated at Cojutepeque

Jan. 28, The Liberal leaders Cabanas and Barrios returned to Salvador

Feb. 2, Vice-President Guzman assumed executive office and captured the barracks

Feb. 22, Guzman defeated Malespin at Montero

April 4, Treaty of peace with Guatemala signed

April 18, Treaty of peace with Honduras signed but not ratified by Honduras

June 2, Salvadorian army under Cabanas defeated in attack on Comayagua, Honduras

June 10, Salvadorians defeated at Sensenti

Aug. 15, General Guardiola defeated by Salvador army in attack at hacienda del Obrajuelo and forced to evacuate San Miguel

Nov. 27, Treaty of peace with Honduras signed. Malespin and Espinosa forbidden to enter Salvador

1846

Feb. 1, J. E. Guzman, Vice-President in executive office, resigned. Senator F. Palacios assumed office

Feb. 20, Eugenio Aguilar appointed President by the Assembly

July 11 and 16, Efforts of Bishop Viteri to overthrow President Aguilar unsuccessful

July 29, Decree of the President prohibited return of Bishop Viteri who had fled to Guatemala

Nov. 1, Invasion of Malespin representing Bishop Viteri

Nov. 25, Malespin defeated, assassinated by the Indians at San Fernando

1848

Feb. 7, Doroteo Vasconcelos assumed office as elected President

July 3, Tomas Miguel Pineda y Zaldana, Bishop of Antigona, given administration of the diocese of Salvador with the right of succession

1849

Nov. 12, Salvador forced by British blockade of port of La Union to accept claims made by Chatfield, British chargé d'affaires

1850

Jan., President Vasconcelos reëlected, began second term

Jan. 2, Treaty of amity, navigation, and commerce with the United States signed

Oct. 16, Second British blockade of La Union which lasted until Feb., 1851

Dec. 4, War with Guatemala begun

1851

Feb. 2, Battle of Arada. Vasconcelos defeated in invasion of Guatemala by Carrera and forced to retreat to Salvador

Feb. 6, Martial law declared and all men called to service for defense against Guatemalans

March 1, J. F. Quiroz assumed executive office as substitute. Vasconcelos deposed

1852

Jan. 1, Francisco Duenas assumed office as elected President

1853

Aug. 17, Treaty of peace with Guatemala concluded

1854

Feb., José Maria San Martin succeeded Dr. Duenas as President

April 16, Earthquake destroyed San Salvador. Capital removed to Cojutepeque

1856

Jan., Rafael Campo took office as President and Francisco Duenas as Vice-President

April 14, Act declared independence of the Republic of Salvador

June 6, General G. Barrios landed at La Libertad and marched on San Salvador

June 11, Manifesto of Barrios proposal to depose President Campo and call Duenas to presidency. Not supported

1858

Jan., Miguel Santin del Castillo succeeded Campo as President

Feb. 15, Treaty of friendship, commerce, and navigation with Belgium signed

Coup d'état of Senator Barrios forced resignation of Campo. Aided by Vice-President Guzman

1859

June 24, New Constitution promulgated

Aug. 9, Convention of Honduras with Guatemala agreed to recognize the constitutional authority in Salvador

1860

Jan. 28, General Gerardo Barrios inaugurated elected President

Oct. 27, Treaty of commerce and navigation with Italy signed

1861

Sept. 15, Bishop Zaldana exiled went to Guatemala with other clergy who refused to take oath of allegiance to the Government

1862

March 25, Treaty of Santa Rosa of friendship and peace signed with Honduras

Oct. 24, Treaty of friendship and commerce with Great Britain signed

1863

Feb. 9, President Carrera invaded Salvador in war against Barrios, reaching Jutiapa

Feb. 21, Santa Ana occupied by troops under Cerna, Guatemalan general

Feb. 24, Battle of Coatepeque. Barrios defeated Carrera. Carrera retreated to Jutiapa and returned to Guatemala

April 29, Martinez of Nicaragua defeated allied Hondurans and Salvadorians at San Felipe

June 16, Battle of Santa Rosa. Allied Guatemalans and Nicaraguans defeated Salvadorians and Hondurans

June 29, Revolt at Sonsonate declared against Barrios proclaiming Duenas provisional President. Revolt joined by Cojutepeque July 27, Zacatecoluca Aug. 14

July 3, Carrera attacked and defeated General Gonzales who had declared himself provisional President and occupied Santa Ana

Sept. 29, Siege of President Barrios in capital begun

Oct. 26, San Salvador surrendered and was occupied by Guatemalans. Barrios escaped. Dr. Duenas assumed office as President

Nov. 18, Barrios embarked for Panama

1864

Feb. 18, Assembly met and confirmed Duenas as provisional President

March 19, Act reaffirmed declaration of independence of Republic of Salvador

1865

Jan. 23, Defensive alliance with Colombia concluded

Feb. 1, President Duenas inaugurated as constitutional President

May 15, Manifesto of General Cabanas in San Miguel against President Duenas

May 24, Treaty of amity, commerce, and navigation with Spain

May 29, Gonzales defeated Cabanas near La Union

June 30, Barrios on shipboard captured by Nicaraguan force and taken to Leon

Aug. 29, Barrios surrendered to Salvador, executed

1868

March 17, Treaty of friendship and commerce with Nicaragua signed

Dec., President Duenas reëlected

1870

May 23, Treaty of extradition with the United States signed

Dec. 6, Treaty of amity, commerce, and consular relations with the United States signed

1871

Jan. 16–21, Conference with Honduras to settle differences not successful

Feb. 7, Honduras suspended treaty relations with Salvador

March 5, Declaration of war by Honduras

March 17, President Medina of Honduras occupied Sensuntepeque and presently Ilobasco

March 19, Government troops under General Tomas Martinez attacked Ilobasco

April 10, Government troops decisively routed at Santa Ana by General Santiago Gonzales in rebellion against President Duenas

April 15, Revolutionists entered the capital proclaiming Gonzales provisional President. Duenas took refuge in the American Legation

April 20, Surrender of Duenas and Martinez. Both permitted to leave the country

July 28, Constituent Assembly met

Oct. 16, New Constitution promulgated

Oct. 19, Treaty of alliance with Costa Rica

1872

Jan. 24, Treaty of amity and alliance with Guatemala signed

Feb. 1, General Santiago Gonzales inaugurated as constitutional President

March 25, Honduras declared war on Salvador. *See* Honduras

April 10, Duenas defeated by General Gonzales at Santa Ana

April 13, Ex-President Duenas declared legally deposed

Sept. 1, Assassination of Vice-President Manuel Mendez

Nov. 9, Constitution amended

1873

March 19, Earthquake destroyed the capital for the eighth time in history

May 12, Extradition Treaty with the United States

Aug. 26, Treaty of alliance with Nicaragua and Guatemala signed

1874

Dec. 30, Adherence to Geneva Convention of 1864

1875

March 14, Insurrection of the Indians of Dolores Izalco who assaulted garrison of city of Izalco

June 20, Insurrection led by religious fanatic Tinoco and Father J. M. Palacio attacked the garrison of the city of San Miguel. Commander Felipe Espinosa killed. Looting and burning continued until the 24th. Suppressed by arrival of government troops on the 24th

Dec. 1, Election of Andres Valle, President, and S. Gonzales, Vice-President

1876

Jan. 12, Inauguration of Andres Valle as President and Santiago Gonzales as Vice-President

Feb. 15, Convention signed by President Valle and President Barrios of Guatemala in conference at Chingo, agreement to support Marco Aurelio Soto, Honduran, in effort to end civil war in Honduras

March 10, Government declared country in state of siege

March 20, Guatemala declared official relations with Salvador ended

March 25, Salvadorians defeated in first battle

March 26, Salvador declared Treaty of Jan., 1872, with Guatemala abrogated, denied that Salvadorian troops had invaded Guatemala and accused Barrios of attempt to conquer Central America beginning with Honduras and Salvador

March 27, Guatemala declared war on Salvador

April 15, Guatemalans defeated in battle near Apaneca

April 17–19, Battle of Pasaquina. General Solares won important victory over Salvadorians commanded by Generals Brioso, Dalgado, Sanchez, and Espinosa

April 25, Peace terms concluded dictated by Guatemalans. President Valle to resign and Rafael Zaldivar chosen provisional President

May 8, Treaty of peace signed with Guatemala to which Honduras adhered on the 27th

July 3, Congress installed and Zaldivar chosen President

July 19, President Zaldivar inaugurated

1878

March 31, Treaty of peace, commerce, and extradition with Honduras signed

1880

Jan. 15, Constituent Congress met

Feb. 16, Amendments to Constitution adopted by Congress and Zaldivar reëlected President for term from Feb. 1 to Feb. 1, 1884

Aug., International Bank founded

Dec. 18, Supplementary Treaty with Honduras concluded

1881

Aug. 23, Boundary Treaty with Honduras signed

1883

Feb. 17, Decimal system adopted

April 16, Insurrection led by Dr. Manuel Gallardo and others attacked garrison at Santa Tecla. Repulsed by Commander Colonel Matias Castro Delgado, and martial law declared

June 1, Revolt suppressed and martial law repealed

Dec. 6, New Constitution adopted

1884

Feb. 1, President Zaldivar inaugurated for third term

March 15, Salvador repudiated Guatemalan dictatorship

1885

March 13, Red Cross Society organized

March 22, Alliance with Costa Rica and Nicaragua against Guatemala

March 28, Guatemalans invaded Salvador in support of President Barrios' declaration of Central American Union

April 2, Battle of Chalchuapa in which Salvadorians victorious and Barrios killed

April 15, Proclamation of peace and general amnesty

May 14, President Zaldivar turned over executive office to General Fernando Figueroa and left for Europe the following day

May 22, General Francisco Menendez leader of insurrection which had broken out in the west entered capital and proclaimed himself provisional President

June 22, The Senate recognized General Menendez as President

1886

Jan. 1, Decimal system made obligatory

Jan. 13, Treaty of peace with Nicaragua ended disputes

Feb. 15, Law for regulation of higher education passed

Aug. 13, New Constitution adopted

Sept. 28, Boundary Treaty with Honduras

Sept. 29, Law as to aliens approved

1887

March 1, President Menendez inaugurated

Sept. 6–10, Rebellion suppressed

1889

Oct. 15, Pact with Honduras and Guatemala. *See* Central America

1890

March 29, Treaty of friendship, commerce, and navigation with Ecuador signed

June 22, Revolution begun which resulted in death of President Menendez and assumption of power by General Ezeta, leader of insurrection

General Barillas of Guatemala mobilized troops on the frontier against Salvador

July 21, Guatemala declared war on Salvador

July 29, General Rivas in revolt against Ezeta seized San Salvador

Aug. 1, Ezeta recaptured San Salvador and executed Rivas

Aug. 3, Guatemalans defeated Salvadorians

Aug. 26, War ended by mediation of diplomatic corps

1891

March 1, General A. Ezeta inaugurated constitutional President

May 6, Rebellion in the Island of Amapala suppressed. General Bardales the leader killed

Sept. 9 and 13, Earthquakes in the capital and at Comasagua

Dec. 30, Commercial Convention with the United States concluded

1892

Sept. 30, Monetary reform law passed adopted gold standard. Peso established as monetary unit

1893

April 24, Treaty of friendship, commerce, and navigation with Mexico signed

1894

May 29, Revolt against President Ezeta headed by General Gutierrez

June 16, Revolutionists seized the capital. Ezeta fled to Panama

June 24, General Rafael Gutierrez proclaimed himself President

1895

Jan. 19, Boundary Treaty with Honduras signed

March 1, President Gutierrez inaugurated constitutional President

1898

Nov. 2, Revolt begun against Confederation of Central America organized at Managua the day before

Nov. 13, Tomas Regalado proclaimed himself provisional President

Nov. 25, Manifesto against the Central American Confederation issued

1899

March 1, Tomas Regalado inaugurated constitutional President

1900

June 2, Decree issued governing copyrights

Sept. 3, Dr. Castro, War Minister, shot ending insurrection against the Government

1901

Jan. 9, Commercial Convention with France signed

Dec. 19, Claims Convention with the United States signed

1902

Jan. 28, Arbitration Treaty with Spain signed

May 2, Decision of arbitrator disallowed claim of Maurice Gelbtrunk and Company, American firm, for property seized during revolt

1903

March 1, Don Pedro José Escalon assumed executive office as President

1906

April 14, Treaty of friendship, commerce, and navigation with Italy signed

April 30, New Tariff law passed

May 27, Forces of Salvador invaded Guatemala. *See* Guatemala

July 20, Preliminary Treaty of peace signed. *See* Central America

Sept. 11, Revolutionary plot against the Government discovered

Sept. 12, State of siege declared

Sept. 25, Final Treaty of Peace with Guatemala signed. *See* Central America

1907

March 1, General Fernando Figueroa inaugurated President

April 23, Treaty of Peace with Nicaragua signed

Nov. 20, Decree of President Figueroa granted amnesty to all political offenders, suspended martial law, and declared the Constitution again in force

Dec. 20, Treaty of peace and amity signed. *See* Central America

1908

March 14, Naturalization Treaty with the United States signed

April 14, Most favored nation commercial Treaty signed with Germany

Dec. 21, Arbitration Treaty with the United States signed

1911

March 1, Manuel Enrique Araujo succeeded Fernando Figueroa as President, Onofre Duran Figueroa, Vice-President

April 18, Extradition Treaty with the United States signed

May 12, Workmen's Compensation Act enacted

1912

Jan. 1, Population 1,161,426

March 11, Secretary Knox from the United States arrived at San Salvador

1913

Feb. 9, President Araujo assassinated by political enemies. Succeeded by Carlos Melendez

May 17, Protest against proposed treaty of Nicaragua with the United States as to interoceanic canal. Bay of Fonseca partly Salvadorian water

Aug. 7, Advancement of Peace Treaty with the United States signed

Oct. 21, Protest to United States against grant of naval station by Nicaragua in Gulf of Fonseca

1914

Aug. 29, Alfonso Quinonez Molina inaugurated as President succeeding Melendez resigned

Dec. 17, Executive decree established normal institute for boys at San Salvador

1915

March 1, Carlos Melendez inaugurated President and A. Quinonez Molina, Vice-President

April 30, Decree imposed general tax on incomes and law enacted June 15

July 27, Treaty with Honduras signed providing for freedom of trade

1916

May 14, College for girls opened at Chalchuapa

June 19, New Income tax passed laid tax on incomes over 2,000 pesos and on professions, salaries, fees, rents of land and houses, and interest on capital. Published Aug. 30

1917

March 2, Central American Court of Justice declared Salvador's rights infringed by Treaty of Aug. 5, 1914 between Nicaragua and the United States

June 7, Earthquake and eruption of Mount Jabali nearly destroyed San Salvador

Aug. 24, Salvador gave the United States permission to use her ports

1918

Feb. 28, Commercial Treaty with Honduras signed

April 5, Boundary Treaty with Honduras signed

Mining law declared mineral deposits the property of the State

1919

March 1, President Carlos Melendez inaugurated for a second term

April 28, City of San Salvador partly destroyed by earthquake

Law against illiteracy enacted

Sept., Currency reform law enacted
Dec. 14, Note to the United States asked interpretation of Monroe Doctrine and Article 21 of the Covenant of the League of Nations

1920

April 22, Railroad between San Vicente and Cojutepeque opened by the President
June 24, Salvador invited Central American States to a conference. *See* Central America
July 16, Law promulgated as to monetary system
July 27, Law established permanent banking commission
Aug. 23, Decree established provisions for protection of persons in domestic service
Aug. 27, Congress passed a resolution in favor of political unity of the five Central American republics

1921

Jan. 19, Salvador signed agreement for Central American Republic. *See* Central America

1922

Feb. 4, Salvador withdrew from Union resuming independent status
Feb. 15, Rising of cadets of the Military Academy against President Melendez
March 17, Railroad between Cojutepeque and San Salvador opened
——, Arrival of first train over international railroad at San Salvador from Zacatecoluca

1923

March 1, Alfonso Quinonez Molina inaugurated President, Pio R. Bosque, Vice-President
May 1, Decree regulated use of wireless telephone and telegraph, and as to concessions granted
Sept. 6, Death of former President Pedro José Escalon
Oct. 9, Loan arranged with banking house of J. F. Lisman of New York for $6,000,000

1924

Feb. 2, Revolt of General Carias at El Paraiso
March 10, Salvador became a member of the League of Nations
April 9, Agreement with France provided for modification of the Treaty of commerce of Jan. 9, 1901
June 6, Commercial agreement concluded with Spain
July 8, Decree of President gave regulations for domestic service
Nov. 7, Arbitration Treaty with Uruguay signed

1925

Aug. 12, Decree revised tariff law reducing taxes from 2 to 40% on valuation of imports, tax $1.15 gold per 100 kilos of imports
Nov. 25, Commission of financial experts created to revise banking laws
Nov. 28, Decree provided for registration of Chinese residents

1926

Feb. 12, Additional Articles to Treaty of commerce with Honduras of 1918 signed
Feb. 22, Treaty of friendship, commerce, and consular rights with the United States signed
May 21, Law provided that 80% of employees of foreign and domestic corporations must be Salvadorians
May 29, Labor law established eight hour day, Sunday rest, and gave 15 days annual vacation
June 10, Act provided for protection of commercial employees
June 22, The President approved legislative decree of May 2 creating a Bureau of Statics
Sept. 23, Immigration law enacted

1927

March 1, Dr. Pio Romero Bosque inaugurated President, Gustavo Vides, Vice-President
May 25, Pact signed by Salvador to act with Honduras and Guatemala in matters affecting general interests
May 31, New law for protection of commercial employees repealed that of 1926
June 30, Law provided for registration of commercial establishment, workshops, &c., worth more than 300 colones
July 6, Treaty signed with Guatemala and Honduras. *See* Central America
July 9, Pharmacy Act provided for School of Chemistry and Pharmacy
Oct. 3, National Industrial School opened in the capital

1928

Jan. 1, Colonel Charles A. Lindbergh flying from Belize reached San Salvador
Jan. 7, Commercial *modus vivendi* established with Great Britain
Feb. 1, Commercial *modus vivendi* concluded with Chile
April 30, Decree reëstablished export tax on coffee and sugar exempted under a decree of Dec. 28, 1923
Oct. 16, First train arrived at Guatemala border on Salvador section of International Railways of Central America
Nov. 26, President Elect Hoover of the United States delivered "good will" speech at La Union
Dec. 3, Formal opening of railroad between Texistepeque and Metapan

1929

June 13, Legislative decree established eight hour day for labor in mills, factories, railroads, ports, and industrial and commercial establishments
Oct. 4, Daily airplane service between Guatemala City and San Salvador inaugurated

1930

April 22, Decree authorized establishment of National School of Mines
May 30, New retirement and pension law signed by President for civil, judicial, and administrative branches of the government service
Dec. 21, Labor riots instigated by communists in towns of Santa Tecla and Sonsonate

SOUTH AMERICA

South America, the southern continent of the western Hemisphere, between the Atlantic and Pacific oceans, and joined to North America by the Isthmus of Panama, situated between 34° and 82° W. Long. and 13° N. and 55° S. Lat.

South America is the fourth largest of the continents with an approximate area of 7,570,000, slightly less than that of North America, and about 14% of the land surface of the globe. The continent is triangular in shape extending north and south about 4,550 miles, the maximum width in the northern part about 3,200 miles. Tierra del Fuego at the southern extremity separated from the continent by the Strait of Magellan is the farthest south inhabited land in the world. Columbus discovered South America on his third voyage (*see* America). The original Spanish colonies revolted from Spain in the early nineteenth century and with Brazil (Portuguese) formed 10 independent republics of Argentina, Bolivia, Brazil, Chile, Colombia, Ecuador, Paraguay, Peru, Uruguay, and Venezuela. Panama declared independence of Colombia in 1903, forming an independent State. The 3 European colonies on the continent are British, Dutch, and French Guiana. For voyages of discovery *see* America.

1503

Jan. 20 and June 5, Decrees established the Casa de Contratacion or House of Trade at Seville, Spain, to have charge of all matters relating to New Spain

1512

Dec. 12, Laws of Burgos for New Spain proclaimed established regulations as to Indians

1516

Sept. 17, Decree declared Bartolomé de Las Casas official protector of the Indians

1524

Aug. 4, Council of the Indies formally reorganized for the government of New Spain

1525

Nov. 17, Decree of Spain for protection of Indians decreasing under cruel exploitation of the Spaniards

1528

Feb. 15, Contract of Spanish Government with 2 Germans who agreed to supply 4,000 negroes to the Indies in 4 years, first actual contract to furnish slaves

1542

Nov. 20, "New Laws," achievement of B. de Las Casas signed by Spanish Emperor made Indians vassals of the Crown of Castile and provided for their release from slavery unless owners could prove a legal title, and no more to be enslaved

1569

Jan. 25, Decree of Philip II of Spain established the tribunal of the Inquisition in New Spain, established Nov. 2, 1571

1570

Nov. 5, Decree of Philip II forbade any trade with foreigners; renewed from time to time

1573

Dec. 1, Cedula of Philip II on colonization promulgated

1576

June 7, The excise tax of the *alcabala* at first 2% later 6% levied on all inheritances or transfers of property, on all sales or barter or exchange of commodities between 2 or more individuals

1713

April 11, By Treaty of Utrecht the English obtained right to furnish negro slaves to Spanish colonies, and the French concessions of trade at ports of Chile and Peru

1741

June 11, George Anson arrived at Juan Fernandez Islands and ravaged coast of South America

1743

Voyage of La Condamine down the Amazon, first scientist to descend the river

1750

Jan. 13, Boundary Treaty between Spain and Portugal defined Spanish and Portuguese lands; replaced by new Agreement Feb. 12, 1761

1764

Aug. 24, Royal Ordinance established postal service between Spain and the Spanish colonies in America

1767

Feb. 27, Decree expelled Jesuits from Spanish colonies

1776

Aug. 22, Northern New Spain established as an independent Viceroyalty separated from Mexico

1777

Oct. 1, Treaty of San Ildefonso between Spain and Portugal established new line of demarcation between Spanish and Portuguese lands

1778

Oct. 12, Ordinance permitted free trade between Spain and 20 ports in New Spain, and reduced duties on traffic; Venezuela excluded but included in 1789

1784

Jan. 20, Royal Decree prohibited foreign ships from entering ports of Spanish colonies

1786

Dec. 4, Royal Ordinance appointed intendants for New Spain

1790

June 18, Casa de Contratacion established in 1503 to have charge of all commerce, navigation, and affairs of the Spanish colonies abolished

1799

July 16, Alexander Humboldt landed at Cumana beginning his exploration, spent 4 months on Orinoco and proved connection with Amazon

1809

Jan. 22, Royal Decree declared South American colonies entitled to direct representation in Spanish Cortes

May 25, First revolt against Spain in Bolivia. *See* Bolivia, and other countries for wars of independence

1813

June 8, Decree of Spanish Cortes published suppressed Inquisition

1814

May 4, Decree of Spanish King Ferdinand, restored to the throne, annulled the liberal Constitution of March 19, 1812 which he had undertaken to support before he entered Madrid May 14

July 21, The Inquisition restored by Ferdinand

1815

Sept. 6, Letter of Simon Bolivar from Jamaica urged Confederation of South American States

1816

March 25, First Congress of United Provinces of South America at Tucuman, representatives of Argentina, Uruguay, and Paraguay

Sept. 7, Royal Order established a Junta at Madrid for the pacification of America

1822

June 19, First recognition of Spanish-American Republic by the United States, President Monroe receiving Manuel Torres as the representative of Colombia

1823

Jan. 27, Recognition of Chile and United Provinces of La Plata by the United States by appointment of Ministers

Oct. 10, England accredited consular representatives to chief towns of Spanish America

Dec. 2, Message of President Monroe to Congress announced "Monroe Doctrine" that the American continents were not to be considered henceforth as subjects for future colonization by European Powers, and any action against the independence of the Spanish American Republics would be regarded as "manifestation of an unfriendly disposition toward the United States"

1824

May 26, Independence of Brazil recognized by the United States

Sept. 24, Encyclical of Pope Leo XII addressed to bishops and archbishops of America asked them to support Ferdinand

Dec. 7, Bolivar issued invitation to a Congress at Panama

1825

Jan. 11, Announcement of Canning to the diplomatic corps in London of his intention to recognize the Spanish-American States

May 13 and 29, Portugal recognized the independence of Brazil

1826

Jan. 8, France recognized the independence of Brazil

Jan. 28, The Pope recognized the independence of Brazil

June 22–July 15, Bolivar's Congress met at Panama City, Great Colombia, Guatemala, Mexico, and Peru represented, signed Treaty of "union, league, and perpetual confederation"; not ratified

1835

Nov. 26, The Pope recognized the independence of New Granada

1836

Dec. 4, Decree of the Spanish Cortes authorized the Government to recognize the independence of the Spanish-American Republics

1847

Dec. 11–March 1, 1848, International Congress met at Lima with representatives from Peru, New Granada, Bolivia, Chile, and Ecuador, and Feb. 8 adopted Treaty of confederation, commerce, and navigation

1856

Sept. 15, International Congress at Santiago, Chile, with representatives from Peru, Chile, and Ecuador signed the "Continental Treaty" to promote union; never effective

1864

Nov. 14–March 13, 1865, Second International Congress met in Lima, Peru, with object of forming a union of the Spanish-American States, attended by representatives from Guatemala, Venezuela, Colombia, Ecuador, Argentina, Bolivia, and Peru, and Jan. 23, 1865, Treaty of Union signed by delegates from Bolivia, Chile, Colombia. Ecuador, Peru, and Salvador

1877

Dec. 9, International Congress of Jurists met at Lima, Peru, with representatives from Peru, Argentina, Bolivia, Chile, Ecuador, Venezuela, Central America, and Cuba and drew up treaties of extradition

1881

Nov. 29, Secretary of State of the United States, James G. Blaine, invited States to a conference to be held in Washington with the object of consideration of "methods of preventing war" between American States; invitation withdrawn by Secretary of State Frelinghuysen

1889

Oct. 2–April 19, 1890, First Pan-American Conference met in Washington to "consider measures for preserving the peace," Secretary of State Blaine of the United States presiding, established Bureau of American Republics later Pan-American Union for collection and distribution of commercial information. The majority of the delegates voted for compulsory arbitration, and recommendations were made for reciprocity in trade, uniform customs regulations, port duties, sanitary regulations, free navigation of rivers, monetary union, uniform weights and measures, patents and trade marks, intercontinental railroad

1890

March 29, International Bureau of American Republics organized

1901

Oct. 22–Jan. 31, 1902, Second Pan-American Conference met in Mexico City; a pact for compulsory arbitration signed by 10 delegates, and agreement that the States should adhere to the Hague Conventions of 1899 which provided for voluntary arbitration, and resolution adopted that financial claims of citizens of one State against the Government of another should be submitted to the Hague Court, the International Bureau of American Republics reorganized, resolutions as to trade marks, patents, and copyrights passed

1903

Jan. 15, First Customs Congress met in New York City with representatives from 13 American States. A commission of jurists created to frame codes of international law, the Drago doctrine against the forcible collection of public debts approved, and resolution adopted that the Second Peace Conference at The Hague should draw up a general arbitration convention and consider the question of forcible collection of public debts. Resolutions adopted at Mexico City reaffirmed

1904

June 12, International Sanitary Convention signed by Argentina, Brazil, Paraguay, and Uruguay

1906

July 21–Aug. 26, Third Pan-American Conference met in Rio de Janeiro, Brazil, with delegates from all American States except Haiti and Venezuela

1907

Hamilton Rice began explorations of the Amazon Basin

1908

Dec. 25–Jan. 5, 1909, First Pan-American Scientific Congress met at Santiago, Chile

1910

July 12–Aug. 30, Fourth Pan-American Conference met at Buenos Aires, Argentina. Conventions drawn up for payment of financial claims, trade marks, copyrights and patents, and 20 resolutions adopted. Name of the Bureau changed to Pan-American Union and scope enlarged

1912

June 26, International Commission of Jurists met at Rio de Janeiro to prepare codes regulating relations between American States

1914

Feb. 27, Theodore Roosevelt reached the River of Doubt, and April 5, the Amazon

1915

May 24, First Pan-American Financial Conference in Washington

May 25, Peace and Arbitration Treaty signed by Argentina, Brazil, and Chile, the "A.B.C." Treaty

Dec. 27–Jan. 1916, Second Pan-American Scientific Congress met at Washington, and appointed an International High Commission to meet in 1916 to promote uniform commercial laws

1916

April 3, International High Commission met at Buenos Aires, improvement of cable, telegraph, and railroad service and merchant marine advocated

April 15, Permanent International High Commission created, Secretary McAdoo, president, John Bassett Moore, vice-president, to frame uniform laws for the American States

1918

Nov. 13, Pan-American Federation of Labor Conference met at Laredo, Texas, with delegates from the United States, Mexico, and Central America, Colombia only of the South American States represented on account of influenza epidemic

1923

Jan. 1, Latin-American Office of League of Nations Secretariat organized with headquarters at Geneva

March 25–May 11, Fourth Pan-American Conference met at Santiago, Chile, with delegates from the United States, and all the Central and South American Republics except Bolivia and Peru, and Mexico was not represented. Four Conventions adopted and signed dealing with investigation and settlement of disputes by a fact-finding commission, trademarks, uniformity of nomenclature of merchandise, and publicity of customs documents, and 72 resolutions adopted on public health, copyrights, agriculture, sanitation, education, parcels post, and 4 permanent committees appointed to study commercial relations, hygiene, organization of labor, and coöperation of universities in the Americas

May 3, Pan-American Treaty for the pacific settlement of disputes (Gondra Pact) signed

Nov. 25–Dec. 6, First Pan-American Red Cross Conference at Buenos Aires

1924

Nov. 14, Sanitary Code signed provided for a Pan-American Sanitary Bureau

1925

Jan., First Pan-American Conference on the uniformity of specifications held at Lima, Peru

1928

Jan. 16–Feb. 20, Sixth Pan-American Conference met at Havana, Cuba, delegations from all American Republics present including the United States. Convention placed the Pan-American Union on a treaty basis, Pan-American Convention on aërial navigation adopted, and 14 conferences arranged for to be held under auspices of the Pan-American Union

Dec. 10–Jan. 6, 1929, Pan-American Conference on arbitration and conciliation in Washington and adopted Conventions on arbitration and conciliation, the Gondra Treaty modified, 2 permanent commissions at Montevideo and Washington, respectively, to deal with disputes, and the temporary commissions continued

1929

Jan. 6–8, Pan-American Commercial Congress met in New York City

Oct. 29, American Academy of International Law inaugurated and Cuba declared the permanent seat

1930

Sept. 8–20, First Pan-American Conference on agriculture met in Washington

ARGENTINA

Argentina (Argentine Republic) second in area and population of the South American States, occupies the largest part of southern South America divided from Chile on the west by the Andes, and bounded by Chile on the south, the Atlantic Ocean and Uruguay, Brazil, and Paraguay on the east, Paraguay and Bolivia on the north. The fourteen provinces, 10 territories and 1 federal district have an area of 1,153,119 square miles, population of 11,192,702 as estimated Jan. 1930. In an official estimate of May 1, 1929 the total population is given as 11,000,000, including 8,400,000 natives and 2,600,000 foreigners.

The Indian population, steadily dwindling, is estimated at from 20,000 to 30,000.

Population of the capital, Buenos Aires, on January 30, 1930, was 2,116,284; Rosario (Santa Fé), June, 1922, 265,000; Córdoba, December 31, 1929, 239,600; La Plata, May, 1928, 165,813; Avellaneda (1914), 46,277; Tucumán, 91,216; Bahía Blanca, 44,143; Santa Fé, 59,574; Mendoza, 58,790; Paraná, 36,089; Salta, 28,436; Lomas de Zamora, 22,231; Río Cuarto, 18,421; Corrientes, 28,681; Quilmes, 19,311; Concordia, 20,107.

Argentina was discovered by Juan Díaz de Solís and Vicente Pinzon. The name is a latinization of the name of the La Plata River, the name taken by the provinces in 1816 declared the

United Provinces of Rio de la Plata (United Provinces of the Silver River). Of the area of 699,278,300 acres, about 250,000,000 is used for cattle raising, and 250,000,000 for agriculture, 92,250,000 are woodland and the remainder 103,028,300 acres are mountain, lake, river, or arid regions.

Lieutenant-General Don José F. Uriburu, Provisional President.

1508

June 29, Voyage of Vicente Pinzon and Juan Diaz de Solis which coasted South American coast as far as the Colorado River, Argentina

1513

Portuguese navigator Nuno Manuele Christovão de Haro entered Rio de la Plata

1516

Feb., On second voyage to South America Juan Diaz de Solis explored the estuary of the Rio de La Plata which he had probably discovered in 1508 in search of a passage to the Spice Islands, naming the estuary "Mare Dulce." He was killed by the Indians

1520

Jan. 11, Magellan examined the estuary of the Rio de La Plata in search of passage to the East Indies

March 31–Aug. 24, Magellan in winter quarters at Port Saint Julian, Argentina

Oct. 21, Magellan arrived at Cabo de las Virgenes and sailed through the straits, which he named Todos los Santos but which later were named after him, to the Pacific Ocean (Mare Pacificum) Nov. 28

1526

Sebastian Cabot in service of Spain entered the Parana River and at the mouth of the Tercero founded first settlement in Argentina which he named San Espiritu. He named the Rio de La Plata (Silver River) because of the silver ornaments he received from the Indians and according to Hirst from the silver color of the River. He also ascended the Paraguay River

1530

Cabot returned to Spain leaving 170 persons under Captain Nuno de Lara at San Espiritu

1534

Sept. 1, Don Pedro de Mendoza granted land in the La Plata region sailed from San Lucar with 2,500 colonists and 100 horses

1535

Feb. 2, Pedro de Mendoza founded city of Santa Maria de Buenos Aires. Hostility of the Indians prevented permanent settlement at this time. Mendoza returned to Spain leaving colony in charge of Juan de Ayolas

1536

Region of the Rio de La Plata made part of the Viceroyalty of Peru

1537

Aug. 15, Juan de Ayolas built fort named Asuncion near junction of the Pilcomayo and the Paraguay rivers and colony moved there

Sept. 12, Juan de Ayolas by royal commission succeeded Mendoza as head of the colony. He was killed by Indians returning from expedition into interior

Domingo Martinez de Irala succeeded Ayolas as Governor

1541

Oct. 18, Alvaro Nunez Cabeza de Vaca led Spanish colonists from Santa Catharina in Brazil overland to Asuncion. Succeeded Irala as Governor

1542

March 11, Cabeza de Vaca, new Governor arrived at Asuncion

July 12, Cabeza de Vaca led successful expedition against the Guaycurus

Cabeza de Vaca with 400 Spaniards made second attempt to establish settlement at Buenos Ayres. Abandoned after a few months

1544

Martinez de Irala Governor a second time. Cabeza de Vaca sent to Spain for trial. Acquitted

1555

Pedro de la Torre appointed bishop. Juan de Barrios had been appointed first bishop but had never assumed duties

1557

Death of Governor Irala. He designated Gonzalo Mendoza as his successor

1558

Death of Governor Mendoza. Francisco Ortiz de Vergara elected Governor by the colonists. Not confirmed by Peru. Juan Ortiz de Zarate appointed by Viceroy

1560

City of Mendoza founded by Pedro del Castillo

1561

Santiago del Estero founded by Francisco de Aguirre

1563

Aug., Philip II separated Tucuman from Chile and appointed Aguirre Governor

1573

Cordoba founded by Geronimo Luis Cabrera, and Santa Fé by de Garay

1575

Death of Governor Ortiz de Zarate. Diego Mendieta *ad interim* Governor. Succeeded by Juan de Garay (1576–84)

1580

June 11, Juan de Garay with colonists from Asuncion made first permanent settlement at Buenos Ayres

1582

Salta founded by Hernando de Lerma

1584

Garay killed by the Indians. Juan de Torres Navarrete *ad interim* Governor

1586

The Jesuits arrived in the Argentine

1587

Juan de Torres de Vera succeeded Garay as Governor (1587–91)

1588

Corrientes founded (Hirst)

1591

Hernando Arias de Saavedra a Colonial elected Governor by the colonists. Confirmed by the Crown (1591–94)

1592

Jujuy founded

1594

Fernando de Zarate succeeded Saavedra as Governor

1595

Feb. 16, Governor Zarate began construction of a fort at Buenos Ayres

Juan Ramirez de Velasco Governor on death of Zarate (1595–97)

1597

Saavedra became Governor a second time (1597–99)

1599

Rodriguez de Valdez appointed Governor by the King (1599–1602)

1602

Saavedra again Governor, appointed Governor and Captain General by the Viceroy of Peru (1602–09)

1608

First school established at Buenos Ayres by Felipe Arias de Mansilla

1609

Diego Martinez Negron, Governor

1614

Feb., University founded by Bishop Trejo at Cordoba in 1613 opened as the Colegio Maximo

1615

Hernando Arias de Saavedra again Governor (1615–18)

1618

All settlements south of the confluence of the Parana and Paraguay rivers formed into the separate province of the Rio de La Plata under the Viceroy of Peru with Buenos Ayres as the capital including Buenos Aires, Santa Fé, Entre Rios, Corrientes, and the present Uruguay, Diego de Gongora the first Governor

1620

Buenos Aires made seat of bishop

1623

Alonso Perez de Salazar *ad interim* Governor of the Rio de La Plata

1624

Francisco de Cespedes, Governor

1629

Portuguese from the Brazilian State of Sao Paulo attacked the Reduction of San Antonio killing and capturing Indians and expelling the Jesuits

1632
Pedro Esteban d'Avilla, Governor

1638
Mendo de la Cueva y Benavides, Governor

1640
Ventura Mujica, Governor

1641
Jeronimo Luis de Cabrera, Governor

1646
Jacinto de Lariz, Governor

1653
Pedro Luis Baegorry, Governor

1656
Indian uprising led by Bahorquez claiming to be descendant and heir of the Incas

1660
Alonso de Mercado y Villacorta, Governor

1662
José Martinez de Salazar, Governor

1665
Audiencia (High Court) established in Buenos Aires

1672
Audiencia abolished

1674
Agustin de Robles, Governor

1678
José de Garro, Governor

1682
José de Herrera, Governor

1691
Agustin de Robles, Governor

1700
Manuelde Prado Maldonado, Governor

1704
Alonso de Valdez Inclan, Governor

1708
Manuel Velazco, Governor

1712
Alonso de Arce Saria, Governor

1713
April 11, By the Peace of Utrecht England obtained contract for supply of African slaves to Spanish colonies, Buenos Aires named as mart for the traffic
Baltasar Garcia Ros, Governor

1717
Bruno Mauricio de Zabala, Governor

1734
Miguel de Salcedo, Governor

1742
Domingo Ortes de Rosas, Governor

1745
José de Andronaigui, Governor

1746
Pedro de Ceballos, Governor
The Jesuit, Quiroga, first to explore shores of Patagonia

1766
Francisco de Buccarelli, Governor

1767
July 13, Royal edict expelling Jesuits published in Buenos Aires, and Jesuits made prisoners on the 22d and deported Aug. 20 and Sept. 29

1770
Juan José Vertiz, Governor

1776
Aug. 1, The La Plata Province with Buenos Aires established as a viceroyalty independent of Peru. Pedro de Ceballos made first Viceroy (1776–78)

1777
April 2, Viceroy Ceballos with 9,000 Spanish soldiers landed at Montevideo from Cadiz, Spain
June 4, The Portuguese settlement of Colonia (Uruguay) surrendered to forces of Ceballos
Oct. 1, By treaty of San Ildefonso between Spain and Portugal, Portugal withdrew from Uruguay
Oct. 27, Royal decree declared viceroyalty of La Plata permanent

1778
Juan José de Vertiz y Salcedo, Viceroy (1778–84)
Trade restrictions relaxed permitting trade with foreign countries

1780
Colony of Carmen de Patagones established near mouth of the Negro river first permanent settlement made in Patagonia

1784
Nicolas del Campo, Marques de Loreto, Viceroy (1784–89)

1785
Aug., Audiencia recreated 1782 formally opened in Buenos Aires

1789
Nicolas de Arredondo, Viceroy (1789–95)

1795
Pedro Melo de Portugal y Villena, Viceroy (1795–97)

1797
Antonio Olagner Feliu, Viceroy (1797–99) and the Royal Audiencia

1799
Gabriel de Aviles y del Fierro, Viceroy (1799–1801)

1801

Joaquin de Pina, Viceroy (1801–04)

April 1, *El Telegrafo Mercantil* first newspaper published in Buenos Aires

1804

Rafael Sobremonte, Marques de Sobremonte, Viceroy (1804–06)

1806

Santiago Liniers, Viceroy (1806–09)

June 27, Buenos Aires captured by English expedition commanded by General Beresford and Sir Home Popham. Viceroy fled to Cordova making no defense

Aug. 12, General Beresford forced to surrender to patriots led by Jacques de Liniers

1807

June 28, English General Whitelock landed at port of Ensenada from Montevideo which they had taken by assault

July 5, English attack on Buenos Aires at first successful but finally driven from city by de Liniers

July 7, Capitulation signed by English

July 12, General Whitelock sailed from Buenos Aires

1808

Aug. 21, Act of fealty to Ferdinand VII

1809

Jan. 1, Insurrection of Alzaga against de Liniers in Buenos Aires suppressed by General Saavedra

May 25, Insurrection at Chuquisaca deposed Spanish government

July 30, Baltasar Hidalgo Cisneros y la Torre, last Viceroy assumed office

1810

May 18, Proclamation of Viceroy Cisneros stated that "within the confines of the American continent the liberty and independence of the Spanish monarchy would be preserved"

May 25, The Cabildo of Buenos Aires deposed Viceroy and replaced him by provisional Junta ostensibly formed to preserve the authority of Ferdinand VII of Spain composed of President General Cornelio de Saavedra, Belgrano, Alberdi, Castelli, Azcuenaga, Matheu Larrea, Paso, and Moreno

June 1, Cisneros and other officials loyal to Spain deported

June, "La Gaceta de Buenos Aires" founded

Aug., "Plan of operations which the provisional government of the United Provinces of the Rio de la Plata should pursue to consolidate the great work of our liberty and independence" ascribed to Mariano Moreno, completed

Nov. 7, Patriots successful in the battle of Suipacha

Dec. 6, Titles and honors formerly accorded to President Saavedra revoked as concession to the democratic ideas of Moreno

Dec., Deputies from the provinces included in the governing Junta

1811

Jan., Mariano Moreno with his brothers Manuel and Tomas Guido sent on diplomatic mission to England to ask for help in revolt against Spain. Moreno died on the way. Mission unsuccessful

Feb. 18, Spanish fleet blockaded Buenos Aires

March 2, First naval battle in front of San Nicolas de los Arroyas

April 5–6, Revolution of the fifth and sixth of April forced reorganization of Junta of Buenos Aires by dismissal of four members

June 20, Argentine army invaded Bolivia. *See* Bolivia

Sept. 23, Junta abdicated and executive power vested in a triumvirate composed of Feliciano Chiclana, Manuel de Sarratea, and Juan J. Paso

Oct. 18, Commercial Convention concluded between Juntas of Buenos Aires and Asuncion

Nov. 22, Provisional statute for the Government of the United Provinces of La Plata promulgated

1812

March 9, José de San Martin landed at Buenos Aires, his native land with Carlos Alvear and Matias Zapiola and established branch of the secret "Gran Reunion Americana" for the revolution which they called the "Logiade Lautaro"

March 16, San Martin appointed lieutenant-colonel of cavalry by the Junta of Buenos Aires

May 15, Prohibition of importation of slaves

Sept. 24, General Belgrano defeated Spanish royalist army commanded by General Pio Tristan at Tucuman

Oct. 7–8, Meeting of citizens elected new triumvirate composed of Juan J. Paso, Rodriguez Pena, and Alvarez Jonte

1813

Jan. 31, Constituent congress met at Buenos Aires. Made declaration abolishing slavery

Feb. 3, First victory of San Martin defeat of Spanish army at San Lorenzo

Feb. 20, General Belgrano forced royalists to capitulate at Salta

Oct. 1, General Belgrano defeated by Spaniards in battle at Vilcapugio

Nov. 26, Belgrano's army routed by royalists on plains of Ayohuma

1814

Jan. 18, San Martin appointed commander-in-chief of army of Buenos Aires which he reorganized

Jan. 31, Congress at Buenos Aires chose Gervasio Posadas as Dictator

March 17, Admiral Brown defeated Spanish fleet and took possession of Island of Martin Garcia in River Plata

April, San Martin resigned as commander-in-chief

April 20, Admiral Brown began blockade of Montevideo

May 16, Admiral Brown defeated Spanish squadron off Montevideo

May 25, Arenales ambushed royalist force at La Florida

June 20, Montevideo, Uruguay captured by Argentine force. *See* Uruguay

Aug. 10, San Martin appointed Governor-Intendant of province of Cuyo where from 1814 to 1821 he trained and organized Army of the Andes

1815

Jan.–April, Carlos Maria de Alvear "Supreme director"

April–April, 1816, José Rondeau "Supreme director"

1816

March 24, Congress composed chiefly of Argentinians met at Tucuman

May 3, Juan Martin Puyrredon of Buenos Aires made "Supreme director" of the Confederation

May 7, Rivadavia and Belgrano arrived in Europe to seek assistance in revolt against Spain. Mission unsuccessful

July 9, Congress of Tucuman declared United Provinces of Rio de la Plata independent of Spain

Aug. 1, Puyrredon appointed San Martin commander-in-chief of Army of the Andes and Dec. 21 signed order for expedition against royalists in Chile

Oct. 2, Manifesto of Congress declared Assembly removed from Tucuman to Buenos Aires

Dec. 3, Prohibition of exportation of slaves

1817

Jan. 18, General San Martin's army began march over the Andes to free Chile from the Spanish rule. *See* Chile

1818

May 11, General San Martin returned to Buenos Aires

1819

May 25, Constitution of United Provinces of South America promulgated modeled on that of the United States

June 10, José Rondeau elected Dictator

Sept. 23, General Soublette, Bolivian general, in indecisive battle with Latorre at Rosario

1820

Feb., Rondeau defeated in battle at Cepeda by Gauchos of Lopez and Ramirez

Feb. 23, Treaty of Pilar recognized the "Litoral Federation" and undertook to pay indemnity

May 27, Junta authorized a gradual issue of paper money

June 20, Death of General Belgrano

Nov. 9, Formal possession taken of the Falkland Islands by Government of Buenos Aires

General Martin Rodriguez named Governor of Buenos Aires. Established some order. Entered into diplomatic relations with foreign nations

1821

April 16, King John VI recognized the United Provinces of La Plata as independent nation in the name of Portugal and Brazil

April 20, Puyrredon landed called from exile by Government

July 29, Figuieredo officially received as Minister from Portugal by Government at Buenos Aires

University of Buenos Aires founded

1822

March 7 and 8, Notes of American Secretary of State John Quincy Adams recognized independence of Argentine Republic

Sept. 16, Notes of Bank of Buenos Aires issued for first time, amount 26,400 pesos

1823

Jan. 27, Appointment of C. A. Rodney as American Minister to the United Provinces confirmed by United States Senate

Oct. 1, First number of the newspaper *Gaceta Mercantil* published which continued until Feb. 3, 1852

Dec. 15, Note of Secretary George Canning by which

Great Britain recognized independence of United Provinces

Dec. 23, General Carlos de Alvear appointed first Minister to the United States

1824

May 9, Juan de Las Heras took office as Governor

Dec. 16, Constituent Assembly of delegates from certain provinces met at Buenos Aires

1825

Jan. 23, Constituent Assembly promulgated a fundamental law providing that the provinces should be governed by their own institutions until a national constitution adopted. National executive power *pro tem* to be vested in the Governor of Buenos Aires

Feb. 2, Commercial Treaty with Great Britain signed at Buenos Aires

Feb. 7, Don Bernardo Rivadavia representing the Centralist party inaugurated as President

Dec. 10, Brazil declared war because of incorporation of Uruguay (Banda Oriental) in Argentine Confederation

1826

Jan. 20, Discount Bank made the national bank

Feb. 6, Congress vested executive power in a President. Bernardino Rivadavia chosen first President

May 5, Law postponed all redemption of notes of National Bank until 1828

May 7, Law made all bank notes full legal tender in settlement of contracts

July 19, Congress adopted a centralistic constitution of the "Argentine Republic." Buenos Aires made the capital

Dec. 24, Constitution submitted to provinces. Rejected by several

1827

Feb. 20, Battle of Itiuzaingo. Alvear returned from exile and given command of army defeated Brazilians

May 24, Preliminary Treaty of peace with Brazil. Not ratified

July 5, Resignation of President Rivadavia, "unitarian," in dispute with Congress in opposition to his centralized constitution and to Buenos Aires as capital

Aug. 13, Manuel Dorrego elected Governor of Buenos Aires. Undertook to organize a new Confederation of United Provinces

1828

Aug. 27, Treaty with Brazil signed by which the independence of Uruguay guaranteed and war ended

Dec. 1, Governor Dorrego, federalist, forced to leave the country because of rebellion of the soldiers under leadership of General Juan Lavalle, unitarian, who seized the government

Dec. 13, Dorrego defeated by Lavalle at Navarro shot without trial by Lavalle

1829

April, Federalists commanded by Lopez and Rosas defeated General Lavalle who fled to Uruguay

June 10, Government of Buenos Aires published decree affirming sovereignty over Falkland Islands

Dec. 8, Juan Manuel de Rosas elected Governor of the province of Buenos Aires beginning the "Age of Rosas"

1832

Dec. 17, General Juan R. Balcarce named Governor of Buenos Aires

1833

Sept. 3, Diplomatic relations severed by United States because of Falkland Islands incidents, capture of American sealing vessels in 1831 for violation of Argentine fishing laws

Nov., Juan J. Viamont, Governor of Buenos Aires

1834

Oct., Manuel V. de Maza, Governor of Buenos Aires

1835

March 7, Juan Manuel de Rosas appointed Governor of Buenos Aires. Twelve provinces gave him authority as national executive

1836

May 30, Decree declared National Bank dissolved, the Casa de Moneda created to issue paper money for expenses

1837

May 12, Sardinia recognized independence of Provinces of the Rio de la Plata

1838

June 20, Notification of blockade of coast of Argentine by French vessels in dispute with General Rosas

1839

Feb. 24, Uruguay declared war on Rosas

Nov. 7, Insurrection led by Beron de Astrada, governor of Province of Corrientes, against Rosas defeated at Chascomus. Astrada captured and executed

General Lavalle organized an expedition against the government of Rosas. Defeated and killed

1841

Jan. 20, Protocol with Denmark signed which recognized independence of Argentina

1843

April 11, Independence of Argentina recognized by Bremen

1844

March 1, Protocol with Hamburg signed recognized independence of Argentina

Oct. 2, Protocol with Prussia signed recognized independence of Argentina

1845

April, English and French fleets blockaded Buenos Aires claiming free navigation of the Rio de la Plata

Sept. 2, Death of Bernardino Rivadavia at Cadiz, Spain

1846

Jan. 3, Independence recognized by Sweden and Norway

Feb. 4, General Urquiza defeated Corrientes insurgents in battle of Vences

1847

Nov. 3, Treaty of commerce with Peru signed

1849

Nov. 24, Treaty of friendship with Great Britain signed

1850

Aug. 17, Death of General San Martin at Bologne, France

1851

May 1, General Justo José de Urquiza, Governor of Entre Rios, in alliance with Virasoro, Governor of Corrientes declared against Rosas

May 25, Proclamation of General Urquiza urged civilians and soldiers to rise against Rosas

May 29, At Montevideo an offensive and defensive treaty signed with Brazil by representatives of Colorados of Uruguay and revolutionists of Entre Rios

1852

Jan. 8, General Urquiza completed passage of the Parana river with 28,000 men and advanced on Buenos Aires

Feb. 3, Forces of Brazil and Uruguay united with General Urquiza defeated Rosas in battle at Monte-Caseros. Rosas fled to England

Feb. 19, General Urquiza and allied armies entered Buenos Aires

Feb. 22, Te Deum in cathedral celebrated overthrow of tyrant Rosas

May 31, Governors of 11 Provinces framed agreement of 19 Articles at San Nicolas providing for election of delegates to a constituent assembly. General Urquiza given title of Provisional Director of the Argentine Confederation. Not accepted by the Province of Buenos Aires

July 15, Treaty of commerce, navigation, and limits with Paraguay signed

Sept. 3, Decree of general amnesty

Sept. 11, Buenos Aires declared independence of the Confederation under leadership of General Mitre

Nov. 20, Constituent Assembly met at Sante Fé

1853

May 1, Constitution modeled on that of the United States adopted by Constituent Assembly. Slavery prohibited

May 5, General Urquiza elected provisional President

May 25, The Constitution dated May 15 adopted by vote

July 10, Treaty with England, France, and the United States declared free navigation of the Parana and other rivers

July 27, Treaty of friendship, commerce, and navigation with the United States signed

Oct. 12, Buenos Aires seceded from Confederation. First Governor Dr. D. Pastor Obligado elected

1854

Jan. 1, Mint transferred into the Provincial Bank

Jan. 9, Concession granted for construction of railroad from Buenos Aires to Flores. Signed by Governor Jan. 12. First railroad law

March 5, General Urquiza inaugurated as first constitutional President of the "Argentine Confederation." Parana made the capital

April 2, Decree granted concession to William Wheelwright for construction of railroad from Rosario to Cordoba

April 12, Buenos Aires adopted a Constitution

Sept. 5, Concession granted by national Government for railroad from Rosario to Cordoba

1855

Jan. 8, Peace concluded between the Province of Buenos Aires and the Confederation

Aug. 30, Treaty of friendship, commerce, and navigation with Chile signed

1856

March 7, Treaty of friendship, commerce, and navigation with Brazil signed. Provided that navigation of the Rio de La Plata system should remain free in time of war

July 29, Treaty of friendship, commerce, and navigation with Paraguay signed

Oct. 1, Declaration of maritime rights signed with France and Great Britain

1857

May, Dr. Valentin Alsina elected Governor of Buenos Aires

Aug. 30, First railroad opened from Buenos Aires to San José de Flores

Sept. 19, Treaty of friendship, commerce, and navigation with Prussia signed

Nov. 20, Convention with Brazil declared rivers Uruguay, Parana, and Paraguay free to ships of all nations

Dec. 14, Boundary Treaty defined frontiers with Brazil in Misiones District, the right bank of the Uruguay recognized as Argentine territory

1858

July 9, Treaty of peace, amity, and recognition signed with Spain

1859

Jan. 2, Supplementary Convention of peace signed to Convention of 1828 with Brazil

Oct. 22, Buenos Aires army commanded by General Mitre defeated by General Urquiza at Cepeda

Nov. 10, Buenos Aires reunited with the Confederation by Treaty of peace and union

1860

Feb. 8, Dr. Santiago Derqui succeeded J. Urquiza as President of Argentina

Sept. 25, New Constitution ratified

Oct. 21, General Mitre, Governor of Buenos Aires, swore to support the Federal Constitution

Nov.–Jan., 1862, Insurrection in San Juan

1861

Sept. 17, Battle of Pavon. National army under Urquiza defeated by forces of Buenos Aires commanded by General Mitre

Nov. 5, Resignation of President Derqui

1862

April 22, General Bartolome Mitre, Governor of Buenos Aires, became Dictator assuming control of the national Government

May 25, National Congress convened by General Mitre met at Buenos Aires

Aug. 27, General Mitre elected President by Congress

Sept. 10, Commercial Code published

Oct. 12, President Mitre inaugurated. The national Government transferred from Parana to Buenos Aires, declared the capital

Oct. 16, Law reorganized the federal courts

1863

April 20, President Mitre broke ground at Rosario for construction of railroad for which concession had been granted to William Wheelwright

June 22, Government seized Uruguayan warship "General Artigas" and blockaded mouth of Uruguay River on account of seizure by Uruguay of contraband munitions of war consigned to revolutionists seized from Argentine steamer "Salto"

June 23, Uruguay severed diplomatic relations

June 29, Protocol of peace signed in which neutrality declared as to revolution in Uruguay

Sept. 14, Law provided for jurisdiction of federal courts

Sept. 21, Treaty of peace and amity with Spain signed by which Spain recognized independence of Argentine Republic

Oct. 28 and Nov. 3, Expeditions publicly left principal wharf in Buenos Aires to join Flores expedition

Dec. 10, Government announced interruption of diplomatic relations with Uruguay

1864

Aug. 22, Agreement with Brazil as to Uruguay

Oct. 11, Law enacted for protection of patents of invention

Nov. 24, Geneva Convention of 1864 ratified

1865

Feb. 9, Note refused to allow Paraguayan troops to cross Argentine territory

April 13, War with Paraguay begun. *See* Paraguay

April 19, Letter of General Urquiza offered his services to the national Government

May 1, Treaty of alliance with Brazil and Uruguay against Paraguay signed

May 2, Treaty of amity, commerce, and navigation with Bolivia signed

May 3, Note of President Lopez of Paraguay dated March 18 declaring war received

May 9, Formal declaration of war against Paraguay

1866

Sept. 12, Amendments to Constitution adopted

Nov. 9, Decree regulated application of patent law

1867

Cholera epidemic

1868

Jan. 2, Death of Vice-President Marcos Paz

July 9, Treaty of friendship, commerce, and navigation with Bolivia signed

Oct. 12, Colonel Domingo Faustino Sarmiento succeeded General Mitre as President

Nov., Insurrection of Corrientes suppressed

1869

Feb. 27, Boundary Treaty with Bolivia

Sept. 29, Civil Code adopted to go into effect Jan. 1, 1871

Oct. 8, Law enacted regulations for citizenship and naturalization

Oct. 18, First issue of newspaper *La Prensa*

Nov. 16, Treaty of extradition with Brazil signed

First census taken. Population 1,830,214

1870

April 12, Murder of Urquiza

May 17, Formal opening of Central Argentine Railroad to Cordoba

June, Treaty ended war with Paraguay

1872

Sept. 8, Law enacted for regulation of State railroads

Oct. 3, Law established the "Banco Nacional"

Dec., Wheelwright completed railroad from Buenos Aires to Ensenada

1873

Jan. 18, Treaty of friendship, commerce, and navigation with Brazil signed

Feb. 4, Decree of President Sarmiento reorganized the curricula for secondary schools

Nov., First section of Buenos Aires and Pacific Railway opened from Villa Nueva to Rio Cuarto

76,332 immigrants arrived during year

1874

March 9, Treaty of friendship, commerce, and navigation with Peru signed

Oct. 12, Dr. Nicolas Avellaneda became President

Dec. 2, Insurrection led by General Mitre at Buenos Aires (Sept.–Nov.) suppressed

1875

Feb. 28, Jesuits' college and palace of the archbishop burned and priests killed by mob. Martial law proclaimed

Aug. 26, Mining law enacted

Oct. 7, Telegraph law enacted

Oct. 22, Buenos Aires and Pacific Railway from Rio Cuarto to Villa Mercedes opened

1876

Jan. 14, Claims Protocol with Uruguay signed

Feb. 3, Treaty with Paraguay signed providing for submission of boundary dispute to the arbitration of the United States

May 16, Suspension of specie payments by Government

Oct. 10, Postal law enacted

Oct. 19, First Immigration and Colonization law enacted

1877

March 14, Death of ex-President Rosas in exile in England

April 28, Site of Indian city discovered in Catamarca

July 13, Law adopted metric system of weights and measures

1878

Jan. 18, Boundary Treaty with Chile signed

Nov. 13, President Hayes as arbitrator gave decision in favor of Paraguay in boundary dispute as to title of region of El Chaco

1880

Feb. 13, President Avellaneda held conference of officers including General Mitre, Colonel Arias, Colonel Julio Campos, Colonel Lagos, and others to question them as to their connection with the revolutionary society the "Tiro Nacional." The officers charged with treason resigned their commissions

Feb. 15, Meeting of the "Tiro Nacional" avoided clash with national troops by changing place of meeting. Demonstration of 2,000 members of the Society in the streets of Buenos Aires

Feb. 16, Meeting of citizens of Buenos Aires appointed a committee to confer with Dr. Carlos Tejedor, Governor of the Province, and arrange for a *modus vivendi* by which the Portenos should be given representation in national affairs

May, Colonel Lisandro Olmos unsuccessful in attempt to start Porteno revolution at Cordoba

June, Attack on escort of the President in Buenos Aires by Portenos brought about civil war

June 13, Red Cross Society founded

July 20–21, Battle outside Buenos Aires for possession of the city. Colonel Racedo commanding national troops attacked Colonel Arias commanding the Portenos and advancing to join General Julio Campos

July 22, Armistice declared and conference of leaders at which the Portenos because of lack of ammunition were obliged to accept terms of National Government

Sept. 21, National Congress divided Buenos Aires from the Province of that name and made it the capital of the Republic as the Federal District and ratified the election of General Julio Roca as President

Oct. 2, Railroad Loan of $12,000,000 authorized

Oct. 12, Inauguration of President Roca

1881

July 23, Treaty with Chile signed which ended quarrel with Chile over boundary. Argentina obtained Patagonia to line made by the Cordilleras and a part of Tierra del Fuego

1882

Feb. 15, Buenos Aires Exposition opened

Oct. 2, Code of criminal procedure for Federal District adopted

Oct. 24, Public land law enacted provided for sales at public auction at fixed minimum price, a certain number of acres allowed each purchaser, and for surveys

1884

Feb. 15, First railroad train from Buenos Aires crossed the Andes

Oct. 16, Organic law for government of national Territories enacted

1885

Jan., President Roca enacted measure declaring banknote currency inconvertible for 2 years

May 30, Treaty of friendship, commerce, and navigation with Chile signed

July 17, Treaty of friendship, commerce, and navigation with Sweden and Norway signed

Sept. 28, Territorial and Fluvial Convention with Brazil signed

Oct. 21, Public Works Loan authorized to amount of £8,400,000

Immigrants during the year 108,722

1886

Sept. 14, Law established National Mortgage Bank

Oct. 9, Central Northern Railway Loan authorized for £4,000,000

Oct. 12, Dr. Miguel Juarez Celman, brother-in-law of Roca, succeeded him as President

Nov., Decree postponed banknote conversion

Dec. 2, Act authorized issue of £2,058,200, the "National Bank Loan"

Dec. 8, Mining Code adopted to come into effect May 1, 1887

1887

March 1, Penal Code enacted Dec. 7, 1886 came into effect

June 21, Act authorized "Treasury Bonds Conversion Loan"

Aug. 15, Act authorized loan to balance debts of National Government and Province of Buenos Aires

Nov. 3, Organic Banking law enacted provided for establishment of banks of issue throughout the Republic whose notes should be guaranteed by national bonds

1888

Aug. 2, "Conversion of Debts Loan" authorized, £5,290,000 at 6%

Aug. 20, Supplementary Convention signed with Chile to Treaty of July, 1881

1889

July 2, "Conversion of Hard Dollars Loan" authorized, $13,403,380 at 3½%

Sept. 7, Arbitration Treaty with Brazil signed provided for arbitration of disputes in the Misiones territory and as to rivers

Oct. 30, Second Railway Loan authorized of £3,000,000

260,000 immigrants arrived during year

1890

April 13, New political party founded the Union Civica

July 5, Customs Tariff Convention with Belgium signed

July 7, Panic on Bourse at Buenos Aires due to failure of loans

July 26, Revolt in Buenos Aires organized by the Union Civica headed by Senators Alcru, Romero, and Del Valle against President Celman and his ministry charged with corruption. Fighting in the streets. Dr. Leandro N. Alem, President of the Union Civica with others formed a Provisional Government

July 27, Captain O'Connor assisting revolt opened naval fire on Buenos Aires

July 28–29, Armistice. Union Civica demand resignation of the President

Aug. 5, President Celman compelled to resign

Aug. 6, Vice-President Carlos Pelligrini assumed the executive office as formal resignation of the President accepted by Congress

Nov. 24, Financial crisis at Buenos Aires

Nov. 28, Salaries of officials of the Government reduced 10%

1891

Jan. 24, "Consolidated Loan" authorized

Feb. 14, Alleged conspiracy discovered in Buenos Aires. Officers of Celman régime arrested and 40 ordered to leave the country

Feb. 20–March 15, State of siege declared at Buenos Aires

March 4, Financial crisis. Banco Nacional and Banco de la Provincia de Buenos Aires closed

March 13, Banks reopened

March 18, General Bartolome Mitre arrived from Europe. Received by 50,000 people. Meeting of citizens petitioned him to become President

April 1, Law 2774 creating an internal revenue went into effect, tax on alcoholic liquors, matches, beer, banking transactions, insurance premiums

April 7, The Banco Nacional and Banco de la Provincia de Buenos Aires suspend payment until June 1

May 22, Insurrection in Cordoba suppressed after 11 hours fighting

June 2, Run on banks of Buenos Aires

June 11, Congress passed bill over President's veto

granting a moratorium and general suspension of debts and obligations for 6 months, later time reduced to 3 months

Oct. 5, Banking Law enacted authorized establishment of "Bank of the Argentine Nation" (Banco de la Nacion)

Nov. 24, The Exchange closed. Gold at 350

——, General railroad law promulgated

Dec. 1, Bank of the Argentine Nation opened

1892

April 2, State of siege declared on discovery of alleged attempt at revolution

April 3, Dr. Alem, General Garcia, and other radicals of the Union Civica arrested

April 9, Dr. Luis Saenz Pena elected President. Radicals abstained from voting. After the election political prisoners released except Dr. Alem who was kept in prison for several weeks longer

June 12, Congress declared President Pena elected

Oct. 12, President Pena inaugurated

1893

Jan., Insurgents took Cas

May 1, Supplementary Article to Convention of Aug., 1888, with Chile signed

June 8, President Pena reconstructed his Cabinet making it a "fusion" of all political parties, Dr. Wenceslao Escalante, Premier, not a success

July 6, New Ministry of Lucio Lopez, Radical

July 20, Radical revolt begun San Luis province, the Governor captured, and the following day in provinces of Santa Fé and Buenos Aires

Aug. 8, Del Valle commanding federal troops entered the port of Ensenada and disarmed contending factions

Aug. 14, Radicals eliminated from Cabinet, Manuel Quintana, Premier

Aug. 15, Congress declared a state of siege

Sept. 20, Government troops in Cordoba, Tucuman, and Corrientes joined revolt

Oct. 1, Rosario, headquarters of the revolution, captured by General Roca

1894

June 1, Commercial Convention providing for most favored nation treatment with Italy signed

June 30, Railroad Convention with Bolivia signed provided for construction of railroad from Atocha to Villazon

1895

Jan. 16, Cabinet resigned because of refusal of President Saenz Pena to issue decree of amnesty for all persons implicated in last revolution

Jan. 22, Resignation of President Saenz Pena

Jan. 23, Vice-President Uribu assumed the executive office and issued the desired decree

Feb. 5, President Cleveland, arbitrator in boundary dispute with Brazil over title of Misiones territory decided in favor of Brazil that boundary line should follow the westerly of the 2 river systems

Aug. 9, Protocol of Arbitration signed with the United States

Sept. 6, Agreement as to demarcation of boundary with Chile signed

Second census gave total population as 3,954,911

1896

April 17, Boundary Agreement with Chile signed

April 17, New Protocol of Arbitration with Great Britain signed

Aug. 8, Law authorized Conversion of Provincial Debts Loan

Sept. 26, Treaty of extradition with the United States signed

1897

Sept. 25, Law authorized Conversion of Municipal Stock Loan

1898

March 15, Amendments to the Constitution adopted

June 12, General J. A. Roca elected President

Sept. 23, Increase of customs duties on imported goods came into effect

Oct. 6, Boundary Convention with Brazil signed

Oct. 11, Law enacted prescribed duties and functions of various executive departments of the Government

Oct. 12, President Roca inaugurated

Nov. 2, Treaty signed with Chile to submit boundary dispute to arbitration

1899

Jan. 5, Law authorized loan of £6,000,000 to balance debts of Treasury

March 24, Award of American minister as regarded the Atacama district in boundary dispute with Chile decided in favor of Chile

June 8, Arbitration Treaty with Uruguay signed

Nov. 3, Law approved provided that nation should redeem paper pesos of 100 centavos for 44 centavos in gold

Nov. 6, Arbitration Treaty with Paraguay signed

1900

Jan. 15, Patent law came into effect

March, Revolt in Entre Rios suppressed by national troops

April 30, Agreement as to Andes boundary line with Chile signed

Oct. 25, Visit of Brazilian President Campos Salles to Buenos Aires

Nov. 23, Trade Marks Law enacted. Regulations issued Dec. 5

1901

July 3, Rioting in Buenos Aires. Government newspaper office wrecked because of opposition to President's proposal to unify the external and internal debt

Dec. 6, Law established compulsory military service

1902

Jan. 28, Treaty of Arbitration with Mexico signed

Feb. 3, Arbitration Treaty with Bolivia signed

May 8, Message of President Roca stated foreign debt to be $386,451,295

May 28, General Arbitration Treaty with Chile signed, one limiting naval armaments and agreement as to boundary marking

Nov. 20, Award of King Edward VII in boundary dispute with Chile as to Patagonia

Dec. 29, Federal Election law enacted

——, Note of Luis M. Drago, Minister of Foreign Affairs, to Argentine Minister in Washington, as to forcible collection of public debts in relation to blockade of Venezuela

Dec. 30, Bankruptcy Law promulgated

1903

Jan. 8, New Land Law enacted

Aug. 22, "Law of Reforms" enacted amended penal code of 1887

1904

June 12, Dr. Manuel Quintana elected President and Dr. José Figueroa Alcorta, Vice-President

——, Sanitary Convention with Brazil, Paraguay, and Uruguay signed

Sept. 10, Law enacted provided for civil pensions for certain government employees

Sept. 29, Banking law amended. Regulations Dec. 9 and Sept. 26, 1905

Sept. 30, Bank of the Argentine Nation made a State bank

Oct. 12, President Quintana inaugurated

Oct. 20, Treaty of peace and friendship with Bolivia signed

Immigrants arrived during the year 125,567

1905

Feb. 4, Revolution in Buenos Aires, Santa Fé, Cordoba, Bahia Blanca, and Mendoza soon suppressed

May, President Quintana proposed plan for electoral reform, gradual decrease of customs duties, abolition of export duties, and Bill fixing "monetary régime"

Sept. 6, Act established compulsory Sunday rest in factories, commercial houses, and workshops

Sept. 11, Agreement as to Pilcomayo River signed with Argentina

Sept. 17, Arbitration Treaty with Brazil signed

Sept. 25, Law enacted governing recruiting

Sept. 29, Consular service reorganized

Dec. 20, New Tariff enacted

1906

Jan. 18, Death of General Bartolome Mitre

March 12, Death of President Quintana. Succeeded by Vice-President Dr. Figueroa Alcorta

July 4, Work begun on railroad from Lima to Oroya, highest railroad in the world 15,665 feet above sea level at summit

Aug. 14, American Secretary of State Elihu Root arrived at Buenos Aires on official visit

Oct. 4, Law enacted for the exploitation of forests

Nov. 8, Regulations for Land Act of 1903 published

Dec. 12, Treaty of amity, commerce, and navigation with Brazil signed

Immigrants arrived during the year 302,000

1907

Feb. 7, Revolt at San Juan of Col. Carlos D. Sarmiento soon suppressed

March 14, National Department of Labor established

May 18, Convention with Bolivia signed under terms of which the North Central Railroad to be extended into Bolivia and a railroad constructed from Tupiza on the frontier

Sept. 18, Arbitration Treaty with Italy signed

Oct. 1, "Mitre Law" enacted gave Government control over all railroads. Regulating decree published April 30, 1908

Oct. 7, Sunday rest law enacted

Oct. 14, Labor Law regulated work of women and children in factories. Minimum age for children fixed at 10 years and all minors limited to 8 hours. Regulating decree published Feb. 20, 1908

1908

Jan., Congress dissolved because of opposition
March 8, Election a victory for the Government
Immigrants during the year 255,710

1909

May 1, Labor riots in Buenos Aires attributed to anarchists, 12 persons killed, 100 injured
July 20, Boundary dispute with Bolivia
Aug. 5, Railroad Act modified. New division in Ministry of Public Works created headed by an inspector general
Aug. 9, Naturalization Treaty with the United States signed
Sept. 30, Railroad Commission created charged with construction of national railway lines
Nov. 14, Assassination of Colonel Falcon, prefect of police at Buenos Aires, by a bomb thrown into his carriage. The Government declared a state of siege
Immigrants during the year 345,275

1910

Jan. 5, Protocol with Uruguay signed settled two year dispute regarding the navigation of the River Plate
March 13, Dr. Roque Saenz Pena elected President
April 5, Trans-Andean tunnel connecting Chile and Argentina by rail formally opened
June 3, Atlantic cable from Europe to Buenos Aires via Ascension Island opened, second longest in the world
Sept. 23, Copyright Act promulgated
Oct. 12, President Saenz Pena inaugurated
Dec. 4, Reëstablishment of diplomatic relations with Bolivia

1911

Jan. 9, Diplomatic relations with Bolivia resumed
Feb. 4, Decree provided regulations for patent law of 1910
June, Congress authorized new loan of $70,000,000 for schools and colleges and federal offices
July 12, Arbitration Treaty with Ecuador signed
July 20, Regulations published for labor law of Aug. 31, 1905
July 22, Arbitration Treaty with Venezuela signed
Aug. 29, New battleship launched in Philadelphia for Argentina, the largest in the world
Sept. 2, Banking Act amended
Nov. 27, Law conferred Argentine nationality on foreign officers in army and navy under a law of July 14

1912

Jan. 10, Arbitration Treaty with Colombia signed
Jan. 24, Ultimatum sent to Paraguay demanding compensation for attack on shipping
Feb. 13, Revision of Federal Electoral Act established a measure of proportional representation. "Aimed to compel every property voter to cast his ballot at national elections." Robertson
Feb. 17, Diplomatic relations resumed with Paraguay
April 7, First election under new law
July 30, Decree provided for registration of trademarks
Aug. 6, Treaty with Chile signed regulating commercial traffic

1913

Sept. 25, Act provided for establishment of national employment exchanges
Immigrants arrived during the year 364,878

1914

Jan. 24, Radio service between Buenos Aires and New York City inaugurated
July 3, Arbitration Treaty with France signed
July 24, Advancement of Peace Treaty with the United States signed
Aug. 5, Decree of neutrality in European War
Aug. 8, Death of President Saenz Pena. Vice-President Victorino de la Plaza assumed the executive office
Sept. 29, Law established postal savings banks
Oct. 2, Act declared wages and salaries not liable to seizure
Nov. 14, National City Bank of New York City established a branch at Buenos Aires
Third Census taken. Population 7,885,237 of which 1,575,814 in the Federal District

1915

March 12, Parcel Post Convention with the United States signed
May 25, Peace and Arbitration Treaty signed with Brazil and Chile
June 30, Law created compulsory retirement fund for all railroad employees
Aug. 17, The Prince of Wales arrived at Buenos Aires
Aug. 28, Act established State supervision of private employment agencies
Oct. 5, Act created a National Cheap Housing Commission
Oct. 11, Act provided for payment of compensation for industrial accidents

1916

Jan. 25, Executive decree regulated law governing employer's liability
April 2, Radical party successful in election
June 12, Dr. Hipolito Irigoyen chosen President and Dr. Pelagio Luna, Vice-President
June 24, Bradley and Zuloaga made first air voyage over the Andes in a balloon
July 9, Arbitration Treaty with Spain signed
July 12, Commercial Treaty with Paraguay concluded
Oct. 12, President Irigoyen inaugurated
Oct., New immigration law with restrictive provisions came into effect
Law number 9,688 enacted governing employers' liability in cases of accident

1917

April 10, Argentina notified the Government of the United States that she recognized the justice of its decision to make war upon Germany
April 11, Declaration of neutrality in war between Germany and the United States
April 13, Argentine ship "Monte Protegido" sunk by German submarine
April 21, Note to German Government demanded satisfaction for sinking vessel
July 4, Protest to German Government regarding torpedoing of vessels "Toro" and "Oriana"
Aug. 5, Note to German Government demanded indemnity
Aug. 28, German Note agreed to payment of indemnity
Sept. 8, Publication of cablegrams by the United States sent by German Minister in Argentina, Count von Luxburg, in which he advised sinking of Argentine ships "without a trace," the "spurlos versenkt" messages of May 19 and July 9

Sept. 12, Government notified Count von Luxburg that he was dismissed and asked for explanation

Sept. 19, Senate declared in favor of breaking off diplomatic relations with Germany. Sept. 25, The Chamber of Deputies voted the same. Nothing done because the President withheld his approval

Sept. 23, German Note disapproved action of Count von Luxburg

Sept. 24–Oct. 18, Serious strike of railroad workers

Oct. 11 and Nov. 21, Decrees regulated labor of railroad employees and fixed hours

1918

Jan. 14, Wheat Convention with Entente Allies signed

Feb., Strike on Argentine Pacific Railroad

Feb. 1, Naval and military attachés recalled from Germany

April 11, Convention re triangulation of Uruguay River signed with Uruguay

Oct. 8, Act regulated labor of home workers

1919

Jan. 7, Strike begun in port of Buenos Aires

Jan. 14, Martial law declared for 30 days because of strike rioting

March 15, Decree nationalized port of Buenos Aires. Government ordered the striking workmen to load and unload vessels

April 30, Workmen's retirement and pension law enacted

May 1, General strike called for

July 5, The Senate ratified the League of Nations Covenant

July 18, Argentina became original member of the League of Nations

Oct. 13, Police and frontier Convention with Chile signed

Nov. 27, Workmen's Compensation Convention with Spain signed

1920

Feb.–May 21, Strike of maritime workers

March 9, Aviator Captain Antonio Parodi made first successful flight over the Andes

March 16, Captain Zami, aviator, flew over the Andes and back again

March 26, Workmen's Compensation Convention with Italy concluded

Dec. 4, Argentine representative at League of Nations Assembly read resolution requesting admittance of all sovereign States to membership in the League. When this motion was rejected the Argentine members withdrew

1921

May 27, Custom house warehouses in Buenos Aires burned in labor dispute

June 9, Death of Dr. L. M. Drago, jurist

July 11, Decree provided for founding of agricultural and pastoral colonies legalizing the situation of thousands of settlers

1922

Jan. 4, Railroad agreement with Bolivia signed

April 25, Convention with Chile provided for transAndean communication between Argentina and Chile

April 29, New Penal Code went into effect

June 3, Decree reorganized petroleum fields of Commodoro Rivadavia

July 22, Arbitration Treaty with Venezuela signed

Aug. 28, Extradition Treaty with Colombia signed

Oct. 12, Dr. Marcelo T. de Alvear inaugurated President

Dec. 22, Decree provided for arbitration tribunal for railroad disputes

1923

March 24 and 29, Minimum wage and eight hour day established, and Decree April 30

April 21, Decree extended operation of rent law to Sept. 1. Rent charges not to be changed

Aug. 28, Anti-trust Bill signed by the President

Sept., Government floated loan of $55,000,000 in the United States

Sept. 28, Three measures regulating livestock and meat industry signed by the President

Sept. 29, Bank employees pension law enacted

Oct. 1, Death of Estanislao Z. Zeballos, jurist, at Liverpool, England

1924

May 3, General strike at Buenos Aires against new pension law

Aug. 25, General strike declared by Maritime Labor Federation

Sept. 9, Resignation of President Arturo Alessandri. Succeeded by General Altamarino

Sept. 24, Senate adopted resolution that the papal nuncio Mgr. Giovanni Beda Cardinale was no longer *persona grata*

Sept. 30, Law governing the labor of women and children passed replacing that of Oct. 14, 1907. Published Oct. 1

——, Eight o'clock closing law passed

Oct. 1, Strike of longshoremen at Buenos Aires

Nov. 1, Trade-mark law of 1923 went into effect

Nov. 4, Diplomatic relations with the Vatican suspended. Discontinuance of funds for support of envoy voted

Nov. 17, Arbitration Treaty with Switzerland signed

1925

Jan. 18, Arrival of General John Pershing and party at Buenos Aires

April 30, Sunday rest law of 1907 amended

May 28, Decree regulated employment of women and minors in dangerous occupations

June 9, Regulations promulgated for enforcement of law respecting the labor of women and children

July 9, Frontier Delimitation Treaty with Bolivia signed ending boundary dispute

Aug. 5, Wage law enacted. *See* Dec. 15

Aug. 17, Arrival of the Prince of Wales at Buenos Aires

Sept. 27, Announcement of new loan of $30,000,000, balance of $150,000,000 authorized by Congress

Dec. 15, Law providing for payment of wages and salaries in the national currency and regulating times of payment went into effect

1926

Jan. 28, Decree created National Bank which absorbed the Bank of Buenos Aires

March 1, Decree promulgated Sunday closing law. Went into effect June 10

——, Air mail and passenger service inaugurated between Buenos Aires and Montevideo

March 22, Convention with Austria signed provided

for reciprocal payment of labor accident compensation

May 1, Loan of $20,000,000 offered by New York City bankers

June 29, Treaty of friendship with Turkey signed

Sept. 22, Law approved granted to women of legal age same civil rights that laws granted to men

Sept. 29, Chamber voted appropriation to reorganize and enlarge the navy

Oct. 5, Fray Bottaro, Archbishop of Buenos Aires, appointed to negotiate with Vatican and end dispute of 2 years over filling of positions

Dec. 20, Law provided for establishment and regulation of coöperative societies

1927

Jan. 26, Agreement with France signed as to military service

April 8, Strike in Buenos Aires against decision of Massachusetts court against retrial for Sacco and Vanzetti

April 17, Law prohibiting night work in bakeries in province of Buenos Aires

April 28, Government loan of $21,000,000 of 6% gold bonds for public works offered by J. P. Morgan and Company of New York City

May 4, Decree created Bureau of Aëronautics (Army)

May 25, Loan of 100,000,000 pesetas from Spain and sale to Argentina of 2 torpedo boat destroyers

Aug. 26, Government decree reopened the Conversion Office closed for 13 years and announced return to the gold standard

Oct. 16, First municipal public library opened at Buenos Aires

Nov. 16, Workmen's Compensation Convention with Denmark signed

Dec. 27, Supplementary Boundary Convention with Brazil signed to Convention of 1898

Population estimated at 10,500,000

1928

Jan. 12, Treaty regarding literary and artistic rights with Mexico signed

Feb. 3, General strike at Tucuman the center of the sugar industry

April 1, Dr. Irigoyen elected President, Francisco Beiro, Vice-President

May 12, National Sugar Commission established

May 22, Riots during strike of dockers at port of Rosario

May 23, Bomb killed 10 persons and injured 40 at dedication of new Italian consulate

July 22, Death of Vice-President Elect Beiro

Oct. 12, Inauguration of Dr. Hipolito Irigoyen, President and Dr. E. Martinez, Vice-President

Oct. 25, Exchange of notes announced respecting British land claims in South Orkney, South Georgia, and Falkland Islands

Dec. 13, President-Elect Herbert Hoover arrived at Buenos Aires from Chile on his "good-will" visit to South America

1929

Jan. 2, Decree regulated loans granted to coöperative societies under law of 1926

Jan. 31, Direct radiotelephone service between Buenos Aires and Paris, France, opened

June 13, The President signed decree setting aside

$2,200,000 for school census and construction of primary schools

July 25, General strike at port of Rosario

Aug. 3 and Sept. 23, The Senate rejected credentials of 3 anti-Irigoyen senators from provinces of Mendoza and San Juan

Aug. 20, British Trade Mission headed by Lord D'Abernon arrived at Buenos Aires

Aug. 29, Decrees for application of eight-hour day promulgated to take effect March 12, 1930

Nov. 2, Decree of the President authorized renewal by Minister of Agriculture without interest of obligations for seed incurred by farmers in planting new crop after long drought

Nov. 8, Decree reduced duties on British rayon and similar textiles in return for free import of Argentine meats and cereals by Great Britain

Nov. 10, Assassination of Dr. Carlos W. Lencinas, former Governor of province of Mendoza, political opponent of Irigoyen elected to Senate and rejected

Nov. 15, Convention with Great Britain providing for compensation of industrial accidents

Nov. 16, Preferential Tariff Agreement with Great Britain signed

Dec. 5, Bank employees' retirement and pension law promulgated

Dec. 14, Strike of students of the Law School against the dean, J. P. Ramos, who later resigned

Dec. 16, Decree suspended gold payments by *Caja de Conversion* which had been resumed in Aug., 1927

Dec. 24, Attempted assassination of President Irigoyen by Italian anarchist, Gualberto Marinelli, who was killed by the President's escort

1930

March 11–22, Railway employees strike for higher wages; settled by intervention of Government

March 12, New eight hour day went into effect

April 5, General strike of stevedores tied up traffic, Buenos Aires

Aug. 10, Manifesto of 44 members of Congress representing 7 opposition groups declared that President Irigoyen disregarded the Constitution

Sept. 2, Resignation of Minister of War stating that he could no longer be held responsible for troops

Sept. 4, Demonstration of university students against the President

Sept. 5, President Irigoyen resigned office under pressure of revolution and delegated executive power to Vice-President Martinez who declared martial law and prohibited public gatherings

Sept. 6, Martinez deposed by soldiers led by General José F. Uriburu who took over the Government

Sept. 8, General Uriburu sworn in as Provisional President with new Cabinet

Sept. 16, Government of Uriburu recognized by Germany and England for business reasons

Sept. 18, New Government recognized by the United States

Oct. 4, Martial law replaced by "state of siege"

Oct. 17, Lacroze subway at Buenos Aires formally opened by President Uriburu

Nov. 14, Former President Dr. Irigoyen committed for trial

Dec. 17, The *Caja de Conversion* (exchange bank) closed by Decree of the President to stop export of gold

BOLIVIA

Bolivia, inland Republic of west central South America and fourth in area, bounded on the north and east by Brazil, on the east by Paraguay, on the south by Argentina, and on the west by Chile and Peru. Boundary disputes make exact calculations of area impossible. An official estimate of 1929 gives the area as 506,467 square miles, exclusive of the area disputed by Paraguay in the Chaco region where Bolivia claims all the Chaco between the Pilcomayo and Paraguay rivers, whereas the Paraguayan claim would cut Bolivia off from the Paraguayan River, including the Chaco area in dispute 514,155. Bolivia has no sea coast since the war with Chile and the Treaty of peace of 1883. The population is estimated at 2,911,283 in 1929, and another official estimate gives 2,974,904. The Republic is divided into 8 departments, 3 territories.

The 1929 estimate showed 1,586,649 Indians, 426,212 whites, and 898,429 mixed races. Other estimates (1930) distribute the population thus: Indians, 57%; mixed, 30%; white, 13%; and 6,000 Chinese, Negroes, &c.

The foreign population numbered 7,425, of whom 2,072 were Peruvians.

The estimated population (1929) of the principal towns: La Paz (the actual seat of government though Sucre is nominally the capital), 146,930; Cochabamba, 36,196; Potosí, 34,083; Sucre (the legal capital and the actual seat of the Judiciary, the University, and the Archbishop), 34,577; Tarija, 11,543; Oruro, 40,700; Santa Cruz, 30,323.

Bolivia was formed from the Province of Upper Peru, in colonial times the Audiencia of Charcas, and named after Simon Bolivar, the Liberator. Potosi in the tin and silver district is the highest city in the world at an elevation of 14,350 feet.

Dr. Hernando Siles, President.

1535

Bolivia, then Upper Peru, divided by Pizarro between his brothers Hernando and Gonzalo Pizarro

1538

Sucre founded on site of Indian village of Chuquisaca and was called Charcas

1539

Diego de Rojas made Governor subject to the Government at Lima, Peru

1548

Oct. 20, La Paz founded under name of Ciudad Nuevo de Nuestra Senora de la Paz by Alonzo de Mendoza

1555

Franciscans established the Colegio de San Andres at La Paz

1559

Audiencia of Charcas established

1622

Feb. 2, Royal decree confirmed by papal bull of Aug. 8, 1623, established the University of Sucre now called University of St. Francis Xavier. Opened 1624

1660

June 1, Silver mines at La Paz discovered by Spaniards

1776

Aug. 1, Detached from Peru and made a province of the newly created Viceroyalty of Buenos Aires

1780

Nov. 4, Revolt of the Indians led by the last of the Incas Tupac Amaru. *See* Peru

1781

June, Siege of 109 days of La Paz by Indians ended
Aug.–Oct. 17, Second siege of La Paz

1809

March 25, Citizens of La Paz deposed Spanish authorities
May 25, Citizens of Chuquisaca, the present Sucre, deposed the Spanish authorities and the Audiencia assumed military and political control, first outbreak of revolution
July 16, Manifesto of revolt published at La Paz

1810

Jan. 29, Execution of General Domingo Murillo, "father of Bolivian independence"

1811

June 20, Patriot army of General Belgrano from Buenos Aires invading Bolivia defeated by royalist General Goyeneche at Huaqui
Oct. 1, Belgrano again defeated by Spaniards at Vilcapuyo and practically annihilated

1813

Feb. 4, Patriots defeated by Blanco
May 25, Royalists defeated at La Florida by Arenales
Oct. 1, Belgrano routed in battle with royalists at Vilcapugio
Nov. 26, Belgrano's army routed on plains of Ayohuma

1814

Feb. 24, La Paz taken by assault by Pinela, patriot
Aug. 29, Pinela entered Puno
Indian uprising in region north of Lake Titicaca led by Munecas

1815

Nov. 15, Spaniards defeated patriots in Battle of Viluma

1823

July 25, Patriot army of Santa Cruz and Miller entered Bolivia from Peru
Aug. 7, Santa Cruz occupied La Paz
Aug. 25, Patriot army from La Paz defeated by Valdez and La Serna

1824

Dec. 9, Battle of Ayacucho, Peru. The victorious General Sucre after this battle began march with army to Upper Peru (Bolivia)

1825

Jan. 29, Spanish evacuated La Paz delivering city to patriot commander, General Joseph M. Lanza

Feb. 9, General Sucre proclaimed the presidency would remain under control of his army until convention he convened at Chuquisaca could form a government

April 1, Battle of Tumusla. General Sucre routed Spanish forces

April 25, General Miller entered Potosi, held by Spanish General Olaneta until March when he was mortally wounded in action with some of his own revolted troops

May 16, Bolivar at Arequipa proclaimed the liberation of Bolivia

July 10, Constituent Congress met at Chuquisaca

Aug. 6, Congress declared independence of Spain and adopted the name of Bolivia in honor of General Simon Bolivar declared supreme executive

Aug. 11, Decree of Congress established the Republic; adopted the name of Republica Bolivar later

Oct. 3, Congress provided that General Sucre should be ruler of Bolivia whenever Bolivar was not in the State

Oct. 5, Bolivar entered Potosi in triumph

Oct. 6, Provisional Congress dissolved

Nov. 1, Bolivar entered the capital

Dec. 29, Bolivar announced that a constituent Congress would meet in May and transferred his authority to General Sucre

1826

Jan., Bolivar left Chuquisaca for Lima, Peru

May 18, Peru recognized the independence of Bolivia

May 25, Constituent Congress met at Chuquisaca to consider Constitution of this date prepared and presented by Bolivar from Lima

Oct. 3, General Sucre made provisional President

Nov. 6, Bolivar's Constitution formally proclaimed adopted

Nov. 15, Treaty of Federation with Peru signed

Nov. 30, Congress declared Bolivar's Constitution adopted and Bolivar elected President for life, General Sucre to represent him   •

Dec. 9, President Antonio José Sucre inaugurated

1828

April 18, Mutiny of soldiers against Sucre due to Peruvian influence at Chuquisaca followed by invasion from Peru

July 6, Sucre forced to sign capitulation which provided for his own resignation and withdrawal of Colombian soldiers

Aug. 2, Resignation of President Sucre. He sailed for Guayaquil. General Blanco succeeded him as President, but was soon assassinated

1829

General Don Andres Santa Cruz chosen President

1830

June 4, Ex-President Sucre assassinated in the forest of Berueros near the town of Pasto, Colombia

1831

Aug. 14, New Constitution adopted

1832

Nov. 17, Treaty of commerce with Peru signed

1834

July 4, Commercial Treaty with France signed

Oct., A "reformed Constitution" adopted

1835

June 24, Treaty with Peru signed. President Santa Cruz agreed to send army to restore order and his plan of a confederation to be adopted. For war with Chile see Peru

1836

March 17, Assembly at Sicuani, Peru. See Peru

Aug. 11, Congress at Huari proclaimed the Confederation and the State of North Peru

Oct. 28, New Constitution promulgated. Santa Cruz proclaimed the Confederation of Bolivia and North and South Peru

1837

May 1, Treaty with North and South Peru signed at Tacna serving as Constitution of the Confederation

1839

Feb. 20, Decree of President Santa Cruz dissolved the Confederation after his defeat by Chileans Jan. 20 in Battle of Jungay

June, General Velasco became President. Santa Cruz exiled

Nov. 16, New Constitution promulgated proclaimed Bolivian Republic against the Peru-Bolivian Confederation

1840

Sept. 29, Treaty of friendship, and extradition with Great Britain signed

1841

President Velasco ousted by Santa Cruz party and General Ballivian became President

July 6, Peru declared war on Bolivia on Ballivian Government

Nov. 20, Battle of Yngavi. Bolivians victorious and Peruvian President Gamarra killed

1842

July 7, Peace Treaty with Peru signed

1843

June 11, Another Constitution adopted

1847

July 21, Treaty of peace and amity with Spain signed by which the independence of Bolivia recognized by Spain

Nov. 3, Treaty of commerce with Peru signed

Dec., Resignation of President Ballivian after revolt. Succeeded by General Velasco

1848

March 30, Independence of Bolivia recognized by the United States

Dec. 6, Defeat of President Velasco in battle with General Manuel I. Belzu at Yamparaez. Belzu became President

Dec. 11, Treaty of friendship and commerce with Peru signed

1851

Sept. 21, Another Constitution promulgated

1852

Aug. 22, Protest against Paraguayan assumption of sovereignty over the Paraguay River

1853

Jan. 27, Decree of President Belzu announced free navigation of all rivers to vessels of all nations

1855

General Jorge Cordova proclaimed President

1857

Sept., Insurrection led by José Maria Linares in Oruro. President Cordova escaped to Peru and Linares became President

1858

March 31, President Linares assumed powers of dictator to bring about reforms

May 8, Patent law promulgated

May 13, Treaty of friendship, commerce, and navigation with the United States signed

1860

Aug. 17, Treaty of commerce and navigation with Belgium signed

1861

Jan., Military revolt forced Linares out and General José Maria de Acha elected President

Aug., New Constitution adopted

1863

Nov. 5, Treaty of friendship and commerce with Peru signed

1864

Dec. 28, Revolt led by General Mariano Melgarejo defeated President de Acha and General Melgarejo became President

1865

March, Insurrection of General Belzu suppressed

1866

Jan. 24, President Melgarejo defeated revolt led by Arguedas at Viacha. Proclaimed amnesty after battle

May 10, Boundary Treaty with Chile signed

Aug. 10, Treaty of Atacama with Chile signed settled boundary dispute

Oct. 17, Revolt suppressed

1867

March 27, Boundary Treaty with Brazil

Dec. 21, Amnesty proclaimed

1868

July 9, Treaty of friendship, commerce, navigation, and boundary with Argentina signed

New Constitution promulgated

1869

Feb. 27, Boundary Treaty with Argentina

1870

Jan., Bank of the "Credito Hipotecario de Bolivia" established

Nov., Successful revolt proclaimed Colonel Agustin Morales, President

1872

June, Banco Nacional de Bolivia organized

Nov., President Morales murdered. Succeeded by Colonel Adolfo Ballivian

Dec. 5, Boundary Treaty with Chile signed

1873

Feb. 6, Treaty of defensive alliance with Peru signed

1874

Feb. 14, Dr. Tomas Frias became President on death of Ballivian

Aug. 6, Boundary Treaty with Chile signed and Bolivia agreed not to impose taxes on Chilean industries on Bolivian territory. This treaty not ratified

Sept., Revolt of Corral suppressed

1875

American company in Valparaiso, Alsop and Company, contracted with Government for settlement of a debt of Bolivian Government in return for certain concessions as to duties

July 21, Boundary Treaty with Chile signed

1876

May 4, General Hilarion Daza became President

1878

Feb. 14, Resolution of Congress that all nitrates exported should be subject to duty of 10 cents the quintal

1879

Jan. 3, Ultimatum from Chile demanded withdrawal of law of Feb. 14, 1878

Feb. 13, Government ordered sale of land belonging to Chilean nitrate company at Antofagasta on the following day because of its refusal to pay tax imposed by Government on nitrates

Feb. 14, Chilean soldiers seized Bolivian port of Antofagasta

March 1, Bolivia declared war on Chile. For war *see* Chile

April 5, Chile declared war on Bolivia and Peru. "War of the Pacific"

May 10, Treaty of commerce, navigation, and extradition with Portugal signed

Oct. 16, Bolivia adhered to Geneva Convention of 1864

1880

Jan. 19, President Daza deposed, General Narciso Campero made President

June 1, President Campero inaugurated constitutional President

Oct. 13, Mining law enacted based on that of Spain of Dec. 29, 1868. Regulations for law promulgated Oct. 28, 1882

Oct. 17, Centralistic Constitution adopted. Promulgated Oct. 28

1881

June 7, Treaty of commerce and customs with Peru signed

Aug. 10, Amendment to Constitution

1883

Dec. 11, Peace with Chile signed by which Bolivia agreed to cede to Chile the province of Antofagasta including the port of Cobija, her entire seacoast

1884

April 4, Treaty of Valparaiso with Chile signed confirming agreement of cession of Dec. 11, the "Pact of Truce"

Aug., Gregorio Pacheco, President (1884–88)

1886

Nov. 30, *Banco Hipotecario Garantizador de Valores* founded

1887

Nov., *Banco de Potosi* opened

1888

Aug. 1, Aniceto Arce, President

Nov. 10 and 20, Constitution amended

1889

Oct. 27, Law enacted regulated concessions as to railroads

1890

May 15, Railroad from Ascotan to Oruro opened

1891

April 18, Military College opened

1892

Jan. 28, First battle at Cururuyuqui in serious revolt of Indians

Aug. 6, Mariano Baptista inaugurated President (1892–96)

1895

May 18, Treaty with Chile signed at Santiago by which Chile agreed if by plebiscite or otherwise she should acquire permanent sovereignty over Tacna and Arica they should be transferred to Bolivia for $5,000,000

May 23, Treaty of peace and commerce with Chile signed

Dec. 9, Protocol to Treaty of May 18 signed by which Chile agreed to cede port to Bolivia

1896

Aug., Severo Fernandez Alonzo inaugurated President (1896–99)

1898

Nov. 6, Revolution of Liberal party led by Colonel Pando

Dec. 6, President Alonzo left Sucre to suppress revolt

1899

Jan. 17, Battle near La Paz a victory for insurgents

April 11, Colonel Pando entered Oruro after defeating government troops. President Alonzo escaped to Chile

April 28, Insurgent provisional government proclaimed, Serapio Reyes Ortez, J. M. Pando, and Marcario Pinilla

July, Rebellion of Brazilian rubber gatherers in Acre against Bolivia

Oct. 26, José M. Pando elected on the 23d inaugurated constitutional President (1899–1904)

1900

April 21, Extradition Treaty with the United States signed

Aug. 18, Rebellion of Brazilian inhabitants of Acre declaring independence of Bolivia suppressed by troops who took Puerto Alonso

Nov. 28, Congress rejected Chilean plan proposed for settlement of questions in dispute unless port on Pacific considered

1901

Nov. 21, Arbitration Treaty with Peru signed for duration of 10 years to settle points in controversy

1902

Feb. 17, Arbitration Treaty with Spain signed

Dec. 2, Constitution amended

Dec. 30, Boundary Treaty with Peru signed

1903

Nov. 17, Treaty of Petropolis signed with Brazil by which the Acre territory ceded to Brazil (73,750 square miles) for $10,000,000, receiving in return 1,200 square miles. Brazil undertook to construct a railroad between Sao Antonio and Bella Vista to connect navigation on Madeira River in Brazil with navigation on the Bolivian River Mamore

1904

Aug. 4, Ismael Montes inaugurated President

Oct. 20, Treaty of peace, friendship, and commerce with Chile signed ceded to Chile the maritime provinces occupied by Chile since the war, definitely relinquishing a seaport, Chile to construct a railroad from Arica to La Paz of which the Bolivian section was to be turned over to Bolivia at end of 15 years

Nov. 15, Supplementary Protocol to Treaty signed by which Bolivia recognized sovereignty of Chile over territory between parallels of 23° and 24° from the Argentine boundary to the Pacific Ocean

1905

Sept. 4, Constitution amended

Nov. 27, Treaty of commerce and customs with Peru signed

1906

Feb. 6, Serious riots in strike of railroad workers in Oruro district

Aug. 27, Law provided that the public exercise of other religions than the Roman Catholic should be permitted

Sept. 14, Law enacted provided for adoption of the gold standard

1907

Jan. 12, Treaty of arbitration and *status quo* as to boundary with Paraguay signed

March 18, Immigration law promulgated

May 18, Convention with Argentina provided for extension of North Central Railroad into Bolivia and construction of railroad from Tupiza on frontier

1908

Jan. 30, Convention with Peru signed provided for free transit through designated ports for Bolivian commerce

May 6, Dr. Guachalla elected President

July 22, Treaty of peace and commerce with Germany signed

July 24, Death of Dr. Fernando Guachalla, President-Elect

Dec. 31, Act of Congress promulgated adoption of gold standard, monetary unit the boliviano

1909

July 9, Award given by President of Argentina in boundary dispute with Peru in favor of Peru

July 10, Mobs attacked consulates of Peru and Argentina

July 14, Announcement of Government that award in boundary dispute with Peru would not be accepted

Aug. 6, Dr. Elidoro Villazon inaugurated President

Sept. 15, Boundary Protocol with Peru signed

Sept. 17, Rectification of frontier and exchange of territory with Peru

1910

Feb. 5, Act provided for permanent army of 3,153 officers and men

Dec. 4, Diplomatic relations with Argentina resumed

Dec. 16, Resignation of Ministry as protest against resumption of diplomatic relations with Argentina

Census gave population of 1,766,451. City of La Paz had 54,713

1911

Jan. 7, Law promulgated provided for establishment of the *Banco de la Nacion*

March 31, Protocol signed with Peru for arbitration of boundary dispute

May 13, Bank of the Nation officially opened

May 17, Arbitration Treaty with Italy signed

Aug. 1, Treaty of commerce with Great Britain signed

Sept. 26, Agreement with Peru signed as to imports into Bolivia by way of Mollendo

1912

March 19, Act provided that all marriages must be celebrated by civil authorities

Aug. 6, Commercial Traffic Convention with Chile signed

Dec. 28, Protocol with Brazil signed released Brazil from pledge of Treaty of Petropolis to build railroad between Villa Murtinho and Villa Bella

1913

April 5, Definitive Boundary Treaty Protocol with Paraguay signed

May 3, Protocol signed with Chile as to transfer of Bolivian section of Arica-La Paz Railroad to Bolivia after 15 years

May 13, Arica-La Paz Railroad from Antofagasta, Chile to Rio Mulato, Bolivia formally opened connecting seaport of Arica, Chile with the capital of Bolivia

Aug. 6, Ismael Montes inaugurated President for second term

Oct. 8, Law prohibited lotteries except for charities allowed by special permit

Oct. 23, Chamber of Deputies passed new banking law

Nov. 29, Law prohibited foreigners from acting as masters of vessels in lakes or rivers, crews to be 50% natives

1914

Jan. 22, Advancement of Peace Treaty with the United States signed

Feb., New banking law promulgated

Feb. 21, Mining town of Challapata destroyed by explosion of 3,500 cases of dynamite. Many persons killed

April 13, Treaty of commerce with Japan signed

Dec. 31, 90 day moratorium declared because of scarcity of money. Extended later to Dec., 1915

1915

April 5, National Postal Savings Bank (Caja Nacional de Ahorro Postal) incorporated

May 14, Loan of $1,000,000 negotiated through the National City Bank of New York

July 19, Boundary Protocol with Paraguay signed

Dec. 15, Law provided for permanent army of 3,577 men

1916

Dec. 2, Patent law enacted

1917

April 13, Bolivia protested against German submarine policy and severed diplomatic relations

May 15, Red Cross Society founded

Aug. 15, José N. Gutierrez Guerra inaugurated President

1918

June 3, Treaty of extradition with Brazil signed

June 30, Potosi to Sucre Railroad opened to Betanzos

Nov. 13, Arbitration Treaty with Colombia signed

Dec. 24, Law divided the country into 6 military districts each under control of Brigadier General or Colonel with staff

1919

April 12, Arbitration Treaty with Venezuela signed

June 28, Bolivia signed the Treaty of Versailles. Ratified Nov. 16

Dec. 3, Treaty of friendship and commerce with China signed

1920

Jan. 10, Bolivia became an original member of the League of Nations

Feb. 3, Law provided for tax on mineral exports

March 1 and 16, Notes to Peru respecting claims in Tacna-Arica settlement

April 11, Commercial Treaty with China signed

May 25, Death of Dr. José Carrasco, statesman

June 23, Presidential decree provided for establishment of School of Military Aviation

July 11, Revolt overthrew President Guerra because of his Chilean policy and a provisional junta took over the Government headed by Dr. Escalier

July 14, President Guerra deported and Bautista Saavedra became provisional President

Sept. 29, Decree provided for regulation of strikes

Nov. 1, Bolivian delegation to League of Nations asked Assembly to consider revision of Treaty of Oct. 20, 1904 with Chile by which Bolivia deprived of access to sea

1921

Jan. 26, Saavedra elected constitutional President

June 11, Petroleum law enacted, concession not more than 100,000 hectares

July 20, Protocol with Germany signed for renewal of diplomatic relations

Oct. 27, Immigration law promulgated

1924

Nov. 21, Eight-hour day law enacted and provision made for overtime at double wages

——, Act regulated contracts for employment

1925

Feb. 13, Mining code adopted

May 2, Election of José Cabino Villaneuva for President and Abdon Saavedra for Vice-President

June 2, Protocol signed with Peru as to survey of boundary line according to Treaty of Sept. 23, 1902

July 9, Convention signed with Argentina as to interpretation of boundary treaty of 1889

July 26, Atocha-Villazon railroad completed

Sept. 1, Congress annulled election of José Villaneuva of May 2 on charges of fraud. Government assumed by President of Senate, Felix Gutzman

Sept. 3, Four Protocols signed with Brazil for execution of the Treaty of Petropolis of Nov. 17, 1903

Sept. 18, Government declared state of siege in provinces of La Paz, Oruro, and Cochabamba. President Villaneuva fled from the country

1926

Jan. 1, Dr. Hernando Siles inaugurated as President

March 6, Law authorized organization of national Labor Bureau

May 1, La Paz to Yungas Railroad opened to Unduavi

Dec. 3, Bolivia expressed willingness to accept proposal of American Secretary of State Kellogg as to Tacna and Arica

1927

Jan., Loan contracted with Dillon, Read and Company of New York for $14,000,000 bonds offered at 7% for 31 years for railroad expansion

Jan. 20, Immigration Act passed

Feb. 12, Act set up General Labor Directorate

March 4, Surtax of 10% duty on all imports except food stuffs and certain textiles made permanent

April 22, Boundary Protocol with Paraguay signed. Agreed to accept offer of Argentina to arbitrate boundary dispute in Chaco region

April 26, Death of Ignacio Calderon, Minister to the United States

May 2, Strike of students in La Paz because of unpaid salaries of teachers

May 3, Clash of students and police

May 6, Martial law proclaimed in La Paz

——, Government agreed to pay salaries of professors

July 5, Edward Kemmerer completed financial mission

Aug., 50,000 Indians in revolt in departments of Cochabamba, Potosi, and Chuquisaca

Sept. 29, New tariff law passed

1928

Jan. 15, Prominent citizens and deputies in plot against the President

May 13, Chile turned over to Bolivia section of Arica-Alto de la Paz Railroad according to Treaty of 1904

July 11, Monetary law provided for adoption of gold standard. Established the boliviano as monetary unit to contain .54917 grams of fine gold. Went into effect Sept. 2

July 13, Conference with Paraguay to adjust Gran Chaco boundary unsuccessful

Aug. 22, Paraguayan patrol took party of Bolivians on frontier prisoners

Aug. 25, Decree established new port, Puerto Siles, at Matucare on right shore of the Mamore River

Sept., Loan of $23,000,000 floated with Dillon Read, New York

Sept. 10, Joseph T. Byrne took office of American Advisor to the Comptroller-General

Sept. 20, First Mining Congress met at La Paz

Dec. 6, Clash between frontier patrols on Paraguayan border in boundary dispute respecting Gran Chaco region at Fort Vanguardia (Bolivian outpost); 22 Bolivians killed

——, President-Elect Hoover arrived at Antofagasta

Dec. 8, Diplomatic relations broken off by Bolivia and Paraguay. See Paraguay Dec. 10, and 14

Dec. 14, E. O. Detlefsen of New York made Superintendent of Banks

Dec. 18, Bolivia accepted mediation of Pan-American Conference in dispute with Paraguay

Dec. 25, Frontier and Railroad Convention with Brazil signed

Dec. 27, Another clash on border at Fort Vanguardia again occupied by Bolivians

1929

Jan. 3, Protocol of conciliation with Paraguay signed provided for arbitration. See Paraguay March 13, July 2, Aug. 31, Sept. 9, Sept. 12, Oct. 1

April 23, Congress ratified Boundary Treaty with Argentina of July 9, 1925

May 7, Bolivia filed protest against proposed solution of Tacna-Arica dispute

May 15, Decree placed duty on all flour imported to come into effect Dec. 4

May 18, Legation at Washington protested against settlement in Tacna-Arica dispute

May 30, Treaty with Netherlands signed

July 1, Central Bank (Banco Central de Bolivia) opened, created by law of April 20, part of program recommended by the Kemmerer Mission

July 2, Mediation of the United States and other Powers accepted. See also Paraguay Aug. 31, Sept. 9, Sept. 12, and Oct. 1

Sept. 21, Presidential decree provided regulations for protection of women and children in industry

Nov. 13, Bolivia accepted proposal of the United States for direct negotiation in boundary dispute with Paraguay

Dec. 14, Bolivia's acceptance of Chaco peace plan announced. Suggestion of Bolivia that Paraguay should reconstruct Fort Vanguardia before Bolivia be required to return Fort Boqueron to Paraguay;

1930

Jan. 16, Most favored nation commercial Treaty with Denmark

——, Skirmish with Paraguayan soldiers in Chaco Boreal near Fort Boqueron

Feb. 2, Decree of the Government that 75% of all employees of foreign corporations must be native Bolivians

March 2, Resignation of Cabinet

March 13, New Cabinet constituted

April 4, Peace Protocol with Paraguay signed

April 26, Decree of the President reduced salaries of government employees from 5 to 20%

May 1, Diplomatic relations with Paraguay resumed

May 16, Cabinet resigned

May 17, New Cabinet constituted the third within the year

May 28, Dr. Hernando Siles, President, resigned government to Council of Ministers, and Cabinet called constituent assembly in order to amend Constitution to extend term of Dr. Siles

June 16, Revolt led by Roberto Hinojosa at Villazon near the southern border spread to other parts of the country

June 22, Street fighting in La Paz, students and workmen in conflict with police, 100 killed

June 25, Revolution in Oruro. Provisional Government formed by General Blanco Galindo

June 25, Cadets of the military college joined the revolution

June 26, Council of Ministers resigned to military Junta led by General Galindo

June 27, Capitulation of La Paz to rebels

June 29, Junta of 6 army officers under General Carlos Blanco Galindo assumed control of the Government

July 15, Commercial Agreement with Switzerland prolonged the Agreement of 1883

July 23, Official exchange of Forts Bouqueron and Vanguardia

Sept. 18, New Government recognized by the United States

BRAZIL

Brazil, the largest Republic of South America, and fifth largest country in the world, has frontiers with all the other South American States except Chile and Ecuador, and borders the 3 Guianas. The total area is 3,275,510 square miles, length greatest north and south 2,660 miles, and maximum width east and west 2,700 miles. The Atlantic Ocean is the boundary on the east, northeast and southeast. The Republic is divided into 20 federated States, the Federal District of Rio de Janeiro, and the Territory of Acre, total population estimated Dec. 31, 1929, 40,272,650. According to the census in 1920 the population consisted of 15,443,818 males and 15,191,787 females. Of these 1,565,961, or 5%, were foreigners, viz., 558,405 Italians, 433,575 Portuguese, 219,142 Spaniards, 52,870 Germans, 50,251 from Asiatic Turkey, 33,621 Uruguayans, 27,976 Japanese, 26,354 Austrians, 22,117 Argentinians, and 141,-650 other nationalities. Some 100,000 Indians are to be found in the Amazon area. The language is Portuguese, though Italian and German are widely used in the Southern States.

In 1929 the estimated population of Rio de Janeiro was 1,468,621; São Paulo, 879,788; S. Salvador, 328,898; Recife, 340,543; Belem, 279,491; Curitybe, 100,135; Porto Alegre, 273,376; Manáos, 83,736; Nictheroy, 108,233; Bello Horizonte, 108,849; Fortaleza, 123,706; Maceió, 103,930; São Luiz, 62,895; Parahyba, 74,104.

The number of immigrants between 1820 and 1928 was 4,351,068, including 1,474,000 Italians, 1,250,000 Portuguese, 574,000 Spaniards, 194,000 Germans, 110,000 Russians, and 89,000 Austrians. In 1929 the number of immigrants was 100,424, including 38,879 Portuguese, 16,648 Japanese, 5,288 Italians, 9,095 Poles, and 4,351 Germans.

The interior of the country is practically as it was when settled by the Portuguese and Spaniards, the fringe of the coast the inhabited section together with the eastern part of the central plateau. The name is derived from the Portuguese word "braza," live coal, named from the native red dye-wood carried to Europe by Pinzon, the discoverer, and the early traders.

Dr. Getulio Vargas, President.

1500

Jan. 20, Expedition of Vicente Yañez Pinzon, a companion of Columbus, Spanish navigator, discovered the east coast of Brazil at Cape St. Augustine

Jan., Diego de Lepe and Amerigo Vespucci explored coast from Cape San Roque to 10° south, "farthest south"

Feb. 28, Pinzon discovered the mouth of the Amazon which he named Marañon. His claim to this region for Spain not valid as land within Portuguese sphere by line of demarcation of the Treaty of Tordesillas of 1493. *See* South America

April 22, Pedro Alvarez Cabral sighted unknown land and anchored in present Bay of Santa Cruz taking formal possession at Puerto Seguro for Portugal May 1 naming the country Santa Cruz ("Terra Sanctæ Crusis"—Land of the True Cross)

1501

Aug. 16, Voyage of Vespucci reached Brazil at the Cape of San Roque named for festival day of the saint

1502

Jan. 1, Portuguese expedition of Andre Gonçalves entered Bay of Guanabara (Bay of Rio de Janeiro) which he believed to be a river and named River of January. Denis gives name as Gonzalo Coelho

1504

French expedition of de Gonneville visited the coast

1506

After this date nearly all Portuguese squadrons bound for the Indies stopped at Brazil

1510

Diego Alvares shipwrecked on coast near present site of Bahia supposed to have taken daughter of Indian chief as his wife and become a patriarchal chief

1512

João Ramalho shipwrecked on coast further south also married an Indian and descendants became the so-called Mamelucos prominent in exploration and conquest of the country

1516

Cristobal Jacques sent to protect coast from the Spanish and French

Jan. 1, Expedition of Juan Diaz de Solis reached the Bay of Rio de Janeiro

1519

Dec. 13, Magellan at Bay of Rio de Janeiro

1525

King John III sent fleet to protect coast against attacks of the French

1526

Cristobal Jacques founded a settlement on the Rio Iguarassu in present State of Pernambuco which was afterwards abandoned

1528

Antonio Ribeiro succeeded Jacques as Captain Major of the coast guard fleet

1530

Settlement made by Duarte Coelho Pereira at Olinda, Pernambuco

1531

Jan., Martin Affonso de Sousa reached Pernambuco and explored coast from mouth of the Gurupy to mouth of the Chuy, at the present boundary between Brazil and Uruguay. Name Rio de Janeiro also attributed to him by some writers

1532

Jan. 22, Affonso de Sousa founded first permanent settlement of São Vicente near site of present port of Santos. Aided in colonization by Ramalho who had great influence with the Indians. *See* 1512

Sept., John III divided Brazil into 12 hereditary feudal districts which were called captaincies to be settled and developed by private grants under the Crown. Martim Affonso de Sousa granted first captaincy. H. G. James "Brazil" describes these divisions, the geographical background of the seacoast States of today, so they can be placed on a modern map

1534

May 27, Grant of captaincy of Puerto Seguro to Pero de Campo Tourinho

Aug. 26, Grant of captaincy of Bahia de Todos os Santos (Bahia) to Francisco Pereira Coutinho

Oct. 6, Captaincy of Santo Amaro and region known as Terras de Sant' Anna to Pero Lopez de Sousa, brother of Martim, and Martim confirmed in possession of the captaincy of São Vicente and São Thome

Oct. 7, Grant of captaincy of Espirito Santo to Vasco Fernandez Coutinho

Oct. 24, Grant of captaincy of Pernambuco to Duarte Coelho Pereira

1535

March 11, Captaincy of Maranhão granted in 3 parcels to João de Barros, Ayres da Cunha, and Fernão Alvares de Andrade

April 1, Grant of captaincy of Ilheos extending to Bay of Todos os Santos (Bahia) to Jorge de Figueiredo Correa

1536

Feb. 29, Captaincy of Parahyba do Sul granted to Pero de Goes da Silveira

1541

Aug. 26, Francisco de Orellana descending the Amazon from the Andes reaching the river by the Napo reached the sea

1548

Powers of captaincies limited by a central government with a captain-general

Dec. 13, Thome de Sousa appointed first governor-general of Brazil by John III

1549

March 29, Governor-General Sousa arrived and proceeded to establish the city of São Salvador later called Bahia as his capital where he formally assumed office Nov. 1. 6 Jesuits came with this expedition

1552

June 22, First Bishop of Brazil, Pedro Fernandes Sardinha, arrived at Bahia

1553

July 13, Duarte da Costa arrived succeeding Thome de Sousa as Governor-General

1554

Jan. 25, Jesuit College of São Paulo founded

1555

Nov. 10, French Huguenot colony of Villegagnon arrived in Bay of Rio de Janeiro and established a settlement on island given his name, and settlement on mainland called Henryville which was to be future capital of "Antarctic France"

1557

March 7, Second French squadron arrived in harbor of Rio de Janeiro

1558

Mem de Sa succeeded Duarte da Costa as Governor-General (1558–72). He established law and order in the captaincies, subjugated the Indians and expelled the French colonists on Guanabara Bay

1559

Nov., Portuguese squadron commanded by Captain-Major Bartholomeu de Vasconcellos da Cunha arrived to aid Mem de Sa in attack on French who were driven to mainland but returned as soon as Portuguese sailed away and restored Fort Coligny in the following year

1565

March, Second Portuguese squadron commanded by Estacio de Sa arrived at Bahia and established settlement on Guanabara Bay

1567

Jan. 20, French driven from settlements by de Sa on feast-day of St. Sebastian and new settlement founded by Portuguese named Sao Sebastiao do Rio de Janeiro

June 20 and March 15, 1568, Edict forbidding Maranos (secret Jews) to settle in Brazil. Repealed for $714,000 May 21, 1577

1570

Luiz de Vasconcellos appointed Governor-General to succeed Mem de Sa, but his fleet of 7 or 8 ships captured by French corsairs who destroyed fleet and massacred all on board

1572

March 2, Luiz de Brito e Almeida, new Governor-General reached Bahia a few days before the death of Mem de Sa

Dec. 10–1577, Government divided into two districts by royal decree with Bahia as capital of the northern and Rio de Janeiro of the southern with Antonio Salema as Governor-General, Brito e Almeida remaining Governor-General at Bahia

1577

April 12, Royal decree united country into one captaincy-general under Luiz de Brito e Almeida

1578

Lourenço da Veiga succeeded Brito e Almeida as Governor-General (1578–81)

1580–1640

Period of Spanish control of Brazil under "personal union" of Portugal with Spain

1583

English fleet under buccaneer Edward Fenton attacked port of Santos

1585

Population of Portuguese colony about 57,000, 25,000 white persons, 8,000 in Pernambuco, 12,000 in Bahia

1587

English buccaneer Wirthington attacked Bahia and ravaged the surrounding country

1591

Thomas Cavendish, English buccaneer sacked Santos

1592

Cavendish repulsed in attack on Espirito Santo

1595

Joint English and French expedition of James Lancaster and Le Noyer captured and looted Recife, Pernambuco

1599

Van Noort, Dutch buccaneer, repulsed in attack on Rio de Janeiro, and attack of Van Corden on Bahia

1609

Supreme Court established in Bahia

1612

French expedition of La Ravardiere established a colony on the Island of Maranhão and built fortified village named St. Louis, the present São Luiz

1615

Nov. 4, Portuguese and Indians compelled French at Maranhão to surrender. They retired to Guiana

1621

State of Maranhão created by the Crown independent of Brazil until 1777

1624

May 8, Dutch fleet commanded by Admiral Willekens and Vice-Admiral Piet Heyn of 26 vessels attacked Bahia, compelled to surrender May 10

1625

April 30, Bahia under siege for a year surrendered to Spanish fleet of 52 ships and 12,000 men which had arrived March 29 for relief of Bahia

1627

Piet Heyn sacked Bahia twice without gaining permanent possession

1630

Feb. 13, Dutch fleet of 65 ships and 7,300 men commanded by Admiral Lonck attacked and within a few days captured Pernambuco beginning 24 year occupation of northern Brazil

1637

Jan. 27, Prince Maurice of Nassau-Siegen arrived as Governor of Dutch Brazil

Oct. 28–Dec. 12, 1639, Expedition of Pedro Teixeira from Para proceeded up the Amazon to highest navigable point and overland to Quito returning by same route completing survey, third navigation of the Amazon River. Name Amazon given to river the name of a supposed race of women warriors Teixeira heard tales about

1640

Dec. 13, The Duke of Braganza crowned as John IV of Portugal and the "Sixty Years Captivity" of Portugal to Spain ended

1644

Prince Maurice returned to Holland

1645

June 13, Uprising of Portuguese of Pernambuco against the Dutch

1648

Aug. 18, Portuguese defeated Dutch at Battle of Guarapes

1653

Arrival of Jesuit Antonio Vieira who preached against enslavement of Indians and eventually secured royal decree placing Indians under guardianship of his order

1654

Jan. 26, Capitulation of Dutch in Pernambuco and surrender of all fortified places to Portuguese ended Dutch occupation

1661

Aug. 6, Treaty of Holland and Portugal signed by which Holland relinquished claim to all territory in Brazil

1673

Negro State of Palmares established in the interior of the present State of Alagoas by escaped negro slaves. Attained population of 30,000 before it was overthrown by force of 6,000 soldiers in 1695

1684

Revolution of Bekman (Bequimão) against the Jesuits in Maranhão

1693

Gold rush begun with discovery by the Paulistas of rich deposits in what is now the State of Minas Geraes

1710

Expedition sent from France to take Rio de Janeiro under command of Jean François du Clerc repulsed by Governor Castro Moraes

1710–11

"War of the *mascates*" native born Brazilians and Portuguese in Pernambuco between Olinda, the seat of government, and Recife, the new town built by Portuguese merchants called *mascates* or hucksters by the improvident aristocrats of Olinda

1711

Sept. 12, Second French expedition under Duguay Trouin entered Bay of Rio de Janeiro and captured the town on the 22d withdrawing after exaction of a heavy ransom

1713

April 11, Treaty between France and Portugal by

which France renounced claim to territory between the Amazon and the River Oyapoc

1721

Diamonds discovered in gold producing center of Minas Geraes near site of city of Diamantina

1730

Diamond mining made a government monopoly

1747

Printing office opened in Rio de Janeiro. Closed by order from Portugal

1750

Jan. 13, Treaty of Madrid signed by Spain and Portugal by which Spain recognized claims of Portugal to territories west of original line of demarcation extending Portuguese possessions in the west to the base of the Andes in the north and to the basin of the Parana in the south

1751

Supreme Court established in Rio de Janeiro

1759

Jesuits expelled by royal edict and their property confiscated

1760

March 12, João Alberto Castello brought first coffee plant to Brazil

1761

Feb. 12, Convention between Spain and Portugal annulled Treaty of Madrid and the boundary line again that of the line of Tordesillas

1762

General Gomes de Andrade appointed Viceroy

1763

Rio de Janeiro made capital city instead of Bahia

1773

Maranhão incorporated into Brazil

1777

Oct. 1, By Treaty of Ildefonso between Spain and Portugal boundary line outlined following practically that of the Treaty of 1750 giving Portugal more than twice as much territory as that conceded by the Treaty of Tordesillas. Island of Santa Catharina given to Portugal

1789

Conspiracy of Minas Geraes under leadership of Joaquim Jose da Silva Xavier, an ensign of cavalry, nicknamed "Tiradentes," to establish a republic independent of Portugal. Discovered and leaders deported except Tiradentes who was hanged in 1792

1808

Jan. 23, Dom João, Regent of Portugal, in flight from Portugal, arrived at Bahia where he was welcomed with enthusiasm

Jan. 28, Decree of Regent opened ports of Brazil to the commerce of all friendly nations

March 7, The royal family arrived at Rio de Janeiro

April 1, Decree of Regent removed prohibition upon free exercise of industries

Royal printing press established

May 1, Expedition dispatched that conquered French Guiana. Given back to France by Treaty of Paris in 1814

Aug. 23, Decree established a commercial court at Rio de Janeiro

Sept. 10, The *Gazeta da Rio de Janeiro* began publication

Sept., Decree established the Bank of Brazil

1811

Scientific expedition of explorer, W. L. von Eschwege (1811–14)

1812

May 26, Armistice concluded with revolutionary government of Buenos Aires by the Regent by which plans to intervene in La Plata provinces renounced

1815

Dec. 16, Decree of the Regent declared Brazil a kingdom, a coördinate member of the "United Kingdom of Portugal, Brazil, and Algarves"

Expedition of Prince Maximilian of Wied-Neuwied, explorer (1815–17)

1816

March 20, Death of Queen Maria. The Prince Regent became King João VI of Portugal

Oct., Uruguayans led by Artigas invaded the Misiones territory in dispute with Brazil and were repulsed with great slaughter

Expedition of Auguste de Sainte-Hilaire, explorer (1816–22)

1817

Jan. 20, Portuguese and Brazilians defeated forces of Uruguay and captured Montevideo, Uruguay

March 6, Republican revolution broke out in Pernambuco

Nov. 5, Archduchess Leopoldina, daughter of Emperor Francis I of Austria, married by proxy to Pedro son of João VI

Expedition of J. B. von Spix and C. F. P. von Martius, explorers (1817–20) crossed area east of 50° W. Long. and made scientific exploration of the Amazon

1818

Feb. 6, João VI formally crowned at Rio de Janeiro

1821

April 21, João adopted Spanish Constitution of 1812 until new Portuguese one should be framed

April 22, King João made his son Pedro Regent of Brazil

April 26, King João sailed for Portugal

Uruguay, the "Banda Oriental" formally annexed to Brazil as the Cisplatine Province

Oct. 1, Decree of Cortes ordered return to Portugal of Dom Pedro

Dec. 9, Decree reduced government to a province

1822

Jan. 9, Prince Pedro defied Cortes announcing his decision to remain in Brazil

Jan. 13, Cortes abolished judicial tribunals in Rio de Janeiro making the Supreme Court a provincial tribunal subordinate to the Supreme Court in Portugal

Jan. 16, José Bonifacio de Andrada appointed chief Minister

Feb. 21, Pedro ordered that no law of the Cortes of Lisbon should be effective in Brazil without his sanction

May 13, Pedro adopted the title of "Perpetual Protector and Defender of Brazil"

June 3, Pedro convoked a legislative and constituent assembly

Sept. 7, Pedro at Sao Paulo declared independence of Portugal, the "Grito de Ypiranga" or "Cry of Ipiranga" from name of plain outside city

Oct. 12, Pedro proclaimed constitutional emperor of Brazil at Rio de Janeiro and all connection with Portugal severed

Dec. 1, Dom Pedro crowned emperor

1823

March, Lord Cochrane arrived to take command of the new Brazilian fleet

May 3, Constituent Assembly met dominated by José Bonifacio de Andrada and his two brothers, patriotic Paulistas

July 17, The Andrada Ministry dismissed by the Emperor because of measure introduced by Andrada that all Portuguese suspected of disloyalty to the new régime should be expelled from the country

Oct. 20, Law declared Spanish ordinances of Philip I (II of Spain) compiled in 1603 in force in Brazil and commercial law of Aug. 18, 1769 should be observed

Nov. 12, Pedro dissolved Assembly because of opposition and selected a commission to frame a constitution

Nov. 18, Portuguese commander at Montevideo surrendered to new régime

Nov. 23, Pedro banished the Andrada brothers

Dec., Revolt in Pernambuco

1824

March 25, Constitution of the Empire promulgated

May 26, Independence of Brazil recognized by the United States. Rebello received as chargé d'affaires by President Monroe

July 2, "Confederation of the Equator" led by Governor Carvalho Peaz against Pedro included besides Pernambuco the States of Parahyba, Rio Grande do Norte, and Ceara

Sept. 17, Government forces with aid of Lord Cochrane captured Pernambuco and suppressed insurrection

First German colony founded of São Leopoldo in province of Rio Grande do Sul

1825

May 13, Proclamation of João VI of Portugal recognized the independence of Brazilian Empire

Aug. 25, Declaration of independence of Uruguay. See Uruguay

Aug. 29, Treaty with Portugal signed which recognized the independence of Brazil

Sept. 24, Battle of Rincon. Brazilians defeated

Oct. 12, Battle of Sarandi. Brazilians defeated

Dec. 10, Brazil declared war on Argentina because of incorporation of Uruguay in the La Plata Confederation

1826

Jan. 8, Treaty with France signed at Rio de Janeiro formally recognized the independence of Brazil

Feb. 9, Brazilian fleet defeated Argentine fleet commanded by Admiral Brown

March 10, Death of King João VI of Portugal. Pedro became King of Portugal as well as Emperor of Brazil

May 2, Pedro resigned the throne of Portugal in favor of his daughter Maria who left for Portugal

May 3, Pedro called Congress

June 7, Treaty of friendship, commerce, and navigation with France signed

July 30, Admiral Lobo defeated Argentine fleet of Admiral Brown

Nov. 23, Convention with Great Britain provided for total abolition of the slave trade at end of 3 years

1827

Feb. 20, Battle of Ituzaingo. The Marquis of Barbacena defeated by Argentine General Carlos Alvear

Feb., Brazilian fleet annihilated in Uruguay River by Admiral Brown, Argentine

May 24, Preliminary Peace Treaty with Argentina which contained provision that Uruguay should be independent

Aug. 17, Treaty of amity and commerce with Great Britain signed which formally recognized the independence of Brazil

Oct. 1, First appearance of the "Journal do Commercio" in Rio de Janeiro

Nov. 17, Treaty of commerce signed with German States of Lubeck, Bremen, and Hamburg

1828

April 18, Treaty of amity, navigation, and commerce with Prussia signed

May, Congress met

Aug. 27, Peace Treaty with Argentina guaranteed the independence of Uruguay

Sept. 18, Act created the Supreme Court

Oct. 1, Law enacted governing municipal organizations

Dec. 12, Treaty of amity, commerce, and navigation with the United States signed

1829

Jan. 20, Supreme Court installed

1831

March 13, The "noite das garrafadas" (night of the bottles). Conflict between native Brazilians and Portuguese in Rio de Janeiro

March 20, Pedro dismissed majority of his cabinet and replaced them with native Brazilians in effort to conciliate disaffected people

April, Pedro dismissed Ministers and replaced them with unpopular aristocrats

April 7, Dom Pedro abdicated in favor of his five year old son Dom Pedro de Alcantara, and provisional regency of 3 members took over the Government, the Marquis of Caravelas, Campos Vergueiro, and General F. de Lima e Silva

April 13, Pedro sailed for Europe

May 16, Congress appointed commission to revise the Constitution

June 17, Permanent regency appointed for 4 years, General Francisco de Lima e Silva, José da Costa Carvalho and João Braulio Muniz which ruled until 1835

Nov. 7, Law passed providing for abolition of African slave trade

1834

Aug. 12, "Acto Addicional" amended Constitution of

1824. Council of State abolished, Provincial assemblies created and a regent to be elected for 4 years

1835

Sept., Federalist revolt begun in the province of Rio Grande do Sul, the war of the "Farrapos" which threatened secession and lasted 10 years

Oct. 1, Law authorized granting of concessions for construction of railroads

Oct. 12, Father Diego Antonio Feijo installed as sole Regent

1836

May 19, Treaty of navigation and commerce with Portugal signed

July 6, Additional Article to Treaty with Great Britain

1837

Sept., Araujo Lima became Regent on resignation of Father Feijo

Military revolt in Bahia suppressed

1838

Nov. 23, American exploring expedition of Lieutenant Charles Wilkes arrived at Rio de Janeiro on way to Antarctic regions

1839

Revolt in Maranhão against the Regency known as the "Balaida" which ended in 1841

1840

July 23, Pedro II proclaimed constitutional Emperor

1841

July 18, Coronation ceremonies of Pedro II

Nov. 23, Law reëstablished the Council of State

Dec. 3, Code of procedure promulgated standardizing legal processes

1845

March 1, The "Farrapos" laid down their arms ending insurrection of the province of Rio Grande do Sul

1848

Sept., Insurrection of Liberals in Pernambuco suppressed by Conservative officials they tried to displace

1849

Jan. 27, Claims Convention with the United States signed

1850

March 22, First steamship line between Brazil and Europe inaugurated

June 25, Commercial Code adopted, first original codification in America. Promulgated Nov. 25

Sept. 4, Domestic slave trade abolished

Sept. 18, Law on public lands enacted created general Department of Public Lands

1851

May 29, Brazil concluded offensive and defensive alliance with Colorados of Uruguay and revolutionists of Entre Rios against the tyrant Rosas. *See* Argentina

Oct. 12, Treaties of alliance and boundary limits signed with Uruguay

Oct. 23, Treaty of commerce, navigation, and boundaries signed with Peru

1852

Feb. 3, Battle of Monte-Caseros. Allies defeated Rosas

May 15, Boundary Treaty with Uruguay

June 26, Railroad law enacted

Aug. 26, Protest against Treaty of July 15 between Argentina and Paraguay as to frontiers in Misiones

1854

April 30, First railroad in Brazil opened between Maua at head of Guanabara Bay to foot of Serra do Mar below Petropolis

1856

March 7, Treaty of commerce and navigation with Argentina

April 6, Treaty of friendship, commerce, and navigation with Paraguay signed

Dec., American whaleship "Canada" seized

1857

Jan. 23, Indemnity of $212,365 demanded by the United States for seizure of ship "Canada"

Jan. 26, Protest to Paraguay against violation of Treaty. *See* Paraguay Decrees of July 15 and Aug. 10

Sept. 4, Treaty of commerce with Uruguay and revision of treaties of 1851 and 1856

Nov. 20, Treaty with Argentina declared rivers Uruguay, Parana, and Paraguay free to ships of all nations

Nov. 28 and Dec. 3, Exchange of notes with Uruguay by which certificates of nationality to be respected

Dec. 14, Boundary Treaty with Argentina defined frontiers in Misiones district. The right bank of the Uruguay River recognized as Argentine territory

Tariff law enacted

1858

Feb. 12, Fluvial Convention with Brazil signed by Paraguay

1859

May 5, Boundary Treaty with Venezuela signed

1860

Aug. 22, Law on checks enacted

1861

June, Seizure by Brazilian citizens of British ship "Prince of Wales" wrecked off coast of Albardas, plundered and some of crew killed

1862

June 17, Arrest of British officers at Rio de Janeiro

Dec. 31, British seized 5 Brazilian merchant ships in reprisal because of refusal of reparation for seizure of "Prince of Wales"

1863

Feb. 26, Brazilian Minister in London paid indemnity of £3,000 under protest

May, Diplomatic intercourse with Great Britain suspended because of refusal of British to express regret for reprisals

June 18, Award of King of the Belgians in dispute with Great Britain as to affair of June 17, 1862 decided in favor of Brazil

1864

Aug. 4, Ultimatum of Saraiva, Foreign Minister, to Uruguay demanded payment of claims and punish-

ment for barbarities against Brazilian subjects in
Uruguay

Aug. 22, Protocol signed with Argentina as to united
policy toward Uruguay

Nov. 12, Seizure of steamer "Marques de Olinda" by
Paraguay. *See* Paraguay and notice from Paraguay
of severance of diplomatic relations

1865

March 18, Paraguayan Congress approved war with
Brazil. *See* Paraguay for war

May 1, Treaty of alliance with Argentina and Uruguay
against Paraguay signed

1866

Dec. 7, Decree announced that after Sept. 7 the navigation of the Amazon should be free to merchant vessels
of all nations

1867

March 27, Boundary Treaty with Bolivia

July 31, Decree extended free navigation of Amazon to
Tabatinga

1869

Nov. 16, Treaty of extradition with Argentina signed

New tariff enacted

1870

March 14, Protocol with the United States signed submitted case of "Canada" steamship seized in 1856
to arbitration

July 11, Award in "Canada" case in favor of the
United States that Brazil should pay $100,740.04

Sept. 29, New ministry under Viscount St. Vincent

Dec. 3, First number of a journal named "A Republica" published, organ of new political party the
Republicans

1871

Sept. 28, The "Rio Branco" law enacted provided that
the children of slaves born after this date should be
free

1872

Jan. 18, Treaty of friendship, commerce, and navigation
with Paraguay signed

March 31, Return of the Emperor and Empress from
visit to Europe

1873

Jan. 18, Treaty of friendship, commerce, and navigation with Argentina signed

April 26, Monopoly granted to British company to
construct a telegraph

1874

Feb. 11, Treaty with Peru provided for mutual cessions
of territory

Feb. 28, Decree regulated railroad franchises and defined spheres of action of the central and provincial
governments and authorized expenditure of up to
100,000,000 milreis for railroad undertakings

New tariff enacted

1875

Feb. 27, Law made military service compulsory

May, Bank failures at Rio de Janeiro

June 25, The Duke de Caixias, president of the Ministry

Nov. 6, Decree created School of Mines at Ouro Preto

1882

Oct. 14, Law and decree of Dec. 30 provided for protection of inventions by patent

1883

June 7, Treaty of commerce and navigation with
Paraguay signed

1884

March 25, Slavery was abolished in the province of
Ceara

1885

Aug., Ministry of Baron de Cotegipe

Sept. 28, Saraiva law provided that all slaves attaining
the age of 60 should be free

1886

June 12, Decree provided for gradual emancipation of
slaves according to law of 1885

1887

March 30, Official return gave number of slaves as
723,419 of legal value of $485,225,212

Dec. 31, Regulations for patent law issued

New tariff enacted

1888

March, New Ministry under Senator de Oliviera

May 13, Law declared slavery abolished, the "lei
aurea," "Golden Law"

May 15, Royal decree declared all slaves free

Aug. 22, Return of the Emperor from visit to Europe

1889

June 7, New Liberal Cabinet under Viscount de Ouro
Preto

June 11, In the House of Deputies a member called out
"Down with the monarchy. Long live the Republic"

Sept. 7, Treaty with Argentina signed provided for
arbitration of dispute as to limitary rivers in the
Misiones territory

Nov. 15, Revolution of Rio de Janeiro. The Emperor
deposed and the Republic proclaimed by troops
headed by Colonel Botelho de Magalhaes. General
Deodoro da Fonseca headed provisional Government

Nov. 17, The Imperial family placed on a steamer sailing for Portugal

Nov. 18, Official announcement that the provisional
Government would recognize all obligations, contracts, treaties and debts of the previous Government

Nov. 19, Government decree extended the suffrage to
all adult male citizens who could read and write
abolishing income qualification existing under imperial régime (James. Robertson, Nov. 21)

Nov. 26, Law provided that all aliens should *ipso facto*
become citizens unless they expressly declared before their national consuls intention to remain aliens

Dec. 3, Decree appointed a commission to frame a constitution for the United States of Brazil

Dec. 18–20, Counter revolution in Rio de Janeiro

Dec. 20, Decree banished the Emperor and his family

Dec. 21, Decree fixed date for election for constituent
assembly as Sept. 15 and meeting Nov. 15

Dec. 23, Decree imposed press restrictions. A military
tribunal established for cases of treason

1890

Jan. 7, Decree proclaimed separation of Church and
State

Jan. 17, Law established banks of issue

Jan. 29, The United States recognized the Republic of
Brazil

Feb., Bank of Brazil established

March 8, Decree gave Banco de Brazil and Banco Nacional the right to issue bank notes

May 1, The first of repeated separatist outbreaks in Rio Grande do Sul

June 13, Decree provided that declaration must be made by resident foreigners who do not wish to be considered citizens of Brazil

June 22, Decree convoked constituent assembly to meet Nov. 15 and draft constitution promulgated

June 28, New regulations for immigrants promulgated

Oct. 11, Decree promulgated new Penal Code replacing that of 1830, and regulations organizing federal judiciary and procedure

Oct. 20, Great Britain recognized the Republic of Brazil

Oct. 24, Bankruptcy law enacted

Nov. 14, Law organized the federal judiciary

Nov. 15, Constituent Assembly met at Rio de Janeiro

1891

Jan. 20, First republican Cabinet, Senator J. C. de Faria Alvim, resigned

Jan. 22, New cabinet formed by Senator Uchoa

Feb. 5, Reciprocal Commercial Treaty with the United States signed

Feb. 21, Act treating of disappropriation of lands along railroads and public highways and rivers for founding of agricultural establishments

Feb. 24, New Constitution promulgated and title of "United States of Brazil"

Feb. 25, General Deodoro da Fonseca elected first constitutional President for four year term and General Floriano Peixoto, Vice-President

March 9, Manifesto of the State of Sao Paulo against intervention of national government in local affairs

March 18, Manifesto signed by 30 senators and deputies representing 14 States and the Federal District protesting against the arbitrary, corrupt, and unconstitutional rule of President Fonseca

June 15, National Congress First of the Republic opened

July 4, Decree governing legal status of stock corporations and for the establishment of banks issued

Oct. 10, Commercial Treaty with Peru signed

Nov. 3, President Fonseca dissolved Congress and assumed powers of a dictator placing Rio de Janeiro under martial law in dispute with Congress over veto

Nov. 9, Revolt of garrisons in State of Rio Grande do Sul against federal Government declared independence

Nov. 23, Revolt of navy commanded by Admiral Custodio José de Mello threatened to bombard Rio de Janeiro and forced resignation of the President. Vice-President Peixoto assumed the executive office

Dec. 5, Death of Pedro II in Paris

1892

April, Matto Grosso declared independence under name of Republica Transatlantica

April 10, Decree of President Peixoto that the Federal District should be considered under martial law

April 11, Insurrection against arbitrary rule of Peixoto in Rio de Janeiro suppressed

May 7, Government troops invested Cubaya, Matto Grosso. Garrison surrendered May 13

June, Insurrection in Rio Grande do Sul led by famous "gaucho," cow-boy Gumercindo Saraiva

July 3, Italian sailors maltreated by police at Santos

Aug. 23, Death of former President Deodoro da Fonseca

1893

March 17, Federals routed in battle near Santa Anna

March 27, State troops defeated at Algrete, Rio Grande do Sul

July 15, Government cruiser forced surrender of insurgent vessel "Jupiter" and captured Admiral Wandenkolk

Sept. 6, Naval revolt begun led by Admiral Mello in harbor of Rio de Janeiro to drive Floriano from office

Sept. 13, Bombardment of Rio de Janeiro by rebel fleet

Oct. 1, Commanders of naval forces of the United States, France, Italy, and Portugal in the harbor notified Admiral Mello that they would oppose by force further bombardment of Rio de Janeiro

Oct. 9, Insurgents occupied Fort Villegaignon

Oct. 23, Admiral de Mello asked American Minister in Brazil for recognition of his provisional Government in State of Santa Catharina (Florianopolis) which was refused

Oct. 24, Provisional Government of De Mello established at Desterro

Nov. 22, Insurgent vessel "Javary" sunk by fire from Fort São João

Nov. 28, Federal insurgents in Rio Grande do Sul won decisive victory over General Isidoro Fernando who surrendered

Dec. 1, Admiral de Mello ran past the government batteries to sea and sailed south to join forces with the insurgents in Rio Grande do Sul leaving Rear Admiral Luis Felippe de Saldanha da Gama in command. He raised the imperial flag

1894

Jan. 1, English occupied Trinidade Island

Jan. 16, Rebels captured Mocangue. They also took and garrisoned Conceição, Velha, and Vianna

Jan. 30, Insurgent fleet trying to maintain the blockade fired on American merchant vessels and the U.S.S. "Detroit." The fire returned

Feb. 3, Blockade raised

Feb. 9, Da Gama defeated at Armacao trying to establish position on mainland

March 1, Dr. Prudente José de Moraes Barros, civilian, elected President and Dr. Manoel Victorino Pereira, Vice-President

March 7, Arrival of fleet purchased in Europe and the United States by the President

March 13, Naval rebellion ended as Da Gama with his men took asylum on Portuguese warships

March 16, Announcement diplomatic relations with Portugal resumed

April 12, Mello repulsed in attack on Rio Grande

April 16, Mello with 5 ships and 1,200 men surrendered at Buenos Aires to the President of Argentina. The "Aquidaban" fired on by government vessel off Destero disabled and abandoned by insurgents. Government troops occupied insurgent headquarters at Desterro, Captain Lorena, President of the Provisional Government shot with many others who had taken part in the rebellion including 3 French engineers who had taken no part in war but had been forced to repair rebel ships for which 900,000 francs indemnity was paid later to France

May 14, Diplomatic relations with Portugal broken off because of refusal of warships to surrender Da

Gama and other refugees. Da Gama escaped to Buenos Aires but returned to join the rebels in Rio Grande do Sul

June 27, Battle near Passo Fundo (Rio Grande do Sul) General Saraiva defeated Government troops under General Lima

Aug. 10, General Saraiva defeated and mortally wounded at Cavary

Nov. 15, President Moraes Barros inaugurated, V. Pereira, Vice-President

1895

Jan. 3, The President granted amnesty to all enlisted men who had taken part in revolt

Jan. 12, Admiral de Mello returned to harbor of Rio de Janeiro

Feb. 5, Dispute with Argentina as to Misiones territory settled in favor of Brazil. Award of President Cleveland established boundary on rivers Pepiri-Guazu and San Antonio

March 1, Rio Grande rebels defeated government troops near Uruguayan frontier

March 15, Demonstration of cadets in the Military School against the President suppressed. The School closed and cadets dismissed

March 16, Diplomatic relations with Portugal resumed

June 24, Decisive battle in which rebel troops in Rio Grande surrounded by government troops defeated. Da Gama wounded committed suicide to avoid capture

June 29, Death of Ex-President Peixoto

Aug. 23, Formal peace agreement with rebels signed

Sept. 1, Law governing life insurance companies enacted

Oct. 30, Law enacted reorganizing legal education

Nov. 1, Decree regulating foreign insurance companies issued so severe that a number of foreign companies including the New York Life and Equitable left the country

1896

Jan. 7, Note protested English occupation of Island of Trinidade in order to facilitate laying of cable

Aug. 22–27, Outbreak at São Paulo against Italians in dispute as to claims for damages during revolution

Aug. 25, British vessel took down British flag at Trinidade

Nov. 10–March 4, 1897, The President transferred executive office to Vice-President Dr. Manoel V. Pereira because of ill-health

1897

Feb. 19 and 21, Fanatics defeated in battle in State of Minas

March 2, Federal troops sent against Antonio Conselheiro, religious fanatic, who had gone to live with the Jagunços and established settlement at Canudos some 300 miles from Bahia, defeated. Quarrel of Conselheiro with the local authorities had become an insurrection

March 7, Government force ambushed and almost annihilated

May 14, Extradition Treaty with the United States signed

July 18, General Oscar repulsed in attempt to take Canudos by assault

Aug. 15, Treaty with France submitted boundary with French Guiana

Oct. 3, General Oscar with 5,500 troops took Canudos.

Conselheiro it was found had been killed during the siege

Nov. 4, Attempt at assassination of President Moraes by his political enemies as he boarded steamer to welcome General Ruy Barbosa, exile of 1893. Later Captain Diocteano and Major Diocletiano Martyr sentenced to 30 years imprisonment for plotting crime

1898

Jan. 31, Ministry of Finance Department reorganized

March 1, Dr. Campos Salles elected President and Dr. Rosa E. Silva, Vice-President

June 15, President Elect Campos Salles in London arranged funding loan which saved Brazil from financial disaster. Cash interest payments suspended from July 1, and bonds issued for amount due

Aug. 1, Copyright law enacted

Nov. 5, Decree consolidated regulations as to federal judiciary

Nov. 15, President Campos Salles inaugurated

Dec. 31, Act authorized Government to provide for consolidation of internal debt and pay interest in bonds

1899

May 18, Arbitration Treaty with Chile

Aug. 8, Visit of President of Argentina

Bubonic plague appeared in Santos

1900

Jan. 22, Decree created federal stamp tax

March 19, Executive decree published new tariff

June 5, Exchange of notes established commercial agreement with Italy

June 26–30, Exchange of notes established commercial *modus vivendi* with France renewing Treaty indefinitely

Oct., Visit of President in Argentina

Dec. 1, Boundary dispute as to frontier with French Guiana settled by award of Swiss President in favor of Brazil as to interpretation of Article VIII of the Treaty of Utrecht of 1713, and that the Japoc was identical with the Oyapoc River as claimed by Brazil

Bubonic plague in Rio de Janeiro

1901

Nov. 6, Treaty with Great Britain submitted boundary of British Guiana to arbitration

1902

Aug. 16, Bankruptcy law enacted

Sept. 6, Claims Convention with the United States signed

Nov. 12, Decree providing for naturalization of foreigners. Regulations for carrying out promulgated Dec. 12, 1907

Nov. 15, Election of Dr. Francisco de Paula Rodrigues Alves as President and Affonso Augusto Moreira Penna, Vice-President

1903

Jan. 6, Decree regulated organization of agricultural and industrial coöperative organizations

Sept., Plan for civic improvement of Rio de Janeiro approved included improvement of water supply, eradication of bubonic plague and yellow fever, construction of quay with warehouses, railroads and electric lights, and construction of modern houses and streets

Nov. 17, Treaty of Petropolis signed by which Bolivia ceded to Brazil her rights over Acre territory for $10,000,000, and Brazil agreed to build railroad connecting the Amazon and Madeira with Bolivia

Dec. 12, New law enacted regulating insurance companies

1904

Jan. 5, Act gave priority to unpaid wages of rural workers before all other creditors of employers

——, Law and decree of Feb. 26 reorganized the Public Health Service

March 8, Decree reorganized administration of the Federal District

——, Decree issued regulations for sanitary measures for prevention of yellow fever

——, The new street in Rio de Janeiro, the "Avenida Central" begun

May 6, Boundary Treaty with Ecuador signed

May 9 and 11, Brazilians and Peruvians in battle in disputed Acre region

June 6, Arbitration award of the King of Italy settled boundary with British Guiana

July 12, Protocol of boundary agreement with Peru signed

Sept. 24, Patent law amended

Oct. 31, Law enacted provided for compulsory vaccination

Nov. 11–13, Rioting in Rio de Janeiro against compulsory vaccination, and against Conservative Government

1905

Jan. 9, Law reorganized judicial organization of the Federal District

Sept. 17, General Arbitration Treaty with Argentina signed

Dec. 9, Protocol with Venezuela signed, demarcation of boundary

1906

March 1, Dr. Affonso Augusto Penna elected President, Nili Peçanha Vice-President

April 30, Brazil ratified the Geneva Convention of 1864

May 5, Convention with Holland fixed boundary with Dutch Guiana

July 27, American Secretary of State Elihu Root arrived at Rio de Janeiro on U.S.S. "Charleston" to attend Pan-American Conference

Nov. 15, President Penna inaugurated

Dec. 6, Law provided for the establishment of a bank for the redemption of paper, the "Caixa de Conversão"

Dec. 12, Treaty of amity, commerce, and navigation with Argentina signed

1907

Jan. 5, Law enacted governing trade unions, coöperative syndicates, coöperative societies, &c.

Jan. 7, Law provided for expulsion of aliens on enumerated grounds

April 11, Decree regulated colonization and immigration

April 24, Treaty with Colombia of boundaries, transit, and inland navigation

May 10, Treaty of commerce and inland navigation with Ecuador signed

Nov. 28, Law authorized establishment of a central agricultural bank designed to assist farmers with capital and credit

Dec. 12, Regulations as to naturalization of foreigners

Dec. 20, Legislative decree as to copyrights

1908

Jan. 4, Army Reorganization Act made military service compulsory for citizens between ages of 21 and 44

Jan. 13, Decree of the President reduced tariff duties to United States in return for favor shown by the United States to Brazilian coffee

April 15, Agreement with Peru signed for navigation of River Japura or Cuqueta

April 27, Naturalization Treaty with the United States signed

May 14, Decree amended law governing naturalization of aliens

Aug. 11, Brazilian National Exposition opened at Rio de Janeiro

Dec. 5, Red Cross Society founded

Dec. 17, Bankruptcy law enacted

Dec. 30, Law on bills of exchange and promissory notes amended and revised

1909

Jan. 23, Arbitration Convention with the United States signed

March 25, Arbitration Treaty with Portugal signed

April 7, Arbitration Treaty with France signed

April 8, Arbitration Treaty with Spain signed

April 11, Arbitration Treaty with Mexico signed

April 26, Arbitration Treaty with Honduras signed

April 30, Arbitration Convention with Venezuela signed

May 18, Arbitration Treaty with Costa Rica signed

June 10, Arbitration Treaty with Cuba signed

June 14, Death of President Penna. Succeeded by Vice-President Nilo Peçanha

June 18, Arbitration Treaty with Great Britain signed

June 25, Arbitration Treaty with Bolivia signed

July 13, Arbitration Treaty with Norway signed

Sept. 3, Arbitration Treaty with Salvador signed

Sept. 8, Boundary Treaty with Peru signed as to dispute over upper course of the Madre de Dios. Peru gained that region and relinquished 6,500 kilometers of territory

Oct. 4, Boundary Treaty with Argentina declared frontiers

Oct. 30, Treaty with Uruguay modified frontiers at Lake Merim and the Jaguaro River

Dec. 7, Treaty of Arbitration with Peru signed

Dec. 14, Arbitration Treaty with Sweden signed

1910

March 1, Marshal Hermes da Fonseca, Conservative, elected President. Ruy Barbosa, Liberal, distinguished publicist, defeated candidate charged election frauds

April 25, Arbitration Treaty with Haiti signed

July 18, Arbitration court settled outstanding differences with Peru

Aug. 12, Treaty of commerce and river navigation with Bolivia

Nov. 3, Decree regulated civil procedure in the Federal District

Nov. 15, President Hermes da Fonseca inaugurated

Nov. 22, Revolt of navy demanding better conditions begun. Mutineers killed their officers, shelled Rio de Janeiro, and sent ultimatum to the Government

Nov. 27, Ships surrendered, demands met, and amnesty granted

Dec. 9, Mutiny of marines stationed on Cobras Island fired on town. 200 mutineers killed, the rest surrendered after 10 hours fighting

1911

Feb. 24, Arbitration Treaty with Paraguay signed

April 1, Transatlantic cable (German) from Monrovia to Pernambuco opened

April 5, New organic law on higher education enacted

May 3, Leland Stanford scientific expedition from the United States arrived at Para

June 28, Extradition law enacted

Nov. 3, Decree of 227 articles published regulating immigration and colonization and including provisions as to public lands

Nov. 27, Arbitration Treaty with Denmark signed

Dec. 28, Decree reorganized judiciary of the Federal District amending law of 1905

1912

Jan. 17, Copyright law extended to provide for protection of scientific, literary, and artistic works published in foreign countries on a reciprocal basis

Feb. 10, Death of Baron of Rio Branco, Minister of Foreign Affairs

Feb. 29, Boundary convention with Venezuela signed

June 26, First meeting International Commission of Jurists at Rio de Janeiro

July, Law passed required States to obtain Federal sanction before contracting new loans

Aug. 7, Law of 1860 regulating cheques modified

Sept., 226.17 miles of Madeira-Mamore River railroad completed

Dec. 7, Law provided for civil responsibility of railroad in transportation of passengers and freight

1913

May, Preferential rates on imports from the United States restored

May 7, Boundary Treaty with Uruguay drew boundary line on the San Miguel River and recognized Brazilian rights on the river

May 12, First section of new port works at Rio de Janeiro inaugurated

June 4, Decree granted concession for colonization to Japanese in states of São Paulo, Rio de Janeiro, and Minas Geraes

——, State of São Paulo made arrangements to introduce 20,000 Japanese colonists for the cultivation of rice

Dec. 28, Liberal party candidates Ruy Barbosa for president, and Alfredo Ellis for vice-president withdrew because of financial crisis

1914

Jan. 1, From this date standard time and longitude of Greenwich instead of that of Rio de Janeiro adopted

Feb. 2, Decree provided regulations for night work in bakeries in the Federal District

Feb. 27, Discovery of "River of Doubt" branch of Amazon named Rio Teodora after the discoverer, Theodore Roosevelt

March 1, Wenceslau Braz Pereira Gomes elected President

March 5, Ceara placed under martial law because of revolt

March 18, Regulations of 357 articles in part revoked organic law of higher education of 1911

——, Executive decree reorganized Public Health Service

June 6, Award of King of Italy gave Brazil 14,000 square miles of territory and Great Britain 19,000 in dispute as to boundary with British Guiana

July 24, Advancement of Peace Convention with the United States signed

Aug. 4, Law adopted general rules of neutralization in case of war between 2 foreign countries

——, Decree of neutrality in European War

Aug. 30, Railroad from Itapara to Puerto Esperanza completed

Oct. 31, Parcel Post Convention with Argentina signed

Nov. 9, Congress approved and the President ratified 15 conventions and resolutions adopted at Fourth Pan-American Conference. *See* South America

Nov. 15, President Wenceslau Braz inaugurated

Dec. 31, Law as to Federal stamp tax revised

1915

Jan. 6, Federal mining law enacted regulated property in mines, concessions, taxation, &c.

Jan. 13, Executive decree reorganized executive departments of the Republic

Jan. 27, Executive decree provided for organization of a "service of pastoral industry" to be attached to the Department of Agriculture, Industry, and Commerce

March 4, Decree provided for taxation of articles of consumption

April 5, Branches of the National City Bank of New York City opened at Rio de Janeiro and at Santos

May 1, Brazilian ship sunk by German submarine

May 25, Argentina, Brazil, and Chile signed treaty ("A.B.C.") agreement to arbitrate disputes and to refrain from hostilities until opportunity had been given for mediation of an international and permanent commission

1916

Jan. 1, Civil Law Code enacted, a general Federal statute superseding the national laws and regulations in such matters as land-holding, contracts, and judicial proceedings and also the respective laws of 21 States. To go into effect Jan. 1, 1917

Jan. 26, Law imposed income tax on official salaries from the President down

April, Decree guaranteed the deposits of savings banks

Dec. 27, Arbitration Treaty with Uruguay signed

——, New election law passed

1917

Jan. 1, New Civil Code came into effect

Feb. 9 and 13, Protest to Germany made against unrestricted submarine warfare

April 4, The Brazilian vessel "Parana" sunk by German submarine

April 11, Diplomatic relations with Germany severed

April 28, Government proclaimed neutrality in war between the United States and Germany

May 29, Chamber of Deputies passed bill authorizing the President to revoke the proclamation of neutrality

June 1, Act signed by the President revoked neutrality in war between the United States and Germany and provided for seizure of German vessels interned in Brazilian ports

June 2, Decree revoked neutrality as to war between the United States and Germany. German ships seized
June 28, Decree revoked neutrality as to Allied Powers
Oct. 26, Brazil declared state of war with Germany
Dec. 27, Decree authorized the President to revise the military service law
Dec. 28, Protocol signed with Bolivia released Brazil from pledge to build railroad. *See* Bolivia

1918

Feb. 28, Decree required establishment of agricultural schools for poor children
March 1, Dr. Rodriguez Alves elected President, Delfim Moreira, Vice-President
April 24, Decree regulated export of food
May 30, Decree provided for incorporation of the national guard into the army
June 3, Treaty of extradition with Bolivia signed
June 12, Decree established Public Food Commission
July 11, Obligatory Arbitration Convention with Peru signed
July 19, Decree placed international exchange under government control
Nov. 15, Inauguration of President Rodriguez Alves. Because of his illness Vice-President temporarily administered the government

1919

Jan. 15, Civil Code amended. Promulgated July 13
———, Workmen's Compensation Act passed
———, Death of President Rodriguez Alves without assuming office
April 4, Treaty with Great Britain provided for establishment of a permanent peace commission of 5 members
April 13, Special election. Dr. Epitacio Pessoa, head of Brazilian delegation at the Paris Peace Conference elected President
June 20, President Epitacio Pessoa landed in New York
June 28, Brazil signed the Treaty of Versailles. Ratified Nov. 11
July 2, Boundary Treaty with Uruguay signed
July 28, Inauguration of the President
Dec. 3, Treaty of friendship with China signed

1920

Jan. 10, Brazil became original member of the League of Nations
Sept. 3, Presidential decree revoked banishment of former Imperial family
Sept. 7, University of Rio de Janeiro founded
Sept. 19, King Albert and Queen Elizabeth of Belgium arrived at Rio de Janeiro, first European sovereigns to visit a South American country
Oct. 20, Arrival of former premier Orlando as Italian ambassador to Brazil
Oct. 30, Code of military justice reorganized
Nov. 13, Commercial Treaty with Belgium signed
Dec. 16, Decree authorized building of houses for workmen under law of Jan. 18, 1911
Census gave population as 30,635,605, including 1,565,951 foreigners. Total number of immigrants registered from 1820 to 1920 was 3,648,382 of which more than a third (1,388,881) were Italians, Portuguese, 1,055,154, Spaniards, 510,514. Total German immigration 1820 to 1920 was 131,441

1921

Jan. 6, New Immigration law enacted
Jan. 17, Repression of anarchy law enacted provided penalties
July 23, Law established Department of Labor
Oct. 8, Immigration Treaty with Italy signed
Nov. 22, Rent law enacted placed limitations on rents because of housing shortage
Dec. 7, Extradition Treaty with Uruguay signed
Dec. 11, Agreement with Germany signed on account of seizure of German ships and reparation due
Dec. 21, Rent law regulations issued

1922

Jan. 7, National Bureau of Sugar Exportation created to stimulate export and maintain prices
Jan. 28, Death of Dr. Amaro Cavalcanti, statesman
Feb. 24, Extradition Treaty with Paraguay signed
March 1, Dr. Arturo da Silva Bernardes elected President defeating Dr. Nilo Peçanha in the most bitterly contested election ever held in Brazil
June 17, Portuguese aviators S. Cabral and G. Coutinho reached Rio de Janeiro after flight from Lisbon in 9 "hops"
July 5–6, Military revolt in São Paulo led by Colonel Isidor Lopes defeated by government troops
July 29, Treaty with Great Britain signed as to dual nationality, questions of literary and artistic property, and immigration and labor
Sept. 7, Centennial exposition opened in Rio de Janeiro. Pension Bureau for workers established
Sept. 26, Treaties signed with Portugal as to dual nationality, literary and artistic property, and immigration and labor
Nov. 6, Contract signed by which the United States agreed to send a rear admiral and naval officers to help reorganize Brazilian navy
Nov. 15, Inauguration of President Bernardes
Dec. 31, Income tax law enacted

1923

Jan. 8, Law vested right to issue paper money in Bank of Brazil
Jan. 24, Decree established superannuation and pension fund for employees of railroads
March 1, Death of Ruy Barbosa, jurist, in Rio de Janeiro
March 11, Emigration and Labor Convention with Italy signed
April 30, Decree created a national council of commerce and industry to act as a consulting body
June 30, Act regulated employment of persons in domestic service. Regulations issued July 30
Oct. 18, Most favored nation commercial Treaty with the United States signed

1924

Feb. 27, Decree exempted certain machinery from import duties to encourage the cultivation of cotton
———, Minor's act prohibited employment of young persons under 18 in occupations dangerous to health or morals and limited night work to 6 hours
Feb. 29, Agreement with Spain concluded provided for commercial reciprocity
March 3, Juvenile Court opened in the Federal District
June 23, Arbitration Treaty with Switzerland signed
July 4, Revolt begun in city of São Paulo led by General Isidor Lopes

July 28, Government troops forced rebels out of São Paulo

Sept. 1, Government suppressed the newspaper the *Correio da Manha* opposed to the administration

Sept. 16, Rebels captured ports of Guayra and Mendez on upper Parana River

Oct., Revolt in State of Rio Grande do Sul

Oct. 18, National Department of Public Health issued regulations for industrial hygiene

Dec. 10, Shooting affray on frontier of Uruguay

Dec. 31, Decree established new code of civil and commercial law for the Federal District

———, Immigration regulations enacted. Went into effect June 30, 1925

1925

Jan., Revolutionary plot discovered by the police in Rio de Janeiro. Country placed under martial law until April 30

March 4, Settlement of boundary difficulties in Amazon effected in United States State Department by Brazil, Peru, and Colombia

March 30, Convention signed with Uruguay as to conduct of the 2 countries in the event of internal disturbances

April 17, Decree published in the official Gazette established national Bureau of Education and Council of Education

Sept. 3, Protocols signed for execution of boundary treaty of Nov. 17, 1903

Dec. 24, Law signed by the President provided for 15 days annual vacation in commercial and industrial establishments, and banks

1926

March 22, 38 persons killed by explosion and sinking of steamer "Paes de Carvalho" on Solimoes River

April 13, Treaty with Venezuela signed for maintenance of order on the frontier

April 22, Boundary Treaty with Great Britain as to British Guiana

June 10, Announcement that Brazil would withdraw from League of Nations because not accorded a permanent seat on Council; formal notice June 14

June 24, Issue of $25,000,000 6½% gold bonds of Brazilian Government offered by a syndicate of New York bankers

Oct. 30, The President signed regulations for law of Dec. 24, 1925 as to 15 days annual vacation for workers

Nov. 14, Rising in Rio Grande do Sul and in Santa Maria on the 17th

Nov. 15, Dr. Washington Luiz Pereira de Souza inaugurated President and Mello Vianna, Vice-President

Nov. 23, Manuel Rivas Vicuna formed Ministry

Dec. 1, Legislative decree published a Minors Code which combined previous laws as to child welfare and juvenile delinquency. 12 years set as minimum age for industrial employment

Dec. 18, Law passed adopted new unit of account called the *cruzeiro*, a gold coin containing 2 grammes of gold .900 fine, to be exchanged for 4 paper milreis

Dec. 20, (Act 5109) Pension law enacted

1927

Jan. 13, Law provided for establishment of an aviation force

Feb. 19, Agreement with Poland as to immigration signed

May 21, Boundary Treaty with Paraguay fixed line between the mouth of the Apa River and Bahia Negra

June 10, Trial of revolutionists of São Paulo of 1924 concluded. 115 found guilty, 167 acquitted. The leader General I. Lopes sentenced to 2 years imprisonment in absence

July 5, Death of Gustao de Cunha

Aug. 13, The President signed act to repress communism by rendering strikes illegal

Sept. 7, University of Minas Geraes organized

Sept. 8, Treaty of friendship with Turkey signed

Nov. 30, Law abolished tax reductions, and exemptions on imports and exports and taxable articles to begin Jan. 1, 1928

Dec. 27, Boundary Agreement with Argentina signed

1928

March 10, Landslide on Mount Serrat destroyed part of city of Santos and killed nearly 100 persons

May 3, Decree of the President fixed value of gold milreis at 4.567 milreis paper

June 14, Withdrawal of Brazil from the League of Nations became effective

July 14, First Congress of Aviation met at Rio de Janeiro

Aug. 18, Frontier Treaty with Venezuela signed

Nov. 15, Boundary Treaty with Colombia signed

Dec. 3, Return of Alberto Santos-Dumont, aviator, to Brazil, his native land. Government decreed a half day holiday in his honor

Dec. 22, President-Elect Herbert Hoover made final speech of his tour of South America at Rio de Janeiro, stressing international affection

Dec. 25, Boundary Treaty with Bolivia settled points not included in treaties of 1867 and 1903

1929

April 22, Agreement with Great Britain signed as to boundary with British Guiana

July 24, Protocol for delimitation of boundary with Venezuela signed

Dec. 9, New bankruptcy law approved

1930

Feb. 5, From this date Brazil subject to compulsory jurisdiction of the Permanent Court of International Justice

Feb. 7, Vice-President Vianna shot and wounded 3 times by political opponent in demonstration in town of Montes Carlos and 5 persons killed and 14 others wounded

March 1, Election of Dr. Julio Prestes (Republican-Conservative) for President and Dr. Vital Soares for Vice-President

March 14, Frontier Protocol with Colombia signed for remarking the boundary line

March 18, Agreement with Great Britain signed for demarcation of the boundary of British Guiana

May 10, Protocol signed with Paraguay settled long standing boundary dispute

May 22, The dirigible "Graf Zeppelin" arrived at Pernambuco after flight of 3,750 miles from Seville, Spain in 61 hours

May, Revolt led by José Pereira in State of Parahyba against President Pessoa

July 26, Liberal President João Pessoa, President of

State of Parahyba, assassinated at Pernambuco by
political rival João Dantas

Oct. 3, Revolt begun in southern States of Minas
Geraes, Parahyba, and Rio Grande do Sul and in
extreme north to prevent the inauguration of Dr.
Julio Prestes as President and to "wipe out the
clique that has dominated Brazil for the past forty
years," the Conservatives and the "coffee ogli-
garchy"

Oct. 4, State of siege declared in 3 southern States in
revolt

Oct. 5, Martial law proclaimed for entire Republic

Oct. 7, Rebels captured Natal and Pernambuco in victorious advance

Oct. 16, Engagement with rebels at Itarare

Oct. 22, Shipment of arms to the rebels prohibited by
the United States

Oct. 24, Military and naval officers headed by General
Fragoso demanded resignation of President

——, The federal fort at Rio de Janeiro fired on German
liner "Baden" killing 21 passengers and wounding 71.
Authorities stated that the ship refused to halt when
signaled

Oct. 26, Military Junta offered Dr. Getulio Vargas,
Liberal rebel leader of Rio Grande do Sul the presidency of which he accepted

Oct. 30, Washington Luis refused to resign as President
and was imprisoned

Nov. 2, New Government recognized by Peru

Nov. 3, Dr. Getulio Vargas inaugurated Provisional
President

Nov. 5, Portuguese Cabinet decided to recognize the
new Government

——, Provisional Government invalidated all laws
passed by Congress after Oct. 3

Nov. 6, Chile, Bolivia, Uruguay, Italy, and Portugal
recognized the new Government

Nov. 8, New Government recognized by the United
States, Great Britain, and the Vatican State

——, Decree granted amnesty to all persons who had
taken part in revolt

Nov. 11, Decree of Provisional Government dissolved
the national Congress, suspended constitutional
guarantees and announced creation of a National
Consultative Council and a Special Tribunal for
prosecution and trial of political and administrative
offenses of the preceding administration

Nov. 20, Former President Luis and Carvalho de Brillo
head of Bank of Brazil allowed to depart for Europe
and other political and military prisoners sent into
exile

Dec. 13, Decree limited immigration for one year to aid
unemployment situation

Dec. 17, Majors Tadeo and Larre-Borges of Uruguay
and Lieutenant Challes of France in flight from
Seville crashed in forest on the coast

CHILE

Chile, republic on west coast, extending between the Pacific and the Andes south of Peru
and bounded on the east by Bolivia and Argentina. The length of this long narrow country is
2,661 miles, and breadth ranges from 46 to 250
miles, total area 290,119 square miles, and population 3,742,799 in 1920, and 4,264,819 by census

of 1931. The capital is Santiago. Chile is seventh
in size among the South American republics and
stands third in the value of its foreign commerce,
exceeded by Brazil and Argentina only. The
northern region is the world's chief source of
nitrate of soda, the excise tax on its export providing the largest item of the revenue.

The great majority of the population is of
European origin. The indigenous inhabitants
are of three branches, the *Fuegians*, mostly
nomadic, living in or near Tierra del Fuego; the
Araucanians (101,118) in the valleys or on the
western slopes of the Andes; the *Changos*, who in-
habit the northern coast region and work as laborers. The total number of foreigners included
in the census of 1920 was 120,436, as against
134,524 in 1907.

The two leading cities, with census population
in 1931, are Santiago, the capital, 538,144, and
Valparaiso, 191,494; Viña del Mar has 52,871.
Other towns with population as estimated in 1929
(census figures of 1920 in parentheses) are:—
Concepcion, 70,645 (64,074); Iquique, 36,547
(37,421); Talca, 37,033 (36,079); Chillan, 31,902
(30,881); Antofagasta, 84,221 (51,531); Temuco,
44,000 (28,546); Magallanes, 32,268 (27,000);
Talcaguano, 39,770 (22,084); Valdivia, 39,905
(26,854).

Colonel Carlos Ibanez, President.

1520

Oct. 21, Magellan discovered and named Cape Virgins
at eastern end of the Straits through which he sailed
to the Pacific Ocean Nov. 28

1534

May 21, A royal grant gave to Diego de Almagro,
lieutenant of Pizarro, the territory south of Peru
to be called New Toledo

1535

July, Almagro started on journey of exploration and
conquest from Cuzco, crossing the Andes and arriving
in Chile in May, 1536, returning to Peru across the
deserts of Atacama and Tarapaco the same year,
forced to give up the subjection of the Araucanian
Indians at the Cachapoal River, the northern boundary of the Purumancian territory, by the determined
resistance of the Indians

1536

Sept., Juan de Saavedra, lieutenant of Almagro,
named Valparaiso Bay

1540

Jan., Pedro de Valdivia, sent by Pizarro, led exploring
expedition from Cuzco and with Francisco de
Aguirre reached the Copiapo Valley in Sept.

1541

Feb. 12, Valdivia founded Santiago de Chile, the first
European settlement

March 7, Municipal government of Santiago organized,
Valdivia elected Governor, Aguirre, *Alcalde*

Sept. 11, Santiago burned by the Indians and settlers driven to the fort

1544

Sept. 3, Valdivia proclaimed the founding of the town of Valparaiso

1546

The Spaniards crossed the Rio Maulé, southern boundary of the Purumancians, but attacked by Araucanians near the Itata River and forced to return to Santiago

La Serena founded in province of Coquimbi by Juan Bohon, lieutenant of Valdivia

1547

Dec. 6, Valdivia sailed from Valparaiso for Peru leaving F. de Villagra as *ad interim* governor

1548

April 23, Valdivia confirmed as Governor of Chile by Las Gasca

Dec., Araucanians began war against Spaniards. Captain Juan Bohon captured and killed

1549

June 20, Valdivia arrived at Santiago from Peru

July 17, Royal decree established audiencia at Santa Fé de Bogota

1550

Feb. 22, Valdivia defeated attack of Araucanians in Battle of Andalien

June 26, City of Chillan founded

Oct. 5, City of Concepcion founded by Valdivia

1552

Feb., City of Valdivia founded by Valdivia and named for himself

Dec. 23, Letter of Francisco de Aguirre to Charles V asked for grant of Tucuman of which Valdivia had made him Governor and which he had taken making Prado a prisoner

1553

Captain Francisco de Ulloa explored province of Chiloe and part of the Chonos Archipelago

1554

Jan. 1, Valdivia captured and defeated in battle with the Araucanian Indians and killed by them. Cabildo proclaimed Francisco de Villagra Governor at Santiago. Aguirre, rival contestant, proclaimed Governor at La Serena

Jan. 29, Don Garcia Hurtado de Mendoza sent from Peru to assume office as Governor

Feb. 28, Villagra defeated by Indians and obliged to abandon Fort Penco at Concepcion

1557

April 23, The new Governor, Hurtado de Mendoza, arrived in Chile. He soon sent Aguirre and Villagra into exile

April 29, Villagra defeated and killed Lautaro, Indian leader

June, Governor Mendoza took the field against the Indians

Nov., Battle of the Laguinallas (Little Lagoons). Mendoza routed the Indians early in the month

Nov. 29, Indians defeated in attack by superior weapons of the Spaniards

Juan de Ladrillero from Valdivia passed through the Straits of Magellan and took possession of the land for Chile and Spain

1558

Jan., Canete founded by Mendoza in Arauco

Jan. 20 and Dec. 14, Araucanians defeated in battles by Mendoza

1561

June 5, Francisco de Villagra appointed Governor to succeed Mendoza arrived in Chile

1562

Dec. 8, Villagra defeated the Indians in battle on the banks of the Bio Bio River

1563

June 22, Death of Villagra. He had designated a cousin Pedro de Villagra to succeed him as Governor *ad interim*

June 30, Arauco Fort evacuated by Commander L. B. de Mercado besieged by Indians since May 26

1564

March 25, Battle near Angol in which Mercado defeated the Indians

1565

Jan., Governor Villagra pacified the district between the Maulé and Bio Bio rivers

Rodrigo de Quiroga appointed *ad interim* Governor of Chile (1565–67)

Aug. 27, Decree established a royal audiencia for Chile. Dissolved in 1573

1567

Sept. 23, Melchor Bravo de Saravia appointed Governor of Chile

1569

Jan. 7, Indians repulsed attack of Spaniards commanded by Saravia

1572

April 2, Melchor Calderon appointed Commissary of the Inquisition for Chile

1574

Nov. 22, Discovery of Juan Fernandez Islands. *See* America

1575

March 17, First recorded earthquake destroyed towns of Santiago and Concepcion

Dec. 16, Earthquake and tidal wave destroyed Valdivia

Rodrigo de Quiroga returned as Captain-General

1578

March 21, Quiroga routed Indians in battle at Andalican (Colcura)

Nov. 27, Indian attack on Quiroga encamped in Valley of Guadva defeated

Dec. 4, Sir Francis Drake arrived in Bay of Valparaiso and captured and looted the city

1580

Feb. 25, Death of Rodrigo de Quiroga. He designated Martin Ruiz de Gamboa *ad interim* Governor

1583

Sept. 17, New Captain-General Alonso de Sotomayor arrived at Santiago (1583–92)

1585

Jan. 16, Indians defeated in battle with Governor and Garcia Ramon on the Cayamcura River

1591

Jan. 23, Fort Ildefonso erected on site of Fort Arauco destroyed by the Indians

1592

Aug., Governor de Sotomayor sailed for Peru for reinforcements

Oct. 6, Don Martin Onez de Loyola took office as Governor succeeding Pedro de Viscarra *ad interim* Governor (1592–98)

1593

Feb., Loyola began unsuccessful campaign against the Indians

April 12, The Jesuits arrived at Santiago and established a school

Valparaiso plundered by Sir Richard Hawkins

1595

Augustinians established a monastery

1598

Dec. 23, De Loyola and his soldiers attacked and killed by Indians at Imperial

Viscarra again *ad interim* Governor

1599

May 28, Francisco de Quinones appointed Governor (May 18) arrived at Concepcion bringing aid to Spaniards

Nov. 24, Indians attacked Fort Valdivia and killed the Spanish garrison

1600

March 30, Quinones brought aid to town of Imperial besieged by Indians. Town abandoned the following day

July 29, Alonso Garcia Ramon appointed Governor arrived at Santiago (1600–01)

1601

Feb. 7, Town of Villarica taken by the Indians

Feb. 9, Alonso de Ribera y Zambrano appointed Governor arrived at Santiago (1601–05)

1605

Nov. 6, Army of 1,000 sent by Spain arrived at Santiago

Dec. 12, Ramon again Governor (1605–10) began unsuccessful campaign against the Indians

1608

March 26, Royal decree of Philip III declared Indians, prisoners of war, slaves. A letter of marque authorized the slave trade

May 26, Royal decree of Philip III pronounced Araucanians slaves

1609

Sept. 8, Royal audiencia established at Santiago subordinated to Viceroy of Peru

Sept. 28, Royal court at Santiago declared forced labor for Indians abolished only in cases of women and minors

Settlement of Jesuits in Chiloe

1610

Aug. 5, Death of Governor Ramon. Luis Merlo de la Fuente designed by him Governor *ad interim*. Succeeded by appointed Governor Juan Zara Quemada (1610–12)

Aug. 20, Decree of Philip III making Araucanians taken in war slaves published

1612

March 27, Alonso de Ribera appointed Governor for the second time arrived in Chile (1612–17)

1617

March 9, Death of Governor de Ribera, Fernando Talaverano *ad interim* Governor

1618

Jan. 12, Governor Lope de Ulloa y Lemos arrived in Chile (1617–20)

1620

March 28, Regulations for Indians of Chile signed by the Viceroy of Peru

Dec. 8, Death of Governor Ulloa y Lemos, Cristobal de la Cerda designated *ad interim* Governor

1621

A mint established in Santa Fé de Bogota

Nov., Appointed Governor Pedro Osores de Ulloa arrived in Chile

1624

Sept. 18, Death of Governor Osores de Ulloa, Alba y Noruena designated *ad interim* Governor

1625

May 29, Luis Ferdinand de Cordoba new Governor assumed office and began offensive war against the Indians

1629

May 15, Battle of Las Cangregeras near Yumbal in which Indian leader Lientur defeated the Spaniards

Dec., New Governor Francisco Laso de la Vega, marquess of Baides, arrived, "one of the best in the whole history of Chile" Elliott (1629–39)

1631

Jan. 13, Battle of Albarrada in which the Spaniards defeated the Indians near Arauco

1639

May 1, New Governor Francisco Lopez de Zuniga, marquess of Baides took oath of office at Concepcion (1639–46)

1641

Jan. 6, Governor Baides held first peace parley with the Indians at Quillin and made treaty with the Indians by which the Bio Bio River was recognized as boundary line between the Spaniards and the Indians, the "Peace of Quillin" which lasted until 1655

1642

Nov. 5, Death of Father Valdivia in Spain after failure of his plan and effort to make peaceful conquest of the Indians

1643

Aug. 7, Dutch fleet took Valdivia but plan for colony abandoned because of failure of alliance with the Indians against the Spaniards

1645
Feb. 6, Spanish expedition reëstablished fortress at Valdivia

1646
May 8, Don Martin de Mujica succeeding Baides as Governor arrived at Concepcion (1646–48)

1647
Feb. 24, Second parley with the Indians held by Governor Mujica at Quillin

May 13, Santiago partly destroyed by earthquake. Over 1,000 persons killed

1649–1650
Alonso de Figueroa y Cordoba Governor *ad interim*

1650
May 7, Arrival of new Governor Antonio de Acuna y Cabrera (1650–55)

1651
Jan. 24, Father Rosales held peace parley with Indians

Feb. 14, Indians rose between the Rio Maulé and the Bio Bio in desperate revolt against the Spaniards

Nov. 16, Concepcion refounded by Valdivia

Governor Cabrera deposed and Francisco de la Fuente Villabos acclaimed Governor

1655
Feb. 14, Indians between the Maulé and Bio Bio Rivers rose in desperate insurrection. "In one day the results of one hundred years of fighting almost disappeared" Elliot

1656
Admiral Pedro Portale de Casanate Governor (1656–62)

1657
March 15, Severe earthquake in Chile

1662
Feb. 27, Death of Governor Casanate. Diego Gonzales Montero Governor for 3 months

May 22, Angel de Peredo Governor (1662–64)

1664
Jan., Francisco de Meneses Governor (1664–68)

1668
Diego Davila Coello y Pacheco, marques de Navamorquende, Governor (1668–70)

1670
Montero again temporary Governor

1671
Oct. 30, Juan Henriquez assumed office as Governor (1670–82)

1674
Dec. 20, Royal decree of Dona Mariana of Austria abolished slavery for Chilean Indians

1679
June 12, Decree of Charles II abolished slavery in Chile

1682
March 25, Arrival of new Governor Marcos José de Garro (1682–91)

1686
Sept. 15, Serena repulsed attack on town by pirates commanded by Captain Davis

1692
Jan. 5, Tomas Marin de Poveda assumed office as Governor

Dec. 15–16, The Governor held peace parleys with the Indians at Choquecheque and at Yumbel

1700
Arrival of Governor Francisco Ibanez y Peralta (1700–06)

1706
Feb. 26, Ibanez deposed. Succeeded by Juan Andres de Ustaritz Governor (1706–17)

1709
Jan. 31, H.M.S. "Duke" rescued Alexander Selkirk (Selcraig) after 4 years and 4 months a castaway on Juan Fernandez Island of Mas a Tierra where he was landed in Sept., 1704 after quarrel with captain of ship of which he was boatswain

1716
Dec. 23, On order of the King the Viceroy of Peru deposed Ustaritz as Governor and appointed Don José de Santiago Concha *ad interim*

1717
Sept. 30, Ustaritz convicted of smuggling on French ships

Nov. 11, Present city of Quillota founded by Concha

Dec. 16, Gabriel Cano de Aponte took office as Governor (1717–33)

Philip V installed viceroyalty at Santa Fé de Bogota which lasted 6 years

1720
July 12, Royal decree ordered that all the Indian *encomiendas* which had lapsed or were unconfirmed should be incorporated in the Royal Exchequer

1722
April 5, Discovery of Easter Island (Paash Eyland) off coast by Dutch Admiral Jacob Roggeveen

1726
Feb. 13, Parley of Negrete with the Indians and peace treaty concluded

1730
July 8, Earthquake at Santiago, Valparaiso, Cordova, and Tucuman

1733
Nov. 11, Death of Governor Cano de Aponte. Francisco Sanchez de la Barreda y Vera appointed *ad interim* Governor

1734
Jan. 29, José A. Manso de Salamanca appointed Governor. Arrived in Santiago Nov. 15, 1737 (1737–45)

1738
July 28, Royal decree established the University of Santiago

Dec. 8, The Governor held parley with the Indians at Tapihue

1739

March 27, Town of Santa Maria de los Angeles founded by Manso

1740

July 26, Don Francisco Garcia Huidobro purchased from Philip V of Spain for 1,000 pesos the entire "corregimiento" of Aconcagua Valley
Aug. 3, City of San Felipe founded by the Governor

1742

Feb. 17, Villa de San Agustin de Talca founded

1743

Oct. 1, Royal decree granted concession for minting money to Don Francisco Garcia Huidobro

1744

April 5, Royal decree reached Santiago by which the Governor authorized to sell 6 titles of marquess or count for 120,000 pesos
Sept. 8, Governor Manso founded city of Copiago
Dec. 24, Governor Manso appointed Viceroy of Peru

1745

Marquess of Obando *ad interim* Governor

1746

March 25, Domingo Ortiz de Rosas new Governor made formal entry into Santiago (1745–55)

1747

March 11, State University installed at Santiago

1748

July 11, First stone of cathedral at Santiago laid by Bishop Juan Gonzales Marmolejo

1751

May 25, Earthquake destroyed Santiago and Concepcion

1755

Nov. 25, Don Manuel de Amat y Junient appointed Governor (1755–61)

1756

June 28, Death of Ortiz de Rosas at sea on voyage to Spain
Dec. 13, Governor Amat held parley with the Indians in the Satto del Laja

1759

Jan. 18, Governor Amat held second parley with the Indians

1760

Feb. 14, Governor Amat held third parley with the Indians

1761

Sept. 9, Amat appointed Viceroy of Peru. Felix de Berroeta *ad interim* Governor

1762

Oct. 4, Governor Antonio de Guill y Gonzaga arrived and assumed office (1762–68)

1764

Dec. 8, Governor Gonzaga held parley with the Indians and induced them to sign agreement to settle in the towns

1766

Dec. 25, Successful revolt of Indians in Araucania

1767

Aug. 7, Royal order to expel the Jesuits of April 1 received in Santiago, and executed Aug. 16

1768

May 7, Jesuits sailed from Callao, Peru
Aug. 24, Death of Governor Gonzaga. Don Juan de Balmaceda y Censano senior judge of Royal Audiencia became *ad interim* Governor

1770

March 3, Francisco Xavier de Morales y Castejon superseded Balmaceda deposed by the Viceroy of Peru because of his inhuman treatment of Araucanians in suppression of revolution (1770–73)
Nov. 19, Chilean squadron took formal possession of Easter Island which they named St. Charles Island
Dec. 31, First public clock on church tower of church of Santa Ana struck the hour. Mackenna "History" states that "the whole city lay awake listening with all its ears and holding its breath"

1771

Feb. 26, Morales held parley with the Indians at Negrete

1772

Nov. 21, Morales held second parley with the Indians at Los Angeles

1773

March 6, Governor Augustin de Jauregui assumed office (1773–80)

1774

Dec. 21, Governor Jauregui held parley with the Indians

1777

Jan. 28, Foundation stone of the Mint laid by Governor Jauregui

1778

Title captain-general adopted as designation of executive

1780

July 6, Jauregui appointed Viceroy of Peru. Don Tomas Alvarez de Acevedo appointed *ad interim*. Ambrosio de Benavides Governor (1780–88)
Conspiracy of Antoine Berney, Antoine Gramuset, and José Antonio Rojas first effort for independence of Spain

1781

Feb. 5, Sentence on Berney and Gramuset

1784

Jan. 3, Parley with the Indians at Longuilmo, Ambrose O'Higgins representing Benavides
June 1, Royal order provided that Chile should be dependent on the Viceroyalty of Peru as to military administration and affairs of royal Treasury

1785

Dec. 8, Royal cedula ordered adoption of mining ordinances of New Spain of May 22, 1783 in Chile

1787

Feb. 6, Decree established intendancies in Chile
April 27, Death of Benavides Acevedo then acting as

ad interim Governor. Tomas Alvarez de Acevedo succeeded him

1788

May 26, Ambrose O'Higgins, most notable colonial Governor, assumed office (1788–96)

Aug. 19, Governor O'Higgins issued his "Declaration of Good Government"

1791

June 10, Royal decree of Charles IV abolished *encomiendas* freeing the Indians from slavery

1793

Jan. 19, Resolution of the *cabildo* of Santiago established "a public playhouse"

March 4, Governor O'Higgins held parley with the Indians at Negrete. Ceremonies lasted 3 days

1794

June 18, Governor O'Higgins founded present Fort Constitucion (Nueva Bilbao) at mouth of the Maulé River

1795

Feb. 26, Royal cedula introduced the *Ordenanza de Bilbao,* Spanish commercial law into Chile and the *Tribunal del Consulado* created for trial of commercial cases

1796

May, O'Higgins left Chile to become Viceroy of Peru. José de Rezabal y Ugarte *ad interim* Governor

Sept. 18, Gabriel de Aviles y del Fierro assumed office as Governor (1796–99)

1797

March 6, The San Luis Academy founded by Governor Aviles

1799

Jan. 21, Aviles left Chile to become Viceroy of Buenos Aires

Jan. 31, Field Marshal Joaquin del Pino y Rosas assumed office as Governor *ad interim*

1801

March 18, Governor del Pino received appointment as Viceroy of Buenos Aires and 12 days later left Chile. José de Santiago Concha *ad interim* Governor, followed by Francisco Diez de Medina *ad interim* Governor

1802

Jan. 31, Lieutenant General Luis Munoz de Guzman assumed office as permanent Governor (1802–08)

March 9, Royal decree made Valparaiso a city and awarded a coat of arms

1803

March 3, Parley with the Indians at Negrete

1806

Oct. 23, Royal decree provided that in case of death of governor the office to be taken by officer next highest in rank not senior judge as heretofore

1808

Feb. 11, Death of Governor Munoz de Guzman. At first illegally succeeded by the president of the Audiencia, Ballesteros

April 22, General Francisco Antonio Garcia Carrasco assumed office as *ad interim* Governor

1809

May 26, Governor Carrasco proclaimed severe penalties against persons engaged in any matter relating to independence of Spain

1810

May 25, Governor Carrasco arrested and imprisoned Don José Antonio Rojas and Don Juan Antonio Ovalle, patriot leaders

July 10, Rojas and Ovalle deported by order of the Governor

July 11, City of Santiago rose against the Governor because of deportations

July 16, Governor Carrasco forced to resign

——, Don Mateo de Toro y Zambrano assumed office as Governor after the insurrection

July 20, Cabildo at Santa Fé de Bogota established Junta declaring allegiance to Ferdinand of Spain

Sept. 18, Toro resigned power to Junta of 7 including Rozas and I. Carrera, Conde de la Conquista, president and office of Captain General abolished. This day celebrated by Chile as Independence Day

1811

Feb. 21, Decree of Provisional Junta announced Chilean ports open to trade with the United States

April 11, Election held for representatives to a national Congress

July 4, First national Congress met at Santiago. Members took oath of fidelity to Ferdinand VII

July 25, Don Bernardo O'Higgins arrived at Valparaiso

Aug. 9, Junta elected, Martin Calvo Encalada, Juan José Aldunate, and F. Javier del Sola

Aug. 14, Constitution promulgated

Aug. 25, Don Juan Martinez de Rozas organized a revolt at Concepcion against the conservative Junta at Santiago

Sept. 4, José M. Carrera in favor of independence from Spain overthrew the Junta. A new Junta of Rozas, Rosales, Encalada, Marin, and Mackenna appointed

Oct. 27, New constitutional statute of 27 articles published. Recognized the authority of Ferdinand

Nov. 15, Resignation of Junta forced by José Carrera and new Junta of Carrera, Bernardo O'Higgins and Gaspar Marin formed

Dec. 2, Carrera dismissed Congress and appointed José Nicolas de la Cerda and Juan José Aldunate as his associates in governing Junta on resignation of O'Higgins and Marin

1812

Feb. 13, *La Aurora,* first periodical published in Chile appeared at Santiago

Feb. 24, Arrival of American "consul," Joel R. Poinsett

July 23, José Carrera again overthrew the Government forming new Junta with Uribe and Urzua as associates

Aug. 21, First school for girls opened in Santiago

1813

March 26, Brigadier-General Don Antonio Pareja with Spanish army sent by Viceroy of Peru to subdue Chile landed on coast

March 31, Carrera issued declaration of war against the Viceroy of Peru

April 5, Carrera established headquarters at Talca

April 15, Pareja reached Chillan and all Chile south of the Maulé River under his control

Aug. 3, Carrera and O'Higgins made successful assault on royalists at Chillan

Aug. 13, Governing Junta authorized creation of a public library and solicited donations of money and books

1814

Jan. 28, O'Higgins proclaimed as Chilean commander-in-chief

Jan. 31, Another Spanish army under General Gavino Gainza landed at Arauco

May 3, Treaty of Lircai signed by which Chileans agreed to acknowledge the sovereignty of Ferdinand and authority of the Supreme Council of the Regency

May 5, Truce of Talca signed by which royalists recognized existing order. Repudiated by Viceroy

Sept. 4, O'Higgins resigned as commander-in-chief in favor of José Carrera

Oct. 1–2, Battle of Rancagua. Carrera and O'Higgins defeated by royalists. This victory made Colonel Mariano Osorio Governor (1814–15)

1815

March 26, New Governor Francisco Casimiro Marco del Pont arrived (1815–17)

1817

Jan. 23, Cabot took Coquimbo

Feb. 7, San Martin's army arrived in Chile over the Andes and took outpost at La Guardia

Feb. 12, Davila Larraona took Copiapo

——, Battle of Chacabuco. General José de San Martin, Argentine general, with army he had trained at Mendoza for liberation of Chile and led across the Andes joined with forces of O'Higgins and won decisive victory against the royalists

Feb. 14, General San Martin entered Santiago. Invited to assume the government he declined in favor of O'Higgins who was elected Supreme Director on the 16th

May 5, Royalist attack defeated in advance on Concepcion

June 9, Decree provided for coinage of money bearing inscription "Liberty, Union, and Strength-Independent Chile"

Oct. 13, O'Higgins and Carrera repulsed attack of royalists at Campo de los Robles

1818

Jan. 1, Declaration of independence signed at Concepcion by O'Higgins and his three ministers

Feb. 12, On first anniversary of Chacabuco O'Higgins formally proclaimed the independence of Chile

March 19, San Martin's army surprised and defeated by royalists commanded by Osorio at Cancha Rayada

April 5, Independence ensured by patriot victory at Battle of Maipu. San Martin defeated royalists commanded by General Osorio

April 26, Chilean men of war defeated Spanish fleet at Valparaiso raising the blockade

May 5, Commission from the United States headed by Theodorick Bland, sent to investigate situation of new republic, arrived at Santiago and were received by O'Higgins

Aug. 10, Constitution published and submitted to popular vote

Oct 23, Constitution adopted. O'Higgins given supreme executive authority

Oct. 28, Chilean squadron captured the Spanish frigate "Maria Isabel" off Quirquina Island sent by Spain to crush American revolt

Nov. 28, Lord Thomas Cochrane arrived to take command of fleet

Dec. 12, Congress of the United Provinces of La Plata the first to recognize Chile as a free and sovereign State

1819

March 4, Edict of Bernardo O'Higgins declared the native Indians citizens of Chile and released them from obligation to pay tribute

1820

Feb. 2, 3, 4, Cochrane in the "O'Higgins" ("Maria Isabel" renamed) captured Valdivia from royalists

Aug. 20, Expedition commanded by General San Martin sailed from Valparaiso in squadron commanded by Lord Thomas Cochrane for liberation of Peru

Nov. 27, Battle of Alameda de Concepcion. Benavides defeated by patriots

1821

Aug. 11, Treaty with Portugal signed by which independence recognized by Portugal

Sept. 4, Carranza betrayed, captured, and shot at Mendoza, Argentina

1822

Jan. 27, Minister from the United States to Chile appointed, constituting recognition of the Republic

Feb. 23, Vicente Benavides renegade patriot and pirate hanged

May 22, O'Higgins published decree calling for elections for a "preparatory convention"

July 6, Lord Cochrane sailed the first steamboat on the Pacific from Valparaiso, "La Estrella Naciente"

July 23, Constitutional Convention met at Santiago

Oct. 23, New Constitution adopted by Convention. O'Higgins to be dictator for 10 years

Nov. 19, Earthquake destroyed Santiago

1823

Jan. 18, General San Martin left Chile for Peru

Jan. 27, Independence of Chile recognized by the United States

Jan. 28, Committee of revolutionists requested resignation of President O'Higgins. General Ramon Freire assumed dictatorship

July 24, Law abolished slavery

Aug. 12, National Congress assembled

Aug. 19, National Library opened

Dec. 29, A third Constitution dated Dec. 28 adopted

1824

April 27, Heman Allen first Minister from the United States arrived at Valparaiso

1825

Jan. 1, Parley held with patriots at Tapihue and new Government recognized

Feb. 2, Independence of Chile recognized by Great Britain

1826

July 14, Proclamation of the President decreed that republic of Chile should be constituted according to the Federal system

Aug. 28, Constitution adopted established Federal system

Nov. 20, Treaty of commerce, friendship, alliance, and navigation with Argentina

1827

May 2, General Freire resigned. General Pinto assumes supreme power

Aug. 10, Don Joaquin Campino appointed first Minister to the United States

1828

March 28, Plebiscite for Tacna-Arica was not held at end of ten-year period

Aug. 6, Political Constitution of 1828 adopted, promulgated by Assembly Aug. 8

1829

April 20, Revolt in Concepcion against the Government of Santiago

1830

April 17, The Battle of Lircay between Liberals and Conservatives. General Prieto defeated General Freire, Liberal, who was banished to Peru

1831

General Joaquin Prieto, President (1831–41)

March 7, Treaty of friendship, commerce, and navigation with Mexico

Oct. 1, Congress passed law convoking a convention to revise the Constitution

Oct. 20, Constitutional Convention assembled

1832

May 16, Treaty of commerce with the United States signed

Juan Godoy at Chanarcillo discovered silver mines

1833

May 25, Constitution of General Prieto dated May 22 adopted giving greater powers to executive

June 11, Mining ordinances of New Spain adopted by decree

Sept. 1, Additional explanatory article to Treaty of commerce with the United States signed

1835

Jan. 20, Treaty of friendship, commerce, and navigation with Peru signed

Feb. 20, Earthquake destroyed city of Concepcion

Aug. 25, Chile granted William Wheelwright, American, concession for monopoly of steam navigation for ten years on the Pacific coast

1836

July, Attempted naval invasion of ex-President Freire from Chiloe Island failed

Aug. 21, Peruvian navy of 3 ships captured by Captain Garrido

Nov. 11, Chile declared war on Peru

1837

June 6, Revolt of regiment stationed near Valparaiso led by Colonel Vidaurre. General Portales assassinated but Vidaurre, defeated by General Encalada, captured and shot

Nov. 17, Chile defeated in war with Peru. General

Blanco Encalada sent to assist the opponents of Santa Cruz, forced to surrender to General Cerdena

1839

Jan. 20, Battle of Jungay. Peruvians defeated by General Bulnes

April 25, Military Code adopted

1840

Sept. 9, Patent law enacted

Oct. 15, William Wheelwright arrived from England at Valparaiso with two steamships and inaugurated the Pacific Steam Navigation Company

1841

Sept. 18, General Manuel Bulnes assumed office as President

1842

Oct. 24, Death of Bernardo O'Higgins in Lima, Peru

Oct. 31, Law provided regulations for exports of guano

Nov. 19, Law provided for the founding of the University of Chile at Santiago. Opened Sept. 17, 1843

1844

April 25, Treaty of peace and amity with Spain signed by which the independence of Chile acknowledged

1845

Nov. 18, Colonization law enacted

1846

President Bulnes reëlected

1848

Dec. 16, Constitution amended

1849

June 19, Government granted William Wheelwright concession to construct a railroad from Santiago to Valparaiso

1851

Jan. 9, New colonization law enacted

July 4, Railroad from Caldera, port on the Pacific, built by William Wheelwright to Monte Amarg opened to traffic

Aug. 28, Constitution amended

Sept. 18, Manuel Montt elected President inaugurated

Dec. 8, Liberals defeated at the battle of Loncomilla

Dec. 25, First locomotive in South America run on railroad from Caldera to Copiapo

1854

Nov. 8, First law on organization of municipalities enacted

1855

Aug. 30, Boundary Treaty with Argentina

Sept. 10, First section of railroad from Santiago to Maulé River opened to San Bernardo by the President

Sept. 29, Law provided for commercial courts, *Tribunales del Consulado* for Santiago and Valparaiso

Dec. 14, Promulgation of the Civil Code

1856

President Montt reëlected

1857

Jan. 1, Civil Code came into effect

1858–59

Insurrection under the leadership of Pedro Leon Gallo
suppressed

1860

July 23, Bank of issue law enacted

1861

Sept. 18, José Joaquin Perez took office as President
Oct. 24, President Perez appointed Colonel Cornelio
Saavedra intendant of new province of Arauco and
commander-in-chief of army there

1862

May 25, The "American Union" Society founded by
Chilean Liberals
Aug. 6, Railroad law enacted
Dec. 7, Saavedra founded town of Angol

1863

July 4, First train entered Santiago from Valparaiso on
completion of railroad
Dec. 8, Jesuit church of the Compania in Santiago
burned. More than 2,000 persons perished

1864

Oct., Diplomatic relations with Bolivia severed

1865

War between Spain and Chile and Peru
Jan., Captain J. W. Rebolledo in the "Esmeralda"
seized Spanish gunboat "Vadonga" and took his
prize into Coquimbo
July 27, Constitution amended provided for freedom
of religious worship for non-Catholic sects and priv-
ilege given to such sects to establish private schools
for their children
Sept. 22, Spanish Admiral Pareja issued ultimatum to
Chile and declared a blockade
Sept. 25, Chile declared war on Spain
Nov. 23, Commercial Code adopted

1866

March 31, Valparaiso bombarded by Spaniards commanded by Admiral Nunez. Property damage by
fires $14,000,000
April 14, End of the blockade
May 10, Boundary Treaty with Bolivia
August 16, Treaty of Atacama with Bolivia signed
fixed boundary between them at 24th degree and
provided for joint jurisdiction of territory between
23rd and 25th degrees. Guano exports to be equally
divided
Dec. 12, Offensive and defensive alliance with Peru
signed

1867

Jan. 1, Commercial Code came into effect

1868

June 23, Law abolished imprisonment for debt except
in certain specified cases
Dec. 25, Railroad from Santiago to Curico opened
War with Araucanian Indians begun which lasted 2
years

1871

Sept. 18, Federico Errazuriz Zanartu took office as
President (1871–76)

1872

Jan. 1, General Urrutia, new intendant of province of
Arauco held peace parley with the Indians
Dec. 5, Boundary Treaty with Bolivia signed
Dec. 26, Law and ordinances as to customs enacted

1873

Feb. 6, Peru and Bolivia formed an alliance against
Chile
April 18, Death of William Wheelwright

1874

March 9, Treaty of commerce and navigation with
Peru signed
Aug. 6, Boundary Agreement with Bolivia signed.
Bolivia agreed not to impose taxes on Chilean in-
dustries in Atacama on the Pacific
Nov. 12, Trade-Mark Law enacted and Penal Code
which came into force March 1, 1875
Nov. 18, First Mining Code adopted which came into
force March 1, 1875

1875

April 7, C. A. Logan, American Minister in Chile, gave
award as arbitrator in dispute with Peru as to expenses of allied naval squadron
July 21, Boundary Treaty with Bolivia signed
Oct. 15, Judiciary Act adopted of 408 articles in effect
a code

1876

Jan. 16, International Exposition opened in Santiago
Sept. 18, Anibal Pinto took office as President (1876–81)

1877

May 9, Tidal wave swept away the town of Arica and
its inhabitants

1877–79

Financial crisis

1878

Feb. 14, Bolivia in violation of agreement of 1874 imposed export tax at Antofagasta of 10 cents a quintal
on all shipments
June 24, Navigation law enacted
July 4, Constitution amended

1879

Jan. 3, Ultimatum to Bolivia that diplomatic relations
would be severed if law of Feb. 14, 1878 was enforced
in violation of treaty of 1874
Jan. 11, Law enacted as to bankruptcy amending the
Commercial Code
Feb. 10, Diplomatic relations with Bolivia severed
Feb. 14, Chilean man-of-war seized the Bolivian port
of Antofagasta on date set by Bolivia for sale of
property of Chilean saltpeter company to pay impost
imposed
March 1, "War of the Pacific." Bolivia declared war
on Chile
March 23, Engagement in which the Chileans defeated
Bolivians and Calama on the Loa River captured
April 5, Chile declared war against Peru, ally of Bolivia,
and Bolivia. Rear-Admiral Rebolledo established
blockade at Iquique with the "Esmeralda" and the
"Covadonga"
April 17, Chilean ships bombarded Mollendo
April 18, Chilean ships bombarded Pisagua, unfortified
town

May 16, Admiral Rebolledo sailed north in search of Peruvian fleet leaving the "Esmeralda" and the "Covadonga" to maintain the blockade at Iquique

May 21, Peruvian ships "Huascar" and "Independencia" attacked Chilean ships at Iquique, the "Esmeralda" sunk, the "Independencia" run ashore in pursuit of the "Covadonga." Chilean commander Arturo Prat killed in action

June 10, Railroad from Concepcion to Chillan opened

July 17, Chilean fleet bombarded Iquique at night. No previous notice given to foreign residents

July 23, The Peruvian warship "Huascar" captured Chilean transport carrying cavalry regiments and 300 horses

Aug. 17, The "Huascar" attacked two Chilean men-of-war at Antofagasta. Repulsed by shore batteries

Oct. 8, Naval engagement at Iquique and Battle of Cape Angamos in which the Peruvian warship "Huascar" destroyed, gave Chile command of the sea. Chilean soldiers took possession of nitrate provinces of Peru

Nov. 2, Pisagua captured by Chilean troops commanded by General O'Higgins. Junin occupied by General Escala, Chilean commander-in-chief

Nov. 6, Colonel José Vergara defeated Peruvians near Agua Santa. Chileans occupied the railroad from Pisagua to Agua Santa

Nov. 15, Government ratified the Geneva Convention of 1864

Nov. 17, Chileans captured the Peruvian warship "Pilcomayo"

Nov. 18, Battle of San Francisco at Dolores in which Chile defeated forces of Bolivia and Peru

Nov. 20, Iquique surrendered to Chileans

Nov. 22, Peruvian army commanded by General Budenia in retreat reached Tarapaca

Nov. 27, Battle of Tarapaca, Chilean victory over forces of Peru and Bolivia

Dec. 18, Peruvian army in retreat from Tarapaca reached Arica

1880

Feb. 24, General Baquedano, new commander-in-chief of Chilean forces, began advance on Tacna and Arica

March 20, Chileans occupied Moquega

March 23, Chileans occupied Torata

April 10, Chilean navy established blockade of Callao, Peru

April 17, Peruvian troops commanded by Colonel Albarracain defeated in engagement with Chilean cavalry commanded by Vergara

April 22 and 23 and May 10, Chileans bombarded Callao

May 20, Death of General Sotomayor, Chilean Minister of War

May 25, Chilean torpedo boat "Janequeo" sunk by Peruvian "Independencia" commanded by Lieutenant Galvez who was taken prisoner

May 26, Battle of Tacna. Defeat of allied Peruvian and Bolivian forces commanded by General Narciso Campero by Chileans commanded by General Manuel Baquedano

June 7, Chileans commanded by Colonel Lagos storm Arica

July 3, Chilean transport "Loa" sunk by a torpedo concealed in a bag of grain and later the "Cavadonga" also lost by explosion

Sept. 10–Nov. 10, Chilean Captain Patricio Lynch laid waste the country and government property between Callao and Payta

Oct. 22, Conference of representatives of Chile, Bolivia, and Peru on board U.S.S. "Lackawanna." No agreement reached

Nov. 19, Chileans occupied Pisco, Peruvian garrison surrendered

Dec. 6, Naval engagement off Callao. Forts bombarded

Dec. 22, Chilean army began landing at Curayaco

1881

Jan. 13, Battle of Chorillos near Callao. Victory of Chilean General Baquedano

Jan. 15, Battle of Miraflores, Chileans broke second line of Peruvian defenses. Lima surrendered to General Pierola

Jan. 17, Chilean General Saavedra occupied Lima

July 23, Boundary Convention with Argentine Republic

Sept. 18, Domingo Santa Maria took office as President (1881–86)

1882

July 9, Chileans routed by Caceres at Concepcion

1883

July, Arequipa captured

July 10, Peruvians defeated with great loss of life at Huamachuco

Oct. 20, Treaty of Ancon with Peru signed. Provided for cession by Peru of province of Tarapaca, Tacna and Arica provinces to be occupied by Chile, and at end of 10 years plebiscite to be held to determine sovereignty

1884

Jan. 16, Law of civil marriage enacted

April 4, Chile forced Bolivia to sign the Pact of Truce (Pacto de Tregua) by which Chile retained coast province of Atacama

Sept. 4, Constitution amended

1885

Feb. 6, City of Ercilla, named for poet, founded in province of Malleco

May 30, Treaty of commerce with Bolivia signed

1886

Jan. 19, Treaty of arbitration with Switzerland signed

Jan. 22, Law enacted reorganizing the internal administration of the country

Jan. 25, Death of Benjamin Vicuna Mackenna

Sept. 18, José Manuel Balmaceda took office as President (1886–91)

Nov. 25, Balmaceda's first national Ministry resigned

Nov. 30, New Liberal Cabinet formed

1887

Sept. 10, Constitution amended

1888

April 12, Ministry of Señor Cuadra took office

Aug. 9, Law passed giving the suffrage to all male citizens of 21 years of age who could read and write

Aug. 20, Supplementary Boundary Convention with Argentina

Nov. 2, Barros Luco Ministry took office

Dec. 20, New Mining Code adopted

1889

June 11, Lastarria Ministry took office
Oct. 23, Ministry of Ramon Donoso Vergara
Nov. 7, Ministry of M. S. Fontecilla

1890

Jan. 1, Ministry of Adolfo Ibanez
Jan., Balmaceda formed a new Cabinet in opposition to Congress. Not accepted
May 30, Ministry of Sanfuentes
Aug. 11, Ministry of Belisario Prats
Oct. 15, Ministry of Claudio Vicuna appointed by President Balmaceda during recess of Congress. Mass meeting held, adopted a resolution stating that the President had shown bad faith in appointment of Cabinet
Dec. 10, Balmaceda notified by committee that after Dec. 31 he would have no authority to maintain the army or the navy unless Congress made appropriations

1891

Jan. 5, Decree of President Balmaceda announced his intention to put the budget of 1890 into effect if new budget not passed
Jan. 6, Leaders of Congress opposed to Balmaceda went on board vessel of Capt. Jorge Montt, the "Blanco Encalada"
Jan. 7, Revolt of part of the navy against Balmaceda dictatorship. Army remained loyal. Revolutionists took possession of Pisagua, Serena, and Coquimbo
——, Congress declared Balmaceda deposed because of violation of the Constitution. Captain Jorge Montt appointed head of Junta
Jan. 19, Pisagua occupied by the Congressists
Jan. 21, Pisagua bombarded, surrendered to Balmacedists
Jan. 26, Insurgents bombarded Coronel
Jan. 29, Government troops recaptured Serena and Coquimbo
Feb. 6, Rebels recaptured Pisagua
Feb. 15, Balmacedist commander General E. Robles defeated on battlefield of San Francisco at Dolores
Feb. 16, Iquique, evacuated by Colonel Soto going to aid General Robles, seized by Congressists
Feb. 17, At Huara General Robles and Colonel Soto defeated Congressists commanded by General Urrutia
Feb. 19, Engagement at Iquique, the President's troops defeated
Feb. 20, Iquique bombarded by Congressists surrendered
March 7, Government troops defeated at Pozo Almonte which gave rebels control of Tarapaca. General Robles mortally wounded and his army dispersed
March 20, General Holley, Congressist commander, occupied Antofagasta evacuated by government troops after mutiny of garrison
March 29, Calama occupied by Congressists which gave them control of province of Atacama
April 7, Insurgents capture Arica evacuated by government troops
April 22, Congressists took Caldera
April 23, Congressists man-of-war "Blanco Encalada" blown up and sunk by torpedo in Caldera harbor in attack of government troops. 200 killed
May 5, American Government ordered seizure of steamer "Itata" at San Diego, California, on representation of Chilean Minister that she was taking arms to insurgents
May 7, "Itata" sailed carrying the United States marshal a prisoner, landed him south of San Diego, and took on cargo of arms and entered Iquique harbor June 3
June 4, Surrender of the "Itata" to the U.S.S. "Charleston"
June 13, The "Itata" left for San Diego under convoy of American warships
July 2, Congressist army occupied Huasco
Aug. 20, "Massacre of Lo Canos." The President had 21 young men shot as sympathisers with the revolution
——, Congressist troops commanded by Colonel Canto landed at Quinteros 20 miles north of Valparaiso
Aug. 21, Battle of Concon. Congressists defeated the Balmacedists
Aug. 23, Congressists defeated in the hills around Vina del Mar
Aug. 28, Battle of Placilla. Soldiers of Balmaceda decisively defeated. Valparaiso surrendered to Congressists
Aug. 29, Santiago taken by Congressists
——, Balmaceda resigned and appointed General Baquedano head of a provisional Government
Sept. 4, Provisional Government established by Congressists with Jorge Montt, President
Sept. 7, New Chilean Government recognized by the United States
Sept. 19, Balmaceda in hiding at the Argentine legation committed suicide
Oct. 16, At Valparaiso street row between the Chileans and sailors from the U.S.S. "Baltimore." An American officer killed and several sailors wounded
Oct. 18, General election a victory for the Liberals
Oct. 26, American Minister Egan demanded satisfaction for Baltimore affair
Nov. 10, New Congress met and revolutionary Junta, Admiral Montt, Señor Waldo Silva, and Ramon Barros Luca resigned. Admiral Montt asked to continue acting as provisional President
Dec. 11, Señor Matta sent to all Chilean ministers for their information and for publication statement as to the Baltimore affair which reflected on American Minister Egan
Dec. 18, Admiral Jorge Montt elected President. Inaugurated Dec. 26
Dec. 22, Organic Law for government of municipalities enacted
Dec. 25, Amnesty granted to the followers of Balmaceda except Cabinet Ministers between Jan. 1 and Aug. 29 and some other officials, about 400 persons

1892

Jan. 20, Chile demanded recall of American Minister Egan. Not answered
Jan. 21, Ultimatum of United States to Chile demanding indemnity
Jan. 25, Chile withdrew note of Dec. 11 and agreed to pay indemnity of $75,000 for the families of the wounded sailors of the U.S.S. "Baltimore"
March 13, New Cabinet headed by Edouardo Matte without Conservatives, Gaspar Toro, Foreign Affairs, Finance, A. Edwards
June 11, New Cabinet headed by Barrios Luco, Isidro Errazuriz, Foreign Affairs
Aug. 7, Claims Convention with United States signed

by which settlement of claims referred to a mixed commission

1893

April 18, New Cabinet headed by I. Errazuriz
June 26, Constitution amended
Aug. 28, Amnesty extended to include all Balmacedists

1894

March 28, End of ten-year period since ratification of Treaty of Ancon. No plebiscite held. Tacna and Arica remained in possession of Chile

1895

Feb. 11, Law established the gold standard to come into effect June 1
May 18, Treaty of commerce with Bolivia signed and for transfer of Tacna and Arica. *See* Bolivia
July 6, Resignation of Ministry of Luco, succeeded July 29 by Ministry formed by Senator Recabarren
Sept. 25, Treaty of friendship, commerce, and navigation with Japan signed; additional Article, May 18, 1899

1896

April 14, National guard established
April 17, Boundary Agreement with Argentina signed
Sept. 18, Federico Errazuris, son of the former President, elected in July, took office as President

1897

March 4, Consular law enacted, regulations April 9
May 24, Claims Convention with the United States signed
June, Financial panic, 4 banks closed
June 25, New coalition Cabinet formed which resigned Aug. 9 and Valdes Cuevas formed Liberal Ministry

1898

March 22, Cabinet resigned and April 15 Carlos Walker Martinez formed Cabinet
July 7, Moratorium ordered for 30 days and all banks closed until the 12th
July 12, Treaty of commerce and navigation with Italy signed
July 31, Law enacted providing for regulation of foreign banks
Sept. 22, Agreement with Argentina provided for submission of boundary dispute to arbitration, Treaty signed Nov. 2

1899

March 24, Award in boundary dispute with Argentina as to Puña de Atacama
May 18, Arbitration Treaty with Brazil signed
May 24, New coalition Cabinet formed by Julio Zegero; resigned June 2
June 27, New Liberal Ministry formed by Silva Cruz
Sept. 3, Rafael Soto Mayor formed new coalition Cabinet

1900

April 17, Extradition Convention with the United States signed
April 30, Agreement with Argentina signed as to boundary line in the Andes
May 12, Claims Convention with the United States revived
Sept. 5, Law enacted provided for compulsory military service
Oct. 12, Cabinet resigned

1901

Jan. 19, Chamber of Deputies rejected proposal of Peru for convention as to Tacna and Arica
Feb. 2, Guano deposits on Huanillos, Punta Lobos, and Pabellon de Pica reverted to Chile
April 21, New Cabinet formed, Anibal Zanartu Prime Minister
July 12, Death of President Errazuriz
Sept. 18, Jerman Riesco proclaimed July 25 took office as President

1902

Jan. 11, Congress authorized loan of $12,500,000
Jan. 18, Law enacted provided for regulation, production, and distilling of alcohol, including taxation and penalties for violation and for drunkenness
May 28, Peace Agreement, general arbitration Treaty, and Agreement for limitation of naval armaments signed with Argentina
Aug. 28, Code of Civil Procedure adopted. Came into force March 1, 1903
Nov. 20, Arbitration award of King Edward VII given in dispute with Argentina as to boundary in Patagonia

1903

March 30, Treaty of friendship and commerce with Persia signed
Dec. 18, Red Cross Society founded

1904

Oct. 20, Treaty of peace, friendship, and commerce with Bolivia signed taking the place of Pact of Truce of 1884
Nov. 17, Law for government of foreign insurance companies enacted. Regulations, Dec. 14

1905

Jan. 1, President Rafael Rayes inaugurated
March 3, New Cabinet formed under Balmaceda
May 23, Bond issue of 1,000,000,000 pesos for railroad construction
Aug. 12, Trade-Mark Law enacted
Oct. 24, Riot and 50 persons killed, 500 wounded and $250,000 in property destroyed as result of mass meeting to protest against high price of meat under protective tariff
Nov. 27, Treaty of commerce and customs with Bolivia signed

1906

Feb. 20, Workers' Dwellings Act passed
June 12, Code of Criminal Procedure adopted
July 25, Pedro Montt elected President by the National party
Aug. 16, Severe earthquake especially affected Valparaiso. 3,000 persons perished, 20,000 injured. Property loss $100,000,000
Sept. 18, President Pedro Montt inaugurated

1907

March 1, Code of Criminal Procedure came into effect
April 5, Labor Office established
Sept. 25, Immigration law enacted
Nov., Financial crisis due to fall of rate of exchange. 4 banks failed

1909

Oct. 19, Regulations for consular fees published
Nov. 27, Tunnels of the trans-Andean railroad linking Argentine and Chile formally opened

Dec. 1, Protocol signed with the United States, agreement to submit claim of Alsop and Company to arbitration of King Edward VII

1910

May 16, Loan of $13,000,000 from Rothschilds of London negotiated

——, First trans-Andean railroad from Valparaiso to Mendoza, Argentina opened

Aug. 16, Death of President Montt at Bremen. Succeeded by the Minister of the Interior, the Vice-President Elias Fernandez Albano

Sept. 6, Death of acting-President Albano. Succeeded by Don Emiliano Figuero as provisional President

1911

July 5, Decision of arbitrator, the King of England, in Alsop claim case in favor of the United States

Aug. 7, Executive decree outlined procedure in payment of mining licenses

Sept. 18, Ramon Barros Luco inaugurated as President

Nov. 13, $935,000 paid to the United States, awarded in Alsop claim

1912

April 2, Arica-La Paz railroad completed

April 23, Revised tariff came into effect

June 12, Railroad opened to terminus at Puerto Montt

Aug. 6, Treaty with Argentina as to regulation of commercial traffic

1913

May 3, Protocol with Bolivia signed as to transfer of section of Arica-La Paz Railroad

June 3, 2 Chilean submarines launched at Seattle, Washington

July 19, British hospital in Valparaiso opened

Aug. 8, Arbitration Treaty with Italy signed

Aug. 22, Cornerstone of new national library in Santiago laid

1914

Jan. 26 and 29, Law of reorganization of the government railways

Feb. 21, New reformed election law enacted

July 24, Treaty of arbitration with the United States signed

Aug. 2, The President authorized to make advances to nitrate producers agreeing to continue operations

Aug. 3, Law provided for issuance of treasury notes by the Government

——, The President authorized to prohibit export of cattle, food products, and coal, and decree the following day published list of prohibited exports

——, The Chilean Secretary notified the German Minister. at Santiago that the Government would maintain "the strictest neutrality" in European War

Aug. 5, Declaration of neutrality in European War

Aug. 7, Moratorium declared for 30 days and later extensions made

Sept., Price of nitrate dropped from 8 shillings in July to 6s. 4d., but no market

Sept. 15, Advancement of Peace Treaty with the United States signed

Nov. 16, Arbitration and Extradition Treaty with Colombia signed

Dec 9, Law authorized plans for irrigation to add to 2,470,000 acres already under irrigation

Dec. 12, Note to Germany protested violation of neutrality by cruiser "Eitel Friedrich"

Dec. 18, Organic law of 1891 governing municipalities amended

1915

Feb. 5, Law established an inheritance tax

Feb. 8, Treaty of friendship with China signed

Feb. 27, Arbitration Treaty with Uruguay signed

March 1, Law reduced salaries of national government officials from 5% to 15% and all pensions

——, Law established a general property tax of 2 to 4 mills based on municipal tax, and tax on borax imposed

March 4, Import duty of 36 cents per 100 pounds on wheat flour suspended until June 30, 1915

March 14, British squadron opened fire on the "Dresden" in Chilean waters. Violation of neutrality protested

March 24, Note to Great Britain protested violation of neutrality in case of the "Dresden" on March 14, fired on by British squadron in Chilean waters

April 16, Great Britain apologized for violation of neutrality in "Dresden" affair

May 25, "A.B.C." Peace Treaty signed

July 25, Juan Luis Sanfuentes elected President

Oct. 29, Resignation of Cabinet; new Liberal Ministry organized Dec. 15

Dec. 23, President Juan Luis Sanfuentes inaugurated and Cabinet of Elias Balmacedo took office

Dec. 31, Balmacedo Cabinet resigned

1916

Jan. 12, Maximiliano Ibanez formed new coalition Cabinet

Feb. 17, Decree provided for compulsory military service

April 1, New tariff of consular fees went into effect

April 10, New tariff law enacted came into effect May 10

Nov. 22, New Ministry of Zanartu Huidobro Iniguez and others appointed

Dec. 30, Workmen's Compensation Act passed

1917

Jan. 1, New law as to fees to be paid by commercial travelers came into effect

Jan. 29, New shipping law promulgated

Feb. 8, Government protested to Germany against submarine policy

April 11, Neutrality proclaimed in the war between the United States and Germany

April 25, Diplomatic relations with Germany broken off

July, New Cabinet, the third within the year, took office

Oct. 13, The "Santa Ana" first of line of nitrate vessels of W. R. Grace and Co. launched in Philadelphia for freight service between New York and Valparaiso

Nov. 5, Act established compulsory Sunday rest for workers in industrial and commercial establishments

1918

Nov. 4, Chile seized 84 interned German merchant ships

Nov. 23, Anti-Peruvian riots at Iquique

Nov. 25, Diplomatic relations with Peru severed in dispute as to Tacna and Arica

1919

March 28, Conciliation Treaty with Great Britain established peace commission

Sept. 6, General strike of 1 day in Santiago

Oct. 13, Police and frontier Convention with Argentina signed

Nov. 4, Chile became original member of League of Nations (Jan. 10, 1920) by adherence to Covenant

1920

May 14, University of Concepcion incorporated by decree of the President

June 25, Election gave Liberal candidate 179 electoral votes to 175 cast for opponent, Barrios. Fraud charged

Aug. 26, Law on compulsory primary instruction promulgated

Oct. 4, Decision of Court of Honor gave the Presidency to Arturo Alessandri in disputed election

Oct. 26, Congress accepted decision of court as to election of Alessandri

Nov. 1, Peruvian delegation to first Assembly of League of Nations invoked Articles 15 and 19 of Covenant, and asked the Assembly to consider revision of the Treaty of Ancon of Oct. 20, 1883

Dec. 23, President Alessandri inaugurated

1921

June 1, Message of President Alessandri outlined program of political and social reform

June 28, General strike of 48 hours begun in Valparaiso in support of cigarette workers

July 25, Cabinet resigned on adverse vote on proposal of concession to English nitrate transportation company. New Ministry organized under H. T. Caso

Aug. 5, Death of Senator Malaquias

Sept. 13, Law regulated nitrate industry and provided for loans because of depression

Nov. 17, President Alessandri resigned. Resignation not accepted

Dec. 12, Government asked Peru to agree to hold plebiscite as to sovereignty of Tacna and Arica according to Article 3 of the Treaty of Ancon

Dec. 17, Peru refused to agree to plebiscite. Proposed submission of question to arbitration of the United States

Dec. 20, Second Note to Government of Peru refused to submit to arbitration entire Treaty of Ancon

——, Bolivia sent identic notes to Chile and Peru asserting right to part in settlement of Treaty of Ancon which deprived her of sea coast

Dec. 26, Third Note to Peruvian Government. Answered Dec. 28

Dec. 29, Fourth and last Note to Peruvian Government as to Tacna and Arica. Answered Dec. 31

1922

Jan. 17, Government of the United States invited Chile and Peru to meet in Washington to discuss Tacna-Arica question. Chile accepted Jan. 18 and Peru Jan. 19

Jan. 23, Bolivia asked for representation in Washington negotiations

Feb. 8, Law enacted on current banking accounts and checks

April 22, Death of Mujica Eduardo Suarez

May 15, Conference of representatives of Chile and Peru opened in Washington

May 22, Bolivia refused participation in Washington conference

June 18, Proposal of Secretary of State Hughes that

Chile and Peru submit Tacna-Arica dispute to arbitration

July 20, Protocol signed by representatives of Chile and Peru nominated the President of the United States as arbiter in the Tacna-Arica dispute as to Article 3 of Treaty of Ancon of Oct. 20, 1883

Aug. 2, Cabinet resigned in dispute as to Tacna-Arica. Antonio Hunewa formed Cabinet at end of month

Oct. 7, Death of Admiral Jorge Montt, former President

Nov. 11, Earthquake and tidal wave on northern coast killed nearly 1,000 people and destroyed property in region from Antofagasta to Coquimbo

1923

Jan. 3, Vicuna Cabinet resigned. Izquierdo named Premier, Aldunate Minister of Foreign Affairs

March 25–May 3, Fifth Pan-American Conference met at Santiago

May 8, Decree established regulations for labor accidents

July 1, New Ministry of Domingo A. Solar

Dec., Senate refused to pass income tax and forced resignation of ministry

Dec. 29, First Income Tax law passed to come into effect Jan. 1, 1924

1924

Jan. 1, Santiago garrison evacuated city as appropriation not passed

Jan. 7, President Alessandri dissolved Congress but compromise effected

Jan. 23, New Cabinet formed by P. A. Cerda

Jan. 30, Decree exempted day wages from income tax

Feb. 9, Senate passed Alessandri reform measures including tax budget

July 20, New radical Cabinet appointed, Señor Aguirre Prime Minister and Minister of the Interior

Aug. 4, Visiting British squadron arrived at Coquimbo

Sept. 5, Committee of army officers attended session of reactionary Senate and demanded immediate passage of reform program. Forced resignation of Cabinet and installed military Junta to direct affairs headed by General Luis Altamirano

Sept. 7, President Alessandri received 6 months leave. Altamirano as head of Ministry became acting President

Sept. 8, Labor Law enacted as to contracts of employment, first in Latin America. Eight hour day established, provision made for tribunals of arbitration and conciliation in labor disputes. New Workmen's Compensation Act passed

Sept. 12, New Cabinet appointed by Altamirano committee

Sept. 29, Law on organization of labor unions passed

Oct. 4, Decree law prohibited night work in bakeries, pastry shops, candy factories, &c.

Oct. 14, Decree established Ministry of Hygiene, Social Assistance, and Welfare and Labor

Dec. 13, Military Junta declared resolution of adherence to Government and resigned. Altamirano remained in executive control

Dec. 19, Rafael Luis Barahona appointed Prime Minister

1925

Jan. 2, New Cabinet formed by Armando Jaramillo

Jan. 9, Convention of National Union proclaimed candidacy of Ladislao Errazuriz, extreme conservative, for President

Jan. 23, Second coup d'état led by Major Carlos Ibanez overthrew provisional Government of Altamirano and President Alessandri recalled
Feb. 13, Decree regulated housing and rents. Courts to have jurisdiction as to repairs, sanitation, demolition, &c.
——, General strike in Valparaiso
Feb. 14, Monster labor meeting in Santiago
March 4, Award of President Coolidge published March 8 gave decision in favor of plebiscite to determine sovereignty of Tacna-Arica and assigned province of Tarata definitely to Peru
March 12, Decree law as to legal capacity of women
March 18, Decree law on Workmen's Compensation replaced law of Sept. 1924
March 20, President Alessandri arrived from Europe and resumed executive office
March 23, General John J. Pershing appointed head of Plebiscite Commission by President Coolidge
June 5, State of siege declared in provinces of Tarapaca and Antofagasta because of riots after suppression of communist newspapers at Iquique
July–Oct., Dr. E. W. Kemmerer of Princeton University and a group of associates made investigation of financial situation and published report of recommended reforms
Aug. 2, General Pershing arrived at Arica
Aug. 5, First formal meeting of Plebiscite Commission: representative for Chile, Augustin Edwards, for Peru, Manuel de Freyre Santander
Aug. 21, Central bank created to administer the finances of the Government, to reduce general rates of interest and regulate other banks of the country
Sept. 1, Tarata province formally transferred to Peru
Sept. 6, The Prince of Wales arrived at Santiago, making 2 weeks visit in Chile
Sept. 12, Decree law created Superior Council of Charity and the Council of Moral and Physical Education
Sept. 16, Law established the gold peso as monetary unit
Sept. 18, New Constitution adopted by plebiscite of Aug. 30 promulgated to come into effect one month later
Sept. 26, Decree law on banks promulgated substantially as prepared by the Kemmerer Commission
Sept. 30, Colonel Ibanez announced his candidacy for office of President and resigned from Cabinet
Oct. 1, President Alessandri resigned, turning over office to Minister of the Interior, Luis Barros Borgono
Oct. 14, Law established gold peso as monetary unit of 0.183057 grammes of fine gold equivalent to $.1217
Oct. 17, Decree provided that 75% of persons employed in any undertaking must be Chileans
Oct. 18, Alessandri's Constitution came into effect. Attempted military revolt suppressed
Oct. 24, Emiliano Figueroa elected President by large majority, receiving over 75% of votes cast
Nov. 21, Senator Augustin Edwards resigned from Tacna-Arica Commission
Dec. 1, Spanish Bank of Chile suspended payment
Dec. 9, Tacna-Arica Plebiscite Commission fixed Feb. 15, 1926 as date of registration, April 15, 1926 as date for taking vote. Resolution censured Chilean authorities in Tacna and Arica for expulsion and deportation of Peruvian voters. Chile appealed against the decision
Dec. 19, New Cabinet formed by M. Ibanez
Dec. 23, President Figueroa inaugurated

1926
Jan. 11, General William Lassiter replaced General Pershing as head of Tacna-Arica Plebiscite Commission
——, Banco Central opened
Jan. 30, Treaty of friendship with Turkey signed
Feb. 8, Chile and Peru protested to President Coolidge against election law adopted by Plebiscite Commission Jan. 27
Feb. 25, President Coolidge upheld decision of Plebiscite Commission as to election regulations
March 10, Peru asked that date for registration of plebiscite be postponed indefinitely
March 14, Registration of voters for Tacna-Arica plebiscite postponed until March 1927
March 26, Announcement that governments of Chile and Peru would settle Tacna-Arica dispute without plebiscite
——, New banking law became effective
April 6, Conference of Chile and Peru as to Tacna and Arica begun in Washington
June 14, Plebiscite Commission voted to abandon plebiscite in Tacna-Arica affair because of obstructionist tactics of Chile and adjourned the following day
July 1, Organic Budget law as recommended by Kemmerer Mission went into effect
July 3, Banco Espanol opened in Santiago
Oct. 27, Strike of 9,000 miners at Potrerillos
Nov. 5, Twenty-four hour strike against enforced contribution to industrial insurance
Nov. 18, Resignation of Premier Maximiliano
Nov. 21, Cabinet organized by Manuel Rivas-Vicuna, Independent Liberal
Nov. 30, Proposal of American Secretary of State that disputed Tacna-Arica territory be ceded to Bolivia

1927
Feb. 9, Vicuna Ministry resigned on seizure of the Government by General Carlos Ibanez
Feb. 24, Treaty of conciliation and judicial settlement of disputes with Italy signed
Feb. 25, Ex-Premier Vicuna and a number of members of Parliament and other officials deported by order of Premier Ibanez
March 18, Decree created Comptrollership of the Republic as recommended by Kemmerer Mission
April 7, President Figueroa granted "leave of absence" and General Ibanez appointed Vice-President and acting President
May 4, President Figueroa resigned
May 22, Colonel Carlos Ibanez elected President
May 28, Arbitration Treaty with Spain signed
July 21, President Ibanez inaugurated
Aug. 29, New organic law for the universities enacted
Dec. 21, Decree announced all claims for petroleum exploitation would be void the following March 28 unless certain minimum production obtained or a certain amount of money spent in digging wells or exploration

1928
Jan. 1, New real estate tax went into effect
Feb. 1, Commercial *modus vivendi* with Salvador concluded
Feb. 27, New tariff law published to go into effect April 27
March 22, Agricultural credit law promulgated

July 6, Loss of Chilean government transport "Angamos" in storm. 291 lives lost, only 4 survivors picked up

July 13, Peru and Chile resumed friendly relations after 17 years of dispute over Tacna-Arica

Oct. 5, Peruvian ambassador received

Nov. 19, First air mail from Europe to Chile arrived at Santiago in 9 days and 20 hours

Nov., Supervisory Council of Education established

Dec. 1, Destruction of towns of Talca, Chillan, and Constitucion by earthquake

Dec. 10, President-Elect Hoover arrived at Valparaiso on visit to country

——, Agricultural Colonization Bank Bill signed by the President

1929

Jan. 8, Decree reorganized secondary education

Feb. 6, First air mail and passenger service inaugurated between Santiago and Arica

May 15, Proposals of President Hoover for settlement of Tacna-Arica dispute submitted to Chile and Peru, and accepted by Chile same day

May 17, Settlement of the Tacna-Arica controversy announced by President Hoover, Chile to retain Arica with its nitrate fields and Peru to receive Tacna and $6,000,000

June 3, Tacna-Arica Treaty settling the boundaries dispute between Chile and Peru signed at Lima. Ratified by Chilean Senate July 1, July 4 by Deputies

July 5, Treaty of friendship with Egypt signed

July 21, First air mail for New York left Chile. Trip took 10 days

July 23, Chile signed Paris Peace Pact

July 28, Exchange of ratification for Treaty of Lima

Aug. 5, Earthquake and storms practically destroyed the $15,000,000 breakwater at Antofagasta

Aug. 28, Tacna, city and province, formally delivered to Peru

Sept. 17, Law and Decree of Dec. 31 provided for religious instruction in schools

Oct. 19, Conciliation Treaty with Poland signed

Oct. 22, Unsuccessful attempt to assassinate President Ibanez

1930

April 29, Agreement with Peru for establishment of boundary police

May 5, Decree made the province of Tarapaca part of the Dept. of Arica from May 1

May 27, Treaty for prevention of smuggling of intoxicating liquors signed with the United States

July 17, Death of Juan Luis Sanfuentes, former President

July 21, Tacna-Arica frontier delimitation completed and Final Act signed at Lima Aug. 5

July 30, Temporary commercial Treaty with France signed

Aug. 1, Air mail service opened between Puerto Aysen and Magallanes (former Punta Arenas)

Sept. 18, Most favored nation commercial Treaty with Czechoslovakia signed

Sept. 21, Revolt of garrison at Concepcion in the south led by General Enrique Bravo and Colonel M. Grove suppressed

Nov. 27, Earthquake, fire, and floods in north central region

COCOS ISLAND

Cocos Island, in East Pacific, distant from Panama about 540 miles, area 18 square miles, about 4½ miles long and 14 miles in circumference, administered by Costa Rica since 1888.

COLOMBIA

Colombia, former New Granada, fifth in area of the Republics of South America, bounded on the north by the Caribbean Sea and Venezuela, on the east by Venezuela and Brazil, on the south by Brazil, Peru, and Ecuador, and on the west by the Caribbean, Panama, and the Pacific Ocean, coast line on the Caribbean 868 miles, on the Pacific, 1,178 miles, greatest length from north to south 1,050 miles, and greatest width 860 miles. The area of the Republic is estimated at about 447,536 miles, exact size not known because of unsettled boundaries. The population according to census of Nov. 16, 1928 of the 14 departments, 3 intendencies, and 7 commissaries is 7,851,000 including 69,867 Indians. Foreigners in 1928 numbered 35,251 including: German, 1,682; English, 1,436; United States, 1,607; Italian, 1,916; Syrian, 2,967; and Venezuelan, 14,743.

The capital, Bogotá (census population, 1928, 235,421), lies 8,600 feet above the sea. The chief commercial towns, with their population in 1928, are Barranquilla (139,974), connected with the coast at Puerto Colombia by 17 miles of railway; Cali (122,847); Medellin (120,044), a mining center; Cartagena (92,494); Manizales (81,091); Ibaque (56,333); Cúcuta (49,279); Bucaramanga (44,083).

Dr. Enrique Olaya Herrera, President.

1509

First settlement of present Colombia made by Alonso de Ojeda granted region of Nueva Andalusia east of the Darien River and the Gulf of Darien and Uraba to Cape de la Vela. Settled colony on the Gulf of Uraba and named the settlement San Sebastian. Colony moved to Panama by Encisco and Vasco Nunez de Balboa. *See* Panama

1510

Ojeda driven from site of Cartago by the Indians

1515

Voyage of Bachiller de Encisco along the coast

1525

July 29, First permanent settlement made at Santa Marta by Roderigo de Bastidas, at first not more than a slave-catching center

1529

Pedro Vadillo, Governor of Santa Marta after death of Bastidas, arrived

Garcia Lerma succeeded Vadillo as Governor of Santa Marta

1533

Jan. 21, Cartagena founded by Pedro de Heredia made Governor of region from Atrato River to the Magdalena and from northern sea to equator
San Sebastian refounded by Alonso de Heredia

1535

Dec., Pedro Fernandez de Lugo appointed Governor of Santa Marta and its provinces in 1533 arrived at Santa Marta

1536

April 6, Gonzalo Jiminez de Quesada commissioned by Lugo left Santa Marta and marched inland to explore the upper Magdalena River valley and conquer the Chibchan Indians
July 25, Sebastian de Benalcazar advancing into this region from Quito founded Cali
Oct., Death of Governor de Lugo. Jeronimo Lebron, Governor of Santa Marta
Dec., Popayan founded by Benalcazar
Expedition of Francisco Cesar from San Sebastian to the Guaca Valley

1537

March 12, Jiminez de Quesada arrived at Guacheta (San Gregorio)
Oct., Quesada defeated the Indians in the Battle of Bonda
Dec. 21, Juan de Badillo with Francisco Cesar left Santa Marta to explore the region south of the Gulf of Uraba

1538

Aug. 6, Santa Fé de Bogotá founded by Jiminez de Quesada and the region he had conquered he called the "New Kingdom of Granada"
Dec. 24, Badillo expedition reached the Cauca River valley

1539

March 17, Jiminez de Quesada, Benalcazar, and Federmann who had entered the country from Venezuela agreed to go together to Spain to present their claims to region discovered to the King

1540

Cartago founded by Jorge de Robledo, lieutenant of Benalcazar
Timana founded by Pedro de Anasco, lieutenant of Benalcazar

1541

Antioquia founded by Robledo
Benalcazar appointed Governor of Popayan returned to his domain

1542

Luis Alonso de Lugo, son of former Governor appointed Governor of Santa Marta and New Granada (1542–45) by the King instead of Jiminez de Quesada

1547

Jan. 17, Miguel Diaz de Armendarez sent by the Council of the Indies to proclaim and introduce the "New Laws" as to the Indians arrived at Bogotá

1549

Pamplona founded
Quesada made Marshal and Alderman of Bogotá by the King

1550

April 7, Royal Audiencia established at Bogotá in which the Government vested until 1564

1554

April 27, Royal decree ordered that school for the Indians be established

1555

Emerald mines of Muzo 75 miles south of Bogotá discovered by Lanchero

1564

The colony made a presidency and Andres Diaz Venero de Leiva appointed first President took over the Government from the Audiencia

1565

March 5, Quesada given title of adelanto but no jurisdiction and leave to return to New Granada

1575

March, Arrival of second President, Francisco Briceno, who took over the administration from the Audiencia who had assumed Government after the death of President de Leiva

1578

Lopez Diaz Aux de Armendariz third President. He was later suspended and Audiencia again resumed the Government

1579

Feb. 16, Death of Jiminez de Quesada of leprosy

1585

Dec., Expedition of Sir Francis Drake sacked and burned Santa Marta

1586

Feb. 9, Drake appeared before Cartagena and took and looted the town
April 2, Drake gave receipt for ransom of 107,000 pecas after he had taken all gold and silver he could find from Cartagena

1590

Jan. 24, Death of Archbishop Zapata
Antonio Gonzales, President (1590–97) brought first Jesuits to New Granada

1597

Francisco de Sande succeeded Gonzales as President

1599

March 28, Archbishop Lobo Guerrero arrived

1602

Oct. 2, Juan de Borja, President, arrived in Bogotá

1604

Sept. 7, First College of the Jesuits the "Seminario de San Bartolome" opened at Bogotá

1610

Feb. 25, Royal decree established the Inquisition at Cartagena
Sept. 26, The Inquisitors formally received at the Cathedral

1614

Feb. 2, Auto-da-fé celebrated by the Inquisition at Cartagena

1622

March 13, Auto-da-fé at Cartagena, an Englishman, Protestant, burned

1626

June 17, Auto-da-fé celebrated at which 22 persons burned

1630

Feb. 1, Sancho Giron, Marquis of Sofraga, assumed office as President, succeeding de Borja

1635

Sept. 8, Archbishop Cristobal de Torres arrived at Bogotá

1637

Oct. 5, Martin de Saavedra Guzman assumed office as President, succeeding Giron

1644

Jan. 16, Earthquake destroyed city of Pamplona

1645

Dec. 25, Juan Fernandez de Cordova y Coalla, Marquis of Auta, succeeded Saavedra as President

1651

Dec. 31, Royal decree founded the "Colegio Mayor de Nuestra Senora del Rosario" at Bogotá

1654

April 25, Dionisio Perez Manrique de Lara, Marquis of Santiago took office as President, succeeding Cordova

July 8, Death of Archbishop Cristobal de Torres

1680

April 15, French and Indian piratical raid on Santa Marta

1686

Gil de Cabrera y Davalos, President

1687

March 9, Severe earthquake

1697

April 14, French fleet under de Pointis attacked and forced surrender of Cartagena. Treaty of ransom signed May 7 and pirates left

1717

May 27, Viceroyalty of New Granada established

1718

Arrival of Antonio de la Pedrosa, first Viceroy. Capital at Santa Fé de Bogotá

1719

Jorge Villalonge, Count de la Cueva, second Viceroy

1723

Viceroyalty abolished

1724

May 17, Antonio Manso Maldonado, President, assumed office

1731

Government by Audiencia (1731–33)

1733

Rafael de Estaba, President (1733–37)

1736

Scientists Jorge Juan and Antonio de Ulloa on royal mission coöperating with the French Academy to measure the equator traveled through the country

1738

Oct. 21, Antonio Gonzales Manrique assumed office as President. Died in 13 days

1739

Aug. 20, Viceroyalty of New Granada reëstablished. Don Sebastian de Eslaba, first Viceroy

1740

April 9, Assault of Admiral Vernon on Cartagena unsuccessful

1741

March 3–April 17, Unsuccessful siege of Cartagena by Vernon. Story of the siege in "Roderick Random" by Smollett

1767

Aug. 1, Jesuits expelled from New Granada

1776

Feb. 10, Manuel Antonio Florez assumed office of Viceroy at Cartagena

1781

March 16, Insurrection at Socorro led by José Delgadillo against abuses, especially the taxes and monopolies

May, Indians led by Ambrosio Pisco joined the insurrection

June 4, Insurgents deceived by agreement providing for abolishing monopolies and a large number of taxes

Aug. 15, 500 veteran soldiers arrived from Cartagena to suppress the insurrection

1782

Jan. 30, Bartolome Galan, leader of insurrection, sentenced to death

March 18, Public announcement of annulment of agreement of June 4 by the Audiencia after execution of leaders of revolt

1789

Don José de Ezpeleta, Viceroy (1789–97)

1791

Jan. 1, First periodical a weekly began publication, the *Periodico de Santa Fé de Bogotá*

1797

Feb. 4, Earthquake devastated the country from Santa Fé to Panama

1810

May 22, Revolutionary Junta formed at Cartagena

June 14, Francisco Montes, Governor, arrested and sent to Havana because of his opposition to the establishment of a "Disputacion provincial"

July 4, Pamplona established a revolutionary Junta

July 21, Junta established by assembly of citizens at Santa Fé de Bogotá declared allegiance to Ferdinand VII. The Viceroy made President

July 23, Don Antonio de Amar y Borbon, Viceroy, deposed by the Junta of Bogotá which assumed the Government. Dr. Lozano made President eventually

1811

March 28, The patriots defeated the royalists at Popayan near Cali

Sept. 19, Lozano deposed in Bogotá ("The State of Cundinamarca") and Narino made dictator

Nov. 11, Revolutionary Junta declared the province of Cartagena independent of Spain

1812

Feb. 19, Viceroy Benito Perez established his government at Panama unable to get to Bogotá

Dec. 15, Bolivar in Cartagena published appeal to patriots for aid in liberation of Venezuela which was granted on condition of future union with New Granada

Dec. 31, Narino defeated royalists under Samano and occupied Popayan

1813

May 15, Bolivar with 800 men started for Venezuela

May, Viceroy Francisco Montalvo established government at Santa Marta

July 16, Congress assembled at Santa Fé de Bogotá adopted a declaration of independence and declared the province of Cundinamarca independent

1814

Jan. 15, Spanish General Samano defeated by Nareno at Calivio

Sept. 25, Bolivar arrived in Cartagena after failure of Venezuelan campaign

Dec. 12, Bolivar took Santa Fé which had revolted for the Federalist Congress

1815

Jan. 13, Bolivar's army entered Santa Fé. Federal capital moved its seat there

May 8, Bolivar resigned command of army and sailed for Jamaica

Aug. 22, Spanish General Morillo entered Cartagena

Oct. 25, Bombardment of Cartagena begun

Nov. 25, Calzada defeated patriots at Balaga and took Popayan

1816

Feb. 22, Torres defeated by royalist General Calzada near Ocana

1819

May 25, General Bolivar with army of Venezuelans, British, and Irish recruited from England started from Venezuela across the Andes for liberation of New Granada

July 6, Bolivar's army reached Sacha

July 11, Bolivar in indecisive battle with Colonel Barreiro on the heights of Gameza

July 25, Bolivar won victory in battle with Barreiro at Pantano de Vargas near the Sagamoso River

Aug. 5, Bolivar took the city of Tunja

Aug. 7, Battle of Boyaca. Bolivar and Santander decisively defeated the royalist army of Barreiro, breaking Spanish power in New Granada

Aug. 10, Bolivar entered the city of Bogotá evacuated by Viceroy Samano

Sept. 11, Bolivar chose General Santander as Vice-President of New Granada

Sept. 20, Bolivar returned to Venezuela

Oct. 11, Colonel Barreiro and 38 officers taken after Boyaca executed by order of Santander

1820

March 14, Bolivar arrived at Bogotá from Venezuela

April 21–23, and April 25, Colombian vessels at Honduras. See Honduras

May 15, Manuel Torres appointed agent and chargé d'affaires to the United States

June 6, Valdez repulsed attack of royalist Calzada at town of Pitayo near Popayan

Nov. 25, Armistice signed at Trujillo by Bolivar and royalist General Morillo which lasted until the following April

1821

Jan. 5, Bolivar again at Bogotá

Feb. 2, Valdez marching on Pasto defeated by royalists under Garcia in pass of Jenay

April 20, Colonel Lara attacked and defeated royalists at Lorica 8 days before time set for end of truce

May 6, Congress installed at Rosario de Cucuta and Bolivar named President and Santander, Vice-President

July 12, Permanent union of New Granada and Venezuela proclaimed and Constitution adopted

July 21, Law enacted provided that children of slaves born after this date should be free

Aug. 3, Death of last Viceroy, Samano, in Panama. Succeeded by General Cruz Murgeon

Aug. 22, Congress declared Inquisition abolished

Aug. 30, Constitution for the new Republic of Colombia adopted and formally ratified. Bolivar proclaimed President

Sept. 7, Bolivar elected President by Congress. Civil authority vested in Vice-President Santander

Oct. 1, Cartagena surrendered to the patriot General Montilla after siege of 14 months

——, First monetary law enacted. Provided that coins should have the same weight and fineness as in the Colonial period

Oct. 3, Bolivar took oath of office as President

Oct. 9, Bolivar procured passage of law which gave him absolute power over the army

Oct. 14, Declaration that Spanish law as to collection of the tenth for the Church be continued

Nov. 28, Fortresses of Chagres and Portobello taken by patriots. Panama and Veraguas declared independence and union with Colombia

Dec. 13, Bolivar left Bogotá for campaign in the South in Peru and Bolivia

1822

Jan. 23, Independence of Colombia recognized by Central America

April 7, Bolivar won battle at Bombona and entered Pasto June 8

April 29, Colombia recognized by Mexico as an independent State

May 29, The "Intendencia de Quito" now Ecuador joined the Colombian Federation

June 19, Manuel Torres, Colombian representative, formally presented by John Quincy Adams to President Monroe, first formal act of recognition of Colombia by the United States

July 6, Treaty of alliance with Peru signed

Oct. 21, Treaty of alliance with Chile signed

1823

Jan. 20, Decree excluded all Spanish products and manufactured articles from Colombian ports

Jan. 27, Appointment of Minister from the United States to Colombia

July 23, General Padilla totally destroyed the Spanish fleet

Oct. 3, Treaty of friendship with Mexico signed

Dec. 16, Arrival of American Minister Richard C. Anderson, first Minister from the United States to serve in a Spanish-American State

1824

April 22, J. M. Hurtado in London signed contract with B. A. Goldschmidt and Company for loan which amounted to £4,750,000

May 19, Law enacted exempted from the tithe all new plantations of cacao, coffee, and indigo for 10, 7, and 4 years respectively

July 28, "Law of the Patronage" enacted as to the Church

Oct. 3, Treaty of amity, commerce, and navigation with the United States signed

1825

Jan. 3, Formal recognition of Colombia by Great Britain

March 15, Treaty of alliance with Central American States

April 18, Treaty of amity, commerce, and navigation with Great Britain signed at Bogotá

Nov. 21, Hurtado, first Minister from Colombia, presented by Mr. Canning to King George IV

1826

July 26, Law of Congress declared monasteries with less than 8 members abolished and property confiscated to the service of public instruction

Nov. 14, Bolivar arrived at Bogotá from Peru but left Nov. 24 to suppress rebellion in Venezuela

1827

May 2, Congress met at Tunja. Moved to Bogotá

Sept. 10, Bolivar arrived at Bogotá and took the oath as President

Nov. 11, Cauca University founded in the city of Popayan

1828

April 9–June 10, Convention summoned by Bolivar met at Ocana to revise Constitution. Dissolved because of non-agreement. First public demonstrations against Bolivar engineered by Santander

June 13, Junta at Bogotá reëstablished Bolivar as Dictator

Aug. 27, "Organic decree" by which Bolivar assumed sovereignty over Colombia proclaiming himself Dictator. He suppressed the Vice-Presidency

Sept. 25, Attempt of political enemies to assassinate Bolivar who escaped

Oct. 29, General José Padilla and Colonel Ramon Guerra executed and a number of other prominent citizens exiled suspected of connection with conspiracy against Bolivar including Santander

Nov. 26, Venezuela seceded from the Federation

1829

May 1, Treaty of friendship, commerce, and navigation with the Netherlands signed

Sept. 5, Cabinet applied to English and French diplomatic agents for a prince to take title of emperor after the death of Bolivar but Bolivar decided the idea could not be carried out

Sept. 12, General Cordova led insurrection at Antioquia

Sept. 22, Boundary Treaty with Peru signed

Oct. 24, Decree of Bolivar reaffirmed Spanish mining law of 1783, substituting Colombian Nation for Spanish Crown. Mines declared property of State

1830

Jan. 20–May 11, The "Admiral Congress" met at Bogotá

April 27, Formal resignation of Bolivar as President presented to Congress which was accepted

April, New Constitution framed to try to preserve the Union, adopted May 5. Don Joaquin Mosquera, Liberal, elected President

May 8, Bolivar left Bogotá for coast

June 4, General Sucre assassinated at Berruecos, province of Pasto, as he passed through the mountains

Sept. 5, Mosquera Government overthrown and civil war begun by Urdaneta

Dec. 17, Death of Simon Bolivar at Santa Marta aged 47

1831

Nov. 17, Convention at Bogotá announced that the central Colombian provinces constituted a State which adopted the title of the Republic of New Granada

Nov. 21, Decree divided new State into provinces

Dec., Decision made that the Constitution of 1830 should govern the State

1832

Jan. 2, Acosta received as chargé d'affaires from New Granada to the United States constituting recognition

Feb. 29, New Constitution adopted of the "State of New Granada"

Oct. 7, General Santander, returned from exile, assumed office as elected President

Nov. 14, Treaty of friendship, commerce, and navigation with France signed

Dec. 8, Treaty with Ecuador

1834

May, Congress enacted that in official documents the name "Republic of New Granada" should be used instead of State of New Granada

Dec. 23, Representatives of New Granada, Venezuela, and Ecuador signed agreement as to division of public debt of the Colombian Confederation, Colombia to take 50%, Venezuela 28½%, Ecuador 21½%

1835

Population 1,686,000

Nov. 26, Recognition of New Granada by the Pope

1837

April 1, José de Marquez inaugurated elected President to succeed Santander. General Ovando the defeated candidate supported by Santander

1838

Congress granted a concession for a canal across Panama to a French company. Lapsed

1839

Decree suppressing certain monasteries resulted in revolt in Pasto

1840

May 26, Death of Francisco de Paula Santander

1841

May 18, Pedro A. Herran elected President (1842–45)

1842

July 23, Treaty of friendship, commerce, and navigation with Venezuela signed

1843

April 20, The "Political Constitution of the Republic of New Granada" promulgated, increased the power and influence of the President

1845

General Tomas de Mosquera became President

1846

Dec. 12, Treaty of peace, amity, navigation, and commerce with the United States signed, guaranteed the United States "right of way or transit across the Isthmus of Panama"

1847

April 28, Law enacted prohibited the importation of slaves into the Republic, all slaves introduced to be free

May, Concession granted to an association of Frenchmen known as the Panama Company represented by Mateo Kline exclusive privilege to build railroad across the Isthmus

1848

Dec. 28, Contract for Panama Railroad Company signed with the Government by Americans, John L. Stephens, Henry Chauncey, and William R. Aspinwall

1849

General José H. Lopez, Liberal, declared President by Congress

1850

April 15, Concession granted to John L. Stephens and William Aspinwall a new revised contract for railroad across the Isthmus of Panama. Signed by the President June 4

May 4, Consular agreement with the United States signed

May 21, Decree of the President expelled the Jesuits from the Republic

1851

May 21, Law enacted that all slaves should be free after Jan. 1, 1852

Sept. 10, Conservative insurrection defeated at Rio Negro

Oct. 1, A work train passed over railroad from Aspinwall to Gatun (8 miles)

1852

Feb. 2, The town of Aspinwall formally established

April, Law announced that rivers of New Granada should be open to navigation by merchant vessels of foreign nations

1853

April, General Obando, Liberal, inaugurated as President

May 23, Insurrection in Bogotá

May 28, New Constitution adopted. Departments granted right to elect their Governors by popular vote and powers of provincial legislatures increased

June, Law decreed separation of Church and State

1854

April, Congress dissolved by revolutionists and President Obando imprisoned as a Dictator. Succeeded by Vice-President Manuel Mallarino

1855

Jan. 28, First railroad train crossed the completed Isthmus railroad from Aspinwall to Panama (47 miles, cost over $8,000,000)

Feb. 27, Constitution amended, the "Granadan Federation" provided that Panama should be a Federal State

1856

April 15, "Panama massacre" riot over non-payment of 10 cents for a slice of watermelon led to killing of many passengers chiefly North Americans in transit across the Isthmus and destruction and looting of property

1857

April 1, Mariano Ospina, Conservative, inaugurated elected President

Sept. 10, Claims Convention with the United States signed by which New Granada admitted responsibility for "Panama massacre" of 1856 and indemnity of about $160,000 paid

1858

April 1, New Constitution adopted for the "Granadan Confederation" under which the Republic became a "Confederation Granadina" of 8 States. Promulgated May 22

1861

July 18, General Mosquera, Liberal Governor of State of Cauca, after a series of conflicts, captured Bogotá and overthrew the Government and became President

Sept. 20, Congress of the States formed union of "United States of New Granada"

1862

Nov. 1, Assassination of chief of Conservative Party, Julio Arboleda

1863

May 8, Congress promulgated a new liberal Constitution the "Political Constitution of the United States of Colombia" at Rio Negro. Moquera elected President until April, 1864

Dec. 6, Invading Ecuador army defeated at Cuaspud

1864

Feb. 10, Claims Convention with the United States signed

Manuel Murillo Toro elected President

1866

March 11, Mosquera elected President for the third time

1867

May 23, Mosquera accused of malfeasance in office deposed by Santos Acosta who becomes provisional President

Aug. 16, Colombia granted concession of exclusive privileges on Isthmus to the Panama Railroad Company. The Panama Canal Company later acquired controlling influence in this company

Nov. 1, Ex-President sentenced to exile for 2 years

1868

General Santos Gutierrez elected President

Rebellion in Panama. *See* Panama

1870

General E. Salgar elected President

Jan. 26, Canal Treaty with the United States signed

Nov. 25, Bank of Bogotá, oldest bank, established. Opened Jan. 2, 1871

1871

April 7, American schooner "Montijo" seized by Colombian revolutionists

Population 2,951,000

1872

April 1, Manuel Murillo Toro became President

1873

Rebellion in Panama. *See* Panama

1874

April 1, Santiago Perez, President

Aug. 17, Arbitration Treaty with the United States signed

Oct. 28, Mining law enacted in 1873 became effective

1875

July 26, Award of $33,401 to the United States in re seizure of American schooner "Montijo" in 1871

1876

April 1, Aquileo Parra became President

May 28, Contract with A. de Gorgoza and General Stephen Turr for opening an interoceanic canal

Aug.–April, 1877, Civil war in Panama

Revolt in Cauca

1878

April 1, General Trujillo inaugurated President

May 18, Government granted French Company exclusive privileges for 99 years for construction of an interoceanic canal. The Universal Interoceanic Canal Company headed by Count de Lesseps purchased concession

July and Dec., Revolts in Panama

1880

April 1, Rafael Nunez became President, supposed to be a Liberal

Dec. 25, Treaty with Costa Rica submitted boundary dispute to arbitration

1881

Jan. 30, Treaty of peace and amity with Spain signed

Feb. 24, French engineers began work on canal

Sept. 4, Agreement with Venezuela to submit boundary dispute to arbitration of King of Spain

1882

April 1, Dr. F. J. Zaldua inaugurated President

Dec., Death of President Zaldua. T. E. Otalora, Vice-President, assumed office

1883

April 1, T. E. Otalora, President

1884

April 1, Rafael Nunez elected President

1885

Jan., Revolution at Tunja

Jan. 18, American marines landed to protect railroad at request of President of Panama

March 2, Insurrection at Barranquilla. *See also* Panama

May 7, Attack of rebels on Cartagena repulsed

May 19, Siege of Cartagena raised by government troops

Aug. 4, Formal surrender of rebels ended revolt of Liberals

Nov. 11, Convention to reform the Constitution, the "National Council" met at Bogotá

Nov. 30, Act promulgated as basis of reforms. Declaration that the nation should be designated as the "Republic of Colombia" and the National Council would act as a constituent assembly

Dec., National Council proclaimed Nunez first President under proposed new Constitution

1886

Jan. 20, Boundary Treaty with Costa Rica

Feb. 15, Boundary dispute with Venezuela referred to arbitration of King of Spain

May, Convention agreed to submit demand for indemnity of Italy in Cerruti case for confiscation of property in 1885 to arbitration of King of Spain

Aug. 4, New Constitution adopted abolished the Federal Union and adopted unitary republican form of Government. The States became Departments with Governors appointed by the President

Aug. 7, Nunez declared himself elected President for ensuing term of 6 years

1887

April, President Nunez promulgated new Civil Code

Dec. 31, Concordat with the Papacy signed agreeing that Catholic Church in Colombia should be independent of the civil power

1888

May 7, Extradition Treaty with the United States signed

May 25, Law provided for registration of foreign companies and firms

Senator Carlos Holguin acted as provisional head of Government for President Nunez

1889

May 15, Work stopped on canal by French company. Company had gone into hands of receiver on Feb. 4

1890

Jan. 2, Gunboat "La Popa" seized 2 American vessels for contravention of customs laws. Released Feb. 24

Jan. 4, Railroad concession for road from Cartagena to Calamar to American S.S. McConnico, of Nov. 19, 1889, confirmed by the President

Oct. 18, Decree provided regulations for naturalization of aliens

1891

March 16, Royal award of Queen Regent of Spain settled boundary with Venezuela

1892

Aug. 7, Nunez reëlected President. Miguel A. Caro elected Vice-President assumed office acting as President because of ill health of Nunez

1893

Jan. 22, Workmen criticized by newspapers seized offices in Bogotá and mob held city for 2 days until dispersed by troops

Feb. 20, March 31, April 5, Temporary extensions of Panama Canal concession granted and April 7 an extension of 10 years

1894

Aug., The railroad from Cartagena to Calamar completed (67 miles)

Aug. 17, Legation in Costa Rica reëstablished

Aug. 18, Agreement signed to submit Cerruti claims to arbitration

Sept. 18, Death of President Nunez. Vice-President Caro became President

Nov. 1, New French company began work on Canal

1895

Jan. 31, Insurrection at Bogotá

March 15, Rebels routed and many surrendered at Ensiso

June 24, Government forces defeated

1896

March 12, President Caro resigned in order to be candidate for President and Quinto Calderon, Vice-President became Acting President

Nov. 4, Boundary Treaty with Costa Rica

1897

March 2, Award of President Cleveland made in case of Ernesto Cerruti, Italian citizen imprisoned during revolution and his property confiscated by Government, gave Cerruti indemnity of $300,000

July, Italian squadron anchored off Cartagena to enforce payment of award

1898

Aug. 7, President M. A. Sanclemente inaugurated, J. M. Maroquin, Vice-President

1899

July 16, Controversy with Italy reported settled

Aug., Liberal revolt begun

Oct. 17, Armed conflict begun between Liberals and Conservative Government

Oct. 24, Armed government steamers destroyed the "Tinsurg," insurgent vessel

Oct. 30, Insurgents defeated government troops in battle

Nov. 12, Revolt ended, suppressed by government forces

1900

March 31, General Herrera, insurgent, occupied David

April, General G. Vargas-Santos proclaimed President by revolutionists

May 11–25, Siege of Bucaramanga by rebels

June 12–14, Insurgents led by General B. Parras defeated government troops in battle near Panama

July 20, Rebels led by General Emilio Herrera defeated government troops at Corazal

July 25, Cucuta taken by General Gonzales Valencia from rebels

July 27, Peace Treaty with rebels signed

July 31, Coup d'état led by Vice-President José M. Marroquin deposed and imprisoned President Sanclemente and Marroquin assumed presidency

Sept. 11, Award of President Loubet of France in boundary dispute with Costa Rica

Oct. 15, Liberals under General Uribe again in revolt captured Corozal but defeated Nov. 3 in assault on Buenaventura

Nov. 25, Engagement with rebels at Tolu Viejo

1901

Jan. 12, Rebels defeated outside Panama

Feb. 20, Rebel General Herrera took Aguadulce

Aug. 4, Venezuelan force led by Colombians invaded Colombia by way of Riottacha

Aug. 12, Colombian Minister left Venezuela

Sept. 14, Venezuelans and Liberals defeated in battle near La Hacha

Oct. 5, Rebels defeated near Ambaleg

Nov. 16, Diplomatic relations with Venezuela severed

Dec. 9, Insurrection, the Liberals attack and capture Colon, Nov. 19; fierce fighting near Colon, the insurgents defeated, Nov. 24; they surrender at Colon, Nov. 29; Honda attacked, fierce fighting, insurgents defeated with loss

Dec. 27, Victory of government troops at Honda

1902

Jan. 4, French Panama Canal Company offered to sell rights to the United States for $40,000,000

Jan. 20, Sinking of steamer "Lautaro" off Panama by rebels. The Governor of Panama drowned in naval battle

Jan. 26, Insurgents repulsed with great loss 20 miles from Bogotá, reported

Feb. 17, Arbitration Treaty with Spain signed

Feb. 23–27, Aguadulce attacked by Gen. Herrera, great slaughter; Gen. Castro abandons the town and breaks through the Liberal lines

Feb. 27, Colombia forbade Panama Canal Company to transfer concessions to the United States until it had fulfilled certain stipulations with Colombia

June 25, Peace treaties signed, general amnesty for political offenses, reported

July 29–31, Fresh outbreak, terrible fighting at Aguadulce; 2,000 men surrender there; desperate fighting elsewhere, and great slaughter, Sept. 5–8

Oct. 25, Surrender of rebel General Uribe-Uribe

Nov. 21, Treaty of peace signed on board U.S.S. "Wisconsin" ended civil war

1903

Jan. 22, Hay-Herran Treaty with the United States signed gave the United States the Canal Zone on payment of $10,000,000 and annual payment of $250,000 to begin 10 years later

June, Liberals finally defeated

June 20, Congress met to consider the Hay-Herran Treaty

Aug. 12, Senate refused to ratify the Hay-Herran Treaty

recommending that no further action be taken until concession of French Canal Company expired and its property and rights forfeited to Colombia

Oct. 22, Act applied fiscal code of 1873 as to national domain to the exploitation of oil deposits. First specific mention of petroleum in national law

Oct. 31, Congress adjourned without ratification of Hay-Herran Treaty

Nov. 3, Insurrection in Panama City declared the Isthmus independent of Colombia the next day

Nov. 6, President Roosevelt received Señor Bunau-Varilla as Minister from the new State of Panama constituting recognition

Nov. 7, Colombia asked permission of the American war vessels to land troops for purpose of maintaining the integrity of her territory which was refused under clause of Treaty of 1846 giving right to maintain neutrality along the railroad which could not be maintained in event of civil war

Nov. 16, Colombia protested action of United States as to Panama

1904

Aug. 7, General Rafael Reyes inaugurated President, Gonzales Valencia, Vice-President

Nov. 4, Treaty for arbitration of boundary disputes with Ecuador signed

1905

Feb. 1, President Reyes issued call for a "National Assembly" to take the place of Congress which he had dissolved assuming dictatorial powers

Feb. 28, Diplomatic relations with the United States resumed

March 27, 28, 30, April 5, 8, 13, 17, 27, The extra-legal Assembly made amendments to the Constitution among others declaring that it should continue to exercise legislative functions until Feb. 1, 1908. The offices of Vice-President and Designado were abolished and the Council of State

May 1, The term of President Reyes extended to Dec. 31, 1914

July, The United States asked to help maintain principle of free navigation of rivers violated by Venezuela to which Acting Secretary of State Adee made a favorable reply Aug. 5

Aug. 10, Treaty of friendship, commerce, and navigation, extradition and arbitration with Ecuador signed

Sept. 12, Boundary Treaty and Arbitration Treaty with Peru signed

Population 4,143,000

1906

Feb. 10, Unsuccessful attempt to assassinate the President

April 7, Government of Venezuela refused to receive Colombian representative General Benjamin Herrera who had arrived at Caracas to negotiate new treaty of commerce and navigation

June 7, Geneva Convention of 1864 adhered to

1907

April 24, Treaty of boundaries, transit, and inland navigation with Brazil signed

June 12, Act established monetary unit as gold dollar equal to one-fifth of a pound sterling and of proportionate weight, the fineness being the same

Aug. 17, Secretary Taft concluded agreement with representatives of Colombia and Panama, settlement of issues growing out of separation of Panama

1908

Jan. 21, Claim of French Government against the Panama Canal Company and Colombia compromised by payment of $1,600,000

March 11, F. J. Urrutia became premier

May 25, Treaty of commerce and navigation with Japan signed

Aug. 11, Law promulgated to become operative Jan. 1 abolished former political divisions and divided the Republic into 34 departments

Aug. 21, Treaty of commerce and navigation with Brazil signed

Sept. 19, Death of ex-President J. M. Marroquin

Marketing of emeralds arranged with an English company

1909

Jan. 9, Root-Cortez Treaty with the United States and Panama concluded by which Colombia was to receive $25,000,000 and recognize the independence of Panama. Congress refused ratification

July 4, Part of army at Barranquilla revolted and seized the town proclaiming Gonzales Valencia President. Soon suppressed

July 8, Resignation of President Reyes who left the country. Vice-President Jorge Holguin assumed the Government

Aug. 3, General Ramon Gonzales Valencia chosen provisional President

1910

Jan. 19, Important contract gave Jesuits control of higher education

March 8, Mob in Bogotá stormed the American legation

July 15, Carlos E. Restrepo elected President

Aug. 7, President Restrepo inaugurated

Oct. 14 and 18, Decrees of the President created office of Inspector-General of Public Instruction bringing all grades of public instruction under supervision of the national government

Oct. 24, Decree of the President directed that instruction in Colombian history and geography should be given in all schools

Oct. 31, Amendments to Constitution adopted limited term of president to 4 years and provided for successor in case of death, resignation, or demotion, abolished capital punishment, citizens able to read and write and with income of 300 pesos or real estate to value of 1,000 pesos to vote in presidential and congressional elections

1911

Jan. 18, Invasion of Peruvian territory in dispute

Nov. 7, Colombian troops occupied Pedrera, Peru

1912

March 4, Census gave population as 5,072,604

Nov. 23, New fiscal code adopted

Dec., Railroad from Buenaventura opened

1913

Jan. 31 and Feb. 15, Offer from the United States to settle Panama claims refused

March 4, New fiscal code published in the *Gazette*

May, Concession to Pearson and Son (Lord Cowdray) granted oil interests of the Republic

Aug. 7, First wireless message received at Colombia through station at Cartagena

Aug. 11, First gold money coined at mint in Medellin

Nov. 4, Resolution affirming isthmean rights adopted by Congress

Nov. 15, Law reaffirmed proprietorship of the nation of all petroleum deposits beneath public lands and made regulations as to concessions

1914

Feb. 9, José V. Concha, clerical Conservative, elected President

April 6, Thompson-Urrutia Treaty signed settled dispute as to Panama between the United States and Colombia, the United States to pay Colombia $25,000,000 and recognize the independence of Panama. Contained expressions of regret by United States for differences which had arisen and was therefore rejected by the United States Senate as a slur on Roosevelt

June 9, Law sanctioned the Treaty of April 7 with the United States

Aug. 7, President José Vicente Concha inaugurated

Aug. 13, Governors of departments ordered to observe neutrality in the European War as to vessels of belligerent nations

Sept. 1, Decree proclaimed neutrality in the European War

Sept. 10, Constitutional Amendment reëstablished Council of State abolished in 1905

Nov. 16, Arbitration Treaty with Chile signed

Nov. 26, Decree provided that standing army for the current year should be 6,000 men

1915

Jan. 8, Executive decree imposed export tax on gold coins, jewelry of 1% ad valorem and on lumber $2 per cubic meter

July 30, National Red Cross Society founded

Nov. 15, Workmen's Compensation Act passed

1916

July 15, Boundary Treaty with Ecuador signed by which Colombia received most of the Putumayo rubber region

Nov. 3, Protest of Colombia as to Nicaraguan Treaty with the United States as to lease of Great and Little Corn Islands to the United States as a denial of Colombian sovereignty under cedula of King of Spain of Nov. 30, 1803. Dispute referred to arbitration of King of Spain

1917

June 2, Announcement declared neutrality in the war between the United States and Germany

Oct. 17, Resolution adopted by Congress protested against German submarine campaign

1918

Census of population gave 5,855,077

Aug. 7, Marco Fidel Suarez inaugurated President whose cabinet as follows: Interior, Dr. Pedro Molina; Foreign Relations, Gen. Jorge Holguim; Finance, Dr. Marcelino Arango; War, Dr. Jorge Roa; Public Instruction, Dr. Emilio Ferrero; Agriculture and Commerce, Dr. Simon Arauja; Public Works, Señor Rafael Del Corral; Treasury, Señor Pedro A. Lopez

Nov. 13, Arbitration Treaty with Bolivia signed

Nov. 21, Banking law passed

Nov. 27, Law established an income tax

1919

April 11, Decree modified income-tax law

June 20, Decree of the President defined ownership in minerals and petroleum

July 19, Final boundary agreement with Ecuador signed

Aug. 15, Contract with Tropical Oil Company by which the company agreed to pay the Government 10% of gross products of mines

Nov. 19, Law respecting strikes provided for arbitration courts

Dec. 30, New law concerning deposits of hydrocarbons promulgated

1920

Feb. 16, Colombia acceded to Covenant becoming an original member of the League of Nations

Oct. 4, Act regarding conciliation and arbitration in labor disputes passed

Nov. 6, Red Cross Society founded

Inauguration of hydroplane service on the Magadalena River greatly shortening the journey to Bogotá, the capital city

1921

April 20, The United States Senate ratified the Thompson-Urrutia Treaty of 1914 amended and modified

Nov. 11, General Jorge Holguin became Acting President on retirement of President Suarez

Nov. 19, Compulsory collective insurance law for employees enacted

Dec. 22, Congress ratified the Thompson-Urrutia Treaty with the United States as modified and on the 24th the President ratified it

Dec. 24, Colombia recognized the independence of Panama

1922

Feb. 12, Pedro Nel Ospina, Conservative, elected President defeating Benjamin Herrera, Liberal

March 24, Award in boundary dispute with Venezuela given by Swiss Federal Council settled boundary ———, Boundary Treaty with Peru signed

Aug. 7, Inauguration of President Pedro Nel Ospina

Sept. 27, Law provided for establishment of commercial offices in foreign countries under control of Colombian diplomatic representatives to give information and promote commerce

Dec. 7, The United States paid first installment of $5,000,000 under Treaty in compensation for loss of Panama

Dec. 14, Railroad law enacted

1923

Jan. 31, New law on exploitation of hydrocarbons enacted

Feb. 21, Diplomatic relations with Mexico resumed after 25 years

March, Commission from the United States headed by E. W. Kemmerer arrived in Colombia to advise on financial reform

June 19, Wireless telegraph with Venezuela inaugurated

July 23 Bank of the Republic established in Bogotá

Oct. 9, 22, 25, and 27, Laws authorized construction of railroad and appropriated money

Nov. 12, Law issued established General Labor Office

Nov., New organic banking law went into effect

Dec. 10, Law authorized the Government to establish an Agricultural Mortgage Bank in Bogotá

1924

Jan. 12, Decree provided regulations for income tax law

Feb. 7, Liberal leader General Justo L. Duran assassinated

Feb. 29, Death of General Benjamin Herrera

April 14, District of El Viento handed over to Venezuela

April 22, End of strike of car employees

May 8, Diplomatic relations with Panama established

May 19, Strike of faculties in the National University

July 30, Colombia took possession of territory ceded under Swiss arbitration award on the frontier of Venezuela

Aug. 20, Treaty with Panama signed for establishment of international boundary by Mixed Commission

Aug. 22, Council of Bogotá approved $6,000,000 loan contract with Dillon, Read and Company

Aug. 26–Sept. 4, Trial of former Minister of the Treasury, Dr. Pomponio Guzman. Acquitted for lack of evidence

Sept. 29–Oct. 3, Trial of former Councillor of State in Senate. Found guilty

Oct. 8, Strike of workers of Barranca Bermeja

Nov. 6, General strike called

Nov. 29, Act passed for protection of child labor

1925

Jan. 31, Social Hygiene Act regulated conditions in factories and commercial establishments

Feb. 28, Law enacted for protection of industrial property and patent rights

March 4, Settlement of boundary dispute in Amazon region effected in State Department of the United States by Colombia, Brazil, and Peru

April 12, Insurrection against the President frustrated and leaders arrested

Nov. 15, Workmen's Compensation Act enacted

Production of Tropical Oil Company 1,006,708 barrels of oil

1926

Feb. 2, Cancellation of De Barco concession (American) of 5,000,000 acres of oil land on ground of alleged non-fulfillment of contract

Feb. 14, Dr. Miguel Abadia Mendez, Conservative, elected President

July 1, Pipe line of Andean National Corporation opened connecting terminal of Mamonal on Cartagena Bay with petroleum lands of Tropical Oil Company

July 3, Decree regulated sale of intoxicating beverages

July 4, First tank oil steamer left Cartagena with 87,500 barrels of oil

Aug. 7, President Abadia Mendez inaugurated

Sept. 4, Strike of employees of government railroads

Nov. 5, Landslide near Previa blocked Otun River killing 100 persons

Nov. 16, Obligatory Sunday Rest Law enacted affecting workers in commerce and industry

Production of Tropical Oil Company 6,443,540 barrels

1927

April 4, Death of M. F. Suarez, former President

May 13, Election a victory for Conservatives

May 20, Minister to Peru recalled and relations severed because of failure of Peru to ratify boundary treaty

Aug. 2, Treaty of conciliation, judicial settlement, and arbitration with Switzerland signed

Sept. 13, Conciliation Treaty with Sweden signed

Sept. 14, Law provided for foreign loan of 12,000,000 pesos for construction of railroad

Nov. 14, Law number 84 relative to hydrocarbons reserved to government ownership and right to exclusive exploitation. Promulgated Jan., 1928. Required presentation of proof of ownership

Nov. 17, Law enacted gave Minister of Industries supreme control to declare title to oil lands when any doubt as to title proved. Promulgated in Jan., 1928

Nov. 25, Law provided for government inspection of insurance companies

Dec. 24, Extradition Treaty with Panama signed

Production of Tropical Oil Company 15,002,175 barrels during year

1928

Jan. 26, Colonel Charles A. Lindbergh, aviator, arrived at Cartagena flying from Colon, and flew to Bogotá the following day

Jan. 28, Decree promulgated regulations for Law 84 of 1927 dealing with petroleum, putting law into operation

Jan. 30, Promulgation of law of 1927 as to proving ownership of oil properties

March 2, Death of Jorge Holguin, former Acting President

March 9, Commercial Treaty with Sweden signed

March 24, Treaty with Nicaragua signed awarded Mosquito Coast and Great and Little Corn Islands to Nicaragua and the islands of San Andres, Providencia, Santa Catalina, and others of the Andres Archipelago to Colombia

March, Loan for $34,000,000 contracted in New York City for public works construction

April 2, Daily aviation service established between Cartagena, Barranquilla, and Girardot

April 10, Exchange of notes with the United States as to sovereignty over Serrana and Quita Sueno Banks and Roncador Cay (Caribbean Sea)

——, Agreement with the United States to keep *status quo* as to Serrano and Quita Sueno Banks and Roncador Cay

May 5, Convention with the Vatican as to missions signed

May 7, Extradition Treaty with Costa Rica signed

June 1, Decree suspended Petroleum Law of 1927 and Decree of 1928 pending decisions of Supreme Court and State Council

June 5, Law enacted gave national Government entire control of contraction of departmental and municipal loans

June 12, Extradition Treaty with Mexico signed

June 26, Executive decree unified practice as to Sunday rest of workers

July 11, Arbitration Treaty with Mexico signed

Oct. 3, Death of Ramon G. Valencia, former President

Oct. 8, Convention signed with Costa Rica provided for mutual recognition of professional decrees

Nov. 11, Strike of employees of United Fruit Company begun against wages and conditions. Government troops sent supported the Company

Nov. 15, Treaty with Brazil defined boundaries ceding territory to Brazil

Dec. 6, Troops fired on crowd at station railroad at Cienaga in strike district killing 410 persons and wounding 40, beginning reign of "terror" in which more than 1,500 persons killed (Rippy)

Dec. 16, Strike in banana region ended when leader Alberto Castrillon killed by troops

Population estimated at 7,993,000 of which 32.8%

counted as pure white, 8.6% pure negro, 6.5% pure Indian, and 52.1% mulattoes and mestizos

1929

May 13, Election a Conservative victory

June 6, Strike at Bogotá over removal of Mayor Luis Augusto Cuervo who had removed managers of city aqueduct and street railways, one a brother-in-law of the President, citizens and students boycotting the railroad

June 7, Demonstration of 30,000 persons in favor of the Mayor charged by police and many injured

Nov. 16, Congress adjourned without passing new oil law or making financial appropriation

——, Note as to ownership of Roncador and Quita Sueno Keys on Atlantic Ocean

1930

Jan. 22, Archbishop Perdomo issued circular recommending support of Dr. Guillermo Valencia, Conservative, for President, but withdrew it Feb. 3 declaring in favor of General Vasquez Cabo

Feb. 9, Enrique Olaya Herrera, Liberal, elected President, the first time a Liberal won in election since 1884

March 14, Protocol signed with Brazil provided for remarking the boundary line

April 4, Cabinet resigned

April 14, Coalition Cabinet of the 2 leading parties sworn in

Aug. 4, Professor Edmund W. Kemmerer arrived heading financial mission to study conditions

Aug. 7, Dr. Enrique Olaya Herrera inaugurated President

Sept. 24, Export of gold prohibited

Dec. 15, Cabinet reorganized

EASTER ISLAND

Easter Island, 2,100 miles west of Coquimbo, Chile, in Pacific Ocean, area about 40 square miles, circumference about 29 miles, discovered April 5, 1722 by Jacob Roggeveen, Hollander, and rediscovered in 1770 by F. Gonzales, Spaniard, and annexed to Chile, formal annexation Nov. 19.

ECUADOR

Ecuador, Republic in the northwest, is bounded on the north and northeast by Colombia and Peru, on west by the Pacific Ocean, on the south and on the east by Peru. The maximum length of the country from north to south is about 100 miles. Since the frontiers of Ecuador have not been settled, no definite figure of the area of the country can be given. Ecuador is said to have more boundaries than any other country, and there are maps of the Republic showing six different frontiers according to six different authorities. Taking the boundaries arranged with Brazil in 1904, with Colombia by the Treaty of July 15, 1916, and those for Peru according to the Royal Decree of 1739, the area of Ecuador is 571,250

square kilometers (220,502 square miles). Taking its Peruvian boundary in accordance with the Protocol Pedemonte-Mosquera of 1830, its area is 443,750 square kilometers (171,287 square miles). According to an estimate made in 1926, the total area is 284,860 square kilometers, or 109,978 square miles. The area of the Archipelago of Colon (Galapagos Islands) adds 7,430 square kilometers (2,868 square miles). The country is divided into 17 provinces and one territory—the Archipelago of Galapagos—officially called "Colon," situated in the Pacific Ocean about 600 miles to the west of Ecuador.

So far no exact census has been taken, but the population has been estimated (1929) at 1,785,800, of which the whites are 10%; Indians, 38%; mixed, 41%; lowland Indians, 1%; Negroes, 5%; others, 5%. The foreign community is composed of about 10,000 persons.

The chief towns are the capital, Quito (82,000), Guayaquil (100,000), Cuenca (40,000), Riobamba (20,000), Ambato (20,000), Loja (10,000), Latacunga (15,000), Bahia (5,000), Esmeraldas (4,000).

The name is derived from the Spanish word for equator, so-called because the equator crosses the country. Ecuador in colonial history was the Presidency of Quito.

Dr. Isidro Ayora, President.

1526

Sept. 21, The Spaniard Bartolome Ruiz in service of Pizarro entered Bay of San Mateo, first European in Ecuador

1532

Jan. 10, Pizarro expedition to Peru reached Bay of San Mateo and proceeded to march along the coast to Gulf of Guyaquil, crossed in boats to Puna where he defeated Indians in battle

1533

Dec.–Dec. 1534, Expedition of Sebastian de Benalcazar, Governor of San Miguel (Peru) sent by Pizarro engaged in exploration and conquest of Quito (later Ecuador) entered the city of Quito May or June, 1533 which he found burned by Indians and took formal possession of it for King of Spain Dec. 6, 1534 becoming Governor. Almagro sent to aid him against Alvarado

1534

March, Pedro de Alvarado with band of adventurers from Central America landed at Caraquez Bay and marched east from coast for conquest of country

Aug. 15, Almagro and Benalcazar founded city of Santiago de Quito near present Riobamba

Aug. 26, Alvarado finding he had arrived too late agreed to retire from the country

Aug. 28, The City of Santiago de Quito moved to present site and name changed to San Francisco de Quito

Dec. 6, Benalcazar took formal possession of Indian city of Quito

1535

Portoviejo founded

July 25, Santiago de Guayaquil founded by Benalcazar at mouth of Rio Babahoyo

1537

Guayaquil refounded by Orellana and permanent settlement made

1540 •

Dec. 1, Francisco Pizarro appointed his brother Gonzalo Governor of Quito succeeding Benalcazar

1541

Feb., Gonzalo Pizarro with Orellana and large company of Spaniards and Indians left Quito in quest of the fabled city of El Dorado and crossed Andes by Guamani pass. Returned in rags and almost alone in June, 1542. Orellana descended the Amazon to its mouth

Nov., Vaca de Castro, sent from Spain to Peru, at Quito

1546

June 18, Battle of Anaquito near Quito. *See* Peru

1557

Cuenca founded on site of Indian town

1563

Nov. 29, Royal ordinance created an Audiencia for city of Quito

1564

Kingdom of Quito made a presidencia subject to Viceroy of New Granada and in judicial matters to Audiencia at Lima

1570

Ambato founded

1592

July, Revolt against imposition of tax of the "alcabala" of 2% on all merchandise sold which was to become effective Aug. 15 forced suspension of tax

Dec., Another alcabala revolt because of information that troops from Peru were to be sent to punish people of Quito

1606

Ibarra founded under direction of Don Miguel de Ibarra

1620

University of San Gregorio Magno formally established

1709

Feb., Captain Woodes Rogers, pirate, took and sacked Guayaquil, forcing inhabitants to pay ransom

1718

Nov. 25, Audiencia of Quito suppressed and administrative authority transferred to Santa Fé de Bogotá

1722

Audiencia of Quito reëstablished under Peru

1741

Town of La Tola founded by Spanish Governor Don Pedro Vicente Maldonado

1746

French Commission headed by Charles M. La Conda-
mine completed work of measuring length of a decree of the meridian in Ecuador

1750

First printing press set up at Ambato

1765

May 22 and June 24, The "Monopoly Revolution" insurrection due to royal decree that alcohol should not be distilled except for account of royal Treasury

1767

Aug. 20, Royal decree of expulsion read to Jesuits who were deported Sept. 17, 25, and Oct. 3

1790

Patriotic Society of Friends of the Country (Sociedad Patriotica de Amigos del Pais) established by Francisco Javier Eugenio de Santa Cruz y Espejo, patriot

1792

Jan. 5, First periodical the *Primiccias de la Cultura de Quito* issued by Espejo

1794

Oct. 4, Seditious posters appeared in Quito inciting the people to revolt

1795

Dec. 27, Death of patriot, Espejo, released from prison

1803

July 7, Royal order transferred province of Guayaquil from New Granada to Peru

1808

March, Unsuccessful insurrection

1809

March, Revolt planned by friends and disciples of Espejo failed

Aug. 10, Colonists in Quito deposed Ruiz de Castilla president of the Audiencia and established an independent Junta headed by the Marquis of Selva Alegre, a descendant of Espejo, which proclaimed allegiance to Ferdinand VII

Oct. 24, Quito forced to capitulate to Count Ruiz de Castilla

1810

Aug. 2, Patriots in prison including leaders of revolution massacred

Sept. 19, Junta installed at Quito under presidency of Ruiz de Castillo, late Captain General who was deposed Dec. 11 and later murdered by mob. Molina had succeeded him as Captain General

Oct. 11, Second attempt at revolution set up the "Eight Provinces of the State of Quito"

1811

Dec. 4, Patriot Congress convened in Quito for better organization of the government

1812

Feb. 15, First Constitution promulgated at Quito by Congress

Sept. 2, Marshal Montes defeated patriots at Mocha

Nov. 3, Spaniards commanded by General Toribio Montes defeated patriots and gained possession of Quito

1817

July 26, Don Juan Ramirez succeeded Montes as President of Quito

1820

Oct. 9, Citizens of Guayaquil proclaimed independence and set up autonomous government

Nov. 11, Guayaquil assembly drafted provisional constitutional regulations, 20 articles

Nov. 15, City of Cuenca which had proclaimed independence Nov. 3 drew up "plan of government"

Nov. 20, Luis Urdaneta advancing on Quito from Guayaquil defeated by royalist Colonel Gonzales on plateau of Ambato

1821

Jan. 3, Garcia rallying army of Urdaneta defeated by royalists and captured and killed

May 6, General Sucre from Colombia sent by Bolivar to aid revolution reached Guayaquil. Quito not included in armistice. See Colombia, Nov. 25, 1820

Aug. 19, Sucre defeated royalists at Yahuachi compelling Aymerich, Captain General to return to Quito

Sept. 12, Sucre defeated on plateau of Ambato by royalist Colonel Gonzales with superior force

Oct. 22, Royalist expedition sailed from Panama commanded by General Murgeon, new Viceroy of New Granada, arriving Dec. 24 at Quito

Dec. 16, The district of Puerto Viejo declared union with Colombia

1822

Feb. 21, Sucre occupied Cuenca

March 24, Bolivar with liberating army the "Colombian Guard" arrived at frontiers of Quito

April 7, Battle of Bombona. Bolivar defeated royalists but with heavy loss

April 22, General Sucre occupied Riobamba evacuated by royalists

May 24, Battle of Pichincha. Decisive victory won by Sucre

May 25, Aymerich surrendered city of Quito to Sucre

May 29, Quito declared for annexation to the Colombian Confederation

June 16, Bolivar entered Quito

July 11, Bolivar entered Guayaquil

July 26–27, Conference of San Martin with Bolivar at Guayaquil which resulted in withdrawal of San Martin from South American affairs

July 31, Formal annexation of Guayaquil to Colombian Confederation

1823

July 18, Battle of Ibarra. Bolivar defeated Agustin de Agualongo

1826

Sept. 12, Bolivar arrived at Guayaquil

1829

Jan., Peruvians aiming to acquire Guayaquil blockaded the port and forced surrender

Feb. 27, General Sucre defeated Peruvians at Tarqui

1830

May 12, Popular assembly called by General Flores at Quito proclaimed independence of the Colombian Confederation and named country Ecuador. Formal resolution signed May 13

Aug. 14–Sept. 28, Constitutional Convention met at Riobamba of the three departments of Azuay,

Guayas, and Quito and announced independent State called "Estado del Ecuador en Colombia"

Sept. 11, General Juan Jose Flores elected President to begin term Sept. 22 (1830–Sept. 10, 1834)

——, Constitution promulgated

Sept. 26, Law enacted to free slaves

1832

Feb. 12, The Government took formal possession of the Galapagos Islands

July 12, Treaty of commerce, friendship, and alliance with Peru signed

Dec. 8, Treaty of commerce and friendship with New Granada signed. Provided that the department of Cauca should belong to New Granada and established Carchi River as boundary line

1834

July, "Pact" between President Flores and Liberal leader Rocafuerte ended insurrection

Dec. 23, Ecuador assumed $21 1/2\%$ of debt of Colombian Confederation

1835

June 22–Aug. 22, Constitutional Convention met at Ambato

Aug. 8, Vicente Rocafuerte, President (1835–Jan. 31, 1839)

Aug. 13, New Constitution promulgated for the "Republic of Ecuador"

1838

June 9, Independence of Ecuador recognized by the United States

1839

Jan. 31, General Flores again President (1839–Jan. 22, 1843)

March 25, Ports opened to Spanish commerce

June 13, Treaty of peace, friendship, navigation, and commerce with the United States signed

1840

Feb. 16, Treaty of peace, amity, and recognition with Spain signed

1841

Aug. 6, The war steamship "San Vicente Guayas" launched at Guayaquil, first vessel of the kind constructed in yards of Spanish America

1843

Jan. 15–June 18, Constitutional Convention in Quito

April 1, New Constitution promulgated. President Flores began his third term in office

June 6, Treaty of commerce and navigation with France signed

1845

March 6, Resolution deposed President Flores

June 25, Flores forced to sign agreement with Liberal leaders recognizing their provisional Government and leave Ecuador

Oct. 3–Feb. 7, 1846, Constitutional Convention in Cuenca

Dec. 8, Vicente Ramon Roca, President (1845–June 10, 1850)

1846

May 29, Agreement with New Granada provided for negotiation of boundary treaty

1851

Feb. 26, Diego Noboa, made President by General Urbina

March, Law permitted return of Jesuits

July 17–Oct. 2, 1852, Constitutional Convention in Guayaquil

Sept. 13, Noboa forced from office by revolution and Urbina became Dictator

1852

July 17–Oct. 2, Constitutional Convention at Guayaquil. José Maria Urbina declared President

Sept. 6, New Constitution promulgated at Guayaquil

Sept. 27, Slavery abolished

1853

Nov. 26, Act of Congress opened the Amazon and its tributaries within the jurisdiction of Ecuador to foreign commerce and navigation

1856

July 9, Treaty of friendship, commerce, and navigation with New Granada signed

Oct. 16, Francisco Robles, President (1856–May 1, 1859)

Dec. 6, French metric system for weights and measures made legal standard for the Government. Not adopted by commerce

1857

Chilean Civil Code adopted

1859

May 1, Revolt led by Garcia Moreno who took possession of Quito. Declared President

Aug. 21, General Franco seized the Government

War with Peru at frontier. Warships blockaded Guayaquil

1860

Jan., President Franco agreed to treaty with Peru which recognized the limits of the vice-royalties of Peru and New Granada according to royal order of 1802. The Peruvian fleet withdrawn

Sept. 24, Port of Guayaquil captured from General Franco by General Garcia Moreno and General Flores

1861

Jan. 10–June, Constitutional Convention at Quito

March 10, New Constitution adopted. Promulgated at Quito one month later

April 2, Gabriel Garcia Moreno, President (1861–65)

1862

Sept. 26, Concordat signed at Rome. The Roman Catholic made sole religion of the Republic

Nov. 25, Claims Convention with the United States referred claims to board organized at Guayaquil Aug. 22, 1864 which settled claims at $94,799.56

1863

Dec. 6, General Flores leading army into New Granada defeated in Battle of Cuaspud

1865

Sept. 7, Jeronimo Carrion, President (1865–Nov. 6, 1867)

1866

Feb. 27, War declared against Spain

1868

Jan. 20, Javier Espinosa, President (1868–Jan. 17, 1869)

Aug. 13–15, Earthquake destroyed public buildings in Quito

1869

Jan. 17, Garcia Moreno *ad interim* President after military revolt

May 16–Aug. 30, Constitutional Convention at Quito

June 9, New Constitution promulgated. Moreno elected President

1875

Aug. 6, President Moreno assassinated at Quito

Dec. 7, Law enacted authorized the Government to sell the public lands

Dec. 9, Antonio Borrero, President (1875–Sept. 8, 1876)

1876

Sept. 8, Liberal revolution headed by General Veintemilla overthrew Borrero

Dec. 14, Insurgents won decisive victory over government troops commanded by General Aparicio near Galte

Dec. 25, General Veintemilla proclaimed himself President

1878

Jan. 26–May 31, Constitutional Convention in Ambato

April 21, Ignacio de Veintemilla made constitutional President (1878–March 26, 1882)

1880

Sept. 20, Treaty of extradition with Great Britain signed

Oct. 18, Treaty of commerce and navigation with Great Britain signed

1882

April 2, President Veintemilla proclaimed himself Dictator

1883

Jan., Revolt against the Government led by Alfaro successful in battle at Gatajo

July 9, President Veintemilla fled from the country

Oct. 11–April 26, 1884, Constitutional Convention at Quito

1884

Feb. 10, José Maria Placido Caamaño, President (1884–June 30, 1888)

Feb. 13, New Constitution promulgated

Liberal revolt led by General Eloy Alfaro

1887

March 28, Treaty of friendship with Germany

July 26, Law modified Constitution of 1884

Aug. 1, Treaty with Peru by which they agreed to submit boundary dispute to King of Spain

1888

Aug. 17, Dr. Antonio Flores, President (1888–July 1, 1892)

1889

Sept. 22, Government order prohibited Chinese immigration

1890

March 29, Treaty of friendship, commerce, and navigation with Salvador signed

Sept. 4, Tariff law enacted

1892

July 1, Luis Cordero, President (1892–April 16, 1895)

Aug. 15, New mining law adopted published Aug. 24 conceded perpetual ownership to private proprietors on condition of annual duty paid on concessions

Aug. 28, Law as to rights of foreigners enacted

1894

"Esmeralda affair." Chilean vessel with aid of Government of Ecuador transferred to Japanese at war with China, breach of international law. The President was censured and uprising against him

1895

April, General Aloy Alfaro in exile in Nicaragua issued manifesto against President Cordero and revolt begun by his followers in province of Carchi

April 24, President Cordero resigned and fled from the country. Succeeded by Vicente Salazar, Vice-President

May 25, Revolt of garrison at Guayaquil

June 6, Revolutionists captured Guayaquil, and Alfaro proclaimed provisional President June 16 on arrival at Guayaquil

Aug. 6, Guaranda occupied by rebels after battle

Aug. 13–14, Government forces under Minister of War, General Savasti, defeated near Riobamba

Sept. 1, Alfaro entered Quito and was proclaimed "Supreme Chief of the Republic"

Nov. 4, President Alfaro named Cabinet

1896

July 24, Conservatives and clergy defeated by Alfaro near San Miguel de Chimbo

Aug. 22, Cuenca captured by Alfaro from General Vega, ending insurrection

Sept. 22, Award given in Santos claim. Decision in favor of the United States against Ecuador

Oct. 9–Nov. 6, and Dec. 9–June 14, 1897, Constitutional Convention at Guayaquil

1897

Jan. 12, New Constitution adopted. Promulgated Jan. 14

Jan. 17, General Eloy Alfaro, constitutional President (1897–Aug. 31, 1901)

June 14, Contract signed with Archer Harman, American, for construction of the Guayaquil and Quito Railroad

Indians who had supported Alfaro in 1895 admitted to citizenship

1899

Jan. 24, Revolt suppressed after battle at San Aneaja

Sept. 27, Law abrogated certain provisions of the Concordat as to jurisdiction of Papal legates, circulation of bulls or rescripts, raising of church revenue, right to appoint bishops

Oct. 12, Law prohibited immigration of Chinese

1900

June 4, Gold standard established by law of 1898 came into effect

1901

Sept. 1, Leonidas Plaza Gutierrez, President (1901–Aug. 31, 1905). His measures of reform continued to lessen the authority and privileges of the Catholic Church

1902

Oct. 3, Act signed making civil marriage compulsory to go into effect Jan. 1, 1903

1904

Feb. 19, Ecuador and Peru signed Protocol referring boundary dispute to King of Spain

May 6, Treaty with Brazil by which Ecuador resigned claim to certain territory between the Caqueta River and the Amazon

Oct. 13, Law provided that any faith not contrary to morals or laws of Ecuador should be tolerated

Nov. 4, Treaty with Colombia provided for arbitration of boundary dispute

1905

Aug. 10, Treaty of friendship, commerce, navigation, and extradition with Colombia signed

Law declared rural property held by the Church the property of the State

Sept. 1, Lizardo Garcia, President (1905–Jan. 15, 1906)

1906

Jan. 1, Revolt against Garcia Government supported by ex-President Alfaro

Jan. 4, Rebels occupied Riobamba barracks. Rebels commanded by Colonel Emilio Maria Reran defeated by Colonel Manuel Andrade

Jan. 6, President Garcia declared the Republic in a state of war

Jan. 17, Alfaro occupied Quito and became again ruler of Ecuador

Oct. 10–Feb. 9, 1907, Constitutional Convention at Quito

Dec. 23, New Constitution promulgated. Public education removed from control of the Church. In general foreigners were to enjoy the same rights as natives but foreigners making contracts with the Government must renounce all recourse to diplomacy

1907

Jan. 1, Alfaro inaugurated constitutional President (1907–Aug. 14, 1911)

May 10, Treaty of commerce and river navigation with Brazil signed

Aug. 3, Government adhered to Geneva Convention of 1864

1908

June 17, Last spike in the Guayaquil and Quito Railroad driven by the President's daughter

June 25, First train entered Quito from Guayaquil

Aug. 29, Treaty of commerce and navigation with Chile signed

Sept. 26, Sanitary Convention with Panama signed

Oct. 29, New sanitary law enacted

1909

Jan. 7, Arbitration Treaty with the United States signed

May 13, Arbitration Treaty with Brazil signed

1910

May 21, Ecuador and Peru accepted American Secretary Knox's offer of mediation of boundary dispute

June 3, Peru and Ecuador agreed to withdraw troops from the border and accept mediation of Brazil, Argentina, and the United States

Nov. 14, Red Cross Society founded

1911

Jan. 20, Ecuador declined to submit boundary dispute with Peru to the Hague Court

Jan. 29, Plan of the lease of Galapagos Islands for 99 years to the United States for $15,000,000 declined because of popular disapproval

July 12, Arbitration Treaty with Argentina signed

Aug. 14, Resignation of President Alfaro

Sept. 1, Emilio Estrada, inaugurated President

Sept. 24, Heavy earthquake at Riobamba

Dec. 22, Death of President Estrada. Succeeded by *interregnum* in which the president of the Senate or of the Chamber of Deputies in charge of executive office

Dec. 27, General Montero had himself proclaimed President by a part of the army and revolution followed

1912

Jan. 13, Rebels led by ex-President Alfaro defeated at Huigra and leaders captured and imprisoned

Jan. 28, Mob at Quito broke into prison and murdered rebel leaders including Alfaro

March 5, Revolutionary outbreak at Quito in favor of Conservative party

March 6, General Julio Andrade assassinated by his troops

April 8, General Leonidas Plaza Gutierrez elected President

Aug. 10, Congress elected Señor Morena to serve as head of the Government until inauguration of President Elect Gutierrez

Sept. 1, Leonidas Plaza Gutierrez inaugurated (1912–Aug. 31, 1916)

1913

June 26, Concession to Pearson and Son (Lord Cowdray) for exploitation of oil

July 21, Extradition Treaty with Bolivia signed

Dec. 15, Rebels led by Carlos Concha took city of Esmeraldes which they held for 4 months

1914

March 12, Federal troops reoccupied Esmeraldes evacuated by rebels

April, Esmeraldes besieged by Concha

Aug. 17, Proclamation of neutrality in European War

Oct. 13, Advancement of Peace Treaty with the United States signed

Oct. 24, Mining Code amended

Nov. 19, Circular defined neutrality in response to charges of England and France that Ecuador had permitted violations within her jurisdiction

1915

Feb., Capture of rebel leader Carlos Concha ended insurrection

1916

Jan. 12, Alfredo Baquerizo Moreno elected President, Liberal candidate, defeating Arizaga, Conservative

July 15, Boundary Treaty with Colombia signed provided for commission to make survey

Aug. 10, Treaty of commerce and navigation with Colombia

Sept. 1, President Moreno inaugurated

Sept. 12, Eight hour day law enacted

Commission of the Rockefeller Foundation under direction of American sanitary expert Colonel Gorgas made investigation of conditions in Guayaquil, chief seaport, which resulted in complete eradication of yellow fever by May, 1920

1917

Oct. 17, Ecuador refused to receive Minister from Germany accredited to Ecuador and Peru which was virtually a suspension of diplomatic relations

Oct. 30, Pension law enacted

Dec. 7, Ecuador severed diplomatic relations with Germany

1918

July 9, Arrival of American Sanitary Commission at Guayaquil

Aug. 26, Treaty of friendship, commerce, and navigation with Japan signed

Oct. 20, Decree abolished peonage and canceled debts of peons

1919

Jan. 1, New law regulating taxes on rum and wine went into effect

June 8, Law enacted abolishing peonage and imprisonment for debt

July 19, Boundary Treaty with Colombia signed

Oct. 18, Law authorized the President to determine taxes to be paid for exploitation of petroleum deposits

1920

Jan. 11, Dr. José Luis Tamayo, Liberal, elected President

Jan. 20, Decree of the President levied tax on oil wells in operation of 6% of their gross production as a license fee

March 30, Decree regulated immigration of Chinese

Sept. 1, President Tamayo inaugurated

Nov. 1, Senate resolved to postpone action for entering League of Nations

Nov. 4, Lieutenant Elia Liut, Italian aviator in service of *El Telegrafo* made successful flight over Andes in 1 hour and 55 minutes at height of about 19,000 feet

Nov. 19, Lieutenant Liut flew from Cuenca to inter-Andean city of Riobamba

Nov. 25, Law promulgated declared petroleum land concessions on which exploitation had not begun within 5 years to be forfeited

1921

May 24, Arbitration Treaty with Venezuela signed

——, Military service made compulsory

Sept. 5, Legislative decree prohibited Sunday sale of beer and alcoholic liquors after Jan. 1, 1922

Sept. 13, Workmen's Compensation Act enacted

Sept. 30, Labor accident law signed by the President

Oct. 8, Eight hour day law of 1916 amended

Oct. 18, Law enacted dealing with alienage, extradition and naturalization, and petroleum law

1922

May 18, Diplomatic relations with Germany reëstablished

Nov. 16, Government took over monopoly and control of all foreign bills of exchange fixing sucre at about 47 cents which was later changed to 25 cents

1923

March 17, Executive decree established immigration station on Island of Puna

Oct. 18, Law passed imposed tax of 5% on teachers' salaries for pensions

Oct. 22, Law established tax on all commercial and industrial sales made in the Republic

Dec. 16, Earthquake destroyed city of Tulcan in province of Carchi

1924

Jan. 17, Gonzalo Cordova elected President

Jan. 19, Agreement with Germany for maintenance of Treaty of friendship of 1887

June 21, Protocol signed with Peru provided for submission of boundary dispute to arbitration

Sept. 1, President Cordova assumed office but delegated power to Dr. Martinez

Oct. 16, Law passed prohibited importation of opium, morphine, &c., by private individuals or corporations

———, Law placed telegraph and wireless telegraph under control of Government

Oct. 28, Shoe factory established in Riobamba. Opened with ceremonies attended by the Governor

1925

July 9, Military coup d'état. President Cordova deposed by General Francisco Gomez de la Torre and sent into exile and Provisional Junta of 7 took over the Government

July 14, Modesto Larrea Jijon formed Cabinet

American Minister withdrawn in accordance with policy of non-recognition of government founded by force

1926

Jan. 13, Military Board of 3 succeeded Provisional Junta in charge of Government

March 15, Floods in the Jubones River caused death of 50 persons and destroyed property valued at $2,000,000

April 1, Military Board dissolved and Dr. Isidro Ayora appointed provisional President

April 10, Financial crisis, 3 banks closed by Government

June 1, New tariff law to be effective July 1 established protection of industries, especially shoe, nail, and textiles

Oct. 19, Kemmerer Financial Mission arrived from the United States to study conditions with view to place finances and currency on more stable basis

1927

March 4, Law authorized establishment of Central Bank

———, New monetary law passed. Monetary unit of sucre established at $.20 gold

Aug. 10, Banco Central officially opened

Dec. 22, Decree established government salt monopoly

1928

Jan. 2, New income tax law as recommended by the Kemmerer Mission published

Jan. 11, Costes-Lebrix expedition (aviators) at Guayaquil

March 4, Mortgage Bank opened (Banco Hipotecario)

March 13, Pension Savings and Coöperative Act passed

April, Death of ex-President Cordova

July 6, First train from Quito arrived at Cayambe on the Quito-Esmeraldes Railroad

July 17, Patent law signed

Aug. 1, Law created office of prosecuting attorney for the Republic

Aug. 2, General Statistical Bureau of the Republic created

Aug. 14, Diplomatic relations resumed by the United States recognizing the Ayora Government

Aug. 28, Law of this date fixed tax on inheritances, legacies, and donations

Sept. 19, Law declared government monopoly of alcohol

Sept. 21, Trade-mark law enacted

Oct. 6, Labor laws passed dealing with labor contracts, hours of labor, weekly rest, employment of women and minors, labor accidents, and suits

———, Act extended the benefits of compulsory retirement fund to employees in banks

Oct. 9, Constitutional Assembly met which had been elected Aug. 30

Oct. 10, Assembly elected Dr. Ayora constitutional President

Nov. 1, Laws promulgated amended codes of civil and criminal procedure

Dec. 1, President-Elect Hoover on good will visit to Latin America arrived at Guayaquil

1929

Jan. 1, Eight hour day and child labor laws came into effect

March 25, New Constitution adopted. Promulgated March 28

March 27, Dr. Isidro Ayora elected constitutional President by the Assembly for five year term

April 12, Dr. Ayora inaugurated President

July 3, Decree provided for support to Gorgas Memorial Laboratory for Tropical Research, Panama

July 9, National Assembly approved changes in the banking laws

Aug. 3–5, Strike of bank clerks because of government taxation of their retirement funds

Sept., Strike of University students for control of Central University of Guayaquil

1930

Aug. 10, First constitutional Congress since 1924 convened

Sept. 29, President Ayora resigned to avert revolution. Congress refused to accept his resignation

Dec. 17, Guayaquil inaugurated city manager plan of government, first trial of plan in a Latin-American city

FALKLAND ISLANDS

Falkland Islands, British Crown Colony, situated in the South Atlantic, 300 miles east of Straits of Magellan: East Falkland, 2,580 square miles; West Falkland, 2,038 square miles, including in each case the adjacent small islands; total, 4,618 square miles; besides South Georgia, 1,000 square miles (estimated). Among other Dependencies are the South Shetlands, the South Orkneys, the Sandwich Group, and Graham's Land. Population: census of 1921, 2,087 (1,182 males and 905 females), exclusive of the Whaling Settlement in South Georgia (population in 1926, 1,895, including only 7 females), population 1928, 2,296 (998 females).

The islands were discovered by John Davis in

1592, explored by Sir Richard Hawkins in June, 1593. On April 5, 1764, the French explorer de Bougainville took possession of the islands but settlers withdrew following a protest by Spain. Jan. 23, 1765 Commodore Byron took possession in the name of Great Britain, and the name Falkland given. The British settlers were expelled by the Spaniards in 1770, restored by Agreement of Jan. 22, 1771 on condition of evacuation, and abandoned settlement May 20, 1774 leaving inscription that the islands were a possession of George III. The Government of Buenos Aires took formal possession of the islands Nov. 9, 1820 and settled at Port St. Louis. This settlement was dispersed in 1831 in dispute with the United States over seizure of American sealing vessels claimed to have violated Argentine fishing laws. Jan. 3, 1833 Captain Onslow took possession for Great Britain claiming the islands by right of discovery and prior occupation. Letters patent declared the Falkland Islands British dependencies, reaffirmed March 28, 1917.

GALAPAGOS ISLANDS

Galapagos Islands, Pacific archipelago, officially called "Colon," consist of 15 large islands and forty smaller ones lying on the equator 600 miles west of Ecuador. They were discovered March 10, 1535 by Thomas de Berlanga, Bishop of Panama, on a voyage to Peru, rediscovered 1546 by Rivadeneira, and formally annexed by the Government of Ecuador Feb. 12, 1832. The area in square miles is 2,868 square miles and estimated population 500. The name is derived from the Spanish *galapago*, tortoise, and was given because of the giant turtles described by Charles Darwin in 1858, some of them weighing nearly 400 pounds, and attaining an age of 300 to 400 years. Albemarle is the largest island, 100 miles in length and 28 wide.

GUIANA, BRITISH

Guiana, British, or Demerara, on the northeastern coast with Atlantic coast line of 220 miles, bounded by Dutch Guiana on the east, Brazil on the south and southwest, and west by Venezuela and northwest, a British Colony. Area, 89,480 square miles. Population at census 1921, 297,691 (excluding about 9,700 aborigines). Population, 1929, 309,676.

This territory, including the counties of Demerara, Essequebo, and Berbice, named from the three rivers, was first partially settled by the Dutch West India Company about 1620. The Dutch retained their hold until 1796, when it was captured by the English, and was finally ceded to Great Britain in 1814.

The capital is Georgetown, population 57,560.

The boundary with Venezuela was settled by award of Oct. 3, 1899, and Agreement of March 18, 1930 (*See* Venezuela); with Brazil by award of June 6, 1904 which gave most of territory in dispute to British Guiana, and Treaty with Brazil of April 22, 1929. The first English settlement was made in 1604 by Captain Charles Leigh on the Oyapok River now a part of French Guiana, but was not successful. In 1613 Robert Harcourt received a grant from King James of "all that part of Guiana or continent of America lying between the river of Amazones and the river of Dessequebe" not in possession of any Christian Power on terms of friendship with England, and May 19, 1627 a royal grant was made to the Duke of Buckingham and 55 other adventurers, Harcourt joining the company, but no permanent settlement made. In 1796 the British captured the Dutch settlements of Essequibo, Demerara, and Berbice, returned to Holland by the Peace of Amiens in 1802, taken again by the British in 1803, and formally ceded to them in Aug., 1814.

Sir Edward Brandis Denham, Governor.

GUIANA, DUTCH

Guiana, Dutch, or Surinam, Colony of the Netherlands, is situated on the north coast of S. America between 2 and 6° N. latitude, and 53° 50′ and 58° 20′ W. longitude, and bounded on the north by the Atlantic Ocean, on the east by the river Marowijne, which separates it from French Guiana, on the west by the river Corantijn, which separates it from British Guiana, and on the south by inaccessible forests and savannas to the Tumac-Humac Mountains, which separates it from Brazil. Area, 54,291 English square miles; population (December 31, 1929) 151,350 inclusive of the negroes and Indians living in the forests. Capital, Paramaribo, 46,953 inhabitants.

At the peace of Breda, in 1667, between England and the United Netherlands, Surinam was assured to the Netherlands in exchange for the colony of New Netherland in North America, and this was confirmed by the Treaty of Westminster of February, 1674. Since then Surinam has been twice in the possession of England, 1799 till 1802, when it was restored at the peace of Amiens, and in 1804 to 1816, when it was returned according to the Convention of London of August 13, 1814, confirmed at the peace of Paris of November 20, 1815, with the other Dutch colonies, except Berbice, Demerara, Essequibo, and the Cape of Good Hope.

The coast was sighted by Columbus in 1498. Dutch traders appeared on the rivers in 1598, and first settlement established on Corantyn River and fort built in 1613. In March, 1667 the Dutch captured the English settlements on the

Surinam River which were ceded to them the same year. The boundary with Brazil was settled by Treaty of May 5, 1906, ratified by the Dutch July 11, 1908, and with French Guiana by award of May, 1891, and Treaty of Sept. 30, 1915.

Dr. A. A. L. Rutgers, Governor, appointed April 1, 1928.

GUIANA, FRENCH

Guiana, French, Cayenne, French Colony, and penal settlement on northeast coast, bounded by the Atlantic Ocean on the north, on the west by Dutch Guiana, and on the east and south by Brazil, lying between 2 and 3° N. Lat. and 51 and 53° W. Long. The total area is about 34,740 square miles, and population according to the census of 1926, 47,341. The port of Cayenne, the capital, has population of 13,936. Since 1852 Cayenne has had a penal settlement, population in 1929, 4,000. The first French settlement was made in 1626 on the Sinnamary River by traders from Rouen. By Treaty with Portugal of April 11, 1713 France renounced all claim to territory between the Amazon River and the Oyapock, the present boundary between Brazil and French Guiana, further boundary agreements June 9, 1815, and Aug. 28, 1817 and award of Dec. 1, 1900 (see Brazil) and boundary with Dutch Guiana by award of May, 1891, of the Czar of Russia, in favor of the Dutch, and Treaty of Sept. 30, 1915 between the Netherlands and France as to boundary line and islands.

JUAN FERNANDEZ ISLANDS

Juan Fernandez Islands, in South Pacific Ocean 400 miles west by south from Valparaiso, Chile. The largest island is Mas-a-Tierra, 13 miles long and 4 miles wide, name from the Spanish "nearer land" to distinguish it from Mas-a-Fuera, "farther out" about 100 miles west, and Santa Clara Island southwest of Mas-a-Tierra. Santa Clara is between 4 and 5 miles in circumference, and Mas-a-Fuera 9 miles long and 6 miles wide. The islands were discovered by Juan Fernandez Nov. 22, 1574, and in 1749 were declared a Spanish possession, and in 1819 passed into possession of Chile when independence declared by Chile. In Sept., 1704 Alexander Selkirk, Scottish sailor, landed on the islands and remained there alone until Jan. 31, 1709, when he was found by Captain Woodes Rogers and taken off; his adventures suggested to Defoe the story of "Robinson Crusoe."

MALPELO ISLAND

Malpelo Island, bare rock, uninhabited, 270 miles southwest of the Gulf of Panama, about 1 mile in length and 700 yards wide, possession of Columbia. Shown on map of "Peru" published in 1530.

PARAGUAY

Paraguay, inland Republic shut in by forests, bounded on the northwest by Bolivia, north and east by Brazil, southeast, south and west by Argentina. The country is divided into 2 sections: the "Oriental" east of the Paraguay River, and the "Occidental" west of the same river. The Oriental section is divided into 12 departments, and the Occidental section (the Chaco) into 3 "commandancias militares." The population in 1930 was estimated at 857,337 including 37,500 in the Chaco.

The approximate area of Paraguay proper or "oriental section," which is situated between the rivers Paraguay and Alto Paraná, is estimated at 159,834 square kilometers, or 61,647 square miles. An area officially stated to be 100,000 square miles in extent, lying between the rivers Paraguay and Pilcomayo, known as the Chaco, is claimed by Paraguay, whose rights, however, are disputed by Bolivia. Serious friction developed in December, 1928, and the two countries broke off diplomatic relations, which were not fully resumed until May, 1930, when a judicial body, chosen by the Pan-American Union, took up the dispute. Boundary with Brazil was determined by treaty in 1929.

In 1929 the total population was estimated at 843,905 (including 37,500 in the Chaco, of whom Indians are roughly estimated at 15,000), with a density of 5 per square mile. The population of Paraguay (oriental section) consists of people of Mestizo, Indian, European (chiefly Spanish) and negro blood, the Mestizo largely predominating. On December 31, 1928, the urban population of the capital, Asunción (founded 1537), was 142,300, or about one-sixth of the total population; including the surrounding district, it was 228,600 or nearly one-fourth; other towns, as estimated in 1926, are Villarrica, 26,000; Concepción, 11,000; Encarnación, 7,500; San Pedro, 8,700; Luque, 13,000; Carapeguà, 12,000; Paraguarì, 10,000; Villa del Pilar, 6,000. These figures include the surrounding districts in each case, and are estimated.

Dr. José Patricio Guggiari, President.

1526

Sebastian Cabot explored the upper Parana and Paraguay rivers

1530

Portuguese expedition sent by the Governor of Brazil headed by Alejo Garcia first to explore the interior of Paraguay. Garcia killed by Indians

1537

Aug. 15, Juan de Ayolas built a fort at Asunción and

the La Plata colony moved to this site. For records of the colony *see* Argentina

1542

First missions established by the Franciscans

1586

Jesuit Fathers Angulo and Alfonso Barcena from Bolivia began mission in Guayra

1588

Francisco Solano made journey from Peru to establish Franciscan mission in Paraguay

1596

Jurisdiction of Governor Ramirez de Velazco of Tucuman (La Plata) extended to Paraguay. He designated de Saavedra substitute

1608

The Jesuits invited by Governor de Saavedra came to Asunción
King Philip III gave Jesuits the task of conversion of the Indians

1609

Oct. 10, Fathers Maceta and Cataldino left Asunción and after journey of 5 months reached the Paranapanema River former Jesuit mission center and founded mission of Loreto on the upper Parana

1618

Separation of the settlements south of the confluence of the Parana and Paraguay rivers made the separate province of the Rio de La Plata. The northern province received the name of Guaira but continued to be known as Paraguay. Manuel de Frias the first Governor

1627

Death of Governor Frias. Succeeded by Luis de Cespedes

1629

20 Jesuit missions had been established and a unique theocratic government of the Indians instituted. In this year the Paulistas from Brazil sacked the missions of San Antonio seizing the Indians to sell as slaves

1631

The reductions of San Miguel and Jesus Maria sacked by Spaniards seeking slaves
Led by Padre Truxillo and Ruiz Montoya 12,000 Indians migrated from the province of Guayra 500 miles to found new settlements distant from the Spaniards on the Upper Parana

1636

Pedro de Lugo Navarra, Governor
Indians defeated the attacks of the Mamelucos

1641

Gregorio de Hinostrosa became Governor on the death of Lugo

1659

Alonso Sarmiento, Governor (1659–63). Suppressed Indian revolt

1717

Diego de los Reyes appointed Governor

1721

Jan. 15, José de Antequera appointed to investigate the charges against Reyes and assume office of Governor at end of his term or sooner if his removal seemed desirable. He deposed and imprisoned Reyes 5 months before his term ended
Jesuit Fathers Patimo and Niebla ascended the Pilcomayo River for more than 250 Spanish leagues on exploring expedition

1722

Feb. 26, Reyes received dispatch from the Viceroy authorizing him to continue Governor until end of his 5 year term. Order resisted by Antequera

1723

Feb. 23 and June 7, Letters of Viceroy commanded Antequera to restore Reyes as Governor. General Garcia Ros charged with execution of this order
Nov. 10, Government at Asunción wrote the King urging the banishment of the Jesuits

1724

Aug. 10, Battle of Tebicuary. Antequera defeated General Ros

1725

March 5, Antequera fled from Paraguay on approach of General Zabala, Governor of Buenos Aires with troops, sent by the Viceroy. Martin de Barua, with this expedition, appointed Governor of Paraguay

1726

April 16, Antequera taken prisoner in Lima, Peru
Nov. 6, Royal decree separated 13 pueblos of the Jesuits of the Misiones district from Paraguay and placed them under the jurisdiction of Buenos Aires
——, Royal decree placed Jesuits again in possession of the College at Asunción

1731

July 5, Public execution of Antequera after long imprisonment

1732

Feb., Paraguayans expelled Jesuits from their College and plundered their property

1733

Sept. 15, Governor Ruiloba assassinated

1735

Jan., General Zabala sent by the Viceroy with troops from Buenos Aires restored order in Paraguay and reinstated Jesuits in their College

1740

Exploring expedition of Colonel José Espinola from Asunción into interior of the Chaco region

1750

Oct. 5, By the Treaty of Madrid Indian villages or reductions established by the Jesuits in Paraguay east of the Uruguay River ceded to Portugal in exchange for the fortified village of Colonia (Uruguay). Resisted by Jesuits

1754

May 21, Governor Andonægui began to move troops toward Indian missions to be ceded to Portugal under the Treaty

Oct. 3, Spaniards and Portuguese in first clash over surrender of missions

Nov. 12, Spanish troops withdrawn and Indians resisted cession

Nov. 18, Truce between Spanish forces and Indians

1756

Jan. 16, Spanish and Portuguese troops met near Rio Negro in second campaign to force Indians to cede villages to Portuguese

Feb. 10, Battle with Indians

May 9, Village of Viana taken by Spanish troops

May 17, Spanish troops entered San Miguel

1768

May 24–Sept. 16, Governor Bucarelli from Buenos Aires on armed expedition to Paraguay to deport Jesuits who made no resistance

1769

Dec. 8, Jesuits from Paraguay deported to Spain from Buenos Aires

1776

Aug. 1, Paraguay included in Viceroyalty of La Plata created

1784

July 14, The 13 pueblos of the Misiones returned to jurisdiction of Paraguay by Viceroy of La Plata

1792

Don Joaquim de Aloz y Bru, Intendente of Paraguay, built Fort Borbon on the Chaco side of the Paraguay River

1803

May 17, Royal decree united the 17 Uruguayan missions and the 13 Paraguayan missions into a separate province of Misiones independent of the Governors of Paraguay and Buenos Aires. B. de Velazco made Governor

1806

May 5, Velazco assumed office as Governor of Misiones province and of Paraguay

1811

Jan. 19, General Belgrano with liberating army from Buenos Aires attacked Spanish Government near Asunción and was defeated

March 9, General Belgrano's army captured

May 14, Don Pedro Juan Caballero attacked and occupied Asunción capturing the Spanish garrison

May 15, Governor Velazco as concession to the Revolution constituted a governing Junta of 3 persons with Fulgencio Yegros as head and Dr. Rodriguez de Francia, Secretary

June 9, Spanish Governor Velazco deposed and de Francia and Zeballos remained in charge of the Government

June 11, Assembly passed resolution renouncing allegiance to Spain

July, Independence declared and Junta at Asunción vested power of Government in two "consuls"

Aug. 14, Independence declared

1813

Oct. 1, Constitutional Convention met at Asunción

Oct. 12, Congress elected Don José Gaspar Rodriguez Francia and Don Fulgencio Yerges Yegros consuls. National flag adopted

Oct. 12, Treaty with Buenos Aires concluded recognized independence of Paraguay and its jurisdiction over part of Misiones

1814

Foreigners excluded and Paraguay shut off from the world commercially and politically until 1840

1816

June 1, Congress declared José de Francia "perpetual Dictator" of the Republic

1840

Sept. 20, Death of Dr. Francia. Provisional Government established under presidency of Don José Manuel Ortiz

1841

Jan. 23, Governing Junta of 4 replaced by a triumvirate

March 12, Triumvirate abolished by Congress and executive authority vested in 2 consuls to serve for 3 years, Carlos Antonio Lopez and Mariano Roque Alonzo

July 31, Treaty of friendship, commerce, and navigation signed in a boundary convention with Governor Ferre of Province of Corrientes in revolt against the Argentine Government

1842

Nov. 24, Decree abolished slavery from Jan. 1, 1843

Nov. 25, Congress of 400 deputies signed formal act declaring independence of Paraguay

1844

March 13, Congress adopted plan providing for 3 departments of Government and a President who should hold office for 10 years

March 14, Carlos Antonio Lopez became first President

March 27, Note from President Rosas of Argentina refused to recognize independence

Sept. 14, Brazil recognized independence of Paraguay

Oct. 7, Treaty of friendship, commerce, navigation, extradition, and boundaries with Brazil signed

Dec. 2, Treaty of navigation and commerce with Corrientes signed

1845

Jan. 8, Decree of President Rosas of Argentina denied right to any vessel to leave any port for Paraguay or Corrientes

Jan. 17 and April 16, Decrees of General Oribe prohibiting Paraguayan commerce

April–Sept. 1852, First periodical published the *Paraguayo Independiente*

Nov. 11, President Lopez concluded offensive and defensive alliance with Corrientes against the Argentine Confederation

Dec. 4, Declaration of war against President Rosas of Argentina

1850

Dec. 25, Secret Treaty of offensive and defensive alliance with Brazil signed

1852

April 27, Independence of Paraguay recognized by the United States

July 15, Treaty with Argentina signed of commerce and navigation and defining boundary. Not ratified by Argentine legislature because of clauses as to frontier in the Chaco region

July 17, Argentina recognized independence of Paraguay

1853

March 4, Treaties of friendship, commerce, and navigation signed with France and Great Britain

1854

March 27, Treaty of amity, commerce, and navigation with Sardinia signed

Aug. 1, Decree prohibited foreigners from purchase of land

1855

Feb. 1, American vessel "Water Witch" in the Parana River fired on by order of the President

April 27, Treaty of friendship, commerce, and navigation with Brazil signed. Boundary settlement postponed. Not ratified by Brazil

1856

April 6, Treaty of friendship, commerce, and navigation with Brazil signed. Provided for appointment of a boundary commission

July 15, Decree issued declared that foreign merchant vessels must have Paraguayan pilot from Asunción to first Brazilian port in Matto Grosso

July 29, Treaty of friendship, commerce, and navigation with Argentina signed

Aug. 10, Decree imposing dues which violated freedom of navigation agreed upon in Treaty with Brazil

1857

Nov. 20, Convention of Parana with Brazil signed

From this period until 1862 various disputes with foreign powers, the United States, France, and England

1859

Feb. 4, Treaty of friendship, commerce, and navigation with the United States signed and a Claims Convention

1861

Sept., First section of Central Railroad opened to Trinidad

1862

Sept. 10, Death of President Lopez. His son constituted Vice-President to act as President until Congress chose successor

Oct. 16, Francisco Solano Lopez elected constitutional President for 10 years by Congress

1863

April 17, General Flores in exile landed at Montevideo and began to gather insurgent army together

1864

June 17, President Lopez accepted position of mediator for Uruguay in dispute with Brazil. Rendered unnecessary by successful Thornton-Saraiva-Elezaldi mediation

Aug. 30, Note to Brazil protested occupation of Uruguay by Brazilian forces

Nov. 12, Brazilian steamer "Marques de Olinda" seized 50 miles above Asunción by Paraguayan war vessel

——, President Lopez notified Brazil that diplomatic relations were broken off and prohibited Brazilian vessels from Paraguayan waters

Nov. 28, Uruguayans united with rebel General Flores captured Salt

Dec. 24, Paraguayan expedition against Matto Grosso, Brazil embarked from Asunción

Dec. 26, Colonel Barrios, brother-in-law of President Lopez, commanding the army reached Coimbra in Matto Grosso near Brazilian frontier and the following day sent note to Brazilian commander demanding surrender

Dec. 27, Bombardment of Coimbra begun by Paraguayans

Dec. 30, Brazilians evacuated Coimbra during the night and Paraguayans occupied the town

1865

Jan. 14, Lopez asked permission of President Mitre for passage of troops across Corrientes, Argentine territory. Presented Feb. 6, refused Feb. 9

March 6, Congress convoked by decree of the President of Feb. 15 met at Asunción

March 18, War declared against Argentina, the entire Misiones territory claimed on basis of decree of May 17, 1803. War with Brazil approved by Congress

April 8, Foundation of "National Order of Merit" for reward for military and civil service

April 13, 5 Paraguayan war vessels made surprise attack on 2 Argentine gunboats in the port of Corrientes, Argentina and began bombardment of Corrientes

April 14, Corrientes occupied by General Robles and Paraguayan cavalry

May 1, Secret Treaty of Alliance signed by Argentina, Brazil, and Uruguay to overthrow Lopez

May 9, Argentine declaration of war against Paraguay

May 25, Corrientes assaulted and captured by Argentinian General Paunero

June 2, Paraguayan fleet retired to Humaita where Lopez joined them June 9

June 10, San Borja taken by Paraguayans commanded by Colonel Estigarribia and Major Duarte

June 11, Battle of Riachuelo. Brazilian fleet defeated Paraguayan squadron attacking near Corrientes

July 23, General Robles surrendered to General Barrios by order of Lopez was imprisoned and later with other officers shot

Aug. 6, Estigarribia entered Uruguayana evacuated by Allies

Aug. 17, Battle of Yatai. Paraguayans defeated by Generals Flores and Paunero. Major Duarte taken prisoner

Sept. 18, Paraguayan Colonel Estigarribia besieged by Allies in Uruguayana surrendered

Nov. 25, Lopez took command of the army in person at Paso La Patria

1866

Jan. 21, Successful raid of Paraguayans on Corrales

Feb. 20, Paraguayan raid sacked Itati

March 21, Allied fleet came up from Corrientes and formed in battle line from Corrales to mouth of the Paraguay

April 16, Crossing of Parana River begun by Allies

April 18, Allies took possession of Itapiru

April 23, Paraguayans burned and evacuated Paso La Patria which was occupied by Allies

May 2, First Battle of Esteros Bellaco (Tuyuti). Paraguayan attack north of Parana River repulsed

May 20, Allies crossing the Bellaco repulsed Paraguayan attack. Second Battle of Esteros Bellaco

May 20, Bombardment of Paso La Patria by Brazilian fleet

May 24, Allies defeated the Paraguayans at Tuyuti
——, Battle of the Bellaco. Paraguayans defeated by General Mitre

July 11, Battle of Yatatity Cora. Paraguayan attack defeated by Generals Mitre, Rivas, and Paunero

July 16, Paraguayan trenches carried in attack by General Souza and Colonel Conessa

July 18, Allied capture of Paraguayan redoubt after battle forced retreat of Paraguayans within the "Lines of Rojas"

Sept. 3, Fortified position of Curuzu taken by Allies after bombardment

Sept. 12, Interview of President Lopez with President Mitre at request of Lopez. No agreement reached

Sept. 22, Allied attack on Curupayty defeated. No engagements of consequence for 14 months after this

1867

Jan. 1, General Asboth, American minister in Buenos Aires, offered mediation of the United States

Aug. 15, Allied blockade of Humaita begun

Nov. 3, Lopez made successful attack on Tuyuti. Forced to retreat as reinforcements arrived from Tuyucue

1868

Feb. 18, Allied vessels forced passage of the river past Huamaita. Caxias captured the Cierva Redoubt

Feb. 20, General Flores shot in his carriage going through the streets of Montevideo

Feb. 22, Asunción bombarded by allied vessels

March 21, Allied General Argollo attacked and took Sauce

March 22, Outer fortifications of Humaita evacuated and occupied by Allies

July 21, Passage of 3 Allied ironclads up river past Humaita

July 24, Paraguayans evacuated Humaita during the night

July 25, Allies occupied Humaita

Aug. 5, Paraguayan army in the forests near Humaita surrendered by General Martinez to General Rivas

Aug. 28, Paraguayans evacuated the Tebicuary trenches on approach of Allies

Sept. 24, Villa del Pilar captured by Allies

Dec. 6, Allied advance took bridge across the Itaroro to Villeta defended by Paraguayans

Dec. 21, The Pikysyry trenches captured by the Allies

Dec. 27, Allies carried Lopez's fortified position on right bank of the Paraguay 50 miles from Asunción. He fled to Cerro-Leon

Dec. 30, Angostura last stronghold of the Paraguayans surrendered to the Marques de Caxias by Major Lucas Carrillo and George Thompson

Dec. 31, Allies occupied Asunción

1869

June 2, Agreement of Argentina, Brazil, and Paraguay as to Provisional Government of Paraguay

Aug. 15, Provisional Government established at Asunción by Allies, C. Laizaga, C. A. Rivarola, and J. D. de Bedoya

Oct. 2, Decree of the Provisional Government declared all slaves free

1870

March 1, Lopez, trying to escape, overtaken by Brazilian soldiers near the Aquidaban River and shot

June 20, Treaty of Peace signed with the Provisional Government

Aug. 15, Constituent Assembly met and a committee of 5 men headed by Juan Silvano Godoi appointed to frame a Constitution

Aug. 17, Decree after his death declared Lopez an outlaw

Nov. 25, Constitution promulgated. It declared dictatorship unlawful

Dec. 10, Cirilio A. Rivarola elected President, Cuyo Miltos, Vice-President

1871

Dec. 12, Salvador Jovellanos elected President

1872

Jan. 9, Boundary Treaty with Brazil signed ceded to Brazil territory north of the Rio Apa

Jan. 18, Treaty of friendship, commerce, and navigation with Great Britain

April 23, Department of Public Instruction created

Nov. 19, Argentina and Brazil signed Protocol on affairs of Paraguay

1873

March 23, Revolution headed by Caballo against Jovellanos Government

1874

Nov. 25, Juan Bautista Gill elected President

1875

April, President Gill assassinated. Succeeded by Señor Candido Bareiro and by Señor Saguier, Vice-President

1876

Feb. 3, Boundary Treaty with Argentina ceded Argentina region on left bank of the Parana River and on the right bank of the Paraguay River between the Bermejo and Pilcomayo rivers. The region between the Verde and Pilcomayo rivers including Villa Occidental to be submitted to arbitration of the President of the United States

1877

March 6, Extradition Treaty with Argentina signed

March 14, Consular Convention with Argentina

April 12, Higinio Uriarte, President

1878

Nov. 9, Treaty of commerce and navigation with Portugal signed

Nov. 12, Award of President Hayes in favor of Paraguay in claim to region of El Chaco between the Pilcomayo and Verde rivers

Nov. 25, Candido Bareiro, President

1879

Oct. 15, Boundary Treaty with Bolivia by which a strip of territory on the Paraguay River between Bahia Negra and the mouth of the Apa River ceded to Bolivia. Not ratified

1880

Sept. 10, Treaty of peace and amity with Spain signed by which Spain acknowledged the independence of Paraguay

1881

Nov. 25, General B. Caballero, President

1882

July 12, Decree authorized first law school. Opened in 1883

1883

April 20, Treaty with Uruguay recognized debt
April 30, Extradition Convention with Uruguay
June 7, Treaty of commerce and navigation with Brazil signed
Oct. 15, Act created a Medical Council of 4 physicians, 2 pharmacists, and a chemist to take care of the public health

1884

March 1, Telegraph from Paso to Asunción completed
Oct. 16, Treaty of friendship, commerce, and navigation with Great Britain signed

1885

Sept. 28, Treaty with Brazil as to Misiones boundary
Dec. 18, Land law promulgated

1886

Nov. 25, General P. Escobar elected President

1887

July 21, Treaty of commerce and navigation with Great Britain signed
Aug. 12, Protocol signed with the United States in claim as to the "Water Witch" by which Paraguay should pay $90,000. Failed to pass Congress. No settlement made
Sept. 2, Law provided for establishment of Agricultural Bank of Paraguay to protect and foster agriculture

1889

Sept. 24, Law established University of Asunción. Opened March 1890

1890

Sept. 25, Juan G. Gonzales elected President

1891

Oct. 22, Liberal revolt led by Major Vera and Deputy Machen suppressed
Dec. 22, Land tax law enacted

1893

Sept., Colonists from Australia arrive
Oct. 11, New Australia officially inaugurated

1894

Feb. 15, Convention of commerce and navigation concluded with Belgium
June 9, Coup d'état by which President Gonzales seized and deported. Vice-President Marinigo assumed executive office
Nov. 25, General J. B. Egusquiza inaugurated President

1895

Financial reforms

1898

Nov. 25, Emilio Aceval, President

1902

Jan. 9–11, Revolution deposed and imprisoned Dr. Emilio Aceval, led by his own Ministers, Colonel Juan Antonio Escurra, and Señor Fulgencio Moreno, all of the Colorado party

Jan. 30, Arbitration and pecuniary claims treaty with the United States signed
Nov. 25, Colonel Escurra inaugurated President

1903

May 18, Arbitration Treaty with Peru signed
Oct. 6, Immigration law enacted

1904

June 24, Law of private colonization enacted
Aug. 11, Revolt of party called the *Azules* or *Civicos* led by Benigno Ferreira was successful and Ferreira became President 4 months later

1905

Sept. 11, Agreement as to Pilcomayo River signed with Argentina

1906

July 24, Treaty of friendship and arbitration with Peru signed

1907

Jan. 12, Treaty of arbitration and *status quo* as to boundary with Bolivia signed
May 31, Adherence to Geneva Convention of 1864

1908

July 2–4, Revolution in Asunción successful led by Colonel Albino Jara, Liberal-Radical
July 4, President Ferreira resigned and Vice-President Emiliano Navero succeeded as President

1909

March 13, Treaty of arbitration with the United States signed

1910

Dec., Manuel Gondra inaugurated elected President

1911

Jan. 19, Coup d'état of Colonel Jara forced resignation of President Gondra. Congress elected Colonel Jara President
Feb. 24, Arbitration Treaty with Brazil signed
March 10, Martial law declared as result of revolt against Colonel Jara
May 10, Arbitration Treaty with Italy signed
July 5, Martial law again declared because of insurrection against Jara who was forced to resign. Congress elected Liberto Rojas to succeed him as provisional President

1912

Feb. 18, Diplomatic relations with Argentina resumed
March 1, Pedro Pena appointed provisional President to succeed Rojas captured by revolutionists
March 22, Rebels overthrew the Government forcing Pena and his Cabinet to take flight
March 25, Emilio Gonzales Navero appointed provisional President
April 27, Jara led revolt in the South but was mortally wounded in engagement at Paraguari
May 13, Rebels defeated near Asunción
Aug. 15, Eduardo Schaerer inaugurated President

1913

March 26, Extradition Treaty with the United States signed, Minister from the United States sent, resuming direct diplomatic relations after 8 years

April 5, Definitive Boundary Treaty Protocol with Bolivia signed providing for direct negotiations regarding disputed territory on right bank Paraguay River below mouth of the Apa

July 9, Electric tram service in Asunción inaugurated

Steam ferry established by the Central Paraguayan Railroad across the Alto Parana River from Encarnacion to Posadas connected with the Argentine Northeastern Railroad

1914

March 2, Convention renewed Arbitration Treaty with the United States

Aug. 2, Advancement of Peace Treaty with the United States

Aug. 24, New mining law enacted

Sept. 25, Bank of the Republic established

1915

Jan., Military revolt led by Escobar unsuccessful

July 19, Boundary Treaty with Bolivia signed

1916

Aug. 15, Manuel Franco elected President inaugurated

Nov. 30, Election law provided for 20 senators and 40 deputies

1917

Jan. 1, Law establishing compulsory military service came into effect

June 7, Act established Sunday rest for workers

1919

June 5, Death of President Franco. Succeeded by Vice-President José P. Montero

Sept. 26, Decree regulating immigration promulgated

Nov. 12, Red Cross Society founded

Nov. 17, Commercial Treaty with Japan signed

Dec. 26, Paraguay declared adherence to Covenant of the League of Nations

1920

Jan. 10, Paraguay became member of the League of Nations

Aug. 15, Manuel Gondra inaugurated elected President

Nov. 16, Financial moratorium declared for 2 months and extended to April

1921

Jan. 21, Decree gave temporary permission to vessels under foreign flags to engage in trade on Upper Parana River

July 22, Act exempted Mennonite settlers from the United States and Canada from military service and granted them 5,000 acres for colonization

July 26, Charter for colonization granted to Mennonites on upper Paraguay River in Chaco region

Oct. 15, Tax on livestock went into effect, 25 pesos each head of cattle slaughtered

Oct., Revolutionists force resignation of President Gondra. Vice-President Paiva assumed office

Oct. 29, Eusebio Hyala assumed office as President

1922

Feb. 24, Extradition Treaty with Brazil signed

Oct., Revolution which began in the summer ended

1923

Jan. 17, Formal opening of new reservoir and sewers at Asunción

April 10, Dr. Eligio Ayala elected provisional President by Congress on resignation of Dr. Eusebio Ayala, and new Cabinet headed by Modeste Cugiari

1924

Jan. 28, Electoral law amended

March 17, Congress elected Dr. Luis A. Riart as provisional President on resignation of Dr. Eligio Ayala

May 11, Eligio Ayala, Liberal, elected President and Manuel Burgos, Vice-President

Aug. 15, President Ayala inaugurated

Sept. 27, Customs tariff law promulgated

Oct. 31, Immigration law amended to restrict admission of undesirable persons

Nov. 14, Law enacted governing election of presidential electors, senators, and deputies

1925

Sept. 3, Law creating patent office promulgated

Oct. 25, Sunday and legal holiday rest law went into effect. Sale of alcoholic liquors prohibited on these days except at mealtimes in restaurants and hotels

1926

July 2, Law enacted for supervision of corporations. Regulating decree June 24, 1930

Sept. 20, Hurricane wrecked city of Encarnacion, 200 killed, $1,000,000 damage

1927

April 22, Diaz-Leon Protocol signed with Bolivia accepted offices of Argentina in delimitation of boundary in Chaco Boreal region

May 21, Boundary Treaty with Brazil

Aug. 30, Agreement with France signed as to military service

Sept. 7, Labor Accident Compensation law signed by the President

1928

July 12, Agreement with Bolivia signed to settle boundary dispute by peaceful means

Aug. 15, Dr. José P. Guggiari inaugurated President

Sept. 25, Treaty of commerce with Great Britain signed

Dec. 6, Bolivian and Paraguan troops in conflict in boundary dispute respecting Gran Chaco region at Fort Vanguardia. 22 Bolivians killed

Dec. 8, Diplomatic relations broken off by Bolivia and Paraguay

Dec. 10, Paraguay appealed to League of Nations for intervention in dispute with Bolivia

——, Pan-American Conference in Washington adopted resolution urging pacific settlement of dispute and appointed a peace committee to plan conciliation between Bolivia and Paraguay

Dec. 14, Pan-American Conference offered to mediate in dispute

Dec. 16, Mobilization ordered

Dec. 17, Mediation of Pan-American Conference accepted by Paraguay

1929

Jan. 3, Protocol of conciliation with Bolivia signed providing for arbitration of questions in dispute

Feb. 21, Direct telegraph connection with Brazil inaugurated

March 13–Sept. 13, Meeting of Commission of inquiry and conciliation in Washington, General Frank McCoy, President

April 23, Dispute with Brazil arising from occupation of Margarita Island by Brazilian troops settled by withdrawal of Brazilian force

June 25, First textile factory in Paraguay, for making of canvas used in shoes, opened by the President of the Republic

June 29, Paraguayan soldiers captured by Bolivians repatriated

July 2, Paraguay and Bolivia accept mediation of the United States, Mexico, Colombia, Cuba, and Uruguay in boundary dispute

Aug. 31, Draft arbitration convention submitted by Commission

Sept. 9, Draft arbitration convention rejected by Paraguay and Bolivia

Sept. 12, Further proposals for settlement of the Commission rejected by Paraguay and Bolivia

Oct. 1, Proposal of the United States, Mexico, Cuba, Colombia, and Uruguay for direct negotiation of the Chaco region boundary dispute. Accepted by Paraguay Oct. 5

1930

Jan. 16, Skirmish with Bolivian forces in Chaco Boreal. Paraguayan soldiers seized Fort Boqueron

Jan. 23, President Zaleski (League of Nations Council) appealed to Paraguay and Bolivia to settle dispute by pacific means

April 4, Peace Protocol with Bolivia signed as to resumption of diplomatic relations and exchange of Forts Boqueron (taken by Bolivians shortly after Paraguayans took Vanguardia) and Vanguardia

May 1, Diplomatic relations with Bolivia resumed

May 10, Boundary Protocol with Brazil signed as to territory in dispute

PERU

Peru, republic on west central coast on the Pacific Ocean north of Chile and south of Ecuador, with Brazil and Bolivia on the east.

There has been no enumeration of the population in recent years. The census returns of 1862 showed a total population of 2,487,916; that of 1876 put the number at 2,660,881, of whom about 13.8% were white, 1.9% negroes, 57.6% Indian, 24.8% mestizos (Cholos and Zambos), and 1.9% Asiatic, chiefly Chinese. An estimate in 1927 gives the population in that year as 6,147,000.

The population of the capital, Lima, according to the official census of December 17, 1920, was 176,467 and of Callao 52,843. The estimated population in 1928 of the principal cities was as follows: Lima city, 265,000; Lima and suburbs, 316,000; Callao, 77,000; Arequipa, 65,000; Cuzco, 40,000; Chiclayo, 35,000; Ica, 20,000; Trujillo, 30,000; Chincha, 20,000; Huancayo, 20,000; Ayacucho, 20,000; Iquitos, 25,000; Huaráz, 20,000; Piura, 15,000.

The areas of the 20 departments and 3 provinces (Callao, Tumbes, and Moquegua), according to estimates supplied by the Lima Geographical Society (1915), according to the census returns of 1867 (the latest official one) area 532,047 square miles, population 2,660,881.

There are, besides, many uncivilized Indians, but their numbers are unknown.

Augusto B. Leguia, President.

1522

Pascual de Andagoya in voyage southward from Panama the first to hear of the Inca Empire

1524

Nov. 14, Francisco Pizarro sailed from Panama to find Biru (Peru) followed by his partner in the enterprise Diego Almagro with supplies. Sailed beyond the point reached by Andagoya but forced to return for want of provisions

1525

Bartolome Ruiz sent by Pizarro discovered Gallo Island and proceeded to Bay of San Mateo and Coaque

1526

March 10, Agreement signed by Pizarro, Almagro, and Hernando Luque representing Gaspar de Espinosa, alcalde mayor of Panama, who advanced funds for second expedition. This voyage of Pizarro and Almagro with Bartolome Ruiz as pilot reached the San Juan. Ruiz on further voyage south from there the first European to cross the line of the equator on the Pacific Ocean. Pizarro eventually reached Tumbez, Peru

1529

July 26, Pizarro in Spain received concession from Juana, the Queen Mother, to conquer and settle Peru of which he was made Governor and Captain General. Almagro received title of Marshal and rank of hidalgo, Ruiz made Grand Pilot of the South Sea, and Luque, Bishop of Tumbez

1530

Jan. 19, Pizarro with his 4 brothers and other adventurers sailed from San Lucar for Panama

Dec. 28, Pizarro expedition sailed from Panama and arrived at Bay of San Mateo in 13 days where he landed troops and marched overland to Tumbez

1532

May 18, Pizarro left Tumbez, leaving garrison under Antonio Navarro and Alonzo Riquelme

May 24, First Spanish town founded of San Miguel de Tangarara on north bank of Chira River. Pizarro introduced system of encomiendas and repartimientos which made Indians on land alloted practically slaves of proprietor

Sept. 24, Pizarro marched from San Miguel to Caxamarca where Atahualpa, Inca Emperor, was encamped

Nov. 15, Pizarro reached Caxamarca. Notified by Atahualpa that he would visit the Spanish camp the following day

Nov. 16, Atahualpa on friendly visit made a prisoner and his attendants butchered by Spaniards

1533

Jan. 5, Hernando Pizarro left Caxamarca making journey to Pachecamac on the coast in search of treasure near site of present Lima

Jan. 30, Hernando Pizarro reached the temple of Pachecamac

March 25, Hernando Pizarro returned to Caxamarca with 27 loads of gold and much silver. Deducting the royal fifth it amounted to $17,500,000

April 14, Almagro reached Caxamarca from the coast with reinforcements of 150 men

Aug. 29, Atahualpa who had bought his freedom with a huge ransom strangled in the public square of Caxamarca by order of Pizarro on charge of murder of his brother Huascar and of planning an uprising. Pizarro named Tupac younger brother of Atahualpa as his successor

Oct. 4, City of Jauja founded by Pizarro

Nov. 15, Pizarro and Almagro entered Cuzco. He had Manco Capac, brother of Atahualpa, crowned Inca Emperor with ceremony

1534

March 24, The "Ayuntamiento" or municipal council installed at Cuzco. Juan and Gonzalo Pizarro among the 8 regidores. Father Valverde made Bishop of Cuzco

May 21, Royal grant to Diego Almagro of territory 200 leagues south of Pizarro's lands to be called New Toledo, its northern boundary the Santiago River. Under this concession Almagro claimed Cuzco

1535

Jan. 18, The first stones of Pizarro's new capital laid at the present Lima, called by him "Ciudad de Los Reyes" (City of the Kings). The first Alcaldes were Nicolas de Ribera and Juan Tello. The first stone of the Cathedral laid by Pizarro (Markham and Moses. Prescott and Winsor give Jan. 6)

April 18, Manco escaped from Cuzco and led revolt of Indians which was for a time successful. Manco besieged Cuzco for 5 months. Titu Yupani slain in attack of Indians on Lima

1537

April 18, Almagro claiming Cuzco took forcible possession of the city imprisoning Hernando and Gonzalo Pizarro

July 12, Almagro defeated Alvarado in battle at the Pachachaca bridge and brought him and his officers prisoners to Cuzco (Prescott. Markham 13)

Nov. 15, Negotiations as to boundaries of grants of Pizarro and Almagro referred to arbitration of friar Bobadilla who decided that Cuzco had been seized unlawfully and should be returned to Pizarro until ship could be sent to ascertain the latitude of the Santiago River. Not accepted by Almagro but the Pizarros freed pending decision of the King

1538

April 26, Battle of Las Salindas. The Pizarros defeated and captured Almagro

July 8, Almagro executed in public square at Cuzco

1539

June 24, Settlement founded at Guamanga by Pizarro

1541

June 26, Francisco assassinated by conspirators led by Juan de la Rada who declared the young son of Almagro Governor of Peru

1542

Sept. 16, Battle of Chupas. Vaca de Castro who had been sent from Spain to investigate affairs in Peru led army against Almagro who was defeated and later captured and executed. Vaca de Castro became Governor

Nov. 20, The "New Laws" due to efforts of Bishop Las Casas providing for abolition of the repartimiento system and forced labor of Indians promulgated by Charles V

1543

The Spaniards began working the silver mines of Porco

1544

May 17, Blasco Nunez Vela appointed first Viceroy of Peru and entrusted with enforcement of the "New Laws" for protection of the Indians, formally installed at Lima

Oct. 28, Gonzalo Pizarro leading revolt against the enforcement of the "New Laws" entered Lima on invitation of the Audiencia. Proclaimed Governor and Captain General of Peru

1545

Jan., The silver mines of Potosi discovered by Indian, Qualca, herding cattle

April 21, First claim registered for Centeno silver mine at Potosi by Villarroel and Guanca and rush begun to this region

May, Rebellion of Diego Centeno against Gonzalo Pizarro begun supporting the Viceroy

Oct. 20, Royal decree revoked the New Laws

Dec., Building of town of Potosi begun

1546

May 26, Pedro de Gasca sent by the King to establish peace sailed from Spain and arrived at Nombre de Dios, Panama July 17

June 18, Battle of Anaquito. Forces of the Viceroy, Blasco Nunez Vela, defeated by Gonzalo Pizarro and Francisco Carbajal. The Viceroy killed

Oct. 14, Letter of the inhabitants of Lima to Gasca said that their troubles had been settled under governorship of Pizarro

1547

June 13, Gasca landed at Tumbez with 1,000 soldiers and 22 ships

July 17, Pizarro left Lima marching to Arequipa

Oct. 26, Battle of Huarina. Gonzalo defeated forces of Centeno

1548

April 8, Battle of Jaguijaguana. Gonzalo defeated by army of Gasca, taken prisoner and executed. Carbajal hanged

April 11, Pedro de Gasca made triumphal entry into Cuzco

1550

Jan., Pedro de Gasca sailed for Spain leaving government in hands of the Audiencia after making redistribution of the *encomiendas* to the loyal

1551

May 12, University of San Marcos founded at Lima

Sept. 23, Second Viceroy, Don Antonio de Mendoza, arrived from Mexico and took charge of the Government

1552

July 21, Death of Viceroy Mendoza. The Audiencia again in charge

1553

Nov. 13, Giron Francisco Hernandez began rebellion

1554

May 20, Giron Francisco Hernandez defeated the government troops commanded by the Marshal Alvarado near Chuquinga

Oct. 24, Giron defeated at Pucara

Dec. 6, Giron captured and brought to Lima and presently executed

1556

June 29, Don Andres Hurtado de Mendoza, Marquis of Canete, assumed office at Lima as Viceroy appointed for 6 year term

1560

April, Don Diego de Acevedo y Zuniga, Count of Nieva, new Viceroy, arrived at Payta

1561

March 30, Death of the Marquis of Canete at Lima

1564

Feb. 20, Death of the Count of Nieva, Viceroy

Sept. 22, Lope Garcia de Castro appointed Governor and Captain General arrived at Lima

1569

Jan. 25, Decree established the Inquisition in Peru

Nov. 26, Lope Garcia de Castro succeeded by the new Viceroy, Francisco de Toledo (1569–81)

1570

Jan. 29, Members of the Inquisition made formal entry into Lima

1571

July 25, Papal Bull confirmed the establishment of the University of Lima

Oct. 4, The young Inca Tupac Amaru captured with many of his chiefs and brought to Cuzco and presently beheaded by order of the Viceroy

1573

Nov. 15, First auto-da-fé held in Lima by the Inquisition

1575

Death of Geronimo de Loaysa first Archbishop of Lima

1578

April 13, Second auto-da-fé

1581

May 24, Arrival of Dr. Toribio Mogrovejo, second Archbishop

Sept. 28, Don Martin Enriquez succeeded Toledo as Viceroy

1583

March 15, Death of Viceroy Enriquez. Government assumed by the Audiencia

1584

First book printed by Jesuits, a catechism by Antonio Ricardo at Lima

1586

Nov. 20, The next Viceroy Don Fernando Torres y Portugal, Count of Villar Don Pardo, reached Lima

1590

Jan. 6, Don Garcia Hurtado de Mendoza, Marquis of Canete, took office as Viceroy

1594

June 17, Don Beltran defeated English off the Bay of San Mateo and brought Sir Richard Hawkins a prisoner to Lima. He was later sent to Spain

1596

July 24, Don Luis de Velasco, Marquis of Salinas, took office as Viceroy (1596–1604)

1598

The University of San Antonio Abad founded at Cuzco

1604

The Count of Monterey, Viceroy, died within the year (1604–05)

1606

March 23, Death of Archbishop Mogrovejo

1607

Don Juan de Mendoza, Marquis of Montes Claros, Viceroy (1607–15)

1615

Don Francisco de Borjay Aragon, Prince of Esquilache, Viceroy (1615–21)

Dutch squadron of George Spilberg defeated Peruvian squadron and spent 3 days in Callao. Also took and sacked Huarmey and Paita

1616

College of San Geronimo founded

1617

Aug. 24, Death of Rosa, nun of Lima, canonized in 1671

1619

Silver mine of San Antonio de Esquilache near Lake of Titicaca opened

Dec. 20, Commercial Court of Esquilache established by ordinance of Viceroy

First settlement on the Maranon beyond the Pongo de Manseriche named Borja

1622

July 25, Arrival of Viceroy Don Diego Fernandez de Cordova, Marquis of Guadalcazar at Lima (1622–29)

Dutch fleet of Jacob L'Heremite which occupied Island of San Lorenzo and threatened Callao repulsed by Peruvians

1625

Oct. 19, The Cathedral at Lima formally dedicated

1628

Discovery of the benefits of the quinine in bark of the Chinchona trees by the Jesuits

1629

Jan., Arrival of Viceroy Luis Geronimo de Cabrera, Count of Chinchon (1629–39)

1630

Nov. 27, Earthquake at Lima

1631

Feb. 27, Auto-da-fé held at Lima

1632

Insurrection of the Urus or Ochozumas in southwest part of Lake of Titicaca led by Pedro Laime, chief, which continued until 1634

1635

Aug. 17, Auto-da-fé at Lima

1639

Jan. 23, Auto-da-fé at Lima. 80 victims
Dec. 18, Arrival of Viceroy Don Pedro de Toledo y Leyva, Marquis of Mancera (1639–48)

1648

Sept. 20, Garcia Sarmiento, Count of Salvatierra succeeded Mancera as Viceroy (1648–55)

1650

March 30, Earthquake destroyed Cuzco

1655

Feb., Luis Henrique de Guzman, Count of Alba de Liste, arrived at Lima as Viceroy (1655–61), founder of scientific studies in Peru
Nov. 13, Earthquake caused great destruction in Lima

1657

Silver mines of Laicacota discovered near Lake Titicaca

1661

Diego Benavides y de la Cueva, Count of Santistevan, Viceroy (1661–66)

1666

March, Death of Count of Santistevan at Lima

1667

Nov. 21, Pedro Fernandez de Castro Andrade y Portugal, Count of Lemos, Viceroy, made public entry into Lima (1667–72)

1668

Viceroy Lemos opened court at Laicacota and judgment passed on 42 persons including José de Salcedo who had amassed great wealth from the silver mines. All executed and the town razed. Descendants of Salcedo had this judgment reversed 40 years later

1672

Dec. 6, Death of Count of Lemos, Viceroy. Government assumed by the Audiencia

1674

Baltazar de la Cueva, Count of Castellar, Viceroy (1674–78)

1678

July 7, Dr. Melchor de Linan y Cisneros, Archbishop, took charge of the Government as the Viceroy was put on trial which lasted 2 years for allowing commercial intercourse with Mexico and introduction of articles from China. He was finally acquitted

1681

Nov. 20, Melchor de Navarra y Rocaful, Duke of La Palata, Viceroy, arrived (1681–89)

1684

Feb. 20, Ordinance of Viceroy regulated treatment of Indians to prevent their spoliation by clergy

1687

Oct. 20, Earthquake destroyed Lima

1689

Aug. 15, Arrival of Don Melchor Portocarrero Laso de la Vega, Count of Monclova, Viceroy (1689–1705)

1705

Sept. 22, Death of Viceroy Monclova

1707

July 7, Arrival of Manuel Oms de Semanat, Marquis of Castel dos Rios, Viceroy (1707–10)

1709

July 16, Peruvian squadron sailed from Callao in search of English pirates but failed to meet enemy

1710

April 22, Death of Viceroy Castel dos Rios
Aug. 30, Dr. Diego Ladron de Guevara, Bishop of Quito succeeded as Viceroy (1710–16)

1713

March 13, By Treaty of Utrecht France and England allowed to trade in ports of Peru and Chile

1716

March 2, Guevara deposed as Viceroy. Succeeded by Audiencia
Oct. 5, Carmine Nicolas Caraccioli, Prince of Santo Bono, entered Lima bringing orders to destroy all foreign trade in the Pacific. Succeeded Guevara as Viceroy (1716–20)

1720

Jan. 26, Dr. Morcillo Rubio de Aunon, Archbishop of Charcas, Viceroy (1720–24)

1724

May 14, Arrival of Don José de Armendariz, Marquis of Castelfuerte, Viceroy (1724–36)

1731

July 5, Execution of Antequera in Lima. *See* Paraguay

1736

Scientific expedition of La Condamine in the Amazon basin
Jan. 4, Arrival of the Marquis of Villa Garcia of the House of Mendoza (1736–45)

1739

Aug. 20, Royal decree made territorial line between vice-royalties of New Granada and Peru

1740

Sept. 18, English Captain Anson sacked and looted Paita

1741

May 19, Don Antonio Ulloa discovered platinum in the sands of the Pinto River

1745

July 12, General Don José Antonio Manso, Count of Superunda, entered Lima as Viceroy (1745–61)

1746

Oct. 28, Earthquake destroyed city of Lima. More than 1,000 persons perished

1761

Oct. 12, Don Manuel de Amat y Junient entered Lima as Viceroy (1761–76)

1767

Aug. 20, Arrival of royal orders for expulsion of Jesuits
Sept. 8, Jesuits deported

1768

Aug. 27, City of Cuzco in report to the King protested against the oppression of the "corregidores" agents in charge of the Indians

1776

July 17, Manuel de Guirion, Viceroy, arrived at Lima (1776–80)

1780

Jan. 10, Augustin de Jaurequi, Viceroy, arrived (1780–84)
Nov. 4, Revolt of Tupac Amaru, descendant of the Incas, against Spaniards. He captured Don Antonio Aliga, corregidor of Tinta, who had cruelly oppressed the Indians and formally tried and executed him
Nov. 13, Indians defeated Spaniards in battle in valley of Vilcamayu
Nov. 18, Battle of Sangarara in which Indians defeated Spaniards. Don Tiburcio Landa, Governor of Paucartambo, Corregidor Cabrera, and Indian ally, Juan Sahuaraura, killed
Nov. 27, From his headquarters at Tinta Tupac Amaru issued edict stating the grievances of his people

1781

Jan. 3, Letter of Tupac Amaru to the cabildo and bishop of Cuzco stating his position and desire to end abuses against Indians
Jan. 8, Indecisive battle near Cuzco
Feb. 11, Indian attack on Paucartambo unsuccessful
March 27–June, First siege of La Paz by Indians
April 6, General del Valle defeated Indians and entered Tinta. Tupac Amaru captured by treachery of Indian soon after this battle
May 9, Diego Tupac Amaru began siege of Puno
May 18, Tupac Amaru executed
May 26, Spaniards evacuated Puno and began retreat to Cuzco
Aug.–Oct. 17, Second siege of La Paz by Indians
Dec. 11, Diego Tupac Amaru, promised full pardon, surrendered to General del Valle

1782

Sept. 4, Death of General del Valle. Succeeded in command by Don Gabriel de Aviles

1783

July 19, Diego Tupac Amaru and other members of the Inca family hanged on trumped up charges by Spaniards who had never intended to keep faith with them

1784

April 3, Arrival of Teodor de Croix, Viceroy (1784–90)
Reforms inaugurated for which Tupac Amaru had striven. The office of corregidor abolished

1785

Jan. 24, Intendente system established, and division of Peru into 7 provinces called *intendencias*
Dec. 8, Royal cedula ordered adoption of mining ordinances of New Spain of May 22, 1783 in Peru

1790

Jan. 8, Francisco Gil de Taboada y Lemus, Viceroy (1790–96)

1791

Jan. 1, First issue of periodical called the *Mercurio Peruano*

1796

June 5, Don Ambrosio O'Higgins, Marquis of Osorno, made public entry into Lima as Viceroy (1796–1801)

1801

Gabriel Aviles, Marquis of Aviles, Viceroy after death of O'Higgins (1801–06)

1802

July 15, Royal cedula for administration of Peru

1806

Don José Fernando Abascal, Viceroy (1806–16)

1813

The Inquisition ended in Peru. The people of Lima forced their way into the palace, liberated the prisoners, and broke the instruments of torture

1814

Aug. 3, Uprising of Indians at Cuzco led by Pumacagua joined by a number of patriots
Dec. 9, Spanish General Ramirez entered Arequipa evacuated by Pumacagua and the patriots

1815

March 11, Ramirez defeated the Indians and patriots in the Battle of Umachiri
March 25, Ramirez entered Cuzco. Pumacagua captured and hanged soon after the battle
Nov. 29, Army under Rondeau defeated by royalists at Sipe Sipe, Upper Peru

1816

July 7, General Don Joaquim de la Pezuela entered Lima as Viceroy

1819

Feb. 28, Lord Cochrane with fleet and soldiers commanded by Major Miller from Chile repulsed by Spanish garrison at Callao
June 27, Patriot troops won battle at Paya
Nov. 16, Ensign Vidal with Chilean troops captured Santa north of Callao, defeating Spaniards

1820

May 26, Patriots including Riva Aguero, Carrasco, and Pezet imprisoned. Released after 3 months because of lack of proof of plot
Aug. 21, Liberating army of General San Martin with Lord Cochrane's fleet sailed from Valparaiso for Peru
Sept. 8, First division of San Martin's army landed at Pisco south of Callao
Oct. 5, General Arenales marching from Pisco entered Yca
Oct. 26, San Martin's army reëmbarked at Pisco and proceeded to Huacho
Nov. 5, Lord Cochrane captured the largest Spanish frigate, the "Esmeralda" off Callao. Renamed the "Valdivia"
Nov. 9, San Martin established headquarters at Huaura
Dec. 6, General Arenales defeated royalists at Cerro Pasco northwest of Lima

1821

Jan. 29, Resignation of Viceroy Pezuela forced by Spanish generals in camp at Asnapuquio. They declared Don José de la Serna Viceroy

May 3, General San Martin offered terms of peace to General Abreu and Viceroy La Serna on condition of recognition of independence of Peru

May 22, Major Miller defeated the Spaniards near Mirabe

May 23, Armistice arranged for peace negotiations. Ended without result in June

July 12, General San Martin made triumphal entrance into Lima evacuated by royalists

July 15, Act of Independence signed by assembly of prominent citizens

July 22, General San Martin formally proclaimed the independence of Peru

Aug. 2, San Martin occupied Pisco

Aug. 3, San Martin declared "Protector" of Peru with supreme military and civil power

Aug. 12, Proclamation of San Martin that all children born after July 28 of slaves declared free

Aug. 28, Decree of San Martin abolished forced labor of Indians

Aug. 29, General San Martin founded a library at Lima

Sept. 21, Callao surrendered to San Martin

Oct. 8, General San Martin issued provisional decree as to government

1822

Jan. 12, General San Martin in Lima founded the Order of the Sun

April 22, Surprise and capture of large body of revolutionists by Canterac at Ica

July 6, Treaty of "perpetual union, league, and confederation" signed at Lima with Colombian Federation

July 26, Meeting of San Martin with Bolivar at Guayaquil which resulted in withdrawal of San Martin from South American affairs in favor of Bolivar

Sept. 20, Constituent Congress met. General San Martin resigned to this body and left Peru, leaving Bolivar in full possession. A "Junta Gubernativa" appointed, the Count of Vista Florida, General Lamar, General Alvarado, Colonel Don José de la Riva Aguero, acting as President

Dec. 16, Congress adopted the "Bases of the Political Constitution"

Dec. 31, Decree of Torre Tagle that all Spaniards not natives should leave the country

1823

Jan. 19, Expedition to southern Peru of General Rudesindo Alvarado reached Moquegua where he failed to dislodge the royalists under Valdez and Canterac encamped on the heights of Torata (Battle of Torata)

Feb. 26, Don José de la Riva Aguero elected first President of the republic by Congress

Feb. 28, President Riva Aguero inaugurated

March 4, Santa Cruz made commander-in-chief of the army

March 18, Agreement signed at Guayaquil by which Bolivar agreed to aid Peruvian patriots

June 16, General Canterac entered Lima evacuated by the patriots

June 19, President Riva Aguero deposed and Don José Bernardo Tagle, Marquis of Torre Tagle, hench-

man of Bolivar, given executive authority as "supreme delegate." General Sucre the real power took office as commander-in-chief

July 17, Canterac evacuated Lima

Aug. 25, Santa Cruz defeated royalists under Valdez at Zepita but obliged to make disastrous retreat as reinforcements arrived

Sept. 1, General Bolivar entered Lima and was given supreme power

Nov. 12, New Constitution promulgated

Nov. 14, Law enacted declaring that any articles of the Constitution incompatible with authority of Bolivar should be suspended

Nov. 25, Riva Aguero, the legitimate President, with the loyal majority of the Congress arrested at Truxillo and presently at instigation of Bolivar sentenced to be executed as a traitor but by intervention of Admiral Guise allowed to retire to Europe

1824

Feb. 7, Revolt of garrison at Callao demanding pay made royalist Colonel Casariego Governor

Feb. 10, The Congress of Sucre dissolved themselves and conferred absolute dictatorship on Bolivar. The Constitution of 1823 abolished

March 3, Spanish General Monet invited by the revolting garrison at Callao took possession of Callao Castle

Aug. 6, Battle of Junin. Bolivar with General Sucre, and Miller defeated the Spanish army of Canterac

Aug. 24, O'Higgins, the Liberator, driven from Chile joined Bolivar's army at Huancayo. He was later granted a pension and an estate by the Peruvian Government

Dec. 3, La Serna and Sucre in engagement in valley of Acrocos

Dec. 7, Famous circular of Bolivar from Lima addressed to Governors of Colombia, Mexico, Argentina, Chile, and Guatemala invitation to Congress at Panama

Dec. 9, Battle of Ayacucho. General Sucre defeated the royalists ending Spanish rule in Peru. General Canterac signed capitulation and with La Serna and the other generals became a prisoner of war

Dec. 25, Patriot army reached Cuzco, marching to liberate Upper Peru (Bolivia)

1825

Feb. 8, Supreme Court founded

Feb. 10, Congress assembled and Bolivar resigned dictatorship but this was not accepted

March 29, Congress made up entirely of supporters of Bolivar made him President for life

Aug. 6, Electoral College voted abrogation of Constitution of 1823

——, Separation of Bolivia from Peru. See Bolivia

Oct. 8, Attack of Admiral Martin Guise on royalist vessels off Callao Castle

1826

Jan. 19, Spanish General Rodil surrendered Callao Castle besieged by the patriots for 13 months

May 2, Appointment of James Cooley as chargé d'affaires to Peru confirmed by the United States Senate

Sept. 3, General Bolivar left Lima for Guayaquil, leaving General Lara in command of his Colombian troops

Nov. 30, Bolivar's Constitution declared adopted and Bolivar elected President. Promulgated Dec. 8

1827

Jan. 26, Revolt headed by Colonel Bustamente arrested Lara and put him and troops on board a vessel for Guayaquil freeing Peru from foreign dictation

June 4, Congress met at Lima. Bolivar's Constitution discarded and the Constitution of 1823 with some modifications declared in force June 27

Aug. 24, General José de Lamar y Cortazar elected President and the Count of Vista Florida, Vice-President by Congress

1828

March 18, Congress adopted the "Political Constitution of the Peruvian Republic"

May 8, General Gamarra sent by President Lamar to reverse Bolivar's arrangements in Bolivia entered La Paz

June 2, Treaty of Piquiza signed by which Bolivia agreed that a new President should be elected in place of General Sucre and all Colombian troops leave the country and a new Constitution be framed to take place of that of Bolivar

July 3, General Bolivar declared war on Peru

1829

Jan. 21, Peruvians captured Guayaquil. Admiral Guise killed in attack

Feb. 27, Battle at Portete de Tarqui. General Sucre with Colombian troops victorious

Feb. 28, Peace signed at Giron after General Sucre had defeated Peruvians. Agreed to surrender Guayaquil.

June 7, Revolt against President Lamar headed by Gamarra

June 9, Lamar put on board steamer and landed in Central America

Aug. 31, General La Fuente who had assumed power assembled a Congress at Lima to which he resigned his authority. Gamarra made Provisional President

——, General Agustin Gamarra took office as President with General La Fuente as Vice-President

Sept. 6, President Gamarra left to subdue revolt in Cuzco leaving General La Fuente in charge

Sept. 22, Boundary Treaty with Colombia signed

1830

Oct. 11, Death of ex-President Lamar in Costa Rica

1831

April 16, Troops made attack on house of Vice-President La Fuente accused of plot against Gamarra. He escaped to vessel and remained in exile

Nov. 8, Treaty of Tiquina signed with Bolivia regulating commerce

1832

July 12, Commercial Treaty with Ecuador signed

Nov. 16, Treaty of amity, commerce, and navigation with Mexico

1833

Dec. 30, Don Luis José Orbegoso inaugurated as President

1834

Jan. 4, Ex-President Gamarra proclaimed General Bermudez provisional President and troops from garrison at Lima took possession of Congress declaring the election of Orbegoso unconstitutional

Jan. 28, Gamarra and Bermudez evacuated Lima, marching to Xauxa

Jan. 29, President Orbegosa entered Lima in triumph

March 10, General Orbegosa took command of army, leaving the Count of Vista Florida in charge of the Government

April 17, Battle near Huaylacucho in which Bermudez forced retreat of army of Orbegosa commanded by General Miller

April 23, The "Embrace of Maquinhuayo," Army of Bermudez made submission to the President. Bermudez and Gamarra fled from the country

June 10, New Constitution promulgated

June 23, Dr. Jorge de Benavente, first republican archbishop installed at Lima

Nov. 9, President Orbegosa left Lima to subdue revolt in the south. Vice-President Count of Vista Florida left in charge

1835

Jan. 1, Revolt of garrison at Callao, declaring in favor of General La Fuente returned from exile to incite revolt

Jan. 2, Callao Castle stormed by General Salaverry and mutiny suppressed

Jan. 20, Treaty of friendship, commerce, and navigation with Chile signed

Feb. 25, General Salaverry led revolt against Orbegoso and proclaimed himself supreme chief

May 20, Ex-President Gamarra with Colonel Lopera occupied Cuzco

June 24, Treaty with Bolivia signed. President Santa Cruz undertook to enter Peru to restore order and Confederation of North and South Peru with Bolivia to be proclaimed

Aug. 13, Santa Cruz defeated Lopera and Gamarra near Cuzco, the Battle of Yanacocha

Oct. 19, Gamarra who had escaped to Lima banished to Costa Rica

Dec. 30, General Vidal in opposition to Salaverry entered Lima

Dec. 31, General Salaverry at head of army entered Moquega

1836

Jan. 30, President Santa Cruz of Bolivia entered Arequipa evacuated by Salaverry

Feb. 4, Salaverry successful in engagements at Uchumayu

Feb. 7, Battle of Socabaya. Salaverry defeated by Santa Cruz

Feb. 9, Salaverry and Cardenas surrendered to General Miller under promise their lives should be spared

Feb. 18, Santa Cruz ordered execution of Salaverry, General Fernandini, Colonels Solar, Cardenas, Rivas, Carillo, Valdivia, Moya, and Picoaga, declaring Miller had no authority to make convention sparing their lives

March 17, Assembly at Sicuani declared establishment of independent State of South Peru of departments of Arequipa, Ayacucho, Cuzco, and Puno with Santa Cruz as "Supreme Protector"

Aug. 11, Assembly at Huari proclaimed State of North Peru with Santa Cruz as "Protector"

Aug. 21, Chilean Captain Victorino Garrido in time of peace and by surprise attack at night captured the Peruvian fleet of 3 vessels lying unarmed off Callao

Oct. 12, Chileans defeated by General Cerdena in attack on Arequipa

Oct. 28, Santa Cruz's Confederation proclaimed at Lima, General Orbegosa to be sub-President of Lima and North Peru and General Herrera of South Peru

Nov. 11, Chile declared war on Peru
Nov. 30, Convention of commerce and navigation signed with the United States and Bolivia

1837

May 1, Date of Constitution of the Confederation signed at Tacna
Aug. 6, Chilean force including Peruvian exiles with Gamarra, La Fuente and Torrico landed at Ancon and marched on Lima. Gamarra in Lima proclaimed provisional President
Sept. 18, Torrico defeated a Bolivian army at Matucana
Nov. 17, Treaty of Paucarpata signed by which Chileans allowed to depart on condition the war should not be renewed and the warships returned by Chilean General Blanco Encalada

1838

Nov. 9, Santa Cruz, the "Protector," entered Lima evacuated on his approach. Orbegosa who had been defeated in engagement with Chileans had taken a vessel to Guayaquil in 1837

1839

Jan. 6, Santa Cruz defeated in engagement at bridge of Buin
Jan. 20, Santa Cruz defeated in Battle of Jungay by General Bulnes, Chilean in command of the allied armies. Santa Cruz escaped to Arequipa
Feb. 20, Decree of Santa Cruz dissolved the Confederation
Feb. 22, General Miller embarked with Santa Cruz on the H.M.S. "Samarang"
Feb. 24, Provisional President Gamarra entered Lima
March 8, Callao Castle surrendered to Gamarra
Aug. 15, Constituent Congress met and declared General Agustin Gamarra constitutional President
Nov. 10, New Constitution proclaimed

1841

Jan. 4, Colonel Manuel Ignacio Vivanco in the south headed revolt against Gamarra, taking the title of "Regenerator"
March 17, Claims Convention with the United States signed
March 25, Vivanco successful in engagement with General Castilla, commanding the government troops at Cachamarca
April 5, Castilla entered Arequipa after defeating the "Regenerator" at Cuevillas
July 6, War declared on Bolivia with object of expelling the adherents of Santa Cruz
Oct. 24, General Roman defeated Bolivian army at Mecapaca
Nov. 20, Battle of Yngavi. Peruvians defeated by Bolivians and Gamarra killed, Don Manuel Menendez became acting President

1842

July 7, Peace with Bolivia signed at Acora
July 28, Generals La Fuente and Vivanco refusing to recognize Menendez proclaimed General Francisco Vidal President
Sept. 26, Vidal troops in encounter with force of General Torrico who had deposed Menendez and proclaimed himself President at Incahuasi
Oct. 17, Troops of Vidal defeated forces of Torrico and San Roman at Agua Santa

1843

April 8, General Manuel I. Vivanco entered Lima and was proclaimed Supreme Director after resignation of Vidal who had handed over government to Justo Figuerola who had been deposed by Colonel Arambu declaring for Vivanco
Oct. 28, General Ramon Castilla declaring against Vivanco in favor of legal President, the first Vice-President of Vidal namely Menendez, met General Guarda at San Antonio and by strategy procured his surrender

1844

July 17, Army of Vidal defeated by Castilla at Carmen Alto
Aug. 10, Don Manuel Menendez, acting-President convoked a Congress for election of a President

1845

April 16, Congress met
April 20, Congress declared General Ramon Castilla President

1847

Dec. 11, International Congress met at Lima

1848

Dec. 11, Treaty of friendship and commerce with Bolivia signed

1850

June 30, President Castilla laid foundation stone of the first railroad in South America, from Callao to Lima

1851

April 5, Railroad from Callao to Lima opened
April 20, José Rufino Echenique elected President
July 26, Treaty of commerce and navigation signed with the United States
Oct. 23, Treaty of commerce and navigation and boundary with Brazil signed

1852

Oct. 23, Note of Secretary of Foreign Affairs to the United States stated claims of Peru to the Lobos Islands
Nov. 16, Note of American Secretary of State, Edward Everett, recognized sovereignty of Peru over Lobos Islands

1854

Jan. 7, Battle of Saraja. Revolt of Don Domingo Elias against the Government defeated
June 1, Ex-President Castilla, joining revolt against Echenique, issued decree accepting position of provisional President
July 5, Castilla decreed abolition of tribute paid by the Indians
Aug. 2, Castilla in engagement at bridge of Iscuchaca forced Echenique to retreat
Nov. 30, Government forces under General Moran repulsed in attack on Arequipa and Moran captured and shot the following morning
Dec. 3, Castilla decreed emancipation of negro slaves

1855

Jan. 5, Battle of La Palma. Castilla victorious proceeded to Lima
July 14, Castilla elected constitutional President by Congress
Oct. 13, New Constitution adopted. Ratified Nov. 25, 1860

1856

July 22, Treaty respecting neutrality at sea signed with the United States

Oct. 31, Revolt begun at Arequipa declaring for Vivanco as President. Suppressed by Castilla

Nov. 16, The fleet joined the revolt but the country remained loyal

1857

July 4, Treaty with the United States as to whaling ships signed

1858

March 5, Castilla attacked Arequipa which had been taken by Montero and Vivanco

March 7, Arequipa capitulated. Vivanco escaped in disguise

1859

Aug. 27, Contract signed providing for introduction of 25,000 Irish immigrants

Nov. 22, Contract signed providing for importation of Spanish immigrants

1860

Nov. 10, Revised Constitution adopted and signed. Promulgated Nov. 13

Dec. 31, Contract signed providing for introduction of German immigrants

1861

Oct. 31, Death of General Miller who had returned to Peru in 1859

1862

Oct. 24, General Miguel San Roman took office as President on resignation of Castilla

Dec. 20, Claims Convention with the United States signed. King of the Belgians named as arbitrator

1863

Jan. 12, Claims Treaty with the United States signed

April 3, Death of President San Roman. Succeeded by second Vice-President General Pedro Diaz Canseco

Aug. 5, First Vice-President General J. A. Pezet returned from Europe took office as President

Nov. 5, Treaty of friendship and commerce with Bolivia signed

1864

Jan. 11, The Government issued invitations to Governments of the American Republics to a Congress at Lima

April 14, Spanish Admiral Pinzon seized the Chincha Islands in settlement of claims

Sept. 5, Commercial and customs treaty with Bolivia signed

Oct. 28, International Congress at Lima opened

1865

Jan. 9, Public Land law enacted

Jan. 27, Negotiations for return of Chincha Islands concluded with Spain. Independence of Peru recognized

Feb. 6, Castilla who had violent quarrel with Pezet because of the humiliating terms of arrangement as to Chincha Islands seized, placed on vessel, and sent to England

Feb. 28, Insurrection in Arequipa begun

Nov. 6, President Echenique resigned and went on board vessel sailing for England to avoid civil war because of revolt organized at Arequipa by Colonel

Mariano I. Prado joined by second Vice-President Canseco

Nov. 8, Prado proclaimed President

Dec. 5, Alliance with Bolivia and Chile and Ecuador against Spain

1866

Jan. 14, Peru declared war against Spain

Feb. 6, Spanish fleet attacking Peruvian and Chilean vessels near Abtao repulsed

April 25, Spanish vessels appeared before Callao and declared blockade on the 27th

May 2, Bombardment of Callao by Admiral Mendez Nunez successfully defended by General Prado. Spanish fleet withdrew after terrific battle

May 9, Spanish fleet sailed for Spain from San Lorenzo

Dec. 12, Offensive and defensive alliance with Chile concluded

1867

April 15, Revolts at Lima against religious toleration

May 30, Ex-President Castilla died of fever leading revolt against President Prado illegally President declaring in favor of legal President Canseco

Aug. 31, New Constitution dated Aug. 29 proclaimed

1868

Jan. 7, Prado defeated in attempt to take Arequipa held by revolutionists Canseco and Balta. Resigned the presidency and escaped to Chile. Canseco assumed executive office

May 4, Concession granted to Henry Meiggs, American, for construction of a railroad between Arequipa and port of Mejia

Aug. 2, Colonel José Balta declared elected President

Dec. 4, Claims Treaty with the United States signed

Dec. 17, Decree proclaimed free navigation to merchant vessels of all nations of all rivers of the Republic

1870

Feb. 10, Treaty of commerce and navigation with Colombia signed

July 23, Treaty of commerce and customs with Bolivia signed

Sept. 6, Treaty of commerce and navigation with the United States signed

Sept. 12, Treaty of extradition with the United States signed

Dec. 31, Formal opening of the railroad from Arequipa to Mejia

1871

May 31, Railroad from Pisco to Yca opened

Oct., Gold mines discovered at Huacho

1872

July 1, National exhibition at Lima opened

July 22, Revolt of the Gutierrez brothers at Cuzco. The President seized and imprisoned

July 23, Tomas Gutierrez proclaimed himself supreme chief

July 26, Silvestre Gutierrez shot by a mob at the railroad station and in reprisal Marceliano Gutierrez murdered the imprisoned President Balta. Tomas and Marceliano then killed by mob

July 28, Vice-President Mariano Zavallos assumed office as President

Aug. 2, Don Manuel Pardo inaugurated constitutional President, first civilian to hold the office

Dec. 17, Decree authorized the establishment of European immigrant associations to facilitate immigration to Peru

1873

Feb. 6, Secret Treaty of defensive alliance with Bolivia signed

May, Armed riots in Lima at execution of Colonels Ganrio and Zevallos as rebels

June 5, Agreement with the United States signed as to Treaty of 1870

1874

Jan. 1, First locomotive arrived at Lake Titicaca over new line crossing the Andes at elevation of 14,660 feet

Feb. 11, Treaty with Brazil signed, mutual cession of territory

March 9, Treaty of friendship, commerce, and navigation with Argentina signed

May 4/16, Treaty of commerce and navigation with Russia signed

June 26, Immigration Treaty with China signed

Nov. 1, Insurgents led by Nicolas de Pierola landed at Pacasmayu

Dec. 3, Pierola defeated at Sorota

Dec. 23, Treaty of friendship, commerce, and navigation with Italy signed

1875

Oct. 27, Fire destroyed a large part of City of Iquique

1876

Aug. 2, Colonel Don Mariano Ignacio Prado inaugurated as constitutional President

Dec. 28, Trujillo Railroad opened between Chocope and Ascope

Census taken gave population as 2,673,075

1877

Sept. 30, Death of Henry Meiggs at Lima

Dec. 9, International Congress of Jurists met at Lima

1878

May 27, Nicolas de Pierola seized warship "Huascar" by a ruse and occupied port of Pisagua in Tarapaca. In 2 hour engagement with Peruvian squadron but escaped

May 29, The "Huascar" surrendered by insurgents

Nov. 16, Assassination of ex-President Pardo

1879

April 5, Chile declared war on Peru and Bolivia. *See* Chile

May 21, The "Huascar" commanded by Michael Grau the one warship left to Peru after battle of this date guarded coasts from attack

Aug. 14, Treaty of peace with Spain signed in Paris

Oct. 8, The "Huascar" destroyed in engagement with Chilean fleet. Admiral Grau killed

Nov. 18, Colonel Espinar killed in Battle of San Francisco. Colonel Suarez led remainder of army to Tarapaca

Nov. 26, President Prado gave command of army to Admiral Montero and returned to Lima

Dec. 17, President Prado sailed for Europe with idea of raising a loan and purchasing iron-clads. General La Puerta, Vice-President in charge of the Government

Dec. 22, Revolt led by Nicolas de Pierola seized Callao

Dec. 23, Pierola entered Lima and was proclaimed Supreme Chief. The Vice-President persuaded to resign

Dec. 26, The entire male population between 18 and 30 called to service

1880

March 17, The "Union" a wooden corvette, the one ship of the Peruvian navy ran the gauntlet of the Chilean navy from Callao and landed guns and ammunition and supplies for the army in Arica

April 22, Government ratified the Geneva Convention of 1864

1881

Jan. 17, Chileans occupied Lima. Pierola had fled to the interior and eventually to Europe. The destruction of the city prevented by firm stand of the foreign ministers and admirals, but the University used as barracks and everything of value destroyed including 8,000 priceless manuscripts in the library. The United States minister reported the proceedings as "violations of the rules of civilized warfare which call for an earnest protest on behalf of all civilized nations"

March 12, Dr. Francisco Garcia Calderon inaugurated as President made the village of Magdalena his capital

June 7, Treaty of commerce and customs with Bolivia signed

June 23, Calderon Government recognized by the United States. Switzerland and the Central American Republics also recognized the Government

July 28 and again Nov. 28, Pierola resigned the presidency

Aug. 4, President Calderon had interview with Chileans seeking peace but their demands seemed too excessive

Sept. 28, Chileans took President Calderon prisoner and abolished his Government and sent him with other leading citizens to Chile in November. The Government carried on by Vice-President Montero

1883

June 6, Congress met at Arequipa and elected Dr. Garcia Calderon President and Admiral Monte Vice-President and General Caceres second Vice-President

Aug., Capture of Arequipa by Chileans

Oct. 20, Treaty of Ancon negotiated by General Iglesias with Chileans signed without consent of constitutional Government. The province of Tarapaca ceded to Chile. The provinces of Tacna and Arica ceded to Chile for a period of 10 years at end of which occupation a plebiscite to be held to determine sovereignty. General Iglesias proclaimed himself President

Oct. 22, Captain Lynch and his troops evacuated Lima

Oct. 25, General Iglesias entered Lima. Admiral Monte forced to retire to Bolivia left General Caceres as constitutional head of State

1884

March 28, Treaty of Ancon ratified by Assembly

Aug. 24, Attempt of General Caceres to seize Lima unsuccessful. Retired to Arequipa to reorganize

1885

May 1, Government troops defeated by Caceres at Ayacucho

Nov. 15, Caceres in battle with Government troops commanded by Colonel Relayze at Huaripampa near Xauxa

Nov. 24, Caceres captured rolling stock at railroad terminus of Chilca and took his army to Lima

Dec. 1, General Caceres entered Lima and persuaded Iglesias to resign. General amnesty proclaimed

Dec. 25, Iglesias left Lima

1886

June 3, President Andres Avelino Caceres elected May 30 inaugurated President, Colonel Bermudez first Vice-President and Aurelio Dengri second Vice-President

1887

April 10, Paita to Piura Railroad opened

Aug. 1, Treaty with Ecuador signed. Agreement to submit boundary dispute to arbitration of King of Spain

Aug. 30, Peruvian Academy corresponding with Spanish Royal Academy inaugurated

Aug. 31, Treaty of commerce and navigation with the United States signed

Oct. 14, Immigration law passed

Nov. 4, Public Land law enacted

1889

Oct. 25, Congress approved the proposal made by Michael Grace of New York, representing foreign bondholders, for creation of Peruvian Corporation to receive railroads, mining privileges, and land grants for a long term of years for settlement of debt which amounted to £51,423,190. Half of the debt to be assumed by Chile

1890

Jan. 8, Protocol with Chile signed which enabled President Caceres to make arrangements as to the foreign debt

Jan. 11, Grace bond-holders signed contract for liquidation of debt

April, The "Peruvian Corporation" formed in London

June 30, The railroads handed over to the Peruvian Corporation

Aug. 10, Colonel Don Remijio Morales Bermudez inaugurated as President, Dr. Pedro Alejandrino, first and Don Justiniano Borgono, second Vice-President

1891

Aug. 24, New Ministry formed by Justiniano Borgono

1892

March 3, New Ministry under General Velarde

1893

Jan. 21, Central Railroad begun by Henry Meiggs completed to La Oroya as the Lima and La Jaiya Railroad

Feb., New Cabinet of Premier General Velarde who also took portfolio of Foreign Affairs

May 12, New Ministry under José Mariano Jiminez

Oct. 25, Railroad law enacted

1894

March 28, Ten year period since ratification of Treaty of Ancon elapsed. Nothing done as to plebiscite

April 1, Death of President Bermudez

July 1, Señor del Solar, first Vice-President constitutional President but the office illegally seized by Colonel Borgono, second Vice-President in interests of Caceres

Aug. 10, Caceres assumed office claiming to be elected President. The election not recognized by his opponents who started revolt

Nov. 17, Cabinet reorganized, Dr. Manuel Yrigoyen, Premier and Minister of Foreign Affairs

1895

March 17–18, Insurgents led by Pierola took Lima by assault

March 19, Caceres took refuge in foreign legation and left the country

March 20, Treaty of friendship, commerce, and navigation with Japan signed

March 21, Pierola organized a provisional government and appointed Señor Candamo provisional President

Sept. 8, Nicolas de Pierola assumed office as elected President

1896

June 3, Patent law enacted

Nov. 11, Battle at Huanta, captured by Colonel Para, 500 revolting Indians killed

Dec. 27, Law made male citizens from 19 to 50 years of age liable for military service

Rising of Caceres and his party suppressed

1897

April 9, Government suspended coinage of silver at Mint and prohibited importation of silver coins after May 10

Dec. 23, Law legalized marriage of non-Catholics before magistrates and decree in 1899 made provision for legalization of marriages already performed by Protestant ministers

Dec. 29, Law established gold currency authorizing mintage of gold coin the "libra" of same weight and value as the English pound. Came into effect by presidential decree of Jan. 10, 1898

1898

May 17 and June 6, Claims Conventions with the United States signed

Dec. 27, Law made military service compulsory

1899

Sept. 8, Eduardo de Romana inaugurated President

Oct. 30, Revolution begun by General Pisco Durand by attack on custom house; soon suppressed

Nov. 28, Extradition Treaty with the United States signed

1901

Feb. 2, Guano deposits on Huanillos, Punta Lobos, and Pabellon de Pica reverted to the Chilean Government

Nov. 21, Arbitration Treaty with Bolivia signed for 10 year period

Dec. 14, Gold standard adopted by Act of Congress

1902

Dec. 30, Boundary Treaty with Bolivia signed

1903

May 30, Miguel Candamo elected President

Aug. 8, Senate passed measure reducing import duty on sugar to an equivalent of 6 francs, the maximum allowed by the Brussels Convention

1904

Feb. 19, Protocol signed with Ecuador by which it was agreed to submit boundary dispute to arbitration of King of Spain

May 7, Death of President Candamo. Vice-President Calderon assumed office

July 12, Protocol with Brazil signed as to boundary

Sept. 23, José Pardo proclaimed elected President. Assumed office the following day

1905

Feb. 19, Formal protest made against treaty between Chile and Bolivia

April 18, Arbitration Treaty with Italy signed

Sept. 12, General Arbitration Treaty with Colombia signed and Special Arbitration Treaty submitting arbitration of boundary to the Pope

Nov. 27, Treaty of commerce and customs with Bolivia signed

1906

July 6, *Modus vivendi* as to Putumayo district signed with Colombia

July 24, Treaty of friendship and arbitration with Paraguay signed

Aug. 10, Decree of the President for encouragement of immigration announced that the State would pay third class passage of immigrants under certain specified conditions

Sept. 10, Secretary Elihu Root arrived at Lima on official visit from the United States

1907

Oct. 15, Naturalization Treaty with the United States signed

Nov., Peruvian troops attacked Brazilian frontier fort at Leticia and subsequently seized town of Tabatinga. Government withdrew troops and made apologies.

Dec. 18, Treaty of amity with Chile signed, the first since the war of 1879

1908

Jan. 30, Protocol with Bolivia signed regulating transit trade as to Mollendo

April 15, Treaty with Brazil signed provided for navigation of the Japura or Cuqueta River

May 8, Revolution in Peru failed

July 8, Wireless telegraph between Iquitos and Masisea and between Iquitos and Puerto Bermudez opened

Sept. 24, Augusto B. Leguia inaugurated elected President

Dec. 5, Arbitration Treaty with the United States signed

1909

May 14, Executive decree prohibited entrance of Chinese immigrants with less than $500 in money

May 29, Revolt of partisans of General Pierola attacked palace and captured the President and his Cabinet. Rescue by loyal troops within an hour and the insurrection suppressed

July 9, Award of President of Argentina in boundary dispute with Bolivia

Sept. 8, Treaty with Brazil settled frontiers and established general principles as to commerce and navigation in Amazon basin

Dec. 7, Treaty of arbitration with Brazil signed

1910

March 21, Diplomatic relations severed with Chile because of expulsion of Peruvian priests from Tacna and Arica

June 3, Peru and Ecuador agreed to withdraw troops from the frontier and accept mediation of Brazil, Argentina, and the United States in boundary dispute

Aug. 6, New Cabinet headed by G. Schreiber

Sept. 8, New altitude record of 8,409 feet made by J. Chavez in France

Sept. 23, Jorge Chavez, Peruvian aviator, first to fly across the Alps in Switzerland

Nov. 26, Plot to overthrow the Government discovered and leaders arrested

1911

Jan. 20, Workmen's Compensation Act passed

March 31, Protocol signed with Bolivia for arbitration of difficulties

Aug. 30, New Cabinet under Austin Ganoza

Sept. 26, Agreement with Bolivia as to imports into Bolivia by way of Mollendo

Nov. 7, Colombians occupied Pedrera

1912

Feb. 25, Arbitration Treaty with Venezuela signed

April 22, The President appointed a committee to form plan for administrative reform of the Putumayo River district

May 3, Hague Tribunal gave decision in favor of Peru in the Canevaro claims case dispute with Italy

July 13, Report of Sir Roger Casement, British consul, on cruel and forced labor of Indians in Putumayo district by rubber companies sent to Peruvian Government

Aug. 8, The Pope issued an encyclical on the Putumayo case

Sept. 13, Resolution of Peruvian Congress demanded punishment of officials in Putumayo district

Sept. 24, Guillermo Billinghurst inaugurated as elected President

Nov. 20, Proposal for holding of plebiscite in Tacna and Arica made to Chile. Chilean occupation of Tacna and Arica continued by agreement

Dec. 17, Julio C. Arana, director of the British Rubber Company proved to have committed atrocities against the Indians in Putumayo district arrested by Peruvian authorities

1913

Feb. 26, F. L. Peralta formed new Ministry

April 30, New Protocol signed with Brazil provided for delimitation of boundary by Mixed Commission

June 23, Death of ex-President Pierola

July, Insurrection in Lima

July 11, Decree created national school of aviation

Oct. 3, Constitutional Amendment passed modified Article 4 of the Constitution to permit the building of Protestant churches, missions, and schools

Nov. 7, Earthquake destroyed the town of Abancay

1914

Feb. 4, Military revolt led by Colonel Oscar Benavides attacked and captured the palace, forcing resignation of President Billinghurst, later sent into exile

Feb. 12, Revolutionary Government formally recognized by the United States

March 26, Vice-President Robert E. Leguia resigned as acting President

May 15, Colonel Benavides elected provisional President by Congress

July 14, Advancement of Peace Treaty with the United States signed

Aug. 6, 30 day financial moratorium declared; extended Sept. 30

Aug. 8, Law prohibited export of gold and minted silver

Aug. 9, The President required employers to give 24 hours notice of dismissal and to file reasons with sub-prefect

Aug. 10, Law authorized the President to take necessary measures to prevent excessive rise in prices

Aug. 18, First naval vessel to use the Panama Canal the Peruvian torpedo boat "Teniente Rodriguez"

Aug. 21, Decree of neutrality in European War

Aug. 22, New Ministry constituted

——, Law authorized banks to issue circular checks payable to bearer to amount not to exceed £1,100,000 and legal reserve fixed at 35% gold, 65% securities

1915

Jan. 8, Ex-President Billinghurst and Dr. Augusto Durand ordered to leave Chile

Jan. 28, Death of ex-President Billinghurst at Iquique, Chile

Feb. 19, New Cabinet took office

Aug. 18, José Pardo inaugurated elected President

Nov. 12, Congress formally promulgated the religious liberty Amendment to the Constitution granting freedom to all denominations

Nov., Mineral export tax passed by Congress, 25 cents per ton on petroleum, $3.75 on copper

1916

March 15, Resignation of President Pardo because of ill health. Succeeded by Vice-President Ricardo Bentin *pro tem*

Sept. 1, Metric system of weights and measures came into effect in Lima and Callao

Oct. 16, Minimum Wage Act for native rural workers passed. Payment to be in current coin

Oct. 20, Workmen's Compensation Act of 1911 amended

1917

Feb. 5, Peruvian bark "Lorton" sunk by German submarine near coast of Spain

Feb. 10, Secretary of Foreign Relations protested to Germany against policy of submarine warfare, beginning exchange of notes as to indemnity for the "Lorton"

July 18, Treaty for general obligatory arbitration with Uruguay signed

July 27, New Cabinet formed with Francisco Tudela as Premier

Oct. 5, Congress voted to sever diplomatic relations with Germany by vote of 105 to 6

Oct. 6, German Minister handed his passports

Oct. 10, Peru notified Great Britain and the United States that ports open to their vessels

1918

Jan. 3, Constitution amended

June 14, Peru seized 8 German ships interned at Callao

July 11, Obligatory Arbitration Convention with Brazil signed

Nov. 23, Act provided funds for railroad construction. Promulgated Nov. 29, 1921

Nov. 25, Act regulating labor of women and children prohibited employment of children under 14

——, Peru withdrew her consuls from Chile in dispute over Tacna-Arica

Dec. 10, Law passed provided for government control of railroads

Dec. 26, Act prohibited work on Sundays and civic holidays in factories, workshops, warehouses, mines, and quarries

Dec. 28, Law provided for building houses for workmen to be sold to government employees receiving certain minimum wages

1919

Jan. 13, General strike called in Lima and Callao

June 9 and Dec. 10, Decrees as to admission of foreigners

July 4, Coup d'état of partisans of Leguia overthrew the Government of President Pardo

July 20, Leguia assumed control as *de facto* President. Pardo imprisoned

Aug. 24, Augusto B. Leguia elected constitutional President

Aug. 29, The United States recognized the Leguia Government

Oct. 12, President Leguia inaugurated

Dec. 27, New Constitution promulgated to go into effect Jan. 18, 1920, prohibition of any other religion than Roman Catholic repealed, primary education made compulsory, compulsory arbitration of disputes between capital and labor, industrial accident compensation to workmen provided for, issue of irredeemable paper money prohibited, graduated income tax established

1920

Jan. 10, Peru became member of League of Nations

Jan. 18, New Constitution came into effect repealing that of Nov. 10, 1860

Jan. 29, Notice given of intention to submit Tacna-Arica claims to League of Nations

Jan. 31, Law established a Council of State of 7 members appointed by the President for terms of 5 years

March 6, Decree provided that labor section of Ministry of Development should act as mediator in industrial disputes

March 18, New Code of criminal procedure became effective

April, National City Bank of New York City established a branch at Lima

May, General strike in Lima and Callao

Aug. 6, Decree as to importation of livestock

1921

Jan., Captain B. Freyer, head of naval mission from the United States to reorganize the Peruvian navy created Chief of the Naval Staff

Feb. 5, New organic education law made elementary education compulsory between the ages of 7 and 14 and created University of Technical Schools

May 2, Decree required all banks to maintain in vaults or in investments within the Republic a sum equal to their capital and the amount of their deposits. A Government Bureau created for inspection of banks (Inspeccion Fiscal de Bancos y Seguros)

May 11, Decree fixed maximum in rate of bank interest at 10%

May 21, Claims Convention with the United States provided for submission of the Landreau claim to arbitration

Aug. 21, Revolt of troops at Iquitos because of 6 months arrears in pay

Aug. 27, Protocol with Great Britain signed provided for submission to arbitration of differences as to mining properties

Oct. 11, Decision of Permanent Court of Arbitration that Peru should pay 25,000,000 francs in settlement of French claims

Dec. 18 and 28, Proposals of Peru to Chile to accept arbitration of the United States as to Tacna and Arica

Dec. 25, Note to Bolivia offered to arbitrate between Bolivia and Chile

1922

Jan. 2, Act regulating granting of petroleum concessions passed, oil lands declared property of nation

Jan. 19, Peru accepted invitation to Washington Conference with Chile

March 1, Law fixed export tax on petroleum. Not to be increased for 20 years

March 2, Agreement with Great Britain signed as to mining properties

March 8, Reserve Bank of Peru authorized. Chartered April 4

March 24, Boundary Treaty with Colombia signed

April 28, Decree created Superior Council of Labor and Social Welfare

Oct. 26, Award in claims case of J. C. Landreau heirs that Peru should pay $125,000

Dec. 26, Budget law enacted

1923

Jan. 14, Note to all South American republics gave instances of alleged mistreatment of Peruvian citizens in Tacna and Arica by Chile

March 14, Arbitration Treaty with Venezuela signed

April 3, Death of Augusto Durand, revolutionist

June 13, New tariff law signed by the President

Aug. 31, Decree of Congress reëstablished the decoration of the Order of the Sun (Orden del Sol)

Sept. 7, Legislation amended Constitution to increase term of office of President from 4 years to 5 making President Leguia eligible for reëlection, and for a second term

Sept. 28, Criminal Code amended

Dec. 12, Law issued provided for stamp duty on titles, contracts, deeds, &c.

1924

April 7, Treaty of friendship, commerce, and navigation with Japan of March 20, 1895 extended

April 12, Case of Tacna-Arica presented to arbitration of the President of the United States

June 21, Protocol with Ecuador signed as to boundary providing for direct negotiations and arbitration of questions in dispute

Oct. 10, New York bankers announced $7,000,000 loan part of the $24,000,000 credit granted to Peru. Customs duties and collection of other revenues and taxes pledged under the loan to be collected by American company

Oct. 13, New Ministry of Alejandrino Maguino took office

Dec. 6–20, American mission headed by General J. J. Pershing in Peru

1925

Jan. 16, Law by which commercial business firms, and merchants obliged to keep their books in the Spanish language

March 4, Settlement of boundary dispute with Brazil and Colombia in Amazon region effected in Department of State of the United States

——, President Coolidge gave award in Tacna-Arica dispute providing for a plebiscite

March 14, Mobs attacked American Legation at Lima in protest against Coolidge award

April 18, Decree established government monopoly in match industry and trade

June 2, Protocol with Bolivia signed as to frontier

1926

April 9, Peru rejected Secretary Kellogg's proposed plan to divide the Tacna-Arica territory with Chile

April 13, Treaty with Venezuela signed provided for maintenance of order in frontier districts

Sept. 1, Province of Tarata (1,922 square miles) restored to Peru by Chile

Sept. 28, Constitution amended

Nov. 19, New tariff law enacted

Nov. 30, Memorandum of American Secretary of State suggested cession to Bolivia of Tacna and Arica

Kemmerer Mission from the United States in Peru to advise on reform of financial affairs

1927

Jan. 12, Peru rejected American proposal of cession of Tacna and Arica to Bolivia

Jan. 27, Decree of the President published regulations of law for granting petroleum concessions

March 16, Agreement as to military service with France signed

Oct. 19, Act placed tax on all native cotton

Dec. 21, Loan of $50,000,000 in 6% 33 year bonds arranged in New York largely to establish gold exchange fund to assist in stabilizing the currency

1928

Jan. 1, New rent law went into effect for 2 years

April 9, Earthquake destroyed Mucasani

May 3, Decree established Institute of International Law

May 19, Earthquake at and near Pimpincos killed over 300 persons

July 11, Leguia Bridge across the Colorado River at Tarma opened

July 13, Diplomatic relations with Chile resumed

July 28, Announcement of the President of organization of Peruvian Institute of International Law

Oct. 1, Loan of $25,000,000 in 6% gold bonds of this date floated in the United States and Europe

Oct. 3, Chilean ambassador received by President Leguia

Dec. 5, President-Elect Hoover arrived at Callao and Lima on good-will visit

1929

May 7, New Cabinet headed by Benjamin Huaman de los Heros assumed office

June 3, Tacna-Arica Treaty signed with Chile. Peru received Tacna and $6,000,000, approved by Congress July 2

June 22, Decree of the President prohibited teaching of doctrines opposed to State (Roman Catholic) religion

June 30, External debt on this date 22,888,592 Peruvian pounds

July 3, Peru signed the Paris Peace Pact

Aug. 3, Cancellation of concession of land to B. T. Lee,

American citizen, on ground of non-fulfillment of contract. Taken up by United States State Department

Aug. 5, Augusto B. Leguia reëlected President

Aug. 29, Tacna formally placed under Peruvian sovereignty

Oct. 12, President Leguia inaugurated

Nov. 19, Bill passed imposed tax of 10% on all salaries of public employees, included members of Congress

Dec. 15, Decree provided that all sales and business contracts should be settled in Peruvian currency

Dec. 31, Law authorized the President to establish government monopoly on importation and sale of explosives

1930

Jan. 2, Act created National Savings Bank

Feb. 10, Law established gold sol as monetary unit of the Republic, value $.40

Feb. 19, Exchange of notes with Japan renewed Treaty of amity, commerce, and navigation

Feb. 22, Act authorized the President to establish a government monopoly on the sale of petroleum

March 6, New Cabinet sworn in

March 27, Peruvian pound replaced by sol as unit of currency, value $.40

April 26, Decree provided for establishment of 3 normal schools

April 29, Agreement with Chile established police guard for international boundary line

Aug. 5, Final Act signed relative to boundary with Chile

Aug. 14, New air service from Lima to Chachapoyas opened

Aug. 22, Revolt broke out in Arequipa against the President led by Lieutenant Colonel Luis Sanchez Cerro

Aug. 25, President Leguia resigned and fled from the country. Military Junta headed by General Ponce took over the Government

Aug. 26, Leguia surrendered by officers on the cruiser on which he had left the country

Aug. 27, Lieutenant Colonel Luis Sanchez Cerro heads second military Junta taking over the Government as provisional President

——, Governor Ricardo Luna of Tacna assassinated when he refused to join southern military junta

Sept. 1, Former President Leguia imprisoned on Island of San Lorenzo in harbor of Callao to await trial for alleged misrule

Sept. 3, Mutual recognition of military juntas of Bolivia and Peru

Sept. 15, Provisional Government arrested General Manuel Ponce and others

Sept. 18, The United States resumed normal relations with new Government

Sept. 20, Formal charge made against former President Leguia of misuse of government funds. Sept. 26, Case dismissed

Nov. 4, "Sanctions Court" announced list of persons to be tried for "illegal enrichment" during the Leguia régime. Included the former President, his 2 sons, sons-in-law, and 20 others

Nov. 12, Riots at Cerro de Pasco copper mines

Nov. 21, Resignation of provisional Cabinet. Succeeded the following day by one headed by Colonel Ernesto Montague

Nov. 24, The newspaper La Prensa suspended for criticism of the Cabinet

URUGUAY

Uruguay, smallest of the South American republics, south of Brazil on the Atlantic coast, the southern boundary the Rio de la Plata, and separated from Argentina on the west by the Uruguay River. The official name is the Oriental Republic of the Uruguay and the country is known locally as the *Banda Oriental*, the "eastern shore." Total population 2,036,884, area 72,153 square miles. Montevideo is the chief seaport and capital.

The last census was taken in 1908, when the total population was 1,042,686, divided into 861,464 native-born and 181,222 immigrants, including 62,357 Italians, 54,885 Spaniards, 27,789 Brazilians, and 18,600 Argentinians.

The census population of Montevideo City (the capital) on January 1, 1930, was 468,634. Of the other cities, Paysandu had 26,000 inhabitants; Salto, 30,000; Mercedes, 23,000.

1512

Juan Diaz de Solis first European to set foot in Uruguay

1516

Feb., Juan Diaz de Solis on second expedition killed by Indians in Colonia

1520

Jan. 15, Ferdinand Magellan named hill overlooking bay Montevideo. Name extended to city later established

1526

Cabot sent expedition under his lieutenant Juan Alvarez Ramon to explore the country along the Uruguay River. Attacked by Indians and leader killed

1527

Cabot directed erection of fort in the "Banda Oriental" east of the Uruguay River on San Salvador River. Destroyed by Indians in 1529

1550

Captain Juan Romero from Asunción (Paraguay) made first settlement in present Uruguay on the San Juan River called San Juan Bautista. Abandoned 2 years later

1574

Settlement begun on site of Cabot's fort on the San Salvador River but abandoned because of hostility of Indians

1603

Spanish troops of Saavedra defeated in battle with the Indians

1624

First permanent settlement made by Jesuits. Bernardo de Guzman established colonists on the Rio Negro calling the settlement Santo Domingo de Soriano

1680

Jan., Portuguese from Rio de Janeiro built fort across the River from Buenos Aires at Sacramento (now Colonia)

1704

Oct. 17, Captain Garcia Ros sent by the Viceroy of Peru seized Colonia from the Portuguese

1723

Portuguese fortified the heights around the Bay of Montevideo

1726

Dec. 24, Montevideo founded by Spanish Governor Zabala of Buenos Aires

1730

Jan. 1, Formal appointment of city government of Montevideo

1735 to Sept., 1737

Colonia besieged by Spaniards without success

1749

Dec., José Joaquin de Viana became Governor of Montevideo subordinate to Government of Buenos Aires

1750

Montevideo made a provincial government independent of Buenos Aires

1761

Colonia surrendered to Spaniards

1763

Feb. 10, Colonia restored to Portugal by the Treaty of Paris

Maldonado settled by colonists led by Pedro Ceballos

1777

Oct. 1, By Treaty of San Ildefonso Uruguay ceded to Spain by Portugal

June 4, Colonia surrendered to Spanish commanded by Ceballos

1778

Santa Lucia founded by immigrants from Asturias and Galicia

1781

Pando founded by immigrants from Asturias

1782

Paysandu founded by 12 families from the Misiones

1783

San José and Minas founded

1793

Rocha founded by immigrants from Asturias and Galicia

1807

Feb. 3, English combined land and sea attack commanded by Sir Samuel Auchmuty took Montevideo

Sept. 9, The British evacuated Montevideo

1810

July 12, Mutiny of garrison at Montevideo soon suppressed by Spanish authorities

1811

Feb. 26, José Artigas, patriot leader, attacked royalists at San José compelling their retreat on Montevideo

Feb. 28, Artigas and others made declaration of independence at Asunción, the "Grito de Ascencio"

April 26, Artigas routed Spaniards at San José

May 18, Artigas defeated Spaniards at Las Piedras just outside Montevideo but did not capture city.

Uruguay declared a part of the United Provinces of the Rio de La Plata

1812

Dec. 3, José Rondeau with Argentine force defeated Spaniards at Cerrito near Montevideo

1813

Jan. 31, Constituent Assembly at Buenos Aires. Delegates sent by Artigas refused admittance. They were instructed to urge adoption of declaration of independence

1814

May 16, Argentine fleet commanded by William Brown defeated Spanish squadron stationed at Montevideo

June 20, Spanish garrison at Montevideo surrendered to General Alvear commanding land forces and William Brown commanding fleet

1815

Jan. 10, The independence of Uruguay recognized by the Governor of Buenos Aires, and José Artigas as head of the republic

1816

Oct., Forces of Artigas invaded the Misiones territory in dispute with Brazil and were repulsed with heavy loss

1817

Jan. 20, The "Banda Oriental del Uruguay" invaded by Portuguese troops from Rio de Janeiro. Artigas defeated at Paso de Catalan and Montevideo captured

1820

Sept. 23, Artigas exiled from Uruguay granted asylum by Dr. Francia in Paraguay

1821

Uruguay annexed to Brazil as the Provincia Cisplatina

1824

May 9, The Emperor of Brazil declared Uruguay incorporated into Brazil as the Cisplatine Province

1825

April 19, Thirty-three patriots, refugees from Uruguay, led by Juan Antonio Lavalleja landed in Uruguay from Buenos Aires

Aug. 25, Assembly called by the "thirty-three immortals" at Florida declared independence and separation from Brazil. They pledged adherence to the United Provinces of La Plata which led to war of Brazil and Argentina for possession of Uruguay

Sept. 24 and Oct. 12, Brazilians defeated. *See* Brazil

1827

Feb. 20, Brazilians defeated. *See* Brazil

1828

Aug. 27, Treaty of Argentina and Brazil ended war and recognized the independence of Uruguay

Nov., Constituent Assembly met at San José and appointed a provisional President

Dec. 13, Decree of provisional President announced that all foreign officials should cease to exercise authority in territory of Uruguay

1829

Sept. 10, Constitution approved by Assembly

1830

May 26, Constitution approved by Argentina and Brazil

July 18, Constitution formally adopted which set up a unitary centralized government

Nov. 6, General Fructuoso Rivera inaugurated first President succeeding Rondeau who had acted as provisional Governor

1831

War with the Charrua Indians

1832

July, Revolt begun by General Lavalleja against President Rivera. Defeated 2 months later at Tupambay and Lavalleja escaped to Brazil

1834

July 1, Independence recognized by the United States

Oct. 29, Treaty of commerce and navigation with Great Britain signed

1835

March, General Manuel Oribe succeeded Rivera as second President

1836

April 7, Commercial Treaty with France signed

Sept. 19, Oribe aided by soldiers of Dictator Rosas from Argentina defeated forces of Rivera in revolt against him at the Battle of Carpinteria. Oribe's soldiers wore red badges and Rivera's white, first appearance of the 2 parties, *Blancos* and *Colorados*

Civil war continued until 1838

1837

June 14, Decree prohibited importation of slaves

1838

May 27, Decree founded University of Montevideo. Not opened until 1849

Nov., Rivera defeated Oribe who escaped to Buenos Aires and Rivera was presently elected President

1839

Feb. 24, President Rivera declared war against the tyrant Rosas, not the people of Argentina

July 17, Amendment to Constitution approved

Dec. 10, Argentine army invading Uruguay defeated in Battle of Cagancha

1840

Oct. 29, Treaty of commerce and navigation with Sardinia signed

1841

Oct. 9, Treaty of peace, friendship, commerce, navigation, and recognition signed with Spain

Argentine fleet commanded by William Brown practically put an end to sea power of Uruguay

Oribe with army from Argentina invaded Entre Rios to attack allies of Rivera

General Urquiza defeated Rivera at India Muerta

1842

Jan., Rivera went to Entre Rios to aid General Paz against Oribe

Aug. 26, Treaty of amity, commerce, and navigation with Great Britain signed

Dec. 6, Rivera and Paz defeated at Arroya Grande

Dec. 12, Decree abolished slavery

1843

"La guerra grande" siege of *Colorados* in Montevideo from 1843–1851 by Oribe with aid of soldiers of Rosas

1849

University of Montevideo opened

1851

May 29, Offensive and defensive Treaty with Brazil and revolutionists of Entre Rios headed by Urquiza who had declared against Rosas signed

July 18, Brazilian troops and fleet joined General Urquiza in relief of Montevideo and defeated troops of Oribe

Oct. 8, General Urquiza made Treaty with Oribe which provided for ending the war and left the *Colorados* in power

Oct. 12, Treaties adjusting boundary and of alliance with Brazil signed

1852

March 1, Juan Francisco Giro elected fourth constitutional President

May 15, Boundary Treaty with Brazil signed

Oct., Giro resigned delegating executive authority to Don Bernardo Berro, a *Blanco*

1853

July, Successful revolt against Government led by General Diaz and Colonel Palleja at Montevideo. Berro first reorganized his Cabinet but was soon forced to leave taking refuge in French legation

Sept., Triumvirate of Generals Lavalleja, Rivera, and Colonel Venancio Flores formed to complete the term of office of Giro. The death of both Lavalleja and Rivera made Flores sole executive

Sept. 16, Treaty of commerce and navigation with Belgium signed

Oct. 10, Decree opened navigation of rivers to foreign commerce

1854

Jan. 13, Death of General Fructuosa Rivera, former President

Venancio Flores, President, a *Colorado*. He asked aid of Brazil to end civil war

March 24, Emancipation of slaves enacted

June 27 and July 11, Constitutional amendments approved

1855

Compromise of *Blancos* and *Colorados* made Manuel Bustamente temporary President

1856

Gabriel A. Pereira, President

June 23, Treaty of friendship, commerce, and navigation with Prussia signed

1857

Invaders from Argentina supporting plan of Juan C. Gomez for annexation of Uruguay to the province of Buenos Aires defeated and leaders shot

Sept. 4, Treaty of commerce and navigation with Brazil signed

1858

Jan. 28, Insurrection of General Cesar Diaz defeated at Cagancha and Diaz subsequently shot

1859

Jan. 2, Alliance concluded with Argentina and Brazil

1860

Bernardo Berro succeeded Pereira as President

1862

May 16, Constitutional amendments approved

1863

April 19, General Venancio Flores in revolt landed at Rincon de las Gallinas and gathered army

June, The "Salto" Argentinian steamer captured with contraband. The captain and ship released, contraband kept at Montevideo and Argentine Government notified and asked to claim property and prove arms not intended for rebels under Flores

June 8, Note of Elizalde (Argentine) to Herrera ignored note and demanded reprisal for capture of the "Salto"

June 12, Uruguay offered to submit dispute to arbitration which Argentina refused June 15

June 22, Argentine warship seized Uruguayan warship "General Artigas" and blockaded mouth of the Uruguay. Flores because of this blockade was able to land troops and ammunition

June 23, Diplomatic relations with Argentina severed

Oct. 20, Protocol of agreement as to Salto signed, the Lamas-Elizalde agreement, referring dispute to arbitration

Nov. 23, Armed expedition surprised in Uruguayan Islands and presently captured

Dec. 10, Argentina suspended diplomatic relations

1864

General Atanasio Aguirre, *Blanco*, became President

Jan. 26–27, 8 *Blanco* leaders arrested preventing revolutionary coup d'état

May 18, Note from Brazil cited claims of Brazil against Uruguay

May 24, Reply of Herrera to Brazilian note

June 13, Uruguay formally requested mediation of Paraguay in dispute with Brazil

June 19, Conference of Puntas del Rosario, Flores, Saraiva (Brazil), Thornton (British), Elizalde (Argentina), and Castellanos and Lamas representing the Montevideo Government. Agreement signed to end war by Flores with certain conditions

June 23, Basis of settlement signed by Montevideo Government

July 3, President Aguirre refused to make change of Ministry agreed on in settlement with Flores

July 7, President Aguirre named new Cabinet of extreme *Blanco* chiefs, and Flores resumed war against the Government

Aug. 4, Ultimatum from Brazil demanded payment of claims for damages to Brazilian citizens resident in Uruguay over a period of 10 years

Aug. 25, Uruguay asked Paraguay to intervene in difficulties with Brazil

Aug. 26, Uruguayan war steamer the "Villa del Salto" going to relief of Mercedes besieged by Flores fired on by Brazilian gunboat

Sept. 14, Brazilian troops crossed the frontier

Oct. 16, Brazilians occupied town of Mello

Oct. 20, General Flores joined forces with Brazilians

Nov. 28, Salto surrendered to Brazilians

Dec. 6, Bombardment of Paysandu by Flores and Brazilians

Dec. 31, Attempt of Colonel Leander Gomez to cut through investing forces from Paysandu failed

1865

Jan. 2, Paysandu carried by assault by Flores and Brazilians in spite of the heroic defense of Colonel Gomez. Colonel Gomez was shot by Colonel Suarez and garrison massacred

Jan. 22, President Aguirre accepted offered mediation of President Mitre of Argentina

Feb. 2, Blockade of Montevideo established by Brazilians

Feb. 15, Tomas Villaba, President of Senate, assumed executive office on expiration of term of President Aguirre

Feb. 22, General Flores supported by Brazilians entered Montevideo and was proclaimed provisional President

May 1, Uruguay signed Treaty of alliance against Paraguay with Brazil and Argentina. For war *see* Paraguay

July 7, Treaty of commerce and navigation with France of 1836 renewed

1866

March 1, F. A. Vidal became President

May 7, Treaty of commerce and navigation with Italy signed

1868

Jan. 23, Civil Code promulgated

Feb. 19, *Blanco* Insurrection led by Senator Bernardo P. Berro took the palace. General Flores assassinated on his way to the palace. The leaders arrested and Berro shot. American marines landed at Montevideo to protect foreign residents, withdrawn Feb. 26

March 1, Congress elected General Lorenzo Batlle, President

Cholera epidemic in this year

1869

Financial crisis

Railroad between Montevideo and Canelones opened

March 11, Constitutional Amendment approved

June 2, Agreement as to provisional government of Paraguay. *See* Paraguay

1870

March 5, *Blanco* insurrection of Colonel Timoteo Aparicio begun in the North-West

Sept. 12, Government troops commanded by Suarez defeated near the river of Santa Lucia Chico

Sept. 29, General Caraballa after defeat by rebels near Corralito escaped during the night

Nov. 28, Rebels took fortress at the Cerro

Nov. 29, President Batlle made sortie from Montevideo defeating rebels

Dec. 23, Suarez succeeded in reaching the capital

Dec. 25, Suarez defeated rebels in battle at Montevideo

1871

July 17, Rebels collected at Manantiales de San Juan defeated and dispersed by General Enrique Castro

Tomas Gomensoro, President of the Senate, took office as President on expiration of term of President Batlle as no elections could be held in disturbed state of country

1872

April 6, Peace agreement signed ended civil war, *Colorados* in power

1873

Feb. 14, Dr. José E. Ellauri chosen president of the

Senate and therefore succeeded Gomensoro as temporary President

March 1, Dr. Ellauri elected constitutional President

Nov. 22, Constitutional Amendment approved

1874

July 20, Constitutional amendments approved

1875

Jan., President Ellauri forced out of office by military revolt

Jan. 22, Pedro Varela elected President by Congress

May, Revolt begun in Department of Maldonado by Colonel Julian de la Llana which was joined by both *Colorados* and *Blancos* "La revolucion tricolor," Colonel Angel Munis commanding rebels defeated "The terrible year," financial panic

1876

Jan. 14, Protocol signed with Argentina as to settlement of claims

March 10, Colonel Lorenzo Latorre supported by the army deposed Varela and proclaimed himself dictator

May 23, Constitutional amendments approved

1877

Aug. 24, Decree of President Latorre reorganized educational system

1879

March 1, Latorre elected constitutional President inaugurated

April 29, Protocol with Great Britain renewed diplomatic relations

Oct. 24, Death of Ex-President Varela

1880

March 13, President Latorre resigned declaring Uruguay "ungovernable." Dr. Francisco A. Vidal elected to fill the unexpired term

1881

May 3, Constitutional Amendment approved

1882

March 1, Vidal resigned, and General Maximo Santos elected constitutional President

July 17, Constitutional amendments approved

1883

Jan. 22 and Oct. 30, Constitutional amendments approved

Oct. 9, Independence of Uruguay finally recognized by Spain as ratifications of treaty exchanged

1885

March 27, Constitutional amendments approved

Sept. 19, Treaty of commerce and navigation with Italy signed

Nov. 13, Treaty of commerce and navigation with Great Britain signed

1886

March 1, Vidal elected President, General Santos made commander-in-chief of the army, and the real ruler

March 28, Revolt led by General Enrique Castro and General José Miguel Arredondo

March 30 and 31, Rebels defeated by General Tajes

May 24, Vidal resigned and Santos who had been made

President of the Senate became President by virtue of his office

Aug. 17, Attempt at assassination of President Santos in new revolution

Nov. 4, New Cabinet of Dr. J. P. Ramirez, opposition leader, the "Ministerio de la conciliacion"

Nov. 18, Resignation of President Santos. General Maximo Tajes made President

Dec. 28, Decree of President dismembered several regiments particularly those whose officers had interfered in political affairs

1889

May 10, Death of General Santos in exile at Buenos Aires

1890

March 1, Julio Herrera y Obes took office as President

June 12, Immigration law promulgated

1891

Aug. 31, Grave financial crisis, Uruguay defaulting on obligations, but conversion of state debt and reduction of interest proposed accepted by creditors in London.

Oct. 11, *Blanco* revolt at Montevideo suppressed. Martial law declared

1892

July 4, Treaty of commerce and navigation with France signed

1894

March 21, Juan I Borda took office as President

1895

May 3, Insurgents defeated troops under General Escobar

1896

Nov., Elections so manipulated that in districts where *Blancos* a known majority the vote falsified in favor of the *Colorados*

Dec. 5, Government announcement that revolution "terminated" and the "bandit Saraiva" defeated

1897

Feb., "Nationalist" insurrection led by *Blancos*, Aparicio Saraiva in the North and Colonel Diego Lamas in the South

March 17, Severe fighting at Paysandu. Retreat of government troops

May 16, Insurgents routed by General Villar near San Fructuoso

May 18, War loan authorized, 4,000,000 pesos at 6%

Aug. 25, President Borda shot and killed as he walked in a procession at the capital. Succeeded by President of the Senate, Juan Lindolfo Cuestas

Sept. 18, Pact of reconciliation signed at Montevideo by Government and insurgent Nationalists

1898

Feb. 10, President Cuestas dissolved Congress which opposed him assuming dictatorial powers

Feb. 12, Council of State installed whose first act to reduce legislative salaries a saving of $250,000 a year

June 23, Treaty of commerce and navigation with Italy signed

July 1, Revolution broke out in Montevideo by mutiny of the 4th regiment of artillery. Suppressed after fight of 48 hours

1899

March 1, New Congress elected Cuestas constitutional President

June 8, Arbitration Treaty with Argentina signed

July 15, Convention with Great Britain renewed Treaty of friendship, commerce, and navigation of 1885

1900

May 3, Uruguay adhered to Geneva Convention of 1864

1902

Jan. 28, Treaty of arbitration with Spain signed

1903

Feb. 17, Claims Convention with United States signed referred claims to arbitration

March 1, José Batlle y Ordonez succeeded Cuestas as President

1904

Jan. 8, "Nationalistic" revolt begun led by General Saraiva

March 6, Engagement at Puntas de Quequaychico

Aug. 23, Revolutionists captured Santa Rosa

Sept. 1, Decisive battle at Masoller ended insurrection. Saraiva mortally wounded

Sept. 24, Peace signed with rebels providing for general amnesty, supervision of elections by party committees

1905

March 11, Extradition Treaty with the United States signed

1906

Feb. 15, Dr. Francis Soca elected president of the Senate and Vice-President of the Republic for one year

Sept. 15, Agronomical Institute of University of Montevideo opened and made a national agricultural college

1907

March 1, Claudio Williman, *Colorado*, inaugurated President

May 13, New land law enacted

Sept. 22, Capital punishment abolished

Nov. 25, General election. Government secured 73 seats the Nationalists 14

1908

Feb. 22, Strike on Central Uruguayan suppressed

Aug. 10, Naturalization Treaty with the United States signed

Oct., Census gave population as 1,042,668, foreigners 181,222

Dec., Supreme Court established

1909

Oct. 30, Boundary Treaty with Brazil modified frontiers at Lake Merim and the Jaguaro River

1910

Jan. 5, Protocol with Argentina signed as to navigation of the Rio de la Plata

Oct. 25, Permanent Court of Arbitration gave award in claims case in dispute with the United States setting Barge award of 1904 of $28,224 aside and increasing it to $64,000 more

1911

Jan. 9, First South American Postal Congress inaugurated at Montevideo

March 1, President Batlle y Ordonez inaugurated for a second term

March 31, Diplomatic relations with the Vatican suspended

July 12, Law set aside 100,000 pesos for encouragement of immigration

1912

Jan. 1, South American Postal Bureau established at Montevideo

March 1, National Insurance Bank with monopoly of insurance of all kinds created by the Government

1913

Jan., Colonization law enacted

May 2, First South American International Conference of Agricultural Defense held at Montevideo

May 7, Boundary Treaty with Brazil signed by which Brazil ceded "the waters and navigation" of Lake Merim and the Jaguaro River

May 16, Montevideo Port Railway opened train service between Montevideo and Porto Allegre

May 28, Decree created National Labor Office

Nov. 30, Election gave Government party a majority

1914

July 20, Advancement of Peace Treaty with the United States signed

July 21, Law made compulsory provisions for prevention of industrial accidents

Aug. 5, Decrees of neutrality in European War

Full political rights given to women

1915

Feb. 13, Act provided for eight hour day for workers in factories, workshops, dock-yards, quarries. Rules and regulations promulgated April 14

Feb. 27, Arbitration Treaty with Chile signed

March 1, Feliciano Viera inaugurated President

1916

Sept. 4, Eight hour day came into effect

Dec. 27, Arbitration Treaty with Brazil signed

1917

May 23, General strike Montevideo

June 3, Uruguayan ship "Rosario" sunk by German torpedo

June 16, Presidential decree announced that no American nation which was forced into a war with "nations of other countries" in defense of her own rights would be considered by Uruguay as a belligerent

July 18, Treaty with Peru provided for obligatory arbitration

Sept. 30, Congress authorized President to sever diplomatic relations with Germany

Oct. 7, Decree severed diplomatic relations with Germany

Oct. 15, New Constitution voted by Congress

Nov. 9, Uruguay seized 8 German steamships in harbor of Montevideo

Nov. 25, Constitution ratified by popular vote

1918

Jan. 3, New Constitution promulgated. Provided for complete separation of Church and State, and decentralization of the Federal Government by division of executive power between the President and the National Administrative Council in elaborate precautions to prevent conversion of presidency into a dictatorship; universal male suffrage granted

A ril 18, Arbitration Convention with France signed and also with Great Britain

Aug. 27, Treaty of Commerce with the United States signed

Oct. 31, Treaty with Paraguay signed as to coasting trade

1919

Feb. 1, Old age pension law promulgated

March 1, New Constitution as amended Jan. 3, 1918 came into effect replacing that of Sept. 10, 1829, adopted July 1830, universal male suffrage to all over 18 able to read and write

——, Baltasar Brum inaugurated President

Oct. 6, Pension law enacted established retirement fund and Pension Bank for employees in the public service

Oct. 29, Aviation pension law promulgated

1920

Jan. 10, Uruguay became original member of the League of Nations

Nov. 15, Act prescribed liability of employers in compensation for industrial accidents

Dec. 10, Day of rest law enacted for labor. Regulations promulgated Jan. 5, 1922

1921

June 20, Rent Control law enacted limited amount of rents to be charged

Dec. 7, Extradition Treaty with Brazil signed

1922

Jan. 29, Striking street car workers at Montevideo won increase in wages

March 23, Arbitration Treaty with Spain signed

1923

Feb. 15, Rural Minimum Wage law enacted

Feb. 28, Compulsory arbitration agreement with Venezuela signed

March 1, José Serrato inaugurated President

1924

Sept. 5, Crown Prince Humbert left Montevideo for Rome after visit to Argentina, Chile and Uruguay

Nov. 7, Arbitration Treaty with Salvador signed

Dec. 10, Shooting affray with Brazilian troops near Rivera on border

1925

Jan. 23, General John J. Pershing arrived at Montevideo

Feb. 6, New pension and retirement law enacted

Feb. 8, Election a victory for the Nationalists for first time in 50 years

Aug. 14, The Prince of Wales at Montevideo

Sept. 14, Decree prohibited sale and manufacture of white phosphorus matches

Nov. 5, Law established regulations for retirement of police on pension at 55

Census gave population as 1,758,334

1926

Aug. 23, Uruguay recognized Soviet Government of Russia, the first Latin-American Republic to grant recognition

Nov. 28, Dr. Juan Campisteguy (Colorado) elected President

1927

Jan. 12, Note to the United States rejected proposals as to Tacna-Arica

March 1, Dr. Juan Campisteguy inaugurated President

1928

Feb. 3, Foreigners granted citizenship in addition to their own on certain conditions

Aug. 16, Law extended pension benefits

Dec. 16, President-Elect Hoover arrived at Montevideo on South American visit

1929

Jan. 4, Treaty of friendship with Turkey signed

Oct. 20, Death of former president, Dr. José Batlle y Ordonez

Dec. 13, Law established official radio broadcasting service under Department of Education

Dec. 15–16, Lieutenant Challe, Uruguayan, started on flight from Spain. *See* Spain

1930

April 26, Senate approved terms of loan of $17,000,000 from American banks

Oct. 6–7, "Business strike" of protest against extension to private business of minimum wage and old-age pension legislation of the government employees

Nov. 30, Dr. Gabriel Terra of the Batllista or radical faction of the Colorado (Liberal) party elected President to succeed President Juan Campisteguy in 1931

VENEZUELA

Venezuela, most northern of the South American republics on the Caribbean Sea, with coastline of about 1,700 miles, bounded on the east by British Guiana, on the west by Colombia and the South by Brazil. Caracas is the seat of government.

Venezuela has an area of 393,874 square miles, according to English geographers, though local estimates put it at 393,976 square miles. It has more than 1,000 rivers, with total navigable length of more than 6,000 miles. According to the census of January, 1926, the population was 3,026,878, not including 10,520 Venezuelans known to be residing abroad. Estimated population on December 31, 1926, was 3,053,497. The language of the country is Spanish.

The country is now divided into a Federal District, 20 States and two Territories.

Some of the more important cities with their population according to the census of 1926, are:

Caracas	135,253	San Cristobal	15,295	Maracay	11,108
Maracaibo	74,767	Ciudad Bolivar	16,762	La Guaira	8,323
Valencia	36,804	Cumana	18,737		
Barquisimeto	23,109	Coro	10,932		

Dr. Juan Bautista Perez, President.

1498

July 31, Columbus discovered and named Trinidad Island off the coast of Venezuela

Aug. 1, Columbus landed on South American continent near mouth of the Orinoco River, Venezuela, and named the land Isla Santa

Aug. 2, Columbus sailed through the Gulf of Paria discovering and naming Margarita Island

1499

Alonso de Ojeda and Vespucci coasted Venezuela and gave it the name "Little Venice" on account of sight of Indian village built on piles over the water of Lake Maracaibo. *See* America May 20, Aug. 24

Voyage of Pedro Alonso Nino to Gulf of Paria. *See* America

1500

Vicente Yañez Pinzon sailing north coasted Venezuela. *See* America Feb. 28

Rodrigo de Bastidas coasted Venezuela. *See* America Oct.

50 adventurers from Hispaniola established a settlement on Island of Cubagua off the northern coast of Venezuela to engage in pearl fishing

1510

Dominican friars Pedro de Cordova and Juan Garces built monastery on the pearl coast. Destroyed by Indians, rebuilt in 1518 and destroyed by Indians again in 1520

1520

May 19, Grant of land between Paria and Santa Marta to Bartolome de Las Casas, bishop of Chiapas, known as the "Protector of the Indians" for establishment of colony of Indians. His plans defeated by the Spanish slave hunters

1521

Jan. 20, Cumana called Nuevo Toledo first founded by Gonzalo de Ocampo sent to punish Indians for destruction of monastery. Soon destroyed by Indians

1523

Cumana refounded by Captain Jacome Castellon near the ruins of New Toledo and called by him New Cordova

1525

Grant of the province of Venezuela by the Spanish crown to Heinrich Ehinger and Hieronymus Sailer creditors; German merchants of the house of the Welsers, to be held as fief of crown of Castile

1527

Coro founded by expedition of Juan de Ampues with colonists from Hispaniola. Called the city of Santa Ana de Coro

1528

Oct. 7, Welser expedition sailed from San Lucar for Venezuela

1529

Feb. 24, Ambrosius Ehinger appointed Governor superseding Ampues arrived at Coro

Oct. 2–March 17, 1530, Journey of exploration of Nicolas Federmann from Coro

1530

Feb. 15, Ordinance conferred rights of Ehinger under concession of 1525 to Anton and B. Welser

Aug. 2, Royal decree abolished Indian slavery

1531

May 10, Decree abolishing slavery of Indians modified. Slaves not to be sold out of the province

June 9, Expedition of Governor Ehinger hunting gold, B. de Santillana, deputy Governor

Sept. 1, Governor Ehinger left Maracaibo on treasure hunting expedition and was killed by poisoned arrow

1533

July 19, Welser Company appointed Nicolas Federmann Governor but appointment annulled on protest of colonists

1534

May 4, Audiencia appointed Bishop Rodrigo de Bastidas provisional Governor

1535

Feb. 7, Governor Jorge de Spira, second nominee of the Welsers confirmed Jan. 28 arrived at Coro

1537

July 6, The Audiencia of Santo Domingo appointed Dr. Antonio Navarro royal judge to investigate the Welser Company agents in Venezuela

1540

June 11, Death of Governor de Spira. Hohermut von Speier and Pedro de Villegas made *ad interim* Governors

Aug. 1, Expedition of Philip von Hutten of the Welser Company on hunt for gold

1545

Grant to the Welsers rescinded and Venezuela made a crown colony

Tocuyo first permanent settlement in the interior made by Caravajal, *ad interim* Governor

Sept. 12, Perez de Tolosa appointed Governor for the Crown (1545–48)

1546

June, Governor de Tolosa arrived at Coro

1549

Juan de Villegas succeeded Tolosa as Governor. He founded the town of Concepcion de Barburata

1550

Venezuela became a captaincy-general

1554

Villacinda succeeded Villegas as Governor (1554–56)

1555

Valencia founded by Alonzo Diaz Moreno

1556

Trujillo founded by acting Governor Paredes

Decision of the Council of the West Indies set aside claims of the Welsers

1559

Pablo Collado, Governor

1567

July 25, Caracas, the capital of Venezuela, founded by Diego de Losada under name of Santiago de Leon de Caracas

1568

May 15, Diego Fernandez de Serpa appointed Governor

1569

Nov. 24, Governor de Serpa reorganized New Cordova and changed name to Cumana

1576

Juan de Pimental arrived as Governor and Captain General and took up residence at Caracas as his capital instead of Coro

1579

April 6, Expedition of Captain Garcia Gonzales de Silva from Caracas in unsuccessful attempt to subdue Indians

1580

Luis de Rojas succeeded Pimental as Governor

1585

Campaign of Christobal de Cobas against the Cuinanagotos Indians unsuccessful

1587

Governor Rojas removed from office. Succeeded by Diego Osorio

1592

June 22, Royal decree ordered establishment of school at Caracas which later became the Seminario Tridentino

1595

March, Sir Walter Raleigh expedition arrived at mouth of Orinoco

May 29–June 4, Caracas taken and looted by English Captains Preston and Sommers

1617

Dec. 31, Sir Walter Raleigh arrived at mouth of the Orinoco River and sent 5 ships up the river in search of El Dorado

1637

Barcelona founded

1654

French buccaneers repelled in attack on Cumana

1669

Henry Morgan, English buccaneer, sacked Maracaibo

1696

College for ecclesiastics founded. Became University by royal charter of 1724

1697

French expedition pillaged Caracas

1721

Dec. 22, Decree of Philip V authorized establishment of University at Caracas

1728

Sept. 25, Royal decree granted special concessions in trade to the Guipuzcoa Company in return for protection of the coast from foreign trade

1749

April 20, Francisco de Leon led company to capital in revolt against the domination of the Guipuzcoa Company

Oct. 11, The director of the Guipuzcoa Company published manifesto detailing the benefits accruing to the colony and to Spain from the Company

1750

Jan., Julian de Arriaga y Rivero arrived succeeding Castellanos as Governor

1752

Aug. 7, Francisco de Leon and his son sent prisoners to Spain by Governor after trial of several months

1777

Sept. 8, Royal decree appointed an intendant for Venezuela organized as a captaincy-general independent of New Granada

1781

Feb. 15, Guipuzcoa Company deprived of special privileges

1786

Audiencia of Caracas established

1793

June 3, Decree established commercial court at Caracas

1797

July 13, First movement for independence. Revolt of José Manuel Espana and Manuel Gual in Caracas

1799

April 29, Espana captured and hanged a few days later

1806

March 25, Liberating Expedition of Miranda, patriot, repulsed by Captain General Vasconcelos at Ocumare. He retired to Trinidad

April 27, Francisco Miranda in ship "Leander" with army recruited in the United States and with the good wishes of the English admiral Sir A. Cochrane attempted to disembark near Puerto Cabello and proclaim the republic

April 29, Spanish ships repulsed Miranda and captured 60 of his recruits on unarmed schooners who were afterwards imprisoned and some of them hanged

Aug. 3, Miranda captured Coro and issued his proclamation to South Americans but Venezuelans failed to come to his support and he evacuated the town on the 13th

1808

July 15, Napoleon's envoys arrived at Caracas. Rejected by people and the municipal council

1810

April 19, Citizens of Caracas, Don Martin Tobar and others, formed an independent Junta "to preserve the rights of Ferdinand VII" and deposed the Spanish Governor Vicente Emparan

April 27, Junta issued address to cabildos at Spanish-American capitals inviting them to join the revolution and form a Spanish-American Confederation

June 9, Simon Bolivar, revolutionary leader, sailed with Lopez Mendez and Andres Bello on diplomatic mission to London

June 26, President Madison appointed Robert Lowery commercial agent for the United States in Caracas

Nov. 28, Marquis del Toro repulsed with heavy loss in attack on Coro, headquarters of royalist reaction

Dec. 5, Return of Bolivar with Francisco de Miranda

1811

March 2, First Congress met at Caracas

June 22, Miranda obtained a seat in Congress

July 5, Independence of Venezuela adopted by Congress and flag raised by Miranda in 1806 adopted as national flag

July 7, Declaration of independence approved and signed

July 11, Royalist counter-revolution at Caracas suppressed

July 19, Miranda appointed commander of army marched to subdue royalist uprising in Valencia which had broken out July 11

July 27, First agent to represent a Latin-American nation in the United States appointed, Telesforo de Orea, as "extraordinary agent of the Venezuelan Confederation"

Aug. 13, Valencia surrendered to Miranda after siege and attack

Dec. 21, Federal Constitution adopted by Congress

1812

March 10, Royalist invasion led by Monteverde

March 23, Monteverde captured Carora

March 25, Royalist squadron attacked and after 2 days destroyed the patriot fleet in the Bay of Lorondo

March 26, Destructive earthquake. 10,000 persons killed in Caracas. Used by priests to make people believe it a judgment of God because of the revolution which did not affect Coro, Maracaibo, and Guayana which had remained faithful to the King

April 23, Congress appointed Miranda commander-in-chief of army

April 26, Miranda appointed Dictator

May 3, Royalists entered Valencia

June 17, Retreat of Miranda to Victoria attacked by Monteverde

June 24, General insurrection of slaves

June 29, Miranda repulsed royalist attack

June 30, Bolivar lost Puerto Cabello by its capture by Spanish prisoners there

July 5, Bolivar embarked for La Guaira after defeat July 4

July 25, Treaty of San Mateo. Capitulation of Miranda surrendering to Monteverde. Property and persons of Venezuelans to be respected

July 30, Miranda reached La Guaira to sail for the United States. Accused by Bolivar and others as a traitor because of the capitulation he was made a prisoner and Spanish authorities in violation of agreement sent him to Spain where he was moved from dungeon to dungeon until his death

——, Royalists entered Caracas

July 31, Spanish flag raised over forts of La Guaira replacing that of the Republic

Aug. 8, Domingo Monteverde entered Caracas as Captain-General

Aug. 27, Bolivar granted a passport by Monteverde sailed for Curacoa

Dec. 3, The "Spanish Constitution" published in Caracas

1813

Jan. 13, Arrival at La Guaira of Don Santiago Marino and other refugees from Trinidad

May 15, Bolivar with liberating army started from Colombia for Venezuela

May 30, Bolivar took Merida and established his government

June 8, Bolivar made his proclamation of "war to the death"

June 14, Bolivar entered Trujillo

June 15, Bolivar again proclaimed "war to the death" against Spaniards

June 19, Patriot General Girardot defeated Spaniards under Manuel de Canas near Agua de Obispos

July 30, Capuchinos surrendered to patriot Colonel Marino

Aug. 4, Bolivar entered Caracas

Aug. 26–Sept. 6, Siege of Puerto Cabello by Bolivar's generals Girardot, Rivas, and Urdaneta until arrival of Spanish warship compelled them to leave

Sept. 16, Royalists defeated near Barquisimeto

Sept. 21, Royalist General Boves defeated patriots commanded by Colonel Thomas Montilla in Calabozo district

Sept. 30, Battle near Naguanagua in Valencia. Girardot killed

Oct. 14, Caracas proclaimed Bolivar "Liberator of Venezuela" and made him Governor and Captain-General of the armies of Venezuela

Nov. 10, Bolivar attacked Colonel José Ceballos at Barquisimeto but his troops retreated at moment of victory

Dec. 5, Bolivar defeated Ceballos and Yanez near Araure

Dec. 14, Boves defeated patriots at San Marcos and occupied Calabozo

1814

Jan. 2, Bolivar declared Dictator by Government at Caracas

Feb. 2, Yanez, royalist, defeated Urdaneta at Ospino

Feb. 3, Battle at La Puerta. Boves defeated patriots commanded by Campo Elias

Feb. 10, Morales repulsed in attack on Victoria by Rivas and Campo Elias

March 31, Battle of General Marino with General Boves, royalist, at Bocachica

April 16, General Marino defeated by royalist General Ceballos in Arado

May 28, Bolivar defeated Spanish Field Marshal Cajigal at Carabobo

June 14, Bolivar decisively defeated at La Puerta by Indians and plainsmen led by Boves

July 6, Bolivar evacuated Caracas and La Guaira

July 7, Royalist Ramon Gonzales occupied Caracas

July 9, Valencia surrendered to Boves

Aug. 14, Don Pablo Morillo appointed Captain-General of Venezuela

Aug. 18, Bolivar and Marino defeated by royalist Morales at Aragua near Barcelona

Sept. 7, General Urdaneta badly defeated at Mucuchies by royalist Calzada and fled to Colombia. Bolivar sailed for Curaçoa

Sept. 8–12, Morales defeated at Maturin, patriots commanded by Bermudez

Sept. 29, General Piar defeated royalists at Cumana

Dec. 5, Royalist victory in valley of Urica but General Boves killed

Dec. 10, Morales defeated Bermudez in decisive battle. General Rivas captured by royalists and beheaded, Bermudez escaped

Dec. 11, Maturin last stronghold of patriots taken by Morales

1815

April 3, Spanish troops sent by Ferdinand VII arrived at Puerto Santo

April 9, Spanish fleet took possession of Island of Margarita

April 10, Governor Morillo arrived from Spain and landed on Margarita Island

May 11, General Morillo entered Caracas

May 26, Patriots at San Diego elected Monagas and Zaraza chiefs of new army

Oct. 31, José Antonio Paez defeated royalists under Calzada in Chire

Nov. 15, Patriot leader Arismendi leading insurgents on Margarita Island laid siege to capital and shut up Governor in the castle of Santa Rosa

1816

March 16, Bolivar with liberating army of 300 men sailed from Cayos de San Luis in ships of Luis Brion, the "admiral of Venezuela"

May 2, Bolivar expedition arrived at the Island of Margarita

May 7, Bolivar named supreme chief with Marino second in command

May 8, Bolivar issued first proclamation to the people of Venezuela, and announced renunciation of his former policy of war to the death under which hundreds had been massacred

July 5, Bolivar landed at Ocumare

July 13, Bolivar and Soublette routed by Morales near Ocumare

July 14, Death of General Francisco Miranda in prison in Cadiz, Spain

——, Bolivar fled to West Indies reaching Island of Bonaire July 16

Aug. 2, General MacGregor and Soublette routed royalists at Quebrada-Honda

Aug. 16, Bolivar arrived at La Guaira, but obliged to return to Haiti as Generals Marino and Bermudez refused to recognize his authority after his flight and abandonment of patriots

Aug. 25, MacGregor and Monagas defeated royalists commanded by Rafael Lopez at Aragua

Sept. 12, Royalists evacuated Barcelona

Sept. 27, Battle of Juncal. MacGregor and Piar defeated royalists

Dec. 21, Bolivar sailed from Haiti for Venezuela and proceeded to Barcelona

1817

Jan. 9, Bolivar and Arismendi defeated in attack on royalists in entrenched position on the Unare River

Jan. 17, General Piar, patriot, repulsed in attack on Angostura

Jan. 19, General Marino attacked royalists at Cumana

Jan. 28, General Paez routed the Spaniards under Morillo in the savannas of Mucuritas

Feb. 1, General Marino at Barcelona recognized Bolivar as "supreme chief of the republic"

Feb. 16–18, Bolivar defeated army of Morillo near Barcelona

April 7, Barcelona taken by royalists and garrison massacred

April 11, General Piar defeated Spanish commanded by La Torre at San Felix

May 8, General Marino who had declared himself independent of Bolivar installed a Federal Congress and provisional Government in Cariaco with Asunción as the capital. Bolivar named one of executive Junta. Marino made general-in-chief

May 19, 2,800 soldiers arrived from Spain with General Juan Canterac

June 10, Morillo and Canterac captured Cariaco

July 15, Spanish troops landed at port of Gumache, Margarita Island

July 17, Angostura surrendered to patriots

July 31, Morillo in severe battle defeated patriots at Matasite, Margarita Island

Aug. 3, Guayana Vieja evacuated by La Torre and occupied by Bolivar

Aug. 8, Morillo attacked and captured Juan Griego, port of Island of Margarita and massacred garrison in lake nearby known today as "The Lake of the Martyrs".

Aug. 17, Spanish General Morillo evacuated Margarita Island and reëstablished headquarters at Caracas Aug. 20

Oct. 16, General Piar who had joined with Marino in effort to have a Junta of War appointed to restrict authority of Bolivar executed by order of Bolivar in the public square at Angostura. Marino banished

Oct. 30, Bolivar presided at opening of Council of State

Dec. 2, Patriots commanded by Zaraza surprised and defeated by La Torre at Hogaza

Dec., The United States recognized the Venezuelan patriots as belligerents

1818

Jan. 31, First meeting of Bolivar and Paez

Feb. 10, Morillo defeated by Bolivar and Paez near Calabozo

Feb. 13, Bolivar and Paez appeared before Calabozo and Morillo forced to withdraw the following day

March 6, General Paez, patriot, captured San Fernando

March 16, Bolivar defeated by Morillo and Morales at La Puerta

April 18, Bolivar defeated by royalists near Rincon de los Toros

May 2, Paez defeated by La Torre on plains of Onoto near Cojedes

May 20, Battle at Los Patos. General Cedeno defeated royalist General Morales

May 28, Paez defeated Morales near the Apure River

Aug. 25, Bermudez and Brion defeated royalists near La Guaira

Sept. 13, Bermudez defeated by royalists near Rio Caribe

Oct. 22, Bolivar proclaimed plan for the union of Venezuela and New Granada

1819

Jan. 21, Two transports with 1,500 English troops recruited by Venezuelan agents in London arrived at the Island of Margarita to join patriot army

Jan. 30, General Morillo advanced on San Fernando. Paez burned the city and retreated southward

Feb. 4, Morillo took Marrero and Caujaral

Feb. 10, Bolivar elected President and Don Francisco Antonia Zea, Vice-President

Feb. 15, Second Congress of Venezuela installed at Angostura. Bolivar resigned his dictatorship to this

body and thereafter consulted them though dictator *de facto*
March 27, Colonel José Pereira defeated troops of Bolivar
April 3, Paez defeated Morillo in action known as Las Queseras del Medio
July 17, General Urdaneta captured Barcelona but attacked by royalists was forced to retire to Paria
Aug. 5, Urdaneta repulsed in attack on royalists at Cumana
Aug. 7, Battle of Boyaca in New Granada isolated Morillo in Venezuela
Aug. 15, Angostura Congress promulgated a provisional Constitution
Dec. 11, Bolivar returned from victorious campaign in New Granada resumed authority
Dec. 14, Congress installed
Dec. 17, Fundamental Law enacted in which Venezuela and New Granada united in the Republic of Colombia. Bolivar made President of "Great Colombia" which also included Quito

1820

Oct. 2, Bolivar occupied Merida
Oct. 22, General Monagas attacked and defeated royalists commanded by Saint Just at Barcelona
Nov. 25, Armistice signed by Bolivar and Morillo
Dec. 17, General Morillo embarked for Spain leaving General La Torre in the chief command

1821

Jan. 28, Province of Maracaibo declared independence of Spain and union with Colombia
April 28, Armistice ended. General Urdaneta occupied Altagracia, Maracaibo
May 11, Coro captured by patriot General Urdaneta
May 15, General Bermudez took Caracas but forced by royalist General Morales to retire on the 26th
May 24, Indecisive battle of Bermudez and Morales in highlands of Cocuisas
June 15, General Bermudez attacked royalists under Pereira at Santa Lucia forcing their retirement
June 24, Battle of Carabobo. Bolivar defeated royalists commanded by La Torre which secured the independence of Venezuela
June 29, Bolivar entered Caracas in triumph
July 3, Pereira with 700 men surrendered to Bolivar
July 11, Royalist attack at Cumarebo defeated by Escalona
July 12, Fundamental Law adopted. *See* Colombia. Permanent union of Venezuela and New Granada proclaimed
Aug. 22, La Torre in attempt to escape from Puerto Cabello defeated in battle with Colonel Manrique
Sept. 2, Commission sent by Bolivar to Spain to treat for peace expelled from the country because of breaches of armistice by patriots
Oct. 16, Cumana with 800 men surrendered by royalist Colonel José Caturla to General Bermudez
Nov. 10, General Morales from Puerto Cabello attacked La Guaira, Catu, and Ocumare

1822

Jan. 9, Royalist General La Torre occupied Coro and defeated Colonel Juan Gomez in 2 battles
Jan. 16, Royalists defeated Colonel Reyes Vargas in valley of Baragua
April 17, Colonel Pinango in battle with royalists

near Coro which resulted in occupation of Coro by patriots
June 7, Royalist army of General Morales defeated General Soublette in Dabajuro
Sept. 7, Morales took Maracaibo
Sept. 8, Fort San Carlos on Lake Maracaibo surrendered to General Morales, royalist
Oct. 16, Cumana surrendered to patriot General Bermudez
Nov. 12, Morales defeated patriot army of Montilla and then occupied the Province of Santa Marta
Dec. 3, Morales occupied Coro
Dec. 5, Morales defeated Colonel Torrellas near Coro
Dec. 28, Morales occupied Trujillo

1823

Jan., Santa Marta retaken by patriot General Montilla and Coro by General Soublette
Jan. 4, Trujillo recaptured by General Clemente
May 1, Naval engagement at Puerto Cabello where Colonel Padilla was maintaining blockade of royalists
June 16, Colonels Padilla and Manrique took royalist fort at Maracaibo and made Governor Moreno a prisoner. Evacuated June 19 on return of Morales
July 24, Colonel Padilla in successful engagement with Spanish squadron sunk 1 boat and captured 10
Aug. 3, Capitulation of Spanish General Morales to Colonel Padilla and surrender of Maracaibo and Fort San Carlos
Nov. 7, Night attack of Padilla on Puerto Bello
Nov. 8, Surrender of Puerto Bello by Spanish General Calzada

1824

April 5, Congress of the Confederation at Bogota, Colombia adopted Constitution. *See* Colombia

1826

April 30, Paez headed insurrection in Valencia proclaiming independence of Venezuela of the Colombian Federation
May 5, Caracas joined the insurrection
Oct. 19, Garrison at Angostura declared for Paez
Nov. 19, Battle at Cumana. Forces of Paez defeated those of Bermudez
Dec. 16, Bolivar arrived at Maracaibo

1827

Jan. 1, Bolivar at Puerto Cabello restored General Paez to his command from which he had been suspended by Congress pending investigation of charges of forcible conscription and proclaimed general amnesty
Jan. 10, Bolivar entered Caracas
July 5, Bolivar left Venezuela for Colombia

1828

Aug. 18, Royalist guerillas in insurrection in the mountains surrendered to General Paez

1829

Nov. 13, Secessionist movement begun in Valencia
Nov. 26, Resolution adopted by convention in Caracas that Venezuela should separate from Colombian Federation
Dec. 8, Decree of General Paez announced dissolution of the Confederation

1830

Jan. 13, General Paez declared the independence of Venezuela and invited convention to meet in April in Valencia

May 6, Constitutional Congress met at Valencia

Sept. 22, Congress adopted Constitution and affirmed separation from Colombia. General Paez elected President

Dec. 17, Death of Simon Bolivar at Santa Marta, Colombia

1831

Jan. 15, Revolt against Paez in province of Barcelona led by General José Tadeo Monagas

April 18, New Congress declared General Paez constitutional President and Dr. Urbaneja Vice-President

May 25, Caracas declared the capital city by Congress

May, Revolt in Caracas suppressed

1833

Jan., Third Congress met

March 11, Preliminary commercial Convention concluded with France

April 6, Law abolished tithes and provided expenses of Church be paid by national Treasury

1834

Feb. 18, Decree proclaimed freedom of worship

Oct. 29, Treaty of commerce and navigation with Great Britain

Dec. 23, Agreement signed to assume part of debt of Colombian Confederation

1835

Feb. 28, Recognition of independence by the United States

José M. Vargas elected President by Congress

July, Insurrection led by General Marino deposed and exiled Vargas. General Paez took the field against the insurgents

1836

Jan. 20, Treaties of commerce and navigation and amity with the United States signed which also recognized independence of Venezuela

March 1, General Paez defeated rebels under General Marino at Puerto Cabello

April, President Vargas who had returned from exile resigned and Vice-President Narvarte assumed executive office

Nov. 30, Archbishop Mendez exiled because of his refusal to obey laws as to exercise of patronage by the civil power

1837

Jan. 20, General Carreno became acting President and a few months later General Carlos Soublette inaugurated as President

March 27, Treaty of friendship, commerce, and navigation with the Hanseatic States signed

March 30, Law provided that Spanish merchant vessels would be admitted to Venezuelan ports

Convents for men abolished and friars granted pensions

1838

Paez reëlected President

March 26, Treaty of commerce and navigation with Denmark signed

1839

April, Law enacted granting further freedom of the press

1840

April 23, Treaty of friendship, commerce, and navigation with Sweden and Norway signed

1841

May, Law provided for establishment of a national bank

1842

July 23, Commercial treaty with Colombia provided for free trade with certain exceptions and free navigation of rivers and lakes

Oct. 15, Decree outlined organization of the missions to the Indians of Guyana placed under a director-general under the Dept. of the Interior, and Oct. 22 for Maracaibo

1843

March 25, Treaty of friendship, commerce, and navigation with France signed

General Soublette elected President

June, Law regulated universities

June 27, Resolution decreed that ecclesiastics were civil employees with civil functions to perform and must act subject to civil authority and give notification if absent from their parishes

1845

March 30, Treaty of friendship and peace and recognition of independence signed with Spain. Recognized right to territory as far east as Essequibo

1846

Insurrection against President Paez led by Antonio L. Guzman suppressed

General José Tadeo Monagas elected President. A. L. Guzman defeated candidate

1848

Jan. 24, President Monagas dissolved Congress by force of arms

April 10, Public land law enacted

April 28, Law provided for manumission of slaves

Aug. 31, Decree prohibited entrance of Jesuits into Venezuela

1849

General Paez led insurrection against President Monagas who defeated him and finally sent him into exile

July 6, Ecclesiastics required to obtain special license for leaving their parishes

1851

General José Gregorio Monagas, brother of the President, elected President

1852

May 1, Claims Convention with the United States signed

Nov. 25, Treaty of friendship and boundary limits with Brazil signed

1854

March 24, Law abolished slavery

April 1, Mint established at Caracas

1855

General José Tadeo Monagas became President for second time

1857

April 10, New Constitution promulgated

1858

Feb. 8, Treaty of commerce and friendship with Belgium signed

March 5, Insurrection in Valencia led by General Julian Castro, Governor of Carabobo, against the Constitution of 1857. General Castro became President

Dec. 24, New Constitution adopted more federalistic than that of 1830. Congress invited Paez to return from exile

Antonio Guzman Blanco, Liberal, exiled

1859

Jan. 14, Claims Convention with the United States signed

Feb. 20, Vote of majority of citizens declared in favor of a Federal Republic

May 5, Boundary Treaty with Brazil

July 24, General Falcon, Liberal, landed in Venezuela and proclaimed the Federal Republic. Castro captured presently and deposed

Aug. 1, President Monagas arrested; Dr. Pedro Gual became President

Aug. 2, The same troops which had arrested Monagas now declared against the Revolution, firing on the people, beginning five year "War of the Federation"

Sept. 30, Battle of Sabana de la Cruz which resulted in the fall of Barquismeto, Liberal victory

Dec., Battle of Santa Ines, Liberal victory

1860

March 31, Treaty of friendship, commerce, and navigation with the Hanseatic Republics

Manuel Felipe Tovar elected President

Aug. 27, Treaty of amity, commerce, and navigation with the United States signed

1861

March, General Paez returned to Venezuela, captured Caracas and deposed President Tovar, became Dictator and with General Juan Falcon succeeded in ending civil war for a time

June 19, Treaty of friendship, commerce, and navigation with Italy signed

Sept. 8, Paez elected President

1862

Oct. 21, Guzman Blanco won the victory of Quebradaseca

Dec. 19, Treaty of friendship, commerce, and navigation with Denmark signed

1863

March 6, President Paez signed Concordat with the Vatican which was not accepted by Congress as not in harmony with the Law of Patronage

April 16-18, Battles which gave the province of Caracas to the Federals

May 22, Peace of Coche, an agreement to end hostilities signed by Paez and Guzman Blanco, representing General Falcon leading revolution, by which Paez agreed to abdicate and an assembly to be nominated by chiefs of both parties. General Falcon named as "provisional President"

July 24, General Falcon, elected President, entered Caracas. Guzman Blanco became Minister of Finance and Foreign Affairs

1864

March 28, New Constitution adopted for the "United States of Venezuela"

1866

April 25, Claims Convention with the United States

1867

Oct. 28, New Civil Code promulgated in May went into effect

1868

May 2, President Falcon in the face of revolt and opposition of Congress resigned in favor of Bruzal and Urrutia and went into exile

July, General José Tadeo Monagas seized the Government

Nov. 18, Death of President Monagas. Pulgar became provisional President

1869

Feb., General Ruperto Monagas, son of former President, elected President by Congress

Aug. 14, Nocturnal attack on house of Guzman Blanco, Federalist. He was exiled

1870

April 27, The *Jaunes* (Liberals) entered Caracas after 3 days conflict and General Antonio Guzman Blanco made President

May 7, Decree of President Blanco ordered redemption of the *censos* (fixed contribution to the church from landed property) by certificates of public indebtedness

June 27, Decree provided that education should be free and compulsory and tax established for support of elementary education

July 13, President Blanco inaugurated as constitutional President and became virtual Dictator for 20 years as either President or through Presidents elected on understanding that all official acts must be submitted for his approval

1871

Jan. 6, Archbishop Guevara left the country, exiled for refusal to celebrate a *Te Deum* as ordered for victory of Blanco over Salazar on Sept. 21, 1870

May, Decree regulated coinage

1872

May, Revolt of General Salazar suppressed and Salazar shot

1873

Jan. 1, Decree made civil marriage legal

May 7, Death of General José A. Paez in New York City

1874

May 5, Convents for nuns extinguished in law and ordered closed, nuns granted a pension

May 27, New Constitution promulgated

June 1, Decree provided that the courts should take cognizance of cases against the clergy

1876

May, Resignation of Archbishop Guevara in exile obtained, the see of Caracas declared vacant by the Pope in June and José Antonio Ponte elected by Congress

Sept., Renunciation of papal authority announced

1877

Feb. 27, General Alcantara elected President. Guzman Blanco went to Europe

May 18, Trade mark law enacted

Aug. 7, Guevara returned to Caracas, decree of exile repealed

1879

Guzman Blanco again President

March 31, Currency law enacted. Coin called bolivar made monetary unit

1881

April 27, Constitution adopted resembling that of Switzerland

Sept. 4, Boundary Agreement with Colombia signed

1882

May 15, Law adopted gave the head of the Government full powers as to granting permission for foreign war vessels to enter ports, not open, for scientific purposes

May 20, Treaty of commerce and navigation with Spain signed

May 25, Patent law enacted

1883

Aug. 27, Treaty of commerce and navigation with Salvador signed

Sept. 15, Concession granted to E. R. Hamilton to exploit forests and asphalt in State of Bermudez

Railroad between Caracas and La Guaira opened

1884

Joaquin Crespo, President. Blanco again accredited Minister Plenipotentiary to France went to Europe, directing Venezuelan affairs from Paris

March 1, Treaty of amity, commerce, and navigation signed with Belgium

1885

Dec. 9, Concession of Hamilton of Sept. 15, 1883 transferred to New York and Bermudez Company (asphalt) incorporated in New York Oct. 24, 1885

1886

Sept. 14, General A. Guzman Blanco elected President

1887

Feb. 20, Announcement of severance of diplomatic relations with Great Britain in dispute over boundary with British Guiana

June 2, New currency law enacted

July, President Blanco transmitted his authority to Manuel Diez, a member of his Council and proceeded to Europe on a diplomatic mission, General Lopez elected President

1888

Jan., Agreement to pay Great Britain indemnity of £10,000

March 15 and Oct. 5, Claims Conventions with the United States signed

June 29, Dr. Juan Pablo Rojas Paul elected President

Nov., Revolt of Joaquin Crespo failed

1889

May 19, President Rojas Paul resigned but subsequently recalled resignation

Oct., Political revolution begun by students of the University which ended in overthrow of Blanco and Rojas Paul his nominee

1890

Feb. 20, Raimundo Andueza Palacio elected President

Sept. 2, Award in claims of the United States against Venezuela $912,036.88

1891

March 16, King of Spain made award in boundary dispute with Colombia

April 9, New Constitution promulgated

June 26, Currency Act

June 30, Mining law promulgated

1892

Jan. 19, Convention with the United States signed to submit to arbitration matter of seizure of 3 American steamships during revolution

March 26, Decision of Supreme Court against continuance in office of President Palacio as unconstitutional. President Palacio sent the judges to prison

March 28, New Cabinet appointed

March 29, Battle on shores of Lake Maracaibo. Government forces led by General Castro forced to retire

April–Aug., Revolt led by General Joaquin Crespo because of refusal of President Andueza Palacio to relinquish his office at end of legal term

June 17, Resignation of President Palacio, Senator Villegas, provisional President assumed office

Oct. 5, Government troops defeated at San Pedro

Oct. 6, General Joaquin Crespo entered Caracas

Oct. 7, Crespo proclaimed himself Dictator

1893

Jan. 7, Immigration and colonization law enacted

June 21, New Constitution adopted which came into effect July 5

1894

March 9, Earthquake in which 10,000 persons perished

March 14, President Crespo inaugurated as elected President

May 12, Law outlined system of missions to the Indians

July 9, Venezuela adhered to Geneva Convention

Aug. 24, New public land law replaced that of 1848

Oct. 10, Venezuelans invaded British Guiana in boundary dispute

1895

Jan. 30, Red Cross Society founded

March 7, French and Belgian Consul Generals handed passports because of attitude on claims of governments for damages in civil war of 1892

March 26, Award in claims of the United States against Venezuela $141,500 for seizure of 3 American steamships during revolution

July 20, Note of American Secretary of State Olney protested to Great Britain, declaring that the boundary dispute as to British Guiana came under the Monroe Doctrine

Oct. 22, Ultimatum of Great Britain to Venezuela on account of arrest of 2 British officials on the Cuyuni River in April charged with illegal exercise of functions as Guiana police in Venezuelan territory

Nov. 10, Revolt against President Crespo begun

Dec. 17, Message of President Cleveland to Congress, intervention in Venezuelan boundary dispute with Great Britain. *See* United States

1896

Jan. 1, Commission appointed to investigate boundary with British Guiana by the President of the United States

Feb. 2, Attempt to assassinate President Crespo failed

May 18, Agreement made to pay Great Britain $8,000 indemnity as personal damages in settlement Yuruan incident, arrest of British officials in 1895

Dec. 30, Swiss arbitration award recognized claim of French merchant Fabiani

1897

Feb. 2, Treaty with Great Britain provided for arbitration of boundary dispute as to British Guiana and resumption of diplomatic relations

April 16, Ex-President Crespo killed in battle with insurgents led by Hernandez

May 17, Pension law enacted

June 28, New Cabinet constituted

Dec. 11, Diplomatic relations with Great Britain formally resumed

1898

Jan. 4, President Crespo decreed Hamilton contract (Bermudez asphalt company) terminated. Decree reversed by Court Aug. 23

March 1, General Ignacio Andrade succeeded Crespo as President

1899

Feb. 20, Revolt begun in new State of Guarico by Ramon Guerra

March 7, Government troops captured Calabozo

March 22, Guerra defeated by Government troops

April 4–7, Visit of American fleet commanded by Admiral W. T. Sampson

May 23, General Cipriano Castro, the "lion of the Andes" began insurrection against Andrade which Hernandez joined

May 24, Manifesto of Castro denounced Congress for authorizing dictatorship

June 15, Boundary Arbitration Commission met in Paris

Aug. 7, Castro defeated by government troops in State of Los Andes

Aug. 23, Castro defeated Government troops near San Cristobal and near Colombian line captured General Sarria and a large number of prisoners

Sept. 14, Valencia taken by rebel General Castro but not held

Oct. 3, Paris Boundary Commission gave decision as to boundary line with British Guiana giving Great Britain large area of inland territory claimed, 60,000 square miles, the Shomburgh line with 2 exceptions taken as boundary, but to Venezuela the entire mouth of the delta of the Orinoco River

Oct. 4, Armistice agreed to for conference which began the following day on board the U.S.S. "Detroit"

Oct. 10, Contract of Maritime Canal Company declared voided because of non-fulfilment within stipulated 10 years

Oct. 20, President Andrade transferred his authority to Vice-President Victor Rodriguez and made his escape to La Guaira and from there eventually to Puerto Rico

Oct. 23, General Castro entered Caracas and assumed the executive office next day as Provisional President

Oct. 26, General José Manuel Hernandez issued manifesto against Castro; proclaiming revolution

Oct. 30, Hernandez defeated at San Casimiro by General Mendoza

Nov. 12, Puerto Cabello taken by General Castro

Nov. 20, The Castro Government recognized by the United States

Dec. 3, Government forces took Maracaibo

1900

Feb. 27, Unsuccessful attempt to assassinate President Castro

March 21–22, Hernandez defeated by J. M. Paredes at Manocal

May 27, Hernandez defeated and captured by General Davilla at Tierra Negra and imprisoned, ending insurrection

Sept. 28, Executive decree reëstablished Seminary of Caracas

Oct. 24, General Pedro Julian Acosta began revolution in Yrapa. Captured after battle

Oct. 29, Earthquake destroyed the town of Guarenas and destroyed part of Caracas

——, Provisional President Castro elected constitutional President

1901

March 26, New Constitution adopted

July 28, Battle of San Cristobal in insurrection led by General Carlos Rangel Gardiras aided by Colombians in effort to open rivers closed by Castro, ruining coffee industry in Santander

Sept. 14, Venezuelans defeated at La Hacha. *See* Colombia

Dec. 21, Revolution is State of Lara led by General Mendoza

1902

Feb. 19, Commercial Treaty with France signed and diplomatic relations renewed

March 1, Colombians under Rangel Gardiras defeated near Lafrias

April 29, Agreement with France to pay certain claims of French citizens and submit others to arbitration

Aug. 12, Barcelona sacked by rebels

Oct. 13, Government troops won victory near Victoria

Nov. 4, Revolt ended with defeat of rebels after many battles

Nov. 13, British ultimatum to Venezuela as to payment of claims, the third in 3 months

Dec. 7, Great Britain and Germany present ultimatum as to claims

Dec. 9, Venezuelan war vessels in port of Caracas seized by British and German vessels

Dec. 11, Blockade of Venezuelan ports established by Great Britain and Germany

Dec. 13, Bombardment of forts at Puerto Bello by British and German cruisers. Venezuela asked President Roosevelt to arbitrate dispute

Dec. 16–17, Great Britain agreed to arbitration except as to certain "first rank" claims

Dec. 20, Formal "pacifist" blockade of ports established by Great Britain, Germany, and Italy, creditor nations; President Roosevelt asked to act as arbitrator

Dec. 29, Note of Luis M. Drago, Argentine Secretary of Foreign Affairs as to blockade. *See* Argentina

1903

Feb. 13, Protocol of settlement signed through mediation of the United States for reference of claims of blockading nations to Hague Tribunal

Feb. 17, The blockade raised

——, Claims Convention with the United States signed

May 7, Treaty signed by which claims conditions agreed

upon, including claims not only of blockading nations but all creditor nations

Feb. 26, Protocol of claims signed with Mexico, with France Feb. 27, with the Netherlands Feb. 28, with Belgium March 7

Sept., Claims of the Powers presented as follows: France, $16,040,000; United States, $10,900,000; Italy, $9,300,000; Belgium, $3,003,000; Great Britain, $2,500,000; Germany, $1,417,300; the Netherlands, $1,048,451; Spain, $600,000; Mexico, $500,000; Sweden, $200,000

1904

Feb. 22, Award of Hague Tribunal given decided in favor of preferential treatment of 3 blockading nations

April 27, New Constitution adopted. President Castro to be provisional President until next constitutional term begun on May 5

May 5, President Castro inaugurated, Juan Vicente Gomez, first Vice-President, José Antonio Velutini, second Vice-President

July 29, President Castro confiscated the property demanding $10,000,000 of the New York and Bermudez Asphalt Company basing demand on alleged support given to Matos revolution of 1902. The same charge was made against the French Cable Company and franchise annulled and property confiscated

Aug. 1, Protest of the United States against seizure of property of the American company asphalt properties

Nov. 12, Decree expelled Jaurett American proprietor of newspaper and resident 8 years and on the 14th escorted to railroad by police and sent out of country

1905

Jan. 1, Population 2,598,063

Feb. 16, Supreme Court reaffirmed decision sequestrating property of American asphalt company

March 20, France presented ultimatum in matter of seizure of property of French Cable Company and French warships ordered to ports

March 21, Agreement to pay $26,000,000 to Great Britain and Germany

March 24, President Castro refused to submit claims of American asphalt company to arbitration

March 31, Supreme Court declared French Cable Company had forfeited its charter through failure to fulfil terms

June 7, General Castro reëlected President

Nov. 16, Refusal to pay second installment of French claims under award

Dec. 9, Protocol signed at Caracas settled boundary dispute with Brazil

1906

Jan. 10, Diplomatic relations with France severed

Jan. 17, Head of French cable office expelled from Venezuela

Jan. 18, Venezuelan chargé d'affaires in France handed his passports and escorted to Belgian frontier

April 9, General Castro temporarily resigned office transferring authority to Vice-President Gomez while he had vacation

May 17, New Cabinet

July 4, President Castro resumed office

1907

Feb., General Antonio Paredes landed near mouth of the Orinoco and announced revolution against Government. Captured at El Rosario and executed

July 1, Award of Hague Tribunal placed British, French, and Italian claims at £691,160. £840,000 still due other nations

Debt to Belgium repudiated

July 27, President Castro refused to submit American claims to arbitration

Nov. 19, Decree increased duties on agricultural products

1908

March 3, President Castro again declined arbitration of American claims

March 17, Court decision annulled Fitzgerald concessions under which several American companies claimed rights in Venezuela

May 14, Decree of President Castro prohibited the transshipment at Curacoa of goods destined for Venezuela in retaliation for Dutch quarantine against yellow fever in port of La Guaira, disrupting West Indian trade

June 23, Secretary of American Legation left Caracas severing diplomatic relations because of refusal of Castro to pay claims or submit them to arbitration

July 1, Court of Cassation confirmed decision of lower courts imposing fine of $5,000,000 on New York and Bermudez Asphalt Company

July 22, Dutch Minister given his passports

Aug. 20, Ultimatum of the Netherlands demanded revocation of decree of May 14

Sept. 12, President Castro refused to revoke decree of May 14

Nov. 7, Netherlands Government revoked Treaty of 1894 and proclaimed blockade of Venezuelan ports

Dec., President Castro left Venezula for Europe for surgical operation, Vice-President Gomez assuming the executive office

Dec. 12, Venezuelan coast guard vessel seized by Dutch cruiser as reprisal

Dec. 17, Mob at Caracas shouted "Down with Castro" and wrecked property of his adherents

Dec. 19, Vice-President Gomez proclaimed himself President

Dec. 20, Castro adherents arrested on charge of plot to kill Gomez

Dec. 21, The United States resumed diplomatic relations

Dec. 22, Trans-shipment decree of May 14 revoked

Dec. 24, Decree of Castro permitting trade with Colombia at only a few points revoked

1909

Jan. 28, Treaty of amity, commerce, and navigation signed with Germany

Feb. 13, Protocol signed with the United States provided that certain claims (the Orinoco corporation and the Critchfield claims) be referred to Hague Tribunal for arbitration

March 24, President Castro in Bordeaux notified that he would be arrested if he returned to Venezuela

April 19, Treaty with the Netherlands

April 30, Arbitration Convention with Brazil signed

May 12, Agreement with French Cable Company settled points in dispute

May 21, Ex-President Castro charged with plotting to kill Gomez, Acting President, acquitted by Court

June 2, Preliminary Treaty with Colombia as basis for

Treaty of frontiers signed renewed diplomatic relations

July 12, General Castro in Spain renounced his claim to the presidency

Aug. 5, New Constitution promulgated

Aug. 12, Gomez formally elected Provisional President and assumed office the next day

Sept. 23, Representative at Colombia recalled in dispute over lands required under Treaty of 1899

Dec. 28, Diplomatic relations severed with France on account of claims on behalf of French citizens

1910

Feb. 10, Discovery of plot of Castro partisans to overthrow the Government. Many arrests made

March 31, $1,030 paid Great Britain for unlawful detention of British trading schooner in 1908

April 27, Gomez elected constitutional President

June 3, President Gomez inaugurated

June 29, Mining Code promulgated

Sept. 23, Colombian representative recalled from Bogota in dispute over lands required by Treaty of 1909

Oct. 25, Award rendered in Orinoco claims case $46,867 with 3% interest since June 6, 1903 and $7,000 costs

1911

June 24–July 24, Centennial celebration of independence of Venezuela

July 22, Arbitration Treaty with Argentina signed

July, Decree converted revolutionary and other public debts into the national internal debt

1912

Feb. 25, Arbitration Treaty with Peru signed

March 21–23, Visit of American Secretary of State, Philander C. Knox

May 18, Decree provided that official system of weights and measures should be the metric system

June 13, Railroad concessions law enacted and Treasury Code

1913

Jan. 1, Population 2,755,638

Feb. 12, Minister from France arrived, renewing diplomatic relations

Feb. 28, Slight revolt against the Government

May 24, New naturalization law promulgated. One year of residence required before naturalization with certain exceptions

June 13, Agreement signed at Caracas restored diplomatic relations with France

——, New Fundamental law adopted

July 1, Board of Mines established

July 3, New pension law enacted

July 27, Manifesto of ex-President Castro who had returned secretly to Island of Trinidad issued began second revolution against President Gomez

July 29, President Gomez issued proclamation of campaign against Castro

Aug. 1, Martial law declared

Aug. 18, Government troops recaptured towns from the Castro insurgents

1914

Jan. 1, President Gomez returned to Caracas at head of his victorious army

March, Insurrection near Marawhanna

March 21, Advancement of Peace Treaty with the United States

April 19, Secretary of War General V. Marquez Bustillos chosen Provisional President to succeed Gomez by Congress, Gomez to be commander-in-chief of the army

June 13, New Constitution adopted May 18 promulgated

Aug. 1, Code of mines revised

Aug. 8, The Government announced that it would maintain strict neutrality during the European War

Aug., Decree decreased official salaries and abolished certain offices

Sept., Revolt in eastern part of the Republic led by General Du Charme

Dec. 19, Law provided that primary instruction should be compulsory and free for children from 7 to 14

1915

Jan. 9, Executive decree presented rules and regulations for fishing for pearls

Jan. 14, Protocol settled claims of France

March 18, Executive decree made it obligatory to send children between the ages of 7 and 14 to primary school

May 3, Congress reëlected Juan Vicente Gomez President for period 1915–1922. The President-Elect did not assume office, but remained in command of the army. Provisional President Bustillos continued to act as President

June 4, Law as to aliens enacted, regulations for foreigners

June 30, Penal Code promulgated and Code of criminal procedure

Aug. 23, Battle at Maturin. Rebel General Du Charme captured and executed, ending revolt begun in Sept. 1914

Nov. 16, Arbitration Treaty with Chile signed

Dec. 19, Decree provided for construction of eastern highway from Caracas through the states of Miranda, Anzoategui, and Bolivia to interior of Guiana

1916

Jan. 3, Decree created naval school at Puerto Cabella. Formally inaugurated April 19

July 16, Ex-President Cipriano Castro excluded from the United States on arrival from Europe on the ground of moral turpitude. Released from detention at Ellis Island by the Secretary of Labor July 18. Sailed for Puerto Rico Aug. 6

Aug. 11, Decree provided for construction of western highway from Caracas to San Cristobal

Nov. 3, Convention as to frontiers with Colombia signed referring dispute to arbitration

Dec. 19, New Civil Code came into effect replacing that of 1904

1917

Feb. 14, Statement of Minister of Foreign Affairs that policy would accord with the principles of international law and with the relations of peace and friendship which Venezuela had with all the belligerents in World War

June 26, Workshop and Public Establishment Act passed

——, Law enacted on the gathering and exploitation of heron feathers

Aug., The President suppressed 2 newspapers favorable to Allies and against Germany

1918

April 12, Decree made study of English obligatory in the public schools

June 4, Organic finance law signed by the President and law on railroad concessions

——, Decree provided that companies organized abroad should be considered as national companies and be required to conform to laws of Venezuela

June 24, New public land law promulgated

June 26, Immigration and colonization law approved

June 27, Mining law promulgated

July 2, Bureau of Mines and of Public Lands, Industries, and Commerce established

First shipment of oil from Venezuela, 800 metric tons, about 2,400 barrels, from Maracaibo

1919

April 12, Arbitration Treaty with Bolivia signed

June 24, New alien law enacted regulating aliens, resident and transient

June 27, Sanitary law enacted, and laws on public lands, forests, and waters

June 29, Code of commerce enacted

Dec. 29, Presidential decree promulgated regulations for the law as to mines

1920

Jan. 2, New Sanitary Code promulgated by decree

March 3, Venezuela joined the League of Nations

March 17, Rules and regulations governing deposits of coal and petroleum promulgated

April 17, Decree provided for establishment of military aviation school at Maracay

May 11, Convention signed for reëstablishment of diplomatic relations with the Netherlands

June 15, Law enacted governing pearl fisheries

June 24, New sanitary law enacted

June 26, Consular service law promulgated repealing that of 1910

——, New mining law promulgated repealed that of June 27, 1918

June 30, New law promulgated as to hydro-carbons and other mineral fuels

July 21, Aviation law promulgated

Dec. 21, Protocol signed for settlement of claims of Italian subjects

1921

May 24, Arbitration Treaty with Ecuador signed

Aug. 25, Death of General José Manuel Hernandez

2,500,000 barrels of oil exported during year

1922

Jan. 19 and 21, Extradition Treaty with the United States signed

Feb. 8, Regulations for exploitation of natural products enacted

March 24, Award of President of Swiss Republic in boundary dispute with Colombia practically upheld decision of King of Spain of 1891

May 3, General Juan Vicente Gomez reëlected President and General José Gomez first Vice-President

June 2, Mining law passed

June 19, New Constitution adopted, promulgated June 24

June 24, President Gomez assumed office as President relieving Acting-President Marquez Bustillos of nominal authority he had exercised since 1914

July 5, Presidential decree opened the Central University, closed for some years

July 10, Alien law approved defined rights of aliens

July 13, Civil Code promulgated

July 22, Arbitration Treaty with Argentina signed

1923

Feb. 28, Arbitration Treaty with Uruguay signed

March 14, Arbitration Treaty with Peru signed

June 15, New financial reform law came into effect

June 19, Wireless telegraph between Venezuela and Colombia inaugurated

June 30, Juan C. Gomez, first Vice-President, brother of the President, assassinated in the palace as a protest against nepotism

July 10, National sanitation law passed

July 15, New law governing the consular service enacted

Aug. 7, Law as to aliens published prescribed conditions to be fulfilled by foreigners living in Venezuela, admission, expulsion, &c.

Oct. 7, Announcement that Mexico had broken off diplomatic relations. Reason given expulsion of Mexican theatrical company

1924

June 20, New land law for distribution, sale, lease, and administration of government lands signed by the President

July 4, Law on import duties published by the President

Dec. 4, Death of Ex-President Castro in Puerto Rico at San Juan

9,000,000 barrels of oil exported during year

1925

Feb. 22, Arrival of General Pershing and staff on U.S.S. "Utah" at La Guaira

May 1, Radio service with the United States inaugurated from Caracas

June 10, Pension law promulgated repealed laws of 1913 and 1897

June 24, New Constitution adopted making minor changes in that of 1922

July 18, Law of mines published included regulations for work hours, compensation for accidents, and prohibited labor of women and children in interior of mines

Aug. 15, Law published as to status of foreigners

Aug. 18, Law published on uncultivated and public lands

1926

April 13, Treaty with Brazil signed as to maintenance of order in frontier district

May 10, Transandean mail service by motor begun between Valencia and San Christobal

June 22, New organic financial law superseded that of 1918

July 6, New Code of criminal procedure promulgated

July 15, New Penal Code promulgated

July 24, International bridge over the La Grita River opened

38,500,000 barrels of oil exported during year

1927

June 27, Act established 8½ hour day for workers in public undertakings

July 5, Professor Edwin Kemmerer and commission on

financial mission completed work and left the country

July 9, Trade-mark law of 1877 as amended June 30 signed by the President and new patent law enacted

July 18, Banking law authorized free establishment of banks

July 20, New tariff law promulgated for increased revenue

July 21, Decree reorganized post-office service

Aug. 15, New regulations for work of minors adopted. Published Aug. 27

1928

Jan. 17, The French aviators D. Costes and J. Lebrix arrived at Maracay in flight from Colon

Jan. 29, Colonel Charles A. Lindbergh arrived at Maracay in flight from Colon

April 7, Mutinous troops and students in clash with government forces at the palace

April 23, Special message of the President advised abolishing of the office of Vice-President and Inspector-General of the Army and announced the resignation of his son of both those offices. Congress abolished the offices

——, Government closed national Military School at Caracas because of student riots

June 5, Law passed established Agricultural and Livestock Bank to finance agricultural and livestock business

July 13, New copyright law signed by the President

——, New naturalization law signed by the President superseding that of 1913

July 23, New labor law signed by the President. Regulations issued Aug. 13

Aug. 6, New passport and entrance regulations for foreigners published

Aug. 18, Boundary Agreement with Brazil to replace Protocol of 1905 provided for commission to complete survey

Oct. 28, Student rioters imprisoned

1929

Jan. 17, Earthquake destroyed seaport of Cumana, oldest existing European settlement in South America, killing 25 persons; rebuilt

Feb. 13, President Gomez fired on by 6 men in environs of Maracay. All killed by escort of the President

April 19, Congress met and on May 3 reëlected President Gomez who declined to serve

April 28, Revolutionists led by General Arevalo Cedeno invaded the country from Colombia

May 29, New Constitution adopted

May 30, Congress elected Juan Bautista Perez, president of the High Court of Cassation, President of the Republic for a 7 year term. The retiring President General Gomez appointed Commander-in-Chief of the army

June 8, Venezuelan exiles raided police headquarters at Willemstad, seat of government of Curacao (Dutch West Indies), seized arms and commandeered ship and forced captain to take them to Venezuelan coast

June 24, Capture of General José Rafael Gabaldon ended revolt in southwest

Aug. 29, Government took over the match industry

Nov. 19, Student rioters imprisoned in 1928 for demonstration against the President freed on peace bonds

Oil production 110,000,000 barrels, surpassing production of both Mexico and Russia

1930

April 2, Strike of street car employees at Caracas

May 24, Statue of Francisco de Miranda presented by French colony of Venezuela unveiled in town of Valmy, France

June 6 and 9, Contracts signed by the President for establishment of air mail lines connecting with Panama and cities of Central, North, and South America

Aug. 11, Decree created new Ministry of Sanitation and Agriculture

Dec. 17, Unsuccessful revolt against the Government

ARCTIC REGIONS

For voyages of discovery *see also* America, United States, and Canada

1472

Alleged expedition of John Scolp, Dane, to Labrador region

1497

May 2–Aug. 6, First voyage of John and Sebastian Cabot (Giovanni Caboto, of Genoa) under English flag with crew of 18 men from Bristol. *See* America

1498

June 24, Second expedition of the Cabots with 5 vessels reached mainland of North America

1500

Voyage of Gaspar de Cortereal (Portuguese) in search of a North West passage

1553

May 20, Sir Hugh Willoughby's and Richard Chancellor's expedition to find a North East passage to China, in the *Edward Bonaventura, Bona Esperanza,* and *Bona Confidentia,* sailed from the Thames

1554

Richard Chancellor, in the *Edward,* reached Archangel and Moscow; the rest perished off the coast of Lapland

1576

Sir Martin Frobisher's attempts to find a North West passage to China, June 7–Oct. 2; May 26–Sept. 23, 1577; May 31–Oct., 1578

1585

Company called the "Fellowship for the discovery of the North West passage" formed in London

1585, 1586, 1587

Capt. Davis's expedition to find a North West passage

1594–95

Barentz's Dutch expeditions (by N.E.)

1602

Waymouth and Knight's expedition

1607–10

Hudson's voyages. April 19, 1607, Henry Hudson reached 80° 23′, farthest north at the time

1612

Sir Thomas Button's voyage

1616

Baffin's Bay discovered by William Baffin

1631

Foxe's expedition. *See* Canada

1728, 1729, 1741

Bering's voyages

1742

Middleton's expedition

1746

Moore's and Smith's expedition

1769

Hearne's land expedition

1773

Captain Phipps, afterwards Lord Mulgrave, his expedition

1776

July, Capt. Cook, in the *Resolution* and *Discovery*

1777

June 8, Lieutenant Walter Young instructed to search for passage westward from Baffin Bay reached 72° 42′ North Lat. Back in England Aug. 26

1789

Mackenzie's expedition

1790

Captain Duncan's voyage

1795

Sept., The *Discovery,* Captain Vancouver, returned from a voyage of survey and discovery on the northwest coast of America

1815

Oct., Lieut. Kotzebue's expedition

1818

May 3, Captain Ross and Lieut. Parry in the *Isabella* and *Alexander*. *See* Canada

Captain Buchan's and Lieut. Franklin's expedition in the *Dorothea* and *Trent*

1819

May 12–Nov. 3, 1820, Expedition of Lieuts. Parry and Liddon, in the *Hecla* and *Griper* in search of the North West passage. Entered Lancaster Sound Aug. 1, Sept. 4 passed the 110th meridian west of Greenwich. Wintered on Melville Island. Aug. 8 sailed west toward Bering Strait and blocked by ice, forced to return to England

1819–22

Franklin's second expedition

1821–23

May 8, Capts. Parry and Lyon in *Fury* and *Hecla;* discovered Hecla and Fury Strait July, 1822

1824

May 8, Parry's third expedition with the *Hecla*

1825

Feb. 16, Capts. Franklin and Lyon, after having attempted a land expedition, again sail from Liverpool

1827

June 22, Capt. Parry again in the *Hecla*, sails from Deptford, and reaches a spot 435 miles from the North Pole; returns Oct. 6

1833

Oct. 18, Capt. Ross arrived at Hull, on his return from his Arctic expedition, after an absence of four years, and when all hope of his return had been nearly abandoned *

1835

Sept. 8, Capt. Back and his companions arrived at Liverpool from their perilous Arctic land expedition (1833), after having visited the Great Fish River and examined its course to the Polar Seas. *See also* Canada, June 7, 1834

1836

June 14, Capt. Back sailed from Chatham in command of his majesty's ship *Terror*, on an exploring adventure to Wager River

1845

May 24, Sir John Franklin, and Capts. Crozier and Fitzjames, in the ships *Erebus* and *Terror*, leave England (*see* Franklin)

1847–48

The NORTH WEST PASSAGE was discovered by Sir John Franklin and his companions, who sailed down Peel and Victoria Straits, since named Franklin Straits. On the monument in Waterloo place is inscribed— "*To Franklin and his brave companions, who sacrificed their lives in completing the discovery of the North West passage*, A.D. 1847-8"

1849

July 17, Commander Moore sailed from Kotzebue Sound, reached Point Barrow July 27, wintered in Grantley Harbor

1850

Jan. 20, Commanders Collinson and M'Clure, in the *Enterprise* and *Investigator*, sailed eastward in search of Sir John Franklin and discovered North West passage †

* In 1830 he discovered Boothia Felix: on June 1, 1831, his nephew, Com. James Clark Ross, discovered the north magnetic Pole, in 70° 5' 17" N. Lat., and 96° 46' 45" W. Long.

† Capt. M'Clure sailed in the *Investigator* in company with Com. Collinson in the *Enterprise* in search of Sir John Franklin, Jan. 20, 1850. On Sept. 6 he discovered high land, which he named Baring's land; on the 9th, other land, which he named after Prince Albert; on the 30th the ship was frozen in. Entertaining a strong conviction that the waters in which the *Investigator* then lay communicated with Barrow Strait, he set out on Oct. 21, with a few men in his sledge, to test his views. On Oct. 26 he reached Point Russell (73° 31' N. Lat., 114° 14' W. Long.), where from an eleva-

Oct. 26, A North West passage discovered by Capt. M'Clure

1869

June 15, A German Arctic expedition (the *Germania* and the *Hansa*) sailed; arrived at Pendulum bay, Greenland, July 18, 1869; the vessels parted; the *Germania* arrived at Bremen, Sept. 11, 1870; the *Hansa* was frozen and sank, Oct. 1869; the crew escaped with provisions and reached Copenhagen Sept. 1, 1870

1871

June 20, Capt. Hall sailed from New York in the U.S. ship *Polaris*; frozen in, Sept.; died, Nov. 8. After much suffering, the crew reached Newfoundland May 9, 1873. *See also* United States

Mr. B. Leigh Smith sailed to Lat. 81° 24', and discovered land to the northeast of Spitzbergen; in other voyages he discovered under-currents of warm water flowing into the polar basin; he relieved the Swedish expedition, 1872–73

1872

A Norwegian Arctic expedition sailed in the spring

July 14, An Austro-Hungarian expedition in the *Admiral Tegethoff*, and the *Isbörjnen*, under Weyprecht and Payer, sailed from Tromsö, in Norway; the ships parted company, and the *Tegethoff* sailed northward and discovered Franz-Josef Land, Aug. 31, 1873; frozen in, abandoned ship, May, 1874; reached Vardöe, Norway, by sledges, Sept. 3; arrived at Vienna Sept. 25, 1874

July 21, A Swedish expedition, under Professor Nordenskjöld, sailed from Tromsö; unsuccessful; returned summer 1873

1875

May 29, Capt. G. S. Nares, of the *Challenger*, appointed to command the *Alert*, and Capt. H. F. Stephenson to command the *Discovery* sailed from Portsmouth; dispatches received from Disco (all well) July 15

June 25, Expedition of Capt. Allen Young in the *Pandora* (aided by Lady Franklin), sailed; returned Oct. 19; sailed again, June 2, 1876; returned Oct. 31

1876

Oct. 27, *Alert* (on return) arrived at Valentia; the *Discovery* at Queenstown, Oct. 29; at Portsmouth Nov. 2. *Results.* Sledges reached 83° 20' 26", May 12, 1876; passage to the Pole declared to be impracticable; no signs of open polar sea; ships wintered, 82° 87' Lat.; sun absent 142 days; no Esquimaux beyond 81° 52'

1878

April, Dutch expedition sailed from Holland

July 4, Another expedition in *Vega*, under Prof. Nordenskjöld, started; at Port Dickson on the Yenisei, Aug. 6; at the mouth of Lena, Aug. 27; at Yakutsk, Sept. 22; imprisoned in ice near Tschuctshe settlement, Sept. 28, 1878–July 18, 1879; passed East Cape, Bering Strait; entered St. Lawrence Bay, in Pacific Ocean, July 20; reached Yokohama Sept. 2. The NORTH EAST PASSAGE from the Atlantic to the

tion of 600 feet he saw Parry or Melville Sound beneath them. The strait connecting the Atlantic and Pacific Oceans he named after the Prince of Wales. The *Investigator* was the first ship which traversed the Polar sea from Bering's straits to Bering island.

Pacific is thus accomplished; chiefly at the expense of Oscar Dickson, a merchant of Gothenburg

1879

May 6, Dutch exploring expedition in *Willem Barents*, sailed for Arctic Ocean; successful; returned to Hammerfest, Norway, Sept. 24

July 8, Mr. James Gordon Bennett's expedition; Lieut. de Long sailed in yacht *Jeannette*

1880

June 22–Oct. 12, Mr. B. Leigh Smith's successful expedition in his yacht *Eira* from and to Peterhead

1881

June 14, Another expedition by him in the *Eira*; *Eira* seen in Straits of Nova Zembla July 8. [The *Eira* injured by ice; at Cape Flora sank in deep water, Aug. 21; stores saved, tent and house erected; the party live on seals, walrus, &c. during winter, 1881–2; return voyage began (boats hauled, &c.), June 21; fell in with a Dutch vessel, *Willem Barents*, and soon after with the *Hope*, near Matotchkin Straits, Nova Zembla, Aug. 3; sail for home, Aug. 6; arrive at Aberdeen, Aug. 20]

July 7, Expedition of A. W. Greely sailed from St. Johns, Newfoundland and reached Discovery Harbor Aug. 12 where he established station. *See also* United States

1882

April 2, Austrian Polar expedition, *Polar* started; returned to Drontheim Aug. 11; to Vienna Aug. 22, 1883

May 11, British circumpolar expedition started; Aug. 30, arrived at Fort Rae; good news Dec. 1

May 15, Greely expedition reached farthest north at Lat. 83° 24½' N. and Long. 40° 46½' W.

June 13, Expedition in the *Jeannette*, which is crushed by ice; two boats with crew received by Russians at mouth of the Lena, March 23; one boat missing, Dec. 1881. Bodies of Capt. de Long and others found near the mouth of the Lena, conveyed to Philadelphia, and buried Feb. 23, 1884

Oct. 23, German Arctic expedition, *Germania* sailed, summer, returned

1883

July 23, Greely's ship the "Proteus" crushed in polar ice. *See also* United States

1884

Feb., The British Government presents the *Alert* to aid the expedition, under Commander Winfield S. Schley, in search for the party under Lieut. Greely, 25 persons (which started for the Polar seas in the summer of 1881); the search expedition starts, May 10, 1884; $25,000 reward offered by U.S. Government for discovery of Lieut. Greely and party, May

June 22, Lieut. Greely's party reached Cape Sabine, Smith's Sound, 83° 24' N. Lat.; 17 persons starved to death; 1 drowned, 6 survivors found by Com. Schley with the *Thetis*; arrive at St. John's, Newfoundland, July 17; at Portsmouth, New Hampshire, Aug. 1

1886

Oct. 2–March 3, 1897, Colonel Gilder's overland expedition from Winnipeg

1892

June 24, Bjorling and Kalstennius, young Swedish naturalists, and a small party, leave St. John's in the *Ripple* for Smith's Sound; reach Disco Island, Greenland, insufficiently equipped, July 31; they crossed Baffins Bay, and arrived at Carey Island, Aug. 16; the vessel is driven on shore, Aug. 17; in a desperate condition with shortness of provisions, embark for Clarence Head, Cape Faraday, Ellesmereland, in a small boat, Oct. 12; not since heard of, reported Dec. 1893; traces of them found on Carey Island, reported Oct. 19, 1894

1893

June 24, Dr. Fridtjof Nansen starts from Christiania in the *Fram* for Arctic regions; Dr. Nansen with Lieut. Johansen, left the *Fram* in charge of Capt. Sverdrup and Lieut. Scott-Hansen, March 14, 1895; after having touched a point 4 degrees further north than any previous explorer. In their journey over the ice they reached 86° 14' Lat., April 8; and arrived at Franz-Josef Land, Aug. 14, and there wintered: Dr. Nansen met Mr. Jackson there, June 17, 1896; and they returned in the *Windward* to Vardöe, Aug. 3; arrival of the *Fram* at Skjervöe, after reaching 85° 57' N. Lat. Aug. 20

July 2, Lieutenant Peary starts from New York, with an expedition in two parties, the expedition fails through bad weather and loss of dogs, returned to St. John's

1894

Feb. 4, Mr. F. G. Jackson arrives at Hull after spending some months within the Arctic circle

July 7, Peary relief expedition in the *Falcon* leaves St. John's; returns there with the members of the expedition, including Mrs. Peary, all well, Sept. 15; Lieut. Peary, Mr. Hugh Lee, and Henson, a servant, remain in Greenland to continue their explorations; Peary relief expedition, in the *Kite*, leaves St. John's for Bowdoin Bay, Inglefield Gulf, July; returns with Lieut. Peary, Mr. Lee, and Henson, who were nearly starved, Sept. 21, 1895

July 12, The Jackson-Harmsworth expedition (33 persons) in the *Windward*, Mr. A. C. Harmsworth defraying all expenses, about 25,000*l.* starts for Franz-Josef-Land from London; left Archangel, Aug. 5; reached Franz-Josef Land, Sept., 1894, frozen in; exploration by Mr. Jackson; he and his party remain; the *Windward* leaves July 3, and arrives at Gravesend, Oct. 22, 1895

Nov. 27, The *Falcon* wrecked off South Greenland, Oct.; all perish; reported

1896

June 15, Herr Andrée and M. Eckholm leave Tromsö in the *Virgo* for a balloon expedition to the North Pole; prevented, and return, Aug. 24

July 15–Sept. 26, Sixth expedition of R. E. Peary. *See* United States

1897

July 11, Andrée ascends in the *Eagle* with Drs. Strindberg and Fraenkel from Danes Island (617 miles from the North Pole), 2.30 P.M.; not heard of afterward; relief expedition in the *Victoria* returns to Tromsö without news, Nov. 21, 1897

July 19–Sept. 20, Seventh expedition of R. E. Peary; returns to St. John's with the Cape York meteorite (45 tons). *See* United States

Sept. 3, Capt. Robertson, of the Dundee whaler *Balæna*, discovers several islands on the south coast of Franz-Josef Land, reported

1898

May 30, Herr Theodor Lerner's North polar expedition in the German steamship *Helgoland* leaves Berlin

June 24, Capt. Sverdrup's polar expedition in the *Fram* leaves Christiania

July 3, Mr. Wellman's expedition to Franz-Josef Land sailed from Tromsö; established an outpost, "Fort McKinley," 81° Lat., autumn, 1898; Mr. Wellman pushed northward, mid Feb. 1899; unknown regions explored, and good scientific results, reported; they return to Tromsö Aug. 17

1899

June 12, The Duke of Abruzzi's expedition in the *Stella Polare* to Franz-Josef Land left Christiania; wintered on Rudolf Land; Capt. Cagni's party (the Duke too severely frost-bitten to go) started for the N. Pole, March 11 (Lieut. Quérini and two men lost since March 22), reached 86° 33' 49" N., April 25, 1900; returned, Sept. 6

June 27, Mr. Walter Wellman's (American) North polar expedition in the *Frithjof* leaves Tromsö

Sept. 12, Andrée search expedition, under Dr. Nathorst, discovers new inlets east of Greenland, and arrives at Malmö

1900

July 11, Andrée's buoy No. 4 found at Skjervöe, containing message: N. 45° east, in excellent spirits; M. Andrée reported by some to have been killed by natives, Aug. 31

1901

June 28, The Baldwin-Ziegler expedition left Dundee; visited Rudolf Land, Nansen's hut, Greely Island, returned with new charts, &c., to Norway, July 31, 1902

1902

July 13, Baron Toll's expedition left Cape Wyssoki for Bennett Land

Lieut. Peary, undaunted by previous suffering, advanced to extremity of Greenland, 83° 50', spring, 1900; was stopped by the ice opening; again he started from Cape Hecla, Grinnell Land, and reached 83° 15', but had to fall back, spring, 1901; he started again, April 1, 1902, with Henson and four Eskimos, &c., but failed to reach the Pole but reached farthest north Lat. 84° 17' 27"; all returned in the *Windward*, to Sydney, Cape Breton Island, Sept. 18

Sept. 19, Capt. Sverdrup, in the *Fram*, was blocked in the ice about 79° N. near Cape Sabine, Aug. 1898; in Aug. 1899, he rounded south end of Ellesmere Land, through Jones Sound and Cardigan Strait; explored new lands, with important scientific results, to 81° 37'; returned to Norway

1903

Jan., Scientific expedition to the region of the North Pole, under the patronage of, and subsidized by, the French Academy of Sciences, in process of organization by M. Jean Charcot

June 23, Ziegler expedition in the *America* leaves Trondhjem for Franz-Josef Land

Aug. 12, The *America* arrives at Cape Flora; fights its way slowly against the ice, reaches Toplitz Bay,

Crown Prince Rudolf Island, the most northern harbor in Franz-Josef Land (which formed the base camp of the expedition during the whole of its stay in the Arctic, and was named Cape Abruzzi in honor of the Italian explorer), end Aug.

Aug. 22, Canadian Arctic expedition in the *Neptune* leaves Halifax for Hudson Bay, and the Arctic seas

Nov. 21, *America* crushed by the ice and completely wrecked; ship's coats and coal sledged ashore from the vessel

1904

Jan. 22, Heavy gale of wind breaks up the old ice in Toplitz Bay, with several miles of the glacier face, and carries it away with the remains of the *America*

March 7, First sledge party leaves Toplitz Bay; stormbound for a number of days at Cape Fligely, and compelled to return owing to injuries sustained by some of the men, and for repair of equipments; second sledge party leaves Toplitz Bay, March 25

May 16, M. Fiala, leader of the Ziegler expedition, leaving a small company of volunteers to stay at Cape Abruzzi through another winter, for the purpose of another attempt further north, conducts a party of 25 men, 16 pony sledges, and 8 dog teams and sledges, to Cape Flora to await the relief ship; Cape Flora reached

Nov. 20, Watch kept for arrival of relief ship, May 16 to Sept. 10; important discovery of coal made; hope of relief given, arrangements made to return to Cape Abruzzi for further attempt to reach the Pole in 1905; party arrives at Camp Abruzzi

1905

March 9, North Pole Commission officially declares that the expedition under Baron Toll to the New Siberian Islands, in the Arctic Ocean, has ended with the death of the members of the party

March 16, Ziegler sledge party, delayed by bad weather and high temperature, start from Camp Abruzzi for their northern expedition

April 1, Fog, high temperature, rough ice, and pressing necessity for sending food supplies to the parties at Cape Flora and Camp Ziegler, the scarcity of dogs, and impossibility of breaking the record under prevailing conditions, determine M. Fiala to return, Camp Abruzzi being reached

May, Expedition organized by the duc d'Orleans, in connection with the international commission for the exploration of the northern seas, sails for Spitzbergen in the *Belgica*

July 16, Peary starts again for the North Pole in the *Roosevelt*; sails from New York

July 30, Preparations made by the Ziegler expedition for work in the ensuing winter; observatories erected in Camp Ziegler, and scientific work carried on continuously; party of men dispatched to Cape Dillon to keep a look-out for the relief ship, *Terra Nova*, early July; party return bringing news of the arrival of the relief expedition, under the command of Mr. Champ

Sept. 13, Death of Capt. J. Wiggins, the discoverer or rediscoverer (1874) of a new ocean highway within the Arctic circle, by which the trade of European Russia obtained for the first time direct maritime access to the great navigable rivers of her Siberian possession in North Asia

Nov. 19, News received from Capt. R. Amundsen, who sailed in 1903, in the *Gjöa*, to the northern magnetic;

letter, dated May 22, 1905, from King William's Land, where the expedition since Nov. 22, 1903, had spent two winters taking magnetic observations

1906

Jan. 20, Mr. Einar Mikkelsen, in conjunction with Mr. Leffingwell, organize an expedition to the Beaufort Sea, sails from Liverpool

Sept. 5, Captain Amundsen reports arrival of the *Gjöa* at Nome, Alaska, having completed the navigation of the North West passage

Nov. 4, Commander Peary reports having reached 87° 6' north latitude, about 200 miles from the Pole on the Greenland side, April 6, and 30 miles farther than has been previously accomplished

1907

June 3, The Wellman polar expedition steamer *Frithjof*, having on board Mr. Wellman and the 35 men of his party, sails for Spitzbergen

1908

Captain Einar Mikkelsen, the Danish explorer who jointly commanded the Anglo-American polar expedition to the Beaufort Sea, arrives at Alaska, having started from Flaxman Island on October 16, 1907, and making a sledge expedition, found the continental shelf, beyond which there is water of great depth, demonstrating that the Beaufort Sea is not a shallow basin; at a distance of 64 miles from land it was impossible to touch bottom with a 320 fathom line, which indicated that the shelf had been passed, April 2

July 6, Commander Robert E. Peary in the "Roosevelt" sailed from New York, left Sydney, N.S., July 17, and wintered at Grant Land

July 28, Canadian Government steamer "Arctic" commanded by Capt. J. E. Bernier left Quebec and proceeded to Etah, Greenland where supplies left for Dr. Cook. Then proceeded to Smith Sound, Lancaster Bay, along Barrow Strait to Erebus Bay and to Beechey Island, to Winter Harbor, Melville Island. Wintered at Winter Harbor

1909

Feb. 15, Peary expedition arrived at Cape Columbia and began dash for the North Pole March 1. *See also* United States

April 6, Discovery of the Pole by Robert E. Peary

June 19, The members of the Wellman North Polar expedition, whose object is to reach the Pole by airship, leave Paris for Tromsö

Commander Peary's message to the Governor of Newfoundland, saying that he planted the stars and stripes at the North Pole on April 6th, received by wireless message from Indian-harbor, Labrador, Sept. 6

Dec. 21, Dr. Cook, who claimed that he had first reached the North Pole April 21, 1908, sent his proofs to the University of Copenhagen, whose decision went against his claim

1913

July 2, MacMillan expedition left New York for 3 year exploration of Arctic

July 29, Canadian Government expedition commanded by Vilhjamur Stefansson sailed from Port Clarence, Alaska for the Arctic seas to explore unknown areas

and to get scientific information. Wintered at Collinson Point

1914

Jan. 11, The "Karluk" of the Stefansson expedition crushed by ice and 8 members of party lost in attempt to reach land. *See* Canada

March 22, Stefansson Canadian expedition. *See* Canada, and Sept. 7, 1914 and Feb. 20, 1915

Sept. 1, Survivors of Russian polar expedition reached Archangel, Lieut. Sedov dead

1917

Aug. 26, MacMillan expedition (Crocker Land) reached Sydney, Cape Breton, reported Crocker Land a mirage

1921

July 8–Sept. 20, 1924, MacMillan expedition engaged in glaciological research Smith Sound

1922

March 19, Stefansson announced taking possession of Wrangel Island in Sept. 1921

Aug. 8, The "Maud" (Amundsen polar expedition) froze in ice near Wrangel Island and drifted until Aug. 1924 when the New Siberian Islands were reached, and the ship emerged from ice

1925

March 31, Captain Roald Amundsen and Lieutenant Lincoln Ellsworth (American) left Oslo for Tromsö to begin airplane expedition to the North Pole from Spitzbergen

April 8, Lieut. Comm. Robert Byrd appointed to command flying unit MacMillan Arctic expedition

May 21, Amundsen-Ellsworth expedition left Spitzbergen in 2 airplanes for polar flight the "N 24" wrecked, the "N 25" obliged to give up flight because of insufficient amount of gasoline after 8 hours, landing at position of 87° 44' N. Lat. and 10° 21' W. Long., where plane was frozen in for 3 weeks; it had been expected that the trip to the Pole would take 7 hours, Spitzbergen reached June 15 after flight of 8 hours and 25 minutes

June 20, MacMillan expedition left Boston for base at Etah, Greenland, reached Aug. 1

June 25, Amundsen-Ellsworth expedition made flight to North Cape on northern extremity of North-East Land

Oct. 5, Amundsen polar expedition in the "Maud" returned to Seattle after 3 years in the Arctic Ocean

Oct. 12, MacMillan expedition returned from Greenland. The planes covered 6,000 miles and discovered uncharted mountain ranges

1926

March 31–April 7, Detroit Arctic expedition commanded by George H. Wilkins with Lieut. Carl B. Eielson, pilot, in plane "Alaskan" made flights from Point Barrow

May 9, Lieutenant Commander Richard E. Byrd, U.S. Navy, retired, and Floyd Bennett, U.S. Navy, left King's Bay, Spitzbergen in triple motored Fokker monoplane, the "Josephine Ford" at 12.30 A.M. and reached the North Pole at 9.04 A.M. Greenwich time and made return flight, total flying time 15½ hours, reaching Spitzbergen at 4.20 P.M., distance about 1,500 miles

May 11, Captain Amundsen, in the "Norge" with

Colonel Nobile, the designer and builder of the "Norge," Lieutenant Ruser-Larsen of the Norwegian Navy, and Lincoln Ellsworth (American) and crew of 14 men left King's Bay for flight to the North Pole reaching the Pole in about 15 hours May 12 at 2.30 P.M., and then proceeded to Point Barrow, Alaska, and from there to Teller, Alaska, 68 hours flight from King's Bay, flight of 3,291 miles May 14

June 27–Oct. 1, Putnam Arctic expedition returned to New York with specimens for American Museum of Natural History from Greenland after 14 weeks voyage in Arctic covering 8,500 miles, George Palmer Putnam, director, Robert E. Peary, Jr., Captain Robert Bartlett and Knud Rasmussen. The University of Michigan expedition headed by Professor William H. Hobbs to study Greenland weather conditions, on the same boat

1927

March 29, Captain G. H. Wilkins with Ben Eielson, pilot, left Point Barrow in airplane to explore polar region north of Asia. Forced landing at 175° W. Long. and 77° 45′ N. Lat. Plane abandoned 83 miles from Point Barrow because of insufficient gasoline. Walking along Alaskan shore they reached Beechey Point April 15

June 25, The 11th Rawson-MacMillan Sub-Arctic scientific expedition left New York for 15 months' exploration of Labrador and Baffin Land

1928

April 15, Wilkins and Eielson left Point Barrow in airplane and reached Green Harbor, Spitzbergen April 21, the flight reduced unexplored area but no land found

May 15, General Nobile in the dirigible "Italia" left Spitzbergen making a survey eastward over Franz-Josef Land and Nicholas II Land (Lenin Land)

May 23, General Nobile started from Spitzbergen at 4.35 A.M. for the North Pole reaching the Pole at 12.20 A.M. May 24

May 25, On return flight the "Italia" wrecked on North-East Land within 225 miles of King's Bay, 6 of party carried away with balloon and lost, the party succeeded in sending radio messages of position

June 18, Captain Roald Amundsen, Lieutenant Dietrichsen, Commander René Guilbaud, and Lieutenant de Cuverville left Tromsö, Norway to go to relief of Nobile and were not heard from again

June 20, The "Italia" sighted by Maddalena in plane but he was unable to land

June 22, General Nobile taken off ice floe by Captain E. Lundborg, Swedish aviator

July 12, Mariano and Zappi who had started with Malgren to walk over the ice May 30 rescued by Russian ice-breaker "Krassin" and the 5 others of crew who had remained with General Nobile at the wreck; Malgren died

Dec. 19, G. H. Wilkins and Eielson made flight from Deception Island 600 miles south across Graham Land discovering several new islands and that Graham Land divided by strait into 2 islands

1929

Dec. 3, The Mawson expedition left Heard Island and reached position at 65° 41′ S. and about 79½° E.

1930

Aug. 6, Norwegian scientific expedition headed by Dr. Gunnar Horn found on White Island bodies of the Swedes, Solomon August Andrée, Nils Strindberg, and Knut Fraenkel who on July 11, 1897, flew from Dane's Island, Spitzbergen, in a balloon to drift across the North Pole to America, and whose fate had been unknown. Brought to Tromsö, Norway

Nov. 12, Announcement made that the Norwegian Government formally recognized sovereignty of Canada over the Sverdrup Islands

ARCTIC REGIONS: SEARCH FOR SIR JOHN FRANKLIN

FRANKLIN, SEARCH FOR. Sir John Franklin, with Captains Crozier and Fitzjames, in H.M.S. *Erebus* and *Terror* (carrying in all 138 persons), sailed on his third Arctic expedition of discovery and survey, from Greenhithe, on May 19, 1845. Their last despatches were from the Whalefish islands, dated July 12, 1845. Their protracted absence caused intense anxiety, and expeditions were sent from England and elsewhere in search of them which remade the map of northern Canada. Coals, provisions, clothing, and other necessaries, were deposited in various places in the Arctic seas by the British and American Governments, by Lady Franklin, and numerous private persons. The *Truelove*, Captain Parker, which arrived at Hull, Oct. 4, 1849, from Davis's Straits, brought intelligence (not afterwards confirmed) that the natives had seen Sir John Franklin's ships in the previous March, frozen up by the ice in Prince Regent's inlet. Other accounts were equally illusory. The English Government, on March 7, 1850, offered a reward of 20,000*l*. to any party of any country, that should render efficient assistance to the crews of the missing ships. Sir John's first winter quarters were found at Beechey island by Captains Ommanney and Penny in 1850. *See infra*

1848

Jan. 1, H.M.S. *Plover*, Capt. Moore (afterwards under Capt. Maguire), sailed from Sheerness to Bering Strait, in search

March 25, Land expedition under Sir John Richardson and Dr. John Rae, of the Hudson Bay Company, left England. Sir John Richardson returned to England in 1849, and Dr. Rae continued his search till 1851. *See also* Canada

1849

Nov. 3, Sir James Ross, with the *Enterprise* and *Investigator* (June 12, 1848), having also sailed in search to Barrow Strait, returned to England (Scarborough)

1850

Jan. 20, The *Enterprise*, Capt. Collinson, and *Investigator*, Commander M'Clure, sailed from Plymouth for Bering Strait. Both ships proceeded through to the eastward

April 13, The *Lady Franklin*, Capt. Penny; and *Sophia*, Capt. Stewart, sailed from Aberdeen for Barrow Strait. Returned home Sept. 1851

April 25, Capt. Austin's expedition, viz.: *Resolute*, Capt. Austin; *Assistance*, Capt. Ommanney; *Intrepid*,

Lieut. Bertie Cator; and *Pioneer*, Lieut. Sherard Osborn, sailed from England for Barrow Strait. Returned Sept., 1851

May 22, The AMERICAN expedition in the *Advance* and *Rescue*, under Lieut. De Haven and Dr. Kane towards which Mr. Grinnell subscribed 30,000 dollars, sailed for Lancaster Sound and Barrow Strait; after drifting in the pack down Baffin's Bay, the ships were released in 1851 uninjured

——, The *Felix*, Sir John Ross, fitted out chiefly by the Hudson Bay Company, sailed to the same locality. Returned in 1851

June 5, *Prince Albert*, Capt. Forsyth, sailed from Aberdeen to Barrow Strait. Returned Oct. 1, 1850

Aug. 23, Capt. Erasmus Ommanney and Capt. Penny found traces of camp of Sir John Franklin on Beechey Island and Cape Riley

Sept. 28, H.M.S. *North Star*, Commander Saunders, which had sailed from England in 1849, wintered in Wolstenholme Sound, and returned to Spithead

1851

H.M.S. *Herald*, Captain Kellett, which had sailed in 1848, made three voyages to Bering Strait, and returned

June 4, The *Prince Albert*, Mr. Kennedy, accompanied by Lieut. Bellot, of the French navy, and John Hepburn, sailed from Stromness to Prince Regent's Inlet. Returned Oct. 1852

Nov. 18, Lieut. Pim went to St. Petersburg with the intention of traveling through Siberia to the mouth of the river Kolyma; but was dissuaded from proceeding by the Russian Government

1852

April 15, Sir Edward Belcher's expedition, consisting of—*Assistance*, Sir Edward Belcher; *Resolute*, Captain Kellett; *North Star*, Capt. Pullen; *Intrepid*, Capt. M'Clintock; and *Pioneer*, Capt. Sherard Osborn, sailed from Woolwich. This expedition arrived at Beechey Island Aug. 14, 1852. The *Assistance* and *Pioneer* proceeded through Wellington Channel, and the *Resolute* and *Intrepid* to Melville Island; the *North Star* remaining at Beechey Island

July 6, The *Isabel*, Commander Inglefield, sailed for the head of Baffin's Bay, Jones's Sound, and the Wellington Channel; and returned Nov.

1853

Mr. Kennedy sailed again in the *Isabel*, on a renewed search to Bering Strait

Dr. Rae, in the spring of 1853, again proceeded towards the magnetic pole; and in July, 1854, he reported to the Admiralty that he had purchased from a party of Esquimaux a number of articles which had belonged to Sir J. Franklin and his party—namely, Sir John's star or order, part of a watch, silver spoons, and forks with crests, &c. He also reported the statement of the natives; that they had met with a party of white men about four winters previous, and had sold them a seal; and that four months later, in the same season, they had found the bodies of thirty men (some buried), who had evidently perished by starvation; the place appears, from the description, to have been in the neighborhood of the Great Fish River of Back. Dr. Rae arrived in England on Oct. 22, 1854, with the relics, which

were deposited in Greenwich hospital. He and his companions were awarded 10,000*l.* for their discovery. Dr. Rae, aged 80, died July 22, 1893

May, The *Phœnix* (with the *Breadalbane* transport), Commander Inglefield, accompanied by Lieut. Bellot, sailed; he returned, bringing dispatches from Sir. E. Belcher, &c. Oct.

The *Investigator* and Sir E. Belcher's squadron were safe; but no traces of Franklin's party had been met with. Lieut. Bellot was unfortunately drowned in August while voluntarily conveying dispatches for Sir E. Belcher. Capt. M'Clure had left the *Herald* at Cape Lisburne, July 31, 1850. On Oct. 8 the ship was frozen in, and so continued for nine months. On Oct. 26, 1850, while on an excursion party, the Captain discovered an entrance into Barrow Strait, and thus established the existence of a North East-North West *passage*. In Sept., 1851, the ship was again fixed in ice, and so remained till Lieut. Pim and a party from Capt. Kellett's ship, the *Resolute*, fell in with them in April, 1853. The position of the *Enterprise* was still unknown

May 30, The second AMERICAN expedition, the *Advance* under Dr. Kane sailed; reached "farthest north" Aug. 29 at 78° 43'

Aug., H.M.S. *Rattlesnake*, Commander Trollope, dispatched to assist the *Plover*, Capt. Maguire (who succeeded Capt. Moore), at Point Barrow in April; met with it

1854

April, Sir E. Belcher, after mature deliberation, determined to abandon his ships, and gave orders to that effect to all the captains under his command; and Capt. Kellett gave similar orders to Capt. M'Clure, of the *Investigator*. The vessels had been abandoned May 15 when the crews of the *Phœnix* and *Talbot* (under Capt. Inglefield) arrived. On their return to England all the captains were tried by court martial and honorably acquitted Oct. 17–19

May, The *Phœnix*, *North Star*, and *Talbot*, under the command of Capt. Inglefield, sailed, and returned in Oct.

Capt. Kellett's ship, the *Resolute*, was found adrift 1,000 miles distant from where she was left, by a Mr. George Henry, commanding an American whaler, who brought her to New York. The British Government having abandoned their claim on the vessel, it was bought by order of the American Congress, thoroughly repaired and equipped, and entrusted to Capt. H. J. Hartstene, to be presented to Queen Victoria. It arrived at Southampton, Dec. 12, 1856

Capt. Collinson's fate was long uncertain, and another expedition was in contemplation, when intelligence came, in Feb. 1855, that he had met the *Rattlesnake* at Fort Clarence on Aug. 21, 1854, and had sailed immediately, in hopes of getting up with Capt. Maguire in the *Plover*, which had sailed two days previously. Capt. Collinson having failed in getting through the ice in 1850 with Capt. M'Clure, returned to Hong-Kong to winter. In 1851 he passed through Prince of Wales's Straits, and remained in the Arctic regions without obtaining any intelligence of Franklin till July, 1854, when, being once more released from the ice, he sailed for Fort Clarence, where he arrived as above mentioned, Captains

Collinson and Maguire arrived in England in May, 1855

1855

May 31, The third AMERICAN expedition in search of Dr. Kane, in the *Advance*, consisted of the *Release* and the steamer *Arctic*, the barque *Eringo*, and another vessel under the command of Lieut. H. J. Hartstene, accompanied by a brother of Dr. Kane as surgeon

[On May 17, 1855, Dr. Kane and his party quitted the *Advance*, and journeyed over the ice, 1,300 miles, to the Danish settlement; on their way home in a Danish vessel, they fell in with Lieut. Hartstene, Sept. 18; and arrived with him at New York, Oct. 11, 1855. Dr. Kane visited England in 1856; he died in 1857]

June, The Hudson Bay Company, under advice of Dr. Rae and Sir G. Back, sent out an overland expedition, which returned Sept. following. Some more remains of Franklin's party were discovered

1857

July 1, The 18th British expedition (equipped by Lady Franklin and her friends, the Government having declined to fit out another)—the *Fox*, screw steamer, under Capt. (since Sir) F. L. M'Clintock, sailed from Aberdeen, returned Sept. 22, 1859

1859

May 6, Lieut. Hobson found at Point Victory, near Cape Victoria, besides a cairn, a tin case, containing a paper, signed April 25, 1848, by Capt. Fitzjames, which certified that the ships *Erebus* and *Terror*, on Sept. 12, 1846, were beset in Lat. 70° 50′ N., and Long. 98° 23′ W.; that Sir John Franklin died June 11, 1847; and that the ships were deserted April 22, 1848. Captain M'Clintock continued the search, and discovered skeletons and other relics

Aug. 1865, Mr. Hall, the Arctic explorer, reported circumstances that led him to hope that Capt. Crozier and others were surviving

ANTARCTIC REGIONS

1773

Jan. 17, The Antarctic Circle crossed for the first time in history by Captain James Cook in the "Resolution" and Captain Tobias Furneaux in the "Adventure" and 67° 15′ S. in 39° 35′ E. reached where ships were stopped by ice

Nov., Captain Cook left New Zealand on second voyage, crossed the Antarctic Circle Dec. 20 reaching Jan. 30, 1774, 71° 10′ S., 106° 54′ W., 1,130 miles from the Pole, "farthest south" of the eighteenth century disproving the existence of the "Great Southern Continent" to be found on all old maps

1774

Nov., Captain Cook left New Zealand and crossed the South Pacific discovering the Isle of Georgia and Sandwich Land after rounding Cape Horn Dec. 29, and crossed the South Atlantic to the Cape of Good Hope

1819

Feb., William Smith rounded Cape Horn and sighted land which on second voyage in October he named New South Shetland

1821

Russian expedition of Fabian von Bellingshausen discovered Peter Island and Alexander Land

1823

James Weddell sailed South to 74° 15′, 945 miles from the Pole

1831

John Biscoe discovered Enderby Land 65° 57′ S. and Biscoe Islands, also Graham Land 67° S.

1838

The French expedition, under D'Urville, discovered Adelie Land and found its advance blocked by a bank extending East and West for 300 miles; La Terre Adélie in 140° E. was named in this voyage

1839

Voyage of John Balleny from New Zealand discovered the Balleny Islands

1839–1843, Sir James Clarke Ross made three voyages and discovered Victoria Land; crossed the Antarctic Circle March 1, 1842 on third and last voyage

1840

Dec. 26, United States expedition (Capt. Wilkes) sailed from New Zealand and discovered land extending from the 100th to the 100th meridian of E. Long. between the parallels of 65° and 67° S.

1845

Lieut. T. E. Moore's expedition

1850

Capt. Tassell's expedition

1874

Feb. 16, The H.M.S. "Challenger" crossed the Circle reaching 66° 40′ S. in 78° 30′ E. south of Kerguelen Land

1875

Capt. Dallmann's expedition

1892

Capt. Larsen's expedition

1893

Capt. Evanson's expedition

1895

Capt. Kristensen's expedition

Feb. 23, Mr. C. E. Borchgrevink, a Norwegian explorer, first to land at Cape Adair, on the Southern continent; a scientific expedition under him, equipped by Sir Geo. Newnes, left London in the *Southern Cross* (Capt. B. Jensen) for South Victoria Land, Aug. 22, 1898; reached Cape Adair, Feb. 17, 1899, which they ascended to 3,670 ft., March 12; valuable collection made at Duke of York island and Geikie Land (so named by Mr. Borchgrevink); magnetic position of the South Pole fixed at about Lat. 73° 20′ S. and 146° E.; furthest point South ever reached 78° 50′, March 17, 1900; they returned to Stewart island, April 4, 1900

1897

Aug. 16, The De Gerlache expedition in the *Belgica* leaves Antwerp; explored the South Shetlands, Jan. 21, 1898; discovered strait Belgica, land to the east, named Danco Land, Jan. 23; ice-bound, Feb. 23, continual night, May 17–July 21; Lieut. Danco died June 5; Punta Arenias, Patagonia, reached March 28, 1899

1901

Aug. 6, Expedition under command of Captain R. F. Scott and including Lieutenant E. H. Shackleton sailed in the "Discovery" from England for exploration of Victoria Land reached in January, 1902, following coast southward discovered King Edward Land, wintered near Mount Erebus and made sledge expeditions attaining latitude of 82° 17′ S. about 500 miles from the South Pole. Jan. 5, 1904 the relief ships arrived and "Discovery" broken out of ice Feb. 16 and reached England by way of Cape Horn Sept. 10

Aug. 11, Expedition under command of Professor Erich von Drygalski (German). The *Gauss*, Capt. Hans Ruser, left Hamburg, Aug. 11, 1901, reached Kerguelén Island, Jan. 2, 1902; a magnetic station founded there. Found bottom at 3,950 fathoms, 18° 15′ W. 0° 11′ S.

Oct., Swedish expedition of Dr. Otto Nordenskjöld, Captain Larsen in command of the ship "Antarctic" reached South Shetlands in Jan. 1902, and penetrated pack in Weddell Sea almost to circle in 50° W.

1903

Aug. 17, Relief expedition for Dr. Nordenskjöld left Sweden. *See* Sweden

Oct., Scottish expedition of Dr. W. S. Bruce, Captain Thomas Robertson in command of the ship, "Scotia" made valuable oceanographical investigations in the Weddell Sea

1904

Jan., French expedition of Dr. Charcot left Fuegan Archipelago and coasted west Graham Land

1908

Jan. 1, Expedition of Lieutenant Ernest H. Shackleton in the "Nimrod" sailed from New Zealand and established headquarters at Cape Royds, Ross Island Feb. 3

March 5, Ascent of Mt. Erebus to edge of active crater by six of the party (13,350 feet above sea level) March 10. The sledge journey of Shackleton and 3 others begun Oct. 29 passed "farthest south" Nov. 26 and reached latitude 88° 23′ S., Jan. 9, 1909, 111 miles from Pole by way of the Beardmore glacier, reaching the "Nimrod" on return journey March 1. Oct. 4, 1908 Professor T. W. E. David led party to the south magnetic Pole, reached Jan. 16, 72° 25′ S. 155° 16′ E. at altitude of over 7,000 feet. Expedition reached New Zealand March 25 and England Aug. 26

Aug. 15, The Charcot expedition in the *Pourgusi pas* left Le Havre for the Antarctic, Aug. 15, 1908; at Punta Arenas, Dec. 17, 1909; Dr. Charcot landed at Rouen, on his return, June 5, 1910

1910

June 1, Expedition of Captain Robert F. Scott in the "Terra Nova" left England, making final departure from New Zealand Nov. 29 and reaching open water in the Ross Sea Jan. 1, 1911, and established winter quarters at Cape Royd

1911

Feb. 11, Japanese expedition of Lieutenant Shirase left New Zealand but obliged to turn back after several months because of insufficient equipment

Oct. 11, Expedition of Captain Roald Amundsen (Norwegian), who had come from Madeira to Ross Sea without calling at any port or announcing intention of south polar exploration, began journey by new route by way of the Axel Heiberg glacier and reached the South Pole Dec. 14, return journey made in 38 days

Oct. 24, Captain Scott started journey to Pole from M'Murdo Sound, Cape Evans, and Dec. 10 began ascent of Beardmore glacier, Captain Scott, Wilson, Bowers, Captain Oates, and Edgar Evans reached the Pole Jan. 18, 1912, and there found tent left by Amundsen who had preceded them

Dec. 2, Australian expedition of Dr. Douglas Mawson in the "Aurora" sailed from Australia and established base in Adélie Land, Queen Mary Land discovered

1912

Feb. 17, Death of Edgar Evans on the Beardmore glacier, and on March 17 of Oates in blizzard, and of Captain Scott, March 29, with Dr. Wilson and Lieutenant Bowers on return journey from the Pole. On Nov. 12 a search party found the tent containing the bodies of Scott, Wilson and Bowers and Scott's diary and records

1913

Jan. 7, German expedition under Filchner returned to Buenos Aires after visit to the Weddell Sea and discovery of Luitpold Land

1914

Aug. 1, Sir Ernest Shackleton in the "Endurance" left England entering ice-pack in the Weddell Sea in December

1915

Jan. 11, Shackleton expedition discovered the Caird coast between Coats Land and Luitpold Land, but no landing place

Oct. 27, The "Endurance" crushed in ice abandoned in 69° 5′ S. and the 28 men camped on ice-floe moving northward drifting until April 9, 1916 when they took to their small boats in 62° S. 54′ W. and made landing after 6 days on Elephant Island

1916

May 31, Sir Ernest Shackleton with 5 companions arrived at Port Stanley, Falkland Islands in small boat

1917

Jan. 10, Sir E. Shackleton arrived at Cape Evans, New Zealand, with survivors of Ross sea expedition

Sept. 3, Sir Ernest Shackleton reached Punta Arenas, Chile, with the 22 members of his expedition who had been marooned on Elephant Island, successful in his fourth attempt in their rescue

1921

Sept. 17, Sir Ernest Shackleton sailed from London on the "Quest" to explore the Enderby quadrant of the Antarctic, and died, off South Georgia

1924

March 27, Decree annexed Adélie Land to France

1928

Aug. 25, Expedition of Commander Byrd left New York, and New Zealand Dec. 2 in the "City of New York" for Ross Sea and Ice Shelf

Oct. 24, Captain G. H. Wilkins (now Sir Hubert) left Montevideo on whaling ship with 2 airplanes reaching base at Deception Island, South Shetlands, Nov. 7

Nov. 16, First flight in airplane in Antarctic made by Sir Hubert Wilkins with C. B. Eielson as pilot

Dec. 20, Main exploring flight of 5 and one-half hours over Graham Land, 600 miles southwest, Graham Land believed to be a peninsula discovered to be a mass of islands

Dec. 25, Byrd expedition reached Ross Ice Shelf 177° 25′ W. Long.

Dec. 28, The Byrd expedition fixed on base in Bay of Whales and began building city of "Little America"

1929

Jan. 10, Second flight of Wilkins and Eielson over same course

Jan. 27, Admiral Byrd made flight northeast to Alexandra Mts. and discovered new range of mountains which he named Rockefeller

Feb. 1, Flight made of 200 miles to 73° S. on 101st W. meridian by Wilkins and Eielson

Feb. 18, Adm. Byrd and Capt. A. B. Parker in 2 planes discovered land beyond the 150th meridian and named it Marie Byrd Land claimed for U. S.

Oct. 19, Expedition of Sir Douglas Mawson in the "Discovery" (the British and Australian and New Zealand Research Expedition) sailed from Cape Town arriving at Heard Island Nov. 26

Nov. 1, Sir Hubert Wilkins sailed from Montevideo arriving at his base on Deception Island Nov. 11, and Dec. 19 made 3 hour flight from south end of Neumayer Channel along the coast to Beaschochea Bay to Richthofen Valley

Nov. 4–Jan. 19, 1930, Geological expedition of Dr. L. M. Gould to mountain border of South Polar Plateau (Byrd expedition)

Nov. 8, Expedition of Commander Riiser-Larsen on the "Norwegia" started from point west of Bouvet Island in 55° S. and 4′ W.

Nov. 28–29, Flight of Admiral Byrd, with Bernt Balchen and Harold June as pilots of 1,600 miles to the South Pole and back, dropping American flag at Pole Nov. 29 about 8.55 A.M. 19 hours

Dec. 7, Riiser-Larsen expedition at point 64° 21′ S. and 53° 14′ E. made airplane flight 40 miles south

Dec. 16, Mawson expedition from Heard Island (Dec. 3) reached point in 65° 41′ S. and about 79° and ½ E.

Dec. 27, Dr. Gould found cairn left by Amundsen 18 years before at foot of Axel Heiburg Glacier

Dec. 29, Wilkins expedition made flight of 450 miles as far as Charcot Island adding some 300 miles of new coast line to the Antarctic Continent

Dec. 31, Mawson expedition made first flight from 66° 10′ S. discovering land he named Mac Robertson, after Dr. Macpherson Robertson of Melbourne, along the 67th parallel between the 60th and 67th meridians

1930

Jan. 5, Flight of Mawson expedition over Mac Robertson Land

——, Flight of Sir Hubert Wilkins from Charcot Island to Deception Island

Jan. 13, Party from Mawson expedition landed on Proclamation Island and reaffirmed British possession

Jan. 14, Flight of Commander Riiser-Larsen along west coast of Enderby Land naming Ice Bay in 68° S. 50° E.

Jan. 16, Flight of Commander Riiser-Larsen from the "Norwegia" to newly discovered land between Ice Bay and 43° E. named Queen Maud Land

Jan. 20, Adm. Byrd made flight west to Discovery Inlet indentation in Ross Ice Shelf

Jan. 25–Feb. 14, Flights of Sir Hubert Wilkins from Deception Island southward, and departure for Montevideo

Jan. 26, Mawson expedition turned back with minimum coal for safe return reaching Adelaide April 1

Feb. 18, The "City of New York" reached "Little America" to bring back Byrd expedition

——, Flight of Commander Riiser-Larsen, Seal Bay and Cape Norwegia named in 71 and $^1/_5$°

Feb. 19, The Byrd expedition sailed for New Zealand reaching Dunedin March 10

Feb. 20, Commander Riiser-Larsen discovered and named land between Seal Bay and Coats Land and named it Crown Princess Martha Land

March 10, Byrd expedition reached Dunedin, New Zealand

Dec. 22, Commander Riiser-Larsen expedition reached 65° 15′ S. and 49° 30′ E. and made flight to Enderby Land a few miles southwest of Biscoe's Cape Ann